RON SHANDLER's
Baseball
Forecaster
2011
Silver Anniversary Edition

TRIUMPH
BOOKS

This book is available in quantity at special discounts for your group or organization. For further information, contact:

Triumph Books
542 South Dearborn Street
Suite 750
Chicago, Illinois 60605
(312) 939-3330
Fax (312) 663-3557

Printed in U.S.A.
ISBN: 978-1-60078-549-8

Rotisserie League Baseball is a registered trademark of the Rotisserie League Baseball Association, Inc.

Statistics provided by Baseball Info Solutions

Cover design by Jon Resh@Go-Undaunted.com
Front cover photograph by Tim Vizer/Icon Sports Media, Inc.
Author photograph by Kevin Hurley

Acknowledgments

Ron Shandler's BASEBALL FORECASTER

Editor
Ray Murphy

Associate Editors
Rod Truesdell
Brent Hershey

Data and Charts
Paul Petera
Brent Hershey
Joshua Randall

Player commentaries
Dave Adler
Andy Andres
Brent Hershey
Joe Hoffer
Bill Macey
Scott Monroe
Ray Murphy
Harold Nichols
Stephen Nickrand
Josh Paley
Joshua Randall
Brian Rudd
Jock Thompson
Rod Truesdell

Research and Articles
Ed DeCaria
Bill Macey
Ray Murphy
Stephen Nickrand
Michael Weddell

Prospects
Rob Gordon
Jeremy Deloney
Tom Mulhall

Injuries
Rick Wilton

Back in 1986, it was just me, a kitchen table and LOTUS 1-2-3 Version 1A on an IBM PC clone. In the 25 years since, much of that has changed, most importantly that it's not just me anymore. While my name is in the book's title — mostly out of stubborn habit and "branding" (whatever) — the fanalytic heroes listed on the left are where your kudos should be directed. Without them, there is no *Baseball Forecaster*.

Those contributors are part of the larger Baseball HQ family. The other fanalytic brothers, uncles and nephews are Randy Appel, Matt Baic, Matt Beagle, Bob Berger, Rob Carroll, Matt Cederholm, Patrick Davitt, Doug Dennis, Pat DiCaprio, Matt Dodge, Jim Driscoll, Neil FitzGerald, Scott Gellman, Dylan Hedges, Phil Hertz, Tom Kephart, Brandon Kruse, Troy Martell, Mike Murray, Frank Noto, Kris Olson, Greg Pyron, Nick Richards, Mike Shears, Peter Sheridan, Skip Snow, Tom Todaro and Jeffrey Tomich. You'd be hard-pressed to assemble this much intelligence in one place, anywhere. These guys are the heart of everything we do here.

Thanks to Mike Krebs, Rob Rosenfeld and Uri Foox, our tech team that keeps the heart pumping.

Lynda Knezovich has been leading our customer service operation for nearly a decade. When Sue and I decided to stop entering orders and stuffing envelopes ourselves, it took three years to find someone as dedicated as Lynda to keep back office operations running smoothly. She has been an invaluable contributor to this milestone.

A generation's worth of gratitude to my industry colleagues, who've helped to shape everything I've done: Greg Ambrosius, Jeff Barton, Matthew Berry, Jim Callis, Tristan Cockcroft, Glen Colton, Don Drooker, Jeff Erickson, Brian Feldman, Steve Gardner, Jason Grey, Tim Heaney, Eric Karabell, Peter Kreutzer, Gene McCaffrey, Lenny Melnick, John Menna, Nick Minnix, Lawr Michaels, Steve Moyer, Alex Patton, Peter Schoenke, Cory Schwartz, Joe Sheehan, Mike Siano, John Sickels, Perry Van Hook, Sam Walker, Brian Walton, Jeff Winick, Rick Wolf, Trace Wood and Todd Zola. There are other folks who I've crossed paths with at various times during this journey, from Rob Neyer, to John Hunt, to Mat Olkin, and hundreds in between. From leading roles, to supporting players, to cameos, every one has played a huge part.

Thank you to the folks at Big Lead Sports/Fantasy Sports Ventures and Triumph Books for providing a light at the end of the tunnel.

Thank you to the folks at USA Today and the Huffington Post for giving me new platforms for my random brain flakes.

Thank you to my ladies, who made me get vanity plates this year (more on that later). Darielle is now a sophomore at Drew University and has added "Stage Manager" and "Playwright" to her resume. She is having way too much fun at college and now only calls me when she needs money or is lost in New Jersey. (I bought her a GPS.)

Justina's songs are getting hits on YouTube ("Salt" is a personal fave.). Inundated in college auditions, she could end up anywhere from Berklee College, to Miami, to USC, though Dad is still skittish about her flying 3,000 miles to visit her boyfriend in Seattle.

The nice thing about this book is it helps me also keep track of how many years Sue has put up with me. For our own special anniversary, we held a summit in Quebec this summer and agreed upon another 25-year contract for the marriage. We'll convene again and renegotiate in 2035.

Finally… thank *you* for still being here. You've made it through four-plus presidential administrations, several labor disputes and a documentary film. Frankly, I can't believe you're still here after all that. But I'm incredibly grateful that you see fit to keep coming back, sharing your successes and reading to the end of the Acknowledgments.

25 years — unbelievable. Thank you. Truly, thank you.

CONTENTS

From ESPN's 30-for-30 documentary, "Silly Little Game":

"There were probably a good two or three dozen people who were just trying their hand to see what they could make out of this industry, and perhaps make a living, perhaps make some money on the side…"
— *Ron Shandler, early Rotisserie entrepreneur*

"That should have been all of our business… if we had figured out a way to capture the market."
— *Dan Okrent, Founder of Rotisserie League Baseball*

AN IMPORTANT CONSUMER ADVISORY FOR FANTASY LEAGUERS
REGARDING PROPER USAGE OF THE BASEBALL FORECASTER
APPEARS IN THE BACK OF THE BOOK

Now

Okay, let's review...

What have we learned after 25 years? After all the auctions and aberrations, balls and strikes (juiced and labor), drafts, dynasties and disabled lists... what have we *really* learned?

Never bet against Albert Pujols?

Well, yes but...

Never count on a healthy season from Nick Johnson?

Of course, but I'm looking for something at a higher level.

Never deploy a starting pitcher in Coors Field?

Um... well, that's not even true anymore. Maybe 10 years ago, but ever since the humidor...

Well, I give up. I'm clueless.

Exactly.

Huh?

The takeaway after 25 years is... No matter how much effort we put into playing this game, we are not nearly as smart as we think we are. We are all pretty much clueless.

Give me a break. I just dropped a bunch of cash on this book and you're telling me that 25 years of evaluating players and playing fantasy baseball has taught you nothing?

Oh, no, it has taught me tons. But as much as we think we are getting closer to nailing this game, we're really not even close. I don't know that we'll ever be.

For years we've been searching for the Holy Grail, some process or strategy that would yield consistent success. We thought the LIMA Plan was a vital point in that quest – and it probably was back in 1998 – but all it really showed us was that competitive advantages have a short shelf life. By 2002, we were back to being clueless.

In 2003, the book *Moneyball* was hailed as a breakthrough analysis on leveraging economic inefficiencies and sabermetrics to win at baseball. Forget the fact that the Athletics were never able to turn that intelligence into a World Series title. But after nearly a decade, the real lesson from the book was that sabermetrics alone is not enough. The optimal approach to player evaluation has to be an integration of sabermetrics and scouting. Why? Because players are human and not stat-producing robots. And we're back to being clueless again.

This past year, I surveyed some of the top fantasy players in the industry and asked them the secret of consistent success. It was tough to get a consensus on any of the six variables I presented. The results of that research appear later in the book.

And we're not learning anything from all this?

Generally, we're not real good at learning from our past mistakes. Consider the case of Brady Anderson. For the first eight years of his career, he hit more than 12 home runs in a season only once; the 21 he hit in 1992. Then in 1996, out of nowhere, he hit 50. We analyzed the phenomenon to death and could not come up with any firm conclusion. In 1997, Anderson hit 18 homers and never hit more than 24 again.

How smart were we? It took several years for that 50-HR season to filter its way out of the historical baseline from which we calculate our projections. It took another decade before we were able to come to terms with the possibility that PEDs might have been involved.

So what have we really learned from that? Not much. In 2010, Jose Bautista came out of nowhere to hit 54 HRs. We've been conditioned to think that PEDs are no longer an issue we need to consider, but can we really be so sure? The bigger question is, how many HRs should we project for Bautista in 2011? Odds are most prognosticators will project a regression, perhaps as low as the mid-30s. Will anyone go out on the limb that 2010 was a complete anomaly and push his HR total below 20? Not likely.

So you're saying we should be projecting Jose Bautista to hit 15 home runs again in 2011?

I am saying we should not dismiss the possibility. Players don't go from 15 home runs to 50 without some underlying change. Just because nobody is willing to fess up doesn't mean that we have to toss it off as random. A 300% increase in HRs is big! If Bautista has really figured out the secret to prodigious power, he wouldn't tell anyone anyway, right? Not when there's always the promise of a huge, lucrative contract down the line.

So we're back to being clueless again?

We don't have enough information to make as informed decisions as we'd like. As much as we think we've accounted for every conceivable variable, there is always one more unknown that is going to mess up our perfect analysis. Heck, it would have been nice to know about Pablo Sandoval's pending divorce before I drafted him in the third round of the NFBC last March.

Stuff happens. There are always going to be outliers.

Sure, you can just resign yourself to that. The problem for fantasy leaguers is that outliers are what usually separate the winners from the losers. Over the past few years, these types of surprise performers have a disproportionate impact on league standings. For instance, of those teams that owned Bautista or Carlos Gonzalez last year, one in five finished in first place, and more than 70% finished no lower than 5th. That's huge.

So shouldn't we just learn from these guys and draft them high next year? Seems pretty simple.

No! That's what everyone is going to be doing and it's wrong. One of the biggest errors we make in this game is our obsession with Now. We've become programmed to jump at the current reality before we've had the chance to examine whether it is, in fact, real at all.

But reality is fluid. There is no way for us to determine

whether Now is permanent unless we exhibit a modicum of patience and evaluate things objectively.

Okay, now you've gone all philosophical on me. What the heck are you talking about?

You are ready to draft Carlos Gonzalez in the first round this spring because he had such a great season in 2010. That makes the assumption that Gonzalez's Now performance is a new reality. But history shows that he is a very poor percentage play to repeat.

Look what happened in 2005… Derrek Lee came out of nowhere to finish as the top-ranked player, then rose to #7 in the 2006 ADP list only to be never heard from as a first-rounder again. Jimmy Rollins finished in the first round in 2007, then repeated in the ADP Top 15 for *two more years,* even though he hasn't cracked the first round since '07.

More recently, Matt Kemp and Joe Mauer finished in the Top 15 in 2009, boosting them into the 2010 pre-season ADP first round. You know the rest.

But CarGo was amazing last year. How could he not finish as one of 2011's top players?

You said that same thing about Mauer coming into 2010. He was last year's Now player.

So are you saying that we should just be staying away from all career years and breakout players? Ignore all Now players?

We don't have to stay away from those players, just value them more appropriately. The two strongest forces in baseball prognosticating are regression and gravity. Every player's future performance is forcefully pulled back to their career mean (regression). For some players, each season is a battle to put up just enough numbers to stay gainfully employed (gravity). No matter how good the player is, projecting a decline is always going to be a stronger percentage play than projecting improvement.

So, in terms of Now, yes, Now is bad. Now anchors us into an expectation that may be unrealistic. But Now is so tough to ignore, because, well, it's happening Now.

And Albert Pujols?

Ha! He's for real. He was Now once but has proven his endurance over many years of Nows.

So how do we get from CarGo to Pujols?

It takes time. Time to observe. Time to create a track record. Time to more accurately analyze. But that's exactly what an obsession with Now steals from us — time.

Sounds like this has taken you time to learn.

It has definitely been a learning process. There was a period when I had it all wrong myself and had to figure out how to get back on the right path.

Do tell.

In 1994, my introduction to the 8th edition of the *Baseball Forecaster* included this passage:

"Information is routinely faulty. It is comprised simply of other people's opinions. A manager who believes a certain player is going to be a regular. A scout whose opinion is that a player

has potential. A team physician whose opinion is that a player is healthy. Words from experts, but still only opinions.

"Now, what do we normally do to process this information? We adjust our own opinions. We upgrade and downgrade players in our mind based on these outside opinions. And that would be fine if the point of fantasy baseball was to form qualitative judgments about players. But it is not.

"Fantasy baseball is a game of numbers. Period. All that matters are the numbers. Period. In fantasy baseball, numbers are everything. The purpose of reality is to feed the numbers. Without numbers, there is nothing."

Back then, I believed that everything was pretty much quantifiable. It was idealistic, written when sabermetrics was still new and exciting, and the possibilities to apply this intelligence seemed endless. This was four years before the LIMA Plan and nearly a decade before *Moneyball.*

Well, we know that everything is not quantifiable, but your general point was on the mark, wasn't it?

True. While the passage did recognize the imprecision of information, it drew the wrong conclusion. Acknowledging faulty information does not mean we need to seek out greater precision. It could also mean quite the opposite — we need to accept the imprecision in our processes, and figure out other ways to improve our chances of winning.

Today, I've come to think the numbers hardly matter at all. Of course, we still measure winning and losing in numbers, but I think attempts to project performance with any precision are generally a waste of effort. I think the best we can hope for is to project general tendencies.

I'm confused. First you said that figuring out the outliers was more important. Then I see all these other sites trying to come up with the most accurate overall projections. I don't see how you can have it both ways.

Admittedly, with all the advanced analytical tools and methods available today, mine is not a terribly popular opinion. The new breed of baseball analysts have the same idealism now that I felt 25 years ago. That is a good thing; idealism breeds innovation.

However, 25 years has just led me to one conclusion: the capabilities of today's projection models are so close that the quest for greater precision is blocked by diminishing returns. It is nearly useless to obsess over precision when a general sense of expectation yields comparable results. In fantasy baseball, Occam's Razor rules.

I don't buy it. Shouldn't we always be striving for the most accurate projections possible?

Look at it this way. Projecting player performance is like painting a room in your house, in white. The natural inclination, of course, is to do the best job possible. But for some, that means finding the exact shade of white and then choosing a one-inch brush. They'll explain this by saying how they need to make sure all the corners and moldings are perfect, and how the small brush allows them to draw out the nuance in their work.

I'm quite content using a roller. I don't care if I get a little paint on the baseboards because, in the end, the room is going to look painted. And from a distance – which is where we sit as the stats accumulate – how much nuance is there, really, in white?

So, you're saying that it's good enough to just toss a can of paint at the walls?

No. That would be like projecting performance from gut feel. You still need to put down drop-cloths and use the roller in correct strokes. The job still needs to look right. But it's not about being perfectly accurate, it's about being accurate enough.

So getting the room painted is like saying the basic projections will take care of themselves? Then we can focus on the outliers?

Sort of. That's the approach we've taken in this year's book. You'll find that the 2011 projections have a lot more regression than in the past. Ed DeCaria's article, "Trending into Trouble," shows why. Those who rely on us for their breakout candidates can find those in the Upside (UP) and Downside (DN) indicators in the player boxes. There are more of those this year as we look harder for the outliers in each player's skills profile. But the formal projections are going with the best percentage play that we can use, and that is going to be largely driven by regression and gravity.

And white paint. Is that all I need to know?

There is one more important element, and unfortunately, it's a fundamental flaw in the entire process. We are not really coating the room in a fine latex paint; it's more like watercolors, and it's doing a lousy job of covering the walls.

In real terms, the flaw is that the quantitative inputs we feed into our models are themselves inherently imprecise, and therefore the outputs of the model must be at least as imprecise, and probably more. Computer engineers sum it up as "garbage in, garbage out."

When Albert Pujols hit 42 HRs this past season, that was interpreted as a finite and accurate measure. When he hits 41, 49, 32, 37 and 47 HRs over a five-year period, those data points are seen as a valid range of values. But they're not.

Pujols' 42 HRs described a unique confluence of events that were shaped by his health, ballpark dimensions, wind currents and the particular assortment of pitchers he faced last season. Of the thousands of pitches he saw, a handful of changes in velocity or location could have shifted that 42 HRs to 41, or 48, or 36. In this book, we define "errant gust of wind" as a standard unit of measure describing the same phenomenon.

The truth is, that 42 was an almost arbitrary stopping point along a continuum of possibilities this year. Yet we use that 42 as absolute input in our projections models.

An irony is that Pujols is considered one of the most consistent power hitters of our time, despite him hitting anywhere from 32 to 49 HRs. That 17-HR range is comparable to the career ranges of power hitters like Lance Berkman, Aubrey Huff, Brandon Inge, Melvin Mora and Vernon Wells – all hitters whose home run output is generally described as inconsistent.

That's why our attempts at precision in projection-model outputs are misguided. It's mostly "garbage out" because it's mostly "garbage in."

It's the same thing with virtually every other statistical gauge — ERA, OBP, BABIP, BPV — you name it. They are all calculated with statistical measures that are highly variable. In this book, we try to filter out as much noise as possible and reduce skill to its component parts. But these efforts have limitations too. Even the most fundamental element — whether a pitch is a strike or a ball — is colored by the particular umpire behind the plate.

Numbers are everything when we look at the actual stats to determine winners and losers. But as counterintuitive as it sounds, nearly everything that leads up to those final October reports is far less precise, far less projectable and far less important.

Wow. Major disillusionment. Makes me wonder why we bother at all. Should we be drafting our fantasy teams just by throwing darts?

As bad as it sounds, it's not *that* bad. It's all about having reasonable expectations. If you are looking for someone to tell you exactly how many home runs Jose Bautista is going to hit in 2011 — in crisp black and white — then you are going to be disappointed, no matter what source you use. But if you are looking for an analysis that provides general expectations and tendencies, percentage plays and lots of shades of grey, then that is highly achievable and you are in the right place.

There is no quick fix, no canned answers, no Holy Grail. And if you want true insight, you are going to have to work a little for it.

And I'll be able to uncover next year's Carlos Gonzalez?

Well, our work has focused on separating underlying skills from surface stats. That often reveals some hidden potential we would not ordinarily have seen. Last year's Mayberry Method got us a little bit closer to identifying the surprises by doing something completely counter-intuitive. Mayberry got us smarter by taking a *simpler* approach to player evaluation.

We got smarter by being more stupid?

In a way, yes. Broad strokes with a roller as opposed to fine strokes with a brush, and the room still gets painted. Twenty-five years of searching for the Holy Grail and we pretty much ended up right where we started.

That's gotta be frustrating.

Actually, it has been enlightening. In the end, there are small gains to be made, but I am convinced our time will be best spent searching for improvements in playing time projections, injury analysis, and game play itself, including the game theory and economics involved in auction and draft management.

And forget about trying to project player performance?

Don't forget about it, just don't obsess over it. And don't obsess over Now. Today's Now is tomorrow's Derrek Lee.

Then

I started out on this journey 25 years ago because I was not cut out to be an employee. After graduating from college, I had nine jobs over 16 years and left only two of them voluntarily.

These books are my legacy, for good or bad. Here is a little taste of each edition, in the form of meaningless trivia, random excerpts and an occasional angry rant...

1986

The Mets win the World Series, and one month later, a publication debuts called *Baseball SuperSTATS*. It would become the *Baseball Forecaster Annual Review* in 1988, *Ron Shandler's Baseball Forecaster Annual Review* in 1993 and *Ron Shandler's Baseball Forecaster* in 2003.

1987

The Minnesota Twins win the World Series despite an 85-77 record, a 79-83 Pythagorean Projection and a 76-86 Linear Weights record. Some of the cutting edge statistics appearing in the second edition are Bill James' offensive winning pct., earned runs prevented average (a forerunner of strand rate) and Rolaids Formula relief points.

1988

The Dodgers win the World Series and the color of the *Forecaster's* cover is Dodger Blue. From now through 1998, the book cover would be color-coordinated with the team colors of that year's World Series winner. So, the 1989 book cover would be green (A's), the 1990 cover red (Reds), all the way to the 1998 cover which would be teal (Marlins).

This edition is the first to acknowledge that fantasy leaguers might be reading the book. The new Player Rating & Rankings section begins, "Welcome Rotisserie Leaguers, Fantasy Leaguers, Statistical Leaguers and Board Gamers." It includes 1989 projections for Linear Weights and a "Rotisserie Rating," which puts performance in the 4x4 categories on a 0-100 scale. Top rated player? Roger Clemens at 98.6 — perfectly normal.

1989

"The members of Shandler Enterprises are all franchise owners in the Baseball Association of the Granite State (BAGS), a New Hampshire-based Rotisserie-style league that is constantly experimenting with progressive rule changes. BAGS will be entering its 6th year in 1990. Ron's team, the RonSue Perbs, is celebrating its first championship despite setting a new BAGS record by having the most players on the D.L. at one time — 7."

1990

"Mostly Sunny, Increasing Darkness Towards Evening" begins the second section of this book, the forerunner of the Forecaster's Toolbox, which has is now the Encyclopedia of Fanalytics. It includes several Bill James concepts (Law of Competitive Balance, Plexiglass Principle, Whirlpool Principle, etc.), a note about peak ages and "the difference between an acceptable or unacceptable performance level may have been one particularly good or bad month."

1991

We have never missed a year since 1986, yet there is no 1991 book. Beginning with the 1992 edition, we start post-dating. The 1990 edition was published in November 1990. The 1992 edition was published in November 1991.

1992

"It has become a battle... analysts look down upon the fantasy leaguers' warped use of numbers. Rotisserians look at sabermetricians with benign tolerance. It is a challenge trying to appeal to the whims of two diverse audiences.

"There are some who might disagree with this scenario. Bill James — the Grand Guru of Sabermetrics — has bridged the gap by designing his own fantasy game. This is more of a marketing ploy than anything else. If my name was Bill James, I'd go where the money is too.

"However, there is still the interesting case of the 1990 SABR membership survey. This is the organization from which James originally coined the term sabermetrics. This is the same group that requested — over 70% of them — that coverage of Rotisserie leagues in their monthly newsletter be decreased or dropped."

1993

"The values and concepts we've grown up with are so much a part of us that we often lose our objectivity. Everything we do tends to be within the framework of our preconceptions. We really need to challenge ourselves to look at things as a child might, with open eyes and a sense of adventure.

"A few months ago during breakfast, I heard a sound from my childhood that I had associated with a very specific circumstance. But in this particular instance, the sound was disturbingly out of place. As I came to grips with the reality, it became my revelation for the day.

"The sound was *snap, crackle and pop*. It was coming from a bowl of Special-K."

1994

Player commentaries appear for the first time. Over the years, these would become many readers' favorite part of the book. For the writers, too. It allows us to reach beyond the cold numbers and find the essence of each player.

Every year, there are always some players that don't lend themselves to much analysis. For these players, we often like to have a little fun, flexing our comedic muscle a bit. Here are some of my favorites from each year.

> Kirt Manwaring: Has peaked. Eye is already in decline. Power might bounce back a bit. I feel like I'm analyzing a piece of lint with an electron microscope.

> Mark Gardner: I'm really getting depressed. It's 6 o'clock, I'm hungry, the wife and kids aren't home yet and I have to write about all these pitchers with horrible trends. I feel like there will be nobody out there to draft next year.

1995

There is no World Series, and so no color for the book cover. I write: "At first I thought, make it black. All black. No art or graphics, just black. If the Beatles can have a White Album, I can have a Black Book. Then I thought, well maybe I should soften it up a bit. A few greys, a little white space. Maybe retain the titles… I finally decided to throw in some red. This was in no way related to Cincy's chances to win the Fall Classic. The red was for the blood that these greedy multi-millionaires have sucked out of all of us."

Player commentaries:

Mike Felder: Here's an exercise… Take a piece of graph paper and plot out his 5-year eye ratios. Connect the dots and what do you get? A squirrel? No, no, connect them consecutively. Use a ruler if you have to.

Tim Wallach: I spent all season yelling, "Fluke! Fluke!" and while he kept getting better and better, people started sending me these fish. It can't happen again. I've got no more room in my freezer.

Mike Perez: Took his opportunity to make big bucks as a major league closer and just ran with it. Luckily, it's only 256 miles from St. Louis to Louisville, so he should be there by now.

Rick Sutcliffe: Dear Rick, I would think that two years in oblivion are more than any one person should be subjected to. Please retire. Your friend, Ron.

"Reports of the demise of Major League Baseball have been greatly exaggerated. They can take away seven weeks of the 1994 season. They can take away the pennant races and the record quests. They can even take away the security of knowing when the next Major League game will be played. But there's one thing they can't take away…

"Baseball, the game, remains. The players still have their skills. They have not taken their bats and balls and gone home. The game is simply undergoing an evolution. Sometimes evolution occurs over eons and sometimes it sputters and lurches forward. What the result of this will be is anyone's guess. (Maybe 1995 will only see minor league ball until the United League debuts in 1996.)

"But we have choices as to how we are going to approach these changes. We could sit here and stew over the outrage that has been thrust upon us. Or we could look for the exciting opportunities this evolution may bring, moving forward — as a baseball fan and as a fantasy leaguer — towards some new adventure."

1996

Top 10 Reasons Why Projecting Playing Time is a Thankless Job

#9: Somewhere inside White Sox management offices…

"We are contenders, but Julio is not our only key to success. Let him go. So we need a designated hitter? No problem. We'll use Chris Sabo as DH. Yes! Great idea!

Okay, that didn't work. No problem. DH's are a dime a dozen. We'll get John Kruk for DH. Even better!

Okay, that didn't work either. No problem. Let's see…

We can use… Thomas at DH, move Martinez to first and put Devereaux in right. No, how about Ventura at first and Grebeck at third? No, no, let's try this kid Snopek at third. Wait, wait… how about Raines at DH and put Martinez back in left? No, let's try the kid Mouton in left. No, right. No, left. No, right again. I got a better one… Make Martinez the DH. No, no, no, how about Norberto? Wait, back to Snopek again. No, Mouton. No, Raines. No, Devereaux. No, berto. No! How about… No, wait, I got it! Let's buy Julio a one-way ticket back to Chicago. No, no, no… does anyone know if Harold Baines is a free agent this year?"

Player commentaries:

Pat Kelly: He lost the 2B job. He looked all over for it, under the grandstand, behind the bleachers, in the far corner of the visitor's dugout… but we're fairly certain it's pretty much lost.

Wayne Kirby: In a perfect world, his BPIs indicate he should have batted much higher than .207. But in a perfect world, he would be eight years younger and his name would be Manny Ramirez.

Jose Oquendo: He wants to come back for one more year. Y'know, you give 'em one year, then they want a spring training invite. Ya give them a look-see and they want a roster spot again. Before you know it, ya got a .185 hitter stuck on your roster for 10 years.

Jose Vizcaino: Try as I might, I cannot find anything intrinsically wrong with his season. (It's my job to look.) Sure, there's not much here, but he fields his position, calls his Mom on Mother's Day and avoids crushing small animals on the highway.

Mike Oquist: He's been abandoned by his control. They had a nice relationship once. You know, flowers, soft music, that sort of thing. But he said "I'm going to BAL" and his control said, "So long, I'm staying in Rochester."

1997

Top 10 Theories Why Brady Anderson Hit 50 HRs in 1996

#9: The Dave Johnson Theory

New manager Dave Johnson returned to the city of some of his greatest successes and decided to impart his "Secret of 1973" to a worthy apprentice. Back in 1973, Johnson was traded from Baltimore to Atlanta. Apparently, he was so angered by the deal that he wanted to show Orioles' management what a mistake they had made. He hit 43 HRs for the Braves that year. He never hit more than 18 in any other season. In fact, Johnson's annual HR totals bear an eerie resemblance to Anderson's trends.

#1: The "It was right there in front of our noses" Theory

STATS Inc. Scouting Report, 1996 (deftly edited and taken out of context, but the words did appear there): Anderson provides unusual power from the lead-off spot. He can drive the ball a long distance when he gets hold of one.

Player commentaries:

Juan Castro: His levels are meager, diminutive. His trends are stable, unexciting. His bouquet is full-bodied, aromatic.

Mark Parent: A backstop who's avoided the scrap heap by selling out and becoming a kept man. Now he's Scott Erickson's personal catcher, providing advice, running errands, putting on the gear every 5th day…

Edgar Renteria: There was talk of sending him and Conine to SF for Bonds, but fans threatened to burn down the stadium. And rightly so… it's a horrible stadium for baseball.

Rusty Meacham: BPIs are improving but LHers ate him for dinner. Reviews were mixed… some found him tender and juicy, others only managed to get through the meal with a bourbon chaser to kill the aftertaste.

1998

"Since 1994, *Baseball Weekly* has used their LABR experts league as an early gauge of player values. I've had the honor of participating in these drafts with some of the brightest baseball minds in the industry.

"At the end of 1997's grueling two-day affair, I offered up a proposition to the group. I suggested that in 1998 we do at least one of the drafts blind. We could bring in absolutely no prep material except for an unmarked list of each team's 25-man rosters. The only thing we could write on that sheet would be a line through each player's name as he came up for bid, and a running total of our finances.

"The response to this proposal was predictable. At first there was quiet consideration. Then there came a few hesitant votes of "that might be interesting." Then, those who were busy gathering up their computer printouts and loose-leaf notebooks began shaking their heads and muttering about the inability to track draft inflation and the loss of control. To my mind, that was the exact reason why we needed to do this.

"It would have been fun to strip away the security of draft lists. It would have been fun to trust my knowledge of the player population and my own instincts. But even among the nation's top experts, there were too many who could not handle the nakedness, and so the motion failed."

Player commentaries:

Archie Cianfrocco: Some Forecaster prose…
> A little pop
> A little speed
> A batting eye
> Is all you need
> Burma Shave.

Don Wengert: I saw one back in '94, I touched it, held it, wanted more. It cajoled me and teased me, led me astray to gaudy stats on SanFran Bay. Its memory lives on every line but now I know that it's not mine.
(The 2.0 Command Ratio Lament)

1999

This book's introduction is entitled, "Crickets." From this edition on, every introductory essay would have a one-word title: Crickets, Revelation, Propaganda, Catharsis, Pilgrimage, Fanalytics, Relevance, Longevity, Watch, Noise, Faith, Billboards and Now.

Pop Quiz: Match Column A with Column B

COLUMN A	COLUMN B
Elbow twinge	Day-to-day
Cracked rib	Interminable day-to-day
Pulled hamstring	15 day DL
Sore shoulder	15 day DL, +/- a few weeks
Back spasms	60 day DL
Fingernail blister	So long, season's over!

I like quizzes like this. No matter how you answer, you're never wrong!

Player commentaries:

Felipe Crespo: "Got to know Syracuse real well. Nice town. Good people. Did well there once. Toronto? Big city. Hockey town. A marginal player could get lost. But Syracuse, I tell ya, THERE was a place to play."

Ricky Gutierrez: Essentially, a replacement level shortstop. Doesn't help you, doesn't hurt you. If he misses a game, you don't miss him. He'll show up at spring training and say, "Hi, I'm back." And we'll say, "Oh, were you gone?"

Andy Benes: Solid second half salvaged a slow start. (Hmm… how alliterative…) Skills set stable. (Don't stop me now.) At 31, it's possible he could post a peak pick-up in his performance. (Wheeeee!)

Mike Morgan: Test of the emergency self-control system (don't worry, it's only a test): Draft Day, 13th round, you hear, "Mike Morgan $1." Do you a) stay silent, b) bid $2, or c) bid $5? Steady now, I know this one's a toughie.

2000

"In the beginning, there was chaos and there was anarchy. The world's populace, driven to the brink of despair, teetered on the edge of mass destruction. The terrified and homeless clung tightly to any warm body as public address systems wailed mournful warnings. For any grain of hope was better than none, and any source of warmth was better than the alternative. It was bad, very bad, and there was no sign that things were going to get any better. It was May 20, 1999 and Greg Maddux had an ERA of 5.02."

Player commentaries:

Manny Alexander: Free swinger. Doesn't get on base. Has no power. Speed skills are gone. OPS was .666, which has to be a bad sign.

Orlando Hernandez: Not quite as dominant a performance as 1998. But then again, in 1998 he was 29 years old, and in 1999 he was 33.

Jim Pittsley: Once upon a time, there was this frog who was drafted in the first round. For years, potential suitors stood in line, hoping that their kiss would reveal the prince inside. But… it was just a frog.

2001

"At last count, there were more hitters on pace for a 50-HR season than at any previous time in the history of Major League Baseball. We polled our readers to find out what they thought the most plausible explanation was:

The strike zone	24.5%
The balls	24.1%
The pitchers	21.7%
The hitters	15.8%
The stadiums	8.8%
An aberration	5.3%

"ESPN.com columnist Jayson Stark wrote a column that addressed the issue of baseball's elevated offense. His advice: "This is baseball in the 21st century. Get used to it.""

"Get used to it? Massive shifts don't just suddenly happen."

Player commentaries:

Mark Sweeney: Had a nice skills set with some upside in 1996, but the last three years have been flat and unimpressive. (Hmm, I once had a girlfriend that was described the same way.)

John Halama: Regressing, and for no good reason. They're calling it a "dead arm" which is the organizational vernacular for "we haven't got a clue, but it sure as hell ain't OUR fault." This is when I recommend a change of scenery.

Matt Clement: Walked 125 batters in 2000, which is an accomplishment in itself and the apex of a 4-year trend. That's the bad news. The good news is that I used the word "apex" in a player note and am rapidly expanding my vocabulary.

2002

"*Why did the September 11 terrorist attack hit us so hard?*

"For our own psychological security, we need to feel like we have some control over our lives. The fact that the attacks occurred in the manner they did put our sense of control at risk. If we decided to fly, would it be safe? Can we even open our mailbox without putting our safety in jeopardy? As much as we've been told to just get on with things, it's tough because we do not feel as much in control of our lives as we did on September 10.

"In a time when our psychological well-being is crying out for some stability, fantasy sports have been able to provide a small reminder that there is a place where we can go to feel like we have some control

"True, it is false control, as it affects nothing but our own fantasy world. But that is often enough to provide a level of catharsis that can help us weather the uncertainty in our lives. We know that the sport itself may be irrelevant, but that is not the point. These days, it serves a purpose far beyond that of mere escapist entertainment."

Player commentaries:

John Flaherty: BA trend tells a story. OB trend tells a story. OPS trend tells a story. RC/G trend tells a story. RAR trend tells a story. It's all the same story, one in which John's career does not live happily ever after.

Randy Knorr: You may not want this guy on your team, but he has two World Series rings and you don't.

Billy McMillon: Opened '01 with a royal opportunity to grab a sizable chunk of playing time… and went THUD. Doesn't matter that he batted .340 in the 2nd half. Once you go THUD, nobody can see past the THUD.

Ed Sprague: Good enough to try, but not good enough to keep. Those that have tried since 1998 are TOR, OAK, PIT, SD, BOS and SEA. Both coasts, two countries and still unemployed.

2003

"In *Wise Guy Baseball 2002,* Gene McCaffrey wrote, "Can we please turf this 'fantasy' word? People ask me what I do, then look at me like I'm peddling webcam shots of Andruw Jones at the club. Who decided to call it this? How could they get it more wrong? The games we play are won by predicting reality… What we play is personal baseball, admittedly not as catchy a moniker. The true appeal of the games is that they provide an arena in which we can be provably correct.""

"From another reader: "*Fantasy* refers to something that is never expected to occur. *Fantasy baseball* deals with events and happenings that *are* expected to occur. We deal with the real world, facts, the manipulation of those facts, the extrapolation of those facts, probabilities, trends, predictability, and expected outcomes. Fantasy leaguers deal with statistics and with real world events, all in the setting of a competition."

"Fantasy sports have spawned a new type of fandom that is, in fact, *more grounded in reality.* With the growth of sabermetric research, today's fan has a better understanding of the intricacies of the game than ever before.

"From yet another reader: "We use game theory principles to construct models of successful performing teams. Specifically, we examine the individual performances of baseball players to predict a successful team model. These models are then tested by the actual performances of players and teams during the current season."

"*Fantasy* is the furthest thing from this."

The following year, "fanalytics" is born. The term draws more wrath than respect. It takes six more years for it to appear on the cover of this book.

Player commentaries:

Jolbert Cabrera: His BPIs have TAILed, which I suppose is fitting for someone recovering from a posterior injury. He was an END-gamer before, BUTT now's he's BEHIND even that. BUMmer.

Mike Morgan: In retrospect, many players find that there's really nothing wrong with retirement. The millions saved tend to get spent a bit slower, the food is better and you don't have to shower with naked men all the time.

2004

"Is the obsession with micro-managing a bad thing? A recent Baseball HQ poll found that nearly one third of all leagues today allow some level of daily roster management. The problem is this often forces us to ignore the analytical end of the decision-making process.

"There is a belief that making frequent roster decisions is empowering, but that perception is flawed. With a microscope on the minutia, there is a great inclination to treat random streaks and slumps as permanent reality. And that leads to over-managing every element of your roster.

"This fosters an obsession with immediate gratification. If I draft a .300 hitter, *he absolutely has to hit .300 from Day One or I've got to find someone else who will.* Every slugger and speedster bears the burden of producing *a consistent stream of HRs and SBs, every day.* And this obsession can get ugly. On April 8, HQ columnist Neil Bonner wrote a sentence that was the most frightening thing I've read in a long time: "In ESPN leagues, Rey Ordonez is now owned in 82% of all AL leagues."

"And as the short-term decision-maker wields his mighty sword, swinging wildly at anything that even marginally looks like an extra home run, save or steal, the game of fantasy baseball suffers. No longer is it a test of knowledge; it becomes a test of reflexes, a statistical video game controlled by the fleeting urges of the person holding the joystick. Power is just another mouse-click away.

"It's easy to get caught up in that type of power. It's captivating, transforming an innocent game into a six-month adrenaline rush. And admittedly, it feels good. But does the inner game suffer?

Player commentaries:

Keith Osik: The ultimate back door slam… On April 3, Mgr Ned Yost said : "I am going to make you the personal catcher for… Glendon Rusch and Todd Ritchie."

Reggie Taylor: A brutal season characterized by a dreadful 62% contact rate. The only thing that managed to put a stop to his plummeting trends was a merciful August shoulder injury. Bottom line was, he HAD to be stopped.

J.C. Romero: One bizarre season…

4/15	Sore shoulder
6/9	Sore groin
7/25	Food poisoning
8/20	Struck in head by foul ball
9/15	Buttock laceration

You can't make this stuff up

2005

"What ends up happening in this world of growing complexity and precision is that we obsess over hundredths of percentage points and treat minute variances as gospel. *For want of confirming that your order of nachos has two more chips than mine does, we miss out on the fact that both plates are delicious… and the beer is missing.*"

Player commentaries:

Javier Valentin: Draft table tactical planning…
- Listen carefully for the opener.
- Gauge the pace of the bidding.
- Carefully time your reactions.
- Drop out when the price hits $1.

Matt Thornton: Tried to resolve his soft-tossing ways by flinging projectiles at warp speed. Boosted his Dom by over 50% but with a 7.2 Ctl, also scared away everyone in the first 10 rows.

2006

In the 20th edition of the book, I identified the five most controversial (read: worst) projections of my career:

1. I projected a strong growth year for pitcher **Frank Castillo** in 1993, then again in 1995 and again in 1997. He bombed all three times.

2. After a minor breakout in 1999, I said pitcher **Todd Ritchie** "could be a steal for under $20." When I dropped out on his bidding at $11 in Tout Wars, there was a huge backlash, despite my explanations about the timing of his availability in the auction. He earned $7.

3. From May of **Albert Pujols'** rookie year, and for 12-15 months afterward, I kept telling readers to bet against him being able to maintain his numbers. We are still waiting for that advice to pan out.

4. After **Alfonso Soriano** hit 18 HRs and batted .268 with a 0.29 batting eye ratio in his 2001 rookie season, I called him a fluke. He went on to hit 39 HRs and bat .300 in 2002. That led to a re-evaluation of batting eye as a projective tool and the development of the Expected Batting Average stat.

5. In 2003, I projected "signs of a major breakout" and a return to 2000 levels for **Brad Fullmer**, based on his rising BPI trends. He got hurt that year, but I projected a big upside again. When he failed a second time, I projected a rebound. He never saw another major league at bat. Two years later, PED allegations put his career into better focus.

"Everyone has their opinion about the steroids controversy. It is a health issue, a legal issue, a political issue, an ethical issue. The problem for me is that I have a job to do, that of attempting to project player performance with some reasonable level of accuracy. The steroid issue has a huge impact on my efforts, and the credibility of what we do here. As long as we don't have real information regarding this issue, much of our prognosticating efforts are like shooting arrows into the dark.

"Here is an unnerving fact: *You cannot look at a single player in this book without wondering, "Can I trust these numbers?"* We do not know whether a player's sudden power drop-off was due to him coming off the juice. We do not know whether a previously reliable player's sudden rash of injuries was related to artificially-bulked muscles pulling at unyielding tendons. We can analyze the statistical data forever, but unless we know all the facts, we can't draw any conclusions about future performance.

"Am I a conspiracy theorist? I don't think so. I see myself as a realist. I believe that there is nothing more important than the truth, but there are too many conflicting messages right now to believe any one reality we are being fed."

Player commentaries:

Darin Erstad: After years of erratic trends, he's finally settled into a comfortable zone. It's a place of generally mediocre skill and below replacement value. But it's HIS place and his bosses are willing to pay him to stay there.

Chris Magruder: 5th OFer on a four OF ballclub. This is the type of player who could get hurt and NOT be placed on the DL because there was no plan to use him for another 15 days anyway.

Omar Quintanilla: Injury call-up who made decent but empty contact. Remarkably similar to Juan Pierre, except without the speed, on base ability or overall skill level.

Ramon Vazquez: No speed, no power and an OB that matched '04's BA. Shows that he is perfectly capable of putting up ugly numbers without the benefit of bad luck.

This edition includes a sadly prophetic player comment: Pitches with a perpetual black cloud over his head. The luck harbingers of H%, S% and hr/f are always casting shadows. xERA shows that there is something good here. Will his luck ever turn? Who knows?

The 2007 follow-up: "Rest in peace, Cory Lidle."

2007

"Baseball's "post-steroid" era began with...
° Chris Shelton hitting 9 HRs in his first 13 games.
° Albert Pujols on pace for 79 HRs on June 1
° Ryan Howard making a late run at 61 HRs.

"What better way to turn around public perception of baseball's credibility than with some good, old-fashioned HR races? In '98, MLB discovered that such a media event could cure all ills. If nothing else, it reinforces the fact that players don't need artificial substances in order to hit HRs.

"The beginning of the "post-steroid" era ended with...
° Chris Shelton hitting 7 HRs in his next 119 games.
° Albert Pujols missing a month and hitting *only* 49 HRs
° Ryan Howard getting pitched around to 58 HRs

"...and the public generally losing interest in Barry Bonds. That was the intent all along, wasn't it?"

Player commentaries:

Sal Fasano:
PRO: Occasional power
CON: Everything else
After extensive and painstaking research, it's been determined that there are no existing fantasy game formats that would benefit from use of this player.

Jose Vizcaino: Somehow managed an 11% walk rate to accompany his robust 51 PX. Question to MLB pitchers: what exactly are you afraid of?

Chad Harville: Home plate is that pentagonal thing in front of the catcher. (The catcher is the crouching one with the mask. No, no, not the one in black.) It's been 3 years. He needs reminding.

2008

"Toronto Blue Jays GM J.P. Ricciardi reported in the spring that B.J. Ryan's back was bothering him. The truth was, Ryan had an elbow injury that was serious enough to require surgery, forcing him to miss most of the 2007 season. The *Toronto Star* reported that "the club's original injury report was an intended fabrication" made in order to buy some time.

"Why is this important? First, this was not just an error of omission. Many baseball sources will obfuscate the truth by not revealing all information. In this case, we were deliberately fed *false information*. That is a huge difference.

"The second reason… *Some of you would not have paid $25 for B.J. Ryan if you had known he had a bum elbow.*

"Reliable sources are drying up but we still need accurate information. But maybe we can't expect absolute accuracy. Let's create a scale:

0% **No truth**
J.P. Ricciardi says that B.J. Ryan is perfectly healthy.

25% **Minor truth**
Ricciardi says that Ryan is hurt (true) but lies about the type of injury.

50% **Mixed truth**
Ricciardi says that Ryan is hurt (true) and says that it's an elbow injury (true) but lies about how serious it is.

75% **Mostly truth**
Ricciardi says that Ryan has a serious elbow injury (true) but lies that team doctors say he could be back by June.

100% **Perfect truth**
Ricciardi says that Ryan is a player on the Toronto Blue Jays. Beyond that, I'm not sure that there is such a thing as perfect truth. But it's good to have a goal."

Player commentaries:

Preston Wilson: Another season-ending knee surgery. Now 33, with the knees of a much older man. Club officials are unsure how he came into possession of these knees but there's one angry geezer up in Peoria.

Mike Maroth: The publisher takes no responsibility for any eye damage suffered by the reader when reviewing the "skills" in the box to the left. For safety's sake, look away. This is no joke. I'm serious. Don't look.

2009

"In *Fantasyland,* Sam Walker separated the Tout Wars experts into two groups — those who use laptops and those who are pen-and-paper drafters. But you know something about us pen-and-paper guys? We are not eschewing technology. I believe we just have greater confidence in our abilities to play this game. After two decades of experience, participating in a Rotisserie auction has evolved into a higher level decision-making process that does not need to rely on the hard data.

"I would better liken the process to when Luke Skywalker blew up the Death Star in *Star Wars.* The Force was a level of faith in his abilities that a higher level decision-making process was at work. For me, it's more of a sixth sense (but without the dead people). I just feel it.

"Perhaps the best description of this process was in Malcolm Gladwell's book, *Blink.* He talks about our abilities to understand and react to situations at a glance, and make better decisions than those who have access to mountains of data. We have the ability to make unconscious adjustments to situations long before we are consciously aware that adjustments need to be made. He shows many case studies that prove our abilities to do this."

Player commentaries:

Nick Johnson: It's Nick's Anatomy, Season 9! After thumb ('01), knee, wrist ('02), hand, back ('03), back, cheek ('04), heel ('05), hand, leg ('06), leg ('07) and wrist woes, you'll thrill to all-new injuries. See what part Nick hurts next!

Fernando Cabrera: He's the "three true outcomes" of pitchers. What would happen if he faced Jack Cust? All the fielders could probably go home.

Franklin Morales: Why he lost the strike zone in '08:
- Unexplained myopic spasms.
- Using metric-based strike zone
- Coors Field too close to satellites for GPS to work
- He left it with his car keys.

2010

"There was an essay in the *1990 Baseball Forecaster* entitled, "Mostly sunny, increasing darkness towards evening." Twenty years ago, we did not know nearly as much as we do now, so our forecasting efforts were far more rudimentary. Often, the best we could do was make projections with a broad brush. We've spent the past two decades designing all these intricate forecasting systems, but maybe we've just been spinning our wheels. I believe that obsessing over "I projected he'd hit 33 HRs, you projected he'd hit 30 HRs and he hit 32 HRs, so I win" is a complete waste of brain cells.

"The Mayberry Method is designed to simplify the player evaluation process to a level that will at first seem fuzzy, flawed and imprecise, but you'll actually find to be fuzzy, warm and comfortable. Like Aunt Bea's apple cobbler."

Player commentaries:

Paul Bako: RAR and BPV say that he's getting slightly less crappy as he pushes 40. That's like saying, "a skunk smells less horrible the farther you're away from it." But it still smells bad and you still need to be far away from it.

Ryan Hanigan: All we ask from a $1 catcher is: first, do no harm. That means high ct% and low AB. It sets a BA floor, and worst case, few AB. Like the old Yiddish joke:
　　Lady #1: This food is terrible.
　　Lady #2: And such small portions.

J.C. Romero: Returned from suspension with awful BPIs before missing two months with forearm strain. Still has a nice GB rate, but that's like telling the ugliest girl in the room that she has nice elbows. She does… but still.

Joel Zumaya: Are you feeling lucky? Or desperate? Must pick one.

Tomorrow

Our cherished game in 25 years? One can only imagine.

Organized baseball will likely continue to trudge forward at its typical snail's pace. Progress is not something that this game readily embraces. I often fear that its dogged insistence on clinging to a colorful past will create a painfully pallid future.

Instant replay? Really? Is this even a decision we have to make? You can try to attribute the demise of buggy-whip manufacturers to the absence of a strong union but I'm certainly not stockpiling 5¼″ floppies in anticipation of a retro-tech revival. (And I am *not* anti-union. I am pro-logic.) Baseball needs to come to terms with the 21st century. Tradition has its place but not as an excuse to avoid progress. Milkmen and blood-letters had to learn a new skill; umpires can too.

Perhaps the motto I have used in running this business for 25 years – and we're still here! – sums it up best:

"To stand still is to move backwards."

Our fantasy game in 25 years? The future will likely continue to be driven by technology and capitalism. This is a self-perpetuating, symbiotic relationship that fosters progress. But I don't know if I particularly like this type of progress. We are not too far from being able to watch our fantasy players live on our iPads, swapping them into and out of our lineups after each pitch, and winning cash after every positive outcome.

While I suppose this does constitute forward movement, it's not a terribly innovative path. It's just more Now and, well, More. Now and More.

Perhaps this is a logical response to trying to maintain vitality in an industry that has become dominated by fantasy football. You might wonder why we should even care, but decision-making at the upper-most levels is now driven more by pigskin than cowhide. Baseball is being left with sloppy seconds.

Advertisers throw their money at fantasy football's bigger audience. When major media organizations create new operational models, they always start with football and then retro-fit to baseball. Even look how Sirius/XM satellite radio introduced their new all-fantasy channel — just in time for football season. Odds are they are a wee bit worried whether they can sustain their audience through those lean months of February through June.

In some ways, we have lost our identity; we are Fantasy Football – The Other Game. But we don't deserve to be retro-fitted; we deserve our own solutions. While the game of baseball might be facing elements of obsolescence, one would think fantasy baseball can be more in control of its own destiny. Shouldn't we be more open to *real* change, even if Major League Baseball is not?

That's what I keep pushing for. I am often chastised for promoting a more cerebral game at the expense of all the rushing adrenaline. But to my way of thinking, the direction fantasy is headed – one driven by real-time decision-making – leads to more random outcomes rather than control, making fantasy baseball one more game of chance. This is the exact antithesis of why we started playing these games in the first place.

It may sound like I'm pushing for a return to our roots, just the thing I am chastising MLB for doing. But I see the roots of fantasy — the cerebral game — as a springboard to something more mentally stimulating, not as a means to cling to tradition.

There is a better experience out there, somewhere. Maybe it's with different stats, or different methods to value players, or a completely new structural model for the game. Maybe it's some integration of Rotisserie and simulation, or maybe it *is* a remote, real-time, head-to-head competition. But Now and More are not enough on their own. It has to be something Richer.

My recent work continues to try to find those richer experiences. That's what the Mayberry Method and the new Rotisserie 500 game format are all about. But this is not the end of the journey. None of this can be considered the Holy Grail. It is just another castle to check out, yet one more place where we might find 160 virgins or get showered with bovine.

As for Ron Shandler in the next 25 years, well, I will be going into retirement, eventually. Odds are pretty close to 100% that you won't see my name on the cover of this book when I'm pushing 80. Odds are also pretty good that, while the information in these pages may still be available, you won't be getting it in book form anyway.

But for now, I am still here, and we keep on moving. Forward, forward, forward.

Progress is good.

In the 25th Anniversary Edition

If you are new to the *Forecaster* (and where have you been all these years?), this tome may seem overwhelming. There is a lot of information here. The best place to start is in the new Encyclopedia of Fanalytics, which explains what we are all about. Then jump in anywhere. Close your eyes, flip to any random page, and take it all in.

What's New in 2011?

Encyclopedia of Fanalytics: I recently received an email asking about the relative dollar value for each snake draft round; I then realized that the research from past years was disappearing into the ether. So we've combined our old glossary and Forecaster's Toolbox, and unearthed years of still-relevant research. Then we cut, pasted, rearranged and assembled over 40 pages of vital intelligence.

The Mayberry Method, Take 2: A review, a tweak and the marriage with Portfolio3.

Rotisserie 500: There are incongruities in the rules of the original game that we've accepted for decades and don't even realize they're flawed. Here's a new game that created a buzz at First Pitch Arizona.

Power and Speed Support Charts: We continue to break skill down into its component parts. With the player boxes filled to capacity, these new charts provide additional insight into two important Rotisserie skills.

What's Old from 2010?

In last year's book, we ran a survey and two contests that were hidden in several of the player commentaries. Here are the results:

JOE THURSTON: We have a choice in this book. We can continue to include analyses for these useless players in the interest of completeness, or opt to use the space in a more productive way. Voice your preference. See p.10.

The vote was close. 43% wanted us to keep the Joe Thurstons; 57% said get rid of them. Unfortunately, this was far too close to make a sweeping decision; those who wanted to keep these players had very persuasive arguments, particularly those in deep leagues. They stay.

MIKE GONZALEZ: Though he avoided the DL, back, forearm and elbow issues dogged him all season. Here is the big question: Will he get 35 saves or 35 IP? Cast your vote. Winners placed in drawing for a free '11 book.

32% said he'd get 35 saves. 63% said he'd get 35 IP. 5% broke from the group and selected a choice that wasn't offered... he would get neither 35 saves nor 35 IP. That rebel group was the winner. The random drawing awarded the free book to Gregory Wise of Tampa, FL.

JUAN CASTRO: Inflated h% propped up BA, but xBA tells the true tale. So how exactly has a career .230 hitter with no power or speed racked up 2,500 major league ABs? Most creative answer gets a free copy of next year's book.

We received hundreds of responses, ranging from sagas about Fidel Castro's love child to random nonsense, like "he bakes three different types of brownies." In the end, the winner was a submission that took the phrase "creative answer" beyond the printed page. Steve Katzenmoyer submitted an original musical composition that you can listen to here: http://www.baseballhq.com/JuanCastro.mp3

No hidden contests this year, but we do have a special event that could net you a free Baseball HQ subscription. Check out the back of the book for **PQS Across America**.

Updates

Content Updates: If there are corrections or clarifications on the information in this book, you will find them here: http://www.baseballhq.com/books/bfupdates.shtml

Free Projections Update: As a buyer of this book, you get one free 2011 projections update, available online at http://www.baseballhq.com/books/freeupdate/index.shtml

These are spreadsheet data files, to be posted on or about March 1, 2011. Remember to keep the book handy when you visit as the access codes are hidden within these pages.

Electronic book: The complete PDF version of the Forecaster – plus MS Excel versions of most key charts – is available free to those who bought the book directly through the BaseballHQ.com website. These files will be available in January 2011; contact us if you do not receive information via e-mail about accessing them. If you purchased the book through an online vendor or bookstore, or would like these files earlier, you can purchase them from us for $9.95. Call 1-800-422-7820 for more information.

Beyond the Forecaster

The *Baseball Forecaster* is just the beginning. The following companion products and services are described in more detail in the back of the book.

BaseballHQ.com is our home website. It provides regular updates to everything in this book, including daily updated statistics and projections. A subscription to HQ gets you more than 1,000 articles over the course of the year, cheat sheets customized to your own league's parameters, access to data going back over a decade, plus a ton more.

First Pitch Forums are a series of conferences we run all over the country, where you can meet some of the top industry analysts and network with fellow fantasy leaguers in your area. In late February and early March, we'll be in cities from coast to coast.

RotoHQ.com is a very, very large online library of fantasy strategy essays and tools.

The 6th edition of the *Minor League Baseball Analyst* is by Rob Gordon and Jeremy Deloney. It is a minor league version of the *Forecaster*, with stat boxes for more than 1,000 prospects, and more. Available in January.

We still have copies available of *How to Value Players for Rotisserie Baseball*, Art McGee's ground-breaking book on valuation theory. They are now on closeout at 50% off.

RotoLab is the best draft software on the market, period.

We're on Facebook! http://www.facebook.com/baseballhq "Like" the Baseball HQ page for updates, photos from First Pitch events and links to other important stuff. I have my own personal page as well, but I reserve that for personal stuff (you don't really want to know about my medical procedures, do you?) so I do not accept friend requests from folks I don't know personally. Sorry, it's nothing personal.

That's it, I've run out of space. Now, go read.   — *Ron*

Encyclopedia of Fanalytics

It's all Bill James' fault.

It was his work in the 1980s that forced us to take a look at the game of baseball through a much more colorful lens. It was his work, along with that of analysts Pete Palmer and Thomas Boswell, that prompted me to create *Baseball SuperSTATS* in 1986. It was because of all of them that we discovered the truth: when a batter came to the plate on our television broadcasts, his value could not be summed up by HR, RBI and batting average *alone*. Pitchers were not *only* about wins, losses and ERA.

During the *Forecaster*'s first few years, we presented the work of many analysts and included some gauges of our own. The 1990 edition included the first semblance of a centralized repository for these "new statistics." It was called "Stats du Jour." The first full-fledged glossary appeared in 1994, titled "Official Glossary of Abbreviations, Acronyms, Obscure Formulas, Arbitrary Concepts, Inside Jokes and Government Secrets." To mess with our readers a little more, we put this glossary in the front of the book.

The section was renamed "Encyclopaedia" the following year; it retained that title until 1999 when it was split into a glossary and the Forecaster's Toolbox. It stayed that way for 12 years, through 2010.

This information represents the core of the research that powers everything we do here. And there is *so much stuff*, even more than we could publish each year. We've been bursting at the seams for awhile; it was time to return to an *encyclopedia*, and spell it the way it sounds.

In the next 40-plus pages, we've merged the glossary and Forecaster's Toolbox, and eliminated a bunch of redundancy. We've organized the new Encyclopedia into several logical sections:

1. Fundamentals
2. Batters
3. Pitchers
4. Prospects
5. Gaming

And we've beefed everything up. The Gaming section, in particular, contains tons of important research and benchmarks for playing fantasy, much of which had been relegated to the archives for years.

Enough talking. Jump in. Remember to breathe.

Abbreviations

Avg	Batting average (also BA)
BA	Batting average (also Avg)
BABIP	Batting average on balls-in-play (also h%, H%)
bb%	Walk rate (hitters)
bb/9	Opposition walks per 9 IP (also Ctl)
BF/G	Batters faced per game
BIP	Balls-in-play
BPI	Base performance indicator
BPV	Base performance value
Cmd	Command ratio (K/BB)
Ct%	Contact rate (AB-K)/AB
Ctl	Control ratio (also bb/9)
DIS%	PQS disaster rate
Dom	Dominance ratio (also k/9)
DOM%	PQS domination rate
ERA	Earned run average
Eye	Batting eye (bb/k)
FAAB	Free agent acquisition budget
FB%	Fly ball percentage
G/L/F:	Ground balls, line drives, and fly balls as a percentages of total balls in play (hits *and* outs)
GB%	Ground ball percentage
H%	Hits allowed per balls in play (pitchers)
h%	Hits per balls in play (batters)
HH%	Hard hit balls as a pct. of total balls in play
hr/9	Opposition home runs per 9 IP
hr/f	Home runs hit (batters), or allowed (pitchers), per fly ball
IP/G	Innings pitched per game appearance
k/9	Dominance ratio (also Dom)
LD%	Line drive percentage
LW	Linear weights
LWPwr	Linear weighted power
MLE	Major league equivalency
OB	On base average (batters)
OBA	Opposition batting average (pitchers)
OOB	Opposition on base average (pitchers)
OPS	On base plus slugging average
PA	Plate appearances
PQR	Pure Quality Relief
PQS	Pure Quality Starts
Pw	Linear weighted power
PX	Linear weighted power index
QC	Quality/Consistency Score
qERA	PQS earned run average
R$	Rotisserie value (also 15$, 12$, etc. for specific league sizes)
RAR	Runs above replacement
RC	Runs created
RC/G	Runs created per game
REff%	Reliever efficiency percentage
S%	Strand rate
SBO	Stolen base opportunity percent
Slg	Slugging average
Spd	Statistically Scouted Speed (see page 62)
Sv%	Saves conversion rate
SX	Speed Index
WHIP	Walks plus hits divided by innings pitched
xBA	Expected batting average
xERA	Expected earned run average
xPX	Expected skills-based power index (see page 60)

Fundamentals

What is Fanalytics?

Fanalytics is the scientific approach to fantasy baseball analysis. A contraction of "fantasy" and "analytics," fanalytic gaming might be considered a mode of play that requires a more strategic and quantitative approach to player analysis and game decisions.

The three key elements of fanalytics are:
1. Performance analysis
2. Performance forecasting
3. Gaming analysis

For **performance analysis**, we tap into the vast knowledge of the sabermetric community. Founded by Bill James, this area of study provides objective and progressive new ways to assess skill. What we do in this book is called "component skills analysis." We break down performance into its component parts, then reverse-engineer it back into the traditional measures with which we are more familiar.

Our **forecasting** methodology is one part science and one part art. We start with a computer-generated baseline for each player. We then make subjective adjustments based on a variety of factors, such as discrepancies in skills indicators and historical guidelines gleaned from more than 20 years of research. We don't rely on a rigid model; our method forces us to get our hands dirty. Literally.

You might say that our brand of forecasting is more about finding logical journeys than blind destinations.

Gaming analysis is an integrated approach designed to help us win our fantasy leagues. It takes the knowledge gleaned from the first two elements and adds the strategic and tactical aspect of each specific fantasy game format.

Definitions

Base Performance Indicator (BPI): A statistical formula that measures an isolated aspect of a player's situation-independent raw skill or a gauge that helps capture the effects that random chance has on skill.

Leading Indicator: A statistical formula that can be used to project potential future performance.

Noise: Irrelevant or meaningless pieces of information that can distort the results of an analysis. In news, this is opinion or rumor that can invalidate valuable information. In forecasting, these are unimportant elements of statistical data that can artificially inflate or depress a set of numbers.

Situation Independent: Describing performance that is separate from the context of team, ballpark, or other outside variables. Strikeouts and Walks, as they are unaffected by the performance of a batter's team, are often considered situation independent stats. Conversely, RBIs are situation *dependent* because individual performance varies greatly by the performance of other batters on the team (you can't drive in runs if there is nobody on base). Situation independent gauges are important for us to be able to isolate and judge performance on its own merits.

Soft Skills: BPIs with levels below established minimums for acceptable performance.

Surface Stats: Traditional gauges that the mainstream media uses to measure performance. Stats like batting average, wins, and ERA only touch the surface of a player's skill and often distort the truth. To uncover a player's *true* skill, you have to look at component skills statistics.

Component Skills Analysis

Familiar gauges like HR and ERA have long been used to measure skill. In fact, these gauges only measure the outcome of an individual event, or series of events. They represent statistical output. They are "surface stats."

Raw skill is the talent beneath the stats, the individual elements of a player's makeup. Players use these skills to create the individual events, or components, that we record using measures like HR and ERA. Our approach:

1. It's not about batting average, it's about seeing the ball and making contact. We target hitters based on elements such as their batting eye (walks to strikeouts ratio), how often they make contact and the type of contact they make. We then combine these components into an "expected batting average." By comparing each hitter's actual BA to how he *should* be performing, we can draw conclusions about the future.

2. It's not about home runs, it's about power. From the perspective of a round bat meeting a round ball, it may be only a fraction of an inch at the point of contact that makes the difference between a HR or a long foul ball. When a ball is hit safely, often it is only a few inches that separate a HR from a double. We tend to neglect these facts in our analyses, although the outcomes — the doubles, triples, long fly balls — may be no less a measure of that batter's raw power skill. We must incorporate all these components to paint a complete picture.

3. It's not about ERA, it's about getting the ball over the plate and keeping it in the park. Forget ERA. You want to draft pitchers who walk few batters (control), strike out many (dominance) and succeed at both in tandem (command). You also want pitchers who keep the ball on the ground (because home runs are bad). All of this translates into an "expected ERA" that you can use to compare to a pitcher's actual performance.

4. It's never about wins. For pitchers, winning ballgames is less about skill than it is about offensive support. As such, projecting wins is nearly pointless and valuing hurlers based on their win history is dangerous. Target skill; wins will come.

5. It's not about saves, it's about opportunity first and skills second. While the highest skilled pitchers have the best potential to succeed as closers, they still have to be given the ball with the game on the line in the 9th inning, and that is a decision left to others. Over the past 10 years, about 40% of relievers drafted for saves failed to hold the role for the entire season. The lesson: Don't take chances on draft day. There will always be saves in the free agent pool.

Accounting for "luck"

Luck has been used as a catch-all term to describe random chance. When we use the term here, we're talking about unexplained variances that shape the statistics. While these variances may be random, they are also often measurable and projectable. To get a better read on "luck," we use formulas that capture the external variability of the data.

Through our research and the work of others, we have learned that when raw skill is separated from statistical output, what's remaining is often unexplained variance. The aggregate totals of many of these variances, for all players, is often a constant. For instance, while a pitcher's ERA might fluctuate, the rate at which his opposition's batted balls fall for hits will always tend to be about 30%. Large variances can be expected to regress towards 30%.

Why is all this important? Analysts complain about the lack of predictability of many traditional statistical gauges. The reason they find it difficult is that they are trying to project performance using gauges that are loaded with external noise. Raw skills gauges are more pure and follow better defined trends during a player's career. Then, as we get a better handle on the variances — explained and unexplained — we can construct a complete picture of what a player's statistics really mean.

Baseball Forecasting

Forecasting in perspective

Forecasts. Projections. Predictions. Prognostications. The crystal ball aura of this process conceals the fact it *is* a process. We might define it as "the systematic process of determining likely end results." At its core, it's scientific.

However, the *outcomes* of forecasted events are what is most closely scrutinized, and are used to judge the success or failure of the forecast. That said, as long as the process is sound, the forecast has done the best job it can do. *In the end, forecasting is about analysis, not prophecy.*

Baseball performance forecasting is inherently a high-risk exercise with a very modest accuracy rate. This is because the process involves not only statistics, but also unscientific elements, from random chance to human volatility. And even from within the statistical aspect there are multiple elements that need to be evaluated, from skill to playing time to a host of external variables.

Every system is comprised of the same core elements:

- Players will tend to perform within the framework of past history and/or trends.
- Skills will develop and decline according to age.
- Statistics will be shaped by a player's health, expected role and venue.

While all systems are built from these same elements, they also are constrained by the same limitations. We are all still trying to project a bunch of human beings, each one...

- with his own individual skill set
- with his own rate of growth and decline
- with his own ability to resist and recover from injury
- limited to opportunities determined by other people
- generating a group of statistics largely affected by external noise. For instance, a pitcher's wins require the analysis of not only skill, but the skills of his team's offense, defense, bullpen and the manager's tendencies.

Based on the research of multiple sources, the best accuracy rate that can be attained by any system is about 70%. In fact, a simple system that uses three-year averages adjusted for age ("Marcel the Monkey") can attain a success rate of 65%. This means all the advanced systems are fighting for occupation of the remaining 5%.

But there is a bigger question... *what exactly are we measuring?* When we search for accuracy, what does that mean? In fact, any quest for accuracy is going to run into a brick wall of paradoxes...

- If a slugging average projection is dead on, but the player hits 10 fewer HRs than expected (and likely, 20 more doubles), is that a success or a failure?
- If a projection of hits and walks allowed by a pitcher is on the mark, but the bullpen and defense implodes, and inflates his ERA by a run, is that a success or a failure?
- If the projection of a speedster's rate of stolen base success is perfect, but his team replaces the manager with one that doesn't run, and the player ends up with half as many SBs as expected, is that a success or a failure?
- If a batter is traded to Texas and all the touts project an increase in production, but he posts a statistical line exactly what would have been projected had he not been traded to a hitters' ballpark, is that a success or a failure?
- If the projection for a bullpen closer's ERA, WHIP and peripheral numbers is perfect, but he saves 20 games instead of 40 because the GM decided to bring in a high-priced free agent at the trading deadline, is that a success or a failure?
- If a player is projected to hit .272 in 550 AB and only hits .249, is that a success or failure? Most will say "failure." But wait a minute! The real difference is only two hits per month. That shortfall of 23 points in batting average is because a fielder might have made a spectacular play, or a screaming liner might have been hit right at someone, or a long shot to the outfield might have been held up by the wind... once every 14 games. Does that constitute "failure?"

Even if we were to isolate a single statistic that measures "overall performance" and run our accuracy tests on it, the results will still be inconclusive.

According to OPS, these players are virtually identical:

BATTER	HR	RBI	SB	BA	OBA	SLG	OPS
Fielder,P	32	83	1	.261	.383	.471	**.854**
Howard,R	31	108	1	.276	.346	.505	**.852**
Crawford	19	90	47	.307	.356	.495	**.851**
Ramirez,H	21	76	32	.300	.374	.475	**.850**

If I were to project Prince Fielder-caliber stats and ended up with Carl Crawford numbers, I'd hardly call that an accurate projection, especially if my fantasy team was already well-stocked with speed.

According to Roto dollars, these players are also dead-on:

BATTER	HR	RBI	Runs	SB	BA	R$
Hart,C	31	102	91	7	.283	**$23**
Pagan,A	11	69	80	37	.290	**$23**
Huff,A	26	86	100	7	.290	**$23**
Weeks,R	29	83	112	11	.269	**$23**

It's not so simple for someone to claim they have accurate projections. And so, it is best to focus on the bigger picture, especially when it comes to winning at fantasy baseball.

More on this: "The Great Myths of Projective Accuracy" http://www.baseballhq.com/books/myths.shtml

Baseball Forecaster's forecasting process

We are all about component skills. Our approach is to assemble these evaluators in such a way that they can be used to validate our observations, analyze the relevance of each gauge and project a likely future direction.

In a perfect world, if a player's raw skills improve, then so should his surface stats. If his skills decline, then his stats should follow as well. But, sometimes a player's skill may increase while his surface stats may decline. These variances may be due to a variety of factors.

Our forecasting process is based on the expectation that events tend to move towards universal order. Surface stats will eventually approach their raw skill levels. Unexplained variances will regress to a mean. And from this, we can identify players whose performance may potentially change.

For most of us, this process begins with the previous year's numbers. Last season provides us with a point of reference, so it's a natural way to begin the process of looking at the future.

Component skills analysis allows us to validate last year's numbers. A batter with few HRs but a high linear weighted power level has a good probability of improving his future HR output. A pitcher whose ERA was solid while his command ratio was poor is a good bet for an ERA spike.

Of course, these leading indicators do not always follow the rules. There are more shades of grey than blacks and whites. When indicators are in conflict – for instance, a pitcher who is displaying both a rising strikeout rate and a rising walk rate – then we have to find ways to sort out what these indicators might be saying.

It is often helpful to look at leading indicators in a hierarchy, of sorts. In fact, a hierarchy of the most important pitching base performance indicators might look like this: command (k/bb), control (bb/9), dominance (k/9) and GB/FB rate. For batters, contact rate might top the list, followed by power, walk rate and speed.

Assimilating additional research

Once we've painted the statistical picture of a player's potential, we then use additional criteria and research results to help us add some color to the analysis. These other criteria include the player's health, age, changes in role, ballpark and a variety of other factors. We also use the research results described in the following pages. This research looks at things like traditional periods of peak performance and breakout profiles.

The final element of the process is assimilating the news into the forecast. This is the element that many fantasy leaguers tend to rely on most since it is the most accessible. However, it is also the element that provides the most noise. Players, management and the media have absolute control over what we are allowed to know. Factors such as hidden injuries, messy divorces and clubhouse unrest are routinely kept from us, while we are fed red herrings and media spam. *We will never know the entire truth.*

And so, as long as we do not know all the facts, we cannot dismiss the possibility that any one fact is true, no matter how often the media assures it, deplores it, or ignores it. Don't believe everything you read; use your own judgment. If your observations conflict with what is being reported, that's powerful insight that should not be ignored.

Quite often, all you are reading is just other people's opinions... a manager who believes that a player has what it takes to be a regular or a team physician whose diagnosis is that a player is healthy enough to play. These words from experts have some element of truth, but cannot be wholly relied upon to provide an accurate expectation of future events. As such, it is often helpful to develop an appropriate cynicism for what you read.

For instance, if a player is struggling for no apparent reason and there are denials about health issues, don't dismiss the possibility that an injury does exist. There are often motives for such news to be withheld from the public.

Also remember that nothing lasts forever in major league baseball. *Reality is fluid.* One decision begets a series of events that lead to other decisions. Any reported action can easily be reversed based on subsequent events. My favorite examples are announcements of a team's new bullpen closer. Those are about the shortest realities known to man.

We need the media to provide us with context for our analyses, and the *real* news they provide is valuable intelligence. But separating the news from the noise is difficult. In most cases, the only thing you can trust is how that player actually performs.

Embracing imprecision

Precision in baseball prognosticating is a fool's quest. There are far too many unexpected variables and noise that can render our projections useless. The truth is, the best we can ever hope for is to accurately forecast general tendencies and percentage plays.

However, even when you follow an 80% percentage play, for instance, you will still lose 20% of the time. That 20% is what skeptics use as justification to dismiss prognosticators. The paradox, of course, is that fantasy league titles are often won or lost by those exceptions. Still, long-term success dictates that you always chase the 80% and accept the fact that you will be wrong 20% of the time. Or, whatever that percentage play happens to be.

For fantasy purposes, playing the percentages can take on an even less precise spin. The best projections are often the ones that are just far enough away from the field of expectation to alter decision-making. In other words, it doesn't matter if I project Player X to bat .320 and he only bats .295; it matters that I project .320 and everyone else projects .280. Those who follow my less-accurate projection will go the extra dollar to acquire him in their draft.

Or, perhaps we should evaluate projections based upon their intrinsic value. For instance, coming into 2010, would it have been more important for me to tell you that Albert Pujols was going to hit 40 HRs or that Carlos Gonzalez would hit 25 HRs? By season's end, the Pujols projection would have been more accurate, but the Gonzalez projection — even though it was off by 9 HR — would have been far more *valuable.*

And that has to be enough. Any tout who projects a player's statistics dead-on will have just been lucky with his dart throws that day.

Perpetuity

Forecasting is not an exercise that produces a single set of numbers. It is dynamic, cyclical and ongoing. Conditions are constantly changing and we must react to those changes by adjusting our expectations. A pre-season projection is just a snapshot in time. Once the first batter steps to the plate on Opening Day, that projection has become obsolete. Its value is merely to provide a starting point, a baseline for what is about to occur.

During the season, if a projection appears to have been invalidated by current performance, the process continues. It is then that we need to ask... What went wrong? What conditions have changed? In fact, has *anything* changed? We need to analyze the situation and revise our expectation, if necessary. This process must be ongoing.

About fantasy baseball touts

As a group, there is a strong tendency for all pundits to provide numbers that are publicly palatable, often at the expense of realism. That's because committing to either end of the range of expectation poses a high risk. Few touts will put their credibility on the line like that, even though we all know that those outliers are inevitable. Among our projections, you will find few .350 hitters and 70-steal speedsters. *Someone* is going to post a 2.25 ERA next year, but damned if any of us will commit to that. So we take an easier road. We'll hedge our numbers or split the difference between two equally possible outcomes.

In the world of prognosticating, this is called the *comfort zone*. This represents the outer tolerances for the public acceptability of a set of numbers. In most circumstances, even if the evidence is outstanding, prognosticators will not stray from within the comfort zone.

As for this book, occasionally we do commit to outlying numbers when we feel the data support it. But on the whole, most of the numbers here can be nearly as cowardly as everyone else's. We get around this by providing "color" to the projections in the capsule commentaries. That is where you will find the players whose projection has the best potential to stray beyond the limits of the comfort zone.

As analyst John Burnson once wrote: "The issue is not the success rate for one player, but the success rate for all players. No system is 100% reliable, and in trying to capture the outliers, you weaken the middle and thereby lose more predictive pull than you gain. At some level, everyone is an exception!"

Validating Performance
Performance validation criteria

The following is a set of support variables that helps determine whether a player's statistical output is an accurate reflection of his skills. From this we can validate or refute stats that vary from expectation, essentially asking, is this performance "fact or fluke?"

1. Age: Is the player at the stage of development when we might expect a change in performance?

2. Health: Is he coming off an injury, reconditioned and healthy for the first time in years, or a habitual resident of the disabled list?

3. Minor league performance: Has he shown the potential for greater things at some level of the minors? Or does his minor league history show a poor skill set that might indicate a lower ceiling?

4. Historical trends: Have his skill levels over time been on an upswing or downswing?

5. Component skills indicators: Looking beyond batting averages and ERAs, what do his support ratios look like?

6. Ballpark, team, league: Pitchers going to Texas will see their ERA spike. Pitchers going to PETCO Park will see their ERA improve.

7. Team performance: Has a player's performance been affected by overall team chemistry or the environment fostered by a winning or losing club?

8. Batting stance, pitching style: Has a change in performance been due to a mechanical adjustment?

9. Usage pattern, lineup position, role: Has a change in RBI opportunities been a result of moving further up or down in the batting order? Has pitching effectiveness been impacted by moving from the bullpen to the rotation?

10. Coaching effects: Has the coaching staff changed the way a player approaches his conditioning, or how he approaches the game itself?

11. Off-season activity: Has the player spent the winter frequenting workout rooms or banquet tables?

12. Personal factors: Has the player undergone a family crisis? Experienced spiritual rebirth? Given up red meat? Taken up testosterone?

Skills ownership

Once a player displays a skill, he owns it. That display could occur at any time – earlier in his career, back in the minors, or even in winter ball play. And while that skill may lie dormant after its initial display, the potential is always there for him to tap back into that skill at some point, barring injury or age. That dormant skill can reappear at any time given the right set of circumstances.

Caveats:

1. The initial display of skill must have occurred over an extended period of time. An isolated 1-hit shut-out in Single-A ball amidst a 5.00 ERA season is not enough. The shorter the display of skill in the past, the more likely it can be attributed to random chance. The longer the display, the more likely that any re-emergence is for real.

2. If a player has been suspected of using performance enhancing drugs at any time, all bets are off.

Corollaries:

1. Once a player displays a vulnerability or skills deficiency, he owns that as well. That vulnerability could be an old injury problem, an inability to hit breaking pitches, or just a tendency to go into prolonged slumps.

2. The probability of a player addressing and correcting a skills deficiency declines with each year he allows that deficiency to continue to exist.

Categories of surprises

When a player has an uncharacteristically good or bad season, the likelihood of a repeat can be assessed by categorizing the performance.

Career year: Players who have established a certain level of performance over several years, then suddenly put up exceptional numbers. Career years may be explained from the list of validation criteria, but are usually one-shot deals.

Maturation: Players who have also established a certain level of performance over time, but the performance spike is truly indicative of a positive change in skills and will likely be maintained.

Off year: Players who have an established performance level, then suddenly drop off. This could be an anomaly, an adjustment period or caused by an injury. These players have the potential to bounce back.

Comedown: Players with an established performance level whose drop is indicative of a new level at which they will likely plateau. You'll see this often with aging players.

Opportunity: Players whose rise or decline is not related to skill but to a change in playing time. Often, a role player moves into a full-time job and experiences a marked change in productivity. This can work both ways — he may rise to the occasion, or find that the regular day-to-day grind has an adverse effect on his numbers. Opportunity surprises are created by events like injuries or changes in managerial strategy and can last as long as the opportunity lasts.

No surprise: Players whose rise or decline might have been anticipated. We often form unrealistic expectations about players due to media hype or small samples of past performance, such as with rookies and injured players. The success or failure of unknown, untested or unproven commodities should not be unexpected.

Aberration: Players whose performances cannot be adequately explained by the validation criteria. Chance occurrences do happen. There are stretches in a player's career when a spray hitter might see a few week's worth of fat, juicy homer balls, or a pitcher might face a string of wiffle bats. It just happens, then it stops. Most times, it will never happen again.

Contract year performance *(Tom Mullooly)*

There is a contention that players step up their game when they are playing for a contract. Research looked at contract year players and their performance during that year as compared to career levels. Of the batters and pitchers studied, 53% of the batters performed as if they were on a salary drive, while only 15% of the pitchers exhibited some level of contract year behavior.

How do players fare *after* signing a large contract (minimum $4 million per year)? Research from 2005-2008 revealed that only 30% of pitchers and 22% of hitters exhibited an increase of more than 15% in base performance values after signing a large deal either with their new team, or re-signing with the previous team. But nearly half of the pitchers (49%) and nearly half of the hitters (47%) saw a drop in BPV of more than 15% in the year after signing.

Risk management and reliability grades

Forecasts are constructed with the best data available, but there are factors that can impact the variability around that projection. One way we manage this risk is to assign each player Reliability Grades. The more certainty we see in a data set, the higher the reliability grades assigned to that player. The following variables are evaluated:

Health: Players with a history of staying healthy and off the disabled list are valuable to own. Unfortunately, while the ability to stay healthy can be considered skill, it is not very projectable. We can track the number of days spent on the disabled list and draw only rough conclusions. The grades in the player boxes also include an adjustment for older players, who have a higher likelihood of getting hurt. That is the only forward-looking element of the grade.

"A" level players would have accumulated fewer than 30 days on the Major League DL over the past five years. "F" grades go to those who've spent more than 120 days on the DL. Recent DL stays are given a heavier weight in the calculation.

Playing Time and Experience (PT/Exp): The greater the pool of Major League history to draw from, the greater our ability to construct a viable forecast. Length of service is important, as is length of consistent service. So players who bounce up and down from the Majors to the minors are higher risk players. And rookies are all high risk.

For batters, we simply track plate appearances. Major league PAs have greater weight than minor league PAs. "A" level players would have averaged at least 550 major league PA per year over the past three years. "F" graded players averaged fewer than 250 major league PA per year.

For pitchers, workload can be a double-edged sword. On one hand, small IP samples are deceptive in providing a read on a pitcher's true potential. Even a consistent 65-inning reliever can be considered higher risk; just one bad outing can skew an entire season's work.

On the flipside, high workload levels also need to be monitored, especially in the formative years of a pitcher's career. Exceeding those levels elevates the risk of injury, burnout, or breakdown. So, tracking workload must be done within a range of innings. The grades capture this.

Consistency: Consistent performers are easier to project and garner higher reliability grades. Players that mix mediocrity with occasional flashes of brilliance or badness generate higher risk projections. Even those who exhibit a consistent upward or downward trend cannot be considered truly consistent as we do not know whether those trends will continue. Typically, they don't.

"A" level players are those whose runs created per game level (xERA for pitchers) has fluctuated by less than half a run during each of the past three years. "F" grades go to those whose RC/G or xERA has fluctuated by two runs or more.

Remember that these grades have nothing to do with *quality* of performance; they strictly refer to confidence in our expectations. So a grade of **AAA** for Joe Saunders, for instance, only means that there is a high probability he will perform as poorly as we've projected.

Reliability and age

Peak batting reliability occurs at ages 29 and 30, followed by a minor decline for four years. So, to draft the most reliable batters, and maximize the odds of returning at least par value on your investments, you should target the age range of 28-34.

The most reliable age range for pitchers is 29-34. While we are forever looking for "sleepers" and hot prospects, it is very risky to draft any pitcher under 27 or over 35.

Health Analysis

Disabled list statistics

Year	#Players	3yr Avg	DL Days	3yr Avg
2002	337		23,724	
2003	351		22,118	
2004	382	357	25,423	23,755
2005	356	363	24,016	23,852
2006	347	362	22,472	23,970
2007	404	369	28,524	25,004
2008	422	391	28,187	26,394
2009	408	411	26,252	27,654
2010	393	408	22,911	25,783

D.L. days as a leading indicator *(Bill Macey)*

Players who are injured in one year are likely to be injured in a subsequent year:

% DL batters in Year 1 who are also DL in year 2	38%
Under age 30	36%
Age 30 and older	41%
% DL batters in Year 1 and 2 who are also DL in year 3	54%
% DL pitchers in Year 1 who are also DL in year 2	43%
Under age 30	45%
Age 30 and older	41%
% DL pitchers in Yr 1 and 2 who are also DL in year 3	41%

Previously injured players also tend to spend a longer time on the DL. The average number of days on the DL was 51 days for batters and 73 days for pitchers. For the subset of these players who get hurt again the following year, the average number of days on the DL was 58 days for batters and 88 days for pitchers.

Spring training spin *(Dave Adler)*

Spring training sound bites raise expectations among fantasy leaguers, but how much of that "news" is really "noise?" Thanks to a summary listed at RotoAuthority.com, we were able to compile the stats for 2009. Verdict: Noise.

BATTERS	No.	IMPROVED	DECLINED
Weight change	30	33%	30%
Fitness program	3	0%	67%
Eye surgery	6	50%	33%
Plans more SB	6	17%	33%

PITCHERS	No.	IMPROVED	DECLINED
Weight change	18	44%	44%
Fitness program	4	50%	50%
Eye surgery	2	0%	50%
New pitch	5	60%	40%

In-Season Analysis

April performance as a leading indicator

We isolated all players who earned at least $10 more or $10 less than we had projected in March. Then we looked at the April stats of these players to see if we could have picked out the $10 outliers after just one month.

	Identifiable in April
Earned $10+ more than projected	
BATTERS	39%
PITCHERS	44%
Earned -$10 less than projected	
BATTERS	56%
PITCHERS	74%

Nearly three out of every four pitchers who earned at least $10 less than projected also struggled in April. For all the other surprises — batters or pitchers — April was not a strong leading indicator. Another look:

	Pct.
Batters who finished +$25	45%
Pitchers who finished +$20	44%
Batters who finished under $0	60%
Pitchers who finished under -$5	78%

April surgers are less than a 50/50 proposition to maintain that level all season. Those who finished April at the bottom of the roto rankings were more likely to continue struggling, especially pitchers. In fact, of those pitchers who finished April with a value *under -$10,* 91% finished the season in the red. Holes are tough to dig out of.

Courtship period

Any time a player is put into a new situation, he enters into what we might call a *courtship period.* This period might occur when a player switches leagues, or switches teams. It could be the first few games when a minor leaguer is called up. It could occur when a reliever moves into the rotation, or when a lead-off hitter is moved to another spot in the lineup. There is a team-wide courtship period when a manager is replaced. Any external situation that could affect a player's performance sets off a new decision point in evaluating that performance.

During this period, it is difficult to get a true read on how a player is going to ultimately perform. He is adjusting to the new situation. Things could be volatile during this time.

For instance, a role change that doesn't work could spur other moves. A rookie hurler might buy himself a few extra starts with a solid debut, even if he has questionable skills.

It is best not to make a decision on a player who is going through a courtship period. Wait until his stats stabilize. Don't cut a struggling pitcher in his first few starts after a managerial change. Don't pick up a hitter who smacks a pair of HRs in his first game after having been traded. Unless, of course, talent and track record say otherwise.

Half-season fallacies

A popular exercise at the midpoint of each season is to analyze those players who are *consistent* first half to second half surgers or faders. There are several fallacies with this analytical approach.

1. Half-season consistency is rare. There are very few players who show consistent changes in performance from one half of the season to the other.

Research results from a three-year study conducted in the late-1990s: The test groups... batters with min. 300 AB full season, 150 AB first half, and pitchers with min. 100 IP full season, 50 IP first half. Of those groups (size noted):

3-year consistency in	BATTERS (98)	PITCHERS (42)
1 stat category	40%	57%
2 stat categories	18%	21%
3 stat categories	3%	5%

When the analysis was stretched to a fourth year, only 1% of all players showed consistency in even one category.

2. Analysts often use false indicators. Situational statistics provide us with tools that can be misused. Several sources offer up 3 and 5-year stats intended to paint a picture of a long-term performance. Some analysts look at a player's half-season swing over that multi-year period and conclude that he is demonstrating consistent performance.

The fallacy is that those multi-year scans may not show any consistency at all. They are not individual season performances but *aggregate* performances. A player whose 5-year batting average shows a 15-point rise in the 2nd half, for instance, may actually have experienced a BA *decline* in several of those years, a fact that might have been offset by a huge BA rise in one of the years.

3. It's arbitrary. The season's midpoint is an arbitrary delineator of performance swings. Some players are slow starters and might be more appropriately evaluated as pre-May 1 and post-May 1. Others bring their game up a notch with a pennant chase and might see a performance swing with August 15 as the cut-off. Each player has his own individual tendency, if, in fact, one exists at all. There's nothing magical about mid-season as the break point, and certainly not over a multi-year period.

Half-season tendencies

Despite the above, it stands to reason *logically* that there might be some underlying tendencies on a more global scale, first half to second half. In fact, one would think that the player population as a whole might *decline in performance* as the season drones on. There are many variables that might contribute to a player wearing down — workload, weather, boredom — and the longer a player is on the field, the higher the likelihood that he is going to get hurt. A recent 5-year study uncovered the following tendencies:

Batting

Overall, batting skills held up pretty well, half to half. There was a 5% erosion of playing time, likely due, in part, to September roster expansion..

Power: First half power studs (20 HRs in 1H) saw a 10% drop-off in the second half. 34% of first half 20+ HR hitters hit 15 or fewer in the second half and only 27% were able to improve on their first half output.

Speed: Second half speed waned as well. About 26% of the 20+ SB speedsters stole *at least 10 fewer bases* in the second half. Only 26% increased their second half SB output at all.

Batting average: 60% of first half .300 hitters failed to hit .300 in the second half. Only 20% showed any second half improvement at all. As for 1H strugglers, managers tended to stick with their full-timers despite poor starts. Nearly one in five of the sub-.250 1H hitters managed to hit *more than .300* in the second half.

Pitching

Overall, there was some slight erosion in innings and ERA despite marginal improvement in some peripherals.

ERA: For those who pitched at least 100 innings in the first half, ERAs rose an average of 0.40 runs in the 2H. Of those with first half ERAs less than 4.00, only 49% were able to maintain a sub-4.00 ERA in the second half.

Wins: Pitchers who won 18 or more games in a season tended to pitch *more* innings in the 2H and had slightly better peripherals.

Saves: Of those closers who saved 20 or more games in the first half, only 39% were able to post 20 or more saves in the 2H, and 26% posted fewer than 15 saves. Aggregate ERAs of these pitchers rose from 2.45 to 3.17, half to half.

Teams

Johnson Effect *(Bryan Johnson)*: Teams whose actual won/loss record exceeds or falls short of their statistically projected record in one season will tend to revert to the level of their projection in the following season.

Law of Competitive Balance *(Bill James)*: The level at which a team (or player) will address its problems is inversely related to its current level of success. Low performers will tend to make changes to improve; high performers will not. This law explains the existence of the Plexiglass and Whirlpool Principles.

Plexiglass Principle *(Bill James)*: If a player or team improves markedly in one season, it will likely decline in the next. The opposite is true but not as often (because a poor performer gets fewer opportunities to rebound).

Whirlpool Principle *(Bill James)*: All team and player performances are forcefully drawn to the center. For teams, that center is a .500 record. For players, it represents their career average level of performance.

Other Diamonds

The Fanalytic Fundamentals

1. This is not a game of accuracy or precision. It is a game of human beings and tendencies.

2. This is not a game of projections. It is a game of market value versus real value.

3. Draft skills, not stats.

4. A player's ability to post acceptable stats despite lousy BPIs will eventually run out.

5. Once you display a skill, you own it.

6. Virtually every player is vulnerable to a month of aberrant performance. Or a year.

7. Exercise excruciating patience.

Aging Axioms

1. Age is the only variable for which we can project a rising trend with 100% accuracy. (Or, age never regresses.)

2. The aging process slows down for those who maintain a firm grasp on the strike zone. Plate patience and pitching command can preserve any waning skill they have left.

3. Negatives tend to snowball as you age.

Steve Avery List: Players who hang onto MLB rosters for six years searching for a skill level they only had for three.

Bylaws of Badness

1. Some players are better than an open roster spot, but not by much.

2. Some players have bad years because they are unlucky. Others have *many* bad years because they are bad... and lucky.

George Brett Path to Retirement: Get out while you're still putting up good numbers and the public perception of you is favorable. Like Mike Mussina. And Billy Wagner.
(See Steve Carlton Path to Retirement.)

Steve Carlton Path to Retirement: Hang around the major leagues long enough for your numbers to become so wretched that people begin to forget your past successes.
(See George Brett Path to Retirement.)

Among the many players who have taken this path include Jose Mesa, Doc Gooden, Matt Morris, Nomar Garciaparra and of course, Steve Carlton. Current players who look to be on the same course include Luis Castillo, Todd Helton, Andruw Jones and Manny Ramirez.

Christie Brinkley Law of Statistical Analysis: Never get married to the model.

Employment Standards

1. If you are right-brain dominant, own a catcher's mitt and are under 40, you will always be gainfully employed.

2. Some teams believe that it is better to employ a player with *any* experience because it has to be better than the devil they don't know.

3. It's not so good to go pffft in a contract year.

Laws of Prognosticating Perspective

- Berkeley's 17th Law: A great many problems do not have accurate answers, but do have approximate answers, from which sensible decisions can be made.
- Ashley-Perry Statistical Axiom #4: A complex system that works is invariably found to have evolved from a simple system that works.
- Baseball Variation of Harvard Law: Under the most rigorously observed conditions of skill, age, environment, statistical rules and other variables, a ballplayer will perform as he damn well pleases.

Brad Fullmer List: Players whose leading indicators indicate upside potential, year after year, but consistently fail to reach that full potential. Ricky Nolasco is at the top of the list right now.

Ceiling: The highest professional level at which a player maintains acceptable BPIs. Also, the peak performance level that a player will likely reach, given his BPIs.

Good Luck Truism: Good luck is rare and everyone has more of it than you do. <u>That's</u> <u>the</u> <u>law</u>.

The Gravity Principles

1. It is easier to be crappy than it is to be good.

2. All performance starts at zero, ends at zero and can drop to zero at any time.

3. The odds of a good performer slumping are far greater than the odds of a poor performer surging.

4. Once a player is in a slump, it takes several 3-for-5 days to get out of it. Once he is on a streak, it takes a single 0-for-4 day to begin the downward spiral.

Corollary: Once a player is in a slump, not only does it take several 3-for-5 days to get out of it, but he also has to get his name back on the lineup card.

5. Eventually all performance comes down to earth. It may take a week, or a month, or may not happen until he's 45, but eventually it's going to happen.

Health Homilies

1. Staying healthy is a skill (and "DL Days" should be a Rotisserie category).

2. A $40 player can get hurt just as easily as a $5 player but is eight times tougher to replace.

3. Chronically injured players never suddenly get healthy.

4. There are two kinds of pitchers: those that are hurt and those that are not hurt... yet.

5. Players with back problems are always worth $10 less.

6. "Opting out of surgery" usually means it's coming anyway, just later.

The Health Hush: Players get hurt and potentially have a lot to lose, so there is an incentive for them to hide injuries. HIPAA laws restrict the disclosure of health information. Team doctors and trainers have been instructed not to talk with the media. So, when it comes to information on a player's health status, we're all pretty much in the dark.

Hidden Injury Syndrome

1. Player's skills implode.

2. Team and player deny injury.

3. More unexplained struggles.

4. Injury revealed; surgery follows.

Law of Injury Estimation (Westheimer's Rule): To calculate an accurate projection of the amount of time a player will be out of action due to injury, first take the published time estimate, double it and change the unit of measure to the next highest unit. Thus, a player estimated to be out two weeks will actually be out four months.

The Livan Level: The point when a player's career Runs Above Replacement level has dropped so far below zero that he has effectively cancelled out any possible remaining future value. (Similarly, the Dontrelle Demarcation.)

Monocarp: A player whose career consists of only one productive season.

Paradoxes and Conundrums

1. Is a player's improvement in performance from one year to the next a point in a growth trend, an isolated outlier or a complete anomaly?

2. A player can play through an injury, post rotten numbers and put his job at risk... or... he can admit that he can't play through an injury, allow himself to be taken out of the lineup/rotation, and put his job at risk.

3. Did irregular playing time take its toll on the player's performance or did poor performance force a reduction in his playing time?

4. Is a player only in the game versus right-handers because he has a true skills deficiency versus left-handers? Or is his poor performance versus left-handers because he's never given a chance to face them?

5. The problem with stockpiling bench players in the hope that one pans out is that you end up evaluating performance using data sets that are too small to be reliable.

6. There are players who could give you 20 stolen bases if they got 400 AB. But if they got 400 AB, they would likely be on a bad team that wouldn't let them steal.

Quack!: An exclamation in response to the educated speculation that a player has used performance enhancing drugs. While it is rare to have absolute proof, there is often enough information to suggest that, "if it looks like a duck and quacks like a duck, then odds are it's a duck."

Tenets of Optimal Timing

1. If a second half fader had put up his second half stats in the first half and his first half stats in the second half, then he probably wouldn't even have had a second half.

2. Fast starters can often buy six months of playing time out of one month of productivity.

3. Poor 2nd halves don't get recognized until it's too late.

4. "Baseball is like this. Have one good year and you can fool them for five more, because for five more years they expect you to have another good one." — Frankie Frisch

The Three True Outcomes

1. Strikeouts
2. Walks
3. Home runs

The Three True Handicaps

1. Has power but can't make contact.
2. Has speed but can't hit safely.
3. Has potential but is too old.

UGLY (Unreasonable Good Luck Year): The driving force behind every winning team. It's what they really mean when they say "winning ugly."

Walbeckian: Possessing below replacement level stats, as in "Brandon Wood's season was downright Walbeckian." *Alternate usage:* "Brandon Wood's stats were so bad that I might as well have had Walbeck in there."

Wasted talent: A player with a high level skill that is negated by a deficiency in another skill. For instance, base path speed can be negated by poor on base ability. Pitchers with strong arms can be wasted because home plate is an elusive concept to them.

Zombie: A player who is indestructible, continuing to get work, year-after-year, no matter how dead his BPIs are. Like Seth McClung.

Batters

Batting Eye, Contact and Batting Average

Batting average (BA, or Avg)

This is where it starts. BA is a grand old nugget that has long outgrown its usefulness. We revere .300 hitting superstars and scoff at .250 hitters, yet the difference between the two is 1 hit every 20 ABs. This 1 hit every five games is not nearly the wide variance that exists in our perceptions of what it means to be a .300 or .250 hitter. BA is a poor evaluator of performance in that it neglects the offensive value of the base on balls and assumes that all hits are created equal.

Batting average perception

Early season batting average strugglers who surge later in the year get no respect because they have to live with the weight of their early numbers all season long. Conversely, quick starters who fade late get far more accolades than they deserve.

For instance, take Julio Borbon's 2010 month-by-month batting averages. Perception, which is typically based solely on a player's cumulative season stat line, was that he struggled with his batting average pretty much all season. Reality is different. He had only one truly horrible month, and it happened to occur in April. How many people knew he batted .292 from May 1 on?

Month	BA	Cum BA
April	.191	.191
May	.278	.236
June	.356	.282
July	.222	.269
August	.255	.267
Sept-Oct	.309	.276

Walk rate (bb%)
(BB / (AB + BB))

A measure of a batter's plate patience. **BENCHMARKS:** The best batters will have levels more than 10%. Those with poor plate patience will have levels of 5% or less.

On base average (OB)
(H + BB) / (AB + BB)

Addressing a key deficiency with BA, OB gives value to events that get batters on base, but are not hits. An OB of .350 can be read as "this batter gets on base 35% of the time." When a run is scored, there is no distinction made as to how that runner reached base. So, two thirds of the time — about how often a batter comes to the plate with the bases empty — a walk really is as good as a hit.

The official version of this formula includes hit batsmen. We do not include it because our focus is on skills-based gauges; research has shown that HBP is not a measure of batting skill but of pitching deficiency. **BENCHMARKS:** We know what a .300 hitter is, but what represents "good" for OB? That comparable level would likely be .400, with .275 representing the comparable level of futility.

Ground ball, fly ball, line drive percentages (G/F/L)

The percentage of all Balls-in-Play that are hit on the ground, in the air and as line drives. For batters, increased fly ball tendency may foretell a rise in power skills; increased line drive tendency may foretell an improvement in batting average. For a pitcher, the ability to keep the ball on the ground can contribute to his statistical output exceeding his demonstrated skill level.

*BIP Type	Total%	Out%
Ground ball	45%	72%
Line drive	20%	28%
Fly ball	35%	85%
TOTAL	*100%*	*69%*

* Data only includes fieldable balls and is net of HRs.

Batting eye (Eye)
(Walks / Strikeouts)

A measure of a player's strike zone judgment. **BENCHMARKS:** The best hitters have eye ratios more than 1.00 (indicating more walks than strikeouts) and are the most likely to be among a league's .300 hitters. Ratios less than 0.50 represent batters who likely also have lower BAs.

Batting eye as a leading indicator

There is a strong correlation between strike zone judgment and batting average. However, research shows that this is more descriptive than predictive:

Batting Eye	Batting Average				
	2006	2007	2008	2009	2010
0.00 - 0.25	.251	.250	.242	.239	.235
0.26 - 0.50	.267	.265	.261	.259	.260
0.51 - 0.75	.279	.276	.273	.272	.264
0.76 - 1.00	.286	.280	.280	.274	.272
1.01 and over	.287	.305	.285	.292	.280

Note that the lower offensive levels in 2010 shifted the trend about 10 points downward. We can create percentage plays for the different levels:

For Eye Levels of	Pct who bat .300+	.250-
0.00 - 0.25	7%	39%
0.26 - 0.50	14%	26%
0.51 - 0.75	18%	17%
0.76 - 1.00	32%	14%
1.01 - 1.50	51%	9%
1.51 +	59%	4%

Any batter with an eye ratio more than 1.50 has about a 4% chance of hitting less than .250 over 500 at bats.

Of all .300 hitters, those with ratios of at least 1.00 have a 65% chance of repeating as .300 hitters. Those with ratios less than 1.00 have less than a 50% chance of repeating.

Only 4% of sub-.250 hitters with ratios less than 0.50 will mature into .300 hitters the following year.

In a 1995-2000 study, only 37 batters hit .300-plus with a sub-0.50 eye ratio over at least 300 AB in a season. Of this group, 30% were able to accomplish this feat on a consistent basis. For the other 70%, this was a short-term aberration.

Contact rate (ct%)

((AB - K) / AB)

Measures a batter's ability to get wood on the ball and hit it into the field of play. **BENCHMARKS:** Those batters with the best contact skill will have levels of 90% or better. The hackers of society will have levels of 75% or less.

Contact rate as a leading indicator

The more often a batter makes contact with the ball, the higher the likelihood that he will hit safely. Note how the lower offense levels in 2010 flattened the trend.

	Batting Average				
Contact Rate	**2006**	**2007**	**2008**	**2009**	**2010**
0% - 60%	.181	.204	.210	.189	.187
61% - 65%	.220	.228	.226	.229	.235
66% - 70%	.251	.237	.235	.241	.236
71% - 75%	.256	.250	.250	.247	.254
76% - 80%	.270	.269	.262	.263	.256
81% - 85%	.274	.277	.273	.275	.271
86% - 90%	.287	.284	.284	.281	.273
Over 90%	.295	.289	.285	.287	.270

Contact rate and walk rate as leading indicators

A matrix of contact rates and walk rates can provide expectation benchmarks for a player's batting average:

		bb%			
		0-5	**6-10**	**11-15**	**16+**
ct%	**65-**	.179	.195	.229	.237
	66-75	.190	.248	.254	.272
	76-85	.265	.267	.276	.283
	86+	.269	.279	.301	.309

A contact rate of 65% or lower offers virtually no chance for a player to hit even .250, no matter how high a walk rate he has. The .300 hitters most often come from the group with a minimum 86% contact and 11% walk rate.

Balls-in-play (BIP)

(AB – K)

The total number of batted balls that are hit fair, both hits and outs. An analysis of how these balls are hit – on the ground, in the air, hits, outs, etc. – can provide analytical insight, from player skill levels to the impact of luck on statistical output.

Batting average on balls in play *(Voros McCracken)*

(H—HR) / (AB – HR - K)

Also called Hit rate (h%). The percent of balls hit into the field of play that fall for hits. **BENCHMARK:** Every hitter establishes his own individual hit rate that stabilizes over time. A batter whose seasonal hit rate varies significantly from the h% he has established over the preceding three seasons (variance of at least +/- 3%) is likely to improve or regress to his individual H% mean (with over-performer declines more likely and sharper than under-performer recoveries). Three-year h% levels strongly predict a player's h% the following year.

P/PA as a leading indicator for BA *(Paul Petera)*

The art of working the count has long been considered one of the more crucial aspects of good hitting. It is common knowledge that the more pitches a hitter sees, the greater opportunity he has to reach base safely.

P/PA	OBA	BA
4.00+	.360	.264
3.75-3.99	.347	.271
3.50-3.74	.334	.274
Under 3.50	.321	.276

Generally speaking, the more pitches seen, the lower the BA, but the higher the OBA. But what about the outliers, those players that bucked the trend in year #1?

	YEAR TWO	
	BA Improved	**BA Declined**
Low P/PA and Low BA	77%	23%
High P/PA and High BA	21%	79%

In these scenarios, there was a strong tendency for performance to normalize in year #2.

Expected batting average *(John Burnson)*

$$xCT\% * [xH1\% + xH2\%]$$
where
$$xH1\% = GB\% \times [0.0004\ PX + 0.062\ ln(SX)]$$
$$+ LD\% \times [0.93 - 0.086\ ln(SX)]$$
$$+ FB\% \times 0.12$$
and
$$xH2\% = FB\% \times [0.0013\ PX - 0.0002\ SX - 0.057]$$
$$+ GB\% \times [0.0006\ PX]$$

A hitter's batting average as calculated by multiplying the percentage of balls put in play (contact rate) by the chance that a ball in play falls for a hit. The likelihood that a ball in play falls for a hit is a product of the speed of the ball and distance it is hit (PX), the speed of the batter (SX), and distribution of ground balls, fly balls, and line drives. We further split it out by non-homerun hit rate (xH1%) and homerun hit rate (xH2%). **BENCHMARKS:** In general, xBA should approximate batting average fairly closely. Those hitters who have large variances between the two gauges are candidates for further analysis. **LIMITATION:** xBA tends to understate a batter's true value if he is an extreme ground ball hitter (G/F ratio over 3.0) with a low PX. These players are not inherently weak, but *choose* to take safe singles rather than swing for the fences.

Expected batting average variance

xBA - BA

The variance between a batter's BA and his xBA is a measure of over or underachievement. A positive variance indicates the potential for a batter's BA to rise. A negative variance indicates the potential for BA to decline. **BENCHMARK:** Discount variances that are less than 20 points. Any variance more than 30 points is regarded as a strong indicator of future change.

Power

Slugging average (Slg)

(Singles + (2 x Doubles) + (3 x Triples) + (4 x HR)) / AB

A measure of the total number of bases accumulated (or the minimum number of runners' bases advanced) per at bat. It is a misnomer; it is not a true measure of a batter's slugging ability because it includes singles. Slg also assumes that each type of hit has proportionately increasing value (i.e. a double is twice as valuable as a single, etc.) which is not true. For instance, with the bases loaded, a HR always scores four runs, a triple always scores three, but a double could score two or three and a single could score one, or two, or even three. **BENCHMARKS:** Top batters will have levels over .500. The bottom batters will have levels less than .300.

Fly ball tendency and power *(Mat Olkin)*

There is a proven connection between a hitter's ground ball-fly ball tendencies and his power production.

1. Extreme ground ball hitters generally do not hit for much power. It's almost impossible for a hitter with a ground/fly ratio over 1.80 to hit enough fly balls to produce even 25 HRs in a season. However, this does not mean that a low G/F ratio necessarily guarantees power production. Some players have no problem getting the ball into the air, but lack the strength to reach the fences consistently.

2. Most batters' ground/fly ratios stay pretty steady over time. Most year-to-year changes are small and random, as they are in any other statistical category. A large, sudden change in G/F, on the other hand, can signal a conscious change in plate approach. And so...

3. If a player posts high G/F ratios in his first few years, he probably isn't ever going to hit for all that much power.

4. When a batter's power suddenly jumps, his G/F ratio often drops at the same time.

5. Every so often, a hitter's ratio will drop significantly even as his power production remains level. In these rare cases, impending power development is likely, since the two factors almost always follow each other.

Home runs to fly ball rate *(HR / F)*

The percent of fly balls that are hit for HRs.

HR/F rate as a leading indicator *(Joshua Randall)*

Each batter establishes an individual home run to fly ball rate that stabilizes over rolling three-year periods; those levels strongly predict the HR/F in the subsequent year. A batter who varies significantly from his HR/F is likely to regress toward his individual HR/F mean, with over-performance decline more likely and more severe than under-performance recovery.

P/PA as a leading indicator for PX *(Paul Petera)*

Working the count has a positive effect on power.

P/PA	PX
4.00+	123
3.75-3.99	108
3.50-3.74	96
Under 3.50	84

As for the year #1 outliers:

	YEAR TWO	
	PX Improved	PX Declined
Low P/PA and High PX	11%	89%
High P/PA and Low PX	70%	30%

In these scenarios, there was a strong tendency for performance to normalize in year #2

Opposite field home runs *(Ed DeCaria)*

From 2001-2008, nearly 75% of all HRs were hit to the batter's pull field, with the remaining 25% distributed roughly evenly between straight away and opposite field. Left-handers accomplished the feat slightly more often than right-handers (including switch-hitters hitting each way), and younger hitters did it significantly more often than older hitters. The trend toward pulled home runs was especially strong after age 36.

Power Quartile	AB/HR	Opp. Field	Straight Away	Pull Field
Top 25%	17.2	15.8%	16.0%	68.2%
2nd 25%	28.0	10.7%	12.2%	77.0%
3rd 25%	44.1	8.9%	10.0%	81.1%
Bot 25%	94.7	5.4%	5.9%	88.7%

Opposite field HRs serve as a strong indicator of overall home run power (AB/HR). Power hitters (smaller AB/HR rates) hit a far higher percentage of their HR to the opposite field or straight away (over 30%). Conversely, non-power hitters hit almost 90% of their home runs to their pull field.

Performance in Y2-Y4 (% of Group)

Y1 Trigger	<=30 AB/HR	5.5+ RC/G	$16+ R$
2+ OppHR	69%	46%	33%
<2 OppHR	29%	13%	12%

Players who hit just two or more OppHR in one season were 2-3 times as likely as those who hit zero or one OppHR to sustain strong AB/HR rates, RC/G levels, or R$ values over the following three seasons.

Y2-Y4 Breakout Performance
(% Breakout by Group, Age <=26 Only)

Y1 Trigger	AB/HR >35 to <=30	RC/G <4.5 to 5.5+	R$ <$8 to $16+
2+ OppHR	32%	21%	30%
<2 OppHR	23%	12%	10%

Roughly one of every 3-4 batters age 26 or younger experiences a *sustained three-year breakout* in AB/HR, RC/G or R$ after a season in which they hit 2+ OppHR, far better odds than the one in 8-10 batters who experience a breakout without the 2+ OppHR trigger.

Linear weighted power (LWPwr)

((Doubles x .8) + (Triples x .8) + (HR x 1.4)) / (At bats- K) x 100

A variation of the linear weights formula that considers only events that are measures of a batter's pure power. **BENCHMARKS:** Top sluggers typically top the 17 mark. Weak hitters will have a LWPwr level of less than 10.

Linear weighted power index (PX)

(Batter's LWPwr / League LWPwr) x 100

LWPwr is presented in this book in its normalized form to get a better read on a batter's accomplishment in each year. For instance, a 30-HR season today is much more of an accomplishment than 30 HRs hit in a higher offense year like 2003. **BENCHMARKS:** A level of 100 equals league average power skills. Any player with a value more than 100 has above average power skills, and those more than 150 are the Slugging Elite.

Power breakout profile

It is not easy to predict which batters will experience a power spike. We can categorize power breakouts to determine the likelihood of a player taking a step up or of a surprise performer repeating his feat. Possibilities:

- Increase in playing time
- History of power skills at some time in the past
- Redistribution of already demonstrated extra base hit power
- Normal skills growth
- Situational breakouts, particularly in hitter-friendly venues
- Increased fly ball tendency
- Use of illegal performance-enhancing substances
- Miscellaneous unexplained variables

Speed

Wasted talent on the base paths

We refer to some players as having "wasted talent," a high level skill that is negated by a deficiency in another skill. Among these types are players who have blazing speed that is negated by a sub-.300 on base average.

These players can have short-term value. However, their stolen base totals are tied so tightly to their "green light" that any change in managerial strategy could completely erase that value. A higher OB mitigates that downside; the good news is that plate patience *can* be taught.

Players in 2010 who had at least 20 SBs with an OB less than .300, and whose SB output could be at risk, are Erick Aybar (22 SB, .299) and Trevor Crowe (20 SB, .297).

Speed score *(Bill James)*

A measure of the various elements that comprise a runner's speed skills. Although this formula (a variation of James' original version) may be used as a leading indicator for stolen base output, SB attempts are controlled by managerial strategy which makes speed score somewhat less valuable. The new Statistically Scouted Speed value (see the Research Abstracts section for more details) is proving to be a more accurate measure of raw speed skill.

Speed score is calculated as the mean value of the following four elements...

1. Stolen base efficiency = $(((SB + 3)/(SB + CS + 7)) - .4) \times 20$
2. Stolen base freq. = *Square root of $((SB + CS)/(Singles + BB))) / .07$*
3. Triples rating = $(3B / (AB - HR - K))$ and the result assigned a value based on the following chart:

< 0.001	0	0.0105	6
0.001	1	0.013	7
0.0023	2	0.0158	8
0.0039	3	0.0189	9
0.0058	4	0.0223+	10
0.008	5		

4. Runs scored as a percentage of times on base = $(((R - HR) / (H + BB - HR)) - .1) / .04$

Speed score index (SX)

(Batter's Spd / League Spd) x 100

Normalized speed scores get a better read on a runner's accomplishment in context. A level of 100 equals league average speed skill. Values more than 100 indicate above average skill, more than 200 represent the Fleet of Feet Elite.

Stolen base opportunity per cent (SBO)

(SB + CS) / (BB + Singles)

A rough approximation of how often a base-runner attempts a stolen base. Provides a comparative measure for players on a given team and, as a team measure, the propensity of a manager to give a "green light" to his runners.

Overall Performance Analysis

On base plus slugging average (OPS)

A simple sum of the two gauges, it is considered one of the better evaluators of overall performance. OPS combines the two basic elements of offensive production — the ability to get on base (OB) and the ability to advance baserunners (Slg). **BENCHMARKS:** The game's top batters will have OPS levels more than .900. The worst batters will have levels less than .600.

Base Performance Value (BPV)

(Walk rate - 5) x 2)
+ ((Contact rate - 75) x 4)
+ ((Power Index - 80) x 0.8)
+ ((Speed Index - 80) x 0.3)

A single value that describes a player's overall raw skill level. This is more useful than traditional statistical gauges to track player performance trends and project future statistical output. The BPV formula combines and weights several BPIs.

This formula combines the individual raw skills of batting eye, contact rate, power and speed. BENCHMARKS: The best hitters will have a BPV of 50 or greater.

Linear weights *(Pete Palmer)*

((Singles x .46) + (Doubles x .8) + (Triples x 1.02) + (Home runs x 1.4) + (Walks x .33) + (Stolen Bases x .3) - (Caught Stealing x .6) - ((At bats - Hits) x Normalizing Factor)

(Also referred to as Batting Runs.) Formula whose premise is that all events in baseball are linear; that is, the output (runs) is directly proportional to the input (offensive events). Each of these events is then weighted according to its relative value in producing runs. Positive events — hits, walks, stolen bases — have positive values. Negative events — outs, caught stealing — have negative values.

The normalizing factor, representing the value of an out, is an offset to the level of offense in a given year. It changes every season, growing larger in high offense years and smaller in low offense years. The value is about .26 and varies by league.

LW is not included in the player forecast boxes, but the LW concept is used with the linear weighted power gauge.

Runs above replacement (RAR)

An estimate of the number of runs a player contributes above a "replacement level" player. "Replacement" is defined as the level of performance at which another player can easily be found at little or no cost to a team. What constitutes replacement level is a topic that is hotly debated. There are a variety of formulas and rules of thumb used to determine this level for each position (replacement level for a shortstop will be very different from replacement level for an outfielder). Our estimates appear below.

One of the major values of RAR for fantasy applications is that it can be used to assemble an integrated ranking of batters and pitchers for drafting purposes.

To calculate RAR for batters:

Start with a batter's runs created per game (RC/G).

Subtract his position's replacement level RC/G.

Multiply by number of games played: (AB - H + CS) / 25.5.

Replacement levels used in this book, for 2010:

POS	AL	NL
C	4.16	4.48
1B	5.77	6.33
2B	4.46	4.82
3B	4.83	4.90
SS	3.96	4.42
LF	4.88	5.07
CF	5.33	4.89
RF	4.95	5.33
DH	6.35	

RAR can also be used to calculate rough projected team won-loss records. *(Roger Miller)* Total the RAR levels for all the players on a team, divide by 10 and add to 53 wins.

Runs created *(Bill James)*

(H + BB - CS) x (Total bases + (.55 x SB)) / (AB + BB)

A formula that converts all offensive events into a total of runs scored. As calculated for individual teams, the result approximates a club's actual run total with great accuracy.

Runs created per game

Bill James version:

Runs Created / ((AB - H + CS) / 25.5)

Neil Bonner version (used in this book):

(SS x 37.96) + (ct% x 10.38) + (bb% x 14.81) – 13.04

where SS, or "swing speed" is defined as

((1B x 0.5) + (2B x 0.8) + (3B x 1.1) + (HR x 1.2)) / (AB - K)

RC expressed on a per-game basis might be considered the hypothetical ERA compiled against a particular batter. Another way to look at it... a batter with a RC/G of 7.00 would be expected to score 7 runs per game if he were cloned nine times and faced an average pitcher in every at bat. Cloning batters is not a practice we recommend.

BENCHMARKS: Few players surpass the level of a 10.00 RC/G, but any level more than 7.50 can still be considered very good. At the bottom are levels less than 3.00.

Handedness

1. While pure southpaws account for about 27% of total ABs (RHers about 55% and switch-hitters about 18%), they hit 31% of the triples and take 30% of the walks.

2. The average lefty posts a batting average about 10 points higher than the average RHer. The on base averages of pure LHers are nearly 20 points higher than RHers, but only 10 points higher than switch-hitters.

3. LHers tend to have a better batting eye ratio than RHers, but about the same as switch-hitters.

4. Pure righties and lefties have virtually identical power skills. Switch-hitters tend to have less power, on average.

5. Switch-hitters tend to have the best speed, followed by LHers, and then RHers.

6. On an overall production basis, LHers have an 8% advantage over RHers and a 14% edge over switch-hitters.

Optimal ages

Every player develops at a different pace, but age can still be helpful to determine where they should be along the developmental curve. Bill James' research said batters peak at about 27. Recent research suggests that average is now closer to 30. More tendencies:

"26 With Experience" *(John Benson):* While batters may peak at about age 27, the players most likely to exhibit the most dramatic spike in performance are those aged 26 who have several years of major league experience.

Power: Batting power tends to grow consistently between 24 and 29. Many batters experience a power peak at about 30-31. Catchers often see a power spike in the mid-30s.

Speed: Base-running and speed are skills of the young. When given the choice of two speedsters of equivalent abilities and opportunity, always go after the younger one. A sharp drop-off in speed skills typically occurs at age 34.

Batting eye: For batters who continue to play into their 30s, this is a skill that can develop and grow throughout their career. A decline in this level, which can occur at any age, often indicates a decline in overall skills.

Thirtysomethings *(Ed Spaulding):* Batters tend to lose points on their BA but draw more walks. While players on the outside of the defensive spectrum (1B, 3B, LF, RF, DH) often have their best seasons in their 30s, players in the middle (2B, SS, CF) tend to fade.

Catchers *(Ed Spaulding):* Many catchers — particularly second line catchers — have their best seasons late in their careers. Some possible reasons why:

1. Catchers, like shortstops, often get to the big leagues for defensive reasons and not their offensive skills. These skills take longer to develop.

2. The heavy emphasis on learning the catching/defense/pitching side of the game detracts from their time to learn about, and practice, hitting.

3. Injuries often curtail their ability to show offensive skills, though these injuries (typically jammed fingers, bruises on the arms, rib injuries from collisions) often don't lead to time on the disabled list.

4. The time spent behind the plate has to impact the ability to recognize, and eventually hit, all kinds of pitches.

Spring training leading indicator *(John Dewan)*

A positive difference between a hitter's spring training slugging pct. and his lifetime slugging pct. of .200 or more is a leading indicator for a better than normal season.

Overall batting breakout profile *(Brandon Kruse)*

We define a breakout performance as one where a player posts a Roto value of $20+ after having never posted a value of $10. These criteria are used to validate an apparent breakout in the current season but may also be used carefully to project a potential upcoming breakout:

- Age 27 or younger.
- An increase in at least two of: H%, PX or SX.
- Minimum league average PX or SX (100)
- Minimum contact rate of 75%
- Minimum xBA of .270

In-Season Analysis

Quality/consistency score (QC)
(PQS DOM% - (2 x PQS DIS%)) x 2)

Using the PQS system and DOM/DIS percentages, this score measures both the quality of performance as well as week–to–week consistency. A week with a BPV level of 50 qualifies as a DOM week; BPVs less than 0 are DIS weeks.

Projecting RBIs *(Patrick Davitt)*

Evaluating players in-season for RBI potential is a function of the interplay among four factors:

- Teammates' ability to reach base ahead of him and to run the bases efficiently
- His own ability to drive them in by hitting, especially XBH
- Number of Games Played
- Place in the batting order

3-4-5 Hitters:
(0.69 x GP x TOB) + (0.30 x ITB) + (0.275 x HR) – (.191 x GP)

6-7-8 Hitters:
(0.63 x GP x TOB) + (0.27 x ITB) + (0.250 x HR) – (.191 x GP)

9-1-2 Hitters:
(0.57 x GP x TOB) + (0.24 x ITB) + (0.225 x HR) – (.191 x GP)

...where GP = games played, TOB = team on-base pct. and ITB = individual total bases (ITB).

Apply this pRBI formula after 70 games played or so (to reduce the variation from small sample size) to find players more than 9 RBIs over or under their projected RBI. There could be a correction coming.

You should also consider other factors, like injury or trade (involving the player or a top-of-the-order speedster) or team SB philosophy and success rate.

Remember: the player himself has an impact on his TOB. When we first did this study, we excluded the player from his TOB and got better results. The formula overestimates projected RBI for players with high OBP who skew his teams' OBP but can't benefit in RBI from that effect.

Other Diamonds

It's a Busy World Short-cut: For marginal utility-type players, scan their PX and Spd history to see if there's anything to mine for. If you see triple digits anywhere, stop and look further. If not, move on.

Chronology of the Classic Free-Swinger with Pop

1. Gets off to a good start.
2. Thinks he's in a groove.
3. Gets lax, careless.
4. Pitchers begin to catch on.
5. Fades down the stretch.

Errant Gust of Wind: A unit of measure used to describe the difference between your home run projection and mine.

Hannahan Admission: Players with a .218 BA rarely get 441 AB, but when they do, it's usually once.

Mendoza Line: Named for Mario Mendoza, it represents the benchmark for batting futility. Usually refers to a .200 batting average, but can also be used for low levels of other statistical categories. Note that Mendoza's lifetime batting average was actually a much more robust .215.

Small Sample Certitude: If players' careers were judged based what they did in a single game performance, then Tuffy Rhodes and Mark Whiten would be in the Hall of Fame.

Esix Snead List: Players with excellent speed and sub-.300 on base averages who get a lot of practice running down the line to first base, and then back to the dugout. Also used as an adjective, as in "Esix-Sneadian."

Pitchers

Strikeouts and Walks

Fundamental skills

Unreliable pitching performance is a fallacy driven by the practice of attempting to project pitching stats using gauges that are poor evaluators of skill.

How can we better evaluate pitching skill? We can start with the three statistical categories that are generally unaffected by external factors. These three stats capture the outcome of an individual pitcher versus batter match-up without regard to supporting offense, defense or bullpen:

Walks Allowed, Strikeouts and Ground Balls

Even with only these stats to observe, there is a wealth of insight that these measures can provide.

Control rate (bb/9), or Opposition walks per game
BB Allowed x 9 / IP

Measures how many walks a pitcher allows per game equivalent. **BENCHMARK:** The best pitchers will have bb/9 levels of 3.0 or less.

Dominance rate (k/9), or Opposition strikeouts/game
Strikeouts Recorded x 9 / IP

Measures how many strikeouts a pitcher allows per game equivalent. **BENCHMARK:** The best pitchers will have k/9 levels of 5.6 or higher.

Command ratio (Cmd)
(Strikeouts / Walks)

A measure of a pitcher's ability to get the ball over the plate. There is no more fundamental a skill than this, and so it is used as a leading indicator to project future rises and falls in other gauges, such as ERA. **BENCHMARKS:** Baseball's best pitchers will have ratios in excess of 3.0. Pitchers with ratios less than 1.0 — indicating that they walk more batters than they strike out — have virtually no potential for long term success. If you make no other changes in your approach to drafting pitchers, limiting your focus to only pitchers with a command ratio of 2.0 or better will substantially improve your odds of success.

Command ratio as a leading indicator

The ability to get the ball over the plate — command of the strike zone — is one of the best leading indicators for future performance. Command ratio (K/BB) can be used to project potential in ERA as well as other skills gauges.

1. Research indicates that there is a high correlation between a pitcher's Cmd ratio and his ERA.

	Earned Run Average				
Command	2006	2007	2008	2009	2010
0.0 - 1.0	6.42	6.48	7.00	6.43	5.86
1.1 - 1.5	5.06	5.12	5.07	5.10	5.14
1.6 - 2.0	4.65	4.58	4.60	4.41	4.34
2.1 - 2.5	4.48	4.28	3.96	4.19	3.95
2.6 - 3.0	4.15	3.89	3.89	3.70	3.71
3.1 +	3.49	3.49	3.35	3.40	3.25

We can create percentage plays for the different levels:

For Cmd	% with ERA of	
Levels of	3.50-	4.50+
0.0 - 1.0	0%	87%
1.1 - 1.5	7%	67%
1.6 - 2.0	7%	57%
2.1 - 2.5	19%	35%
2.6 - 3.0	26%	25%
3.1 +	53%	5%

Pitchers who maintain a Cmd of over 2.5 have a high probability of long-term success. For fantasy drafting purposes, it is best to avoid pitchers with sub-2.0 ratios. Avoid bullpen closers if they have a ratio less than 2.5.

2. A pitcher's command in tandem with dominance (strikeout rate) provides even greater predictive abilities.

	Earned Run Average	
Command	-5.6 Dom	5.6+ Dom
0.0-0.9	5.36	5.99
1.0-1.4	4.94	5.03
1.5-1.9	4.67	4.47
2.0-2.4	4.32	4.08
2.5-2.9	4.21	3.88
3.0-3.9	4.04	3.46
4.0+	4.12	2.96

This helps to highlight the limited upside potential of soft-tossers with pinpoint control. The extra dominance makes a huge difference.

3. Research also suggests that there is a strong correlation between a pitcher's command ratio and his propensity to win ballgames. Over three quarters of those with ratios over 3.0 post winning records, and the collective W/L record of those command artists is nearly .600.

The command/winning correlation holds up in both leagues, although the effect was more pronounced in the NL. Over four times more NL hurlers than AL hurlers had Cmd over 3.0, and higher ratios were required in the NL to maintain good winning percentages. A ratio between 2.0 and 2.9 was good enough for a winning record for over 70% of AL pitchers, but that level in the NL generated an above-.500 mark slightly more than half the time.

In short, in order to have at least a 70% chance of drafting a pitcher with a winning record, you must target NL pitchers with at least a 3.0 command ratio. To achieve the same odds in the AL, a 2.0 command ratio will suffice.

Power/contact rating
(BB + K) / IP

Measures the level by which a pitcher allows balls to be put into play. In general, extreme power pitchers can be successful even with poor defensive teams. Power pitchers tend to have greater longevity in the game. Contact pitchers with poor defenses behind them are high risks to have poor W-L records and ERA. **BENCHMARKS:** A level of 1.13+ describes pure throwers. A level of .93 or less describes high contact pitchers.

Balls in Play

Balls-in-play (BIP)
((IP x 2.82)) + H – K

The total number of batted balls that are hit fair, both hits and outs. An analysis of how these balls are hit – on the ground, in the air, hits, outs, etc. – can provide analytical insight, from player skill levels to the impact of luck on statistical output.

Batting average on balls in play *(Voros McCracken)*
(H—HR) / ((IP x 2.82) + H - K - HR)

Also called **Hit rate** (H%). The percent of balls hit into the field of play that fall for hits. **BENCHMARK:** The league average is 30%, which is also the level that individual performances will regress to on a year to year basis. Any +/- variance of 3% or more can affect a pitcher's ERA.

BABIP rate as a leading indicator *(Voros McCracken)*

In 2000, Voros McCracken published a study that concluded that "there is little if any difference among major league pitchers in their ability to prevent hits on balls hit in the field of play." His assertion was that, while a Johan Santana would have a better ability to prevent a batter from getting wood on a ball, or perhaps keeping the ball in the park, once that ball was hit in the field of play, the probability of it falling for a hit was virtually no different than for any other pitcher.

Among the findings in his study were:

- There is little correlation between what a pitcher does one year in the stat and what he will do the next. This is not true with other significant stats (BB, K, HR).
- You can better predict a pitcher's hits per balls in play from the rate of the rest of the pitcher's team than from the pitcher's own rate.

This last point brings a team's defense into the picture. It begs the question, when a batter gets a hit, is it because the pitcher made a bad pitch, the batter took a good swing, or the defense was not positioned correctly?

Pitchers will often post hit rates per balls-in-play that are far off from the league average, but then revert to the mean the following year. As such, we can use that mean to project the direction of a pitcher's ERA.

Subsequent research has shown that ground ball or fly ball propensity may have a small impact on this rate.

Hit rate *(See Batting average on balls in play)*

Opposition batting average (OBA)
(Hits Allowed / ((IP x 2.82) + Hits Allowed))

A close approximation of the batting average achieved by opposing batters against a pitcher. **BENCHMARKS:** The best pitchers will have levels less than .250; the worst pitchers levels more than .300.

Opposition on base average (OOB)
(Hits Allowed + BB) / ((IP x 2.82) + H + BB)

A close approximation of the on base average achieved by opposing batters against a pitcher. **BENCHMARK:** The best pitchers will have levels less than .300; the worst pitchers levels more than .375.

Walks plus hits divided by innings pitched (WHIP)

Essentially the same measure as opposition on base average, but used for Rotisserie purposes. **BENCHMARKS:** A WHIP of less than 1.20 is considered top level; more than 1.50 indicative of poor performance. Levels less than 1.00 — allowing fewer runners than IP — represent extraordinary performance and are rarely maintained over time.

Ground ball, fly ball, line drive pcts. (G/F/L)

The percentage of all balls-in-play that are hit on the ground, in the air and as line drives. For a pitcher, the ability to keep the ball on the ground can contribute to his statistical output exceeding his demonstrated skill level.

Ground ball tendency as a leading indicator
(John Burnson)

Ground ball pitchers tend to give up fewer HRs than do fly ball pitchers. There is also evidence that GB pitchers have higher hit rates. In other words, a ground ball has a higher chance of being a hit than does a fly ball that is not out of the park.

GB pitchers have lower strikeout rates. We should be more forgiving of a low strikeout rate (under 5.5 K/9) if it belongs to an extreme ground ball pitcher.

GB pitchers have a lower ERA but a higher WHIP than do fly ball pitchers. On balance, GB pitchers come out ahead, even when considering strikeouts, because a lower ERA also leads to more wins.

Groundball and strikeout tendencies as indicators
(Mike Dranchak)

Pitchers were assembled into 9 groups based on the following profiles (minimum 23 starts in 2005):

Profile	Ground Ball Rate
Ground Ball	higher than 47%
Neutral	42% to 47%
Fly Ball	less than 42%

Profile	Strikeout Rate (k/9)
Strikeout	higher than 6.6 k/9
Average	5.4 to 6.6 k/9
Soft-Tosser	less than 5.4 k/9

Findings: Pitchers with higher strikeout rates had better ERAs and WHIPs than pitchers with lower strikeout rates, regardless of ground ball profile. However, for pitchers with similar strikeout rates, those with higher ground ball rates had better ERAs and WHIPs than those with lower ground ball rates.

Pitchers with higher strikeout rates tended to strand more baserunners than those with lower K rates. Fly ball pitchers tended to strand fewer runners than their GB or neutral counterparts within their strikeout profile.

Ground ball pitchers (especially those who lacked high-dominance) yielded more home runs per fly ball than did fly ball pitchers. However, the ERA risk was mitigated by the fact that ground ball pitchers (by definition) gave up fewer fly balls to begin with.

Line Drive Pct. as a Leading Indicator *(Seth Samuels)*

Also beyond a pitcher's control is the percentage of balls-in-play that are line drives. Line drives do the most damage; from 1994-2003, here were the expected hit rates and number of total bases per type of BIP.

	|—— Type of BIP ——|	
	GB	FB	LD
H%	26%	23%	56%
Total bases	0.29	0.57	0.80

Despite the damage done by LDs, pitchers do not have any innate skill to avoid them. There is little relationship between a pitcher's LD% one year and his rate the next year. All rates tend to regress towards a mean of 22.6%.

However, GB pitchers do have a slight ability to prevent line drives (21.7%) and extreme GB hurlers even moreso (18.5%). Extreme FB pitchers have a slight ability to prevent LDs (21.1%) as well.

Home run to fly ball rate
HR / FB
The percent of fly balls that are hit for home runs.

HR/FB rate as a leading indicator *(John Burnson)*

McCracken's work focused on "balls in play," omitting home runs from the study. However, pitchers also do not have much control over the percentage of fly balls that turn into HR. Research shows that there is an underlying rate of HR as a percentage of fly balls of about 10%. A pitcher's HR/FB rate will vary each year but always tends to regress to that 10%. The element that pitchers *do* have control over is the number of fly balls they allow. That is the underlying skill or deficiency that controls their HR rate.

Pitchers who keep the ball out of the air more often correlate well with Roto value.

Opposition home runs per game (hr/9)
(HR Allowed x 9 / IP)
Also, expected opposition HR rate = (FB x 0.10) x 9 / IP

Measures how many HR a pitcher allows per game equivalent. Since FB tend to go yard at about a 10% rate, we can also estimate this rate off of fly balls. **BENCHMARK:** The best pitchers will have hr/9 levels of less than 1.0.

Runs

Expected earned run average
Gill and Reeve version:
(.575 x H [per 9 IP]) + (.94 x HR [per 9 IP]) + (.28 x BB [per 9 IP]) - (.01 x K [per 9 IP]) - Normalizing Factor

John Burnson version (used in this book)
(xER x 9)/IP, where xER is defined as
xER% x (FB/10) + (1-xS%) x [(0.3 x BIP - (FB/10)) + BB]
where
xER% = 0.96 - (0.0284 x (GB/FB))
and
xS% = (64.5 + (K/9 x 1.2) - (BB/9 x (BB/9 + 1)) / 20)
* + ((0.0012 x (GB%^2)) - (0.001 x GB%) - 2.4)*

xERA represents the an equivalent of what a pitcher's real ERA might be, calculated solely with skills-based measures. It is not influenced by situation-dependent factors.

Expected ERA variance
xERA - ERA

The variance between a pitcher's ERA and his xERA is a measure of over or underachievement. A positive variance indicates the potential for a pitcher's ERA to rise. A negative variance indicates the potential for ERA improvement. **BENCHMARK:** Discount variances that are less than 0.50. Any variance more than 1.00 (one run per game) is regarded as a indicator of future change.

Projected xERA or projected ERA?

Which should we be using to forecast a pitcher's ERA? Projected xERA is more accurate for looking ahead on a purely skills basis. Projected ERA includes situation-*dependent* events — bullpen support, park factors, etc. — which are reflected better by ERA. The optimal approach is to use both gauges as a *range of the expectation* for forecasting purposes.

Strand rate (S%)
(H + BB - ER) / (H + BB - HR)

Measures the percentage of allowed runners a pitcher strands (earned runs only), which incorporates both individual pitcher skill and bullpen effectiveness. **BENCHMARKS:** The most adept at stranding runners will have S% levels over 75%. Those with rates over 80% will have artificially low ERAs which will be prone to relapse. Levels below 65% will inflate ERA but have a high probability of regression.

Strand rate as a leading indicator *(Ed DeCaria)*

Strand Rate often regresses/rebounds toward past rates (usually 69-74%), resulting in Year 2 ERA changes:

% of Pitchers with Year 2 Regression/Rebound

Y1 S%	RP	SP	LR
<60%	100%	94%	94%
65	81%	74%	88%
70	53%	48%	65%
75	55%	85%	100%
80	80%	100%	100%
85	100%	100%	100%

Typical ERA Regression/Rebound in Year 2

Y1 S%	RP	SP	LR
<60%	-2.54	-2.03	-2.79
65	-1.00	-0.64	-0.93
70	-0.10	-0.05	-0.44
75	0.24	0.54	0.75
80	1.15	1.36	2.29
85	1.71	2.21	n/a

Starting pitchers (SP) have a narrower range of strand rate outcomes than do relievers (RP) or swingmen/long relievers (LR). **Relief pitchers** with Y1 strand rates of <=67% or >=78% are likely to experience a +/- ERA regression in Y2. **Starters and swingmen/long relievers** with Y1 strand rates of <=65% or >=75% are likely to experience a +/- ERA regression in Y2. Pitchers with strand rates that deviate more than a few points off of their individual expected strand rates are likely to experience some degree of ERA regression in Y2. Over-performing (or "lucky") pitchers are more likely than underperforming (or "unlucky") pitchers to see such a correction.

Wins

Projecting/chasing wins

There are five events that need to occur in order for a pitcher to post a single win...

1. He must pitch well, allowing few runs.
2. The offense must score enough runs.
3. The defense must successfully field all batted balls.
4. The bullpen must hold the lead.
5. The manager must leave the pitcher in for 5 innings, and not remove him if the team is still behind.

Of these five events, only one is within the control of the pitcher. As such, projecting, or chasing wins can be an exercise in futility.

Home field advantage (John Burnson)

Based on a 2006 study, the home starting pitcher got a win in 38% of his outings. The visiting team starter got a win in 33% of his outings.

Usage

Batters faced per game (Craig Wright)

$((IP \times 2.82) + H + BB) / G$

A measure of pitcher usage and one of the leading indicators for potential pitcher burnout.

Workload

Research suggests that there is a finite number of innings in a pitcher's arm. This number varies by pitcher, by development cycle, and by pitching style and repertoire. We can measure a pitcher's potential for future arm problems and/or reduced effectiveness (burnout):

Sharp increases in usage from one year to the next... Any pitcher who significantly increases his workload from one year to another is a candidate for burnout symptoms in a future year. That threshold may be 50 IP or 100 IP, depending upon the pitcher, and the result may not be seen for several seasons after the increase.

Starters' overuse... Consistent "batters faced per game" (BF/G) levels of 28.0 or higher, combined with consistent seasonal IP totals of 200 or more may indicate burnout potential. Within a season, a BF/G of more than 30.0 with a projected IP total of 200 may indicate a late season fade.

Relievers' overuse... Warning flags should be up for relievers who post in excess of 100 IP in a season, while averaging fewer than 2 IP per outing.

When focusing solely on minor league pitchers, research results are striking:

Stamina: Virtually every minor league pitcher who had a BF/G of 28.5 or more in one season experienced a drop-off in BF/G the following year. Many were unable to ever duplicate that previous level of durability.

Performance: Most pitchers experienced an associated drop-off in their BPVs in the years following the 28.5 BF/G season. Some were able to salvage their effectiveness later on by moving to the bullpen.

Protecting young pitchers (Craig Wright)

There is a link between some degree of eventual arm trouble and a history of heavy workloads in a pitcher's formative years. Some recommendations from this research:

Teenagers (A-ball): No 200 IP seasons and no BF/G over 28.5 in any 150 IP span. No starts on three days rest.

Ages 20-22: Average no more than 105 pitches per start with a single game ceiling of 130 pitches.

Ages 23-24: Average no more than 110 pitches per start with a single game ceiling of 140 pitches.

When possible, a young starter should be introduced to the majors in long relief before he goes into the rotation.

Overall Performance Analysis

Base Performance Value (BPV)

$((Dominance\ Rate - 5.0) \times 18)$
$+ (4.0 - Walk\ Rate) \times 27))$
$+ (Ground\ ball\ rate - 40\%)$

A single value that describes a player's overall raw skill level. This is more useful than traditional statistical gauges to track player performance trends and project future statistical output. The formula combines the individual raw skills of power, control and the ability to keep the ball down in the zone, all characteristics that are unaffected by most external factors. In tandem with a pitcher's strand rate, it provides a more complete picture of the elements that contribute to ERA, and therefore serves as an accurate tool to project likely changes in ERA. **BENCHMARKS:** A BPV of 50 is the minimum level required for long-term success. The elite of the bullpen aces will have BPVs in excess of 100 and it is rare for these stoppers to enjoy long term success with consistent levels under 75.

Runs above replacement (RAR)

An estimate of the number of runs a player contributes above a "replacement level" player.

Batters create runs; pitchers save runs. But are batters and pitchers who have comparable RAR levels truly equal in value? Pitchers might be considered to have higher value. Saving an additional run is more important than producing an additional run. A pitcher who throws a shutout is guaranteed to win that game, whereas no matter how many runs a batter produces, his team can still lose given poor pitching support.

To calculate RAR for pitchers:

Start with the replacement level league ERA.

Subtract the pitcher's ERA. (To calculate *projected* RAR, use the pitcher's xERA.)

Multiply by number of games played, calculated as plate appearances (IP x 4.34) divided by 38.

Multiply the resulting RAR level by 1.08 to account for the variance between earned runs and total runs.

Handedness

1. LHers tend to peak about a year after RHers.

2. LHers post only 15% of the total saves. Typically, LHers are reserved for specialist roles so few are frontline closers.

3. RHers have slightly better command and HR rate.

4. There is no significant variance in ERA.

5. On an overall skills basis, RHers have about a 6% advantage.

Optimal ages

As with batters, each pitcher develops at a different pace, but a look at their age can help determine where they should be along the developmental curve. Tendencies:

While peaks vary, most all pitchers (who are still around) tend to experience a sharp drop-off in their skills at age 38.

Thirtysomethings (*Ed Spaulding*): Older pitchers, as they lose velocity and movement on the ball, must rely on more variety and better location. Thus, if strikeouts are a priority, you don't want many pitchers over 30. The over-30 set that tends to be surprising includes finesse types, career minor leaguers who break through for 2-3 seasons often in relief, and knuckleballers (a young knuckleballer is 31).

The first 20-save season for a relief ace arrives at about age 26. About three of every four relievers who begin a run of 20-save seasons in their 20s will likely sustain that level for about four years, with their value beginning to decline at the beginning of the third year.

Many aces achieve a certain level of maturity in their 30s and can experience a run of 20-save seasons between ages 33 and 36. For some, this may be their first time in the role of bullpen closer. However, those who achieve their first 20-save season after age 34 are unlikely to repeat.

Catchers' effect on pitching (*Thomas Hanrahan*)

A typical catcher handles a pitching staff better after having been with a club for a few years. Research has shown that there is an improvement in team ERA of approximately 0.37 runs from a catcher's rookie season to his prime years with a club. Expect a pitcher's ERA to be higher than expected if he is throwing to a rookie backstop.

First productive season (*Michael Weddell*)

To find those starting pitchers who are about to post their first productive season in the majors (10 wins, 150 IP, ERA of 4.00 or less), look for:

- Pitchers entering their age 23-26 seasons, especially those about to pitch their age 25 season.
- Pitchers who already have good skills, shown by an xERA in the prior year of 4.25 or less.
- Pitchers coming off of at least a partial season in the majors without a major health problem.
- To the extent that one speculates on pitchers who are one skill away, look for pitchers who only need to improve their control (bb/9).

Overall pitching breakout profile (*Brandon Kruse*)

A breakout performance is defined here as one where a player posts a Rotisserie value of $20 or higher after having never posted a value of $10 previously. These criteria are primarily used to validate an apparent breakout in the current season but may also be used carefully to project a potential breakout for an upcoming season.

- Age 27 or younger
- Minimum 5.6 Dom, 2.0 Cmd, 1.1 hr/9 and 50 BPV
- Maximum 30% hit rate
- Minimum 71% strand rate
- Starters should have a hit rate no greater than the previous year's hit rate. Relievers should show improved command
- Maximum xERA of 4.00

Career year drop-off (*Rick Wilton*)

Research shows that a pitcher's post-career year drop-off, on average, looks like this...

- ERA increases by 1.00
- WHIP increases by 0.14.
- Nearly 6 fewer wins

Closers

Saves

There are six events that need to occur in order for a relief pitcher to post a single save...

1. The starting pitcher and middle relievers must pitch well.
2. The offense must score enough runs.
3. It must be a reasonably close game.
4. The manager must put the pitcher in for a save opportunity.
5. The pitcher must pitch well and hold the lead.
6. The manager must let him finish the game.

Of these six events, only one is within the control of the relief pitcher. As such, projecting saves for a reliever has little to do with skill and a lot to do with opportunity. However, pitchers with excellent skills may create opportunity for themselves.

Saves conversion rate (Sv%)

Saves / Save Opportunities

The percentage of save opportunities that are successfully converted. **BENCHMARK:** We look for a minimum 80% for long-term success.

Saves chances and wins (*Craig Neuman*)

Should the quality of a pitcher's MLB team be a consideration in drafting a closer? One school of thought says that more wins means more save opportunities. The flipside is that when poor teams win they do so by a small margin, which means more save opportunities.

A 6-season correlation yielded these results for saves, save opportunities, save percentage, wins, quality starts and run differential. (Any value above .50 suggests at least a moderate correlation.)

	Sv	**SvO**	**W**	**Sv%**	**RD**	**QS**
SV	1					
SVO	.78	1				
W	.66	.41	1			
S%	.66	.05	.56	1		
RD	.48	.26	.92	.44	1	
QS	.41	.24	.58	.34	.60	1

Saves do correlate with wins. As for the theory that teams who play in close games would accumulate more saves, the low correlation between saves and run differential seems to dispel that a bit.

On average, teams registered one save for every two wins. However, there is a relationship between wins and the number of saves per win a team achieves:

Win Total	Saves/Win
>90	.494
80-89	.492
70-79	.505
<69	.525

Teams with fewer wins end up with more saves per win. So, when poor teams do win games, they are more likely to get a save in their wins.

Origin of closers

History has long maintained that ace closers are not easily recognizable early on in their careers, so that every season does see its share of the unexpected. John Axford, Jon Rauch, Alfredo Simon, Juan Gutierrez... who would have thought it a year ago?

Accepted facts, all of which have some element of truth:

* You cannot find major league closers from pitchers who were closers in the minors.
* Closers begin their careers as starters.
* Closers are converted set-up men.
* Closers are pitchers who were unable to develop a third effective pitch.

More simply, closers are a product of circumstance.

Are the minor leagues a place to look at all?

From 1990-2004, there were 280 twenty-save seasons in Double-A and Triple-A, accomplished by 254 pitchers.

Of those 254, only 46 ever made it to the majors at all.

Of those 46, only 13 ever saved 20 games in a season.

Of those 13, only 5 ever posted more than one 20-save season in the majors: John Wetteland, Mark Wohlers, Ricky Bottalico, Braden Looper and Francisco Cordero.

Five out of 254 pitchers, over 15 years, a rate of 2%.

One of the reasons that minor league closers rarely become major league closers is because, in general, they do not get enough innings in the minors to sufficiently develop their arms into big-league caliber.

In fact, organizations do not look at minor league closing performance seriously, assigning that role to pitchers who they do not see as legitimate prospects.

Year	Avg age of all AA and AAA pitchers who posted 20-plus saves
2005	28
2006	27
2007	28
2008	27
2009	27
2010	28

Elements of saves success

The task of finding future closing potential comes down to looking at two elements:

Talent: The raw skills to mow down hitters for short periods of time. Optimal BPVs over 100, but not under 75.

Opportunity: The more important element, yet the one that pitchers have no control over.

There are pitchers that have *Talent, but not Opportunity.* These pitchers are not given a chance to close for a variety of reasons (e.g. being blocked by a solid front-liner in the pen, being left-handed, etc.), but are good to own because they will not likely hurt your pitching staff. You just can't count on them for saves, at least not in the near term.

There are pitchers that have *Opportunity, but not Talent.* MLB managers decide who to give the ball to in the 9th inning based on their own perceptions about what skills are required to succeed, even if those perceived "skills" don't translate into acceptable BPI levels. Those pitchers without the BPIs may have some initial short-term success, but their long-term prognosis is poor and they are high risks to your roster. Classic examples of the short life span of these types of pitchers include Matt Karchner, Heath Slocumb, Ryan Kohlmeier, Dan Miceli and Danny Kolb.

Closers' job retention *(Michael Weddell)*

Of pitchers with 20 or more saves in one year, only 67.5% of these closers earned 20 or more saves the following year. The variables that best predicted whether a closer would avoid this attrition:

* **Saves history:** Career saves was the most important factor.
* **Age:** Closers are most likely to keep their jobs at age 27. For long-time closers, their growing career saves totals more than offset the negative impact of their advanced ages. Older closers without a long history of racking up saves tend to be bad candidates for retaining their roles.
* **Performance:** Actual performance, measured by ERA+, was of only minor importance.
* **Being Right-Handed** increased the odds of retaining the closer's role by 9% over lefthanders.

How well can we predict which closers will keep their jobs? Of the 10 best closers during 1989-2007, 90% saved at least 20 games during the following season. Of the 10 worst bets, only 20% saved at least 20 games the next year.

BPV as a leading indicator *(Doug Dennis)*

Research has shown that base performance value (BPV) is an excellent indicator of long-term success as a closer. Here are 20-plus saves seasons, by year:

Year	B P V (Pct.) No.	100+	75+	<75
1999	26	27%	54%	46%
2000	24	25	54	46
2001	25	56	80	20
2002	25	60	72	28
2003	25	36	64	36
2004	23	61	61	39
2005	25	36	64	36
2006	25	52	72	28
2007	23	52	74	26
MEAN	**25**	**45**	**66**	**34**

Though 20-saves success with a 75+ BPV is only a 66% percentage play in any given year, the below-75 group is composed of closers who are rarely able to repeat the feat in the following season:

Year	No. with BPV < 75	No. who followed up 20+ saves <75 BPV
1999	12	2
2000	11	2
2001	5	2
2002	7	3
2003	9	3
2004	9	2
2005	9	1
2006	7	3
2007	6	0

Other Relievers

Projecting holds (Doug Dennis)

Here are some general rules of thumb for identifying pitchers who might be in line to accumulate Holds. The percentages represent the portion of 2003's top Holds leaders who fell into the category noted.

1. Left-handed set-up men with excellent BPIs. (43%)

2. A "go-to" right-handed set-up man with excellent BPIs. This is the one set-up RHer that a manager turns to with a small lead in the 7th or 8th innings. These pitchers also tend to vulture wins. (43%, but 6 of the top 9)

3. Excellent BPIs, but not a firm role as the main LHed or RHed set-up man. Roles change during the season; cream rises to the top. Relievers projected to post great BPIs often overtake lesser set-up men during the season. (14%)

Reliever efficiency per cent (REff%)

(Wins + Saves + Holds) / (Wins + Losses + SaveOpps + Holds)

This is a measure of how often a reliever contributes positively to the outcome of a game. A record of consistent, positive impact on game outcomes breeds managerial confidence, and that confidence could pave the way to save opportunities. For those pitchers suddenly thrust into a closer's role, this formula helps gauge their potential to succeed based on past successes in similar roles. **BENCHMARK:** Minimum of 80%.

Vulture

A pitcher, typically a middle reliever, who accumulates an unusually high number of wins by preying on other pitchers' misfortunes. More accurately, this is a pitcher typically brought into a game after a starting pitcher has put his team behind, and then pitches well enough and long enough to allow his offense to take the lead, thereby "vulturing" a win from the starter.

In-Season Analysis
Pure Quality Starts

We've always approached performance measures on an aggregate basis. Each individual event that our statistics chronicle gets dumped into a huge pool of data. We then use our formulas to try to sort and slice and manipulate the data into more usable information.

Pure Quality Starts (PQS) take a different approach. It says that the smallest unit of measure should not be the "event" but instead be the "game." Within that game, we can accumulate all the strikeouts, hits and walks, and evaluate that outing as a whole. After all, when a pitcher takes the mound, he is either "on" or "off" his game; he is either dominant or struggling, or somewhere in between.

In PQS, we give a starting pitcher credit for exhibiting certain skills in each of his starts. Then by tracking his "PQS Score" over time, we can follow his progress. A starter earns one point for each of the following criteria...

1. The pitcher must go a minimum of 6 innings. This measures stamina. If he goes less than 5 innings, he automatically gets a total PQS score of zero, no matter what other stats he produces.

2. He must allow no more than an equal number of hits to the number of innings pitched. This measures hit prevention.

3. His number of strikeouts must be no fewer than two less than his innings pitched. This measures dominance.

4. He must strike out at least twice as many batters as he walks. This measures command.

5. He must allow no more than one home run. This measures his ability to keep the ball in the park.

A perfect PQS score would be 5. Any pitcher who averages 3 or more over the course of the season is probably performing admirably. The nice thing about PQS is it allows you to approach each start as more than an all-or-nothing event.

Note the absence of earned runs. No matter how many runs a pitcher allows, if he scores high on the PQS scale, he has hurled a good game in terms of his base skills. The number of runs allowed — a function of not only the pitcher's ability but that of his bullpen and defense — will tend to even out over time.

It doesn't matter if a few extra balls got through the infield, or the pitcher was given the hook in the fourth or sixth inning, or the bullpen was able to strand their inherited baserunners. When we look at performance in the aggregate, *those events do matter*, and will affect a pitcher's BPIs and ERA. But with PQS, the minutia is less relevant than the overall performance.

In the end, a dominating performance is a dominating performance, whether Cole Hamels is hurling a 1-hit shutout or giving up 4 runs while striking out 10 in 7 IP. And a disaster is still a disaster, whether Kyle Kendrick gets a second inning hook after giving up 6 runs, or "takes one for the team" getting shelled for 7 runs in 5 IP.

Skill versus consistency

Two pitchers have identical 4.50 ERAs and identical 3.0 PQS averages. Their PQS logs look like this:

```
PITCHER A:   3   3   3   3   3
PITCHER B:   5   0   5   0   5
```

Which pitcher would you rather have on your team? The risk-averse manager would choose Pitcher A as he represents the perfectly known commodity. Many fantasy leaguers might opt for Pitcher B because his occasional dominating starts show that there is an upside. His Achilles Heel is inconsistency — he is unable to sustain that high level. Is there any hope for Pitcher B?

• If a pitcher's inconsistency is characterized by more poor starts than good starts, his upside is limited.

• Pitchers with extreme inconsistency rarely get a full season of starts.

• However, inconsistency is neither chronic nor fatal.

The outlook for Pitcher A is actually worse. Disaster avoidance might buy these pitchers more starts, but history shows that the lack of dominating outings is more telling of future potential. In short, consistent mediocrity is bad.

PQS DOMination and DISaster rates

(Gene McCaffrey)

DOM% is the percentage of a starting pitcher's outings that rate as a PQS-4 or PQS-5. DIS% is the percentage that rate as a PQS-0 or PQS-1.

DOM/DIS percentages open up a new perspective, providing us with two separate scales of performance. In tandem, they measure consistency.

PQS ERA (qERA)

A pitcher's DOM/DIS split can be converted back to an equivalent ERA. By creating a grid of individual DOM% and DIS% levels, we can determine the average ERA at each cross point. The result is an ERA based purely on PQS.

Quality/consistency score (QC)

(PQS DOM% - (2 x PQS DIS%)) x 2

Using PQS and DOM/DIS percentages, this score measures both the quality of performance as well as start-to-start consistency.

PQS correlation with Quality Starts *(Paul Petera)*

PQS	QS%
0	0%
1	3%
2	21%
3	51%
4	75%
5	95%

Forward-looking PQS *(John Burnson)*

PQS says whether a pitcher performed ably in a *past* start – it doesn't say anything about how he'll do in the *next* start. We built a version of PQS that attempts to do that. For each series of five starts for a pitcher, we looked at his average IP, K/9, HR/9, H/9, and K/BB, and then whether the pitcher won his next start. We catalogued the results by indicator and calculated the observed future winning percentage for each data point.

This research suggested that a forward-looking version of PQS should have *these* criteria:

• The pitcher must have lasted at least 6.2 innings.

• He must have recorded at least IP-1 strikeouts.

• He must have allowed zero home runs.

• He must have allowed no more hits than IP+2.

• He must have had a Command (K/BB) of at least 2.5.

Pure Quality Relief *(Patrick Davitt)*

A system for evaluating reliever outings. The scoring :

1. Two points for the first out, and one point for each subsequent out, to a maximum of four points.

2. One point for having at least one strikeout for every four full outs (one K for 1-4 outs, two Ks for 5-8 outs, etc.).

3. One point for zero baserunners, minus one point for each baserunner, though allowing the pitcher one unpenalized runner for each three full outs (one baserunner for 3-5 outs, two for 6-8 outs, three for nine outs)

4. Minus one point for each earned run, though allowing one ER for 8– or 9-out appearances.

5. An automatic PQR-0 for allowing a home run.

Pitching streaks

It is possible to find predictive value in strings of DOMinating (PQS 4/5) or DISaster (PQS 0/1) starts:

Once a pitcher enters into a DOM streak of any length, the probability is that his subsequent start is going to be a better-than-average outing. The further a player is into a DOM streak, the *higher the likelihood* that the subsequent performance will be of high quality. In fact, once a pitcher has posted six DOM starts in a row, there is greater than a 70% probability that the streak will continue. When it does end, there is less than a 10% probability that the streak-breaker is going to be a DISaster.

Once a pitcher enters into a DIS streak of any length, the probability is that his next start is going to be below average, even if it breaks the streak. However, DIS streaks end quickly. Once a pitcher hits the skids, odds are low for him to start posting good numbers in the short term, though the duration of the plummet itself should be brief.

Pitch counts as a leading indicator

Long-term analysis of workload is an ongoing science. However, there have also been questions whether we can draw any conclusions from short-term trends. For this analysis, all pitching starts from 2005-2006 were isolated — looking at pitch counts and PQS scores — and compared side-by-side with each pitcher's subsequent outing. We examined two-start trends, the immediate impact that the length of one performance would have on the next start.

		NEXT START			
Pitch Ct	**Pct.**	**PQS**	**DOM**	**DIS**	**qERA**
< 80	13%	2.5	33%	28%	4.90
80-89	14%	2.6	35%	29%	4.82
90-99	28%	2.7	37%	26%	4.82
100-109	30%	2.9	41%	23%	4.56
110-119	13%	3.1	46%	18%	4.40
120+	3%	3.0	43%	20%	4.56

There does appear to be merit to the concern over limiting hurlers to 120 pitches per start. The research shows a slight drop-off in performance in those starts following a 120+ pitch outing. However, the impact does not appear to be all that great and the fallout might just affect those pitchers who have no business going that deep into games anyway. Additional detail to this research (not displayed) showed that higher-skilled pitchers were more successful throwing over 120 pitches but less-skilled pitchers were not.

Days of rest as a leading indicator

Workload is only part of the equation. The other part is how often a pitcher is sent out to the mound. For instance, it's possible that a hurler might see no erosion in skill after a 120+ pitch outing if he had enough rest between starts.

PITCH COUNTS	NEXT START				
Three days rest	**Pct.**	**PQS**	**DOM**	**DIS**	**qERA**
< 100	72%	2.8	35%	17%	4.60
100-119	28%	2.3	44%	44%	5.21
Four Days rest					
< 100	52%	2.7	36%	27%	4.82
100-119	45%	2.9	42%	22%	4.56
120+	3%	3.0	42%	20%	4.44
Five Days rest					
< 100	54%	2.7	38%	25%	4.79
100-119	43%	3.0	44%	19%	4.44
120+	3%	3.2	48%	14%	4.28
Six Days rest					
< 100	58%	2.7	39%	30%	5.00
100-119	40%	2.8	40%	26%	4.82
120+	3%	1.8	20%	60%	7.98
20+ Days rest					
< 100	85%	1.8	20%	46%	6.12
100-119	15%	2.3	33%	33%	5.08

Managers are reluctant to put a starter on the mound with any fewer than four days rest, and the results for those who pitched deeper into games shows why. Four days rest is the most common usage pattern and even appears to mitigate the drop-off at 120+ pitches.

Perhaps most surprising is that an extra day of rest improves performance across the board and squeezes even more productivity out of the 120+ pitch outings.

Performance begins to erode at six days (and continues at 7-20 days, though those are not displayed). The 20+ Days chart represents pitchers who were primarily injury rehabs and failed call-ups, and the length of the "days rest" was occasionally well over 100 days. This chart shows the result of their performance in their first start back. The good news is that the workload was limited for 85% of these returnees. The bad news is that these are not pitchers you want active. So for those who obsess over getting your DL returnees activated in time to catch every start, the better percentage play is to avoid that first outing.

Other Diamonds

The Pitching Postulates

1. Never sign a soft-tosser to a long-term contract.
2. Right-brain dominance has a very long shelf life.
3. A fly ball pitcher who gives up many HRs is expected. A GB pitcher who gives up many HRs is making mistakes.

4. Never draft a contact fly ball pitcher who plays in a hitter's park.
5. Only bad teams ever have a need for an inning-eater.
6. Never chase wins.

Ricky Bones List: Pitchers with BPIs so incredibly horrible that you have to wonder how they can possibly draw a major league paycheck year after year. (Given that Bones was named in the Mitchell Report for taking steroids/HGH and was a pitching coach in the Arizona Fall League — think about those two facts for a second — we may need to rename this the Dontrelle Willis List.)

Chaconian: Having the ability to post many saves despite sub-Mendoza BPIs and an ERA in the stratosphere.

Vintage Eck Territory: A BPV greater than 200, a level achieved by Dennis Eckersley for four consecutive years.

Edwhitsonitis: A dreaded malady marked by the sudden and unexplained loss of pitching ability upon a trade to the New York Yankees.

ERA Benchmark: A half run of ERA over 200 innings comes out to just one earned run every four starts.

Gopheritis (also, Acute Gopheritis and Chronic Gopheritis): The dreaded malady in which a pitcher is unable to keep the ball in the park. Pitchers with gopheritis have a FB rate of at least 40%. More severe cases have a FB% over 45%

Jason Jennings Rationalization: Occasional nightmares (2/3 inning, 11 ER) are just a part of the game.

The Knuckleballers Rule: Knuckleballers don't follow no stinkin' rules.

Brad Lidge Lament: When a closer posts a 62% strand rate, he has nobody to blame but himself.

LOOGY (Lefty One Out GuY): A left-handed reliever whose job it is to get one out in important situations.

Meltdown: Any game in which a starting pitcher allows more runs than innings pitched.

Lance Painter Lesson: Six months of solid performance can be screwed up by one bad outing. (In 2000, Painter finished with an ERA of 4.76. However, prior to his final appearance of the year — in which he pitched 1 inning and gave up 8 earned runs — his ERA was 3.70.)

The Five Saves Certainties:

1. On every team, there *will* be save opportunities and *someone* will get them. At a bare minimum, there will be at least 30 saves to go around, and not unlikely more than 45.

2. *Any* pitcher could end up being the chief beneficiary. Bullpen management is a fickle endeavor.

3. Relief pitchers are often the ones that require the most time at the start of the season to find a groove. The weather is cold, the schedule is sparse and their usage is erratic.

4. Despite the talk about "bullpens by committee," managers prefer a go-to guy. It makes their job easier.

5. As many as 50% of the saves in any year will come from pitchers who are unselected at the end of Draft Day.

Soft-tosser: A pitcher with a strikeout rate of 5.5 or less.

Soft-tosser land: The place where feebler arms leave their fortunes in the hands of the defense, variable hit and strand rates, and park dimensions. It's a place where many live, but few survive.

Prospects

Minor League Prospecting in Perspective

In our perpetual quest to be the genius who uncovers the next Albert Pujols when he is in A-ball, there is an obsessive fascination with minor league prospects. That's not to say that prospecting is not important. The issue is perspective:

1. During the 10 year period of 1996 to 2005, only 8% of players selected in the first round of the Major League Baseball First Year Player Draft went on to become stars.

2. Some prospects are going to hit the ground running (Ryan Braun) and some are going to immediately struggle (Alex Gordon), no matter what level of hype follows them.

3. Some prospects are going to start fast (since the league is unfamiliar with them) and then fade (as the league figures them out). Others will start slow (since they are unfamiliar with the opposition) and then improve (as they adjust to the competition). So if you make your free agent and roster decisions based on small early samples sizes, you are just as likely to be an idiot as a genius.

4. How any individual player will perform relative to his talent is largely unknown because there is a psychological element that is vastly unexplored. Some make the transition to the majors seamlessly, some not, completely regardless of how talented they are.

5. Still, talent is the best predictor of future success, so major league equivalent base performance indicators still have a valuable role in the process. As do scouting reports, carefully filtered.

6. Follow the player's path to the majors. Did he have to repeat certain levels? Was he allowed to stay at a level long enough to learn how to adjust to the level of competition? A player with only two great months at Double-A is a good bet to struggle if promoted directly to the majors because he was never fully tested at Double-A, let alone Triple-A.

7. Younger players holding their own against older competition is a good thing. Older players reaching their physical peak, regardless of their current address, can be a good thing too. The Jorge Campillos and Ryan Ludwicks can have some very profitable years.

8. Remember team context. A prospect with superior potential often will not unseat a steady but unspectacular incumbent, especially one with a large contract.

9. Don't try to anticipate how a team is going to manage their talent, both at the major and minor league level. You might think it's time to promote Dustin Ackley and give him an everyday role. You are not running the Mariners.

10. Those who play in shallow, one-year leagues should have little cause to be looking at the minors at all. The risk versus reward is so skewed against you, and there is so much talent available with a track record, that taking a chance on an unproven commodity makes no sense.

11. Decide where your priorities really are. If your goal is to win, prospect analysis is just a *part* of the process, not the entire process.

Factors Affecting Minor League Stats *(Terry Linhart)*

1. Often, there is an exaggerated emphasis on short-term performance in an environment that is supposed to focus on the long-term. Two poor outings don't mean a 21-year-old pitcher is washed up.

2. Ballpark dimensions and altitude create hitters parks and pitchers parks, but a factor rarely mentioned is that many parks in the lower minors are inconsistent in their field quality. Minor league clubs have limited resources to maintain field conditions, and this can artificially depress defensive statistics while inflating stats like batting average.

3. Some players' skills are so superior to the competition at their level that you can't get a true picture of what they're going to do from their stats alone.

4. Many pitchers are told to work on secondary pitches in unorthodox situations just to gain confidence in the pitch. The result is an artificially increased number of walks.

5. The #3, #4, and #5 pitchers in the lower minors are truly longshots to make the majors. They often possess only two pitches and are unable to disguise the off-speed offerings. Hitters can see inflated statistics in these leagues.

Minor League Level versus Age

When evaluating minor leaguers, look at the age of the prospect in relation to the median age of the league he is in:

Low level A	Between 19-20
Upper level A	Around 20
Double-A	21
Triple-A	22

These are the ideal ages for prospects at the particular level. If a prospect is younger than most and holds his own against older and more experienced players, elevate his status. If he is older than the median, reduce his status.

Triple-A Experience as a Leading Indicator

The probability that a minor leaguer will immediately succeed in the Majors can vary depending upon the level of Triple-A experience he has amassed at the time of call-up.

	BATTERS		PITCHERS	
	≤ 1 Yr	Full	≤1 Yr	Full
Performed well	57%	56%	16%	56%
Performed poorly	21%	38%	77%	33%
2nd half drop-off	21%	7%	6%	10%

The odds of a batter achieving immediate MLB success was slightly more than 50-50. More than 80% of all pitchers promoted with less than a full year at Triple-A struggled in their first year in the majors. Those pitchers with a year in Triple-A succeeded at a level equal to that of batters.

Major League Equivalency (Bill James)

A formula that converts a player's minor or foreign league statistics into a comparable performance in the major leagues. These are not projections, but conversions of current performance. Contains adjustments for the level of play in individual leagues and teams. Works best with Triple-A stats, not quite as well with Double-A stats, and hardly at all with the lower levels. Foreign conversions are still a work in process. James' original formula only addressed batting. Our research has devised conversion formulas for pitchers, however, their best use comes when looking at BPIs, not traditional stats.

Adjusting to the Competition

All players must "adjust to the competition" at every level of professional play. Players often get off to fast or slow starts. During their second tour at that level is when we get to see whether the slow starters have caught up or whether the league has figured out the fast starters. That second half "adjustment" period is a good baseline for projecting the subsequent season, in the majors or minors.

Premature major league call-ups often negate the ability for us to accurately evaluate a player due to the lack of this adjustment period. For instance, a hotshot Double-A player might open the season in Triple-A. After putting up solid numbers for a month, he gets a call to the bigs, and struggles. The fact is, we do not have enough evidence that the player has mastered the Triple-A level. We don't know whether the rest of the league would have caught up to him during his second tour of the league. But now he's labeled as an underperformer in the bigs when in fact he has never truly proven his skills at the lower levels.

Bull Durham Prospects

There is some potential talent in older players — age 26, 27 or higher — who, for many reasons (untimely injury, circumstance, bad luck, etc.), don't reach the majors until they have already been downgraded from prospect to suspect. Equating potential with age is an economic reality for Major League clubs, but not necessarily a skills reality.

Skills growth and decline is universal, whether it occurs at the major league level or in the minors. So a high skills journeyman in Triple-A is just as likely to peak at age 27 as a major leaguer of the same age. The question becomes one of opportunity — will the parent club see fit to reap the benefits of that peak performance?

Prospecting these players for your fantasy team is, admittedly, a high risk endeavor, though there are some criteria you can use. Look for a player who is/has:

- Optimally, age 27-28 for overall peak skills, age 30-31 for power skills, or age 28-31 for pitchers.
- At least two seasons of experience at Triple-A. Career Double-A players are generally not good picks.
- Solid base skills levels.
- Shallow organizational depth at their position.
- Notable winter league or spring training performance.

Players who meet these conditions are not typically draftable players, but worthwhile reserve or FAAB picks.

Batters

MLE PX as a leading indicator (Bill Macey)

Looking at minor league performance (as MLE) in one year and the corresponding MLB performance the subsequent year:

	Year 1 MLE	Year 2 MLB
Observations	496	496
Median PX	95	96
Percent PX > 100	43%	46%

In addition, 53% of the players had a MLB PX in year 2 that exceeded their MLE PX in year 1. A slight bias towards improved performance in year 2 is consistent with general career trajectories.

Year 1 MLE PX	Year 2 MLB PX	Pct. Incr	Pct. MLB PX > 100
<= 50	61	70.3%	5.4%
51-75	85	69.6%	29.4%
76-100	93	55.2%	39.9%
101-125	111	47.4%	62.0%
126-150	119	32.1%	66.1%
> 150	142	28.6%	76.2%

Slicing the numbers by performance level, there is a good amount of regression to the mean.

Players rarely suddenly develop power at the MLB level if they didn't previously display that skill at the minor league level. However, the relatively large gap between the median MLE PX and MLB PX for these players, 125 to 110, confirms the notion that the best players continue to improve once they reach the major leagues.

MLE contact rate as a leading indicator (Bill Macey)

There is a strong positive correlation (0.63) between a player's MLE ct% in Year 1 and his actual ct% at the MLB level in Year 2.

MLE ct%	Year 1 MLE ct%	Year 2 MLB ct%
< 70%	69%	68%
70% - 74%	73%	72%
75% - 79%	77%	75%
80% - 84%	82%	77%
85% - 89%	87%	82%
90% +	91%	86%
TOTAL	**84%**	**79%**

There is very little difference between the median MLE BA in Year 1 and the median MLB BA in Year 2:

MLE ct%	Year 1 MLE BA	Year 2 MLB BA
< 70%	.230	.270
70% - 74%	.257	.248
75% - 79%	.248	.255
80% - 84%	.257	.255
85% - 89%	.266	.270
90% +	.282	.273
TOTAL	**.261**	**.262**

Excluding the <70% cohort (which was a tiny sample size), there is a positive relationship between MLE ct% and MLB BA.

Pitchers

BPIs as a Leading Indicator for Pitching Success

The percentage of hurlers that were good investments in the year that they were called up varied by the level of their historical minor league BPIs *prior* to that year.

Pitchers who had:	Fared well	Fared poorly
Good indicators	79%	21%
Marginal or poor indicators	18%	82%

The data used here were MLE levels from the previous two years, not the season in which they were called up. The significance? Solid current performance is what merits a call-up, but this is not a good indicator of short-term MLB success, because a) the performance data set is too small, typically just a few month's worth of statistics, and b) for those putting up good numbers at a new minor league level, there has typically not been enough time for the scouting reports to make their rounds.

Minor League BPV as a Leading Indicator

(Al Melchior)

There is a link between minor league skill and how a pitching prospect will fare in his first 5 starts upon call-up.

	MLE BPV		
PQS Avg	**< 50**	**50-99**	**100+**
0.0-1.9	60%	28%	19%
2.0-2.9	32%	40%	29%
3.0-5.0	8%	33%	52%

Pitchers who demonstrate sub-par skills in the minors (sub-50 BPV) tend to fare poorly in their first big league starts. Three-fifths of these pitchers register a PQS average below 2.0, while only 8% average over 3.0.

Fewer than 1 out of 5 minor leaguers with a 100+ MLE BPV go on to post a sub-2.0 PQS average in their initial major league starts, but more than half average 3.0 or better.

Late Season Performance of Rookie Starting

Pitchers *(Ray Murphy)*

Given that a rookie's second tour of the league provides insight as to future success, do rookie pitchers typically run out of gas? We studied 2002-2005, identified 56 rookies who threw at least 75 IP and analyzed their PQS logs. The group:

All rookies	#	#GS/P	DOM%	DIS%	qERA
before 7/31	56	13.3	42%	21%	4.56
after 7/31	56	9.3	37%	29%	4.82

There is some erosion, but a 0.26 run rise in qERA is hardly cause for panic. If we re-focus our study class, the qERA variance increased to 4.44-5.08 for those who made at least 16 starts before July 31. The variance also was larger (3.97-4.56) for those who had a PQS-3 average prior to July 31. The pitchers who intersected these two sub-groups:

PQS>3+GS>15	#	#GS/P	DOM%	DIS%	qERA
before 7/31	8	19.1	51%	12%	4.23
after 7/31	8	9.6	34%	30%	5.08

While the sample size is small, the degree of flameout by these guys (0.85 runs) is more significant.

Japanese Baseball *(Tom Mulhall)*

Comparing MLB and Japanese *Besuboru*

The Japanese major leagues are generally considered to be equivalent to very good Triple-A ball and the pitching may be even better. However, statistics are difficult to convert due to differences in the way the game is played in Japan.

1. While strong on fundamentals, Japanese baseball's guiding philosophy is risk avoidance. Mistakes are not tolerated. Runners rarely take extra bases, batters focus on making contact rather than driving the ball, and managers play for one run at a time. As a result, offenses score fewer runs than they should given the number of hits. Pitching stats tend to look better than the talent behind them.

2. Stadiums in Japan usually have shorter fences. Normally this would mean more HRs, but given #1 above, it is the American players who make up the majority of Japan's power elite. Power hitters do not make an equivalent transition to the MLB.

3. There are more artificial turf fields, which increases the number of ground ball singles. Only a few stadiums have infield grass and some still use dirt infields.

4. The quality of umpiring is questionable; there are no sanctioned umpiring schools in Japan. Fewer errors are called, reflecting the cultural philosophy of low tolerance for mistakes and the desire to avoid publicly embarrassing a player. Moreover, umpires are routinely intimidated.

5. Teams have smaller pitching staffs, sometimes no more than about seven deep. Three-man pitching rotations are not uncommon and the best starters often work out of the pen between starts. Despite superior conditioning, Japanese pitchers tend to burn out early due to overuse.

6. Japanese leagues use a slightly smaller baseball, making it easier for pitchers to grip and control.

7. Tie games are allowed. If the score remains even after 12 innings, the game goes into the books as a tie.

Japanese Players as Fantasy Farm Selections

Many fantasy leagues have large reserve or farm teams with rules allowing them to draft foreign players before they sign with a MLB team. With increased coverage by fantasy experts, the internet, and exposure from the World Baseball Classic, anyone willing to do a modicum of research can compile an adequate list of good players.

However, the key is not to identify the *best* Japanese players – the key is to identify impact players who have the desire and opportunity to sign with a MLB team. It is easy to overestimate the value of drafting these players. Since 1995, only about three dozen Japanese players have made a big league roster, and about half of them were middle relievers. But for owners who are allowed to carry a large reserve or farm team at reduced salaries, these players could be a real windfall, especially if your competitors do not do their homework.

A list of Japanese League players who could jump to the Majors appears in the Prospects section.

Other Diamonds

Age 26 Paradox: 26 is when a player begins to reach his peak skill, no matter what his address is. If circumstances have him celebrating that birthday in the majors, he is a breakout candidate. If circumstances have him celebrating that birthday in the minors, he is washed up.

A-Rod 10-Step Path to Stardom: Not all well-hyped prospects hit the ground running. More often they follow an alternative path...

1. Prospect puts up phenomenal minor league numbers.
2. The media machine gets oiled up.
3. Prospect gets called up, but struggles, Year 1.
4. Prospect gets demoted.
5. Prospect tears it up in the minors, Year 2.
6. Prospect gets called up, but struggles, Year 2.
7. Prospect gets demoted.
8. The media turns their backs. Fantasy leaguers reduce their expectations.
9. Prospect tears it up in the minors, Year 3. The public shrugs its collective shoulders.
10. Prospect is promoted in Year 3 and explodes. Some lucky fantasy leaguer lands a franchise player for under $5.

Some players that are currently stuck at one of the interim steps, and may or may not ever reach Step 10, include Matt Gamel, Max Ramirez and Travis Snider.

Developmental Dogmata

1. Defense is what gets a minor league prospect to the majors; offense is what keeps him there. *(Deric McKamey)*

2. The reason why rapidly promoted minor leaguers often fail is that they are never given the opportunity to master the skill of "adjusting to the competition."

3. Rookies who are promoted in-season often perform better than those that make the club out of spring training. Inferior March competition can inflate the latter group's perceived talent level.

4. Young players rarely lose their inherent skills. Pitchers may uncover weaknesses and the players may have difficulty adjusting. These are bumps along the growth curve, but they do not reflect a loss of skill.

5. Late bloomers have smaller windows of opportunity and much less chance for forgiveness.

6. The greatest risk in this game is to pay for performance that a player has never achieved.

7. Some outwardly talented prospects simply have a ceiling that's spelled AAA.

Bull Durham List: Older minor leaguers who sneak onto major league rosters and shine for brief periods, showing what a mistake it is to pigeon-hole talented players just because they are not 24 and beautiful.

Rule 5 Reminder: Don't ignore the Rule 5 draft lest you ignore the 1% possibility of a Johan Santana.

Gaming

Standard Rules and Variations

Rotisserie Baseball was invented as an elegant confluence of baseball and economics. Whether by design or accident, the result has lasted for three decades. But what would Rotisserie and fantasy have been like if the Founding Fathers knew then what we know now about statistical analysis and game design? You can be sure things would be different.

The world has changed since the original game was introduced yet many leagues use the same rules today. New technologies have opened up opportunities to improve elements of the game that might have been limited by the capabilities of the 1980s. New analytical approaches have revealed areas where the original game falls short.

As such, there are good reasons to tinker and experiment; to find ways to enhance the experience.

Following are the basic elements of fantasy competition, those that provide opportunities for alternative rules and experimentation. This is by no means an exhaustive list, but at minimum provides some interesting food-for-thought.

Player pool

Standard: American League-only, National League-only or Mixed League. AL typically drafts 8-12 teams (pool penetration of 52% to 79%). NL typically drafts 8-13 teams (46% to 75% penetration). Mixed leagues draft 10-18 teams (31% to 55% penetration), though 15 teams (46%) is a common number.

Drafting of reserve players will increase the penetration percentages. A 12-team AL-only league adding 6 reserves onto 23-man rosters would draft 99% of the available pool of players on all AL teams' 25-man rosters.

The draft penetration level determines which fantasy management skills are most important to your league. The higher the penetration, the more important it is to draft a good team. The lower the penetration, the greater the availability of free agents and the more important in-season roster management becomes.

There is no generally-accepted optimal penetration level, but we have often suggested that 75% provides a good balance between the skills required for both draft prep and in-season management.

Alternative pools: There is a wide variety of options here. Certain leagues draft from within a small group of Major League divisions or teams. Some competitions, like home run leagues, only draft batters.

Bottom-tier pool: Drafting from the entire Major League population, the only players available are those who posted a Rotisserie dollar value of $5 or less in the previous season. Best used as a pick-a-player contest with any number of teams participating.

Positional structure

Standard: 23 players. One at each defensive position (though three outfielders may be from any of LF, CF or RF), plus one additional catcher, one middle infielder (2B or SS), one corner infielder (1B or 3B), two additional outfielders and a utility player/designated hitter (which often can be a player who qualifies anywhere). Nine pitchers, typically holding any starting or relief role.

Open: 25 players. One at each defensive position (plus DH), 5-man starting rotation and two relief pitchers. Nine additional players at any position, which may be a part of the active roster or constitute a reserve list.

40-man: Standard 23 plus 17 reserves. Used in many keeper and dynasty leagues.

Reapportioned: In recent years, new obstacles are being faced by 12-team A.L. leagues and 13-team N.L. leagues thanks to changes in the real game. The 14/9 split between batters and pitchers no longer reflects how MLB teams structure their rosters. Of the 30 teams, each with 25-man rosters, not one contains 14 batters for any length of time. In fact, many spend a good part of the season with only 12 batters, which means teams often have more pitchers than hitters.

For fantasy purposes in AL- and NL-only leagues, that leaves a disproportionate draft penetration into the batter and pitcher pools:

	BATTERS	PITCHERS
On AL rosters	180	170
Drafted, AL	168	108
Pct.	93%	64%
On NL rosters	201	199
Drafted, NL	182	117
Pct.	91%	59%

These drafts are now depleting about 30% more batters out of the pool than pitchers. Add in those leagues with reserve lists — perhaps an additional 6 players per team removing another 72-78 players — and post-draft free agent pools are very thin, especially on the batting side.

The impact is less in 15-team mixed leagues, though the FA pitching pool is still disproportionately deep.

	BATTERS	PITCHERS
On all rosters	381	369
Drafted	210	135
Pct.	55%	37%

One solution is to reapportion the number of batters and pitchers that are rostered. Adding one pitcher slot and eliminating one batter slot may be enough to provide better balance. The batting slot most often removed is the second catcher, since it is the position with the least depth.

Selecting players

Standard: The three most prevalent methods for stocking fantasy rosters are...

Snake/Straight/Serpentine draft: Players are selected in order with seeds reversed in alternating rounds. This method has become the most popular due to its speed, ease of implementation and ease of automation.

Auction: Players are sold to the highest bidder from a fixed budget, typically $260. Auctions provide the team owner with the most control over which players will be on his team, but can take twice as long as snake drafts.

Pick-a-player / Salary cap: Players are assigned fixed values and owners assemble their roster within a fixed cap. This type of roster-stocking is an individual exercise which results in teams typically having some of the same players.

Hybrid snake-auction: Each draft begins as an auction. Each team has to fill its first seven roster slots from a budget of $154. Opening bid for any player is $15. This assures that player values will be close to reality. After each team has filled seven slots, it becomes a snake draft.

If you like, you can assign fixed salaries to the snake-drafted players in such a way that each roster will still add up to about $260.

Round	Salary
8	$14
9	$13
10	$12
11	$11
12	$10
13	$9
14	$8
15	$7
16	$6
17	$5
18	$4
19	$3
20	$2
21	$1
22	$1
23	$1

You can also use this chart to decide how deep into the rosters you want to auction. If you want to auction the first 15 players, for instance, you'd use a budget of $238. Though not shown, if you only wanted to auction the first 5 players, your budget would be $121.

This method is intended to reduce draft time while still providing an economic component for selecting players.

Stat categories

Standard: The standard statistical categories for Rotisserie leagues are:

4x4: HR, RBI, SB, BA, W, Sv, ERA, WHIP

5x5: HR, R, RBI, SB, BA, W, Sv, K, ERA, WHIP

6x6: Categories typically added are Holds and OPS.

7x7, etc.: Any number of categories may be added.

In general, the more categories you add, the more complicated it is to isolate individual performance and manage the categorical impact on your roster. There is also the danger of redundancy; with multiple categories measuring like stats, certain skills can get over-valued. For instance, home runs are double-counted when using the categories of both HR and slugging average.

If the goal is to have categories that create a more encompassing picture of player performance, it is actually possible to accomplish more with less:

Retro 4x4: HR, (RBI+R-HR), SB, BA, W, Sv, K, ERA. This provides a better balance between batting and pitching in that each has three counting categories and one ratio category. You may also opt to replace BA with OBA.

Advanced 4x4:

Extra bases: Enhances the excitement of the big hit by adding doubles and triples.

Runs Produced (RBI + R—HR): In 5x5, two categories are devoted to situational stats. This combines them.

Net SB: Players should not get credit for steals without incurring the penalty for CS.

OBA: Walks are far too valuable to ignore.

Innings Pitched: A pitcher has to be good and have stamina to run up innings.

Net saves: You can't get credit for the good stuff without also being responsible for the bad.

Strikeouts - (HR x 4): A convoluted statistic but it captures the opposite ends of the spectrum of pitching outcomes.

WHIP: Oddly enough, the only original category to stay. Essentially, the pitching equivalent of OBA.

Keeping score

Standard: These are the most common scoring methods...

Rotisserie: Players are evaluated in several statistical categories. Totals of these statistics are ranked by team. The winner is the team with the highest cumulative ranking.

Points: Players receive points for events that they contribute to in each game. Points are totaled for each team and teams are then ranked.

Head-to-Head (H2H): Using Rotisserie or points scoring, teams are scheduled in weekly matchups. The winner of that week's match-up is the team that finishes higher in more categories (Rotisserie) or scores the most points.

Hybrid H2H-Rotisserie: Rotisserie's category ranking system can be converted into a weekly won-loss record. Depending upon where your team finishes for that week's statistics determines how many games you win for that week. Each week, your team will play seven games.

*Place	Record	*Place	Record
1st	7-0	7th	3-4
2nd	6-1	8th	2-5
3rd	6-1	9th	2-5
4th	5-2	10th	1-6
5th	5-2	11th	1-6
6th	4-3	12th	0-7

* Based on overall Rotisserie category ranking for the week.

At the end of each week, all the statistics revert to zero and you start over. You never dig a hole in any category that you can't climb out of, because all categories themselves are incidental to the standings.

The regular season lasts for 23 weeks, which equals 161 games. Weeks 24, 25 and 26 are for play-offs.

Free agent acquisition

Standard: Two methods are the most common for acquiring free agent players during the season.

<u>Reverse order of standings</u>: Access to the free agent pool is typically in a snake draft fashion with the last place team getting the first pick, and each successive team higher in the standings picking afterwards.

<u>Free agent acquisition budget (FAAB)</u>: Teams are given a set budget at the beginning of the season (typically, $100 or $1000) from which they bid on free agents in a closed auction process.

Vickrey FAAB: Research has shown that more than 50% of FAAB dollars are overbid on an annual basis. Given that this is a scarce commodity, one would think that a system to better manage these dollars might be desirable. The Vickrey system conducts a closed auction in the same way as standard FAAB, but the price of the winning bid is set at the amount of the second highest bid, plus $1. In some cases, gross overbids (at least $10 over) are reduced to the second highest bid plus $5.

This method was designed by William Vickrey, a Professor of Economics at Columbia University. His theory was that this process reveals the true value of the commodity. For his work, Vickrey was awarded the Nobel Prize for Economics (and $1.2 Million) in 1996.

Double-Bid FAAB: One of the inherent difficulties in the current FAAB system is that we have so many options for setting a bid amount. You can bid $47, or $51, or $23. You might agonize over whether to go $38 or $39. With a $100 budget, there are 100 decision points. And while you may come up with a rough guesstimate of the range in which your opponents might bid, the results for any individual player bidding are typically random within that range.

The first part of this process reduces the number of decision points. Owners must categorize their interest by bidding a fixed number of pre-set dollar amounts for each player. In a $100 FAAB league, for instance, those levels might be $1, $5, $10, $15, $20, $30, $40 or $50. All owners would set the general market value for free agents in these eight levels of interest. (This system sets a $50 maximum, but that is not absolutely necessary.)

The initial stage of the bidding process serves to screen out those who are not interested in a player at the appropriate market level. That leaves a high potential for tied owners, those who share the same level of interest.

The tied owners must then submit a second bid of equal or greater value than their first bid. These bids can be in $1 increments. The winning owner gets the player; if there is still a tie, then the player would go to the owner lower in the standings.

An advantage of this second bid is that it gives owners an opportunity to see who they are going up against, and adjust. If you are bidding against an owner close to you in the standings, you may need to be more aggressive in that second bid. If you see that the tied owner(s) wouldn't hurt you by acquiring that player, then maybe you resubmit the

original bid and be content to potentially lose out on the player. If you're ahead in the standings, it's actually a way to potentially opt out on that player completely by resubmitting your original bid and forcing another owner to spend his FAAB.

Some leagues will balk at adding another layer to the weekly deadline process; it's a trade-off to having more control over managing your FAAB.

The season

Standard: Leagues are played out during the course of the entire Major League Baseball season.

Split-season: Leagues are conducted from Opening Day through the All-Star break, then re-drafted to play from the All-Star break through the end of the season.

50-game split-season: Leagues are divided into three 50-game split-seasons. There would be a one-week break in between each segment. The advantages:

- With dwindling attention spans over the long 162-game season, 50 games is a more accessible time frame to maintain interest. There would be fewer abandoned teams.
- There would be four shots at a title each year; the first place team from each split, plus the team with the best overall record for the entire year.
- Given that drafting is considered the most fun aspect of the game, these splits triple the opportunities to participate in some type of draft. Leagues may choose to do complete re-drafts and treat the year as three distinct mini-seasons. Or, leagues might allow teams to drop their five worst players and conduct a restocking draft at each break.

Single game (Quint-Inning Lite format): Played with five owners drafting from the active rosters of the two Major League teams in a single game. Prior to the game, rosters are snake-drafted (no positional requirements). Points are awarded based on how players perform during the game. Batters accumulate points for bases gained:

Single	+1
Double	+2
Triple	+3
HR	+4
BB	+1
HBP	+1
SB	+1

Pitchers get +1 point for each full inning completed (3 outs) and lose 1 point for each run allowed (both earned and unearned).

A deck of standard playing cards may be used as an aid for scorekeeping and to break ties.

Players may be dropped, added or traded after the first inning. However, an owner must always have 5 players by the beginning of each half inning. Any player can be cut from an owner's roster. Free agents (players not rostered by any of the owners) can be claimed by any owner, between half-innings, in reverse order of the current standings. If two owners are tied and both want to place a claim, the tie is broken by drawing high card from the scorekeeping deck. Trades can be consummated at any time, between any two or more owners.

At the beginning of the 5th inning, each owner has the option of doubling the points (positive and negative) for any one player on his roster for the remainder of the game (the "Quint"). Should that player be traded, or dropped and then re-acquired, his "Quint" status remains for the game.

Beginning in the 9th inning, all batting points are doubled.

Quint-Inning can be played as a low stakes, moderate or higher stakes competition.

- It costs ($1/$5/$55) to get in the game.
- It costs (25 cents/$1/$5) per inning to stay in the game for the first four innings.
- Beginning with the 5th inning, the stakes go up to (50 cents/$2/$10) per inning to stay in the game.
- Should the game go into extra innings, the stakes rise to ($1/$5/$25) to stay in the game until its conclusion.

Each owner has to decide whether he is still in the game at the end of each full inning. Owners can drop out at the end of any inning, thus forfeiting any monies they've already contributed to the pot. When an owner drops, his players go back into the pool and can be acquired as free agents by the other owners.

The winner is the owner who finishes the game with the most points.

Post-season league: Some leagues re-draft teams from among the MLB post-season contenders and play out a separate competition. It is possible, however, to make a post-season competition that is an extension of the regular season.

Start by designating a set number of regular season finishers as qualifying for the post-season. The top four teams is a good number.

These four teams would designate a fixed 23-man roster for all post-season games, starting by freezing all currently-owned players on MLB post-season teams.

In order to fill the roster holes that will likely exist, these four teams would then pick players off the non-play-off teams (for the sake of the post-season only). This would be in the form of a snake draft done on the day following the end of the regular season. Draft order would be regular season finish, so the play-off team with the most regular season points would get first pick. Picks would continue until all four rosters are filled with as close to 23 men as possible.

Regular scoring would be used for all games during October. The team with the best play-off stats at the end of the World Series is the overall champ.

Snake Drafting
Snake draft first round history

The following tables record the comparison between pre-season projected player rankings (using Average Draft Position data from Mock Draft Central) and actual end-of-season results. The 7-year success rate of identifying each season's top talent is only 37%.

2004	ADP		ACTUAL = 6
1	Alex Rodriguez	1	Ichiro Suzuki
2	Albert Pujols	2	Vlad Guerrero (5)
3	Carlos Beltran	3	Randy Johnson
4	Todd Helton	4	Albert Pujols (2)
5	Vlad Guerrero	5	Johan Santana
6	Alfonso Soriano	6	Bobby Abreu
7	N. Garciaparra	7	Adrian Beltre
8	Barry Bonds	8	Barry Bonds (8)
9	Pedro Martinez	9	Carlos Beltran (3)
10	Mark Prior	10	Ben Sheets
11	Manny Ramirez	11	Melvin Mora
12	Roy Halladay	12	Carl Crawford
13	Magglio Ordonez	13	Manny Ramirez (11)
14	Edgar Renteria	14	Miguel Tejada
15	Sammy Sosa	15	Todd Helton (4)

2005	ADP		ACTUAL = 7
1	Alex Rodriguez	1	Derrek Lee
2	Carlos Beltran	2	Alex Rodriguez (1)
3	Albert Pujols	3	Albert Pujols (3)
4	Vlad Guerrero	4	David Ortiz
5	Manny Ramirez	5	Mark Teixeira
6	Bobby Abreu	6	Carl Crawford (12)
7	Miguel Tejada	7	Chone Figgins
8	Johan Santana	8	Jason Bay
9	Todd Helton	9	Miguel Cabrera
10	Jason Schmidt	10	Manny Ramirez (5)
11	Randy Johnson	11	Michael Young
12	Carl Crawford	12	Vlad Guerrero (4)
13	Alfonso Soriano	13	Ichiro Suzuki
14	Ben Sheets	14	Bobby Abreu (6)
15	Curt Schilling	15	Johan Santana (8)

2006	ADP		ACTUAL = 4
1	Albert Pujols	1	Jose Reyes
2	Alex Rodriguez	2	Derek Jeter
3	Vlad Guerrero	3	Albert Pujols (1)
4	Mark Teixeira	4	Ryan Howard
5	Manny Ramirez	5	Johan Santana
6	Miguel Cabrera	6	Alfonso Soriano
7	Derrek Lee	7	Carl Crawford (10)
8	Bobby Abreu	8	Matt Holliday
9	Miguel Tejada	9	Vlad Guerrero (3)
10	Carl Crawford	10	Miguel Cabrera (6)
11	Michael Young	11	Ichiro Suzuki
12	Carlos Beltran	12	Chase Utley
13	Jason Bay	13	Garrett Atkins
14	David Ortiz	14	Jermaine Dye
15	David Wright	15	Lance Berkman

2007	ADP		ACTUAL = 5
1	Albert Pujols	1	Alex Rodriguez (4)
2	Alfonso Soriano	2	Hanley Ramirez
3	Jose Reyes	3	Matt Holliday
4	Alex Rodriguez	4	Magglio Ordonez
5	Ryan Howard	5	David Wright (12)
6	Johan Santana	6	Jimmy Rollins
7	Carl Crawford	7	Ichiro Suzuki
8	Chase Utley	8	Jose Reyes (3)
9	Carlos Beltran	9	Jake Peavy
10	David Ortiz	10	David Ortiz (10)
11	Vlad Guerrero	11	Carl Crawford (7)
12	David Wright	12	Eric Byrnes
13	Miguel Cabrera	13	Brandon Phillips
14	Lance Berkman	14	Chipper Jones
15	Carlos Lee	15	Prince Fielder

2008	ADP		ACTUAL = 7
1	Alex Rodriguez	1	Albert Pujols (10)
2	Hanley Ramirez	2	Jose Reyes (4)
3	David Wright	3	Hanley Ramirez (2)
4	Jose Reyes	4	Manny Ramirez
5	Matt Holliday	5	Matt Holliday (5)
6	Jimmy Rollins	6	David Wright (3)
7	Miguel Cabrera	7	Lance Berkman
8	Chase Utley	8	Dustin Pedroia
9	Ryan Howard	9	Roy Halladay
10	Albert Pujols	10	Josh Hamilton
11	Prince Fielder	11	Alex Rodriguez (1)
12	Ryan Braun	12	C.C. Sabathia
13	Johan Santana	13	Carlos Beltran
14	Carl Crawford	14	Grady Sizemore
15	Alfonso Soriano	15	Chase Utley (8)

2009	ADP		ACTUAL = 5
1	Hanley Ramirez	1	Albert Pujols (2)
2	Albert Pujols	2	Hanley Ramirez (1)
3	Jose Reyes	3	Tim Lincecum
4	David Wright	4	Dan Haren
5	Grady Sizemore	5	Carl Crawford
6	Miguel Cabrera	6	Matt Kemp
7	Ryan Braun	7	Joe Mauer
8	Jimmy Rollins	8	Derek Jeter
9	Ian Kinsler	9	Zach Greinke
10	Josh Hamilton	10	Ryan Braun (7)
11	Ryan Howard	11	Jacoby Ellsbury
12	Mark Teixeira	12	Mark Reynolds
13	Alex Rodriguez	13	Prince Fielder
14	Matt Holliday	14	Chase Utley (15)
15	Chase Utley	15	Miguel Cabrera (6)

2010	ADP		ACTUAL = 5
1	Albert Pujols	1	Carlos Gonzalez
2	Hanley Ramirez	2	Albert Pujols (1)
3	Alex Rodriguez	3	Joey Votto
4	Chase Utley	4	Roy Halladay
5	Ryan Braun	5	Carl Crawford (15)
6	Mark Teixeira	6	Miguel Cabrera (9)
7	Matt Kemp	7	Josh Hamilton
8	Prince Fielder	8	Adam Wainwright
9	Miguel Cabrera	9	Felix Hernandez
10	Ryan Howard	10	Robinson Cano
11	Evan Longoria	11	Jose Bautista
12	Tom Lincecum	12	Paul Konerko
13	Joe Mauer	13	Matt Holliday
14	David Wright	14	Ryan Braun (5)
15	Carl Crawford	15	Hanley Ramirez (2)

ADP attrition

Why are there such large variances in the above lists? We rank and draft players based on the expectation that those ranked higher will return greater value, both from a productivity and playing time perspective. However, there are many variables affecting where players finish.

Of the players projected to finish in the top 300 coming into 2010, 44% lost playing time due to injuries, demotions and suspensions. That was actually an improvement over 2009 when the attrition rate was 51%. When you consider that about half of the best players had fewer at-bats or innings pitched than we projected, it shows how tough it is to rank players each year.

The fallout? Consider: it is nearly a foregone conclusion that Carlos Gonzalez will rank as a first round pick in 2011. The above data provide a strong argument against Gonzalez returning first-round value.

Yes, he is an excellent player, one of the best in the game, in 2010 anyway. But the issue is not his skills profile. The issue is the profile of what makes a worthy first rounder. Note:

- Over the past 6 years, two thirds of players finishing in the Top 15 were not in the Top 15 the previous year. There is a great deal of turnover in the first round, year-to-year.
- Of those who were first-timers, only 14.7% repeated in the first round the following year.
- Established superstars who finished in the Top 15 were no guarantee to repeat. These were players like David Ortiz (twice in 1st round, twice unable to repeat), Mark Teixeira (#5, 2005), Ryan Howard (#4, 2006) and Chase Utley (3 times in 1st round, only repeated once). Gonzalez is a first-time star; those types, like Josh Hamilton (2008), Matt Kemp and Joe Mauer (2009) are even less likely to repeat.
- From 2004 to 2009 (6 seasons), five of the six players who finished ranked #1 overall did repeat in the Top 15 the following year. However, none of them were coming off their first full season in the Majors as Gonzalez is. All of them were already established regulars.
- From 2005 to 2007, 14 of the top 15 players were batters. In 2008, that dropped to 13. The past two years, only 12. As player value shifts toward pitching, more arms are appearing the in first round, leaving fewer spots for the top batters.

As such, the odds of repeating in the first round, regardless of skill, are steep.

What is the best seed to draft from?

Most drafters like mid-round so they never have to wait too long for their next player. Some like the swing pick, suggesting that getting two players at 15 and 16 is better than a 1 and a 30. Many drafters assume that the swing pick means you'd be getting something like two $30 players instead of a $40 and $20.

Equivalent auction dollar values reveal the following facts about the first two snake draft rounds:

In an AL-only league, the top seed would get a $44 player (at #1) and a $24 player (at #24) for a total of $68; the 12th seed would get two $29s (at #12 and #13) for $58.

In an NL-only league, the top seed would get a $48 and a $28 ($76); the 13th seed would get two $30s ($60).

In a mixed league, the top seed would get a $47 and a $24 ($71); the 15th seed would get two $28s ($56).

Since the talent level flattens out after the 2nd round, low seeds never get a chance to catch up:

Dollar value difference between first player selected and last player selected.		
Round	12-team	15-team
1	$15	$19
2	$7	$8
3	$5	$4
4	$3	$3
5	$2	$2
6	$2	$1
7-17	$1	$1
18-23	$0	$0

The total value each seed accumulates at the end of the draft is hardly equitable:

Seed	AL	NL	Mixed
1	$266	$274	$273
2	$264	$265	$269
3	$263	$265	$261
4	$262	$266	$262
5	$259	$259	$260
6	$261	$260	$260
7	$260	$261	$260
8	$261	$260	$260
9	$261	$258	$258
10	$257	$259	$260
11	$257	$257	$257
12	$258	$255	$257
13		$254	$257
14			$255
15			$256

Of course, the draft is just the starting point for managing your roster and player values are variable. Still, it's tough to imagine a scenario where the #1 seed wouldn't have an advantage over the bottom seed.

Using ADPs to determine when to select players
(Bill Macey)

Although average draft position (ADP) data gives us a good idea of where in the draft each player is selected, it can be misleading when trying to determine how early to target a player. This chart summarizes the percentage of players drafted within 15 picks of his ADP as well as the average standard deviation by grouping of players.

ADP Rank	% within 15 picks	Standard Deviation
1-25	100%	2.5
26-50	97%	6.1
51-100	87%	9.6
100-150	72%	14.0
150-200	61%	17.4
200-250	53%	20.9

As the draft progresses, the picks for each player become more widely dispersed and less clustered around the average. Most top 100 players will go within one round of their ADP-converted round. However, as you reach the mid-to-late rounds, there is much more uncertainty as to when a player will be selected. Pitchers have slightly smaller standard deviations than do batters (i.e. they tend to be drafted in a narrower range). This suggests that drafters may be more likely to reach for a batter than for a pitcher.

Using the ADP and corresponding standard deviation, we can to estimate the likelihood that a given player will be available at a certain draft pick. We estimate the predicted standard deviation for each player as follows:

Stdev = -0.42 + 0.42*(ADP - Earliest Pick)

(That the figure 0.42 appears twice is pure coincidence; the numbers are not equal past two decimal points.)

If we assume that the picks are normally distributed, we can use a player's ADP and estimated standard deviation to estimate the likelihood that the player is available with a certain pick (MS Excel formula):

=1-normdist(x,ADP,Standard Deviation,True)

where «x» represents the pick number to be evaluated.

We can use this information to prepare for a snake draft by determining how early we may need to reach in order to roster a player. Suppose you have the 8th pick in a 15-team league draft and your target is 2009 sleeper candidate Nelson Cruz. His ADP is 128.9 and his earliest selection was with the 94th pick. This yields an estimated standard deviation of 14.2. You can then enter these values into the formula above to estimate the likelihood that he is still available at each of the following picks:

Pick	Likelihood Available
83	100%
98	99%
113	87%
128	53%
143	16%
158	2%

Mapping ADPs to auction value *(Bill Macey)*

Reliable average auction values (AAV) are often tougher to come by than ADP data for snake drafts. However, we can estimate predicted auction prices as a function of ADP, arriving at the following equation:

$$y = -9.8\ln(x) + 57.8$$

where $\ln(x)$ is the natural log function, x represents the actual ADP, and y represents the predicted AAV.

This equation does an excellent job estimating auction prices (r^2=0.93), though deviations are unavoidable. The asymptotic nature of the logarithmic function, however, causes the model to predict overly high prices for the top players. So be aware of that, and adjust.

Auction Value Analysis

Auction values (R$) in perspective

R$ is the dollar value placed on a player's statistical performance in a Rotisserie league, and designed to measure the impact that player has on the standings.

There are a several of methods to calculate a player's value from his projected (or actual) statistics.

The method we use here is a variation of the Standings Gain Points method described in the book, *How to Value Players for Rotisserie Baseball*, by Art McGee. (2nd edition available now). SGP converts a player's statistics in each Rotisserie category into the number of points those stats will allow you to gain in the standings. These are then converted back into dollars.

Another popular method is the Percentage Valuation Method. In PVM, a least valuable, or replacement performance level is set for each category (given league size) and then values are calculated representing the incremental improvement from that base. A player is then awarded value in direct proportion to the level he contributes to each category.

As much as these methods serve to attach a firm number to projected performance, the winning bid for any player is still highly variable depending upon many factors:

- the salary cap limit
- the number of teams in the league
- each team's roster size
- the impact of any protected players
- each team's positional demands at the time of bidding
- the statistical category demands at the time of bidding
- external factors, e.g. media inflation or deflation of value

In other words, **a *$30 player is only a $30 player if someone in your draft pays $30 for him.***

Since we currently have no idea who is going to close games for the Braves, or whether Dustin Ackley is going to break camp with Seattle, all the projected values in this book are slightly inflated. They are roughly based on a 12-team AL and 13-team NL league. The formula we use is applied across the board to all seasons so that each player's annual performance can be compared using a common base. The dollar values listed for past seasons are likely different (the actual values are on BaseballHQ.com).

We've attempted to take some contingencies into account, but the values will not total to anywhere near $3120, so don't bother adding them up. A $25 player in this book might actually be worth $21. Or $28. This level of precision is irrelevant in a process that is driven by market forces anyway. *So, don't obsess over it.*

Beware of other sources that publish perfectly calibrated Rotisserie values over the winter. They are likely making arbitrary decisions as to where free agents are going to sign and who is going to land jobs in the spring. We do not make those massive leaps of faith here. Bottom line... Some things you can predict, to other things you have to react. As roles become more defined over the winter, our online updates will provide better approximations of playing time, and projected Roto values that add up to $3120.

Roster slot valuation *(John Burnson)*

Tenets of player valuation say that the number of ballplayers with positive value – either positive *projected* value (before the season) or positive *actual* value (after the season) – must equal the total number of roster spots, and that, before the season, the value of a player must match his expected production. These propositions are wrong.

The unit of production in Rotisserie is not "the player" or "the statistic" but the *player-week*. If you own a player, you must own him for at least one week, and if you own him for more than one week, you must own him for multiples of one week. Moreover, you cannot break down his production – everything that a player does in a given week, you earn. (In leagues that allow daily transactions, the unit is the *player-day*. The point stays.)

When you draft a player, what have you bought?

"You have bought the stats generated by this player."

No. You have bought the stats generated by his *slot*. Initially, the drafted player fills the slot, but he need not fill the slot for the season, and he need not contribute from Day One. If you trade the player during the season, then your bid on Draft Day paid for the stats of the original player *plus* the stats of the new player. If the player misses time due to injury or demotion, then you bought the stats of whomever fills the weeks while the drafted player is missing. At season's end, there will be more players providing positive value than there are roster slots.

Before the season, the number of players projected for positive value has to equal the total number of roster slots – after all, we can't order owners to draft more players than can fit on their rosters. However, the projected productivity

should be adjusted by the potential to capture extra value in the slot. This is especially important for injury-rehab cases and late-season call-ups. For example, if we think that a player will miss half the season, then we would augment his projected stats with a half-year of stats from a replacement-level player at his position. Only then would we calculate prices. Essentially, we want to apportion $260 per team among the *slots*, not the players.

Average player value by draft round

Rd	AL	NL	Mxd	Avg
1	$34	$35	$34	$35
2	$26	$29	$26	$27
3	$23	$25	$23	$24
4	$20	$22	$20	$21
5	$18	$19	$18	$18
6	$17	$17	$16	$17
7	$16	$16	$15	$15
8	$15	$15	$13	$14
9	$13	$14	$12	$13
10	$12	$12	$11	$12
11	$11	$11	$10	$11
12	$10	$9	$9	$9
13	$9	$8	$8	$8
14	$8	$7	$8	$7
15	$7	$6	$7	$7
16	$6	$4	$6	$6
17	$5	$4	$5	$5
18	$4	$3	$4	$4
19	$3	$2	$3	$3
20	$2	$1	$2	$2
21	$1	$1	$2	$2
22	$1	$1	$1	$1
23	$1	$1	$1	$1

Benchmarks for auction players:
° All $30 players will go in the first round.
° All $20-plus players will go in the first four rounds.
° Double-digit value ends pretty much after Round 11.
° The $1 end game starts at about Round 20 or 21.

Dollar values by lineup position *(Michael Roy)*

How much value is derived from batting order position?

Pos	PA	R	RBI	R$
#1	747	107	72	$18.75
#2	728	102	84	$19.00
#3	715	95	100	$19.45
#4	698	93	104	$19.36
#5	682	86	94	$18.18
#6	665	85	82	$17.19
#7	645	81	80	$16.60
#8	623	78	80	$16.19
#9	600	78	73	$15.50

So, a batter moving from the bottom of the order to the clean-up spot, with no change in performance, would gain nearly $4 in value from runs and RBIs alone.

Dollar values: expected projective accuracy

There is a 65% chance that a player projected for a certain dollar value will finish the season with a final value within plus-or-minus $5 of that projection. That means, if you value a player at $25, you only have about a 2-in-3 shot of him finishing between $20 and $30.

If you want to get your odds up to 80%, the range now becomes +/- $9. You have an 80% shot that your $25 player will finish somewhere between $16 and $34.

How likely is it that a $30 player will repeat?

(Matt Cederholm)

From 2003-2008, there were 205 players who earned $30 or more (using single-league 5x5 values). Only 70 of them (34%) earned $30 or more in the next season. Not good.

In fact, the odds of repeating a $30 season aren't good no matter how you slice it. As seen below, the best odds during that period were 42%, hardly something you would stake your future on. And as we would expect, pitchers fare far worse than hitters.

	Total>$30	# Repeat	% Repeat
Hitters	167	64	38%
Pitchers	38	6	16%
Total	205	70	34%
High-Reliability*			
Hitters	42	16	38%
Pitchers	7	0	0%
Total	49	16	33%
100+ BPV			
Hitters	60	25	42%
Pitchers	31	6	19%
Total	91	31	19%
High-Reliability and 100+ BPV*			
Hitters	12	5	42%
Pitchers	6	0	0%
Total	18	5	28%

*Reliability figures are from 2006-2008

Maybe one season isn't enough. What if we looked at players with multiple seasons of $30 or more in value? The numbers do get better. For players with consecutive $30 seasons, 2003-2008:

	Total>$30	# Repeat	% Repeat
Two Years	62	29	55%
Three+ Years	29	19	66%

Still, a player with two consecutive seasons at $30 in value is barely a 50/50 proposition. And three consecutive seasons is only a 2/3 shot. Small sample sizes aside, this does illustrate the nature of the beast. Even the most consistent, reliable players fail 1/3 of the time. Of course, this is true whether they are kept or drafted anew, so this alone shouldn't prevent you from keeping a player.

How well do elite pitchers retain their value?

(Michael Weddell)

An elite pitcher (one who earns at least $24 in a season) on average keeps 80% of his R$ value from year 1 to year 2. This compares to the baseline case of only 52%.

Historically, 36% of elite pitchers improve, returning a greater R$ in the second year than they did the first year. That is an impressive performance considering they already were at an elite level. 17% collapse, returning less than a third of their R$ in the second year. The remaining 47% experience a middling outcome, keeping more than a third but less than all of their R$ from one year to the next.

Profiling the end game

What types of players are typically the most profitable in the end-game? First, our overall track record on $1 picks:

Avg Return	%Profitable	Avg Prof	Avg. Loss
$1.89	51%	$10.37	($7.17)

On aggregate, the hundreds of players drafted in the end-game earned $1.89 on our $1 investments. While they were profitable overall, only 51% of them actually turned a profit. Those that did cleared more than $10 on average. Those that didn't — the other 49% — lost about $7 apiece.

Pos	Pct.of tot	Avg Val	%Profit	Avg Prof	Avg Loss
CA	12%	($1.68)	41%	$7.11	($7.77)
CO	9%	$6.12	71%	$10.97	($3.80)
MI	9%	$3.59	53%	$10.33	($4.84)
OF	22%	$2.61	46%	$12.06	($5.90)
SP	29%	$1.96	52%	$8.19	($7.06)
RP	19%	$0.35	50%	$11.33	($10.10)

These results bear out the danger of leaving catchers to the end game. They were the only position that returned negative value. Corner infielder returns beg the tactic of leaving open a 1B or 3B spot for the end.

Age	Pct.of tot	Avg Val	%Profit	Avg Prof	Avg Loss
< 25	15%	($0.88)	33%	$8.25	($8.71)
25-29	48%	$2.59	56%	$11.10	($8.38)
30-35	28%	$2.06	44%	$10.39	($5.04)
35+	9%	$2.15	41%	$8.86	($5.67)

The practice of speculating on younger players – mostly rookies – in the end game was a washout. Part of the reason was that those that even made it to the end game were often of the long-term type. The better prospects were typically drafted earlier.

	Pct.of tot	Avg Val	%Profit	Avg Prof	Avg Loss
Injury rehabs	20%	$3.63	36%	$15.07	($5.65)

One in five end-gamers were players coming back from injury. While only 36% of them were profitable, the healthy ones returned a healthy profit. The group's losses were small, likely because they weren't healthy enough to play.

Advanced Draft Strategies

Stars & Scrubs v. Spread the Risk

Stars & Scrubs (S&S): A Rotisserie auction strategy in which a roster is anchored by a core of high priced stars and the remaining positions filled with low-cost players.

Spread the Risk (STR): An auction strategy in which available dollars are spread evenly among all roster slots.

Both approaches have benefits and risks. An experiment was conducted in 2004 whereby a league was stocked with four teams assembled as S&S, four as STR and four as a control group. Rosters were then frozen for the season.

The Stars & Scrubs teams won all three ratio categories. Those deep investments ensured stability in the categories that are typically most difficult to manage. On the batting side, however, S&S teams amassed the least amount of playing time, which in turn led to bottom-rung finishes in HRs, RBIs and Runs.

One of the arguments for the S&S approach is that it is easier to replace end-game losers (which, in turn, may help resolve the playing time issues). Not only is this true, but the results of this experiment show that replacing those bottom players is critical to success.

The Spread the Risk teams stockpiled playing time, which in turn led to strong finishes in many of the counting stats, including clear victories in RBIs, Wins and Strikeouts. This is a key tenet in drafting philosophy; we often say that the team that compiles the most ABs will undoubtedly be among the top teams in RBI and Runs.

The danger is on the pitching side. More innings did yield more wins and Ks, but also destroyed ERA/WHIP.

So, what approach makes the most sense? **The optimal strategy might be to STR on offense and go S&S with your pitching staff.** STR buys more ABs, so you immediately position yourself well in four of the five batting categories. On pitching, it might be more advisable to roster a few core arms, though that immediately elevates your risk exposure. Admittedly, it's a balancing act, which is why we need to pay more attention to risk analysis and look closer at strategies like the RIMA Plan and Portfolio3.

The LIMA Plan

The LIMA Plan is a strategy for Rotisserie leagues (though the underlying concept can be used in other formats) that allows you to target high skills pitchers at very low cost, thereby freeing up dollars for offense. LIMA is an acronym for Low Investment Mound Aces, and also pays tribute to Jose Lima, a $1 pitcher in 1998 who exemplified the power of the strategy. In a $260 league:

1. *Budget a maximum of $60 for your pitching staff.*
2. *Allot no more than $30 of that budget for acquiring saves.* In 5x5 leagues, it is reasonable to forego saves at the draft (and acquire them during the season) and re-allocate this $30 to starters ($20) and offense ($10).
3. *Draft only pitchers with:*
   - Command ratio (K/BB) of 2.0 or better.
   - Strikeout rate of 5.6 or better.
   - Expected home run rate of 1.0 or less.
4. *Draft as few innings as your league rules will allow.* This is intended to manage risk. For some game formats, this should be a secondary consideration.
5. *Maximize your batting slots.* Target batters with:
   - Contact rate of at least 80%
   - Walk rate of at least 10%
   - PX or SX level of at least 100

Spend no more than $29 for any player and try to keep the $1 picks to a minimum.

The goal is to ace the batting categories and carefully pick your pitching staff so that it will finish in the upper third in ERA, WHIP and saves (and IP or Ks in 5x5), and an upside of perhaps 9th in wins. In a competitive league, that should be enough to win, and definitely enough to finish in the money. Worst case, you should have an excess of offense available that you can deal for pitching.

The strategy works because it better allocates resources. Fantasy leaguers who spend a lot for pitching are not only paying for expected performance, they are also paying for better defined roles – #1 and #2 rotation starters, ace closers, etc. – which are expected to translate into more IP, wins and saves. But roles are highly variable. A pitcher's role will usually come down to his skill and performance; if he doesn't perform, he'll lose the role.

The LIMA Plan says, let's invest in skill and let the roles fall where they may. In the long run, better skills should translate into more innings, wins and saves. And as it turns out, pitching skill costs less than pitching roles do.

In *snake draft leagues*, don't start drafting starting pitchers until Rd 10. In *shallow mixed leagues*, the LIMA Plan may not be necessary; just focus on the BPI benchmarks. In *simulation leagues*, build your staff around BPI benchmarks.

8 Myths of the LIMA Plan

The LIMA Plan was introduced in 1998. During that time, its basic tenets have spread throughout the internet until it has become mostly mainstream. However, like the game of "telephone," time often distorts the message. Here are the most common misconceptions we've come across:

MYTH #1: LIMA means... Low Innings Mound Aces

Minimizing innings is intended to help manage risk, but fantasy leaguers have been interpreting this to mean that you should avoid starting pitchers. This is not true.

MYTH #2: LIMA means... Fill your staff with middle relievers.

Stocking your pitching staff with middle relievers may be an end result if you cannot acquire other more valuable arms, but it is certainly not the intent of LIMA.

MYTH #3: LIMA means... you have to punt wins.

It's true that the lack of innings does put a strain on the Wins category. There's less margin for error. However, the focus on skill tends to uncover hidden innings upside, which leads to more wins.

MYTH #4: LIMA means... don't spend for saves.

The riskiness of the Wins category requires that you do spend for saves, but admittedly, acquiring those precious saves is probably the biggest challenge to pulling off LIMA.

MYTH #5: If you don't spend $200 on offense, you've blown it.

Or alternatively, "blow the rules, punt the plan." LIMA provides a series of targets, but just because you miss a few doesn't mean that your efforts have gone to waste.

MYTH #6: LIMA will not work in a 5x5 league.

The innings restriction and budget allocations may be a problem, so you move them. Don't use the foundation to weigh you down, use it as a springboard. There are several 5x5 variations that are very doable.

MYTH #7: LIMA only works in Rotisserie leagues.

The budget framework may be roto-specific, but the core concepts are applicable to just about any fantasy game. The focus on skills is what provides the greatest benefit and is what sets LIMA apart from any other strategy

MYTH #8: It won't work if more than one person is doing it.

There are plenty of LIMA-caliber pitchers and more than enough offense, so a few owners using it will make little difference. However, as more and more owners build large offenses and wait for pitching bargains, LIMA drafters will need to be cognizant of the economic shift.

Variations on the LIMA Plan

LIMA Extrema: Limit your total pitching budget to only $30, or less. This can be particularly effective in shallow leagues where LIMA-caliber starting pitcher free agents are plentiful during the season.

SANTANA Plan: Instead of spending $30 on saves, you spend it on a starting pitcher anchor. In 5x5 leagues where you can reasonably punt saves at the draft table, allocating those dollars to a high-end LIMA-caliber starting pitcher can work well as long as you pick the right anchor.

One way to approach that selection is...

RIMA Plan: LIMA is based on optimal resource allocation. These days, however, no matter how good of a team you draft, player inconsistency, injuries and unexpected *risk factors* can wreak havoc with your season. The RIMA Plan adds the element of **RI**sk **MA**nagement.

Players are not risks by virtue of their price tags alone. A $35 Roy Halladay, for example, might be a very good buy since he is a healthy, stable commodity. But most LIMA drafters would not consider him because of the price.

The RIMA Plan involves setting up two pools of players. The first pool consists of those who meet the LIMA criteria. The second pool includes players with high Reliability grades. The set of players who appear in both pools are our prime draft targets. We then evaluate the two pools further, integrating different levels of skill and risk.

RIMA was introduced in 2004; the specifics of the plan have since been assimilated into Portfolio3.

Total Control Drafting (TCD)

Part of the reason we play this game is the aura of "control," our ability to create a team of players we want and manage them to a title. We make every effort to control as many elements as possible, but in reality, the players that end up on our teams are largely controlled by the other owners. *Their* bidding affects your ability to roster the players you want. In a snake draft, the other owners control your roster even more. We are really only able to get the players we want within the limitations set by others.

However, an optimal roster can be constructed from a fanalytic assessment of skill and risk. We can create our teams from that "perfect player pool" and not be forced to roster players that don't fit our criteria. It's now possible. It's just a matter of taking *Total Control*.

Why this makes sense

1. Our obsession with projected player values is holding us back. If a player on your draft list is valued at $20 and you agonize when the bidding hits $23, odds are about two chances in three that he could really earn anywhere from $15 to $25. What this means is, in some cases, and within reason, you should just pay what it takes to get the players you want.

2. There is no such thing as a bargain. Most of us *don't* just pay what it takes because we are always on the lookout for players who go under value. But we really don't know which players will cost less than they will earn because

prices are still driven by the draft table. The concept of "bargain" assumes that we even know what a player's true value is. To wit: If we target a player at $23 and land him for $20, we might *think* we got a bargain. In reality, this player might earn anywhere from $19 to $26, making that $3 in perceived savings virtually irrelevant.

The point is, a "bargain" is defined by your particular marketplace at the time of your particular draft, not by any list of canned values, or an "expectation" of what the market value of any player might be. So any contention that TCD forces you to overpay for your players is false.

3. "Control" is there for the taking. Most owners are so focused on their own team that they really don't pay much attention to what you're doing. There are some exceptions, and bidding wars do happen, but in general, other owners will not provide that much resistance.

How it's done

1. Create your optimal draft pool.

2. Get those players.

Start by identifying which players will be draftable based on the LIMA or Portfolio3 criteria. Then, at the draft, your focus has to be on your roster only. When it's your bid opener, toss a player you need at about 50%-75% of your projected value. Bid aggressively. Forget about bargain-hunting; just pay what you need to pay. Of course, don't spend $40 for a $25 player, but it's okay to exceed your projected value within reason.

Mix up the caliber of openers. Instead of tossing out an Albert Pujols at $35 in the first round, toss out a Denard Span at $8. *Wise Guy Baseball's* Gene McCaffrey suggests tossing all lower-end players early, which makes sense. It helps you bottom-fill your roster with players most others won't chase early, and you can always build the top end of your roster with players others toss out.

Another good early tactic is to gauge the market value of scarce commodities with a $19 opener for Heath Bell (saves) or a $29 opener for Carlos Crawford (stolen bases).

At the end of the draft, you may have rostered 23 players who could have been purchased at somewhat lower cost. It's tough to say. Those extra dollars likely won't mean much anyway; in fact, you might have just left them on the table. TCD almost ensures that you spend all your money.

In the end, it's okay to pay a slight premium to make sure you get the players with the highest potential to provide a good return on your investment. It's no different than the premium you'd pay to get the last valuable shortstop, or for the position flexibility a player like Jerry Hairston provides. With TCD, you're just spending those extra dollars up front on players with high skill and low risk.

The best part is that you take more control of your destiny. You build your roster with what you consider are the best assemblage of players. You keep the focus on your team. And you don't just roster whatever bargains the rest of the table leaves for you, because a bargain is just a fleeting perception of value we have in March.

The Portfolio3 Plan

The previously discussed strategies have had important roles in furthering our potential for success. The problem is that they all take a broad-stroke approach to the draft. The $35 first round player is evaluated and integrated into the plan in the same way that the end-gamer is. But each player has a different role on your team by virtue of his skill set, dollar value, position and risk profile. When it comes to a strategy for how to approach a specific player, one size does not fit all.

We need some players to return fair value more than others. When you spend $40 on a player, you are buying the promise of putting more than 15% of your budget in the hands of 4% of your roster. By contrast, the $1 players are easily replaceable. If you're in a snake draft league, you know that a first-rounder going belly-up is going to hurt you far more than a 23rd round bust.

We rely on some players for profit more than others. Those first-rounders are not where we are likely going to see the most profit potential. The $10-$20 players are likely to return more pure dollar profit; the end-gamers are most likely to return the highest profit percentage.

We can afford to weather more risk with some players than with others. Since those high-priced early-rounders need to return at least fair value, we cannot afford to take on excessive risk. Since we need more profit potential from the lower priced, later-round picks, that means opening up our tolerance for risk more with those players.

Players have different risk profiles based solely on what roster spot they are going to fill. Catchers are more injury prone. A closer's value is highly dependent on fickle managerial whim. These types of players are high risk even if they have the best skills on the planet. That needs to affect their draft price or draft round.

For some players, the promise of providing a scarce skill, or productivity at a scarce position, may trump risk. Not always, but sometimes. At minimum, we need to be open to the possibility. The determining factor is usually price. An $8, 14th round Koji Uehara is not something you pass up, even with a Reliability Grade of FCC.

In the end, we need a way to integrate all these different types of players, roles and needs. We need to put some form to the concept of a diversified draft approach. Thus:

The **Portfolio3 Plan** provides a three-tiered approach to the draft. Just like most folks prefer to diversify their stock portfolio, P3 advises to diversify your roster with three different types of players. Depending upon the stage of the draft (and budget constraints in auction leagues), P3 uses a different set of rules for each tier that you'll draft from. The three tiers are:

1. Core Players
2. Mid-Game Players
3. End-Game Players

TIER 1: CORE PLAYERS

Roster Slots	Budget	BATTERS Rel	Ct%	PX or Sp		PITCHERS Rel	BPV
5-8	Max $160	BBB	80%	100	100	BBB	75

These are the players who will provide the foundation to your roster. These are your prime stat contributors and where you will invest the largest percentage of your budget. In snake drafts, these are the names you pick in the early rounds. There is no room for risk here. Given their price tags, there is usually little potential for profit. The majority of your core players should be batters.

The above chart shows general roster goals. In a snake draft, you need to select core-caliber players in the first 5-8 rounds. In an auction, any player purchased for $20 or more should meet the Tier 1 filters.

The filters are not strict, but they are important, so you should stick to them as best as possible. An 80% contact rate ensures that your batting average category is covered. PX and Spd ensure that you draft players with a minimum league average power or speed. On the pitching side, a BPV of 75 ensures that, if you must draft a pitcher in your core, it will be one with high-level skill. For both batters and pitchers, minimum reliability grades of BBB cover risk.

Since these are going to be the most important players on your roster, the above guidelines help provide a report card, of sorts, for your draft. For instance, if you leave the table with only three Tier 1 players, then you know you have likely rostered too much risk or not enough skill. If you manage to draft nine Tier 1 players, that doesn't necessarily mean you've got a better roster, just a better core. There still may be more work to do in the other tiers.

Tier 1 remains the most important group of players as they are the blue chips that allow you to take chances elsewhere. However, there can be some play within this group on the batting side.

The 80% contact rate is important to help protect the batting average category. However, with some care, you can roster a few BA Suzuki-esque studs to allow you the flexibility to take on some low-contact hitters who excel in other areas (typically power). The tactic would work like this... If you are short on Tier 1 players and have exhausted the pool of those who meet all the filters, you can work your way down the following list...

TIER 1 BATTERS

	Rel	Ct%	PX	or	Spd
Primary group	BBB	80%	100		100
Secondary	BBB	75%	110		110
Tertiary	BBB	70%	120		120

...knowing full well that, for every player you roster from these lower groups, you are putting your batting average at greater risk. You should only do this if you think the power/speed gains will sufficiently offset any BA shortfalls.

These two sub-groups are not fixed filters; they form a continuum. So if you have a player with a 78% contact rate, your PX/Spd requirement would probably be somewhere around 105. I would not go anywhere near a player with a contact rate less than 70%.

TIER 2: MID-GAME PLAYERS

Roster		BATTERS				PITCHERS	
Slots	Budget	Rel	Ct% or	PX or Sp		Rel	BPV
7-13	$50-$100	BBB	80%	100	100	BBB	50

All players must be less than $20
Batters must be projected for at least 500 AB

In an early 2008 column, I noted how fellow Tout combatant, Jason Grey, was consistently able to assemble offensive juggernauts by the singular tactic of accumulating massive amounts of often-cheap playing time. Intrinsic skill was irrelevant. On the offensive side, this makes sense.

Runs and RBIs are only tangentially related to skill. If a player is getting 500 AB, he is likely going to provide positive value in those categories just from opportunity alone. And given that his team is seeing fit to give him those AB, he is probably also contributing somewhere else.

These players have value to us. And we can further filter this pool of full-timers who miss the P3 skills criteria by skimming off those with high REL grades.

There are two dangers in this line of thinking. First, it potentially puts the batting average category at risk. You don't want to accumulate bad AB; when you dig yourself into a hole in BA, it is the one category that is nearly impossible to dig out of. However, this just means we need to approach it tactically; if we decide to roster a Mark Reynolds, we must also roster an Ichiro Suzuki.

Second, this line of thinking assumes we can accurately project playing time. But if we focus on those players who are locked into firm roles, there is still a decent-sized pool to draw from.

Tier 2 is often where the biggest auction bargains tend to be found as the blue-chippers are already gone and owners are reassessing their finances. It is in that mid-draft lull where you can scoop up tons of profit. In a snake draft, these players should take you down to about round 16-18.

TIER 3: END-GAME PLAYERS

Roster		BATTERS			PITCHERS	
Slots	Budget	Rel	Ct%	PX or Sp	Rel	BPV
5-10	Up to $50	n/a	80%	100 100	n/a	75

All players must be less than $10

For some fantasy leaguers, the end game is when the beer is gone and you have to complete your roster with any warm body. In P3, these are gambling chips, but every end-gamer must provide the promise of upside. For that reason, the focus must remain on skill and conditional opportunity. P3 drafters should fill the majority of their pitching slots from this group.

By definition, end-gamers are typically high risk players, but risk is something you'll want to embrace here. You probably don't want a Jeff Francoeur-type player at the end of the draft. His AAB reliability grade would provide stability, but there is no upside, so there is little profit potential. This is where you need to look for profit so it is better here to ignore reliability; instead, take a few chances in your quest for those pockets of possible profit. If the player does not pan out, he can be easily replaced.

As such, a Tier 3 end-gamer should possess the BPI skill levels noted above, and...

- playing time upside as a back-up to a risky front-liner
- an injury history that has depressed his value
- solid skills demonstrated at some point in the past
- minor league potential even if he has been more recently a major league bust

Notes on draft implementation...

Auction leagues: Tier 1 player acquisition should be via the Total Control Drafting method. Simply, pay whatever it takes, within reason. Be willing to pay a small premium for the low risk and high skills combination.

Snake drafters will have choices in the first six rounds or so. There are no guarantees — a swing-pick seed might negate any chance you have for rostering some players — but at least there are some options. If you miss out on the cream, you can either drop down and select a lower round player early, or relax the filters a bit to grab someone who might have higher value but perhaps greater risk.

Position scarcity: While we still promote the use of position scarcity in snake drafts, it may be more important to have solid foundation players in the early rounds.

Drafting pitchers early is still something we advise against. However, if you are going to grab a pitcher in the first six rounds, at least make sure it's a Tier 1 name. It is still a viable strategy to hold off on starting pitchers until as late as Round 10 or 11; however, if it's Round 7 and Justin Verlander is still sitting out there, by all means jump.

LIMA Plan: Although LIMA says no starting pitchers over $20, Tier 1 provides a few options where it would be okay to break the rules. You can adjust your $60 pitching budget up to accommodate, or downgrade saves targets.

Punting saves: Still viable, unless a Tier 1 closer falls into your lap. These are extremely rare commodities anyway.

Keeper leagues: When you decide upon your freeze list, you should be looking for two types of keepers — the best values *and* the most valuable players. Freezing a $15 Tim Lincecum is a no-brainer; where some drafters struggle is with the $25 Ryan Zimmerman. Given that TCD says that we should be willing to pay a premium for Tier 1 players, any name on that list should be a freeze consideration.

Adding in the variable of potential draft inflation, you should be more flexible with the prices you'd be willing to freeze players at. For instance, if you currently own a $40 Miguel Cabrera, you might be tempted to throw him back. However, between draft inflation and the premium you should be willing to pay for a Tier 1 commodity, his real value could be well over $50.

In-Season Analyses

The efficacy of streaming *(John Burnson)*

In leagues that allow weekly or daily transactions, many owners flit from hot player to hot player. But published dollar values don't capture this traffic – they assume that players are owned from April to October. For many leagues, this may be unrealistic.

We decided to calculate these "investor returns." For each week, we identified the top players by one statistic – BA for hitters, ERA for pitchers – and took the top 100 hitters and top 50 pitchers. We then said that, at the end of the week, the #1 player was picked up (or already owned) by 100% of teams, the #2 player was picked up or owned by 99% of teams, and so on, down to the 100th player, who was on 1% of teams. (For pitchers, we stepped by 2%.) Last, we tracked each player's performance in the *next* week, when ownership matters.

We ran this process anew for every week of the season, tabulating each player's "investor returns" along the way. If a player was owned by 100% of teams, then we awarded him 100% of his performance. If the player was owned by half the teams, we gave him half his performance. If he was owned by no one (that is, he was not among the top players in the prior week), his performance was ignored. A player's cumulative stats over the season was his investor return.

The results...

60% of pitchers had poorer investor returns, with an aggregate ERA 0.40 *higher* than their true ERA.

55% of batters had poorer investor returns, but with an aggregate batting average virtually identical to the true BA.

Sitting stars and starting scrubs *(Ed DeCaria)*

In setting your pitching rotation, conventional wisdom suggests sticking with trusted stars despite difficult matchups. But does this hold up? And can you carefully start inferior pitchers against weaker opponents? Here are the ERA's posted by varying skilled pitchers facing a range of different strength offenses:

Pitcher (ERA)	OPPOSING OFFENSE (RC/G)				
	5.25+	**5.00**	**4.25**	**4.00**	**<4.00**
3.00-	3.46	3.04	3.04	2.50	2.20
3.50	3.98	3.94	3.44	3.17	2.87
4.00	4.72	4.57	3.96	3.66	3.24
4.50	5.37	4.92	4.47	4.07	3.66
5.00+	6.02	5.41	5.15	4.94	4.42

Recommendations:

1. Never start below replacement-level pitchers.

2. Always start elite pitchers.

3. Other than that, never say never or always.

Playing matchups can pay off when the difference in opposing offense is severe.

Two-start pitcher weeks *(Ed DeCaria)*

A two-start pitcher is a prized possession. But those starts can mean two DOMinant outings, two DISasters, or anything else in between, as shown by these results:

PQS Pair	% Weeks	ERA	WHIP	Win/Wk	K/Wk
DOM-DOM	20%	2.53	1.02	1.1	12.0
DOM-AVG	28%	3.60	1.25	0.8	9.2
AVG-AVG	14%	4.44	1.45	0.7	6.8
DOM-DIS	15%	5.24	1.48	0.6	7.9
AVG-DIS	17%	6.58	1.74	0.5	5.7
DIS-DIS	6%	8.85	2.07	0.3	5.0

Weeks that include even one DISaster start produce terrible results. Unfortunately, avoiding such disasters is much easier in hindsight. But what is the actual impact of this decision on the stat categories?

ERA and WHIP: When the difference between opponents is extreme, inferior pitchers can actually be a better percentage play. This is true both for one-start pitchers and two-start pitchers, and for choosing inferior one-start pitchers over superior two-start pitchers.

Strikeouts per Week: Unlike the two rate stats, there is a massive shift in the balance of power between one-start and two-start pitchers in the strikeout category. Even stars with easy one-start matchups can only barely keep pace with two-start replacement-level arms in strikeouts per week.

Wins per week are also dominated by the two-start pitchers. Even the very worst two-start pitchers will earn a half of a win on average, which is the same rate as the very best one-start pitchers.

The bottom line… If strikeouts and wins are the strategic priority, use as many two-start weeks as the rules allow, even if it means using a replacement-level pitcher with two tough starts instead of a mid-level arm with a single easy start. But if ERA and/or WHIP management are the priority, two-start pitchers can be very powerful, as a single week might impact the standings by over 1.5 points in ERA/WHIP, positively or negatively.

Consistency *(Dylan Hedges)*

Few things are as valuable to head-to-head league success as filling your roster with players who can produce a solid baseline of stats, week in and week out. In traditional leagues, while consistency is not as important — all we care about are aggregate numbers — filling your team with consistent players can make roster management easier.

Consistent batters have good plate discipline, walk rates and on base percentages. These are foundation skills. Those who add power to the mix are obviously more valuable, however, the ability to hit home runs consistently is rare.

Consistent pitchers demonstrate similar skills in each outing; if they also produce similar results, they are even more valuable.

We can *track* consistency but *predicting* it is difficult. Many fantasy leaguers try to predict a batter's hot or cold streaks, or individual pitcher starts, but that is typically a fool's errand. The best we can do is find players who demonstrate seasonal consistency over time; in-season, we want to manage players and consistency tactically.

Gaming Demographics

Each year at BaseballHQ.com, we keep tabs on ongoing fantasy baseball industry trends by means of our weekly HQ Poll, which we've been running since December 1998. We've been tracking dozens of trends.

Since these questions are asked at Baseball HQ, they only represent the opinions of folks who a) visit Baseball HQ, and b) respond to online polls. So these are clearly not scientific representations of the industry as a whole. However, even this group can reveal some interesting tidbits about how fantasy leaguers play the game. Note that all poll results had at least 500 responses.

Here is a profile of these respondents — who very well might be an accurate reflection of *you* — by the numbers:

74% say their primary league is a keeper league.

72% participate in an auction draft.

69% of those in keeper leagues will fill only slots where they can protect good value, even if it's less than the allowable limit.

65% of keeper leaguers have an August trading deadline.

64% would not trade Miguel Cabrera even up for Roy Halladay.

57% prefer 5x5 Rotisserie as their favorite fantasy format.

56% of weekly transaction leagues have a Monday deadline.

53% have one or two primary leagues they focus the most on. They manage other leagues whenever they find extra time.

45% would ride a struggling frontline starting pitcher (Round 1-6, $20+ draft pick) all year because the odds of a turnaround are greater than any free agent option.

44% think doing mock drafts in November is absurd.

43% start getting into the upcoming baseball season at the end of the fantasy football season.

43% believe that the largest deficit that can be overcome in July and still win their league is 15 points.

42% of leagues use an in-season salary cap.

42% of leagues have daily transactions.

41% of leagues allow September roster expansion.

40% say their core motivation for playing fantasy sports is the challenge of proving their knowledge.

40% buy spring annual magazines because they can't help themselves – it is like a drug.

37% of NL-only and AL-only leagues allow owners to keep a player who is traded out of the league.

34% would want to find ways to keep interest alive all season if they could make just one change to improve their leagues.

34% don't bother calculating draft inflation.

32% will quit on a struggling team before the season is over.

25% typically watch at least one game every day, on average, during the baseball season.

25% say that "dump deals" are *never* okay under any condition.

24% play in a mixed league with 10 or fewer teams.

24% prefer more than 6 starting pitchers on a 9-man 5x5 staff.

24% don't start taking the standings seriously until June or later.

21% say it is impossible to contend in their league without a constant pulse on all levels of the minor leagues.

21% of keeper leagues allow five or fewer players to be protected from one season to the next.

17% say that there are certain owners in their league that they dislike and work harder to beat.

17% play in a league that uses the category of Holds.

12% would not play in a fantasy league without cash stakes.

4% play in a fantasy competition based on the MLB post-season.

2% of leagues do not allow trades.

Other Diamonds

Cellar value: The dollar value at which a player cannot help but earn more than he costs. Always profit here.

Crickets: The sound heard when someone's opening draft bid on a player is also the only bid.

Scott Elarton List: Players you drop out on when the bidding reaches $1.

End-game wasteland: Home for players undraftable in the deepest of leagues, who stay in the free agent pool all year. It's the place where even crickets keep quiet when a name is called at the draft.

FAAB Forewarnings

1. Spend early and often.

2. Emptying your budget for one prime league-crosser is a tactic that should be reserved for the desperate.

3. If you chase two rabbits, you will lose them both.

Fantasy Economics 101: The market value for a player is generally based on the aura of past performance, not the promise of future potential. Your greatest advantage is to leverage the variance between market value and real value.

Fantasy Economics 102: The variance between market value and real value is far more important than the absolute accuracy of any individual player projection.

Hope: A commodity that routinely goes for $5 over value at the draft table.

JA$G: Just Another Dollar Guy.

Professional Free Agent (PFA): Player whose name will never come up on draft day but will always end up on a roster at some point during the season as an injury replacement.

RUM pick: A player who is rosterable only as a Reserve, Ultra or Minors pick.

Standings Vantage Points

First Place: It's lonely at the top, but it's comforting to look down upon everyone else.

Sixth Place: The toughest position to be in is mid-pack at dump time.

Last Place in April: The sooner you fall behind, the more time you will have to catch up.

Last Place, Yet Again: If you can't learn to do something well, learn to enjoy doing it badly.

Mike Timlin List: Players who you are unable to resist drafting even though they have burned you multiple times in the past.

Seasonal Assessment Standard: If you still have reason to be reading the boxscores during the last weekend of the season, then your year has to be considered a success.

The Three Cardinal Rules for Winners: If you cherish this hobby, you will live by them or die by them...

1. Revel in your success; fame is fleeting.

2. Exercise excruciating humility.

3. 100% of winnings must be spent on significant others.

Statistical Research Abstracts

Our changing statistical pool

by Ray Murphy

2010 was branded by the mainstream media as the "Year of the Pitcher," thanks mainly to the season's binge of no-hitters. In fact, there are some interesting multi-year trends afoot regarding the statistical balance between pitcher and hitter, and between the American and National Leagues.

First, let's look at home runs totals.

Year	AL	NL
2004	2605	2846
2005	2437	2580
2006	2546	2840
2007	2252	2705
2008	2270	2608
2009	2560	2482
2010	2209	2404

On the NL side, we see a consistent, gradual decline over the past four years, with an end result of 15% fewer HR in 2010 than in 2006. The AL shows more abrupt changes, as the bottom fell out between 2006-07, and has stayed there (other than an unsustained recovery in 2009). The AL's 2006/2010 delta is similar to the NL's at 13%.

In light of the above power outage, are we seeing a return to small-ball tactics? If so, it should be evidenced in the stolen base numbers:

Year	AL	NL
2004	1253	1336
2005	1217	1349
2006	1252	1515
2007	1354	1564
2008	1317	1482
2009	1541	1429
2010	1505	1454

While HRs have dropped off in both leagues, only the AL seems to be reacting with an increased focus on the running game. AL SBs are up nearly 20% over the last five years, while the NL total has stayed stable and in fact dropped off from a 2007 peak. The end result of those differing trends is a surprising one in that the AL's 14 teams have out-stolen the NL's 16 teams in each of the past two seasons.

And while we wouldn't expect SB to correlate directly with ERA, the above HR results make the following ERA trends unsurprising:

Year	AL	NL
2004	4.64	4.31
2005	4.36	4.23
2006	4.56	4.49
2007	4.52	4.44
2008	4.36	4.30
2009	4.46	4.20
2010	4.14	4.02

It appears that 2010 was in fact the "Year of the Pitcher," as ERAs in both leagues dipped to their lowest levels yet in the (supposed) post-steroids era. The narrowing of the ERA gap between leagues, which has been a consistent 0.10 or less in four of the last five years, suggests that the adage "buy American League hitters and National League pitchers" is less applicable than in the past, and that individual team environments (i.e. park factors, divisional strength) are the factors to be weighed more heavily.

Possible explanations

What's causing this disparity? We have a few theories:

1. Talent disparities. Are the better players concentrated in the AL? Certainly, payroll doesn't perfectly correspond with talent, but it can at least inform the conversation. If you eliminate the Yankees, there doesn't seem to be a wide disparity in payrolls between the two leagues. The top 15 payroll teams in 2009 were split 8-7 between the leagues.

But a look at the bottom of the payroll spectrum tells a slightly different story. Of the 10 teams that had a sub-$75M payroll in 2009, seven of those teams are NL teams. Furthermore, the bottom four MLB payrolls were all in the NL. Put another way, the combined payroll of 1/4 of the NL (WAS, PIT, SD, FLA) falls short of the Yankees' 2009 payroll.

2. Park factors. There has been some subtle shift over time in the profile of the ballparks that compose each league. The 2009 openings of the two New York stadiums extended the disparity in parks between leagues: while Yankee Stadium is fairly neutral in terms of overall runs scored, the gap between the two parks in terms of HR production is more of a chasm.

Oddly, Target Field in Minnesota and the new Yankee Stadium were the AL's first new parks since Comerica Park opened in Detroit in 2000. In that same time span, the NL has seen 11 new parks, only two of which (Philadelphia and Cincinnati) can be rated as consistently hitter-friendly. Add in the humidor's muting effect on Coors Field, and the NL on the whole has become a more pitcher-friendly environment over the last decade. With the rumored introduction of a humidor into Arizona's Chase Field in 2011, that trend may continue.

Trending into trouble

by Ed DeCaria

It is almost irresistibly tempting to look at three numbers moving in one direction and expect that the fourth will continue that progression. While such pattern recognition serves us well in other endeavors, it can lead to some dreadful decision-making in the world of fantasy baseball.

In this analysis, we will isolate batters and pitchers who exhibited rising three-year trends (+3YT) during any subset of years from 2003-2009 in any of 10 statistics. For each, we will study player performance in the next season (Y4) to see how often the rising trend predicted even better things to come, and how often it proved to be a mirage. Coming out of this, we can guide our future decision-making by 1) determining the historical odds against continued growth among last year's +3YT players and 2) establishing a baseline percentage of previous gains that a +3YT player should expect to "give back" in the upcoming season.

The following tables show the average performance trend for all +3YT performers in each of ten hitting and pitching categories. "Odds of Trend Continuation" counts the number of +3YT players who regress in Y4 for every one who continues a rising trend; odds are *not* weighted by playing time because we are calculating the likelihood of trend reversion on a per-player basis. "% Giveback" shows the average percentage of Y2 to Y3 gains lost from Y3 to Y4 (among all +3YT players regardless of trend continuation).

Here are the Year 4 results for +3YT hitters:

Statistic	# +3YT Players	Avg Y1	Avg Y2	Avg Y3	Odds of Trend Continuation	Result Y4	Typical Giveback
AB	201	331	452	519	3.0 : 1	441	-115%
BB%	129	7	9	11	4.5 : 1	10	-79%
CT%	143	79	82	85	5.5 : 1	83	-71%
XBA	47	252	268	285	9.5 : 1	262	-135%
FB%	110	34	38	41	2.0 : 1	39	-62%
PX	143	90	110	129	4.0 : 1	106	-121%
HR/F	60	8	10	12	2.5 : 1	10	-118%
SX	137	67	81	95	4.0 : 1	77	-129%
SBO	154	6	9	12	3.5 : 1	10	-84%
$15	215	2	7	12	4.0 : 1	9	-60%

We see a forceful trend disruption in all ten metrics. What had been clean, beautifully-formed trend lines six months ago quickly become mangled, tangled unintelligible question marks. Part-timer finally gets a full-time shot? He's only a 3-to-1 bet to keep his gig. Promising player shows plus power? He's likely to give it all back and then some. Sleeper speedster gets more aggressive on the bases? 80% chance he mails it in next year. At best, we see only 2-to-1 odds of continuing a 3-year trend another year.

Separating players by age (not shown), we find that "Growth" players (<=27) and "Peak" players (28-32) hold their gains *slightly* better than "Decline" players (33+), but the numbers do not fundamentally differ versus the above.

For +3YT pitchers, the odds of extending a 3-year trend into a fourth year are somewhat better than for hitters, but the % giveback among +3YT pitchers is still awfully steep:

Statistic	# +3YT Players	Avg Y1	Avg Y2	Avg Y3	Odds of Trend Continuation	Result Y4	Typical Giveback
IP	137	100	139	171	2.0 : 1	152	-61%
xERA	119	4.86	4.40	4.05	2.5 : 1	4.50	-127%
BABIP	86	33	30	27	3.0 : 1	30	-122%
S%	104	67	73	78	3.5 : 1	73	-90%
GB%	47	40	44	50	2.5 : 1	44	-100%
BB/9	147	4.1	3.4	2.7	3.0 : 1	3.3	-85%
K/9	134	6.0	7.0	8.1	1.5 : 1	7.6	-41%
CMD	132	1.9	2.5	3.2	3.0 : 1	2.7	-73%
BPV	122	36	62	84	2.0 : 1	68	-73%
$15	206	-1	3	7	2.0 : 1	6	-17%

Take xERA, for example. How many times do we see a trend like that and immediately mentally project an ERA in the 3.00s? In reality, over 70% of pitchers go backwards from that point, and on average give back everything that had made us optimistic in the first place. The story is the same with other statistics: spiking ground ball pitchers give up fly balls again, improving control artists lose their finesse, and good fortunes (BABIP and S%) soon turn bad.

There are at least a few bright spots. About one-third of pitchers with 3-year IP increases manage to increase their innings further in Y4. Strikeout trends also tend to hold up, as does overall dollar value (though that is likely due to the entrenchment of innings pitched once established).

Among age cohorts, we still cannot readily find a 50% play for trend continuation; there is nothing magical about young, emerging players that can avoid these givebacks.

The reality is that regression to established performance levels is a powerful force. So much so, in fact, that most regression-based projection systems effectively *ignore* trends altogether. By projecting every player to a weighted historical average (with adjustments for age, skill set, etc.), these systems basically say: "We know that a quarter of these guys are going to significantly outperform this projection, a quarter are going to fall well short, and half are going to come pretty close ... but we don't know which specific players will do what." That's perfectly okay; but in doing so, systems like this will always fail to identify players who defy the odds and continue growth into Y4.

Such conservatism can be problematic for fantasy GMs. No one wants foolish forecasts that assume continuation of every positive trend, but projecting universal regression has little practical value if not supplemented with player-specific trend analysis. A review of recent Baseball HQ projections for all twenty of the statistics above indicates a willingness to selectively break from baseline forecasts as situations warrant. Our implied odds of trend continuation generally range from 6:1 to 20:1 – this significantly stretches typical forecasting boundaries (as regression-based odds would be incalculably high), but in no way aims to peg the exact list of odds-defying +3YT players to the point that validity of the core system is compromised.

Projections aside, this analysis highlights the harsh reality of trend disruption and quantifies the severity of regression. So, although it's okay to look at a +3YT player and hope for that next number in line, fantasy GMs still need to be very careful not to pay even money for it.

Long-term contracts and injury avoidance

by Bill Macey

One of the common themes in fantasy baseball strategy articles is the importance of risk mitigation, particularly for your team's high-dollar or early draft round selections.

In theory, professional baseball teams should act no differently. It seems a reasonable hypothesis that teams would perform more due diligence on a player that they are signing to a long-term contract. This could range anywhere from increased scouting to subjecting potential signees to more extensive medical tests. If this theory is true, we'd expect that such players should be injured less frequently... at least for the first year of their contract.

To test this hypothesis, we looked at all MLB players signed to multi-year contracts after the 2006, 2007, or 2008 seasons and examined if any subsets of those players were less likely to spend time on the DL during the first year of the contract.

All free agents signed to multi-year contracts:

	Count	On DL	DL Pct	Avg DL Days
Batters	64	34	53%	43
Pitchers	55	21	38%	63
Total	119	55	46%	51

Beginning with the full sample of 119 multi-year contracts, we see that newly signed free agents are actually a little more likely to spend time on the DL than the general population (in 2008, approximately 33% of batters and 37% of pitchers ended up on the DL). Of course, injury rates can vary from year to year, and we are also dealing with different populations, so let's consider this our baseline for the remainder of this article.

We can continue to look at the effect of longer-term contracts, although sample size begins to become an issue. The next two tables (players signed to contracts greater than 3 years and greater than 4 years, respectively) show a general trend that players signed to longer-term contracts end up on the DL less frequently during their first season:

Free agents signed to multi-year contracts, 3 years or longer:

	Count	On DL	DL Pct	Avg DL Days
Batters	30	14	47%	52
Pitchers	30	11	37%	60
Total	60	25	42%	56

Free agents signed to multi-year contracts, 4 years or longer:

	Count	On DL	DL Pct	Avg DL Days
Batters	13	5	38%	43
Pitchers	14	4	29%	39
Total	27	9	33%	41

One might argue that the length of the contract is less important than the dollar value; it's reasonable that a team might perform more due diligence on a player to whom they offer a 2-year, $20 million contract than a player to whom they offer a 5-year, $10 million contract. Here's what the numbers say. Free agents signed to multi-year contracts, annual value > $5M:

	Count	On DL	DL Pct	Avg DL Days
Batters	33	14	42%	39
Pitchers	30	11	37%	69
Total	63	25	40%	52

Free agents signed to multi-year contracts, annual value > $10M:

	Count	On DL	DL Pct	Avg DL Days
Batters	18	7	39%	44
Pitchers	17	6	35%	63
Total	35	13	37%	53

This theory does seem to be valid, as both batters and pitchers signed to high-dollar, multi-year contracts are placed on the DL during their first season of that contract less frequently than the general population.

Finally, let's consider one more subset of the data. In theory, teams should know more about their own players than potential free agents from other teams and make use of this inside information by not re-signing their players that posed an increased injury risk.

So, do teams that re-sign their own free agents fare better? Free agents signed to multi-year contracts, same team:

	Count	On DL	DL Pct	Avg DL Days
Batters	22	14	64%	42
Pitchers	13	8	62%	81
Total	35	22	63%	56

This is a resounding "no!" We are once again dealing with a small sample size, but it appears that teams re-signing their own free agents either don't go through enough due diligence or that they are forced (or choose) to accept increased risk in order to retain popular players and keep the fan base happy.

In fact, this may also explain some of the findings above. When looking through the 27 players signed to contracts 4 years or longer, only five of these contracts are for players that stayed with the same team. And in *all* five cases, the player spent time on the DL during their first year on the new contract.

An unexpected trend across all the results is that pitchers signed to multi-year contracts end up on the DL less frequently than do batters (although their average stay on the DL usually lasts longer). This goes against previous research showing pitchers are more frequently injured and suggests that it may be easier to screen for pitchers likely to get injured than to do so for batters. For example, a team may be able to use MRIs to pick up warning signs that a pitcher's labrum is starting to fray, perhaps even before the pitcher may feel any pain. A recent loss in velocity would present similar warnings. But no medical test tells you which batter will foul a ball off his shin or break his finger sliding into second base.

From a fanalytic standpoint, this should give you comfort to share the confidence of a MLB team that signs a free agent to a high-dollar, multi-year contract. There are never any guarantees that a player won't get injured, even the healthiest can get hurt. But even reducing the risk of significant lost time due to injury by 10% may be worth drafting a player a round earlier or paying the extra buck.

Peak age and BPV

by Bill Macey

It's not only important to see when players peak, but also to quantify the expected trajectory. Let's look at the career path of players using BPV, which measures total skill level.

General Population Results - Batters

For batters with a minimum 50 AB in any season from 2006 to 2009 and median BPV for each age 23-40:

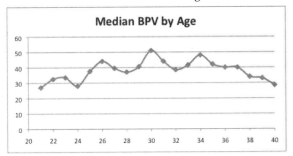

BPV reaches an absolute peak around age 30 (median BPV of 51) with local peaks at 26 (median 44) and 34 (median 48). Perhaps what is most interesting is that median BPV is remarkably flat between ages 25-37. The difference between a 44 BPV and a 39 BPV is practically a rounding error. For example, a 5-point difference in BPV is the equivalent of a difference between a PX of 100 and 108, all else being equal.

A possible reason for the flat distribution is due to the multi-skill nature of BPV. For example, previous research suggests that a batter's power typically improves with age (until a certain point), but often at the expense of speed. As these trends would individually push BPV in the opposite direction, they may cancel each other out as a player ages.

Individual Player Career Trends - Batters

We also examined how the BPVs of individual players changed over their careers. We identified 119 batters with at least 50 AB in each season between 2002-2009. To control for different skill levels between players, we compared the difference between a player's BPV in each year with their average BPV over the 8-year period, referred to as "BPV+". For example, Jimmy Rollins had an average BPV of 90 over the period and a BPV of 92 in 2009 at the age of 31. Therefore, his BPV+ for his age-31 season equaled +2.

We then aligned each player-year with the corresponding age and calculated the median BPV+ at each age across the sample. Remarkably, the trends were still relatively flat:

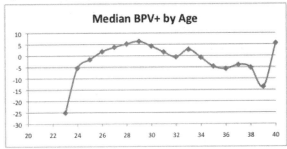

Batters between the ages of 25 and 34 tended to post BPVs better than their period average while those younger than

25 and older than 34 tended to under-perform their average BPVs for the period. Peak performance for the group came at the age-29 season. However, again notice the relative flatness of the curve - despite these trends, the median BPV+ between the ages of 24 and 38 were all generally within the range of -5 to +5.

General Population Results - Pitchers

For pitchers with at least 20 IP in any season from 2006 to 2009 and median BPV for each age 23-40.

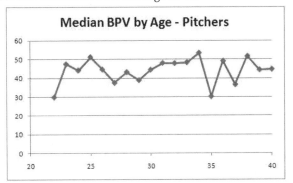

Unlike the graph for batters, there is no discernible trend for pitchers. The mild peak in the early 30s seems reasonable; by this age, struggling pitchers have probably pitched themselves out of a job and you're left with the serviceable remainder. However, the absolute peak at 34 is temporary, and the rest of the trend is erratic. Looking at this so broadly tells us more about the skill level necessary to play in the Majors than what to expect from a pitcher at any particular age. Again, performance seems to dictate playing time, not age.

Individual Player Career Trends - Pitchers

We again examined how the BPVs of individual pitchers changed over their careers using BPV+. Our sample included 85 pitchers with at least 20 IP, 2003-2009.

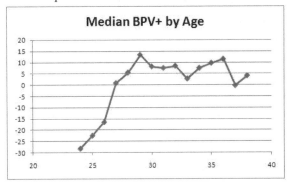

Consistent with the results for batters, the trends were still relatively flat, especially between the ages of 28 and 36.

Comparing the above chart to the one for batters, it does seem that pitchers either take a few extra years to develop or benefit from additional seasoning. The "peak period" for pitchers starts later (~28) than it does for batters (~25-26).

What does this all mean? The key take-away is not to put too much emphasis on age. Neither pay a premium for players entering their peak years nor avoid players in their mid-30s. On an actuarial basis, these rises and falls are likely to be soft. Instead, let skills trends shape decisions.

Estimating PX using hard-hit ball data

by Bill Macey

One of the most powerful and often-used tools to evaluate batters at Baseball HQ is the linear weighted power index (PX), which measures a player's ability to hit for power. A wonderful attribute of PX is that it is scaled such that a PX of 100 is league average, which makes it very intuitive to evaluate how a player is performing: anything above 100 is above average; above 150 is elite; below 50 is quite poor. The biggest shortcoming of PX, however, it that it is still ultimately a metric determined by results and not skills. It is calculated with the number of doubles, triples and HR a player hits as compared to the rest of the league.

Over the last two years, we have begun using hard-hit ball data to evaluate player performance. Our previous research has shown that hard-hit balls are more likely to result in hits and hard-hit fly balls are more likely to end up as home runs. We decided to use the hard-hit ball data to calculate an expected skills-based PX (xPX). This metric provides the best of both worlds: it starts with hard-hit ball data, which measures a player's fundamental skill of making solid contact; and then places it on the same scale as PX, which is an easily recognizable measure of a player's total power compared to the rest of the league.

Using player data during the 2005-2009 seasons (minimum 100 AB), we found that hard-hit fly balls and hard-hit line drives are excellent predictors of PX. Using statistical techniques, we calculated the xPX equation as:

xPX = 2.6 + 269*HHLD% + 724*HHFB%

HHLD% is calculated as the number of hard hit-line drives divided by the total number of balls put in play. HHFB% is similarly calculated. For example, a player for whom HHLD and HHFB each accounted for 10% of his balls put in a play would have an xPX of 102.

To see if xPX does a good job of predicting future performance changes, we examined historical data over the two half-seasons of 2009. We isolated players with large differences between their first-half PX and their first-half xPX and examined how their actual PX changed between the first and second halves.

We identified 23 batters (min 100 AB) for whom their PX was less than their xPX by at least 30 points over the first half of 2009 (under-performers) and 29 for whom their PX exceeded their xPX by at least 30 points (over-performers).

Among the sample of 23 under-performers, 18 posted a higher PX during the second half with a median increase of 21.5 points. Among the sample of 29 over-performers, 23 posted a lower PX during the second half with a median decrease of 27 points. Overall, approximately 80% of the players saw their second half PX move in the direction predicted by xPX.

With that in mind, the tables below present the batters who under-performed and over-performed in 2010.

Underperformers, 200+ AB, xPX > PX by 30 pts

Name	AB	PX	xPX	Diff
Bengie Molina	377	48	103	55
Troy Glaus	412	110	164	54
Alex Avila	294	82	133	51
Jason Bay	348	106	157	51
Todd Helton	398	80	126	46
Gerald Laird	270	70	112	42
Brandon Wood	226	44	85	41
Mike Lowell	218	89	130	41
Rusty Ryal	207	70	110	40
Yadier Molina	465	53	93	40
Justin Smoak	348	108	148	40
Alex Gordon	242	101	140	39
Jim Edmonds	246	169	208	39
Matt Treanor	237	61	99	38
Jeremy Hermida	222	104	141	37
Gabe Gross	222	57	92	35
Brian Roberts	230	83	118	35
Jonathan Lucroy	277	51	85	34
Joe Mauer	510	99	132	33
Geovany Soto	322	152	185	33
Gaby Sanchez	572	116	149	33
Carlos Lee	605	98	130	32
Nate McLouth	242	95	126	31
Chase Utley	425	103	134	31
Derrek Lee	547	123	154	31
Alcides Escobar	506	53	84	31

Overperformers, 200+ AB, xPX > PX by 30 pts

Name	AB	PX	xPX	Diff
Mike Stanton	359	191	145	-46
Jose Bautista	569	221	178	-43
Jim Thome	276	240	199	-41
Mark Reynolds	499	194	153	-41
Josh Hamilton	518	177	141	-36
Russell Branyan	376	193	158	-35
Shelley Duncan	229	144	109	-35
Colby Rasmus	464	168	136	-32
Andres Torres	507	155	124	-31
Brett Gardner	477	72	42	-30

Please consider the following important caveats when applying this analysis.

1. Consider sample size. Just one additional hard-hit fly ball out of 100 balls in play translates to an increased xPX of more than 7 points. When you consider that not all at bats end with a ball put in play (strikeouts), this is an important reminder that results based on small sample sizes should be taken with a heavy dose of skepticism.

2. As with other "expected" stats such as xERA, xBA, etc., this is not an exact prognosis for future performance. Rather, it's a translation of past performance after stripping out various components of luck - events outside the control of the batter. While players with large differences between xPX and PX are more likely to see a correction, it's also possible that their HH% rates have for whatever reason diverged and those may also correct. These two phenomena are not mutually exclusive; for some batters they may counteract each other, but for other batters, they may compound.

Predicting SB and SBO

by Bill Macey

One of the tenets of Baseball HQ is to focus on skills, not surface stats. Rather than look at previous HR output when projecting future HR totals, we look at metrics such as PX and Eye, which measure a player's underlying skills and ability rather than the results.

Similarly, we use the metric SX to measure a player's speed. But using SX to determine a player's SB totals can be somewhat misleading; other skills that go into the calculation of SX include triples and runs scored. And other factors that we can't measure, such as quickness (think first step speed), leadoff distance, and most importantly, player and managerial tendencies, might affect stolen base totals just as much.

So, if we are solely concerned about predicting SB, is there a better way?

To better understand how SB totals can fluctuate from year to year, we considered several variables related to SB: stolen base success rate (SB%), Stolen Base Opportunities (SBO), SX, and SB totals themselves. So that we could isolate any long term trends, we used a sample of 119 players who had at least 50 AB in each year 2002-2009.

We began by looking at how these statistics were correlated from year to year. Recall that correlation is measured on a scale from 0 to 1 (on an absolute basis), where a value of 1 indicates perfect correlation (like height in inches vs. height in cm) and a value of 0 indicates no relationship at all.

Variable	Correlation
SBO	0.82
SB	0.81
SB/AB	0.80
SX	0.76
SB%	0.20

Each of the variables except for SB% are strongly correlated on a year-to-year basis and there is no meaningful difference between the correlations for SB, SB/AB or SBO. This helps us confirm that speed just doesn't vanish and that players who stole bases previously are likely to continue doing so in the future.

We performed a regression analysis to determine the best fit for predicting future SB based on prior totals and arrived at the following:

$$xSB = 11 + 0.77 \cdot SB\_PY - 0.3 \cdot AGE$$

where SB_PY represents the SB total in the prior year and AGE represents the age of the player in the predicted year.

The trouble with projecting future totals is that it highly relies on accurate estimates of playing time. Playing time has been an important focus at Baseball HQ recently and for good reason - more than anything, it's playing time that affects total stat line at the end of the year. So, rather than focus on a total amount that's tied to a particular AB total, we can instead look at predicted SBO (xSBO), which is more easily scaled and fluid to changes in playing time:

$$xSBO = 0.07 + 0.79 \cdot SBO\_Y1 - 0.0017 \cdot Age\_Y2$$

In both equations, we see that predicted SB totals and SBO rates are closely tied to previous levels, with only a small adjustment for age. All else being equal, we expect SB and SBO to decrease from each year to the next, while a player's actual age only seems to slightly affect the rate of that decline.

There are two variables worth discussing that we evaluated but did not ultimately include in the regression.

SB%: Including stolen base success rate did not improve the goodness of fit, nor was it statistically significant at the 95% confidence interval. In other words, there's reasonable statistical doubt whether or not SB% influences SB totals or SBO, and even if we include it, it doesn't improve the accuracy of the projections.

SX: While there is a close relationship between SX and SB totals (particularly since SB totals are used to help determine SX), adding this as a variable to predict SB and SBO only very marginally improves the accuracy of the estimate, while inviting statistical complications (multi-colinearity).

One oddity is that the formulas predict non-zero stolen bases and SBO even for players that didn't attempt a single steal in the previous year. While potentially counter-intuitive, the data bears these results out. For example, the xSBO equation predicts an SBO% of 2.4% for a 25 year old player with a SBO of 0% in the previous year. This expected rate decreases to 1.6% if the player is 30 years old, rather than 25.

Our sample had 93 player-seasons with a SBO of 0%. In only 43 of the subsequent seasons did the player also not attempt a SB in year 2, and the average SBO in year 2 for the subsample was 1.9%. So, the predicted rate seems reasonable; just because a player didn't attempt any steals previously doesn't mean they won't in the future.

Conclusion

Whether a player is fast or slow, their tendency to steal bases previously is a much better predictor of their future SB totals than their speed. SX remains a powerful tool, but it is better used to validate past performance than to predict future performance.

Statistically Scouted Speed

by Ed DeCaria

Derived from Bill James' speed score metric, Speed Index (SX) combines four statistics -- SB attempt rate, SB success rate, triples per ball in play, and runs scored per time on base -- that together are an appropriate substitute for "speed." However, when trying to predict or validate stolen base output, relying on SX alone is problematic because the metric itself is heavily influenced by stolen base attempts and successes. Fantasy GMs need an independent measure of speed to use alongside SB attempt rate and success rate (in conjunction with on-base ability and playing time) to holistically assess player performance and potential on the base paths.

To craft this new speed measure, we first obtained scouting reports for over 400 top prospects of the past decade. For those that went on to earn significant MLB playing time within three years of their last report, we converted observed "home-to-first" times (generally 3.9 to 4.5 seconds) to a standard 20-80 scouting scale to account for the fact that LHBs have faster average times than RHBs. We then plotted the scores against various major league (not minor league or MLE) stats, from which nine emerged with notable individual correlations to observed speed:

Metric Name (or Calculation)	Correlation w/ Home-to-First Time
Stolen Base Attempt Rate	0.65
Triples / (Doubles + Triples)*	0.54
Runs Scored per Time on Base	0.47
(Runs - HR) / (RBI - HR)	0.46
Stolen Base Success Rate	0.44
Hit Rate on Soft/Med Grounders	0.41
Triples per Ball in Play	0.41
Body Mass Index	-0.39
GIDP / Ball in Play	0.29

*Compared to League Average by Batter Hand (LHB = 11.2%, RHB = 7.7%)

From these options, we constructed a composite metric that largely explains observed speed despite the self-enforced exclusion of SB attempt rate (the #1 ranking factor) and success rate (#5). The components are:

(Runs - HR) / (RBI - HR): Unlike Runs Scored per Time on Base, this metric aims to minimize the influence of extra base hit power and team run-scoring rates on perceived speed.

3B / (2B + 3B): No one can deny that triples are a fast runner's stat; dividing them by 2B+3B instead of all balls in play dampens the power aspect of extra base hits.

(Soft + Medium Ground Ball Hits) / (Soft + Medium Ground Balls): Faster runners are more likely than slower runners to beat out routine grounders. Hard hit balls are excluded from numerator and denominator.

Body Mass Index (BMI): Calculated as Weight (lbs) / Height (in)^2 * 703. All other factors considered, leaner players run faster than heavier ones.

Components are calculated as indices vs. league average (lg_av). To stabilize the first three components when sample size is low (e.g., April), a small age-specific weight (age_wt) is added before running each index.

The full calculation for *Statistically Scouted Speed* (Spd) is:

$$104 + \{[(\text{Runs-HR}+10^*\text{age\_wt})/(\text{RBI-HR}+10)]/\text{lg\_av}^*100\} / 5$$
$$+ \{[(3B+5^*\text{age\_wt})/(2B+3B+5)]/\text{lg\_av}^*100\} / 5$$
$$+ \{[(\text{SoftMedGBhits}+25^*\text{age\_wt})/(\text{SoftMedGB}+25)]/\text{lg\_av}^*100\} / 2$$
$$- \{[\text{Weight (Lbs)}/\text{Height (In)}^2 * 703]/\text{lg\_av}^*100\}$$

Statistically Scouted Speed correlates with observed home-to-first times in our initial sample (n=159) at a rate of R=0.72. When correlating Spd for all players with 300+ plate appearances for any consecutive pair of seasons from 2002-2009, the result (R=0.75, similar to Bill James' speed score and SX) inspires confidence that Spd is measuring a true skill over time. The Spd "aging curve" backs this up:

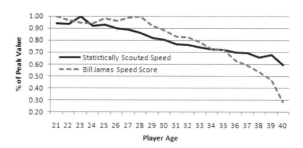

Spd declines fairly consistently after age 23 (measured as aggregate year-over-year change in Spd among players in each pair of consecutive years, weighted by PA); the James score also shows a decline by age but peaks much later.

By keeping this new speed score separate from attempt rate and success rate, we can now determine which "fast" players may have hidden SB potential if they become more aggressive (i.e., increase in attempt rate) or improve their timing/technique (i.e., increase in success rate), and we can assess which players might have lost a step (i.e., decrease in Spd) that hasn't yet manifested itself in a SB decline due to inflated attempt and success rates vs. personal averages.

After the 2009 season, we used Spd to identify players having SB upside or downside vs. what SX had suggested. Among those with 2010 upside recommended by Spd:

Ichiro Suzuki: 153 Spd in 2009 suggested he was still as fast as ever, rewarding 2010 owners with 40+ SB

Rafael Furcal: 132 Spd masked in SX by low attempt rate; delivered 20+ SB in 2010 as attempt rate rebounded

Hunter Pence: 121 Spd suggested increased SB potential with improved success rate, which he achieved in 2010

Among those with downside as warned by Spd:

Ian Kinsler: 100 Spd in '09 not bad, but low for someone with 30 SB hype; as attempt rate fell, so did SBs in 2010

Torii Hunter: 82 Spd not fooled by inflated attempt and success rates; Hunter's SB total dropped by half in 2010

Ryan Howard: 67 Spd buried by 2009 noise of improved physique and 8 SB supported by 94 SX; slow again in 2010

Spd replaces SX in this year's player boxes. For ease of transition and interpretation, Spd has been scaled to a midpoint of 100 (instead of the 20-80 scouting scale as originally defined). Use Spd with SBO (a.k.a. attempt rate) and SB success rate to form a complete picture of stolen base potential and risk heading into 2011.

Debunking pitcher burnout effects

by Michael Weddell

Tom Verducci writes an annual column for *Sports Illustrated* listing those pitchers age 25 or younger whose innings pitched totals have increased by 30+ compared to the prior year. Verducci believes that these pitchers bear increased risks of injury and ineffectiveness. Originally dubbed the "Year-After Effect," others have renamed the oft-cited rule of thumb as the "Verducci Effect."

How strong is the Verducci Effect? Should it impact our risk tolerance for drafting these pitchers? J.C. Bradbury, David Gassko and Jeremy Greenhouse have all been unable to detect a statistically significant Effect. However, those researchers have not looked at pitchers' effectiveness using xERA or a comparable ERA estimator, or examined data over a 20+ year period, as we're about to do.

Testing for the Verducci Effect

We found 163 Verducci Effect pitchers who met these filters, using data from www.baseball-reference.com:

- Pitched in the majors for two consecutive years during 1988-2008
- Pitched at least 100 innings during the second year
- Age 25 or younger during the second year
- Increased their workload by at least 30 IP
- Pitched a non-zero number of innings in Year 3

The filters amp up the Verducci Effect criteria just a bit to focus on the pitchers we're really interested in. We required 100 IP for the second year to eliminate most relievers (who have different workload and usage patterns) and so that we're focused on real major leaguers.

For each pitcher who met the above set of filters, we then identified the nearest match who did not meet the filters. We assembled this as a control group. The results:

	Verducci Eff group		Control group	
Year	IP	xERA	IP	xERA
1	97.1	4.31	170.1	4.09
2	193.2	4.06	193.2	4.06
3	162.0	4.19	161.2	4.25

The Verducci Effect group increased their major league workload by 96.1 IP on average. Naturally, they pitched well in year 2, which explains why their managers wanted to pitch them so much, with an xERA of 4.06 and an actual ERA even better than that.

What happened in year 3, the year after the innings were increased? Both the Verducci Effect pitchers and our control group fell off almost identically. Innings pitched dropped by a little over 30 IP. The Verducci pitchers actually did a touch better in ERA and xERA in year 3, but we wouldn't read much into that difference.

Our research indicates that there is no increased risk by rostering the Verducci Effect group instead of a control group. Both groups fell off in terms of the quantity and quality of their pitching, but the Verducci Effect pitchers did not fare worse than our control group did.

Looking for Other Year-After Effects

While debunking accepted wisdom may be fun, we would prefer to find an actionable rule that helps fantasy leaguers avoid risky pitchers. Using the same database, we considered the following variables as we tried to construct a useful injury-risk filter:

- We switched from filtering on IP to filtering on pitch counts. This is a better gauge of workload.
- We considered increases in pitch counts from the prior year to the current one. Our working hypothesis was that if a pitcher throws a large number of pitches, that might not be a danger sign if he already is accustomed to a heavy workload or at least gradually eases into a heavy workload.
- We continued to focus on starters aged 25 or younger. However, we considered each age group separately, allowing us to relax our filters year-by-year if needed.

We limited ourselves to filtering on pitch counts and increases in pitch counts by multiples of 100 pitches. We allowed our workload filters to remain steady or increase as young pitchers grew older. We examined numerous injury-risk filters based on age, pitch count, and pitch count increases to find the best fit for predicting loss of durability and effectiveness in the following year. We compared various "injury risk" groups with a control group of starters age 25 or under who pitched a similar number of innings, 190 or more, but fell outside of the injury risk filters.

Knowing Nothing is Something

And we found nothing. Again. No matter how we tried to slice off those with the highest pitch counts and/or increased pitch counts from the year before, even when we varied the filters by each age group, we found no actionable injury risk filters.

The best filters we constructed yielded such meager results that they were not actionable. Among the 1200+ starting pitching seasons with 190+ IP during 1989-2008, their xERAs declined from 4.07 to 4.24. The best injury risk filter we constructed resulted in a decline of just a couple points more. We did find filters that produced a moderately higher decline in the next year's pitch count but it was only equivalent to an average decline of about 20 fewer batters faced the following season. Given that the group we thought would have higher risk always threw substantially more pitches than the control group, this decline in workload can probably be explained by regression further toward an average major league workload.

It's difficult to prove a negative, to prove that there are no useful workload and age related filters that can identify which group of pitchers bears a greater burn out or injury effect. However, we reluctantly conclude that there is no burnout effect at the workload levels that starting pitchers have experienced during the past two decades. We are better off to ignore workload concerns and let our opponents irrationally shy away from young starters who have had heavy workloads.

Note that this research only tested for pitcher burnout effects in the following season. There still is considerable evidence that throwing too many pitches at a young age can harm pitchers' long-term durability.

Strand rates revisited

by Michael Weddell

It's been a few years since we last revised our expected strand rate formula. The formula has held up surprisingly well over time, especially considering that we are experiencing significantly lower levels of offense than when the formula was last revised.

Nonetheless, let's revisit the formula to see if we can improve it. Expected strand rate or xS% is a key input to our widely used xERA metric, so it's worth looking at again even if the current xS% formula works fairly well.

Our current expected strand rate formula is based on three core skills: strikeouts per nine innings, walks per nine innings, and groundballs per balls in play. Mathematically, the current formula is:

$$xS\% = 62.1 + (1.2 * K/9) - 0.05 * (BB/9*(BB/9+1)) + (0.0012 * GB\%^2 - 0.001 * GB\%)$$

Deriving a New Expected Strand Rate Formula

Our new xS% formula will start with those same three skills. Based on a new regression analysis using 2005-09 data from www.baseball-reference.com with a minimum of 40 IP per season, we'll give a lower weight to strikeouts and a heavier weight to avoiding walks and inducing groundballs. In addition, we will add two new variables.

First, we know that relievers have an advantage over starters because of the way we allocate earned runs. If a starter leaves a runner on base, exits in the middle of the inning, but the reliever lets the runner score, the earned run is allocated entirely to the starter. This scorekeeping effect is significant, creating about a 3% point spread in strand rates between starters and relievers.

Second, let's also consider whether the pitcher is left or right-handed. Because lefthanders face first base during their wind-ups, they tend to control the running game (and limit runners' leads even when they aren't attempting to steal). Also, because they tend to have smaller platoon differentials, left-handers probably are less disadvantaged if pinch hitters are used when there are runners on base. In any case, the difference is significant, accounting for nearly a one percentage point spread in expected strand rates.

Here is our new expected strand rate formula:

$$xS\% = 73.935 + K/9 - 0.116 * (BB/9*(BB/9+1)) + (0.0047 * GB\%^2 - 0.3385 * GB\%) + (MAX(2,MIN(4,IP/G))/2-1) + (0.82 \text{ if left-handed})$$

The new formula represents a moderate improvement over our current formula. On a scale where 1 means expected strand rate and actual strand rate are perfectly correlated and 0 means there is no correlation at all between the two statistics, the current xS% formula showed a 0.38 correlation but the new xS% formula bumped that up to a 0.44 correlation.

Considering the Outliers

Who are the starting pitchers who seem to consistently have actual strand rates during the 2005-09 period better or worse than we would expect? At least some of these deviations are due to random variation, but we'll also speculate on some possible reasons.

Pitchers who stranded more baserunners than expected were Mark Buehrle, Paul Byrd, Chris Carpenter, Roger Clemens, Tom Glavine, Ray Halladay, Rich Harden, John Lackey, Cliff Lee, Jeff Suppan, Adam Wainwright, and Carlos Zambrano.

Pitchers who let more baserunners score than expected were Jeremy Bonderman, David Bush, Jorge de la Rosa, Luke Hochevar, Greg Maddux, Joel Pineiro, Javier Vazquez, and Jeff Weaver.

Perhaps the most obvious explanation for a pitcher's actual strand rate differing from expectations is that the pitcher's effectiveness is worse when he pitches from the stretch. Greg Maddux is the clearest example of a pitcher who performed worse with runners on base. The effect is not just a worse H% with runners on base but also fewer strikeouts, more walks, and more home runs. A current pitcher with this same tendency is Jeff Weaver. Luke Hochevar looks like he may have this same problem, but it may be too early in his career to tell.

Another possible reason for having a strand rate worse than expected is because the pitcher habitually is prone to having a bad inning so that his baserunners are clustered together more than usual. Jeremy Bonderman and David Bush have had considerable first inning problems throughout their careers. To some extent, nearly all starters yield more earned runs in the first inning and less in the second inning because of opponents' batting orders, but Bonderman and Bush have had problems beyond the norm.

Javier Vazquez has the opposite problem. His first few innings are fine but he has hit the wall in the sixth inning throughout his career. The end result is the same: a pitcher who allows more baserunners than expected to score.

Mark Buehrle is well known for shutting down the running game, unless umpires continue calling more balks on him. This is a clear explanation for his actual strand rate consistently being better than xS% predicts. In case you are curious, Andy Pettitte, another pitcher renowned for stopping the running game, also tends to fare better than expected, although he wasn't consistent enough to make our above list of over-performers.

Lastly, Tom Glavine became known throughout his career for stranding more baserunners than expected. With runners on, Glavine refused to give batters good pitches to hit. His walk rate jumped much higher than normal with runners on base, but he yielded many fewer homers in those situations. This was a unique adaptation, but worth remembering in case we see the same pattern again.

As with most of our skill-based metrics, there is a balancing act. It's important that we trust the metric to work for most players, especially when we are dealing with small sample sizes. On the other hand, a model that works well for the pitching population as a whole sometimes misses the unique skills that a specific player may possess.

Are PQS trends predictive?

by Bill Macey

What pitchers to start in a given week? The Encyclopedia recalls previous research finding that streaks of dominating or disaster starts tend to continue. This all begs the question - how instructive are a pitcher's last 5 starts really?

The research summarized is very helpful if you can find a pitcher on a prolonged hot or cold streak - you certainly never want to sit your studs - but what to do when trying to decide between two pitchers, each of whose performance over their last few starts is somewhat uneven?

We looked at 10,528 starts over the years 2007-2009 and compared the 5 game rolling average PQS (5G PQS) with the PQS score in the subsequent sixth game to see if the 5G PQS had any predictive effect.

5-Game AVG PQS	No.	Avg PQS	DOM%	DIS%
Less than 1	93	2.1	27%	40%
Between 1 and 2	1214	2.4	32%	32%
Between 2 and 3	3681	2.6	36%	26%
Between 3 and 4	3896	3.0	47%	19%
4 or greater	1644	3.5	61%	12%

On the basis of these summary statistics, the 5G PQS game does seem to have some mild predictive power as pitchers with higher PQS scores in their previous 5 starts tended to pitch better in their next start. But the relative parity of subsequent DOM and DIS starts for all but the hottest of streaks warn us not to put too much effort into predicting any given start. That more than a quarter of pitchers who had been awful over their previous 5 starts still put up a dominating start next shows that anything can happen in a single game.

It's easy to buy into hype and be misled by small sample sizes and recent trends. By focusing on recent trends, do we ignore better information? For example, is 5G PQS a better predictor of future performance than the full season year-to-date PQS score? How much do recent stats matter in the face of a larger body of work?

To answer this, we compared both the 5G PQS as well as the YTD average PQS score with the subsequent game 6 PQS score to see which was more accurate as a measure of future performance in the next start.

Measure	AVG Difference	Std Dev
5G PQS	1.42	1.01
YTD PQS	1.35	0.96

Using the absolute value of the difference between the predicted and actual PQS as the measure, over the sample of 10,528 games, the YTD PQS score was a more accurate predictor - both the average difference and the standard deviation were slightly lower.

Of course, skills aren't static - pitchers may markedly improve over the course of the year as they learn a new pitch or develop better control. Their skills can dissolve just as quickly. Surely using year-long data will miss out on these trends, right?

There were 861 starts in which the difference between the preceding YTD PQS and 5G PQS was greater than 1.0 (in absolute value). In theory, when a pitcher's 5G PQS exceeds the YTD PQS (which is inclusive of the last 5 games) by more than 1, this suggests that he is pitching much better as of late. Likewise, a 5G PGS significantly lower than the YTD PQS hints at a decline in skills and perhaps poor results going forward.

Isolating these times when the YTD PQS and 5G PQS are so divergent allows us to test this hypothesis. Once again, despite any recent trends, we find that the YTD PQS is a better predictor of future performance. The average difference between YTD PQS and subsequent PQS is 1.4, whereas the average difference between the 5 game rolling average and subsequent is 1.7. Over these 861 samples, the YTD PQS score was closer to the subsequent PQS 559 times (65%).

We then considered two further subsets of this: both where the pitcher's performance has recently improved and the 5-game rolling average exceeds the YTD average, as well as the reverse case. In 345 cases where the 5G PQS exceeds the YTD PQS, the 5Q PQS is more accurate 163 times (47%). But in the 515 cases where the YTD PQS exceeds the 5G PQS, the 5G PQS was more accurate only 138 times (27%).

It's easy to get lost in trying to see which measure more accurately predicts a pitcher's performance in their next game. And while YTD consistently beats out 5G PQS, the difference is rather small. But this result obfuscates a more important point - that regardless of the method, it's likely to be quite wrong! When an error of 1.4 on a scale that only goes up to 5 represents relative improvement, any hopes for accurate predictions about a single game are folly. Instead, the most prudent course of action - whether picking up a pitcher for a single start or the remainder of the season - is to focus on a player's longer track record of skills. But prepare for a bumpy ride.

Pitcher skill by time through lineup

by Stephen Nickrand

There's a danger in analyzing a pitcher's skills using small data samples. Drawing too much optimism from a few good weeks—or reading too much into a few bad weeks—can force you into making incorrect judgments about a pitcher.

That said, if you play in a competitive league, you probably need to draw premature conclusions from incomplete data to gain an edge. The keys are to know which skill flashes can be precursors to bigger things.

Here, let's take a look at the skills pitchers display by time through lineup:

	Pitcher Skills by Time Through Lineup					
Yr	Time Thru Lineup	bb/9	k/9	hr/9	GB%	BPV
'08	1st	3.6	7.4	1.0	46	61
	2nd	3.2	6.4	1.1	45	53
	3rd	3.3	5.9	1.2	44	40
'09	1st	3.6	7.5	1.0	45	60
	2nd	3.2	6.5	1.1	45	55
	3rd	3.3	6.2	1.3	44	43
'10	1st	3.5	7.8	0.9	46	70
	2nd	3.0	7.0	0.9	46	70
	3rd	3.1	6.3	1.1	45	50

In each of the last three seasons, skills of pitchers reduce dramatically between the first and third times they go through a lineup.

The primary reason for this is a reduction in dominance (K/9) rate. It becomes more difficult for pitchers to strike out hitters the more times a pitcher goes through a lineup during a game.

In general, pitchers also are more prone to allow home runs (HR/9) the more times they go through a lineup.

While these trends are interesting, most of us are not able to manage our staffs in a manner that would enable us to take advantage of them. However, this kind of analysis can help us spot pitchers who may be an adjustment or two away from righting the ship or breaking out…

C.C. Sabathia suffered some significant skill erosion this season compared to previous years. His command (K/BB) ratio during the last four seasons: 5.6, 4.3, 2.9, 2.7. A closer look reveals that he had an elite BPV of 129 and 127 the first and second times he went through lineups. His skills fell through the floor his third time through lineups: 5.8 Dom, 4.3 Ctl, 22 BPV. His significant workload over the years may be catching up to him. So far those worries are evident only late in games.

Justin Verlander threw a lot of pitches this year. But he was a workhorse who got better the more times he went through lineups. His BPV by time through lineup: 87, 102, 131. He's the anti-Sabathia.

Gio Gonzalez had surface stats in '10 that were much better than the skills he displayed. That said, don't label him as overvalued too quickly. His skills were poor the first two times he went through lineups (44 BPV, 32 BPV), but they were close to elite the third time through lineups: 8.5 Dom, 3.3 Ctl, 49% GB%, 90 BPV.

Ricky Romero struggled through another poor second half after looking like an elite SP in the 1H. He posted an elite 115 BPV his first time through lineups. That mark plummeted to a negative BPV the second time through lineups, then rebounded to an 87 BPV the third time through lineups. In the end, the elite skill flashes he keeps displaying are well worth bidding on. Consistency is the remaining piece. He's almost there.

Ervin Santana posted a solid 72 BPV the first time through lineups, and followed that up with a 71 BPV his next time through lineups. He really struggles late in games though, as shown by his 15 BPV the third time through lineups. Be careful here, given his previous injury concerns.

Shaun Marcum might not have his arm strength back. His BPV by time through lineup: 130, 116, 48. He showed a 9.6 Dom the first time through lineups, a mark that dropped below 6.0 his second and third time through lineups. That said, there's a sub-3.50 ERA lurking here.

Max Scherzer looked like a staff ace in the second half, and it does not appear to be a fluke. Lineups were not successful in sustaining their adjustments the more times they saw him. His BPV by time through lineup: 91, 69, 104.

Edwin Jackson is the master of teasing us with skill flashes. He had a fantastic 2nd half, in large part due to a monster August. A deeper look reveals that he gets better the more times he faces a lineup during a game. His BPV by time through lineup: 67, 88, 102. It seems to take him a while to iron out his control. His Ctl by time through lineup: 4.2, 3.2, 2.2.

Jonathon Niese is really close to becoming an elite pitcher. He needs to fix these third time through lineup skills: 5.7 Dom, 4.5 Ctl, 1.8 HR/9, 0 BPV. He owns an elite 130 and 90 BPV his first and second time through lineups.

Jason Hammel might not fly under the radar again next season, but his skills could. He flashed a 100+ BPV in both his first and third times through lineups. His 41 BPV the second time through lineups kept his surface stats worse than they should have been. He's closer to becoming an impact pitcher than it may seem.

Rick Porcello has yet to translate his raw stuff into strikeouts. But he is showing flashes of being able to do that, at least early in games. His BPV by time through lineup: 102, 62, 17. His Dom by time through lineup: 6.6, 5.3, 2.3.

Jhoulys Chacin posted an elite 141 BPV the first time through lineups, due to these electric skills: 10.9 Dom, 3.0 Ctl, 48% GB%. A near-50% GB% combined with a 10.0+ Dom is a filthy combination. The missing piece is learning how to adjust as he goes through lineups, given his 53 and 12 BPV his second and third time through.

Manny Parra seems destined to end up in a relief role. He has a 128 BPV the first time through lineups, but a horrible 21 and -31 BPV his second and third time through lineups.

Pitcher skill by base situation

by Stephen Nickrand

It is interesting to analyze how pitchers perform with the bases empty vs. with runners on. Perhaps skills are better with runners on because those situations require more focus. Or maybe skills decline with runners on since throwing from the stretch gets a pitcher out of his normal wind-up.

Over the last two seasons, the verdict has been clear. Skills of pitchers consistently have been much better with the bases empty. Finding pitchers with wide skill splits in this area can help us spot premium buying opportunities...

Pitcher Skills with None On/Runners On						
Yr	Bases	bb/9	k/9	hr/9	GB%	BPV
'09	None On	3.2	7.4	1.1	45%	70
	Runners On	3.8	6.6	0.9	45%	39
'10	None On	3.0	7.7	1.0	46%	79
	Runners On	3.6	6.6	0.9	46%	46

Max Scherzer owns a reverse none on/runners on split. He becomes an elite pitcher with runners on base: 7.9 Dom, 2.1 Ctl, 44% GB%, 107 BPV. By contrast, he has an elevated 4.2 Ctl with the bases empty. Perhaps pitching from the stretch simplifies his delivery and allows him to maintain a consistent arm slot.

Anibal Sanchez shows a similar none on/runners on split. He is fantastic while pitching from the stretch: 7.7 Dom, 2.6 Ctl, 51% GB%, 97 BPV. His skills are mediocre with the bases empty: 6.9 Dom, 3.8 Ctl, 45% GB%, 46 BPV.

Tim Stauffer is heading into 2011 as a premium end-game target. Only five starting pitchers posted *better* skills than Stauffer with the bases empty: Stephen Strasburg, Roy Halladay, Josh Johnson, Francisco Liriano and Mat Latos. Stauffer had a 7.6 Dom, 1.0 Ctl, and 55% GB% with none on, good for a 141 BPV. Problem is, he was hopeless with runners on base (-16 BPV). He's no longer an elite prospect, but this former first round pick could make a big splash in a starting role if he stays healthy and can pitch better from the stretch.

Daniel Hudson ended the year with a flourish after his trade from CHW to ARI, posting these skills after July 1: 7.9 Dom, 2.5 Ctl, 87 BPV. A closer look shows that he was unhittable with the bases empty: 9.0 Dom, 2.0 Ctl, 124 BPV. His skills were mediocre while pitching from the stretch: 6.3 Dom, 3.4 Ctl, 37 BPV. If he can get more groundouts and improve this split, he could make a big impact in 2011.

Madison Bumgarner didn't seem focused or healthy while trying to earn a rotation spot in the spring, but he emerged as an impact SP in the second half: 7.0 Dom, 2.2 Ctl, 45% GB%, 91 BPV. He was great with the bases empty (7.1 Dom, 1.5 Ctl, 110 BPV) but not nearly as good with runners on (7.0 Dom, 2.9 Ctl, 73 BPV). He might be overvalued due to his quick emergence, but he remains a young pitcher worth owning.

Avoiding relief disasters

by Ed DeCaria

"Nooooooooooooooooooooooooooooooooooooooooooooooooooooo!"

Somewhere, four times per night across the majors, a relief pitcher gets shelled; and, somehow, none of us ever see it coming. Can we do *anything* to avoid relief disasters?

Relief disasters (defined here as ER>=3 except if IP>=3), occur in 5%+ of all appearances. The chance of a disaster exceeds 13% in any 7-day period. Note the impact of just one disaster appearance at any given point in the season:

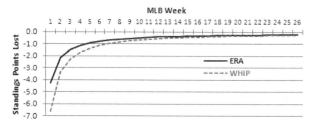

As innings accumulate, the effects of a disaster are more easily washed out. Still, measured at season's end, a single disaster will have stolen away a half point in the standings based on typical Standings Gain Points (SGP) thresholds. The wreckage is magnified 10X in the early season, where disasters can throw us off course by five standings points or more. It can take weeks to recover, and that assumes we can avoid the *next* disaster looming around the corner.

Can we? We analyzed the nearly 110,000 MLB relief appearances from 2002-2009 to determine what factors most heavily influenced a reliever's propensity to implode, with a particular focus on those factors that would have been knowable and actionable when it was time to set our rosters each week or day.

We split our sample randomly into two and applied a logistic regression to Group A in an attempt to model the probability of a disaster appearance occurring in the next seven days. The final model produced the following list of factors, in order of influence:

1. Strength of opposing offense
2. Park factor of home stadium
3. BB/9 over latest 31 days (more walks is bad)
4. Pitch count over previous 7 days (more pitches is bad)
5. Latest 31 Days ERA>xERA (recent bad luck continues)

Daily league owners who can slot relievers by individual game should also pay attention to days of rest: pitching on less rest than one is accustomed to increases disaster risk.

Applying these guidelines to our Group B sample showed that, by avoiding relievers who pitch in difficult environments or who have recently been overworked or plagued by control problems, we can cut our exposure to relief disasters in half.

Make no mistake, though: we cannot prevent disasters, and overactive decision-making can backfire if it means frequently starting inferior pitchers. But we should at least *consider* taking shelter when the warning bells sound.

Projecting team saves

by Michael Weddell

We spend most of our fanalytic baseball energy trying to predict individual players' performances. However, saves work differently, right? For saves, we try to predict whether a reliever will become a closer and do well enough to keep that role. Then we hope that the team hands enough save opportunities to its closer over the course of the season to generate a large number of saves. To a considerable extent, projecting a closer's saves depends on how many saves a team earns during a season. How should we project team saves?

Team Saves as a Function of Team Wins

Let's start with a simple rule of thumb. On average, a team earns about one save for every two wins. If you want more precision, during the 2000-09 decade, a save was recorded in 49.74% of the games.

Of course, predicting team wins is a challenge unto itself. Even the best set of team win predictions will differ from year-end results by about 6-8 wins per team. We're going to sidestep this problem and keep pressing on.

Once we agree on a predicted number of team wins, we can get a bit more precise than simply dividing by two. As a percentage of their wins, excellent teams tend to outscore their opponents by 4+ runs more often than lousy teams do. Because it's nearly impossible to record saves in those blowout victories, the best teams will average somewhat less than one save for every two wins and the worst teams will average somewhat more than one save for every two wins.

Predicted team saves =
   32.984 * LN (team wins) -104.31

Factors Affecting Team Saves

So far, so good, but we didn't need research to tell us that there's a close relationship between team wins and team saves. What else is there?

Listed in descending order of importance, let's discuss the other factors detected by our research, focusing more in depth on team saves during 2005-09.

Predicted team saves =

Team wins
   1.0562 * (32.984 * LN (team wins) -104.31)
Runs per game
   -1.7897 * (runs per gm + opponents runs per game)
Managerial tendency #1
   4.7325 * past 3 yrs history of Svs / predicted Svs
Managerial tendency #2
   2.6130 if past 3 yrs saves / predicted saves ≥ 115%
Expected closer quality
   0.4331 * opening day closer's historical xERA

Runs Per Game: If a team habitually plays in games with a low number of runs scored, then a greater percentage of the time the game will be decided by 1-3 runs, yielding more save opportunities. This is a fairly big impact, adjusting projected team saves by about 5 saves per team.

Managerial Tendencies: At least since Francisco Rodriguez set the individual saves record as an Angel back in 2008, we have noticed that Mike Scioscia's teams tend to earn a large number of saves. It's not a matter of avoiding complete games: The Angels were 4th in the majors in that category last year. Perhaps Scioscia's focus on contact hitting and aggressive baserunning allows his team to score a consistent number of runs, keeping more victories within the 1-3 run margin needed to generate save opportunities. Whatever the reasons are for Scioscia's influence, let's call it a managerial tendency and research whether it persists.

In general, there was a lot of noise in the managerial tendency factor and very little year-to-year persistence, with one notable exception. Of the managers whose teams recorded 15% or more saves than expected (based on their three most recent prior complete years of managing), 10 out of 10 of these managers continued to record more saves than expected during the next year. If a manager has a three year track record at recording more saves than expected, this bumps up his team's future projected saves total by about 3 saves.

Closer Quality: We also guessed that having a very good closer to start the season would be correlated with more team saves. An excellent closer should blow fewer save opportunities and his manager might be less inclined to let starters pitch complete games. We tested for this by designating the pitcher who recorded a team's first save of the season, excluding extra inning wins and the rare save with a greater than 3-run margin of victory, as the "opening day closer." It's not a perfect method of identification, but it's very close.

We looked for a correlation between the opening day closer's quality (using the most recent three years' base skills) and team saves. After adjusting for other factors, the correlation was surprisingly weak. A two-run improvement in xERA led to just one extra team save during the entire season. Perhaps the level of closer turnover within each season is so high that the identity of the opening day closer has little impact on the number of team saves.

In short, we now have both a simple version for predicting team saves based on wins and a more complicated formula that reflects other variables.

References
Sources include:
Inspiration from a BaseballHQ forum discussion led by "Patioboater".
Data from www.baseball-reference.com, which means that indirectly the data was obtained free of charge from and is copyrighted by RetroSheet. Interested parties may contact Retrosheet at "www.retrosheet.org".
Observations regarding Mike Scioscia from an April 5, 2010 article on HardballTimes.com and the book <u>Evaluating Baseball's Managers, 1876-2008</u>, both by Chris Jaffe.

A look at rookie playing time

by Ed DeCaria

Rookies elicit more excitement and anxiety in fantasy GMs than any other type of player. While translated minor league statistics can help us to gauge *how well* rookies might perform in the majors, they do not provide any clues as to *how many* plate appearances or innings pitched we can reasonably expect a player to earn in his debut season.

MLB teams have awarded more playing time to debut rookies in recent years, increasing from an average of 269 plate appearances and 114 innings pitched per team in the late 1970s to 344 plate appearances (+28%) and 136 innings pitched (+19%) per team in the late 2000s. With newcomers now playing more prominent roles, fantasy GMs can gain a competitive edge by knowing which players in which situations are most likely to see significant playing time.

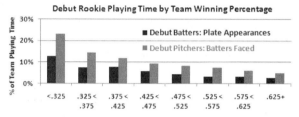

The above chart shows that weaker-performing teams have historically (1976-2009) been far more dependent on debut rookies than stronger-performing teams. This makes sense, as non-contenders have greater incentive and flexibility to allow young players to gain experience at the MLB level. Which individual teams have given the most playing time to debut rookies in recent years?

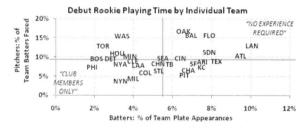

From 2006-2009, decision-makers of the A's, Orioles, Marlins, and Dodgers have depended more on debut batters and pitchers than their average MLB competitor. Conversely, the Mets, Phillies, Brewers, Rockies, and Yankees have kept debut playing time to a minimum. The Nationals and Blue Jays also stand out for their heavy use of first-year pitchers, as do the Pirates, White Sox, and Royals for their relative focus on first-year batters.

Clearly, team success and individual club management can impact debut rookie playing time. Additionally, individual player characteristics can provide clues as to which debut rookies will earn significant PA or IP:

- Rookies who can play up-the-middle (CF, 2B, SS) or on the left side (LF, 3B) are likely to see more debut playing time than those at 1B, RF, C, or DH.
- LH batters and pitchers are slightly more likely than righties to earn significant PA or IP in their debuts.

- Rookies under age 22 earn nearly twice the PAs of those aged 25-26 in their debut season. Pitchers under age 23 earn twice the innings of those aged 26-27.

Now knowing which teams are more likely to use debut rookies and which types of players are more likely to get an early look, exactly when during the season do most players actually receive their first call-up to the majors?

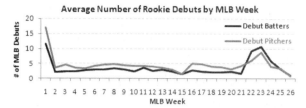

For hitters, there are about 12 players per year who debut during MLB's opening week. After that, there is a sharp drop-off down to 2-3 players per week, with upticks near the typical service time thresholds, and then one final spike due to September roster expansion.

For pitchers, the pattern is similar to that of hitters, but on a slightly higher scale, starting with about 17 pitchers per year who debut on Opening Day followed by a steady stream of 3-5 pitchers per week until the All-Star break. Debuts spike again approaching the trade deadline and one last time upon expansion of team rosters in September.

Now knowing what drives debut rookie playing time potential, how many big debuts should we expect in 2011?

# of Debut Rookies Who Reach Major PA/IP Thresholds

	PA	# Players	Cumulative		IP	# Players	Cumulative
Batters	600+	0.7	0.7	**Pitchers**	200+	0.3	0.3
	500-600	1.3	2.8		150-200	1.6	2.7
	400-500	1.8	5.8		100-150	3.2	8.3
	300-400	1.5	8.2		75-100	6.2	14.4
	200-300	3.3	13.4		50-75	11.4	25.8
	100-200	7.8	26.2		25-50	23.3	49.2

Not many. These are the average number of debuts per season for hitters by PA and for pitchers by IP, 1998-2009. Very few reach playing time levels that can yield significant fantasy value, especially in shallower leagues. But those who do can make an impact, such as these from 2010:

Batter Name	PA	Key 2010 Stats	Pitcher Name	IP	Key 2010 Stats
Jackson, A	675	103R, 27SB	Leake, M	138.1	4.23ERA, 50%GB
Heyward, J	623	.393OBP, 83R	Takahashi, H	122.0	3.61ERA, 8.4K/9
Davis, I	601	19HR, 71RBI	Wood, T	102.2	3.51ERA, 3.3K/BB
Boesch, B	512	14HR, 67RBI	Arrieta, J	100.1	4.66ERA, 4.7K/BB
Castro, S	506	.300BA, 10SB	Ely, J	100.0	6.8K/BB, 46%GB
Tabata, J	441	.299BA, 19SB	Enright, B	99.0	3.91ERA, 1.27WHIP
Smoak, J	397	13HR, 48RBI	Monasterios, C	88.1	4.38ERA, 1.8K/BB
Stanton, M	396	22HR, .507SLG	Atilano, L	85.2	5.15ERA, 1.3K/BB
Alvarez, P	386	16HR, 64RBI	Venters, J	83.0	1.95ERA, 10.1K/9
Donald, J	325	39R, 5SB, @2B+SS	Tomlin, J	73.0	4.56ERA, 2.3K/BB
Jay, J	323	.300BA, 47R	Sanabia, A	72.1	3.73ERA, 2.9K/BB
Valencia, D	322	.311BA, 40RBI	Strasburg, S	68.0	2.91ERA, 12.2K/9

Some very strong debuts, especially among batters. The trick for fantasy GMs is to identify such players while looking forward rather than backward. Because projecting playing time is so difficult for debut rookies, however, the best that we can do is to adhere to the guidelines above and then consider each player's individual opportunity with a critical eye and an open mind.

Gaming Research Abstracts

The Mayberry Method, Take 2

The Mayberry Method – named after the fictional TV village where life was simpler – was introduced last year in this book. It is a player evaluation method that embraces the imprecision of the forecasting process and projects performance in broad strokes rather than with precise statistics. Mayberry creates player ratings that are outwardly simple but inwardly powerful.

MM reduces every player to a 7-character code. Three of those characters are our reliability grades. The other four characters describe individual elements of the player's skill set, each on a simple scale of 0 to 5.

Kelly Johnson's MM code is "4235 BBD." Tommy Hanson's MM code is "3405 ABA." Here is how these codes are determined:

MM Power: The first character in the MM code refers to the batter's power skills. It is assigned using the following table:

PX	MM	Rough HR Approx
0 - 49	0	0
50 - 79	1	up to 10
80 - 99	2	up to 20
100 - 119	3	up to 30
120 - 159	4	up to 40
160+	5	up to 50+

I provide a rough approximation of what these codes equate to for a full-time player in order to get you comfortable with the code. Knowing that a player with a "3" means he has up to 30-HR power makes it easier to understand and connect with the system.

MM Speed: The second character in the MM code refers to the batter's speed skills.

Spd	MM	Rough SB Approx
0 - 49	0	0
50 - 79	1	up to 10
80 - 99	2	up to 20
100 - 119	3	up to 30
120 - 139	4	up to 40
140+	5	up to 50+

The rough SB approximation is probably a little bit rougher here, since a good deal of SB output is driven by opportunity, but it still instills some familiarity into the system. We've also replaced SX with Spd.

MM Batting Average: The third character in the MM code refers to batting average, and uses Expected Batting Average to measure it.

xBA	MM
.000 - .239	0
.240 - .254	1
.255 - .269	2
.270 - .284	3
.285 - .299	4
.300+	5

MM Playing Time: Each draft day, we come to the table with a ranked list of players defined by statistical projections. While it is nice to see that stat line, it is a combination of two very separate elements — skill and opportunity. When we combine those elements to create the projection, we impede our ability to evaluate the elements independently.

That ability is more important than ever before. Skill and playing time each requires separate analysis. So MM keeps plate appearances (PA) and innings-pitched (IP) separate from skill, though we will combine them at the proper time.

Playing time remains the biggest challenge in projecting performance. From injuries to managerial whim, PA and IP are the toughest variables to project and manage. In last year's version of Mayberry, we handled playing time like any of the other skills-based variables. We tiered batters within five 100-AB stratas, and pitchers within 40-IP stratas.

As it turned out, those five stratas were just not wide enough. Playing time is *highly* variable, moreso than a 100-AB or 40-IP break could expect to capture.

So I decided that we needed to expand the error bars. The best we can reasonably expect is to label players as "potential full-timers," "mid-timers" and "fringe/bench players." The number of at-bats or innings within those three levels is far too variable to pin down.

Role	PA	MM
Potential full-timers	450+	5
Mid-timers	250-449	3
Fringe/bench	100-249	1
Non-factors	0-99	0

For batters who could be expected to amass 550 plate appearances, 600 PA or more, the broad "5" level serves to mitigate any downside due to injury. Playing time, in tandem with the skills indicators, also serves as a proxy for situationally-dependent Rotisserie categories, such as Runs and RBIs.

The PA character is now used as a multiplier to create an overall score for ranking purposes. Simply:

MM Score =
(PX score + Spd score + xBA score + PA score)
x PA score

The highest score you can get is 100, so this becomes an easy scale to evaluate.

Note that the PA variable becomes a "lever" for manipulating a player's score. If a DL stay will significantly impact a player's future playing time, you can just adjust that digit downward and recalculate the overall score in your head (try doing that with any other overall performance evaluator!). If a part-time player backs into more ABs, you can adjust upward for similar effect.

MM Overall Pitching Skill: The first character in the pitching MM refers to xERA, which captures a pitcher's overall ability and is a proxy for ERA, and even WHIP.

xERA	MM
4.81+	0
4.41 - 4.80	1
4.01 - 4.40	2
3.61 - 4.00	3
3.21 - 3.60	4
3.20-	5

MM Dominance measures strikeout ability.

K/9	MM
0.0 - 4.9	0
5.0 - 5.9	1
6.0 - 6.9	2
7.0 - 7.9	3
8.0 - 8.9	4
9.0+	5

MM Saves: This is the only part of MM score that is somewhat subjective. Saves are tough to project so the best we can do is position ourselves to grab them when we can.

Description	Saves est.	MM
No hope for saves; starting pitchers	0	0
Speculative closer	1-9	1
Closer in a pen with alternatives	10-24	2
Frontline closer with firm bullpen role	25+	3

This code only goes to "3" in order to soften the overall impact that relief pitchers have.

MM Playing Time: Like batters, the playing time code for pitchers - innings pitched - serves multiple purposes...

Role	IP	MM
Potential #1-2 starters	180+	5
Potential #3-4 starters	130-179	3
#5 starters/swingmen	70-129	1
Relievers	0-69	0

This system penalizes relievers for amassing fewer innings. We've taken that into account in the calculation of the overall score by including the saves variable as a part of the multiplier:

MM Score =
((xERA score x 2) + K/9 score + Saves score + IP score)
x (IP score + Saves score)

Except in exceedingly rare cases, that multiplier should never add up to more than 5.

Here, as in the batting formula, IP does double duty and greatly affects the MM score. Saves also do the same, so if a reliever moves into a closing role, that too can have an immediate and dramatic impact on the score.

Integrating Mayberry and Portfolio3

The Portfolio3 Plan debuted in 2007 as a means to provide a structure to balancing skill and risk at the draft table. Just like most folks prefer to diversify their stock portfolio, P3 advises to diversify your roster with three types of players. This is the basic structure:

	Roster		BATTERS				PITCHERS	
Tr	Slots	Budget	Rel	Ct%		PX or Sp	Rel	BPV
1	5-8	Max $160	BBB	80%		100 100	BBB	75
2	7-13	$50-$100	BBB	80% or		100 100	BBB	50
3	5-10	Up to $50	n/a	80%		100 100	n/a	75

Tier 1 remains the most important group as they are the lowest-risk, highest-skill players. Any player who costs $20 or more, or is drafted in the first few rounds, needs to meet the Tier 1 filters.

Tier 2 contains low-risk players but with slightly less skill. For batters, the focus is on players who contribute playing time. At-bats are necessary to compete in the external productivity categories - Runs and RBIs.

Tier 3's are the high-skilled, higher-risk speculations. With the smallest budget, these players potentially provide the most profit, but worst case, can also be the most easily replaceable.

The Mayberry scores can be used as a proxy for the BPI filters in the above chart. And the simplicity of Mayberry carries over to make P3 easier to implement. Pretty much all you need to remember is the number "3".

	Roster		BATTERS				PITCHERS	
Tr	Slots	Budget	Rel	PA	xBA	PX or Sp	Rel	xERA
1	5-8	Max $160	BBB	n/a	3	3 3	BBB	3
2	7-13	$50-$100	BBB	5	3 or	3 3	BBB	2
3	5-10	Up to $50	n/a	n/a	3	3 3	n/a	3

The conversion to Mayberry is pretty straightforward. On the batting side, xBA provides a good proxy for contact rate (since ct% drives xBA), and PX and Spd stay. For pitching, xERA easily replaces BPV.

The number of P3-worthy players in the higher tiers is similar. But Mayberry significantly opens up more possibilities for Tier 3 sleepers. Going into 2010, the numbers looked like this:

	Number of Players			
BATTERS	T1	T2	T3	TOTAL
Portfolio3	36	38	74	148
Mayberry/P3	44	26	102	172

PITCHERS	T1	T2	T3	TOTAL
Portfolio3	24	24	67	115
Mayberry/P3	22	26	112	160

Bumping the Portfolio3-eligible pool from 263 to 332 made drafting a bit easier.

The formula for consistent success

Has winning at fantasy baseball evolved into a game where having good projections is trumped by other factors?

Did knowing about Carlos Silva's new changeup give credit to contextual factors outside of the standard projected stats line; is "context" more important now? Is LIMA losing steam, and if so, does that mean we can no longer get an edge by gaming the draft? Is FAABing the right players the real key to success? Or is it just luck – being the guy who happened to draft Jose Bautista?

What does it really take to be successful at this game? Or better, what does it take to be *really* successful at this game?

This is a difficult question to answer for several reasons. First, we need to define "success."

Success is not just winning a league. Anyone can win a league in any given season. Winning once proves very little, especially in redraft leagues.

Success has to be defined as the ability to win *consistently*. Granted, it is a feat in itself to reach the mountaintop. But the battle isn't truly won unless you can stay atop that peak while others keep trying to knock you off.

What does it take to win that battle? I decided to conduct a little study.

I defined six variables, each of which could be considered as providing a competitive edge in playing this game. Then I contacted about a dozen high profile fantasy leaguers who have managed to win consistently at some point in their gaming career. I asked these players to rank the variables based on how each one impacted their own success. Then, based on their responses, we would come up with a consensus answer to our question.

The Variables

The contenders in your league this year will be the ones who have a little bit of each of the following six variables. The eventual winner will be the one who has a little bit more. But which is the most important? That's the question.

1. Better player projections: This is where it all begins and where many fantasy leaguers place the greatest emphasis. We'll define this variable as "the raw number of HRs, Ks, etc. each player would compile."

It would seem intuitive that the owner with the best projections would be the one with the best shot at winning, but it's not that clear cut. I once wrote that you could have 100% accurate projections and still lose at this game — for which I was duly chastised — but I think this is still an open question. There is no such thing as 100% accuracy — even 70% accuracy is a stretch — so "better projections" might not have much intrinsic value at all.

Still, you can't go into battle unarmed.

2. Better grasp of contextual elements that affect players: We'll define this as "team environment, potential usage based on conditional variables, etc." but that's really just scratching the surface.

Having the knowledge of Silva's new change-up — whether or not you used that knowledge to change his projections — is a tidbit you would have tucked away that provided unforeseen profit. Having knowledge about the Nationals' plans for Stephen Strasburg, or the short leashes Texas would have with Chris Davis and Frank Francisco, or Grady Sizemore's real health status... these are huge pieces of information had you known about them back in March.

But it is difficult to quantify this insight and incorporate it into our projections. Do these tidbits affect playing time? Performance baselines? Or do you just notate a little UP or DOWN arrow to show upside or downside potential? Still, it seems that knowing, and speculating, on this information could have great value in getting a competitive advantage.

3. Better sense of value, or knowing your marketplace. We'll define this as "projected value versus market value, based on more accurate dollar projections or ADPs."

This variable says that specific projections and contextual knowledge have less value than just knowing where the profit lies. How do your fellow owners value each player? This is the intelligence that allows you to target the most profitable commodities. If the marketplace thinks Prince Fielder is a $30/2nd round player and you consider him less valuable, then that's all you need to know. But is it the key determining factor to winning?

4. Better in-draft strategy and tactics: This is the "ability to budget dollars or plan picks, and the flexibility to react to changing conditions on the fly."

Perhaps all the pre-draft knowledge in the world is not as important as the actual task of leaving your draft with the best roster. It is true that you can't win your league on Draft Day (though you can lose it), but you have to set yourself up to contend. Perhaps it comes down to one question: "Which is more important, the knowledge or the application of that knowledge?"

5. Better in-season roster management: We'll define this as the ability to maximize "activations versus reserves, FAAB bidding, etc." This would also include trading, at least in leagues that allow trading.

With the rising tide of disabled list visits, it would seem that the game we play during the season may have as much impact as anything else we do. However, the randomness of FAAB bidding actually takes some control out of our hands. Still, given that teams can overcome huge deficits to win leagues, even late in the season, we can't discount the importance of what we do from April to September.

6. Better luck: There is no denying the impact of luck. In redraft leagues and for single, isolated championships, luck has a huge role. But for a fantasy player who manages to win consistently, one would think that some other skill has to transcend the impact of luck.

That doesn't mean luck is irrelevant. In fact, a case could be made that luck has just as much impact in multiple championships as with single titles. The question is, how much? Let's ask.

The Players

The fantasy players I selected to participate in this study were those who have won multiple expert or national competition titles within a short period of time. In alphabetical order, here they are, along with their league championships:

Shawn Childs
- NFBC: 4 main events, two AL auctions and one NL auction.
- Finished 3rd overall three times and 5th once in six years

Jason Grey (*ESPN.com*)
- Tout Wars-AL: 2002, 2003, 2010
- LABR: 2007, 2009

Peter Kreutzer/Alex Patton
(*AskRotoman.com/AlexPatton.com*)
- XFL: Lifetime standings leader

Mike Lombardo
- Tout Wars-NL: 2005, 2007, 2008

Gene McCaffrey (*Wise Guy Baseball*)
- CDM Challenge games: More than 30 league titles

Lenny Melnick/Irwin Zwilling (*FantasyPros911.com*)
- LABR: 1995, 1996
- Tout Wars: 2002

Larry Schechter (*Sandlot Shrink*)
- Tout Wars-Mixed: 2005, 2006, 2007

Sam Walker (*Fantasyland*)
- Tout Wars-AL: 2005, 2008

Scott Wilderman
- Tout Wars-NL: 2004, 2006

Jeff Winick
- XFL: 2004, 2006, 2010

Trace Wood (*LongGhandi.com*)
- Tout Wars-AL: 2004, 2006

And me...
- Tout Wars-AL: 1998, 2000, 1999 (2nd place)
- Tout Wars-NL: 1998
- LABR: 2001
- FSTA: 1999 (tied), 2001 (2nd place), 2010

This exercise proved to be difficult. I personally found the thought process to be a challenge, and I ended up ranking and re-ranking the variables at least four times. The other participants found it equally challenging; some of them dispensed with the 1 to 6 ranking, opting instead to group the variables and rank them within a narrower range.

Peter Kretuzer wrote: "These are hard to rank, especially because it's very hard to define where skill ends and luck begins (or vice versa)." Sam Walker concurred: "Really tough to rank these things since the relative importance of all of these factors falls into a pretty narrow range (in other words, they're all damn important)."

For Trace Wood, the question was one that had no answer at all: "I've given this a great deal of thought and I'm not sure I can help you because I never presume where I will gain an advantage. I set forth a plan based on data and observation but allow that circumstances will influence its direction and execution."

Still, in the end, a dozen expert players, many of whom play different game formats, came to a near consensus.

Here are the six variables, and the percentage of responses that were ranked in each of three groups — top two, middle two and bottom two. The "score" is the mean of all responses, where a "1" received 6 points, a "2" received 5 points, and so on.

Better player projections

Per cent ranked			
1-2	**3-4**	**5-6**	**Score**
12%	31%	54%	2.62

It will probably come to the surprise of nobody that I ranked this 6th. However, there are two ways to interpret the effect of better projections. You can approach it from the perspective that better accuracy is attainable and any edge you get provides value. Or your starting point can be that accuracy has an inherently low ceiling so any value will always be limited. Most of the participants in the study chose the latter approach and so it ranked as the lowest-scoring variable.

Kreutzer: "I think projections are important as a reality check, but they are not important when it comes to deciding what players should cost and what you will pay for them." For Jeff Winick, projections "don't provide an advantage; they simply prevent going into a draft at a disadvantage."

Better grasp of contextual elements that affected players

Per cent ranked			
1-2	**3-4**	**5-6**	**Score**
31%	38%	31%	3.62

The more I think about this variable, the more I realize how it can make or break a season, and the more important I think it has become. I ranked it 2nd.

Take the Texas Rangers. If you were to look back at the "formal" pre-season projections for Frank Francisco and Neftali Feliz, or Chris Davis and Justin Smoak, you'd see a bunch of hedging. On Opening Day, nobody knew who would emerge as the closer or 1Bman, or when a switchover might occur. Given how things turned out, projections for all four of these players were likely completely invalidated by the beginning of May.

However, if we had even the tiniest contextual knowledge that the Rangers would have a short leash with their underperformers, it would have influenced our perceptions of all four players. It would not have likely changed the projections — because we still would not have known that Francisco and Davis would fail — but it *would* have shaped our draft day behavior.

In the end, our expert players were split across the board on this variable. Overall, it ranked 4th.

Better sense of value

Per cent ranked			
1-2	**3-4**	**5-6**	**Score**
46%	46%	7%	4.15

I was the only one of the participants to rank this 1st. To my way of thinking, everything comes back to the marketplace. Getting the players you want at the draft is dependent upon how others value those players. Lucking into the correct FAAB bid is dependent upon how others value those players. Negotiating trades, same thing. It's all about leveraging what you believe with what others believe. Nearly all decisions are made within those limitations.

Scott Wilderman said that knowing "which of my projections differ significantly from everyone else's and the uncertainty/risk level in those projections" is important, but "then I need to be right about enough of them to make a difference."

Overall, the expert players ranked this 2nd.

Better in-draft strategy and tactics

Per cent ranked

1-2	3-4	5-6	Score
77%	15%	7%	5.00

I ranked this variable 3rd. After you have a sense of the marketplace and contextual factors that impact value, then you need to set your team's foundation at the draft. You can have a plan and strategies to game the table, but you can't have a good draft without that arsenal of knowledge. My opinion.

The expert consensus was much more definitive about the importance of the draft. This was the top-ranked variable by a large margin.

Walker felt that "the years I won, the momentum started at the draft. If there was value sitting out there, I took it, even if it didn't fit the plan (hence, draft strategy is #1 and value is #2)." Winick was even more definitive: "I've never won a league when I merely winged it at the draft."

I suppose I also question whether you can really evaluate how good a draft you had. Pro-forma standings projections are completely useless. The only way to know whether you had a good draft is if your players perform well.

Better in-season roster management

Per cent ranked

1-2	3-4	5-6	Score
31%	38%	31%	3.54

I ranked this 5th for pretty much the same reason I ranked "better projections" 6th. I don't believe we have much control over it. FAAB bidding is highly random and most of our decision-making is influenced by small sample sizes. We manage our rosters by trying to time streaks and slumps, and play pitching matchups. In deep leagues, we've reached the point where any breathing entity generates a lemming rush to be claimed. In the end, good roster management is often just about getting lucky on short-term decisions.

I'd rank this much higher if I thought we really had more control, though I suppose in-season managers whose moves pan out will rank this variable high.

But some disagreed. "The difference between winning and losing is what you do once you leave the draft room" is how Winick summed it up. Shawn Childs wrote, "(You have to) understand what you have as a team. If they are playing poorly, will they come around? What areas do you need to improve on? The battle is grinding it out."

The expert players were split. They ranked this 5th.

Better luck

Per cent ranked

1-2	3-4	5-6	Score
46%	23%	31%	3.85

For me, luck constitutes as much as 50%-60% of success for a single title, but that percentage drops for each successive title. Perhaps 35% for two consecutive titles, 25% for three, but probably never drops much below 20%. I ranked it 4th, but I can see that level varying up or down each season; first one season, sixth the next.

Gene McCaffrey wrote, "There is no doubt that luck plays a larger role than it used to, if only because people know more. Still, there wasn't much difference in March between Ellsbury and Crawford, but one was right and one was wrong. And the pitchers... you take Javier Vazquez, my money's on Livan Hernandez. You can have Beckett and I'll destroy you with Mat Latos."

Alex Patton had described the stages of competition in his books: "One of my refrains is, the more skilled we all become, the more it becomes a game of luck." And Jason Grey: "I believe you can do certain things that put yourself in a position to take full advantage of good luck, or minimize the effects of some bad luck."

Larry Schechter wrote that luck depends upon context: "For example, the luck element is much greater for a draft/auction league than for a salary cap game like CDM/Fanball. When your $30 player or #1 pick is hurt, it's a killer for an auction/draft team. But for salary cap, it's no big deal if Pujols goes on the DL for 3 months or Johan needs TJS."

Overall, the study participants ranked luck 3rd.

I asked readers and visitors to Baseball HQ to participate in a poll that asked the same question, though I asked them just to pick their #1 variable. Here are the results, as compared with the #1 picks of our participants in the study:

	Poll	Experts
Better player projections	10%	7%
Better sense of contextual elements	11%	7%
Better sense of market value v. projected value	24%	7%
Better in-draft strategy and tactics	14%	40%
Better in-season roster management	28%	13%
Better luck	13%	27%

How do you interpret these widely divergent results? The only variables where there is some agreement are the player projections and context. Small sample sizes might explain the experts' results, but these study participants still represent some of the best fantasy players today. Can we ignore their opinions?

Every variable is important and has its own contribution to success. That contribution probably does vary each year, making Trace Wood's comment more telling. But there are overall tendencies that we can identify. If nothing else, this may refute arguments that place undue importance on the role of player projections in determining consistent success. I think we are all little bit smarter already.

Projecting playing time

by Ed DeCaria

In "real baseball," playing time is fluid. Especially in the early winter, there is great uncertainty regarding rosters and roles for the upcoming season. So for fantasy leaguers, rather than guessing the outcome of every roster decision made three months in advance of Opening Day, we choose instead to hedge: and when we do, we hedge high.

The following charts show the pre-season progression of Baseball HQ's playing time projections, using pre-season 2010 as an example (the process is similar year-to-year).

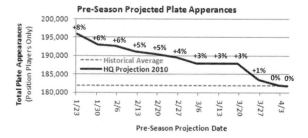

In January, we over-projected hitters by about 8% (amounting to about 14,000 extra plate appearances or the equivalent of 25 extra full-time hitters). However, this gap between projection and historical benchmark (1998-2009) was gradually narrowed each week to the point that it was completely closed by Opening Day.

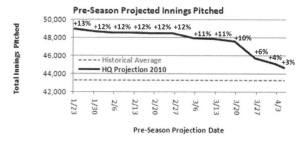

Similarly, we over-projected pitchers by about 13% (amounting to over 5,000 extra innings or the equivalent of 25 extra full-time starters) in the early off-season. This gap also narrowed over time, but in a later and more compressed fashion, as pitching roles were not clarified until closer to Opening Day or even after.

These downward chronological trends are typical of the annual playing time projection process at the league level. Still, even after matching expected league PA and IP totals, the *distribution* of playing time at the individual player level is still subject to variance vs. historical benchmarks.

Realistically, we know that players are going to be injured. But as forecasters, it is impossible to know in advance exactly who will miss time and how much. Other factors come into play as well: team success, service time and contract considerations, position or role flexibility, presence of viable replacements, and performance. Yet despite these projection obstacles, forecasters are obligated to offer an opinion on how each team's plate appearances and innings will be distributed among its players.

Here was our pre-season (Opening Day) 2010 outlook:

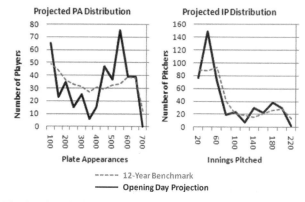

The height of each line indicates the number of hitters or pitchers who end the season at the level of PA or IP shown.

Among hitters, we projected many more players to land in the 450-600 PA range than recent MLB averages would suggest, made up for by an under-projection of players falling into the 250-450 PA range. Why? Because it was the most logical assignment that could be made in a world where Casey Kotchman "had won the 1B job outright" in Seattle, where Conor Jackson "was now healthy," and where Jason Heyward "hoped to say goodbye to the minors for good" without the benefit of hindsight to tell us which of those statements would turn out to be laughably wrong by season's end (it was Jackson). 1-in-3 actually is the playing time projection failure rate at the 450-600 PA level; a harsh truth, but one that we must embrace.

Among pitchers, history told us that 14 starters (+/- five) would finish with 220+ IP; we conservatively projected only three as of Opening Day, just as we projected zero 700+ PA hitters despite a historical average of 12 +/- two. At the next level down, we more aggressively projected nearly 100 starters to remain in the rotation for close to the full season (about 20% more than typically do). We offset this by under projecting swingmen and SPs expected to finish with 80-140 IP, the level at which predictable cases like 5th starters, rookies on pitch limits, and rehabs are joined by unexpected underperformers and healthy pitchers derailed by unforeseen physical problems.

The other primary differences between pitcher IP projections and reality come in the relief pool. Bullpen roles (and often relievers themselves) are interchangeable such that we project many RPs to finish with 40-60 IP -- mainly those with little experience, low reliability, and/or remaining minor league options who made the Opening Day roster. In reality, those innings will be split by a committee of relievers in a usage pattern unknown even to team GMs and field managers at the start of the season.

Projecting playing time is increasingly becoming a key differentiator among fantasy forecasters. The projections in this book are only a starting point. Baseball HQ employs dedicated playing time analysts to cover every MLB team, and together with subscriber input, we quantify *and qualify* our projections in real time to provide the best possible picture of playing time probability and potential.

Fantasy impact of batting order

by Ed DeCaria

Sabermetric analysts have studied optimal MLB lineup construction on countless occasions. Yet among all of these analyses of "protecting" star hitters, balancing OBP and power, strategically alternating LHBs/RHBs, slotting pitchers 8th vs. 9th, and making other tweaks that yield mere tenths of real-life runs per game, fantasy GMs have been left in the dark to guess how they can exploit such managerial lineup decisions to help win their own leagues.

Game logs reveal interesting patterns in lineup construction and stability over time (both game-to-game and season-to-season), and enable us to isolate the effects of batting order on skills indicators and surface statistics. Applying these insights through a fantasy lens can make us smarter and more nimble when trying to anticipate and respond to lineup changes across MLB.

Part 1: Lineup Construction and Stability Over Time

Among everyday players (starting 75%+ of team games), fewer than 1/3 hold a "dominant" lineup slot each year, of which 90% hold the leadoff, 2nd, 3rd, or cleanup positions:

Lineup Consistency	% of Players	Highest Frequency Lineup Slot								
		1	2	3	4	5	6	7	8	9
Dominant Slot (75%+)	31%	30%	14%	25%	22%	5%	1%	1%	2%	1%
Majority Slot (50-75%)	36%	10%	12%	18%	20%	16%	9%	5%	6%	4%
Fluid Slot (<50%)	33%	7%	14%	13%	9%	21%	17%	10%	7%	3%

Based on annual games started totals 1954-2009.

Another 1/3 of everyday players have a "majority" lineup slot (usually 1st thru 6th) in which they appear in 50%+ of their starts, but they also frequently bat in other slots. The final 1/3 of everyday players have no firm hold on any one lineup slot (i.e., subject to matchups, off days, or injuries).

With almost 70% of everyday players (and nearly all part-timers) lacking a dominant lineup slot, how quickly do lineup shifts occur and at what specific slots?

Lineup Slot "Today"	% of Players* Still in Same Lineup Slot After [n] Games			Next Most Likely Lineup Slot(s) After 50 Games
	Next Gm	+10 Gms	+50 Gms	
1st	88%	78%	68%	2nd
2nd	76%	59%	46%	1st|3rd
3rd	86%	72%	56%	4th|2nd|5th
4th	82%	69%	54%	3rd|5th|6th
5th	66%	49%	34%	4th|6th|3rd
6th	56%	39%	27%	5th|7th
7th	53%	37%	26%	6th|8th|5th
8th	64%	49%	37%	7th|9th
9th	70%	52%	36%	8th|2nd|7th

Based on daily game logs 2002-2009.

* Includes all players. Players with significant experience in a given slot "last year" show more game-to-game stability in that slot "this year".

88% of today's leadoff hitters bat leadoff again in their next game, 78% still bat leadoff 10 games later, and 68% still bat leadoff 50 games later. Despite this level of turnover after 50 games, leadoff hitters actually have the best chance of retaining their role over time; as a slot that requires special talent (perceived or real), this makes sense. After leadoff, #3 and #4 hitters are the next most likely to retain their lineup slots.

The picture then becomes much muddier, so much so that today's #5 through #9 hitters are 2-3 times more likely to bat in a different slot than to retain their current slot after 50 games. When players do move, they tend to move up or down only 1-2 slots, though bigger jumps (e.g., from #7-#9 to #1-#2 slots) do happen.

On a season-to-season basis, leadoff hitters are again the most stable, with 69% of last year's primary leadoff hitters retaining the #1 slot next year:

		Highest Frequency Lineup Slot Next Season ...								
		1	2	3	4	5	6	7	8	9
Highest Frequency Lineup Slot This Season	1	69%	12%	5%	1%	2%	2%	3%	4%	1%
	2	14%	50%	12%	2%	4%	4%	6%	6%	2%
	3	3%	8%	57%	15%	9%	4%	2%	1%	0%
	4	1%	1%	13%	60%	17%	6%	2%	0%	0%
	5	2%	4%	10%	24%	36%	17%	5%	1%	0%
	6	4%	6%	7%	13%	18%	31%	17%	5%	0%
	7	3%	12%	4%	3%	9%	18%	28%	19%	3%
	8	8%	8%	1%	1%	1%	6%	12%	52%	10%
	9	6%	11%	1%	0%	3%	3%	4%	18%	55%

Read chart horizontally. Based on annual games started totals 1954-2009.

Players with primary #2, #3, #4, #8, and #9 slots are slightly better than an even bet to retain the same slot next year. The #5, #6, and #7 slots are much more volatile across seasons. Similar to the game-by-game results, players usually only move 1-2 places as their primary lineup slot, illustrated by the stair step shading pattern on the chart.

Part 2: Impact of Batting Order on Player Statistics

Now knowing that lineups change frequently within and across seasons, does batting order itself have any real impact on fantasy baseball statistics and skills indicators?

To find out, we unearthed daily batting data for every player from 2002-2009, representing 300,000+ individual games started. We then carefully aggregated these games by player (to control for ability), by season (to control for aging effects), by team (to control for quality of surrounding lineup in-season), by home team's league (to control for games in which the pitcher batted), by opposing starting pitcher handedness (to control for player platoon splits), and finally by lineup slot (excluding the NL #9 slot), which is the elusive variable that we wished to isolate.

From this, we conducted a modified version of Tom Tango's **W**ith **O**r **W**ithout **Y**ou (WOWY) analysis that effectively compares a player to himself to determine net statistical performance "with" each lineup slot vs."without" that lineup slot (e.g., batting "6th" vs. "not 6th") in otherwise similar circumstances. Player WOWY pairs (weighted by harmonic mean of plate appearances "with" and "without") are then aggregated, and indices are calculated as:

WOWY Index =
"With" Lineup Slot / "Without" Lineup Slot * 100

For each statistic below, a WOWY Index >100 means that lineup slot alone contributes positively to player value (e.g., 110 index = +10% and 90 index = -10% change):

Plate Appearances per Game Started										
Lineup Slot:	1st	2nd	3rd	4th	5th	6th	7th	8th	9th	Chart
AL With	4.5	4.4	4.3	4.2	4.1	4.0	3.9	3.7	3.5	
Without	4.0	4.0	4.2	4.2	4.1	4.0	4.0	3.9	3.9	
Index	112	108	103	102	100	99	97	96	90	
NL With	4.5	4.4	4.3	4.2	4.1	4.0	3.8	3.7		
Without	4.1	4.1	4.2	4.2	4.1	4.1	4.0	4.0		
Index	110	106	102	101	99	98	96	91		

Plate appearances decline linearly by lineup slot. Leadoff batters receive 10-12% more PAs than when batting lower in the lineup. AL #9 batters and NL #8 batters get 9-10% fewer PAs. These results mirror play-by-play data showing a 15-20 PA drop by lineup slot over a full season.

Walk Rate										
Lineup Slot:	1st	2nd	3rd	4th	5th	6th	7th	8th	9th	Chart
AL With	8%	8%	10%	10%	9%	9%	8%	7%	7%	
Without	8%	8%	10%	10%	9%	9%	8%	7%	7%	
Index	99	96	99	101	102	100	102	100	96	
NL With	8%	8%	10%	11%	9%	8%	8%	9%		
Without	8%	9%	10%	11%	10%	9%	8%	7%		
Index	99	91	98	105	98	99	97	123		

Walk rate is largely unaffected by lineup slot in the AL. In the NL, the WOWY indices seem to highlight common managerial tactics with #2 and #8 hitters, emphasizing sacrifice bunts from the #2 slot (NL WOWY Index for bunts = 164, not shown) and avoiding #8 hitters to face pitchers. Beware strong BB% rates by NL #8 hitters, as much of this "skill" will disappear if ever moved from the #8 slot.

Contact Rate										
Lineup Slot:	1st	2nd	3rd	4th	5th	6th	7th	8th	9th	Chart
AL With	84%	83%	82%	81%	81%	81%	81%	81%	82%	
Without	84%	83%	83%	81%	81%	81%	81%	81%	81%	
Index	99	100	99	100	101	100	100	100	101	
NL With	84%	84%	82%	81%	80%	81%	81%	82%		
Without	83%	83%	83%	81%	81%	81%	81%	81%		
Index	101	100	99	100	99	100	100	100		

Batting order has no discernable effect on contact rate. Though players atop the order have better CT% (see "With" row), they exhibit similar rates in other slots, illustrated by the WOWY index flat line from #1 to #9.

Batting Average on Balls in Play										
Lineup Slot:	1st	2nd	3rd	4th	5th	6th	7th	8th	9th	Chart
AL With	30%	30%	30%	30%	29%	30%	29%	29%	31%	
Without	31%	31%	31%	30%	30%	30%	29%	29%	29%	
Index	96	100	95	101	99	100	100	102	107	
NL With	30%	31%	30%	30%	30%	30%	30%	30%		
Without	31%	31%	32%	30%	30%	30%	29%	29%		
Index	97	100	96	101	99	100	102	104		

After contact is made, hit rate slopes gently upward as hitters are slotted deeper in the lineup. This uptick is not due to G/L/F rate changes (not shown) as one might expect.

Home Runs per Fly Ball										
Lineup Slot:	1st	2nd	3rd	4th	5th	6th	7th	8th	9th	Chart
AL With	7%	8%	12%	13%	12%	11%	10%	9%	8%	
Without	7%	8%	12%	14%	12%	11%	10%	8%	7%	
Index	97	101	95	91	96	104	104	106	111	
NL With	8%	9%	12%	15%	13%	12%	10%	9%		
Without	7%	9%	14%	15%	13%	11%	10%	7%		
Index	110	97	92	97	101	101	102	114		

Similarly, HR/FB seems to suffer for heart-of-the-order hitters vs. when they occupy other lineup slots. Despite the BABIP and HR/FB troubles, RBI opportunities still abound:

"Other" Runs Batted In per Total Base										
Lineup Slot:	1st	2nd	3rd	4th	5th	6th	7th	8th	9th	Chart
AL With	0.19	0.22	0.26	0.27	0.25	0.23	0.24	0.25	0.24	
Without	0.23	0.24	0.24	0.24	0.25	0.25	0.24	0.24	0.24	
Index	83	94	107	109	102	93	100	105	102	
NL With	0.17	0.19	0.24	0.25	0.25	0.24	0.24	0.24		
Without	0.21	0.23	0.23	0.23	0.24	0.24	0.24	0.23		
Index	81	85	105	107	107	101	102	105		

The #3-4-5 slots are ideal for "Other" RBI (excluding HR), seemingly at the expense of #6 hitters. RBIs are worst for players in the #1-2 slots. (Consider this impact on star players like Hanley Ramirez or Carl Crawford who alternate between the #1 and #3 slots). However, the top of the order does have a few other statistical benefits:

Runs Scored per Time on Base										
Lineup Slot:	1st	2nd	3rd	4th	5th	6th	7th	8th	9th	Chart
AL With	0.38	0.37	0.32	0.30	0.30	0.30	0.31	0.31	0.34	
Without	0.35	0.33	0.32	0.30	0.31	0.31	0.32	0.33	0.35	
Index	108	111	101	100	99	96	97	95	98	
NL With	0.38	0.37	0.32	0.30	0.30	0.27	0.26	0.27		
Without	0.34	0.31	0.31	0.29	0.29	0.30	0.30	0.31		
Index	112	119	104	102	100	91	86	85		

Batting atop the order sharply increases the probability of scoring runs, especially in the NL. Because this is measured per time on base, these benefits exist over and above the PA boost shown in the first WOWY.

Stolen Base Attempt Rate										
Lineup Slot:	1st	2nd	3rd	4th	5th	6th	7th	8th	9th	Chart
AL With	14.2	10.5	6.7	4.7	5.6	6.4	6.9	7.1	10.2	
Without	13.8	11.0	7.7	4.6	5.2	6.0	6.9	7.3	10.4	
Index	103	96	87	102	108	107	100	97	98	
NL With	15.9	11.0	7.4	5.9	6.4	7.4	6.4	5.1		
Without	14.0	10.5	7.3	5.7	6.1	6.8	7.2	8.6		
Index	113	105	100	103	104	109	88	60		

The leadoff slot easily has the highest SB attempt rate in raw terms. Interestingly, the #4-5-6 holes have positive WOWY indices, meaning that hitters attempt steals more often when batting out of those slots than they do batting elsewhere. Impossible to miss on the chart is the lowest WOWY index of this or any other chart, which is the SB attempt sink hole known as the NL #8 hitter. A change in batting order from #8 to #1 in the NL could nearly double a player's SB output due to lineup slot alone.

Conclusion

Real-life changes in batting order can significantly impact fantasy statistics. Understanding lineup dynamics and batting order impact can help fantasy GMs to squeak out a few extra standings points by more tightly managing active rosters, opportunistically working the waiver wire, or capitalizing on misplaced competitor expectations of certain players in certain situations.

The daily lineup data used in this analysis was obtained free of charge from and is copyrighted by Retrosheet. Interested parties may contact Retrosheet at www.retrosheet.org.

ADP and scarcity

by Bill Macey

Previous research concerning a player's average draft positions (ADP) revealed that most players are selected within a round or two of their ADP with tight clustering around the average. But as experienced drafters will attest, every draft is unique and every pick in the draft seemingly affects the ordering of subsequent picks. In fact, deviations from "expected" sequences can sometimes start a chain reaction at that position. This is most often seen in runs at scarce positions such as the closer; once the first one goes, the next seems sure to closely follow. But do these effects really exist or is it just perception?

To investigate this, we looked at 121 league drafts for the 2009 season held at Mock Draft Central. Actual league drafts (as opposed to mock drafts) were selected as they tended to have very few computer or AI drafters that could skew the results of the analysis.

For each of the 121 drafts, we analyzed the sequencing of picks at each position. Rather than look at specific players (who different drafters may value differently), we examined the draft position of the first SS taken, the second SS taken, etc. and the relationship of those picks. This allows us to look past the valuation of specific players and focus on the effects of positional scarcity.

We found that some positions are more influenced by early selections at that position than others. A good example of this is at RP. In 2009, the ADP of the first RP selected (usually Jonathan Papelbon but occasionally Joe Nathan or others) was 58.2 and the ADP of the second RP selected was 65.4. However, the earlier the first RP was selected, the earlier the second RP was selected as well. For example, the ADP for the 10 earliest selections of a RP equaled 38.9. In those 10 drafts, the ADP of the second-selected RP was 55.3 (a 15% increase). The earlier the first RP goes, the earlier the next follows.

Other positions are more independent. For example, the ADP of the first SP selected was 18.5, but in the 13 drafts in which a SP went earliest, the ADP of the first SP taken was a low 7.9. Over those same 13 drafts, the ADP of the second SP drafted was 23.3, which isn't substantially different from the overall ADP of 25.0 for the second SP taken (an approx. 7% increase). The scarcer the position, the greater the interrelationship between picks. Deep positions like SP and OF are more independent that scarce positions like RP.

A closer examination suggests that within each position, there is a correlation within tiers of players (as defined by ADP) but that those tiers can be somewhat independent of each other. At each position, we can calculate the correlation between each two consecutive ranked draft picks. That is, the correlation between the first selected 1B and the second selected 1B; the correlation between the second selected 1B and the third selected 1B; etc. (While these correlations necessarily approach 1 as we progress later into the draft, they can be quite telling over the first hundred picks or so and reveal the effects of tiering).

The following shows the correlation between picks at 1B:

Rank	Correlation with next pick	Rank	Correlation
1	0.32	9	0.06
2	0.42	10	0.65
3	0.54	11	0.64
4	0.09	12	0.44
5	0.50	13	0.48
6	0.46	14	0.55
7	0.37	15	0.66
8	0.22		

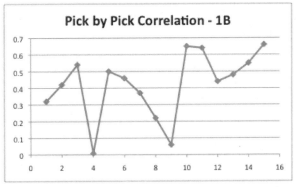

Overlaying this with ADP data, we can see a clear connection. The sooner players within a generally accepted tier are selected, the sooner other players within the same tier will be taken. However, once that tier is exhausted, the draft order tends to revert to normal. Continuing with 1B in 2009, per ADP data, the generally accepted tiers were:

Name	ADP	Tier
Albert Pujols	2.6	1
Miguel Cabrera	6.3	1
Ryan Howard	10.8	1
Mark Teixeira	11.6	1
Lance Berkman	21.6	2
Prince Fielder	25.3	2
Justin Morneau	28.5	2
Adrian Gonzalez	40.9	2
Joey Votto	53.4	2
Carlos Pena	87.0	3
Derrek Lee	88.3	3

Within the first tier, Pujols was the first 1B taken and Cabrera usually the second, but Howard and Teixeira were interchangeable. We can see from the above data and graph that the sooner the first three 1B went off the board, the sooner did the fourth, regardless of who that 1B was.

By comparison, the timing of when the fourth 1B (the last of the first tier) was selected had very little effect on how soon the fifth 1B (the first among the second tier) was selected. Again, we see fairly strong correlations within the second tier through the last player in that tier. But once Tier 2 is exhausted, Tier 3 seems to start anew.

Another observation is that all these effects eventually settle and do not reverberate through the remainder of the draft. Recall the earlier example of how the timing of the first selected RP affected how the next RP was selected. But by the time we get to the tenth selected RP, much of that effect has worn off. Unlike the second ranked RP which saw a 15% increase in ADP, the tenth ranked RP only gets a boost from 113 to 108, an increase of less than 5%.

How can we use this information? If you notice a reach pick, you can expect that other drafters may follow suit. If your draft plan is to get a similar player within that tier, you'll need to adjust your picks accordingly.

The value of consistency in H2H play

by Bill Macey

One of the often-stated assumptions is that consistent players are more valuable in Head-to-Head games than players with more volatile weekly performances. But is weekly consistency a repeatable skill?

At Baseball HQ, we maintain weekly consistency charts for batters that show the number and percentage of DOMinant, DISaster and NEUTral weeks for each player. For each week of play, a player earns a DOM week if their weekly BPV was greater or equal to 50; a NEUT if their BPV was between 0 and 50, and a DIS if their weekly BPV was less than or equal to 0. The percentage of Dominant weeks, DOM%, is simply calculated as the number of DOM weeks divided by the total number of weeks that player played.

To test whether a consistent performance was a repeatable skill for batters, we examined how closely related a player's DOM% was from year to year. To make sure our results weren't skewed by small sample sizes, we looked at players that played in at least 24 weeks during each season 2007-2009.

We found that batters with higher DOM% in year 1 were more likely to post high DOM% in year 2. Splitting the sample into roughly equal cohorts, the following chart compares DOM% rates in subsequent years:

YR1 DOM%	AVG YR2 DOM%
< 35%	37%
35% - 45%	40%
46% - 55%	45%
56% +	56%

These results are not unexpected. Annual BPV results tend to be strongly correlated from year to year (which is why we preach drafting skills, not stats). Furthermore, players with high annual BPVs tended to have high DOM% rates; mathematically, it's fairly difficult to post a high BPV over an entire year and still have many DIS weeks, unless your DOM weeks are obscenely good to compensate.

There are four individual skills that comprise BPV: contact rate, walk rate, power, and speed. We examined the relationship of each of these skills with a player's level of consistency.

CT%: Controlling for differences in the other three skills, contact rate has the strongest relationship with a player's level of consistency. A plausible story can be told to explain this: holding other skills constant, the more often a player puts the ball into play, the more chances he has for "something good" to happen. Conversely, every strikeout is a missed opportunity to get on base or drive in a run. Anecdotally, it does seem that a player who swings for the fences but strikes out frequently is more prone to slumps.

BB%: This metric has the second strongest relationship amongst the four skill components; a higher walk rate seems to moderately help a player smooth out his week-to-week performances.

PX: Players with a high Power Index do tend to post more consistent weekly performances, but the relationship overall is surprisingly mild.

SX: Not unexpectedly, Speed Index had the weakest relationship with consistency. Conventional wisdom says that SB often come in clumps, and given that SB is a major component of SX, this result is not surprising.

So, why does consistency matter?

Consider two teams playing a simple H2H contest with a single category — HR. Team 1 will be the consistent team; it hits exactly 20 HR per week. Team 2 will be the inconsistent team. Let's say that, *on average*, Team 2 hits 20 HR per week, but the actual amount is subject to a normal distribution (i.e., bell curve) with a standard deviation of 3 HR.

Under these circumstances, we'd expect Team 1 and 2 to each win 50% of the time. In the short-term, there would be some deviations from the 50/50 split, but the more times we repeat the game, the closer we'll converge to 50/50.

Now suppose that our consistent team (Team 1) continues to hit a guaranteed 20 HR each week, but our inconsistent team (Team 2) hits fewer HR on average (18 HR per week on average) with a standard deviation of 3 HR. In this case, Team 1 will win the contest approximately 75% of the time and Team 2 will win the other 25%.

As the standard deviation for Team 2 increases — as the team's performance becomes more inconsistent — Team 2 will win more frequently. For example, increasing the standard deviation for Team 2 from 3 HR to 4 HR increases Team 2's expected winning percentage from approximately 25% to approximately 31%.

The converse is equally true — when the inconsistent team's average HR is greater than the consistent team's average HR, increasing the level of inconsistency only serves to lower its expected winning percentage.

There are even times when a team may prefer a lower expected average output if it came with increased consistency. If and when this trade-off would occur depends entirely on the distribution of expected performance for the two teams.

These principles continue to apply when *each* team has elements of inconsistency. The team with the lower expected total benefits from increased inconsistency while the team with the higher expected total prefers more consistent performances. Note that each team's preferences apply to both teams; that is, the favored team benefits from more consistent performances from both teams and the underdog benefits from inconsistency from both teams.

Conclusion

The analysis presented here lays the foundation for embracing consistency in head-to-head play. When you are favored, there is less benefit to the potential upside performances and more risk associated with the downside; reducing inconsistency around those weekly performances should result in more overall wins.

However, there are times where inconsistency could be the ally of the savvy owner. During those weeks when you play the role of the underdog, consider starting some of your risky but high upside players in hopes of achieving upside. You want to swing for the fences when you'd likely lose otherwise anyway.

Psychologies of high stakes leagues

I don't play in any big money leagues. I prefer to play this game for the competition and camaraderie, and for me, money adds a component that distorts the experience. This is just my opinion. But I have often been challenged on it, so I decided to do some research.

Last winter at BaseballHQ.com, we ran a poll to see what our readers' attitudes were towards money leagues:

* I play for the competition and camaraderie. Cash winnings are irrelevant. (31%)
* Competition and camaraderie are important, but I am at least somewhat motivated by cash. (38%)
* The potential for cash winnings is at least equally important as competition and camaraderie. (15%)
* Money is a major motivator. (3%)
* I would not play in a league that didn't have cash winnings. (13%)

About 7 in 10 had at least some cash motivation. The idea that 13% would not play *at all* if not for the cash is foreign to me. Wouldn't money as sole motivation potentially change how you play the game, even your core behavior?

There is a ton of research available about the psychology of "playing for fun" versus "playing for money." Here is a profile compiled from several online sources:

Those playing for the competition, or for "fun"...

* are more likely to experiment with new tools and strategies.
* play looser (which may be good or bad).
* may take wild risks since there is less at stake.
* are more forgiving.
* are less likely to have the game interfere with their other life priorities.
* say they play to win, even if their behavior says otherwise.
* don't mind paying an entry fee just to be entertained.
* measure success by the number of competitions they've won.

Those playing for money...

* tend to play in games they are most experienced in.
* tend to rely on proven strategies.
* take fewer risks.
* demand fairness.
* are more likely to find the game stressing their other life priorities.
* say they play to win, and mean it.
* find it incomprehensible that someone would pay an entry fee just to be entertained.
* measure success by the amount of cash they've won.

One report, entitled *Winning Expectancies and Arousal*, went so far as to conclude: "According to self-reports, it is the expectancy of winning money that is exciting, not playing the game. Regardless of the level of risk-taking, expectancy of winning is a cognitive factor influencing levels of arousal. Playing for fun is significantly less stimulating than playing for money."

The above research focused mostly on other gaming applications, from poker to backgammon, but the results are probably still relevant. The behaviors described do mirror our experiences playing fantasy.

Still, these are just logical analyses. It's no surprise to conclude that money players are more intense and gravitate to competitions they'd do better in. One might also expect higher stakes games to exacerbate the effect. Perhaps the most insightful item is how each group measures success.

However, one research study found that there are underlying personality tendencies that cut deeper.

The article appeared in the November 17, 2006 issue of *Science Magazine* entitled, "The Psychological Consequences of Money." Nine behavioral experiments were conducted, using random samples of students and non-students from three universities. The test group engaged in activities while being given "mental priming techniques, which heightened the accessibility of the idea of money but at a level below participants' conscious awareness." The control group participated in the same activities but received no such priming. All experiments yielded consistent results.

From a commentary about the article, at bankrate.com:

"(The) study finds that folks with money on their minds are less helpful, less considerate and less willing to ask for assistance or engage with others than those who have not been preconditioned to money. On the bright side, the money-minded tend to be more independent and focused and tend to work longer on a task before asking for help.

"Money may not be the root of all evil, but it might be the root of indifference to others."

This is concerning because fantasy sports was designed to be a social game. The rise of online competition, which has driven the growth of the industry, has in many ways isolated us. Most agree that private local leagues and live drafts provide a more enriching experience. If money makes us indifferent to others, we might as well sit behind our computer monitors to play... which most of us now do.

But what about those people who play in big money leagues only because, well, they have the financial means to do so? It is not a matter of taking a high stakes risk for the thrill of the win, but simply because $1,000 is their definition of pocket change.

HQ subscriber Josh Turin responded:

"I play in two private high stakes leagues. Most of the participants are highly knowledgeable. We are accountants, lawyers, programmers, engineers — analytical people who enjoy a challenge. For some of us, playing for "high stakes" serves a number of not-unworthy functions: It is a less-harmful surrogate for gambling. It is a way to provide a "prize" for hard work. And this "high stakes" commitment to Roto in many cases motivates some of us to develop analytical skills we otherwise would not have.

"What actually happens in our high stakes leagues is that people display behaviors opposite to those of these gambling studies. Most gambling is 'anonymous.' If I play poker at Bellagio, I do not know my opponents. But my league opponents are my friends *and* competitors. While we each insist on 'fairness,' we innately provide it ourselves."

Fair enough.

Rotisserie 500

The book that started it all – the 1984 edition of *Rotisserie League Baseball* – described a game that is different from the one we play today. The original Rotisserie game was a 4x4 contest with AL-only and NL-only leagues, no reserve lists and (heavens!) no daily transactions.

Real-time stats? Heck, the Founding Fathers relied on *The Sporting News*, whose published updates were 10 days old by time they reached their mailboxes. Postal mailboxes.

Three decades have passed since that first constitution was written. One would expect that there would be some evolution; 5x5, mixed leagues and Free Agent Acquisition Budgets (FAAB) have all helped to move the game forward. Still, even with these changes, the foundation of the original game remains. This is both good and bad.

We've come to accept certain elements of the game and its rules that, from an objective perspective, are somewhat incongruous. These are not things that we typically think about. The game has rules; we play by them without questioning.

Heck, we accept incongruities all the time, even with the real game of baseball. To wit…

1. I'm a starting pitcher hurling a fine 6-2 game but put two runners on with two outs in the 9th inning. A reliever comes in and promptly gives up a 3-run homerun before retiring the last batter. I get my win but have two extra runs charged to me, inflating my ERA. The reliever gets a save despite nearly blowing the game.

2. In a late-inning tie game, I come to bat with runners on first and third and nobody out. I hit into a double play which scores the go-ahead run. I do not get credit for an RBI, even though I might have just driven in the game-winning run. Why is that run different from any other run?

In fantasy, when we run into these types of inconsistencies, we simply change the rules. We close the loopholes and add another Band-Aid to our constitution. And while this can snowball, creating monster rules documents, the thought process behind it is sound. If something is broke, don't ignore it — fix it.

So, I am here to fix some things with Rotisserie Baseball that I consider, if not fully broke, then at minimum in need of objective consideration.

Rotisserie 500 (Roto500) addresses three areas in particular:

- Valuing of players
- Selection of players
- Statistical categories

It starts as a 12-team mixed league with 23-man active rosters.

Valuing of players

How do we measure what is a player worth? We all know that a player's draft dollar value will vary depending upon a variety of factors, from size of the league, to stage of the draft, to personal bias. That, in itself, is an inconsistency, but there are player valuing issues at an even higher level.

Within an individual league, there are several different "currencies" for valuing players. For the active roster in an auction league, the currency is a $260 budget. For the reserve roster, the currency is snake picks. For free agents, the currency might be FAAB dollars or first guy to the computer.

Shouldn't the currency we use to value and purchase players be the same no matter how we acquire them? After all, a player is a player is a player. Ike Davis shouldn't be valued using one unit of measure if he's drafted, another if he's a reserve pick and yet another if he's FAABed. There should be a standard, consistent unit of measure used for all players, for every aspect of the game.

In Roto500, that standard unit of measure is dollars. Every owner gets a $500 budget at the beginning of the season. This goes to pay for everything — the draft roster, reserves and any free agents acquired during the season.

There are fascinating strategic implications to giving owners a flat $500 for the entire season and complete freedom to spend it as they see fit.

Since there is no $260 limit for the draft, you have to decide how you are going to budget your money. If you spend $260 on your active roster, that will leave you $240 for reserve players and free agents. You can opt to stock up with the very best players for your active roster — perhaps $300 worth, or more, limited only by what players are available to you — but that will limit your options for reserves and free agents. If you excel at in-season management, perhaps you draft a $200 team, or less, and leave yourself with more money during the season. Each owner has to decide how he is going to play it.

Selection of players

In assembling our roster during a fantasy draft, we're trying to find value. The draft methods we typically use define and rank value in different ways. Each has its advantages and disadvantages.

In a snake draft, the underlying assumption is that value can be ranked relative to a linear baseline. Pick #1 is better than pick #2, which is better than pick #3... and the difference between each pick is assumed to be somewhat equivalent. We know that this is not true. However, snake drafting has the advantage of being quick to play, and easy to automate and administer.

In an auction, the baseline is $0 at the beginning of each player put up for bid. The final purchase price for each player is shaped by many factors and can vary wildly from one league to another. While auctions provide owners with the greatest control over the players they roster, the draft events can run very long and online automation has not yet been perfected.

In a salary cap league, each player has his own fixed value. This is pre-set based on some formula that looks at past season performance. These type of leagues are typically pick-a-player contests with multiple teams rostering the same players.

In Roto500, all three methods are combined, taking elements from each. From salary cap games, we assign each player his own baseline value based on past season performances. From auctions, we permit owners to bid up players with undervalued baselines, though selectively. From snake, well, that's how we will select the players.

Each player has a list price in Roto500. This pre-set dollar amount is calculated as the average of his end-of-season values from the past two years (rounded up, if necessary). Seasons in which a player maintained his rookie eligibility are valued at $10. Negative valued years revert to $0, but every player must have a list price of at least $1.

For 2011, Albert Pujols would be listed at about par for $52 (average of $54 in 2009 and $49 in 2010). Josh Hamilton would be possibly undervalued at $20 ($4 + $35). Zach Greinke would be possibly overvalued at $21 ($37 + $5).

This method creates value decisions for owners. Where do you draft a consistently productive yet expensive player, like a $37 Miguel Cabrera ($30 + $43). Where do you draft a potentially undervalued injury rehab, like a $20 Jacoby Ellsbury ($39 + $0)? Maybe a $33 Felix Hernandez ($34 + $31) is not the best early-round staff anchor. Maybe the $14 David Price ($3 + $25) provides more profit there. The drafting process in Roto500 is not just finding the best player available but balancing value and profit. Since this is a snake draft, these decisions are made with every pick.

As the owners fill their rosters, they use up some portion of their $500 budget. But auction dynamics also play a part: **owners can bid up players they believe are undervalued**. However, each owner can purchase no more than three players above list price, so they have to pick their spots.

Further complicating the decision-making process is, if you toss out a player during your turn and another owner bids him up and wins, you've potentially lost your pick in that round. There are two remedies to counter this.

1. The owner who originally tossed out the player has "topper rights" for that bid. If he selected the $13 Adrian Beltre and others bid the player up to a final price of $22, the original owner has the option to purchase Beltre for $23. However, that would constitute one of the three players he is allowed to purchase above list price.

2. The original owner always has the option to bid on another player in the same round.

So there is a lot at stake when you toss out a name. You have to consider how well a player's list price reflects his true value and the likelihood that the player will generate bidding from other owners. At some point in the draft, owners will begin running out of their three allowable purchases and the dynamic will change.

After all teams have rostered their 23 active players, the snake draft will continue to fill each **reserve list.** Reserve lists can be as large as 17 players – and constitute each team's bench as well as its disabled list – however, owners need not fill all the slots at the draft. The advantage of stocking at least some of the reserve at the draft is that these players can be rostered at their draft prices. After the draft, any further reserve players must be acquired via FAAB.

Roto500 levels the playing field a bit in **keeper leagues**. In most leagues today, a superstar drafted as a farm player may remain undervalued for many seasons (in the XFL, I currently own Tim Lincecum at $13). In Roto500, the baseline value for each player changes each season. Since that baseline is based on a two-year average, a young star will never be undervalued for more than two years. To wit:

Let's say we expect Jason Heyward to be a consistent $25 player. We would have rostered him in 2010 for $10 and kept him in 2011 at $18 ($10 + $25). By 2012 his cost would be up to his par value ($25) but we would have already benefited by owning him at a discount for two years.

During the season, the player value unit of measure shifts to FAAB, though still under the $500 cap. You can use the standard FAAB procedure, though adding Vickrey or Double-bid FAAB will aid greatly in the budgeting process.

Statistical Categories

My contention is that more is not necessarily better. 5x5 may have been an improvement over 4x4 but not for the reasons we may think. It did not really capture that much more of a player's productivity than 4x4 did. The purpose that 5x5 really served was to close off some of the loopholes that allowed 4x4 owners to game the system.

Some bright 4x4 player realized he could assemble a winning pitching staff of just relievers, so leagues instituted minimum innings requirements. These became unnecessary with the addition of strikeouts as a pitching category. Runs were added on the batting side to provide balance. But the last thing that 5x5, or even 4x4, provide is balance.

With one ratio category on the batting side (batting average) and two on the pitching side (ERA and WHIP), there has always been an inherent imbalance in how batters and pitchers are valued. Adding Runs on the batting side only serves to double the number of categories that are situation-dependent. RBI and Runs provide less a measure of individual skill than a measure of a player's surrounding cast. (In addition, including both R and RBI means that we have been triple-counting the impact of home runs!) In the end, 40% of a batter's value in 5x5 is composed of stats that are only marginally skills-related.

While the natural inclination is to add categories to make up for these types of deficiencies, we can actually capture just as much by going back to a 4x4 format. An added advantage is that players and categories are easier to manage when there are fewer moving parts.

Our Roto500 categories would be:
* Home Runs
* Stolen Bases
* On Base Percentage (better than Batting Average)
* We'd combine Runs and RBIs into one category — Runs Produced (R + RBI – HR) – to minimize effects of team environment (and remove some redundant HR).
* Wins
* Strikeouts
* Earned Run Average
* We'd change Saves to (Saves + Holds - Blown Saves) to reduce the impact that closers have on 4x4 values.

WHIP goes away. Who really manages their pitchers using WHIP anyway?

In the end, we're back to 4x4 but with more balance. One ratio category on each side and we largely maintain most of the categories we've come to love.

Constructing player values for the draft poses its own set of challenges. If we calculate values based on the above categories, a $500 budget and 40-man rosters, the resulting dollars run higher than the levels we are familiar with. Albert Pujols becomes a $69 player ($72 in 2009 and $65 in 2010), Felix Hernandez tops all pitchers at $42, and nearly two dozen players finish at $40 or higher.

To move these values back to familiar levels, we have to calculate the pool with a $400 budget. This is not entirely a bad thing as it assumes that there will be some new value coming into the league during the season (purchased with FAAB), and we will need that room under the $500 cap.

A complete list of player values for a 2011 draft appears in the back of the book.

First Pitch Arizona Mock Draft

We conducted an abbreviated mock draft of Roto500 in November at First Pitch Arizona. Twelve members of the fantasy baseball media community, including several Baseball HQ writers, took the game out for a test run.

There were many different opinions about how the game should be played. Albert Pujols was bid up to $115. Several other players were bid into the $70s and $80s. There was an undercurrent of expectation that the $500 cap was far more than enough to accommodate the available talent in the league so you should pay whatever it takes to roster the best three biddable players.

That's not how I envisioned this. Using the price list in the back, taking the first seed and picking eligible players at each turn, I could put together the following team:

CA	Posey	10	P	Lester	22
CA	Posada	10	P	J.Johnson	22
1B	Pujols	52	P	Latos	15
3B	Beltre	13	P	Beckett	9
CO	Prado	11	P	B.Myers	9
2B	Utley	26	P	Cueto	7
SS	Furcal	13	P	Niese	7
MI	Pedroia	22	P	R.Soriano	12
OF	C.Gonzalz	26	P	B.Wilson	15
OF	Heyward	22			
OF	Stanton	9			
OF	Ad.Jones	9			
OF	A.Soriano	8			
UT	Kendrick	8			

The total list price of these 23 players is $357. But odds are I would not be able to get all these players as some would get bid up. Assuming I'd have to go off list price for Posey, Beltre and Gonzalez, I'd probably be looking at spending closer to $400 for this group. Then let's say I spend another $10-$20 to fill half my reserve roster and suddenly my available FAAB seems painfully thin.

It's not as easy as it looks.

Shortly after the weekend, I received an email from HQ's Dave Adler. He wrote: "I'll be honest with you...when I first heard of this idea, I figured the experts would scoff and laugh it off as a gimmick. But while playing poker Saturday night — there were about a dozen of them waiting to play — they were going through the pros and cons of various strategies for the game. It was actually getting pretty animated." The Tuesday after the trip, Jeff Erickson had me on his Rotowire Fantasy Sports radio show on Sirius/XM to talk about Roto500. The game was generating a buzz.

So I emailed the dozen participants and asked them for their thoughts. Here are a few of their ideas and points:

Josh Paley: It might be better if the number of "toppers" were around eight, not three.

With the current system, 36 players (3 toppers x 12 owners) get to have their list prices corrected. While that might not be the optimal number, if we raise the limit too high, then the draft will just devolve into a regular auction. We need to find the right number.

Paley: FAAB dollars are less valuable than auction dollars, perhaps by a factor of 5 or 10 to 1.

I think that is something that the market will eventually self-correct once teams start pushing up against the cap.

Derek Van Riper: Would you consider either adding more owners and/or cutting the reserve roster spots from 17? This could leave a more desirable crop of free agents during the season and make the strategy of saving extra FAAB a better one (drafting 420 Players - a 14-team league with 30-man rosters v. 480 players - 12-team league, 40-man).

Given that AL and NL-only leagues draft to even greater penetration, I think supply and demand alone will be enough to determine how free agents are priced.

Steve Gardner: If everyone thinks Derek Jeter is too expensive at $27, is there a chance he might go undrafted? Then, he could be purchased at a lower price with FAAB?

That definitely could occur. And given that this is a snake draft, you'd have to decide whether to wait it out and take the chance that someone else won't grab him, even at $27.

Neil Fitzgerald: Open up the market to more closely simulate the GM's world by allowing owners to trade draft picks (for future years), FAAB, etc. In this way, non-competing teams could trade outstanding FAAB for minor leaguers/keepers/draft picks/etc. Then perhaps allow the roll-over of unspent $500 budget to subsequent years - again in the spirit of making strategic GM type decisions.

All great ideas. In time.

We need to play this thing out. The Baseball HQ staff will be doing just that in 2011, as part of a year-long laboratory league. But you don't have to wait. Should you decide to take Roto500 out for a test run, go to the Contact page at BaseballHQ.com and keep me posted with your progress. If you have any suggestions for fine-tuning the concept, I'd love to hear them.

The Teams

The following four pages contain stat boxes for all 30 major league teams plus summary boxes for both leagues. The stats themselves will be mostly familiar to you from the player boxes, however, we have included both batter and pitcher BPIs on each line.

Each team box is divided into three sections.

At Home represents all batting and pitching statistics accumulated by that team in its home ballpark.

Away represents all batting and pitching statistics accumulated by that team in its games on the road.

Opp@ represents all batting and pitching statistics accumulated by all visiting teams when they played at the home ballpark.

Within each section are BPIs from the past three years, 2008-2010. Teams that have changed ballparks during that time may cause some inconsistent data.

To get a sense of ballpark effects, look at both the At Home and Opp@ sections in tandem. If the levels are similar, then it may indicate a particular ballpark tendency. If the levels are not similar, then it may be team dependent. You can compare this data from one team's box to another for additional insight.

As an example, the Dodgers' batters have a contact rate at home around 80% but the opposition at Dodger Stadium has posted levels consistently 4% lower. This could indicate the success of the Dodgers pitching staff as opposed to any park effects. In contrast, Cincinnati's At Home and Opp@ contact rates are both in the high 70%'s, which might be more telling of Great American Ballpark park effects.

In the pitching section of each chart, we also show the number of wins (W) each team had, the Pythagorean projected wins (Py) they should have had based on their runs scored and runs allowed, and the percentage of save opportunities successfully converted. The Blue Jays under-performed in road games in 2009 by a massive 10 games, winning only 31 while they should have won 41. As Bill James' Plexiglass Principle tells us, phenomena like that tend to correct quickly. And it did in 2010.

The save opportunities data are interesting. We don't typically consider that a closer's success might hinge on the friendliness of his environment. However, one of the reasons the Angels did so poorly this year might have been their offense's inability to get to opposition bullpens. Visiting teams in Angels Stadium were able to close out 92% of their save opportunities. Over the past six years, only the 2007 Royals exhibited this level of futility at home (93%). The Atlanta bullpen has been showing some improvement over the past three years, closing out their opposition at home by the rates of 58%, 68% and 77% this past year.

Other things to look at include a team's SX and SBO rates, which provide insight into which teams are running more or less, or which teams are easier or more difficult to run on. The White Sox have been running more each of the past three years, with SBO rates increasing from 7% in 2008 to 10% in 2009 and 14% in 2010 at home (and 7%, 11% and 18% on the road). The opposition has been running more on Giants' backstops (9%, 11%, 13% the past three years); compare that to the Cardinals, where opposing runners test Yadier Molina only 5% of the time.

Some other interesting tidbits…

Humidor or not, opposing pitchers are having a tougher time in Coors Field lately, their ERA rising over the past three years from 4.96, to 5.54, to 5.76. The Red Sox home offense continues to brutalize opposing pitchers, yielding a 5.00-plus ERA for all eight years we've run this chart.

Home runs per fly ball tend to regress to 10%, but there are a few ballparks where the base rate has been consistently higher, including U.S. Cellular Field, Cincinnati, Colorado, Milwaukee, Yankee Stadium, Philadelphia, Tampa and Texas. Consistent sub-10% rates can be found in KC, Dodger Stadium, Oakland, Pittsburgh, San Diego and Seattle.

It's interesting how two completely different stadiums are just a subway ride apart. CitiField was the stingiest park for visitors, allowing just 7% of fly balls to go yard over the past two years. By comparison, Yankee Stadium was the most visitor-friendly, allowing 15% home runs per fly ball.

BATTING / PITCHING

ARI	Yr	Avg	OB	Slg	OPS	bb%	ct%	h%	Eye	G	L	F	PX	SX	SBO	xBA	RC/G	W	Py	Sv%	ERA	WHIP	H%	S%	xERA	Ctl	Dom	Cmd	hr/f	hr/9	BPV
At Home	08	268	341	446	786	10	78	32	0.49	40	21	39	114	106	6%	260	5.36	48	43	74%	4.10	1.27	31%	70%	4.04	2.6	7.8	2.9	11%	1.0	92
	09	270	340	451	791	10	78	32	0.49	42	19	39	119	104	8%	262	5.38	36	36	62%	4.78	1.38	31%	67%	4.71	3.1	7.3	2.3	10%	1.1	69
	10	262	339	446	786	10	72	33	0.42	41	20	39	130	104	8%	252	5.41	40	38	77%	4.53	1.35	30%	70%	4.43	2.8	6.9	2.4	12%	1.3	67
Away	08	234	308	385	693	10	75	28	0.43	39	21	40	101	85	5%	239	4.09	34	39	52%	3.88	1.32	31%	72%	3.94	3.0	7.7	2.5	9%	0.8	79
	09	237	306	385	691	9	75	29	0.40	44	17	39	99	96	11%	235	4.02	34	39	68%	4.09	1.37	30%	73%	4.13	3.4	7.1	2.1	10%	1.0	56
	10	238	306	386	692	9	72	30	0.35	42	16	42	109	88	10%	223	4.06	25	31	41%	5.10	1.52	30%	70%	4.92	4.1	6.5	1.6	12%	1.4	27
Opp @ ARI	08	254	307	404	712	7	78	30	0.34	46	19	35	98	93	9%	249	4.21	33	38	62%	4.78	1.46	32%	69%	4.77	3.8	7.8	2.0	10%	1.0	55
	09	266	326	428	755	8	79	31	0.43	44	19	37	104	116	10%	259	4.82	45	45	72%	4.64	1.46	32%	71%	4.56	3.7	7.6	2.1	10%	1.1	57
	10	267	323	441	764	8	80	30	0.41	42	19	39	110	109	10%	263	4.86	41	43	68%	4.72	1.46	33%	71%	4.32	4.1	9.6	2.4	13%	1.3	81

ATL	Yr	Avg	OB	Slg	OPS	bb%	ct%	h%	Eye	G	L	F	PX	SX	SBO	xBA	RC/G	W	Py	Sv%	ERA	WHIP	H%	S%	xERA	Ctl	Dom	Cmd	hr/f	hr/9	BPV
At Home	08	278	353	411	764	10	82	32	0.65	46	22	32	83	91	5%	263	5.09	43	39	58%	4.44	1.41	30%	70%	4.38	3.7	6.8	1.8	11%	1.0	48
	09	257	333	392	725	10	80	30	0.58	43	21	36	88	78	7%	253	4.55	40	42	68%	3.43	1.28	30%	74%	3.70	3.3	7.8	2.4	7%	0.7	75
	10	270	344	423	767	10	80	31	0.56	44	20	36	101	97	6%	261	5.08	56	51	77%	3.20	1.20	29%	76%	3.38	3.0	8.1	2.7	9%	0.7	93
Away	08	263	332	405	737	9	81	30	0.56	44	22	34	91	79	5%	264	4.70	29	40	60%	4.50	1.40	30%	70%	4.39	3.6	6.7	1.8	12%	1.0	49
	09	269	338	418	756	9	81	31	0.56	44	19	37	97	81	3%	258	4.91	46	49	62%	3.73	1.36	31%	74%	3.81	3.2	7.3	2.3	9%	0.8	70
	10	247	327	380	707	11	78	29	0.55	46	17	37	93	76	5%	239	4.36	35	42	63%	3.96	1.35	31%	72%	3.96	3.4	7.4	2.2	10%	0.9	71
Opp @ ATL	08	263	334	426	761	10	80	30	0.54	47	21	32	103	109	9%	272	4.99	38	42	57%	4.58	1.55	32%	71%	4.60	4.1	6.4	1.5	8%	0.8	27
	09	245	313	370	683	9	77	30	0.42	46	19	34	85	93	9%	239	3.99	41	39	66%	3.63	1.39	29%	76%	3.86	3.8	6.6	1.7	9%	0.9	37
	10	237	299	355	655	8	76	29	0.37	50	17	33	84	83	10%	230	3.53	25	30	45%	4.59	1.48	31%	71%	4.61	3.9	7.0	1.8	10%	1.0	41

BAL	Yr	Avg	OB	Slg	OPS	bb%	ct%	h%	Eye	G	L	F	PX	SX	SBO	xBA	RC/G	W	Py	Sv%	ERA	WHIP	H%	S%	xERA	Ctl	Dom	Cmd	hr/f	hr/9	BPV
At Home	08	275	338	444	782	9	83	30	0.56	42	19	38	103	94	7%	268	5.15	37	36	63%	5.14	1.54	30%	70%	4.96	4.1	5.9	1.4	12%	1.3	17
	09	288	348	455	804	8	83	32	0.54	44	18	38	106	82	7%	265	5.40	39	40	59%	4.71	1.49	32%	72%	4.54	3.1	5.8	1.9	11%	1.3	42
	10	269	322	403	725	7	82	31	0.43	45	18	37	88	74	7%	246	4.38	37	31	52%	4.66	1.40	30%	70%	4.58	3.1	6.6	2.1	11%	1.3	55
Away	08	260	325	414	739	9	81	30	0.52	43	19	38	98	95	8%	259	4.68	31	37	55%	5.17	1.60	31%	69%	5.29	4.6	5.8	1.3	9%	1.0	3
	09	249	312	376	688	8	81	29	0.48	44	19	38	87	78	8%	246	4.02	25	28	58%	5.66	1.56	31%	66%	5.43	3.8	5.9	1.5	12%	1.4	23
	10	250	302	370	672	7	80	29	0.37	47	18	36	81	89	8%	240	3.72	29	32	61%	4.52	1.42	30%	70%	4.72	3.4	6.0	1.8	9%	1.0	36
Opp @ BAL	08	277	352	448	801	10	83	30	0.70	45	18	37	101	102	10%	269	5.46	43	44	65%	4.91	1.46	31%	69%	4.84	3.4	6.0	1.8	11%	1.2	38
	09	289	345	467	812	8	84	32	0.53	42	19	40	112	95	10%	273	5.46	42	41	78%	5.08	1.51	32%	69%	4.90	3.3	6.1	1.8	11%	1.2	43
	10	271	330	440	770	8	81	30	0.48	43	17	40	107	94	8%	257	4.95	44	50	65%	3.83	1.34	31%	74%	4.02	2.7	6.3	2.3	9%	0.9	63

BOS	Yr	Avg	OB	Slg	OPS	bb%	ct%	h%	Eye	G	L	F	PX	SX	SBO	xBA	RC/G	W	Py	Sv%	ERA	WHIP	H%	S%	xERA	Ctl	Dom	Cmd	hr/f	hr/9	BPV
At Home	08	292	371	468	839	11	82	33	0.70	43	20	38	115	115	9%	276	6.06	56	52	70%	3.78	1.34	30%	74%	4.04	3.4	7.2	2.1	8%	0.8	60
	09	284	360	498	858	11	80	32	0.59	38	19	43	142	105	12%	276	6.22	56	52	66%	4.07	1.35	32%	72%	4.29	3.0	7.4	2.5	8%	0.9	71
	10	275	346	455	801	10	80	31	0.54	39	18	43	122	86	5%	260	5.47	46	43	74%	4.25	1.36	30%	70%	4.45	3.5	7.3	2.1	8%	0.9	61
Away	08	268	338	428	766	10	80	31	0.52	40	20	39	99	94	10%	256	5.00	39	43	66%	4.26	1.31	29%	70%	4.35	3.4	7.5	2.2	10%	1.0	65
	09	257	335	414	749	11	80	29	0.59	40	19	42	102	98	9%	250	4.83	39	41	74%	4.64	1.47	32%	71%	4.43	3.6	8.0	2.2	11%	1.2	65
	10	261	327	447	775	9	80	29	0.49	40	17	43	121	99	6%	258	5.07	43	45	62%	4.14	1.36	30%	72%	4.27	3.7	7.6	2.1	10%	1.0	57
Opp @ BOS	08	253	321	398	719	9	79	30	0.47	44	19	37	99	86	8%	250	4.45	25	29	57%	5.53	1.65	33%	68%	5.44	4.5	6.4	1.4	9%	1.0	15
	09	262	321	412	732	8	79	31	0.40	40	18	41	105	106	9%	249	4.54	25	29	60%	5.90	1.60	32%	66%	5.52	4.3	7.3	1.7	12%	1.5	32
	10	254	323	399	722	9	79	30	0.48	45	17	38	102	110	15%	251	4.48	35	38	67%	5.12	1.51	32%	69%	5.04	3.9	7.2	1.9	10%	1.3	42

CHW	Yr	Avg	OB	Slg	OPS	bb%	ct%	h%	Eye	G	L	F	PX	SX	SBO	xBA	RC/G	W	Py	Sv%	ERA	WHIP	H%	S%	xERA	Ctl	Dom	Cmd	hr/f	hr/9	BPV
At Home	08	272	340	481	821	9	82	29	0.57	38	20	42	123	77	7%	273	5.57	54	52	57%	3.75	1.23	29%	73%	3.81	2.8	7.5	2.7	11%	1.0	83
	09	252	322	415	737	9	82	27	0.56	42	17	41	100	86	10%	252	4.59	43	39	68%	4.22	1.36	30%	72%	4.21	3.4	7.5	2.2	11%	1.1	64
	10	272	337	453	790	9	83	29	0.58	44	18	38	110	98	14%	271	5.22	45	44	74%	4.38	1.36	31%	70%	4.47	3.1	7.4	2.4	9%	1.0	71
Away	08	253	316	414	730	8	81	28	0.49	42	19	39	100	84	7%	257	4.50	35	36	72%	4.50	1.43	32%	70%	4.42	2.9	6.6	2.3	9%	0.9	65
	09	264	327	408	735	8	81	30	0.49	45	18	38	94	87	11%	250	4.57	36	41	66%	4.09	1.34	30%	72%	4.18	2.9	6.5	2.2	10%	1.0	61
	10	263	313	388	702	7	83	30	0.44	47	17	35	81	96	18%	250	4.11	43	42	77%	3.80	1.35	31%	73%	3.98	3.0	6.9	2.3	8%	0.7	68
Opp @ CHW	08	242	300	388	688	8	78	28	0.38	46	19	35	95	109	12%	252	3.93	28	30	60%	5.63	1.46	29%	66%	5.26	3.6	6.3	1.8	15%	1.8	33
	09	258	325	413	738	9	78	30	0.46	44	18	38	105	97	13%	252	4.63	38	42	67%	4.46	1.35	28%	71%	4.56	3.5	6.3	1.8	12%	1.3	38
	10	264	325	410	734	8	79	31	0.42	44	17	39	101	85	9%	245	4.56	36	37	63%	4.94	1.42	29%	69%	4.78	3.4	5.8	1.7	13%	1.4	35

CHC	Yr	Avg	OB	Slg	OPS	bb%	ct%	h%	Eye	G	L	F	PX	SX	SBO	xBA	RC/G	W	Py	Sv%	ERA	WHIP	H%	S%	xERA	Ctl	Dom	Cmd	hr/f	hr/9	BPV
At Home	08	290	365	471	836	11	79	33	0.57	44	20	36	111	86	6%	266	5.92	55	51	76%	3.77	1.26	30%	73%	3.87	3.1	8.2	2.6	10%	1.0	83
	09	265	340	423	763	10	80	30	0.57	42	19	39	102	83	6%	255	5.02	46	44	75%	3.94	1.32	29%	73%	4.12	3.6	7.9	2.2	10%	1.0	65
	10	265	323	416	739	8	79	31	0.41	44	20	36	102	86	7%	258	4.62	35	33	74%	4.55	1.46	32%	71%	4.46	3.8	8.1	2.1	10%	1.1	63
Away	08	267	340	417	757	10	78	32	0.51	42	23	35	99	88	8%	261	4.96	40	45	53%	4.07	1.35	29%	73%	4.22	3.8	7.4	2.0	10%	1.0	51
	09	245	315	392	707	9	77	29	0.44	44	20	36	98	75	6%	247	4.27	37	39	65%	3.74	1.33	29%	75%	3.82	3.7	7.9	2.2	10%	1.0	64
	10	248	309	387	696	8	76	30	0.37	45	18	38	96	82	5%	236	4.06	40	40	74%	3.91	1.34	30%	73%	4.09	3.8	7.8	2.1	9%	0.9	60
Opp @ CHC	08	242	305	391	696	8	76	29	0.38	42	20	38	98	87	8%	243	4.08	26	30	57%	5.51	1.61	33%	68%	4.97	4.2	7.4	1.8	14%	1.4	41
	09	245	318	387	706	10	76	29	0.46	42	18	39	94	93	8%	236	4.26	34	36	73%	4.81	1.46	31%	69%	4.86	4.0	7.0	1.8	10%	1.1	38
	10	266	338	415	753	10	77	32	0.47	42	19	39	99	107	9%	243	4.87	46	48	78%	4.02	1.36	31%	73%	4.02	3.0	7.4	2.5	10%	0.9	73

CIN	Yr	Avg	OB	Slg	OPS	bb%	ct%	h%	Eye	G	L	F	PX	SX	SBO	xBA	RC/G	W	Py	Sv%	ERA	WHIP	H%	S%	xERA	Ctl	Dom	Cmd	hr/f	hr/9	BPV
At Home	08	253	327	428	755	10	80	28	0.54	45	19	36	106	84	8%	262	4.85	43	38	69%	4.51	1.41	31%	72%	4.15	3.3	7.7	2.3	13%	1.3	70
	09	252	323	418	741	10	79	29	0.50	42	19	39	105	87	10%	254	4.68	40	37	80%	4.06	1.33	29%	73%	4.15	3.4	7.0	2.0	11%	1.1	54
	10	278	339	454	793	8	79	32	0.43	43	19	39	114	94	9%	259	5.27	49	46	73%	3.98	1.34	30%	73%	4.09	3.3	7.3	2.2	10%	1.0	62
Away	08	241	308	388	696	9	79	28	0.46	45	20	36	92	79	10%	250	4.09	31	33	55%	4.59	1.50	33%	72%	4.27	3.7	7.6	2.1	12%	1.2	59
	09	242	305	371	676	8	80	28	0.44	45	18	37	86	91	9%	243	3.84	38	39	75%	4.30	1.41	29%	73%	4.38	3.7	6.2	1.7	11%	1.2	31
	10	265	329	419	748	9	78	31	0.42	43	19	38	102	97	8%	251	4.74	42	45	64%	4.06	1.32	29%	72%	4.31	3.2	6.7	2.1	9%	1.0	56
Opp @ CIN	08	272	335	456	791	9	78	32	0.43	42	21	37	116	90	8%	264	5.27	38	43	56%	4.40	1.38	28%	72%	4.23	3.7	6.9	1.9	14%	1.3	46
	09	254	323	414	736	9	79	29	0.49	43	19	38	102	81	10%	253	4.61	41	44	75%	3.76	1.34	29%	76%	3.76	3.6	7.1	2.0	12%	1.2	52
	10	255	321	395	716	9	79	30	0.46	43	19	38	92	83	8%	246	4.33	32	35	60%	4.77	1.45	32%	71%	4.45	3.3	7.5	2.3	12%	1.3	68

CLE	Yr	Avg	OB	Slg	OPS	bb%	ct%	h%	Eye	G	L	F	PX	SX	SBO	xBA	RC/G	W	Py	Sv%	ERA	WHIP	H%	S%	xERA	Ctl	Dom	Cmd	hr/f	hr/9	BPV
At Home	08	272	346	439	785	10	79	32	0.55	40	20	40	109	97	7%	257	5.31	45	47	58%	4.03	1.34	31%	71%	4.17	2.8	6.4	2.3	8%	0.8	63
	09	255	326	388	713	9	79	30	0.49	45	20	36	93	87	7%	249	4.37	35	37	67%	4.40	1.47	32%	71%	4.51	3.5	6.3	1.8	9%	0.9	42
	10	249	321	384	705	10	78	30	0.48	45	19	36	94	96	8%	247	4.28	38	37	72%	3.84	1.34	29%	73%	4.10	3.3	5.9	1.8	9%	0.9	44
Away	08	254	314	410	724	8	77	30	0.39	40	21	39	105	88	7%	252	4.42	36	38	64%	4.92	1.41	31%	69%	4.69	2.7	5.9	2.2	12%	1.4	54
	09	272	341	445	785	9	78	32	0.47	43	20	37	116	97	8%	264	5.27	30	35	54%	5.80	1.56	31%	66%	5.60	4.0	6.0	1.5	12%	1.4	20
	10	248	312	373	684	8	79	29	0.44	44	18	38	87	81	8%	238	3.95	31	33	64%	4.79	1.52	31%	70%	4.73	4.0	6.3	1.6	10%	1.0	32
Opp @ CLE	08	268	324	394	717	8	81	31	0.44	46	21	33	82	79	6%	254	4.33	36	34	65%	5.13	1.50	32%	68%	5.07	4.0	7.4	1.8	10%	1.1	42
	09	277	343	418	761	9	82	32	0.56	45	19	36	94	89	9%	259	4.96	46	44	69%	4.15	1.37	31%	71%	4.30	3.6	7.4	2.0	9%	0.8	58
	10	258	323	401	724	9	83	29	0.55	48	17	35	94	93	14%	260	4.50	43	44	79%	3.72	1.35	30%	74%	3.92	3.6	7.5	2.1	8%	0.8	60

BATTING | PITCHING

COL	Yr	Avg	OB	Slg	OPS	bb%	ct%	h%	Eye	G	L	F	PX	SX	SBO	xBA	RC/G	W	Py	Sv%	ERA	WHIP	H%	S%	xERA	Ctl	Dom	Cmd	hr/f	hr/9	BPV
At Home	08	278	346	454	801	10	80	32	0.52	42	23	35	110	111	11%	275	5.46	43	40	61%	4.83	1.43	32%	68%	4.64	3.1	6.3	2.1	11%	1.0	56
	09	287	367	483	849	11	80	33	0.62	42	20	38	123	112	11%	274	6.17	51	48	65%	4.41	1.40	31%	70%	4.30	3.4	7.2	2.1	10%	0.9	66
	10	298	367	498	864	10	79	35	0.51	41	21	38	125	117	8%	274	6.27	52	49	61%	4.25	1.31	31%	70%	4.17	2.8	7.7	2.7	10%	1.0	86
Away	08	249	317	377	694	9	77	30	0.43	45	20	35	86	88	12%	239	4.09	31	34	61%	4.70	1.49	31%	69%	4.75	4.0	6.7	1.7	9%	0.8	37
	09	235	316	399	715	11	73	29	0.44	41	19	40	112	91	10%	237	4.43	41	41	83%	4.06	1.32	30%	71%	4.19	3.2	7.2	2.2	9%	0.9	66
	10	226	299	351	651	9	75	28	0.42	44	17	39	86	96	11%	225	3.53	31	35	65%	4.02	1.37	31%	72%	4.17	3.8	7.7	2.0	9%	0.8	62
Opp @ COL	08	280	337	435	772	8	82	32	0.48	47	21	31	95	98	7%	273	5.03	38	41	51%	4.96	1.49	32%	69%	4.69	3.7	7.1	1.9	12%	1.2	48
	09	266	331	419	750	9	79	31	0.47	49	20	32	99	120	10%	266	4.82	30	33	62%	5.54	1.60	32%	68%	5.26	4.4	7.1	1.6	12%	1.3	28
	10	263	319	414	732	8	78	31	0.37	46	20	34	103	86	7%	255	4.51	29	32	58%	5.76	1.62	34%	67%	5.17	3.9	7.6	2.0	13%	1.4	51

DET	Yr	Avg	OB	Slg	OPS	bb%	ct%	h%	Eye	G	L	F	PX	SX	SBO	xBA	RC/G	W	Py	Sv%	ERA	WHIP	H%	S%	xERA	Ctl	Dom	Cmd	hr/f	hr/9	BPV
At Home	08	287	349	478	827	9	83	31	0.56	42	19	38	112	103	6%	274	5.68	40	41	63%	4.84	1.48	31%	70%	4.82	3.7	6.4	1.7	10%	1.1	37
	09	270	339	432	771	10	81	31	0.54	41	18	40	102	91	6%	254	5.05	51	46	73%	4.05	1.33	28%	73%	4.30	3.6	6.9	1.9	10%	1.1	49
	10	282	347	427	774	9	82	32	0.54	43	20	37	96	95	5%	260	5.11	52	49	86%	3.62	1.28	29%	74%	3.98	3.0	6.5	2.2	8%	0.9	59
Away	08	256	327	411	738	10	79	30	0.51	44	18	38	98	90	6%	250	4.67	34	37	47%	4.98	1.54	30%	69%	5.18	4.4	5.9	1.4	9%	1.0	8
	09	252	314	402	716	8	79	29	0.44	43	18	39	97	89	7%	246	4.30	35	35	55%	4.64	1.50	31%	72%	4.47	3.8	6.8	1.8	12%	1.2	40
	10	255	320	404	723	9	78	30	0.42	43	19	39	101	84	7%	247	4.44	29	33	57%	5.03	1.47	31%	67%	5.16	3.8	6.7	1.8	9%	0.9	40
Opp @ DET	08	276	344	437	781	9	82	31	0.58	44	19	38	100	94	6%	261	5.20	41	40	57%	5.23	1.52	31%	69%	4.90	3.4	6.2	1.8	13%	1.4	39
	09	249	320	402	722	10	80	28	0.51	42	17	41	100	85	9%	243	4.45	30	35	61%	4.75	1.47	31%	71%	4.69	3.7	6.9	1.9	11%	1.2	43
	10	252	311	381	692	8	81	29	0.46	44	17	39	82	90	10%	238	4.03	29	32	57%	4.77	1.51	33%	70%	4.81	3.5	6.5	1.8	8%	0.9	43

FLA	Yr	Avg	OB	Slg	OPS	bb%	ct%	h%	Eye	G	L	F	PX	SX	SBO	xBA	RC/G	W	Py	Sv%	ERA	WHIP	H%	S%	xERA	Ctl	Dom	Cmd	hr/f	hr/9	BPV
At Home	08	247	319	419	738	10	73	30	0.39	42	19	39	114	102	8%	242	4.69	45	39	63%	4.31	1.39	31%	71%	4.46	3.6	7.6	2.1	9%	0.9	57
	09	273	344	428	772	10	78	32	0.49	41	20	40	101	88	7%	248	5.11	43	38	58%	4.51	1.44	32%	71%	4.42	3.9	8.2	2.1	10%	1.0	64
	10	247	320	388	708	10	73	32	0.39	46	17	36	103	103	8%	234	4.35	39	38	53%	3.88	1.38	32%	73%	4.14	3.6	8.0	2.2	7%	0.7	68
Away	08	261	323	446	769	8	77	30	0.40	42	20	38	118	81	7%	258	4.97	39	42	58%	4.58	1.41	29%	70%	4.63	3.7	6.5	1.7	11%	1.1	37
	09	263	327	403	731	9	78	31	0.44	43	20	37	95	85	7%	248	4.55	44	44	73%	4.12	1.35	30%	72%	4.27	3.6	7.3	2.1	10%	1.0	56
	10	256	312	409	721	8	77	30	0.36	44	19	37	103	110	9%	252	4.36	39	41	71%	4.30	1.39	30%	71%	4.46	3.3	6.5	2.0	9%	1.0	49
Opp @ FLA	08	257	328	400	727	9	78	31	0.47	40	21	39	93	94	9%	246	4.53	36	42	62%	4.47	1.35	31%	70%	4.21	3.7	9.4	2.6	13%	1.2	90
	09	261	336	409	745	10	77	32	0.48	44	19	37	100	101	10%	245	4.80	38	43	59%	4.61	1.48	32%	71%	4.51	3.8	7.7	2.0	10%	1.1	56
	10	255	327	384	711	10	77	31	0.45	44	18	39	91	96	11%	234	4.37	39	40	68%	4.16	1.36	33%	71%	4.10	3.7	9.4	2.6	9%	0.8	94

HOU	Yr	Avg	OB	Slg	OPS	bb%	ct%	h%	Eye	G	L	F	PX	SX	SBO	xBA	RC/G	W	Py	Sv%	ERA	WHIP	H%	S%	xERA	Ctl	Dom	Cmd	hr/f	hr/9	BPV
At Home	08	277	332	451	783	8	82	31	0.44	46	19	36	105	99	13%	268	5.10	47	40	78%	4.28	1.36	30%	72%	4.11	3.2	7.3	2.3	12%	1.2	67
	09	269	330	418	748	8	82	30	0.50	48	17	34	92	99	11%	257	4.73	44	39	67%	4.01	1.38	32%	74%	3.84	3.0	7.4	2.5	11%	1.0	77
	10	248	300	375	675	7	81	28	0.40	48	16	36	82	99	11%	243	3.77	42	37	75%	3.51	1.30	30%	75%	3.72	3.4	7.9	2.3	8%	0.8	74
Away	08	254	311	389	700	8	80	29	0.42	45	20	34	85	83	11%	251	4.09	39	38	70%	4.48	1.38	30%	71%	4.34	3.1	6.6	2.1	12%	1.2	56
	09	252	304	383	687	7	82	29	0.41	48	18	34	85	93	11%	252	3.93	30	29	50%	5.12	1.51	32%	68%	4.88	3.9	6.9	1.8	12%	1.2	43
	10	247	301	349	651	7	81	29	0.41	47	19	34	70	93	9%	240	3.51	34	31	75%	4.71	1.48	33%	70%	4.64	3.4	7.2	2.1	9%	1.0	58
Opp @ HOU	08	261	323	438	761	8	79	30	0.44	44	19	37	110	83	6%	261	4.88	31	38	55%	4.60	1.40	31%	70%	4.36	2.9	6.5	2.3	12%	1.2	63
	09	273	331	424	755	8	79	32	0.41	46	19	35	98	73	5%	252	4.79	37	42	61%	3.99	1.37	30%	74%	4.02	3.1	6.2	2.0	10%	1.0	54
	10	244	313	380	693	9	77	30	0.43	45	18	37	94	101	10%	241	4.09	39	44	64%	3.32	1.23	29%	76%	3.61	2.6	6.4	2.5	8%	0.8	73

KC	Yr	Avg	OB	Slg	OPS	bb%	ct%	h%	Eye	G	L	F	PX	SX	SBO	xBA	RC/G	W	Py	Sv%	ERA	WHIP	H%	S%	xERA	Ctl	Dom	Cmd	hr/f	hr/9	BPV
At Home	08	275	323	396	719	7	83	32	0.42	46	21	33	79	87	7%	260	4.34	38	37	76%	4.13	1.33	30%	71%	4.43	3.1	6.2	2.0	8%	0.9	51
	09	276	338	421	760	9	83	31	0.55	46	17	36	92	110	7%	260	4.94	33	34	58%	4.86	1.49	33%	68%	4.87	3.5	7.2	2.0	8%	0.8	56
	10	280	336	414	750	8	84	32	0.51	45	18	37	85	107	11%	256	4.77	38	36	66%	4.57	1.42	32%	70%	4.66	3.1	6.5	2.1	9%	1.0	55
Away	08	263	310	398	708	6	81	30	0.36	47	19	34	86	93	9%	252	4.15	37	35	71%	4.89	1.42	32%	68%	4.85	3.4	7.3	2.2	10%	1.1	59
	09	242	292	390	682	7	78	28	0.32	45	19	37	99	101	10%	249	3.81	32	32	63%	4.80	1.43	30%	70%	4.71	4.1	7.4	1.8	12%	1.3	45
	10	267	325	385	710	8	84	30	0.53	44	18	38	77	79	10%	246	4.28	29	28	70%	5.41	1.52	31%	66%	5.33	3.9	6.5	1.7	11%	1.2	32
Opp @ KC	08	260	320	402	722	8	82	30	0.49	43	19	38	89	94	7%	253	4.43	43	44	70%	3.92	1.35	32%	72%	4.14	2.5	6.0	2.4	7%	0.6	64
	09	280	346	423	769	9	80	33	0.49	44	18	37	96	106	8%	252	5.06	48	47	74%	4.40	1.44	31%	71%	4.57	3.3	6.1	1.8	8%	0.8	44
	10	275	333	425	758	8	82	31	0.47	43	18	39	99	97	12%	257	4.84	43	45	69%	4.30	1.41	31%	70%	4.60	2.9	5.6	1.9	7%	0.8	47

LA	Yr	Avg	OB	Slg	OPS	bb%	ct%	h%	Eye	G	L	F	PX	SX	SBO	xBA	RC/G	W	Py	Sv%	ERA	WHIP	H%	S%	xERA	Ctl	Dom	Cmd	hr/f	hr/9	BPV
At Home	08	266	332	397	729	9	81	31	0.52	46	21	33	81	95	12%	255	4.53	48	51	72%	3.01	1.13	29%	75%	3.31	2.6	8.0	3.1	7%	0.6	103
	09	265	330	407	737	9	81	31	0.51	45	21	34	90	99	11%	260	4.63	50	51	66%	3.10	1.19	28%	76%	3.53	3.1	7.9	2.5	7%	0.7	80
	10	258	327	385	711	9	79	31	0.49	46	20	34	86	80	9%	248	4.34	45	39	74%	3.81	1.23	29%	71%	4.09	3.2	8.0	2.5	9%	0.8	80
Away	08	263	328	400	729	9	82	30	0.53	47	21	32	85	96	10%	263	4.56	36	37	57%	4.40	1.45	32%	72%	4.16	3.4	6.9	2.0	11%	0.9	60
	09	275	352	416	769	11	81	32	0.62	46	21	33	90	101	9%	262	5.14	45	48	61%	3.74	1.32	28%	74%	4.04	4.0	7.7	1.9	9%	0.9	49
	10	246	311	374	685	9	77	30	0.42	45	21	35	88	101	11%	245	3.98	35	39	66%	4.24	1.36	31%	70%	4.37	3.5	7.9	2.3	9%	0.9	69
Opp @ LA	08	228	284	333	617	7	76	28	0.32	50	18	32	73	89	8%	225	3.01	33	30	73%	4.09	1.40	30%	73%	4.13	3.4	6.5	1.9	10%	0.9	49
	09	229	295	343	638	9	76	28	0.40	45	18	38	79	83	10%	224	3.34	31	30	58%	4.23	1.39	30%	71%	4.34	3.3	6.5	2.0	9%	0.9	50
	10	234	302	354	656	9	76	29	0.41	46	17	37	83	88	9%	227	3.57	36	42	75%	3.72	1.35	30%	74%	3.90	3.4	7.1	2.0	9%	0.8	58

LAA	Yr	Avg	OB	Slg	OPS	bb%	ct%	h%	Eye	G	L	F	PX	SX	SBO	xBA	RC/G	W	Py	Sv%	ERA	WHIP	H%	S%	xERA	Ctl	Dom	Cmd	hr/f	hr/9	BPV
At Home	08	277	329	414	744	7	83	31	0.45	46	18	36	85	99	11%	254	4.62	50	43	76%	4.07	1.28	30%	71%	4.21	2.5	6.6	2.6	10%	1.0	73
	09	288	353	450	803	9	83	32	0.57	44	18	38	102	103	11%	264	5.43	49	46	70%	4.44	1.40	31%	72%	4.39	3.1	6.7	2.1	11%	1.3	54
	10	247	307	378	685	8	80	28	0.44	46	17	37	87	83	10%	241	3.92	43	40	68%	3.55	1.28	29%	75%	3.93	3.3	7.2	2.2	8%	0.8	60
Away	08	260	324	411	736	9	82	29	0.52	47	18	35	93	104	12%	258	4.59	50	44	73%	3.92	1.36	31%	74%	3.92	3.2	7.2	2.3	10%	1.0	65
	09	283	345	434	778	9	80	33	0.48	45	20	36	100	108	15%	261	5.13	48	46	76%	4.47	1.41	31%	70%	4.60	3.4	6.5	1.9	9%	1.0	48
	10	250	307	402	710	8	81	28	0.43	46	17	37	100	95	12%	254	4.21	37	39	72%	4.58	1.47	31%	71%	4.63	3.7	6.9	1.8	9%	1.0	44
Opp @ LAA	08	260	310	404	714	7	81	30	0.38	45	18	37	89	100	10%	249	4.21	31	38	54%	4.47	1.39	31%	69%	4.54	2.8	6.1	2.2	9%	0.9	59
	09	273	333	439	772	8	81	31	0.47	40	19	41	106	90	10%	257	4.98	32	35	66%	5.29	1.53	32%	67%	5.16	3.5	6.2	1.7	11%	1.2	37
	10	243	309	369	678	9	79	29	0.46	42	19	39	86	92	11%	239	3.88	38	41	92%	3.76	1.25	28%	72%	4.07	2.9	6.6	2.3	9%	0.9	64

MIL	Yr	Avg	OB	Slg	OPS	bb%	ct%	h%	Eye	G	L	F	PX	SX	SBO	xBA	RC/G	W	Py	Sv%	ERA	WHIP	H%	S%	xERA	Ctl	Dom	Cmd	hr/f	hr/9	BPV
At Home	08	251	324	433	756	10	77	29	0.47	42	18	40	114	94	10%	253	4.89	49	45	63%	3.51	1.32	29%	76%	3.56	3.4	7.1	2.1	11%	0.9	59
	09	257	334	437	772	10	77	30	0.51	43	18	39	115	88	6%	253	5.12	40	38	64%	4.43	1.39	30%	72%	4.38	3.6	7.6	2.1	11%	1.2	59
	10	259	328	430	758	9	79	30	0.48	43	18	40	111	95	7%	253	4.88	40	36	67%	4.51	1.43	32%	72%	4.34	3.6	8.1	2.3	11%	1.2	69
Away	08	254	317	429	746	8	79	29	0.44	42	19	39	110	102	11%	259	4.71	41	42	64%	4.26	1.35	29%	73%	4.10	3.1	6.6	2.1	13%	1.3	58
	09	268	338	415	753	10	78	32	0.48	43	19	38	97	91	8%	246	4.87	40	39	70%	5.28	1.54	31%	69%	4.99	4.0	6.2	1.6	13%	1.4	25
	10	265	328	418	745	8	78	32	0.42	46	19	35	102	103	7%	256	4.71	37	40	59%	4.67	1.44	32%	69%	4.66	3.7	7.6	2.0	10%	1.0	57
Opp @ MIL	08	252	321	386	706	9	79	29	0.48	46	21	33	83	76	9%	250	4.24	32	36	52%	4.33	1.36	29%	72%	4.25	3.7	7.7	2.1	12%	1.3	60
	09	258	328	437	766	9	78	30	0.48	42	17	41	118	97	7%	255	5.01	41	43	64%	4.51	1.42	30%	72%	4.34	4.0	7.8	2.0	12%	1.3	54
	10	267	334	431	765	9	77	32	0.44	41	20	40	113	93	9%	252	5.00	41	45	58%	4.43	1.40	30%	72%	4.31	3.6	7.5	2.1	12%	1.3	58

BATTING / PITCHING

MIN	Yr	Avg	OB	Slg	OPS	bb%	ct%	h%	Eye	G	L	F	PX	SX	SBO	xBA	RC/G	W	Py	Sv%	ERA	WHIP	H%	S%	xERA	Ctl	Dom	Cmd	hr/f	hr/9	BPV
At Home	08	289	348	429	777	8	84	33	0.55	46	21	33	87	115	9%	271	5.15	53	53	83%	3.27	1.22	29%	77%	3.45	2.2	6.3	2.9	9%	1.0	75
	09	278	348	448	795	10	82	31	0.60	47	17	36	105	112	9%	269	5.37	49	44	69%	4.49	1.35	31%	69%	4.55	2.6	6.6	2.6	9%	1.1	69
	10	282	353	422	775	10	84	32	0.70	46	20	35	92	104	5%	269	5.24	53	49	76%	3.53	1.27	31%	74%	3.77	2.3	6.5	2.8	8%	0.8	78
Away	08	269	333	388	722	9	82	31	0.53	47	19	34	76	103	9%	248	4.48	35	37	50%	5.12	1.50	32%	68%	4.89	2.9	6.0	2.1	11%	1.3	50
	09	271	338	411	749	9	81	31	0.55	45	19	36	91	85	6%	253	4.81	38	42	82%	4.51	1.41	30%	71%	4.58	3.2	6.4	2.0	10%	1.2	47
	10	265	327	421	748	8	81	30	0.49	47	18	35	101	89	7%	260	4.72	41	43	62%	4.39	1.32	30%	70%	4.37	2.4	6.5	2.7	11%	1.1	73
Opp @ MIN	08	255	299	396	694	6	82	29	0.35	43	20	37	87	82	9%	254	3.93	28	28	66%	5.19	1.49	33%	65%	5.24	3.2	5.8	1.8	8%	0.7	42
	09	273	322	426	749	7	81	31	0.39	41	19	41	99	107	11%	254	4.63	33	38	52%	5.10	1.49	31%	68%	4.94	3.7	6.2	1.7	12%	1.2	36
	10	263	309	397	706	6	81	30	0.36	46	18	36	91	85	8%	252	4.13	28	32	69%	4.77	1.53	32%	69%	5.04	3.9	5.6	1.4	7%	0.7	19

NYM	Yr	Avg	OB	Slg	OPS	bb%	ct%	h%	Eye	G	L	F	PX	SX	SBO	xBA	RC/G	W	Py	Sv%	ERA	WHIP	H%	S%	xERA	Ctl	Dom	Cmd	hr/f	hr/9	BPV
At Home	08	267	348	430	778	11	82	30	0.68	46	22	32	96	97	9%	273	5.23	48	45	57%	3.78	1.27	28%	73%	3.96	3.5	7.4	2.1	10%	0.9	62
	09	274	339	408	747	9	83	32	0.57	46	19	35	84	109	11%	259	4.83	41	40	70%	3.98	1.34	29%	73%	4.27	3.6	6.9	1.9	9%	1.0	47
	10	255	323	393	715	9	81	29	0.53	41	18	41	87	118	11%	245	4.40	47	47	65%	3.12	1.30	29%	77%	3.65	3.5	6.9	2.0	6%	0.6	54
Away	08	265	330	411	741	9	82	30	0.54	46	24	30	88	112	12%	275	4.70	41	45	62%	4.39	1.48	32%	73%	4.25	3.8	7.1	1.9	11%	1.1	45
	09	266	330	381	711	9	83	31	0.57	47	21	32	76	98	10%	259	4.38	29	33	60%	4.99	1.57	32%	70%	5.02	4.2	6.1	1.5	9%	1.0	17
	10	243	302	373	675	8	79	29	0.40	44	17	39	88	98	13%	239	3.81	32	35	73%	4.36	1.44	31%	72%	4.23	3.3	6.8	2.1	11%	1.1	56
Opp @ NYM	08	236	307	369	676	9	78	28	0.47	44	21	36	86	66	5%	243	3.85	33	36	62%	4.47	1.51	30%	74%	4.23	4.3	6.4	1.5	13%	1.2	23
	09	248	319	396	715	9	80	28	0.52	42	17	41	96	80	7%	244	4.39	40	41	80%	4.08	1.41	31%	71%	4.43	3.3	5.9	1.8	6%	0.6	40
	10	243	314	350	664	9	80	29	0.50	46	17	37	74	86	5%	229	3.77	34	34	75%	4.00	1.35	29%	72%	4.48	3.4	6.4	1.9	7%	0.8	43

NYY	Yr	Avg	OB	Slg	OPS	bb%	ct%	h%	Eye	G	L	F	PX	SX	SBO	xBA	RC/G	W	Py	Sv%	ERA	WHIP	H%	S%	xERA	Ctl	Dom	Cmd	hr/f	hr/9	BPV
At Home	08	281	342	440	783	9	82	31	0.53	45	19	36	98	103	10%	265	5.15	48	45	82%	4.11	1.30	30%	70%	4.26	3.1	7.4	2.4	9%	0.8	73
	09	284	364	490	854	11	83	30	0.72	44	20	37	126	88	9%	287	6.10	57	50	76%	4.03	1.34	29%	74%	3.94	3.6	7.8	2.2	12%	1.2	64
	10	279	354	472	826	11	80	31	0.58	45	18	37	122	109	8%	274	5.77	52	50	68%	4.22	1.31	28%	72%	4.18	3.3	7.2	2.2	12%	1.3	61
Away	08	262	328	414	743	9	81	30	0.52	47	20	33	95	93	11%	264	4.69	41	42	83%	4.47	1.43	33%	71%	4.36	3.0	6.9	2.3	10%	1.0	66
	09	283	353	466	819	10	82	32	0.59	43	19	38	118	109	8%	276	5.67	46	46	79%	4.54	1.37	31%	69%	4.58	3.5	7.9	2.2	10%	1.0	66
	10	256	336	402	738	11	79	30	0.58	45	17	38	95	96	8%	246	4.72	43	47	69%	3.91	1.31	29%	72%	4.14	3.4	7.2	2.1	9%	0.9	60
Opp @ NYY	08	253	315	387	702	8	78	30	0.42	46	19	35	88	89	11%	246	4.16	33	36	55%	4.83	1.48	32%	70%	4.64	3.3	6.3	1.9	11%	1.2	46
	09	249	321	404	725	10	77	29	0.46	43	19	38	102	94	12%	248	4.46	24	31	38%	5.60	1.62	30%	70%	4.99	4.5	6.2	1.4	16%	1.7	13
	10	249	316	413	728	9	79	28	0.46	44	16	40	105	94	11%	246	4.44	29	31	68%	5.88	1.58	32%	66%	5.34	4.2	7.2	1.7	14%	1.5	39

OAK	Yr	Avg	OB	Slg	OPS	bb%	ct%	h%	Eye	G	L	F	PX	SX	SBO	xBA	RC/G	W	Py	Sv%	ERA	WHIP	H%	S%	xERA	Ctl	Dom	Cmd	hr/f	hr/9	BPV
At Home	08	243	314	368	682	9	78	29	0.47	40	19	41	85	93	7%	234	3.97	42	40	67%	3.53	1.27	28%	75%	4.03	3.5	6.5	1.9	8%	0.8	44
	09	259	329	403	732	9	81	30	0.55	41	20	39	95	102	10%	256	4.61	40	46	77%	3.88	1.32	31%	72%	4.06	2.9	7.1	2.4	8%	0.8	71
	10	261	329	380	709	9	81	31	0.53	41	20	39	82	120	13%	246	4.36	47	50	78%	3.04	1.16	27%	76%	3.46	3.0	6.9	2.3	8%	0.8	68
Away	08	241	313	367	681	10	77	29	0.46	43	18	38	84	100	8%	234	3.95	32	34	63%	4.55	1.44	31%	70%	4.78	3.8	6.7	1.8	8%	0.9	36
	09	265	323	392	715	8	81	31	0.46	42	19	39	87	92	14%	248	4.32	35	35	75%	4.71	1.46	31%	70%	4.69	3.6	6.9	1.9	10%	1.1	49
	10	252	315	376	691	8	81	29	0.47	43	18	38	84	94	13%	243	4.05	34	36	71%	4.16	1.40	30%	74%	4.14	3.5	6.6	1.9	11%	1.2	48
Opp @ OAK	08	240	311	368	679	9	80	28	0.53	42	18	40	82	81	8%	238	3.94	37	39	64%	3.77	1.32	30%	73%	4.21	3.6	7.5	2.1	7%	0.8	57
	09	260	318	393	711	8	79	31	0.41	44	20	37	90	90	9%	249	4.25	41	35	88%	4.76	1.40	30%	67%	5.06	3.6	6.5	1.8	8%	0.9	39
	10	225	289	338	627	8	79	26	0.43	47	18	35	75	94	11%	233	3.20	34	31	65%	4.17	1.39	31%	70%	4.67	3.5	6.7	1.9	5%	0.6	45

PHI	Yr	Avg	OB	Slg	OPS	bb%	ct%	h%	Eye	G	L	F	PX	SX	SBO	xBA	RC/G	W	Py	Sv%	ERA	WHIP	H%	S%	xERA	Ctl	Dom	Cmd	hr/f	hr/9	BPV
At Home	08	262	336	447	784	10	80	29	0.57	41	23	36	111	116	13%	276	5.23	48	48	68%	3.67	1.33	30%	75%	3.67	3.0	6.7	2.2	11%	1.0	61
	09	263	336	455	791	10	79	30	0.53	41	21	38	121	110	10%	273	5.32	45	44	75%	4.29	1.36	31%	72%	4.15	3.0	7.4	2.5	12%	1.2	71
	10	264	331	430	761	9	83	29	0.57	44	19	38	103	111	8%	267	4.93	52	49	70%	3.53	1.20	29%	74%	3.56	2.4	7.5	3.1	11%	1.0	96
Away	08	249	318	429	747	9	79	28	0.49	44	19	37	109	108	9%	264	4.73	44	45	81%	4.13	1.40	30%	73%	4.12	3.6	6.7	1.9	11%	1.0	48
	09	253	322	439	762	9	79	28	0.49	40	19	41	116	105	10%	260	4.91	48	47	61%	4.03	1.35	30%	74%	4.08	3.1	6.9	2.2	10%	1.1	59
	10	256	324	397	721	9	79	30	0.49	45	18	37	94	111	9%	250	4.45	43	43	65%	3.90	1.31	30%	73%	3.89	2.7	7.1	2.6	10%	1.0	78
Opp @ PHI	08	258	318	400	718	8	81	30	0.45	44	23	33	89	86	10%	266	4.35	33	33	64%	4.91	1.44	29%	70%	4.65	3.9	6.9	1.8	14%	1.4	38
	09	267	325	430	755	8	79	31	0.40	41	21	38	106	84	8%	260	4.77	36	37	58%	4.95	1.45	30%	70%	4.67	3.8	7.3	1.9	13%	1.4	46
	10	247	297	395	692	7	78	29	0.32	48	16	36	99	92	8%	244	3.92	29	32	57%	4.70	1.42	30%	70%	4.72	3.5	6.1	1.8	11%	1.2	38

PIT	Yr	Avg	OB	Slg	OPS	bb%	ct%	h%	Eye	G	L	F	PX	SX	SBO	xBA	RC/G	W	Py	Sv%	ERA	WHIP	H%	S%	xERA	Ctl	Dom	Cmd	hr/f	hr/9	BPV
At Home	08	263	318	410	728	8	83	30	0.47	42	21	36	91	87	5%	264	4.47	39	36	75%	4.52	1.53	31%	72%	4.58	3.9	5.6	1.4	9%	0.9	16
	09	270	332	420	752	8	81	31	0.50	45	19	36	95	100	8%	259	4.80	40	41	63%	4.03	1.37	29%	72%	4.36	3.3	5.8	1.7	8%	0.8	36
	10	254	314	394	707	8	79	30	0.43	48	17	35	94	97	8%	249	4.23	40	34	84%	4.56	1.41	31%	68%	4.81	3.3	6.3	1.9	8%	0.8	47
Away	08	254	314	396	710	8	80	29	0.44	43	20	38	90	83	5%	251	4.24	28	31	46%	5.73	1.61	32%	66%	5.38	4.2	6.3	1.5	12%	1.3	23
	09	234	298	354	652	8	76	29	0.39	45	18	37	85	89	9%	231	3.54	22	26	61%	5.22	1.54	31%	68%	5.21	3.8	5.9	1.5	10%	1.1	25
	10	231	291	354	645	8	76	28	0.35	46	17	37	87	87	11%	228	3.39	17	20	43%	5.49	1.58	33%	68%	5.00	3.6	6.8	1.9	13%	1.3	47
Opp @ PIT	08	282	355	434	789	10	84	31	0.70	44	22	34	94	77	8%	275	5.38	42	45	64%	4.26	1.32	30%	70%	4.49	2.8	6.0	2.1	9%	0.9	52
	09	265	330	407	738	9	83	30	0.58	44	20	36	92	92	8%	263	4.69	41	40	74%	4.26	1.40	31%	72%	4.33	3.2	6.4	2.0	9%	1.0	52
	10	268	332	420	751	9	82	31	0.52	44	18	37	102	113	10%	264	4.85	41	47	67%	3.85	1.30	30%	72%	4.03	3.0	7.0	2.3	9%	0.8	71

SD	Yr	Avg	OB	Slg	OPS	bb%	ct%	h%	Eye	G	L	F	PX	SX	SBO	xBA	RC/G	W	Py	Sv%	ERA	WHIP	H%	S%	xERA	Ctl	Dom	Cmd	hr/f	hr/9	BPV
At Home	08	239	311	366	677	9	77	29	0.46	43	19	38	81	74	4%	232	3.88	35	35	53%	3.65	1.27	29%	73%	3.95	3.1	7.0	2.2	9%	0.8	63
	09	219	307	342	649	11	77	26	0.55	44	17	39	81	87	6%	227	3.61	42	35	71%	3.44	1.26	28%	75%	3.77	3.6	7.7	2.1	8%	0.8	63
	10	242	317	358	675	10	78	29	0.49	46	18	36	77	99	11%	230	3.89	45	48	74%	2.92	1.18	28%	78%	3.14	3.2	8.4	2.6	9%	0.8	89
Away	08	260	316	412	729	8	78	31	0.37	43	20	37	97	69	3%	248	4.44	28	33	54%	5.24	1.53	32%	68%	5.03	3.9	6.6	1.7	12%	1.2	34
	09	264	325	416	741	8	79	31	0.44	44	20	36	99	96	9%	256	4.64	33	33	62%	5.40	1.54	32%	67%	5.13	3.9	7.0	1.8	12%	1.3	42
	10	251	311	384	695	8	79	29	0.41	45	19	37	89	95	12%	245	4.05	45	43	78%	3.91	1.33	31%	73%	3.99	3.2	7.6	2.4	9%	0.9	74
Opp @ SD	08	246	310	368	677	8	79	29	0.45	43	20	37	75	98	14%	240	3.84	46	46	73%	3.38	1.28	29%	76%	3.69	3.5	7.7	2.2	8%	0.8	64
	09	233	308	353	662	10	77	28	0.47	44	18	38	79	85	9%	228	3.68	39	46	56%	3.31	1.25	26%	76%	3.83	4.1	7.5	1.8	8%	0.8	44
	10	223	292	345	636	9	75	28	0.38	47	18	35	84	85	9%	227	3.30	36	33	71%	3.88	1.31	29%	72%	4.19	3.7	7.5	2.0	8%	0.7	59

SEA	Yr	Avg	OB	Slg	OPS	bb%	ct%	h%	Eye	G	L	F	PX	SX	SBO	xBA	RC/G	W	Py	Sv%	ERA	WHIP	H%	S%	xERA	Ctl	Dom	Cmd	hr/f	hr/9	BPV
At Home	08	271	320	398	718	7	84	30	0.46	46	19	35	80	92	7%	256	4.33	35	36	69%	4.40	1.47	31%	72%	4.50	4.0	6.8	1.7	9%	0.9	38
	09	255	313	395	708	8	80	30	0.41	44	18	38	93	82	8%	246	4.19	48	38	68%	3.62	1.26	28%	74%	3.94	3.2	6.6	2.1	9%	1.0	52
	10	235	298	322	621	8	77	29	0.40	45	19	36	63	94	13%	221	3.14	35	32	78%	3.40	1.19	27%	74%	3.94	2.7	6.1	2.3	8%	0.8	58
Away	08	260	312	381	692	7	84	29	0.47	47	20	33	75	85	9%	256	4.02	26	31	40%	5.08	1.56	32%	69%	4.94	3.9	5.9	1.5	11%	1.1	25
	09	260	307	409	716	6	81	30	0.36	45	17	39	98	90	10%	250	4.22	37	37	60%	4.15	1.35	28%	73%	4.33	3.4	6.3	1.8	10%	1.2	40
	10	236	292	356	648	7	79	28	0.38	45	17	39	81	89	13%	230	3.42	26	28	61%	4.55	1.39	30%	70%	4.53	3.0	6.0	2.0	11%	1.1	51
Opp @ SEA	08	268	343	409	751	10	80	31	0.58	45	19	37	91	84	9%	250	4.89	46	45	72%	3.85	1.34	31%	73%	4.14	2.6	5.5	2.2	7%	0.7	54
	09	243	308	376	684	9	81	28	0.48	42	20	39	87	72	9%	247	3.93	33	43	67%	3.67	1.30	30%	75%	3.80	2.9	7.0	2.4	9%	1.0	70
	10	238	295	367	662	7	82	27	0.44	42	17	40	86	76	7%	241	3.64	46	49	75%	2.76	1.20	29%	78%	3.34	3.0	7.5	2.5	5%	0.4	78

BATTING / PITCHING

SF	Yr	Avg	OB	Slg	OPS	bb%	ct%	h%	Eye	G	L	F	PX	SX	SBO	xBA	RC/G	W	Py	Sv%	ERA	WHIP	H%	S%	xERA	Ctl	Dom	Cmd	hr/f	hr/9	BPV
At Home	08	264	322	391	712	8	82	31	0.47	50	18	31	82	99	11%	254	4.34	37	32	62%	4.45	1.44	31%	71%	4.62	4.0	7.6	1.9	9%	0.9	45
	09	268	322	412	734	7	79	32	0.39	45	20	35	92	114	8%	256	4.52	52	48	77%	3.27	1.21	29%	75%	3.52	3.0	8.1	2.7	9%	0.8	88
	10	265	325	417	742	8	81	30	0.46	47	17	35	99	89	6%	256	4.66	49	49	82%	3.07	1.22	28%	77%	3.45	3.5	8.3	2.4	8%	0.8	76
Away	08	260	314	374	688	7	81	31	0.40	47	19	34	75	88	10%	243	3.98	35	37	74%	4.30	1.43	31%	72%	4.44	4.1	7.9	1.9	9%	0.9	48
	09	247	292	368	660	6	78	30	0.30	46	18	37	83	88	7%	235	3.54	36	38	63%	3.85	1.36	29%	74%	4.06	4.3	8.1	1.9	10%	1.0	49
	10	250	311	400	711	8	79	29	0.42	42	18	39	98	79	6%	246	4.23	43	45	74%	3.67	1.33	30%	75%	3.95	3.6	8.1	2.2	8%	0.9	67
Opp @ SF	08	259	336	412	749	10	78	31	0.53	39	21	39	99	106	9%	251	4.89	44	49	60%	3.54	1.33	31%	74%	3.82	2.9	6.3	2.1	7%	0.6	62
	09	234	296	361	658	8	76	29	0.37	44	20	36	88	91	11%	237	3.57	29	33	71%	4.39	1.33	31%	68%	4.45	2.7	7.1	2.6	9%	0.9	77
	10	225	300	348	648	10	75	28	0.42	44	17	40	85	95	13%	222	3.50	32	32	59%	4.23	1.35	30%	71%	4.30	3.1	6.6	2.2	10%	1.0	61

STL	Yr	Avg	OB	Slg	OPS	bb%	ct%	h%	Eye	G	L	F	PX	SX	SBO	xBA	RC/G	W	Py	Sv%	ERA	WHIP	H%	S%	xERA	Ctl	Dom	Cmd	hr/f	hr/9	BPV
At Home	08	285	350	430	780	9	83	32	0.58	43	22	35	85	79	6%	265	5.16	46	42	61%	4.06	1.35	29%	72%	4.18	3.1	5.8	1.9	10%	1.0	43
	09	263	330	404	734	9	81	30	0.54	47	18	35	91	90	8%	252	4.64	46	43	79%	3.44	1.28	30%	74%	3.65	2.9	6.7	2.3	8%	0.7	71
	10	270	346	406	752	10	82	31	0.66	45	19	36	88	88	8%	257	4.93	52	52	78%	2.92	1.19	29%	78%	3.24	2.6	6.8	2.6	8%	0.7	79
Away	08	277	346	436	783	10	82	31	0.59	45	21	34	96	86	7%	268	5.21	40	44	54%	4.35	1.42	31%	72%	4.26	3.0	6.1	2.0	11%	1.0	52
	09	263	325	425	751	9	81	30	0.48	43	19	39	102	90	7%	257	4.75	45	47	71%	3.89	1.32	30%	73%	3.99	2.9	6.4	2.2	10%	0.9	65
	10	256	311	398	709	7	81	29	0.41	47	18	35	93	78	8%	251	4.18	34	39	74%	4.27	1.42	31%	72%	4.14	3.3	6.8	2.0	11%	1.0	60
Opp @ STL	08	261	322	416	738	8	83	29	0.54	44	21	34	95	83	5%	272	4.63	35	39	74%	4.47	1.50	32%	72%	4.40	3.5	6.1	1.7	10%	1.0	36
	09	254	313	366	678	8	80	30	0.43	50	19	31	74	73	5%	241	3.86	35	38	73%	4.13	1.39	30%	72%	4.32	3.4	6.4	1.9	9%	0.9	47
	10	243	297	355	653	7	80	29	0.38	49	18	33	76	68	5%	235	3.50	29	29	67%	4.55	1.48	31%	71%	4.75	4.0	6.1	1.5	8%	0.9	23

TAM	Yr	Avg	OB	Slg	OPS	bb%	ct%	h%	Eye	G	L	F	PX	SX	SBO	xBA	RC/G	W	Py	Sv%	ERA	WHIP	H%	S%	xERA	Ctl	Dom	Cmd	hr/f	hr/9	BPV
At Home	08	273	353	440	793	11	78	32	0.57	42	20	38	105	119	13%	257	5.44	54	48	79%	3.33	1.22	27%	75%	3.75	3.2	7.1	2.2	8%	0.9	61
	09	273	349	462	811	10	77	32	0.51	39	21	40	126	125	19%	265	5.64	52	49	71%	3.72	1.28	29%	74%	3.95	3.1	7.3	2.4	9%	1.0	68
	10	243	328	395	723	11	76	29	0.54	44	17	39	102	111	15%	243	4.55	49	47	81%	3.42	1.18	28%	75%	3.71	2.8	7.6	2.7	9%	1.0	78
Away	08	248	319	405	724	9	78	29	0.47	46	19	35	102	96	11%	254	4.48	40	42	72%	4.34	1.37	30%	72%	4.41	3.3	7.1	2.2	10%	1.2	57
	09	252	331	418	749	11	78	29	0.53	42	19	39	110	98	14%	254	4.84	32	37	59%	5.04	1.43	31%	68%	4.85	3.4	6.9	2.0	12%	1.3	51
	10	251	331	411	742	11	76	30	0.50	42	18	41	113	122	13%	248	4.81	47	49	71%	4.17	1.33	30%	72%	4.20	3.1	7.1	2.3	11%	1.2	65
Opp @ TAM	08	231	299	367	665	9	79	27	0.45	41	19	39	88	86	7%	240	3.72	24	30	44%	4.86	1.53	32%	71%	4.67	4.3	7.6	1.8	12%	1.2	41
	09	247	309	395	704	8	79	29	0.42	41	18	41	99	96	9%	244	4.17	29	32	65%	5.19	1.52	32%	69%	4.87	4.1	8.0	2.0	12%	1.3	51
	10	232	292	389	681	8	77	27	0.37	40	18	42	105	106	11%	244	3.86	32	34	68%	4.34	1.39	29%	71%	4.48	4.3	7.9	1.9	10%	1.0	49

TEX	Yr	Avg	OB	Slg	OPS	bb%	ct%	h%	Eye	G	L	F	PX	SX	SBO	xBA	RC/G	W	Py	Sv%	ERA	WHIP	H%	S%	xERA	Ctl	Dom	Cmd	hr/f	hr/9	BPV
At Home	08	297	369	494	863	10	79	34	0.55	42	23	35	125	115	7%	284	6.29	40	39	50%	5.47	1.55	32%	66%	5.28	3.6	6.2	1.7	11%	1.2	33
	09	273	336	479	815	9	78	31	0.43	39	20	42	134	120	14%	268	5.54	48	46	80%	4.27	1.37	29%	72%	4.34	3.2	6.3	2.0	11%	1.1	47
	10	288	350	447	797	9	84	32	0.58	45	19	36	98	97	10%	270	5.33	51	49	60%	3.65	1.29	29%	75%	3.87	3.2	7.1	2.2	9%	1.0	61
Away	08	268	331	431	762	9	79	31	0.44	42	21	37	108	92	6%	262	4.94	39	37	62%	5.26	1.61	32%	68%	5.19	4.2	5.8	1.4	10%	1.0	14
	09	248	301	412	714	7	77	29	0.33	41	19	40	112	99	13%	250	4.19	39	39	75%	4.51	1.37	29%	69%	4.70	3.4	6.4	1.9	9%	1.0	44
	10	265	323	391	714	8	81	30	0.46	46	18	36	83	97	11%	248	4.30	39	41	81%	4.24	1.33	29%	71%	4.47	3.7	7.5	2.1	9%	1.0	56
Opp @ TEX	08	289	354	468	822	9	83	32	0.59	42	21	37	110	120	10%	278	5.70	41	42	61%	5.77	1.66	35%	68%	5.09	4.1	7.6	1.8	14%	1.4	44
	09	262	325	425	750	9	82	29	0.51	42	20	38	104	94	10%	266	4.75	33	35	68%	5.17	1.44	31%	68%	4.75	3.3	7.7	2.3	14%	1.6	65
	10	247	311	387	698	8	79	29	0.45	41	20	39	94	86	11%	247	4.10	30	32	59%	5.01	1.51	32%	69%	4.81	3.4	5.8	1.7	11%	1.2	36

TOR	Yr	Avg	OB	Slg	OPS	bb%	ct%	h%	Eye	G	L	F	PX	SX	SBO	xBA	RC/G	W	Py	Sv%	ERA	WHIP	H%	S%	xERA	Ctl	Dom	Cmd	hr/f	hr/9	BPV
At Home	08	264	329	413	742	9	83	30	0.55	44	21	36	93	110	6%	266	4.73	47	48	83%	3.12	1.21	29%	76%	3.39	3.0	7.7	2.5	8%	0.7	84
	09	259	328	439	767	9	81	29	0.54	40	19	41	118	92	7%	266	4.99	44	42	57%	4.11	1.32	30%	72%	4.05	3.2	7.4	2.3	11%	1.1	70
	10	254	314	487	801	8	79	27	0.42	37	18	45	146	93	7%	270	5.26	45	43	78%	4.08	1.32	30%	72%	4.08	3.1	7.7	2.4	10%	1.0	77
Away	08	264	326	386	712	8	83	30	0.56	44	20	36	79	90	8%	252	4.36	39	44	74%	3.89	1.28	30%	73%	3.92	2.8	7.0	2.5	11%	1.0	74
	09	273	333	441	774	8	83	30	0.52	38	18	44	108	76	6%	257	5.03	31	41	65%	4.85	1.52	33%	71%	4.51	3.6	7.3	2.0	12%	1.2	55
	10	243	303	426	729	8	78	28	0.39	42	16	42	123	82	6%	253	4.44	39	41	71%	4.35	1.38	30%	70%	4.52	3.6	7.1	2.0	9%	0.9	55
Opp @ TOR	08	234	298	361	659	8	77	29	0.39	48	19	33	87	91	9%	241	3.64	34	33	53%	4.20	1.39	30%	71%	4.42	3.4	6.1	1.8	9%	0.9	40
	09	255	319	417	736	9	78	30	0.43	46	19	35	110	88	9%	261	4.59	37	39	66%	4.68	1.40	29%	70%	4.68	3.6	6.6	1.8	11%	1.3	41
	10	254	316	408	724	8	78	30	0.41	46	18	37	105	95	7%	250	4.44	33	35	76%	4.93	1.32	27%	70%	4.50	3.0	7.2	2.4	16%	2.0	63

WAS	Yr	Avg	OB	Slg	OPS	bb%	ct%	h%	Eye	G	L	F	PX	SX	SBO	xBA	RC/G	W	Py	Sv%	ERA	WHIP	H%	S%	xERA	Ctl	Dom	Cmd	hr/f	hr/9	BPV
At Home	08	251	323	368	691	10	81	30	0.54	49	21	29	74	82	9%	250	4.12	34	29	55%	4.57	1.42	30%	71%	4.49	3.4	6.3	1.9	12%	1.2	44
	09	257	334	408	742	10	79	30	0.54	44	19	37	96	99	8%	250	4.78	33	35	57%	4.69	1.42	29%	69%	4.91	3.6	5.5	1.5	10%	1.0	23
	10	260	324	405	729	9	79	31	0.45	47	18	36	96	94	10%	248	4.52	41	37	67%	3.97	1.32	31%	72%	4.04	2.9	7.1	2.4	9%	0.9	74
Away	08	250	311	378	689	8	80	29	0.44	46	21	33	82	80	7%	250	4.00	25	33	47%	4.76	1.49	31%	71%	4.61	4.0	7.0	1.8	12%	1.2	38
	09	258	331	404	736	10	77	31	0.48	45	19	36	97	70	7%	245	4.65	26	31	57%	5.37	1.62	32%	69%	5.17	4.3	6.0	1.4	11%	1.1	14
	10	241	304	376	679	8	76	29	0.38	48	17	35	90	102	12%	237	3.84	28	35	62%	4.31	1.45	31%	72%	4.40	3.5	6.2	1.8	9%	1.0	38
Opp @ WAS	08	269	334	434	768	9	82	30	0.54	43	21	36	100	94	9%	270	5.00	46	51	72%	3.71	1.33	29%	73%	3.93	3.5	6.5	1.8	8%	0.6	50
	09	263	333	431	764	9	84	29	0.66	44	19	37	105	82	6%	272	5.03	48	46	61%	4.31	1.42	30%	72%	4.40	4.0	7.3	1.8	10%	1.0	47
	10	260	318	398	716	8	79	31	0.41	46	18	36	91	100	9%	248	4.31	40	44	68%	3.87	1.35	30%	74%	3.92	3.2	7.2	2.2	10%	0.9	67

AL	Yr	Avg	OB	Slg	OPS	bb%	ct%	h%	Eye	G	L	F	PX	SX	SBO	xBA	RC/G	W	Py	Sv%	ERA	WHIP	H%	S%	xERA	Ctl	Dom	Cmd	hr/f	hr/9	BPV
At Home	08	273	335	424	759	9	82	31	0.51	44	20	36	100	100	9%	266	4.89	44	43	72%	4.00	1.34	30%	72%	4.19	3.2	6.8	2.1	9%	0.9	56
	09	270	339	440	779	9	81	30	0.54	43	19	38	100	100	10%	258	5.15	47	44	71%	4.09	1.34	30%	72%	4.18	3.2	7.1	2.2	10%	1.1	61
	10	264	331	411	742	9	81	30	0.52	44	19	38	100	100	10%	258	4.70	47	45	73%	3.66	1.26	29%	74%	3.91	2.9	6.9	2.4	9%	0.9	67
Away	08	258	321	399	720	9	81	30	0.48	45	19	35	100	100	9%	262	4.41	37	38	64%	4.62	1.45	31%	70%	4.62	3.5	6.6	1.9	10%	1.0	45
	09	264	325	420	745	8	80	30	0.46	43	19	39	100	100	10%	254	4.68	39	40	68%	4.55	1.41	30%	71%	4.55	3.5	6.9	2.0	10%	1.1	50
	10	253	318	393	711	9	80	29	0.47	44	18	38	100	100	10%	252	4.29	36	39	68%	4.38	1.38	30%	71%	4.44	3.3	6.8	2.0	10%	1.1	54

NL	Yr	Avg	OB	Slg	OPS	bb%	ct%	h%	Eye	G	L	F	PX	SX	SBO	xBA	RC/G	W	Py	Sv%	ERA	WHIP	H%	S%	xERA	Ctl	Dom	Cmd	hr/f	hr/9	BPV
At Home	08	263	330	414	745	9	80	30	0.51	44	21	35	100	100	9%	265	4.74	43	41	65%	3.99	1.34	30%	73%	4.10	3.3	6.8	2.1	10%	0.9	56
	09	263	333	415	749	10	80	30	0.53	45	19	37	100	100	9%	258	4.82	44	41	68%	3.97	1.34	30%	73%	4.13	3.3	7.1	2.1	9%	0.9	60
	10	260	327	403	730	9	80	30	0.49	45	18	37	100	100	9%	255	4.56	46	43	71%	3.63	1.29	30%	74%	3.86	3.1	7.4	2.4	8%	0.8	73
Away	08	259	321	405	727	8	80	30	0.46	45	20	35	100	100	8%	263	4.47	35	38	59%	4.73	1.47	31%	70%	4.60	3.7	6.7	1.8	11%	1.1	43
	09	257	322	398	721	9	79	30	0.46	44	19	36	100	100	9%	256	4.42	35	37	65%	4.69	1.46	31%	70%	4.69	3.8	6.7	1.8	10%	1.1	40
	10	247	309	382	691	8	78	29	0.41	45	18	37	100	100	10%	251	4.01	35	37	67%	4.37	1.41	31%	71%	4.35	3.3	7.1	2.1	10%	1.0	60

The Batters

QUALIFICATION: Nearly all batters who had at least 100 at bats in the majors in 2010 are included. Beyond that, the decision comes down to whether they will have an impact in 2011. Those who may have a role but have battled injuries for several years may not be included, though all of these players will appear at Baseball HQ as roles become clearer.

POSITIONS: Up to three positions are listed for each batter and represent those for which he appeared a minimum of 20 games in 2010. Positions are shown with their numeric designation (2=CA, 3=1B, 7=LF, 0=DH, etc.)

AGE: Each batter's age as of Opening Day 2011 is shown.

BATS: Shows which side of the plate he bats from — Left, Right or Both.

Ht/Wt: Each batter's height (in inches) and weight (in pounds). Reminder benchmark: 72 inches is 6 feet.

RELIABILITY GRADES: An analysis of each player's forecast risk, on an A-F scale. High grades go to those batters who have accumulated few disabled list days (Health), have a history of substantial and regular major league playing time (PT/Exp) and have displayed consistent performance over the past three years, using RC/G (Consist).

LIMA PLAN GRADE: Rating that evaluates how well a batter would fit into a team using the LIMA Plan. Best grades go to batters who have excellent base skills, are expected to see a good amount of playing time, and are in the $10-$30 Rotisserie dollar range. Lowest grades will go to poor skills, few AB and values less than $5 or more than $30.

RAND VAR: A score that measures the impact random variance had on the batter's 2010 stats and the probability that his 2011 performance will exceed or fall short of 2010. The variables tracked are levels for h%, hr/f and xBA that would be prone to regression. Players are rated on a scale of –5 to +5 with positive scores indicating rebounds and negative scores indicate corrections.

PLAYER STAT LINES: The past five years' statistics represent the total accumulated in the majors as well as in Triple-A, Double-A ball and various foreign leagues during each year. All non-major league stats used have been converted to a major league equivalent (MLE) performance level. Minor league levels below AA are not included.

Nearly all baseball publications separate a player's statistical experiences in the major leagues from the minor leagues and outside leagues. While this may be appropriate for the sake of official record-keeping, it is not an accurate snapshot of a player's complete performance for the year.

Bill James has proven that minor league statistics (converted to MLEs), at Double-A level or above, provide as accurate a record of a player's performance as Major League statistics. Other researchers have also devised conversion factors for foreign leagues. Since these are accurate barometers, we include them in the pool of historical data.

TEAM DESIGNATIONS: An asterisk (*) appearing with a team name means that Triple-A (aaa) and/or Double-A (aa) numbers are included in that year's stat line. A designation of "a/a" means the stats were accumulated at both levels that year. Other designations: JPN (Japan), MEX (Mexico), KOR (Korea), CUB (Cuba) and ind (independent league). All of these statistics are converted to major league equivalents.

The designation "2TM" appears whenever a player was on more than one major league team, crossing leagues, in a season. "2AL" and "2NL" represent more than one team in the same league. Complete season stats are presented for players who crossed leagues during the season.

SABERMETRIC CATEGORIES: Descriptions of all the categories appear in the Encyclopedia. The decimal point has been suppressed on some categories to conserve space.
- Platoon data (vL, vR) and Ball-in-play data (G/L/F) are for major league performance only.
- xBA only appears for years in which G/L/F data is available.

2011 FORECASTS: It is far too early to be making definitive projections for 2011, especially on playing time. Focus on the skill levels and trends, then consult Baseball HQ for playing time revisions as players change teams and roles become finalized. A free projections update will be available online in March.

Forecasts are computed from a player's trends over the past five years. Adjustments were made for leading indicators and variances between skill and statistical output. After reviewing the leading indicators, you might opt to make further adjustments.

Although each year's numbers include all playing time at the Double-A level or above, the 2011 forecast only represents potential playing time at the major league level, and again is highly preliminary.

CAPSULE COMMENTARIES: For each player, a brief analysis of their BPI's and the potential impact on performance in 2011 is provided. For those who played only a portion of 2010 at the major league level, and whose isolated MLB stats are significantly different from their full-season total, their MLB stats are listed here. Note that these commentaries generally look at performance related issues only. Playing time expectations may impact these analyses, so you will have to adjust accordingly. Upside (UP) and downside (DN) statistical potential appears for some players. These are less grounded in hard data and more speculative of skills potential.

DO-IT-YOURSELF ANALYSIS: Here are some data points you can look at in doing your own player analysis:
- Variance between vLH and vRH batting averages
- Growth or decline in walk rate (bb%)
- Growth or decline in contact rate (ct%)
- Variance in 2010 hit rate (h%) to 2007-2009 three-year avg
- Variance between Avg and xBA each year
- Growth or decline in power index (PX) rate
- Variance in 2010 hr/f rate to 2007-2009 three-year average
- Growth or decline in statistically scouted speed (Spd) score
- Concurrent growth/decline of gauges like ct%, PX, F
- Concurrent growth/decline of gauges like Spd, SBO, OB

Additional power and speed gauges are in the support charts.

Abreu,Bobby			AB	R	HR	RBI	SB	Avg	vL	vR	OB	Slg	OPS	bb%	ct%	h%	Eye	xBA	G	L	F	PX	hr/f	Spd	SBO	RC/G	RAR	BPV	R$
Pos	79	06 2TM	548	98	15	107	30	297	293	299	427	462	889	18	75	37	0.90	271	45	26	29	117	13%	71	16%	7.23	30.8	53	$27
Age/B	37 Left	07 NYY	605	123	16	101	25	283	262	289	370	445	815	12	81	33	0.73	279	46	20	34	109	9%	76	17%	5.83	13.6	60	$26
Ht/Wt	72 210	08 NYY	609	100	20	100	22	296	315	287	371	471	842	11	82	33	0.67	290	48	23	30	114	13%	73	17%	6.03	20.4	65	$27
Health	A	09 LAA	563	96	15	103	30	293	267	305	394	435	829	14	80	34	0.83	261	48	19	33	90	10%	86	18%	6.11	17.5	48	$27
PT/Exp	A	10 LAA	573	88	20	78	24	255	228	267	353	435	788	13	77	30	0.66	277	47	17	36	132	13%	71	20%	5.50	10.6	63	$23
Consist	A	1st Half	309	47	8	43	14	259			355	405	759	13	78	31	0.67	268	48	18	34	107	10%	77	20%	5.15	2.5	47	$12
LIMA Plan	C+	2nd Half	264	41	12	35	10	250			351	470	821	13	76	29	0.65	288	47	14	39	161	15%	66	19%	5.92	8.2	83	$10
Rand Var	+3	11 Proj	442	72	15	69	17	274			371	449	820	13	78	32	0.71	276	47	19	34	121	12%	76	17%	5.93	12.8	62	$19

Had never hit lower than .283 in any previous season... until now. 1H BA issues led to opening of 2H swing and power surge. BA will rebound some with h%, but age is showing. Plus, he'll likely lose some AB vs. LHP.

Abreu,Tony			AB	R	HR	RBI	SB	Avg	vL	vR	OB	Slg	OPS	bb%	ct%	h%	Eye	xBA	G	L	F	PX	hr/f	Spd	SBO	RC/G	RAR	BPV	R$
Pos	5	06 aa	457	64	6	53	8	269			316	365	681	6	85	31	0.45	0				62		78	10%	3.90	-17.8	27	$11
Age/B	26 Both	07 LA	* 400	60	4	32	4	300	214	290	332	435	767	5	88	34	0.38	285	52	15	32	91	4%	102	4%	4.89	-7.9	65	$11
Ht/Wt	69 200	08 LA	0	0	0	0	0	0							0			0											
Health	F	09 a/a	307	38	10	44	3	294			319	463	782	4	85	32	0.25	0				104		77	8%	4.87	-0.4	56	$11
PT/Exp	F	10 ARI	* 287	26	2	26	3	251	257	220	269	345	614	2	79	31	0.11	251	46	21	33	75	3%	69	7%	2.83	-17.6	2	$4
Consist	F	1st Half	124	14	0	7	2	250			273	323	596	3	81	31	0.17	272	54	22	24	67	0%	66	12%	2.72	-8.0	7	$2
LIMA Plan	F	2nd Half	163	12	2	19	1	252			265	362	627	2	77	32	0.08	224	34	19	47	81	3%	84	3%	2.93	-9.4	2	$3
Rand Var	0	11 Proj	169	19	1	18	2	272			297	370	667	3	82	33	0.20	255	48	19	33	75	3%	73	7%	3.57	-7.4	19	$4

1-13-.233 in 193 AB at ARI. PX trend, playing time opps raised 2010 hopes. Relapse, eroding Eye and bb%, more health issues have dashed them. "Growth age" doesn't always mean growth.

Ackley,Dustin			AB	R	HR	RBI	SB	Avg	vL	vR	OB	Slg	OPS	bb%	ct%	h%	Eye	xBA	G	L	F	PX	hr/f	Spd	SBO	RC/G	RAR	BPV	R$
Pos	4	06	0	0	0	0	0	0							0			0											
Age/B	23 Left	07	0	0	0	0	0	0							0			0											
Ht/Wt	73 185	08	0	0	0	0	0	0							0			0											
Health	A	09	0	0	0	0	0	0							0			0											
PT/Exp	F	10 a/a	501	61	5	39	8	230			312	337	649	11	87	25	0.94	275	45	20	35	74	3%	117	9%	3.91	-11.1	66	$7
Consist	F	1st Half	253	31	2	19	6	217			327	320	647	14	88	24	1.32	0				73		111	11%	4.10	-4.2	72	$3
LIMA Plan	D+	2nd Half	248	30	3	20	2	242			296	355	651	7	87	27	0.58	274	45	20	35	74	4%	120	7%	3.69	-7.1	59	$4
Rand Var	+3	11 Proj	347	42	4	27	5	233			309	347	656	10	87	26	0.85	271	45	20	35	74	4%	118	9%	3.94	-7.7	65	$5

Showed patience, contact and speed in AA/AAA stint, but none of the power or base-stealing skills expected from second pick in the '09 draft. Age gives him time, pedigree will give him opportunity.

Allen,Brandon			AB	R	HR	RBI	SB	Avg	vL	vR	OB	Slg	OPS	bb%	ct%	h%	Eye	xBA	G	L	F	PX	hr/f	Spd	SBO	RC/G	RAR	BPV	R$
Pos	7	06	0	0	0	0	0	0							0			0											
Age/B	25 Left	07	0	0	0	0	0	0							0			0											
Ht/Wt	74 235	08 aa	153	27	15	29	3	268			345	614	959	11	76	26	0.49	0				208		83	11%	7.32	9.7	118	$8
Health	A	09 ARI	* 551	70	20	69	5	255	91	232	316	430	746	8	81	28	0.48	261	44	17	39	111	11%	62	5%	4.69	-14.1	51	$15
PT/Exp	D	10 ARI	* 416	50	17	60	9	220	143	289	321	399	720	13	80	24	0.75	285	27	31	42	114	12%	68	12%	4.55	-6.7	60	$11
Consist	C	1st Half	170	18	6	22	3	220			323	401	724	13	83	23	0.92	0				114		84	17%	4.75	-1.7	79	$4
LIMA Plan	D	2nd Half	246	32	12	38	6	220			320	397	717	13	78	24	0.66	279	27	31	42	113	14%	59	8%	4.43	-4.8	47	$7
Rand Var	+5	11 Proj	312	41	13	45	5	240			323	428	751	11	80	26	0.61	274	36	23	40	118	13%	71	9%	4.85	-3.9	59	$9

1-6-.267 in 45 AB at ARI. Hints of growth after rebound from early season shoulder injury. BB%, Eye and xBA gains point way to acceptable BA with big power upside intact. Still a work in progress.

Alvarez,Pedro			AB	R	HR	RBI	SB	Avg	vL	vR	OB	Slg	OPS	bb%	ct%	h%	Eye	xBA	G	L	F	PX	hr/f	Spd	SBO	RC/G	RAR	BPV	R$
Pos	5	06	0	0	0	0	0	0							0			0											
Age/B	24 Left	07	0	0	0	0	0	0							0			0											
Ht/Wt	75 235	08	0	0	0	0	0	0							0			0											
Health	A	09 aa	222	35	10	33	1	306			382	523	904	11	79	35	0.57	0				145		68	1%	6.81	11.5	75	$9
PT/Exp	F	10 PIT	* 589	74	26	105	3	249	228	270	319	450	769	9	71	31	0.35	257	46	15	40	149	16%	60	5%	5.12	3.9	41	$20
Consist	D	1st Half	304	38	12	50	3	234			298	421	719	8	74	28	0.36	250	41	14	46	133	12%	69	12%	4.36	-5.1	43	$9
LIMA Plan	C	2nd Half	285	36	14	55	-0	266			341	480	821	10	67	35	0.35	258	47	15	38	167	19%	60	-0%	6.04	9.3	44	$11
Rand Var	0	11 Proj	535	74	25	90	2	275			348	487	835	10	74	33	0.42	265	46	15	39	151	16%	60	3%	5.98	13.6	56	$20

16-64-.256 in 347 AB at PIT. Struggles vs. LHP, borderline contact were the only flaws in a nice MLB debut. Streaky, but saved the best for last with .939 OPS in September. More growth coming.

Anderson,Garret			AB	R	HR	RBI	SB	Avg	vL	vR	OB	Slg	OPS	bb%	ct%	h%	Eye	xBA	G	L	F	PX	hr/f	Spd	SBO	RC/G	RAR	BPV	R$
Pos	7	06 LAA	543	63	17	85	1	280	248	294	327	433	760	7	83	31	0.40	263	41	22	37	94	10%	55	1%	4.75	-6.5	37	$14
Age/B	38 Left	07 LAA	417	67	16	80	1	297	288	300	340	492	832	6	87	31	0.50	297	40	19	41	121	11%	58	1%	5.59	6.3	77	$16
Ht/Wt	75 225	08 LAA	557	66	15	84	7	293	290	293	328	433	760	5	86	32	0.38	271	42	21	36	86	9%	80	7%	4.70	-2.4	49	$18
Health	B	09 ATL	496	52	13	61	1	268	283	262	306	401	707	5	85	29	0.37	260	41	20	38	86	8%	47	1%	4.09	-21.0	37	$12
PT/Exp	C	10 LA	155	8	2	12	1	181	133	192	206	271	477	3	78	22	0.15	232	42	20	38	65	4%	74	4%	1.11	-19.7	-5	($1)
Consist	D	1st Half	127	6	2	11	1	189			208	291	499	2	77	23	0.10	230	38	20	42	73	5%	74	5%	1.32	-15.2	-4	($0)
LIMA Plan	F	2nd Half	28	2	0	1	0	143			200	179	379	7	82	17	0.40	244	61	17	22	33	0%	76	0%	0.27	-4.5	-7	($1)
Rand Var	+5	11 Proj	67	7	1	9	0	254			287	350	638	5	83	29	0.28	244	41	20	39	66	5%	66	3%	3.22	-4.0	16	$1

Toast, at least from a fantasy perspective. May even retire. Part-time play and age clearly do not agree with him. Surprisingly consistent and effective player until health issues took over in 2004.

Andrus,Elvis			AB	R	HR	RBI	SB	Avg	vL	vR	OB	Slg	OPS	bb%	ct%	h%	Eye	xBA	G	L	F	PX	hr/f	Spd	SBO	RC/G	RAR	BPV	R$
Pos	6	06	0	0	0	0	0	0							0			0											
Age/B	22 Right	07	0	0	0	0	0	0							0			0											
Ht/Wt	72 185	08 aa	482	66	3	53	43	271			314	335	649	6	86	31	0.44	0				44		103	46%	3.53	-13.8	23	$20
Health	A	09 TEX	480	72	6	40	33	267	279	262	323	373	696	8	84	31	0.52	278	55	22	23	61	6%	136	28%	4.17	-3.9	43	$17
PT/Exp	B	10 TEX	588	88	0	35	32	265	268	264	337	301	638	10	84	32	0.67	263	61	19	20	28	0%	132	23%	3.60	-6.3	18	$17
Consist	B	1st Half	305	55	0	25	22	289			369	328	697	11	82	35	0.70	262	58	22	20	30	0%	134	27%	4.37	3.6	16	$13
LIMA Plan	C+	2nd Half	283	33	0	10	10	240			302	272	574	8	86	28	0.63	262	64	16	19	25	0%	124	18%	2.81	-9.9	19	$4
Rand Var	0	11 Proj	610	88	3	44	38	264			325	325	650	8	84	31	0.58	269	59	20	21	41	3%	128	27%	3.67	-9.3	27	$19

Almost the same season as 2009, with a few more GBs and zero power. Young enough to resume growth, but power isn't his game, even in Texas. Pay only for the SBs, hope for more upside.

Ankiel,Rick			AB	R	HR	RBI	SB	Avg	vL	vR	OB	Slg	OPS	bb%	ct%	h%	Eye	xBA	G	L	F	PX	hr/f	Spd	SBO	RC/G	RAR	BPV	R$
Pos	8	06	0	0	0	0	0	0							0			0											
Age/B	31 Left	07 STL	* 559	72	31	97	3	236	391	246	275	445	720	5	77	25	0.23	259	44	15	41	125	18%	86	6%	4.06	-7.9	44	$16
Ht/Wt	73 210	08 STL	413	65	25	71	2	264	224	279	332	506	838	9	76	29	0.42	267	36	19	45	154	18%	87	3%	5.84	13.1	73	$16
Health	D	09 STL	372	50	11	38	4	231	234	230	281	387	669	7	73	29	0.26	228	40	15	45	113	9%	82	9%	3.64	-12.4	24	$7
PT/Exp	C	10 2TM	* 278	36	9	30	3	222	164	256	291	387	677	9	69	29	0.31	249	53	14	33	134	14%	72	7%	3.92	-10.1	23	$5
Consist	C	1st Half	84	10	4	12	1	226			270	452	722	6	65	29	0.17	274	54	15	32	191	23%	70	8%	4.53	-1.5	49	$2
LIMA Plan	C	2nd Half	194	26	5	18	2	220			299	358	658	10	70	29	0.37	239	53	14	33	111	10%	79	6%	3.69	-8.5	14	$3
Rand Var	+1	11 Proj	420	56	17	53	4	233			292	423	715	8	71	29	0.29	252	45	16	39	138	14%	75	7%	4.31	-8.0	36	$10

6-24-.232 in 211 AB at KC and ATL. More injuries (quad) and deteriorating ct% combine with futility vs. LHP to make him a part-time player. Power remains solid, but at his age, it won't get much better.

Arencibia,JP			AB	R	HR	RBI	SB	Avg	vL	vR	OB	Slg	OPS	bb%	ct%	h%	Eye	xBA	G	L	F	PX	hr/f	Spd	SBO	RC/G	RAR	BPV	R$
Pos	2	06	0	0	0	0	0	0							0			0											
Age/B	25 Right	07	0	0	0	0	0	0							0			0											
Ht/Wt	73 215	08 aa	262	26	13	35	0	260			273	458	731	2	82	27	0.11	0				120		67	0%	4.05	-1.1	52	$7
Health	A	09 aaa	466	49	17	55	0	202			233	374	607	4	81	22	0.21	0				112		72	1%	2.75	-22.2	42	$5
PT/Exp	F	10 TOR	* 447	48	21	54	0	224		217	265	437	702	5	85	22	0.37	269	29	13	58	135	10%	64	0%	3.99	-2.2	79	$9
Consist	C	1st Half	260	27	11	29	0	236			271	439	711	5	85	24	0.32	0				132		76	0%	4.10	-0.5	80	$5
LIMA Plan	D	2nd Half	187	21	11	25	0	206			256	434	690	6	84	19	0.42	271	29	13	58	140	12%	63	0%	3.85	-1.8	82	$4
Rand Var	+4	11 Proj	325	35	16	40	0	218			253	431	684	4	83	22	0.27	257	29	13	58	132	10%	64	0%	3.68	-5.3	67	$6

2-4-.143 in 35 AB at TOR. Nice growth year in AAA, and the power is legit. But poor bb%, LD% suggest that pitch selection needs improvement for BA to survive at higher levels. Intriguing #2 CA flyer.

JOCK THOMPSON

Arias,Joaquin			AB	R	HR	RBI	SB	Avg	vL	vR	OB	Slg	OPS	bb%	ct%	h%	Eye	xBA	G	L	F	PX	hr/f	Spd	SBO	RC/G	RAR	BPV	R$
Pos	4	06 aaa	493	56	4	48	26	281			308	383	691	4	89	31	0.34	0				53		196	29%	3.97	-5.6	66	$15
Age/B	26 Right	07 aaa	432	44	6	36	17	256			280	358	637	3	90	27	0.34	0				56		183	23%	3.35	-12.8	69	$9
Ht/Wt	73 165	08 TEX	* 542	59	6	45	21	263	417	256	291	368	659	4	90	28	0.39	273	48	20	32	60	4%	194	22%	3.65	-19.8	76	$13
Health	B	09 aaa	504	48	4	39	19	228			250	287	537	3	92	24	0.36	0				35		130	20%	2.30	-37.4	42	$7
PT/Exp	D	10 2TM	128	23	0	13	1	258	333	232	280	320	601	3	82	31	0.17	231	43	18	39	50	0%	141	3%	2.76	-7.0	19	$3
Consist	B	1st Half	91	16	0	5	1	264			287	297	584	3	84	32	0.20	235	44	22	34	30	0%	126	4%	2.54	-5.5	4	$2
LIMA Plan	F	2nd Half	37	7	0	8	0	243			263	378	642	3	78	31	0.13	242	41	12	46	104	0%	142	0%	3.34	-1.4	46	$1
Rand Var	-3	11 Proj	34	4	0	3	1	265			289	310	600	3	88	30	0.29	222	43	16	41	32	1%	116	15%	2.85	-1.8	23	$1

Can't hit for power
Doesn't get on base
If the red light continues
Good-bye roster space.

Flexing those creative muscles early this year. Don't cringe.

Atkins,Garrett			AB	R	HR	RBI	SB	Avg	vL	vR	OB	Slg	OPS	bb%	ct%	h%	Eye	xBA	G	L	F	PX	hr/f	Spd	SBO	RC/G	RAR	BPV	R$
Pos	3	06 COL	602	117	29	120	4	329	341	327	407	556	963	12	87	34	1.04	301	37	22	41	131	13%	83	2%	7.44	22.8	104	$32
Age/B	31 Right	07 COL	605	83	25	111	3	301	286	307	371	486	856	10	84	32	0.70	282	31	24	44	111	11%	75	2%	6.09	-0.7	70	$24
Ht/Wt	75 215	08 COL	611	86	21	99	1	286	357	265	330	452	782	6	84	31	0.40	265	37	22	41	101	10%	88	1%	4.99	-12.7	56	$21
Health	A	09 COL	354	37	9	48	0	226	268	199	306	342	648	10	84	25	0.71	234	42	16	42	71	7%	90	0%	3.65	-30.7	41	$5
PT/Exp	C	10 BAL	140	5	1	9	0	214	204	220	276	286	562	8	79	27	0.40	219	42	16	42	60	2%	75	0%	2.43	-14.4	3	($0)
Consist	C	1st Half	140	5	1	9	0	214			276	286	562	8	79	27	0.40	219	42	16	42	60	2%	75	0%	2.43	-14.4	3	($0)
LIMA Plan	F	2nd Half	0	0	0	0	0	0																					
Rand Var	+2	11 Proj	128	14	3	17	0	258			322	392	714	9	83	29	0.54	256	39	19	42	89	8%	75	1%	4.34	-4.8	44	$3

Plate discipline and FB rates remain steady, but declining PX and hr/f show he's not hitting much other than singles. Unless there's a hidden injury, no reason to expect a rebound. Avoid.

Avila,Alex			AB	R	HR	RBI	SB	Avg	vL	vR	OB	Slg	OPS	bb%	ct%	h%	Eye	xBA	G	L	F	PX	hr/f	Spd	SBO	RC/G	RAR	BPV	R$
Pos	2	06	0	0	0	0	0	0							0			0											
Age/B	24 Left	07	0	0	0	0	0	0							0			0											
Ht/Wt	71 210	08	0	0	0	0	0	0							0			0											
Health	A	09 DET	* 390	52	15	60	2	246	400	255	336	431	767	12	79	27	0.66	255	43	14	43	117	11%	78	3%	5.14	10.0	61	$10
PT/Exp	F	10 DET	294	28	7	31	2	228	182	234	312	340	652	11	76	28	0.51	246	43	22	35	82	9%	45	5%	3.60	-5.0	6	$4
Consist	D	1st Half	127	11	3	11	2	228			315	339	653	11	76	28	0.52	239	46	19	35	81	9%	58	5%	3.62	-2.1	9	$2
LIMA Plan	D	2nd Half	167	17	4	20	0	228			310	341	651	11	76	28	0.50	252	42	24	35	83	9%	53	4%	3.58	-3.0	10	$2
Rand Var	+1	11 Proj	390	43	11	49	2	249			334	382	716	11	77	30	0.56	253	43	21	36	94	10%	46	4%	4.46	2.9	23	$8

Nice walk rate, but mediocre ct% and subpar speed limit BA. potential. He hit the ball quite hard (38% hard hit rate and xPX of 133 in 2010), so if he can hit a few more FB...
UP: 20 HR

Aviles,Mike			AB	R	HR	RBI	SB	Avg	vL	vR	OB	Slg	OPS	bb%	ct%	h%	Eye	xBA	G	L	F	PX	hr/f	Spd	SBO	RC/G	RAR	BPV	R$
Pos	4	06 aaa	469	46	6	42	12	245			283	340	623	5	91	26	0.60	0				56		89	15%	3.34	-14.3	48	$7
Age/B	30 Right	07 aa	538	58	11	57	3	239			270	362	632	4	90	25	0.40	0				71		107	8%	3.31	-16.9	57	$8
Ht/Wt	69 203	08 KC	* 633	100	17	83	11	313	348	313	341	495	836	4	88	34	0.34	301	46	20	33	113	9%	115	9%	5.57	11.7	85	$25
Health	D	09 KC	120	10	1	8	1	183	195	177	210	250	460	3	78	23	0.15	217	45	19	36	43	3%	91	5%	0.90	-15.5	-17	($1)
PT/Exp	D	10 KC	* 494	68	9	37	14	291	263	319	322	398	720	4	88	31	0.40	266	43	19	38	66	5%	129	14%	4.25	-3.0	56	$16
Consist	F	1st Half	262	34	3	18	2	294			320	385	705	4	88	33	0.31	269	40	23	36	60	4%	125	8%	4.06	-3.0	46	$7
LIMA Plan	D+	2nd Half	232	34	6	19	12	287			324	412	735	5	89	30	0.50	266	45	15	39	72	7%	119	20%	4.46	0.0	62	$10
Rand Var	-3	11 Proj	474	59	8	40	11	262			292	369	662	4	86	29	0.31	257	45	18	37	66	5%	112	12%	3.55	-14.5	41	$11

8-32-.304 with 14 SB in 424 AB at KC. Finished the year hot but has struggled with consistency before. xBA, PX and DDF reliability rating all imply that a repeat performance is doubtful.

Aybar,Erick			AB	R	HR	RBI	SB	Avg	vL	vR	OB	Slg	OPS	bb%	ct%	h%	Eye	xBA	G	L	F	PX	hr/f	Spd	SBO	RC/G	RAR	BPV	R$
Pos	6	06 LAA	* 379	56	5	39	27	259	250	250	291	370	660	4	91	27	0.48	265	70	3	27	66	6%	120	58%	3.70	-8.5	63	$13
Age/B	27 Both	07 LAA	194	18	1	19	4	237	304	216	275	289	563	5	84	28	0.31	221	52	12	36	35	2%	138	16%	2.40	-11.3	15	$2
Ht/Wt	70 170	08 LAA	346	53	3	39	7	277	286	274	306	384	690	4	87	31	0.31	271	52	18	30	69	3%	150	11%	3.94	-3.8	58	$9
Health	B	09 LAA	504	70	5	58	14	312	325	305	350	423	773	6	89	34	0.56	273	46	21	33	63	3%	152	14%	5.01	7.8	66	$18
PT/Exp	B	10 LAA	534	69	5	29	22	253	252	253	299	330	628	6	85	29	0.43	244	49	15	36	51	3%	148	21%	3.28	-10.9	39	$13
Consist	C	1st Half	297	48	2	15	12	283			343	364	706	8	84	33	0.57	255	53	15	32	59	2%	137	19%	4.34	3.3	44	$9
LIMA Plan	C+	2nd Half	237	21	3	14	10	215			241	287	528	3	86	24	0.24	229	44	16	41	42	4%	153	24%	1.94	-14.9	30	$3
Rand Var	0	11 Proj	550	71	5	46	19	271			308	361	669	5	87	30	0.40	254	48	17	35	56	3%	146	19%	3.74	-7.1	48	$15

2nd half hampered by multiple leg injuries and bad luck. There's nothing to suggest a sudden burst of power, but with elite speed, rising SBO and health...
UP: 30 SB

Aybar,Willy			AB	R	HR	RBI	SB	Avg	vL	vR	OB	Slg	OPS	bb%	ct%	h%	Eye	xBA	G	L	F	PX	hr/f	Spd	SBO	RC/G	RAR	BPV	R$
Pos	0	06 2NL	* 450	57	11	62	2	278	328	263	346	420	766	9	87	30	0.82	254	44	14	42	86	7%	72	6%	5.10	-17.2	61	$12
Age/B	28 Both	07	0	0	0	0	0	0							0			0											
Ht/Wt	71 205	08 TAM	324	33	10	33	2	253	266	245	320	410	731	9	86	27	0.73	273	40	21	40	95	9%	78	5%	4.62	-2.9	65	$6
Health	B	09 TAM	296	38	12	41	1	253	265	247	330	416	746	10	82	27	0.63	268	42	22	36	95	14%	65	1%	4.74	-3.8	45	$7
PT/Exp	D	10 TAM	270	22	6	43	0	230	246	212	307	344	651	10	77	28	0.49	241	42	18	39	85	7%	48	0%	3.58	-22.6	14	$4
Consist	B	1st Half	134	12	5	22	0	246			294	396	689	6	78	28	0.31	258	41	20	39	99	12%	53	0%	3.80	-10.1	23	$3
LIMA Plan	F	2nd Half	136	10	1	21	0	213			318	294	613	13	76	27	0.66	226	43	17	40	71	2%	59	0%	3.30	-12.8	9	$1
Rand Var	+1	11 Proj	189	19	5	27	0	243			320	372	692	10	81	28	0.59	252	42	19	39	86	9%	57	2%	4.12	-9.7	31	$4

Abnormally low hr/f in 2H depressed power, but ct%, xBA and BPV all going in the wrong direction. Could return to 2009 levels, but needs to get out of TAM to get more AB. DH-only eligibility hurts fanalytic value.

Baker,Jeff			AB	R	HR	RBI	SB	Avg	vL	vR	OB	Slg	OPS	bb%	ct%	h%	Eye	xBA	G	L	F	PX	hr/f	Spd	SBO	RC/G	RAR	BPV	R$
Pos	45	06 COL	* 539	65	22	101	7	292	438	341	335	497	832	6	83	32	0.38	306	44	28	28	120	17%	85	6%	5.59	14.9	68	$21
Age/B	29 Right	07 COL	144	17	4	12	0	222	246	205	287	347	634	8	72	28	0.33	219	40	20	39	75	10%	143	0%	3.20	-6.6	10	$1
Ht/Wt	74 210	08 COL	299	55	12	48	4	268	290	256	326	468	794	8	72	34	0.31	268	43	24	33	148	17%	92	6%	5.44	5.7	51	$12
Health	C	09 2NL	226	27	4	24	1	288	279	291	340	425	765	7	77	36	0.34	249	45	19	35	102	7%	112	2%	4.99	2.9	38	$6
PT/Exp	D	10 CHC	206	29	4	21	1	272	350	106	324	413	737	7	76	34	0.32	260	42	22	36	106	7%	99	2%	4.62	-1.2	34	$6
Consist	A	1st Half	117	14	3	12	0	239			282	393	675	6	74	30	0.23	245	46	16	38	107	9%	119	0%	3.72	-3.8	29	$2
LIMA Plan	D	2nd Half	89	15	1	9	1	315			378	438	816	9	79	39	0.47	283	38	29	33	104	4%	79	4%	5.76	2.2	42	$3
Rand Var	0	11 Proj	226	33	5	26	2	279			334	432	766	8	76	35	0.34	263	42	23	35	112	9%	100	3%	5.01	1.8	40	$7

Mediocre ct% limits BA upside despite sustained ability to hit line drives. Stable BPIs make him a good short-term injury replacement, but there's not much profit potential here.

Baker,John			AB	R	HR	RBI	SB	Avg	vL	vR	OB	Slg	OPS	bb%	ct%	h%	Eye	xBA	G	L	F	PX	hr/f	Spd	SBO	RC/G	RAR	BPV	R$
Pos	2	06 aaa	293	39	3	30	5	240			312	338	650	9	79	29	0.51	0				72		76	6%	3.65	-6.4	18	$4
Age/B	30 Left	07 aaa	270	26	6	30	2	226			283	338	622	7	77	27	0.36	0				79		71	3%	3.07	-10.6	11	$3
Ht/Wt	73 228	08 FLA	* 390	58	10	55	1	281	213	327	361	424	785	11	79	33	0.60	277	49	25	26	101	12%	81	2%	5.38	13.0	46	$12
Health	F	09 FLA	373	59	9	50	0	271	171	281	343	410	753	10	76	33	0.46	253	49	20	31	105	10%	60	0%	4.92	7.1	28	$11
PT/Exp	D	10 FLA	78	7	0	6	0	218	125	229	299	282	581	10	77	28	0.50	244	53	22	25	50	0%	91	0%	2.80	-4.0	-2	$0
Consist	C	1st Half	78	7	0	6	0	218			299	282	581	10	77	28	0.50	244	53	22	25	50	0%	91	0%	2.80	-4.0	-2	$0
LIMA Plan	F	2nd Half	0	0	0	0	0	0																					
Rand Var	+5	11 Proj	32	4	0	4	0	250			324	359	682	10	78	31	0.49	260	51	22	27	85	7%	71	2%	4.03	-0.3	21	$1

Tried to rehab forearm injury all season before succumbing to Tommy John surgery in Sept. Even if he returns in late 2011, his low xBA and high GB rate limit any long-term value.

Baldelli,Rocco			AB	R	HR	RBI	SB	Avg	vL	vR	OB	Slg	OPS	bb%	ct%	h%	Eye	xBA	G	L	F	PX	hr/f	Spd	SBO	RC/G	RAR	BPV	R$
Pos	0	06 TAM	* 411	66	16	61	10	311	297	303	340	527	867	4	81	36	0.22	287	51	16	34	134	14%	139	13%	5.96	-5.2	81	$18
Age/B	29 Right	07 TAM	137	16	5	12	4	204	156	219	253	358	611	6	74	24	0.26	238	38	18	44	106	13%	114	19%	2.78	-14.9	31	$2
Ht/Wt	76 200	08 TAM	80	12	4	13	0	263	292	219	322	475	797	8	69	33	0.28	255	49	15	36	159	20%	84	0%	5.50	1.3	46	$3
Health	F	09 BOS	150	23	7	23	1	253	290	193	304	433	738	7	75	29	0.30	252	46	18	36	106	17%	121	3%	4.42	-3.3	38	$5
PT/Exp	F	10 TAM	* 68	8	3	10	1	213		278	234	385	619	3	77	24	0.12	275	42	21	37	120	14%	98	10%	2.75	-7.6	42	$2
Consist	C	1st Half	0	0	0	0	0	0																					
LIMA Plan	F	2nd Half	68	8	3	10	1	213			234	385	619	3	77	24	0.12	275	42	21	37	120	14%	98	10%	2.75	-7.6	42	$2
Rand Var	+5	11 Proj	138	18	7	18	1	246			284	431	715	5	76	28	0.22	262	43	18	39	121	16%	98	4%	4.03	-7.4	43	$4

1-5-.208 in 24 AB at TAM
Odd that his h% and Avg have been highest in the years where he's hit the fewest LD. PX and Spd both say he can still contribute if he can overcome health woes.

BILL MACEY

Barajas,Rod			AB	R	HR	RBI	SB	Avg	vL	vR	OB	Slg	OPS	bb%	ct%	h%	Eye	xBA	G	L	F	PX	hr/f	Spd	SBO	RC/G	RAR	BPV	R$
Pos	2	06 TEX	344	49	11	41	0	256	156	279	291	410	701	5	85	27	0.33	244	32	17	51	94	7%	64	0%	3.97	-4.4	47	$7
Age/B	35 Right	07 PHI	122	16	4	10	0	230	226	231	343	393	736	15	80	26	0.88	240	31	15	54	109	8%	59	3%	4.91	1.8	57	$2
Ht/Wt	74 250	08 TOR	349	44	11	49	0	249	204	270	284	410	694	5	83	27	0.28	255	37	17	46	107	8%	45	0%	3.87	-3.3	40	$8
Health	B	09 TOR	429	43	19	71	1	226	267	213	261	403	664	4	82	23	0.26	233	29	14	57	103	9%	32	1%	3.42	-11.1	32	$9
PT/Exp	C	10 2NL	313	39	17	47	0	240	190	256	270	447	717	4	83	24	0.24	248	19	14	66	127	10%	44	0%	4.00	-4.5	56	$9
Consist	B	1st Half	213	28	11	31	0	244			271	451	722	4	85	24	0.26	250	19	14	68	125	9%	52	0%	4.08	-2.5	66	$6
LIMA Plan	D	2nd Half	100	11	6	16	0	230			267	440	707	5	77	24	0.22	242	21	17	63	131	12%	46	0%	3.84	-1.9	38	$3
Rand Var	+1	11 Proj	309	36	15	46	0	236			274	423	697	5	81	25	0.28	241	26	15	59	116	10%	42	1%	3.82	-5.1	42	$8

Hit even more fly balls than usual, resulting in a PX jump. Both will likely regress a bit in 2011, though he should still provide solid power from the catcher position. Just beware the BA drag that comes with it.

Bard,Josh			AB	R	HR	RBI	SB	Avg	vL	vR	OB	Slg	OPS	bb%	ct%	h%	Eye	xBA	G	L	F	PX	hr/f	Spd	SBO	RC/G	RAR	BPV	R$
Pos	2	06 2TM	249	30	9	40	1	333	333	333	405	522	927	11	83	37	0.71	295	52	21	27	120	16%	56	1%	7.05	17.4	69	$10
Age/B	33 Both	07 SD	389	42	5	51	0	285	376	250	367	404	770	11	85	33	0.86	274	52	18	30	81	5%	71	1%	5.31	9.6	51	$9
Ht/Wt	75 225	08 SD	178	11	1	16	0	202	135	230	276	270	545	9	86	23	0.72	247	47	22	31	51	2%	40	0%	2.55	-9.2	17	($0)
Health	D	09 WAS	* 314	22	6	32	0	217	240	228	278	334	612	8	81	25	0.45	238	40	19	41	84	6%	39	1%	3.08	-11.5	21	$2
PT/Exp	F	10 SEA	* 197	13	5	19	0	195	283	167	249	324	573	7	78	23	0.33	238	38	16	46	96	7%	48	0%	2.45	-10.6	18	$1
Consist	B	1st Half	113	10	3	13	0	186			246	327	573	7	81	20	0.43	229	21	17	63	100	5%	71	0%	2.57	-5.7	44	$1
LIMA Plan	F	2nd Half	84	3	2	6	0	208			254	319	573	6	73	26	0.23	227	44	16	39	89	7%	49	0%	2.34	-4.8	-8	$0
Rand Var	+4	11 Proj	194	13	4	19	0	216			277	328	604	8	80	25	0.41	243	43	18	38	81	6%	45	1%	2.94	-7.6	15	$1

3-10-.214 in 112 AB at SEA. Spent most of 1H in minors and on DL, struggled in backup role during 2H. Got power back to respectable level, but bb%, ct% continue to slip. Really no reason to expect a rebound.

Barmes,Clint			AB	R	HR	RBI	SB	Avg	vL	vR	OB	Slg	OPS	bb%	ct%	h%	Eye	xBA	G	L	F	PX	hr/f	Spd	SBO	RC/G	RAR	BPV	R$
Pos	46	06 COL	478	57	7	56	5	220	267	209	254	335	589	4	85	25	0.31	231	34	18	48	72	4%	91	10%	2.75	-27.4	35	$5
Age/B	32 Right	07 COL	* 465	50	8	30	6	229	444	143	255	337	592	3	86	25	0.26	198	21	17	63	64	3%	152	12%	2.73	-28.2	51	$4
Ht/Wt	73 210	08 COL	393	47	11	44	13	290	307	283	320	468	788	4	82	33	0.25	255	29	22	49	112	7%	116	19%	5.01	2.7	64	$14
Health	A	09 COL	550	69	23	76	12	245	245	246	286	440	726	5	78	28	0.26	253	31	20	49	128	11%	86	20%	4.25	-4.6	53	$17
PT/Exp	B	10 COL	387	43	8	50	3	235	280	214	299	351	650	8	83	27	0.53	247	30	21	49	82	5%	55	5%	3.59	-14.4	32	$8
Consist	B	1st Half	249	28	7	41	2	257			307	410	717	7	83	29	0.43	266	29	21	50	106	7%	49	5%	4.29	-3.9	47	$7
LIMA Plan	F	2nd Half	138	15	1	9	1	196			284	246	530	11	83	23	0.71	212	31	21	48	38	2%	80	5%	2.29	-11.1	9	$0
Rand Var	+2	11 Proj	293	34	7	33	4	239			292	369	661	7	82	27	0.41	242	30	21	49	87	6%	76	11%	3.62	-9.8	36	$6

Keeps hitting the ball in the air, but '09 power display looks like an aberration. Slowed down on the bases, after just a 55% success rate in '09. Has little value without speed, and that trend doesn't look good.

Bartlett,Jason			AB	R	HR	RBI	SB	Avg	vL	vR	OB	Slg	OPS	bb%	ct%	h%	Eye	xBA	G	L	F	PX	hr/f	Spd	SBO	RC/G	RAR	BPV	R$
Pos	6	06 MIN	* 568	85	3	51	16	303	314	307	339	407	746	5	87	35	0.42	267	44	22	34	72	2%	119	15%	4.69	4.4	52	$16
Age/B	31 Right	07 MIN	510	75	5	43	23	265	319	245	330	361	691	9	86	30	0.68	256	44	20	36	60	3%	164	17%	4.23	-0.9	60	$14
Ht/Wt	72 190	08 TAM	454	48	1	37	20	286	379	248	319	361	681	5	85	34	0.32	257	49	21	30	56	1%	122	21%	3.84	-6.3	32	$12
Health	B	09 TAM	500	90	14	66	30	320	338	312	386	490	876	10	82	37	0.61	272	35	26	39	102	9%	138	23%	6.42	26.8	74	$26
PT/Exp	B	10 TAM	468	71	4	47	11	254	273	244	320	350	670	9	82	30	0.54	261	45	21	34	73	3%	99	13%	3.92	-0.6	36	$12
Consist	F	1st Half	229	31	2	29	3	223			307	328	635	11	83	26	0.70	262	44	20	36	78	3%	87	8%	3.63	-2.3	42	$4
LIMA Plan	C+	2nd Half	239	40	2	18	8	285			332	372	704	7	82	34	0.40	261	45	21	33	67	3%	110	17%	4.18	1.5	30	$8
Rand Var	+2	11 Proj	580	89	7	59	22	281			339	391	729	8	83	33	0.51	264	43	22	35	76	4%	116	18%	4.58	6.8	46	$19

2009 may have been a career year, but '10 was not as bad as it seems. xBA was comparable with past years; h% explains some of the shortfall. BA v. LHP and Spd are key to a rebound. Power? Pipe dream, likely.

Barton,Daric			AB	R	HR	RBI	SB	Avg	vL	vR	OB	Slg	OPS	bb%	ct%	h%	Eye	xBA	G	L	F	PX	hr/f	Spd	SBO	RC/G	RAR	BPV	R$
Pos	3	06 aaa	147	22	2	19	1	247			366	367	732	16	88	27	1.51	0				68		113	2%	5.16	-2.4	72	$3
Age/B	25 Left	07 OAK	* 588	87	11	67	4	279	296	378	360	423	784	11	89	30	1.12	285	32	24	44	96	5%	95	5%	5.50	4.1	84	$15
Ht/Wt	72 218	08 OAK	451	59	9	47	2	224	273	208	322	344	665	13	78	27	0.66	221	35	19	46	78	6%	115	2%	3.93	-18.5	36	$6
Health	B	09 OAK	* 413	65	9	58	1	232	333	257	326	376	702	12	86	25	1.03	258	31	20	48	91	5%	78	3%	4.55	-14.5	68	$8
PT/Exp	B	10 OAK	556	79	10	57	7	273	310	259	393	405	798	17	82	32	1.08	267	39	21	39	92	6%	104	5%	5.90	2.1	67	$16
Consist	B	1st Half	295	35	4	31	0	288			397	410	807	15	83	34	1.04	259	36	20	44	90	4%	98	2%	5.97	1.7	64	$7
LIMA Plan	B+	2nd Half	261	44	6	26	7	257			390	398	788	18	80	30	1.12	276	43	23	34	95	8%	112	8%	5.81	0.3	69	$8
Rand Var	-2	11 Proj	537	79	15	61	5	263			371	421	792	15	83	29	1.00	270	38	21	41	102	6%	101	4%	5.68	0.7	74	$15

Showing little sign of much power growth at this point, and FB rate dropped. High BA vs LH fueled by 36 percent hit rate. Major step up not likely, though walk rate and defense give him plenty of value in sim formats.

Bautista,Jose			AB	R	HR	RBI	SB	Avg	vL	vR	OB	Slg	OPS	bb%	ct%	h%	Eye	xBA	G	L	F	PX	hr/f	Spd	SBO	RC/G	RAR	BPV	R$
Pos	59	06 PIT	* 501	70	18	60	4	243	283	216	323	420	743	11	74	29	0.46	230	40	13	47	117	10%	103	7%	4.79	-10.6	45	$11
Age/B	30 Right	07 PIT	532	75	15	63	6	254	256	253	338	414	752	11	81	29	0.67	257	40	16	43	106	8%	84	6%	4.97	-10.0	59	$13
Ht/Wt	72 195	08 2TM	370	45	15	54	1	238	250	233	312	405	718	10	75	28	0.44	243	46	15	39	113	14%	83	2%	4.34	-8.7	38	$9
Health	A	09 TOR	336	54	13	40	4	235	293	202	344	408	752	14	75	28	0.66	239	41	17	42	107	12%	115	4%	5.04	3.6	50	$8
PT/Exp	B	10 TOR	569	109	54	124	9	260	222	269	371	617	988	15	80	24	0.86	330	31	14	54	221	22%	85	7%	7.84	49.9	152	$33
Consist	D	1st Half	284	50	21	52	3	236			350	532	882	15	77	23	0.76	297	29	17	55	193	18%	91	6%	6.63	15.5	121	$12
LIMA Plan	B+	2nd Half	285	59	33	72	6	284			391	702	1093	15	82	24	1.00	363	33	12	54	246	26%	80	8%	8.97	33.1	183	$21
Rand Var	+5	11 Proj	575	98	38	101	7	270			369	530	898	14	78	29	0.71	282	37	15	48	163	17%	91	5%	6.79	32.8	98	$26

Hit 10 HR from Sept. 6 on in '09, but nobody predicted this. Huge jump in FB, improved ct% fueled success. Won't repeat, but how much will he regress? xBA and 2H suggest a strong follow-up. My gut takes the under on 35 HR.

Bay,Jason			AB	R	HR	RBI	SB	Avg	vL	vR	OB	Slg	OPS	bb%	ct%	h%	Eye	xBA	G	L	F	PX	hr/f	Spd	SBO	RC/G	RAR	BPV	R$
Pos	7	06 PIT	570	101	35	109	11	286	304	280	394	532	926	15	73	34	0.65	257	41	15	44	155	19%	95	7%	7.43	35.0	75	$27
Age/B	32 Right	07 PIT	538	78	21	84	4	247	227	254	322	418	740	10	74	30	0.42	237	38	17	45	114	12%	95	3%	4.68	-10.8	37	$14
Ht/Wt	74 205	08 2TM	577	111	31	101	10	286	252	296	374	522	896	12	76	33	0.59	266	38	17	46	154	15%	127	6%	6.80	26.9	93	$27
Health	C	09 BOS	531	103	36	119	13	267	292	257	378	537	914	15	69	32	0.58	260	33	18	49	179	20%	91	10%	7.38	36.4	81	$27
PT/Exp	A	10 NYM	348	48	6	47	10	259	259	258	342	402	744	11	74	33	0.48	236	36	19	46	106	5%	141	10%	4.97	-1.0	47	$11
Consist	C	1st Half	290	46	6	41	10	276			362	445	807	12	75	35	0.54	250	36	19	45	122	6%	142	11%	5.83	6.3	67	$12
LIMA Plan	C+	2nd Half	58	2	0	6	0	172			238	190	428	8	67	26	0.26	166	36	21	44	19	0%	91	0%	0.27	-9.0	-70	($1)
Rand Var	0	11 Proj	464	63	15	74	8	265			350	422	772	12	71	34	0.46	227	36	18	46	112	10%	109	6%	5.29	0.2	33	$16

Concussion in July put him out for rest of year. Before that, it looked like ugly '07 season. He still hit fly balls, but not very far, as shown by hr/f. Should be better, but it all depends upon recovery.

Beckham,Gordon			AB	R	HR	RBI	SB	Avg	vL	vR	OB	Slg	OPS	bb%	ct%	h%	Eye	xBA	G	L	F	PX	hr/f	Spd	SBO	RC/G	RAR	BPV	R$
Pos	4	06	0	0	0	0	0	0							0			0											
Age/B	24 Right	07	0	0	0	0	0	0							0			0											
Ht/Wt	72 190	08	0	0	0	0	0	0							0			0											
Health	A	09 CHW	* 553	83	18	85	9	278	318	250	342	467	809	9	84	30	0.61	277	40	17	43	121	9%	76	9%	5.55	9.7	76	$19
PT/Exp	B	10 CHW	444	58	9	49	4	252	224	261	310	378	688	8	79	30	0.40	257	46	17	37	92	7%	92	9%	3.99	-6.3	36	$10
Consist	D	1st Half	257	31	2	20	4	206			264	280	544	7	80	25	0.39	236	49	16	35	57	3%	98	12%	2.21	-18.3	12	$2
LIMA Plan	C+	2nd Half	187	27	7	29	0	316			373	513	886	8	78	37	0.41	285	41	19	40	141	12%	92	6%	6.49	10.4	71	$8
Rand Var	0	11 Proj	514	73	17	69	5	272			332	451	783	8	81	31	0.47	276	43	17	40	121	8%	84	9%	5.18	8.5	64	$16

Huge disappointment in 1H, but prior to suffering bruised hand, 2H showed his potential. Sure, the inflated hit rate helped, but there is a lot to like here. Can't completely discount 1H, but... UP: .290 BA, 25 HR

Belliard,Ronnie			AB	R	HR	RBI	SB	Avg	vL	vR	OB	Slg	OPS	bb%	ct%	h%	Eye	xBA	G	L	F	PX	hr/f	Spd	SBO	RC/G	RAR	BPV	R$
Pos	4	06 2TM	544	63	13	67	2	272	220	295	317	403	720	6	85	30	0.44	258	46	19	35	81	8%	57	4%	4.31	-0.7	37	$12
Age/B	36 Right	07 WAS	511	57	11	58	3	290	329	275	334	427	761	6	86	32	0.47	266	44	17	39	89	6%	72	2%	4.83	1.8	51	$13
Ht/Wt	70 212	08 WAS	296	37	11	46	3	287	307	279	366	473	839	11	80	33	0.64	281	42	23	35	125	13%	49	6%	6.01	10.4	61	$11
Health	B	09 2NL	264	39	10	39	3	277	282	275	327	451	778	7	79	32	0.36	266	42	22	36	114	13%	70	4%	5.00	3.5	44	$10
PT/Exp	D	10 LA	162	24	2	19	2	216	167	250	294	327	622	10	78	26	0.51	247	40	20	40	86	4%	72	10%	3.30	-7.7	26	$3
Consist	C	1st Half	102	15	2	14	1	235			328	382	710	12	81	27	0.74	269	39	20	40	104	6%	76	11%	4.56	-0.8	58	$2
LIMA Plan	F	2nd Half	60	9	0	5	1	183			234	233	468	6	73	25	0.25	210	42	20	38	51	0%	63	8%	1.02	-7.3	-32	$0
Rand Var	+5	11 Proj	128	18	3	16	2	242			306	368	674	8	79	29	0.43	252	42	21	37	93	7%	58	7%	3.83	-3.4	25	$3

Traded contact for increased power in '08-09. Unfortunately, didn't do either well in 2010, nor could he sustain success vs LH. He'll likely find part-time gig somewhere, but at his age, any rebound will be minimal.

BRIAN RUDD

Bell,Josh

Bell,Josh			AB	R	HR	RBI	SB	Avg	vL	vR	OB	Slg	OPS	bb%	ct%	h%	Eye	xBA	G	L	F	PX	hr/f	Spd	SBO	RC/G	RAR	BPV	R$
Pos	5	06	0	0	0	0	0	0							0			0											
Age/B	24 Both	07	0	0	0	0	0	0							0			0											
Ht/Wt	75 235	08	0	0	0	0	0	0							0			0											
Health	A	09 aa	448	65	22	76	3	297			379	525	903	12	79	33	0.63	0				148		66	6%	6.82	24.0	80	$19
PT/Exp	F	10 BAL	* 475	49	15	52	2	239	217	212	269	388	657	4	76	29	0.17	271	57	17	26	110	16%	75	9%	3.32	-21.7	23	$9
Consist	F	1st Half	286	30	9	35	2	240			275	404	679	5	79	28	0.23	0				120		64	9%	3.68	-10.0	42	$6
LIMA Plan	D	2nd Half	189	19	6	17	0	237			260	363	623	3	70	31	0.11	243	57	17	26	93	17%	87	8%	2.80	-11.7	-10	$3
Rand Var	+2	11 Proj	307	37	9	40	1	254			305	404	710	7	76	31	0.31	267	57	17	26	108	15%	72	7%	4.16	-6.0	28	$7

3-12-.214 in 159 AB at BAL. Wrote the book on how NOT to impress the new manager -- 1% bb%, 67% ct% in majors. 2009 hints he'll get a shot to pen another chapter, but likely not before more AAA seasoning.

Beltran,Carlos

Beltran,Carlos			AB	R	HR	RBI	SB	Avg	vL	vR	OB	Slg	OPS	bb%	ct%	h%	Eye	xBA	G	L	F	PX	hr/f	Spd	SBO	RC/G	RAR	BPV	R$
Pos	8	06 NYM	510	127	41	116	18	275	247	288	388	594	983	16	81	27	0.96	305	37	17	47	186	21%	76	14%	7.87	50.2	127	$31
Age/B	33 Both	07 NYM	554	93	33	112	23	276	304	265	356	525	882	11	80	29	0.62	291	38	19	43	150	17%	75	16%	6.44	30.1	87	$28
Ht/Wt	73 199	08 NYM	606	116	27	112	25	284	326	266	378	500	878	13	84	30	0.96	300	45	22	33	131	16%	92	15%	6.57	31.4	97	$32
Health	F	09 NYM	308	50	10	48	11	325	326	324	414	500	914	13	86	35	1.09	289	45	20	35	112	11%	101	11%	7.05	19.0	92	$17
PT/Exp	C	10 NYM	220	21	7	27	3	255	292	244	344	427	771	12	82	28	0.77	275	42	19	39	109	10%	91	6%	5.25	2.3	69	$6
Consist	C	1st Half	0	0	0	0	0	0																					
LIMA Plan	B	2nd Half	220	21	7	27	3	255			344	427	771	12	82	28	0.77	275	42	19	39	109	10%	91	6%	5.25	2.3	69	$6
Rand Var	+3	11 Proj	401	64	18	67	9	282			374	490	864	13	83	30	0.86	292	42	20	38	130	14%	88	8%	6.37	18.0	90	$18

A 5-HR, .964-OPS September clouded by (more) right knee pain in the season's final week. Health, skills trend and contract-year pressure in NYC together breed caution. Spd number still solid, but SB value waning.

Beltre,Adrian

Beltre,Adrian			AB	R	HR	RBI	SB	Avg	vL	vR	OB	Slg	OPS	bb%	ct%	h%	Eye	xBA	G	L	F	PX	hr/f	Spd	SBO	RC/G	RAR	BPV	R$
Pos	5	06 SEA	620	88	25	89	11	268	280	264	319	465	784	7	81	30	0.40	270	37	21	42	121	12%	66	11%	5.07	1.1	57	$19
Age/B	32 Right	07 SEA	595	87	26	99	14	276	280	274	319	482	801	6	83	30	0.37	288	44	17	39	132	13%	63	12%	5.21	5.7	69	$23
Ht/Wt	71 222	08 SEA	556	74	25	77	8	266	338	240	327	457	784	8	84	28	0.56	283	40	22	39	116	14%	52	7%	5.09	3.4	62	$18
Health	C	09 SEA	449	54	8	44	13	265	298	253	295	379	673	4	84	30	0.26	247	46	16	38	76	6%	71	15%	3.64	-13.5	26	$11
PT/Exp	A	10 BOS	589	84	28	102	2	321	328	318	364	553	918	6	86	34	0.49	318	40	18	42	149	14%	43	2%	6.57	27.4	91	$29
Consist	F	1st Half	302	40	12	53	1	341			378	546	924	6	84	38	0.37	315	41	23	36	137	13%	51	2%	6.65	14.2	73	$15
LIMA Plan	C	2nd Half	287	44	16	49	1	300			350	561	910	7	89	29	0.67	323	40	15	45	160	14%	41	2%	6.51	13.3	111	$14
Rand Var	-2	11 Proj	530	73	21	78	4	291			334	485	819	6	85	31	0.44	290	42	18	40	123	12%	53	4%	5.43	9.2	68	$19

Impressive rebound with skills support. Solving RHP, 2H gains in ct% and FB% raise possiblity of a 30-HR future. Avoided DL, but nagging injuries (hamstrings, ankle, wrist) and Health grade serve as a risk reminder.

Berkman,Lance

Berkman,Lance			AB	R	HR	RBI	SB	Avg	vL	vR	OB	Slg	OPS	bb%	ct%	h%	Eye	xBA	G	L	F	PX	hr/f	Spd	SBO	RC/G	RAR	BPV	R$
Pos	30	06 HOU	536	95	45	136	3	315	266	335	421	621	1042	15	80	32	0.92	302	39	19	42	173	25%	52	3%	8.58	37.4	107	$32
Age/B	35 Both	07 HOU	561	95	34	102	7	278	265	282	382	510	891	14	78	30	0.75	280	44	18	38	139	21%	63	5%	6.75	9.9	72	$24
Ht/Wt	73 220	08 HOU	554	114	29	106	18	312	276	327	417	567	983	15	81	35	0.92	298	43	18	39	163	17%	80	11%	8.03	34.7	109	$33
Health	B	09 HOU	460	73	25	80	7	274	231	291	400	509	909	17	79	30	0.99	283	43	18	39	153	18%	58	7%	7.19	9.0	92	$20
PT/Exp	A	10 2TM	404	48	14	58	3	248	171	267	368	413	781	16	79	28	0.91	267	48	16	36	114	12%	58	4%	5.54	-6.2	59	$11
Consist	C	1st Half	239	27	8	37	3	243			356	414	770	15	76	29	0.74	269	45	19	36	124	12%	63	5%	5.36	-4.9	55	$7
LIMA Plan	B	2nd Half	165	21	6	21	0	255			385	412	797	17	83	27	1.25	264	51	12	36	102	12%	58	2%	5.82	-1.1	68	$4
Rand Var	+4	11 Proj	410	61	19	67	5	271			390	474	864	16	80	30	0.97	278	46	17	38	132	15%	61	5%	6.57	7.4	78	$16

Anything left in this cat?
PRO: bb%/ct% still strong; 2010 xBA doesn't fully support BA dip.
CON: Power trends sliding, injuries mounting, borderline useless vs. LHP.
Might be on his eighth life.

Bernadina,Roger

Bernadina,Roger			AB	R	HR	RBI	SB	Avg	vL	vR	OB	Slg	OPS	bb%	ct%	h%	Eye	xBA	G	L	F	PX	hr/f	Spd	SBO	RC/G	RAR	BPV	R$
Pos	789	06	0	0	0	0	0	0							0			0											
Age/B	26 Left	07 a/a	413	56	5	33	35	232			300	317	617	9	80	28	0.49	0				58		115	45%	3.19	-26.3	22	$12
Ht/Wt	74 198	08 WAS	* 533	74	7	45	37	278			334	388	722	8	79	34	0.41	0				72		125	33%	4.45	-15.1	30	$21
Health	F	09 WAS	4	1	0	0	1	250			400	500	900	20	75	33	1.00	0				244		98	100%	7.83	0.3	167	$0
PT/Exp	D	10 WAS	* 475	58	13	53	22	255	250	246	313	395	707	8	80	30	0.41	248	47	13	39	92	9%	105	20%	4.19	-12.4	40	$17
Consist	F	1st Half	229	22	7	30	13	293			347	450	797	8	83	33	0.50	275	51	15	34	95	11%	121	25%	5.28	1.4	63	$11
LIMA Plan	C	2nd Half	246	36	6	23	9	221			281	344	625	8	76	27	0.35	226	44	13	43	88	7%	92	15%	3.11	-14.7	19	$6
Rand Var	0	11 Proj	419	56	12	40	25	258			316	400	716	8	79	30	0.41	241	47	13	40	91	9%	112	29%	4.31	-12.0	42	$16

11-47-.246 w/ 16 SB in 414 AB at WAS. Waiver-wire find surprised w/ HR/SB combo, but low LD% and HH% (34%) will hinder BA for now. 89% success rate points to SB upside if given opps. A fanalytic 4th outfielder.

Betancourt,Yuniesky

Betancourt,Yuniesky			AB	R	HR	RBI	SB	Avg	vL	vR	OB	Slg	OPS	bb%	ct%	h%	Eye	xBA	G	L	F	PX	hr/f	Spd	SBO	RC/G	RAR	BPV	R$
Pos	6	06 SEA	558	68	8	47	11	289	240	303	310	403	713	3	90	31	0.31	265	46	18	36	67	4%	117	14%	4.16	-3.9	58	$13
Age/B	29 Right	07 SEA	536	72	9	67	5	289	333	277	309	418	726	3	91	30	0.31	286	43	19	38	84	5%	79	7%	4.31	0.3	62	$14
Ht/Wt	70 195	08 SEA	559	66	7	51	4	279	273	281	300	392	692	3	92	29	0.40	272	40	20	40	72	3%	93	6%	4.01	-5.1	64	$12
Health	A	09 2AL	470	40	6	49	3	245	283	231	277	351	628	4	91	26	0.48	252	42	17	41	60	3%	102	6%	3.36	-15.4	51	$6
PT/Exp	B	10 KC	556	60	16	78	2	259	289	250	288	405	693	4	88	27	0.36	275	40	18	42	90	8%	64	4%	3.92	-0.7	55	$14
Consist	B	1st Half	278	36	5	33	0	255			281	374	655	3	86	28	0.26	270	42	19	39	81	5%	72	2%	3.46	-4.1	41	$6
LIMA Plan	C	2nd Half	278	24	11	45	2	263			296	435	731	4	91	26	0.50	282	38	16	46	100	10%	62	7%	4.37	3.3	72	$8
Rand Var	+1	11 Proj	558	58	12	68	4	262			290	393	682	4	90	27	0.40	269	41	18	41	79	6%	82	6%	3.86	-5.1	57	$12

BA should rebound some, but if ct% continues to fall, all bets are off. Fluky 2H hr/f rate responsible for power surge; a repeat is unlikely. And OBP leaguers should cross him off your list now. DN: 2009

Betemit,Wilson

Betemit,Wilson			AB	R	HR	RBI	SB	Avg	vL	vR	OB	Slg	OPS	bb%	ct%	h%	Eye	xBA	G	L	F	PX	hr/f	Spd	SBO	RC/G	RAR	BPV	R$
Pos	5	06 2NL	373	49	18	53	3	263	189	281	328	469	797	9	73	32	0.35	260	42	21	37	139	18%	66	4%	5.40	-1.0	41	$11
Age/B	29 Both	07 2TM	240	33	14	50	0	229	239	227	335	454	789	14	66	28	0.46	252	42	18	40	167	22%	66	0%	5.64	2.9	46	$7
Ht/Wt	75 230	08 NYY	189	24	6	25	0	265	233	274	287	429	716	3	70	35	0.11	256	43	25	33	129	14%	76	3%	4.17	-3.9	16	$5
Health	A	09 CHW	* 306	32	10	43	2	206			259	372	631	7	72	25	0.26	240	47	16	38	121	12%	53	3%	3.13	-14.7	16	$4
PT/Exp	D	10 KC	* 389	42	14	54	1	272	312	291	351	448	799	11	76	33	0.51	257	40	15	45	129	10%	72	2%	5.54	7.9	52	$12
Consist	D	1st Half	153	15	4	18	1	248			315	405	721	9	82	28	0.54	236	33	10	57	109	6%	92	5%	4.48	-1.6	61	$3
LIMA Plan	D	2nd Half	236	27	10	36	0	287			373	476	850	12	72	36	0.50	258	42	16	43	143	14%	63	-0%	6.33	9.9	49	$9
Rand Var	-1	11 Proj	311	35	11	44	1	251			316	425	741	9	73	31	0.36	253	41	18	41	128	12%	65	2%	4.67	-1.3	35	$8

13-43-.297 in 276 AB at KC. The issue is not the individual skills... ~10% bb%, decent ct%, solid FB and hr/f%. It's whether they show up together, as in 2010. History doubts a repeat, and xBA is non-committal.

Blake,Casey

Blake,Casey			AB	R	HR	RBI	SB	Avg	vL	vR	OB	Slg	OPS	bb%	ct%	h%	Eye	xBA	G	L	F	PX	hr/f	Spd	SBO	RC/G	RAR	BPV	R$
Pos	5	06 CLE	401	63	19	68	6	282	272	286	354	479	833	10	77	33	0.48	267	40	23	37	124	17%	86	5%	5.84	9.4	54	$15
Age/B	37 Right	07 CLE	588	81	18	78	4	270	256	276	332	437	769	8	79	32	0.44	259	39	18	43	113	9%	85	6%	5.01	2.4	51	$16
Ht/Wt	74 204	08 2TM	536	71	21	81	3	274	287	270	335	463	798	8	78	32	0.41	267	38	22	40	129	13%	69	2%	5.35	3.4	53	$17
Health	A	09 LA	485	84	18	79	3	280	320	270	363	468	831	11	76	34	0.54	266	42	23	35	124	14%	100	5%	5.99	11.8	58	$19
PT/Exp	A	10 LA	509	56	17	64	0	248	314	222	312	407	719	9	73	31	0.35	255	43	20	37	119	12%	70	3%	4.39	-7.8	27	$12
Consist	C	1st Half	253	27	8	33	0	261			330	423	753	9	77	31	0.44	266	41	21	38	116	11%	78	4%	4.85	-0.4	44	$7
LIMA Plan	C	2nd Half	256	29	9	31	0	234			295	391	686	8	69	30	0.28	244	45	20	36	122	14%	65	2%	3.93	-7.5	11	$5
Rand Var	+1	11 Proj	463	57	15	60	0	251			320	411	731	9	75	31	0.40	255	42	21	37	115	13%	78	2%	4.58	-7.1	34	$11

Read the signs:
- 3-yr ct% slide picking up pace
- hitting more GB, less FB
- platoon splits widening
- no longer replacement level
- all the above worsened in 2H

At 38, all that's left is a bit of pop.

Blanco,Andres

Blanco,Andres			AB	R	HR	RBI	SB	Avg	vL	vR	OB	Slg	OPS	bb%	ct%	h%	Eye	xBA	G	L	F	PX	hr/f	Spd	SBO	RC/G	RAR	BPV	R$
Pos	4	06 aaa	283	28	2	19	5	234			284	312	596	7	88	26	0.60	0				45		108	13%	3.06	-11.2	37	$2
Age/B	26 Both	07 aaa	97	8	0	8	0	186			225	206	432	5	87	21	0.38	0				17		95	0%	1.01	-10.3	0	($1)
Ht/Wt	70 190	08 aaa	298	22	1	27	7	242			268	283	551	3	92	26	0.42	0				27		90	14%	2.48	-21.2	24	$4
Health	C	09 CHC	* 353	39	7	36	5	264	250	253	305	391	696	6	89	28	0.54	283	53	19	28	83	8%	59	9%	4.12	-4.3	53	$8
PT/Exp	F	10 TEX	166	17	0	13	0	277	220	302	322	349	671	6	86	32	0.46	264	44	22	34	58	0%	95	4%	3.87	-2.8	32	$3
Consist	B	1st Half	57	4	0	1	0	211			274	228	502	8	88	24	0.71	223	40	21	40	15	0%	111	6%	2.04	-4.4	15	($0)
LIMA Plan	F	2nd Half	109	13	0	12	0	312			348	413	761	5	84	37	0.35	284	46	23	31	82	0%	85	3%	4.87	1.2	41	$3
Rand Var	-4	11 Proj	132	13	1	11	1	258			300	353	653	6	88	29	0.49	271	45	21	34	64	3%	93	8%	3.64	-3.7	43	$2

With so few AB, the passable BA hardly matters. There's no power here, and though he's had a couple of league-average speed seasons, SBO has not been cooperative. Move along.

BRENT HERSHEY

Blanco,Gregor			AB	R	HR	RBI	SB	Avg	vL	vR	OB	Slg	OPS	bb%	ct%	h%	Eye	xBA	G	L	F	PX	hr/f	Spd	SBO	RC/G	RAR	BPV	R$
Pos	8	06 a/a	520	84	0	27	30	281			390	344	734	15	79	35	0.87	0				51		128	22%	5.07	8.0	29	$15
Age/B	27 Left	07 aaa	464	73	3	31	21	267			346	341	687	11	83	32	0.72	0				49		142	26%	4.23	-4.2	38	$12
Ht/Wt	71 170	08 ATL	430	52	1	38	13	251	248	252	361	309	670	15	77	32	0.75	233	50	24	26	43	1%	120	11%	4.15	-7.5	10	$8
Health	A	09 aaa	333	42	2	24	8	195			280	240	520	11	81	23	0.63	0				31		106	11%	2.09	-27.6	5	$2
PT/Exp	D	10 2TM	* 391	51	2	22	18	263	179	315	343	338	681	11	81	32	0.62	258	54	20	26	54	2%	134	18%	4.13	-11.2	30	$11
Consist	F	1st Half	182	26	1	10	7	269			354	335	690	12	82	32	0.73	266	45	27	27	49	2%	123	14%	4.29	-4.3	29	$5
LIMA Plan	D	2nd Half	209	25	1	12	11	258			333	340	673	10	79	32	0.54	256	57	18	26	59	2%	134	22%	3.99	-6.9	27	$6
Rand Var	-1	11 Proj	**367**	**48**	**1**	**24**	**14**	**245**			**332**	**309**	**641**	**12**	**80**	**30**	**0.66**	**249**	**52**	**22**	**26**	**46**	**2%**	**124**	**16%**	**3.65**	**-14.2**	**20**	**$7**

1-14-.283-11 SB in 237 AB at ATL/KC. Owns the tools for a breakout: Spd, GB%, bb%, all point to emerging SB source. 2H SBO shows he got green light in KC. Healthy bb% means he's an OBP league asset, too.

Blanco,Henry			AB	R	HR	RBI	SB	Avg	vL	vR	OB	Slg	OPS	bb%	ct%	h%	Eye	xBA	G	L	F	PX	hr/f	Spd	SBO	RC/G	RAR	BPV	R$
Pos	2	06 CHC	241	23	6	37	0	266	325	236	306	419	725	5	84	29	0.37	273	38	24	38	93	8%	51	0%	4.35	0.1	40	$5
Age/B	39 Right	07 CHC	54	3	0	4	0	167	50	235	196	222	419	4	78	21	0.17	189	29	17	55	51	0%	60	0%	0.44	-7.0	-21	($1)
Ht/Wt	71 220	08 CHC	120	15	3	12	0	292	316	270	325	392	717	5	82	34	0.27	221	42	17	42	61	7%	85	0%	4.08	-0.4	12	$3
Health	C	09 SD	204	21	6	16	0	235	322	200	322	382	704	11	75	28	0.52	232	41	16	43	107	9%	54	0%	4.31	0.3	28	$3
PT/Exp	F	10 NYM	130	10	2	8	1	215	167	239	277	300	577	8	80	25	0.42	207	34	15	51	61	4%	62	3%	2.59	-7.6	5	$1
Consist	B	1st Half	74	9	2	7	1	284			354	419	773	10	78	34	0.50	229	25	19	56	97	6%	66	4%	5.11	1.3	32	$2
LIMA Plan	F	2nd Half	56	1	0	1	0	125			169	143	312	5	82	15	0.30	175	45	11	45	16	0%	63	0%	-0.62	-9.8	-27	($2)
Rand Var	+1	11 Proj	**102**	**9**	**2**	**8**	**0**	**225**			**284**	**320**	**604**	**8**	**80**	**27**	**0.41**	**214**	**38**	**15**	**46**	**66**	**5%**	**63**	**1%**	**2.90**	**-4.6**	**8**	**$1**

Clearly, it was the stress of maintaining a .284 BA over a 74-AB workload at age 38 in the first half that wore him down, leading to the 2nd half disaster. They just don't make players as resilient as they used to.

Blanks,Kyle			AB	R	HR	RBI	SB	Avg	vL	vR	OB	Slg	OPS	bb%	ct%	h%	Eye	xBA	G	L	F	PX	hr/f	Spd	SBO	RC/G	RAR	BPV	R$
Pos	7	06	0	0	0	0	0	0							0			0											
Age/B	24 Right	07	0	0	0	0	0	0							0			0											
Ht/Wt	78 285	08 aa	492	65	16	92	4	287			344	439	783	8	83	32	0.52	0				90		72	6%	5.11	-0.3	45	$18
Health	F	09 SD	* 381	51	19	52	1	241	220	262	328	436	764	11	71	29	0.45	224	37	13	51	134	14%	50	2%	5.07	-5.6	33	$11
PT/Exp	F	10 SD	102	14	3	15	1	157	174	152	265	324	588	13	55	25	0.33	203	41	14	45	164	12%	71	5%	3.03	-6.9	-0	$1
Consist	C	1st Half	102	14	3	15	1	157			265	324	588	13	55	25	0.33	203	41	14	45	164	12%	71	5%	3.03	-6.9	-0	$1
LIMA Plan	D+	2nd Half	0	0	0	0	0	0																					
Rand Var	+5	11 Proj	**393**	**53**	**15**	**63**	**3**	**232**			**313**	**406**	**719**	**11**	**70**	**29**	**0.40**	**227**	**40**	**14**	**46**	**125**	**12%**	**65**	**5%**	**4.49**	**-9.2**	**24**	**$10**

3-15-.157 in 102 AB at SD. PRO: Small sample PX, FB%, hr/f, bb% demonstrate power. CON: horrible ct%, xBA show BA downside. Right age for skills growth, but PETCO curbs our enthusiasm.

Bloomquist,Willie			AB	R	HR	RBI	SB	Avg	vL	vR	OB	Slg	OPS	bb%	ct%	h%	Eye	xBA	G	L	F	PX	hr/f	Spd	SBO	RC/G	RAR	BPV	R$
Pos	9	06 SEA	251	36	1	15	16	247	253	243	313	299	612	9	84	29	0.60	218	46	17	37	32	1%	130	25%	3.22	-18.4	21	$6
Age/B	33 Right	07 SEA	173	28	2	13	7	277	238	290	317	329	646	5	80	34	0.29	246	61	19	20	35	7%	97	23%	3.28	-11.3	-11	$5
Ht/Wt	71 195	08 SEA	165	32	0	9	14	279	351	220	374	285	659	13	82	34	0.86	226	56	20	24	5	0%	137	24%	3.97	-6.7	3	$7
Health	B	09 KC	434	52	4	29	25	265	248	275	308	355	663	6	83	31	0.37	246	46	21	33	50	3%	162	26%	3.65	-21.4	35	$12
PT/Exp	D	10 2TM	187	31	3	17	8	267	289	250	301	380	681	5	85	30	0.32	271	44	21	35	77	5%	83	29%	3.80	-7.5	38	$7
Consist	A	1st Half	74	18	2	10	5	243			291	392	683	6	85	26	0.45	278	55	14	31	90	10%	89	47%	3.90	-2.9	54	$4
LIMA Plan	F	2nd Half	113	13	1	7	3	283			308	372	679	3	85	33	0.24	268	38	25	38	69	3%	80	18%	3.72	-4.6	27	$3
Rand Var	+1	11 Proj	**196**	**31**	**2**	**15**	**11**	**270**			**317**	**360**	**678**	**6**	**84**	**31**	**0.43**	**254**	**47**	**20**	**32**	**57**	**4%**	**116**	**27%**	**3.86**	**-7.5**	**31**	**$7**

Poster boy for replacement level utility guy. Played all over (except C and P) in 2010. SB is his only value, but Spd and 2H SBO cast doubt there, too. Never exhibited BA, OBP, or pop -- don't expect it at age 33.

Blum,Geoff			AB	R	HR	RBI	SB	Avg	vL	vR	OB	Slg	OPS	bb%	ct%	h%	Eye	xBA	G	L	F	PX	hr/f	Spd	SBO	RC/G	RAR	BPV	R$
Pos	6	06 SD	276	27	4	34	0	254	167	267	297	366	663	6	82	30	0.33	245	36	23	41	77	4%	80	2%	3.62	-6.0	25	$4
Age/B	37 Both	07 SD	330	34	5	33	0	252	238	256	318	367	684	9	84	29	0.62	251	36	20	44	79	4%	81	0%	4.10	-3.4	44	$4
Ht/Wt	75 205	08 HOU	325	36	14	53	1	240	229	242	286	418	705	6	83	25	0.39	261	36	20	44	105	12%	80	4%	4.02	-5.9	56	$8
Health	B	09 HOU	381	34	10	49	0	247	345	239	307	367	674	8	84	27	0.54	233	36	18	46	74	7%	69	1%	3.83	-9.3	34	$7
PT/Exp	D	10 HOU	202	22	2	22	0	267	138	289	318	356	674	7	84	31	0.45	256	44	21	35	64	3%	78	0%	3.86	-3.3	25	$4
Consist	A	1st Half	137	15	0	14	0	241			307	307	613	9	88	28	0.76	256	48	18	33	50	0%	80	0%	3.41	-4.1	34	$2
LIMA Plan	F	2nd Half	65	7	2	8	0	323			343	462	805	3	75	40	0.13	257	35	27	39	99	11%	81	0%	5.14	1.2	13	$3
Rand Var	-1	11 Proj	**169**	**17**	**4**	**21**	**0**	**266**			**312**	**384**	**696**	**6**	**82**	**31**	**0.37**	**249**	**38**	**21**	**41**	**79**	**7%**	**68**	**1%**	**3.98**	**-2.6**	**26**	**$4**

Willie Bloomquist without the speed. Utility IF with fading power (see PX, Slg, HR, fb%) and age trending in the wrong direction. When the best skill is consistent ct%, but xBA can't break .260, we've got issues.

Boesch,Brennan			AB	R	HR	RBI	SB	Avg	vL	vR	OB	Slg	OPS	bb%	ct%	h%	Eye	xBA	G	L	F	PX	hr/f	Spd	SBO	RC/G	RAR	BPV	R$
Pos	79	06	0	0	0	0	0	0							0			0											
Age/B	25 Left	07	0	0	0	0	0	0							0			0											
Ht/Wt	78 210	08	0	0	0	0	0	0							0			0											
Health	A	09 aa	527	71	23	75	9	242			278	439	717	5	80	26	0.24	0				118		113	10%	4.09	-18.8	58	$15
PT/Exp	F	10 DET	* 522	54	17	80	9	264	337	233	320	431	751	8	78	31	0.38	264	45	15	40	115	10%	96	8%	4.73	-2.3	51	$17
Consist	B	1st Half	281	33	15	59	4	342			383	598	981	6	79	39	0.32	305	42	17	41	168	16%	116	5%	7.50	19.0	99	$16
LIMA Plan	D	2nd Half	241	21	2	21	5	173			248	236	484	9	78	22	0.44	214	48	14	38	52	3%	78	13%	1.44	-27.1	-4	$0
Rand Var	0	11 Proj	**327**	**37**	**8**	**46**	**6**	**242**			**292**	**384**	**676**	**7**	**79**	**28**	**0.33**	**247**	**46**	**15**	**39**	**95**	**8%**	**105**	**9%**	**3.75**	**-11.5**	**37**	**$8**

14-67-.256 in 464 AB at DET. Three most important things in 2010: 1H/2H splits, 1H/2H splits, 1H/2H splits.Scary truth... a rookie's 2H is the baseline going into next year. Could be the 21st century Kevin Maas.

Bonifacio,Emilio			AB	R	HR	RBI	SB	Avg	vL	vR	OB	Slg	OPS	bb%	ct%	h%	Eye	xBA	G	L	F	PX	hr/f	Spd	SBO	RC/G	RAR	BPV	R$
Pos	8	06	0	0	0	0	0	0							0			0											
Age/B	25 Both	07 aa	574	72	2	36	34	265			308	326	634	6	84	31	0.40	283	63	21	16	42	3%	134	31%	3.34	-20.4	26	$15
Ht/Wt	71 195	08 2NL	* 567	76	1	40	24	264	163	270	311	343	653	6	82	32	0.37	258	55	21	23	53	1%	138	25%	3.59	-19.5	26	$14
Health	A	09 FLA	461	72	1	27	21	252	315	223	303	308	611	7	79	32	0.36	230	53	19	28	37	1%	152	23%	3.02	-23.7	9	$11
PT/Exp	C	10 FLA	* 344	43	0	18	18	243	348	231	302	308	611	8	80	30	0.42	254	52	22	26	48	0%	152	23%	3.11	-18.5	20	$8
Consist	A	1st Half	184	14	0	9	9	223			270	283	553	6	82	27	0.36	281	58	25	17	45	0%	121	32%	2.37	-14.6	15	$2
LIMA Plan	D	2nd Half	160	29	0	9	9	267			338	337	675	10	77	35	0.47	246	51	22	27	51	0%	156	16%	4.01	-4.0	18	$5
Rand Var	+1	11 Proj	**259**	**37**	**0**	**15**	**13**	**255**			**310**	**325**	**635**	**7**	**80**	**32**	**0.40**	**248**	**53**	**21**	**27**	**48**	**1%**	**144**	**23%**	**3.39**	**-10.8**	**19**	**$7**

0-10-.261-12 SB in 180 AB at FLA. Speed is elite, defensive versatility will earn him ABs. But OBP is intolerable with no signs of growth, so SB surge unlikely. FLA told him to learn to bunt for hits, which might help a bit.

Borbon,Julio			AB	R	HR	RBI	SB	Avg	vL	vR	OB	Slg	OPS	bb%	ct%	h%	Eye	xBA	G	L	F	PX	hr/f	Spd	SBO	RC/G	RAR	BPV	R$
Pos	8	06	0	0	0	0	0	0							0			0											
Age/B	25 Left	07	0	0	0	0	0	0							0			0											
Ht/Wt	73 180	08 aa	255	31	4	17	13	306			335	412	746	4	90	33	0.44	0				63		123	36%	4.58	-3.5	58	$10
Health	A	09 TEX	* 564	87	6	48	39	288	125	333	337	367	704	7	89	32	0.67	269	54	19	27	43	4%	178	28%	4.28	-5.8	60	$22
PT/Exp	B	10 TEX	438	60	3	42	15	276	247	284	306	340	647	4	87	31	0.32	249	56	13	31	40	3%	139	18%	3.40	-24.5	31	$13
Consist	B	1st Half	235	33	3	24	8	285			311	383	694	4	88	32	0.31	266	54	15	31	56	5%	146	22%	3.94	-9.5	48	$8
LIMA Plan	C	2nd Half	203	27	0	18	7	266			300	291	591	5	85	31	0.33	226	58	12	30	22	0%	114	14%	2.75	-15.1	4	$5
Rand Var	-1	11 Proj	**465**	**65**	**4**	**40**	**23**	**284**			**321**	**352**	**673**	**5**	**88**	**32**	**0.45**	**253**	**56**	**14**	**30**	**42**	**3%**	**144**	**24%**	**3.79**	**-17.4**	**40**	**$15**

Speed has roto value, elite CF defense will keep him playing. PRO: Right age, strong ct%, high gb% point to OB, SB gains. CON: 2H drop in Spd and SBO, low bb%, no PX. With a bit more OB... UP: 40 SB

Bourgeois,Jason			AB	R	HR	RBI	SB	Avg	vL	vR	OB	Slg	OPS	bb%	ct%	h%	Eye	xBA	G	L	F	PX	hr/f	Spd	SBO	RC/G	RAR	BPV	R$
Pos	78	06 aa	411	59	4	34	21	247			307	347	653	8	83	29	0.51	0				64		106	25%	3.68	-19.0	33	$10
Age/B	29 Right	07 a/a	500	67	10	48	33	277			332	399	731	8	87	30	0.62	0				75		103	30%	4.58	-9.0	55	$18
Ht/Wt	69 190	08 aaa	510	67	8	39	24	245			284	343	627	5	88	27	0.45	0				59		101	29%	3.26	-29.1	41	$13
Health	A	09 aaa	424	44	2	30	26	253			282	316	598	4	91	27	0.47	0				39		103	32%	3.02	-28.7	37	$11
PT/Exp	D	10 HOU	* 358	42	4	22	24	252	250	190	305	331	636	7	89	28	0.66	251	45	18	37	49	3%	102	35%	3.52	-16.8	40	$11
Consist	A	1st Half	152	27	4	20	15	447			509	612	1121	11	82	53	0.68	262	43	14	43	109	8%	94	31%	9.53	15.9	66	$15
LIMA Plan	F	2nd Half	206	15	-0	2	9	109			142	123	265	4	94	12	0.62	236	45	19	36	11	-1%	107	46%	-0.36	-39.8	25	($4)
Rand Var	0	11 Proj	**165**	**19**	**1**	**11**	**10**	**248**			**292**	**323**	**615**	**6**	**89**	**27**	**0.56**	**247**	**45**	**18**	**37**	**47**	**3%**	**93**	**33%**	**3.24**	**-10.2**	**35**	**$5**

0-3-.220-12 SB in 123 AB at HOU. Certainly not baseball bourgeois - definitely proletariat. SB history looks attractive, but Spd screams average. No future beyond a replacement-level 5th OF/pinch-run role.

ANDY ANDRES

Bourjos,Peter		AB	R	HR	RBI	SB	Avg	vL	vR	OB	Slg	OPS	bb%	ct%	h%	Eye	xBA	G	L	F	PX	hr/f	Spd	SBO	RC/G	RAR	BPV	R$
Pos 8	06	0	0	0	0	0	0							0			0											
Age/B 24 Right	07	0	0	0	0	0	0							0			0											
Ht/Wt 73 180	08	0	0	0	0	0	0							0			0											
Health A	09 aa	437	65	5	46	29	268			333	384	718	9	84	31	0.63	0				67		175	33%	4.54	-1.9	64	$16
PT/Exp F	10 LAA *	595	78	15	50	29	245	182	214	273	383	655	4	84	27	0.24	256	51	10	39	81	8%	173	31%	3.40	-34.7	63	$18
Consist C	1st Half	282	31	4	18	14	212			241	295	536	4	86	23	0.27	0				46		187	30%	2.09	-28.8	46	$5
LIMA Plan B	2nd Half	313	46	11	33	15	275			301	462	763	4	83	30	0.22	278	51	10	39	113	11%	155	31%	4.64	-6.3	77	$13
Rand Var 0	11 Proj	457	64	13	43	25	256			299	411	710	6	84	28	0.39	258	51	10	39	88	10%	173	33%	4.17	-12.5	72	$16

6-15-.204-10 SB in 181 AB at LAA. PRO: elite speed with hints of developing power. CON: BA/OBP woes limit short-term SB potential. Buy the speed/power skills, but expect a bumpy ride for a while.

Bourn,Michael		AB	R	HR	RBI	SB	Avg	vL	vR	OB	Slg	OPS	bb%	ct%	h%	Eye	xBA	G	L	F	PX	hr/f	Spd	SBO	RC/G	RAR	BPV	R$
Pos 8	06 a/a	470	91	5	39	42	274			345	379	724	10	81	33	0.56	0				56		216	31%	4.61	0.8	54	$20
Age/B 28 Left	07 PHI	119	29	1	6	18	277	154	312	348	378	727	10	82	33	0.62	267	58	18	24	56	4%	208	49%	4.67	0.5	59	$7
Ht/Wt 71 180	08 HOU	467	57	5	29	41	229	190	242	286	300	586	7	76	29	0.33	221	54	17	29	46	5%	167	41%	2.61	-30.9	9	$14
Health A	09 HOU	606	97	3	35	61	285	287	285	353	384	737	9	77	37	0.45	258	58	21	22	69	3%	188	38%	4.80	1.2	40	$28
PT/Exp A	10 HOU	535	84	2	38	52	265	229	276	338	346	684	10	80	33	0.54	263	59	17	23	61	2%	143	38%	4.14	-12.0	32	$23
Consist C	1st Half	296	48	1	20	25	260			334	341	676	10	79	33	0.53	266	62	17	21	66	2%	124	36%	4.03	-7.6	29	$12
LIMA Plan C+	2nd Half	239	36	1	18	27	272			343	351	695	10	80	34	0.55	257	56	18	25	54	2%	158	41%	4.26	-4.4	33	$12
Rand Var 0	11 Proj	571	90	3	38	48	266			335	353	688	9	79	33	0.49	255	58	18	24	60	3%	171	33%	4.14	-11.0	35	$22

One-trick pony returns nice value from his wheels alone. bb%, strong GB% and elite Spd suggest big SBs will continue for awhile. 2009 H% now an outlier, so set BA expectations against consistent xBA history.

Bowker,John		AB	R	HR	RBI	SB	Avg	vL	vR	OB	Slg	OPS	bb%	ct%	h%	Eye	xBA	G	L	F	PX	hr/f	Spd	SBO	RC/G	RAR	BPV	R$
Pos 9	06	0	0	0	0	0	0							0			0											
Age/B 27 Left	07 aa	522	63	16	71	2	266			308	437	745	6	83	29	0.36	0				107		116	8%	4.58	-9.4	66	$13
Ht/Wt 74 200	08 SF	326	31	10	43	1	255	152	266	296	408	704	6	77	30	0.26	252	37	25	38	99	11%	110	3%	4.01	-11.3	34	$7
Health A	09 aa	366	66	16	67	8	294			393	493	886	14	84	32	1.00	0				118		89	11%	6.71	16.7	85	$18
PT/Exp D	10 2NL *	439	48	17	53	1	237	133	228	292	413	704	7	82	26	0.42	275	48	15	37	114	13%	78	4%	4.10	-16.3	57	$10
Consist F	1st Half	179	23	8	24	1	235			275	413	689	5	79	25	0.27	281	51	18	31	116	18%	71	10%	3.73	-8.8	44	$5
LIMA Plan F	2nd Half	260	25	9	29	0	239			303	412	715	8	83	26	0.54	268	46	12	42	112	9%	92	0%	4.35	-7.6	69	$5
Rand Var +3	11 Proj	96	12	4	13	1	260			323	443	766	9	82	29	0.51	277	43	20	37	114	12%	104	7%	4.95	-0.5	68	$3

5-21-.219 in 151 AB at SF/PIT. Quad-A slugger ripped up Triple-A, then flailed (again) in majors, chances now waning. UP: One more shot to show pop in MLB and beat the Quad-A rap. DN: selling kitchen appliances.

Bradley,Milton		AB	R	HR	RBI	SB	Avg	vL	vR	OB	Slg	OPS	bb%	ct%	h%	Eye	xBA	G	L	F	PX	hr/f	Spd	SBO	RC/G	RAR	BPV	R$
Pos 70	06 OAK	351	53	14	52	10	276	293	270	368	447	815	13	81	31	0.78	263	52	15	33	99	15%	90	10%	5.75	5.7	60	$13
Age/B 32 Both	07 2TM	209	37	13	37	5	306	304	307	396	545	941	13	80	33	0.76	286	39	19	43	141	18%	86	10%	7.25	11.8	88	$11
Ht/Wt 72 225	08 TEX	414	78	22	77	5	321	341	312	431	563	994	16	73	40	0.71	290	41	25	34	173	21%	82	5%	8.51	40.7	89	$22
Health F	09 CHC	393	61	12	40	2	257	333	231	364	397	761	14	76	31	0.69	245	47	20	33	70	9%	70	4%	5.19	-4.3	32	$10
PT/Exp C	10 SEA	244	28	8	29	8	205	235	190	287	348	635	10	69	26	0.37	224	37	18	45	107	11%	75	17%	3.29	-12.2	8	$5
Consist F	1st Half	208	24	8	28	6	212			290	370	660	10	70	26	0.37	232	35	18	47	120	12%	59	16%	3.60	-8.3	14	$5
LIMA Plan D+	2nd Half	36	4	0	1	2	167			268	222	491	12	67	25	0.42	183	48	17	35	31	0%	113	20%	1.38	-4.1	-48	$0
Rand Var +5	11 Proj	300	46	10	45	6	270			366	425	791	13	75	33	0.59	250	41	20	39	109	10%	73	8%	5.55	5.4	35	$11

It's one thing to be a clubhouse cancer when your skills are intact. It's another when your BA, xBA, OB, SLG, bb%, ct% and Eye are all in steep decline. Upside? Yes. A good bet for recovery? No.

Brantley,Michael		AB	R	HR	RBI	SB	Avg	vL	vR	OB	Slg	OPS	bb%	ct%	h%	Eye	xBA	G	L	F	PX	hr/f	Spd	SBO	RC/G	RAR	BPV	R$
Pos 8	06	0	0	0	0	0	0							0			0											
Age/B 23 Left	07 aa	187	25	0	19	15	241			338	286	624	13	88	27	1.25	0				32		123	27%	3.78	-4.3	43	$5
Ht/Wt 74 200	08 aa	420	65	3	32	22	284			349	346	696	9	95	29	1.95	0				39		111	23%	4.53	-6.2	64	$14
Health A	09 CLE *	569	76	5	41	42	255	462	267	325	325	650	9	90	28	1.00	280	47	26	27	45	4%	109	30%	3.87	-13.1	48	$17
PT/Exp C	10 CLE *	570	79	6	45	20	260	172	266	318	342	661	8	89	28	0.80	273	48	20	32	52	4%	109	17%	3.88	-24.4	50	$15
Consist A	1st Half	273	40	2	23	9	256			319	318	637	8	89	28	0.86	274	56	19	26	41	3%	107	17%	3.65	-13.7	42	$7
LIMA Plan C+	2nd Half	297	39	4	22	11	264			318	364	682	7	89	28	0.75	280	47	21	32	62	5%	115	17%	4.09	-10.7	58	$8
Rand Var +1	11 Proj	419	58	5	33	22	260			326	340	666	9	90	28	0.99	273	48	21	31	50	4%	104	22%	4.03	-13.1	48	$12

3-22-10-.246 in 297 AB at CLE. ct%, Eye, and Spd make nice building blocks, while lack of power limits his ceiling. xBA says he's a fairly low-risk SB source, but Spd suggests he lacks elite SB upside.

Branyan,Russell		AB	R	HR	RBI	SB	Avg	vL	vR	OB	Slg	OPS	bb%	ct%	h%	Eye	xBA	G	L	F	PX	hr/f	Spd	SBO	RC/G	RAR	BPV	R$
Pos 30	06 2TM	241	37	18	36	2	228	220	230	324	498	822	12	63	28	0.38	241	29	19	52	194	23%	52	3%	6.18	3.4	50	$7
Age/B 35 Left	07 2NL	163	22	10	26	1	196	158	201	314	423	737	15	58	26	0.41	214	29	18	53	178	20%	83	2%	5.25	-4.5	29	$3
Ht/Wt 75 230	08 MIL *	285	40	21	44	4	262		280	345	548	892	11	69	31	0.40	265	22	21	57	206	18%	50	6%	6.92	9.9	79	$12
Health C	09 SEA	431	64	31	76	2	251	222	267	339	520	859	12	65	31	0.39	250	33	17	50	188	22%	60	2%	6.63	11.6	56	$16
PT/Exp C	10 2AL	376	47	25	57	1	237	190	254	320	487	807	11	65	29	0.35	252	35	13	52	193	19%	54	1%	5.83	0.6	55	$12
Consist B	1st Half	191	28	12	31	0	267			327	503	830	8	71	31	0.31	262	36	15	49	166	18%	70	0%	5.78	0.0	57	$8
LIMA Plan C	2nd Half	185	19	13	26	1	205			313	470	783	14	59	26	0.38	243	33	11	56	227	21%	46	2%	5.91	0.8	60	$5
Rand Var +1	11 Proj	313	42	22	49	2	240			329	498	826	12	65	30	0.38	250	32	15	53	195	20%	53	2%	6.18	5.1	55	$11

Look up "three true outcomes" in dictionary and you will find his picture. PX is intact and top-of-the-line, but so are his struggles with BA and ct%. Useful end-game power source if you can build a BA cushion.

Braun,Ryan		AB	R	HR	RBI	SB	Avg	vL	vR	OB	Slg	OPS	bb%	ct%	h%	Eye	xBA	G	L	F	PX	hr/f	Spd	SBO	RC/G	RAR	BPV	R$
Pos 7	06 aa	231	40	15	38	11	294			353	580	933	8	81	31	0.47	0				173		88	20%	6.92	10.9	105	$13
Age/B 27 Right	07 MIL *	568	116	43	116	19	322	450	282	370	637	1007	7	79	35	0.35	310	39	16	45	190	21%	116	19%	7.78	37.3	117	$37
Ht/Wt 73 200	08 MIL	611	92	37	106	14	285	287	284	331	553	884	6	79	31	0.33	286	39	17	44	166	17%	127	14%	6.24	14.3	101	$29
Health A	09 MIL	635	113	32	114	20	320	395	302	376	551	927	8	81	35	0.47	296	47	19	34	144	18%	116	14%	6.86	22.4	92	$37
PT/Exp A	10 MIL	619	101	25	103	14	304	271	315	361	501	862	8	83	33	0.53	300	48	17	35	131	14%	88	10%	6.08	17.3	82	$31
Consist B	1st Half	325	50	11	51	11	295			349	474	823	8	84	33	0.51	293	47	17	35	119	11%	94	14%	5.60	4.8	76	$16
LIMA Plan D	2nd Half	294	51	14	52	3	313			375	531	905	9	82	34	0.56	307	50	16	34	144	17%	83	6%	6.62	12.4	89	$16
Rand Var 0	11 Proj	621	105	28	108	16	306			362	519	880	8	81	34	0.47	293	46	17	36	137	17%	99	12%	6.29	17.4	84	$32

When your down year is still worth $31, that's pretty good. But three years of declining HR and PX paired with two years of Spd deterioration should not be ignored. Until he reverses GB% spike, 40 HR not in future.

Brignac,Reid		AB	R	HR	RBI	SB	Avg	vL	vR	OB	Slg	OPS	bb%	ct%	h%	Eye	xBA	G	L	F	PX	hr/f	Spd	SBO	RC/G	RAR	BPV	R$
Pos 46	06 aa	110	20	3	18	3	315			358	496	854	6	71	42	0.23	0				123		132	10%	6.26	5.6	38	$5
Age/B 25 Left	07 aa	527	77	15	69	13	235			299	387	686	8	84	25	0.59	0				93		125	15%	4.04	-4.9	68	$13
Ht/Wt 75 195	08 aaa	352	36	7	36	4	222			265	358	623	6	78	27	0.27	0				99		100	9%	3.08	-19.0	34	$4
Health A	09 TAM *	505	54	8	44	6	259	50	343	296	388	684	5	84	30	0.32	255	34	23	43	84	4%	119	12%	3.87	-15.9	50	$9
PT/Exp D	10 TAM	301	39	8	45	3	256	227	261	302	385	688	6	74	32	0.26	237	38	19	42	94	8%	106	8%	3.84	-5.5	19	$9
Consist A	1st Half	177	23	2	24	2	277			330	384	714	7	74	36	0.30	243	38	24	39	89	4%	109	6%	4.36	-0.5	17	$5
LIMA Plan D	2nd Half	124	16	6	21	1	226			262	387	649	5	75	25	0.19	231	39	14	47	101	14%	101	12%	3.10	-5.2	23	$4
Rand Var -3	11 Proj	382	47	10	50	5	249			291	386	677	6	78	30	0.27	240	38	18	44	94	8%	110	10%	3.70	-10.4	32	$9

Post-hype breakout candidate or bench warmer? For now, struggles with ct%, PX, BA vLH outweigh speed and power upside flashed in the minors. May yet figure it out, but don't expect that to happen in 2011.

Brown,Domonic		AB	R	HR	RBI	SB	Avg	vL	vR	OB	Slg	OPS	bb%	ct%	h%	Eye	xBA	G	L	F	PX	hr/f	Spd	SBO	RC/G	RAR	BPV	R$
Pos 9	06	0	0	0	0	0	0							0			0											
Age/B 23 Left	07	0	0	0	0	0	0							0			0											
Ht/Wt 77 204	08	0	0	0	0	0	0							0			0											
Health A	09 aa	147	17	3	17	7	252			304	395	698	7	79	30	0.35	0				94		124	23%	4.10	-4.4	44	$4
PT/Exp F	10 PHI *	405	60	20	68	16	281	77	245	338	497	835	8	79	32	0.40	294	41	22	37	141	17%	107	24%	5.73	4.7	77	$20
Consist D	1st Half	343	52	18	55	14	294			350	523	873	8	82	32	0.47	0				143		114	24%	6.15	8.1	93	$19
LIMA Plan C	2nd Half	62	8	2	13	2	210			269	355	623	7	61	31	0.21	222	41	22	37	128	14%	93	23%	3.22	-4.1	-8	$2
Rand Var +1	11 Proj	421	54	15	67	17	259			314	430	743	7	73	32	0.30	257	41	22	37	120	13%	106	22%	4.66	-6.1	39	$16

2-13-.210 in 62 AB at PHI. Legitimate five-tool talent now primed for MLB opportunity following near-full season in the minors. Borderline ct% may lead to rookie struggles, but a nice longer-term investment.

JOE HOFFER

Bruce,Jay

		Year	AB	R	HR	RBI	SB	Avg	vL	vR	OB	Slg	OPS	bb%	ct%	h%	Eye	xBA	G	L	F	PX	hr/f	Spd	SBO	RC/G	RAR	BPV	R$
Pos	9	06	0	0	0	0	0	0																					
Age/B	24 Left	07 a/a	253	36	15	39	3	322			376	600	976	8	79	36	0.41					177		91	10%	7.51	15.9	102	$12
Ht/Wt	75 225	08 CIN	* 597	91	30	82	11	281	190	286	329	487	817	7	75	33	0.29	267	45	21	34	131	20%	92	12%	5.47	4.7	50	$25
Health	B	09 CIN	345	47	22	58	3	223	210	229	300	470	770	10	78	22	0.51	263	39	13	49	150	17%	84	8%	4.93	0.6	81	$11
PT/Exp	B	10 CIN	509	80	25	70	5	281	277	283	354	493	848	10	73	34	0.43	264	36	20	44	144	15%	111	6%	6.15	11.8	64	$21
Consist	B	1st Half	296	49	10	36	5	277			355	463	818	11	75	34	0.48	265	37	22	41	131	11%	113	8%	5.85	4.4	61	$11
LIMA Plan	C+	2nd Half	213	31	15	34	0	286			353	535	888	9	71	34	0.36	263	35	18	48	164	21%	100	3%	6.59	7.6	68	$10
Rand Var	-2	11 Proj	508	75	30	86	5	272			339	508	847	9	75	31	0.41	267	38	17	45	152	17%	94	7%	5.99	12.3	71	$22

PRO: Improvement vLHP; Spd increase; maintained bb% gain. CON: ct% drop; hr/f on a 2-yr. decline; declining SBO (no SB after May). 2H shows that 30 HR within reach, and if 2H hr/f is maintained... UP: 40 HR

Buck,John

		Year	AB	R	HR	RBI	SB	Avg	vL	vR	OB	Slg	OPS	bb%	ct%	h%	Eye	xBA	G	L	F	PX	hr/f	Spd	SBO	RC/G	RAR	BPV	R$
Pos	2	06 KC	371	37	11	50	0	245	246	245	295	396	691	7	77	29	0.31	252	45	20	35	101	11%	65	2%	3.91	-5.5	25	$6
Age/B	30 Right	07 KC	347	41	18	48	0	222	189	231	295	429	724	9	73	25	0.39	253	43	13	44	142	16%	52	1%	4.39	1.1	44	$7
Ht/Wt	75 230	08 KC	370	48	9	48	0	224	236	219	297	365	661	9	74	28	0.40	233	43	16	41	106	8%	70	3%	3.69	-5.7	22	$5
Health	B	09 KC	* 213	18	9	39	1	240	213	259	284	463	747	6	71	30	0.21	253	37	18	45	148	13%	74	5%	4.72	2.9	40	$5
PT/Exp	D	10 TOR	409	53	20	66	0	281	409	246	308	489	797	4	73	34	0.14	264	39	16	45	152	15%	64	0%	5.14	11.3	42	$16
Consist	B	1st Half	219	26	13	40	0	274			303	511	814	4	71	33	0.14	268	39	14	47	174	18%	56	0%	5.42	7.9	49	$9
LIMA Plan	D+	2nd Half	190	27	7	26	0	289			315	463	778	4	75	35	0.15	261	39	18	43	128	11%	79	0%	4.85	3.7	36	$7
Rand Var	-4	11 Proj	392	46	16	61	0	263			303	456	760	5	73	32	0.22	255	40	17	43	138	13%	67	2%	4.77	6.4	36	$11

HR spike due more to increase in AB than any PX or hr/f boost. BA will fall because:
- BA vLHP is an anomaly;
- bb% and Eye in 2-yr decline;
- h% should regress

Pay for the power, not the BA.

Burrell,Pat

		Year	AB	R	HR	RBI	SB	Avg	vL	vR	OB	Slg	OPS	bb%	ct%	h%	Eye	xBA	G	L	F	PX	hr/f	Spd	SBO	RC/G	RAR	BPV	R$
Pos	70	06 PHI	462	80	29	95	0	258	290	244	388	502	890	18	72	30	0.75	256	31	21	48	158	18%	65	0%	7.03	24.0	69	$18
Age/B	34 Right	07 PHI	472	77	30	97	0	256	255	257	401	502	903	19	75	28	0.95	266	31	18	51	158	17%	50	0%	7.21	25.5	81	$18
Ht/Wt	76 235	08 PHI	536	74	33	86	0	250	279	238	370	507	877	16	75	28	0.75	274	34	20	45	169	18%	65	0%	6.73	20.7	87	$18
Health	B	09 TAM	412	45	14	64	2	221	202	229	316	367	682	12	71	28	0.48	215	34	18	48	99	10%	60	2%	4.01	-12.6	8	$7
PT/Exp	B	10 2TM	373	50	20	64	0	252	213	264	351	469	820	13	72	30	0.54	259	34	17	49	157	15%	45	2%	5.91	10.3	55	$13
Consist	F	1st Half	157	19	7	24	0	255			335	439	775	11	70	32	0.40	245	35	19	46	138	14%	51	2%	5.25	1.3	30	$5
LIMA Plan	D+	2nd Half	216	31	13	40	0	250			362	491	853	15	73	28	0.66	270	34	15	51	170	16%	51	2%	6.38	9.0	76	$8
Rand Var	0	11 Proj	387	51	18	66	0	258			362	457	819	14	72	31	0.58	247	34	18	48	139	14%	55	1%	5.95	9.6	47	$13

2008-10 performance by league:

Lg	BA	OPS	bb%	ct%
AL	218	672	12	70
NL	259	889	15	74

Full PX recovery brings 30 HR back in play. See where he ends up and judge accordingly.

Butera,Drew

		Year	AB	R	HR	RBI	SB	Avg	vL	vR	OB	Slg	OPS	bb%	ct%	h%	Eye	xBA	G	L	F	PX	hr/f	Spd	SBO	RC/G	RAR	BPV	R$
Pos	2	06	0	0	0	0	0	0																					
Age/B	27 Right	07 aa	167	8	1	6	0	176			199	228	427	3	86	20	0.20					32		110	0%	0.79	-19.3	8	($2)
Ht/Wt	73 205	08 aa	302	30	5	30	0	184			249	286	535	8	83	21	0.52					70		84	2%	2.23	-19.1	32	($0)
Health	A	09 aaa	298	18	2	19	0	176			219	247	466	5	84	20	0.35					51		84	2%	1.36	-28.1	16	($3)
PT/Exp	F	10 MIN	142	12	2	13	0	197	183	207	219	296	515	3	82	23	0.16	243	40	19	41	68	4%	76	0%	1.69	-11.0	14	$0
Consist	B	1st Half	45	3	1	4	0	178			196	267	462	2	78	21	0.10					59		90	0%	0.78	-4.9	-8	($0)
LIMA Plan	F	2nd Half	97	9	1	9	0	206			230	309	539	3	85	23	0.20	252	40	19	41	71	3%	79	0%	2.10	-6.2	27	$0
Rand Var	+2	11 Proj	100	8	1	8	0	190			232	288	519	5	84	22	0.34	244	40	19	41	66	3%	89	1%	1.98	-7.1	28	($0)

2-13-.197 in 142 AB in MIN. MLEs show a sub-.200 BA at every step along the way. Dad Sal was a career .227 hitter in 9 MLB seasons, proving that the apple doesn't fall very far from the tree.

Butler,Billy

		Year	AB	R	HR	RBI	SB	Avg	vL	vR	OB	Slg	OPS	bb%	ct%	h%	Eye	xBA	G	L	F	PX	hr/f	Spd	SBO	RC/G	RAR	BPV	R$
Pos	30	06 aa	477	67	11	79	1	308			354	447	801	7	90	33	0.71					84		58	1%	5.34	-4.7	60	$16
Age/B	24 Right	07 KC	* 532	72	18	92	1	282	340	272	360	457	817	11	85	31	0.79	294	47	21	33	110	12%	53	1%	5.73	7.0	66	$17
Ht/Wt	74 240	08 KC	* 544	60	15	66	0	283	340	244	338	421	759	8	88	30	0.71	270	49	17	35	84	9%	64	1%	4.89	-5.9	57	$14
Health	A	09 KC	608	78	21	93	1	301	330	289	362	492	854	9	83	33	0.56	286	47	18	35	122	12%	53	1%	6.05	5.7	65	$21
PT/Exp	A	10 KC	595	77	15	78	0	318	267	330	389	469	857	10	87	35	0.88	293	48	18	34	104	9%	50	0%	6.22	7.1	69	$22
Consist	B	1st Half	309	40	8	42	0	320			386	476	862	10	88	35	0.87	302	48	19	33	106	9%	53	0%	6.22	3.7	73	$12
LIMA Plan	C	2nd Half	286	37	7	36	0	315			391	462	853	11	86	35	0.90	285	47	17	35	102	8%	54	0%	6.22	3.4	66	$10
Rand Var	-3	11 Proj	602	77	17	83	0	306			371	469	841	9	86	33	0.75	288	48	18	34	107	10%	54	0%	5.94	5.0	67	$20

A BPV scan reveals skills that have been treading water for 5 years, albeit at a fairly decent level. An almost imperceptible uptick in '10, but he still profiles out as a .300 hitter with only moderate power.

Byrd,Marlon

		Year	AB	R	HR	RBI	SB	Avg	vL	vR	OB	Slg	OPS	bb%	ct%	h%	Eye	xBA	G	L	F	PX	hr/f	Spd	SBO	RC/G	RAR	BPV	R$
Pos	8	06 WAS	* 352	44	10	42	6	223	188	242	293	361	654	9	78	26	0.44	245	45	21	34	87	11%	59	11%	3.54	-9.8	18	$6
Age/B	33 Right	07 TEX	* 590	78	14	89	7	286	327	300	328	432	761	6	79	34	0.30	265	47	20	33	94	9%	99	7%	4.79	4.4	35	$18
Ht/Wt	72 245	08 TEX	403	70	10	53	7	298	277	308	370	462	831	10	85	33	0.74	287	46	21	33	106	9%	71	7%	5.92	6.4	67	$15
Health	A	09 TEX	547	66	20	89	8	283	244	300	323	479	802	6	82	31	0.33	278	41	19	41	124	11%	51	10%	5.23	9.1	56	$19
PT/Exp	B	10 CHC	580	84	12	66	5	293	357	267	329	429	758	5	83	34	0.32	277	52	17	30	96	8%	59	4%	4.71	-2.9	39	$20
Consist	B	1st Half	307	43	9	35	4	309			338	482	820	4	86	34	0.30	300	48	19	33	119	10%	41	7%	5.34	3.8	60	$12
LIMA Plan	C	2nd Half	273	41	3	31	1	275			320	370	690	6	80	33	0.33	253	57	16	27	69	5%	82	1%	3.95	-7.3	15	$7
Rand Var	-1	11 Proj	529	75	13	69	6	285			331	434	765	6	82	33	0.38	271	48	18	33	101	9%	61	6%	4.86	1.1	43	$18

1H continued promise of '09, but rising GB rate eventually drove down his power output. OPS has dropped last two years as AB increased, suggesting a fatigue issue.

Cabrera,Asdrubal

		Year	AB	R	HR	RBI	SB	Avg	vL	vR	OB	Slg	OPS	bb%	ct%	h%	Eye	xBA	G	L	F	PX	hr/f	Spd	SBO	RC/G	RAR	BPV	R$
Pos	6	06 aaa	393	58	5	39	13	269			332	375	706	9	80	33	0.47					76		102	22%	4.31	-0.9	31	$10
Age/B	25 Both	07 CLE	* 565	108	9	75	23	295	340	259	365	423	788	10	87	33	0.86	278	44	20	36	84	5%	102	18%	5.44	18.3	69	$23
Ht/Wt	72 170	08 CLE	* 493	71	10	59	6	274	349	230	344	394	738	10	80	33	0.52	254	46	21	34	85	8%	85	8%	4.71	5.4	33	$13
Health	C	09 CLE	523	81	6	68	17	308	306	309	362	438	799	8	83	36	0.49	280	48	22	30	91	5%	115	14%	5.44	14.3	56	$20
PT/Exp	B	10 CLE	381	39	3	29	6	276	264	281	320	346	667	6	84	32	0.42	252	52	17	31	52	3%	98	9%	3.71	-2.7	23	$8
Consist	C	1st Half	136	16	1	7	1	287			322	368	689	5	85	33	0.35	276	56	19	25	57	3%	119	8%	3.93	-0.1	34	$3
LIMA Plan	C	2nd Half	245	23	2	22	5	269			319	335	654	7	84	32	0.45	238	50	16	35	50	3%	88	10%	3.58	-2.7	17	$5
Rand Var	0	11 Proj	519	67	6	52	11	285			338	382	720	7	83	33	0.47	262	50	19	31	70	4%	101	11%	4.42	3.6	36	$14

Missed two months with broken arm, which could explain drop in xBA/PX. H% spike in '09 came back to earth, and BA fell accordingly. Expect a rebound if fully healthy, but .300 seems off the table now.

Cabrera,Everth

		Year	AB	R	HR	RBI	SB	Avg	vL	vR	OB	Slg	OPS	bb%	ct%	h%	Eye	xBA	G	L	F	PX	hr/f	Spd	SBO	RC/G	RAR	BPV	R$
Pos	6	06	0	0	0	0	0	0																					
Age/B	24 Both	07	0	0	0	0	0	0																					
Ht/Wt	70 176	08	0	0	0	0	0	0																					
Health	D	09 SD	* 404	63	2	31	26	257	239	261	335	361	696	10	77	33	0.51	253	63	15	23	74	3%	155	28%	4.33	-4.0	37	$13
PT/Exp	D	10 SD	212	22	1	22	10	208	214	206	273	278	551	8	75	27	0.35	243	54	22	23	51	3%	102	30%	2.23	-14.9	-12	$3
Consist	F	1st Half	120	11	0	13	7	208			269	275	544	8	76	27	0.34	237	46	23	31	58	0%	82	36%	2.19	-8.6	-9	$2
LIMA Plan	D	2nd Half	92	11	1	9	3	207			277	283	560	9	73	27	0.36	252	66	22	13	42	12%	135	24%	2.30	-6.3	-15	$1
Rand Var	+2	11 Proj	318	40	3	29	16	242			312	337	649	9	75	31	0.41	251	59	19	21	64	5%	132	27%	3.59	-9.0	12	$8

Hamstring woes likely caused decrease in Spd, but 63% SB success rate not a good sign. To have any value, needs to increase Spd and OB back up to '09 levels. Still young, so buy low and hope.

Cabrera,Melky

		Year	AB	R	HR	RBI	SB	Avg	vL	vR	OB	Slg	OPS	bb%	ct%	h%	Eye	xBA	G	L	F	PX	hr/f	Spd	SBO	RC/G	RAR	BPV	R$
Pos	789	06 NYY	* 582	93	11	73	15	301	286	278	372	423	795	10	89	33	0.98	267	49	17	33	73	7%	93	11%	5.50	5.2	63	$20
Age/B	26 Both	07 NYY	545	66	8	73	13	273	250	282	327	391	717	7	88	30	0.63	283	51	20	29	71	6%	110	12%	4.46	-9.2	56	$14
Ht/Wt	71 200	08 NYY	414	42	8	37	9	249	213	265	298	341	639	7	86	27	0.50	246	46	19	35	55	6%	88	10%	3.39	-17.9	30	$8
Health	A	09 NYY	485	66	13	68	10	274	268	277	333	416	750	8	88	29	0.73	288	50	21	30	85	10%	68	9%	4.82	-2.6	58	$15
PT/Exp	B	10 ATL	458	50	4	42	7	255	233	266	318	354	672	8	86	29	0.66	270	49	19	32	70	3%	79	6%	3.99	-14.4	43	$9
Consist	C	1st Half	250	27	2	23	3	256			314	328	642	8	86	29	0.60	251	53	15	31	51	3%	92	6%	3.57	-11.0	29	$5
LIMA Plan	C	2nd Half	208	23	2	19	4	255			323	385	708	9	86	29	0.72	293	43	23	33	94	3%	70	8%	4.50	-3.4	61	$4
Rand Var	+1	11 Proj	349	41	6	37	7	264			324	380	704	8	87	29	0.67	275	48	20	32	77	6%	80	8%	4.34	-9.5	51	$9

Empty skill set benefitted from Yankee Stadium in '09 but reverted to irrelevance upon his departure. GB hitter shows no power, low OB depresses non-speed. But he gets tons of ABs. That may finally end.

SCOTT MONROE

Cabrera,Miguel			AB	R	HR	RBI	SB	Avg	vL	vR	OB	Slg	OPS	bb%	ct%	h%	Eye	xBA	G	L	F	PX	hr/f	Spd	SBO	RC/G	RAR	BPV	R$
Pos	3	06 FLA	576	112	26	114	9	339	321	344	424	568	992	13	81	38	0.80	300	40	24	35	144	16%	71	7%	8.02	30.6	89	$32
Age/B	27 Right	07 FLA	588	91	34	119	2	320	364	309	400	565	965	12	78	36	0.62	294	40	21	39	153	19%	69	2%	7.59	23.0	83	$29
Ht/Wt	76 240	08 DET	616	85	37	127	1	292	311	286	351	537	889	8	80	32	0.44	291	41	20	39	153	19%	65	1%	6.36	18.6	79	$27
Health	A	09 DET	611	96	34	103	6	324	315	326	392	547	938	10	82	35	0.64	291	43	20	37	129	18%	64	4%	7.02	21.4	74	$30
PT/Exp	A	10 DET	548	111	38	126	3	328	313	333	422	622	1045	14	83	34	0.94	334	39	19	42	187	20%	49	3%	8.56	40.6	125	$36
Consist	C	1st Half	289	59	20	69	2	339			419	630	1049	12	83	35	0.82	335	43	18	40	186	21%	48	5%	8.48	20.6	121	$20
LIMA Plan	D+	2nd Half	259	52	18	57	1	317			425	614	1039	16	82	33	1.07	334	36	20	44	190	19%	60	1%	8.63	19.9	132	$16
Rand Var	0	11 Proj	606	108	40	125	4	320			403	592	995	12	82	34	0.76	316	40	20	40	168	20%	57	3%	7.86	36.1	105	$34

Answered off-season questions with gaudy numbers fully backed by PX, xBA. Trends in bb%, Eye, FB% hint at further power. Just entering prime years, owns elite skills, so bid with confidence. UP: 50HR, 140RBI

Cabrera,Orlando			AB	R	HR	RBI	SB	Avg	vL	vR	OB	Slg	OPS	bb%	ct%	h%	Eye	xBA	G	L	F	PX	hr/f	Spd	SBO	RC/G	RAR	BPV	R$
Pos	6	06 LAA	607	95	9	72	27	282	243	297	337	404	741	8	90	30	0.88	258	39	17	43	79	4%	92	18%	4.82	7.0	70	$20
Age/B	36 Right	07 LAA	638	101	8	86	20	301	308	299	346	397	743	6	90	33	0.69	263	43	18	39	64	4%	98	13%	4.71	7.4	55	$23
Ht/Wt	69 185	08 CHW	661	93	8	57	19	281	273	284	338	371	708	8	89	31	0.79	267	46	21	33	59	4%	86	13%	4.40	1.3	48	$18
Health	B	09 2AL	656	83	9	77	13	284	271	290	321	389	710	5	89	31	0.51	265	46	19	36	65	4%	91	10%	4.25	-3.8	48	$18
PT/Exp	B	10 CIN	494	64	4	42	11	263	326	240	303	354	657	5	89	29	0.53	268	45	18	37	68	2%	73	12%	3.71	-10.3	46	$12
Consist	A	1st Half	321	40	3	31	10	252			292	343	635	5	88	28	0.49	269	44	20	36	67	3%	68	14%	3.43	-9.4	40	$8
LIMA Plan	D	2nd Half	173	24	1	11	1	283			322	376	698	5	91	31	0.63	268	46	16	38	70	2%	83	9%	4.23	-1.0	57	$4
Rand Var	+1	11 Proj	376	51	4	35	8	271			314	371	686	6	90	29	0.60	267	45	18	37	69	3%	85	12%	4.07	-4.8	53	$10

Age-related decline in full force across the BPI spectrum. Speed that once drove his value is now plummeting. Ct% remains a strength, but age sounds klaxons that his days as a full-timer are nearing an end.

Cain,Lorenzo			AB	R	HR	RBI	SB	Avg	vL	vR	OB	Slg	OPS	bb%	ct%	h%	Eye	xBA	G	L	F	PX	hr/f	Spd	SBO	RC/G	RAR	BPV	R$
Pos	8	06	0	0	0	0	0	0							0			0											
Age/B	24 Right	07	0	0	0	0	0	0							0			0											
Ht/Wt	74 185	08 a/a	167	16	3	15	5	228			303	365	668	10	77	28	0.47	0				91		145	17%	3.86	-6.1	47	$3
Health	A	09 aa	145	14	3	12	2	189			236	284	520	6	79	22	0.29	0				63		99	17%	1.72	-14.0	9	$0
PT/Exp	F	10 MIL	* 478	61	3	34	27	279	289	314	342	369	710	9	82	34	0.51	245	43	21	37	62	2%	163	22%	4.40	-6.7	44	$16
Consist	F	1st Half	237	35	2	14	15	271			348	348	696	11	81	33	0.61	0						186	21%	4.29	-4.1	39	$9
LIMA Plan	D	2nd Half	241	27	1	20	12	286			335	389	724	7	82	34	0.41	259	43	21	37	77	1%	134	22%	4.49	-2.7	47	$8
Rand Var	-5	11 Proj	296	32	1	23	11	240			298	315	613	8	80	30	0.41	232	43	21	37	56	1%	135	19%	3.12	-15.0	22	$5

1-13-.306, 7 SB in 147 AB at MIL. PRO: monster Spd, good defense helps him stay in lineup. CON: complete lack of power, xBA suggests .300 was a fluke, shaky ct% endangers job. If he stays in lineup... UP: 40 SB.

Cairo,Miguel			AB	R	HR	RBI	SB	Avg	vL	vR	OB	Slg	OPS	bb%	ct%	h%	Eye	xBA	G	L	F	PX	hr/f	Spd	SBO	RC/G	RAR	BPV	R$
Pos	5	06 NYY	222	28	0	30	13	239	279	221	281	320	601	6	86	28	0.42	250	53	16	31	55	0%	120	27%	3.05	-13.1	37	$5
Age/B	36 Right	07 2TM	174	20	0	15	10	253	254	252	297	328	625	6	86	29	0.46	228	43	14	43	53	0%	108	27%	3.34	-9.8	33	$4
Ht/Wt	73 210	08 SEA	221	34	0	23	5	249	267	237	305	330	636	8	86	29	0.56	261	49	20	31	62	0%	113	12%	3.56	-8.7	42	$4
Health	A	09 PHI	* 341	38	5	26	6	232			256	322	579	3	87	25	0.24	219	43	13	45	55	4%	115	9%	2.56	-26.6	34	$5
PT/Exp	F	10 CIN	200	30	4	28	4	290	262	304	346	410	756	8	86	33	0.57	288	44	25	31	84	7%	73	7%	4.85	-0.3	47	$8
Consist	D	1st Half	97	14	2	10	1	278			307	371	678	4	86	31	0.29	288	49	27	24	59	10%	87	4%	3.65	-3.4	25	$3
LIMA Plan	F	2nd Half	103	16	2	18	3	301			379	447	826	11	84	34	0.81	291	38	24	38	108	6%	65	9%	5.94	2.9	68	$5
Rand Var	-2	11 Proj	163	23	2	19	2	264			313	372	685	7	86	30	0.49	270	44	22	33	73	5%	94	6%	4.00	-5.2	45	$4

Journeyman backup has done nice job providing owners with profits on $1 bids for several years. H% inflated by high LD% and Spd, SBO now in free fall, so don't expect a repeat of $8 in value. Stick to $1 bid level.

Callaspo,Alberto			AB	R	HR	RBI	SB	Avg	vL	vR	OB	Slg	OPS	bb%	ct%	h%	Eye	xBA	G	L	F	PX	hr/f	Spd	SBO	RC/G	RAR	BPV	R$
Pos	5	06 ARI	* 532	74	6	59	6	305	278	208	362	427	789	8	95	31	1.78	242	46	8	46	63	3%	146	8%	5.50	0.2	93	$16
Age/B	27 Both	07 ARI	* 370	48	5	31	2	271	219	214	329	380	709	8	92	28	1.11	289	47	21	32	68	4%	98	5%	4.53	-11.6	70	$7
Ht/Wt	69 180	08 KC	213	21	0	16	2	305	333	291	362	371	733	8	93	33	1.36	285	47	26	28	40	0%	124	4%	4.87	-0.1	62	$5
Health	B	09 KC	576	79	11	73	2	300	361	273	358	457	815	8	91	32	1.02	278	41	17	42	61	5%	113	2%	5.69	16.1	90	$17
PT/Exp	B	10 2AL	562	61	10	56	5	265	233	274	304	374	677	5	93	27	0.74	278	45	18	38	67	5%	87	6%	3.97	-14.1	63	$13
Consist	C	1st Half	311	37	7	36	3	273			309	415	724	5	91	28	0.55	279	43	15	42	89	6%	96	4%	4.41	-3.8	75	$9
LIMA Plan	B	2nd Half	251	24	3	20	2	255			297	323	620	6	95	26	1.15	277	48	20	32	42	4%	75	7%	3.46	-10.2	49	$4
Rand Var	+2	11 Proj	522	60	7	52	4	282			330	387	717	7	93	29	1.00	278	45	19	36	64	4%	102	5%	4.53	-4.1	68	$12

PRO: xBA and elite ct% foretell a BA rebound, still at prime age. CON: Drops in PX and Spd, multi-years struggles vLHP all suggest that his holes are being exposed by full-time work. 2009 was likely his career year.

Cameron,Mike			AB	R	HR	RBI	SB	Avg	vL	vR	OB	Slg	OPS	bb%	ct%	h%	Eye	xBA	G	L	F	PX	hr/f	Spd	SBO	RC/G	RAR	BPV	R$
Pos	8	06 SD	552	88	22	83	25	268	252	273	352	482	833	11	74	32	0.50	250	38	17	45	137	12%	132	22%	6.08	26.5	71	$23
Age/B	38 Right	07 SD	571	88	21	78	18	242	294	222	321	431	752	11	72	30	0.42	246	37	19	44	131	12%	127	16%	4.96	7.5	54	$17
Ht/Wt	74 205	08 MIL	444	69	25	70	17	243	282	231	325	477	803	11	68	30	0.38	249	33	22	46	169	18%	91	20%	5.71	12.9	58	$18
Health	D	09 MIL	544	78	24	70	7	250	271	244	341	452	793	12	71	31	0.48	240	35	17	48	145	13%	97	7%	5.57	13.5	57	$17
PT/Exp	C	10 BOS	162	24	4	15	0	259	357	225	318	401	719	8	73	33	0.32	222	29	16	55	115	6%	110	2%	4.42	-4.3	34	$4
Consist	B	1st Half	106	14	1	9	0	264			316	358	674	7	78	33	0.35	209	28	16	57	80	2%	107	4%	3.81	-4.7	25	$2
LIMA Plan	C+	2nd Half	56	10	3	6	0	250			323	482	805	10	63	34	0.29	248	31	17	53	199	16%	91	0%	6.05	1.2	58	$2
Rand Var	-3	11 Proj	396	61	17	47	5	253			328	452	780	10	70	32	0.37	241	32	17	51	149	12%	107	7%	5.34	3.0	53	$12

Hernia wiped out bulk of season. Despite small '10 sample, at this age we need to take PX and bb% drops seriously, rather than give injury-related passes. Days as an everyday player may well be over.

Cano,Robinson			AB	R	HR	RBI	SB	Avg	vL	vR	OB	Slg	OPS	bb%	ct%	h%	Eye	xBA	G	L	F	PX	hr/f	Spd	SBO	RC/G	RAR	BPV	R$
Pos	4	06 NYY	482	62	15	78	5	342	287	363	366	525	891	4	89	36	0.33	308	52	20	28	112	12%	70	6%	6.10	24.8	75	$20
Age/B	28 Left	07 NYY	617	93	19	97	4	306	328	296	348	488	835	6	86	33	0.46	303	52	17	31	112	12%	100	6%	5.66	28.2	78	$23
Ht/Wt	72 205	08 NYY	597	70	14	72	2	271	292	263	302	410	712	4	89	29	0.40	284	47	19	33	86	8%	90	4%	4.18	-12.1	62	$14
Health	A	09 NYY	637	103	25	85	5	320	309	326	351	520	870	4	90	33	0.48	312	47	20	33	114	13%	82	8%	5.91	17.0	87	$26
PT/Exp	A	10 NYY	626	103	29	109	3	319	285	340	376	534	910	8	88	33	0.74	318	44	19	36	130	14%	81	3%	6.59	35.7	98	$31
Consist	A	1st Half	318	59	16	55	2	343			391	569	960	7	88	35	0.66	327	46	19	36	137	16%	93	4%	7.06	21.5	107	$19
LIMA Plan	C+	2nd Half	308	44	13	54	1	295			362	497	859	9	87	30	0.82	310	43	20	37	123	13%	71	1%	6.10	13.9	90	$13
Rand Var	-1	11 Proj	622	95	24	106	3	310			355	504	860	7	88	32	0.60	309	46	19	35	116	13%	80	4%	5.93	22.5	86	$27

What changed? Incredibly stable skill set aided by 1H uptick in PX, which led to better lineup position, which in turn led to spike in bb% and RBI. PX and h% corrected in 2H, so set expectations against 2009 line.

Cantu,Jorge			AB	R	HR	RBI	SB	Avg	vL	vR	OB	Slg	OPS	bb%	ct%	h%	Eye	xBA	G	L	F	PX	hr/f	Spd	SBO	RC/G	RAR	BPV	R$
Pos	35	06 TAM	413	40	14	62	1	249	233	256	294	404	698	6	78	29	0.29	246	42	20	38	97	11%	87	2%	3.93	-18.1	29	$8
Age/B	29 Right	07 2TM	* 300	33	4	33	0	255	232	283	308	374	682	7	81	31	0.39	266	45	22	34	89	5%	65	0%	3.94	-15.4	29	$4
Ht/Wt	75 207	08 FLA	628	92	29	95	6	277	293	272	320	481	801	6	82	30	0.36	273	34	21	45	128	13%	81	6%	5.17	-9.9	70	$24
Health	A	09 FLA	585	67	16	100	3	289	322	278	342	443	785	7	86	31	0.58	271	36	21	43	102	7%	69	3%	5.16	-22.1	64	$20
PT/Exp	A	10 2TM	472	50	11	56	0	256	234	266	299	392	691	6	80	30	0.31	263	40	21	39	98	7%	59	0%	3.91	-29.4	29	$10
Consist	B	1st Half	306	34	10	50	0	261			311	428	739	7	80	30	0.37	270	36	19	44	118	9%	56	0%	4.52	-13.5	48	$9
LIMA Plan	C	2nd Half	166	16	1	6	0	247			277	325	603	4	79	31	0.20	256	46	24	30	62	3%	90	0%	2.76	-16.1	2	$1
Rand Var	0	11 Proj	527	59	12	64	1	266			309	401	710	6	82	31	0.34	263	39	22	39	94	7%	68	2%	4.16	-27.1	36	$12

5-23-.311 in April, but you focused on skills, not RBI, and weren't fooled. Small-sample 2H decline can be discounted, and pre-2010 success vs. LHP should ensure at least a platoon role going forward.

Carroll,Jamey			AB	R	HR	RBI	SB	Avg	vL	vR	OB	Slg	OPS	bb%	ct%	h%	Eye	xBA	G	L	F	PX	hr/f	Spd	SBO	RC/G	RAR	BPV	R$
Pos	46	06 COL	463	84	5	36	10	300	359	283	376	404	780	11	86	34	0.85	271	49	23	29	64	4%	153	14%	5.39	10.3	64	$15
Age/B	37 Right	07 COL	227	45	2	22	6	225	262	194	310	300	609	11	85	26	0.82	261	44	25	32	50	3%	105	12%	3.35	-9.4	35	$4
Ht/Wt	69 170	08 CLE	347	60	1	36	7	277	261	284	341	346	687	9	81	34	0.52	255	45	27	27	49	1%	152	9%	4.12	-7.7	29	$9
Health	B	09 CLE	315	53	2	26	4	276	271	278	350	340	690	10	80	34	0.57	241	46	24	30	43	3%	113	6%	4.18	-6.8	11	$7
PT/Exp	C	10 LA	351	48	0	23	12	291	295	289	381	339	720	13	82	36	0.80	252	53	21	26	42	0%	116	12%	4.75	-0.7	23	$11
Consist	A	1st Half	173	28	0	11	6	289			394	329	724	15	80	36	0.86	244	55	20	25	38	0%	110	8%	4.88	0.3	14	$6
LIMA Plan	D	2nd Half	178	20	0	12	6	292			367	348	715	11	84	35	0.72	259	51	21	27	45	0%	111	16%	4.60	-1.1	27	$5
Rand Var	-4	11 Proj	311	48	1	24	8	283			363	343	706	11	82	34	0.69	251	49	23	28	45	1%	124	10%	4.47	-2.2	25	$9

Reasons why an $11 season ain't happening again...
- xBA doesn't support Avg
- Falling LD% means more outs.
- Spd doesn't support SB rise.
- Rand Var screams regression.
- New skills at 37? Really now.

JOSH PALEY

Carter,V.Chris

	Year	AB	R	HR	RBI	SB	Avg	vL	vR	OB	Slg	OPS	bb%	ct%	h%	Eye	xBA	G	L	F	PX	hr/f	Spd	SBO	RC/G	RAR	BPV	R$
Pos 7	06	0	0	0	0	0	0							0			0											
Age/B 24 Right	07	0	0	0	0	0	0							0			0											
Ht/Wt 76 225	08	0	0	0	0	0	0							0			0											
Health A	09 a/a	544	86	20	86	10	279			354	461	816	10	83	31	0.66	0				116		78	11%	5.66	5.9	69	$21
PT/Exp F	10 OAK	* 535	72	23	72	2	204	200	180	282	380	662	10	78	22	0.49	239	34	12	54	118	10%	75	2%	3.62	-21.0	50	$11
Consist F	1st Half	287	35	10	37	0	184			260	348	608	9	78	20	0.46	0				115		87	0%	2.97	-17.5	49	$3
LIMA Plan C	2nd Half	248	36	13	34	2	226			306	417	723	10	78	24	0.53	243	34	12	54	121	12%	73	5%	4.37	-3.8	55	$7
Rand Var +2	11 Proj	441	64	19	64	4	238			315	426	741	10	80	26	0.56	244	34	12	54	121	10%	76	7%	4.67	-3.4	61	$12

3-7-.186 in 70 AB at OAK. Brief MLB sample showed both the upside and the warts from his minors skill set. 2011 should bring extended opportunity, but MLB pitchers will likely exploit those warts for a while.

Carter,W.Chris

	Year	AB	R	HR	RBI	SB	Avg	vL	vR	OB	Slg	OPS	bb%	ct%	h%	Eye	xBA	G	L	F	PX	hr/f	Spd	SBO	RC/G	RAR	BPV	R$
Pos 7	06 aaa	509	67	16	75	8	275			354	434	788	11	90	28	1.19	0				90		68	8%	5.45	3.5	75	$15
Age/B 28 Left	07 a/a	548	65	14	72	1	288			340	449	789	7	88	31	0.64	0				103		72	1%	5.25	0.8	71	$15
Ht/Wt 72 230	08 aaa	470	51	17	63	0	260			306	423	729	6	84	28	0.42	0				101		62	0%	4.37	-10.4	50	$11
Health A	09 aaa	428	44	13	54	1	273			332	425	757	8	84	30	0.57	0				97		54	1%	4.85	-5.3	50	$11
PT/Exp F	10 NYM	* 280	26	8	38	1	258	143	269	301	402	703	6	91	26	0.73	263	39	14	47	88	6%	49	5%	4.24	-6.9	65	$7
Consist B	1st Half	179	18	6	27	0	257			282	441	723	3	92	25	0.45	274	39	10	51	109	8%	66	0%	4.30	-4.0	85	$5
LIMA Plan F	2nd Half	101	7	1	11	1	260			332	333	665	10	90	28	1.10	233	38	16	45	49	3%	39	9%	4.07	-3.0	33	$2
Rand Var +1	11 Proj	213	20	4	27	1	263			318	376	695	7	88	28	0.68	242	39	15	46	75	5%	49	4%	4.18	-6.8	44	$5

4-24-.263 in 167 AB at NYM. Mired in AAA since 2006, and with 84 career HR at that level, finally got a decent MLB trial and didn't do much. Age, lack of a true plus skill may limit future opportunities.

Cash,Kevin

	Year	AB	R	HR	RBI	SB	Avg	vL	vR	OB	Slg	OPS	bb%	ct%	h%	Eye	xBA	G	L	F	PX	hr/f	Spd	SBO	RC/G	RAR	BPV	R$
Pos 2	06 aaa	240	15	2	18	1	159			225	225	450	8	69	22	0.27	0				53		89	6%	0.65	-29.8	-39	($3)
Age/B 33 Right	07 aaa	176	18	5	20	0	155			234	290	524	9	69	19	0.33	0				100		68	0%	1.65	-15.8	-4	($1)
Ht/Wt 72 200	08 BOS	142	11	3	15	0	225	361	179	313	338	651	11	65	33	0.36	211	50	18	32	97	10%	68	0%	3.69	-2.2	-18	$1
Health A	09 aaa	68	6	2	7	0	175			250	263	513	9	62	25	0.26	0				65		82	0%	1.40	-6.3	-55	($0)
PT/Exp F	10 2TM	* 152	7	2	8	0	170	250	140	234	222	456	8	74	22	0.32	206	46	19	35	37	5%	66	0%	0.81	-17.4	-38	($2)
Consist C	1st Half	95	5	2	7	0	189			242	263	505	7	76	23	0.30	225	45	21	34	47	8%	66	0%	1.45	-8.7	-22	($0)
LIMA Plan F	2nd Half	57	2	0	2	0	138			220	155	375	10	70	20	0.35	178	49	16	35	19	0%	77	0%	-0.35	-9.0	-61	($1)
Rand Var +4	11 Proj	100	6	1	7	0	180			255	253	508	9	70	24	0.33	204	48	18	34	58	6%	68	0%	1.49	-9.0	-34	($1)

2-5-.167 in 114 AB at HOU/BOS. Over 641 career ABs, has a .183/.248/.278 slash line, making him one of the worst hitters of the live-ball era. If we could type "Avoid" in a 48-pt red font here, we would do that.

Casilla,Alexi

	Year	AB	R	HR	RBI	SB	Avg	vL	vR	OB	Slg	OPS	bb%	ct%	h%	Eye	xBA	G	L	F	PX	hr/f	Spd	SBO	RC/G	RAR	BPV	R$
Pos 46	06 aa	170	26	1	12	18	282			348	371	718	9	88	32	0.85	0				59		107	42%	4.63	1.3	53	$7
Age/B 26 Both	07 MIN	* 509	67	3	29	35	248	274	181	302	308	611	7	84	29	0.50	263	62	16	22	43	3%	121	34%	3.13	-13.5	25	$13
Ht/Wt 69 178	08 MIN	* 481	67	7	52	10	262	264	289	325	343	668	8	87	29	0.72	244	52	15	34	52	5%	90	10%	3.90	-13.9	37	$12
Health C	09 MIN	* 384	42	2	31	19	240	182	205	295	310	606	7	85	28	0.53	227	51	12	36	40	2%	159	24%	3.13	-21.1	37	$7
PT/Exp D	10 MIN	152	26	1	20	6	276	364	252	333	395	728	8	89	31	0.76	267	50	13	37	71	2%	144	16%	4.71	1.1	73	$6
Consist C	1st Half	39	7	0	2	0	256			370	333	703	15	87	29	1.40	218	61	0	39	44	0%	139	7%	4.85	0.5	58	$1
LIMA Plan C	2nd Half	113	19	1	18	6	283			319	416	735	5	89	31	0.50	281	46	17	37	80	3%	130	21%	4.61	0.5	73	$5
Rand Var -1	11 Proj	418	59	3	45	25	263			315	348	664	7	87	30	0.59	252	50	15	35	54	2%	129	25%	3.84	-9.4	47	$14

Elbow, ankle injuries shortened his season. Still hasn't seized a job despite opportunities, but ct%, GB%, Spd, SBO point to an impact SB source lurking here. If he finally wins a job...
UP: 40 SB.

Castillo,Luis

	Year	AB	R	HR	RBI	SB	Avg	vL	vR	OB	Slg	OPS	bb%	ct%	h%	Eye	xBA	G	L	F	PX	hr/f	Spd	SBO	RC/G	RAR	BPV	R$
Pos 4	06 MIN	584	84	3	49	25	296	256	316	358	370	728	9	90	33	0.97	280	61	18	21	44	3%	142	18%	4.74	10.2	58	$18
Age/B 35 Both	07 2TM	548	91	1	38	19	301	296	303	363	359	722	9	92	33	1.18	291	67	15	18	37	1%	155	13%	4.73	5.8	63	$17
Ht/Wt 71 197	08 NYM	298	46	3	28	17	245	211	257	353	305	659	14	88	27	1.43	262	66	16	18	36	6%	95	17%	4.21	-5.0	41	$9
Health C	09 NYM	486	77	1	40	20	302	264	319	389	346	735	12	88	34	1.19	272	59	23	19	29	1%	127	13%	5.00	6.4	40	$18
PT/Exp C	10 NYM	247	28	0	17	8	235	243	232	339	267	606	14	90	26	1.56	275	70	14	15	20	0%	127	12%	3.68	-8.6	43	$4
Consist C	1st Half	141	13	0	14	7	241			352	277	628	15	93	26	2.40	286	71	14	15	17	0%	153	15%	4.12	-3.0	62	$3
LIMA Plan D+	2nd Half	106	15	0	3	1	226			322	255	577	12	86	26	1.00	256	70	15	15	25	0%	75	8%	3.09	-5.7	12	$1
Rand Var +5	11 Proj	331	46	1	23	12	269			362	312	674	13	89	30	1.30	272	66	17	17	28	1%	118	13%	4.34	-3.7	40	$9

Tale of an aging speedster:
- Spd still a plus, but not elite.
- SBO erosion well underway.
- tough to keep old legs healthy, bruised foot cost him six weeks. Still capable of a random good month or two, but that's about it.

Castro,Jason

	Year	AB	R	HR	RBI	SB	Avg	vL	vR	OB	Slg	OPS	bb%	ct%	h%	Eye	xBA	G	L	F	PX	hr/f	Spd	SBO	RC/G	RAR	BPV	R$
Pos 2	06	0	0	0	0	0	0							0			0											
Age/B 23 Left	07	0	0	0	0	0	0							0			0											
Ht/Wt 75 210	08	0	0	0	0	0	0							0			0											
Health A	09 aa	239	29	2	22	2	259			314	335	649	7	89	29	0.70	0				49		102	4%	3.70	-3.9	41	$4
PT/Exp F	10 HOU	* 406	50	5	28	1	217	70	243	296	292	588	10	83	25	0.66	246	41	22	37	52	4%	85	2%	2.96	-19.1	22	$3
Consist B	1st Half	244	31	4	21	1	221			303	298	601	10	84	25	0.72	273	43	29	29	51	7%	85	3%	3.12	-10.2	24	$3
LIMA Plan D	2nd Half	162	19	1	7	0	210			285	284	569	9	82	25	0.59	241	41	21	38	55	2%	100	0%	2.71	-8.9	23	$0
Rand Var +2	11 Proj	333	40	4	24	1	231			299	313	613	9	85	26	0.66	248	41	22	37	55	4%	89	3%	3.25	-11.3	31	$4

2-8-.205 in 195 AB at HOU. Some promise in decent bb%, and near-Avg speed is good for a CA. But lack of pop and utter ineptitude vs. LHP highlight need for patience. Check back in a few years.

Castro,Juan

	Year	AB	R	HR	RBI	SB	Avg	vL	vR	OB	Slg	OPS	bb%	ct%	h%	Eye	xBA	G	L	F	PX	hr/f	Spd	SBO	RC/G	RAR	BPV	R$
Pos 6	06 2TM	251	18	3	28	1	251	268	244	282	351	633	4	86	28	0.31	261	49	21	29	59	5%	90	5%	3.25	-8.4	27	$3
Age/B 38 Right	07 CIN	89	5	0	5	0	180	226	155	215	236	451	4	76	24	0.19	205	39	17	43	52	0%	87	0%	0.83	-10.4	-16	($1)
Ht/Wt 71 190	08 2TM	* 213	23	3	18	0	207	185	196	259	286	545	7	84	23	0.44	222	49	13	38	54	4%	79	0%	2.28	-14.6	18	$1
Health A	09 LA	112	18	1	9	0	277	240	287	314	339	653	5	78	35	0.24	211	34	23	43	48	3%	77	0%	3.37	-4.1	-15	$3
PT/Exp F	10 2NL	129	7	0	13	0	194	233	182	241	233	473	6	81	24	0.32	206	50	13	37	36	0%	61	4%	1.30	-12.8	-17	($1)
Consist D	1st Half	115	7	0	12	0	209			242	252	494	4	82	26	0.24	209	50	13	38	40	0%	60	0%	1.51	-10.4	-13	($0)
LIMA Plan F	2nd Half	14	0	0	1	0	71			235	71	307	18	71	10	0.75	185	50	20	30	0	0%	83	25%	-1.11	-3.0	-52	($1)
Rand Var +2	11 Proj	66	7	0	6	0	227			268	287	555	5	82	27	0.31	223	46	16	37	48	2%	73	1%	2.30	-4.4	2	$0

Thanks to Cash above, Castro's .596 career OPS makes him only the second-worst hitter on this page. With PX and Spd at a 5-year low, he's mounting a serious challenge to "you can't fall off the floor."

Castro,Ramon

	Year	AB	R	HR	RBI	SB	Avg	vL	vR	OB	Slg	OPS	bb%	ct%	h%	Eye	xBA	G	L	F	PX	hr/f	Spd	SBO	RC/G	RAR	BPV	R$
Pos 2	06 NYM	126	13	4	12	0	238	269	230	319	389	708	11	68	32	0.38	223	36	22	42	112	11%	77	0%	4.40	0.2	9	$2
Age/B 35 Right	07 NYM	144	24	11	31	0	285	276	287	331	556	887	6	73	32	0.26	274	36	18	46	171	23%	60	0%	6.34	7.7	62	$7
Ht/Wt 75 246	08 NYM	143	15	7	24	0	245	277	218	308	441	748	8	76	27	0.38	263	36	24	40	128	16%	55	0%	4.64	1.8	42	$4
Health D	09 2TM	* 285	28	9	34	0	222	222	218	284	366	650	8	78	26	0.39	247	35	22	42	97	9%	37	1%	3.43	-7.3	18	$4
PT/Exp F	10 CHW	115	18	8	21	1	278	286	275	331	504	835	7	77	30	0.35	282	42	20	38	136	24%	52	3%	5.54	4.5	50	$6
Consist D	1st Half	38	6	2	8	1	316			409	500	909	14	71	40	0.55	263	37	26	37	126	20%	54	7%	7.18	3.1	30	$2
LIMA Plan F	2nd Half	77	12	6	13	0	260			287	506	794	4	81	25	0.20	293	44	17	38	140	25%	62	0%	4.75	1.3	62	$3
Rand Var -1	11 Proj	149	19	8	24	0	248			300	458	757	7	77	27	0.31	270	39	20	41	133	18%	52	0%	4.63	1.8	44	$5

Consistently impressive PX, hr/f in minimal AB highlights his utility as a 2nd CA option. And if his front-liner gets hurt and he gets to start for a few weeks, you absolutely want to pick him up for that stretch.

Castro,Starlin

	Year	AB	R	HR	RBI	SB	Avg	vL	vR	OB	Slg	OPS	bb%	ct%	h%	Eye	xBA	G	L	F	PX	hr/f	Spd	SBO	RC/G	RAR	BPV	R$
Pos 6	06	0	0	0	0	0	0							0			0											
Age/B 21 Right	07	0	0	0	0	0	0							0			0											
Ht/Wt 72 190	08	0	0	0	0	0	0							0			0											
Health A	09 aa	111	9	0	13	5	284			334	378	713	7	91	31	0.88	0				59		122	17%	4.56	0.0	66	$3
PT/Exp F	10 CHC	* 572	68	4	56	13	310	339	286	351	426	777	6	86	35	0.46	289	51	20	29	81	3%	132	17%	5.08	10.6	63	$19
Consist B	1st Half	282	32	3	33	4	302			363	421	784	9	87	34	0.76	292	51	21	29	78	4%	140	14%	5.34	7.4	73	$9
LIMA Plan B	2nd Half	290	36	1	23	9	317			338	431	769	3	85	37	0.21	286	52	19	29	84	1%	123	20%	4.81	3.1	53	$11
Rand Var -1	11 Proj	521	55	3	54	17	286			329	400	729	6	88	32	0.55	286	51	19	29	75	3%	131	18%	4.58	1.0	66	$16

3-41-.300-10 SB in 463 AB at CHC. Toolsy rookie flashed a decent plate approach. SBO highlights his aggression, with 8 CS as a consequence. Expect bumpy ride before he emerges as a solid BA/speed contributor.

RAY MURPHY

Cedeno,Ronny

			AB	R	HR	RBI	SB	Avg	vL	vR	OB	Slg	OPS	bb%	ct%	h%	Eye	xBA	G	L	F	PX	hr/f	Spd	SBO	RC/G	RAR	BPV	R$
Pos	6	06 CHC	534	51	6	41	8	245	230	251	269	339	608	3	80	30	0.16	224	47	16	37	58	4%	157	14%	2.76	-25.8	20	$7
Age/B	28 Right	07 CHC	* 361	48	13	42	7	294	176	225	343	451	794	7	84	32	0.45	261	33	23	44	92	9%	114	12%	5.16	7.3	58	$13
Ht/Wt	72 180	08 CHC	216	36	2	28	4	269	257	282	325	352	677	8	81	32	0.44	243	52	18	30	64	4%	91	8%	3.88	-4.7	20	$6
Health	A	09 2TM	341	32	10	38	5	208	193	213	250	337	587	5	77	24	0.24	224	51	11	38	78	10%	137	10%	2.48	-22.1	23	$4
PT/Exp	C	10 PIT	468	42	8	38	12	256	291	246	291	382	674	5	77	32	0.22	256	49	16	35	95	6%	121	15%	3.66	-10.4	33	$10
Consist	C	1st Half	228	12	4	16	7	219			255	311	567	5	75	27	0.20	219	46	15	40	70	6%	91	17%	2.20	-15.6	-4	$3
LIMA Plan	D	2nd Half	240	30	4	22	5	292			325	450	775	5	79	35	0.24	288	52	18	30	118	7%	137	13%	4.99	3.9	64	$8
Rand Var	0	11 Proj	412	44	8	41	8	250			290	372	662	5	78	30	0.26	247	50	16	35	86	7%	121	12%	3.53	-12.0	31	$9

PRO: Above-average Spd, high SB%, rising SBO. Power drifting in right direction.
CON: poor plate approach limits BA upside.
Even with the positive trends, no real cause for optimism.

Cervelli,Francisco

			AB	R	HR	RBI	SB	Avg	vL	vR	OB	Slg	OPS	bb%	ct%	h%	Eye	xBA	G	L	F	PX	hr/f	Spd	SBO	RC/G	RAR	BPV	R$
Pos	2	06	0	0	0	0	0	0							0			0											
Age/B	25 Right	07	0	0	0	0	0	0							0			0											
Ht/Wt	73 210	08 aa	78	8	0	8	0	282			364	346	710	11	77	37	0.56	0				60		79	0%	4.54	0.7	5	$1
Health	A	09 NYY	* 221	27	4	24	0	255	345	277	290	353	644	5	83	29	0.30	253	46	20	34	63	6%	88	9%	3.30	-6.5	22	$4
PT/Exp	F	10 NYY	266	27	0	38	1	271	322	246	351	335	686	11	84	32	0.79	246	47	18	34	47	0%	110	2%	4.30	1.1	32	$5
Consist	C	1st Half	166	15	0	29	0	271			339	343	682	9	86	32	0.71	243	48	16	36	48	0%	127	0%	4.19	0.2	39	$4
LIMA Plan	F	2nd Half	100	12	0	9	1	270			371	320	691	14	82	33	0.89	252	46	23	31	46	0%	80	5%	4.46	0.9	18	$2
Rand Var	-1	11 Proj	191	22	1	23	1	262			328	335	664	9	83	31	0.60	248	47	20	33	52	3%	95	5%	3.85	-2.0	24	$3

Draft him with eyes open: no power, no SB potential, but a solid plate approach that yields a BA that won't kill you. Unlikely to see full-time ABs, which also helps. He's fine as a low-risk end-game backup catcher.

Chavez,Eric

			AB	R	HR	RBI	SB	Avg	vL	vR	OB	Slg	OPS	bb%	ct%	h%	Eye	xBA	G	L	F	PX	hr/f	Spd	SBO	RC/G	RAR	BPV	R$
Pos	0	06 OAK	485	74	22	72	3	241	197	257	353	435	788	15	79	26	0.84	255	39	18	44	118	13%	73	2%	5.50	-13.4	65	$12
Age/B	33 Left	07 OAK	341	43	15	46	4	240	234	244	309	446	755	9	78	27	0.45	266	36	17	46	136	12%	73	8%	4.82	-14.5	62	$8
Ht/Wt	73 220	08 OAK	89	10	2	14	0	247	333	215	295	393	688	6	80	29	0.33	252	42	17	41	108	7%	55	0%	3.93	-2.6	37	$2
Health	F	09 OAK	30	0	0	1	0	100	111	83	129	133	262	3	77	13	0.14	178	43	13	43	30	0%	62	0%	-1.63	-7.2	-42	($1)
PT/Exp	F	10 OAK	111	10	1	10	0	234	111	245	286	333	619	7	72	32	0.26	239	49	19	32	92	4%	53	0%	3.08	-10.9	-7	$1
Consist	F	1st Half	111	10	1	10	0	234			286	333	619	7	72	32	0.26	239	49	19	32	92	4%	53	0%	3.08	-10.9	-7	$1
LIMA Plan	F	2nd Half	0	0	0	0	0	0																					
Rand Var	-2	11 Proj	63	8	1	8	0	238			318	358	675	10	76	29	0.50	238	42	18	41	92	6%	61	3%	3.95	-3.6	20	$1

Remember the days of 500+ AB and 25-35 HR? Neither do we. Chronic injury woes have rendered him a non-factor for years. Gotta applaud OAK's steadfast, unrelenting loyalty, though.

Choo,Shin-Soo

			AB	R	HR	RBI	SB	Avg	vL	vR	OB	Slg	OPS	bb%	ct%	h%	Eye	xBA	G	L	F	PX	hr/f	Spd	SBO	RC/G	RAR	BPV	R$
Pos	9	06 2AL	* 532	84	14	63	27	288	278	281	358	444	801	10	78	35	0.50	286	56	24	20	102	17%	106	22%	5.53	-2.0	48	$21
Age/B	28 Left	07 aaa	208	29	2	23	9	233			297	324	620	8	83	27	0.53	0				64		115	22%	3.29	-12.1	36	$4
Ht/Wt	71 200	08 CLE	* 359	69	15	69	5	299	286	317	382	523	905	12	74	37	0.53	284	41	23	36	161	15%	106	10%	7.08	17.4	84	$17
Health	B	09 CLE	583	87	20	86	21	300	275	312	383	489	872	12	74	38	0.52	264	42	22	36	127	13%	100	12%	6.64	21.0	54	$25
PT/Exp	B	10 CLE	550	81	22	90	22	300	264	319	392	484	875	13	79	35	0.70	283	45	20	35	125	15%	69	15%	6.58	25.1	63	$28
Consist	A	1st Half	301	48	13	43	12	286			384	475	859	14	80	32	0.81	286	47	18	35	121	15%	95	15%	6.36	12.1	76	$15
LIMA Plan	C+	2nd Half	249	33	9	47	10	317			401	494	895	12	76	39	0.59	281	43	22	35	130	13%	48	15%	6.87	13.1	50	$14
Rand Var	-1	11 Proj	554	85	21	90	20	298			383	484	867	12	77	36	0.59	277	44	21	35	128	14%	82	14%	6.48	20.3	60	$26

2010 eerily similar to 2009; mixed a lower h% with better patience, the results are the same. The power is there, but low FB% suppresses the HR totals, making a step forward in power tough to project.

Church,Ryan

			AB	R	HR	RBI	SB	Avg	vL	vR	OB	Slg	OPS	bb%	ct%	h%	Eye	xBA	G	L	F	PX	hr/f	Spd	SBO	RC/G	RAR	BPV	R$
Pos	79	06 WAS	* 390	47	17	60	10	232	265	279	316	425	741	11	72	28	0.44	241	39	18	43	130	14%	65	12%	4.76	-5.8	35	$11
Age/B	32 Left	07 WAS	470	57	15	70	3	272	229	287	341	464	805	9	77	32	0.46	286	43	22	35	138	12%	63	4%	5.58	2.9	59	$13
Ht/Wt	74 218	08 NYM	319	54	12	49	2	276	264	282	344	439	783	9	74	34	0.40	256	45	24	31	110	16%	86	5%	5.23	-1.8	30	$12
Health	C	09 2NL	359	46	4	40	6	273	213	290	334	384	719	8	84	32	0.57	262	46	20	33	85	4%	61	8%	4.50	-10.9	41	$9
PT/Exp	D	10 2NL	219	25	5	25	1	201	122	219	255	352	607	7	70	26	0.25	239	36	19	45	125	7%	62	3%	2.88	-15.0	16	$2
Consist	C	1st Half	145	15	3	14	1	193			235	331	566	5	77	23	0.24	246	40	18	42	103	6%	73	4%	2.31	-12.6	23	$1
LIMA Plan	F	2nd Half	74	10	2	11	0	216			293	392	685	10	58	34	0.26	225	28	21	51	183	9%	62	0%	4.59	-1.1	19	$1
Rand Var	+5	11 Proj	201	26	5	26	2	259			322	409	730	9	72	33	0.34	246	40	20	40	121	9%	57	5%	4.61	-3.8	22	$5

Low h% hurt his Avg, and two years of low hr/f have snuffed the HRs. Primed for a rebound? Unlikely. He's already a platoon player; with eroding ct% and newfound struggles vs RHP, he could be toast.

Clement,Jeff

			AB	R	HR	RBI	SB	Avg	vL	vR	OB	Slg	OPS	bb%	ct%	h%	Eye	xBA	G	L	F	PX	hr/f	Spd	SBO	RC/G	RAR	BPV	R$
Pos	3	06 aaa	304	26	5	36	0	237			284	342	626	6	82	27	0.36	0				69		77	3%	3.18	-23.3	20	$3
Age/B	27 Left	07 aa	455	62	16	66	0	236			315	420	734	10	81	26	0.61	0				120		91	0%	4.67	-13.9	71	$9
Ht/Wt	73 215	08 SEA	* 375	48	15	56	0	253	289	209	330	448	778	10	76	29	0.48	263	41	18	40	135	13%	65	1%	5.21	-0.7	55	$10
Health	B	09 aa	470	62	15	69	2	231			292	399	691	8	80	26	0.43	0				112		77	3%	4.02	-29.7	51	$10
PT/Exp	D	10 PIT	* 312	27	12	35	1	223	257	183	252	398	650	4	75	26	0.16	270	46	20	33	122	16%	58	10%	3.20	-30.3	26	$5
Consist	C	1st Half	204	16	8	21	0	201			237	378	615	4	75	23	0.19	276	48	21	31	125	16%	61	6%	2.81	-22.8	30	$2
LIMA Plan	F	2nd Half	108	11	5	15	1	263			281	435	716	2	76	31	0.10	238	36	14	50	117	12%	79	16%	3.93	-7.8	26	$3
Rand Var	+2	11 Proj	179	20	7	24	1	240			286	413	699	6	77	27	0.28	262	43	19	38	118	13%	59	7%	3.93	-12.6	36	$4

7-12-.201 in 144 AB at PIT. Consistently low h% sets low BA ceiling. Strong PX and hr/f show the seeds of HR potential; If 2H FB% spike (warning: small sample size!) is real, power could emerge. UP: 20 HR.

Coghlan,Chris

			AB	R	HR	RBI	SB	Avg	vL	vR	OB	Slg	OPS	bb%	ct%	h%	Eye	xBA	G	L	F	PX	hr/f	Spd	SBO	RC/G	RAR	BPV	R$
Pos	7	06	0	0	0	0	0	0							0			0											
Age/B	25 Left	07	0	0	0	0	0	0							0			0											
Ht/Wt	72 198	08 aa	483	68	6	61	27	264			342	375	718	11	88	29	0.98	0				73		106	27%	4.70	-6.3	65	$17
Health	C	09 FLA	* 595	103	12	67	15	323	316	323	388	472	860	10	85	36	0.72	287	48	23	30	97	8%	110	11%	6.23	10.8	72	$26
PT/Exp	C	10 FLA	358	60	5	28	10	268	261	270	330	383	713	8	77	34	0.39	272	51	24	25	87	7%	117	13%	4.37	-7.3	30	$11
Consist	D	1st Half	302	53	5	27	9	281			346	414	760	9	76	35	0.42	281	50	25	25	100	9%	115	13%	5.03	-0.3	40	$11
LIMA Plan	C	2nd Half	56	7	0	1	1	196			237	214	452	5	77	26	0.23	217	56	19	26	17	0%	103	15%	0.80	-7.7	-36	($0)
Rand Var	0	11 Proj	436	67	7	36	12	273			333	386	719	8	81	32	0.48	271	51	22	27	78	7%	110	15%	4.43	-10.7	39	$13

2009 NL ROY couldn't repeat; bb%, ct% regression scuttled his 1st half, then he tore up his knee. Skill set is soft to begin with so there is little reason to expect much of a rebound, even if healthy.

Colvin,Tyler

			AB	R	HR	RBI	SB	Avg	vL	vR	OB	Slg	OPS	bb%	ct%	h%	Eye	xBA	G	L	F	PX	hr/f	Spd	SBO	RC/G	RAR	BPV	R$
Pos	79	06	0	0	0	0	0	0							0			0											
Age/B	25 Left	07 aa	247	29	8	26	6	271			283	425	708	2	81	31	0.09	0				93		134	14%	3.82	-9.8	46	$7
Ht/Wt	75 190	08 aa	540	51	11	60	5	223			267	358	625	6	85	24	0.40	0				81		142	9%	3.23	-31.8	61	$7
Health	A	09 aa	307	41	12	40	4	269			297	463	760	4	83	29	0.24	0				110		135	7%	4.59	-6.1	70	$10
PT/Exp	D	10 CHC	358	60	20	56	6	254	250	256	312	500	812	8	72	30	0.30	280	43	17	40	169	19%	128	9%	5.58	5.3	79	$15
Consist	C	1st Half	162	27	12	32	2	278			324	568	892	6	70	32	0.23	303	44	20	36	204	30%	107	6%	6.59	7.0	91	$9
LIMA Plan	C+	2nd Half	196	33	8	24	4	235			302	444	746	9	73	28	0.37	260	42	15	43	141	13%	143	11%	4.78	-1.7	69	$6
Rand Var	+1	11 Proj	409	59	19	56	6	254			298	466	765	6	78	29	0.28	271	43	17	40	133	15%	131	9%	4.78	-5.9	71	$14

1H hr/f spike wasn't sustainable, but his power profile is legit. 2H Spd/SBO combo points to SB upside as well. Combine that power/speed blend with regular playing time, and...
UP: 30 HR, 15 SB

Conrad,Brooks

			AB	R	HR	RBI	SB	Avg	vL	vR	OB	Slg	OPS	bb%	ct%	h%	Eye	xBA	G	L	F	PX	hr/f	Spd	SBO	RC/G	RAR	BPV	R$
Pos	5	06 aaa	532	81	19	76	12	237			294	458	751	7	78	27	0.37	0				134		138	18%	4.79	-7.5	79	$14
Age/B	31 Both	07 aaa	533	58	16	48	8	164			225	308	533	7	73	19	0.29	0				104		100	13%	1.82	-60.1	20	$1
Ht/Wt	71 190	08 aaa	465	58	18	62	3	182			233	356	588	6	78	20	0.29	0				113		96	5%	2.56	-38.3	44	$5
Health	A	09 ATL	* 452	54	11	54	9	209	222	200	276	334	610	8	73	26	0.34	206	29	18	53	91	6%	81	10%	2.93	-31.1	9	$7
PT/Exp	D	10 ATL	156	31	8	33	5	250	278	242	320	487	807	9	71	30	0.36	265	32	16	52	176	14%	89	17%	5.64	3.4	72	$8
Consist	D	1st Half	69	16	4	16	4	261			311	536	847	7	70	32	0.24	282	28	15	57	219	15%	82	33%	6.17	2.5	93	$4
LIMA Plan	F	2nd Half	87	15	4	17	1	241			327	448	775	11	72	29	0.46	252	35	17	48	143	13%	102	9%	5.24	0.9	59	$3
Rand Var	-2	11 Proj	160	26	6	27	4	225			291	415	706	9	73	27	0.35	239	32	17	51	134	11%	91	13%	4.19	-4.4	46	$5

PRO: PX/FB% combo points to decent HR potential.
CON: low ct% puts BA at risk; low Spd negates rising SBO; minor league power doesn't support current level. This was likely his career year.

DAVE ADLER

Cora,Alex

Cora,Alex			AB	R	HR	RBI	SB	Avg	vL	vR	OB	Slg	OPS	bb%	ct%	h%	Eye	xBA	G	L	F	PX	hr/f	Spd	SBO	RC/G	RAR	BPV	R$
Pos	4	06 BOS	235	31	1	18	6	238	333	219	295	298	593	7	88	27	0.66	238	51	16	32	37	2%	109	12%	3.06	-7.5	30	$3
Age/B	35 Left	07 BOS	207	30	3	18	1	246	179	257	271	386	658	3	89	27	0.30	280	43	20	37	81	4%	124	5%	3.60	-2.4	66	$3
Ht/Wt	72 200	08 BOS	152	14	0	9	1	270	286	266	339	349	688	10	91	29	1.23	277	42	25	33	53	0%	92	4%	4.44	-2.0	56	$2
Health	C	09 NYM	271	31	1	18	8	251	292	238	314	310	624	8	90	28	0.89	249	47	20	33	41	1%	76	14%	3.55	-7.9	34	$5
PT/Exp	F	10 2TM	176	14	0	20	4	210	161	221	253	278	531	5	91	23	0.63	270	48	21	31	42	0%	91	13%	2.44	-12.1	38	$1
Consist	C	1st Half	128	14	0	17	2	227			277	305	582	7	91	25	0.82	273	52	18	30	45	0%	106	10%	3.10	-6.1	49	$2
LIMA Plan	F	2nd Half	48	0	0	3	2	167			184	208	392	2	90	19	0.20	270	37	28	35	35	0%	57	29%	0.62	-6.3	10	($0)
Rand Var	+5	11 Proj	97	11	0	9	2	247			302	335	638	7	90	27	0.81	272	44	23	33	53	1%	100	9%	3.71	-2.8	50	$1

There are keeper leagues that often have flawed rules where there is an incentive to finish lower in the standings to get better draft picks. But any rule that makes a player like this valuable needs to be changed.

Counsell,Craig

Counsell,Craig			AB	R	HR	RBI	SB	Avg	vL	vR	OB	Slg	OPS	bb%	ct%	h%	Eye	xBA	G	L	F	PX	hr/f	Spd	SBO	RC/G	RAR	BPV	R$
Pos	56	06 ARI	372	56	4	30	15	255	256	255	313	347	659	8	87	28	0.66	258	48	20	31	53	4%	128	22%	3.81	-18.7	48	$9
Age/B	40 Left	07 MIL	282	31	3	24	4	220	157	234	319	309	627	13	83	25	0.87	235	46	15	38	58	3%	107	7%	3.61	-17.4	40	$2
Ht/Wt	72 179	08 MIL	248	31	1	14	3	226	190	229	347	302	649	16	83	27	1.10	254	47	23	30	59	2%	95	5%	4.07	-9.8	41	$2
Health	A	09 MIL	404	61	4	39	3	285	237	290	352	408	760	9	87	32	0.78	267	44	21	35	77	3%	121	6%	5.12	-0.2	66	$11
PT/Exp	D	10 MIL	204	16	2	21	1	250	206	259	320	319	639	9	86	28	0.72	242	42	19	39	49	3%	70	3%	3.60	-7.8	24	$3
Consist	C	1st Half	120	10	1	12	1	258			310	333	643	7	83	30	0.45	258	44	23	33	58	3%	78	3%	3.48	-5.0	19	$2
LIMA Plan	F	2nd Half	84	6	1	9	0	238			333	298	631	12	89	26	1.33	218	39	14	46	37	3%	74	3%	3.80	-2.8	36	$1
Rand Var	0	11 Proj	125	13	1	12	1	248			330	332	662	11	86	28	0.88	246	43	19	37	55	3%	96	5%	4.00	-4.1	41	$2

xBA confirms '09 BA spike was a fluke, even though he still controls plate well. And speed is a skill of the young, so days of double-digit SB are long gone.

Craig,Allen

Craig,Allen			AB	R	HR	RBI	SB	Avg	vL	vR	OB	Slg	OPS	bb%	ct%	h%	Eye	xBA	G	L	F	PX	hr/f	Spd	SBO	RC/G	RAR	BPV	R$
Pos	9	06	0	0	0	0	0	0							0			0											
Age/B	26 Right	07 aa	24	4	2	2	0	243			272	566	838	4	79	23	0.19	0				204		111	0%	5.46	0.2	120	$1
Ht/Wt	74 190	08 aa	506	64	15	65	2	256			306	397	703	7	86	27	0.52	0				86		85	2%	4.13	-16.9	55	$12
Health	A	09 aaa	472	58	18	62	2	267			307	430	737	5	84	29	0.35	0				98		89	2%	4.39	-9.8	52	$13
PT/Exp	D	10 STL *	420	51	12	73	1	248	208	273	302	403	705	7	83	27	0.44	279	38	22	39	105	9%	74	2%	4.16	-14.6	53	$12
Consist	A	1st Half	213	26	6	37	1	238			281	384	665	6	84	26	0.37	0				99		81	2%	3.64	-10.8	51	$5
LIMA Plan	D+	2nd Half	207	25	7	36	0	260			322	423	745	8	82	29	0.50	281	38	22	39	112	10%	79	2%	4.69	-3.9	59	$6
Rand Var	+2	11 Proj	392	48	12	60	1	258			307	409	716	7	83	28	0.43	272	38	22	39	98	9%	82	2%	4.25	-10.2	52	$11

4-18-.246 in 114 AB at STL. Four recalls from Triple-A later, still not much hope of becoming a regular. Mediocre skill base, shaky glove will prevent that. PX says we can't write him off yet, but at age 27, time's running out.

Crawford,Carl

Crawford,Carl			AB	R	HR	RBI	SB	Avg	vL	vR	OB	Slg	OPS	bb%	ct%	h%	Eye	xBA	G	L	F	PX	hr/f	Spd	SBO	RC/G	RAR	BPV	R$
Pos	7	06 TAM	600	89	18	77	58	305	288	311	345	482	827	6	86	33	0.44	285	52	18	30	92	12%	153	40%	5.55	6.2	77	$33
Age/B	29 Left	07 TAM	584	93	11	80	50	315	318	314	351	466	816	5	81	38	0.29	278	48	20	32	101	7%	111	38%	5.46	6.8	50	$31
Ht/Wt	74 215	08 TAM	443	69	8	57	25	273	248	285	319	400	719	6	86	30	0.50	271	49	21	30	69	7%	136	26%	4.38	-6.1	56	$17
Health	A	09 TAM	606	96	15	68	60	305	269	322	359	452	811	8	84	35	0.52	279	52	19	29	85	10%	130	41%	5.49	8.3	60	$33
PT/Exp	A	10 TAM	600	110	19	90	47	307	256	332	356	495	851	7	83	35	0.44	290	47	16	36	116	11%	145	34%	5.94	17.7	83	$37
Consist	B	1st Half	301	62	7	41	29	316			376	488	864	9	84	36	0.59	301	53	16	30	112	9%	139	40%	6.25	11.5	85	$20
LIMA Plan	D	2nd Half	299	48	12	49	18	298			335	502	837	5	82	33	0.31	278	41	17	42	121	12%	143	26%	5.62	6.2	79	$17
Rand Var	-2	11 Proj	610	102	17	84	49	300			348	466	814	7	83	34	0.44	281	49	18	33	98	10%	138	35%	5.48	9.3	70	$33

Maybe he hasn't peaked yet...
- Solid PX growth, spike in 2H
- Wheels show no sign of wear
- Elite durability

At minimum, a .300 BA/50 SB lock, but if he lands in the right park... UP: 25 HR

Crisp,Coco

Crisp,Coco			AB	R	HR	RBI	SB	Avg	vL	vR	OB	Slg	OPS	bb%	ct%	h%	Eye	xBA	G	L	F	PX	hr/f	Spd	SBO	RC/G	RAR	BPV	R$
Pos	8	06 BOS	413	58	8	36	22	264	277	259	315	385	700	7	84	30	0.46	251	48	16	36	77	6%	121	24%	4.14	-6.3	49	$12
Age/B	31 Both	07 BOS	526	85	6	60	28	268	270	267	332	382	714	9	84	31	0.60	260	47	17	36	75	4%	116	23%	4.47	-1.0	51	$17
Ht/Wt	72 180	08 BOS	361	55	7	41	20	283	295	278	346	407	753	9	84	32	0.59	252	41	20	39	80	6%	105	25%	4.88	-4.9	50	$14
Health	F	09 KC	180	30	3	14	13	228	222	231	335	378	713	14	87	25	1.26	276	48	18	34	81	6%	148	28%	4.84	1.1	88	$5
PT/Exp	D	10 OAK	290	51	8	38	32	279	329	261	347	438	785	9	83	31	0.61	277	47	17	37	100	9%	127	41%	5.28	-0.5	72	$17
Consist	A	1st Half	43	12	2	10	4	302			375	605	980	10	74	37	0.45	319	45	18	36	200	17%	135	45%	8.09	3.4	121	$4
LIMA Plan	B	2nd Half	247	39	6	28	28	275			342	409	751	9	85	31	0.66	269	47	16	37	85	8%	116	41%	4.86	-3.3	61	$14
Rand Var	-1	11 Proj	429	67	11	45	27	266			337	418	755	10	85	29	0.71	273	46	17	37	93	9%	122	27%	4.96	-1.7	71	$17

Speed skills remain enticing, but they don't matter much if he can't stay on field. And even if healthy, bid on 20-30 SB, not 30+. Only a constant green light helped him break that threshold. He'll be overvalued due to 2H.

Crosby,Bobby

Crosby,Bobby			AB	R	HR	RBI	SB	Avg	vL	vR	OB	Slg	OPS	bb%	ct%	h%	Eye	xBA	G	L	F	PX	hr/f	Spd	SBO	RC/G	RAR	BPV	R$
Pos	6	06 OAK	358	42	9	40	8	229	185	242	299	338	637	9	79	27	0.47	232	47	18	35	69	9%	85	9%	3.34	-11.6	16	$6
Age/B	31 Right	07 OAK	349	40	8	31	10	226	222	228	274	341	615	6	82	25	0.37	263	48	20	32	77	9%	79	15%	3.01	-13.6	28	$6
Ht/Wt	75 203	08 OAK	559	66	7	61	7	238	222	244	299	349	648	8	83	28	0.51	250	48	16	36	82	4%	80	7%	3.61	-12.1	39	$9
Health	C	09 OAK	238	35	6	29	2	223	265	184	294	357	651	9	82	25	0.55	241	44	15	40	81	8%	100	5%	3.61	-6.2	41	$4
PT/Exp	C	10 2NL	168	9	1	13	0	220	217	222	292	298	590	9	77	28	0.45	229	51	15	35	68	2%	75	7%	2.84	-8.3	6	$0
Consist	A	1st Half	139	8	1	11	0	245			314	324	637	9	80	30	0.50	238	50	15	35	66	3%	82	5%	3.48	-4.0	17	$1
LIMA Plan	F	2nd Half	29	1	0	2	0	103			187	172	360	9	66	16	0.30	195	55	10	35	79	0%	77	25%	-0.66	-5.4	-31	($1)
Rand Var	0	11 Proj	96	10	1	10	1	229			294	316	610	8	81	27	0.49	237	48	16	36	65	4%	81	7%	3.10	-4.1	20	$1

From ROY to out of baseball in six seasons? Could happen. Power is long gone. He's a slap hitter with no wheels. There are no signs of a resurrection here. But at least OAK finally gave up on this one.

Crowe,Trevor

Crowe,Trevor			AB	R	HR	RBI	SB	Avg	vL	vR	OB	Slg	OPS	bb%	ct%	h%	Eye	xBA	G	L	F	PX	hr/f	Spd	SBO	RC/G	RAR	BPV	R$
Pos	78	06 aa	154	18	1	12	15	214			301	292	593	11	86	24	0.86	0				51		102	49%	3.21	-10.0	38	$4
Age/B	27 Both	07 aa	518	74	4	43	24	230			305	309	614	10	87	26	0.84	0				54		108	24%	3.42	-28.6	46	$10
Ht/Wt	72 190	08 a/a	344	61	8	36	15	271			344	424	768	10	80	32	0.55	0				109		102	24%	5.15	0.1	59	$13
Health	A	09 CLE *	368	43	3	32	17	245	255	228	311	339	650	9	82	29	0.53	255	56	16	27	63	4%	113	25%	3.68	-14.9	32	$8
PT/Exp	D	10 CLE *	561	63	3	45	25	239	202	266	283	318	601	6	84	28	0.39	263	53	18	29	59	2%	101	24%	2.96	-32.7	27	$12
Consist	C	1st Half	307	39	2	28	15	231			277	310	588	6	87	26	0.47	256	49	17	34	54	2%	103	24%	2.89	-18.7	34	$7
LIMA Plan	D	2nd Half	254	24	1	17	10	248			290	327	617	6	81	30	0.31	266	56	19	25	65	2%	98	25%	3.08	-13.9	19	$5
Rand Var	+2	11 Proj	453	55	3	38	18	245			302	331	634	8	83	29	0.48	261	54	18	28	64	3%	101	23%	3.43	-20.7	29	$10

2-36-.251-20 in 442 AB at CLE. The 20 SB were nice, but Spd, eroding OB say they're no given. With no power and tendency to hit everything on ground, he's really limited. Former 1st round pick more likely bust than boom.

Cruz,Nelson

Cruz,Nelson			AB	R	HR	RBI	SB	Avg	vL	vR	OB	Slg	OPS	bb%	ct%	h%	Eye	xBA	G	L	F	PX	hr/f	Spd	SBO	RC/G	RAR	BPV	R$
Pos	9	06 2TM *	501	75	25	87	16	265	217	226	327	465	792	8	75	31	0.36	245	46	12	42	126	16%	95	18%	5.23	0.3	48	$20
Age/B	30 Right	07 TEX *	469	57	21	66	3	249	212	245	303	441	743	7	74	29	0.30	249	38	16	46	129	13%	90	8%	4.58	-12.9	44	$12
Ht/Wt	75 230	08 TEX *	498	83	34	95	20	287	419	298	357	551	908	10	79	30	0.52	297	40	22	38	160	23%	101	21%	6.66	18.6	95	$27
Health	C	09 TEX	462	75	33	76	20	260	235	270	331	524	855	10	74	28	0.42	270	38	16	46	161	21%	77	21%	6.04	9.6	71	$22
PT/Exp	B	10 TEX	399	60	22	78	17	318	330	314	378	576	954	9	80	35	0.47	307	37	18	45	172	15%	86	19%	7.26	25.0	102	$25
Consist	B	1st Half	150	22	10	39	8	313			383	613	997	10	75	36	0.45	318	34	23	42	205	21%	76	24%	8.08	12.9	108	$11
LIMA Plan	C+	2nd Half	249	38	12	39	9	321			374	554	928	8	83	35	0.49	299	39	15	46	154	13%	92	16%	6.83	12.6	99	$14
Rand Var	-2	11 Proj	469	72	33	96	16	292			356	577	933	9	78	31	0.44	300	38	18	45	180	20%	84	18%	6.99	24.0	100	$27

Don't be fooled by HR dip; bum hammy nagged him all year. He'll give back some BA after h% corrects, but you'll buy him for power. And there's more of that to come if PX growth, health align. UP: 40 HR

Cuddyer,Michael

Cuddyer,Michael			AB	R	HR	RBI	SB	Avg	vL	vR	OB	Slg	OPS	bb%	ct%	h%	Eye	xBA	G	L	F	PX	hr/f	Spd	SBO	RC/G	RAR	BPV	R$
Pos	39	06 MIN	557	102	24	109	6	284	297	276	355	504	860	10	77	33	0.48	279	44	21	35	145	16%	86	4%	6.28	13.4	70	$22
Age/B	32 Right	07 MIN	547	87	16	81	5	276	308	263	352	433	785	10	80	32	0.60	269	45	19	36	102	10%	114	3%	5.32	1.0	60	$17
Ht/Wt	74 215	08 MIN	249	30	3	36	5	249	250	249	318	369	687	9	84	29	0.63	263	46	21	33	78	4%	110	9%	4.18	-8.0	51	$5
Health	C	09 MIN	588	93	32	94	6	276	307	264	336	520	857	8	80	30	0.46	286	44	16	40	144	17%	95	5%	6.02	5.1	82	$23
PT/Exp	B	10 MIN	609	93	14	81	7	271	285	265	334	417	751	9	85	30	0.62	286	50	17	33	97	8%	89	6%	4.87	-15.8	63	$19
Consist	C	1st Half	300	45	7	36	2	263			328	413	742	9	85	29	0.63	285	45	19	36	99	8%	103	4%	4.77	-8.7	68	$8
LIMA Plan	B	2nd Half	309	48	7	45	5	278			340	421	761	9	85	31	0.62	285	54	16	30	96	9%	78	8%	4.97	-7.0	58	$11
Rand Var	+1	11 Proj	561	85	17	82	7	271			335	441	776	9	83	30	0.56	281	48	18	35	108	10%	95	6%	5.14	-8.1	66	$18

Why 20+ HR may be history...
- hr/f drove last two HR spikes
- High GB rate and growing
- No power against RHers

Versatility is his primary calling card now. As an OF/1B, his lack of thump stands out even more.

STEPHEN NICKRAND

Cunningham,Aaron

			AB	R	HR	RBI	SB	Avg	vL	vR	OB	Slg	OPS	bb%	ct%	h%	Eye	xBA	G	L	F	PX	hr/f	Spd	SBO	RC/G	RAR	BPV	R$
Pos	7	06	0	0	0	0	0	0							0			0											
Age/B	24 Right	07 aa	118	21	5	17	1	271			328	517	845	8	81	30	0.45	0				148		138	15%	5.93	2.6	103	$4
Ht/Wt	71 203	08 OAK	* 506	75	13	65	15	283	208	268	340	435	775	8	79	34	0.42	227	34	14	52	102	6%	117	15%	5.08	3.3	51	$18
Health	A	09 OAK	* 387	51	9	41	8	236	176	139	285	368	653	6	82	27	0.38	247	49	14	38	86	7%	92	15%	3.50	-17.8	38	$8
PT/Exp	D	10 SD	* 403	39	6	49	3	228	364	250	278	348	627	7	79	28	0.33	246	46	15	39	91	5%	95	17%	3.19	-23.8	31	$6
Consist	B	1st Half	215	19	4	22	1	207			251	320	571	6	77	25	0.25	228	46	13	42	84	6%	94	19%	2.37	-18.8	16	$2
LIMA Plan	F	2nd Half	188	21	2	26	2	251			308	381	689	8	80	30	0.42	261	46	16	38	100	3%	95	16%	4.11	-5.5	47	$4
Rand Var	+2	11 Proj	260	32	5	32	4	246			299	377	676	7	80	29	0.38	246	45	15	40	92	6%	98	15%	3.83	-11.4	40	$6

1-15-.288 in 132 AB at SD. BA in SD was a mirage caused by 36% hit rate. 2nd half suggests he might return to '07-'08 skills. Still young, but it's time for some real growth if he's to have a career.

Cust,Jack

			AB	R	HR	RBI	SB	Avg	vL	vR	OB	Slg	OPS	bb%	ct%	h%	Eye	xBA	G	L	F	PX	hr/f	Spd	SBO	RC/G	RAR	BPV	R$
Pos	0	06 aaa	441	71	19	57	0	233			384	405	789	20	76	26	1.02	0				109		57	2%	5.73	-9.4	49	$9
Age/B	32 Left	07 OAK	* 475	73	32	96	0	250	218	273	400	507	906	20	58	35	0.60	254	42	23	35	214	34%	32	1%	8.25	28.2	55	$17
Ht/Wt	73 240	08 OAK	485	79	35	80	0	233	235	229	376	489	864	19	59	31	0.56	244	40	21	39	204	33%	49	0%	7.33	35.0	54	$16
Health	A	09 OAK	513	88	25	70	4	240	221	247	356	417	774	15	64	32	0.50	217	37	20	43	127	18%	54	3%	5.57	6.1	6	$15
PT/Exp	B	10 OAK	* 459	63	16	63	2	253	221	285	374	406	779	16	66	35	0.57	237	40	22	39	125	13%	45	2%	5.71	-8.7	14	$13
Consist	B	1st Half	227	32	5	25	0	252			372	362	734	16	71	33	0.67	249	39	28	34	90	8%	49	0%	4.99	-9.1	6	$5
LIMA Plan	C	2nd Half	232	31	11	38	2	254			375	448	824	16	62	36	0.51	236	40	19	41	165	19%	50	5%	6.59	1.7	28	$8
Rand Var	0	11 Proj	408	62	21	60	2	245			371	441	812	17	64	33	0.56	239	39	21	40	151	20%	46	2%	6.22	4.6	27	$13

13-52-.272 in 349 AB at OAK. Low 1st half PX, hr/f probably an anomaly, as 2nd half shows power is still there. Expect a rebound, but struggles vs LHP will limit playing time.

Damon,Johnny

			AB	R	HR	RBI	SB	Avg	vL	vR	OB	Slg	OPS	bb%	ct%	h%	Eye	xBA	G	L	F	PX	hr/f	Spd	SBO	RC/G	RAR	BPV	R$
Pos	70	06 NYY	593	115	24	80	25	285	297	280	358	482	840	10	86	30	0.79	281	41	19	40	113	12%	112	20%	5.93	12.8	89	$26
Age/B	37 Left	07 NYY	533	93	12	63	27	270	281	266	351	396	746	11	85	30	0.84	274	48	18	33	81	8%	120	18%	4.93	-1.6	65	$20
Ht/Wt	74 205	08 NYY	555	95	17	71	29	303	258	321	375	461	836	10	85	33	0.78	281	44	22	34	95	11%	130	20%	5.92	16.6	79	$26
Health	A	09 NYY	550	107	24	82	12	282	269	288	364	489	853	11	82	31	0.72	276	41	16	42	125	13%	115	7%	6.16	17.8	88	$23
PT/Exp	A	10 DET	539	81	8	51	11	271	275	270	354	401	754	11	83	31	0.73	273	44	19	37	92	5%	121	7%	5.10	3.4	68	$15
Consist	B	1st Half	269	48	4	22	7	264			357	394	751	13	84	30	0.91	277	47	17	36	93	5%	115	9%	5.15	2.1	73	$8
LIMA Plan	B+	2nd Half	270	33	4	29	4	278			350	407	757	10	83	32	0.64	269	41	20	38	91	5%	122	5%	5.05	1.3	62	$7
Rand Var	+1	11 Proj	516	85	13	61	14	279			358	434	792	11	83	31	0.75	274	43	19	38	101	8%	117	10%	5.47	8.0	73	$18

Leaving the Bronx for Comerica yielded a HR dip, though more extreme than expected. Other BPIs are holding up well, even Spd, which is admirable given his age. But his age is still 37 so it's tough to bet on a rebound.

Davis,Chris

			AB	R	HR	RBI	SB	Avg	vL	vR	OB	Slg	OPS	bb%	ct%	h%	Eye	xBA	G	L	F	PX	hr/f	Spd	SBO	RC/G	RAR	BPV	R$
Pos	3	06	0	0	0	0	0	0							0			0											
Age/B	25 Left	07 aa	109	18	11	21	0	275			342	642	984	9	80	25	0.50	0				218		81	0%	7.42	5.4	138	$5
Ht/Wt	76 235	08 TEX	* 592	104	36	112	6	294	279	287	339	557	896	6	76	34	0.28	296	35	25	40	176	20%	75	7%	6.49	20.1	80	$28
Health	A	09 TEX	* 556	70	26	84	0	255	189	260	311	449	759	7	67	33	0.24	233	35	21	44	136	16%	86	1%	5.00	-11.6	20	$15
PT/Exp	A	10 TEX	* 518	57	12	64	5	263	148	204	319	407	726	8	76	33	0.34	267	42	22	36	111	8%	62	5%	4.48	-19.4	29	$13
Consist	C	1st Half	279	26	7	35	2	273			320	418	739	7	77	33	0.31	260	42	19	39	105	8%	80	4%	4.55	-9.7	33	$7
LIMA Plan	D	2nd Half	239	31	5	29	3	251			318	393	711	9	74	32	0.38	270	42	24	34	118	8%	59	7%	4.38	-9.8	29	$6
Rand Var	+1	11 Proj	258	34	10	38	2	244			302	429	732	8	74	30	0.32	265	37	22	40	134	13%	76	4%	4.52	-8.6	42	$7

1-4-.192 in 120 AB at TEX. Crashed and burned in third attempt to win 1B job, despite superb AAA stats. You know the story... we HAVE to project a down year but he'll go out in 2011 and hit 45 HRs.

Davis,Ike

			AB	R	HR	RBI	SB	Avg	vL	vR	OB	Slg	OPS	bb%	ct%	h%	Eye	xBA	G	L	F	PX	hr/f	Spd	SBO	RC/G	RAR	BPV	R$
Pos	3	06	0	0	0	0	0	0							0			0											
Age/B	24 Left	07	0	0	0	0	0	0							0			0											
Ht/Wt	77 195	08	0	0	0	0	0	0							0			0											
Health	A	09 aa	207	24	10	35	0	275			342	483	825	9	76	32	0.43	0				138		87	0%	5.71	-2.3	62	$7
PT/Exp	F	10 NYM	* 556	79	21	74	3	268	295	254	359	449	807	12	74	33	0.56	262	43	16	41	133	12%	95	3%	5.74	-9.5	60	$18
Consist	A	1st Half	286	47	12	41	1	268			350	453	803	11	75	32	0.50	265	44	17	40	132	14%	90	1%	5.57	-6.3	57	$10
LIMA Plan	B	2nd Half	270	32	9	33	2	267			367	444	812	14	74	33	0.61	260	42	16	41	135	11%	103	5%	5.92	-3.2	63	$8
Rand Var	0	11 Proj	559	72	20	82	2	261			344	436	781	11	75	32	0.51	255	43	16	41	126	12%	90	2%	5.32	-15.2	53	$17

19-71-.264 in 523 AB at NYM.
PRO:
- Solid PX, FB rate
- Walk rate showed growth
CON:
- Low ct% limits BA upside
Feels like he's still a year away.

Davis,Rajai

			AB	R	HR	RBI	SB	Avg	vL	vR	OB	Slg	OPS	bb%	ct%	h%	Eye	xBA	G	L	F	PX	hr/f	Spd	SBO	RC/G	RAR	BPV	R$
Pos	789	06 aaa	385	50	2	20	44	278			323	345	668	6	85	32	0.46	0				47		95	50%	3.77	-16.5	22	$16
Age/B	30 Right	07 2NL	* 401	55	4	32	43	269	299	258	329	372	701	8	87	30	0.69	252	43	17	40	66	3%	134	51%	4.35	-12.3	59	$17
Ht/Wt	71 195	08 2TM	218	31	3	20	30	248	232	250	278	358	635	4	82	29	0.23	254	48	22	30	62	6%	194	72%	3.19	-13.0	44	$11
Health	A	09 OAK	390	65	3	48	41	305	316	299	353	423	776	7	82	37	0.41	260	46	20	34	81	3%	126	47%	5.13	1.3	47	$21
PT/Exp	C	10 OAK	525	66	5	52	50	284	304	276	318	377	695	5	85	33	0.33	255	48	16	37	67	3%	116	44%	3.99	-13.6	40	$24
Consist	C	1st Half	258	33	2	21	26	256			289	345	634	4	83	30	0.27	251	49	15	35	65	3%	127	51%	3.23	-12.7	33	$10
LIMA Plan	D+	2nd Half	267	33	3	31	24	311			345	408	753	5	87	35	0.41	259	46	16	38	69	3%	98	38%	4.69	-1.4	46	$14
Rand Var	-2	11 Proj	482	67	5	49	46	284			323	387	710	5	84	33	0.36	257	47	18	35	69	3%	131	45%	4.21	-10.2	44	$22

Declining Spd would not be a concern as long as SBO and OB hold up. But, ah, OB is the rub with that minuscule bb%. Note xBA's. Do you want to bid on a BA repeat?
DN: 300 AB, 30 SB

DeJesus,David

			AB	R	HR	RBI	SB	Avg	vL	vR	OB	Slg	OPS	bb%	ct%	h%	Eye	xBA	G	L	F	PX	hr/f	Spd	SBO	RC/G	RAR	BPV	R$
Pos	9	06 KC	491	83	8	56	6	295	307	291	352	446	798	8	86	33	0.61	290	49	22	29	95	7%	125	7%	5.45	-2.9	75	$14
Age/B	31 Left	07 KC	605	101	7	58	10	260	240	267	330	372	702	10	86	29	0.77	265	46	19	36	71	4%	142	8%	4.42	-19.1	65	$13
Ht/Wt	72 190	08 KC	518	70	12	73	11	307	302	310	363	452	815	8	86	34	0.65	290	46	25	29	87	9%	120	12%	5.58	3.2	69	$19
Health	C	09 KC	558	74	13	71	4	281	290	277	342	434	775	8	84	31	0.59	273	46	20	34	88	8%	123	8%	5.13	-3.1	64	$15
PT/Exp	B	10 KC	352	46	5	37	3	318	258	340	378	443	821	9	87	36	0.72	291	47	21	32	86	5%	113	5%	5.75	7.6	69	$12
Consist	B	1st Half	306	40	5	35	3	327			387	467	854	9	87	36	0.75	299	48	20	32	96	6%	117	6%	6.14	9.7	79	$12
LIMA Plan	B	2nd Half	46	6	0	2	0	261			320	283	603	8	85	31	0.57	241	41	26	33	19	0%	85	0%	3.08	-2.5	-2	$1
Rand Var	-3	11 Proj	530	75	7	64	7	291			352	417	769	9	86	33	0.68	282	47	21	32	82	5%	118	8%	5.13	-0.5	64	$16

Thumb injury ended season before h% regression could bring BA back to usual level. xBA says he's not really a .300 hitter. Spd in decline so days of double digit SB probably over.

Denorfia,Chris

			AB	R	HR	RBI	SB	Avg	vL	vR	OB	Slg	OPS	bb%	ct%	h%	Eye	xBA	G	L	F	PX	hr/f	Spd	SBO	RC/G	RAR	BPV	R$
Pos	78	06 CIN	* 418	57	8	49	15	318	317	262	380	437	817	9	85	36	0.69	276	59	17	24	75	9%	98	12%	5.66	4.6	51	$17
Age/B	30 Right	07 OAK	0	0	0	0	0	0							0			0											
Ht/Wt	72 204	08 OAK	* 251	33	2	22	6	247	241	333	287	331	617	5	83	29	0.33	270	61	18	20	62	4%	105	17%	3.08	-13.4	27	$4
Health	D	09 aaa	432	40	5	31	9	195			230	273	503	4	90	21	0.46	0				45		114	20%	1.95	-46.4	41	$2
PT/Exp	D	10 SD	* 405	52	10	44	13	255	295	257	315	404	720	8	83	29	0.52	295	59	17	24	97	12%	108	17%	4.43	-7.7	60	$12
Consist	D	1st Half	215	22	1	19	7	239			293	325	618	7	84	28	0.48	297	65	21	14	62	3%	118	19%	3.26	-11.8	36	$4
LIMA Plan	F	2nd Half	190	30	9	25	6	274			340	495	834	9	82	29	0.56	310	56	15	29	138	20%	96	16%	5.78	3.9	88	$9
Rand Var	0	11 Proj	195	24	4	19	6	246			299	379	678	7	85	27	0.50	284	59	16	25	84	10%	107	17%	3.91	-8.0	55	$5

9-36-.271-8 in 284 AB at SD. Most MLB AB of his career, and he celebrated with Pujols-like hr/f in 2nd half. History says bet against a repeat of either skills or opportunity.

DeRosa,Mark

			AB	R	HR	RBI	SB	Avg	vL	vR	OB	Slg	OPS	bb%	ct%	h%	Eye	xBA	G	L	F	PX	hr/f	Spd	SBO	RC/G	RAR	BPV	R$
Pos	7	06 TEX	520	78	13	74	4	296	342	278	351	456	807	8	80	35	0.43	281	49	23	29	109	11%	84	6%	5.48	4.3	51	$16
Age/B	36 Right	07 CHC	502	64	10	72	1	293	283	297	366	420	786	10	81	34	0.62	262	42	22	36	84	7%	94	2%	5.37	0.1	44	$14
Ht/Wt	73 205	08 CHC	505	103	21	87	6	285	310	275	371	481	852	12	79	33	0.65	273	40	22	38	126	14%	85	4%	6.22	11.3	69	$23
Health	F	09 2TM	515	78	23	78	3	250	278	242	313	433	746	8	77	29	0.39	250	43	17	40	117	15%	71	4%	4.63	-10.0	39	$16
PT/Exp	C	10 SF	93	9	1	10	0	194	280	162	265	258	523	9	83	22	0.56	235	44	19	36	46	4%	69	9%	2.09	-9.0	8	$0
Consist	F	1st Half	93	9	1	10	0	194			265	258	523	9	83	22	0.56	235	44	19	36	46	4%	69	9%	2.09	-9.0	8	$0
LIMA Plan	D+	2nd Half	0	0	0	0	0	0																					
Rand Var	+5	11 Proj	379	55	11	54	2	253			325	393	718	10	80	29	0.54	259	43	20	37	94	10%	74	5%	4.43	-9.4	39	$10

Wrist problems began in '09. Even with off-season surgery he struggled in '10 before getting shut down again. Is his wrist finally healed? No matter what you hear, we won't know for sure until well into the '11 season.

Desmond,Ian

			AB	R	HR	RBI	SB	Avg	vL	vR	OB	Slg	OPS	bb%	ct%	h%	Eye	xBA	G	L	F	PX	hr/f	Spd	SBO	RC/G	RAR	BPV	R$
Pos	6	06 aa	121	7	0	3	4	165			192	215	407	3	74	22	0.13	0				39		115	26%	0.10	-17.1	-32	($1)
Age/B	25 Right	07 a	0	0	0	0	0	0																					
Ht/Wt	74 210	08 aa	323	32	9	34	10	212			266	334	600	7	80	24	0.37	0				79		78	28%	2.78	-17.6	23	$5
Health	A	09 WAS	* 430	55	10	39	19	295	300	278	349	449	797	8	82	34	0.46	263	54	12	34	104	8%	104	21%	5.35	8.4	60	$17
PT/Exp	C	10 WAS	525	59	10	65	17	269	300	257	306	392	698	5	79	32	0.26	260	53	16	32	87	8%	107	17%	3.96	-6.9	31	$17
Consist	D	1st Half	255	28	4	34	6	255			288	380	669	4	80	31	0.23	262	50	17	32	89	6%	102	13%	3.61	-6.1	31	$7
LIMA Plan	C	2nd Half	270	31	6	31	11	281			322	404	725	6	79	34	0.28	258	55	14	31	86	9%	106	21%	4.30	-0.9	30	$10
Rand Var	-2	11 Proj	546	60	11	56	20	258			302	385	686	6	79	31	0.30	255	53	15	32	87	8%	106	21%	3.86	-10.5	33	$15

Held up under full-time AB. Double-digit HR/SB from a MI ain't bad, but gives little vs. RHP, isn't super-young, and skills contain lots of "meh". Still, if his club believes in him, 500 AB = consistent rate stats.

DeWitt,Blake

			AB	R	HR	RBI	SB	Avg	vL	vR	OB	Slg	OPS	bb%	ct%	h%	Eye	xBA	G	L	F	PX	hr/f	Spd	SBO	RC/G	RAR	BPV	R$
Pos	4	06 aa	104	6	1	6	0	173			225	212	437	6	80	21	0.33	0				23		86	4%	0.75	-12.3	-22	($1)
Age/B	25 Left	07 aa	178	17	5	17	0	253			277	416	693	3	88	26	0.27	0				101		96	3%	3.89	-2.4	68	$3
Ht/Wt	71 204	08 LA	* 479	58	12	66	4	264	286	257	337	386	723	10	83	30	0.66	251	47	19	34	74	9%	94	3%	4.54	-3.2	42	$12
Health	A	09 LA	* 401	57	8	42	2	219	200	205	295	354	649	10	88	23	0.91	240	49	7	44	82	5%	116	4%	3.84	-8.5	74	$6
PT/Exp	C	10 2NL	440	47	5	52	3	261	253	263	333	373	705	10	80	32	0.55	256	46	19	35	80	4%	91	4%	4.38	-5.7	34	$9
Consist	B	1st Half	206	22	1	29	0	272			351	379	729	11	82	33	0.68	266	46	21	33	79	2%	96	2%	4.81	-0.1	43	$5
LIMA Plan	D+	2nd Half	234	25	4	23	3	252			316	368	684	9	79	30	0.45	248	45	18	37	81	6%	88	6%	3.99	-5.7	27	$5
Rand Var	-2	11 Proj	409	47	6	46	3	252			320	366	687	9	83	29	0.59	254	46	18	36	76	5%	94	4%	4.12	-7.3	41	$8

Nice Eye and ok Spd give some hope for Runs, SB. Otherwise, he really doesn't do anything that well. The best scenario? A manager who'll give him a much greener light. As is, he's just pulling your team into mediocrity.

Diaz,Matt

			AB	R	HR	RBI	SB	Avg	vL	vR	OB	Slg	OPS	bb%	ct%	h%	Eye	xBA	G	L	F	PX	hr/f	Spd	SBO	RC/G	RAR	BPV	R$
Pos	7	06 ATL	297	37	7	32	5	327	295	358	351	475	825	4	84	37	0.22	283	50	24	27	87	11%	127	12%	5.39	1.1	51	$11
Age/B	33 Right	07 ATL	358	44	12	45	4	338	356	318	366	497	864	4	82	39	0.25	280	46	21	34	101	12%	92	4%	5.82	4.3	49	$15
Ht/Wt	73 215	08 ATL	* 173	13	3	18	4	231	319	159	253	295	548	3	77	28	0.13	234	52	25	24	39	10%	73	15%	1.83	-19.0	-32	$2
Health	F	09 ATL	371	56	13	58	12	313	412	255	372	488	860	9	76	38	0.39	274	48	25	27	117	17%	108	15%	6.22	6.7	48	$18
PT/Exp	D	10 ATL	224	27	7	31	3	250	273	223	291	438	729	5	80	28	0.30	300	44	23	33	130	12%	78	9%	4.38	-4.6	62	$6
Consist	F	1st Half	80	5	0	5	2	175			224	250	474	6	71	25	0.22	221	47	19	33	66	0%	107	14%	1.09	-10.3	-16	($0)
LIMA Plan	D	2nd Half	144	22	7	26	1	292			329	542	871	5	85	30	0.38	343	43	25	32	160	18%	60	7%	5.99	3.7	100	$7
Rand Var	+5	11 Proj	297	36	8	40	6	286			327	443	770	6	79	34	0.28	277	47	23	30	107	12%	84	11%	4.87	-3.4	38	$11

Again tanked vs righties, which probably seals his fate as a platoon player. But what a platoon player! -- note PX, xBA. Not for shallow leagues, but say, in sim leagues, do what ATL did, and let him tear up LHers.

Dickerson,Chris

			AB	R	HR	RBI	SB	Avg	vL	vR	OB	Slg	OPS	bb%	ct%	h%	Eye	xBA	G	L	F	PX	hr/f	Spd	SBO	RC/G	RAR	BPV	R$
Pos	8	06 aa	389	58	11	43	19	217			316	376	692	13	68	29	0.44	0				116		109	23%	4.29	-2.3	22	$9
Age/B	28 Left	07 a/a	468	57	12	46	25	231			304	355	659	9	69	31	0.33	0				87		131	25%	3.64	-12.9	4	$12
Ht/Wt	75 228	08 CIN	* 451	69	15	55	24	254	286	309	339	435	774	11	72	32	0.46	234	37	18	45	125	10%	127	27%	5.32	7.9	50	$17
Health	F	09 CIN	255	31	2	15	11	275	243	280	371	373	743	13	74	36	0.59	239	49	22	29	76	4%	134	15%	5.07	2.5	26	$7
PT/Exp	D	10 2NL	* 140	20	3	10	8	256		225	319	387	706	9	67	37	0.28	254	52	26	21	104	13%	120	25%	4.45	-1.8	6	$5
Consist	A	1st Half	44	9	0	0	3	205			222	273	495	2	57	36	0.05	193	57	22	22	60	0%	156	38%	1.39	-4.8	-72	$1
LIMA Plan	D	2nd Half	96	11	3	10	5	280			360	439	799	11	71	37	0.44	282	50	29	21	121	18%	80	21%	5.71	2.2	30	$4
Rand Var	-2	11 Proj	208	27	3	21	11	260			345	376	721	11	71	35	0.45	246	48	24	28	89	8%	109	21%	4.66	-0.8	14	$7

0-5-.206-4 in 97 AB at CIN/MIL. Leg woes cut into otherwise enticing Spd. The injuries are getting no fewer, and he's not a kid anymore. Still... the wheels, the walks, the 2H BA, maybe?... Nah, he's just not a good hitter.

Dobbs,Greg

			AB	R	HR	RBI	SB	Avg	vL	vR	OB	Slg	OPS	bb%	ct%	h%	Eye	xBA	G	L	F	PX	hr/f	Spd	SBO	RC/G	RAR	BPV	R$
Pos	5	06 SEA	* 406	51	7	47	11	270			321	385	706	7	85	30	0.51	275	52	22	26	70	8%	105	16%	4.23	-9.2	45	$10
Age/B	32 Left	07 PHI	324	45	10	55	3	272	214	277	331	451	782	8	79	32	0.43	255	38	16	46	115	9%	111	4%	5.18	-3.9	61	$10
Ht/Wt	73 210	08 PHI	226	30	9	40	3	301	111	309	333	491	824	5	82	33	0.28	272	30	25	45	119	11%	69	7%	5.39	0.2	57	$10
Health	A	09 PHI	154	15	5	20	1	247	429	238	297	383	680	7	81	28	0.38	231	29	20	51	86	8%	67	3%	3.75	-6.3	29	$3
PT/Exp	F	10 PHI	* 225	21	7	22	3	188	188	197	245	327	572	7	77	21	0.33	220	33	14	53	96	7%	74	9%	2.39	-18.1	23	$2
Consist	D	1st Half	84	4	1	7	1	167			231	250	481	8	76	21	0.35	189	31	13	56	67	3%	68	6%	1.29	-9.9	-4	($1)
LIMA Plan	F	2nd Half	141	17	6	15	2	200			253	373	626	7	77	22	0.32	241	35	15	50	113	10%	84	10%	3.03	-8.3	40	$2
Rand Var	+5	11 Proj	112	11	4	14	1	223			275	365	640	7	79	25	0.35	233	32	18	50	94	8%	64	7%	3.25	-6.3	27	$2

5-15-.196 in 163 AB at PHI. Explain again how a playoff team gave this many AB to this skills set? Oh, okay, he's only a couple of seasons into his Frankie Frisch Five Years. He'll do well to get all five.

Donald,Jason

			AB	R	HR	RBI	SB	Avg	vL	vR	OB	Slg	OPS	bb%	ct%	h%	Eye	xBA	G	L	F	PX	hr/f	Spd	SBO	RC/G	RAR	BPV	R$
Pos	46	06	0	0	0	0	0	0							0			0											
Age/B	26 Right	07	0	0	0	0	0	0							0			0											
Ht/Wt	73 190	08 aa	362	40	12	38	8	260			321	411	732	8	81	29	0.48	0				95		108	10%	4.51	-3.4	52	$10
Health	A	09 aaa	243	27	2	13	6	201			245	290	535	5	77	25	0.25	0				70		109	12%	1.96	-21.1	9	$1
PT/Exp	F	10 CLE	* 433	58	5	36	12	243	286	243	304	359	662	8	77	30	0.38	267	49	22	30	90	5%	125	14%	3.73	-9.5	37	$10
Consist	F	1st Half	265	33	3	22	7	239			297	359	656	8	80	29	0.41	277	47	23	31	90	4%	127	16%	3.67	-6.4	48	$5
LIMA Plan	D+	2nd Half	168	25	2	14	5	250			315	357	672	9	73	33	0.35	251	50	21	29	90	6%	114	11%	3.88	-2.9	16	$4
Rand Var	0	11 Proj	454	57	5	35	12	240			295	346	641	7	77	30	0.34	256	49	21	29	80	5%	119	12%	3.40	-16.4	24	$8

4-24-.253-5 in 296 AB at CLE. Cliff Lee trade chip flashed a little speed and, as past skills suggested, little else. At 27, there's not a lot to build on either. Only consider if in dire need of SB, and can take BA hit.

Doumit,Ryan

			AB	R	HR	RBI	SB	Avg	vL	vR	OB	Slg	OPS	bb%	ct%	h%	Eye	xBA	G	L	F	PX	hr/f	Spd	SBO	RC/G	RAR	BPV	R$
Pos	2	06 PIT	* 171	18	6	24	0	222	208	208	292	397	689	9	73	27	0.37	243	46	17	38	118	13%	82	0%	4.01	-1.7	32	$2
Age/B	30 Both	07 PIT	* 305	44	12	47	4	286	246	282	346	487	833	8	77	34	0.40	278	42	21	38	136	13%	79	9%	5.85	12.4	59	$11
Ht/Wt	73 215	08 PIT	431	71	15	69	2	318	330	314	352	501	854	5	87	34	0.42	298	41	23	35	116	11%	50	4%	5.77	18.1	69	$19
Health	F	09 PIT	280	31	10	38	4	250	266	244	300	414	714	7	83	27	0.41	261	42	18	40	106	11%	68	6%	4.20	-0.5	51	$8
PT/Exp	C	10 PIT	406	42	13	45	1	251	186	282	320	406	726	9	79	29	0.47	252	41	16	43	108	9%	64	1%	4.48	0.0	40	$9
Consist	B	1st Half	245	22	7	28	1	257			323	408	732	9	82	29	0.55	254	44	13	43	102	8%	66	2%	4.58	0.7	49	$6
LIMA Plan	D+	2nd Half	161	20	6	17	0	242			315	404	718	10	73	29	0.40	249	35	21	44	118	12%	69	0%	4.38	-0.5	29	$4
Rand Var	+1	11 Proj	405	49	14	51	2	259			318	428	746	8	80	29	0.42	263	41	19	40	114	11%	66	3%	4.67	3.4	47	$11

Despite the apparent downturn in his numbers, skills are not much different from '07 and '08. Injuries have worn him down some, but it appears that this is a safe level at which he's plateaued. Still a health risk, tho.

Drew,J.D.

			AB	R	HR	RBI	SB	Avg	vL	vR	OB	Slg	OPS	bb%	ct%	h%	Eye	xBA	G	L	F	PX	hr/f	Spd	SBO	RC/G	RAR	BPV	R$
Pos	9	06 LA	494	84	20	100	2	283	244	296	393	498	891	15	79	33	0.84	277	45	19	36	133	14%	100	3%	6.94	30.4	83	$19
Age/B	35 Left	07 BOS	466	84	11	64	4	270	224	286	376	423	799	14	79	32	0.79	264	46	18	37	107	8%	115	4%	5.77	3.7	65	$13
Ht/Wt	73 200	08 BOS	368	79	19	64	4	280	284	279	407	519	926	18	78	31	0.99	285	42	18	40	153	17%	118	4%	7.47	22.0	108	$16
Health	A	09 BOS	452	84	24	68	2	279	272	281	390	522	912	15	76	32	0.75	279	39	20	41	154	17%	92	5%	7.20	24.4	87	$18
PT/Exp	B	10 BOS	478	69	22	68	3	255	208	277	338	452	790	11	78	28	0.57	276	44	16	39	130	15%	83	3%	5.34	5.5	66	$16
Consist	C	1st Half	242	43	10	41	1	281			367	496	863	12	76	34	0.56	283	41	17	42	155	13%	89	3%	6.46	10.4	79	$10
LIMA Plan	B	2nd Half	236	26	12	27	2	229			308	407	715	10	81	24	0.59	269	48	16	37	107	17%	72	3%	4.27	-4.9	52	$6
Rand Var	+2	11 Proj	454	75	22	68	3	264			363	476	839	13	78	30	0.70	278	43	18	39	136	16%	93	4%	6.11	12.4	77	$16

Signs of decline?... BA vs LHP, PX, Spd, Eye all down. And with 3rd-most AB of career, now there's room for rate stats to dip. Our trend analysis points to a rebound, but if that 2H is real: DN: 15 HR, platoon player

Drew,Stephen

			AB	R	HR	RBI	SB	Avg	vL	vR	OB	Slg	OPS	bb%	ct%	h%	Eye	xBA	G	L	F	PX	hr/f	Spd	SBO	RC/G	RAR	BPV	R$
Pos	6	06 ARI	* 551	69	16	62	4	279	350	308	328	452	780	7	84	31	0.45	267	36	24	40	98	9%	155	6%	5.07	11.2	77	$15
Age/B	28 Left	07 ARI	543	60	12	60	9	238	246	235	313	370	684	10	82	27	0.60	239	38	16	46	85	6%	114	6%	4.07	-6.1	50	$9
Ht/Wt	72 185	08 ARI	611	91	21	67	3	291	267	300	336	502	838	6	82	33	0.38	278	35	23	43	132	10%	138	4%	5.76	19.3	90	$20
Health	A	09 ARI	533	71	12	65	5	261	200	282	323	428	751	8	84	29	0.56	259	39	19	42	102	6%	151	4%	4.88	3.3	80	$14
PT/Exp	A	10 ARI	565	83	15	61	10	278	255	287	349	458	808	10	81	32	0.57	274	40	19	41	117	8%	156	9%	5.63	19.7	86	$19
Consist	A	1st Half	276	36	4	28	5	268			331	409	741	9	82	32	0.51	263	43	18	39	93	5%	138	8%	4.78	2.9	61	$8
LIMA Plan	A	2nd Half	289	47	11	33	5	287			366	505	871	11	80	33	0.63	285	37	20	43	140	11%	166	11%	6.46	16.8	107	$12
Rand Var	-1	11 Proj	542	77	15	61	7	275			340	457	797	9	82	31	0.54	270	39	20	42	115	8%	148	7%	5.43	14.4	84	$17

Let your eyes feast on those Spd numbers. Now, the SBO. Now hope Kirk Gibson reads this book. More raw speed than... Carl Crawford? If nothing else, speculating on the upside alone is worth an extra $1 in March.

ROD TRUESDELL

Duda,Lucas			AB	R	HR	RBI	SB	Avg	vL	vR	OB	Slg	OPS	bb%	ct%	h%	Eye	xBA	G	L	F	PX	hr/f	Spd	SBO	RC/G	RAR	BPV	R$
Pos	7	06	0	0	0	0	0	0																					
Age/B	25 Left	07	0	0	0	0	0	0																					
Ht/Wt	76 225	08	0	0	0	0	0	0																					
Health	A	09 aa	395	38	7	42	2	243			327	365	691	11	81	29	0.65					86		77	4%	4.24	-12.3	39	$6
PT/Exp	F	10 NYM	* 509	64	21	75	1	243	158	215	307	450	757	8	82	26	0.53	289	35	19	46	139	11%	52	1%	4.84	-3.5	75	$14
Consist	B	1st Half	213	26	8	33	1	239			316	437	753	10	87	24	0.85	0				128		78	2%	4.98	-0.6	96	$6
LIMA Plan	D	2nd Half	296	38	14	43	0	246			301	459	759	7	79	27	0.38	284	35	19	46	148	13%	52	0%	4.77	-2.6	67	$9
Rand Var	+3	11 Proj	235	27	10	31	1	264			334	464	798	10	82	29	0.58	277	35	19	46	132	11%	64	2%	5.37	0.7	73	$7

4-13-.202 in 84 AB at NYM. Power finally blossomed, and carried over (156 PX) in small MLB sample. Shaky 74% ct% in majors raises the BA risk, but could have value as an end-game power source.

Duncan,Shelley			AB	R	HR	RBI	SB	Avg	vL	vR	OB	Slg	OPS	bb%	ct%	h%	Eye	xBA	G	L	F	PX	hr/f	Spd	SBO	RC/G	RAR	BPV	R$
Pos	7	06 a/a	394	39	17	53	3	205			262	382	644	7	75	23	0.32					114		68	5%	3.26	-24.0	30	$5
Age/B	31 Right	07 NYY	* 410	65	29	84	2	260	303	220	333	520	853	10	75	28	0.44	292	35	24	41	164	23%	61	4%	6.00	11.5	72	$17
Ht/Wt	77 225	08 aaa	205	29	9	34	4	193			296	386	682	13	72	22	0.53					136		85	11%	3.98	-7.5	51	$5
Health	A	09 aaa	452	69	26	81	2	228			307	459	766	10	77	24	0.50					145		72	2%	4.94	-4.7	69	$14
PT/Exp	F	10 CLE	* 375	43	14	58	1	230	264	211	300	394	695	9	73	28	0.37	228	29	16	56	121	9%	64	1%	4.04	-9.5	27	$9
Consist	B	1st Half	206	20	7	34	0	239			303	397	700	8	75	28	0.37	243	23	23	54	114	9%	69	0%	4.07	-5.0	32	$5
LIMA Plan	D	2nd Half	169	23	7	24	1	219			298	391	688	10	70	27	0.37	221	30	13	56	129	11%	72	2%	4.00	-4.5	27	$4
Rand Var	-1	11 Proj	211	28	13	34	1	237			314	470	783	10	74	26	0.42	256	30	16	54	156	15%	70	3%	5.18	1.6	63	$7

11-36-.231 in 229 AB at CLE. Huge OPS split (.857 vLH, .661 vRH) highlights his platoon usefulness. PX and FB% combo say his power is legit, but that platoon split limits opportunities and lowers his ceiling.

Dunn,Adam			AB	R	HR	RBI	SB	Avg	vL	vR	OB	Slg	OPS	bb%	ct%	h%	Eye	xBA	G	L	F	PX	hr/f	Spd	SBO	RC/G	RAR	BPV	R$
Pos	7	06 CIN	561	99	40	92	7	234	270	215	361	490	851	17	65	28	0.58	249	28	24	49	176	22%	33	4%	6.63	10.6	48	$20
Age/B	31 Left	07 CIN	522	101	40	106	9	264	239	278	384	554	937	16	68	31	0.61	274	35	19	47	197	24%	51	6%	7.76	24.7	81	$26
Ht/Wt	78 287	08 2NL	517	79	40	100	2	236	195	253	382	513	894	19	68	26	0.74	260	36	18	46	190	25%	45	2%	7.19	22.6	79	$20
Health	A	09 WAS	546	81	38	105	0	267	268	267	396	529	925	18	68	33	0.66	259	31	20	49	189	21%	40	1%	7.71	18.9	71	$24
PT/Exp	A	10 WAS	558	85	38	103	0	260	199	286	350	536	885	12	64	33	0.39	270	33	18	49	218	22%	50	1%	7.18	13.8	73	$24
Consist	B	1st Half	298	44	17	49	0	275			355	544	899	11	67	36	0.37	281	32	20	47	214	18%	61	0%	7.28	8.0	81	$12
LIMA Plan	B	2nd Half	260	41	21	54	0	242			343	527	870	13	62	30	0.40	257	34	15	51	224	26%	40	1%	7.07	5.7	66	$12
Rand Var	0	11 Proj	535	83	39	102	1	254			367	528	895	15	66	31	0.52	263	33	19	49	204	23%	46	1%	7.28	16.1	72	$23

PRO: Elite power profile: big PX, lots of FBs and BBs.
CON:abysmal ct%, LHPs are his kryptonite.
In other words, nothing new here. Remarkable consistency makes this an easy projection.

Eckstein,David			AB	R	HR	RBI	SB	Avg	vL	vR	OB	Slg	OPS	bb%	ct%	h%	Eye	xBA	G	L	F	PX	hr/f	Spd	SBO	RC/G	RAR	BPV	R$
Pos	4	06 STL	500	68	2	23	7	292	280	298	333	344	677	6	92	32	0.76	264	49	22	29	34	1%	112	8%	4.00	-8.4	41	$10
Age/B	36 Right	07 STL	434	58	3	31	10	309	298	314	345	382	727	5	95	32	1.09	275	41	22	37	49	2%	80	8%	4.59	-1.3	55	$13
Ht/Wt	67 177	08 2TM	324	32	2	27	2	265	313	246	330	349	678	9	90	29	0.97	273	51	20	28	61	2%	66	3%	4.20	-5.9	48	$5
Health	C	09 SD	503	64	2	50	3	260	244	268	314	334	648	7	91	28	0.85	257	46	19	34	52	1%	80	3%	3.79	-10.9	45	$9
PT/Exp	B	10 SD	442	49	1	29	8	267	265	268	309	326	635	6	92	29	0.77	270	48	20	32	46	1%	66	7%	3.58	-15.8	38	$9
Consist	A	1st Half	296	29	1	22	5	280			317	355	672	5	96	29	1.33	285	48	19	33	55	1%	63	8%	4.08	-6.2	59	$7
LIMA Plan	D	2nd Half	146	20	0	7	3	240			293	267	560	7	84	28	0.48	240	48	22	30	24	0%	76	7%	2.51	-10.0	-5	$2
Rand Var	0	11 Proj	312	38	1	23	4	263			313	320	633	7	90	29	0.73	260	48	20	32	44	1%	71	6%	3.55	-10.6	32	$6

If there was a "Scrappy" BPI, he would lead the Majors. Until there is, xBA says .300 BA is ancient history, his speed is waning and RAR trend could not be clearer. Good for MLB clubhouses, not for your team.

Edmonds,Jim			AB	R	HR	RBI	SB	Avg	vL	vR	OB	Slg	OPS	bb%	ct%	h%	Eye	xBA	G	L	F	PX	hr/f	Spd	SBO	RC/G	RAR	BPV	R$
Pos	8	06 STL	350	52	19	70	4	257	156	295	355	471	826	13	71	31	0.52	247	35	20	44	142	17%	58	4%	6.00	15.9	44	$13
Age/B	40 Left	07 STL	365	39	12	53	0	252	198	268	328	403	730	10	79	29	0.55	245	36	19	44	93	9%	62	2%	4.57	0.4	33	$8
Ht/Wt	73 212	08 2NL	340	53	20	55	2	235	146	250	342	479	821	14	76	25	0.67	268	37	18	45	157	17%	70	4%	5.86	11.5	80	$11
Health	C	09	0	0	0	0	0	0																					
PT/Exp	F	10 2NL	246	44	11	23	2	276	239	285	341	504	845	9	76	33	0.40	300	28	28	43	170	14%	73	3%	6.04	8.1	80	$9
Consist	A	1st Half	166	28	4	11	2	265			322	440	762	8	75	33	0.33	285	30	30	40	145	8%	79	5%	5.02	0.6	56	$5
LIMA Plan	F	2nd Half	80	16	7	12	0	300			378	637	1015	11	78	31	0.56	333	25	25	49	221	23%	64	0%	8.10	7.0	130	$5
Rand Var	-4	11 Proj	186	30	6	26	1	263			346	436	782	11	76	32	0.53	260	32	23	45	125	10%	61	3%	5.33	2.9	48	$6

Surprisingly effective after a a year away, and validated by xBA, PX and RAR. But age, plus Achilles injury that shelved him for postseason, may make this a single encore performance.

Ellis,Mark			AB	R	HR	RBI	SB	Avg	vL	vR	OB	Slg	OPS	bb%	ct%	h%	Eye	xBA	G	L	F	PX	hr/f	Spd	SBO	RC/G	RAR	BPV	R$
Pos	4	06 OAK	441	64	11	52	4	249	278	242	312	385	697	8	83	28	0.53	249	39	19	42	87	7%	79	4%	4.15	0.3	43	$9
Age/B	33 Right	07 OAK	583	84	19	76	9	276	313	263	327	441	768	7	84	30	0.47	256	32	18	50	104	8%	88	9%	4.90	15.0	61	$18
Ht/Wt	71 193	08 OAK	442	55	12	41	14	233	176	256	315	373	688	11	85	25	0.82	249	34	20	46	85	7%	101	13%	4.22	-9.0	63	$10
Health	D	09 OAK	377	52	10	61	10	263	260	264	305	403	708	6	86	28	0.43	267	40	20	39	87	8%	68	15%	4.16	-8.5	46	$12
PT/Exp	B	10 OAK	436	45	5	49	7	291	330	279	351	381	732	8	87	33	0.71	265	42	21	37	65	4%	72	9%	4.66	2.5	41	$12
Consist	A	1st Half	163	20	2	22	3	288			352	374	726	9	87	32	0.76	270	45	22	33	61	4%	71	8%	4.62	0.7	38	$5
LIMA Plan	D+	2nd Half	273	25	3	27	4	293			350	385	735	8	87	33	0.69	263	41	20	39	67	3%	76	11%	4.69	1.7	44	$7
Rand Var	-3	11 Proj	396	47	8	49	8	273			331	390	721	8	86	30	0.63	263	40	20	40	78	6%	78	11%	4.49	-1.4	48	$11

Reasons for pessimism despite rising BA trend:
1. xBA doesn't support BA
2. Declining PX and Spd
3. Health is always in issue
4. Mid-30s are a tough time for middle infielders.

Ellsbury,Jacoby			AB	R	HR	RBI	SB	Avg	vL	vR	OB	Slg	OPS	bb%	ct%	h%	Eye	xBA	G	L	F	PX	hr/f	Spd	SBO	RC/G	RAR	BPV	R$
Pos	8	06 aa	198	25	3	16	14	289			358	407	765	10	89	32	0.94	0				70		112	35%	5.17	3.7	65	$7
Age/B	27 Left	07 BOS	* 552	89	5	53	44	312	346	356	358	418	776	7	89	35	0.63	286	52	19	29	70	4%	128	31%	5.12	9.0	64	$25
Ht/Wt	73 185	08 BOS	554	98	9	47	50	280	295	275	329	394	723	7	86	31	0.51	274	52	20	28	69	7%	147	39%	4.44	-14.7	57	$25
Health	F	09 BOS	624	94	8	60	70	301	318	294	352	415	767	7	88	33	0.66	269	50	18	32	65	5%	145	43%	5.03	6.9	64	$33
PT/Exp	B	10 BOS	78	10	0	5	7	192	235	180	232	244	475	5	88	22	0.44	248	49	16	35	44	0%	92	53%	1.65	-9.2	28	$2
Consist	D	1st Half	44	7	0	3	2	250			267	341	608	2	86	29	0.17	273	50	16	34	79	0%	100	25%	2.95	-3.1	45	$1
LIMA Plan	C+	2nd Half	34	3	0	2	5	118			189	118	307	8	91	13	1.00	218	48	16	35	0	0%	96	86%	0.07	-6.4	12	$0
Rand Var	+5	11 Proj	583	91	7	54	52	290			342	400	742	7	88	32	0.66	279	51	19	30	69	5%	133	38%	4.75	-5.6	63	$27

Series of rib injuries rendered him useless in 2010.
PRO: elite speed returns intact.
CON: SBO is maxed out, xBA didn't support 2009 BA.
Set your expectations against 2008. Anything more is gravy.

Encarnacion,Edwin			AB	R	HR	RBI	SB	Avg	vL	vR	OB	Slg	OPS	bb%	ct%	h%	Eye	xBA	G	L	F	PX	hr/f	Spd	SBO	RC/G	RAR	BPV	R$
Pos	5	06 CIN	406	60	15	72	6	276	248	287	342	473	815	9	81	31	0.53	280	41	21	37	127	12%	65	9%	5.62	1.5	64	$14
Age/B	28 Right	07 CIN	* 548	77	19	82	9	297	284	291	345	456	801	7	84	33	0.44	261	38	19	43	97	10%	66	6%	5.25	-5.5	47	$21
Ht/Wt	74 231	08 CIN	506	75	26	68	1	251	292	235	332	466	798	11	80	27	0.60	257	34	16	50	135	13%	74	1%	5.39	0.3	73	$15
Health	D	09 2TM	293	35	13	39	2	225	250	219	312	410	722	11	77	25	0.55	243	37	17	46	113	13%	62	4%	4.45	-4.1	42	$6
PT/Exp	C	10 TOR	* 364	52	23	58	1	252	234	246	309	489	798	8	83	25	0.49	290	32	17	51	144	15%	50	1%	5.14	3.3	80	$14
Consist	B	1st Half	160	22	11	29	1	224			306	469	775	11	83	20	0.70	279	30	14	56	146	15%	40	3%	5.00	0.8	84	$6
LIMA Plan	C	2nd Half	204	30	12	29	0	275			312	505	817	5	83	28	0.32	295	33	19	47	142	15%	70	0%	5.23	2.3	80	$8
Rand Var	+4	11 Proj	465	64	25	69	2	260			326	472	798	9	81	27	0.51	271	34	18	48	130	14%	56	2%	5.26	6.1	65	$16

21-51-.244 in 332 BA at TOR. Consecutive injury-filled years raise questions, but xBA shows BA upside and PX/FB% combo underscores power potential. Put it all together and...
UP: .30 HR, 85 RBI, .275 BA

Escobar,Alcides			AB	R	HR	RBI	SB	Avg	vL	vR	OB	Slg	OPS	bb%	ct%	h%	Eye	xBA	G	L	F	PX	hr/f	Spd	SBO	RC/G	RAR	BPV	R$
Pos	6	06	0	0	0	0	0	0																					
Age/B	24 Right	07 aa	226	24	1	25	3	274			306	339	646	4	86	31	0.33					38		138	10%	3.42	-6.3	27	$4
Ht/Wt	73 182	08 aa	547	77	7	61	28	292			324	384	708	5	88	32	0.39					58		107	25%	4.14	-5.3	41	$21
Health	A	09 MIL	* 555	81	4	38	37	274	480	260	312	359	671	5	87	31	0.43	257	52	17	31	56	3%	155	34%	3.80	-14.1	52	$20
PT/Exp	C	10 MIL	506	57	4	41	10	235	236	235	286	326	612	7	86	27	0.51	259	44	21	34	53	3%	148	11%	3.20	-18.7	47	$8
Consist	A	1st Half	266	33	2	24	6	244			300	331	630	7	87	28	0.60	263	48	20	32	50	3%	154	10%	3.47	-7.6	51	$5
LIMA Plan	C+	2nd Half	240	24	2	17	4	225			271	321	591	6	85	26	0.43	256	40	23	37	57	3%	128	13%	2.90	-11.3	39	$3
Rand Var	+4	11 Proj	538	66	4	45	19	257			299	344	642	6	87	29	0.45	255	44	21	34	53	3%	138	19%	3.49	-16.4	43	$13

Two reasons why he'll improve:
1. ct% and xBA say BA will head north.
2. Speed is elite. SBO says all he needs are the opps.
With a better lineup position...
UP: Back to 30+ SB

JOE HOFFER

Escobar,Yunel			AB	R	HR	RBI	SB	Avg	vL	vR	OB	Slg	OPS	bb%	ct%	h%	Eye	xBA	G	L	F	PX	hr/f	Spd	SBO	RC/G	RAR	BPV	R$
Pos	6	06 aa	428	51	2	43	7	249			337	322	658	12	82	30	0.73					51		110	11%	3.93	-5.9	27	$6
Age/B	28 Right	07 ATL	*499	72	7	54	11	323	355	303	373	443	816	7	86	36	0.58	299	56	21	23	81	7%	105	11%	5.58	15.2	58	$18
Ht/Wt	74 200	08 ATL	514	71	10	60	2	288	262	299	361	401	762	10	88	31	0.95	278	58	17	25	69	9%	104	4%	5.12	7.1	61	$15
Health	A	09 ATL	528	89	14	76	5	299	232	327	368	436	803	10	88	32	0.92	282	50	20	30	82	10%	84	5%	5.53	12.8	66	$21
PT/Exp	A	10 2TM	497	60	4	35	6	256	274	251	331	318	649	10	89	28	0.98	263	54	18	28	44	3%	77	5%	3.86	-4.8	35	$9
Consist	C	1st Half	237	27	0	19	5	241			341	287	628	13	87	28	1.16	253	51	19	30	40	0%	75	7%	3.80	-2.8	31	$4
LIMA Plan	C+	2nd Half	260	33	4	16	1	269			321	346	668	7	90	29	0.77	273	55	17	27	48	6%	87	3%	3.88	-2.3	41	$5
Rand Var	+3	11 Proj	524	72	10	52	5	275			345	377	722	10	88	30	0.90	276	54	18	28	65	7%	84	5%	4.63	4.3	51	$14

Odd, ugly season in his prime, although it got a little better in TOR. Plate approach stayed intact, which is reassuring even as PX/xBA crashed. Has rebound potential, especially if HR-happy TOR can reduce GBs.

Espinosa,Danny			AB	R	HR	RBI	SB	Avg	vL	vR	OB	Slg	OPS	bb%	ct%	h%	Eye	xBA	G	L	F	PX	hr/f	Spd	SBO	RC/G	RAR	BPV	R$
Pos	4	06	0	0	0	0	0	0																					
Age/B	23 Both	07	0	0	0	0	0	0																					
Ht/Wt	72 190	08	0	0	0	0	0	0																					
Health	A	09	0	0	0	0	0	0																					
PT/Exp	F	10 WAS	*584	85	25	74	22	237	200	218	291	416	707	7	78	27	0.34	244	46	8	46	113	12%	120	27%	4.07	-13.4	54	$21
Consist	F	1st Half	261	37	8	24	12	225			289	372	661	8	77	27	0.38	0				99		123	30%	3.60	-10.0	41	$7
LIMA Plan	D+	2nd Half	323	47	17	50	10	247			293	452	744	6	79	27	0.30	256	46	8	46	124	14%	120	24%	4.45	-3.7	65	$13
Rand Var	0	11 Proj	391	57	15	51	14	238			291	406	697	7	78	27	0.34	234	46	8	46	106	11%	115	26%	3.95	-9.3	46	$13

6-15-.214 in 103 AB at WAS.
PRO: Above-average and still-developing power/speed blend.
CON: lack of consistent ct% creates BA drag. If he gets 400 AB and holds 2H gains...
UP: 20 HR, 20 SB

Ethier,Andre			AB	R	HR	RBI	SB	Avg	vL	vR	OB	Slg	OPS	bb%	ct%	h%	Eye	xBA	G	L	F	PX	hr/f	Spd	SBO	RC/G	RAR	BPV	R$
Pos	9	06 LA	*482	62	12	64	7	307	351	298	366	469	835	9	81	36	0.50	261	41	22	37	95	8%	139	9%	5.87	14.6	62	$17
Age/B	28 Left	07 LA	447	50	13	64	0	284	279	286	351	452	803	9	85	31	0.68	284	46	18	36	106	10%	84	3%	5.50	7.8	70	$12
Ht/Wt	74 210	08 LA	525	90	20	77	6	305	243	326	375	510	885	10	83	34	0.67	302	41	27	32	129	14%	101	6%	6.51	19.1	89	$23
Health	A	09 LA	596	92	31	106	6	272	194	302	350	508	859	11	81	29	0.62	289	38	20	42	151	16%	82	6%	6.18	22.3	91	$25
PT/Exp	A	10 LA	517	71	23	82	2	292	233	318	365	493	858	10	80	33	0.58	290	39	22	40	134	14%	77	2%	6.15	11.8	74	$21
Consist	A	1st Half	247	39	13	49	1	320			378	559	936	9	86	33	0.66	322	39	21	40	151	15%	72	1%	6.91	10.4	105	$14
LIMA Plan	C+	2nd Half	270	32	10	33	1	267			353	433	786	12	75	32	0.54	261	38	22	40	116	12%	89	2%	5.39	0.5	46	$8
Rand Var	0	11 Proj	596	86	27	98	4	287			361	500	861	10	81	32	0.60	291	39	22	39	138	15%	85	4%	6.19	17.6	81	$24

Skills growth was continuing until broken pinkie in May interrupted him. Continues to struggle vLH, but pre-injury skills say we haven't yet seen his peak...
UP: 35-115-.300

Evans,Nick			AB	R	HR	RBI	SB	Avg	vL	vR	OB	Slg	OPS	bb%	ct%	h%	Eye	xBA	G	L	F	PX	hr/f	Spd	SBO	RC/G	RAR	BPV	R$
Pos	7	06	0	0	0	0	0	0																					
Age/B	25 Right	07	0	0	0	0	0	0																					
Ht/Wt	74 219	08 NYM	*405	62	13	54	2	274	319	135	323	462	784	7	81	31	0.37	282	44	23	33	121	12%	115	3%	5.12	-3.5	69	$13
Health	A	09 NYM	*407	38	11	37	2	203	321	162	258	355	614	7	80	23	0.37	248	49	13	38	103	9%	90	3%	3.02	-32.3	43	$3
PT/Exp	C	10 NYM	*523	67	18	62	0	252	333	267	305	435	739	7	85	27	0.49	295	50	15	35	122	12%	70	1%	4.59	-7.4	73	$13
Consist	D	1st Half	277	35	10	28	0	236			290	417	707	7	85	24	0.52	0				119		76	2%	4.20	-7.2	76	$6
LIMA Plan	F	2nd Half	246	33	8	34	0	271			321	455	776	7	84	30	0.45	294	50	15	35	125	11%	75	0%	5.03	-0.3	73	$8
Rand Var	+3	11 Proj	144	17	5	16	0	264			315	442	757	7	82	29	0.42	281	48	17	35	118	11%	90	2%	4.79	-2.0	66	$4

1-5-.306 in 36 AB at NYM. Bounced back from lost 2009 with improved ct% and PX recovery, putting him back on our radar screen. Upside lurking if given a chance, at least in a platoon role vLHP.

Feliz,Pedro			AB	R	HR	RBI	SB	Avg	vL	vR	OB	Slg	OPS	bb%	ct%	h%	Eye	xBA	G	L	F	PX	hr/f	Spd	SBO	RC/G	RAR	BPV	R$
Pos	5	06 SF	603	75	22	98	1	244	212	253	283	428	711	5	81	27	0.29	256	40	16	43	110	10%	81	2%	4.10	-25.0	50	$14
Age/B	35 Right	07 SF	557	61	20	72	2	253	257	252	290	418	708	5	87	26	0.41	268	43	15	42	95	10%	73	3%	4.10	-24.7	59	$12
Ht/Wt	73 210	08 PHI	425	43	14	58	0	249	288	231	303	402	706	7	87	26	0.61	264	47	16	37	89	10%	82	0%	4.22	-14.4	61	$9
Health	A	09 PHI	580	62	12	82	0	266	208	282	307	386	694	6	88	28	0.51	270	44	21	35	76	7%	68	1%	4.05	-18.2	47	$14
PT/Exp	B	10 2NL	409	36	5	40	1	218	240	208	242	293	535	3	90	23	0.32	232	44	13	43	46	3%	96	2%	2.20	-34.0	34	$3
Consist	C	1st Half	246	18	3	24	1	224			251	309	560	4	90	24	0.38	236	42	13	44	55	3%	83	4%	2.53	-17.9	39	$2
LIMA Plan	F	2nd Half	163	18	2	16	0	209			228	270	497	2	90	22	0.24	225	48	12	40	33	3%	111	0%	1.71	-16.1	25	$1
Rand Var	+3	11 Proj	215	22	4	26	0	237			271	345	616	4	89	25	0.40	250	45	16	40	64	6%	84	1%	3.10	-12.8	42	$3

Reasons he is not rosterable:
1. BA and xBA plummeting toward Mendoza levels.
2. ct% still good, but PX shows that it's increasingly hollow.
3. bb% and Eye are atrocious
4. RAR screams "stay away."

Fielder,Prince			AB	R	HR	RBI	SB	Avg	vL	vR	OB	Slg	OPS	bb%	ct%	h%	Eye	xBA	G	L	F	PX	hr/f	Spd	SBO	RC/G	RAR	BPV	R$
Pos	3	06 MIL	569	82	28	81	7	271	247	280	339	483	822	9	78	30	0.47	264	42	18	39	132	16%	31	6%	5.66	-5.6	48	$19
Age/B	26 Left	07 MIL	573	109	50	119	2	288	261	301	385	618	1002	14	79	29	0.74	316	35	19	46	196	24%	26	2%	8.01	30.2	109	$31
Ht/Wt	71 268	08 MIL	588	86	34	102	3	276	239	295	366	507	873	13	77	30	0.63	269	41	19	40	146	19%	35	3%	6.44	11.9	63	$24
Health	A	09 MIL	591	103	46	141	2	299	292	303	409	602	1012	16	77	32	0.80	293	41	16	43	191	24%	36	2%	8.39	30.7	104	$35
PT/Exp	A	10 MIL	578	94	32	83	1	261	226	280	383	471	854	16	76	29	0.83	263	42	18	40	138	18%	13	0%	6.39	1.1	54	$22
Consist	D	1st Half	305	50	18	36	1	262			366	482	848	14	74	30	0.63	261	41	16	42	148	19%	24	1%	6.24	-0.8	51	$11
LIMA Plan	C+	2nd Half	273	44	14	47	0	260			401	458	858	19	79	28	1.10	272	44	19	37	127	18%	18	0%	6.58	2.0	62	$10
Rand Var	+1	11 Proj	592	97	37	106	2	275			387	515	902	15	77	30	0.79	275	42	18	41	153	20%	22	2%	6.96	11.8	70	$26

PRO: PX still strong despite dip, ct% and Eye stable.
CON: BA dip supported by xBA, serious struggles vLHP (.668 OPS vLH, .976 vRH).
Verdict: nothing wrong here that a hr/f recovery won't fix.

Fields,Josh			AB	R	HR	RBI	SB	Avg	vL	vR	OB	Slg	OPS	bb%	ct%	h%	Eye	xBA	G	L	F	PX	hr/f	Spd	SBO	RC/G	RAR	BPV	R$
Pos	5	06 aaa	482	82	21	66	26	290	167	143	362	500	862	10	72	36	0.41	253	58	8	33	143	18%	78	22%	6.42	15.9	50	$23
Age/B	28 Right	07 CHW	*578	79	34	100	8	251	321	213	333	481	814	11	69	31	0.39	256	41	17	43	166	20%	47	9%	5.82	16.3	45	$20
Ht/Wt	74 225	08 CHW	*308	37	9	31	7	212	273	95	290	361	651	10	65	29	0.32	225	67	7	27	118	18%	107	11%	3.62	-12.1	9	$5
Health	F	09 CHW	*337	43	11	41	3	228	243	213	305	365	670	10	70	29	0.37	216	41	18	41	89	11%	103	9%	5.12	-9.6	4	$6
PT/Exp	F	10 KC	*88	12	3	12	1	334	364	259	348	518	866	2	86	36	0.15	320	58	18	25	124	16%	64	4%	5.71	2.0	69	$4
Consist	C	1st Half	0	0	0	0	0	0																					
LIMA Plan	F	2nd Half	88	12	3	12	1	334			348	518	866	2	86	36	0.15	320	58	18	25	124	16%	64	4%	5.71	2.0	69	$4
Rand Var	-3	11 Proj	166	22	7	22	3	247			305	433	738	8	74	30	0.32	264	49	17	34	129	16%	81	11%	4.58	-1.1	40	$5

3-6-.306 in 49 AB at KC. Lost most of 2010 to hip surgery. Since 23 HR in '07, only 320 AB in Majors. PX is legit, but so is unacceptable ct%, which makes it unlikely he'll ever deliver on the promise of that PX.

Figgins,Chone			AB	R	HR	RBI	SB	Avg	vL	vR	OB	Slg	OPS	bb%	ct%	h%	Eye	xBA	G	L	F	PX	hr/f	Spd	SBO	RC/G	RAR	BPV	R$
Pos	4	06 LAA	604	93	9	62	52	267	233	280	338	376	714	10	83	31	0.65	247	44	21	36	65	5%	148	37%	4.48	6.5	52	$24
Age/B	33 Both	07 LAA	442	81	3	58	41	330	326	331	400	432	832	10	82	40	0.63	279	47	26	26	72	3%	114	32%	6.00	24.2	41	$25
Ht/Wt	68 180	08 LAA	453	72	1	22	34	276	272	277	363	318	681	12	82	33	0.78	238	46	24	30	33	1%	116	27%	4.21	-9.1	16	$15
Health	B	09 LAA	615	114	5	54	42	298	246	323	397	393	790	14	81	36	0.89	248	41	24	36	64	3%	133	24%	5.70	13.6	47	$26
PT/Exp	A	10 SEA	602	62	1	35	42	259	286	247	340	306	646	11	81	32	0.65	238	47	21	32	38	1%	114	28%	3.70	-13.8	13	$17
Consist	D	1st Half	293	35	0	19	23	239			340	280	620	13	79	30	0.73	216	44	19	37	36	0%	103	26%	3.46	-8.9	4	$8
LIMA Plan	C+	2nd Half	309	27	1	16	19	278			340	330	670	9	83	33	0.56	258	50	23	27	40	1%	114	29%	3.89	-5.2	18	$9
Rand Var	0	11 Proj	557	76	2	39	35	268			352	331	683	12	82	32	0.71	245	45	22	32	47	2%	118	26%	4.21	-6.5	25	$17

Batted .211 in April/May but solid .280 mark the rest of the way couldn't make up for it.
PRO: Still collecting SBs.
CON: It's mostly driven by SBO. If on-base skills continue to erode, his value could plummet.

Fontenot,Mike			AB	R	HR	RBI	SB	Avg	vL	vR	OB	Slg	OPS	bb%	ct%	h%	Eye	xBA	G	L	F	PX	hr/f	Spd	SBO	RC/G	RAR	BPV	R$
Pos	4	06 aaa	362	49	8	32	5	271			348	418	766	11	83	31	0.70					96		100	8%	5.15	8.3	63	$8
Age/B	30 Left	07 CHC	*445	64	8	53	7	269	212	297	319	409	728	7	83	31	0.43	272	47	19	34	88	6%	129	11%	4.50	-2.6	57	$12
Ht/Wt	68 170	08 CHC	243	42	9	40	2	305	333	302	390	514	904	12	79	36	0.67	286	38	24	38	146	12%	87	3%	6.96	14.5	85	$11
Health	A	09 CHC	377	38	9	43	4	236	212	240	301	377	678	8	78	28	0.42	245	44	18	38	99	8%	90	5%	3.88	-7.4	37	$7
PT/Exp	D	10 2NL	240	24	1	25	1	283	214	288	325	375	700	6	83	34	0.37	277	46	26	28	67	2%	111	8%	4.14	-4.7	32	$5
Consist	D	1st Half	148	11	1	16	1	297			338	419	756	6	88	33	0.50	301	43	27	30	79	3%	106	5%	4.87	0.2	60	$4
LIMA Plan	F	2nd Half	92	13	0	9	0	261			306	304	610	6	75	35	0.26	238	52	23	25	43	0%	99	12%	2.91	-5.3	-21	$2
Rand Var	0	11 Proj	194	24	2	22	1	268			325	378	704	8	80	33	0.42	261	45	23	32	82	5%	91	7%	4.23	-2.8	30	$4

PRO: One of the best mullets in baseball
CON: can't hit LH, bb% and Eye trends say plate discipline is waning, PX has flown the coop and RAR says the end is near. At least he has cool hair.

JOE HOFFER

Fowler,Dexter

			AB	R	HR	RBI	SB	Avg	vL	vR	OB	Slg	OPS	bb%	ct%	h%	Eye	xBA	G	L	F	PX	hr/f	Spd	SBO	RC/G	RAR	BPV	R$
Pos	8	06	0	0	0	0	0	0																					
Age/B	25 Both	07	0	0	0	0	0	0																					
Ht/Wt	76 185	08 aa	421	66	7	46	14	304			373	449	822	10	86	34	0.77					93		125	18%	5.83	9.3	76	$16
Health	A	09 COL	433	73	4	34	27	266	321	240	364	406	770	13	73	35	0.58	240	42	21	37	106	3%	156	27%	5.52	10.2	53	$15
PT/Exp	C	10 COL	* 545	87	7	44	14	266	260	260	347	418	765	11	78	33	0.56	269	45	22	33	102	5%	160	13%	5.26	5.9	65	$16
Consist	A	1st Half	269	40	2	15	9	263			364	413	776	14	77	33	0.70	261	44	20	36	101	3%	169	16%	5.60	5.6	70	$7
LIMA Plan	B+	2nd Half	276	47	5	29	5	268			329	424	753	8	78	33	0.41	275	45	23	32	104	7%	144	10%	4.91	0.2	56	$9
Rand Var	+1	11 Proj	527	86	6	45	31	271			354	416	771	11	77	34	0.57	259	44	21	35	100	5%	152	25%	5.35	8.7	60	$20

6-36-.260-13 SB in 439 AB at COL. xBA growth reflective of improvement in ct%, and raises SB ceiling. Combine solidifying plate approach with elite Spd, SBO rebound, and...
UP: 50 SB.

Fox,Jake

			AB	R	HR	RBI	SB	Avg	vL	vR	OB	Slg	OPS	bb%	ct%	h%	Eye	xBA	G	L	F	PX	hr/f	Spd	SBO	RC/G	RAR	BPV	R$
Pos	0	06	0	0	0	0	0	0																					
Age/B	28 Right	07	0	0	0	0	0	0																					
Ht/Wt	72 210	08 aa	505	65	23	74	5	237			284	443	726	6	82	25	0.37					130		69	7%	4.30	-9.5	68	$13
Health	A	09 CHC	* 380	56	25	85	2	299	250	263	351	574	924	7	80	32	0.39	291	34	19	47	171	18%	70	3%	6.73	16.4	94	$20
PT/Exp	D	10 2AL	198	21	7	22	0	217	209	227	248	384	631	4	75	25	0.16	241	39	13	48	118	10%	95	0%	2.99	-20.4	34	$3
Consist	F	1st Half	110	13	3	14	0	209			250	336	586	5	73	26	0.20	224	47	11	42	97	9%	88	0%	2.44	-13.3	7	$1
LIMA Plan	D	2nd Half	88	8	4	8	0	227			244	443	688	2	78	25	0.11	261	30	14	55	142	11%	97	0%	3.63	-7.3	63	$2
Rand Var	+3	11 Proj	232	28	12	35	1	250			289	469	758	5	78	27	0.25	266	36	15	49	142	13%	83	2%	4.62	-8.4	64	$7

Brief 2H PX spike reminded us that there is real power here, but dwindling ct%, weak Eye, odd reverse platoon split all conspiring against chances of an expanded role. Potentially useful if he regains CA eligibility.

Francisco,Ben

			AB	R	HR	RBI	SB	Avg	vL	vR	OB	Slg	OPS	bb%	ct%	h%	Eye	xBA	G	L	F	PX	hr/f	Spd	SBO	RC/G	RAR	BPV	R$
Pos	79	06 aaa	515	76	14	56	24	260			318	416	734	8	86	28	0.63					93		98	22%	4.62	-9.0	67	$17
Age/B	29 Right	07 CLE	* 439	61	13	56	19	287	286	273	340	452	792	8	82	33	0.45	283	47	19	35	112	10%	88	26%	5.24	2.6	62	$17
Ht/Wt	73 190	08 CLE	* 539	72	16	60	7	255	269	265	318	411	730	9	79	30	0.45	244	34	18	48	109	8%	111	7%	4.52	-5.3	56	$13
Health	A	09 2TM	405	58	15	46	14	257	247	260	321	447	767	9	80	29	0.46	265	38	18	44	127	11%	82	22%	4.98	-3.6	63	$14
PT/Exp	C	10 PHI	179	24	6	28	8	268	284	253	321	441	763	7	80	30	0.40	269	38	17	45	122	9%	71	19%	4.85	-1.1	57	$8
Consist	A	1st Half	88	9	1	11	2	250			290	364	654	5	82	30	0.31	248	33	19	48	91	3%	68	11%	3.52	-4.0	33	$2
LIMA Plan	D	2nd Half	91	15	5	17	6	286			350	516	866	9	79	31	0.47	291	43	15	42	154	17%	85	25%	6.15	2.8	85	$6
Rand Var	0	11 Proj	225	32	8	31	9	267			325	450	775	8	80	30	0.44	266	38	18	45	125	10%	77	19%	5.02	-1.6	62	$9

Healthy PX with FB% tilt speaks to power potential, SBO shows baserunning aggression even without plus Spd. 4th OF role trapped him in 2010, but one injury doubles his AB, and then...
UP: 20 HR, 20 SB

Francisco,Juan

			AB	R	HR	RBI	SB	Avg	vL	vR	OB	Slg	OPS	bb%	ct%	h%	Eye	xBA	G	L	F	PX	hr/f	Spd	SBO	RC/G	RAR	BPV	R$
Pos	5	06	0	0	0	0	0	0																					
Age/B	23 Left	07	0	0	0	0	0	0																					
Ht/Wt	74 180	08	0	0	0	0	0	0																					
Health	A	09 a/a	529	69	26	79	5	276			304	486	789	4	81	30	0.21					127		105	6%	4.89	-0.3	68	$19
PT/Exp	F	10 CIN	* 363	39	17	53	1	260	222	283	293	482	774	4	76	30	0.19	299	60	11	29	154	21%	112	3%	4.86	-0.4	72	$11
Consist	A	1st Half	158	17	5	19	0	242			269	434	703	4	80	27	0.19	0				138		100	0%	3.98	-4.3	70	$3
LIMA Plan	D	2nd Half	205	23	12	34	1	274			310	518	829	5	73	32	0.19	297	60	11	29	168	28%	118	5%	5.63	4.3	73	$8
Rand Var	+3	11 Proj	278	33	15	41	2	252			283	494	777	4	78	27	0.20	303	60	11	29	156	25%	110	5%	4.79	-2.5	80	$9

1-7-.273 in 55 AB at CIN. Owns legit power and some sneaky speed, but poor ct%/Eye combo threatens to undermine it all. No signs of growth right now, so until further notice he profiles as a low-BA power source.

Francoeur,Jeff

			AB	R	HR	RBI	SB	Avg	vL	vR	OB	Slg	OPS	bb%	ct%	h%	Eye	xBA	G	L	F	PX	hr/f	Spd	SBO	RC/G	RAR	BPV	R$
Pos	9	06 ATL	651	83	29	103	1	260	292	248	285	449	733	3	80	29	0.17	261	45	18	37	107	15%	101	5%	4.20	-11.0	44	$18
Age/B	27 Right	07 ATL	642	84	19	105	5	293	317	281	336	444	780	6	80	34	0.33	263	43	19	37	101	10%	75	4%	4.99	2.0	38	$22
Ht/Wt	76 220	08 ATL	599	70	11	71	0	239	210	251	285	359	644	6	81	28	0.35	253	45	21	34	82	7%	73	1%	3.39	-32.2	27	$9
Health	A	09 2NL	593	72	15	76	6	280	344	256	307	423	730	4	84	31	0.25	258	38	21	41	91	7%	91	7%	4.28	-10.2	47	$18
PT/Exp	A	10 2TM	454	52	13	65	8	249	300	231	295	383	679	6	82	28	0.37	243	41	14	45	86	8%	86	10%	3.75	-18.7	38	$13
Consist	B	1st Half	276	33	8	42	7	261			306	406	712	6	82	29	0.35	250	42	14	44	97	8%	86	13%	4.16	-7.9	44	$9
LIMA Plan	F	2nd Half	178	19	5	23	1	230			279	348	627	6	83	25	0.40	233	39	15	46	70	7%	93	5%	3.14	-10.8	31	$3
Rand Var	0	11 Proj	288	34	8	39	3	264			304	404	709	5	83	30	0.33	252	41	17	42	89	8%	90	6%	4.09	-8.9	41	$8

Another year, another team gives up on this once-promising bat. Flails helplessly against RHP, so bad-side platoon work is his only future, and there's little fantasy value in that role.

Frandsen,Kevin

			AB	R	HR	RBI	SB	Avg	vL	vR	OB	Slg	OPS	bb%	ct%	h%	Eye	xBA	G	L	F	PX	hr/f	Spd	SBO	RC/G	RAR	BPV	R$
Pos	5	06 SF	* 386	47	4	30	5	256	200	217	279	368	647	3	90	28	0.32	255	48	13	39	71	3%	94	14%	3.49	-23.0	55	$6
Age/B	28 Right	07 SF	* 331	36	6	36	7	282	262	274	337	392	729	8	91	30	0.92	293	53	21	26	66	7%	82	12%	4.65	-9.1	58	$9
Ht/Wt	72 184	08 SF	1	0	0	0	0	0			0	0	0	0	100	0	0.00	274	100	0	0			104			-0.3	33	($0)
Health	D	09 SF	* 477	56	9	44	3	237	154	135	269	340	609	4	92	24	0.58	263	55	14	32	59	6%	95	6%	3.16	-28.6	56	$7
PT/Exp	F	10 LAA	* 359	45	2	24	5	224	226	262	257	301	559	4	92	24	0.59	284	56	15	28	56	2%	97	8%	2.70	-23.3	54	$4
Consist	F	1st Half	198	29	1	14	3	269			306	351	657	5	96	28	1.42	302	57	16	27	60	2%	97	8%	3.94	-5.1	74	$4
LIMA Plan	F	2nd Half	161	16	1	9	2	168			196	240	436	3	88	19	0.28	259	56	14	30	51	2%	98	7%	1.09	-19.6	30	($1)
Rand Var	+2	11 Proj	100	12	1	8	1	230			265	311	576	5	91	24	0.55	275	55	17	29	55	4%	89	9%	2.82	-6.1	47	$1

0-14-.250 in 160 AB at LAA. Elite ct% is only an asset when you can actually hit the ball with some authority. Piles of GBs to SS aren't much better than piles of strikeouts. And often much worse.

Freeman,Freddie

			AB	R	HR	RBI	SB	Avg	vL	vR	OB	Slg	OPS	bb%	ct%	h%	Eye	xBA	G	L	F	PX	hr/f	Spd	SBO	RC/G	RAR	BPV	R$
Pos	3	06	0	0	0	0	0	0																					
Age/B	21 Left	07	0	0	0	0	0	0																					
Ht/Wt	77 220	08	0	0	0	0	0	0																					
Health	A	09 aa	149	14	2	23	0	242			291	332	623	6	88	26	0.59					59		80	0%	3.32	-12.3	39	$2
PT/Exp	F	10 ATL	* 485	65	16	75	5	283	667	95	336	454	790	7	84	31	0.48	287	44	19	38	114	11%	80	6%	5.17	-15.8	66	$18
Consist	D	1st Half	250	28	7	34	1	250			309	416	725	8	87	26	0.65	0				109		84	4%	4.53	-13.3	78	$6
LIMA Plan	D+	2nd Half	235	36	9	40	4	318			364	494	858	7	80	37	0.37	279	44	19	38	119	13%	79	7%	5.95	-2.4	56	$12
Rand Var	0	11 Proj	451	55	15	70	3	271			321	429	750	7	85	29	0.50	276	44	19	38	101	11%	74	4%	4.68	-20.5	59	$14

Heir apparent for Braves' 1B job took off in 2H, rode hot streak all the way to ATL. Good plate approach should allow him to stick in ATL for good, but it may take some time before 20+ power emerges in bigs.

Freese,David

			AB	R	HR	RBI	SB	Avg	vL	vR	OB	Slg	OPS	bb%	ct%	h%	Eye	xBA	G	L	F	PX	hr/f	Spd	SBO	RC/G	RAR	BPV	R$
Pos	5	06	0	0	0	0	0	0																					
Age/B	27 Right	07	0	0	0	0	0	0																					
Ht/Wt	74 220	08 aa	464	62	18	68	4	251			295	427	723	6	80	28	0.32					112		78	6%	4.24	-12.1	48	$13
Health	D	09 STL	* 247	30	8	37	1	257	176	500	311	418	729	7	79	29	0.38	240	44	12	44	111	10%	70	2%	4.41	-5.2	42	$7
PT/Exp	F	10 STL	240	28	4	36	1	296	357	271	352	404	757	8	75	38	0.36	254	49	22	29	83	8%	84	3%	4.89	-0.0	11	$8
Consist	A	1st Half	240	28	4	36	1	296			352	404	757	8	75	38	0.36	254	49	22	29	83	8%	84	3%	4.89	-0.0	11	$8
LIMA Plan	D+	2nd Half	0	0	0	0	0	0																					
Rand Var	-5	11 Proj	391	49	8	58	2	269			320	388	707	7	78	33	0.35	258	48	21	30	86	8%	77	3%	4.17	-10.4	21	$11

Missed 2H with ankle and toe injuries. Surgery on both ankles now clouds his 2011 readiness. PX and ct% from minors haven't yet carried over, and elevated GB% works against any power growth. Low short-term ceiling.

Fukudome,Kosuke

			AB	R	HR	RBI	SB	Avg	vL	vR	OB	Slg	OPS	bb%	ct%	h%	Eye	xBA	G	L	F	PX	hr/f	Spd	SBO	RC/G	RAR	BPV	R$
Pos	9	06 JPN	578	114	19	101	10	281			349	485	834	10	85	30	0.69					123		100	8%	5.91	11.4	88	$22
Age/B	33 Left	07 JPN	269	62	8	47	5	274			398	441	839	17	77	33	0.89					123		91	7%	6.43	9.6	69	$11
Ht/Wt	72 187	08 CHC	501	79	10	58	12	257	276	251	361	379	740	14	79	31	0.78	253	51	19	30	83	8%	112	9%	4.97	-3.2	47	$14
Health	B	09 CHC	499	79	11	54	6	259	164	270	375	421	796	16	78	31	0.83	276	46	24	30	118	10%	108	10%	5.83	14.2	70	$13
PT/Exp	B	10 CHC	358	45	13	44	7	263	262	263	374	439	813	15	81	29	0.96	280	49	16	35	115	13%	91	12%	5.90	6.1	77	$12
Consist	A	1st Half	199	24	6	24	4	261			361	412	773	13	82	29	0.89	276	53	16	31	94	12%	112	12%	5.33	0.0	67	$6
LIMA Plan	C+	2nd Half	159	21	7	20	3	264			391	472	862	17	80	29	1.03	287	45	16	40	143	14%	68	13%	6.61	6.1	91	$6
Rand Var	+1	11 Proj	386	57	12	48	7	277			387	449	836	15	80	32	0.89	277	48	18	34	117	12%	94	10%	6.24	12.2	73	$14

Too old to learn new skills? 2H FB% spike raises some hope for late-career power spike. Rest of skill set is stable, good plate patience creates value in OBP leagues. If those FBs continue...
UP: 20 HR

RAY MURPHY

Furcal,Rafael

Furcal,Rafael			AB	R	HR	RBI	SB	Avg	vL	vR	OB	Slg	OPS	bb%	ct%	h%	Eye	xBA	G	L	F	PX	hr/f	Spd	SBO	RC/G	RAR	BPV	R$
Pos	6	06 LA	654	113	15	63	37	300	324	293	370	445	815	10	85	33	0.74	278	50	21	29	83	9%	122	23%	5.70	24.8	65	$28
Age/B	33 Both	07 LA	581	87	6	47	25	270	313	254	333	355	688	9	88	30	0.81	263	50	19	32	52	4%	110	17%	4.21	-4.0	47	$16
Ht/Wt	68 187	08 LA	143	34	5	16	8	357	365	352	436	573	1009	12	88	38	1.18	315	49	19	32	130	12%	120	21%	8.11	13.0	119	$10
Health	F	09 LA	613	92	9	47	12	269	296	261	335	375	711	9	85	30	0.69	267	53	19	28	68	6%	112	10%	4.43	-4.1	50	$16
PT/Exp	C	10 LA	383	66	8	43	22	300	277	310	366	460	826	9	84	34	0.67	291	47	20	33	102	8%	112	22%	5.83	15.1	74	$19
Consist	F	1st Half	213	43	4	28	12	338			390	502	892	8	86	38	0.60	303	46	23	31	102	7%	113	22%	6.51	11.8	77	$13
LIMA Plan	C	2nd Half	170	23	4	15	10	253			339	406	744	11	82	29	0.73	276	49	17	35	102	8%	100	22%	4.93	2.6	66	$6
Rand Var	-1	11 Proj	**481**	**82**	**9**	**47**	**23**	**293**			**364**	**432**	**796**	**10**	**85**	**33**	**0.75**	**281**	**49**	**19**	**32**	**89**	**7%**	**112**	**19%**	**5.51**	**13.6**	**68**	**$20**

Two DL stints cost him plenty of ABs, yet SB total soared as SBO returned to normal. Injury history has caused AB totals to yo-yo; REL grades show you can't count on consistency. Bid on speed, the rest is gravy.

Gamel,Mat

Gamel,Mat			AB	R	HR	RBI	SB	Avg	vL	vR	OB	Slg	OPS	bb%	ct%	h%	Eye	xBA	G	L	F	PX	hr/f	Spd	SBO	RC/G	RAR	BPV	R$
Pos	5	06	0	0	0	0	0	0																					
Age/B	25 Left	07	0	0	0	0	0	0																					
Ht/Wt	72 200	08 a/a	529	76	16	76	5	280			337	443	780	8	81	32	0.46					106		91	10%	5.12	-0.0	54	$17
Health	C	09 MIL *	401	43	14	56	2	238	304	229	320	403	723	11	68	32	0.37	222	23	27	51	127	10%	90	2%	4.66	-5.8	23	$9
PT/Exp	D	10 MIL *	354	46	10	55	2	261	500	154	325	415	740	9	79	30	0.47	297	43	29	29	111	13%	66	3%	4.66	-2.5	46	$11
Consist	A	1st Half	123	16	2	16	1	260			331	367	698	10	78	32	0.48	0				85		80	3%	4.22	-2.4	23	$3
LIMA Plan	F	2nd Half	231	30	8	39	1	261			322	441	763	8	80	29	0.46	309	43	29	29	124	16%	66	3%	4.89	-0.1	60	$8
Rand Var	+3	11 Proj	**190**	**24**	**6**	**28**	**1**	**258**			**328**	**434**	**762**	**9**	**75**	**31**	**0.42**	**252**	**23**	**27**	**51**	**125**	**9%**	**84**	**4%**	**4.99**	**-0.6**	**48**	**$5**

0-1-.200 in 15 AB at MIL. It's all about potential at this point. PRO: .341/.412/.602 in 2H AAA. CON: Low ct% in '09/'10 and defense are holding him back in the majors. Still a work in progress.

Gardner,Brett

Gardner,Brett			AB	R	HR	RBI	SB	Avg	vL	vR	OB	Slg	OPS	bb%	ct%	h%	Eye	xBA	G	L	F	PX	hr/f	Spd	SBO	RC/G	RAR	BPV	R$
Pos	78	06 aa	217	39	0	13	26	255			330	291	620	10	81	31	0.60					23		136	42%	3.34	-12.2	7	$9
Age/B	27 Left	07 a/a	384	75	1	24	36	260			343	341	684	11	80	32	0.64					56		150	34%	4.23	-11.1	36	$15
Ht/Wt	70 183	08 NYY *	468	75	3	43	44	251	125	252	343	338	681	12	78	32	0.64	225	48	17	35	58	2%	153	35%	4.19	-9.3	31	$18
Health	B	09 NYY	248	48	3	23	26	270	291	264	339	379	718	9	84	31	0.65	251	49	19	33	58	4%	167	40%	4.55	-3.3	53	$12
PT/Exp	C	10 NYY	477	97	5	47	47	277	252	287	379	379	759	14	79	34	0.78	261	53	19	28	72	5%	142	31%	5.29	5.7	46	$25
Consist	B	1st Half	251	53	5	29	24	319			398	434	832	12	84	37	0.80	271	50	20	30	67	8%	155	30%	5.99	7.6	60	$16
LIMA Plan	B	2nd Half	226	44	0	18	23	230			360	319	679	17	73	31	0.77	250	58	17	25	77	0%	122	33%	4.41	-3.3	28	$9
Rand Var	-2	11 Proj	**445**	**85**	**4**	**40**	**40**	**263**			**356**	**361**	**718**	**13**	**80**	**32**	**0.71**	**252**	**52**	**18**	**30**	**65**	**3%**	**151**	**32%**	**4.70**	**-3.1**	**42**	**$19**

This breakout was all about opportunity, but the regular PT may have also exposed his flaws. 2H warning signs are ominous -- diving ct% and BA cut into productivity. If that carries into '11, his value could drop fast.

Getz,Chris

Getz,Chris			AB	R	HR	RBI	SB	Avg	vL	vR	OB	Slg	OPS	bb%	ct%	h%	Eye	xBA	G	L	F	PX	hr/f	Spd	SBO	RC/G	RAR	BPV	R$
Pos	4	06 aa	508	63	2	34	17	244			310	304	614	9	91	27	1.02					34		128	15%	3.49	-13.3	48	$8
Age/B	27 Left	07 aa	278	35	3	26	11	270			346	338	684	10	89	29	1.10					42		110	19%	4.30	-0.4	47	$7
Ht/Wt	72 185	08 aaa	404	51	10	43	10	265			323	398	721	8	88	28	0.71					81		86	13%	4.48	-4.1	60	$11
Health	B	09 CHW	375	49	2	31	25	261	246	265	316	347	663	7	86	30	0.56	253	47	19	33	55	2%	111	26%	3.82	-12.1	37	$11
PT/Exp	D	10 KC	224	23	0	18	15	237	304	219	296	277	573	8	88	27	0.68	252	52	18	30	35	0%	94	27%	2.86	-10.9	24	$5
Consist	B	1st Half	107	12	0	10	8	234			299	262	561	9	85	27	0.63	229	52	15	32	25	0%	103	28%	2.64	-5.9	10	$3
LIMA Plan	D	2nd Half	117	11	0	8	7	239			294	291	584	7	90	27	0.75	273	52	20	28	43	0%	92	26%	3.05	-5.0	37	$2
Rand Var	+2	11 Proj	**304**	**35**	**1**	**25**	**17**	**250**			**309**	**305**	**614**	**8**	**88**	**28**	**0.68**	**254**	**51**	**19**	**31**	**41**	**1%**	**99**	**23%**	**3.33**	**-11.5**	**31**	**$7**

Oblique strain, concussion limited his ABs. Good ct% but nothing much happens when he hits the ball. On those rare occsions when he manages to reach 1B, SBO will yield SBs, even without much speed skill.

Giambi,Jason

Giambi,Jason			AB	R	HR	RBI	SB	Avg	vL	vR	OB	Slg	OPS	bb%	ct%	h%	Eye	xBA	G	L	F	PX	hr/f	Spd	SBO	RC/G	RAR	BPV	R$
Pos	3	06 NYY	446	92	37	113	2	253	213	270	401	558	959	20	76	25	1.04	280	30	16	53	185	20%	45	1%	7.84	31.6	108	$21
Age/B	40 Left	07 NYY	254	31	14	39	1	236	239	235	340	433	773	14	74	26	0.61	237	30	16	53	127	14%	41	1%	5.18	-0.6	39	$6
Ht/Wt	75 240	08 NYY	458	68	32	96	2	247	231	253	354	502	856	14	76	26	0.68	266	33	17	50	160	18%	66	2%	6.25	13.3	81	$18
Health	B	09 2TM	293	43	13	51	0	201	213	196	331	382	714	16	73	23	0.71	226	33	15	51	123	12%	53	0%	4.55	-14.4	40	$6
PT/Exp	C	10 COL	176	17	6	35	2	244	277	233	370	398	767	17	73	30	0.74	239	31	20	49	113	10%	35	3%	5.38	-4.9	30	$5
Consist	C	1st Half	88	10	3	16	1	216			361	375	736	19	75	25	0.91	230	29	16	56	116	8%	48	3%	5.02	-3.5	47	$2
LIMA Plan	F	2nd Half	88	7	3	19	1	273			379	420	799	15	72	35	0.60	248	34	25	41	110	12%	42	3%	5.77	-1.4	18	$3
Rand Var	-1	11 Proj	**118**	**14**	**5**	**23**	**1**	**237**			**359**	**425**	**783**	**16**	**74**	**28**	**0.71**	**244**	**32**	**19**	**49**	**131**	**13%**	**49**	**2%**	**5.51**	**-2.7**	**47**	**$4**

I'll take "Riding into the sunset" for $600, Alex. He still walks, but low ct%, drop in PX and high FB% mean all that's left are a bunch of harmless fly-outs. It's not even warning track power, it's "shagging flies" power.

Gillespie,Cole

Gillespie,Cole			AB	R	HR	RBI	SB	Avg	vL	vR	OB	Slg	OPS	bb%	ct%	h%	Eye	xBA	G	L	F	PX	hr/f	Spd	SBO	RC/G	RAR	BPV	R$
Pos	7	06	0	0	0	0	0	0																					
Age/B	26 Right	07	0	0	0	0	0	0																					
Ht/Wt	73 205	08 aa	462	55	11	60	12	237			323	384	707	11	81	27	0.67					103		81	11%	4.45	-9.6	55	$11
Health	A	09 a/a	374	43	9	38	9	229			306	387	693	10	82	25	0.63					93		123	16%	4.21	-12.4	62	$7
PT/Exp	D	10 ARI *	368	43	7	41	6	230	204	255	295	363	658	8	83	26	0.54	279	55	16	29	89	7%	114	15%	3.74	-15.1	56	$7
Consist	A	1st Half	208	23	4	20	3	240			314	376	690	10	81	28	0.56	303	59	23	18	93	12%	115	14%	4.17	-5.8	53	$4
LIMA Plan	F	2nd Half	160	20	3	22	3	217			269	347	616	7	86	24	0.50	251	51	8	41	84	5%	105	17%	3.21	-9.3	57	$3
Rand Var	+4	11 Proj	**159**	**19**	**3**	**18**	**3**	**245**			**314**	**386**	**700**	**9**	**83**	**28**	**0.58**	**264**	**54**	**13**	**33**	**90**	**8%**	**107**	**14%**	**4.26**	**-4.8**	**55**	**$4**

2-12-.231 in 104 AB at ARI. If he was 22, we'd say, "good Eye and decent BA in minors hasn't translated to majors yet." But at 26, what might have been a 15 HR, 15 SB upside looks much more bleak.

Glaus,Troy

Glaus,Troy			AB	R	HR	RBI	SB	Avg	vL	vR	OB	Slg	OPS	bb%	ct%	h%	Eye	xBA	G	L	F	PX	hr/f	Spd	SBO	RC/G	RAR	BPV	R$
Pos	3	06 TOR	540	105	38	104	3	252	292	238	355	513	868	14	75	27	0.64	264	34	17	49	162	19%	65	3%	6.40	15.6	79	$21
Age/B	34 Right	07 TOR	385	60	20	62	0	262	361	235	363	473	836	14	74	31	0.60	263	34	21	45	142	16%	61	1%	6.11	9.5	56	$12
Ht/Wt	77 240	08 STL	544	69	27	99	0	270	221	290	371	483	854	14	81	29	0.84	271	38	19	43	133	14%	62	1%	6.28	8.5	78	$19
Health	F	09 STL *	89	10	2	9	1	161		192	270	241	511	13	73	20	0.54	199	19	29	52	56	5%	68	4%	1.67	-14.2	-17	($0)
PT/Exp	C	10 ATL	412	52	16	71	0	240	234	243	341	400	742	13	76	28	0.63	241	40	16	45	111	11%	56	0%	4.83	-18.4	37	$12
Consist	F	1st Half	277	41	14	56	0	260			363	458	822	14	76	29	0.68	265	40	18	43	133	16%	57	0%	5.88	-3.6	58	$11
LIMA Plan	D	2nd Half	135	11	2	15	0	200			294	281	576	12	75	25	0.53	190	40	11	49	63	4%	65	0%	2.63	-15.7	-5	$1
Rand Var	0	11 Proj	**304**	**39**	**13**	**49**	**0**	**250**			**349**	**426**	**775**	**13**	**76**	**29**	**0.65**	**245**	**38**	**16**	**46**	**119**	**12%**	**57**	**1%**	**5.26**	**-8.9**	**46**	**$9**

1H power display made it look like he was back; 2H power/BA outage, caused by knee injury, reminds us of the health risk. If you buy at a discount; know that you are buying his 300 AB plus another 200 replacement AB.

Gload,Ross

Gload,Ross			AB	R	HR	RBI	SB	Avg	vL	vR	OB	Slg	OPS	bb%	ct%	h%	Eye	xBA	G	L	F	PX	hr/f	Spd	SBO	RC/G	RAR	BPV	R$
Pos	3	06 CHW	156	22	3	18	6	327	308	333	352	462	813	4	90	35	0.40	293	51	21	27	76	8%	107	14%	5.29	-0.5	64	$6
Age/B	35 Left	07 KC	320	37	7	51	2	288	388	269	321	441	762	5	88	31	0.41	298	50	19	31	97	8%	91	5%	4.79	-4.2	68	$9
Ht/Wt	73 190	08 KC	388	46	3	37	3	273	263	277	314	348	662	6	90	30	0.59	267	46	22	32	51	3%	89	7%	3.77	-16.8	40	$7
Health	B	09 FLA	230	33	6	30	0	261	194	271	328	400	728	9	87	28	0.77	263	40	21	39	82	8%	106	0%	4.62	-12.6	66	$6
PT/Exp	D	10 PHI	128	16	6	22	1	281	273	282	324	484	808	6	88	28	0.53	284	42	12	47	123	11%	83	3%	5.26	-3.9	90	$5
Consist	B	1st Half	66	5	3	12	1	242			242	424	667	0	94	22	0.00	271	44	8	48	100	10%	74	10%	3.45	-5.7	80	$2
LIMA Plan	F	2nd Half	62	11	3	10	0	323			400	548	948	11	82	35	0.73	296	39	16	45	151	13%	96	0%	7.31	1.6	103	$3
Rand Var	0	11 Proj	**98**	**13**	**3**	**14**	**1**	**286**			**335**	**443**	**779**	**7**	**88**	**30**	**0.60**	**275**	**42**	**17**	**41**	**99**	**9%**	**84**	**3%**	**5.04**	**-3.3**	**70**	**$3**

The danger of small sample sizes - plenty of 1H/2H swings, none of which mean much. What does matter - he's now a pinch hitter with occasional pop and decent BA. Ignorable in all but the deepest leagues.

Gomes,Jonny

Gomes,Jonny			AB	R	HR	RBI	SB	Avg	vL	vR	OB	Slg	OPS	bb%	ct%	h%	Eye	xBA	G	L	F	PX	hr/f	Spd	SBO	RC/G	RAR	BPV	R$
Pos	7	06 TAM	385	53	20	59	1	216	297	187	323	431	754	14	70	25	0.53	232	29	17	54	149	14%	51	6%	5.04	-1.6	43	$8
Age/B	30 Right	07 TAM *	391	54	18	56	16	247	313	218	326	451	777	10	64	34	0.32	231	26	21	53	163	14%	82	21%	5.58	6.4	33	$14
Ht/Wt	73 225	08 TAM *	261	37	10	32	8	190	182	182	258	364	622	8	71	23	0.32	211	34	10	56	127	9%	75	20%	3.05	-15.1	26	$5
Health	A	09 CIN *	412	52	28	71	6	257	307	244	315	525	840	8	71	30	0.29	271	34	20	46	187	21%	58	9%	5.93	4.5	68	$17
PT/Exp	C	10 CIN	511	77	18	86	5	266	285	257	318	431	749	7	76	32	0.32	243	29	21	50	113	9%	88	6%	4.66	-6.1	37	$19
Consist	F	1st Half	251	34	10	56	2	287			335	490	825	7	74	35	0.28	266	27	24	49	147	11%	84	8%	5.70	4.5	55	$11
LIMA Plan	C	2nd Half	260	43	8	30	3	246			302	373	676	7	78	29	0.36	218	31	17	52	82	8%	95	4%	3.70	-10.5	21	$7
Rand Var	-2	11 Proj	**469**	**67**	**20**	**73**	**7**	**247**			**308**	**435**	**742**	**8**	**73**	**30**	**0.32**	**240**	**31**	**19**	**51**	**131**	**11%**	**76**	**9%**	**4.63**	**-8.9**	**38**	**$16**

Larger 2010 sample size makes 2009 PX, hr/f look like outliers. Did better vs RHP, but platoon role makes sense. ct% "bump" unlikely to last. He's a free swinger who hits plenty of FBs; expect HRs, not much else.

DAVE ADLER

Gomez,Carlos

		Year	AB	R	HR	RBI	SB	Avg	vL	vR	OB	Slg	OPS	bb%	ct%	h%	Eye	xBA	G	L	F	PX	hr/f	Spd	SBO	RC/G	RAR	BPV	R$
Pos	8	06 aa	430	54	6	48	42	283			326	410	736	6	80	34	0.31					84		116	46%	4.54	-0.2	35	$19
Age/B	25 Right	07 NYM	*265	34	4	23	26	245	254	212	301	336	637	7	83	28	0.46	234	45	16	39	58	5%	113	48%	3.37	-9.5	28	$9
Ht/Wt	76 215	08 MIN	577	79	7	59	33	258	270	254	289	360	650	4	75	33	0.18	221	44	17	39	73	4%	158	32%	3.32	-34.9	17	$18
Health	C	09 MIN	315	51	3	28	14	229	204	239	279	337	615	7	77	29	0.31	236	45	19	36	72	3%	138	30%	3.06	-15.5	23	$7
PT/Exp	C	10 MIL	291	38	5	24	18	247	196	273	289	357	646	6	75	31	0.24	235	48	16	36	78	6%	128	30%	3.32	-13.7	15	$10
Consist	A	1st Half	183	27	5	18	9	235			271	377	648	5	79	27	0.24	250	46	15	39	92	9%	121	26%	3.29	-8.9	38	$6
LIMA Plan	D	2nd Half	108	11	0	6	9	269			319	324	643	7	69	39	0.24	211	52	19	29	51	0%	125	34%	3.45	-4.6	-32	$4
Rand Var	-1	11 Proj	315	42	3	26	20	251			295	347	642	6	75	33	0.25	228	47	18	35	70	4%	135	33%	3.33	-13.8	11	$10

Injuries factored into PT dip; inability to hit LHP didn't help. Poor plate approach limits SB opportunities - as they say, you can't steal first base. With signs of growth lacking... DN: 10 SB

Gonzalez,Adrian

		Year	AB	R	HR	RBI	SB	Avg	vL	vR	OB	Slg	OPS	bb%	ct%	h%	Eye	xBA	G	L	F	PX	hr/f	Spd	SBO	RC/G	RAR	BPV	R$
Pos	3	06 SD	570	83	24	82	0	304	312	301	362	500	862	8	80	34	0.46	282	44	23	33	122	16%	54	1%	6.10	1.5	53	$21
Age/B	28 Left	07 SD	646	101	30	100	0	282	263	290	347	502	849	9	78	32	0.46	278	37	19	44	143	14%	72	0%	6.02	-2.1	69	$23
Ht/Wt	74 225	08 SD	616	103	36	119	0	279	213	320	357	510	866	11	77	31	0.52	277	43	20	37	146	21%	57	0%	6.26	9.2	65	$27
Health	A	09 SD	552	90	40	99	1	277	234	305	405	551	956	18	80	28	1.09	298	39	21	40	164	22%	59	1%	7.67	18.2	107	$26
PT/Exp	A	10 SD	591	87	31	101	0	298	337	278	393	511	904	14	81	33	0.82	293	39	21	39	137	16%	46	0%	6.87	8.8	76	$27
Consist	C	1st Half	296	43	16	51	0	291			386	517	903	13	80	32	0.78	295	38	20	41	149	16%	49	0%	6.86	4.3	83	$13
LIMA Plan	C+	2nd Half	295	44	15	50	0	305			401	505	906	14	81	33	0.85	291	40	22	38	126	17%	54	0%	6.88	4.4	72	$14
Rand Var	0	11 Proj	574	89	33	100	0	291			388	521	909	14	80	31	0.79	291	40	21	39	144	18%	53	0%	6.93	10.7	80	$26

Crushed LHP for a change, thanks in part to a 38% h%. PX, hr/f couldn't hold at 2008-09 peak levels. Still, this is a solid patience/power combo, bid to value while imagining what he could do if he left PETCO.

Gonzalez,Alberto

		Year	AB	R	HR	RBI	SB	Avg	vL	vR	OB	Slg	OPS	bb%	ct%	h%	Eye	xBA	G	L	F	PX	hr/f	Spd	SBO	RC/G	RAR	BPV	R$
Pos	45	06 a/a	449	58	5	43	4	272			322	363	685	7	92	29	0.94					53		104	4%	4.17	-2.4	58	$9
Age/B	27 Right	07 a/a	493	58	1	48	12	244			289	338	627	6	87	28	0.49					63		139	15%	3.42	-13.9	55	$7
Ht/Wt	70 194	08 2TM	*322	33	5	34	3	230	219	275	275	328	603	6	86	25	0.44	279	44	28	29	68	6%	53	8%	2.99	-18.1	27	$4
Health	A	09 WAS	*381	36	1	41	2	268	397	228	316	346	663	7	85	31	0.48	251	43	23	34	56	1%	97	4%	3.78	-8.3	30	$7
PT/Exp	D	10 WAS	186	19	0	5	0	247	254	244	275	301	576	4	84	29	0.23	240	55	14	31	43	0%	108	0%	2.53	-12.6	12	$1
Consist	C	1st Half	73	8	0	3	0	288			325	342	667	5	82	35	0.31	239	65	10	25	50	0%	82	0%	3.66	-2.4	6	$1
LIMA Plan	F	2nd Half	113	11	0	2	0	221			241	274	516	3	85	26	0.18	238	49	16	34	39	0%	119	0%	1.82	-10.4	14	($0)
Rand Var	0	11 Proj	133	14	0	9	1	248			286	318	604	5	85	29	0.35	248	51	17	31	50	1%	99	3%	2.97	-6.9	22	$1

Outer space is empty, but it can't hold a candle to this bat. Bereft of power and not enough plate patience to take advantage of his average speed, even a decent ct% doesn't help much.

Gonzalez,Alex

		Year	AB	R	HR	RBI	SB	Avg	vL	vR	OB	Slg	OPS	bb%	ct%	h%	Eye	xBA	G	L	F	PX	hr/f	Spd	SBO	RC/G	RAR	BPV	R$
Pos	6	06 BOS	388	48	9	50	1	255	278	244	295	397	692	5	83	29	0.33	250	37	20	43	91	6%	77	1%	3.93	-5.4	40	$7
Age/B	34 Right	07 CIN	393	55	16	55	0	272	234	287	314	468	782	6	81	30	0.32	278	34	22	44	125	12%	66	1%	4.97	5.9	57	$11
Ht/Wt	71 216	08 CIN	0	0	0	0	0	0																					
Health	F	09 2TM	391	42	8	41	2	238	212	247	275	355	630	5	83	27	0.31	231	37	16	47	79	5%	53	4%	3.17	-16.2	24	$6
PT/Exp	D	10 2TM	595	74	23	88	1	250	224	260	288	447	735	5	80	28	0.26	274	33	19	49	134	10%	52	3%	4.37	3.2	56	$17
Consist	C	1st Half	306	44	15	42	1	258			297	484	781	5	80	28	0.28	289	30	20	49	151	12%	54	2%	4.91	6.4	70	$10
LIMA Plan	D+	2nd Half	289	30	8	46	0	242			277	408	686	5	80	28	0.25	258	35	17	49	117	7%	56	4%	3.80	-3.4	43	$6
Rand Var	-2	11 Proj	479	58	15	65	1	251			288	419	707	5	81	28	0.29	259	34	18	47	112	8%	60	3%	4.06	-4.0	45	$11

240 PX, 18% hr/f, 55% FB% in April got his power rebound started but it was too airborne to sustain. He returned to Earth in 2H. Could approach 20 HR again, but injury history says to bet the under on 500 AB.

Gonzalez,Carlos

		Year	AB	R	HR	RBI	SB	Avg	vL	vR	OB	Slg	OPS	bb%	ct%	h%	Eye	xBA	G	L	F	PX	hr/f	Spd	SBO	RC/G	RAR	BPV	R$
Pos	789	06	0	0	0	0	0	0																					
Age/B	25 Left	07 aa	500	60	16	71	8	272			316	454	770	6	82	30	0.36					119		91	13%	4.89	-4.5	66	$15
Ht/Wt	73 215	08 OAK	*475	49	7	48	5	242	188	263	280	358	638	5	77	30	0.23	245	49	18	33	88	6%	74	7%	3.23	-23.0	14	$7
Health	A	09 COL	*470	87	22	77	21	297	276	286	360	544	904	9	80	33	0.48	288	38	23	39	148	15%	143	22%	6.71	15.2	100	$26
PT/Exp	B	10 COL	587	111	34	117	26	336	320	345	378	598	976	6	77	39	0.30	307	43	21	37	170	21%	110	21%	7.48	37.6	92	$42
Consist	C	1st Half	298	49	14	52	12	295			329	493	822	5	76	35	0.21	272	43	20	37	124	17%	133	22%	5.43	3.0	55	$17
LIMA Plan	D+	2nd Half	289	62	20	65	14	377			427	706	1133	8	78	43	0.39	343	42	22	37	217	24%	91	20%	9.55	32.1	130	$26
Rand Var	-5	11 Proj	596	102	32	103	22	302			350	559	909	7	78	34	0.34	302	42	21	37	162	19%	111	20%	6.65	22.9	92	$34

What to make of this monster? PRO: Increase in PX and hr/f drove HR outburst; blasted LHP. CON: High h% spurred 2H BA. Verdict: Power gains legit, BA not so much, but some level of regression is pretty much a given.

Gordon,Alex

		Year	AB	R	HR	RBI	SB	Avg	vL	vR	OB	Slg	OPS	bb%	ct%	h%	Eye	xBA	G	L	F	PX	hr/f	Spd	SBO	RC/G	RAR	BPV	R$
Pos	7	06 aa	486	87	20	79	17	286			361	490	851	10	83	31	0.67					127		72	15%	6.09	12.1	76	$21
Age/B	27 Left	07 KC	543	60	15	60	14	247	217	258	300	411	710	7	75	30	0.30	251	37	19	44	120	8%	76	15%	4.24	-12.9	34	$12
Ht/Wt	73 220	08 KC	493	72	16	59	9	260	234	273	347	432	779	12	76	31	0.55	249	31	21	48	125	9%	73	8%	5.34	7.1	51	$14
Health	D	09 KC	*261	44	9	37	5	250	163	261	339	407	746	12	77	29	0.58	238	44	14	42	100	10%	91	6%	4.86	-1.2	41	$8
PT/Exp	C	10 KC	*502	76	17	51	6	239	200	220	333	406	739	12	76	28	0.59	270	38	23	39	119	11%	67	9%	4.81	-1.1	47	$13
Consist	A	1st Half	235	38	8	27	5	268			364	446	810	13	77	32	0.66	282	35	26	39	126	12%	80	9%	5.78	6.2	62	$8
LIMA Plan	C	2nd Half	267	38	9	25	1	214			305	371	676	12	75	25	0.53	262	38	23	39	113	11%	71	9%	3.93	-8.0	38	$4
Rand Var	+3	11 Proj	406	62	14	48	6	259			346	422	768	12	76	31	0.57	255	38	20	42	114	11%	72	8%	5.16	2.7	44	$12

8-20-.215 in 242 AB at KC. Finally ready to reach potential? PRO: improved xBA, PX, LD%; good bb%. CON: falling FB%, no ct% growth. Some signs of life, but there's much more work to be done.

Granderson,Curtis

		Year	AB	R	HR	RBI	SB	Avg	vL	vR	OB	Slg	OPS	bb%	ct%	h%	Eye	xBA	G	L	F	PX	hr/f	Spd	SBO	RC/G	RAR	BPV	R$
Pos	8	06 DET	596	90	19	68	8	260	218	274	334	438	772	10	71	34	0.38	240	39	22	39	122	12%	142	8%	5.28	10.8	45	$15
Age/B	30 Left	07 DET	612	122	23	74	26	302	160	337	357	552	909	8	77	36	0.37	279	34	21	45	158	11%	208	18%	6.89	39.6	114	$29
Ht/Wt	73 185	08 DET	553	112	22	66	12	280	259	288	362	494	856	11	80	32	0.64	271	40	19	41	128	12%	197	10%	6.26	14.3	106	$22
Health	B	09 DET	631	91	30	71	20	249	180	275	326	453	779	10	78	28	0.51	248	30	21	49	119	12%	131	15%	5.15	9.6	67	$20
PT/Exp	A	10 NYY	466	76	24	67	12	247	234	253	324	468	792	10	75	28	0.46	264	33	20	47	142	15%	133	12%	5.34	0.1	77	$18
Consist	B	1st Half	199	30	7	22	6	226			300	402	702	10	76	26	0.44	255	32	23	45	116	10%	133	13%	4.19	-6.9	57	$6
LIMA Plan	B+	2nd Half	267	46	17	45	6	262			341	517	858	11	75	29	0.47	273	34	18	49	162	17%	127	11%	6.20	6.8	89	$13
Rand Var	+2	11 Proj	547	91	26	71	15	256			332	471	803	10	76	29	0.48	260	34	20	46	133	13%	146	12%	5.50	6.7	78	$20

Move to NY helped PX and hr/f; injuries cut back on the ABs. Traditionally struggles vs LHP, but some 2H tweaks led to better numbers. If he stays healthy and holds the gains vLH: UP: 30 HR, 20 SB again

Griffey Jr.,Ken

		Year	AB	R	HR	RBI	SB	Avg	vL	vR	OB	Slg	OPS	bb%	ct%	h%	Eye	xBA	G	L	F	PX	hr/f	Spd	SBO	RC/G	RAR	BPV	R$
Pos	0	06 CIN	428	62	27	72	0	252	204	278	315	486	801	8	82	25	0.50	268	42	15	43	130	18%	51	0%	5.21	-15.3	65	$14
Age/B	41 Left	07 CIN	528	78	30	93	6	277	236	300	377	496	873	14	81	29	0.86	266	35	16	49	128	14%	74	4%	6.46	3.2	80	$21
Ht/Wt	75 230	08 2TM	486	66	18	71	0	247	202	272	350	422	772	14	82	27	0.87	264	38	20	42	112	11%	67	1%	5.30	5.3	66	$12
Health	A	09 SEA	387	44	19	57	0	214	213	215	324	411	735	14	79	22	0.79	251	37	16	47	118	13%	47	0%	4.75	-5.0	56	$7
PT/Exp	C	10 SEA	98	6	0	7	0	184	250	174	252	204	456	8	83	22	0.53	179	34	15	51	19	0%	74	0%	1.28	-15.9	-13	($1)
Consist	F	1st Half	98	6	0	7	0	184			252	204	456	8	83	22	0.53	179	34	15	51	19	0%	74	0%	1.28	-15.9	-13	($1)
LIMA Plan		2nd Half	0	0	0	0	0	0																					
Rand Var		11 Proj	0	0	0	0	0	0																					

Announced retirement in June, so it's time to book that 2016 hotel room in Cooperstown. 630 total home runs (5th all-time), never a whiff of scandal. Baseball done right.

Gross,Gabe

		Year	AB	R	HR	RBI	SB	Avg	vL	vR	OB	Slg	OPS	bb%	ct%	h%	Eye	xBA	G	L	F	PX	hr/f	Spd	SBO	RC/G	RAR	BPV	R$
Pos	79	06 MIL	208	42	9	38	1	274	95	294	381	476	857	15	71	35	0.60	253	34	23	42	143	14%	69	1%	6.61	8.1	51	$8
Age/B	31 Left	07 MIL	*259	39	11	33	5	258	91	244	351	470	822	13	80	28	0.74	280	39	20	41	128	13%	121	8%	5.87	3.9	88	$8
Ht/Wt	75 220	08 2TM	345	46	13	40	4	238	191	249	334	414	749	13	76	28	0.61	244	41	17	43	115	12%	118	6%	4.93	-2.1	60	$8
Health	A	09 TAM	282	31	6	36	6	227	172	233	327	355	682	13	72	29	0.53	237	40	23	36	94	8%	84	11%	4.13	-7.6	17	$5
PT/Exp	D	10 OAK	222	27	1	25	5	239	167	253	293	311	604	7	82	29	0.44	250	46	20	34	57	2%	83	11%	3.02	-12.4	16	$4
Consist	B	1st Half	146	13	1	15	2	260			299	329	627	5	81	32	0.29	247	45	23	33	50	3%	106	8%	3.13	-7.5	7	$3
LIMA Plan	F	2nd Half	76	14	0	10	3	197			282	276	559	11	86	23	0.82	255	50	15	35	70	0%	60	17%	2.84	-4.9	39	$1
Rand Var	+2	11 Proj	152	21	2	19	3	230			313	351	664	11	79	28	0.57	252	44	19	36	87	6%	89	10%	3.86	-4.9	35	$3

Things are not looking good...- Only 13 XBH, power declining for 4 straight years, can't hit LH, too many GB, no speed. At 31, young to have already slid into irrelevance, but that just makes our job as analysts easier.

DAVE ADLER

Guerrero,Vladimir

			AB	R	HR	RBI	SB	Avg	vL	vR	OB	Slg	OPS	bb%	ct%	h%	Eye	xBA	G	L	F	PX	hr/f	Spd	SBO	RC/G	RAR	BPV	R$
Pos	0	06 LAA	607	92	33	116	15	329	401	307	381	552	932	8	89	33	0.74	297	44	19	37	121	16%	51	11%	6.73	4.9	85	$32
Age/B	36 Right	07 LAA	574	89	27	125	2	324	321	325	398	547	945	11	89	33	1.15	317	48	16	36	133	15%	70	3%	7.19	14.6	108	$28
Ht/Wt	75 235	08 LAA	541	85	27	91	5	303	286	309	363	521	884	9	86	31	0.66	297	47	17	36	128	16%	80	5%	6.30	20.4	89	$24
Health	C	09 LAA	383	59	15	50	2	295	250	311	328	460	788	5	85	31	0.34	266	42	18	40	92	11%	72	3%	4.93	-2.6	48	$14
PT/Exp	B	10 TEX	593	83	29	115	4	300	338	287	339	496	835	6	90	30	0.58	305	45	18	37	111	15%	50	6%	5.52	-13.7	77	$28
Consist	B	1st Half	297	52	18	70	4	330			372	566	938	6	91	32	0.74	323	40	20	40	130	17%	57	8%	6.67	2.5	99	$19
LIMA Plan	D+	2nd Half	296	31	11	45	0	270			305	426	731	5	89	27	0.45	287	50	17	33	93	13%	47	3%	4.34	-17.1	55	$9
Rand Var	+1	11 Proj	**488**	**70**	**21**	**83**	**3**	**289**			**332**	**469**	**801**	**6**	**88**	**29**	**0.54**	**289**	**45**	**18**	**37**	**104**	**13%**	**59**	**5%**	**5.19**	**-8.9**	**67**	**$19**

Once you display a skill... At least for 1H, he reclaimed his 2006-08 skill set. Texas heat brought him back to reality in 2H, resuming his expected late-30s skill fade. 500+ AB seasons can no longer be assumed, either.

Guillen,Carlos

			AB	R	HR	RBI	SB	Avg	vL	vR	OB	Slg	OPS	bb%	ct%	h%	Eye	xBA	G	L	F	PX	hr/f	Spd	SBO	RC/G	RAR	BPV	R$
Pos	4	06 DET	543	100	19	85	20	320	291	332	399	519	918	12	84	35	0.82	285	42	20	38	122	11%	101	16%	7.01	42.9	89	$26
Age/B	35 Both	07 DET	564	86	21	102	13	296	302	295	359	502	860	9	84	32	0.59	289	39	20	41	126	11%	118	13%	6.14	34.0	90	$24
Ht/Wt	73 213	08 DET	420	68	10	54	9	286	287	285	375	436	811	13	84	32	0.90	277	45	20	35	100	8%	100	9%	5.80	10.9	73	$14
Health	F	09 DET	277	36	11	41	1	242	244	245	335	419	754	12	80	27	0.70	252	37	20	43	102	11%	105	5%	4.97	0.3	58	$7
PT/Exp	C	10 DET	253	26	6	34	1	273	234	286	328	419	747	8	84	31	0.51	274	50	14	36	101	8%	73	5%	4.74	2.0	56	$7
Consist	B	1st Half	176	19	5	22	1	284			347	438	785	9	84	31	0.61	279	50	14	36	106	9%	72	4%	5.23	3.8	62	$5
LIMA Plan	D	2nd Half	77	7	1	12	0	247			284	377	661	5	83	29	0.31	262	48	14	38	91	4%	80	6%	3.61	-2.0	41	$1
Rand Var	0	11 Proj	**290**	**36**	**8**	**42**	**2**	**266**			**333**	**417**	**750**	**9**	**83**	**30**	**0.59**	**266**	**45**	**17**	**38**	**99**	**8%**	**86**	**7%**	**4.85**	**2.1**	**56**	**$8**

Stable skills say he can still hit, but can he get in the lineup and stay there? Declining AB trend highlights ongoing injuries, and is unlikely to reverse thanks to knee surgery that puts Opening Day readiness in doubt.

Guillen,Jose

			AB	R	HR	RBI	SB	Avg	vL	vR	OB	Slg	OPS	bb%	ct%	h%	Eye	xBA	G	L	F	PX	hr/f	Spd	SBO	RC/G	RAR	BPV	R$
Pos	90	06 WAS	241	28	9	40	1	216	200	221	262	398	660	6	80	23	0.31	247	41	14	45	113	10%	63	2%	3.50	-9.4	44	$4
Age/B	34 Right	07 SEA	593	84	23	99	5	290	362	268	336	460	796	6	80	33	0.35	271	48	16	36	108	14%	108	4%	5.16	-5.6	54	$21
Ht/Wt	72 195	08 KC	598	66	20	97	2	264	305	248	291	438	730	4	82	29	0.22	277	47	18	35	116	12%	69	3%	4.24	-19.3	52	$16
Health	C	09 KC	281	30	9	40	1	242	181	273	297	367	664	7	82	27	0.44	232	46	14	40	72	10%	69	1%	3.59	-14.6	23	$6
PT/Exp	B	10 2TM	524	55	19	77	1	258	215	269	300	416	716	6	78	30	0.28	258	45	17	39	105	12%	75	1%	4.14	-15.3	34	$15
Consist	B	1st Half	310	42	14	52	1	274			322	458	780	7	77	32	0.31	264	41	18	40	118	15%	93	1%	4.97	-1.5	46	$12
LIMA Plan	F	2nd Half	214	13	5	25	0	234			268	355	623	4	80	27	0.24	246	49	14	37	86	8%	56	0%	2.98	-13.9	18	$3
Rand Var	0	11 Proj	**259**	**26**	**9**	**38**	**1**	**251**			**293**	**396**	**689**	**6**	**80**	**28**	**0.31**	**251**	**46**	**16**	**38**	**95**	**11%**	**64**	**1%**	**3.81**	**-10.2**	**30**	**$6**

Socked 7 HR in April, then crashed back to earth. Shaky plate approach has long been an issue, but now that it's combined with merely average power, there's nothing left to hold our interest.

Gutierrez,Franklin

			AB	R	HR	RBI	SB	Avg	vL	vR	OB	Slg	OPS	bb%	ct%	h%	Eye	xBA	G	L	F	PX	hr/f	Spd	SBO	RC/G	RAR	BPV	R$
Pos	8	06 CLE	* 485	81	9	44	12	266	262	277	336	396	732	10	77	33	0.46	256	43	23	34	97	7%	104	15%	4.66	-0.1	39	$12
Age/B	28 Right	07 CLE	* 400	66	16	50	14	283	330	232	329	463	792	7	76	34	0.29	255	43	15	42	120	13%	118	19%	5.17	7.3	51	$16
Ht/Wt	74 190	08 CLE	399	54	8	41	9	248	252	246	296	383	679	6	78	30	0.31	243	42	17	41	98	6%	106	13%	3.81	-18.2	38	$9
Health	A	09 SEA	565	85	18	70	16	283	335	262	337	425	762	8	78	33	0.38	251	45	19	36	89	11%	103	13%	4.82	2.8	33	$20
PT/Exp	A	10 SEA	568	61	12	64	25	245	248	244	306	363	669	8	76	30	0.36	233	42	16	42	86	7%	110	19%	3.71	-27.4	23	$16
Consist	C	1st Half	285	34	8	36	10	277			354	421	775	11	75	35	0.47	242	41	18	41	99	9%	143	12%	5.24	-0.7	44	$11
LIMA Plan	C	2nd Half	283	27	4	28	15	212			254	304	558	5	77	26	0.25	221	44	14	42	73	4%	78	29%	2.19	-27.7	2	$6
Rand Var	0	11 Proj	**560**	**71**	**14**	**63**	**19**	**255**			**310**	**385**	**696**	**7**	**77**	**31**	**0.35**	**241**	**43**	**17**	**40**	**91**	**8%**	**104**	**16%**	**4.02**	**-17.6**	**29**	**$16**

Couldn't hold 2009 BA gains (as xBA foretold), but SB spike propped up value. Despite near-average Spd, 25/3 SB/CS says he's a good base-stealer. But xBA says BA hasn't hit bottom yet, which would cut SB opps.

Guzman,Cristian

			AB	R	HR	RBI	SB	Avg	vL	vR	OB	Slg	OPS	bb%	ct%	h%	Eye	xBA	G	L	F	PX	hr/f	Spd	SBO	RC/G	RAR	BPV	R$
Pos	46	06 WAS	0	0	0	0	0	0																					
Age/B	33 Both	07 WAS	174	31	2	14	2	328	357	318	381	466	846	8	88	36	0.71	302	60	17	23	72	6%	207	3%	6.02	6.1	89	$6
Ht/Wt	72 211	08 WAS	579	77	9	55	6	316	354	299	342	440	783	4	90	34	0.40	299	53	23	25	77	7%	114	7%	4.98	3.3	66	$19
Health	F	09 WAS	531	74	6	52	4	284	307	277	305	390	695	3	86	32	0.21	264	54	17	29	67	5%	131	7%	3.89	-9.7	44	$14
PT/Exp	B	10 2TM	365	48	2	26	4	266	317	241	304	337	641	5	83	32	0.32	253	52	19	29	49	2%	123	6%	3.34	-13.7	19	$7
Consist	B	1st Half	268	38	1	21	3	299			333	377	710	5	85	35	0.34	265	53	19	28	52	2%	138	6%	4.20	-3.3	34	$8
LIMA Plan	F	2nd Half	97	10	1	5	1	175			223	227	450	6	77	22	0.27	218	47	20	33	38	4%	54	5%	0.81	-12.0	-31	($0)
Rand Var	0	11 Proj	**285**	**38**	**3**	**22**	**3**	**263**			**299**	**354**	**653**	**5**	**84**	**31**	**0.32**	**261**	**52**	**19**	**29**	**59**	**4%**	**121**	**6%**	**3.48**	**-9.8**	**30**	**$6**

At his peak, he used high ct% and good Spd to produce high Avg, but he doesn't own either of those skills anymore. Still hits LHPs, and that may earn him more paychecks, but not a spot on your roster.

Gwynn,Tony

			AB	R	HR	RBI	SB	Avg	vL	vR	OB	Slg	OPS	bb%	ct%	h%	Eye	xBA	G	L	F	PX	hr/f	Spd	SBO	RC/G	RAR	BPV	R$
Pos	8	06 MIL	* 524	71	4	42	30	277	167	268	329	361	690	7	82	33	0.44	257	50	23	27	54	3%	128	28%	4.05	-6.0	27	$16
Age/B	28 Left	07 MIL	* 249	30	0	21	12	261	316	250	316	317	633	7	85	31	0.54	246	53	18	29	34	0%	158	21%	3.47	-7.8	32	$6
Ht/Wt	71 193	08 aaa	375	33	2	18	14	218			260	263	523	5	88	25	0.45					27		135	22%	2.10	-34.6	25	$3
Health	A	09 SD	* 545	84	3	27	22	265	215	290	342	339	681	10	85	31	0.76	253	46	24	30	47	2%	163	17%	4.19	-8.7	48	$14
PT/Exp	D	10 SD	289	30	3	20	17	204	325	185	303	287	590	12	83	24	0.82	244	46	19	35	54	4%	120	25%	3.12	-16.3	37	$5
Consist	D	1st Half	211	21	2	16	13	227			324	318	641	12	85	26	0.94	256	45	21	35	57	3%	117	26%	3.82	-7.0	47	$5
LIMA Plan	D	2nd Half	78	9	1	4	4	141			247	205	452	12	77	17	0.61	209	52	12	36	47	5%	102	21%	1.08	-10.0	3	$0
Rand Var	+5	11 Proj	**251**	**30**	**2**	**15**	**15**	**243**			**321**	**311**	**633**	**10**	**83**	**29**	**0.67**	**235**	**48**	**18**	**34**	**44**	**3%**	**121**	**23%**	**3.52**	**-9.6**	**25**	**$6**

Seemingly forgot how to hit RHP, although h% a big culprit. Combo of walks, GBs, and Spd/SBO point to SB upside if that h% moves north a bit. He got 400 AB in 2009, if that happens again... UP: 40 SB

Hafner,Travis

			AB	R	HR	RBI	SB	Avg	vL	vR	OB	Slg	OPS	bb%	ct%	h%	Eye	xBA	G	L	F	PX	hr/f	Spd	SBO	RC/G	RAR	BPV	R$
Pos	0	06 CLE	454	100	42	117	0	308	321	300	433	659	1092	18	76	33	0.90	316	39	21	40	216	30%	44	0%	9.57	38.7	126	$28
Age/B	33 Left	07 CLE	545	80	24	100	1	266	274	261	382	451	833	16	79	30	0.89	274	48	17	35	118	16%	74	1%	6.14	-1.6	65	$18
Ht/Wt	75 240	08 CLE	198	21	5	24	1	197	220	189	293	323	617	12	72	25	0.49	242	42	25	33	96	11%	39	4%	3.14	-11.3	3	$1
Health	D	09 CLE	338	46	16	49	0	272	210	292	351	470	821	11	80	30	0.61	274	39	21	40	121	15%	63	0%	5.70	5.1	60	$11
PT/Exp	C	10 CLE	396	46	13	50	2	278	273	279	360	449	810	11	76	34	0.54	272	43	19	38	129	11%	48	3%	5.72	-7.1	48	$12
Consist	C	1st Half	225	26	8	29	0	244			331	413	744	11	77	28	0.57	266	46	16	37	121	12%	50	2%	4.82	-10.3	46	$5
LIMA Plan	D+	2nd Half	171	20	5	21	2	322			399	497	896	11	75	41	0.51	280	38	23	39	140	10%	54	4%	6.95	2.7	52	$7
Rand Var	-2	11 Proj	**366**	**46**	**14**	**51**	**2**	**284**			**369**	**463**	**833**	**12**	**77**	**34**	**0.57**	**270**	**41**	**21**	**38**	**126**	**13%**	**49**	**2%**	**6.00**	**1.7**	**47**	**$12**

Persistent shoulder issues make 2006 a distant memory, but he retains some utility vs. RHP. 2H PX was a flash of the good ol' days, but don't get sucked in: chronically injured players don't suddenly get healthy.

Hairston,Jerry

			AB	R	HR	RBI	SB	Avg	vL	vR	OB	Slg	OPS	bb%	ct%	h%	Eye	xBA	G	L	F	PX	hr/f	Spd	SBO	RC/G	RAR	BPV	R$
Pos	46	06 2TM	170	25	0	10	5	206	153	245	262	253	515	7	80	26	0.38	203	42	17	41	36	0%	112	17%	1.87	-13.4	-2	$1
Age/B	34 Right	07 TEX	159	22	3	16	5	189	228	150	241	289	530	6	85	20	0.46	219	35	14	52	66	4%	86	19%	2.13	-9.5	33	$2
Ht/Wt	70 190	08 CIN	* 340	55	9	48	16	324	345	316	371	502	873	7	87	35	0.57	291	32	27	41	113	7%	98	21%	6.18	12.9	84	$18
Health	C	09 2TM	383	62	10	39	7	251	242	255	308	394	703	8	86	27	0.59	266	34	23	43	90	7%	85	12%	4.23	-5.7	59	$10
PT/Exp	C	10 SD	430	53	10	50	9	244	244	244	295	353	648	7	87	26	0.57	245	40	16	44	65	6%	91	14%	3.55	-16.4	44	$11
Consist	C	1st Half	259	26	5	30	5	239			281	344	625	5	85	27	0.38	237	40	17	44	64	5%	94	13%	3.15	-13.1	31	$5
LIMA Plan	F	2nd Half	171	27	5	20	4	251			316	368	684	9	92	25	1.14	257	41	16	44	66	7%	79	14%	4.16	-3.4	63	$5
Rand Var	0	11 Proj	**297**	**43**	**7**	**33**	**8**	**256**			**310**	**382**	**692**	**7**	**87**	**27**	**0.62**	**256**	**37**	**19**	**43**	**78**	**6%**	**85**	**15%**	**4.09**	**-5.5**	**53**	**$9**

No longer owns any above-average skill, except perhaps versatility. SBO says he still tries to run, but effectiveness is waning (16 SB/10 CS last two years), so that won't last much longer, either.

Hairston,Scott

			AB	R	HR	RBI	SB	Avg	vL	vR	OB	Slg	OPS	bb%	ct%	h%	Eye	xBA	G	L	F	PX	hr/f	Spd	SBO	RC/G	RAR	BPV	R$
Pos	7	06 aaa	396	64	20	63	2	292	375	429	358	510	868	9	83	31	0.62	326	50	30	20	126	31%	108	2%	6.15	10.3	88	$16
Age/B	30 Right	07 2NL	263	37	11	36	2	243	235	247	311	452	764	9	79	27	0.47	261	34	15	50	134	10%	87	3%	4.95	-3.2	70	$7
Ht/Wt	72 196	08 SD	326	42	17	31	3	248	280	224	308	479	786	8	74	28	0.33	251	38	14	48	151	15%	130	6%	5.19	-2.3	75	$9
Health	C	09 2TM	430	50	17	64	11	265	318	243	305	456	761	5	81	29	0.30	250	34	15	51	121	10%	91	15%	4.70	-7.3	60	$15
PT/Exp	C	10 SD	295	34	10	36	6	210	233	198	285	346	631	10	77	24	0.45	221	34	15	51	91	9%	80	10%	3.21	-17.1	24	$6
Consist	B	1st Half	186	25	8	25	4	226			311	387	698	11	75	26	0.49	229	38	13	49	108	12%	97	10%	4.10	-5.5	38	$5
LIMA Plan	D	2nd Half	109	9	2	11	2	183			239	275	515	7	80	21	0.36	208	28	17	55	65	4%	63	9%	1.76	-11.6	5	$1
Rand Var	+3	11 Proj	**295**	**34**	**11**	**36**	**5**	**247**			**306**	**413**	**719**	**8**	**78**	**28**	**0.39**	**235**	**34**	**15**	**51**	**109**	**9%**	**93**	**9%**	**4.28**	**-8.6**	**46**	**$8**

Nagging injuries continue to, well, nag him. In 2010 it was hamstring, calf, and shoulder at various times, with effects now seen in PX and xBA trends. May return to mashing LHPs, but that's his ceiling.

RAY MURPHY

Hall,Bill

Hall,Bill		AB	R	HR	RBI	SB	Avg	vL	vR	OB	Slg	OPS	bb%	ct%	h%	Eye	xBA	G	L	F	PX	hr/f	Spd	SBO	RC/G	RAR	BPV	R$
Pos 47	06 MIL	537	101	35	85	8	270	300	261	347	553	900	11	70	32	0.39	268	33	19	48	192	19%	99	13%	7.01	37.9	85	$23
Age/B 31 Right	07 MIL	452	59	14	63	4	254	270	247	315	425	740	8	72	33	0.31	255	36	23	41	131	10%	54	8%	4.72	0.3	26	$11
Ht/Wt 72 210	08 MIL	404	50	15	55	5	225	306	174	290	396	686	8	69	29	0.30	235	39	21	40	127	13%	81	12%	3.96	-10.1	22	$9
Health A	09 2TM	334	32	8	36	2	201	223	186	260	338	599	7	64	29	0.23	207	39	18	43	117	9%	53	6%	2.82	-20.1	-17	$2
PT/Exp C	10 BOS	344	44	18	46	9	247	199	283	315	456	771	9	70	30	0.33	257	38	18	44	152	17%	62	12%	5.10	6.5	40	$12
Consist D	1st Half	141	21	6	19	3	227			327	404	731	13	67	29	0.46	226	32	18	51	131	13%	85	7%	4.78	1.4	28	$4
LIMA Plan D+	2nd Half	203	23	12	27	6	261			306	493	798	6	71	31	0.22	277	42	18	40	167	21%	53	16%	5.27	4.8	49	$8
Rand Var 0	11 Proj	352	43	15	45	6	250			314	437	751	8	68	32	0.29	242	38	19	43	140	14%	63	10%	4.90	3.1	24	$10

Resurgence of PX and Avg vRH drove this recovery. Can he hold those gains? Still owns the prior skills, and neither h% nor hr/f was out of line. Added bonus: he regained 2B eligibility. This should be repeatable.

Hamilton,Josh

Hamilton,Josh		AB	R	HR	RBI	SB	Avg	vL	vR	OB	Slg	OPS	bb%	ct%	h%	Eye	xBA	G	L	F	PX	hr/f	Spd	SBO	RC/G	RAR	BPV	R$
Pos 78	06	0	0	0	0	0	0																					
Age/B 29 Left	07 CIN	* 338	60	23	54	6	295	222	314	364	563	927	10	78	32	0.50	309	45	22	33	161	26%	106	10%	6.93	14.9	96	$17
Ht/Wt 76 235	08 TEX	624	98	32	130	9	304	288	313	369	530	900	9	80	34	0.51	295	46	21	33	141	20%	85	5%	6.60	29.8	78	$30
Health C	09 TEX	336	43	10	54	8	268	327	239	317	426	742	7	76	32	0.30	249	36	22	42	104	9%	78	13%	4.59	-4.1	28	$11
PT/Exp B	10 TEX	518	95	32	100	8	359	271	402	408	633	1041	8	82	39	0.45	334	42	22	36	177	21%	84	6%	8.17	42.9	111	$35
Consist F	1st Half	313	55	20	61	6	339			384	617	1001	7	79	38	0.35	324	40	22	38	183	21%	91	8%	7.71	23.1	105	$20
LIMA Plan C+	2nd Half	205	40	12	39	2	390			444	659	1103	9	86	41	0.69	348	44	22	34	167	20%	77	3%	8.86	19.5	120	$15
Rand Var -5	11 Proj	515	86	29	94	9	307			363	555	917	8	80	33	0.45	310	42	22	36	156	19%	81	8%	6.72	25.3	89	$26

You don't need any sabermetric analysis to tell you how good this season was. Okay, fortunate h% may have helped a bit. But Health and Consistency grades tell the real tale; R$ column shows the variability in your ROI.

Hanigan,Ryan

Hanigan,Ryan		AB	R	HR	RBI	SB	Avg	vL	vR	OB	Slg	OPS	bb%	ct%	h%	Eye	xBA	G	L	F	PX	hr/f	Spd	SBO	RC/G	RAR	BPV	R$
Pos 2	06 a/a	139	16	0	13	0	207			310	220	530	13	81	26	0.78					11		88	0%	2.32	-8.9	-13	($0)
Age/B 30 Right	07 a/a	324	35	3	27	0	226			312	311	624	11	86	25	0.91					58		94	2%	3.57	-7.8	44	$2
Ht/Wt 72 201	08 CIN	* 357	35	6	34	1	264	237	298	318	348	667	7	87	29	0.63	263	51	21	28	54	6%	96	1%	3.82	-4.0	38	$6
Health B	09 CIN	251	22	3	11	0	263	291	255	358	331	688	13	88	29	1.19	262	48	24	27	41	5%	89	0%	4.43	1.2	38	$3
PT/Exp D	10 CIN	* 249	29	5	42	0	279	291	304	369	394	763	12	89	30	1.32	288	48	21	31	75	7%	68	0%	5.30	5.8	64	$8
Consist B	1st Half	77	9	2	17	0	351			457	506	963	16	92	36	2.50	319	44	23	33	100	9%	68	0%	7.87	6.7	104	$4
LIMA Plan D	2nd Half	172	20	3	25	0	247			327	343	671	11	88	27	0.98	274	50	19	30	64	7%	74	0%	4.09	-2.0	48	$4
Rand Var 0	11 Proj	352	38	6	43	0	281			367	374	742	12	88	31	1.15	273	48	22	30	60	6%	65	0%	5.00	6.2	46	$9

5-40-.300 in 203 AB at CIN. Was off to great start before fracturing thumb in May. Great ct%-Eye combo point to BA upside, small-sample 1H PX hints at something more... UP: 15 HR, .300 BA

Hardy,J.J.

Hardy,J.J.		AB	R	HR	RBI	SB	Avg	vL	vR	OB	Slg	OPS	bb%	ct%	h%	Eye	xBA	G	L	F	PX	hr/f	Spd	SBO	RC/G	RAR	BPV	R$
Pos 6	06 MIL	128	13	5	14	1	242	294	223	297	398	696	7	82	26	0.43	261	47	19	34	90	14%	99	6%	3.96	-1.5	46	$2
Age/B 28 Right	07 MIL	592	89	26	80	2	277	316	264	323	463	786	6	88	28	0.55	282	41	17	42	105	12%	98	3%	5.03	9.8	79	$19
Ht/Wt 74 189	08 MIL	569	78	24	74	2	283	304	276	343	478	821	8	83	31	0.53	277	48	15	36	118	14%	127	2%	5.58	15.2	82	$19
Health C	09 MIL	* 485	58	14	55	0	226	169	245	292	355	648	9	81	25	0.49	235	46	14	40	82	9%	109	1%	3.48	-17.4	41	$8
PT/Exp B	10 MIN	340	44	6	38	1	268	210	294	323	394	717	8	84	30	0.52	274	49	17	34	86	6%	114	2%	4.41	4.4	56	$8
Consist D	1st Half	146	14	3	13	0	219			265	336	600	6	84	24	0.39	266	50	16	33	75	7%	102	0%	2.89	-4.8	41	$1
LIMA Plan C+	2nd Half	194	30	3	25	1	304			366	438	804	9	84	35	0.61	281	49	17	34	94	5%	121	3%	5.55	8.5	67	$7
Rand Var 0	11 Proj	502	65	15	59	1	273			331	421	752	8	83	30	0.51	269	48	16	36	94	10%	111	2%	4.76	8.4	59	$13

Plagued all year by wrist issues, still managed to improve on '09 nightmare. High GB% stifles power, but xBA shows that he has minimal BA downside. And if wrist issues were holding back power... UP: 20 HR.

Harris,Brendan

Harris,Brendan		AB	R	HR	RBI	SB	Avg	vL	vR	OB	Slg	OPS	bb%	ct%	h%	Eye	xBA	G	L	F	PX	hr/f	Spd	SBO	RC/G	RAR	BPV	R$
Pos 5	06 CIN	* 409	55	11	54	4	269			329	421	750	8	80	31	0.44	217	37	9	54	101	6%	95	5%	4.79	-8.3	47	$11
Age/B 30 Right	07 TAM	521	72	12	59	4	286	345	264	339	434	773	7	82	33	0.44	276	43	21	35	102	8%	83	4%	5.04	2.4	49	$14
Ht/Wt 73 210	08 MIN	434	57	7	49	1	265	265	265	326	394	720	8	77	33	0.40	255	53	16	30	96	7%	102	2%	4.45	-5.4	36	$9
Health A	09 MIN	414	44	6	37	0	261	302	239	309	362	672	7	81	31	0.37	243	51	15	34	69	5%	102	2%	3.74	-11.3	26	$6
PT/Exp C	10 MIN	* 340	31	4	24	1	168	178	143	210	243	453	5	82	19	0.30	250	58	15	27	55	5%	77	1%	1.06	-41.8	8	($2)
Consist D	1st Half	108	11	1	4	0	157			222	213	435	8	79	19	0.39	230	58	15	27	42	4%	78	0%	0.78	-14.5	-11	($1)
LIMA Plan F	2nd Half	232	20	3	20	1	172			204	256	461	4	84	19	0.25					60		87	2%	1.18	-27.5	19	($1)
Rand Var +5	11 Proj	206	22	3	17	0	252			300	355	655	6	81	30	0.35	251	53	16	31	72	6%	96	2%	3.53	-7.8	24	$3

1-4-.222 in 108 AB at MIN. Hit an obscene number of GBs in '10 but lacked the speed, power or luck (h%) to reach first base. Forget '10's BA; there are at least 30 pts of hidden BA in his skill set. End-game flyer.

Harris,Willie

Harris,Willie		AB	R	HR	RBI	SB	Avg	vL	vR	OB	Slg	OPS	bb%	ct%	h%	Eye	xBA	G	L	F	PX	hr/f	Spd	SBO	RC/G	RAR	BPV	R$
Pos 79	06 BOS	* 263	45	7	16	15	193			273	307	580	10	75	23	0.44	234	68	9	24	74	14%	111	33%	2.58	-22.3	14	$5
Age/B 32 Left	07 ATL	* 402	70	3	37	22	277	191	283	351	408	760	10	81	34	0.60	260	42	21	37	88	2%	143	30%	5.16	-2.3	59	$14
Ht/Wt 69 191	08 WAS	367	58	13	43	13	251	240	255	341	417	757	12	82	27	0.76	258	43	18	38	98	11%	133	14%	5.03	-4.2	72	$12
Health A	09 WAS	323	47	7	27	11	235	121	248	350	393	743	15	81	27	0.92	239	39	15	47	102	6%	124	15%	5.12	-4.4	74	$8
PT/Exp C	10 WAS	224	25	10	32	5	183	222	180	288	362	650	13	73	20	0.55	243	41	16	43	117	14%	88	13%	3.52	-11.2	40	$4
Consist B	1st Half	116	10	4	18	2	155			246	310	556	11	76	17	0.50	231	44	11	45	102	10%	73	17%	2.30	-10.9	31	$1
LIMA Plan D+	2nd Half	108	15	6	14	3	213			331	417	747	15	70	24	0.59	253	39	21	40	133	20%	101	9%	4.92	-0.5	50	$3
Rand Var +5	11 Proj	208	28	8	24	7	240			341	423	764	13	77	28	0.65	251	41	17	42	116	12%	110	14%	5.16	-0.7	60	$6

Sneaky little power/speed skill set emerging here over past few years. Early-season knee injury likely sapped Spd, still-rising PX validates recent HR surge. With a bit of an h% correction... UP: see 2008.

Hart,Corey

Hart,Corey		AB	R	HR	RBI	SB	Avg	vL	vR	OB	Slg	OPS	bb%	ct%	h%	Eye	xBA	G	L	F	PX	hr/f	Spd	SBO	RC/G	RAR	BPV	R$
Pos 9	06 MIL	* 337	47	13	50	14	279	304	272	332	474	806	7	75	34	0.32	253	42	17	41	128	12%	106	29%	5.47	6.9	52	$14
Age/B 29 Right	07 MIL	505	86	24	81	23	295	331	278	342	539	881	7	80	33	0.36	283	37	17	46	147	13%	142	25%	6.26	19.6	97	$25
Ht/Wt 78 229	08 MIL	612	76	20	91	23	268	281	263	299	459	758	4	82	30	0.25	274	40	19	40	123	10%	101	25%	4.65	-9.6	68	$23
Health A	09 MIL	419	64	12	48	11	260	248	264	329	418	747	9	78	31	0.47	245	41	17	42	107	9%	119	15%	4.79	-1.2	54	$14
PT/Exp A	10 MIL	558	91	31	102	7	283	318	271	337	525	862	7	75	33	0.32	283	38	18	44	165	17%	99	10%	6.13	12.7	79	$27
Consist B	1st Half	276	42	19	61	4	286			350	572	922	9	78	31	0.44	302	35	17	48	187	18%	95	10%	6.86	12.0	108	$15
LIMA Plan B	2nd Half	282	49	12	41	3	280			323	479	802	6	72	35	0.23	264	42	18	40	143	15%	104	9%	5.39	0.5	49	$12
Rand Var -1	11 Proj	552	86	29	85	8	279			331	516	847	7	77	32	0.34	280	40	18	43	155	16%	109	12%	5.89	11.9	81	$24

Traded off ct% for PX, and boy did that ever work out. 2H PX slide likely caused by July wrist injury. A healthy Hart will give you power, help you breathe easier and add longevity to your roster.

Hawpe,Brad

Hawpe,Brad		AB	R	HR	RBI	SB	Avg	vL	vR	OB	Slg	OPS	bb%	ct%	h%	Eye	xBA	G	L	F	PX	hr/f	Spd	SBO	RC/G	RAR	BPV	R$
Pos 9	06 COL	499	67	22	84	5	293	232	302	384	515	899	13	75	35	0.60	274	42	22	36	142	16%	102	6%	6.98	31.0	74	$19
Age/B 31 Left	07 COL	516	80	29	116	0	291	214	315	387	539	926	14	73	35	0.59	279	36	21	43	165	18%	79	1%	7.37	35.9	78	$23
Ht/Wt 75 205	08 COL	488	69	25	85	2	283	282	283	379	498	877	13	73	34	0.57	259	38	23	39	144	18%	93	2%	6.73	21.2	62	$19
Health B	09 COL	501	82	23	86	1	285	243	303	383	519	902	14	71	36	0.54	276	43	20	36	175	18%	91	3%	7.23	33.3	81	$21
PT/Exp B	10 2TM	298	31	9	44	2	245	258	239	338	419	758	12	71	31	0.49	259	41	20	40	137	11%	59	4%	5.17	0.3	40	$7
Consist C	1st Half	191	17	5	31	1	272			356	455	812	12	75	34	0.53	279	41	21	38	140	9%	64	4%	5.86	3.9	58	$6
LIMA Plan C+	2nd Half	107	14	4	13	1	196			306	355	662	14	64	26	0.45	223	39	17	43	131	13%	67	3%	3.83	-4.4	12	$2
Rand Var +3	11 Proj	425	57	19	67	2	278			373	484	856	13	71	35	0.52	262	40	20	39	153	16%	69	3%	6.56	17.0	53	$15

Stat line cratered and earned him a release, but skills largely intact and still attractive. Career home/road splits (60 HR each home/road) say he's not just a Coors-made product. Bet on a nice rebound.

Hayes,Brett

Hayes,Brett		AB	R	HR	RBI	SB	Avg	vL	vR	OB	Slg	OPS	bb%	ct%	h%	Eye	xBA	G	L	F	PX	hr/f	Spd	SBO	RC/G	RAR	BPV	R$
Pos 2	06	0	0	0	0	0	0																					
Age/B 27 Right	07 aa	273	18	2	25	2	206			249	281	529	5	83	24	0.33					57		83	4%	2.03	-19.8	14	($0)
Ht/Wt 73 202	08 a/a	297	32	9	28	2	220			249	346	595	4	80	25	0.19					79		100	13%	2.54	-15.4	21	$4
Health A	09 aaa	321	23	3	31	2	208			248	275	523	5	80	25	0.26					50		68	3%	1.81	-24.5	-8	$1
PT/Exp F	10 FLA	* 136	11	3	10	0	192	143	222	236	336	572	5	75	23	0.23	214	32	10	58	109	5%	95	0%	2.38	-9.1	30	$0
Consist B	1st Half	84	5	1	4	0	180			225	258	482	5	83	21	0.23	225	39	17	44	58	3%	92	0%	1.45	-8.2	17	($1)
LIMA Plan F	2nd Half	52	6	2	6	0	212			255	462	716	5	63	29	0.16	243	28	6	66	216	9%	100	0%	4.71	0.4	69	$1
Rand Var +2	11 Proj	133	11	4	12	0	203			243	372	616	5	76	24	0.22	212	30	8	62	119	7%	95	4%	2.89	-6.2	39	$1

2-6-.208 in 77 AB at FLA. Defense-first catcher benefitted from several injuries to get a big-league call, and... reminded us that "defense first" is just another way of saying "can't hit worth a lick".

RAY MURPHY

Headley,Chase			AB	R	HR	RBI	SB	Avg	vL	vR	OB	Slg	OPS	bb%	ct%	h%	Eye	xBA	G	L	F	PX	hr/f	Spd	SBO	RC/G	RAR	BPV	R$
Pos	5	06	0	0	0	0	0	0																					
Age/B	26 Both	07 aa	451	73	17	69	1	288	167	250	382	495	877	13	74	36	0.58	269	36	21	43	145	12%	99	1%	6.75	19.1	71	$16
Ht/Wt	74 211	08 SD	* 590	74	19	71	4	263	276	265	326	432	758	9	72	34	0.33	251	38	25	37	125	12%	78	3%	4.98	-6.7	31	$16
Health	A	09 SD	543	62	12	64	10	262	244	270	337	392	729	10	76	33	0.47	233	45	17	38	96	8%	81	8%	4.64	-7.9	26	$14
PT/Exp	A	10 SD	610	77	11	58	17	264	217	285	326	375	701	8	77	33	0.40	244	46	18	36	82	6%	94	13%	4.17	-12.9	21	$18
Consist	A	1st Half	322	44	5	27	11	267			320	357	677	7	79	32	0.37	242	46	19	35	67	6%	86	15%	3.79	-10.4	13	$10
LIMA Plan	C+	2nd Half	288	33	6	31	6	260			332	396	728	10	75	33	0.43	246	47	17	37	99	8%	100	10%	4.62	-2.4	31	$8
Rand Var	0	11 Proj	588	74	15	66	13	260			331	401	731	10	75	32	0.43	245	45	18	37	102	9%	87	10%	4.62	-8.2	30	$17

Minor-league power still MIA, some of that is PETCO's fault (8 of 11 HR on road), but GB%, PX trend, BA vLH all say it's not just park factors. Surprising SB spike props up value, but Spd cautions against a repeat there.

Heisey,Chris			AB	R	HR	RBI	SB	Avg	vL	vR	OB	Slg	OPS	bb%	ct%	h%	Eye	xBA	G	L	F	PX	hr/f	Spd	SBO	RC/G	RAR	BPV	R$
Pos	789	06	0	0	0	0	0	0																					
Age/B	26 Right	07	0	0	0	0	0	0																					
Ht/Wt	72 200	08	0	0	0	0	0	0																					
Health	A	09 a/a	516	75	21	63	17	283			335	474	809	7	87	29	0.59					113		85	15%	5.38	1.4	79	$21
PT/Exp	F	10 CIN	* 280	38	12	30	3	239	169	321	294	418	712	7	72	29	0.28	247	35	19	45	127	13%	93	8%	4.18	-7.5	36	$8
Consist	C	1st Half	138	17	8	15	2	232			305	450	755	10	74	26	0.40	263	34	20	45	143	17%	91	9%	4.79	-1.2	58	$4
LIMA Plan	F	2nd Half	142	21	4	15	1	246			282	387	669	5	71	32	0.17	232	36	19	45	111	9%	94	7%	3.57	-6.4	13	$4
Rand Var	0	11 Proj	195	27	8	22	4	256			308	445	753	7	78	29	0.34	258	35	19	45	123	12%	94	11%	4.66	-3.5	54	$6

8-21-.254 in 201 AB at CIN. PRO: plus PX and FB bias point to a legit power source, especially in friendly home park. CON: poor ct% kills Avg Speculate in the end-game.

Helms,Wes			AB	R	HR	RBI	SB	Avg	vL	vR	OB	Slg	OPS	bb%	ct%	h%	Eye	xBA	G	L	F	PX	hr/f	Spd	SBO	RC/G	RAR	BPV	R$
Pos	5	06 FLA	240	30	10	47	0	329	336	323	383	575	958	8	77	39	0.38	293	38	26	36	155	15%	85	6%	7.48	12.9	75	$11
Age/B	34 Right	07 PHI	280	21	5	39	0	246	282	221	294	368	662	6	78	30	0.31	245	39	20	41	90	6%	71	0%	3.59	-16.7	20	$4
Ht/Wt	76 227	08 FLA	251	28	5	31	0	243	258	234	291	347	638	6	74	31	0.26	221	42	20	38	77	7%	64	0%	3.20	-16.1	-8	$4
Health	A	09 FLA	214	18	3	33	1	271	273	270	313	364	677	6	75	35	0.24	216	43	18	39	74	5%	73	4%	3.73	-8.7	-6	$5
PT/Exp	D	10 FLA	254	25	4	39	0	220	324	180	293	346	639	9	70	30	0.34	229	45	18	37	97	6%	102	3%	3.46	-11.3	9	$4
Consist	A	1st Half	105	11	3	13	0	257			304	419	723	6	69	35	0.21	240	39	23	38	117	11%	102	8%	4.49	-1.3	13	$2
LIMA Plan	F	2nd Half	149	14	1	26	0	195			286	295	581	11	71	27	0.44	220	48	15	37	83	3%	96	0%	2.75	-10.1	4	$1
Rand Var	+1	11 Proj	194	19	3	29	0	242			301	366	667	8	73	32	0.31	231	43	19	38	93	6%	88	3%	3.74	-7.9	9	$3

Managed to halt multi-year PX and SX declines, even nudged BPV back into positive territory. Sadly, at this point such "achievement" in support of a .220 BA in 250 AB does not make him any more roster-worthy

Helton,Todd			AB	R	HR	RBI	SB	Avg	vL	vR	OB	Slg	OPS	bb%	ct%	h%	Eye	xBA	G	L	F	PX	hr/f	Spd	SBO	RC/G	RAR	BPV	R$
Pos	3	06 COL	546	94	15	81	3	302	326	295	402	476	878	14	88	32	1.42	285	35	24	41	102	8%	85	3%	6.74	11.2	91	$20
Age/B	37 Left	07 COL	557	86	17	91	0	320	285	334	437	494	931	17	87	35	1.57	300	40	24	36	109	10%	72	0%	7.53	20.8	92	$22
Ht/Wt	74 210	08 COL	299	39	7	29	0	264	246	270	389	388	777	17	83	30	1.22	257	38	23	38	82	7%	60	0%	5.61	-1.0	53	$6
Health	C	09 COL	544	79	15	86	0	325	311	332	420	489	909	14	87	36	1.22	290	40	24	36	104	9%	82	0%	7.07	8.1	85	$23
PT/Exp	B	10 COL	398	48	8	37	0	256	272	248	363	367	730	14	77	31	0.74	239	34	23	43	80	6%	73	0%	4.84	-17.3	27	$8
Consist	D	1st Half	248	29	2	16	0	246			337	310	647	12	79	31	0.64	232	37	24	39	52	3%	74	0%	3.70	-19.3	4	$3
LIMA Plan	D+	2nd Half	150	19	6	21	0	273			404	460	864	18	75	33	0.89	253	28	21	51	129	10%	75	0%	6.76	1.8	66	$5
Rand Var	0	11 Proj	355	47	9	44	0	270			383	411	795	15	81	31	0.97	261	36	23	41	95	8%	72	0%	5.73	-5.4	56	$10

Finally went on DL with back problems in July, 1H line shows he was diminished long before then. 2009 now looks like a mirage, His 40+ HR seasons a decade ago are science fiction. Steve Carlton Path to Retirement?

Hermida,Jeremy			AB	R	HR	RBI	SB	Avg	vL	vR	OB	Slg	OPS	bb%	ct%	h%	Eye	xBA	G	L	F	PX	hr/f	Spd	SBO	RC/G	RAR	BPV	R$
Pos	79	06 FLA	307	37	5	28	4	251	219	261	324	368	692	10	77	31	0.47	241	45	20	35	84	6%	79	6%	4.15	-10.0	21	$5
Age/B	27 Left	07 FLA	429	54	18	63	3	296	292	297	366	501	867	10	76	36	0.45	280	44	21	35	141	16%	70	6%	6.37	12.2	58	$15
Ht/Wt	75 222	08 FLA	502	74	17	61	6	249	240	252	315	406	721	9	73	31	0.35	237	46	18	36	109	13%	99	5%	4.41	-14.9	26	$14
Health	C	09 FLA	429	48	13	47	5	259	189	282	344	392	736	12	76	31	0.55	233	41	20	39	86	10%	101	5%	4.71	-10.7	30	$11
PT/Exp	C	10 2AL	* 312	26	7	42	1	219	176	223	267	336	603	6	77	26	0.28	242	39	20	41	88	7%	51	2%	2.76	-20.2	6	$4
Consist	C	1st Half	138	13	5	27	1	217			270	384	654	7	74	26	0.28	259	36	22	42	124	12%	57	4%	3.41	-6.2	28	$3
LIMA Plan	F	2nd Half	174	13	2	15	0	220			265	297	562	6	79	27	0.28	228	44	18	39	61	4%	64	0%	2.29	-13.8	-4	$1
Rand Var	+5	11 Proj	275	29	7	34	2	240			303	374	677	8	76	29	0.37	244	42	20	39	94	9%	77	4%	3.81	-9.2	20	$5

6-29-.216 in 222 AB at BOS and OAK. Showed a glimpse of long-lost power in 1H, then broke five ribs in OF collision. Combo of below-average PX and ct%, plus no Spd means no appreciable value.

Hernandez,Anderson			AB	R	HR	RBI	SB	Avg	vL	vR	OB	Slg	OPS	bb%	ct%	h%	Eye	xBA	G	L	F	PX	hr/f	Spd	SBO	RC/G	RAR	BPV	R$
Pos	6	06 NYM	* 480	47	1	25	15	229	211	128	261	277	539	4	84	27	0.27	213	49	15	36	30	1%	102	18%	2.09	-33.3	-1	$4
Age/B	28 Both	07 aa	554	67	4	33	12	259			291	334	625	4	87	29	0.35					51		119	16%	3.20	-19.2	35	$9
Ht/Wt	69 186	08 WAS	* 560	56	4	45	8	193	366	300	247	269	515	7	84	22	0.44	258	39	30	31	51	3%	110	14%	1.97	-48.0	24	$1
Health	A	09 2NL	366	39	3	37	7	251	273	245	313	339	652	8	83	30	0.52	257	55	20	25	59	4%	93	12%	3.67	-10.8	24	$7
PT/Exp	C	10 2TM	* 309	26	1	16	6	197	143	239	244	234	477	6	86	23	0.43	241	52	18	30	29	1%	82	14%	1.53	-26.3	4	$0
Consist	D	1st Half	224	15	1	14	3	194			229	231	460	4	88	22	0.36	260	49	23	28	28	2%	83	15%	1.34	-20.7	8	($0)
LIMA Plan	F	2nd Half	85	11	0	2	3	205			280	240	520	9	81	25	0.54	218	55	14	32	33	0%	91	12%	2.05	-5.7	-3	$1
Rand Var	+5	11 Proj	125	13	1	8	3	232			287	293	580	7	83	27	0.47	245	54	18	28	42	2%	98	13%	2.75	-6.1	13	$1

0-3-.220-3 SB in 109 AB at CLE and HOU. Stop us if you've heard this before: lacks power, hits lots of grounders but lacks Spd to beat them out. Makes decent contact, but rarely does it lead to anything interesting.

Hernandez,Ramon			AB	R	HR	RBI	SB	Avg	vL	vR	OB	Slg	OPS	bb%	ct%	h%	Eye	xBA	G	L	F	PX	hr/f	Spd	SBO	RC/G	RAR	BPV	R$
Pos	2	06 BAL	501	66	23	91	1	275	291	270	333	479	812	8	84	29	0.54	280	44	19	38	119	14%	49	1%	5.42	14.4	64	$16
Age/B	34 Right	07 BAL	364	40	9	62	1	258	250	261	325	382	707	9	84	29	0.61	253	49	16	35	81	8%	37	4%	4.30	0.1	31	$8
Ht/Wt	72 225	08 BAL	467	49	15	65	0	257	283	245	305	407	711	6	87	27	0.51	276	47	20	33	91	11%	50	0%	4.22	0.4	48	$10
Health	D	09 CIN	287	25	5	37	1	258	288	246	334	362	697	10	88	28	0.97	261	49	19	32	66	6%	55	1%	4.39	1.1	44	$6
PT/Exp	C	10 CIN	313	30	7	48	0	297	303	295	357	428	785	8	84	33	0.59	284	52	18	29	89	9%	65	0%	5.22	6.4	47	$10
Consist	B	1st Half	181	16	3	23	0	287			361	403	765	10	82	34	0.64	281	50	23	27	82	8%	77	0%	5.12	3.2	39	$5
LIMA Plan	D	2nd Half	132	14	4	25	0	311			350	462	812	6	88	33	0.50	287	53	15	31	97	11%	54	0%	5.34	3.1	59	$5
Rand Var	-3	11 Proj	321	32	8	49	0	265			325	398	723	8	86	29	0.64	275	50	19	31	85	9%	57	1%	4.50	1.1	48	$8

Typical mid-30s CA value spike? Not so fast, mostly just a case of inflated h%. Soaring GB% trend kills hope of a return to double-digit HRs and h% regression will chop BA again. Low risk, low reward.

Herrera,Jonathan			AB	R	HR	RBI	SB	Avg	vL	vR	OB	Slg	OPS	bb%	ct%	h%	Eye	xBA	G	L	F	PX	hr/f	Spd	SBO	RC/G	RAR	BPV	R$
Pos	4	06	0	0	0	0	0	0																					
Age/B	26 Both	07 aa	509	54	3	33	15	248			291	322	613	6	90	27	0.58					49		127	22%	3.25	-17.0	49	$7
Ht/Wt	69 150	08 aaa	226	28	2	22	11	273			315	325	640	6	91	29	0.67					33		107	20%	3.53	-8.5	36	$7
Health	A	09 aaa	381	50	2	26	12	242			311	302	614	9	89	27	0.95					35		145	16%	3.46	-14.7	49	$7
PT/Exp	F	10 COL	* 444	52	2	31	4	248	292	280	311	298	610	8	88	28	0.74	248	50	18	32	33	2%	133	7%	3.29	-20.4	35	$6
Consist	A	1st Half	256	24	1	16	2	256			298	289	587	6	88	29	0.48	240	51	18	32	25	1%	105	9%	2.83	-15.2	15	$3
LIMA Plan	F	2nd Half	188	28	1	16	2	236			328	310	639	12	88	27	1.11	258	49	19	32	44	2%	149	5%	3.88	-5.3	57	$3
Rand Var	0	11 Proj	160	20	1	12	4	250			314	302	615	8	89	28	0.82	247	49	19	32	33	2%	126	12%	3.40	-6.4	38	$3

1-21-.284 in 222 AB at COL. Low SBO kept SB total down (2 in COL), but Spd says he's a rabbit. Good ct%, GBs, strong defense and versatility should allow him to start showing it. Worth a speculative buck.

Heyward,Jason			AB	R	HR	RBI	SB	Avg	vL	vR	OB	Slg	OPS	bb%	ct%	h%	Eye	xBA	G	L	F	PX	hr/f	Spd	SBO	RC/G	RAR	BPV	R$
Pos	9	06	0	0	0	0	0	0																					
Age/B	21 Left	07	0	0	0	0	0	0																					
Ht/Wt	76 220	08	0	0	0	0	0	0																					
Health	A	09 a/a	173	32	6	29	5	339			431	554	985	14	89	35	1.51					121		106	10%	7.92	12.7	116	$10
PT/Exp	F	10 ATL	520	83	18	72	11	277	249	291	385	456	840	15	75	34	0.71	282	55	18	27	125	17%	103	9%	6.32	14.8	64	$21
Consist	D	1st Half	255	41	11	45	5	251			357	455	812	14	73	30	0.62	273	52	14	34	141	18%	107	11%	5.88	4.2	69	$10
LIMA Plan	B+	2nd Half	265	42	7	27	6	302			411	457	867	16	77	37	0.82	292	58	21	21	111	16%	101	8%	6.73	10.2	62	$11
Rand Var	0	11 Proj	538	91	19	79	15	296			398	491	889	15	81	34	0.90	301	55	18	26	125	17%	106	11%	6.86	25.8	88	$25

Sterling debut for 20-year old, especially in light of nagging thumb/knee injuries. What's next? High GB% sets a short-term cap on power, but small 2H ct% growth keeps '09 MLE Avg in his future sights.

Hill,Aaron

			AB	R	HR	RBI	SB	Avg	vL	vR	OB	Slg	OPS	bb%	ct%	h%	Eye	xBA	G	L	F	PX	hr/f	Spd	SBO	RC/G	RAR	BPV	R$
Pos	4	06 TOR	546	70	6	50	5	291	298	288	342	386	728	7	88	32	0.64	257	46	19	35	61	4%	106	4%	4.57	6.9	48	$12
Age/B	29 Right	07 TOR	608	87	17	78	4	291	317	283	336	459	795	6	83	33	0.40	285	40	21	39	114	9%	78	5%	5.21	20.7	62	$18
Ht/Wt	71 205	08 TOR	205	19	2	20	4	263	286	258	317	361	678	7	85	30	0.52	233	35	17	47	73	2%	83	11%	3.95	-5.6	40	$4
Health	C	09 TOR	682	103	36	108	6	286	298	282	327	499	826	6	86	29	0.43	288	39	20	41	119	15%	74	5%	5.40	9.1	74	$27
PT/Exp	B	10 TOR	528	70	26	68	2	205	125	228	262	394	656	7	84	20	0.48	251	35	11	54	115	11%	62	4%	3.49	-16.1	63	$11
Consist	D	1st Half	265	30	11	30	1	189			266	355	621	10	85	18	0.68	240	38	8	53	102	9%	69	2%	3.25	-10.2	61	$3
LIMA Plan	C	2nd Half	263	40	15	38	1	221			257	433	691	5	83	21	0.30	263	32	13	55	128	12%	63	7%	3.72	-6.0	66	$8
Rand Var	+5	11 Proj	589	79	27	77	5	258			307	447	754	7	85	27	0.45	265	37	15	48	114	11%	69	6%	4.63	0.5	65	$18

Turned 2009 LDs into 2010 FBs, which killed h% and Avg, but propped up HR total. Expect a better LD/FB balance in 2011, which should raise BA toward xBA at the expense of a few HR.

Hill,Koyie

			AB	R	HR	RBI	SB	Avg	vL	vR	OB	Slg	OPS	bb%	ct%	h%	Eye	xBA	G	L	F	PX	hr/f	Spd	SBO	RC/G	RAR	BPV	R$
Pos	2	06 aaa	70	4	1	5	0	129			187	200	387	7	74	16	0.28					50		89	0%	-0.11	-10.7	-21	($1)
Age/B	32 Both	07 CHC	* 242	22	4	28	1	211			257	326	583	6	82	24	0.35					82		65	3%	2.67	-13.2	28	$1
Ht/Wt	72 190	08 aaa	364	37	12	42	2	210			263	366	629	7	81	23	0.37					101		75	5%	3.15	-11.9	42	$4
Health	A	09 CHC	253	26	2	24	0	237	256	233	311	324	635	10	69	34	0.35	222	50	22	28	73	4%	98	0%	3.42	-6.4	-14	$3
PT/Exp	F	10 CHC	215	18	1	17	1	214	297	197	256	298	553	5	72	29	0.20	242	51	22	26	77	2%	77	2%	2.13	-15.6	-16	$1
Consist	B	1st Half	86	6	0	7	0	221			264	291	554	5	74	30	0.23	266	54	29	17	59	0%	102	0%	2.20	-6.0	-12	$0
LIMA Plan	F	2nd Half	129	12	1	10	1	209			250	302	552	5	70	29	0.18	228	49	18	33	90	3%	65	4%	2.09	-9.6	-17	$1
Rand Var	+1	11 Proj	140	13	1	13	0	221			273	310	583	7	73	30	0.27	242	51	22	27	74	3%	86	2%	2.60	-7.6	-6	$1

His hitting can be described by the following: impuissant, lackadaisical, sluggish, anemic, languid, rickety, forceless, destitute, suffering, substandard, ineffective, undesirable, amiss. These also describe his upside.

Hinske,Eric

			AB	R	HR	RBI	SB	Avg	vL	vR	OB	Slg	OPS	bb%	ct%	h%	Eye	xBA	G	L	F	PX	hr/f	Spd	SBO	RC/G	RAR	BPV	R$
Pos	37	06 2AL	277	43	13	34	2	271	167	293	353	487	840	11	71	34	0.44	248	40	16	43	148	15%	74	5%	6.18	6.1	51	$8
Age/B	33 Left	07 BOS	186	25	6	21	3	204	200	205	308	398	706	13	71	25	0.52	246	45	11	44	142	10%	100	7%	4.49	-4.5	55	$3
Ht/Wt	73 235	08 TAM	381	59	20	60	10	247	143	262	329	465	794	11	77	27	0.52	272	39	20	40	142	17%	54	13%	5.37	1.1	61	$14
Health	A	09 2TM	190	31	8	25	1	242	244	242	336	432	768	12	73	29	0.52	246	37	18	45	135	13%	81	2%	5.20	-5.1	50	$5
PT/Exp	D	10 ATL	281	38	11	51	0	256	381	246	334	456	790	11	73	31	0.44	266	33	20	47	150	11%	38	0%	5.45	-7.2	48	$9
Consist	A	1st Half	164	24	5	32	0	280			348	482	830	9	74	35	0.40	280	34	22	44	158	9%	56	0%	6.00	-1.5	62	$6
LIMA Plan	D	2nd Half	117	14	6	19	0	222			316	419	735	12	72	26	0.48	245	32	18	50	138	14%	31	0%	4.64	-6.0	33	$3
Rand Var	0	11 Proj	266	38	12	42	0	244			331	447	778	11	73	29	0.48	257	36	19	45	145	13%	58	1%	5.29	-7.6	51	$8

PX, bb%, and xBA show us that he is still a useful hitter. Success vLH is an outlier; Spd won't be coming back. Otherwise stable skills set ensures double-digit HR for your end-game investment.

Holliday,Matt

			AB	R	HR	RBI	SB	Avg	vL	vR	OB	Slg	OPS	bb%	ct%	h%	Eye	xBA	G	L	F	PX	hr/f	Spd	SBO	RC/G	RAR	BPV	R$
Pos	7	06 COL	602	119	34	114	10	326	327	325	374	586	961	7	82	35	0.43	307	45	21	34	153	20%	92	9%	7.19	31.2	94	$33
Age/B	31 Right	07 COL	636	120	36	137	11	340	301	351	399	607	1006	9	80	38	0.50	314	44	20	36	166	20%	107	8%	7.92	42.5	105	$38
Ht/Wt	76 235	08 COL	539	107	25	88	28	321	293	329	403	538	941	12	81	36	0.71	294	46	22	33	139	18%	105	16%	7.30	27.1	92	$34
Health	A	09 2TM	581	94	24	109	14	313	289	322	389	515	904	11	83	35	0.71	279	44	16	39	125	13%	90	11%	6.76	23.5	81	$29
PT/Exp	A	10 STL	596	95	28	103	9	312	344	301	383	532	915	10	84	33	0.74	302	42	17	41	142	14%	64	8%	6.82	28.5	93	$31
Consist	A	1st Half	302	45	11	39	6	298			369	493	862	10	83	33	0.68	298	43	19	38	132	12%	69	8%	6.23	9.7	82	$13
LIMA Plan	D+	2nd Half	294	50	17	64	3	327			398	571	970	11	85	34	0.81	307	41	15	44	152	15%	65	8%	7.41	18.5	106	$18
Rand Var	0	11 Proj	595	101	28	109	10	318			390	540	930	11	83	34	0.70	297	43	18	39	141	15%	79	8%	7.02	28.3	92	$32

Declining Spd reduces him to a four-category player, but he's still really good in those four. 2H shows strong, stable, still-peak skill set, RBI column shows benefits of batting behind Pujols.

Howard,Ryan

			AB	R	HR	RBI	SB	Avg	vL	vR	OB	Slg	OPS	bb%	ct%	h%	Eye	xBA	G	L	F	PX	hr/f	Spd	SBO	RC/G	RAR	BPV	R$
Pos	3	06 PHI	581	104	58	149	0	313	279	331	421	659	1080	16	69	36	0.60	295	42	22	36	220	40%	59	0%	9.69	57.7	102	$36
Age/B	31 Left	07 PHI	529	94	47	136	1	268	225	297	392	584	976	17	62	34	0.54	278	31	24	44	233	32%	34	1%	8.78	40.2	82	$27
Ht/Wt	76 259	08 PHI	610	105	48	146	1	251	224	268	339	543	881	12	67	29	0.41	276	41	22	36	200	32%	59	1%	6.80	19.2	73	$29
Health	B	09 PHI	616	105	45	141	8	279	207	320	357	571	929	11	70	33	0.40	285	36	23	41	204	26%	60	6%	7.38	15.1	84	$34
PT/Exp	A	10 PHI	550	87	31	108	1	276	264	283	346	505	852	10	71	33	0.38	277	40	23	37	157	21%	92	1%	6.20	-2.0	60	$25
Consist	B	1st Half	317	52	15	59	0	293			347	502	849	8	74	35	0.32	278	40	24	37	141	17%	97	1%	6.00	-2.9	56	$15
LIMA Plan	C+	2nd Half	233	35	16	49	1	253			346	511	857	12	68	30	0.44	276	40	23	38	180	27%	79	2%	6.48	1.0	66	$10
Rand Var	0	11 Proj	581	95	36	107	1	272			354	518	873	11	69	33	0.42	272	39	23	38	172	23%	75	1%	6.65	6.5	62	$25

Long thought of as having a skill profile that won't age well; is it true? Lots of low HR totals in the 'Year of the Pitcher' but PX normalized many of them. Not here. Don't assume a return to 40 HR level. In fact: DN: -30 HR

Hudson,Orlando

			AB	R	HR	RBI	SB	Avg	vL	vR	OB	Slg	OPS	bb%	ct%	h%	Eye	xBA	G	L	F	PX	hr/f	Spd	SBO	RC/G	RAR	BPV	R$
Pos	4	06 ARI	579	87	15	67	9	287	338	270	355	454	809	10	87	31	0.78	285	49	19	32	95	9%	121	9%	5.62	16.8	80	$18
Age/B	33 Both	07 ARI	517	69	10	63	10	294	281	298	378	441	819	12	83	34	0.80	286	52	20	28	90	8%	137	7%	5.90	17.3	72	$16
Ht/Wt	72 191	08 ARI	407	54	8	41	4	305	269	321	367	450	817	9	85	34	0.65	287	48	23	29	96	8%	100	4%	5.68	10.1	66	$13
Health	C	09 LA	551	74	9	62	8	283	293	280	356	417	773	10	82	33	0.63	276	56	19	26	92	8%	104	5%	5.24	11.0	55	$16
PT/Exp	B	10 MIN	497	80	6	37	10	268	261	272	335	372	707	9	82	31	0.57	270	49	21	31	73	5%	123	9%	4.37	-1.4	45	$13
Consist	B	1st Half	263	46	3	19	6	274			339	373	712	9	85	31	0.65	277	47	22	31	69	4%	112	9%	4.45	-0.1	48	$8
LIMA Plan	C	2nd Half	234	34	3	18	4	261			329	372	701	9	80	32	0.51	262	50	19	31	78	5%	122	9%	4.29	-1.2	39	$6
Rand Var	+1	11 Proj	493	72	8	46	8	278			347	402	748	10	83	32	0.61	276	51	20	29	83	6%	111	7%	4.90	4.1	52	$13

Sometimes the BPV says it all, heading in the wrong direction as his skills gently fade with age. Spd remains a plus, but he has never turned that into SBs. Subpar PX seals his status as a replacement-level hitter.

Huff,Aubrey

			AB	R	HR	RBI	SB	Avg	vL	vR	OB	Slg	OPS	bb%	ct%	h%	Eye	xBA	G	L	F	PX	hr/f	Spd	SBO	RC/G	RAR	BPV	R$
Pos	379	06 2TM	454	57	21	66	0	267	233	278	339	469	808	10	86	27	0.78	286	45	19	36	114	15%	79	0%	5.51	-2.6	80	$13
Age/B	34 Left	07 BAL	550	68	15	72	1	280	305	272	338	442	780	8	84	31	0.55	275	46	16	38	103	9%	92	1%	5.14	-1.8	65	$14
Ht/Wt	76 234	08 BAL	598	96	32	108	4	304	270	321	361	552	913	8	85	31	0.60	305	41	17	42	152	15%	71	3%	6.62	22.0	102	$27
Health	A	09 2AL	536	59	15	85	0	241	232	245	307	384	691	9	84	26	0.59	255	48	15	36	89	9%	51	4%	4.09	-26.2	41	$10
PT/Exp	A	10 SF	569	100	26	86	7	290	296	287	380	506	887	13	84	31	0.91	303	45	18	37	134	15%	89	4%	6.63	4.8	98	$26
Consist	F	1st Half	285	46	15	47	3	288			370	526	896	11	86	29	0.95	314	43	18	39	141	16%	94	4%	6.63	2.4	111	$13
LIMA Plan	C+	2nd Half	284	54	11	39	4	292			391	486	877	14	82	33	0.88	293	47	18	35	127	14%	83	4%	6.63	2.4	83	$13
Rand Var	0	11 Proj	544	83	22	84	4	278			355	473	828	11	84	30	0.75	286	45	17	37	122	13%	75	4%	5.83	-6.7	79	$21

Huge bounceback year featured xBA and PX reverting to 2008 levels. 2009 now looks like an outlier, but age starting to work against him. Doubling his 2H sets a nice 2011 baseline.

Hundley,Nick

			AB	R	HR	RBI	SB	Avg	vL	vR	OB	Slg	OPS	bb%	ct%	h%	Eye	xBA	G	L	F	PX	hr/f	Spd	SBO	RC/G	RAR	BPV	R$
Pos	2	06	0	0	0	0	0	0																					
Age/B	27 Right	07 aa	373	47	17	61	0	211			281	402	683	9	80	22	0.48					118		90	2%	3.87	-5.7	61	$7
Ht/Wt	73 205	08 SD	* 422	47	13	55	0	211			253	348	602	5	77	24	0.25					90		92	0%	2.68	-19.9	22	$5
Health	B	09 SD	256	23	8	30	5	238	159	267	313	406	720	10	70	31	0.37	230	31	22	47	126	9%	93	9%	4.53	2.1	32	$6
PT/Exp	D	10 SD	273	33	8	43	0	249	274	242	312	418	730	8	76	30	0.38	264	41	19	40	123	10%	87	8%	4.55	0.5	47	$7
Consist	B	1st Half	166	24	5	25	0	253			330	416	745	10	76	31	0.48	256	41	19	40	112	10%	117	11%	4.83	1.7	51	$5
LIMA Plan	D	2nd Half	107	9	3	18	0	243			283	421	704	5	76	29	0.23	276	41	20	40	141	9%	57	0%	4.09	-1.3	46	$2
Rand Var	0	11 Proj	323	34	10	47	2	251			309	415	724	8	75	31	0.34	251	38	20	42	118	10%	85	5%	4.44	0.6	38	$8

Defense keeps him employed, while PX and hr/f say double-digt HR power is legit. xBA confirms BA growth and offers more room for growth. No real platoon split; can play every day. If he does... UP: 20 HR.

Hunter,Torii

			AB	R	HR	RBI	SB	Avg	vL	vR	OB	Slg	OPS	bb%	ct%	h%	Eye	xBA	G	L	F	PX	hr/f	Spd	SBO	RC/G	RAR	BPV	R$
Pos	89	06 MIN	557	86	31	98	12	278	319	262	332	490	822	7	81	30	0.42	271	45	18	37	121	18%	89	12%	5.46	12.7	63	$23
Age/B	35 Right	07 MIN	600	94	28	107	18	287	314	276	331	505	836	6	83	31	0.40	296	49	14	37	140	15%	68	20%	5.62	18.8	79	$27
Ht/Wt	74 225	08 LAA	551	85	21	78	19	278	304	268	338	466	804	8	80	31	0.46	280	46	19	35	125	14%	90	17%	5.41	0.9	67	$22
Health	B	09 LAA	451	74	22	90	18	299	336	287	365	508	873	9	80	34	0.51	275	47	16	36	127	17%	71	17%	6.27	20.5	62	$24
PT/Exp	A	10 LAA	573	76	23	90	9	281	257	292	350	464	814	10	82	31	0.58	291	48	18	34	123	15%	59	13%	5.57	4.1	64	$23
Consist	B	1st Half	289	49	14	60	7	294			374	522	897	11	81	32	0.67	316	45	21	34	156	17%	50	18%	6.70	11.4	89	$15
LIMA Plan	C	2nd Half	284	27	9	30	2	268			325	405	730	8	82	30	0.47	266	52	16	33	90	12%	72	8%	4.43	-7.5	39	$7
Rand Var	+1	11 Proj	574	82	21	93	9	284			348	456	804	9	81	32	0.51	276	48	17	35	113	13%	70	11%	5.42	5.4	55	$22

Was he tired or hiding injury? 2H drop in LD%, PX were harsh, xBA validates BA dip. Age and Spd/SBO drops say that days of high-teens SB are over. BA vLH should recover, so BA/power form skill base now.

JOSH PALEY

Iannetta,Chris

Iannetta,Chris			AB	R	HR	RBI	SB	Avg	vL	vR	OB	Slg	OPS	bb%	ct%	h%	Eye	xBA	G	L	F	PX	hr/f	Spd	SBO	RC/G	RAR	BPV	R$
Pos	2	06 COL	* 384	59	14	47	1	307	231	266	386	495	880	11	85	33	0.88	306	52	23	25	108	17%	96	2%	6.51	22.7	82	$14
Age/B	27 Right	07 COL	* 251	29	5	33	0	228	204	223	322	354	676	12	75	29	0.55	228	41	18	41	85	6%	103	0%	4.03	-3.0	25	$3
Ht/Wt	72 225	08 COL	333	50	18	65	0	264	275	261	370	505	875	14	72	31	0.61	270	38	21	41	166	18%	73	0%	6.75	24.4	75	$13
Health	A	09 COL	289	41	16	52	0	228	296	202	328	460	789	13	74	25	0.57	250	32	16	52	154	14%	76	1%	5.42	10.2	70	$9
PT/Exp	D	10 COL	* 251	30	13	40	1	216	222	184	313	420	732	12	78	23	0.65	262	41	13	45	132	14%	60	2%	4.62	1.1	63	$6
Consist	C	1st Half	139	17	8	21	1	238			331	463	794	12	77	26	0.61	276	39	16	45	152	16%	49	3%	5.41	3.9	71	$4
LIMA Plan	D+	2nd Half	112	13	5	19	0	187			289	366	655	12	79	19	0.70	247	42	12	46	107	12%	88	0%	3.67	-2.9	57	$2
Rand Var	+5	11 Proj	305	40	15	51	0	252			348	467	815	13	77	28	0.63	260	38	16	46	139	14%	72	1%	5.75	12.3	67	$10

9-27-.197 in 188 AB at COL. Hard to get job back when neither defense nor bat is good as competition. FB% and hr/f will keep HR up. With some h% recovery, he'll get his job back and.... UP: 25 HR.

Ibanez,Raul

Ibanez,Raul			AB	R	HR	RBI	SB	Avg	vL	vR	OB	Slg	OPS	bb%	ct%	h%	Eye	xBA	G	L	F	PX	hr/f	Spd	SBO	RC/G	RAR	BPV	R$
Pos	7	06 SEA	626	103	33	123	2	289	243	308	356	516	872	9	82	31	0.57	282	42	19	39	132	17%	95	3%	6.22	18.4	81	$25
Age/B	38 Left	07 SEA	573	80	21	105	0	291	256	305	351	480	831	8	83	32	0.55	282	42	18	40	118	11%	99	0%	5.74	11.2	75	$20
Ht/Wt	74 225	08 SEA	635	85	23	110	2	293	305	288	358	479	836	9	83	32	0.58	276	41	19	40	120	11%	73	3%	5.85	17.8	69	$23
Health	B	09 PHI	500	93	34	93	4	272	285	267	345	552	897	10	76	29	0.47	289	43	15	42	182	21%	80	3%	6.64	15.5	96	$24
PT/Exp	A	10 PHI	561	75	16	83	4	275	268	277	353	444	797	11	81	32	0.63	278	45	18	37	116	9%	83	4%	5.52	7.2	64	$19
Consist	B	1st Half	266	31	6	37	2	241			331	391	722	12	82	27	0.75	266	44	17	39	101	7%	80	4%	4.69	-3.1	59	$6
LIMA Plan	B	2nd Half	295	44	10	46	2	305			373	492	865	10	80	36	0.53	288	45	19	36	129	12%	86	4%	6.29	9.9	69	$13
Rand Var	0	11 Proj	521	78	20	87	3	280			353	476	829	10	80	32	0.56	277	43	18	39	129	12%	82	4%	5.84	8.4	70	$20

2009 PX and hr/f weren't going to stick, rest of skill set held up pretty well, especially in light of slow recovery from off-season surgery that likely impacted 1H. Skill set stable, but at this age injuries are a potent enemy.

Infante,Omar

Infante,Omar			AB	R	HR	RBI	SB	Avg	vL	vR	OB	Slg	OPS	bb%	ct%	h%	Eye	xBA	G	L	F	PX	hr/f	Spd	SBO	RC/G	RAR	BPV	R$
Pos	457	06 DET	224	35	4	25	3	277	286	273	319	415	735	6	80	33	0.31	236	38	19	43	86	5%	153	9%	4.50	2.5	48	$6
Age/B	29 Right	07 DET	* 204	27	2	21	5	284	281	265	326	362	688	6	85	33	0.42	227	33	21	47	53	2%	119	10%	3.96	-0.2	31	$5
Ht/Wt	72 180	08 ATL	317	45	3	40	0	293	325	273	339	416	756	6	86	33	0.50	276	33	30	37	85	3%	122	1%	4.87	0.9	64	$9
Health	D	09 ATL	203	24	2	27	2	305	323	298	365	389	754	9	86	35	0.68	247	32	27	41	56	3%	113	3%	4.92	2.2	43	$7
PT/Exp	C	10 ATL	471	65	8	47	7	321	276	342	360	416	776	6	87	36	0.47	262	47	19	34	59	6%	141	8%	4.94	1.6	50	$18
Consist	A	1st Half	165	23	1	22	3	309			345	376	721	5	82	37	0.31	247	43	22	35	54	2%	107	10%	4.26	-2.5	17	$6
LIMA Plan	C+	2nd Half	306	42	7	25	4	327			368	438	806	6	89	35	0.61	270	49	17	34	61	8%	162	8%	5.31	4.0	69	$12
Rand Var	-5	11 Proj	504	68	7	57	6	308			353	404	757	7	86	35	0.50	256	40	23	37	63	4%	125	6%	4.80	1.1	47	$17

Is this BA sustainable? Combo of Spd/GB/ct% say yes. Weak Eye, xBA, and low LD say no. Tiebreaking vote goes to PX and Rand Var, which say: NO.

Inge,Brandon

Inge,Brandon			AB	R	HR	RBI	SB	Avg	vL	vR	OB	Slg	OPS	bb%	ct%	h%	Eye	xBA	G	L	F	PX	hr/f	Spd	SBO	RC/G	RAR	BPV	R$
Pos	5	06 DET	542	83	27	83	7	253	243	256	308	463	771	7	76	28	0.34	250	40	14	46	133	14%	95	9%	4.90	-1.8	57	$17
Age/B	33 Right	07 DET	508	64	14	71	9	236	333	209	301	376	677	8	70	31	0.31	234	37	22	41	105	10%	87	9%	3.85	-15.6	11	$11
Ht/Wt	71 188	08 DET	347	41	11	51	4	205	232	196	292	369	661	11	73	25	0.46	228	37	16	46	113	9%	108	8%	3.72	-12.7	39	$5
Health	B	09 DET	562	71	27	84	2	230	243	225	297	404	701	9	70	28	0.32	221	41	15	44	112	16%	106	5%	4.07	-10.5	20	$13
PT/Exp	B	10 DET	514	47	13	70	4	247	254	245	319	397	716	10	74	31	0.40	240	38	17	45	111	8%	96	5%	4.43	-6.1	34	$11
Consist	A	1st Half	278	21	6	33	0	259			333	399	733	10	76	32	0.46	253	37	21	42	110	7%	71	3%	4.69	-1.1	33	$5
LIMA Plan	C	2nd Half	236	26	7	37	4	233			301	394	695	9	72	29	0.35	225	39	12	49	112	8%	127	9%	4.13	-5.0	36	$6
Rand Var	-1	11 Proj	494	55	15	72	3	235			306	388	694	9	72	29	0.37	228	39	16	46	108	9%	104	5%	4.10	-10.7	28	$10

Stable PX and FB% leave HR to track with hr/f, which makes 2009 the outlier. Narrow multi-year range of xBA sets BA expectation. Combine the PX and BA outlooks, and the result is an unappealing proposition.

Inglett,Joe

Inglett,Joe			AB	R	HR	RBI	SB	Avg	vL	vR	OB	Slg	OPS	bb%	ct%	h%	Eye	xBA	G	L	F	PX	hr/f	Spd	SBO	RC/G	RAR	BPV	R$
Pos	9	06 CLE	* 422	59	5	39	13	288	217	292	341	390	731	7	83	34	0.47	264	47	24	29	67	4%	112	14%	4.56	-13.2	37	$12
Age/B	32 Left	07 aaa	392	35	3	45	5	209			270	293	562	8	85	24	0.54					52		141	20%	2.63	-32.4	40	$2
Ht/Wt	70 185	08 TOR	* 398	54	4	44	10	301	276	298	355	416	771	8	87	34	0.65	287	49	25	26	68	4%	145	11%	5.12	-2.7	63	$13
Health	A	09 TOR	* 250	30	2	22	6	273		291	323	369	692	7	85	32	0.49	245	35	23	42	65	2%	118	13%	4.11	-8.9	43	$5
PT/Exp	F	10 MIL	142	15	1	8	1	254	105	276	325	401	726	10	76	33	0.44	240	34	20	45	102	2%	148	3%	4.74	-2.5	52	$2
Consist	B	1st Half	57	8	0	1	1	333			397	544	941	10	84	40	0.67	292	36	17	47	141	0%	146	6%	7.47	3.2	114	$2
LIMA Plan	D	2nd Half	85	7	1	7	0	200			277	306	582	10	71	27	0.36	208	33	23	44	72	4%	129	0%	2.66	-7.1	-0	$0
Rand Var	-2	11 Proj	128	15	1	10	2	266			327	394	721	8	81	32	0.48	249	38	22	41	85	3%	127	8%	4.55	-2.2	48	$3

Spd is is only plus skill, but lack of SBO keeps it a latent one. Can't hit lefties, strikes out too much and lacks power. Other than that, how was the play Mrs. Lincoln?

Ishikawa,Travis

Ishikawa,Travis			AB	R	HR	RBI	SB	Avg	vL	vR	OB	Slg	OPS	bb%	ct%	h%	Eye	xBA	G	L	F	PX	hr/f	Spd	SBO	RC/G	RAR	BPV	R$
Pos	3	06 aa	298	33	10	42	0	225			306	391	697	10	70	29	0.38					112		113	0%	4.22	-13.5	25	$4
Age/B	27 Left	07 aa	173	13	2	13	1	181			240	242	481	7	76	23	0.32					39		121	2%	1.24	-24.8	-11	($1)
Ht/Wt	75 225	08 SF	* 500	70	21	94	9	263		280	329	471	800	9	80	29	0.49	294	56	18	26	138	20%	81	13%	5.40	-4.8	74	$19
Health	A	09 SF	326	49	9	39	2	261	278	259	323	387	710	8	73	33	0.34	223	45	18	37	86	10%	124	4%	4.24	-21.6	15	$9
PT/Exp	D	10 SF	158	18	3	22	0	266	111	286	322	392	714	8	82	31	0.45	283	42	25	32	94	7%	59	0%	4.33	-9.1	37	$4
Consist	B	1st Half	45	8	2	9	0	311			367	556	923	8	80	35	0.44	341	39	31	31	177	18%	65	0%	6.91	0.7	100	$2
LIMA Plan	F	2nd Half	113	10	1	13	0	248			303	327	631	7	82	29	0.45	259	44	23	33	62	3%	68	0%	3.33	-10.0	16	$2
Rand Var	+1	11 Proj	179	20	5	23	1	240			303	390	693	8	78	28	0.40	262	45	21	34	102	11%	89	4%	4.02	-12.0	37	$4

Slick-fielding 1Bman's woes vLHPs means his upside is limited to bad side of platoon. .769 OPS vs RHPs is no great shakes, either. He's not young at 27; time may have run out to prove he can be a starter.

Iwamura,Akinori

Iwamura,Akinori			AB	R	HR	RBI	SB	Avg	vL	vR	OB	Slg	OPS	bb%	ct%	h%	Eye	xBA	G	L	F	PX	hr/f	Spd	SBO	RC/G	RAR	BPV	R$
Pos	4	06 JPN	546	82	19	75	7	290			357	456	813	9	78	34	0.47	0				104		86	4%	5.59	18.7	41	$19
Age/B	32 Left	07 TAM	491	82	7	34	12	285	323	268	361	411	772	11	77	36	0.51	251	46	20	34	84	6%	183	13%	5.27	17.9	52	$14
Ht/Wt	69 200	08 TAM	627	91	6	48	8	274	260	280	347	380	727	10	79	34	0.53	245	47	20	33	73	4%	154	7%	4.66	-4.1	43	$13
Health	D	09 TAM	231	28	1	22	9	290	386	248	357	390	746	9	81	35	0.55	250	44	21	36	74	2%	97	14%	4.92	-0.1	33	$7
PT/Exp	C	10 2TM	* 359	38	4	23	3	185	100	192	294	267	561	13	81	22	0.80	236	56	12	32	60	4%	89	6%	2.73	-22.2	26	$0
Consist	C	1st Half	165	18	2	9	3	182			293	267	560	14	81	21	0.84	241	56	13	31	59	5%	89	9%	2.73	-10.2	28	$0
LIMA Plan	F	2nd Half	194	20	2	14	0	187			295	267	562	13	80	22	0.78	213	57	5	38	60	3%	91	3%	2.73	-12.0	25	($0)
Rand Var	+5	11 Proj	186	22	2	15	3	237			325	333	658	12	80	29	0.66	244	49	17	34	68	3%	105	8%	3.88	-4.4	32	$3

2-13-.173 in 196 AB at PIT/OAK. Journeyman 2B always lacked pop, then knee injury claimed his speed. With those gone, there's little reason left to give him regular ABs.

Izturis,Cesar

Izturis,Cesar			AB	R	HR	RBI	SB	Avg	vL	vR	OB	Slg	OPS	bb%	ct%	h%	Eye	xBA	G	L	F	PX	hr/f	Spd	SBO	RC/G	RAR	BPV	R$
Pos	6	06 2NL	252	21	1	20	1	240	206	253	296	308	603	7	94	25	1.23	262	52	16	31	43	1%	107	8%	3.41	-7.3	57	$1
Age/B	31 Both	07 2NL	314	31	0	16	3	258	186	285	300	315	616	6	94	27	1.00	284	49	23	28	39	0%	136	7%	3.46	-9.1	61	$3
Ht/Wt	69 155	08 STL	414	50	1	24	24	263	304	237	312	309	621	7	94	28	1.12	259	47	22	31	27	1%	147	24%	3.53	-13.4	56	$11
Health	C	09 BAL	387	34	2	30	12	256	290	238	289	328	617	4	90	28	0.47	266	49	20	30	43	2%	135	16%	3.23	-13.9	46	$6
PT/Exp	C	10 BAL	473	42	1	28	11	230	205	240	269	268	538	5	89	26	0.47	242	46	19	35	28	1%	103	13%	2.32	-23.8	21	$5
Consist	B	1st Half	229	21	0	12	5	245			279	279	559	5	89	28	0.42	239	46	18	36	30	0%	86	17%	2.52	-10.0	15	$3
LIMA Plan	D	2nd Half	244	21	1	16	6	217			260	258	518	5	89	24	0.52	245	46	20	34	27	1%	120	10%	2.12	-13.8	26	$2
Rand Var	+1	11 Proj	393	37	1	25	11	249			289	300	589	5	90	27	0.58	255	47	20	33	33	1%	118	15%	2.97	-14.2	36	$6

Drop in Spd, SBO cripples core fanalytic value. Lacks any other plus skill and Avg is following xBA south. Will land a job as long as his defense is perceived as exceptional enough to offset horrid RAR.

Izturis,Maicer

Izturis,Maicer			AB	R	HR	RBI	SB	Avg	vL	vR	OB	Slg	OPS	bb%	ct%	h%	Eye	xBA	G	L	F	PX	hr/f	Spd	SBO	RC/G	RAR	BPV	R$
Pos	45	06 LAA	352	64	5	44	14	293	247	307	362	412	773	10	90	31	1.09	278	49	19	32	73	5%	112	18%	5.31	11.9	73	$13
Age/B	30 Both	07 LAA	336	47	6	51	7	289	280	291	352	405	757	9	88	31	0.85	267	45	17	38	73	5%	106	8%	5.00	9.4	63	$11
Ht/Wt	68 170	08 LAA	290	44	3	37	11	269	258	272	329	362	691	8	91	29	0.96	283	49	23	29	59	4%	112	15%	4.30	-4.9	62	$9
Health	F	09 LAA	387	74	8	65	13	300	380	288	358	434	792	8	89	32	0.85	272	43	19	38	78	6%	110	15%	5.37	4.7	72	$17
PT/Exp	D	10 LAA	212	27	3	27	7	250	280	241	318	363	681	9	87	27	0.78	268	42	18	40	79	4%	94	18%	4.14	-2.0	60	$6
Consist	C	1st Half	103	15	2	15	4	233			319	369	688	11	87	25	1.00	274	42	16	42	96	5%	79	19%	4.35	-0.3	75	$3
LIMA Plan	C	2nd Half	109	12	1	12	3	266			316	358	674	7	87	30	0.57	262	43	20	37	62	3%	110	17%	3.93	-1.7	46	$3
Rand Var	+3	11 Proj	320	48	5	44	11	272			334	385	719	9	88	30	0.81	271	44	19	37	73	5%	102	16%	4.57	-0.3	62	$11

Shoulder, hamstring, forearm... What he's missing is a trip to the DL with a sticky eyelid a la José Cardenal, Spring 1976. Injuries obfuscate data for 2010 so expect across-the-board recovery toward 2009 levels.

JOSH PALEY

Jackson,Austin			AB	R	HR	RBI	SB	Avg	vL	vR	OB	Slg	OPS	bb%	ct%	h%	Eye	xBA	G	L	F	PX	hr/f	Spd	SBO	RC/G	RAR	BPV	R$
Pos	8	06	0	0	0	0	0	0																					
Age/B	24 Right	07	0	0	0	0	0	0																					
Ht/Wt	73 185	08 aa	520	73	9	67	18	276			342	400	742	9	79	33	0.49					88		107	16%	4.77	-4.1	41	$17
Health	A	09 aaa	504	64	4	62	23	286			336	377	713	7	77	37	0.32					65		131	18%	4.31	-5.4	14	$17
PT/Exp	C	10 DET	618	103	4	41	27	293	226	317	343	400	743	7	72	40	0.28	255	48	24	27	86	3%	185	18%	4.81	-9.0	30	$22
Consist	A	1st Half	292	47	1	19	13	305			347	401	748	6	72	42	0.23	258	48	27	25	86	2%	150	19%	4.87	-3.7	14	$11
LIMA Plan	C+	2nd Half	326	56	3	22	14	282			339	399	738	8	73	38	0.32	253	49	22	29	86	4%	200	18%	4.76	-5.3	40	$11
Rand Var	-5	11 Proj	616	92	4	59	26	287			340	384	725	7	75	38	0.32	252	48	24	28	73	3%	160	18%	4.52	-9.9	24	$21

Huge Spd limits downside, as SBs will set a value floor. But how many SB? Inflated h% and poor Eye scream for BA correction and resulting dip in SB opportunities.
DN: .250 BA, under 20 SB

Jackson,Conor			AB	R	HR	RBI	SB	Avg	vL	vR	OB	Slg	OPS	bb%	ct%	h%	Eye	xBA	G	L	F	PX	hr/f	Spd	SBO	RC/G	RAR	BPV	R$
Pos	7	06 ARI	485	75	15	79	1	291	296	288	362	441	803	10	85	32	0.74	260	38	21	41	89	9%	78	1%	5.50	3.4	56	$16
Age/B	28 Right	07 ARI	415	56	15	60	2	284	320	270	365	467	833	11	88	29	1.06	288	38	20	43	110	10%	91	3%	5.96	7.1	91	$13
Ht/Wt	74 215	08 ARI	540	87	12	75	10	300	315	295	369	446	815	10	89	32	0.97	274	40	22	38	87	7%	114	7%	5.73	4.7	81	$21
Health	F	09 ARI	99	8	1	14	5	182	172	186	264	253	516	10	84	21	0.69	221	41	18	41	51	3%	55	21%	2.13	-10.9	14	$1
PT/Exp	D	10 2TM	208	25	2	16	6	236	243	234	335	327	662	13	87	26	1.15	281	37	27	36	69	3%	76	11%	4.16	-5.1	54	$4
Consist	F	1st Half	196	24	1	15	5	245			333	327	660	12	88	27	1.08	283	37	28	35	64	2%	79	10%	4.12	-5.0	52	$4
LIMA Plan	C+	2nd Half	12	1	1	1	1	83			353	333	686	29	75	0	1.67	264	44	11	44	146	25%	87	20%	4.16	-0.4	104	$0
Rand Var	+4	11 Proj	405	56	7	51	5	277			356	397	753	11	88	30	0.99	274	39	22	39	81	5%	81	5%	5.09	-0.2	63	$12

Reasons to expect a rebound:
- Eye validates plate approach.
- xBA and LD% say BA will rise.
- Rand Var shows he was unlucky on field as well as off.
Mounting DL time a concern, but if healthy... UP: see 2008.

Janish,Paul			AB	R	HR	RBI	SB	Avg	vL	vR	OB	Slg	OPS	bb%	ct%	h%	Eye	xBA	G	L	F	PX	hr/f	Spd	SBO	RC/G	RAR	BPV	R$
Pos	6	06	0	0	0	0	0	0																					
Age/B	28 Right	07 a/a	523	55	4	33	10	210			283	289	572	9	86	24	0.71					56		117	10%	2.86	-24.7	43	$2
Ht/Wt	74 193	08 CIN *	398	39	7	38	2	211			261	319	580	6	80	25	0.34					75		91	2%	2.58	-25.3	22	$3
Health	A	09 CIN	256	36	1	16	2	211	230	203	284	305	588	9	84	25	0.65	240	37	19	44	77	1%	97	3%	3.06	-12.7	49	$1
PT/Exp	D	10 CIN	200	23	5	25	1	260	308	237	333	385	718	10	85	28	0.73	243	30	19	51	83	6%	87	7%	4.51	0.5	54	$5
Consist	B	1st Half	50	7	2	9	0	280			379	460	839	14	88	29	1.33	253	12	21	67	111	7%	84	6%	6.16	2.5	95	$2
LIMA Plan	D	2nd Half	150	16	3	16	1	253			317	360	677	9	84	28	0.58	240	35	18	46	73	5%	95	7%	3.93	-2.2	42	$3
Rand Var	-3	11 Proj	258	31	4	27	2	236			309	345	654	10	84	27	0.67	234	30	19	51	76	4%	86	6%	3.76	-5.8	46	$4

Decent on-base skills plus steady glove may open door to more AB. Unfortunately, lack of power and speed says that more AB not necessarily a good thing for fantasy owners.
DN: .225 in 400 AB.

Jaso,John			AB	R	HR	RBI	SB	Avg	vL	vR	OB	Slg	OPS	bb%	ct%	h%	Eye	xBA	G	L	F	PX	hr/f	Spd	SBO	RC/G	RAR	BPV	R$
Pos	2	06	0	0	0	0	0	0																					
Age/B	27 Left	07 aa	380	50	10	58	2	273			356	413	769	12	88	29	1.09					85		102	3%	5.27	10.0	76	$10
Ht/Wt	74 205	08 a/a	392	51	9	52	2	230			327	355	682	13	89	24	1.36					73		96	2%	4.38	2.1	72	$7
Health	A	09 aaa	331	34	4	24	1	225			304	306	610	10	86	25	0.81					51		110	1%	3.34	-9.3	40	$2
PT/Exp	D	10 TAM	339	57	5	44	4	263	191	274	372	378	749	15	88	28	1.51	272	46	17	37	75	5%	104	3%	5.33	11.4	77	$10
Consist	D	1st Half	157	24	3	26	3	274			394	389	782	16	89	29	1.82	272	41	20	39	71	5%	96	5%	5.79	7.3	78	$6
LIMA Plan	C	2nd Half	182	33	2	18	1	253			352	368	721	13	88	28	1.27	273	51	14	35	78	4%	111	2%	4.92	4.0	76	$4
Rand Var	0	11 Proj	401	57	6	46	3	257			353	361	714	13	88	28	1.22	259	47	16	37	66	4%	102	2%	4.77	6.5	63	$9

High bb% made him viable leadoff hitter; Eye says more to come. Rest of skill set is pretty hollow, but when your resume starts with "CA offers plus on-base skills", nothing else matters... you've got the job.

Jay,Jon			AB	R	HR	RBI	SB	Avg	vL	vR	OB	Slg	OPS	bb%	ct%	h%	Eye	xBA	G	L	F	PX	hr/f	Spd	SBO	RC/G	RAR	BPV	R$
Pos	89	06	0	0	0	0	0	0																					
Age/B	26 Left	07 aa	102	14	2	9	3	206			270	314	584	8	85	22	0.60					62		131	17%	2.86	-5.4	48	$1
Ht/Wt	72 200	08 a/a	430	51	9	44	8	269			323	385	708	7	90	28	0.78					68		110	15%	4.36	-8.7	63	$11
Health	A	09 aaa	505	55	7	40	15	236			273	317	591	5	90	25	0.51					50		90	21%	2.91	-27.5	39	$9
PT/Exp	D	10 STL *	452	69	7	50	11	284	308	297	336	409	745	7	85	32	0.53	285	49	19	32	90	6%	99	13%	4.74	-1.9	59	$16
Consist	D	1st Half	209	31	5	27	9	270			310	412	722	6	89	29	0.51	0				96		78	19%	4.38	-3.0	67	$8
LIMA Plan	D	2nd Half	243	38	2	23	2	296			357	407	764	9	82	35	0.53	272	49	19	32	84	3%	112	8%	5.07	1.2	49	$8
Rand Var	-2	11 Proj	359	48	5	35	9	262			312	366	678	7	87	29	0.56	270	49	19	32	69	5%	105	15%	3.96	-8.8	50	$9

4-27-.300 in 287 AB at STL. Value is in Avg, Spd, defense. 2010 Minor League Baseball Analyst: "Power output in the PCL doesn't suggest enough upside to start." Still the case as PX and Eye confirm.

Jennings,Desmond			AB	R	HR	RBI	SB	Avg	vL	vR	OB	Slg	OPS	bb%	ct%	h%	Eye	xBA	G	L	F	PX	hr/f	Spd	SBO	RC/G	RAR	BPV	R$
Pos	9	06	0	0	0	0	0	0																					
Age/B	24 Right	07	0	0	0	0	0	0																					
Ht/Wt	74 180	08	0	0	0	0	0	0																					
Health	A	09 a/a	497	83	10	56	47	296			373	447	819	11	88	32	1.00					89		146	34%	5.87	10.7	90	$27
PT/Exp	F	10 TAM *	420	70	2	30	31	238	273	100	303	329	633	9	86	27	0.65	243	47	12	41	65	1%	148	35%	3.57	-17.7	58	$13
Consist	F	1st Half	196	34	1	17	15	265			323	380	703	8	85	31	0.58	0				83		142	31%	4.36	-3.3	68	$8
LIMA Plan	B+	2nd Half	224	35	1	14	17	215			287	285	572	9	86	25	0.72	230	47	12	41	49	1%	145	38%	2.87	-14.8	47	$6
Rand Var	0	11 Proj	520	86	2	46	43	260			330	352	683	10	87	30	0.78	240	47	12	41	63	1%	147	34%	4.23	-14.5	61	$20

2-2-.190 in 21 AB at TAM. Carl Crawford heir-apparent and clone: great defense, Spd with big Avg, SB, R upside. Moderate power will come, but 2011 too soon for that. If his arrival is now, UP: 50+ SB.

Jeter,Derek			AB	R	HR	RBI	SB	Avg	vL	vR	OB	Slg	OPS	bb%	ct%	h%	Eye	xBA	G	L	F	PX	hr/f	Spd	SBO	RC/G	RAR	BPV	R$
Pos	6	06 NYY	623	118	14	97	34	343	390	328	409	483	892	10	84	39	0.68	298	59	22	18	90	15%	110	17%	6.61	35.7	61	$34
Age/B	36 Right	07 NYY	639	102	12	73	15	322	317	324	377	452	829	8	84	37	0.56	296	56	20	24	87	9%	129	11%	5.75	25.2	64	$25
Ht/Wt	75 195	08 NYY	596	88	11	69	11	300	302	300	356	408	764	8	86	34	0.61	278	58	18	24	68	9%	127	8%	4.96	10.4	53	$20
Health	A	09 NYY	634	107	18	66	30	334	395	311	402	465	868	10	86	37	0.80	290	57	20	23	76	15%	100	15%	6.26	30.3	57	$31
PT/Exp	A	10 NYY	663	111	10	67	18	270	321	246	333	370	703	9	84	31	0.59	289	66	16	18	68	10%	111	12%	4.28	6.1	43	$21
Consist	D	1st Half	338	55	8	39	9	281			341	405	747	8	85	31	0.61	307	67	18	16	82	18%	100	12%	4.76	7.7	54	$13
LIMA Plan	C	2nd Half	325	56	2	28	9	258			325	332	657	9	83	31	0.58	270	65	14	21	54	4%	118	11%	3.77	-1.8	31	$9
Rand Var	+3	11 Proj	605	100	11	64	19	284			349	397	746	9	85	32	0.64	289	61	18	21	73	11%	114	13%	4.81	10.8	51	$21

His skills are amazingly stable for a 37-year-old, but lofty GB% and BA vRH erosion suggest no more 18 HR years. H% drop says .300+ Avg years possibly gone as well. Fortunately, his intangibles are still off the charts.

Johnson,Chris			AB	R	HR	RBI	SB	Avg	vL	vR	OB	Slg	OPS	bb%	ct%	h%	Eye	xBA	G	L	F	PX	hr/f	Spd	SBO	RC/G	RAR	BPV	R$
Pos	5	06	0	0	0	0	0	0																					
Age/B	26 Right	07	0	0	0	0	0	0																					
Ht/Wt	75 220	08 aa	431	38	10	48	4	249			280	370	650	4	84	28	0.27					78		80	4%	3.35	-22.5	33	$8
Health	A	09 HOU *	406	37	11	32	2	232		133	262	371	633	4	81	26	0.21	258	81	0	19	89	17%	103	4%	3.09	-25.2	34	$5
PT/Exp	D	10 HOU *	490	59	17	76	3	299	286	316	328	475	803	4	78	36	0.20	283	41	24	35	123	13%	74	3%	5.20	4.0	42	$19
Consist	A	1st Half	211	26	6	32	1	300			328	467	795	4	84	34	0.26	311	44	27	29	111	11%	98	2%	5.07	1.0	65	$8
LIMA Plan	C	2nd Half	279	33	11	44	2	297			329	480	809	4	72	38	0.17	269	41	23	36	135	15%	65	3%	5.40	3.8	28	$11
Rand Var	-4	11 Proj	532	56	21	64	3	269			299	453	752	4	79	30	0.21	281	43	23	34	119	15%	78	3%	4.49	-9.2	47	$16

11-52-.308 in 341 AB at HOU. Free-swinger hit for power and Avg, but only one of those skills looks real. Hr/f and PX validate power, while xBA, low ct% and GB% (without speed) indict the BA. Pay for the power only.

Johnson,Dan			AB	R	HR	RBI	SB	Avg	vL	vR	OB	Slg	OPS	bb%	ct%	h%	Eye	xBA	G	L	F	PX	hr/f	Spd	SBO	RC/G	RAR	BPV	R$
Pos	0	06 OAK *	458	56	14	70	0	246	217	238	338	398	736	12	85	26	0.95	261	49	15	36	91	10%	67	1%	4.86	-21.4	61	$9
Age/B	31 Left	07 OAK	416	53	18	62	0	236	234	237	348	418	767	15	81	25	0.94	274	43	18	39	113	14%	69	0%	5.24	-12.5	69	$9
Ht/Wt	74 216	08 aaa	394	61	18	59	0	236			337	419	756	13	81	25	0.82					112		68	1%	5.01	0.9	64	$10
Health	A	09 JPN	325	42	14	56	0	201			292	362	654	11	77	21	0.57					93		99	0%	3.55	-16.6	39	$6
PT/Exp	D	10 TAM *	451	61	27	88	1	220	235	191	333	441	774	14	79	22	0.80	271	38	15	47	139	16%	54	1%	5.19	-16.0	73	$15
Consist	D	1st Half	250	31	12	45	0	224			305	411	716	10	78	24	0.52	0				124		66	0%	4.32	-15.5	53	$7
LIMA Plan	D	2nd Half	201	29	16	43	1	215			364	478	843	19	80	19	1.18	290	38	15	47	157	20%	59	1%	6.20	-1.0	104	$8
Rand Var	+2	11 Proj	207	28	10	38	0	232			339	418	756	14	79	24	0.79	255	41	16	44	113	15%	63	1%	4.99	-5.3	57	$6

7-23-.198 in 111 AB at TAM. Classic Quad-A career includes trip to Japan. PX begs for more PT, but he hasn't hit over .240 from either side of the plate since 2005. The power is worth a $1 bid, hope ABs find him.

JOSH PALEY

Johnson,Kelly			AB	R	HR	RBI	SB	Avg	vL	vR	OB	Slg	OPS	bb%	ct%	h%	Eye	xBA	G	L	F	PX	hr/f	Spd	SBO	RC/G	RAR	BPV	R$
Pos	4	06 aaa	*39	3	1	7	1	308			400	487	887	13	85	34	1.00					121		77	8%	6.81	2.6	87	$2
Age/B	29 Left	07 ATL	521	91	16	68	9	276	272	278	372	457	828	13	78	33	0.68	262	43	19	39	113	10%	121	8%	6.07	20.6	65	$18
Ht/Wt	73 205	08 ATL	547	86	12	69	11	287	333	270	349	446	795	9	79	34	0.46	267	39	25	36	110	8%	89	11%	5.42	10.1	51	$19
Health	B	09 ATL	*355	54	10	41	8	230	325	188	298	396	694	9	83	25	0.56	258	39	18	43	107	8%	85	12%	4.17	-3.9	61	$9
PT/Exp	B	10 ARI	585	93	26	71	13	284	310	272	369	496	865	12	75	34	0.53	281	41	21	38	148	16%	96	11%	6.47	27.5	72	$25
Consist	D	1st Half	288	49	13	36	7	264			365	479	844	14	75	31	0.63	284	43	18	39	160	15%	78	12%	6.28	12.3	79	$12
LIMA Plan	C+	2nd Half	297	44	13	35	6	303			373	512	885	10	75	37	0.44	277	40	23	37	138	16%	116	11%	6.63	15.0	66	$14
Rand Var	-2	11 Proj	563	89	22	68	12	279			355	478	833	11	78	33	0.53	275	40	21	39	132	13%	94	11%	5.94	19.7	68	$22

Move to ARI alone can't explain gains of this magnitude; hr/f correction should be on horizon. But 2009 h% now an outlier, and 2H Spd suggests SB gains are real. Even with reduced power, this is a worthy skill profile.

Johnson,Nick			AB	R	HR	RBI	SB	Avg	vL	vR	OB	Slg	OPS	bb%	ct%	h%	Eye	xBA	G	L	F	PX	hr/f	Spd	SBO	RC/G	RAR	BPV	R$
Pos	0	06 WAS	500	100	23	77	10	290	303	285	418	520	938	18	80	32	1.11	296	42	22	36	148	16%	59	7%	7.65	17.1	95	$22
Age/B	32 Left	07 WAS	0	0	0	0	0	0																					
Ht/Wt	75 236	08 WAS	109	15	5	20	0	220	167	247	401	431	833	23	77	24	1.32	278	38	24	39	144	15%	58	0%	6.49	5.2	89	$3
Health	F	09 2NL	457	71	8	62	2	291	316	281	417	405	822	18	82	34	1.18	254	43	22	34	78	6%	81	3%	6.26	14.0	51	$15
PT/Exp	D	10 NYY	72	12	2	8	0	167	190	157	375	306	681	25	68	21	1.04	236	37	22	41	116	10%	61	3%	4.39	-4.7	35	$0
Consist	C	1st Half	72	12	2	8	0	167			375	306	681	25	68	21	1.04	236	37	22	41	116	10%	61	3%	4.39	-4.7	35	$0
LIMA Plan	D	2nd Half	0	0	0	0	0	0																					
Rand Var	+5	11 Proj	191	30	7	28	0	267			428	439	866	22	76	32	1.16	269	39	23	38	124	12%	57	2%	7.00	6.4	65	$6

Still owns elite bb% and Eye, so to quote Joaquin Andujar, "One word: youneverknow." But other skills eroding in between injuries, and age now an enemy. Any meaningful comeback is now is a longshot play at best.

Johnson,Reed			AB	R	HR	RBI	SB	Avg	vL	vR	OB	Slg	OPS	bb%	ct%	h%	Eye	xBA	G	L	F	PX	hr/f	Spd	SBO	RC/G	RAR	BPV	R$
Pos	79	06 TOR	461	86	12	49	8	319	323	316	364	479	844	7	82	37	0.41	276	47	20	33	105	10%	110	8%	5.83	8.0	62	$18
Age/B	34 Right	07 TOR	275	31	2	14	4	236	325	202	278	320	598	5	80	29	0.29	241	47	19	34	62	3%	102	9%	2.80	-18.6	12	$2
Ht/Wt	70 180	08 CHC	333	52	6	50	5	303	333	280	341	420	761	5	80	37	0.28	254	41	24	35	86	7%	89	12%	4.76	-6.2	26	$13
Health	F	09 CHC	165	23	4	22	2	255	324	206	309	412	721	7	84	28	0.48	273	50	17	33	101	9%	97	8%	4.43	-5.5	61	$4
PT/Exp	F	10 LA	202	24	2	15	2	262	301	222	280	366	647	2	75	34	0.10	237	43	19	37	81	4%	126	9%	3.22	-11.0	11	$4
Consist	B	1st Half	124	15	0	7	1	282			299	379	678	2	77	37	0.10	246	44	21	35	79	0%	133	11%	3.69	-4.9	16	$2
LIMA Plan	F	2nd Half	78	9	2	8	1	231			250	346	596	2	73	29	0.10	223	43	16	41	86	9%	90	7%	2.44	-6.2	-5	$1
Rand Var	-2	11 Proj	167	22	3	18	2	251			285	371	656	4	78	31	0.21	247	45	19	36	86	6%	102	9%	3.41	-9.2	23	$4

Platoon splits tell his story: .790 OPS vLH, .520 OPS vRH. Glimmers of Spd remain, but low SBO% and Age are stifling. No other plus skills remain, so expect him to be confined to bad-side platoon work.

Johnson,Rob			AB	R	HR	RBI	SB	Avg	vL	vR	OB	Slg	OPS	bb%	ct%	h%	Eye	xBA	G	L	F	PX	hr/f	Spd	SBO	RC/G	RAR	BPV	R$
Pos	2	06 aaa	337	24	3	28	12	205			230	267	497	3	80	25	0.17					39		92	30%	1.41	-32.1	-11	$2
Age/B	28 Right	07 aaa	422	47	5	32	6	230			286	317	603	7	86	26	0.55					62		83	13%	3.09	-16.5	34	$4
Ht/Wt	73 215	08 aaa	417	42	7	38	6	257			306	365	671	7	86	28	0.52					74		62	12%	3.83	-4.6	39	$8
Health	A	09 SEA	258	21	2	27	1	213	171	233	285	326	611	9	77	27	0.43	249	46	21	33	86	3%	64	3%	3.15	-9.0	15	$1
PT/Exp	F	10 SEA	*242	30	3	18	1	199	184	193	292	298	590	12	76	25	0.56	232	52	12	36	83	4%	64	3%	2.91	-9.6	16	$1
Consist	A	1st Half	140	23	2	13	1	200			304	307	611	13	73	26	0.55	233	52	14	34	92	6%	69	5%	3.19	-4.3	14	$2
LIMA Plan	F	2nd Half	102	7	1	5	0	197			275	284	560	10	81	23	0.57	219	52	7	41	71	3%	69	0%	2.58	-5.1	23	($0)
Rand Var	+3	11 Proj	159	16	2	13	1	214			287	306	594	9	79	26	0.50	238	49	16	35	74	4%	62	6%	2.93	-6.4	16	$1

2-13-.191 in 178 AB for SEA. What looks like a horrible year at the plate was really average on 2010 Mariners. Off-season hip surgery likely hampered him, but even when healthy, bb% is his only redeeming skill.

Jones,Adam			AB	R	HR	RBI	SB	Avg	vL	vR	OB	Slg	OPS	bb%	ct%	h%	Eye	xBA	G	L	F	PX	hr/f	Spd	SBO	RC/G	RAR	BPV	R$
Pos	8	06 SEA	*454	71	16	66	15	273	235	211	317	441	758	6	81	31	0.34	284	44	27	29	102	15%	91	19%	4.69	0.3	48	$16
Age/B	25 Right	07 SEA	*485	81	23	77	9	280	310	194	330	499	829	7	75	33	0.30	283	34	27	39	145	16%	110	15%	5.69	16.3	66	$19
Ht/Wt	74 210	08 BAL	480	61	9	57	10	269	256	275	304	398	701	5	77	33	0.22	243	47	18	35	86	7%	129	11%	4.01	-18.6	28	$13
Health	B	09 BAL	473	83	19	70	10	277	246	295	328	457	785	7	80	31	0.39	279	55	17	28	107	18%	97	11%	5.06	5.7	52	$18
PT/Exp	B	10 BAL	581	76	19	69	7	284	259	293	311	442	754	4	80	33	0.19	267	46	17	37	103	11%	108	10%	4.51	-13.6	43	$20
Consist	B	1st Half	322	37	13	37	3	270			290	441	731	3	78	31	0.13	266	47	17	36	107	14%	116	10%	4.13	-11.2	41	$10
LIMA Plan	C+	2nd Half	259	39	6	32	4	301			337	444	781	5	81	35	0.29	268	45	17	37	99	8%	97	10%	4.97	-2.6	45	$10
Rand Var	-1	11 Proj	573	84	21	75	10	272			310	444	755	5	79	31	0.27	272	49	17	34	109	13%	107	12%	4.61	-8.0	50	$20

Has been returning value via high AB of good avg, but xBA, Eye and ct% all say Avg is unsustainable. hr/f figures to recover, so if he can hold 2010 FB gains, then...
UP: 25 HR, 90 RBI.

Jones,Andruw			AB	R	HR	RBI	SB	Avg	vL	vR	OB	Slg	OPS	bb%	ct%	h%	Eye	xBA	G	L	F	PX	hr/f	Spd	SBO	RC/G	RAR	BPV	R$
Pos	9	06 ATL	565	107	41	129	4	262	260	263	355	531	886	13	78	27	0.65	280	39	19	42	158	22%	33	3%	6.54	29.0	74	$26
Age/B	33 Right	07 ATL	572	83	26	94	5	222	225	221	307	413	719	11	76	25	0.51	251	39	17	44	122	14%	54	5%	4.41	-8.2	41	$14
Ht/Wt	73 240	08 LA	209	21	3	14	0	158	178	147	254	249	503	11	64	23	0.36	179	48	13	39	77	6%	62	2%	1.42	-26.1	-40	($2)
Health	C	09 TEX	281	43	17	43	5	214	218	210	322	459	781	14	74	22	0.63	263	34	16	50	159	16%	58	9%	5.32	-0.1	72	$8
PT/Exp	D	10 CHW	278	41	19	48	9	230	256	219	337	486	823	14	74	24	0.62	275	44	11	44	170	21%	56	14%	5.84	7.6	78	$12
Consist	F	1st Half	165	19	10	22	7	194			304	424	728	14	76	19	0.65	262	44	10	46	148	17%	65	22%	4.55	-2.1	70	$5
LIMA Plan	D+	2nd Half	113	22	9	26	2	283			386	575	962	14	71	32	0.58	293	44	14	42	205	27%	51	6%	7.88	9.3	93	$7
Rand Var	+1	11 Proj	303	46	18	50	6	224			328	457	785	13	72	25	0.56	259	42	14	44	158	18%	55	9%	5.38	2.0	60	$10

PRO: 2H skills set with nice power and bb% helped him chew up LHP (.931 OPS).
CON: Avg is quite the turn-off, even if xBA says it wasn't really that bad. Remaining career value is RH side of platoon.

Jones,Chipper			AB	R	HR	RBI	SB	Avg	vL	vR	OB	Slg	OPS	bb%	ct%	h%	Eye	xBA	G	L	F	PX	hr/f	Spd	SBO	RC/G	RAR	BPV	R$
Pos	5	06 ATL	411	87	26	86	6	324	293	332	411	596	1007	13	82	34	0.84	301	41	19	40	156	19%	100	5%	8.07	28.2	112	$24
Age/B	38 Both	07 ATL	513	108	29	102	5	337	274	378	429	604	1033	14	85	35	1.09	325	44	19	37	157	18%	93	3%	8.42	37.6	124	$30
Ht/Wt	76 210	08 ATL	439	82	22	75	4	364	394	349	473	574	1047	17	86	39	1.48	303	43	24	33	121	18%	97	2%	8.78	37.3	107	$27
Health	D	09 ATL	488	80	18	71	4	264	289	252	390	430	821	17	82	29	1.13	268	45	20	35	104	13%	84	3%	6.09	13.4	71	$17
PT/Exp	B	10 ATL	317	47	10	46	5	265	245	275	384	426	809	16	85	28	1.30	276	38	18	44	107	8%	73	4%	5.97	9.7	83	$11
Consist	C	1st Half	221	30	5	32	5	249			385	380	765	18	83	28	1.32	262	40	18	41	93	7%	70	6%	5.55	4.2	66	$7
LIMA Plan	C+	2nd Half	96	17	5	14	0	302			380	531	911	11	90	30	1.20	308	33	18	48	137	12%	87	0%	6.78	4.9	118	$5
Rand Var	+4	11 Proj	272	46	12	42	0	276			385	477	862	15	85	29	1.21	291	40	20	40	123	13%	86	1%	6.48	10.7	97	$10

ACL surgery means best case is he starts season on DL, only missing April. Worst case is he misses first half. Declines in skills are function of his age. Don't be surprised if he doesn't make it back from this one.

Jones,Garrett			AB	R	HR	RBI	SB	Avg	vL	vR	OB	Slg	OPS	bb%	ct%	h%	Eye	xBA	G	L	F	PX	hr/f	Spd	SBO	RC/G	RAR	BPV	R$
Pos	39	06 aaa	525	71	21	91	3	230			294	421	714	8	76	27	0.37					125		68	6%	4.28	-22.8	41	$12
Age/B	29 Left	07 MIN	*477	61	14	72	3	254			305	426	730	7	77	30	0.32					120		81	6%	4.47	-11.1	45	$11
Ht/Wt	76 245	08 aaa	527	62	16	69	7	225			275	376	651	6	82	25	0.38					96		70	8%	3.44	-33.2	40	$10
Health	A	09 PIT	*591	78	29	80	21	272	208	333	331	484	815	8	80	30	0.44	274	40	18	41	137	15%	68	18%	5.48	-17.7	68	$25
PT/Exp	B	10 PIT	592	64	21	86	7	247	220	262	309	414	722	8	79	28	0.43	264	44	17	39	115	11%	52	7%	4.37	-34.5	43	$17
Consist	D	1st Half	301	33	10	50	6	276			347	432	779	10	79	32	0.53	267	47	18	36	108	12%	56	10%	5.18	-10.0	43	$11
LIMA Plan	C	2nd Half	291	31	11	36	1	216			267	395	662	6	79	24	0.33	262	41	15	43	121	11%	55	2%	3.53	-25.1	45	$5
Rand Var	+1	11 Proj	513	60	19	72	8	246			303	421	724	8	80	27	0.40	261	43	17	40	117	12%	58	10%	4.36	-29.0	46	$15

Couldn't hold 2009's PX surge, and BA vLH is still a problem that will relegate him to platoon work. That would help his rate stats, but .774 OPS vRHP is still iffy, and may not be enough to hold off competition.

Joyce,Matt			AB	R	HR	RBI	SB	Avg	vL	vR	OB	Slg	OPS	bb%	ct%	h%	Eye	xBA	G	L	F	PX	hr/f	Spd	SBO	RC/G	RAR	BPV	R$
Pos	9	06	0	0	0	0	0	0																					
Age/B	26 Left	07 aa	456	57	15	66	4	236			308	408	717	9	73	29	0.39					124		104	9%	4.43	-10.6	44	$9
Ht/Wt	74 185	08 DET	*442	69	23	67	2	244			323	482	805	10	73	28	0.43					162		121	7%	5.60	3.2	82	$13
Health	B	09 TAM	*449	63	16	62	12	233	250	179	323	419	742	12	78	27	0.60	242	38	12	50	122	9%	95	16%	4.82	-7.0	63	$12
PT/Exp	D	10 TAM	*308	44	12	49	3	241	80	262	358	445	803	16	76	28	0.77	269	33	18	49	145	10%	88	9%	5.83	8.3	80	$9
Consist	B	1st Half	115	18	3	13	2	227			354	366	719	16	80	26	1.00	250	47	11	42	101	7%	91	17%	4.82	-0.5	65	$3
LIMA Plan	B	2nd Half	193	26	9	36	1	249			361	492	853	15	74	29	0.67	279	31	19	50	174	13%	96	4%	6.52	9.0	94	$7
Rand Var	+2	11 Proj	460	66	17	69	6	246			345	441	787	13	76	29	0.63	257	33	18	49	136	10%	93	10%	5.50	4.6	69	$13

10-40-.241 in 216 AB at TAM. Can't hit lefties at all, but mashes righties (.910 OPS). Even in a platoon, elite and still-emerging PX is begging for an opportunity. If it comes... UP: 30 HR.

JOSH PALEY

Ka'aihue,Kila

			AB	R	HR	RBI	SB	Avg	vL	vR	OB	Slg	OPS	bb%	ct%	h%	Eye	xBA	G	L	F	PX	hr/f	Spd	SBO	RC/G	RAR	BPV	R$
Pos	3	06 aa	327	31	4	35	0	171			258	251	508	10	83	19	0.70					53		66	1%	2.03	-39.2	19	($2)
Age/B	27 Left	07 aa	244	31	9	33	0	219			316	378	694	13	86	22	1.03					96		77	0%	4.36	-10.0	71	$4
Ht/Wt	75 230	08 a/a	401	76	29	84	3	282			412	536	948	18	85	27	1.51					139		67	3%	7.52	23.0	111	$20
Health	A	09 aaa	441	61	12	42	0	215			332	360	692	15	85	23	1.13					91		81	1%	4.48	-22.2	67	$6
PT/Exp	D	10 KC	* 503	70	24	81	2	246	250	206	358	436	793	15	81	26	0.93	261	35	15	49	118	12%	60	2%	5.55	-3.3	69	$16
Consist	F	1st Half	219	34	9	37	0	252			391	441	832	18	82	27	1.27	319	33	33	33	125	15%	69	0%	6.29	3.3	89	$7
LIMA Plan	C+	2nd Half	284	36	14	44	2	241			330	431	761	12	80	25	0.68	253	35	15	50	113	13%	76	3%	4.95	-7.0	60	$9
Rand Var	0	11 Proj	358	51	17	53	1	251			362	443	805	15	83	26	1.02	259	35	15	50	115	11%	65	2%	5.72	0.8	75	$11

8-25-.217 in 180 AB at KC. xPX of 148 hints at hidden power potential. Excellent Eye, low h% and xBA all support a BA rebound, but this is not a .300 hitter either. If he can find AB, a sleeper in OBP leagues.

Kalish,Ryan

			AB	R	HR	RBI	SB	Avg	vL	vR	OB	Slg	OPS	bb%	ct%	h%	Eye	xBA	G	L	F	PX	hr/f	Spd	SBO	RC/G	RAR	BPV	R$
Pos	8	06	0	0	0	0	0	0																					
Age/B	23 Left	07	0	0	0	0	0	0																					
Ht/Wt	73 205	08	0	0	0	0	0	0																					
Health	A	09 aa	391	54	10	47	12	263			326	411	737	9	82	30	0.52					93		95	14%	4.64	-0.6	50	$12
PT/Exp	F	10 BOS	* 456	71	14	61	30	268	233	258	333	436	770	9	83	30	0.58	290	46	18	36	115	10%	95	29%	5.06	-3.6	72	$21
Consist	A	1st Half	198	33	7	27	13	268			353	449	802	12	87	28	1.04	0				114		91	24%	5.63	1.7	94	$10
LIMA Plan	D+	2nd Half	258	38	7	34	17	267			318	426	744	7	79	31	0.36	278	46	18	36	115	10%	94	34%	4.63	-5.3	54	$12
Rand Var	+1	11 Proj	288	43	7	37	15	267			331	420	751	9	82	30	0.54	274	46	18	36	101	9%	98	23%	4.83	-2.1	59	$11

4-24-.252 with 10 SB in 163 AB at BOS. High SB success rate (91%) bodes well for future SB despite average speed. PX also encouraging given age. Don't pay for it in 2011, but he could be a 20/20 guy eventually.

Kapler,Gabe

			AB	R	HR	RBI	SB	Avg	vL	vR	OB	Slg	OPS	bb%	ct%	h%	Eye	xBA	G	L	F	PX	hr/f	Spd	SBO	RC/G	RAR	BPV	R$
Pos	9	06 BOS	* 155	23	2	14	1	244	265	242	313	359	672	9	86	27	0.73	250	47	14	38	76	4%	105	5%	4.04	-7.5	58	$2
Age/B	35 Right	07	0	0	0	0	0	0																					
Ht/Wt	74 205	08 MIL	229	36	8	38	3	301	354	272	339	498	837	5	83	34	0.33	283	46	18	36	125	12%	101	7%	5.64	2.8	75	$10
Health	C	09 TAM	205	26	8	32	5	239	276	150	333	439	772	12	81	26	0.74	281	36	22	41	126	12%	66	13%	5.25	-0.5	71	$6
PT/Exp	F	10 TAM	124	19	2	14	1	210	206	222	274	290	564	8	81	24	0.46	232	42	19	40	57	5%	70	6%	2.46	-9.7	7	$2
Consist	D	1st Half	89	18	1	10	1	225			289	292	581	8	80	27	0.44	218	39	18	43	50	3%	78	8%	2.66	-6.3	2	$2
LIMA Plan	F	2nd Half	35	1	1	4	0	171			237	286	523	8	83	18	0.50	267	48	21	31	72	11%	69	0%	1.97	-3.4	27	($0)
Rand Var	+5	11 Proj	78	13	2	11	1	256			317	409	726	8	82	29	0.50	267	42	18	40	103	9%	79	9%	4.47	-1.6	53	$2

Whatever skills he had been clinging to abandoned him in 2010. Nevertheless, a 35 year old platoon player who has already retired once is not the smartest place to speculate.

Kearns,Austin

			AB	R	HR	RBI	SB	Avg	vL	vR	OB	Slg	OPS	bb%	ct%	h%	Eye	xBA	G	L	F	PX	hr/f	Spd	SBO	RC/G	RAR	BPV	R$
Pos	79	06 2NL	537	86	24	86	9	264	336	236	356	467	823	12	75	31	0.56	259	42	19	39	132	15%	69	8%	5.91	10.3	52	$19
Age/B	30 Right	07 WAS	587	84	16	74	2	266	292	258	345	411	756	11	82	30	0.67	270	45	20	35	95	10%	65	2%	4.98	-6.5	46	$14
Ht/Wt	75 243	08 WAS	313	40	7	32	2	217	153	241	296	316	612	10	80	25	0.56	239	47	21	32	64	9%	60	5%	3.10	-22.4	11	$4
Health	D	09 WAS	174	20	3	17	1	195	122	224	320	305	625	16	71	26	0.63	214	46	19	36	79	7%	83	4%	3.42	-11.8	4	$1
PT/Exp	D	10 2AL	403	55	10	49	4	263	252	270	339	395	733	10	71	35	0.40	251	44	23	33	104	11%	57	4%	4.72	-1.9	8	$11
Consist	B	1st Half	247	36	7	35	4	271			350	417	767	11	73	34	0.45	271	44	26	30	114	13%	44	7%	5.17	2.0	21	$9
LIMA Plan	F	2nd Half	156	19	3	14	0	250			320	359	679	9	68	35	0.32	219	45	19	36	87	8%	85	0%	3.99	-4.1	-12	$3
Rand Var	-4	11 Proj	274	35	6	30	2	248			335	368	702	12	73	32	0.47	236	45	21	34	88	9%	65	3%	4.33	-4.9	5	$6

1H resurgence due to LD bump that wasn't sustainable. When G/L/F rates reverted to historical levels, it was 2009 all over again. Let someone else pay.
DN: sub-.200 Avg

Kelly,Don

			AB	R	HR	RBI	SB	Avg	vL	vR	OB	Slg	OPS	bb%	ct%	h%	Eye	xBA	G	L	F	PX	hr/f	Spd	SBO	RC/G	RAR	BPV	R$
Pos	37	06 a/a	444	45	0	36	20	215			284	280	564	9	87	25	0.78					44		117	26%	2.86	-40.1	40	$5
Age/B	31 Left	07 aaa	150	14	0	7	4	194			255	232	488	8	89	22	0.74					27		109	20%	1.95	-18.3	27	($0)
Ht/Wt	76 190	08 aaa	436	46	6	41	2	232			273	341	614	5	91	24	0.60					65		117	3%	3.27	-29.3	62	$5
Health	A	09 DET	* 427	51	4	34	22	266			324	366	691	8	86	30	0.60	266	47	22	31	61	4%	115	21%	4.16	-19.2	44	$12
PT/Exp	D	10 DET	238	30	9	27	3	244	217	247	268	374	642	3	82	26	0.19	237	32	19	49	76	9%	94	6%	3.06	-19.1	27	$6
Consist	B	1st Half	95	11	1	8	1	221			253	274	526	4	85	25	0.29	208	30	19	51	35	2%	105	5%	1.94	-11.1	11	$1
LIMA Plan	F	2nd Half	143	19	8	19	2	259			279	441	719	3	80	27	0.14	256	33	19	47	105	15%	91	6%	3.86	-7.9	40	$5
Rand Var	0	11 Proj	265	31	8	26	6	245			285	371	656	5	85	26	0.37	241	33	19	48	74	7%	102	12%	3.46	-17.2	42	$6

Surprising power in 2H a result of inflated hr/f rate. SBO seems to come and go, so no telling whether he'll get the green light in 2011. The off chance of putting it all together for a year makes him worth a flier.

Kemp,Matt

			AB	R	HR	RBI	SB	Avg	vL	vR	OB	Slg	OPS	bb%	ct%	h%	Eye	xBA	G	L	F	PX	hr/f	Spd	SBO	RC/G	RAR	BPV	R$
Pos	8	06 LA	* 535	93	16	84	28	293	229	264	343	464	806	7	79	34	0.36	268	40	24	36	107	10%	89	24%	5.40	14.5	46	$25
Age/B	26 Right	07 LA	* 453	73	14	58	18	324	390	318	359	505	863	5	80	38	0.28	273	45	17	37	113	10%	145	20%	5.99	17.9	68	$22
Ht/Wt	75 226	08 LA	606	93	18	76	35	290	369	260	340	459	799	7	75	36	0.30	262	45	23	32	119	12%	115	29%	5.40	11.4	44	$28
Health	B	09 LA	606	97	26	101	34	297	362	278	353	490	843	8	77	35	0.37	261	40	21	38	121	15%	113	24%	5.88	19.5	57	$34
PT/Exp	A	10 LA	602	82	28	89	19	249	295	233	310	450	760	8	72	30	0.31	261	41	20	39	139	16%	87	24%	4.90	0.1	42	$23
Consist	B	1st Half	321	56	15	47	10	268			329	483	811	8	72	33	0.32	273	42	21	37	151	18%	93	25%	5.64	7.2	54	$15
LIMA Plan	C+	2nd Half	281	26	13	42	9	228			289	413	701	8	72	27	0.30	248	40	19	42	125	15%	82	22%	4.04	-7.4	30	$9
Rand Var	+2	11 Proj	600	85	28	89	21	270			326	477	802	8	74	32	0.32	267	41	21	38	136	17%	99	21%	5.39	10.6	53	$26

The Good: Rising PX, hr/f, age 26
The Bad: Declining ct%, speed, seemingly bailed in 2nd half.
Future bleak because he doesn't have the "grit and wily veteranship of S.Podsednik."
We disagree. UP: 35 HR

Kendall,Jason

			AB	R	HR	RBI	SB	Avg	vL	vR	OB	Slg	OPS	bb%	ct%	h%	Eye	xBA	G	L	F	PX	hr/f	Spd	SBO	RC/G	RAR	BPV	R$
Pos	2	06 OAK	552	76	1	50	11	295	331	285	357	342	699	9	90	33	0.98	269	50	24	26	35	1%	93	8%	4.41	0.1	36	$13
Age/B	36 Right	07 2TM	466	45	3	41	3	242	198	259	290	309	599	6	91	26	0.74	252	44	19	38	45	2%	89	6%	3.17	-16.7	41	$4
Ht/Wt	72 192	08 MIL	516	46	2	49	8	246	250	245	313	324	636	9	91	27	1.11	253	46	18	37	54	1%	88	8%	3.80	-6.4	55	$7
Health	B	09 MIL	452	48	2	43	7	241	218	246	311	305	617	9	87	27	0.79	241	44	20	36	46	1%	94	7%	3.43	-11.3	34	$6
PT/Exp	B	10 KC	434	39	0	37	12	256	323	237	314	297	611	8	90	29	0.82	243	46	18	36	35	0%	68	15%	3.37	-10.2	25	$8
Consist	A	1st Half	280	23	0	29	5	264			322	314	637	8	90	29	0.89	255	47	18	34	42	0%	65	14%	3.69	-3.9	32	$5
LIMA Plan	F	2nd Half	154	16	0	8	7	240			299	266	566	8	88	27	0.72	223	45	17	39	22	0%	83	15%	2.78	-6.3	13	$3
Rand Var	-1	11 Proj	128	13	0	11	2	250			312	295	608	8	89	28	0.83	241	45	18	36	35	1%	80	8%	3.33	-3.4	27	$2

Season cut short by September shoulder surgery, which will keep him out for at least the first half of 2011. Position, age and lack of PX or Spd make a counting stat comeback less likely.

Kendrick,Howie

			AB	R	HR	RBI	SB	Avg	vL	vR	OB	Slg	OPS	bb%	ct%	h%	Eye	xBA	G	L	F	PX	hr/f	Spd	SBO	RC/G	RAR	BPV	R$
Pos	4	06 LAA	* 557	70	14	79	15	307	264	295	329	476	804	3	85	34	0.22	280	52	15	33	107	9%	83	15%	5.14	15.6	60	$20
Age/B	27 Right	07 LAA	* 388	63	8	49	6	315	325	322	332	451	783	3	82	37	0.14	276	54	16	30	94	8%	101	10%	4.83	8.8	41	$14
Ht/Wt	70 200	08 LAA	340	43	3	37	11	306	300	308	330	421	750	3	83	36	0.21	276	54	20	26	86	4%	79	18%	4.57	-3.0	33	$11
Health	C	09 LAA	* 452	70	12	70	15	294	313	278	332	449	780	5	82	34	0.31	279	54	19	27	97	12%	91	18%	4.98	0.6	44	$18
PT/Exp	B	10 LAA	616	67	10	75	14	279	264	286	311	407	718	4	85	32	0.30	289	53	19	28	90	7%	74	12%	4.23	-4.1	44	$19
Consist	B	1st Half	328	38	7	50	8	271			301	399	701	4	86	30	0.31	289	54	18	28	86	9%	73	13%	3.99	-4.4	46	$11
LIMA Plan	D+	2nd Half	288	29	3	25	6	288			321	417	738	5	83	34	0.29	288	53	19	28	96	4%	79	12%	4.52	0.5	43	$8
Rand Var	+2	11 Proj	603	76	10	75	16	292			323	425	748	4	83	34	0.27	283	54	19	28	92	8%	79	14%	4.56	-0.7	42	$20

Has tantalized us before with flashes of brilliance, but remarkably stable multiyear BPI advise us to expect more of the same in 2011. The window for the long-awaited breakout is closing.

Kennedy,Adam

			AB	R	HR	RBI	SB	Avg	vL	vR	OB	Slg	OPS	bb%	ct%	h%	Eye	xBA	G	L	F	PX	hr/f	Spd	SBO	RC/G	RAR	BPV	R$
Pos	34	06 LAA	451	50	4	55	16	273	193	291	331	384	714	8	84	32	0.54	270	41	27	32	72	3%	80	21%	4.44	-12.9	36	$11
Age/B	35 Left	07 STL	279	27	3	18	6	219	122	235	276	290	566	7	88	24	0.67	237	43	17	40	44	3%	105	11%	2.73	-29.3	36	$2
Ht/Wt	73 195	08 STL	339	42	2	36	7	280	270	283	322	372	694	6	87	32	0.49	267	43	25	32	60	2%	100	9%	4.12	-15.5	41	$9
Health	B	09 OAK	* 611	74	14	70	22	280	241	307	337	402	739	8	84	32	0.53	266	41	24	36	78	7%	81	16%	4.63	-18.8	39	$19
PT/Exp	C	10 WAS	342	43	3	31	14	249	316	240	322	327	649	10	87	28	0.84	257	43	20	37	56	3%	94	16%	3.82	-25.5	43	$9
Consist	B	1st Half	167	22	2	16	9	240			317	329	647	10	87	26	0.90	264	46	19	34	59	4%	101	18%	3.81	-12.5	50	$5
LIMA Plan	D	2nd Half	175	21	1	15	5	257			326	326	652	9	87	29	0.78	251	40	21	39	53	2%	85	13%	3.83	-13.0	36	$4
Rand Var	+1	11 Proj	352	43	4	35	12	261			324	351	674	8	86	29	0.67	258	42	22	36	61	4%	87	15%	3.99	-23.4	39	$9

Drop off from career year was inevitable, but ct% rebound and rise in bb% say there's still something left in the tank. Scrappy reputation and left handedness will help ensure he gets AB somewhere.

BILL MACEY

Keppinger,Jeff			AB	R	HR	RBI	SB	Avg	vL	vR	OB	Slg	OPS	bb%	ct%	h%	Eye	xBA	G	L	F	PX	hr/f	Spd	SBO	RC/G	RAR	BPV	R$
Pos	4	06 KC	*510	67	6	50	0	298	222	303	354	378	732	8	93	31	1.25	282	58	19	23	48	5%	82	2%	4.77	9.3	53	$11
Age/B	30 Right	07 CIN	*469	66	7	47	3	331	362	320	387	450	837	8	95	34	1.67	301	47	21	32	71	5%	116	3%	5.97	15.8	89	$16
Ht/Wt	72 184	08 CIN	459	45	3	43	3	266	360	225	311	346	657	6	95	28	1.25	284	51	21	28	52	2%	92	3%	3.95	-10.9	62	$8
Health	B	09 HOU	305	35	7	29	0	256	314	227	316	387	703	8	89	27	0.82	281	53	18	29	76	9%	108	2%	4.34	-1.7	68	$6
PT/Exp	B	10 HOU	514	62	6	59	4	288	304	282	352	393	745	9	93	30	1.42	298	51	20	30	71	4%	76	3%	5.02	2.8	72	$15
Consist	B	1st Half	291	31	1	28	2	278			335	361	696	8	92	30	1.09	294	52	21	28	64	1%	70	4%	4.42	-3.3	58	$6
LIMA Plan	B	2nd Half	223	31	5	31	2	300			373	435	808	10	94	30	2.00	305	50	18	32	81	7%	90	3%	5.78	5.9	91	$8
Rand Var	0	11 Proj	**416**	**50**	**6**	**45**	**2**	**281**			**342**	**392**	**735**	**8**	**93**	**29**	**1.25**	**291**	**51**	**19**	**30**	**69**	**6%**	**89**	**3%**	**4.83**	**1.3**	**71**	**$11**

PRO: Good plate discipline and excellent ct%; 2H bump in FB and hr/f mildly encouraging. CON: Power and speed still subpar; 2010 spike due to increased AB. He might repeat 2010, but don't expect more.

Kinsler,Ian			AB	R	HR	RBI	SB	Avg	vL	vR	OB	Slg	OPS	bb%	ct%	h%	Eye	xBA	G	L	F	PX	hr/f	Spd	SBO	RC/G	RAR	BPV	R$
Pos	4	06 TEX	423	65	14	55	11	286	271	292	348	454	802	9	85	31	0.63	265	35	21	44	103	9%	75	13%	5.40	15.4	64	$15
Age/B	28 Right	07 TEX	483	96	20	61	23	263	339	239	347	441	788	11	83	28	0.75	266	35	20	46	108	11%	94	17%	5.34	18.8	71	$20
Ht/Wt	72 200	08 TEX	518	102	18	71	26	319	281	332	373	517	890	8	87	34	0.67	293	32	24	43	124	9%	111	19%	6.42	21.3	99	$28
Health	F	09 TEX	566	101	31	86	31	253	310	230	323	488	811	9	86	24	0.77	272	30	16	54	129	12%	100	27%	5.49	9.4	99	$26
PT/Exp	B	10 TEX	391	73	9	45	15	286	376	258	376	412	788	13	85	32	0.98	263	40	18	42	83	6%	94	14%	5.51	11.7	63	$17
Consist	A	1st Half	214	44	3	26	8	299			398	411	809	14	85	34	1.06	262	36	21	43	84	4%	83	14%	5.92	8.7	61	$10
LIMA Plan	C+	2nd Half	177	29	6	19	7	271			348	412	761	11	86	29	0.88	266	45	16	39	81	10%	113	16%	5.02	2.9	68	$7
Rand Var	-2	11 Proj	**479**	**87**	**20**	**61**	**21**	**280**			**356**	**471**	**826**	**11**	**86**	**29**	**0.84**	**279**	**37**	**18**	**45**	**113**	**11%**	**97**	**18%**	**5.77**	**16.0**	**86**	**$22**

Made two trips to DL for ankle and groin injuries. Speed and hr/f returned to normal levels in 2H, so counting stats should rebound in 2011. But that "F" health rating casts a long, dark shadow.

Konerko,Paul			AB	R	HR	RBI	SB	Avg	vL	vR	OB	Slg	OPS	bb%	ct%	h%	Eye	xBA	G	L	F	PX	hr/f	Spd	SBO	RC/G	RAR	BPV	R$
Pos	30	06 CHW	566	97	35	113	1	313	318	310	379	551	930	10	82	33	0.58	289	33	25	42	139	18%	59	1%	6.88	22.2	76	$27
Age/B	35 Right	07 CHW	549	71	31	90	0	259	296	244	351	490	841	12	81	27	0.76	287	38	17	45	145	16%	45	1%	5.99	11.7	82	$17
Ht/Wt	74 215	08 CHW	438	59	22	62	2	240	236	241	338	438	776	13	82	25	0.81	279	41	22	38	119	16%	63	2%	5.23	-0.6	69	$12
Health	A	09 CHW	546	75	28	88	1	277	338	253	346	489	835	10	84	29	0.65	275	36	19	46	122	13%	54	1%	5.77	0.9	70	$19
PT/Exp	A	10 CHW	548	89	39	111	0	312	339	304	392	584	976	12	80	33	0.65	309	35	20	45	171	20%	63	1%	7.58	26.9	101	$31
Consist	C	1st Half	270	46	20	57	0	296			383	563	946	12	81	30	0.73	305	33	20	46	163	20%	46	0%	7.20	10.6	94	$15
LIMA Plan	C+	2nd Half	278	43	19	54	0	327			401	604	1005	11	79	36	0.59	313	37	19	44	179	20%	80	1%	7.97	16.2	108	$16
Rand Var	-3	11 Proj	**515**	**77**	**32**	**93**	**1**	**282**			**362**	**525**	**887**	**11**	**81**	**29**	**0.67**	**294**	**36**	**20**	**44**	**148**	**17%**	**59**	**1%**	**6.46**	**12.0**	**86**	**$22**

A great reminder that once you display a skill, you own it. Just remember that he also had 2007-2009. h% and hr/f both above career averages, so BA and HR corrections are likely. Don't pay full price.

Kotchman,Casey			AB	R	HR	RBI	SB	Avg	vL	vR	OB	Slg	OPS	bb%	ct%	h%	Eye	xBA	G	L	F	PX	hr/f	Spd	SBO	RC/G	RAR	BPV	R$
Pos	3	06 LAA	79	6	1	6	0	152	214	138	221	215	436	8	84	17	0.54	234	67	11	23	40	7%	91	6%	1.04	-11.7	12	($1)
Age/B	28 Left	07 LAA	443	64	11	68	2	296	315	292	371	467	838	11	90	31	1.23	307	51	16	33	109	8%	83	5%	6.09	10.2	96	$14
Ht/Wt	75 215	08 2TM	525	65	14	74	2	272	303	261	319	410	729	6	93	27	0.92	290	53	18	30	80	10%	74	2%	4.57	-13.9	71	$14
Health	B	09 2TM	385	37	7	48	1	268	250	275	335	382	717	9	89	29	0.93	276	51	19	29	73	7%	58	1%	4.58	-17.0	53	$8
PT/Exp	B	10 SEA	414	37	9	51	0	217	179	231	278	336	614	8	86	23	0.61	281	55	17	27	78	9%	61	0%	3.22	-32.4	43	$5
Consist	B	1st Half	194	17	4	25	0	206			280	325	605	9	88	22	0.83	284	53	18	29	75	8%	74	0%	3.27	-15.1	54	$2
LIMA Plan	D	2nd Half	220	20	5	26	0	227			277	345	622	6	85	25	0.45	279	58	17	25	80	11%	58	0%	3.18	-17.2	36	$3
Rand Var	+5	11 Proj	**257**	**26**	**6**	**33**	**0**	**257**			**317**	**385**	**702**	**8**	**88**	**27**	**0.75**	**286**	**54**	**18**	**29**	**80**	**9%**	**72**	**1%**	**4.31**	**-9.9**	**57**	**$5**

xBA suggests BA will improve, but high GB rate and low PX say the extra hits will mostly be singles. MLB teams unlikely to tolerate subpar power at 1B, so downward PX trend will probably affect his playing time.

Kotsay,Mark			AB	R	HR	RBI	SB	Avg	vL	vR	OB	Slg	OPS	bb%	ct%	h%	Eye	xBA	G	L	F	PX	hr/f	Spd	SBO	RC/G	RAR	BPV	R$
Pos	30	06 OAK	502	57	7	59	6	275	265	278	333	386	720	8	89	30	0.80	263	46	19	35	70	4%	82	6%	4.56	-12.3	54	$10
Age/B	35 Left	07 OAK	*243	21	1	21	2	207	130	238	276	280	556	9	91	22	1.08	246	45	15	41	54	1%	70	6%	2.90	-17.9	49	$0
Ht/Wt	72 204	08 2TM	402	45	6	49	2	276	250	288	329	403	732	7	89	30	0.71	276	42	22	36	80	5%	95	6%	4.67	-9.6	65	$9
Health	F	09 2AL	187	16	4	23	3	278	219	290	332	390	722	7	89	30	0.71	267	47	19	34	67	7%	67	9%	4.48	-6.6	46	$5
PT/Exp	D	10 CHW	327	30	8	31	1	239		258	306	376	683	9	89	25	0.89	272	44	16	40	86	7%	72	5%	4.16	-15.9	66	$5
Consist	A	1st Half	175	18	6	19	1	229			325	389	714	13	89	23	1.32	280	41	16	43	99	9%	52	6%	4.68	-5.8	79	$3
LIMA Plan	D	2nd Half	152	12	2	12	0	250			283	362	645	4	89	27	0.41	264	47	15	38	70	4%	97	3%	3.50	-10.3	51	$2
Rand Var	+3	11 Proj	**226**	**21**	**4**	**24**	**2**	**257**			**313**	**376**	**689**	**8**	**89**	**27**	**0.75**	**268**	**45**	**17**	**38**	**75**	**6%**	**73**	**6%**	**4.17**	**-9.8**	**55**	**$4**

Another high-contact, low power first baseman. BA should bounce back as 3-year xBA sets expectations for 2011. 0-25 vs. RH in '10 may mean he's a strict platoon player now, which would only help his value.

Kottaras,George			AB	R	HR	RBI	SB	Avg	vL	vR	OB	Slg	OPS	bb%	ct%	h%	Eye	xBA	G	L	F	PX	hr/f	Spd	SBO	RC/G	RAR	BPV	R$
Pos	2	06 a/a	376	46	7	43	0	223			321	359	680	13	77	27	0.61					97		97	1%	4.14	-2.7	40	$4
Age/B	27 Left	07 aaa	294	29	8	35	1	238			304	401	706	9	78	28	0.44					119		87	3%	4.26	-0.9	54	$4
Ht/Wt	72 185	08 aaa	395	50	16	52	0	214			302	383	685	11	75	24	0.51					114		80	0%	3.98	-2.7	42	$7
Health	A	09 BOS	*117	16	1	10	0	243	111	267	337	394	731	12	73	32	0.52	249	30	23	48	134	2%	81	0%	4.96	2.4	50	$1
PT/Exp	F	10 MIL	212	24	9	26	2	203	200	204	310	396	706	13	79	21	0.75	264	43	12	45	128	12%	88	4%	4.41	-0.5	75	$4
Consist	B	1st Half	114	15	6	19	2	202			355	439	793	19	78	20	1.08	287	40	14	46	164	15%	74	6%	5.75	4.5	106	$3
LIMA Plan	D	2nd Half	98	9	3	7	0	204			250	347	597	6	81	22	0.32	238	47	10	43	88	9%	118	0%	2.72	-5.4	42	$1
Rand Var	+5	11 Proj	**186**	**22**	**5**	**20**	**1**	**215**			**305**	**377**	**681**	**11**	**77**	**25**	**0.56**	**246**	**40**	**15**	**45**	**117**	**8%**	**90**	**2%**	**4.07**	**-1.8**	**54**	**$2**

Unable to find playing time, but above average PX and FB rate, and acceptable xBA say he could succeed if given the chance.
UP: 15 HR, .250 BA and 350 AB

Kouzmanoff,Kevin			AB	R	HR	RBI	SB	Avg	vL	vR	OB	Slg	OPS	bb%	ct%	h%	Eye	xBA	G	L	F	PX	hr/f	Spd	SBO	RC/G	RAR	BPV	R$
Pos	5	06 CLE	*402	65	20	78	4	321	167	227	376	546	922	8	85	34	0.61	288	59	9	32	132	18%	61	7%	6.71	18.5	84	$19
Age/B	29 Right	07 SD	484	57	18	74	1	275	356	240	320	457	776	6	81	31	0.34	269	41	18	41	116	11%	62	1%	4.93	-9.3	48	$14
Ht/Wt	73 210	08 SD	624	71	23	84	0	260	237	269	286	433	719	4	78	30	0.17	256	40	22	39	112	12%	95	0%	4.07	-23.6	38	$16
Health	A	09 SD	529	50	18	88	1	255	291	241	291	420	711	5	80	29	0.25	262	44	20	36	110	12%	48	1%	4.06	-16.8	34	$14
PT/Exp	A	10 OAK	551	59	16	71	2	247	261	242	278	396	674	4	83	27	0.25	268	43	17	40	101	9%	59	3%	3.61	-19.9	39	$12
Consist	A	1st Half	316	34	8	39	1	266			297	386	683	4	84	29	0.28	258	45	17	38	79	8%	59	1%	3.72	-10.1	28	$8
LIMA Plan	C	2nd Half	235	25	8	32	1	221			253	409	662	4	80	24	0.22	281	41	17	42	132	10%	66	6%	3.46	-9.9	57	$4
Rand Var	+3	11 Proj	**554**	**60**	**19**	**80**	**2**	**253**			**287**	**424**	**711**	**5**	**81**	**28**	**0.25**	**271**	**42**	**18**	**39**	**113**	**11%**	**62**	**2%**	**4.05**	**-12.4**	**44**	**$14**

The move out of SD didn't help as OAK park also limits HR and BA for RH batters. 2H xBA shows that there's some upside here, especially if he can pair it with his 1H ct%. AAA reliability rating limits downside.

Kubel,Jason			AB	R	HR	RBI	SB	Avg	vL	vR	OB	Slg	OPS	bb%	ct%	h%	Eye	xBA	G	L	F	PX	hr/f	Spd	SBO	RC/G	RAR	BPV	R$
Pos	90	06 MIN	*340	41	12	48	4	253	243	240	302	415	717	7	80	29	0.35	264	49	21	31	99	14%	68	5%	4.21	-14.5	33	$8
Age/B	28 Left	07 MIN	418	49	13	65	5	273	236	280	338	450	787	9	81	31	0.52	289	43	22	35	121	11%	69	5%	5.28	-2.6	61	$12
Ht/Wt	72 218	08 MIN	463	74	20	78	0	272	232	283	339	471	810	9	80	30	0.52	270	40	20	41	122	13%	96	1%	5.50	1.9	68	$16
Health	A	09 MIN	514	73	28	103	1	300	245	322	368	539	907	10	79	33	0.53	285	39	20	41	147	17%	53	1%	6.73	19.8	72	$22
PT/Exp	A	10 MIN	518	68	21	92	0	249	225	260	322	427	749	10	78	28	0.48	263	38	19	43	118	12%	63	1%	4.76	-2.9	45	$16
Consist	D	1st Half	253	27	10	44	0	261			348	439	787	12	79	29	0.64	269	35	21	44	119	11%	60	0%	5.37	3.1	55	$8
LIMA Plan	C+	2nd Half	265	41	11	48	0	238			296	415	711	8	76	27	0.35	257	40	18	42	117	13%	74	2%	4.16	-6.3	38	$8
Rand Var	+2	11 Proj	**503**	**70**	**22**	**90**	**1**	**266**			**335**	**462**	**797**	**9**	**79**	**30**	**0.48**	**270**	**39**	**19**	**41**	**125**	**14%**	**64**	**1%**	**5.34**	**2.4**	**54**	**$17**

It's clear now that 2009 was an outlier buoyed by high h% and hr/f rates. Struggles vs. LH will probably limit future at bats and limit his upside. BPI stable, but be careful not to overpay.

Laird,Gerald			AB	R	HR	RBI	SB	Avg	vL	vR	OB	Slg	OPS	bb%	ct%	h%	Eye	xBA	G	L	F	PX	hr/f	Spd	SBO	RC/G	RAR	BPV	R$
Pos	2	06 TEX	243	46	7	22	3	296	400	241	329	473	803	5	78	36	0.22	252	34	19	46	124	8%	89	7%	5.27	5.8	48	$8
Age/B	31 Right	07 TEX	407	48	9	47	6	224	239	218	277	349	626	7	75	28	0.29	202	33	12	55	89	5%	99	9%	3.10	-14.9	15	$6
Ht/Wt	73 225	08 TEX	344	54	6	41	2	276	245	288	322	398	720	6	82	32	0.37	254	38	22	41	90	5%	61	7%	4.32	1.3	31	$9
Health	A	09 DET	413	49	4	33	5	225	248	222	294	320	613	9	84	26	0.59	224	41	14	45	65	3%	81	5%	3.25	-12.7	30	$4
PT/Exp	C	10 DET	270	22	5	25	3	207	183	224	257	304	561	6	79	25	0.32	224	43	15	42	70	6%	56	7%	2.28	-15.9	3	$2
Consist	C	1st Half	160	13	2	13	2	188			249	263	511	8	78	23	0.37	222	43	18	40	57	4%	55	9%	1.71	-12.6	-8	$0
LIMA Plan	F	2nd Half	110	9	3	12	1	236			270	364	633	4	80	27	0.23	229	43	11	46	88	7%	70	4%	3.07	-3.6	22	$2
Rand Var	+2	11 Proj	**196**	**21**	**4**	**19**	**2**	**230**			**280**	**335**	**615**	**7**	**80**	**27**	**0.36**	**228**	**41**	**15**	**44**	**75**	**5%**	**61**	**6%**	**3.02**	**-7.1**	**15**	**$3**

There's not much to like here as BPIs are all slowly trending downwards. A bit of a BA rebound is likely, but PX, xBA and declining AB say it won't really matter.

BILL MACEY

Langerhans,Ryan			AB	R	HR	RBI	SB	Avg	vL	vR	OB	Slg	OPS	bb%	ct%	h%	Eye	xBA	G	L	F	PX	hr/f	Spd	SBO	RC/G	RAR	BPV	R$
Pos	7	06 ATL	315	46	7	28	1	241	308	232	345	378	723	14	71	32	0.55	228	41	21	38	96	8%	95	3%	4.76	-4.6	19	$5
Age/B	31 Left	07 2TM	* 261	37	7	25	4	181	219	157	275	314	590	11	63	26	0.35	198	44	13	43	105	10%	102	8%	2.74	-20.7	-7	$2
Ht/Wt	75 221	08 WAS	* 324	47	5	36	11	243	217	239	351	367	718	14	73	32	0.62	243	44	25	31	93	6%	91	13%	4.75	-6.5	24	$8
Health	A	09 SEA	* 306	37	9	39	5	221	212	221	304	378	681	11	75	27	0.47	232	37	16	47	108	8%	74	16%	3.99	-9.8	32	$5
PT/Exp	F	10 SEA	* 146	21	3	6	6	196	91	243	330	309	638	17	58	32	0.47	189	38	20	43	104	8%	129	16%	3.81	-5.0	-12	$2
Consist	A	1st Half	79	13	2	5	5	198			361	330	690	20	64	28	0.70	215	45	14	41	118	10%	99	19%	4.53	-0.9	22	$2
LIMA Plan	F	2nd Half	67	8	1	1	1	194			289	284	573	12	51	36	0.27	157	32	24	44	83	7%	129	11%	3.02	-4.0	-66	$0
Rand Var	-2	11 Proj	121	16	3	9	3	207			315	329	644	14	64	30	0.44	206	38	20	42	99	8%	103	14%	3.66	-4.9	-3	$2

3-4-.196 in 107 at SEA. Still can draw a walk with the best of 'em, but the other 83% of AB are problematic, to say the least. Has the wheels once he gets on, and he's not powerless, but at age 31, AB will be scarce.

LaPorta,Matt			AB	R	HR	RBI	SB	Avg	vL	vR	OB	Slg	OPS	bb%	ct%	h%	Eye	xBA	G	L	F	PX	hr/f	Spd	SBO	RC/G	RAR	BPV	R$
Pos	3	06	0	0	0	0	0	0																					
Age/B	26 Right	07	0	0	0	0	0	0																					
Ht/Wt	74 210	08	0	0	0	0	0	0																					
Health	A	09 CLE	* 519	79	20	68	3	257	211	266	318	443	761	8	83	27	0.54	272	40	18	42	113	11%	69	5%	4.86	-13.0	62	$14
PT/Exp	D	10 CLE	* 445	47	16	53	0	233	216	223	318	386	704	11	80	26	0.61	243	42	13	45	101	10%	70	1%	4.27	-20.2	44	$9
Consist	B	1st Half	217	22	8	26	0	257			332	404	736	10	81	29	0.59	255	43	16	41	96	11%	74	1%	4.62	-7.3	45	$5
LIMA Plan	D+	2nd Half	228	25	8	27	0	211			305	368	673	12	79	23	0.63	237	41	10	48	105	9%	76	0%	3.92	-13.0	47	$3
Rand Var	0	11 Proj	445	55	17	55	1	240			317	411	728	10	81	26	0.59	253	42	14	45	109	10%	70	2%	4.53	-14.8	54	$10

12-41-.221 in 376 AB at CLE. Awful start (.209 on 6/3) erased spring training buzz. Plate skills remained stable throughout, but advertised power has not yet materialized (.388 career SLG). BPIs preach patience.

Larish,Jeff			AB	R	HR	RBI	SB	Avg	vL	vR	OB	Slg	OPS	bb%	ct%	h%	Eye	xBA	G	L	F	PX	hr/f	Spd	SBO	RC/G	RAR	BPV	R$
Pos	3	06	0	0	0	0	0	0																					
Age/B	28 Left	07 aa	454	66	25	93	5	241			354	460	815	15	76	26	0.74					139		91	5%	5.82	1.7	76	$15
Ht/Wt	74 200	08 DET	* 488	51	18	67	2	223	250	260	292	388	680	9	74	27	0.37	247	44	19	37	114	13%	101	4%	3.84	-21.5	36	$8
Health	A	09 DET	* 285	44	9	28	2	227		235	341	374	715	15	73	28	0.63	228	46	14	40	101	10%	101	5%	4.60	-9.7	33	$5
PT/Exp	D	10 OAK	* 401	37	14	56	2	205	91	196	273	358	631	9	76	24	0.39	249	60	9	30	109	15%	54	3%	3.18	-32.4	27	$6
Consist	C	1st Half	215	24	9	31	0	218			302	389	692	11	76	24	0.51	0				118		78	0%	4.04	-11.4	46	$4
LIMA Plan	F	2nd Half	186	13	5	25	2	190			237	321	558	6	76	23	0.25	242	60	9	30	99	11%	56	9%	2.16	-21.4	12	$2
Rand Var	+4	11 Proj	116	13	4	16	1	216			297	359	656	10	75	26	0.46	243	53	12	35	103	12%	79	5%	3.61	-7.3	28	$2

2-9-.179 in 67 AB at DET/OAK. A player like this has to make the most of every opportunity, and he whiffed with 2 teams in 2010. Double-digit HRs look good, but hr/f primarily responsible. Let that second half be your guide.

LaRoche,Adam			AB	R	HR	RBI	SB	Avg	vL	vR	OB	Slg	OPS	bb%	ct%	h%	Eye	xBA	G	L	F	PX	hr/f	Spd	SBO	RC/G	RAR	BPV	R$
Pos	3	06 ATL	492	89	32	90	0	285	241	297	356	561	917	10	74	33	0.43	286	38	21	41	180	21%	61	2%	7.02	14.1	80	$21
Age/B	31 Left	07 PIT	563	71	21	88	1	272	299	262	344	458	802	10	77	32	0.47	265	36	21	44	130	11%	58	1%	5.51	-9.9	50	$16
Ht/Wt	75 203	08 PIT	492	66	25	85	1	270	241	282	342	500	842	10	75	31	0.44	269	37	20	43	154	16%	68	2%	6.02	4.1	66	$18
Health	A	09 2TM	555	78	25	83	2	277	243	293	357	488	846	11	74	33	0.49	264	35	22	43	145	14%	71	3%	6.17	0.9	59	$19
PT/Exp	A	10 ARI	560	75	25	100	0	261	264	259	319	468	787	8	69	33	0.28	258	38	18	44	160	15%	65	1%	5.38	-15.5	42	$20
Consist	A	1st Half	275	42	12	53	0	251			331	455	786	11	69	32	0.39	255	38	17	45	157	14%	67	0%	5.47	-6.9	47	$10
LIMA Plan	C+	2nd Half	285	33	13	47	0	270			307	481	787	5	69	35	0.17	261	38	19	43	163	15%	71	2%	5.26	-8.8	40	$10
Rand Var	0	11 Proj	556	76	26	94	1	270			335	485	820	9	72	33	0.35	264	37	20	43	157	15%	65	2%	5.77	-7.8	53	$20

Year-to-year consistency and reliability his strongest asset. Given his age and BPI, drop in Eye is not yet a concern. BA should rebound, and power numbers... let's just say you know what you're getting.

LaRoche,Andy			AB	R	HR	RBI	SB	Avg	vL	vR	OB	Slg	OPS	bb%	ct%	h%	Eye	xBA	G	L	F	PX	hr/f	Spd	SBO	RC/G	RAR	BPV	R$
Pos	5	06 a/a	432	66	17	69	8	282			363	461	824	11	87	29	0.96					102		74	10%	5.81	7.0	75	$16
Age/B	27 Right	07 LA	* 358	60	16	48	4	258	200	235	351	455	806	13	83	27	0.83	281	41	19	40	119	14%	90	6%	5.62	0.1	80	$11
Ht/Wt	73 210	08 2NL	* 368	47	9	40	4	198	143	175	302	293	595	13	85	21	1.00	232	49	16	35	56	8%	63	4%	3.19	-25.4	32	$4
Health	A	09 PIT	524	64	12	64	3	258	285	249	322	401	723	9	84	29	0.60	264	49	17	34	91	8%	80	3%	4.52	-9.4	53	$12
PT/Exp	C	10 PIT	247	26	4	16	1	206	256	180	263	287	551	7	83	24	0.44	244	50	17	33	55	6%	81	3%	2.30	-20.1	15	$1
Consist	D	1st Half	198	24	3	13	1	232			290	313	603	7	85	26	0.55	258	49	20	31	54	6%	83	4%	3.04	-11.2	27	$2
LIMA Plan	D	2nd Half	49	2	1	3	0	102			154	184	338	6	71	12	0.21	187	56	6	39	59	7%	86	0%	-0.98	-10.1	-28	($1)
Rand Var	+4	11 Proj	202	27	5	22	2	238			316	354	670	10	85	26	0.75	260	49	18	33	73	8%	84	5%	3.96	-6.9	45	$4

Supposed to have more tools than his brother, but has beaten each opportunity into the ground (at a 50% clip). 2007 (pitch selectivity, swing loft) showed potential, but it's buried deeper with each subsquent season.

Lee,Carlos			AB	R	HR	RBI	SB	Avg	vL	vR	OB	Slg	OPS	bb%	ct%	h%	Eye	xBA	G	L	F	PX	hr/f	Spd	SBO	RC/G	RAR	BPV	R$
Pos	37	06 2TM	624	102	37	116	19	300	313	296	359	540	899	9	90	29	0.89	304	40	20	40	128	16%	57	12%	6.42	12.2	97	$31
Age/B	34 Right	07 HOU	627	93	32	119	10	303	338	292	357	528	885	8	90	30	0.84	297	38	16	46	126	12%	48	9%	6.26	2.3	93	$29
Ht/Wt	74 240	08 HOU	436	61	28	100	4	314	330	309	368	569	937	8	89	30	0.76	308	35	21	44	142	17%	45	4%	6.77	12.2	100	$24
Health	B	09 HOU	610	65	26	102	5	300	325	293	344	489	833	6	92	29	0.80	288	36	20	44	107	11%	58	5%	5.61	-15.2	84	$24
PT/Exp	A	10 HOU	605	67	24	89	3	246	274	238	290	417	706	6	90	24	0.63	275	39	16	46	99	10%	48	5%	4.18	-38.8	68	$17
Consist	C	1st Half	306	31	10	41	1	232			279	379	658	6	88	23	0.56	261	37	17	47	87	8%	57	6%	3.64	-25.2	54	$6
LIMA Plan	C	2nd Half	299	36	14	48	2	261			301	455	755	5	92	24	0.74	289	40	14	45	110	11%	44	3%	4.71	-14.0	83	$10
Rand Var	+5	11 Proj	599	72	23	92	3	277			323	451	775	6	91	28	0.72	280	38	18	45	101	10%	52	4%	4.98	-21.8	73	$20

The blame for 2010 goes to:
- 24% hit rate
- lower than expected hr/f
- advancing age

Only two of those will revert to previous levels; bb%, ct%, FB% all fine. 2H is the new baseline.

Lee,Derrek			AB	R	HR	RBI	SB	Avg	vL	vR	OB	Slg	OPS	bb%	ct%	h%	Eye	xBA	G	L	F	PX	hr/f	Spd	SBO	RC/G	RAR	BPV	R$
Pos	3	06 CHC	175	30	8	30	8	286	292	283	375	474	849	13	77	33	0.61	257	41	20	38	118	16%	67	21%	6.19	1.0	48	$8
Age/B	35 Right	07 CHC	567	91	22	82	6	317	339	312	393	513	907	11	80	37	0.62	284	41	21	38	129	13%	69	6%	6.86	11.3	68	$24
Ht/Wt	77 245	08 CHC	623	93	20	90	8	291	306	286	363	462	825	10	81	33	0.60	274	45	21	34	113	12%	67	5%	5.81	1.3	57	$23
Health	B	09 CHC	532	91	35	111	1	306	300	308	393	579	972	13	80	33	0.70	293	35	19	46	172	18%	73	1%	7.65	16.6	104	$29
PT/Exp	A	10 2NL	547	80	19	80	1	260	270	256	347	428	775	12	76	31	0.54	270	40	23	38	124	12%	60	2%	5.25	-17.2	45	$17
Consist	F	1st Half	300	36	10	36	1	227			324	367	690	13	74	27	0.56	244	39	21	40	99	11%	59	3%	4.12	-20.2	22	$6
LIMA Plan	C+	2nd Half	247	44	9	44	0	300			375	502	877	11	77	36	0.53	300	41	24	35	153	14%	64	1%	6.58	1.7	73	$11
Rand Var	+2	11 Proj	504	80	20	84	3	286			369	477	846	12	78	33	0.59	276	40	22	39	133	13%	65	3%	6.14	-1.7	62	$20

Couldn't sustain FB, hr/f spikes from 2009 and his value took a dive. BA rebounded in 2H, but h% responsible. Back issues continued and at his age, that's the real story. Remains risky.

Lewis,Fred			AB	R	HR	RBI	SB	Avg	vL	vR	OB	Slg	OPS	bb%	ct%	h%	Eye	xBA	G	L	F	PX	hr/f	Spd	SBO	RC/G	RAR	BPV	R$
Pos	7	06 aaa	439	64	9	43	14	241			320	379	698	10	82	28	0.64					80		140	20%	4.31	-12.2	57	$10
Age/B	30 Left	07 SF	* 328	57	8	42	11	259	276	289	327	413	739	9	80	30	0.50	266	55	15	30	92	10%	137	14%	4.71	-6.2	53	$11
Ht/Wt	74 198	08 SF	468	81	9	40	21	282	270	285	353	440	793	10	74	37	0.41	257	54	18	28	109	9%	160	20%	5.58	2.1	51	$18
Health	A	09 SF	295	49	4	20	8	258	164	279	338	390	728	11	72	35	0.43	253	52	21	27	108	7%	138	14%	4.79	-6.7	37	$8
PT/Exp	C	10 TOR	* 450	74	9	40	19	264	247	266	326	424	750	8	77	33	0.39	275	47	18	34	120	8%	118	23%	4.89	0.1	57	$16
Consist	A	1st Half	256	39	4	20	7	277			332	430	762	8	74	36	0.31	276	48	21	31	124	7%	123	16%	5.07	1.4	48	$8
LIMA Plan	C	2nd Half	194	35	5	20	12	247			319	416	735	10	80	28	0.54	272	47	14	39	116	8%	101	32%	4.71	-1.0	65	$8
Rand Var	+1	11 Proj	389	66	8	34	13	267			337	423	760	10	76	34	0.44	268	50	18	32	112	8%	132	18%	5.08	1.7	54	$12

8-36-.262 with 17 SB in 428 AB in TOR. Carries most of value in his legs, though declining Spd and mediocre success rate (74%) say it's fleeting. Repeating 2nd half bb% and ct% gains, though, would be a great next step.

Lillibridge,Brent			AB	R	HR	RBI	SB	Avg	vL	vR	OB	Slg	OPS	bb%	ct%	h%	Eye	xBA	G	L	F	PX	hr/f	Spd	SBO	RC/G	RAR	BPV	R$
Pos	4	06	0	0	0	0	0	0																					
Age/B	27 Right	07 a/a	525	67	11	50	36	257			302	371	673	6	79	31	0.30					75		112	36%	3.68	-10.5	23	$17
Ht/Wt	71 190	08 ATL	* 435	46	4	39	21	190	171	222	241	291	532	6	76	24	0.28	203	45	11	44	73	3%	100	35%	1.96	-39.7	7	$5
Health	A	09 CHW	* 341	38	3	23	20	200	214	134	282	263	545	10	76	26	0.47	214	47	19	34	43	3%	102	25%	2.22	-29.4	-9	$5
PT/Exp	D	10 CHW	* 283	38	6	28	19	218	303	185	259	331	590	5	73	28	0.20	238	36	25	39	85	7%	100	43%	2.53	-17.3	1	$8
Consist	A	1st Half	197	22	5	18	14	231			278	354	631	6	78	27	0.29	224	22	22	56	85	5%	98	39%	3.14	-8.0	24	$6
LIMA Plan	F	2nd Half	86	16	1	10	5	186			213	279	493	3	60	29	0.09	201	38	26	36	83	5%	108	57%	1.18	-9.4	-50	$2
Rand Var	0	11 Proj	122	16	1	11	7	221			270	308	579	6	72	30	0.24	222	40	23	37	68	4%	100	36%	2.47	-8.2	-13	$3

2-16-.224 with 5 SB in 98 AB in CHW. Positional versatility, but serious ct% issues, 3 seasons of sub-.600 OPS. Strong SB history, but OBP-challenged and SBO (not Spd) is the source. 1 step forward; 2 steps back.

BRENT HERSHEY

Lind,Adam

			AB	R	HR	RBI	SB	Avg	vL	vR	OB	Slg	OPS	bb%	ct%	h%	Eye	xBA	G	L	F	PX	hr/f	Spd	SBO	RC/G	RAR	BPV	R$
Pos	0	06 TOR	* 517	66	26	91	3	331	444	353	389	559	948	9	79	38	0.44	272	35	19	46	148	14%	70	3%	7.21	10.6	73	$23
Age/B	27 Left	07 TOR	* 464	51	17	70	1	254	194	251	297	420	717	6	78	29	0.28	262	45	19	37	109	13%	60	3%	4.15	-28.5	31	$11
Ht/Wt	73 215	08 TOR	* 515	69	15	83	3	288	253	294	330	458	788	6	82	33	0.34	281	51	19	30	110	12%	90	3%	5.11	2.6	55	$17
Health	A	09 TOR	587	93	35	114	1	305	275	317	367	562	930	9	81	33	0.53	305	43	20	37	157	20%	50	1%	6.90	27.7	85	$27
PT/Exp	A	10 TOR	569	57	23	72	0	237	117	275	285	425	710	6	75	28	0.26	266	41	19	40	134	13%	54	0%	4.13	-37.9	36	$13
Consist	F	1st Half	302	30	10	37	0	205			266	351	617	8	73	25	0.30	237	39	18	42	105	11%	62	0%	2.93	-32.1	10	$4
LIMA Plan	C+	2nd Half	267	27	13	35	0	273			307	509	817	5	77	31	0.21	299	43	19	38	164	16%	54	0%	5.39	-7.3	67	$9
Rand Var	+4	11 Proj	587	71	28	90	1	273			322	490	812	7	78	31	0.33	285	43	19	38	144	16%	58	1%	5.41	-7.3	60	$19

Slogged through the 1H a shell of 2009's budding superstar, then h% and hr/f% returned. Chalk up ineptitude vs. LHP to a 17% h%. Reasons for optimism include 2H xBA, rising FB%. Buy low if you can.

Loney,James

			AB	R	HR	RBI	SB	Avg	vL	vR	OB	Slg	OPS	bb%	ct%	h%	Eye	xBA	G	L	F	PX	hr/f	Spd	SBO	RC/G	RAR	BPV	R$
Pos	3	06 LA	* 468	73	10	74	8	333	350	268	379	503	882	7	92	35	0.96	279	49	12	39	96	6%	83	11%	6.32	4.0	87	$21
Age/B	26 Left	07 LA	* 577	63	16	93	2	295	319	336	350	455	805	8	84	33	0.54	281	42	22	36	98	9%	76	2%	5.41	-11.5	57	$18
Ht/Wt	75 220	08 LA	595	66	13	90	7	289	249	305	339	434	773	7	86	32	0.53	275	44	22	34	90	7%	85	7%	5.03	-11.8	57	$19
Health	A	09 LA	576	73	13	90	7	281	274	283	359	399	758	11	88	30	1.03	268	43	22	35	72	7%	68	5%	5.10	-23.0	54	$19
PT/Exp	A	10 LA	588	67	10	88	10	267	222	286	327	395	721	8	84	30	0.55	288	43	25	32	92	6%	61	10%	4.49	-31.5	45	$17
Consist	A	1st Half	311	44	5	56	9	305			357	434	791	7	85	35	0.54	305	42	29	29	93	6%	70	14%	5.29	-9.0	53	$14
LIMA Plan	C	2nd Half	277	23	5	32	1	224			293	350	643	9	82	26	0.55	268	45	20	36	91	6%	58	3%	3.56	-23.4	40	$3
Rand Var	+2	11 Proj	562	64	11	83	7	274			337	405	741	9	85	30	0.65	279	43	23	34	87	7%	68	7%	4.76	-24.2	51	$17

Lost more than 100 pts of SLG from age 22 to 26. When you can't count on either .300 BA nor 15 HR from a corner IF, get ready to play catchup. He'll rebound a a little, but sim gamers: stay far away from RARs like this.

Longoria,Evan

			AB	R	HR	RBI	SB	Avg	vL	vR	OB	Slg	OPS	bb%	ct%	h%	Eye	xBA	G	L	F	PX	hr/f	Spd	SBO	RC/G	RAR	BPV	R$
Pos	5	06 aa	105	15	6	20	2	257			264	476	740	1	80	27	0.05					128		77	18%	4.08	-3.6	50	$4
Age/B	25 Right	07 a/a	485	91	25	90	4	292			382	507	889	13	80	32	0.73					134		82	3%	6.63	18.7	80	$22
Ht/Wt	74 210	08 TAM	448	67	27	85	7	272	242	284	340	531	871	9	73	32	0.38	281	39	20	42	180	20%	79	6%	6.42	19.7	79	$19
Health	A	09 TAM	584	100	33	113	9	281	289	277	360	526	885	11	76	32	0.51	282	39	19	42	160	18%	67	6%	6.59	31.5	76	$26
PT/Exp	A	10 TAM	574	96	22	104	15	294	324	281	373	507	880	11	78	34	0.58	290	37	20	43	150	11%	97	12%	6.59	28.3	87	$28
Consist	A	1st Half	315	49	12	59	12	298			370	511	881	10	78	35	0.53	293	35	22	43	150	11%	94	16%	6.56	15.1	84	$16
LIMA Plan	B	2nd Half	259	47	10	45	3	290			376	502	878	12	78	34	0.64	287	39	18	44	151	11%	98	8%	6.63	13.2	90	$12
Rand Var	0	11 Proj	595	100	31	110	11	286			361	526	887	11	77	32	0.51	290	38	19	43	162	16%	85	9%	6.59	30.0	86	$28

Five-category blueprint:
- stable FB rate (30-HR return)
- lineup support (100 R and RBI)
- Double-digit SBO (15 SB)
- rising xBA (.300 w/in reach)

Ct% improving; at a growth age. Thank 2010 hr/f for buying opp.

Lopez,Felipe

			AB	R	HR	RBI	SB	Avg	vL	vR	OB	Slg	OPS	bb%	ct%	h%	Eye	xBA	G	L	F	PX	hr/f	Spd	SBO	RC/G	RAR	BPV	R$
Pos	456	06 2NL	617	98	11	52	44	274	246	285	358	381	739	12	80	33	0.64	246	50	20	30	69	7%	99	27%	4.83	4.2	28	$24
Age/B	30 Both	07 WAS	603	70	9	50	24	245	269	235	306	352	658	8	82	29	0.49	260	50	20	30	67	6%	106	20%	3.68	-18.5	31	$13
Ht/Wt	72 203	08 2NL	481	64	6	46	8	283	306	270	342	387	728	8	83	33	0.52	255	50	19	31	73	5%	92	11%	4.57	-2.8	37	$13
Health	A	09 2TM	604	88	9	57	6	310	320	306	382	427	809	11	83	36	0.71	279	52	22	26	80	7%	94	6%	5.69	15.9	49	$19
PT/Exp	B	10 2TM	391	52	8	37	8	233	258	221	310	345	656	10	79	27	0.54	252	48	18	34	80	8%	76	9%	3.68	-11.4	26	$8
Consist	D	1st Half	184	26	4	18	5	272			346	402	749	10	79	32	0.55	262	47	18	35	93	8%	94	11%	4.88	1.2	42	$6
LIMA Plan	D	2nd Half	207	26	4	19	3	198			278	295	573	10	79	23	0.53	243	49	18	33	69	7%	63	8%	2.61	-13.3	13	$2
Rand Var	+3	11 Proj	347	47	6	32	7	259			333	369	702	10	81	31	0.58	259	50	19	31	77	7%	83	10%	4.29	-3.8	32	$9

2H h% collapse led the way, but there were other culprits: drop in ct%, continued below avg power and speed. Very telling... over the past 5 years, the only team that saw fit to keep him for a whole season was WAS.

Lopez,Jose

			AB	R	HR	RBI	SB	Avg	vL	vR	OB	Slg	OPS	bb%	ct%	h%	Eye	xBA	G	L	F	PX	hr/f	Spd	SBO	RC/G	RAR	BPV	R$
Pos	5	06 SEA	603	78	10	79	5	282	331	265	312	405	716	4	87	31	0.33	263	49	18	33	72	6%	116	5%	4.21	-13.6	49	$15
Age/B	27 Right	07 SEA	524	58	11	62	2	252	244	254	279	355	634	4	88	27	0.31	255	46	17	37	61	6%	99	4%	3.22	-25.6	39	$9
Ht/Wt	72 205	08 SEA	644	80	17	89	6	297	298	296	325	443	767	4	90	31	0.40	286	44	20	36	91	8%	79	6%	4.77	-2.0	65	$21
Health	A	09 SEA	613	69	25	96	3	272	286	266	300	463	763	4	89	27	0.35	288	41	19	41	110	11%	51	5%	4.66	-0.4	68	$18
PT/Exp	A	10 SEA	593	49	10	58	3	239	277	226	268	339	607	4	89	26	0.35	264	43	18	38	67	5%	56	4%	2.98	-32.8	35	$8
Consist	B	1st Half	322	27	5	31	3	242			272	332	604	4	89	26	0.35	263	45	19	36	60	5%	64	7%	2.94	-18.2	31	$5
LIMA Plan	C	2nd Half	271	22	5	27	0	236			263	347	610	4	89	25	0.34	266	41	18	41	74	5%	57	0%	3.03	-14.6	43	$3
Rand Var	+3	11 Proj	544	54	13	66	3	268			296	401	697	4	89	28	0.35	274	43	19	39	82	7%	65	4%	3.96	-13.3	50	$13

Just as he had clawed himself into a replacement-level 2Bman, he switched to 3B and -- BAM -- started hitting like a utility IFer. Some power and BA should return, but he has quite the cliff to scale to become a 3B asset.

Lowell,Mike

			AB	R	HR	RBI	SB	Avg	vL	vR	OB	Slg	OPS	bb%	ct%	h%	Eye	xBA	G	L	F	PX	hr/f	Spd	SBO	RC/G	RAR	BPV	R$
Pos	3	06 BOS	573	79	20	80	2	284	241	302	339	475	813	8	89	29	0.77	295	38	22	41	114	10%	68	3%	5.53	1.7	86	$17
Age/B	37 Right	07 BOS	589	79	21	120	3	324	323	325	380	501	881	8	88	34	0.75	279	36	18	46	107	9%	83	3%	6.29	16.1	81	$25
Ht/Wt	75 210	08 BOS	419	58	17	73	2	274	318	263	335	461	795	8	85	29	0.62	275	32	21	47	116	10%	63	4%	5.28	0.1	72	$14
Health	D	09 BOS	445	54	17	75	2	290	301	285	339	474	813	7	86	31	0.54	284	39	21	41	108	11%	66	3%	5.41	-3.7	67	$15
PT/Exp	C	10 BOS	218	23	5	26	0	239	224	250	311	367	678	10	84	26	0.68	250	31	18	51	89	5%	55	0%	4.03	-11.4	47	$4
Consist	B	1st Half	80	5	2	12	0	213			308	350	658	12	88	22	1.10	278	41	19	40	92	7%	51	0%	4.01	-4.3	65	$1
LIMA Plan		2nd Half	138	18	3	14	0	254			313	377	690	8	83	29	0.50	232	25	18	57	88	5%	74	0%	4.05	-7.0	41	$3
Rand Var		11 Proj	0	0	0	0	0	0																					

Health issues brought this formidable career to an end quickly. Resume includes two World Series titles, 4 All Star appearances, 1 Gold Glove. And a Fenway fan base forever.

Lowrie,Jed

			AB	R	HR	RBI	SB	Avg	vL	vR	OB	Slg	OPS	bb%	ct%	h%	Eye	xBA	G	L	F	PX	hr/f	Spd	SBO	RC/G	RAR	BPV	R$
Pos	46	06	0	0	0	0	0	0																					
Age/B	26 Both	07 a/a	497	71	10	60	4	288			371	471	842	12	84	33	0.85					126		107	6%	6.22	26.2	96	$14
Ht/Wt	72 180	08 BOS	* 458	62	6	72	2	253	338	222	340	395	734	12	77	32	0.57	254	32	25	43	111	4%	90	2%	4.88	-0.2	50	$10
Health	F	09 BOS	* 136	13	5	19	0	156	211	122	256	305	561	12	75	17	0.54	189	24	10	66	97	7%	81	0%	2.36	-11.6	28	($0)
PT/Exp	F	10 BOS	171	31	9	24	1	287	338	250	378	526	904	13	85	29	1.00	298	29	16	54	154	11%	78	4%	6.81	11.3	115	$8
Consist	F	1st Half	0	0	0	0	0	0																					
LIMA Plan	C+	2nd Half	171	31	9	24	1	287			378	526	904	13	85	29	1.00	298	29	16	54	154	11%	78	4%	6.81	11.3	115	$8
Rand Var	0	11 Proj	400	57	14	57	2	275			362	467	830	12	80	31	0.69	263	29	18	52	131	8%	81	3%	5.97	15.6	76	$13

Diagnosed with mono in spring training, didn't get an AB in BOS until July. Kissed performance concerns goodbye with notable gains in ct%, Eye and hr/f. Shaking the injury-prone label, securing AB the next tasks.

Lucroy,Jonathan

			AB	R	HR	RBI	SB	Avg	vL	vR	OB	Slg	OPS	bb%	ct%	h%	Eye	xBA	G	L	F	PX	hr/f	Spd	SBO	RC/G	RAR	BPV	R$
Pos	2	06	0	0	0	0	0	0																					
Age/B	24 Right	07	0	0	0	0	0	0																					
Ht/Wt	72 185	08	0	0	0	0	0	0																					
Health	A	09 aa	419	49	8	53	1	236			341	365	706	14	86	26	1.17					85		85	2%	4.68	5.2	69	$7
PT/Exp	F	10 MIL	* 399	36	6	38	4	257	284	241	299	339	638	6	85	29	0.41	246	44	19	38	55	5%	78	6%	3.33	-13.5	22	$8
Consist	C	1st Half	201	23	4	17	2	272			302	374	676	4	87	30	0.33	265	45	19	36	67	6%	85	8%	3.70	-4.5	37	$5
LIMA Plan	D	2nd Half	198	13	2	21	2	242			296	303	599	7	84	28	0.47	231	43	19	38	43	3%	83	4%	2.93	-9.1	11	$3
Rand Var	0	11 Proj	391	39	6	43	3	248			316	339	655	9	86	28	0.69	248	43	19	38	63	4%	77	4%	3.77	-7.0	36	$7

4-26-.253 in 277 AB at MIL. PRO: Sustained strong ct% upon promotion; improved bb% as year went on. CON: Poor power metrics got worse in 2H; xBA only lukewarm. Still young -- check back in a year or two.

Ludwick,Ryan

			AB	R	HR	RBI	SB	Avg	vL	vR	OB	Slg	OPS	bb%	ct%	h%	Eye	xBA	G	L	F	PX	hr/f	Spd	SBO	RC/G	RAR	BPV	R$
Pos	9	06 aaa	508	71	23	70	2	233			291	434	725	8	68	30	0.25					145		78	7%	4.51	-10.9	27	$11
Age/B	32 Right	07 STL	* 409	59	19	75	5	257	221	298	311	459	770	7	77	29	0.34	261	37	16	47	134	13%	72	10%	4.90	0.2	54	$14
Ht/Wt	75 218	08 STL	538	104	37	113	4	299	266	316	372	591	963	10	73	35	0.42	288	27	26	47	198	20%	82	6%	7.69	37.4	97	$30
Health	B	09 STL	486	63	22	97	4	265	269	264	323	447	769	8	78	30	0.39	243	33	18	49	115	12%	72	5%	4.87	-0.2	44	$18
PT/Exp	A	10 2NL	490	63	17	69	0	251	194	275	318	418	736	9	75	30	0.40	255	32	23	45	119	10%	91	3%	4.61	-10.5	44	$13
Consist	D	1st Half	264	40	11	42	0	273			331	485	816	8	77	32	0.38	275	30	22	48	149	11%	107	5%	5.59	2.0	77	$10
LIMA Plan	C	2nd Half	226	23	6	27	0	226			303	341	643	10	73	28	0.42	232	35	23	42	84	9%	69	2%	3.40	-13.3	3	$3
Rand Var	+1	11 Proj	424	58	16	70	2	257			323	429	752	9	75	31	0.39	248	32	22	46	119	11%	80	4%	4.78	-4.6	39	$13

Best to release 2008 to its h% and hr/f% party in the sky. What remains? Strong FB hitter with eroding contact. Awful 2nd half and SD disaster (.631 OPS) will reduce his suitors. Could struggle to repeat even 2010.

BRENT HERSHEY

Lugo,Julio

			AB	R	HR	RBI	SB	Avg	vL	vR	OB	Slg	OPS	bb%	ct%	h%	Eye	xBA	G	L	F	PX	hr/f	Spd	SBO	RC/G	RAR	BPV	R$
Pos	46	06 2TM	435	69	12	37	24	278	263	284	338	421	758	8	83	31	0.51	263	47	20	34	87	10%	136	27%	4.86	6.3	59	$16
Age/B	35 Right	07 BOS	570	71	8	73	33	237	226	241	296	349	645	8	86	26	0.59	263	46	17	37	78	4%	102	28%	3.62	-6.6	53	$15
Ht/Wt	73 175	08 BOS	261	27	1	22	12	268	283	264	353	330	682	12	80	33	0.67	247	60	18	23	51	2%	92	18%	4.18	-5.5	16	$6
Health	C	09 2TM	257	40	3	21	9	280	278	281	353	405	758	10	82	33	0.64	251	40	21	38	78	4%	167	11%	5.08	2.6	65	$8
PT/Exp	D	10 BAL	241	26	0	20	5	249	306	210	293	282	575	6	79	31	0.30	224	49	20	31	24	0%	148	17%	2.49	-14.5	-6	$4
Consist	D	1st Half	143	17	0	8	5	231			281	245	526	7	80	29	0.36	204	46	18	36	13	0%	109	24%	1.92	-11.5	-20	$2
LIMA Plan	F	2nd Half	98	9	0	12	0	276			311	337	647	5	78	36	0.23	250	53	24	24	40	0%	153	7%	3.37	-3.1	-0	$2
Rand Var	-1	11 Proj	194	23	1	18	5	263			320	334	655	8	80	32	0.43	243	49	20	31	50	2%	135	15%	3.63	-5.6	20	$4

Held out for most of Sept. with head injury after errant pickoff throw. Once a BA-and-SB guy, infrequent AB and age have sapped his value. Speed looks fine, but 42% success rate the true story. A non-factor.

Maier,Mitch

			AB	R	HR	RBI	SB	Avg	vL	vR	OB	Slg	OPS	bb%	ct%	h%	Eye	xBA	G	L	F	PX	hr/f	Spd	SBO	RC/G	RAR	BPV	R$
Pos	89	06 aa	543	70	10	68	10	257			297	385	681	5	86	28	0.40					78		98	19%	3.89	-10.9	49	$12
Age/B	28 Left	07 aa	544	58	10	48	5	233			268	349	617	5	85	26	0.32					73		114	6%	3.06	-24.2	44	$6
Ht/Wt	74 211	08 KC	* 436	54	6	41	9	279	273	293	320	387	707	6	87	31	0.46	276	48	22	30	71	6%	97	12%	4.20	-14.4	48	$11
Health	A	09 KC	* 387	48	4	39	10	245	299	224	330	339	669	11	78	31	0.58	224	42	18	40	65	3%	114	11%	3.95	-8.0	22	$7
PT/Exp	C	10 KC	373	41	5	39	3	263	221	274	336	375	711	10	82	31	0.60	238	39	17	44	74	4%	142	4%	4.46	-9.5	50	$8
Consist	A	1st Half	187	22	2	26	0	257			338	358	696	11	82	30	0.70	229	39	16	46	66	3%	132	2%	4.35	-5.4	46	$4
LIMA Plan	D	2nd Half	186	19	3	13	3	269			333	392	726	9	81	32	0.51	246	39	18	43	81	5%	139	7%	4.56	-4.1	51	$4
Rand Var	-2	11 Proj	287	33	4	28	5	261			328	368	696	9	82	31	0.55	238	40	18	42	71	4%	119	8%	4.21	-7.4	40	$6

Got more AB than expected due to injury and late-season deals. Maintained bb% and bumped up ct%, but xBA, BPV aren't impressed. Spd ascent begs for '07-'08 SBO to return; at 29, it's the best hope for future value.

Manzella,Tommy

			AB	R	HR	RBI	SB	Avg	vL	vR	OB	Slg	OPS	bb%	ct%	h%	Eye	xBA	G	L	F	PX	hr/f	Spd	SBO	RC/G	RAR	BPV	R$
Pos	6	06	0	0	0	0	0	0																					
Age/B	27 Right	07 aa	228	28	1	12	8	250			297	325	622	6	84	29	0.42					53		141	16%	3.24	-7.7	36	$4
Ht/Wt	74 190	08 a/a	452	32	3	35	3	210			249	291	540	5	87	24	0.39					54		119	13%	2.30	-31.3	38	$0
Health	B	09 aaa	530	48	6	40	8	234			273	333	607	5	84	27	0.34					65		122	10%	2.96	-25.6	37	$6
PT/Exp	D	10 HOU	* 299	23	2	25	0	236	290	201	272	288	560	5	74	31	0.19	220	53	18	29	44	3%	89	4%	2.13	-20.8	-29	$2
Consist	B	1st Half	189	13	1	16	0	212			251	254	505	5	70	30	0.18	200	53	17	30	38	3%	90	2%	1.34	-18.1	-51	$0
LIMA Plan	D	2nd Half	110	10	1	9	0	278			308	345	654	4	82	33	0.25	260	51	22	27	52	4%	98	6%	3.39	-3.3	10	$2
Rand Var	-3	11 Proj	399	35	3	30	3	241			278	315	593	5	81	29	0.27	249	52	19	28	55	3%	110	8%	2.72	-21.6	13	$4

1-21-.225 in 258 AB at HOU. Fractured finger interrupted his season; bat showed a little life upon return. He'll need every bit of that 2H ct% spike and h% help to provide value in the majors. The glove better be good.

Markakis,Nick

			AB	R	HR	RBI	SB	Avg	vL	vR	OB	Slg	OPS	bb%	ct%	h%	Eye	xBA	G	L	F	PX	hr/f	Spd	SBO	RC/G	RAR	BPV	R$
Pos	9	06 BAL	491	72	16	62	2	291	286	293	348	448	796	8	85	32	0.60	282	51	20	29	92	13%	99	1%	5.29	-5.0	63	$15
Age/B	27 Left	07 BAL	637	97	23	112	18	300	274	311	361	485	846	9	82	33	0.54	286	45	18	37	120	12%	101	13%	5.94	7.8	76	$28
Ht/Wt	74 195	08 BAL	599	106	20	88	10	304	297	310	403	487	890	14	81	35	0.87	289	46	21	33	126	12%	90	8%	6.86	24.9	82	$25
Health	A	09 BAL	642	94	18	101	6	293	262	314	350	453	803	8	85	32	0.57	268	43	17	41	100	8%	103	4%	5.41	1.4	68	$22
PT/Exp	A	10 BAL	629	79	12	60	7	297	361	269	370	436	806	10	85	33	0.78	283	46	18	36	97	6%	116	5%	5.65	12.1	76	$19
Consist	B	1st Half	303	34	4	27	2	307			400	436	836	13	84	36	0.96	281	44	19	36	98	4%	107	3%	6.23	10.6	75	$9
LIMA Plan	C+	2nd Half	326	45	8	33	5	288			341	436	776	7	87	31	0.59	285	47	17	37	96	8%	123	7%	5.08	1.2	77	$11
Rand Var	0	11 Proj	599	85	15	75	7	295			365	450	815	10	84	33	0.70	280	45	18	37	103	8%	104	6%	5.68	8.5	73	$20

Plate-skills rebound (bb%, Eye, xBA) encouraging, but power erosion at 26 continues to baffle. 1H hr/f partly to blame, but FB/ PX trends say a lot. Has to rebound some, but 10 SB more likely than 20 HR at this point.

Marson,Lou

			AB	R	HR	RBI	SB	Avg	vL	vR	OB	Slg	OPS	bb%	ct%	h%	Eye	xBA	G	L	F	PX	hr/f	Spd	SBO	RC/G	RAR	BPV	R$
Pos	2	06	0	0	0	0	0	0																					
Age/B	24 Right	07	0	0	0	0	0	0																					
Ht/Wt	73 198	08 aa	322	41	4	34	2	276			374	363	737	13	84	32	0.94					62		92	5%	4.97	7.2	40	$7
Health	A	09 CLE	* 375	42	2	30	3	246	111	269	324	328	652	10	81	30	0.61	250	46	22	32	62	2%	93	4%	3.77	-5.5	25	$4
PT/Exp	D	10 CLE	* 386	43	6	33	12	184	286	161	265	289	554	10	81	21	0.57	260	56	15	29	78	7%	89	15%	2.46	-21.0	33	$4
Consist	C	1st Half	186	22	2	14	4	181			263	271	535	10	73	24	0.42	240	58	15	27	79	5%	89	10%	2.04	-12.7	5	$1
LIMA Plan	F	2nd Half	200	22	4	19	8	187			266	305	572	10	87	20	0.86	278	54	15	31	77	7%	93	20%	2.91	-8.0	60	$3
Rand Var	+5	11 Proj	206	24	2	18	4	243			323	330	653	11	82	29	0.65	251	55	16	30	66	5%	83	8%	3.76	-2.8	28	$3

3-22-.195 with 8 SB in 262 AB at CLE. Despite proven bb%/ct% skills, he'll struggle for a second chance due to flimsy FB, PX and 2010's h% debacle. Then there's that uber-prospect issue. Finding AB will be a challenge.

Marte,Andy

			AB	R	HR	RBI	SB	Avg	vL	vR	OB	Slg	OPS	bb%	ct%	h%	Eye	xBA	G	L	F	PX	hr/f	Spd	SBO	RC/G	RAR	BPV	R$
Pos	35	06 CLE	* 521	69	19	69	1	246	227	225	310	433	742	8	78	28	0.42	250	34	17	48	125	9%	56	1%	4.66	-11.6	49	$11
Age/B	27 Right	07 CLE	* 409	44	14	60	0	237	278	154	274	396	671	5	84	25	0.32	252	29	19	52	99	8%	69	0%	3.60	-20.3	47	$7
Ht/Wt	73 205	08 CLE	235	21	3	17	1	221	293	198	265	315	580	6	78	27	0.27	206	34	16	49	69	3%	92	6%	2.51	-20.0	8	$1
Health	B	09 CLE	* 455	58	20	77	2	263	167	244	311	463	774	7	84	28	0.43	257	31	16	53	117	10%	76	2%	4.90	-10.7	66	$14
PT/Exp	D	10 CLE	170	18	5	19	0	229	290	194	299	382	682	9	79	26	0.49	239	35	15	50	99	7%	114	7%	3.94	-9.6	51	$3
Consist	A	1st Half	44	7	1	8	0	205			314	341	655	14	77	24	0.70	195	31	9	60	83	5%	122	8%	3.82	-2.7	42	$1
LIMA Plan	F	2nd Half	126	11	4	11	0	238			294	397	691	7	80	27	0.40	254	36	18	47	105	9%	103	7%	3.96	-7.0	52	$2
Rand Var	0	11 Proj	131	14	4	15	0	237			286	392	678	6	81	27	0.36	246	34	17	48	101	7%	94	4%	3.78	-7.3	47	$2

After '09 tease, reality returned:
- sub-80% contact rate
- lots of harmless fly balls
- clueless vs. righthanders

Walk rate trending the right way, but he's got to reach mediocrity first before setting the bar higher.

Martinez,Fernando

			AB	R	HR	RBI	SB	Avg	vL	vR	OB	Slg	OPS	bb%	ct%	h%	Eye	xBA	G	L	F	PX	hr/f	Spd	SBO	RC/G	RAR	BPV	R$
Pos	7	06	0	0	0	0	0	0																					
Age/B	22 Left	07 aa	236	31	3	20	2	278			333	380	713	8	85	32	0.54					68		115	12%	4.35	-5.9	44	$5
Ht/Wt	73 200	08 aa	352	43	6	39	5	271			318	397	715	6	83	31	0.42					82		112	8%	4.29	-8.5	48	$9
Health	C	09 NYM	* 267	31	7	32	4	234	158	181	272	398	671	5	85	25	0.35	265	52	10	38	110	8%	77	11%	3.72	-14.9	63	$5
PT/Exp	F	10 NYM	* 275	31	9	27	1	217		167	255	367	622	5	79	24	0.25	260	50	14	36	103	12%	75	4%	2.95	-18.0	34	$4
Consist	B	1st Half	147	14	3	13	1	227			247	357	605	3	82	26	0.16					95		84	4%	2.75	-10.4	39	$2
LIMA Plan	F	2nd Half	128	17	6	14	0	205			263	379	642	7	76	22	0.33	257	50	14	36	113	17%	84	4%	3.18	-7.6	36	$2
Rand Var	+5	11 Proj	132	16	5	14	1	250			293	419	712	6	82	27	0.33	262	51	12	37	109	13%	82	7%	4.09	-4.6	51	$3

0-2-.167 in 18 AB at NYM. Power is still promised, though injuries and several callups in '10 prevented an AB comfort zone. 2H PX, hr/f hint at the upside, though Eye needs work. Best case: a full year of AAA at-bats.

Martinez,Victor

			AB	R	HR	RBI	SB	Avg	vL	vR	OB	Slg	OPS	bb%	ct%	h%	Eye	xBA	G	L	F	PX	hr/f	Spd	SBO	RC/G	RAR	BPV	R$
Pos	2	06 CLE	572	82	16	93	0	316	290	332	392	465	857	11	86	35	0.91	278	44	22	34	92	9%	55	0%	6.23	27.9	60	$20
Age/B	32 Both	07 CLE	562	78	25	114	0	301	289	307	370	505	876	10	86	31	0.82	304	42	20	38	126	13%	49	0%	6.31	31.2	83	$22
Ht/Wt	74 210	08 CLE	266	30	2	35	0	278	339	260	338	365	703	8	88	31	0.75	266	45	22	33	64	3%	66	0%	4.37	1.4	41	$5
Health	C	09 2AL	588	88	23	108	1	303	273	316	382	480	861	11	87	32	1.01	290	43	21	35	101	13%	67	1%	6.25	31.8	75	$23
PT/Exp	B	10 BOS	493	64	20	79	1	302	400	257	355	493	847	8	89	31	0.77	300	41	17	42	116	11%	72	1%	5.85	22.8	89	$20
Consist	C	1st Half	246	36	9	38	1	289			347	480	827	8	90	29	0.88	317	44	19	37	122	11%	55	2%	5.71	10.6	92	$9
LIMA Plan	B	2nd Half	247	28	11	41	0	316			362	506	868	7	89	32	0.67	283	38	15	47	111	11%	98	0%	5.99	12.2	90	$11
Rand Var	0	11 Proj	506	67	19	83	1	300			362	480	842	9	88	31	0.83	293	42	19	39	108	11%	68	0%	5.88	23.1	80	$19

Expect CA-vs-1B talk to continue to escalate as he ages--though his desire to remain behind the plate is cause for fanalytic rejoicing. BPIs stable, though FB spike opens the door for a HR increase. A lock to return value.

Martin,Russell

			AB	R	HR	RBI	SB	Avg	vL	vR	OB	Slg	OPS	bb%	ct%	h%	Eye	xBA	G	L	F	PX	hr/f	Spd	SBO	RC/G	RAR	BPV	R$
Pos	2	06 LA	* 489	76	10	72	10	278	366	265	351	425	776	10	87	31	0.83	283	50	20	30	90	8%	71	12%	5.30	13.5	62	$16
Age/B	28 Right	07 LA	540	87	19	87	21	293	357	273	371	469	839	11	84	32	0.75	283	48	18	34	108	12%	86	18%	5.99	24.0	70	$24
Ht/Wt	70 210	08 LA	553	87	13	69	18	280	253	291	381	396	777	14	85	31	1.08	262	51	19	30	73	9%	67	12%	5.46	19.7	49	$21
Health	C	09 LA	505	63	7	53	11	250	275	243	340	329	668	12	84	28	0.86	247	49	21	31	54	5%	75	10%	4.05	-3.2	28	$11
PT/Exp	B	10 LA	331	45	5	26	6	248	235	252	343	332	675	13	82	29	0.79	256	51	21	28	60	7%	64	7%	4.11	-3.7	21	$7
Consist	B	1st Half	261	40	4	18	6	245			346	326	671	13	82	29	0.83	252	52	20	29	56	7%	75	9%	4.08	-3.1	23	$6
LIMA Plan	D+	2nd Half	70	5	1	8	0	257			333	357	690	10	81	30	0.62	277	49	25	26	76	7%	55	0%	4.19	-0.6	25	$1
Rand Var	+1	11 Proj	418	51	7	45	7	258			347	357	704	12	83	30	0.80	262	50	21	29	69	7%	59	8%	4.45	0.9	31	$10

Avoided surgery on hip injury that ended his season in Aug. 2010 rates a copy of 2009 -- which was the bottom of a 2-yr skills slide. Assuming health, no reason to expect anything different in 2011.

BRENT HERSHEY

Mathis,Jeff

			AB	R	HR	RBI	SB	Avg	vL	vR	OB	Slg	OPS	bb%	ct%	h%	Eye	xBA	G	L	F	PX	hr/f	Spd	SBO	RC/G	RAR	BPV	R$
Pos	2	06 LAA	* 439	57	6	41	2	241	133	150	285	364	650	6	83	28	0.37	211	29	12	59	85	3%	77	3%	3.52	-11.6	39	$5
Age/B	28 Right	07 LAA	* 421	57	8	45	3	214	242	203	265	332	597	6	78	26	0.32	228	42	13	45	87	5%	88	6%	2.77	-19.8	23	$4
Ht/Wt	72 200	08 LAA	283	35	9	42	2	194	224	184	272	318	590	10	68	25	0.33	183	36	11	53	90	9%	84	6%	2.58	-14.5	-9	$4
Health	B	09 LAA	237	26	5	28	2	211	228	203	278	308	586	8	69	28	0.30	193	37	17	46	71	7%	90	8%	2.55	-12.8	-20	$2
PT/Exp	D	10 LAA	* 238	23	4	21	3	195	204	192	223	289	512	4	72	25	0.13	196	39	13	48	69	5%	117	7%	1.40	-20.8	-13	$1
Consist	B	1st Half	75	10	2	7	2	253			291	373	664	5	72	33	0.19	216	43	13	44	91	8%	100	11%	3.48	-1.5	3	$2
LIMA Plan	F	2nd Half	163	13	2	14	1	167			191	250	441	3	72	22	0.10	186	37	13	49	59	3%	120	4%	0.44	-19.8	-22	($1)
Rand Var	0	11 Proj	197	21	4	21	2	208			256	316	572	6	72	27	0.23	200	38	14	48	78	6%	102	7%	2.30	-11.8	-6	$2

3-18.195 in 205 AB at LAA. Two months off for a broken wrist and still got 150 AB too many. Woeful LD and declining Eye says that, even at 28, a rebound is unlikely. Profile has "Future Managerial Candidate" written all over it.

Matsui,Hideki

			AB	R	HR	RBI	SB	Avg	vL	vR	OB	Slg	OPS	bb%	ct%	h%	Eye	xBA	G	L	F	PX	hr/f	Spd	SBO	RC/G	RAR	BPV	R$
Pos	0	06 NYY	172	32	8	29	1	302	226	336	397	494	891	14	87	31	1.17	270	39	17	44	108	12%	80	2%	6.70	1.3	86	$7
Age/B	36 Left	07 NYY	547	100	25	103	4	285	274	290	369	488	857	12	87	29	1.00	292	43	17	40	117	13%	100	3%	6.21	-0.4	96	$22
Ht/Wt	74 210	08 NYY	337	43	9	45	0	294	315	284	365	424	790	10	86	32	0.81	265	47	19	34	82	9%	55	0%	5.36	4.1	49	$10
Health	C	09 NYY	456	62	28	90	0	274	282	271	363	509	872	12	84	27	0.85	288	38	20	42	130	17%	66	1%	6.32	15.0	84	$18
PT/Exp	B	10 LAA	482	55	21	84	0	274	236	289	362	459	821	12	80	31	0.68	273	39	19	42	121	13%	57	1%	5.79	-7.8	59	$17
Consist	B	1st Half	277	24	10	46	0	260			337	415	752	10	76	31	0.48	244	37	17	46	110	10%	47	0%	4.84	-12.1	28	$8
LIMA Plan	C+	2nd Half	205	31	11	38	0	293			396	517	913	15	85	30	1.13	313	43	20	37	136	17%	74	1%	7.01	3.8	101	$9
Rand Var	0	11 Proj	430	58	20	76	0	281			370	476	846	12	83	30	0.83	282	41	19	40	118	14%	64	1%	6.08	2.9	72	$16

A repeat of 2009 minus a bit of thump. Second half showed what a return of ct% can do for BA, but increase in GB wiped out hopes of a power surge. Similar season in 2011 plausible, but don't overcommit.

Mauer,Joe

			AB	R	HR	RBI	SB	Avg	vL	vR	OB	Slg	OPS	bb%	ct%	h%	Eye	xBA	G	L	F	PX	hr/f	Spd	SBO	RC/G	RAR	BPV	R$
Pos	20	06 MIN	521	86	13	84	8	347	331	356	433	507	940	13	90	37	1.46	312	49	25	26	94	11%	100	5%	7.38	40.0	92	$24
Age/B	27 Left	07 MIN	406	62	7	60	7	293	283	299	380	426	806	12	87	32	1.12	296	55	18	28	87	7%	110	6%	5.80	17.1	79	$13
Ht/Wt	77 225	08 MIN	536	98	9	85	1	328	361	312	419	451	871	14	91	35	1.68	296	49	23	28	76	7%	95	1%	6.66	34.9	81	$21
Health	B	09 MIN	523	94	28	96	4	365	345	376	446	587	1033	13	88	38	1.21	319	48	22	30	121	20%	75	2%	8.26	52.1	99	$31
PT/Exp	A	10 MIN	510	88	9	75	1	327	272	365	403	469	872	11	90	35	1.23	320	47	24	29	99	7%	75	3%	6.52	32.1	85	$22
Consist	D	1st Half	271	44	3	34	1	303			378	432	810	11	90	33	1.22	317	45	25	30	94	4%	72	3%	5.83	12.5	80	$9
LIMA Plan	B+	2nd Half	239	44	6	41	0	356			432	510	942	12	89	38	1.23	324	49	23	27	105	10%	83	2%	7.30	19.2	91	$13
Rand Var	0	11 Proj	509	90	12	82	2	334			415	481	896	12	89	36	1.28	310	48	23	29	94	9%	82	3%	6.81	34.8	83	$23

A testament to the affects of hr/f. Impeccable overall hitting skills, but '09 power an abberation. Multiple injuries (shoulder, heel hip, knee) highlight positional risk. Still a star in growth mode, but G/L/F caps value for now.

Maxwell,Justin

			AB	R	HR	RBI	SB	Avg	vL	vR	OB	Slg	OPS	bb%	ct%	h%	Eye	xBA	G	L	F	PX	hr/f	Spd	SBO	RC/G	RAR	BPV	R$
Pos	89	06	0	0	0	0	0	0																					
Age/B	27 Right	07	0	0	0	0	0	0																					
Ht/Wt	77 235	08 aa	146	27	5	21	10	191			301	348	649	14	84	19	1.01					89		128	37%	3.86	-5.7	76	$4
Health	A	09 WAS	* 473	68	14	43	34	217	242	250	299	355	654	10	68	29	0.36	212	48	14	38	97	12%	149	35%	3.60	-16.8	16	$15
PT/Exp	D	10 WAS	* 334	44	8	29	18	213	155	130	320	343	663	14	67	30	0.47	211	35	16	49	115	7%	84	28%	3.92	-10.3	13	$8
Consist	A	1st Half	197	22	4	15	8	226			340	335	675	15	69	31	0.55	214	29	24	48	93	6%	91	26%	4.12	-4.9	8	$4
LIMA Plan	D	2nd Half	137	21	4	14	9	194			290	355	645	12	64	27	0.37	218	38	12	50	148	9%	79	31%	3.66	-5.3	23	$4
Rand Var	-2	11 Proj	123	18	4	12	8	211			308	366	674	12	69	27	0.45	219	39	14	46	116	9%	107	32%	3.96	-3.2	28	$4

3-12-.144 with 5 SB in 104 AB in WAS. Poor ct% in majors (59%) mars potential results. Ability to take a walk provides SB opps, but Spd trend says those skills waning. OK flyer in the end-game, nothing more.

Maybin,Cameron

			AB	R	HR	RBI	SB	Avg	vL	vR	OB	Slg	OPS	bb%	ct%	h%	Eye	xBA	G	L	F	PX	hr/f	Spd	SBO	RC/G	RAR	BPV	R$
Pos	8	06	0	0	0	0	0	0																					
Age/B	24 Right	07 DET	* 69	17	4	10	5	203		200	298	436	733	12	61	26	0.35	243	54	4	43	191	22%	106	33%	4.97	0.9	56	$3
Ht/Wt	75 206	08 FLA	* 422	70	11	43	22	272	375	542	358	423	782	12	72	35	0.48	265	50	29	21	101	17%	200	22%	5.46	9.0	55	$17
Health	A	09 FLA	* 474	69	7	47	8	281	254	248	352	424	776	10	78	35	0.50	263	55	17	28	100	7%	141	9%	5.30	7.7	55	$14
PT/Exp	C	10 FLA	* 421	62	11	45	13	252	222	238	308	377	685	7	74	32	0.30	239	53	14	33	85	11%	150	14%	3.88	-12.6	24	$13
Consist	B	1st Half	182	31	5	19	6	225			281	341	621	7	69	30	0.25	227	57	14	30	82	13%	130	16%	2.98	-10.7	-2	$5
LIMA Plan	B	2nd Half	239	31	6	26	7	273			329	405	734	8	77	33	0.36	241	47	15	38	87	8%	153	13%	4.53	-2.5	40	$8
Rand Var	0	11 Proj	446	66	12	46	13	267			332	417	749	9	75	33	0.39	253	53	15	31	100	12%	152	14%	4.82	0.4	45	$15

8-28-.234 with 9 SB in 291 AB in FLA. Over the last 2 seasons, ct% has been his nemesis: 81% in AAA; 70% in MLB. Tools still ooze, and Spd confirms he has elite wheels. But still 24; be prepared to wait.

May,Lucas

			AB	R	HR	RBI	SB	Avg	vL	vR	OB	Slg	OPS	bb%	ct%	h%	Eye	xBA	G	L	F	PX	hr/f	Spd	SBO	RC/G	RAR	BPV	R$
Pos	2	06	0	0	0	0	0	0																					
Age/B	26 Right	07	0	0	0	0	0	0																					
Ht/Wt	72 190	08 aa	392	41	11	41	5	200			249	348	596	6	76	24	0.27					106		89	9%	2.68	-18.7	30	$4
Health	A	09 aa	235	26	5	26	2	270			342	404	747	10	77	33	0.48					98		92	4%	4.86	4.0	35	$5
PT/Exp	F	10 KC	* 412	48	10	48	3	234	100	222	280	366	646	6	82	26	0.35	231	39	11	50	89	6%	87	6%	3.37	-9.9	38	$8
Consist	D	1st Half	224	24	7	25	1	235			272	361	633	5	84	25	0.32					80		84	8%	3.15	-6.9	38	$4
LIMA Plan	F	2nd Half	188	24	4	23	2	232			289	373	662	7	78	28	0.37	232	39	11	50	102	5%	98	5%	3.66	-2.8	41	$4
Rand Var	0	11 Proj	129	15	2	15	1	240			298	364	662	8	79	29	0.39	218	39	11	50	87	5%	103	5%	3.67	-2.1	32	$2

0-6-.189 in 37 AB in KC. Overmatched in first exposure, but can't dismiss power history and improving contact. Unlikely to help in 2011, and a longshot even after that.

McCann,Brian

			AB	R	HR	RBI	SB	Avg	vL	vR	OB	Slg	OPS	bb%	ct%	h%	Eye	xBA	G	L	F	PX	hr/f	Spd	SBO	RC/G	RAR	BPV	R$
Pos	2	06 ATL	442	61	24	93	2	333	266	351	389	572	962	8	88	34	0.76	304	35	22	43	135	14%	46	2%	7.16	32.6	92	$23
Age/B	27 Left	07 ATL	504	51	18	92	0	270	264	273	317	452	770	6	85	29	0.47	281	39	19	43	115	10%	42	1%	4.90	6.8	61	$14
Ht/Wt	75 230	08 ATL	509	68	23	87	5	301	299	301	371	523	894	10	87	31	0.89	298	37	20	43	135	12%	56	3%	6.55	32.7	97	$22
Health	A	09 ATL	488	63	21	94	4	281	225	308	346	486	832	9	83	30	0.59	284	38	21	41	131	13%	50	4%	5.76	20.8	72	$20
PT/Exp	A	10 ATL	479	63	21	77	5	269	263	272	367	453	820	13	80	30	0.76	272	37	20	43	122	13%	51	4%	5.84	18.7	60	$18
Consist	A	1st Half	234	38	10	34	3	265			370	449	819	14	80	29	0.85	272	34	21	46	122	12%	64	5%	5.88	9.5	68	$9
LIMA Plan	C	2nd Half	245	25	11	43	2	273			364	457	821	12	79	31	0.67	271	40	20	40	121	14%	51	4%	5.80	9.3	55	$9
Rand Var	0	11 Proj	498	63	22	87	4	265			347	462	809	11	82	28	0.70	281	37	20	42	127	13%	47	4%	5.58	17.4	69	$18

HR/RBI numbers tell familiar story, but BA and xBA are on a two-year slide. Unless ct% reverses course, his .300 BA days are over. Power indicators consistent, but this skill set has lost some of its luster.

McCutchen,Andrew

			AB	R	HR	RBI	SB	Avg	vL	vR	OB	Slg	OPS	bb%	ct%	h%	Eye	xBA	G	L	F	PX	hr/f	Spd	SBO	RC/G	RAR	BPV	R$
Pos	8	06	0	0	0	0	0	0																					
Age/B	24 Right	07 aa	513	68	9	47	19	260			316	373	688	8	86	29	0.57					72		119	17%	4.06	-7.1	52	$13
Ht/Wt	71 175	08 aa	512	66	7	44	30	270			345	371	716	10	86	30	0.80					67		110	32%	4.58	-7.3	52	$17
Health	A	09 PIT	* 634	108	15	71	30	284	310	279	353	456	809	10	84	32	0.67	268	42	19	39	105	7%	176	20%	5.65	16.6	94	$27
PT/Exp	B	10 PIT	570	94	16	56	33	286	324	273	364	449	813	11	84	32	0.79	284	43	19	38	106	9%	143	24%	5.72	13.6	89	$27
Consist	B	1st Half	302	50	7	24	20	295			374	444	817	11	81	34	0.68	265	43	18	39	98	7%	177	26%	5.80	7.9	82	$15
LIMA Plan	B+	2nd Half	268	44	9	32	13	276			353	455	809	11	88	29	0.97	304	44	20	37	114	10%	102	22%	5.65	5.9	96	$12
Rand Var	0	11 Proj	566	89	17	58	30	290			362	460	822	10	85	32	0.75	280	43	19	38	105	9%	146	23%	5.77	15.8	90	$26

First full MLB season capped by an eye-opening Sept (.965 OPS, 1.89 Eye). Second half spike in ct% points to possible .300 BA future. The explosion is still a year or two away, but impressive breadth of skills in place already.

McDonald,Darnell

			AB	R	HR	RBI	SB	Avg	vL	vR	OB	Slg	OPS	bb%	ct%	h%	Eye	xBA	G	L	F	PX	hr/f	Spd	SBO	RC/G	RAR	BPV	R$
Pos	789	06 aaa	538	71	12	50	27	260			312	387	699	7	79	31	0.36					85		77	28%	4.05	-18.7	22	$16
Age/B	32 Right	07 aaa	491	65	7	67	31	269			328	381	708	8	78	33	0.39					80		108	27%	4.29	-13.0	25	$18
Ht/Wt	71 208	08 aaa	369	38	8	41	14	212			262	343	605	6	78	25	0.30					91		89	22%	2.85	-26.3	25	$6
Health	A	09 CIN	* 385	43	10	39	7	254	365	170	285	418	703	4	77	31	0.19	258	47	18	35	114	9%	116	13%	4.02	-17.6	44	$9
PT/Exp	D	10 BOS	* 360	44	11	40	10	272	294	247	331	449	780	8	74	34	0.34	268	42	19	39	131	10%	100	12%	5.23	3.6	51	$12
Consist	C	1st Half	218	23	7	26	7	266			315	430	745	7	76	32	0.30	267	44	18	37	121	11%	83	13%	4.63	-1.6	41	$7
LIMA Plan	F	2nd Half	142	21	4	14	3	282			354	479	833	10	72	37	0.40	268	39	21	40	148	10%	113	10%	6.19	5.3	62	$5
Rand Var	-2	11 Proj	195	24	6	21	6	262			314	430	744	7	75	32	0.31	259	42	19	39	118	10%	97	15%	4.68	-1.5	42	$6

9-34-.270 with 9 SB in 319 AB in BOS. Almost DFA'd, he ended up as part of BOS OF rotation and extended his career in the process. Ct% shows limits, but pop, speed and success vs. LH are assets in a reserve role.

BRENT HERSHEY

McDonald,John			AB	R	HR	RBI	SB	Avg	vL	vR	OB	Slg	OPS	bb%	ct%	h%	Eye	xBA	G	L	F	PX	hr/f	Spd	SBO	RC/G	RAR	BPV	R$
Pos	4	06 TOR	260	35	3	23	7	223	230	220	268	308	576	6	84	25	0.39	238	48	18	34	49	4%	125	15%	2.63	-11.9	27	$3
Age/B	36 Right	07 TOR	327	32	1	31	7	251	329	223	275	333	608	3	85	29	0.23	259	40	23	37	62	1%	103	13%	2.95	-10.2	30	$5
Ht/Wt	70 177	08 TOR	186	21	1	18	3	210	250	184	250	269	519	5	87	24	0.40	219	42	15	43	44	1%	77	10%	2.03	-16.6	17	$1
Health	B	09 TOR	151	18	4	13	0	258	260	257	263	384	647	1	88	27	0.06	239	32	17	50	73	6%	93	7%	3.16	-7.9	42	$3
PT/Exp	F	10 TOR	152	27	6	23	2	250	250	250	278	454	732	4	83	27	0.23	286	34	20	45	129	11%	108	11%	4.29	-0.8	77	$5
Consist	C	1st Half	60	9	1	5	0	217			242	383	625	3	85	24	0.22	282	38	18	44	115	4%	93	0%	3.18	-2.4	68	$1
LIMA Plan	F	2nd Half	92	18	5	18	2	272			302	500	802	4	82	29	0.24	288	32	22	46	138	14%	113	16%	5.05	1.6	81	$5
Rand Var	+1	11 Proj	135	20	4	16	2	244			269	394	663	3	85	26	0.23	260	36	19	45	93	7%	99	10%	3.48	-4.5	52	$3

Impressive power/speed combo in 2nd half... but had he posted those 92 AB at age 25 instead of 35, he might have ended up as more than a Professional Free Agent in fantasy leagues.

McGehee,Casey			AB	R	HR	RBI	SB	Avg	vL	vR	OB	Slg	OPS	bb%	ct%	h%	Eye	xBA	G	L	F	PX	hr/f	Spd	SBO	RC/G	RAR	BPV	R$
Pos	5	06 aaa	497	51	11	62	0	266			318	390	708	7	87	29	0.58					76		82	2%	4.27	-14.1	49	$9
Age/B	28 Right	07 a/a	436	45	9	48	1	229			283	355	639	7	83	26	0.44					85		102	4%	3.41	-24.4	46	$5
Ht/Wt	73 195	08 aaa	497	49	9	66	0	248			288	357	646	5	85	28	0.38					73		77	3%	3.41	-25.4	35	$8
Health	A	09 MIL	355	58	16	66	0	301	303	301	362	499	861	9	81	33	0.51	274	38	22	40	125	14%	93	2%	6.07	9.1	71	$16
PT/Exp	C	10 MIL	610	70	23	104	1	285	316	274	339	464	803	8	83	31	0.49	287	47	17	36	117	13%	72	1%	5.33	7.3	66	$22
Consist	D	1st Half	300	35	13	52	1	270			336	460	796	9	82	29	0.57	281	47	15	38	124	14%	66	3%	5.31	3.5	68	$11
LIMA Plan	C	2nd Half	310	35	10	52	0	300			342	468	810	6	84	33	0.41	293	48	19	33	111	12%	83	0%	5.34	3.7	64	$12
Rand Var	0	11 Proj	593	73	24	97	0	282			334	465	799	7	83	30	0.47	282	44	19	37	116	13%	78	2%	5.25	2.6	66	$21

Proved '09 power jump was no fluke, despite hitting a lot more ground balls. If that doesn't change, power upside will be limited. But he kills lefties (.947 OPS in 2010), and can still provide solid value.

McLouth,Nate			AB	R	HR	RBI	SB	Avg	vL	vR	OB	Slg	OPS	bb%	ct%	h%	Eye	xBA	G	L	F	PX	hr/f	Spd	SBO	RC/G	RAR	BPV	R$
Pos	8	06 PIT	270	50	7	16	10	233	260	227	281	385	666	6	78	27	0.31	259	39	25	35	99	9%	138	20%	3.63	-6.6	48	$6
Age/B	29 Left	07 PIT	329	62	13	38	22	258	269	256	337	459	796	11	77	30	0.51	246	31	16	53	132	10%	134	26%	5.47	9.1	75	$14
Ht/Wt	71 180	08 PIT	597	113	26	94	23	276	261	282	347	497	845	10	84	29	0.70	280	35	19	47	137	11%	98	17%	5.98	21.2	98	$28
Health	C	09 2TM	507	86	20	70	19	256	230	269	344	436	780	12	80	28	0.69	255	40	16	43	112	11%	86	17%	5.28	8.9	63	$20
PT/Exp	B	10 ATL	* 370	43	10	37	12	189	135	205	280	313	593	11	79	21	0.61	234	40	16	44	82	8%	86	15%	2.89	-23.7	32	$6
Consist	D	1st Half	170	20	3	14	4	176			286	282	568	13	73	22	0.57	217	38	17	45	86	5%	81	14%	2.56	-13.0	13	$1
LIMA Plan	C+	2nd Half	200	23	7	23	8	199			275	339	614	10	84	20	0.67	252	45	15	40	79	11%	103	17%	3.16	-10.9	52	$5
Rand Var	+5	11 Proj	437	65	15	52	16	254			334	415	750	11	80	29	0.62	251	39	17	44	104	10%	93	15%	4.86	0.9	56	$16

6-24-.190 with 7 SB in 242 AB at ATL. Got off to terrible start, then missed 6 weeks with a concussion before demotion to minors. Strong Sept. (156 PX), and young enough to rebound, but questions vs LH remain.

Michaels,Jason			AB	R	HR	RBI	SB	Avg	vL	vR	OB	Slg	OPS	bb%	ct%	h%	Eye	xBA	G	L	F	PX	hr/f	Spd	SBO	RC/G	RAR	BPV	R$
Pos	7	06 CLE	494	77	9	55	9	267	291	252	326	391	717	8	80	32	0.43	250	40	23	38	87	6%	80	11%	4.37	-11.6	30	$12
Age/B	34 Right	07 CLE	267	43	7	39	3	270	287	252	321	397	718	7	81	31	0.40	237	37	17	46	82	7%	104	10%	4.27	-6.0	38	$8
Ht/Wt	72 206	08 2TM	286	28	8	53	2	224	187	241	291	360	651	9	77	26	0.42	234	38	19	43	92	8%	68	4%	3.49	-14.4	22	$5
Health	A	09 HOU	135	17	4	16	1	237	268	215	318	430	748	11	72	30	0.42	249	31	21	48	151	9%	76	10%	4.99	-2.4	54	$3
PT/Exp	F	10 HOU	186	23	8	26	0	253	275	232	298	468	766	6	84	26	0.41	291	34	18	48	138	11%	65	0%	4.82	-1.4	82	$5
Consist	B	1st Half	93	10	5	14	0	247			255	473	728	1	84	25	0.07	278	36	14	49	132	13%	77	0%	4.00	-2.9	69	$3
LIMA Plan	F	2nd Half	93	13	3	12	0	258			337	462	799	11	85	28	0.79	304	31	21	48	145	8%	67	0%	5.56	1.3	99	$3
Rand Var	+3	11 Proj	188	24	6	26	1	245			306	431	737	8	80	28	0.44	266	34	19	47	128	9%	70	4%	4.60	-3.7	61	$5

Drew just 1 walk in first half, but eventually managed to raise Eye to remarkably consistent level. Showed '09 power wasn't total fluke, but regression is likely, and regular at-bats could be hard to come by.

Miles,Aaron			AB	R	HR	RBI	SB	Avg	vL	vR	OB	Slg	OPS	bb%	ct%	h%	Eye	xBA	G	L	F	PX	hr/f	Spd	SBO	RC/G	RAR	BPV	R$
Pos	4	06 STL	426	48	2	30	2	263	291	256	323	347	671	8	90	29	0.90	279	55	20	25	51	2%	120	2%	4.09	-6.3	56	$5
Age/B	34 Both	07 STL	414	55	2	32	2	290	286	292	330	348	678	6	90	32	0.63	264	54	18	28	39	2%	106	2%	3.96	-8.6	38	$8
Ht/Wt	68 180	08 STL	379	49	4	31	3	317	315	317	356	398	754	6	90	34	0.62	277	54	21	25	51	5%	118	5%	4.78	0.1	50	$12
Health	B	09 CHC	* 244	23	0	11	4	189	206	179	220	239	459	4	86	22	0.28	243	50	20	30	40	0%	81	13%	1.27	-25.5	8	($1)
PT/Exp	F	10 STL	* 200	22	0	18	0	259	281	280	295	297	591	5	89	29	0.49	234	54	13	34	32	0%	87	3%	2.94	-11.1	21	$3
Consist	F	1st Half	91	11	0	10	0	239			288	289	577	6	89	27	0.62	215	59	4	37	42	0%	80	4%	2.88	-5.3	28	$1
LIMA Plan	F	2nd Half	109	11	0	8	0	275			301	303	604	4	90	31	0.36	235	52	15	33	23	0%	90	3%	2.98	-5.8	14	$2
Rand Var	-1	11 Proj	128	14	0	9	0	250			287	296	583	5	89	28	0.45	246	53	17	30	36	1%	84	4%	2.81	-7.3	20	$1

0-9-.281 in 139 AB at STL. Keeps finding a job, despite the fact that the only thing he does well is make contact. It's been 321 at-bats since his last home run, and speed isn't coming back.

Milledge,Lastings			AB	R	HR	RBI	SB	Avg	vL	vR	OB	Slg	OPS	bb%	ct%	h%	Eye	xBA	G	L	F	PX	hr/f	Spd	SBO	RC/G	RAR	BPV	R$
Pos	79	06 NYM	* 473	70	11	61	15	275	241	241	355	429	783	11	79	33	0.60	263	44	22	34	99	8%	119	20%	5.39	1.9	57	$15
Age/B	26 Right	07 NYM	* 246	41	10	40	8	289	317	250	330	472	801	6	78	34	0.27	283	47	24	29	113	18%	127	16%	5.21	-1.0	53	$11
Ht/Wt	72 203	08 WAS	523	65	14	61	24	268	258	272	317	402	719	7	82	31	0.40	255	45	20	35	85	9%	88	24%	4.28	-17.5	37	$19
Health	A	09 2TM	* 383	35	4	30	15	270	327	265	309	358	667	5	82	32	0.31	240	41	21	38	65	3%	72	22%	3.64	-18.5	14	$9
PT/Exp	C	10 PIT	379	38	4	34	5	277	320	256	327	380	707	7	84	32	0.45	264	49	19	33	73	4%	94	8%	4.25	-8.9	37	$9
Consist	B	1st Half	239	21	1	24	4	268			335	364	699	9	81	33	0.52	259	49	19	32	77	2%	88	10%	4.31	-5.3	31	$5
LIMA Plan	D+	2nd Half	140	17	3	10	1	293			312	407	720	3	89	31	0.25	272	48	18	34	68	7%	106	3%	4.13	-3.7	48	$4
Rand Var	0	11 Proj	419	47	8	39	11	277			319	397	716	6	83	32	0.37	262	46	19	34	79	7%	90	14%	4.24	-12.5	37	$12

The only thing good about '10 was the small sign of life in the 2nd half. For a player who does have some talent, allegedly, that might be enough to project productive stats in '11. But I'm not ready to take a leap of faith.

Molina,Bengie			AB	R	HR	RBI	SB	Avg	vL	vR	OB	Slg	OPS	bb%	ct%	h%	Eye	xBA	G	L	F	PX	hr/f	Spd	SBO	RC/G	RAR	BPV	R$
Pos	2	06 TOR	433	44	19	57	1	284	358	246	314	467	781	4	89	28	0.40	290	39	23	38	99	13%	39	2%	4.84	5.3	58	$12
Age/B	36 Right	07 SF	497	38	19	81	0	276	271	277	297	433	729	3	89	28	0.28	269	37	19	44	85	10%	49	0%	4.20	-3.3	48	$13
Ht/Wt	71 225	08 SF	530	47	16	95	0	292	297	291	317	445	762	3	93	29	0.50	266	35	18	47	90	7%	35	0%	4.72	7.4	62	$17
Health	A	09 SF	491	52	20	80	0	265	277	261	284	442	726	3	86	27	0.19	252	31	17	53	106	9%	35	0%	4.10	-2.3	47	$15
PT/Exp	B	10 2TM	377	27	5	36	0	249	350	213	294	326	621	6	91	26	0.71	232	35	17	48	48	3%	46	0%	3.34	-10.8	30	$5
Consist	B	1st Half	211	17	3	17	0	256			305	327	632	7	91	27	0.75	235	38	18	45	44	4%	39	0%	3.48	-5.2	25	$3
LIMA Plan	D	2nd Half	166	10	2	19	0	241			280	325	605	5	92	25	0.64	228	32	15	52	52	3%	58	0%	3.17	-5.7	38	$2
Rand Var	0	11 Proj	368	30	10	49	0	261			293	387	681	4	90	27	0.46	249	34	17	49	75	6%	42	0%	3.84	-4.9	43	$8

Contact rate bounced back, but typical, consistent power fell off a cliff. Still hit the ball in air, but it rarely left the park. Expect some rebound, though at his age, can't bank on full return to form.

Molina,Jose			AB	R	HR	RBI	SB	Avg	vL	vR	OB	Slg	OPS	bb%	ct%	h%	Eye	xBA	G	L	F	PX	hr/f	Spd	SBO	RC/G	RAR	BPV	R$
Pos	2	06 LAA	225	18	4	22	1	240	218	254	269	369	638	4	78	29	0.18	240	42	18	39	96	6%	45	2%	3.18	-8.3	13	$2
Age/B	35 Right	07 2AL	191	18	1	19	2	257	360	220	276	340	616	3	77	33	0.12	253	48	23	29	73	2%	60	8%	2.84	-8.1	-7	$2
Ht/Wt	74 235	08 NYY	268	32	3	18	0	216	188	230	250	313	563	4	81	26	0.23	246	48	19	33	75	4%	54	0%	2.32	-15.4	9	$1
Health	B	09 NYY	138	15	1	11	0	217	220	216	289	268	558	9	80	27	0.50	205	39	19	42	36	2%	70	0%	2.43	-7.8	-11	$0
PT/Exp	F	10 TOR	167	13	6	12	1	246	174	273	284	377	661	5	78	28	0.25	258	43	22	35	84	13%	61	3%	3.36	-3.9	11	$3
Consist	B	1st Half	75	6	0	4	0	280			325	333	658	6	81	34	0.36	250	45	23	32	49	0%	69	0%	3.61	-1.2	0	$1
LIMA Plan	F	2nd Half	92	7	6	8	1	217			250	413	663	4	76	22	0.18	266	41	21	37	113	23%	63	6%	3.18	-2.8	24	$2
Rand Var	0	11 Proj	170	16	4	13	1	235			279	344	623	6	79	28	0.29	243	43	21	36	72	8%	60	2%	2.99	-6.2	5	$2

Impressive power in second half, but 35-year-olds don't repeat anomalies. He has been helpless against lefties 4 of the last 5 years, below replacement level for the last 9. 'nuff said.

Molina,Yadier			AB	R	HR	RBI	SB	Avg	vL	vR	OB	Slg	OPS	bb%	ct%	h%	Eye	xBA	G	L	F	PX	hr/f	Spd	SBO	RC/G	RAR	BPV	R$
Pos	2	06 STL	417	29	6	49	1	216	213	217	262	321	583	6	90	23	0.63	253	42	18	39	67	4%	30	4%	2.94	-18.0	37	$2
Age/B	28 Right	07 STL	353	30	6	40	1	275	288	269	339	368	707	9	88	30	0.79	254	46	19	35	58	6%	45	2%	4.38	-0.5	31	$7
Ht/Wt	71 230	08 STL	444	37	7	56	0	304	323	296	351	392	743	7	93	31	1.10	268	46	21	33	53	5%	52	1%	4.77	6.9	47	$12
Health	A	09 STL	481	45	6	54	9	293	248	307	360	383	742	9	92	31	1.28	270	51	20	29	57	5%	51	7%	4.95	9.3	49	$14
PT/Exp	B	10 STL	465	34	6	62	8	262	217	281	323	342	665	8	89	28	0.82	271	51	21	28	53	5%	40	9%	3.93	-7.5	29	$11
Consist	B	1st Half	245	16	3	31	6	229			300	302	602	9	88	25	0.83	264	52	20	28	50	5%	45	13%	3.23	-9.4	25	$4
LIMA Plan	D+	2nd Half	220	18	3	31	2	300			350	386	737	7	90	32	0.81	282	50	22	28	57	5%	46	4%	4.68	1.2	38	$7
Rand Var	+1	11 Proj	478	39	7	60	6	278			337	363	700	8	91	30	0.94	269	49	21	30	55	5%	41	6%	4.34	-0.4	37	$12

Provided value on basepaths for second year in row, despite lack of speed. BA vs LH not a concern, as 24% hit rate over last 2 years is to blame. There is value in reliability, and high ct% provides solid BA baseline.

BRIAN RUDD

Montero,Miguel			AB	R	HR	RBI	SB	Avg	vL	vR	OB	Slg	OPS	bb%	ct%	h%	Eye	xBA	G	L	F	PX	hr/f	Spd	SBO	RC/G	RAR	BPV	R$
Pos	2	06 a/a	439	38	15	66	1	269	333	231	338	426	764	9	87	28	0.81	251	38	15	46	91	9%	67	5%	5.02	8.2	62	$10
Age/B	27 Left	07 ARI	214	30	10	37	0	224	286	218	291	397	688	9	84	22	0.57	249	39	14	47	97	12%	86	0%	3.93	-3.3	57	$5
Ht/Wt	71 190	08 ARI	184	24	5	18	0	255	286	250	325	435	760	9	73	32	0.39	255	36	22	41	138	9%	86	0%	5.07	4.6	50	$4
Health	C	09 ARI	425	61	16	59	1	294	329	286	352	478	830	8	82	33	0.49	278	44	20	36	122	13%	79	3%	5.70	17.0	67	$16
PT/Exp	D	10 ARI	297	36	9	43	0	266	213	286	331	438	769	9	76	32	0.41	261	38	19	43	125	9%	76	1%	5.08	5.1	47	$9
Consist	B	1st Half	71	9	2	12	0	394			463	577	1040	11	85	45	0.82	330	39	31	30	131	11%	87	0%	8.47	6.7	94	$4
LIMA Plan	C	2nd Half	226	27	7	31	0	226			289	394	682	8	73	28	0.33	239	37	15	48	123	9%	76	2%	3.91	-4.0	33	$4
Rand Var	-1	11 Proj	**441**	**56**	**15**	**62**	**0**	**283**			**348**	**465**	**814**	**9**	**79**	**33**	**0.47**	**273**	**39**	**21**	**40**	**126**	**11%**	**76**	**1%**	**5.61**	**15.4**	**60**	**$14**

Missed 2 months after tearing meniscus during first week of season. When he came back, power was there, but contact rate dropped, and he couldn't hit lefties. Should bounce back, so now's a good time to buy.

Moore,Adam			AB	R	HR	RBI	SB	Avg	vL	vR	OB	Slg	OPS	bb%	ct%	h%	Eye	xBA	G	L	F	PX	hr/f	Spd	SBO	RC/G	RAR	BPV	R$
Pos	2	06	0	0	0	0	0	0																					
Age/B	26 Right	07	0	0	0	0	0	0																					
Ht/Wt	75 220	08 aa	428	47	11	56	0	276			329	426	755	7	84	31	0.48					102		74	1%	4.80	7.4	55	$10
Health	B	09 a/a	435	46	9	47	1	249			307	361	668	8	83	28	0.51					73		60	2%	3.76	-6.5	28	$7
PT/Exp	F	10 SEA	* 339	25	6	26	1	218	212	190	248	312	561	4	75	27	0.16	238	57	15	28	70	8%	78	3%	2.09	-21.5	-10	$2
Consist	C	1st Half	100	9	2	9	0	266			294	372	666	4	76	34	0.16	238	54	14	32	82	8%	78	0%	3.45	-2.1	1	$2
LIMA Plan	D	2nd Half	239	16	4	17	1	198			230	287	517	4	75	25	0.16	238	59	15	26	65	8%	85	4%	1.53	-19.9	-12	$0
Rand Var	+2	11 Proj	**330**	**30**	**6**	**32**	**1**	**242**			**286**	**343**	**629**	**6**	**79**	**29**	**0.29**	**245**	**57**	**15**	**28**	**72**	**8%**	**67**	**2%**	**3.11**	**-10.8**	**8**	**$4**

4-15-.195 in 205 AB at SEA. Big league pitchers found his weaknesses, as contact rate dropped to 69 percent. Still has time to live up to expectations, but nowhere close at this point.

Morales,Kendry			AB	R	HR	RBI	SB	Avg	vL	vR	OB	Slg	OPS	bb%	ct%	h%	Eye	xBA	G	L	F	PX	hr/f	Spd	SBO	RC/G	RAR	BPV	R$
Pos	3	06 LAA	* 453	53	14	63	1	263	229	235	306	413	718	6	87	28	0.47	262	52	15	34	86	11%	57	6%	4.28	-15.2	48	$10
Age/B	27 Both	07 LAA	* 374	48	8	47	0	302	241	311	335	445	779	5	87	33	0.37	262	47	11	42	96	6%	75	3%	4.95	-3.2	58	$11
Ht/Wt	73 225	08 LAA	* 378	44	14	60	1	283	214	213	317	446	764	5	88	29	0.42	260	41	15	44	96	10%	58	5%	4.70	-6.2	58	$12
Health	F	09 LAA	566	86	34	108	3	306	296	309	358	569	927	8	79	33	0.39	294	42	17	41	162	18%	68	7%	6.82	17.5	84	$26
PT/Exp	C	10 LAA	193	29	11	39	0	290	208	339	332	487	819	6	84	30	0.39	298	48	21	31	113	22%	47	2%	5.26	-2.8	54	$9
Consist	D	1st Half	193	29	11	39	0	290			332	487	819	6	84	30	0.39	298	48	21	31	113	22%	47	2%	5.26	-2.8	54	$9
LIMA Plan	D+	2nd Half	0	0	0	0	0	0																					
Rand Var	0	11 Proj	**547**	**74**	**24**	**94**	**1**	**291**			**331**	**479**	**810**	**6**	**85**	**31**	**0.40**	**286**	**46**	**18**	**36**	**113**	**15%**	**52**	**4%**	**5.25**	**-6.0**	**59**	**$21**

Suffered broken ankle and leg in late May celebrating walk-off homer. Before that, BPIs were short of '09 breakout, as power and success vs LH declined. Should be ready for March, but hedge your bets on full recovery.

Mora,Melvin			AB	R	HR	RBI	SB	Avg	vL	vR	OB	Slg	OPS	bb%	ct%	h%	Eye	xBA	G	L	F	PX	hr/f	Spd	SBO	RC/G	RAR	BPV	R$
Pos	35	06 BAL	624	96	16	83	11	274	253	282	332	391	723	8	84	30	0.55	243	39	20	41	71	7%	67	7%	4.41	-18.0	31	$18
Age/B	39 Right	07 BAL	467	67	14	58	9	274	254	280	340	418	758	9	82	31	0.57	258	40	19	42	93	9%	83	9%	4.89	-5.0	48	$14
Ht/Wt	71 200	08 BAL	513	77	23	104	3	285	314	272	333	483	816	7	86	29	0.53	293	42	21	37	117	14%	60	8%	5.40	2.0	73	$21
Health	B	09 BAL	450	44	8	48	3	260	242	270	312	358	670	7	87	29	0.57	247	43	19	38	61	5%	59	5%	3.82	-24.9	29	$8
PT/Exp	B	10 COL	316	39	7	45	2	285	296	276	349	421	770	9	83	32	0.58	261	44	18	38	83	7%	100	3%	5.08	-11.2	50	$10
Consist	F	1st Half	131	12	0	12	1	244			327	328	655	11	86	28	0.89	245	42	18	41	60	0%	88	3%	4.01	-9.0	43	$2
LIMA Plan	F	2nd Half	185	27	7	33	1	314			365	486	851	7	81	36	0.43	272	47	18	35	101	13%	105	3%	5.90	-2.2	54	$9
Rand Var	-2	11 Proj	**257**	**32**	**7**	**36**	**2**	**276**			**335**	**414**	**748**	**8**	**85**	**31**	**0.57**	**261**	**43**	**19**	**38**	**84**	**8%**	**80**	**5%**	**4.75**	**-11.1**	**48**	**$8**

Lousy '09 and first half of '10 made it look like he was done. Inflated second half h%, hr/f may help him land job in '11. Sustaining that success not likely, and won't find anything close to a full-time role.

Moreland,Mitch			AB	R	HR	RBI	SB	Avg	vL	vR	OB	Slg	OPS	bb%	ct%	h%	Eye	xBA	G	L	F	PX	hr/f	Spd	SBO	RC/G	RAR	BPV	R$
Pos	3	06	0	0	0	0	0	0																					
Age/B	25 Left	07	0	0	0	0	0	0																					
Ht/Wt	74 230	08	0	0	0	0	0	0																					
Health	A	09 aa	301	40	7	46	1	287			328	431	758	6	88	31	0.50					86		83	2%	4.79	-11.1	59	$9
PT/Exp	F	10 TEX	* 498	58	18	72	5	248	200	264	327	423	751	11	83	27	0.68	290	40	23	38	115	12%	50	5%	4.88	-13.2	60	$14
Consist	A	1st Half	253	24	5	34	1	234			299	372	671	8	85	26	0.61					98		67	3%	3.94	-14.0	57	$4
LIMA Plan	D	2nd Half	245	34	14	38	4	262			355	477	832	13	80	28	0.72	294	40	23	38	133	18%	58	7%	5.88	0.8	71	$10
Rand Var	+3	11 Proj	**287**	**36**	**12**	**43**	**2**	**265**			**330**	**455**	**785**	**9**	**84**	**28**	**0.62**	**293**	**40**	**23**	**38**	**115**	**13%**	**68**	**4%**	**5.19**	**-3.7**	**70**	**$9**

9-25-.255 in 145 AB at TEX. Impressive debut, as power and patience in majors were better than expected. Rarely played against LH, but youth and second half suggest he could be worth an investment.

Morgan,Nyjer			AB	R	HR	RBI	SB	Avg	vL	vR	OB	Slg	OPS	bb%	ct%	h%	Eye	xBA	G	L	F	PX	hr/f	Spd	SBO	RC/G	RAR	BPV	R$
Pos	8	06 aa	219	31	1	8	17	254			294	322	615	5	87	29	0.42					37		159	46%	3.16	-9.4	38	$6
Age/B	30 Left	07 PIT	* 271	37	1	14	25	262	259	313	310	332	642	7	83	31	0.41	246	57	16	27	41	2%	142	45%	3.46	-8.8	21	$9
Ht/Wt	72 175	08 PIT	* 482	67	1	33	42	264	240	304	297	331	628	5	84	31	0.30	262	50	25	26	51	1%	133	45%	3.21	-22.1	28	$17
Health	B	09 2NL	464	74	3	39	42	308	175	344	363	390	753	8	84	36	0.55	257	54	19	26	51	3%	148	37%	4.87	1.9	40	$24
PT/Exp	B	10 WAS	509	60	0	24	34	253	200	273	308	314	622	7	83	31	0.45	261	53	22	25	43	0%	155	35%	3.28	-25.1	28	$14
Consist	D	1st Half	307	37	0	13	18	254			310	322	633	8	83	31	0.47	275	54	24	22	47	0%	158	34%	3.43	-13.8	33	$8
LIMA Plan	C	2nd Half	202	23	0	11	16	252			304	302	606	7	83	31	0.43	240	50	19	31	36	0%	131	36%	3.04	-11.3	14	$6
Rand Var	+1	11 Proj	**498**	**66**	**1**	**30**	**35**	**269**			**319**	**334**	**653**	**7**	**83**	**32**	**0.45**	**255**	**53**	**20**	**27**	**44**	**1%**	**146**	**35%**	**3.62**	**-17.3**	**29**	**$17**

Hit rate normalized, so not as many chances to run, and his success rate dipped to 67%. Just 5 SB in 115 at-bats after return from hip injury. Stable skills, though, so if healthy, you can take 30+ SB to the bank.

Morneau,Justin			AB	R	HR	RBI	SB	Avg	vL	vR	OB	Slg	OPS	bb%	ct%	h%	Eye	xBA	G	L	F	PX	hr/f	Spd	SBO	RC/G	RAR	BPV	R$
Pos	3	06 MIN	592	97	34	130	3	321	315	325	377	559	936	8	84	34	0.57	298	36	24	41	137	17%	75	4%	6.85	22.8	88	$29
Age/B	29 Left	07 MIN	590	84	31	111	1	271	228	294	343	492	834	10	85	28	0.70	293	45	16	39	130	16%	66	1%	5.77	8.6	83	$21
Ht/Wt	76 235	08 MIN	623	97	23	129	0	300	284	310	376	499	875	11	86	32	0.89	295	43	19	38	124	11%	68	1%	6.43	19.9	89	$25
Health	C	09 MIN	508	85	30	100	0	274	277	272	364	516	880	12	83	28	0.84	285	41	16	43	139	17%	56	0%	6.45	10.7	87	$20
PT/Exp	B	10 MIN	296	53	18	56	0	345	325	358	439	618	1058	14	79	39	0.81	318	33	22	45	185	17%	75	0%	8.94	24.1	118	$18
Consist	C	1st Half	288	51	17	55	0	344			439	615	1054	15	79	39	0.82	317	33	22	45	185	16%	79	0%	8.90	23.2	119	$17
LIMA Plan	B	2nd Half	8	2	1	1	0	375			444	750	1194	11	75	40	0.50	344	33	33	33	220	50%	79	0%	10.31	0.9	124	$1
Rand Var	-5	11 Proj	**511**	**83**	**27**	**101**	**0**	**305**			**388**	**540**	**928**	**12**	**83**	**33**	**0.79**	**301**	**39**	**19**	**41**	**146**	**15%**	**66**	**1%**	**7.05**	**19.8**	**95**	**$24**

Was having best year of career before concussion ended it in July. Hit rate was inflated, but huge power uptick made up for dip in ct%. There is risk due to the severity of concussion, but that 1H shows his HR upside.

Morrison,Logan			AB	R	HR	RBI	SB	Avg	vL	vR	OB	Slg	OPS	bb%	ct%	h%	Eye	xBA	G	L	F	PX	hr/f	Spd	SBO	RC/G	RAR	BPV	R$
Pos	7	06	0	0	0	0	0	0																					
Age/B	23 Left	07	0	0	0	0	0	0																					
Ht/Wt	74 215	08	0	0	0	0	0	0																					
Health	A	09 aa	278	42	7	41	8	259			387	410	797	17	85	29	1.35					95		88	12%	5.92	5.2	77	$9
PT/Exp	F	10 FLA	* 482	69	6	51	1	273	342	257	375	423	798	14	83	32	0.98	289	48	20	32	102	5%	105	2%	5.84	10.7	77	$12
Consist	A	1st Half	165	18	3	21	1	273			364	422	786	12	86	30	1.05					99		93	6%	5.58	2.4	80	$4
LIMA Plan	A	2nd Half	317	52	3	31	0	273			380	424	805	15	82	33	0.96	285	48	20	32	104	4%	115	1%	5.99	8.3	77	$8
Rand Var	+1	11 Proj	**534**	**77**	**12**	**66**	**7**	**268**			**379**	**432**	**811**	**15**	**84**	**30**	**1.13**	**288**	**48**	**20**	**32**	**106**	**8%**	**96**	**7%**	**6.00**	**11.4**	**82**	**$16**

2-18-.283 in 244 AB at FLA. PRO: Age, elite plate discipline, 29 extra base hits after callup. CON: Ground ball rate, major league ct% dipped to 79%. Promising future, but doubles may not turn into HR just yet.

Morse,Mike			AB	R	HR	RBI	SB	Avg	vL	vR	OB	Slg	OPS	bb%	ct%	h%	Eye	xBA	G	L	F	PX	hr/f	Spd	SBO	RC/G	RAR	BPV	R$
Pos	9	06 SEA	* 249	25	4	40	1	249			292	382	673	6	81	29	0.31	242	42	16	42	94	5%	85	4%	3.75	-14.1	37	$4
Age/B	29 Right	07 aa	291	38	5	31	4	254			303	374	677	7	83	29	0.42					88		92	9%	3.87	-11.3	46	$5
Ht/Wt	77 230	08 SEA	0	0	0	0	0	0																					
Health	F	09 WAS	* 477	51	16	78	2	271			315	430	745	6	81	31	0.35	264	61	11	28	103	14%	78	2%	4.54	-4.6	45	$14
PT/Exp	F	10 WAS	* 317	45	18	47	0	276	295	287	335	499	834	8	77	31	0.38	281	46	16	38	144	19%	97	1%	5.73	3.6	69	$13
Consist	C	1st Half	110	14	6	12	0	251			320	429	749	9	81	26	0.53	273	48	17	35	107	18%	95	0%	4.64	-2.2	57	$3
LIMA Plan	D+	2nd Half	207	31	12	35	0	290			344	536	880	8	74	34	0.32	287	46	15	39	166	20%	96	2%	6.38	6.1	76	$9
Rand Var	-4	11 Proj	**325**	**41**	**15**	**47**	**1**	**268**			**320**	**463**	**784**	**7**	**79**	**30**	**0.38**	**272**	**47**	**16**	**37**	**126**	**15%**	**85**	**3%**	**5.04**	**-1.0**	**60**	**$11**

15-41-.289 in 266 AB at WAS. Second half power was much better than he had previously shown. OPS of .999 in 88 AB against LH. Hr/f will drop, but could provide some power, and may still fly under the radar.

BRIAN RUDD

Murphy,Daniel

Murphy,Daniel		AB	R	HR	RBI	SB	Avg	vL	vR	OB	Slg	OPS	bb%	ct%	h%	Eye	xBA	G	L	F	PX	hr/f	Spd	SBO	RC/G	RAR	BPV	R$
Pos 37	06	0	0	0	0	0	0																					
Age/B 26 Left	07 aa	361	48	11	56	12	271			333	432	765	8	89	28	0.84					97		82	18%	5.03	-7.0	77	$12
Ht/Wt 74 215	08 NYM	* 492	72	13	73	12	283	400	306	350	443	793	9	86	31	0.76	313	41	33	25	100	12%	93	14%	5.42	-4.5	74	$18
Health F	09 NYM	508	60	12	63	4	266	223	275	317	427	744	7	86	29	0.55	272	40	19	41	105	7%	72	5%	4.72	-26.4	67	$13
PT/Exp D	10 aaa	34	3	1	6	1	249			269	415	684	3	94	24	0.44					105		82	17%	3.92	-2.1	91	$1
Consist B	1st Half	34	3	1	6	1	249			269	415	684	3	94	24	0.44					105		82	17%	3.92	-2.1	91	$1
LIMA Plan D	2nd Half	0	0	0	0	0	0																					
Rand Var +3	11 Proj	253	33	8	36	1	273			332	437	769	8	87	29	0.70	288	40	21	39	103	9%	74	5%	5.05	-6.6	73	$7

Had the inside edge on 1B AB after '09 2H surge; knee injury delayed, then ended his year in early June. Now seeking AB off the bench, look for return of FB, PX trends and PT opp before you buy.

Murphy,David

Murphy,David		AB	R	HR	RBI	SB	Avg	vL	vR	OB	Slg	OPS	bb%	ct%	h%	Eye	xBA	G	L	F	PX	hr/f	Spd	SBO	RC/G	RAR	BPV	R$
Pos 79	06 a/a	490	59	10	61	6	259			327	422	749	9	85	29	0.67					106		79	9%	4.93	-4.1	69	$10
Age/B 29 Left	07 2AL	* 512	56	10	51	7	267	409	325	318	405	723	7	85	30	0.49	290	42	26	32	89	7%	114	7%	4.45	-8.8	60	$10
Ht/Wt 76 205	08 TEX	415	64	15	74	7	275	258	282	325	465	790	7	83	30	0.44	277	42	18	40	121	11%	102	9%	5.17	3.8	76	$15
Health B	09 TEX	432	61	17	57	9	269	235	279	343	447	790	10	75	32	0.46	249	38	19	43	117	12%	92	11%	5.35	4.3	45	$14
PT/Exp B	10 TEX	419	54	12	65	14	291	272	298	360	449	809	10	83	33	0.63	284	44	19	36	106	9%	89	13%	5.57	8.1	65	$18
Consist A	1st Half	195	24	2	23	3	262			311	364	675	7	80	32	0.36	261	40	23	37	85	3%	83	8%	3.82	-6.0	28	$5
LIMA Plan C+	2nd Half	224	30	10	42	11	317			400	522	922	12	86	34	0.97	305	48	17	36	124	15%	97	15%	7.01	12.9	97	$13
Rand Var -1	11 Proj	444	60	15	67	12	282			349	450	799	9	82	32	0.56	274	43	19	39	110	10%	91	11%	5.41	6.0	62	$17

BA spike fueled by improved ct% and more GBs; 2H power surge fueled by inflated hr/f. RC/G, OPS say BA / HR tradeoff didn't hurt productivity. 85% SB% was a revelation; should retain his value in 2011.

Nady,Xavier

Nady,Xavier		AB	R	HR	RBI	SB	Avg	vL	vR	OB	Slg	OPS	bb%	ct%	h%	Eye	xBA	G	L	F	PX	hr/f	Spd	SBO	RC/G	RAR	BPV	R$
Pos 39	06 2NL	468	57	17	63	3	280	336	263	323	453	776	6	82	31	0.35	264	46	17	37	106	12%	84	5%	4.91	-14.5	51	$14
Age/B 32 Right	07 PIT	431	55	20	72	3	278	295	274	315	476	791	5	77	32	0.23	268	39	21	40	127	15%	76	4%	5.03	-13.4	43	$15
Ht/Wt 73 185	08 2TM	555	76	25	97	2	305	262	317	350	510	860	7	81	34	0.38	294	41	25	34	131	16%	72	2%	5.93	6.6	68	$23
Health F	09 NYY	28	4	0	2	0	286	333	273	310	429	739	3	79	36	0.17	291	41	27	32	127	0%	86	0%	4.60	-0.9	50	$1
PT/Exp D	10 CHC	317	33	6	33	0	256	242	265	293	353	647	5	73	33	0.20	232	47	20	33	76	8%	73	0%	3.26	-28.4	-12	$6
Consist C	1st Half	127	10	4	19	0	236			281	370	652	6	75	29	0.25	255	45	22	33	95	13%	69	0%	3.31	-11.5	10	$2
LIMA Plan D	2nd Half	190	23	2	14	0	268			302	342	644	5	72	36	0.17	218	48	18	34	63	4%	88	0%	3.23	-16.9	-24	$4
Rand Var -1	11 Proj	331	39	10	44	1	269			309	412	721	6	77	32	0.25	255	44	21	35	101	11%	72	2%	4.22	-19.4	22	$9

Two TJ surgeries sandwiched a lost '09, contributing to PX plunge and other issues. Now two years off last productive season at age 32, he has much to prove. Worth a flyer, but not much more.

Napoli,Mike

Napoli,Mike		AB	R	HR	RBI	SB	Avg	vL	vR	OB	Slg	OPS	bb%	ct%	h%	Eye	xBA	G	L	F	PX	hr/f	Spd	SBO	RC/G	RAR	BPV	R$
Pos 23	06 LAA	* 346	57	18	51	3	225	185	241	337	434	770	14	65	29	0.48	218	34	14	52	155	15%	85	7%	5.47	11.3	39	$9
Age/B 29 Right	07 LAA	219	40	10	34	5	247	291	232	345	443	788	13	71	30	0.52	248	36	19	46	139	14%	85	11%	5.52	8.0	49	$7
Ht/Wt 72 215	08 LAA	227	39	20	49	7	273	286	270	370	586	956	13	69	31	0.50	272	31	17	52	209	24%	96	15%	7.80	23.8	102	$13
Health B	09 LAA	382	60	20	56	3	272	330	253	341	492	833	9	73	32	0.39	259	38	19	43	145	17%	88	6%	5.90	18.0	55	$14
PT/Exp C	10 LAA	453	60	26	68	4	238	305	208	303	468	771	8	70	28	0.31	270	38	20	42	168	19%	43	6%	5.07	12.3	45	$15
Consist C	1st Half	242	33	14	36	3	256			316	492	807	8	68	32	0.27	278	40	23	37	176	23%	57	9%	5.64	10.6	49	$9
LIMA Plan C+	2nd Half	211	27	12	32	1	218			289	441	730	9	72	24	0.35	261	36	16	48	160	17%	41	2%	4.45	1.9	47	$6
Rand Var +3	11 Proj	409	61	23	65	5	249			325	476	801	10	71	30	0.38	259	36	18	45	159	18%	65	7%	5.53	16.1	51	$15

Set personal HR high but AB spike exposed limitations. Ct% remains an issue, bb% is no longer a strength, struggled vs. RHP. Won't play every day, but elite power keeps 20+ HR upside intact.

Navarro,Dioner

Navarro,Dioner		AB	R	HR	RBI	SB	Avg	vL	vR	OB	Slg	OPS	bb%	ct%	h%	Eye	xBA	G	L	F	PX	hr/f	Spd	SBO	RC/G	RAR	BPV	R$
Pos 2	06 2TM	* 308	30	6	29	3	241	286	245	315	336	651	10	82	28	0.59	235	35	24	41	60	6%	46	4%	3.62	-6.9	10	$4
Age/B 27 Both	07 TAM	388	46	9	44	3	227	226	227	287	356	643	8	83	25	0.49	250	42	17	41	84	7%	64	4%	3.47	-9.6	35	$5
Ht/Wt 69 205	08 TAM	427	43	7	54	0	295	257	308	347	407	755	7	89	32	0.69	284	46	23	30	76	6%	54	3%	4.87	8.8	48	$11
Health A	09 TAM	376	38	8	32	5	218	279	182	254	322	576	5	86	23	0.35	243	37	20	43	62	6%	52	9%	2.58	-19.7	22	$4
PT/Exp C	10 TAM	* 265	25	3	23	2	212	184	200	289	291	580	10	84	24	0.68	238	47	16	37	59	3%	52	4%	2.89	-10.4	21	$2
Consist C	1st Half	105	11	1	7	0	210			284	286	570	9	87	23	0.79	246	45	17	38	56	3%	64	4%	2.87	-4.3	32	$0
LIMA Plan F	2nd Half	160	14	2	16	2	214			292	294	586	10	83	25	0.63	229	62	8	31	60	5%	59	4%	2.92	-6.1	19	$1
Rand Var +3	11 Proj	143	14	2	13	1	231			292	328	620	8	85	26	0.59	252	42	19	38	66	5%	58	5%	3.28	-4.0	29	$2

1-7-.194 in 124 AB at TAM. Plenty of catchers lack speed, some lack power, he has neither. A sub-.250 xBA and a bb% that looks like it's being chased by bees say look elsewhere for a #2 CA.

Nava,Daniel

Nava,Daniel		AB	R	HR	RBI	SB	Avg	vL	vR	OB	Slg	OPS	bb%	ct%	h%	Eye	xBA	G	L	F	PX	hr/f	Spd	SBO	RC/G	RAR	BPV	R$
Pos 7	06	0	0	0	0	0	0																					
Age/B 28 Both	07	0	0	0	0	0	0																					
Ht/Wt 70 200	08	0	0	0	0	0	0																					
Health A	09 aa	118	19	3	17	0	327			422	499	921	14	91	34	1.78					106		83	0%	7.27	6.2	103	$5
PT/Exp F	10 BOS	* 445	54	8	62	4	247	207	250	309	379	688	8	77	30	0.39	242	39	16	45	102	5%	66	6%	4.03	-11.3	28	$10
Consist F	1st Half	259	30	6	41	2	268			310	432	742	6	79	32	0.29	267	36	18	45	124	7%	67	7%	4.58	-2.3	48	$8
LIMA Plan F	2nd Half	186	24	2	21	2	219			308	305	613	11	74	29	0.50	209	41	14	44	70	3%	78	5%	3.18	-9.8	1	$3
Rand Var 0	11 Proj	93	13	2	13	0	258			340	404	745	11	82	30	0.69	255	40	15	45	103	5%	83	3%	4.97	0.1	59	$2

1-26-.242 in 162 AB at BOS. Nice story, but only saw this much MLB PT due to injuries. Good patience, avg power, FB% suggests he could hit a few out. But age says this is a part-timer profile at best.

Nelson,Chris

Nelson,Chris		AB	R	HR	RBI	SB	Avg	vL	vR	OB	Slg	OPS	bb%	ct%	h%	Eye	xBA	G	L	F	PX	hr/f	Spd	SBO	RC/G	RAR	BPV	R$
Pos 45	06	0	0	0	0	0	0																					
Age/B 25 Right	07	0	0	0	0	0	0																					
Ht/Wt 71 175	08 aa	283	26	2	29	4	208			271	291	562	8	83	24	0.52					62		94	8%	2.60	-19.7	29	$2
Health F	09 aa	107	16	4	13	4	251			313	440	752	8	84	27	0.58					106		123	22%	4.81	0.3	78	$4
PT/Exp F	10 COL	* 344	44	8	34	6	258	444	188	297	373	670	5	89	27	0.50	287	52	19	29	69	9%	95	11%	3.75	-10.8	52	$9
Consist D	1st Half	132	13	4	12	1	256			301	399	700	6	89	27	0.57					84		108	12%	4.13	-2.7	69	$3
LIMA Plan F	2nd Half	212	31	4	22	5	259			294	357	651	5	89	28	0.45	280	52	19	29	60	7%	95	11%	3.52	-8.1	44	$6
Rand Var +1	11 Proj	98	13	2	11	2	245			295	353	648	7	87	27	0.53	273	52	19	29	66	6%	111	14%	3.59	-3.4	48	$2

0-0-.280 in 25 AB at COL. Former '04 #1 pick touted for raw power, speed. Didn't develop as planned, with injuries a contributing factor. Trying to catch on as 2B / UT; pedigree and venue make him watchable.

Nieves,Wil

Nieves,Wil		AB	R	HR	RBI	SB	Avg	vL	vR	OB	Slg	OPS	bb%	ct%	h%	Eye	xBA	G	L	F	PX	hr/f	Spd	SBO	RC/G	RAR	BPV	R$
Pos 2	06 aaa	321	24	5	28	2	221			255	298	553	4	91	23	0.49					45		66	4%	2.49	-18.6	30	$1
Age/B 33 Right	07 NYY	* 151	11	1	14	1	199			234	265	499	4	86	22	0.33	233	52	13	35	44	2%	82	3%	1.75	-12.1	15	($0)
Ht/Wt 70 182	08 WAS	* 201	18	1	22	1	250	304	242	301	324	625	7	83	30	0.42	251	54	20	26	55	2%	99	3%	3.26	-5.6	20	$2
Health A	09 WAS	224	20	1	26	1	259	186	276	311	299	610	7	80	32	0.38	235	62	19	19	32	3%	73	1%	2.98	-8.3	-17	$3
PT/Exp F	10 WAS	158	10	3	16	0	203	212	200	241	310	551	5	82	23	0.28	254	54	15	31	77	8%	60	0%	2.18	-11.4	18	$1
Consist B	1st Half	109	5	1	9	0	174			211	239	449	4	81	21	0.24	229	54	15	31	49	4%	67	0%	0.91	-12.6	-7	($1)
LIMA Plan F	2nd Half	49	5	2	7	0	265			308	469	777	6	84	28	0.38	313	54	17	29	137	17%	69	0%	4.92	0.6	79	$1
Rand Var +5	11 Proj	113	8	2	11	0	221			264	304	568	6	83	25	0.34	249	56	17	27	56	7%	75	2%	2.44	-6.7	12	$1

Power surge more than doubled his career-to-date HR total. With a more appropriate hit rate, he could have matched '09's BA and called this a career year. I'm really trying hard to keep a straight face right now.

Nix,Jayson

Nix,Jayson		AB	R	HR	RBI	SB	Avg	vL	vR	OB	Slg	OPS	bb%	ct%	h%	Eye	xBA	G	L	F	PX	hr/f	Spd	SBO	RC/G	RAR	BPV	R$
Pos 45	06 aaa	358	29	2	19	11	235			283	293	576	6	88	26	0.56					39		96	16%	2.80	-17.1	26	$3
Age/B 28 Right	07 aa	439	59	9	43	18	252			290	387	677	5	85	28	0.35					90		101	28%	3.78	-7.5	53	$12
Ht/Wt 71 185	08 aa	264	41	12	34	7	251			297	460	757	6	82	26	0.37					131		92	24%	4.68	-1.2	76	$9
Health A	09 CHW	255	36	12	32	10	224	256	194	300	408	708	10	75	25	0.44	233	39	13	48	117	13%	92	19%	4.19	-5.8	42	$7
PT/Exp D	10 2AL	331	32	14	34	1	224	233	220	268	396	664	6	74	26	0.23	239	36	15	49	122	12%	86	5%	3.44	-10.4	32	$6
Consist B	1st Half	79	5	2	8	0	203			284	329	613	10	77	24	0.50	211	34	10	56	93	6%	92	0%	3.09	-3.4	33	$0
LIMA Plan D	2nd Half	252	27	12	26	1	230			262	417	679	4	73	27	0.16	248	37	16	47	132	14%	87	7%	3.56	-6.9	33	$6
Rand Var +1	11 Proj	315	36	15	34	6	235			291	427	718	7	77	26	0.34	246	37	13	50	125	13%	87	13%	4.19	-4.0	51	$8

Can loft FBs, but not BA. Pop gave him most of CLE 3B AB in 2H; poor ct% and patience will likely take them away soon enough. 3B defense also a minus. Power-without-BA profiles better at 2B.

JOCK THOMPSON

Nix,Laynce

Nix,Laynce			AB	R	HR	RBI	SB	Avg	vL	vR	OB	Slg	OPS	bb%	ct%	h%	Eye	xBA	G	L	F	PX	hr/f	Spd	SBO	RC/G	RAR	BPV	R$
Pos	7	06 2TM	* 421	53	17	72	4	261	125	169	296	440	736	5	72	33	0.17	231	43	15	43	120	13%	77	5%	4.43	-9.6	18	$12
Age/B	30 Left	07 a/a	358	49	20	63	4	226			279	447	726	7	70	26	0.24					154		74	5%	4.36	-9.1	41	$10
Ht/Wt	73 220	08 aaa	380	43	16	41	4	223			273	407	680	6	80	24	0.34					116		86	10%	3.72	-16.6	51	$7
Health	B	09 CIN	309	42	15	46	0	239	156	249	290	476	766	7	74	28	0.27	275	38	20	43	171	15%	58	2%	4.91	-6.0	65	$9
PT/Exp	B	10 CIN	165	16	4	18	0	291	313	289	350	455	805	8	76	36	0.38	270	40	22	37	119	9%	85	2%	5.55	2.2	45	$5
Consist	B	1st Half	104	8	4	12	0	240			269	423	692	4	75	28	0.15	260	40	19	41	125	13%	77	5%	3.76	-4.1	32	$2
LIMA Plan	F	2nd Half	61	8	0	6	0	377			472	508	980	15	79	48	0.85	286	42	27	31	109	0%	95	0%	8.38	4.9	63	$3
Rand Var	-5	11 Proj	192	23	6	24	0	271			333	451	784	9	76	33	0.39	269	40	22	38	129	10%	80	3%	5.28	0.1	51	$5

First good BA in years was produced by incremental gains everywhere - but the inflated h% was key. bb% trend looks promising, power is intact, but small sample (only 16 AB vs. LHP) doesn't lock in repeat.

Olivo,Miguel

Olivo,Miguel			AB	R	HR	RBI	SB	Avg	vL	vR	OB	Slg	OPS	bb%	ct%	h%	Eye	xBA	G	L	F	PX	hr/f	Spd	SBO	RC/G	RAR	BPV	R$
Pos	2	06 FLA	430	52	16	58	2	263	273	258	278	440	717	2	76	31	0.09	250	42	19	39	112	13%	73	6%	3.99	-4.4	22	$11
Age/B	32 Right	07 FLA	452	43	16	60	3	237	295	221	260	405	665	3	73	29	0.11	239	43	17	40	112	12%	62	6%	3.39	-14.1	8	$8
Ht/Wt	72 229	08 KC	306	29	12	41	7	255	262	251	272	444	716	2	73	31	0.09	251	38	17	44	140	12%	62	14%	4.04	-1.3	30	$8
Health	A	09 KC	390	51	23	65	5	249	265	238	284	490	773	5	68	31	0.15	248	45	14	40	159	22%	73	10%	5.04	8.9	31	$13
PT/Exp	C	10 COL	394	55	14	58	7	269	295	259	316	449	765	6	70	35	0.23	246	42	18	40	129	13%	104	11%	5.01	6.0	30	$15
Consist	B	1st Half	212	37	11	39	4	307			364	538	901	8	72	38	0.32	268	38	22	40	149	18%	134	13%	6.86	14.1	65	$12
LIMA Plan	D+	2nd Half	182	18	3	19	3	225			258	346	604	4	69	31	0.14	215	46	13	41	103	6%	65	9%	2.76	-9.5	-13	$3
Rand Var	-3	11 Proj	377	46	15	54	6	255			289	443	733	5	70	32	0.16	243	43	16	41	134	14%	82	11%	4.45	0.8	24	$12

BA surged in Coors (.318), died on the road (.211). 2nd half problems fueled by impatience and GB spike, but overall profile unchanged. Double-digit HR from CA spot, but BA still a risk, especially outside of COL.

Ordonez,Magglio

Ordonez,Magglio			AB	R	HR	RBI	SB	Avg	vL	vR	OB	Slg	OPS	bb%	ct%	h%	Eye	xBA	G	L	F	PX	hr/f	Spd	SBO	RC/G	RAR	BPV	R$
Pos	9	06 DET	593	82	24	104	1	298	294	300	348	477	825	7	85	32	0.52	272	45	18	38	104	13%	64	3%	5.53	-2.2	60	$21
Age/B	37 Right	07 DET	595	117	28	139	4	363	410	351	435	595	1030	11	87	39	0.96	319	42	19	39	146	14%	65	2%	8.22	40.5	108	$36
Ht/Wt	72 215	08 DET	561	72	21	103	1	317	328	314	376	494	870	9	86	34	0.70	286	44	20	36	107	12%	67	3%	6.17	12.4	70	$23
Health	D	09 DET	465	54	9	50	3	310	352	289	378	428	806	10	86	35	0.78	276	51	21	28	73	8%	69	3%	5.58	3.2	45	$14
PT/Exp	B	10 DET	323	56	12	59	1	303	371	285	380	474	854	11	88	32	1.05	309	47	22	32	103	13%	63	1%	6.16	10.6	78	$15
Consist	B	1st Half	266	46	10	50	1	312			386	489	875	11	89	32	1.10	316	44	23	33	107	13%	67	1%	6.38	10.3	85	$13
LIMA Plan	C	2nd Half	57	10	2	9	0	263			354	404	757	12	84	28	0.89	275	58	15	27	86	15%	59	0%	5.04	0.1	50	$2
Rand Var	+1	11 Proj	407	62	13	65	1	290			365	445	810	11	86	31	0.85	288	50	19	31	95	12%	64	2%	5.61	5.0	63	$15

Power rebounded to playable level before broken ankle ended season in late July. Other skills holding up but G/L/F trend is losing the battle with age. Should produce, but glory days have passed him by.

Ortiz,David

Ortiz,David			AB	R	HR	RBI	SB	Avg	vL	vR	OB	Slg	OPS	bb%	ct%	h%	Eye	xBA	G	L	F	PX	hr/f	Spd	SBO	RC/G	RAR	BPV	R$
Pos	0	06 BOS	558	115	54	137	1	287	278	292	412	636	1048	18	79	27	1.02	309	36	17	47	200	26%	62	1%	8.76	36.3	132	$31
Age/B	35 Left	07 BOS	549	116	35	117	3	332	308	343	444	621	1065	17	81	36	1.08	320	38	17	45	188	17%	70	2%	9.09	41.2	132	$32
Ht/Wt	76 230	08 BOS	416	74	23	89	1	264	221	279	370	507	878	14	82	27	0.95	291	37	19	45	152	15%	58	1%	6.58	19.8	99	$17
Health	B	09 BOS	541	77	28	99	0	238	212	250	330	462	792	12	75	27	0.55	256	32	17	50	145	14%	55	1%	5.43	4.2	60	$15
PT/Exp	B	10 BOS	518	86	32	102	0	270	222	297	370	529	899	14	72	32	0.57	287	38	17	45	188	19%	54	1%	7.02	10.0	84	$23
Consist	C	1st Half	232	43	17	54	0	259			365	556	921	14	69	30	0.55	297	36	16	48	224	22%	48	2%	7.45	7.4	102	$12
LIMA Plan	B	2nd Half	286	43	15	48	0	280			374	507	881	13	74	33	0.58	280	39	18	43	161	17%	65	0%	6.71	2.9	73	$12
Rand Var	0	11 Proj	462	76	26	91	0	266			367	510	876	14	75	30	0.64	279	36	18	46	166	16%	56	1%	6.62	10.4	80	$19

Rebounded from horrific April to re-affirm elite power and patience. But ct% and ability vs. LHP (.324 Slg) aren't apt to reverse course at his age. Buy the HR, but be aware of the BA and PT downside.

Overbay,Lyle

Overbay,Lyle			AB	R	HR	RBI	SB	Avg	vL	vR	OB	Slg	OPS	bb%	ct%	h%	Eye	xBA	G	L	F	PX	hr/f	Spd	SBO	RC/G	RAR	BPV	R$
Pos	3	06 TOR	581	82	22	92	5	312	284	322	371	508	879	9	83	34	0.57	294	46	22	32	124	14%	45	5%	6.32	14.2	66	$22
Age/B	34 Left	07 TOR	425	49	10	44	2	240	287	224	316	391	706	10	82	27	0.60	283	49	21	31	105	9%	54	2%	4.37	-11.3	48	$6
Ht/Wt	74 235	08 TOR	544	74	15	69	1	270	215	291	366	411	777	12	79	32	0.64	266	44	23	33	103	11%	65	2%	5.31	0.6	43	$14
Health	A	09 TOR	423	57	16	64	0	265	190	282	374	466	840	15	78	31	0.78	276	42	20	37	136	13%	41	0%	6.28	6.9	63	$12
PT/Exp	A	10 TOR	534	75	20	67	1	243	222	250	328	433	760	11	75	29	0.51	270	45	16	39	139	13%	54	1%	5.04	-11.5	53	$14
Consist	C	1st Half	291	39	8	29	1	241			318	392	710	10	76	29	0.46	257	46	17	37	110	10%	77	1%	4.36	-12.3	36	$6
LIMA Plan	C	2nd Half	243	36	12	38	0	247			339	481	821	12	75	28	0.57	286	44	15	42	173	16%	35	0%	5.87	0.7	77	$8
Rand Var	+2	11 Proj	461	64	17	63	1	256			347	444	790	12	77	30	0.61	273	44	19	37	133	13%	48	1%	5.48	-2.1	56	$12

FB, hr/f spikes and a tad more patience produced 2H power surge. BA decline continued with ct%, though more AB vs. LHP played a role. FB% trend says buy power, but a mix of 2009-10 is more likely.

Pagan,Angel

Pagan,Angel			AB	R	HR	RBI	SB	Avg	vL	vR	OB	Slg	OPS	bb%	ct%	h%	Eye	xBA	G	L	F	PX	hr/f	Spd	SBO	RC/G	RAR	BPV	R$
Pos	789	06 CHC	170	28	5	18	4	247	196	272	308	394	702	8	84	27	0.54	256	51	15	34	81	10%	124	14%	4.18	-5.4	55	$4
Age/B	29 Both	07 CHC	* 264	34	7	28	8	237	236	289	283	391	674	6	80	27	0.33	245	36	18	46	96	7%	128	18%	3.74	-12.9	52	$6
Ht/Wt	74 195	08 NYM	91	12	0	13	4	275	250	294	353	374	727	11	80	34	0.61	240	36	23	41	79	0%	104	14%	4.79	-1.6	39	$3
Health	F	09 NYM	343	54	6	32	14	306	280	316	353	487	840	7	84	35	0.45	275	41	21	38	111	5%	140	23%	5.90	3.2	81	$14
PT/Exp	C	10 NYM	579	80	11	69	37	290	261	300	340	425	765	7	83	33	0.45	256	36	20	44	89	5%	125	28%	4.93	-2.3	58	$27
Consist	C	1st Half	272	43	4	38	15	301			365	441	806	9	85	34	0.66	270	35	23	42	91	4%	131	24%	5.59	4.0	72	$13
LIMA Plan	C+	2nd Half	307	37	7	31	22	280			318	410	728	5	82	32	0.30	243	38	16	46	87	6%	111	33%	4.33	-6.5	43	$14
Rand Var	-3	11 Proj	517	74	9	56	26	280			329	420	749	7	83	32	0.43	254	39	19	42	90	5%	131	24%	4.75	-7.7	58	$20

Seized full-time AB w/ defense and new-found running game, legitimized by 80% SB%. Fell off some in 2H with impatience and ct% issues - swinging for the fences? He'll likely beat his xBA again with his legs.

Parra,Gerardo

Parra,Gerardo			AB	R	HR	RBI	SB	Avg	vL	vR	OB	Slg	OPS	bb%	ct%	h%	Eye	xBA	G	L	F	PX	hr/f	Spd	SBO	RC/G	RAR	BPV	R$
Pos	79	06	0	0	0	0	0	0																					
Age/B	23 Left	07	0	0	0	0	0	0																					
Ht/Wt	71 197	08 aa	265	30	4	28	14	267			319	408	727	7	90	29	0.73					80		121	36%	4.62	-4.1	75	$8
Health	A	09 ARI	* 563	78	8	70	11	300	220	310	351	417	768	7	82	35	0.44	259	53	18	29	74	6%	112	13%	4.99	-9.1	38	$20
PT/Exp	D	10 ARI	* 400	36	4	35	3	269	283	257	311	387	697	6	80	33	0.30	270	51	20	29	84	4%	92	4%	4.07	-11.5	29	$8
Consist	B	1st Half	192	18	3	19	2	275			314	425	739	5	83	32	0.34	292	52	19	29	104	6%	85	7%	4.58	-2.7	54	$5
LIMA Plan	F	2nd Half	208	18	1	16	1	264			308	351	659	6	77	34	0.28	250	51	21	28	64	2%	102	2%	3.58	-9.0	5	$3
Rand Var	0	11 Proj	262	29	3	27	5	279			325	392	717	6	82	33	0.38	266	52	20	29	76	5%	101	12%	4.35	-6.9	34	$7

3-30-.261 in 364 AB at ARI. Received more AB than he should have. Zero power, decent speed but no SB skills. Empty skill set tabs him as a fourth outfielder at best.

Patterson,Corey

Patterson,Corey			AB	R	HR	RBI	SB	Avg	vL	vR	OB	Slg	OPS	bb%	ct%	h%	Eye	xBA	G	L	F	PX	hr/f	Spd	SBO	RC/G	RAR	BPV	R$
Pos	7	06 BAL	463	75	16	53	45	276	207	301	308	443	751	4	80	32	0.22	252	39	21	40	99	11%	126	50%	4.51	-9.1	46	$23
Age/B	31 Left	07 BAL	461	65	8	45	37	269	310	251	301	386	687	4	86	30	0.32	254	44	15	41	78	5%	111	42%	3.86	-16.0	50	$18
Ht/Wt	70 173	08 CIN	366	46	10	34	14	205	188	209	238	344	582	4	84	22	0.28	251	46	15	38	85	8%	89	37%	2.58	-33.4	43	$7
Health	A	09 aaa	387	37	9	42	15	220			249	354	603	4	78	26	0.18					92		91	35%	2.70	-31.5	21	$7
PT/Exp	D	10 BAL	* 365	47	8	34	23	272	207	292	316	403	719	6	78	33	0.29	254	43	18	38	96	7%	109	33%	4.26	-6.6	34	$14
Consist	B	1st Half	228	29	4	15	17	290			332	404	736	6	78	36	0.29	248	46	17	37	85	6%	113	35%	4.49	-2.6	28	$10
LIMA Plan	F	2nd Half	137	18	4	19	6	241			288	401	689	6	77	29	0.28	264	40	20	39	115	10%	101	28%	3.89	-4.1	43	$5
Rand Var	-4	11 Proj	166	20	4	18	9	241			279	381	661	5	79	28	0.25	253	43	18	39	96	8%	98	35%	3.48	-7.3	34	$5

8-32-.269, 21 SB in 308 AB at BAL. Fine job as injury fill-in fueled by h% and 85% SB%. With with base-stealing his only real skill, his value depends on playing time. The 2H numbers provide the 2011 benchmark.

Patterson,Eric

Patterson,Eric			AB	R	HR	RBI	SB	Avg	vL	vR	OB	Slg	OPS	bb%	ct%	h%	Eye	xBA	G	L	F	PX	hr/f	Spd	SBO	RC/G	RAR	BPV	R$
Pos	78	06 a/a	508	79	11	59	46	270			339	411	750	9	81	32	0.54					85		129	39%	4.87	-5.1	51	$23
Age/B	27 Left	07 aa	516	75	12	52	19	261			317	401	718	7	85	29	0.55					85		119	21%	4.40	-12.3	62	$15
Ht/Wt	71 170	08 2TM	* 445	54	8	50	24	242	217	187	294	361	656	7	79	29	0.35	232	39	18	43	84	5%	99	26%	3.55	-21.1	29	$13
Health	A	09 OAK	* 560	77	8	50	35	247	375	269	308	368	676	8	84	28	0.56	239	34	20	46	74	4%	138	31%	3.97	-17.6	56	$16
PT/Exp	D	10 2AL	187	26	6	16	11	214	219	213	269	406	675	7	67	29	0.23	227	33	16	51	142	9%	153	34%	3.92	-5.6	43	$5
Consist	C	1st Half	113	17	4	9	6	204			256	389	646	7	72	25	0.25	243	37	16	47	130	11%	123	30%	3.35	-5.4	43	$3
LIMA Plan	D	2nd Half	74	9	2	7	5	230			287	432	720	7	59	36	0.20	203	27	15	59	163	8%	166	40%	5.11	0.5	35	$2
Rand Var	0	11 Proj	157	21	4	15	10	236			293	393	686	7	73	30	0.30	220	32	16	52	107	7%	133	32%	3.96	-4.6	36	$5

Power spike coupled with solid speed metrics are intriguing, but other numbers tell a different story. Needs to think patience, contact, GBs, but there's nothing to suggest he will ever read this box.

JOCK THOMPSON

Paulino,Ronny

Paulino,Ronny		Yr	AB	R	HR	RBI	SB	Avg	vL	vR	OB	Slg	OPS	bb%	ct%	h%	Eye	xBA	G	L	F	PX	hr/f	Spd	SBO	RC/G	RAR	BPV	R$
Pos	2	06 PIT	* 471	39	6	59	1	306	339	300	356	390	747	7	82	36	0.42	248	47	23	31	58	5%	75	1%	4.68	4.4	12	$12
Age/B	29 Right	07 PIT	457	56	11	55	2	263	407	218	312	389	702	7	83	30	0.42	257	47	17	36	83	8%	76	3%	4.09	-4.5	36	$10
Ht/Wt	75 210	08 PIT	* 229	21	5	32	0	235	235	202	299	377	676	8	76	29	0.39	246	43	19	38	107	7%	80	3%	3.88	-2.3	34	$3
Health	A	09 FLA	239	24	8	27	1	272	290	250	341	423	764	9	80	31	0.52	252	39	21	39	96	11%	91	1%	4.95	4.7	45	$6
PT/Exp	D	10 FLA	316	31	4	37	1	259	358	217	314	354	668	7	84	30	0.49	247	42	18	40	71	4%	68	1%	3.80	-6.3	29	$6
Consist	C	1st Half	214	25	3	28	1	299			345	407	752	7	86	34	0.48	254	40	17	43	79	4%	75	2%	4.75	1.6	43	$7
LIMA Plan	F	2nd Half	102	6	1	9	0	176			250	245	495	9	80	21	0.50	235	48	18	34	53	4%	73	0%	1.67	-9.2	5	($1)
Rand Var	0	11 Proj	**257**	**23**	**5**	**29**	**1**	**245**			**308**	**353**	**660**	**8**	**81**	**29**	**0.47**	**245**	**43**	**19**	**38**	**76**	**6%**	**70**	**1%**	**3.67**	**-5.4**	**24**	**$4**

What little power he had is ticking south. Otherwise stable skill set isn't enough to earn regular AB. Defense, ability vs. LHP keep him employed. Unlikely to be a category killer while you seek alternatives.

Paul,Xavier

Paul,Xavier		Yr	AB	R	HR	RBI	SB	Avg	vL	vR	OB	Slg	OPS	bb%	ct%	h%	Eye	xBA	G	L	F	PX	hr/f	Spd	SBO	RC/G	RAR	BPV	R$
Pos	7	06	0	0	0	0	0	0																					
Age/B	26 Left	07 aa	422	53	10	42	15	263			328	384	712	9	77	32	0.43					83		88	20%	4.30	-11.3	22	$12
Ht/Wt	69 203	08 aaa	443	65	8	53	14	277			330	398	728	7	82	32	0.43					83		92	18%	4.49	-8.3	37	$14
Health	A	09 aaa	116	11	2	13	7	290			339	430	769	7	82	34	0.41					97		85	28%	5.00	-0.9	48	$4
PT/Exp	F	10 LA	* 349	43	7	34	7	239	238	230	277	367	645	5	85	27	0.35	281	41	23	36	90	6%	84	16%	3.41	-17.6	49	$7
Consist	C	1st Half	241	35	7	27	7	266			305	420	724	5	84	29	0.35	286	40	23	38	103	9%	89	19%	4.31	-5.4	58	$8
LIMA Plan	F	2nd Half	108	8	0	7	0	180			215	251	466	4	87	21	0.34	267	42	23	35	62	0%	73	6%	1.47	-12.6	29	($1)
Rand Var	+5	11 Proj	**131**	**14**	**1**	**13**	**4**	**260**			**305**	**375**	**679**	**6**	**83**	**30**	**0.39**	**267**	**41**	**23**	**36**	**83**	**3%**	**89**	**18%**	**3.90**	**-5.3**	**41**	**$3**

0-11-.231 in 121 AB at LA. 1H MLB stint better than 2H, due largely to h%. No standout skills here. Career .300 BA in PCL won't follow him to LA without better selectivity and patience. A 5th OF profile.

Pearce,Steve

Pearce,Steve		Yr	AB	R	HR	RBI	SB	Avg	vL	vR	OB	Slg	OPS	bb%	ct%	h%	Eye	xBA	G	L	F	PX	hr/f	Spd	SBO	RC/G	RAR	BPV	R$
Pos	3	06	0	0	0	0	0	0																					
Age/B	27 Right	07 PIT	* 480	74	15	78	12	293	429	259	342	482	823	7	87	31	0.57	308	48	20	32	117	11%	79	12%	5.59	-7.2	81	$19
Ht/Wt	71 214	08 PIT	* 495	45	13	64	11	229	321	222	274	378	652	6	82	26	0.34	245	38	17	45	100	7%	67	15%	3.44	-34.6	41	$10
Health	F	09 PIT	* 438	48	13	57	3	227	268	174	300	393	693	9	81	25	0.55	257	38	19	43	113	9%	51	10%	4.15	-32.1	50	$8
PT/Exp	D	10 PIT	* 158	22	2	16	5	261	294	250	356	406	762	13	82	31	0.82	282	44	20	36	108	4%	91	15%	5.33	-4.7	70	$5
Consist	B	1st Half	158	22	2	16	5	261			356	406	762	13	82	31	0.82	282	44	20	36	108	4%	91	15%	5.33	-4.7	70	$5
LIMA Plan	F	2nd Half	0	0	0	0	0	0																					
Rand Var	+1	11 Proj	**96**	**11**	**2**	**12**	**2**	**250**			**316**	**416**	**732**	**9**	**83**	**28**	**0.55**	**271**	**41**	**19**	**41**	**112**	**7%**	**85**	**14%**	**4.65**	**-4.6**	**65**	**$3**

0-5-.276 in 29 AB at PIT. Patience and Eye advances made BA respectable again, but power remains stagnant, unremarkable. At 28, a bench role vs. LHP appears to be his upside.

Pedroia,Dustin

Pedroia,Dustin		Yr	AB	R	HR	RBI	SB	Avg	vL	vR	OB	Slg	OPS	bb%	ct%	h%	Eye	xBA	G	L	F	PX	hr/f	Spd	SBO	RC/G	RAR	BPV	R$
Pos	4	06 BOS	* 512	56	7	53	1	283	162	212	349	404	754	9	94	29	1.68	299	48	23	30	75	5%	73	4%	5.16	15.1	78	$10
Age/B	27 Right	07 BOS	520	86	8	50	7	317	348	303	374	442	816	8	92	33	1.12	287	43	18	38	83	4%	109	5%	5.70	23.8	85	$17
Ht/Wt	69 180	08 BOS	653	118	17	83	20	326	313	331	374	493	867	7	92	34	0.96	306	43	21	36	104	8%	103	11%	6.14	21.7	99	$30
Health	D	09 BOS	626	115	15	72	20	296	277	302	370	447	817	11	93	30	1.64	289	39	20	41	90	6%	99	14%	5.87	16.5	96	$24
PT/Exp	A	10 BOS	302	53	12	41	9	288	236	304	366	493	859	11	87	30	0.97	318	39	22	39	131	12%	83	11%	6.23	15.0	104	$14
Consist	A	1st Half	295	52	12	41	8	292			369	502	870	11	88	30	1.00	321	38	22	39	134	12%	83	11%	6.36	15.6	107	$14
LIMA Plan	B+	2nd Half	7	1	0	0	1	143			250	143	393	12	71	20	0.50	204	60	20	20	0	0%	96	50%	0.02	-1.0	-59	$0
Rand Var	+2	11 Proj	**603**	**103**	**19**	**73**	**19**	**303**			**368**	**483**	**852**	**9**	**91**	**31**	**1.15**	**309**	**41**	**21**	**38**	**110**	**9%**	**95**	**12%**	**6.11**	**24.9**	**102**	**$26**

Foot injury cut season short. Until then, had traded a touch of ct% successfully for power, helped by three Coors Field HR. We'd take either version going forward. If healthy, he'll be rock-solid again.

Pena,Brayan

Pena,Brayan		Yr	AB	R	HR	RBI	SB	Avg	vL	vR	OB	Slg	OPS	bb%	ct%	h%	Eye	xBA	G	L	F	PX	hr/f	Spd	SBO	RC/G	RAR	BPV	R$
Pos	2	06 ATL	* 366	39	2	36	6	287	200	308	327	361	688	6	91	31	0.69	289	58	22	19	48	3%	72	11%	4.11	-2.4	39	$8
Age/B	29 Both	07 aaa	345	38	5	43	5	284			317	387	705	5	90	31	0.48					66		66	14%	4.16	-2.0	43	$9
Ht/Wt	71 247	08 aaa	234	26	5	25	6	267			328	405	733	8	93	27	1.39					85		55	13%	4.84	4.4	77	$6
Health	A	09 KC	* 253	25	9	31	2	267	258	282	307	438	745	5	90	27	0.57	304	51	22	28	97	14%	40	5%	4.61	2.5	62	$6
PT/Exp	F	10 KC	158	11	1	19	2	253	204	275	306	335	641	7	83	30	0.44	238	45	16	39	68	2%	35	5%	3.48	-3.2	12	$3
Consist	B	1st Half	28	1	0	3	1	179			303	214	517	15	79	23	0.83	186	52	9	39	34	0%	56	11%	2.19	-1.8	-9	$0
LIMA Plan	D	2nd Half	130	10	1	16	1	269			307	362	668	5	84	31	0.33	250	43	18	39	74	2%	35	3%	3.70	-1.7	18	$3
Rand Var	-2	11 Proj	**390**	**38**	**7**	**45**	**5**	**259**			**303**	**384**	**687**	**6**	**89**	**28**	**0.58**	**278**	**46**	**19**	**35**	**81**	**6%**	**40**	**9%**	**4.05**	**-1.9**	**47**	**$8**

Offense stagnated with 1H bench time, rebounded with more regular AB. Playing time peaked in Sept, producing .848 OPS, 86% ct%, 112 PX. PT agrees with him; 400 AB vs. RHP look profitable.

Pena,Carlos

Pena,Carlos		Yr	AB	R	HR	RBI	SB	Avg	vL	vR	OB	Slg	OPS	bb%	ct%	h%	Eye	xBA	G	L	F	PX	hr/f	Spd	SBO	RC/G	RAR	BPV	R$
Pos	3	06 BOS	* 451	66	21	68	4	249	273	273	339	433	772	12	76	28	0.57	254	48	17	35	115	18%	67	3%	5.13	-3.8	43	$12
Age/B	32 Left	07 TAM	490	99	46	121	1	282	271	286	406	627	1033	17	71	30	0.73	311	37	18	45	233	30%	60	1%	8.96	51.0	125	$28
Ht/Wt	74 225	08 TAM	490	76	31	102	1	247	190	280	370	494	864	16	66	31	0.58	246	32	18	50	181	19%	72	1%	6.86	23.1	65	$18
Health	B	09 TAM	471	91	39	100	3	227	211	236	348	537	885	16	65	25	0.53	263	29	17	54	215	23%	59	5%	7.09	19.8	85	$19
PT/Exp	A	10 TAM	484	64	28	84	5	196	179	204	319	407	726	15	67	22	0.55	246	45	14	41	155	21%	40	4%	4.65	-17.1	38	$13
Consist	C	1st Half	280	39	16	50	2	200			311	407	718	14	69	23	0.51	245	47	12	41	149	20%	53	4%	4.47	-11.5	39	$8
LIMA Plan	C+	2nd Half	204	25	12	34	3	191			329	407	736	17	66	22	0.60	250	42	18	40	163	22%	40	5%	4.89	-5.7	41	$5
Rand Var	+5	11 Proj	**434**	**67**	**28**	**82**	**4**	**235**			**355**	**475**	**830**	**16**	**67**	**28**	**0.57**	**252**	**38**	**16**	**46**	**172**	**21%**	**54**	**3%**	**6.25**	**8.1**	**56**	**$16**

Power remains Elite, but LHPs carve him up, and sub-70% contact have made him a BA killer since '08. FB% and h% should bounce, but not enough to alter profile. OBP outlook now iffy; so are fulltime AB.

Pena,Ramiro

Pena,Ramiro		Yr	AB	R	HR	RBI	SB	Avg	vL	vR	OB	Slg	OPS	bb%	ct%	h%	Eye	xBA	G	L	F	PX	hr/f	Spd	SBO	RC/G	RAR	BPV	R$
Pos	56	06 aa	86	6	1	6	0	186			231	244	475	5	76	23	0.24					40		104	6%	1.05	-11.7	-21	($1)
Age/B	25 Both	07 aa	203	23	0	10	7	246			317	291	608	9	84	29	0.64					34		139	16%	3.23	-12.3	25	$3
Ht/Wt	71 165	08 aa	443	53	2	42	8	250			308	327	636	8	81	30	0.45					54		143	11%	3.42	-22.6	28	$7
Health	A	09 NYY	* 271	33	3	19	9	242	120	333	297	336	633	7	83	28	0.45	246	37	24	39	65	3%	123	16%	3.37	-10.6	36	$5
PT/Exp	D	10 NYY	154	18	0	18	7	227	161	244	256	247	503	4	82	28	0.22	203	41	19	40	12	0%	141	21%	1.58	-15.3	-9	$3
Consist	B	1st Half	73	11	0	9	3	192			234	205	439	5	81	24	0.29	202	40	20	40	13	0%	102	18%	0.82	-9.3	-24	$1
LIMA Plan	F	2nd Half	81	7	0	9	4	259			277	284	561	2	84	31	0.15	204	42	18	40	11	0%	155	23%	2.23	-6.2	-2	$2
Rand Var	-1	11 Proj	**99**	**11**	**0**	**9**	**4**	**242**			**286**	**306**	**592**	**6**	**83**	**29**	**0.35**	**225**	**40**	**20**	**40**	**43**	**1%**	**131**	**18%**	**2.78**	**-6.0**	**17**	**$2**

PRO: Speed, SBO, defensive versatility, almost certain PX spike on the horizon.
CON: Everything else
He's also less wretched vs. RHP than LHP, though he should probably avoid both.

Pence,Hunter

Pence,Hunter		Yr	AB	R	HR	RBI	SB	Avg	vL	vR	OB	Slg	OPS	bb%	ct%	h%	Eye	xBA	G	L	F	PX	hr/f	Spd	SBO	RC/G	RAR	BPV	R$
Pos	9	06 aa	523	81	24	79	15	254			317	471	788	8	82	27	0.51					124		124	16%	5.19	-0.3	83	$18
Age/B	27 Right	07 HOU	* 551	70	20	86	13	315	354	314	354	531	885	6	80	36	0.31	301	49	19	32	135	14%	144	13%	6.31	21.5	86	$24
Ht/Wt	76 210	08 HOU	595	78	25	83	11	269	250	275	315	466	781	6	79	30	0.32	271	52	14	34	125	15%	119	15%	4.98	-3.6	67	$21
Health	A	09 HOU	585	76	25	72	14	282	294	279	347	472	819	9	81	31	0.53	276	53	15	33	115	16%	126	15%	5.58	11.8	75	$23
PT/Exp	A	10 HOU	614	93	25	91	18	282	292	279	327	461	788	6	83	31	0.39	288	53	15	32	112	15%	108	17%	5.03	-5.3	68	$28
Consist	B	1st Half	303	45	11	37	9	254			300	413	713	6	86	27	0.47	299	60	15	25	96	17%	97	19%	4.19	-10.4	64	$11
LIMA Plan	C+	2nd Half	311	48	14	54	9	309			352	508	860	6	80	35	0.34	278	46	14	40	128	14%	121	15%	5.93	5.2	74	$17
Rand Var	+1	11 Proj	**586**	**83**	**26**	**84**	**15**	**283**			**334**	**480**	**814**	**7**	**82**	**31**	**0.41**	**285**	**52**	**15**	**33**	**121**	**16%**	**116**	**16%**	**5.40**	**4.2**	**74**	**$25**

Was 2H FB spike telling, or a blip mixed with a h% surge? Three-year BPIs, performance point to stabilizing skill set aided by RHB-friendly home venue. Either he is what he is, or more power is coming.

Pennington,Cliff

Pennington,Cliff		Yr	AB	R	HR	RBI	SB	Avg	vL	vR	OB	Slg	OPS	bb%	ct%	h%	Eye	xBA	G	L	F	PX	hr/f	Spd	SBO	RC/G	RAR	BPV	R$
Pos	6	06	0	0	0	0	0	0																					
Age/B	26 Both	07 aa	271	34	2	17	7	222			302	294	595	10	89	24	1.08					48		117	11%	3.32	-8.7	53	$3
Ht/Wt	71 188	08 OAK	* 539	80	1	34	27	233	289	213	334	284	617	13	87	27	1.14	212	36	19	46	36	0%	139	19%	3.65	-11.2	46	$11
Health	A	09 OAK	* 568	60	6	48	26	235	200	307	296	334	630	8	85	27	0.58	244	42	18	39	64	3%	112	25%	3.45	-17.5	42	$11
PT/Exp	B	10 OAK	508	64	6	46	29	250	258	247	317	368	685	9	81	30	0.52	249	36	21	43	82	3%	128	25%	4.10	2.2	48	$15
Consist	A	1st Half	271	34	3	27	12	262			336	380	716	10	81	31	0.58	249	35	21	44	84	3%	114	18%	4.54	4.6	46	$8
LIMA Plan	C+	2nd Half	237	30	3	19	17	236			296	354	650	8	81	28	0.45	250	36	22	42	79	4%	137	34%	3.61	-2.5	48	$7
Rand Var	-1	11 Proj	**539**	**67**	**6**	**44**	**31**	**243**			**314**	**342**	**656**	**9**	**84**	**28**	**0.63**	**243**	**37**	**21**	**42**	**66**	**3%**	**122**	**25%**	**3.80**	**-6.1**	**45**	**$14**

PX uptick unlikely to continue. Legs look profitable, but ct%, bb%, and FB% aren't helping. Decent value at SS now, 30+ SB possible with reasonable skills upticks. But if they don't materialize, a bench role will.

JOCK THOMPSON

Peralta,Jhonny			AB	R	HR	RBI	SB	Avg	vL	vR	OB	Slg	OPS	bb%	ct%	h%	Eye	xBA	G	L	F	PX	hr/f	Spd	SBO	RC/G	RAR	BPV	R$
Pos	56	06 CLE	569	84	13	68	0	257	267	252	323	385	708	9	73	33	0.37	234	48	19	34	91	9%	106	1%	4.30	-11.9	17	$11
Age/B	28 Right	07 CLE	574	87	21	72	4	270	275	269	340	430	770	10	75	33	0.42	256	47	19	35	111	14%	76	5%	5.07	3.3	31	$17
Ht/Wt	73 210	08 CLE	605	104	23	89	3	276	247	285	329	473	802	7	79	32	0.38	280	44	20	36	132	13%	94	3%	5.35	8.1	67	$21
Health	A	09 CLE	582	57	11	83	0	254	235	261	314	375	689	8	77	31	0.38	249	50	19	31	86	8%	67	1%	4.01	-11.5	15	$10
PT/Exp	A	10 2AL	551	60	15	81	1	249	241	251	315	392	707	9	81	28	0.51	265	34	22	43	98	8%	78	1%	4.26	-9.3	47	$13
Consist	B	1st Half	281	30	5	34	1	253			320	395	715	9	78	31	0.45	257	34	21	45	109	5%	79	1%	4.45	-3.1	43	$6
LIMA Plan	C+	2nd Half	270	30	10	47	0	244			308	389	697	8	85	26	0.61	272	35	24	42	87	10%	77	0%	4.10	-5.9	51	$7
Rand Var	+3	11 Proj	**559**	**67**	**19**	**82**	**1**	**259**			**322**	**425**	**747**	**8**	**80**	**30**	**0.45**	**270**	**41**	**21**	**38**	**110**	**11%**	**78**	**1%**	**4.69**	**-1.9**	**48**	**$15**

HRs plummeted from '08 to '09. He responded by swinging for the fences in 1H, pumping up his FB rate by 14% to ill result. Then the Aha! moment - make better contact! 2nd half flyballs suddenly started going yard.

Phillips,Brandon			AB	R	HR	RBI	SB	Avg	vL	vR	OB	Slg	OPS	bb%	ct%	h%	Eye	xBA	G	L	F	PX	hr/f	Spd	SBO	RC/G	RAR	BPV	R$
Pos	4	06 CIN	536	65	17	75	25	276	299	268	320	427	748	6	84	30	0.40	265	46	19	35	90	11%	75	20%	4.58	-0.2	43	$20
Age/B	29 Right	07 CIN	650	107	30	94	32	288	341	262	322	485	807	5	83	31	0.30	286	47	18	35	111	16%	133	25%	5.15	8.3	73	$31
Ht/Wt	72 195	08 CIN	559	80	21	78	23	261	296	247	309	442	751	7	83	28	0.42	274	50	16	34	105	13%	125	25%	4.65	-2.0	70	$22
Health	A	09 CIN	584	78	20	98	25	276	301	267	326	447	773	7	87	29	0.59	283	50	17	33	101	12%	99	23%	4.99	7.7	75	$25
PT/Exp	A	10 CIN	626	100	18	59	16	275	291	268	324	430	754	7	87	29	0.55	288	51	15	33	96	10%	113	17%	4.77	-0.9	73	$22
Consist	A	1st Half	334	63	11	28	10	308			364	485	849	8	86	33	0.63	298	48	16	35	113	11%	121	19%	5.92	10.4	89	$16
LIMA Plan	C	2nd Half	292	37	7	31	6	236			278	366	645	6	87	25	0.46	277	55	14	31	77	9%	108	15%	3.46	-12.1	56	$7
Rand Var	+1	11 Proj	**598**	**87**	**19**	**75**	**15**	**276**			**323**	**436**	**760**	**7**	**86**	**29**	**0.50**	**281**	**51**	**16**	**33**	**96**	**11%**	**105**	**16%**	**4.79**	**1.2**	**68**	**$22**

Maintained ct% gains, but PX, hr/f, and SBO all trending in wrong direction. SB success rate was just 57%, even more reason to doubt that Spd, SBO will return to '07-'08 level. 20/20 is no longer a sure thing.

Pierre,Juan			AB	R	HR	RBI	SB	Avg	vL	vR	OB	Slg	OPS	bb%	ct%	h%	Eye	xBA	G	L	F	PX	hr/f	Spd	SBO	RC/G	RAR	BPV	R$
Pos	7	06 CHC	699	87	3	40	58	292	293	291	323	388	711	4	95	31	0.84	300	55	21	24	52	2%	159	41%	4.40	-17.1	79	$26
Age/B	33 Left	07 LA	668	96	0	41	64	293	274	301	327	353	680	5	94	31	0.89	286	53	21	26	36	0%	150	40%	4.08	-24.5	63	$27
Ht/Wt	70 187	08 LA	375	44	1	28	40	283	346	257	322	328	650	6	94	30	0.92	281	53	24	23	28	1%	124	45%	3.76	-18.3	47	$16
Health	A	09 LA	380	57	0	31	30	308	320	304	354	392	746	7	93	33	1.00	293	51	24	24	50	0%	158	35%	4.91	-7.0	74	$17
PT/Exp	B	10 CHW	651	96	1	47	68	275	297	268	322	316	638	6	93	30	0.96	282	59	19	23	28	1%	121	43%	3.67	-23.3	45	$29
Consist	C	1st Half	313	42	0	13	30	259			305	288	593	6	92	28	0.88	263	62	14	24	21	0%	118	41%	3.15	-16.4	36	$11
LIMA Plan	C+	2nd Half	338	54	1	34	38	290			337	343	680	7	93	31	1.04	299	56	23	21	35	1%	116	44%	4.15	-7.2	51	$18
Rand Var	+1	11 Proj	**577**	**83**	**1**	**44**	**46**	**288**			**332**	**346**	**678**	**6**	**93**	**31**	**0.96**	**289**	**55**	**21**	**23**	**36**	**1%**	**126**	**35%**	**4.11**	**-13.8**	**54**	**$23**

Back in F/T role, set career high in SBs despite eroding speed skill. It's all in the opps. And given that, at 33, odds are that Spd will more likely decline than improve, his complete value will be tied to playing time.

Pierzynski,A.J.			AB	R	HR	RBI	SB	Avg	vL	vR	OB	Slg	OPS	bb%	ct%	h%	Eye	xBA	G	L	F	PX	hr/f	Spd	SBO	RC/G	RAR	BPV	R$
Pos	2	06 CHW	509	65	16	64	1	295	270	304	324	436	760	4	86	32	0.31	274	44	23	33	84	11%	61	1%	4.60	2.7	39	$14
Age/B	34 Left	07 CHW	472	54	14	50	1	263	252	266	300	403	702	5	86	28	0.38	266	43	18	39	88	9%	49	2%	4.02	-3.7	41	$10
Ht/Wt	75 230	08 CHW	534	66	13	60	1	281	286	279	306	416	721	3	87	30	0.27	264	44	18	38	86	7%	63	1%	4.18	-0.2	44	$13
Health	A	09 CHW	504	57	13	49	1	300	277	307	331	425	756	5	90	31	0.46	277	47	20	33	70	9%	69	1%	4.65	5.3	47	$14
PT/Exp	B	10 CHW	474	43	9	56	3	270	250	276	292	388	681	3	92	28	0.38	276	49	16	36	78	6%	41	7%	3.83	-4.5	50	$11
Consist	B	1st Half	242	20	4	21	0	244			265	355	620	3	92	25	0.37	278	45	18	38	74	5%	46	2%	3.21	-6.9	50	$3
LIMA Plan	D+	2nd Half	232	23	5	35	3	297			321	422	743	3	91	31	0.40	276	53	14	34	81	7%	46	10%	4.49	2.2	53	$8
Rand Var	+1	11 Proj	**433**	**46**	**9**	**50**	**1**	**277**			**304**	**393**	**696**	**4**	**90**	**29**	**0.38**	**270**	**48**	**17**	**35**	**74**	**6%**	**49**	**3%**	**3.98**	**-2.8**	**43**	**$10**

High contact rate should keep BA strong, but with all of the ground balls, can't count on double digit HR anymore. Used to be a 2nd tier choice for #1 catcher; now becoming a 1st tier choice for #2 catcher.

Pie,Felix			AB	R	HR	RBI	SB	Avg	vL	vR	OB	Slg	OPS	bb%	ct%	h%	Eye	xBA	G	L	F	PX	hr/f	Spd	SBO	RC/G	RAR	BPV	R$
Pos	7	06 aaa	559	78	17	57	18	295			350	468	818	8	81	34	0.44					107		137	20%	5.60	6.1	68	$20
Age/B	26 Left	07 CHC	* 406	69	10	57	16	283	111	241	333	436	769	7	81	33	0.39	272	48	20	32	92	9%	158	22%	4.94	-4.9	61	$16
Ht/Wt	74 170	08 CHC	* 418	51	9	51	11	249	91	264	290	381	671	5	83	28	0.33	256	49	17	34	83	8%	128	21%	3.68	-22.0	49	$11
Health	C	09 BAL	252	38	9	29	1	266	250	269	330	437	766	9	77	31	0.41	253	41	21	38	103	12%	147	6%	4.97	-0.3	54	$7
PT/Exp	D	10 BAL	288	39	5	31	5	274	230	286	306	413	719	4	82	32	0.25	285	51	20	29	92	7%	136	10%	4.23	-5.4	53	$8
Consist	C	1st Half	20	4	1	1	0	400			455	650	1105	9	75	50	0.40	330	47	27	27	189	25%	123	0%	9.50	2.2	108	$1
LIMA Plan	C+	2nd Half	268	35	4	30	5	265			294	396	689	4	82	31	0.23	281	51	19	29	85	6%	136	12%	3.87	-7.9	49	$7
Rand Var	0	11 Proj	**456**	**64**	**12**	**54**	**10**	**268**			**312**	**421**	**733**	**6**	**81**	**31**	**0.34**	**275**	**48**	**20**	**33**	**97**	**10%**	**134**	**15%**	**4.45**	**-6.4**	**56**	**$14**

Missed nearly 3 months with lat injury; PX was down when he returned. Speed is legit, but OBP, SBO, and LHP holding him back. Power should return, and if he gets green light:
UP: 20 HR, 20 SB

Podsednik,Scott			AB	R	HR	RBI	SB	Avg	vL	vR	OB	Slg	OPS	bb%	ct%	h%	Eye	xBA	G	L	F	PX	hr/f	Spd	SBO	RC/G	RAR	BPV	R$
Pos	7	06 CHW	524	86	3	45	40	261	216	278	330	353	684	9	82	32	0.56	257	49	23	28	63	2%	133	38%	4.12	-16.9	38	$18
Age/B	35 Left	07 CHW	* 287	40	3	16	14	244	279	229	296	363	659	7	82	29	0.41	278	53	19	28	83	4%	156	32%	3.69	-11.9	57	$6
Ht/Wt	74 190	08 COL	162	22	1	15	12	253	167	264	320	333	653	9	83	30	0.57	264	51	24	24	58	3%	110	34%	3.73	-8.3	30	$5
Health	C	09 CHW	* 579	79	7	50	31	296	320	297	345	402	747	7	86	33	0.54	269	53	18	30	65	5%	143	25%	4.75	-4.2	56	$21
PT/Exp	C	10 2TM	539	63	6	51	35	297	289	300	345	382	728	7	85	34	0.48	259	50	19	31	52	4%	173	29%	4.47	-7.8	48	$23
Consist	B	1st Half	309	39	3	33	24	301			353	372	725	7	84	35	0.50	256	52	19	28	41	4%	185	31%	4.46	-4.5	41	$15
LIMA Plan	C	2nd Half	230	24	3	18	11	291			335	396	730	6	86	33	0.45	263	48	18	35	66	4%	139	25%	4.48	-3.3	51	$8
Rand Var	-4	11 Proj	**455**	**57**	**5**	**40**	**26**	**286**			**337**	**379**	**716**	**7**	**85**	**33**	**0.51**	**263**	**51**	**19**	**30**	**60**	**4%**	**146**	**27%**	**4.38**	**-9.5**	**46**	**$16**

Flirted with .300 for second straight year, but xBA says he's been fortunate. Displayed elite speed in 1H, but just 1 SB in last 108 at-bats. Without speed he's worthless, so don't get too carried away on the bidding.

Polanco,Placido			AB	R	HR	RBI	SB	Avg	vL	vR	OB	Slg	OPS	bb%	ct%	h%	Eye	xBA	G	L	F	PX	hr/f	Spd	SBO	RC/G	RAR	BPV	R$
Pos	5	06 DET	461	58	4	52	1	295	272	305	320	364	685	4	94	31	0.63	276	51	21	28	42	3%	90	2%	3.98	-13.3	46	$10
Age/B	35 Right	07 DET	587	105	9	67	7	341	326	345	380	458	838	6	95	35	1.23	310	45	24	31	72	5%	122	5%	5.79	14.1	88	$23
Ht/Wt	70 194	08 DET	580	90	8	58	7	307	321	301	346	417	764	6	93	32	0.81	278	47	19	35	69	4%	104	5%	4.95	1.1	70	$18
Health	B	09 DET	618	82	10	72	7	285	266	294	324	396	721	6	93	30	0.78	274	43	20	37	64	5%	95	5%	4.46	-3.8	63	$16
PT/Exp	A	10 PHI	554	76	6	52	5	298	280	305	336	386	722	5	92	32	0.68	276	45	20	35	58	3%	92	3%	4.46	-6.8	53	$17
Consist	A	1st Half	261	39	5	27	3	318			348	433	781	4	90	34	0.48	291	45	22	33	75	6%	74	4%	4.96	0.4	55	$10
LIMA Plan	C+	2nd Half	293	37	1	25	2	280			326	345	671	6	92	30	0.91	262	45	19	36	44	1%	107	2%	4.02	-7.3	52	$7
Rand Var	-1	11 Proj	**534**	**74**	**7**	**54**	**5**	**296**			**335**	**395**	**729**	**5**	**92**	**31**	**0.76**	**276**	**45**	**20**	**35**	**62**	**4%**	**99**	**4%**	**4.56**	**-8.0**	**61**	**$16**

Contact rate remains elite, and as long as that continues, there will be value here. Some age-related skills erosion, but continues to post just enough counting stats to justify a double-digit bid.

Posada,Jorge			AB	R	HR	RBI	SB	Avg	vL	vR	OB	Slg	OPS	bb%	ct%	h%	Eye	xBA	G	L	F	PX	hr/f	Spd	SBO	RC/G	RAR	BPV	R$
Pos	20	06 NYY	465	65	23	93	3	277	263	284	365	492	857	12	79	31	0.66	270	38	20	42	132	15%	78	2%	6.24	24.1	72	$17
Age/B	39 Both	07 NYY	506	91	20	90	2	338	331	341	422	543	966	13	81	39	0.76	298	40	22	37	140	13%	78	1%	7.70	44.9	85	$24
Ht/Wt	74 215	08 NYY	168	18	3	22	0	268	255	274	359	411	770	13	77	33	0.63	253	40	21	40	108	6%	73	0%	5.34	5.5	45	$5
Health	D	09 NYY	383	55	22	81	1	285	290	282	364	522	886	11	74	33	0.48	272	36	21	43	157	18%	63	1%	6.67	25.8	63	$16
PT/Exp	C	10 NYY	383	49	18	57	3	248	257	243	348	454	803	13	74	29	0.60	276	43	19	38	147	16%	58	4%	5.67	17.1	61	$12
Consist	C	1st Half	176	26	9	28	0	267			368	483	851	14	76	30	0.67	290	41	21	38	151	18%	55	0%	6.27	10.7	71	$7
LIMA Plan	C	2nd Half	207	23	9	29	3	232			332	430	762	13	72	28	0.54	264	45	16	39	145	15%	68	7%	5.14	6.2	54	$6
Rand Var	+4	11 Proj	**367**	**48**	**15**	**61**	**1**	**264**			**357**	**461**	**817**	**13**	**75**	**31**	**0.57**	**269**	**40**	**20**	**40**	**138**	**14%**	**64**	**1%**	**5.85**	**17.4**	**56**	**$12**

Power holding up well, but two reasons to be cautious:
1. Ct% trending downward (and just 62% in final 77 AB)
2. Hit just .205 on the road.
Still holding value but bottom could drop out at any time.

Posey,Buster			AB	R	HR	RBI	SB	Avg	vL	vR	OB	Slg	OPS	bb%	ct%	h%	Eye	xBA	G	L	F	PX	hr/f	Spd	SBO	RC/G	RAR	BPV	R$
Pos	23	06	0	0	0	0	0	0																					
Age/B	24 Right	07	0	0	0	0	0	0																					
Ht/Wt	73 205	08	0	0	0	0	0	0																					
Health	A	09 SF	* 148	19	4	19	0	277		167	344	426	769	9	84	31	0.63	261	62	8	31	94	10%	103	2%	5.07	3.4	62	$4
PT/Exp	F	10 SF	* 578	81	22	91	1	306	309	304	361	494	855	8	87	32	0.64	305	49	18	33	115	13%	87	2%	5.96	23.5	83	$24
Consist	B	1st Half	282	36	6	35	1	305			360	445	805	8	87	33	0.69	295	52	18	30	88	8%	104	2%	5.48	7.7	70	$10
LIMA Plan	C+	2nd Half	296	45	16	56	0	307			361	541	902	8	86	32	0.60	320	47	18	34	142	18%	75	3%	6.44	15.9	97	$15
Rand Var	0	11 Proj	**499**	**68**	**20**	**74**	**0**	**289**			**348**	**479**	**828**	**8**	**85**	**31**	**0.63**	**295**	**49**	**17**	**33**	**116**	**14%**	**89**	**2%**	**5.67**	**18.2**	**80**	**$18**

18-67-.305 in 406 AB at SF. Just 1 home run in 97 AB in 1H, then exploded. Maintaining 2H hr/f will be tough. But combo of power, ct%, age, and position bodes well for 2011. And he's golden in keeper leagues.

BRIAN RUDD

Powell,Landon

			AB	R	HR	RBI	SB	Avg	vL	vR	OB	Slg	OPS	bb%	ct%	h%	Eye	xBA	G	L	F	PX	hr/f	Spd	SBO	RC/G	RAR	BPV	R$
Pos	2	06 aa	41	4	1	4	0	244			295	317	613	7	68	33	0.23					43		71	0%	2.79	-1.9	-55	$1
Age/B	29 Both	07 aa	236	38	11	32	1	240			318	419	738	10	83	25	0.68					103		78	1%	4.63	1.9	60	$6
Ht/Wt	75 260	08 aaa	300	29	10	37	0	178			283	310	593	13	78	19	0.66					84		54	1%	2.87	-12.9	21	$1
Health	A	09 OAK	140	19	7	30	0	229	128	267	299	429	727	9	74	26	0.39	250	38	18	44	129	15%	48	0%	4.41	0.6	35	$4
PT/Exp	F	10 OAK	* 157	17	3	12	1	192	167	232	288	284	572	12	77	23	0.59	215	37	17	46	67	5%	57	2%	2.63	-7.6	5	$1
Consist	D	1st Half	108	10	2	7	1	196			295	292	587	12	75	24	0.57	237	39	23	39	75	6%	61	3%	2.82	-4.6	5	$0
LIMA Plan	F	2nd Half	49	7	1	5	0	184			273	265	538	11	82	21	0.67	188	35	10	55	52	5%	63	0%	2.27	-3.0	11	$0
Rand Var	+2	11 Proj	124	14	4	16	0	218			308	360	668	12	77	25	0.57	228	37	15	48	95	9%	54	2%	3.79	-1.6	25	$2

2-11-.214 in 112 AB at OAK Ability to take a walk and rarity of switch-hitting catchers make him a nice bench player for an MLB team, but here's no reason for him to be on your roster. Pass.

Prado,Martin

			AB	R	HR	RBI	SB	Avg	vL	vR	OB	Slg	OPS	bb%	ct%	h%	Eye	xBA	G	L	F	PX	hr/f	Spd	SBO	RC/G	RAR	BPV	R$
Pos	45	06 ATL	* 459	48	4	45	4	270	310	154	315	349	664	6	85	31	0.44	229	49	14	37	49	3%	114	6%	3.70	-12.0	29	$8
Age/B	27 Right	07 aaa	395	55	4	37	5	301			351	397	748	7	90	33	0.79					63		106	7%	4.84	5.4	60	$11
Ht/Wt	73 190	08 ATL	228	36	2	33	3	320	283	349	378	461	838	8	87	36	0.72	281	42	23	35	93	3%	110	6%	5.99	7.4	75	$9
Health	B	09 ATL	450	64	11	49	1	307	301	309	358	464	822	7	87	33	0.61	285	44	20	37	107	8%	85	3%	5.63	13.6	76	$15
PT/Exp	B	10 ATL	599	100	15	66	5	307	275	320	351	459	810	6	86	34	0.47	300	48	21	31	101	10%	103	5%	5.38	9.2	69	$24
Consist	A	1st Half	346	57	7	36	4	335			377	480	856	6	86	37	0.49	305	50	22	29	98	8%	109	7%	5.94	10.3	72	$15
LIMA Plan	C+	2nd Half	253	43	8	30	1	269			315	431	746	6	85	29	0.44	293	47	20	33	105	11%	94	2%	4.60	-1.6	65	$8
Rand Var	-1	11 Proj	572	89	16	66	4	301			349	465	814	7	86	33	0.54	294	46	21	33	106	10%	98	4%	5.47	11.9	75	$21

Differences between 1H and 2H mostly h% related as skills were stable. At 27, power growth wouldn't be surprising given stable PX and rising hr/f. Hip injury casts shadow on early '11. UP: 20 HR, more if healthy.

Pujols,Albert

			AB	R	HR	RBI	SB	Avg	vL	vR	OB	Slg	OPS	bb%	ct%	h%	Eye	xBA	G	L	F	PX	hr/f	Spd	SBO	RC/G	RAR	BPV	R$
Pos	3	06 STL	535	119	49	137	7	331	336	329	429	671	1100	15	91	29	1.84	334	37	18	45	170	23%	69	5%	8.98	42.0	151	$38
Age/B	31 Right	07 STL	565	99	32	103	2	327	367	313	428	568	996	15	90	32	1.71	317	42	19	39	133	16%	68	4%	7.98	28.1	118	$29
Ht/Wt	75 230	08 STL	524	100	37	116	7	357	411	333	463	653	1116	17	90	35	1.93	341	40	22	37	167	21%	54	5%	9.43	49.4	144	$37
Health	A	09 STL	568	124	47	135	16	327	338	324	441	658	1099	17	89	30	1.80	335	39	16	46	186	20%	66	10%	9.21	40.8	159	$43
PT/Exp	A	10 STL	587	115	42	118	14	312	306	314	414	596	1011	15	87	30	1.36	327	38	17	46	167	18%	53	9%	8.10	28.3	129	$38
Consist	B	1st Half	298	48	20	60	9	305			415	567	982	16	86	30	1.37	314	35	18	46	155	17%	58	11%	7.84	12.4	120	$19
LIMA Plan	C	2nd Half	289	67	22	58	5	318			414	626	1040	14	88	30	1.34	341	41	16	43	179	20%	56	6%	8.36	15.8	141	$20
Rand Var	+2	11 Proj	562	115	40	121	12	317			423	607	1030	16	88	30	1.57	328	39	18	43	166	19%	59	8%	8.36	32.0	137	$37

The perennial All-Star's shine will have to dim eventually, but elite BPIs suggest that it won't be anytime soon. SB totals are impressive given the subpar speed; 77% success rate over '07-'09 should keep him running.

Punto,Nick

			AB	R	HR	RBI	SB	Avg	vL	vR	OB	Slg	OPS	bb%	ct%	h%	Eye	xBA	G	L	F	PX	hr/f	Spd	SBO	RC/G	RAR	BPV	R$
Pos	56	06 MIN	459	73	1	45	17	290	331	267	356	373	728	9	85	34	0.69	259	46	24	30	53	1%	118	15%	4.72	-3.7	39	$13
Age/B	33 Both	07 MIN	472	53	1	25	16	210	175	226	292	271	563	10	81	26	0.61	226	51	15	35	46	1%	111	17%	2.67	-32.7	16	$3
Ht/Wt	69 190	08 MIN	338	43	2	28	15	284	302	274	346	382	728	9	83	34	0.56	252	45	21	35	69	2%	105	20%	4.64	-2.4	38	$10
Health	D	09 MIN	359	56	1	38	16	228	236	225	340	284	625	15	81	28	0.87	227	48	19	33	43	1%	79	15%	3.61	-11.7	11	$7
PT/Exp	C	10 MIN	252	24	1	20	6	238	253	231	314	302	616	10	80	29	0.56	230	52	15	33	51	1%	75	11%	3.26	-11.9	6	$4
Consist	B	1st Half	186	18	1	18	5	253			332	323	654	11	78	32	0.55	224	52	14	35	56	2%	83	8%	3.75	-5.9	7	$4
LIMA Plan	F	2nd Half	66	6	0	2	1	197			264	242	506	8	85	23	0.60	250	52	19	29	40	0%	67	19%	2.02	-6.1	10	($0)
Rand Var	0	11 Proj	251	30	1	19	8	235			315	295	611	11	82	28	0.65	237	49	18	32	47	1%	83	15%	3.28	-11.8	14	$4

Hip and hamstring injuries limited his ability to get the stolen bases that kept him (barely) rosterable. Speed trend says SBO should continue to decline even if he regains his health.

Quentin,Carlos

			AB	R	HR	RBI	SB	Avg	vL	vR	OB	Slg	OPS	bb%	ct%	h%	Eye	xBA	G	L	F	PX	hr/f	Spd	SBO	RC/G	RAR	BPV	R$
Pos	90	06 ARI	* 484	74	16	72	5	262	171	280	331	469	800	9	86	28	0.72	287	46	16	38	125	10%	66	4%	5.51	10.3	83	$14
Age/B	28 Right	07 ARI	* 344	52	9	52	2	242	172	230	294	400	694	7	80	28	0.37	260	43	16	41	110	8%	61	7%	4.03	-8.8	44	$7
Ht/Wt	73 230	08 CHW	480	96	36	100	7	288	246	303	374	571	944	12	83	28	0.83	303	41	15	43	164	21%	72	7%	7.14	24.0	113	$26
Health	C	09 CHW	351	47	21	56	3	236	213	245	298	456	754	8	85	22	0.60	270	37	16	47	118	15%	44	4%	4.67	-6.9	67	$10
PT/Exp	B	10 CHW	453	73	26	87	2	243	211	253	318	479	797	10	82	24	0.60	284	37	14	49	148	14%	61	4%	5.31	4.9	85	$17
Consist	D	1st Half	249	41	13	50	0	229			302	450	752	9	83	23	0.62	286	35	16	49	141	13%	46	0%	4.76	-1.4	80	$8
LIMA Plan	C+	2nd Half	204	32	13	37	2	260			338	515	852	11	80	27	0.59	283	39	12	50	156	16%	86	8%	6.01	6.4	93	$9
Rand Var	+4	11 Proj	474	75	28	86	4	262			333	500	834	10	83	26	0.62	282	38	15	47	142	15%	61	5%	5.73	7.7	84	$19

Two straight years of subpar h% may suppress market value, but solid xBA, ct%, and rising FB rate make him a nice buy-low candidate. Chronic injuries the only impediment to: UP: Return to 2008

Quintero,Humberto

			AB	R	HR	RBI	SB	Avg	vL	vR	OB	Slg	OPS	bb%	ct%	h%	Eye	xBA	G	L	F	PX	hr/f	Spd	SBO	RC/G	RAR	BPV	R$
Pos	2	06 HOU	* 313	33	3	31	3	262			298	366	664	5	86	30	0.36	309	61	28	11	69	10%	74	4%	3.68	-6.0	32	$5
Age/B	31 Right	07 HOU	* 230	17	3	16	0	240			254	336	590	2	85	27	0.12	305	55	30	15	63	11%	62	4%	2.57	-12.9	13	$1
Ht/Wt	69 215	08 HOU	* 298	25	4	24	0	205	273	215	230	277	507	3	84	23	0.20	226	59	12	29	46	5%	74	3%	1.64	-24.1	3	$0
Health	B	09 HOU	157	11	4	14	0	236	273	226	268	376	644	4	74	29	0.17	226	57	10	32	101	11%	54	0%	3.21	-4.9	3	$2
PT/Exp	F	10 HOU	265	13	4	20	0	234	165	263	256	317	573	3	78	29	0.14	231	47	19	34	62	6%	43	0%	2.24	-17.8	-19	$2
Consist	C	1st Half	151	9	3	9	0	232			266	338	604	4	75	29	0.18	225	50	14	37	81	7%	59	0%	2.67	-8.2	-7	$1
LIMA Plan	F	2nd Half	114	4	1	11	0	237			243	289	533	1	82	28	0.05	247	43	26	31	38	3%	41	0%	1.72	-9.4	-27	$1
Rand Var	0	11 Proj	179	11	3	15	0	235			258	327	585	3	79	28	0.15	232	51	17	32	65	7%	46	1%	2.40	-10.6	-10	$1

Mild improvement in FB and ct% rates didn't help as BPV continued its downward trend. On the wrong side of 30, there's no upside here. Avoid.

Raburn,Ryan

			AB	R	HR	RBI	SB	Avg	vL	vR	OB	Slg	OPS	bb%	ct%	h%	Eye	xBA	G	L	F	PX	hr/f	Spd	SBO	RC/G	RAR	BPV	R$
Pos	79	06 aaa	451	62	18	73	15	257			328	454	782	10	75	30	0.43					127		99	16%	5.25	0.5	53	$15
Age/B	29 Right	07 DET	* 453	81	19	84	14	277	259	338	353	489	842	11	78	32	0.54	283	41	19	39	141	13%	116	14%	6.05	13.2	82	$20
Ht/Wt	72 185	08 DET	182	26	4	20	3	236	238	235	298	368	666	8	73	30	0.33	228	47	14	39	99	8%	104	9%	3.71	-6.3	21	$4
Health	A	09 DET	* 308	53	20	52	7	279	278	298	345	535	880	9	76	31	0.42	266	38	14	47	152	18%	105	14%	6.34	11.8	79	$14
PT/Exp	D	10 DET	371	54	15	62	2	280	295	273	329	474	804	7	75	34	0.29	269	39	18	44	141	12%	93	4%	5.38	5.2	57	$14
Consist	D	1st Half	117	14	2	16	1	214			270	359	629	7	72	28	0.27	229	29	18	54	121	4%	91	5%	3.24	-5.9	28	$2
LIMA Plan	C+	2nd Half	254	40	13	46	1	311			357	528	884	7	77	36	0.31	286	43	17	40	150	17%	92	4%	6.30	9.9	70	$13
Rand Var	-1	11 Proj	470	71	22	74	7	268			326	476	802	8	75	31	0.34	263	39	16	44	142	14%	97	9%	5.39	6.2	61	$18

High hit rate helped fuel 2H breakout but xBA and BPV show it wasn't all luck. Hr/f is volatile, but PX history suggests power is real. Be aware, though, that ct% limits his BA upside.

Ramirez,Alexei

			AB	R	HR	RBI	SB	Avg	vL	vR	OB	Slg	OPS	bb%	ct%	h%	Eye	xBA	G	L	F	PX	hr/f	Spd	SBO	RC/G	RAR	BPV	R$
Pos	6	06 CUB	212	28	7	30	3	274			345	420	764	10	92	27	1.44							108	8%	5.15			
Age/B	29 Right	07 CUB	340	51	20	68	7	335			418	562	979	12	89	33	1.30							105	8%	7.58			
Ht/Wt	74 170	08 CHW	480	65	21	77	13	290	312	281	315	475	790	4	87	30	0.30	285	47	17	37	106	14%	114	20%	4.89	7.7	77	$20
Health	A	09 CHW	542	71	15	68	14	277	370	248	337	389	726	8	88	29	0.74	248	46	16	38	60	8%	106	11%	4.51	0.9	50	$17
PT/Exp	A	10 CHW	585	83	18	70	13	282	278	283	314	431	744	4	86	30	0.33	290	48	19	33	94	11%	112	15%	4.46	8.4	63	$21
Consist	A	1st Half	277	31	7	31	2	278			313	412	724	5	86	30	0.36	283	47	19	34	86	9%	107	12%	4.28	2.6	56	$8
LIMA Plan	C	2nd Half	308	52	11	39	11	286			315	448	763	4	86	30	0.30	296	49	18	33	100	13%	117	18%	4.63	5.8	70	$14
Rand Var	0	11 Proj	593	83	21	79	14	285			327	440	767	6	87	30	0.49	281	47	17	35	90	11%	110	14%	4.80	10.5	67	$22

PX and xBA rebounded to 2008 levels making 2009 look like an adjustment year. Continued 2H improvement a good sign that the gains can stick. GB rate will limit HRs, but he will continue to be a middle infield asset.

Ramirez,Aramis

			AB	R	HR	RBI	SB	Avg	vL	vR	OB	Slg	OPS	bb%	ct%	h%	Eye	xBA	G	L	F	PX	hr/f	Spd	SBO	RC/G	RAR	BPV	R$
Pos	5	06 CHC	594	93	38	119	2	291	261	301	346	561	907	8	89	27	0.79	303	35	18	47	141	15%	69	2%	6.46	16.1	109	$27
Age/B	32 Right	07 CHC	506	72	26	101	0	310	395	286	364	549	914	8	87	32	0.65	302	39	18	44	136	13%	78	0%	6.60	13.6	98	$22
Ht/Wt	73 215	08 CHC	554	97	27	111	2	289	239	305	373	518	891	12	83	31	0.79	283	31	20	48	145	12%	69	2%	6.62	19.5	94	$25
Health	B	09 CHC	306	46	15	65	2	317	350	312	374	516	891	8	86	33	0.65	278	35	21	44	115	13%	73	3%	6.33	9.8	76	$16
PT/Exp	B	10 CHC	465	61	25	83	0	241	259	235	293	452	744	7	81	25	0.38	259	27	16	57	131	12%	49	0%	4.48	-5.8	58	$15
Consist	C	1st Half	209	19	6	23	0	177			242	297	539	8	76	20	0.35	207	26	17	57	83	7%	47	0%	1.94	-20.0	1	$1
LIMA Plan	C	2nd Half	256	42	19	60	0	293			335	578	913	6	85	28	0.41	301	28	15	57	167	15%	62	0%	6.36	10.3	105	$15
Rand Var	+4	11 Proj	515	75	27	91	0	285			343	505	847	8	83	30	0.52	273	31	18	51	132	12%	65	1%	5.81	10.3	76	$22

Thumb injuries and bad luck in 1H help to hide a complete recovery in 2H. FB rate likely unsustainable, but he plays in the right park to take advantage of strong FB history. If the bidding stalls, go the extra buck.

BILL MACEY

Ramirez,Hanley			AB	R	HR	RBI	SB	Avg	vL	vR	OB	Slg	OPS	bb%	ct%	h%	Eye	xBA	G	L	F	PX	hr/f	Spd	SBO	RC/G	RAR	BPV	R$
Pos	6	06 FLA	633	119	17	59	51	292	307	288	350	480	830	8	80	34	0.44	274	44	21	35	118	10%	147	40%	5.83	26.6	76	$31
Age/B	27 Right	07 FLA	639	125	29	81	51	332	399	312	382	562	944	8	85	36	0.55	300	40	18	42	137	13%	115	36%	6.98	43.8	102	$41
Ht/Wt	75 225	08 FLA	589	125	33	67	35	301	258	313	395	540	935	14	79	33	0.75	287	46	17	37	148	19%	134	24%	7.29	44.2	105	$35
Health	A	09 FLA	576	101	24	106	27	342	316	352	405	543	948	10	82	38	0.60	280	39	20	42	131	12%	103	18%	7.21	38.7	87	$37
PT/Exp	A	10 FLA	543	92	21	76	32	300	286	305	374	475	849	11	83	33	0.69	288	51	16	33	111	14%	101	24%	6.05	24.9	74	$31
Consist	B	1st Half	299	47	13	52	15	298			379	498	877	12	85	32	0.87	308	54	15	31	123	17%	106	21%	6.44	17.0	95	$17
LIMA Plan	D+	2nd Half	244	45	8	24	17	303			368	447	815	9	80	35	0.52	265	47	18	35	96	12%	95	28%	5.56	7.9	47	$14
Rand Var	0	11 Proj	574	104	22	79	30	303			375	484	859	10	82	34	0.63	279	46	18	36	117	13%	104	22%	6.18	26.8	75	$32

The risks to the former stud... Power: PX decline in tandem with sudden GB spike puts 20 HR at risk. But odds are he'll hold onto that.
Speed: League avg Spd needs SBO to keep 30 SB. More risky.

Ramirez,Manny			AB	R	HR	RBI	SB	Avg	vL	vR	OB	Slg	OPS	bb%	ct%	h%	Eye	xBA	G	L	F	PX	hr/f	Spd	SBO	RC/G	RAR	BPV	R$
Pos	70	06 BOS	449	79	35	102	0	321	326	319	444	619	1064	18	77	35	0.98	299	36	22	42	181	24%	72	1%	9.19	48.1	114	$24
Age/B	38 Right	07 BOS	483	84	20	88	0	296	344	279	386	493	879	13	81	33	0.77	286	38	22	41	129	13%	59	0%	6.58	20.5	73	$19
Ht/Wt	72 200	08 2TM	552	102	37	121	3	332	308	339	423	601	1024	14	78	37	0.70	300	38	23	39	173	22%	71	2%	8.45	47.9	99	$33
Health	C	09 LA	352	62	19	63	0	290	270	295	409	531	940	17	77	33	0.88	286	33	25	42	160	17%	72	1%	7.62	20.3	93	$16
PT/Exp	B	10 2TM	265	38	9	42	1	298	260	307	402	460	862	15	77	36	0.75	276	43	23	34	117	13%	54	2%	6.56	11.6	49	$11
Consist	B	1st Half	183	31	8	39	1	322			415	525	940	14	81	36	0.85	303	45	21	34	136	16%	59	3%	7.37	11.8	82	$10
LIMA Plan	C	2nd Half	82	7	1	3	0	244			374	317	691	17	67	35	0.63	217	38	27	35	65	5%	66	0%	4.47	-1.2	-24	$1
Rand Var	-1	11 Proj	354	53	14	54	0	291			402	476	878	16	75	35	0.75	271	38	24	38	129	14%	67	1%	6.83	17.0	57	$13

Skills were solid in 1H, though ground ball rate limited power. Calf and hamstring issues led to 3 DL stints. LD% consistent and strong, but health is a big question mark. Best chance for future success is likely as DH.

Ramirez,Max			AB	R	HR	RBI	SB	Avg	vL	vR	OB	Slg	OPS	bb%	ct%	h%	Eye	xBA	G	L	F	PX	hr/f	Spd	SBO	RC/G	RAR	BPV	R$
Pos	2	06	0	0	0	0	0	0																					
Age/B	26 Right	07	0	0	0	0	0	0																					
Ht/Wt	71 175	08 TEX	* 326	49	18	52	2	289	71	281	361	515	876	10	78	32	0.52	261	33	17	50	141	14%	104	4%	6.34	19.7	80	$13
Health	B	09 aaa	274	23	4	34	1	203			274	287	562	9	73	26	0.37					65		83	1%	2.32	-16.7	-10	$1
PT/Exp	F	10 TEX	* 258	25	4	29	0	237	158	240	320	323	643	11	75	30	0.50	212	51	10	39	67	5%	80	0%	3.51	-5.0	3	$4
Consist	F	1st Half	118	12	2	11	0	223			319	323	642	12	71	30	0.50	213	51	10	39	83	6%	87	0%	3.55	-2.2	5	$1
LIMA Plan	F	2nd Half	140	13	2	18	0	248			321	322	644	10	79	30	0.50					55		90	0%	3.50	-2.7	7	$2
Rand Var	-2	11 Proj	229	23	6	28	0	231			309	359	668	10	75	28	0.45	225	48	11	40	90	9%	82	1%	3.75	-3.2	20	$4

2-8-.217 in 69 AB at TEX. Wrist injury sapped his power in '09 and it obviously hasn't come back. These things often do take time. Upside of 2008 remains but no sign of it yet.

Ramos,Wilson			AB	R	HR	RBI	SB	Avg	vL	vR	OB	Slg	OPS	bb%	ct%	h%	Eye	xBA	G	L	F	PX	hr/f	Spd	SBO	RC/G	RAR	BPV	R$
Pos	2	06	0	0	0	0	0	0																					
Age/B	23 Right	07	0	0	0	0	0	0																					
Ht/Wt	72 220	08	0	0	0	0	0	0																					
Health	A	09 aa	205	28	3	26	0	293			310	410	719	2	90	31	0.24					79		67	0%	4.18	-0.5	49	$6
PT/Exp	F	10 WAS	* 436	38	8	37	1	239	563	206	264	350	614	3	85	26	0.23	242	43	13	43	75	5%	69	3%	2.94	-20.2	31	$6
Consist	C	1st Half	224	18	3	15	0	193			214	285	499	3	85	21	0.18	218	46	8	46	66	3%	58	3%	1.61	-20.4	20	($0)
LIMA Plan	F	2nd Half	212	21	5	23	1	288			316	418	735	4	85	32	0.28	258	42	16	42	85	7%	87	4%	4.34	-0.8	45	$6
Rand Var	0	11 Proj	204	22	4	21	0	250			272	368	640	3	87	27	0.24	247	43	14	43	79	5%	66	2%	3.26	-6.7	39	$4

1-5-.278 in 79 AB at WAS. He was blocked in MIN, but is now catcher of the future for Nats. Ct% is already a strength, but patience and power are works in progress. Bright future, but temper expectations for 2011.

Rasmus,Colby			AB	R	HR	RBI	SB	Avg	vL	vR	OB	Slg	OPS	bb%	ct%	h%	Eye	xBA	G	L	F	PX	hr/f	Spd	SBO	RC/G	RAR	BPV	R$
Pos	8	06	0	0	0	0	0	0																					
Age/B	24 Left	07 aa	472	76	22	59	15	239			323	456	778	11	82	25	0.67					136		108	17%	5.20	9.6	91	$15
Ht/Wt	74 200	08 aaa	331	44	8	28	12	218			298	329	627	10	83	24	0.69					71		94	18%	3.40	-17.0	41	$6
Health	A	09 STL	474	72	16	52	3	251	160	277	304	407	711	7	80	28	0.38	243	35	20	46	100	9%	98	3%	4.17	-7.9	46	$13
PT/Exp	C	10 STL	464	85	23	66	12	276	270	278	362	498	860	12	68	36	0.43	254	32	19	49	169	15%	110	15%	6.65	23.7	67	$22
Consist	D	1st Half	245	48	16	40	9	278			368	547	915	13	67	35	0.43	265	31	18	51	202	19%	115	18%	7.50	18.5	89	$14
LIMA Plan	C+	2nd Half	219	37	7	26	3	274			356	443	799	11	70	36	0.42	243	33	21	46	134	10%	104	11%	5.74	5.4	42	$8
Rand Var	-5	11 Proj	493	81	24	70	11	258			334	469	803	10	75	30	0.46	259	33	20	47	143	14%	97	13%	5.50	10.3	65	$19

Trading contact for power led to huge 1H. Tanked in 2H for second straight year, though inflated h% saved him. Major improvements in PX, vs LH are encouraging, but he's a BA risk due to strikeout spike.

Reddick,Josh			AB	R	HR	RBI	SB	Avg	vL	vR	OB	Slg	OPS	bb%	ct%	h%	Eye	xBA	G	L	F	PX	hr/f	Spd	SBO	RC/G	RAR	BPV	R$
Pos	8	06	0	0	0	0	0	0																					
Age/B	24 Left	07	0	0	0	0	0	0																					
Ht/Wt	74 180	08 aa	117	18	4	20	2	199			262	354	616	8	83	21	0.51					91		127	13%	3.11	-7.2	61	$2
Health	A	09 BOS	* 386	49	13	36	5	231	200	167	295	415	709	8	78	26	0.42	240	31	17	52	117	8%	129	13%	4.26	-4.6	65	$7
PT/Exp	D	10 BOS	* 513	53	15	57	4	243	400	175	272	410	682	4	86	26	0.28	276	45	13	43	108	8%	101	13%	3.77	-24.3	69	$11
Consist	B	1st Half	255	23	6	27	2	192			237	331	568	5	83	21	0.34	245	53	5	42	89	7%	126	18%	2.47	-23.7	54	$2
LIMA Plan	F	2nd Half	258	30	9	30	2	293			309	487	796	2	88	31	0.19	305	39	18	43	126	9%	92	8%	4.96	-2.6	88	$9
Rand Var	+1	11 Proj	160	19	5	18	2	250			294	420	714	6	83	27	0.37	259	38	15	47	109	8%	109	12%	4.20	-4.3	66	$4

1-5-.194 in 62 AB at BOS. Got off to terrible start, but despite lack of patience, bat came alive in 2H. May need more time to develop, but if he gets chance, power/speed combo makes him intriguing right away.

Reimold,Nolan			AB	R	HR	RBI	SB	Avg	vL	vR	OB	Slg	OPS	bb%	ct%	h%	Eye	xBA	G	L	F	PX	hr/f	Spd	SBO	RC/G	RAR	BPV	R$
Pos	7	06	0	0	0	0	0	0																					
Age/B	27 Right	07 aa	186	24	10	28	2	271			324	501	825	7	79	30	0.37					150		91	12%	5.56	1.9	80	$6
Ht/Wt	76 205	08 aa	507	73	22	70	6	252			322	441	764	9	86	26	0.75					111		99	7%	4.96	-2.5	83	$15
Health	A	09 BAL	* 467	67	23	69	14	299	271	284	381	517	898	12	79	34	0.62	276	48	14	37	134	17%	106	11%	6.74	22.4	78	$21
PT/Exp	C	10 BAL	* 453	48	11	42	6	211	265	164	291	319	610	10	83	23	0.66	237	49	12	39	70	8%	74	7%	3.15	-24.3	32	$6
Consist	F	1st Half	221	18	6	19	0	189			257	302	559	8	80	21	0.46	232	47	13	41	75	8%	77	0%	2.35	-17.8	23	$1
LIMA Plan	C	2nd Half	232	30	6	22	6	232			321	337	658	12	86	25	0.92	246	54	11	36	65	8%	85	12%	3.89	-7.0	46	$5
Rand Var	+4	11 Proj	399	50	17	47	7	253			330	430	760	10	82	27	0.64	269	49	13	38	108	14%	94	9%	4.91	-0.2	66	$12

3-14-.207 in 116 AB at BAL. Is this the fallout from 2009's Achilles injury? Slow start resulted in demotion to Triple-A, where he had just a .738 OPS. We know he owns some skill so should merit a speculative bid.

Renteria,Edgar			AB	R	HR	RBI	SB	Avg	vL	vR	OB	Slg	OPS	bb%	ct%	h%	Eye	xBA	G	L	F	PX	hr/f	Spd	SBO	RC/G	RAR	BPV	R$
Pos	6	06 ATL	598	100	14	70	17	293	333	281	359	436	796	9	85	33	0.70	282	47	22	31	90	9%	87	13%	5.43	18.0	59	$22
Age/B	35 Right	07 ATL	494	87	12	57	11	332	349	323	389	470	859	9	84	38	0.60	285	46	23	31	89	9%	93	8%	6.09	21.3	56	$22
Ht/Wt	73 200	08 DET	503	69	10	55	6	270	366	239	320	382	702	7	87	29	0.58	272	46	22	32	69	7%	105	6%	4.19	-2.0	51	$12
Health	C	09 SF	460	50	5	48	7	250	231	257	309	328	637	8	85	28	0.57	250	48	21	31	54	4%	72	7%	3.47	-16.1	22	$9
PT/Exp	C	10 SF	243	26	3	22	3	276	286	272	333	374	708	8	82	32	0.49	247	48	16	37	68	4%	117	4%	4.29	-0.9	37	$6
Consist	B	1st Half	128	10	1	12	3	305			360	375	735	8	84	36	0.55	252	52	17	31	54	3%	93	7%	4.62	0.7	26	$4
LIMA Plan	D	2nd Half	115	16	2	10	0	243			304	374	678	8	80	29	0.43	239	42	14	43	86	5%	124	0%	3.92	-1.7	44	$2
Rand Var	-2	11 Proj	346	42	5	34	3	269			326	371	697	8	84	31	0.52	254	47	19	35	69	5%	103	4%	4.16	-3.5	38	$8

You can see the skills erosion in Ct%, xBA, and hr/f. His body is following the same path, as he landed on DL three times, then missed another couple of weeks in Sept. He's become an end-game pick at this point.

Repko,Jason			AB	R	HR	RBI	SB	Avg	vL	vR	OB	Slg	OPS	bb%	ct%	h%	Eye	xBA	G	L	F	PX	hr/f	Spd	SBO	RC/G	RAR	BPV	R$
Pos	9	06 LA	130	21	3	16	10	254	239	262	331	377	708	10	82	29	0.63	249	44	21	35	73	8%	122	36%	4.37	-1.6	44	$5
Age/B	30 Right	07	0	0	0	0	0	0																					
Ht/Wt	70 192	08 aa	459	64	9	36	14	225			284	345	630	8	78	27	0.38					81		123	19%	3.23	-29.0	33	$9
Health	C	09 aa	393	53	12	35	18	222			263	365	628	5	79	25	0.27					90		96	31%	3.03	-25.4	29	$10
PT/Exp	F	10 MIN	* 355	45	7	28	10	217	196	250	284	318	601	8	77	26	0.39	214	38	15	47	71	6%	89	17%	2.84	-23.5	9	$6
Consist	A	1st Half	233	26	4	19	7	215			277	304	581	8	80	25	0.43	140	25	0	75	58	3%	99	18%	2.62	-17.0	14	$4
LIMA Plan	F	2nd Half	122	19	3	9	3	221			296	344	641	10	70	29	0.35	217	39	16	45	100	8%	82	16%	3.39	-5.9	4	$2
Rand Var	0	11 Proj	129	18	3	11	5	225			286	341	627	8	77	27	0.37	227	40	17	43	80	8%	86	22%	3.13	-8.2	14	$3

3-9-.228 in 127 AB at MIN. Got opportunity in 2H, but recent minor league stats suggest he didn't earn it. Strong defensive reputation, but low ct%, below average power/speed don't provide much hope offensively.

BRIAN RUDD

Reyes,Jose			AB	R	HR	RBI	SB	Avg	vL	vR	OB	Slg	OPS	bb%	ct%	h%	Eye	xBA	G	L	F	PX	hr/f	Spd	SBO	RC/G	RAR	BPV	R$
Pos	6	06 NYM	647	122	19	81	64	300	330	288	353	487	840	8	87	32	0.65	288	45	21	34	98	10%	135	45%	5.85	27.4	86	$37
Age/B	27 Both	07 NYM	681	119	12	57	78	280	318	266	354	421	775	10	89	30	0.99	270	42	18	40	81	5%	151	48%	5.33	17.6	87	$35
Ht/Wt	73 200	08 NYM	688	113	16	68	56	297	280	303	358	475	833	9	88	32	0.80	294	44	23	33	100	8%	156	36%	5.90	24.8	99	$35
Health	D	09 NYM	147	18	2	15	11	279	400	248	358	395	752	11	87	31	0.95	252	41	19	40	71	4%	136	27%	5.09	1.8	70	$6
PT/Exp	B	10 NYM	563	83	11	54	30	282	309	274	320	428	748	5	89	30	0.49	278	43	18	40	87	6%	121	29%	4.69	4.3	74	$23
Consist	B	1st Half	310	51	6	32	19	277			319	419	739	6	88	30	0.50	266	42	16	42	84	5%	126	27%	4.60	1.6	69	$14
LIMA Plan	B	2nd Half	253	32	5	22	11	289			321	439	759	5	90	30	0.48	292	44	19	37	91	6%	110	31%	4.79	2.8	78	$10
Rand Var	0	11 Proj	**560**	**81**	**13**	**55**	**32**	**286**			**339**	**441**	**780**	**7**	**88**	**31**	**0.69**	**280**	**43**	**19**	**38**	**91**	**7%**	**134**	**29%**	**5.18**	**10.8**	**83**	**$24**

Poor April and oblique issues in 2H marred solid rebound season. Skill set intact, with bb%, durability being the only exceptions. Value is in his legs, with fragility adding risk and capping upside.

Reynolds,Mark			AB	R	HR	RBI	SB	Avg	vL	vR	OB	Slg	OPS	bb%	ct%	h%	Eye	xBA	G	L	F	PX	hr/f	Spd	SBO	RC/G	RAR	BPV	R$
Pos	5	06 aa	114	20	8	18	0	264			322	528	849	8	70	31	0.29					177		76	4%	6.08	2.8	63	$4
Age/B	27 Right	07 ARI *	500	84	23	79	3	278	278	279	347	495	842	10	69	36	0.34	251	36	20	44	153	15%	113	4%	6.29	9.7	53	$18
Ht/Wt	74 220	08 ARI	539	87	28	97	11	239	279	226	320	458	778	11	62	33	0.31	229	36	19	45	172	19%	92	10%	5.67	4.8	37	$20
Health	A	09 ARI	578	98	44	102	24	260	235	266	346	543	889	12	61	34	0.34	252	35	17	47	223	26%	83	22%	7.40	38.7	74	$31
PT/Exp	A	10 ARI	499	79	32	85	7	198	218	191	313	433	746	14	58	26	0.39	222	32	13	55	195	20%	68	8%	5.37	7.4	38	$16
Consist	D	1st Half	271	46	19	54	5	221			319	487	806	13	59	29	0.35	236	26	13	61	223	20%	83	11%	6.33	11.9	65	$11
LIMA Plan	B	2nd Half	228	33	13	31	2	171			305	368	674	16	57	22	0.44	205	38	14	48	161	21%	71	6%	4.17	-5.4	11	$4
Rand Var	+5	11 Proj	**467**	**75**	**29**	**78**	**9**	**223**			**322**	**461**	**783**	**13**	**60**	**30**	**0.37**	**231**	**35**	**16**	**50**	**189**	**21%**	**80**	**11%**	**5.82**	**10.5**	**44**	**$17**

Value took a dive along with h% and SBO, deteriorating further as season progressed. He'll rebound some, but '09 BA looks unattainable with downward drifting ct%. Frankly, a 58% contact rate is obscene.

Rhymes,Will			AB	R	HR	RBI	SB	Avg	vL	vR	OB	Slg	OPS	bb%	ct%	h%	Eye	xBA	G	L	F	PX	hr/f	Spd	SBO	RC/G	RAR	BPV	R$
Pos	4	06	0	0	0	0	0	0																					
Age/B	28 Left	07 aa	155	19	1	19	5	239			266	294	560	4	87	27	0.29					39		104	16%	2.40	-9.1	20	$3
Ht/Wt	69 155	08 a/a	541	62	2	47	13	261			306	328	635	6	89	29	0.61					42		136	13%	3.52	-20.9	45	$10
Health	A	09 aaa	404	40	3	34	17	225			278	305	583	7	87	25	0.54					49		127	25%	2.88	-23.3	39	$6
PT/Exp	D	10 DET *	555	73	3	45	16	270	351	292	319	366	685	7	92	29	0.85	290	44	23	33	62	2%	136	16%	4.21	-4.1	72	$14
Consist	B	1st Half	256	31	0	19	13	243			290	302	592	6	93	26	0.96					37		139	23%	3.23	-9.5	58	$6
LIMA Plan	D	2nd Half	299	43	3	26	4	293			344	421	765	7	90	32	0.78	303	44	23	33	83	3%	128	11%	5.08	5.3	82	$9
Rand Var	0	11 Proj	**328**	**40**	**3**	**29**	**10**	**271**			**318**	**367**	**684**	**6**	**89**	**30**	**0.64**	**277**	**44**	**23**	**33**	**59**	**3%**	**126**	**17%**	**4.09**	**-5.0**	**58**	**$8**

1-19-.304 in 191 AB at DET. Seized AB down the stretch with high-ct% game. Lacks power, but Spd, 80% SB% in minors hint at untapped SBs. Though at age 28, time is limited. UP: 20 SB

Rios,Alex			AB	R	HR	RBI	SB	Avg	vL	vR	OB	Slg	OPS	bb%	ct%	h%	Eye	xBA	G	L	F	PX	hr/f	Spd	SBO	RC/G	RAR	BPV	R$
Pos	8	06 TOR	450	68	17	82	15	302	295	305	353	516	868	7	80	35	0.39	276	37	22	42	134	11%	100	18%	6.18	19.0	74	$20
Age/B	30 Right	07 TOR	643	114	24	85	17	297	345	283	352	498	850	8	84	32	0.53	285	36	20	44	125	10%	114	12%	5.94	25.2	88	$27
Ht/Wt	77 215	08 TOR	635	91	15	79	32	291	289	292	337	461	799	6	82	33	0.39	276	41	21	38	113	7%	101	25%	5.32	-0.6	65	$26
Health	A	09 2AL	582	63	17	71	24	247	261	242	292	395	688	6	82	28	0.35	250	43	16	41	92	9%	81	22%	3.86	-13.5	38	$16
PT/Exp	A	10 CHW	567	89	21	88	34	284	259	292	329	457	786	6	84	31	0.41	282	45	17	38	109	12%	94	33%	5.03	-4.9	65	$29
Consist	C	1st Half	287	49	13	45	22	303			351	509	859	7	86	31	0.54	299	42	16	42	127	13%	98	39%	5.91	4.7	92	$18
LIMA Plan	C	2nd Half	280	40	8	43	12	264			306	404	710	6	81	30	0.31	266	49	17	34	90	10%	93	26%	4.10	-10.3	36	$11
Rand Var	0	11 Proj	**567**	**81**	**20**	**81**	**28**	**275**			**321**	**452**	**772**	**6**	**82**	**30**	**0.38**	**276**	**43**	**18**	**39**	**111**	**11%**	**94**	**27%**	**4.90**	**-3.1**	**62**	**$24**

Another good half / bad half split, but didn't approach '09 disaster. Skill set remained same, with h%, ct% upticks and SBO hike adding to bottom line. Expect something similar in 2011.

Rivera,Juan			AB	R	HR	RBI	SB	Avg	vL	vR	OB	Slg	OPS	bb%	ct%	h%	Eye	xBA	G	L	F	PX	hr/f	Spd	SBO	RC/G	RAR	BPV	R$
Pos	79	06 LAA	448	65	23	85	0	310	351	293	358	525	882	7	87	32	0.56	292	51	16	33	121	18%	55	3%	6.13	11.7	77	$18
Age/B	32 Right	07 LAA *	104	6	2	19	0	224	276	286	247	341	588	3	90	23	0.30	261	44	15	41	77	5%	61	0%	2.78	-7.1	46	$1
Ht/Wt	74 230	08 LAA	256	31	12	45	1	246	233	253	290	438	728	6	87	24	0.48	263	37	14	48	111	11%	55	4%	4.33	-4.0	68	$7
Health	C	09 LAA	529	72	25	88	0	287	333	271	333	478	811	6	89	28	0.63	286	44	18	38	101	14%	68	1%	5.31	4.5	73	$19
PT/Exp	C	10 LAA	416	53	15	52	2	252	264	246	307	409	716	7	86	26	0.57	274	46	16	39	97	11%	54	4%	4.30	-7.1	55	$11
Consist	B	1st Half	234	38	10	34	1	239			296	423	720	8	82	25	0.46	274	40	16	44	119	12%	66	4%	4.28	-4.2	62	$7
LIMA Plan	F	2nd Half	182	15	5	18	1	269			321	390	712	7	91	27	0.82	276	52	16	32	72	9%	50	4%	4.35	-2.8	51	$4
Rand Var	+1	11 Proj	**294**	**35**	**12**	**43**	**1**	**265**			**314**	**430**	**744**	**7**	**88**	**27**	**0.59**	**276**	**45**	**16**	**39**	**97**	**11%**	**56**	**3%**	**4.59**	**-2.9**	**61**	**$9**

BPIs declined at least slightly almost across the board; GB trend coupled with poor speed looking particularly ominous. Poor defense contributed to 2H PT loss. Rebound possible, just don't bet on a big one.

Roberts,Brian			AB	R	HR	RBI	SB	Avg	vL	vR	OB	Slg	OPS	bb%	ct%	h%	Eye	xBA	G	L	F	PX	hr/f	Spd	SBO	RC/G	RAR	BPV	R$
Pos	4	06 BAL	563	85	10	55	36	286	235	308	350	410	760	9	88	31	0.83	271	44	21	35	77	6%	105	25%	5.04	14.8	66	$21
Age/B	33 Both	07 BAL	621	103	12	57	50	290	268	299	379	432	810	13	84	33	0.90	261	36	20	45	95	5%	110	27%	5.83	32.2	73	$28
Ht/Wt	69 175	08 BAL	614	107	9	57	40	295	313	289	379	448	827	12	83	34	0.80	281	40	24	36	107	5%	109	26%	6.05	20.1	76	$26
Health	D	09 BAL	632	110	16	79	30	283	294	278	358	451	809	10	82	32	0.66	273	36	22	42	114	7%	88	21%	5.67	13.4	70	$26
PT/Exp	A	10 BAL	230	28	4	15	12	278	288	275	352	391	743	10	83	32	0.65	254	34	22	45	83	5%	86	19%	4.83	2.4	45	$8
Consist	B	1st Half	14	1	0	0	2	143			250	214	464	13	86	17	1.00	259	50	17	33	63	0%	82	67%	1.82	-1.2	45	$0
LIMA Plan	C+	2nd Half	216	27	4	15	10	287			358	403	761	10	82	33	0.63	254	33	22	46	85	5%	88	17%	5.03	3.5	46	$8
Rand Var	-1	11 Proj	**473**	**74**	**7**	**44**	**23**	**281**			**359**	**413**	**772**	**11**	**83**	**32**	**0.73**	**266**	**37**	**22**	**41**	**93**	**5%**	**99**	**19%**	**5.28**	**9.1**	**61**	**$17**

Returned from 1H back woes with 86% SB% and most skills intact, only power MIA. But age and health are now legit issues.
UP: 35 SB
DN: More DL time

Rodriguez,Alex			AB	R	HR	RBI	SB	Avg	vL	vR	OB	Slg	OPS	bb%	ct%	h%	Eye	xBA	G	L	F	PX	hr/f	Spd	SBO	RC/G	RAR	BPV	R$
Pos	5	06 NYY	572	113	35	121	15	290	294	289	387	523	909	14	76	33	0.65	267	42	18	40	143	20%	83	10%	6.99	31.9	71	$29
Age/B	35 Right	07 NYY	583	143	54	156	24	314	272	327	410	645	1055	14	79	32	0.79	325	41	17	42	199	28%	70	15%	8.64	59.8	128	$45
Ht/Wt	75 228	08 NYY	510	104	35	103	18	302	263	316	381	573	953	11	77	33	0.56	295	42	18	40	175	22%	81	14%	7.39	35.4	97	$31
Health	C	09 NYY	444	78	30	100	14	286	277	289	395	532	927	15	78	31	0.82	283	42	20	38	141	23%	60	10%	7.20	31.5	76	$24
PT/Exp	A	10 NYY	522	74	30	125	4	270	217	290	344	506	850	10	81	28	0.60	294	46	14	40	149	18%	58	5%	5.97	17.2	83	$24
Consist	B	1st Half	286	43	12	62	2	276			351	486	837	10	81	30	0.62	297	44	18	38	139	14%	63	5%	5.93	9.0	79	$12
LIMA Plan	C+	2nd Half	236	31	18	63	2	263			336	530	866	10	81	25	0.58	291	48	9	43	160	22%	53	5%	6.03	8.3	89	$12
Rand Var	+4	11 Proj	**502**	**83**	**32**	**117**	**7**	**285**			**370**	**527**	**897**	**12**	**79**	**30**	**0.66**	**287**	**44**	**16**	**40**	**149**	**20%**	**61**	**7%**	**6.65**	**26.1**	**81**	**$26**

Nagging injuries (groin, calf) contributed to disappearance of speed game, perhaps also to OPS plunge. GB% and bb% are eye-openers. Health, age are becoming issues, but still among the very best 3B plays.

Rodriguez,Ivan			AB	R	HR	RBI	SB	Avg	vL	vR	OB	Slg	OPS	bb%	ct%	h%	Eye	xBA	G	L	F	PX	hr/f	Spd	SBO	RC/G	RAR	BPV	R$
Pos	2	06 DET	547	74	13	69	8	300	340	284	332	437	769	5	84	34	0.30	276	50	21	28	83	10%	90	8%	4.77	5.5	42	$17
Age/B	39 Right	07 DET	502	50	11	63	2	281	302	274	294	420	714	2	81	33	0.09	278	52	19	28	96	10%	77	4%	3.97	-4.6	29	$11
Ht/Wt	69 190	08 2AL	398	44	7	35	10	276	289	272	316	394	710	5	83	32	0.34	275	56	20	24	78	9%	80	11%	4.17	-0.3	32	$10
Health	B	09 2TM	425	55	10	47	1	249	283	240	280	384	663	4	78	30	0.20	258	54	18	28	91	11%	74	3%	3.46	-10.2	19	$8
PT/Exp	C	10 WAS	398	32	4	49	2	266	292	258	295	347	641	4	83	31	0.24	267	61	18	21	59	6%	62	5%	3.26	-14.1	9	$8
Consist	A	1st Half	196	18	1	25	2	306			333	403	736	4	85	36	0.27	294	60	21	19	76	3%	69	10%	4.45	-0.2	30	$6
LIMA Plan	D	2nd Half	202	14	3	24	0	228			257	292	549	4	82	26	0.22	240	63	15	23	42	8%	59	0%	2.07	-14.8	-11	$2
Rand Var	0	11 Proj	**307**	**31**	**4**	**35**	**2**	**257**			**288**	**345**	**632**	**4**	**82**	**30**	**0.23**	**258**	**58**	**18**	**24**	**62**	**6%**	**68**	**5%**	**3.14**	**-11.2**	**8**	**$6**

Still holding onto PT, but age, 2H surface stat decline and GB% spikes say he won't for much longer. Profit is possible as your team's #2 CA, but so is another mid-year flameout. High-risk, minimal reward.

Rodriguez,Sean			AB	R	HR	RBI	SB	Avg	vL	vR	OB	Slg	OPS	bb%	ct%	h%	Eye	xBA	G	L	F	PX	hr/f	Spd	SBO	RC/G	RAR	BPV	R$
Pos	48	06	0	0	0	0	0	0																					
Age/B	25 Right	07 aa	508	76	15	66	14	236			302	386	688	9	77	28	0.40					104		94	19%	3.97	-5.9	37	$13
Ht/Wt	72 190	08 LAA *	415	75	20	53	6	247	178	213	311	461	772	8	77	28	0.41	258	41	12	47	141	13%	99	8%	4.99	1.2	71	$13
Health	A	09 a/a	385	75	26	84	8	264			346	534	879	11	70	31	0.42					176		127	9%	6.67	21.7	84	$19
PT/Exp	D	10 TAM	343	53	9	40	13	251	292	229	294	397	690	6	72	32	0.22	244	42	19	39	113	9%	90	21%	3.93	-5.4	18	$12
Consist	F	1st Half	192	31	6	29	6	276			298	438	735	3	71	36	0.11	248	40	17	43	129	10%	75	20%	4.40	-0.3	20	$8
LIMA Plan	C	2nd Half	151	22	3	11	7	219			289	344	634	9	72	28	0.36	240	44	21	36	92	8%	118	22%	3.31	-5.4	17	$3
Rand Var	-2	11 Proj	**482**	**80**	**14**	**67**	**17**	**247**			**309**	**405**	**714**	**8**	**73**	**31**	**0.33**	**245**	**42**	**18**	**39**	**113**	**11%**	**98**	**18%**	**4.34**	**-3.9**	**29**	**$16**

PRO: Plus power, 81% SB%, versatility, improved 2H bb%.
CON: Ct%, struggles vs. RHP. Without better contact, his PT could be at the mercy of h% vagaries again. There's both risk and reward here.

JOCK THOMPSON

Rolen,Scott

Rolen,Scott			AB	R	HR	RBI	SB	Avg	vL	vR	OB	Slg	OPS	bb%	ct%	h%	Eye	xBA	G	L	F	PX	hr/f	Spd	SBO	RC/G	RAR	BPV	R$
Pos	5	06 STL	521	94	22	95	7	296	259	310	364	518	882	10	87	31	0.81	289	33	20	48	133	10%	67	8%	6.42	13.6	95	$23
Age/B	36 Right	07 STL	392	55	8	58	5	265	204	287	329	398	727	9	86	29	0.66	260	38	20	43	85	6%	68	7%	4.59	-11.6	50	$10
Ht/Wt	76 250	08 TOR	408	58	11	50	5	262	250	266	337	431	768	10	83	29	0.65	268	36	21	44	113	7%	71	5%	5.14	3.1	64	$11
Health	C	09 2TM	475	76	11	67	5	305	374	283	365	455	820	9	87	33	0.73	277	37	23	41	97	7%	76	6%	5.69	10.2	68	$18
PT/Exp	B	10 CIN	471	66	20	83	1	285	260	295	353	497	850	10	83	31	0.61	293	37	19	44	139	12%	63	2%	6.03	15.0	82	$19
Consist	A	1st Half	265	42	17	56	0	302			366	577	944	9	83	31	0.61	314	36	18	46	169	17%	68	3%	7.03	15.7	110	$14
LIMA Plan	C	2nd Half	206	24	3	27	1	262			336	393	729	10	82	31	0.61	269	38	22	40	99	4%	61	2%	4.71	-1.1	46	$5
Rand Var	0	11 Proj	444	64	13	67	3	279			347	450	798	9	84	31	0.65	278	37	21	43	114	8%	66	4%	5.45	4.4	67	$15

3 reasons he'll be overvalued...
- Inflated hr/f drove HR spike
- 2H PX in line with 3-year norm
- Big 1H masked 2H collapse

Given age and spotty health record, odds of sustaining 1H are slim. Stop bidding at $15.

Rollins,Jimmy

Rollins,Jimmy			AB	R	HR	RBI	SB	Avg	vL	vR	OB	Slg	OPS	bb%	ct%	h%	Eye	xBA	G	L	F	PX	hr/f	Spd	SBO	RC/G	RAR	BPV	R$
Pos	6	06 PHI	689	127	25	83	36	277	277	277	332	478	810	8	88	28	0.71	294	44	19	37	111	11%	124	24%	5.49	22.2	97	$30
Age/B	32 Both	07 PHI	716	139	30	94	41	296	321	286	341	531	872	6	88	30	0.58	294	36	20	44	124	11%	180	27%	6.10	33.1	121	$37
Ht/Wt	68 170	08 PHI	556	76	11	59	47	277	288	272	345	437	782	9	90	29	1.05	302	45	24	31	95	7%	115	32%	5.40	12.3	92	$25
Health	C	09 PHI	672	100	21	77	31	250	230	257	296	423	719	6	90	25	0.63	282	40	19	41	103	8%	101	27%	4.40	-5.3	85	$24
PT/Exp	A	10 PHI	350	48	8	41	17	243	297	218	321	374	695	10	91	25	1.25	279	46	17	37	78	7%	99	18%	4.44	0.2	78	$12
Consist	B	1st Half	89	16	4	14	2	270			375	494	869	14	85	28	1.15	296	39	16	45	138	12%	92	7%	6.55	5.4	110	$4
LIMA Plan	B	2nd Half	261	32	4	27	15	234			301	333	634	9	93	24	1.32	275	48	17	35	59	5%	101	23%	3.76	-5.2	68	$8
Rand Var	+4	11 Proj	559	83	15	67	29	275			342	437	779	9	90	29	0.97	286	43	19	38	95	8%	105	20%	5.27	12.2	87	$24

Why there's hope for rebound... Eye spike, gradual ct% gains, SB returned with 2H green light. Calf problem zapped Spd in 1H. xBA supports '06-'08 BA. With h% help and some health...
UP: 20 HR, 30 SB, .280 BA

Rosales,Adam

Rosales,Adam			AB	R	HR	RBI	SB	Avg	vL	vR	OB	Slg	OPS	bb%	ct%	h%	Eye	xBA	G	L	F	PX	hr/f	Spd	SBO	RC/G	RAR	BPV	R$
Pos	4	06	0	0	0	0	0	0																					
Age/B	27 Right	07 aa	255	41	11	25	3	242			321	462	783	10	77	27	0.50					143		138	13%	5.27	7.1	86	$6
Ht/Wt	74 195	08 aaa	432	54	9	44	6	246			274	387	662	4	84	28	0.24					92		138	8%	3.51	-17.0	58	$9
Health	A	09 CIN	* 339	44	9	35	4	242	255	200	315	381	696	10	82	27	0.60	248	45	16	40	90	8%	117	6%	4.20	-3.4	58	$7
PT/Exp	D	10 OAK	255	31	7	31	2	271	289	261	321	400	721	7	75	34	0.29	255	38	28	34	88	11%	125	6%	4.31	-1.1	22	$7
Consist	A	1st Half	204	23	6	24	1	265			310	407	725	7	75	33	0.31	257	38	27	35	97	11%	129	2%	4.39	-0.4	31	$5
LIMA Plan	D	2nd Half	51	8	1	7	1	294			333	373	706	6	75	38	0.23	250	38	32	30	55	9%	98	19%	4.01	-0.7	-16	$2
Rand Var	-4	11 Proj	293	40	7	34	4	256			309	382	691	7	78	31	0.35	259	40	26	34	84	9%	120	11%	3.95	-5.7	32	$7

Carved out utility niche before stress fracture in ankle shelved him in August. Problem is, that .270 BA came from fortunate h%. Given that and dwindling ct% OB dip is big risk, meaning his Spd will remain a wasted skill.

Ross,Cody

Ross,Cody			AB	R	HR	RBI	SB	Avg	vL	vR	OB	Slg	OPS	bb%	ct%	h%	Eye	xBA	G	L	F	PX	hr/f	Spd	SBO	RC/G	RAR	BPV	R$
Pos	789	06 2NL	* 319	45	16	52	1	244	245	216	317	447	764	10	76	27	0.45	253	36	21	43	122	15%	86	5%	4.91	-3.2	49	$9
Age/B	30 Right	07 FLA	173	35	12	39	2	335	385	306	404	653	1057	10	78	37	0.53	334	41	21	38	211	23%	79	4%	8.71	15.1	127	$11
Ht/Wt	70 194	08 FLA	461	59	22	73	6	260	285	249	310	488	798	7	75	30	0.28	266	36	21	43	152	15%	89	7%	5.30	-1.6	63	$16
Health	A	09 FLA	559	73	24	90	5	270	284	266	312	469	781	6	78	31	0.28	259	33	19	48	134	12%	69	6%	4.96	-9.7	54	$20
PT/Exp	B	10 2NL	525	71	14	65	9	269	287	263	317	413	730	7	77	33	0.31	265	46	21	34	103	10%	88	8%	4.43	-9.7	32	$17
Consist	A	1st Half	304	40	7	43	8	289			335	431	766	6	78	35	0.31	276	48	22	29	102	10%	88	11%	4.90	-1.4	34	$12
LIMA Plan	D+	2nd Half	221	31	7	22	1	240			291	389	680	7	76	29	0.30	249	42	18	40	104	10%	89	4%	3.76	-8.7	29	$5
Rand Var	0	11 Proj	410	56	13	58	5	266			315	429	744	7	77	32	0.31	256	40	20	40	113	10%	81	6%	4.60	-7.9	38	$13

3 signs he's on a 4th OF track...
- Another year of skill decline
- Stagnant bb%, ct%, Eye
- 3 yr Slg vs. RH: .451 .424, .371

Post season heroics will give him longer leash, but you'll see these risks and side w/caution.

Ross,David

Ross,David			AB	R	HR	RBI	SB	Avg	vL	vR	OB	Slg	OPS	bb%	ct%	h%	Eye	xBA	G	L	F	PX	hr/f	Spd	SBO	RC/G	RAR	BPV	R$
Pos	2	06 CIN	247	37	21	52	0	255	316	228	352	579	931	13	70	28	0.49	276	32	17	51	211	24%	49	0%	7.44	22.4	90	$10
Age/B	34 Right	07 CIN	311	32	17	39	0	203	248	175	273	399	671	9	70	23	0.33	236	34	19	48	129	16%	41	0%	3.61	-7.9	17	$4
Ht/Wt	74 238	08 2TM	142	18	3	13	0	225	206	241	368	352	720	18	73	29	0.82	240	38	25	37	100	8%	54	2%	4.88	3.0	25	$2
Health	B	09 ATL	128	18	7	20	0	273	250	284	376	508	884	14	70	34	0.54	257	30	22	49	175	16%	58	0%	6.97	9.9	65	$5
PT/Exp	F	10 ATL	121	15	2	28	0	289	308	256	390	479	869	14	77	36	0.71	285	38	21	41	149	5%	66	3%	6.83	8.0	77	$5
Consist	C	1st Half	65	8	0	16	0	277			390	354	743	16	82	34	1.00	228	39	16	45	71	0%	54	4%	5.25	1.5	32	$2
LIMA Plan	D	2nd Half	56	7	2	12	0	304			391	625	1016	12	71	39	0.50	339	37	27	37	253	14%	74	0%	9.04	7.0	137	$3
Rand Var	-2	11 Proj	120	15	5	22	0	275			378	508	886	14	73	34	0.62	282	35	22	43	174	13%	61	1%	7.00	9.0	80	$4

Blueprint for how mid-30's backup catcher can extend career. Elite power in flashes... how 'bout that 2H! Blame a tiny hr/f for his HR outage. Still a nice reserve backstop in very deep leagues, even without many AB.

Rowand,Aaron

Rowand,Aaron			AB	R	HR	RBI	SB	Avg	vL	vR	OB	Slg	OPS	bb%	ct%	h%	Eye	xBA	G	L	F	PX	hr/f	Spd	SBO	RC/G	RAR	BPV	R$
Pos	8	06 PHI	405	59	12	47	10	262	222	275	293	425	718	4	81	30	0.24	270	44	22	34	101	11%	96	16%	4.15	-3.5	45	$12
Age/B	33 Right	07 PHI	612	105	27	89	6	309	315	306	358	515	873	7	81	35	0.39	288	43	20	38	133	15%	75	5%	6.15	27.0	67	$26
Ht/Wt	72 219	08 SF	549	57	13	70	2	271	286	266	325	410	735	7	77	33	0.35	252	49	19	32	102	10%	59	4%	4.55	-2.9	24	$13
Health	B	09 SF	499	61	15	64	4	261	213	276	302	419	721	6	75	32	0.24	242	45	16	39	114	10%	76	4%	4.28	-6.6	27	$13
PT/Exp	B	10 SF	331	42	11	34	5	230	211	237	265	378	643	5	78	26	0.22	251	48	15	37	97	12%	93	12%	3.16	-17.5	27	$7
Consist	B	1st Half	223	27	7	26	2	238			264	399	663	3	78	28	0.16	262	50	15	35	109	11%	88	10%	3.40	-10.0	34	$5
LIMA Plan	F	2nd Half	108	15	4	8	3	213			267	333	601	7	77	24	0.32	224	46	14	40	72	12%	83	15%	2.64	-7.6	6	$2
Rand Var	+4	11 Proj	245	31	8	27	4	245			289	394	683	6	77	29	0.27	247	47	16	37	100	11%	81	9%	3.74	-7.6	26	$6

Further Eye erosion, marginal power, mediocre Spd combine to give him plenty of downside. Yes, BA will come back a bit with h%, but the writing's on the wall. (I'd like to see this wall and what exactly does it say on it?)

Ruiz,Carlos

Ruiz,Carlos			AB	R	HR	RBI	SB	Avg	vL	vR	OB	Slg	OPS	bb%	ct%	h%	Eye	xBA	G	L	F	PX	hr/f	Spd	SBO	RC/G	RAR	BPV	R$
Pos	2	06 PHI	* 437	58	20	76	4	289	263	260	354	488	842	9	85	30	0.68	287	47	19	34	113	16%	69	5%	5.85	18.5	72	$17
Age/B	32 Right	07 PHI	374	42	6	54	6	259	189	282	334	396	730	10	87	29	0.86	279	46	18	36	91	5%	87	7%	4.79	3.9	68	$8
Ht/Wt	70 204	08 PHI	320	47	4	31	1	219	212	220	313	300	613	12	88	24	1.16	252	54	17	29	54	5%	63	3%	3.55	-6.5	41	$3
Health	B	09 PHI	322	32	9	43	3	255	293	242	350	425	775	13	88	27	1.21	284	42	19	39	111	8%	59	5%	5.44	11.2	85	$8
PT/Exp	C	10 PHI	371	43	8	53	0	302	327	291	392	447	839	13	85	34	1.02	289	45	20	35	102	7%	67	1%	6.20	17.5	71	$13
Consist	C	1st Half	153	16	2	13	0	275			393	366	759	16	84	32	1.20	272	48	23	29	67	5%	60	0%	5.43	4.1	41	$3
LIMA Plan	C	2nd Half	218	27	6	40	0	321			391	505	896	10	87	35	0.86	302	43	18	39	125	8%	76	1%	6.68	12.9	92	$10
Rand Var	-4	11 Proj	399	47	10	54	2	288			376	442	818	12	87	31	1.04	285	46	19	35	102	8%	63	3%	5.89	17.0	73	$12

There's no such thing as a 2H player, right? His OPS last 3 yrs:
1H: .576, .720, .759
2H: .654, .822, .896
He's an outlier to that edict. That aside, plate control is rock solid, and he still has... UP: 15 HR

Ryal,Rusty

Ryal,Rusty			AB	R	HR	RBI	SB	Avg	vL	vR	OB	Slg	OPS	bb%	ct%	h%	Eye	xBA	G	L	F	PX	hr/f	Spd	SBO	RC/G	RAR	BPV	R$
Pos	37	06	0	0	0	0	0	0																					
Age/B	28 Right	07 aa	178	17	6	17	3	224			252	374	626	4	80	25	0.19					89		136	17%	2.94	-15.2	41	$2
Ht/Wt	74 200	08 aa	460	52	14	53	3	245			290	396	687	6	82	27	0.35					93		115	6%	3.85	-22.8	51	$9
Health	A	09 ARI	* 463	61	18	62	4	259			307	483	790	6	78	30	0.31	275	36	21	44	150	11%	109	7%	5.21	-17.6	79	$14
PT/Exp	D	10 ARI	207	19	3	11	0	261	274	248	288	348	636	4	68	37	0.12	202	45	16	39	71	6%	136	6%	3.15	-19.4	-22	$3
Consist	D	1st Half	92	8	2	6	0	293			316	402	718	3	70	40	0.11	219	44	20	36	76	9%	143	0%	4.20	-5.4	-10	$2
LIMA Plan	F	2nd Half	115	11	1	5	0	235			267	304	571	4	66	35	0.13	188	46	13	41	67	3%	113	12%	2.28	-14.5	-38	$1
Rand Var	-5	11 Proj	148	16	3	13	1	243			279	371	650	5	73	31	0.19	230	45	16	39	93	8%	119	8%	3.32	-13.1	16	$2

Looked overmatched by MLB hurlers. With brutal bb% and ct%, his Spd skills are useless. Heck, even inflated h% could only net a .261 BA. Still owns that '09 PX, so we can't write him off yet. We'll likely do that next year.

Ryan,Brendan

Ryan,Brendan			AB	R	HR	RBI	SB	Avg	vL	vR	OB	Slg	OPS	bb%	ct%	h%	Eye	xBA	G	L	F	PX	hr/f	Spd	SBO	RC/G	RAR	BPV	R$
Pos	6	06 a/a	69	9	1	8	1	217			250	275	525	4	86	24	0.30					32		99	13%	1.92	-5.3	8	$1
Age/B	29 Right	07 STL	* 501	71	5	23	20	240	354	238	288	311	599	6	89	26	0.63	254	47	19	34	42	3%	158	20%	3.09	-20.6	53	$9
Ht/Wt	74 195	08 STL	197	30	0	10	7	244	261	229	300	289	590	8	84	29	0.52	241	52	19	28	39	0%	113	16%	2.92	-10.1	19	$4
Health	A	09 STL	390	55	3	37	14	292	265	306	333	400	733	6	86	34	0.43	266	51	19	30	68	3%	147	19%	4.55	-1.2	55	$13
PT/Exp	C	10 STL	439	50	2	36	11	223	224	223	278	294	571	7	86	25	0.55	251	47	18	35	50	2%	117	14%	2.76	-22.5	37	$6
Consist	D	1st Half	212	20	2	15	7	198			267	292	560	9	83	23	0.56	256	45	20	35	66	3%	102	17%	2.59	-12.3	35	$2
LIMA Plan	D	2nd Half	227	30	0	21	4	247			287	295	583	5	89	28	0.54	245	49	16	35	37	0%	123	12%	2.90	-10.4	37	$4
Rand Var	+4	11 Proj	397	52	2	31	12	252			301	324	625	7	86	29	0.52	252	49	18	32	50	2%	124	16%	3.35	-13.8	38	$8

On surface, a huge drop-off. But plate control is still solid; blame h% for BA drop. You'll buy him for speed, and 20 SB still possible if he keeps getting F/T work. He'll provide profit if you can stomach the iffy BA and PT risk.

STEPHEN NICKRAND

Salazar,Oscar

Salazar,Oscar			AB	R	HR	RBI	SB	Avg	vL	vR	OB	Slg	OPS	bb%	ct%	h%	Eye	xBA	G	L	F	PX	hr/f	Spd	SBO	RC/G	RAR	BPV	R$
Pos	7	06 VNZ	229	36	7	42	1	262			324	419	743	8	87	27	0.72					88		102	5%	4.75	-3.1	69	$7
Age/B	32 Right	07 aa	532	47	14	61	2	197			222	330	551	3	84	21	0.20					84		84	6%	2.15	-51.4	37	$3
Ht/Wt	72 195	08 BAL	*527	66	15	76	6	250	211	349	308	409	716	8	87	26	0.65	276	40	19	40	100	8%	92	7%	4.41	-6.8	74	$13
Health	B	09 2TM	*338	40	14	59	0	305	357	265	352	506	858	7	86	32	0.50	280	48	13	39	119	12%	86	3%	5.92	5.9	79	$13
PT/Exp	D	10 SD	131	19	3	19	1	237	235	238	320	336	656	11	82	27	0.70	229	43	15	42	64	7%	72	8%	3.74	-5.3	26	$3
Consist	D	1st Half	102	13	2	15	1	235			328	304	632	12	80	28	0.70	210	43	16	41	41	6%	77	9%	3.43	-5.1	4	$2
LIMA Plan	F	2nd Half	29	6	1	4	0	241			290	448	739	6	90	24	0.67	303	42	12	46	137	8%	81	0%	4.67	-0.3	107	$1
Rand Var	0	11 Proj	119	14	3	18	1	252			313	382	695	8	84	27	0.57	241	44	13	43	81	8%	71	6%	4.09	-4.2	42	$3

Nickname "Chaci," Spanish for small part (insert your own joke here). His '09 PX gave a bit of hope he'd get a new nickname, but at 33, it still seems apt. Also wants to be on Dancing with the Stars (insert your own joke here).

Saltalamacchia,Jarrc

Saltalamacchia,Jarrc			AB	R	HR	RBI	SB	Avg	vL	vR	OB	Slg	OPS	bb%	ct%	h%	Eye	xBA	G	L	F	PX	hr/f	Spd	SBO	RC/G	RAR	BPV	R$
Pos	2	06 aa	313	29	8	38	0	220			335	358	693	15	78	26	0.78					91		75	1%	4.36	-0.2	39	$3
Age/B	25 Both	07 2TM	*389	55	16	44	2	270	226	290	322	450	772	7	77	31	0.33	260	44	17	39	118	14%	87	2%	4.92	6.3	44	$11
Ht/Wt	76 235	08 TEX	*253	35	5	36	0	252	158	311	345	381	726	12	66	36	0.42	223	31	27	42	112	7%	73	3%	4.91	5.4	2	$5
Health	B	09 TEX	283	34	9	34	0	233	229	235	289	371	660	7	66	32	0.23	216	36	23	41	104	12%	86	3%	3.61	-5.7	-12	$5
PT/Exp	D	10 2AL	*298	35	9	32	1	218	143	200	287	383	670	9	79	25	0.45					119		78	2%	3.79	-3.4	52	$5
Consist	B	1st Half	170	17	7	17	0	210			263	360	623	7	80	23	0.36	175	25	0	75	95	6%	75	0%	3.01	-6.1	34	$2
LIMA Plan	D	2nd Half	128	18	2	15	1	228			318	413	731	12	77	28	0.56					151		85	4%	4.84	2.6	78	$2
Rand Var	+5	11 Proj	222	28	6	26	1	248			320	407	727	10	73	31	0.39	252	38	21	40	121	9%	85	2%	4.60	2.5	35	$5

0-2-.167 in 24 AB at TEX/BOS. Made better contact, but unlucky h% hid progress. Excellent power potential, still owns the promising '07-'08 skills. Fresh start with BOS may help. Young as CA's go, so there's hope.

Sanchez,Angel

Sanchez,Angel			AB	R	HR	RBI	SB	Avg	vL	vR	OB	Slg	OPS	bb%	ct%	h%	Eye	xBA	G	L	F	PX	hr/f	Spd	SBO	RC/G	RAR	BPV	R$
Pos	6	06 aa	542	80	3	43	6	242			286	301	587	6	91	26	0.70					39		102	12%	3.01	-22.7	40	$7
Age/B	27 Right	07	0	0	0	0	0	0																					
Ht/Wt	74 185	08 a/a	372	33	2	29	4	220			278	280	559	7	86	25	0.57					42		117	11%	2.59	-22.0	28	$2
Health	C	09 aaa	449	46	5	41	1	248			290	346	636	6	87	28	0.46					65		109	3%	3.43	-14.9	47	$6
PT/Exp	D	10 2TM	*476	49	0	38	5	259	284	274	301	319	620	6	85	30	0.40	262	44	25	31	44	0%	141	5%	3.21	-13.6	31	$7
Consist	B	1st Half	233	19	0	13	5	232			287	282	570	7	88	26	0.65	305	67	22	11	40	0%	108	9%	2.82	-9.7	33	$2
LIMA Plan	D	2nd Half	243	30	0	25	0	284			315	354	669	4	82	35	0.25	253	43	25	32	49	0%	156	1%	3.66	-3.7	24	$5
Rand Var	-1	11 Proj	330	35	0	28	1	252			295	312	607	6	86	29	0.44	260	44	25	31	44	0%	129	4%	3.10	-12.1	31	$4

0-25-.277 in 253 AB at BOS/HOU Spd would suggest SB upside, but they won't let him run. A four-year 54% success rate might have something to do with that! BPV, RAR vividly reveal the rest of his "skills." No SB = no value.

Sanchez,Freddy

Sanchez,Freddy			AB	R	HR	RBI	SB	Avg	vL	vR	OB	Slg	OPS	bb%	ct%	h%	Eye	xBA	G	L	F	PX	hr/f	Spd	SBO	RC/G	RAR	BPV	R$
Pos	4	06 PIT	582	85	6	85	3	344	442	316	377	473	849	5	91	37	0.60	297	37	28	36	85	3%	78	3%	5.85	18.8	68	$23
Age/B	33 Right	07 PIT	602	77	11	81	0	304	364	282	339	442	781	5	87	33	0.42	281	39	22	38	88	5%	96	1%	5.02	5.2	61	$17
Ht/Wt	70 189	08 PIT	569	75	9	52	0	271	289	266	297	371	667	4	89	29	0.33	275	45	24	30	62	6%	100	1%	3.64	-18.4	45	$12
Health	C	09 2NL	457	56	7	41	5	293	323	282	326	416	741	5	83	34	0.29	272	45	24	31	85	6%	109	5%	4.50	-0.3	46	$13
PT/Exp	B	10 SF	431	55	7	47	3	292	343	276	341	397	738	7	84	33	0.47	267	44	22	34	73	6%	83	3%	4.58	-2.9	36	$13
Consist	A	1st Half	157	19	1	20	0	287			349	357	706	9	85	33	0.63	258	53	18	28	55	3%	72	2%	4.35	-2.1	24	$4
LIMA Plan	D+	2nd Half	274	36	6	27	3	296			337	420	756	6	84	33	0.39	271	38	24	38	83	7%	90	4%	4.71	-0.8	43	$9
Rand Var	-2	11 Proj	429	55	7	45	3	280			321	390	711	6	85	32	0.41	272	44	23	33	75	5%	94	3%	4.22	-6.1	43	$11

Stats look good, but closer look says '06-'07 glory days are gone. His remaining value lies in BA, and falling xBA says that could collapse at any time. Use that, not BA, as a baseline.
DN: .260 BA

Sanchez,Gaby

Sanchez,Gaby			AB	R	HR	RBI	SB	Avg	vL	vR	OB	Slg	OPS	bb%	ct%	h%	Eye	xBA	G	L	F	PX	hr/f	Spd	SBO	RC/G	RAR	BPV	R$
Pos	3	06	0	0	0	0	0	0																					
Age/B	27 Right	07	0	0	0	0	0	0																					
Ht/Wt	73 234	08 aa	478	55	13	72	13	265			344	429	773	11	86	29	0.87					107		57	16%	5.25	-3.5	71	$15
Health	A	09 aaa	318	45	13	46	4	246			321	399	720	10	86	25	0.78					85		52	4%	4.45	-15.6	50	$9
PT/Exp	C	10 FLA	572	72	19	85	5	273	324	256	339	448	786	9	82	30	0.56	269	37	17	46	117	9%	75	3%	5.25	-17.7	65	$19
Consist	B	1st Half	289	41	9	38	3	308			373	481	854	9	84	34	0.64	280	38	20	43	114	9%	97	3%	6.10	-1.8	76	$12
LIMA Plan	C+	2nd Half	283	31	10	47	2	237			303	413	717	9	81	26	0.50	256	36	14	50	120	9%	56	3%	4.36	-16.7	56	$7
Rand Var	-1	11 Proj	538	69	21	80	5	258			329	433	763	10	84	27	0.66	261	37	17	47	109	10%	63	4%	4.96	-20.4	64	$17

Mixed signals in debut.
PRO: Decent power now, FB trend may signal PX upside.
CON: Falling Eye; overall 2H skills dip; now age 28, so that may have been his peak.
UP: 25 HR; DN: .240 BA

Sandoval,Pablo

Sandoval,Pablo			AB	R	HR	RBI	SB	Avg	vL	vR	OB	Slg	OPS	bb%	ct%	h%	Eye	xBA	G	L	F	PX	hr/f	Spd	SBO	RC/G	RAR	BPV	R$
Pos	5	06	0	0	0	0	0	0																					
Age/B	24 Both	07	0	0	0	0	0	0																					
Ht/Wt	71 246	08 SF	*320	50	9	57	0	328	237	383	350	491	841	3	90	34	0.35	311	45	26	29	99	11%	85	1%	5.54	1.4	75	$14
Health	A	09 SF	572	79	25	90	5	330	379	314	386	556	942	8	85	35	0.63	302	45	19	36	139	14%	74	6%	7.02	28.6	94	$28
PT/Exp	B	10 SF	563	61	13	63	3	268	227	282	325	409	733	8	86	29	0.58	269	44	17	38	93	7%	50	3%	4.60	-4.9	49	$14
Consist	D	1st Half	308	39	6	32	2	269			328	399	728	8	87	29	0.69	267	47	15	38	85	6%	61	5%	4.60	-2.7	54	$8
LIMA Plan	C	2nd Half	255	22	7	31	1	267			320	420	740	7	84	30	0.48	273	42	19	39	103	8%	44	2%	4.60	-2.2	46	$6
Rand Var	+3	11 Proj	487	60	16	68	3	287			339	465	804	7	86	31	0.55	287	44	19	37	112	10%	61	4%	5.37	3.7	68	$16

Disappointment, especially PX, but monthly data (125, 79, 67, 59, 145, 74) shows he still owns the skill. Should rebound given past, but there's a big range:
UP: 25 HR, .300 BA
DN: 10 HR, .260 BA

Santana,Carlos

Santana,Carlos			AB	R	HR	RBI	SB	Avg	vL	vR	OB	Slg	OPS	bb%	ct%	h%	Eye	xBA	G	L	F	PX	hr/f	Spd	SBO	RC/G	RAR	BPV	R$
Pos	2	06	0	0	0	0	0	0																					
Age/B	24 Both	07	0	0	0	0	0	0																					
Ht/Wt	71 188	08	0	0	0	0	0	0																					
Health	A	09 aa	429	81	21	87	2	267			388	482	870	16	81	29	1.06					134		83	3%	6.63	29.3	93	$18
PT/Exp	F	10 CLE	*346	52	15	60	8	263	146	314	389	469	858	17	82	28	1.17	296	35	21	44	138	12%	66	6%	6.56	24.0	96	$14
Consist	A	1st Half	266	41	13	53	5	274			394	504	898	16	83	29	1.14	315	37	23	40	153	14%	68	5%	7.01	21.6	108	$12
LIMA Plan	B+	2nd Half	80	11	2	7	3	225			374	350	724	19	81	25	1.27	246	33	20	47	87	7%	87	10%	5.01	2.1	61	$2
Rand Var	+2	11 Proj	405	66	15	66	8	272			398	449	847	17	82	30	1.15	269	34	20	46	116	10%	71	6%	6.47	26.2	78	$15

6-22-.260 in 150 AB at CLE. Knee injury cut short a splendid debut. Excellent patience and power profile that stayed solid in majors, with 1H xBA showing BA upside. A star in the making.
UP: 25 HR, .300 BA

Santiago,Ramon

Santiago,Ramon			AB	R	HR	RBI	SB	Avg	vL	vR	OB	Slg	OPS	bb%	ct%	h%	Eye	xBA	G	L	F	PX	hr/f	Spd	SBO	RC/G	RAR	BPV	R$
Pos	46	06 DET	*163	20	1	14	3	227			267	294	562	5	80	28	0.27	233	58	15	27	47	3%	117	11%	2.32	-9.0	4	$1
Age/B	31 Both	07 DET	*432	44	3	33	10	240	300	281	265	329	595	3	84	28	0.22	261	39	26	35	61	2%	139	21%	2.75	-16.5	36	$5
Ht/Wt	71 175	08 DET	124	30	4	18	1	282	320	273	390	460	850	15	86	30	1.29	293	44	23	33	102	11%	146	2%	6.41	5.3	103	$5
Health	A	09 DET	262	29	7	35	1	267	270	267	312	385	697	6	78	32	0.30	235	47	17	35	69	10%	122	4%	3.93	-7.6	19	$6
PT/Exp	D	10 DET	320	38	3	22	2	263	313	249	326	325	651	9	83	31	0.54	251	49	21	30	44	4%	120	4%	3.61	-8.0	20	$6
Consist	C	1st Half	175	22	2	12	1	274			342	331	673	9	84	32	0.64	257	53	21	26	39	5%	100	2%	3.93	-2.7	17	$4
LIMA Plan	D	2nd Half	145	16	1	10	1	248			306	317	623	8	81	30	0.43	243	45	21	34	50	3%	128	7%	3.22	-5.4	19	$2
Rand Var	0	11 Proj	224	30	4	22	2	263			325	361	686	8	82	31	0.50	253	47	20	32	61	6%	132	5%	4.01	-3.9	34	$5

Lots of fluctuation in this skill set, but over the past four seasons, he's produced almost exactly the same $ value. So you know what to expect. Which isn't a lot, frankly.
UP: Sorry, no upside here...

Saunders,Michael

Saunders,Michael			AB	R	HR	RBI	SB	Avg	vL	vR	OB	Slg	OPS	bb%	ct%	h%	Eye	xBA	G	L	F	PX	hr/f	Spd	SBO	RC/G	RAR	BPV	R$
Pos	7	06	0	0	0	0	0	0																					
Age/B	24 Left	07	0	0	0	0	0	0																					
Ht/Wt	76 212	08 aa	343	47	9	38	11	247			314	398	712	9	76	30	0.41					106		105	23%	4.32	-8.5	40	$10
Health	A	09 SEA	*370	65	11	33	9	265	200	239	318	416	735	7	77	32	0.34	240	47	15	39	94	10%	140	13%	4.50	-5.5	41	$11
PT/Exp	D	10 SEA	*369	34	10	37	9	202	202	215	287	327	614	11	74	25	0.45	218	36	16	48	87	8%	96	13%	3.04	-21.4	17	$5
Consist	B	1st Half	199	22	7	25	4	195			264	330	594	9	73	23	0.35	219	35	16	49	94	10%	67	11%	2.63	-14.2	8	$3
LIMA Plan	C	2nd Half	170	12	3	12	5	212			313	324	636	13	74	27	0.57	214	36	17	47	79	5%	125	14%	3.51	-7.3	25	$2
Rand Var	+3	11 Proj	412	52	13	39	10	250			321	399	720	9	75	30	0.42	230	38	16	46	99	9%	111	13%	4.41	-6.5	34	$11

10-33-.211-6 in 289 AB at SEA. Enough speed and power to produce double-digit HR & SB, but ct% and xBA say they will come with BA damage. Young and touted enough to improve, but a risky investment for '11.

HAROLD NICHOLS

Schierholtz,Nate			AB	R	HR	RBI	SB	Avg	vL	vR	OB	Slg	OPS	bb%	ct%	h%	Eye	xBA	G	L	F	PX	hr/f	Spd	SBO	RC/G	RAR	BPV	R$
Pos	9	06 aa	470	56	14	55	8	270			310	445	755	5	83	30	0.33					103		100	10%	4.68	-7.3	56	$12
Age/B	27 Left	07 SF	* 523	63	12	65	11	299	500	266	319	463	782	3	87	33	0.23	272	44	15	41	97	6%	118	14%	4.89	0.1	69	$17
Ht/Wt	74 217	08 SF	* 425	65	14	67	8	294	333	315	326	503	828	5	87	31	0.38	329	46	30	24	121	16%	92	12%	5.51	3.8	85	$17
Health	A	09 SF	285	33	5	29	3	267	370	242	306	400	706	5	80	32	0.28	257	45	21	35	96	6%	91	6%	4.11	-6.4	35	$7
PT/Exp	D	10 SF	227	34	3	17	4	242	294	227	304	366	669	8	83	28	0.53	263	44	18	37	84	4%	107	16%	3.89	-10.0	51	$5
Consist	B	1st Half	146	23	2	11	4	267			327	390	717	8	87	30	0.68	273	47	17	36	80	4%	105	18%	4.52	-3.5	62	$4
LIMA Plan	D	2nd Half	81	11	1	6	0	198			261	321	582	8	77	25	0.37	247	39	21	40	94	4%	101	13%	2.70	-6.9	29	$0
Rand Var	+4	11 Proj	**215**	**29**	**4**	**21**	**3**	**265**			**313**	**414**	**727**	**6**	**82**	**31**	**0.38**	**268**	**43**	**20**	**37**	**99**	**7%**	**100**	**11%**	**4.45**	**-4.4**	**51**	**$6**

2008's xBA, PX and hr/f once got our attention, but have since proven to be outliers. Now there isn't enough contact or power here to hold our interest. Reverse platoon split reduces chances of a meaningful role.

Schneider,Brian			AB	R	HR	RBI	SB	Avg	vL	vR	OB	Slg	OPS	bb%	ct%	h%	Eye	xBA	G	L	F	PX	hr/f	Spd	SBO	RC/G	RAR	BPV	R$
Pos	2	06 WAS	410	30	4	55	2	256	271	251	319	329	648	8	84	30	0.57	249	47	23	30	50	4%	50	3%	3.62	-8.7	9	$6
Age/B	34 Left	07 WAS	408	33	6	54	0	235	212	244	328	336	663	12	86	26	1.00	247	48	15	36	66	5%	54	0%	4.08	-4.3	40	$4
Ht/Wt	73 210	08 NYM	335	30	9	38	0	257	187	277	340	367	707	11	84	28	0.79	278	53	26	21	66	15%	55	0%	4.39	1.7	30	$6
Health	C	09 NYM	170	11	3	24	0	218	0	230	293	335	628	10	88	23	0.86	258	57	13	30	80	7%	49	0%	3.56	-3.6	50	$1
PT/Exp	F	10 PHI	125	17	4	15	0	240	56	271	340	384	724	13	80	27	0.76	254	45	17	38	90	11%	86	0%	4.66	0.7	46	$3
Consist	B	1st Half	63	9	2	6	0	254			338	381	719	11	84	27	0.80	273	47	21	32	78	12%	76	0%	4.52	0.1	46	$2
LIMA Plan	D	2nd Half	62	8	2	9	0	226			342	387	730	15	76	27	0.73	235	43	13	45	104	10%	93	0%	4.81	0.6	46	$1
Rand Var	0	11 Proj	**216**	**23**	**6**	**28**	**0**	**245**			**335**	**376**	**710**	**12**	**83**	**27**	**0.77**	**257**	**50**	**17**	**33**	**82**	**10%**	**67**	**0%**	**4.48**	**0.7**	**42**	**$4**

PRO: PX trend hints at a mini edition of mid-30s CA spike, still effective vRHP (.802 OPS) CON: despite growth, PX still below average; GB% stifles any hope for HR or Avg upside. A marginal 2nd CA at this point.

Schumaker,Skip			AB	R	HR	RBI	SB	Avg	vL	vR	OB	Slg	OPS	bb%	ct%	h%	Eye	xBA	G	L	F	PX	hr/f	Spd	SBO	RC/G	RAR	BPV	R$
Pos	4	06 aaa	369	42	3	23	10	281			319	350	668	5	88	31	0.46					42		97	13%	3.75	-6.4	27	$8
Age/B	31 Left	07 STL	* 409	42	6	40	3	272	375	327	317	385	702	6	86	30	0.48	279	54	19	27	73	6%	80	7%	4.18	-6.2	42	$8
Ht/Wt	70 195	08 STL	540	87	8	46	8	302	168	340	358	406	763	8	89	33	0.78	290	58	22	20	62	8%	104	6%	5.02	3.7	54	$18
Health	A	09 STL	532	85	4	35	2	303	220	322	365	393	758	9	87	34	0.75	293	61	22	17	66	5%	98	2%	5.03	7.3	51	$15
PT/Exp	A	10 STL	476	66	5	42	5	265	211	275	326	338	664	8	87	30	0.67	284	59	22	20	51	6%	76	6%	3.85	-13.4	28	$11
Consist	B	1st Half	263	40	2	19	4	255			315	327	642	8	86	29	0.62	291	57	25	19	51	5%	87	8%	3.59	-9.6	29	$6
LIMA Plan	D	2nd Half	213	26	3	23	1	277			339	352	691	9	87	31	0.74	273	61	18	21	49	8%	66	3%	4.17	-3.9	28	$5
Rand Var	+2	11 Proj	**386**	**55**	**4**	**32**	**4**	**282**			**341**	**364**	**705**	**8**	**87**	**32**	**0.69**	**284**	**59**	**21**	**20**	**55**	**6%**	**82**	**5%**	**4.34**	**-4.2**	**36**	**$10**

PRO: makes consistent contact; h% and xBA point to a mild rebound in Avg. CON: nothing interesting happens after contact, not enough Spd to beat out GBs. Hollow BA is his only upside.

Scott,Luke			AB	R	HR	RBI	SB	Avg	vL	vR	OB	Slg	OPS	bb%	ct%	h%	Eye	xBA	G	L	F	PX	hr/f	Spd	SBO	RC/G	RAR	BPV	R$
Pos	0	06 HOU	* 532	79	26	85	7	287	240	366	369	517	887	11	81	31	0.68	284	36	24	40	133	15%	113	5%	6.58	2.3	89	$21
Age/B	32 Left	07 HOU	369	49	18	64	3	255	271	252	348	504	852	13	74	30	0.56	284	41	19	40	167	16%	68	4%	6.36	1.3	78	$12
Ht/Wt	72 210	08 BAL	476	67	23	65	2	256	215	269	331	471	801	10	79	28	0.52	268	39	17	44	139	14%	69	3%	5.43	7.0	68	$14
Health	B	09 BAL	449	61	25	77	0	258	260	257	339	488	827	11	77	28	0.53	268	40	17	43	143	17%	58	0%	5.78	8.0	63	$14
PT/Exp	B	10 BAL	447	70	27	72	2	284	240	297	368	535	902	12	78	31	0.60	302	40	19	41	167	19%	56	2%	6.77	5.2	88	$20
Consist	B	1st Half	223	35	12	30	1	274			347	520	867	10	75	32	0.45	298	40	19	41	176	18%	64	2%	6.36	0.1	82	$9
LIMA Plan	C+	2nd Half	224	35	15	42	1	295			388	549	937	13	81	31	0.81	307	41	18	41	159	20%	55	1%	7.17	5.1	97	$11
Rand Var	0	11 Proj	**443**	**65**	**25**	**72**	**2**	**264**			**348**	**505**	**853**	**11**	**78**	**29**	**0.59**	**288**	**40**	**18**	**42**	**155**	**17%**	**62**	**2%**	**6.13**	**3.8**	**80**	**$16**

Career-best BA and HR levels driven by bumps in h% and hr/f rather than skills growth. Skill set is stable, but as age passes power peak, we need to expect regression. Pay only for 2008-09 levels.

Scutaro,Marco			AB	R	HR	RBI	SB	Avg	vL	vR	OB	Slg	OPS	bb%	ct%	h%	Eye	xBA	G	L	F	PX	hr/f	Spd	SBO	RC/G	RAR	BPV	R$
Pos	6	06 OAK	365	52	5	41	5	266	218	279	354	397	751	12	82	31	0.76	256	44	21	36	84	5%	114	5%	5.11	7.3	55	$8
Age/B	35 Right	07 OAK	338	49	7	41	2	260	309	245	330	361	691	9	88	28	0.88	256	39	20	41	62	6%	79	3%	4.23	-0.6	47	$7
Ht/Wt	70 185	08 TOR	517	76	7	60	7	267	268	267	340	356	696	10	87	29	0.88	261	43	23	35	59	4%	95	5%	4.34	0.2	47	$12
Health	A	09 TOR	574	100	12	60	14	282	269	287	380	409	789	14	87	31	1.20	256	37	19	44	80	6%	91	9%	5.64	19.4	68	$19
PT/Exp	A	10 BOS	632	92	11	56	5	275	282	273	331	388	719	8	89	30	0.75	266	41	17	42	77	5%	89	5%	4.50	9.8	61	$17
Consist	C	1st Half	332	49	4	25	1	280			345	380	725	9	89	31	0.87	272	41	20	39	72	4%	93	4%	4.67	6.7	60	$8
LIMA Plan	B	2nd Half	300	43	7	31	4	270			316	397	712	6	89	28	0.61	259	40	14	46	83	6%	82	6%	4.30	3.0	61	$9
Rand Var	0	11 Proj	**502**	**77**	**9**	**51**	**5**	**275**			**345**	**389**	**734**	**10**	**88**	**30**	**0.87**	**260**	**40**	**19**	**41**	**75**	**5%**	**91**	**5%**	**4.77**	**8.5**	**59**	**$13**

Other than a drop in bb%, this was a credible followup to '09 "career year". Beware, though: big AB totals have propped up his value, and 550+ AB gets tougher to repeat in mid-30s. DN: See 2006-07.

Shoppach,Kelly			AB	R	HR	RBI	SB	Avg	vL	vR	OB	Slg	OPS	bb%	ct%	h%	Eye	xBA	G	L	F	PX	hr/f	Spd	SBO	RC/G	RAR	BPV	R$
Pos	2	06 CLE	* 188	18	6	25	0	247	314	213	298	409	708	7	63	36	0.20	213	43	15	42	137	12%	66	2%	4.51	0.6	-3	$3
Age/B	30 Right	07 CLE	161	26	7	30	0	261	265	260	308	472	780	6	65	36	0.20	255	46	15	39	176	17%	77	0%	5.45	5.4	40	$5
Ht/Wt	72 220	08 CLE	352	67	21	55	0	261	304	246	330	517	847	9	62	36	0.27	256	38	19	43	213	22%	61	0%	6.72	25.8	58	$13
Health	B	09 CLE	271	33	12	40	0	214	304	191	299	399	698	11	64	29	0.34	233	41	22	37	141	19%	60	0%	4.32	0.4	10	$5
PT/Exp	D	10 TAM	158	17	5	17	0	196	261	114	287	342	628	11	55	32	0.28	193	44	11	44	145	13%	71	0%	3.68	-2.4	-18	$2
Consist	D	1st Half	48	4	1	5	0	229			362	354	716	17	56	38	0.48	188	50	7	43	133	9%	74	0%	5.33	1.7	-10	$1
LIMA Plan	F	2nd Half	110	13	4	12	0	182			250	336	586	8	55	29	0.20	195	42	13	45	151	15%	72	0%	2.90	-4.4	-21	$1
Rand Var	+1	11 Proj	**192**	**27**	**8**	**27**	**0**	**224**			**291**	**405**	**696**	**9**	**61**	**32**	**0.24**	**225**	**41**	**17**	**42**	**158**	**16%**	**65**	**0%**	**4.44**	**1.3**	**9**	**$4**

1H ruined by knee surgery, but balance of good power/bad ct% has moved from tolerable to intolerable. Completely inept vs. RHP (38 K in 70 AB!), so future appears typecast as a lefty-bashing 2nd CA.

Sizemore,Grady			AB	R	HR	RBI	SB	Avg	vL	vR	OB	Slg	OPS	bb%	ct%	h%	Eye	xBA	G	L	F	PX	hr/f	Spd	SBO	RC/G	RAR	BPV	R$
Pos	8	06 CLE	655	134	28	76	22	290	214	329	366	533	898	11	77	34	0.51	271	33	20	47	158	12%	118	16%	6.86	40.6	92	$28
Age/B	28 Left	07 CLE	628	118	24	78	33	277	284	274	377	462	839	14	75	33	0.65	254	33	21	47	125	11%	100	20%	6.22	30.7	61	$28
Ht/Wt	74 200	08 CLE	634	101	33	90	38	268	224	286	366	502	868	13	79	29	0.75	278	35	19	46	147	14%	91	23%	6.44	20.1	92	$30
Health	F	09 CLE	436	73	18	64	13	248	216	262	339	445	784	12	79	28	0.65	249	36	16	48	116	11%	100	17%	5.35	9.4	65	$15
PT/Exp	B	10 CLE	128	15	0	13	4	211	122	266	263	289	552	7	73	29	0.26	212	39	19	42	65	0%	100	21%	2.21	-12.6	-12	$2
Consist	F	1st Half	128	15	0	13	4	211			263	289	552	7	73	29	0.26	212	39	19	42	65	0%	100	21%	2.21	-12.6	-12	$2
LIMA Plan	C+	2nd Half	0	0	0	0	0	0																					
Rand Var	+2	11 Proj	**468**	**74**	**17**	**59**	**9**	**250**			**332**	**441**	**773**	**11**	**76**	**29**	**0.52**	**258**	**36**	**19**	**45**	**127**	**11%**	**98**	**13%**	**5.20**	**1.5**	**60**	**$14**

Microfracture knee surgery in June ended season. Aiming to be ready for spring training, but pre-injury skills warts (BA vLH, borderline ct%, sliding PX) plus health questions make a return to 2006-08 levels very unlikely.

Sizemore,Scott			AB	R	HR	RBI	SB	Avg	vL	vR	OB	Slg	OPS	bb%	ct%	h%	Eye	xBA	G	L	F	PX	hr/f	Spd	SBO	RC/G	RAR	BPV	R$
Pos	4	06	0	0	0	0	0	0																					
Age/B	26 Right	07	0	0	0	0	0	0																					
Ht/Wt	72 185	08	0	0	0	0	0	0																					
Health	A	09 a/a	520	73	14	55	17	275			342	439	781	9	84	30	0.63					104		102	15%	5.24	7.6	70	$18
PT/Exp	F	10 DET	* 442	57	11	42	2	247	224	223	307	383	690	8	76	30	0.36	256	38	22	40	103	8%	84	3%	4.00	-6.1	30	$9
Consist	C	1st Half	224	29	4	16	1	245			316	356	672	9	77	30	0.46	253	37	24	39	88	6%	89	5%	3.86	-4.1	28	$4
LIMA Plan	D	2nd Half	218	28	7	27	1	249			298	411	709	7	75	31	0.27	258	41	19	40	120	10%	89	2%	4.16	-1.9	36	$5
Rand Var	0	11 Proj	**344**	**46**	**9**	**35**	**8**	**259**			**320**	**413**	**733**	**8**	**79**	**30**	**0.43**	**264**	**38**	**22**	**40**	**107**	**8%**	**94**	**12%**	**4.58**	**-0.2**	**49**	**$9**

3-14-.224 in 143 AB at DET. Broke ankle at 2009 AFL, likely hampered him all season. Weak ct% in majors (72%) a concern, but if he can hold the 2H PX and push Spd/SBO back to '09 levels: UP: 15 HR, 20 SB

Smith,Seth			AB	R	HR	RBI	SB	Avg	vL	vR	OB	Slg	OPS	bb%	ct%	h%	Eye	xBA	G	L	F	PX	hr/f	Spd	SBO	RC/G	RAR	BPV	R$
Pos	79	06 aa	524	61	13	55	3	279			329	452	781	7	90	29	0.74					104		86	6%	5.19	-0.4	85	$12
Age/B	28 Left	07 aa	451	50	14	61	5	275			320	447	767	6	86	30	0.47					104		107	8%	4.89	-4.0	74	$12
Ht/Wt	75 215	08 COL	* 356	50	11	50	8	265		289	348	421	769	11	84	29	0.80	274	45	21	34	98	11%	96	8%	5.17	-2.5	68	$12
Health	A	09 COL	335	61	15	55	4	293	259	300	378	510	888	12	80	33	0.69	275	39	19	42	137	13%	103	5%	6.67	10.4	87	$15
PT/Exp	C	10 COL	358	55	17	52	2	246	154	261	313	469	782	9	81	26	0.52	279	36	16	48	138	12%	94	4%	5.14	0.8	84	$12
Consist	D	1st Half	195	34	11	35	2	282			340	533	873	8	85	29	0.57	299	37	18	45	142	15%	106	4%	6.13	5.8	102	$10
LIMA Plan	C+	2nd Half	163	21	6	17	0	202			282	393	674	10	77	22	0.49	255	35	14	51	134	9%	84	3%	3.87	-6.2	64	$2
Rand Var	+4	11 Proj	**378**	**57**	**17**	**53**	**4**	**270**			**343**	**484**	**827**	**10**	**82**	**29**	**0.60**	**275**	**37**	**17**	**45**	**133**	**12%**	**93**	**5%**	**5.76**	**5.3**	**82**	**$14**

Was showing nice skills consolidation in 1H (see ct%, xBA, FB%) before h% dried up in 2H and opportunity shrank accordingly. All he needs is 450 AB vs. RHP, and... UP: 25 HR (still)

R.MURPHY / H.NICHOLS

Smoak,Justin

			AB	R	HR	RBI	SB	Avg	vL	vR	OB	Slg	OPS	bb%	ct%	h%	Eye	xBA	G	L	F	PX	hr/f	Spd	SBO	RC/G	RAR	BPV	R$
Pos	3	06	0	0	0	0	0	0																					
Age/B	24 Both	07	0	0	0	0	0	0																					
Ht/Wt	75 200	08	0	0	0	0	0	0																					
Health	A	09 aa	380	45	9	43	0	261			363	384	747	14	83	30	0.92					81		84	0%	5.06	-11.6	51	$8
PT/Exp	F	10 2AL	* 531	65	20	71	1	224	215	220	322	383	705	13	77	26	0.62	266	38	23	39	110	12%	53	1%	4.32	-23.4	38	$11
Consist	B	1st Half	270	36	10	38	1	217			335	383	718	15	78	24	0.81	277	41	22	37	116	13%	62	1%	4.64	-9.4	56	$6
LIMA Plan	C+	2nd Half	261	29	10	33	0	231			307	383	690	10	75	27	0.44	252	32	24	44	104	11%	63	0%	3.98	-14.1	25	$5
Rand Var	+3	11 Proj	515	61	21	64	0	258			353	430	783	13	79	29	0.69	270	37	23	40	112	13%	58	0%	5.34	-4.5	50	$13

13-48-.218 in 348 AB at TEX/SEA. Key to TEX's Cliff Lee deal was a bit unlucky in ML debut; note xBA. PX growth, bb% give hope. Struck out too much, but has shown better. Still some growing pains in store, but a solid future.

Snider,Travis

			AB	R	HR	RBI	SB	Avg	vL	vR	OB	Slg	OPS	bb%	ct%	h%	Eye	xBA	G	L	F	PX	hr/f	Spd	SBO	RC/G	RAR	BPV	R$
Pos	79	06	0	0	0	0	0	0																					
Age/B	23 Left	07	0	0	0	0	0	0																					
Ht/Wt	72 235	08 TOR	* 499	74	21	87	2	271	286	305	340	458	799	9	72	34	0.38	287	37	35	29	137	20%	48	2%	5.50	9.3	35	$17
Health	C	09 TOR	* 416	58	20	59	3	268	225	244	347	486	833	11	72	33	0.44	256	44	15	41	146	16%	65	7%	6.01	12.1	50	$13
PT/Exp	C	10 TOR	* 379	47	18	45	8	256	254	255	299	464	763	6	75	30	0.24	292	41	24	35	151	18%	60	16%	4.76	-1.3	51	$13
Consist	B	1st Half	116	16	6	15	3	241			323	483	806	11	75	27	0.48	320	45	12	44	178	24%	56	15%	5.59	2.5	83	$4
LIMA Plan	C	2nd Half	263	31	12	30	5	262			287	456	743	3	75	31	0.13	277	38	23	39	139	16%	69	16%	4.37	-4.0	38	$9
Rand Var	+4	11 Proj	454	61	22	62	6	262			324	476	800	8	74	31	0.34	280	42	22	36	151	18%	61	10%	5.41	6.4	52	$15

14-32-.255 in 298 AB at TOR. Kinda more of the same, which is good and bad -- great power growth, lots of K's (holding back the HR). So young, xBA shows promise. In this post-quack era, PX makes him worth waiting for.

Snyder,Chris

			AB	R	HR	RBI	SB	Avg	vL	vR	OB	Slg	OPS	bb%	ct%	h%	Eye	xBA	G	L	F	PX	hr/f	Spd	SBO	RC/G	RAR	BPV	R$
Pos	2	06 ARI	184	19	6	32	0	277	246	294	354	424	778	11	79	32	0.56	257	45	22	33	93	13%	52	0%	5.20	4.5	28	$5
Age/B	30 Right	07 ARI	326	37	13	47	0	252	316	215	333	433	766	11	79	28	0.60	254	40	15	45	117	11%	47	0%	5.05	5.9	49	$7
Ht/Wt	76 245	08 ARI	334	47	16	64	0	237	250	231	346	452	798	14	70	29	0.55	248	38	18	44	158	16%	50	0%	5.76	15.5	51	$10
Health	C	09 ARI	165	20	6	22	0	200	161	220	330	352	681	16	72	24	0.68	219	37	17	46	109	11%	69	0%	4.12	-0.7	28	$2
PT/Exp	D	10 2NL	319	34	15	48	0	207	192	212	318	376	694	14	71	24	0.55	229	42	15	43	117	15%	55	0%	4.15	-3.3	23	$6
Consist	B	1st Half	176	19	9	28	0	239			353	438	790	15	68	30	0.55	238	45	12	44	148	17%	55	0%	5.65	6.1	40	$5
LIMA Plan	D	2nd Half	143	15	6	20	0	168			274	301	575	13	73	18	0.55	221	39	18	43	82	13%	70	0%	2.44	-9.5	8	$1
Rand Var	+2	11 Proj	361	42	16	55	0	233			341	398	739	14	72	28	0.59	230	40	17	43	114	14%	54	0%	4.81	4.8	25	$9

Gotta love the power & patience, but spent another year flirting with Mendoza. That said, 2H h% should regress, taking BA from horrid to okay. Rand Var also points to rebound. PT uncertain, but small profit potential exists.

Sogard,Eric

			AB	R	HR	RBI	SB	Avg	vL	vR	OB	Slg	OPS	bb%	ct%	h%	Eye	xBA	G	L	F	PX	hr/f	Spd	SBO	RC/G	RAR	BPV	R$
Pos	4	06	0	0	0	0	0	0																					
Age/B	24 Left	07	0	0	0	0	0	0																					
Ht/Wt	70 180	08	0	0	0	0	0	0																					
Health	A	09 aa	458	63	4	40	8	244			313	321	634	9	91	26	1.10					49		102	11%	3.73	-13.8	53	$8
PT/Exp	F	10 OAK	* 521	56	3	44	10	240	1000	200	311	313	624	9	90	26	1.08	391	50	50	0	50		112	15%	3.65	-13.1	56	$8
Consist	A	1st Half	279	30	1	22	5	237			302	289	591	9	92	26	1.13					36		100	12%	3.27	-10.2	45	$4
LIMA Plan	D	2nd Half	242	26	2	22	5	242			321	342	662	10	89	27	1.03	391	50	50	0	66		116	18%	4.10	-2.7	65	$4
Rand Var	+5	11 Proj	118	14	0	10	2	246			317	305	622	9	90	27	1.08	382	50	50	0	41	0%	107	13%	3.64	-3.5	47	$2

0-0-.429 in 7 AB at OAK. Hit well at one of the tougher hitter's park in PCL, then got his cup of coffee. Solid Eye and ok Spd point to SB upside, but BA won't play with that little pop. Watch, don't draft, for now.

Soriano,Alfonso

			AB	R	HR	RBI	SB	Avg	vL	vR	OB	Slg	OPS	bb%	ct%	h%	Eye	xBA	G	L	F	PX	hr/f	Spd	SBO	RC/G	RAR	BPV	R$
Pos	7	06 WAS	647	119	46	95	41	277	293	271	345	560	904	9	75	30	0.42	272	29	20	51	175	18%	100	37%	6.70	27.6	92	$36
Age/B	35 Right	07 CHC	579	97	33	70	19	299	254	311	334	560	894	5	78	34	0.24	287	34	20	46	166	16%	123	20%	6.35	15.9	92	$27
Ht/Wt	73 180	08 CHC	453	76	29	75	19	280	351	252	343	532	875	9	77	31	0.42	277	29	23	48	160	17%	68	19%	6.23	10.5	77	$24
Health	C	09 CHC	477	64	20	55	9	241	184	256	300	423	723	8	75	28	0.34	241	33	19	48	124	12%	89	10%	4.33	-17.5	45	$14
PT/Exp	B	10 CHC	496	67	24	79	5	258	295	243	320	496	816	8	75	30	0.37	273	29	16	54	171	12%	89	6%	5.63	8.0	83	$18
Consist	D	1st Half	252	41	13	39	4	274			344	532	876	10	75	32	0.43	285	26	20	54	185	13%	90	7%	6.50	10.3	97	$11
LIMA Plan	B	2nd Half	244	26	11	40	1	242			294	459	753	7	75	28	0.30	259	32	13	55	156	11%	88	4%	4.72	-2.6	69	$7
Rand Var	+2	11 Proj	502	71	25	74	5	267			325	494	819	8	76	31	0.35	264	31	18	51	156	13%	87	7%	5.60	4.8	71	$19

Surface stats didn't show it, but this was a nice skills rebound. xBA, PX at vintage levels. Don't expect '06-'07, certainly. But with two "down" years in a row, most will underbid. He still shows '08 skills. Go the extra buck.

Soto,Geovany

			AB	R	HR	RBI	SB	Avg	vL	vR	OB	Slg	OPS	bb%	ct%	h%	Eye	xBA	G	L	F	PX	hr/f	Spd	SBO	RC/G	RAR	BPV	R$
Pos	2	06 aaa	367	32	6	37	0	253			323	360	683	9	80	30	0.52	214	60	5	35	75	6%	62	1%	4.02	-3.8	19	$4
Age/B	28 Right	07 CHC	* 439	73	26	95	0	325	444	333	390	588	978	10	78	37	0.48	307	41	22	37	170	21%	87	0%	7.68	37.8	94	$23
Ht/Wt	73 225	08 CHC	494	66	23	86	0	285	312	276	365	504	869	11	76	34	0.51	269	38	21	41	150	15%	65	1%	6.45	31.1	65	$19
Health	D	09 CHC	331	27	11	47	1	218	205	221	320	381	701	13	77	25	0.65	245	41	18	41	113	10%	45	1%	4.34	0.8	39	$5
PT/Exp	C	10 CHC	322	47	17	53	0	280	367	235	396	497	893	16	74	33	0.75	284	36	24	40	153	18%	57	1%	7.00	23.0	71	$13
Consist	B	1st Half	184	25	8	21	0	266			400	451	851	18	76	31	0.91	277	40	24	36	129	16%	60	0%	6.54	10.9	62	$6
LIMA Plan	C+	2nd Half	138	22	9	32	0	297			390	558	948	13	72	35	0.55	294	30	25	44	186	20%	67	2%	7.64	12.1	87	$8
Rand Var	0	11 Proj	402	51	20	68	0	276			374	496	870	14	75	32	0.63	277	37	22	41	150	16%	55	1%	6.55	24.9	67	$15

Terrific bounce-back, but more health woes again robbed him of lots of AB. Shoulder surgery is supposed to fix things, but that's about as iffy for a CA as for a pitcher. He's no Tier 1 pick, but RAR's show the huge upside.

Span,Denard

			AB	R	HR	RBI	SB	Avg	vL	vR	OB	Slg	OPS	bb%	ct%	h%	Eye	xBA	G	L	F	PX	hr/f	Spd	SBO	RC/G	RAR	BPV	R$
Pos	8	06 aa	536	75	2	42	23	272			319	332	651	6	86	32	0.48					37		115	22%	3.60	-14.9	22	$14
Age/B	27 Left	07 aaa	487	58	3	54	25	261			313	345	658	7	81	32	0.40					57		112	29%	3.65	-12.9	20	$13
Ht/Wt	72 205	08 MIN	* 503	96	8	59	30	294	283	299	381	424	805	12	81	35	0.75	290	54	26	20	85	9%	116	26%	5.76	5.9	55	$23
Health	A	09 MIN	578	97	8	68	23	311	330	304	386	415	801	11	85	36	0.79	263	53	19	28	57	6%	149	15%	5.60	15.4	52	$24
PT/Exp	A	10 MIN	629	85	3	58	26	264	279	256	328	348	676	9	88	30	0.81	276	54	18	28	53	2%	118	16%	4.13	-21.9	50	$18
Consist	B	1st Half	335	49	3	35	16	275			341	379	721	9	88	31	0.83	288	58	17	24	62	4%	125	16%	4.65	-6.5	59	$12
LIMA Plan	B	2nd Half	294	36	0	23	10	252			312	313	625	8	89	28	0.79	263	50	19	31	43	0%	103	15%	3.54	-15.6	39	$6
Rand Var	+3	11 Proj	570	85	6	57	25	279			347	378	725	9	86	32	0.74	273	53	19	27	60	4%	124	18%	4.67	-6.9	50	$19

Hit rate pendulum swung back, took BA with it. But another h% correction says '11 BA ends up between '10 and '08-'09. Overall 2H decline, late sore foot hints at nagging injury. Add in Rand Var, and all points to partial rebound.

Spilborghs,Ryan

			AB	R	HR	RBI	SB	Avg	vL	vR	OB	Slg	OPS	bb%	ct%	h%	Eye	xBA	G	L	F	PX	hr/f	Spd	SBO	RC/G	RAR	BPV	R$
Pos	79	06 COL	* 436	62	8	46	11	295	323	267	348	422	770	7	85	33	0.53	274	51	21	29	78	7%	109	11%	5.01	-2.9	51	$14
Age/B	31 Right	07 COL	* 388	57	14	62	6	282	356	271	349	452	801	9	84	31	0.63	291	50	21	30	101	15%	98	9%	5.40	0.5	65	$14
Ht/Wt	73 190	08 COL	233	38	6	36	7	313	326	306	410	468	877	14	82	36	0.93	288	55	21	24	100	13%	111	12%	6.70	8.3	73	$11
Health	B	09 COL	352	55	8	48	9	241	230	250	308	395	703	9	78	29	0.43	255	46	18	36	110	8%	108	17%	4.25	-13.9	50	$10
PT/Exp	D	10 COL	341	41	10	39	4	279	257	296	353	437	790	10	76	34	0.47	268	42	23	35	115	11%	79	9%	5.41	3.4	41	$11
Consist	D	1st Half	160	21	8	17	0	269			339	469	808	10	72	33	0.38	271	45	22	33	137	21%	94	9%	5.58	2.4	46	$5
LIMA Plan	D+	2nd Half	181	20	2	22	4	287			365	409	773	11	79	35	0.58	267	40	24	37	97	4%	74	9%	5.31	1.2	39	$6
Rand Var	-1	11 Proj	345	47	9	44	5	264			340	418	758	10	78	31	0.53	269	46	21	33	107	10%	91	10%	4.99	-2.8	49	$10

Another guy who never comes out of the spring with a job, but still manages 300+ AB, steady value. Hit rate may regress a little, but really, '10 is who he is. Get him for single-digit dollars late, and enjoy a small profit.

Stairs,Matt

			AB	R	HR	RBI	SB	Avg	vL	vR	OB	Slg	OPS	bb%	ct%	h%	Eye	xBA	G	L	F	PX	hr/f	Spd	SBO	RC/G	RAR	BPV	R$
Pos	7	06 2AL	348	42	13	51	0	247	217	252	325	420	744	10	75	29	0.47	244	43	17	39	117	13%	44	0%	4.76	-4.3	31	$7
Age/B	43 Left	07 TOR	357	58	21	64	2	289	289	288	367	549	916	11	82	30	0.67	307	40	18	42	166	17%	44	3%	6.86	18.2	96	$15
Ht/Wt	69 215	08 2TM	337	46	13	49	1	252	235	254	335	409	745	11	73	31	0.47	238	43	20	37	105	14%	67	2%	4.78	-3.5	22	$9
Health	B	09 PHI	103	15	5	17	0	194	0	200	341	379	720	18	71	22	0.77	222	47	11	42	128	16%	43	0%	4.66	-2.9	37	$2
PT/Exp	F	10 SD	99	14	6	16	2	232	0	240	309	475	784	10	68	28	0.34	267	38	18	44	185	20%	57	9%	5.38	0.9	58	$4
Consist	A	1st Half	49	6	1	7	2	184			273	306	579	11	55	31	0.27	194	43	18	39	132	9%	57	18%	2.87	-3.4	-33	$1
LIMA Plan	D	2nd Half	50	8	5	9	0	280			345	640	985	9	80	26	0.50	339	35	18	48	220	26%	60	0%	7.43	3.3	134	$3
Rand Var	+2	11 Proj	106	16	6	17	0	255			343	480	823	12	76	28	0.56	271	41	17	42	150	17%	52	1%	5.77	1.6	66	$4

The venerable slugger has one job: pinch hit vs. a righty, and hit a homer. Or walk. He does both just enough that he'll probably get big league money one more year. Random note: no hits off a lefty since '08! (0-6 over 2 years)

ROD TRUESDELL

Stanton,Mike

		Yr	AB	R	HR	RBI	SB	Avg	vL	vR	OB	Slg	OPS	bb%	ct%	h%	Eye	xBA	G	L	F	PX	hr/f	Spd	SBO	RC/G	RAR	BPV	R$
Pos	9	06	0	0	0	0	0	0																					
Age/B	21 Right	07	0	0	0	0	0	0																					
Ht/Wt	77 225	08	0	0	0	0	0	0																					
Health	A	09 aa	299	45	14	49	1	225			296	425	721	9	71	27	0.35					138		100	3%	4.44	-6.1	43	$8
PT/Exp	F	10 FLA	* 551	81	40	104	6	272	218	272	358	555	913	12	69	32	0.44	292	43	16	41	205	26%	93	5%	7.21	29.7	95	$27
Consist	F	1st Half	274	46	20	58	4	269			374	546	920	14	71	31	0.57	298	52	15	33	192	30%	119	5%	7.36	15.9	102	$14
LIMA Plan	B	2nd Half	277	35	20	46	2	274			341	563	904	9	68	33	0.32	293	41	17	42	218	25%	74	6%	7.05	13.7	90	$13
Rand Var	+1	11 Proj	519	76	30	92	4	262			340	500	840	11	70	32	0.39	266	42	17	41	171	20%	94	4%	6.15	15.1	67	$21

22-59-.259 in 359 AB at FLA. Explosive, elite power and solid bb% both contributed to terrific rookie year. BA limited by ct% right now, but that's the only real downside. The best part? He did it at age 20. Don't hesitate here.

Stavinoha,Nick

		Yr	AB	R	HR	RBI	SB	Avg	vL	vR	OB	Slg	OPS	bb%	ct%	h%	Eye	xBA	G	L	F	PX	hr/f	Spd	SBO	RC/G	RAR	BPV	R$
Pos	9	06 aa	417	43	9	57	2	255			292	383	675	5	83	29	0.31					81		69	3%	3.72	-18.3	31	$8
Age/B	28 Right	07 aaa	499	37	9	36	5	206			241	287	528	4	86	22	0.32					49		70	6%	1.98	-49.9	14	$1
Ht/Wt	74 240	08 aaa	427	50	11	54	2	274			298	403	701	3	90	28	0.35					75		91	3%	3.99	-15.7	56	$11
Health	A	09 STL	* 346	34	9	57	3	224	262	200	267	368	635	5	84	24	0.36	243	34	18	49	95	7%	61	4%	3.27	-17.0	42	$7
PT/Exp	F	10 STL	* 221	23	6	27	0	276	262	250	299	409	708	3	81	32	0.18	269	48	20	33	90	9%	70	0%	3.95	-8.7	26	$6
Consist	B	1st Half	80	8	2	7	0	275			310	375	685	5	71	36	0.17	223	43	21	36	72	10%	78	0%	3.72	-3.7	-22	$2
LIMA Plan	F	2nd Half	141	15	4	20	0	276			294	428	721	2	87	30	0.19	296	56	17	28	99	10%	67	0%	4.14	-4.8	53	$4
Rand Var	-3	11 Proj	82	8	2	11	0	256			286	366	652	4	83	29	0.25	252	44	19	37	75	7%	64	2%	3.35	-4.3	22	$2

2-9.256 in 121 AB at STL. If you can do one thing really, really well, it can offset a lot of shortcomings. Unfortunately, he doesn't do even one thing particularly well, and he's been not doing it for a long time.

Stewart,Ian

		Yr	AB	R	HR	RBI	SB	Avg	vL	vR	OB	Slg	OPS	bb%	ct%	h%	Eye	xBA	G	L	F	PX	hr/f	Spd	SBO	RC/G	RAR	BPV	R$
Pos	5	06 aa	462	58	9	55	2	255			312	424	736	8	84	29	0.51					109		109	11%	4.69	-7.8	73	$8
Age/B	26 Left	07 COL	* 457	63	14	63	9	284	100	242	346	442	788	9	81	33	0.48	271	46	19	35	101	11%	108	8%	5.24	-4.8	55	$15
Ht/Wt	75 205	08 COL	* 523	79	24	81	6	254	370	231	323	471	794	9	73	30	0.39	258	31	25	44	147	14%	120	8%	5.42	0.8	68	$18
Health	A	09 COL	425	74	25	70	7	228	178	244	318	464	782	12	68	27	0.41	243	40	14	46	168	19%	91	10%	5.42	3.6	57	$15
PT/Exp	C	10 COL	386	54	18	61	5	256	231	264	334	443	777	10	72	31	0.41	253	37	22	41	129	16%	100	6%	5.21	3.5	42	$14
Consist	A	1st Half	240	36	9	35	5	250			336	417	752	11	69	32	0.42	246	37	25	38	121	14%	109	8%	5.03	0.9	31	$8
LIMA Plan	C+	2nd Half	146	18	9	26	0	267			331	486	818	9	75	30	0.39	265	37	18	46	141	18%	85	3%	5.50	2.5	60	$6
Rand Var	0	11 Proj	472	69	26	75	5	252			327	473	800	10	73	29	0.41	259	37	19	44	148	17%	96	7%	5.47	5.2	60	$17

Not a lot of skills growth, with PX step-back a disappointment. Did seem to be turning it around when he strained an oblique. A strong pedigree and young, so worth patience. Trivia: now the son-in-law of his A-ball manager.

Stubbs,Drew

		Yr	AB	R	HR	RBI	SB	Avg	vL	vR	OB	Slg	OPS	bb%	ct%	h%	Eye	xBA	G	L	F	PX	hr/f	Spd	SBO	RC/G	RAR	BPV	R$
Pos	8	06	0	0	0	0	0	0																					
Age/B	26 Right	07	0	0	0	0	0	0																					
Ht/Wt	76 205	08 a/a	167	20	2	14	5	264			319	374	693	7	79	32	0.39					81		109	13%	4.08	-4.7	32	$4
Health	A	09 CIN	* 591	74	11	49	47	247	286	261	314	355	669	9	76	31	0.41	231	42	21	37	78	7%	134	37%	3.77	-17.2	26	$21
PT/Exp	C	10 CIN	514	91	22	77	30	255	240	262	327	444	770	10	67	34	0.33	241	44	16	40	138	16%	157	26%	5.27	5.9	48	$25
Consist	B	1st Half	271	44	11	41	16	240			311	417	728	9	69	31	0.33	238	45	16	39	122	15%	178	27%	4.59	-2.4	46	$12
LIMA Plan	B	2nd Half	243	47	11	36	14	272			344	473	818	10	66	37	0.33	244	42	16	42	156	16%	123	25%	6.07	8.3	47	$13
Rand Var	-2	11 Proj	509	81	19	59	31	250			318	424	742	9	72	31	0.36	243	43	17	40	122	13%	142	29%	4.72	-0.9	48	$22

Power/speed surprise -- not the speed part, of course. But free-swinging has its cost, in BA. The trade-off isn't all bad, but the low OB that results hit does cap SB. It's also the difference between a good player and a true star.

Suzuki,Ichiro

		Yr	AB	R	HR	RBI	SB	Avg	vL	vR	OB	Slg	OPS	bb%	ct%	h%	Eye	xBA	G	L	F	PX	hr/f	Spd	SBO	RC/G	RAR	BPV	R$
Pos	9	06 SEA	695	110	9	49	45	322	352	312	367	416	783	7	90	35	0.69	274	51	22	28	50	5%	195	20%	5.15	-9.6	73	$30
Age/B	37 Left	07 SEA	678	111	6	68	37	351	331	358	395	431	825	7	89	39	0.64	286	56	20	24	48	4%	180	18%	5.62	2.2	63	$33
Ht/Wt	71 172	08 SEA	686	103	6	42	43	310	287	321	358	386	745	7	91	34	0.78	285	57	20	23	44	4%	188	20%	4.77	-11.0	70	$27
Health	A	09 SEA	639	88	11	46	26	352	339	359	383	465	848	5	89	38	0.45	288	56	18	26	66	7%	159	17%	5.71	6.3	68	$28
PT/Exp	A	10 SEA	680	74	6	43	42	315	309	318	357	394	751	6	87	35	0.52	280	57	17	25	55	4%	130	23%	4.74	-3.9	47	$27
Consist	B	1st Half	332	33	3	24	22	328			381	419	799	8	87	37	0.67	281	56	17	27	63	4%	117	25%	5.41	4.2	53	$15
LIMA Plan	C+	2nd Half	348	41	3	19	20	302			334	371	705	5	87	34	0.39	278	58	18	24	48	4%	133	21%	4.10	-8.2	39	$13
Rand Var	-1	11 Proj	659	85	7	44	32	310			350	396	746	6	88	34	0.54	282	57	18	25	55	5%	148	19%	4.66	-9.2	56	$24

His key skill is speed, which despite SBO-fueled SB spike has dropped from super-elite to merely above average. It's also a skill of the young, so he's not going to get any faster. The first sign of his baseball mortality?

Suzuki,Kurt

		Yr	AB	R	HR	RBI	SB	Avg	vL	vR	OB	Slg	OPS	bb%	ct%	h%	Eye	xBA	G	L	F	PX	hr/f	Spd	SBO	RC/G	RAR	BPV	R$
Pos	2	06 aa	376	52	6	45	4	250			333	366	699	11	89	27	1.10					74		81	6%	4.51	1.5	62	$7
Age/B	27 Right	07 OAK	* 424	53	9	61	0	249	151	281	315	363	679	9	83	28	0.57	238	39	16	45	78	6%	78	0%	3.95	-4.2	37	$8
Ht/Wt	71 199	08 OAK	534	54	7	42	2	279	246	291	335	369	704	8	87	31	0.65	252	45	19	36	60	4%	99	3%	4.29	1.6	44	$10
Health	A	09 OAK	570	74	15	88	8	274	250	283	308	421	729	5	90	28	0.47	283	44	19	36	88	8%	70	8%	4.40	2.2	61	$17
PT/Exp	A	10 OAK	495	55	13	71	3	242	213	253	290	366	655	6	90	25	0.67	266	42	17	41	72	7%	72	4%	3.68	-7.1	54	$11
Consist	A	1st Half	222	26	10	35	1	252			288	423	711	5	90	24	0.50	274	46	12	43	92	12%	94	2%	4.11	-0.3	74	$7
LIMA Plan	C+	2nd Half	273	29	3	36	2	234			292	319	610	7	90	25	0.81	263	40	21	40	56	3%	60	6%	3.33	-6.9	40	$4
Rand Var	+3	11 Proj	556	65	16	75	4	273			321	416	736	7	89	28	0.64	275	43	18	39	84	9%	77	5%	4.56	5.6	61	$16

Biggest skills change was 2H PX dip, which began just after his grandfather's death in June. May be coincidence, but players ARE human beings. No other signs of skills issues, so a return to '08-'09 levels seems likely.

Sweeney,Mike

		Yr	AB	R	HR	RBI	SB	Avg	vL	vR	OB	Slg	OPS	bb%	ct%	h%	Eye	xBA	G	L	F	PX	hr/f	Spd	SBO	RC/G	RAR	BPV	R$
Pos	0	06 KC	217	23	8	33	2	258	266	255	343	438	781	11	78	30	0.58	256	35	21	44	121	11%	55	3%	5.29	-7.2	49	$5
Age/B	37 Right	07 KC	265	26	7	38	0	260	301	242	305	404	709	6	89	27	0.59	271	35	20	45	88	7%	88	0%	4.25	-15.3	67	$5
Ht/Wt	75 225	08 OAK	126	13	2	12	0	286	321	260	323	397	720	5	95	29	1.17	267	42	17	41	70	4%	61	0%	4.52	-1.4	68	$3
Health	F	09 SEA	242	25	8	34	0	281	235	340	328	442	770	7	87	30	0.55	268	38	18	44	96	9%	65	0%	4.92	-1.7	60	$6
PT/Exp	F	10 2TM	* 192	25	10	32	4	255	224	280	323	446	769	9	88	25	0.82	274	43	12	45	109	13%	63	8%	4.98	-7.7	78	$7
Consist	A	1st Half	99	11	6	18	2	263			324	475	799	8	86	25	0.64	267	40	10	50	119	14%	65	8%	5.19	-3.3	77	$4
LIMA Plan	F	2nd Half	93	14	4	14	2	248			322	416	738	10	90	24	1.08	294	49	16	36	99	12%	70	7%	4.77	-4.3	82	$3
Rand Var	+2	11 Proj	111	13	4	16	1	270			328	441	769	8	89	27	0.75	275	41	16	43	101	10%	66	4%	4.98	-2.7	73	$4

8-26-.252 in 151 AB at SEA/PHI. Clubhouse chemist was hurt a lot, and showed some pop when not hurt. In other words, a lot like most recent seasons. Saw very little PT down the stretch, which will be another continuing trend.

Sweeney,Ryan

		Yr	AB	R	HR	RBI	SB	Avg	vL	vR	OB	Slg	OPS	bb%	ct%	h%	Eye	xBA	G	L	F	PX	hr/f	Spd	SBO	RC/G	RAR	BPV	R$
Pos	9	06 CHW	* 484	65	15	75	7	310			357	469	825	7	86	34	0.52	344	50	39	11	94	35%	89	10%	5.55	-1.5	61	$18
Age/B	26 Left	07 CHW	* 442	52	13	50	7	263			339	397	737	10	85	29	0.77	322	60	28	13	84	27%	75	10%	4.74	-9.9	52	$11
Ht/Wt	76 221	08 OAK	* 421	57	6	49	9	289	216	307	354	393	747	9	83	34	0.59	255	45	21	34	72	5%	94	7%	4.83	-6.2	38	$13
Health	D	09 OAK	484	68	6	53	6	293	268	301	347	407	754	8	86	33	0.60	279	45	24	31	74	5%	95	8%	4.89	-6.0	50	$13
PT/Exp	C	10 OAK	303	41	1	36	1	294	246	307	346	383	728	7	86	34	0.59	283	52	20	28	68	1%	94	2%	4.61	-2.8	45	$8
Consist	A	1st Half	285	38	1	35	1	298			351	386	737	7	86	34	0.59	282	52	20	28	67	1%	97	2%	4.71	-1.9	45	$8
LIMA Plan	D	2nd Half	18	3	0	1	0	222			263	333	596	5	89	25	0.50	302	50	19	31	94	0%	85	0%	3.13	-1.0	69	$0
Rand Var	0	11 Proj	321	43	4	39	4	290			348	399	747	8	85	33	0.61	277	48	22	30	74	5%	94	7%	4.82	-3.2	47	$9

More knee problems are casting a long shadow on his career. Season ended with one surgery, and another possible. BA is his only contributing category, and if the knees kill his Spd, even that could go. Risky business.

Swisher,Nick

		Yr	AB	R	HR	RBI	SB	Avg	vL	vR	OB	Slg	OPS	bb%	ct%	h%	Eye	xBA	G	L	F	PX	hr/f	Spd	SBO	RC/G	RAR	BPV	R$
Pos	9	06 OAK	556	106	35	95	1	254	291	241	364	493	857	15	73	29	0.64	252	33	19	48	152	18%	77	2%	6.42	12.4	67	$20
Age/B	30 Both	07 OAK	539	84	22	78	3	262	291	250	377	455	832	16	76	31	0.76	261	37	18	46	136	12%	64	3%	6.19	10.8	64	$16
Ht/Wt	71 210	08 CHW	497	86	24	69	3	219	197	227	330	410	740	14	73	25	0.61	246	35	21	45	129	15%	70	4%	4.82	-8.3	46	$12
Health	A	09 NYY	498	84	29	82	0	249	244	251	371	498	869	16	75	28	0.77	271	38	16	46	162	17%	56	0%	6.66	19.5	80	$16
PT/Exp	A	10 NYY	566	91	29	89	1	288	294	285	354	511	865	9	75	34	0.42	279	36	20	45	153	15%	71	2%	6.26	20.8	66	$24
Consist	C	1st Half	287	49	13	47	1	293			368	505	873	11	77	34	0.51	278	33	22	45	143	13%	91	2%	6.44	11.9	72	$13
LIMA Plan	B	2nd Half	279	42	16	42	0	283			340	516	856	8	74	33	0.33	278	38	17	45	164	17%	54	1%	6.07	8.8	62	$12
Rand Var	-3	11 Proj	522	86	28	81	1	272			361	499	860	12	75	32	0.55	270	36	19	45	153	16%	66	2%	6.36	17.8	67	$20

Other than '08, skills a broken record; for you kids with MP3's, they're set on "repeat" (can't be too careful...). BA up, as xBA foretold, and looks mostly sustainable. Reliable contributor in all fanalytic formats.

ROD TRUESDELL

Tabata,Jose

		Year	AB	R	HR	RBI	SB	Avg	vL	vR	OB	Slg	OPS	bb%	ct%	h%	Eye	xBA	G	L	F	PX	hr/f	Spd	SBO	RC/G	RAR	BPV	R$
Pos	7	06	0	0	0	0	0	0																					
Age/B	22 Right	07	0	0	0	0	0	0																					
Ht/Wt	71 160	08 aa	383	50	5	44	16	264			317	350	666	7	86	30	0.54					56		111	17%	3.78	-15.0	37	$12
Health	A	09 aa	362	43	4	29	9	273			319	371	690	6	91	29	0.72					64		111	19%	4.16	-12.0	62	$9
PT/Exp	D	10 PIT	* 629	94	6	50	39	289	247	315	338	386	724	7	87	33	0.55	287	59	16	25	67	4%	151	29%	4.50	-10.4	61	$26
Consist	A	1st Half	318	44	3	21	26	264			322	355	677	8	87	30	0.66	291	62	17	21	66	5%	109	39%	4.03	-9.9	51	$12
LIMA Plan	C+	2nd Half	311	50	3	29	13	315			355	418	773	6	86	36	0.45	286	58	16	26	68	4%	169	19%	4.98	-0.8	64	$14
Rand Var	-1	11 Proj	**561**	**77**	**6**	**49**	**25**	**283**			**330**	**377**	**707**	**7**	**88**	**31**	**0.58**	**281**	**59**	**16**	**25**	**63**	**5%**	**134**	**22%**	**4.30**	**-15.8**	**57**	**$19**

4-35-.299-19 in 405 AB at PIT
Elite Spd but big 1H SB was all SBO, not skill. 73% SB success rate at PIT says he's more runner than base stealer, which may cap his upside, for now. But down the road, UP: 50 SB

Tatis,Fernando

		Year	AB	R	HR	RBI	SB	Avg	vL	vR	OB	Slg	OPS	bb%	ct%	h%	Eye	xBA	G	L	F	PX	hr/f	Spd	SBO	RC/G	RAR	BPV	R$
Pos	3	06 BAL	* 382	47	8	41	7	260	286	214	329	387	716	9	80	31	0.51	231	44	15	41	83	7%	95	8%	4.41	-11.2	35	$8
Age/B	36 Right	07 aa	120	13	9	22	0	184			258	432	690	9	81	15	0.53					141		79	0%	3.85	-7.1	82	$2
Ht/Wt	71 187	08 NYM	* 393	46	20	69	3	262	311	287	332	468	800	9	79	29	0.50	286	42	26	32	128	19%	89	3%	5.34	-4.4	67	$13
Health	D	09 NYM	340	42	8	48	4	282	278	285	326	438	764	6	84	32	0.41	274	47	19	34	100	8%	95	6%	4.86	-15.8	59	$11
PT/Exp	D	10 NYM	65	6	2	6	0	185	250	48	254	338	592	8	71	23	0.32	244	39	20	41	122	11%	66	0%	2.65	-7.6	20	$0
Consist	C	1st Half	65	6	2	6	0	185			254	338	592	8	71	23	0.32	244	39	20	41	122	11%	67	0%	2.65	-7.6	20	$0
LIMA Plan	F	2nd Half	0	0	0	0	0	0																					
Rand Var	+5	11 Proj	**55**	**6**	**2**	**8**	**0**	**236**			**300**	**398**	**698**	**8**	**78**	**27**	**0.42**	**265**	**42**	**21**	**36**	**110**	**13%**	**74**	**3%**	**4.06**	**-3.6**	**41**	**$1**

Surgery for torn labrum puts 2011 in doubt given his age and 2010 struggles. A bit of trivia: he's the only player in MLB history to hit two grand slams in one inning!

Tatum,Craig

		Year	AB	R	HR	RBI	SB	Avg	vL	vR	OB	Slg	OPS	bb%	ct%	h%	Eye	xBA	G	L	F	PX	hr/f	Spd	SBO	RC/G	RAR	BPV	R$
Pos	2	06	0	0	0	0	0	0																					
Age/B	28 Right	07 aa	173	17	2	18	0	198			255	291	546	7	75	25	0.31					71		95	3%	2.11	-12.3	2	($0)
Ht/Wt	73 224	08 a/a	332	24	7	45	1	207			251	320	571	6	81	24	0.31					77		69	3%	2.45	-18.1	20	$2
Health	A	09 aaa	213	17	3	17	0	203			251	289	541	6	76	25	0.27					66		61	0%	1.99	-15.2	-11	$0
PT/Exp	F	10 BAL	114	11	0	9	1	281	214	319	349	316	665	10	82	34	0.57	244	52	22	27	32	0%	74	3%	3.86	-1.0	-4	$2
Consist	C	1st Half	48	4	0	4	0	229			327	271	598	13	85	27	1.00	262	41	27	32	37	0%	69	0%	3.36	-1.2	19	$0
LIMA Plan	F	2nd Half	66	7	0	5	1	318			366	348	715	7	79	40	0.36	233	60	17	23	29	0%	85	4%	4.28	0.2	-20	$2
Rand Var	-5	11 Proj	**98**	**9**	**0**	**10**	**1**	**224**			**274**	**265**	**539**	**6**	**78**	**29**	**0.32**	**232**	**60**	**17**	**23**	**38**	**0%**	**69**	**3%**	**2.07**	**-6.4**	**-20**	**$1**

Red flag! Red flag! History, 2nd half xBA and GB rate all say this is NOT the guy you want as your #2 catcher. As h% regresses, things WILL get ugly.

Taylor,Michael

		Year	AB	R	HR	RBI	SB	Avg	vL	vR	OB	Slg	OPS	bb%	ct%	h%	Eye	xBA	G	L	F	PX	hr/f	Spd	SBO	RC/G	RAR	BPV	R$
Pos	89	06	0	0	0	0	0	0																					
Age/B	25 Right	07	0	0	0	0	0	0																					
Ht/Wt	78 250	08	0	0	0	0	0	0																					
Health	A	09 a/a	428	61	19	70	18	291			350	495	845	8	86	30	0.64					119		86	20%	5.86	14.3	83	$20
PT/Exp	F	10 aaa	464	54	4	53	11	213			268	298	566	7	86	24	0.52	249	47	16	36	58	3%	103	16%	2.65	-35.8	36	$7
Consist	F	1st Half	229	24	2	26	6	197			248	289	537	6	85	22	0.46					61		113	21%	2.29	-20.7	39	$2
LIMA Plan	F	2nd Half	235	30	2	27	5	229			287	306	593	8	86	26	0.58	247	47	16	36	55	3%	88	13%	3.00	-15.2	31	$4
Rand Var	+3	11 Proj	**162**	**21**	**5**	**22**	**5**	**247**			**304**	**405**	**709**	**8**	**86**	**26**	**0.57**	**275**	**47**	**16**	**36**	**96**	**10%**	**89**	**18%**	**4.26**	**-3.3**	**63**	**$5**

OAK prospect took a big step back. Injuries a factor, but PX disappearance troubling. Let's see if late hot streak carries into '11, which suddenly is big for his prospect status. All that said, he still owns skills of '09.

Teagarden,Taylor

		Year	AB	R	HR	RBI	SB	Avg	vL	vR	OB	Slg	OPS	bb%	ct%	h%	Eye	xBA	G	L	F	PX	hr/f	Spd	SBO	RC/G	RAR	BPV	R$
Pos	2	06	0	0	0	0	0	0																					
Age/B	27 Right	07 aa	102	16	6	14	0	266			318	466	784	7	68	34	0.24					137		101	0%	5.22	2.5	27	$3
Ht/Wt	73 200	08 TEX	* 293	34	13	33	1	202	91	389	278	382	660	10	71	24	0.37	230	25	25	50	122	12%	109	3%	3.56	-5.8	36	$4
Health	A	09 TEX	198	26	6	24	0	217	288	192	269	374	643	7	62	32	0.18	214	42	17	41	134	12%	107	0%	3.54	-4.4	1	$3
PT/Exp	F	10 TEX	* 297	32	8	31	0	186	185	136	256	301	557	9	62	27	0.25	189	41	14	46	97	9%	102	0%	2.16	-19.0	-24	$2
Consist	B	1st Half	174	18	3	17	0	180			256	265	521	9	60	28	0.26	151	50	0	50	75	5%	102	0%	1.67	-14.0	-48	$0
LIMA Plan	F	2nd Half	123	14	5	14	0	193			257	352	608	8	65	25	0.24	222	37	19	44	125	14%	98	0%	2.82	-5.2	7	$2
Rand Var	+2	11 Proj	**161**	**19**	**5**	**18**	**0**	**217**			**280**	**360**	**640**	**8**	**64**	**30**	**0.24**	**212**	**40**	**17**	**43**	**115**	**12%**	**93**	**0%**	**3.36**	**-4.2**	**-5**	**$2**

4-6-.155 in 71 AB at TEX
Hope: flashed 163 PX in TEX.
Reality: 52% MLB contact rate.
Remember, catchers mature late, so there is always hope, but right now we have to live in the real world.

Teahen,Mark

		Year	AB	R	HR	RBI	SB	Avg	vL	vR	OB	Slg	OPS	bb%	ct%	h%	Eye	xBA	G	L	F	PX	hr/f	Spd	SBO	RC/G	RAR	BPV	R$
Pos	5	06 KC	* 472	83	20	82	10	298	274	296	374	527	900	11	80	34	0.60	283	49	16	35	136	15%	144	7%	6.78	23.0	95	$20
Age/B	29 Left	07 KC	544	78	7	60	13	285	255	297	351	410	761	9	77	36	0.43	263	50	21	29	90	6%	131	11%	5.06	3.0	38	$15
Ht/Wt	75 210	08 KC	572	66	15	59	4	255	262	252	311	402	713	7	77	31	0.35	262	49	21	31	101	11%	102	5%	4.26	-10.4	37	$12
Health	C	09 KC	524	69	12	50	8	271	287	262	319	408	727	7	77	33	0.30	260	51	20	29	97	10%	90	7%	4.42	-3.9	26	$13
PT/Exp	B	10 CHW	233	31	4	25	3	258	162	276	329	382	711	10	74	33	0.41	260	47	23	30	97	8%	102	12%	4.42	-2.8	24	$6
Consist	A	1st Half	137	16	3	14	3	255			342	387	729	12	79	30	0.62	269	45	22	33	93	8%	92	17%	4.70	-0.5	42	$3
LIMA Plan	D	2nd Half	96	15	1	11	0	260			311	375	686	7	67	38	0.22	248	51	25	25	103	6%	111	4%	4.14	-2.0	-2	$2
Rand Var	0	11 Proj	**294**	**40**	**6**	**32**	**3**	**265**			**325**	**401**	**726**	**8**	**74**	**34**	**0.34**	**260**	**49**	**22**	**29**	**101**	**10%**	**99**	**8%**	**4.51**	**-2.6**	**25**	**$7**

Best thing about this skill set is consistency, which obviously is damning with faint praise. Should be celebrating peak seasons, but lost starting job to a 43 year-old.
Enough said.

Teixeira,Mark

		Year	AB	R	HR	RBI	SB	Avg	vL	vR	OB	Slg	OPS	bb%	ct%	h%	Eye	xBA	G	L	F	PX	hr/f	Spd	SBO	RC/G	RAR	BPV	R$
Pos	3	06 TEX	628	99	33	110	2	282	302	275	371	514	885	12	80	31	0.70	282	39	20	41	146	16%	64	1%	6.61	21.0	81	$23
Age/B	30 Both	07 2TM	494	86	30	105	0	306	357	282	394	563	957	13	77	34	0.64	296	39	20	41	165	19%	81	0%	7.56	25.1	93	$24
Ht/Wt	75 220	08 2TM	574	102	33	121	2	308	303	311	408	552	961	14	84	32	1.04	307	43	21	36	149	19%	74	1%	7.58	32.3	107	$29
Health	A	09 NYY	609	103	39	122	2	292	305	287	375	565	940	12	81	30	0.71	300	36	20	44	161	18%	69	1%	7.18	24.9	100	$28
PT/Exp	A	10 NYY	601	113	33	108	0	256	278	247	356	481	837	13	80	27	0.76	289	36	19	45	148	15%	54	1%	6.01	4.1	82	$24
Consist	B	1st Half	313	55	13	53	0	243			343	428	772	13	82	26	0.84	283	37	20	42	123	12%	52	1%	5.25	-4.9	70	$10
LIMA Plan	B	2nd Half	288	58	20	55	0	271			369	538	908	14	77	29	0.69	296	33	18	49	176	18%	64	0%	6.89	9.2	99	$14
Rand Var	+5	11 Proj	**600**	**109**	**36**	**115**	**1**	**285**			**378**	**532**	**910**	**13**	**80**	**30**	**0.76**	**296**	**37**	**19**	**44**	**155**	**17%**	**64**	**1%**	**6.90**	**21.3**	**93**	**$27**

Looks like a nice bell-shaped curve with '08-'09 as peak, but 2nd half rebound says growth may not be done yet. If he can approach 2nd half PX and FB rate... UP: 40 HR

Tejada,Miguel

		Year	AB	R	HR	RBI	SB	Avg	vL	vR	OB	Slg	OPS	bb%	ct%	h%	Eye	xBA	G	L	F	PX	hr/f	Spd	SBO	RC/G	RAR	BPV	R$
Pos	56	06 BAL	648	99	24	100	6	330	335	329	375	498	873	7	88	35	0.58	299	51	22	27	98	16%	63	4%	6.06	17.9	63	$27
Age/B	36 Right	07 BAL	514	72	18	81	2	296	323	287	348	442	789	7	89	30	0.75	284	52	17	31	82	13%	60	2%	5.17	4.3	58	$18
Ht/Wt	69 213	08 HOU	632	92	13	66	7	283	282	284	309	415	724	4	89	30	0.33	288	48	23	29	82	8%	62	9%	4.28	-19.7	48	$18
Health	A	09 HOU	635	83	14	86	5	313	326	310	333	455	788	3	92	32	0.40	296	49	20	31	89	8%	53	4%	4.99	-2.7	65	$24
PT/Exp	A	10 2TM	636	71	15	71	2	269	282	264	302	381	682	5	89	28	0.45	275	49	19	32	69	8%	40	1%	3.84	-18.7	36	$16
Consist	B	1st Half	319	31	6	32	0	279			301	376	677	3	91	29	0.33	274	47	19	33	61	6%	56	0%	3.72	-10.3	36	$7
LIMA Plan	C	2nd Half	317	40	9	39	2	259			303	385	688	6	88	27	0.54	277	50	19	31	77	10%	31	3%	3.95	-8.4	38	$8
Rand Var	+1	11 Proj	**555**	**65**	**12**	**63**	**1**	**276**			**307**	**398**	**705**	**4**	**90**	**29**	**0.45**	**284**	**49**	**20**	**31**	**76**	**8%**	**52**	**2%**	**4.12**	**-13.3**	**46**	**$14**

Skills continued their slow decline, but something always rescues surface stats. This year it was 8 Aug/Sept HR. One day soon the house of cards will topple.
DN: .260 BA, under 10 HR

Tejada,Ruben

		Year	AB	R	HR	RBI	SB	Avg	vL	vR	OB	Slg	OPS	bb%	ct%	h%	Eye	xBA	G	L	F	PX	hr/f	Spd	SBO	RC/G	RAR	BPV	R$
Pos	46	06	0	0	0	0	0	0																					
Age/B	21 Right	07	0	0	0	0	0	0																					
Ht/Wt	71 165	08	0	0	0	0	0	0																					
Health	A	09 aa	488	49	4	38	15	262			306	342	648	6	90	28	0.66					52		113	15%	3.66	-15.3	51	$10
PT/Exp	F	10 NYM	* 434	47	2	27	3	229	296	185	282	294	577	7	85	27	0.48	251	41	23	36	52	2%	88	8%	2.74	-27.8	23	$4
Consist	F	1st Half	249	32	1	13	1	247			282	303	585	5	85	29	0.33	264	39	28	33	45	1%	104	5%	2.71	-15.7	20	$3
LIMA Plan	D	2nd Half	185	15	1	14	2	206			284	282	565	10	84	24	0.57	246	42	19	39	62	2%	83	13%	2.75	-12.2	31	$1
Rand Var	+1	11 Proj	**395**	**40**	**2**	**28**	**7**	**243**			**296**	**314**	**610**	**7**	**87**	**28**	**0.57**	**250**	**41**	**21**	**37**	**53**	**2%**	**96**	**12%**	**3.20**	**-18.1**	**34**	**$5**

1-15-.213 in 216 AB at NYM
Clearly still a work in progress. Flashes of patience, Spd bodes well for the future, but any real productivity is still at least a couple of years away.

HAROLD NICHOLS

Thames,Marcus

		AB	R	HR	RBI	SB	Avg	vL	vR	OB	Slg	OPS	bb%	ct%	h%	Eye	xBA	G	L	F	PX	hr/f	Spd	SBO	RC/G	RAR	BPV	R$
Pos 70	06 DET	348	61	26	60	1	256	238	266	327	549	876	10	74	27	0.40	261	26	15	59	185	17%	96	3%	6.38	12.3	92	$13
Age/B 34 Right	07 DET	269	37	18	54	2	242	310	209	277	498	775	5	73	26	0.18	275	38	16	46	173	20%	60	7%	4.80	-1.9	60	$9
Ht/Wt 74 220	08 DET	316	50	25	56	0	241	234	245	294	516	810	7	70	26	0.25	261	32	17	51	184	22%	71	5%	5.42	5.4	64	$12
Health C	09 DET	* 307	37	15	40	0	242	257	248	315	428	743	10	72	29	0.38	231	35	18	47	119	14%	83	2%	4.67	-3.1	29	$7
PT/Exp D	10 NYY	212	22	12	33	0	288	302	268	346	491	837	8	71	35	0.31	241	32	16	52	140	15%	63	0%	5.88	5.9	34	$8
Consist B	1st Half	77	7	2	11	0	286			389	416	804	14	70	38	0.57	199	25	14	61	105	6%	82	0%	5.94	2.3	20	$2
LIMA Plan D	2nd Half	135	15	10	22	0	289			319	533	852	4	72	33	0.16	263	37	16	47	159	22%	54	0%	5.77	3.4	42	$6
Rand Var -5	11 Proj	225	27	13	35	0	253			315	459	774	8	71	30	0.32	239	33	16	51	138	16%	66	2%	5.01	0.5	34	$7

BA will trend back toward historic levels, but BA's not the reason you buy him. With solid PX and FB%, he's a double-digit HR lock and a worthy end-game target.

Theriot,Ryan

		AB	R	HR	RBI	SB	Avg	vL	vR	OB	Slg	OPS	bb%	ct%	h%	Eye	xBA	G	L	F	PX	hr/f	Spd	SBO	RC/G	RAR	BPV	R$
Pos 46	06 CHC	* 414	71	3	35	26	294	346	317	358	399	756	9	88	33	0.81	290	50	27	24	62	3%	146	23%	5.06	5.4	64	$16
Age/B 31 Right	07 CHC	537	80	3	45	28	266	286	260	328	346	674	8	91	29	0.98	278	49	21	30	54	2%	116	20%	4.14	-8.7	60	$15
Ht/Wt 71 175	08 CHC	580	85	1	38	22	307	305	308	384	359	743	11	90	34	1.26	279	57	23	20	34	1%	139	15%	5.07	4.9	53	$19
Health A	09 CHC	602	81	7	54	21	284	306	279	340	369	709	8	85	33	0.55	252	50	20	30	54	5%	134	16%	4.31	-3.9	39	$19
PT/Exp A	10 2NL	586	72	2	29	20	270	286	264	317	312	630	7	87	31	0.55	260	54	20	26	30	1%	133	16%	3.38	-24.7	29	$14
Consist B	1st Half	304	37	0	17	15	276			313	306	618	5	88	32	0.42	257	56	19	25	23	0%	131	20%	3.16	-14.5	19	$9
LIMA Plan C+	2nd Half	282	35	2	12	5	262			322	319	642	8	87	30	0.69	263	52	20	28	38	3%	123	13%	3.61	-10.2	35	$5
Rand Var 0	11 Proj	548	73	3	35	19	270			328	329	657	8	87	31	0.68	262	53	20	27	39	2%	132	17%	3.79	-15.0	38	$14

Value comes from BA and SB, but note small warning signs. Eye and xBA predict BA drop. Spd in slow decline. Got green light less in LA than CHC. Bidding on past 20 SB seasons now risky business.

Thole,Josh

		AB	R	HR	RBI	SB	Avg	vL	vR	OB	Slg	OPS	bb%	ct%	h%	Eye	xBA	G	L	F	PX	hr/f	Spd	SBO	RC/G	RAR	BPV	R$
Pos 2	06	0	0	0	0	0	0																					
Age/B 24 Left	07	0	0	0	0	0	0																					
Ht/Wt 73 205	08	0	0	0	0	0	0																					
Health A	09 NYM	* 437	41	1	46	7	293	200	349	352	373	725	8	92	32	1.21	321	46	34	20	58	1%	80	9%	4.78	6.4	59	$11
PT/Exp F	10 NYM	* 367	32	5	30	1	254	143	299	327	370	697	10	88	28	0.87	288	44	23	33	80	5%	104	1%	4.39	-0.9	67	$5
Consist A	1st Half	174	15	2	17	0	243			309	389	698	9	88	27	0.82	275	44	11	44	108	3%	86	0%	4.43	-0.2	85	$2
LIMA Plan D+	2nd Half	193	17	3	13	1	264			343	352	695	11	87	29	0.92	270	44	23	32	55	6%	119	2%	4.35	-0.7	51	$3
Rand Var +2	11 Proj	445	40	5	40	4	270			337	373	711	9	90	29	0.97	288	45	24	31	71	4%	96	4%	4.57	2.5	64	$8

3-17-.277 in 202 AB at NYM. Not much pop, yet, but solid ct% limits BA downside. Sometimes that's all you want from an end-game, #2 catcher. $1 bid could net $5 profit.

Thome,Jim

		AB	R	HR	RBI	SB	Avg	vL	vR	OB	Slg	OPS	bb%	ct%	h%	Eye	xBA	G	L	F	PX	hr/f	Spd	SBO	RC/G	RAR	BPV	R$
Pos 0	06 CHW	490	108	42	109	0	288	236	321	415	598	1013	18	70	33	0.73	282	37	20	43	204	28%	57	0%	8.80	32.4	98	$26
Age/B 40 Left	07 CHW	432	79	35	96	0	275	196	315	406	563	969	18	69	32	0.71	283	43	18	39	197	30%	45	1%	8.22	24.3	85	$21
Ht/Wt 75 250	08 CHW	503	93	34	90	1	245	233	249	360	503	863	15	71	28	0.62	269	40	18	42	180	23%	32	1%	6.57	24.4	69	$19
Health A	09 2TM	362	55	23	77	0	249	209	262	369	481	850	16	66	31	0.56	250	44	20	36	165	27%	37	0%	6.60	15.3	41	$14
PT/Exp B	10 MIN	276	48	25	59	0	283	241	302	411	627	1038	18	70	31	0.73	325	41	21	38	240	34%	55	0%	9.13	21.6	127	$16
Consist C	1st Half	128	20	10	27	0	266			394	594	987	17	70	30	0.69	319	38	21	41	242	27%	51	0%	8.53	8.0	124	$6
LIMA Plan C+	2nd Half	148	28	15	32	0	297			425	655	1081	18	71	32	0.77	330	43	22	35	239	41%	64	0%	9.64	13.4	133	$10
Rand Var +1	11 Proj	303	53	21	63	0	261			387	532	919	17	69	31	0.67	283	42	20	38	190	27%	47	0%	7.50	14.6	79	$13

PX like this at age 40 is Bonds territory. Awesome power intact, but a balky back in Aug/Sept limited playing time. Those types of problems are here to stay, so only pay for 20 HR; anything more is gravy.

Torrealba,Yorvit

		AB	R	HR	RBI	SB	Avg	vL	vR	OB	Slg	OPS	bb%	ct%	h%	Eye	xBA	G	L	F	PX	hr/f	Spd	SBO	RC/G	RAR	BPV	R$
Pos 2	06 COL	* 259	23	7	44	4	234	246	247	273	407	680	5	79	27	0.25	272	63	13	25	112	14%	87	15%	3.76	-4.6	42	$5
Age/B 32 Right	07 COL	396	47	8	47	2	255	264	252	314	376	690	8	82	30	0.47	264	53	18	29	81	8%	78	3%	4.04	-4.6	33	$7
Ht/Wt 71 200	08 COL	236	19	6	31	0	246	279	234	282	394	676	5	81	28	0.27	263	50	17	33	103	10%	64	9%	3.69	-3.7	39	$4
Health B	09 COL	213	27	2	31	1	291	220	318	355	380	735	9	80	36	0.50	254	50	23	28	66	4%	97	3%	4.68	2.5	23	$6
PT/Exp D	10 SD	325	31	7	37	7	271	227	287	338	378	716	9	79	32	0.49	264	55	20	25	76	11%	65	12%	4.38	-1.0	18	$9
Consist B	1st Half	139	14	1	15	3	273			336	345	681	9	80	34	0.46	266	58	22	20	59	5%	72	9%	3.97	-2.0	8	$4
LIMA Plan D	2nd Half	186	17	6	22	4	269			340	403	743	10	79	31	0.51	264	52	19	29	89	14%	66	14%	4.68	1.1	29	$6
Rand Var -1	11 Proj	321	33	6	41	4	268			328	381	709	8	80	32	0.45	262	53	20	27	79	9%	78	9%	4.27	-1.0	25	$8

Consistent but just-okay xBA's set BA ceiling. Too many GB to help much with HR, and too few AB to boost other counting stats. And with that Spd, don't bet on 7 steals again. Another backup CA with minimal upside. Yawn.

Torres,Andres

		AB	R	HR	RBI	SB	Avg	vL	vR	OB	Slg	OPS	bb%	ct%	h%	Eye	xBA	G	L	F	PX	hr/f	Spd	SBO	RC/G	RAR	BPV	R$
Pos 789	06 aaa	348	43	2	28	18	214			303	318	621	11	72	29	0.46					74		147	26%	3.34	-20.5	15	$5
Age/B 33 Both	07 a/a	473	58	7	40	17	232			289	381	670	7	76	29	0.33					91		210	24%	3.82	-20.1	54	$9
Ht/Wt 70 190	08 aaa	409	60	8	33	19	233			294	370	664	8	77	29	0.37					94		136	24%	3.72	-17.6	41	$10
Health B	09 SF	* 195	37	7	25	7	272	338	210	330	508	838	8	67	37	0.26	229	34	16	49	159	11%	179	17%	6.43	4.9	66	$8
PT/Exp D	10 SF	507	84	16	63	26	268	226	283	341	479	820	10	75	33	0.44	285	39	22	39	156	11%	104	26%	5.90	12.3	77	$23
Consist D	1st Half	242	39	4	24	16	285			380	463	843	13	77	36	0.67	286	38	25	38	136	6%	111	27%	6.40	9.3	80	$11
LIMA Plan B	2nd Half	265	45	12	39	10	253			303	494	797	7	72	31	0.26	285	40	19	41	176	15%	97	26%	5.42	2.7	75	$12
Rand Var 0	11 Proj	447	74	14	52	19	251			317	455	772	9	73	32	0.35	258	38	20	42	143	10%	133	24%	5.23	-0.5	65	$16

Reasons to be skeptical:
- MLB PX 60% above minor league PX
--Falling Spd, FB%
- Past peak years
Make him do it again before you sing "I'm a Believer."

Towles,J.R.

		AB	R	HR	RBI	SB	Avg	vL	vR	OB	Slg	OPS	bb%	ct%	h%	Eye	xBA	G	L	F	PX	hr/f	Spd	SBO	RC/G	RAR	BPV	R$
Pos 2	06	0	0	0	0	0	0																					
Age/B 27 Right	07 HOU	* 299	52	11	54	9	293	333	387	347	466	813	8	87	31	0.64	283	34	24	42	99	10%	103	22%	5.46	8.9	76	$13
Ht/Wt 74 190	08 HOU	* 314	30	10	36	3	198	222	118	259	335	594	8	79	22	0.39	216	41	11	48	86	8%	88	10%	2.72	-15.0	30	$3
Health A	09 HOU	* 193	24	5	19	2	217	286	147	287	366	653	9	80	25	0.50	247	53	9	38	103	8%	100	4%	3.62	-3.8	53	$3
PT/Exp F	10 HOU	* 61	6	1	11	2	178	111	211	237	291	528	7	73	23	0.29	202	33	11	56	95	4%	87	17%	1.83	-5.2	12	$1
Consist C	1st Half	61	6	1	11	2	178			237	291	528	7	73	23	0.29	202	33	11	56	95	4%	87	17%	1.83	-5.2	12	$1
LIMA Plan F	2nd Half	0	0	0	0	0	0																					
Rand Var +4	11 Proj	125	14	4	17	2	224			284	366	650	8	79	26	0.39	226	38	12	50	99	7%	82	12%	3.45	-3.6	37	$3

1-8-.191 in 47 AB at HOU. Opened season as starting CA, demoted to AA, broke hand in May. Has yet to fulfill 2007 promise. OPS, ct%, BPV are in free-fall. May need change of scenery.

Tracy,Chad

		AB	R	HR	RBI	SB	Avg	vL	vR	OB	Slg	OPS	bb%	ct%	h%	Eye	xBA	G	L	F	PX	hr/f	Spd	SBO	RC/G	RAR	BPV	R$
Pos 5	06 ARI	597	91	20	80	5	281	231	304	341	451	792	8	78	33	0.42	254	36	21	43	112	10%	65	4%	5.27	-3.7	41	$19
Age/B 30 Left	07 ARI	227	30	7	35	0	264	174	287	348	454	801	11	81	30	0.67	270	37	18	45	125	8%	74	0%	5.61	0.0	71	$6
Ht/Wt 74 215	08 ARI	* 322	29	8	43	0	265	243	271	302	395	696	5	84	30	0.32	250	29	24	47	85	6%	63	0%	3.93	-13.3	34	$7
Health C	09 ARI	* 292	32	8	42	1	238	146	258	306	381	687	9	85	26	0.64	245	35	18	48	91	7%	75	3%	4.08	-9.3	54	$6
PT/Exp F	10 2NL	* 305	37	10	42	0	269	200	248	309	427	736	6	83	29	0.35	271	39	19	42	105	10%	57	1%	4.40	-4.4	47	$9
Consist A	1st Half	135	19	3	16	0	283			325	417	742	6	83	32	0.36	252	43	14	43	93	7%	72	2%	4.53	-1.4	41	$4
LIMA Plan F	2nd Half	170	19	7	26	0	257			296	435	731	5	83	27	0.34	283	38	21	41	114	12%	58	0%	4.30	-3.0	55	$5
Rand Var 0	11 Proj	229	26	7	32	0	262			311	415	726	7	83	29	0.43	260	35	20	45	100	9%	62	1%	4.36	-4.9	47	$6

1-15-.247 in 146 AB at FLA. Consistent production means what you see is what you get, proportional to however many AB they give him. Decent PX, ct% minimize risk. Another guy on whom a $1 bid can net $5.

Treanor,Matt

		AB	R	HR	RBI	SB	Avg	vL	vR	OB	Slg	OPS	bb%	ct%	h%	Eye	xBA	G	L	F	PX	hr/f	Spd	SBO	RC/G	RAR	BPV	R$
Pos 2	06 FLA	157	12	2	14	0	229	268	216	313	318	631	11	78	28	0.56	220	44	18	38	59	4%	104	2%	3.42	-4.4	15	$1
Age/B 35 Right	07 FLA	171	16	4	19	0	269	245	280	342	392	734	10	83	30	0.66	267	42	24	34	75	8%	100	0%	4.68	1.2	44	$3
Ht/Wt 72 210	08 FLA	206	18	2	23	1	238	197	255	299	301	600	8	74	31	0.34	221	55	20	25	50	5%	68	2%	2.81	-8.6	-25	$2
Health F	09 DET	13	0	0	0	0	0	0	0	71	0	71	7	69	0	0.25	252	44	44	11		0%	68	0%	-4.80	-4.6	-86	($1)
PT/Exp F	10 TEX	237	22	5	27	1	211	137	244	278	308	586	8	82	24	0.51	241	43	19	38	61	7%	64	5%	2.76	-10.4	15	$3
Consist F	1st Half	159	17	5	23	1	233			299	371	670	9	82	26	0.52	255	41	18	40	86	10%	74	5%	3.76	-1.9	37	$3
LIMA Plan F	2nd Half	78	5	0	4	0	167			235	179	415	8	82	20	0.50	215	47	20	33	12	0%	54	5%	0.73	-8.9	-28	($1)
Rand Var 0	11 Proj	192	16	2	19	0	229			297	304	601	9	80	28	0.48	234	46	20	33	49	5%	82	3%	2.94	-7.4	3	$2

Returned from a season lost to injury with typical results. Unlucky h% should rebound but xBA says that won't help much.

UP: He gets to go home to a beach volleyball icon each night.

HAROLD NICHOLS

Tuiasosopo,Matt			AB	R	HR	RBI	SB	Avg	vL	vR	OB	Slg	OPS	bb%	ct%	h%	Eye	xBA	G	L	F	PX	hr/f	Spd	SBO	RC/G	RAR	BPV	R$
Pos	7	06 aa	216	16	1	9	2	180			253	214	466	9	72	24	0.35					27		83	6%	0.98	-29.6	-45	($2)
Age/B	24 Right	07 aa	446	64	8	49	3	235			337	359	695	13	77	29	0.65					89		106	9%	4.36	-11.5	38	$7
Ht/Wt	74 225	08 aaa	437	71	10	60	3	249			312	389	701	8	79	29	0.44					99		83	3%	4.19	-12.2	41	$11
Health	B	09 aaa	226	37	10	30	3	234			330	425	755	13	65	32	0.41					151		65	6%	5.24	-0.3	26	$6
PT/Exp	F	10 SEA *	270	31	8	26	2	192	133	195	280	315	595	11	71	24	0.42	232	44	19	37	93	11%	84	6%	2.74	-18.5	7	$3
Consist	D	1st Half	113	14	3	11	1	241			333	353	685	12	70	32	0.46	228	39	23	39	85	9%	96	11%	4.08	-2.8	5	$2
LIMA Plan	F	2nd Half	157	18	5	16	1	156			241	288	529	10	71	18	0.39	235	47	17	36	98	12%	76	0%	1.78	-16.0	9	$0
Rand Var	+5	11 Proj	125	17	4	14	1	224			309	360	668	11	71	29	0.42	235	44	19	37	102	11%	80	5%	3.79	-4.4	14	$2

4-11-.173 in 127 AB at SEA. A pinch of pop but not a promising BA. Saw time at five positions, so might have a career as utility player.

Tulowitzki,Troy			AB	R	HR	RBI	SB	Avg	vL	vR	OB	Slg	OPS	bb%	ct%	h%	Eye	xBA	G	L	F	PX	hr/f	Spd	SBO	RC/G	RAR	BPV	R$
Pos	6	06 COL *	519	73	12	53	8	268	150	263	326	410	737	8	85	29	0.59	282	49	21	30	89	9%	102	10%	4.65	4.4	61	$13
Age/B	26 Right	07 COL	609	104	24	99	7	291	333	278	351	479	831	9	79	34	0.44	271	42	20	38	119	13%	119	8%	5.76	22.5	64	$24
Ht/Wt	75 205	08 COL	377	48	8	46	1	263	330	242	330	401	731	9	85	29	0.68	266	42	20	37	90	7%	98	7%	4.66	0.4	62	$9
Health	C	09 COL	543	101	32	92	20	297	269	307	380	552	932	12	79	32	0.65	286	42	18	40	153	19%	142	18%	7.15	38.4	108	$31
PT/Exp	B	10 COL	470	89	27	95	11	315	342	302	378	568	946	9	83	33	0.62	313	45	15	40	157	17%	101	10%	7.09	33.9	110	$29
Consist	C	1st Half	235	47	9	34	7	306			373	502	875	10	83	34	0.63	291	44	16	40	130	12%	91	13%	6.34	12.4	84	$13
LIMA Plan	B	2nd Half	235	42	18	61	4	323			384	634	1018	9	84	32	0.61	336	46	14	40	185	23%	114	6%	7.83	21.3	137	$17
Rand Var	-1	11 Proj	501	88	26	91	11	299			368	530	898	10	83	32	0.62	295	44	17	39	141	16%	107	11%	6.57	28.7	97	$26

Reasons for caution:
-15 HR, 40 RBI in Sept, rest of season less remarkable
- Two straight growth years; some regression likely
- Health grade
Elite yes, but not without risk.

Uggla,Dan			AB	R	HR	RBI	SB	Avg	vL	vR	OB	Slg	OPS	bb%	ct%	h%	Eye	xBA	G	L	F	PX	hr/f	Spd	SBO	RC/G	RAR	BPV	R$
Pos	4	06 FLA	611	105	27	90	6	282	307	273	334	480	813	7	80	31	0.39	256	41	17	42	113	13%	134	8%	5.42	14.4	67	$23
Age/B	31 Right	07 FLA	632	113	31	88	2	245	245	245	319	479	798	10	74	29	0.41	263	34	16	51	162	13%	82	2%	5.48	14.6	70	$19
Ht/Wt	71 213	08 FLA	531	97	32	92	5	260	191	283	354	514	868	13	68	32	0.45	254	36	16	48	189	18%	87	7%	6.74	30.8	75	$22
Health	A	09 FLA	564	84	31	90	2	243	208	253	349	459	808	14	73	28	0.61	250	37	17	46	145	16%	67	2%	5.72	20.1	60	$19
PT/Exp	A	10 FLA	589	100	33	105	4	287	306	281	370	508	878	12	75	33	0.52	273	40	18	43	151	18%	67	3%	6.53	28.3	65	$28
Consist	B	1st Half	299	53	16	49	2	271			359	482	840	12	73	32	0.51	257	45	12	43	147	17%	63	2%	6.09	10.9	56	$13
LIMA Plan	C+	2nd Half	290	47	17	56	2	303			382	534	917	11	76	35	0.54	288	35	23	42	155	18%	76	3%	6.97	17.1	77	$15
Rand Var	-3	11 Proj	563	94	31	96	4	263			352	489	841	12	74	30	0.52	265	38	18	45	154	17%	74	3%	6.09	22.3	67	$23

2nd half shows what happens when ct% meets inflated LD rate. Latter will regress, taking BA back down with it. Other skills solid, so could have a couple more years at this level. Except BA, of course.

Upton,B.J.			AB	R	HR	RBI	SB	Avg	vL	vR	OB	Slg	OPS	bb%	ct%	h%	Eye	xBA	G	L	F	PX	hr/f	Spd	SBO	RC/G	RAR	BPV	R$
Pos	8	06 TAM *	573	90	8	50	56	258	298	227	345	357	702	12	79	31	0.63	248	54	19	27	65	7%	131	41%	4.38	-5.0	33	$23
Age/B	26 Right	07 TAM	474	86	24	82	22	300	281	306	384	508	892	12	68	40	0.42	257	43	20	38	156	20%	122	19%	7.13	34.7	57	$25
Ht/Wt	75 185	08 TAM	531	85	9	67	44	273	269	275	385	401	786	15	75	35	0.72	252	51	19	31	101	7%	111	31%	5.72	5.8	46	$24
Health	A	09 TAM	560	79	11	55	42	241	190	262	311	373	684	9	73	31	0.38	227	44	15	40	96	7%	133	39%	4.03	-10.5	29	$19
PT/Exp	A	10 TAM	536	89	18	62	42	237	278	218	322	424	745	11	69	31	0.41	253	40	17	44	149	11%	119	38%	4.98	-5.7	57	$23
Consist	C	1st Half	268	48	7	29	24	228			317	399	716	12	73	29	0.48	262	45	16	38	133	9%	118	45%	4.57	-6.3	58	$11
LIMA Plan	B	2nd Half	268	41	11	33	18	246			327	448	774	11	66	33	0.35	244	34	17	50	167	12%	119	31%	5.47	1.2	57	$12
Rand Var	+3	11 Proj	545	86	19	63	37	248			333	427	760	11	71	32	0.44	251	42	17	41	135	12%	118	33%	5.13	0.8	52	$22

The Good: rising power metrics say he could be on the verge of a power breakout. Not as Good: falling ct%, BA vs RHP conspire to increase BA risk. The net:
UP: 25 HR
DN: .225 BA

Upton,Justin			AB	R	HR	RBI	SB	Avg	vL	vR	OB	Slg	OPS	bb%	ct%	h%	Eye	xBA	G	L	F	PX	hr/f	Spd	SBO	RC/G	RAR	BPV	R$
Pos	9	06	0	0	0	0	0	0																					
Age/B	23 Right	07 ARI *	399	59	15	57	10	278	200	230	350	486	836	10	81	31	0.58	264	36	16	48	127	9%	133	17%	5.95	12.4	86	$15
Ht/Wt	74 205	08 ARI	356	52	15	42	1	250	253	249	349	463	812	13	66	34	0.45	238	37	21	42	157	15%	143	5%	6.15	10.2	61	$9
Health	B	09 ARI	526	84	26	86	20	300	377	277	367	532	899	9	74	36	0.40	275	45	19	36	155	19%	128	17%	6.81	28.3	79	$28
PT/Exp	B	10 ARI	495	73	17	69	18	273	276	272	356	442	798	11	69	36	0.42	247	41	19	39	131	13%	107	17%	5.73	5.8	39	$21
Consist	B	1st Half	300	48	14	39	11	260			343	457	800	11	65	35	0.37	245	45	17	38	151	19%	120	18%	5.85	4.6	43	$13
LIMA Plan	B	2nd Half	195	25	3	30	7	292			376	421	796	12	75	37	0.54	250	36	23	41	103	5%	92	15%	5.67	1.9	37	$8
Rand Var	-2	11 Proj	529	78	23	77	16	280			360	490	850	11	72	35	0.45	264	41	20	39	148	15%	121	15%	6.33	18.0	67	$23

Small labrum tear flared up and wiped out Sept, maybe affected Aug PX (64). He's almost there; ct% still holding him back. *If* 2H ct% is sign of change (likely not), and the shoulder's okay (not a given): UP: 30 HR, 30 SB

Uribe,Juan			AB	R	HR	RBI	SB	Avg	vL	vR	OB	Slg	OPS	bb%	ct%	h%	Eye	xBA	G	L	F	PX	hr/f	Spd	SBO	RC/G	RAR	BPV	R$
Pos	456	06 CHW	463	53	21	71	1	235	224	244	256	441	697	3	82	24	0.16	266	38	17	45	123	12%	66	3%	3.76	-5.1	55	$10
Age/B	32 Right	07 CHW	513	55	20	68	1	234	257	225	282	394	675	6	78	26	0.30	234	35	15	50	101	10%	88	9%	3.62	-5.9	34	$9
Ht/Wt	72 230	08 CHW	324	38	7	40	1	247	254	245	295	386	681	6	80	29	0.34	248	34	20	45	99	6%	74	6%	3.84	-10.2	37	$6
Health	A	09 SF	398	50	16	55	3	289	255	299	331	495	826	6	79	33	0.30	275	39	21	40	134	13%	90	4%	5.55	11.4	66	$15
PT/Exp	C	10 SF	521	64	24	85	1	248	231	252	307	440	747	8	82	26	0.49	270	40	15	44	119	13%	61	2%	4.62	-3.1	61	$16
Consist	C	1st Half	271	39	12	46	1	255			327	446	773	10	82	27	0.59	281	42	18	39	122	14%	58	4%	5.05	1.8	64	$9
LIMA Plan	C	2nd Half	250	25	12	39	0	240			286	432	718	6	83	25	0.37	257	38	13	50	116	12%	67	0%	4.15	-5.0	58	$7
Rand Var	+2	11 Proj	472	56	21	70	2	246			296	445	741	7	81	26	0.38	269	38	17	44	125	12%	75	4%	4.49	-3.2	62	$13

Yes, we already knew what he could do with full-time ABs. Free agent loved AT&T Park (.307/.384/.521 over two years) but struggled on the road (.227/.306/.410). His home could determine his value.

Utley,Chase			AB	R	HR	RBI	SB	Avg	vL	vR	OB	Slg	OPS	bb%	ct%	h%	Eye	xBA	G	L	F	PX	hr/f	Spd	SBO	RC/G	RAR	BPV	R$
Pos	4	06 PHI	658	131	32	102	15	309	301	312	369	527	896	9	80	35	0.48	269	37	20	43	131	14%	111	10%	6.53	34.8	77	$32
Age/B	32 Left	07 PHI	530	104	22	103	9	332	318	340	390	566	956	9	83	37	0.56	301	38	20	42	147	12%	104	7%	7.27	35.8	101	$29
Ht/Wt	73 190	08 PHI	607	113	33	104	14	292	277	301	359	535	895	10	83	31	0.62	295	33	24	42	147	15%	94	10%	6.51	29.4	99	$31
Health	C	09 PHI	571	112	31	93	23	282	288	279	378	508	886	13	81	30	0.80	267	34	18	48	137	14%	120	12%	6.62	33.6	97	$31
PT/Exp	A	10 PHI	425	75	16	65	13	275	294	266	369	445	814	13	85	29	1.00	283	41	20	39	104	11%	101	11%	5.78	11.6	82	$19
Consist	A	1st Half	264	49	11	37	5	277			372	466	838	13	86	29	1.08	294	42	20	39	113	13%	116	7%	6.08	9.5	98	$12
LIMA Plan	B	2nd Half	161	26	5	28	8	273			364	410	774	12	84	30	0.88	265	40	20	40	87	9%	75	16%	5.28	2.1	55	$8
Rand Var	+2	11 Proj	585	107	28	96	15	284			370	488	858	12	83	30	0.81	282	38	20	42	124	13%	100	9%	6.22	24.7	88	$28

Rebound hopes from thumb injury can look to Sept as key indicator: 123 PX, .293 xBA, 86 BPV. He should be fine.

Valaika,Chris			AB	R	HR	RBI	SB	Avg	vL	vR	OB	Slg	OPS	bb%	ct%	h%	Eye	xBA	G	L	F	PX	hr/f	Spd	SBO	RC/G	RAR	BPV	R$
Pos	4	06	0	0	0	0	0	0																					
Age/B	25 Right	07	0	0	0	0	0	0																					
Ht/Wt	73 180	08 aa	379	44	10	38	5	264			303	390	694	5	84	29	0.36					79		104	10%	3.93	-10.1	45	$9
Health	B	09 aaa	366	26	6	30	1	210			238	312	550	4	81	24	0.20					70		97	1%	2.11	-29.8	19	$1
PT/Exp	F	10 CIN *	462	41	5	42	2	260	400	174	285	350	634	3	84	30	0.22	268	41	24	34	67	4%	87	5%	3.18	-22.2	26	$8
Consist	C	1st Half	277	23	0	20	1	248			277	312	589	4	85	29	0.28					54		102	4%	2.77	-16.9	25	$2
LIMA Plan	F	2nd Half	185	18	5	23	1	278			296	406	702	3	83	31	0.15	278	41	24	34	87	9%	82	7%	3.83	-5.3	33	$5
Rand Var	0	11 Proj	116	10	3	11	1	250			277	371	648	4	83	28	0.22	269	41	24	34	82	8%	92	5%	3.27	-5.0	34	$2

1-2-.263 in 38 AB at CIN. Broken wrist in 2009 has scuttled the progress of this former prospect. Will need a standout season in '11 to re-establish himself, but there are little signs of that happening.

Valbuena,Luis			AB	R	HR	RBI	SB	Avg	vL	vR	OB	Slg	OPS	bb%	ct%	h%	Eye	xBA	G	L	F	PX	hr/f	Spd	SBO	RC/G	RAR	BPV	R$
Pos	4	06	0	0	0	0	0	0																					
Age/B	25 Left	07 aa	444	47	9	38	9	214			283	331	614	9	83	24	0.57					76		104	15%	3.19	-16.1	43	$5
Ht/Wt	70 195	08 SEA *	501	75	9	50	15	267			339	373	712	10	86	30	0.76					69		113	16%	4.47	-6.2	54	$14
Health	A	09 CLE *	446	64	12	42	4	257	205	255	318	420	738	8	79	30	0.42	265	41	22	37	107	9%	104	10%	4.64	-3.9	50	$10
PT/Exp	C	10 CLE *	371	39	6	39	3	210	318	169	291	313	604	10	79	25	0.54	245	47	18	35	77	6%	58	5%	3.05	-16.3	17	$4
Consist	B	1st Half	172	17	3	16	2	179			272	271	543	11	77	22	0.55	229	52	15	33	69	7%	51	9%	2.22	-12.6	2	$1
LIMA Plan	D	2nd Half	199	22	3	23	1	237			308	349	658	9	81	28	0.53	258	41	21	38	84	5%	80	2%	3.74	-4.3	34	$3
Rand Var	+4	11 Proj	344	42	8	35	4	247			318	384	702	9	80	29	0.53	261	44	20	36	93	8%	81	9%	4.26	-3.6	41	$7

2-24-.193 in 275 AB at CLE. CLE tries to give him a job, he keeps giving it back. But h% will normalize, and with it BA. He still owns prior Spd, that '09 PX, and still only 25. Speculate, but only at the right price.

HAROLD NICHOLS

Valdez,Wilson

Valdez,Wilson			AB	R	HR	RBI	SB	Avg	vL	vR	OB	Slg	OPS	bb%	ct%	h%	Eye	xBA	G	L	F	PX	hr/f	Spd	SBO	RC/G	RAR	BPV	R$
Pos	46	06 aaa	528	67	5	38	19	236			289	298	586	7	92	25	0.89					38		97	27%	3.07	-21.3	42	$8
Age/B	32 Right	07 aaa	361	51	3	18	9	235			289	299	589	7	89	26	0.72					42		117	15%	3.03	-14.6	42	$5
Ht/Wt	71 170	08 JPN	78	8	1	8	1	239			297	275	572	8	83	28	0.49					23		98	4%	2.59	-5.2	-3	$1
Health	A	09 NYM *	321	33	0	16	5	206	115	317	254	241	496	6	88	24	0.53	264	64	19	17	24	0%	125	10%	1.88	-26.7	22	$1
PT/Exp	F	10 PHI *	355	39	4	38	9	266	242	265	312	362	674	6	87	30	0.51	292	60	19	21	63	6%	110	11%	3.87	-9.7	46	$9
Consist	C	1st Half	148	21	4	21	3	264			278	405	684	2	88	28	0.17	314	62	18	19	87	16%	105	10%	3.67	-4.9	58	$5
LIMA Plan	F	2nd Half	207	18	0	17	6	268			334	331	665	9	86	31	0.72	275	58	19	22	46	0%	111	11%	3.98	-5.1	35	$4
Rand Var	0	11 Proj	131	15	1	11	3	267			314	342	656	6	88	30	0.56	281	61	19	20	49	4%	109	12%	3.71	-3.9	38	$3

4-35-.258-7 in 333 AB at PHI. There's a reason these MI utility types are always available... this one's xBA hints at some BA upside. But as an extreme GBer with only okay wheels, that's not enough to bid.

Valencia,Danny

Valencia,Danny			AB	R	HR	RBI	SB	Avg	vL	vR	OB	Slg	OPS	bb%	ct%	h%	Eye	xBA	G	L	F	PX	hr/f	Spd	SBO	RC/G	RAR	BPV	R$
Pos	5	06	0	0	0	0	0	0																					
Age/B	26 Right	07	0	0	0	0	0	0																					
Ht/Wt	74 200	08 aa	266	33	8	26	2	249			285	411	697	5	76	30	0.21					114		109	5%	3.92	-9.4	40	$5
Health	A	09 a/a	487	65	10	57	0	247			292	392	684	6	85	27	0.42					95		98	4%	3.94	-14.2	59	$9
PT/Exp	D	10 MIN *	484	46	7	57	4	281	374	280	324	391	714	6	84	32	0.40	263	43	19	38	80	4%	74	3%	4.27	-7.7	37	$12
Consist	A	1st Half	233	20	0	19	3	254			300	310	610	6	84	30	0.39	246	49	18	33	50	0%	95	5%	3.07	-12.0	17	$3
LIMA Plan	D	2nd Half	251	26	7	38	1	307			346	466	812	6	85	34	0.41	286	42	19	39	107	8%	71	1%	5.35	3.6	61	$9
Rand Var	-2	11 Proj	372	42	6	44	2	266			308	390	698	6	83	31	0.37	261	43	19	39	86	5%	89	3%	4.06	-8.0	43	$8

7-40-.311 in 299 AB at MIN. Solid debut; now for the downer:

	BA	OB	Slg
vs LH	.374	.441	.525
vs RH	.280	.303	.410

Glove will get him AB, but he's a part-timer vs LH for you, for now.

Varitek,Jason

Varitek,Jason			AB	R	HR	RBI	SB	Avg	vL	vR	OB	Slg	OPS	bb%	ct%	h%	Eye	xBA	G	L	F	PX	hr/f	Spd	SBO	RC/G	RAR	BPV	R$
Pos	2	06 BOS	365	46	12	55	1	238	229	244	324	400	724	11	76	28	0.53	244	45	17	38	106	11%	81	3%	4.55	1.6	38	$7
Age/B	38 Both	07 BOS	435	57	17	68	1	255	264	252	360	421	780	14	72	32	0.58	240	42	18	40	112	14%	92	2%	5.45	14.8	35	$11
Ht/Wt	74 230	08 BOS	423	37	13	43	0	220	284	201	305	359	665	11	71	28	0.43	213	42	14	45	104	10%	52	1%	3.74	-5.9	7	$4
Health	C	09 BOS	364	41	14	51	0	209	231	200	311	390	701	13	75	24	0.60	241	38	15	47	123	11%	49	0%	4.31	0.4	42	$5
PT/Exp	D	10 BOS	112	18	7	16	0	232	222	235	295	473	768	8	69	27	0.29	254	27	16	57	179	16%	59	0%	5.02	2.9	54	$4
Consist	B	1st Half	95	18	7	16	0	263			327	547	874	9	69	31	0.31	276	24	17	59	209	18%	63	0%	6.50	6.4	83	$4
LIMA Plan	D	2nd Half	17	0	0	0	0	59			111	59	170	6	65	9	0.17	124	45	9	45	0	0%	65	0%	-3.78	-5.0	******	($1)
Rand Var	+1	11 Proj	218	29	10	31	0	248			331	437	769	11	72	30	0.45	242	36	16	48	136	13%	55	1%	5.14	6.0	38	$6

Flashed early season power by lofting everything in Apr - May. Then broken foot got in way. PX +FB% trends would be reasons to predict big power spike... if he was five years younger. Still, a good end-game HR stash at CA.

Velez,Eugenio

Velez,Eugenio			AB	R	HR	RBI	SB	Avg	vL	vR	OB	Slg	OPS	bb%	ct%	h%	Eye	xBA	G	L	F	PX	hr/f	Spd	SBO	RC/G	RAR	BPV	R$
Pos	7	06	0	0	0	0	0	0																					
Age/B	28 Both	07 aa	394	45	1	19	41	247			284	322	606	5	84	29	0.33					48		196	61%	3.00	-27.2	46	$12
Ht/Wt	73 162	08 SF *	446	52	5	42	26	265	235	268	308	398	706	6	84	31	0.39	278	59	15	26	85	5%	168	39%	4.25	-15.8	69	$14
Health	A	09 SF *	467	63	7	52	24	261	200	286	300	391	690	5	83	30	0.33	269	54	17	29	84	6%	152	35%	3.97	-22.4	57	$15
PT/Exp	D	10 SF *	376	40	6	31	20	225	167	163	266	328	595	5	86	25	0.38	259	61	9	30	64	7%	125	46%	2.84	-27.0	43	$9
Consist	B	1st Half	206	24	3	16	14	232			274	322	596	6	85	26	0.39	248	57	11	32	56	5%	126	45%	2.86	-14.4	36	$6
LIMA Plan	F	2nd Half	170	16	4	15	6	217			256	336	593	5	86	23	0.38	289	86	0	14	72	17%	129	46%	2.82	-12.6	52	$3
Rand Var	+4	11 Proj	161	18	3	14	9	242			282	374	656	5	85	27	0.36	276	57	15	28	81	9%	136	44%	3.54	-8.7	56	$5

2-8-.164 in 55 AB at SF. Had just 9 AB after getting hit in head by foul ball in July. You used to be able to mine for SB here. Given Spd trend and horrible OB, that's more of a risk, but at 28, he can't be written off.

Venable,Will

Venable,Will			AB	R	HR	RBI	SB	Avg	vL	vR	OB	Slg	OPS	bb%	ct%	h%	Eye	xBA	G	L	F	PX	hr/f	Spd	SBO	RC/G	RAR	BPV	R$
Pos	789	06	0	0	0	0	0	0																					
Age/B	28 Left	07 aa	515	56	7	58	18	238			284	314	598	6	84	27	0.40					48		107	15%	2.86	-36.2	20	$10
Ht/Wt	74 210	08 SD *	552	72	12	57	7	245	324	237	305	374	679	8	78	29	0.39	234	49	13	37	86	8%	123	7%	3.87	-25.6	36	$11
Health	A	09 SD *	493	63	20	60	7	234	225	266	291	417	708	7	73	28	0.30	242	44	16	40	123	14%	106	7%	4.14	-21.0	40	$13
PT/Exp	C	10 SD	392	60	13	51	29	245	154	259	323	408	731	10	67	33	0.35	221	39	17	44	116	11%	171	33%	4.76	-3.6	36	$18
Consist	A	1st Half	214	35	8	32	14	238			312	416	728	10	64	33	0.30	218	36	18	46	130	13%	168	30%	4.80	-1.8	34	$10
LIMA Plan	C	2nd Half	178	25	5	19	15	253			335	399	734	11	71	33	0.42	224	42	15	42	100	9%	147	35%	4.76	-1.6	31	$8
Rand Var	-4	11 Proj	369	51	12	44	17	238			306	397	703	9	73	30	0.36	230	41	16	43	106	10%	141	23%	4.20	-11.9	37	$12

Spd spike, basepath freedom created perfect storm for SBs. Still needs to improve ct% and BA vLH to become a full-timer. But this was Jose Reyes' HR/SB in 200 fewer AB; daily gamers could have found big profit there.

Viciedo,Dayan

Viciedo,Dayan			AB	R	HR	RBI	SB	Avg	vL	vR	OB	Slg	OPS	bb%	ct%	h%	Eye	xBA	G	L	F	PX	hr/f	Spd	SBO	RC/G	RAR	BPV	R$
Pos	5	06 CUB	323	53	8	57	3	315			349	481	829	5	87	34	0.41								8%	5.54			
Age/B	22 Right	07 CUB	301	38	5	34	2	235			324	360	684	12	84	27	0.80							117	7%	4.26			
Ht/Wt	71 240	08 CUB	177	40	6	37	2	274			356	422	778	11	86	29	0.88							98	5%	5.25			
Health	A	09 aa	504	65	12	70	4	268			298	378	676	4	85	29	0.29					67		49	5%	3.63	-18.6	19	$14
PT/Exp	D	10 CHW *	447	50	23	50	2	264	340	278	281	464	746	2	80	28	0.13	284	42	19	39	127	16%	53	4%	4.24	-7.6	46	$14
Consist	C	1st Half	260	26	13	28	2	260			280	458	738	3	82	27	0.16	296	56	17	28	124	22%	44	6%	4.17	-5.0	49	$8
LIMA Plan	D	2nd Half	187	24	10	22	0	269			284	473	757	2	78	30	0.10	275	38	20	43	133	16%	66	0%	4.36	-2.5	43	$6
Rand Var	+1	11 Proj	295	41	16	41	2	261			296	475	771	5	82	27	0.28	285	40	19	41	126	17%	69	5%	4.67	-1.2	62	$10

5-13-.308 in 104 AB at CHW. Power is unquestioned in this Cuban prospect, but pitch recognition (13 BB in 447 AB) is another story. Pitchers will carve him up until he changes approach. Patience needed.

Victorino,Shane

Victorino,Shane			AB	R	HR	RBI	SB	Avg	vL	vR	OB	Slg	OPS	bb%	ct%	h%	Eye	xBA	G	L	F	PX	hr/f	Spd	SBO	RC/G	RAR	BPV	R$
Pos	8	06 PHI	415	70	6	46	4	287	273	293	326	414	740	5	87	32	0.44	266	45	21	34	72	5%	155	6%	4.60	1.9	65	$12
Age/B	30 Both	07 PHI	456	78	12	46	37	281	291	276	335	423	758	8	86	30	0.60	272	47	17	36	85	8%	127	32%	4.85	4.2	68	$21
Ht/Wt	69 187	08 PHI	570	102	14	58	36	293	282	298	345	447	792	7	88	31	0.65	276	45	19	36	90	8%	160	29%	5.28	8.8	88	$27
Health	A	09 PHI	620	102	10	62	25	292	314	283	354	445	800	9	89	32	0.85	288	45	23	32	93	5%	143	18%	5.55	14.3	91	$24
PT/Exp	A	10 PHI	587	84	18	69	34	259	321	235	320	429	750	8	87	27	0.67	285	45	17	38	100	9%	132	26%	4.82	-1.2	84	$24
Consist	A	1st Half	321	51	12	46	17	255			315	452	767	8	87	26	0.68	286	44	15	41	107	11%	154	24%	5.00	1.0	99	$14
LIMA Plan	B	2nd Half	266	33	6	23	17	263			326	402	729	9	86	29	0.66	284	46	20	34	90	8%	99	29%	4.60	-2.2	64	$10
Rand Var	+3	11 Proj	611	94	16	64	33	275			334	440	774	8	87	29	0.69	287	45	19	35	98	9%	136	25%	5.13	6.0	86	$25

PRO:
PX surge, HR spike w/o fluky hr/f hint at more power upside
CON:
Further decline vs RHers could raise part-time whispers
UP: 20+ HR, keeps his SB

Vizquel,Omar

Vizquel,Omar			AB	R	HR	RBI	SB	Avg	vL	vR	OB	Slg	OPS	bb%	ct%	h%	Eye	xBA	G	L	F	PX	hr/f	Spd	SBO	RC/G	RAR	BPV	R$
Pos	5	06 SF	579	88	4	58	24	295	340	281	357	389	746	9	91	32	1.10	257	40	22	38	51	2%	150	16%	4.99	-8.2	70	$19
Age/B	43 Both	07 SF	513	54	4	51	14	246	243	247	305	316	621	8	91	26	0.92	243	41	18	40	43	2%	101	14%	3.50	-32.5	45	$9
Ht/Wt	69 175	08 SF	266	24	0	23	5	222	121	250	286	267	553	8	89	25	0.83	235	42	18	40	34	0%	76	13%	2.74	-21.8	24	$2
Health	B	09 TEX	177	17	1	14	4	266	485	215	316	345	660	7	85	31	0.48	231	34	22	43	50	2%	116	8%	3.73	-4.8	29	$3
PT/Exp	D	10 CHW	344	36	2	30	11	276	207	290	341	331	673	9	87	31	0.76	254	46	21	33	39	2%	100	16%	4.02	-8.2	29	$9
Consist	B	1st Half	128	17	1	14	2	242			297	320	617	7	85	28	0.53	250	48	17	35	54	3%	111	12%	3.25	-6.2	33	$2
LIMA Plan	F	2nd Half	216	19	1	16	9	296			367	338	705	10	88	33	0.92	258	46	23	31	31	2%	85	17%	4.46	-2.3	24	$7
Rand Var	-3	11 Proj	225	23	1	20	6	253			315	313	628	8	87	29	0.69	245	42	21	37	41	2%	97	14%	3.48	-8.9	29	$4

Ageless veteran still can control plate with the best of them. 2H SB came from opportunities not skill, so we can't expect a repeat there. And xBA history says to bet against BA repeat. Very little value as a CI.

Votto,Joey

Votto,Joey			AB	R	HR	RBI	SB	Avg	vL	vR	OB	Slg	OPS	bb%	ct%	h%	Eye	xBA	G	L	F	PX	hr/f	Spd	SBO	RC/G	RAR	BPV	R$
Pos	3	06 aa	508	78	21	71	22	300			383	517	901	12	79	34	0.65					143		70	19%	6.86	16.3	78	$23
Age/B	27 Left	07 CIN *	580	77	26	99	16	284	269	345	359	469	828	10	81	32	0.59	269	28	26	46	112	12%	71	15%	5.74	-6.5	56	$24
Ht/Wt	75 233	08 CIN	526	69	24	84	7	297	292	299	368	506	873	10	81	33	0.58	295	44	25	31	131	18%	81	8%	6.33	8.8	74	$22
Health	A	09 CIN	469	82	25	84	4	322	329	319	410	567	977	13	77	37	0.66	292	39	22	39	167	18%	62	3%	7.90	17.4	90	$25
PT/Exp	A	10 CIN	547	106	37	113	16	324	283	347	420	600	1020	14	77	36	0.73	317	45	20	35	183	25%	73	11%	8.45	31.2	107	$38
Consist	C	1st Half	285	53	19	57	7	312			408	572	980	14	77	35	0.71	302	46	18	36	164	24%	96	11%	7.88	12.2	99	$18
LIMA Plan	D+	2nd Half	262	53	18	56	9	336			433	630	1063	15	77	38	0.75	333	44	23	33	202	27%	58	11%	9.07	18.8	119	$20
Rand Var	-3	11 Proj	548	96	33	103	8	318			407	579	985	13	78	36	0.68	308	43	22	35	171	22%	70	6%	7.93	24.8	98	$31

The breakout we've waited for. Another year of PX growth puts 40 HR as a possible next step. And with bb% gains + elite xBA, bank on a solid BA follow-up. Only fluke was SB, given way below average Spd.

STEPHEN NICKRAND

Walker,Neil

Walker,Neil			AB	R	HR	RBI	SB	Avg	vL	vR	OB	Slg	OPS	bb%	ct%	h%	Eye	xBA	G	L	F	PX	hr/f	Spd	SBO	RC/G	RAR	BPV	R$
Pos	4	06	0	0	0	0	0	0																					
Age/B	25 Both	07 a/a	495	71	10	56	8	259			320	394	714	8	85	29	0.63					89		95	11%	4.43	1.2	60	$12
Ht/Wt	75 215	08 aaa	505	59	13	69	9	223			258	367	625	4	82	25	0.26					90		98	17%	3.07	-27.6	42	$10
Health	A	09 aaa	356	30	11	55	4	232			273	407	680	5	86	24	0.40					113		86	9%	3.86	-9.4	73	$7
PT/Exp	D	10 PIT *	594	76	16	85	10	288	295	296	341	457	798	7	82	33	0.45	283	36	22	41	118	8%	88	9%	5.34	8.8	65	$22
Consist	C	1st Half	287	37	7	31	10	279			329	447	775	7	82	32	0.42	266	33	17	49	120	6%	105	18%	5.06	2.0	73	$10
LIMA Plan	C+	2nd Half	307	39	9	54	0	296			353	466	819	8	81	34	0.47	287	38	24	38	116	9%	80	1%	5.61	6.8	61	$12
Rand Var	-3	11 Proj	556	65	17	80	8	270			318	443	762	7	83	30	0.43	282	37	23	40	115	9%	86	9%	4.83	1.8	66	$17

12-66-.296 in 426 AB at PIT. Light finally went on for this former first rounder. No LH/RH splits, growing PX, age 26 give hope for further growth. And as a 2B, he's an impact bat already. UP: 25 HR

Wallace,Brett

Wallace,Brett			AB	R	HR	RBI	SB	Avg	vL	vR	OB	Slg	OPS	bb%	ct%	h%	Eye	xBA	G	L	F	PX	hr/f	Spd	SBO	RC/G	RAR	BPV	R$
Pos	3	06	0	0	0	0	0	0																					
Age/B	24 Left	07	0	0	0	0	0	0																					
Ht/Wt	73 245	08 aa	49	12	2	9	0	306			333	510	844	4	84	33	0.25					133		69	0%	5.58	0.1	71	$2
Health	A	09 a/a	532	55	14	46	1	243			288	361	649	6	84	27	0.40					73		59	3%	3.42	-42.8	27	$8
PT/Exp	F	10 HOU *	529	51	13	49	1	227	240	218	261	354	615	4	80	26	0.23	242	39	17	44	87	7%	70	2%	2.88	-55.4	21	$7
Consist	C	1st Half	306	29	9	25	0	229			261	370	632	4	84	25	0.28					94		59	0%	3.14	-29.5	41	$4
LIMA Plan	D	2nd Half	223	23	4	25	1	225			261	331	592	5	74	29	0.19	216	39	17	44	76	5%	86	4%	2.56	-25.7	-6	$3
Rand Var	+2	11 Proj	465	47	13	43	1	245			283	376	659	5	81	28	0.27	238	39	17	44	86	8%	66	3%	3.43	-39.1	23	$8

2-13-.222 in 144 AB at HOU. Recent first rounder has a lot of work to do. See RAR. That PX from '08 was in a tiny sample, so we can't draw much hope from it. He's nothing more than an end-game stash for now.

Weeks,Rickie

Weeks,Rickie			AB	R	HR	RBI	SB	Avg	vL	vR	OB	Slg	OPS	bb%	ct%	h%	Eye	xBA	G	L	F	PX	hr/f	Spd	SBO	RC/G	RAR	BPV	R$
Pos	4	06 MIL	359	73	8	34	19	279	271	280	334	404	738	8	74	36	0.33	236	46	20	33	83	9%	118	23%	4.62	0.2	16	$14
Age/B	28 Right	07 MIL	409	87	16	36	25	235	258	225	357	433	790	16	72	29	0.67	250	42	17	41	133	13%	139	21%	5.72	12.6	69	$15
Ht/Wt	70 213	08 MIL	475	89	14	46	19	234	250	227	327	398	725	12	76	28	0.57	241	46	15	39	107	10%	129	18%	4.66	-1.6	54	$15
Health	F	09 MIL	147	28	9	24	2	272	276	271	327	517	844	8	73	31	0.31	260	38	19	44	154	19%	133	11%	5.90	5.8	74	$7
PT/Exp	B	10 MIL	651	112	29	83	11	269	329	251	345	464	809	10	72	33	0.41	262	49	15	36	139	17%	89	8%	5.69	16.4	48	$26
Consist	B	1st Half	332	53	14	49	5	271			346	458	804	10	73	33	0.42	263	48	17	35	132	17%	82	8%	5.59	7.4	43	$13
LIMA Plan	B	2nd Half	319	59	15	34	6	266			345	470	815	11	71	33	0.41	262	50	13	37	147	18%	97	8%	5.80	9.0	53	$13
Rand Var	-2	11 Proj	521	96	26	66	9	263			338	479	817	10	73	31	0.42	263	45	16	38	144	18%	115	10%	5.72	15.2	63	$21

With health came the $25 year we knew was possible. ct% dip reminds us to use xBA as BA barometer. 20+ SB requires green light, which is gone. Bid on power only. And don't bank on repeat of health.

Wells,Casper

Wells,Casper			AB	R	HR	RBI	SB	Avg	vL	vR	OB	Slg	OPS	bb%	ct%	h%	Eye	xBA	G	L	F	PX	hr/f	Spd	SBO	RC/G	RAR	BPV	R$
Pos	9	06	0	0	0	0	0	0																					
Age/B	26 Right	07	0	0	0	0	0	0																					
Ht/Wt	74 210	08 aa	270	46	13	40	6	250			311	486	797	8	81	27	0.46					142		114	17%	5.30	0.2	90	$10
Health	A	09 aa	311	41	12	33	7	228			304	417	720	10	72	28	0.39					128		103	21%	4.45	-6.4	43	$7
PT/Exp	F	10 DET *	480	56	21	52	6	225	265	395	273	431	704	6	77	25	0.28	279	42	19	39	138	15%	128	17%	4.03	-13.8	69	$11
Consist	B	1st Half	255	22	8	20	3	181			216	336	552	4	76	20	0.18	266	57	14	29	106	15%	99	20%	1.99	-24.8	28	$1
LIMA Plan	D+	2nd Half	225	35	12	32	3	275			334	539	873	8	77	31	0.39	306	40	19	40	174	18%	130	15%	6.29	8.8	106	$9
Rand Var	+5	11 Proj	290	39	14	34	6	248			308	472	780	8	76	28	0.36	277	41	19	40	144	16%	119	19%	5.09	-0.7	72	$9

4-17-.323 in 93 AB at DET. Mashed RHers in late season callup. Solid, consistent power-speed skills give hope he can make F/T impact, assuming no further Eye erosion. With consistency: UP: 20 HR, 20 SB

Wells,Vernon

Wells,Vernon			AB	R	HR	RBI	SB	Avg	vL	vR	OB	Slg	OPS	bb%	ct%	h%	Eye	xBA	G	L	F	PX	hr/f	Spd	SBO	RC/G	RAR	BPV	R$
Pos	8	06 TOR	611	91	32	106	17	303	333	292	359	542	901	8	85	31	0.60	294	42	18	40	136	15%	82	13%	6.48	30.7	93	$28
Age/B	32 Right	07 TOR	584	85	16	80	10	245	311	226	303	402	706	8	85	27	0.55	265	39	17	44	101	7%	78	10%	4.26	-4.7	61	$14
Ht/Wt	73 230	08 TOR	427	63	20	78	4	300	333	290	344	496	841	6	89	30	0.63	294	47	17	36	111	15%	65	5%	5.65	3.6	80	$18
Health	B	09 TOR	630	84	15	66	17	260	206	278	313	400	713	7	86	28	0.56	253	43	15	42	85	6%	80	13%	4.33	-5.8	53	$17
PT/Exp	A	10 TOR	590	79	31	88	6	273	195	291	330	515	845	8	86	27	0.60	314	42	16	42	151	15%	60	8%	5.81	8.2	99	$23
Consist	C	1st Half	307	45	19	48	4	274			326	544	870	7	84	27	0.49	328	45	16	39	170	19%	68	8%	6.04	6.2	109	$14
LIMA Plan	C	2nd Half	283	34	12	40	2	272			333	484	817	8	88	28	0.74	299	39	16	45	131	11%	54	7%	5.58	2.1	90	$10
Rand Var	+2	11 Proj	583	79	25	83	9	280			334	484	817	7	87	29	0.60	291	42	16	41	123	12%	68	9%	5.50	6.8	82	$21

Hello 2006! It's amazing what a little health can do. He's young enough to do it again, but a return to form vs. LHers would help. Problem is, last time he had consecutive 20+ HR years was '05-'06. Be conservative.

Werth,Jayson

Werth,Jayson			AB	R	HR	RBI	SB	Avg	vL	vR	OB	Slg	OPS	bb%	ct%	h%	Eye	xBA	G	L	F	PX	hr/f	Spd	SBO	RC/G	RAR	BPV	R$
Pos	89	06	0	0	0	0	0	0																					
Age/B	31 Right	07 PHI	255	43	8	49	7	298	375	257	401	459	860	15	71	39	0.60	254	40	27	33	109	13%	123	8%	6.71	15.4	41	$11
Ht/Wt	77 212	08 PHI	418	73	24	67	20	273	303	255	360	498	858	12	72	33	0.48	259	39	23	38	147	21%	113	16%	6.37	19.5	64	$22
Health	A	09 PHI	571	98	36	99	20	268	302	256	369	506	875	14	73	31	0.58	261	36	20	44	159	20%	87	13%	6.61	31.1	73	$29
PT/Exp	A	10 PHI	554	106	27	85	13	296	287	300	387	532	919	13	73	36	0.56	282	37	18	45	175	15%	101	9%	7.30	37.2	92	$29
Consist	A	1st Half	269	49	13	48	4	283			371	532	903	12	70	36	0.48	281	34	18	48	197	14%	85	7%	7.23	17.8	91	$13
LIMA Plan	B+	2nd Half	285	57	14	37	9	309			401	533	935	13	76	36	0.66	284	40	17	43	156	15%	113	11%	7.40	19.6	94	$16
Rand Var	-1	11 Proj	577	105	32	93	13	284			379	523	901	13	73	34	0.56	274	38	20	43	165	18%	101	9%	7.03	36.5	83	$29

Thank that h% spike for his nice BA. Even if BA falls, his HRs won't, given rising flyball rate and PX. Extending BPV gains one more season, there's a $30 year here...if he still has a hitter cozy home park. UP: 40 HR

Whiteside,Eli

Whiteside,Eli			AB	R	HR	RBI	SB	Avg	vL	vR	OB	Slg	OPS	bb%	ct%	h%	Eye	xBA	G	L	F	PX	hr/f	Spd	SBO	RC/G	RAR	BPV	R$
Pos	2	06 aaa	315	36	11	46	1	231			254	394	648	3	77	27	0.13					107		74	7%	3.17	-11.6	22	$5
Age/B	31 Right	07 a/a	202	18	5	29	1	207			233	340	573	3	78	24	0.16					81		108	13%	2.28	-13.3	19	$2
Ht/Wt	74 215	08 a/a	175	11	2	16	2	176			215	236	452	5	84	20	0.31					41		73	5%	1.08	-17.6	2	($1)
Health	A	09 SF *	243	27	6	31	0	211	83	262	243	354	596	4	71	27	0.14	222	41	17	42	105	9%	78	0%	2.57	-12.7	3	$3
PT/Exp	F	10 SF	126	19	4	10	1	238	172	258	284	397	680	6	72	30	0.23	237	46	12	42	115	11%	108	11%	3.77	-2.7	27	$3
Consist	C	1st Half	87	12	4	9	1	253			301	471	772	6	71	31	0.24	258	44	11	45	157	14%	103	17%	5.05	1.5	57	$3
LIMA Plan	F	2nd Half	39	7	0	1	0	205			244	231	475	5	74	28	0.20	192	52	14	34	26	0%	96	0%	1.03	-4.2	-41	$0
Rand Var	-2	11 Proj	114	12	3	13	1	228			265	360	625	5	76	28	0.21	223	43	13	44	91	7%	91	9%	2.99	-4.8	16	$2

Caddies like these get lost behind young upstarts like the Poseys of the world. There's a reason for it, as shown by RAR. Occasional pop vs. RHers, PX trend say he'll probably have a few more years in a similar role.

Wieters,Matt

Wieters,Matt			AB	R	HR	RBI	SB	Avg	vL	vR	OB	Slg	OPS	bb%	ct%	h%	Eye	xBA	G	L	F	PX	hr/f	Spd	SBO	RC/G	RAR	BPV	R$
Pos	2	06	0	0	0	0	0	0																					
Age/B	24 Both	07	0	0	0	0	0	0																					
Ht/Wt	77 230	08 aa	208	36	11	45	1	341			434	572	1006	14	88	35	1.42					131		82	1%	8.06	20.8	114	$12
Health	A	09 BAL *	495	58	14	70	0	287	248	313	347	426	773	8	77	35	0.41	239	42	19	40	89	9%	75	0%	5.05	10.8	22	$14
PT/Exp	D	10 BAL	446	37	11	55	0	249	210	263	320	377	697	10	79	29	0.50	247	46	15	38	91	8%	65	1%	4.16	-0.1	29	$8
Consist	D	1st Half	254	21	6	26	0	236			307	343	650	9	78	28	0.46	233	47	15	37	75	8%	69	1%	3.50	-5.1	11	$4
LIMA Plan	D+	2nd Half	192	16	5	29	0	266			338	422	760	10	81	31	0.57	268	45	15	40	111	8%	69	0%	5.00	4.7	54	$5
Rand Var	+2	11 Proj	473	51	14	70	0	268			341	419	760	10	80	31	0.55	256	45	16	39	100	10%	70	1%	4.96	10.2	43	$12

PRO: PX, ct% spikes in 2nd half
CON: xBA, negative RAR
Guys with his ceiling can emerge quickly. And as a post-hyper, there's profit here anyway.
UP: 20 HR

Wigginton,Ty

Wigginton,Ty			AB	R	HR	RBI	SB	Avg	vL	vR	OB	Slg	OPS	bb%	ct%	h%	Eye	xBA	G	L	F	PX	hr/f	Spd	SBO	RC/G	RAR	BPV	R$
Pos	345	06 TAM	444	55	24	79	4	275	316	260	324	498	821	7	78	30	0.33	271	40	19	41	138	17%	68	7%	5.46	0.6	59	$15
Age/B	33 Right	07 2TM	547	71	22	67	3	278	284	276	328	459	787	7	79	32	0.36	271	44	18	38	119	13%	86	5%	5.09	-9.5	54	$16
Ht/Wt	72 190	08 HOU	386	50	23	58	4	285	340	265	340	526	866	8	82	30	0.46	288	45	16	39	144	19%	85	10%	5.99	2.9	86	$16
Health	B	09 BAL	410	44	11	41	1	273	252	285	312	400	712	5	86	30	0.40	255	43	18	39	75	8%	76	3%	4.15	-18.4	40	$9
PT/Exp	B	10 BAL	581	63	22	76	0	248	237	252	307	415	722	8	80	28	0.43	270	47	16	37	111	13%	76	1%	4.34	-24.6	50	$14
Consist	C	1st Half	272	30	14	43	0	246			321	445	766	10	82	25	0.63	291	50	16	34	123	18%	65	1%	4.93	-6.8	69	$8
LIMA Plan	D	2nd Half	309	33	8	33	0	249			295	388	683	6	78	30	0.29	251	45	15	40	100	8%	90	0%	3.80	-17.9	33	$6
Rand Var	+3	11 Proj	358	40	14	45	1	268			319	441	760	7	82	29	0.41	270	45	17	38	109	12%	82	3%	4.75	-9.2	54	$10

With positional flexibility and consistent 20 HR pop, he's undervalued every year. Don't worry about BA; .270-.280 days are just a small h% uptick away. If they say he won't get AB due to lack of role, bid and enjoy profit.

STEPHEN NICKRAND

Willingham,Josh

			AB	R	HR	RBI	SB	Avg	vL	vR	OB	Slg	OPS	bb%	ct%	h%	Eye	xBA	G	L	F	PX	hr/f	Spd	SBO	RC/G	RAR	BPV	R$
Pos	7	06 FLA	502	62	26	74	2	277	299	269	347	496	843	10	78	31	0.50	265	43	16	41	132	16%	98	1%	5.92	9.6	70	$17
Age/B	32 Right	07 FLA	521	75	21	89	8	265	218	281	348	463	810	11	77	31	0.54	265	36	21	43	130	12%	84	6%	5.68	4.8	60	$18
Ht/Wt	74 215	08 FLA	351	54	15	51	3	254	242	258	343	470	813	12	77	29	0.59	265	39	19	42	140	13%	119	5%	5.77	3.6	81	$11
Health	D	09 WAS	427	70	24	61	4	260	300	251	352	496	849	13	76	29	0.59	277	36	22	42	161	17%	79	6%	6.18	7.8	82	$16
PT/Exp	C	10 WAS	370	54	16	56	8	268	277	264	380	459	839	15	77	31	0.79	260	31	20	49	129	12%	82	6%	6.23	12.3	68	$15
Consist	A	1st Half	263	43	15	46	7	281			402	513	915	17	76	32	0.85	274	28	22	50	150	15%	79	7%	7.25	16.2	85	$14
LIMA Plan	B	2nd Half	107	11	1	10	1	234			322	327	649	12	79	29	0.61	227	38	16	46	78	3%	85	3%	3.74	-4.3	27	$1
Rand Var	0	11 Proj	458	65	23	77	4	269			362	489	851	13	77	30	0.64	273	36	19	45	147	15%	79	4%	6.24	12.8	76	$18

In aggregate, a disappointment. But knee problems were the culprit behind that 2H. His 1H PX and flyball rate are what you want to speculate on, even with injury history. If healthy (a big if).. UP: 30 HR, .280 BA

Willits,Reggie

			AB	R	HR	RBI	SB	Avg	vL	vR	OB	Slg	OPS	bb%	ct%	h%	Eye	xBA	G	L	F	PX	hr/f	Spd	SBO	RC/G	RAR	BPV	R$
Pos	78	06 LAA	* 397	78	2	33	28	285			391	352	743	15	88	32	1.41	285	39	35	26	45	2%	134	30%	5.25	0.9	58	$15
Age/B	29 Both	07 LAA	430	74	0	34	27	293	333	276	391	344	735	14	81	36	0.83	248	49	23	28	44	0%	114	20%	5.00	-0.5	22	$15
Ht/Wt	71 185	08 LAA	* 145	26	0	10	3	226	200	193	338	278	616	15	78	29	0.78	205	44	16	40	43	0%	137	9%	3.46	-6.2	20	$2
Health	A	09 aaa	234	32	1	21	9	218			297	275	572	10	81	27	0.60					42		101	18%	2.74	-18.6	11	$4
PT/Exp	F	10 LAA	159	23	0	8	2	258	255	259	337	302	639	11	84	31	0.73	221	35	20	45	40	0%	104	11%	3.67	-5.8	21	$3
Consist	B	1st Half	69	11	0	5	1	246			350	275	625	14	87	28	1.22	211	31	20	48	25	0%	105	12%	3.78	-2.3	29	$1
LIMA Plan	F	2nd Half	90	12	0	3	1	267			327	322	649	8	81	33	0.47	228	38	20	42	52	0%	100	11%	3.61	-3.4	14	$1
Rand Var	-3	11 Proj	124	19	0	8	3	250			335	293	628	11	82	30	0.72	220	40	20	40	37	0%	99	14%	3.53	-5.3	13	$2

Few control plate better, but with literally no pop, he's a part-timer at best unless he can tap into those '06/'07 speed skills again. No signs of that happening soon. And recent xBA history gives little hope of a BA rebound.

Wilson,Jack

			AB	R	HR	RBI	SB	Avg	vL	vR	OB	Slg	OPS	bb%	ct%	h%	Eye	xBA	G	L	F	PX	hr/f	Spd	SBO	RC/G	RAR	BPV	R$
Pos	6	06 PIT	543	70	8	35	4	273	301	262	314	370	684	6	88	30	0.51	271	47	23	30	61	6%	95	5%	3.96	-6.3	43	$10
Age/B	33 Right	07 PIT	477	67	12	56	2	296	320	289	348	440	788	7	90	31	0.83	276	39	19	42	86	7%	106	5%	5.25	10.7	79	$14
Ht/Wt	72 200	08 PIT	305	24	1	22	2	272	228	282	302	348	649	4	91	30	0.48	260	41	22	37	54	1%	82	5%	3.61	-9.0	43	$4
Health	F	09 2TM	373	37	5	39	3	255	240	260	294	362	656	5	87	28	0.44	246	42	16	42	72	4%	81	5%	3.63	-10.2	43	$6
PT/Exp	D	10 SEA	193	17	0	14	1	249	264	243	275	316	591	4	82	30	0.20	238	40	20	40	57	0%	100	7%	2.68	-7.4	12	$2
Consist	A	1st Half	108	9	0	9	0	250			257	333	590	1	81	31	0.05	236	40	15	45	77	0%	93	5%	2.54	-4.6	19	$1
LIMA Plan	D	2nd Half	85	8	0	5	1	247			297	294	591	7	82	30	0.40	243	40	26	34	32	0%	107	8%	2.83	-2.9	3	$1
Rand Var	0	11 Proj	367	35	2	29	3	245			281	327	608	5	85	28	0.34	250	41	20	39	60	2%	98	7%	3.02	-12.7	30	$4

Has reached fantasy irrelevance..
- Eroding Eye, ct% mean BA free fall won't stop
- No hope of power
- No latent speed upside

No longer viable, even in deep leagues. (See next player box.)

Wilson,Josh

			AB	R	HR	RBI	SB	Avg	vL	vR	OB	Slg	OPS	bb%	ct%	h%	Eye	xBA	G	L	F	PX	hr/f	Spd	SBO	RC/G	RAR	BPV	R$
Pos	6	06 aaa	335	46	8	34	11	287			341	426	767	8	91	30	0.95					77		123	16%	5.06	6.5	80	$11
Age/B	30 Right	07 2TM	282	28	2	24	6	238	256	230	281	333	614	6	80	29	0.30	220	43	13	44	69	2%	125	13%	3.03	-11.4	25	$3
Ht/Wt	72 175	08 a/a	405	32	5	32	10	222			262	318	579	5	84	25	0.34					68		95	18%	2.66	-22.9	33	$4
Health	A	09 2TM	* 295	30	5	24	3	214	188	234	262	327	589	6	80	25	0.32	237	41	19	41	77	5%	111	9%	2.70	-17.1	30	$2
PT/Exp	D	10 SEA	* 442	26	2	33	5	230	196	239	254	308	562	3	80	28	0.16	227	35	20	45	62	1%	96	7%	2.25	-22.9	7	$3
Consist	A	1st Half	263	17	1	22	3	258			288	354	642	4	83	31	0.25	260	38	23	39	73	1%	103	7%	3.35	-4.7	32	$4
LIMA Plan	D	2nd Half	179	9	1	11	2	190			203	240	444	2	75	25	0.07	184	32	16	51	43	1%	84	7%	0.52	-19.6	-33	($1)
Rand Var	0	11 Proj	335	26	3	25	5	221			254	313	567	4	81	27	0.23	226	36	18	45	67	3%	102	10%	2.37	-18.7	17	$2

2-25-.227 in 361 AB at SEA. Hit over 50% of balls in air in 2H and for that was rewarded with... one HR. His only potential value is speed. Given OB trend, it's not a place to invest. Rule of thumb: avoid all J.Wilsons.

Winn,Randy

			AB	R	HR	RBI	SB	Avg	vL	vR	OB	Slg	OPS	bb%	ct%	h%	Eye	xBA	G	L	F	PX	hr/f	Spd	SBO	RC/G	RAR	BPV	R$
Pos	79	06 SF	573	82	11	56	10	262	219	278	319	396	715	8	89	28	0.76	275	50	17	33	79	6%	119	12%	4.48	-13.0	72	$13
Age/B	36 Both	07 SF	593	73	14	65	15	300	351	277	349	445	794	7	86	33	0.52	288	51	19	31	94	9%	94	11%	5.24	-1.9	62	$20
Ht/Wt	74 193	08 SF	598	84	10	64	25	306	289	313	368	426	795	9	85	35	0.67	271	51	19	30	81	7%	103	14%	5.41	-0.1	57	$24
Health	A	09 SF	538	65	2	51	16	262	158	292	321	353	675	8	83	31	0.51	255	46	22	32	68	1%	116	12%	3.97	-24.9	38	$13
PT/Exp	B	10 2TM	205	23	4	25	6	239	184	256	310	356	666	9	82	27	0.57	267	48	20	31	76	8%	100	11%	3.82	-7.0	39	$5
Consist	B	1st Half	114	12	1	10	3	228			302	316	617	10	77	29	0.46	252	51	21	28	66	4%	103	10%	3.20	-6.1	14	$2
LIMA Plan	F	2nd Half	91	11	3	15	3	253			320	407	727	9	88	26	0.82	286	45	20	35	87	11%	92	12%	4.58	-1.0	69	$3
Rand Var	+4	11 Proj	123	15	2	14	4	252			317	366	683	9	84	29	0.60	267	48	20	32	75	6%	99	12%	4.07	-3.7	45	$3

Quoted on the 2009 season, he said: "I was horrible, the numbers showed it. I was terrible and there's no two ways about it." Turns out that was both descriptive AND projective.

Wise,DeWayne

			AB	R	HR	RBI	SB	Avg	vL	vR	OB	Slg	OPS	bb%	ct%	h%	Eye	xBA	G	L	F	PX	hr/f	Spd	SBO	RC/G	RAR	BPV	R$
Pos	8	06 CIN	* 242	34	6	24	6	240			278	395	673	5	80	28	0.26	313	72	22	6	102	49%	107	16%	3.68	-5.6	46	$5
Age/B	33 Left	07 aaa	207	27	6	16	6	211			235	382	617	3	73	26	0.12					113		155	26%	2.82	-11.1	39	$3
Ht/Wt	73 190	08 CHW	* 320	49	14	35	20	251	154	268	306	450	755	7	80	28	0.38	268	35	23	42	122	13%	129	37%	4.72	-6.1	72	$13
Health	C	09 CHW	142	17	2	11	4	225	400	205	241	366	608	2	81	27	0.11	235	36	17	47	88	4%	140	41%	2.80	-8.3	42	$2
PT/Exp	F	10 TOR	* 249	33	6	23	6	229	231	253	258	388	647	4	77	27	0.17	266	41	22	37	107	9%	148	17%	3.26	-15.7	48	$5
Consist	C	1st Half	162	18	4	16	4	215			248	399	647	4	78	25	0.19	290	53	18	29	125	12%	134	22%	3.33	-10.1	60	$3
LIMA Plan	D	2nd Half	87	15	2	7	2	253			278	368	646	3	76	31	0.14	238	38	23	38	74	8%	133	10%	3.15	-5.6	11	$2
Rand Var	+2	11 Proj	168	24	7	15	5	238			267	443	710	4	78	27	0.18	271	38	20	41	128	13%	141	26%	4.01	-5.5	67	$5

3-14-.250 in 112 AB at TOR. A good OF glove can only get you so far. Can't steal 1B, so all he can do is pinch run. And even a constant green light (see '09) won't help much there. Given age, flyer days are over.

Wood,Brandon

			AB	R	HR	RBI	SB	Avg	vL	vR	OB	Slg	OPS	bb%	ct%	h%	Eye	xBA	G	L	F	PX	hr/f	Spd	SBO	RC/G	RAR	BPV	R$
Pos	56	06 aa	453	55	18	61	14	236			297	446	743	8	76	27	0.35					143		84	20%	4.67	-8.0	60	$12
Age/B	26 Right	07 LAA	* 470	68	21	73	9	247			306	440	746	8	74	29	0.33	257	52	10	38	134	16%	85	9%	4.65	-3.1	47	$14
Ht/Wt	75 210	08 LAA	* 545	81	30	83	9	247	94	229	300	457	757	7	76	28	0.31	245	36	14	50	135	14%	95	12%	4.67	-3.4	55	$18
Health	A	09 LAA	* 427	62	19	65	1	259	217	167	314	473	787	7	78	29	0.36	302	45	27	27	134	21%	99	2%	5.13	5.6	67	$13
PT/Exp	D	10 LAA	* 277	23	5	15	1	146	169	134	170	207	377	3	70	19	0.10	164	35	13	52	41	5%	90	2%	-0.60	-50.3	-52	($3)
Consist	F	1st Half	214	18	4	13	1	166			188	226	414	3	73	21	0.10	174	34	15	50	38	5%	91	3%	-0.02	-34.0	-44	($1)
LIMA Plan	F	2nd Half	63	5	1	2	0	79			108	143	251	3	62	11	0.08	136	38	5	56	53	5%	97	0%	-2.75	-17.2	-73	($2)
Rand Var	+5	11 Proj	123	14	7	12	1	236			275	431	706	5	71	27	0.19	225	37	10	53	130	14%	87	5%	3.93	-3.2	28	$3

4-14-.146 in 226 AB at LAA. Had lowest OPS in MLB of anyone w/200+ AB, and it was not close. With his PX history, we can't write him off yet. But he's got some HUGE holes to close down in his swing.

Worth,Danny

			AB	R	HR	RBI	SB	Avg	vL	vR	OB	Slg	OPS	bb%	ct%	h%	Eye	xBA	G	L	F	PX	hr/f	Spd	SBO	RC/G	RAR	BPV	R$
Pos	6	06	0	0	0	0	0	0																					
Age/B	25 Right	07	0	0	0	0	0	0																					
Ht/Wt	73 180	08 a/a	297	35	4	26	6	224			286	337	622	8	84	25	0.54					74		129	8%	3.33	-10.4	52	$4
Health	C	09 a/a	436	35	0	24	6	209			262	265	527	7	78	27	0.32					45		123	13%	1.95	-35.9	-0	$0
PT/Exp	F	10 DET	* 270	24	4	22	11	253	283	233	289	333	622	5	86	28	0.37	265	47	21	32	54	5%	88	21%	3.12	-6.8	27	$6
Consist	C	1st Half	229	18	2	20	11	250			281	314	594	4	86	29	0.29	244	49	16	35	47	3%	88	22%	2.77	-8.1	16	$5
LIMA Plan	F	2nd Half	41	6	2	2	0	268			333	439	772	9	90	26	0.99	325	44	28	28	92	19%	110	17%	5.02	1.3	87	$1
Rand Var	0	11 Proj	159	15	4	13	4	239			287	371	658	6	83	27	0.40	263	49	16	35	83	9%	113	15%	3.56	-3.0	47	$3

2-8-.255 in 106 AB at DET. Held down full-time gig late in year. Owns some good speed skills, so repeating that 2H ct% and bb% will help him stick in a full time role. Given previous skill void, be pessimistic though.

Wright,David

			AB	R	HR	RBI	SB	Avg	vL	vR	OB	Slg	OPS	bb%	ct%	h%	Eye	xBA	G	L	F	PX	hr/f	Spd	SBO	RC/G	RAR	BPV	R$
Pos	5	06 NYM	582	96	26	116	20	311	285	321	381	531	912	10	81	35	0.58	272	36	19	44	133	13%	89	14%	6.85	21.6	78	$30
Age/B	28 Right	07 NYM	604	113	30	107	34	325	361	311	415	546	962	13	81	36	0.82	298	39	23	38	139	16%	78	18%	7.62	32.6	87	$37
Ht/Wt	72 208	08 NYM	626	115	33	124	15	302	382	275	393	534	927	13	81	33	0.80	295	36	26	38	145	17%	79	10%	7.14	30.6	92	$34
Health	A	09 NYM	535	88	10	72	27	307	416	277	391	447	838	12	74	40	0.53	251	38	26	36	110	7%	98	19%	6.27	16.9	39	$26
PT/Exp	A	10 NYM	587	87	29	103	19	283	339	267	358	503	861	11	73	35	0.43	271	38	19	43	158	16%	73	18%	6.38	25.0	62	$29
Consist	A	1st Half	305	49	14	64	15	315			396	541	937	12	69	42	0.43	273	39	20	41	181	16%	74	23%	7.80	24.5	67	$20
LIMA Plan	C+	2nd Half	282	38	15	39	4	248			316	461	777	9	77	27	0.43	269	38	18	44	136	16%	85	11%	5.03	1.1	62	$10
Rand Var	0	11 Proj	590	94	28	98	21	275			356	491	847	11	75	32	0.52	276	38	22	40	148	16%	82	17%	6.15	18.0	69	$28

PRO:
- '09 HR outage was hr/f fluke
- AAA reliability

CON:
- Eroding ct%, Eye put BA at further risk

Still $25 lock; $30, not so much.

STEPHEN NICKRAND

Youkilis,Kevin

Youkilis,Kevin			AB	R	HR	RBI	SB	Avg	vL	vR	OB	Slg	OPS	bb%	ct%	h%	Eye	xBA	G	L	F	PX	hr/f	Spd	SBO	RC/G	RAR	BPV	R$
Pos	3	06 BOS	569	100	13	72	5	279	270	283	379	429	808	14	79	33	0.76	251	31	24	45	104	6%	80	4%	5.85	6.9	53	$16
Age/B	32 Right	07 BOS	528	85	16	83	4	288	290	287	379	453	831	13	80	33	0.73	264	34	21	45	113	8%	77	3%	6.04	11.5	61	$18
Ht/Wt	73 220	08 BOS	538	91	29	115	3	312	288	318	383	569	952	10	80	35	0.57	297	34	22	44	166	15%	84	5%	7.34	30.5	100	$27
Health	C	09 BOS	491	99	27	94	7	305	309	304	400	548	948	14	75	36	0.62	276	35	21	44	160	17%	73	6%	7.63	25.8	77	$25
PT/Exp	B	10 BOS	362	77	19	62	4	307	404	275	402	564	966	14	81	33	0.87	304	37	16	47	164	14%	109	4%	7.71	19.1	120	$20
Consist	A	1st Half	274	65	17	54	2	299			407	584	991	15	81	32	0.96	307	37	13	50	179	15%	105	3%	8.09	17.5	132	$16
LIMA Plan	B+	2nd Half	88	12	2	8	2	330			385	500	885	8	83	38	0.53	299	36	27	37	119	7%	104	7%	6.48	1.6	77	$4
Rand Var	0	11 Proj	520	94	28	84	7	310			391	560	951	12	80	34	0.66	300	35	21	43	162	15%	90	6%	7.43	25.4	101	$26

On the way to career year before Aug. thumb surgery. With health, FB% spike and elite PX make this a place to mine for HR profit. xBA confirms you can bank on a .300 BA. Not much upside at 32, but just maybe... UP: 35 HR

Young Jr.,Eric

Young Jr.,Eric			AB	R	HR	RBI	SB	Avg	vL	vR	OB	Slg	OPS	bb%	ct%	h%	Eye	xBA	G	L	F	PX	hr/f	Spd	SBO	RC/G	RAR	BPV	R$
Pos	4	06	0	0	0	0	0	0																					
Age/B	25 Both	07	0	0	0	0	0	0																					
Ht/Wt	70 180	08 aa	403	52	2	24	32	255			326	336	661	9	87	29	0.79					56		126	43%	3.97	-10.8	51	$13
Health	C	09 COL	* 529	100	7	35	49	270	304	206	329	375	705	8	86	30	0.62	282	59	20	22	64	7%	180	44%	4.33	-3.2	66	$24
PT/Exp	D	10 COL	* 308	41	1	14	24	231	238	248	294	284	578	8	82	28	0.48	240	54	17	29	40	1%	143	34%	2.73	-19.9	20	$8
Consist	B	1st Half	89	13	1	4	6	206			277	282	559	9	86	23	0.69	267	53	20	27	45	5%	139	30%	2.67	-6.1	41	$2
LIMA Plan	C	2nd Half	219	28	0	10	18	241			300	285	586	8	80	30	0.42	229	54	16	30	37	0%	128	36%	2.77	-13.8	6	$6
Rand Var	+1	11 Proj	343	52	3	18	23	245			309	325	633	8	84	28	0.58	257	55	17	28	52	4%	152	34%	3.47	-13.2	43	$10

0-8-.244-17 in 172 AB at COL. Young burner's wheels held back by eroding ct%, no OB. Pitchers know they can knock bat out of his hands; just six extra base hits with COL. Still young, but he's heading in the wrong direction.

Young,Chris

Young,Chris			AB	R	HR	RBI	SB	Avg	vL	vR	OB	Slg	OPS	bb%	ct%	h%	Eye	xBA	G	L	F	PX	hr/f	Spd	SBO	RC/G	RAR	BPV	R$
Pos	8	06 ARI	* 472	67	18	66	14	241	360	178	307	440	747	9	86	25	0.66	288	42	20	37	116	12%	88	20%	4.78	4.9	81	$14
Age/B	27 Right	07 ARI	569	85	32	68	27	237	246	234	291	467	758	7	75	26	0.30	259	37	15	48	146	15%	109	29%	4.71	3.2	67	$21
Ht/Wt	74 200	08 ARI	625	85	22	85	14	248	285	236	316	443	759	9	74	30	0.38	251	38	19	43	137	11%	112	13%	4.99	4.6	58	$19
Health	A	09 ARI	* 487	67	18	49	13	225	262	196	318	421	739	12	70	28	0.46	228	26	18	56	146	9%	117	15%	4.89	2.4	60	$12
PT/Exp	A	10 ARI	584	94	27	91	28	257	264	255	340	452	792	11	75	30	0.51	255	34	17	50	137	12%	77	21%	5.40	8.9	58	$28
Consist	A	1st Half	299	44	15	57	14	264			327	482	809	9	75	30	0.38	267	37	15	48	154	14%	70	22%	5.49	5.2	64	$15
LIMA Plan	B	2nd Half	285	50	12	34	14	249			353	421	775	14	75	29	0.65	241	30	19	51	119	11%	93	21%	5.29	3.4	53	$12
Rand Var	0	11 Proj	561	85	28	74	25	253			335	474	809	11	74	29	0.48	258	33	18	50	152	13%	98	22%	5.64	14.3	72	$24

Superb resurgence differed from 2007 in two main ways...
- bb% gains, especially in 2H
- Stable, higher h% bodes well

While Spd says to temper enthusiasm, Eye, OB gains say there's more growth here.

Young,Delmon

Young,Delmon			AB	R	HR	RBI	SB	Avg	vL	vR	OB	Slg	OPS	bb%	ct%	h%	Eye	xBA	G	L	F	PX	hr/f	Spd	SBO	RC/G	RAR	BPV	R$
Pos	7	06 TAM	* 468	68	11	71	25	325	379	299	348	485	834	3	83	38	0.20	292	47	26	27	102	10%	116	26%	5.51	4.1	56	$22
Age/B	25 Right	07 TAM	645	65	13	93	10	288	299	285	316	408	724	4	80	34	0.20	265	46	21	33	86	8%	75	8%	4.19	-15.4	22	$18
Ht/Wt	75 200	08 MIN	575	80	10	69	14	290	300	286	331	405	736	6	82	34	0.33	262	55	17	28	77	8%	115	12%	4.48	-6.1	36	$18
Health	A	09 MIN	395	50	12	60	2	284	310	272	305	425	730	3	77	34	0.13	246	50	16	34	90	12%	109	7%	4.18	-9.4	19	$12
PT/Exp	B	10 MIN	570	77	21	112	5	298	312	292	331	493	824	5	86	32	0.35	299	45	15	40	129	11%	69	7%	5.42	8.5	79	$25
Consist	B	1st Half	258	35	9	55	3	298			337	488	825	5	86	32	0.43	309	46	17	36	128	11%	71	10%	5.50	4.4	82	$12
LIMA Plan	D+	2nd Half	312	42	12	57	2	298			326	497	823	4	85	32	0.28	292	43	14	43	130	11%	75	4%	5.35	4.1	78	$13
Rand Var	0	11 Proj	603	80	24	101	8	294			324	484	808	4	82	32	0.25	286	48	16	36	122	13%	84	9%	5.17	4.1	63	$24

Ct% gains, power spike fueled this mini-breakout. xBA supports potential .300 upside. And with flyball and PX gains, there's more power on the horizon. He's still a growth stock. For '11... UP: 30 HR, .300 BA

Young,Delwyn

Young,Delwyn			AB	R	HR	RBI	SB	Avg	vL	vR	OB	Slg	OPS	bb%	ct%	h%	Eye	xBA	G	L	F	PX	hr/f	Spd	SBO	RC/G	RAR	BPV	R$
Pos	9	06 aaa	532	58	14	75	2	233			277	378	654	6	85	25	0.39					92		60	7%	3.52	-27.4	43	$8
Age/B	28 Both	07 LA	* 524	85	16	77	4	281	333	421	322	470	791	6	80	33	0.30	273	34	21	45	129	8%	96	6%	5.18	4.4	65	$17
Ht/Wt	70 191	08 LA	126	10	1	7	0	246	231	253	321	341	663	10	73	33	0.41	226	50	17	33	84	3%	81	0%	3.82	-5.1	6	$1
Health	A	09 PIT	354	40	7	43	2	266	233	282	321	381	703	8	75	34	0.32	238	46	22	33	84	8%	85	2%	4.15	-7.5	8	$8
PT/Exp	F	10 PIT	191	22	7	28	1	236	333	224	284	414	698	6	73	29	0.25	249	47	13	40	131	13%	63	3%	4.01	-7.6	29	$5
Consist	A	1st Half	111	9	3	18	1	234			274	414	688	5	72	30	0.19	254	47	12	41	143	9%	68	5%	3.93	-4.7	35	$2
LIMA Plan	F	2nd Half	80	13	4	10	0	237			299	412	711	8	74	27	0.33	244	47	14	39	114	17%	73	0%	4.11	-2.9	27	$2
Rand Var	+1	11 Proj	130	15	4	16	0	246			302	385	687	7	74	30	0.31	239	47	16	37	102	10%	64	2%	3.89	-4.8	15	$3

Sometimes, all you need to know can be gleaned from context clues. Peak-aged switch-hitting OFer cannot even earn 200 AB on a team that hasn't had a winning season in 18 years. See? No stats required.

Young,Michael

Young,Michael			AB	R	HR	RBI	SB	Avg	vL	vR	OB	Slg	OPS	bb%	ct%	h%	Eye	xBA	G	L	F	PX	hr/f	Spd	SBO	RC/G	RAR	BPV	R$
Pos	5	06 TEX	691	93	14	103	7	314	295	320	359	459	817	6	86	35	0.50	297	48	25	27	94	9%	94	5%	5.52	9.5	63	$23
Age/B	34 Right	07 TEX	639	80	9	94	13	315	309	316	362	418	779	7	83	37	0.44	290	48	27	24	74	7%	80	8%	5.07	3.5	32	$22
Ht/Wt	73 200	08 TEX	645	102	12	82	10	284	305	276	340	402	742	8	83	33	0.50	269	47	23	31	80	7%	89	5%	4.67	-3.7	41	$20
Health	A	09 TEX	541	76	22	68	8	322	297	331	376	518	893	8	83	35	0.52	297	45	22	33	118	15%	91	7%	6.43	25.3	73	$23
PT/Exp	A	10 TEX	656	99	21	91	4	284	322	270	334	444	778	7	82	32	0.43	283	47	18	34	106	11%	80	3%	5.01	3.3	54	$23
Consist	D	1st Half	339	55	11	51	3	307			354	487	841	7	83	34	0.43	300	47	20	33	122	12%	78	5%	5.78	8.8	68	$15
LIMA Plan	C	2nd Half	317	44	10	40	1	259			313	397	710	7	82	29	0.44	265	48	17	35	89	11%	82	1%	4.18	-6.0	40	$9
Rand Var	+1	11 Proj	616	90	19	82	6	294			346	448	794	7	83	33	0.47	283	47	21	32	100	11%	82	5%	5.23	7.2	53	$22

You can almost ink in 600 AB, which is a feat in itself. But there are some chinks in the armor:
- 16 of 21 HR came at home
- 2nd half PX dip
- At 34, rising odds of erosion

Quibbles, really. Gimme a pen!

Zaun,Gregg

Zaun,Gregg			AB	R	HR	RBI	SB	Avg	vL	vR	OB	Slg	OPS	bb%	ct%	h%	Eye	xBA	G	L	F	PX	hr/f	Spd	SBO	RC/G	RAR	BPV	R$
Pos	2	06 TOR	290	39	12	40	0	272	373	251	363	462	825	12	86	28	0.98	277	38	20	42	113	11%	70	2%	5.88	12.2	81	$8
Age/B	39 Both	07 TOR	331	43	10	52	0	242	290	229	343	411	754	13	83	26	0.93	276	42	17	41	113	9%	70	0%	5.13	8.3	73	$7
Ht/Wt	70 170	08 TOR	245	29	6	30	2	237	163	255	339	359	698	13	84	26	1.00	245	44	15	40	79	7%	75	4%	4.47	2.0	53	$4
Health	F	09 2AL	262	34	8	27	0	260	217	269	338	416	754	11	82	29	0.65	260	42	18	40	101	9%	90	3%	4.93	5.1	58	$6
PT/Exp	F	10 MIL	102	11	2	14	0	265	161	310	336	392	728	10	88	28	0.92	286	48	19	33	87	7%	58	0%	4.73	0.7	62	$2
Consist	A	1st Half	102	11	2	14	0	265			336	392	728	10	88	28	0.92	286	48	19	33	87	7%	58	0%	4.73	0.7	62	$2
LIMA Plan	F	2nd Half	0	0	0	0	0	0																					
Rand Var	+1	11 Proj	31	4	1	4	0	258			344	402	746	12	85	28	0.88	270	44	18	38	96	8%	82	2%	4.96	0.5	67	$1

Torn labrum ended season in May, and with it, maybe his career. Few end-game catchers controlled bat better at his age.

Zimmerman,Ryan

Zimmerman,Ryan			AB	R	HR	RBI	SB	Avg	vL	vR	OB	Slg	OPS	bb%	ct%	h%	Eye	xBA	G	L	F	PX	hr/f	Spd	SBO	RC/G	RAR	BPV	R$
Pos	5	06 WAS	614	84	20	110	11	287	280	289	351	471	822	9	80	33	0.51	276	42	22	36	119	11%	77	11%	5.71	3.8	60	$23
Age/B	26 Right	07 WAS	653	99	24	91	4	266	374	235	329	458	787	9	81	30	0.49	276	44	17	40	121	11%	109	3%	5.22	-7.3	72	$19
Ht/Wt	75 228	08 WAS	428	51	14	51	1	283	333	259	331	442	773	7	83	31	0.44	272	46	20	34	100	12%	89	2%	4.92	-5.4	56	$12
Health	B	09 WAS	610	110	33	106	2	292	270	298	367	525	891	11	80	32	0.61	283	40	19	42	146	16%	92	1%	6.54	23.8	89	$28
PT/Exp	A	10 WAS	525	85	25	85	4	307	331	300	387	510	898	12	81	34	0.70	285	41	18	41	133	14%	69	3%	6.69	25.6	78	$25
Consist	B	1st Half	266	49	14	44	1	286			379	504	883	13	79	32	0.70	287	46	15	38	145	17%	76	2%	6.61	12.8	81	$12
LIMA Plan	C+	2nd Half	259	36	11	41	3	328			396	517	913	10	84	36	0.71	285	37	20	44	121	12%	66	3%	6.77	12.7	76	$13
Rand Var	-3	11 Proj	597	93	29	94	4	298			370	509	879	10	82	32	0.62	286	41	19	40	134	15%	78	3%	6.37	21.0	80	$27

PROs:
- Surging bb%, Eye
- Another solid power year

CONs:
- BA came from h% jump
- Still too many GB for a slugger

More HR upside, but not yet.

Zobrist,Ben

Zobrist,Ben			AB	R	HR	RBI	SB	Avg	vL	vR	OB	Slg	OPS	bb%	ct%	h%	Eye	xBA	G	L	F	PX	hr/f	Spd	SBO	RC/G	RAR	BPV	R$
Pos	49	06 TAM	* 567	68	5	48	12	265	212	229	340	372	712	10	86	30	0.82	270	47	22	30	67	3%	125	13%	4.58	7.8	58	$10
Age/B	29 Both	07 TAM	* 319	47	8	29	10	226	182	147	320	358	677	12	81	26	0.74	259	43	20	37	85	8%	112	14%	4.08	0.8	54	$6
Ht/Wt	75 200	08 TAM	* 269	44	15	41	6	260	269	242	350	491	840	12	79	28	0.66	273	44	13	42	141	17%	114	9%	5.99	8.6	90	$11
Health	B	09 TAM	501	91	27	91	17	297	319	287	405	543	948	15	79	33	0.88	288	41	20	39	144	18%	133	13%	7.60	37.4	105	$26
PT/Exp	B	10 TAM	541	77	10	75	24	238	247	235	349	353	702	15	80	28	0.86	252	44	18	38	83	6%	92	15%	4.53	1.1	46	$17
Consist	F	1st Half	292	38	5	41	14	288			375	404	779	12	79	35	0.68	261	45	21	34	84	6%	110	16%	5.41	7.8	45	$12
LIMA Plan	B+	2nd Half	249	39	5	34	10	181			320	293	613	17	81	20	1.09	240	43	15	43	81	6%	73	14%	3.52	-7.6	47	$5
Rand Var	+2	11 Proj	540	84	21	79	18	256			362	440	802	14	80	28	0.85	272	43	18	39	117	12%	109	13%	5.70	17.5	78	$20

Quest to put together two impact halves in same year continues. HR will rebound with hr/f, but BA is less likely, since that '09 h% seems like a clear outlier. And given Spd drop, we can't bank on 20+ SB again. A wildcard.

STEPHEN NICKRAND

The Pitchers

QUALIFICATION: Nearly all pitchers who had at least 40 IP in the majors in 2010 are included. Beyond that, the decision comes down to whether they will have an impact in 2011. Those who may have a role but have battled injuries for several years may not be included, though all of these players will appear at Baseball HQ as roles become clearer.

THROWS: Right (RH) or left (LH). **ROLE:** Starters (SP) are those projected to face 18+ batters per game, the rest are Relievers (RP).

AGE: Each pitcher's age as of Opening Day 2011 is shown.

TYPE evaluates the extent to which a pitcher allows the ball to be put into play and his ground ball or flyball tendency. CON (contact) represents pitchers who allow the ball to be put into play a great deal. PWR (power) represents those with high strikeout and/or walk totals who keep the ball out of play. GB are those who have a ground ball rate more than 50%; xGB are those who have a GB rate more than 55%. FB are those who have a fly ball rate more than 40%; xFB are those who have a FB rate more than 45%.

RELIABILITY GRADES: An analysis of each player's forecast risk, on an A-F scale. High grades go to pitchers who have accumulated few disabled list days (Health), have a history of substantial and regular major league playing time (PT/Exp) and have displayed consistent performance over the past three years, using xERA (Consist).

LIMA PLAN GRADE: Rating that evaluates how well that pitcher would be a good fit for a team employing the LIMA Plan. Best grades will go to pitchers who have excellent base skills and had a 2010 dollar value less than $20. Lowest grades will go to poor skills and values more than $20.

RAND VAR: A score that measures the impact random variance had on the pitcher's 2010 stats and the probability that his 2011 performance will exceed or fall short of 2010. The variables tracked are levels for H%, S%, hr/f and xERA that would be prone to regression. Players are rated on a scale of –5 to +5 with positive scores indicating rebounds and negative scores indicate corrections.

PLAYER STAT LINES: The past five years' statistics represent the total accumulated in the majors as well as in Triple-A, Double-A ball and various foreign leagues during each year. All non-major league stats used have been converted to a major league equivalent (MLE) performance level. Minor league levels below AA are not included.

Nearly all baseball publications separate a player's statistical experiences in the major leagues from the minor leagues and outside leagues. While this may be appropriate for the sake of official record-keeping, it is not an accurate snapshot of a player's complete performance for the year.

Bill James has proven that minor league statistics (converted to MLEs), at Double-A level or above, provide as accurate a record of a player's performance as Major League statistics. Other researchers have also devised conversion factors for foreign leagues. Since these are accurate barometers, we include them in the pool of historical data.

TEAM DESIGNATIONS: An asterisk (*) appearing with a team name means that major league equivalent Triple-A (aaa) and/or Double-A (aa) numbers are included in that year's stat line. A designation of "a/a" means the stats were accumulated at both levels that year. Other designations: JPN (Japan), MEX (Mexico), KOR (Korea), CUB (Cuba) and ind (independent league). All these stats are converted to major league equivalents.

The designation "2TM" appears whenever a player was on more than one major league team, crossing leagues, in a season. "2AL" and "2NL" represent more than one team in the same league. Complete season stats are presented for players who crossed leagues during the season.

SABERMETRIC CATEGORIES: Descriptions of all the categories appear in the Encyclopedia. The decimal point has been suppressed on several categories to conserve space.

- Platoon data (vL, vR) and Ball-in-play data (G/L/F) are for major league performance only.
- The xERA2 and new BPV formulas are used when G/L/F data is available. The old formulas are used otherwise.

2011 FORECASTS: It is far too early to be making definitive projections for 2011, especially on playing time. Focus on the skill levels and trends, then consult Baseball HQ for playing time revisions as players change teams and roles become finalized. A free projections update will be available online in March.

Forecasts are computed from a player's trends over the past five years. Adjustments were made for leading indicators and variances between skill and statistical output. After reviewing the leading indicators, you might opt to make further adjustments.

Although each year's numbers include all playing time at the Double-A level or above, the 2011 forecast only represents potential playing time at the major league level, and again is highly preliminary.

CAPSULE COMMENTARIES provide a brief analysis of each player's BPIs and the potential impact on performance in 2011. For those who played only a portion of 2010 in the Majors, and whose isolated MLB stats are significantly different from their full-season total, their MLB stats are listed here. Note that these commentaries generally look at performance related issues only. Playing time expectations may impact these analyses, so you will have to adjust accordingly. Upside (UP) and downside (DN) statistical potential appears for some players. These are less grounded in hard data and more speculative of skills potential.

DO-IT-YOURSELF ANALYSIS: Here are some data points you can look at in doing your own player analysis:

- Variance between vLH and vRH opposition batting avg
- Variance in 2010 hr/f rate from 10%
- Variance in 2010 hit rate (H%) from 30%
- Variance in 2010 strand rate (S%) to tolerances (65% - 75%)
- Variance between ERA and xERA each year
- Growth or decline in Base Performance Value (BPV)
- Spikes in innings pitched

Aardsma,David

		Yr	Tm	W	L	Sv	IP	K	ERA	WHIP	OBA	vL	vR	BF/G	H%	S%	xERA	G	L	F	Ctl	Dom	Cmd	hr/f	hr/9	RAR	BPV	R$
RH RP	29	06	CHC *	5	3	8	89	81	4.24	1.38	239	190	225	5.2	29%	72%	4.44	37	19	44	4.4	8.2	**1.8**	9%	1.0	2.7	42	$10
Ht/Wt	76 205	07	CHW *	5	3	15	67	76	6.17	1.49	273			5.6	33%	63%	3.86	37	21	42	3.9	10.1	**2.6**	18%	1.9	-13.9	92	$9
Type	Pwr xFB	08	BOS	4	2	0	49	49	5.54	1.72	263	289	250	4.8	34%	68%	4.64	44	18	38	6.5	9.1	**1.4**	8%	0.7	-7.2	10	$1
Health	A	09	SEA	3	6	38	71	80	2.52	1.16	196	197	183	4.0	27%	80%	3.99	25	21	54	4.3	10.1	**2.4**	4%	0.5	17.0	69	$23
PT/Exp	B	10	SEA	0	6	31	50	49	3.44	1.17	191	244	148	3.8	23%	74%	3.84	36	19	45	4.5	8.9	**2.0**	9%	0.9	4.3	51	$14
Consist	A	1st Half		0	5	16	25	24	5.34	1.26	236			3.8	28%	61%	4.00	31	19	49	3.6	8.5	**2.4**	12%	1.4	-3.7	67	$6
LIMA Plan	B	2nd Half		0	1	15	24	25	1.48	1.07	138			3.9	19%	88%	3.64	41	20	39	5.5	9.2	**1.7**	5%	0.4	8.0	36	$8
Rand Var	-3	**11**	**Proj**	**2**	**5**	**25**	**65**	**67**	**4.00**	**1.33**	**220**			**4.2**	**28%**	**72%**	**4.10**	**35**	**20**	**45**	**4.8**	**9.2**	**1.9**	**8%**	**0.8**	**1.5**	**49**	**$13**

2nd year in a row that favorable H% made him look like a stud, especially in 2H. BPV tells true story; he's been racking up saves despite mediocre skills. He defied fate for 2 years. Are you feeling lucky for 3 in a row?

Aceves,Alfredo

		Yr	Tm	W	L	Sv	IP	K	ERA	WHIP	OBA	vL	vR	BF/G	H%	S%	xERA	G	L	F	Ctl	Dom	Cmd	hr/f	hr/9	RAR	BPV	R$
RH RP	28	06	MEX	8	5	0	124	90	4.86	1.28	271			27.4	31%	64%	4.54				2.1	6.5	**3.1**		1.2	-5.2	70	$10
Ht/Wt	75 220	07	MEX	11	5	0	106	65	4.33	1.32	254			25.0	29%	67%	3.97				3.2	5.5	**1.7**		0.7	1.7	53	$10
Type		08	NYY *	5	5	0	123	78	3.66	1.27	265	238	213	22.4	29%	76%	4.27	42	17	41	2.3	5.7	**2.5**	10%	1.2	10.4	61	$10
Health	F	09	NYY *	12	1	1	108	84	3.67	1.04	226	212	228	9.1	26%	69%	3.95	35	17	48	1.9	7.0	**3.7**	9%	1.1	10.5	87	$17
PT/Exp	D	10	NYY *	3	0	1	23	11	5.48	1.70	302	235	194	6.2	33%	68%	4.86	50	20	30	4.3	4.3	**1.0**	8%	0.8	-3.8	-11	$1
Consist	B	1st Half		3	0	1	12	2	3.00	1.17	228			4.9	22%	77%	4.73	50	20	30	3.0	1.5	**0.5**	8%	0.8	1.7	-26	$3
LIMA Plan	B+	2nd Half		0	0	0	11	9	8.18	2.27	367			8.2	44%	63%	8.07				5.7	7.4	**1.3**		0.8	-5.5	28	($2)
Rand Var	0	**11**	**Proj**	**3**	**2**	**0**	**44**	**30**	**4.14**	**1.22**	**251**			**16.4**	**28%**	**69%**	**3.89**	**45**	**19**	**36**	**2.5**	**6.2**	**2.5**	**10%**	**1.0**	**2.1**	**68**	**$4**

3-0, 3.00 ERA in 12 IP at NYY. Only in Majors until early May when bulging disc effectively ended his season. Unusually poor Command likely related to injury. Even with mulligan for '10, he's of little interest.

Acosta,Manny

		Yr	Tm	W	L	Sv	IP	K	ERA	WHIP	OBA	vL	vR	BF/G	H%	S%	xERA	G	L	F	Ctl	Dom	Cmd	hr/f	hr/9	RAR	BPV	R$
RH RP	29	06	a/a	1	6	21	60	48	4.89	1.86	255			5.6	30%	75%	5.64				8.1	7.1	**0.9**		0.9	-2.8	37	$6
Ht/Wt	76 170	07	ATL *	10	4	12	82	69	2.69	1.47	229	250	93	5.9	29%	81%	4.06	61	11	29	5.7	7.5	**1.3**	3%	0.2	17.6	20	$14
Type	Pwr	08	ATL	3	5	3	53	31	3.57	1.40	243	280	218	5.0	26%	79%	4.35	53	19	28	4.4	5.3	**1.2**	15%	1.2	4.6	7	$5
Health	A	09	ATL *	2	4	0	59	47	4.12	1.64	287	297	302	5.3	33%	79%	4.61	44	19	37	4.6	7.2	**1.6**	12%	1.2	0.5	28	$1
PT/Exp	D	10	NYM *	5	5	6	76	69	3.43	1.32	235	163	245	4.7	29%	77%	3.90	42	18	41	4.0	8.2	**2.0**	9%	0.9	5.5	58	$9
Consist	A	1st Half		2	3	3	39	35	3.46	1.41	236			5.3	29%	78%	4.38	38	15	46	4.8	8.1	**1.7**	8%	0.9	2.7	31	$4
LIMA Plan	C+	2nd Half		3	2	3	37	34	3.41	1.22	235			4.1	28%	76%	3.55	43	19	39	3.2	8.3	**2.6**	10%	1.0	2.8	84	$5
Rand Var	-1	**11**	**Proj**	**4**	**5**	**0**	**65**	**54**	**3.72**	**1.44**	**252**			**4.9**	**30%**	**77%**	**4.14**	**46**	**18**	**35**	**4.4**	**7.4**	**1.7**	**10%**	**1.0**	**-0.0**	**39**	**$4**

3-2, 2.95 ERA in 39 IP at NYM. Showed how good he could be with lower 2H Ctl, but past says to bet against. Overall 2.0 Cmd gets our attention briefly, before we remember he's a 29-year-old journeyman.

Adams,Mike

		Yr	Tm	W	L	Sv	IP	K	ERA	WHIP	OBA	vL	vR	BF/G	H%	S%	xERA	G	L	F	Ctl	Dom	Cmd	hr/f	hr/9	RAR	BPV	R$
RH RP	32	06	aaa	1	3	2	60	39	4.84	1.68	311			5.8	36%	70%	5.59				3.7	5.9	**1.6**		0.5	-2.4	47	$1
Ht/Wt	77 204	07		0	0	0	0	0	0.00	0.00							0.00											
Type	Pwr FB	08	SD *	5	4	0	80	84	3.65	1.43	267	228	190	5.2	35%	76%	3.73	42	18	40	3.6	9.5	**2.6**	8%	0.8	6.0	94	$7
Health	F	09	SD *	1	0	0	46	49	1.57	0.74	145	130	88	3.7	19%	84%	2.73	51	7	42	2.3	9.6	**4.1**	7%	0.6	14.9	138	$9
PT/Exp	D	10	SD	4	1	0	67	73	1.75	1.06	203	185	206	3.8	29%	84%	3.08	41	20	39	3.1	9.9	**3.2**	3%	0.3	18.6	112	$10
Consist	B	1st Half		2	1	0	40	44	2.25	0.95	193			3.9	27%	76%	2.79	43	20	37	2.5	9.9	**4.0**	3%	0.2	8.7	132	$6
LIMA Plan	B+	2nd Half		2	0	0	27	29	1.01	1.24	218			3.7	30%	94%	3.52	38	20	42	4.0	9.8	**2.4**	4%	0.3	9.9	82	$4
Rand Var	-5	**11**	**Proj**	**3**	**1**	**8**	**58**	**60**	**2.48**	**1.14**	**216**			**4.1**	**29%**	**79%**	**3.36**	**43**	**16**	**41**	**3.3**	**9.3**	**2.9**	**5%**	**0.5**	**5.6**	**101**	**$10**

Continued ridiculously good ERA thanks to strand rate help. But that takes nothing away from his elite skills. Could be a dominant closer if ever given the opportunity. But health grade looms as a caveat.

Affeldt,Jeremy

		Yr	Tm	W	L	Sv	IP	K	ERA	WHIP	OBA	vL	vR	BF/G	H%	S%	xERA	G	L	F	Ctl	Dom	Cmd	hr/f	hr/9	RAR	BPV	R$
LH RP	31	06	2TM	8	8	1	97	48	6.21	1.62	271	212	289	8.2	28%	63%	5.32	50	17	33	5.1	4.4	**0.9**	12%	1.2	-20.2	-30	$1
Ht/Wt	77 226	07	COL	4	3	0	59	46	3.51	1.36	220	250	211	3.4	27%	74%	4.21	53	14	33	5.0	7.0	**1.4**	6%	0.5	6.7	21	$6
Type	Pwr xGB	08	CIN	1	1	0	78	80	3.33	1.32	261	269	255	4.5	33%	79%	3.03	54	18	28	2.9	9.2	**3.2**	15%	1.0	9.0	120	$6
Health	B	09	SF	2	2	0	62	55	1.73	1.17	193	211	187	3.4	24%	87%	2.93	65	17	18	4.5	7.9	**1.8**	10%	0.4	18.9	65	$8
PT/Exp	C	10	SF	4	3	4	50	44	4.14	1.60	284	290	290	4.3	35%	75%	3.60	56	19	26	4.3	7.9	**1.8**	10%	0.7	-0.8	60	$4
Consist	A	1st Half		2	3	2	30	26	4.85	1.85	295			4.6	36%	75%	4.26	53	22	25	6.1	7.9	**1.3**	13%	0.9	-3.1	9	$0
LIMA Plan	B+	2nd Half		2	0	2	20	18	3.10	1.23	268			3.8	34%	75%	2.78	60	15	26	1.8	8.0	**4.5**	6%	0.4	2.3	133	$3
Rand Var	+3	**11**	**Proj**	**4**	**2**	**3**	**58**	**51**	**3.26**	**1.40**	**252**			**4.0**	**31%**	**78%**	**3.39**	**58**	**17**	**25**	**4.0**	**7.9**	**2.0**	**9%**	**0.6**	**5.4**	**69**	**$6**

Without H% and S% help like in '09, he's revealed for what he is: a barely average pitcher (check that RAR). Fluky half-season Ctl swing shouldn't distract from fact that he made no gains there overall.

Albers,Matt

		Yr	Tm	W	L	Sv	IP	K	ERA	WHIP	OBA	vL	vR	BF/G	H%	S%	xERA	G	L	F	Ctl	Dom	Cmd	hr/f	hr/9	RAR	BPV	R$
RH RP	28	06	HOU *	12	5	0	156	113	3.23	1.38	258	333	267	24.9	31%	77%	4.20	43	26	30	3.6	6.5	**1.8**	5%	0.5	24.2	41	$15
Ht/Wt	72 205	07	HOU *	6	14	0	164	105	5.43	1.59	288	280	298	18.5	31%	69%	4.72	48	17	35	4.0	5.8	**1.4**	13%	1.4	-20.4	22	$1
Type	GB	08	BAL	3	3	0	49	26	3.49	1.33	237	163	312	7.4	26%	75%	4.53	53	12	34	4.0	4.8	**1.2**	7%	0.7	5.2	8	$4
Health	B	09	BAL	3	6	0	67	49	5.51	1.73	297	342	273	5.6	35%	66%	4.71	48	20	31	4.8	6.6	**1.4**	4%	0.4	-8.7	14	($0)
PT/Exp	C	10	BAL	5	3	0	76	49	4.52	1.48	268	297	250	5.4	30%	70%	4.03	56	15	29	4.0	5.8	**1.4**	9%	0.7	-3.5	30	$3
Consist	A	1st Half		3	3	0	37	22	5.07	1.58	270			4.9	28%	72%	4.29	59	14	27	4.8	5.3	**1.1**	18%	1.4	-4.3	2	$1
LIMA Plan	C+	2nd Half		2	0	0	38	27	3.98	1.38	265			5.9	32%	68%	3.77	54	15	31	3.3	6.3	**1.9**	0%	0.0	0.7	57	$2
Rand Var	0	**11**	**Proj**	**3**	**4**	**0**	**65**	**43**	**4.55**	**1.52**	**273**			**6.2**	**32%**	**69%**	**4.28**	**53**	**16**	**31**	**4.1**	**5.9**	**1.4**	**6%**	**0.6**	**0.0**	**26**	**$2**

Lefties still cause him prob- (.819 OPS), although with... *snnk* Hunh? Sorry, must have dozed off. Say, did you know he was voted Double-A's Most Spectacular Pitcher back in '06?

Ambriz,Hector

		Yr	Tm	W	L	Sv	IP	K	ERA	WHIP	OBA	vL	vR	BF/G	H%	S%	xERA	G	L	F	Ctl	Dom	Cmd	hr/f	hr/9	RAR	BPV	R$
RH RP	26	06		0	0	0	0	0	0.00	0.00							0.00											
Ht/Wt	74 235	07		0	0	0	0	0	0.00	0.00							0.00											
Type	FB	08	aa	5	13	0	152	100	6.72	1.60	311			25.5	33%	61%	6.52				2.9	5.9	**2.0**		1.7	-45.4	18	($3)
Health	B	09	a/a	12	11	0	156	113	5.94	1.65	326			25.5	38%	64%	6.10				2.6	6.5	**2.5**		0.9	-31.4	54	$2
PT/Exp	D	10	CLE	0	2	0	48	37	5.59	1.76	333	324	354	6.6	37%	73%	4.57	42	16	42	3.2	6.9	**2.2**	14%	1.9	-8.6	58	($2)
Consist	B	1st Half		0	1	0	32	29	4.23	1.70	324			6.2	40%	77%	4.05	46	14	40	3.1	8.0	**2.6**	7%	0.8	-0.4	85	($0)
LIMA Plan	D	2nd Half		0	1	0	16	8	8.26	1.88	349			7.8	32%	66%	5.49	38	17	45	3.3	4.6	**1.4**	25%	3.9	-8.3	10	($2)
Rand Var	+5	**11**	**Proj**	**0**	**1**	**0**	**9**	**6**	**6.00**	**1.78**	**339**			**10.6**	**36%**	**71%**	**4.95**	**40**	**16**	**44**	**3.0**	**6.0**	**2.0**	**14%**	**2.0**	**-0.7**	**45**	**($0)**

TJS will likely keep him out of action until 2012.
Skills made decent transition to Majors, but he was hurt by unlucky H%, S%, and hr/f. Keep his name tucked away for next season.

Anderson,Brett

		Yr	Tm	W	L	Sv	IP	K	ERA	WHIP	OBA	vL	vR	BF/G	H%	S%	xERA	G	L	F	Ctl	Dom	Cmd	hr/f	hr/9	RAR	BPV	R$
LH SP	23	06		0	0	0	0	0	0.00	0.00							0.00											
Ht/Wt	76 215	07		0	0	0	0	0	0.00	0.00							0.00											
Type	GB	08	aa	2	1	0	31	34	2.49	1.14	240			21.0	32%	82%	3.30				2.2	9.8	**4.4**		0.8	7.0	133	$5
Health	D	09	OAK	11	11	0	175	150	4.06	1.28	267	313	247	24.6	32%	71%	3.52	51	15	34	2.3	7.7	**3.3**	11%	1.0	8.6	105	$17
PT/Exp	C	10	OAK	7	6	0	112	75	2.80	1.19	261	299	243	24.3	30%	77%	3.30	55	17	28	1.8	6.0	**3.4**	6%	0.5	18.5	93	$12
Consist	A	1st Half		2	1	0	31	22	2.35	1.04	244			20.3	30%	75%	3.01	52	21	28	1.2	6.4	**5.5**	0%	0.0	6.8	114	$4
LIMA Plan	B+	2nd Half		5	5	0	82	53	2.98	1.25	267			26.2	31%	78%	3.41	56	16	28	2.0	5.8	**2.9**	8%	0.7	11.7	85	$8
Rand Var	-2	**11**	**Proj**	**11**	**9**	**0**	**174**	**139**	**3.16**	**1.20**	**258**			**23.1**	**31%**	**76%**	**3.27**	**53**	**17**	**30**	**2.0**	**7.2**	**3.7**	**8%**	**0.7**	**21.9**	**107**	**$20**

PRO: Skills held up despite elbow injury that cost him three months; outstanding Ctl / GB; 58% PQS DOM in 19 GS.
CON: That injury; Dom decline.
VERDICT: Still a keeper as long as you heed his Health rating.

Arrieta,Jake

		Yr	Tm	W	L	Sv	IP	K	ERA	WHIP	OBA	vL	vR	BF/G	H%	S%	xERA	G	L	F	Ctl	Dom	Cmd	hr/f	hr/9	RAR	BPV	R$
RH SP	25	06		0	0	0	0	0	0.00	0.00							0.00											
Ht/Wt	76 225	07		0	0	0	0	0	0.00	0.00							0.00											
Type		08		0	0	0	0	0	0.00	0.00							0.00											
Health	A	09	a/a	11	11	0	150	124	4.91	1.57	295			24.1	35%	71%	5.59				3.5	7.4	**2.1**		1.1	-11.1	51	$7
PT/Exp	D	10	BAL *	12	8	0	173	106	3.64	1.40	248	315	213	24.9	28%	75%	4.63	42	19	39	4.2	5.5	**1.3**	6%	0.7	10.8	6	$12
Consist	B	1st Half		8	4	0	99	67	3.17	1.32	227			24.8	26%	77%	4.44	44	17	39	4.4	6.1	**1.4**	5%	0.5	11.8	11	$10
LIMA Plan	D+	2nd Half		4	4	0	74	39	4.26	1.50	275			25.2	30%	73%	4.88	42	20	38	3.9	4.7	**1.2**	7%	0.9	-1.1	-0	$3
Rand Var	-2	**11**	**Proj**	**13**	**11**	**0**	**189**	**129**	**4.25**	**1.48**	**271**			**24.4**	**31%**	**73%**	**4.58**	**42**	**20**	**39**	**3.9**	**6.2**	**1.6**	**8%**	**0.9**	**-6.8**	**26**	**$11**

6-6, 4.66 ERA in 100 IP at BAL. Struggled to adjust to Majors (4.7 Dom, 1.1 Cmd) and couldn't get lefties out. Also, he's trying to rehab a sore elbow instead of having surgery. Does that ever work?

JOSHUA RANDALL

Arroyo,Bronson

		Yr	Tm	W	L	Sv	IP	K	ERA	WHIP	OBA	vL	vR	BF/G	H%	S%	xERA	G	L	F	Ctl	Dom	Cmd	hr/f	hr/9	RAR	BPV	R$
RH SP	34	06	CIN	14	11	0	240	184	3.30	1.19	247	282	206	28.2	28%	78%	4.05	38	21	41	2.4	6.9	2.9	11%	1.2	35.3	76	$26
Ht/Wt	76 194	07	CIN	9	15	0	211	156	4.23	1.40	281	274	285	26.8	32%	73%	4.50	35	21	44	2.7	6.7	2.5	10%	1.2	5.1	61	$12
Type	Con	08	CIN	15	11	0	200	163	4.77	1.44	280	314	254	25.6	32%	70%	4.05	41	23	36	3.1	7.3	2.4	13%	1.3	-12.3	69	$12
Health	A	09	CIN	15	13	0	220	127	3.84	1.27	256	278	236	27.9	27%	75%	4.29	45	19	37	2.7	5.2	2.0	12%	1.3	9.5	44	$17
PT/Exp	A	10	CIN	17	10	0	216	121	3.88	1.15	236	285	185	26.6	25%	71%	4.16	43	16	40	2.5	5.0	2.1	11%	1.2	3.6	46	$19
Consist	A	1st Half		8	4	0	112	55	4.25	1.26	240			27.6	25%	68%	4.59	44	16	40	3.3	4.4	1.3	8%	1.0	-3.2	13	$7
LIMA Plan	D	2nd Half		9	6	0	103	66	3.48	1.03	232			25.5	24%	74%	3.72	43	17	41	1.6	5.7	3.7	13%	1.5	6.8	82	$12
Rand Var	-2	11	Proj	15	11	0	210	133	4.02	1.22	250			26.4	27%	72%	4.14	43	18	39	2.5	5.7	2.3	12%	1.3	0.0	55	$17

2010 eerily similar to 2009.
PRO: dominated RH; good Ctl; 2H Cmd spike.
CON: low H% helped out; Dom sliding into irrelevance.
xERA shows he's a consistent workhorse.

Atchison,Scott

		Yr	Tm	W	L	Sv	IP	K	ERA	WHIP	OBA	vL	vR	BF/G	H%	S%	xERA	G	L	F	Ctl	Dom	Cmd	hr/f	hr/9	RAR	BPV	R$
RH RP	35	06	aaa	4	0	1	50	32	3.00	1.56	302			7.5	35%	81%	5.02				3.0	5.7	1.9		0.4	9.4	56	$5
Ht/Wt	74 200	07	SF *	3	2	4	84	62	3.27	1.31	277			5.9	33%	77%	4.17	37	23	41	2.1	6.7	3.2	6%	0.7	12.0	79	$8
Type	FB	08	JPN	7	6	0	104	81	4.62	1.38	276			10.7	31%	70%	4.95				2.8	7.0	2.5		1.3	-4.0	56	$7
Health	A	09	JPN	5	3	0	90	77	2.11	0.99	202			4.7	25%	81%	2.12				2.5	7.7	3.1		0.5	24.4	111	$14
PT/Exp	C	10	BOS *	3	3	0	73	55	4.73	1.34	264	290	220	5.8	30%	67%	3.98	48	11	41	3.0	6.8	2.3	10%	1.1	-5.3	68	$4
Consist	F	1st Half		2	1	0	39	37	4.89	1.37	259			6.3	33%	64%	3.68	49	9	42	3.5	8.5	2.4	6%	0.7	-3.7	86	$2
LIMA Plan	B+	2nd Half		1	2	0	34	18	4.54	1.31	269			5.3	27%	71%	4.33	47	12	41	2.4	4.8	2.0	13%	1.6	-1.7	47	$1
Rand Var	+1	11	Proj	3	2	0	58	43	4.03	1.26	255			5.9	29%	70%	3.99	45	14	41	2.6	6.7	2.5	8%	0.9	2.1	72	$5

2-3, 4.50 ERA in 60 IP at BOS. Journeyman dominated RHers in middle relief. Decent Dom didn't carry into 2H, fortunate LD avoidance did. Simply put, there's not enough here to justify a bigger role.

Atilano,Luis

		Yr	Tm	W	L	Sv	IP	K	ERA	WHIP	OBA	vL	vR	BF/G	H%	S%	xERA	G	L	F	Ctl	Dom	Cmd	hr/f	hr/9	RAR	BPV	R$
RH SP	25	06		0	0	0	0	0	0.00	0.00							0.00											
Ht/Wt	75 215	07		0	0	0	0	0	0.00	0.00							0.00											
Type	Con FB	08		0	0	0	0	0	0.00	0.00							0.00											
Health	C	09	a/a	9	8	0	125	55	5.41	1.73	347			25.3	36%	71%	6.99				2.1	4.0	1.9		1.2	-17.0	14	($0)
PT/Exp	D	10	WAS *	8	8	0	99	48	5.29	1.55	294	275	286	23.2	31%	67%	4.96	41	21	38	3.4	4.4	1.3	9%	1.1	-15.6	6	$1
Consist	F	1st Half		8	5	0	87	45	4.44	1.42	279			23.7	30%	70%	4.59	42	21	37	3.0	4.6	1.5	8%	0.9	-4.5	23	$4
LIMA Plan	C	2nd Half		0	3	0	12	3	11.79	2.53	394			20.9	38%	54%	8.10	30	22	49	6.3	2.3	0.4	12%	2.3	-11.0	-120	($3)
Rand Var	0	11	Proj	5	4	0	65	31	5.02	1.55	308			24.0	33%	69%	5.18	35	21	44	2.7	4.3	1.6	7%	1.0	-8.3	19	$1

6-7, 5.15 ERA in 86 IP at WAS. 3-0 start got tongues wagging; low Dom combined with too many baserunners made them stop talking. Look elsewhere until he improves the 19/38 PQS DOM/DIS.

Axford,John

		Yr	Tm	W	L	Sv	IP	K	ERA	WHIP	OBA	vL	vR	BF/G	H%	S%	xERA	G	L	F	Ctl	Dom	Cmd	hr/f	hr/9	RAR	BPV	R$
RH RP	28	06		0	0	0	0	0	0.00	0.00							0.00											
Ht/Wt	77 195	07		0	0	0	0	0	0.00	0.00							0.00											
Type	Pwr	08		0	0	0	0	0	0.00	0.00							0.00											
Health	A	09	a/a	5	0	1	40	38	4.48	1.52	244			6.9	31%	71%	4.31				5.5	8.5	1.5		0.7	-0.8	67	$4
PT/Exp	F	10	MIL *	11	4	26	71	92	2.43	1.27	224	225	183	4.8	34%	80%	2.79	48	19	33	4.1	11.7	2.9	2%	0.1	13.9	126	$21
Consist	D	1st Half		6	3	11	35	44	2.60	1.43	254			4.9	38%	80%	2.86	48	25	27	4.2	11.3	2.7	0%	0.0	6.1	117	$9
LIMA Plan	C+	2nd Half		5	1	15	36	48	2.25	1.11	191			4.7	30%	79%	2.65	48	16	36	4.0	12.0	3.0	4%	0.2	7.8	134	$12
Rand Var	-2	11	Proj	8	4	33	73	84	3.21	1.32	229			4.8	32%	75%	3.22	48	19	33	4.3	10.4	2.4	5%	0.4	8.3	96	$20

24 Sv, 2.48 ERA in 58 IP at MIL. Reasons numbers can't be fully repeated: shaky Ctl, low hr/f, high S%. Still, BPV shows this is a great skill set, led by Dom and GB%. Should be able to hold onto the closer role for awhile.

Badenhop,Burke

		Yr	Tm	W	L	Sv	IP	K	ERA	WHIP	OBA	vL	vR	BF/G	H%	S%	xERA	G	L	F	Ctl	Dom	Cmd	hr/f	hr/9	RAR	BPV	R$
RH RP	28	06		0	0	0	0	0	0.00	0.00							0.00											
Ht/Wt	77 204	07	aa	2	0	0	18	10	2.50	0.94	191			23.2	20%	80%	2.45				2.5	5.0	2.0		1.0	4.4	59	$3
Type	xGB	08	FLA *	3	3	0	53	38	5.39	1.57	294	298	281	17.1	33%	67%	3.95	54	20	26	3.5	6.4	1.8	16%	1.2	-7.4	51	$1
Health	C	09	FLA	7	4	0	72	57	3.75	1.32	259	250	269	8.7	31%	72%	3.43	54	20	26	3.0	7.1	2.4	9%	0.6	3.9	79	$7
PT/Exp	D	10	FLA *	2	6	1	84	55	3.79	1.29	253	238	252	5.4	29%	71%	3.66	57	14	29	3.1	5.9	1.9	7%	0.5	2.3	58	$4
Consist	A	1st Half		0	6	1	35	22	5.21	1.58	293			6.3	34%	66%	4.16	52	20	28	3.7	5.6	1.5	6%	0.5	-5.2	31	($1)
LIMA Plan	B	2nd Half		2	0	0	49	33	2.77	1.09	221			4.9	26%	76%	3.33	59	12	30	2.6	6.1	2.4	7%	0.6	7.5	76	$5
Rand Var	0	11	Proj	4	5	0	73	51	3.97	1.34	260			7.2	30%	71%	3.64	55	17	27	3.1	6.3	2.0	8%	0.6	4.5	63	$5

2-5, 3.99 ERA in 68 IP at FLA. Seeds for success are here: extreme GBer, consistently solid xERA. Don't expect a repeat of 2H; low H% and LD% helped. A reasonable LIMA option in deep leagues.

Baez,Danys

		Yr	Tm	W	L	Sv	IP	K	ERA	WHIP	OBA	vL	vR	BF/G	H%	S%	xERA	G	L	F	Ctl	Dom	Cmd	hr/f	hr/9	RAR	BPV	R$
RH RP	33	06	2NL	5	6	9	59	39	4.56	1.30	264	295	244	4.4	31%	64%	4.50	40	17	43	2.6	5.9	2.3	4%	0.5	-0.5	55	$8
Ht/Wt	73 233	07	BAL	0	6	3	50	29	6.44	1.57	261	346	200	4.3	27%	61%	4.97	51	17	32	5.2	5.2	1.0	15%	1.4	-12.0	-17	($0)
Type	xGB	08	BAL	0	0	0	0	0	0.00	0.00							0.00											
Health	F	09	BAL	4	6	0	72	40	4.02	1.13	226	248	197	4.9	24%	67%	3.63	61	13	26	2.8	5.0	1.8	14%	1.0	3.8	55	$7
PT/Exp	D	10	PHI	3	4	0	48	28	5.47	1.64	290	306	297	4.3	32%	68%	4.47	56	13	31	4.3	5.3	1.2	12%	1.1	-8.6	12	($0)
Consist	B	1st Half		2	3	0	31	16	4.69	1.56	264			4.2	28%	73%	4.78	55	13	32	5.0	4.7	0.9	12%	1.2	-2.6	-18	$0
LIMA Plan	D	2nd Half		1	1	0	17	12	6.88	1.76	334			4.4	38%	61%	3.93	59	12	29	3.2	6.4	2.0	12%	1.1	-6.0	66	($1)
Rand Var	+2	11	Proj	3	4	0	51	31	4.79	1.50	278			4.5	30%	70%	4.22	56	14	31	3.7	5.5	1.5	12%	1.1	-0.5	32	$1

Return to the NL didn't help. While he's still a GB machine, new-found struggles vs RHers and too many walks did him in. Combined with sliding Dom, it's getting hard to think of a reason to draft him.

Bailey,Andrew

		Yr	Tm	W	L	Sv	IP	K	ERA	WHIP	OBA	vL	vR	BF/G	H%	S%	xERA	G	L	F	Ctl	Dom	Cmd	hr/f	hr/9	RAR	BPV	R$
RH RP	26	06		0	0	0	0	0	0.00	0.00							0.00											
Ht/Wt	75 234	07		0	0	0	0	0	0.00	0.00							0.00											
Type	Pwr xFB	08	aa	5	9	0	110	89	4.73	1.47	263			13.1	31%	70%	4.73				4.2	7.3	1.7		1.0	-5.8	52	$5
Health	B	09	OAK	6	3	26	83	91	1.84	0.88	173	146	185	4.7	23%	82%	3.07	42	13	45	2.6	9.8	3.8	6%	0.5	26.9	127	$26
PT/Exp	C	10	OAK	1	3	25	49	42	1.47	0.96	197	195	202	4.0	24%	89%	3.47	39	16	45	2.4	7.7	3.2	5%	0.6	16.1	92	$16
Consist	C	1st Half		0	2	17	34	23	1.59	0.94	200			4.0	23%	87%	3.74	38	19	43	2.1	6.1	2.9	5%	0.5	10.7	68	$10
LIMA Plan	B	2nd Half		1	1	8	15	19	1.20	1.00	191			4.2	28%	93%	2.84	44	6	50	3.0	11.4	3.8	6%	0.6	5.4	146	$6
Rand Var	-5	11	Proj	3	4	33	65	67	2.48	1.07	210			4.9	27%	80%	3.40	42	13	46	2.9	9.2	3.2	7%	0.7	7.1	108	$20

Elbow injury slowed him in 2H; eventually led to surgery. H%, S%, hr/f point to an ERA bump, but Cmd, OBA, BPV point to continued success. Should be healthy next spring, if so he's an elite closer at a discount.

Bailey,Homer

		Yr	Tm	W	L	Sv	IP	K	ERA	WHIP	OBA	vL	vR	BF/G	H%	S%	xERA	G	L	F	Ctl	Dom	Cmd	hr/f	hr/9	RAR	BPV	R$
RH SP	24	06	aa	7	1	0	68	68	2.02	1.25	230			21.8	31%	83%	2.79				3.7	9.0	2.5		0.1	21.0	111	$12
Ht/Wt	75 210	07	CIN *	10	5	0	112	83	4.51	1.37	232	284	233	22.9	27%	67%	4.45	47	18	35	4.6	6.6	1.4	6%	0.6	-1.1	19	$9
Type	Pwr	08	CIN *	4	13	0	147	106	6.14	1.70	312	305	423	25.2	35%	65%	4.51	43	25	31	3.8	6.5	1.7	13%	1.2	-34.0	36	($4)
Health	C	09	CIN *	16	10	0	203	158	4.09	1.47	276	283	248	26.2	32%	76%	4.26	43	21	37	3.6	7.0	2.0	11%	1.2	2.5	51	$13
PT/Exp	C	10	CIN	4	3	0	109	100	4.46	1.37	262	238	272	24.6	32%	69%	3.71	42	21	37	3.3	8.3	2.5	9%	0.9	-6.0	79	$5
Consist	A	1st Half		1	2	0	51	41	5.50	1.48	274			24.8	32%	65%	4.29	39	20	41	3.7	7.3	2.0	11%	1.2	-9.3	48	($0)
LIMA Plan	B+	2nd Half		3	1	0	58	59	3.55	1.27	251			24.4	33%	73%	3.22	44	23	33	2.9	9.1	3.1	7%	0.6	3.3	107	$5
Rand Var	+1	11	Proj	10	7	0	174	152	3.98	1.41	269			24.3	32%	74%	3.89	42	21	36	3.4	7.9	2.3	10%	0.9	5.3	71	$11

After two months on the DL, his 2H got our attention... just like 2009's Sept/Oct (2.08 ERA) got our attention coming into this year. Cmd, GB%, xERA, BPV all made impressive gains but beware the risk.

Baker,Scott

		Yr	Tm	W	L	Sv	IP	K	ERA	WHIP	OBA	vL	vR	BF/G	H%	S%	xERA	G	L	F	Ctl	Dom	Cmd	hr/f	hr/9	RAR	BPV	R$
RH SP	29	06	MIN *	10	12	0	167	119	5.19	1.54	310	349	299	26.6	35%	68%	4.79	34	19	47	2.4	6.4	2.6	8%	1.2	-13.0	62	$7
Ht/Wt	76 220	07	MIN *	12	11	1	186	134	4.39	1.29	282	323	257	25.3	32%	68%	4.21	35	22	43	1.7	6.5	3.9	7%	0.9	2.6	85	$16
Type	xFB	08	MIN	11	4	0	172	141	3.45	1.18	249	263	230	25.2	29%	75%	3.98	33	21	46	2.2	7.4	3.4	9%	1.0	19.1	84	$20
Health	B	09	MIN	15	9	0	194	160	4.36	1.19	252	221	271	24.9	29%	67%	4.05	34	19	47	2.1	7.4	3.5	10%	1.3	2.2	88	$21
PT/Exp	A	10	MIN	12	9	0	170	148	4.49	1.34	279	277	277	25.0	33%	70%	3.85	36	21	43	2.3	7.8	3.4	10%	1.2	-7.4	93	$13
Consist	A	1st Half		7	7	0	103	91	4.72	1.32	287			25.7	34%	68%	3.64	35	23	42	1.7	8.0	4.8	11%	1.3	-7.4	111	$7
LIMA Plan	B	2nd Half		5	2	0	67	57	4.15	1.38	267			24.1	31%	73%	4.17	37	17	47	3.2	7.6	2.4	9%	1.1	-0.1	65	$5
Rand Var	+1	11	Proj	14	7	0	174	145	3.98	1.29	267			25.3	31%	73%	4.04	35	20	45	2.4	7.5	3.2	10%	1.2	5.4	84	$17

A member of the Brad Fullmer List, thanks to chronic gopheritis and elbow issues. Otherwise, skills are superb. Most of us have given up waiting for the breakout. That means he'll win the Cy Young Award in '11.

DAVE ADLER

Balester,Collin

		Yr	Tm	W	L	Sv	IP	K	ERA	WHIP	OBA	vL	vR	BF/G	H%	S%	xERA	G	L	F	Ctl	Dom	Cmd	hr/f	hr/9	RAR	BPV	R$
RH RP	24	06		0	0	0	0	0	0.00	0.00							0.00											
Ht/Wt	77 199	07	a/a	4	10	0	150	103	4.45	1.40	280			24.0	32%	68%	4.57				2.7	6.2	2.3		0.7	0.2	63	$7
Type	Pwr GB	08	WAS *	12	10	0	158	107	4.85	1.41	280	278	298	22.8	31%	69%	4.41	40	22	39	2.8	6.1	2.2	12%	1.3	-11.2	52	$9
Health	A	09	WAS *	8	14	0	137	81	5.90	1.71	322	315	254	23.6	36%	66%	5.36	37	17	47	3.3	5.3	1.6	7%	1.0	-28.9	20	($2)
PT/Exp	D	10	WAS *	3	4	0	90	72	6.20	1.60	285	257	154	7.8	33%	62%	3.96	57	11	32	4.3	7.2	1.7	12%	1.1	-24.2	48	($2)
Consist	C	1st Half		1	3	0	41	21	10.10	1.95	334			11.7	35%	47%	7.44				4.8	4.6	1.0		1.5	-30.8	-10	($7)
LIMA Plan	B	2nd Half		2	1	0	49	51	2.94	1.31	237			5.9	31%	80%	3.12	57	11	32	3.9	9.4	2.4	10%	0.7	6.5	99	$4
Rand Var	+5	11	Proj	2	3	0	44	37	4.14	1.45	268			7.0	32%	74%	3.84	51	14	34	3.7	7.7	2.1	11%	1.0	1.6	67	$2

0-1, 2.57 ERA in 21 IP at WAS. AAA food for thought:

	IP	ERA	WHIP	BAA
starter	21	11.57	2.38	.385
reliever	48	3.38	1.17	.215

Success in same role in majors (see 2H BPV) holds our interest.

Balfour,Grant

		Yr	Tm	W	L	Sv	IP	K	ERA	WHIP	OBA	vL	vR	BF/G	H%	S%	xERA	G	L	F	Ctl	Dom	Cmd	hr/f	hr/9	RAR	BPV	R$
RH RP	33	06		0	0	0	0	0	0.00	0.00							0.00											
Ht/Wt	74 195	07	2TM *	2	3	7	68	81	4.57	1.55	255			5.3	36%	70%	3.79	42	22	36	5.2	10.7	2.0	7%	0.6	-0.9	71	$6
Type	Pwr xFB	08	TAM *	7	2	12	82	113	1.23	0.86	131	120	159	4.7	21%	89%	2.87	29	19	52	3.9	12.4	3.2	5%	0.5	31.4	126	$24
Health	C	09	TAM	5	4	4	67	69	4.81	1.37	237	240	232	4.0	30%	65%	4.11	36	21	43	4.4	9.2	2.1	8%	0.8	-3.0	61	$7
PT/Exp	D	10	TAM	2	1	0	55	56	2.28	1.08	216	267	174	3.9	29%	81%	3.55	31	20	50	2.8	9.1	3.3	4%	0.5	12.7	98	$8
Consist	B	1st Half		1	1	0	34	33	2.10	1.02	218			4.0	29%	79%	3.31	35	21	45	2.1	8.7	4.1	2%	0.3	8.6	112	$5
LIMA Plan	B+	2nd Half		1	0	0	21	23	2.57	1.19	213			3.8	28%	83%	3.90	24	18	58	3.9	9.9	2.6	7%	0.9	4.1	75	$3
Rand Var	-5	11	Proj	4	2	0	65	72	3.03	1.18	214			4.1	29%	76%	3.68	31	20	49	3.7	9.9	2.7	6%	0.7	4.9	87	$9

Elite skills have been somewhat consistent, but more important is that they've maintained at his age. S% drives his ERA, but there is nothing you can do about that. FB% creates some risk. But still a solid LIMA option.

Bannister,Brian

		Yr	Tm	W	L	Sv	IP	K	ERA	WHIP	OBA	vL	vR	BF/G	H%	S%	xERA	G	L	F	Ctl	Dom	Cmd	hr/f	hr/9	RAR	BPV	R$
RH SP	30	06	NYM *	5	4	0	68	40	4.78	1.52	285	286	185	21.6	31%	71%	5.22	40	15	45	3.6	5.3	1.5	9%	1.2	-2.5	16	$3
Ht/Wt	74 217	07	KC *	13	10	0	185	87	3.84	1.22	254	281	219	24.7	27%	71%	4.66	41	19	40	2.4	4.2	1.8	8%	1.0	15.2	32	$18
Type		08	KC	9	16	0	183	113	5.76	1.49	294	313	274	25.2	32%	64%	4.72	37	22	41	2.9	5.6	1.9	12%	1.4	-31.9	39	$4
Health	B	09	KC	7	12	0	154	98	4.73	1.37	270	266	270	25.4	30%	66%	4.21	50	17	34	2.9	5.7	2.0	9%	0.9	-5.4	52	$8
PT/Exp	A	10	KC	7	12	0	128	77	6.34	1.63	305	273	330	24.2	32%	64%	4.68	43	20	37	3.5	5.4	1.5	14%	1.6	-34.7	24	($2)
Consist	A	1st Half		7	6	0	89	55	5.46	1.53	297			24.7	32%	67%	4.40	44	20	36	3.0	5.6	1.8	13%	1.4	-14.5	40	$2
LIMA Plan	D	2nd Half		0	6	0	39	22	8.37	1.86	323			23.1	33%	57%	5.34	42	20	38	4.7	5.1	1.1	17%	2.1	-20.2	-14	($5)
Rand Var	+5	11	Proj	5	13	0	131	78	5.38	1.56	295			24.4	32%	68%	4.73	43	19	37	3.4	5.4	1.6	11%	1.2	-7.1	25	$1

One would think, with all the stat analysis that he does personally, he'd figure out how to take his game up a notch. Skills are not good, but S% is the ERA killer. BPIs are not showing any upside here.

Bard,Daniel

		Yr	Tm	W	L	Sv	IP	K	ERA	WHIP	OBA	vL	vR	BF/G	H%	S%	xERA	G	L	F	Ctl	Dom	Cmd	hr/f	hr/9	RAR	BPV	R$
RH RP	25	06		0	0	0	0	0	0.00	0.00							0.00											
Ht/Wt	76 200	07		0	0	0	0	0	0.00	0.00							0.00											
Type	Pwr	08	aa	4	1	7	49	53	2.45	1.26	202			6.6	27%	82%	2.87				4.9	9.8	2.0		0.6	11.3	98	$10
Health	A	09	BOS *	3	2	7	65	88	3.18	1.17	211	263	200	4.4	30%	78%	2.78	45	19	36	3.7	12.2	3.3	15%	1.1	10.2	141	$12
PT/Exp	D	10	BOS	1	2	3	75	76	1.93	1.00	176	141	215	4.0	22%	86%	3.14	47	15	38	3.6	9.2	2.5	9%	0.7	20.4	92	$12
Consist	A	1st Half		1	2	3	40	42	2.04	0.86	164			3.8	20%	83%	2.81	48	12	40	2.7	9.5	3.5	11%	0.9	10.3	124	$8
LIMA Plan	B+	2nd Half		0	0	0	35	34	1.80	1.17	189			4.2	25%	87%	3.55	45	20	36	4.6	8.7	1.9	6%	0.5	10.1	55	$4
Rand Var	-5	11	Proj	2	2	8	65	74	2.48	1.12	193			4.5	26%	82%	3.14	46	17	37	4.0	10.2	2.6	11%	0.8	9.2	100	$12

High Dom, GB% and ridiculous OBA scream FUTURE CLOSER! ERA will rise, but still has a very low ceiling. This a valuable skill set that's worth an investment whether or not he's the closer.

Bastardo,Antonio

		Yr	Tm	W	L	Sv	IP	K	ERA	WHIP	OBA	vL	vR	BF/G	H%	S%	xERA	G	L	F	Ctl	Dom	Cmd	hr/f	hr/9	RAR	BPV	R$
LH RP	25	06		0	0	0	0	0	0.00	0.00							0.00											
Ht/Wt	71 194	07		0	0	0	0	0	0.00	0.00							0.00											
Type	Pwr xFB	08	aa	1	5	0	67	50	4.15	1.48	247			21.0	25%	81%	5.55				5.0	6.8	1.4		2.1	1.3	13	$2
Health	A	09	a/a	3	2	3	49	44	2.27	1.01	221			14.8	28%	78%	2.28				1.9	8.0	4.2		0.4	12.3	136	$9
PT/Exp	F	10	PHI *	3	1	3	36	49	3.53	1.35	247	200	300	3.4	38%	72%	3.32	32	15	53	3.8	12.3	3.2	2%	0.3	2.1	128	$5
Consist	F	1st Half		0	0	0	12	13	5.12	1.22	147			3.2	19%	57%	4.52	30	10	60	6.6	9.5	1.4	6%	0.7	-1.7	1	$0
LIMA Plan	A	2nd Half		3	1	3	24	36	2.70	1.41	291			3.5	47%	79%	2.58	35	24	41	2.3	13.7	5.9	0%	0.0	3.8	197	$4
Rand Var	+1	11	Proj	3	3	0	51	54	3.19	1.32	255			7.2	33%	79%	3.95	32	14	54	3.2	9.6	3.0	7%	0.9	1.2	96	$5

2-0, 4.34 ERA in 19 IP at PHI. Move to pen agreed with him; 33 K/6 BB in 20 AAA IP. There will be ERA fluctuation as hr/f, H% normalize. With high Dom and success vs LHers, should find a niche in late relief.

Batista,Miguel

		Yr	Tm	W	L	Sv	IP	K	ERA	WHIP	OBA	vL	vR	BF/G	H%	S%	xERA	G	L	F	Ctl	Dom	Cmd	hr/f	hr/9	RAR	BPV	R$
RH RP	40	06	ARI	11	8	0	206	110	4.59	1.53	284	321	257	27.0	31%	71%	4.57	52	20	28	3.7	4.8	1.3	9%	0.8	-2.5	17	$7
Ht/Wt	73 208	07	SEA	16	11	0	193	133	4.29	1.52	277	295	258	26.0	32%	73%	4.75	44	17	39	4.0	6.2	1.6	7%	0.8	5.1	27	$13
Type	Pwr	08	SEA	4	14	1	115	73	6.26	1.86	294	293	298	12.5	32%	69%	5.52	46	20	34	6.2	5.7	0.9	14%	1.5	-27.1	-40	($4)
Health	A	09	SEA	7	4	1	71	52	4.04	1.65	282	331	242	5.8	33%	77%	4.83	47	18	35	4.9	6.6	1.3	9%	0.9	3.6	10	$5
PT/Exp	C	10	WAS	1	2	2	83	55	3.70	1.33	233	243	229	6.1	26%	75%	4.20	50	15	35	4.2	6.0	1.4	10%	1.0	3.2	22	$4
Consist	B	1st Half		0	2	1	44	29	4.06	1.35	219			6.1	24%	73%	4.63	47	14	39	5.1	5.9	1.2	10%	1.0	-0.3	-6	$1
LIMA Plan	C	2nd Half		1	0	1	38	26	3.28	1.30	249			6.0	28%	78%	3.74	54	16	30	3.3	6.1	1.9	11%	0.9	3.5	53	$3
Rand Var	-2	11	Proj	2	2	0	45	30	4.18	1.50	261			7.1	29%	75%	4.54	49	17	34	4.6	6.0	1.3	10%	1.0	-2.2	11	$1

PRO: High GB%; only a myth that he's been pitching since the Truman administration. CON: weak Cmd, H% kept ERA under 4.00 last year. He simply doesn't do enough to have him on your radar.

Bautista,Denny

		Yr	Tm	W	L	Sv	IP	K	ERA	WHIP	OBA	vL	vR	BF/G	H%	S%	xERA	G	L	F	Ctl	Dom	Cmd	hr/f	hr/9	RAR	BPV	R$
RH RP	30	06	2TM *	3	12	0	121	79	7.90	2.02	336	272	294	21.4	38%	59%	5.35	49	19	32	5.3	5.9	1.1	8%	0.8	-50.6	-10	($11)
Ht/Wt	77 195	07	COL *	5	3	0	73	54	5.80	1.90	322			5.9	39%	67%	5.63	30	27	42	5.1	6.7	1.3	1%	0.1	-12.3	-8	($1)
Type	Pwr xFB	08	2TM	4	4	0	60	44	5.22	1.71	264	279	275	5.5	30%	70%	5.68	37	17	46	6.3	6.6	1.0	7%	0.9	-6.8	-36	$1
Health	A	09	PIT *	3	4	1	62	59	6.14	2.01	320			6.1	41%	68%	5.12	39	22	39	6.2	8.6	1.4	4%	0.5	-14.8	5	($3)
PT/Exp	D	10	SF *	5	2	9	56	65	3.86	1.39	209	204	205	4.8	28%	74%	4.20	33	12	55	5.8	10.4	1.8	7%	0.8	1.0	43	$8
Consist	B	1st Half		3	1	6	39	45	2.40	1.32	204			5.1	29%	81%	4.04	35	10	55	5.4	10.4	1.9	2%	0.2	7.7	54	$7
LIMA Plan	C	2nd Half		2	1	3	17	20	7.19	1.53	221			4.2	25%	57%	4.56	28	17	56	6.6	10.5	1.6	18%	2.2	-6.7	17	$1
Rand Var	-1	11	Proj	3	2	0	40	39	5.01	1.59	249			5.2	31%	69%	4.80	35	16	49	5.9	8.9	1.5	7%	0.9	-3.2	13	$1

2-0, 3.74 ERA in 34 IP at SF. Rising Dom, but it's tough to get past all the walks. Low hr/f kept high FB% from being a problem. He's been trying to stick in the majors since 2004; Ctl is standing in the way.

Beckett,Josh

		Yr	Tm	W	L	Sv	IP	K	ERA	WHIP	OBA	vL	vR	BF/G	H%	S%	xERA	G	L	F	Ctl	Dom	Cmd	hr/f	hr/9	RAR	BPV	R$
RH SP	30	06	BOS	16	11	0	204	158	5.02	1.30	249	251	238	26.1	27%	66%	4.09	45	17	38	3.3	7.0	2.1	16%	1.6	-11.8	60	$18
Ht/Wt	77 222	07	BOS	20	7	0	201	194	3.27	1.14	250	255	235	27.2	32%	74%	3.21	47	16	37	1.8	8.7	4.9	8%	0.8	30.5	133	$31
Type	Pwr	08	BOS	12	10	0	174	172	4.03	1.19	260	260	252	26.5	33%	68%	3.15	41	25	34	1.8	8.9	5.1	11%	0.9	6.9	131	$20
Health	D	09	BOS	17	6	0	212	199	3.86	1.19	249	258	226	27.3	30%	71%	3.26	47	21	32	2.3	8.4	3.6	13%	1.1	15.6	114	$26
PT/Exp	A	10	BOS	6	6	0	128	116	5.78	1.53	295	310	267	27.1	35%	65%	3.74	46	19	35	3.2	8.2	2.6	14%	1.4	-25.8	85	$2
Consist	A	1st Half		1	1	0	46	40	7.29	1.66	307			26.2	36%	56%	3.96	43	26	31	3.7	7.9	2.1	13%	1.2	-17.7	62	($2)
LIMA Plan	A+	2nd Half		5	5	0	82	76	4.94	1.46	289			27.6	34%	71%	3.62	47	15	38	2.9	8.3	2.9	15%	1.5	-8.1	99	$4
Rand Var	+5	11	Proj	14	9	0	196	181	4.09	1.26	254			26.4	31%	71%	3.43	45	20	34	2.7	8.3	3.1	13%	1.1	20.8	100	$20

Missed two months with back strain; injury probably affected him all year. xERA, BPV show that while he wasn't as good as 2007-09, skills were still solid. With h% reversion and full health, he could be a bargain.

Bedard,Erik

		Yr	Tm	W	L	Sv	IP	K	ERA	WHIP	OBA	vL	vR	BF/G	H%	S%	xERA	G	L	F	Ctl	Dom	Cmd	hr/f	hr/9	RAR	BPV	R$
LH RP	32	06	BAL	15	11	0	196	171	3.76	1.35	262	200	272	25.4	32%	73%	3.62	49	21	30	3.2	7.8	2.5	9%	0.7	19.2	83	$21
Ht/Wt	73 200	07	BAL	13	5	0	182	221	3.16	1.09	216	229	208	26.1	29%	75%	2.77	48	17	35	2.8	10.9	3.9	13%	0.9	30.1	146	$29
Type	Pwr	08	SEA	6	4	0	81	72	3.67	1.32	235	253	224	22.9	28%	76%	4.17	40	17	43	4.1	8.0	1.9	9%	1.0	6.8	51	$9
Health	F	09	SEA	5	3	0	83	90	2.82	1.19	217	214	211	22.8	28%	80%	3.49	42	17	40	3.7	9.8	2.6	9%	0.9	16.7	96	$12
PT/Exp	D	10	SEA	0	0	0	0	0	0.00	0.00							0.00											
Consist	B	1st Half		0	0	0	0	0	0.00	0.00							0.00											
LIMA Plan	C	2nd Half		0	0	0	0	0	0.00	0.00							0.00											
Rand Var	+5	11	Proj	4	5	0	87	82	4.03	1.32	239			24.6	29%	72%	3.76	45	18	37	3.9	8.5	2.2	11%	1.0	5.7	69	$7

Didn't make it back from 8/09 rotator cuff surgery. When healthy, dominates with stellar Cmd, GB%, and OBA. But he's never topped 200 IP. Let others chase the dream.

Beimel,Joe			W	L	Sv	IP	K	ERA	WHIP	OBA	vL	vR	BF/G	H%	S%	xERA	G	L	F	Ctl	Dom	Cmd	hr/f	hr/9	RAR	BPV	R$
LH RP 33	06	LA *	5	1	2	83	37	2.73	1.26	252	234	277	4.8	27%	81%	4.32	57	11	32	2.8	4.0	1.5	8%	0.8	18.0	33	$9
Ht/Wt 75 215	07	LA	4	2	1	67	39	3.88	1.29	249	188	294	3.4	29%	67%	4.39	48	18	35	3.2	5.2	1.6	1%	0.1	4.5	33	$6
Type Con	08	LA	5	1	0	49	32	2.02	1.45	266	278	263	3.0	32%	85%	4.45	47	19	34	3.9	5.9	1.5	0%	0.0	13.6	27	$6
Health A	09	2NL	1	6	1	55	35	3.58	1.37	268	258	282	3.3	30%	76%	4.73	39	15	46	3.1	5.7	1.8	6%	0.8	4.2	36	$3
PT/Exp D	10	COL	1	2	0	45	21	3.40	1.36	266	221	329	2.7	28%	79%	4.72	43	16	40	3.0	4.2	1.4	8%	1.0	3.4	16	$2
Consist A	1st Half		1	0	0	26	12	2.40	0.99	204			2.8	22%	76%	4.17	49	9	42	2.4	4.1	1.7	3%	0.3	5.3	36	$3
LIMA Plan C+	2nd Half		0	2	0	19	9	4.81	1.87	339			2.6	34%	81%	5.49	37	24	39	3.9	4.3	1.1	15%	1.9	-1.8	-11	($1)
Rand Var -3	11	Proj	2	3	0	51	27	4.08	1.46	278			3.0	30%	75%	4.84	43	18	40	3.4	4.8	1.4	9%	1.1	-4.4	16	$2

Inconsistencies abound... He might get help from S% one year, or GB rate another year, or his value might rest in getting LHers out. But to wager a roto bid that his ERA will continue to clear xERA by a run... not for me.

Belisario,Ronald			W	L	Sv	IP	K	ERA	WHIP	OBA	vL	vR	BF/G	H%	S%	xERA	G	L	F	Ctl	Dom	Cmd	hr/f	hr/9	RAR	BPV	R$
RH RP 28	06		0	0	0	0	0	0.00	0.00							0.00											
Ht/Wt 75 237	07	aa	1	0	0	25	21	3.96	1.60	269			6.3	31%	81%	5.67				5.0	7.6	1.5		1.4	1.6	35	$1
Type xGB	08	aa	4	4	9	57	27	6.49	1.91	335			7.2	36%	66%	6.93				4.4	4.3	1.0		0.9	-15.4	8	$0
Health A	09	LA	4	3	0	71	64	2.04	1.15	207	270	157	4.2	26%	84%	3.20	56	16	28	3.7	8.1	2.2	8%	0.5	18.8	81	$10
PT/Exp D	10	LA	3	1	2	55	38	5.05	1.28	250	257	246	3.9	28%	62%	3.26	61	17	22	3.1	6.2	2.0	16%	1.0	-7.0	67	$3
Consist D	1st Half		1	1	1	33	23	4.13	1.28	239			4.0	28%	68%	3.33	60	18	22	3.6	6.3	1.8	9%	0.6	-0.5	56	$2
LIMA Plan B	2nd Half		2	0	1	23	15	6.37	1.28	265			3.8	28%	52%	3.15	63	15	22	2.4	6.0	2.5	25%	1.6	-6.6	84	$1
Rand Var +5	11	Proj	4	2	0	65	47	3.86	1.33	252			4.3	29%	73%	3.47	60	16	24	3.4	6.5	1.9	12%	0.8	5.4	61	$5

Season shortened by non-injury issues (visa, personal reasons). xERA shows a classic example of small-sample volatility in RP: same xERA in 2009-10 yields ERAs three runs apart. Use xERA to set 2011 expectations.

Belisle,Matt			W	L	Sv	IP	K	ERA	WHIP	OBA	vL	vR	BF/G	H%	S%	xERA	G	L	F	Ctl	Dom	Cmd	hr/f	hr/9	RAR	BPV	R$
RH RP 30	06	CIN	2	0	0	40	26	3.60	1.55	276	240	295	6.0	30%	81%	4.77	48	17	35	4.3	5.9	1.4	11%	1.1	4.4	16	$2
Ht/Wt 76 231	07	CIN	8	9	0	178	125	5.32	1.44	297	298	303	25.8	33%	66%	4.20	42	22	36	2.2	6.3	2.9	12%	1.3	-19.6	75	$0
Type Con	08	CIN *	7	5	4	77	36	6.13	1.73	345	296	419	10.8	38%	63%	4.34	51	26	23	2.2	4.2	1.9	8%	0.6	-17.6	45	$1
Health B	09	COL *	4	2	9	89	58	4.25	1.37	291			6.7	33%	70%	4.26	40	21	40	1.9	5.9	3.0	7%	0.8	-0.7	71	$7
PT/Exp D	10	COL	7	5	1	92	91	2.93	1.09	245	232	253	4.9	31%	75%	2.85	46	20	33	1.6	8.9	5.7	8%	0.7	12.3	142	$12
Consist B	1st Half		3	3	1	50	53	2.70	1.06	230			5.2	31%	76%	2.76	49	16	35	2.0	9.5	4.8	7%	0.5	8.1	146	$7
LIMA Plan B	2nd Half		4	2	0	42	38	3.21	1.12	262			4.5	32%	74%	2.95	43	25	32	1.1	8.1	7.6	10%	0.9	4.2	139	$5
Rand Var 0	11	Proj	5	3	0	65	46	3.72	1.24	270			5.0	31%	73%	3.65	45	22	33	1.8	6.3	3.5	10%	1.0	3.9	89	$6

Picked an odd age for a huge Dom spike, with no evidence of a new pitch to explain it. Maybe some old dogs can learn new tricks. This one just learned how to become closer-worthy in his 30s.

Bell,Heath			W	L	Sv	IP	K	ERA	WHIP	OBA	vL	vR	BF/G	H%	S%	xERA	G	L	F	Ctl	Dom	Cmd	hr/f	hr/9	RAR	BPV	R$
RH RP 33	06	NYM *	3	3	12	72	79	3.59	1.49	301	308	348	6.1	39%	78%	2.93	51	26	23	2.5	9.8	4.0	15%	0.9	8.0	139	$10
Ht/Wt 75 250	07	SD	6	4	2	94	102	2.02	0.96	185	216	157	4.5	26%	79%	2.43	59	19	23	2.9	9.8	3.4	6%	0.3	27.8	135	$18
Type Pwr	08	SD	6	6	0	78	71	3.58	1.21	231	207	254	4.3	29%	71%	3.56	46	20	35	3.2	8.2	2.5	7%	0.6	6.7	84	$9
Health A	09	SD	6	4	42	70	79	2.71	1.12	216	275	138	4.1	30%	76%	2.94	48	18	35	3.1	10.2	3.3	5%	0.4	12.7	126	$25
PT/Exp A	10	SD	6	1	47	70	86	1.93	1.20	221	200	241	4.3	33%	83%	2.96	44	18	38	3.6	11.1	3.1	2%	0.1	18.0	124	$27
Consist A	1st Half		4	0	23	37	49	1.72	1.34	253			4.2	38%	88%	2.78	44	21	35	3.4	12.0	3.5	3%	0.2	10.4	146	$14
LIMA Plan C+	2nd Half		2	1	24	33	37	2.16	1.05	183			4.4	27%	77%	3.15	44	14	42	3.8	10.0	2.6	0%	0.0	7.6	100	$13
Rand Var -5	11	Proj	6	3	40	75	85	2.75	1.17	220			4.3	30%	78%	3.05	46	18	36	3.3	10.2	3.0	7%	0.6	10.1	117	$24

Everything you want in a closer: rock-solid and fully closer-worthy skill set, top-notch Reliability. This is not a PETCO-created mirage. Nary a wart to be found in this box, bid with confidence.

Bell,Trevor			W	L	Sv	IP	K	ERA	WHIP	OBA	vL	vR	BF/G	H%	S%	xERA	G	L	F	Ctl	Dom	Cmd	hr/f	hr/9	RAR	BPV	R$
RH RP 24	06		0	0	0	0	0	0.00	0.00							0.00											
Ht/Wt 74 185	07		0	0	0	0	0	0.00	0.00							0.00											
Type Con	08		0	0	0	0	0	0.00	0.00							0.00											
Health A	09	a/a	7	7	0	140	75	3.15	1.21	256			26.3	29%	74%	3.35				2.2	4.8	2.2		0.4	20.1	67	$13
PT/Exp D	10	LAA *	4	5	0	91	61	4.15	1.47	296	308	316	12.9	34%	71%	4.12	42	23	35	2.6	6.0	2.3	5%	0.5	-0.2	60	$4
Consist B	1st Half		2	1	0	36	24	4.31	1.46	310			9.2	36%	71%	3.71	46	25	29	1.8	6.1	3.4	8%	0.8	-0.7	86	$2
LIMA Plan C+	2nd Half		2	4	0	56	37	4.05	1.48	287			17.4	34%	71%	4.35	41	22	38	3.1	6.0	1.9	3%	0.3	0.6	43	$2
Rand Var 0	11	Proj	4	5	0	91	56	4.05	1.34	276			15.5	31%	71%	4.16	42	23	35	2.4	5.5	2.3	8%	0.8	1.4	56	$6

2-5, 4.72 ERA in 61 IP at LAA. Young sinkerballer showing slight Dom growth, but walk rate ballooned upon promotion. Small signs of something good here but not enough of a track record to invest in.

Benoit,Joaquin			W	L	Sv	IP	K	ERA	WHIP	OBA	vL	vR	BF/G	H%	S%	xERA	G	L	F	Ctl	Dom	Cmd	hr/f	hr/9	RAR	BPV	R$
RH RP 33	06	TEX	1	1	0	79	85	4.89	1.34	233	191	245	6.0	31%	62%	3.94	37	19	44	4.3	9.7	2.2	5%	0.6	-3.2	73	$5
Ht/Wt 75 220	07	TEX	7	4	6	82	87	2.85	1.17	227	172	268	4.8	30%	78%	3.44	37	24	39	3.1	9.5	3.1	7%	0.7	16.7	104	$15
Type Pwr xFB	08	TEX	3	2	1	45	43	5.00	1.67	240	184	282	4.7	29%	72%	5.58	27	17	56	7.0	8.6	1.2	9%	1.2	-3.6	-29	$2
Health F	09	TEX	0	0	0	0	0	0.00	0.00							0.00											
PT/Exp D	10	TAM	1	2	1	60	75	1.34	0.68	150	144	150	3.4	20%	91%	2.43	39	12	49	1.6	11.2	6.8	10%	0.9	20.8	174	$13
Consist F	1st Half		0	0	1	24	34	0.76	0.55	119			3.3	18%	100%	1.98	42	7	51	1.5	12.9	8.5	9%	0.8	9.9	211	$6
LIMA Plan B+	2nd Half		1	2	0	37	41	1.72	0.77	169			3.5	21%	88%	2.74	38	15	48	1.7	10.1	5.9	10%	1.0	10.9	150	$7
Rand Var -5	11	Proj	3	2	18	65	74	2.90	1.06	210			4.1	28%	77%	3.28	35	16	49	2.8	10.2	3.7	9%	1.0	8.1	122	$15

Rousingly successful comeback from 2009 rotator cuff surgery. Health will continue to be the overriding issue going forward, Rel grades underscore the risk. But in between DL stints, there is a legitimate reward here.

Bergesen,Brad			W	L	Sv	IP	K	ERA	WHIP	OBA	vL	vR	BF/G	H%	S%	xERA	G	L	F	Ctl	Dom	Cmd	hr/f	hr/9	RAR	BPV	R$
RH SP 25	06		0	0	0	0	0	0.00	0.00							0.00											
Ht/Wt 74 215	07		0	0	0	0	0	0.00	0.00							0.00											
Type Con	08	aa	15	6	0	148	61	4.07	1.33	290			26.2	31%	71%	4.58				1.6	3.7	2.3		0.8	4.2	43	$12
Health B	09	BAL	7	5	0	123	65	3.43	1.28	266	263	267	27.3	29%	76%	4.19	50	18	32	2.3	4.7	2.0	8%	0.8	15.5	50	$11
PT/Exp B	10	BAL	8	12	0	170	81	4.98	1.44	287	303	266	24.7	30%	69%	4.50	49	15	37	2.7	4.3	1.6	12%	1.4	-17.6	31	$4
Consist A	1st Half		4	5	0	80	29	6.20	1.60	318			21.3	32%	63%	4.89	50	14	36	2.6	3.3	1.3	11%	1.4	-20.4	17	($2)
LIMA Plan C+	2nd Half		4	7	0	90	52	3.89	1.28	257			29.1	27%	76%	4.16	48	15	37	2.8	5.2	1.9	13%	1.4	2.8	44	$6
Rand Var +1	11	Proj	10	10	0	174	86	4.24	1.36	278			25.7	29%	72%	4.36	49	16	35	2.4	4.4	1.8	10%	1.1	-1.6	42	$10

Owns GB skill, but half-season splits show importance of pairing GBs with even marginal Dom. Despite 2H gains, Sept fade (1.4 Cmd) keeps us skeptical. Treading a fine line between bad and less bad.

Berg,Justin			W	L	Sv	IP	K	ERA	WHIP	OBA	vL	vR	BF/G	H%	S%	xERA	G	L	F	Ctl	Dom	Cmd	hr/f	hr/9	RAR	BPV	R$
RH RP 26	06		0	0	0	0	0	0.00	0.00							0.00											
Ht/Wt 75 230	07		0	0	0	0	0	0.00	0.00							0.00											
Type GB	08	aa	4	9	0	118	48	6.09	1.70	294			17.1	30%	65%	5.86				4.7	3.6	0.8		1.0	-26.0	3	($4)
Health A	09	aaa	6	2	0	55	30	2.96	1.41	234			6.5	27%	79%	3.50				4.9	4.8	1.0		0.3	9.2	48	$6
PT/Exp D	10	CHC *	4	2	0	69	28	4.73	1.49	269	235	300	4.9	28%	68%	4.68	54	17	29	4.1	3.6	0.9	7%	0.7	-6.1	-14	$1
Consist D	1st Half		3	1	0	34	13	4.26	1.52	247			5.6	26%	72%	5.58	43	20	37	5.3	3.3	0.6	5%	0.5	-1.0	-63	$1
LIMA Plan F	2nd Half		1	1	0	35	15	5.20	1.47	290			4.4	31%	64%	4.06	59	16	25	2.8	3.8	1.3	10%	0.8	-5.1	29	($0)
Rand Var 0	11	Proj	2	3	0	44	20	4.97	1.61	285			6.2	30%	70%	4.73	55	17	28	4.3	4.1	1.0	9%	0.8	-3.2	-10	($0)

0-1, 5.18 ERA in 40 IP at CHC. Gets GBs, but with absolutely no complementary skills, his fate lies in the skills of the defense. Basically, this is just a batting practice pitcher throwing infield practice. Okay, let's turn two!

Berken,Jason			W	L	Sv	IP	K	ERA	WHIP	OBA	vL	vR	BF/G	H%	S%	xERA	G	L	F	Ctl	Dom	Cmd	hr/f	hr/9	RAR	BPV	R$
RH RP 27	06		0	0	0	0	0	0.00	0.00							0.00											
Ht/Wt 72 210	07		0	0	0	0	0	0.00	0.00							0.00											
Type	08	aa	12	4	0	145	104	4.63	1.44	294			24.4	34%	68%	4.83				2.4	6.4	2.7		0.7	-5.8	69	$9
Health B	09	BAL *	9	13	0	153	85	5.80	1.65	311	335	318	22.5	33%	67%	5.11	39	24	37	3.4	5.0	1.5	11%	1.3	-25.5	15	$1
PT/Exp D	10	BAL	3	3	0	62	45	3.03	1.33	267	253	279	6.5	31%	79%	3.88	47	16	37	2.7	6.5	2.4	7%	0.7	8.5	68	$5
Consist B	1st Half		1	1	0	46	34	1.75	1.12	230			6.7	27%	88%	3.70	45	15	39	2.5	6.6	2.6	6%	0.6	13.6	74	$6
LIMA Plan C	2nd Half		2	2	0	16	11	6.75	1.94	357			6.0	40%	66%	4.39	51	19	31	3.4	6.2	1.8	11%	1.1	-5.2	49	($0)
Rand Var -3	11	Proj	3	3	0	44	28	4.55	1.49	290			6.4	32%	72%	4.36	45	20	35	3.1	5.8	1.9	10%	1.0	-0.4	44	$2

PRO: Found a home in bullpen, rediscovered his minor-league skill set and became relevant.
CON: Tore labrum in Aug, chose rehab over surgery, which often means surgery will be coming anyway. Major risk for 2011.

RAY MURPHY

Betancourt,Rafael

Betancourt,Rafael		Yr	Tm	W	L	Sv	IP	K	ERA	WHIP	OBA	vL	vR	BF/G	H%	S%	xERA	G	L	F	Ctl	Dom	Cmd	hr/f	hr/9	RAR	BPV	R$
RH RP	35	06	CLE	3	4	3	56	48	3.84	1.12	247	221	254	4.5	29%	70%	4.20	26	17	57	1.8	7.7	4.4	8%	1.1	5.0	95	$8
Ht/Wt	74 200	07	CLE	5	1	3	79	80	1.48	0.76	186	241	147	4.3	25%	84%	3.20	27	20	54	1.0	9.1	8.9	4%	0.5	29.6	141	$19
Type	Pwr xFB	08	CLE	3	4	4	71	64	5.07	1.42	275	252	295	4.5	32%	68%	4.40	29	21	50	3.2	8.1	2.6	10%	1.4	-6.3	67	$5
Health	C	09	2TM	4	3	2	56	61	2.73	1.11	210	265	169	3.7	28%	78%	3.74	30	16	54	3.2	9.8	3.1	5%	0.6	10.9	98	$9
PT/Exp	C	10	COL	5	1	1	62	89	3.61	0.96	228	279	187	3.4	33%	69%	2.50	26	22	52	1.2	12.9	11.1	12%	1.3	3.1	204	$10
Consist	B	1st Half		1	1	1	31	37	4.69	1.30	288			3.6	38%	67%	3.19	26	26	48	1.5	10.8	7.4	10%	1.2	-2.6	160	$2
LIMA Plan	A	2nd Half		4	0	0	32	52	2.56	0.63	160			3.1	24%	73%	1.89	25	15	59	0.9	14.8	17.3	16%	1.4	5.7	247	$8
Rand Var	+3	11	Proj	4	2	3	58	67	3.41	1.09	231			3.7	30%	75%	3.34	27	19	53	2.2	10.4	4.8	10%	1.2	5.7	134	$9

Paid an unlikely visit to Vintage Eck territory. Soak in that Cmd for a minute: that's 8 BB/89 K. The "non-closer" tag is firmly affixed, and HR issues aren't going away, but he's a Holds machine and LIMA HOFer.

Billingsley,Chad

Billingsley,Chad		Yr	Tm	W	L	Sv	IP	K	ERA	WHIP	OBA	vL	vR	BF/G	H%	S%	xERA	G	L	F	Ctl	Dom	Cmd	hr/f	hr/9	RAR	BPV	R$
RH SP	26	06	LA *	13	7	0	160	128	3.79	1.47	247	328	213	22.7	29%	76%	4.48	48	16	36	4.9	7.2	1.5	8%	0.8	13.7	25	$13
Ht/Wt	73 245	07	LA	12	5	0	147	141	3.31	1.33	240	277	210	14.5	30%	78%	3.92	41	20	39	3.9	8.6	2.2	10%	0.9	20.3	69	$17
Type	Pwr	08	LA	16	10	0	201	201	3.14	1.34	249	274	225	24.4	32%	78%	3.40	49	20	31	3.6	9.0	2.5	8%	0.6	28.0	92	$22
Health	A	09	LA	12	11	0	196	179	4.03	1.32	238	257	229	25.2	29%	71%	3.82	45	18	36	3.9	8.2	2.1	9%	0.8	3.8	65	$16
PT/Exp	A	10	LA	12	11	0	192	171	3.57	1.28	246	252	236	26.0	31%	71%	3.41	50	18	32	3.2	8.0	2.5	5%	0.4	10.6	85	$16
Consist	A	1st Half		6	4	0	89	80	4.06	1.38	269			25.4	33%	71%	3.55	47	18	34	3.0	8.1	2.7	8%	0.7	-0.5	89	$6
LIMA Plan	C+	2nd Half		6	7	0	103	91	3.15	1.19	224			26.5	29%	71%	3.29	52	18	30	3.4	8.0	2.3	1%	0.1	11.1	81	$10
Rand Var	-1	11	Proj	16	8	0	203	185	3.37	1.28	242			24.3	30%	76%	3.51	48	19	33	3.4	8.2	2.4	9%	0.8	15.9	83	$21

Reasons he breaks out in 2011:
- Dom dip balanced by better Ctl and uptick in GB rate.
- Has always shredded RHers, still improving v. LHers.

Others think he's peaked, but you see... UP: sub-3.00 ERA.

Blackburn,Nick

Blackburn,Nick		Yr	Tm	W	L	Sv	IP	K	ERA	WHIP	OBA	vL	vR	BF/G	H%	S%	xERA	G	L	F	Ctl	Dom	Cmd	hr/f	hr/9	RAR	BPV	R$
RH SP	29	06	aa	7	8	0	132	66	6.38	1.70	327			20.3	35%	62%	6.44				2.9	4.5	1.5		1.0	-30.3	18	($2)
Ht/Wt	76 227	07	a/a	10	4	0	148	58	3.26	1.26	282			24.8	30%	75%	4.13				1.3	3.5	2.6		0.6	22.0	57	$14
Type	Con	08	MIN	11	11	0	193	96	4.05	1.36	291	295	289	25.1	31%	73%	4.33	45	21	34	1.8	4.5	2.5	10%	1.1	7.1	54	$12
Health	A	09	MIN	11	11	0	206	98	4.03	1.37	293	300	277	26.7	31%	74%	4.51	46	18	37	1.8	4.3	2.4	9%	1.1	10.8	53	$13
PT/Exp	A	10	MIN	10	12	0	161	68	5.42	1.45	299	285	318	25.1	30%	66%	4.37	51	17	32	2.2	3.8	1.7	13%	1.4	-25.5	37	$3
Consist	A	1st Half		7	6	0	93	33	6.00	1.65	326			26.5	33%	66%	4.92	48	17	35	2.5	3.2	1.3	12%	1.5	-21.4	15	($1)
LIMA Plan	C+	2nd Half		3	6	0	68	35	4.63	1.19	259			23.3	27%	65%	3.62	55	16	29	1.9	4.6	2.5	16%	1.3	-4.1	67	$4
Rand Var	+3	11	Proj	11	12	0	189	87	4.20	1.38	291			24.6	30%	73%	4.33	49	18	34	2.0	4.2	2.1	11%	1.2	-1.0	47	$10

Got tattooed in 1H, reinvented himself as an extreme GB guy in 2H. Rediscovered his Cmd after a brief exile to minors in August. GBs are nice, but lack of Dom limits upside. If Cmd holds, he can repeat 2008-09.

Blanton,Joe

Blanton,Joe		Yr	Tm	W	L	Sv	IP	K	ERA	WHIP	OBA	vL	vR	BF/G	H%	S%	xERA	G	L	F	Ctl	Dom	Cmd	hr/f	hr/9	RAR	BPV	R$
RH SP	30	06	OAK	16	12	0	194	107	4.82	1.54	306	314	304	27.1	34%	69%	4.78	43	20	37	2.7	5.0	1.8	7%	0.8	-6.3	38	$10
Ht/Wt	75 252	07	OAK	14	10	0	230	140	3.95	1.22	270	291	248	28.0	31%	68%	3.85	47	21	32	1.6	5.5	3.5	7%	0.6	15.7	81	$22
Type		08	2TM	9	12	0	198	111	4.69	1.40	275	256	286	25.9	30%	68%	4.52	44	20	35	3.0	5.1	1.7	9%	1.0	-9.3	32	$8
Health	A	09	PHI	12	8	0	195	163	4.06	1.32	264	252	271	26.7	30%	74%	3.91	41	20	39	2.7	7.5	2.8	13%	1.4	3.2	80	$15
PT/Exp	A	10	PHI	9	6	0	176	134	4.82	1.42	294	266	314	26.3	33%	70%	3.94	42	19	39	2.2	6.9	3.1	12%	1.4	-17.3	84	$6
Consist	A	1st Half		3	5	0	75	44	6.27	1.43	302			27.1	32%	59%	4.37	44	14	42	1.9	5.3	2.8	13%	1.7	-20.7	65	($1)
LIMA Plan	B	2nd Half		6	1	0	101	90	3.74	1.41	288			25.7	34%	78%	3.62	40	24	36	2.4	8.0	3.3	12%	1.2	3.4	98	$7
Rand Var	+3	11	Proj	10	8	0	189	139	4.30	1.36	278			26.0	31%	72%	4.01	42	20	38	2.4	6.6	2.7	12%	1.2	3.1	74	$11

Conditioning holding him back? Big guy whose splits show that he turns into a batting practice pitcher after 75 pitches. Expect him to continue underachieving vs. his skills until he lays off the donuts, or gets quicker hooks.

Blevins,Jerry

Blevins,Jerry		Yr	Tm	W	L	Sv	IP	K	ERA	WHIP	OBA	vL	vR	BF/G	H%	S%	xERA	G	L	F	Ctl	Dom	Cmd	hr/f	hr/9	RAR	BPV	R$
LH RP	27	06		0	0	0	0	0	0.00	0.00							0.00											
Ht/Wt	78 181	07	aa	4	5	4	54	57	2.81	1.17	249			5.4	33%	77%	3.29				2.1	9.5	4.5		0.5	11.0	141	$10
Type	Pwr FB	08	OAK *	3	5	10	70	63	3.11	1.25	259	193	256	4.5	32%	77%	3.59	43	18	38	2.4	8.1	3.4	7%	0.7	10.7	103	$11
Health	A	09	OAK *	5	3	2	85	74	4.43	1.34	275	250	218	5.6	34%	67%	4.32	32	17	52	2.4	7.9	3.3	5%	0.8	0.2	87	$8
PT/Exp	D	10	OAK	2	1	1	49	46	3.70	1.48	282	231	311	3.4	34%	80%	3.85	38	23	39	3.3	8.5	2.6	12%	1.3	2.7	79	$3
Consist	B	1st Half		2	1	0	28	31	4.18	1.61	295			3.5	38%	76%	3.74	37	24	39	3.9	10.0	2.6	9%	1.0	-0.1	90	$2
LIMA Plan	A	2nd Half		0	0	1	21	15	3.04	1.30	265			3.2	28%	87%	3.99	39	22	39	2.6	6.5	2.5	16%	1.7	2.8	64	$2
Rand Var	0	11	Proj	2	2	0	51	46	3.55	1.30	263			4.0	32%	77%	3.76	38	22	40	2.7	8.2	3.1	10%	1.1	3.3	91	$5

Minor-league BPIs held great promise, but he's proven to be just another lefty specialist who can't get enough righties out to escape the specialist role. Had hip labrum surgery in October, clouding Opening Day outlook.

Boggs,Mitchell

Boggs,Mitchell		Yr	Tm	W	L	Sv	IP	K	ERA	WHIP	OBA	vL	vR	BF/G	H%	S%	xERA	G	L	F	Ctl	Dom	Cmd	hr/f	hr/9	RAR	BPV	R$
RH RP	27	06		0	0	0	0	0	0.00	0.00							0.00											
Ht/Wt	76 215	07	aa	11	7	0	152	100	4.45	1.65	307			26.7	35%	75%	5.88				3.6	5.9	1.6		0.9	0.2	36	$6
Type	Pwr GB	08	STL *	12	5	0	159	79	4.68	1.44	267	321	283	23.9	28%	69%	4.53	52	19	29	3.7	4.4	1.2	10%	0.9	-8.0	9	$7
Health	A	09	STL *	8	7	0	134	91	5.09	1.82	321	410	234	21.2	37%	72%	4.58	53	18	29	4.4	6.1	1.4	8%	0.7	-14.9	22	($1)
PT/Exp	C	10	STL	2	3	0	67	52	3.61	1.29	240	253	238	4.6	29%	73%	3.65	53	16	31	3.6	7.0	1.9	8%	0.7	3.4	58	$4
Consist	A	1st Half		1	2	0	35	27	2.55	1.13	220			4.5	26%	79%	3.40	54	14	31	3.1	6.9	2.3	6%	0.5	6.4	74	$4
LIMA Plan	C+	2nd Half		1	1	0	32	25	4.78	1.47	262			4.8	31%	68%	3.92	51	18	30	4.2	7.0	1.7	10%	0.8	-3.0	42	$1
Rand Var	0	11	Proj	4	3	0	73	51	4.22	1.43	263			7.9	30%	71%	4.03	52	17	30	3.8	6.3	1.6	9%	0.7	1.0	41	$3

In 1H, fixed 2009 Ctl issues, and saw ERA improvement. In 2H, Ctl deserted him again, and ERA spiked accordingly. Dom and Ctl are an appealing combination, but, oh, those bases on balls.

Bonderman,Jeremy

Bonderman,Jeremy		Yr	Tm	W	L	Sv	IP	K	ERA	WHIP	OBA	vL	vR	BF/G	H%	S%	xERA	G	L	F	Ctl	Dom	Cmd	hr/f	hr/9	RAR	BPV	R$
RH SP	28	06	DET	14	8	0	214	202	4.08	1.30	262	284	235	26.6	33%	70%	3.41	48	20	32	2.7	8.5	3.2	9%	0.8	12.6	106	$23
Ht/Wt	74 220	07	DET	11	9	0	174	145	5.01	1.38	282	268	291	26.8	33%	66%	3.76	48	18	34	2.5	7.5	3.0	12%	1.2	-10.8	94	$12
Type		08	DET	3	4	0	71	44	4.29	1.56	272	291	255	26.6	30%	75%	4.89	47	16	37	4.5	5.6	1.2	10%	1.1	0.5	3	$3
Health	F	09	DET *	1	5	1	44	26	6.43	1.82	344	278	423	9.5	36%	69%	5.24	32	32	37	3.1	5.4	1.7	15%	1.9	-10.8	22	($2)
PT/Exp	C	10	DET	8	10	0	171	112	5.53	1.44	279	303	250	24.9	30%	64%	4.34	45	16	39	3.2	5.9	1.9	11%	1.3	-29.3	44	$3
Consist	B	1st Half		4	6	0	92	66	4.81	1.35	275			24.5	31%	66%	4.12	39	19	41	2.6	6.5	2.5	9%	1.1	-7.6	65	$4
LIMA Plan	C+	2nd Half		4	4	0	79	46	6.36	1.55	285			25.3	30%	61%	4.61	50	13	37	3.9	5.2	1.4	14%	1.6	-21.7	18	($1)
Rand Var	+3	11	Proj	9	10	0	174	115	4.55	1.41	275			26.0	30%	71%	4.32	45	17	38	3.1	5.9	1.9	12%	1.3	-0.7	47	$9

xERA says this wasn't all bad. Faded badly in 2H, unsurprising after two injury-shortened years. Decent skills in 1H, GB% rose every month, and he still owns 2006-07 skills. If health allows... UP: sub-4.00 ERA.

Bonine,Eddie

Bonine,Eddie		Yr	Tm	W	L	Sv	IP	K	ERA	WHIP	OBA	vL	vR	BF/G	H%	S%	xERA	G	L	F	Ctl	Dom	Cmd	hr/f	hr/9	RAR	BPV	R$
RH RP	29	06		0	0	0	0	0	0.00	0.00							0.00											
Ht/Wt	77 220	07	a/a	15	5	0	162	60	5.67	1.54	326			27.8	34%	63%	5.96				1.6	3.3	2.1		0.9	-24.2	26	$5
Type	Con	08	a/a	12	5	0	110	54	5.45	1.49	315			27.0	34%	64%	5.54				1.8	4.4	2.5		0.9	-15.6	42	$5
Health	A	09	DET *	5	6	0	136	60	5.75	1.57	324			22.6	34%	65%	4.31	56	16	28	1.9	4.0	2.1	13%	1.2	-21.8	53	($0)
PT/Exp	D	10	DET	4	1	0	68	26	4.63	1.56	305	275	329	6.5	32%	72%	4.80	48	18	34	2.9	3.4	1.2	8%	0.9	-4.1	10	$1
Consist	B	1st Half		3	0	0	37	18	2.70	1.14	219			5.5	23%	82%	4.03	53	16	32	3.2	4.4	1.4	11%	1.0	6.5	24	$4
LIMA Plan	C+	2nd Half		1	1	0	31	8	6.90	2.04	384			7.8	39%	66%	5.71	44	20	35	2.6	2.3	0.9	6%	0.9	-10.7	-6	($4)
Rand Var	0	11	Proj	3	3	0	63	25	4.75	1.50	307			10.2	32%	70%	4.66	48	18	33	2.3	3.6	1.6	9%	1.0	-2.9	29	$1

Skills went from mediocre to terrible in 2H, when he said he stopped throwing his knuckler much because he "lost the feel". Funny, it doesn't look like he has much of a feel for any of his other pitches either.

Bowden,Michael

Bowden,Michael		Yr	Tm	W	L	Sv	IP	K	ERA	WHIP	OBA	vL	vR	BF/G	H%	S%	xERA	G	L	F	Ctl	Dom	Cmd	hr/f	hr/9	RAR	BPV	R$
RH RP	24	06		0	0	0	0	0	0.00	0.00							0.00											
Ht/Wt	75 215	07	aa	8	6	0	96	69	5.33	1.60	308			22.9	36%	67%	5.71				3.1	6.5	2.1		0.8	-10.3	51	$4
Type	xFB	08	a/a	9	7	0	144	111	3.25	1.10	241			22.2	29%	72%	3.04				1.8	6.9	3.8		0.6	18.8	110	$18
Health	A	09	BOS *	5	7	0	142	88	5.38	1.53	285	395	258	19.8	31%	66%	5.06	42	14	44	3.7	5.6	1.5	8%	1.1	-16.3	21	$2
PT/Exp	D	10	BOS *	6	5	1	121	79	4.71	1.32	258	379	273	11.4	28%	67%	4.80	29	18	53	3.1	5.9	1.9	8%	1.2	-8.4	30	$6
Consist	C	1st Half		3	3	0	78	47	5.07	1.34	257			22.2	27%	66%	4.48				3.3	5.4	1.6		1.4	-9.0	29	$3
LIMA Plan	C+	2nd Half		3	2	1	42	32	4.03	1.27	260			5.9	30%	70%	4.40	29	18	53	2.5	6.8	2.7	6%	0.8	0.6	60	$4
Rand Var	0	11	Proj	3	2	0	52	36	4.35	1.37	270			5.8	30%	72%	4.77	31	18	51	3.0	6.3	2.1	8%	1.2	-3.1	42	$3

0-1, 4.70 ERA in 15 IP at BOS. Transitioned to bullpen mid-year with some success. xFB is a scary trait for a reliever, but 2H Cmd gains suggest pen is his best road to the show. Best to watch this experiment from afar.

RAY MURPHY

Boyer,Blaine		Yr	Tm	W	L	Sv	IP	K	ERA	WHIP	OBA	vL	vR	BF/G	H%	S%	xERA	G	L	F	Ctl	Dom	Cmd	hr/f	hr/9	RAR	BPV	R$
RH RP	29	06	ATL	0	0	0	0	0	0.00	0.00				2.8		40%	0.00	67	0	33	45.0	0.0	**0.0**	0%	0.0	0.1		
Ht/Wt	75 215	07	aaa	4	3	2	73	51	5.71	2.02	310			17.2	37%	69%	6.14				6.7	6.3	**0.9**		0.1	-11.3	47	($2)
Type	xGB	08	ATL	2	6	1	72	67	5.88	1.36	264	271	256	4.1	32%	58%	3.72	46	16	38	3.1	8.4	**2.7**	13%	1.3	-14.3	90	$2
Health	A	09	2NL	0	2	0	55	29	4.11	1.39	266	240	290	4.9	31%	68%	3.77	60	19	21	3.3	4.8	**1.5**	3%	0.2	0.5	35	$1
PT/Exp	C	10	ARI	3	2	0	57	29	4.26	1.54	268	352	198	4.7	30%	72%	4.01	66	13	21	4.6	4.6	**1.0**	7%	0.5	-1.7	3	$1
Consist	A	1st Half		1	2	0	25	10	5.40	2.00	319			5.3	35%	71%	5.56	59	13	28	6.1	3.6	**0.6**	4%	0.4	-4.3	-64	($2)
LIMA Plan	C+	2nd Half		2	0	0	32	19	3.37	1.19	224			4.2	25%	72%	2.83	73	13	15	3.4	5.3	**1.6**	14%	0.6	2.5	56	$3
Rand Var	0	11	Proj	**2**	**2**	**0**	**54**	**30**	**4.50**	**1.44**	**269**			**4.9**	**30%**	**69%**	**3.88**	**61**	**15**	**23**	**3.7**	**5.0**	**1.4**	**10%**	**0.7**	**1.8**	**30**	**$1**

Improved over ugly 1H, but that was really just a string of 4 ugly outings (4.1 IP, 9 ER). Ctl, Dom and Cmd are unappealing, but elite GB% and 2H Cmd gains give a glimmer of hope. Still, consider us skeptical.

Braddock,Zach		Yr	Tm	W	L	Sv	IP	K	ERA	WHIP	OBA	vL	vR	BF/G	H%	S%	xERA	G	L	F	Ctl	Dom	Cmd	hr/f	hr/9	RAR	BPV	R$
LH RP	23	06		0	0	0	0	0	0.00	0.00							0.00											
Ht/Wt	76 230	07		0	0	0	0	0	0.00	0.00							0.00											
Type	Pwr xFB	08		0	0	0	0	0	0.00	0.00							0.00											
Health	B	09	aa	2	1	0	16	19	5.06	1.38	274			5.7	36%	65%	4.70				2.8	10.7	**3.8**		1.1	-1.5	110	$2
PT/Exp	F	10	MIL *	1	2	1	50	66	3.62	1.37	222	151	284	3.7	34%	73%	3.56	30	22	49	5.1	12.0	**2.4**	4%	0.4	2.4	86	$4
Consist	C	1st Half		1	1	1	30	46	5.10	1.40	249			4.8	41%	61%	2.93	29	26	45	4.2	13.8	**3.3**	3%	0.3	-4.0	142	$2
LIMA Plan	B	2nd Half		0	1	0	20	20	1.37	1.32	178			2.8	24%	92%	4.55	30	18	52	6.4	9.1	**1.4**	4%	0.5	6.4	-0	$2
Rand Var	0	11	Proj	**1**	**2**	**0**	**51**	**63**	**3.69**	**1.35**	**208**			**3.4**	**30%**	**73%**	**3.92**	**30**	**20**	**50**	**5.4**	**11.1**	**2.0**	**5%**	**0.5**	**1.4**	**60**	**$4**

1-2, 2.94 ERA in 38 IP at MIL. Elite Dom and success vLH are attractive, but 2H success was reliant on fortuitous H%, S% and hr/f trio that won't repeat. Exciting arm, if he can conquer Ctl and health issues.

Braden,Dallas		Yr	Tm	W	L	Sv	IP	K	ERA	WHIP	OBA	vL	vR	BF/G	H%	S%	xERA	G	L	F	Ctl	Dom	Cmd	hr/f	hr/9	RAR	BPV	R$
LH SP	27	06	aa	0	0	0	3	2	18.00	3.00	515			17.8	55%	38%	16.54				0.0	6.0			3.0	-5.0	******	($1)
Ht/Wt	73 198	07	OAK *	4	11	0	148	125	5.13	1.39	275	214	324	19.3	33%	64%	4.27	37	18	45	2.9	7.6	**2.7**	8%	0.9	-11.4	75	$7
Type	Con FB	08	OAK *	8	5	0	125	82	3.58	1.37	277	319	272	17.8	31%	78%	4.52	38	18	44	2.6	5.9	**2.3**	8%	1.1	11.8	53	$11
Health	A	09	OAK	8	9	0	137	81	3.88	1.36	272	203	290	26.6	31%	72%	4.77	36	21	43	2.8	5.3	**1.9**	5%	0.6	9.6	36	$10
PT/Exp	B	10	OAK	11	14	0	193	113	3.50	1.16	249	271	242	26.2	27%	72%	4.07	41	18	41	2.0	5.3	**2.6**	7%	0.8	15.1	60	$18
Consist	A	1st Half		4	7	0	94	58	3.83	1.19	266			25.8	29%	71%	3.81	42	21	37	1.5	5.6	**3.6**	9%	1.0	3.6	79	$7
LIMA Plan	D+	2nd Half		7	7	0	99	55	3.19	1.12	232			26.6	26%	73%	4.31	39	16	45	2.5	5.0	**2.0**	5%	0.6	11.5	41	$11
Rand Var	-1	11	Proj	**10**	**12**	**0**	**181**	**113**	**4.02**	**1.29**	**266**			**26.3**	**29%**	**71%**	**4.38**	**39**	**19**	**42**	**2.4**	**5.6**	**2.3**	**8%**	**1.0**	**-2.0**	**52**	**$14**

Entered spotlight with perfection. PRO: elite Ctl led to career best ERA and WHIP. CON: low Dom means even a minor Ctl spike can ruin Cmd. xERA points to regression, IP spike adds another wrinkle.

Bray,Bill		Yr	Tm	W	L	Sv	IP	K	ERA	WHIP	OBA	vL	vR	BF/G	H%	S%	xERA	G	L	F	Ctl	Dom	Cmd	hr/f	hr/9	RAR	BPV	R$
LH RP	27	06	2NL *	7	3	7	81	77	4.42	1.39	273	333	252	5.1	33%	71%	3.61	44	25	31	3.0	8.5	**2.9**	13%	1.1	0.7	94	$10
Ht/Wt	75 222	07	CIN *	4	5	1	33	39	5.95	1.50	293	158	342	4.0	40%	58%	3.53	37	23	40	3.0	10.5	**3.5**	5%	0.5	-6.2	125	$3
Type	Pwr xFB	08	CIN *	2	2	1	56	67	3.06	1.54	265	260	274	3.5	36%	83%	3.75	35	27	37	4.7	10.7	**2.3**	9%	0.8	8.4	81	$5
Health	F	09	CIN	0	0	0	0	0	0.00	0.00							0.00											
PT/Exp	F	10	CIN *	0	2	1	34	36	3.49	1.02	197	106	271	3.2	25%	70%	3.50	37	7	57	3.0	9.6	**3.2**	9%	1.1	2.2	107	$3
Consist	A	1st Half		0	0	1	8	10	2.20	0.63	151			3.2	19%	76%	1.84	57	14	29	1.2	10.6	**9.2**	20%	1.1	1.8	196	$2
LIMA Plan	A	2nd Half		0	2	0	25	26	3.91	1.15	210			3.2	26%	69%	3.90	35	6	59	3.6	9.2	**2.6**	8%	1.1	0.3	83	$2
Rand Var	-2	11	Proj	**3**	**4**	**0**	**44**	**46**	**4.14**	**1.31**	**246**			**3.7**	**31%**	**71%**	**3.74**	**37**	**17**	**46**	**3.5**	**9.5**	**2.7**	**9%**	**1.0**	**2.2**	**91**	**$4**

LIMA favorite made victorious return from TJ surgery. Very limited sample size, but carved up LHers, improved Ctl and Cmd while retaining most of Dom. Not a bullpen foundation, but BPV says still LIMA-worthy.

Breslow,Craig		Yr	Tm	W	L	Sv	IP	K	ERA	WHIP	OBA	vL	vR	BF/G	H%	S%	xERA	G	L	F	Ctl	Dom	Cmd	hr/f	hr/9	RAR	BPV	R$
LH RP	30	06	BOS *	7	3	7	79	77	3.86	1.35	252			6.5	33%	71%	4.01	31	29	40	3.6	8.8	**2.4**	5%	0.5	6.8	70	$12
Ht/Wt	73 181	07	aaa	2	3	1	68	59	5.84	1.72	318			6.4	38%	66%	6.29				3.6	7.8	**2.2**		1.0	-11.6	54	($0)
Type	Pwr xFB	08	2AL	0	2	1	47	39	1.91	1.13	204	183	221	3.9	26%	83%	3.95	42	17	42	3.6	7.5	**2.1**	2%	0.2	14.1	56	$6
Health	A	09	2AL	8	7	0	70	55	3.36	1.10	196	204	191	3.6	22%	74%	4.38	33	19	48	3.7	7.1	**1.9**	9%	1.0	9.4	37	$11
PT/Exp	C	10	OAK	4	4	5	75	71	3.01	1.10	201	181	201	4.0	24%	78%	3.97	30	15	56	3.5	8.6	**2.4**	8%	1.1	10.4	67	$11
Consist	A	1st Half		3	2	0	38	40	2.84	1.00	170			3.7	22%	74%	3.90	23	13	64	3.8	9.5	**2.5**	5%	0.7	6.1	69	$6
LIMA Plan	C	2nd Half		1	2	5	37	31	3.19	1.20	230			4.3	26%	82%	4.03	36	16	49	3.2	7.6	**2.4**	12%	1.5	4.3	64	$5
Rand Var	-5	11	Proj	**3**	**4**	**6**	**58**	**51**	**3.72**	**1.21**	**223**			**4.1**	**26%**	**73%**	**4.19**	**33**	**17**	**50**	**3.6**	**7.9**	**2.2**	**9%**	**1.1**	**0.7**	**57**	**$8**

PRO: Uptick in Dom and Cmd shut down both LHers and RHers. CON: continues to thrive off abnormally low H%; uses home park to survive high FB%. xERA has long called for regression, heed its warning.

Broxton,Jonathan		Yr	Tm	W	L	Sv	IP	K	ERA	WHIP	OBA	vL	vR	BF/G	H%	S%	xERA	G	L	F	Ctl	Dom	Cmd	hr/f	hr/9	RAR	BPV	R$
RH RP	26	06	LA *	5	1	8	87	113	2.27	1.18	213	244	196	4.5	31%	84%	3.10	39	20	40	3.7	11.6	**3.1**	9%	0.7	23.8	127	$16
Ht/Wt	76 294	07	LA	4	4	2	82	99	2.85	1.15	230	200	247	4.0	32%	77%	2.68	49	22	29	2.7	10.9	**4.0**	10%	0.7	15.9	148	$12
Type	Pwr	08	LA	3	5	14	69	88	3.13	1.17	217	270	181	4.0	33%	72%	2.80	45	23	32	3.5	11.5	**3.3**	4%	0.3	9.7	134	$13
Health	A	09	LA	7	2	36	76	114	2.61	0.96	170	138	190	4.0	29%	74%	1.96	56	16	28	3.4	13.5	**3.9**	10%	0.5	14.9	184	$27
PT/Exp	B	10	LA	5	6	22	62	73	4.04	1.48	267	243	292	4.3	37%	73%	3.20	47	20	33	4.0	10.5	**2.6**	8%	0.6	-0.2	105	$12
Consist	C	1st Half		3	0	17	36	52	2.02	1.06	235			4.0	38%	81%	2.06	47	20	33	1.8	13.1	**7.4**	4%	0.3	8.8	213	$12
LIMA Plan	B+	2nd Half		2	6	5	27	21	6.77	2.03	306			4.7	36%	67%	5.23	46	23	30	7.1	7.1	**1.0**	11%	1.0	-9.0	-40	($0)
Rand Var	+3	11	Proj	**5**	**6**	**30**	**65**	**77**	**3.59**	**1.26**	**230**			**4.1**	**32%**	**73%**	**2.95**	**48**	**21**	**31**	**3.7**	**10.6**	**2.9**	**10%**	**0.7**	**9.6**	**117**	**$17**

A tale of two seasons. 1H, he was as untouchable as ever. 2H, Ctl flew the coop and ERA, WHIP, Dom and Cmd followed. Hidden injury? Overuse? BPV says still closer worthy, so... UP: 40 Sv... finally.

Buchholz,Clay		Yr	Tm	W	L	Sv	IP	K	ERA	WHIP	OBA	vL	vR	BF/G	H%	S%	xERA	G	L	F	Ctl	Dom	Cmd	hr/f	hr/9	RAR	BPV	R$
RH SP	26	06	aa	9	4	0	103	70	4.62	1.65	307			22.4	34%	75%	6.19				3.6	6.1	**1.7**		1.2	-1.3	28	$5
Ht/Wt	75 190	07	BOS *	11	6	0	148	168	2.92	1.10	219	217	133	21.2	30%	75%	2.99	38	29	33	2.8	10.2	**3.7**	8%	0.6	28.9	125	$24
Type	Pwr GB	08	BOS *	7	11	0	134	122	5.14	1.52	276	293	305	22.1	34%	67%	3.85	48	21	31	4.0	8.2	**2.1**	11%	0.9	-13.1	66	$6
Health	B	09	BOS *	14	6	0	191	144	3.93	1.30	249	284	228	24.4	28%	73%	3.71	54	18	29	3.3	6.8	**2.1**	13%	1.0	12.3	66	$18
PT/Exp	B	10	BOS	17	7	0	174	120	2.33	1.20	225	230	221	25.6	26%	82%	3.75	51	18	31	3.5	6.2	**1.8**	6%	0.5	38.7	47	$24
Consist	A	1st Half		10	4	0	92	64	2.45	1.25	229			25.6	27%	80%	3.81	51	18	31	3.7	6.3	**1.7**	4%	0.3	19.2	41	$13
LIMA Plan	D	2nd Half		7	3	0	82	56	2.20	1.15	220			25.6	25%	84%	3.68	51	17	32	3.2	6.2	**1.9**	8%	0.7	19.5	53	$12
Rand Var	-5	11	Proj	**14**	**11**	**0**	**196**	**149**	**3.72**	**1.29**	**243**			**24.2**	**28%**	**73%**	**3.75**	**51**	**18**	**31**	**3.4**	**6.9**	**2.0**	**10%**	**0.8**	**13.0**	**59**	**$19**

Reasons why he won't repeat 2010 breakout season:
1. xERA says ERA gains are a mirage.
2. Ctl, Dom and Cmd continue to slip.
Pay for 2010 xERA, not ERA.

Buehrle,Mark		Yr	Tm	W	L	Sv	IP	K	ERA	WHIP	OBA	vL	vR	BF/G	H%	S%	xERA	G	L	F	Ctl	Dom	Cmd	hr/f	hr/9	RAR	BPV	R$
LH SP	32	06	CHW	12	13	0	204	98	4.99	1.45	300	238	322	27.8	31%	70%	4.70	44	19	37	2.1	4.3	**2.0**	13%	1.6	-10.8	43	$9
Ht/Wt	74 230	07	CHW	10	9	0	201	115	3.63	1.26	268	314	258	28.0	29%	74%	4.32	43	18	39	2.0	5.1	**2.6**	9%	1.0	21.8	60	$18
Type	Con	08	CHW	15	12	0	219	140	3.79	1.34	280	293	277	27.4	31%	74%	3.88	50	19	31	2.1	5.8	**2.7**	10%	0.9	15.1	74	$19
Health	A	09	CHW	13	10	0	213	105	3.84	1.25	270	298	267	27.0	28%	73%	4.36	45	19	36	1.9	4.4	**2.3**	10%	1.1	16.1	52	$18
PT/Exp	A	10	CHW	13	13	0	210	99	4.28	1.40	293	275	303	27.5	32%	70%	4.47	46	16	38	2.1	4.2	**2.0**	6%	0.7	-3.7	43	$10
Consist	A	1st Half		7	7	0	103	49	4.53	1.44	297			26.5	32%	70%	4.53	46	16	38	2.3	4.3	**1.9**	7%	0.9	-5.0	39	$4
LIMA Plan	C	2nd Half		6	6	0	107	50	4.04	1.36	290			28.7	32%	71%	4.41	46	16	39	1.9	4.2	**2.2**	5%	0.6	1.3	47	$6
Rand Var	-1	11	Proj	**12**	**13**	**0**	**210**	**102**	**4.28**	**1.36**	**284**			**27.3**	**30%**	**71%**	**4.45**	**46**	**17**	**37**	**2.2**	**4.4**	**2.0**	**9%**	**1.0**	**-4.2**	**44**	**$12**

2010 was shaky, but should have been worse. Ctl still elite, but Dom dragging Cmd in wrong direction. Two year trend of xERA and BPV erosion but it'll probably stabilizes a bit. Still... DN: ERA closer to 5.00 than 4.00

Bullington,Bryan		Yr	Tm	W	L	Sv	IP	K	ERA	WHIP	OBA	vL	vR	BF/G	H%	S%	xERA	G	L	F	Ctl	Dom	Cmd	hr/f	hr/9	RAR	BPV	R$
RH SP	30	06		0	0	0	0	0	0.00	0.00							0.00											
Ht/Wt	76 220	07	aa	11	9	0	150	62	5.85	1.80	322			27.3	34%	67%	6.39				4.2	3.7	**0.9**		0.7	-25.7	10	($2)
Type		08	a/a	5	9	1	128	81	7.94	2.05	374			25.4	41%	62%	8.53				3.3	5.7	**1.7**		1.4	-57.4	8	($12)
Health	B	09	aaa	3	1	3	38	34	4.15	1.50	315			6.0	39%	72%	5.12				1.8	8.0	**4.4**		0.5	0.7	116	$4
PT/Exp	D	10	KC *	9	6	0	145	87	4.20	1.37	274	330	256	18.8	30%	71%	4.20	46	17	36	2.8	5.4	**2.0**	8%	0.9	-1.0	47	$8
Consist	F	1st Half		4	2	0	73	42	3.60	1.36	261			17.4	28%	77%	4.57	40	20	40	3.3	5.2	**1.6**	8%	0.9	4.9	21	$5
LIMA Plan	B	2nd Half		5	4	0	72	45	4.81	1.38	288			20.5	32%	65%	4.01	47	17	36	2.2	5.7	**2.6**	7%	0.8	-5.9	68	$4
Rand Var	0	11	Proj	**3**	**5**	**0**	**73**	**46**	**4.97**	**1.56**	**308**			**16.2**	**34%**	**70%**	**4.40**	**46**	**17**	**36**	**2.7**	**5.7**	**2.1**	**9%**	**1.0**	**-1.0**	**53**	**$1**

1-4, 6.12 ERA in 42 IP at KC. Former #1 pick dominated at AAA, then got destroyed at KC. PRO: decent Ctl
CON: everything else.
30 years old = not rosterable.

JOE HOFFER

Bumgarner,Madison

		W	L	Sv	IP	K	ERA	WHIP	OBA	vL	vR	BF/G	H%	S%	xERA	G	L	F	Ctl	Dom	Cmd	hr/f	hr/9	RAR	BPV	R$
LH SP 21	06	0	0	0	0	0	0.00	0.00							0.00											
Ht/Wt 76 215	07	0	0	0	0	0	0.00	0.00							0.00											
Type	08	0	0	0	0	0	0.00	0.00							0.00											
Health A	09 SF *	9	1	0	117	72	2.28	1.10	228	83	304	19.6	26%	82%	3.46	58	15	27	2.4	5.5	2.3	8%	0.6	27.6	70	$16
PT/Exp D	10 SF *	14	7	0	193	140	3.04	1.29	273	243	283	25.4	32%	79%	3.80	45	17	38	2.1	6.5	3.2	7%	0.7	23.3	85	$18
Consist A	1st Half	7	3	0	96	64	3.29	1.24	268			25.0	31%	75%	3.90	48	11	41	1.9	6.0	3.2	6%	0.7	8.6	82	$9
LIMA Plan C	2nd Half	7	4	0	97	76	2.78	1.33	277			25.8	33%	82%	3.74	45	18	38	2.2	7.1	3.2	7%	0.7	14.7	89	$9
Rand Var -3	11 Proj	11	6	0	174	119	3.47	1.25	262			25.9	30%	75%	3.90	46	17	37	2.2	6.2	2.8	8%	0.9	5.2	75	$15

7-6, 3.00 ERA in 111 IP at SF. 4 things we like in young SP's:
- Elite Ctl and Cmd
- Still-emerging Dom
- GB bias
- No signs of 2nd half fade

Sign us up.

Burnett,Alex

		W	L	Sv	IP	K	ERA	WHIP	OBA	vL	vR	BF/G	H%	S%	xERA	G	L	F	Ctl	Dom	Cmd	hr/f	hr/9	RAR	BPV	R$
RH RP 23	06	0	0	0	0	0	0.00	0.00							0.00											
Ht/Wt 72 190	07	0	0	0	0	0	0.00	0.00							0.00											
Type Pwr	08	0	0	0	0	0	0.00	0.00							0.00											
Health A	09 aa	1	2	9	55	43	2.78	1.11	213			5.5	26%	75%	2.39				3.1	7.0	2.3		0.3	10.4	92	$9
PT/Exp F	10 MIN *	2	4	2	67	52	5.52	1.66	298	351	258	5.6	35%	67%	4.30	47	19	34	4.2	7.0	1.7	9%	0.9	-11.4	38	($0)
Consist D	1st Half	1	1	0	36	27	3.53	1.43	269			5.0	32%	76%	3.99	46	20	34	3.5	6.8	1.9	5%	0.5	2.7	51	$2
LIMA Plan C+	2nd Half	1	3	2	31	25	7.79	1.92	328			6.3	38%	60%	4.66	50	14	36	4.9	7.2	1.5	13%	1.4	-14.0	25	($2)
Rand Var +3	11 Proj	1	2	0	29	23	4.66	1.48	268			5.6	31%	70%	4.15	47	18	35	4.0	7.1	1.8	10%	0.9	0.5	45	$1

2-2, 5.29 ERA in 47 IP at MIN. Followed decent 1H with 2H meltdown that earned demotion. 2H bb, h% and hr/9 left a bad taste, but xERA, Dom, GB% form the foundation of a LIMA-worthy skill set.

Burnett,A.J.

		W	L	Sv	IP	K	ERA	WHIP	OBA	vL	vR	BF/G	H%	S%	xERA	G	L	F	Ctl	Dom	Cmd	hr/f	hr/9	RAR	BPV	R$
RH SP 34	06 TOR	10	8	0	135	118	3.99	1.31	266	261	267	27.2	32%	72%	3.42	50	20	29	2.6	7.9	3.0	12%	0.9	9.4	100	$15
Ht/Wt 76 230	07 TOR	10	8	0	166	176	3.75	1.19	219	200	231	27.2	27%	74%	3.05	55	15	30	3.6	9.6	2.7	18%	1.2	15.5	108	$21
Type Pwr	08 TOR	18	10	0	221	231	4.07	1.34	253	262	231	26.9	33%	71%	3.32	49	19	32	3.5	9.4	2.7	10%	0.8	7.7	101	$23
Health B	09 NYY	13	9	0	207	195	4.04	1.40	248	217	282	27.1	30%	74%	4.09	43	18	39	4.2	8.5	2.0	11%	1.1	10.4	60	$18
PT/Exp A	10 NYY	10	15	0	187	145	5.25	1.51	279	286	285	25.1	32%	67%	4.20	45	18	37	3.8	7.0	1.9	11%	1.2	-25.7	47	$5
Consist A	1st Half	6	7	0	101	78	4.90	1.50	275			26.3	31%	70%	4.18	46	18	36	3.9	7.0	1.8	11%	1.2	-9.5	43	$4
LIMA Plan C+	2nd Half	4	8	0	86	67	5.67	1.52	284			23.8	32%	64%	4.21	44	17	39	3.6	7.0	2.0	11%	1.3	-16.2	52	$1
Rand Var +2	11 Proj	11	12	0	189	155	4.68	1.43	265			25.6	31%	70%	4.06	45	18	37	3.7	7.4	2.0	11%	1.1	5.2	56	$11

Reasons not to expect the 2006-08 version to return:
- 33% PQS-DIS shows volatility.
- 3-year Dom decline
- BPV in death spiral.

Age makes anything close to a major turnaround unlikely.

Burnett,Sean

		W	L	Sv	IP	K	ERA	WHIP	OBA	vL	vR	BF/G	H%	S%	xERA	G	L	F	Ctl	Dom	Cmd	hr/f	hr/9	RAR	BPV	R$
LH RP 28	06 aaa	8	11	0	120	39	7.27	1.81	332			22.7	34%	60%	7.02				3.7	2.9	0.8		1.2	-40.7	-13	($6)
Ht/Wt 73 200	07 aaa	4	5	0	70	23	5.99	2.11	348			23.5	37%	71%	7.53				5.4	3.0	0.6		0.6	-13.2	-2	($5)
Type Pwr GB	08 PIT *	2	2	3	74	53	3.94	1.51	248	171	328	4.7	28%	77%	4.63	48	19	33	5.3	6.5	1.2	11%	1.0	3.0	1	$4
Health A	09 2NL	2	3	1	58	43	3.12	1.11	181	186	176	3.3	20%	76%	3.81	49	21	30	4.4	6.7	1.5	13%	0.9	7.6	30	$6
PT/Exp D	10 WAS	1	7	3	63	62	2.14	1.14	226	273	182	3.5	30%	83%	2.75	54	21	24	2.9	8.9	3.1	7%	0.4	14.6	115	$8
Consist B	1st Half	0	4	0	28	26	2.92	1.41	271			3.2	35%	79%	3.18	54	20	26	3.2	8.4	2.6	5%	0.3	3.7	96	$1
LIMA Plan B+	2nd Half	1	3	3	35	36	1.53	0.93	188			3.8	25%	87%	2.41	55	23	22	2.5	9.2	3.6	10%	0.5	10.8	129	$7
Rand Var -4	11 Proj	2	6	6	73	65	3.35	1.27	247			4.0	30%	76%	3.25	52	21	27	3.1	8.1	2.6	11%	0.7	8.0	91	$8

Four reasons we're buying:
- xERA says ERA is for real
- Dramatic Ctl gains make for elite WHIP
- Miniscule FB% limit HR's
- Elite Cmd and BPV

These skills are closer-worthy.

Burres,Brian

		W	L	Sv	IP	K	ERA	WHIP	OBA	vL	vR	BF/G	H%	S%	xERA	G	L	F	Ctl	Dom	Cmd	hr/f	hr/9	RAR	BPV	R$
LH SP 29	06 aaa	10	6	0	139	98	5.43	1.64	298			24.4	33%	69%	6.00				3.9	6.3	1.6		1.2	-15.6	30	$4
Ht/Wt 73 181	07 BAL	6	8	0	121	96	5.95	1.70	291	306	281	15.1	34%	66%	5.02	38	22	40	4.9	7.1	1.5	9%	1.0	-21.6	12	$0
Type	08 BAL	7	10	0	130	63	6.04	1.66	311	321	306	19.2	33%	65%	5.37	36	24	40	3.5	4.4	1.3	9%	1.2	-27.0	-1	($1)
Health A	09 aaa	6	7	0	107	68	5.42	1.58	315			25.4	35%	67%	5.82				2.6	5.7	2.2		1.0	-14.6	42	$1
PT/Exp C	10 PIT *	9	9	0	161	91	5.15	1.51	279	308	265	20.4	30%	67%	4.80	42	19	39	3.8	5.1	1.3	9%	1.1	-22.6	10	$2
Consist B	1st Half	3	5	0	67	45	6.01	1.60	289			20.2	32%	64%	4.78	40	20	40	4.1	6.1	1.5	11%	1.3	-16.5	16	($1)
LIMA Plan C	2nd Half	6	4	0	94	46	4.54	1.45	272			20.6	29%	70%	4.78	45	17	38	3.6	4.4	1.2	8%	0.9	-6.2	6	$3
Rand Var 0	11 Proj	4	4	0	67	39	5.24	1.54	290			21.3	31%	68%	4.89	39	22	40	3.5	5.2	1.5	10%	1.2	-6.2	17	$1

'4-5, 4.99 ERA in 79 IP at PIT. Looked *almost* rosterable after his '09 stint in AAA, but that was just an anomaly. There's really nothing here worth analyzing, except perhaps why he still keeps getting work.

Bush,David

		W	L	Sv	IP	K	ERA	WHIP	OBA	vL	vR	BF/G	H%	S%	xERA	G	L	F	Ctl	Dom	Cmd	hr/f	hr/9	RAR	BPV	R$
RH SP 31	06 MIL	12	11	0	210	166	4.41	1.14	253	258	246	25.1	29%	64%	3.49	47	19	34	1.6	7.1	4.4	12%	1.1	1.9	109	$20
Ht/Wt 74 204	07 MIL	12	10	0	186	134	5.12	1.40	292	246	324	24.4	33%	66%	4.14	43	19	38	2.1	6.5	3.0	12%	1.3	-16.0	80	$10
Type FB	08 MIL	9	10	0	185	109	4.18	1.14	238	244	224	24.2	25%	69%	4.28	41	18	41	2.3	5.3	2.3	12%	1.4	2.0	51	$15
Health D	09 MIL	5	9	0	114	89	6.38	1.47	289	293	295	22.8	32%	58%	4.48	34	21	45	2.9	7.0	2.4	12%	1.5	-30.9	60	$0
PT/Exp A	10 MIL	8	13	0	174	107	4.54	1.51	287	277	293	24.1	31%	74%	4.74	39	18	42	3.4	5.5	1.6	11%	1.4	-11.4	26	$3
Consist A	1st Half	3	6	0	83	43	4.43	1.55	281			23.3	30%	74%	4.98	43	19	39	4.0	4.6	1.2	9%	1.1	-4.3	-3	$1
LIMA Plan C+	2nd Half	5	7	0	91	64	4.65	1.47	292			25.0	31%	75%	4.51	36	18	45	2.8	6.3	2.3	13%	1.8	-7.1	54	$3
Rand Var 0	11 Proj	9	13	0	181	122	4.47	1.41	279			23.8	31%	72%	4.49	39	19	42	2.9	6.1	2.1	11%	1.3	-7.7	48	$8

Finally put up a normal S%, but no longer displays the skill set of five years ago. GBs turned into FBs (and HRs), Dom and Cmd dried up. Slight sign of life in 2H gives hope that there may still be something left... Nah.

Byrdak,Tim

		W	L	Sv	IP	K	ERA	WHIP	OBA	vL	vR	BF/G	H%	S%	xERA	G	L	F	Ctl	Dom	Cmd	hr/f	hr/9	RAR	BPV	R$
LH RP 37	06 BAL	1	0	0	7	2	12.86	3.14	415			2.7	40%	60%	8.88	52	26	23	10.3	2.6	0.3	28%	2.6	-7.2	******	($2)
Ht/Wt 71 196	07 DET	3	0	1	45	49	3.20	1.42	230			5.0	31%	79%	3.97	41	21	38	5.2	9.8	1.9	7%	0.6	7.2	55	$6
Type Pwr xFB	08 HOU *	2	1	0	62	55	3.97	1.34	236	135	289	4.0	27%	76%	4.11	43	19	39	4.2	7.9	1.9	15%	1.4	2.3	50	$4
Health B	09 HOU	1	2	0	61	58	3.23	1.22	184	184	172	3.3	20%	82%	4.19	42	14	45	5.3	8.5	1.6	15%	1.5	7.3	30	$5
PT/Exp D	10 HOU	2	2	0	39	29	3.49	1.55	268	213	333	2.7	31%	80%	5.17	29	18	53	4.7	6.7	1.5	6%	0.9	2.5	2	$2
Consist B	1st Half	1	0	0	20	18	5.03	1.57	284			3.1	34%	71%	4.66	29	19	53	4.1	8.2	2.0	10%	1.4	-2.5	44	$0
LIMA Plan C	2nd Half	1	2	0	19	11	1.89	1.53	251			2.4	29%	89%	5.73	28	18	53	5.2	5.2	1.0	3%	0.5	5.0	-41	$1
Rand Var -5	11 Proj	2	2	0	58	48	4.03	1.59	272			3.2	31%	79%	4.87	36	18	46	4.8	7.4	1.5	10%	1.2	-5.2	18	$2

Continues to post solid ERAs despite the utter lack of control and periodic gopheritis. H% and S% have often swooped in to save the day, but how long can that last? Heed that 1st half... DN: 5.00 ERA

Cahill,Trevor

		W	L	Sv	IP	K	ERA	WHIP	OBA	vL	vR	BF/G	H%	S%	xERA	G	L	F	Ctl	Dom	Cmd	hr/f	hr/9	RAR	BPV	R$
RH SP 23	06	0	0	0	0	0	0.00	0.00							0.00											
Ht/Wt 75 211	07	0	0	0	0	0	0.00	0.00							0.00											
Type GB	08 aa	6	1	0	37	29	2.08	1.08	186			21.1	23%	83%	2.14				3.9	7.2	1.8		0.5	10.1	85	$8
Health A	09 OAK	10	13	0	179	90	4.63	1.44	269	286	252	24.3	28%	72%	4.80	48	18	34	3.6	4.5	1.3	13%	1.4	-4.0	10	$8
PT/Exp B	10 OAK	18	8	0	197	118	2.97	1.11	218	237	198	26.4	24%	77%	3.57	56	15	29	2.9	5.4	1.9	11%	0.9	28.3	53	$25
Consist D	1st Half	8	2	0	82	56	2.74	1.05	209			25.0	23%	78%	3.43	54	14	32	2.7	6.1	2.2	11%	0.9	14.1	69	$12
LIMA Plan F	2nd Half	10	6	0	115	62	3.14	1.15	225			27.5	24%	76%	3.66	57	16	27	3.0	4.9	1.6	11%	0.9	14.1	42	$13
Rand Var -3	11 Proj	17	11	0	203	121	3.64	1.32	257			25.3	28%	76%	4.04	52	16	31	3.1	5.4	1.7	11%	1.0	6.1	43	$19

Superior results backed by mediocre skills. Throws GB with the best of them, but 2H Dom, Cmd and BPV are uninspiring. As H% and S% regress, ERA is going to soar... DN: 4.50 ERA.

Cain,Matt

		W	L	Sv	IP	K	ERA	WHIP	OBA	vL	vR	BF/G	H%	S%	xERA	G	L	F	Ctl	Dom	Cmd	hr/f	hr/9	RAR	BPV	R$
RH SP 26	06 SF	13	12	0	190	179	4.16	1.28	226	217	227	25.0	28%	69%	4.30	36	16	48	4.1	8.5	2.1	7%	0.9	7.6	55	$18
Ht/Wt 75 246	07 SF	7	16	0	200	163	3.65	1.26	235	248	224	26.1	28%	72%	4.29	39	16	45	3.6	7.3	2.1	5%	0.6	19.3	53	$17
Type FB	08 SF	8	14	0	218	186	3.76	1.36	251	268	235	27.4	30%	74%	4.38	33	23	44	3.8	7.7	2.0	7%	0.8	13.6	48	$14
Health A	09 SF	14	8	0	218	171	2.89	1.18	231	233	231	27.1	27%	80%	4.04	39	19	42	3.0	7.1	2.3	8%	0.9	34.8	63	$20
PT/Exp A	10 SF	13	11	0	223	177	3.14	1.08	223	225	217	27.1	26%	75%	3.85	36	17	47	2.5	7.1	2.9	7%	0.9	24.0	76	$24
Consist A	1st Half	6	7	0	115	82	2.98	1.16	225			27.5	26%	76%	4.31	32	20	48	3.1	6.4	2.1	5%	0.6	14.6	43	$11
LIMA Plan C	2nd Half	7	4	0	109	95	3.31	1.00	221			26.6	26%	73%	3.39	41	14	45	1.8	7.9	4.3	10%	1.2	9.4	112	$13
Rand Var -3	11 Proj	15	8	0	218	178	3.26	1.16	240			27.0	28%	76%	3.89	37	18	45	2.4	7.3	3.0	8%	0.9	6.7	82	$24

Combined good 1H luck with brilliant 2H skills for super season. Multi-year Ctl, Cmd and BPV trends are for real. May not hold all of those 2H gains, but this is a AAA-reliability workhorse.

JOE HOFFER

Camp,Shawn			W	L	Sv	IP	K	ERA	WHIP	OBA	vL	vR	BF/G	H%	S%	xERA	G	L	F	Ctl	Dom	Cmd	hr/f	hr/9	RAR	BPV	R$
RH RP	35	06 TAM	7	4	4	75	53	4.68	1.49	305	370	284	4.4	35%	71%	3.58	57	18	24	2.3	6.4	**2.8**	15%	1.1	-1.1	88	$7
Ht/Wt	72 204	07 TAM	0	3	0	40	36	7.20	2.03	358			4.0	42%	66%	3.86	57	21	22	4.1	8.1	**2.0**	23%	1.6	-13.3	72	($3)
Type	GB	08 TOR *	4	1	4	49	41	3.29	1.14	246	356	204	4.3	31%	71%	3.06	54	19	27	2.0	7.6	**3.8**	5%	0.4	6.5	114	$8
Health	A	09 TOR	2	6	1	80	58	3.50	1.28	245	260	230	5.7	28%	75%	3.69	55	17	28	3.3	6.5	**2.0**	10%	0.8	9.4	63	$7
PT/Exp	D	10 TOR	4	3	2	72	46	2.99	1.23	258	299	234	4.3	29%	80%	3.63	52	17	31	2.2	5.7	**2.6**	11%	1.0	10.3	73	$8
Consist	A	1st Half	2	1	0	44	26	2.47	1.01	221			4.5	23%	84%	3.36	55	14	31	1.9	5.4	**2.9**	15%	1.2	9.0	79	$6
LIMA Plan	B	2nd Half	2	2	2	29	20	3.78	1.57	309			4.0	36%	77%	4.03	48	20	32	2.8	6.3	**2.2**	6%	0.6	1.3	63	$2
Rand Var	-2	11 Proj	**4**	**4**	**0**	**73**	**52**	**3.60**	**1.34**	**271**			**4.5**	**31%**	**76%**	**3.64**	**53**	**18**	**29**	**2.6**	**6.5**	**2.5**	**10%**	**0.9**	**5.8**	**77**	**$6**

Lots of GBs and just enough Dom have kept his xERA in the '3's and R$ in the black. Despite solid BPIs, he typically never gets drafted but often ends up as an injury replacement to preserve ERA in deep leagues.

Capps,Matt			W	L	Sv	IP	K	ERA	WHIP	OBA	vL	vR	BF/G	H%	S%	xERA	G	L	F	Ctl	Dom	Cmd	hr/f	hr/9	RAR	BPV	R$
RH RP	27	06 PIT	9	1	1	80	56	3.82	1.16	264	250	275	3.8	29%	73%	3.91	41	20	40	1.3	6.3	**4.7**	12%	1.3	6.6	95	$11
Ht/Wt	74 245	07 PIT	4	7	18	79	64	2.28	1.01	223	281	181	4.1	27%	80%	3.94	31	19	50	1.8	7.3	**4.0**	4%	0.6	20.9	91	$18
Type		08 PIT	2	3	21	54	39	3.02	0.97	237	222	245	4.3	27%	72%	3.75	31	23	46	0.8	6.5	**7.8**	7%	0.8	8.3	104	$14
Health	B	09 PIT	4	8	27	54	46	5.80	1.66	323	342	306	4.4	37%	69%	4.31	41	19	41	2.8	7.6	**2.7**	14%	1.7	-10.8	80	$9
PT/Exp	B	10 2TM	5	3	42	73	59	2.47	1.26	267	248	280	4.1	32%	84%	3.32	50	19	31	2.1	7.3	**3.5**	9%	0.7	14.5	102	$22
Consist	B	1st Half	2	3	22	37	32	3.19	1.39	298			4.2	36%	81%	3.37	47	19	34	1.7	7.8	**4.6**	10%	1.0	4.0	120	$10
LIMA Plan	C	2nd Half	3	0	20	36	27	1.74	1.13	232			4.1	28%	87%	3.26	53	19	28	2.5	6.7	**2.7**	7%	0.5	10.5	84	$12
Rand Var	-5	11 Proj	**5**	**5**	**25**	**73**	**58**	**3.33**	**1.22**	**259**			**4.1**	**30%**	**77%**	**3.64**	**44**	**19**	**37**	**2.1**	**7.2**	**3.4**	**10%**	**1.0**	**5.1**	**94**	**$16**

Bounced back from 2009's h%-induced meltdown, and then some. Growth of GB% along with elite Cmd validates closer-worthiness; Sv total earns him the "proven closer" label that should help him keep the role.

Capuano,Chris			W	L	Sv	IP	K	ERA	WHIP	OBA	vL	vR	BF/G	H%	S%	xERA	G	L	F	Ctl	Dom	Cmd	hr/f	hr/9	RAR	BPV	R$
LH RP	32	06 MIL	11	12	0	221	174	4.03	1.25	269	273	264	27.1	31%	72%	3.93	40	20	40	1.9	7.1	**3.7**	11%	1.2	12.5	94	$19
Ht/Wt	74 220	07 MIL	5	12	0	150	132	5.10	1.49	287	259	293	22.8	34%	68%	4.12	43	18	39	3.2	7.9	**2.4**	11%	1.2	-12.5	76	$5
Type		08 MIL	0	0	0	0	0	0.00	0.00							0.00											
Health	F	09 MIL	0	0	0	0	0	0.00	0.00							0.00											
PT/Exp	F	10 MIL *	5	5	0	91	68	3.39	1.26	258	224	272	13.6	30%	76%	3.87	43	17	40	2.5	6.8	**2.7**	8%	0.9	7.0	75	$7
Consist	F	1st Half	1	2	0	33	21	2.53	1.26	275			15.3	33%	78%	3.79	48	15	37	1.7	5.8	**3.4**	0%	0.0	6.1	85	$3
LIMA Plan	C+	2nd Half	4	3	0	58	47	3.88	1.26	248			12.8	28%	75%	3.85	42	17	41	2.9	7.3	**2.5**	13%	1.4	1.0	72	$5
Rand Var	-1	11 Proj	**9**	**8**	**0**	**152**	**121**	**4.08**	**1.31**	**264**			**23.8**	**31%**	**71%**	**3.92**	**43**	**18**	**39**	**2.7**	**7.2**	**2.7**	**9%**	**1.0**	**4.2**	**77**	**$11**

4-4, 3.95 ERA in 66 IP at MIL. Made it all the way back from two Tommy John surgeries, fully reclaimed his prior skills in 2H. Once you display a skill you own it, so if health allows... UP: 15 wins, sub-3.75 ERA.

Carmona,Fausto			W	L	Sv	IP	K	ERA	WHIP	OBA	vL	vR	BF/G	H%	S%	xERA	G	L	F	Ctl	Dom	Cmd	hr/f	hr/9	RAR	BPV	R$
RH SP	27	06 CLE *	2	13	0	102	85	5.75	1.55	294	299	298	10.4	35%	63%	3.64	60	13	27	3.4	7.5	**2.2**	12%	1.0	-15.0	80	$2
Ht/Wt	76 230	07 CLE	19	8	0	215	137	3.06	1.21	247	275	216	27.7	28%	77%	3.27	64	14	22	2.6	5.7	**2.2**	11%	0.7	38.4	77	$27
Type	xGB	08 CLE	8	7	0	121	58	5.44	1.62	270	303	230	24.9	30%	65%	4.49	63	15	22	5.2	4.3	**0.8**	8%	0.5	-16.3	-22	$1
Health	B	09 CLE *	7	15	0	165	107	5.82	1.64	295	331	245	25.1	32%	66%	4.38	55	18	27	4.2	5.8	**1.4**	16%	1.3	-28.0	25	$0
PT/Exp	B	10 CLE	13	14	0	210	124	3.77	1.31	255	269	244	26.9	28%	72%	3.88	56	14	31	3.1	5.3	**1.7**	8%	0.7	9.7	46	$15
Consist	A	1st Half	7	7	0	110	57	3.69	1.29	248			27.1	27%	72%	3.92	58	13	29	3.2	4.7	**1.5**	7%	0.6	6.0	34	$8
LIMA Plan	D	2nd Half	6	7	0	101	67	3.85	1.33	263			26.7	30%	73%	3.83	53	14	33	3.0	6.0	**2.0**	10%	0.9	3.6	59	$7
Rand Var	0	11 Proj	**13**	**13**	**0**	**199**	**121**	**4.22**	**1.40**	**270**			**26.0**	**30%**	**71%**	**3.90**	**57**	**15**	**28**	**3.2**	**5.5**	**1.7**	**10%**	**0.9**	**9.4**	**48**	**$13**

Nice recovery toward the skills he displayed in his 2007 career year, although neither Ctl nor GB% quite made it back to those peak levels. Still, if he can hold onto the 2H Cmd gains, he can repeat to 2010 levels.

Carpenter,Chris			W	L	Sv	IP	K	ERA	WHIP	OBA	vL	vR	BF/G	H%	S%	xERA	G	L	F	Ctl	Dom	Cmd	hr/f	hr/9	RAR	BPV	R$
RH SP	35	06 STL	15	8	0	221	184	3.09	1.07	237	266	210	27.6	28%	75%	3.08	53	18	28	1.7	7.5	**4.3**	12%	0.9	38.1	119	$30
Ht/Wt	78 230	07 STL	0	1	0	6	3	7.50	1.67	347	375	300	27.5	39%	50%	2.82	65	26	9	1.5	4.5	**3.0**	0%	0.0	-2.3	84	($0)
Type	GB	08 STL	0	1	0	15	7	1.76	1.31	271	158	351	16.2	31%	85%	4.01	51	24	24	2.4	4.1	**1.8**	0%	0.0	4.7	40	$1
Health	F	09 STL	17	4	0	193	144	2.24	1.01	223	239	214	27.0	27%	78%	3.08	55	17	28	1.8	6.7	**3.8**	4%	0.3	46.3	106	$30
PT/Exp	A	10 STL	16	9	0	235	179	3.22	1.18	244	239	248	27.5	29%	75%	3.41	51	17	32	2.4	6.9	**2.8**	9%	0.8	23.1	87	$23
Consist	B	1st Half	9	2	0	120	105	3.16	1.21	244			27.5	29%	79%	3.23	52	17	31	2.7	7.9	**2.9**	13%	1.1	12.7	99	$13
LIMA Plan	C	2nd Half	7	7	0	115	74	3.28	1.14	244			27.6	28%	72%	3.60	51	16	33	2.1	5.8	**2.7**	6%	0.5	10.5	76	$11
Rand Var	0	11 Proj	**13**	**7**	**0**	**189**	**142**	**3.10**	**1.18**	**247**			**26.6**	**29%**	**75%**	**3.32**	**53**	**19**	**28**	**2.3**	**6.8**	**3.0**	**9%**	**0.7**	**19.1**	**91**	**$20**

Defied injury history with second straight healthy season and only minor skill erosion. Skills are not in question at this point, but can you bet on third straight healthy year? Health grade is really the only data point that matters here.

Carrasco,Carlos			W	L	Sv	IP	K	ERA	WHIP	OBA	vL	vR	BF/G	H%	S%	xERA	G	L	F	Ctl	Dom	Cmd	hr/f	hr/9	RAR	BPV	R$
RH SP	24	06	0	0	0	0	0	0.00	0.00							0.00											
Ht/Wt	75 215	07 aa	6	4	0	70	44	5.50	1.63	263			22.8	28%	69%	5.58				5.6	5.7	**1.0**		1.3	-9.0	17	$2
Type	Pwr xGB	08 a/a	9	9	0	151	138	4.14	1.39	266			25.0	32%	72%	4.48				3.3	8.2	**2.5**		1.0	3.1	74	$12
Health	A	09 CLE *	11	14	0	179	152	5.69	1.42	283	367	431	25.1	33%	61%	3.48	48	27	25	2.7	7.6	**2.8**	17%	1.2	-27.5	90	$4
PT/Exp	C	10 CLE *	12	8	0	195	156	3.93	1.31	264	193	356	25.7	31%	73%	3.29	57	14	29	2.7	7.2	**2.7**	12%	1.0	5.1	92	$16
Consist	B	1st Half	7	3	0	91	70	4.54	1.45	278			26.6	31%	73%	5.02				3.3	6.9	**2.1**		1.4	-4.5	44	$5
LIMA Plan	C+	2nd Half	5	5	0	104	86	3.39	1.19	251			25.0	31%	72%	3.04	57	14	29	2.2	7.5	**3.4**	8%	0.6	9.6	111	$10
Rand Var	+1	11 Proj	**12**	**10**	**0**	**189**	**153**	**4.06**	**1.35**	**263**			**25.1**	**31%**	**71%**	**3.45**	**55**	**17**	**28**	**3.1**	**7.3**	**2.4**	**11%**	**0.8**	**19.5**	**82**	**$15**

2-2, 3.83 ERA in 45 IP at CLE. Shook off 1.5 years of struggle with big 2H breakout, acquitted self well in Sept callup (97 BPV in CLE). Now inked into 2011 rotation, has the Cmd and GB% to make a smooth transition.

Carrasco,D.J.			W	L	Sv	IP	K	ERA	WHIP	OBA	vL	vR	BF/G	H%	S%	xERA	G	L	F	Ctl	Dom	Cmd	hr/f	hr/9	RAR	BPV	R$
RH RP	33	06 JPN	0	3	0	10	9	15.30	3.20	438			20.4	50%	52%	14.49				9.0	8.1	**0.9**		2.7	-13.3	-46	($4)
Ht/Wt	75 220	07 aaa	5	14	0	137	89	7.81	2.13	365			20.4	40%	64%	8.62				4.6	5.8	**1.3**		1.3	-56.6	4	($14)
Type	Pwr	08 CHW *	3	1	1	64	51	4.10	1.27	244	186	244	6.8	30%	66%	3.54	51	21	28	3.2	7.2	**2.2**	4%	0.3	2.0	71	$6
Health	A	09 CHW	5	1	0	93	62	3.76	1.41	281	317	251	8.3	33%	73%	4.19	47	20	33	2.8	6.0	**2.1**	5%	0.5	7.9	57	$7
PT/Exp	C	10 2NL	3	2	0	78	65	3.68	1.30	235	260	227	5.2	29%	72%	3.70	48	21	32	3.9	7.5	**1.9**	7%	0.6	3.3	54	$5
Consist	B	1st Half	1	2	0	42	32	3.88	1.32	244			4.9	30%	70%	3.82	46	23	31	3.7	6.9	**1.9**	5%	0.4	0.7	49	$2
LIMA Plan	C+	2nd Half	2	0	0	37	33	3.44	1.28	225			5.7	28%	75%	3.56	50	18	32	4.2	8.1	**1.9**	9%	0.7	2.6	61	$3
Rand Var	-1	11 Proj	**3**	**2**	**0**	**73**	**57**	**4.19**	**1.40**	**262**			**6.7**	**31%**	**71%**	**3.90**	**48**	**20**	**32**	**3.6**	**7.0**	**2.0**	**8%**	**0.7**	**2.2**	**56**	**$4**

His Ctl and Dom bounce around seemingly in tandem, but in all cases his grip on the 2.0 Cmd level is about as secure as on a wet bar of soap. May get a SP look in 2011, but until he owns that Cmd level, stay clear.

Cashner,Andrew			W	L	Sv	IP	K	ERA	WHIP	OBA	vL	vR	BF/G	H%	S%	xERA	G	L	F	Ctl	Dom	Cmd	hr/f	hr/9	RAR	BPV	R$
RH RP	24	06	0	0	0	0	0	0.00	0.00							0.00											
Ht/Wt	78 210	07	0	0	0	0	0	0.00	0.00							0.00											
Type	Pwr	08	0	0	0	0	0	0.00	0.00							0.00											
Health	A	09 aa	3	4	0	58	34	4.47	1.46	250			21.2	30%	66%	3.51				4.6	5.3	**1.1**		0.0	-1.1	60	$2
PT/Exp	D	10 CHC *	8	7	0	111	99	3.51	1.29	240	300	246	7.3	30%	74%	3.52	48	19	33	3.6	8.0	**2.2**	9%	0.7	6.9	74	$10
Consist	A	1st Half	6	4	0	72	58	2.30	1.09	226			12.6	28%	80%	3.26	53	13	34	2.4	7.3	**3.0**	4%	0.4	15.2	97	$10
LIMA Plan	C+	2nd Half	2	3	0	39	41	5.73	1.65	265			4.4	33%	68%	3.98	46	21	32	5.7	9.4	**1.6**	17%	1.4	-8.3	39	($0)
Rand Var	0	11 Proj	**4**	**5**	**0**	**73**	**58**	**3.97**	**1.43**	**250**			**8.3**	**30%**	**73%**	**4.11**	**47**	**20**	**33**	**4.5**	**7.2**	**1.6**	**9%**	**0.7**	**0.3**	**34**	**$4**

2-6, 4.80 ERA in 54 IP at CHC. SP prospect transitioned to pen to help CHC. Ctl struggles (5.0 Ctl in CHC) overshadowed nice GB/Dom skill base in debut, but that base gives him longer-term promise. Worth tucking away.

Casilla,Santiago			W	L	Sv	IP	K	ERA	WHIP	OBA	vL	vR	BF/G	H%	S%	xERA	G	L	F	Ctl	Dom	Cmd	hr/f	hr/9	RAR	BPV	R$
RH RP	30	06 OAK *	2	0	4	35	29	4.10	1.14	227	400		5.3	28%	63%	3.25	40	40	20	2.8	7.4	**2.6**	10%	0.5	2.0	76	$5
Ht/Wt	72 202	07 OAK *	5	2	5	75	73	4.75	1.38	235	212	230	4.7	29%	66%	4.52	33	16	51	4.7	8.8	**1.9**	7%	0.9	-2.3	43	$8
Type	Pwr	08 OAK	2	1	2	50	43	3.94	1.59	297	308	291	4.4	36%	77%	4.19	43	20	36	3.6	7.7	**2.2**	9%	0.9	2.6	63	$3
Health	B	09 OAK	1	2	0	48	35	5.96	1.78	309	354	257	4.9	35%	68%	4.65	50	20	30	4.7	6.5	**1.4**	12%	1.1	-9.0	20	($1)
PT/Exp	D	10 SF	7	2	2	55	56	1.95	1.19	204	203	211	4.4	28%	84%	3.16	51	21	29	4.2	9.1	**2.2**	5%	0.3	14.1	79	$10
Consist	B	1st Half	1	2	2	15	25	2.35	1.57	232			3.8	40%	87%	2.98	33	33	33	6.5	14.7	**2.3**	10%	0.6	3.1	101	$2
LIMA Plan	C+	2nd Half	6	0	0	40	31	1.80	1.05	193			4.7	24%	83%	3.20	56	17	27	3.4	7.0	**2.1**	3%	0.2	10.9	69	$8
Rand Var	-5	11 Proj	**4**	**2**	**3**	**58**	**56**	**3.88**	**1.40**	**245**			**4.5**	**31%**	**74%**	**3.68**	**47**	**21**	**32**	**4.3**	**8.7**	**2.0**	**10%**	**0.8**	**3.3**	**64**	**$5**

What's real here? Certainly not 2010 ERA, as xERA screams "he's not THIS good". But 2009 was injury-plagued, and once we discount that, the skills look worthy of supporting another sub-4.00 ERA.

RAY MURPHY

Cecil,Brett	Yr	Tm	W	L	Sv	IP	K	ERA	WHIP	OBA	vL	vR	BF/G	H%	S%	xERA	G	L	F	Ctl	Dom	Cmd	hr/f	hr/9	RAR	BPV	R$
LH SP 24	06		0	0	0	0	0	0.00	0.00							0.00											
Ht/Wt 73 235	07		0	0	0	0	0	0.00	0.00							0.00											
Type	08	a/a	8	5	0	108	98	3.75	1.39	263			19.4	33%	73%	3.99				3.4	8.2	2.4		0.5	7.5	86	$10
Health A	09	TOR *	8	9	0	142	97	5.57	1.62	301	295	314	23.9	34%	67%	4.77	43	20	38	3.6	6.1	1.7	11%	1.2	-19.5	34	$2
PT/Exp C	10	TOR	15	7	0	173	117	4.22	1.33	264	224	275	26.2	30%	70%	4.08	44	18	38	2.8	6.1	2.2	9%	0.9	-1.8	56	$14
Consist B	1st Half		9	5	0	97	75	3.90	1.21	245			25.0	29%	69%	3.75	44	17	40	2.6	7.0	2.7	7%	0.7	2.9	77	$11
LIMA Plan D+	2nd Half		6	2	0	76	42	4.64	1.48	287			27.8	31%	72%	4.52	45	18	37	3.1	5.0	1.6	11%	1.2	-4.6	29	$3
Rand Var 0	11	Proj	13	8	0	180	125	4.41	1.40	271			24.3	30%	71%	4.28	44	18	38	3.2	6.3	2.0	10%	1.1	0.1	48	$12

Took what appeared to be a step forward in 1H, but followed with a big 2H fade for second straight year. GB tilt offers a foundation skill, if 2009-10 1H's represent his true skill level... UP: 3.75 ERA, 15 Wins.

Ceda,Jose	Yr	Tm	W	L	Sv	IP	K	ERA	WHIP	OBA	vL	vR	BF/G	H%	S%	xERA	G	L	F	Ctl	Dom	Cmd	hr/f	hr/9	RAR	BPV	R$
RH RP 24	06		0	0	0	0	0	0.00	0.00							0.00											
Ht/Wt 76 275	07		0	0	0	0	0	0.00	0.00							0.00											
Type Pwr xFB	08	aa	2	1	9	30	36	2.69	1.43	255			5.9	36%	83%	4.04				4.2	10.8	2.6		0.6	6.0	105	$7
Health F	09		0	0	0	0	0	0.00	0.00							0.00											
PT/Exp F	10	FLA *	4	1	6	41	49	2.47	1.53	205	333	133	5.2	29%	86%	4.59	29	17	54	7.2	10.8	1.5	6%	0.7	7.8	6	$6
Consist B	1st Half		1	0	0	4	6	0.00	0.77	155			4.9	27%	100%	0.46				2.3	13.1	5.6		0.0	2.0	221	$1
LIMA Plan C+	2nd Half		3	1	6	37	43	2.74	1.61	210			5.2	29%	86%	4.88	29	17	54	7.7	10.5	1.4	6%	0.7	5.8	-13	$5
Rand Var -5	11	Proj	3	1	5	44	51	4.14	1.49	227			5.5	30%	75%	4.43	29	17	54	6.0	10.6	1.8	9%	1.0	-1.5	35	$5

0-0, 5.19 ERA in 9 IP at FLA. PRO: Dom returned intact after 2009 layoff (labrum surgery). CON: Ctl issues pre-date injury, preclude closer work for now. Big arm could emerge quickly, watch for Ctl improvement.

Chacin,Gustavo	Yr	Tm	W	L	Sv	IP	K	ERA	WHIP	OBA	vL	vR	BF/G	H%	S%	xERA	G	L	F	Ctl	Dom	Cmd	hr/f	hr/9	RAR	BPV	R$
LH RP 30	06	TOR	9	4	0	87	47	5.06	1.47	268	268	266	22.5	26%	72%	5.35	35	21	44	3.9	4.9	1.2	15%	2.0	-5.4	-6	$6
Ht/Wt 71 193	07	TOR *	2	3	0	37	15	6.73	1.49	302	269	265	20.1	30%	57%	5.21	40	19	41	2.5	3.7	1.5	13%	1.7	-10.0	17	($0)
Type FB	08		0	0	0	0	0	0.00	0.00							0.00											
Health C	09	a/a	9	4	0	115	48	4.60	1.80	322			27.2	34%	77%	6.65				4.1	3.7	0.9		1.1	-4.1	-1	$1
PT/Exp F	10	HOU *	3	3	1	63	42	4.56	1.68	308	323	310	5.8	34%	76%	4.99	36	21	44	3.8	6.0	1.6	9%	1.2	-4.3	19	$0
Consist D	1st Half		2	2	0	45	30	3.62	1.43	285			7.8	32%	79%	4.30	42	18	40	2.7	6.0	2.2	9%	1.1	2.2	54	$2
LIMA Plan F	2nd Half		1	1	1	18	12	6.88	2.29	360			3.8	40%	72%	6.54	30	23	46	6.4	5.9	0.9	9%	1.5	-6.5	-58	($2)
Rand Var 0	11	Proj	2	1	0	29	16	5.28	1.69	300			7.4	32%	71%	5.50	35	21	44	4.3	5.0	1.1	9%	1.2	-4.9	-14	($0)

2-2, 4.70 ERA in 38 IP at HOU. His "breakout" season was a 13-9, 3.72 rookie year with TOR in 2005, which was supported by a BPV of 32... a level that he hasn't regained since. Keep him far away from your roster.

Chacin,Jhoulys	Yr	Tm	W	L	Sv	IP	K	ERA	WHIP	OBA	vL	vR	BF/G	H%	S%	xERA	G	L	F	Ctl	Dom	Cmd	hr/f	hr/9	RAR	BPV	R$
RH SP 23	06		0	0	0	0	0	0.00	0.00							0.00											
Ht/Wt 75 200	07		0	0	0	0	0	0.00	0.00							0.00											
Type Pwr	08		0	0	0	0	0	0.00	0.00							0.00											
Health A	09	COL *	9	9	0	128	95	4.21	1.40	251	263	59	17.8	28%	73%	4.49	48	9	43	4.1	6.7	1.6	9%	1.1	-0.4	36	$8
PT/Exp D	10	COL *	12	13	0	173	168	2.91	1.25	224	266	201	20.5	29%	78%	3.35	47	22	32	3.9	8.8	2.3	8%	0.6	23.6	78	$19
Consist C	1st Half		8	7	0	94	95	3.15	1.25	219			23.0	28%	76%	3.38	46	21	33	4.1	9.1	2.2	9%	0.7	10.0	77	$11
LIMA Plan D+	2nd Half		4	6	0	79	74	2.62	1.25	230			18.2	30%	80%	3.32	48	23	30	3.6	8.4	2.3	6%	0.5	13.6	79	$8
Rand Var -2	11	Proj	13	10	0	199	174	3.62	1.33	241			24.9	29%	75%	3.72	47	21	32	3.9	7.9	2.0	9%	0.8	10.4	60	$17

9-11, 3.28 ERA in 137 IP at COL. Brilliant rookie campaign shows skill set built for long-term success, even in Coors: strong Dom, enough Cmd, healthy GB bias, stable 1H/2H split. UP: Sub-3.00 ERA

Chamberlain,Joba	Yr	Tm	W	L	Sv	IP	K	ERA	WHIP	OBA	vL	vR	BF/G	H%	S%	xERA	G	L	F	Ctl	Dom	Cmd	hr/f	hr/9	RAR	BPV	R$
RH RP 25	06		0	0	0	0	0	0.00	0.00							0.00											
Ht/Wt 74 230	07	NYY *	7	2	1	72	104	2.62	1.11	219	132	156	9.7	34%	80%	2.63	37	22	41	2.9	13.0	4.5	9%	0.7	16.8	171	$15
Type Pwr	08	NYY	4	3	0	100	118	2.60	1.26	235	247	219	10.0	33%	80%	2.98	52	14	34	3.5	10.6	3.0	6%	0.4	21.6	126	$13
Health A	09	NYY	9	6	0	157	133	4.75	1.54	274	266	282	21.9	32%	72%	4.39	43	21	36	4.3	7.6	1.8	12%	1.2	-5.8	41	$8
PT/Exp B	10	NYY	3	4	3	72	77	4.39	1.30	260	246	258	4.1	34%	67%	3.17	46	17	37	2.8	9.7	3.5	8%	0.8	-2.3	123	$6
Consist C	1st Half		1	3	2	34	38	5.25	1.49	282			4.2	39%	62%	3.21	49	18	33	3.4	10.0	2.9	3%	0.3	-4.7	114	$2
LIMA Plan A	2nd Half		2	1	1	37	39	3.61	1.12	238			4.1	30%	73%	3.11	42	16	41	2.2	9.4	4.3	12%	1.2	2.4	131	$5
Rand Var +3	11	Proj	4	3	8	73	77	3.72	1.26	241			4.8	31%	73%	3.29	45	18	37	3.2	9.6	3.0	10%	0.9	8.9	108	$10

Returned to bullpen and once again displayed a closer-worthy skill set, seemingly showing that '09 skills dip was rooted in role change. Consider him a closer-in-waiting, whether that chance comes in 2011 or later.

Chapman,Aroldis	Yr	Tm	W	L	Sv	IP	K	ERA	WHIP	OBA	vL	vR	BF/G	H%	S%	xERA	G	L	F	Ctl	Dom	Cmd	hr/f	hr/9	RAR	BPV	R$
LH RP 23	06	CUB	3	5	0	54	53	5.38	2.20	253			18.4	30%	78%	6.93				11.2	8.9	0.8		1.4	-5.7	33	($2)
Ht/Wt 76 185	07	CUB	4	3	7	81	95	3.45	1.55	217			15.7	30%	79%	4.07				6.9	10.5	1.5		0.7	10.1	85	$9
Type Pwr	08	CUB	6	7	0	74	75	4.83	1.42	220			20.1	29%	65%	3.57				5.6	9.1	1.6		0.6	-4.8	82	$6
Health A	09	CUB	11	4	0	118	123	5.02	1.64	260			24.5	33%	70%	4.99				5.9	9.4	1.6		0.9	-10.3	67	$6
PT/Exp C	10	CIN *	11	8	8	109	135	3.80	1.35	231	154	212	8.6	33%	73%	2.22	73	8	19	4.5	11.2	2.5	17%	0.7	2.8	130	$14
Consist F	1st Half		5	6	0	70	78	4.89	1.54	258			19.5	34%	69%	4.50				5.0	10.0	2.0		0.9	-7.6	79	$3
LIMA Plan B+	2nd Half		6	2	8	38	57	1.82	1.01	177			4.0	29%	84%	1.55	73	8	19	3.6	13.3	3.7	13%	0.4	10.4	193	$11
Rand Var +4	11	Proj	8	5	5	83	98	3.36	1.30	228			5.2	31%	76%	3.08	49	20	31	4.2	10.6	2.5	11%	0.8	10.9	104	$12

2-2, 2.03 ERA in 13 IP at CIN. PRO: His Dom will play in any role; Ctl stabilized in bullpen. Con: Role uncertainty makes it hard to pin down his value. Buy these skills, wait for role to settle. Our bet: future closer.

Chavez,Jesse	Yr	Tm	W	L	Sv	IP	K	ERA	WHIP	OBA	vL	vR	BF/G	H%	S%	xERA	G	L	F	Ctl	Dom	Cmd	hr/f	hr/9	RAR	BPV	R$
RH RP 27	06	a/a	4	6	4	78	74	5.42	1.58	281			6.9	35%	65%	5.00				4.3	8.5	2.0		0.7	-8.7	71	$4
Ht/Wt 74 170	07	aa	3	3	2	80	51	4.97	1.64	333			7.9	38%	69%	5.87				2.1	5.8	2.7		0.5	-5.0	66	$2
Type FB	08	PIT *	2	7	14	83	69	5.53	1.53	287			5.6	33%	66%	5.47				3.6	7.5	2.1		1.2	-12.9	51	$5
Health A	09	PIT	1	4	0	67	47	4.01	1.35	267	228	299	3.9	29%	76%	4.36	39	20	41	2.9	6.3	2.1	13%	1.5	1.5	51	$3
PT/Exp D	10	2TM	5	5	0	63	45	5.89	1.47	281	260	292	5.4	31%	63%	4.66	34	17	48	3.3	6.5	2.0	11%	1.6	-14.0	40	$1
Consist B	1st Half		0	1	0	31	27	5.81	1.29	262			6.2	30%	57%	4.18	27	20	53	2.6	7.8	3.0	10%	1.5	-6.6	75	$0
LIMA Plan C+	2nd Half		5	4	0	32	18	5.96	1.64	298			4.8	31%	67%	5.16	41	15	44	4.0	5.1	1.3	12%	1.7	-7.4	3	$1
Rand Var +4	11	Proj	3	3	0	44	31	4.97	1.47	281			5.0	31%	70%	4.64	37	18	45	3.3	6.4	1.9	11%	1.4	-2.3	41	$2

PRO: xERA says this wasn't as bad as it looked; Dom and Cmd rank as "acceptable". CON: No plus skill, combined with scary FB rate, leaves HRs as his downfall. Despite age, little hope of improvement.

Chen,Bruce	Yr	Tm	W	L	Sv	IP	K	ERA	WHIP	OBA	vL	vR	BF/G	H%	S%	xERA	G	L	F	Ctl	Dom	Cmd	hr/f	hr/9	RAR	BPV	R$
LH SP 33	06	BAL	0	7	0	98	70	6.97	1.75	331	328	337	11.5	35%	67%	5.22	33	21	47	3.2	6.4	2.0	17%	2.6	-29.2	39	($5)
Ht/Wt 73 215	07	TEX *	1	1	0	26	19	6.23	1.42	276			12.5	29%	61%	5.93				3.1	6.6	2.1		2.1	-5.5	21	$1
Type xFB	08		0	0	0	0	0	0.00	0.00							0.00											
Health F	09	KC *	5	8	0	144	97	5.14	1.38	267	292	305	20.0	29%	66%	5.02	31	17	51	3.2	6.0	1.9	9%	1.3	-12.2	32	$6
PT/Exp D	10	KC *	12	8	1	161	114	3.82	1.33	250	259	253	18.9	28%	74%	4.56	34	18	48	3.5	6.4	1.8	7%	1.0	6.3	33	$14
Consist A	1st Half		5	3	1	69	58	2.89	1.18	204			14.1	25%	77%	4.28	30	20	50	4.1	7.6	1.9	5%	0.7	10.6	34	$9
LIMA Plan C	2nd Half		7	5	0	92	56	4.52	1.44	281			25.0	31%	72%	4.79	36	17	47	3.0	5.5	1.8	8%	1.2	-4.3	30	$5
Rand Var -2	11	Proj	7	8	0	140	97	4.65	1.41	271			17.8	30%	71%	4.78	33	18	48	3.3	6.3	1.9	10%	1.4	-8.4	35	$7

12-7, 4.17 ERA in 140 IP at KC. 11 Wins in 23 GS, while rest of KC SPs won 35 in 139 GS. So, Chen = '72 Steve Carlton? Not exactly. Skills more like the washed-up late '80s Carlton; you don't want any part of that.

Choate,Randy	Yr	Tm	W	L	Sv	IP	K	ERA	WHIP	OBA	vL	vR	BF/G	H%	S%	xERA	G	L	F	Ctl	Dom	Cmd	hr/f	hr/9	RAR	BPV	R$
LH RP 35	06	aaa	6	0	8	45	37	2.72	1.26	267			4.4	34%	76%	3.24				2.1	7.4	3.5		0.0	10.0	120	$10
Ht/Wt 73 200	07	aaa	3	1	3	62	45	4.60	1.78	343			5.4	40%	74%	6.63				2.7	6.5	2.4		0.7	-1.0	55	$2
Type Pwr xGB	08	aaa	0	4	2	39	27	5.83	1.75	301			7.0	34%	67%	6.01				4.9	6.1	1.3		1.0	-7.3	29	($1)
Health A	09	TAM *	4	0	5	55	40	3.98	1.22	231	141	321	2.8	27%	68%	3.34	65	10	25	3.3	6.6	2.0	10%	0.6	3.2	72	$8
PT/Exp D	10	TAM	4	3	0	45	40	4.23	1.30	245	202	410	2.2	31%	67%	3.03	60	15	24	3.4	8.1	2.4	10%	0.6	-0.5	91	$4
Consist C	1st Half		1	2	0	21	22	5.57	1.10	223			2.1	29%	48%	2.16	66	16	18	2.6	9.4	3.7	21%	0.9	-3.7	144	$2
LIMA Plan B+	2nd Half		3	1	0	24	18	3.04	1.48	264			2.4	32%	79%	3.86	55	15	30	4.2	6.8	1.6	5%	0.4	3.2	43	$3
Rand Var +1	11	Proj	4	3	0	58	46	3.72	1.38	258			2.9	31%	74%	3.39	61	14	25	3.6	7.1	2.0	9%	0.6	6.4	71	$5

Remains highly effective v LH batters (.529 OPS). RH split is probably something of a sample-size fluke (only 39 AB), and as long as that sample stays small, he's a low-risk source of a few vulture wins.

RAY MURPHY

Clippard,Tyler

		Yr	Tm	W	L	Sv	IP	K	ERA	WHIP	OBA	vL	vR	BF/G	H%	S%	xERA	G	L	F	Ctl	Dom	Cmd	hr/f	hr/9	RAR	BPV	R$
RH RP	26	06	aa	12	10	0	166	145	4.61	1.23	235			24.6	28%	64%	3.68				3.3	7.9	2.4		1.0	-1.8	77	$16
Ht/Wt	75 200	07	NYY *	9	6	0	123	88	6.15	1.80	309			22.4	34%	69%	6.93				4.9	6.4	1.3		1.5	-24.9	13	($0)
Type	Pwr xFB	08	aaa	6	13	0	143	105	5.10	1.42	258			23.0	30%	64%	4.32				4.0	6.6	1.7		0.8	-14.0	54	$5
Health	A	09	WAS *	8	3	1	99	103	2.08	1.07	174	122	234	6.1	21%	87%	4.03	30	13	57	4.3	9.3	2.2	8%	1.0	25.8	61	$17
PT/Exp	D	10	WAS	11	8	1	91	112	3.07	1.21	212	242	188	4.8	30%	77%	3.59	28	17	56	4.1	11.1	2.7	7%	0.8	10.7	96	$14
Consist	A	1st Half		8	5	1	51	57	2.65	1.20	213			5.0	29%	79%	3.77	28	17	55	3.9	10.1	2.6	4%	0.5	8.6	82	$9
LIMA Plan	B	2nd Half		3	3	0	40	55	3.60	1.22	210			4.6	30%	75%	3.35	27	16	57	4.3	12.4	2.9	10%	1.1	2.1	112	$5
Rand Var	-2	11	Proj	6	5	10	73	81	3.60	1.31	233			6.5	30%	77%	4.05	28	15	56	4.1	10.1	2.5	9%	1.1	0.8	77	$11

Was a vulture-win machine in 1H, then pushed skills to even higher levels in 2H. Scary FB%, bb%, and big relief workload are concerning, but that Dom covers a lot of ills. Expect regression of W and ERA, but not a crash.

Coffey,Todd

		Yr	Tm	W	L	Sv	IP	K	ERA	WHIP	OBA	vL	vR	BF/G	H%	S%	xERA	G	L	F	Ctl	Dom	Cmd	hr/f	hr/9	RAR	BPV	R$
RH RP	30	06	CIN	6	7	8	78	60	3.58	1.44	279	347	242	4.2	33%	77%	3.79	52	21	27	3.1	6.9	2.2	10%	0.8	8.8	71	$10
Ht/Wt	76 241	07	CIN *	4	1	1	78	63	4.41	1.48	293	343	313	4.5	33%	75%	3.54	58	16	27	2.8	7.3	2.6	18%	1.4	0.1	91	$4
Type	Pwr GB	08	2NL *	4	3	2	66	50	5.14	1.74	329			5.1	38%	73%	6.82				3.3	6.9	2.1		1.3	-7.1	36	$1
Health	A	09	MIL	4	4	2	84	65	2.90	1.16	244	282	223	4.4	28%	79%	3.37	52	17	31	2.3	7.0	3.1	11%	0.9	13.3	95	$10
PT/Exp	D	10	MIL	2	4	0	62	56	4.77	1.41	270	275	267	3.9	32%	69%	3.67	48	17	36	3.3	8.1	2.4	12%	1.2	-5.8	82	$2
Consist	D	1st Half		2	2	0	30	19	3.94	1.38	257			4.0	29%	72%	4.37	46	15	39	3.6	5.8	1.6	6%	0.6	0.3	30	$2
LIMA Plan	A	2nd Half		0	2	0	33	37	5.52	1.44	281			3.8	35%	66%	3.07	49	18	33	3.0	10.2	3.4	20%	1.7	-6.1	129	$0
Rand Var	+2	11	Proj	3	4	0	65	56	3.72	1.33	261			4.1	31%	75%	3.54	51	17	32	3.0	7.7	2.5	11%	1.0	4.8	86	$5

Thumb injury shelved him most of June, 2H skill set was elite upon his retun, done in by silly h% and hr/f. Healthy GB% plus rising Dom make him a stable relief option, even if 2H gains regress. LIMA grade agrees.

Coke,Phil

		Yr	Tm	W	L	Sv	IP	K	ERA	WHIP	OBA	vL	vR	BF/G	H%	S%	xERA	G	L	F	Ctl	Dom	Cmd	hr/f	hr/9	RAR	BPV	R$
LH RP	28	06		0	0	0	0	0	0.00	0.00							0.00											
Ht/Wt	73 210	07		0	0	0	0	0	0.00	0.00							0.00											
Type	Pwr FB	08	NYY *	12	6	0	151	118	3.75	1.50	290			13.6	35%	76%	4.72				3.2	7.0	2.2		0.6	11.0	68	$12
Health	A	09	NYY	4	3	2	60	49	4.50	1.07	206	195	227	3.3	22%	63%	4.02	35	20	45	3.0	7.4	2.5	13%	1.5	-0.4	65	$8
PT/Exp	C	10	DET	7	5	2	65	53	3.76	1.44	269	273	276	3.8	33%	73%	4.31	35	21	43	3.6	7.4	2.0	2%	0.3	3.1	48	$7
Consist	A	1st Half		5	0	0	33	25	2.75	1.38	258			3.8	32%	80%	4.36	36	20	44	3.6	6.9	1.9	2%	0.3	5.6	41	$5
LIMA Plan	C	2nd Half		2	5	2	32	28	4.78	1.50	279			3.8	35%	66%	4.24	34	23	43	3.7	7.9	2.2	2%	0.3	-2.5	55	$2
Rand Var	-2	11	Proj	12	10	0	145	114	4.41	1.39	259			24.1	30%	71%	4.46	35	21	44	3.7	7.1	1.9	9%	1.1	-3.1	42	$11

Reports say he's going to transition this unremarkable skill set into a starting role for 2011. Lack of L/R split is a good sign for that change, but unless he can allow only 2 HR per 65 IP again, expect ERA over 4.00.

Coleman,Casey

		Yr	Tm	W	L	Sv	IP	K	ERA	WHIP	OBA	vL	vR	BF/G	H%	S%	xERA	G	L	F	Ctl	Dom	Cmd	hr/f	hr/9	RAR	BPV	R$
RH SP	23	06		0	0	0	0	0	0.00	0.00							0.00											
Ht/Wt	73 180	07		0	0	0	0	0	0.00	0.00							0.00											
Type	Con	08		0	0	0	0	0	0.00	0.00							0.00											
Health	A	09	aa	14	6	0	149	72	4.71	1.53	284			24.6	31%	69%	4.82				3.7	4.3	1.2		0.6	-7.3	31	$7
PT/Exp	D	10	CHC *	14	9	0	174	78	4.29	1.31	257	278	250	22.3	28%	67%	4.43	49	17	34	3.0	4.0	1.3	6%	0.7	-5.9	19	$10
Consist	A	1st Half		6	7	0	88	42	4.80	1.26	262			24.6	28%	62%	3.87				2.3	4.3	1.8		0.8	-8.5	42	$4
LIMA Plan	C	2nd Half		8	2	0	86	36	3.77	1.36	253			20.5	27%	72%	4.69	49	17	34	3.7	3.8	1.0	5%	0.5	2.6	-4	$6
Rand Var	-1	11	Proj	7	8	0	116	53	4.50	1.49	284			23.3	30%	72%	4.76	49	17	34	3.3	4.1	1.2	9%	1.0	-8.8	11	$3

4-2, 4.11 ERA in 57 IP at CHC. Helpful GB% punched his ticket to the show, but that GB level isn't elite enough to cover for the intolerable Dom and Cmd. He just goes out there and waits for his fielders to make plays.

Contreras,Jose

		Yr	Tm	W	L	Sv	IP	K	ERA	WHIP	OBA	vL	vR	BF/G	H%	S%	xERA	G	L	F	Ctl	Dom	Cmd	hr/f	hr/9	RAR	BPV	R$
RH RP	39	06	CHW	13	9	0	196	134	4.27	1.27	260	267	248	27.4	29%	68%	4.17	45	16	39	2.5	6.2	2.4	8%	0.9	6.9	65	$18
Ht/Wt	76 255	07	CHW	10	17	0	189	113	5.57	1.56	303	333	270	26.4	33%	65%	4.68	45	19	36	3.0	5.4	1.8	9%	1.0	-24.9	40	$4
Type	Pwr	08	CHW	7	6	0	121	70	4.54	1.36	276	286	258	25.9	30%	68%	4.04	51	19	30	2.6	5.2	2.0	10%	0.9	-2.8	52	$7
Health	C	09	2TM *	9	14	0	165	129	4.74	1.43	262	252	292	21.7	31%	68%	4.20	47	17	36	3.9	7.0	1.8	9%	0.9	-8.6	48	$8
PT/Exp	C	10	PHI	6	4	4	57	57	3.33	1.22	249	253	256	3.5	32%	75%	3.18	45	19	36	2.5	9.0	3.6	9%	0.8	4.8	117	$8
Consist	B	1st Half		3	3	3	25	30	3.24	1.12	221			3.4	31%	73%	2.75	43	22	34	2.9	10.8	3.8	10%	0.7	2.4	138	$5
LIMA Plan	B+	2nd Half		3	1	1	32	27	3.41	1.29	270			3.6	32%	76%	3.53	46	17	37	2.3	7.7	3.4	9%	0.9	2.4	100	$4
Rand Var	0	11	Proj	5	4	0	58	51	3.72	1.29	255			6.1	31%	74%	3.59	46	19	35	2.9	7.9	2.7	10%	0.9	4.0	87	$6

Carried over late-2009 career rebirth as an RP, reversing Dom slide while maintaining Ctl and GBs. How long can he keep this up? Heck, we likely don't even know how old he really is.

Cook,Aaron

		Yr	Tm	W	L	Sv	IP	K	ERA	WHIP	OBA	vL	vR	BF/G	H%	S%	xERA	G	L	F	Ctl	Dom	Cmd	hr/f	hr/9	RAR	BPV	R$
RH SP	32	06	COL	9	15	0	212	92	4.24	1.40	288	314	258	28.6	31%	70%	4.08	58	18	24	2.3	3.9	1.7	10%	0.7	6.4	43	$10
Ht/Wt	75 215	07	COL	8	7	0	166	61	4.12	1.34	275	263	295	28.3	29%	71%	4.13	58	19	24	2.4	3.3	1.4	11%	0.8	6.3	31	$9
Type	Con xGB	08	COL	16	9	0	211	96	3.96	1.34	284	297	276	28.2	31%	70%	3.88	56	20	24	2.0	4.1	2.0	7%	0.6	8.1	52	$15
Health	D	09	COL	11	6	0	158	78	4.16	1.41	282	282	285	25.3	30%	73%	3.98	57	19	25	2.7	4.4	1.7	14%	1.1	0.6	42	$9
PT/Exp	A	10	COL	6	8	0	128	62	5.07	1.56	290	337	258	24.9	31%	68%	4.22	58	17	25	3.7	4.4	1.2	10%	0.8	-16.7	16	($0)
Consist	A	1st Half		3	5	0	95	43	4.66	1.45	268			25.8	29%	67%	4.27	58	16	27	3.7	4.1	1.1	7%	0.6	-7.5	9	$1
LIMA Plan	D	2nd Half		3	3	0	33	19	6.27	1.88	345			22.6	37%	68%	4.08	60	19	21	3.5	5.2	1.5	19%	1.4	-9.2	35	($1)
Rand Var	+1	11	Proj	11	9	0	160	79	4.34	1.48	289			25.1	31%	72%	4.01	58	18	24	3.0	4.5	1.5	11%	0.8	2.6	35	$6

Here, we have an elite GB% that can somewhat compensate for the lack of Dom/Cmd. There is no upside here, but he can often be found on waiver wire for a spot start and a shot at a Win without terrible ERA risk.

Cordero,Francisco

		Yr	Tm	W	L	Sv	IP	K	ERA	WHIP	OBA	vL	vR	BF/G	H%	S%	xERA	G	L	F	Ctl	Dom	Cmd	hr/f	hr/9	RAR	BPV	R$
RH RP	35	06	2TM	10	5	22	75	84	3.72	1.34	246	286	219	4.2	33%	74%	3.60	40	21	39	3.8	10.1	2.6	9%	0.8	7.5	96	$18
Ht/Wt	75 238	07	MIL	0	4	44	63	86	2.99	1.11	226	225	212	3.9	34%	74%	2.74	41	17	42	2.6	12.2	4.8	7%	0.6	11.2	170	$22
Type	Pwr	08	CIN	5	4	34	70	78	3.33	1.41	235	212	252	4.2	31%	78%	3.77	41	22	37	4.9	10.0	2.1	9%	0.8	8.2	67	$19
Health	A	09	CIN	2	6	39	67	58	2.16	1.32	236	228	256	4.2	30%	84%	3.98	41	23	36	4.0	7.8	1.9	3%	0.3	16.7	51	$20
PT/Exp	A	10	CIN	6	5	40	73	59	3.84	1.43	249	274	226	4.2	30%	74%	4.20	43	20	37	4.5	7.3	1.6	6%	0.6	1.6	32	$18
Consist	A	1st Half		3	3	22	38	34	4.03	1.50	267			4.2	32%	75%	3.89	50	15	35	4.3	8.1	1.9	10%	0.9	-0.1	57	$10
LIMA Plan	D	2nd Half		3	2	18	35	25	3.63	1.35	229			4.2	28%	72%	4.51	37	25	38	4.7	6.5	1.4	3%	0.3	1.6	5	$9
Rand Var	-1	11	Proj	4	5	35	65	57	4.00	1.41	249			4.2	30%	73%	4.11	41	22	37	4.3	7.9	1.8	9%	0.8	0.3	45	$16

Another outwardly-solid year of closing, but Dom now in three-year decline with 2H acceleration. Cmd has slipped to substandard levels, and BPV free-fall reaching critical levels. Buy skills, not role.

Cormier,Lance

		Yr	Tm	W	L	Sv	IP	K	ERA	WHIP	OBA	vL	vR	BF/G	H%	S%	xERA	G	L	F	Ctl	Dom	Cmd	hr/f	hr/9	RAR	BPV	R$
RH RP	30	06	ATL *	8	8	0	127	66	5.23	1.77	323	271	351	15.7	35%	71%	4.96	50	21	29	3.8	4.7	1.2	10%	0.9	-11.7	8	($0)
Ht/Wt	73 200	07	ATL *	7	9	0	106	55	6.10	1.73	323			22.3	33%	69%	4.81	51	19	30	3.4	4.7	1.4	20%	1.9	-21.8	20	($1)
Type	GB	08	BAL *	4	4	1	92	57	3.33	1.46	266	240	308	7.3	31%	77%	3.92	57	21	22	3.9	5.6	1.4	6%	0.4	11.5	29	$7
Health	A	09	TAM	3	3	2	77	36	3.26	1.29	256	239	261	6.1	27%	77%	4.35	52	17	30	2.9	4.2	1.4	8%	0.7	11.4	27	$7
PT/Exp	C	10	TAM	4	3	0	62	30	3.92	1.65	280	252	320	4.7	30%	79%	5.00	50	19	32	4.9	4.4	0.9	10%	1.0	1.7	-27	$2
Consist	B	1st Half		3	1	0	32	12	4.50	1.78	307			5.0	33%	75%	5.15	53	19	28	4.8	3.4	0.7	6%	0.6	-1.4	-37	$0
LIMA Plan	C	2nd Half		1	2	0	30	18	3.30	1.50	249			4.4	26%	85%	4.85	45	19	36	5.1	5.4	1.1	15%	1.5	3.1	-17	$1
Rand Var	-2	11	Proj	3	3	0	58	30	4.34	1.57	281			5.8	30%	74%	4.71	51	19	30	4.2	4.7	1.1	10%	0.9	-3.0	-0	$2

Yet another case where a nice GB rate can only cover up so many ills. Poor Dom is survivable, sub-1.0 Cmd is not. Reverse platoon split further limits his utility. Even if Ctl returns, no reason to roster.

Corpas,Manny

		Yr	Tm	W	L	Sv	IP	K	ERA	WHIP	OBA	vL	vR	BF/G	H%	S%	xERA	G	L	F	Ctl	Dom	Cmd	hr/f	hr/9	RAR	BPV	R$
RH RP	28	06	COL *	3	3	19	77	63	2.22	1.06	238	281	290	4.0	29%	81%	3.38	45	20	34	1.6	7.3	4.5	5%	0.5	21.6	112	$17
Ht/Wt	75 170	07	COL	4	2	19	78	58	2.08	1.06	223	234	214	4.0	26%	84%	3.25	57	14	28	2.3	6.7	2.9	9%	0.7	22.6	94	$18
Type		08	COL	3	4	4	80	50	4.52	1.46	293	285	308	4.6	33%	70%	4.00	50	23	28	2.6	5.6	2.2	9%	0.8	-2.4	59	$4
Health	B	09	COL	1	3	1	34	24	5.88	1.51	316	400	267	4.3	37%	60%	3.79	49	22	30	1.9	6.4	3.4	9%	0.8	-7.0	92	$0
PT/Exp	C	10	COL	3	5	10	62	47	4.62	1.41	273	326	239	4.8	31%	69%	4.11	43	19	39	3.2	6.8	2.1	9%	1.0	-4.7	57	$6
Consist	A	1st Half		2	5	10	44	28	4.91	1.25	248			4.7	28%	61%	4.20	43	16	41	2.9	5.7	2.0	7%	0.8	-4.8	47	$5
LIMA Plan	C	2nd Half		1	0	0	18	19	3.93	1.80	326			5.1	40%	83%	3.86	42	25	33	3.9	9.3	2.4	16%	1.5	0.2	82	$0
Rand Var	0	11	Proj	0	0	0	7	5	4.97	1.66	306			4.7	34%	73%	4.43	46	21	33	3.7	6.2	1.7	12%	1.2	-0.3	35	($0)

Had Tommy John surgery in September, so absolute best-case scenario would be a token return in September 2011. Check back next year.

RAY MURPHY

Correia,Kevin				W	L	Sv	IP	K	ERA	WHIP	OBA	vL	vR	BF/G	H%	S%	xERA	G	L	F	Ctl	Dom	Cmd	hr/f	hr/9	RAR	BPV	R$
RH SP	30	06	SF	2	0	0	69	57	3.51	1.24	247	275	218	6.0	30%	73%	4.21	34	22	44	2.9	7.4	2.6	6%	0.7	8.3	68	$6
Ht/Wt	75 200	07	SF	4	7	0	102	80	3.45	1.32	247	217	257	7.3	29%	76%	4.22	45	15	40	3.5	7.1	2.0	7%	0.8	12.2	55	$9
Type	Pwr	08	SF	* 4	8	0	122	76	5.74	1.63	307	307	312	20.6	34%	66%	4.89	38	25	37	3.5	5.6	1.6	10%	1.2	-22.1	24	($2)
Health	A	09	SD	12	11	0	198	142	3.91	1.30	258	247	269	25.3	30%	71%	4.04	45	19	36	2.9	6.5	2.2	8%	0.8	6.9	60	$15
PT/Exp	B	10	SD	10	10	0	145	115	5.40	1.49	271	248	290	22.8	31%	66%	3.90	49	21	30	4.0	7.1	1.8	15%	1.2	-24.8	48	$4
Consist	A	1st Half		5	6	0	87	65	5.05	1.48	266			24.0	30%	68%	4.00	48	23	29	4.1	6.7	1.6	14%	1.1	-11.2	36	$2
LIMA Plan	B	2nd Half		5	4	0	58	50	5.93	1.51	279			21.3	32%	63%	3.75	50	19	32	3.7	7.8	2.1	16%	1.4	-13.6	67	$1
Rand Var	+4	11	Proj	9	11	0	160	122	4.51	1.38	260			24.5	30%	70%	4.01	45	20	34	3.5	6.9	2.0	11%	1.1	2.5	53	$8

Despite ERA, this was a worthy follow-up to 2009 breakout. Actually added Dom and GBs, unfortunately BB and HR too. Net result is still-borderline Cmd, which mutes our enthusiasm despite xERA trend.

Crain,Jesse				W	L	Sv	IP	K	ERA	WHIP	OBA	vL	vR	BF/G	H%	S%	xERA	G	L	F	Ctl	Dom	Cmd	hr/f	hr/9	RAR	BPV	R$
RH RP	29	06	MIN	4	5	1	76	60	3.54	1.27	269	259	263	4.7	32%	74%	3.22	55	21	24	2.1	7.1	3.3	11%	0.7	9.5	103	$9
Ht/Wt	73 215	07	MIN	1	2	0	16	10	5.52	1.41	292	269	308	3.9	29%	68%	4.30	48	14	38	2.2	5.5	2.5	19%	2.2	-2.0	66	$1
Type	Pwr FB	08	MIN	5	4	0	63	50	3.59	1.37	260	259	261	4.1	31%	76%	4.28	41	17	42	3.4	7.2	2.1	8%	0.9	5.9	55	$6
Health	C	09	MIN	* 8	4	1	67	61	4.28	1.47	246	297	221	4.4	31%	70%	4.46	43	16	41	4.9	8.2	1.6	4%	0.4	1.4	34	$7
PT/Exp	D	10	MIN	1	1	1	68	62	3.04	1.18	217	196	228	3.9	27%	76%	3.78	39	17	44	3.6	8.2	2.3	6%	0.7	9.2	68	$7
Consist	A	1st Half		1	0	0	32	28	4.18	1.39	266			4.1	32%	71%	4.11	37	13	45	3.3	7.8	2.3	7%	0.8	-0.2	65	$2
LIMA Plan	C+	2nd Half		0	1	1	36	34	2.02	0.98	166			3.8	21%	82%	3.46	42	15	43	3.8	8.6	2.3	5%	0.5	9.3	72	$5
Rand Var	-2	11	Proj	4	3	0	68	60	3.84	1.34	247			4.2	30%	73%	4.02	42	16	42	3.7	7.9	2.1	7%	0.8	2.2	63	$6

Best BPV since 2007 injury, but still short of pre-injury peak. PRO: Cmd safely back above 2.0 threshold; improved vs. LHP; 2nd half Dom uptick. CON: Shaky Ctl; FB tilt; and xERA all say ERA repeat unlikely.

Cueto,Johnny				W	L	Sv	IP	K	ERA	WHIP	OBA	vL	vR	BF/G	H%	S%	xERA	G	L	F	Ctl	Dom	Cmd	hr/f	hr/9	RAR	BPV	R$
RH SP	25	06		0	0	0	0	0	0.00	0.00							0.00											
Ht/Wt	70 201	07	a/a	8	4	0	83	88	3.41	1.15	261			24.1	33%	74%	3.92				1.3	9.6	7.1		1.0	10.8	179	$13
Type		08	CIN	9	14	0	174	158	4.81	1.41	266	249	275	24.3	31%	71%	4.09	39	21	41	3.5	8.2	2.3	14%	1.5	-11.6	69	$9
Health	A	09	CIN	11	11	0	171	132	4.41	1.36	263	250	274	24.4	30%	71%	4.22	42	18	41	3.2	6.9	2.2	11%	1.5	-4.7	58	$11
PT/Exp	A	10	CIN	12	7	0	186	138	3.63	1.28	257	234	276	25.1	30%	74%	3.93	42	19	39	2.7	6.7	2.5	9%	0.9	8.7	67	$15
Consist	A	1st Half		8	2	0	104	76	3.56	1.31	259			25.8	30%	74%	4.05	39	22	38	3.0	6.6	2.2	7%	0.7	5.8	56	$9
LIMA Plan	C+	2nd Half		4	5	0	82	62	3.73	1.23	255			24.3	29%	74%	3.78	45	16	39	2.4	6.8	2.8	11%	1.2	2.9	80	$6
Rand Var	0	11	Proj	14	9	0	193	156	3.78	1.30	260			24.7	30%	74%	3.93	42	19	40	2.8	7.3	2.6	10%	1.0	5.1	75	$16

Maturating before our eyes? Concurrent Ctl/Dom declines suggest he's pitching, not just throwing. 2H GB% and Cmd spikes suggest he might have found the right formula. If so... UP: 15 Wins, 3.25 ERA.

Danks,John				W	L	Sv	IP	K	ERA	WHIP	OBA	vL	vR	BF/G	H%	S%	xERA	G	L	F	Ctl	Dom	Cmd	hr/f	hr/9	RAR	BPV	R$
LH SP	25	06	a/a	9	9	0	140	140	5.69	1.59	296			23.4	35%	69%	6.45				3.6	9.0	2.5		1.9	-20.3	45	$5
Ht/Wt	73 205	07	CHW	6	13	0	139	109	5.50	1.54	290	281	292	23.8	32%	69%	4.78	35	19	46	3.5	7.1	2.0	14%	1.8	-17.1	45	$4
Type		08	CHW	12	9	0	195	159	3.32	1.23	249	264	240	24.5	30%	75%	3.71	43	22	35	2.6	7.3	2.8	7%	0.7	24.6	82	$22
Health	A	09	CHW	13	11	0	200	149	3.77	1.28	246	244	246	26.3	27%	76%	4.26	44	15	41	3.3	6.7	2.0	11%	1.3	16.7	54	$19
PT/Exp	A	10	CHW	15	11	0	213	162	3.72	1.22	239	273	221	27.5	28%	71%	3.81	45	16	39	3.0	6.8	2.3	7%	0.8	11.0	67	$21
Consist	B	1st Half		7	7	0	103	79	3.58	1.21	233			26.6	28%	71%	3.84	47	13	39	3.2	6.9	2.1	6%	0.6	7.1	62	$10
LIMA Plan	D+	2nd Half		8	4	0	110	83	3.85	1.22	246			28.5	28%	71%	3.79	44	18	38	2.7	6.8	2.5	9%	0.9	4.0	71	$11
Rand Var	-1	11	Proj	15	9	0	203	158	3.86	1.30	255			26.8	29%	73%	4.01	43	17	40	3.0	7.0	2.3	10%	1.0	7.0	66	$19

Regained 2008's skill set, and offers cause for more optimism:
- Handling RH batters easily
- Promising 2H Ctl, Cmd gains.
- Rising BF/G trend shows an emerging workhorse.

Rock-solid with profit potential.

Davies,Kyle				W	L	Sv	IP	K	ERA	WHIP	OBA	vL	vR	BF/G	H%	S%	xERA	G	L	F	Ctl	Dom	Cmd	hr/f	hr/9	RAR	BPV	R$
RH SP	27	06	ATL	3	7	0	63	51	8.42	1.95	336	333	331	21.9	37%	59%	5.23	37	24	39	4.7	7.3	1.5	17%	2.0	-30.6	19	($5)
Ht/Wt	74 218	07	2TM	7	15	0	136	99	6.09	1.65	288	275	293	22.2	32%	66%	5.08	39	21	41	4.6	6.6	1.4	12%	1.5	-27.3	10	$0
Type	Pwr FB	08	KC	* 15	9	0	170	101	3.70	1.46	275	251	300	23.3	31%	76%	4.84	39	22	40	3.5	5.3	1.5	6%	0.8	13.7	18	$14
Health	A	09	KC	* 12	11	0	169	120	4.63	1.55	276	239	284	25.2	31%	73%	4.90	42	17	41	4.3	6.4	1.5	10%	1.1	-3.7	19	$9
PT/Exp	B	10	KC	8	12	0	184	126	5.34	1.56	285	279	288	25.7	32%	67%	4.70	41	17	42	3.9	6.2	1.6	8%	1.0	-27.2	24	$2
Consist	A	1st Half		4	6	0	89	55	5.64	1.53	276			24.9	31%	63%	4.89	42	15	43	4.1	5.5	1.3	7%	0.9	-16.6	8	$0
LIMA Plan	C	2nd Half		4	6	0	94	71	5.05	1.58	292			26.5	34%	70%	4.52	40	19	42	3.7	6.8	1.8	9%	1.0	-10.6	39	$1
Rand Var	0	11	Proj	8	9	0	131	90	4.97	1.52	277			24.2	31%	70%	4.76	40	18	41	4.0	6.2	1.6	10%	1.2	-7.6	22	$5

Here's yet another way to express how bad things have gotten in KC. This guy and his never-above-25 BPV have logged nearly 500 IP over last three years. Royals fans, you deserve better.

Davis,Doug				W	L	Sv	IP	K	ERA	WHIP	OBA	vL	vR	BF/G	H%	S%	xERA	G	L	F	Ctl	Dom	Cmd	hr/f	hr/9	RAR	BPV	R$
LH SP	35	06	MIL	11	11	0	203	159	4.92	1.52	265	307	253	26.5	31%	68%	4.56	44	20	36	4.5	7.0	1.6	9%	0.8	-10.8	27	$8
Ht/Wt	76 213	07	ARI	13	12	0	193	144	4.25	1.59	280	252	290	26.3	32%	75%	4.55	47	19	34	4.4	6.7	1.5	10%	1.0	4.2	26	$10
Type	Pwr	08	ARI	6	8	0	146	112	4.32	1.53	280	321	269	25.0	33%	73%	4.21	47	22	31	3.9	6.9	1.8	9%	0.8	-0.8	43	$5
Health	F	09	ARI	9	14	0	203	146	4.12	1.51	261	264	268	26.5	29%	76%	4.60	43	22	35	4.6	6.5	1.4	11%	1.1	1.8	14	$8
PT/Exp	B	10	MIL	1	4	0	38	34	7.52	1.98	337	265	351	23.5	40%	63%	4.48	47	21	33	4.9	8.0	1.6	14%	1.4	-16.6	35	($4)
Consist	A	1st Half		1	4	0	33	32	7.57	1.98	338			23.3	42%	61%	4.17	50	19	31	4.9	8.6	1.8	12%	1.1	-14.6	52	($3)
LIMA Plan	D	2nd Half		0	0	0	5	2	7.20	2.00	332			24.6	29%	75%	6.49	26	32	42	5.4	3.6	0.7	25%	3.6	-2.0	-77	($1)
Rand Var	+5	11	Proj	6	11	0	145	118	4.72	1.53	268			23.9	32%	71%	4.41	39	24	36	4.5	7.3	1.6	10%	1.0	-4.9	29	$4

Made only one start after May due to illness, elbow issues. No years in this box with a WHIP under 1.50.

Need we say more?

Davis,Wade				W	L	Sv	IP	K	ERA	WHIP	OBA	vL	vR	BF/G	H%	S%	xERA	G	L	F	Ctl	Dom	Cmd	hr/f	hr/9	RAR	BPV	R$
RH SP	25	06		0	0	0	0	0	0.00	0.00							0.00											
Ht/Wt	77 220	07	aa	7	3	0	80	71	3.83	1.44	271			24.9	34%	72%	4.16				3.5	8.0	2.3		0.3	6.3	87	$8
Type	FB	08	a/a	13	8	0	160	117	3.99	1.40	260			24.7	30%	73%	4.21				3.7	6.6	1.8		0.7	6.3	58	$13
Health	A	09	TAM	* 12	10	0	195	159	4.12	1.37	260	238	250	24.6	31%	71%	4.15	39	25	36	3.4	7.4	2.1	9%	0.8	8.0	57	$16
PT/Exp	C	10	TAM	12	10	0	168	113	4.07	1.35	258	260	250	24.7	28%	74%	4.44	39	17	44	3.3	6.1	1.8	10%	1.3	1.4	37	$12
Consist	A	1st Half		5	9	0	87	58	4.86	1.48	271			23.9	29%	73%	4.71	40	16	43	3.9	6.0	1.5	13%	1.7	-7.8	20	$3
LIMA Plan	D+	2nd Half		7	1	0	81	55	3.22	1.21	245			25.7	28%	77%	4.16	38	18	44	2.7	6.1	2.3	7%	0.9	9.2	54	$9
Rand Var	0	11	Proj	14	9	0	189	139	3.96	1.38	264			25.4	30%	75%	4.42	39	18	43	3.3	6.6	2.0	10%	1.1	-3.0	46	$15

Monthly BPV trend: 9. -7, 60, 43, 46, 67. Great sign to see rookie adjust and improve as year went on. But 2H xERA isn't fully convinced. Mild FB bias says HR issues are legit, Dom is borderline. Don't overbid.

de la Rosa,Jorge				W	L	Sv	IP	K	ERA	WHIP	OBA	vL	vR	BF/G	H%	S%	xERA	G	L	F	Ctl	Dom	Cmd	hr/f	hr/9	RAR	BPV	R$
LH SP	30	06	2TM	* 8	7	0	109	85	5.72	1.66	286	250	269	14.7	33%	67%	4.90	41	20	39	4.7	7.0	1.5	11%	1.2	-16.1	17	$3
Ht/Wt	73 210	07	KC	8	12	0	130	82	5.82	1.64	304	234	321	22.8	33%	67%	5.01	41	20	39	3.7	5.7	1.5	12%	1.4	-21.0	22	$2
Type	Pwr	08	COL	* 13	8	0	152	145	4.56	1.47	263	289	253	20.9	33%	70%	3.90	46	20	34	4.2	8.6	2.1	9%	0.8	-5.4	65	$11
Health	D	09	COL	16	9	0	185	193	4.38	1.38	248	204	262	24.1	32%	70%	3.56	45	21	34	4.0	9.4	2.3	12%	1.0	-4.3	83	$16
PT/Exp	B	10	COL	8	7	0	122	113	4.22	1.31	234	206	244	25.8	28%	71%	3.38	52	19	29	4.1	8.4	2.1	15%	1.1	-3.0	71	$9
Consist	A	1st Half		3	1	0	23	26	3.91	1.43	236			25.0	33%	72%	2.73	61	21	18	5.1	10.2	2.0	10%	0.4	0.3	85	$2
LIMA Plan	B	2nd Half		5	6	0	99	87	4.29	1.29	234			26.0	27%	71%	3.51	50	18	31	3.8	7.9	2.1	16%	1.3	-3.3	68	$6
Rand Var	+3	11	Proj	13	10	0	167	161	4.05	1.38	249			23.1	31%	72%	3.51	49	20	31	4.0	8.7	2.2	11%	0.8	13.0	76	$13

Finger injury ruined 1H, but still lots to like in this profile: Big GB% plus healthy Dom is a foundation to build on. Ctl a bit shaky, but as long as Cmd stays over 2.0, he still has... UP: 18 Wins, 3.75 ERA.

Delcarmen,Manny				W	L	Sv	IP	K	ERA	WHIP	OBA	vL	vR	BF/G	H%	S%	xERA	G	L	F	Ctl	Dom	Cmd	hr/f	hr/9	RAR	BPV	R$
RH RP	29	06	BOS	* 2	1	0	70	62	4.62	1.44	283	319	302	5.1	36%	66%	3.69	45	26	30	3.0	8.0	2.7	3%	0.3	-0.6	86	$4
Ht/Wt	74 205	07	BOS	* 3	2	1	73	73	3.10	1.29	232	167	194	4.8	30%	77%	3.75	45	17	38	4.0	8.9	2.3	7%	0.6	12.7	77	$9
Type	Pwr	08	BOS	1	2	2	74	72	3.27	1.12	208	190	218	4.1	27%	72%	3.28	52	13	35	3.4	8.7	2.6	7%	0.6	9.9	95	$9
Health	A	09	BOS	5	2	0	60	44	4.52	1.64	275	221	322	4.3	32%	73%	5.09	42	17	40	5.1	6.6	1.3	7%	0.8	-0.5	1	$3
PT/Exp	C	10	2TM	3	4	0	52	38	4.99	1.47	234	194	255	4.0	25%	70%	4.67	45	17	38	5.5	6.5	1.2	14%	1.4	-5.9	-8	$1
Consist	C	1st Half		2	2	0	33	23	4.59	1.41	223			4.4	24%	70%	4.67	45	16	38	5.4	6.2	1.2	11%	1.1	-2.1	-11	$1
LIMA Plan	C	2nd Half		1	2	0	19	15	5.68	1.58	251			3.6	27%	69%	4.67	44	18	38	5.7	7.1	1.3	19%	1.9	-3.8	-3	($0)
Rand Var	0	11	Proj	3	3	0	58	46	4.66	1.48	248			4.1	29%	71%	4.49	45	17	38	5.0	7.1	1.4	11%	1.1	-2.0	17	$2

Complete loss of Cmd caused BOS to give up on him. BPV freefall shows the scope of his problems. He still owns those near closer-worthy skills, but make him show them again before you bid.

RAY MURPHY

Demel,Sam

Demel,Sam		W	L	Sv	IP	K	ERA	WHIP	OBA	vL	vR	BF/G	H%	S%	xERA	G	L	F	Ctl	Dom	Cmd	hr/f	hr/9	RAR	BPV	R$
RH RP 25	06	0	0	0	0	0	0.00	0.00							0.00											
Ht/Wt 72 200	07	0	0	0	0	0	0.00	0.00							0.00											
Type Pwr GB	08	0	0	0	0	0	0.00	0.00							0.00											
Health A	09 a/a	2	5	14	61	50	2.21	1.27	232			4.7	29%	83%	3.05				3.8	7.4	**1.9**		0.3	15.9	84	$11
PT/Exp F	10 ARI *	4	1	8	65	57	3.59	1.29	258	237	304	4.7	31%	74%	3.30	53	16	31	2.8	7.9	**2.9**	10%	0.8	3.4	98	$8
Consist A	1st Half	2	0	6	36	31	1.74	1.07	227			5.0	29%	84%	2.84	59	14	27	2.2	7.7	**3.4**	4%	0.2	10.2	115	$7
LIMA Plan B	2nd Half	2	1	2	29	26	5.92	1.56	294			4.3	34%	65%	3.66	51	17	32	3.4	8.1	**2.4**	17%	1.6	-6.8	82	$1
Rand Var 0	11 Proj	3	3	10	58	50	3.88	1.33	255			4.6	31%	73%	3.53	52	16	32	3.3	7.8	2.4	11%	0.9	4.4	82	$8

2-1, 2 Sv, 5.35 ERA in 37 IP at ARI. Sub-2.00 ERA in AAA but struggled in MLB, although problems mainly due to h% and hr/f issues. His GB bias and increased Cmd bode well for potential save opportunities.

Dempster,Ryan

Dempster,Ryan		W	L	Sv	IP	K	ERA	WHIP	OBA	vL	vR	BF/G	H%	S%	xERA	G	L	F	Ctl	Dom	Cmd	hr/f	hr/9	RAR	BPV	R$
RH SP 33	06 CHC	1	9	24	75	67	4.80	1.51	267	310	226	4.5	33%	68%	3.94	52	18	30	4.3	8.0	**1.9**	7%	0.6	-2.9	58	$10
Ht/Wt 74 215	07 CHC	2	7	28	67	55	4.72	1.33	239	259	224	4.3	28%	67%	3.98	47	20	32	4.0	7.4	**1.8**	13%	1.1	-2.4	49	$13
Type Pwr	08 CHC	17	6	0	207	187	2.96	1.21	230	243	213	25.9	29%	77%	3.47	48	20	32	3.3	8.1	**2.5**	8%	0.6	33.4	83	$26
Health B	09 CHC	11	9	0	200	172	3.65	1.31	258	281	241	27.3	31%	75%	3.65	47	18	34	2.9	7.7	**2.6**	11%	1.0	13.4	86	$17
PT/Exp A	10 CHC	15	12	0	215	208	3.85	1.32	246	234	252	26.8	30%	74%	3.53	47	16	37	3.6	8.7	**2.4**	11%	1.0	4.5	85	$17
Consist A	1st Half	6	7	0	117	114	3.54	1.17	224			28.2	27%	75%	3.31	49	13	38	3.2	8.8	**2.7**	13%	1.2	6.9	98	$11
LIMA Plan C	2nd Half	9	5	0	98	94	4.21	1.50	271			25.5	34%	73%	3.78	46	19	36	4.0	8.6	**2.1**	9%	0.8	-2.4	70	$6
Rand Var 0	11 Proj	13	11	0	203	186	3.96	1.33	251			26.9	31%	73%	3.63	47	18	35	3.5	8.3	2.4	10%	0.9	12.9	79	$16

Third straight year of rock-solid skills, as shown by consistent BPV. Cmd struggles in 2H hint at possible fatigue issues. Age and 2H fade raise the risk level, but should be good for another go-round.

Dessens,Elmer

Dessens,Elmer		W	L	Sv	IP	K	ERA	WHIP	OBA	vL	vR	BF/G	H%	S%	xERA	G	L	F	Ctl	Dom	Cmd	hr/f	hr/9	RAR	BPV	R$
RH RP 40	06 2TM	5	8	2	77	52	4.56	1.40	284	267	292	5.4	32%	69%	4.10	45	23	31	2.6	6.1	**2.4**	10%	0.9	-0.4	63	$6
Ht/Wt 71 200	07 2NL *	5	2	0	60	41	4.95	1.32	274			10.6	31%	63%	4.48				2.3	6.2	**2.7**		0.9	-3.9	67	$4
Type Con FB	08 ATL	0	1	0	4	2	22.50	3.50	470			6.4	49%	31%	15.58				9.0	4.5	**0.5**		2.3	-9.0	-69	($3)
Health A	09 NYM *	3	2	11	68	35	3.16	1.15	230	193	228	5.0	24%	77%	4.73	38	14	48	2.7	4.7	**1.7**	7%	1.0	8.6	27	$10
PT/Exp F	10 NYM *	9	2	6	64	30	2.28	1.29	259	232	243	4.1	28%	84%	4.68	42	14	44	2.7	4.3	**1.6**	4%	0.6	13.7	24	$11
Consist F	1st Half	7	1	6	33	22	1.97	1.28	268			4.5	33%	83%	4.14	38	19	43	2.2	6.1	**2.7**	0%	0.0	8.3	65	$8
LIMA Plan C+	2nd Half	2	1	0	31	8	2.61	1.29	249			3.7	24%	86%	5.30	44	12	44	3.2	2.3	**0.7**	8%	1.2	5.4	-22	$2
Rand Var -5	11 Proj	3	4	0	51	26	4.08	1.36	274			4.9	29%	73%	4.70	42	16	42	2.7	4.6	1.7	8%	1.1	-3.5	31	$3

4-2, 2.30 ERA in 47 IP at NYM. Appears to have found fountain of youth, but extreme S% and hr/f say not so fast. Middling Cmd, xERA and BPV do not support low ERA. 4.00 ERA in '11? Take the over and bet the bank.

Detwiler,Ross

Detwiler,Ross		W	L	Sv	IP	K	ERA	WHIP	OBA	vL	vR	BF/G	H%	S%	xERA	G	L	F	Ctl	Dom	Cmd	hr/f	hr/9	RAR	BPV	R$
LH SP 25	06	0	0	0	0	0	0.00	0.00							0.00											
Ht/Wt 77 174	07	0	0	0	0	0	0.00	0.00							0.00											
Type	08	0	0	0	0	0	0.00	0.00							0.00											
Health D	09 WAS *	5	11	0	152	103	4.50	1.64	303	288	289	22.3	35%	72%	4.55	43	25	32	3.7	6.1	**1.6**	5%	0.5	-5.9	30	$1
PT/Exp D	10 WAS *	4	5	0	67	44	3.69	1.61	312	381	268	18.9	35%	79%	4.44	43	20	37	3.0	5.9	**2.0**	7%	0.8	2.7	47	$2
Consist A	1st Half	0	0	0	7	7	1.32	2.05	384			17.9	48%	93%	7.10				2.6	8.3	**3.2**		0.0	2.4	95	$0
LIMA Plan C+	2nd Half	4	5	0	60	38	3.97	1.56	302			19.1	34%	77%	4.47	43	20	37	3.0	5.7	**1.9**	8%	0.9	0.3	41	$2
Rand Var -1	11 Proj	6	9	0	109	70	4.47	1.51	291			20.1	33%	72%	4.42	43	22	35	3.1	5.8	1.8	9%	0.9	-3.7	40	$3

1-3, 4.25 ERA in 30 IP at WAS.
3 reasons for pessimism:
- xERA foreshadows ERA spike
- Minimal progress with Cmd
- Poor Dom (5.2) in MLB career.

Has had success at AAA, but not carrying over... time running out?

Dickey,R.A.

Dickey,R.A.		W	L	Sv	IP	K	ERA	WHIP	OBA	vL	vR	BF/G	H%	S%	xERA	G	L	F	Ctl	Dom	Cmd	hr/f	hr/9	RAR	BPV	R$
RH SP 36	06 aaa	9	8	1	131	50	7.87	1.77	327			28.0	32%	57%	7.53				3.6	3.5	**1.0**		1.9	-54.2	-26	($7)
Ht/Wt 74 216	07 aaa	13	6	0	169	103	4.99	1.56	291			24.4	32%	70%	5.65				3.6	5.5	**1.5**		1.2	-10.9	26	$7
Type Con GB	08 SEA *	7	13	0	162	81	5.00	1.61	304	260	306	18.8	33%	70%	4.96	46	17	36	3.4	4.5	**1.3**	8%	1.0	-13.0	15	$2
Health A	09 MIN *	3	2	0	97	56	5.19	1.64	305	246	326	11.1	34%	69%	4.89	47	18	35	3.6	5.2	**1.4**	8%	0.8	-8.9	20	$0
PT/Exp C	10 NYM *	15	11	0	235	133	2.76	1.18	255	226	269	27.5	28%	79%	3.51	55	17	28	1.9	5.1	**2.6**	8%	0.6	36.4	73	$23
Consist B	1st Half	10	3	0	119	71	2.57	1.21	261			28.8	30%	79%	3.51	55	16	29	1.9	5.4	**2.8**	5%	0.4	21.1	79	$13
LIMA Plan C	2nd Half	5	8	0	116	62	2.95	1.15	248			26.2	27%	78%	3.53	55	17	27	1.9	4.8	**2.5**	11%	0.9	15.3	67	$10
Rand Var -3	11 Proj	10	9	0	185	102	3.89	1.35	281			27.3	31%	74%	4.02	51	17	31	2.2	5.0	2.2	10%	0.9	2.7	58	$11

11-9, 2.84 ERA in 174 IP at NYM. Success came from knuckleball with more velocity. H% and S% correction may bump ERA but GB%, Ctl will maintain success. However, knuckleballers don't follow rules, so be forewarned.

Dotel,Octavio

Dotel,Octavio		W	L	Sv	IP	K	ERA	WHIP	OBA	vL	vR	BF/G	H%	S%	xERA	G	L	F	Ctl	Dom	Cmd	hr/f	hr/9	RAR	BPV	R$
RH RP 37	06 NYY	0	0	0	10	7	10.80	2.90	390	333	414	4.2	43%	63%	8.46	37	20	44	9.9	6.3	**0.6**	12%	1.8	-7.7	******	($3)
Ht/Wt 72 215	07 2TM	2	1	11	31	41	4.10	1.34	251	265	225	4.0	35%	73%	3.25	38	16	46	3.5	12.0	**3.4**	12%	1.2	1.4	137	$7
Type Pwr xFB	08 CHW	4	4	1	67	92	3.76	1.21	216	240	194	3.8	29%	77%	3.06	38	16	46	3.9	12.4	**3.2**	18%	1.6	4.8	133	$9
Health C	09 CHW	3	3	0	62	75	3.32	1.44	235	268	226	4.4	32%	81%	4.19	30	19	51	5.2	10.8	**2.1**	9%	1.0	8.7	62	$6
PT/Exp C	10 2NL	3	4	22	64	75	4.08	1.31	224	301	166	4.0	29%	73%	3.84	32	14	54	4.5	10.5	**2.3**	11%	1.3	-0.5	78	$12
Consist B	1st Half	2	1	19	34	41	4.27	1.31	221			4.2	30%	70%	3.75	30	16	54	4.5	10.9	**2.4**	9%	1.1	-1.1	83	$9
LIMA Plan C+	2nd Half	1	3	3	30	34	3.86	1.32	226			3.8	28%	77%	3.94	33	12	54	4.5	10.1	**2.3**	12%	1.5	0.6	73	$3
Rand Var 0	11 Proj	3	4	8	65	75	4.28	1.36	230			4.1	30%	73%	3.97	33	16	51	4.7	10.3	2.2	11%	1.2	1.4	71	$7

Improved Cmd and consistent Dom suggest that he can keep Father Time at bay for another year. But BA vLH is a concern, and rising FB% raises the risk of an ERA spike. Still LIMA-useful, but the clock is ticking fast.

Doubront,Felix

Doubront,Felix		W	L	Sv	IP	K	ERA	WHIP	OBA	vL	vR	BF/G	H%	S%	xERA	G	L	F	Ctl	Dom	Cmd	hr/f	hr/9	RAR	BPV	R$
LH RP 23	06	0	0	0	0	0	0.00	0.00							0.00											
Ht/Wt 74 165	07	0	0	0	0	0	0.00	0.00							0.00											
Type Pwr GB	08	0	0	0	0	0	0.00	0.00							0.00											
Health A	09 aa	8	6	0	121	87	4.31	1.59	291			21.0	34%	73%	5.04				3.9	6.5	**1.7**		0.6	-0.0	53	$5
PT/Exp D	10 BOS *	10	5	2	105	85	3.60	1.47	274	189	317	15.9	34%	75%	4.15	47	10	42	3.6	7.3	**2.0**	3%	0.3	7.0	59	$10
Consist B	1st Half	8	2	0	74	55	3.15	1.37	264			21.2	33%	75%	4.73	30	15	55	3.3	6.7	**2.0**	0%	0.0	9.0	40	$8
LIMA Plan B	2nd Half	2	3	2	31	30	4.68	1.69	299			10.1	37%	75%	3.92	53	9	38	4.4	8.8	**2.0**	11%	1.2	-2.0	71	$2
Rand Var -1	11 Proj	4	4	0	58	47	4.34	1.48	272			9.5	32%	73%	4.16	51	9	39	3.9	7.3	1.9	9%	0.9	0.9	56	$4

2-2, 2 Sv, 4.32 ERA in 25 IP at BOS. Small MLB sample, but reasons why he might be suited for a specialist role in pen:
- Large variance in splits;
- Extreme GB% in 2H.

Speculate if he lands a RP job.

Downs,Scott

Downs,Scott		W	L	Sv	IP	K	ERA	WHIP	OBA	vL	vR	BF/G	H%	S%	xERA	G	L	F	Ctl	Dom	Cmd	hr/f	hr/9	RAR	BPV	R$
LH RP 35	06 TOR	6	2	1	77	61	4.09	1.34	252	232	258	5.6	29%	72%	3.59	56	18	26	3.5	7.1	**2.0**	15%	1.1	4.4	67	$8
Ht/Wt 74 209	07 TOR	4	2	1	58	57	2.17	1.22	223	209	238	3.0	29%	84%	2.94	60	18	22	3.7	8.8	**2.4**	9%	0.5	16.7	97	$9
Type xGB	08 TOR	0	3	5	71	57	1.78	1.15	213	194	226	4.4	26%	86%	3.00	66	12	22	3.4	7.3	**2.1**	7%	0.4	22.4	81	$10
Health B	09 TOR	1	3	9	47	43	3.08	1.26	259	263	246	4.1	32%	78%	2.99	56	21	24	2.5	8.3	**3.3**	13%	0.8	7.9	115	$8
PT/Exp C	10 TOR	5	5	0	61	48	2.64	1.00	214	152	243	3.6	26%	74%	2.93	58	13	29	2.1	7.0	**3.4**	6%	0.4	11.3	107	$9
Consist A	1st Half	2	5	0	35	28	2.80	0.99	220			3.5	27%	73%	2.89	55	17	28	1.8	7.1	**4.0**	7%	0.5	5.8	113	$5
LIMA Plan A	2nd Half	3	0	0	26	20	2.42	1.00	206			3.6	25%	76%	2.97	62	8	30	2.4	6.9	**2.9**	5%	0.3	5.5	99	$5
Rand Var -3	11 Proj	4	4	8	65	54	3.17	1.15	233			3.9	28%	74%	3.04	59	15	26	2.6	7.4	2.8	10%	0.7	10.0	100	$11

The makings of a quality closer?
- Ctl and Cmd improvement
- Extreme GB profile
- xERA consistency
- Low OBA and elite BPV

Just needs to overcome the LHP bias. Pay for the skills, then hope

Drabek,Kyle

Drabek,Kyle		W	L	Sv	IP	K	ERA	WHIP	OBA	vL	vR	BF/G	H%	S%	xERA	G	L	F	Ctl	Dom	Cmd	hr/f	hr/9	RAR	BPV	R$
RH SP 23	06	0	0	0	0	0	0.00	0.00							0.00											
Ht/Wt 72 185	07	0	0	0	0	0	0.00	0.00							0.00											
Type xGB	08	0	0	0	0	0	0.00	0.00							0.00											
Health A	09 aa	8	2	0	96	64	4.40	1.42	279			27.8	31%	71%	4.84				2.9	6.0	**2.1**		1.0	-1.1	48	$7
PT/Exp D	10 TOR *	14	12	0	179	127	3.27	1.25	231	292	308	24.9	27%	76%	3.40	62	12	26	3.6	6.4	**1.8**	10%	0.7	19.2	57	$18
Consist C	1st Half	7	8	0	98	67	3.67	1.36	248			26.2	28%	74%	3.77				3.9	6.2	**1.6**		0.7	5.6	54	$8
LIMA Plan C	2nd Half	7	4	0	81	60	2.78	1.12	211			23.4	25%	78%	3.18	62	12	26	3.3	6.7	**2.0**	10%	0.7	13.6	70	$11
Rand Var -1	11 Proj	11	6	0	131	94	4.00	1.34	257			24.2	30%	71%	3.66	57	14	28	3.3	6.5	2.0	10%	0.8	10.1	62	$12

0-3, 4.76 ERA in 17 IP at TOR. Spent full season at AA before late-season callup. Lots to like, including 2H Cmd, ERA/xERA agreement, and GB profile. Still young and learning, but definitely one to stash if possible.

SCOTT MONROE

Duchscherer,Justin			W	L	Sv	IP	K	ERA	WHIP	OBA	vL	vR	BF/G	H%	S%	xERA	G	L	F	Ctl	Dom	Cmd	hr/f	hr/9	RAR	BPV	R$
RH SP 33	06	OAK	2	1	9	55	51	2.93	1.11	250	248	241	4.2	31%	75%	3.34	37	26	38	1.5	8.3	5.7	7%	0.7	11.1	125	$11
Ht/Wt 74 201	07	OAK	3	3	0	16	13	4.97	1.60	281	400	176	4.3	31%	74%	4.48	47	17	36	4.4	7.2	1.6	16%	1.7	-0.9	35	$2
Type	08	OAK	10	8	0	142	95	2.54	1.00	211	227	188	25.2	24%	78%	3.79	41	20	39	2.2	6.0	2.8	7%	0.7	31.6	70	$22
Health F	09	OAK	0	0	0	0	0	0.00	0.00							0.00											
PT/Exp D	10	OAK	2	1	0	28	18	2.89	1.36	248	192	320	24.0	27%	83%	4.28	46	18	36	3.9	5.8	1.5	10%	1.0	4.3	24	$3
Consist A	1st Half		2	1	0	28	18	2.89	1.36	248			24.0	27%	83%	4.28	46	18	36	3.9	5.8	1.5	10%	1.0	4.3	24	$3
LIMA Plan B	2nd Half		0	0	0	0	0	0.00	0.00							0.00											
Rand Var -5	11	Proj	3	2	0	58	41	3.57	1.31	258			8.8	29%	76%	4.06	44	19	37	2.9	6.4	2.2	9%	0.9	1.6	57	$5

After missing most or all of 3 of the past 4 seasons, his main hurdle is proving to teams that he is healthy and able to pitch. If hip and elbow and any other issues are resolved, then he may be worth an end-game bid.

Duensing,Brian			W	L	Sv	IP	K	ERA	WHIP	OBA	vL	vR	BF/G	H%	S%	xERA	G	L	F	Ctl	Dom	Cmd	hr/f	hr/9	RAR	BPV	R$
LH RP 28	06	aa	1	2	0	49	24	5.10	1.72	316			22.8	33%	74%	6.82				3.8	4.4	1.2		1.5	-3.5	-2	($1)
Ht/Wt 71 195	07	a/a	15	6	0	167	98	4.11	1.43	296			26.0	33%	73%	5.16				2.2	5.3	2.4		0.9	7.3	49	$13
Type Con GB	08	aaa	5	11	0	138	62	5.07	1.48	303			24.3	32%	67%	5.44				2.3	4.1	1.8		1.1	-12.9	24	$2
Health A	09	MIN	* 9	8	0	159	88	4.55	1.48	292	244	269	18.9	33%	69%	4.80	45	15	40	2.9	5.0	1.7	4%	0.5	-1.9	36	$7
PT/Exp C	10	MIN	10	3	0	131	78	2.62	1.20	249	162	282	10.2	28%	82%	3.70	53	16	31	2.4	5.4	2.2	8%	0.8	24.5	63	$15
Consist B	1st Half		2	1	0	36	23	1.75	0.89	191			3.9	21%	86%	3.45	48	15	37	2.0	5.8	2.9	8%	0.8	10.6	76	$6
LIMA Plan D+	2nd Half		8	2	0	95	55	2.95	1.32	268			22.3	30%	80%	3.79	55	16	30	2.6	5.2	2.0	9%	0.8	13.9	57	$9
Rand Var -4	11	Proj	12	8	0	189	106	3.82	1.35	275			24.5	30%	74%	4.18	50	15	34	2.5	5.1	2.0	9%	0.9	2.4	51	$14

Favorable H%, S% and hr/f combined to produce an ERA a full run off his xERA. GB% does help to make up for low Dom, but he's demonstrated that tendency for only half a season. Don't bank on a repeat.

Duke,Zach			W	L	Sv	IP	K	ERA	WHIP	OBA	vL	vR	BF/G	H%	S%	xERA	G	L	F	Ctl	Dom	Cmd	hr/f	hr/9	RAR	BPV	R$
LH SP 27	06	PIT	10	15	0	215	117	4.48	1.50	296	264	310	28.0	33%	71%	4.38	51	20	29	2.8	4.9	1.7	8%	0.7	0.3	40	$8
Ht/Wt 74 205	07	PIT	3	8	0	107	41	5.54	1.73	347	341	363	25.0	36%	70%	4.83	51	20	29	2.1	3.4	1.6	11%	1.2	-14.7	34	($3)
Type Con	08	PIT	5	14	0	185	87	4.82	1.50	306	279	308	26.4	33%	69%	4.48	48	21	31	2.3	4.2	1.9	9%	0.9	-12.5	41	$2
Health B	09	PIT	11	16	0	213	106	4.06	1.31	278	284	285	28.2	30%	72%	4.22	48	20	33	2.1	4.5	2.2	10%	1.0	3.5	50	$12
PT/Exp A	10	PIT	8	15	0	159	96	5.72	1.65	321	328	319	25.1	35%	68%	4.36	48	20	33	2.9	5.4	1.9	14%	1.4	-33.4	46	($3)
Consist A	1st Half		3	8	0	80	50	5.49	1.72	329			26.6	36%	71%	4.27	49	21	30	3.0	5.6	1.9	14%	1.3	-14.6	47	($2)
LIMA Plan D	2nd Half		5	7	0	79	46	5.95	1.59	313			23.7	33%	65%	4.44	46	18	35	2.7	5.3	1.9	13%	1.5	-18.7	45	($1)
Rand Var +5	11	Proj	9	16	0	189	107	4.63	1.43	289			25.6	31%	70%	4.21	48	20	32	2.5	5.1	2.0	11%	1.1	-1.5	50	$6

Bad luck played a part, but he also gave back many gains in Cmd, xERA, and BPV from '09. On the plus side, Dom now has risen for 3 straight years, but still doesn't miss enough bats to be worth more than a gamble.

Durbin,Chad			W	L	Sv	IP	K	ERA	WHIP	OBA	vL	vR	BF/G	H%	S%	xERA	G	L	F	Ctl	Dom	Cmd	hr/f	hr/9	RAR	BPV	R$
RH RP 33	06	aaa	11	8	0	185	120	4.34	1.44	292			28.8	33%	72%	5.12				2.5	5.8	2.4		1.0	4.1	52	$12
Ht/Wt 74 222	07	DET	8	7	1	128	66	4.72	1.43	270	281	255	15.4	28%	71%	4.99	44	16	40	3.5	4.7	1.3	12%	1.5	-3.4	12	$7
Type Pwr	08	PHI	5	4	1	88	63	2.87	1.32	247	311	214	5.2	29%	79%	4.14	46	20	34	3.6	6.5	1.8	6%	0.5	15.1	43	$9
Health B	09	PHI	2	2	2	70	62	4.39	1.48	222	223	218	5.2	26%	73%	4.75	39	18	42	6.1	8.0	1.3	10%	1.0	-1.7	-2	$3
PT/Exp C	10	PHI	4	1	0	69	63	3.80	1.31	245	324	195	4.5	30%	73%	3.78	42	17	41	3.5	8.3	2.3	9%	0.9	1.8	73	$5
Consist B	1st Half		0	1	0	35	31	3.31	1.19	237			5.0	29%	74%	3.55	47	11	41	2.8	7.9	2.8	7%	0.8	3.1	92	$2
LIMA Plan C	2nd Half		4	0	0	33	32	4.31	1.44	254			4.2	31%	73%	4.02	37	22	40	4.3	8.6	2.0	11%	1.1	-1.2	54	$3
Rand Var 0	11	Proj	4	2	0	65	56	4.00	1.38	246			5.2	29%	73%	4.16	42	18	40	4.1	7.7	1.9	9%	1.0	-0.1	47	$4

The yo-yo continues...
PRO: 3 straight years of Dom gain; regained Ctl and boosted Cmd; skills support ERA drop.
CON: Troubles vLHers return; 2H Ctl problems raise flags.
Low bid = low risk, low reward.

Ely,John			W	L	Sv	IP	K	ERA	WHIP	OBA	vL	vR	BF/G	H%	S%	xERA	G	L	F	Ctl	Dom	Cmd	hr/f	hr/9	RAR	BPV	R$
RH SP 24	06		0	0	0	0	0	0.00	0.00							0.00											
Ht/Wt 73 200	07		0	0	0	0	0	0.00	0.00							0.00											
Type	08		0	0	0	0	0	0.00	0.00							0.00											
Health A	09	aa	14	2	0	156	107	3.86	1.45	281			25.2	32%	74%	4.64				3.1	6.2	2.0		0.7	8.6	56	$13
PT/Exp D	10	LA	* 9	14	0	168	122	5.30	1.40	264	240	299	23.4	30%	63%	4.04	46	20	34	3.5	6.5	1.9	11%	1.0	-26.7	47	$4
Consist B	1st Half		6	6	0	93	65	3.40	1.18	237			25.3	27%	73%	3.74	44	22	34	2.7	6.3	2.3	7%	0.7	7.1	63	$9
LIMA Plan C+	2nd Half		3	8	0	75	57	7.65	1.67	295			21.6	33%	54%	4.37	49	16	34	4.4	6.8	1.5	14%	1.4	-33.8	31	($5)
Rand Var +4	11	Proj	9	8	0	131	96	4.55	1.42	268			23.6	31%	70%	4.09	46	20	34	3.4	6.6	1.9	10%	1.0	0.9	51	$7

4-10, 5.49 ERA in 100 IP at LA. Promising 1H undercut by bad luck in 2H with H%, S%, hr/f, but Ctl was his own undoing. Dom growth a plus, but BA vRH is a concern and shaky Ctl limits his short-term upside.

Enright,Barry			W	L	Sv	IP	K	ERA	WHIP	OBA	vL	vR	BF/G	H%	S%	xERA	G	L	F	Ctl	Dom	Cmd	hr/f	hr/9	RAR	BPV	R$
RH SP 25	06		0	0	0	0	0	0.00	0.00							0.00											
Ht/Wt 75 220	07		0	0	0	0	0	0.00	0.00							0.00											
Type Con xFB	08		0	0	0	0	0	0.00	0.00							0.00											
Health A	09	aa	10	9	0	156	88	5.35	1.58	321			26.0	35%	68%	6.18				2.2	5.1	2.3		1.2	-20.0	32	$3
PT/Exp D	10	ARI	* 10	8	0	192	117	4.03	1.27	270	241	279	26.0	28%	74%	4.52	35	15	50	2.1	5.5	2.6	10%	1.5	-0.4	55	$11
Consist D	1st Half		5	1	0	98	73	4.05	1.29	279			27.6	32%	72%	4.25	29	21	50	1.8	6.7	3.7	7%	1.1	-0.4	79	$6
LIMA Plan C	2nd Half		5	7	0	94	44	4.02	1.26	260			24.5	25%	78%	4.88	35	15	50	2.4	4.2	1.8	13%	1.9	-0.1	25	$5
Rand Var 0	11	Proj	8	7	0	145	84	4.53	1.39	290			26.1	31%	72%	4.83	35	15	50	2.2	5.2	2.4	10%	1.5	-12.3	49	$6

6-7, 3.91 ERA in 99 IP at ARI. Most of 1H spent in AA, so the disparity between 1H/2H Dom and Cmd is concerning. His low Dom/high FB profile makes him the perfect rooting target when your power hitter comes to bat.

Eveland,Dana			W	L	Sv	IP	K	ERA	WHIP	OBA	vL	vR	BF/G	H%	S%	xERA	G	L	F	Ctl	Dom	Cmd	hr/f	hr/9	RAR	BPV	R$
LH RP 27	06	MIL	* 6	8	0	132	135	4.43	1.35	243			19.4	32%	67%	3.51	44	27	29	3.9	9.2	2.3	9%	0.6	1.0	81	$10
Ht/Wt 73 216	07	aaa	2	0	0	33	16	4.64	1.76	301			11.9	34%	72%	4.97	55	20	25	4.9	4.4	0.9	3%	0.3	-0.7	-21	$0
Type GB	08	OAK	9	9	0	168	118	4.34	1.48	266	248	275	25.5	31%	70%	4.22	49	22	29	4.1	6.3	1.5	7%	0.5	0.2	29	$9
Health A	09	OAK	* 10	10	0	168	93	5.80	1.76	318	373	362	23.1	35%	67%	4.58	56	18	25	4.0	5.0	1.2	10%	0.8	-28.0	16	($1)
PT/Exp C	10	2TM	* 3	7	0	80	45	7.48	1.92	341	319	326	16.9	37%	60%	5.02	50	16	34	4.2	5.1	1.2	9%	1.0	-33.8	7	($7)
Consist A	1st Half		3	5	0	54	24	6.80	1.92	320			21.9	34%	63%	5.59	50	16	34	5.3	4.0	0.8	6%	0.7	-18.2	-44	($4)
LIMA Plan C+	2nd Half		0	2	0	26	21	8.92	1.94	382			11.5	44%	55%	8.48				1.8	7.4	4.1		1.8	-15.5	56	($4)
Rand Var +5	11	Proj	2	3	0	44	28	5.17	1.56	290			16.3	32%	68%	4.34	50	19	31	3.7	5.8	1.6	11%	1.0	-0.7	32	$0

3-5, 6.79 ERA in 54 IP at TOR and PIT. The last two years show what kind of pitcher he is, and there is not a lot of call for a soft-tossing LH with poor Ctl, despite his GB%. Bad luck? Yes, but also a bad pitcher.

Farnsworth,Kyle			W	L	Sv	IP	K	ERA	WHIP	OBA	vL	vR	BF/G	H%	S%	xERA	G	L	F	Ctl	Dom	Cmd	hr/f	hr/9	RAR	BPV	R$
RH RP 34	06	NYY	3	6	6	66	75	4.36	1.36	250	215	264	3.9	33%	71%	3.76	34	22	44	3.8	10.2	2.7	11%	1.1	1.6	93	$8
Ht/Wt 76 233	07	NYY	2	1	0	60	48	4.80	1.45	262	273	242	4.1	30%	71%	4.95	30	19	51	4.1	7.2	1.8	10%	1.4	-2.2	29	$3
Type Pwr	08	2AL	2	3	1	60	61	4.48	1.53	292	275	318	4.4	34%	81%	4.11	35	19	46	3.3	9.1	2.8	18%	2.2	-1.0	88	$3
Health A	09	KC	1	5	0	37	42	4.58	1.53	290	277	294	4.0	39%	70%	3.44	46	21	34	3.4	10.1	3.0	8%	0.7	-0.6	115	$2
PT/Exp D	10	2TM	3	2	0	65	61	3.34	1.14	232	264	202	4.4	30%	71%	3.30	41	22	36	2.6	8.5	3.2	6%	0.6	5.9	101	$7
Consist A	1st Half		1	0	0	34	26	2.10	1.08	224			5.1	27%	83%	3.47	41	25	33	2.4	6.8	2.9	6%	0.5	8.4	78	$4
LIMA Plan A	2nd Half		2	2	0	30	35	4.74	1.22	240			3.8	33%	60%	3.10	41	19	40	3.0	10.4	3.5	6%	0.6	-2.5	126	$3
Rand Var -1	11	Proj	3	4	0	65	67	3.86	1.26	246			4.1	31%	72%	3.44	41	21	39	3.0	9.2	3.0	10%	1.0	6.2	103	$6

Seems to be improving with age. Luck finally balanced out, and an ERA correction resulted. FB% spike in 2H is a concern, but as long as he still has that elite Dom, he remains a nice LIMA play.

Feldman,Scott			W	L	Sv	IP	K	ERA	WHIP	OBA	vL	vR	BF/G	H%	S%	xERA	G	L	F	Ctl	Dom	Cmd	hr/f	hr/9	RAR	BPV	R$
RH SP 28	06	TEX	* 2	4	4	68	52	3.57	1.26	259	280	259	4.8	30%	76%	3.18	59	19	22	2.5	6.8	2.7	18%	1.1	8.3	93	$8
Ht/Wt 77 210	07	TEX	* 2	3	2	69	39	5.87	1.79	288			6.5	32%	66%	4.98	59	15	26	5.8	5.1	0.9	7%	0.5	-11.6	-29	($1)
Type Con	08	TEX	* 8	8	0	164	77	5.33	1.42	274	291	269	23.7	28%	64%	4.87	44	19	37	3.2	4.2	1.3	11%	1.2	-19.8	11	$5
Health A	09	TEX	17	8	0	190	113	4.08	1.28	250	226	277	23.4	27%	70%	4.26	47	21	33	3.1	5.4	1.7	9%	0.9	8.7	38	$18
PT/Exp B	10	TEX	7	11	0	141	75	5.48	1.60	312	302	323	22.0	34%	67%	4.71	43	20	37	2.9	4.8	1.7	10%	1.1	-23.3	29	($0)
Consist B	1st Half		5	8	0	101	61	5.51	1.63	316			27.1	35%	67%	4.48	45	20	35	2.9	5.4	1.8	9%	1.0	-17.1	41	($0)
LIMA Plan F	2nd Half		2	3	0	40	14	5.40	1.52	303			14.8	30%	69%	5.26	37	21	42	2.7	3.1	1.2	11%	1.6	-6.2	-1	($0)
Rand Var +2	11	Proj	8	9	0	145	74	4.72	1.47	286			21.2	30%	70%	4.72	43	20	36	3.0	4.6	1.5	10%	1.1	-7.7	22	$5

Another low-Dom pitcher with not much margin for error. With good luck (and a high GB%), 2009 was possible. With bad luck (and more FBs), 2010 is the downside. To bid is essentially to roll the dice and hope.

SCOTT MONROE

Feliciano,Pedro

Feliciano,Pedro		W	L	Sv	IP	K	ERA	WHIP	OBA	vL	vR	BF/G	H%	S%	xERA	G	L	F	Ctl	Dom	Cmd	hr/f	hr/9	RAR	BPV	R$
LH RP 34	06 NYM	7	2	0	60	54	2.10	1.26	248	231	266	3.9	31%	86%	3.44	49	21	29	3.0	8.1	2.7	8%	0.6	17.7	92	$10
Ht/Wt 70 192	07 NYM	2	2	2	64	61	3.09	1.22	207	168	221	3.4	27%	75%	3.34	56	17	27	4.4	8.6	2.0	7%	0.4	10.5	70	$7
Type Pwr xGB	08 NYM	3	4	2	53	50	4.05	1.56	275	210	357	2.8	33%	78%	3.69	53	19	27	4.4	8.4	1.9	16%	1.2	1.4	65	$3
Health A	09 NYM	6	4	0	59	59	3.04	1.16	234	215	264	2.8	29%	79%	2.88	57	16	28	2.7	9.0	3.3	16%	1.1	8.4	122	$9
PT/Exp C	10 NYM	3	6	0	63	56	3.30	1.53	272	211	336	3.0	35%	77%	3.36	56	23	21	4.3	8.0	1.9	3%	0.1	5.5	62	$3
Consist B	1st Half	2	4	0	34	33	2.40	1.57	280			3.2	37%	85%	3.24	54	26	21	4.3	8.8	2.1	5%	0.3	6.7	75	$3
LIMA Plan A	2nd Half	1	2	0	29	23	4.34	1.48	262			2.8	33%	67%	3.49	59	20	22	4.3	7.1	1.6	0%	0.0	-1.2	48	$1
Rand Var 0	11 Proj	4	5	3	63	56	3.74	1.31	248			3.0	31%	73%	3.19	56	20	24	3.5	8.1	2.3	11%	0.7	7.3	86	$6

He's still great against lefties (.574 OPS), but righties maul him, so he stays pigeon-holed as a specialist. Ctl worries are false alarm, as 20% of his 2010 BBs were intentional. Still some LIMA value here.

Feliz,Neftali

Feliz,Neftali		W	L	Sv	IP	K	ERA	WHIP	OBA	vL	vR	BF/G	H%	S%	xERA	G	L	F	Ctl	Dom	Cmd	hr/f	hr/9	RAR	BPV	R$
RH RP 22	06	0	0	0	0	0	0.00	0.00							0.00											
Ht/Wt 75 190	07	0	0	0	0	0	0.00	0.00							0.00											
Type Pwr xFB	08 aa	4	3	0	45	42	3.23	1.25	217			18.8	29%	72%	2.67				4.2	8.4	2.0		0.2	6.0	98	$6
Health A	09 TEX *	5	6	2	108	104	3.50	1.20	232	155	85	9.9	30%	70%	4.15	38	5	57	3.2	8.7	2.7	2%	0.3	12.7	87	$13
PT/Exp C	10 TEX	4	3	40	69	71	2.73	0.88	180	127	220	3.8	23%	71%	3.15	37	15	48	2.3	9.2	3.9	6%	0.6	12.1	118	$25
Consist C	1st Half	1	2	22	36	40	3.00	0.97	191			3.8	26%	70%	3.15	33	20	47	2.8	10.0	3.6	5%	0.5	5.1	116	$12
LIMA Plan C+	2nd Half	3	1	18	33	31	2.43	0.78	168			3.7	20%	74%	3.14	41	9	49	1.9	8.4	4.4	7%	0.8	7.0	119	$13
Rand Var -4	11 Proj	4	3	38	65	64	3.31	1.12	220			4.1	28%	73%	3.68	38	13	50	2.9	8.8	3.0	7%	0.8	4.8	96	$21

Transition to closer was very smooth. Ate up lefties and very good against righties. H% will level off, and that FB% in TEX will yield more HR and drag ERA a bit. TEX may be tempted to make him a starter - a mistake.

Figueroa,Nelson

Figueroa,Nelson		W	L	Sv	IP	K	ERA	WHIP	OBA	vL	vR	BF/G	H%	S%	xERA	G	L	F	Ctl	Dom	Cmd	hr/f	hr/9	RAR	BPV	R$
RH RP 36	06 aaa	3	5	0	76	35	5.48	1.50	297			21.0	30%	67%	5.88				2.7	4.2	1.5		1.5	-9.0	8	$1
Ht/Wt 73 180	07 MEX	8	6	0	153	84	4.46	1.39	286			34.8	31%	70%	4.89				2.3	4.9	2.1		0.9	-0.0	43	$8
Type	08 NYM *	7	10	0	159	107	5.65	1.71	316	371	200	20.4	35%	68%	4.89	41	21	39	3.6	6.1	1.7	10%	1.2	-26.9	31	($2)
Health A	09 NYM *	10	13	0	182	130	3.32	1.36	277	274	294	23.6	32%	77%	4.22	37	24	39	2.5	6.4	2.5	6%	0.7	19.5	62	$14
PT/Exp C	10 2NL *	10	4	1	112	87	2.99	1.19	234	280	217	13.6	27%	79%	3.84	42	18	40	3.0	7.0	2.3	8%	0.9	14.2	66	$13
Consist B	1st Half	4	1	1	41	26	2.89	1.07	215			11.7	25%	73%	3.86	41	23	36	2.7	5.8	2.2	5%	0.5	5.7	51	$6
LIMA Plan C+	2nd Half	6	3	0	71	61	3.04	1.27	245			14.9	29%	81%	3.81	43	16	41	3.2	7.7	2.4	11%	1.1	8.5	74	$8
Rand Var -3	11 Proj	7	7	0	116	83	3.88	1.34	263			17.0	30%	74%	4.20	41	20	40	2.9	6.4	2.2	9%	1.0	-0.9	55	$8

7-4, 3.29 ERA in 93 IP at PHI, MIL. Better suited to bullpen:

	Ctl	Dom	Cmd
Starting	4.0	7.3	1.8
Relief	2.2	6.8	3.1

That's the difference between marginal and very good.

Fister,Doug

Fister,Doug		W	L	Sv	IP	K	ERA	WHIP	OBA	vL	vR	BF/G	H%	S%	xERA	G	L	F	Ctl	Dom	Cmd	hr/f	hr/9	RAR	BPV	R$
RH SP 27	06	0	0	0	0	0	0.00	0.00							0.00											
Ht/Wt 80 193	07 aa	7	8	0	131	74	5.52	1.64	328			24.9	36%	68%	6.39				2.4	5.1	2.1		1.1	-17.2	32	$1
Type Con	08 aa	6	14	0	134	88	6.43	1.70	321			20.0	36%	61%	6.07				3.2	5.9	1.8		0.8	-35.1	39	($3)
Health A	09 SEA *	10	8	0	173	104	4.69	1.52	324	237	298	22.0	35%	72%	4.51	41	20	39	1.5	5.4	3.5	10%	1.2	-5.2	75	$7
PT/Exp C	10 SEA	6	14	0	171	93	4.11	1.28	279	274	279	25.7	31%	68%	3.96	47	18	35	1.7	4.9	2.9	7%	0.7	0.7	68	$9
Consist C	1st Half	3	4	0	78	38	3.22	1.05	235			25.9	25%	71%	3.72	53	13	34	1.6	4.4	2.7	7%	0.7	8.9	66	$8
LIMA Plan C+	2nd Half	3	10	0	93	55	4.85	1.48	313			25.5	35%	67%	4.14	43	22	35	1.7	5.3	3.1	6%	0.7	-8.2	70	$2
Rand Var 0	11 Proj	8	13	0	174	101	4.40	1.37	290			23.3	32%	70%	4.16	46	19	36	2.0	5.2	2.7	9%	1.0	2.7	65	$9

High Cmd, low Dom soft-tosser got fabulous 1H results due to low LD% and H%. Skills grew in 2H as stat line regressed. Value lies in Safeco (3.60 home ERA, 5.06 road), there are better skill sets to chase.

Flores,Randy

Flores,Randy		W	L	Sv	IP	K	ERA	WHIP	OBA	vL	vR	BF/G	H%	S%	xERA	G	L	F	Ctl	Dom	Cmd	hr/f	hr/9	RAR	BPV	R$
LH RP 35	06 STL	1	1	0	41	40	5.68	1.72	297	258	329	2.9	37%	68%	4.57	39	22	39	4.8	8.7	1.8	10%	1.1	-6.1	45	($0)
Ht/Wt 72 190	07 STL	3	0	1	55	47	4.25	1.56	314	326	299	3.5	39%	71%	4.07	41	23	37	2.5	7.7	3.1	3%	0.3	1.2	91	$3
Type Pwr	08 STL	1	0	1	26	17	5.25	2.10	319	314	316	3.0	37%	75%	5.73	51	19	31	7.0	6.0	0.9	7%	0.7	-3.1	-53	($1)
Health A	09 aaa	0	2	0	31	27	4.86	1.69	324			3.8	39%	71%	5.85				3.0	7.7	2.5		0.6	-2.1	71	($0)
PT/Exp D	10 2TM	2	0	0	31	20	3.19	1.52	268	295	246	2.4	28%	88%	4.95	35	22	43	4.4	5.8	1.3	14%	1.7	3.4	-0	$2
Consist B	1st Half	2	0	0	20	11	3.20	1.07	190			2.3	20%	74%	4.77	33	15	53	3.7	5.0	1.4	7%	0.9	2.1	3	$3
LIMA Plan C+	2nd Half	0	0	0	11	9	3.19	2.30	374			2.5	40%	100%	5.23	37	33	30	5.6	7.2	1.3	32%	3.2	1.2	-6	($1)
Rand Var -5	11 Proj	2	0	0	29	21	4.66	1.48	268			3.0	31%	70%	4.45	41	24	36	4.0	6.5	1.6	9%	0.9	-0.9	27	$1

High hr/9, low Dom, high Ctl... his ERA wasn't a fluke, it was a strand rate-fed miracle. LH specialists who don't retire LHers often end up retiring themselves.

Floyd,Gavin

Floyd,Gavin		W	L	Sv	IP	K	ERA	WHIP	OBA	vL	vR	BF/G	H%	S%	xERA	G	L	F	Ctl	Dom	Cmd	hr/f	hr/9	RAR	BPV	R$
RH SP 28	06 PHI *	11	7	0	169	105	6.81	1.74	317	306	323	28.1	34%	62%	5.19	39	24	37	3.9	5.6	1.4	13%	1.5	-48.5	13	($4)
Ht/Wt 77 230	07 CHW *	8	8	0	176	134	4.70	1.44	285	314	286	23.3	32%	72%	4.33	42	17	41	2.8	6.8	2.4	13%	1.5	-4.2	67	$10
Type	08 CHW	17	8	0	206	145	3.84	1.26	246	259	226	26.1	27%	75%	4.22	41	19	40	3.1	6.3	2.1	12%	1.3	12.9	51	$21
Health A	09 CHW	11	11	0	193	163	4.06	1.23	246	232	256	26.7	29%	69%	3.64	44	22	33	2.8	7.6	2.8	11%	1.0	9.4	85	$19
PT/Exp A	10 CHW	10	13	0	187	151	4.08	1.37	274	259	292	25.9	33%	71%	3.57	50	18	32	2.8	7.3	2.6	8%	0.7	1.3	83	$12
Consist A	1st Half	3	7	0	97	82	4.65	1.34	268			25.8	33%	65%	3.47	50	18	32	2.8	7.6	2.7	7%	0.7	-6.1	90	$5
LIMA Plan C+	2nd Half	7	6	0	91	69	3.48	1.40	279			26.1	33%	77%	3.68	50	18	32	2.8	6.9	2.5	8%	0.7	7.4	76	$8
Rand Var 0	11 Proj	13	10	0	189	148	3.82	1.34	266			25.9	31%	74%	3.79	47	19	34	2.9	7.1	2.5	10%	1.0	11.5	75	$17

Carbon copy of 2009 (now with more GBs!) confirms his skill level. Ended year with sore right shoulder, which perhaps explains 2H Dom dip, and ups the 2011 risk level a bit. If healthy, expect carbon copy #3.

Francisco,Frank

Francisco,Frank		W	L	Sv	IP	K	ERA	WHIP	OBA	vL	vR	BF/G	H%	S%	xERA	G	L	F	Ctl	Dom	Cmd	hr/f	hr/9	RAR	BPV	R$
RH RP 31	06 TEX *	0	1	0	22	25	3.26	1.22	243		444	4.4	31%	79%	3.10	50	13	38	2.9	10.2	3.6	14%	1.2	3.5	134	$2
Ht/Wt 75 230	07 TEX	1	1	0	59	49	4.55	1.60	254	221	286	4.5	31%	71%	5.15	35	22	43	5.8	7.4	1.3	4%	0.5	-0.3	-9	$2
Type Pwr FB	08 TEX	3	5	5	63	83	3.13	1.15	208	193	207	4.4	30%	77%	3.20	33	19	48	3.7	11.8	3.2	10%	1.0	9.5	123	$11
Health D	09 TEX	2	3	25	49	57	3.83	1.12	223	238	186	3.9	29%	69%	3.45	29	21	50	2.7	10.4	3.8	10%	1.1	3.8	121	$15
PT/Exp C	10 TEX	6	4	2	53	60	3.76	1.27	248	205	275	3.9	33%	73%	3.21	39	20	40	3.1	10.2	3.3	9%	0.9	2.5	119	$8
Consist A	1st Half	6	3	2	37	46	3.89	1.32	257			4.0	37%	70%	3.07	39	22	40	3.2	11.2	3.5	5%	0.5	1.1	133	$6
LIMA Plan A	2nd Half	0	1	0	16	14	3.44	1.15	227			3.8	25%	80%	3.55	41	18	41	2.9	8.0	2.8	17%	1.7	1.4	86	$1
Rand Var +1	11 Proj	3	4	13	58	63	3.57	1.19	234			4.0	30%	74%	3.42	36	20	44	2.9	9.8	3.3	11%	1.1	6.2	111	$11

Still has closer-worthy skills, but lost his gig due to poor start (7.30 ERA through May 6). Dip in FB% is encouraging, leaving Arlington as FA could be more encouraging. Health risk is real but so are skills... UP: 35 SV

Francis,Jeff

Francis,Jeff		W	L	Sv	IP	K	ERA	WHIP	OBA	vL	vR	BF/G	H%	S%	xERA	G	L	F	Ctl	Dom	Cmd	hr/f	hr/9	RAR	BPV	R$
LH SP 30	06 COL	13	11	0	199	117	4.16	1.29	250	241	252	26.2	28%	69%	4.49	45	19	36	3.1	5.3	1.7	8%	0.8	8.0	34	$16
Ht/Wt 77 205	07 COL	17	9	0	215	165	4.22	1.38	278	242	289	27.2	32%	72%	4.07	44	18	37	2.6	6.9	2.6	10%	1.0	5.4	75	$18
Type	08 COL	4	10	0	144	94	5.01	1.48	288	248	295	26.4	31%	69%	4.46	44	20	36	3.1	5.9	1.9	12%	1.3	-13.1	45	$2
Health F	09 COL	0	0	0	0	0	0.00	0.00							0.00											
PT/Exp C	10 COL	4	6	0	104	67	5.00	1.36	288	309	290	22.3	32%	64%	3.82	47	21	32	2.0	5.8	2.9	10%	0.9	-12.7	76	$2
Consist B	1st Half	2	3	0	65	30	4.42	1.40	293			25.6	32%	67%	4.10	52	18	30	2.0	4.1	2.0	5%	0.5	-3.2	50	$1
LIMA Plan B+	2nd Half	2	3	0	39	37	5.98	1.30	279			18.4	32%	58%	3.27	42	24	34	1.9	8.5	4.4	19%	1.8	-9.5	121	$1
Rand Var +3	11 Proj	6	8	0	138	98	4.31	1.36	277			23.6	31%	71%	3.95	44	21	35	2.5	6.4	2.6	10%	1.0	3.3	71	$7

The BPIs show a portrait of a very good pitcher in between DL stints. 2H sample is tiny, but skills appear intact, or even improved. IF (a BIG BIG IF) he can stay healthy...
UP: 3.75 ERA, 15 Wins.

Franklin,Ryan

Franklin,Ryan		W	L	Sv	IP	K	ERA	WHIP	OBA	vL	vR	BF/G	H%	S%	xERA	G	L	F	Ctl	Dom	Cmd	hr/f	hr/9	RAR	BPV	R$
RH RP 38	06 2NL	6	7	0	77	43	4.55	1.54	283	265	294	5.2	30%	75%	4.91	47	18	35	3.9	5.0	1.3	14%	1.5	-0.6	11	$4
Ht/Wt 75 190	07 STL	4	4	1	80	44	3.04	1.01	237	238	231	4.6	25%	74%	3.71	48	18	34	1.2	5.0	4.0	9%	0.9	13.7	82	$10
Type Con	08 STL	6	6	17	79	51	3.55	1.47	279	268	285	4.7	31%	80%	4.61	43	19	38	3.4	5.8	1.7	10%	1.1	7.0	33	$12
Health A	09 STL	4	3	38	61	44	1.92	1.20	222	196	238	4.1	27%	85%	3.98	46	20	34	3.5	6.5	1.8	3%	0.3	17.1	45	$21
PT/Exp B	10 STL	6	2	27	65	42	3.46	1.03	237	250	215	4.4	26%	70%	3.60	45	17	39	1.4	5.8	4.2	9%	1.0	4.4	90	$17
Consist B	1st Half	3	0	15	33	19	2.16	0.99	230			4.3	26%	78%	3.56	48	16	36	1.4	5.1	3.8	3%	0.3	7.6	82	$10
LIMA Plan C	2nd Half	3	2	12	32	23	4.83	1.07	245			4.4	26%	61%	3.62	41	17	42	1.4	6.5	4.6	15%	1.7	-3.2	98	$7
Rand Var -2	11 Proj	5	3	23	65	43	4.00	1.24	258			4.5	28%	71%	4.00	44	18	38	2.3	5.9	2.5	10%	1.1	1.1	66	$13

Used pinpoint Ctl to drive Cmd spike and hold closer role for 2nd straight year. But also 2nd straight year of dramatic 2H fade, which along with poor Dom continues to suggest that he isn't long for the closer role.

JOSH PALEY

Frasor,Jason

		Yr	Tm	W	L	Sv	IP	K	ERA	WHIP	OBA	vL	vR	BF/G	H%	S%	xERA	G	L	F	Ctl	Dom	Cmd	hr/f	hr/9	RAR	BPV	R$
RH RP	33	06	TOR *	6	3	1	70	81	4.50	1.49	265	211	262	4.5	34%	73%	3.56	43	23	34	4.2	10.4	2.5	16%	1.3	0.5	94	$7
Ht/Wt	70 175	07	TOR	1	5	3	57	59	4.58	1.23	226	245	200	4.6	30%	61%	3.45	45	19	36	3.6	9.3	2.6	6%	0.5	-0.5	93	$6
Type	Pwr	08	TOR	1	2	0	47	42	4.19	1.44	213	266	174	4.2	26%	72%	4.62	38	24	38	6.1	8.0	1.3	8%	0.8	0.9	-4	$3
Health	A	09	TOR	7	3	11	58	56	2.50	1.02	209	274	140	3.7	27%	78%	3.47	38	18	43	2.5	8.7	3.5	6%	0.6	13.9	106	$15
PT/Exp	C	10	TOR	3	4	4	64	65	3.67	1.38	253	248	247	4.0	33%	74%	3.45	46	19	35	3.8	9.2	2.4	7%	0.6	3.7	87	$6
Consist	B	1st Half		3	1	3	32	35	4.78	1.69	291			4.2	39%	71%	3.54	51	20	30	4.8	9.8	2.1	7%	0.6	-2.5	77	$3
LIMA Plan	A	2nd Half		0	3	1	32	30	2.56	1.07	212			3.7	27%	78%	3.34	42	18	40	2.8	8.5	3.0	6%	0.6	6.2	96	$4
Rand Var	0	11	Proj	4	4	18	65	64	3.45	1.23	233			3.9	30%	73%	3.51	43	20	38	3.3	8.8	2.7	7%	0.7	6.2	90	$13

Won the closer's job out of camp and was so excited he overthrew himself out of a job (7.4 Ctl, 12.1 Dom, 8.38 ERA in April). Settled down after that, maintaining closer-worthy BPIs. Hopefully we all learned a valuable lesson.

French,Luke

		Yr	Tm	W	L	Sv	IP	K	ERA	WHIP	OBA	vL	vR	BF/G	H%	S%	xERA	G	L	F	Ctl	Dom	Cmd	hr/f	hr/9	RAR	BPV	R$
LH SP	25	06		0	0	0	0	0	0.00	0.00							0.00											
Ht/Wt	76 220	07		0	0	0	0	0	0.00	0.00							0.00											
Type	Con xFB	08	aa	9	11	0	170	76	4.58	1.63	314			28.7	33%	73%	5.83				3.1	4.0	1.3		0.9	-5.8	18	$3
Health	A	09	2AL *	8	9	0	149	104	4.55	1.48	291	322	310	23.3	33%	72%	4.94	29	23	48	2.9	6.3	2.2	8%	1.1	-1.7	42	$8
PT/Exp	C	10	SEA *	16	10	0	201	92	3.83	1.27	265	256	264	25.5	28%	72%	4.97	32	16	51	2.3	4.1	1.8	5%	0.9	7.7	23	$16
Consist	A	1st Half		9	3	0	104	48	2.97	1.21	262			25.2	29%	76%	4.47	33	26	41	1.8	4.1	2.2	4%	0.5	15.0	36	$11
LIMA Plan	C	2nd Half		7	7	0	97	45	4.74	1.34	268			25.8	28%	68%	5.20	32	15	53	2.8	4.2	1.5	7%	1.2	-7.2	10	$5
Rand Var	-3	11	Proj	6	7	0	102	55	4.34	1.41	283			25.8	30%	72%	5.11	31	19	50	2.7	4.9	1.8	7%	1.1	-10.3	25	$5

5-7, 4.83 ERA in 87.2 IP at SEA. Extreme soft-tosser had 3.0 Ctl in majors, which won't cut it. Unusually low LD% and Safeco Field shielded his ERA from a worse fate. Even with pinpoint control... DN: ERA over 5.00

Frieri,Ernesto

		Yr	Tm	W	L	Sv	IP	K	ERA	WHIP	OBA	vL	vR	BF/G	H%	S%	xERA	G	L	F	Ctl	Dom	Cmd	hr/f	hr/9	RAR	BPV	R$
RH RP	25	06		0	0	0	0	0	0.00	0.00							0.00											
Ht/Wt	74 190	07		0	0	0	0	0	0.00	0.00							0.00											
Type	Pwr xFB	08		0	0	0	0	0	0.00	0.00							0.00											
Health	A	09	aa	10	9	0	140	97	3.85	1.44	259			22.6	30%	74%	4.31				4.1	6.2	1.5		0.7	7.9	51	$10
PT/Exp	D	10	SD *	4	2	17	69	85	1.58	0.96	142	176	156	4.0	20%	87%	3.53	25	13	62	4.5	11.0	2.5	5%	0.5	20.7	81	$18
Consist	B	1st Half		3	1	15	32	35	1.69	0.88	118			4.1	15%	85%	0.92				4.5	9.7	2.1		0.6	9.2	118	$11
LIMA Plan	C+	2nd Half		1	1	2	37	50	1.47	1.04	162			3.9	25%	89%	3.32	25	13	62	4.4	12.2	2.8	4%	0.5	11.5	104	$6
Rand Var	-5	11	Proj	4	3	0	65	67	3.45	1.23	210			6.3	27%	73%	4.36	25	13	62	4.3	9.2	2.2	5%	0.7	-1.8	54	$7

1-1, 1.71 ERA in 31.2 IP at SD. LD% and strand rate were both abnormally low, Ctl issues say that he does not currently own closer-worthy skills. Huge FB% shows how much PETCO, not a dog, is a pitcher's best friend.

Fuentes,Brian

		Yr	Tm	W	L	Sv	IP	K	ERA	WHIP	OBA	vL	vR	BF/G	H%	S%	xERA	G	L	F	Ctl	Dom	Cmd	hr/f	hr/9	RAR	BPV	R$
LH RP	35	06	COL	3	4	30	65	73	3.46	1.17	214	186	217	4.0	28%	75%	3.71	35	16	50	3.6	10.1	2.8	10%	1.1	8.3	97	$18
Ht/Wt	76 230	07	COL	3	5	20	61	56	3.08	1.13	210	204	207	3.9	25%	76%	3.88	36	21	43	3.4	8.2	2.4	9%	0.9	10.2	71	$14
Type	Pwr xFB	08	COL	1	5	30	63	82	2.73	1.10	210	184	211	3.8	32%	76%	3.04	33	22	46	3.2	11.8	3.7	5%	0.4	11.9	137	$19
Health	F	09	LAA	1	5	48	55	46	3.93	1.40	255	239	261	3.7	30%	75%	4.60	36	17	47	3.9	7.5	1.9	8%	1.0	3.6	43	$20
PT/Exp	B	10	2AL	4	1	24	48	47	2.81	1.06	186	128	202	4.0	23%	78%	4.02	23	19	59	3.8	8.8	2.4	7%	0.9	7.9	58	$15
Consist	C	1st Half		3	1	15	24	28	4.44	1.28	235			4.1	28%	73%	3.81	21	24	56	3.7	10.4	2.8	15%	1.9	-0.9	85	$8
LIMA Plan	D	2nd Half		1	0	9	24	19	1.14	0.84	130			3.9	17%	85%	4.21	25	13	62	3.8	7.2	1.9	0%	0.0	8.8	30	$7
Rand Var	-5	11	Proj	3	3	23	58	52	3.72	1.33	241			4.0	29%	75%	4.46	29	18	53	3.9	8.1	2.1	7%	0.9	-1.3	48	$13

He's had brief brushes with closer-worthiness but not since 2008. xERA tells one part of the story. The other part... isn't an extreme flyball power pitcher exactly NOT what you want with a game on the line in the 9th?

Fujikawa,Kyuji

		Yr	Tm	W	L	Sv	IP	K	ERA	WHIP	OBA	vL	vR	BF/G	H%	S%	xERA	G	L	F	Ctl	Dom	Cmd	hr/f	hr/9	RAR	BPV	R$
RH RP	30	06	JPN	5	0	17	79	116	0.85	0.97	181			4.9	29%	97%	1.84				3.1	13.2	4.2		0.6	35.8	170	$24
Ht/Wt	72 183	07	JPN	5	5	46	83	109	2.02	0.92	186			4.5	29%	79%	1.61				2.4	11.8	4.9		0.4	25.0	180	$32
Type	Pwr	08	JPN	8	1	38	67	85	0.83	0.79	162			3.9	24%	94%	1.02				2.2	11.5	5.3		0.4	28.7	189	$31
Health	A	09	JPN	5	3	25	57	82	1.57	0.93	176			4.5	26%	93%	2.13				2.9	12.9	4.4		1.0	19.3	158	$21
PT/Exp	B	10	JPN	3	4	28	62	77	2.52	1.21	224			4.4	28%	91%	3.98				3.6	11.2	3.1		1.7	11.8	92	$17
Consist	C	1st Half		0	0	0	0	0	0.00	0.00							0.00											
LIMA Plan	C	2nd Half		3	4	28	62	77	2.52	1.21	224			4.4	28%	91%	3.98				3.6	11.2	3.1		1.7	11.8	92	$17
Rand Var	-5	11	Proj	4	2	13	58	67	3.26	1.33	245			4.7	30%	85%	4.66				3.7	10.4	2.8		1.7	-3.2	76	$11

Elite Dom makes him attractive as possible MLB closer should the posting price be right. S% won't persist (nobody does that in MLB), but he has closer skills even with high hr/9 and Ctl. Heed the ERA - xERA range.

Fulchino,Jeff

		Yr	Tm	W	L	Sv	IP	K	ERA	WHIP	OBA	vL	vR	BF/G	H%	S%	xERA	G	L	F	Ctl	Dom	Cmd	hr/f	hr/9	RAR	BPV	R$
RH RP	31	06	aaa	6	10	0	140	96	4.84	1.54	285			25.0	33%	69%	5.03				3.7	6.2	1.7		0.7	-5.5	48	$5
Ht/Wt	77 252	07	aaa	6	2	0	88	42	8.13	2.20	370			28.2	39%	64%	9.23				4.9	4.2	0.9		1.6	-39.8	-24	($10)
Type	Pwr	08	aaa	3	4	6	64	42	7.89	2.24	375			12.3	43%	62%	8.02				4.9	5.8	1.2		0.4	-28.3	29	($6)
Health	B	09	HOU	6	4	0	82	71	3.40	1.18	232	261	209	5.5	28%	73%	3.62	47	14	38	3.0	7.8	2.6	8%	0.8	8.0	86	$9
PT/Exp	D	10	HOU	2	1	0	47	46	5.52	1.59	284	257	292	4.3	34%	68%	4.02	40	22	38	4.2	8.8	2.1	13%	1.3	-8.8	63	$0
Consist	F	1st Half		0	0	0	29	28	6.83	1.79	317			4.7	38%	64%	4.08	46	20	35	4.3	8.7	2.0	16%	1.6	-10.1	63	($2)
LIMA Plan	B	2nd Half		2	1	0	18	18	3.44	1.26	225			3.6	28%	76%	3.87	31	25	44	3.9	8.9	2.3	9%	1.0	1.3	62	$2
Rand Var	+5	11	Proj	5	3	0	73	67	4.47	1.42	258			5.3	31%	71%	4.01	41	19	39	4.0	8.3	2.1	10%	1.0	1.2	62	$4

2009 2H Dom spike persisted through 2010, so that appears to be his new level. Wildness also persisted, but keeping his Cmd over 2.0 means that he merits at least some attention as a LIMA option with role upside.

Galarraga,Armando

		Yr	Tm	W	L	Sv	IP	K	ERA	WHIP	OBA	vL	vR	BF/G	H%	S%	xERA	G	L	F	Ctl	Dom	Cmd	hr/f	hr/9	RAR	BPV	R$
RH SP	29	06	aa	1	6	0	41	31	7.63	2.05	379			22.7	43%	64%	8.98				3.0	6.9	2.3		1.6	-15.7	20	($4)
Ht/Wt	76 180	07	aa	11	8	0	152	104	5.98	1.68	308			25.9	34%	66%	6.32				3.8	6.1	1.6		1.2	-28.5	26	$1
Type	FB	08	DET	13	7	0	179	126	3.73	1.19	232	267	174	24.5	25%	75%	4.11	44	17	40	3.1	6.3	2.1	13%	1.4	13.7	53	$19
Health	A	09	DET	6	10	0	144	95	5.64	1.57	281	309	257	22.2	30%	67%	4.97	40	22	39	4.2	5.9	1.4	13%	1.5	-21.0	12	$2
PT/Exp	B	10	DET *	8	11	0	188	106	4.57	1.37	266	241	276	24.5	28%	70%	4.89	37	14	49	3.2	5.0	1.6	9%	1.3	-10.0	21	$7
Consist	A	1st Half		7	4	0	89	48	4.81	1.33	264			23.6	28%	65%	4.66	42	12	46	2.8	4.8	1.7	8%	1.0	-7.4	31	$5
LIMA Plan	C+	2nd Half		1	7	0	99	58	4.35	1.41	268			25.3	28%	74%	5.02	35	15	50	3.5	5.2	1.5	10%	1.5	-2.6	14	$2
Rand Var	0	11	Proj	4	6	0	87	54	4.76	1.44	273			23.7	29%	70%	4.79	39	17	44	3.4	5.6	1.6	10%	1.2	-5.4	25	$3

4-9, 4.49 ERA in 144.1 IP at DET. He will be remembered for the perfect game that wasn't. Avoids LDs, instead yields FBs in bunches that too frequently clear the fence. Low Dom seals his fate. Pass.

Gallagher,Sean

		Yr	Tm	W	L	Sv	IP	K	ERA	WHIP	OBA	vL	vR	BF/G	H%	S%	xERA	G	L	F	Ctl	Dom	Cmd	hr/f	hr/9	RAR	BPV	R$
RH RP	25	06	aa	7	5	0	86	84	4.28	1.81	280			27.2	36%	77%	5.52				6.5	8.8	1.4		0.6	2.5	62	$4
Ht/Wt	74 235	07	CHC *	10	3	1	116	81	4.50	1.47	269			18.8	31%	69%	4.89	39	16	45	3.9	6.3	1.6	5%	0.6	-1.1	26	$8
Type	Pwr	08	2TM *	7	9	0	144	129	4.80	1.44	257	266	259	22.5	31%	68%	4.38	36	22	43	4.2	8.0	1.9	8%	0.9	-8.8	46	$7
Health	D	09	SD *	4	2	0	40	27	3.86	1.39	254	323	327	9.1	30%	70%	4.72	34	25	40	3.9	6.0	1.6	2%	0.2	1.6	16	$3
PT/Exp	D	10	2NL *	2	3	0	69	54	5.63	1.76	282	208	333	6.6	33%	68%	4.98	43	18	39	5.9	7.1	1.2	8%	0.9	-13.7	-11	($3)
Consist	A	1st Half		0	2	0	34	32	5.25	1.78	282			9.0	34%	73%	5.03	35	18	47	6.0	8.4	1.4	10%	1.3	-5.2	1	($1)
LIMA Plan	C	2nd Half		2	1	0	34	22	6.02	1.74	281			5.2	32%	64%	5.05	48	19	34	5.8	5.8	1.0	5%	0.5	-8.5	-26	($1)
Rand Var	+1	11	Proj	3	2	0	44	33	4.76	1.56	264			6.7	31%	69%	4.75	41	20	39	5.0	6.8	1.4	6%	0.6	-3.3	8	$1

2-1, 5.77 ERA in 57.2 IP at PIT. Traded Dom for GB% in 2H and the results were equally bad. Control has always been a chronic problem, and is officially a career-threatening one at this point.

Gallardo,Yovani

		Yr	Tm	W	L	Sv	IP	K	ERA	WHIP	OBA	vL	vR	BF/G	H%	S%	xERA	G	L	F	Ctl	Dom	Cmd	hr/f	hr/9	RAR	BPV	R$
RH SP	25	06	aa	5	2	0	77	80	2.22	1.15	214			24.1	29%	81%	2.52				3.4	9.3	2.7		0.3	21.8	115	$12
Ht/Wt	74 222	07	MIL *	17	8	0	188	211	3.56	1.19	232	247	244	23.4	32%	71%	3.30	38	24	38	3.1	10.1	3.3	7%	0.6	20.1	115	$26
Type	Pwr	08	MIL *	0	1	0	39	37	3.33	1.42	280	324	204	24.3	34%	81%	4.10	40	12	48	2.9	8.4	2.9	9%	1.1	4.5	91	$2
Health	D	09	MIL	13	12	0	186	204	3.73	1.31	223	213	225	26.2	29%	75%	3.52	45	19	36	4.6	9.9	2.2	12%	1.0	10.5	78	$18
PT/Exp	B	10	MIL	14	7	0	185	200	3.84	1.37	254	280	228	25.6	34%	72%	3.30	43	24	33	3.6	9.7	2.7	7%	0.6	3.9	98	$15
Consist	A	1st Half		8	4	0	112	122	2.58	1.26	228			26.0	31%	81%	3.20	44	23	33	3.9	9.8	2.5	6%	0.5	19.8	95	$13
LIMA Plan	B	2nd Half		6	3	0	73	78	5.77	1.55	291			25.1	38%	61%	3.44	41	26	33	3.3	9.6	2.9	9%	0.7	-15.9	102	$2
Rand Var	+1	11	Proj	13	7	0	189	204	3.49	1.29	243			25.6	32%	75%	3.33	43	22	36	3.5	9.7	2.8	10%	0.8	18.8	102	$19

2H stat line was depressingly deceptive due to ridiculously low S% and high H%, but BPIs were solid and stable. If he can maintain 2H gains, normalized H% and S% could yield...
UP: sub-3.00 ERA

JOSH PALEY

Garcia,Freddy		Yr	Tm	W	L	Sv	IP	K	ERA	WHIP	OBA	vL	vR	BF/G	H%	S%	xERA	G	L	F	Ctl	Dom	Cmd	hr/f	hr/9	RAR	BPV	R$
RH SP	34	06	CHW	17	9	0	216	135	4.54	1.28	272	262	271	27.5	29%	68%	4.32	41	18	41	2.0	5.6	2.8	11%	1.3	0.5	66	$20
Ht/Wt	76 260	07	PHI	1	5	0	58	50	5.90	1.60	312	292	339	23.9	35%	68%	4.28	36	27	38	2.9	7.8	2.6	17%	1.9	-10.5	74	($0)
Type	Con	08	DET	1	1	0	15	12	4.20	1.13	206	100	265	20.3	21%	71%	4.11	40	14	45	3.6	7.2	2.0	16%	1.8	0.3	51	$2
Health	C	09	CHW *	3	7	0	73	50	5.30	1.34	280	196	316	25.9	32%	60%	4.26	45	14	41	2.2	6.2	2.8	7%	0.9	-7.6	74	$3
PT/Exp	C	10	CHW	12	6	0	157	89	4.64	1.38	279	271	287	24.1	29%	70%	4.38	41	21	38	2.6	5.1	2.0	11%	1.3	-9.8	41	$9
Consist	A	1st Half		8	3	0	91	54	4.65	1.34	270			25.8	29%	69%	4.40	39	21	40	2.7	5.3	2.0	11%	1.3	-5.7	41	$6
LIMA Plan	C	2nd Half		4	3	0	66	35	4.64	1.42	290			22.1	30%	71%	4.36	43	21	35	2.5	4.8	1.9	12%	1.4	-4.1	41	$3
Rand Var	0	11	Proj	8	9	0	142	86	4.71	1.40	285			24.4	31%	70%	4.42	42	19	39	2.5	5.5	2.2	11%	1.3	-2.3	51	$7

It's a real tribute to him that he came back from three straight years of injury to post a near-full season at age 34. However, he's now a soft-tosser who gives up too many HR to be anything more than an innings-eater.

Garcia,Jaime		Yr	Tm	W	L	Sv	IP	K	ERA	WHIP	OBA	vL	vR	BF/G	H%	S%	xERA	G	L	F	Ctl	Dom	Cmd	hr/f	hr/9	RAR	BPV	R$
LH SP	24	06		0	0	0	0	0	0.00	0.00							0.00											
Ht/Wt	74 200	07	aa	5	9	0	103	85	4.19	1.42	262			24.8	30%	74%	4.85				3.8	7.4	2.0		1.2	3.5	52	$7
Type	Pwr xGB	08	STL *	8	7	0	122	94	4.13	1.38	262			18.1	31%	70%	4.18				3.4	6.9	2.0		0.7	2.1	67	$9
Health	A	09	aaa	2	0	0	21	20	6.00	1.38	243			22.6	25%	65%	5.73				4.3	8.6	2.0		2.6	-4.4	23	$1
PT/Exp	C	10	STL	13	8	0	163	132	2.70	1.32	247	211	251	24.7	30%	81%	3.36	56	19	26	3.5	7.3	2.1	7%	0.5	26.5	70	$17
Consist	D	1st Half		8	4	0	94	77	2.10	1.22	222			24.4	28%	84%	3.22	58	18	24	3.7	7.3	2.0	6%	0.4	22.3	67	$12
LIMA Plan	C	2nd Half		5	4	0	69	55	3.52	1.45	278			25.1	33%	77%	3.53	54	19	27	3.3	7.2	2.2	9%	0.7	4.2	73	$5
Rand Var	-3	11	Proj	12	10	0	174	138	3.57	1.37	260			22.0	31%	75%	3.52	55	19	26	3.5	7.1	2.1	10%	0.7	13.4	68	$14

Brilliant rookie season, but Ctl does not support sub-3.00 ERA. xERA shows 1H/2H split was mostly just h%/s% variance, and GB% is a great skill base. Use 2H line as your guide in assessing sophomore value.

Garland,Jon		Yr	Tm	W	L	Sv	IP	K	ERA	WHIP	OBA	vL	vR	BF/G	H%	S%	xERA	G	L	F	Ctl	Dom	Cmd	hr/f	hr/9	RAR	BPV	R$
RH SP	31	06	CHW	18	7	0	211	112	4.52	1.36	293	290	297	27.4	31%	69%	4.47	42	20	38	1.7	4.8	2.7	9%	1.1	1.0	59	$17
Ht/Wt	78 210	07	CHW	10	13	0	208	98	4.23	1.33	272	259	281	27.6	29%	69%	4.75	39	23	38	2.5	4.2	1.7	7%	0.8	7.0	27	$13
Type		08	LAA	14	8	0	197	90	4.90	1.50	299	300	307	27.2	32%	69%	4.42	50	22	28	2.7	4.1	1.5	12%	1.1	-13.3	29	$7
Health	A	09	2NL	11	13	0	204	109	4.01	1.40	281	271	293	26.7	30%	74%	4.47	46	19	35	2.7	4.8	1.8	10%	1.0	4.4	38	$10
PT/Exp	A	10	SD	14	12	0	200	136	3.47	1.32	238	254	228	25.7	27%	77%	3.92	52	18	30	3.9	6.1	1.6	11%	0.9	13.6	34	$16
Consist	A	1st Half		8	5	0	103	65	3.24	1.36	247			25.9	28%	78%	4.04	52	19	29	3.9	5.7	1.4	9%	0.7	9.8	26	$8
LIMA Plan	D	2nd Half		6	7	0	97	71	3.70	1.26	228			25.4	25%	75%	3.80	52	16	32	3.9	6.6	1.7	13%	1.1	3.8	43	$8
Rand Var	-2	11	Proj	13	12	0	203	131	3.99	1.38	267			26.5	30%	74%	4.11	49	19	32	3.2	5.8	1.8	11%	1.0	0.8	44	$12

Dom became respectable while Ctl decayed, yielding a near-identical BPV to '09. The gains were in fickle H% and S%, and some PETCO help (3.00 ERA at home; 4.01 on road). It's a house of cards; tread carefully.

Garza,Matt		Yr	Tm	W	L	Sv	IP	K	ERA	WHIP	OBA	vL	vR	BF/G	H%	S%	xERA	G	L	F	Ctl	Dom	Cmd	hr/f	hr/9	RAR	BPV	R$
RH SP	27	06	MIN *	12	9	0	141	123	4.15	1.30	255	245	356	23.8	31%	68%	4.03	35	25	40	3.0	7.8	2.6	6%	0.6	7.2	73	$16
Ht/Wt	76 215	07	MIN *	9	13	0	175	144	4.53	1.59	300	314	276	24.7	36%	72%	4.29	48	15	38	3.4	7.4	2.1	7%	0.7	-0.4	66	$8
Type	FB	08	TAM	11	9	0	185	128	3.70	1.24	246	244	245	25.6	28%	73%	4.19	42	18	40	2.9	6.2	2.2	8%	0.9	14.7	54	$18
Health	A	09	TAM	8	12	0	203	189	3.95	1.26	236	196	271	26.5	28%	72%	3.96	40	18	43	3.5	8.4	2.4	10%	1.1	12.7	74	$19
PT/Exp	A	10	TAM	15	10	1	205	150	3.91	1.25	251	241	255	25.9	28%	73%	4.17	36	19	45	2.8	6.6	2.4	10%	1.2	5.7	58	$19
Consist	A	1st Half		9	5	0	104	83	4.08	1.30	253			27.4	29%	72%	4.10	35	22	43	3.1	7.2	2.3	10%	1.1	0.8	58	$9
LIMA Plan	D+	2nd Half		6	5	1	101	67	3.74	1.20	248			24.5	27%	75%	4.22	37	17	46	2.4	6.0	2.5	10%	1.3	4.9	57	$9
Rand Var	0	11	Proj	13	11	0	210	159	3.98	1.29	254			26.1	29%	73%	4.23	38	19	43	3.0	6.8	2.3	9%	1.1	1.5	58	$18

Pitched with more precision yet yielded virtually identical results to '09. But 7 more wins makes '10 look that much better. It wasn't. Rising FB%, concurrent gopheritis raises caution too. 4.00 ERA? It could go either way.

Gaudin,Chad		Yr	Tm	W	L	Sv	IP	K	ERA	WHIP	OBA	vL	vR	BF/G	H%	S%	xERA	G	L	F	Ctl	Dom	Cmd	hr/f	hr/9	RAR	BPV	R$
RH RP	28	06	OAK *	7	2	2	88	58	2.45	1.31	210	253	201	6.3	25%	81%	5.05	39	16	45	5.0	5.9	1.2	3%	0.3	22.9	-11	$12
Ht/Wt	70 188	07	OAK	11	13	0	199	154	4.43	1.53	267	282	250	26.1	31%	73%	4.24	51	19	30	4.5	7.0	1.5	12%	0.9	8.3	32	$11
Type	Pwr FB	08	2TM	9	5	0	90	71	4.40	1.32	266	273	258	7.6	31%	69%	4.08	39	21	40	2.7	7.1	2.6	10%	1.1	-1.0	72	$9
Health	A	09	2TM	6	10	0	147	139	4.64	1.51	260	296	224	21.0	32%	70%	4.13	44	20	36	4.6	8.5	1.8	9%	0.9	-6.0	49	$7
PT/Exp	B	10	2AL	1	4	0	65	53	5.65	1.50	284	283	287	6.9	30%	70%	4.37	39	15	46	3.4	7.3	2.1	17%	2.2	-12.2	56	($0)
Consist	A	1st Half		0	3	0	34	32	6.94	1.66	306			7.4	34%	64%	4.27	38	18	45	3.7	8.5	2.3	19%	2.4	-11.7	69	($2)
LIMA Plan	D+	2nd Half		1	1	0	32	21	4.27	1.33	258			6.4	26%	77%	4.46	41	13	47	3.1	6.0	1.9	15%	2.0	-0.5	42	$2
Rand Var	+4	11	Proj	3	4	0	64	52	4.82	1.45	269			8.7	31%	70%	4.30	41	17	42	3.7	7.4	2.0	11%	1.3	-0.1	52	$3

His gopheritis is not chronic; it was acute. Gave up HRs in bunches: 6 in 4 gms in May, 4 in 2 gms in Sept. The other 6 HRs scattered thru the other 36 gms. Still, volatile control, borderline BPIs make him undraftable.

Gee,Dillon		Yr	Tm	W	L	Sv	IP	K	ERA	WHIP	OBA	vL	vR	BF/G	H%	S%	xERA	G	L	F	Ctl	Dom	Cmd	hr/f	hr/9	RAR	BPV	R$
RH SP	24	06		0	0	0	0	0	0.00	0.00							0.00											
Ht/Wt	73 195	07		0	0	0	0	0	0.00	0.00							0.00											
Type	FB	08		0	0	0	0	0	0.00	0.00							0.00											
Health	A	09	aaa	1	3	0	48	37	5.24	1.52	292			23.7	34%	67%	5.40				3.2	6.9	2.2		1.1	-5.5	50	$1
PT/Exp	D	10	NYM *	15	10	0	194	155	4.64	1.36	276	170	239	25.2	32%	68%	3.92	47	10	43	2.6	7.2	2.8	9%	1.1	-14.9	86	$12
Consist	C	1st Half		7	5	0	90	71	5.20	1.39	285			24.2	32%	65%	4.97				2.4	7.1	3.0		1.3	-13.1	64	$4
LIMA Plan	B+	2nd Half		8	5	0	104	84	4.15	1.34	269			26.1	32%	71%	3.89	47	10	43	2.7	7.3	2.7	8%	1.0	-1.7	83	$7
Rand Var	0	11	Proj	4	4	0	81	63	4.36	1.38	275			24.7	32%	71%	4.08	47	10	43	2.8	7.0	2.5	9%	1.1	0.6	76	$4

2-2, 2.18 ERA in 33 IP for NYM. Former marginal prospect has growth year, rises all the way to Big Apple. This new skill set is now worthy of our attention, but we need to see him hold those gains before investing.

Germano,Justin		Yr	Tm	W	L	Sv	IP	K	ERA	WHIP	OBA	vL	vR	BF/G	H%	S%	xERA	G	L	F	Ctl	Dom	Cmd	hr/f	hr/9	RAR	BPV	R$
RH RP	28	06	aaa	10	6	0	155	77	5.11	1.50	321			27.4	34%	68%	5.89				1.5	4.5	3.1		1.1	-11.2	49	$6
Ht/Wt	75 205	07	SD *	11	10	0	165	93	4.02	1.24	258	244	272	22.2	28%	69%	4.13	49	17	33	2.4	5.1	2.2	8%	0.8	8.3	55	$14
Type	Con	08	SD *	2	12	0	142	67	6.66	1.72	336	268	330	22.7	35%	62%	4.85	49	18	33	2.7	4.2	1.6	12%	1.3	-41.8	32	($8)
Health	A	09	JPN	5	4	0	76	40	5.44	1.46	315			23.8	34%	64%	5.70				1.5	4.7	3.2		1.2	-10.6	52	$2
PT/Exp	D	10	CLE *	5	6	1	108	69	3.85	1.27	269	213	200	9.6	29%	74%	4.13	40	17	42	2.0	5.8	2.8	10%	1.2	3.9	67	$8
Consist	C	1st Half		4	3	1	53	31	4.19	1.26	265			12.3	29%	68%	3.84				2.2	5.2	2.4		0.8	-0.3	59	$4
LIMA Plan	B	2nd Half		1	3	0	54	38	3.51	1.27	273			7.9	29%	80%	3.97	40	17	42	1.9	6.3	3.3	13%	1.6	4.2	81	$4
Rand Var	0	11	Proj	3	3	0	58	34	4.19	1.34	284			8.5	31%	73%	4.15	46	17	36	2.0	5.3	2.6	11%	1.2	1.0	65	$4

0-3, 3.31 ERA in 35.1 IP at CLE. Got mashed everywhere from PETCO to Japan, but most of the damage was from H% and S% rates. Those finally normalized in '10 and BPIs showed growth, but at 28, he has to move fast.

Gervacio,Sammy		Yr	Tm	W	L	Sv	IP	K	ERA	WHIP	OBA	vL	vR	BF/G	H%	S%	xERA	G	L	F	Ctl	Dom	Cmd	hr/f	hr/9	RAR	BPV	R$
RH RP	26	06		0	0	0	0	0	0.00	0.00							0.00											
Ht/Wt	72 170	07	aa	3	2	0	23	22	2.74	1.35	217			7.6	27%	83%	3.61				5.1	8.6	1.7		0.8	4.9	75	$4
Type	Pwr FB	08	aa	3	5	5	73	80	4.19	1.50	283			6.4	37%	74%	5.07				3.4	9.8	2.9		1.0	1.0	87	$6
Health	A	09	HOU *	3	3	0	73	73	4.50	1.28	238	250	208	4.5	30%	65%	3.10	57	15	28	3.6	8.9	2.5	11%	0.8	-2.8	100	$5
PT/Exp	F	10	HOU *	0	1	0	14	12	5.90	1.46	205	143	375	4.6	25%	58%	4.93	42	8	50	6.6	7.8	1.2	5%	0.7	-3.2	-17	($0)
Consist	D	1st Half		0	1	0	14	12	5.90	1.46	205			4.6	25%	58%	4.93	42	8	50	6.6	7.8	1.2	5%	0.7	-3.2	-17	($0)
LIMA Plan	A	2nd Half		0	0	0	0	0	0.00	0.00						0%	0.00											
Rand Var	+1	11	Proj	2	3	3	58	57	4.19	1.36	255			5.2	31%	72%	3.75	47	10	43	3.6	8.8	2.5	10%	1.1	2.8	88	$4

0-1, 12.27 ERA in 3.1 IP in HOU. Here is a sad combination of words: shoulder strain, age 25, cortisone shots. Age, Dom, and S% point to some upside. If health returns, worth chasing this skill set in a shaky pen.

Gomez,Jeanmar		Yr	Tm	W	L	Sv	IP	K	ERA	WHIP	OBA	vL	vR	BF/G	H%	S%	xERA	G	L	F	Ctl	Dom	Cmd	hr/f	hr/9	RAR	BPV	R$
RH SP	23	06		0	0	0	0	0	0.00	0.00							0.00											
Ht/Wt	76 190	07		0	0	0	0	0	0.00	0.00							0.00											
Type		08		0	0	0	0	0	0.00	0.00							0.00											
Health	A	09	aa	10	4	0	123	99	4.61	1.49	287			24.7	34%	71%	5.07				3.1	7.2	2.3		1.0	-4.5	61	$8
PT/Exp	D	10	CLE *	12	13	0	174	106	5.11	1.53	295	268	360	24.9	32%	68%	4.27	47	20	33	3.1	5.5	1.8	11%	1.1	-20.8	40	$5
Consist	B	1st Half		5	7	0	85	50	5.73	1.54	296			25.3	32%	64%	5.38				3.2	5.3	1.7		1.2	-16.8	26	$0
LIMA Plan	C	2nd Half		7	6	0	89	56	4.50	1.51	295			24.5	33%	72%	4.19	47	20	33	3.0	5.7	1.9	10%	1.0	-4.0	46	$4
Rand Var	+1	11	Proj	8	10	0	139	92	4.55	1.47	285			24.3	32%	71%	4.20	47	20	33	3.1	6.0	1.9	11%	1.0	1.6	48	$7

4-5, 4.68 ERA in 57.2 IP at CLE. Soft-tosser had four good starts to begin his MLB career, but then melted down. Showed Cmd in minors, forgot to bring it to the show. Avoid now, check back in a few years.

JOSH PALEY

Gonzalez,Gio

		Yr	Tm	W	L	Sv	IP	K	ERA	WHIP	OBA	vL	vR	BF/G	H%	S%	xERA	G	L	F	Ctl	Dom	Cmd	hr/f	hr/9	RAR	BPV	R$
LH SP	25	06	aa	7	12	0	154	139	6.36	1.64	281			26.0	32%	65%	6.41				4.8	8.1	1.7		1.9	-35.0	25	$1
Ht/Wt	71 197	07	aa	9	7	0	150	165	4.44	1.35	251			23.7	33%	69%	4.19				3.7	9.9	2.7		0.9	0.4	94	$13
Type	Pwr	08	OAK *	9	11	0	157	140	5.27	1.46	251	194	260	20.8	30%	66%	4.32	42	18	40	4.6	8.0	1.7	11%	1.2	-17.8	39	$8
Health	A	09	OAK *	10	8	0	160	167	4.56	1.53	260	340	271	22.2	33%	72%	3.97	46	18	36	4.9	9.4	1.9	12%	1.0	-2.1	62	$11
PT/Exp	B	10	OAK	15	9	0	201	171	3.23	1.31	232	209	235	25.7	28%	77%	3.77	49	15	35	4.1	7.7	1.9	8%	0.7	22.5	54	$21
Consist	A	1st Half		7	5	0	103	84	3.50	1.31	230			25.6	28%	75%	3.95	47	16	37	4.2	7.3	1.8	7%	0.7	8.2	44	$10
LIMA Plan	D+	2nd Half		8	4	0	98	87	2.95	1.31	234			25.8	29%	79%	3.58	52	15	33	4.1	8.0	2.0	8%	0.6	14.4	64	$11
Rand Var	-2	11	Proj	13	10	0	196	181	3.82	1.38	246			23.4	30%	75%	3.80	48	16	35	4.2	8.3	2.0	10%	0.9	11.8	63	$17

Is this a $20 starter?
PRO: Heavy and improving GB tendency; lotsa Ks; across-the-board growth in 2H.
CON: Fortunate H% and W total; yet to reach 2.0 Cmd or 65 BPV. Promising, but unlikely profitable.

Gonzalez,Mike

		Yr	Tm	W	L	Sv	IP	K	ERA	WHIP	OBA	vL	vR	BF/G	H%	S%	xERA	G	L	F	Ctl	Dom	Cmd	hr/f	hr/9	RAR	BPV	R$
LH RP	32	06	PIT	3	4	24	54	64	2.17	1.35	216	163	227	4.3	32%	83%	3.70	37	27	36	5.2	10.7	2.1	2%	0.2	15.5	67	$16
Ht/Wt	74 213	07	ATL	2	0	2	17	13	1.59	1.35	238	333	189	4.0	30%	87%	4.55	39	20	41	4.2	6.9	1.6	0%	0.0	6.0	26	$3
Type	Pwr FB	08	ATL *	1	3	15	45	52	3.47	1.31	257	259	196	4.2	34%	79%	3.53	31	25	44	3.1	10.5	3.4	11%	1.2	4.4	114	$9
Health	F	09	ATL	5	4	10	74	90	2.42	1.20	211	194	218	3.8	29%	84%	3.35	38	18	44	4.0	10.9	2.7	9%	0.8	16.2	105	$14
PT/Exp	D	10	BAL	1	3	1	25	31	4.01	1.30	205	324	130	3.6	31%	68%	3.51	33	22	45	5.1	11.3	2.2	4%	0.4	0.4	76	$3
Consist	A	1st Half		0	2	1	2	3	18.00	4.50	470			4.9	65%	56%	15.22				18.0	13.5	0.8		0.0	-3.4	58	($1)
LIMA Plan	A+	2nd Half		1	1	0	23	28	2.78	1.01	169			3.4	25%	73%	3.04	37	18	45	4.0	11.1	2.8	5%	0.4	3.8	108	$4
Rand Var	-1	11	Proj	2	3	10	48	57	3.38	1.25	219			3.9	30%	76%	3.44	36	21	43	4.1	10.7	2.6	10%	0.9	5.0	95	$9

Surprise! Lasted 2 IP in Mar before hurting his back; 2 IP in Apr before straining his shoulder. Finally got 23 IP in 2H, w/ usual results: excellent Dom, OK Ctl, many FB. FDA reliability grade screams high risk, high reward.

Gorzelanny,Tom

		Yr	Tm	W	L	Sv	IP	K	ERA	WHIP	OBA	vL	vR	BF/G	H%	S%	xERA	G	L	F	Ctl	Dom	Cmd	hr/f	hr/9	RAR	BPV	R$
LH SP	28	06	PIT *	8	10	0	160	120	3.53	1.20	227	239	223	24.5	27%	70%	3.90	49	18	33	3.4	6.7	2.0	5%	0.4	18.8	57	$16
Ht/Wt	74 202	07	PIT	14	10	0	202	135	3.88	1.40	273	217	284	27.2	31%	74%	4.51	42	18	40	3.0	6.0	2.0	7%	0.8	13.5	47	$15
Type	Pwr FB	08	PIT *	9	10	0	140	91	5.74	1.65	284	261	299	22.9	31%	67%	5.34	40	16	44	4.8	5.9	1.2	10%	1.4	-25.5	-5	$0
Health	B	09	2NL *	11	6	0	134	105	4.21	1.45	276	244	252	15.8	33%	71%	4.26	41	21	38	3.4	7.1	2.1	6%	0.6	-0.4	54	$9
PT/Exp	C	10	CHC	7	9	1	136	119	4.09	1.50	261	286	251	20.8	32%	74%	4.27	41	19	40	4.5	7.9	1.8	7%	0.7	-1.3	39	$6
Consist	B	1st Half		2	5	1	63	65	3.14	1.37	243			16.9	32%	77%	3.49	44	22	34	4.1	9.3	2.2	5%	0.4	6.8	78	$5
LIMA Plan	C	2nd Half		5	4	0	73	54	4.91	1.61	277			25.5	32%	71%	4.96	38	17	45	4.8	6.6	1.4	8%	1.0	-8.1	6	$1
Rand Var	-1	11	Proj	10	10	0	160	126	4.40	1.50	268			20.1	31%	73%	4.49	41	19	41	4.2	7.1	1.7	9%	1.0	-6.9	34	$7

Was certainly "hittable": took 3 body shots from batted balls (2 - fingers, 1 - shoulder) in 2010. Was a 1H revelation, but neither Dom nor Ctl lasted. Skill swings make him a moving target.

Gregerson,Luke

		Yr	Tm	W	L	Sv	IP	K	ERA	WHIP	OBA	vL	vR	BF/G	H%	S%	xERA	G	L	F	Ctl	Dom	Cmd	hr/f	hr/9	RAR	BPV	R$
RH RP	26	06		0	0	0	0	0	0.00	0.00							0.00											
Ht/Wt	75 200	07		0	0	0	0	0	0.00	0.00							0.00											
Type	Pwr	08	aa	7	6	10	75	64	3.78	1.28	250			5.5	31%	71%	3.63				3.0	7.6	2.5		0.6	4.8	85	$12
Health	A	09	SD	2	4	1	75	93	3.24	1.24	227	285	161	4.3	33%	73%	2.94	46	21	33	3.7	11.2	3.0	5%	0.4	8.8	124	$8
PT/Exp	C	10	SD	4	7	2	78	89	3.22	0.83	176	180	162	3.7	23%	65%	2.50	48	15	37	2.1	10.2	4.9	12%	0.9	7.7	155	$12
Consist	B	1st Half		2	3	1	40	51	2.23	0.60	137			3.7	20%	64%	2.09	42	18	40	1.3	11.4	8.5	6%	0.4	8.9	189	$9
LIMA Plan	B+	2nd Half		2	4	1	38	38	4.26	1.08	213			3.6	25%	66%	2.96	53	12	35	2.8	9.0	3.2	18%	1.4	-1.2	117	$4
Rand Var	0	11	Proj	4	6	8	73	81	3.35	1.13	224			4.2	30%	72%	2.93	48	17	35	2.9	10.1	3.5	9%	0.7	10.8	130	$11

Strand rate giveth and hit rate taketh away, but top-flight skills remaineth. Strong and improving GB tilt, impeccable Ctl and Cmd highlight this pen gem. Should the opportunity arise...
UP: sub-3.00 ERA, 35 saves

Gregg,Kevin

		Yr	Tm	W	L	Sv	IP	K	ERA	WHIP	OBA	vL	vR	BF/G	H%	S%	xERA	G	L	F	Ctl	Dom	Cmd	hr/f	hr/9	RAR	BPV	R$
RH RP	32	06	LAA	3	4	0	78	71	4.15	1.40	285	298	268	10.5	34%	74%	4.12	36	18	46	2.4	8.2	3.4	9%	1.2	3.9	96	$6
Ht/Wt	78 238	07	FLA	0	5	32	84	87	3.54	1.23	210	162	247	4.7	27%	73%	4.25	29	16	55	4.3	9.3	2.2	6%	0.8	9.2	59	$18
Type	Pwr FB	08	FLA	7	8	29	69	58	3.41	1.28	208	181	222	4.0	26%	73%	4.13	45	20	35	4.8	7.6	1.6	5%	0.4	7.3	29	$18
Health	A	09	CHC	5	6	23	69	71	4.72	1.31	236	195	257	4.0	28%	70%	3.85	38	18	44	3.9	9.3	2.4	16%	1.7	-4.5	77	$13
PT/Exp	B	10	TOR	2	6	37	59	58	3.51	1.39	238	225	248	4.0	31%	76%	3.89	42	17	40	4.6	8.8	1.9	6%	0.6	4.6	56	$17
Consist	A	1st Half		0	3	18	31	36	4.06	1.48	243			4.4	33%	74%	3.45	50	15	35	5.2	10.5	2.0	11%	0.9	0.3	75	$7
LIMA Plan	D+	2nd Half		2	3	19	28	22	2.89	1.29	233			3.7	29%	77%	4.32	35	19	46	3.9	7.1	1.8	3%	0.3	4.3	36	$9
Rand Var	-1	11	Proj	3	6	30	58	55	3.88	1.40	248			4.2	30%	76%	4.08	40	18	42	4.2	8.5	2.0	10%	1.1	1.5	58	$15

Career high in saves, but reasons not to count on a repeat:
- 2.0 Cmd a struggle
- xERA consistently ~4.00
- Fortunate hr/f history
- Notable 2H skills slide

Closer on 2nd tier team at best.

Greinke,Zack

		Yr	Tm	W	L	Sv	IP	K	ERA	WHIP	OBA	vL	vR	BF/G	H%	S%	xERA	G	L	F	Ctl	Dom	Cmd	hr/f	hr/9	RAR	BPV	R$
RH SP	27	06	KC *	9	3	0	111	87	4.69	1.23	260	400	200	22.0	30%	63%	3.70	35	35	30	2.2	7.0	3.2	11%	0.9	-1.8	81	$12
Ht/Wt	74 192	07	KC	7	7	1	122	106	3.69	1.30	262	266	263	9.9	32%	74%	4.15	32	22	46	2.7	7.8	2.9	7%	0.9	12.3	79	$13
Type	Pwr	08	KC	13	10	0	202	183	3.47	1.28	261	287	232	26.5	32%	76%	3.63	43	19	38	2.5	8.1	3.3	9%	0.9	21.9	100	$22
Health	A	09	KC	16	8	0	229	242	2.16	1.07	232	250	211	27.7	31%	81%	3.18	40	19	41	2.0	9.5	4.7	5%	0.4	64.9	135	$38
PT/Exp	A	10	KC	10	14	0	220	181	4.17	1.25	261	280	235	27.8	31%	67%	3.51	46	18	36	2.3	7.4	3.3	8%	0.7	-0.9	97	$17
Consist	A	1st Half		4	8	0	112	92	3.94	1.20	265			27.1	31%	70%	3.48	44	17	40	1.6	7.4	4.6	10%	1.0	2.8	111	$9
LIMA Plan	B	2nd Half		6	6	0	108	89	4.42	1.30	256			28.5	32%	64%	3.52	49	19	33	2.9	7.4	2.5	5%	0.4	-3.7	81	$8
Rand Var	0	11	Proj	13	11	0	218	194	3.60	1.21	253			25.0	31%	73%	3.52	43	19	38	2.3	8.0	3.5	9%	0.9	20.7	103	$23

Can hang most of 2-run ERA jump on S%. But he wasn't as sharp, either: 55%/9% PQS DOM/DIS, down from 87%/0% in '09. BPV and xERA still ace-worthy, but just hope that he's not losing interest (see 2H).

Guerrier,Matt

		Yr	Tm	W	L	Sv	IP	K	ERA	WHIP	OBA	vL	vR	BF/G	H%	S%	xERA	G	L	F	Ctl	Dom	Cmd	hr/f	hr/9	RAR	BPV	R$
RH RP	32	06	MIN	1	0	1	69	37	3.38	1.43	286	333	256	7.7	30%	81%	4.65	45	18	37	2.7	4.8	1.8	10%	1.2	10.0	36	$4
Ht/Wt	75 195	07	MIN	2	4	1	88	68	2.35	1.05	222	264	187	4.8	26%	83%	3.55	47	16	36	2.1	7.0	3.2	10%	0.9	23.4	93	$13
Type	Con	08	MIN	6	9	1	76	59	5.19	1.59	281	282	272	4.5	32%	71%	4.45	47	18	35	4.4	7.0	1.6	14%	1.4	-7.9	32	$3
Health	A	09	MIN	5	1	1	76	47	2.26	0.94	211	194	213	3.7	22%	84%	3.84	42	18	40	1.7	5.6	3.4	10%	1.1	20.5	76	$13
PT/Exp	C	10	MIN	5	7	1	71	42	3.17	1.10	219	236	210	3.9	24%	75%	3.98	47	15	38	2.8	5.3	1.9	9%	0.9	8.5	45	$9
Consist	A	1st Half		1	4	1	38	27	2.82	1.12	223			4.1	26%	78%	3.92	41	18	41	2.8	6.3	2.3	6%	0.7	6.2	57	$4
LIMA Plan	C+	2nd Half		4	3	0	33	15	3.58	1.07	213			3.6	21%	71%	4.03	52	13	35	2.8	4.1	1.5	11%	1.1	2.3	30	$4
Rand Var	-4	11	Proj	4	4	1	58	36	3.72	1.28	258			4.2	28%	75%	4.16	46	16	37	2.6	5.6	2.1	10%	1.1	0.9	53	$6

Again, fortunate h% inflated his value. Again, in the top 3 in AL appearances (3rd yr in a row). GB rate a plus, but Dom trend (esp. 2H) points to a tired pitcher. Will probably get a bunch of holds--and one save. Again.

Guthrie,Jeremy

		Yr	Tm	W	L	Sv	IP	K	ERA	WHIP	OBA	vL	vR	BF/G	H%	S%	xERA	G	L	F	Ctl	Dom	Cmd	hr/f	hr/9	RAR	BPV	R$
RH SP	32	06	CLE *	9	5	0	142	88	4.61	1.55	275			21.2	32%	70%	4.62	50	19	31	4.3	5.6	1.3	6%	0.5	-1.0	13	$7
Ht/Wt	73 196	07	BAL	7	5	0	175	123	3.70	1.21	250	255	243	22.6	28%	74%	4.05	42	19	38	2.4	6.3	2.6	11%	1.2	17.5	69	$17
Type	Con FB	08	BAL	10	12	0	191	120	3.63	1.23	247	241	243	26.4	27%	75%	4.20	44	18	38	2.7	5.7	2.1	11%	1.1	16.8	50	$17
Health	A	09	BAL	10	17	0	200	110	5.04	1.42	284	289	274	26.3	29%	69%	5.09	35	19	47	2.7	5.0	1.8	11%	1.6	-14.5	29	$8
PT/Exp	A	10	BAL	11	14	0	209	119	3.83	1.16	246	253	234	26.7	26%	71%	4.20	42	14	43	2.2	5.1	2.4	9%	1.1	8.0	54	$17
Consist	B	1st Half		3	10	0	107	56	4.64	1.26	259			26.2	27%	66%	4.42	41	17	42	2.4	4.7	1.9	10%	1.2	-6.6	38	$5
LIMA Plan	D	2nd Half		8	4	0	103	63	2.98	1.06	233			27.2	25%	77%	3.97	44	11	45	1.8	5.5	3.0	8%	1.0	14.6	71	$13
Rand Var	-2	11	Proj	11	13	0	203	119	4.03	1.30	267			26.0	29%	73%	4.50	41	16	43	2.5	5.3	2.1	9%	1.2	-5.2	47	$14

Sub-30% hit rates have resulted sub-4 ERAs in three recent seasons. Pitched better in the 2H, but history is skeptical Ctl gains can continue. At 32, there are no other favorable signs. Will give you 200 IP, but DN: '09

Gutierrez,Juan

		Yr	Tm	W	L	Sv	IP	K	ERA	WHIP	OBA	vL	vR	BF/G	H%	S%	xERA	G	L	F	Ctl	Dom	Cmd	hr/f	hr/9	RAR	BPV	R$
RH RP	27	06	aa	8	4	0	103	87	3.78	1.42	277			22.4	33%	76%	4.81				3.1	7.6	2.5		1.0	9.5	68	$10
Ht/Wt	75 210	07	aaa	5	10	0	156	86	5.22	1.61	295			27.2	32%	70%	5.89				3.8	5.0	1.3		1.2	-14.6	17	$1
Type	Pwr xFB	08	aaa	5	11	0	116	69	8.86	2.14	379			23.5	42%	58%	8.69				3.8	5.4	1.4		1.2	-65.3	5	($15)
Health	A	09	ARI	4	3	9	71	66	4.06	1.37	251	297	207	4.7	33%	68%	3.96	40	20	39	3.8	8.4	2.2	3%	0.3	1.2	66	$8
PT/Exp	C	10	ARI	0	6	15	57	47	5.08	1.38	256	286	228	4.2	27%	71%	4.43	35	14	51	3.7	7.5	2.0	15%	2.1	-7.4	49	$5
Consist	F	1st Half		0	5	1	27	25	7.67	1.67	302			4.4	31%	63%	4.69	29	19	52	4.0	8.3	2.1	23%	3.3	-12.2	49	($2)
LIMA Plan	C	2nd Half		0	1	14	30	22	2.73	1.11	208			4.0	24%	80%	4.16	41	10	49	3.3	6.7	2.0	7%	0.9	4.7	49	$7
Rand Var	+2	11	Proj	2	4	25	58	46	4.66	1.48	275			5.6	31%	72%	4.57	38	16	46	3.7	7.1	1.9	10%	1.2	-3.1	44	$10

Terrible hr/f luck ruined his 1H; fortunate h% saved his 2H -- when the saves opps arrived. Made mechanical adjustment in June... and BPV says is didn't make a difference. A closer option worth chasring? Not really.

BRENT HERSHEY

Haeger,Charlie

Haeger,Charlie		W	L	Sv	IP	K	ERA	WHIP	OBA	vL	vR	BF/G	H%	S%	xERA	G	L	F	Ctl	Dom	Cmd	hr/f	hr/9	RAR	BPV	R$
RH SP 27	06	0	0	0	0	0	0.00	0.00							0.00											
Ht/Wt 73 211	07 aaa	5	16	0	147	112	5.63	1.62	288			27.9	32%	68%	6.06				4.3	6.8	**1.6**		1.5	-21.1	28	$1
Type Pwr	08 aaa	10	13	0	178	103	5.87	1.57	285			28.6	31%	63%	5.24				4.0	5.2	**1.3**		0.9	-34.4	29	$1
Health B	09 LA *	12	7	0	163	95	4.76	1.63	291	125	222	26.5	31%	74%	5.03	48	13	39	4.3	5.2	**1.2**	11%	1.4	-11.5	6	$4
PT/Exp D	10 LA *	4	7	0	83	62	6.10	1.73	255	354	257	19.4	30%	64%	5.32	41	21	38	6.9	6.7	**1.0**	7%	0.8	-21.4	-46	($3)
Consist A	1st Half	1	5	0	40	37	7.21	1.96	272			17.8	33%	63%	5.49	41	21	38	8.2	8.2	**1.0**	11%	1.1	-15.8	-54	($4)
LIMA Plan F	2nd Half	3	2	0	43	26	5.07	1.52	238			21.2	27%	65%	3.84				5.7	5.4	**0.9**		0.4	-5.6	46	$1
Rand Var +1	11 Proj	**2**	**2**	**0**	**29**	**19**	**5.28**	**1.69**	**275**			**22.3**	**30%**	**71%**	**5.26**	**42**	**20**	**38**	**5.6**	**5.9**	**1.1**	**11%**	**1.2**	**-4.0**	**-25**	**($0)**

0-4, 8.40 ERA in 30 IP at LA. Knuckeballer broke camp as 5th starter, but season was cruel: APR: 7.45 ERA, 4 PQS-DIS MAY: DL'd w/ foot injury JUN: Designated for assignment JUL-SEP: Rooted for RA Dickey

Halladay,Roy

Halladay,Roy		W	L	Sv	IP	K	ERA	WHIP	OBA	vL	vR	BF/G	H%	S%	xERA	G	L	F	Ctl	Dom	Cmd	hr/f	hr/9	RAR	BPV	R$
RH SP 33	06 TOR	16	5	0	220	132	3.19	1.10	251	259	244	27.6	28%	74%	3.18	57	21	22	1.4	5.4	**3.9**	12%	0.8	37.1	95	$29
Ht/Wt 78 230	07 TOR	16	7	0	225	139	3.72	1.24	267	265	270	30.3	30%	71%	3.70	53	18	29	1.9	5.6	**2.9**	7%	0.6	22.0	79	$23
Type GB	08 TOR	20	11	0	246	206	2.78	1.05	241	243	230	28.7	29%	76%	2.88	54	19	27	1.4	7.5	**5.3**	9%	0.7	47.5	129	$37
Health A	09 TOR	17	10	0	239	208	2.79	1.13	258	240	278	30.2	31%	79%	3.04	50	20	29	1.3	7.8	**5.9**	11%	0.8	49.1	134	$34
PT/Exp A	10 PHI	21	10	0	251	219	2.44	1.04	246	259	231	30.1	30%	81%	2.79	51	19	30	1.1	7.9	**7.3**	11%	0.9	48.7	142	$35
Consist A	1st Half	9	7	0	130	112	2.42	1.11	257			30.8	31%	81%	2.89	51	20	30	1.2	7.8	**6.6**	9%	0.7	25.5	136	$17
LIMA Plan C	2nd Half	12	3	0	121	107	2.46	0.97	234			29.3	28%	82%	2.68	52	18	30	1.0	8.0	**8.2**	14%	1.0	23.2	147	$20
Rand Var -2	11 Proj	**19**	**9**	**0**	**232**	**195**	**2.87**	**1.07**	**248**			**29.9**	**30%**	**77%**	**2.91**	**52**	**19**	**29**	**1.2**	**7.6**	**6.1**	**11%**	**0.8**	**35.3**	**132**	**$31**

Season was remarkably similar to CY year in 2003: 266 IP, 22 W, 3.25 ERA, 6.9 Cmd, 143 BPV. Owners can only hope for a healthier followup (133 IP, 4.20 ERA in 2004). A-list stuff and makeup reduce the risk.

Hamels,Cole

Hamels,Cole		W	L	Sv	IP	K	ERA	WHIP	OBA	vL	vR	BF/G	H%	S%	xERA	G	L	F	Ctl	Dom	Cmd	hr/f	hr/9	RAR	BPV	R$
LH SP 27	06 PHI *	11	8	0	155	177	3.59	1.15	228	207	244	24.3	30%	73%	3.34	39	18	43	2.8	10.2	**3.6**	11%	1.1	17.1	125	$21
Ht/Wt 75 190	07 PHI	15	5	0	183	177	3.39	1.12	240	247	236	26.5	29%	76%	3.36	42	19	39	2.1	8.7	**4.1**	13%	1.2	23.5	119	$25
Type Pwr	08 PHI	14	10	0	227	196	3.09	1.08	231	262	215	27.6	27%	77%	3.52	40	22	39	2.1	7.8	**3.7**	11%	1.1	33.1	101	$28
Health A	09 PHI	10	11	0	194	168	4.32	1.29	274	242	282	25.5	32%	69%	3.67	40	21	39	2.0	7.8	**3.9**	11%	1.1	-3.1	105	$14
PT/Exp A	10 PHI	12	11	0	209	211	3.06	1.18	239	196	247	25.9	30%	80%	3.19	45	17	38	2.6	9.1	**3.5**	12%	1.1	24.6	116	$22
Consist A	1st Half	6	7	0	97	96	4.07	1.34	259			25.9	30%	77%	3.57	43	17	40	3.1	8.9	**2.8**	16%	1.7	-0.7	95	$7
LIMA Plan C+	2nd Half	6	4	0	111	115	2.18	1.04	221			26.0	29%	82%	2.86	48	16	36	2.2	9.3	**4.3**	8%	0.6	25.2	135	$16
Rand Var 0	11 Proj	**14**	**8**	**0**	**210**	**201**	**3.47**	**1.18**	**246**			**26.1**	**30%**	**75%**	**3.36**	**43**	**19**	**38**	**2.4**	**8.6**	**3.7**	**11%**	**1.1**	**20.3**	**112**	**$23**

Emotional maturation as promising as ERA rebound. Only poor run support (PHI scored 2 runs or less in 8 of his losses) tamed otherwise brilliant season. Phenomenal 2H (GB, Cmd, xERA) hints at further upside.

Hammel,Jason

Hammel,Jason		W	L	Sv	IP	K	ERA	WHIP	OBA	vL	vR	BF/G	H%	S%	xERA	G	L	F	Ctl	Dom	Cmd	hr/f	hr/9	RAR	BPV	R$
RH SP 28	06 TAM *	5	15	0	171	132	6.10	1.62	311	372	299	23.5	36%	62%	4.44	44	19	38	3.1	6.9	**2.2**	9%	1.0	-32.5	63	$1
Ht/Wt 78 220	07 TAM *	7	10	0	161	129	5.50	1.52	278	310	277	19.3	33%	64%	4.64	41	16	43	3.9	7.2	**1.8**	7%	0.9	-19.7	43	$5
Type	08 TAM	4	4	2	78	44	4.60	1.51	273	281	265	8.7	29%	73%	4.67	47	21	32	4.0	5.1	**1.3**	13%	1.3	-2.4	7	$4
Health A	09 COL	10	8	0	177	133	4.33	1.39	289	289	290	22.4	34%	70%	3.72	46	23	31	2.1	6.8	**3.2**	10%	0.9	-3.0	88	$10
PT/Exp A	10 COL	10	9	0	178	141	4.81	1.40	286	282	291	25.6	34%	67%	3.64	47	20	33	2.4	7.1	**3.0**	10%	0.9	-17.4	89	$7
Consist B	1st Half	6	3	0	84	68	4.18	1.36	280			25.7	33%	71%	3.49	47	22	31	2.4	7.3	**3.1**	11%	1.0	-1.7	92	$5
LIMA Plan B	2nd Half	4	6	0	94	73	5.38	1.43	292			25.5	34%	62%	3.77	47	18	35	2.4	7.0	**2.9**	9%	0.9	-15.8	86	$1
Rand Var +3	11 Proj	**10**	**10**	**0**	**181**	**135**	**4.32**	**1.40**	**281**			**24.5**	**32%**	**71%**	**3.86**	**46**	**21**	**33**	**2.7**	**6.7**	**2.5**	**10%**	**0.9**	**6.2**	**73**	**$9**

Sleeper (again) or just sleepy? PRO: Maintained Dom/Cmd gains; GB%, BPV still strong. CON: S% looks chronic (career OppOPS .855 w/ runners on); hitters connect (LD%, OBA). UP: sub-4 ERA DN: repeat

Hanrahan,Joel

Hanrahan,Joel		W	L	Sv	IP	K	ERA	WHIP	OBA	vL	vR	BF/G	H%	S%	xERA	G	L	F	Ctl	Dom	Cmd	hr/f	hr/9	RAR	BPV	R$
RH RP 29	06 a/a	11	5	0	140	91	4.32	1.57	260			24.2	29%	74%	4.81				5.2	5.9	**1.1**		0.8	3.4	37	$8
Ht/Wt 76 251	07 WAS *	10	7	0	126	101	5.24	1.67	276	267	305	21.5	31%	72%	5.33	31	25	44	5.4	7.2	**1.3**	12%	1.4	-12.6	-6	$4
Type Pwr	08 WAS	6	3	9	84	93	3.95	1.36	235	228	237	5.2	31%	74%	3.61	43	22	36	4.5	9.9	**2.2**	12%	1.0	3.3	78	$11
Health A	09 2NL	1	4	5	64	72	4.78	1.67	288	269	293	4.4	39%	70%	4.07	36	25	39	4.8	10.1	**2.1**	4%	0.4	-4.7	68	$2
PT/Exp C	10 PIT	4	1	6	70	100	3.62	1.21	228	219	222	4.0	35%	72%	2.61	42	18	40	3.4	12.9	**3.8**	10%	0.8	3.4	162	$10
Consist B	1st Half	2	1	0	35	49	3.89	1.04	197			3.8	30%	64%	2.63	37	17	46	3.1	12.7	**4.1**	9%	0.8	0.5	160	$4
LIMA Plan A	2nd Half	2	0	6	35	51	3.34	1.37	256			4.2	39%	78%	2.57	47	19	35	3.6	13.1	**3.6**	11%	0.8	2.9	163	$5
Rand Var +3	11 Proj	**4**	**2**	**30**	**73**	**90**	**3.48**	**1.27**	**224**			**4.5**	**31%**	**75%**	**3.20**	**40**	**21**	**39**	**4.1**	**11.2**	**2.7**	**10%**	**0.9**	**8.5**	**109**	**$18**

Thrived as co-closer when given shot, but this was a season-long surge. Elite Dom still on the rise, but gains in GB% and Ctl were the real keys. And xERA says it should have been better. Closer inexperience the only drawback.

Hanson,Tommy

Hanson,Tommy		W	L	Sv	IP	K	ERA	WHIP	OBA	vL	vR	BF/G	H%	S%	xERA	G	L	F	Ctl	Dom	Cmd	hr/f	hr/9	RAR	BPV	R$
RH SP 24	06	0	0	0	0	0	0.00	0.00							0.00											
Ht/Wt 78 220	07	0	0	0	0	0	0.00	0.00							0.00											
Type Pwr FB	08 aa	8	4	0	98	99	3.49	1.21	220			22.5	28%	74%	3.25				3.8	9.1	**2.4**		0.8	9.9	91	$12
Health A	09 ATL *	14	7	0	194	195	2.51	1.10	215	256	192	24.3	28%	80%	3.42	40	18	42	2.9	9.1	**3.1**	7%	0.7	40.2	102	$28
PT/Exp B	10 ATL	10	11	0	203	173	3.33	1.17	242	226	251	24.4	30%	73%	3.63	42	17	42	2.5	7.7	**3.1**	6%	0.6	17.1	91	$19
Consist A	1st Half	8	5	0	97	98	4.19	1.37	266			24.4	34%	70%	3.68	38	18	44	3.1	9.1	**3.0**	6%	0.7	-2.1	97	$8
LIMA Plan C+	2nd Half	2	6	0	106	75	2.55	1.00	217			24.4	25%	77%	3.57	45	15	40	2.0	6.4	**3.3**	6%	0.6	19.2	85	$11
Rand Var -1	11 Proj	**12**	**9**	**0**	**203**	**186**	**3.24**	**1.20**	**239**			**24.6**	**29%**	**76%**	**3.63**	**42**	**17**	**41**	**2.8**	**8.2**	**3.0**	**8%**	**0.8**	**12.8**	**93**	**$21**

As expected, an excellent first full season. 2H Dom dive curious, though simultaneous gains in GB% and Ctl are huge positives. Even solved 1H consistency concerns (no PQS-DIS in 2H). A repeat, at least.

Happ,J.A.

Happ,J.A.		W	L	Sv	IP	K	ERA	WHIP	OBA	vL	vR	BF/G	H%	S%	xERA	G	L	F	Ctl	Dom	Cmd	hr/f	hr/9	RAR	BPV	R$
LH SP 28	06 a/a	7	2	0	80	71	3.70	1.35	252			26.3	32%	72%	3.70				3.6	8.0	**2.2**		0.4	8.1	86	$9
Ht/Wt 78 200	07 aaa	4	6	0	118	100	6.40	1.72	293			22.8	35%	63%	6.06				5.0	7.6	**1.5**		1.1	-28.2	40	($2)
Type Pwr FB	08 PHI *	9	7	0	167	153	4.52	1.39	261	209	247	22.5	31%	71%	4.21	31	27	43	3.5	8.2	**2.3**	11%	1.2	-5.1	62	$10
Health C	09 PHI	12	4	0	166	119	2.93	1.23	241	216	253	19.7	27%	82%	4.28	38	19	43	3.0	6.5	**2.1**	9%	1.1	25.8	51	$18
PT/Exp C	10 2NL *	7	5	0	122	93	4.74	1.64	276	179	244	23.1	31%	74%	4.92	39	18	43	5.1	6.9	**1.4**	10%	1.2	-10.9	4	$1
Consist A	1st Half	2	0	0	26	15	5.88	2.17	350			22.4	37%	78%	6.32	36	18	45	5.9	5.3	**0.9**	13%	2.0	-6.1	-49	($2)
LIMA Plan C	2nd Half	5	5	0	95	78	4.43	1.49	252			23.3	30%	72%	4.57	39	18	43	4.9	7.4	**1.5**	9%	1.0	-4.8	18	$3
Rand Var 0	11 Proj	**8**	**4**	**0**	**128**	**98**	**4.43**	**1.55**	**275**			**22.0**	**31%**	**75%**	**4.77**	**38**	**19**	**43**	**4.4**	**6.9**	**1.6**	**10%**	**1.2**	**-9.9**	**23**	**$5**

6-4, 3.40 ERA in 87 IP at PHI and HOU. Forearm strain and lost velocity torpedoed his 1H; 2H better but still filled with issues. Gets strikeouts and shuts down LHers, but Ctl, gopheritis are ongoing cautions.

Harang,Aaron

Harang,Aaron		W	L	Sv	IP	K	ERA	WHIP	OBA	vL	vR	BF/G	H%	S%	xERA	G	L	F	Ctl	Dom	Cmd	hr/f	hr/9	RAR	BPV	R$
RH SP 32	06 CIN	16	11	0	234	216	3.77	1.27	268	267	270	27.3	33%	74%	3.71	39	22	40	2.2	8.3	**3.9**	10%	1.1	20.8	108	$24
Ht/Wt 79 261	07 CIN	16	6	0	232	218	3.73	1.14	246	237	246	27.7	30%	71%	3.52	40	18	42	2.0	8.5	**4.2**	10%	1.1	19.9	116	$27
Type FB	08 CIN	6	17	0	184	153	4.79	1.38	283	298	274	26.4	32%	71%	4.20	34	22	44	2.4	7.5	**3.1**	14%	1.7	-11.7	81	$8
Health F	09 CIN	6	14	0	162	142	4.21	1.41	289	285	289	27.0	34%	75%	4.00	35	24	41	2.4	7.9	**3.3**	12%	1.3	-0.5	90	$8
PT/Exp A	10 CIN	6	7	0	112	82	5.32	1.58	306	283	323	22.9	35%	69%	4.48	37	22	41	3.1	6.6	**2.2**	10%	1.3	-17.9	51	$0
Consist A	1st Half	6	7	0	100	75	5.02	1.46	294			25.8	33%	69%	4.14	38	23	40	2.5	6.7	**2.7**	12%	1.3	-12.5	69	$3
LIMA Plan A	2nd Half	0	0	0	11	7	7.89	2.72	395			12.9	44%	70%	7.85	30	17	52	7.9	5.5	**0.7**	4%	0.8	-5.5	-105	($3)
Rand Var +3	11 Proj	**8**	**10**	**0**	**149**	**125**	**4.47**	**1.30**	**268**			**26.2**	**31%**	**70%**	**3.93**	**36**	**21**	**43**	**2.4**	**7.6**	**3.2**	**12%**	**1.4**	**3.8**	**87**	**$10**

Back problem wiped out Jul and Aug, and he was, um, rusty upon return. Overall, still plus-Cmd, and H% / S% gods unfair, but hitters like him more and more (OBA, LD%). Priority #1: Putting a stop to that IP trend.

Harden,Rich

Harden,Rich		W	L	Sv	IP	K	ERA	WHIP	OBA	vL	vR	BF/G	H%	S%	xERA	G	L	F	Ctl	Dom	Cmd	hr/f	hr/9	RAR	BPV	R$
RH SP 29	06 OAK	4	0	0	46	49	4.29	1.23	192	176	211	21.3	24%	67%	3.62	43	24	32	5.1	9.5	**1.9**	14%	1.0	1.6	57	$6
Ht/Wt 73 195	07 OAK	1	2	0	26	27	2.45	1.13	199	292	98	14.9	25%	85%	3.60	39	19	42	3.9	9.5	**2.5**	11%	1.1	6.5	83	$4
Type Pwr xFB	08 2TM	10	2	0	148	181	2.07	1.06	187	200	167	23.6	26%	84%	3.34	30	21	49	3.7	11.0	**3.0**	7%	0.7	40.9	106	$26
Health F	09 CHC	9	9	0	141	171	4.09	1.34	235	251	220	23.1	30%	75%	3.54	38	18	44	4.3	10.9	**2.6**	15%	1.5	1.8	97	$13
PT/Exp B	10 TEX *	5	7	0	115	102	5.38	1.62	263	273	238	20.9	30%	71%	4.97	35	14	51	5.5	8.0	**1.4**	12%	1.7	-17.6	7	$1
Consist B	1st Half	3	3	0	65	59	5.68	1.68	265			23.0	29%	72%	5.17	33	13	54	6.0	8.2	**1.4**	14%	1.9	-12.3	-3	($0)
LIMA Plan C+	2nd Half	2	4	0	50	43	5.00	1.54	260			18.6	30%	71%	4.61	38	16	45	5.0	7.7	**1.6**	11%	1.3	-5.3	21	$1
Rand Var +1	11 Proj	**6**	**5**	**0**	**102**	**105**	**4.43**	**1.39**	**243**			**20.8**	**30%**	**72%**	**4.07**	**36**	**17**	**47**	**4.3**	**9.3**	**2.1**	**11%**	**1.2**	**2.7**	**64**	**$8**

5-5, 5.58 ERA in 92 IP at TEX. Pre-'10, there were 2 absolutes:
1) He would get injured, but
2) His IP would be effective.
Ctl, Cmd and FB trends, along with 2010 xERA and BPV, say we might be down to one.

BRENT HERSHEY

Haren,Dan

	Yr	Tm	W	L	Sv	IP	K	ERA	WHIP	OBA	vL	vR	BF/G	H%	S%	xERA	G	L	F	Ctl	Dom	Cmd	hr/f	hr/9	RAR	BPV	R$
RH SP 30	06	OAK	14	13	0	223	176	4.12	1.21	263	246	268	27.1	30%	70%	3.63	45	19	36	1.8	7.1	3.9	13%	1.3	12.1	102	$24
Ht/Wt 77 215	07	OAK	15	9	0	223	192	3.07	1.21	254	230	264	27.0	30%	79%	3.63	44	17	38	2.2	7.8	3.5	10%	1.0	39.4	102	$28
Type Pwr	08	ARI	16	8	0	216	206	3.33	1.13	251	241	253	26.5	31%	73%	3.14	44	21	35	1.7	8.6	5.2	9%	0.8	25.0	132	$27
Health A	09	ARI	14	10	0	229	223	3.14	1.00	229	229	219	27.3	28%	74%	3.00	43	20	37	1.5	8.8	5.9	12%	1.1	29.7	138	$31
PT/Exp A	10	2TM	12	12	0	235	216	3.91	1.27	270	258	274	28.1	32%	74%	3.51	40	19	41	2.1	8.3	4.0	11%	1.2	4.8	112	$18
Consist A	1st Half		7	6	0	123	119	4.38	1.31	283			28.9	34%	71%	3.36	41	19	40	1.8	8.7	5.0	13%	1.4	-4.7	129	$9
LIMA Plan B	2nd Half		5	6	0	112	97	3.38	1.24	255			27.3	31%	76%	3.67	39	19	42	2.4	7.8	3.2	9%	1.0	9.5	93	$10
Rand Var 0	11	Proj	14	9	0	218	201	3.52	1.17	254			27.8	31%	74%	3.37	42	19	39	1.9	8.3	4.4	10%	1.0	22.7	118	$24

Fickle hr/f and H% in the 1H hid the fact that his skills aligned exactly to 2008-09. More walks slowed his 2H, but looks like a blip. Elite Cmd, xERA and BPV consistency all point to an easy return to the $20+ level.

Harrison,Matt

	Yr	Tm	W	L	Sv	IP	K	ERA	WHIP	OBA	vL	vR	BF/G	H%	S%	xERA	G	L	F	Ctl	Dom	Cmd	hr/f	hr/9	RAR	BPV	R$
LH RP 25	06	aa	3	4	0	77	48	5.14	1.57	319			26.6	36%	68%	5.76				2.2	5.6	2.5		0.8	-5.9	53	$1
Ht/Wt 76 225	07	aa	5	7	0	116	67	4.34	1.49	296			25.6	33%	70%	4.92				2.7	5.2	1.9		0.5	1.8	51	$5
Type	08	TEX	* 15	6	0	168	88	4.73	1.55	298	310	297	25.0	32%	71%	4.90	40	23	36	3.2	4.7	1.5	9%	1.0	-7.9	17	$8
Health F	09	TEX	4	5	0	63	34	6.11	1.64	312	210	351	26.3	33%	64%	4.75	47	23	31	3.3	4.8	1.5	13%	1.3	-13.0	24	($0)
PT/Exp C	10	TEX	3	2	2	78	46	4.71	1.52	266	235	273	9.4	29%	72%	4.62	47	21	33	4.5	5.3	1.2	12%	1.1	-5.5	-1	$2
Consist A	1st Half		1	1	1	50	29	4.47	1.37	257			16.6	27%	71%	4.25	47	21	32	3.6	5.2	1.5	14%	1.3	-2.1	22	$2
LIMA Plan C	2nd Half		2	1	1	28	17	5.14	1.79	282			5.5	31%	72%	5.33	45	20	34	6.1	5.5	0.9	9%	1.0	-3.5	-43	$0
Rand Var 0	11	Proj	4	3	0	73	41	4.97	1.61	291			11.3	31%	71%	4.80	46	22	33	4.1	5.1	1.2	11%	1.1	-4.5	5	$1

Struggled in 6 starts in Apr/May (5.29 ERA, 1.4 Cmd), but really no better out of the pen (4.26 ERA, 1.0 Cmd). Without adequate Dom, those GB are going to waste, but ballooning Ctl is the more pressing problem.

Hawkins,LaTroy

	Yr	Tm	W	L	Sv	IP	K	ERA	WHIP	OBA	vL	vR	BF/G	H%	S%	xERA	G	L	F	Ctl	Dom	Cmd	hr/f	hr/9	RAR	BPV	R$
RH RP 38	06	BAL	3	2	0	60	27	4.49	1.46	301	323	285	4.4	33%	69%	4.73	44	21	35	2.2	4.0	1.8	5%	0.6	0.5	34	$3
Ht/Wt 77 215	07	COL	2	5	0	55	29	3.42	1.23	250	237	266	3.7	27%	76%	3.51	63	16	21	2.6	4.7	1.8	16%	1.0	6.9	56	$5
Type Con	08	2TM	3	1	1	62	48	3.92	1.21	233	293	189	4.5	28%	67%	3.88	46	17	37	3.2	7.0	2.2	5%	0.4	3.0	63	$6
Health F	09	HOU	1	4	11	63	45	2.13	1.20	252	203	303	4.0	28%	88%	3.66	45	24	31	2.3	6.4	2.8	12%	1.0	16.1	77	$10
PT/Exp D	10	MIL	0	3	0	16	18	8.44	1.69	318	269	359	4.1	41%	48%	3.35	47	21	32	3.4	10.1	3.0	13%	1.1	-8.7	116	($1)
Consist A	1st Half		0	3	0	12	15	9.23	1.71	298			4.2	42%	42%	3.28	52	13	35	4.6	11.5	2.5	9%	0.8	-7.5	113	($1)
LIMA Plan D+	2nd Half		0	0	0	4	3	6.28	1.63	366			3.9	40%	67%	3.45	38	38	25	0.0	6.3		25%	2.1	-1.2	128	($0)
Rand Var +5	11	Proj	2	3	0	44	27	3.72	1.31	268			4.1	30%	74%	3.94	44	26	30	2.5	5.6	2.3	9%	0.8	1.1	56	$3

Shoulder stiffness in March led to a long DL stint and eventual surgery in August. Expected to be ready for spring training, but waning age and health are a dubious duo. Saves speculation dollars best spent elsewhere.

Hawksworth,Blake

	Yr	Tm	W	L	Sv	IP	K	ERA	WHIP	OBA	vL	vR	BF/G	H%	S%	xERA	G	L	F	Ctl	Dom	Cmd	hr/f	hr/9	RAR	BPV	R$
RH RP 28	06	aa	4	2	0	79	55	3.98	1.43	270			26.5	31%	75%	4.70				3.5	6.3	1.8		0.9	5.2	48	$5
Ht/Wt 75 195	07	aaa	4	13	0	129	74	6.31	1.66	323			23.7	34%	65%	6.97				2.9	5.2	1.8		1.7	-29.4	9	($3)
Type GB	08	aaa	5	7	0	88	64	7.37	1.95	349			23.9	40%	63%	7.63				4.0	6.5	1.6		1.2	-33.3	21	($6)
Health A	09	STL	* 9	4	0	113	63	3.55	1.24	248	246	176	11.2	28%	71%	4.04	54	14	32	2.8	5.0	1.8	5%	0.4	8.8	45	$11
PT/Exp D	10	STL	4	8	0	90	61	4.98	1.64	307	304	315	9.1	34%	74%	4.20	51	17	31	3.5	6.1	1.7	16%	1.5	-10.8	45	($0)
Consist D	1st Half		2	5	0	43	30	5.02	1.63	312			8.1	34%	73%	4.00	54	15	31	3.1	6.3	2.0	16%	1.5	-5.3	60	($0)
LIMA Plan D	2nd Half		2	3	0	47	31	4.95	1.65	303			10.3	33%	74%	4.38	49	19	32	3.8	5.9	1.6	16%	1.5	-5.4	30	($0)
Rand Var +4	11	Proj	5	6	0	87	58	4.66	1.53	290			11.4	32%	72%	4.17	52	17	32	3.4	6.0	1.8	11%	1.0	-0.3	45	$2

Better in relief (4.25 ERA, 2.4 Cmd) than as starter (5.83, 1.3), but needs to cap walks and simply find an out pitch to succeed. GB% is a good foundation, but the big picture doesn't inspire.

Heilman,Aaron

	Yr	Tm	W	L	Sv	IP	K	ERA	WHIP	OBA	vL	vR	BF/G	H%	S%	xERA	G	L	F	Ctl	Dom	Cmd	hr/f	hr/9	RAR	BPV	R$
RH RP 32	06	NYM	4	5	0	87	73	3.62	1.16	229	231	231	4.8	28%	69%	3.77	45	17	38	2.9	7.6	2.6	5%	0.5	9.3	81	$9
Ht/Wt 77 227	07	NYM	7	7	1	86	63	3.03	1.07	229	234	218	4.2	26%	75%	3.62	45	21	34	2.1	6.6	3.2	9%	0.8	14.8	85	$13
Type Pwr	08	NYM	3	8	3	76	80	5.21	1.59	259	308	222	4.4	33%	69%	4.15	41	24	35	5.4	9.5	1.7	14%	1.2	-8.8	42	$3
Health A	09	CHC	4	4	1	72	65	4.11	1.41	250	210	288	4.5	30%	74%	4.13	41	21	39	4.2	8.1	1.9	11%	1.1	0.7	50	$5
PT/Exp C	10	ARI	5	8	6	72	55	4.50	1.38	264	229	291	4.4	30%	70%	4.33	36	20	45	3.3	6.9	2.1	9%	1.1	-4.3	50	$6
Consist A	1st Half		2	3	3	36	26	3.72	1.43	265			4.3	30%	77%	4.79	28	23	48	3.7	6.4	1.7	7%	1.0	1.3	22	$3
LIMA Plan C+	2nd Half		3	5	3	36	29	5.29	1.32	263			4.6	30%	62%	3.85	43	16	41	2.8	7.3	2.6	11%	1.3	-5.6	78	$3
Rand Var 0	11	Proj	4	6	0	58	49	4.34	1.38	255			4.5	30%	71%	4.12	41	20	40	3.7	7.6	2.0	10%	1.1	0.1	55	$4

Dom and Ctl both decreased for second straight season, and he might have found that elusive balance in 2H. But S% ruined it all; saves opps disappeared in Sept. Only chance for impact is with 2.5+ Cmd.

Hellickson,Jeremy

	Yr	Tm	W	L	Sv	IP	K	ERA	WHIP	OBA	vL	vR	BF/G	H%	S%	xERA	G	L	F	Ctl	Dom	Cmd	hr/f	hr/9	RAR	BPV	R$
RH SP 23	06		0	0	0	0	0	0.00	0.00							0.00											
Ht/Wt 73 185	07		0	0	0	0	0	0.00	0.00							0.00											
Type Pwr xFB	08	aa	4	4	0	75	68	4.55	1.44	305			25.2	35%	76%	6.16				1.8	8.1	4.5		1.9	-2.3	81	$4
Health A	09	a/a	9	2	0	114	116	3.08	1.00	207			22.3	27%	71%	2.40				2.4	9.2	3.9		0.7	17.3	128	$18
PT/Exp D	10	TAM	* 16	3	0	154	138	2.87	1.21	250	301	154	20.5	31%	78%	3.82	37	13	50	2.5	8.1	3.3	5%	0.6	24.0	94	$21
Consist F	1st Half		10	2	0	99	86	2.63	1.19	257			24.0	32%	78%	3.10				1.9	7.8	4.1		0.4	18.4	125	$14
LIMA Plan B	2nd Half		6	1	0	54	52	3.31	1.25	235			16.2	29%	77%	3.90	37	13	50	3.5	8.6	2.5	8%	1.0	5.5	76	$7
Rand Var -4	11	Proj	13	5	0	145	138	3.79	1.23	251			23.1	31%	73%	3.82	37	13	50	2.5	8.6	3.4	8%	1.1	8.4	101	$17

4-0, 3.47 ERA in 36 IP at TAM. After 4 starts (all PQS-DOM) in Aug, TAM moved him to bullpen to keep IP low. With 4.1 Cmd, 109 BPV in MLB, he looks ready. FBs bear watching (1.2 hr/9), but that's the only caution. Invest.

Hendrickson,Mark

	Yr	Tm	W	L	Sv	IP	K	ERA	WHIP	OBA	vL	vR	BF/G	H%	S%	xERA	G	L	F	Ctl	Dom	Cmd	hr/f	hr/9	RAR	BPV	R$
LH RP 36	06	2TM	6	15	0	164	99	4.22	1.43	272	287	264	23.0	30%	72%	4.59	48	16	36	3.4	5.4	1.6	9%	0.9	6.1	32	$8
Ht/Wt 81 240	07	LA	4	8	0	123	92	5.21	1.39	291	258	300	13.6	33%	64%	3.89	44	23	33	2.1	6.7	3.2	12%	1.1	-11.8	86	$4
Type	08	FLA	7	8	0	134	81	5.45	1.47	282	248	296	16.3	31%	64%	4.55	44	20	35	3.2	5.5	1.7	11%	1.1	-19.5	33	$3
Health A	09	BAL	6	5	1	105	61	4.37	1.42	281	275	282	8.6	30%	74%	4.52	45	20	35	2.8	5.2	1.8	13%	1.4	1.0	40	$6
PT/Exp B	10	BAL	1	6	0	75	55	5.26	1.55	314	317	311	6.5	36%	68%	4.02	43	22	35	2.4	6.6	2.8	10%	1.1	-10.4	75	($0)
Consist A	1st Half		1	3	0	41	29	5.27	1.51	314			6.7	36%	67%	3.89	44	22	33	2.0	6.4	3.2	11%	1.1	-5.7	83	$0
LIMA Plan D+	2nd Half		0	3	0	34	26	5.25	1.60	313			6.2	36%	69%	4.17	41	22	36	2.9	6.8	2.4	10%	1.0	-4.7	64	($1)
Rand Var +4	11	Proj	2	5	0	73	49	4.59	1.39	279			8.0	31%	70%	4.14	44	21	35	2.7	6.1	2.2	11%	1.1	1.3	57	$3

Seen wearning this T-shirt: "I had by far my best skills season in three years and all I got was this lousy 5.26 ERA." Age 37 and in a contract year, this H%/S% debacle was ill-timed. Is a lefty, though.

Hensley,Clay

	Yr	Tm	W	L	Sv	IP	K	ERA	WHIP	OBA	vL	vR	BF/G	H%	S%	xERA	G	L	F	Ctl	Dom	Cmd	hr/f	hr/9	RAR	BPV	R$
RH RP 31	06	SD	11	12	0	187	122	3.71	1.34	248	263	239	21.5	28%	74%	4.11	54	17	30	3.7	5.9	1.6	9%	0.7	18.0	39	$15
Ht/Wt 71 185	07	SD	* 3	10	0	121	65	8.68	2.34	378	287	324	24.5	41%	63%	6.28	49	15	36	5.6	4.8	0.9	11%	1.4	-63.5	-38	($19)
Type Pwr GB	08	SD	* 2	3	0	87	48	5.55	1.71	295	288	221	8.4	32%	69%	5.04	51	18	31	4.8	4.9	1.0	11%	1.0	-13.8	-12	($3)
Health D	09	aaa	9	4	0	124	71	4.35	1.56	289			22.2	32%	73%	5.09				3.7	5.2	1.4		0.7	-0.7	36	$5
PT/Exp D	10	FLA	3	4	7	75	77	2.16	1.11	203	216	184	4.4	27%	81%	2.96	53	15	32	3.5	9.2	2.7	5%	0.4	17.2	104	$12
Consist C	1st Half		1	3	0	35	44	2.33	1.10	197			4.8	30%	78%	2.64	49	16	34	3.6	11.4	3.1	4%	0.3	7.2	135	$5
LIMA Plan C+	2nd Half		2	1	7	40	33	2.01	1.12	209			4.2	26%	84%	3.25	56	14	30	3.3	7.4	2.2	6%	0.4	10.0	76	$8
Rand Var -5	11	Proj	3	3	15	73	62	3.60	1.37	252			4.9	31%	75%	3.65	53	16	32	3.7	7.7	2.1	9%	0.7	4.4	69	$10

Always had GB, but move to relief led to more Ks and fueled this breakout. Ctl held up during the season; Dom didn't, but converted all 7 save opps in Sept. A full skills repeat unlikely, but should be in closer mix.

Hernandez,David

	Yr	Tm	W	L	Sv	IP	K	ERA	WHIP	OBA	vL	vR	BF/G	H%	S%	xERA	G	L	F	Ctl	Dom	Cmd	hr/f	hr/9	RAR	BPV	R$
RH RP 25	06		0	0	0	0	0	0.00	0.00							0.00											
Ht/Wt 75 215	07		0	0	0	0	0	0.00	0.00							0.00											
Type Pwr xFB	08	aa	10	4	0	141	141	3.42	1.45	251			22.8	32%	78%	4.24				4.5	9.0	2.0		0.8	15.4	77	$13
Health B	09	BAL	* 7	12	0	162	136	5.21	1.49	276	280	297	22.4	30%	71%	4.92	29	18	53	3.7	7.5	2.0	13%	1.9	-15.2	43	$6
PT/Exp C	10	BAL	8	8	2	79	72	4.31	1.44	244	198	271	8.4	29%	72%	4.62	28	21	51	4.8	8.2	1.7	8%	1.6	-1.7	24	$7
Consist A	1st Half		3	6	2	56	43	4.52	1.47	238			12.2	28%	70%	5.10	29	20	51	5.3	6.9	1.3	6%	0.8	-2.6	-12	$3
LIMA Plan C+	2nd Half		5	2	0	24	29	3.81	1.36	257			4.8	34%	79%	3.58	24	24	52	3.4	11.1	3.2	13%	1.5	0.9	109	$4
Rand Var -1	11	Proj	6	4	5	58	56	4.03	1.40	258			10.0	31%	76%	4.35	27	21	52	3.7	8.7	2.3	11%	1.4	-0.5	61	$8

Another role-switcher. Missed most of Aug w/ ankle sprain that interrupted tidy move to bullpen:
As SP: 5.7 Dom, 1.0 Cmd
As RP: 10.9 Dom, 3.5 Cmd
Watch FB%, but if Dom sticks...
UP: 3.50 ERA, 15 saves

BRENT HERSHEY

Hernandez,Felix

		Yr	Tm	W	L	Sv	IP	K	ERA	WHIP	OBA	vL	vR	BF/G	H%	S%	xERA	G	L	F	Ctl	Dom	Cmd	hr/f	hr/9	RAR	BPV	R$
RH SP	24	06	SEA	12	14	0	191	176	4.52	1.34	266	281	241	26.2	32%	69%	3.11	58	18	25	2.8	8.3	2.9	17%	1.1	0.8	109	$18
Ht/Wt	75 225	07	SEA	14	7	0	190	165	3.93	1.38	280	299	262	27.3	34%	74%	3.08	61	16	23	2.5	7.8	3.1	15%	0.9	13.6	112	$19
Type	Pwr GB	08	SEA	9	11	0	201	175	3.45	1.39	259	275	242	27.9	32%	77%	3.59	52	18	29	3.6	7.8	2.2	10%	0.8	22.1	75	$17
Health	A	09	SEA	19	5	0	239	217	2.49	1.14	229	228	226	28.5	29%	80%	3.17	53	17	30	2.7	8.2	3.1	8%	0.6	57.8	106	$36
PT/Exp	A	10	SEA	13	12	0	250	232	2.27	1.06	216	213	212	29.2	27%	81%	2.88	54	16	30	2.5	8.4	3.3	9%	0.6	57.5	114	$35
Consist	A	1st Half		6	5	0	122	116	3.03	1.14	227			29.1	29%	75%	2.99	54	15	31	2.8	8.6	3.1	9%	0.7	16.6	110	$14
LIMA Plan	C	2nd Half		7	7	0	128	116	1.55	0.98	205			29.3	26%	88%	2.77	54	17	29	2.2	8.2	3.6	8%	0.6	40.9	118	$21
Rand Var	-3	11	Proj	15	11	0	247	224	2.99	1.15	231			28.7	29%	76%	3.07	54	17	29	2.7	8.2	3.0	9%	0.7	37.0	106	$31

Full-blown encore seemed impossible after '09 breakout and workload spike. But he improved, even in the face of historically poor offensive support. IP still a worry, but for now he's one of the AL's best.

Hernandez,Livan

		Yr	Tm	W	L	Sv	IP	K	ERA	WHIP	OBA	vL	vR	BF/G	H%	S%	xERA	G	L	F	Ctl	Dom	Cmd	hr/f	hr/9	RAR	BPV	R$
RH SP	36	06	2NL	13	13	0	216	128	4.83	1.50	288	302	275	28.1	31%	71%	5.11	37	20	44	3.3	5.3	1.6	9%	1.2	-9.2	23	$9
Ht/Wt	74 245	07	ARI	11	11	0	204	90	4.93	1.60	300	295	320	28.0	30%	73%	5.50	38	21	41	3.5	4.0	1.1	11%	1.5	-12.8	-6	$3
Type	Con	08	2TM	13	11	0	180	67	6.05	1.67	336	340	344	26.6	34%	65%	5.04	44	22	34	2.2	3.4	1.6	11%	1.3	-38.7	25	($2)
Health	A	09	2NL	9	12	0	184	102	5.44	1.56	298	287	330	26.6	33%	66%	4.87	41	22	37	3.3	5.0	1.5	8%	0.9	-28.3	20	$1
PT/Exp	A	10	WAS	10	12	0	212	114	3.66	1.32	266	295	248	27.2	29%	73%	4.51	39	21	40	2.7	4.8	1.8	6%	0.7	9.4	31	$12
Consist	A	1st Half		6	4	0	106	51	2.98	1.26	253			27.6	27%	79%	4.41	44	18	37	2.7	4.3	1.6	7%	0.8	13.5	27	$8
LIMA Plan	D+	2nd Half		4	8	0	106	63	4.33	1.39	278			26.9	31%	69%	4.60	34	23	43	2.7	5.3	2.0	5%	0.6	-4.1	35	$3
Rand Var	-2	11	Proj	8	10	0	160	83	4.63	1.46	289			26.9	31%	71%	4.76	40	21	39	2.8	4.7	1.7	9%	1.1	-12.2	26	$4

Improved Ctl, 1H H% and S%, and 2H hr/f produced the ERA. But 2010 luck aside, his newfound ability to avoid HRs over the past two years is still baffling. And we still wouldn't take him on a dare.

Herndon,David

		Yr	Tm	W	L	Sv	IP	K	ERA	WHIP	OBA	vL	vR	BF/G	H%	S%	xERA	G	L	F	Ctl	Dom	Cmd	hr/f	hr/9	RAR	BPV	R$
RH RP	25	06		0	0	0	0	0	0.00	0.00							0.00											
Ht/Wt	77 230	07		0	0	0	0	0	0.00	0.00							0.00											
Type	Con xGB	08		0	0	0	0	0	0.00	0.00							0.00											
Health	A	09	aa	5	6	11	65	28	4.22	1.57	322			5.8	33%	78%	6.39				2.0	3.8	1.9		1.5	0.7	9	$6
PT/Exp	D	10	PHI	1	3	0	52	29	4.30	1.61	312	328	317	5.0	35%	72%	4.04	57	17	27	2.9	5.0	1.7	4%	0.3	-1.8	46	($0)
Consist	F	1st Half		0	1	0	28	11	3.57	1.59	327			5.0	36%	75%	4.08	58	17	25	1.9	3.6	1.8	0%	0.0	1.5	48	($0)
LIMA Plan	D	2nd Half		1	2	0	25	18	5.12	1.63	295			5.1	34%	68%	3.98	56	16	28	4.0	6.6	1.6	9%	0.7	-3.4	43	($0)
Rand Var	0	11	Proj	1	2	0	29	15	4.34	1.59	312			5.2	34%	74%	4.17	57	16	27	2.8	4.7	1.7	11%	0.9	-0.1	43	$0

Has the GB% thing working all the time, but it's accompanied by mid-30% H% and too much inconsistency elsewhere. 2H Dom spike negated by Ctl issues. Upside limited unless Cmd improves.

Herrera,Daniel

		Yr	Tm	W	L	Sv	IP	K	ERA	WHIP	OBA	vL	vR	BF/G	H%	S%	xERA	G	L	F	Ctl	Dom	Cmd	hr/f	hr/9	RAR	BPV	R$
LH RP	26	06		0	0	0	0	0	0.00	0.00							0.00											
Ht/Wt	66 165	07	aa	5	2	0	52	55	5.01	1.36	258			6.6	34%	63%	4.10				3.5	9.5	2.8		0.7	-3.5	97	$5
Type		08	a/a	7	4	6	72	52	3.24	1.16	248			5.1	29%	73%	3.31				2.1	6.5	3.1		0.6	9.5	90	$12
Health	A	09	CIN	4	4	0	62	44	3.06	1.41	266			3.8	31%	80%	3.98	50	20	30	3.5	6.4	1.8	9%	0.7	8.6	49	$5
PT/Exp	D	10	CIN *	3	5	5	60	44	4.67	1.29	281	316	328	4.1	33%	63%	3.53	43	26	31	1.7	6.5	4.0	7%	0.6	-4.8	94	$5
Consist	B	1st Half		1	3	0	23	14	3.91	1.61	323			2.9	36%	77%	4.22	43	26	31	2.3	5.5	2.3	8%	0.8	0.3	56	$0
LIMA Plan	B+	2nd Half		2	2	5	37	30	5.13	1.09	252			5.7	31%	50%	2.95				1.2	7.2	5.9		0.5	-5.1	157	$4
Rand Var	+3	11	Proj	2	2	0	29	21	4.03	1.31	268			4.2	31%	71%	3.72	45	24	30	2.5	6.5	2.6	11%	0.9	1.5	74	$2

1-3, 3.91 ERA in 23 IP at CIN. Spent 2H at AAA after inflated H% fueled 5.58 ERA during May and June. BPV and xERA say promise remains, but he needs to re-establish GB% and Dom at MLB level.

Herrmann,Frank

		Yr	Tm	W	L	Sv	IP	K	ERA	WHIP	OBA	vL	vR	BF/G	H%	S%	xERA	G	L	F	Ctl	Dom	Cmd	hr/f	hr/9	RAR	BPV	R$
RH RP	26	06		0	0	0	0	0	0.00	0.00							0.00											
Ht/Wt	76 220	07		0	0	0	0	0	0.00	0.00							0.00											
Type	Con xFB	08	a/a	11	8	0	144	86	5.21	1.61	315			26.1	35%	68%	5.66				2.8	5.4	1.9		0.8	-16.1	41	$4
Health	A	09	a/a	4	4	2	106	53	3.93	1.46	310			9.5	34%	74%	5.15				1.7	4.5	2.7		0.7	5.1	54	$5
PT/Exp	D	10	CLE *	3	1	3	73	43	2.60	1.12	239	310	241	5.0	27%	80%	4.21	36	20	45	2.1	5.4	2.5	6%	0.7	13.9	52	$9
Consist	B	1st Half		3	0	3	41	26	0.89	0.90	187			4.9	22%	92%	3.56	46	16	38	2.3	5.8	2.6	2%	0.2	16.4	68	$9
LIMA Plan	C+	2nd Half		0	1	0	32	17	4.78	1.41	296			5.1	31%	70%	4.76	32	21	47	2.0	4.8	2.4	10%	1.4	-2.5	43	$0
Rand Var	-5	11	Proj	2	2	0	58	32	4.03	1.34	284			7.1	31%	73%	4.69	34	20	46	2.0	5.0	2.5	8%	1.1	-2.9	47	$3

0-1, 4.03 ERA in 45 IP at CLE. Forte is Ctl and work vs. RHers, aided by fortunate H% and S%. With a G/L/F this volatile, he won't repeat his MLB debut without hiking his dominance.

Hill,Shawn

		Yr	Tm	W	L	Sv	IP	K	ERA	WHIP	OBA	vL	vR	BF/G	H%	S%	xERA	G	L	F	Ctl	Dom	Cmd	hr/f	hr/9	RAR	BPV	R$
RH SP	29	06	WAS *	4	6	0	91	44	3.95	1.36	290			23.0	32%	70%	4.28	50	19	31	1.9	4.3	2.2	4%	0.4	6.1	54	$5
Ht/Wt	74 225	07	WAS	4	5	0	97	65	3.42	1.14	239	288	189	24.7	27%	73%	3.53	55	17	28	2.3	6.0	2.6	11%	0.8	12.0	78	$10
Type	Con	08	WAS	1	5	0	63	39	5.83	1.75	330	294	374	24.7	37%	66%	4.54	46	25	28	3.3	5.5	1.7	8%	0.7	-12.2	36	($3)
Health	F	09	WAS	1	1	0	12	7	5.25	1.50	307			17.7	34%	65%	4.94	30	23	47	2.3	5.3	2.3	5%	0.8	-1.6	42	$0
PT/Exp	D	10	TOR *	4	4	0	49	23	2.46	1.20	256	302	262	20.1	28%	82%	3.89	49	21	30	2.1	4.3	2.0	7%	0.6	10.1	47	$6
Consist	B	1st Half		0	0	0	0	0	0.00	0.00							0.00											
LIMA Plan	C+	2nd Half		4	4	0	49	23	2.46	1.20	256			20.1	28%	82%	3.89	49	21	30	2.1	4.3	2.0	7%	0.6	10.1	47	$6
Rand Var	-5	11	Proj	5	7	0	108	62	3.83	1.31	271			22.9	30%	73%	4.10	46	21	32	2.4	5.2	2.1	10%	0.9	2.5	52	$7

1-2, 2.61 ERA in 21 IP at TOR. Second TJS in 6 years delayed sinkerballer's season. Flashed trademark GB% and Ctl in four starts, but his Dom and health grade tell the story. Flyer material only.

Hochevar,Luke

		Yr	Tm	W	L	Sv	IP	K	ERA	WHIP	OBA	vL	vR	BF/G	H%	S%	xERA	G	L	F	Ctl	Dom	Cmd	hr/f	hr/9	RAR	BPV	R$
RH SP	27	06		0	0	0	0	0	0.00	0.00							0.00											
Ht/Wt	77 210	07	KC *	4	10	0	165	121	6.03	1.59	310	273	208	23.9	35%	64%	3.68	63	10	27	2.9	6.6	2.3	18%	1.4	-31.0	83	$0
Type		08	KC *	7	13	0	146	82	5.28	1.44	276	314	244	25.5	30%	64%	4.36	52	17	32	3.3	5.0	1.5	9%	0.9	-16.8	31	$4
Health	D	09	KC *	12	14	0	191	134	5.39	1.46	290	292	289	25.3	32%	65%	4.25	47	18	36	2.8	6.3	2.3	11%	1.2	-22.1	63	$8
PT/Exp	C	10	KC	6	6	0	103	76	4.81	1.43	275	288	255	24.9	32%	67%	3.95	46	21	33	3.2	6.6	2.1	8%	0.8	-8.5	56	$5
Consist	A	1st Half		5	4	0	78	57	4.96	1.38	267			25.8	31%	64%	3.89	46	22	32	3.2	6.6	2.0	8%	0.7	-7.9	55	$4
LIMA Plan	B	2nd Half		1	2	0	25	19	4.32	1.56	298			22.4	34%	75%	4.10	46	18	36	3.2	6.8	2.1	10%	1.1	-0.6	60	$1
Rand Var	+1	11	Proj	9	14	0	189	139	4.54	1.41	273			24.0	31%	70%	4.00	47	18	34	3.1	6.6	2.1	11%	1.1	6.6	61	$10

Both Dom and xERA trends along with 41% PQS-DOM% suggest there's still something decent here. Missed all of July and Aug with strained elbow. Another end-of-draft flyer if he's healthy.

Hoffman,Trevor

		Yr	Tm	W	L	Sv	IP	K	ERA	WHIP	OBA	vL	vR	BF/G	H%	S%	xERA	G	L	F	Ctl	Dom	Cmd	hr/f	hr/9	RAR	BPV	R$
RH RP	43	06	SD	0	2	46	63	50	2.14	0.97	213	194	214	3.8	25%	84%	3.82	32	22	45	1.9	7.1	3.8	8%	0.9	18.2	89	$24
Ht/Wt	72 221	07	SD	4	5	42	57	44	2.98	1.12	233	299	169	3.8	29%	73%	4.31	31	18	52	2.4	6.9	2.9	2%	0.3	10.2	69	$22
Type	xFB	08	SD	3	6	30	45	46	3.77	1.04	229	291	165	3.7	27%	72%	3.33	39	14	47	1.8	9.1	5.1	14%	1.6	2.8	133	$16
Health	B	09	MIL	3	2	37	54	48	1.83	0.91	187	222	149	3.8	24%	81%	3.49	39	14	46	2.3	8.0	3.4	3%	0.3	15.7	98	$22
PT/Exp	B	10	MIL	2	7	10	47	30	5.90	1.44	269	298	242	4.1	28%	62%	5.03	32	17	51	3.6	5.7	1.6	10%	1.5	-11.0	15	$3
Consist	B	1st Half		2	4	5	25	16	8.28	1.64	299			4.4	30%	53%	5.74	20	19	61	4.0	5.8	1.5	14%	2.5	-13.2	-5	$0
LIMA Plan	C+	2nd Half		0	3	5	22	14	3.23	1.21	232			3.8	27%	73%	4.17	46	15	40	3.2	5.6	1.8	4%	0.4	2.2	38	$3
Rand Var	+3	11	Proj	2	5	8	51	33	4.26	1.44	274			4.2	30%	74%	4.87	36	16	48	3.4	5.9	1.7	9%	1.2	-4.6	28	$4

Salvaged season by mixing in more breaking stuff, becoming GBer in 2H. But Ctl is rising along with age while Dom is crashing, leaving reprise of 2H in doubt. Value is limited to a potential handful of saves.

Holland,Derek

		Yr	Tm	W	L	Sv	IP	K	ERA	WHIP	OBA	vL	vR	BF/G	H%	S%	xERA	G	L	F	Ctl	Dom	Cmd	hr/f	hr/9	RAR	BPV	R$
LH SP	24	06		0	0	0	0	0	0.00	0.00							0.00											
Ht/Wt	74 185	07		0	0	0	0	0	0.00	0.00							0.00											
Type	Pwr FB	08	aa	3	0	0	26	24	1.38	0.96	188			25.2	24%	88%	1.72				2.8	8.3	3.0		0.3	9.4	120	$6
Health	C	09	TEX	8	13	0	138	107	6.12	1.50	291	287	289	18.5	32%	62%	4.37	41	19	39	3.1	7.0	2.3	15%	1.7	-28.4	62	$3
PT/Exp	C	10	TEX *	9	6	0	120	98	3.09	1.26	246	130	277	20.0	29%	79%	3.91	42	15	43	3.1	7.4	2.4	7%	0.8	15.5	70	$13
Consist	D	1st Half		6	2	0	58	48	2.19	1.17	250			21.4	30%	85%	3.84	39	10	51	2.0	7.5	3.7	6%	0.8	13.8	98	$9
LIMA Plan	C	2nd Half		3	4	0	62	50	3.92	1.35	243			18.9	29%	73%	4.07	44	18	38	4.1	7.3	1.8	9%	0.9	1.7	43	$4
Rand Var	-3	11	Proj	10	10	0	145	116	4.34	1.37	264			22.2	30%	72%	4.10	42	18	40	3.2	7.2	2.3	11%	1.2	3.3	64	$11

3-4, 4.08 ERA in 57 IP at TEX. Health a consideration after missing June / July with knee and rotator cuff issues. 2H Ctl showed rust, but held Dom, hr/9 gains all year. Remains a promising work-in-progress.

JOCK THOMPSON

Howell,J.P.

		Yr	Tm	W	L	Sv	IP	K	ERA	WHIP	OBA	vL	vR	BF/G	H%	S%	xERA	G	L	F	Ctl	Dom	Cmd	hr/f	hr/9	RAR	BPV	R$
LH RP	27	06	TAM	* 9	8	0	133	103	4.60	1.53	298	400	281	22.8	36%	70%	3.99	45	26	29	3.0	7.0	2.3	7%	0.6	-0.7	68	$8
Ht/Wt	72 180	07	TAM	* 8	14	0	179	177	5.43	1.45	286	296	325	25.2	35%	66%	3.50	46	23	31	2.9	8.9	3.1	17%	1.4	-20.4	106	$9
Type	Pwr	08	TAM	6	1	3	89	92	2.22	1.13	198	188	197	5.7	26%	83%	3.08	54	17	30	3.9	9.3	2.4	9%	0.6	23.5	93	$15
Health	F	09	TAM	7	5	17	67	79	2.83	1.20	200	284	158	4.0	27%	81%	3.18	49	16	35	4.5	10.7	2.4	13%	0.9	13.3	99	$17
PT/Exp	C	10	TAM	0	0	0	0	0	0.00	0.00							0.00											
Consist	A	1st Half		0	0	0	0	0	0.00	0.00							0.00											
LIMA Plan	C	2nd Half		0	0	0	0	0	0.00	0.00							0.00											
Rand Var	+5	11	Proj	3	3	0	44	43	4.14	1.36	246			7.8	31%	71%	3.47	50	19	32	3.9	8.9	2.3	10%	0.8	4.4	82	$4

Was a save-opps dark horse until May surgery for torn labrum erased 2010, putting future in question. Had been a mixed bag of rising Dom vs. rising Ctl and hr/9. Short-term, he's best watched from afar.

Hudson,Dan

		Yr	Tm	W	L	Sv	IP	K	ERA	WHIP	OBA	vL	vR	BF/G	H%	S%	xERA	G	L	F	Ctl	Dom	Cmd	hr/f	hr/9	RAR	BPV	R$
RH SP	24	06		0	0	0	0	0	0.00	0.00							0.00											
Ht/Wt	76 220	07		0	0	0	0	0	0.00	0.00							0.00											
Type	Pwr xFB	08		0	0	0	0	0	0.00	0.00							0.00											
Health	A	09	CHW	* 10	1	0	99	91	2.82	1.17	238	194	257	20.2	30%	77%	4.24	30	12	58	2.6	8.3	3.1	4%	0.5	19.8	86	$16
PT/Exp	D	10	2TM	* 19	6	0	188	180	3.30	1.15	230	203	201	24.7	28%	77%	3.60	35	19	45	2.8	8.6	3.1	10%	1.1	18.1	93	$25
Consist	B	1st Half		11	3	0	88	91	4.19	1.33	262			23.4	32%	75%	4.64				3.0	9.3	3.1		1.5	-1.3	78	$10
LIMA Plan	C+	2nd Half		8	3	0	100	89	2.51	1.00	201			26.2	24%	79%	3.55	35	19	45	2.6	8.0	3.1	7%	0.8	19.3	87	$15
Rand Var	0	11	Proj	11	12	0	189	175	3.53	1.20	242			22.9	29%	75%	3.84	34	18	47	2.7	8.4	3.1	10%	1.1	8.7	89	$20

8-2, 2.45 ERA in 95 IP at CHW and ARI. Stunning 2H aided by fortunate H% and 0.6 hr/9 at Chase Field. FB% says ERA will rise, but Dom and Ctl say 2010 wasn't all luck. A promising future.

Hudson,Tim

		Yr	Tm	W	L	Sv	IP	K	ERA	WHIP	OBA	vL	vR	BF/G	H%	S%	xERA	G	L	F	Ctl	Dom	Cmd	hr/f	hr/9	RAR	BPV	R$
RH SP	35	06	ATL	13	12	0	218	141	4.87	1.44	276	281	265	27.2	31%	68%	3.86	58	18	24	3.3	5.8	1.8	15%	1.0	-10.3	52	$10
Ht/Wt	73 170	07	ATL	16	10	0	224	132	3.33	1.22	259	261	261	27.3	30%	72%	3.34	62	17	22	2.1	5.3	2.5	6%	0.4	30.3	78	$23
Type	xGB	08	ATL	11	7	0	142	85	3.17	1.16	238	255	223	25.2	27%	75%	3.38	59	19	22	2.5	5.4	2.1	11%	0.7	19.3	66	$16
Health	F	09	ATL	2	1	0	42	30	3.62	1.47	291	329	271	26.5	34%	78%	3.29	62	18	20	2.8	6.4	2.3	14%	0.9	3.0	80	$2
PT/Exp	B	10	ATL	17	9	0	229	139	2.83	1.15	227	233	225	27.4	25%	79%	3.22	64	14	22	2.9	5.5	1.9	13%	0.8	33.3	62	$24
Consist	A	1st Half		8	4	0	114	58	2.44	1.15	218			27.3	23%	82%	3.36	68	11	22	3.2	4.6	1.4	12%	0.7	22.2	41	$13
LIMA Plan	D+	2nd Half		9	5	0	114	81	3.23	1.15	235			27.4	27%	75%	3.08	60	17	23	2.6	6.4	2.5	14%	0.9	11.1	83	$12
Rand Var	-2	11	Proj	14	8	0	203	130	3.37	1.27	255			26.6	29%	75%	3.31	62	16	22	2.7	5.8	2.1	11%	0.7	20.9	70	$18

Model of consistency despite borderline Dom. Health risk is elevated with advancing age after another workhorse year. Lots of GBs, good Ctl, helpful ERA and less IP are solid bets. Don't pay for a repeat.

Huff,David

		Yr	Tm	W	L	Sv	IP	K	ERA	WHIP	OBA	vL	vR	BF/G	H%	S%	xERA	G	L	F	Ctl	Dom	Cmd	hr/f	hr/9	RAR	BPV	R$
LH SP	26	06		0	0	0	0	0	0.00	0.00							0.00											
Ht/Wt	74 190	07		0	0	0	0	0	0.00	0.00							0.00											
Type	Con FB	08	a/a	11	5	0	146	123	3.37	1.16	250			22.1	30%	74%	3.64				2.0	7.6	3.9		1.0	16.9	103	$18
Health	A	09	CLE	* 16	9	0	167	94	5.50	1.53	296	317	292	24.8	32%	65%	5.08	38	20	42	3.1	5.0	1.6	9%	1.1	-21.6	23	$7
PT/Exp	D	10	CLE	* 10	13	0	154	82	5.57	1.62	310	342	300	25.9	33%	68%	5.09	36	21	43	3.2	4.8	1.5	9%	1.2	-27.2	14	$0
Consist	B	1st Half		4	9	0	82	43	5.48	1.67	313			25.2	33%	69%	5.26	36	21	43	3.5	4.7	1.3	9%	1.2	-13.6	3	($1)
LIMA Plan	C+	2nd Half		6	4	0	72	39	5.67	1.56	307			26.7	33%	66%	4.78	41	18	41	2.8	4.9	1.7	10%	1.3	-13.5	30	$1
Rand Var	+1	11	Proj	7	9	0	116	68	4.97	1.47	289			24.3	31%	69%	4.81	37	20	42	2.9	5.3	1.8	10%	1.2	-7.4	31	$4

2-11, 6.21 ERA in 80 IP at CLE. Ongoing flammability is illustrated by ERA / xERA in lock-step. The absence of an advantage over LHers doesn't help. Not a skill set worth chasing; '08 BPV is history.

Hughes,Dustin

		Yr	Tm	W	L	Sv	IP	K	ERA	WHIP	OBA	vL	vR	BF/G	H%	S%	xERA	G	L	F	Ctl	Dom	Cmd	hr/f	hr/9	RAR	BPV	R$
LH RP	28	06		0	0	0	0	0	0.00	0.00							0.00											
Ht/Wt	70 187	07	aa	6	2	1	108	61	4.26	1.62	292			19.6	33%	73%	5.11				4.1	5.1	1.3		0.5	2.7	40	$4
Type	FB	08	aa	8	4	3	108	61	5.94	1.84	333			16.1	36%	69%	6.96				3.9	5.1	1.3		1.1	-21.7	12	($1)
Health	A	09	aaa	3	3	1	87	64	4.79	1.62	285			11.6	33%	71%	5.20				4.5	6.6	1.5		0.8	-5.1	46	$2
PT/Exp	D	10	KC	1	3	0	56	34	3.84	1.47	271	260	283	4.3	31%	74%	4.85	36	22	42	3.8	5.4	1.4	4%	0.5	2.1	8	$2
Consist	C	1st Half		1	1	0	27	17	3.71	1.54	285			3.8	32%	79%	4.81	40	16	44	3.7	5.7	1.5	8%	1.0	1.4	21	$1
LIMA Plan	C	2nd Half		0	2	0	30	17	3.95	1.42	258			4.9	30%	69%	4.87	32	28	40	4.0	5.2	1.3	0%	0.0	0.7	-4	$1
Rand Var	-3	11	Proj	1	2	0	44	27	4.76	1.54	277			6.7	31%	71%	5.06	35	23	42	4.1	5.6	1.4	8%	1.0	-4.2	2	$1

Journeyman alert. Lefty specialist whose 15/13 K/BB vs. LHers isn't at all special. Most RPs with mediocre skills only end their MLB careers in places like KC. He may both start and finish there.

Hughes,Phil

		Yr	Tm	W	L	Sv	IP	K	ERA	WHIP	OBA	vL	vR	BF/G	H%	S%	xERA	G	L	F	Ctl	Dom	Cmd	hr/f	hr/9	RAR	BPV	R$
RH SP	24	06	aa	10	3	0	116	120	2.96	1.02	206			21.8	28%	71%	2.18				2.6	9.3	3.6		0.4	22.4	132	$20
Ht/Wt	77 240	07	NYY	* 9	4	0	108	93	3.88	1.18	224	264	210	22.1	27%	68%	4.09	37	18	45	3.3	7.7	2.3	6%	0.7	8.4	65	$14
Type	Pwr xFB	08	NYY	* 1	4	0	63	51	6.57	1.71	313	333	299	20.9	37%	61%	4.70	34	27	39	3.9	7.3	1.9	7%	0.9	-17.3	39	($2)
Health	D	09	NYY	* 11	3	3	105	112	3.00	1.14	231	257	184	7.9	30%	78%	3.48	34	22	44	2.7	9.6	3.6	9%	0.9	18.9	113	$18
PT/Exp	C	10	NYY	18	8	0	176	146	4.19	1.25	246	235	253	23.7	28%	71%	4.05	36	16	47	3.0	7.5	2.5	10%	1.3	-1.0	68	$18
Consist	B	1st Half		10	2	0	94	86	3.83	1.20	241			25.8	29%	72%	3.77	34	20	46	2.8	8.2	3.0	9%	1.1	3.6	85	$12
LIMA Plan	C	2nd Half		8	6	0	82	60	4.59	1.30	252			21.7	27%	70%	4.38	39	13	49	3.2	6.6	2.1	12%	1.5	-4.6	49	$7
Rand Var	0	11	Proj	15	8	0	174	154	4.09	1.28	251			25.2	30%	72%	4.03	36	18	46	3.1	8.0	2.6	10%	1.1	5.6	75	$18

Fast start began to fade in June as falling Dom and gopheritis became issues. Late-season time off didn't help much; still looked wobbly at year-end. Upside remains, but short-term IP trend now looks ominous.

Hunter,Tommy

		Yr	Tm	W	L	Sv	IP	K	ERA	WHIP	OBA	vL	vR	BF/G	H%	S%	xERA	G	L	F	Ctl	Dom	Cmd	hr/f	hr/9	RAR	BPV	R$
RH SP	24	06		0	0	0	0	0	0.00	0.00							0.00											
Ht/Wt	75 255	07		0	0	0	0	0	0.00	0.00							0.00											
Type	Con FB	08	aa	8	4	0	105	48	3.77	1.36	285			28.1	30%	76%	4.80				2.1	4.1	1.9		1.0	7.0	32	$8
Health	B	09	TEX	* 13	8	0	183	107	4.54	1.45	290	288	228	25.0	32%	71%	4.85	37	20	42	2.6	5.2	2.0	8%	1.0	-1.9	39	$11
PT/Exp	D	10	TEX	* 14	6	0	154	80	3.91	1.30	265	272	231	22.5	27%	75%	4.47	42	18	40	2.6	4.7	1.8	11%	1.3	4.3	35	$13
Consist	A	1st Half		6	2	0	63	32	3.17	1.34	266			22.2	30%	77%	4.57	38	24	38	2.9	4.6	1.6	4%	0.4	7.5	21	$6
LIMA Plan	C	2nd Half		8	4	0	92	48	4.42	1.28	265			22.6	26%	74%	4.39	43	15	41	2.4	4.7	2.0	16%	2.0	-3.1	42	$7
Rand Var	0	11	Proj	9	9	0	145	77	4.41	1.40	284			24.1	30%	72%	4.69	40	19	41	2.5	4.8	1.9	10%	1.2	-7.1	36	$8

13-4, 3.73 ERA in 128 IP at TEX. Oblique strain put him on DL to begin the year, then over-achieved again in partial MLB season. The odds of this happening again aren't good. DN: 4.75 ERA, bullpen spot.

Iwakuma,Hisashi

		Yr	Tm	W	L	Sv	IP	K	ERA	WHIP	OBA	vL	vR	BF/G	H%	S%	xERA	G	L	F	Ctl	Dom	Cmd	hr/f	hr/9	RAR	BPV	R$
RH SP	29	06	JPN	1	2	0	38	15	4.71	1.61	301			28.7	30%	76%	6.32				3.5	3.6	1.0		1.6	-0.9	-9	$0
Ht/Wt	75 170	07	JPN	5	5	0	90	80	4.22	1.45	287			24.6	35%	73%	5.08				2.9	8.0	2.8		1.0	2.7	74	$6
Type		08	JPN	21	4	0	201	151	2.34	1.08	234			28.7	29%	78%	2.51				2.0	6.8	3.4		0.2	48.9	113	$32
Health	A	09	JPN	13	6	0	169	115	4.03	1.45	287			30.8	32%	77%	5.35				2.8	6.1	2.1		1.3	5.8	40	$12
PT/Exp	A	10	JPN	10	9	0	201	145	3.50	1.20	258			29.6	30%	73%	3.63				2.0	6.5	3.2		0.8	14.1	86	$17
Consist	F	1st Half		0	0	0	0	0	0.00	0.00							0.00											
LIMA Plan	D+	2nd Half		10	9	0	201	145	3.50	1.20	258			29.6	30%	73%	3.63				2.0	6.5	3.2		0.8	14.1	86	$17
Rand Var	-3	11	Proj	8	8	0	116	78	4.11	1.34	267			29.0	30%	72%	4.36				2.8	6.1	2.2		1.0	-2.1	53	$8

PRO: Ctl; age; health.
CON: Dom transition to MLB in question; volatile hr/9.
GBer who appears to be the Japanese import most likely to make 2011 MLB debut. Back-end rotation candidate at best.

Jackson,Edwin

		Yr	Tm	W	L	Sv	IP	K	ERA	WHIP	OBA	vL	vR	BF/G	H%	S%	xERA	G	L	F	Ctl	Dom	Cmd	hr/f	hr/9	RAR	BPV	R$
RH SP	27	06	TAM	* 3	7	5	109	83	6.60	1.86	314	233	333	11.6	37%	64%	4.76	52	17	31	5.1	6.8	1.3	9%	0.8	-27.5	15	($2)
Ht/Wt	75 210	07	TAM	5	15	0	161	128	5.76	1.76	300	313	285	23.5	35%	68%	4.82	45	19	36	4.9	7.2	1.5	10%	1.1	-24.9	19	($1)
Type	Pwr	08	TAM	14	11	0	183	108	4.42	1.51	278	295	268	25.4	30%	74%	4.97	39	21	40	3.8	5.3	1.4	9%	1.1	-1.6	11	$10
Health	A	09	DET	13	9	0	214	161	3.62	1.26	249	247	248	27.1	28%	76%	4.27	39	18	42	2.9	6.8	2.3	10%	1.1	22.0	59	$21
PT/Exp	A	10	2TM	10	12	0	209	181	4.47	1.40	266	271	258	28.2	32%	69%	3.58	49	19	32	3.4	7.8	2.3	11%	0.9	-10.3	77	$11
Consist	B	1st Half		6	6	0	112	89	4.74	1.41	258			28.5	31%	67%	3.86	49	19	32	3.9	7.2	1.9	9%	0.8	-9.2	51	$5
LIMA Plan	C	2nd Half		4	6	0	97	92	4.16	1.38	275			27.9	34%	72%	3.28	50	18	32	2.8	8.5	3.1	12%	1.0	-1.1	106	$6
Rand Var	+1	11	Proj	11	11	0	203	162	4.17	1.42	269			25.2	31%	73%	4.04	45	19	36	3.4	7.2	2.1	10%	1.0	4.4	60	$12

Strong 2H largely unnoticed due to elevated H%, hr/f. Dom trend, 2H Ctl, and return of GB% are piquing our interest. Could be just a continuation of his streakiness, but if not...
UP: 18 wins, 3.75 ERA

JOCK THOMPSON

Jansen,Kenley		W	L	Sv	IP	K	ERA	WHIP	OBA	vL	vR	BF/G	H%	S%	xERA	G	L	F	Ctl	Dom	Cmd	hr/f	hr/9	RAR	BPV	R$
RH RP 23	06	0	0	0	0	0	0.00	0.00							0.00											
Ht/Wt 74 220	07	0	0	0	0	0	0.00	0.00							0.00											
Type Pwr xFB	08	0	0	0	0	0	0.00	0.00							0.00											
Health A	09	0	0	0	0	0	0.00	0.00							0.00											
PT/Exp F	10 LA *	5	0	12	54	82	1.17	1.07	151	205	63	4.6	28%	88%	2.85	34	16	50	5.2	13.7	**2.6**	0%	0.0	19.0	119	$15
Consist F	1st Half	4	0	6	19	25	1.42	1.16	157			5.2	26%	86%	1.48				5.7	11.8	**2.1**		0.0	6.1	138	$7
LIMA Plan B+	2nd Half	1	0	6	35	57	1.03	1.03	147			4.3	29%	89%	2.55	34	16	50	4.9	14.7	**3.0**	0%	0.0	12.9	144	$8
Rand Var -5	11 Proj	**4**	**3**	**10**	**73**	**94**	**3.10**	**1.26**	**200**			**4.8**	**29%**	**77%**	**3.53**	**34**	**16**	**50**	**5.0**	**11.7**	**2.4**	**6%**	**0.6**	**5.5**	**88**	**$12**

1-0, 0.67 ERA, 4 Svs in 27 IP at LA. Made transformation from minor league CA to MLB RP in less than two seasons. Ctl, FB%, experience are still issues; Dom and upside aren't.
UP: 25 saves

Janssen,Casey		W	L	Sv	IP	K	ERA	WHIP	OBA	vL	vR	BF/G	H%	S%	xERA	G	L	F	Ctl	Dom	Cmd	hr/f	hr/9	RAR	BPV	R$
RH RP 29	06 TOR *	7	15	0	136	72	5.64	1.40	295	292	261	21.0	32%	60%	4.16	53	16	31	2.0	4.7	**2.4**	11%	1.1	-18.2	62	$5
Ht/Wt 76 210	07 TOR	2	3	6	73	39	2.35	1.20	246	257	241	4.3	28%	82%	4.13	49	18	33	2.5	4.8	**2.0**	5%	0.5	19.3	47	$10
Type	08 TOR	0	0	0	0	0	0.00	0.00							0.00											
Health F	09 TOR	2	4	1	40	24	5.85	1.83	343	313	367	9.0	38%	69%	4.52	50	24	26	3.2	5.4	**1.7**	13%	1.1	-6.9	40	($1)
PT/Exp D	10 TOR	5	2	0	69	63	3.67	1.38	276	283	264	5.3	34%	77%	3.37	47	22	31	2.8	8.3	**3.0**	13%	1.0	4.0	99	$6
Consist C	1st Half	4	0	0	37	38	4.34	1.21	244			5.1	32%	64%	2.94	50	19	31	2.7	9.2	**3.5**	10%	0.7	-0.9	121	$4
LIMA Plan B	2nd Half	1	2	0	31	25	2.87	1.59	311			5.4	36%	89%	3.90	43	25	32	2.9	7.2	**2.5**	15%	1.4	4.9	73	$2
Rand Var +2	11 Proj	**4**	**4**	**3**	**73**	**55**	**4.10**	**1.39**	**276**			**6.1**	**32%**	**73%**	**3.75**	**48**	**22**	**30**	**2.9**	**6.8**	**2.4**	**12%**	**1.0**	**4.8**	**72**	**$6**

Pitched without shoulder pain all season, and it showed up in the results. Hiked 1H Dom and Cmd to new levels. Faded in in 2H, but inflated S% worked wonders for ERA. Serviceable only if he can stay healthy.

Jenks,Bobby		W	L	Sv	IP	K	ERA	WHIP	OBA	vL	vR	BF/G	H%	S%	xERA	G	L	F	Ctl	Dom	Cmd	hr/f	hr/9	RAR	BPV	R$
RH RP 30	06 CHW	3	4	41	69	80	4.03	1.40	253	227	268	4.5	35%	72%	2.81	59	19	22	4.0	10.4	**2.6**	13%	0.7	4.5	115	$20
Ht/Wt 75 275	07 CHW	3	5	40	65	56	2.77	0.89	197	237	169	3.8	25%	68%	2.91	54	16	31	1.8	7.8	**4.3**	4%	0.3	13.9	123	$24
Type Pwr xGB	08 CHW	3	1	30	62	38	2.63	1.10	227	219	241	4.4	26%	77%	3.51	58	14	28	2.5	5.5	**2.2**	6%	0.4	13.1	68	$18
Health B	09 CHW	3	4	29	53	49	3.71	1.28	257	309	202	4.3	30%	78%	3.46	49	18	33	2.7	8.3	**3.1**	18%	1.5	4.8	103	$15
PT/Exp B	10 CHW	1	3	27	53	61	4.44	1.37	267	243	277	4.1	37%	67%	2.47	58	21	21	3.1	10.4	**3.4**	10%	0.5	-2.0	141	$12
Consist B	1st Half	1	1	17	29	35	4.03	1.48	275			4.1	38%	73%	2.55	56	24	19	3.7	10.9	**2.9**	13%	0.6	0.4	129	$7
LIMA Plan B+	2nd Half	0	2	10	24	26	4.94	1.22	256			4.1	35%	57%	2.37	61	17	23	2.3	9.9	**4.3**	7%	0.4	-2.3	155	$5
Rand Var +5	11 Proj	**2**	**3**	**35**	**51**	**50**	**3.72**	**1.26**	**251**			**4.2**	**32%**	**72%**	**2.92**	**56**	**18**	**26**	**2.8**	**8.9**	**3.1**	**11%**	**0.7**	**8.5**	**117**	**$16**

Shut down with ulner (forearm) neuritis over final 4 weeks. Inflated H%, poor 1H Ctl and unfortunate 2H S% masked a nice skills bump almost across the board at age 29. He could come cheap in your league.

Jepsen,Kevin		W	L	Sv	IP	K	ERA	WHIP	OBA	vL	vR	BF/G	H%	S%	xERA	G	L	F	Ctl	Dom	Cmd	hr/f	hr/9	RAR	BPV	R$
RH RP 26	06	0	0	0	0	0	0.00	0.00							0.00											
Ht/Wt 75 215	07	0	0	0	0	0	0.00	0.00							0.00											
Type Pwr xGB	08 aa	3	4	13	54	46	2.27	1.44	233			5.9	29%	86%	3.72				5.2	7.6	**1.4**		0.5	13.6	69	$10
Health A	09 LAA *	7	4	3	73	63	7.02	1.92	334	373	208	5.2	41%	62%	4.16	57	16	27	4.6	7.8	**1.7**	10%	0.8	-23.0	53	($1)
PT/Exp D	10 LAA	2	4	0	59	61	3.97	1.41	245	239	263	3.8	33%	70%	3.16	56	18	26	4.4	9.3	**2.1**	5%	0.3	1.3	82	$4
Consist B	1st Half	0	1	0	27	32	4.95	1.54	260			3.7	37%	66%	2.96	58	18	24	4.9	10.5	**2.1**	6%	0.3	-2.7	93	$1
LIMA Plan B+	2nd Half	2	3	0	32	29	3.12	1.29	232			3.8	30%	75%	3.33	53	19	28	4.0	8.2	**2.1**	4%	0.3	4.0	72	$3
Rand Var 0	11 Proj	**4**	**4**	**5**	**65**	**61**	**3.72**	**1.38**	**246**			**4.3**	**31%**	**74%**	**3.37**	**56**	**17**	**27**	**4.1**	**8.4**	**2.0**	**10%**	**0.7**	**7.4**	**74**	**$7**

Fixed issues vs. LHers, Dom and GB% still point to closer upside. But Ctl, inconsistency aren't cooperating. 1H H% and and S% didn't help. If he puts it together...
UP: 20 saves

Jimenez,Ubaldo		W	L	Sv	IP	K	ERA	WHIP	OBA	vL	vR	BF/G	H%	S%	xERA	G	L	F	Ctl	Dom	Cmd	hr/f	hr/9	RAR	BPV	R$
RH SP 27	06 a/a	14	4	0	151	128	4.88	1.48	254			25.6	31%	67%	4.37				4.7	7.6	**1.6**		0.7	-6.7	63	$11
Ht/Wt 76 200	07 COL *	12	9	0	185	145	6.51	1.67	285	244	212	25.0	33%	61%	4.77	46	17	37	4.9	7.0	**1.4**	10%	1.1	-47.6	19	($0)
Type Pwr GB	08 COL	12	12	0	199	172	3.99	1.43	245	248	241	25.4	31%	72%	3.80	54	18	28	4.7	7.8	**1.7**	7%	0.5	7.0	47	$13
Health A	09 COL	15	12	0	218	198	3.47	1.23	229	251	206	27.4	29%	72%	3.31	53	20	28	3.5	8.2	**2.3**	8%	0.5	19.4	83	$23
PT/Exp A	10 COL	19	8	0	222	214	2.88	1.15	208	191	227	27.4	27%	75%	3.32	49	16	35	3.7	8.7	**2.3**	5%	0.4	31.0	82	$28
Consist A	1st Half	14	1	0	119	107	2.27	1.08	200			28.0	25%	80%	3.25	52	14	34	3.3	8.1	**2.4**	6%	0.5	25.6	85	$20
LIMA Plan D+	2nd Half	5	7	0	103	107	3.59	1.25	216			26.7	29%	70%	3.41	46	19	36	4.2	9.4	**2.2**	4%	0.4	5.4	79	$9
Rand Var -2	11 Proj	**16**	**11**	**0**	**218**	**202**	**3.56**	**1.27**	**231**			**26.8**	**29%**	**73%**	**3.49**	**50**	**18**	**32**	**3.8**	**8.4**	**2.2**	**8%**	**0.7**	**17.5**	**75**	**$21**

Stuff affirmed by H% and 0.4 hr/9 in Coors, but Ctl bit him again in 2H. Dom and GB% keep him in upper echelon of SPs, but note the near identical '09 xERA and BPV. 2009 is your 2011 benchmark.

Johnson,Josh		W	L	Sv	IP	K	ERA	WHIP	OBA	vL	vR	BF/G	H%	S%	xERA	G	L	F	Ctl	Dom	Cmd	hr/f	hr/9	RAR	BPV	R$
RH SP 27	06 FLA	12	7	0	157	133	3.10	1.30	235	246	227	21.4	28%	79%	4.02	46	19	36	3.9	7.6	**2.0**	9%	0.8	27.0	56	$18
Ht/Wt 79 252	07 FLA	0	3	0	16	14	7.45	2.42	370	419	361	21.0	45%	68%	5.69	44	22	33	6.9	8.0	**1.2**	5%	0.6	-5.9	-19	($2)
Type Pwr	08 FLA *	8	2	0	106	89	3.73	1.38	279	288	259	26.9	34%	74%	3.63	48	21	31	2.6	7.5	**2.9**	8%	0.7	7.1	90	$9
Health F	09 FLA	15	5	0	209	191	3.23	1.16	238	242	231	25.8	30%	73%	3.20	50	18	32	2.5	8.2	**3.3**	8%	0.6	24.7	109	$25
PT/Exp A	10 FLA	11	6	0	184	186	2.30	1.11	230	223	235	26.4	31%	80%	2.96	46	21	34	2.4	9.1	**3.9**	4%	0.3	38.8	124	$24
Consist A	1st Half	8	3	0	114	115	1.82	0.96	205			26.1	28%	82%	2.76	48	19	33	2.1	9.1	**4.3**	4%	0.3	30.9	132	$19
LIMA Plan C+	2nd Half	3	3	0	70	71	3.10	1.33	268			27.0	35%	77%	3.28	43	23	35	2.7	9.2	**3.4**	4%	0.4	7.9	113	$6
Rand Var -4	11 Proj	**12**	**6**	**0**	**196**	**190**	**3.22**	**1.21**	**247**			**26.1**	**31%**	**75%**	**3.19**	**46**	**20**	**33**	**2.5**	**8.7**	**3.5**	**8%**	**0.7**	**22.9**	**113**	**$21**

2010 Forecaster call proved spot-on: A CY contender until Aug fade and Sept shutdown; could it be workload related? Elite skill set, only questions are about health and durability.
DN: Shoulder woes, DL time.

Jurrjens,Jair		W	L	Sv	IP	K	ERA	WHIP	OBA	vL	vR	BF/G	H%	S%	xERA	G	L	F	Ctl	Dom	Cmd	hr/f	hr/9	RAR	BPV	R$
RH SP 25	06 aa	4	3	0	67	48	4.22	1.52	300			24.8	34%	75%	5.50				2.8	6.5	**2.3**		1.0	2.5	52	$4
Ht/Wt 73 200	07 DET *	10	6	0	143	94	4.47	1.42	284	262	167	23.9	32%	69%	4.70	38	18	44	2.7	5.9	**2.2**	6%	0.8	0.6	50	$10
Type	08 ATL	13	10	0	188	139	3.68	1.37	261	261	260	26.1	31%	73%	3.75	52	22	27	3.3	6.6	**2.0**	7%	0.5	13.7	59	$15
Health C	09 ATL	14	10	0	215	152	2.60	1.21	235	264	212	26.1	27%	81%	4.13	43	18	39	3.1	6.4	**2.0**	6%	0.6	42.3	51	$24
PT/Exp A	10 ATL	7	6	0	116	86	4.64	1.39	268	294	250	25.1	31%	68%	4.28	40	18	42	3.3	6.7	**2.0**	9%	1.0	-9.0	50	$5
Consist A	1st Half	2	4	0	42	29	5.79	1.64	297			21.3	33%	66%	5.10	35	17	48	4.1	6.2	**1.5**	7%	1.1	-9.2	15	($1)
LIMA Plan C+	2nd Half	5	2	0	74	57	4.00	1.25	250			28.2	29%	71%	3.89	42	19	40	2.8	6.9	**2.5**	9%	1.0	0.2	69	$6
Rand Var 0	11 Proj	**12**	**10**	**0**	**189**	**137**	**4.01**	**1.36**	**262**			**25.2**	**30%**	**73%**	**4.21**	**43**	**19**	**39**	**3.2**	**6.5**	**2.0**	**9%**	**1.0**	**-1.5**	**52**	**$13**

Leg issues (hamstring, torn meniscus) sidelined him for May, June and most of Sept. Skills showed little change while bottom line deteriorated as expected. Serviceable SP, but don't look for 2009 again.

Karstens,Jeff		W	L	Sv	IP	K	ERA	WHIP	OBA	vL	vR	BF/G	H%	S%	xERA	G	L	F	Ctl	Dom	Cmd	hr/f	hr/9	RAR	BPV	R$
RH SP 28	06 NYY *	13	6	0	189	108	4.33	1.40	277	253	233	24.8	30%	72%	5.18	33	16	51	2.8	5.1	**1.8**	7%	1.1	5.2	28	$14
Ht/Wt 75 185	07 NYY *	5	4	0	51	31	5.06	1.69	309			16.7	34%	73%	5.78	27	21	52	3.8	5.4	**1.4**	8%	1.3	-3.5	-0	$2
Type Con FB	08 PIT *	8	10	0	120	68	4.61	1.38	288	265	293	24.5	31%	70%	4.48	42	20	39	2.1	5.1	**2.4**	11%	1.3	-4.9	53	$6
Health D	09 PIT	4	6	0	108	52	5.42	1.48	274	263	294	12.2	29%	64%	5.38	39	16	46	3.8	4.3	**1.2**	7%	1.0	-16.3	-7	$0
PT/Exp C	10 PIT *	4	12	0	139	81	5.32	1.44	304	364	249	19.5	32%	67%	4.33	42	18	40	1.9	5.3	**2.8**	13%	1.6	-22.4	64	$0
Consist B	1st Half	3	5	0	89	45	5.38	1.48	311			18.6	32%	68%	4.53	41	20	39	1.8	4.6	**2.5**	14%	1.7	-15.0	52	($0)
LIMA Plan C+	2nd Half	1	7	0	50	36	5.22	1.38	291			21.5	33%	65%	3.98	44	15	41	2.0	6.5	**3.3**	11%	1.3	-7.4	85	$0
Rand Var +2	11 Proj	**2**	**5**	**0**	**58**	**34**	**4.81**	**1.43**	**291**			**18.0**	**31%**	**69%**	**4.60**	**41**	**17**	**42**	**2.5**	**5.3**	**2.1**	**10%**	**1.2**	**-3.3**	**47**	**$1**

3-10, 4.92 ERA in 123 IP at LA. Stayed healthy until sore shoulder shelved him in Sept; put up 2H Cmd that gives us pause. But history of too many HR and DL days, not enough Ks and GBs, moves us along.

Kawakami,Kenshin		W	L	Sv	IP	K	ERA	WHIP	OBA	vL	vR	BF/G	H%	S%	xERA	G	L	F	Ctl	Dom	Cmd	hr/f	hr/9	RAR	BPV	R$
RH SP 35	06 JPN	17	7	0	215	184	3.12	1.05	227			29.5	25%	80%	3.66				2.0	7.7	**3.8**		1.5	37.1	90	$32
Ht/Wt 71 200	07 JPN	12	8	0	167	138	4.42	1.30	285			27.1	32%	72%	5.26				1.5	7.4	**4.8**		1.6	0.9	95	$15
Type	08 JPN	9	5	0	117	106	2.87	1.17	244			23.9	28%	84%	4.03				2.4	8.2	**3.4**		1.4	20.8	85	$16
Health C	09 ATL	7	12	1	156	105	3.86	1.34	258	252	268	20.8	29%	73%	4.39	42	19	39	3.3	6.0	**1.8**	8%	0.9	6.4	40	$10
PT/Exp B	10 ATL	1	10	0	87	59	5.15	1.49	285	299	271	21.4	32%	67%	4.42	40	22	38	3.3	6.1	**1.8**	9%	1.0	-12.3	38	($1)
Consist A	1st Half	1	9	0	82	57	4.48	1.40	273			23.7	31%	70%	4.27	39	22	39	3.1	6.2	**2.0**	9%	1.0	-4.8	47	$1
LIMA Plan D	2nd Half	0	1	0	5	2	16.20	3.00	438			9.9	45%	43%	7.21	43	30	26	7.2	3.6	**0.5**	17%	1.8	-7.5	******	($2)
Rand Var +1	11 Proj	**7**	**10**	**0**	**140**	**94**	**4.13**	**1.38**	**267**			**24.0**	**30%**	**72%**	**4.19**	**42**	**25**	**33**	**3.2**	**6.1**	**1.9**	**10%**	**1.0**	**-0.9**	**42**	**$7**

Demoted to pen, minors after 25%/32% PQS-DOM/DIS in 1H as SP. Skills mostly unchanged; H%, LD% did most of the damage. Sub-par S% didn't help. Can't survive as a SP without better command.

JOCK THOMPSON

Kazmir,Scott			W	L	Sv	IP	K	ERA	WHIP	OBA	vL	vR	BF/G	H%	S%	xERA	G	L	F	Ctl	Dom	Cmd	hr/f	hr/9	RAR	BPV	R$
LH SP	27	06 TAM	10	8	0	144	163	3.25	1.28	245	227	242	25.2	32%	78%	3.37	42	19	39	3.2	10.2	3.1	10%	0.9	23.3	115	$20
Ht/Wt	72 190	07 TAM	13	9	0	207	239	3.48	1.38	252	217	263	26.1	34%	77%	3.57	43	16	41	3.9	10.4	2.7	8%	0.8	26.1	104	$24
Type	Pwr xFB	08 TAM	12	8	0	152	166	3.49	1.27	223	198	227	23.6	28%	79%	3.92	31	20	49	4.1	9.8	2.4	12%	1.4	16.2	74	$19
Health	D	09 2AL	10	9	0	147	117	4.89	1.42	264	261	258	24.6	31%	67%	4.71	34	19	48	3.7	7.1	2.0	8%	1.0	-7.9	42	$9
PT/Exp	A	10 LAA	9	15	0	150	93	5.94	1.58	272	274	271	24.1	29%	65%	5.14	39	17	44	4.7	5.6	1.2	12%	1.5	-33.3	-10	$0
Consist	B	1st Half	7	7	0	81	55	5.67	1.56	271			24.2	30%	65%	4.83	41	18	42	4.6	6.1	1.3	10%	1.2	-15.3	6	$2
LIMA Plan	C+	2nd Half	2	8	0	69	38	6.26	1.61	273			24.0	27%	65%	5.52	37	16	46	5.0	5.0	1.0	13%	1.8	-18.1	-29	($2)
Rand Var	+2	11 Proj	10	12	0	156	121	4.92	1.50	267			24.6	30%	71%	4.75	37	18	45	4.3	7.0	1.6	11%	1.3	-9.0	25	$7

No matter how you slice it, skills slide is downright ugly:
- Command is in freefall
- He's caught gopheritis
- Doesn't control LH anymore

Still 27, but don't roster without a bench slot.

Kelley,Shawn			W	L	Sv	IP	K	ERA	WHIP	OBA	vL	vR	BF/G	H%	S%	xERA	G	L	F	Ctl	Dom	Cmd	hr/f	hr/9	RAR	BPV	R$
RH RP	26	06	0	0	0	0	0	0.00	0.00							0.00											
Ht/Wt	74 215	07	0	0	0	0	0	0.00	0.00							0.00											
Type	Pwr xFB	08 aa	3	1	9	42	38	2.47	1.27	231			6.1	29%	82%	3.19				3.8	8.1	2.1		0.4	9.6	89	$9
Health	F	09 SEA	5	4	0	46	41	4.50	1.17	258	209	303	4.6	29%	69%	3.98	31	17	51	1.8	8.0	4.6	13%	1.8	-0.3	106	$6
PT/Exp	D	10 SEA	3	1	0	25	26	3.96	1.52	269	261	269	5.0	32%	82%	4.60	23	16	61	4.3	9.4	2.2	12%	1.8	0.6	53	$2
Consist	B	1st Half	3	1	0	25	26	3.96	1.52	269			5.0	32%	82%	4.60	23	16	61	4.3	9.4	2.2	12%	1.8	0.6	53	$2
LIMA Plan	C+	2nd Half	0	0	0	0	0	0.00	0.00							0.00											
Rand Var	-2	11 Proj	2	2	0	29	27	4.34	1.41	255			5.5	30%	75%	4.66	26	16	57	4.0	8.4	2.1	11%	1.6	-1.3	46	$2

Elbow injury knocked him out in June, and he had "partial" TJ surgery in Sept. Hoping for 2H return in '11, but Ctl a concern, and fly ball rate says home run issues are probably not going away.

Kendrick,Kyle			W	L	Sv	IP	K	ERA	WHIP	OBA	vL	vR	BF/G	H%	S%	xERA	G	L	F	Ctl	Dom	Cmd	hr/f	hr/9	RAR	BPV	R$
RH SP	26	06	0	0	0	0	0	0.00	0.00							0.00											
Ht/Wt	75 205	07 PHI *	14	11	0	202	91	3.88	1.33	283	321	241	26.8	30%	73%	4.38	47	21	32	1.9	4.0	2.1	9%	0.9	13.7	45	$15
Type	Con	08 PHI	11	9	0	156	68	5.49	1.61	306	334	271	22.8	32%	68%	4.88	44	27	29	3.3	3.9	1.2	14%	1.3	-23.5	4	$1
Health	A	09 PHI *	12	8	0	169	66	4.08	1.35	278	267	278	21.9	29%	70%	4.00	56	22	22	2.4	3.5	1.5	9%	0.6	2.4	32	$10
PT/Exp	B	10 PHI	11	10	0	181	84	4.73	1.37	281	312	254	23.5	29%	69%	4.55	45	17	38	2.4	4.2	1.7	11%	1.3	-16.0	32	$6
Consist	B	1st Half	5	3	0	96	45	4.70	1.35	274			24.0	28%	69%	4.54	44	18	38	2.5	4.2	1.7	11%	1.3	-8.1	29	$3
LIMA Plan	C	2nd Half	6	7	0	85	39	4.76	1.40	288			23.0	30%	69%	4.54	46	16	38	2.3	4.1	1.8	11%	1.3	-7.9	35	$3
Rand Var	0	11 Proj	10	8	0	145	64	4.59	1.40	285			23.2	30%	70%	4.59	45	20	35	2.5	4.0	1.6	10%	1.1	-8.0	28	$6

PRO: Small Cmd steps; team provides win potential.
CON: Cmd still subpar; LH love him (.913 career OPS).
1H/2H nearly identical, and provide a good idea of what to expect in 2011. Not much.

Kennedy,Ian			W	L	Sv	IP	K	ERA	WHIP	OBA	vL	vR	BF/G	H%	S%	xERA	G	L	F	Ctl	Dom	Cmd	hr/f	hr/9	RAR	BPV	R$
RH SP	26	06	0	0	0	0	0	0.00	0.00							0.00											
Ht/Wt	72 195	07 NYY *	7	2	0	102	91	3.00	1.13	209	161	216	23.0	26%	74%	4.25	26	23	51	3.4	8.0	2.3	4%	0.5	19.0	56	$15
Type	Pwr FB	08 NYY *	5	7	0	109	87	4.89	1.43	266	236	397	20.5	32%	66%	4.54	41	12	48	3.6	7.2	2.0	6%	0.8	-7.2	50	$6
Health	A	09 NYY *	1	0	0	23	22	2.35	1.35	253			19.6	34%	81%	3.19				3.5	8.6	2.4		0.0	6.0	107	$3
PT/Exp	C	10 ARI	9	10	0	194	168	3.80	1.20	230	218	238	25.0	27%	73%	3.88	37	19	44	3.2	7.8	2.4	11%	1.2	5.1	68	$15
Consist	C	1st Half	3	6	0	100	89	3.77	1.23	227			26.0	25%	76%	3.98	35	19	46	3.6	8.0	2.2	13%	1.5	3.1	60	$7
LIMA Plan	C	2nd Half	6	4	0	94	79	3.84	1.17	232			24.0	28%	69%	3.77	39	18	42	2.9	7.6	2.6	8%	0.9	2.0	76	$9
Rand Var	-1	11 Proj	11	9	0	203	176	3.68	1.29	250			25.1	30%	75%	4.04	38	17	45	3.1	7.8	2.5	9%	1.1	2.4	71	$16

Performance rooted in 2009's small-sample size gains. 2010 more consistent than it seems due to 9-BB start on 6/26. IP jump could be an issue, but showed no signs of tiring, as 8 of last 10 GS were PQS-DOM.

Kershaw,Clayton			W	L	Sv	IP	K	ERA	WHIP	OBA	vL	vR	BF/G	H%	S%	xERA	G	L	F	Ctl	Dom	Cmd	hr/f	hr/9	RAR	BPV	R$
LH SP	23	06	0	0	0	0	0	0.00	0.00							0.00											
Ht/Wt	75 223	07 aa	1	2	0	24	26	4.88	1.63	228			21.8	26%	76%	5.57				7.1	9.8	1.4		1.9	-1.2	40	$1
Type	Pwr FB	08 LA *	7	8	0	169	157	3.48	1.30	240	250	269	20.4	30%	74%	3.57	48	21	31	3.7	8.4	2.2	8%	0.6	16.4	76	$14
Health	A	09 LA	8	8	0	171	185	2.79	1.23	198	173	208	22.9	27%	77%	3.74	39	19	42	4.8	9.7	2.0	4%	0.4	29.5	63	$19
PT/Exp	A	10 LA	13	10	0	204	212	2.91	1.18	217	200	218	26.2	29%	77%	3.46	40	18	42	3.6	9.3	2.6	6%	0.6	27.9	90	$23
Consist	A	1st Half	8	4	0	104	116	3.02	1.23	210			25.4	29%	76%	3.54	40	15	45	4.3	10.0	2.3	5%	0.5	12.8	82	$12
LIMA Plan	C	2nd Half	5	6	0	100	96	2.79	1.13	225			27.0	29%	77%	3.38	40	20	40	2.8	8.6	3.1	7%	0.6	15.1	98	$11
Rand Var	-2	11 Proj	13	8	0	209	214	3.15	1.23	225			26.2	29%	77%	3.58	41	19	40	3.7	9.2	2.5	8%	0.7	14.5	85	$22

Developing nicely: Ugly 6.8 Ctl in April, then just 3.0 the rest of the way. Worked deeper into games, resulting in more wins. If control gains continue...
UP: 20 wins, NL strikeout leader

Kimbrel,Craig			W	L	Sv	IP	K	ERA	WHIP	OBA	vL	vR	BF/G	H%	S%	xERA	G	L	F	Ctl	Dom	Cmd	hr/f	hr/9	RAR	BPV	R$
RH RP	22	06	0	0	0	0	0	0.00	0.00							0.00											
Ht/Wt	71 205	07	0	0	0	0	0	0.00	0.00							0.00											
Type	Pwr FB	08	0	0	0	0	0	0.00	0.00							0.00											
Health	A	09 a/a	2	1	6	14	19	1.29	1.50	168			4.4	28%	90%	2.53				8.4	12.2	1.5		0.0	5.2	125	$5
PT/Exp	F	10 ATL *	7	2	24	76	119	1.47	1.16	153	176	79	4.5	27%	89%	3.00	28	22	50	5.8	14.1	2.4	4%	0.3	23.8	102	$22
Consist	A	1st Half	3	0	9	34	53	1.01	1.07	145			4.9	27%	90%	2.90	38	6	56	5.4	13.9	2.6	0%	0.0	12.7	120	$10
LIMA Plan	D+	2nd Half	4	2	15	42	66	1.85	1.23	159			4.2	27%	88%	3.06	19	38	44	6.2	14.3	2.3	9%	0.6	11.1	85	$12
Rand Var	-5	11 Proj	7	2	18	73	89	2.73	1.38	212			4.7	30%	83%	3.77	38	17	45	5.6	11.0	2.0	8%	0.7	3.3	64	$15

4-0, 0.44 ERA in 21 IP at ATL. A closer candidate, but:
- Ctl high (but better in Sept)
- Strand rate in ATL was 96%
- FB% should be monitored
- 2010 still a miniscule sample

Exciting arm, but no sure thing.

Kirkman,Michael			W	L	Sv	IP	K	ERA	WHIP	OBA	vL	vR	BF/G	H%	S%	xERA	G	L	F	Ctl	Dom	Cmd	hr/f	hr/9	RAR	BPV	R$
LH RP	24	06	0	0	0	0	0	0.00	0.00							0.00											
Ht/Wt	76 195	07	0	0	0	0	0	0.00	0.00							0.00											
Type	Pwr FB	08	0	0	0	0	0	0.00	0.00							0.00											
Health	A	09 aa	5	7	0	96	53	5.30	1.60	287			24.1	31%	68%	5.39				4.1	5.0	1.2		1.0	-11.8	24	$1
PT/Exp	D	10 TEX *	13	3	0	147	128	3.30	1.44	247	214	107	16.9	31%	78%	4.14	49	10	41	4.6	7.8	1.7	5%	0.5	15.2	42	$14
Consist	C	1st Half	7	2	0	84	69	3.53	1.51	255			24.8	31%	77%	4.05				4.9	7.4	1.5		0.5	6.3	64	$6
LIMA Plan	C+	2nd Half	6	1	0	63	59	2.99	1.34	236			11.7	30%	79%	3.83	49	10	41	4.3	8.4	2.0	6%	0.6	9.0	63	$8
Rand Var	-3	11 Proj	5	3	0	73	55	4.34	1.48	260			17.7	30%	73%	4.48	49	10	41	4.3	6.8	1.6	9%	1.0	-1.7	32	$4

0-0, 1.65 ERA in 16 IP at TEX. Worked out of bullpen following August call up, but starting is his future. Significant step up in Dom, particularly in 2H. Ctl is an issue, though, so impact in 2011 likely minimal.

Kuo,Hong-Chih			W	L	Sv	IP	K	ERA	WHIP	OBA	vL	vR	BF/G	H%	S%	xERA	G	L	F	Ctl	Dom	Cmd	hr/f	hr/9	RAR	BPV	R$
LH RP	29	06 LA *	5	8	1	112	123	3.70	1.45	255	241	246	9.6	34%	75%	3.67	44	21	34	4.3	9.9	2.3	8%	0.6	10.8	83	$9
Ht/Wt	73 242	07 LA *	1	5	0	50	49	6.32	1.61	290	240	296	15.2	36%	60%	4.69	31	20	49	4.2	8.8	2.1	7%	0.9	-11.8	54	($1)
Type	Pwr FB	08 LA	5	3	1	80	96	2.14	1.01	210	202	205	7.5	30%	81%	2.63	46	20	34	2.4	10.8	4.6	6%	0.5	21.0	155	$14
Health	F	09 LA	2	0	0	30	32	3.00	1.13	199	152	219	3.5	27%	75%	3.35	46	15	39	3.9	9.6	2.5	7%	0.6	4.4	91	$4
PT/Exp	C	10 LA	3	2	12	60	73	1.20	0.78	146	95	159	4.0	23%	85%	2.79	36	14	51	2.7	11.0	4.1	2%	0.2	20.8	138	$16
Consist	B	1st Half	3	1	2	26	36	1.03	0.72	129			3.8	21%	89%	2.41	35	17	48	2.7	12.3	4.5	4%	0.3	9.7	161	$7
LIMA Plan	B	2nd Half	0	1	10	34	37	1.34	0.83	159			4.1	24%	82%	3.10	36	12	53	2.7	9.9	3.7	0%	0.0	11.1	120	$9
Rand Var	-5	11 Proj	3	2	18	65	75	2.62	1.06	203			4.6	28%	78%	3.13	40	16	44	3.0	10.3	3.4	7%	0.7	8.1	122	$15

Health an ongoing issue, as he began the season on DL with tender elbow. Returned with elite BPIs, excelled when given opportunity as closer. Health grade should be noted, but:
UP: 2008 plus 30 saves.

Kuroda,Hiroki			W	L	Sv	IP	K	ERA	WHIP	OBA	vL	vR	BF/G	H%	S%	xERA	G	L	F	Ctl	Dom	Cmd	hr/f	hr/9	RAR	BPV	R$
RH SP	36	06 JPN	13	6	1	189	137	2.31	1.10	254			29.2	29%	85%	3.58				1.2	6.5	5.2		0.9	51.6	125	$28
Ht/Wt	73 220	07 JPN	12	8	0	180	117	4.41	1.34	271			29.5	28%	74%	5.23				2.6	5.8	2.2		1.7	1.2	33	$13
Type	GB	08 LA	9	10	0	183	116	3.73	1.22	259	260	246	24.5	30%	70%	3.65	51	20	29	2.1	5.7	2.8	8%	0.6	12.2	76	$15
Health	C	09 LA	8	7	0	117	87	3.76	1.14	250	233	253	22.7	29%	70%	3.47	49	17	33	1.8	6.7	3.6	10%	0.9	6.2	98	$12
PT/Exp	A	10 LA	11	13	0	196	159	3.39	1.16	245	245	241	25.8	29%	72%	3.26	51	17	32	2.2	7.3	3.3	8%	0.7	15.1	101	$18
Consist	A	1st Half	7	6	0	95	78	3.78	1.41	281			25.8	34%	75%	3.40	54	18	28	2.7	7.4	2.7	10%	0.8	2.8	90	$7
LIMA Plan	B	2nd Half	4	7	0	101	81	3.03	0.93	208			25.9	25%	69%	3.11	48	16	36	1.7	7.2	4.3	7%	0.6	12.3	111	$12
Rand Var	0	11 Proj	11	11	0	189	142	3.49	1.15	248			25.6	29%	72%	3.40	50	17	32	2.0	6.8	3.4	9%	0.8	17.1	96	$18

BPV trending in right direction, headlined by another step up in Dom. Very consistent, with triple-digit BPV in every month but May. With high GB rate, excellent Ctl, will likely be a worthy investment once again.

BRIAN RUDD

Lackey,John			W	L	Sv	IP	K	ERA	WHIP	OBA	vL	vR	BF/G	H%	S%	xERA	G	L	F	Ctl	Dom	Cmd	hr/f	hr/9	RAR	BPV	R$
RH SP	32	06 LAA	13	11	0	217	190	3.56	1.27	249	263	231	27.6	31%	72%	3.84	43	18	39	3.0	7.9	2.6	6%	0.6	26.6	82	$25
Ht/Wt	78 245	07 LAA	19	9	0	224	179	3.01	1.21	257	280	229	28.0	31%	77%	3.68	45	19	36	2.1	7.2	3.4	7%	0.7	41.2	96	$30
Type		08 LAA	12	5	0	163	130	3.75	1.23	259	221	301	28.2	29%	76%	3.62	45	20	35	2.2	7.2	3.3	15%	1.4	12.1	93	$18
Health	C	09 LAA	11	8	0	176	139	3.83	1.27	263	276	247	27.4	31%	72%	3.79	45	20	35	2.4	7.1	3.0	9%	0.9	13.6	86	$17
PT/Exp	A	10 BOS	14	11	0	215	156	4.40	1.42	278	298	251	28.3	32%	70%	4.02	46	18	36	3.0	6.5	2.2	7%	0.8	-6.8	60	$12
Consist	A	1st Half	9	4	0	108	66	4.49	1.54	294			28.4	33%	72%	4.51	46	17	37	3.3	5.5	1.7	7%	0.7	-4.7	33	$5
LIMA Plan	C+	2nd Half	5	7	0	107	90	4.30	1.29	261			28.1	32%	67%	3.54	45	20	34	2.7	7.6	2.8	8%	0.8	-2.1	87	$7
Rand Var	0	11 Proj	13	10	0	209	162	3.84	1.32	267			27.7	31%	74%	3.83	45	19	36	2.7	7.0	2.6	10%	0.9	11.8	77	$18

Got off to slow start, but righted ship, despite what ERA says: First 19 starts- 5.3 Dom, 3.6 Ctl Last 14 starts- 8.1 Dom, 2.3 Ctl 2H BPIs mirror recent history, so bid with confidence. UP: 3.50 ERA, 18 wins

Laffey,Aaron			W	L	Sv	IP	K	ERA	WHIP	OBA	vL	vR	BF/G	H%	S%	xERA	G	L	F	Ctl	Dom	Cmd	hr/f	hr/9	RAR	BPV	R$
LH RP	25	06 aa	8	3	0	112	54	4.34	1.54	305			26.3	33%	73%	5.37				2.7	4.3	1.6		0.7	2.6	32	$5
Ht/Wt	72 185	07 CLE *	17	6	0	180	115	3.79	1.29	271	322	271	24.5	31%	70%	3.17	62	19	19	2.1	5.7	2.7	8%	0.4	15.9	86	$20
Type	Con GB	08 CLE *	11	9	0	155	85	4.88	1.54	302	244	292	25.6	33%	68%	4.37	51	19	30	2.9	4.9	1.7	7%	0.7	-10.2	40	$6
Health	C	09 CLE *	7	11	1	139	68	5.22	1.74	305	255	310	21.6	33%	70%	5.21	49	21	30	4.5	4.4	1.0	7%	0.7	-13.2	-15	($0)
PT/Exp	D	10 CLE *	2	4	0	84	38	4.37	1.69	291	308	270	9.6	32%	72%	5.02	49	21	30	4.8	4.1	0.9	2%	0.2	-2.4	-29	($1)
Consist	B	1st Half	1	3	0	56	29	5.18	1.71	287			9.9	32%	68%	4.99	49	22	29	5.2	4.7	0.9	4%	0.3	-7.2	-29	($2)
LIMA Plan	C	2nd Half	1	1	0	28	10	2.75	1.66	299			9.1	33%	82%	5.09	50	20	30	4.1	3.1	0.8	0%	0.0	4.8	-27	$1
Rand Var	-3	11 Proj	3	4	0	70	33	4.76	1.61	291			7.2	31%	71%	4.84	50	20	30	4.1	4.2	1.0	8%	0.8	-4.8	-7	$1

2-3, 4.53 ERA in 56 IP at CLE. Failed to earn rotation spot, and wasn't effective out of pen either. If not for lucky hr/f, it would have been even worse. While BPIs are bad, the trends are more concerning.

Lannan,John			W	L	Sv	IP	K	ERA	WHIP	OBA	vL	vR	BF/G	H%	S%	xERA	G	L	F	Ctl	Dom	Cmd	hr/f	hr/9	RAR	BPV	R$
LH SP	26	06	0	0	0	0	0	0.00	0.00							0.00											
Ht/Wt	76 215	07 WAS *	8	5	0	109	43	3.31	1.38	257	273	273	24.6	28%	76%	4.98	51	14	35	3.6	3.6	1.0	5%	0.5	14.9	-5	$9
Type	Con GB	08 WAS	9	15	0	182	117	3.91	1.34	251	259	250	25.0	27%	75%	3.93	54	19	27	3.6	5.8	1.6	15%	1.1	8.2	40	$12
Health	A	09 WAS	9	13	0	206	89	3.88	1.35	265	290	259	26.7	28%	74%	4.42	52	18	30	3.0	3.9	1.3	10%	1.0	7.8	20	$10
PT/Exp	A	10 WAS *	9	12	0	184	93	4.94	1.63	316	287	307	26.1	34%	70%	4.31	51	21	27	2.9	4.5	1.5	10%	0.9	-20.9	32	($1)
Consist	A	1st Half	2	5	0	75	24	5.76	1.85	330			25.6	34%	69%	5.34	50	21	29	4.2	2.9	0.7	8%	0.8	-16.1	-33	($5)
LIMA Plan	C	2nd Half	7	7	0	109	69	4.37	1.48	307			26.5	35%	72%	3.62	53	22	25	2.1	5.7	2.7	11%	0.9	-4.7	77	$4
Rand Var	+2	11 Proj	9	11	0	174	97	4.34	1.43	283			25.2	31%	71%	4.08	52	20	28	2.8	5.0	1.8	10%	0.9	1.3	44	$7

8-8, 4.65 ERA in 143 IP at WAS. Disastrous 1H resulted in ticket back to AA. Came back strong, with 3.4 Cmd, 45%/0% PQS-DOM/DIS in 11 starts. GB% will be high, but the issue is whether he can repeat that 2H or not.

Latos,Mat			W	L	Sv	IP	K	ERA	WHIP	OBA	vL	vR	BF/G	H%	S%	xERA	G	L	F	Ctl	Dom	Cmd	hr/f	hr/9	RAR	BPV	R$
RH SP	23	06	0	0	0	0	0	0.00	0.00							0.00											
Ht/Wt	78 225	07	0	0	0	0	0	0.00	0.00							0.00											
Type	Pwr FB	08	0	0	0	0	0	0.00	0.00							0.00											
Health	A	09 SD *	9	6	0	98	79	3.32	1.11	216	271	200	20.7	26%	71%	4.00	36	19	45	2.9	7.3	2.5	6%	0.6	10.5	66	$13
PT/Exp	C	10 SD	14	10	0	185	189	2.92	1.08	224	220	214	23.8	29%	76%	3.12	45	15	40	2.4	9.2	3.8	8%	0.8	24.9	123	$24
Consist	B	1st Half	9	4	0	100	91	2.62	0.96	199			24.2	24%	77%	3.14	47	14	39	2.3	8.2	3.5	9%	0.8	17.2	109	$16
LIMA Plan	C+	2nd Half	5	6	0	85	98	3.28	1.22	250			23.5	34%	75%	3.09	42	16	42	2.5	10.4	4.1	7%	0.7	7.7	138	$9
Rand Var	0	11 Proj	15	11	0	189	180	3.39	1.14	230			23.9	29%	73%	3.48	42	16	42	2.7	8.6	3.2	8%	0.9	15.3	102	$23

After mixed results in '09 debut, quickly lived up to potential. Solid growth across the board: GB rate, Dom, success vs LH (.580 OPS against). IP spike a concern, but given that 2H, we may see more years like 2010.

League,Brandon			W	L	Sv	IP	K	ERA	WHIP	OBA	vL	vR	BF/G	H%	S%	xERA	G	L	F	Ctl	Dom	Cmd	hr/f	hr/9	RAR	BPV	R$
RH RP	28	06 TOR *	4	4	9	96	66	2.80	1.33	275	276	178	6.4	33%	78%	2.68	73	13	14	2.3	6.2	2.6	7%	0.3	20.9	99	$13
Ht/Wt	74 205	07 TOR	0	0	0	12	7	6.15	2.22	365			4.3	41%	72%	5.03	59	18	23	5.4	5.4	1.0	10%	0.8	-2.4	-11	($1)
Type	xGB	08 TOR *	3	5	3	67	50	3.78	1.45	274	263	200	5.8	32%	75%	2.98	67	19	14	3.5	6.7	1.9	17%	0.7	4.7	70	$5
Health	B	09 TOR	3	6	0	75	76	4.58	1.24	255	270	245	4.6	32%	65%	2.89	56	18	26	2.5	9.2	3.6	15%	1.0	-1.2	130	$7
PT/Exp	C	10 SEA	9	7	6	79	56	3.42	1.19	231	243	218	4.6	26%	74%	3.06	63	16	21	3.1	6.4	2.1	14%	0.8	7.0	73	$12
Consist	A	1st Half	5	5	2	43	32	2.93	1.09	219			4.5	25%	79%	2.82	64	16	20	2.7	6.7	2.5	20%	1.0	6.4	89	$7
LIMA Plan	B	2nd Half	4	2	4	36	24	4.00	1.31	245			4.8	29%	69%	3.35	62	17	21	3.5	6.0	1.7	8%	0.5	0.6	53	$5
Rand Var	0	11 Proj	6	6	10	80	60	3.39	1.27	250			4.9	30%	74%	3.15	61	17	22	2.9	6.8	2.3	10%	0.6	11.2	82	$12

2009 Dom proved to be a fluke, but RH success was, too. Thanks to hr/f, ERA hasn't caught up to xERA. But with elite GB rate, a 2.0 command still produces good results.

Leake,Mike			W	L	Sv	IP	K	ERA	WHIP	OBA	vL	vR	BF/G	H%	S%	xERA	G	L	F	Ctl	Dom	Cmd	hr/f	hr/9	RAR	BPV	R$
RH SP	23	06	0	0	0	0	0	0.00	0.00							0.00											
Ht/Wt	73 190	07	0	0	0	0	0	0.00	0.00							0.00											
Type	GB	08	0	0	0	0	0	0.00	0.00							0.00											
Health	A	09	0	0	0	0	0	0.00	0.00							0.00											
PT/Exp	D	10 CIN	8	4	0	138	91	4.23	1.50	288	292	291	25.5	32%	76%	4.08	50	18	32	3.2	5.9	1.9	13%	1.2	-3.7	49	$5
Consist	F	1st Half	6	1	0	101	67	3.38	1.42	269			27.5	30%	80%	4.05	50	18	32	3.5	6.0	1.7	11%	1.0	8.0	41	$6
LIMA Plan	B	2nd Half	2	3	0	37	24	6.57	1.70	337			21.4	36%	65%	4.15	51	17	32	2.4	5.8	2.4	19%	1.9	-11.6	69	($2)
Rand Var	+1	11 Proj	10	9	0	174	114	4.50	1.48	292			22.5	32%	73%	4.07	51	17	32	2.8	5.9	2.1	12%	1.2	1.5	58	$7

Zero minor league experience, and more than held his own in majors. Shut down in August after h%, hr/f led to 12.41 ERA in last 4 outings. Expect some growing pains, but GB%, Cmd, low IP bode well for future.

LeBlanc,Wade			W	L	Sv	IP	K	ERA	WHIP	OBA	vL	vR	BF/G	H%	S%	xERA	G	L	F	Ctl	Dom	Cmd	hr/f	hr/9	RAR	BPV	R$
LH SP	26	06	0	0	0	0	0	0.00	0.00							0.00											
Ht/Wt	75 202	07 aa	7	3	0	57	47	4.23	1.34	257			20.2	29%	74%	4.82				3.3	7.4	2.3		1.5	1.6	51	$7
Type	xFB	08 SD *	12	12	0	160	127	6.40	1.53	291			22.9	33%	60%	5.85				3.3	7.1	2.1		1.5	-42.0	39	$3
Health	A	09 SD *	7	10	0	167	111	4.01	1.20	244	235	203	20.9	27%	70%	4.45	36	17	47	2.7	6.0	2.3	8%	1.0	3.7	50	$12
PT/Exp	C	10 SD	8	12	0	146	110	4.25	1.42	276	308	269	24.4	31%	76%	4.45	35	19	46	3.1	6.8	2.2	11%	1.5	-4.3	50	$7
Consist	B	1st Half	4	6	0	87	58	3.10	1.40	266			25.1	30%	81%	4.52	38	20	42	3.4	6.0	1.8	8%	0.9	9.8	32	$5
LIMA Plan	C+	2nd Half	4	6	0	59	52	5.95	1.46	290			23.5	32%	66%	4.33	30	18	52	2.7	7.9	2.9	16%	2.3	-14.1	77	$1
Rand Var	0	11 Proj	8	9	0	122	93	4.44	1.37	270			22.7	30%	73%	4.47	34	18	48	3.0	6.9	2.3	11%	1.5	-4.9	56	$7

PRO: 2H command growth; 2.71 ERA at home. CON: FB% led to 2.0 hr/9, 6.11 ERA on road; lefties eat him up (career .844 OPS against). Unlikely to take a step up until he reins in the fly balls.

Lecure,Sam			W	L	Sv	IP	K	ERA	WHIP	OBA	vL	vR	BF/G	H%	S%	xERA	G	L	F	Ctl	Dom	Cmd	hr/f	hr/9	RAR	BPV	R$
RH SP	26	06	0	0	0	0	0	0.00	0.00							0.00											
Ht/Wt	73 190	07 aa	7	5	0	110	86	5.31	1.72	313			24.3	36%	71%	6.50				3.9	7.1	1.8		1.3	-11.5	35	$2
Type		08 aa	9	7	0	155	106	4.16	1.49	282			25.3	32%	74%	4.91				3.5	6.2	1.8		0.9	2.9	47	$8
Health	A	09 aaa	10	8	0	143	109	5.91	1.53	299			25.4	34%	64%	5.86				2.9	6.9	2.3		1.5	-28.2	42	$4
PT/Exp	D	10 CIN *	10	8	0	146	112	4.47	1.45	284	304	252	21.3	33%	71%	3.92	46	20	34	3.0	6.9	2.3	10%	1.0	-8.1	66	$7
Consist	C	1st Half	6	6	0	93	66	3.73	1.48	281			27.4	32%	78%	4.21	44	21	35	3.4	6.3	1.9	10%	1.0	3.3	44	$5
LIMA Plan	B+	2nd Half	4	2	0	53	46	5.78	1.40	289			15.2	35%	59%	3.39	50	18	33	2.3	7.9	3.5	12%	1.1	-11.5	108	$2
Rand Var	+1	11 Proj	4	3	0	58	45	4.34	1.40	275			20.9	32%	72%	3.86	47	19	34	2.9	7.0	2.4	12%	1.1	2.0	71	$3

2-5, 4.50 ERA in 48 IP at CIN. Got 6 starts in May/June, with 5.41 xERA, 1.1 Cmd. Solid out of pen after 2H recall, with 9.2 Dom, 111 BPV. Whatever his role, needs to find a way to get LH out (.928 OPS against).

Lee,Cliff			W	L	Sv	IP	K	ERA	WHIP	OBA	vL	vR	BF/G	H%	S%	xERA	G	L	F	Ctl	Dom	Cmd	hr/f	hr/9	RAR	BPV	R$
LH SP	32	06 CLE	14	11	0	200	129	4.41	1.41	284	261	282	26.3	31%	73%	4.90	33	19	48	2.6	5.8	2.2	9%	1.3	3.8	45	$15
Ht/Wt	75 190	07 CLE *	7	11	0	143	109	5.73	1.59	283	327	267	22.3	32%	65%	5.20	35	15	50	4.3	6.8	1.6	8%	1.1	-21.6	19	$3
Type		08 CLE	22	3	0	223	170	2.54	1.11	254	272	245	29.0	31%	78%	3.43	46	19	35	1.4	6.9	5.0	5%	0.5	49.8	110	$34
Health	B	09 2TM	14	13	0	232	181	3.22	1.24	273	241	283	28.4	33%	76%	3.70	41	22	36	1.7	7.0	4.2	7%	0.7	31.1	101	$24
PT/Exp	A	10 2AL	12	9	0	212	185	3.18	1.00	246	281	227	29.7	30%	70%	3.10	42	18	40	0.8	7.8	10.3	7%	0.7	25.1	140	$27
Consist	A	1st Half	8	3	0	104	89	2.34	0.95	239			30.8	30%	76%	3.05	42	17	41	0.5	7.7	14.8	4%	0.4	23.0	144	$17
LIMA Plan	C+	2nd Half	4	6	0	109	96	3.98	1.06	252			28.8	30%	64%	3.14	42	18	40	1.0	8.0	8.0	9%	0.9	2.2	137	$11
Rand Var	-1	11 Proj	14	10	0	225	180	3.36	1.16	259			28.6	30%	74%	3.57	42	19	39	1.6	7.2	4.6	8%	0.9	19.9	107	$26

Battled abdominal strain, balky back, but his BPIs were better than ever. Took elite Ctl to new level, while posting best Dom since '04. Just 1 PQS-Disaster, and he dominated RH. All signs point to repeat, or close to it.

BRIAN RUDD

Lester,Jon

		Yr	Tm	W	L	Sv	IP	K	ERA	WHIP	OBA	vL	vR	BF/G	H%	S%	xERA	G	L	F	Ctl	Dom	Cmd	hr/f	hr/9	RAR	BPV	R$
LH SP	27	06	BOS	*10	6	0	127	100	4.39	1.64	283	397	271	22.3	33%	75%	4.83	41	22	38	4.8	7.1	1.5	8%	0.9	2.7	16	$8
Ht/Wt	74 190	07	BOS	*9	5	0	140	97	4.69	1.52	270	231	267	23.1	31%	70%	5.20	34	19	47	4.3	6.2	1.4	7%	0.9	-3.1	8	$7
Type	Pwr GB	08	BOS	16	6	0	210	152	3.21	1.27	254	217	273	26.7	30%	76%	3.81	47	21	32	2.8	6.5	2.3	7%	0.6	29.5	66	$23
Health	B	09	BOS	15	8	0	203	225	3.41	1.23	245	257	237	26.4	32%	75%	3.11	48	18	34	2.8	10.0	3.5	11%	0.9	26.2	129	$27
PT/Exp	A	10	BOS	19	9	0	208	225	3.25	1.20	222	226	219	26.8	30%	74%	2.89	54	17	30	3.6	9.7	2.7	9%	0.6	22.9	110	$28
Consist	A	1st Half		10	3	0	114	118	2.76	1.10	205			26.9	28%	75%	2.85	53	18	30	3.3	9.3	2.8	6%	0.4	19.3	109	$17
LIMA Plan	C+	2nd Half		9	6	0	94	107	3.83	1.33	241			26.6	32%	73%	2.93	54	16	30	3.9	10.2	2.6	13%	0.9	3.6	111	$11
Rand Var	0	11	Proj	17	9	0	203	220	3.24	1.20	226			25.4	30%	75%	3.04	50	18	32	3.4	9.8	2.9	10%	0.8	31.2	111	$28

Maintained '09 Dom gains while GB% continued to rise and BA vs RHers continued to fall. In one 16-start stretch, he recorded 15 PQS-DOMs. A mature 27, so don't be surprised if...
UP: 1H times two, Cy Young

Lewis,Colby

		Yr	Tm	W	L	Sv	IP	K	ERA	WHIP	OBA	vL	vR	BF/G	H%	S%	xERA	G	L	F	Ctl	Dom	Cmd	hr/f	hr/9	RAR	BPV	R$
RH SP	31	06	aaa	6	7	0	147	86	5.47	1.57	317			27.6	35%	66%	5.88				2.4	5.2	2.2		1.0	-17.3	40	$2
Ht/Wt	76 230	07	OAK	*8	5	0	133	89	3.86	1.40	278			14.0	31%	77%	4.70	38	16	46	2.8	6.1	2.2	9%	1.2	10.6	49	$11
Type	Pwr xFB	08	JPN	15	8	0	178	174	3.33	1.10	244			27.5	30%	74%	3.44				1.7	8.8	5.2		1.0	21.5	137	$25
Health	A	09	JPN	11	9	0	176	176	3.68	1.09	252			24.3	31%	70%	3.61				1.2	9.0	7.5		1.1	13.6	183	$22
PT/Exp	A	10	TEX	12	13	0	201	196	3.72	1.19	235	239	216	25.8	29%	72%	3.58	38	17	45	2.9	8.8	3.0	9%	0.9	10.5	95	$21
Consist	A	1st Half		7	5	0	105	97	3.35	1.11	213			26.4	26%	73%	3.52	41	17	42	3.1	8.3	2.7	9%	0.9	10.2	86	$13
LIMA Plan	C+	2nd Half		5	8	0	96	99	4.11	1.28	257			25.3	32%	71%	3.63	35	17	48	2.7	9.3	3.4	9%	1.0	0.3	106	$8
Rand Var	0	11	Proj	12	11	0	196	187	3.86	1.23	250			24.6	31%	72%	3.72	37	17	46	2.6	8.6	3.3	9%	1.0	13.7	99	$20

Strikeout rate in Japan carried over, even if walk rate didn't. 66%/3% PQS-DOM/DIS showcased his effectiveness. FB rate the only concern. Look for a solid encore in 2011.

Lewis,Jensen

		Yr	Tm	W	L	Sv	IP	K	ERA	WHIP	OBA	vL	vR	BF/G	H%	S%	xERA	G	L	F	Ctl	Dom	Cmd	hr/f	hr/9	RAR	BPV	R$
RH RP	26	06	aa	1	2	0	39	39	4.83	1.51	299			24.7	38%	69%	5.32				2.8	9.0	3.3		0.9	-1.5	90	$2
Ht/Wt	75 210	07	CLE	*4	1	2	81	89	2.10	1.11	216			5.5	30%	83%	3.55	32	19	48	3.0	9.9	3.3	4%	0.4	24.1	107	$14
Type	Pwr xFB	08	CLE	*1	6	14	86	70	4.19	1.44	264	267	264	6.1	31%	74%	4.42	35	25	40	3.9	7.3	1.9	10%	1.0	1.7	41	$8
Health	A	09	CLE	2	4	1	66	62	4.62	1.37	249	299	205	6.1	28%	73%	4.33	37	16	48	3.9	8.4	2.1	15%	1.8	-1.3	60	$4
PT/Exp	D	10	CLE	*6	3	2	66	55	3.02	1.31	243	264	182	4.6	30%	77%	4.20	30	26	43	3.7	7.5	2.0	4%	0.4	9.1	43	$8
Consist	A	1st Half		2	2	1	33	26	3.00	1.43	263			5.0	33%	77%	4.28	32	31	37	3.8	7.0	1.8	0%	0.0	4.7	33	$3
LIMA Plan	C+	2nd Half		4	1	1	33	30	3.05	1.20	221			4.3	27%	78%	4.27	26	18	56	3.6	8.0	2.2	6%	0.8	4.5	52	$5
Rand Var	-4	11	Proj	4	3	0	58	51	3.88	1.38	255			5.4	30%	76%	4.28	34	21	45	3.7	7.9	2.1	11%	1.2	0.0	53	$5

4-2, 2.97 ERA in 36 IP at CLE. Allowed just 1 HR in majors, but unfortunately, that's just a FB pitcher getting lucky. Success vs RH the past 2 years helped by 24% hit rate. Little chance of another sub-3.00 ERA.

Lidge,Brad

		Yr	Tm	W	L	Sv	IP	K	ERA	WHIP	OBA	vL	vR	BF/G	H%	S%	xERA	G	L	F	Ctl	Dom	Cmd	hr/f	hr/9	RAR	BPV	R$
RH RP	34	06	HOU	1	5	32	75	104	5.28	1.40	246	286	201	4.2	35%	64%	2.99	44	23	33	4.3	12.5	2.9	17%	1.2	-7.3	130	$15
Ht/Wt	77 215	07	HOU	5	3	19	67	88	3.36	1.25	222	184	243	4.2	31%	79%	3.18	42	15	43	4.0	11.8	2.9	13%	1.2	8.8	124	$15
Type	Pwr FB	08	PHI	2	0	41	69	92	1.95	1.23	204	273	105	4.0	32%	84%	2.89	46	22	32	4.5	11.9	2.6	4%	0.3	19.9	117	$24
Health	C	09	PHI	0	8	31	59	61	7.21	1.81	303	319	285	4.1	37%	62%	4.55	39	19	42	5.2	9.4	1.8	15%	1.7	-21.8	45	$6
PT/Exp	B	10	PHI	1	1	27	46	52	2.95	1.23	199	214	173	3.8	26%	80%	3.66	37	15	48	4.7	10.2	2.2	10%	1.0	6.0	72	$13
Consist	C	1st Half		1	0	5	12	17	5.25	1.33	262			3.6	35%	69%	2.84	39	16	45	3.0	12.8	4.3	23%	2.3	-1.8	165	$3
LIMA Plan	C+	2nd Half		0	1	22	34	35	2.14	1.19	174			3.8	23%	84%	3.98	37	15	49	5.3	9.3	1.8	5%	0.5	7.8	39	$11
Rand Var	-4	11	Proj	1	3	33	58	64	3.88	1.36	227			4.1	30%	74%	3.82	40	17	43	4.8	9.9	2.1	9%	0.9	2.3	67	$14

2H results say he recovered from elbow, knee injuries, but H%, S% and hr/f scream "Fluke!" Risky FB trend and Ctl, and struggled w/ men on base (1.4 Cmd, .798 OPS against). Will get Svs, but...
DN: 4.50 ERA, more DL time.

Lilly,Ted

		Yr	Tm	W	L	Sv	IP	K	ERA	WHIP	OBA	vL	vR	BF/G	H%	S%	xERA	G	L	F	Ctl	Dom	Cmd	hr/f	hr/9	RAR	BPV	R$
LH SP	35	06	TOR	15	13	0	181	160	4.32	1.43	259	202	265	24.7	30%	75%	4.40	38	19	43	4.0	7.9	2.0	12%	1.4	5.3	50	$17
Ht/Wt	73 190	07	CHC	15	8	0	207	174	3.83	1.14	237	258	230	24.7	27%	71%	4.07	34	17	49	2.4	7.6	3.2	10%	1.2	15.3	83	$24
Type	xFB	08	CHC	17	9	0	205	184	4.09	1.23	245	307	219	25.0	28%	72%	3.95	34	22	44	2.8	8.1	2.9	12%	1.4	4.6	81	$21
Health	B	09	CHC	12	9	0	177	151	3.10	1.06	232	219	233	26.1	27%	76%	3.84	32	17	51	1.8	7.7	4.2	9%	1.1	23.8	99	$23
PT/Exp	A	10	2NL	10	12	0	194	166	3.62	1.08	232	301	213	25.8	26%	74%	3.86	30	18	53	2.0	7.7	3.8	11%	1.5	9.4	91	$19
Consist	A	1st Half		3	7	0	93	64	3.76	1.10	235			26.8	25%	73%	4.20	32	17	51	2.1	6.2	2.9	11%	1.4	2.9	64	$7
LIMA Plan	C+	2nd Half		7	5	0	100	102	3.50	1.06	229			24.9	27%	75%	3.55	26	19	55	2.0	9.1	4.6	12%	1.5	6.4	116	$12
Rand Var	-1	11	Proj	11	10	0	178	156	3.79	1.17	247			26.0	29%	74%	3.95	31	19	50	2.2	7.9	3.5	10%	1.4	4.2	91	$17

Missed most of April following shoulder and knee surgeries. Took awhile for Dom to come around, but 12 of final 15 starts were PQS-DOM. Despite BA, had 9.3 Cmd vs LHers. Repeat is the most likely scenario.

Lincecum,Tim

		Yr	Tm	W	L	Sv	IP	K	ERA	WHIP	OBA	vL	vR	BF/G	H%	S%	xERA	G	L	F	Ctl	Dom	Cmd	hr/f	hr/9	RAR	BPV	R$
RH SP	26	06		0	0	0	0	0	0.00	0.00							0.00											
Ht/Wt	71 170	07	SF	*11	5	0	177	188	3.35	1.20	214	214	238	25.2	29%	73%	3.45	47	15	38	3.9	9.5	2.5	7%	0.6	23.5	92	$22
Type	Pwr	08	SF	18	5	0	227	265	2.62	1.17	221	221	221	27.3	31%	78%	3.06	44	21	35	3.3	10.5	3.2	6%	0.4	46.3	121	$33
Health	A	09	SF	15	7	0	225	261	2.48	1.05	209	209	203	27.9	30%	77%	2.75	48	19	33	2.7	10.4	3.8	6%	0.4	47.6	140	$34
PT/Exp	A	10	SF	16	10	0	212	231	3.43	1.27	245	254	229	27.0	32%	75%	3.01	49	20	32	3.2	9.8	3.0	10%	0.8	15.2	116	$22
Consist	A	1st Half		8	4	0	110	121	3.28	1.30	239			27.3	32%	76%	3.11	47	22	31	3.8	9.9	2.6	8%	0.6	9.9	102	$11
LIMA Plan	C+	2nd Half		8	6	0	103	110	3.60	1.24	251			26.7	32%	74%	2.91	51	17	32	2.6	9.6	3.7	12%	1.0	5.3	131	$11
Rand Var	0	11	Proj	17	8	0	203	226	2.97	1.16	225			26.7	30%	77%	2.95	48	19	33	3.1	10.0	3.2	9%	0.7	29.7	122	$27

Had 6 PQS-DIS starts, after a total of 2 in 08-09. Fixed May Ctl issues (5.7), then Cmd and BPV returned to typical, elite level. ERA rebound very likely, and this could be the year he reaches 20 wins.

Lincoln,Brad

		Yr	Tm	W	L	Sv	IP	K	ERA	WHIP	OBA	vL	vR	BF/G	H%	S%	xERA	G	L	F	Ctl	Dom	Cmd	hr/f	hr/9	RAR	BPV	R$
RH SP	25	06		0	0	0	0	0	0.00	0.00							0.00											
Ht/Wt	72 215	07		0	0	0	0	0	0.00	0.00							0.00											
Type	Con xFB	08		0	0	0	0	0	0.00	0.00							0.00											
Health	A	09	a/a	7	7	0	136	86	4.09	1.35	290			23.2	33%	71%	4.56				1.8	5.7	3.2		0.7	3.7	76	$9
PT/Exp	D	10	PIT	*8	9	0	147	94	5.24	1.32	275	299	319	22.2	30%	61%	4.32	37	19	44	2.3	5.8	2.5	8%	1.0	-22.2	58	$5
Consist	A	1st Half		7	4	0	99	60	3.84	1.15	247			25.2	28%	68%	3.97	40	22	38	2.0	5.4	2.7	7%	0.7	2.2	61	$9
LIMA Plan	B	2nd Half		1	5	0	48	35	8.17	1.69	327			18.3	36%	52%	4.90	34	16	51	2.9	6.6	2.3	11%	1.7	-24.4	53	($4)
Rand Var	+3	11	Proj	3	4	0	58	38	4.66	1.33	278			20.5	30%	69%	4.48	36	17	47	2.2	5.9	2.7	10%	1.4	-2.4	61	$3

1-4, 6.66 ERA in 53 IP at PIT. Resurrected prospect status with 8.0 Dom at AAA after TJ surgery in 2007. But strikeout rate dropped to 3.7 in a 9-start MLB trial; it doesn't appear that he is ready yet.

Lindstrom,Matt

		Yr	Tm	W	L	Sv	IP	K	ERA	WHIP	OBA	vL	vR	BF/G	H%	S%	xERA	G	L	F	Ctl	Dom	Cmd	hr/f	hr/9	RAR	BPV	R$
RH RP	31	06	aa	2	4	11	40	40	6.18	1.89	341			5.5	43%	66%	6.66				3.9	9.0	2.3		0.5	-8.2	74	$3
Ht/Wt	75 218	07	FLA	3	4	0	67	62	3.09	1.30	259	263	255	4.0	34%	75%	3.59	47	16	36	2.8	8.3	3.0	3%	0.3	11.0	99	$7
Type	Pwr	08	FLA	3	3	5	57	43	3.14	1.45	261	324	214	3.8	32%	77%	4.16	46	23	30	4.1	6.8	1.7	2%	0.2	8.0	36	$6
Health	B	09	FLA	2	1	15	47	39	5.90	1.65	288	278	284	4.0	34%	64%	4.46	45	20	35	4.6	7.4	1.6	10%	1.0	-10.0	33	$4
PT/Exp	C	10	HOU	2	5	23	53	43	4.39	1.65	311	268	336	4.2	37%	75%	3.98	49	19	32	3.4	7.3	2.2	9%	0.8	-2.5	66	$8
Consist	A	1st Half		2	1	19	33	28	2.97	1.50	288			4.5	36%	80%	3.51	52	20	27	3.2	7.6	2.3	4%	0.3	4.3	79	$9
LIMA Plan	C+	2nd Half		0	4	4	20	15	6.75	1.90	347			3.9	39%	68%	4.73	44	16	40	3.6	6.7	1.9	14%	1.8	-6.7	46	($1)
Rand Var	+3	11	Proj	3	6	10	73	59	4.47	1.46	268			3.9	32%	71%	4.06	46	19	35	3.8	7.3	1.9	10%	1.0	0.8	52	$6

Never got closer job back after back spasms led to August DL stint. Ctl improved in 1H, but skills still not closer-worthy. Has lost job 2 years in a row, and may not get another chance.

Linebrink,Scott

		Yr	Tm	W	L	Sv	IP	K	ERA	WHIP	OBA	vL	vR	BF/G	H%	S%	xERA	G	L	F	Ctl	Dom	Cmd	hr/f	hr/9	RAR	BPV	R$
RH RP	34	06	SD	7	4	2	75	68	3.59	1.22	248	204	294	4.3	30%	75%	3.83	39	19	42	2.6	8.1	3.1	10%	1.1	8.3	93	$10
Ht/Wt	74 210	07	2NL	5	6	1	70	50	3.71	1.32	255	215	284	4.2	27%	79%	4.27	42	21	37	3.2	6.4	2.0	15%	1.5	6.2	49	$7
Type	Pwr xFB	08	CHW	2	2	1	46	40	3.69	1.08	239	200	263	3.7	27%	74%	3.55	39	18	43	1.7	7.8	4.4	14%	1.6	3.7	110	$6
Health	B	09	CHW	3	7	2	56	55	4.66	1.66	307	297	310	4.5	37%	76%	4.24	37	24	39	3.7	8.8	2.4	13%	1.4	-1.4	75	$3
PT/Exp	D	10	CHW	3	2	0	57	52	4.40	1.33	267	288	234	4.7	30%	74%	4.01	32	19	49	2.7	8.2	3.1	13%	1.7	-1.8	85	$4
Consist	A	1st Half		1	0	0	28	30	5.09	1.45	273			4.9	33%	71%	3.78	37	18	45	3.5	9.5	2.7	17%	1.9	-3.3	92	$1
LIMA Plan	A	2nd Half		2	2	0	29	22	3.72	1.21	262			4.4	29%	77%	4.21	28	19	53	1.9	6.8	3.7	11%	1.6	1.5	78	$3
Rand Var	+1	11	Proj	3	4	0	58	52	4.19	1.33	265			4.4	31%	74%	4.00	35	20	45	2.8	8.1	2.9	12%	1.4	2.1	83	$5

PRO: Corrected Ctl issues in 2H; more effective against RH.
CON: GB rate dropping; FB keep leaving park at elevated rate; can't contain LH anymore. Ongoing HR issues make a sub-4.00 ERA unlikely.

BRIAN RUDD

Liriano,Francisco

Liriano,Francisco		W	L	Sv	IP	K	ERA	WHIP	OBA	vL	vR	BF/G	H%	S%	xERA	G	L	F	Ctl	Dom	Cmd	hr/f	hr/9	RAR	BPV	R$
LH SP 27	06 MIN	12	3	1	121	144	2.16	1.00	207	202	206	16.9	29%	82%	2.29	55	21	23	2.4	10.7	**4.5**	13%	0.7	35.8	162	$26
Ht/Wt 74 225	07 MIN	0	0	0	0	0	0.00	0.00							0.00											
Type Pwr	08 MIN	* 16	6	0	194	160	3.85	1.30	256	217	266	24.8	31%	71%	3.98	42	18	40	3.0	7.4	**2.5**	6%	0.7	11.9	73	$20
Health D	09 MIN	5	13	0	137	122	5.79	1.55	276	255	287	21.1	32%	65%	4.48	40	19	41	4.3	8.0	**1.9**	12%	1.4	-22.6	47	$3
PT/Exp B	10 MIN	14	10	0	192	201	3.62	1.26	254	218	262	25.9	34%	71%	2.80	54	19	27	2.7	9.4	**3.5**	6%	0.4	12.4	128	$21
Consist C	1st Half	6	6	0	106	116	3.32	1.22	253			27.4	35%	71%	2.70	51	20	29	2.4	9.9	**4.1**	2%	0.2	10.7	142	$12
LIMA Plan C+	2nd Half	8	4	0	86	85	3.98	1.31	255			24.3	33%	71%	2.93	57	18	26	3.1	8.9	**2.8**	11%	0.7	1.7	110	$9
Rand Var +1	11 Proj	**15**	**9**	**0**	**189**	**185**	**3.87**	**1.27**	**251**			**26.3**	**32%**	**71%**	**3.22**	**49**	**19**	**32**	**2.9**	**8.8**	**3.0**	**10%**	**0.8**	**24.8**	**108**	**$21**

Elevated hit rate helped hide dominant season as GB, Dom and Cmd were all at elite levels. Given slowdown in 2H, IP spike a concern, especially after 49 IP in winter ball. With health... UP: 18 wins, sub-3.00 ERA

Litsch,Jesse

Litsch,Jesse		W	L	Sv	IP	K	ERA	WHIP	OBA	vL	vR	BF/G	H%	S%	xERA	G	L	F	Ctl	Dom	Cmd	hr/f	hr/9	RAR	BPV	R$
RH SP 26	06 aa	3	4	0	69	47	7.29	1.74	352			26.8	40%	57%	7.03				1.8	6.1	**3.4**		1.0	-23.6	61	($3)
Ht/Wt 73 215	07 TOR	* 15	11	0	187	98	3.42	1.29	264	308	229	24.6	28%	77%	4.36	48	18	34	2.5	4.7	**1.8**	9%	1.0	25.2	42	$19
Type Con	08 TOR	13	9	0	176	99	3.58	1.23	264	270	250	25.2	28%	75%	3.94	49	20	32	2.0	5.1	**2.5**	11%	1.0	16.7	64	$18
Health F	09 TOR	0	1	0	9	8	9.00	1.67	356	261	471	20.6	37%	55%	4.34	34	16	50	1.0	8.0	**8.0**	25%	4.0	-5.0	129	($1)
PT/Exp C	10 TOR	* 1	8	0	69	27	6.05	1.50	306	276	300	23.4	31%	61%	4.90	44	16	40	2.4	3.5	**1.5**	10%	1.3	-16.2	22	($2)
Consist A	1st Half	0	6	0	41	18	6.79	1.58	322			23.2	34%	57%	5.02	38	20	42	2.2	3.9	**1.8**	8%	1.1	-13.5	27	($3)
LIMA Plan C+	2nd Half	1	2	0	27	9	4.93	1.39	280			23.6	27%	70%	4.83	48	13	38	2.6	3.0	**1.1**	13%	1.6	-2.7	9	$0
Rand Var +4	11 Proj	**3**	**5**	**0**	**58**	**27**	**4.50**	**1.41**	**291**			**25.1**	**30%**	**72%**	**4.66**	**43**	**19**	**38**	**2.3**	**4.2**	**1.8**	**10%**	**1.2**	**-2.7**	**34**	**$2**

1-5, 5.79 ERA in 47 IP at TOR. Hip surgery in August was the second major operation in two years (Tommy John surgery in 2009). History of low Dom means he needs to return to '07-'08 GB rates to be roster-worthy.

Loe,Kameron

Loe,Kameron		W	L	Sv	IP	K	ERA	WHIP	OBA	vL	vR	BF/G	H%	S%	xERA	G	L	F	Ctl	Dom	Cmd	hr/f	hr/9	RAR	BPV	R$
RH RP 29	06 TEX	3	6	0	78	34	5.88	1.63	323	313	321	23.7	34%	65%	4.73	51	19	30	2.5	3.9	**1.5**	11%	1.2	-12.7	31	($1)
Ht/Wt 80 240	07 TEX	6	11	0	136	78	5.36	1.60	297	328	262	22.0	33%	67%	4.34	56	18	26	3.7	5.2	**1.4**	11%	0.9	-14.3	27	$2
Type xGB	08 TEX	* 4	5	1	89	42	6.13	1.80	340	400	200	10.5	36%	68%	4.98	50	16	33	3.1	4.3	**1.4**	11%	1.3	-19.5	21	($3)
Health A	09 JPN	0	4	0	27	19	7.87	1.98	337			26.5	38%	60%	7.37				5.0	6.3	**1.3**		1.1	-11.8	19	($3)
PT/Exp D	10 MIL	* 7	8	0	121	78	3.31	1.31	264	274	228	8.1	29%	78%	3.42	59	16	25	2.7	5.8	**2.2**	13%	0.9	10.4	70	$9
Consist F	1st Half	4	3	0	82	48	3.13	1.28	251			13.7	28%	78%	3.67	54	21	25	3.0	5.3	**1.8**	12%	0.8	8.9	47	$6
LIMA Plan B	2nd Half	3	5	0	39	30	3.69	1.38	290			4.4	33%	78%	3.09	61	14	24	2.1	6.9	**3.3**	16%	1.2	1.6	108	$3
Rand Var 0	11 Proj	**4**	**6**	**0**	**78**	**49**	**3.81**	**1.38**	**276**			**4.8**	**31%**	**75%**	**3.74**	**57**	**16**	**27**	**2.8**	**5.7**	**2.0**	**12%**	**0.9**	**3.9**	**62**	**$4**

2-5, 2.78 ERA in 58 IP at MIL. Transition to bullpen fit him well: 2H rise in Dom coincided with drop in BF/G. If he remains in short relief, newfound Ks and strong GB% pair for a nice LIMA pick.

Logan,Boone

Logan,Boone		W	L	Sv	IP	K	ERA	WHIP	OBA	vL	vR	BF/G	H%	S%	xERA	G	L	F	Ctl	Dom	Cmd	hr/f	hr/9	RAR	BPV	R$
LH RP 26	06 CHW	* 3	1	12	59	66	5.46	1.49	267			4.4	37%	61%	3.73	44	17	39	4.2	10.1	**2.4**	5%	0.4	-6.6	91	$7
Ht/Wt 77 215	07 CHW	2	1	0	51	35	4.97	1.56	292	221	357	3.3	33%	71%	4.42	51	14	35	3.6	6.2	**1.8**	12%	1.2	-2.9	45	$1
Type Pwr	08 CHW	2	3	0	42	42	5.96	1.68	323	291	351	3.5	39%	67%	3.78	43	23	34	3.0	8.9	**3.0**	15%	1.5	-8.4	102	$0
Health A	09 ATL	* 5	3	2	52	44	4.34	1.46	255			4.7	31%	70%	3.18	64	20	16	4.5	7.5	**1.7**	12%	0.5	-0.9	56	$4
PT/Exp D	10 NYY	* 2	1	0	61	58	2.83	1.31	244	190	279	4.0	31%	80%	3.53	46	17	37	3.6	8.6	**2.4**	6%	0.6	9.9	83	$6
Consist A	1st Half	0	0	0	32	28	2.87	1.34	241			5.2	31%	78%	3.55	47	25	28	4.0	7.9	**2.0**	4%	0.3	4.9	59	$2
LIMA Plan B	2nd Half	2	1	0	30	31	2.77	1.27	247			3.2	32%	82%	3.50	45	8	47	3.1	9.4	**3.1**	8%	0.9	5.0	109	$4
Rand Var -4	11 Proj	**4**	**2**	**0**	**64**	**59**	**3.69**	**1.37**	**254**			**3.9**	**31%**	**75%**	**3.63**	**49**	**18**	**34**	**3.7**	**8.4**	**2.3**	**10%**	**0.9**	**5.1**	**78**	**$6**

2-0, 2.93 ERA in 40 IP at NYY. MLB-only numbers dampen what look like promising BPVs:

- 4.11 xERA in 2010
- '08-'10 Dom: 10.2 vL; 5.0 vR
- 1.8 Cmd for his career

A lefty specialist at best.

Lohse,Kyle

Lohse,Kyle		W	L	Sv	IP	K	ERA	WHIP	OBA	vL	vR	BF/G	H%	S%	xERA	G	L	F	Ctl	Dom	Cmd	hr/f	hr/9	RAR	BPV	R$
RH SP 32	06 2TM	* 7	11	0	150	106	5.30	1.48	287	288	304	17.4	33%	65%	4.44	43	20	37	3.1	6.4	**2.1**	9%	1.0	-14.4	52	$5
Ht/Wt 74 210	07 2NL	9	12	0	193	122	4.62	1.37	276	276	282	24.3	31%	68%	4.61	37	22	41	2.7	5.7	**2.1**	8%	1.0	-4.7	46	$10
Type	08 STL	15	6	0	200	119	3.78	1.30	272	254	285	25.6	30%	73%	4.05	46	22	32	2.2	5.4	**2.4**	9%	0.8	12.1	61	$17
Health F	09 STL	6	10	0	118	77	4.74	1.37	274	251	285	21.9	30%	68%	4.22	45	19	36	2.8	5.9	**2.1**	12%	1.2	-8.0	54	$5
PT/Exp B	10 STL	4	8	0	92	54	6.55	1.78	332	344	330	24.0	37%	63%	4.92	43	19	38	3.4	5.3	**1.5**	7%	0.9	-28.8	24	($5)
Consist A	1st Half	1	4	0	47	25	5.90	1.71	321			24.3	36%	63%	5.06	41	20	39	3.4	4.8	**1.4**	3%	0.4	-11.0	12	($2)
LIMA Plan D	2nd Half	3	4	0	45	29	7.25	1.86	344			23.7	38%	62%	4.76	46	18	37	3.4	5.8	**1.7**	12%	1.4	-17.8	36	($3)
Rand Var +5	11 Proj	**6**	**8**	**0**	**108**	**67**	**4.75**	**1.48**	**289**			**22.6**	**32%**	**70%**	**4.45**	**44**	**20**	**37**	**3.0**	**5.6**	**1.9**	**9%**	**1.0**	**-4.1**	**41**	**$3**

Lost significant time to forearm injury for second consecutive year. While easy to make h% and s% scapegoats, what he can control got worse (Cmd, FB rate). If health recovers, xERA sets expectations for rebound.

Lopez,Javier

Lopez,Javier		W	L	Sv	IP	K	ERA	WHIP	OBA	vL	vR	BF/G	H%	S%	xERA	G	L	F	Ctl	Dom	Cmd	hr/f	hr/9	RAR	BPV	R$
LH RP 33	06 BOS	* 3	1	17	65	41	2.96	1.56	294	250	208	4.4	34%	82%	3.28	65	22	13	3.5	5.6	**1.6**	15%	0.6	12.9	51	$10
Ht/Wt 76 220	07 BOS	* 4	2	0	57	38	3.80	1.55	277	293	176	3.3	33%	75%	4.34	53	20	28	4.3	6.0	**1.4**	4%	0.3	5.0	23	$4
Type xGB	08 BOS	2	0	0	59	38	2.43	1.35	241	182	311	3.6	27%	84%	3.76	60	18	22	4.1	5.8	**1.4**	10%	0.6	14.0	31	$6
Health A	09 BOS	* 1	3	0	51	24	6.18	1.78	318			4.6	34%	64%	5.02	49	26	26	4.2	4.2	**1.0**	9%	0.7	-10.9	-10	($2)
PT/Exp D	10 2NL	4	2	0	58	38	2.34	1.21	235	162	306	3.1	28%	81%	3.27	62	16	23	3.1	5.9	**1.9**	5%	0.3	11.9	62	$7
Consist D	1st Half	1	1	0	30	16	2.67	1.35	233			3.5	26%	80%	4.13	58	16	26	4.5	4.8	**1.1**	4%	0.3	5.0	2	$2
LIMA Plan C+	2nd Half	3	1	0	27	22	1.97	1.06	237			2.7	29%	82%	2.40	66	16	18	1.6	7.2	**4.4**	7%	0.3	6.9	130	$5
Rand Var -5	11 Proj	**3**	**2**	**0**	**51**	**32**	**3.37**	**1.34**	**263**			**3.4**	**30%**	**75%**	**3.49**	**60**	**17**	**22**	**3.0**	**5.7**	**1.9**	**8%**	**0.5**	**4.1**	**59**	**$4**

Tantalizing 2H, but few pitchers sustain such dramatic Ctl gains at his age. Has gotten equal time against righties and lefties but splits show he's best used as a LOOGY. Heed Rand Var and let somebody else speculate.

Lopez,Rodrigo

Lopez,Rodrigo		W	L	Sv	IP	K	ERA	WHIP	OBA	vL	vR	BF/G	H%	S%	xERA	G	L	F	Ctl	Dom	Cmd	hr/f	hr/9	RAR	BPV	R$
RH SP 35	06 BAL	9	18	0	189	136	5.90	1.55	305	308	296	23.5	34%	65%	4.36	43	22	35	2.8	6.5	**2.3**	14%	1.5	-31.4	61	$4
Ht/Wt 73 185	07 COL	5	4	0	79	43	4.43	1.31	271	270	276	24.0	29%	70%	4.51	47	13	40	2.4	4.9	**2.0**	10%	1.2	-0.0	49	$5
Type Con	08	0	0	0	0	0	0.00	0.00							0.00											
Health B	09 aaa	7	5	0	100	57	5.68	1.64	346			25.4	38%	66%	6.58				1.3	5.1	**3.9**		1.0	-16.9	67	$1
PT/Exp C	10 ARI	7	16	0	200	116	5.00	1.42	287	293	280	26.3	30%	70%	4.53	38	21	41	2.5	5.2	**2.1**	13%	1.7	-24.2	42	$3
Consist F	1st Half	4	7	0	110	59	4.43	1.39	279			27.8	29%	73%	4.60	36	23	40	2.6	4.8	**1.8**	12%	1.5	-5.6	31	$3
LIMA Plan B	2nd Half	3	9	0	90	57	5.68	1.45	296			24.7	31%	66%	4.44	39	19	42	2.4	5.7	**2.4**	15%	1.9	-18.5	55	($0)
Rand Var +1	11 Proj	**5**	**7**	**0**	**102**	**60**	**4.79**	**1.38**	**287**			**24.2**	**31%**	**69%**	**4.39**	**42**	**18**	**40**	**2.2**	**5.3**	**2.4**	**11%**	**1.3**	**-3.1**	**56**	**$4**

Other than good control, doesn't bring anything to the fanalytic table. His best chance to help your team is by serving up home runs to your batters.

Lopez,Wilton

Lopez,Wilton		W	L	Sv	IP	K	ERA	WHIP	OBA	vL	vR	BF/G	H%	S%	xERA	G	L	F	Ctl	Dom	Cmd	hr/f	hr/9	RAR	BPV	R$
RH RP 27	06	0	0	0	0	0	0.00	0.00							0.00											
Ht/Wt 72 199	07	0	0	0	0	0	0.00	0.00							0.00											
Type Con xGB	08 a/a	0	2	0	39	19	6.14	1.62	317			6.3	35%	60%	5.48				2.8	4.4	**1.5**		0.5	-8.8	35	($2)
Health A	09 HOU	* 4	7	0	129	61	6.30	1.71	352			16.1	38%	63%	4.08	58	17	25	1.6	4.3	**2.7**	11%	0.9	-33.7	70	($6)
PT/Exp D	10 HOU	5	2	1	67	50	2.96	1.06	259	284	245	3.9	31%	73%	2.85	56	16	28	0.7	6.7	**10.0**	7%	0.5	8.8	136	$9
Consist C	1st Half	5	1	0	38	23	4.10	1.29	295			4.5	34%	67%	3.66	48	18	34	1.0	5.5	**5.7**	5%	0.5	-0.4	99	$4
LIMA Plan A	2nd Half	0	1	1	29	27	1.49	0.77	207			3.3	26%	86%	1.99	64	14	22	0.3	8.3	**27.1**	12%	0.6	9.1	183	$5
Rand Var 0	11 Proj	**3**	**3**	**5**	**73**	**46**	**3.72**	**1.27**	**284**			**5.7**	**32%**	**72%**	**3.32**	**58**	**16**	**26**	**1.4**	**5.7**	**4.2**	**10%**	**0.7**	**7.4**	**102**	**$7**

Even in small sample sizes, a 2H like this is rare, but season xERA and BPV show 2010 was no fluke. Makes nice end-game pick, but not quite the sustained dominance you'd want to see in a future closer.

Lowe,Derek

Lowe,Derek		W	L	Sv	IP	K	ERA	WHIP	OBA	vL	vR	BF/G	H%	S%	xERA	G	L	F	Ctl	Dom	Cmd	hr/f	hr/9	RAR	BPV	R$
RH SP 37	06 LA	16	8	0	218	123	3.63	1.27	264	270	255	26.1	30%	72%	3.18	67	16	17	2.3	5.1	**2.2**	11%	0.6	23.0	75	$20
Ht/Wt 78 230	07 LA	12	14	0	199	147	3.88	1.27	257	271	239	25.3	30%	72%	3.03	65	16	19	2.7	6.6	**2.5**	17%	0.9	13.3	91	$18
Type xGB	08 LA	14	11	0	211	147	3.24	1.13	246	251	240	25.2	29%	72%	3.07	60	17	23	1.9	6.3	**3.3**	10%	0.6	26.8	99	$23
Health A	09 ATL	15	10	0	195	111	4.67	1.52	297	300	303	25.4	33%	70%	4.02	56	18	26	2.9	5.1	**1.8**	9%	0.7	-11.5	48	$8
PT/Exp A	10 ATL	16	12	0	194	136	4.00	1.37	272	287	259	25.2	31%	72%	3.32	59	19	23	2.8	6.3	**2.2**	13%	0.8	0.5	74	$13
Consist B	1st Half	9	6	0	101	60	4.53	1.41	263			25.8	30%	68%	3.73	60	17	23	3.6	5.3	**1.5**	9%	0.6	-6.4	35	$5
LIMA Plan C+	2nd Half	7	6	0	92	76	3.41	1.32	281			24.5	33%	78%	2.90	58	20	22	1.9	7.4	**3.8**	18%	1.1	6.9	116	$8
Rand Var +2	11 Proj	**15**	**13**	**0**	**203**	**137**	**3.95**	**1.33**	**270**			**25.4**	**31%**	**71%**	**3.37**	**59**	**18**	**23**	**2.6**	**6.1**	**2.4**	**11%**	**0.7**	**19.4**	**77**	**$15**

1H Cmd and BPV in line with down year in 2009; returned to form in 2H. Age says he can't do this for much longer. But for now, it's worth paying full value for history of consistency and reliability.

BILL MACEY

Lowe,Mark		Yr	Tm	W	L	Sv	IP	K	ERA	WHIP	OBA	vL	vR	BF/G	H%	S%	xERA	G	L	F	Ctl	Dom	Cmd	hr/f	hr/9	RAR	BPV	R$
RH RP	27	06	SEA *	1	1	3	32	28	1.98	1.13	225	167	205	5.4	29%	83%	3.43	49	19	33	2.8	7.8	**2.8**	3%	0.3	10.2	91	$6
Ht/Wt	75 210	07	SEA	0	0	0	3	3	6.67	1.85	208			3.2	18%	75%	7.35				10.0	10.0	**1.0**		3.3	-0.7	-6	($0)
Type	Pwr FB	08	SEA	1	5	1	64	55	5.37	1.76	303	354	250	5.2	37%	70%	4.53	45	21	35	4.8	7.8	**1.6**	9%	0.8	-8.0	33	($0)
Health	F	09	SEA	2	7	3	80	69	3.26	1.25	239	253	213	4.4	29%	76%	4.00	39	21	40	3.3	7.8	**2.4**	8%	0.8	11.7	68	$9
PT/Exp	D	10	2AL	1	3	0	13	12	5.41	1.80	324	440	241	4.5	39%	73%	4.86	24	27	49	4.1	8.1	**2.0**	9%	1.4	-2.1	39	($0)
Consist	B	1st Half		1	3	0	10	7	3.50	1.55	275			4.2	31%	80%	5.37	23	23	55	4.4	6.1	**1.4**	6%	0.9	0.8	-7	$1
LIMA Plan	C	2nd Half		0	0	0	3	5	12.00	2.67	453			5.6	63%	57%	3.11	30	40	30	3.0	15.0	**5.0**	32%	3.0	-2.9	197	($1)
Rand Var	+4	11	Proj	**2**	**4**	**3**	**65**	**56**	**4.00**	**1.36**	**252**			**5.1**	**30%**	**73%**	**4.20**	**37**	**21**	**42**	**3.7**	**7.7**	**2.1**	**9%**	**1.0**	**0.7**	**53**	**$5**

Back injury cost him most of 2010; "F" health rating shows that he's too familiar with the DL. The Dom is nice, but without an improvement in Ctl, he's only rosterable in very deep leagues.

Luebke,Cory		Yr	Tm	W	L	Sv	IP	K	ERA	WHIP	OBA	vL	vR	BF/G	H%	S%	xERA	G	L	F	Ctl	Dom	Cmd	hr/f	hr/9	RAR	BPV	R$
LH SP	26	06		0	0	0	0	0	0.00	0.00							0.00											
Ht/Wt	76 200	07		0	0	0	0	0	0.00	0.00							0.00											
Type		08		0	0	0	0	0	0.00	0.00							0.00											
Health	A	09	aa	3	2	0	41	27	3.92	1.38	266			19.7	31%	71%	4.01				3.2	5.8	**1.8**		0.5	2.0	61	$3
PT/Exp	D	10	SD *	11	2	0	132	92	2.99	1.09	226	333	222	23.0	26%	75%	3.58	50	14	36	2.4	6.3	**2.6**	7%	0.7	16.6	76	$16
Consist	A	1st Half		4	0	0	44	26	2.49	1.06	222			21.9	25%	78%	2.48				2.3	5.3	**2.3**		0.5	8.3	78	$6
LIMA Plan	C+	2nd Half		7	2	0	88	66	3.24	1.11	228			23.5	26%	74%	3.50	50	14	36	2.5	6.8	**2.7**	9%	0.8	8.3	82	$10
Rand Var	-3	11	Proj	**9**	**3**	**0**	**116**	**78**	**3.72**	**1.31**	**260**			**22.3**	**29%**	**74%**	**4.01**	**50**	**14**	**36**	**2.9**	**6.1**	**2.1**	**9%**	**0.9**	**1.9**	**59**	**$10**

1-1, 4.08 ERA in 18 IP at SD. Flashed 9.0 Dom in MLB but MLEs say it won't last. Good GB rate in minors and growing Cmd set solid foundation for the future. May need additional AAA seasoning first, though.

Lyon,Brandon		Yr	Tm	W	L	Sv	IP	K	ERA	WHIP	OBA	vL	vR	BF/G	H%	S%	xERA	G	L	F	Ctl	Dom	Cmd	hr/f	hr/9	RAR	BPV	R$
RH RP	31	06	ARI	2	4	0	69	46	3.91	1.30	259	244	270	4.3	29%	72%	4.19	43	24	33	2.9	6.0	**2.1**	10%	0.9	4.9	51	$5
Ht/Wt	73 195	07	ARI	6	4	2	74	40	2.68	1.24	251	233	267	4.2	29%	78%	4.50	43	19	38	2.7	4.9	**1.8**	2%	0.2	16.0	36	$10
Type		08	ARI	3	5	26	59	44	4.70	1.48	310	278	321	4.3	36%	70%	4.15	40	22	38	2.0	6.7	**3.4**	9%	1.1	-3.2	85	$11
Health	A	09	DET	6	5	3	77	56	2.92	1.12	205	207	209	4.9	23%	77%	4.00	46	17	36	3.5	6.5	**1.9**	9%	0.8	14.5	48	$12
PT/Exp	B	10	HOU	6	6	20	78	54	3.12	1.27	236	195	257	4.1	28%	74%	4.27	40	20	40	3.6	6.2	**1.7**	2%	0.2	8.7	33	$14
Consist	A	1st Half		5	3	1	37	29	3.62	1.39	250			4.1	31%	73%	4.38	40	17	43	4.1	7.0	**1.7**	2%	0.2	1.8	33	$4
LIMA Plan	D+	2nd Half		1	3	19	41	25	2.65	1.15	223			4.1	26%	76%	4.16	40	22	38	3.1	5.5	**1.8**	2%	0.2	6.8	34	$10
Rand Var	-4	11	Proj	**5**	**5**	**30**	**73**	**50**	**3.72**	**1.32**	**255**			**4.4**	**29%**	**74%**	**4.26**	**42**	**20**	**38**	**3.2**	**6.2**	**1.9**	**8%**	**0.9**	**-1.0**	**44**	**$16**

Seized closer's role in 2H and suffered just 2 blown saves. That will buy him a longer leash; mediocre BPV, Cmd and xERA say he's going to need every inch. Especially when hr/f climbs back up.

Madson,Ryan		Yr	Tm	W	L	Sv	IP	K	ERA	WHIP	OBA	vL	vR	BF/G	H%	S%	xERA	G	L	F	Ctl	Dom	Cmd	hr/f	hr/9	RAR	BPV	R$
RH RP	30	06	PHI	11	9	2	134	99	5.70	1.69	318	306	336	12.4	36%	68%	4.61	43	22	35	3.4	6.6	**2.0**	12%	1.3	-20.1	50	$3
Ht/Wt	78 200	07	PHI	2	2	1	56	43	3.05	1.27	233	170	275	6.2	27%	79%	3.96	47	21	32	3.7	6.9	**1.9**	10%	0.8	9.5	50	$6
Type	Pwr GB	08	PHI	4	2	1	83	67	3.05	1.23	253	268	243	4.5	31%	77%	3.44	51	19	30	2.5	7.3	**2.9**	8%	0.7	12.5	93	$9
Health	D	09	PHI	5	5	10	77	78	3.26	1.23	251	257	245	4.1	32%	76%	3.16	46	22	32	2.6	9.1	**3.5**	10%	0.8	8.9	118	$12
PT/Exp	C	10	PHI	6	2	5	53	64	2.55	1.04	219	217	208	3.8	31%	78%	2.55	50	13	37	2.2	10.9	**4.9**	9%	0.7	9.6	164	$11
Consist	A	1st Half		1	0	4	9	10	7.00	1.78	339			4.7	42%	64%	2.75	62	17	21	3.0	10.0	**3.3**	34%	2.0	-3.3	139	$1
LIMA Plan	B+	2nd Half		5	2	1	44	54	1.64	0.89	189			3.6	28%	84%	2.49	47	12	41	2.0	11.0	**5.4**	5%	0.4	12.9	169	$10
Rand Var	-1	11	Proj	**5**	**3**	**3**	**73**	**70**	**3.10**	**1.17**	**238**			**4.6**	**30%**	**76%**	**3.09**	**51**	**18**	**32**	**2.6**	**8.7**	**3.3**	**10%**	**0.7**	**9.4**	**115**	**$10**

Broke toe in frustration in April. Returned in July to frustrate the NL. Has struggled in closer role before, but GB rate and rising Dom and BPV trends show that he has closer-worthy stuff.
UP: 30 Saves

Maholm,Paul		Yr	Tm	W	L	Sv	IP	K	ERA	WHIP	OBA	vL	vR	BF/G	H%	S%	xERA	G	L	F	Ctl	Dom	Cmd	hr/f	hr/9	RAR	BPV	R$
LH SP	28	06	PIT	8	10	0	176	117	4.76	1.61	289	233	313	26.6	33%	72%	4.36	53	20	27	4.1	6.0	**1.4**	12%	1.0	-5.8	27	$4
Ht/Wt	74 224	07	PIT	10	15	0	178	105	5.01	1.42	289	238	305	26.6	31%	67%	4.07	53	17	30	2.5	5.3	**2.1**	12%	1.1	-12.9	60	$7
Type	Con GB	08	PIT	9	9	0	206	139	3.71	1.28	257	183	279	27.9	29%	74%	3.69	54	19	28	2.7	6.1	**2.2**	12%	0.9	14.3	67	$15
Health	A	09	PIT	8	9	0	195	119	4.44	1.44	287	182	316	27.4	32%	69%	4.06	52	18	30	2.8	5.5	**2.0**	7%	0.6	-6.0	54	$7
PT/Exp	A	10	PIT	9	15	0	185	102	5.10	1.57	304	231	316	26.0	34%	67%	4.28	51	19	30	3.0	5.0	**1.6**	8%	0.7	-24.8	37	$0
Consist	A	1st Half		5	7	0	98	52	4.50	1.59	299			26.0	33%	72%	4.50	50	19	31	3.5	4.8	**1.4**	8%	0.7	-5.9	20	$1
LIMA Plan	C+	2nd Half		4	8	0	87	50	5.77	1.53	309			25.9	34%	61%	4.03	52	19	29	2.5	5.2	**2.1**	8%	0.7	-18.9	56	($1)
Rand Var	+2	11	Proj	**9**	**13**	**0**	**189**	**112**	**4.54**	**1.45**	**287**			**26.6**	**32%**	**69%**	**4.07**	**52**	**19**	**29**	**2.9**	**5.3**	**1.9**	**9%**	**0.8**	**1.6**	**49**	**$6**

PRO: Consistently elite GB rate, previous history of 2.0+ Cmd.
CON: 2-year decline in Dom, ERA/xERA gap a continuing concern.
A shoo-in for lots of IP, but wins will again be hard to come by.

Maine,John		Yr	Tm	W	L	Sv	IP	K	ERA	WHIP	OBA	vL	vR	BF/G	H%	S%	xERA	G	L	F	Ctl	Dom	Cmd	hr/f	hr/9	RAR	BPV	R$
RH SP	29	06	NYM *	9	10	0	146	112	4.14	1.31	250	231	191	23.8	29%	71%	4.57	38	15	47	3.3	6.9	**2.1**	8%	1.0	6.2	49	$12
Ht/Wt	76 200	07	NYM	15	10	0	191	180	3.91	1.27	238	237	234	25.0	29%	73%	4.05	37	18	45	3.5	8.5	**2.4**	10%	1.1	12.1	72	$20
Type	Pwr xFB	08	NYM	10	8	0	140	122	4.18	1.35	236	238	229	23.9	28%	72%	4.20	41	20	39	4.3	7.8	**1.8**	10%	1.0	1.6	43	$11
Health	F	09	NYM	7	6	0	81	55	4.43	1.29	226	159	304	22.8	25%	67%	4.75	35	21	44	4.2	6.1	**1.4**	8%	0.9	-2.4	9	$6
PT/Exp	C	10	NYM	1	3	0	40	39	6.12	1.81	296	200	357	20.9	35%	70%	5.11	26	21	52	5.7	8.8	**1.6**	13%	1.8	-10.3	11	($2)
Consist	A	1st Half		1	3	0	40	39	6.12	1.81	296			20.9	35%	70%	5.11	26	21	52	5.7	8.8	**1.6**	13%	1.8	-10.3	11	($2)
LIMA Plan	D	2nd Half		0	0	0	0	0	0.00	0.00							0.00											
Rand Var	+4	11	Proj	**4**	**4**	**0**	**58**	**50**	**4.81**	**1.47**	**255**			**23.1**	**30%**	**70%**	**4.57**	**34**	**20**	**46**	**4.5**	**7.8**	**1.7**	**10%**	**1.2**	**-3.1**	**30**	**$3**

Plagued by shoulder problems for years, he finally succumbed and went under the knife in July. Perhaps the surgery will fix the multiyear skills decline, but let somebody else take that gamble.

Maloney,Matt		Yr	Tm	W	L	Sv	IP	K	ERA	WHIP	OBA	vL	vR	BF/G	H%	S%	xERA	G	L	F	Ctl	Dom	Cmd	hr/f	hr/9	RAR	BPV	R$
LH SP	27	06		0	0	0	0	0	0.00	0.00							0.00											
Ht/Wt	76 220	07	a/a	13	10	0	170	151	4.65	1.31	259			25.7	30%	68%	4.57				2.9	8.0	**2.7**		1.3	-4.0	71	$15
Type	xFB	08	aaa	11	5	0	140	115	5.72	1.46	293			24.5	34%	64%	5.60				2.6	7.4	**2.9**		1.5	-24.4	57	$6
Health	A	09	CIN *	11	13	0	191	137	4.27	1.37	295	286	280	27.3	33%	73%	4.55	34	13	53	1.7	6.5	**3.8**	8%	1.2	-1.8	83	$11
PT/Exp	D	10	CIN *	12	9	0	155	102	3.94	1.34	284	148	314	21.3	32%	72%	4.22	36	22	42	2.0	5.9	**3.0**	6%	0.8	1.4	68	$11
Consist	B	1st Half		6	4	0	75	54	4.33	1.39	286			23.1	34%	69%	4.33				2.4	6.5	**2.8**		0.6	-2.9	77	$4
LIMA Plan	B+	2nd Half		6	5	0	80	48	3.58	1.29	283			19.8	31%	75%	4.23	36	22	42	1.6	5.4	**3.4**	7%	0.9	4.3	68	$6
Rand Var	-1	11	Proj	**4**	**3**	**0**	**58**	**42**	**4.03**	**1.31**	**278**			**22.3**	**31%**	**74%**	**4.25**	**35**	**19**	**46**	**2.0**	**6.5**	**3.2**	**9%**	**1.2**	**-0.7**	**76**	**$4**

2-2, 3.05 ERA in 21 IP at CIN. Declining Dom and low GB rate a concern, but with consistently good Cmd and improving xERA, he's likely to find a role somewhere. Worth keeping on your radar.

Marcum,Shaun		Yr	Tm	W	L	Sv	IP	K	ERA	WHIP	OBA	vL	vR	BF/G	H%	S%	xERA	G	L	F	Ctl	Dom	Cmd	hr/f	hr/9	RAR	BPV	R$
RH SP	29	06	TOR *	7	4	0	130	117	4.90	1.48	283	303	256	14.7	33%	71%	4.40	36	18	46	3.3	8.1	**2.4**	12%	1.5	-5.6	70	$8
Ht/Wt	72 180	07	TOR	12	6	1	159	122	4.13	1.25	249	259	237	17.4	27%	73%	4.15	40	18	42	2.8	6.9	**2.5**	13%	1.5	7.3	68	$17
Type	FB	08	TOR	9	7	0	151	123	3.39	1.16	228	244	200	24.7	26%	77%	3.82	43	17	40	3.0	7.3	**2.5**	12%	1.2	17.9	73	$18
Health	F	09	TOR	0	0	0	0	0	0.00	0.00							0.00											
PT/Exp	B	10	TOR	13	8	0	195	165	3.64	1.15	247	189	299	25.6	29%	73%	3.60	38	18	43	2.0	7.6	**3.8**	10%	1.1	12.0	100	$21
Consist	A	1st Half		7	4	0	107	88	3.44	1.16	245			25.8	29%	74%	3.64	41	18	41	2.3	7.4	**3.3**	9%	1.0	9.3	91	$12
LIMA Plan	C	2nd Half		6	4	0	88	77	3.89	1.12	251			25.4	29%	70%	3.56	35	19	46	1.6	7.9	**4.8**	10%	1.2	2.7	111	$10
Rand Var	0	11	Proj	**12**	**8**	**0**	**189**	**157**	**3.82**	**1.22**	**252**			**25.2**	**29%**	**73%**	**3.84**	**39**	**18**	**43**	**2.4**	**7.5**	**3.1**	**10%**	**1.1**	**10.4**	**87**	**$19**

Returned from Tommy John surgery without skipping a beat; BPV continued to improve in each half. Mid-season trip to DL for elbow shows health still a concern. Bid, but don't overpay.
UP: 15+ Wins

Marmol,Carlos		Yr	Tm	W	L	Sv	IP	K	ERA	WHIP	OBA	vL	vR	BF/G	H%	S%	xERA	G	L	F	Ctl	Dom	Cmd	hr/f	hr/9	RAR	BPV	R$
RH RP	28	06	CHC *	8	9	0	138	117	5.21	1.59	252	229	263	19.5	30%	68%	5.52	29	18	53	5.8	7.6	**1.3**	7%	1.0	-12.2	-12	$4
Ht/Wt	74 180	07	CHC *	9	2	1	110	134	2.87	1.14	200	209	146	6.7	28%	77%	3.58	31	16	52	3.9	10.9	**2.8**	6%	0.7	21.1	101	$18
Type	Pwr xFB	08	CHC	2	4	7	87	114	2.68	0.93	140	180	98	4.1	18%	77%	3.20	35	10	55	4.2	11.8	**2.8**	10%	1.0	17.1	110	$16
Health	A	09	CHC	2	4	15	74	93	3.41	1.46	171	136	200	4.1	26%	75%	4.45	36	16	48	7.9	11.3	**1.4**	3%	0.2	7.2	4	$10
PT/Exp	B	10	CHC	2	3	38	78	138	2.55	1.18	154	130	161	4.1	32%	77%	2.53	35	17	48	6.0	16.0	**2.7**	2%	0.1	14.1	138	$23
Consist	D	1st Half		2	1	15	38	69	2.13	1.24	157			4.2	33%	83%	2.42	38	21	41	6.4	16.3	**2.6**	4%	0.2	8.8	137	$11
LIMA Plan	C	2nd Half		0	2	23	40	69	2.95	1.13	152			4.1	32%	71%	2.61	33	13	54	5.7	15.6	**2.8**	0%	0.0	5.2	139	$12
Rand Var	-3	11	Proj	**2**	**3**	**33**	**73**	**109**	**3.60**	**1.30**	**180**			**4.5**	**30%**	**73%**	**3.31**	**35**	**15**	**50**	**6.1**	**13.5**	**2.2**	**7%**	**0.6**	**7.4**	**92**	**$18**

In 78 innings, he walked 52 and struck out 138. The same wildness that causes all the walks also keeps batters from making solid contact. Just watch out if Dom falls. Roster along with a large bottle of antacid.

BILL MACEY

Marquis,Jason		Yr	Tm	W	L	Sv	IP	K	ERA	WHIP	OBA	vL	vR	BF/G	H%	S%	xERA	G	L	F	Ctl	Dom	Cmd	hr/f	hr/9	RAR	BPV	R$
RH SP	32	06	STL	14	16	0	194	96	6.03	1.52	288	288	291	26.1	29%	64%	5.23	43	17	40	3.5	4.5	1.3	13%	1.6	-36.9	7	$3
Ht/Wt	73 210	07	CHC	12	9	0	192	109	4.60	1.39	260	274	242	24.3	28%	69%	4.51	50	17	33	3.6	5.1	1.4	11%	1.0	-4.1	23	$11
Type	GB	08	CHC	11	9	0	167	91	4.53	1.45	268	244	287	25.2	29%	70%	4.64	48	20	33	3.8	4.9	1.3	8%	0.8	-5.3	12	$8
Health	D	09	COL	15	13	0	216	115	4.04	1.38	264	275	258	28.1	29%	71%	4.13	56	17	27	3.3	4.8	1.4	8%	0.6	3.9	30	$13
PT/Exp	A	10	WAS	2	9	0	59	31	6.59	1.70	315	336	296	20.9	33%	63%	4.50	53	18	29	3.7	4.8	1.3	15%	1.4	-18.7	17	($3)
Consist	A	1st Half		0	3	0	8	3	20.60	2.89	435			16.1	44%	23%	6.17	51	32	16	6.5	3.3	0.5	32%	2.2	-17.0	-88	($4)
LIMA Plan	D	2nd Half		2	6	0	50	28	4.29	1.51	290			22.3	31%	75%	4.24	54	15	31	3.2	5.0	1.6	13%	1.2	-1.7	35	$1
Rand Var	+5	11	Proj	9	11	0	145	79	4.53	1.46	275			24.4	30%	70%	4.23	52	21	27	3.5	4.9	1.4	11%	0.9	-1.6	24	$5

Sidelined until August after elbow surgery (bone chips), was vintage upon return. Of course, "vintage" is relative here. If your league values GBs & mediocre stat consistency, he is your guy.

Marshall,Sean		Yr	Tm	W	L	Sv	IP	K	ERA	WHIP	OBA	vL	vR	BF/G	H%	S%	xERA	G	L	F	Ctl	Dom	Cmd	hr/f	hr/9	RAR	BPV	R$
LH RP	28	06	CHC *	6	11	0	146	95	5.48	1.55	271	256	273	23.4	29%	67%	4.89	47	17	36	4.6	5.8	1.3	12%	1.3	-17.9	7	$2
Ht/Wt	79 220	07	CHC *	9	8	0	128	79	3.65	1.36	264	203	280	21.8	29%	77%	4.38	48	16	36	3.1	5.6	1.8	11%	1.2	12.3	43	$11
Type	Pwr	08	CHC *	4	6	1	97	76	4.01	1.28	255	269	236	9.9	30%	72%	4.09	41	17	42	2.8	7.1	2.6	9%	1.1	3.2	72	$7
Health	A	09	CHC	3	7	0	85	68	4.33	1.44	274	243	289	6.8	32%	73%	3.77	49	23	28	3.4	7.2	2.1	14%	1.1	-1.4	65	$3
PT/Exp	C	10	CHC	7	5	1	75	90	2.65	1.11	216	196	218	3.8	31%	76%	2.41	52	23	25	3.0	10.8	3.6	7%	0.4	12.6	144	$12
Consist	B	1st Half		5	2	1	38	44	2.11	1.12	212			3.9	30%	81%	2.61	53	20	27	3.3	10.3	3.1	4%	0.2	9.0	128	$7
LIMA Plan	B+	2nd Half		2	3	0	36	46	3.21	1.10	220			3.7	32%	71%	2.21	52	26	23	2.7	11.4	4.2	10%	0.5	3.6	161	$5
Rand Var	0	11	Proj	5	6	3	80	79	3.50	1.25	243			5.4	31%	74%	3.13	49	22	29	3.2	8.9	2.8	11%	0.8	9.9	103	$9

Transitioned to fulltime RP role in spectacular fashion, with across-the-board breakout built on '09 2H. Skills improved again in 2H, though luck didn't. GB% says hr/9 gains are real. There's little not to like here.

Marte,Damaso		Yr	Tm	W	L	Sv	IP	K	ERA	WHIP	OBA	vL	vR	BF/G	H%	S%	xERA	G	L	F	Ctl	Dom	Cmd	hr/f	hr/9	RAR	BPV	R$
LH RP	36	06	PIT	1	7	0	58	63	3.72	1.41	237	225	258	3.4	31%	75%	4.08	34	25	41	4.8	9.8	2.0	8%	0.8	5.5	58	$4
Ht/Wt	74 213	07	PIT	2	0	0	45	51	2.38	1.10	200	94	271	2.8	28%	79%	3.38	43	13	44	3.6	10.1	2.8	4%	0.4	11.4	106	$7
Type	Pwr xFB	08	2TM	5	3	5	65	71	4.02	1.20	221	247	196	3.7	30%	67%	3.62	33	23	44	3.6	9.8	2.7	7%	0.7	2.3	91	$9
Health	F	09	NYY	1	3	0	13	13	9.69	1.62	290			2.8	34%	39%	4.80	29	15	56	4.2	9.0	2.2	14%	2.1	-8.4	57	($1)
PT/Exp	D	10	NYY	0	0	0	18	12	4.07	1.19	167	146	190	2.4	17%	68%	5.13	31	13	56	5.6	6.1	1.1	7%	1.0	0.2	-32	$1
Consist	B	1st Half		0	0	0	17	12	4.31	1.26	175			2.4	19%	68%	5.18	31	14	55	5.9	6.5	1.1	8%	1.1	-0.4	-35	$1
LIMA Plan	C+	2nd Half		0	0	0	1	0	0.00	0.00	0			2.9	0%		3.65	33	0	67	0.0	0.0		0%		0.5	11	$0
Rand Var	-5	11	Proj	0	0	0	10	9	4.50	1.40	242			3.1	29%	69%	4.52	33	17	50	4.5	8.1	1.8	7%	0.9	-0.3	35	$0

More shoulder problems ended season in July; late Oct labrum surgery puts 2011 in doubt. Health woes obviously factor into poor Dom and Ctl trends, but you have better bets than his post-surgery comeback.

Martin,J.D.		Yr	Tm	W	L	Sv	IP	K	ERA	WHIP	OBA	vL	vR	BF/G	H%	S%	xERA	G	L	F	Ctl	Dom	Cmd	hr/f	hr/9	RAR	BPV	R$
RH SP	28	06		0	0	0	0	0	0.00	0.00							0.00											
Ht/Wt	76 200	07	aa	2	3	0	42	20	5.40	1.60	299			21.1	32%	67%	5.62				3.6	4.3	1.2		0.9	-4.9	19	$0
Type	Con FB	08	a/a	12	3	0	89	67	3.29	1.37	282			10.9	33%	79%	4.58				2.3	6.7	2.9		0.8	11.2	74	$11
Health	C	09	WAS *	13	7	0	165	89	3.93	1.27	273	307	252	22.3	29%	72%	4.62	37	17	46	1.9	4.9	2.6	7%	1.0	5.3	52	$14
PT/Exp	D	10	WAS *	3	7	0	89	51	4.35	1.39	294	337	245	24.0	32%	72%	4.47	38	20	43	2.0	5.2	2.6	9%	1.2	-3.7	55	$2
Consist	A	1st Half		2	6	0	76	42	4.05	1.35	295			24.8	32%	72%	4.41	36	20	44	1.5	5.0	3.4	7%	1.0	-0.3	64	$3
LIMA Plan	B	2nd Half		1	1	0	13	9	6.09	1.65	286			20.3	28%	72%	4.96	41	18	41	4.7	6.1	1.3	22%	2.7	-3.4	1	($0)
Rand Var	0	11	Proj	2	2	0	29	17	4.34	1.38	288			17.8	31%	72%	4.52	39	18	43	2.2	5.3	2.4	10%	1.2	-1.4	53	$2

1-5, 4.13 ERA in 48 IP at WAS. Year ended in July with surgery for season-long back issues. Health joins Dom and GB% as reasons not to chase him. Ctl keeps him watchable.

Masset,Nick		Yr	Tm	W	L	Sv	IP	K	ERA	WHIP	OBA	vL	vR	BF/G	H%	S%	xERA	G	L	F	Ctl	Dom	Cmd	hr/f	hr/9	RAR	BPV	R$
RH RP	28	06	a/a	6	7	3	115	88	5.32	1.75	314			16.8	38%	68%	5.79				4.1	6.9	1.7		0.5	-11.4	54	$2
Ht/Wt	76 235	07	CHW *	2	7	0	84	50	6.75	1.79	325			10.5	35%	63%	5.32	43	17	40	3.8	5.3	1.4	9%	1.2	-23.4	12	($4)
Type	Pwr	08	2TM	2	0	1	62	43	3.92	1.56	289	262	316	6.6	33%	78%	4.14	53	20	28	3.8	6.2	1.7	12%	1.0	3.0	41	$3
Health	A	09	CIN	5	1	0	76	70	2.37	1.03	201	219	194	4.1	25%	81%	3.07	54	14	32	2.8	8.3	2.9	9%	0.7	17.1	105	$12
PT/Exp	C	10	CIN	4	4	2	77	85	3.40	1.26	228	196	242	3.9	30%	76%	3.16	47	19	34	3.9	10.0	2.6	10%	0.8	5.8	100	$8
Consist	B	1st Half		3	3	1	37	40	5.35	1.68	292			4.0	37%	70%	3.65	46	23	31	4.6	9.7	2.1	15%	1.2	-6.1	75	$1
LIMA Plan	B+	2nd Half		1	1	1	40	45	1.59	0.88	158			3.8	22%	85%	2.72	48	14	38	3.2	10.2	3.2	6%	0.5	11.9	124	$7
Rand Var	0	11	Proj	4	2	5	73	71	3.48	1.27	236			4.6	30%	74%	3.37	50	17	33	3.6	8.8	2.4	9%	0.7	6.9	89	$8

Poor Ctl, bad H% and hr/f luck fueled miserable 1H. Put it all back together gradually as the season progressed. Dom still on uptick, volatility remains an issue. Consistency, more Cmd would give him closer upside.

Masterson,Justin		Yr	Tm	W	L	Sv	IP	K	ERA	WHIP	OBA	vL	vR	BF/G	H%	S%	xERA	G	L	F	Ctl	Dom	Cmd	hr/f	hr/9	RAR	BPV	R$
RH SP	26	06		0	0	0	0	0	0.00	0.00							0.00											
Ht/Wt	78 250	07	aa	4	3	0	58	43	6.21	1.50	287			25.6	34%	57%	4.98				3.3	6.6	2.0		0.7	-12.5	57	$1
Type	Pwr xGB	08	BOS *	8	8	0	136	106	3.79	1.29	236	238	196	11.9	28%	72%	3.63	54	18	27	3.8	7.0	1.9	10%	0.7	9.4	57	$13
Health	A	09	2AL	4	10	0	129	119	4.52	1.45	260	323	203	13.5	32%	70%	3.77	54	15	31	4.2	8.3	2.0	10%	0.8	-1.2	68	$7
PT/Exp	B	10	CLE	6	13	0	180	140	4.70	1.50	280	290	263	23.4	33%	69%	3.49	60	15	25	3.7	7.0	1.9	10%	0.7	-12.5	65	$5
Consist	A	1st Half		3	7	0	95	77	4.85	1.56	284			26.5	34%	68%	3.27	64	15	21	4.0	7.3	1.8	10%	0.6	-8.3	66	$2
LIMA Plan	C+	2nd Half		3	6	0	85	63	4.54	1.43	274			20.6	32%	69%	3.69	55	15	30	3.3	6.6	2.0	10%	0.8	-4.2	64	$3
Rand Var	+3	11	Proj	8	13	0	189	152	4.39	1.42	263			24.1	31%	70%	3.63	56	15	28	3.7	7.3	1.9	10%	0.8	15.3	65	$10

Upside remains; role still iffy. Dom, xERA fell all year until Sept move to pen. H% and 4.3 Ctl vs. LHers remain issues. Can't give up on this skill set at this age, but 28% PQS-DIS is troubling.

Mathieson,Scott		Yr	Tm	W	L	Sv	IP	K	ERA	WHIP	OBA	vL	vR	BF/G	H%	S%	xERA	G	L	F	Ctl	Dom	Cmd	hr/f	hr/9	RAR	BPV	R$
RH RP	27	06	PHI *	11	7	0	164	141	5.54	1.40	271			25.3	32%	62%	4.24	35	24	41	3.1	7.7	2.5	11%	1.3	-21.3	68	$9
Ht/Wt	75 190	07	aa	0	0	0	2	1	9.28	2.58	354			5.5	31%	75%	12.95				9.3	4.4	0.5		4.6	-1.2	******	($0)
Type	Pwr FB	08		0	0	0	0	0	0.00	0.00							0.00											
Health	F	09	aa	2	0	1	19	16	3.32	1.05	183			5.8	21%	72%	2.49				3.8	7.6	2.0		0.9	2.3	77	$3
PT/Exp	F	10	PHI *	3	6	26	66	70	3.97	1.42	260			5.1	32%	77%	2.86	63	13	25	3.8	9.6	2.5	23%	1.4	0.3	110	$13
Consist	A	1st Half		3	2	14	35	36	3.71	1.36	245			4.8	30%	78%	2.37	80	0	20	4.0	9.3	2.3	27%	1.3	1.3	117	$8
LIMA Plan	B+	2nd Half		0	4	12	31	34	4.27	1.48	276			5.4	35%	77%	3.48	33	33	33	3.7	10.0	2.7	18%	1.5	-1.0	92	$5
Rand Var	+5	11	Proj	2	3	0	44	43	4.34	1.36	255			7.4	31%	72%	3.83	35	24	41	3.5	8.9	2.5	12%	1.2	1.7	79	$3

0-0, 10.80 ERA in 2 IP at PHI. Health grade reflects two career-stunting TJ surgeries; logged more DL time (strained back) in Sept with PHI. Dom is still intriguing, but durability is the issue.

Matsuzaka,Daisuke		Yr	Tm	W	L	Sv	IP	K	ERA	WHIP	OBA	vL	vR	BF/G	H%	S%	xERA	G	L	F	Ctl	Dom	Cmd	hr/f	hr/9	RAR	BPV	R$
RH SP	30	06	JPN	17	5	0	186	211	2.64	1.02	220			29.4	29%	80%	2.96				2.0	10.2	5.0		1.0	43.2	146	$34
Ht/Wt	72 185	07	BOS	15	12	0	205	201	4.40	1.32	249	238	253	27.1	31%	70%	3.96	38	18	44	3.5	8.8	2.5	10%	1.1	2.7	80	$20
Type	Pwr FB	08	BOS	18	3	0	168	154	2.90	1.32	213	225	195	24.5	27%	80%	4.33	39	18	43	5.0	8.3	1.6	6%	0.6	30.0	29	$23
Health	F	09	BOS	4	6	0	59	54	5.77	1.87	326	340	304	23.7	39%	72%	4.99	34	23	43	4.6	8.2	1.8	12%	1.5	-9.6	37	($0)
PT/Exp	B	10	BOS	9	6	0	154	133	4.68	1.37	240	265	211	26.4	29%	66%	4.35	33	22	45	4.3	7.8	1.8	7%	0.8	-10.3	34	$9
Consist	B	1st Half		5	3	0	60	50	4.50	1.35	228			25.6	28%	65%	4.53	31	22	47	4.7	7.5	1.6	4%	0.5	-2.7	18	$5
LIMA Plan	C	2nd Half		4	3	0	94	83	4.80	1.39	248			26.9	30%	67%	4.23	34	21	44	4.1	8.0	1.9	8%	1.0	-7.7	44	$5
Rand Var	0	11	Proj	10	8	0	146	132	4.57	1.47	259			25.6	31%	72%	4.41	35	21	44	4.3	8.2	1.9	10%	1.2	-2.1	43	$9

The upside he once showed in Japan is as far away as his homeland. Third straight year of arm woes; FB% and Ctl keep him combustible. Let's just admit it was an expensive mistake and move on.

Matusz,Brian		Yr	Tm	W	L	Sv	IP	K	ERA	WHIP	OBA	vL	vR	BF/G	H%	S%	xERA	G	L	F	Ctl	Dom	Cmd	hr/f	hr/9	RAR	BPV	R$
LH SP	24	06		0	0	0	0	0	0.00	0.00							0.00											
Ht/Wt	77 200	07		0	0	0	0	0	0.00	0.00							0.00											
Type	Pwr xFB	08		0	0	0	0	0	0.00	0.00							0.00											
Health	A	09	BAL *	12	2	0	91	77	3.47	1.30	264	200	315	23.9	32%	76%	4.26	31	21	48	2.6	7.6	3.0	7%	0.9	11.0	77	$13
PT/Exp	C	10	BAL	10	12	0	176	143	4.30	1.34	259	218	266	23.4	30%	70%	4.17	36	19	45	3.2	7.3	2.3	8%	1.0	-3.6	59	$12
Consist	A	1st Half		3	9	0	101	78	4.56	1.39	272			25.5	32%	69%	4.32	35	18	46	3.0	7.0	2.3	8%	1.0	-5.2	57	$4
LIMA Plan	C+	2nd Half		7	3	0	75	65	3.96	1.28	241			21.0	29%	72%	3.97	37	20	43	3.5	7.8	2.2	9%	1.0	1.7	62	$8
Rand Var	0	11	Proj	13	14	0	189	158	3.92	1.32	258			25.0	30%	74%	4.16	35	20	45	3.0	7.5	2.5	9%	1.1	2.9	68	$17

PRO: Seven PQS-5s, six wins in final ten starts; dominance. CON: 2H Ctl and BF/G; an xFBer pitching in the AL East. Impressive last-ditch rebound by rookie after miserable start. A consolidation year is likely.

JOCK THOMPSON

Maya,Yunesky

		W	L	Sv	IP	K	ERA	WHIP	OBA	vL	vR	BF/G	H%	S%	xERA	G	L	F	Ctl	Dom	Cmd	hr/f	hr/9	RAR	BPV	R$
RH SP 29	06	0	0	0	0	0	0.00	0.00							0.00											
Ht/Wt 71 170	07	0	0	0	0	0	0.00	0.00							0.00											
Type FB	08	0	0	0	0	0	0.00	0.00							0.00											
Health A	09	0	0	0	0	0	0.00	0.00							0.00											
PT/Exp F	10 WAS *	1	4	0	36	19	4.51	1.56	282	333	250	23.1	31%	72%	5.30	33	23	44	4.1	4.8	**1.2**	6%	0.7	-2.2	-14	($0)
Consist F	1st Half	0	0	0	0	0	0.00	0.00							0.00											
LIMA Plan C	2nd Half	1	4	0	36	19	4.51	1.56	282			23.1	31%	72%	5.30	33	23	44	4.1	4.8	**1.2**	6%	0.7	-2.2	-14	($0)
Rand Var -2	11 Proj	**3**	**8**	**0**	**87**	**51**	**4.76**	**1.49**	**281**			**22.6**	**30%**	**71%**	**5.05**	**33**	**23**	**44**	**3.5**	**5.3**	**1.5**	**9%**	**1.2**	**-9.8**	**11**	**$1**

0-3, 5.88 ERA in 26 IP at WAS. Cuban defector signed in July, fast-tracked to majors. Not projected to dominate; expected Ctl didn't flash until final start. Rotation back-end fodder at best; avoid for now.

Mazzaro,Vin

		W	L	Sv	IP	K	ERA	WHIP	OBA	vL	vR	BF/G	H%	S%	xERA	G	L	F	Ctl	Dom	Cmd	hr/f	hr/9	RAR	BPV	R$
RH SP 24	06	0	0	0	0	0	0.00	0.00							0.00											
Ht/Wt 73 215	07	0	0	0	0	0	0.00	0.00							0.00											
Type	08 aa	15	6	0	171	112	2.84	1.25	265			25.5	31%	77%	3.44				2.1	5.9	**2.8**		0.3	30.9	88	$20
Health A	09 OAK *	6	11	0	148	97	4.27	1.48	284	321	316	24.1	32%	73%	4.74	39	21	40	3.3	5.9	**1.8**	7%	0.9	3.3	35	$7
PT/Exp D	10 OAK *	9	9	0	159	112	3.95	1.42	265	289	246	22.3	29%	76%	4.26	43	21	37	3.7	6.3	**1.7**	12%	1.2	3.7	36	$9
Consist B	1st Half	7	3	0	87	64	3.42	1.43	264			22.2	30%	79%	4.22	43	19	38	3.7	6.6	**1.8**	9%	0.9	7.7	40	$7
LIMA Plan C	2nd Half	2	6	0	73	48	4.59	1.42	265			22.5	28%	73%	4.32	43	21	36	3.6	6.0	**1.7**	14%	1.5	-4.0	31	$2
Rand Var 0	11 Proj	**7**	**8**	**0**	**131**	**88**	**4.07**	**1.42**	**271**			**23.6**	**30%**	**74%**	**4.40**	**42**	**21**	**38**	**3.3**	**6.1**	**1.8**	**10%**	**1.0**	**-1.7**	**39**	**$8**

6-8, 4.27 ERA in 122 IP at OAK. Put up a 66%/7% PQS-DOM/DIS over 15 starts before late Aug crash sent him to the pen. Inflated hr/f was a reason, but marginal Cmd keeps his rotation outlook iffy.

McClellan,Kyle

		W	L	Sv	IP	K	ERA	WHIP	OBA	vL	vR	BF/G	H%	S%	xERA	G	L	F	Ctl	Dom	Cmd	hr/f	hr/9	RAR	BPV	R$
RH RP 26	06	0	0	0	0	0	0.00	0.00							0.00											
Ht/Wt 74 215	07 aa	2	0	0	30	25	2.77	1.09	239			5.0	29%	77%	3.06				1.8	7.5	**4.1**		0.6	6.3	119	$4
Type Pwr GB	08 STL	2	7	1	76	59	4.04	1.39	270	238	291	4.8	32%	72%	3.83	48	21	31	3.1	7.0	**2.3**	10%	0.8	2.1	69	$4
Health B	09 STL	4	4	3	67	51	3.37	1.35	229	198	252	4.3	27%	76%	4.07	50	19	31	4.6	6.9	**1.5**	7%	0.5	6.7	28	$7
PT/Exp C	10 STL	1	4	2	75	60	2.27	1.08	215	204	214	4.4	24%	86%	3.41	51	13	36	2.7	7.2	**2.6**	12%	1.1	16.2	84	$9
Consist A	1st Half	0	2	1	37	33	2.43	1.03	217			4.6	26%	82%	3.22	45	16	38	2.2	8.0	**3.7**	10%	1.0	7.2	109	$4
LIMA Plan B	2nd Half	1	2	1	38	27	2.11	1.12	212			4.3	23%	89%	3.58	56	11	33	3.3	6.3	**1.9**	14%	1.2	9.0	59	$4
Rand Var -5	11 Proj	**2**	**4**	**0**	**73**	**57**	**3.35**	**1.27**	**244**			**4.6**	**29%**	**76%**	**3.69**	**51**	**16**	**33**	**3.2**	**7.1**	**2.2**	**10%**	**0.9**	**4.1**	**69**	**$5**

Shaved almost 2 bb/9 off Ctl; fortunate H%, S% made it a career year. Some regression on these fronts is inevitable. But with consistent Dom and GB%, he'll remain valuable if he consolidates Ctl gains.

McCutchen,Daniel

		W	L	Sv	IP	K	ERA	WHIP	OBA	vL	vR	BF/G	H%	S%	xERA	G	L	F	Ctl	Dom	Cmd	hr/f	hr/9	RAR	BPV	R$
RH RP 28	06	0	0	0	0	0	0.00	0.00							0.00											
Ht/Wt 74 214	07 aa	3	2	0	41	27	3.90	1.36	262			25.0	30%	72%	4.22				3.2	5.9	**1.9**		0.7	2.8	55	$4
Type Con xFB	08 a/a	11	12	0	171	113	4.85	1.45	303			26.7	33%	72%	5.86				2.0	6.0	**2.9**		1.6	-11.5	44	$8
Health A	09 PIT *	14	8	0	179	105	4.31	1.41	295	262	280	25.7	33%	71%	4.45	40	20	40	2.0	5.3	**2.6**	7%	0.8	-2.6	59	$11
PT/Exp D	10 PIT *	6	13	0	147	69	5.33	1.45	286	315	286	15.6	29%	67%	5.13	36	16	48	2.8	4.2	**1.5**	10%	1.5	-23.8	14	$0
Consist C	1st Half	5	8	0	84	35	5.72	1.46	295			22.8	30%	63%	4.98	40	17	43	2.5	3.8	**1.5**	10%	1.4	-17.6	19	$0
LIMA Plan C+	2nd Half	1	5	0	63	33	4.81	1.43	274			11.0	28%	72%	5.17	34	15	50	3.3	4.8	**1.4**	11%	1.6	-6.2	8	$0
Rand Var 0	11 Proj	**3**	**4**	**0**	**58**	**32**	**4.81**	**1.43**	**288**			**13.3**	**30%**	**70%**	**4.92**	**37**	**16**	**47**	**2.6**	**5.0**	**1.9**	**10%**	**1.4**	**-5.6**	**33**	**$2**

2-5, 6.12 ERA in 68 IP at PIT. Once Cmd goes this far south, the rest of his skill set looks like one big glaring weakness. A slightly less fortunate 2H H% turns this into a disaster. And FWIW, that was sarcasm.

McDonald,James

		W	L	Sv	IP	K	ERA	WHIP	OBA	vL	vR	BF/G	H%	S%	xERA	G	L	F	Ctl	Dom	Cmd	hr/f	hr/9	RAR	BPV	R$
RH SP 26	06	0	0	0	0	0	0.00	0.00							0.00											
Ht/Wt 77 195	07 aa	7	2	0	52	56	1.72	1.19	238			21.4	30%	93%	3.70				2.8	9.7	**3.5**		1.0	17.6	108	$11
Type Pwr FB	08 a/a	7	4	0	141	124	3.75	1.32	248			22.1	30%	75%	4.12				3.5	7.9	**2.3**		1.1	9.7	69	$12
Health A	09 LA *	6	5	0	93	90	3.78	1.40	238	213	282	7.9	30%	75%	4.02	44	17	39	4.7	8.7	**1.9**	8%	0.8	4.7	53	$7
PT/Exp D	10 2NL *	10	7	0	135	115	3.82	1.33	256	250	271	21.2	32%	71%	4.20	30	23	46	3.3	7.6	**2.3**	4%	0.5	3.2	57	$11
Consist A	1st Half	4	1	0	46	39	4.14	1.38	276			22.0	34%	70%	4.13				2.8	7.5	**2.7**		0.6	-0.7	85	$3
LIMA Plan C	2nd Half	6	6	0	89	76	3.66	1.31	245			20.8	31%	71%	4.21	30	23	46	3.6	7.7	**2.2**	3%	0.4	3.9	51	$7
Rand Var -2	11 Proj	**10**	**13**	**0**	**189**	**170**	**4.11**	**1.34**	**250**			**23.6**	**30%**	**72%**	**4.09**	**35**	**21**	**44**	**3.6**	**8.1**	**2.3**	**9%**	**1.0**	**1.3**	**63**	**$13**

4-6, 4.02 ERA in 72 IP at PIT. PRO: Dom; rising Cmd; 42% PQS-DOM in first legit rotation shot. CON: Volatile Ctl; rising FB%. Sleeper. If things break right... UP: 14 wins, 3.80 ERA.

Meche,Gil

		W	L	Sv	IP	K	ERA	WHIP	OBA	vL	vR	BF/G	H%	S%	xERA	G	L	F	Ctl	Dom	Cmd	hr/f	hr/9	RAR	BPV	R$
RH RP 32	06 SEA	11	8	0	186	156	4.50	1.43	258	240	271	25.3	30%	72%	4.30	43	18	38	4.1	7.5	**1.9**	11%	1.2	1.4	47	$14
Ht/Wt 75 214	07 KC	9	13	0	216	156	3.67	1.30	264	242	284	26.8	30%	74%	3.98	47	18	35	2.6	6.5	**2.5**	9%	0.9	22.3	72	$19
Type	08 KC	14	11	0	210	183	3.98	1.32	256	238	273	26.2	31%	71%	3.92	39	22	39	3.1	7.8	**2.5**	8%	0.8	9.5	74	$20
Health F	09 KC	6	10	0	129	95	5.09	1.57	284	268	292	25.2	32%	70%	4.46	49	17	34	4.0	6.6	**1.6**	12%	1.2	-10.2	37	$4
PT/Exp B	10 KC	0	5	0	62	41	5.69	1.67	272	273	274	14.2	30%	68%	5.03	45	18	38	5.5	6.0	**1.1**	12%	1.3	-11.8	-19	($2)
Consist B	1st Half	0	4	0	49	30	6.65	1.85	290			25.8	31%	65%	5.55	45	18	38	6.3	5.5	**0.9**	11%	1.3	-15.1	-47	($4)
LIMA Plan D+	2nd Half	0	1	0	13	11	2.08	1.00	197			4.6	21%	91%	3.30	45	18	36	2.8	7.6	**2.8**	16%	1.4	3.3	86	$2
Rand Var +1	11 Proj	**2**	**3**	**0**	**44**	**33**	**4.14**	**1.38**	**264**			**6.9**	**30%**	**73%**	**4.07**	**45**	**18**	**37**	**3.3**	**6.8**	**2.1**	**10%**	**1.0**	**1.1**	**57**	**$3**

Rebound shot now murky at best given durability issues. 2H BPIs came from intriguing Sept bullpen audition. But now two years from last effective / healthy stretch, he has a lot to prove, regardless of role.

Medlen,Kris

		W	L	Sv	IP	K	ERA	WHIP	OBA	vL	vR	BF/G	H%	S%	xERA	G	L	F	Ctl	Dom	Cmd	hr/f	hr/9	RAR	BPV	R$
RH RP 25	06	0	0	0	0	0	0.00	0.00							0.00											
Ht/Wt 70 190	07	0	0	0	0	0	0.00	0.00							0.00											
Type Pwr	08 aa	7	8	1	120	102	4.17	1.39	291			14.4	36%	70%	4.53				2.1	7.6	**3.7**		0.6	2.0	101	$9
Health B	09 ATL *	8	5	0	105	111	3.26	1.22	229	183	328	9.7	31%	73%	3.36	41	23	36	3.4	9.5	**2.8**	5%	0.4	12.0	98	$13
PT/Exp C	10 ATL	6	2	0	108	83	3.68	1.20	262	281	257	14.3	30%	73%	3.50	43	22	35	1.8	6.9	**4.0**	11%	1.1	4.5	98	$9
Consist B	1st Half	5	1	0	81	59	3.01	1.13	253			14.2	29%	78%	3.57	43	19	38	1.6	6.6	**4.2**	10%	1.0	10.0	97	$9
LIMA Plan A	2nd Half	1	1	0	27	24	5.67	1.41	289			14.6	34%	62%	3.25	44	30	26	2.3	8.0	**3.4**	19%	1.3	-5.5	103	$0
Rand Var 0	11 Proj	**1**	**1**	**0**	**15**	**13**	**4.34**	**1.17**	**241**			**11.9**	**30%**	**63%**	**3.31**	**43**	**25**	**32**	**2.5**	**8.1**	**3.3**	**8%**	**0.6**	**1.5**	**99**	**$1**

Season ended in mid-August with TJ surgery; will be out for at least 12 months. 3.04 ERA in 23 IP as RP; 7 PQS-DOMs over 10-game stretch from from May-July as SP. Fine 2012 keeper-league stash.

Meek,Evan

		W	L	Sv	IP	K	ERA	WHIP	OBA	vL	vR	BF/G	H%	S%	xERA	G	L	F	Ctl	Dom	Cmd	hr/f	hr/9	RAR	BPV	R$
RH RP 27	06	0	0	0	0	0	0.00	0.00							0.00											
Ht/Wt 72 220	07 aa	2	1	1	67	58	5.51	1.87	319			7.3	40%	68%	6.03				4.9	7.8	**1.6**		0.3	-8.7	62	($1)
Type Pwr xGB	08 a/a	1	1	4	57	39	3.50	1.32	260			7.6	31%	73%	3.65				3.0	6.1	**2.0**		0.4	5.7	72	$5
Health B	09 PIT	1	1	0	47	42	3.45	1.34	204	250	176	4.9	26%	74%	3.89	52	19	29	5.6	8.0	**1.4**	6%	0.4	4.3	25	$3
PT/Exp D	10 PIT	5	4	4	80	70	2.14	1.05	190	168	199	4.5	24%	82%	3.03	57	16	27	3.5	7.9	**2.3**	9%	0.6	18.5	82	$13
Consist B	1st Half	4	2	1	47	42	0.96	0.85	180			4.7	23%	92%	2.72	52	18	30	2.1	8.0	**3.8**	6%	0.4	17.7	118	$10
LIMA Plan C	2nd Half	1	2	3	33	28	3.82	1.33	205			4.4	24%	73%	3.47	63	13	24	5.5	7.6	**1.4**	14%	0.8	0.8	31	$3
Rand Var -5	11 Proj	**3**	**3**	**20**	**73**	**61**	**3.48**	**1.34**	**236**			**5.2**	**29%**	**75%**	**3.55**	**56**	**17**	**27**	**4.2**	**7.6**	**1.8**	**9%**	**0.6**	**5.3**	**56**	**$12**

Breakthrough season until Ctl monster reappeared in 2H. It's the only flaw in a fine skill set. Dom+GB combos like this don't grow on trees, and he can be unhittable at times. Poster-boy for volatile value.

Mejia,Jenrry

		W	L	Sv	IP	K	ERA	WHIP	OBA	vL	vR	BF/G	H%	S%	xERA	G	L	F	Ctl	Dom	Cmd	hr/f	hr/9	RAR	BPV	R$
RH RP 21	06	0	0	0	0	0	0.00	0.00							0.00											
Ht/Wt 72 162	07	0	0	0	0	0	0.00	0.00							0.00											
Type Pwr xGB	08	0	0	0	0	0	0.00	0.00							0.00											
Health A	09 aa	0	5	0	44	43	4.66	1.51	269			19.5	35%	68%	4.28				4.3	8.8	**2.1**		0.4	-1.9	85	$1
PT/Exp F	10 NYM *	2	4	0	74	54	2.98	1.37	247	203	340	7.9	29%	79%	3.57	61	13	26	4.0	6.5	**1.6**	7%	0.5	9.5	49	$4
Consist B	1st Half	0	2	0	28	17	3.25	1.59	271			4.2	31%	81%	3.89	66	12	22	4.9	5.5	**1.1**	10%	0.6	2.6	12	$0
LIMA Plan C+	2nd Half	2	2	0	46	37	2.82	1.24	233			19.3	29%	77%	3.67	50	15	35	3.4	7.2	**2.1**	4%	0.4	6.8	64	$4
Rand Var -3	11 Proj	**4**	**7**	**0**	**116**	**92**	**3.96**	**1.41**	**257**			**19.3**	**31%**	**72%**	**3.49**	**61**	**13**	**26**	**3.9**	**7.1**	**1.8**	**9%**	**0.6**	**9.3**	**63**	**$6**

0-4, 4.62 ERA in 39 IP at NYM. Rushed to NYM pen, but flashed GB skills before being demoted for rotation grooming. Year ended with three poor Sept starts and shoulder issues. Fine upside, but needs time.

JOCK THOMPSON

Mijares,Jose

	Yr	W	L	Sv	IP	K	ERA	WHIP	OBA	vL	vR	BF/G	H%	S%	xERA	G	L	F	Ctl	Dom	Cmd	hr/f	hr/9	RAR	BPV	R$
LH RP 26	06	0	0	0	0	0	0.00	0.00							0.00											
Ht/Wt 72 231	07 a/a	5	4	9	69	66	5.07	1.66	229			6.2	27%	73%	5.25				7.4	8.6	1.2		1.4	-5.2	42	$6
Type Pwr xFB	08 MIN *	1	2	2	26	20	2.77	1.15	223			5.0	26%	79%	2.94				3.1	6.9	2.2		0.7	5.1	78	$4
Health B	09 MIN	2	2	0	62	55	2.33	1.17	220	147	283	3.6	26%	86%	4.16	37	12	51	3.4	8.0	2.4	8%	1.0	16.1	69	$8
PT/Exp D	10 MIN	1	1	0	33	28	3.30	1.31	269	268	268	2.9	32%	79%	4.22	31	14	55	2.5	7.7	3.1	7%	1.1	3.4	81	$3
Consist B	1st Half	0	0	0	17	11	2.65	1.29	262			3.1	27%	89%	4.87	30	9	60	2.6	5.8	2.2	9%	1.6	3.1	42	$1
LIMA Plan B	2nd Half	1	1	0	16	17	4.01	1.34	277			2.8	37%	70%	3.52	33	20	48	2.3	9.7	4.3	5%	0.6	0.2	124	$1
Rand Var -3	11 Proj	2	2	0	51	46	3.72	1.34	251			3.4	30%	77%	4.33	34	14	52	3.5	8.2	2.3	9%	1.2	-0.3	63	$4

Ten weeks lost to DL (elbow in Apr; knee in Aug) and bereavement interrupted 2010. H%, S% say he was lucky in 1H, but deserved better in 2H. More Cmd consistency is best shot at any upside from here.

Miller,Andrew

	Yr	W	L	Sv	IP	K	ERA	WHIP	OBA	vL	vR	BF/G	H%	S%	xERA	G	L	F	Ctl	Dom	Cmd	hr/f	hr/9	RAR	BPV	R$
LH SP 25	06 DET	0	1	0	10	6	6.24	1.78	219			5.9	26%	61%	4.85	64	24	12	8.9	5.3	0.6	0%	0.0	-2.1	******	($0)
Ht/Wt 79 207	07 DET *	7	5	0	100	85	4.67	1.56	275	175	312	23.6	33%	71%	4.11	49	21	30	4.4	7.6	1.7	11%	0.9	-2.0	46	$6
Type Pwr	08 FLA	6	10	0	107	89	5.87	1.64	284	226	307	16.9	35%	63%	4.40	46	22	33	4.7	7.5	1.6	6%	0.6	-21.2	31	$0
Health B	09 FLA *	4	7	0	98	79	5.05	1.62	266	309	261	18.5	32%	68%	4.45	48	22	30	5.4	7.3	1.3	8%	0.6	-10.4	10	$1
PT/Exp C	10 FLA *	2	13	0	118	82	8.31	2.33	347	405	360	22.9	39%	64%	6.21	38	28	34	7.5	6.3	0.8	10%	1.1	-62.4	-74	($19)
Consist B	1st Half	0	4	0	37	22	9.19	2.34	304			21.6	35%	57%	6.73				10.0	5.3	0.5		0.3	-23.6	29	($8)
LIMA Plan F	2nd Half	2	9	0	81	60	7.91	2.33	365			23.6	41%	67%	5.73	38	28	34	6.4	6.7	1.1	13%	1.4	-38.8	-34	($12)
Rand Var +5	11 Proj	1	4	0	44	33	5.79	1.79	277			20.5	32%	68%	4.89	48	23	29	6.4	6.8	1.1	10%	0.8	-4.0	-24	($2)

1-5, 8.54 ERA in 33 IP at FLA. Never good to see spiking Ctl crossing Dom on the downswing. The good news is that he's likely to tick up from here. The bad news is that at these levels, it doesn't matter.

Miller,Trever

	Yr	W	L	Sv	IP	K	ERA	WHIP	OBA	vL	vR	BF/G	H%	S%	xERA	G	L	F	Ctl	Dom	Cmd	hr/f	hr/9	RAR	BPV	R$
LH RP 37	06 HOU	2	3	1	50	56	3.05	1.10	229	224	225	2.9	29%	79%	3.45	33	18	49	2.3	10.0	4.3	11%	1.3	8.9	128	$7
Ht/Wt 75 185	07 HOU	0	0	1	46	46	4.86	1.47	256	209	289	2.7	32%	69%	4.45	34	18	48	4.5	8.9	2.0	10%	1.2	-2.5	52	$2
Type Pwr FB	08 TAM	2	0	2	43	44	4.16	1.36	242	209	286	2.7	32%	68%	4.05	32	25	44	4.2	9.1	2.2	4%	0.4	1.0	62	$4
Health A	09 STL	4	1	0	44	46	2.06	0.96	201	135	295	2.4	25%	86%	3.21	35	20	45	2.3	9.5	4.2	10%	1.0	11.5	122	$8
PT/Exp D	10 STL	0	1	0	36	22	4.00	1.28	228	203	273	2.7	26%	68%	4.44	41	21	37	4.0	5.5	1.4	5%	0.5	0.1	10	$1
Consist C	1st Half	0	1	0	20	13	3.15	1.05	187			2.7	20%	74%	4.13	42	16	42	3.6	5.9	1.6	8%	0.9	2.1	28	$2
LIMA Plan C	2nd Half	0	0	0	16	9	5.06	1.56	274			2.6	32%	64%	4.83	40	27	33	4.5	5.1	1.1	0%	0.0	-2.1	-12	($0)
Rand Var -4	11 Proj	1	1	0	44	31	4.34	1.40	255			2.7	29%	71%	4.55	38	22	40	3.9	6.4	1.6	9%	1.0	-2.2	25	$1

Is age taking its toll? Couldn't find Dom all season while Ctl issues returned. GB spike helped, and he kept split strength vs LHers, but 2H was disturbing, even with bad luck. If you buy, have an exit plan.

Mills,Brad

	Yr	W	L	Sv	IP	K	ERA	WHIP	OBA	vL	vR	BF/G	H%	S%	xERA	G	L	F	Ctl	Dom	Cmd	hr/f	hr/9	RAR	BPV	R$
LH SP 26	06	0	0	0	0	0	0.00	0.00							0.00											
Ht/Wt 71 185	07	0	0	0	0	0	0.00	0.00							0.00											
Type Pwr xFB	08 aa	3	2	0	32	26	1.44	1.25	235			22.4	29%	92%	3.30				3.5	7.3	2.1		0.6	11.4	79	$5
Health A	09 aaa	8	4	0	84	62	4.28	1.46	273			26.3	32%	71%	4.48				3.6	6.6	1.8		0.6	0.3	59	$3
PT/Exp D	10 TOR *	9	6	0	134	104	4.39	1.37	258	273	220	21.3	30%	69%	4.36	41	11	48	3.4	7.0	2.0	7%	0.9	-4.1	52	$9
Consist B	1st Half	4	4	0	71	57	3.84	1.42	261			23.7	31%	74%	4.12				3.8	7.3	1.9		0.8	2.7	63	$5
LIMA Plan C+	2nd Half	5	2	0	63	47	5.01	1.30	256			19.1	29%	63%	4.29	41	11	48	3.0	6.6	2.2	8%	1.0	-6.8	58	$4
Rand Var -1	11 Proj	3	4	0	58	44	4.19	1.38	262			22.7	30%	73%	4.48	39	14	47	3.4	6.8	2.0	8%	1.1	-1.4	48	$4

1-0, 5.64 ERA in 22 IP at TOR. Dom gives him a shot, but needs better Ctl to survive, particularly as xFBer. Avoided gopheritis in minors (career 0.7 hr/9), but has a 1.8 hr/9 in 30 MLB IP.

Millwood,Kevin

	Yr	W	L	Sv	IP	K	ERA	WHIP	OBA	vL	vR	BF/G	H%	S%	xERA	G	L	F	Ctl	Dom	Cmd	hr/f	hr/9	RAR	BPV	R$
RH SP 36	06 TEX	16	12	0	215	157	4.52	1.31	273	285	258	26.7	31%	67%	3.91	45	21	34	2.2	6.6	3.0	10%	1.0	1.0	81	$20
Ht/Wt 76 230	07 TEX	10	14	0	173	123	5.16	1.62	304	288	311	25.3	35%	69%	4.42	46	21	32	3.5	6.4	1.8	10%	1.0	-13.9	46	$5
Type	08 TEX	9	10	0	169	125	5.07	1.59	316	273	354	26.3	37%	69%	4.23	41	25	34	2.6	6.7	2.6	9%	1.0	-15.0	68	$5
Health C	09 TEX	13	10	0	199	123	3.67	1.34	258	240	272	27.3	28%	77%	4.56	42	19	39	3.2	5.6	1.7	11%	1.2	19.2	34	$17
PT/Exp A	10 BAL	4	16	0	191	132	5.10	1.51	293	307	276	27.3	32%	70%	4.48	37	22	41	3.1	6.2	2.0	12%	1.4	-22.5	45	$2
Consist A	1st Half	2	8	0	107	83	5.40	1.54	303			28.0	34%	69%	4.15	39	23	38	2.8	7.0	2.5	15%	1.7	-16.6	68	$0
LIMA Plan C+	2nd Half	2	8	0	84	49	4.71	1.48	280			26.4	30%	70%	4.91	35	20	45	3.4	5.2	1.5	8%	1.1	-6.0	15	$1
Rand Var +1	11 Proj	9	13	0	189	126	4.44	1.44	281			26.5	31%	72%	4.47	40	21	39	3.1	6.0	2.0	10%	1.2	-4.1	43	$9

A lesson on luck and circumstance. Improved a tick of Cmd, xERA and BPV, but without '09 H%, S% and team. Add a 5% drop in GBs, and $15 of value disappears. 2009 is the value outlier. Avoid.

Minor,Mike

	Yr	W	L	Sv	IP	K	ERA	WHIP	OBA	vL	vR	BF/G	H%	S%	xERA	G	L	F	Ctl	Dom	Cmd	hr/f	hr/9	RAR	BPV	R$
LH SP 23	06	0	0	0	0	0	0.00	0.00							0.00											
Ht/Wt 75 210	07	0	0	0	0	0	0.00	0.00							0.00											
Type Pwr xFB	08	0	0	0	0	0	0.00	0.00							0.00											
Health A	09	0	0	0	0	0	0.00	0.00							0.00											
PT/Exp D	10 ATL *	9	9	0	161	175	4.48	1.33	257	293	320	22.8	34%	67%	3.64	35	17	48	3.2	9.8	3.1	7%	0.8	-9.2	103	$11
Consist F	1st Half	2	6	0	87	99	4.66	1.34	253			24.7	34%	66%	3.92				3.5	10.2	2.9		0.8	-6.9	102	$4
LIMA Plan B	2nd Half	7	3	0	74	76	4.27	1.31	262			20.8	34%	69%	3.69	35	17	48	2.8	9.3	3.3	7%	0.9	-2.3	104	$7
Rand Var +2	11 Proj	12	9	0	174	182	4.19	1.26	247			22.0	31%	70%	3.69	35	17	48	3.0	9.4	3.1	9%	1.1	9.7	101	$16

3-2, 5.98 ERA in 41 IP at ATL. MLB debut marred by horrific 40% H% and 64% S% - mixed in with a 1.3 hr/9. FB% will be an ongoing concern. But this is a Dom / Ctl combo worth buying while the price is low.

Mitre,Sergio

	Yr	W	L	Sv	IP	K	ERA	WHIP	OBA	vL	vR	BF/G	H%	S%	xERA	G	L	F	Ctl	Dom	Cmd	hr/f	hr/9	RAR	BPV	R$
RH RP 30	06 FLA	1	5	0	41	31	5.71	1.56	276	344	232	12.2	30%	67%	4.23	52	20	28	4.4	6.8	1.6	20%	1.5	-6.2	34	($0)
Ht/Wt 75 225	07 FLA	5	8	0	149	80	4.65	1.48	300	271	332	24.3	33%	68%	3.85	60	17	23	2.5	4.8	2.0	8%	0.5	-4.1	58	$4
Type Con GB	08 FLA	0	0	0	0	0	0.00	0.00							0.00											
Health F	09 NYY *	6	4	0	97	60	5.33	1.47	312	421	246	22.3	34%	66%	3.60	58	18	24	1.7	5.6	3.3	18%	1.3	-10.5	90	$4
PT/Exp D	10 NYY	0	3	1	54	29	3.33	1.09	220	226	218	8.0	23%	75%	3.82	51	17	32	2.7	4.8	1.8	13%	1.2	5.4	44	$4
Consist A	1st Half	0	1	0	25	15	2.88	1.00	185			8.2	19%	77%	3.90	49	13	38	3.2	5.4	1.7	11%	1.1	3.9	37	$3
LIMA Plan B	2nd Half	0	2	1	29	14	3.72	1.17	248			7.9	25%	73%	3.75	52	20	28	2.2	4.3	2.0	15%	1.2	1.5	50	$2
Rand Var -2	11 Proj	1	3	0	58	33	3.88	1.33	272			9.5	30%	73%	3.85	54	18	28	2.5	5.1	2.1	11%	0.9	3.1	57	$3

PRO: Consistent GB%, Ctl.
CON: Consistently marginal Dom; a regular DL visitor.
Always has a shot with right team, good infield defense, etc. But health is always a requirement.

Moehler,Brian

	Yr	W	L	Sv	IP	K	ERA	WHIP	OBA	vL	vR	BF/G	H%	S%	xERA	G	L	F	Ctl	Dom	Cmd	hr/f	hr/9	RAR	BPV	R$
RH RP 39	06 FLA	7	11	0	122	58	6.57	1.66	323	351	297	19.2	34%	62%	4.96	45	22	33	2.8	4.3	1.5	13%	1.4	-31.3	25	($2)
Ht/Wt 75 235	07 HOU	1	4	1	60	36	4.07	1.41	285	303	268	6.2	31%	75%	4.13	52	16	32	2.6	5.4	2.1	13%	1.2	2.6	59	$3
Type	08 HOU	11	8	0	150	82	4.56	1.35	282	307	255	20.6	30%	69%	4.34	44	21	35	2.2	4.9	2.3	11%	1.2	-5.4	52	$9
Health F	09 HOU	8	12	0	155	91	5.47	1.54	300	280	316	23.8	32%	66%	4.59	44	20	36	3.0	5.3	1.8	11%	1.2	-24.4	38	$1
PT/Exp B	10 HOU	1	4	0	57	28	4.92	1.62	292	282	314	12.9	32%	70%	5.08	42	22	36	4.1	4.4	1.1	7%	0.8	-6.3	-12	($1)
Consist A	1st Half	1	4	0	54	25	5.20	1.64	294			12.9	31%	69%	5.13	42	23	35	4.2	4.2	1.0	8%	0.8	-7.8	-17	($2)
LIMA Plan F	2nd Half	0	0	0	3	3	0.00	1.33	262			12.8	35%	100%	4.14	25	13	63	3.0	9.0	3.0	0%	0.0	1.5	84	$0
Rand Var -1	11 Proj	1	2	0	29	15	4.97	1.62	294			14.6	32%	70%	4.97	45	21	34	4.0	4.7	1.2	9%	0.9	-3.0	-2	($0)

Ctl is the only skill that hasn't retired, but now trend says it will soon join the others. He can't be far behind. One more year at best as pen fodder -- with 0%/38% PQS-DOM/DIS, his swingman days are over.

Monasterios,Carlos

	Yr	W	L	Sv	IP	K	ERA	WHIP	OBA	vL	vR	BF/G	H%	S%	xERA	G	L	F	Ctl	Dom	Cmd	hr/f	hr/9	RAR	BPV	R$
RH RP 25	06	0	0	0	0	0	0.00	0.00							0.00											
Ht/Wt 74 175	07	0	0	0	0	0	0.00	0.00							0.00											
Type	08	0	0	0	0	0	0.00	0.00							0.00											
Health A	09 aa	0	0	0	7	4	3.86	1.71	313			16.2	36%	75%	5.17				3.9	5.1	1.3		0.0	0.4	51	($0)
PT/Exp D	10 LA	3	5	0	88	52	4.38	1.45	284	242	313	12.1	30%	75%	4.49	42	20	38	3.0	5.3	1.8	13%	1.5	-4.0	35	$2
Consist B	1st Half	3	2	0	46	21	3.89	1.34	261			11.6	26%	78%	4.86	41	17	42	3.1	4.1	1.3	12%	1.6	0.7	8	$3
LIMA Plan C+	2nd Half	0	3	0	42	31	4.93	1.57	309			12.6	34%	73%	4.09	43	23	34	2.8	6.6	2.4	15%	1.5	-4.7	66	($1)
Rand Var 0	11 Proj	2	4	0	73	47	4.10	1.43	284			6.9	31%	76%	4.36	42	20	37	2.9	5.8	2.0	11%	1.2	-2.0	48	$2

As SP: 53 IP, 4.9 Dom, 1.4 Cmd, 2.0 hr/9, 5.91 ERA.
As RP: 35 IP, 5.9 Dom, 2.6 Cmd, 0.8 hr/9, 2.06 ERA
Rookie miscast as swingman due to lack of SP depth. Has some value in the right role.

JOCK THOMPSON

Morales,Franklin		W	L	Sv	IP	K	ERA	WHIP	OBA	vL	vR	BF/G	H%	S%	xERA	G	L	F	Ctl	Dom	Cmd	hr/f	hr/9	RAR	BPV	R$
LH RP 25	06	0	0	0	0	0	0.00	0.00							0.00											
Ht/Wt 72 170	07 COL *	8	6	0	152	109	4.46	1.48	262	129	273	23.8	30%	71%	4.07	55	19	27	4.3	6.5	1.5	11%	0.8	-0.6	34	$8
Type Pwr xFB	08 COL *	11	7	0	135	80	6.18	1.76	278	200	295	24.4	30%	66%	5.83	40	20	40	6.0	5.3	0.9	9%	1.1	-31.9	-50	($2)
Health C	09 COL *	5	4	7	81	72	4.11	1.48	259	205	265	7.4	31%	74%	4.76	27	23	50	4.4	8.0	1.8	7%	0.9	0.8	29	$7
PT/Exp D	10 COL *	3	4	4	59	56	4.44	1.51	228	171	293	4.4	27%	74%	4.66	39	14	47	6.1	8.6	1.4	11%	1.2	-3.1	6	$3
Consist B	1st Half	0	3	3	21	15	6.76	1.88	268			4.4	30%	65%	6.12	37	16	46	7.6	6.3	0.8	10%	1.3	-7.2	-76	($1)
LIMA Plan C+	2nd Half	3	1	1	38	41	3.12	1.31	203			4.4	25%	82%	3.91	44	6	50	5.3	9.8	1.9	11%	1.2	4.1	56	$4
Rand Var 0	11 Proj	2	2	0	36	31	4.72	1.57	255			6.5	30%	73%	4.90	36	18	46	5.5	7.7	1.4	10%	1.2	-3.4	5	$1

0-4, 6.28 ERA in 29 IP at COL. Missed a month with shoulder weakness. The strikeouts are enticing, but poor control and tendency to give up the long ball will lead to many disastrous innings. Pass.

Morrow,Brandon		W	L	Sv	IP	K	ERA	WHIP	OBA	vL	vR	BF/G	H%	S%	xERA	G	L	F	Ctl	Dom	Cmd	hr/f	hr/9	RAR	BPV	R$
RH SP 26	06	0	0	0	0	0	0.00	0.00							0.00											
Ht/Wt 75 195	07 SEA	3	4	0	63	66	4.12	1.67	239	278	221	4.8	32%	75%	5.13	35	18	47	7.1	9.4	1.3	4%	0.4	3.0	-10	$3
Type Pwr xFB	08 SEA *	4	6	10	95	104	3.77	1.21	191	198	149	6.9	24%	73%	3.99	33	16	51	4.9	9.9	2.0	11%	1.1	6.7	57	$14
Health A	09 SEA *	7	7	6	125	99	4.06	1.48	252	277	212	15.2	30%	74%	4.85	37	20	43	4.8	7.1	1.5	8%	0.9	6.1	14	$10
PT/Exp C	10 TOR	10	7	0	146	178	4.49	1.38	248	245	253	24.2	35%	68%	3.35	40	18	42	4.1	11.0	2.7	7%	0.7	-6.4	106	$12
Consist C	1st Half	5	6	0	96	107	4.69	1.42	252			24.5	34%	67%	3.50	43	19	38	4.2	10.0	2.4	7%	0.7	-6.5	88	$6
LIMA Plan B	2nd Half	5	1	0	50	71	4.12	1.31	241			23.7	37%	69%	3.07	35	15	50	3.8	12.7	3.4	7%	0.7	0.1	141	$6
Rand Var +2	11 Proj	12	9	0	189	210	3.82	1.29	228			24.1	30%	73%	3.70	37	17	45	4.2	10.0	2.4	8%	0.9	13.6	84	$20

Despite high h%, unlikely to fly under the radar thanks to 17 K performance on August 8. Elite Dom, improving Ctl and carefully monitored workload make it worth paying full price anyway.
UP: 16 wins, 3.25 ERA

Morton,Charlie		W	L	Sv	IP	K	ERA	WHIP	OBA	vL	vR	BF/G	H%	S%	xERA	G	L	F	Ctl	Dom	Cmd	hr/f	hr/9	RAR	BPV	R$
RH SP 27	06	0	0	0	0	0	0.00	0.00							0.00											
Ht/Wt 76 190	07 aa	4	6	0	79	55	5.62	1.72	300			9.0	36%	65%	5.40				4.6	6.3	1.4		0.4	-11.3	51	($0)
Type	08 ATL *	9	10	0	154	111	4.27	1.34	241	306	245	22.6	29%	68%	4.08	50	18	31	4.0	6.5	1.6	6%	0.5	-0.1	38	$10
Health B	09 PIT *	12	11	0	168	112	3.76	1.32	259	316	236	24.6	30%	72%	4.02	49	18	33	3.0	6.0	2.0	6%	0.5	9.0	54	$14
PT/Exp C	10 PIT *	6	16	0	160	102	5.93	1.62	313	329	335	23.4	34%	65%	4.19	47	24	29	3.0	5.7	1.9	13%	1.2	-37.6	46	($4)
Consist A	1st Half	2	11	0	70	52	7.61	1.74	328			21.8	37%	57%	4.14	46	24	30	3.2	6.7	2.1	18%	1.7	-31.2	57	($5)
LIMA Plan C+	2nd Half	4	5	0	89	49	4.60	1.53	300			24.8	33%	71%	4.20	48	23	29	2.9	5.0	1.7	9%	0.8	-6.5	38	$1
Rand Var +5	11 Proj	7	11	0	131	86	4.55	1.39	274			23.5	31%	69%	4.01	48	21	31	3.0	5.9	2.0	10%	0.9	2.1	53	$6

2-12, 7.57 ERA in 80 IP at PIT. Murphy's Law got him in 2010:
- June DL trip for shoulder injury
- Unlucky h%, s% and hr/f rates
- Poor run support (2.6 runs/gm)

Rand Var and xERA say it will get better. Not good - just better.

Moseley,Dustin		W	L	Sv	IP	K	ERA	WHIP	OBA	vL	vR	BF/G	H%	S%	xERA	G	L	F	Ctl	Dom	Cmd	hr/f	hr/9	RAR	BPV	R$
RH SP 29	06 aaa	13	8	0	149	96	4.95	1.49	294			25.3	33%	68%	5.34				2.9	5.8	2.0		1.0	-7.8	42	$9
Ht/Wt 76 215	07 LAA	4	3	0	92	50	4.40	1.35	272	224	323	8.5	30%	68%	4.37	48	18	34	2.6	4.9	1.9	7%	0.7	1.2	43	$6
Type Con	08 LAA *	9	14	0	167	100	8.76	1.94	361	366	300	25.3	39%	55%	4.81	48	21	31	3.1	5.4	1.7	16%	1.8	-90.7	38	($15)
Health F	09 LAA	1	0	0	15	8	4.20	1.53	321			22.3	33%	80%	4.68	39	24	37	1.8	4.8	2.7	15%	1.8	0.5	55	$1
PT/Exp D	10 NYY *	8	8	0	138	80	5.31	1.57	304	281	256	22.0	32%	69%	4.40	49	16	35	3.0	5.2	1.7	13%	1.4	-19.9	39	$2
Consist A	1st Half	4	4	0	74	49	5.48	1.65	330			26.1	37%	68%		100	0	0	2.3	5.9	2.5		1.0	-12.3	121	($0)
LIMA Plan C+	2nd Half	4	4	0	63	31	5.12	1.47	270			18.5	26%	71%	4.71	48	17	35	3.8	4.4	1.1	17%	1.8	-7.6	2	$1
Rand Var +2	11 Proj	3	3	0	44	25	4.97	1.49	290			21.3	31%	69%	4.51	45	20	35	3.1	5.2	1.7	12%	1.2	-1.2	33	$2

4-4, 4.96 ERA in 65 IP at NYY. Low Dom pitchers can survive if they have pinpoint control; he doesn't, and xERA shows the result. Relatively stable BPIs say that's unlikely to change. Avoid.

Mota,Guillermo		W	L	Sv	IP	K	ERA	WHIP	OBA	vL	vR	BF/G	H%	S%	xERA	G	L	F	Ctl	Dom	Cmd	hr/f	hr/9	RAR	BPV	R$
RH RP 37	06 2TM	4	3	0	55	46	4.57	1.43	261	252	261	4.6	29%	75%	4.71	34	18	48	3.9	7.5	1.9	14%	1.8	-0.3	41	$4
Ht/Wt 77 233	07 NYM *	2	3	0	67	52	6.26	1.52	291	235	284	5.0	33%	60%	4.32	44	18	38	3.2	7.1	2.2	11%	1.2	-15.0	62	($0)
Type Pwr FB	08 MIL	5	6	1	57	50	4.11	1.40	244	287	216	4.2	29%	74%	4.03	45	22	33	4.4	7.9	1.8	13%	1.1	1.2	46	$5
Health B	09 LA	3	4	0	65	39	3.45	1.18	223	202	238	4.4	24%	73%	4.69	36	17	47	3.3	5.4	1.6	6%	0.8	6.0	22	$6
PT/Exp C	10 SF	1	3	1	54	38	4.33	1.31	243	247	240	4.1	28%	67%	4.44	38	17	44	3.7	6.3	1.7	6%	0.7	-2.1	31	$2
Consist A	1st Half	0	3	1	32	17	3.07	1.30	241			3.9	27%	76%	4.87	37	18	45	3.6	4.7	1.3	2%	0.3	3.8	2	$2
LIMA Plan C+	2nd Half	1	0	0	22	21	6.22	1.34	246			4.4	30%	54%	3.83	41	16	44	3.7	8.7	2.3	11%	1.2	-5.9	75	$0
Rand Var -1	11 Proj	2	3	0	51	38	4.61	1.42	263			4.4	30%	70%	4.50	39	18	43	3.7	6.7	1.8	9%	1.1	-2.2	38	$2

Why you can safely ignore him:
- Sub-2.0 Cmd in 4 of last 5 years
- H%, hr/f likely to correct
- Too old to be closer-in-waiting

He's been on 6 MLB teams in 5 years, but there's no reason for him to be on yours.

Motte,Jason		W	L	Sv	IP	K	ERA	WHIP	OBA	vL	vR	BF/G	H%	S%	xERA	G	L	F	Ctl	Dom	Cmd	hr/f	hr/9	RAR	BPV	R$
RH RP 28	06	0	0	0	0	0	0.00	0.00							0.00											
Ht/Wt 72 200	07 aa	3	3	8	49	50	2.45	1.38	243			4.7	32%	84%	3.88				4.3	9.1	2.1		0.6	12.2	87	$9
Type Pwr xFB	08 aaa	4	3	9	66	82	4.06	1.61	298			4.8	41%	76%	5.36				3.8	11.1	3.0		0.8	2.0	101	$7
Health A	09 STL	4	4	0	57	54	4.76	1.41	263	341	214	3.6	31%	71%	4.11	38	17	45	3.7	8.6	2.3	14%	1.6	-4.0	72	$3
PT/Exp D	10 STL	4	2	2	52	54	2.24	1.13	218	267	198	3.8	28%	85%	3.46	40	13	47	3.1	9.3	3.0	8%	0.9	11.5	101	$8
Consist B	1st Half	3	2	2	32	36	2.25	1.06	203			3.7	26%	87%	3.22	41	10	49	3.1	10.1	3.3	11%	1.1	7.0	118	$6
LIMA Plan B+	2nd Half	1	0	0	20	18	2.22	1.23	239			3.8	30%	83%	3.84	38	18	45	3.1	8.0	2.6	4%	0.4	4.5	75	$2
Rand Var -5	11 Proj	5	3	18	73	74	3.23	1.30	244			3.9	31%	79%	3.78	39	16	46	3.5	9.2	2.6	9%	1.0	3.3	88	$13

Spent a month on the DL with a sore shoulder. Rand Var says h% and s% regression will drive his ERA back up, but BPV will play regardless. If improving Ctl trends continues...
UP: 30 SV

Moyer,Jamie		W	L	Sv	IP	K	ERA	WHIP	OBA	vL	vR	BF/G	H%	S%	xERA	G	L	F	Ctl	Dom	Cmd	hr/f	hr/9	RAR	BPV	R$
LH SP 48	06 2TM	11	14	0	211	108	4.31	1.32	277	251	285	27.1	29%	72%	4.66	40	21	39	2.2	4.6	2.1	12%	1.4	5.6	42	$14
Ht/Wt 72 185	07 PHI	14	12	0	199	133	5.01	1.45	283	309	279	26.4	31%	69%	4.59	39	21	39	3.0	6.0	2.0	12%	1.4	-14.4	45	$10
Type Con FB	08 PHI	16	7	0	196	123	3.71	1.33	264	240	270	25.3	29%	75%	4.27	44	21	35	2.8	5.6	2.0	9%	0.9	13.5	47	$17
Health D	09 PHI	12	10	0	162	94	4.94	1.36	279	243	290	23.1	29%	68%	4.49	41	19	40	2.4	5.2	2.2	13%	1.5	-15.1	49	$8
PT/Exp A	10 PHI	9	9	0	112	63	4.83	1.10	246	194	249	23.6	25%	61%	3.96	44	15	41	1.6	5.1	3.2	14%	1.6	-11.3	70	$9
Consist A	1st Half	9	7	0	102	59	4.13	1.06	236			25.4	24%	66%	3.83	46	14	40	1.7	5.2	3.1	12%	1.3	-1.5	72	$10
LIMA Plan C	2nd Half	0	2	0	9	4	12.45	1.60	346			14.2	29%	20%	5.27	29	18	53	1.0	3.8	4.0	26%	4.8	-9.8	50	($2)
Rand Var +2	11 Proj	7	9	0	116	64	5.04	1.40	280			26.4	30%	66%	4.77	38	18	44	2.7	5.0	1.8	9%	1.2	-9.0	32	$4

Rehabbed torn ligament in elbow rather than undergoing Tommy John surgery. Health, age and propensity for blowouts (27% PQS-DIS in '09-'10 combined) all red flags; bid cautiously.

Moylan,Peter		W	L	Sv	IP	K	ERA	WHIP	OBA	vL	vR	BF/G	H%	S%	xERA	G	L	F	Ctl	Dom	Cmd	hr/f	hr/9	RAR	BPV	R$
RH RP 32	06 ATL *	1	7	1	71	60	8.33	2.02	323			7.0	39%	57%	4.61	58	17	25	6.1	7.5	1.2	11%	0.8	-33.7	8	($7)
Ht/Wt 74 200	07 ATL	5	3	1	90	63	1.80	1.07	204	242	184	4.5	24%	87%	3.30	62	13	25	3.1	6.3	2.0	9%	0.6	29.2	70	$14
Type Pwr xGB	08 ATL	0	1	1	6	5	1.58	1.05	237	273	167	3.2	27%	100%	2.47	67	11	22	1.6	7.9	5.0	28%	1.6	1.9	144	$1
Health D	09 ATL	6	2	0	73	61	2.84	1.37	240	309	211	3.6	31%	77%	3.24	62	18	20	4.3	7.5	1.7	0%	0.0	12.2	59	$8
PT/Exp D	10 ATL	6	2	1	64	52	2.97	1.41	228	308	214	3.2	27%	81%	3.35	68	11	21	5.2	7.3	1.4	13%	0.7	8.2	37	$6
Consist A	1st Half	3	1	1	33	30	3.00	1.52	250			3.3	32%	81%	3.01	71	11	18	5.2	8.2	1.6	12%	0.5	4.1	56	$3
LIMA Plan C	2nd Half	3	1	0	31	22	2.93	1.30	203			3.2	23%	81%	3.69	64	11	25	5.3	6.4	1.2	14%	0.9	4.1	16	$3
Rand Var -1	11 Proj	5	2	0	65	52	3.45	1.46	246			3.8	30%	77%	3.47	65	13	22	4.8	7.2	1.5	10%	0.6	5.4	42	$5

Able to overcome free passes with terrific GB rate; led relief pitchers with 13 induced double plays. Could be dominant with 2.0 Cmd, but the likelihood of its return fading quickly.

Mujica,Edward		W	L	Sv	IP	K	ERA	WHIP	OBA	vL	vR	BF/G	H%	S%	xERA	G	L	F	Ctl	Dom	Cmd	hr/f	hr/9	RAR	BPV	R$
RH RP 26	06 CLE *	4	2	13	69	53	2.21	1.28	275	324	341	6.6	34%	83%	4.60	26	18	55	1.9	6.9	3.5	2%	0.3	20.1	75	$14
Ht/Wt 74 215	07 CLE *	2	1	14	50	47	6.63	1.39	294			4.9	35%	52%	4.41	26	16	58	2.0	8.4	4.3	8%	1.3	-13.2	102	$6
Type FB	08 CLE *	3	4	4	65	51	6.26	1.58	307	277	318	5.7	36%	60%	4.68	30	23	46	2.9	7.1	2.4	7%	1.0	-15.3	57	$2
Health A	09 SD	3	5	2	94	76	3.94	1.28	277	300	247	5.9	32%	75%	3.92	39	17	44	1.8	7.3	4.0	11%	1.3	2.9	99	$7
PT/Exp C	10 SD	2	1	0	70	72	3.62	0.93	231	202	243	4.6	27%	73%	2.75	45	13	42	0.8	9.3	12.0	18%	1.8	3.4	169	$8
Consist B	1st Half	2	1	0	40	42	3.17	0.91	222			4.7	24%	85%	2.85	41	12	47	0.9	9.5	10.5	21%	2.3	4.1	166	$6
LIMA Plan A	2nd Half	0	0	0	30	30	4.20	0.97	242			4.3	30%	60%	2.62	49	15	36	0.6	9.0	15.0	14%	1.2	-0.7	173	$2
Rand Var +2	11 Proj	2	2	0	73	67	3.35	1.10	250			5.0	30%	76%	3.34	41	16	43	1.5	8.3	5.6	11%	1.2	7.2	129	$7

Out of this world BPIs, especially in 2H. Even if skills come back to earth some, hr/f rate should also regress and cushion the fall. Remains an ideal LIMA candidate with closer upside.

BILL MACEY

Myers,Brett

	Yr	Tm	W	L	Sv	IP	K	ERA	WHIP	OBA	vL	vR	BF/G	H%	S%	xERA	G	L	F	Ctl	Dom	Cmd	hr/f	hr/9	RAR	BPV	R$
RH SP 30	06	PHI	12	7	0	198	189	3.91	1.30	258	259	254	26.9	31%	75%	3.60	46	18	36	2.9	8.6	3.0	14%	1.3	14.1	101	$19
Ht/Wt 76 238	07	PHI	5	7	21	69	83	4.32	1.28	239	183	274	5.7	32%	70%	3.11	46	19	35	3.5	10.9	3.1	15%	1.2	0.9	124	$14
Type Pwr	08	PHI	10	13	0	190	163	4.55	1.38	269	235	293	27.2	31%	71%	3.72	47	20	32	3.1	7.7	2.5	16%	1.4	-6.5	81	$11
Health D	09	PHI	4	3	0	71	50	4.84	1.37	271	233	320	16.9	27%	75%	4.05	47	18	35	2.9	6.4	2.2	23%	2.3	-5.6	61	$3
PT/Exp A	10	HOU	14	8	0	224	180	3.14	1.24	252	240	254	28.2	30%	78%	3.54	49	16	35	2.7	7.2	2.7	9%	0.8	24.2	85	$21
Consist A	1st Half		5	6	0	113	84	3.57	1.36	266			28.5	31%	76%	3.78	48	19	32	3.0	6.7	2.2	10%	0.9	6.2	65	$7
LIMA Plan D+	2nd Half		9	2	0	110	96	2.69	1.12	236			27.9	29%	79%	3.30	49	14	37	2.3	7.8	3.4	8%	0.7	18.0	106	$14
Rand Var -1	11	Proj	13	10	0	218	179	3.81	1.29	257			26.9	30%	73%	3.65	48	17	35	2.8	7.4	2.6	11%	1.0	13.2	83	$17

Reasons to believe:
- At least 6 IP in 32 of 33 starts
- GB%, Ctl and Dom growth
- 2H was even better than 1H
- 1 PQS-DIS start all year

If he can survive IP roller coaster, 2010 is repeatable.

Narveson,Chris

	Yr	Tm	W	L	Sv	IP	K	ERA	WHIP	OBA	vL	vR	BF/G	H%	S%	xERA	G	L	F	Ctl	Dom	Cmd	hr/f	hr/9	RAR	BPV	R$
LH SP 29	06	aaa	8	5	0	80	50	3.60	1.46	269			23.4	29%	79%	4.97				3.8	5.6	1.5		1.1	9.1	32	$8
Ht/Wt 75 205	07	aaa	3	2	0	45	28	7.30	1.60	282			22.7	30%	54%	5.76				4.4	5.6	1.3		1.3	-15.8	19	($1)
Type Pwr FB	08	aaa	6	13	0	136	110	6.00	1.57	289			21.8	33%	65%	5.91				3.8	7.3	1.9		1.6	-28.5	34	$1
Health A	09	MIL *	6	4	5	122	113	4.19	1.28	248	313	224	10.9	31%	68%	4.11	31	21	47	3.2	8.3	2.6	6%	0.7	-0.0	72	$11
PT/Exp C	10	MIL	12	9	0	168	137	4.99	1.38	267	226	280	19.5	31%	66%	4.07	40	18	42	3.2	7.4	2.3	10%	1.1	-20.2	65	$8
Consist B	1st Half		7	5	0	83	68	5.29	1.50	281			16.7	33%	66%	4.10	45	16	39	3.6	7.3	2.1	10%	1.1	-13.1	59	$3
LIMA Plan C+	2nd Half		5	4	0	84	69	4.69	1.26	252			23.5	29%	65%	4.02	34	21	45	2.8	7.4	2.7	10%	1.2	-7.0	70	$5
Rand Var +2	11	Proj	10	9	0	167	137	4.53	1.39	264			23.9	31%	70%	4.25	37	19	43	3.3	7.4	2.2	10%	1.1	-2.3	58	$9

Due to poor S%, he's closer than you might think. Improving xERA, solid Cmd, and 50%/18% PQS-DOM/DIS all good starting points. If he can keep the HR in check and the bullpen helps out: UP: 15 wins, sub-4.00 ERA

Nathan,Joe

	Yr	Tm	W	L	Sv	IP	K	ERA	WHIP	OBA	vL	vR	BF/G	H%	S%	xERA	G	L	F	Ctl	Dom	Cmd	hr/f	hr/9	RAR	BPV	R$
RH RP 36	06	MIN	7	0	36	68	95	1.59	0.79	165	193	130	4.0	27%	82%	2.36	36	22	42	2.1	12.6	5.9	5%	0.4	25.0	183	$29
Ht/Wt 76 225	07	MIN	4	2	37	72	77	1.88	1.02	211	221	199	4.2	29%	84%	3.09	40	21	39	2.4	9.7	4.1	6%	0.5	23.2	128	$26
Type Pwr FB	08	MIN	1	2	39	68	74	1.33	0.90	184	167	192	3.8	25%	91%	2.69	47	19	33	2.4	9.8	4.1	9%	0.7	25.2	138	$25
Health F	09	MIN	2	2	47	67	87	2.15	0.93	175	145	187	3.7	24%	84%	2.82	41	12	47	3.0	11.7	4.0	11%	0.9	19.0	150	$28
PT/Exp B	10	MIN	0	0	0	0	0	0.00	0.00							0.00											
Consist A	1st Half		0	0	0	0	0	0.00	0.00							0.00											
LIMA Plan ******	2nd Half		0	0	0	-0	0	0.00	0.00							0.00											
Rand Var +5	11	Proj	2	2	25	58	64	3.41	1.12	216			4.1	28%	73%	3.20	41	18	40	3.1	9.9	3.2	10%	0.9	7.8	114	$15

Given a full year to recover from TJS, he should be ready to close again in March. Due to age and layoff, a slow start would not surprise. But an eventual return to form wouldn't, either.

Neshek,Pat

	Yr	Tm	W	L	Sv	IP	K	ERA	WHIP	OBA	vL	vR	BF/G	H%	S%	xERA	G	L	F	Ctl	Dom	Cmd	hr/f	hr/9	RAR	BPV	R$
RH RP 30	06	MIN *	10	4	14	97	125	2.65	1.02	219	244	140	5.9	29%	84%	3.07	32	14	54	2.1	11.6	5.5	13%	1.4	22.8	162	$25
Ht/Wt 75 210	07	MIN	7	2	0	70	74	2.94	1.01	182	181	185	3.7	23%	75%	3.71	32	16	52	3.5	9.5	2.7	8%	0.9	13.5	87	$13
Type Pwr xFB	08	MIN	0	1	0	13	15	4.74	1.20	242	250	233	3.7	31%	64%	3.33	31	28	42	2.7	10.2	3.8	14%	1.4	-0.6	118	$1
Health F	09	MIN	0	0	0	0	0	0.00	0.00							0.00											
PT/Exp F	10	MIN *	5	2	1	48	28	4.68	1.58	288	286	185	5.3	31%	72%	5.30	32	20	48	4.0	5.2	1.3	7%	1.0	-3.2	-4	$2
Consist D	1st Half		1	0	0	17	13	5.94	1.25	261			4.9	31%	50%	3.96	36	18	45	2.3	7.1	3.1	5%	0.6	-3.7	80	$1
LIMA Plan C+	2nd Half		4	2	1	32	15	4.02	1.75	301			5.5	31%	81%	6.12	29	21	50	4.9	4.2	0.9	8%	1.2	0.5	-49	$2
Rand Var -2	11	Proj	4	2	0	44	32	4.14	1.43	264			4.8	30%	75%	4.76	31	22	47	3.7	6.6	1.8	9%	1.2	-2.6	28	$4

0-1, 5.00 ERA in 9 IP at MIN. Elbow was cleared in March after missing 2009 from TJS, but a finger injury affected velocity all season. Five IP in Sept (6 BB, 3 ER) raised more questions. No value until proven healthy.

Niemann,Jeff

	Yr	Tm	W	L	Sv	IP	K	ERA	WHIP	OBA	vL	vR	BF/G	H%	S%	xERA	G	L	F	Ctl	Dom	Cmd	hr/f	hr/9	RAR	BPV	R$
RH SP 28	06	aa	5	5	0	77	70	4.09	1.39	252			23.7	31%	73%	4.34				4.0	8.2	2.1		1.0	4.1	68	$7
Ht/Wt 81 260	07	aaa	12	6	0	131	108	5.43	1.72	321			24.3	38%	70%	6.48				3.4	7.4	2.2		1.1	-15.6	48	$4
Type	08	aaa	9	5	0	133	110	4.17	1.23	233			23.0	27%	69%	3.75				3.3	7.4	2.2		1.1	2.2	67	$13
Health A	09	TAM	13	6	0	181	125	3.93	1.35	266	274	258	24.9	30%	73%	4.40	41	20	39	2.9	6.2	2.1	8%	0.8	11.5	51	$16
PT/Exp B	10	TAM	12	8	0	174	131	4.39	1.26	244	244	239	24.3	27%	69%	3.95	44	16	39	3.1	6.8	2.1	12%	1.3	-5.4	59	$14
Consist B	1st Half		6	2	0	106	75	2.80	1.08	219			26.5	24%	81%	3.79	44	15	41	2.5	6.4	2.5	11%	1.2	17.5	68	$13
LIMA Plan C+	2nd Half		6	6	0	68	56	6.85	1.55	280			21.8	32%	57%	4.19	45	18	37	4.1	7.4	1.8	14%	1.4	-22.9	45	$0
Rand Var +1	11	Proj	14	9	0	187	144	3.95	1.31	259			23.2	29%	74%	4.00	43	18	39	2.9	6.9	2.4	11%	1.2	6.7	68	$17

Took step up in 1H, though not as big as ERA suggests. 2H was marred by shoulder strain that caused DL trip and ugly results afterward (33 IP, 9.82 ERA, 4.6 Ctl). Assuming health, there's profit potential lurking.

Niese,Jonathon

	Yr	Tm	W	L	Sv	IP	K	ERA	WHIP	OBA	vL	vR	BF/G	H%	S%	xERA	G	L	F	Ctl	Dom	Cmd	hr/f	hr/9	RAR	BPV	R$
LH SP 24	06		0	0	0	0	0	0.00	0.00							0.00											
Ht/Wt 76 215	07		0	0	0	0	0	0.00	0.00							0.00											
Type Pwr	08	aa	11	8	0	164	124	3.68	1.38	270			24.3	32%	73%	4.08				3.1	6.8	2.2		0.5	12.7	74	$14
Health C	09	NYM *	6	7	0	120	94	4.62	1.40	283	333	242	24.6	34%	67%	3.79	48	19	33	2.5	7.0	2.8	7%	0.6	-6.4	48	$6
PT/Exp C	10	NYM	9	10	0	174	148	4.20	1.46	282	266	283	25.4	33%	74%	3.68	48	21	32	3.2	7.7	2.4	12%	1.0	-3.9	77	$8
Consist A	1st Half		6	2	0	82	65	3.62	1.40	276			25.3	33%	76%	3.65	50	19	31	3.0	7.1	2.4	9%	0.8	4.0	76	$6
LIMA Plan B	2nd Half		3	8	0	92	83	4.71	1.52	287			25.4	34%	72%	3.70	46	22	32	3.4	8.1	2.4	14%	1.3	-7.9	77	$2
Rand Var +2	11	Proj	11	10	0	189	154	3.82	1.38	271			24.6	32%	74%	3.70	48	20	32	3.0	7.4	2.5	10%	0.9	10.3	78	$13

Slowed by another hamstring injury, though didn't require surgery. Consistent BPI (GB%, Cmd, xERA) flying under the radar due to two years of slightly inflated H%. If hammys heal... UP: 15 wins, 3.50 ERA

Nieve,Fernando

	Yr	Tm	W	L	Sv	IP	K	ERA	WHIP	OBA	vL	vR	BF/G	H%	S%	xERA	G	L	F	Ctl	Dom	Cmd	hr/f	hr/9	RAR	BPV	R$
RH RP 28	06	HOU	3	3	0	96	70	4.21	1.33	243	262	224	10.2	26%	75%	4.64	41	15	44	3.8	6.6	1.7	14%	1.7	3.2	33	$6
Ht/Wt 72 195	07	aaa	1	3	0	22	12	6.55	2.18	340			22.4	37%	70%	7.81				6.5	4.9	0.8		0.8	-5.7	8	($2)
Type Pwr xFB	08	HOU *	2	6	6	83	59	6.93	1.85	344			8.4	38%	66%	7.92				3.3	6.4	1.9		1.8	-27.3	10	($3)
Health C	09	NYM *	6	4	0	79	55	4.52	1.48	264	200	351	20.4	30%	71%	4.98	36	18	46	4.3	6.3	1.5	7%	0.8	-3.2	12	$4
PT/Exp D	10	NYM *	4	5	0	82	62	6.14	1.57	287	240	231	7.7	32%	63%	4.71	37	18	45	3.9	6.8	1.7	11%	1.5	-21.5	31	($1)
Consist D	1st Half		2	3	0	34	27	5.61	1.42	228			4.2	23%	68%	4.63	41	16	44	5.3	7.2	1.4	19%	2.1	-6.6	4	$1
LIMA Plan C	2nd Half		2	2	0	48	35	6.51	1.67	323			17.1	37%	61%	5.09	22	26	52	3.0	6.6	2.2	6%	1.0	-14.9	37	($2)
Rand Var +4	11	Proj	1	2	0	29	21	5.28	1.52	275			9.2	31%	68%	4.81	38	17	45	4.0	6.5	1.6	10%	1.2	-2.4	24	$0

2-4, 6.00 ERA in 42 IP at NYM. Finally mustered a 2.0+ Cmd (in 2H) - but compiled it in AAA after he was DFA'd in July. BPV, R$ trends point to a former prospect that has run out of chances.

Nippert,Dustin

	Yr	Tm	W	L	Sv	IP	K	ERA	WHIP	OBA	vL	vR	BF/G	H%	S%	xERA	G	L	F	Ctl	Dom	Cmd	hr/f	hr/9	RAR	BPV	R$
RH RP 29	06	ARI *	13	10	0	150	123	6.11	1.69	317	333	375	25.7	37%	64%	4.10	56	12	32	3.4	7.4	2.1	11%	1.0	-30.0	73	$2
Ht/Wt 80 225	07	ARI *	1	4	0	81	74	6.15	1.49	256	238	290	7.8	31%	59%	4.28	38	28	34	4.7	8.2	1.7	12%	1.1	-17.3	36	($0)
Type Pwr	08	TEX *	9	7	0	135	86	5.98	1.73	320	263	354	19.6	35%	68%	5.09	37	24	39	3.7	5.7	1.6	11%	1.4	-27.1	19	($1)
Health F	09	TEX	5	3	0	70	54	3.87	1.33	246	257	231	14.8	29%	73%	4.38	41	18	41	3.7	7.0	1.9	8%	0.9	5.0	44	$7
PT/Exp C	10	TEX	4	5	0	57	47	4.29	1.68	276	305	261	6.9	32%	77%	4.90	32	27	41	5.4	7.5	1.4	10%	1.1	-1.0	-1	$2
Consist B	1st Half		3	3	0	38	38	4.93	1.88	294			7.4	37%	75%	4.64	38	28	34	6.3	8.9	1.4	10%	0.9	-3.8	5	$0
LIMA Plan C	2nd Half		1	2	0	18	9	2.93	1.25	236			5.9	23%	85%	5.31	21	24	55	3.4	4.4	1.3	9%	1.5	2.7	-15	$2
Rand Var -1	11	Proj	4	5	0	65	47	4.41	1.50	270			9.0	30%	73%	4.66	38	23	39	4.1	6.5	1.6	10%	1.1	-3.0	21	$3

Spent six weeks on DL after taking line drive off his head in July. His health notwithstanding, line drives are a common issue. Poor Cmd and a touch of gopheritis don't help, either. A non-factor.

Nolasco,Ricky

	Yr	Tm	W	L	Sv	IP	K	ERA	WHIP	OBA	vL	vR	BF/G	H%	S%	xERA	G	L	F	Ctl	Dom	Cmd	hr/f	hr/9	RAR	BPV	R$
RH SP 28	06	FLA	11	11	0	140	99	4.82	1.41	285	338	240	17.3	32%	69%	4.46	39	21	40	2.6	6.4	2.4	11%	1.3	-5.8	60	$9
Ht/Wt 74 230	07	FLA *	1	5	0	39	26	10.18	1.96	361	293	350	19.2	39%	48%	5.43	37	19	44	3.3	6.0	1.8	14%	2.1	-28.0	35	($6)
Type Pwr FB	08	FLA	15	8	0	212	186	3.52	1.10	243	238	239	25.1	28%	73%	3.57	39	19	42	1.8	7.9	4.4	11%	1.2	19.7	111	$25
Health C	09	FLA	13	9	0	185	195	5.06	1.25	265	251	268	24.9	34%	61%	3.33	38	22	40	2.1	9.5	4.4	11%	1.1	-19.8	129	$15
PT/Exp A	10	FLA	14	9	0	158	147	4.51	1.28	275	283	263	25.5	33%	69%	3.48	40	19	41	1.9	8.4	4.5	13%	1.4	-9.6	118	$13
Consist A	1st Half		8	6	0	104	88	4.69	1.29	282			25.7	32%	70%	3.68	40	17	43	1.6	7.6	4.6	15%	1.7	-8.6	111	$7
LIMA Plan B+	2nd Half		6	3	0	54	59	4.17	1.26	262			25.1	35%	67%	3.10	41	22	37	2.3	9.8	4.2	7%	0.7	-1.0	133	$6
Rand Var +2	11	Proj	15	10	0	181	174	4.72	1.29	271			23.8	33%	66%	3.52	39	20	40	2.1	8.6	4.0	11%	1.2	14.0	115	$15

Must be Javier Vazquez's long lost little brother, yet another member of the Brad Fullmer list. Repeated 3.50 xERA, 100+ BPV, elite Cmd, yet results disappoint. If knee is healthy and 2H gains are real, then... UP: 3.00 ERA

BRENT HERSHEY

Norris,Bud

	Yr	Tm	W	L	Sv	IP	K	ERA	WHIP	OBA	vL	vR	BF/G	H%	S%	xERA	G	L	F	Ctl	Dom	Cmd	hr/f	hr/9	RAR	BPV	R$
RH SP 26	06		0	0	0	0	0	0.00	0.00							0.00											
Ht/Wt 72 195	07		0	0	0	0	0	0.00	0.00							0.00											
Type Pwr	08	aa	3	8	0	80	70	4.29	1.59	300			19.0	36%	75%	5.50				3.4	7.9	2.3		0.9	0.1	63	$3
Health B	09	HOU *	10	12	0	176	151	3.64	1.47	265	200	323	25.7	32%	77%	4.42	37	20	43	4.0	7.7	1.9	7%	0.8	12.0	45	$12
PT/Exp D	10	HOU *	10	10	0	168	170	4.77	1.50	262	241	269	24.7	33%	70%	3.87	43	18	39	4.5	9.1	2.0	10%	1.0	-15.7	65	$7
Consist B	1st Half		3	5	0	70	77	5.41	1.66	289			22.9	38%	68%	3.90	39	24	37	4.6	9.9	2.1	9%	0.9	-12.1	69	($0)
LIMA Plan B	2nd Half		7	5	0	98	93	4.32	1.38	242			26.3	29%	72%	3.85	45	15	40	4.3	8.5	2.0	11%	1.1	-3.6	61	$6
Rand Var +1	11	Proj	10	12	0	178	167	4.30	1.44	259			23.5	32%	73%	4.03	42	19	40	4.1	8.4	2.0	10%	1.0	2.4	60	$10

9-10, 4.92 ERA in 154 IP at HOU. Enjoyed Dom spike even thru a battle with biceps tendinitis. Ctl still a concern, which make the HRs especially crippling. But xERA, 2H GB% provide a glimpse of his upside.

Nova,Ivan

	Yr	Tm	W	L	Sv	IP	K	ERA	WHIP	OBA	vL	vR	BF/G	H%	S%	xERA	G	L	F	Ctl	Dom	Cmd	hr/f	hr/9	RAR	BPV	R$
RH SP 24	06		0	0	0	0	0	0.00	0.00							0.00											
Ht/Wt 76 210	07		0	0	0	0	0	0.00	0.00							0.00											
Type GB	08		0	0	0	0	0	0.00	0.00							0.00											
Health A	09	a/a	6	8	0	139	77	5.18	1.66	300			26.5	34%	68%	5.38				4.1	5.0	1.2		0.6	-14.8	33	($0)
PT/Exp D	10	NYY *	13	5	0	187	130	3.75	1.42	275	276	258	24.6	32%	75%	3.83	51	18	30	3.1	6.3	2.0	9%	0.8	8.9	58	$13
Consist D	1st Half		5	2	0	87	59	3.62	1.51	292			24.1	34%	77%	3.42	55	27	18	3.1	6.1	2.0	11%	0.6	5.6	59	$5
LIMA Plan C	2nd Half		8	3	0	100	71	3.87	1.34	260			25.1	29%	74%	3.77	51	17	31	3.1	6.4	2.0	11%	1.0	3.3	59	$8
Rand Var 0	11	Proj	7	5	0	116	77	4.19	1.44	276			25.3	31%	72%	4.04	51	18	31	3.3	6.0	1.8	9%	0.8	3.5	49	$7

1-2, 4.50 ERA in 42 IP at NYY. Lived up to GB reputation, though erratic in his first MLB exposure (43%/43% PQS-DOM/DIS; 1.5 Cmd). Needs start-to-start consistency; at 23, more AAA time would not surprise.

Nunez,Leo

	Yr	Tm	W	L	Sv	IP	K	ERA	WHIP	OBA	vL	vR	BF/G	H%	S%	xERA	G	L	F	Ctl	Dom	Cmd	hr/f	hr/9	RAR	BPV	R$
RH RP 27	06	KC *	3	4	8	72	55	3.62	1.44	272	211	355	7.0	31%	79%	4.12	41	30	30	3.5	6.9	2.0	14%	1.1	8.3	48	$8
Ht/Wt 74 182	07	KC *	4	6	0	87	64	3.17	1.11	236	275	248	14.6	26%	78%	4.24	32	19	49	2.1	6.6	3.1	10%	1.3	14.3	71	$11
Type Pwr	08	KC	4	1	0	48	26	2.98	1.24	248	272	230	4.5	28%	76%	4.66	39	18	43	2.8	4.8	1.7	3%	0.4	8.1	29	$6
Health C	09	FLA	4	6	26	69	60	4.06	1.25	233	234	225	3.8	26%	75%	4.02	41	15	44	3.5	7.9	2.2	15%	1.7	1.1	65	$14
PT/Exp B	10	FLA	4	3	30	65	71	3.46	1.28	253	214	291	4.0	34%	74%	2.84	54	16	30	2.9	9.8	3.4	10%	0.7	4.4	130	$16
Consist B	1st Half		3	2	17	34	34	3.20	1.10	228			3.9	31%	69%	2.80	51	19	30	2.4	9.1	3.8	4%	0.3	3.4	128	$10
LIMA Plan C+	2nd Half		1	1	13	31	37	3.74	1.47	278			4.2	37%	79%	2.87	57	13	30	3.5	10.6	3.1	16%	1.2	1.1	133	$6
Rand Var +2	11	Proj	4	4	25	73	67	3.60	1.28	250			4.3	30%	75%	3.54	47	16	37	3.1	8.3	2.7	11%	1.0	5.3	91	$15

Had his best skills season by far, though managerial usage suggested otherwise. 1H S%, 2H H% and hr/f obscured growth in GB%, Ctl and Dom. Even with regression, likely to succeed if trusted; depends on Sv opps.

O'Day,Darren

	Yr	Tm	W	L	Sv	IP	K	ERA	WHIP	OBA	vL	vR	BF/G	H%	S%	xERA	G	L	F	Ctl	Dom	Cmd	hr/f	hr/9	RAR	BPV	R$
RH RP 28	06		0	0	0	0	0	0.00	0.00							0.00											
Ht/Wt 76 220	07	aa	3	4	10	29	18	5.21	1.66	291			4.6	32%	70%	5.74				4.6	5.6	1.2		1.0	-2.7	27	$4
Type FB	08	LAA *	2	3	7	76	52	4.43	1.41	285	275	290	6.5	33%	68%	3.73	55	17	28	2.6	6.2	2.4	8%	0.6	-0.8	75	$6
Health A	09	2TM	2	1	2	59	56	1.84	1.01	199	239	180	3.4	26%	84%	3.43	41	17	42	2.8	8.6	3.1	5%	0.5	17.9	99	$10
PT/Exp D	10	TEX	6	2	0	62	45	2.03	0.89	197	229	181	3.3	23%	82%	3.51	37	21	42	1.7	6.5	3.8	7%	0.7	16.1	86	$11
Consist A	1st Half		3	2	0	33	24	1.65	0.92	200			3.5	24%	83%	3.38	40	23	37	1.9	6.6	3.4	3%	0.3	10.0	85	$6
LIMA Plan B	2nd Half		3	0	0	29	21	2.46	0.85	195			3.1	21%	81%	3.64	34	18	48	1.5	6.5	4.2	10%	1.2	6.1	86	$5
Rand Var -5	11	Proj	4	1	0	58	46	3.10	1.14	241			3.7	28%	77%	3.74	40	19	41	2.2	7.1	3.3	9%	0.9	3.9	88	$7

Continued to school RHers on his way to another successful season. H% and hr/f will snap back at some point, and his declining GB% will be disguised no longer. Still a relief asset, but that ERA/xERA gap is wide.

O'Flaherty,Eric

	Yr	Tm	W	L	Sv	IP	K	ERA	WHIP	OBA	vL	vR	BF/G	H%	S%	xERA	G	L	F	Ctl	Dom	Cmd	hr/f	hr/9	RAR	BPV	R$
LH RP 26	06	SEA *	3	2	7	54	44	1.83	1.52	283			5.7	35%	89%	4.37				3.7	7.3	2.0		0.3	18.1	74	$9
Ht/Wt 74 220	07	SEA	7	1	0	52	36	4.47	1.24	234	183	277	3.9	28%	61%	4.25	45	18	37	3.4	6.2	1.8	2%	0.2	0.2	41	$7
Type Pwr GB	08	SEA *	1	1	2	25	23	9.00	2.20	368			5.8	44%	59%	4.40	50	25	25	5.0	8.3	1.6	18%	1.4	-14.3	41	($3)
Health B	09	ATL	2	1	0	56	39	3.05	1.25	248	215	282	3.0	30%	75%	3.59	55	17	28	2.9	6.3	2.2	4%	0.3	7.8	68	$5
PT/Exp D	10	ATL	3	2	0	44	36	2.45	1.25	230	231	229	3.3	28%	81%	3.19	57	20	23	3.7	7.4	2.0	7%	0.4	8.5	69	$5
Consist B	1st Half		2	1	0	30	26	2.40	1.27	228			3.2	29%	81%	2.98	60	20	20	3.9	7.8	2.0	6%	0.3	6.0	74	$3
LIMA Plan B	2nd Half		1	1	0	14	10	2.57	1.21	233			3.4	27%	81%	3.58	51	20	29	3.2	6.4	2.0	8%	0.6	2.5	58	$2
Rand Var -4	11	Proj	5	2	0	65	50	3.31	1.32	249			3.6	30%	76%	3.60	53	19	28	3.4	6.9	2.0	7%	0.6	4.4	62	$6

Out 5 weeks with mono, returned in late Aug with most skills intact. Final line helped by fortunate H% / S%, but xERA shows steady improvement over last two seasons. Elite GB%, good Cmd bode well for followup.

O'Sullivan,Sean

	Yr	Tm	W	L	Sv	IP	K	ERA	WHIP	OBA	vL	vR	BF/G	H%	S%	xERA	G	L	F	Ctl	Dom	Cmd	hr/f	hr/9	RAR	BPV	R$
RH SP 23	06		0	0	0	0	0	0.00	0.00							0.00											
Ht/Wt 74 230	07		0	0	0	0	0	0.00	0.00							0.00											
Type Con FB	08		0	0	0	0	0	0.00	0.00							0.00											
Health A	09	LAA *	11	8	0	139	81	6.22	1.45	299	263	324	21.0	32%	59%	4.84	37	20	44	2.3	5.2	2.3	11%	1.4	-30.3	48	$4
PT/Exp D	10	2AL *	9	11	0	169	92	5.12	1.46	283	247	302	21.7	30%	67%	4.76	41	17	42	3.1	4.9	1.6	9%	1.2	-20.5	24	$4
Consist A	1st Half		5	4	0	84	45	4.61	1.40	280			21.4	31%	67%	5.07	38	8	54	2.8	4.8	1.7	4%	0.6	-4.9	27	$4
LIMA Plan C+	2nd Half		4	7	0	85	47	5.63	1.51	287			22.1	29%	67%	4.81	41	18	41	3.4	5.0	1.5	14%	1.7	-15.6	17	$0
Rand Var 0	11	Proj	5	6	0	87	49	5.07	1.46	290			21.2	31%	68%	4.79	40	18	43	2.8	5.1	1.8	10%	1.3	-5.4	33	$3

4-6, 5.49 in 84 IP at LAA and KC. Is this a big-league starter?
- 28 GS, 5.08 ERA (career, AAA)
- Marked BPI decline from 2009
- '10 MLB: 5.22 xERA; 12 BPV

Bonus: Your answer doubles as the response to "Should I bid?"

Ogando,Alexi

	Yr	Tm	W	L	Sv	IP	K	ERA	WHIP	OBA	vL	vR	BF/G	H%	S%	xERA	G	L	F	Ctl	Dom	Cmd	hr/f	hr/9	RAR	BPV	R$
RH RP 27	06		0	0	0	0	0	0.00	0.00							0.00											
Ht/Wt 76 185	07		0	0	0	0	0	0.00	0.00							0.00											
Type Pwr	08		0	0	0	0	0	0.00	0.00							0.00											
Health A	09		0	0	0	0	0	0.00	0.00							0.00											
PT/Exp F	10	TEX *	4	1	1	72	71	1.86	1.07	194	229	198	4.6	26%	84%	3.29	44	18	38	3.5	8.9	2.5	4%	0.4	20.2	87	$12
Consist F	1st Half		3	0	1	41	41	1.94	0.92	152			6.1	21%	79%	2.94	52	15	33	3.8	9.0	2.4	3%	0.2	11.2	91	$8
LIMA Plan B+	2nd Half		1	1	0	31	30	1.76	1.27	244			3.6	31%	89%	3.54	41	19	40	3.2	8.8	2.7	6%	0.6	9.0	90	$4
Rand Var -5	11	Proj	3	1	0	65	64	3.31	1.21	227			4.3	29%	74%	3.55	43	18	39	3.4	8.8	2.6	7%	0.7	5.9	86	$7

4-1, 1.30 ERA in 42 IP at TEX. Converted OFer came up in mid-June and pummelled hitters. A closer look, though, reveals an enviable H% / S% / hr/f trifecta. But w/ good GB+Cmd and elite Dom, impact potential lurks.

Ohlendorf,Ross

	Yr	Tm	W	L	Sv	IP	K	ERA	WHIP	OBA	vL	vR	BF/G	H%	S%	xERA	G	L	F	Ctl	Dom	Cmd	hr/f	hr/9	RAR	BPV	R$
RH SP 28	06	a/a	10	8	0	182	111	4.33	1.40	305			28.1	34%	70%	5.07				1.5	5.5	3.7		0.8	4.3	80	$11
Ht/Wt 76 235	07	aaa	3	4	0	68	41	6.67	1.93	356			15.0	39%	66%	7.80				3.3	5.4	1.6		1.2	-18.6	14	($4)
Type FB	08	2TM *	6	8	0	132	98	5.66	1.72	327	370	273	14.5	37%	69%	4.40	43	24	33	3.1	6.7	2.1	12%	1.2	-21.9	58	($1)
Health C	09	PIT	11	10	0	177	109	3.92	1.23	249	286	221	25.3	26%	73%	4.39	41	17	42	2.7	5.6	2.1	11%	1.3	5.8	46	$14
PT/Exp B	10	PIT	1	11	0	108	79	4.07	1.39	258	273	250	22.2	29%	73%	4.61	31	22	46	3.7	6.6	1.8	8%	1.0	-0.8	29	$3
Consist A	1st Half		1	6	0	68	45	4.39	1.45	263			24.6	29%	71%	4.76	35	22	43	4.0	6.0	1.5	8%	0.9	-3.1	13	$1
LIMA Plan C+	2nd Half		0	5	0	41	34	3.55	1.28	249			19.0	29%	77%	4.35	25	23	53	3.1	7.5	2.4	8%	1.1	2.3	55	$2
Rand Var -1	11	Proj	6	10	0	139	98	4.29	1.41	273			20.0	30%	73%	4.57	35	21	45	3.1	6.4	2.0	10%	1.2	-7.4	43	$6

Dom see-sawed back up, but Ctl (1H) and FB (2H) took turns mitigating the extra Ks. Along the way, separate back and shoulder injuries provided more resistance. If health checks out, expect more of the same.

Ohman,Will

	Yr	Tm	W	L	Sv	IP	K	ERA	WHIP	OBA	vL	vR	BF/G	H%	S%	xERA	G	L	F	Ctl	Dom	Cmd	hr/f	hr/9	RAR	BPV	R$
LH RP 33	06	CHC	1	1	0	65	74	4.15	1.31	217	158	243	3.5	29%	70%	3.91	34	23	44	4.7	10.2	2.2	9%	0.8	2.7	69	$5
Ht/Wt 74 210	07	CHC *	2	4	1	43	39	5.14	1.80	308	236	325	3.1	38%	71%	4.85	41	18	42	4.9	8.2	1.7	5%	0.6	-3.8	34	$0
Type Pwr FB	08	ATL	4	1	1	59	53	3.68	1.24	236	200	256	2.9	30%	70%	3.77	36	29	35	3.4	8.1	2.4	5%	0.5	4.3	70	$6
Health D	09	LA	1	0	1	12	7	6.00	1.67	262			2.6	23%	75%	6.02	26	29	45	6.0	5.3	0.9	23%	3.0	-2.7	-63	$0
PT/Exp D	10	2TM	0	2	0	42	43	3.21	1.50	252	229	288	2.7	32%	81%	3.92	46	14	40	4.9	9.2	1.9	9%	0.9	4.4	57	$2
Consist F	1st Half		0	0	0	25	26	2.88	1.48	246			2.7	32%	83%	3.81	48	14	38	5.0	9.4	1.9	8%	0.7	3.7	58	$1
LIMA Plan B	2nd Half		0	2	0	17	17	3.71	1.53	262			2.8	33%	79%	4.04	44	14	42	4.8	9.0	1.9	10%	1.1	0.8	55	$0
Rand Var -3	11	Proj	1	3	3	48	47	4.17	1.47	256			2.9	32%	74%	4.12	38	21	41	4.5	8.9	2.0	9%	0.9	0.5	54	$3

Coming off shoulder surgery in Sept 2009, he put together a decent season. But when a reliever with BF/G this low has a Ctl rate this high, it seems trouble won't be far behind. He'll soon run out of chances.

BRENT HERSHEY

Okajima,Hideki			W	L	Sv	IP	K	ERA	WHIP	OBA	vL	vR	BF/G	H%	S%	xERA	G	L	F	Ctl	Dom	Cmd	hr/f	hr/9	RAR	BPV	R$
LH RP 35	06	JPN	2	2	4	55	60	2.85	1.21	241			4.1	30%	84%	4.09				2.8	9.8	3.4		1.4	11.4	97	$8
Ht/Wt 73 194	07	BOS	3	2	5	69	63	2.22	0.97	204	236	182	4.1	25%	82%	3.34	45	15	41	2.2	8.2	3.7	8%	0.8	19.5	111	$13
Type Pwr FB	08	BOS	3	2	1	62	60	2.61	1.16	219	184	234	4.0	27%	82%	3.88	32	20	48	3.3	8.7	2.6	8%	0.9	13.3	77	$9
Health B	09	BOS	6	0	0	61	53	3.39	1.26	246	167	309	3.8	29%	78%	4.45	30	16	54	3.1	7.8	2.5	8%	1.2	8.0	66	$8
PT/Exp D	10	BOS	4	4	0	46	33	4.50	1.72	313	284	340	3.8	35%	77%	4.88	35	23	42	3.9	6.5	1.7	9%	1.2	-2.1	23	$1
Consist A	1st Half		2	2	0	26	21	5.82	1.83	327			3.8	38%	70%	5.05	31	22	47	4.1	7.2	1.8	9%	1.4	-5.4	27	($0)
LIMA Plan B	2nd Half		2	2	0	20	12	2.74	1.57	293			3.8	33%	86%	4.58	41	25	34	3.7	5.5	1.5	9%	0.9	3.4	19	$2
Rand Var +1	11	Proj	5	3	0	58	47	3.88	1.43	265			3.8	31%	76%	4.46	35	20	44	3.7	7.3	2.0	9%	1.1	-1.3	44	$5

Reasons to be concerned:
- xERA continued steady rise
- LHers had success against him
- RHers lit him up last 2 years
- Dom, Ctl headed wrong way

No longer a lock to help in ratio categories.

Oliver,Andrew			W	L	Sv	IP	K	ERA	WHIP	OBA	vL	vR	BF/G	H%	S%	xERA	G	L	F	Ctl	Dom	Cmd	hr/f	hr/9	RAR	BPV	R$
LH SP 23	06		0	0	0	0	0	0.00	0.00							0.00											
Ht/Wt 75 209	07		0	0	0	0	0	0.00	0.00							0.00											
Type Pwr	08		0	0	0	0	0	0.00	0.00							0.00											
Health A	09		0	0	0	0	0	0.00	0.00							0.00											
PT/Exp D	10	DET *	9	12	0	152	120	4.56	1.44	269	269	328	23.7	31%	71%	4.04	43	21	36	3.6	7.1	2.0	11%	1.1	-7.8	52	$8
Consist F	1st Half		6	6	0	89	70	4.04	1.38	276			23.9	32%	73%	4.01	41	18	41	2.7	7.1	2.6	9%	1.0	1.1	73	$6
LIMA Plan C	2nd Half		3	6	0	63	50	5.29	1.52	259			23.3	30%	67%	4.17	45	24	30	4.9	7.1	1.5	14%	1.1	-8.9	21	$1
Rand Var +1	11	Proj	5	7	0	83	66	4.45	1.43	259			24.1	30%	71%	4.12	44	22	34	4.0	7.2	1.8	11%	1.0	1.7	43	$5

0-4, 7.36 ERA in 22 IP at DET. Small MLB sample aside, not bad for first pro season. Held LH to .143 BA in 9 AAA starts. Shut down in Sept. to limit IP. Youth and inexperience raise risk, but ... UP: 4.00 ERA

Oliver,Darren			W	L	Sv	IP	K	ERA	WHIP	OBA	vL	vR	BF/G	H%	S%	xERA	G	L	F	Ctl	Dom	Cmd	hr/f	hr/9	RAR	BPV	R$
LH RP 40	06	NYM	4	1	0	81	60	3.44	1.12	235	208	244	7.3	25%	77%	3.72	48	17	35	2.3	6.7	2.9	16%	1.4	10.4	83	$9
Ht/Wt 74 200	07	LAA	3	1	0	64	51	3.78	1.26	242	289	209	4.4	29%	71%	4.01	48	12	40	3.2	7.1	2.2	7%	0.7	5.8	68	$6
Type Pwr	08	LAA	7	1	0	72	48	2.88	1.15	248	229	271	5.4	29%	77%	3.82	47	16	37	2.0	6.0	3.0	6%	0.6	13.1	79	$10
Health A	09	LAA	5	1	0	73	65	2.71	1.14	229	263	217	4.7	28%	78%	3.67	44	14	41	2.7	8.0	3.0	6%	0.6	15.7	93	$11
PT/Exp C	10	TEX	1	2	1	62	65	2.48	1.10	233	200	281	3.9	31%	80%	2.77	48	20	32	2.2	9.5	4.3	8%	0.6	12.6	138	$8
Consist B	1st Half		0	0	1	37	41	1.45	0.86	179			3.9	25%	87%	2.42	53	15	32	2.2	9.9	4.6	7%	0.5	12.4	151	$7
LIMA Plan A	2nd Half		1	2	0	24	24	4.06	1.48	304			3.8	38%	74%	3.28	42	27	31	2.2	8.9	4.0	9%	0.7	0.2	120	$1
Rand Var -2	11	Proj	3	2	0	65	60	3.31	1.20	249			4.4	31%	75%	3.33	46	19	35	2.3	8.3	3.5	9%	0.8	7.7	110	$7

Talk about a late career skill surge. Logged 13.3 Cmd vs. LH over last 2 years, and went 41 straight games with no HR allowed. Some regression is to be expected, but showing no signs that the end is near.

Olsen,Scott			W	L	Sv	IP	K	ERA	WHIP	OBA	vL	vR	BF/G	H%	S%	xERA	G	L	F	Ctl	Dom	Cmd	hr/f	hr/9	RAR	BPV	R$
LH SP 27	06	FLA	12	10	0	180	166	4.05	1.30	239	182	255	24.6	29%	73%	3.88	45	18	37	3.7	8.3	2.2	12%	1.1	9.8	71	$17
Ht/Wt 76 211	07	FLA	10	15	0	177	133	5.81	1.76	312	331	311	25.1	35%	70%	5.03	38	24	39	4.3	6.8	1.6	13%	1.5	-30.1	21	($1)
Type	08	FLA	8	11	0	202	113	4.19	1.31	255	187	266	25.8	27%	73%	4.78	37	20	42	3.1	5.0	1.6	11%	1.3	1.9	23	$11
Health F	09	WAS	2	4	0	63	42	6.03	1.72	319	309	324	26.5	35%	68%	5.04	37	22	41	3.6	6.0	1.7	12%	1.6	-14.2	26	($2)
PT/Exp B	10	WAS	4	8	0	81	53	5.56	1.48	289	289	289	21.0	32%	64%	4.18	46	19	34	3.0	5.9	2.0	11%	1.1	-15.4	49	$0
Consist B	1st Half		2	2	0	43	32	3.77	1.37	271			23.1	32%	73%	3.91	43	22	34	2.9	6.7	2.3	7%	0.6	1.3	63	$2
LIMA Plan C+	2nd Half		2	6	0	38	21	7.58	1.61	309			19.1	32%	54%	4.49	50	16	34	3.1	5.0	1.6	15%	1.7	-16.7	34	($2)
Rand Var +3	11	Proj	4	8	0	87	59	4.86	1.43	277			22.2	31%	69%	4.33	43	20	38	3.1	6.1	2.0	11%	1.2	-2.0	47	$3

Better than expected start was derailed by shoulder tightness. Out for 2 months, then typical skills, bad luck bumped him from rotation. It's been awhile since '06, so 8 starts in 1H doesn't make him worth a bid.

Olson,Garrett			W	L	Sv	IP	K	ERA	WHIP	OBA	vL	vR	BF/G	H%	S%	xERA	G	L	F	Ctl	Dom	Cmd	hr/f	hr/9	RAR	BPV	R$
LH RP 27	06	aa	6	5	0	84	76	4.71	1.51	286			26.6	36%	69%	4.85				3.4	8.1	2.4		0.6	-2.0	77	$5
Ht/Wt 73 205	07	BAL *	10	10	0	160	133	5.11	1.42	260			24.0	30%	66%	4.68	34	17	49	3.8	7.5	2.0	9%	1.2	-11.9	43	$10
Type Pwr FB	08	BAL *	10	12	0	169	117	5.97	1.69	304	310	309	23.6	35%	65%	4.91	42	19	39	4.1	6.2	1.5	8%	1.0	-33.8	21	$0
Health A	09	SEA *	5	8	0	127	80	5.43	1.39	251	275	251	13.7	26%	64%	5.16	34	19	47	4.0	5.7	1.4	11%	1.5	-15.3	5	$4
PT/Exp D	10	SEA *	2	8	1	84	74	4.25	1.33	255	245	284	7.6	30%	71%	3.90	37	22	41	3.3	7.9	2.4	10%	1.1	-1.2	69	$5
Consist B	1st Half		2	7	0	56	47	4.32	1.27	239			10.6	29%	66%	3.99	41	15	44	3.5	7.6	2.2	6%	0.7	-1.2	61	$4
LIMA Plan B+	2nd Half		0	1	1	28	27	4.12	1.44	285			5.0	33%	80%	3.77	36	24	40	2.9	8.6	3.0	18%	1.9	0.1	91	$1
Rand Var 0	11	Proj	2	5	0	73	60	4.19	1.37	270			7.1	31%	73%	4.14	37	21	42	3.0	7.4	2.5	11%	1.2	1.3	68	$4

0-3, 4.54 ERA in 38 IP at SEA. Failed as a SP, but decent as RP the last 2 years (4.27 ERA, 6.9 Dom). Cmd rebound was a plus, and in last 16 games, had 9.3 Dom, 2.00 ERA. Should stay in relief role.

Ondrusek,Logan			W	L	Sv	IP	K	ERA	WHIP	OBA	vL	vR	BF/G	H%	S%	xERA	G	L	F	Ctl	Dom	Cmd	hr/f	hr/9	RAR	BPV	R$
RH RP 26	06		0	0	0	0	0	0.00	0.00							0.00											
Ht/Wt 79 205	07		0	0	0	0	0	0.00	0.00							0.00											
Type Con	08		0	0	0	0	0	0.00	0.00							0.00											
Health A	09	a/a	2	1	19	52	30	2.32	1.17	236			5.0	28%	79%	2.73				2.7	5.2	1.9		0.2	12.8	74	$12
PT/Exp F	10	CIN *	5	1	1	78	51	4.06	1.24	250	205	236	4.4	28%	69%	3.96	48	14	38	2.7	5.9	2.2	8%	0.8	-0.4	60	$6
Consist C	1st Half		0	1	1	41	27	5.14	1.34	284			4.7	33%	61%	3.83	46	19	34	2.0	6.0	3.0	7%	0.7	-5.6	78	$0
LIMA Plan C+	2nd Half		5	0	0	37	24	2.89	1.12	210			4.1	23%	79%	4.04	49	11	40	3.4	5.8	1.7	9%	1.0	5.2	40	$6
Rand Var 0	11	Proj	5	1	0	73	45	3.85	1.26	252			4.6	28%	71%	4.15	48	13	39	2.7	5.6	2.0	8%	0.9	-0.0	53	$6

5-0, 3.68 ERA in 59 IP at CIN. 15.0 Cmd vs LHers but just 1.3 vs RHers. Had 20-gm scoreless streak but got big assist from 11% hit rate during that span. Upside limited due to marginal Dom.

Oswalt,Roy			W	L	Sv	IP	K	ERA	WHIP	OBA	vL	vR	BF/G	H%	S%	xERA	G	L	F	Ctl	Dom	Cmd	hr/f	hr/9	RAR	BPV	R$
RH SP 33	06	HOU	15	8	0	220	166	2.98	1.17	262	264	262	27.3	31%	77%	3.47	49	20	31	1.6	6.8	4.4	9%	0.7	40.8	107	$27
Ht/Wt 72 185	07	HOU	14	7	0	212	154	3.18	1.33	270	272	259	27.3	32%	77%	3.75	53	16	31	2.5	6.5	2.6	7%	0.6	32.5	80	$21
Type	08	HOU	17	10	0	209	165	3.54	1.18	253	262	243	26.7	29%	74%	3.33	50	20	29	2.0	7.1	3.5	13%	1.0	18.9	102	$23
Health B	09	HOU	8	6	0	181	138	4.12	1.24	264	279	252	25.1	31%	69%	3.73	43	21	36	2.1	6.9	3.3	10%	0.9	1.6	88	$13
PT/Exp A	10	2NL	13	13	0	212	193	2.76	1.03	213	232	196	25.3	26%	77%	3.16	46	18	37	2.3	8.2	3.5	9%	0.8	32.7	108	$27
Consist A	1st Half		5	10	0	111	104	3.32	1.11	227			26.3	28%	73%	3.23	44	20	36	2.5	8.4	3.4	10%	0.9	9.5	106	$11
LIMA Plan C+	2nd Half		8	3	0	101	89	2.14	0.93	198			24.3	24%	81%	3.07	48	15	37	2.1	8.0	3.7	8%	0.7	23.2	111	$16
Rand Var -2	11	Proj	15	8	0	210	176	3.17	1.16	246			26.0	29%	76%	3.40	47	19	35	2.2	7.5	3.5	9%	0.9	19.2	101	$24

Recorded highest Dom since rookie year, and posted 11 straight PQS-DOM outings down the stretch. Can't count on ERA repeat, but consistent BPIs and IP totals provide excellent year-to-year value.

Owings,Micah			W	L	Sv	IP	K	ERA	WHIP	OBA	vL	vR	BF/G	H%	S%	xERA	G	L	F	Ctl	Dom	Cmd	hr/f	hr/9	RAR	BPV	R$
RH RP 28	06	a/a	16	2	0	162	112	4.41	1.54	301			26.8	35%	71%	5.12				2.9	6.2	2.1		0.6	2.2	59	$12
Ht/Wt 77 220	07	ARI	8	8	0	153	106	4.30	1.28	253	265	240	22.1	28%	70%	4.44	37	20	42	2.9	6.2	2.1	10%	1.2	2.3	48	$11
Type Pwr FB	08	ARI	6	9	0	105	87	5.93	1.38	260	268	242	20.5	30%	58%	4.38	34	23	43	3.5	7.5	2.1	10%	1.2	-21.5	51	$3
Health A	09	CIN	7	12	1	120	68	5.34	1.59	272	272	271	20.8	29%	69%	5.45	37	21	42	4.8	5.1	1.1	11%	1.4	-17.0	-23	$1
PT/Exp C	10	CIN *	3	2	0	53	45	4.44	1.64	257	357	163	8.1	31%	73%	5.19	31	20	49	6.0	7.7	1.3	5%	0.7	-2.8	-15	$1
Consist B	1st Half		3	2	0	33	34	4.40	1.53	226			6.9	30%	71%	4.61	31	21	48	6.3	9.4	1.5	5%	0.6	-1.6	7	$2
LIMA Plan C	2nd Half		0	0	0	21	11	4.48	1.82	302			10.9	33%	77%	5.97				5.4	5.0	0.9		0.9	-1.2	17	($1)
Rand Var -2	11	Proj	2	2	0	44	31	4.97	1.61	273			12.3	30%	72%	5.17	34	22	44	5.0	6.4	1.3	10%	1.2	-5.5	-6	$0

3-2, 5.40 ERA in 33 IP at CIN.
PRO: He can hit (.293 BA, 9 HR in 184 career AB).
CON: Everything on the mound the past 2 seasons.
It may be time to give Rick Ankiel a call.

Padilla,Vicente			W	L	Sv	IP	K	ERA	WHIP	OBA	vL	vR	BF/G	H%	S%	xERA	G	L	F	Ctl	Dom	Cmd	hr/f	hr/9	RAR	BPV	R$
RH SP 33	06	TEX	15	10	0	200	156	4.50	1.38	268	305	228	26.1	31%	69%	4.05	44	22	34	3.2	7.0	2.2	10%	0.9	1.4	63	$17
Ht/Wt 74 220	07	TEX	6	10	0	120	71	5.76	1.63	301	329	271	23.8	33%	66%	4.84	46	21	34	3.7	5.3	1.4	11%	1.2	-18.6	18	$1
Type	08	TEX	14	8	0	171	127	4.74	1.46	277	312	240	25.8	31%	71%	4.35	43	19	38	3.4	6.7	2.0	13%	1.4	-8.2	49	$11
Health F	09	2TM	12	6	0	147	97	4.46	1.43	273	303	246	24.6	31%	71%	4.22	48	20	32	3.3	5.9	1.8	11%	1.0	-2.7	44	$10
PT/Exp B	10	LA	6	5	0	95	84	4.07	1.08	228	167	267	23.8	26%	67%	3.48	40	18	42	2.3	8.0	3.5	13%	1.3	-0.7	100	$9
Consist A	1st Half		2	2	0	41	39	5.05	1.17	252			24.0	28%	64%	3.53	36	18	47	2.0	8.6	4.3	17%	2.0	-5.2	115	$3
LIMA Plan B	2nd Half		4	3	0	54	45	3.33	1.02	208			23.6	25%	70%	3.42	43	18	39	2.5	7.5	3.0	9%	0.8	4.5	89	$7
Rand Var 0	11	Proj	10	7	0	141	111	4.15	1.30	259			24.8	30%	71%	3.90	43	19	38	2.8	7.1	2.5	11%	1.1	4.3	73	$11

Built on excellent '09 finish with highest Dom, lowest Ctl of career. Improvement vs. LH was also key. Health still an issue, as he hit DL twice. He'll end up there again, but Cmd jump suggests going an extra buck.

BRIAN RUDD

Palmer,Matt	Yr	Tm	W	L	Sv	IP	K	ERA	WHIP	OBA	vL	vR	BF/G	H%	S%	xERA	G	L	F	Ctl	Dom	Cmd	hr/f	hr/9	RAR	BPV	R$
RH RP 32	06	a/a	11	7	0	153	85	4.26	1.54	305			22.8	34%	74%	5.44				2.7	5.0	1.9		0.8	5.0	39	$8
Ht/Wt 74 225	07	aaa	11	8	0	155	69	6.75	1.91	346			25.0	36%	66%	7.76				3.8	4.0	1.1		1.4	-43.7	-9	($7)
Type GB	08	aaa	6	10	0	142	91	7.01	2.18	349			27.8	39%	67%	7.92				6.0	5.8	1.0		0.9	-47.4	12	($13)
Health A	09	LAA	11	2	0	121	69	3.93	1.32	235	279	197	12.9	25%	72%	4.55	51	16	34	4.1	5.1	1.3	9%	0.9	7.8	11	$12
PT/Exp C	10	LAA *	3	5	2	80	46	3.58	1.39	244	268	291	12.7	27%	75%	4.54	49	15	36	4.3	5.1	1.2	6%	0.6	5.5	4	$5
Consist D	1st Half		0	1	0	23	11	6.26	2.04	323			12.7	36%	67%	5.78	51	16	33	6.3	4.3	0.7	4%	0.4	-6.0	-62	($2)
LIMA Plan C+	2nd Half		3	4	2	57	35	2.49	1.12	207			12.7	23%	81%	4.39	43	10	47	3.5	5.5	1.6	5%	0.7	11.5	26	$7
Rand Var -3	11	Proj	6	6	0	123	74	4.56	1.53	275			14.7	31%	71%	4.62	50	15	34	4.2	5.4	1.3	8%	0.8	-5.0	13	$4

1-2, 4.54 ERA in 33 IP at LAA. Shoulder sprain cost him chance to prove that '09 was no fluke. Don't be fooled by sexy 2H ERA and WHIP. They were H% and S% induced. Without some Cmd, his nice GB% is useless. Pass.

Papelbon,Jonathan	Yr	Tm	W	L	Sv	IP	K	ERA	WHIP	OBA	vL	vR	BF/G	H%	S%	xERA	G	L	F	Ctl	Dom	Cmd	hr/f	hr/9	RAR	BPV	R$
RH RP 30	06	BOS	4	2	35	68	75	0.93	0.78	172	203	128	4.3	24%	92%	2.89	37	17	46	1.7	9.9	5.8	4%	0.4	30.5	147	$28
Ht/Wt 76 225	07	BOS	1	3	37	58	84	1.85	0.77	154	104	200	3.6	24%	83%	2.56	29	16	55	2.3	13.0	5.6	8%	0.8	19.1	178	$25
Type Pwr FB	08	BOS	5	4	41	69	77	2.34	0.95	229	235	210	4.0	31%	77%	2.43	49	20	31	1.0	10.0	9.6	7%	0.5	17.2	179	$26
Health A	09	BOS	1	1	38	68	76	1.85	1.15	220	187	242	4.2	30%	88%	3.73	27	21	52	3.2	10.1	3.2	6%	0.7	21.8	100	$23
PT/Exp A	10	BOS	5	7	37	67	76	3.90	1.27	232	255	189	4.3	31%	72%	3.44	38	18	44	3.8	10.2	2.7	9%	0.9	2.0	98	$20
Consist B	1st Half		3	4	19	34	30	3.71	1.15	220			4.2	24%	76%	4.02	33	15	53	3.2	7.9	2.5	12%	1.6	1.8	68	$10
LIMA Plan B	2nd Half		2	3	18	33	46	4.09	1.39	244			4.4	38%	69%	2.81	45	21	34	4.4	12.5	2.9	4%	0.3	0.2	131	$9
Rand Var 0	11	Proj	4	5	38	68	79	3.31	1.16	223			4.2	30%	74%	3.26	37	19	44	3.2	10.5	3.3	8%	0.8	8.6	118	$22

Some pitchers think that the way to fix any problem is to just throw harder. Took something off his pitches in 1H and FB, HR spiked. In 2H, threw harder... Dom rose but so did Ctl and H%. It's a mess, but skills are still there.

Park,Chan Ho	Yr	Tm	W	L	Sv	IP	K	ERA	WHIP	OBA	vL	vR	BF/G	H%	S%	xERA	G	L	F	Ctl	Dom	Cmd	hr/f	hr/9	RAR	BPV	R$
RH RP 37	06	SD	7	7	0	136	96	4.82	1.40	275	266	278	24.5	30%	69%	4.35	44	18	38	2.9	6.3	2.2	12%	1.3	-5.6	57	$7
Ht/Wt 74 212	07	aa	6	14	0	135	86	8.38	1.97	365			27.5	38%	61%	9.29				3.1	5.7	1.8		2.4	-65.3	-18	($12)
Type Pwr	08	LA	4	4	2	95	79	3.40	1.40	265	301	237	7.6	31%	80%	3.73	51	19	30	3.4	7.5	2.2	14%	1.1	10.2	71	$8
Health B	09	PHI	3	3	0	83	73	4.43	1.40	263	280	248	8.0	33%	68%	3.82	44	24	33	3.6	7.9	2.2	6%	0.5	-2.5	68	$4
PT/Exp C	10	2TM	4	3	0	64	52	4.66	1.32	266	270	246	5.1	30%	68%	3.66	49	14	37	2.7	7.3	2.7	13%	1.3	-4.6	87	$4
Consist A	1st Half		1	1	0	27	21	6.40	1.46	298			5.8	32%	61%	4.07	40	18	42	2.4	7.1	3.0	17%	2.0	-7.7	81	($0)
LIMA Plan B+	2nd Half		3	2	0	37	31	3.41	1.22	240			4.6	29%	74%	3.33	56	11	33	2.9	7.5	2.6	8%	0.7	3.0	91	$4
Rand Var +2	11	Proj	2	2	0	44	36	4.55	1.40	273			5.7	32%	70%	3.82	48	17	35	3.1	7.4	2.4	11%	1.0	2.1	76	$2

Has found a home in short relief. That 2H BPV and accompanying elite GB% would've pegged him as a bullpen sleeper in deep leagues...10 years ago. Today, he's a potential sub-4.00 ERA LIMA arm nearing retirement.

Parnell,Bobby	Yr	Tm	W	L	Sv	IP	K	ERA	WHIP	OBA	vL	vR	BF/G	H%	S%	xERA	G	L	F	Ctl	Dom	Cmd	hr/f	hr/9	RAR	BPV	R$
RH RP 26	06		0	0	0	0	0	0.00	0.00							0.00											
Ht/Wt 76 200	07	aa	5	5	0	89	62	5.63	1.70	311			24.2	36%	67%	6.12				3.9	6.3	1.6		0.9	-12.8	36	$0
Type Pwr GB	08	a/a	12	8	0	148	93	5.70	1.66	299			23.4	33%	66%	5.65				4.1	5.7	1.4		0.9	-25.4	31	$2
Health A	09	NYM	4	8	1	88	74	5.30	1.66	289	270	290	6.0	35%	68%	4.50	47	16	37	4.7	7.5	1.6	8%	0.8	-12.1	34	$1
PT/Exp D	10	NYM *	1	2	4	76	67	3.74	1.39	272	327	276	5.0	34%	73%	2.91	56	26	18	3.0	7.9	2.6	10%	0.5	2.6	95	$4
Consist C	1st Half		1	1	4	50	45	4.09	1.40	259			6.5	33%	71%	3.22	56	20	24	3.7	8.1	2.2	9%	0.6	-0.4	80	$3
LIMA Plan B+	2nd Half		0	1	0	26	22	3.08	1.37	295			3.5	37%	77%	2.67	56	28	16	1.7	7.5	4.4	7%	0.3	3.0	124	$1
Rand Var +3	11	Proj	3	3	8	73	63	3.85	1.31	260			5.2	32%	72%	3.30	51	21	27	2.9	7.8	2.7	10%	0.7	7.5	93	$8

0-1, 2.83 ERA in 35 IP at NYM. The makings of an impact RP...
- Rising Dom, improving Ctl
- ground baller
- Continued xERA improvement

If elbow is ok and out pitch vs. LHers comes... UP: 30 SV

Parra,Manny	Yr	Tm	W	L	Sv	IP	K	ERA	WHIP	OBA	vL	vR	BF/G	H%	S%	xERA	G	L	F	Ctl	Dom	Cmd	hr/f	hr/9	RAR	BPV	R$
LH RP 28	06	aa	3	0	0	31	25	4.18	1.36	273			22.2	35%	66%	3.61				2.7	7.3	2.7		0.0	1.3	101	$3
Ht/Wt 75 216	07	MIL *	10	5	0	133	119	3.34	1.32	254	174	280	21.6	33%	74%	4.17	33	23	44	3.3	8.1	2.5	2%	0.3	17.8	68	$14
Type Pwr	08	MIL	10	8	0	166	147	4.39	1.54	279	233	288	23.1	34%	74%	3.74	52	22	27	4.1	8.0	2.0	13%	1.0	-2.5	63	$8
Health A	09	MIL *	12	13	0	164	132	5.93	1.75	299	287	311	24.8	35%	67%	4.59	48	18	34	5.0	7.3	1.5	11%	1.0	-35.3	23	($1)
PT/Exp B	10	MIL	3	10	0	122	129	5.02	1.62	282	326	264	13.2	35%	72%	3.74	47	18	34	4.6	9.5	2.0	15%	1.3	-15.1	71	$0
Consist B	1st Half		3	5	0	65	66	4.45	1.65	294			11.8	37%	76%	3.68	49	19	32	4.3	9.2	2.1	13%	1.1	-3.5	76	$1
LIMA Plan B	2nd Half		0	5	0	57	63	5.65	1.59	267			15.2	33%	68%	3.81	45	18	37	5.0	9.9	2.0	17%	1.6	-11.6	65	($1)
Rand Var +5	11	Proj	7	10	0	145	138	4.84	1.59	279			17.2	34%	71%	3.96	48	19	33	4.5	8.6	1.9	11%	1.0	3.2	57	$4

Starter or reliever? You decide...

BPV by Time Through Lineup

1st	128
2nd	21
3rd	-31

Growing problems vs. LHers cement it. He'll kill you as a SP.

Pauley,David	Yr	Tm	W	L	Sv	IP	K	ERA	WHIP	OBA	vL	vR	BF/G	H%	S%	xERA	G	L	F	Ctl	Dom	Cmd	hr/f	hr/9	RAR	BPV	R$
RH SP 27	06	a/a	3	6	0	110	63	5.31	1.59	309			26.1	32%	71%	6.46				2.9	5.1	1.8		1.6	-10.7	12	$1
Ht/Wt 74 210	07	aaa	6	6	0	153	94	5.87	1.63	314			25.8	34%	66%	6.29				3.1	5.5	1.8		1.2	-26.7	26	($1)
Type Con GB	08	aaa	14	4	0	147	87	4.51	1.46	294			25.7	33%	69%	4.78				2.5	5.3	2.1		0.6	-3.8	54	$10
Health A	09	aaa	9	12	0	152	87	6.16	1.72	333			26.1	36%	66%	6.80				2.8	5.2	1.8		1.3	-34.7	20	($3)
PT/Exp D	10	SEA *	5	15	0	176	99	4.04	1.35	267	247	261	22.1	29%	72%	4.07	50	19	31	2.9	5.0	1.7	10%	0.9	2.2	41	$8
Consist F	1st Half		1	6	0	88	51	3.87	1.40	275			22.4	31%	72%	4.90	22	33	44	3.0	5.2	1.7	4%	0.5	3.0	12	$3
LIMA Plan C+	2nd Half		4	9	0	88	48	4.21	1.29	258			21.7	27%	72%	3.98	51	18	31	2.8	4.9	1.8	15%	1.3	-0.7	43	$5
Rand Var 0	11	Proj	5	7	0	94	54	4.77	1.47	293			24.4	32%	70%	4.21	51	18	31	2.8	5.2	1.9	11%	1.1	0.9	47	$3

4-9, 4.07 ERA in 90 IP at SEA. Journeyman didn't blow up in MLB debut, but with sub-tipping point Dom, he's got a razor-thin margin of error. He's one of those "fifth starter in big park" flyers that never seem to help.

Paulino,Felipe	Yr	Tm	W	L	Sv	IP	K	ERA	WHIP	OBA	vL	vR	BF/G	H%	S%	xERA	G	L	F	Ctl	Dom	Cmd	hr/f	hr/9	RAR	BPV	R$
RH SP 27	06		0	0	0	0	0	0.00	0.00							0.00											
Ht/Wt 74 180	07	aa	4	5	0	112	90	4.47	1.53	276			22.6	33%	70%	4.73				4.1	7.2	1.8		0.6	-0.1	63	$5
Type Pwr FB	08	HOU	0	0	0	0	0	0.00	0.00							0.00											
Health F	09	HOU *	5	12	0	132	117	5.70	1.70	304	354	286	20.3	36%	69%	4.45	42	19	39	4.2	8.0	1.9	13%	1.4	-24.5	51	($1)
PT/Exp D	10	HOU	1	9	0	92	83	5.10	1.54	269	306	248	21.5	34%	65%	4.26	42	16	42	4.5	8.1	1.8	4%	0.4	-12.3	45	($0)
Consist A	1st Half		1	8	0	86	76	4.40	1.51	264			27.2	34%	69%	4.29	42	16	42	4.5	8.0	1.8	2%	0.2	-4.0	41	$1
LIMA Plan D+	2nd Half		0	1	0	6	7	15.79	1.93	332			5.5	40%	11%	3.84	47	11	42	4.7	11.1	2.3	28%	3.2	-8.3	96	($2)
Rand Var +1	11	Proj	5	9	0	131	116	4.55	1.53	273			23.2	33%	72%	4.27	44	15	41	4.3	8.0	1.9	8%	0.9	-2.0	51	$4

Shoulder inflammation shelved upside arm in 2H. While overall skills didn't grow like we hoped, they did in flashes. Had an 81 BPV w/none on vs. a 10 BPV with runners on. There's still profit potential here... at $1.

Pavano,Carl	Yr	Tm	W	L	Sv	IP	K	ERA	WHIP	OBA	vL	vR	BF/G	H%	S%	xERA	G	L	F	Ctl	Dom	Cmd	hr/f	hr/9	RAR	BPV	R$
RH SP 35	06	a/a	2	0	0	17	15	1.59	1.12	250			17.2	33%	84%	2.62				1.6	7.9	5.0		0.0	6.1	158	$3
Ht/Wt 77 240	07	NYY	1	0	0	11	4	4.78	1.24	274	208	350	23.5	28%	62%	4.56	46	18	36	1.6	3.2	2.0	7%	0.8	-0.4	38	$1
Type Con	08	NYY *	5	3	0	48	26	5.40	1.47	295	324	283	21.2	30%	68%	4.84	40	17	42	2.6	4.8	1.9	13%	1.7	-6.3	35	$2
Health F	09	2AL	14	12	0	199	147	5.10	1.37	295	271	317	25.9	33%	65%	3.98	43	19	37	1.8	6.6	3.8	11%	1.2	-16.0	93	$13
PT/Exp A	10	MIN	17	11	0	221	117	3.75	1.19	267	292	242	28.4	29%	72%	3.68	51	18	31	1.5	4.8	3.2	11%	1.0	10.7	74	$20
Consist B	1st Half		9	6	0	112	63	3.30	1.05	241			27.7	26%	72%	3.55	48	20	33	1.4	5.1	3.7	10%	0.9	11.5	80	$14
LIMA Plan D+	2nd Half		8	5	0	109	54	4.20	1.34	292			29.1	31%	72%	3.81	55	16	29	1.6	4.4	2.7	12%	1.1	-0.8	68	$7
Rand Var 0	11	Proj	15	10	0	189	106	4.11	1.32	284			26.6	31%	72%	4.03	48	18	34	1.8	5.1	2.9	11%	1.1	6.0	69	$15

Conjured up memories of '04 with this gem. As an emerging GBer with pinpoint control, he has found his niche. Problem is, with that K rate, any regression in GB or Ctl is trouble. Use 2H ERA, WHIP as your baseline.

Peavy,Jake	Yr	Tm	W	L	Sv	IP	K	ERA	WHIP	OBA	vL	vR	BF/G	H%	S%	xERA	G	L	F	Ctl	Dom	Cmd	hr/f	hr/9	RAR	BPV	R$
RH SP 29	06	SD	11	14	0	202	215	4.10	1.23	247	242	243	26.2	32%	69%	3.58	38	18	44	2.8	9.6	3.5	10%	1.0	9.7	114	$20
Ht/Wt 73 193	07	SD	19	6	0	223	240	2.54	1.06	212	242	174	26.1	29%	78%	3.16	44	17	39	2.7	9.7	3.5	6%	0.5	52.0	122	$37
Type Pwr FB	08	SD	10	11	0	174	166	2.85	1.18	230	263	194	26.4	28%	80%	3.54	41	21	38	3.1	8.6	2.8	10%	0.9	30.4	91	$21
Health F	09	2TM	9	6	0	102	110	3.45	1.12	218	249	178	25.7	29%	71%	3.26	42	18	40	3.0	9.7	3.2	8%	0.7	10.8	114	$15
PT/Exp B	10	CHW	7	6	0	107	93	4.63	1.23	245	275	209	26.1	29%	65%	3.73	41	18	42	2.9	7.8	2.7	10%	1.1	-6.4	82	$9
Consist A	1st Half		7	6	0	105	91	4.70	1.23	246			27.3	29%	64%	3.73	41	18	42	2.8	7.8	2.8	10%	1.1	-7.3	83	$8
LIMA Plan B+	2nd Half		0	0	0	2	2	0.00	1.18	173			7.0	26%	100%	3.79	33	0	67	5.3	10.6	2.0	0%	0.0	0.9	59	$0
Rand Var +2	11	Proj	9	7	0	131	121	3.79	1.21	240			27.0	29%	72%	3.61	41	19	40	2.9	8.3	2.9	10%	1.0	10.9	91	$14

Detached muscle in shoulder ended year in July, casts doubt upon '11. Blame most of ERA spike on S%. xERA confirms he's still a legit sub-4.00 ERA pitcher. But given health grade, he's gone from ace to wildcard.

STEPHEN NICKRAND

Pelfrey,Mike		W	L	Sv	IP	K	ERA	WHIP	OBA	vL	vR	BF/G	H%	S%	xERA	G	L	F	Ctl	Dom	Cmd	hr/f	hr/9	RAR	BPV	R$
RH SP 27	06 NYM *	7	3	0	95	84	4.16	1.57	279	278	326	23.7	35%	73%	4.00	49	23	29	4.3	7.9	1.9	6%	0.5	3.9	55	$6
Ht/Wt 79 230	07 NYM *	6	14	0	147	92	5.16	1.60	292	321	279	22.9	33%	68%	4.54	48	23	28	4.0	5.6	1.4	9%	0.7	-13.4	20	$2
Type Con	08 NYM	13	11	0	201	110	3.72	1.36	270	307	245	26.8	30%	73%	4.20	50	21	30	2.9	4.9	1.7	6%	0.5	13.6	39	$14
Health A	09 NYM	10	12	0	184	107	5.03	1.51	291	284	294	26.4	32%	67%	4.31	51	19	30	3.2	5.2	1.6	10%	0.9	-19.1	36	$4
PT/Exp A	10 NYM	15	9	1	204	113	3.66	1.38	270	279	272	25.8	30%	74%	4.20	48	20	32	3.0	5.0	1.7	6%	0.5	8.9	35	$13
Consist A	1st Half	10	2	1	104	66	2.93	1.29	254			25.9	29%	78%	3.88	49	21	30	3.0	5.7	1.9	6%	0.5	13.9	48	$11
LIMA Plan D+	2nd Half	5	7	0	100	47	4.42	1.46	287			25.7	31%	69%	4.54	47	20	33	3.0	4.2	1.4	5%	0.5	-5.0	21	$2
Rand Var -2	11 Proj	**11**	**10**	**0**	**174**	**99**	**4.19**	**1.44**	**279**			**26.2**	**31%**	**72%**	**4.29**	**49**	**20**	**31**	**3.2**	**5.1**	**1.6**	**9%**	**0.8**	**-3.2**	**34**	**$8**

3 reasons he'll be overvalued...
- BPV remains far below average
- Skill erosion in 2nd half
- hr/f, S% drove improved ERA
Some will see sub 4.00 ERA and expect repeat, you'll note similarities to '09 and heed risk.

Pena,Tony		W	L	Sv	IP	K	ERA	WHIP	OBA	vL	vR	BF/G	H%	S%	xERA	G	L	F	Ctl	Dom	Cmd	hr/f	hr/9	RAR	BPV	R$
RH RP 29	06 ARI *	8	5	14	76	53	3.33	1.22	266			4.8	30%	75%	4.07	39	22	39	1.8	6.2	3.5	7%	0.8	10.9	81	$15
Ht/Wt 74 219	07 ARI	5	4	2	85	63	3.27	1.10	208	245	176	4.6	24%	73%	3.99	48	12	40	3.3	6.6	2.0	8%	0.8	12.2	57	$11
Type	08 ARI	3	2	3	73	52	4.33	1.33	281	296	267	4.3	33%	67%	3.79	47	20	32	2.1	6.4	3.1	7%	0.6	-0.6	84	$5
Health A	09 2TM	6	5	2	70	55	3.99	1.44	291	288	280	4.2	34%	74%	3.83	46	23	31	2.6	7.1	2.8	10%	0.9	2.8	82	$6
PT/Exp C	10 CHW	5	3	0	101	56	5.09	1.52	276	244	308	8.6	30%	67%	4.57	49	18	33	4.0	5.0	1.2	9%	0.9	-11.9	8	$1
Consist A	1st Half	1	1	0	37	26	5.31	1.39	255			5.7	28%	64%	4.06	50	16	34	3.9	6.3	1.6	13%	1.2	-5.4	37	$1
LIMA Plan B+	2nd Half	4	2	0	63	30	4.97	1.59	287			11.9	31%	69%	4.88	48	19	33	4.1	4.3	1.0	7%	0.7	-6.5	-9	$1
Rand Var 0	11 Proj	**5**	**3**	**0**	**80**	**57**	**4.18**	**1.38**	**277**			**4.6**	**32%**	**72%**	**3.91**	**48**	**19**	**33**	**2.7**	**6.4**	**2.4**	**10%**	**0.9**	**3.7**	**68**	**$6**

5-3, 5.10 ERA in 100 IP at CHW. Getting stretched out as a SP didn't work out well. Growing problems vs. RHers put his effectiveness into question regardless of role. As RP, he'll have LIMA value. As SP, avoid.

Penny,Brad		W	L	Sv	IP	K	ERA	WHIP	OBA	vL	vR	BF/G	H%	S%	xERA	G	L	F	Ctl	Dom	Cmd	hr/f	hr/9	RAR	BPV	R$
RH SP 32	06 LA	16	9	0	189	148	4.33	1.38	279	275	283	23.9	33%	70%	4.03	44	20	36	2.6	7.0	2.7	9%	0.9	3.6	79	$16
Ht/Wt 76 240	07 LA	16	4	0	208	135	3.03	1.31	253	229	286	26.6	30%	77%	4.09	49	20	31	3.2	5.8	1.8	4%	0.4	35.8	47	$22
Type	08 LA	6	9	0	95	51	6.27	1.63	295	328	284	22.7	31%	62%	4.80	49	20	31	4.0	4.8	1.2	13%	1.2	-23.4	7	($1)
Health F	09 2TM	11	9	0	173	109	4.88	1.40	281	259	299	24.9	31%	67%	4.42	44	18	39	2.6	5.7	2.1	10%	1.1	-12.2	52	$9
PT/Exp B	10 STL	3	4	0	56	35	3.23	1.29	286	360	248	26.1	33%	76%	3.50	53	18	29	1.5	5.7	3.9	7%	0.6	5.4	93	$4
Consist B	1st Half	3	4	0	56	35	3.23	1.29	286			26.1	33%	76%	3.50	53	18	29	1.5	5.7	3.9	7%	0.6	5.4	93	$4
LIMA Plan B	2nd Half	0	0	0	0	0	0.00	0.00							0.00											
Rand Var -1	11 Proj	**8**	**8**	**0**	**123**	**77**	**4.41**	**1.41**	**282**			**25.3**	**32%**	**70%**	**4.09**	**48**	**19**	**32**	**2.7**	**5.7**	**2.1**	**9%**	**0.9**	**0.8**	**55**	**$6**

Strained lat sidelined him after May. When healthy, Cmd spike and strong GB% tilt gave him best skills in a long time. Just don't bet on a repeat. Horrible health record, marginal Dom give him risk, no room for error.

Peralta,Joel		W	L	Sv	IP	K	ERA	WHIP	OBA	vL	vR	BF/G	H%	S%	xERA	G	L	F	Ctl	Dom	Cmd	hr/f	hr/9	RAR	BPV	R$
RH RP 35	06 KC	1	3	1	73	57	4.43	1.24	264	338	234	4.8	30%	68%	4.22	32	22	46	2.1	7.0	3.4	10%	1.2	1.2	79	$6
Ht/Wt 71 193	07 KC	1	3	1	88	66	3.80	1.28	273	248	290	5.9	32%	73%	4.10	36	22	42	1.9	6.8	3.5	8%	0.9	7.7	83	$7
Type xFB	08 KC *	2	2	2	71	52	4.44	1.27	256	247	294	5.9	27%	73%	4.38	35	17	48	2.7	6.7	2.5	15%	1.9	-0.8	61	$5
Health A	09 COL *	6	3	4	61	48	4.20	1.38	263			4.5	31%	71%	4.69	25	26	49	3.3	7.0	2.1	7%	0.9	-0.1	39	$6
PT/Exp D	10 WAS *	3	0	20	82	79	1.78	0.92	204	212	145	4.7	26%	85%	3.49	26	18	56	1.8	8.7	4.9	5%	0.7	22.6	112	$19
Consist B	1st Half	2	0	20	40	35	1.19	1.10	240			4.9	31%	90%	3.79	20	30	50	1.9	8.0	4.2	2%	0.2	13.9	91	$13
LIMA Plan B+	2nd Half	1	0	0	42	44	2.34	0.76	167			4.6	20%	78%	3.15	27	16	57	1.7	9.4	5.5	9%	1.1	8.7	128	$7
Rand Var -5	11 Proj	**3**	**1**	**0**	**66**	**57**	**3.70**	**1.22**	**254**			**5.0**	**30%**	**74%**	**4.00**	**31**	**19**	**49**	**2.3**	**7.8**	**3.4**	**8%**	**1.1**	**1.1**	**87**	**$6**

1-0, 2.02 ERA in 49 IP at WAS. He has shown these flashes before, but nothing like this. H% and S% helped a lot, and sky high FB% gives him more risk than other LIMA gems. Still, take profit here on a couple buck bid.

Perez,Chris		W	L	Sv	IP	K	ERA	WHIP	OBA	vL	vR	BF/G	H%	S%	xERA	G	L	F	Ctl	Dom	Cmd	hr/f	hr/9	RAR	BPV	R$
RH RP 25	06	0	0	0	0	0	0.00	0.00							0.00											
Ht/Wt 76 230	07 aa	2	1	36	54	68	3.33	1.19	141			4.1	19%	75%	2.29				6.5	11.3	1.7		0.8	7.5	106	$19
Type Pwr xFB	08 STL *	4	4	18	67	74	3.51	1.36	223	220	231	4.3	28%	79%	3.89	39	20	41	5.0	10.0	2.0	13%	1.2	6.3	62	$13
Health A	09 2TM	1	2	2	57	68	4.26	1.19	203	188	207	3.8	26%	68%	3.56	35	18	47	4.3	10.7	2.5	13%	1.3	0.3	91	$6
PT/Exp C	10 CLE	2	2	23	63	61	1.71	1.08	184	216	154	4.0	24%	88%	3.73	34	20	46	4.0	8.7	2.2	6%	0.6	18.8	61	$17
Consist A	1st Half	0	2	7	32	26	2.81	1.19	217			4.0	25%	82%	4.21	32	20	48	3.7	7.3	2.0	9%	1.1	5.2	43	$5
LIMA Plan C+	2nd Half	2	0	16	31	35	0.58	0.97	146			4.0	22%	93%	3.23	37	19	43	4.4	10.2	2.3	0%	0.0	13.6	81	$12
Rand Var -5	11 Proj	**2**	**2**	**35**	**58**	**63**	**3.26**	**1.17**	**208**			**4.0**	**27%**	**76%**	**3.61**	**35**	**19**	**46**	**3.9**	**9.8**	**2.5**	**9%**	**0.9**	**4.8**	**85**	**$18**

Took hold of CLE closer job in 2H and ran with it. Another year of improved control suggests there's more upside to come. Just ignore sexy ERA and WHIP; they'll regress as H% and S% correct.

Perez,Oliver		W	L	Sv	IP	K	ERA	WHIP	OBA	vL	vR	BF/G	H%	S%	xERA	G	L	F	Ctl	Dom	Cmd	hr/f	hr/9	RAR	BPV	R$
LH RP 29	06 2NL *	5	18	0	163	152	7.08	1.71	288	260	300	23.6	33%	61%	5.07	30	23	47	5.1	8.4	1.7	14%	1.8	-52.2	22	($5)
Ht/Wt 75 205	07 NYM	15	10	0	177	174	3.56	1.31	235	206	235	25.8	29%	77%	4.28	33	17	50	4.0	8.8	2.2	9%	1.1	18.9	62	$20
Type Pwr xFB	08 NYM	10	7	0	194	180	4.22	1.40	234	158	258	24.7	28%	73%	4.54	32	22	46	4.9	8.4	1.7	10%	1.1	1.2	29	$13
Health F	09 NYM	3	4	0	66	62	6.82	1.92	270	200	306	22.8	31%	67%	6.07	28	20	52	7.9	8.5	1.1	12%	1.6	-21.4	-55	($4)
PT/Exp B	10 NYM	0	5	0	46	37	6.80	2.07	293	214	317	13.6	32%	70%	6.27	35	19	46	8.2	7.2	0.9	13%	1.7	-15.9	-78	($5)
Consist B	1st Half	0	3	0	39	30	6.28	1.96	283			17.2	31%	71%	5.90	39	18	43	7.7	7.0	0.9	13%	1.6	-10.8	-64	($4)
LIMA Plan F	2nd Half	0	2	0	8	7	9.47	2.63	339			7.0	38%	67%	8.07	19	22	59	10.7	8.3	0.8	13%	2.4	-5.1	******	($2)
Rand Var +2	11 Proj	**3**	**6**	**0**	**86**	**77**	**5.53**	**1.69**	**261**			**20.9**	**31%**	**70%**	**5.41**	**28**	**21**	**51**	**6.3**	**8.0**	**1.3**	**10%**	**1.4**	**-13.5**	**-19**	**($1)**

Just when you thought it couldn't get any worse...it did. More knee problems played a part, but his issues are deeper than that. Rising Ctl, continued flyball approach are a lethal combo, healthy or not. Stay far away.

Perez,Rafael		W	L	Sv	IP	K	ERA	WHIP	OBA	vL	vR	BF/G	H%	S%	xERA	G	L	F	Ctl	Dom	Cmd	hr/f	hr/9	RAR	BPV	R$
LH RP 28	06 CLE *	4	8	0	106	90	3.65	1.28	246			10.4	31%	71%	3.57	58	9	33	3.2	7.6	2.4	5%	0.4	11.9	85	$11
Ht/Wt 75 195	07 CLE *	4	5	1	107	90	2.97	1.19	252	145	213	8.5	31%	77%	3.30	53	17	30	2.2	7.6	3.4	9%	0.7	20.3	107	$13
Type GB	08 CLE	4	4	2	76	86	3.54	1.18	237	222	243	4.3	31%	73%	2.54	57	19	24	2.7	10.1	3.7	17%	0.9	7.6	144	$10
Health A	09 CLE	4	3	0	48	32	7.31	1.90	328	412	277	4.3	37%	60%	4.84	49	24	27	4.7	6.0	1.3	11%	0.9	-16.9	8	($2)
PT/Exp C	10 CLE	6	1	0	61	36	3.25	1.59	295	306	295	3.9	34%	80%	4.09	55	19	26	3.7	5.3	1.4	6%	0.4	6.7	29	$4
Consist D	1st Half	1	0	0	27	18	4.29	1.76	319			3.8	38%	73%	4.07	54	23	23	4.0	5.9	1.5	0%	0.0	-0.5	32	($0)
LIMA Plan C+	2nd Half	5	1	0	34	18	2.40	1.45	275			4.1	30%	87%	4.09	57	15	28	3.5	4.8	1.4	10%	0.8	7.2	28	$4
Rand Var -2	11 Proj	**4**	**3**	**0**	**58**	**41**	**4.34**	**1.48**	**275**			**4.3**	**32%**	**72%**	**3.88**	**54**	**20**	**26**	**3.7**	**6.4**	**1.7**	**10%**	**0.8**	**2.9**	**46**	**$3**

ERA rekindled '07-'08 promise, but this version is much different. All that remains is his elite GB%. As a lefty reliever, he'll keep getting more chances. Don't follow suit. ERA will regress, and he's far from getting save opps.

Perry,Ryan		W	L	Sv	IP	K	ERA	WHIP	OBA	vL	vR	BF/G	H%	S%	xERA	G	L	F	Ctl	Dom	Cmd	hr/f	hr/9	RAR	BPV	R$
RH RP 24	06	0	0	0	0	0	0.00	0.00							0.00											
Ht/Wt 76 200	07	0	0	0	0	0	0.00	0.00							0.00											
Type Pwr FB	08	0	0	0	0	0	0.00	0.00							0.00											
Health A	09 DET *	1	1	3	76	71	3.69	1.49	247	294	206	5.5	30%	78%	4.40	42	19	39	5.1	8.4	1.7	10%	1.0	7.2	33	$5
PT/Exp D	10 DET	3	5	2	63	45	3.59	1.24	237	167	284	4.4	27%	74%	4.07	44	15	41	3.3	6.5	2.0	8%	0.9	4.3	49	$6
Consist A	1st Half	1	4	1	23	19	5.55	1.54	256			4.1	31%	64%	4.47	43	17	40	5.2	7.5	1.5	7%	0.8	-4.0	18	$1
LIMA Plan C+	2nd Half	2	1	1	40	26	2.47	1.07	226			4.6	25%	82%	3.85	45	14	41	2.2	5.8	2.6	8%	0.9	8.2	67	$5
Rand Var -1	11 Proj	**2**	**4**	**3**	**73**	**59**	**3.85**	**1.38**	**255**			**4.7**	**30%**	**75%**	**4.17**	**43**	**17**	**40**	**3.7**	**7.3**	**2.0**	**9%**	**1.0**	**1.0**	**53**	**$5**

Biceps problem caused horrible 1H. His 2H skills show more command than upside, but with his elite raw stuff, his Dom potential remains high. Next: pairing '09 Dom with '10 2H Ctl. UP: 20 SV

Pettitte,Andy		W	L	Sv	IP	K	ERA	WHIP	OBA	vL	vR	BF/G	H%	S%	xERA	G	L	F	Ctl	Dom	Cmd	hr/f	hr/9	RAR	BPV	R$
LH SP 38	06 HOU	14	13	0	214	178	4.20	1.44	283	259	290	25.9	33%	74%	3.71	50	22	29	2.9	7.5	2.5	14%	1.1	7.5	83	$15
Ht/Wt 77 225	07 NYY	15	9	0	215	141	4.05	1.43	282	298	282	26.0	32%	72%	4.23	48	19	33	2.9	5.9	2.0	7%	0.7	12.0	54	$16
Type Pwr	08 NYY	14	14	0	204	158	4.54	1.41	288	203	325	26.8	34%	69%	3.59	51	20	29	2.4	7.0	2.9	10%	0.8	-4.9	89	$14
Health C	09 NYY	14	8	0	195	148	4.16	1.38	260	282	249	26.2	30%	72%	4.31	43	19	38	3.5	6.8	1.9	9%	0.9	7.0	49	$16
PT/Exp A	10 NYY	11	3	0	129	101	3.28	1.27	253	186	283	25.7	30%	77%	3.79	44	18	38	2.9	7.0	2.5	9%	0.9	13.7	72	$14
Consist B	1st Half	10	2	0	105	78	2.82	1.15	233			26.8	27%	80%	3.74	44	18	38	2.6	6.7	2.5	9%	0.9	17.1	70	$14
LIMA Plan C	2nd Half	1	1	0	24	23	5.32	1.81	331			22.4	41%	71%	3.97	45	20	35	3.8	8.7	2.3	8%	0.8	-3.4	78	($0)
Rand Var -1	11 Proj	**12**	**7**	**0**	**174**	**138**	**4.29**	**1.39**	**263**			**24.2**	**31%**	**71%**	**3.98**	**46**	**19**	**35**	**3.5**	**7.1**	**2.1**	**9%**	**0.9**	**6.6**	**59**	**$13**

Groin injury wiped out two months. In the end, he's as consistent a $15 pitcher as they come, even as age 40 draws near. Just don't bid on a sub 3.50 ERA or 200 IP again.
DN: More DL time

STEPHEN NICKRAND

Pineiro,Joel

				W	L	Sv	IP	K	ERA	WHIP	OBA	vL	vR	BF/G	H%	S%	xERA	G	L	F	Ctl	Dom	Cmd	hr/f	hr/9	RAR	BPV	R$
RH SP	32	06	SEA	8	13	1	165	87	6.37	1.65	310	287	332	18.9	33%	62%	4.76	47	23	29	3.5	4.7	1.4	13%	1.3	-37.0	17	($1)
Ht/Wt	73 200	07	2TM	7	5	0	98	60	4.33	1.39	285	250	308	10.0	31%	73%	4.22	49	17	34	2.4	5.5	2.3	13%	1.3	1.6	61	$7
Type	Con GB	08	STL	7	7	1	149	81	5.14	1.45	300	297	304	25.0	32%	67%	4.17	49	22	30	2.1	4.9	2.3	14%	1.3	-16.0	58	$4
Health	C	09	STL	15	12	0	214	105	3.49	1.14	265	272	266	27.2	29%	69%	3.34	60	16	24	1.1	4.4	3.9	6%	0.5	18.5	87	$21
PT/Exp	A	10	LAA	10	7	0	152	92	3.84	1.24	265	239	284	27.6	29%	71%	3.54	55	16	29	2.0	5.4	2.7	10%	0.9	5.6	77	$13
Consist	B	1st Half		9	6	0	111	71	3.96	1.29	268			27.6	30%	71%	3.55	55	16	28	2.3	5.7	2.4	11%	0.9	2.4	74	$9
LIMA Plan	C	2nd Half		1	1	0	41	21	3.51	1.10	257			27.5	28%	71%	3.53	53	15	31	1.1	4.6	4.2	9%	0.9	3.2	85	$3
Rand Var	0	11	Proj	**9**	**8**	**0**	**174**	**94**	**3.93**	**1.25**	**273**			**26.9**	**30%**	**71%**	**3.70**	**54**	**17**	**29**	**1.7**	**4.9**	**2.8**	**10%**	**0.9**	**12.6**	**74**	**$13**

A strained oblique, not any arm problems, cut into IP. That's two years of high GB skills under his belt. Regresssion analysis calls for ERA to rise, but xERA and recent history suggest:
UP: 200 IP, 3.50 ERA, 15 W

Porcello,Rick

				W	L	Sv	IP	K	ERA	WHIP	OBA	vL	vR	BF/G	H%	S%	xERA	G	L	F	Ctl	Dom	Cmd	hr/f	hr/9	RAR	BPV	R$
RH SP	22	06		0	0	0	0	0	0.00	0.00							0.00											
Ht/Wt	77 200	07		0	0	0	0	0	0.00	0.00							0.00											
Type	Con GB	08		0	0	0	0	0	0.00	0.00							0.00											
Health	A	09	DET	14	9	0	165	81	4.04	1.35	270	281	255	23.5	28%	74%	4.20	54	17	28	2.7	4.4	1.6	14%	1.2	8.5	38	$14
PT/Exp	C	10	DET	* 11	14	0	191	102	4.72	1.36	283	303	272	26.3	31%	66%	4.03	50	18	32	2.2	4.8	2.2	9%	0.8	-13.6	55	$9
Consist	A	1st Half		5	8	0	84	39	5.71	1.59	314			25.4	34%	64%	4.65	47	19	34	2.7	4.1	1.5	8%	0.9	-16.3	25	($1)
LIMA Plan	C	2nd Half		6	6	0	106	63	3.93	1.18	257			27.2	28%	68%	3.55	53	17	31	1.8	5.3	2.9	10%	0.8	2.7	78	$9
Rand Var	+1	11	Proj	**12**	**11**	**0**	**199**	**108**	**3.98**	**1.35**	**277**			**25.0**	**30%**	**73%**	**4.03**	**52**	**17**	**30**	**2.4**	**4.9**	**2.0**	**11%**	**1.0**	**6.4**	**53**	**$13**

10-12, 4.92 in 163 IP at DET. Skills, PQS both show rebound after the 21-year-old's demotion:

	Starts	DOM	DIS
1H	13	0	3
2H	14	8	2

UP: 2nd half times two.

Price,David

				W	L	Sv	IP	K	ERA	WHIP	OBA	vL	vR	BF/G	H%	S%	xERA	G	L	F	Ctl	Dom	Cmd	hr/f	hr/9	RAR	BPV	R$
LH SP	25	06		0	0	0	0	0	0.00	0.00							0.00											
Ht/Wt	78 225	07		0	0	0	0	0	0.00	0.00							0.00											
Type	Pwr FB	08	TAM	* 8	1	0	89	74	2.73	1.22	242	158	188	20.5	29%	81%	3.68	50	13	38	2.9	7.5	2.6	8%	0.8	17.8	84	$13
Health	A	09	TAM	* 11	11	0	162	133	4.49	1.37	248	236	242	22.5	28%	71%	4.33	41	19	39	4.0	7.4	1.8	12%	1.3	-0.7	44	$13
PT/Exp	B	10	TAM	19	6	0	209	188	2.72	1.19	224	211	224	26.8	28%	79%	3.62	44	17	40	3.4	8.1	2.4	7%	0.6	36.6	76	$28
Consist	B	1st Half		11	4	0	108	90	2.42	1.20	223			27.7	27%	83%	3.61	47	17	35	3.5	7.5	2.1	8%	0.7	22.8	66	$16
LIMA Plan	D+	2nd Half		8	2	0	101	98	3.03	1.19	226			25.9	29%	76%	3.61	40	16	44	3.3	8.7	2.6	6%	0.6	13.8	86	$13
Rand Var	-4	11	Proj	**17**	**8**	**0**	**210**	**183**	**3.51**	**1.30**	**245**			**26.1**	**29%**	**76%**	**3.93**	**43**	**17**	**40**	**3.5**	**7.8**	**2.2**	**9%**	**0.9**	**9.3**	**67**	**$23**

Don't let '08, '10 strand rates fool you: '08 was relieving & sample size; '10 was fortune, as xERA highlights. Don't misunderstand; this was a solid growth season. Just heed the warning of Rand Var, xERA when setting value.

Purcey,David

				W	L	Sv	IP	K	ERA	WHIP	OBA	vL	vR	BF/G	H%	S%	xERA	G	L	F	Ctl	Dom	Cmd	hr/f	hr/9	RAR	BPV	R$
LH RP	28	06	a/a	6	12	0	140	106	8.02	2.03	326			24.7	37%	61%	7.72				6.0	6.8	1.1		1.5	-60.4	11	($11)
Ht/Wt	77 235	07	aa	3	5	0	62	42	7.42	1.67	329			25.9	38%	53%	6.19				2.6	6.1	2.4		0.8	-22.6	52	($2)
Type	Pwr xFB	08	TOR	* 11	12	0	182	154	4.37	1.40	268	284	261	25.4	32%	71%	4.38	32	23	45	3.3	7.6	2.3	8%	1.0	-0.6	57	$13
Health	A	09	TOR	* 10	9	0	187	128	5.28	1.67	277	156	329	26.0	32%	68%	5.75	32	19	49	5.3	6.2	1.2	5%	0.6	-19.2	-22	$3
PT/Exp	D	10	TOR	* 3	3	1	55	52	4.21	1.43	228	163	235	4.5	28%	73%	4.69	29	16	55	5.3	8.6	1.6	8%	1.1	-0.5	17	$4
Consist	C	1st Half		2	2	0	31	28	3.04	1.33	201			4.7	23%	83%	4.84	28	14	58	5.5	8.0	1.5	9%	1.2	4.2	1	$3
LIMA Plan	C	2nd Half		1	1	1	24	25	5.69	1.56	260			4.3	33%	63%	4.54	30	18	53	5.1	9.2	1.8	7%	0.9	-4.6	37	$1
Rand Var	-1	11	Proj	**3**	**3**	**3**	**58**	**50**	**4.81**	**1.53**	**262**			**5.9**	**31%**	**72%**	**4.96**	**30**	**18**	**52**	**4.8**	**7.8**	**1.6**	**9%**	**1.2**	**-4.8**	**18**	**$3**

1-1, 3.71 ERA in 34 IP at TOR. Once the hit rate dust, or magic beans, or whatever he was using ran out, the final stats bore out that he's still an archetypal, hard throwing, no-idea-where-it'll-go lefty. Or, succinctly: don't draft.

Putz,J.J.

				W	L	Sv	IP	K	ERA	WHIP	OBA	vL	vR	BF/G	H%	S%	xERA	G	L	F	Ctl	Dom	Cmd	hr/f	hr/9	RAR	BPV	R$
RH RP	34	06	SEA	4	1	36	78	104	2.30	0.92	211	211	204	4.2	32%	76%	2.17	51	16	33	1.5	12.0	8.0	7%	0.5	21.7	204	$27
Ht/Wt	77 250	07	SEA	6	1	40	72	82	1.38	0.70	155	148	158	3.8	21%	89%	2.56	42	17	41	1.6	10.3	6.3	9%	0.8	27.6	161	$32
Type	Pwr	08	SEA	6	5	15	46	56	3.89	1.60	261	258	253	4.5	36%	77%	3.92	40	20	40	5.4	10.9	2.0	8%	0.8	2.6	67	$10
Health	F	09	NYM	1	4	2	29	19	5.22	1.64	260	296	220	4.6	31%	66%	5.11	47	19	34	5.8	5.8	1.0	3%	0.3	-3.7	-28	$0
PT/Exp	D	10	CHW	7	5	3	54	65	2.83	1.04	212	253	164	3.6	30%	75%	2.65	49	13	39	2.5	10.8	4.3	8%	0.7	8.7	154	$11
Consist	D	1st Half		5	2	2	31	35	1.74	0.77	171			3.8	23%	82%	2.35	53	10	37	1.7	10.2	5.8	8%	0.6	9.2	167	$9
LIMA Plan	B+	2nd Half		2	3	1	23	30	4.30	1.39	262			3.3	38%	70%	3.04	43	16	41	3.5	11.7	3.3	8%	0.8	-0.5	137	$3
Rand Var	0	11	Proj	**6**	**5**	**20**	**58**	**67**	**3.26**	**1.16**	**223**			**3.8**	**30%**	**74%**	**3.01**	**46**	**17**	**38**	**3.1**	**10.4**	**3.4**	**9%**	**0.8**	**9.1**	**127**	**$16**

Why the saves may return:
- Skills as good as SEA heyday
- '10 injuries not arm-related
- Has "proven closer" label.

Why there's risk:
- Health grade says it all.

UP: 2007 DN: 2009

Qualls,Chad

				W	L	Sv	IP	K	ERA	WHIP	OBA	vL	vR	BF/G	H%	S%	xERA	G	L	F	Ctl	Dom	Cmd	hr/f	hr/9	RAR	BPV	R$
RH RP	32	06	HOU	7	3	0	88	56	3.78	1.18	234	229	251	4.5	26%	71%	3.58	60	14	26	2.9	5.7	2.0	14%	1.0	7.7	64	$10
Ht/Wt	77 220	07	HOU	6	5	5	83	78	3.05	1.32	265	248	289	4.3	32%	82%	3.20	57	14	29	2.7	8.5	3.1	14%	1.1	14.1	114	$11
Type	xGB	08	ARI	4	8	9	74	71	2.81	1.07	227	220	229	3.8	29%	75%	2.62	58	19	23	2.2	8.7	3.9	9%	0.5	13.3	133	$13
Health	B	09	ARI	2	2	24	52	45	3.63	1.15	265	298	214	4.2	32%	71%	2.71	57	20	23	1.2	7.8	6.4	14%	0.9	3.6	142	$13
PT/Exp	C	10	2TM	3	4	12	59	49	7.32	1.80	338	392	292	4.0	40%	59%	3.77	55	17	28	3.2	7.5	2.3	12%	1.1	-23.6	81	$1
Consist	B	1st Half		1	4	12	28	27	7.95	2.08	371			4.2	45%	61%	3.74	54	22	24	3.8	8.6	2.3	12%	1.0	-13.5	83	$1
LIMA Plan	A+	2nd Half		2	0	0	31	22	6.74	1.53	305			3.8	34%	56%	3.77	56	12	32	2.6	6.4	2.4	12%	1.2	-10.1	79	($0)
Rand Var	+5	11	Proj	**3**	**3**	**8**	**59**	**49**	**3.85**	**1.28**	**263**			**3.8**	**32%**	**71%**	**3.16**	**56**	**17**	**27**	**2.5**	**7.5**	**3.1**	**11%**	**0.8**	**7.5**	**104**	**$7**

Whatever he did to his fielders and/or the baseball gods to warrant this H%, S% nightmare, he must've done it in both ARI and TAM. Chalk this one up to "that's baseball," talk up that ERA, and grab a huge bargain.

Ramirez,Ramon

				W	L	Sv	IP	K	ERA	WHIP	OBA	vL	vR	BF/G	H%	S%	xERA	G	L	F	Ctl	Dom	Cmd	hr/f	hr/9	RAR	BPV	R$
RH RP	29	06	COL	4	3	0	67	61	3.48	1.26	234	274	194	4.6	29%	74%	4.13	41	14	45	3.6	8.2	2.3	6%	0.7	8.3	68	$7
Ht/Wt	71 190	07	COL	* 12	3	1	91	83	4.83	1.49	264	240	357	5.9	32%	69%	4.78	31	17	52	4.3	8.2	1.9	7%	1.0	-4.5	41	$9
Type	Pwr xFB	08	KC	3	2	1	72	70	2.64	1.23	220	300	153	4.2	29%	78%	3.55	46	19	35	3.9	8.8	2.3	3%	0.3	15.1	77	$9
Health	A	09	BOS	7	4	0	70	52	2.84	1.33	237	244	220	4.2	27%	83%	4.82	35	18	48	4.1	6.7	1.6	7%	0.9	13.9	22	$9
PT/Exp	C	10	2TM	1	3	3	69	46	2.99	1.14	210	231	190	4.1	23%	78%	4.42	36	16	48	3.5	6.0	1.7	7%	0.9	9.3	27	$7
Consist	B	1st Half		0	1	1	32	24	4.74	1.30	254			4.0	28%	68%	4.28	34	21	45	3.1	6.7	2.2	11%	1.4	-2.6	50	$1
LIMA Plan	C	2nd Half		1	2	2	37	22	1.46	1.00	168			4.1	19%	89%	4.52	38	12	50	3.9	5.4	1.4	4%	0.5	11.9	7	$6
Rand Var	-5	11	Proj	**3**	**3**	**0**	**58**	**44**	**3.88**	**1.38**	**255**			**4.4**	**29%**	**75%**	**4.54**	**37**	**17**	**46**	**3.7**	**6.8**	**1.8**	**9%**	**1.1**	**-2.4**	**38**	**$4**

Consider: a game of Russian roulette, only with H%, S%. But it's not one bullet, it's more like five. And yet, he's survived with a lucky spin for three years now. Care to try for four? No? Ahh, our work here is not in vain.

Rapada,Clay

				W	L	Sv	IP	K	ERA	WHIP	OBA	vL	vR	BF/G	H%	S%	xERA	G	L	F	Ctl	Dom	Cmd	hr/f	hr/9	RAR	BPV	R$
LH RP	30	06	a/a	6	4	21	67	55	2.54	1.57	286			4.9	36%	83%	4.51				4.0	7.4	1.9		0.1	16.4	77	$14
Ht/Wt	77 200	07	a/a	7	2	17	58	41	5.69	1.90	328			4.9	38%	70%	6.86				4.7	6.4	1.4		0.9	-8.8	31	$6
Type	Pwr FB	08	DET	* 3	1	2	56	53	3.47	1.53	265			4.7	34%	77%	3.76	51	21	29	4.6	8.5	1.8	5%	0.3	6.1	57	$5
Health	A	09	aaa	4	2	5	45	37	3.85	1.83	336			5.1	41%	78%	6.06				3.6	7.4	2.0		0.2	2.6	69	$3
PT/Exp	D	10	TEX	* 1	2	2	68	53	2.56	1.08	188	53	385	4.3	23%	77%	4.38	32	12	56	3.8	7.0	1.8	3%	0.4	13.2	33	$8
Consist	D	1st Half		1	0	1	36	26	2.19	1.03	192			4.9	24%	76%	1.55				3.3	6.6	2.0		0.0	8.7	98	$5
LIMA Plan	C+	2nd Half		0	2	1	32	27	2.98	1.13	184			3.8	21%	77%	4.41	32	12	56	4.4	7.5	1.7	7%	0.9	4.6	26	$3
Rand Var	-5	11	Proj	**2**	**1**	**0**	**36**	**29**	**3.72**	**1.38**	**255**			**4.6**	**30%**	**74%**	**4.29**	**41**	**16**	**43**	**3.7**	**7.2**	**1.9**	**7%**	**0.7**	**-0.0**	**48**	**$3**

0-0, 4.00 ERA in 9 IP at TEX. Took sidearming lefty 13 G to get 9 IP in majors, even with 3 IP over two late-season mop-ups. Only tough on LHB, so '11 role looks similar. At least he should be good for a few holds.

Rauch,Jon

				W	L	Sv	IP	K	ERA	WHIP	OBA	vL	vR	BF/G	H%	S%	xERA	G	L	F	Ctl	Dom	Cmd	hr/f	hr/9	RAR	BPV	R$
RH RP	32	06	WAS	4	5	2	91	86	3.36	1.25	233	254	216	4.5	28%	79%	4.23	30	21	49	3.6	8.5	2.4	11%	1.3	12.7	65	$10
Ht/Wt	83 291	07	WAS	8	4	4	87	71	3.61	1.10	234	208	249	4.0	28%	69%	4.16	33	13	53	2.2	7.3	3.4	5%	0.7	8.8	85	$13
Type	FB	08	2NL	4	8	18	72	66	4.14	1.19	254	268	242	4.0	30%	70%	3.77	31	23	46	2.0	8.3	4.1	12%	1.4	1.1	104	$13
Health	A	09	2TM	7	3	2	69	49	3.64	1.34	264	239	284	4.0	30%	75%	4.50	37	20	43	3.0	6.4	2.1	6%	0.8	5.8	48	$8
PT/Exp	C	10	MIN	3	1	21	58	46	3.12	1.30	273	288	248	4.1	33%	76%	3.93	38	18	44	2.2	7.2	3.3	4%	0.5	7.3	86	$12
Consist	B	1st Half		2	1	18	32	23	2.53	1.16	268			4.3	31%	82%	3.81	38	16	46	1.1	6.5	5.8	6%	0.8	6.3	102	$10
LIMA Plan	C+	2nd Half		1	0	3	26	23	3.85	1.48	279			3.9	36%	71%	4.08	37	21	42	3.5	8.1	2.3	0%	0.0	0.9	65	$2
Rand Var	-2	11	Proj	**4**	**2**	**5**	**58**	**47**	**3.72**	**1.31**	**265**			**4.0**	**31%**	**74%**	**4.12**	**36**	**20**	**45**	**2.6**	**7.3**	**2.8**	**8%**	**0.9**	**1.2**	**74**	**$7**

Solid 1H imploded in July, when 5.40 ERA and -62 BPV cost him the closer's job. Ignore the ERA, and overall year was what we've come to expect, and should continue to expect in '11. But that may be it for the Sv opps.

ROD TRUESDELL

Ray,Chris		Yr	Tm	W	L	Sv	IP	K	ERA	WHIP	OBA	vL	vR	BF/G	H%	S%	xERA	G	L	F	Ctl	Dom	Cmd	hr/f	hr/9	RAR	BPV	R$
RH RP	29	06	BAL	4	4	33	66	51	2.73	1.09	195	184	202	4.3	21%	84%	4.37	35	16	48	3.7	7.0	1.9	11%	1.4	14.9	39	$20
Ht/Wt	75 223	07	BAL	5	6	16	43	44	4.43	1.24	225	233	212	4.1	28%	67%	3.57	45	18	38	3.8	9.3	2.4	12%	1.1	0.4	87	$11
Type	FB	08	BAL	0	0	0	0	0	0.00	0.00							0.00											
Health	F	09	BAL *	0	5	1	58	53	6.02	1.75	305	449	279	4.8	36%	67%	4.62	41	21	38	4.6	8.2	1.8	11%	1.2	-11.3	41	($1)
PT/Exp	D	10	2TM	5	0	2	56	31	3.72	1.31	234	279	203	3.7	25%	74%	4.94	38	15	47	4.0	5.0	1.2	6%	0.8	2.5	-3	$5
Consist	A	1st Half		2	0	1	34	17	3.18	1.18	200			3.8	20%	78%	5.10	37	11	51	4.2	4.5	1.1	8%	1.1	3.8	-18	$3
LIMA Plan	C	2nd Half		3	0	1	22	14	4.56	1.52	282			3.7	33%	69%	4.65	40	21	40	3.7	5.8	1.6	4%	0.4	-1.3	21	$2
Rand Var	-5	11	Proj	3	2	0	44	29	4.55	1.47	264			4.2	29%	72%	4.82	40	18	42	4.1	6.0	1.5	10%	1.2	-3.3	14	$2

A favorable confluence of all the random chance indicators -- H%, S% and hr/f -- made him look like a draftable player. Plummeting Dom and BPV tell the real story.

Reyes,Dennys		Yr	Tm	W	L	Sv	IP	K	ERA	WHIP	OBA	vL	vR	BF/G	H%	S%	xERA	G	L	F	Ctl	Dom	Cmd	hr/f	hr/9	RAR	BPV	R$
LH RP	33	06	MIN *	6	0	0	68	59	0.80	1.01	208	148	244	3.8	26%	95%	2.52	69	11	20	2.4	7.8	3.2	8%	0.4	31.6	122	$15
Ht/Wt	75 250	07	MIN	2	1	0	29	21	3.99	1.88	292	273	364	2.8	35%	78%	4.56	64	13	22	6.5	6.5	1.0	5%	0.3	1.9	-16	$1
Type	Pwr GB	08	MIN	3	0	0	46	39	2.33	1.19	235	202	276	2.5	28%	84%	3.02	60	17	23	2.9	7.6	2.6	13%	0.8	11.5	95	$7
Health	B	09	STL	0	2	1	41	33	3.29	1.37	232	207	276	2.3	29%	76%	3.94	53	16	31	4.6	7.2	1.6	5%	0.4	4.5	37	$2
PT/Exp	D	10	STL	3	1	1	38	25	3.55	1.45	241	307	177	2.8	28%	75%	4.16	50	25	25	5.0	5.9	1.2	7%	0.5	2.2	1	$3
Consist	B	1st Half		2	1	0	23	17	2.74	1.26	198			2.7	24%	79%	3.59	56	23	21	5.1	6.7	1.3	7%	0.4	3.6	17	$3
LIMA Plan	C+	2nd Half		1	0	1	15	8	4.80	1.73	298			3.0	33%	72%	4.99	43	27	29	4.8	4.8	1.0	7%	0.6	-1.5	-22	$0
Rand Var	-2	11	Proj	1	2	0	36	26	3.97	1.43	255			2.8	30%	73%	3.96	52	21	27	4.2	6.5	1.5	10%	0.7	0.8	33	$1

Four reasons for pessimism:
- Four year GB% decline
- Shoddy control last two years
- xERA says 4.00, not 3.00.
- Stopped getting lefties out

He won't be as bad as his 2H, nor nearly as good as his 1H.

Rhodes,Arthur		Yr	Tm	W	L	Sv	IP	K	ERA	WHIP	OBA	vL	vR	BF/G	H%	S%	xERA	G	L	F	Ctl	Dom	Cmd	hr/f	hr/9	RAR	BPV	R$
LH RP	41	06	PHI	0	5	4	45	48	5.38	1.70	269	290	246	3.8	36%	67%	4.68	36	22	41	6.0	9.6	1.6	4%	0.4	-5.0	25	$1
Ht/Wt	74 212	07	SEA	0	0	0	0	0	0.00	0.00							0.00											
Type	Pwr FB	08	2TM	4	1	2	35	40	2.04	1.25	220	157	309	2.4	32%	82%	3.75	27	28	45	4.1	10.2	2.5	0%	0.0	9.9	78	$7
Health	C	09	CIN	1	1	0	53	48	2.53	1.07	198	141	245	3.2	25%	78%	3.70	41	17	42	3.4	8.1	2.4	5%	0.5	10.9	73	$6
PT/Exp	D	10	CIN	4	4	0	55	50	2.29	1.02	197	214	182	3.1	24%	81%	3.52	36	21	43	2.9	8.2	2.8	6%	0.7	11.7	82	$8
Consist	A	1st Half		3	2	0	33	32	1.09	0.91	162			3.4	22%	90%	3.21	39	22	39	3.3	8.7	2.7	3%	0.3	11.9	86	$7
LIMA Plan	C+	2nd Half		1	2	0	22	18	4.09	1.18	244			2.7	28%	70%	3.96	33	19	48	2.5	7.4	3.0	10%	1.2	-0.2	77	$2
Rand Var	-5	11	Proj	2	3	0	46	39	3.34	1.27	237			3.1	29%	76%	4.12	35	21	44	3.5	7.7	2.2	7%	0.8	0.1	56	$4

He does one thing, and he does it VERY well: murders LHers, in '10 to the tune of 26 K / 1 BB. (Against RH he had only a 1.4 Cmd.) As long as he keeps doing that, he'll have a job until he's 60.

Richard,Clayton		Yr	Tm	W	L	Sv	IP	K	ERA	WHIP	OBA	vL	vR	BF/G	H%	S%	xERA	G	L	F	Ctl	Dom	Cmd	hr/f	hr/9	RAR	BPV	R$
LH SP	27	06		0	0	0	0	0	0.00	0.00							0.00											
Ht/Wt	77 240	07		0	0	0	0	0	0.00	0.00							0.00											
Type		08	CHW *	14	11	0	175	102	4.19	1.27	274	274	320	22.2	31%	67%	3.70	50	23	27	1.8	5.3	2.9	8%	0.6	3.3	74	$16
Health	A	09	2TM	9	5	0	153	114	4.41	1.47	263	229	279	17.7	30%	72%	4.32	48	18	34	4.2	6.7	1.6	11%	1.0	-1.9	34	$8
PT/Exp	A	10	SD	14	9	0	202	153	3.75	1.41	266	228	281	26.5	31%	75%	3.97	46	20	34	3.5	6.8	2.0	8%	0.7	6.7	53	$13
Consist	A	1st Half		6	4	0	102	81	2.74	1.27	242			26.7	29%	80%	3.55	52	17	31	3.4	7.1	2.1	6%	0.5	16.1	69	$10
LIMA Plan	D+	2nd Half		8	5	0	100	72	4.78	1.54	288			26.2	33%	70%	4.39	40	23	37	3.6	6.5	1.8	8%	0.9	-9.5	38	$3
Rand Var	-1	11	Proj	12	11	0	208	150	4.16	1.42	269			22.0	31%	73%	4.13	46	20	34	3.5	6.5	1.9	10%	1.0	0.4	48	$11

After an excellent 1H, he tired:

	GS	DOM	DIS
1H	16	63%	16%
2H	17	41%	24%

BPIs improved overall but are still unexciting. Heed the projections.

Rivera,Mariano		Yr	Tm	W	L	Sv	IP	K	ERA	WHIP	OBA	vL	vR	BF/G	H%	S%	xERA	G	L	F	Ctl	Dom	Cmd	hr/f	hr/9	RAR	BPV	R$
RH RP	41	06	NYY	5	5	34	75	55	1.80	0.96	224	194	248	4.6	27%	83%	3.13	54	16	30	1.3	6.6	5.0	5%	0.4	25.5	115	$25
Ht/Wt	74 185	07	NYY	3	4	30	71	74	3.16	1.12	253	255	241	4.3	33%	72%	2.69	53	19	29	1.5	9.3	6.2	7%	0.5	11.9	158	$20
Type	Con	08	NYY	6	5	39	71	77	1.40	0.66	171	147	183	4.0	23%	84%	2.12	55	15	31	0.8	9.8	12.8	8%	0.5	25.7	188	$30
Health	A	09	NYY	3	3	44	66	72	1.76	0.90	204	182	211	3.8	26%	89%	2.43	51	22	27	1.6	9.8	6.0	16%	1.0	22.0	161	$27
PT/Exp	A	10	NYY	3	3	33	60	45	1.80	0.83	187	214	155	3.7	23%	79%	3.00	51	15	33	1.7	6.8	4.1	4%	0.3	17.3	106	$21
Consist	A	1st Half		2	1	18	32	32	1.11	0.68	149			3.6	20%	86%	2.46	53	11	35	1.7	8.9	5.3	4%	0.3	12.0	147	$13
LIMA Plan	C	2nd Half		1	2	15	28	13	2.60	1.01	227			3.8	25%	74%	3.68	49	19	31	1.6	4.2	2.6	4%	0.3	5.3	60	$8
Rand Var	-5	11	Proj	3	3	30	58	39	3.26	1.12	245			4.1	28%	72%	3.62	46	20	34	1.9	6.1	3.3	7%	0.6	4.8	83	$16

Complaints of sore right knee and left oblique borne out by lower Dom and higher xERA in 2H. Expect more nagging injuries as he ages. It was bound to happen sometime...
DN: DL, under 30 Sv, 3.50+ ERA

Robertson,David		Yr	Tm	W	L	Sv	IP	K	ERA	WHIP	OBA	vL	vR	BF/G	H%	S%	xERA	G	L	F	Ctl	Dom	Cmd	hr/f	hr/9	RAR	BPV	R$
RH RP	25	06		0	0	0	0	0	0.00	0.00							0.00											
Ht/Wt	71 190	07		0	0	0	0	0	0.00	0.00							0.00											
Type	Pwr	08	NYY *	8	0	3	84	101	3.34	1.22	211	259	254	6.3	30%	72%	3.30	43	16	41	4.2	10.9	2.6	5%	0.4	10.4	103	$14
Health	A	09	NYY *	2	4	3	58	84	3.11	1.33	227	189	237	4.6	36%	78%	3.09	36	23	41	4.5	13.1	2.9	8%	0.6	9.6	127	$8
PT/Exp	D	10	NYY	4	5	1	61	71	3.82	1.50	254	268	250	4.2	35%	76%	3.59	40	25	36	4.8	10.4	2.2	9%	0.7	2.4	74	$5
Consist	A	1st Half		1	3	0	27	29	5.93	1.90	313			4.5	40%	69%	4.21	41	26	33	5.6	9.6	1.7	11%	1.0	-6.0	40	($1)
LIMA Plan	A	2nd Half		3	2	1	34	42	2.12	1.18	200			4.0	29%	84%	3.11	38	23	39	4.2	11.1	2.6	7%	0.5	8.5	102	$6
Rand Var	+1	11	Proj	4	5	0	73	92	3.85	1.34	227			4.5	32%	73%	3.30	38	23	38	4.6	11.4	2.5	9%	0.7	8.8	98	$8

His impressive Dom allows him to get away with less than impressive Ctl. Stubbornly high H% finally relented in 2H, giving us a glimpse of ERA upside when luck is with him. Can't count on a repeat, though.

Robertson,Nate		Yr	Tm	W	L	Sv	IP	K	ERA	WHIP	OBA	vL	vR	BF/G	H%	S%	xERA	G	L	F	Ctl	Dom	Cmd	hr/f	hr/9	RAR	BPV	R$
LH SP	33	06	DET	13	13	0	208	137	3.85	1.31	260	181	284	27.5	28%	75%	4.13	47	20	33	2.9	5.9	2.0	13%	1.3	18.2	53	$19
Ht/Wt	74 225	07	DET	9	13	0	178	119	4.76	1.47	284	296	278	26.0	32%	70%	4.51	45	18	37	3.2	6.0	1.9	10%	1.1	-5.6	45	$9
Type		08	DET	7	11	0	169	108	6.35	1.66	314	323	311	24.1	34%	63%	4.71	44	19	37	3.3	5.8	1.7	12%	1.4	-41.6	37	($2)
Health	C	09	DET	2	3	0	50	35	5.43	1.75	296	295	295	8.3	34%	69%	5.35	41	18	41	5.1	6.3	1.3	6%	0.7	-6.0	-4	($0)
PT/Exp	C	10	2NL *	9	10	0	132	77	6.89	1.65	310	269	295	20.7	34%	59%	4.88	42	18	40	3.5	5.3	1.5	10%	1.3	-46.6	22	($4)
Consist	B	1st Half		5	6	0	83	52	4.97	1.50	279			23.0	31%	67%	4.66	42	18	40	3.7	5.6	1.5	6%	0.8	-9.8	22	$2
LIMA Plan	F	2nd Half		4	4	0	48	25	10.21	1.91	357			17.9	37%	46%	5.32	43	14	43	3.1	4.7	1.5	14%	2.1	-36.8	23	($6)
Rand Var	+5	11	Proj	3	8	0	87	52	5.79	1.67	308			14.8	33%	67%	4.98	43	18	40	3.7	5.4	1.4	10%	1.2	-9.0	17	($2)

6-8, 5.95 ERA in 101 IP at PHI, FLA. Only right brain dominance keeps him employed as he possesses the perfect storm of no discernibly useful pitching skill... and unrelenting bad luck. You think he'd get the hint.

Rodney,Fernando		Yr	Tm	W	L	Sv	IP	K	ERA	WHIP	OBA	vL	vR	BF/G	H%	S%	xERA	G	L	F	Ctl	Dom	Cmd	hr/f	hr/9	RAR	BPV	R$
RH RP	34	06	DET	7	4	7	71	65	3.54	1.19	203	202	192	4.6	25%	72%	3.51	57	12	31	4.3	8.2	1.9	10%	0.8	8.9	66	$13
Ht/Wt	71 218	07	DET	2	6	1	51	54	4.26	1.32	243	247	231	4.5	32%	69%	3.48	45	19	35	3.7	9.6	2.6	11%	0.9	1.5	95	$5
Type	Pwr GB	08	DET	0	6	13	40	49	4.91	1.59	230	256	186	4.8	32%	69%	3.98	40	26	33	6.7	10.9	1.6	9%	0.7	-2.8	34	$5
Health	D	09	DET	2	4	37	73	60	4.33	1.43	244	265	219	4.4	29%	72%	3.99	57	11	31	4.7	7.4	1.6	12%	1.0	1.1	42	$16
PT/Exp	B	10	LAA	4	3	14	68	53	4.24	1.54	267	273	254	4.2	32%	72%	4.06	51	19	30	4.6	7.0	1.5	6%	0.5	-0.8	30	$8
Consist	A	1st Half		4	0	6	33	20	3.24	1.47	236			4.1	27%	79%	4.57	54	14	32	5.4	5.4	1.0	6%	0.5	3.7	-17	$5
LIMA Plan	C	2nd Half		0	3	8	35	33	5.19	1.61	295			4.4	38%	67%	3.60	48	24	28	3.9	8.6	2.2	7%	0.5	-4.5	75	$2
Rand Var	0	11	Proj	3	5	10	73	61	4.47	1.50	255			4.4	31%	71%	4.06	51	18	31	4.8	7.6	1.6	9%	0.7	2.1	34	$7

On a pure skills basis, turned his season around in 2H, but that nice Cmd was obscured by bad luck. However, 67% Sv% isn't going to fly for long.
DN: 9th innings become a part of his past

Rodriguez,Francisco		Yr	Tm	W	L	Sv	IP	K	ERA	WHIP	OBA	vL	vR	BF/G	H%	S%	xERA	G	L	F	Ctl	Dom	Cmd	hr/f	hr/9	RAR	BPV	R$
RH RP	28	06		0	0	0	0	0	0.00	0.00							0.00											
Ht/Wt	73 220	07		0	0	0	0	0	0.00	0.00							0.00											
Type	Pwr	08	aa	5	5	2	75	54	5.02	1.75	311			7.0	35%	74%	6.40				4.3	6.5	1.5		1.2	-6.6	27	$1
Health	A	09	aaa	5	4	0	77	49	4.33	1.46	255			7.7	28%	72%	4.41				4.5	5.7	1.3		0.8	-0.2	39	$4
PT/Exp	D	10	LAA *	3	4	0	69	51	4.21	1.42	255	338	192	5.4	30%	71%	4.07	48	18	34	4.1	6.6	1.6	7%	0.6	-0.6	36	$3
Consist	C	1st Half		2	2	0	40	34	3.92	1.18	242			5.7	30%	66%	3.49	44	19	38	2.5	7.7	3.0	5%	0.4	1.1	92	$4
LIMA Plan	C	2nd Half		1	2	0	29	17	4.61	1.74	273			5.1	30%	75%	5.15	51	18	32	6.1	5.2	0.9	10%	0.9	-1.7	-43	($0)
Rand Var	0	11	Proj	2	3	0	44	29	4.34	1.54	268			6.3	30%	73%	4.52	49	18	33	4.6	6.0	1.3	9%	0.8	-1.3	12	$2

1-3, 4.37 ERA in 47 IP at LAA. Small sample size warning here, but that 1H to 2H Cmd drop is NOT a good sign. Difficulties w' lefties limit Mgr's options. There are loads of really good relief choices. This isn't one of them.

JOSHUA RANDALL

Rodriguez,Francisco J.				W	L	Sv	IP	K	ERA	WHIP	OBA	vL	vR	BF/G	H%	S%	xERA	G	L	F	Ctl	Dom	Cmd	hr/f	hr/9	RAR	BPV	R$
RH RP	29	06	LAA	2	3	47	73	98	1.73	1.10	202	215	179	4.2	30%	89%	3.01	39	14	47	3.5	12.1	**3.5**	8%	0.7	25.5	141	$28
Ht/Wt	72 195	07	LAA	5	2	40	67	90	2.81	1.25	209	187	217	4.4	32%	78%	3.13	43	17	40	4.5	12.0	**2.6**	5%	0.4	14.1	115	$24
Type	Pwr	08	LAA	2	3	62	68	77	2.24	1.29	219	227	205	3.8	30%	85%	3.51	42	20	38	4.5	10.1	**2.3**	6%	0.5	17.8	82	$29
Health	B	09	NYM	3	6	35	68	73	3.71	1.31	210	185	223	4.1	27%	74%	4.06	35	19	46	5.0	9.7	**1.9**	9%	0.9	4.1	51	$17
PT/Exp	A	10	NYM	4	2	25	57	67	2.20	1.15	218	245	188	4.4	31%	83%	3.03	42	19	39	3.3	10.5	**3.2**	5%	0.5	12.8	120	$17
Consist	B	1st Half		2	2	20	42	52	2.57	1.29	243			4.4	35%	82%	3.17	40	17	44	3.4	11.1	**3.3**	7%	0.6	7.5	126	$11
LIMA Plan	B	2nd Half		2	0	5	15	15	1.18	0.78	140			4.4	20%	83%	2.62	49	24	27	2.9	8.8	**3.0**	0%	0.0	5.4	106	$5
Rand Var	-5	11	Proj	5	3	35	73	81	2.73	1.20	215			4.3	29%	79%	3.32	42	20	39	3.8	10.1	2.6	7%	0.6	7.3	97	$21

Outstanding rebound season was cut short by domestic violence incident in August. He could be undervalued by those concerned about his potential legal issues, or who look only at '10 saves total.

Rodriguez,Henry				W	L	Sv	IP	K	ERA	WHIP	OBA	vL	vR	BF/G	H%	S%	xERA	G	L	F	Ctl	Dom	Cmd	hr/f	hr/9	RAR	BPV	R$
RH RP	24	06		0	0	0	0	0	0.00	0.00							0.00											
Ht/Wt	73 175	07		0	0	0	0	0	0.00	0.00							0.00											
Type	Pwr FB	08	aa	2	7	0	41	37	7.90	2.27	318			15.2	40%	62%	6.90				8.6	8.1	**0.9**		0.2	-18.2	53	($5)
Health	A	09	aaa	2	1	4	43	64	5.95	1.65	243			5.3	38%	63%	4.64				6.7	13.3	**2.0**		0.8	-8.7	104	$2
PT/Exp	F	10	OAK *	1	2	11	49	60	3.32	1.15	203	283	207	4.1	29%	72%	3.12	39	17	44	3.9	11.1	**2.9**	6%	0.6	4.9	112	$9
Consist	D	1st Half		0	2	9	23	28	2.69	1.15	185			4.5	25%	80%	3.33	38	19	44	4.6	10.8	**2.3**	9%	0.8	4.2	85	$6
LIMA Plan	B+	2nd Half		1	0	2	25	32	3.90	1.14	218			3.7	32%	64%	2.94	40	16	44	3.2	11.3	**3.6**	4%	0.4	0.8	136	$4
Rand Var	0	11	Proj	2	3	3	58	74	4.03	1.33	220			4.9	31%	71%	3.43	40	17	44	4.8	11.5	2.4	8%	0.8	6.2	94	$6

1-0, 4.55 ERA in 27 IP at OAK.
PRO: Sexy Dom; huge Ctl improvement; triple digit BPV.
CON: Ctl gain sketchy due to small samples; FB% plus hr/f reversion will hurt ERA.
Invest, a little, for the long term.

Rodriguez,Wandy				W	L	Sv	IP	K	ERA	WHIP	OBA	vL	vR	BF/G	H%	S%	xERA	G	L	F	Ctl	Dom	Cmd	hr/f	hr/9	RAR	BPV	R$
LH SP	32	06	HOU *	11	12	0	161	110	5.97	1.65	294	262	298	21.0	33%	65%	4.79	45	22	33	4.3	6.1	**1.4**	11%	1.1	-29.6	17	$1
Ht/Wt	71 160	07	HOU	9	13	0	183	158	4.58	1.32	258	252	254	25.0	31%	68%	3.99	41	19	40	3.1	7.8	**2.5**	10%	1.1	-3.5	77	$13
Type	Pwr	08	HOU	9	7	0	137	131	3.54	1.31	260	282	248	23.2	32%	76%	3.62	40	23	36	2.9	8.6	**3.0**	10%	0.9	12.4	95	$13
Health	A	09	HOU	14	12	0	206	193	3.02	1.24	249	192	264	25.9	31%	79%	3.50	45	18	37	2.8	8.4	**3.1**	10%	0.9	29.7	101	$23
PT/Exp	A	10	HOU	11	12	0	195	178	3.60	1.29	250	247	250	25.6	31%	74%	3.38	48	20	32	3.1	8.2	**2.6**	9%	0.7	10.0	89	$16
Consist	A	1st Half		5	10	0	88	61	5.30	1.61	299			25.0	34%	67%	4.11	49	22	28	3.7	6.2	**1.7**	10%	0.8	-14.0	40	($0)
LIMA Plan	B	2nd Half		6	2	0	107	117	2.19	1.02	204			26.3	27%	82%	2.83	47	17	36	2.7	9.9	**3.7**	8%	0.7	24.0	129	$16
Rand Var	0	11	Proj	13	11	0	203	187	3.55	1.26	251			24.9	31%	74%	3.44	45	20	35	2.8	8.3	3.0	9%	0.8	17.5	97	$19

Dramatic 2H turnaround was partially driven by H%/S% shift, but he also recaptured sub-3.0 Ctl and cranked Dom to new heights. xERA trend is very encouraging. Play up awful 1H and buy him at a discount.

Rogers,Esmil				W	L	Sv	IP	K	ERA	WHIP	OBA	vL	vR	BF/G	H%	S%	xERA	G	L	F	Ctl	Dom	Cmd	hr/f	hr/9	RAR	BPV	R$
RH RP	25	06		0	0	0	0	0	0.00	0.00							0.00											
Ht/Wt	73 146	07		0	0	0	0	0	0.00	0.00							0.00											
Type	GB	08		0	0	0	0	0	0.00	0.00							0.00											
Health	A	09	a/a	11	7	0	155	106	5.39	1.56	303			25.7	35%	65%	5.33				3.0	6.1	**2.1**		0.8	-20.6	51	$4
PT/Exp	D	10	COL *	5	6	0	133	111	5.98	1.51	297	370	278	14.7	36%	59%	3.46	52	21	27	2.9	7.5	**2.6**	10%	0.7	-32.3	88	($1)
Consist	D	1st Half		2	5	0	62	43	6.17	1.50	285			14.4	32%	59%	4.05	47	22	31	3.4	6.2	**1.9**	11%	1.0	-16.4	46	($1)
LIMA Plan	B	2nd Half		3	1	0	71	68	5.82	1.52	307			15.1	39%	60%	3.03	55	20	24	2.4	8.6	**3.6**	7%	0.5	-15.9	122	$0
Rand Var	+5	11	Proj	6	5	0	120	93	4.58	1.40	278			23.6	33%	68%	3.52	53	21	26	2.9	7.0	2.4	10%	0.8	9.3	79	$5

2-3, 6.13 ERA in 72 IP at COL. Rookie who more than held his own, though you wouldn't know it due to shellacking by H% and S%. Stats will normalize some, but with better luck...
UP: 10 wins, 4.00 ERA

Romero,J.C.				W	L	Sv	IP	K	ERA	WHIP	OBA	vL	vR	BF/G	H%	S%	xERA	G	L	F	Ctl	Dom	Cmd	hr/f	hr/9	RAR	BPV	R$
LH RP	34	06	LAA	1	2	0	48	31	6.74	1.77	296	202	382	3.5	34%	60%	4.70	57	16	27	5.2	5.8	**1.1**	7%	0.6	-12.9	-2	($2)
Ht/Wt	71 203	07	2TM	2	2	1	56	42	1.92	1.40	197	208	198	3.3	24%	88%	4.41	60	11	29	6.4	6.7	**1.1**	7%	0.5	17.7	-14	$6
Type	Pwr xGB	08	PHI	4	4	1	59	52	2.75	1.34	198	102	282	3.1	24%	82%	3.59	62	16	22	5.8	7.9	**1.4**	14%	0.8	11.1	26	$7
Health	C	09	PHI	0	0	0	17	12	2.69	1.56	216	308	156	3.6	24%	88%	4.87	54	15	30	7.0	6.5	**0.9**	14%	1.1	3.1	-40	$1
PT/Exp	D	10	PHI	1	0	3	37	28	3.68	1.61	225	217	231	2.8	26%	79%	4.40	61	12	26	7.1	6.9	**1.0**	11%	0.7	1.5	-29	$2
Consist	B	1st Half		1	0	3	17	12	2.16	1.50	203			3.1	24%	88%	4.96	47	18	35	7.0	6.5	**0.9**	6%	0.5	3.8	-48	$2
LIMA Plan	C	2nd Half		0	0	0	20	16	4.95	1.70	242			2.6	28%	72%	3.79	74	7	19	7.2	7.2	**1.0**	18%	0.9	-2.3	-13	($1)
Rand Var	-3	11	Proj	2	1	0	51	40	4.43	1.64	243			3.0	29%	73%	4.35	60	13	27	6.6	7.1	1.1	10%	0.7	-1.3	-11	$1

If you walk more batters than you strike out, the only way to survive is with an extreme GB%. But survival is relative, and success is tenuous. xERA and 2H show the downside; do you even want to go there for a relief pitcher?

Romero,Ricky				W	L	Sv	IP	K	ERA	WHIP	OBA	vL	vR	BF/G	H%	S%	xERA	G	L	F	Ctl	Dom	Cmd	hr/f	hr/9	RAR	BPV	R$
LH SP	26	06		0	0	0	0	0	0.00	0.00							0.00											
Ht/Wt	72 210	07	aa	3	6	0	88	68	6.03	1.87	313			23.5	36%	69%	6.78				5.3	6.9	**1.3**		1.1	-17.0	28	($3)
Type	Pwr GB	08	a/a	8	8	0	164	96	5.65	1.76	312			27.4	35%	68%	6.08				4.3	5.3	**1.2**		0.8	-27.2	25	($3)
Health	A	09	TOR	13	9	0	178	141	4.30	1.52	277	297	278	27.3	33%	74%	3.91	54	19	27	4.0	7.1	**1.8**	12%	0.9	3.4	52	$12
PT/Exp	A	10	TOR	14	9	0	210	174	3.73	1.29	242	276	231	27.6	29%	72%	3.32	55	18	27	3.5	7.5	**2.1**	9%	0.6	10.6	73	$19
Consist	C	1st Half		6	5	0	114	106	3.39	1.28	243			28.2	31%	74%	3.05	56	18	26	3.4	8.4	**2.5**	9%	0.6	10.5	93	$11
LIMA Plan	D+	2nd Half		8	4	0	96	68	4.12	1.30	241			27.0	28%	69%	3.65	54	18	27	3.7	6.4	**1.7**	10%	0.7	0.2	48	$8
Rand Var	0	11	Proj	13	10	0	204	165	3.98	1.43	265			26.8	32%	73%	3.62	55	19	27	3.7	7.3	2.0	10%	0.8	16.8	64	$15

Second season in which he's had 69% PQS DOM in 1H; at least in '10 it was 38% in 2H (not 13% like in '09). He has proven he's not a fluke. If he finally maintains stamina into 2H...
UP: 3.50 ERA, 200 K

Romo,Sergio				W	L	Sv	IP	K	ERA	WHIP	OBA	vL	vR	BF/G	H%	S%	xERA	G	L	F	Ctl	Dom	Cmd	hr/f	hr/9	RAR	BPV	R$
RH RP	28	06		0	0	0	0	0	0.00	0.00							0.00											
Ht/Wt	71 191	07		0	0	0	0	0	0.00	0.00							0.00											
Type	Pwr xFB	08	SF *	4	4	11	67	61	3.31	0.99	203	83	176	4.7	26%	67%	3.81	33	14	53	2.4	8.2	**3.4**	4%	0.6	7.9	92	$13
Health	B	09	SF	5	2	2	34	41	3.97	1.21	238	188	259	3.1	35%	65%	3.48	32	15	53	2.9	10.9	**3.7**	2%	0.3	0.9	127	$6
PT/Exp	D	10	SF	5	3	0	62	70	2.18	0.97	208	241	185	3.5	28%	83%	3.08	35	14	51	2.0	10.2	**5.0**	8%	0.9	14.1	141	$11
Consist	A	1st Half		2	3	0	33	33	2.43	0.93	204			3.7	24%	85%	3.46	30	14	57	1.9	8.9	**4.7**	10%	1.4	6.5	117	$5
LIMA Plan	B+	2nd Half		3	0	0	29	37	1.88	1.01	214			3.4	32%	82%	2.61	42	14	43	2.2	11.6	**5.3**	3%	0.3	7.6	170	$6
Rand Var	-5	11	Proj	6	3	3	58	66	3.26	1.10	227			3.5	30%	74%	3.33	35	14	51	2.5	10.2	4.1	8%	0.9	5.8	130	$10

Skills mostly unchanged from '09, so a third season along the same lines is a reasonable bet. Of course, H%, S% regression will mean an ERA spike. Still, superb Cmd makes him a fine LIMA pick.

Ross,Tyson				W	L	Sv	IP	K	ERA	WHIP	OBA	vL	vR	BF/G	H%	S%	xERA	G	L	F	Ctl	Dom	Cmd	hr/f	hr/9	RAR	BPV	R$
RH RP	23	06		0	0	0	0	0	0.00	0.00							0.00											
Ht/Wt	77 215	07		0	0	0	0	0	0.00	0.00							0.00											
Type	Pwr GB	08		0	0	0	0	0	0.00	0.00							0.00											
Health	A	09	aa	5	4	0	50	27	3.78	1.16	225			22.7	25%	67%	2.93				3.1	4.9	**1.6**		0.5	3.3	56	$6
PT/Exp	F	10	OAK *	3	5	1	64	58	4.61	1.43	251	258	282	8.8	31%	68%	3.57	53	18	29	4.3	8.1	**1.9**	9%	0.7	-3.8	60	$4
Consist	B	1st Half		1	4	1	37	30	5.79	1.50	270			6.6	32%	62%	3.84	52	18	30	4.1	7.2	**1.8**	12%	1.0	-7.6	49	$0
LIMA Plan	B	2nd Half		2	1	0	27	28	2.99	1.33	224			16.4	30%	77%		100	0	0	4.6	9.3	**2.0**		0.3	3.8	120	$3
Rand Var	+1	11	Proj	3	3	0	44	34	4.34	1.40	255			13.4	30%	70%	3.85	52	18	30	3.9	7.0	1.8	10%	0.8	2.3	50	$3

1-4, 5.49 ERA in 39 IP at OAK. Back-to-back PQS 0s in two spot starts probably dooms him to the bullpen, at least for now. Don't count on that 2H Dom being sustainable, but the seeds of something good are here.

Rowland-Smith,Ryan				W	L	Sv	IP	K	ERA	WHIP	OBA	vL	vR	BF/G	H%	S%	xERA	G	L	F	Ctl	Dom	Cmd	hr/f	hr/9	RAR	BPV	R$
LH SP	28	06	aa	1	3	4	41	42	3.84	1.63	286			8.1	37%	76%	4.97				4.5	9.1	**2.0**		0.5	3.5	82	$3
Ht/Wt	75 240	07	SEA *	4	4	1	80	85	4.29	1.49	262			6.9	34%	72%	4.25	34	21	46	4.4	9.5	**2.2**	6%	0.7	2.2	64	$6
Type	Con FB	08	SEA *	7	3	2	136	88	3.50	1.36	251	311	224	11.7	28%	78%	4.74	39	19	42	3.8	5.8	**1.5**	8%	1.0	14.3	20	$12
Health	D	09	SEA *	10	7	0	152	85	4.01	1.25	263	195	253	25.4	29%	70%	4.58	39	18	43	2.2	5.0	**2.3**	7%	0.8	8.4	48	$13
PT/Exp	D	10	SEA *	3	14	0	146	69	6.47	1.65	317	342	304	20.2	32%	64%	5.26	37	19	44	3.0	4.2	**1.4**	12%	1.8	-42.1	10	($6)
Consist	A	1st Half		1	7	0	73	31	5.92	1.67	302			19.7	29%	70%	5.62	35	22	43	4.1	3.8	**0.9**	14%	2.0	-16.0	-28	($3)
LIMA Plan	C+	2nd Half		2	7	0	73	38	7.02	1.62	332			20.8	35%	58%	4.97	40	13	47	2.0	4.7	**2.3**	10%	1.6	-26.0	48	($4)
Rand Var	+3	11	Proj	4	8	0	116	64	4.97	1.49	292			16.5	31%	70%	4.96	38	18	44	2.9	5.0	1.7	10%	1.3	-9.6	26	$2

1-10, 6.75 ERA in 109 IP at SEA. Starter or reliever? You choose:

Career	IP	Dom	Cmd	ERA
as SP	270	4.4	1.4	4.87
as RP	93	8.6	2.3	3.68

Move back to 'pen might return higher Dom. Until then, avoid.

JOSHUA RANDALL

Runzler,Dan

		Year	W	L	Sv	IP	K	ERA	WHIP	OBA	vL	vR	BF/G	H%	S%	xERA	G	L	F	Ctl	Dom	Cmd	hr/f	hr/9	RAR	BPV	R$
LH RP	26	06	0	0	0	0	0	0.00	0.00							0.00											
Ht/Wt	76 230	07	0	0	0	0	0	0.00	0.00							0.00											
Type	Pwr GB	08	0	0	0	0	0	0.00	0.00							0.00											
Health	B	09 a/a	3	0	1	11	7	2.45	0.91	205			4.7	23%	78%	2.27				1.6	5.7	3.5		0.8	2.5	97	$3
PT/Exp	F	10 SF	3	0	0	33	37	3.03	1.50	239	260	232	3.5	34%	79%	3.35	52	21	27	5.5	10.2	1.9	4%	0.3	4.0	65	$3
Consist	C	1st Half	2	0	0	28	29	3.50	1.59	246			3.8	33%	77%	3.75	53	19	27	6.0	9.2	1.5	5%	0.3	1.8	34	$2
LIMA Plan	A	2nd Half	1	0	0	4	8	0.00	0.91	195			2.4	40%	100%	1.37	38	38	25	2.0	16.4	8.0	0%	0.0	2.2	255	$1
Rand Var	-2	11 Proj	3	0	0	44	47	3.93	1.56	251			3.4	33%	75%	3.57	53	19	27	5.6	9.7	1.7	9%	0.6	3.0	56	$3

Dislocated knee kept him out of action for two months. Still an impressive debut for a player with only 11 IP above Single-A prior to '10. GB% plus Dom sets strong foundation while he reigns in Ctl.

Russell,Adam

		Year	W	L	Sv	IP	K	ERA	WHIP	OBA	vL	vR	BF/G	H%	S%	xERA	G	L	F	Ctl	Dom	Cmd	hr/f	hr/9	RAR	BPV	R$
RH RP	27	06 aa	3	3	0	55	39	7.09	1.76	327			25.8	37%	60%	6.93				3.5	6.3	1.8		1.3	-17.4	25	($2)
Ht/Wt	80 255	07 aa	9	11	1	138	81	6.99	1.95	344			17.7	38%	63%	7.25				4.3	5.3	1.2		0.8	-43.1	19	($7)
Type	Pwr	08 CHW *	7	2	0	63	47	4.44	1.48	262			5.9	31%	70%	4.63	45	13	41	4.3	6.7	1.5	6%	0.7	-0.8	27	$5
Health	A	09 SD *	5	3	9	80	63	3.92	1.30	233			5.8	28%	70%	4.17	42	22	36	4.0	7.0	1.7	6%	0.6	2.7	38	$9
PT/Exp	D	10 SD *	4	9	14	67	61	4.77	1.68	287	143	324	5.0	36%	71%	3.74	49	30	22	4.9	8.2	1.7	7%	0.4	-6.2	41	$5
Consist	A	1st Half	3	5	2	37	36	5.85	1.58	306			5.4	38%	62%	2.83	48	39	13	3.1	8.7	2.9	21%	0.8	-8.4	100	$1
LIMA Plan	C+	2nd Half	1	4	12	30	25	3.43	1.81	263			4.6	34%	79%	5.02	50	14	36	7.2	7.5	1.0	0%	0.0	2.2	-32	$4
Rand Var	+3	11 Proj	3	4	0	41	33	4.64	1.52	272			5.7	32%	71%	4.15	46	21	33	4.2	7.3	1.7	10%	0.9	-0.1	42	$2

0-0, 4.02 ERA in 15 IP at SD. His four-year rising Dom trend is encouraging, but after seven seasons in the minors and three cups of coffee, he still hasn't cut down on the walks. This old dog isn't learning, so we'll pass.

Russell,James

		Year	W	L	Sv	IP	K	ERA	WHIP	OBA	vL	vR	BF/G	H%	S%	xERA	G	L	F	Ctl	Dom	Cmd	hr/f	hr/9	RAR	BPV	R$
LH RP	25	06	0	0	0	0	0	0.00	0.00							0.00											
Ht/Wt	76 205	07	0	0	0	0	0	0.00	0.00							0.00											
Type	xFB	08 aa	4	8	0	86	53	7.11	1.71	334			22.1	35%	62%	7.56				2.6	5.5	2.1		2.1	-29.8	3	($4)
Health	A	09 a/a	5	6	0	102	62	5.11	1.60	319			12.5	35%	71%	6.19				2.6	5.5	2.1		1.2	-10.0	32	$1
PT/Exp	D	10 CHC *	1	1	0	60	51	5.25	1.37	284	238	308	4.1	30%	71%	4.13	31	20	49	2.3	7.7	3.4	18%	2.4	-9.1	86	$1
Consist	D	1st Half	0	1	0	34	26	4.99	1.43	298			5.3	29%	81%	4.61	22	23	54	2.1	6.8	3.3	20%	3.1	-4.1	66	($0)
LIMA Plan	B+	2nd Half	1	0	0	26	25	5.60	1.28	264			3.2	32%	59%	3.56	40	16	44	2.5	8.8	3.6	12%	1.4	-5.0	110	$1
Rand Var	+4	11 Proj	2	2	0	58	43	4.81	1.41	288			6.0	32%	71%	4.47	34	18	48	2.5	6.7	2.7	11%	1.6	-2.4	65	$2

1-1, 4.96 ERA in 49 IP at CHC. Struggled mightily against RH, allowing an 89% ct% in 117 AB. Without a pitch to miss righty bats, he could be limited to specialist duty. Even so, his Cmd gives reason for hope.

Rzepczynski,Marc

		Year	W	L	Sv	IP	K	ERA	WHIP	OBA	vL	vR	BF/G	H%	S%	xERA	G	L	F	Ctl	Dom	Cmd	hr/f	hr/9	RAR	BPV	R$
LH SP	25	06	0	0	0	0	0	0.00	0.00							0.00											
Ht/Wt	75 205	07	0	0	0	0	0	0.00	0.00							0.00											
Type	Pwr GB	08	0	0	0	0	0	0.00	0.00							0.00											
Health	B	09 TOR *	11	9	0	149	147	3.43	1.52	267	220	226	24.5	35%	78%	3.67	51	20	28	4.4	8.9	2.0	7%	0.5	18.8	70	$14
PT/Exp	D	10 TOR *	9	9	0	131	109	4.98	1.55	288	262	298	22.5	34%	70%	3.84	51	16	32	3.7	7.5	2.0	12%	1.1	-13.6	64	$5
Consist	A	1st Half	4	3	0	48	37	5.66	1.59	308			24.2	36%	65%	5.44				3.0	6.8	2.3		0.9	-9.0	54	$1
LIMA Plan	C+	2nd Half	5	6	0	83	73	4.59	1.53	275			21.6	33%	73%	3.80	51	16	32	4.2	7.9	1.9	14%	1.2	-4.6	60	$4
Rand Var	+4	11 Proj	10	9	0	137	122	3.94	1.43	266			22.9	32%	74%	3.66	51	17	31	3.7	8.0	2.2	10%	0.9	10.6	74	$11

4-4, 4.95 ERA in 63 IP at TOR. Broken finger in Spring set him back, but he closed out season with three PQS DOM starts. His xERA shows sub-4.00 upside; expected H% regression would help him get there.

Sabathia,CC

		Year	W	L	Sv	IP	K	ERA	WHIP	OBA	vL	vR	BF/G	H%	S%	xERA	G	L	F	Ctl	Dom	Cmd	hr/f	hr/9	RAR	BPV	R$
LH SP	30	06 CLE	12	11	0	192	172	3.23	1.18	251	271	242	28.1	31%	75%	3.43	45	19	36	2.1	8.1	3.9	9%	0.8	31.5	112	$25
Ht/Wt	79 290	07 CLE	19	7	0	241	209	3.21	1.14	259	203	275	28.8	32%	74%	3.36	45	18	37	1.4	7.8	5.6	8%	0.7	38.5	126	$33
Type	Pwr	08 2TM	17	10	0	253	251	2.70	1.11	238	205	247	29.2	31%	78%	3.00	47	22	32	2.1	8.9	4.3	9%	0.7	50.0	129	$35
Health	A	09 NYY	19	8	0	230	197	3.37	1.15	233	198	242	27.5	28%	72%	3.65	43	20	37	2.6	7.7	2.9	7%	0.7	30.8	89	$31
PT/Exp	A	10 NYY	21	7	0	238	197	3.18	1.19	238	261	232	28.7	29%	76%	3.41	51	15	34	2.8	7.5	2.7	9%	0.8	28.1	87	$29
Consist	A	1st Half	10	3	0	116	93	3.33	1.13	225			27.7	26%	74%	3.46	51	14	35	2.9	7.2	2.5	10%	0.9	11.6	81	$15
LIMA Plan	C	2nd Half	11	4	0	121	104	3.04	1.24	250			29.7	31%	77%	3.35	51	16	33	2.7	7.7	2.8	7%	0.6	16.5	94	$15
Rand Var	0	11 Proj	19	8	0	232	196	3.34	1.23	248			29.2	30%	76%	3.54	48	18	35	2.7	7.6	2.8	9%	0.9	21.4	89	$27

PRO: Apparent struggles vs. LH was due to 36% H%, not lack of skill; higher GB%.
CON: Dom didn't rebound to '08 level; high BF/G in 2H. Remains an ace, but workload could hasten eventual decline.

Saito,Takashi

		Year	W	L	Sv	IP	K	ERA	WHIP	OBA	vL	vR	BF/G	H%	S%	xERA	G	L	F	Ctl	Dom	Cmd	hr/f	hr/9	RAR	BPV	R$
RH RP	41	06 LA	6	2	24	78	107	2.07	0.91	179	229	129	4.2	28%	78%	2.73	36	16	49	2.7	12.3	4.7	4%	0.3	23.2	164	$24
Ht/Wt	74 214	07 LA	2	1	39	64	78	1.40	0.72	154	186	114	3.7	21%	88%	2.44	46	13	41	1.8	10.9	6.0	9%	0.7	24.0	171	$27
Type	Pwr FB	08 LA	4	4	18	47	60	2.49	1.19	232	244	209	4.3	35%	78%	2.81	47	17	36	3.1	11.5	3.8	2%	0.2	10.3	149	$14
Health	B	09 BOS	3	3	2	56	52	2.42	1.35	241	195	304	4.2	30%	87%	4.52	31	17	52	4.0	8.4	2.1	7%	1.0	13.9	51	$7
PT/Exp	C	10 ATL	2	3	1	54	69	2.83	1.07	212	244	172	3.9	31%	76%	2.70	44	16	41	2.8	11.5	4.1	8%	0.7	7.9	152	$7
Consist	D	1st Half	1	3	0	30	40	3.56	1.09	205			3.9	29%	70%	2.81	43	11	46	3.3	11.9	3.6	10%	0.9	1.7	147	$3
LIMA Plan	A	2nd Half	1	0	1	24	29	1.90	1.05	221			3.8	32%	83%	2.55	44	21	34	2.3	11.0	4.8	5%	0.4	6.2	159	$4
Rand Var	0	11 Proj	3	3	0	65	72	3.31	1.23	237			4.1	31%	76%	3.38	40	17	43	3.2	9.9	3.1	8%	0.8	6.2	111	$7

Returned to form despite a couple of DL stints, and flashed skills of old (or is that of young?). But he's in rarified air now; passing 40, it's likely his body betrays him before his skills depart.

Sale,Chris

		Year	W	L	Sv	IP	K	ERA	WHIP	OBA	vL	vR	BF/G	H%	S%	xERA	G	L	F	Ctl	Dom	Cmd	hr/f	hr/9	RAR	BPV	R$
LH RP	22	06	0	0	0	0	0	0.00	0.00							0.00											
Ht/Wt	77 170	07	0	0	0	0	0	0.00	0.00							0.00											
Type	Pwr GB	08	0	0	0	0	0	0.00	0.00							0.00											
Health	A	09	0	0	0	0	0	0.00	0.00							0.00											
PT/Exp	F	10 CHW	2	1	4	23	32	1.93	1.07	186	290	120	4.4	28%	87%	2.49	51	12	37	3.9	12.4	3.2	11%	0.8	6.3	147	$6
Consist	F	1st Half	0	0	0	0	0	0.00	0.00							0.00											
LIMA Plan	B+	2nd Half	2	1	4	23	32	1.93	1.07	186			4.4	28%	87%	2.49	51	12	37	3.9	12.4	3.2	11%	0.8	6.3	147	$6
Rand Var	-5	11 Proj	4	4	0	58	63	4.03	1.34	238			4.3	31%	71%	3.41	51	12	37	4.2	9.8	2.3	9%	0.8	6.3	92	$6

Called up after just 10 IP in the minors, he lived up to his first round selection in '10 amateur draft. Owns the strong GB% and high Dom combination we crave, but he's SO unproven. Temper your expectations.

Samardzija,Jeff

		Year	W	L	Sv	IP	K	ERA	WHIP	OBA	vL	vR	BF/G	H%	S%	xERA	G	L	F	Ctl	Dom	Cmd	hr/f	hr/9	RAR	BPV	R$
RH RP	26	06	0	0	0	0	0	0.00	0.00							0.00											
Ht/Wt	77 218	07 aa	3	3	0	34	17	4.22	1.38	283			24.4	26%	84%	6.52				2.4	4.5	1.9		2.6	1.0	-14	$3
Type	Pwr FB	08 CHC *	8	6	1	141	95	4.47	1.53	261	167	276	13.1	30%	72%	4.67	46	22	32	4.8	6.1	1.3	9%	0.8	-3.4	4	$6
Health	A	09 CHC *	7	9	0	124	82	5.97	1.63	313	361	304	14.8	34%	67%	4.76	41	18	40	3.1	6.0	1.9	13%	1.6	-27.1	42	($1)
PT/Exp	D	10 CHC *	13	5	0	130	97	5.29	1.52	237	103	367	13.8	27%	66%	5.36	30	17	52	5.8	6.7	1.2	7%	0.9	-20.4	-27	$5
Consist	A	1st Half	5	2	0	42	33	4.92	1.52	223			7.5	25%	70%	5.44	33	13	53	6.4	6.9	1.1	8%	1.1	-4.7	-37	$2
LIMA Plan	C	2nd Half	8	3	0	88	64	5.46	1.51	243			22.9	28%	64%	5.32	30	19	52	5.5	6.6	1.2	6%	0.8	-15.7	-21	$2
Rand Var	0	11 Proj	7	8	0	112	77	5.06	1.55	269			23.9	30%	70%	5.05	38	18	44	4.7	6.2	1.3	10%	1.2	-12.5	1	$2

2-2, 8.38 ERA in 19 IP at CHC. Five reasons to run far away:
- Escalating xERA
- Certified WHIP killer
- Vague on strike zone concept
- Many minus signs in RAR/BPV
- Name is too hard to pronounce

Sampson,Chris

		Year	W	L	Sv	IP	K	ERA	WHIP	OBA	vL	vR	BF/G	H%	S%	xERA	G	L	F	Ctl	Dom	Cmd	hr/f	hr/9	RAR	BPV	R$
RH RP	32	06 aaa	12	3	4	125	54	3.17	1.19	274			19.0	29%	78%	4.20				1.1	3.9	3.6		1.0	20.9	69	$17
Ht/Wt	73 190	07 HOU	7	8	0	122	51	4.59	1.38	287	291	292	21.8	29%	72%	4.70	47	17	36	2.2	3.8	1.7	13%	1.5	-2.4	33	$6
Type	Con GB	08 HOU	6	4	0	117	61	4.22	1.20	263	273	261	9.0	29%	65%	3.73	56	15	29	1.8	4.7	2.7	7%	0.6	0.7	71	$8
Health	C	09 HOU	4	2	3	55	33	5.05	1.57	297	315	272	5.1	34%	66%	4.30	52	20	28	3.4	5.4	1.6	4%	0.3	-5.8	34	$2
PT/Exp	C	10 HOU *	2	2	0	46	25	4.96	1.67	329	306	354	4.4	35%	75%	4.15	52	22	26	2.6	4.8	1.8	18%	1.6	-5.4	47	($1)
Consist	A	1st Half	1	0	0	24	13	6.00	1.71	328			4.1	35%	68%	4.11	57	18	25	3.0	4.9	1.6	18%	1.5	-5.9	42	($1)
LIMA Plan	C+	2nd Half	1	2	0	22	12	3.84	1.64	330			4.6	35%	83%	4.49	35	35	30	2.2	4.8	2.2	16%	1.7	0.5	39	$0
Rand Var	+5	11 Proj	2	2	0	44	23	4.34	1.47	298			5.3	32%	73%	4.13	51	20	29	2.5	4.8	1.9	11%	1.0	0.0	48	$1

1-0, 5.93 ERA in 30 IP at HOU. List of injuries includes partially torn labrum, bone bruise, arm fatigue, shoulder sorness, and tweaking his back while playing with his son. Sampson, meet Delilah.

JOSHUA RANDALL

Sanabia,Alex

		Yr	W	L	Sv	IP	K	ERA	WHIP	OBA	vL	vR	BF/G	H%	S%	xERA	G	L	F	Ctl	Dom	Cmd	hr/f	hr/9	RAR	BPV	R$
RH SP	22	06	0	0	0	0	0	0.00	0.00							0.00											
Ht/Wt	73 165	07	0	0	0	0	0	0.00	0.00							0.00											
Type	Con xFB	08	0	0	0	0	0	0.00	0.00							0.00											
Health	A	09	0	0	0	0	0	0.00	0.00							0.00											
PT/Exp	D	10 FLA *	11	4	0	170	110	2.85	1.09	238	204	313	22.1	28%	74%	4.06	36	19	45	1.9	5.8	**3.1**	3%	0.4	24.5	67	$19
Consist	F	1st Half	5	1	0	84	59	2.46	1.01	223			23.6	27%	75%	2.13				1.8	6.3	**3.5**		0.2	16.1	115	$11
LIMA Plan	B	2nd Half	6	3	0	86	51	3.23	1.17	252			20.8	28%	74%	4.28	36	19	45	2.0	5.3	**2.7**	5%	0.6	8.3	56	$8
Rand Var	-4	11 Proj	**6**	**5**	**0**	**116**	**74**	**3.72**	**1.21**	**258**			**22.8**	**29%**	**72%**	**4.30**	**36**	**19**	**45**	**2.0**	**5.7**	**2.8**	**8%**	**1.0**	**-2.3**	**63**	**$9**

5-3, 3.73 ERA in 72 IP at FLA. Command artist used changeup to dominate LH bats in debut. With FB tilt and marginal Dom, his room for error is slim at best. Late elbow strain adds further reason to temper enthusiasm.

Sanches,Brian

		Yr	W	L	Sv	IP	K	ERA	WHIP	OBA	vL	vR	BF/G	H%	S%	xERA	G	L	F	Ctl	Dom	Cmd	hr/f	hr/9	RAR	BPV	R$
RH RP	32	06 aaa	3	2	19	43	41	3.14	1.12	215			4.8	27%	74%	2.81				3.1	8.5	**2.7**		0.7	7.4	100	$13
Ht/Wt	72 189	07 aaa	2	3	16	47	40	6.72	1.70	350			6.0	41%	61%	7.11				1.7	7.7	**4.6**		1.3	-13.1	89	$4
Type	Pwr xFB	08 aaa	2	1	13	33	34	3.01	1.17	236			4.2	31%	76%	3.12				2.7	9.3	**3.4**		0.6	5.3	117	$9
Health	A	09 FLA *	5	3	4	74	68	2.68	1.34	246	245	227	5.0	31%	83%	4.31	33	17	50	3.8	8.3	**2.2**	6%	0.8	13.7	60	$9
PT/Exp	D	10 FLA	2	2	0	64	54	2.26	1.10	193	192	195	4.2	22%	86%	4.16	33	15	52	3.8	7.6	**2.0**	8%	1.0	13.8	45	$7
Consist	B	1st Half	0	1	0	25	18	3.60	1.44	246			3.9	29%	76%	5.02	30	20	50	4.7	6.5	**1.4**	5%	0.7	1.3	-2	$1
LIMA Plan	C+	2nd Half	2	1	0	39	36	1.40	0.88	155			4.5	17%	97%	3.63	35	12	54	3.3	8.4	**2.6**	10%	1.2	12.5	76	$7
Rand Var	-5	11 Proj	**3**	**3**	**0**	**73**	**65**	**3.60**	**1.35**	**252**			**4.6**	**30%**	**78%**	**4.36**	**33**	**16**	**51**	**3.6**	**8.1**	**2.2**	**8%**	**1.1**	**-1.9**	**59**	**$5**

Might have been the luckiest pitcher in MLB in the 2H, given H% and S% from heaven. As an extreme FBer with eroding Cmd, this isn't the making of a future closer. Or a dominant setup man. Expect a ton of regression.

Sanchez,Anibal

		Yr	W	L	Sv	IP	K	ERA	WHIP	OBA	vL	vR	BF/G	H%	S%	xERA	G	L	F	Ctl	Dom	Cmd	hr/f	hr/9	RAR	BPV	R$
RH SP	27	06 FLA *	13	9	0	199	155	3.48	1.33	252	229	202	25.7	30%	76%	4.31	45	14	41	3.5	7.0	**2.0**	7%	0.8	24.8	55	$19
Ht/Wt	72 219	07 FLA	2	1	0	30	14	4.80	2.07	337	329	357	24.9	36%	78%	6.41	45	15	40	5.7	4.2	**0.7**	7%	0.9	-1.4	-55	($1)
Type	Pwr	08 FLA	2	5	0	52	50	5.57	1.57	270	340	188	23.2	33%	66%	4.09	40	27	32	4.7	8.7	**1.9**	14%	1.2	-8.3	48	$1
Health	F	09 FLA	4	8	0	86	71	3.87	1.51	257	231	276	23.8	30%	78%	4.50	42	20	38	4.8	7.4	**1.5**	10%	1.0	3.4	24	$4
PT/Exp	B	10 FLA	13	12	0	195	157	3.55	1.34	259	262	252	26.0	32%	73%	3.90	45	17	38	3.2	7.2	**2.2**	4%	0.5	11.1	66	$15
Consist	B	1st Half	7	5	0	99	69	3.35	1.38	263			26.7	31%	75%	4.17	43	20	37	3.4	6.3	**1.9**	4%	0.4	8.1	43	$7
LIMA Plan	C	2nd Half	6	7	0	96	88	3.76	1.31	254			25.3	32%	71%	3.62	47	13	40	3.1	8.3	**2.7**	5%	0.6	3.0	90	$8
Rand Var	-2	11 Proj	**12**	**10**	**0**	**174**	**144**	**3.98**	**1.43**	**264**			**24.4**	**31%**	**74%**	**4.10**	**44**	**19**	**38**	**3.7**	**7.4**	**2.0**	**9%**	**0.9**	**1.0**	**55**	**$12**

Put shoulder problems behind him on way to best year since '06 debut. xERA suggests caution, as does health grade. On flip side, big 2H reminds us that he hasn't reached ceiling yet. High risk, high reward.

Sanchez,Jonathan

		Yr	W	L	Sv	IP	K	ERA	WHIP	OBA	vL	vR	BF/G	H%	S%	xERA	G	L	F	Ctl	Dom	Cmd	hr/f	hr/9	RAR	BPV	R$
LH SP	28	06 SF *	7	4	2	95	96	3.79	1.22	210	256	248	8.6	28%	67%	4.01	36	20	45	4.3	9.1	**2.1**	3%	0.3	8.2	62	$12
Ht/Wt	74 189	07 SF *	1	5	0	72	84	5.03	1.54	269	197	321	8.3	36%	69%	3.84	39	22	39	4.5	10.5	**2.3**	11%	1.0	-5.3	83	$2
Type	Pwr FB	08 SF	9	12	0	158	157	5.01	1.45	257	235	263	23.8	33%	66%	3.96	41	21	37	4.3	8.9	**2.1**	8%	0.8	-14.5	65	$8
Health	A	09 SF	8	12	0	163	177	4.24	1.37	227	223	220	21.9	29%	72%	3.91	41	16	43	4.8	9.8	**2.0**	11%	1.0	-1.1	63	$12
PT/Exp	A	10 SF	13	9	0	193	205	3.07	1.23	207	181	210	23.6	26%	79%	3.65	41	15	44	4.5	9.5	**2.1**	10%	1.0	22.5	71	$21
Consist	A	1st Half	6	6	0	94	92	3.26	1.23	211			24.4	27%	76%	3.78	42	15	43	4.3	8.8	**2.0**	8%	0.8	8.8	62	$9
LIMA Plan	D+	2nd Half	7	3	0	99	113	2.90	1.23	202			22.9	26%	83%	3.52	41	15	44	4.6	10.2	**2.2**	12%	1.2	13.7	79	$12
Rand Var	-3	11 Proj	**10**	**10**	**0**	**174**	**185**	**3.78**	**1.34**	**228**			**22.7**	**29%**	**74%**	**3.81**	**41**	**17**	**42**	**4.6**	**9.6**	**2.1**	**9%**	**0.9**	**7.2**	**68**	**$15**

Third straight year of ERA and WHIP improvement. Can we expect a fourth? He's the same pitcher he was a few years ago. H% and S% are the difference, and were very lucky in '10. Set value based on '09 stats.

Santana,Ervin

		Yr	W	L	Sv	IP	K	ERA	WHIP	OBA	vL	vR	BF/G	H%	S%	xERA	G	L	F	Ctl	Dom	Cmd	hr/f	hr/9	RAR	BPV	R$
RH SP	28	06 LAA	16	8	0	204	141	4.28	1.23	239	254	229	25.7	27%	67%	4.47	38	17	44	3.1	6.2	**2.0**	8%	0.9	7.0	45	$21
Ht/Wt	74 185	07 LAA *	9	15	0	182	152	5.94	1.60	302	284	292	24.9	35%	65%	4.69	36	19	46	3.4	7.5	**2.2**	11%	1.5	-32.3	57	$4
Type	FB	08 LAA	16	7	0	219	214	3.49	1.12	243	240	234	27.6	30%	72%	3.36	39	20	42	1.9	8.8	**4.6**	9%	1.2	23.1	123	$29
Health	B	09 LAA	8	8	0	140	107	5.03	1.47	288	323	248	25.6	32%	70%	4.50	38	20	42	3.0	6.9	**2.3**	13%	1.5	-9.9	59	$7
PT/Exp	A	10 LAA	17	10	0	223	169	3.92	1.32	260	271	246	28.6	30%	74%	4.17	35	22	43	3.0	6.8	**2.3**	9%	1.1	6.0	57	$19
Consist	B	1st Half	8	6	0	114	96	3.95	1.34	272			28.6	32%	75%	4.00	33	24	44	2.6	7.6	**2.9**	10%	1.2	2.7	77	$9
LIMA Plan	D+	2nd Half	9	4	0	109	73	3.89	1.30	248			28.7	28%	73%	4.35	38	20	42	3.3	6.0	**1.8**	9%	1.0	3.3	35	$10
Rand Var	0	11 Proj	**14**	**9**	**0**	**203**	**159**	**4.26**	**1.33**	**265**			**27.0**	**30%**	**72%**	**4.18**	**37**	**21**	**42**	**2.9**	**7.0**	**2.4**	**10%**	**1.2**	**2.7**	**64**	**$16**

'09 elbow issues looked like thing of past in 1H, but huge skill decline in 2H adds worry again. Five year scan shows '08 breakout was an anomaly. You'll get burned if you pay for a sub 4.00 ERA. DN: DL

Santana,Johan

		Yr	W	L	Sv	IP	K	ERA	WHIP	OBA	vL	vR	BF/G	H%	S%	xERA	G	L	F	Ctl	Dom	Cmd	hr/f	hr/9	RAR	BPV	R$
LH SP	32	06 MIN	19	6	0	233	245	2.78	1.00	220	254	206	26.9	28%	77%	3.06	41	20	40	1.8	9.5	**5.2**	10%	0.9	51.2	140	$41
Ht/Wt	72 208	07 MIN	15	13	0	219	235	3.33	1.07	229	197	234	26.5	28%	76%	3.26	38	18	44	2.1	9.7	**4.5**	13%	1.4	31.8	132	$33
Type	FB	08 NYM	16	7	0	234	206	2.54	1.15	238	247	227	28.0	29%	83%	3.52	41	22	36	2.4	7.9	**3.3**	10%	0.9	50.1	96	$30
Health	C	09 NYM	13	9	0	167	146	3.13	1.21	249	267	235	27.6	30%	79%	3.96	36	17	48	2.5	7.9	**3.2**	9%	1.1	21.8	88	$19
PT/Exp	A	10 NYM	11	9	0	199	144	2.98	1.18	242	273	229	28.1	28%	77%	4.09	35	20	45	2.5	6.5	**2.6**	6%	0.7	25.3	63	$19
Consist	A	1st Half	5	5	0	111	73	3.41	1.24	248			27.2	28%	74%	4.34	36	20	44	2.8	5.9	**2.1**	5%	0.6	8.4	44	$8
LIMA Plan	C	2nd Half	6	4	0	88	71	2.45	1.09	234			29.4	28%	82%	3.78	33	21	46	2.0	7.3	**3.6**	7%	0.8	16.9	87	$11
Rand Var	-3	11 Proj	**9**	**6**	**0**	**131**	**103**	**3.59**	**1.24**	**255**			**28.6**	**29%**	**75%**	**4.05**	**36**	**20**	**44**	**2.5**	**7.1**	**2.9**	**9%**	**1.1**	**1.5**	**75**	**$12**

Surface stats remain elite, but warning signs abound...
- Steep Cmd, BPV erosion
- Gives up a lot of fly balls
- Ominous xERA trend

Late season shoulder surgery multiplies these risk factors.

Santos,Sergio

		Yr	W	L	Sv	IP	K	ERA	WHIP	OBA	vL	vR	BF/G	H%	S%	xERA	G	L	F	Ctl	Dom	Cmd	hr/f	hr/9	RAR	BPV	R$
RH RP	27	06	0	0	0	0	0	0.00	0.00							0.00											
Ht/Wt	74 240	07	0	0	0	0	0	0.00	0.00							0.00											
Type	Pwr	08	0	0	0	0	0	0.00	0.00							0.00											
Health	A	09 a/a	0	1	0	14	13	9.64	2.43	336			7.5	43%	56%	7.43				9.0	8.4	**0.9**		0.0	-9.2	57	($3)
PT/Exp	F	10 CHW	2	2	1	52	56	2.96	1.53	267	207	298	4.1	36%	81%	3.67	43	21	36	4.5	9.7	**2.2**	4%	0.3	7.5	74	$4
Consist	F	1st Half	0	0	0	25	30	2.13	1.46	236			3.8	35%	84%	3.43	42	27	31	5.3	10.7	**2.0**	0%	0.0	6.3	68	$2
LIMA Plan	A	2nd Half	2	2	1	26	26	3.75	1.59	294			4.4	37%	78%	3.90	44	16	40	3.7	8.9	**2.4**	6%	0.7	1.3	80	$2
Rand Var	-2	11 Proj	**3**	**3**	**10**	**58**	**62**	**3.72**	**1.43**	**255**			**4.1**	**33%**	**76%**	**3.65**	**43**	**20**	**37**	**4.2**	**9.6**	**2.3**	**9%**	**0.8**	**4.6**	**81**	**$8**

Former SS looked like future closer at times in rookie splash. But not yet. All of his success came against LH (.513 OPS). And that hr/f isn't sustainable. HR risk, coupled with wobbly control, foretells ERA spike.

Saunders,Joe

		Yr	W	L	Sv	IP	K	ERA	WHIP	OBA	vL	vR	BF/G	H%	S%	xERA	G	L	F	Ctl	Dom	Cmd	hr/f	hr/9	RAR	BPV	R$
LH SP	29	06 LAA *	17	7	0	205	132	3.48	1.27	254	220	274	25.3	29%	75%	4.05	48	20	32	2.8	5.8	**2.1**	8%	0.8	27.2	54	$23
Ht/Wt	75 210	07 LAA *	12	12	0	193	131	5.78	1.58	313	274	304	27.2	35%	64%	4.37	45	21	34	2.7	6.1	**2.3**	10%	1.1	-30.5	61	$5
Type	Con	08 LAA	17	7	0	198	103	3.41	1.21	251	260	250	26.4	27%	75%	4.32	47	15	38	2.4	4.7	**1.9**	9%	1.0	22.9	44	$22
Health	A	09 LAA	16	7	0	186	101	4.60	1.43	278	257	287	26.1	29%	72%	4.66	47	17	36	3.1	4.9	**1.6**	13%	1.4	-3.3	29	$12
PT/Exp	A	10 2TM	9	17	0	203	114	4.47	1.46	288	259	301	27.0	31%	72%	4.47	44	19	37	2.8	5.0	**1.8**	10%	1.1	-10.0	36	$6
Consist	A	1st Half	6	8	0	102	52	4.59	1.48	273			26.4	29%	71%	4.90	43	18	39	3.8	4.6	**1.2**	9%	1.1	-6.5	1	$3
LIMA Plan	C	2nd Half	3	9	0	101	62	4.35	1.43	303			27.5	33%	73%	4.05	45	20	35	1.9	5.5	**3.0**	11%	1.2	-3.5	72	$3
Rand Var	0	11 Proj	**12**	**12**	**0**	**190**	**108**	**4.35**	**1.38**	**281**			**26.4**	**30%**	**72%**	**4.35**	**45**	**18**	**37**	**2.5**	**5.1**	**2.0**	**10%**	**1.1**	**-3.3**	**48**	**$10**

Mid-year trade to NL didn't net much better results despite better BPIs. Pinpoint Ctl in 2H says he's got another 4.00 ERA in him. But that's it. With long history of struggles vs. RH bats, don't mine for upside here.

Scherzer,Max

		Yr	W	L	Sv	IP	K	ERA	WHIP	OBA	vL	vR	BF/G	H%	S%	xERA	G	L	F	Ctl	Dom	Cmd	hr/f	hr/9	RAR	BPV	R$
RH SP	26	06	0	0	0	0	0	0.00	0.00							0.00											
Ht/Wt	75 213	07 aa	4	4	0	73	65	5.20	1.62	272			23.7	34%	67%	4.84				5.1	8.0	**1.6**		0.5	-6.6	66	$2
Type	Pwr	08 ARI *	1	5	0	109	133	3.39	1.24	229	319	167	15.6	32%	74%	2.98	42	28	30	3.6	10.9	**3.0**	10%	0.7	11.8	118	$10
Health	A	09 ARI	9	11	0	170	174	4.12	1.34	257	265	239	24.2	32%	72%	3.65	42	18	40	3.3	9.2	**2.8**	11%	1.1	1.4	95	$13
PT/Exp	C	10 DET *	14	11	0	211	199	3.29	1.19	232	239	250	26.3	29%	75%	3.52	40	20	40	3.1	8.5	**2.8**	9%	0.9	22.0	88	$24
Consist	A	1st Half	7	6	0	102	97	4.25	1.25	243			25.0	29%	69%	3.59	39	20	40	3.1	8.5	**2.8**	11%	1.2	-1.4	87	$9
LIMA Plan	C	2nd Half	7	5	0	109	102	2.39	1.14	221			27.6	28%	81%	3.46	41	19	40	3.1	8.4	**2.8**	6%	0.6	23.5	88	$15
Rand Var	0	11 Proj	**14**	**8**	**0**	**203**	**202**	**3.41**	**1.25**	**241**			**22.9**	**30%**	**76%**	**3.54**	**41**	**20**	**39**	**3.2**	**9.0**	**2.8**	**9%**	**0.9**	**18.7**	**94**	**$23**

Early season demotion turned light on and he never looked back. Skills, xERA confirm that 1H and 2H were more similar than surface stats suggest. He went three months w/o anything lower than a PQS-3. A new ace.

STEPHEN NICKRAND

Schlereth,Daniel

	Yr	Tm	W	L	Sv	IP	K	ERA	WHIP	OBA	vL	vR	BF/G	H%	S%	xERA	G	L	F	Ctl	Dom	Cmd	hr/f	hr/9	RAR	BPV	R$
LH RP 24	06		0	0	0	0	0	0.00	0.00							0.00											
Ht/Wt 72 210	07		0	0	0	0	0	0.00	0.00							0.00											
Type Pwr GB	08		0	0	0	0	0	0.00	0.00							0.00											
Health A	09	ARI *	1	4	3	45	53	3.38	1.48	210	222	220	4.7	30%	77%	3.59	59	9	33	6.6	10.5	1.6	6%	0.4	4.5	49	$4
PT/Exp F	10	DET *	3	3	1	68	70	2.92	1.61	257	310	244	5.5	35%	81%	4.05	48	14	38	5.7	9.3	1.6	3%	0.3	10.2	39	$5
Consist A	1st Half		1	2	0	36	38	3.25	1.72	262			5.8	36%	79%	5.00	40	0	60	6.5	9.5	1.5	0%	0.0	3.9	14	$1
LIMA Plan A	2nd Half		2	1	1	32	32	2.55	1.48	251			5.2	33%	84%	3.73	49	16	35	4.8	9.1	1.9	6%	0.6	6.2	60	$3
Rand Var -4	11	Proj	2	3	0	44	44	3.72	1.43	237			5.0	31%	75%	3.71	52	14	34	5.0	9.1	1.8	7%	0.6	3.1	60	$3

2-0, 2.89 ERA in 19 IP at DET. Another case of skills falling short of stats. Here, it's that ever-elusive home plate. Maybe 2H is a step in the right direction -- the power arm is there. But don't bid until or unless Cmd hits 2.0.

Sheets,Ben

	Yr	Tm	W	L	Sv	IP	K	ERA	WHIP	OBA	vL	vR	BF/G	H%	S%	xERA	G	L	F	Ctl	Dom	Cmd	hr/f	hr/9	RAR	BPV	R$
RH SP 32	06	MIL	6	7	0	106	116	3.82	1.09	260	248	266	25.0	34%	66%	2.99	40	19	40	0.9	9.8	10.5	8%	0.8	8.7	170	$13
Ht/Wt 73 226	07	MIL	12	5	0	141	106	3.82	1.24	257	200	300	24.5	29%	73%	4.23	37	19	45	2.4	6.8	2.9	9%	1.1	10.5	72	$15
Type	08	MIL	13	9	0	198	158	3.09	1.15	245	256	226	26.0	29%	76%	3.79	41	18	41	2.1	7.2	3.4	7%	0.8	29.0	90	$23
Health F	09		0	0	0	0	0	0.00	0.00							0.00											
PT/Exp B	10	OAK	4	9	0	119	84	4.53	1.39	268	255	278	25.7	29%	72%	4.19	44	16	39	3.2	6.3	2.0	12%	1.4	-5.7	49	$5
Consist A	1st Half		3	7	0	99	74	4.98	1.47	275			25.6	30%	70%	4.26	45	16	39	3.6	6.7	1.9	13%	1.5	-10.4	45	$2
LIMA Plan	2nd Half		1	2	0	20	10	2.25	1.00	232			26.1	24%	83%	3.87	44	17	39	1.3	4.5	3.3	8%	0.9	4.7	66	$3
Rand Var +1	11	Proj	0	0	0	0	0	0.00	0.00																		

Another year, another surgery. This time it was two surgeries in one: a repeat of flexor tendon surgery AND ulnar collateral ligament reconstruction (aka TJ). His career may be over; will definitely miss all of 2011.

Sherrill,George

	Yr	Tm	W	L	Sv	IP	K	ERA	WHIP	OBA	vL	vR	BF/G	H%	S%	xERA	G	L	F	Ctl	Dom	Cmd	hr/f	hr/9	RAR	BPV	R$
LH RP 33	06	SEA	2	4	1	40	42	4.28	1.43	210	143	297	2.4	30%	67%	4.71	30	19	51	6.1	9.5	1.6	0%	0.0	1.4	14	$4
Ht/Wt 72 230	07	SEA	2	0	3	46	56	2.36	0.98	178	156	212	2.4	25%	80%	3.40	25	21	55	3.3	11.0	3.3	7%	0.8	12.1	111	$9
Type Pwr FB	08	BAL	3	5	31	53	58	4.73	1.50	238	190	254	4.1	31%	70%	4.52	34	13	53	5.6	9.8	1.8	8%	1.0	-2.5	38	$13
Health B	09	2TM	1	1	21	69	61	1.70	1.12	214	128	244	3.9	27%	88%	3.89	37	18	45	3.1	8.0	2.5	5%	0.5	22.3	74	$16
PT/Exp C	10	LA	2	2	0	36	25	6.69	1.93	310	192	427	2.7	35%	65%	5.53	40	20	40	6.0	6.2	1.0	8%	1.0	-12.0	-31	($3)
Consist C	1st Half		0	1	0	19	11	6.99	2.18	323			3.1	36%	68%	6.35	43	21	36	7.5	5.1	0.7	8%	0.9	-7.1	-88	($3)
LIMA Plan F	2nd Half		2	1	0	17	14	6.35	1.65	294			2.4	35%	62%	4.69	36	19	45	4.2	7.4	1.8	8%	1.1	-4.9	33	$0
Rand Var +4	11	Proj	2	2	0	44	37	4.76	1.54	264			3.0	31%	71%	4.67	37	19	44	4.8	7.7	1.6	9%	1.0	-2.8	24	$1

And it all crashed down. It was far too late to matter, but he did regain some of the lost Cmd in the 2nd half, showing he didn't completely forget how to pitch. He'll get a no-roster deal, but no saves = no fanalytic value.

Shields,James

	Yr	Tm	W	L	Sv	IP	K	ERA	WHIP	OBA	vL	vR	BF/G	H%	S%	xERA	G	L	F	Ctl	Dom	Cmd	hr/f	hr/9	RAR	BPV	R$
RH SP 29	06	TAM *	9	10	0	185	159	4.37	1.38	289	266	309	25.7	34%	71%	3.70	43	23	34	2.1	7.7	3.6	11%	1.0	4.3	102	$15
Ht/Wt 76 220	07	TAM	12	8	0	215	184	3.85	1.11	250	243	250	27.9	29%	70%	3.50	43	16	40	1.5	7.7	5.1	11%	1.2	17.3	119	$26
Type	08	TAM	14	8	0	215	160	3.56	1.15	255	255	253	26.5	29%	73%	3.63	46	16	37	1.7	6.7	4.0	10%	1.0	20.9	100	$24
Health A	09	TAM	11	12	0	220	167	4.14	1.32	278	272	279	28.3	32%	73%	3.97	42	20	37	2.1	6.8	3.2	11%	1.2	8.5	86	$17
PT/Exp A	10	TAM	13	15	0	203	187	5.18	1.46	300	286	304	26.2	35%	68%	3.64	41	20	38	2.3	8.3	3.7	14%	1.5	-26.1	107	$10
Consist A	1st Half		7	8	0	110	100	4.83	1.38	290			26.3	34%	69%	3.50	41	22	37	2.0	8.2	4.0	14%	1.4	-9.3	111	$7
LIMA Plan A	2nd Half		6	7	0	93	87	5.59	1.55	311			26.1	37%	68%	3.82	41	18	40	2.5	8.4	3.3	14%	1.6	-16.8	102	$2
Rand Var +5	11	Proj	15	10	0	206	175	3.98	1.30	273			26.3	32%	73%	3.67	42	19	38	2.1	7.7	3.6	11%	1.2	15.7	100	$19

Seemed like every GB missed a glove, and every FB cleared the wall, all year. We can't state this strongly enough: skills are as good as ever. If confidence is intact, it says here he'll be the draft-day bargain of 2011.

Shields,Scot

	Yr	Tm	W	L	Sv	IP	K	ERA	WHIP	OBA	vL	vR	BF/G	H%	S%	xERA	G	L	F	Ctl	Dom	Cmd	hr/f	hr/9	RAR	BPV	R$
RH RP 35	06	LAA	7	7	2	87	84	2.89	1.08	222	207	227	4.7	28%	77%	3.10	52	15	33	2.5	8.7	3.5	10%	0.8	17.9	119	$15
Ht/Wt 73 180	07	LAA	4	5	2	77	77	3.86	1.23	222	214	226	4.5	28%	70%	3.60	45	19	36	3.9	9.0	2.3	10%	0.8	6.2	80	$9
Type Pwr	08	LAA	6	4	4	63	64	2.70	1.34	239	209	262	4.2	30%	84%	3.37	54	16	31	4.1	9.1	2.2	11%	0.9	12.9	84	$10
Health D	09	LAA	1	3	1	18	12	6.61	1.75	243	250	229	4.1	28%	60%	6.28	37	19	44	7.6	6.1	0.8	4%	0.5	-4.7	-81	($0)
PT/Exp D	10	LAA	0	3	0	46	39	5.28	1.72	258	172	333	5.0	30%	71%	4.71	48	19	33	6.7	7.6	1.1	13%	1.2	-6.5	-17	($1)
Consist F	1st Half		0	3	0	27	25	5.27	1.79	267			4.8	33%	70%	4.37	52	21	27	6.9	8.2	1.2	9%	0.7	-3.8	-8	($1)
LIMA Plan F	2nd Half		0	0	0	19	14	5.29	1.60	244			5.3	25%	73%	5.12	41	17	42	6.3	6.7	1.1	17%	1.9	-2.7	-29	($0)
Rand Var +2	11	Proj	2	2	0	44	34	4.97	1.68	260			5.0	30%	72%	5.02	45	18	37	6.2	7.0	1.1	10%	1.0	-3.9	-18	$1

Showed rust after missing '09 2H, but only got worse as year went on. Then got hurt again (an arm strain). Even in unlikely case of a rebound, he'll probably just get re-hurt. He's considering retirement, which might be best.

Silva,Carlos

	Yr	Tm	W	L	Sv	IP	K	ERA	WHIP	OBA	vL	vR	BF/G	H%	S%	xERA	G	L	F	Ctl	Dom	Cmd	hr/f	hr/9	RAR	BPV	R$
RH SP 31	06	MIN	11	15	0	180	70	5.95	1.54	326	329	320	22.3	32%	66%	4.83	44	22	34	1.6	3.5	2.2	16%	1.9	-30.9	41	$2
Ht/Wt 76 250	07	MIN	13	14	0	202	89	4.19	1.31	287	294	280	25.9	30%	70%	4.36	48	19	34	1.6	4.0	2.5	8%	0.9	7.9	54	$15
Type	08	SEA	4	15	0	153	69	6.46	1.60	330	348	312	24.7	35%	60%	4.68	44	23	33	1.9	4.1	2.2	10%	1.2	-39.9	44	($4)
Health F	09	SEA	1	3	0	30	10	8.61	1.72	324	380	250	17.6	32%	49%	5.47	45	22	33	3.3	3.0	0.9	13%	1.5	-15.6	-12	($3)
PT/Exp C	10	CHC	10	6	0	113	80	4.22	1.27	274	259	282	22.6	31%	68%	3.58	48	19	33	1.9	6.4	3.3	9%	0.9	-2.9	89	$9
Consist C	1st Half		8	2	0	94	67	2.96	1.08	247			25.2	28%	76%	3.36	48	18	34	1.4	6.4	4.5	8%	0.8	12.3	102	$12
LIMA Plan C+	2nd Half		2	4	0	19	13	10.59	2.25	385			16.1	43%	51%	4.71	49	25	25	4.3	6.3	1.4	16%	1.4	-15.2	23	($3)
Rand Var 0	11	Proj	11	13	0	149	96	4.95	1.46	289			22.5	32%	68%	4.11	47	22	31	2.8	5.8	2.0	12%	1.1	0.6	53	$6

Threw more off-speed pitches than ever, posted best skills in years. Neither heart rate nor elbow issues expected to linger. Dom up, stayed up even during apparent slump. It'll be intriguing to see if he's truly a new pitcher.

Simon,Alfredo

	Yr	Tm	W	L	Sv	IP	K	ERA	WHIP	OBA	vL	vR	BF/G	H%	S%	xERA	G	L	F	Ctl	Dom	Cmd	hr/f	hr/9	RAR	BPV	R$
RH RP 29	06	aaa	0	6	0	52	30	7.34	1.94	361			25.3	39%	62%	7.94				3.1	5.1	1.6		1.2	-18.1	11	($5)
Ht/Wt 76 230	07	aa	5	10	0	119	54	9.56	2.18	381			27.6	39%	57%	9.89				4.0	4.1	1.0		2.1	-74.9	-38	($17)
Type	08	MEX	7	2	0	81	64	3.31	1.18	237			22.1	28%	75%	3.49				2.8	7.1	2.6		0.9	9.9	77	$10
Health F	09	BAL	0	1	0	6	3	10.50	1.67	321			13.8	18%	60%	12.65				3.0	4.5	1.5		7.5	-4.5	******	($1)
PT/Exp D	10	BAL *	5	3	17	66	48	4.26	1.51	280	269	284	5.5	31%	77%	4.18	47	19	34	3.7	6.5	1.7	15%	1.5	-1.0	41	$9
Consist F	1st Half		3	2	10	37	29	2.75	1.51	274			6.6	33%	83%	3.68	57	16	27	4.0	7.0	1.8	7%	0.5	6.4	53	$7
LIMA Plan C+	2nd Half		2	1	7	29	19	6.21	1.52	287			4.6	28%	69%	4.53	40	21	39	3.4	5.9	1.7	24%	2.8	-7.4	32	$2
Rand Var +1	11	Proj	4	3	0	58	39	4.66	1.48	281			8.5	31%	72%	4.40	44	19	36	3.4	6.1	1.8	12%	1.2	-0.8	39	$3

17 Sv, 4.93 ERA in 49 IP at BAL O, the irony: lost closer's job in Aug, his best month of the year (121 BPV). 'Twas poetic justice; doesn't own skills for job. Or as the Bard* wrote, this denoted a foregone conclusion. (*not Josh)

Sipp,Tony

	Yr	Tm	W	L	Sv	IP	K	ERA	WHIP	OBA	vL	vR	BF/G	H%	S%	xERA	G	L	F	Ctl	Dom	Cmd	hr/f	hr/9	RAR	BPV	R$
LH RP 27	06	aa	4	2	3	60	69	4.01	1.25	237			8.6	33%	66%	3.07				3.4	10.3	3.0		0.3	3.8	124	$8
Ht/Wt 72 190	07		0	0	0	0	0	0.00	0.00							0.00											
Type Pwr xFB	08	aa	0	3	1	22	27	4.50	1.41	262			6.0	33%	77%	5.51				3.7	11.0	3.0		2.0	-0.5	71	$1
Health C	09	CLE *	3	0	1	57	67	3.35	1.36	225	208	179	4.2	30%	79%	4.01	35	14	51	4.9	10.6	2.2	9%	1.0	7.7	72	$7
PT/Exp D	10	CLE	2	2	1	63	69	4.14	1.38	213	212	223	3.9	25%	77%	4.31	31	14	55	5.6	9.9	1.8	14%	1.7	-0.0	36	$5
Consist B	1st Half		1	2	0	28	30	5.79	1.82	262			3.7	31%	73%	4.86	38	19	42	7.4	9.6	1.3	18%	1.9	-5.7	-10	($1)
LIMA Plan B	2nd Half		1	0	1	35	39	2.83	1.03	168			4.1	19%	83%	3.88	24	10	66	4.1	10.0	2.4	11%	1.5	5.7	71	$5
Rand Var -1	11	Proj	3	1	5	58	66	4.19	1.43	238			4.4	31%	75%	4.21	32	14	54	5.0	10.2	2.1	10%	1.2	0.5	60	$6

Combine an extreme flyballer with shaky Ctl, add in a dash of high hr/f, and voila! ERA spikes due to many multi-run homers. Past (and 2H) skills say he's still LIMA-worthy. But a combustible lefty, so he'll rarely see the 9th.

Slama,Anthony

	Yr	Tm	W	L	Sv	IP	K	ERA	WHIP	OBA	vL	vR	BF/G	H%	S%	xERA	G	L	F	Ctl	Dom	Cmd	hr/f	hr/9	RAR	BPV	R$
RH RP 27	06		0	0	0	0	0	0.00	0.00							0.00											
Ht/Wt 75 207	07		0	0	0	0	0	0.00	0.00							0.00											
Type Pwr	08		0	0	0	0	0	0.00	0.00							0.00											
Health A	09	a/a	4	4	29	81	87	3.39	1.36	230			5.6	31%	76%	3.54				4.7	9.7	2.1		0.6	9.2	93	$17
PT/Exp F	10	MIN *	2	3	17	70	65	2.78	1.27	207	333	273	5.0	26%	81%	4.41	27	20	53	4.8	8.4	1.8	6%	0.8	11.7	27	$13
Consist B	1st Half		0	1	15	45	42	1.65	0.94	145			4.7	19%	85%	1.16				4.1	8.3	2.0		0.4	13.9	106	$12
LIMA Plan B+	2nd Half		2	2	2	25	23	4.84	1.86	299			5.4	36%	78%	5.34	27	20	53	6.0	8.5	1.4	10%	1.5	-2.1	-2	$1
Rand Var -5	11	Proj	2	2	0	44	43	3.93	1.43	241			5.3	30%	75%	4.18				4.8	8.9	1.9		1.0	0.6	68	$3

0-1, 7.71 ERA in 5 IP at MIN. More sparkly skills before callup, then five bad games in majors basically sank 2H. Has torn it up for four minor league seasons; eventually, that'll play in the Show too. End-game LIMA sleeper.

ROD TRUESDELL

Slaten,Doug

Slaten,Doug		Yr	Tm	W	L	Sv	IP	K	ERA	WHIP	OBA	vL	vR	BF/G	H%	S%	xERA	G	L	F	Ctl	Dom	Cmd	hr/f	hr/9	RAR	BPV	R$
LH RP	31	06	a/a	4	4	10	63	63	2.06	1.23	231			4.5	31%	83%	2.81				3.5	9.0	**2.6**		0.2	19.1	112	$13
Ht/Wt	77 210	07	ARI	3	2	0	36	28	2.73	1.52	286	268	284	2.6	33%	86%	4.43	44	17	39	3.5	6.9	**2.0**	9%	1.0	7.6	53	$4
Type	Pwr FB	08	ARI	0	3	0	32	20	4.74	1.46	266	232	282	3.1	29%	70%	4.96	39	19	43	3.9	5.6	**1.4**	9%	1.1	-1.9	12	$0
Health	A	09	ARI *	3	2	9	50	36	3.91	1.47	291			4.3	34%	75%	4.04	44	24	32	2.8	6.5	**2.3**	8%	0.8	1.7	64	$6
PT/Exp	D	10	WAS *	5	1	0	58	50	2.18	1.21	233	151	295	4.0	30%	82%	3.63	48	12	40	3.1	7.7	**2.5**	3%	0.3	13.0	80	$8
Consist	B	1st Half		3	1	0	33	24	1.38	1.18	255			4.2	31%	87%	3.43	51	16	33	2.0	6.5	**3.3**	0%	0.0	10.6	93	$5
LIMA Plan	B+	2nd Half		2	0	0	25	26	3.24	1.24	203			3.7	26%	76%	3.71	45	9	45	4.7	9.4	**2.0**	7%	0.7	2.4	65	$3
Rand Var	-5	11	Proj	**3**	**2**	**0**	**51**	**42**	**3.51**	**1.33**	**253**			**3.8**	**30%**	**76%**	**4.02**	**44**	**15**	**41**	**3.3**	**7.4**	**2.2**	**8%**	**0.9**	**0.8**	**65**	**$4**

4-1, 3.10 ERA in 40 IP at WAS. The ultimate LOOGY:

	BA	Slg	OPS
LH bats	.151	.151	.385
RH bats	.295	.436	.844

That's right, no xB hits vs. LHers. But no chance of role expansion.

Slowey,Kevin

Slowey,Kevin		Yr	Tm	W	L	Sv	IP	K	ERA	WHIP	OBA	vL	vR	BF/G	H%	S%	xERA	G	L	F	Ctl	Dom	Cmd	hr/f	hr/9	RAR	BPV	R$
RH SP	26	06	aa	4	3	0	59	44	4.42	1.29	268			27.6	30%	69%	4.56				2.3	6.7	**2.9**		1.2	0.8	67	$5
Ht/Wt	75 195	07	MIN *	14	6	0	200	134	3.42	1.26	281	267	309	25.3	32%	76%	4.53	29	21	50	1.4	6.0	**4.2**	6%	0.9	26.7	77	$22
Type	xFB	08	MIN	12	11	0	160	123	3.99	1.15	263	277	246	24.2	30%	70%	3.86	36	19	45	1.3	6.9	**5.1**	10%	1.2	7.1	102	$18
Health	D	09	MIN	10	3	0	91	75	4.86	1.41	306	354	267	24.6	35%	70%	4.26	32	20	48	1.5	7.4	**5.0**	11%	1.5	-4.6	104	$8
PT/Exp	B	10	MIN	13	6	0	156	116	4.45	1.29	281	275	284	21.9	32%	69%	4.23	28	21	51	1.7	6.7	**4.0**	8%	1.2	-6.0	82	$13
Consist	A	1st Half		8	5	0	89	63	4.57	1.36	292			23.8	32%	70%	4.44	28	21	51	1.8	6.4	**3.5**	9%	1.3	-4.7	72	$6
LIMA Plan	B	2nd Half		5	1	0	67	53	4.30	1.19	268			19.7	31%	67%	3.96	29	21	50	1.5	7.1	**4.8**	8%	1.1	-1.3	95	$6
Rand Var	0	11	Proj	**15**	**7**	**0**	**174**	**134**	**3.98**	**1.22**	**272**			**24.0**	**31%**	**72%**	**4.10**	**31**	**20**	**49**	**1.6**	**6.9**	**4.5**	**9%**	**1.2**	**4.0**	**92**	**$18**

Strike-throwing extreme FBer yields lots of HRs, but with wrist, triceps, and elbow issues, big issue is health. The difference between an ERA over or under 4.00 is a league-average strand rate. Let's try one out for size.

Smith,Greg

Smith,Greg		Yr	Tm	W	L	Sv	IP	K	ERA	WHIP	OBA	vL	vR	BF/G	H%	S%	xERA	G	L	F	Ctl	Dom	Cmd	hr/f	hr/9	RAR	BPV	R$
LH SP	27	06	aa	5	4	0	60	33	5.55	1.77	324			25.6	36%	69%	6.45				3.8	5.0	**1.3**		0.9	-7.6	21	$0
Ht/Wt	74 190	07	aa	9	5	0	122	82	4.64	1.50	304			24.5	34%	71%	5.60				2.4	6.1	**2.5**		1.1	-2.7	51	$7
Type	FB	08	OAK	8	16	0	197	113	4.01	1.34	236	232	247	25.5	25%	72%	5.14	34	20	46	4.2	5.2	**1.2**	7%	1.0	8.1	-8	$12
Health	D	09	a/a	1	3	0	37	16	9.17	1.78	343			19.4	34%	50%	8.15				2.8	3.9	**1.4**		2.3	-22.3	-30	($4)
PT/Exp	C	10	COL *	3	7	0	114	71	6.20	1.69	308	179	355	22.8	32%	67%	4.82	41	23	36	3.9	5.6	**1.4**	16%	1.8	-30.7	13	($5)
Consist	F	1st Half		1	3	0	69	47	6.06	1.74	309			23.0	34%	68%	4.80	41	23	36	4.3	6.2	**1.4**	14%	1.6	-17.4	13	($4)
LIMA Plan	F	2nd Half		2	4	0	45	23	6.42	1.61	306			22.6	31%	65%	6.62				3.3	4.7	**1.4**		2.1	-13.3	-11	($2)
Rand Var	+4	11	Proj	**1**	**2**	**0**	**29**	**16**	**5.59**	**1.59**	**300**			**21.8**	**31%**	**68%**	**5.07**	**37**	**21**	**41**	**3.4**	**5.0**	**1.5**	**12%**	**1.6**	**-3.3**	**13**	**($1)**

1-2, 6.23 ERA in 39 IP at COL. On April 13, pitched a 7-inning PQS-5 vs the Mets. In his other 7 starts in COL, he never made it past 5.2 innings or posted a PQS score higher than 3. BPIs, trends, health... all very bad. Pass.

Smith,Joe

Smith,Joe		Yr	Tm	W	L	Sv	IP	K	ERA	WHIP	OBA	vL	vR	BF/G	H%	S%	xERA	G	L	F	Ctl	Dom	Cmd	hr/f	hr/9	RAR	BPV	R$
RH RP	27	06		0	0	0	0	0	0.00	0.00							0.00											
Ht/Wt	74 205	07	NYM *	3	2	2	53	50	3.38	1.50	268	298	266	3.8	34%	78%	3.23	62	17	21	4.2	8.4	**2.0**	9%	0.5	6.9	78	$5
Type	Pwr xGB	08	NYM	6	3	0	63	52	3.55	1.30	222	320	192	3.3	27%	73%	3.18	63	20	18	4.4	7.4	**1.7**	13%	0.6	5.6	55	$7
Health	B	09	CLE	0	0	0	34	30	3.44	1.26	238	355	198	3.8	28%	77%	3.38	55	17	28	3.4	7.9	**2.3**	15%	1.1	4.2	83	$3
PT/Exp	D	10	CLE *	4	3	2	63	48	3.16	1.32	215	342	160	3.7	26%	77%	3.76	56	16	28	4.9	6.9	**1.4**	8%	0.6	7.6	27	$7
Consist	A	1st Half		2	2	2	35	26	3.61	1.38	235			4.2	27%	76%	4.31	41	24	35	4.7	6.8	**1.4**	8%	0.8	2.3	14	$3
LIMA Plan	C+	2nd Half		2	1	0	28	22	2.60	1.23	187			3.1	23%	79%	3.41	64	12	24	5.2	7.1	**1.4**	6%	0.3	5.3	30	$3
Rand Var	-3	11	Proj	**3**	**2**	**0**	**64**	**52**	**3.40**	**1.39**	**241**			**3.6**	**29%**	**77%**	**3.54**	**59**	**16**	**25**	**4.4**	**7.4**	**1.7**	**11%**	**0.7**	**5.9**	**51**	**$5**

2-2, 3.83 ERA in 40 IP at CLE. Extreme GB, Dom history is a good start, but Ctl keeps holding him back. Plus, as a sidearmer with lefty issues, he's on the specialist track. That makes him a LIMA end gamer, but no more.

Smith,Jordan

Smith,Jordan		Yr	Tm	W	L	Sv	IP	K	ERA	WHIP	OBA	vL	vR	BF/G	H%	S%	xERA	G	L	F	Ctl	Dom	Cmd	hr/f	hr/9	RAR	BPV	R$
RH RP	25	06		0	0	0	0	0	0.00	0.00							0.00											
Ht/Wt	75 206	07		0	0	0	0	0	0.00	0.00							0.00											
Type	Con GB	08	aa	2	6	0	55	37	6.22	1.76	340			23.4	38%	66%	6.88				2.8	6.1	**2.2**		1.1	-13.0	35	($2)
Health	A	09	aa	5	3	0	73	33	4.57	1.59	313			25.4	34%	71%	5.48				2.8	4.1	**1.5**		0.6	-2.3	28	$2
PT/Exp	D	10	CIN *	4	5	10	73	38	5.00	1.57	314	333	241	4.9	33%	72%	4.34	50	18	32	2.5	4.6	**1.9**	14%	1.5	-8.9	44	$4
Consist	C	1st Half		2	4	10	37	19	5.52	1.70	335			4.9	36%	70%	4.72	43	21	36	2.5	4.7	**1.9**	10%	1.3	-6.9	37	$2
LIMA Plan	C+	2nd Half		2	1	0	36	18	4.46	1.43	290			4.9	29%	76%	4.13	52	17	31	2.5	4.6	**1.9**	18%	1.7	-2.0	46	$1
Rand Var	+2	11	Proj	**2**	**3**	**0**	**44**	**22**	**4.55**	**1.47**	**294**			**8.0**	**31%**	**71%**	**4.35**	**51**	**17**	**32**	**2.7**	**4.6**	**1.7**	**10%**	**1.0**	**-1.1**	**38**	**$1**

3-2, 3.86 ERA in 42 IP at CIN. Nice GB is all he's got working for him. He'll have a short leash as a righty reliever with no Dom, and he's a liability vs LH so far. Even if ERA follows xERA, it won't make him roster-worthy.

Snell,Ian

Snell,Ian		Yr	Tm	W	L	Sv	IP	K	ERA	WHIP	OBA	vL	vR	BF/G	H%	S%	xERA	G	L	F	Ctl	Dom	Cmd	hr/f	hr/9	RAR	BPV	R$
RH SP	29	06	PIT	14	11	0	186	169	4.74	1.46	274	305	251	25.5	32%	72%	4.04	43	21	36	3.6	8.2	**2.3**	15%	1.4	-5.8	71	$13
Ht/Wt	71 198	07	PIT	9	12	0	208	177	3.76	1.33	263	284	245	27.6	31%	75%	3.88	46	17	37	2.9	7.7	**2.6**	9%	1.0	17.0	82	$17
Type	Pwr	08	PIT	7	12	0	164	135	5.42	1.77	303	314	295	24.8	36%	70%	4.88	38	25	37	4.9	7.4	**1.5**	9%	1.0	-23.4	17	($1)
Health	A	09	2TM *	9	12	0	182	126	4.12	1.52	261	265	267	24.5	30%	74%	4.98	38	22	40	4.7	6.2	**1.3**	6%	0.7	4.4	1	$8
PT/Exp	C	10	SEA *	3	9	0	95	59	6.93	1.83	320	302	313	21.4	35%	64%	5.43	34	24	43	4.5	5.6	**1.2**	11%	1.5	-32.6	-10	($6)
Consist	A	1st Half		1	6	0	55	36	6.07	1.87	312			18.9	34%	71%	5.56	34	24	43	5.3	5.9	**1.1**	12%	1.6	-13.2	-25	($3)
LIMA Plan	C	2nd Half		2	3	0	39	22	8.15	1.78	332			26.3	36%	53%	6.60				3.5	5.1	**1.5**		1.2	-19.4	14	($3)
Rand Var	+5	11	Proj	**3**	**5**	**0**	**58**	**40**	**5.12**	**1.60**	**284**			**23.9**	**32%**	**70%**	**4.89**	**38**	**22**	**39**	**4.3**	**6.2**	**1.4**	**9%**	**1.1**	**-4.3**	**11**	**$1**

0-5, 6.41 ERA in 46 IP at SEA. Free falling Dom, surging xERA predicted this blowup. With FB% on the rise, there's little chance he gets back to '09, let alone '07.
UP: Signed in Japan

Sonnanstine,Andy

Sonnanstine,Andy		Yr	Tm	W	L	Sv	IP	K	ERA	WHIP	OBA	vL	vR	BF/G	H%	S%	xERA	G	L	F	Ctl	Dom	Cmd	hr/f	hr/9	RAR	BPV	R$
RH RP	28	06	aa	15	8	0	185	127	4.11	1.27	274			27.7	31%	70%	4.36				1.9	6.2	**3.2**		1.0	9.4	77	$18
Ht/Wt	75 190	07	TAM *	12	14	0	202	155	5.09	1.31	283	318	266	25.8	32%	64%	4.09	39	18	43	1.8	6.9	**3.9**	10%	1.2	-14.5	93	$14
Type	Con	08	TAM	13	9	0	193	124	4.38	1.29	280	265	289	25.4	31%	68%	4.16	42	17	41	1.7	5.8	**3.4**	8%	1.0	-0.7	78	$15
Health	A	09	TAM *	11	12	0	157	91	6.32	1.62	323	275	367	23.0	35%	63%	4.82	43	19	38	2.5	5.2	**2.1**	11%	1.4	-36.1	48	$1
PT/Exp	B	10	TAM	3	1	1	81	50	4.44	1.36	267	267	253	8.5	29%	71%	4.21	45	19	36	3.0	5.6	**1.9**	12%	1.2	-3.1	42	$4
Consist	B	1st Half		1	0	1	42	27	3.67	1.13	244			6.8	26%	73%	3.80	44	18	39	1.9	5.8	**3.0**	12%	1.3	2.4	74	$4
LIMA Plan	C+	2nd Half		2	1	0	39	23	5.27	1.60	289			11.1	31%	69%	4.66	46	21	33	4.1	5.3	**1.3**	11%	1.1	-5.5	7	$0
Rand Var	0	11	Proj	**4**	**3**	**0**	**73**	**45**	**4.34**	**1.38**	**276**			**13.0**	**30%**	**71%**	**4.33**	**44**	**19**	**37**	**2.7**	**5.6**	**2.0**	**10%**	**1.1**	**-0.3**	**48**	**$4**

PROs:
- Emerging ground ball profile
- '09 vs RHers regressed to norm

CONs:
- Eroding command
- Stagnant xERA

2H more likely to repeat than 1H.

Soriano,Rafael

Soriano,Rafael		Yr	Tm	W	L	Sv	IP	K	ERA	WHIP	OBA	vL	vR	BF/G	H%	S%	xERA	G	L	F	Ctl	Dom	Cmd	hr/f	hr/9	RAR	BPV	R$
RH RP	31	06	SEA	1	2	2	60	65	2.25	1.08	206	244	179	4.5	27%	85%	3.77	27	19	54	3.2	9.8	**3.1**	7%	0.9	17.1	96	$10
Ht/Wt	73 220	07	ATL	3	3	9	72	70	3.00	0.86	188	164	197	3.8	21%	76%	3.41	33	16	51	1.9	8.8	**4.7**	13%	1.5	12.7	118	$14
Type	Pwr xFB	08	ATL	0	1	3	14	16	2.57	1.14	151	222	103	4.1	20%	80%	4.30	23	16	61	5.8	10.3	**1.8**	5%	0.6	2.9	30	$3
Health	D	09	ATL	1	6	27	76	102	2.97	1.06	199	258	138	3.9	30%	74%	2.97	31	21	48	3.2	12.1	**3.8**	8%	0.7	11.4	140	$18
PT/Exp	B	10	TAM	3	2	45	62	57	1.73	0.80	170	196	132	3.6	21%	83%	3.34	33	16	52	2.0	8.2	**4.1**	5%	0.6	18.5	104	$26
Consist	B	1st Half		2	0	21	31	28	1.47	0.75	172			3.6	21%	86%	3.20	37	10	53	1.5	8.2	**5.6**	5%	0.6	10.1	123	$13
LIMA Plan	C+	2nd Half		1	2	24	32	29	1.99	0.85	168			3.6	21%	80%	3.47	29	21	50	2.6	8.3	**3.2**	5%	0.6	8.4	86	$13
Rand Var	-5	11	Proj	**2**	**3**	**40**	**65**	**68**	**3.03**	**1.06**	**217**			**3.9**	**27%**	**76%**	**3.51**	**31**	**18**	**51**	**2.5**	**9.4**	**3.8**	**8%**	**1.0**	**6.3**	**111**	**$22**

Elite, yes, but don't cast it in stone quite yet. Tiny ERA was driven by miniscule H%. As an extreme FBer, he needs a comfy home park and pinpoint control to avoid blowups. Health grade confirms he's still a risk.

Soria,Joakim

Soria,Joakim		Yr	Tm	W	L	Sv	IP	K	ERA	WHIP	OBA	vL	vR	BF/G	H%	S%	xERA	G	L	F	Ctl	Dom	Cmd	hr/f	hr/9	RAR	BPV	R$
RH RP	26	06	MEX	0	0	15	37	28	4.38	1.43	277			4.1	33%	70%	4.60				3.2	6.8	**2.2**		0.7	0.6	64	$6
Ht/Wt	75 204	07	KC	2	3	17	69	75	2.48	0.94	191	167	200	4.3	26%	74%	3.06	39	20	40	2.5	9.8	**3.9**	4%	0.4	17.3	126	$17
Type	Pwr	08	KC	2	3	42	67	66	1.60	0.86	170	167	171	4.0	22%	87%	3.10	45	14	41	2.5	8.8	**3.5**	7%	0.7	22.8	113	$26
Health	A	09	KC	3	2	30	53	69	2.21	1.13	227	224	213	4.6	33%	85%	2.90	40	18	42	2.7	11.7	**4.3**	10%	0.8	14.7	155	$19
PT/Exp	A	10	KC	1	2	43	66	71	1.78	1.05	222	231	196	4.0	30%	86%	2.76	48	17	35	2.2	9.7	**4.4**	7%	0.5	19.1	142	$24
Consist	A	1st Half		0	1	22	32	38	2.56	1.10	232			4.1	31%	84%	2.86	40	18	42	2.3	10.8	**4.8**	12%	1.1	6.2	151	$11
LIMA Plan	C+	2nd Half		1	1	21	34	33	1.06	1.00	213			3.8	29%	88%	2.66	55	16	29	2.1	8.7	**4.1**	0%	0.0	12.9	133	$13
Rand Var	-5	11	Proj	**2**	**2**	**40**	**58**	**64**	**2.64**	**1.14**	**234**			**4.2**	**31%**	**80%**	**3.00**	**45**	**17**	**38**	**2.5**	**9.9**	**4.0**	**9%**	**0.8**	**9.2**	**135**	**$21**

Strand rate has helped, but great Cmd, added GB% give him even more upside. xERA says sub-3.00 ERA is sustainable. On a better club... UP: 50 SV

STEPHEN NICKRAND

Stammen,Craig			W	L	Sv	IP	K	ERA	WHIP	OBA	vL	vR	BF/G	H%	S%	xERA	G	L	F	Ctl	Dom	Cmd	hr/f	hr/9	RAR	BPV	R$
RH RP	27	06	0	0	0	0	0	0.00	0.00							0.00											
Ht/Wt	75 200	07	0	0	0	0	0	0.00	0.00							0.00											
Type		08 a/a	4	5	0	81	53	5.03	1.45	286			23.6	34%	63%	4.36				2.9	5.9	2.1		0.3	-7.3	66	$3
Health	A	09 WAS *	8	9	0	146	60	4.33	1.25	268	290	247	23.4	27%	68%	4.32	47	21	32	2.0	3.7	1.9	11%	1.1	-2.5	38	$8
PT/Exp	C	10 WAS	4	4	0	128	85	5.13	1.50	295	291	301	16.2	33%	66%	3.78	51	23	26	2.9	6.0	2.1	12%	0.9	-17.6	59	$0
Consist	A	1st Half	4	3	0	97	47	5.12	1.43	295			24.8	31%	65%	3.99	51	23	26	2.2	4.3	1.9	12%	1.0	-13.2	47	$1
LIMA Plan	B	2nd Half	0	1	0	31	38	5.17	1.72	294			8.0	41%	69%	3.16	51	24	25	4.9	11.1	2.3	9%	0.6	-4.4	96	($1)
Rand Var	+4	11 Proj	3	4	0	80	57	4.40	1.38	272			14.3	31%	69%	3.72	50	23	27	2.9	6.4	2.2	10%	0.8	4.2	64	$3

There's a sleeper lurking here...
- Steady ground ball profile
- Improved xERA again
- Skills spiked in 2nd half

Inflated H% in 2H hid huge Dom spike, sabotaged surface stats. For '11... UP: 3.50 ERA

Stauffer,Tim			W	L	Sv	IP	K	ERA	WHIP	OBA	vL	vR	BF/G	H%	S%	xERA	G	L	F	Ctl	Dom	Cmd	hr/f	hr/9	RAR	BPV	R$
RH RP	28	06 aaa	7	12	0	153	78	5.35	1.65	320			25.0	35%	68%	6.05				2.9	4.6	1.6		0.9	-15.7	25	$1
Ht/Wt	73 205	07 aa	8	5	0	130	76	5.76	1.74	336			24.3	37%	68%	6.72				2.8	5.2	1.8		1.0	-20.8	28	($1)
Type	GB	08 SD	0	0	0	0	0	0.00	0.00							0.00											
Health	F	09 SD *	7	8	1	115	74	3.17	1.30	247	239	279	16.2	28%	78%	4.30	44	20	36	3.4	5.8	1.7	8%	0.8	14.5	35	$10
PT/Exp	D	10 SD *	6	5	0	100	68	2.40	1.22	244	197	236	10.9	29%	80%	3.61	55	15	31	2.8	6.1	2.1	3%	0.3	19.9	65	$10
Consist	B	1st Half	2	1	0	41	26	2.37	1.37	277			10.8	33%	82%	3.20	68	10	22	2.6	5.7	2.2	3%	0.2	8.2	79	$3
LIMA Plan	C+	2nd Half	4	4	0	59	42	2.42	1.13	219			10.9	26%	78%	3.66	49	16	34	3.0	6.4	2.1	3%	0.3	11.7	60	$7
Rand Var	-5	11 Proj	8	7	0	131	84	3.59	1.36	268			14.3	30%	75%	4.02	51	16	33	3.0	5.8	2.0	8%	0.8	2.0	53	$9

6-5, 1.85 ERA in 82 IP at SD. Former 1st rounder had huge year in spot starter role. Inflated S% helped ERA but xERA confirms he was good. Elite GB profile gives him SP upside now. UP: 15 wins, 3.50 ERA

Storen,Drew			W	L	Sv	IP	K	ERA	WHIP	OBA	vL	vR	BF/G	H%	S%	xERA	G	L	F	Ctl	Dom	Cmd	hr/f	hr/9	RAR	BPV	R$
RH RP	23	06	0	0	0	0	0	0.00	0.00							0.00											
Ht/Wt	74 180	07	0	0	0	0	0	0.00	0.00							0.00											
Type	Pwr FB	08	0	0	0	0	0	0.00	0.00							0.00											
Health	A	09 aa	1	0	0	9	11	4.00	2.22	339			4.6	47%	80%	6.90				7.0	11.0	1.6		0.0	0.3	86	$0
PT/Exp	F	10 WAS *	4	4	9	72	65	3.15	1.22	235	247	238	4.4	30%	75%	3.66	40	20	40	3.1	8.2	2.6	5%	0.5	7.7	80	$10
Consist	F	1st Half	2	1	4	39	32	1.62	1.08	209			4.6	26%	85%	3.60	46	13	41	3.0	7.4	2.5	2%	0.2	11.5	76	$7
LIMA Plan	C+	2nd Half	2	3	5	33	33	4.97	1.38	264			4.2	34%	64%	3.66	35	25	40	3.3	9.1	2.8	8%	0.8	-3.8	88	$3
Rand Var	-2	11 Proj	4	5	28	73	68	3.60	1.27	244			4.4	30%	74%	3.74	38	22	40	3.2	8.4	2.6	9%	0.9	3.6	81	$16

5 Sv, 3.58 ERA in 55 IP at WAS. Need only 30 IP in high minors before making MLB splash. Blame H% and S% for 2H ERA. Handcuffs both LH and RH bats, so he'll have less growing pains than most. UP: 40 SV

Strasburg,Stephen			W	L	Sv	IP	K	ERA	WHIP	OBA	vL	vR	BF/G	H%	S%	xERA	G	L	F	Ctl	Dom	Cmd	hr/f	hr/9	RAR	BPV	R$
RH SP	22	06	0	0	0	0	0	0.00	0.00							0.00											
Ht/Wt	76 220	07	0	0	0	0	0	0.00	0.00							0.00											
Type	Pwr	08	0	0	0	0	0	0.00	0.00							0.00											
Health	C	09	0	0	0	0	0	0.00	0.00							0.00											
PT/Exp	F	10 WAS *	12	5	0	123	148	2.34	0.99	209	241	207	20.9	30%	78%	2.43	48	20	32	2.2	10.8	4.9	7%	0.4	25.4	161	$21
Consist	F	1st Half	9	4	0	92	109	1.96	0.96	201			20.9	29%	80%	2.29	51	22	27	2.3	10.7	4.7	5%	0.3	23.3	160	$17
LIMA Plan	A+	2nd Half	3	1	0	31	39	3.45	1.09	234			20.9	33%	71%	2.54	45	19	36	2.0	11.2	5.6	11%	0.9	2.2	171	$5
Rand Var	-1	11 Proj	1	1	0	15	16	3.72	1.17	227			19.8	31%	69%	3.03	46	19	35	3.1	9.9	3.2	8%	0.6	2.0	119	$2

5-3, 2.91 ERA in 68 IP at WAS. To say he was dominant in MLB debut would be putting it mildly. Before TJ surgery, he already was among game's best, with a GB% tilt to boot. Remains a keeper league gem.

Street,Huston			W	L	Sv	IP	K	ERA	WHIP	OBA	vL	vR	BF/G	H%	S%	xERA	G	L	F	Ctl	Dom	Cmd	hr/f	hr/9	RAR	BPV	R$
RH RP	27	06 OAK	4	4	37	70	67	3.33	1.10	244	274	211	4.1	31%	70%	3.42	37	21	42	1.7	8.6	5.2	5%	0.5	10.6	125	$22
Ht/Wt	72 200	07 OAK	5	2	16	50	63	2.88	0.94	199	224	162	4.0	28%	74%	2.77	40	15	45	2.2	11.3	5.3	10%	0.9	10.0	164	$16
Type	Pwr xFB	08 OAK	7	5	18	71	70	3.80	1.23	231	200	250	4.6	29%	70%	3.71	36	23	41	3.4	8.9	2.6	8%	0.8	4.8	81	$15
Health	D	09 COL	4	1	35	62	70	3.06	0.91	198	167	217	3.7	26%	71%	2.86	38	19	43	1.9	10.2	5.4	11%	1.0	8.6	149	$22
PT/Exp	B	10 COL	4	4	20	47	45	3.62	1.06	226	208	238	4.3	28%	69%	3.44	37	16	48	2.1	8.6	4.1	8%	1.0	2.3	112	$13
Consist	B	1st Half	0	1	2	8	7	2.17	0.60	176			4.2	20%	75%	3.00	32	14	55	0.0	7.6		9%	1.1	1.9	146	$2
LIMA Plan	B+	2nd Half	4	3	18	39	38	3.92	1.15	236			4.3	29%	68%	3.52	38	16	46	2.5	8.8	3.5	8%	0.9	0.4	105	$11
Rand Var	0	11 Proj	5	3	30	58	61	3.57	1.12	231			4.2	30%	71%	3.39	36	18	46	2.5	9.5	3.8	9%	0.9	5.4	118	$18

Rebounded from 1H shoulder, groin problems and showed elite Cmd again. Owns the skills you want from a top tier closer, save FB%. What's missing is health. That's not likely to correct itself. If you can take risk... UP: 40 SV

Suppan,Jeff			W	L	Sv	IP	K	ERA	WHIP	OBA	vL	vR	BF/G	H%	S%	xERA	G	L	F	Ctl	Dom	Cmd	hr/f	hr/9	RAR	BPV	R$
RH RP	36	06 STL	12	7	0	190	104	4.12	1.45	279	302	257	26.0	30%	74%	4.56	47	23	31	3.3	4.9	1.5	11%	1.0	8.6	25	$11
Ht/Wt	74 230	07 MIL	12	12	0	207	114	4.62	1.50	294	334	271	26.9	32%	70%	4.68	45	20	35	3.0	5.0	1.7	7%	0.8	-4.8	33	$8
Type	Con	08 MIL	10	10	0	178	90	4.96	1.54	292	288	308	25.6	30%	72%	4.79	44	23	32	3.4	4.6	1.3	15%	1.5	-15.2	13	$4
Health	C	09 MIL	7	12	0	162	80	5.29	1.69	305	311	306	24.9	32%	72%	5.06	49	18	33	4.1	4.5	1.1	13%	1.4	-21.9	-4	($2)
PT/Exp	A	10 2NL	3	8	0	101	51	5.06	1.65	313	302	339	15.4	33%	71%	5.01	40	21	39	3.3	4.5	1.4	9%	1.2	-13.1	11	($2)
Consist	A	1st Half	0	4	0	50	29	6.44	1.93	352			12.8	38%	68%	5.17	41	22	38	3.6	5.2	1.5	10%	1.3	-15.1	15	($5)
LIMA Plan	F	2nd Half	3	4	0	51	22	3.71	1.37	269			19.9	28%	77%	4.84	40	21	39	3.0	3.9	1.3	9%	1.1	1.9	7	$3
Rand Var	+1	11 Proj	4	6	0	90	45	4.93	1.60	302			22.5	32%	72%	4.92	44	21	36	3.4	4.5	1.3	11%	1.2	-8.6	11	$0

Even STL's Duncan couldn't fix this mess. Those late season surface stats had absolutely no skill support. With marginal Cmd and ominous xERA, even a non-pitching coach magician couldn't wand away these ills.

Sweeney,Brian			W	L	Sv	IP	K	ERA	WHIP	OBA	vL	vR	BF/G	H%	S%	xERA	G	L	F	Ctl	Dom	Cmd	hr/f	hr/9	RAR	BPV	R$
RH RP	36	06 SD *	4	1	2	86	41	3.73	1.30	267	263	237	8.3	29%	73%	4.84	39	20	40	2.4	4.3	1.8	7%	0.8	8.0	29	$7
Ht/Wt	74 200	07 JPN	6	8	0	109	59	4.61	1.48	276			22.9	28%	74%	5.55				3.7	4.9	1.3		1.5	-2.0	12	$5
Type	Con FB	08 JPN	12	5	0	163	95	4.32	1.46	245			25.5	24%	79%	5.45				4.9	5.2	1.1		2.0	-0.3	-1	$9
Health	A	09 JPN	5	8	0	118	61	6.63	1.86	317			26.8	34%	65%	6.87				4.9	4.7	0.9		1.3	-33.8	2	($6)
PT/Exp	B	10 SEA *	3	3	1	65	41	2.96	1.07	231	308	198	6.7	26%	76%	4.11	37	16	47	2.0	5.6	2.8	6%	0.8	9.5	62	$8
Consist	F	1st Half	3	1	1	36	34	2.11	0.93	199			7.7	26%	77%	3.66	26	16	58	2.1	8.4	4.0	2%	0.3	9.0	99	$7
LIMA Plan	C	2nd Half	0	2	0	29	7	3.99	1.23	266			5.8	25%	74%	5.08	39	16	45	1.8	2.2	1.2	10%	1.5	0.5	6	$1
Rand Var	-4	11 Proj	1	2	0	29	15	4.34	1.48	288			10.6	30%	74%	5.05	38	18	44	3.1	4.7	1.5	9%	1.2	-2.7	16	$1

1-2, 3.16 ERA in 37 IP at SEA. Journeyman went to Japan, got blown up there, then showed enough in Triple-A to merit recall. Don't buy surface stats; he can't strike out MLB bats. Use 2H xERA as baseline.

Takahashi,Hisanori			W	L	Sv	IP	K	ERA	WHIP	OBA	vL	vR	BF/G	H%	S%	xERA	G	L	F	Ctl	Dom	Cmd	hr/f	hr/9	RAR	BPV	R$
LH RP	36	06	0	0	0	0	0	0.00	0.00							0.00											
Ht/Wt	70 170	07 JPN	14	4	0	187	134	3.41	1.30	255			28.2	27%	83%	4.89				3.0	6.4	2.2		1.7	24.4	38	$20
Type	Pwr FB	08 JPN	8	5	0	122	89	5.13	1.42	284			23.0	30%	71%	5.83				2.7	6.6	2.4		2.0	-12.4	29	$6
Health	A	09 JPN	10	6	0	144	120	3.65	1.41	280			24.9	31%	82%	5.43				2.8	7.5	2.7		1.7	11.8	50	$12
PT/Exp	B	10 NYM	10	6	8	122	114	3.61	1.30	252	217	264	9.7	31%	75%	3.84	38	16	45	3.2	8.4	2.7	8%	1.0	6.0	82	$14
Consist	B	1st Half	7	3	0	75	70	4.32	1.44	269			13.6	33%	73%	4.11	36	18	46	3.6	8.4	2.3	9%	1.1	-2.8	68	$5
LIMA Plan	C+	2nd Half	3	3	8	47	44	2.49	1.09	223			6.5	28%	81%	3.40	42	15	43	2.5	8.4	3.4	7%	0.8	8.8	104	$9
Rand Var	0	11 Proj	5	3	5	73	62	3.85	1.31	260			12.8	30%	75%	4.00	40	16	45	2.9	7.7	2.7	10%	1.2	1.2	79	$8

Starter or reliever? You decide...

	Dom	HR/9	ERA
As SP	7.6	1.5	5.01
As RP	9.5	0.3	2.04

And that second half skill spike came in relief. Closer material? Not likely as lefty with RH probs.

Talbot,Mitch			W	L	Sv	IP	K	ERA	WHIP	OBA	vL	vR	BF/G	H%	S%	xERA	G	L	F	Ctl	Dom	Cmd	hr/f	hr/9	RAR	BPV	R$
RH SP	27	06 aa	10	7	1	156	133	3.40	1.38	276			24.0	34%	75%	4.12				2.8	7.7	2.8		0.4	21.6	92	$16
Ht/Wt	74 200	07 aaa	13	9	0	161	109	6.15	1.67	311			25.5	35%	63%	5.99				3.6	6.1	1.7		0.9	-33.5	38	$2
Type		08 aaa	13	9	0	161	122	4.47	1.36	288			24.6	35%	66%	4.31				2.0	6.8	3.5		0.5	-3.3	96	$12
Health	A	09 aaa	4	4	0	54	34	5.66	1.81	342			25.6	39%	67%	6.43				3.1	5.6	1.8		0.5	-9.0	43	($1)
PT/Exp	C	10 CLE	10	13	0	159	88	4.41	1.49	273	255	295	25.1	30%	71%	4.61	48	17	35	3.9	5.0	1.3	7%	0.7	-5.3	10	$6
Consist	D	1st Half	8	7	0	103	50	3.86	1.36	255			27.5	28%	73%	4.46	50	17	33	3.6	4.4	1.2	7%	0.7	3.6	10	$7
LIMA Plan	C	2nd Half	2	6	0	57	38	5.41	1.73	305			21.9	35%	69%	4.86	45	17	38	4.5	6.0	1.4	7%	0.8	-8.8	11	($1)
Rand Var	-1	11 Proj	8	13	0	164	106	4.79	1.50	285			24.1	32%	70%	4.46	47	17	37	3.4	5.8	1.7	9%	1.0	-3.4	37	$6

That first half lulled the bidders in, then he went kaboom in 2H. He needs at least a 2.0+ Cmd to survive. He owns that ability, but with this Cmd slide, chances of it returning soon are remote. Especially since RH kill him.

STEPHEN NICKRAND

Tallet,Brian

		Yr	Tm	W	L	Sv	IP	K	ERA	WHIP	OBA	vL	vR	BF/G	H%	S%	xERA	G	L	F	Ctl	Dom	Cmd	hr/f	hr/9	RAR	BPV	R$
LH RP	33	06	TOR *	4	2	3	79	53	5.36	1.65	282	220	246	5.7	31%	70%	5.26	41	18	41	4.9	6.1	**1.2**	10%	1.2	-7.8	-4	$2
Ht/Wt	78 220	07	TOR	2	4	0	62	54	3.47	1.24	218	247	194	5.4	28%	70%	4.11	40	19	40	4.0	7.8	**1.9**	1%	0.1	8.0	50	$6
Type	Pwr FB	08	TOR	1	2	0	56	47	2.88	1.31	247	257	230	4.7	30%	80%	3.94	43	22	36	3.5	7.5	**2.1**	7%	0.6	10.2	61	$5
Health	C	09	TOR	7	9	0	161	120	5.32	1.50	272	290	259	19.2	31%	66%	4.84	36	21	43	4.0	6.7	**1.7**	9%	1.1	-17.2	26	$5
PT/Exp	C	10	TOR	2	6	0	77	53	6.40	1.58	278	176	320	10.2	28%	66%	5.09	35	17	48	4.4	6.2	**1.4**	17%	2.3	-21.6	4	($2)
Consist	B	1st Half		1	3	0	40	31	5.89	1.49	258			14.6	27%	66%	4.74	37	15	48	4.5	7.0	**1.6**	16%	2.0	-8.6	19	($0)
LIMA Plan	D	2nd Half		1	3	0	38	22	6.94	1.68	298			7.9	29%	65%	5.45	33	19	48	4.3	5.3	**1.2**	18%	2.6	-13.0	-11	($2)
Rand Var	+4	11	Proj	**1**	**3**	**0**	**44**	**31**	**4.97**	**1.52**	**273**			**9.7**	**30%**	**71%**	**4.87**	**36**	**19**	**44**	**4.1**	**6.4**	**1.6**	**11%**	**1.4**	**-3.1**	**18**	**$1**

Injury log: 2009 bone bruise, foot contusion. 2010 forearm and shoulder problems. These now overshadow the promise from 2007-08 skill set. Some upside if healthy enough to get back on track, but more risk than reward.

Tazawa,Junichi

		Yr	Tm	W	L	Sv	IP	K	ERA	WHIP	OBA	vL	vR	BF/G	H%	S%	xERA	G	L	F	Ctl	Dom	Cmd	hr/f	hr/9	RAR	BPV	R$
RH RP	24	06		0	0	0	0	0	0.00	0.00							0.00											
Ht/Wt	71 180	07		0	0	0	0	0	0.00	0.00							0.00											
Type	xFB	08		0	0	0	0	0	0.00	0.00							0.00											
Health	F	09	BOS *	11	10	0	134	94	4.35	1.39	284	323	440	22.3	32%	70%	4.95	25	23	53	2.5	6.3	**2.5**	6%	0.9	1.6	49	$11
PT/Exp	F	10	BOS	0	0	0	0	0	0.00	0.00							0.00											
Consist	F	1st Half		0	0	0	0	0	0.00	0.00							0.00											
LIMA Plan	D	2nd Half		0	0	0	0	0	0.00	0.00							0.00											
Rand Var	+5	11	Proj	**5**	**5**	**0**	**58**	**42**	**4.81**	**1.41**	**278**			**20.9**	**30%**	**71%**	**4.86**	**25**	**23**	**53**	**2.9**	**6.5**	**2.2**	**10%**	**1.6**	**-4.1**	**40**	**$4**

Tommy John surgery in April cost him 2010 season and will likely need first half of 2011 to shake rust. Has yet to succeed at major league level, but 2009 AAA Dom and good Ctl point to success... in 2012.

Tejeda,Robinson

		Yr	Tm	W	L	Sv	IP	K	ERA	WHIP	OBA	vL	vR	BF/G	H%	S%	xERA	G	L	F	Ctl	Dom	Cmd	hr/f	hr/9	RAR	BPV	R$
RH RP	29	06	TEX *	11	7	0	153	108	4.52	1.56	271	331	250	23.7	30%	74%	5.20	37	18	45	4.6	6.3	**1.4**	10%	1.2	0.6	6	$9
Ht/Wt	75 248	07	TEX *	6	12	0	114	84	7.49	1.96	313	317	264	23.1	35%	62%	6.15	35	14	51	6.1	6.7	**1.1**	9%	1.3	-41.8	-31	($7)
Type	Pwr xFB	08	2AL *	3	3	1	78	74	3.49	1.12	191	225	115	8.1	24%	70%	4.03	33	20	47	4.1	8.5	**2.1**	7%	0.7	8.3	53	$10
Health	B	09	KC	4	2	0	74	87	3.54	1.26	171	209	125	8.8	24%	72%	4.13	35	15	50	6.1	10.6	**1.7**	5%	0.5	8.3	39	$9
PT/Exp	D	10	KC	3	5	0	61	56	3.54	1.33	242	252	234	4.8	30%	75%	4.29	28	21	51	3.8	8.3	**2.2**	6%	0.7	4.5	51	$5
Consist	A	1st Half		3	3	0	39	36	3.49	1.32	221			5.0	29%	72%	4.34	27	24	49	4.7	8.4	**1.8**	2%	0.2	3.1	31	$4
LIMA Plan	C	2nd Half		0	2	0	22	20	3.63	1.35	276			4.5	32%	81%	4.19	28	16	55	2.4	8.1	**3.3**	11%	1.6	1.4	86	$1
Rand Var	-2	11	Proj	**2**	**3**	**0**	**44**	**42**	**4.14**	**1.40**	**246**			**6.5**	**30%**	**75%**	**4.42**	**31**	**18**	**51**	**4.3**	**8.7**	**2.0**	**10%**	**1.2**	**-0.7**	**48**	**$3**

2H IP limited by biceps injury, but small sample did yield:
- Possible step forward in Ctl
- Continued solid Dom
- LD turning into FB over fence

xERA says he has been lucky; still worth a speculative buck.

Texeira,Kanekoa

		Yr	Tm	W	L	Sv	IP	K	ERA	WHIP	OBA	vL	vR	BF/G	H%	S%	xERA	G	L	F	Ctl	Dom	Cmd	hr/f	hr/9	RAR	BPV	R$
RH RP	25	06		0	0	0	0	0	0.00	0.00							0.00											
Ht/Wt	72 210	07		0	0	0	0	0	0.00	0.00							0.00											
Type	GB	08	aa	3	2	1	22	20	2.86	1.27	244			6.1	29%	84%	4.12				3.3	8.2	**2.5**		1.2	3.9	71	$4
Health	A	09	aa	9	6	2	101	73	4.13	1.61	286			11.2	33%	76%	5.27				4.3	6.5	**1.5**		0.8	2.3	43	$6
PT/Exp	D	10	2AL	1	1	0	61	33	4.85	1.60	297	300	308	6.4	33%	68%	4.33	52	20	27	3.7	4.8	**1.3**	5%	0.4	-5.3	18	($1)
Consist	C	1st Half		1	1	0	33	23	3.85	1.50	275			5.8	33%	73%	3.83	51	25	25	3.9	6.3	**1.6**	4%	0.3	1.2	39	$1
LIMA Plan	F	2nd Half		0	0	0	29	10	5.98	1.71	320			7.4	34%	64%	4.92	53	17	30	3.5	3.1	**0.9**	6%	0.6	-6.5	-5	($2)
Rand Var	0	11	Proj	**1**	**1**	**0**	**29**	**17**	**4.66**	**1.55**	**281**			**7.6**	**32%**	**70%**	**4.37**	**53**	**19**	**28**	**4.0**	**5.3**	**1.3**	**7%**	**0.6**	**-0.3**	**17**	**$1**

Rule 5 pick clearly needs more seasoning in the minors. Right elbow strain in 2H did not help, but his ERA was over 5.00 in four of five months he pitched. 2008 says he has a MLB future, but 2011 is not his time.

Thatcher,Joe

		Yr	Tm	W	L	Sv	IP	K	ERA	WHIP	OBA	vL	vR	BF/G	H%	S%	xERA	G	L	F	Ctl	Dom	Cmd	hr/f	hr/9	RAR	BPV	R$
LH RP	29	06		0	0	0	0	0	0.00	0.00							0.00											
Ht/Wt	74 229	07	a/a	4	1	1	46	53	1.64	1.23	262			4.2	38%	85%	3.11				2.1	10.4	**5.1**		0.0	16.1	171	$9
Type	Pwr	08	aaa	5	2	3	39	32	3.61	1.61	310			4.8	37%	78%	5.35				3.1	7.3	**2.4**		0.6	3.3	70	$5
Health	A	09	SD *	2	2	1	64	74	2.67	1.30	240	182	267	3.8	34%	80%	3.28	44	18	38	3.7	10.4	**2.8**	5%	0.4	12.0	111	$7
PT/Exp	F	10	SD *	1	1	0	40	48	1.61	0.99	207	197	172	2.2	30%	84%	2.66	41	21	38	2.3	10.8	**4.7**	3%	0.2	11.9	151	$6
Consist	C	1st Half		1	1	0	21	23	2.18	0.97	194			2.8	28%	75%	2.93	41	21	38	2.6	9.6	**3.7**	0%	0.0	4.8	121	$3
LIMA Plan	A	2nd Half		0	0	0	19	25	0.96	1.02	221			1.8	34%	94%	2.36	41	22	37	1.9	12.0	**6.3**	6%	0.5	7.0	184	$3
Rand Var	-5	11	Proj	**2**	**1**	**0**	**54**	**61**	**2.52**	**1.14**	**230**			**2.8**	**31%**	**81%**	**2.99**	**42**	**20**	**37**	**2.7**	**10.3**	**3.8**	**8%**	**0.7**	**7.6**	**132**	**$7**

1-0, 1.29 ERA in 35 IP at SD. Can we get tours of the SD reliever factory? The brilliant craftsmanship shows in all their products. 2H S% yielded superhuman stats which can't repeat, 1H line is more legit.

Thomas,Brad

		Yr	Tm	W	L	Sv	IP	K	ERA	WHIP	OBA	vL	vR	BF/G	H%	S%	xERA	G	L	F	Ctl	Dom	Cmd	hr/f	hr/9	RAR	BPV	R$
LH RP	33	06		0	0	0	0	0	0.00	0.00							0.00											
Ht/Wt	76 235	07	aa	8	6	2	116	68	7.55	2.29	387			17.8	43%	66%	9.01				4.5	5.2	**1.2**		0.8	-44.1	8	($11)
Type	Con	08	KOR	0	0	0	0	0	0.00	0.00							0.00											
Health	A	09	KOR	0	0	0	0	0	0.00	0.00							0.00											
PT/Exp	D	10	DET	6	2	0	69	30	3.90	1.53	283	252	322	6.3	31%	75%	4.77	50	17	33	3.8	3.9	**1.0**	5%	0.5	2.1	-3	$3
Consist	F	1st Half		4	0	0	36	15	4.29	1.71	289			8.3	32%	73%	5.11	54	16	30	5.0	3.8	**0.8**	3%	0.3	-0.6	-36	$1
LIMA Plan	C	2nd Half		2	2	0	34	15	3.48	1.34	275			4.9	29%	76%	4.43	46	17	36	2.4	4.0	**1.7**	7%	0.8	2.7	32	$2
Rand Var	-3	11	Proj	**3**	**2**	**0**	**44**	**21**	**4.34**	**1.59**	**290**			**8.2**	**31%**	**75%**	**4.90**	**50**	**17**	**34**	**3.9**	**4.3**	**1.1**	**10%**	**1.0**	**-3.3**	**-0**	**$1**

Had not pitched in the majors since 2004 and his Cmd shows why. Can't get righties out but can strike out lefties (6.4 DOM vLH), so his tenuous chance of sticking in the bigs depends on succeeding in specialist role.

Thornton,Matt

		Yr	Tm	W	L	Sv	IP	K	ERA	WHIP	OBA	vL	vR	BF/G	H%	S%	xERA	G	L	F	Ctl	Dom	Cmd	hr/f	hr/9	RAR	BPV	R$
LH RP	34	06	CHW	5	3	2	54	49	3.33	1.24	232	211	240	3.6	28%	76%	3.55	49	19	32	3.5	8.2	**2.3**	10%	0.8	8.2	80	$8
Ht/Wt	78 235	07	CHW	4	4	2	56	55	4.80	1.51	271	283	260	3.7	35%	68%	3.89	47	19	34	4.2	8.8	**2.1**	7%	0.6	-2.0	71	$5
Type	Pwr	08	CHW	5	3	1	67	77	2.67	1.00	202	170	218	3.6	28%	76%	2.48	53	20	27	2.5	10.3	**4.1**	11%	0.7	13.9	148	$12
Health	A	09	CHW	6	3	4	72	87	2.74	1.08	221	208	223	4.1	31%	77%	2.79	46	17	36	2.5	10.8	**4.4**	8%	0.6	15.3	152	$14
PT/Exp	C	10	CHW	5	4	8	61	81	2.67	1.00	193	175	203	3.9	30%	74%	2.52	40	23	37	3.0	12.0	**4.1**	6%	0.4	11.0	154	$14
Consist	A	1st Half		2	3	5	35	48	2.85	1.01	190			4.0	31%	71%	2.28	45	23	32	3.1	12.4	**4.0**	4%	0.3	5.5	163	$7
LIMA Plan	B+	2nd Half		3	1	3	26	33	2.42	1.00	197			3.8	28%	79%	2.80	33	23	44	2.8	11.4	**4.1**	8%	0.7	5.5	142	$6
Rand Var	-1	11	Proj	**6**	**3**	**15**	**65**	**80**	**2.90**	**1.07**	**210**			**3.9**	**30%**	**75%**	**2.76**	**43**	**21**	**36**	**2.9**	**11.0**	**3.8**	**9%**	**0.7**	**12.3**	**142**	**$16**

Everything about his stat line is supported by superb skills. GB turned into FB in 2H, but elite Dom/Cmd helped to limit damage. We'd be waving the "Let Him Close!" banner if he wasn't 34 and LHed, but still...

Tillman,Chris

		Yr	Tm	W	L	Sv	IP	K	ERA	WHIP	OBA	vL	vR	BF/G	H%	S%	xERA	G	L	F	Ctl	Dom	Cmd	hr/f	hr/9	RAR	BPV	R$
RH SP	22	06		0	0	0	0	0	0.00	0.00							0.00											
Ht/Wt	77 195	07		0	0	0	0	0	0.00	0.00							0.00											
Type		08	aa	11	4	0	135	141	3.74	1.37	248			20.7	32%	74%	3.97				4.0	9.4	**2.3**		0.8	9.4	88	$14
Health	A	09	BAL *	10	11	0	162	130	4.19	1.35	272	254	341	23.1	31%	73%	4.32	37	18	45	2.7	7.2	**2.7**	10%	1.2	5.3	72	$13
PT/Exp	D	10	BAL *	13	12	0	175	114	4.45	1.37	269	274	238	23.5	30%	70%	4.17	43	22	36	3.0	5.9	**1.9**	10%	1.1	-6.7	45	$11
Consist	A	1st Half		7	7	0	85	55	4.40	1.37	283			22.8	31%	71%	4.27	34	26	40	2.4	5.8	**2.5**	10%	1.2	-2.8	54	$6
LIMA Plan	C+	2nd Half		6	5	0	90	59	4.50	1.37	256			24.1	29%	69%	4.16	47	19	34	3.6	5.9	**1.6**	9%	0.9	-4.0	32	$5
Rand Var	0	11	Proj	**8**	**11**	**0**	**145**	**111**	**4.34**	**1.37**	**266**			**23.0**	**31%**	**71%**	**4.18**	**40**	**20**	**40**	**3.1**	**6.9**	**2.2**	**10%**	**1.1**	**2.0**	**59**	**$10**

2-5, 5.87 ERA in 54 IP at BAL. 5.2 Ctl, 1.0 Cmd at BAL shows how his AAA skills didn't accompany him to bigs. RHers smacked him (.940 OPS). Nice longer-term investment, but plan on more short-term bumps.

Tomlin,Josh

		Yr	Tm	W	L	Sv	IP	K	ERA	WHIP	OBA	vL	vR	BF/G	H%	S%	xERA	G	L	F	Ctl	Dom	Cmd	hr/f	hr/9	RAR	BPV	R$
RH SP	26	06		0	0	0	0	0	0.00	0.00							0.00											
Ht/Wt	73 195	07		0	0	0	0	0	0.00	0.00							0.00											
Type	Con xFB	08		0	0	0	0	0	0.00	0.00							0.00											
Health	A	09	aa	14	9	0	145	102	6.14	1.59	327			25.2	36%	65%	6.78				2.0	6.3	**3.2**		1.7	-32.7	42	$3
PT/Exp	D	10	CLE *	14	8	0	180	113	3.62	1.19	243	236	296	23.1	27%	73%	4.53	28	21	50	2.6	5.7	**2.2**	7%	1.0	11.6	39	$18
Consist	F	1st Half		7	2	0	81	48	2.91	1.12	223			20.5	25%	76%	2.79				2.8	5.3	**1.9**		0.7	12.2	61	$10
LIMA Plan	C+	2nd Half		7	6	0	99	66	4.19	1.25	258			25.8	28%	71%	4.48	28	21	50	2.4	6.0	**2.5**	9%	1.3	-0.6	50	$8
Rand Var	-3	11	Proj	**9**	**12**	**0**	**149**	**98**	**4.48**	**1.35**	**280**			**24.4**	**31%**	**71%**	**4.72**	**28**	**21**	**50**	**2.3**	**5.9**	**2.6**	**9%**	**1.3**	**-7.8**	**51**	**$9**

6-4, 4.56 ERA in 73 IP at CLE. Reverse split with righties hitting him hard (.881 OPS) while he held lefties in check. Cmd gives hope for his future, but lofty FB% plus borderline Dom makes him too volatile for now.

JOSH PALEY

Troncoso,Ramon

Troncoso,Ramon		Yr	Tm	W	L	Sv	IP	K	ERA	WHIP	OBA	vL	vR	BF/G	H%	S%	xERA	G	L	F	Ctl	Dom	Cmd	hr/f	hr/9	RAR	BPV	R$
RH RP	28	06		0	0	0	0	0	0.00	0.00							0.00											
Ht/Wt 73	220	07	aa	7	3	7	52	32	3.83	1.54	294			6.6	34%	75%	5.02				3.3	5.6	**1.7**		0.5	4.1	49	$7
Type	xGB	08	LA *	5	1	0	68	52	5.16	1.74	317	254	278	5.9	38%	69%	3.57	61	22	18	3.9	6.9	**1.8**	8%	0.4	-7.5	57	$1
Health	A	09	LA	5	4	6	83	55	2.72	1.41	262	289	251	4.9	31%	81%	3.91	55	19	26	3.7	6.0	**1.6**	4%	0.3	15.0	41	$9
PT/Exp	D	10	LA *	2	5	1	76	49	4.45	1.38	265	244	274	4.9	29%	72%	3.97	53	14	33	3.3	5.8	**1.8**	14%	1.3	-4.1	48	$2
Consist	A	1st Half		1	2	0	37	25	5.15	1.31	263			4.0	28%	64%	3.76	52	15	33	2.7	6.1	**2.3**	16%	1.5	-5.1	67	$1
LIMA Plan	C+	2nd Half		1	3	1	39	24	3.80	1.44	266			6.1	29%	78%	4.11	57	12	32	3.8	5.5	**1.5**	13%	1.2	1.1	33	$2
Rand Var	+2	11	Proj	**3**	**4**	**0**	**65**	**43**	**4.00**	**1.46**	**276**			**5.3**	**31%**	**74%**	**3.95**	**55**	**17**	**28**	**3.4**	**5.9**	**1.7**	**10%**	**0.8**	**1.6**	**47**	**$3**

2-3, 4.33 ERA in 54 IP at LA. ERA spike was not a surprise. With xGB style & middling Cmd, he's subject to whims of chance, infielders. Once again, xERA pegs true level. A strikeout pitch would get us more geeked.

Uehara,Koji

Uehara,Koji		Yr	Tm	W	L	Sv	IP	K	ERA	WHIP	OBA	vL	vR	BF/G	H%	S%	xERA	G	L	F	Ctl	Dom	Cmd	hr/f	hr/9	RAR	BPV	R$
RH RP	36	06	JPN	8	9	0	168	143	3.99	1.16	262			28.5	28%	78%	5.04				1.4	7.7	**5.5**		2.1	10.9	100	$18
Ht/Wt 73	190	07	JPN	4	3	32	62	63	2.16	0.89	224			4.3	28%	83%	2.65				0.7	9.1	**12.6**		1.0	17.6	301	$23
Type	xFB	08	JPN	6	5	1	90	68	4.72	1.29	276			14.6	30%	70%	5.23				2.0	6.8	**3.4**		1.8	-4.6	58	$7
Health	F	09	BAL	2	4	0	67	48	4.05	1.24	274	273	266	23.1	31%	70%	4.48	30	17	53	1.6	6.5	**4.0**	6%	0.9	3.3	81	$5
PT/Exp	C	10	BAL	1	2	13	44	55	2.86	0.95	230	263	185	4.0	32%	76%	2.93	24	18	58	1.0	11.3	**11.0**	8%	1.0	6.9	177	$11
Consist	C	1st Half		0	0	0	7	8	2.57	1.43	262			3.8	37%	80%	3.76	26	26	47	3.9	10.3	**2.7**	0%	0.0	1.4	85	$1
LIMA Plan	B+	2nd Half		1	2	13	37	47	2.92	0.86	223			4.0	30%	74%	2.78	23	16	60	0.5	11.4	**23.5**	9%	1.2	5.6	194	$10
Rand Var	0	11	Proj	**3**	**3**	**20**	**58**	**55**	**3.57**	**1.10**	**252**			**7.5**	**30%**	**75%**	**3.70**	**27**	**19**	**54**	**1.4**	**8.5**	**6.1**	**10%**	**1.4**	**4.2**	**121**	**$14**

PRO:
- Vintage Eck Cmd, gaudy BPV

CON:
- Ultra-xFB means HR risk
- More elbow pain; Health = F
- Dom regression seems likely

Too many risks to bid on repeat.

Valdes,Raul

Valdes,Raul		Yr	Tm	W	L	Sv	IP	K	ERA	WHIP	OBA	vL	vR	BF/G	H%	S%	xERA	G	L	F	Ctl	Dom	Cmd	hr/f	hr/9	RAR	BPV	R$
LH RP	33	06	aaa	1	3	0	32	17	11.19	2.18	387			23.3	40%	48%	10.02				3.6	4.7	**1.3**		2.1	-26.3	-30	($6)
Ht/Wt 71	190	07	aa	0	1	1	29	24	5.28	1.31	255			6.1	29%	62%	4.49				3.1	7.4	**2.4**		1.2	-2.9	62	$1
Type Pwr	xFB	08		0	0	0	0	0	0.00	0.00							0.00											
Health	A	09		0	0	0	0	0	0.00	0.00							0.00											
PT/Exp	F	10	NYM *	5	4	1	95	85	4.24	1.41	266	330	216	8.7	32%	72%	4.24	34	18	48	3.5	8.0	**2.3**	8%	1.0	-2.6	63	$5
Consist	F	1st Half		2	2	1	30	33	5.10	1.57	287			6.7	38%	67%	3.81	38	19	43	3.9	9.9	**2.5**	5%	0.6	-4.0	89	$1
LIMA Plan	C+	2nd Half		3	2	0	65	52	3.84	1.33	256			10.2	29%	75%	4.55	29	17	54	3.3	7.2	**2.2**	8%	1.1	1.4	48	$4
Rand Var	0	11	Proj	**2**	**3**	**0**	**49**	**38**	**4.78**	**1.51**	**285**			**10.9**	**32%**	**73%**	**4.67**	**35**	**18**	**47**	**3.5**	**7.0**	**2.0**	**11%**	**1.5**	**-3.2**	**44**	**$1**

3-3, 4.91 ERA in 59 IP at NYM. Ex-Mexican Leaguer showed enough to maybe get another pot of coffee next year. But that's not the cool part: possibly the only guy in the book with exactly neutral luck (ERA = xERA)!

Valverde,Jose

Valverde,Jose		Yr	Tm	W	L	Sv	IP	K	ERA	WHIP	OBA	vL	vR	BF/G	H%	S%	xERA	G	L	F	Ctl	Dom	Cmd	hr/f	hr/9	RAR	BPV	R$
RH RP	33	06	ARI	2	3	18	49	69	5.87	1.47	265	323	192	4.9	39%	61%	3.26	35	24	41	4.0	12.6	**3.1**	12%	1.1	-8.3	132	$8
Ht/Wt 76	254	07	ARI	1	4	47	64	78	2.66	1.12	202	202	189	4.0	27%	82%	3.37	36	17	47	3.6	10.9	**3.0**	10%	1.0	14.0	112	$24
Type	Pwr	08	HOU	6	3	44	72	83	3.38	1.18	234	190	252	4.0	30%	77%	3.22	39	20	41	2.9	10.4	**3.6**	13%	1.3	8.0	126	$25
Health	B	09	HOU	4	2	25	54	56	2.33	1.13	208	281	144	4.2	27%	84%	3.59	41	13	46	3.5	9.3	**2.7**	8%	0.8	12.4	92	$16
PT/Exp	B	10	DET	2	4	26	63	63	3.00	1.16	188	165	204	4.3	24%	76%	3.24	55	13	32	4.6	9.0	**2.0**	10%	0.7	8.8	71	$16
Consist	A	1st Half		1	1	18	35	33	0.51	0.71	100			3.6	13%	96%	2.58	61	11	28	3.6	8.5	**2.4**	5%	0.3	15.6	94	$13
LIMA Plan	C+	2nd Half		1	3	8	28	30	6.11	1.71	275			5.2	35%	66%	4.04	49	15	37	5.8	9.6	**1.7**	14%	1.3	-6.8	44	$2
Rand Var	-3	11	Proj	**4**	**4**	**28**	**73**	**76**	**3.48**	**1.26**	**227**			**4.4**	**29%**	**75%**	**3.39**	**49**	**13**	**37**	**3.8**	**9.4**	**2.5**	**10%**	**0.9**	**8.1**	**93**	**$17**

Comforting: Reliable, consistent xERA; that growing GB trend. Worrisome: Another BPV fall, esp. 2H when elbow & Ctl issues cropped up. Expected to be ok, but two years of nagging injuries have a way of turning into three.

VandenHurk,Rick

VandenHurk,Rick		Yr	Tm	W	L	Sv	IP	K	ERA	WHIP	OBA	vL	vR	BF/G	H%	S%	xERA	G	L	F	Ctl	Dom	Cmd	hr/f	hr/9	RAR	BPV	R$
RH SP	25	06		0	0	0	0	0	0.00	0.00							0.00											
Ht/Wt 77	219	07		0	0	0	0	0	0.00	0.00							0.00											
Type	xFB	08	aa	5	4	0	73	68	4.96	1.41	257			22.6	30%	69%	4.84				3.9	8.4	**2.1**		1.4	-5.9	57	$5
Health	B	09	FLA *	8	4	0	118	95	3.74	1.20	238	273	224	22.1	27%	72%	4.32	27	23	50	2.8	7.3	**2.6**	8%	1.1	6.5	59	$12
PT/Exp	D	10	2TM *	9	6	0	136	96	5.21	1.46	279	346	179	19.2	32%	66%	4.68	35	17	48	3.3	6.4	**1.9**	8%	1.1	-19.1	38	$4
Consist	A	1st Half		4	4	0	66	53	6.72	1.77	312			19.4	37%	61%	4.73	43	14	43	4.4	7.3	**1.7**	6%	0.8	-21.6	33	($2)
LIMA Plan	C	2nd Half		5	2	0	70	43	3.78	1.17	244			19.0	26%	73%	4.40	34	17	49	2.3	5.5	**2.4**	10%	1.3	2.5	48	$6
Rand Var	0	11	Proj	**7**	**4**	**0**	**102**	**78**	**4.34**	**1.36**	**263**			**20.7**	**30%**	**72%**	**4.59**	**30**	**21**	**50**	**3.2**	**6.9**	**2.2**	**9%**	**1.2**	**-4.8**	**46**	**$7**

0-1, 5.09 ERA in 18 IP at 2TM. A bit of a step back. 2H Dom slide will likely turn around, but it has to, or that many more FB will leave the yard. Did manage to stay healthy, at least. Same as last yr's book: watch-list him.

Vargas,Jason

Vargas,Jason		Yr	Tm	W	L	Sv	IP	K	ERA	WHIP	OBA	vL	vR	BF/G	H%	S%	xERA	G	L	F	Ctl	Dom	Cmd	hr/f	hr/9	RAR	BPV	R$
LH SP	28	06	FLA *	4	8	0	112	71	7.55	1.89	328	262	302	21.6	36%	61%	6.15	32	17	51	4.7	5.7	**1.2**	9%	1.5	-42.4	-13	($8)
Ht/Wt 72	215	07	NYM *	9	8	0	135	92	6.67	1.70	325		370	24.1	36%	61%	5.74	27	13	60	3.1	6.1	**2.0**	7%	1.2	-37.5	30	($2)
Type Con	xFB	08		0	0	0	0	0	0.00	0.00							0.00											
Health	F	09	SEA *	7	9	0	143	94	4.32	1.32	271	290	277	18.9	30%	71%	4.50	37	21	42	2.5	5.9	**2.4**	10%	1.2	2.4	54	$10
PT/Exp	C	10	SEA	9	12	0	193	116	3.78	1.25	256	200	268	25.9	28%	72%	4.48	36	17	47	2.5	5.4	**2.1**	6%	0.8	8.5	44	$14
Consist	A	1st Half		6	4	0	101	65	3.22	1.16	243			25.7	27%	74%	4.35	35	14	50	2.3	5.8	**2.5**	5%	0.7	11.4	55	$10
LIMA Plan	D+	2nd Half		3	8	0	92	51	4.40	1.35	270			26.2	29%	69%	4.62	37	19	43	2.7	5.0	**1.8**	8%	1.0	-3.0	31	$4
Rand Var	-2	11	Proj	**9**	**12**	**0**	**189**	**118**	**4.58**	**1.40**	**280**			**25.5**	**30%**	**71%**	**4.71**	**36**	**18**	**46**	**2.7**	**5.6**	**2.1**	**9%**	**1.2**	**-9.8**	**42**	**$9**

Another finesse lefty who lives on the edge (pitching-wise, that is). Contact, high FB mix is a potentially explosive one -- won't get by with sub-tipping point Dom again. Let others bid to $10, suffer the ERA spike.

Vasquez,Esmerling

Vasquez,Esmerling		Yr	Tm	W	L	Sv	IP	K	ERA	WHIP	OBA	vL	vR	BF/G	H%	S%	xERA	G	L	F	Ctl	Dom	Cmd	hr/f	hr/9	RAR	BPV	R$
RH RP	27	06		0	0	0	0	0	0.00	0.00							0.00											
Ht/Wt 73	173	07	aa	10	6	0	165	129	3.93	1.29	244			23.9	29%	71%	3.83				3.4	7.0	**2.1**		0.8	10.8	69	$15
Type Pwr	FB	08	aaa	3	6	0	83	48	9.25	2.12	297			17.4	31%	56%	7.54				8.3	5.3	**0.6**		1.6	-50.6	-8	($12)
Health	A	09	ARI	3	3	0	53	45	4.42	1.53	258	196	304	4.4	31%	71%	4.54	43	17	40	4.9	7.6	**1.6**	6%	0.7	-1.5	25	$2
PT/Exp	D	10	ARI	1	6	0	54	55	5.20	1.56	233	224	247	4.2	29%	68%	4.57	32	26	43	6.4	9.2	**1.4**	10%	1.0	-7.8	4	($0)
Consist	D	1st Half		1	2	0	28	30	5.14	1.36	218			4.6	28%	63%	3.86	36	24	40	5.1	9.6	**1.9**	10%	1.0	-3.9	49	$1
LIMA Plan	F	2nd Half		0	4	0	26	25	5.25	1.79	249			3.9	31%	72%	5.41	28	28	45	7.7	8.8	**1.1**	9%	1.1	-3.9	-45	($1)
Rand Var	+1	11	Proj	**2**	**5**	**0**	**58**	**51**	**5.12**	**1.64**	**252**			**5.3**	**30%**	**70%**	**4.98**	**36**	**22**	**42**	**6.2**	**7.9**	**1.3**	**10%**	**1.1**	**-6.0**	**-11**	**$0**

Another "real good arm" for whom home plate is but a vague concept. Apparently has decided that throwing hard is way more fun than, you know, actually pitching well.

Vazquez,Javier

Vazquez,Javier		Yr	Tm	W	L	Sv	IP	K	ERA	WHIP	OBA	vL	vR	BF/G	H%	S%	xERA	G	L	F	Ctl	Dom	Cmd	hr/f	hr/9	RAR	BPV	R$
RH SP	34	06	CHW	11	12	0	202	184	4.85	1.30	265	256	261	25.8	32%	64%	3.81	40	20	41	2.5	8.2	**3.3**	10%	1.0	-7.3	98	$17
Ht/Wt 74	210	07	CHW	15	8	0	217	213	3.74	1.14	244	230	253	27.5	30%	72%	3.49	40	17	43	2.1	8.8	**4.3**	11%	1.2	20.5	121	$28
Type Pwr	FB	08	CHW	12	16	0	208	200	4.67	1.32	267	259	266	26.8	33%	67%	3.73	38	20	42	2.6	8.6	**3.3**	10%	1.1	-8.2	101	$17
Health	A	09	ATL	15	10	0	219	238	2.87	1.03	226	235	212	27.0	30%	76%	2.83	42	24	35	1.8	9.8	**5.4**	10%	0.8	35.6	147	$32
PT/Exp	A	10	NYY	10	10	0	157	121	5.32	1.40	259	275	240	21.9	28%	68%	4.50	36	17	47	3.7	6.9	**1.9**	14%	1.8	-22.9	38	$7
Consist	C	1st Half		6	7	0	81	71	5.11	1.31	240			22.8	27%	66%	4.16	35	19	47	3.8	7.9	**2.1**	14%	1.7	-9.7	53	$5
LIMA Plan	B+	2nd Half		4	3	0	76	50	5.54	1.49	278			21.0	29%	69%	4.86	36	16	47	3.7	5.9	**1.6**	14%	2.0	-13.2	22	$1
Rand Var	+2	11	Proj	**12**	**9**	**0**	**170**	**151**	**3.97**	**1.28**	**254**			**23.8**	**30%**	**73%**	**3.90**	**38**	**19**	**43**	**2.9**	**8.0**	**2.7**	**10%**	**1.2**	**8.1**	**81**	**$17**

Edwhitsonitis? We may have to rename it Vazquezitis. Return to NYY got the blame, but sudden Cmd implosion, FB jump may point to a different culprit: a hidden injury. Still, getting out of New York wouldn't hurt, right?

Venters,Jonny

Venters,Jonny		Yr	Tm	W	L	Sv	IP	K	ERA	WHIP	OBA	vL	vR	BF/G	H%	S%	xERA	G	L	F	Ctl	Dom	Cmd	hr/f	hr/9	RAR	BPV	R$
LH RP	26	06		0	0	0	0	0	0.00	0.00							0.00											
Ht/Wt 75	188	07		0	0	0	0	0	0.00	0.00							0.00											
Type Pwr	xGB	08		0	0	0	0	0	0.00	0.00							0.00											
Health	A	09	a/a	8	11	0	156	83	5.70	1.78	307			25.3	34%	67%	5.81				4.8	4.8	**1.0**		0.6	-26.8	26	($3)
PT/Exp	D	10	ATL	4	4	1	83	93	1.95	1.20	207	198	207	4.3	30%	83%	2.28	68	15	17	4.2	10.1	**2.4**	3%	0.1	21.1	114	$11
Consist	F	1st Half		4	0	1	44	46	1.24	1.10	175			5.3	25%	87%	2.56	63	19	19	4.6	9.5	**2.1**	0%	0.0	14.9	89	$8
LIMA Plan	B	2nd Half		0	4	0	40	47	2.73	1.32	239			3.6	35%	78%	2.04	73	13	15	3.9	10.7	**2.8**	7%	0.2	6.3	139	$3
Rand Var	-5	11	Proj	**3**	**5**	**23**	**73**	**70**	**3.10**	**1.30**	**230**			**4.8**	**30%**	**76%**	**2.58**	**70**	**14**	**16**	**4.1**	**8.7**	**2.1**	**10%**	**0.4**	**14.0**	**93**	**$14**

Wagner's successor? Terrific & surprising, and completely skills-supported. Power sinker/slider combo ate up righties too, also fitting closer profile. Odds are his so-so SP days are over. UP: Wagner-esque save totals.

ROD TRUESDELL

Veras,Jose		Yr	Tm	W	L	Sv	IP	K	ERA	WHIP	OBA	vL	vR	BF/G	H%	S%	xERA	G	L	F	Ctl	Dom	Cmd	hr/f	hr/9	RAR	BPV	R$
RH RP	30	06	aaa	5	3	21	59	55	3.07	1.31	256			5.0	32%	78%	3.84				3.1	8.4	**2.7**		0.6	10.6	93	$15
Ht/Wt	77 235	07	NYY	0	0	2	9	7	5.81	1.40	186			4.5	24%	54%	5.20	41	19	41	6.8	6.8	**1.0**	0%	0.0	-1.5	-42	$1
Type	Pwr FB	08	NYY *	5	3	9	71	80	3.33	1.34	236	217	254	4.1	31%	79%	3.60	41	18	41	4.2	10.2	**2.4**	11%	1.0	8.9	88	$12
Health	A	09	2AL	4	3	0	50	40	5.19	1.39	228	259	198	4.6	25%	66%	4.92	36	16	47	5.0	7.2	**1.4**	12%	1.4	-4.6	8	$3
PT/Exp	D	10	FLA *	4	4	2	77	85	4.39	1.53	250	155	221	4.8	33%	73%	3.88	40	23	37	5.3	9.9	**1.9**	9%	0.8	-3.5	53	$4
Consist	C	1st Half		2	1	2	41	46	5.64	1.79	306			5.8	41%	68%	3.82	30	44	26	5.0	10.1	**2.0**	10%	0.7	-8.2	56	($0)
LIMA Plan	B+	2nd Half		2	3	0	36	39	2.98	1.24	177			3.9	22%	80%	3.77	43	16	41	5.7	9.7	**1.7**	11%	1.0	4.7	41	$4
Rand Var	+1	11	Proj	**5**	**4**	**0**	**73**	**73**	**4.59**	**1.43**	**241**			**4.6**	**30%**	**70%**	**4.10**	**39**	**18**	**42**	**4.8**	**9.1**	**1.9**	**10%**	**1.0**	**0.3**	**50**	**$4**

3-3, 3.75 ERA in 48 IP at FLA. Stop me if you've heard this one before: guy has great Dom but can't find the plate, and he never seems to learn. It's maddening. He's been DFA twice in two years, which sums up the story.

Verlander,Justin		Yr	Tm	W	L	Sv	IP	K	ERA	WHIP	OBA	vL	vR	BF/G	H%	S%	xERA	G	L	F	Ctl	Dom	Cmd	hr/f	hr/9	RAR	BPV	R$
RH SP	28	06	DET	17	9	0	186	124	3.63	1.33	263	279	253	26.3	29%	76%	4.27	42	23	35	2.9	6.0	**2.1**	10%	1.0	21.3	49	$21
Ht/Wt	77 225	07	DET	18	6	0	202	183	3.66	1.23	241	232	234	26.2	29%	73%	3.78	41	19	40	3.0	8.2	**2.7**	9%	0.9	21.1	85	$26
Type	Pwr FB	08	DET	11	17	0	201	163	4.84	1.40	256	254	254	26.3	30%	66%	4.39	40	18	42	3.9	7.3	**1.9**	7%	0.8	-12.1	44	$12
Health	A	09	DET	19	9	0	240	269	3.45	1.18	244	248	237	28.1	33%	73%	3.31	36	21	43	2.4	10.1	**4.3**	7%	0.8	29.7	132	$33
PT/Exp	A	10	DET	18	9	0	224	219	3.37	1.16	231	230	225	27.8	30%	72%	3.39	41	19	40	2.8	8.8	**3.1**	6%	0.6	21.3	100	$28
Consist	B	1st Half		10	5	0	110	103	3.85	1.15	225			26.4	29%	67%	3.51	42	16	42	3.0	8.4	**2.8**	6%	0.6	4.0	90	$13
LIMA Plan	C+	2nd Half		8	4	0	114	116	2.91	1.17	237			29.2	31%	76%	3.26	40	22	39	2.7	9.1	**3.4**	6%	0.6	17.3	110	$15
Rand Var	-1	11	Proj	**17**	**10**	**0**	**225**	**219**	**3.60**	**1.21**	**241**			**27.3**	**30%**	**73%**	**3.56**	**40**	**20**	**41**	**2.9**	**8.8**	**3.0**	**8%**	**0.8**	**20.3**	**98**	**$27**

In "Fantasyland," Jed Latkin drafts him as the anchor of his Tout Wars pitching staff. A scan of this data shows that it was a good choice but bad timing. The year was 2008.

Villanueva,Carlos		Yr	Tm	W	L	Sv	IP	K	ERA	WHIP	OBA	vL	vR	BF/G	H%	S%	xERA	G	L	F	Ctl	Dom	Cmd	hr/f	hr/9	RAR	BPV	R$
RH RP	27	06	MIL *	13	8	0	181	146	4.22	1.22	246	226	204	23.5	28%	69%	4.00	43	16	41	2.7	7.2	**2.7**	11%	1.1	6.0	77	$18
Ht/Wt	74 228	07	MIL	8	5	1	114	99	3.94	1.35	239	250	227	8.3	28%	75%	4.51	36	17	47	4.2	7.8	**1.9**	11%	1.5	6.9	42	$11
Type	Pwr FB	08	MIL	4	7	1	108	93	4.07	1.31	268	227	300	9.7	31%	75%	3.63	47	19	35	2.5	7.7	**3.1**	16%	1.5	2.6	96	$8
Health	A	09	MIL	4	10	3	96	83	5.34	1.43	274	257	278	6.5	32%	65%	4.04	40	22	38	3.3	7.8	**2.4**	12%	1.2	-13.7	69	$4
PT/Exp	C	10	MIL	2	0	1	53	67	4.61	1.33	244	232	243	4.5	33%	68%	3.15	34	27	39	3.8	11.4	**3.0**	14%	1.2	-3.9	116	$3
Consist	B	1st Half		0	0	1	42	54	4.26	1.32	242			4.6	34%	69%	3.07	35	29	36	3.8	11.5	**3.0**	11%	0.9	-1.3	116	$2
LIMA Plan	A	2nd Half		2	0	0	10	13	6.06	1.35	254			4.0	30%	64%	3.48	30	19	52	3.5	11.2	**3.3**	22%	2.6	-2.6	117	$1
Rand Var	+5	11	Proj	**3**	**3**	**0**	**73**	**71**	**4.22**	**1.34**	**255**			**7.0**	**31%**	**72%**	**3.80**	**37**	**22**	**42**	**3.4**	**8.8**	**2.6**	**11%**	**1.1**	**3.1**	**83**	**$5**

Strong Dom, but iffy Ctl, some gopheritis, and crummy surface stats got him sent down for a month. Dom will regress, but so will ERA; he's top-tier LIMA material, and +5 Rand Var highlights that he'll be a bargain.

Volquez,Edinson		Yr	Tm	W	L	Sv	IP	K	ERA	WHIP	OBA	vL	vR	BF/G	H%	S%	xERA	G	L	F	Ctl	Dom	Cmd	hr/f	hr/9	RAR	BPV	R$
RH SP	27	06	TEX *	7	12	0	153	127	5.40	1.68	273			24.3	32%	70%	5.56				5.6	7.5	**1.3**		1.2	-16.0	36	$3
Ht/Wt	72 210	07	TEX *	16	3	0	143	133	3.72	1.25	233	222	299	23.9	28%	73%	3.93	38	22	40	3.6	8.3	**2.3**	10%	1.0	13.9	69	$20
Type	Pwr	08	CIN	17	6	0	196	206	3.21	1.33	232	248	214	25.2	31%	77%	3.54	46	20	34	4.3	9.5	**2.2**	8%	0.6	25.5	79	$23
Health	F	09	CIN	4	2	0	50	47	4.35	1.33	195	202	181	23.5	23%	70%	4.07	45	21	34	5.8	8.5	**1.5**	14%	1.1	-1.0	20	$4
PT/Exp	C	10	CIN *	7	3	0	86	84	3.81	1.34	229	229	273	22.8	29%	73%	3.42	54	15	31	4.6	8.8	**1.9**	10%	0.7	2.1	68	$7
Consist	B	1st Half		1	0	0	11	7	3.44	0.86	192			20.8	21%	63%	2.00				1.7	5.4	**3.2**		0.9	0.8	90	$2
LIMA Plan	C	2nd Half		6	3	0	75	77	3.87	1.41	234			23.1	30%	74%	3.45	54	15	31	5.0	9.3	**1.9**	10%	0.7	1.4	66	$6
Rand Var	0	11	Proj	**12**	**6**	**0**	**145**	**143**	**4.03**	**1.39**	**237**			**24.0**	**30%**	**73%**	**3.69**	**48**	**19**	**33**	**4.6**	**8.9**	**1.9**	**11%**	**0.9**	**8.1**	**62**	**$12**

4-3, 4.31 ERA in 62 IP at CIN. Returned from last year's TJS and remained all or nothing, with 50%/33% PQS DOM/DIS split. A 2.6 Ctl in Sept. corresponded to four DOM starts, which offers glimmer of hope for optimists.

Volstad,Chris		Yr	Tm	W	L	Sv	IP	K	ERA	WHIP	OBA	vL	vR	BF/G	H%	S%	xERA	G	L	F	Ctl	Dom	Cmd	hr/f	hr/9	RAR	BPV	R$
RH SP	24	06		0	0	0	0	0	0.00	0.00							0.00											
Ht/Wt	80 227	07	aa	4	2	0	42	23	3.63	1.33	279			25.6	30%	75%	4.53				2.1	4.9	**2.3**		0.9	4.4	51	$4
Type	Con	08	FLA *	10	8	0	175	102	3.39	1.36	258	243	236	25.0	30%	73%	4.15	53	18	29	3.4	5.2	**1.5**	2%	0.2	19.1	33	$13
Health	A	09	FLA	9	13	0	159	107	5.21	1.43	274	255	302	23.9	29%	68%	4.21	49	17	34	3.3	6.1	**1.8**	17%	1.6	-20.0	46	$5
PT/Exp	B	10	FLA	12	9	0	175	102	4.58	1.41	275	292	263	25.3	30%	69%	4.25	48	18	34	3.1	5.2	**1.7**	9%	0.9	-12.1	37	$7
Consist	A	1st Half		4	7	0	95	64	4.45	1.35	260			25.3	30%	68%	3.98	49	18	33	3.2	6.1	**1.9**	8%	0.8	-5.1	49	$4
LIMA Plan	C	2nd Half		8	2	0	80	38	4.72	1.49	292			25.2	31%	70%	4.57	47	18	34	2.9	4.3	**1.5**	9%	1.0	-7.0	23	$3
Rand Var	0	11	Proj	**13**	**10**	**0**	**184**	**108**	**4.40**	**1.42**	**277**			**25.0**	**30%**	**71%**	**4.30**	**49**	**18**	**34**	**3.1**	**5.3**	**1.7**	**10%**	**1.0**	**-3.6**	**39**	**$9**

While others see improvement in W-L record from 1H to 2H (which roughly corresponds to before and after he was briefly demoted to Triple-A), you notice the worsening xERA, Dom, and Cmd and pass.

Wagner,Billy		Yr	Tm	W	L	Sv	IP	K	ERA	WHIP	OBA	vL	vR	BF/G	H%	S%	xERA	G	L	F	Ctl	Dom	Cmd	hr/f	hr/9	RAR	BPV	R$
LH RP	39	06	NYM	3	2	40	72	94	2.25	1.11	225	161	234	4.2	32%	85%	2.47	53	16	31	2.6	11.7	**4.5**	13%	0.9	19.9	171	$25
Ht/Wt	71 203	07	NYM	2	2	34	68	80	2.64	1.13	222	241	209	4.2	30%	80%	3.28	37	18	45	2.9	10.5	**3.6**	8%	0.8	15.1	126	$20
Type		08	NYM	2	1	27	47	52	2.30	0.89	194	220	174	4.0	26%	79%	2.91	38	20	42	1.9	10.0	**5.2**	8%	0.8	11.4	144	$16
Health	F	09	2TM	1	1	0	16	26	1.72	1.02	153	111	176	3.6	28%	87%	2.79	23	15	62	4.6	14.9	**3.3**	6%	0.6	5.0	146	$3
PT/Exp	C	10	ATL	7	2	37	69	104	1.43	0.87	163	71	186	3.7	27%	89%	2.25	38	18	44	2.9	13.5	**4.7**	9%	0.6	22.1	182	$28
Consist	A	1st Half		5	0	17	33	52	1.35	0.93	168			3.8	28%	93%	2.40	32	17	51	3.2	14.1	**4.3**	10%	0.8	10.9	175	$14
LIMA Plan		2nd Half		2	2	20	36	52	1.50	0.81	158			3.6	26%	85%	2.10	43	18	39	2.5	13.0	**5.2**	8%	0.5	11.2	188	$14
Rand Var	-5	11	Proj	**0**	**0**	**0**	**0**	**0**	**0.00**	**0.00**							**0.00**											

Took the George Brett Path to Retirement, going out on top in a big way:
- Monthly Dom never below 10.9
- Murdered LHers (.246 OPS)
- Not too shabby vs. RHers (.569)
- Career 159 BPV

Wainwright,Adam		Yr	Tm	W	L	Sv	IP	K	ERA	WHIP	OBA	vL	vR	BF/G	H%	S%	xERA	G	L	F	Ctl	Dom	Cmd	hr/f	hr/9	RAR	BPV	R$
RH SP	29	06	STL	2	1	3	75	72	3.12	1.15	232	301	182	5.0	29%	75%	3.34	48	17	35	2.6	8.6	**3.3**	8%	0.7	12.7	110	$10
Ht/Wt	79 228	07	STL	14	12	0	202	136	3.70	1.40	271	249	283	27.2	31%	74%	4.24	48	18	34	3.1	6.1	**1.9**	6%	0.6	18.1	51	$16
Type	Pwr	08	STL	11	3	0	132	91	3.20	1.18	247	264	234	27.1	28%	76%	3.83	46	19	35	2.3	6.2	**2.7**	9%	0.8	17.4	73	$15
Health	B	09	STL	19	8	0	233	212	2.63	1.21	247	275	217	28.3	31%	81%	3.21	51	19	30	2.5	8.2	**3.2**	9%	0.7	44.9	107	$30
PT/Exp	A	10	STL	20	11	0	230	213	2.42	1.05	223	226	222	27.7	28%	79%	2.90	52	18	31	2.2	8.3	**3.8**	8%	0.6	45.2	120	$33
Consist	A	1st Half		12	5	0	128	123	2.24	1.00	210			27.9	26%	81%	2.81	52	16	32	2.2	8.6	**3.8**	9%	0.7	28.0	125	$21
LIMA Plan	C	2nd Half		8	6	0	102	90	2.65	1.12	238			27.5	30%	77%	3.00	51	19	30	2.1	7.9	**3.8**	6%	0.4	17.2	115	$13
Rand Var	-2	11	Proj	**17**	**9**	**0**	**218**	**189**	**2.94**	**1.16**	**241**			**27.0**	**29%**	**77%**	**3.23**	**50**	**18**	**32**	**2.4**	**7.8**	**3.3**	**9%**	**0.7**	**24.5**	**105**	**$26**

You can trace his evolution into a stud by noting his four-year PQS DOM trend: 38%, 55%, 65%, 82%. Solved LHers too, at least for 230 IP. The prudent bet is to expect a little pullback, but he'll still be great. Pay up.

Wakefield,Tim		Yr	Tm	W	L	Sv	IP	K	ERA	WHIP	OBA	vL	vR	BF/G	H%	S%	xERA	G	L	F	Ctl	Dom	Cmd	hr/f	hr/9	RAR	BPV	R$
RH SP	44	06	BOS	7	11	0	140	90	4.63	1.33	255	221	265	25.9	28%	68%	4.72	39	16	44	3.3	5.8	**1.8**	10%	1.2	-1.2	33	$10
Ht/Wt	74 210	07	BOS	17	12	0	189	110	4.76	1.35	264	247	276	26.0	29%	67%	4.80	39	19	42	3.0	5.2	**1.7**	8%	1.0	-6.0	29	$15
Type	Con xFB	08	BOS	10	11	0	181	117	4.13	1.18	232	244	218	24.8	25%	69%	4.59	36	16	49	3.0	5.8	**2.0**	9%	1.2	4.9	38	$16
Health	C	09	BOS	11	5	0	130	72	4.58	1.44	272	280	263	26.9	30%	69%	5.25	36	17	47	3.5	5.0	**1.4**	6%	0.8	-2.0	10	$8
PT/Exp	A	10	BOS	4	10	0	140	84	5.34	1.35	279	273	271	18.7	30%	62%	4.54	37	16	47	2.3	5.4	**2.3**	9%	1.2	-20.7	50	$3
Consist	B	1st Half		3	6	0	94	51	4.96	1.29	277			23.4	29%	65%	4.60	34	18	48	1.9	4.9	**2.6**	9%	1.3	-9.6	48	$3
LIMA Plan	C	2nd Half		1	4	0	46	33	6.10	1.47	284			13.4	32%	58%	4.37	43	13	44	3.2	6.5	**2.1**	8%	1.0	-11.1	53	($0)
Rand Var	+2	11	Proj	**5**	**6**	**0**	**94**	**54**	**5.06**	**1.44**	**279**			**20.6**	**30%**	**67%**	**4.95**	**38**	**16**	**46**	**3.2**	**5.2**	**1.6**	**9%**	**1.2**	**-7.7**	**24**	**$3**

He can sometimes reel off the occassional string of great games (like 3 PQS DOM starts with 5.0 Cmd in mid-June). However, you pay for the whole package, which as xERA shows is consistently mediocre.

Walden,Jordan		Yr	Tm	W	L	Sv	IP	K	ERA	WHIP	OBA	vL	vR	BF/G	H%	S%	xERA	G	L	F	Ctl	Dom	Cmd	hr/f	hr/9	RAR	BPV	R$
RH RP	23	06		0	0	0	0	0	0.00	0.00							0.00											
Ht/Wt	77 220	07		0	0	0	0	0	0.00	0.00							0.00											
Type	Pwr xGB	08		0	0	0	0	0	0.00	0.00							0.00											
Health	A	09	aa	1	5	0	60	48	6.90	1.93	337			22.4	40%	63%	6.73				4.5	7.2	**1.6**		0.6	-19.2	46	($4)
PT/Exp	F	10	LAA *	1	2	9	65	58	3.35	1.52	275	214	233	4.8	35%	78%	3.15	60	20	20	4.0	8.1	**2.0**	8%	0.4	6.3	74	$6
Consist	F	1st Half		0	0	5	31	27	4.34	1.64	297			5.3	37%	73%	5.02				4.1	7.8	**1.9**		0.6	-0.8	66	$2
LIMA Plan	B	2nd Half		1	2	4	33	31	2.43	1.41	254			4.4	33%	83%	3.01	60	20	20	4.0	8.4	**2.1**	5%	0.3	7.1	79	$4
Rand Var	0	11	Proj	**2**	**3**	**15**	**65**	**56**	**4.00**	**1.44**	**258**			**6.8**	**32%**	**72%**	**3.26**	**60**	**20**	**20**	**4.1**	**7.7**	**1.9**	**10%**	**0.6**	**8.3**	**65**	**$9**

0-1, 1 Sv, 2.35 ERA in 15 IP at LAA. Rumored closer-in-waiting got our attention by smoking MLB hitters (23 K). He owns a minor league career 1.6 G/F ratio, so he doesn't need all that Dom to be effective. Speculate.

JOSHUA RANDALL

Walker,Tyler	Yr	Tm	W	L	Sv	IP	K	ERA	WHIP	OBA	vL	vR	BF/G	H%	S%	xERA	G	L	F	Ctl	Dom	Cmd	hr/f	hr/9	RAR	BPV	R$
RH RP 34	06	2TM	1	4	10	25	19	7.17	1.55	276	333	226	4.3	33%	50%	4.78	35	28	37	4.3	6.8	1.6	3%	0.4	-8.2	19	$3
Ht/Wt 75 262	07	SF *	3	2	7	37	26	4.46	1.63	299	182	308	4.8	33%	77%	5.22	35	18	48	3.8	6.3	1.6	10%	1.4	-0.1	23	$4
Type Pwr FB	08	SF	5	8	0	53	49	4.56	1.28	238	319	186	3.4	28%	67%	3.53	48	21	31	3.5	8.3	2.3	15%	1.2	-1.9	79	$5
Health F	09	PHI *	4	2	3	54	43	2.68	0.97	209	229	230	4.5	24%	77%	3.76	38	15	48	2.0	7.1	3.5	7%	0.8	10.1	90	$9
PT/Exp D	10	WAS	1	0	0	35	30	3.57	1.22	260	245	277	6.1	30%	76%	3.66	42	13	44	2.0	7.6	3.8	11%	1.3	1.9	103	$3
Consist A	1st Half		1	0	0	35	30	3.57	1.22	260			6.1	30%	76%	3.66	42	13	44	2.0	7.6	3.8	11%	1.3	1.9	103	$3
LIMA Plan B+	2nd Half		0	0	0	0	0	0.00	0.00							0.00											
Rand Var 0	11	Proj	2	2	0	36	30	3.97	1.30	260			4.5	30%	74%	3.88	42	18	40	2.7	7.4	2.7	11%	1.2	1.2	80	$3

Surgery on labrum and rotator cuff in 2H puts '11 in doubt. If healthy, a solid LIMA reliever with improving control and sustained skill growth. But not one to count on for more than 50 IP, given spotty health history.

Wang,Chien-Ming	Yr	Tm	W	L	Sv	IP	K	ERA	WHIP	OBA	vL	vR	BF/G	H%	S%	xERA	G	L	F	Ctl	Dom	Cmd	hr/f	hr/9	RAR	BPV	R$
RH RP 31	06	NYY	19	6	1	218	76	3.63	1.31	275	275	279	27.1	29%	72%	3.83	63	17	20	2.1	3.1	1.5	8%	0.5	24.9	39	$21
Ht/Wt 75 230	07	NYY	19	7	0	199	104	3.70	1.29	261	286	242	28.0	29%	71%	3.78	58	18	23	2.7	4.7	1.8	6%	0.4	19.7	49	$21
Type Con xGB	08	NYY	8	2	0	95	54	4.07	1.32	251	261	238	26.8	29%	68%	3.83	55	22	23	3.3	5.1	1.5	6%	0.4	3.2	36	$8
Health F	09	NYY	1	6	0	42	29	9.64	2.02	358	394	329	17.3	40%	51%	4.66	53	20	27	4.1	6.2	1.5	17%	1.5	-26.9	33	($6)
PT/Exp D	10	WAS	0	0	0	0	0	0.00	0.00							0.00											
Consist B	1st Half		0	0	0	0	0	0.00	0.00							0.00											
LIMA Plan F	2nd Half		0	0	0	0	0	0.00	0.00							0.00											
Rand Var +5	11	Proj	4	4	0	58	32	4.50	1.43	278			22.9	31%	69%	3.89	57	19	24	3.1	5.0	1.6	11%	0.8	1.8	40	$3

Season wiped out due to rehab from shoulder surgery. With rising Ctl before surgery, health or even hr/f fix won't be enough to right ship. Needs a 2.0 Cmd, and that's not coming. A low upside GBer with big health risk.

Weaver,Jeff	Yr	Tm	W	L	Sv	IP	K	ERA	WHIP	OBA	vL	vR	BF/G	H%	S%	xERA	G	L	F	Ctl	Dom	Cmd	hr/f	hr/9	RAR	BPV	R$
RH RP 34	06	2TM	8	14	0	172	107	5.76	1.51	305	340	267	24.6	32%	66%	4.65	39	23	38	2.5	5.6	2.3	15%	1.8	-26.2	51	$3
Ht/Wt 77 200	07	SEA	7	13	0	147	80	6.20	1.53	315	324	306	24.2	33%	61%	5.12	36	17	47	2.1	4.9	2.3	9%	1.4	-30.6	44	$1
Type FB	08	aaa	4	6	0	84	49	8.78	1.94	353			18.6	37%	57%	8.56				3.6	5.3	1.5		2.1	-46.4	-17	($9)
Health B	09	LA	6	4	0	79	64	3.65	1.52	281	286	277	12.5	34%	78%	4.27	41	23	36	3.8	7.3	1.9	8%	0.8	5.3	49	$5
PT/Exp D	10	LA	5	1	0	44	26	6.09	1.53	278	321	275	4.5	30%	60%	5.07	36	20	44	4.1	5.3	1.3	8%	1.0	-11.4	-1	$1
Consist F	1st Half		5	1	0	25	17	4.01	1.38	264			3.7	31%	70%	4.42	37	21	42	3.3	6.2	1.9	3%	0.4	0.0	38	$3
LIMA Plan C	2nd Half		0	0	0	20	9	8.72	1.73	294			6.1	29%	50%	5.95	35	20	45	5.1	4.1	0.8	13%	1.8	-11.4	-49	($3)
Rand Var +3	11	Proj	3	1	0	36	23	5.46	1.57	286			7.4	31%	67%	4.99	37	21	42	4.0	5.7	1.4	10%	1.2	-3.8	11	$1

Ctl waning, Dom fading, and now more flyball problems for Weaver the elder. xERA tells the tale. Only hope now is to stick in long relief. And with chronic problems vs. LH bats, even that's not likely.

Weaver,Jered	Yr	Tm	W	L	Sv	IP	K	ERA	WHIP	OBA	vL	vR	BF/G	H%	S%	xERA	G	L	F	Ctl	Dom	Cmd	hr/f	hr/9	RAR	BPV	R$
RH SP 28	06	LAA *	17	3	0	200	184	2.43	1.02	222	250	174	25.4	27%	82%	3.78	30	18	52	1.9	8.3	4.4	8%	1.0	52.5	106	$36
Ht/Wt 79 205	07	LAA	13	7	0	161	115	3.91	1.39	282	291	269	24.8	32%	74%	4.60	36	17	47	2.5	6.4	2.6	7%	1.0	11.8	61	$15
Type Pwr xFB	08	LAA	11	10	0	177	152	4.33	1.28	258	243	266	24.8	31%	69%	4.11	33	22	46	2.8	7.7	2.8	8%	1.0	0.4	76	$16
Health A	09	LAA	16	8	0	211	174	3.75	1.24	248	276	208	26.6	29%	74%	4.38	31	19	50	2.8	7.4	2.6	8%	1.1	18.2	66	$23
PT/Exp A	10	LAA	13	12	0	224	233	3.01	1.07	228	223	220	26.4	29%	76%	3.31	36	16	48	2.2	9.3	4.3	8%	0.9	31.2	124	$30
Consist B	1st Half		8	3	0	109	124	2.82	1.06	225			25.4	30%	78%	3.05	36	17	47	2.2	10.3	4.8	9%	0.9	17.7	141	$17
LIMA Plan C+	2nd Half		5	9	0	116	109	3.19	1.09	231			27.3	28%	75%	3.55	36	15	49	2.2	8.5	3.9	8%	0.9	13.5	108	$14
Rand Var -1	11	Proj	14	11	0	218	202	3.43	1.19	245			26.3	30%	75%	3.82	34	18	49	2.4	8.4	3.4	8%	1.0	12.6	96	$25

Dom spike, excellent control, out pitch vs. LHers turned him from good to great. High FB% still is a risk factor, but it's never bitten him in past. Even with some S% regression, he's a sub 3.50 ERA lock. And a legit ace now.

Webb,Brandon	Yr	Tm	W	L	Sv	IP	K	ERA	WHIP	OBA	vL	vR	BF/G	H%	S%	xERA	G	L	F	Ctl	Dom	Cmd	hr/f	hr/9	RAR	BPV	R$
RH RP 31	06	ARI	16	8	0	235	178	3.10	1.13	246	261	231	28.9	29%	74%	2.63	66	17	16	1.9	6.8	3.6	13%	0.6	40.2	115	$29
Ht/Wt 75 228	07	ARI	18	10	0	236	194	3.01	1.19	239	272	199	28.6	29%	75%	2.93	62	18	20	2.7	7.4	2.7	9%	0.5	41.3	99	$29
Type xGB	08	ARI	22	7	0	227	183	3.30	1.20	244	265	219	27.4	30%	73%	2.86	64	15	20	2.6	7.3	2.8	10%	0.5	27.3	103	$28
Health F	09	ARI	0	0	0	4	2	13.50	2.00	347	222	500	19.7	30%	33%	5.32	53	13	33	4.5	4.5	1.0	39%	4.5	-4.6	-9	($1)
PT/Exp C	10	ARI	0	0	0	0	0	0.00	0.00							0.00											
Consist F	1st Half		0	0	0	0	0	0.00	0.00							0.00											
LIMA Plan C	2nd Half		0	0	0	-0	0	0.00	0.00							0.00											
Rand Var +5	11	Proj	3	2	0	44	33	3.72	1.24	246			22.6	30%	69%	3.21	58	18	23	2.9	6.8	2.4	7%	0.4	5.0	81	$4

That 230 IP average from '05 to '08 did him in. Hasn't been able to recover from Aug '09 shoulder surgery. As an xGBer who has succeeded w/o mid 90s stuff, we can't write him off. But he's nothing more than a flyer now.

Webb,Ryan	Yr	Tm	W	L	Sv	IP	K	ERA	WHIP	OBA	vL	vR	BF/G	H%	S%	xERA	G	L	F	Ctl	Dom	Cmd	hr/f	hr/9	RAR	BPV	R$
RH RP 25	06		0	0	0	0	0	0.00	0.00							0.00											
Ht/Wt 78 214	07	aa	0	4	0	25	14	11.07	1.94	354			24.5	33%	47%	10.54				3.6	5.0	1.4		3.9	-20.5	-74	($4)
Type xGB	08	aa	9	8	0	130	80	5.40	1.65	323			23.7	36%	67%	5.89				2.7	5.5	2.1		0.8	-17.5	44	$2
Health A	09	aaa	7	1	2	49	35	4.39	1.63	316			6.4	37%	73%	5.50				2.9	6.4	2.2		0.5	-0.5	60	$4
PT/Exp D	10	SD *	4	1	1	79	64	2.39	1.26	254	333	239	4.7	32%	81%	2.73	62	21	17	2.7	7.3	2.7	5%	0.2	15.9	98	$8
Consist D	1st Half		3	1	1	42	33	1.29	0.98	203			4.8	26%	88%	2.39	69	14	17	2.4	7.1	3.0	5%	0.2	14.0	111	$7
LIMA Plan B+	2nd Half		1	0	0	38	31	3.60	1.57	303			4.6	38%	76%	3.10	56	27	17	3.1	7.4	2.4	5%	0.2	1.9	84	$1
Rand Var -4	11	Proj	5	1	0	58	43	3.57	1.34	268			5.8	32%	73%	3.00	61	22	17	2.8	6.7	2.4	10%	0.5	8.2	83	$5

3-1, 2.90 ERA in 59 IP at SD. Deep bullpen kept him on AAA shuttle, but he's got the goods to stick. Rising Dom, elite GB% point to late inning upside. At minimum, a premium LIMA reliever target. UP: 20 saves

Wellemeyer,Todd	Yr	Tm	W	L	Sv	IP	K	ERA	WHIP	OBA	vL	vR	BF/G	H%	S%	xERA	G	L	F	Ctl	Dom	Cmd	hr/f	hr/9	RAR	BPV	R$
RH SP 32	06	2TM	1	4	1	78	54	4.15	1.51	236	208	265	7.5	27%	73%	5.01	49	14	37	5.8	6.2	1.1	7%	0.7	3.6	-17	$3
Ht/Wt 75 225	07	2TM	3	3	0	79	60	4.54	1.48	256	311	200	10.9	29%	73%	4.79	40	18	41	4.5	6.8	1.5	11%	1.2	-0.8	18	$4
Type Pwr FB	08	STL	13	9	0	192	134	3.71	1.25	248	256	237	25.0	27%	75%	4.25	39	21	40	2.9	6.3	2.2	11%	1.2	13.3	52	$17
Health D	09	STL	7	10	0	122	78	5.89	1.77	317	351	305	20.5	35%	69%	5.35	37	21	42	4.2	5.7	1.4	11%	1.4	-25.6	5	($3)
PT/Exp B	10	SF	3	5	0	59	41	5.67	1.57	256	316	216	20.3	27%	69%	5.32	34	17	49	5.4	6.3	1.2	13%	1.8	-12.0	-20	($0)
Consist B	1st Half		3	5	0	59	41	5.52	1.50	243			21.6	25%	68%	5.26	34	15	50	5.4	6.3	1.2	13%	1.8	-10.9	-19	$0
LIMA Plan F	2nd Half		0	0	0	0	0	0.00	0.00				4.0		75%	0.00				0.0	0.0			0.0	0.0	55	$1
Rand Var 0	11	Proj	1	2	0	29	20	4.97	1.52	268			16.1	30%	70%	4.90	38	18	43	4.3	6.2	1.4	10%	1.2	-2.7	11	$0

6 reasons to head for the hills...
- Rising Ctl
- Surging FB%
- Long history of gopheritis
- No command
- Horrible xERA
- '08 magic is long gone

Wells,Randy	Yr	Tm	W	L	Sv	IP	K	ERA	WHIP	OBA	vL	vR	BF/G	H%	S%	xERA	G	L	F	Ctl	Dom	Cmd	hr/f	hr/9	RAR	BPV	R$
RH SP 28	06	a/a	9	7	0	131	97	5.17	1.63	318			23.8	37%	69%	5.98				2.8	6.7	2.4		0.9	-10.5	53	$4
Ht/Wt 75 230	07	aaa	5	6	2	95	77	6.30	1.84	324			11.3	37%	68%	7.25				4.4	7.2	1.6		1.5	-21.6	24	($2)
Type	08	aaa	10	4	0	118	76	5.16	1.69	326			20.2	36%	73%	6.69				3.0	5.8	1.9		1.4	-12.5	23	$3
Health A	09	CHC *	15	10	0	191	119	3.20	1.29	262	310	221	25.1	30%	77%	4.03	48	19	33	2.6	5.6	2.2	7%	0.7	23.3	57	$18
PT/Exp B	10	CHC	8	14	0	194	144	4.26	1.40	276	261	280	26.2	32%	71%	3.86	47	20	33	2.9	6.7	2.3	9%	0.9	-5.9	66	$8
Consist C	1st Half		4	6	0	98	76	4.67	1.42	290			25.1	35%	67%	3.69	45	25	31	2.5	7.0	2.8	7%	0.6	-7.9	81	$3
LIMA Plan C+	2nd Half		4	8	0	96	68	3.84	1.37	262			27.5	29%	76%	4.02	49	15	36	3.4	6.4	1.9	11%	1.1	2.0	51	$5
Rand Var 0	11	Proj	10	11	0	174	121	4.14	1.37	273			22.6	31%	72%	3.98	48	19	34	2.8	6.3	2.2	10%	1.0	3.4	61	$10

As expected, couldn't repeat rookie buzz. But 1H H% partly to blame, and Cmd growth gives a bit of hope. All that said, he's really just not all that skilled. Hey, he's useful at the right price. Just don't bid expecting '09 stats.

Westbrook,Jake	Yr	Tm	W	L	Sv	IP	K	ERA	WHIP	OBA	vL	vR	BF/G	H%	S%	xERA	G	L	F	Ctl	Dom	Cmd	hr/f	hr/9	RAR	BPV	R$
RH SP 33	06	CLE	15	10	0	211	109	4.18	1.43	293	290	300	28.7	32%	71%	3.75	61	17	22	2.3	4.6	2.0	9%	0.6	9.9	59	$15
Ht/Wt 75 215	07	CLE	6	9	0	152	93	4.32	1.41	271	288	263	26.3	30%	70%	4.05	54	20	27	3.3	5.5	1.7	10%	0.8	3.4	43	$9
Type Con xGB	08	CLE	1	2	0	35	19	3.11	1.15	252	238	273	28.3	26%	80%	3.61	55	17	28	1.8	4.9	2.7	16%	1.3	5.3	73	$3
Health F	09	aa *	0	1	0	9	5	3.00	1.22	262			12.4	28%	80%	4.05				2.0	5.0	2.5		1.0	1.5	55	$1
PT/Exp C	10	2TM	10	11	0	203	128	4.22	1.34	262	268	256	26.1	29%	70%	3.65	56	17	26	3.0	5.7	1.9	12%	0.9	-3.6	55	$11
Consist A	1st Half		5	4	0	102	55	4.59	1.43	277			26.1	30%	69%	4.08	53	19	28	3.2	4.9	1.5	11%	0.9	-6.5	32	$3
LIMA Plan C	2nd Half		5	7	0	101	73	3.84	1.24	247			26.2	28%	71%	3.22	60	15	25	2.9	6.5	2.3	13%	0.9	2.9	79	$8
Rand Var +1	11	Proj	11	9	0	174	105	4.03	1.32	266			27.3	30%	71%	3.69	57	17	26	2.7	5.4	2.0	11%	0.8	11.1	60	$12

3 reasons he'll be undervalued...
- Previous Cmd returned in 2H
- Still an extreme groundballer
- Nice xERA

The Duncan Effect helped and that may be the only thing to keep him afloat at his age.

Wheeler,Dan

Wheeler,Dan				W	L	Sv	IP	K	ERA	WHIP	OBA	vL	vR	BF/G	H%	S%	xERA	G	L	F	Ctl	Dom	Cmd	hr/f	hr/9	RAR	BPV	R$
RH RP	33	06	HOU	3	5	9	71	68	2.53	1.15	224	273	183	3.9	29%	81%	3.79	37	20	44	3.0	8.6	2.8	6%	0.6	17.2	87	$13
Ht/Wt	75 220	07	2TM	1	9	11	75	82	5.30	1.30	260	260	253	4.5	33%	62%	3.61	37	18	45	2.8	9.9	3.6	12%	1.3	-7.7	118	$8
Type	Pwr xFB	08	TAM	5	6	13	66	53	3.12	1.00	191	215	163	3.7	20%	77%	4.21	28	17	54	3.0	7.2	2.4	10%	1.4	10.0	55	$14
Health	A	09	TAM	4	5	2	58	45	3.28	0.87	201	305	156	3.2	20%	74%	3.91	31	13	56	1.4	7.0	5.0	12%	1.7	8.4	97	$10
PT/Exp	C	10	TAM	2	4	3	48	46	3.35	1.08	209	154	222	3.0	24%	76%	3.56	35	20	45	3.0	8.6	2.9	12%	1.3	4.7	86	$7
Consist	A	1st Half		2	0	0	25	28	3.28	1.05	205			3.0	26%	74%	3.26	30	22	48	2.9	10.2	3.5	10%	1.1	2.6	113	$4
LIMA Plan	B+	2nd Half		0	4	3	24	18	3.43	1.10	213			3.1	22%	77%	3.87	39	18	42	3.1	6.9	2.3	14%	1.5	2.1	59	$3
Rand Var	-1	11	Proj	3	6	18	65	57	3.31	1.10	224			3.3	26%	76%	3.88	34	18	49	2.6	7.9	3.0	10%	1.2	3.3	82	$14

PRO: Elite Cmd, consistently eats up RH batters.
CON: xFB profile means HR issues aren't going away; 2009 Ctl and Cmd look like outliers.
A nice LIMA option in an unsettled pen, never a bad play.

White,Sean

White,Sean				W	L	Sv	IP	K	ERA	WHIP	OBA	vL	vR	BF/G	H%	S%	xERA	G	L	F	Ctl	Dom	Cmd	hr/f	hr/9	RAR	BPV	R$
RH RP	29	06	aa	5	6	1	102	58	6.95	2.18	371			24.8	42%	66%	7.94				4.6	5.1	1.1		0.4	-30.7	23	($9)
Ht/Wt	76 210	07	SEA *	2	3	0	48	24	5.06	1.50	262			11.8	29%	65%	4.43				4.5	4.5	1.0		0.6	-3.3	34	$1
Type		08	aa	6	11	0	125	39	7.37	2.28	397			29.6	41%	68%	9.32				3.8	2.8	0.7		1.0	-47.3	-23	($16)
Health	A	09	SEA	3	2	1	64	28	2.80	1.09	216	191	238	5.0	23%	75%	4.43	48	16	36	2.8	3.9	1.4	4%	0.4	13.1	21	$8
PT/Exp	D	10	SEA *	1	1	0	47	23	3.81	1.53	283	357	321	4.4	31%	77%	4.71	45	23	32	3.8	4.4	1.2	8%	0.8	1.9	0	$1
Consist	F	1st Half		0	0	0	19	6	7.58	2.11	359			4.2	37%	63%	5.93	46	23	31	4.7	2.8	0.6	8%	0.9	-8.1	-53	($3)
LIMA Plan	C	2nd Half		1	1	0	28	17	1.27	1.15	221			4.6	25%	93%	3.99	43	23	34	3.1	5.5	1.8	7%	0.6	10.0	35	$4
Rand Var	-2	11	Proj	2	2	0	58	31	4.03	1.52	284			5.8	31%	76%	4.68	46	20	34	3.6	4.8	1.3	9%	0.9	-2.8	15	$2

0-1, 5.24 ERA in 34 IP at SEA. 2009 move into positive BPV territory proved to not be sustainable. Not to be confused with Olympic champion Shaun, who might also be able to post a 0 BPV if given the chance.

Willis,Dontrelle

Willis,Dontrelle				W	L	Sv	IP	K	ERA	WHIP	OBA	vL	vR	BF/G	H%	S%	xERA	G	L	F	Ctl	Dom	Cmd	hr/f	hr/9	RAR	BPV	R$
LH SP	29	06	FLA	12	12	0	223	160	3.87	1.42	271	231	281	28.5	31%	75%	4.21	48	20	33	3.3	6.5	1.9	9%	0.8	16.9	51	$15
Ht/Wt	76 225	07	FLA	10	15	0	205	146	5.17	1.60	294	123	320	26.5	33%	70%	4.47	46	21	32	3.8	6.4	1.7	13%	1.3	-18.9	37	$4
Type	Pwr	08	DET *	3	3	0	52	36	7.27	2.06	276	125	242	18.5	31%	65%	6.84	43	12	46	8.8	6.2	0.7	9%	1.2	-18.7	-106	($4)
Health	F	09	DET *	3	6	0	64	33	7.03	1.90	281	306	289	23.7	30%	62%	6.01	52	17	31	7.2	4.6	0.6	9%	0.9	-20.3	-81	($4)
PT/Exp	D	10	2TM	2	3	0	66	47	5.62	1.95	280	216	322	21.3	32%	71%	5.44	46	26	28	7.7	6.4	0.8	10%	0.8	-12.5	-68	($4)
Consist	B	1st Half		2	3	0	66	47	5.62	1.95	280			21.3	32%	71%	5.44	46	26	28	7.7	6.4	0.8	10%	0.8	-12.5	-68	($4)
LIMA Plan	F	2nd Half		0	0	0	0	0	0.00	0.00							0.00											
Rand Var	0	11	Proj	2	3	0	53	35	6.00	1.87	281			22.8	32%	68%	5.48	47	21	32	6.9	6.0	0.9	11%	1.0	-8.2	-53	($2)

In 25 years of player profiles, this may just be the worst 3-year BPV line ever. 255 points of negative BPV in three years?

Clearly, all hope is lost here.

Wilson,Brian

Wilson,Brian				W	L	Sv	IP	K	ERA	WHIP	OBA	vL	vR	BF/G	H%	S%	xERA	G	L	F	Ctl	Dom	Cmd	hr/f	hr/9	RAR	BPV	R$
RH RP	29	06	SF *	3	6	8	58	50	4.50	1.60	252			4.8	31%	72%	4.56	45	26	29	5.9	7.8	1.3	8%	0.6	-0.1	3	$5
Ht/Wt	73 196	07	SF *	2	4	17	58	47	2.66	1.38	220	304	145	4.5	28%	80%	4.03	56	15	29	5.2	7.3	1.4	2%	0.2	12.6	24	$11
Type	Pwr	08	SF	3	2	41	62	67	4.62	1.44	261	202	320	4.3	34%	70%	3.34	52	19	30	4.0	9.7	2.4	14%	1.0	-2.7	95	$18
Health	A	09	SF	5	6	38	72	83	2.74	1.20	227	189	255	4.4	32%	77%	3.10	46	18	36	3.4	10.3	3.1	5%	0.4	12.9	119	$22
PT/Exp	A	10	SF	3	3	48	75	93	1.81	1.18	227	206	231	4.4	33%	86%	2.78	49	13	38	3.1	11.2	3.6	4%	0.4	20.3	144	$26
Consist	A	1st Half		2	0	22	35	49	2.04	1.36	249			4.6	39%	85%	2.63	50	17	33	3.8	12.5	3.3	4%	0.3	8.6	150	$12
LIMA Plan	C+	2nd Half		1	3	26	39	44	1.60	1.02	207			4.2	29%	87%	2.90	48	10	43	2.5	10.1	4.0	5%	0.5	11.7	139	$15
Rand Var	-5	11	Proj	3	4	43	65	75	2.62	1.21	224			4.3	31%	80%	3.07	48	16	36	3.6	10.3	2.9	7%	0.6	8.6	116	$22

So much to like: led league in Svs, top-notch Reliability, and skills, skills, skills. 2H and post-season workload are mildly concerning, but he is elite and legit. Fear the beard, indeed.

Wilson,C.J.

Wilson,C.J.				W	L	Sv	IP	K	ERA	WHIP	OBA	vL	vR	BF/G	H%	S%	xERA	G	L	F	Ctl	Dom	Cmd	hr/f	hr/9	RAR	BPV	R$
LH SP	30	06	TEX	2	4	1	44	43	4.08	1.29	239	155	292	4.2	28%	74%	3.42	49	21	30	3.7	8.8	2.4	20%	1.4	2.6	86	$5
Ht/Wt	73 215	07	TEX	2	1	12	68	63	3.03	1.22	206	112	275	4.3	26%	76%	3.51	49	24	27	4.3	8.3	1.9	8%	0.5	12.4	59	$12
Type	Pwr GB	08	TEX	2	2	24	46	41	6.03	1.64	273	265	269	4.2	31%	66%	4.36	49	16	35	5.2	8.0	1.5	17%	1.6	-9.6	29	$8
Health	B	09	TEX	5	6	14	74	84	2.81	1.33	241	206	249	4.2	34%	79%	2.91	55	20	25	3.9	10.3	2.6	6%	0.4	14.9	113	$15
PT/Exp	B	10	TEX	15	8	0	204	170	3.35	1.25	219	144	236	25.7	27%	73%	3.69	49	17	34	4.1	7.5	1.8	5%	0.4	19.8	51	$22
Consist	C	1st Half		6	4	0	102	73	3.34	1.26	219			26.7	26%	74%	3.99	51	15	34	4.2	6.4	1.5	6%	0.5	10.0	31	$9
LIMA Plan	D+	2nd Half		9	4	0	102	97	3.36	1.23	218			24.8	29%	72%	3.41	47	20	33	4.0	8.6	2.2	5%	0.4	9.7	72	$12
Rand Var	-2	11	Proj	12	9	0	183	172	3.64	1.35	239			26.0	30%	74%	3.57	51	19	31	4.2	8.5	2.0	9%	0.7	16.2	68	$18

Transitioned to SP role with great results, if not great skills. 2H Dom and Cmd gains are promising signs. But he threw more IP in 2010 than in 2007-09 combined (not incl. playoffs) which has to be a concern.

Wolf,Randy

Wolf,Randy				W	L	Sv	IP	K	ERA	WHIP	OBA	vL	vR	BF/G	H%	S%	xERA	G	L	F	Ctl	Dom	Cmd	hr/f	hr/9	RAR	BPV	R$
LH SP	34	06	PHI	4	0	0	56	44	5.60	1.71	284	86	323	21.7	30%	73%	5.33	37	19	44	5.3	7.0	1.3	17%	2.1	-7.7	-1	$1
Ht/Wt	70 202	07	LA	9	6	0	103	94	4.73	1.45	275	250	278	24.9	34%	68%	4.09	41	19	40	3.4	8.2	2.4	8%	0.9	-3.9	75	$8
Type	FB	08	2NL	12	12	0	190	162	4.30	1.38	262	283	258	24.8	31%	71%	4.10	39	23	39	3.4	7.7	2.3	10%	1.0	-0.8	64	$13
Health	B	09	LA	11	7	0	214	160	3.23	1.10	228	159	246	25.3	26%	75%	3.91	40	18	42	2.4	6.7	2.8	9%	1.0	25.3	73	$23
PT/Exp	A	10	MIL	13	12	0	216	142	4.17	1.39	259	286	250	27.3	28%	74%	4.54	39	19	42	3.6	5.9	1.6	10%	1.2	-4.2	26	$11
Consist	A	1st Half		6	7	0	103	61	4.70	1.52	267			27.0	27%	75%	4.91	41	20	39	4.4	5.3	1.2	15%	1.7	-8.8	-5	$2
LIMA Plan	D+	2nd Half		7	5	0	112	81	3.68	1.27	252			27.7	29%	73%	4.22	38	17	45	2.9	6.5	2.3	7%	0.8	4.6	55	$9
Rand Var	0	11	Proj	12	10	0	203	149	4.12	1.33	254			26.1	29%	72%	4.30	39	19	42	3.3	6.6	2.0	10%	1.1	-4.0	48	$13

Fell into a too-many-BB-and-HR rut in 1H, but mostly righted things in 2H. Despite mild 2H recovery, three-year Dom drop is worrisome. 2009 may end up being his last foray into sub-4.00 ERA territory.

Wood,Blake

Wood,Blake				W	L	Sv	IP	K	ERA	WHIP	OBA	vL	vR	BF/G	H%	S%	xERA	G	L	F	Ctl	Dom	Cmd	hr/f	hr/9	RAR	BPV	R$
RH RP	25	06		0	0	0	0	0	0.00	0.00							0.00											
Ht/Wt	76 225	07		0	0	0	0	0	0.00	0.00							0.00											
Type	GB	08		0	0	0	0	0	0.00	0.00							0.00											
Health	A	09	aa	2	8	0	78	41	7.15	1.71	327			21.3	36%	57%	6.36				3.0	4.7	1.6		1.0	-27.4	21	($5)
PT/Exp	F	10	KC *	3	4	5	66	41	4.38	1.44	265	286	286	4.6	30%	71%	4.29	51	15	34	3.8	5.6	1.5	8%	0.8	-1.9	26	$4
Consist	F	1st Half		2	2	5	39	18	3.22	1.25	231			4.7	25%	74%	4.67	45	16	38	3.7	4.1	1.1	4%	0.5	4.4	-2	$5
LIMA Plan	C+	2nd Half		1	2	0	27	23	6.07	1.72	311			4.4	36%	67%	3.85	56	13	31	4.0	7.8	1.9	15%	1.3	-6.4	64	($1)
Rand Var	0	11	Proj	2	5	0	58	36	4.97	1.52	284			6.6	32%	68%	4.32	53	14	33	3.6	5.6	1.6	10%	0.9	-0.2	35	$1

1-3, 5.07 ERA in 50 IP at KC. GB rate is a good start toward a useful skill set, but needs to pair it with something else. 2H Dom spike may be the answer. Can't buy into that small sample, but worth keeping an eye on.

Wood,Kerry

Wood,Kerry				W	L	Sv	IP	K	ERA	WHIP	OBA	vL	vR	BF/G	H%	S%	xERA	G	L	F	Ctl	Dom	Cmd	hr/f	hr/9	RAR	BPV	R$
RH RP	33	06	CHC	1	2	0	19	13	4.22	1.41	260	206	293	20.8	25%	82%	5.06	39	10	51	3.8	6.1	1.6	16%	2.3	0.6	26	$1
Ht/Wt	77 211	07	CHC	1	1	0	24	24	3.33	1.28	208	148	233	4.6	29%	71%	4.31	34	18	48	4.8	8.9	1.8	0%	0.0	3.3	42	$2
Type	Pwr FB	08	CHC	5	4	34	66	84	3.26	1.09	224	209	227	4.1	33%	70%	2.82	39	20	41	2.4	11.4	4.7	5%	0.4	8.3	157	$22
Health	F	09	CLE	3	3	20	55	63	4.25	1.38	236	255	208	4.1	31%	72%	3.85	40	15	45	4.6	10.3	2.3	11%	1.1	1.3	80	$12
PT/Exp	B	10	2AL	3	4	8	46	49	3.13	1.39	212	211	209	4.2	28%	80%	4.04	39	18	43	5.7	9.6	1.7	8%	0.8	5.7	36	$7
Consist	B	1st Half		1	3	8	19	18	6.26	1.50	265			3.9	32%	60%	3.92	45	16	39	4.3	8.7	2.0	14%	1.4	-4.9	62	$3
LIMA Plan	B	2nd Half		2	1	0	27	31	0.99	1.32	172			4.5	25%	94%	4.14	34	19	47	6.6	10.2	1.6	3%	0.3	10.6	18	$4
Rand Var	-3	11	Proj	4	4	5	58	65	3.88	1.36	227			4.1	30%	74%	3.82	39	17	44	4.8	10.1	2.1	9%	0.9	3.3	69	$8

xERA and BPV agree that this is no longer a closer-worthy skill set, despite ERA. Ctl, Dom, Cmd all trending badly, even in 2H "surge". Others will keep chasing value here, but you'll seek better options elsewhere.

Wood,Travis

Wood,Travis				W	L	Sv	IP	K	ERA	WHIP	OBA	vL	vR	BF/G	H%	S%	xERA	G	L	F	Ctl	Dom	Cmd	hr/f	hr/9	RAR	BPV	R$
LH SP	24	06		0	0	0	0	0	0.00	0.00							0.00											
Ht/Wt	71 166	07		0	0	0	0	0	0.00	0.00							0.00											
Type	xFB	08	aa	4	9	0	80	50	8.21	1.85	309			22.4	34%	55%	6.67				5.3	5.6	1.1		1.2	-38.5	12	($6)
Health	A	09	a/a	13	5	0	167	119	2.31	1.18	233			25.4	28%	82%	2.97				3.0	6.4	2.2		0.4	41.2	79	$22
PT/Exp	D	10	CIN *	10	10	0	203	173	3.55	1.14	242	136	240	25.0	29%	72%	3.84	31	21	48	2.2	7.7	3.5	7%	0.9	11.6	87	$18
Consist	F	1st Half		5	6	0	105	89	3.60	1.16	245			26.8	29%	72%	3.95	28	22	50	2.2	7.6	3.4	7%	0.9	5.4	83	$9
LIMA Plan	C	2nd Half		5	4	0	98	84	3.50	1.13	238			23.3	29%	71%	3.80	31	21	48	2.2	7.7	3.5	7%	0.8	6.2	88	$9
Rand Var	-1	11	Proj	11	9	0	178	137	3.89	1.29	255			25.0	30%	72%	4.40	31	21	48	2.9	6.9	2.4	7%	0.9	-5.7	54	$14

5-4, 3.51 ERA in 103 IP at CIN.
PRO: Carried over, even extended, minors skills in MLB debut.
CON: xFB profile with GABP as a home field was a dangerous combo.

ANDY ANDRES

Wright,Jamey				W	L	Sv	IP	K	ERA	WHIP	OBA	vL	vR	BF/G	H%	S%	xERA	G	L	F	Ctl	Dom	Cmd	hr/f	hr/9	RAR	BPV	R$
RH RP	36	06	SF	6	10	0	156	79	5.19	1.48	275	261	300	20.2	29%	66%	4.27	58	18	23	3.7	4.6	1.2	13%	0.9	-13.6	18	$3
Ht/Wt	77 225	07	TEX *	6	6	0	97	48	4.29	1.59	286	268	253	18.2	31%	75%	4.71	55	17	28	4.1	4.5	1.1	10%	0.9	2.6	2	$4
Type	xGB	08	TEX	8	7	0	84	60	5.12	1.52	281	286	280	5.0	33%	65%	3.46	62	20	19	3.7	6.4	1.7	10%	0.5	-8.1	54	$5
Health	B	09	KC	3	5	0	79	60	4.33	1.48	247	200	285	5.3	29%	72%	3.96	59	17	24	5.0	6.8	1.4	14%	0.9	1.2	25	$4
PT/Exp	C	10	2AL *	2	3	1	72	41	5.06	1.56	280	227	280	5.8	31%	67%	4.03	62	13	25	4.2	5.1	1.2	8%	0.6	-8.3	20	$0
Consist	A	1st Half		1	2	0	21	9	5.49	1.60	294			5.3	32%	64%	4.45	61	12	28	3.8	3.8	1.0	5%	0.4	-3.6	4	($0)
LIMA Plan	C+	2nd Half		1	1	1	51	32	4.89	1.54	274			6.0	31%	68%	3.83	63	14	23	4.3	5.7	1.3	11%	0.7	-4.7	27	$1
Rand Var	+1	11	Proj	3	3	0	58	36	4.97	1.52	272			5.8	31%	67%	3.97	60	16	24	4.2	5.6	1.3	11%	0.8	2.2	26	$2

1-3, 4.17 in 58 IP at CLE/SEA. Another pitcher who's made a career out of inducing ground balls, with virtually no other command of the strike zone. Others have done it with ERAs under 5.00, though.

Wright,Wesley				W	L	Sv	IP	K	ERA	WHIP	OBA	vL	vR	BF/G	H%	S%	xERA	G	L	F	Ctl	Dom	Cmd	hr/f	hr/9	RAR	BPV	R$
LH RP	26	06	aa	1	1	1	21	25	5.14	1.33	202			6.0	26%	64%	3.81				5.6	10.7	1.9		1.3	-1.6	81	$2
Ht/Wt	71 160	07	a/a	7	4	2	78	75	4.50	1.68	272			8.2	33%	75%	5.51				5.7	8.7	1.5		1.0	-0.4	54	$5
Type	Pwr	08	HOU	4	3	1	56	57	5.01	1.42	223	207	220	3.4	27%	68%	4.17	40	21	39	5.5	9.2	1.7	14%	1.3	-5.1	35	$4
Health	A	09	HOU *	5	5	0	64	64	4.95	1.63	275	359	265	4.7	34%	73%	4.14	43	23	34	5.1	9.0	1.8	14%	1.3	-5.9	46	$2
PT/Exp	D	10	HOU *	5	3	0	102	64	5.23	1.61	292	206	316	16.0	32%	70%	4.71	44	20	37	4.0	5.6	1.4	11%	1.2	-15.3	15	($0)
Consist	A	1st Half		3	0	0	58	28	5.50	1.71	317			16.7	33%	70%	4.77	50	19	31	3.6	4.3	1.2	12%	1.3	-10.6	8	($2)
LIMA Plan	C+	2nd Half		2	3	0	44	36	4.88	1.47	256			15.0	29%	70%	4.36	41	20	39	4.5	7.3	1.6	12%	1.2	-4.8	28	$1
Rand Var	+1	11	Proj	7	6	0	108	91	4.83	1.56	267			21.0	31%	71%	4.41	42	22	37	4.8	7.6	1.6	11%	1.1	-3.5	28	$3

1-2, 5.73 ERA in 33 IP at HOU. Not much to like here beyond age, mild gb% tilt, and strength vs. LHers. Had brief trial as SP; BA vRH and Cmd say that's a bad idea. Luckily, LH specialists make a good living.

Wuertz,Mike				W	L	Sv	IP	K	ERA	WHIP	OBA	vL	vR	BF/G	H%	S%	xERA	G	L	F	Ctl	Dom	Cmd	hr/f	hr/9	RAR	BPV	R$
RH RP	32	06	CHC *	9	1	10	81	98	2.61	1.22	241	184	245	4.7	33%	83%	2.75	54	16	30	2.9	10.8	3.7	13%	0.9	18.9	148	$17
Ht/Wt	75 205	07	CHC	2	3	0	72	79	3.49	1.37	239	238	233	4.2	31%	78%	3.76	44	15	41	4.4	9.8	2.3	10%	1.0	8.4	81	$6
Type	Pwr	08	CHC *	1	2	4	65	55	3.74	1.48	247	230	288	4.6	29%	78%	4.16	46	25	29	5.0	7.6	1.5	13%	1.0	4.3	26	$4
Health	B	09	OAK	6	1	4	79	102	2.63	0.95	190	183	193	4.1	28%	75%	2.63	45	14	40	2.6	11.7	4.4	9%	0.7	17.7	162	$17
PT/Exp	D	10	OAK	2	3	6	40	40	4.31	1.41	238	265	227	3.6	29%	74%	3.90	41	18	40	4.8	9.1	1.9	14%	1.4	-0.8	54	$5
Consist	C	1st Half		2	1	1	16	12	5.73	1.85	300			3.6	35%	70%	5.16	36	26	38	5.7	6.9	1.2	10%	1.1	-3.1	-17	$0
LIMA Plan	A	2nd Half		0	2	5	24	28	3.37	1.12	191			3.6	23%	78%	3.15	46	11	43	4.1	10.5	2.5	17%	1.5	2.3	102	$4
Rand Var	+1	11	Proj	4	3	3	65	70	3.72	1.24	227			3.9	29%	73%	3.42	43	18	39	3.7	9.7	2.6	11%	1.0	7.0	95	$8

1H is explained by early-season shoulder tendinitis. 2H shows skills are intact and closer-worthy when health cooperates. Whether or not he ever sees a 9th inning with a game on the line, still a classic LIMA gem.

Young,Chris				W	L	Sv	IP	K	ERA	WHIP	OBA	vL	vR	BF/G	H%	S%	xERA	G	L	F	Ctl	Dom	Cmd	hr/f	hr/9	RAR	BPV	R$
RH SP	31	06	SD	11	5	0	179	164	3.47	1.13	210	175	234	23.4	24%	77%	4.39	25	18	56	3.5	8.2	2.4	10%	1.4	22.5	58	$22
Ht/Wt	82 278	07	SD	9	8	0	173	167	3.12	1.10	195	231	155	23.2	25%	72%	4.16	29	16	54	3.7	8.7	2.3	4%	0.5	27.8	62	$22
Type	Pwr xFB	08	SD	7	6	0	102	93	3.96	1.29	226	259	189	23.9	27%	73%	4.62	22	25	53	4.2	8.2	1.9	9%	1.1	3.9	33	$9
Health	F	09	SD	4	6	0	76	50	5.21	1.45	246	210	297	23.7	26%	67%	5.41	30	18	52	4.7	5.9	1.3	10%	1.4	-9.6	-13	$2
PT/Exp	C	10	SD	2	0	0	20	15	0.90	1.05	151	167	130	19.9	18%	95%	4.64	29	16	55	5.0	6.8	1.4	4%	0.5	7.7	-5	$4
Consist	B	1st Half		1	0	0	6	5	0.00	0.67	56			21.5	8%	100%	3.82	27	20	53	4.5	7.5	1.7	0%	0.0	3.0	18	$2
LIMA Plan	C+	2nd Half		1	0	0	14	10	1.29	1.21	186			19.3	21%	94%	4.97	30	15	55	5.1	6.4	1.3	5%	0.6	4.7	-15	$2
Rand Var	-5	11	Proj	7	6	0	116	99	4.11	1.34	238			23.5	28%	73%	4.67	27	19	54	4.1	7.7	1.9	8%	1.2	-7.5	33	$8

Since skull fracture in May '08, has had a rash of arm injuries (forearm, elbow, shoulder last two years). PRO: extreme FB% plays well in PETCO (career 2.85 ERA). CON: rising Ctl. UP: See 2006-07

Zambrano,Carlos				W	L	Sv	IP	K	ERA	WHIP	OBA	vL	vR	BF/G	H%	S%	xERA	G	L	F	Ctl	Dom	Cmd	hr/f	hr/9	RAR	BPV	R$
RH RP	29	06	CHC	16	7	0	214	210	3.41	1.29	212	247	174	27.3	27%	76%	3.89	47	17	36	4.8	8.8	1.8	10%	0.8	28.5	53	$24
Ht/Wt	77 255	07	CHC	18	13	0	216	177	3.95	1.33	235	268	200	27.0	27%	73%	4.15	47	17	37	4.2	7.4	1.8	10%	1.0	12.6	44	$21
Type	Pwr	08	CHC	14	6	0	189	130	3.91	1.29	244	235	247	26.5	28%	72%	4.15	47	18	35	3.4	6.2	1.8	9%	0.9	8.4	44	$16
Health	B	09	CHC	9	7	0	169	152	3.77	1.38	245	258	235	26.0	31%	73%	3.98	45	18	37	4.1	8.1	1.9	6%	0.5	8.7	56	$12
PT/Exp	A	10	CHC	11	6	0	130	117	3.33	1.45	245	279	221	15.7	31%	77%	4.07	44	20	37	4.8	8.1	1.7	5%	0.5	11.0	38	$11
Consist	A	1st Half		3	6	0	56	53	5.66	1.69	305			11.7	38%	67%	4.03	43	22	36	4.0	8.6	2.1	10%	1.0	-11.3	66	($1)
LIMA Plan	D+	2nd Half		8	0	0	74	64	1.58	1.27	193			22.1	25%	87%	4.09	45	18	37	5.4	7.8	1.5	1%	0.1	22.2	18	$11
Rand Var	-3	11	Proj	9	9	0	153	133	4.12	1.42	248			23.7	30%	73%	4.08	45	19	36	4.4	7.8	1.8	9%	0.9	1.2	44	$9

Reasons not to buy into 2nd half:
- BPV OF 18!!
- H%, S%, hr/f anomalies
- Multi- year Ctl issues spiked

From 2002-05, he had BPV's in the 70s and 80s; his excessive workload has worn him down.

Ziegler,Brad				W	L	Sv	IP	K	ERA	WHIP	OBA	vL	vR	BF/G	H%	S%	xERA	G	L	F	Ctl	Dom	Cmd	hr/f	hr/9	RAR	BPV	R$
RH RP	31	06	a/a	9	7	0	162	74	4.78	1.71	336			27.8	35%	75%	6.89				2.6	4.1	1.6		1.3	-5.3	8	$2
Ht/Wt	76 205	07	aa	12	3	2	78	44	3.47	1.40	288			6.8	34%	73%	4.02				2.4	5.1	2.1		0.0	9.6	73	$11
Type	xGB	08	OAK *	5	0	19	85	43	0.88	1.14	222	280	198	5.1	25%	93%	3.39	65	16	19	3.0	4.5	1.5	4%	0.2	36.2	43	$19
Health	A	09	OAK	2	4	7	73	54	3.07	1.50	284	336	265	4.7	34%	79%	3.44	62	18	20	3.4	6.6	1.9	4%	0.2	12.5	67	$7
PT/Exp	C	10	OAK	3	7	0	61	41	3.26	1.35	240	317	213	4.1	28%	77%	3.84	54	19	27	4.2	6.1	1.5	8%	0.6	6.6	30	$5
Consist	A	1st Half		2	4	0	38	25	3.52	1.41	255			4.1	28%	78%	3.94	54	18	28	4.0	5.9	1.5	12%	0.9	2.9	30	$2
LIMA Plan	C+	2nd Half		1	3	0	22	16	2.81	1.25	212			3.9	26%	75%	3.67	55	19	26	4.4	6.4	1.5	0%	0.0	3.7	29	$2
Rand Var	-1	11	Proj	3	5	0	65	43	3.59	1.39	258			4.7	30%	75%	3.69	59	18	23	3.7	5.9	1.6	8%	0.6	4.8	43	$5

Why save opps won't return:
- extreme splits (.565 OPS vRH, .901 vLH)
- Yet to post 2.0 Cmd in majors
- GB bias and Ctl both eroding

Consistently xERA shows he is a pen asset, just not a closer.

Zimmermann,Jordan				W	L	Sv	IP	K	ERA	WHIP	OBA	vL	vR	BF/G	H%	S%	xERA	G	L	F	Ctl	Dom	Cmd	hr/f	hr/9	RAR	BPV	R$
RH RP	24	06		0	0	0	0	0	0.00	0.00							0.00											
Ht/Wt	74 218	07		0	0	0	0	0	0.00	0.00							0.00											
Type	Pwr	08	aa	7	2	0	106	86	3.22	1.21	237			22.0	29%	75%	3.26				3.1	7.3	2.4		0.6	14.2	84	$12
Health	F	09	WAS	3	5	0	91	92	4.63	1.36	270	279	263	24.4	34%	68%	3.37	44	24	32	2.9	9.1	3.2	12%	1.0	-5.0	108	$5
PT/Exp	D	10	WAS *	2	2	0	52	40	3.11	1.10	223	276	238	17.5	24%	80%	3.58	49	13	38	2.6	6.8	2.6	14%	1.4	5.8	79	$5
Consist	A	1st Half		0	0	0	0	0	0.00	0.00							0.00											
LIMA Plan	B	2nd Half		2	2	0	52	40	3.11	1.10	223			17.5	24%	80%	3.58	49	13	38	2.6	6.8	2.6	14%	1.4	5.8	79	$5
Rand Var	-3	11	Proj	7	5	0	149	125	3.93	1.28	254			20.8	30%	72%	3.65	46	19	35	2.8	7.6	2.7	10%	1.0	9.1	83	$11

1-2, 4.94 ERA in 31 IP at WAS. Returned from TJS in August, flashed good skills, headlined by xERA, Cmd, GBs. Still need to see him handle full workload post-surgery, but...
UP: 15 Wins, 3.00 ERA.

Zito,Barry				W	L	Sv	IP	K	ERA	WHIP	OBA	vL	vR	BF/G	H%	S%	xERA	G	L	F	Ctl	Dom	Cmd	hr/f	hr/9	RAR	BPV	R$
LH SP	32	06	OAK	16	10	0	221	151	3.83	1.40	253	260	257	28.1	28%	76%	4.92	38	17	45	4.0	6.1	1.5	9%	1.1	19.9	18	$20
Ht/Wt	76 215	07	SF	11	13	0	197	131	4.53	1.35	247	242	244	24.7	27%	69%	4.70	39	20	41	3.8	6.0	1.6	10%	1.1	-2.5	22	$12
Type	Pwr FB	08	SF	10	17	0	180	120	5.15	1.60	268	213	285	25.4	30%	68%	5.27	36	23	40	5.1	6.0	1.2	7%	0.8	-19.5	-15	$3
Health	A	09	SF	10	13	0	192	154	4.03	1.35	248	230	256	24.9	29%	73%	4.30	38	22	40	3.8	7.2	1.9	9%	1.0	3.8	43	$13
PT/Exp	A	10	SF	9	14	0	199	150	4.15	1.34	247	232	255	25.0	28%	71%	4.45	36	19	45	3.8	6.8	1.8	7%	0.9	-3.4	34	$10
Consist	B	1st Half		7	4	0	110	74	3.75	1.25	240			27.1	28%	71%	4.35	39	18	44	3.3	6.0	1.9	5%	0.7	3.6	37	$8
LIMA Plan	D+	2nd Half		2	10	0	89	76	4.65	1.46	255			22.9	30%	71%	4.56	33	20	47	4.4	7.7	1.7	10%	1.2	-7.0	29	$2
Rand Var	-1	11	Proj	11	13	0	189	143	4.34	1.41	252			24.7	29%	72%	4.59	36	20	43	4.1	6.8	1.7	9%	1.1	-10.3	26	$10

PRO: Held on to 2009's skills rebound; 2H Dom gain.
CON: Ugly combo of poor Ctl and too many FBs in 2H, still can't find the right side of 2.0 Cmd line.
OAK heyday isn't coming back.

Zumaya,Joel				W	L	Sv	IP	K	ERA	WHIP	OBA	vL	vR	BF/G	H%	S%	xERA	G	L	F	Ctl	Dom	Cmd	hr/f	hr/9	RAR	BPV	R$
RH RP	26	06	DET	6	3	1	83	97	1.95	1.18	193	183	188	5.5	27%	87%	3.66	34	21	45	4.5	10.5	2.3	7%	0.6	26.7	78	$15
Ht/Wt	75 210	07	DET	2	3	1	34	27	4.27	1.19	195	271	135	4.9	23%	65%	4.56	36	16	48	4.5	7.2	1.6	7%	0.8	1.0	22	$4
Type	Pwr xFB	08	DET	0	2	1	23	22	3.48	1.97	268	161	317	5.4	32%	86%	5.76	40	20	40	8.5	8.5	1.0	11%	1.2	2.5	-58	$0
Health	F	09	DET	3	3	1	31	30	4.94	1.81	280	344	206	5.1	34%	76%	5.44	34	14	52	6.4	8.7	1.4	11%	1.5	-1.8	-3	$1
PT/Exp	D	10	DET	2	1	1	38	34	2.58	1.12	229	215	240	5.0	30%	76%	3.70	37	16	47	2.6	8.0	3.1	2%	0.2	7.3	89	$5
Consist	C	1st Half		2	1	1	38	34	2.58	1.12	229			5.0	30%	76%	3.70	37	16	47	2.6	8.0	3.1	2%	0.2	7.3	89	$5
LIMA Plan	C+	2nd Half		0	0	0	0	0	0.00	0.00							0.00											
Rand Var	-4	11	Proj	3	3	0	44	38	3.72	1.40	255			5.2	30%	77%	4.35	37	17	46	3.9	7.9	2.0	9%	1.0	-0.3	50	$4

Head, shoulders, knees and toes? No, just finger, elbow and shoulder surgeries in last 4 years. Risk and reward easily evident here: skills are tantalizing, but can't justify buying until we see a healthy season from him.

ANDY ANDRES

Batter Support Charts

The following expanded charts contain these sections:

- Consistency
- Power Skills
- Speed Skills

Consistency

For this section, we use the Base Performance Value (BPV) gauge. This measures walk rate, contact rate, power and speed. BPV levels of 50 or above in a given week are defined as "DOMinating" weeks. Levels less than zero are defined as "DISaster" weeks. By comparing the DOM and DIS levels in individual weeks, we can analyze batters , both in their skill and consistency.

This section includes:

1. Three years of data for all batters who had at least five weeks of stats in 2010
2. Base Performance Value for the year (BPV)
3. Total number of weeks he accumulated stats (#Wks)
4. Domination and Disaster percentages (DOM, DIS)

In the power and speed sections of the chart, the metrics form a kind of funnel that guides us toward a more informed projection via a series of questions.

Power

1. **CT%:** Does he make contact?
2. **xPX:** When he makes contact, does he hit the ball with authority? [1]
3. **FB%:** Does he hit the ball in the air?

Used as a trio, these skills summarize the elements of a player's power potential.

It's a prerequisite that he put the ball in play at a reasonable rate. From there, his power output depends on how often the ball is hit hard, and in the air.

Weaknesses in any of these areas for an existing slugger may be a warning sign, both for power output and potentially for playing time (see Manny Ramirez).

Similarly, strength in all three of these areas from a player who has not yet had a power breakout would strongly suggest a buying opportunity (see Ryan Raburn).

Speed

1. **OBP:** Does he get on base?
2. **Spd:** Is he fast enough to steal bases? Should he (or his manager) consider attempting a steal? [2]
3. **SBO:** Does he attempt to steal bases?
4. **SB%:** When he attempts, what is his rate of success?

Again, the combination of these metrics can paint a compelling picture.

A player with a history of high stolen base totals but weakness in one (or more) of these areas may indicate that his steals totals are at risk going forward (see Torii Hunter).

Similarly, a player who does not have a history of high stolen base totals, but appears to be strong (or improving) in these areas, may be a candidate for a stolen base surge (see Stephen Drew).

[1] For more information on the new xPX gauge, see page 60.

[2] For more information on the new Spd gauge, see page 62.

BATTER SUPPORT SKILLS

		CONSISTENCY			POWER			SPEED			
Name	Yr	#Wk	DOM	DIS	ct%	xPX	FB	OB	Sp	SBO	SB%
Abreu,Bobby	08	27	59%	15%	82%	98	30%	371	73	17%	67%
	09	27	44%	33%	80%	132	33%	394	86	18%	79%
	10	27	59%	19%	77%	143	36%	353	71	20%	71%
Abreu,Tony	09	3	33%	67%	0%	0	0%	319	77	0%	50%
	10	22	23%	68%	79%	49	33%	269	69	7%	75%
Allen,Brandon	09	7	43%	57%	81%	18	39%	316	62	5%	71%
	10	6	33%	67%	80%	14	42%	321	68	12%	64%
Alvarez,Pedro	10	16	38%	50%	71%	78	40%	319	60	5%	38%
Anderson,Garret	08	27	33%	22%	86%	81	36%	328	80	7%	64%
	09	26	35%	23%	85%	110	38%	306	47	1%	100%
	10	18	28%	61%	78%	94	38%	206	74	4%	100%
Andrus,Elvis	09	27	37%	37%	84%	57	23%	323	136	28%	85%
	10	27	7%	48%	84%	40	20%	337	132	23%	68%
Ankiel,Rick	08	24	50%	21%	76%	133	45%	332	87	3%	67%
	09	25	20%	56%	73%	105	45%	281	82	9%	57%
	10	17	35%	59%	69%	82	33%	291	72	7%	75%
Arencibia,JP	10	8	13%	75%	85%	13	58%	265	64	0%	0%
Arias,Joaquin	08	7	43%	43%	90%	10	32%	291	194	22%	76%
	09	2	0%	50%	0%	0	0%	250	130	0%	87%
	10	23	13%	57%	82%	57	39%	280	141	3%	100%
Atkins,Garrett	08	27	41%	19%	84%	113	41%	330	88	1%	50%
	09	26	35%	50%	84%	101	42%	306	90	0%	0%
	10	12	8%	67%	79%	52	42%	276	75	0%	0%
Avila,Alex	09	9	56%	33%	79%	30	43%	336	78	3%	67%
	10	27	19%	52%	76%	133	35%	312	45	5%	50%
Aviles,Mike	08	19	63%	21%	88%	53	33%	341	115	9%	78%
	09	7	14%	86%	78%	58	36%	210	91	5%	100%
	10	24	33%	33%	88%	67	38%	322	129	14%	74%
Aybar,Erick	08	22	36%	32%	87%	60	30%	306	150	11%	78%
	09	27	37%	30%	89%	65	33%	350	152	14%	67%
	10	26	27%	42%	85%	56	36%	299	148	21%	73%
Aybar,Willy	08	21	48%	19%	86%	82	40%	320	78	5%	50%
	09	27	41%	33%	82%	86	36%	330	65	1%	100%
	10	27	26%	56%	77%	90	39%	307	48	0%	0%
Baker,Jeff	08	26	38%	46%	72%	141	33%	326	92	6%	100%
	09	19	32%	47%	77%	113	35%	340	112	2%	100%
	10	27	41%	37%	76%	100	36%	324	99	2%	100%
Baker,John	08	13	69%	15%	79%	42	26%	361	81	2%	33%
	09	27	33%	37%	76%	98	31%	343	60	0%	0%
	10	6	0%	50%	77%	45	25%	299	91	0%	0%
Baldelli,Rocco	08	8	50%	38%	69%	113	36%	322	84	0%	0%
	09	24	33%	54%	75%	118	36%	304	121	3%	100%
	10	5	40%	60%	77%	46	37%	234	98	10%	100%
Barajas,Rod	08	24	50%	33%	83%	109	46%	284	45	0%	0%
	09	27	41%	37%	82%	142	57%	261	32	1%	100%
	10	23	39%	48%	83%	138	66%	270	44	0%	0%
Bard,Josh	08	16	25%	50%	86%	59	31%	276	40	0%	0%
	09	25	32%	40%	81%	92	41%	278	39	1%	0%
	10	15	33%	60%	78%	59	46%	249	48	0%	0%
Barmes,Clint	08	23	48%	17%	82%	93	49%	320	116	19%	76%
	09	26	50%	31%	78%	114	49%	286	86	20%	55%
	10	27	37%	52%	83%	102	49%	299	55	5%	60%
Bartlett,Jason	08	24	38%	29%	85%	66	30%	319	122	21%	77%
	09	24	58%	25%	82%	111	39%	386	138	23%	81%
	10	24	29%	29%	82%	84	34%	320	99	13%	65%
Barton,Daric	08	27	33%	41%	78%	90	46%	322	115	2%	67%
	09	13	54%	23%	86%	47	48%	326	78	3%	32%
	10	27	48%	26%	82%	98	39%	393	104	5%	70%
Bautista,Jose	08	27	30%	48%	75%	96	39%	312	83	2%	50%
	09	27	22%	48%	75%	121	42%	344	115	4%	100%
	10	27	81%	15%	80%	180	54%	371	85	7%	82%
Bay,Jason	08	27	59%	7%	76%	155	46%	374	127	6%	100%
	09	27	67%	26%	69%	181	49%	378	91	10%	81%
	10	17	41%	47%	74%	159	45%	342	141	10%	100%
Beckham,Gord	09	19	58%	32%	84%	94	43%	342	76	9%	69%
	10	26	42%	46%	79%	97	37%	310	92	9%	40%
Belliard,Ronnie	08	20	50%	25%	80%	114	35%	366	49	6%	60%
	09	26	35%	46%	79%	120	36%	327	70	4%	100%
	10	23	26%	48%	78%	91	40%	294	72	10%	50%
Bell,Josh	10	14	7%	86%	76%	31	26%	269	75	9%	25%
Beltran,Carlos	08	27	63%	11%	84%	106	33%	378	92	15%	89%
	09	17	47%	6%	86%	110	35%	414	101	11%	92%
	10	12	42%	17%	82%	140	39%	344	91	6%	75%
Beltre,Adrian	08	25	44%	16%	84%	131	39%	327	52	7%	80%
	09	21	29%	29%	84%	106	38%	295	71	15%	87%
	10	26	65%	8%	86%	145	40%	364	43	2%	67%
Berkman,Lance	08	27	63%	11%	81%	132	39%	417	80	11%	82%
	09	25	72%	8%	79%	149	39%	400	58	7%	64%
	10	23	39%	52%	79%	120	36%	368	58	4%	60%
Bernadina,Rog	08	7	29%	57%	0%	0	0%	334	125	0%	71%
	09	1	100%	0%	0%	0	0%	400	98	0%	100%
	10	25	44%	32%	80%	94	39%	313	105	20%	85%
Betancourt,Yun	08	27	33%	30%	92%	73	40%	300	93	6%	50%
	09	24	21%	13%	91%	74	41%	277	102	6%	50%
	10	27	44%	26%	88%	92	42%	288	64	4%	40%

BATTER SUPPORT SKILLS

		CONSISTENCY			POWER			SPEED			
Name	Yr	#Wk	DOM	DIS	ct%	xPX	FB	OB	Sp	SBO	SB%
Betemit,Wilson	08	22	45%	32%	70%	152	33%	287	76	3%	0%
	09	9	44%	33%	0%	0	0%	259	53	0%	100%
	10	19	42%	37%	76%	114	45%	351	72	2%	50%
Blake,Casey	08	27	56%	22%	78%	123	40%	335	69	2%	100%
	09	27	52%	26%	76%	136	35%	363	100	5%	43%
	10	27	33%	48%	73%	119	37%	312	70	3%	0%
Blanco,Andres	09	16	38%	25%	89%	24	28%	305	59	9%	62%
	10	24	33%	50%	86%	79	34%	322	95	4%	0%
Blanco,Gregor	08	26	35%	38%	77%	38	26%	361	120	11%	72%
	09	6	17%	67%	0%	0	0%	280	106	0%	73%
	10	19	26%	47%	81%	41	26%	343	134	18%	79%
Blanco,Henry	08	25	32%	44%	82%	55	42%	325	85	0%	0%
	09	23	35%	48%	75%	100	43%	322	54	0%	0%
	10	23	17%	70%	80%	88	51%	277	62	3%	100%
Blanks,Kyle	09	11	45%	36%	71%	61	51%	328	50	2%	50%
	10	7	14%	57%	55%	101	45%	265	71	5%	100%
Bloomquist,Will	08	18	11%	67%	82%	18	24%	374	137	24%	82%
	09	27	15%	52%	83%	49	33%	308	162	26%	81%
	10	27	26%	56%	85%	82	35%	301	83	29%	62%
Blum,Geoff	08	26	35%	35%	83%	93	44%	286	80	4%	33%
	09	24	33%	38%	84%	81	46%	307	69	1%	0%
	10	22	32%	50%	84%	40	35%	318	78	0%	0%
Boesch,Brenn	10	25	36%	40%	78%	93	40%	320	96	8%	82%
Bonifacio,Emil	08	14	29%	43%	82%	12	23%	311	138	25%	60%
	09	27	19%	70%	79%	29	28%	303	152	23%	70%
	10	20	20%	55%	80%	29	26%	302	152	23%	79%
Borbon,Julio	09	10	20%	50%	89%	16	27%	337	178	28%	77%
	10	27	19%	48%	87%	37	31%	306	139	18%	68%
Bourgeois,Jas	08	2	50%	50%	0%	0	0%	284	101	0%	68%
	09	9	11%	56%	0%	0	0%	282	103	0%	78%
	10	16	31%	56%	89%	23	37%	305	102	35%	71%
Bourjos,Peter	10	10	50%	20%	84%	28	39%	273	173	31%	74%
Bourn,Michael	08	27	19%	44%	76%	55	29%	286	167	41%	80%
	09	27	30%	37%	77%	54	22%	353	188	38%	84%
	10	25	28%	52%	80%	58	23%	338	143	38%	81%
Bowker,John	08	24	38%	46%	77%	114	38%	296	110	3%	50%
	09	11	27%	27%	0%	0	0%	393	89	0%	56%
	10	14	43%	50%	82%	39	37%	292	78	4%	24%
Bradley,Milton	08	27	67%	15%	73%	136	34%	431	82	5%	63%
	09	24	33%	46%	76%	98	33%	364	70	4%	40%
	10	16	25%	63%	69%	103	45%	287	75	17%	80%
Brantley,M	09	6	0%	67%	90%	8	27%	325	109	30%	81%
	10	17	35%	47%	89%	34	32%	318	109	17%	72%
Branyan,Russ	08	13	54%	31%	69%	82	57%	345	50	6%	81%
	09	21	48%	24%	65%	153	50%	339	60	2%	100%
	10	21	38%	24%	65%	159	52%	320	54	1%	100%
Braun,Ryan	08	27	70%	15%	79%	147	44%	331	127	14%	78%
	09	27	59%	22%	81%	124	34%	376	116	14%	77%
	10	27	52%	15%	83%	118	35%	361	88	10%	82%
Brignac,Reid	08	2	0%	100%	0%	0	0%	265	100	0%	67%
	09	11	27%	27%	84%	17	43%	296	119	12%	43%
	10	27	22%	56%	74%	90	42%	302	106	8%	50%
Brown,Domonic	10	9	33%	56%	79%	24	37%	338	107	24%	64%
Bruce,Jay	08	19	53%	37%	75%	73	34%	329	92	12%	61%
	09	18	56%	33%	78%	154	49%	300	84	8%	50%
	10	26	50%	46%	73%	145	44%	354	111	6%	56%
Buck,John	08	27	41%	37%	74%	88	41%	297	70	3%	0%
	09	22	32%	59%	71%	109	45%	284	74	5%	50%
	10	25	36%	56%	73%	146	45%	308	64	0%	0%
Burrell,Pat	08	26	62%	19%	75%	154	45%	370	65	0%	0%
	09	24	25%	67%	71%	123	48%	316	60	2%	100%
	10	25	48%	40%	72%	144	49%	351	45	2%	0%
Butera,Drew	10	26	23%	58%	82%	60	41%	219	76	0%	0%
Butler,Billy	08	23	43%	39%	88%	67	35%	338	64	1%	0%
	09	27	48%	26%	83%	124	35%	362	53	1%	100%
	10	27	52%	19%	87%	120	34%	389	50	0%	0%
Byrd,Marlon	08	24	50%	17%	85%	104	33%	370	71	7%	78%
	09	26	46%	19%	82%	125	41%	323	51	10%	67%
	10	27	41%	37%	83%	97	30%	329	59	4%	83%
Cabrera,Asdrub	08	23	30%	39%	80%	60	34%	344	85	8%	50%
	09	23	52%	26%	83%	94	30%	362	115	14%	81%
	10	18	11%	44%	84%	63	31%	320	98	9%	60%
Cabrera,Everth	09	20	30%	35%	77%	56	23%	335	155	28%	76%
	10	22	18%	55%	75%	72	23%	273	102	30%	63%
Cabrera,Melky	08	24	25%	38%	86%	64	35%	298	88	10%	82%
	09	27	56%	30%	88%	83	30%	333	68	9%	83%
	10	26	35%	27%	86%	68	32%	318	79	6%	88%
Cabrera,Miguel	08	27	63%	15%	80%	123	39%	351	65	1%	100%
	09	27	56%	15%	82%	147	37%	392	64	4%	75%
	10	26	73%	12%	83%	177	42%	422	49	3%	50%
Cabrera,Orlando	08	27	37%	26%	89%	66	33%	338	86	13%	76%
	09	27	41%	19%	89%	70	36%	321	91	10%	76%
	10	24	33%	29%	89%	69	37%	303	73	12%	73%
Cain,Lorenzo	10	12	42%	33%	82%	35	37%	342	163	22%	85%

BATTER SUPPORT SKILLS

		CONSISTENCY			POWER			SPEED			
Name	Yr	#Wk	DOM	DIS	ct%	xPX	FB	OB	Sp	SBO	SB%
Cairo,Miguel	08	26	19%	50%	86%	59	31%	305	113	12%	71%
	09	12	25%	50%	87%	15	45%	256	115	9%	88%
	10	26	31%	42%	85%	84	31%	346	73	7%	100%
Callaspo,Alb	08	20	30%	35%	93%	49	28%	362	124	4%	67%
	09	27	56%	11%	91%	100	42%	358	113	2%	67%
	10	27	44%	11%	93%	72	38%	304	87	6%	63%
Cameron,Mike	08	23	43%	22%	68%	148	46%	325	91	20%	77%
	09	27	41%	26%	71%	138	48%	341	97	7%	70%
	10	13	38%	54%	73%	179	55%	318	110	2%	0%
Cano,Robinson	08	27	41%	33%	89%	87	33%	302	90	4%	33%
	09	27	63%	19%	90%	97	33%	351	82	8%	42%
	10	27	59%	19%	88%	133	36%	376	81	3%	60%
Cantu,Jorge	08	27	56%	26%	82%	115	45%	320	81	6%	75%
	09	26	46%	15%	86%	114	43%	342	69	3%	75%
	10	27	33%	41%	80%	102	39%	299	59	0%	0%
Carroll,Jamey	08	26	38%	42%	81%	75	27%	341	152	9%	70%
	09	21	33%	57%	80%	60	30%	350	113	6%	67%
	10	27	22%	44%	82%	45	26%	381	116	12%	75%
Cash,Kevin	08	27	26%	63%	65%	101	32%	313	68	0%	0%
	09	3	33%	67%	0%	0	0%	250	82	0%	0%
	10	19	16%	74%	74%	51	35%	234	66	0%	0%
Casilla,Alexi	08	19	37%	26%	87%	37	34%	325	90	10%	67%
	09	21	24%	57%	85%	26	36%	295	159	24%	74%
	10	20	30%	55%	89%	45	37%	333	144	16%	86%
Castillo,Luis	08	20	30%	35%	88%	33	18%	353	95	17%	89%
	09	27	41%	30%	88%	32	19%	389	127	13%	77%
	10	20	20%	35%	90%	32	15%	339	127	12%	73%
Castro,Jason	10	15	20%	33%	83%	33	37%	296	85	2%	50%
Castro,Juan	08	15	0%	60%	84%	41	38%	259	79	0%	0%
	09	23	17%	57%	78%	70	43%	314	77	0%	0%
	10	15	7%	73%	81%	60	37%	241	61	4%	0%
Castro,Ramon	08	20	40%	40%	76%	105	40%	308	55	0%	0%
	09	25	36%	48%	78%	77	42%	284	37	1%	0%
	10	22	41%	45%	77%	98	38%	331	52	3%	100%
Castro,Starlin	10	22	32%	45%	86%	69	29%	351	132	17%	48%
Cedeno,Ronny	08	27	26%	44%	81%	55	30%	325	91	8%	80%
	09	24	25%	67%	77%	103	38%	250	137	10%	71%
	10	27	30%	41%	77%	82	35%	291	121	15%	80%
Cervelli,Francis	08	3	0%	100%	0%	0	0%	364	79	0%	0%
	09	16	31%	44%	83%	43	34%	290	88	9%	0%
	10	26	31%	54%	84%	60	34%	351	110	2%	50%
Chavez,Eric	08	6	17%	33%	80%	117	41%	295	55	0%	0%
	09	3	0%	100%	77%	120	43%	129	62	0%	0%
	10	7	14%	43%	72%	121	32%	286	53	0%	0%
Choo,Shin-Soo	08	18	61%	17%	74%	126	36%	382	106	10%	46%
	09	26	58%	23%	74%	137	36%	383	100	12%	91%
	10	24	63%	25%	79%	141	35%	392	69	15%	76%
Church,Ryan	08	18	61%	28%	74%	104	31%	344	86	5%	40%
	09	24	38%	42%	84%	99	33%	334	61	8%	75%
	10	26	31%	50%	70%	116	45%	255	62	3%	100%
Clement,Jeff	08	15	33%	47%	76%	64	40%	330	65	1%	0%
	10	14	21%	50%	75%	55	33%	252	58	10%	17%
Coghlan,Chris	09	23	39%	22%	85%	74	30%	388	110	11%	68%
	10	17	29%	47%	77%	73	25%	330	117	13%	77%
Colvin,Tyler	10	25	64%	28%	72%	153	40%	312	128	9%	86%
Conrad,Brooks	08	2	50%	50%	0%	0	0%	233	96	0%	75%
	09	10	20%	50%	73%	21	53%	276	81	10%	92%
	10	27	41%	48%	71%	142	52%	320	89	17%	83%
Cora,Alex	08	23	30%	35%	91%	43	33%	339	92	4%	50%
	09	18	39%	28%	90%	42	33%	314	76	14%	73%
	10	20	30%	50%	91%	34	31%	253	91	13%	80%
Counsell,Craig	08	27	30%	59%	83%	66	30%	347	95	5%	75%
	09	27	44%	26%	87%	61	35%	352	121	6%	43%
	10	27	33%	56%	86%	53	39%	320	70	3%	50%
Craig,Allen	10	13	38%	46%	83%	40	39%	302	74	2%	48%
Crawford,Carl	08	21	33%	43%	86%	63	30%	319	136	26%	78%
	09	26	50%	27%	84%	84	29%	359	130	41%	79%
	10	27	56%	19%	83%	104	36%	356	145	34%	82%
Crisp,Coco	08	28	54%	32%	84%	85	39%	346	105	25%	74%
	09	10	50%	30%	87%	94	34%	335	148	28%	87%
	10	14	64%	21%	83%	105	37%	347	127	41%	91%
Crosby,Bobby	08	27	33%	33%	83%	83	36%	299	80	7%	70%
	09	26	31%	35%	82%	105	40%	294	100	5%	67%
	10	19	26%	68%	77%	64	35%	292	75	7%	0%
Crowe,Trevor	09	19	32%	47%	82%	33	27%	311	113	25%	70%
	10	22	45%	41%	84%	60	29%	283	101	24%	76%
Cruz,Nelson	08	6	83%	0%	79%	32	38%	357	101	21%	67%
	09	25	44%	20%	74%	158	46%	331	77	21%	83%
	10	21	52%	24%	80%	157	45%	378	86	19%	81%
Cuddyer,M	08	15	40%	47%	84%	81	33%	318	110	9%	83%
	09	27	59%	30%	80%	129	40%	336	95	5%	86%
	10	27	56%	19%	85%	98	33%	334	89	6%	70%
Cunningham,A	08	4	50%	0%	79%	19	52%	340	117	15%	71%
	09	8	0%	75%	82%	16	38%	285	92	15%	62%
	10	13	46%	38%	79%	42	39%	278	95	17%	20%

BATTER SUPPORT SKILLS

		CONSISTENCY			POWER			SPEED			
Name	Yr	#Wk	DOM	DIS	ct%	xPX	FB	OB	Sp	SBO	SB%
Cust,Jack	08	28	54%	18%	59%	166	39%	376	49	0%	0%
	09	27	26%	44%	64%	167	43%	356	54	3%	80%
	10	22	32%	45%	66%	112	39%	374	45	2%	50%
Damon,Johnny	08	25	44%	16%	85%	68	34%	375	130	20%	78%
	09	27	67%	15%	82%	97	42%	364	115	7%	100%
	10	27	44%	30%	83%	74	37%	354	121	7%	92%
Davis,Chris	08	15	67%	13%	76%	69	40%	339	75	7%	67%
	09	21	19%	57%	67%	109	44%	311	86	1%	0%
	10	11	9%	64%	76%	19	36%	319	62	5%	72%
Davis,Ike	10	25	36%	28%	74%	127	41%	359	95	3%	60%
Davis,Rajai	08	25	28%	60%	82%	51	30%	278	194	72%	83%
	09	27	41%	30%	82%	79	34%	353	126	47%	77%
	10	27	41%	30%	85%	65	37%	318	116	44%	82%
DeJesus,Dav	08	25	52%	20%	86%	81	29%	363	120	12%	58%
	09	25	56%	12%	84%	101	34%	342	123	8%	31%
	10	16	38%	19%	87%	101	32%	378	113	5%	50%
Denorfia,Chris	08	10	40%	30%	83%	19	20%	287	105	17%	56%
	09	2	0%	0%	0%	0	0%	230	114	0%	58%
	10	21	29%	38%	83%	53	24%	315	108	17%	73%
DeRosa,Mark	08	26	50%	27%	79%	122	38%	371	85	4%	100%
	09	26	27%	42%	77%	126	40%	313	71	4%	60%
	10	5	20%	60%	83%	67	36%	265	69	9%	0%
Desmond,Ian	09	5	40%	40%	82%	30	34%	349	104	21%	77%
	10	27	30%	48%	79%	90	32%	306	107	17%	77%
DeWitt,Blake	08	23	30%	48%	83%	60	34%	337	94	3%	100%
	09	13	38%	38%	88%	14	44%	295	116	4%	50%
	10	27	22%	37%	80%	80	35%	333	91	4%	60%
Diaz,Matt	08	10	10%	60%	77%	47	24%	253	73	15%	67%
	09	26	38%	38%	76%	109	27%	372	108	15%	71%
	10	21	33%	38%	80%	114	33%	291	78	9%	75%
Dickerson,C	08	6	83%	17%	72%	31	45%	339	127	27%	70%
	09	21	33%	62%	74%	76	29%	371	134	15%	79%
	10	12	8%	75%	67%	47	21%	319	120	25%	91%
Dobbs,Greg	08	26	58%	23%	82%	126	45%	333	69	7%	75%
	09	24	21%	63%	81%	93	51%	297	67	3%	100%
	10	25	40%	56%	77%	94	53%	245	74	9%	73%
Donald,Jason	10	17	29%	59%	77%	56	30%	304	125	14%	81%
Doumit,Ryan	08	25	48%	24%	87%	115	35%	352	50	4%	50%
	09	16	50%	31%	83%	110	40%	300	68	6%	100%
	10	26	38%	42%	79%	123	43%	320	64	1%	100%
Drew,J.D.	08	23	52%	17%	78%	144	40%	407	118	4%	80%
	09	27	56%	19%	76%	142	41%	390	92	5%	25%
	10	27	44%	33%	78%	117	39%	338	83	3%	75%
Drew,Stephen	08	27	63%	15%	82%	131	43%	336	138	4%	50%
	09	25	44%	24%	84%	113	42%	323	151	4%	83%
	10	26	54%	31%	81%	115	41%	349	156	9%	67%
Duda,Lucas	10	6	50%	50%	82%	23	46%	307	52	1%	100%
Duncan,Shell	08	8	13%	50%	0%	0	0%	296	85	0%	83%
	09	5	0%	100%	0%	0	0%	307	72	0%	100%
	10	21	33%	52%	73%	63	56%	300	64	1%	100%
Dunn,Adam	08	27	74%	11%	68%	175	46%	382	45	2%	67%
	09	27	52%	22%	68%	164	49%	396	40	1%	0%
	10	27	52%	30%	64%	202	49%	350	50	1%	0%
Eckstein,David	08	24	29%	25%	90%	39	28%	330	66	3%	67%
	09	25	40%	20%	91%	37	34%	314	80	3%	75%
	10	24	29%	29%	92%	42	32%	309	66	7%	89%
Edmonds,Jim	08	26	58%	35%	76%	141	45%	342	70	4%	50%
	10	21	52%	29%	76%	209	43%	341	73	3%	100%
Ellis,Mark	08	23	39%	22%	85%	77	46%	315	101	13%	88%
	09	19	37%	26%	86%	77	39%	305	68	15%	77%
	10	24	33%	29%	87%	73	37%	351	72	9%	54%
Ellsbury,Jacoby	08	28	29%	25%	86%	55	28%	329	147	39%	82%
	09	27	56%	11%	88%	90	32%	352	145	43%	85%
	10	6	17%	33%	88%	42	35%	232	92	53%	88%
Encarnacion,E	08	27	56%	26%	80%	91	50%	332	74	1%	100%
	09	18	39%	33%	77%	114	46%	312	62	4%	67%
	10	21	48%	29%	83%	126	51%	309	50	1%	100%
Escobar,Alcid	08	4	50%	50%	0%	0	0%	324	107	0%	74%
	09	9	22%	56%	87%	12	31%	312	155	34%	73%
	10	27	30%	41%	86%	83	34%	286	148	11%	71%
Escobar,Yunel	08	25	36%	24%	88%	85	25%	361	104	4%	29%
	09	27	52%	15%	88%	93	30%	368	84	5%	56%
	10	24	21%	29%	89%	71	28%	331	77	5%	75%
Espinosa,Dan	10	6	50%	50%	78%	24	46%	291	120	27%	61%
Ethier,Andre	08	27	48%	7%	83%	110	32%	375	101	6%	67%
	09	27	52%	22%	81%	139	42%	350	82	6%	60%
	10	25	56%	28%	80%	150	40%	365	77	2%	67%
Evans,Nick	08	16	44%	50%	81%	26	33%	323	115	3%	67%
	09	9	33%	44%	80%	17	38%	258	90	3%	100%
	10	5	20%	60%	85%	6	35%	305	70	1%	0%
Feliz,Pedro	08	23	39%	22%	87%	93	37%	303	82	0%	0%
	09	27	33%	22%	88%	84	35%	307	68	1%	0%
	10	27	26%	44%	90%	68	43%	242	96	2%	50%

BATTER SUPPORT SKILLS

		CONSISTENCY			POWER			SPEED			
Name	**Yr**	**#Wk**	**DOM**	**DIS**	**ct%**	**xPX**	**FB**	**OB**	**Sp**	**SBO**	**SB%**
Fielder,Prince	08	27	59%	19%	77%	141	40%	366	35	3%	60%
	09	27	74%	7%	77%	184	43%	409	36	2%	40%
	10	27	52%	33%	76%	140	40%	383	13	0%	100%
Fields,Josh	08	7	0%	86%	65%	8	27%	290	107	11%	78%
	09	22	23%	73%	70%	74	41%	305	103	9%	38%
	10	5	20%	60%	86%	49	25%	348	64	4%	100%
Figgins,Chone	08	23	22%	26%	82%	43	30%	363	116	27%	72%
	09	27	33%	33%	81%	56	36%	397	133	24%	71%
	10	27	15%	63%	81%	31	32%	340	114	28%	74%
Fontenot,Mike	08	26	62%	27%	79%	126	38%	390	87	3%	100%
	09	26	38%	46%	78%	100	38%	301	90	5%	80%
	10	27	33%	44%	83%	81	28%	325	111	8%	20%
Fowler,Dexter	08	5	0%	100%	0%	0	0%	373	125	0%	58%
	09	26	42%	38%	73%	86	37%	364	156	27%	73%
	10	24	38%	29%	78%	80	33%	347	160	13%	67%
Fox,Jake	09	20	40%	40%	80%	91	47%	351	70	3%	67%
	10	26	27%	50%	75%	109	48%	248	95	0%	0%
Francisco,Ben	08	23	48%	26%	79%	112	48%	318	111	7%	69%
	09	27	52%	33%	80%	128	44%	321	82	22%	67%
	10	27	37%	37%	80%	143	45%	321	71	19%	100%
Francisco,Juan	09	4	50%	50%	0%	0	0%	304	105	0%	71%
	10	10	20%	60%	76%	9	29%	293	112	3%	49%
Francoeur,Jeff	08	27	30%	37%	81%	69	34%	285	73	1%	0%
	09	26	46%	27%	84%	114	41%	307	91	7%	60%
	10	27	37%	37%	82%	116	45%	295	86	10%	73%
Frandsen,Kevin	08	1	0%	100%	0%	0	0%	0	104	0%	0%
	09	9	22%	44%	92%	15	32%	269	95	6%	43%
	10	16	44%	19%	92%	27	28%	257	97	8%	84%
Freeman,Fred	10	5	20%	40%	84%	7	38%	336	80	6%	71%
Freese,David	09	4	25%	50%	79%	21	44%	311	70	2%	100%
	10	13	23%	54%	75%	109	29%	352	84	3%	50%
Fukudome,K	08	26	50%	35%	79%	80	30%	361	112	9%	75%
	09	26	54%	23%	78%	124	30%	375	108	10%	38%
	10	26	42%	35%	81%	114	35%	374	91	12%	47%
Furcal,Rafael	08	7	57%	14%	88%	85	32%	436	120	21%	73%
	09	26	35%	31%	85%	78	28%	335	112	10%	67%
	10	21	57%	33%	84%	83	33%	366	112	22%	85%
Gamel,Mat	08	2	50%	50%	0%	0	0%	337	91	0%	36%
	09	16	25%	69%	68%	42	51%	320	90	2%	100%
	10	4	0%	75%	79%	4	29%	325	66	3%	67%
Gardner,Brett	08	12	25%	58%	78%	21	35%	343	153	35%	81%
	09	21	33%	48%	84%	49	33%	339	167	40%	84%
	10	27	41%	19%	79%	41	28%	379	142	31%	84%
Getz,Chris	08	5	0%	80%	0%	0	0%	323	86	0%	73%
	09	24	33%	38%	86%	53	33%	316	111	26%	93%
	10	23	35%	30%	88%	35	30%	296	94	27%	88%
Giambi,Jason	08	27	63%	19%	76%	165	50%	354	66	2%	67%
	09	22	36%	18%	73%	159	51%	331	53	0%	0%
	10	26	38%	42%	73%	139	49%	370	35	3%	100%
Gillespie,Cole	10	16	25%	50%	83%	20	29%	295	114	15%	43%
Glaus,Troy	08	27	67%	22%	81%	135	43%	371	62	1%	0%
	09	4	0%	50%	73%	38	52%	270	68	4%	100%
	10	25	20%	52%	76%	166	45%	341	56	0%	0%
Gload,Ross	08	25	24%	44%	90%	72	32%	314	89	7%	43%
	09	27	44%	37%	87%	128	39%	328	106	0%	0%
	10	25	40%	32%	88%	118	47%	324	83	3%	100%
Gomes,Jonny	08	23	35%	52%	71%	90	56%	258	75	20%	81%
	09	20	65%	25%	71%	111	46%	315	58	9%	75%
	10	27	37%	41%	76%	135	50%	318	88	6%	63%
Gomez,Carlos	08	27	37%	30%	75%	66	39%	289	158	32%	75%
	09	27	33%	44%	77%	60	36%	279	138	30%	67%
	10	24	25%	50%	75%	51	36%	289	128	30%	86%
Gonzalez,Adr	08	27	52%	15%	77%	149	37%	357	57	0%	0%
	09	27	67%	15%	80%	171	40%	405	59	1%	50%
	10	27	59%	19%	81%	157	39%	393	46	0%	0%
Gonzalez,Alb	08	17	24%	71%	86%	27	29%	275	53	8%	49%
	09	24	38%	29%	85%	48	34%	316	97	4%	50%
	10	27	33%	48%	84%	44	31%	275	108	0%	0%
Gonzalez,Alex	09	23	35%	30%	83%	107	47%	275	53	4%	67%
	10	27	48%	26%	80%	122	49%	288	52	3%	33%
Gonzalez,Carlos	08	17	35%	29%	77%	53	33%	280	74	7%	71%
	09	18	56%	33%	80%	66	39%	360	143	22%	75%
	10	26	54%	31%	77%	148	37%	378	110	21%	76%
Gordon,Alex	08	24	50%	25%	76%	118	48%	347	73	8%	82%
	09	13	31%	46%	77%	82	42%	339	91	6%	100%
	10	15	27%	47%	76%	68	39%	333	67	9%	45%
Granderson,Curt	08	24	58%	13%	80%	118	41%	362	197	10%	75%
	09	27	56%	26%	78%	137	49%	326	131	15%	77%
	10	24	50%	38%	75%	156	47%	324	133	12%	86%
Griffey Jr.,Ken	08	27	44%	15%	82%	116	42%	350	67	1%	0%
	09	27	41%	30%	79%	116	47%	324	47	0%	0%
	10	9	11%	67%	83%	82	51%	252	74	0%	0%
Gross,Gabe	08	27	44%	37%	76%	103	43%	334	118	6%	67%
	09	27	33%	56%	72%	110	36%	327	84	11%	67%
	10	27	22%	63%	82%	93	34%	293	83	11%	83%

BATTER SUPPORT SKILLS

		CONSISTENCY			POWER			SPEED			
Name	**Yr**	**#Wk**	**DOM**	**DIS**	**ct%**	**xPX**	**FB**	**OB**	**Sp**	**SBO**	**SB%**
Guerrero,Vlad	08	26	65%	8%	86%	115	36%	363	80	5%	63%
	09	18	56%	28%	85%	113	40%	328	72	3%	67%
	10	27	52%	15%	90%	116	37%	339	50	6%	44%
Guillen,Carlos	08	22	59%	14%	84%	93	35%	375	100	9%	75%
	09	17	29%	29%	80%	123	43%	335	105	5%	25%
	10	14	43%	21%	84%	107	36%	328	73	5%	33%
Guillen,Jose	08	27	48%	41%	82%	108	35%	291	69	3%	67%
	09	16	25%	50%	82%	98	40%	297	69	1%	100%
	10	27	22%	41%	78%	115	39%	300	75	1%	100%
Gutierrez,Frank	08	27	48%	33%	78%	104	41%	296	106	13%	75%
	09	27	37%	33%	78%	118	36%	337	103	13%	76%
	10	27	26%	41%	76%	116	42%	306	110	19%	89%
Guzman,Cristian	08	26	31%	19%	90%	75	25%	342	114	7%	55%
	09	26	31%	50%	86%	51	29%	305	131	7%	44%
	10	21	19%	52%	83%	61	29%	304	123	6%	67%
Gwynn,Tony	08	9	11%	56%	0%	0	0%	260	135	0%	68%
	09	21	24%	38%	85%	39	30%	342	163	17%	74%
	10	23	26%	48%	83%	43	35%	303	120	25%	81%
Hafner,Travis	08	13	23%	38%	72%	107	33%	293	39	4%	50%
	09	22	41%	27%	80%	128	40%	351	63	0%	0%
	10	25	40%	44%	76%	114	38%	360	48	3%	67%
Hairston,Jerry	08	20	45%	25%	87%	55	41%	371	98	21%	80%
	09	27	41%	41%	86%	80	43%	308	85	12%	64%
	10	22	41%	32%	87%	79	44%	295	91	14%	60%
Hairston,Scott	08	22	45%	36%	74%	130	48%	308	130	6%	75%
	09	23	48%	17%	81%	108	51%	305	91	15%	79%
	10	25	20%	40%	77%	88	51%	285	80	10%	86%
Hall,Bill	08	26	38%	38%	69%	112	40%	290	81	12%	45%
	09	27	30%	59%	64%	126	43%	260	53	6%	50%
	10	26	42%	38%	70%	157	44%	315	62	12%	90%
Hamilton,Josh	08	27	67%	19%	80%	101	33%	369	85	5%	90%
	09	18	28%	39%	76%	124	42%	317	78	13%	73%
	10	24	75%	4%	82%	143	36%	408	84	6%	89%
Hanigan,Ryan	08	8	25%	25%	87%	13	28%	318	96	1%	100%
	09	26	23%	42%	88%	70	27%	358	89	0%	0%
	10	21	57%	19%	89%	72	31%	369	68	0%	0%
Hardy,J.J.	08	27	44%	22%	83%	107	36%	343	127	2%	67%
	09	25	36%	40%	81%	110	40%	292	109	1%	0%
	10	23	48%	30%	84%	97	34%	323	114	2%	50%
Harris,Brendan	08	27	37%	33%	77%	90	30%	326	102	2%	50%
	09	27	26%	48%	81%	78	34%	309	102	2%	0%
	10	11	9%	73%	82%	16	27%	210	77	1%	100%
Harris,Willie	08	26	35%	35%	82%	85	38%	341	133	14%	81%
	09	25	40%	40%	81%	107	47%	350	124	15%	73%
	10	27	30%	48%	73%	115	43%	288	88	13%	71%
Hart,Corey	08	27	52%	22%	82%	122	40%	299	101	25%	77%
	09	21	43%	29%	78%	123	42%	329	119	15%	65%
	10	27	56%	26%	75%	165	44%	337	99	10%	54%
Hawpe,Brad	08	26	54%	19%	73%	135	39%	379	93	2%	50%
	09	27	59%	22%	71%	144	36%	383	91	3%	25%
	10	24	50%	46%	71%	150	40%	338	59	4%	67%
Hayes,Brett	09	8	25%	50%	0%	0	0%	248	68	0%	100%
	10	14	43%	50%	75%	64	58%	236	95	0%	0%
Headley,Chase	08	16	38%	13%	72%	70	37%	326	78	3%	80%
	09	27	30%	37%	76%	117	38%	337	81	8%	83%
	10	27	30%	33%	77%	92	36%	326	94	13%	77%
Heisey,Chris	10	23	39%	43%	72%	97	45%	294	93	8%	59%
Helms,Wes	08	26	27%	54%	74%	106	38%	291	64	0%	0%
	09	27	19%	67%	75%	109	39%	313	73	4%	50%
	10	27	19%	56%	70%	95	37%	293	102	3%	0%
Helton,Todd	08	16	56%	31%	83%	107	38%	389	60	0%	0%
	09	26	62%	15%	87%	106	36%	420	82	0%	0%
	10	23	17%	57%	77%	128	43%	363	73	0%	0%
Hermida,Jer	08	26	38%	31%	73%	94	36%	315	99	5%	86%
	09	23	26%	57%	76%	97	39%	344	101	5%	71%
	10	17	29%	53%	77%	98	41%	267	51	2%	100%
Hernandez,A	08	7	29%	14%	84%	12	31%	247	110	14%	50%
	09	26	35%	54%	83%	42	25%	313	93	12%	58%
	10	16	31%	56%	86%	22	30%	244	82	14%	56%
Hernandez,Ram	08	27	33%	26%	87%	114	33%	305	50	0%	0%
	09	17	41%	29%	88%	101	32%	334	55	1%	100%
	10	26	42%	50%	84%	88	29%	357	65	0%	0%
Herrera,Jon	08	7	14%	71%	0%	0	0%	315	107	0%	79%
	10	17	18%	53%	88%	18	32%	311	133	7%	40%
Heyward,Jason	10	25	56%	36%	75%	108	27%	385	103	9%	65%
Hill,Aaron	08	9	22%	33%	85%	90	47%	317	83	11%	67%
	09	27	48%	11%	86%	127	41%	327	74	5%	75%
	10	25	56%	24%	84%	137	54%	262	62	4%	50%
Hill,Koyie	08	4	25%	75%	0%	0	0%	263	75	0%	50%
	09	26	23%	73%	69%	74	28%	311	98	0%	0%
	10	26	27%	69%	72%	84	26%	256	77	2%	100%
Hinske,Eric	08	27	52%	37%	77%	105	41%	329	54	13%	77%
	09	27	41%	52%	73%	120	45%	336	81	2%	100%
	10	27	44%	41%	73%	135	47%	334	38	0%	0%

BATTER SUPPORT SKILLS

		CONSISTENCY			POWER			SPEED			
Name	Yr	#Wk	DOM	DIS	ct%	xPX	FB	OB	Sp	SBO	SB%
Holliday,Matt	08	24	67%	17%	81%	100	33%	403	105	16%	93%
	09	27	52%	19%	83%	127	39%	389	90	11%	67%
	10	27	67%	7%	84%	139	41%	383	64	8%	64%
Howard,Ryan	08	27	56%	7%	67%	192	36%	339	59	1%	50%
	09	26	58%	15%	70%	209	41%	357	60	6%	89%
	10	26	38%	38%	71%	160	37%	346	92	1%	50%
Hudson,Orlando	08	19	42%	16%	85%	89	29%	367	100	4%	80%
	09	27	37%	30%	82%	81	26%	356	104	5%	89%
	10	24	42%	38%	82%	96	31%	335	123	9%	77%
Huff,Aubrey	08	27	67%	15%	85%	135	42%	361	71	3%	100%
	09	27	37%	37%	84%	110	36%	307	51	4%	0%
	10	27	63%	11%	84%	128	37%	380	89	4%	100%
Hundley,Nick	08	14	29%	36%	0%	0	0%	253	92	0%	0%
	09	20	30%	50%	70%	135	47%	313	93	9%	83%
	10	26	27%	50%	76%	126	40%	312	87	8%	0%
Hunter,Torii	08	27	56%	19%	80%	120	35%	338	90	17%	79%
	09	22	55%	27%	80%	140	36%	365	71	17%	82%
	10	27	44%	26%	82%	109	34%	350	59	13%	43%
Iannetta,Chris	08	27	48%	15%	72%	156	41%	370	73	0%	0%
	09	24	54%	42%	74%	161	52%	328	76	1%	0%
	10	22	32%	36%	78%	95	45%	313	60	2%	100%
Ibanez,Raul	08	27	48%	22%	83%	131	40%	358	73	3%	33%
	09	25	56%	20%	76%	185	42%	345	80	3%	100%
	10	27	52%	30%	81%	130	37%	353	83	4%	57%
Infante,Omar	08	20	45%	15%	86%	86	37%	339	122	1%	0%
	09	16	38%	31%	86%	85	41%	365	113	3%	100%
	10	27	33%	41%	87%	71	34%	360	141	8%	54%
Inge,Brandon	08	26	35%	31%	73%	118	46%	292	108	8%	57%
	09	27	26%	63%	70%	117	44%	297	106	5%	29%
	10	26	35%	50%	74%	124	45%	319	96	5%	57%
Inglett,Joe	08	25	44%	20%	87%	51	26%	355	145	11%	73%
	09	13	8%	54%	85%	16	42%	323	118	13%	61%
	10	27	37%	33%	76%	119	45%	325	148	3%	100%
Ishikawa,Travis	08	8	38%	25%	80%	22	26%	329	81	13%	63%
	09	26	15%	54%	73%	114	37%	323	124	4%	50%
	10	26	38%	46%	82%	122	32%	322	59	0%	0%
Iwamura,Akinori	08	27	30%	19%	79%	89	33%	347	154	7%	57%
	09	14	21%	21%	81%	94	36%	357	97	14%	90%
	10	14	43%	57%	81%	61	32%	294	89	6%	53%
Izturis,Cesar	08	25	16%	40%	94%	22	31%	312	147	24%	80%
	09	22	50%	41%	90%	30	30%	289	135	16%	75%
	10	27	19%	48%	89%	34	35%	269	103	13%	69%
Izturis,Maicer	08	19	37%	32%	91%	57	29%	329	112	15%	85%
	09	26	58%	23%	89%	85	38%	358	110	15%	72%
	10	15	60%	33%	87%	92	40%	318	94	18%	70%
Jackson,Austin	10	27	26%	48%	72%	100	27%	343	185	18%	82%
Jackson,Conor	08	26	46%	12%	89%	87	38%	369	114	7%	83%
	09	6	17%	17%	84%	67	41%	264	55	21%	100%
	10	13	31%	38%	87%	99	36%	335	76	11%	86%
Janish,Paul	08	11	36%	45%	0%	0	0%	261	91	0%	100%
	09	27	33%	26%	84%	73	44%	284	97	3%	100%
	10	27	33%	44%	85%	74	51%	333	87	7%	25%
Jaso,John	08	4	0%	75%	0%	0	0%	327	96	0%	67%
	10	25	60%	16%	88%	88	37%	372	104	3%	100%
Jay,Jon	10	21	24%	43%	85%	51	32%	336	99	13%	74%
Jennings,Desm	10	6	33%	50%	86%	9	41%	303	148	35%	82%
Jeter,Derek	08	26	42%	23%	86%	83	24%	356	127	8%	69%
	09	27	41%	26%	86%	92	23%	402	100	15%	86%
	10	27	26%	26%	84%	64	18%	333	111	12%	78%
Johnson,Chris	09	4	0%	100%	81%	3	19%	262	103	4%	67%
	10	18	39%	50%	78%	83	35%	328	74	3%	100%
Johnson,Dan	08	5	40%	60%	0%	0	0%	337	68	0%	0%
	10	10	40%	50%	79%	27	47%	333	54	1%	100%
Johnson,Kelly	08	27	52%	7%	79%	108	36%	349	89	11%	65%
	09	25	48%	40%	83%	91	43%	298	85	12%	80%
	10	26	58%	23%	75%	145	38%	369	96	11%	65%
Johnson,Nick	08	7	43%	14%	77%	134	39%	401	58	0%	0%
	09	26	46%	31%	82%	108	34%	417	81	3%	33%
	10	5	40%	60%	68%	84	41%	375	61	3%	0%
Johnson,Reed	08	26	38%	38%	80%	81	35%	341	89	12%	45%
	09	18	39%	39%	84%	96	33%	309	97	8%	67%
	10	24	29%	63%	75%	81	37%	280	126	9%	50%
Johnson,Rob	08	5	20%	80%	0%	0	0%	306	62	0%	46%
	09	27	30%	52%	77%	71	33%	285	64	3%	50%
	10	18	39%	50%	76%	62	36%	292	64	3%	50%
Jones,Adam	08	23	22%	22%	77%	89	35%	304	129	11%	77%
	09	22	36%	36%	80%	111	28%	328	97	11%	71%
	10	27	26%	33%	80%	104	37%	311	108	10%	50%
Jones,Andruw	08	15	13%	67%	64%	99	39%	254	62	2%	0%
	09	25	48%	44%	74%	153	50%	322	58	9%	83%
	10	26	50%	38%	74%	149	44%	337	56	14%	82%
Jones,Chipper	08	26	69%	4%	86%	112	33%	473	97	2%	100%
	09	27	63%	37%	82%	128	35%	390	84	3%	80%
	10	19	63%	16%	85%	123	44%	384	73	4%	100%

BATTER SUPPORT SKILLS

		CONSISTENCY			POWER			SPEED			
Name	Yr	#Wk	DOM	DIS	ct%	xPX	FB	OB	Sp	SBO	SB%
Jones,Garrett	09	15	53%	20%	80%	78	41%	331	68	18%	76%
	10	27	41%	33%	79%	124	39%	309	52	7%	70%
Joyce,Matt	08	18	50%	28%	73%	73	47%	323	121	7%	28%
	09	3	67%	33%	78%	17	50%	323	95	16%	69%
	10	16	63%	31%	76%	129	49%	358	88	9%	34%
Kalish,Ryan	10	11	45%	45%	83%	42	36%	333	95	29%	86%
Kapler,Gabe	08	24	58%	21%	83%	86	36%	339	101	7%	75%
	09	27	41%	37%	81%	118	41%	333	66	13%	71%
	10	17	29%	59%	81%	50	40%	274	70	6%	50%
Kearns,Austin	08	16	25%	44%	80%	95	32%	296	60	5%	50%
	09	18	17%	67%	71%	107	36%	320	83	4%	50%
	10	26	19%	50%	71%	111	33%	339	57	4%	80%
Kelly,Don	09	11	27%	45%	86%	10	31%	324	115	21%	86%
	10	27	30%	56%	82%	98	49%	268	94	6%	100%
Kemp,Matt	08	27	48%	19%	75%	119	32%	340	115	29%	76%
	09	27	48%	22%	77%	130	38%	353	113	24%	81%
	10	27	48%	33%	72%	154	39%	310	87	24%	56%
Kendall,Jason	08	27	30%	33%	91%	62	37%	313	88	8%	73%
	09	27	33%	33%	87%	66	36%	311	94	7%	78%
	10	22	18%	41%	90%	44	36%	314	68	15%	63%
Kendrick,Howie	08	19	37%	26%	83%	83	26%	330	79	18%	73%
	09	25	44%	20%	82%	75	27%	332	91	18%	72%
	10	27	33%	37%	85%	98	28%	311	74	12%	78%
Kennedy,Adam	08	27	30%	37%	87%	54	32%	322	100	9%	88%
	09	23	26%	35%	84%	84	36%	337	81	16%	76%
	10	27	37%	26%	87%	71	37%	322	94	16%	88%
Keppinger,Jeff	08	21	29%	24%	95%	51	28%	311	92	3%	75%
	09	26	35%	31%	89%	82	29%	316	108	2%	0%
	10	26	54%	12%	93%	86	30%	352	76	3%	80%
Kinsler,Ian	08	21	57%	5%	87%	125	43%	373	111	19%	93%
	09	26	69%	8%	86%	137	54%	323	100	27%	86%
	10	20	55%	25%	85%	96	42%	376	94	14%	75%
Konerko,Paul	08	24	42%	17%	82%	114	38%	338	63	2%	100%
	09	26	54%	23%	84%	147	46%	346	54	1%	100%
	10	27	56%	26%	80%	172	45%	392	63	1%	0%
Kotchman,C	08	26	31%	31%	93%	83	30%	319	74	2%	67%
	09	26	42%	23%	89%	87	29%	335	58	1%	100%
	10	26	31%	50%	86%	79	27%	278	61	0%	0%
Kotsay,Mark	08	23	43%	26%	89%	93	36%	329	95	6%	33%
	09	18	39%	28%	89%	93	34%	332	67	9%	60%
	10	27	48%	37%	89%	107	40%	306	72	5%	25%
Kottaras,G	08	3	33%	67%	0%	0	0%	302	80	0%	0%
	09	22	36%	50%	73%	112	48%	337	81	0%	0%
	10	27	52%	37%	79%	127	45%	310	88	4%	100%
Kouzmanoff,Kev	08	27	41%	22%	78%	111	39%	286	95	0%	0%
	09	25	28%	40%	80%	137	36%	291	48	1%	100%
	10	26	35%	38%	83%	112	40%	278	59	3%	67%
Kubel,Jason	08	27	59%	11%	80%	136	41%	339	96	1%	0%
	09	27	56%	22%	79%	145	41%	368	53	1%	50%
	10	27	37%	41%	78%	135	43%	322	63	1%	0%
Laird,Gerald	08	22	45%	23%	82%	84	41%	322	61	7%	33%
	09	27	22%	41%	84%	71	45%	294	81	5%	100%
	10	25	20%	48%	79%	110	42%	257	56	7%	75%
Langerhans,Ry	08	18	33%	56%	73%	39	31%	351	91	13%	80%
	09	12	25%	58%	75%	53	47%	304	74	16%	42%
	10	22	14%	77%	58%	64	43%	330	129	16%	75%
LaPorta,Matt	09	12	50%	25%	83%	40	42%	318	69	5%	44%
	10	24	38%	50%	80%	98	45%	318	70	1%	0%
Larish,Jeff	08	12	42%	33%	74%	16	37%	292	101	4%	40%
	09	9	33%	56%	73%	36	40%	341	101	5%	39%
	10	9	22%	56%	76%	17	30%	273	54	3%	68%
LaRoche,Adam	08	26	46%	19%	75%	131	43%	342	68	2%	50%
	09	27	52%	41%	74%	164	43%	357	71	3%	50%
	10	26	38%	46%	69%	178	44%	319	65	1%	0%
LaRoche,Andy	08	17	35%	53%	85%	49	35%	302	63	4%	80%
	09	27	48%	26%	84%	100	34%	322	80	3%	75%
	10	27	33%	59%	83%	85	33%	263	81	3%	50%
Lee,Carlos	08	19	68%	5%	89%	150	44%	368	45	4%	80%
	09	27	67%	7%	92%	128	44%	344	58	5%	63%
	10	27	59%	22%	90%	131	46%	290	48	5%	50%
Lee,Derrek	08	27	59%	22%	81%	120	34%	363	67	5%	80%
	09	27	70%	15%	80%	160	46%	393	73	1%	100%
	10	27	44%	41%	76%	155	38%	347	60	2%	25%
Lewis,Fred	08	24	46%	17%	74%	89	28%	353	160	20%	75%
	09	26	42%	42%	72%	88	27%	338	138	14%	67%
	10	23	35%	35%	77%	102	34%	326	118	23%	73%
Lillibridge,Brent	08	13	31%	62%	76%	21	44%	241	100	35%	73%
	09	16	13%	69%	76%	16	34%	282	102	25%	83%
	10	19	21%	58%	73%	30	39%	259	100	43%	74%
Lind,Adam	08	18	39%	33%	82%	73	30%	330	90	3%	76%
	09	26	65%	15%	81%	148	37%	367	50	1%	50%
	10	27	33%	37%	75%	142	40%	285	54	0%	0%

BATTER SUPPORT SKILLS

Name	Yr	#Wk	DOM	DIS	ct%	xPX	FB	OB	Sp	SBO	SB%
Loney,James	08	27	33%	15%	86%	82	34%	339	85	7%	64%
	09	27	44%	26%	88%	73	35%	359	68	5%	70%
	10	27	41%	33%	84%	87	32%	327	61	10%	67%
Longoria,Evan	08	22	50%	9%	73%	156	42%	340	79	6%	100%
	09	27	44%	22%	76%	155	42%	360	67	6%	100%
	10	25	68%	8%	78%	150	43%	373	97	12%	75%
Lopez,Felipe	08	27	41%	37%	83%	94	31%	342	92	11%	50%
	09	27	44%	26%	83%	95	26%	382	94	6%	50%
	10	23	26%	30%	79%	93	34%	310	76	9%	80%
Lopez,Jose	08	27	48%	19%	90%	88	36%	325	79	6%	67%
	09	27	56%	15%	89%	110	41%	300	51	5%	50%
	10	27	30%	26%	89%	87	38%	268	56	4%	60%
Lowell,Mike	08	23	52%	26%	85%	120	47%	335	63	4%	50%
	09	24	50%	21%	86%	96	41%	339	66	3%	67%
	10	21	33%	38%	84%	132	51%	311	55	0%	0%
Lowrie,Jed	08	17	47%	29%	77%	73	43%	340	90	2%	100%
	09	10	20%	60%	75%	79	66%	256	81	0%	0%
	10	12	58%	25%	85%	170	54%	378	78	4%	50%
Lucroy,Jon	10	20	20%	55%	85%	59	38%	299	78	6%	67%
Ludwick,Ryan	08	27	74%	15%	73%	176	47%	372	82	6%	50%
	09	26	35%	50%	78%	132	49%	323	72	5%	67%
	10	24	38%	46%	75%	134	45%	318	91	3%	0%
Lugo,Julio	08	16	19%	31%	80%	48	23%	353	92	18%	75%
	09	23	48%	39%	82%	85	38%	353	167	11%	100%
	10	25	0%	72%	79%	52	31%	293	148	17%	42%
Maier,Mitch	08	9	11%	56%	87%	8	30%	320	97	12%	66%
	09	26	23%	54%	78%	61	40%	330	114	11%	77%
	10	26	31%	46%	82%	71	44%	336	142	4%	60%
Manzella,Tom	09	4	0%	100%	0%	0	0%	273	122	0%	69%
	10	20	5%	80%	74%	49	29%	272	89	4%	0%
Markakis,Nick	08	27	63%	4%	81%	99	33%	403	90	8%	59%
	09	27	52%	22%	85%	126	41%	350	103	4%	75%
	10	27	44%	19%	85%	90	36%	370	116	5%	78%
Marson,Lou	08	1	100%	0%	0%	0	0%	374	92	0%	33%
	09	7	29%	43%	81%	18	32%	324	93	4%	75%
	10	19	32%	42%	81%	51	29%	265	89	15%	92%
Marte,Andy	08	24	17%	46%	78%	103	49%	265	92	6%	33%
	09	11	36%	45%	84%	48	53%	311	76	2%	100%
	10	24	33%	42%	79%	113	50%	299	114	7%	0%
Martinez,Ferndo	09	6	33%	50%	85%	25	38%	272	77	11%	80%
	10	3	0%	67%	79%	7	36%	255	75	4%	50%
Martinez,Victor	08	16	31%	13%	88%	66	33%	338	66	0%	0%
	09	27	67%	19%	87%	115	35%	382	67	1%	100%
	10	23	57%	26%	89%	119	42%	355	72	1%	100%
Martin,Russell	08	27	52%	19%	85%	85	30%	381	67	12%	75%
	09	26	27%	38%	84%	88	31%	340	75	10%	65%
	10	18	39%	44%	82%	77	28%	343	64	7%	75%
Mathis,Jeff	08	26	23%	58%	68%	89	53%	272	84	6%	50%
	09	27	19%	67%	69%	82	46%	278	90	8%	40%
	10	19	5%	74%	72%	65	48%	223	117	7%	100%
Matsui,Hideki	08	18	39%	11%	86%	96	34%	365	55	0%	0%
	09	27	56%	7%	84%	128	42%	363	66	1%	0%
	10	27	52%	26%	80%	127	42%	362	57	1%	0%
Mauer,Joe	08	27	63%	4%	91%	101	28%	419	95	1%	50%
	09	24	67%	13%	88%	125	30%	446	75	2%	80%
	10	27	63%	19%	90%	134	29%	403	75	3%	20%
Maxwell,Justin	09	10	30%	70%	68%	24	38%	299	149	35%	78%
	10	18	22%	56%	67%	35	49%	320	84	28%	68%
Maybin,Cam	08	3	67%	0%	72%	9	21%	358	200	22%	73%
	09	12	50%	50%	78%	30	28%	352	141	9%	62%
	10	16	25%	56%	74%	66	33%	308	150	14%	81%
May,Lucas	10	5	0%	100%	82%	6	50%	280	87	6%	49%
McCann,Brian	08	27	59%	7%	87%	126	43%	371	56	3%	100%
	09	26	58%	19%	83%	144	41%	346	50	4%	80%
	10	27	52%	33%	80%	151	43%	367	51	4%	71%
McCutchen,A	09	19	63%	16%	84%	80	39%	353	176	20%	81%
	10	27	63%	22%	84%	123	38%	364	143	24%	77%
McDonald,D	09	13	23%	62%	77%	28	35%	285	116	13%	73%
	10	24	38%	38%	74%	105	36%	331	100	12%	91%
McDonald,J	08	23	9%	70%	87%	74	43%	250	77	10%	75%
	09	27	15%	56%	88%	82	50%	263	93	7%	0%
	10	23	43%	43%	83%	104	45%	278	108	11%	67%
McGehee,C	08	4	0%	75%	0%	0	0%	288	77	0%	0%
	09	27	37%	44%	81%	145	40%	362	93	2%	0%
	10	27	41%	19%	83%	113	36%	339	72	1%	50%
McLouth,Nate	08	27	56%	22%	84%	130	47%	347	98	17%	88%
	09	25	56%	12%	80%	105	43%	344	86	17%	76%
	10	18	33%	44%	79%	80	44%	280	86	15%	86%
Michaels,Jas	08	27	37%	48%	77%	116	43%	291	68	4%	67%
	09	26	38%	54%	72%	167	48%	318	76	10%	33%
	10	27	48%	30%	84%	134	48%	298	65	0%	0%
Miles,Aaron	08	27	41%	19%	90%	45	25%	356	118	5%	50%
	09	19	16%	53%	86%	25	30%	220	81	13%	69%
	10	19	21%	42%	89%	23	34%	295	87	3%	0%
Milledge,L	08	24	38%	33%	82%	85	35%	317	88	24%	73%
	09	13	23%	54%	82%	47	38%	309	72	22%	68%
	10	24	25%	33%	84%	80	33%	327	94	8%	63%
Molina,Bengie	08	27	41%	30%	93%	108	47%	317	35	0%	0%
	09	26	46%	31%	86%	145	53%	284	35	0%	0%
	10	27	26%	44%	91%	104	48%	294	46	0%	0%
Molina,Jose	08	27	19%	59%	81%	74	33%	250	54	0%	0%
	09	19	32%	63%	80%	76	42%	289	70	0%	0%
	10	26	23%	58%	78%	129	35%	284	61	3%	100%
Molina,Yadier	08	26	27%	27%	93%	70	33%	351	52	1%	0%
	09	27	44%	33%	92%	77	29%	360	51	7%	75%
	10	25	32%	44%	89%	94	28%	323	40	9%	67%
Montero,Miguel	08	24	42%	38%	73%	132	41%	325	86	0%	0%
	09	27	52%	26%	82%	131	36%	352	79	3%	33%
	10	18	28%	39%	76%	142	43%	331	76	1%	0%
Moore,Adam	09	3	33%	0%	0%	0	0%	307	60	0%	50%
	10	15	0%	73%	75%	51	28%	248	78	3%	48%
Morales,Kend	08	7	14%	71%	88%	13	44%	317	58	5%	20%
	09	27	59%	19%	79%	166	41%	358	68	7%	30%
	10	8	50%	0%	84%	116	31%	332	47	2%	0%
Mora,Melvin	08	26	50%	15%	86%	104	37%	333	60	8%	30%
	09	26	19%	35%	87%	85	38%	312	59	5%	50%
	10	26	38%	35%	83%	85	38%	349	100	3%	67%
Moreland,Mitch	10	11	36%	36%	83%	45	38%	327	50	5%	72%
Morgan,Nyjer	08	14	29%	36%	84%	23	26%	297	133	45%	77%
	09	21	29%	29%	84%	46	26%	363	148	37%	71%
	10	26	27%	42%	83%	56	25%	308	155	35%	67%
Morneau,Justin	08	27	63%	11%	86%	107	38%	376	68	1%	0%
	09	23	61%	13%	83%	149	43%	364	56	0%	0%
	10	14	71%	7%	79%	194	45%	439	75	0%	0%
Morrison,Logan	10	11	45%	36%	83%	53	32%	375	105	2%	25%
Morse,Mike	09	8	38%	38%	81%	15	28%	315	78	2%	67%
	10	22	45%	41%	77%	123	38%	335	97	1%	0%
Murphy,David	08	19	63%	21%	83%	103	40%	325	102	9%	78%
	09	27	44%	41%	75%	106	43%	343	92	11%	69%
	10	26	58%	27%	83%	103	36%	360	89	13%	88%
Nady,Xavier	08	26	62%	8%	81%	120	34%	350	72	2%	67%
	09	2	50%	0%	79%	72	32%	310	86	0%	0%
	10	27	19%	63%	73%	103	33%	293	73	0%	0%
Napoli,Mike	08	22	68%	23%	69%	151	52%	370	96	15%	70%
	09	27	44%	33%	73%	145	43%	341	88	6%	50%
	10	26	54%	31%	70%	154	42%	303	43	6%	67%
Navarro,Dioner	08	24	38%	17%	89%	75	30%	347	54	3%	0%
	09	26	27%	46%	86%	64	43%	254	52	9%	71%
	10	18	28%	44%	84%	25	37%	289	52	4%	65%
Nava,Daniel	10	16	25%	63%	77%	38	45%	309	66	6%	57%
Nelson,Chris	10	8	13%	38%	89%	6	29%	297	95	11%	60%
Nieves,Wil	08	23	35%	57%	83%	60	26%	301	99	3%	46%
	09	25	16%	72%	80%	68	19%	311	73	1%	100%
	10	26	19%	50%	82%	83	31%	241	60	0%	0%
Nix,Jayson	08	6	0%	83%	0%	0	0%	297	92	0%	57%
	09	23	39%	39%	75%	124	48%	300	92	19%	83%
	10	26	31%	50%	74%	110	49%	268	86	5%	33%
Nix,Laynce	08	3	0%	67%	0%	0	0%	273	86	0%	50%
	09	26	50%	35%	74%	115	43%	290	58	2%	0%
	10	24	29%	58%	76%	140	37%	350	85	2%	0%
Olivo,Miguel	08	25	52%	36%	73%	111	44%	272	62	14%	100%
	09	26	38%	42%	68%	121	40%	284	73	10%	71%
	10	26	35%	46%	70%	112	40%	316	104	11%	64%
Ordonez,Mag	08	25	40%	4%	86%	102	36%	376	67	3%	17%
	09	27	30%	30%	86%	75	28%	378	69	3%	75%
	10	16	56%	19%	88%	114	32%	380	63	1%	100%
Ortiz,David	08	21	57%	19%	82%	144	45%	370	58	1%	100%
	09	27	44%	37%	75%	160	50%	330	55	1%	0%
	10	27	63%	22%	72%	173	45%	370	54	1%	0%
Overbay,Lyle	08	27	52%	22%	79%	109	33%	358	65	2%	33%
	09	27	52%	41%	78%	131	37%	374	41	0%	0%
	10	27	37%	30%	75%	136	39%	328	54	1%	100%
Pagan,Angel	08	7	29%	29%	80%	62	41%	353	104	14%	100%
	09	18	61%	17%	84%	108	38%	353	140	23%	67%
	10	27	41%	33%	83%	101	44%	340	125	28%	80%
Parra,Gerardo	09	22	32%	45%	82%	84	29%	351	112	13%	48%
	10	26	31%	54%	80%	88	29%	311	92	4%	75%
Patterson,Cor	08	27	15%	52%	84%	75	38%	238	89	37%	61%
	09	8	0%	88%	0%	0	0%	249	91	0%	64%
	10	22	45%	45%	78%	64	38%	316	109	33%	75%
Patterson,Eric	08	12	17%	58%	79%	15	43%	294	99	26%	89%
	09	11	18%	64%	84%	14	46%	308	138	31%	81%
	10	26	27%	58%	67%	136	51%	269	153	34%	92%
Paulino,Ronny	08	13	23%	62%	76%	63	38%	299	80	3%	0%
	09	26	27%	67%	82%	121	39%	341	91	1%	100%
	10	20	20%	45%	84%	92	40%	314	68	1%	100%
Paul,Xavier	09	3	33%	33%	0%	0	0%	339	85	0%	78%
	10	12	33%	58%	85%	25	36%	277	84	16%	59%

BATTER SUPPORT SKILLS

		CONSISTENCY			POWER			SPEED			
Name	Yr	#Wk	DOM	DIS	ct%	xPX	FB	OB	Sp	SBO	SB%
Pearce,Steve	08	12	33%	33%	82%	24	45%	274	67	15%	75%
	09	15	53%	33%	81%	50	43%	300	51	10%	28%
	10	4	25%	75%	82%	20	36%	356	91	15%	75%
Pedroia,Dustin	08	28	57%	11%	92%	96	36%	374	103	11%	95%
	09	27	78%	4%	93%	99	41%	370	99	14%	71%
	10	13	62%	15%	87%	106	39%	366	83	11%	90%
Pena,Brayan	08	5	40%	40%	0%	0	0%	328	55	0%	67%
	09	22	50%	27%	90%	46	28%	307	40	5%	67%
	10	24	21%	58%	83%	99	39%	306	35	5%	100%
Pena,Carlos	08	24	67%	13%	66%	172	50%	370	72	1%	50%
	09	23	48%	26%	65%	203	54%	348	59	5%	50%
	10	25	40%	32%	67%	154	41%	319	40	4%	83%
Pena,Ramiro	09	21	19%	57%	83%	31	39%	297	123	16%	82%
	10	27	4%	70%	82%	38	40%	256	141	21%	88%
Pence,Hunter	08	27	52%	19%	79%	106	34%	315	119	15%	52%
	09	27	44%	15%	81%	106	33%	347	126	15%	56%
	10	27	56%	30%	83%	103	32%	327	108	17%	67%
Pennington,Cliff	08	8	25%	38%	87%	9	46%	334	139	19%	78%
	09	11	36%	36%	85%	25	39%	296	112	25%	73%
	10	27	44%	41%	81%	76	43%	317	128	25%	85%
Peralta,Jhonny	08	27	56%	19%	79%	125	36%	329	94	3%	75%
	09	27	26%	59%	77%	85	31%	314	67	1%	0%
	10	26	35%	35%	81%	108	43%	315	78	1%	100%
Phillips,Brandon	08	24	42%	17%	83%	100	34%	309	125	25%	70%
	09	27	59%	19%	87%	110	33%	326	99	23%	74%
	10	27	56%	7%	87%	103	33%	324	113	17%	57%
Pierre,Juan	08	25	20%	44%	94%	21	23%	322	124	45%	77%
	09	27	44%	22%	93%	51	24%	354	158	35%	71%
	10	27	30%	4%	93%	28	23%	322	121	43%	79%
Pierzynski,A.J.	08	27	44%	41%	87%	101	38%	306	63	1%	100%
	09	26	42%	35%	90%	88	33%	331	69	1%	50%
	10	27	33%	22%	92%	87	36%	292	41	7%	43%
Pie,Felix	08	10	30%	40%	83%	19	34%	290	128	21%	55%
	09	25	32%	56%	77%	95	38%	330	147	6%	25%
	10	16	50%	44%	82%	87	29%	306	136	10%	71%
Podsednik,S	08	24	21%	46%	83%	66	24%	320	110	34%	75%
	09	24	38%	33%	86%	58	30%	345	143	25%	70%
	10	23	26%	35%	85%	63	31%	345	173	29%	70%
Polanco,P	08	26	50%	23%	93%	43	35%	346	104	5%	88%
	09	27	59%	26%	93%	57	37%	324	95	5%	78%
	10	25	36%	20%	92%	47	35%	336	92	3%	100%
Posada,Jorge	08	11	45%	27%	77%	96	40%	359	73	0%	0%
	09	24	50%	29%	74%	135	43%	364	63	1%	100%
	10	26	42%	42%	74%	131	38%	348	58	4%	75%
Posey,Buster	09	4	0%	75%	84%	8	31%	344	103	2%	0%
	10	20	55%	30%	87%	90	33%	361	87	2%	25%
Powell,Landon	09	25	40%	44%	74%	95	44%	299	48	0%	0%
	10	20	20%	65%	77%	70	46%	288	57	2%	100%
Prado,Martin	08	20	50%	35%	87%	109	35%	378	110	6%	75%
	09	27	48%	19%	87%	115	37%	358	85	3%	25%
	10	24	46%	25%	86%	99	31%	351	103	5%	63%
Pujols,Albert	08	26	85%	0%	90%	142	37%	463	54	5%	70%
	09	27	85%	7%	89%	163	46%	441	66	10%	80%
	10	27	81%	7%	87%	154	44%	414	53	9%	78%
Punto,Nick	08	22	32%	23%	83%	50	35%	346	105	20%	71%
	09	26	31%	46%	81%	38	33%	340	79	15%	84%
	10	21	19%	57%	80%	28	33%	314	75	11%	75%
Quentin,Carlos	08	23	83%	9%	83%	138	43%	374	72	7%	70%
	09	20	50%	25%	85%	149	47%	298	44	4%	100%
	10	26	54%	4%	82%	132	49%	318	61	4%	50%
Quintero,Humb	08	16	19%	56%	84%	43	29%	230	74	3%	0%
	09	25	24%	44%	74%	93	32%	268	54	0%	0%
	10	27	19%	70%	78%	55	34%	256	43	0%	0%
Raburn,Ryan	08	26	31%	35%	73%	103	39%	298	104	9%	75%
	09	25	48%	40%	76%	124	47%	345	105	14%	58%
	10	27	41%	41%	75%	134	44%	329	93	4%	50%
Ramirez,Alexei	08	27	44%	26%	87%	99	37%	315	114	20%	59%
	09	27	41%	33%	88%	78	38%	337	106	11%	74%
	10	27	44%	26%	86%	88	33%	314	112	15%	62%
Ramirez,Aramis	08	27	59%	15%	83%	131	48%	373	69	2%	50%
	09	18	50%	28%	86%	111	44%	374	73	3%	67%
	10	26	54%	31%	81%	154	57%	293	49	0%	0%
Ramirez,Hanley	08	26	65%	12%	79%	119	37%	395	134	24%	74%
	09	26	62%	27%	82%	112	42%	405	103	18%	77%
	10	26	54%	38%	83%	116	33%	374	101	24%	76%
Ramirez,Manny	08	27	70%	11%	78%	161	39%	423	71	2%	100%
	09	19	68%	16%	77%	150	42%	409	72	1%	0%
	10	20	35%	50%	77%	129	34%	402	54	2%	50%
Ramirez,Max	08	8	38%	63%	78%	20	50%	361	104	4%	50%
	10	10	30%	60%	75%	26	39%	320	80	0%	0%
Ramos,Wilson	10	8	25%	50%	85%	24	43%	264	69	3%	33%
Rasmus,Colby	09	27	33%	48%	80%	119	46%	304	98	3%	75%
	10	27	44%	41%	68%	137	49%	362	110	15%	60%
Reddick,Josh	09	9	22%	56%	78%	25	52%	295	129	13%	45%
	10	9	44%	44%	86%	10	43%	272	101	13%	33%

BATTER SUPPORT SKILLS

		CONSISTENCY			POWER			SPEED			
Name	Yr	#Wk	DOM	DIS	ct%	xPX	FB	OB	Sp	SBO	SB%
Reimold,Nolan	09	19	53%	26%	79%	81	37%	381	106	11%	82%
	10	11	27%	55%	83%	20	39%	291	74	7%	78%
Renteria,Edgar	08	27	41%	33%	87%	71	32%	320	105	6%	67%
	09	24	25%	42%	85%	79	31%	309	72	7%	78%
	10	20	30%	35%	82%	87	37%	333	117	4%	100%
Repko,Jason	08	6	17%	67%	0%	0	0%	284	123	0%	70%
	09	6	0%	67%	0%	0	0%	263	96	0%	71%
	10	15	27%	60%	77%	40	47%	284	89	17%	64%
Reyes,Jose	08	27	59%	22%	88%	77	33%	358	156	36%	79%
	09	7	57%	14%	87%	83	40%	358	136	27%	85%
	10	25	52%	20%	89%	73	40%	320	121	29%	75%
Reynolds,Mark	08	27	56%	22%	62%	147	45%	320	92	10%	85%
	09	27	63%	22%	61%	174	47%	346	83	22%	73%
	10	26	42%	38%	58%	156	55%	313	68	8%	64%
Rhymes,Will	10	11	73%	27%	92%	16	33%	319	136	16%	66%
Rios,Alex	08	27	44%	22%	82%	129	38%	337	101	25%	80%
	09	27	41%	37%	82%	111	41%	292	81	22%	83%
	10	26	54%	19%	84%	114	38%	329	94	33%	71%
Rivera,Juan	08	25	32%	44%	87%	100	48%	290	55	4%	50%
	09	26	54%	12%	89%	118	38%	333	68	1%	0%
	10	26	50%	35%	86%	105	39%	307	54	4%	50%
Roberts,Brian	08	27	63%	15%	83%	91	36%	379	109	26%	80%
	09	27	63%	19%	82%	112	42%	358	88	21%	81%
	10	12	50%	33%	83%	118	45%	352	86	19%	86%
Rodriguez,Alex	08	25	68%	8%	77%	145	40%	381	81	14%	86%
	09	23	57%	26%	78%	144	38%	395	60	10%	88%
	10	25	60%	28%	81%	148	40%	344	58	5%	57%
Rodriguez,Ivan	08	27	41%	37%	83%	77	24%	316	80	11%	91%
	09	26	31%	46%	78%	113	28%	280	74	3%	33%
	10	25	24%	56%	83%	80	21%	295	62	5%	40%
Rodriguez,Sean	08	15	27%	67%	77%	32	47%	311	99	8%	75%
	09	6	17%	50%	0%	0	0%	346	127	0%	80%
	10	27	37%	48%	72%	120	39%	294	90	21%	81%
Rolen,Scott	08	22	55%	27%	83%	106	44%	337	71	5%	100%
	09	25	56%	20%	87%	126	41%	365	76	6%	56%
	10	26	54%	23%	83%	138	44%	353	63	2%	33%
Rollins,Jimmy	08	24	54%	21%	90%	90	31%	345	115	32%	94%
	09	26	58%	12%	90%	102	41%	296	101	27%	79%
	10	17	59%	12%	91%	90	37%	321	99	18%	94%
Rosales,Adam	08	8	13%	88%	0%	0	0%	274	138	0%	86%
	09	22	23%	59%	82%	62	40%	315	117	6%	65%
	10	19	32%	47%	75%	76	34%	321	125	6%	50%
Ross,Cody	08	27	52%	19%	75%	133	43%	310	89	7%	86%
	09	25	52%	32%	78%	134	48%	312	69	6%	71%
	10	27	26%	44%	77%	102	34%	317	88	8%	82%
Ross,David	08	20	35%	50%	73%	131	37%	368	54	2%	0%
	09	22	41%	36%	70%	111	49%	376	58	0%	0%
	10	26	35%	50%	77%	130	41%	390	66	3%	0%
Rowand,Aaron	08	27	52%	33%	77%	97	32%	325	59	4%	33%
	09	27	33%	41%	75%	105	39%	302	76	4%	80%
	10	24	29%	54%	78%	102	37%	265	93	12%	63%
Ruiz,Carlos	08	26	27%	54%	88%	69	29%	313	63	3%	33%
	09	24	58%	21%	88%	103	39%	350	59	5%	60%
	10	25	56%	32%	85%	95	35%	392	67	1%	0%
Ryal,Rusty	09	8	38%	50%	78%	24	44%	307	109	7%	57%
	10	27	15%	74%	68%	110	39%	288	136	6%	0%
Ryan,Brendan	08	21	24%	57%	84%	35	28%	300	113	16%	78%
	09	25	52%	36%	86%	53	30%	333	147	19%	67%
	10	27	33%	37%	86%	50	35%	278	117	14%	73%
Salazar,Oscar	08	8	50%	38%	87%	24	40%	308	92	7%	69%
	09	18	39%	44%	86%	48	39%	352	86	3%	0%
	10	22	27%	36%	82%	98	42%	320	72	8%	33%
Saltalamacchia	08	19	53%	32%	66%	91	42%	345	73	3%	0%
	09	20	15%	70%	66%	105	41%	289	86	3%	0%
	10	6	67%	33%	79%	4	0%	287	78	2%	100%
Sanchez,Angel	10	15	7%	53%	85%	27	31%	301	141	5%	70%
Sanchez,Fred	08	27	33%	37%	89%	67	30%	297	100	1%	0%
	09	23	39%	43%	83%	59	31%	326	109	5%	83%
	10	21	29%	29%	84%	86	34%	341	83	3%	75%
Sanchez,Gaby	08	2	50%	50%	0%	0	0%	344	57	0%	61%
	09	8	25%	38%	0%	0	0%	321	52	0%	100%
	10	27	48%	15%	82%	149	46%	339	75	3%	100%
Sandoval,Pablo	08	8	63%	13%	90%	35	29%	350	85	1%	0%
	09	27	67%	19%	85%	121	36%	386	74	6%	50%
	10	27	44%	22%	86%	114	38%	325	50	3%	60%
Santana,Carlos	10	9	67%	33%	82%	68	44%	389	66	6%	100%
Santiago,Ram	08	21	48%	29%	86%	62	33%	390	146	2%	100%
	09	27	19%	56%	78%	101	35%	312	122	4%	33%
	10	26	15%	62%	83%	37	30%	326	120	4%	50%
Saunders,M	09	12	8%	67%	77%	18	39%	318	140	13%	69%
	10	22	32%	55%	74%	63	48%	287	96	13%	75%
Schierholtz,Nate	08	5	60%	20%	87%	15	24%	326	92	12%	66%
	09	25	32%	52%	80%	110	35%	306	91	6%	75%
	10	27	30%	48%	83%	93	37%	304	107	16%	44%

BATTER SUPPORT SKILLS

		CONSISTENCY			POWER			SPEED			
Name	**Yr**	**#Wk**	**DOM**	**DIS**	**ct%**	**xPX**	**FB**	**OB**	**Sp**	**SBO**	**SB%**
Schneider,Brian	08	26	23%	27%	84%	52	21%	340	55	0%	0%
	09	21	43%	38%	88%	85	30%	293	49	0%	0%
	10	23	30%	57%	80%	81	38%	340	86	0%	0%
Schumaker,S	08	27	33%	19%	89%	57	20%	358	104	6%	80%
	09	27	37%	19%	87%	48	17%	365	98	2%	50%
	10	27	33%	33%	87%	66	20%	326	76	6%	63%
Scott,Luke	08	27	52%	26%	79%	109	44%	331	69	3%	50%
	09	26	46%	42%	77%	143	43%	339	58	0%	0%
	10	25	64%	16%	78%	155	41%	368	56	2%	100%
Scutaro,Marco	08	27	37%	30%	87%	86	35%	340	95	5%	78%
	09	25	48%	12%	87%	98	44%	380	91	9%	74%
	10	26	35%	19%	89%	75	42%	331	89	5%	56%
Shoppach,K	08	27	52%	33%	62%	154	43%	330	61	0%	0%
	09	26	35%	54%	64%	129	37%	299	60	0%	0%
	10	20	15%	75%	55%	179	44%	287	71	0%	0%
Sizemore,G	08	27	63%	15%	79%	133	46%	366	91	23%	88%
	09	19	63%	26%	79%	131	48%	339	100	17%	62%
	10	7	14%	57%	73%	123	42%	263	100	21%	67%
Sizemore,S	10	12	33%	50%	76%	31	40%	307	84	3%	50%
Smith,Seth	08	17	35%	41%	84%	32	34%	348	96	8%	100%
	09	27	70%	30%	80%	119	42%	378	103	5%	80%
	10	27	59%	37%	81%	139	48%	313	94	4%	67%
Smoak,Justin	10	19	26%	47%	77%	95	39%	322	53	1%	100%
Snider,Travis	08	6	50%	17%	72%	23	29%	340	48	2%	67%
	09	15	27%	40%	72%	71	41%	347	65	7%	37%
	10	16	38%	25%	75%	105	35%	299	60	16%	67%
Snyder,Chris	08	24	50%	29%	70%	116	44%	346	50	0%	0%
	09	15	33%	60%	72%	130	46%	330	69	0%	0%
	10	25	24%	48%	71%	125	43%	318	55	0%	0%
Sogard,Eric	10	3	33%	33%	90%	4	0%	311	112	15%	43%
Soriano,Alfonso	08	21	57%	19%	77%	127	48%	343	68	19%	86%
	09	22	41%	36%	75%	115	48%	300	89	10%	82%
	10	27	59%	19%	75%	165	54%	320	89	6%	83%
Soto,Geovany	08	26	58%	15%	76%	143	41%	365	65	1%	0%
	09	24	38%	54%	77%	156	41%	320	45	1%	100%
	10	22	55%	36%	74%	187	40%	396	57	1%	0%
Span,Denard	08	17	47%	24%	81%	44	20%	381	116	26%	66%
	09	26	42%	38%	85%	45	28%	386	149	15%	70%
	10	27	44%	33%	88%	55	28%	328	118	16%	87%
Spilborghs,Ry	08	20	60%	30%	82%	75	24%	410	111	12%	64%
	09	27	52%	37%	78%	122	36%	308	108	17%	64%
	10	27	37%	56%	76%	132	35%	353	79	9%	44%
Stairs,Matt	08	27	41%	22%	73%	93	37%	335	67	2%	50%
	09	27	37%	52%	71%	140	42%	341	43	0%	0%
	10	24	33%	54%	68%	160	44%	309	57	9%	100%
Stanton,Mike	10	18	39%	44%	69%	91	41%	358	93	5%	75%
Stavinoha,Nick	08	8	13%	75%	0%	0	0%	298	91	0%	67%
	09	10	40%	30%	84%	27	49%	267	61	4%	100%
	10	24	21%	58%	81%	43	33%	299	70	0%	0%
Stewart,Ian	08	17	41%	41%	73%	73	44%	323	120	8%	60%
	09	27	48%	48%	68%	156	46%	318	91	10%	64%
	10	24	33%	54%	72%	134	41%	334	100	6%	71%
Stubbs,Drew	09	8	13%	38%	76%	43	37%	314	134	37%	79%
	10	27	52%	30%	67%	142	40%	327	157	26%	83%
Suzuki,Ichiro	08	27	37%	19%	91%	48	23%	358	188	20%	91%
	09	26	38%	31%	89%	54	26%	383	159	17%	74%
	10	27	30%	37%	87%	50	25%	357	130	23%	82%
Suzuki,Kurt	08	28	29%	18%	87%	68	36%	335	99	3%	40%
	09	27	63%	26%	90%	107	36%	308	70	8%	80%
	10	24	42%	25%	90%	94	41%	290	72	4%	60%
Sweeney,Mike	08	11	18%	18%	95%	73	41%	323	61	0%	0%
	09	25	48%	36%	87%	140	44%	328	65	0%	0%
	10	19	47%	32%	88%	97	45%	323	63	8%	100%
Sweeney,Ryan	08	26	31%	31%	83%	75	34%	354	94	7%	90%
	09	25	32%	40%	86%	92	31%	347	95	8%	55%
	10	15	47%	20%	86%	45	28%	346	94	2%	50%
Swisher,Nick	08	27	30%	22%	73%	121	45%	330	70	4%	50%
	09	27	56%	26%	75%	152	46%	371	56	0%	0%
	10	27	59%	26%	75%	168	45%	354	71	2%	33%
Tabata,Jose	10	18	39%	28%	87%	57	25%	338	151	29%	74%
Tatis,Fernando	08	19	53%	16%	79%	67	32%	332	89	3%	100%
	09	26	42%	31%	84%	106	34%	326	95	6%	80%
	10	14	36%	50%	71%	136	41%	254	66	0%	0%
Tatum,Craig	09	11	18%	45%	0%	0	0%	251	61	0%	0%
	10	23	13%	61%	82%	68	27%	349	74	3%	100%
Teagarden,T	08	6	67%	17%	71%	38	50%	278	109	3%	50%
	09	27	33%	52%	62%	116	41%	269	107	0%	0%
	10	14	21%	71%	62%	28	46%	256	102	0%	0%
Teahen,Mark	08	27	41%	37%	77%	100	31%	311	102	5%	57%
	09	26	31%	42%	77%	93	29%	319	90	7%	89%
	10	18	39%	39%	74%	88	30%	329	102	12%	38%
Teixeira,Mark	08	27	70%	7%	84%	133	36%	408	74	1%	100%
	09	27	63%	15%	81%	163	44%	375	69	1%	100%
	10	27	67%	22%	80%	155	45%	356	54	1%	0%

BATTER SUPPORT SKILLS

		CONSISTENCY			POWER			SPEED			
Name	**Yr**	**#Wk**	**DOM**	**DIS**	**ct%**	**xPX**	**FB**	**OB**	**Sp**	**SBO**	**SB%**
Tejada,Miguel	08	27	37%	26%	89%	96	29%	309	62	9%	50%
	09	27	52%	15%	92%	104	31%	333	53	4%	71%
	10	27	26%	30%	89%	85	32%	302	40	1%	100%
Tejada,Ruben	10	19	37%	47%	85%	38	36%	282	88	8%	33%
Thames,M	08	27	59%	30%	70%	146	51%	294	71	5%	0%
	09	19	42%	53%	72%	115	47%	315	83	2%	0%
	10	24	29%	63%	71%	167	52%	346	63	0%	0%
Theriot,Ryan	08	27	44%	19%	90%	49	20%	384	139	15%	63%
	09	27	30%	41%	85%	66	30%	340	134	16%	68%
	10	27	19%	44%	87%	42	26%	317	133	16%	69%
Thole,Josh	09	6	50%	17%	92%	14	20%	352	80	9%	58%
	10	16	31%	31%	88%	45	33%	327	104	1%	100%
Thome,Jim	08	27	67%	7%	71%	157	42%	360	32	1%	100%
	09	27	33%	56%	66%	156	36%	369	37	0%	0%
	10	27	59%	37%	70%	201	38%	411	55	0%	0%
Torrealba,Yorv	08	22	36%	36%	81%	94	33%	282	64	9%	0%
	09	22	27%	45%	80%	101	28%	355	97	3%	50%
	10	27	15%	44%	79%	82	25%	338	65	12%	58%
Torres,Andres	09	20	35%	40%	67%	126	49%	330	179	17%	88%
	10	26	50%	27%	75%	122	39%	341	104	26%	79%
Towles,J.R.	08	18	11%	72%	79%	27	48%	259	88	10%	43%
	09	8	13%	88%	80%	32	38%	287	100	4%	100%
	10	5	0%	40%	73%	35	56%	237	87	17%	100%
Tracy,Chad	08	19	47%	32%	84%	92	47%	302	63	0%	0%
	09	23	52%	39%	85%	92	48%	306	75	3%	54%
	10	18	22%	56%	83%	36	42%	309	57	1%	0%
Treanor,Matt	08	21	29%	57%	74%	47	25%	299	68	2%	100%
	09	3	33%	67%	0%	0	0%	71	68	0%	0%
	10	22	14%	55%	82%	100	38%	278	64	5%	33%
Tuiasosopo,M	08	5	40%	40%	0%	0	0%	312	83	0%	100%
	09	3	67%	33%	0%	0	0%	330	65	0%	75%
	10	20	15%	75%	71%	48	37%	280	84	6%	50%
Tulowitzki,Troy	08	19	37%	26%	85%	102	37%	330	98	7%	14%
	09	26	62%	23%	79%	141	40%	380	142	18%	65%
	10	21	52%	5%	83%	149	40%	378	101	10%	85%
Uggla,Dan	08	26	62%	23%	68%	146	48%	354	87	7%	50%
	09	27	41%	37%	73%	142	46%	349	67	2%	67%
	10	27	48%	26%	75%	153	43%	370	67	3%	80%
Upton,B.J.	08	27	48%	22%	75%	89	31%	385	111	31%	73%
	09	26	31%	50%	73%	117	40%	311	133	39%	75%
	10	27	41%	33%	69%	125	44%	322	119	38%	82%
Upton,Justin	08	21	57%	14%	66%	126	42%	349	143	5%	20%
	09	25	60%	28%	74%	128	36%	367	128	17%	80%
	10	25	36%	40%	69%	142	39%	356	107	17%	69%
Uribe,Juan	08	24	38%	38%	80%	86	45%	295	74	6%	25%
	09	27	44%	33%	79%	124	40%	331	90	4%	75%
	10	27	56%	33%	82%	123	44%	307	61	2%	33%
Utley,Chase	08	26	58%	12%	83%	149	42%	359	94	10%	88%
	09	26	65%	19%	81%	159	48%	378	120	12%	100%
	10	21	48%	14%	85%	136	39%	369	101	11%	87%
Valaika,Chris	10	7	14%	57%	84%	8	34%	285	87	5%	33%
Valbuena,Luis	08	5	40%	60%	0%	0	0%	339	113	0%	63%
	09	23	48%	30%	79%	79	37%	318	104	10%	36%
	10	23	17%	65%	79%	54	35%	291	58	5%	59%
Valdez,Wilson	09	12	25%	42%	88%	14	17%	254	125	10%	65%
	10	26	38%	46%	87%	50	21%	312	110	11%	84%
Valencia,Danny	10	19	53%	37%	84%	61	38%	324	74	3%	100%
Varitek,Jason	08	28	36%	46%	71%	108	45%	305	52	1%	0%
	09	27	48%	33%	75%	124	47%	311	49	0%	0%
	10	18	50%	39%	69%	154	57%	295	59	0%	0%
Velez,Eugenio	08	21	38%	52%	84%	44	26%	308	168	39%	63%
	09	18	28%	50%	83%	61	29%	300	152	35%	63%
	10	11	18%	45%	86%	15	30%	266	125	46%	53%
Venable,Will	08	6	50%	33%	78%	21	37%	305	123	7%	63%
	09	18	28%	44%	73%	71	40%	291	106	7%	87%
	10	25	36%	48%	67%	114	44%	323	171	33%	81%
Viciedo,Dayan	10	13	38%	46%	80%	31	39%	281	53	4%	67%
Victorino,Shane	08	24	42%	38%	88%	87	36%	345	160	29%	77%
	09	27	70%	22%	89%	67	33%	354	143	18%	76%
	10	26	62%	19%	87%	93	38%	320	132	26%	85%
Vizquel,Omar	08	22	36%	50%	89%	31	37%	286	76	13%	56%
	09	25	36%	52%	85%	52	43%	316	116	8%	100%
	10	26	19%	46%	87%	45	33%	341	100	16%	61%
Votto,Joey	08	27	48%	11%	81%	122	31%	368	81	8%	58%
	09	24	54%	25%	77%	158	39%	410	62	3%	80%
	10	27	81%	11%	77%	156	35%	420	73	11%	76%
Walker,Neil	09	6	17%	67%	0%	0	0%	273	86	0%	67%
	10	20	40%	20%	82%	94	41%	341	88	9%	71%
Wallace,Brett	10	11	18%	73%	80%	31	44%	261	70	2%	50%
Weeks,Rickie	08	24	42%	25%	76%	91	39%	327	129	18%	79%
	09	7	43%	29%	73%	144	44%	327	133	11%	50%
	10	27	33%	33%	72%	122	36%	345	89	8%	73%
Wells,Casper	10	9	56%	22%	77%	35	39%	273	128	17%	37%

BATTER SUPPORT SKILLS

Name	Yr	#Wk	DOM	DIS	ct%	xPX	FB	OB	Sp	SBO	SB%
Wells, Vernon	08	20	50%	5%	89%	103	36%	344	65	5%	67%
	09	27	44%	19%	86%	98	42%	313	80	13%	81%
	10	26	62%	4%	86%	134	42%	330	60	8%	60%
Werth, Jayson	08	26	62%	19%	72%	122	38%	360	113	16%	95%
	09	27	44%	44%	73%	150	44%	369	87	13%	87%
	10	27	63%	22%	73%	171	45%	387	101	9%	81%
Whiteside, Eli	09	20	20%	60%	71%	43	42%	243	78	0%	0%
	10	24	33%	46%	72%	69	42%	284	108	11%	33%
Wieters, Matt	09	20	25%	65%	77%	77	40%	347	75	0%	0%
	10	25	28%	48%	79%	116	38%	320	65	1%	0%
Wigginton, Ty	08	23	43%	13%	82%	126	39%	340	85	10%	40%
	09	26	38%	31%	86%	83	39%	312	76	3%	33%
	10	27	37%	44%	80%	124	37%	307	76	1%	0%
Willingham, J	08	20	45%	30%	77%	120	42%	343	119	5%	60%
	09	27	52%	37%	76%	154	42%	352	79	6%	57%
	10	20	45%	35%	77%	157	49%	380	82	6%	100%
Willits, Reggie	08	23	17%	74%	78%	5	40%	338	137	9%	60%
	09	17	12%	59%	0%	0	0%	297	101	0%	71%
	10	26	27%	42%	84%	37	45%	337	104	11%	33%
Wilson, Jack	08	18	28%	44%	91%	48	37%	302	82	5%	50%
	09	21	29%	38%	87%	51	42%	294	81	5%	75%
	10	12	17%	50%	82%	58	40%	275	100	7%	33%
Wilson, Josh	09	19	16%	53%	80%	51	41%	262	111	9%	49%
	10	22	14%	64%	80%	54	45%	254	96	7%	85%
Winn, Randy	08	27	48%	19%	85%	92	30%	368	103	14%	93%
	09	27	52%	44%	83%	83	32%	321	116	12%	89%
	10	26	31%	46%	82%	82	31%	310	100	11%	100%
Wise, DeWayne	08	17	35%	53%	80%	48	42%	306	129	37%	75%
	09	20	35%	45%	81%	116	47%	241	140	41%	44%
	10	18	22%	61%	77%	36	37%	258	148	17%	77%
Wood, Brandon	08	12	8%	50%	76%	22	50%	300	95	12%	60%
	09	9	11%	78%	78%	13	27%	314	99	2%	50%
	10	22	5%	73%	70%	69	52%	170	90	2%	100%

BATTER SUPPORT SKILLS

Name	Yr	#Wk	DOM	DIS	ct%	xPX	FB	OB	Sp	SBO	SB%
Worth, Danny	10	11	45%	18%	86%	33	32%	289	88	21%	73%
Wright, David	08	27	59%	7%	81%	125	38%	393	79	10%	75%
	09	25	40%	36%	74%	121	36%	391	98	19%	75%
	10	27	56%	30%	73%	157	43%	358	73	18%	63%
Youkilis, Kevin	08	28	64%	18%	80%	140	44%	383	84	5%	38%
	09	26	62%	31%	75%	168	44%	400	73	6%	78%
	10	18	67%	11%	81%	174	47%	402	109	4%	80%
Young Jr., Eric	09	7	43%	57%	86%	9	22%	329	180	44%	72%
	10	11	36%	45%	82%	34	29%	294	143	34%	80%
Young, Chris	08	27	52%	11%	74%	112	43%	316	112	13%	74%
	09	26	35%	38%	70%	9	56%	318	117	15%	69%
	10	26	54%	19%	75%	141	50%	340	77	21%	80%
Young, Delmon	08	27	41%	22%	82%	78	28%	331	115	12%	74%
	09	25	28%	56%	77%	102	34%	305	109	7%	29%
	10	27	67%	9%	86%	126	40%	331	69	7%	56%
Young, Delwyn	08	21	43%	43%	73%	72	33%	321	81	0%	0%
	09	26	19%	46%	75%	79	33%	321	85	2%	100%
	10	26	38%	50%	73%	95	40%	284	63	3%	100%
Young, Michael	08	27	41%	22%	83%	99	31%	340	89	5%	100%
	09	24	50%	29%	83%	147	33%	376	91	7%	73%
	10	27	37%	30%	82%	112	34%	334	80	3%	67%
Zaun, Gregg	08	24	38%	38%	84%	102	40%	339	75	4%	67%
	09	27	44%	48%	82%	117	40%	338	90	3%	0%
	10	7	43%	0%	88%	72	33%	336	58	0%	0%
Zimmerman, Ry	08	19	53%	32%	83%	107	34%	331	89	2%	50%
	09	27	52%	22%	80%	138	42%	367	92	1%	100%
	10	25	52%	28%	81%	146	41%	387	69	3%	80%
Zobrist, Ben	08	17	47%	24%	79%	94	42%	350	114	9%	86%
	09	27	59%	26%	79%	138	39%	405	133	13%	74%
	10	27	33%	37%	80%	101	38%	349	92	15%	89%

Starting Pitcher Consistency Charts

The following charts include:

- Up to five years of data for all pitchers who had at least five starts in 2010
- Total number of starts in that year (#)
- Average pitch counts for all starts (PC)
- Domination and Disaster percentages (DOM, DIS) for first half, second half and total season
- Quality-Consistency Score (QC)
- PQS Earned Run Average (qERA)

Some observations...

The ability to maintain positive QC scores is rarer than we would think. That's why you have to take notice of a pitcher like **Bronson Arroyo**, who has posted positive QC scores for five straight years.

In his three healthy seasons, **Jeremy Bonderman** has had solid first halves, only to collapse in each second half.

After five full seasons in the Majors, you have to like **Matt Cain's** qERA trend (4.50, 4.10, 3.68. 3.50, 3.38) and his consistency (QC scores of 12, 36, 76, 86, 109).

Those who invested long-term in **Johnny Cueto** may finally be seeing the fruits of their patience. Beyond the improvement in his per-game pitch count, qERA and QC, he finally was able to sustain his skill into the second half of a season.

Ditto for fellow Sox **John Danks** and **Gavin Floyd**, who have even more notable across-the-board trends.

"Improvement" comes in all shapes and sizes. Though **Kyle Davies** is not going to be on many drafts lists, his skill and consistency have improved in each of the last four years.

Further proof that **Jon Garland's** 2010 season was a fluke and he is no more draftable this spring than he was in any previous spring.

For the past four half-seasons, exactly one out of every two **Matt Garza** starts has been dominating, without fail. That will make him a draftable commodity but he needs more to be consistently valuable.

There are rising trends everywhere you look in **Felix Hernandez's** profile.

Livan Hernandez's minor turnaround? There was no skill involved, just disaster avoidance.

John Lackey's "off-year" looks like just a half season of getting acclimated to his new environment. His second half (67/7%) was solid and his season xERA (3.97) was in line with prior years. But be aware of that elevated pitch count.

As much as **Kevin Millwood** has shown a consistently mediocre qERA for five years, and posted a 5.00+ ERA in three of the past four years, his 2010 performance was far inferior. With a 26% DOM rate, he could easily fall completely off the cliff in 2011.

Ricky Nolasco has posted excellent BPIs over the past few years but his QC and qERA trends are somewhat less optimistic.

Rick Porcello's ERA may have risen by a full run from 2009 to 2010, but QC and qERA are further proof that his skills actually improved. His 57/14% second half split alone equates to a qERA under 4.00.

After the awful first half that **Wandy Rodriguez** endured, his final qERA and QC netted out virtually identical to his 2009 levels.

STARTING PITCHER CONSISTENCY CHART

Pitcher	Yr	#	PC	First Half DOM	First Half DIS	2nd Half DOM	2nd Half DIS	Full Season DOM	Full Season DIS	QC	qERA
Anderson,Brett	09	30	94	38%	38%	64%	0%	50%	20%	20	4.50
	10	19	95	67%	17%	54%	8%	58%	11%	74	3.97
Arrieta,Jake	10	18	95	14%	29%	18%	36%	17%	33%	-100	5.29
Arroyo,Bronson	06	34	110	79%	11%	47%	13%	65%	12%	82	3.61
	07	34	101	50%	11%	44%	13%	47%	12%	46	4.28
	08	34	101	40%	30%	64%	0%	50%	18%	28	4.37
	09	33	103	22%	33%	73%	0%	45%	18%	18	4.40
	10	33	99	44%	22%	60%	20%	52%	21%	18	4.50
Atilano,Luis	10	16	91	20%	33%	0%	100%	19%	38%	-113	5.45
Bailey,Homer	07	9	90	17%	33%	33%	0%	22%	22%	-44	4.75
	08	8	85	25%	50%	0%	50%	13%	50%	-174	7.08
	09	20	101	50%	25%	25%	19%	30%	20%	-20	4.71
	10	19	102	44%	33%	70%	10%	58%	21%	32	4.23
Baker,Scott	06	16	90	22%	56%	0%	43%	13%	50%	-174	7.08
	07	23	90	22%	22%	43%	7%	35%	13%	18	4.41
	08	28	96	43%	14%	57%	14%	50%	14%	44	4.23
	09	32	99	53%	18%	67%	13%	59%	16%	54	4.10
	10	29	92	50%	22%	45%	36%	48%	28%	-14	4.67
Bannister,Brian	06	6	100	40%	20%	100%	0%	50%	17%	32	4.37
	07	27	96	38%	15%	36%	29%	37%	22%	-14	4.64
	08	32	98	42%	21%	31%	46%	38%	31%	-48	5.00
	09	26	97	44%	6%	30%	20%	38%	12%	28	4.41
	10	23	93	39%	33%	0%	40%	30%	35%	-78	5.19
Beckett,Josh	06	33	98	56%	17%	47%	13%	52%	15%	44	4.37
	07	30	103	63%	13%	86%	0%	73%	7%	118	3.25
	08	27	100	65%	12%	80%	10%	70%	11%	96	3.51
	09	32	105	89%	11%	64%	0%	78%	6%	132	3.13
	10	21	103	25%	38%	54%	8%	43%	19%	10	4.44
Bell,Trevor	10	7	85			43%	29%	43%	29%	-29	4.74
Bergesen,Brad	09	19	98	44%	6%	33%	0%	42%	5%	64	4.11
	10	28	92	8%	54%	47%	13%	29%	32%	-71	5.13
Billingsley,Chad	06	16	95	0%	60%	36%	18%	25%	31%	-74	5.13
	07	20	95	25%	50%	50%	13%	45%	20%	10	4.53
	08	32	101	58%	5%	54%	8%	56%	6%	88	3.68
	09	32	100	68%	0%	54%	23%	63%	9%	90	3.50
	10	31	101	50%	13%	47%	7%	48%	10%	58	4.28
Blackburn,Nick	08	33	87	47%	21%	29%	50%	39%	33%	-54	5.00
	09	33	94	28%	17%	33%	40%	30%	27%	-48	4.90
	10	26	90	18%	41%	33%	11%	23%	31%	-77	5.21
Blanton,Joe	06	31	101	28%	22%	23%	8%	26%	16%	-12	4.62
	07	34	102	63%	0%	40%	13%	53%	6%	82	3.85
	08	33	98	30%	15%	38%	23%	33%	18%	-6	4.60
	09	31	105	47%	18%	64%	14%	55%	16%	46	4.10
	10	28	97	31%	15%	67%	13%	50%	14%	43	4.23
Bonderman,Jer	06	34	97	61%	11%	38%	25%	50%	18%	28	4.37
	07	28	97	81%	0%	33%	33%	61%	14%	66	3.71
	08	12	98	33%	25%			33%	25%	-34	4.90
	10	29	94	56%	19%	15%	54%	38%	34%	-62	5.00
Braden,Dallas	07	14	85	25%	75%	10%	60%	14%	64%	-228	8.46
	08	10	89			40%	20%	40%	20%	0	4.56
	09	22	97	50%	0%	0%	25%	41%	5%	62	4.11
	10	30	95	60%	13%	47%	13%	53%	13%	53	4.23
Buchholz,Clay	08	15	91	22%	33%	17%	50%	20%	40%	-120	5.50
	09	16	95			38%	25%	38%	25%	-24	4.82
	10	28	100	33%	27%	54%	15%	43%	21%	0	4.56
Buehrle,Mark	06	32	97	28%	11%	21%	43%	25%	25%	-50	4.93
	07	30	103	41%	6%	31%	15%	37%	10%	34	4.41
	08	34	100	47%	11%	60%	20%	53%	15%	46	4.37
	09	33	97	39%	11%	27%	27%	33%	18%	-6	4.60
	10	33	100	33%	22%	33%	7%	33%	15%	6	4.60
Bullington,Bryan	10	5	94			40%	40%	40%	40%	-80	5.21
Bumgarner,Mad	10	18	96	75%	0%	43%	29%	50%	22%	11	4.50
Burnett,A.J.	06	21	103	33%	33%	67%	13%	57%	19%	38	4.10
	07	25	106	60%	27%	70%	0%	64%	16%	64	3.83
	08	34	107	50%	20%	71%	0%	59%	12%	70	3.97
	09	33	105	59%	12%	56%	13%	58%	12%	68	3.97
	10	33	94	39%	22%	53%	47%	45%	33%	-42	4.82
Burres,Brian	10	13	88	0%	57%	67%	17%	31%	38%	-92	5.19
Bush,David	06	32	96	63%	11%	46%	23%	56%	16%	48	4.10
	07	31	95	59%	6%	36%	21%	48%	13%	44	4.28
	08	29	92	35%	24%	42%	8%	38%	17%	8	4.52
	09	21	88	36%	21%	29%	57%	33%	33%	-66	5.08
	10	31	95	29%	12%	21%	21%	26%	16%	-13	4.62
Cahill,Trevor	09	32	94	28%	33%	14%	36%	22%	34%	-92	5.21
	10	30	101	53%	0%	40%	20%	47%	10%	53	4.28
Cain,Matt	06	31	106	38%	38%	67%	7%	52%	23%	12	4.50
	07	32	105	53%	12%	60%	27%	56%	19%	36	4.10
	08	34	106	60%	10%	50%	7%	56%	9%	76	3.68
	09	33	102	61%	11%	60%	7%	61%	9%	86	3.50
	10	33	106	50%	6%	87%	7%	67%	6%	109	3.38

STARTING PITCHER CONSISTENCY CHART

Pitcher	Yr	#	PC	First Half DOM	First Half DIS	2nd Half DOM	2nd Half DIS	Full Season DOM	Full Season DIS	QC	qERA
Capuano,Chris	10	9	81	0%	100%	50%	25%	44%	33%	-44	4.92
Carmona,Fausto	06	7	87	33%	33%	25%	25%	29%	29%	-58	4.93
	07	32	98	53%	12%	47%	0%	50%	6%	76	3.85
	08	22	92	10%	40%	25%	25%	18%	32%	-92	5.29
	09	24	94	8%	25%	25%	25%	17%	25%	-66	5.03
	10	33	100	33%	6%	47%	27%	39%	15%	18	4.52
Carpenter,Chris	06	32	102	65%	0%	67%	7%	66%	3%	120	3.14
	09	28	95	77%	8%	67%	4%	71%	4%	126	2.99
	10	35	101	58%	5%	56%	6%	57%	6%	91	3.68
Carrasco,Carlos	09	5	80			0%	80%	0%	80%	-320	12.14
	10	7	97			57%	0%	57%	0%	114	3.38
Cecil,Brett	09	17	94	38%	38%	33%	44%	35%	41%	-94	5.25
	10	28	97	53%	20%	46%	15%	50%	18%	29	4.37
Chacin,Jhoulys	10	21	101	58%	8%	56%	11%	57%	10%	76	3.97
Chen,Bruce	09	9	93	25%	50%	20%	20%	22%	33%	-88	5.21
	10	23	96	38%	25%	33%	27%	35%	26%	-35	4.82
Coleman,Casey	10	8	95			38%	13%	38%	13%	25	4.41
Cook,Aaron	06	32	97	39%	6%	21%	21%	31%	13%	10	4.49
	07	25	96	32%	11%	67%	0%	40%	8%	48	4.11
	08	32	96	25%	0%	25%	17%	25%	6%	26	4.48
	09	27	89	22%	22%	22%	33%	22%	26%	-60	4.98
	10	23	86	29%	29%	17%	50%	26%	35%	-87	5.27
Correia,Kevin	07	8	88			63%	13%	63%	13%	74	3.71
	08	19	90	40%	40%	33%	22%	37%	32%	-54	5.00
	09	33	96	50%	17%	53%	13%	52%	15%	44	4.37
	10	26	94	41%	12%	22%	33%	35%	19%	-8	4.52
Cueto,Johnny	08	31	98	47%	21%	42%	25%	45%	23%	-2	4.53
	09	30	97	56%	17%	33%	17%	47%	17%	26	4.40
	10	31	101	56%	11%	62%	15%	58%	13%	65	3.97
Danks,John	07	26	93	25%	25%	20%	40%	23%	31%	-78	5.21
	08	33	95	58%	16%	50%	29%	55%	21%	26	4.23
	09	32	100	65%	12%	33%	13%	50%	13%	48	4.23
	10	32	106	59%	12%	67%	7%	63%	9%	88	3.50
Davies,Kyle	06	14	89	25%	38%	17%	67%	21%	50%	-158	6.74
	07	28	88	31%	50%	17%	50%	25%	50%	-150	6.56
	08	21	94	11%	33%	33%	33%	24%	33%	-84	5.21
	09	22	99	36%	43%	50%	13%	41%	32%	-46	4.92
	10	32	98	29%	24%	40%	27%	34%	25%	-31	4.90
Davis,Doug	06	34	103	21%	16%	47%	13%	32%	15%	4	4.60
	07	33	102	44%	22%	40%	27%	42%	24%	-12	4.56
	08	26	95	58%	17%	36%	43%	46%	31%	-32	4.82
	09	34	102	47%	21%	27%	20%	38%	21%	-8	4.64
	10	8	98	13%	63%			13%	63%	-225	8.46
Davis,Wade	09	6	100			33%	17%	33%	17%	-2	4.60
	10	29	96	18%	24%	50%	8%	31%	17%	-7	4.60
de la Rosa,Jorge	06	13	84	0%	100%	10%	30%	8%	46%	-168	6.53
	07	23	91	33%	28%	0%	60%	26%	35%	-88	5.27
	08	23	92	27%	45%	58%	17%	43%	30%	-34	4.92
	09	32	95	47%	24%	53%	13%	50%	19%	24	4.37
	10	20	101	40%	20%	67%	7%	60%	10%	80	3.71
Dempster,Ryan	08	33	101	55%	5%	77%	0%	64%	3%	116	3.29
	09	31	102	65%	12%	64%	0%	65%	6%	106	3.38
	10	34	106	67%	0%	56%	31%	62%	15%	65	3.83
Detwiler,Ross	09	14	88	40%	30%	25%	25%	36%	29%	-44	4.82
	10	5	83			0%	60%	0%	60%	-240	9.02
Dickey,R.A.	10	26	100	60%	0%	44%	6%	50%	4%	85	3.47
Duchscherer,Jus	08	22	93	63%	6%	17%	17%	50%	9%	64	3.85
	10	5	88	20%	20%			20%	20%	-40	4.75
Duensing,Brian	09	9	89			33%	33%	33%	33%	-66	5.08
	10	13	96			54%	8%	54%	8%	77	3.85
Duke,Zach	06	34	96	32%	21%	33%	13%	32%	18%	-6	4.60
	07	19	88	6%	41%	0%	50%	5%	42%	-158	5.80
	08	31	94	21%	26%	50%	8%	32%	19%	-12	4.60
	09	32	96	56%	11%	29%	29%	44%	19%	12	4.44
	10	29	91	29%	36%	33%	33%	31%	34%	-76	5.08
Ely,John	10	18	91	57%	36%	25%	50%	50%	50%	-56	4.87
Enright,Barry	10	17	87	33%	0%	29%	21%	29%	18%	-12	4.62
Eveland,Dana	06	5	97	0%	40%			0%	40%	-160	5.90
	08	29	93	32%	21%	30%	40%	31%	28%	-50	4.90
	09	9	86	17%	67%	0%	67%	11%	67%	-246	9.15
	10	10	85	10%	60%			10%	60%	-220	8.46
Feldman,Scott	08	25	94	21%	21%	27%	18%	24%	20%	-32	4.75
	09	31	98	13%	7%	56%	19%	35%	13%	18	4.41
	10	22	99	33%	22%	0%	100%	27%	36%	-91	5.27
Figueroa,Nelson	08	6	98	33%	33%			33%	33%	-66	5.08
	09	10	99	0%	0%	44%	22%	40%	20%	0	4.56
	10	11	97	100%	0%	40%	30%	45%	27%	-18	4.67
Fister,Doug	09	10	94			50%	20%	50%	20%	20	4.50
	10	28	96	38%	23%	40%	13%	39%	18%	7	4.52

STARTING PITCHER CONSISTENCY CHART

Pitcher	Yr	#	PC	First Half DOM	First Half DIS	2nd Half DOM	2nd Half DIS	Full Season DOM	Full Season DIS	QC	qERA
Floyd,Gavin	06	11	91	9%	55%			9%	55%	-202	7.99
	07	10	96	0%	100%	67%	22%	60%	30%	0	4.39
	08	33	98	39%	17%	47%	7%	42%	12%	36	4.32
	09	30	99	44%	11%	67%	17%	53%	13%	54	4.23
	10	31	97	72%	11%	46%	8%	61%	10%	84	3.71
Francis,Jeff	06	32	99	35%	18%	33%	13%	34%	16%	4	4.60
	07	34	103	56%	6%	50%	13%	53%	9%	70	3.85
	08	24	99	35%	24%	71%	14%	46%	21%	8	4.53
	10	19	86	36%	18%	38%	38%	37%	26%	-32	4.82
French,Luke	09	12	91	50%	50%	10%	30%	17%	33%	-98	5.29
	10	13	90	0%	100%	8%	25%	8%	31%	-108	5.45
Galarraga,Arman	08	28	97	27%	7%	38%	15%	32%	11%	20	4.49
	09	25	93	33%	33%	29%	29%	32%	32%	-64	5.08
	10	24	96	11%	44%	33%	27%	25%	33%	-83	5.13
Gallardo,Yovani	07	17	96	67%	0%	64%	14%	65%	12%	82	3.61
	09	30	107	61%	6%	67%	0%	63%	3%	114	3.29
	10	31	103	89%	6%	69%	23%	81%	13%	110	3.31
Garcia,Freddy	06	33	101	44%	17%	60%	0%	52%	9%	68	3.85
	07	11	95	36%	36%			36%	36%	-72	5.13
	09	9	92			67%	11%	67%	11%	90	3.61
	10	28	88	44%	19%	33%	33%	39%	25%	-21	4.82
Garcia,Jaime	10	28	93	65%	6%	55%	18%	61%	11%	79	3.71
Garland,Jon	06	32	104	35%	18%	53%	7%	44%	13%	36	4.32
	07	32	103	29%	6%	40%	27%	34%	16%	4	4.60
	08	32	100	16%	16%	15%	31%	16%	22%	-56	4.77
	09	33	99	44%	17%	53%	13%	48%	15%	36	4.40
	10	33	99	22%	6%	40%	13%	30%	9%	24	4.48
Garza,Matt	06	9	89			22%	56%	22%	56%	-180	7.36
	07	15	95	100%	0%	29%	36%	33%	33%	-66	5.08
	08	30	98	41%	29%	31%	15%	37%	23%	-18	4.64
	09	32	107	50%	0%	50%	14%	50%	6%	76	3.85
	10	32	102	50%	11%	50%	21%	50%	16%	38	4.37
Gee,Dillon	10	5	98			20%	0%	20%	0%	40	4.47
Gomez,Jeanmar	10	11	91			18%	36%	18%	36%	-109	5.45
Gonzalez,Gio	08	7	89			29%	57%	29%	57%	-170	7.14
	09	17	94	33%	33%	43%	29%	41%	29%	-34	4.74
	10	33	102	44%	28%	73%	7%	58%	18%	42	4.10
Gorzelanny,Tom	06	11	92	0%	50%	56%	22%	45%	27%	-18	4.67
	07	32	104	50%	6%	36%	14%	44%	9%	52	4.11
	08	21	91	6%	35%	25%	75%	10%	43%	-152	5.70
	09	7	77			43%	29%	43%	29%	-30	4.74
	10	23	96	50%	8%	45%	27%	48%	17%	26	4.40
Greinke,Zack	07	14	86	29%	29%	29%	43%	29%	36%	-86	5.27
	08	32	101	58%	16%	77%	8%	66%	13%	80	3.61
	09	33	105	83%	0%	93%	0%	88%	0%	176	2.54
	10	33	104	61%	6%	47%	13%	55%	9%	73	3.68
Guthrie,Jeremy	07	26	96	77%	0%	23%	38%	50%	19%	24	4.37
	08	30	102	50%	5%	50%	20%	50%	10%	60	4.23
	09	33	102	28%	22%	27%	21%	27%	21%	-30	4.73
	10	32	104	44%	22%	71%	0%	56%	13%	63	3.97
Haeger,Charlie	10	6	87	17%	83%			17%	83%	-300	10.80
Halladay,Roy	06	32	95	56%	0%	57%	14%	56%	6%	88	3.68
	07	31	107	50%	13%	47%	7%	48%	10%	56	4.28
	08	33	107	68%	0%	86%	0%	76%	0%	152	2.84
	09	32	106	82%	12%	73%	0%	78%	6%	132	3.13
	10	33	108	74%	5%	64%	0%	70%	3%	127	2.99
Hamels,Cole	06	23	95	22%	33%	64%	14%	48%	22%	8	4.53
	07	28	100	61%	6%	70%	10%	64%	7%	100	3.50
	08	33	104	70%	5%	69%	8%	70%	6%	116	3.25
	09	32	97	53%	35%	53%	13%	53%	25%	6	4.61
	10	33	102	50%	11%	73%	13%	61%	12%	73	3.71
Hammel,Jason	06	9	89	0%	50%	14%	57%	11%	56%	-202	7.77
	07	14	89			21%	36%	21%	36%	-102	5.36
	08	5	89	40%	20%			40%	20%	0	4.56
	09	30	88	53%	33%	47%	13%	50%	23%	8	4.50
	10	30	95	53%	20%	40%	20%	47%	20%	13	4.53
Hanson,Tommy	09	21	95	29%	14%	71%	7%	57%	10%	74	3.97
	10	34	96	61%	22%	69%	0%	65%	12%	82	3.61
Happ,J.A.	09	23	100	60%	20%	31%	15%	43%	17%	18	4.44
	10	16	99	0%	0%	64%	21%	56%	19%	38	4.10
Harang,Aaron	06	34	106	63%	11%	47%	7%	56%	9%	76	3.68
	07	34	106	58%	5%	67%	7%	62%	6%	100	3.50
	08	29	103	53%	21%	60%	30%	55%	24%	14	4.23
	09	26	103	53%	26%	71%	0%	58%	19%	40	4.10
	10	20	100	47%	35%	0%	100%	40%	45%	-100	5.67
Harden,Rich	06	9	89	33%	33%	33%	67%	33%	44%	-110	5.29
	08	25	98	79%	7%	64%	0%	72%	4%	128	2.99
	09	26	96	50%	36%	67%	17%	58%	27%	8	4.39
	10	18	95	8%	38%	20%	60%	11%	44%	-156	5.70

STARTING PITCHER CONSISTENCY CHART

Pitcher	Yr	#	PC	First Half DOM	First Half DIS	2nd Half DOM	2nd Half DIS	Full Season DOM	Full Season DIS	QC	qERA
Haren,Dan	06	34	103	53%	5%	53%	7%	53%	6%	82	3.85
	07	34	107	68%	0%	80%	7%	74%	3%	136	2.99
	08	33	101	89%	5%	71%	14%	82%	9%	128	3.00
	09	33	105	89%	0%	67%	0%	79%	0%	158	2.84
	10	35	107	58%	5%	63%	6%	60%	6%	97	3.50
Harrison,Matt	08	15	91	0%	50%	23%	38%	20%	40%	-120	5.50
	09	11	97	27%	45%			27%	45%	-126	5.98
	10	6	104	33%	17%			33%	17%	0	4.60
Hawksworth,Blake	10	8	88	20%	40%	0%	33%	13%	38%	-125	5.54
Hernandez,David	09	19	98	0%	20%	36%	50%	26%	42%	-116	5.40
	10	8	99	13%	25%			13%	25%	-75	5.08
Hernandez,Felix	06	31	99	47%	18%	50%	7%	48%	13%	44	4.28
	07	30	100	36%	14%	50%	0%	43%	7%	58	4.11
	08	31	103	59%	12%	57%	14%	58%	13%	64	3.97
	09	34	107	72%	11%	75%	6%	74%	9%	112	3.25
	10	34	110	79%	11%	73%	0%	76%	6%	129	3.13
Hernandez,Livan	06	34	103	16%	11%	40%	7%	26%	9%	16	4.48
	07	33	102	22%	22%	20%	33%	21%	27%	-66	4.98
	08	31	90	35%	30%	18%	36%	29%	32%	-70	5.13
	09	31	96	18%	24%	50%	29%	32%	26%	-40	4.90
	10	33	98	28%	0%	33%	20%	30%	9%	24	4.82
Hochevar,Luke	08	22	94	44%	31%	17%	17%	36%	27%	-36	4.82
	09	25	94	20%	40%	47%	27%	36%	32%	-56	5.00
	10	17	93	46%	23%	25%	0%	41%	18%	12	4.44
Holland,Derek	09	21	90	29%	14%	14%	43%	19%	33%	-94	5.29
	10	10	88	50%	50%	33%	50%	40%	50%	-120	6.13
Hudson,Daniel	10	14	103	0%	100%	85%	0%	79%	7%	129	3.13
Hudson,Tim	06	35	98	32%	21%	31%	19%	31%	20%	-18	4.71
	07	34	93	53%	21%	47%	7%	50%	15%	40	4.37
	08	22	91	45%	25%	50%	0%	45%	23%	-2	4.53
	09	7	86			29%	29%	29%	29%	-58	4.93
	10	34	98	50%	11%	50%	6%	50%	9%	65	3.85
Huff,David	09	23	98	18%	36%	17%	25%	17%	30%	-46	5.29
	10	15	93	23%	46%	0%	100%	20%	53%	-173	6.74
Hughes,Phil	07	13	95	50%	50%	36%	27%	38%	31%	-48	5.00
	08	8	79	17%	83%	50%	50%	25%	75%	-250	9.46
	09	7	89	43%	43%			43%	43%	-86	5.21
	10	29	103	56%	6%	54%	23%	55%	14%	55	3.97
Hunter,Tommy	09	19	91	25%	25%	40%	20%	37%	21%	-10	4.64
	10	22	86	43%	14%	7%	27%	18%	23%	-55	4.77
Jackson,Edwin	07	31	95	44%	38%	40%	20%	42%	29%	-32	4.74
	08	31	97	33%	17%	23%	38%	29%	26%	-46	4.93
	09	33	105	78%	0%	20%	27%	52%	12%	56	4.23
	10	32	105	39%	17%	71%	0%	53%	9%	69	3.85
Jimenez,Ubaldo	07	15	90			40%	33%	40%	33%	-52	4.92
	08	34	99	40%	20%	71%	7%	53%	15%	46	4.37
	09	33	102	72%	17%	87%	7%	79%	12%	110	3.41
	10	33	109	94%	0%	67%	13%	82%	6%	139	3.00
Johnson,Josh	06	24	99	58%	0%	67%	17%	63%	8%	94	3.50
	08	14	101	0%	0%	54%	0%	50%	0%	100	3.47
	09	33	100	79%	11%	57%	21%	70%	15%	80	3.63
	10	28	107	78%	0%	60%	10%	71%	4%	129	2.99
Jurrjens,Jair	07	7	68			14%	43%	14%	43%	-144	5.70
	08	31	99	56%	11%	46%	15%	52%	13%	52	4.23
	09	34	97	47%	11%	60%	7%	53%	9%	70	3.85
	10	20	91	29%	29%	46%	8%	40%	15%	20	4.44
Karstens,Jeff	06	6	86			17%	17%	17%	17%	-34	4.65
	08	9	92			22%	22%	22%	22%	-44	4.75
	09	13	80	10%	30%	0%	67%	8%	38%	-136	5.63
	10	17	83	18%	9%	50%	25%	32%	16%	0	4.60
Kawakami,Ken	09	25	91	50%	31%	33%	22%	44%	28%	-24	4.74
	10	16	89	27%	33%	0%	100%	25%	38%	-100	5.27
Kazmir,Scott	06	24	101	47%	16%	100%	0%	58%	13%	64	3.97
	07	34	106	47%	11%	80%	7%	62%	9%	88	3.50
	08	27	102	57%	14%	62%	23%	59%	19%	42	4.10
	09	26	101	42%	42%	79%	7%	62%	23%	32	3.95
	10	28	98	18%	47%	18%	45%	18%	46%	-150	6.25
Kendrick,Kyle	07	20	88	20%	0%	33%	27%	30%	20%	-20	4.71
	08	30	87	26%	32%	9%	64%	20%	43%	-132	5.50
	10	31	90	24%	29%	43%	36%	32%	32%	-65	5.08
Kennedy,Ian	08	9	82	25%	50%	0%	100%	22%	56%	-180	7.36
	10	32	99	61%	11%	64%	14%	63%	13%	75	3.71
Kershaw,Clayton	08	21	88	13%	38%	62%	31%	43%	33%	-46	4.92
	09	30	100	44%	17%	58%	33%	50%	23%	8	4.50
	10	32	106	83%	11%	79%	14%	81%	13%	113	3.31
Kuroda,Hiroki	08	31	88	41%	18%	71%	21%	55%	19%	34	4.10
	09	20	89	44%	11%	64%	18%	55%	15%	50	4.10
	10	31	98	59%	18%	79%	7%	68%	13%	84	3.61

STARTING PITCHER CONSISTENCY CHART

Pitcher	Yr	#	PC	First Half DOM	First Half DIS	2nd Half DOM	2nd Half DIS	Full Season DOM	Full Season DIS	QC	qERA
Lackey, John	06	33	106	61%	11%	60%	27%	61%	18%	50	3.83
	07	33	103	61%	6%	60%	7%	61%	6%	98	3.50
	08	24	101	82%	0%	38%	8%	58%	4%	100	3.38
	09	27	102	50%	25%	67%	20%	59%	22%	30	4.23
	10	33	109	44%	17%	67%	7%	55%	12%	61	3.97
Laffey, Aaron	07	9	80			11%	22%	11%	22%	-66	4.79
	08	16	93	43%	7%	0%	100%	38%	19%	0	4.52
	09	19	95	0%	20%	14%	21%	11%	21%	-62	4.79
	10	5	97	25%	75%	0%	0%	20%	60%	-200	7.98
Lannan, John	07	6	94			0%	17%	0%	17%	-68	4.69
	08	31	95	28%	17%	31%	23%	29%	19%	-18	4.62
	09	33	95	17%	17%	40%	20%	27%	18%	-18	4.62
	10	25	94	21%	50%	45%	0%	32%	28%	-48	4.90
Latos, Mat	09	10	87			30%	50%	30%	50%	-140	6.37
	10	31	96	65%	12%	64%	14%	65%	13%	77	3.61
Leake, Mike	10	22	93	41%	6%	40%	40%	41%	14%	27	4.32
LeBlanc, Wade	09	9	86	0%	100%	29%	0%	22%	22%	-44	4.75
	10	25	95	25%	19%	56%	22%	36%	20%	-8	4.64
Lecure, Sam	10	6	100	17%	17%			17%	17%	-33	4.65
Lee, Cliff	06	33	102	39%	11%	40%	27%	39%	18%	6	4.52
	07	16	97	23%	23%	33%	33%	25%	25%	-50	4.93
	08	31	106	72%	6%	62%	0%	68%	3%	124	3.14
	09	34	104	58%	5%	60%	13%	59%	9%	82	3.68
	10	28	106	71%	0%	57%	7%	64%	4%	114	3.29
Lerew, Anthony	10	6	77	40%	40%	0%	100%	33%	50%	-133	6.37
Lester, Jon	06	15	101	33%	17%	0%	22%	13%	20%	-54	4.79
	07	11	97			36%	27%	36%	27%	-36	4.82
	08	33	100	50%	15%	69%	8%	58%	12%	68	3.97
	09	32	106	61%	11%	79%	14%	69%	13%	86	3.61
	10	32	105	72%	0%	64%	14%	69%	6%	113	3.38
Lewis, Colby	10	32	103	65%	0%	67%	7%	66%	3%	119	3.14
Lilly, Ted	06	32	100	50%	22%	50%	14%	50%	19%	24	4.37
	07	34	95	78%	17%	50%	19%	65%	18%	58	3.73
	08	34	95	55%	30%	86%	7%	68%	21%	52	3.85
	09	27	99	72%	0%	78%	11%	74%	4%	132	2.99
	10	30	97	47%	7%	80%	13%	63%	10%	87	3.71
Lincecum, Tim	07	24	99	58%	33%	75%	8%	67%	21%	50	3.85
	08	33	109	74%	0%	86%	14%	79%	6%	134	3.13
	09	32	107	83%	6%	79%	7%	81%	6%	138	3.00
	10	33	104	67%	17%	60%	20%	64%	18%	55	3.83
Lincoln, Brad	10	9	90	14%	29%	0%	100%	11%	44%	-156	5.70
Liriano, Francisco	06	16	93	80%	0%	50%	33%	69%	13%	86	3.61
	08	14	91	0%	67%	64%	18%	50%	29%	-16	4.61
	09	24	92	39%	28%	33%	50%	38%	33%	-56	5.00
	10	31	97	71%	12%	57%	14%	65%	13%	77	3.61
Litsch, Jesse	07	20	89	20%	60%	27%	20%	25%	30%	-70	5.13
	08	28	97	28%	17%	50%	10%	36%	14%	16	4.41
	10	9	86	33%	50%	0%	67%	22%	56%	-178	7.36
Lohse, Kyle	06	19	89	25%	63%	45%	18%	37%	37%	-74	5.13
	07	32	94	39%	22%	36%	29%	38%	25%	-24	4.82
	08	33	96	50%	15%	54%	15%	52%	15%	44	4.37
	09	22	89	45%	45%	45%	36%	45%	41%	-74	5.14
	10	18	90	33%	44%	11%	33%	22%	39%	-111	5.36
Lopez, Rodrigo	09	5	85	100%	0%	33%	33%	60%	20%	40	3.95
	10	33	96	44%	17%	20%	27%	33%	21%	-18	4.71
Lowe, Derek	06	34	96	32%	26%	47%	20%	38%	24%	-20	4.64
	07	32	94	53%	16%	62%	31%	56%	22%	24	4.23
	08	34	92	65%	5%	64%	14%	65%	9%	94	3.38
	09	34	95	32%	21%	20%	27%	26%	24%	-44	4.73
	10	33	96	32%	11%	50%	7%	39%	9%	42	4.29
Maholm, Paul	06	30	97	28%	28%	42%	0%	33%	17%	-2	4.60
	07	29	91	39%	28%	36%	18%	38%	24%	-20	4.64
	08	31	98	56%	17%	46%	8%	52%	13%	52	4.23
	09	31	98	33%	17%	23%	8%	29%	13%	6	4.50
	10	32	96	39%	22%	29%	43%	34%	31%	-56	5.08
Maine, John	06	15	100	0%	33%	42%	8%	33%	13%	14	4.49
	07	32	102	76%	18%	33%	33%	56%	25%	12	4.39
	08	25	102	63%	21%	17%	33%	52%	24%	8	4.50
	09	15	92	36%	27%	25%	50%	33%	33%	-66	5.08
	10	9	87	22%	33%			22%	33%	-89	5.21
Marcum, Shaun	06	14	88			21%	50%	21%	50%	-158	6.74
	07	25	91	45%	18%	43%	29%	44%	24%	-8	4.56
	08	25	94	67%	7%	30%	50%	52%	24%	8	4.50
	10	31	98	53%	12%	71%	14%	61%	13%	71	3.71
Marquis, Jason	06	33	93	28%	22%	27%	40%	27%	30%	-66	5.13
	07	33	91	44%	17%	40%	33%	42%	24%	-12	4.56
	08	28	94	29%	18%	18%	18%	25%	18%	-22	4.62
	09	33	98	33%	17%	40%	27%	36%	21%	-12	4.64
	10	13	79	0%	100%	30%	40%	23%	54%	-169	6.74

STARTING PITCHER CONSISTENCY CHART

Pitcher	Yr	#	PC	First Half DOM	First Half DIS	2nd Half DOM	2nd Half DIS	Full Season DOM	Full Season DIS	QC	qERA
Martin, J.D.	09	15	86			20%	40%	20%	40%	-120	5.50
	10	9	90	29%	29%	0%	100%	22%	44%	-133	5.50
Masterson, Justin	08	9	96	56%	0%			56%	0%	112	3.38
	09	16	97	50%	0%	30%	40%	38%	25%	-24	4.82
	10	29	101	39%	33%	45%	18%	41%	28%	-28	4.74
Matsuzaka, D	07	32	109	72%	0%	50%	14%	63%	6%	102	3.50
	08	29	100	44%	13%	54%	15%	48%	14%	40	4.28
	09	12	92	13%	50%	50%	0%	25%	33%	-82	5.13
	10	25	105	42%	25%	54%	8%	48%	16%	32	4.40
Matusz, Brian	09	8	93			25%	13%	25%	13%	-2	4.50
	10	32	94	39%	22%	50%	29%	44%	25%	-13	4.74
Maya, Yunesky	10	5	88			0%	40%	0%	40%	-160	5.90
Mazzaro, Vin	09	17	98	63%	25%	0%	67%	29%	47%	-130	5.98
	10	18	97	50%	13%	60%	30%	56%	22%	22	4.23
McCutchen, Daniel	09	6	95			33%	17%	33%	17%	-2	4.60
	10	9	82	0%	50%	33%	67%	11%	56%	-200	7.77
McDonald, James	10	12	97			42%	17%	42%	17%	17	4.44
Meche, Gil	06	32	103	56%	11%	43%	36%	50%	22%	12	4.50
	07	34	105	58%	11%	47%	13%	53%	12%	58	4.23
	08	34	105	45%	0%	86%	0%	62%	6%	100	3.50
	09	23	99	47%	26%	0%	75%	39%	35%	-62	5.13
	10	9	104	11%	33%			11%	33%	-111	5.37
Medlen, Kris	10	14	89	64%	18%	0%	33%	50%	21%	14	4.50
Mendez, Adalberto	10	5	81			20%	60%	20%	60%	-200	7.98
Miller, Andrew	07	13	94	17%	0%	0%	57%	8%	31%	-108	5.45
	08	20	91	30%	40%			30%	40%	-100	5.29
	09	14	91	31%	31%	0%	100%	29%	36%	-86	5.27
	10	7	80			0%	71%	0%	71%	-286	10.58
Millwood, Kevin	06	34	97	56%	11%	63%	13%	59%	12%	70	3.97
	07	31	95	40%	20%	38%	25%	39%	23%	-14	4.64
	08	29	93	33%	17%	73%	27%	48%	21%	12	4.53
	09	31	106	53%	11%	33%	33%	45%	19%	14	4.40
	10	31	104	28%	22%	23%	8%	26%	16%	-13	4.62
Minor, Mike	10	8	93			50%	25%	50%	25%	0	4.61
Misch, Pat	08	7	88	29%	43%			29%	43%	-114	5.40
	09	7	80			0%	29%	0%	29%	-116	5.18
	10	6	86			50%	33%	50%	33%	-33	4.71
Moehler, Brian	06	21	81	27%	47%	0%	67%	19%	52%	-170	6.90
	08	26	84	42%	17%	36%	21%	38%	19%	0	4.52
	09	29	87	33%	20%	21%	43%	28%	31%	-68	5.13
	10	8	83	0%	38%			0%	38%	-150	5.72
Monasterios, Carl	10	13	74	17%	50%	0%	71%	8%	62%	-231	8.72
Morrow, Brandon	08	5	101			40%	40%	40%	40%	-80	5.21
	09	10	85	17%	67%	25%	0%	20%	40%	-120	5.50
	10	26	97	56%	22%	63%	25%	58%	23%	23	4.23
Morton, Charlie	08	15	88	33%	17%	33%	44%	33%	33%	-66	5.08
	09	18	89	40%	40%	38%	23%	39%	28%	-34	4.82
	10	17	84	30%	50%	57%	29%	41%	41%	-82	5.21
Moseley, Dustin	10	9	89			33%	33%	33%	33%	-67	5.08
Moyer, Jamie	06	33	99	39%	6%	27%	27%	33%	15%	6	4.60
	07	33	95	39%	22%	33%	13%	36%	18%	0	4.52
	08	33	96	32%	16%	29%	7%	30%	12%	12	4.49
	09	25	96	35%	29%	38%	13%	36%	24%	-24	4.64
	10	19	92	41%	24%	0%	100%	37%	32%	-53	5.00
Myers, Brett	06	31	104	56%	19%	73%	7%	65%	13%	78	3.61
	08	30	101	29%	29%	77%	15%	50%	23%	8	4.50
	09	10	102	30%	20%			30%	20%	-20	4.71
	10	33	105	56%	0%	67%	7%	61%	3%	109	3.29
Narveson, Chris	10	28	97	29%	21%	71%	14%	50%	18%	29	4.37
Niemann, Jeff	09	30	95	19%	44%	64%	14%	40%	30%	-40	4.92
	10	29	90	59%	6%	9%	27%	34%	14%	14	4.49
Niese, Jonathon	09	5	80	50%	50%	0%	33%	20%	40%	-120	5.50
	10	30	98	40%	20%	40%	27%	40%	23%	-13	4.56
Nolasco, Ricky	06	22	87	30%	40%	25%	33%	27%	36%	-90	5.27
	08	32	99	61%	33%	79%	0%	69%	19%	62	3.73
	09	31	98	44%	25%	73%	13%	58%	19%	40	4.10
	10	26	95	50%	28%	63%	13%	54%	23%	15	4.50
Norris, Bud	09	10	90			50%	10%	50%	10%	60	4.23
	10	27	101	42%	33%	60%	27%	52%	30%	-15	4.71
Nova, Ivan	10	7	80			43%	43%	43%	43%	-86	5.21
O Sullivan, Sean	09	10	87	50%	25%	17%	67%	30%	50%	-140	6.37
	10	14	94			21%	29%	21%	29%	-71	4.98
Ohlendorf, Ross	08	5	86			0%	60%	0%	60%	-240	9.02
	09	29	93	28%	11%	55%	9%	38%	10%	36	4.41
	10	21	84	23%	23%	50%	38%	33%	29%	-48	4.90
Oliver, Andrew	10	5	83	50%	50%	0%	100%	40%	60%	-160	7.05

STARTING PITCHER CONSISTENCY CHART

Pitcher	Yr	#	PC	First Half DOM	DIS	2nd Half DOM	DIS	Full Season DOM	DIS	QC	qERA
Olsen,Scott	06	31	93	50%	19%	60%	13%	55%	16%	46	4.10
	07	33	93	26%	21%	21%	43%	24%	30%	-72	5.21
	08	33	94	42%	21%	36%	14%	39%	18%	6	4.52
	09	11	95	27%	36%			27%	36%	-90	5.27
	10	15	82	50%	25%	29%	43%	40%	33%	-53	4.92
Oswalt,Roy	06	32	101	41%	6%	73%	0%	56%	3%	100	3.38
	07	32	103	60%	0%	50%	17%	56%	6%	88	3.68
	08	32	97	58%	16%	69%	9%	63%	9%	90	3.50
	09	30	93	68%	5%	45%	18%	60%	10%	80	3.71
	10	32	99	67%	17%	79%	7%	72%	13%	94	3.51
Padilla,Vicente	06	33	100	56%	17%	33%	13%	45%	15%	30	4.40
	07	23	89	13%	40%	50%	25%	26%	35%	-88	5.27
	08	29	100	22%	17%	27%	9%	24%	14%	-8	4.51
	09	25	97	13%	13%	60%	0%	32%	8%	32	4.48
	10	16	92	67%	22%	29%	57%	50%	38%	-50	4.87
Parra,Manny	08	29	93	44%	39%	45%	18%	45%	31%	-34	4.82
	09	27	95	29%	36%	31%	23%	30%	30%	-60	5.08
	10	16	97	22%	33%	14%	0%	19%	19%	-38	4.65
Pauley,David	10	15	90	0%	0%	43%	14%	40%	13%	27	4.32
Paulino,Felipe	09	17	89	40%	50%	29%	14%	35%	35%	-70	5.13
	10	14	109	43%	14%			43%	14%	29	4.32
Pavano,Carl	08	7	81			0%	43%	0%	43%	-172	5.90
	09	33	94	56%	17%	47%	20%	52%	18%	32	4.37
	10	32	98	61%	11%	50%	14%	56%	13%	63	3.97
Peavy,Jake	06	32	105	59%	12%	60%	13%	59%	13%	66	3.97
	07	34	106	72%	0%	81%	6%	76%	3%	140	2.84
	08	27	106	73%	20%	50%	17%	63%	19%	50	3.83
	09	16	98	69%	8%	100%	0%	75%	6%	126	3.13
	10	17	101	59%	18%			59%	18%	47	4.10
Pelfrey,Mike	07	13	94	13%	25%	40%	20%	23%	23%	-46	4.75
	08	32	104	33%	28%	36%	21%	34%	25%	-32	4.90
	09	31	102	35%	29%	36%	21%	35%	26%	-34	4.82
	10	33	103	44%	22%	47%	27%	45%	24%	-6	4.53
Penny,Brad	06	33	98	61%	6%	20%	13%	42%	9%	48	4.11
	07	33	98	56%	11%	33%	13%	45%	12%	42	4.28
	08	17	98	40%	20%	0%	50%	35%	24%	-26	4.64
	09	30	98	29%	18%	54%	23%	40%	20%	0	4.56
	10	9	90	56%	11%			56%	11%	67	3.97
Perez,Oliver	06	22	96	40%	47%	43%	43%	41%	45%	-98	5.67
	07	29	104	73%	13%	57%	21%	66%	17%	64	3.73
	08	34	99	42%	26%	73%	13%	56%	21%	28	4.23
	09	14	94	17%	67%	25%	13%	21%	36%	-102	5.36
	10	7	95	14%	43%			14%	43%	-143	5.70
Pettitte,Andy	06	35	100	35%	20%	47%	13%	40%	17%	12	4.44
	07	34	99	39%	22%	50%	13%	44%	18%	16	4.44
	08	33	99	45%	20%	46%	23%	45%	21%	6	4.53
	09	32	103	39%	22%	57%	7%	47%	16%	30	4.40
	10	21	95	65%	12%	25%	75%	57%	24%	19	4.23
Pineiro,Joel	06	25	96	33%	33%	14%	43%	28%	36%	-88	5.27
	07	11	90			36%	36%	36%	36%	-72	5.13
	08	25	87	27%	20%	20%	30%	24%	24%	-48	4.75
	09	32	92	29%	6%	60%	13%	44%	9%	52	4.11
	10	23	108	44%	11%	80%	0%	52%	9%	70	3.85
Porcello,Rick	09	30	88	38%	38%	36%	29%	37%	33%	-58	5.00
	10	27	96	0%	23%	57%	14%	30%	19%	-15	4.60
Price,David	09	23	99	22%	44%	50%	14%	39%	26%	-26	4.82
	10	31	108	65%	6%	71%	0%	68%	3%	123	3.14
Richard,Clayton	08	8	81			38%	63%	38%	63%	-176	7.25
	09	26	91	25%	58%	36%	21%	31%	38%	-90	5.19
	10	33	97	56%	11%	47%	20%	52%	15%	42	4.37
Robertson,Nate	06	32	97	39%	17%	36%	7%	38%	13%	24	4.41
	07	30	96	20%	27%	60%	13%	40%	20%	0	4.56
	08	28	90	26%	16%	33%	44%	29%	25%	-42	4.93
	09	6	79			33%	50%	33%	50%	-134	6.37
	10	18	87	12%	29%	0%	0%	11%	28%	-89	5.08
Rodriguez,Wandy	06	24	92	37%	26%	20%	40%	29%	33%	-50	4.90
	07	31	98	59%	0%	36%	29%	48%	13%	44	4.28
	08	25	91	46%	31%	42%	33%	44%	32%	-40	4.92
	09	33	102	67%	22%	67%	13%	67%	18%	62	3.73
	10	32	100	44%	28%	93%	0%	66%	16%	69	3.73
Rogers,Esmil	10	8	85	0%	100%	17%	33%	13%	50%	-175	7.08
Romero,Ricky	09	29	103	69%	15%	13%	25%	38%	21%	-8	4.64
	10	32	101	61%	11%	43%	7%	53%	9%	69	3.85
Rowland-Smith,R	08	12	99	0%	50%	40%	20%	33%	25%	-34	4.90
	09	15	100	0%	100%	57%	14%	53%	20%	26	4.63
	10	20	84	0%	50%	25%	50%	5%	50%	-190	7.26
Rzepczynski,Marc	09	11	99	100%	0%	67%	22%	73%	18%	74	3.63
	10	12	89	0%	0%	36%	45%	33%	42%	-100	5.29

STARTING PITCHER CONSISTENCY CHART

Pitcher	Yr	#	PC	First Half DOM	DIS	2nd Half DOM	DIS	Full Season DOM	DIS	QC	qERA
Sabathia,C.C.	06	28	105	64%	21%	71%	7%	68%	14%	80	3.61
	07	34	105	74%	5%	73%	0%	74%	3%	136	2.99
	08	35	109	70%	15%	80%	0%	74%	0%	112	3.25
	09	34	106	58%	11%	60%	7%	59%	9%	82	3.68
	10	34	106	58%	5%	53%	0%	56%	3%	100	3.38
Sanabia,Alex	10	12	82	0%	100%	27%	18%	25%	25%	-50	4.93
Sanchez,Anibal	06	17	99	0%	50%	60%	13%	53%	18%	34	4.37
	07	6	95	0%	17%			0%	17%	-68	4.69
	08	10	88			40%	20%	40%	20%	0	4.56
	09	16	92	29%	43%	56%	22%	44%	31%	-36	4.92
	10	32	101	53%	18%	67%	13%	59%	16%	56	4.10
Sanchez,Jonathan	08	29	98	53%	21%	30%	50%	45%	31%	-34	4.82
	09	29	96	21%	36%	60%	13%	41%	24%	-14	4.56
	10	33	98	33%	22%	67%	13%	48%	18%	24	4.40
Santana,Ervin	06	33	97	50%	11%	27%	33%	39%	21%	-6	4.64
	07	26	97	56%	33%	38%	13%	50%	27%	-8	4.61
	08	32	107	79%	0%	69%	0%	75%	0%	150	2.84
	09	23	99	13%	50%	67%	7%	48%	22%	8	4.53
	10	33	108	61%	6%	47%	7%	55%	6%	85	3.68
Santana,Johan	06	34	102	74%	0%	80%	7%	76%	3%	140	2.84
	07	33	101	89%	0%	60%	7%	76%	3%	140	2.84
	08	34	106	79%	0%	80%	7%	79%	3%	146	2.84
	09	25	103	56%	6%	57%	0%	56%	4%	96	3.38
	10	29	104	58%	5%	70%	0%	62%	3%	110	3.29
Saunders,Joe	06	13	89			54%	31%	54%	31%	-16	4.71
	07	18	99	20%	0%	23%	8%	22%	6%	20	4.49
	08	31	97	39%	11%	23%	23%	32%	16%	0	4.60
	09	31	97	28%	22%	15%	23%	23%	23%	-46	4.75
	10	44	100	44%	33%	40%	13%	42%	24%	-12	4.56
Scherzer,Max	08	7	94	33%	33%	50%	0%	43%	14%	30	4.32
	09	30	102	53%	24%	46%	15%	50%	20%	20	4.50
	10	31	106	56%	19%	73%	7%	65%	13%	77	3.61
Sheets,Ben	06	17	92	50%	25%	85%	8%	76%	12%	104	3.41
	07	24	94	67%	11%	50%	50%	63%	21%	42	3.95
	08	31	99	72%	0%	54%	15%	65%	6%	106	3.38
	10	20	98	47%	11%	0%	0%	45%	10%	50	4.28
Shields,James	06	21	95	50%	0%	46%	15%	48%	10%	56	4.28
	07	31	102	61%	0%	77%	8%	68%	3%	124	3.14
	08	33	95	63%	11%	50%	7%	58%	9%	80	3.68
	09	33	101	63%	5%	43%	7%	55%	6%	86	3.68
	10	33	101	50%	11%	47%	27%	48%	18%	24	4.40
Silva,Carlos	06	31	84	13%	33%	31%	38%	23%	35%	-94	5.36
	07	33	93	33%	17%	40%	20%	36%	18%	0	4.52
	08	28	88	35%	25%	0%	63%	25%	36%	-94	5.27
	09	6	86	17%	83%			17%	83%	-298	10.80
	10	21	83	71%	12%	25%	50%	62%	19%	48	3.83
Slowey,Kevin	07	11	94	0%	29%	75%	0%	27%	18%	-18	4.62
	08	27	93	50%	21%	46%	15%	48%	19%	20	4.40
	09	16	89	44%	31%			44%	31%	-36	4.92
	10	28	94	35%	35%	45%	36%	39%	36%	-64	5.13
Smith,Greg	10	8	88	13%	25%			13%	25%	-75	5.08
Snell,Ian	06	32	95	39%	28%	50%	0%	44%	16%	24	4.44
	07	32	98	65%	0%	53%	13%	59%	6%	94	3.68
	08	31	97	39%	33%	38%	31%	39%	32%	-50	5.00
	09	27	94	27%	20%	17%	17%	22%	19%	-32	4.63
	10	8	85	25%	38%			25%	38%	-100	5.27
Stammen,Craig	09	19	83	40%	20%	22%	44%	32%	32%	-64	5.08
	10	19	87	27%	40%	75%	0%	37%	32%	-53	5.00
Stauffer,Tim	09	14	90	100%	0%	31%	38%	36%	36%	-72	5.13
	10	7	81	0%	0%	67%	33%	57%	29%	0	4.39
Strasburg,Stephen	10	12	89	71%	0%	40%	40%	58%	17%	50	4.10
Suppan,Jeff	06	32	96	6%	41%	40%	27%	22%	34%	-92	5.21
	07	34	98	32%	11%	27%	7%	29%	9%	22	4.48
	08	31	91	28%	28%	8%	31%	19%	29%	-78	5.03
	09	30	91	22%	39%	8%	42%	17%	40%	-126	5.60
	10	15	81	0%	71%	38%	13%	20%	40%	-120	5.50
Takahashi,H	10	12	93	44%	22%	67%	33%	50%	25%	0	4.61
Talbot,Mitch	10	28	94	24%	12%	18%	45%	21%	25%	-57	4.98
Tallet,Brian	09	25	93	41%	18%	25%	38%	36%	24%	-24	4.64
	10	5	89	20%	40%			20%	40%	-120	5.50
Tillman,Chris	09	12	97			0%	33%	0%	33%	-132	5.53
	10	11	87	20%	60%	17%	50%	18%	55%	-182	7.55
Tomlin,Josh	10	12	93			50%	17%	50%	17%	33	4.37
Vargas,Jason	09	14	90	18%	36%	0%	67%	14%	43%	-144	5.70
	10	31	97	47%	6%	29%	21%	39%	13%	26	4.41

STARTING PITCHER CONSISTENCY CHART

Pitcher	Yr	#	PC	First Half DOM	DIS	2nd Half DOM	DIS	Full Season DOM	DIS	QC	qERA
Vazquez,Javier	06	32	103	47%	6%	53%	20%	50%	13%	48	4.23
	07	32	108	82%	0%	67%	0%	75%	0%	150	2.84
	08	33	102	53%	16%	50%	29%	52%	21%	20	4.50
	09	32	104	83%	0%	86%	0%	84%	0%	168	2.69
	10	26	96	44%	31%	10%	80%	31%	50%	-138	6.37
Verlander,Justin	06	30	99	47%	6%	38%	23%	43%	13%	34	4.32
	07	32	105	76%	6%	67%	13%	72%	9%	108	3.25
	08	33	107	50%	10%	46%	31%	48%	18%	24	4.40
	09	35	112	79%	11%	75%	0%	77%	6%	130	3.13
	10	33	114	56%	6%	87%	0%	70%	3%	127	2.99
Volquez,Edinson	06	8	81			13%	63%	13%	63%	-226	8.46
	07	6	99			33%	17%	33%	17%	-2	4.60
	08	32	105	74%	11%	54%	8%	66%	9%	96	3.38
	09	9	94	44%	33%			44%	33%	-44	4.92
	10	12	92			50%	33%	50%	33%	-33	4.71
Volstad,Chris	08	14	92	100%	0%	31%	15%	36%	14%	16	4.41
	09	29	89	50%	22%	9%	64%	34%	38%	-84	5.19
	10	30	94	35%	18%	31%	31%	33%	23%	-27	4.71
Wainwright,Adam	07	32	99	18%	12%	60%	7%	38%	9%	40	4.29
	08	20	98	62%	0%	43%	14%	55%	5%	90	3.68
	09	34	106	53%	0%	80%	0%	65%	0%	130	3.14
	10	33	102	84%	5%	79%	0%	82%	3%	152	2.69
Wakefield,Tim	06	23	98	61%	6%	0%	60%	48%	17%	28	4.40
	07	31	93	35%	18%	36%	29%	35%	23%	-22	4.64
	08	30	93	42%	11%	45%	36%	43%	20%	6	4.56
	09	21	96	35%	12%	50%	25%	38%	14%	20	4.41
	10	19	96	50%	7%	20%	20%	42%	11%	42	4.32
Weaver,Jered	06	19	102	100%	0%	38%	15%	58%	11%	72	3.97
	07	28	98	50%	29%	50%	14%	50%	21%	16	4.50
	08	30	101	63%	16%	45%	18%	57%	17%	46	4.10
	09	33	103	67%	6%	47%	27%	58%	15%	56	4.10
	10	34	109	84%	11%	73%	0%	79%	6%	135	3.13

STARTING PITCHER CONSISTENCY CHART

Pitcher	Yr	#	PC	First Half DOM	DIS	2nd Half DOM	DIS	Full Season DOM	DIS	QC	qERA
Wellemeyer,Todd	07	11	77	25%	38%	67%	33%	36%	36%	-72	5.13
	08	32	97	67%	11%	57%	0%	63%	6%	102	3.50
	09	21	93	22%	28%	0%	100%	19%	38%	-114	5.45
	10	11	85	27%	45%			27%	45%	-127	5.98
Wells,Randy	09	27	94	75%	8%	27%	33%	48%	22%	8	4.53
	10	32	96	50%	17%	43%	14%	47%	16%	31	4.40
Westbrook,Jake	06	32	102	61%	17%	21%	14%	44%	16%	24	4.44
	07	25	99	44%	33%	31%	6%	36%	16%	8	4.52
	08	5	101	20%	0%			20%	0%	40	4.47
	10	33	101	28%	28%	47%	7%	36%	18%	0	4.52
Willis,Dontrelle	06	34	106	33%	17%	44%	19%	38%	18%	4	4.52
	07	35	100	47%	11%	19%	38%	34%	23%	-24	4.56
	08	7	71	0%	75%	0%	33%	0%	57%	-228	8.24
	09	7	88	14%	57%			14%	57%	-200	7.77
	10	13	93	23%	46%			23%	46%	-138	6.12
Wilson,C.J.	10	33	104	33%	11%	60%	13%	45%	12%	42	4.28
Wolf,Randy	06	12	88			17%	33%	17%	33%	-98	3.68
	07	18	99	33%	11%			33%	11%	22	4.49
	08	33	96	60%	30%	38%	23%	52%	27%	-4	4.61
	09	34	97	53%	11%	80%	0%	65%	6%	106	3.38
	10	34	105	21%	21%	60%	7%	38%	15%	18	4.52
Wood,Travis	10	17	95	33%	33%	64%	7%	59%	12%	71	3.97
Zambrano,Carlos	06	33	110	68%	11%	71%	14%	70%	12%	92	3.51
	07	34	109	68%	16%	47%	13%	59%	15%	58	4.10
	08	30	101	56%	6%	33%	33%	47%	17%	26	4.40
	09	28	102	56%	13%	50%	25%	54%	18%	36	4.37
	10	20	99	33%	33%	55%	9%	45%	20%	10	4.53
Zimmermann,J	09	16	98	60%	7%	0%	0%	56%	6%	88	3.68
	10	7	79			43%	57%	43%	57%	-143	6.59
Zito,Barry	06	34	108	47%	5%	33%	20%	41%	12%	34	4.32
	07	33	103	22%	22%	60%	27%	39%	24%	-18	4.64
	08	32	100	26%	42%	31%	23%	28%	34%	-80	5.13
	09	33	97	33%	22%	67%	27%	48%	24%	0	4.53
	10	33	98	50%	28%	33%	40%	42%	33%	-48	4.92

Bullpen Indicator Charts

Closer Volatility Chart

CLOSERS DRAFTED refers to the number of saves sources purchased in both LABR and Tout Wars experts leagues each year. These only include relievers drafted for at least $10, specifically for saves speculation. **AVG R$** refers to the average purchase price of these pitchers in the AL-only and NL-only leagues. **FAILED** is the number (and percentage) of closers drafted that did not return at least 50% of their value that year. The Failures include those that lost their value due to ineffectiveness, injury or managerial decision. **NEW SOURCES** are arms that were drafted for less than $10 (if they were drafted at all) but finished with at least double-digit saves.

Bullpen Indicators Chart

These charts offer insight for those looking to speculate on future closer candidates. The charts help focus on many of the statistical and situational factors that might go into a manager's decision to grant any individual pitcher a save opportunity. It's not all-encompassing, but it's a good start. The chart provides a five-year scan for nearly all pitchers who posted at least two saves and/or five holds in 2010.

Saves Percentage: What it says is simple... "Who is getting it done?" Intuitively, this percentage should be a major factor in determining which closers might be in danger of losing their jobs. However, a Doug Dennis study showed little correlation between saves success rate alone and future opportunity. Better to prospect for pitchers who have *both* a high saves percentage (80% or better) *and* high skills, as measured by base performance value.

Base Performance Value: The components of BPV are evaluated in many ways. Big league managers tend to look for a pitcher who can strike out eight or nine batters per 9 IP, sometimes even if he's also walking that many. In using BPV, we set a benchmark of 75 as the minimum necessary for success. BPV's more than 100 are much better, however.

Situational Performance is the last piece of the puzzle. The chart includes opposition batting averages for each pitcher versus right-handed and left-handed hitters, with runners on base, in his first 15 pitches, etc. which are all good indicators. We'll set a benchmark of a .250 BA; anything over and the risk level increases.

There are other variables that come into play as well. Left-handed relievers rarely move into a closer's role unless the team's bullpen has sufficient southpaw depth. Some managers do see the value of having a high-skills arm available for the middle innings, so those pitchers don't get promoted into a closer's role either.

The tools are here. Whether or not a manager will make a decision reflective of this information remains to be seen. But the data can help us increase our odds of uncovering those elusive saves and minimizing some of the risk.

NOTE: In the Bullpen Indicators Chart, BPV values for 2006-07 use the previous version of the BPV formula. 2008-10 values use the new version.

2010 Closer Volatility Report

Closer values dropped 60 cents in 2010, the largest decline since 2006. The $16.96 average value is also a new all-time low. The percentage of closers that failed dropped to 25%, the lowest failure rate in over a decade.

Six drafted closers managed to return 30% or more in profit, double the number from last year: Billy Wagner ($30 return on $18 average draft price), Brian Wilson and Heath Bell (both $28 on $19), Carlos Marmol ($24 on $15), Rafael Soriano ($28 on $20) and Matt Capps ($22 on $13). Eleven drafted closers (39%) returned any type of profit, up 10% from last year. Four returned $0 on their investments (which averaged $15.75) — Mike Gonzalez, Trevor Hoffman, Joe Nathan and Chad Qualls. In all, 17 of 28 pitchers drafted for saves (61%) realized a loss on their purchase price. Saves remain very high risk investments.

The accompanying chart lists the seven 2010 closers who returned less than 50% of their draft value; these are classified as the "failures." However, the list does not include others who also lost their jobs but managed to return at least half their value. These pitchers were Octavio Dotel, Brian Fuentes, Bobby Jenks, Leo Nunez and Huston Street. So, in some sense, the failure rate was even greater than indicated.

While the rate of failed closers plummeted, the number of new sources of 10+ saves remained stable, an indication that teams are running through more options in their efforts to fill that role. Note that both Baltimore and Houston each have two pitchers on the New Sources List. Kevin Gregg appears as a new source even though Jason Frasor is not on the Failures list. Frasor was the closer coming into the season but not did not generate enough draft bidding activity to be considered a failure based on our definition.

Of the 13 new sources that amassed at least 10 saves in 2010, few would be considered strong front-line closer candidates for 2011. In fact, beyond John Axford, Neftali Feliz (who might still be a rotation candidate) and Chris Perez, it is possible that none of the remaining 10 will open 2011 as a closer.

As we go to press, there are four unsettled bullpen situations in the American League and seven in the National League. Five potential closers are free agents — Koji Uehara, Mariano Rivera, Rafael Soriano, and both Kevin Gregg and Jason Frasor in Toronto. There is no guarantee that all these arms will find closing jobs, and in fact, several are good bets to end up in other roles. Still, their signings may create possible ripple effects for all closers.

There will always be volatility here, but this winter likely will not have nearly as much impact as recent seasons. As such, it is reasonable to expect closer prices to rise somewhat in 2011.

CLOSER VOLATILITY CHART

FAILURES

	2004	2005	2006	2007	2008	2009	2010
	Biddle	Adams	Benitez	Benitez	Accardo	Capps	Broxton
	Borowski	Affeldt	Dempster	Dotel	Isringhausen	Devine	Francisco,F
	Guardado	Benitez	Foulke	Fuentes	Jones,T	Hanrahan	Gonzalez,M
	Koch	Dotel	Gagne	Gagne	Soriano,R	Lidge	Hoffman
	Lopez,Aq	Foulke	Guardado	Gonzalez,M	Borowski	Lindstrom	Nathan
	MacDougal	Gagne	MacDougal	Gordon	Corpas	Marmol	Qualls
	Mantei	Graves	Orvella	Ray	Cordero,C	Motte	Wood
	Nen	Kolb	Reitsma	Ryan	Gagne	Perez,C	
	Rhodes	Mota	Turnbow	Torres	Putz	Ryan,BJ	
	Riske	Percival	Valverde	Wickman	Wilson,CJ	Wood	
	Wagner	Speier					
		Takatsu					

NEW SOURCES

	2004	2005	2006	2007	2008	2009	2010
	Affeldt	Brazoban	Burgos	Accardo	Broxton	Aardsma	Axford
	Aquino	Bruney	Duchscherer	Capps	Franklin,R	Bailey,A	Corpas
	Chacon	Dempster	Julio,J	Corpas	Fuentes	Franklin	Feliz,N
	Cordero	Farnsworth	Nelson,J	Embree	Gonzalez,M	Frasor	Gregg
	Frasor	Fuentes	Otsuka	Gregg	Lewis,J	Hawkins	Gutierrez
	Herges	Hermanson	Papelbon	Hennessy	Morrow	Howell,JP	Kuo
	Hermanson	Jones,T	Putz	Myers,B	Rauch	Johnson,J	Lindstrom
	Hawkins	Lyon	Saito,T	Reyes,A	Rodney	MacDougal	Lyon
	Lidge	MacDougal	Timlin	Soria	Torres,S	Madson	Perez,C
	Putz	Reitsma	Torres,S	Wheeler	Wheeler	Nunez,L	Rauch
	Rodriguez,Fr	Rodney	Walker,T	Wilson,CJ	Ziegler	Rodney	Rodney
	Takatsu	Street	Wheeler			Soriano,R	Simon,A
	Wickman	Turnbow				Wilson,CJ	Uehara
	Worrell	Walker,T					
	Yan	Weathers					

SUMMARY

YEAR	NUMBER OF CLOSERS Drafted	Avg R$	Failed	Failure %	New Sources
1999	23	$25	5	22%	7
2000	27	$25	10	37%	9
2001	25	$26	7	28%	7
2002	28	$22	8	29%	12
2003	29	$21.97	17	59%	14
2004	29	$19.78	11	38%	15
2005	28	$20.79	12	43%	15
2006	30	$17.80	10	33%	12
2007	28	$17.67	10	36%	11
2008	32	$17.78	10	31%	11
2009	28	$17.56	9	32%	13
2010	28	$16.96	7	25%	13

BULLPEN INDICATORS

			BPIs			Results		Runners		Pitch Ct		Platoon	
Pitcher			IP/g	bpv	S%	Sv%	Eff%	Emp	On	1-15	16-30	vLH	vRH
Aardsma,David	R	06	1.2	41	75%	0%	100%	189	247	219	197	190	225
		07	1.3	66	63%	0%	56%	262	338	274	356	283	310
		08	1.0	4	68%	0%	73%	202	298	223	316	253	245
		09	1.0	63	80%	90%	82%	185	180	178	185	190	175
		10	0.9	52	74%	86%	74%	271	292	260	381	356	203
Abad,Fernando	L	10	0.9	48	81%	0%	86%	257	263	295	125	238	273
Adams,Mike	R	08	1.2	130	82%	0%	71%	158	273	220	188	225	181
		09	1.0	170	90%	0%	94%	98	158	110	150	138	91
		10	1.0	113	84%	0%	89%	223	371	281	261	280	278
Affeldt,Jeremy	L	06	1.8	9	62%	33%	58%	165	315	260	180	213	240
		07	0.8	58	74%	0%	65%	240	213	241	129	250	211
		08	1.1	116	79%	0%	75%	268	258	277	224	269	261
		09	0.8	62	87%	0%	95%	226	182	187	281	207	198
		10	0.9	60	75%	57%	71%	363	388	371	414	392	365
Albers,Matt	R	08	1.8	10	75%	0%	64%	226	233	203	227	159	292
		09	1.2	11	66%	0%	57%	321	306	296	358	342	289
		10	1.2	30	70%	0%	71%	327	310	333	319	333	307
Atchison,Scott	R	10	1.4	60	69%	0%	75%	333	280	357	241	368	265
Axford,John	R	10	1.2	125	78%	89%	88%	338	300	330	333	344	297
Badenhop,Burke	R	09	2.1	78	72%	0%	64%	257	253	231	277	257	254
		10	1.3	72	68%	33%	61%	245	352	266	298	282	304
Baez,Danys	R	09	1.2	56	67%	0%	70%	196	265	200	306	250	205
		10	0.9	12	68%	0%	60%	368	310	316	414	382	315
Bailey,Andrew	R	09	1.2	124	82%	87%	83%	180	157	174	173	149	188
		10	1.0	91	89%	89%	81%	303	208	284	208	242	284
Balfour,Grant	R	08	1.1	128	86%	80%	89%	120	169	100	213	122	156
		09	0.9	56	65%	44%	75%	197	275	226	246	242	235
		10	1.0	98	81%	0%	90%	316	290	321	241	364	253
Bard,Daniel	R	09	1.0	115	74%	25%	76%	222	238	262	156	263	202
		10	1.0	92	86%	30%	80%	273	228	253	250	183	351
Batista,Miguel	R	09	1.3	8	77%	20%	73%	309	259	284	293	328	247
		10	1.4	21	75%	100%	67%	250	331	343	254	279	297
Beimel,Joe	L	06	1.1	26	79%	100%	93%	258	267	286	185	232	279
		07	0.8	42	67%	100%	91%	250	256	256	235	188	294
		08	0.7	25	85%	0%	94%	268	260	265	250	278	250
		09	0.8	36	76%	17%	58%	263	269	232	412	244	282
		10	0.6	16	79%	0%	88%	300	314	314	200	263	357
Belisario,Ronald	R	09	1.0	78	84%	0%	62%	218	178	184	250	268	156
		10	0.9	67	62%	50%	88%	295	321	288	333	295	314
Belisle,Matt	R	09	1.3	95	62%	0%	80%	246	315	333	162	241	308
		10	1.2	142	75%	50%	83%	349	317	323	324	338	335
Bell,Heath	R	07	1.2	134	79%	33%	84%	162	214	182	206	216	157
		08	1.1	83	71%	0%	69%	234	197	234	159	197	242
		09	1.0	122	76%	88%	83%	241	175	239	141	278	132
		10	1.0	124	83%	94%	93%	361	288	325	353	310	341
Benoit,Joaquin	R	10	1.0	174	91%	25%	84%	253	178	190	421	275	192
Berg,Justin	R	10	1.0	-33	68%	0%	83%	230	365	292	371	250	337
Berken,Jason	R	10	1.5	68	79%	0%	59%	333	333	330	375	323	339
Betancourt,Rafae	R	06	1.1	104	71%	50%	65%	214	278	248	236	221	254
		07	1.2	223	84%	50%	91%	190	173	191	157	239	148
		08	1.0	64	68%	50%	70%	275	270	303	200	243	295
		09	0.9	94	78%	33%	79%	242	184	238	143	268	174
		10	0.9	204	69%	20%	85%	329	403	368	313	444	310
Blevins,Jerry	L	10	0.8	79	80%	50%	88%	370	343	354	444	328	379
Boggs,Mitchell	R	10	1.1	59	73%	0%	73%	337	281	263	460	279	328
Boyer,Blaine	R	08	0.9	89	58%	20%	63%	228	313	230	357	271	256
		09	1.1	36	68%	0%	67%	206	327	263	345	240	288
		10	1.1	3	72%	0%	57%	295	352	292	357	381	256
Braddock,Zach	L	10	0.7	68	79%	0%	80%	390	289	347	300	258	382
Breslow,Craig	L	08	1.0	56	83%	50%	67%	214	200	196	229	190	224
		09	0.9	36	74%	0%	72%	224	160	190	220	206	185
		10	1.0	68	78%	71%	81%	259	247	262	244	250	256
Broxton,Jonathar	R	06	1.1	106	83%	43%	79%	253	172	234	192	244	196
		07	1.0	137	77%	25%	79%	228	220	245	152	200	247
		08	1.0	130	72%	64%	70%	173	255	199	238	260	177
		09	1.0	176	74%	86%	85%	151	196	149	232	142	194
		10	1.0	106	73%	76%	70%	375	408	367	452	371	404
Burnett,Sean	L	09	0.8	28	76%	33%	74%	198	161	176	217	186	176
		10	0.9	114	83%	75%	75%	333	292	336	256	409	253
Byrdak,Tim	L	06	0.4	-56	60%	0%	100%	412	467	444	400	381	545
		07	1.2	80	79%	50%	92%	231	230	193	290	176	268
		08	0.9	28	78%	0%	91%	232	218	235	105	138	295
		09	0.8	26	82%	0%	71%	180	176	177	208	186	171
		10	0.6	3	80%	0%	87%	322	356	353	250	286	387
Camp,Shawn	R	06	1.0	64	71%	67%	79%	316	310	300	365	370	284
		07	0.8	54	66%	0%	69%	382	362	397	212	370	368
		08	1.0	92	67%	0%	91%	228	301	279	167	356	204
		09	1.4	62	75%	100%	60%	256	237	243	273	268	228
		10	1.0	73	80%	50%	79%	325	300	315	325	340	295

BULLPEN INDICATORS

			BPIs			Results		Runners		Pitch Ct		Platoon	
Pitcher			IP/g	bpv	S%	Sv%	Eff%	Emp	On	1-15	16-30	vLH	vRH
Capps,Matt	R	06	1.0	95	72%	10%	70%	265	268	266	288	250	275
		07	1.0	99	80%	86%	79%	228	207	197	364	281	181
		08	1.1	106	72%	81%	74%	233	253	248	235	229	253
		09	1.0	79	69%	84%	71%	353	294	311	380	339	311
		10	1.0	102	84%	88%	84%	339	340	346	310	324	353
Carrasco,D.J.	R	10	1.2	55	72%	0%	77%	267	356	279	315	338	293
Cashner,Andrew	R	10	1.0	41	73%	0%	72%	329	394	330	421	397	333
Casilla,Santiago	R	07	1.1	73	68%	40%	81%	216	233	208	266	212	230
		08	1.0	60	77%	67%	85%	344	257	328	230	308	291
		09	1.1	17	68%	0%	75%	250	354	326	178	366	243
		10	1.1	79	84%	67%	87%	333	295	329	300	444	278
Chacin,Gustavo	L	10	0.9	18	75%	100%	80%	393	377	386	457	442	356
Chamberlain,Job.	R	10	1.0	123	67%	43%	80%	376	315	353	327	349	339
Chavez,Jesse	R	09	0.9	50	76%	0%	67%	256	277	270	255	230	301
		10	1.2	39	63%	0%	65%	303	402	331	327	307	372
Choate,Randy	L	09	0.6	94	71%	100%	100%	213	210	213	200	149	306
		10	0.5	91	67%	0%	81%	381	293	327	500	287	471
Clippard,Tyler	R	09	1.5	53	85%	0%	70%	165	190	186	197	114	247
		10	1.2	96	77%	9%	66%	315	314	349	224	362	276
Coffey,Todd	R	09	1.1	95	79%	33%	80%	226	273	258	206	292	213
		10	0.9	82	69%	0%	71%	247	447	350	324	354	341
Coke,Phil	L	09	0.8	63	63%	29%	77%	235	184	196	243	197	229
		10	0.9	48	73%	50%	79%	326	352	338	345	360	324
Contreras,Jose	R	10	0.8	117	75%	80%	82%	382	338	354	421	344	373
Cordero,Francisc	R	06	1.0	90	74%	67%	75%	229	266	260	231	286	219
		07	1.0	156	74%	86%	80%	187	260	191	340	225	212
		08	1.0	61	78%	85%	80%	213	261	245	203	212	252
		09	1.0	48	84%	91%	80%	241	253	230	327	230	260
		10	1.0	32	74%	83%	78%	311	333	323	293	360	291
Corpas,Manny	R	06	0.9	91	76%	0%	67%	282	291	311	150	281	290
		07	1.0	90	84%	86%	89%	211	245	213	300	234	214
		08	1.0	59	70%	31%	67%	275	295	271	315	267	301
		09	1.0	93	60%	33%	64%	286	369	348	217	400	267
		10	1.1	57	69%	71%	63%	318	352	347	378	368	311
Crain,Jesse	R	06	1.1	91	74%	25%	65%	243	289	250	256	259	263
		07	0.9	47	68%	0%	78%	200	440	224	500	269	308
		08	0.9	55	76%	0%	76%	276	233	256	255	247	258
		09	0.9	26	67%	0%	73%	255	241	243	275	296	218
		10	1.0	68	76%	25%	85%	292	257	275	270	250	298
Daley,Matt	R	09	0.9	97	67%	0%	76%	178	280	216	256	260	198
		10	0.8	37	74%	0%	86%	326	419	377	308	385	354
Delcarmen,Mann	R	06	1.1	91	66%	0%	80%	273	345	283	371	319	302
		07	1.0	93	85%	50%	92%	193	169	195	143	164	196
		08	1.0	92	72%	40%	81%	199	215	209	200	197	214
		09	0.9	-2	73%	0%	69%	288	252	229	361	221	322
		10	0.9	-8	70%	0%	61%	274	297	304	219	261	300
Demel,Sam	R	10	1.0	97	65%	100%	89%	361	364	368	235	311	394
Dessens,Elmer	R	10	0.9	-8	85%	0%	83%	296	219	252	304	260	260
Dotel,Octavio	R	07	0.9	117	73%	73%	74%	322	164	278	133	265	225
		08	0.9	127	77%	20%	76%	242	188	235	167	250	201
		09	1.0	56	81%	0%	76%	228	250	238	232	268	226
		10	0.9	78	73%	79%	74%	319	338	360	256	394	271
Doubront,Felix	L	10	2.1	77	74%	67%	63%	429	300	400	250	364	385
Downs,Scott	L	06	1.3	54	72%	25%	72%	246	134	199	203	177	208
		07	0.7	97	84%	25%	85%	198	250	233	184	209	238
		08	1.1	82	86%	56%	81%	200	229	209	203	194	226
		09	1.0	114	78%	69%	74%	295	205	259	222	263	246
		10	0.9	107	74%	0%	82%	274	273	271	269	207	307
Duensing,Brian	L	09	3.5	36	75%	0%	75%	266	286	341	220	227	303
		10	2.5	63	82%	0%	86%	325	196	244	400	151	349
Durbin,Chad	R	09	1.2	-8	73%	67%	80%	210	240	207	276	229	217
		10	1.1	73	73%	0%	90%	385	272	328	340	418	266
Farnsworth,Kyle	R	09	0.9	111	70%	0%	46%	232	353	288	289	277	294
		10	1.1	100	71%	0%	71%	316	308	358	171	337	289
Feliciano,Pedro	L	06	0.9	87	86%	0%	77%	255	242	270	173	231	266
		07	0.8	87	75%	67%	88%	233	165	199	208	168	221
		08	0.6	60	78%	50%	81%	292	268	297	115	198	368
		09	0.7	120	79%	0%	83%	274	184	228	238	216	264
		10	0.7	62	77%	0%	79%	370	344	311	586	287	421
Feliz,Neftali	R	09	1.6	152	79%	67%	92%	134	114	154	93	161	87
		10	1.0	118	71%	93%	89%	231	288	242	289	200	295
Flores,Randy	L	06	0.6	58	68%	0%	90%	286	293	306	182	258	329
		07	0.8	72	71%	50%	95%	261	360	307	333	326	299
		08	0.6	-56	75%	33%	89%	273	344	286	435	314	316
		09	0.4	164	64%	0%	91%	320	250	268	375	273	313
		10	0.5	0	88%	0%	90%	306	362	341	250	360	304

BULLPEN INDICATORS

			BPIs			Results		Runners		Pitch Ct		Platoon	
Pitcher			IP/g	bpv	S%	Sv%	Eff%	Emp	On	1-15	16-30	vLH	vRH
Francisco,Frank	R	07	1.0	42	71%	0%	96%	309	220	245	284	221	286
		08	1.1	117	77%	45%	65%	189	212	196	216	193	205
		09	1.0	116	69%	86%	82%	167	300	203	250	240	190
		10	0.9	119	73%	33%	74%	329	393	391	174	281	407
Franklin,Ryan	R	07	1.2	92	74%	17%	77%	227	244	256	172	238	231
		08	1.1	33	80%	68%	72%	269	284	283	278	258	287
		09	1.0	44	85%	88%	84%	231	192	221	182	194	230
		10	1.1	90	70%	93%	89%	291	264	296	255	310	258
Frasor,Jason	R	06	1.0	75	71%	0%	83%	207	293	248	235	211	262
		07	1.1	93	61%	50%	50%	217	222	213	224	245	200
		08	1.0	-10	72%	0%	63%	230	186	194	267	266	174
		09	0.9	104	78%	79%	79%	198	227	217	186	274	140
		10	0.9	86	74%	50%	72%	302	348	314	375	329	324
Frieri,Ernesto	R	10	1.0	82	88%	0%	89%	297	233	289	238	316	250
Fuentes,Brian	L	06	1.0	86	75%	83%	77%	240	173	216	184	183	218
		07	1.0	82	76%	74%	72%	167	271	190	275	204	207
		08	0.9	131	76%	88%	80%	188	235	180	300	184	210
		09	0.8	41	75%	87%	80%	264	247	268	205	229	271
		10	1.0	58	78%	86%	86%	205	320	216	385	207	266
Fulchino,Jeff	R	09	1.3	84	73%	0%	72%	226	233	235	280	254	208
		10	0.9	62	68%	0%	78%	373	352	367	364	367	360
Gonzalez,Mike	L	06	1.0	102	83%	100%	88%	168	267	223	184	163	227
		07	0.9	51	87%	100%	100%	290	200	235	300	333	189
		08	0.9	115	71%	88%	74%	221	205	253	77	269	200
		09	0.9	98	84%	59%	74%	258	142	233	138	198	219
		10	0.9	77	68%	33%	71%	269	370	357	182	455	226
Grabow,John	L	06	1.0	70	73%	0%	79%	223	307	259	214	275	251
		07	0.8	63	71%	50%	80%	263	291	293	231	238	303
		08	1.0	28	83%	50%	79%	259	176	228	227	239	214
		09	1.0	11	77%	0%	93%	200	265	254	154	213	242
		10	0.9	23	63%	0%	67%	465	326	388	333	370	403
Gregerson,Luke	R	09	1.0	119	73%	14%	75%	214	239	233	200	291	162
		10	1.0	154	65%	29%	79%	198	355	228	450	275	235
Gregg,Kevin	R	07	1.1	76	73%	89%	81%	194	220	166	276	162	247
		08	1.0	27	73%	76%	70%	182	228	206	200	179	224
		09	1.0	73	70%	77%	69%	242	212	233	222	195	257
		10	0.9	56	76%	86%	78%	360	271	313	325	338	308
Guerrier,Matt	R	06	1.8	31	81%	100%	100%	304	273	276	318	337	258
		07	1.2	92	83%	25%	71%	218	224	232	195	264	187
		08	1.0	30	71%	20%	68%	266	287	264	273	280	272
		09	1.0	70	84%	25%	91%	250	165	224	160	198	221
		10	1.0	46	75%	14%	69%	264	265	249	350	280	255
Gutierrez,Juan	R	09	1.1	63	68%	90%	83%	211	301	264	240	297	212
		10	1.0	49	71%	88%	74%	337	308	318	342	351	302
Hanrahan,Joel	R	08	1.2	72	74%	69%	72%	215	252	257	230	228	237
		09	1.0	61	70%	50%	63%	293	279	302	274	271	297
		10	1.0	162	72%	60%	85%	337	387	349	407	362	353
Harrison,Matt	L	10	2.1	-1	72%	67%	73%	311	324	382	214	333	311
Hawkins,LaTroy	R	06	1.0	44	69%	0%	76%	313	287	314	278	323	285
		07	0.9	53	76%	0%	67%	262	237	222	433	237	266
		08	1.1	62	67%	50%	89%	178	303	219	250	287	185
		09	1.0	77	88%	73%	79%	279	198	266	167	204	289
		10	0.9	116	48%	0%	55%	429	474	389	600	412	467
Heilman,Aaron	R	06	1.2	85	69%	0%	76%	205	267	228	239	231	231
		07	1.1	87	75%	17%	71%	197	261	211	237	234	218
		08	1.0	38	69%	38%	62%	216	309	262	240	308	225
		09	1.0	47	74%	14%	60%	257	256	270	261	214	286
		10	1.0	50	70%	43%	59%	319	337	303	397	294	361
Hendrickson,Mar	L	09	2.0	42	74%	33%	56%	292	240	232	305	247	283
		10	1.4	75	68%	0%	53%	373	377	364	397	410	356
Hensley,Clay	R	10	1.1	103	81%	70%	82%	305	256	241	413	311	258
Hernandez,David	R	10	1.9	24	72%	33%	50%	378	320	353	348	235	410
Herrera,Daniel R.	L	09	0.9	48	80%	0%	76%	263	291	261	360	185	362
		10	0.6	56	77%	0%	71%	333	425	373	429	375	380
Herrmann,Frank	R	10	1.1	52	73%	50%	80%	272	388	343	267	380	273
Hoffman,Trevor	R	06	1.0	98	84%	90%	87%	257	122	212	133	194	214
		07	0.9	70	73%	86%	79%	215	247	230	211	299	169
		08	0.9	130	72%	88%	77%	211	268	217	333	299	170
		09	1.0	97	81%	90%	87%	180	200	209	43	227	151
		10	0.9	15	62%	67%	54%	323	317	279	467	373	279
Hughes,Dustin	L	09	1.8	54	68%	0%	50%	222	190	357	111	250	182
		10	1.0	8	74%	0%	73%	453	235	378	212	325	330
Jansen,Kenley	R	10	1.1	123	93%	100%	100%	286	143	235	273	333	120
Jenks,Bobby	R	06	1.0	97	72%	91%	85%	241	266	254	261	227	268
		07	1.0	131	68%	87%	80%	149	269	202	176	237	169
		08	1.1	69	77%	88%	87%	244	209	244	156	219	240
		09	1.0	101	78%	83%	76%	268	224	265	190	309	202
		10	1.0	141	67%	87%	80%	361	375	357	452	377	359

BULLPEN INDICATORS

			BPIs			Results		Runners		Pitch Ct		Platoon	
Pitcher			IP/g	bpv	S%	Sv%	Eff%	Emp	On	1-15	16-30	vLH	vRH
Jepsen,Kevin	R	09	1.0	91	65%	50%	83%	263	296	280	292	356	204
		10	0.9	82	70%	0%	78%	349	360	339	400	329	388
Johnson,Jim	R	08	1.3	27	79%	100%	85%	236	200	198	250	227	212
		09	1.1	63	73%	63%	70%	285	239	278	224	248	279
		10	1.0	118	77%	17%	68%	381	405	339	500	333	459
Kuo,Hong-Chih	L	08	1.9	149	81%	33%	78%	204	181	214	188	167	207
		09	0.9	87	75%	0%	94%	236	167	209	167	156	225
		10	1.1	138	85%	92%	92%	221	200	224	156	171	227
Laffey,Aaron	L	09	4.9	-8	73%	100%	0%	200	286	130	353	176	276
		10	1.9	-14	70%	0%	70%	327	321	290	343	378	283
League,Brandon	R	08	1.1	46	85%	100%	78%	246	211	235	219	250	210
		09	1.1	128	65%	0%	57%	252	258	239	296	263	246
		10	1.1	73	74%	50%	68%	241	333	266	375	287	288
Lidge,Brad	R	06	1.0	100	64%	84%	78%	224	256	242	236	286	201
		07	1.0	116	79%	70%	74%	223	212	213	234	184	243
		08	1.0	109	84%	100%	100%	209	170	207	137	261	108
		09	0.9	39	62%	74%	63%	279	336	316	286	322	289
		10	0.9	72	80%	84%	82%	246	333	256	391	309	250
Lindstrom,Matt	R	07	0.9	87	75%	0%	79%	230	289	247	280	263	255
		08	0.9	34	77%	83%	85%	276	270	288	152	327	218
		09	0.9	30	64%	88%	89%	267	299	270	310	276	287
		10	0.9	66	75%	79%	73%	380	373	366	400	329	414
Loe,Kameron	R	10	1.1	102	81%	0%	78%	296	319	319	290	306	306
Logan,Boone	L	06	0.8	37	59%	50%	75%	194	378	302	176	357	244
		07	0.7	40	71%	0%	81%	301	295	248	465	221	357
		08	0.8	97	67%	0%	56%	264	371	315	379	291	351
		09	0.9	8	69%	0%	67%	290	278	316	111	237	345
		10	0.8	56	80%	0%	100%	327	302	303	385	313	317
Lopez,Javier	L	10	0.7	62	81%	0%	88%	320	257	295	292	229	337
Lopez,Wilton	R	10	1.0	137	73%	33%	83%	364	278	308	410	322	327
Lyon,Brandon	R	06	1.0	52	72%	0%	69%	290	226	294	143	244	270
		07	1.0	39	78%	40%	86%	294	210	278	146	233	267
		08	1.0	85	70%	84%	76%	294	318	301	314	283	323
		09	1.2	46	78%	50%	75%	203	207	206	153	209	201
		10	1.0	34	74%	91%	85%	284	298	266	410	258	312
Madson,Ryan	R	06	2.7	41	68%	50%	63%	344	256	342	235	296	311
		07	1.5	64	79%	50%	77%	198	280	222	200	170	275
		08	1.1	92	77%	33%	85%	244	258	267	225	257	244
		09	1.0	116	76%	63%	79%	277	220	247	268	259	243
		10	1.0	164	78%	50%	79%	320	309	330	259	328	304
Marmol,Carlos	R	07	1.2	123	89%	50%	92%	183	154	150	208	209	146
		08	1.1	103	77%	78%	87%	126	151	128	162	187	94
		09	0.9	-6	75%	79%	85%	221	131	175	162	138	201
		10	1.0	138	77%	88%	83%	276	324	244	462	286	316
Marshall,Sean	L	08	1.9	74	74%	50%	54%	269	150	242	95	219	217
		09	1.6	63	73%	0%	59%	276	235	260	310	230	277
		10	0.9	144	76%	33%	81%	297	337	292	421	313	317
Marte,Damaso	L	06	0.8	78	75%	0%	56%	257	230	238	206	225	258
		07	0.7	107	79%	0%	100%	202	197	211	160	94	271
		08	0.9	86	67%	71%	88%	197	224	220	146	235	197
		09	0.6	52	39%	0%	60%	286	290	286	300	130	414
		10	0.6	-32	68%	0%	82%	143	273	162	308	200	200
Masset,Nick	R	08	1.5	39	78%	33%	71%	327	263	346	176	263	311
		09	1.0	102	81%	0%	89%	168	255	223	104	217	198
		10	0.9	100	76%	40%	79%	313	341	329	314	284	346
McClellan,Kyle	R	08	1.1	67	72%	17%	73%	298	238	280	253	238	291
		09	1.0	26	76%	50%	76%	187	265	219	210	186	244
		10	1.1	84	86%	67%	81%	243	312	245	315	247	281
Meche,Gil	R	10	3.1	-19	68%	0%	55%	304	222	231	600	214	333
Meek,Evan	R	09	1.1	20	74%	0%	71%	225	189	192	261	250	176
		10	1.1	83	82%	40%	71%	214	280	228	245	200	290
Melancon,Mark	R	10	1.0	100	68%	0%	91%	212	478	289	357	200	419
Mijares,Jose	L	09	0.9	67	86%	0%	91%	248	168	217	188	122	280
		10	0.7	81	79%	0%	91%	309	368	333	333	366	308
Miller,Trever	L	06	0.7	113	79%	33%	75%	271	176	234	161	221	228
		07	0.6	61	69%	33%	87%	205	290	242	333	209	289
		08	0.6	56	68%	67%	94%	313	173	248	250	209	299
		09	0.6	120	86%	0%	89%	188	188	184	231	121	293
		10	0.6	10	68%	0%	85%	254	326	278	333	268	306
Morales,Franklin	L	09	1.0	26	72%	88%	85%	182	263	225	185	152	253
		10	0.8	-34	68%	50%	36%	286	357	273	389	231	362
Mota,Guillermo	R	06	1.1	32	75%	0%	81%	261	253	237	300	252	261
		07	1.1	65	59%	0%	62%	225	317	264	215	235	284
		08	1.0	43	74%	25%	65%	236	253	229	291	291	210
		09	1.1	22	73%	0%	45%	185	283	230	207	207	239
		10	1.0	31	67%	33%	67%	312	313	302	297	317	309
Motte,Jason	R	08	0.9	185	88%	100%	100%	111	167	130	143	71	188
		09	0.8	69	71%	0%	73%	315	202	250	316	341	208
		10	0.9	102	85%	67%	86%	315	310	308	364	364	287

BULLPEN INDICATORS

		BPIs			Results		Runners		Pitch Ct		Platoon	
Pitcher		**IP/g**	**bpv**	**S%**	**Sv%**	**Eff%**	**Emp**	**On**	**1-15**	**16-30**	**vLH**	**vRH**
Moylan,Peter R	07	1.1	76	87%	50%	78%	215	199	223	171	242	184
	08	0.8	144	100%	50%	71%	273	167	217	0	273	167
	09	0.8	56	77%	0%	82%	242	246	263	167	304	211
	10	0.7	37	81%	25%	85%	317	300	322	167	327	301
Nieve,Fernando R	10	1.1	34	63%	0%	57%	277	314	274	412	289	295
Nippert,Dustin R	09	3.5	42	73%	0%	67%	167	241	182	182	125	296
	10	1.5	-1	77%	0%	60%	435	241	364	293	382	301
Nunez,Leo R	08	1.1	29	76%	0%	73%	231	253	246	237	266	221
	09	0.9	63	75%	79%	77%	253	204	246	196	236	229
	10	1.0	130	74%	79%	78%	351	372	371	333	295	442
O Day,Darren R	09	0.9	97	84%	100%	96%	180	221	194	194	246	174
	10	0.9	86	82%	0%	88%	252	242	260	174	267	239
O Flaherty,Eric L	09	0.7	67	75%	0%	85%	221	290	234	379	219	293
	10	0.8	68	81%	0%	80%	323	270	296	222	305	288
Ogando,Alexi R	10	0.9	80	91%	0%	79%	218	358	305	231	268	299
Ohman,Will L	10	0.6	57	81%	0%	86%	309	397	371	250	328	382
Okajima,Hideki L	07	1.0	112	82%	71%	90%	230	168	219	155	236	182
	08	1.0	75	82%	11%	73%	182	269	213	241	188	242
	09	0.9	63	78%	0%	94%	199	305	229	294	167	309
	10	0.8	24	77%	0%	65%	313	464	388	355	352	407
Oliver,Darren L	06	1.8	57	77%	0%	88%	215	259	259	161	208	244
	07	1.1	63	71%	0%	92%	222	263	219	221	289	209
	08	1.3	80	77%	0%	86%	252	263	247	229	231	275
	09	1.2	91	78%	0%	93%	235	235	271	186	250	222
	10	1.0	138	80%	25%	76%	329	369	368	226	328	360
Ondrusek,Logan R	10	1.0	51	73%	0%	85%	219	397	259	394	254	292
Papelbon,Jonath R	06	1.2	169	92%	85%	83%	199	112	180	132	203	128
	07	1.0	189	82%	92%	87%	123	187	161	83	104	200
	08	1.0	178	77%	89%	84%	186	263	206	255	227	202
	09	1.0	96	88%	93%	91%	258	177	257	123	192	246
	10	1.0	98	72%	82%	74%	252	438	341	194	387	244
Parnell,Bobby R	09	1.3	31	68%	20%	64%	253	272	253	280	250	270
	10	0.9	131	79%	0%	75%	328	487	368	474	405	375
Peralta,Joel R	09	0.9	26	61%	0%	60%	318	245	250	273	348	216
	10	1.3	121	82%	0%	83%	244	227	256	233	302	203
Perez,Chris R	08	1.0	46	78%	64%	70%	267	169	202	258	245	207
	09	0.9	85	68%	40%	67%	163	242	193	245	185	209
	10	1.0	61	88%	85%	85%	295	197	267	205	284	224
Perez,Rafael L	07	1.4	137	86%	50%	82%	185	191	147	254	145	213
	08	1.0	140	73%	29%	78%	202	276	230	236	216	244
	09	0.9	7	60%	0%	71%	312	348	322	414	392	283
	10	0.9	29	80%	0%	79%	404	308	351	364	347	358
Perry,Ryan R	09	1.2	23	78%	0%	60%	250	257	252	277	306	210
	10	1.0	49	74%	40%	75%	326	288	323	255	224	350
Putz,J.J. R	06	1.1	226	76%	84%	85%	176	257	200	229	211	204
	07	1.1	194	89%	95%	94%	180	109	173	26	148	158
	08	1.0	61	77%	65%	62%	239	274	279	222	261	250
	09	1.0	-30	66%	50%	68%	228	286	263	242	296	220
	10	0.9	154	75%	43%	73%	299	310	295	364	383	240
Qualls,Chad R	06	1.1	46	71%	0%	77%	242	242	258	181	227	253
	07	1.0	96	82%	50%	76%	292	252	264	333	248	289
	08	1.0	131	75%	53%	69%	212	248	242	176	225	234
	09	1.0	142	71%	83%	79%	223	295	281	150	298	214
	10	0.8	81	59%	63%	70%	333	514	387	610	470	388
Ramirez,Ramon R	06	1.1	76	74%	0%	74%	241	218	265	141	274	194
	07	0.8	51	44%	0%	71%	321	308	316	300	240	357
	08	1.0	73	78%	20%	81%	218	225	226	222	294	157
	09	1.0	20	83%	0%	70%	248	220	217	276	244	220
	10	1.0	27	78%	100%	77%	273	232	247	295	293	231
Rauch,Jon R	06	1.1	63	79%	40%	75%	215	252	257	180	254	216
	07	1.0	81	69%	40%	82%	200	278	230	232	208	249
	08	1.0	103	70%	75%	67%	233	296	252	267	268	242
	09	0.9	47	75%	40%	81%	270	256	283	215	241	282
	10	1.0	86	76%	84%	84%	342	324	342	296	368	305
Ray,Chris R	06	1.1	41	84%	87%	80%	188	202	221	119	184	202
	07	1.0	90	67%	80%	68%	190	276	218	216	233	212
	09	0.9	32	66%	0%	46%	346	337	367	286	442	265
	10	0.9	-3	74%	50%	89%	213	342	242	400	329	228
Resop,Chris R	10	0.9	62	70%	0%	100%	286	333	313	222	375	250
Reyes,Dennys L	06	0.8	105	96%	0%	95%	229	151	205	143	148	244
	07	0.6	38	78%	0%	91%	302	319	293	455	273	364
	08	0.6	95	84%	0%	87%	222	250	240	182	198	284
	09	0.5	34	76%	100%	90%	205	254	234	125	202	268
	10	0.6	0	75%	25%	71%	264	339	330	83	418	193
Rhodes,Arthur L	06	0.8	79	67%	57%	77%	224	305	243	333	286	248
	08	0.6	73	82%	67%	94%	206	250	219	333	162	309
	09	0.8	71	78%	0%	90%	182	227	204	167	141	245
	10	0.8	82	81%	0%	83%	279	246	276	200	316	233

BULLPEN INDICATORS

		BPIs			Results		Runners		Pitch Ct		Platoon	
Pitcher		**IP/g**	**bpv**	**S%**	**Sv%**	**Eff%**	**Emp**	**On**	**1-15**	**16-30**	**vLH**	**vRH**
Rivera,Mariano R	06	1.2	132	83%	92%	83%	258	174	237	194	192	250
	07	1.1	168	72%	88%	80%	245	252	257	208	255	241
	08	1.1	186	84%	98%	88%	178	149	178	130	155	183
	09	1.0	158	89%	96%	90%	243	139	194	224	185	213
	10	1.0	106	79%	87%	82%	255	203	226	300	247	221
Robertson,David R	09	1.0	111	78%	100%	89%	198	231	177	276	203	222
	10	1.0	75	76%	33%	73%	437	310	355	357	400	347
Rodney,Fernand R	06	1.1	67	72%	64%	80%	185	208	176	214	202	192
	07	1.1	92	69%	33%	65%	200	276	262	207	247	231
	08	1.1	25	69%	68%	60%	222	237	261	186	260	197
	09	1.0	32	72%	97%	87%	252	230	238	260	261	213
	10	0.9	30	72%	67%	80%	362	304	331	321	350	311
Rodriguez,Franci R	06	1.1	124	89%	92%	88%	201	191	202	176	215	179
	07	1.1	116	78%	87%	85%	205	204	230	138	187	217
	08	0.9	75	85%	90%	86%	252	183	235	160	228	208
	09	1.0	45	74%	83%	75%	233	171	219	169	186	223
	10	1.1	120	83%	83%	81%	278	354	282	395	329	297
Romero,J.C. L	06	0.7	41	60%	0%	73%	225	363	300	333	202	382
	07	0.8	57	88%	50%	90%	250	158	209	176	208	198
	08	0.7	21	82%	20%	78%	228	174	209	138	101	287
	09	0.8	-45	88%	0%	86%	208	235	283	0	308	156
	10	0.6	-29	79%	50%	81%	212	360	281	308	300	262
Romo,Sergio R	08	1.2	109	76%	0%	89%	123	186	100	242	91	188
	09	0.8	122	65%	100%	89%	210	277	229	261	188	263
	10	0.9	141	83%	0%	79%	265	343	301	296	300	300
Runzler,Dan L	10	0.8	65	79%	0%	100%	354	364	343	429	361	356
Rupe,Josh R	10	0.9	-17	75%	0%	86%	444	400	478	300	313	529
Russell,James L	10	0.9	93	71%	0%	70%	370	350	340	486	373	353
Saito,Takashi R	06	1.1	161	78%	92%	90%	159	206	170	164	227	129
	07	1.0	192	88%	91%	89%	143	169	155	135	186	114
	08	1.0	143	78%	82%	73%	188	288	226	255	250	213
	09	1.0	48	87%	50%	62%	265	222	254	224	200	297
	10	1.0	152	76%	50%	83%	280	333	317	231	313	288
Sale,Chris L	10	1.1	147	87%	100%	89%	222	389	281	333	421	192
Sampson,Chris R	08	2.2	73	65%	0%	74%	203	256	179	295	303	183
	09	1.1	35	66%	50%	81%	241	349	265	350	315	272
	10	0.9	51	70%	0%	75%	429	339	398	333	375	389
Sanches,Brian R	09	1.2	42	85%	0%	72%	255	208	236	236	242	224
	10	1.0	45	86%	0%	82%	272	243	271	231	244	274
Santos,Sergio R	10	0.9	74	81%	33%	81%	365	362	362	385	309	398
Sherrill,George L	06	0.6	89	67%	100%	83%	194	232	217	158	143	297
	07	0.6	122	80%	43%	87%	222	143	174	208	156	212
	08	0.9	31	70%	84%	76%	233	242	259	176	194	257
	09	1.0	72	88%	81%	85%	238	181	222	188	132	250
	10	0.6	-31	65%	0%	60%	340	403	363	474	259	471
Simon,Alfredo R	10	1.0	38	74%	81%	79%	290	415	342	343	325	358
Sipp,Tony L	09	0.9	48	83%	0%	100%	229	172	206	188	211	190
	10	0.9	36	77%	33%	82%	272	382	333	243	313	329
Smith,Joe R	07	0.8	83	79%	0%	87%	203	327	274	257	298	266
	08	0.8	53	73%	0%	80%	195	262	212	293	340	196
	09	0.9	81	77%	0%	91%	210	262	253	208	355	198
	10	0.8	18	74%	0%	86%	228	288	261	250	343	216
Soria,Joakim R	07	1.1	131	74%	81%	80%	173	211	168	246	167	200
	08	1.1	112	87%	93%	88%	154	209	146	267	169	171
	09	1.1	150	85%	91%	87%	252	181	236	163	224	213
	10	1.0	142	86%	93%	90%	344	233	312	222	290	303
Soriano,Rafael R	06	1.1	97	85%	33%	78%	214	192	232	121	244	179
	07	1.0	132	76%	75%	84%	165	221	190	154	164	197
	08	1.0	23	80%	75%	60%	200	111	152	143	222	103
	09	1.0	134	74%	87%	77%	220	155	201	170	258	138
	10	1.0	105	83%	94%	91%	186	276	221	217	241	195
Storen,Drew R	10	1.0	74	72%	71%	76%	333	329	356	270	352	318
Street,Huston R	06	1.0	144	70%	77%	74%	205	276	238	242	274	211
	07	1.0	164	74%	76%	79%	179	213	184	222	224	162
	08	1.1	76	71%	72%	72%	217	250	228	219	200	250
	09	1.0	146	71%	95%	93%	151	303	205	143	172	218
	10	1.1	113	69%	80%	73%	283	361	299	333	313	300
Takahashi,Hisan L	10	2.3	82	75%	100%	78%	262	333	272	300	290	292
Tankersley,Taylo L	10	0.4	-43	60%	0%	67%	385	250	333	0	261	333
Tejeda,Robinson R	09	2.1	32	72%	0%	75%	138	250	158	250	235	150
	10	1.1	51	75%	0%	58%	264	385	318	333	300	341
Thatcher,Joe L	08	1.0	1	61%	0%	42%	400	364	343	405	387	380
	09	0.9	117	77%	0%	91%	200	263	223	227	184	271
	10	0.5	179	86%	0%	100%	238	333	282	286	342	225
Thornton,Matt L	06	0.9	73	76%	40%	81%	223	235	213	316	211	240
	07	0.8	71	68%	29%	72%	245	289	303	146	283	260
	08	0.9	145	76%	17%	76%	148	248	188	186	176	211
	09	1.0	147	77%	44%	81%	218	222	219	230	208	227
	10	1.0	154	74%	80%	85%	359	269	317	308	321	308

BULLPEN INDICATORS

Pitcher			BPIs			Results		Runners		Pitch Ct		Platoon	
			IP/g	bpv	S%	Sv%	Eff%	Emp	On	1-15	16-30	vLH	vRH
Troncoso, Ramon	R	09	1.1	40	81%	86%	83%	281	246	290	226	285	251
		10	1.0	52	71%	0%	71%	256	372	331	278	317	312
Uehara, Koji	R	10	1.0	177	76%	87%	83%	303	341	318	318	422	242
Valverde, Jose	R	06	1.1	109	61%	82%	75%	245	268	270	246	323	192
		07	1.0	112	82%	87%	81%	197	194	203	173	202	189
		08	1.0	122	77%	86%	83%	231	200	228	190	174	253
		09	1.0	89	84%	86%	83%	238	151	230	93	279	129
		10	1.1	72	76%	90%	80%	232	280	250	257	244	266
Vasquez, Esmerli	R	09	1.0	22	71%	0%	50%	247	268	270	232	198	309
		10	0.9	4	68%	0%	47%	294	352	366	194	323	324
Venters, Jonny	L	10	1.1	113	83%	20%	78%	337	232	282	275	362	260
Veras, Jose	R	07	1.0	48	54%	100%	100%	250	111	130	125	154	190
		08	1.0	69	78%	0%	75%	250	214	248	174	202	256
		09	1.1	4	66%	0%	77%	158	299	223	242	263	196
		10	1.0	53	73%	0%	81%	306	216	287	118	204	322
Villanueva, Carlos	R	07	1.9	57	75%	33%	78%	209	278	229	219	230	243
		08	2.3	95	75%	100%	70%	238	185	211	260	206	228
		09	1.5	67	65%	38%	52%	221	293	233	306	242	254
		10	1.1	117	68%	25%	85%	403	313	409	226	404	324
Wagner, Billy	L	06	1.0	138	85%	89%	86%	248	171	250	136	161	234
		07	1.0	119	80%	87%	84%	229	198	223	150	241	209
		08	1.0	142	79%	79%	77%	143	250	170	250	233	169
		09	0.9	135	87%	0%	88%	148	200	189	0	125	194
		10	1.0	182	89%	84%	83%	326	159	284	125	129	314
Walden, Jordan	R	10	1.0	170	84%	100%	88%	412	364	435	200	400	385
Weaver, Jeff	R	10	1.0	-1	60%	0%	83%	274	424	337	317	360	337
Webb, Ryan	R	09	0.9	49	77%	0%	89%	298	234	234	304	233	294
		10	1.1	83	78%	0%	80%	305	371	331	315	395	296
Weinhardt, Robbi	R	10	1.0	84	61%	0%	64%	388	417	397	409	265	476

BULLPEN INDICATORS

Pitcher			BPIs			Results		Runners		Pitch Ct		Platoon	
			IP/g	bpv	S%	Sv%	Eff%	Emp	On	1-15	16-30	vLH	vRH
Wheeler, Dan	R	06	1.0	92	81%	75%	82%	204	245	232	200	273	183
		07	1.1	103	62%	61%	65%	179	371	239	284	260	253
		08	0.9	53	77%	72%	80%	170	214	204	114	217	166
		09	0.8	98	74%	33%	71%	202	205	206	182	310	160
		10	0.8	87	76%	50%	67%	342	191	318	63	200	312
White, Sean	R	09	1.2	23	75%	33%	83%	200	231	233	167	191	238
		10	0.9	16	69%	0%	56%	412	353	380	389	385	373
Wilson, Brian	R	06	1.0	55	67%	50%	64%	404	177	280	294	348	235
		07	1.0	90	77%	86%	84%	218	133	178	182	304	145
		08	1.0	92	70%	87%	85%	234	271	240	288	194	308
		09	1.1	114	77%	84%	77%	238	213	247	175	192	259
		10	1.1	144	86%	91%	86%	290	392	308	400	342	327
Wood, Blake	R	10	1.0	22	69%	0%	70%	333	359	347	351	342	350
Wood, Kerry	R	09	0.9	74	72%	77%	72%	212	263	247	200	257	213
		10	1.0	36	80%	67%	73%	253	372	284	318	327	275
Wright, Jamey	R	09	1.2	22	72%	0%	65%	207	287	221	284	200	285
		10	1.3	14	69%	0%	71%	269	311	275	300	278	298
Wuertz, Mike	R	06	1.0	78	85%	0%	82%	200	253	207	231	184	245
		07	1.0	84	78%	0%	77%	255	210	246	203	241	232
		08	1.0	23	77%	0%	50%	216	357	309	209	233	306
		09	1.1	157	75%	67%	92%	215	165	222	113	183	200
		10	0.8	54	74%	100%	86%	370	288	305	417	371	310
Ziegler, Brad	R	08	1.3	36	93%	85%	92%	283	159	237	222	286	175
		09	1.1	65	79%	70%	77%	294	295	309	238	343	262
		10	0.9	29	77%	0%	66%	309	281	284	324	345	273
Zumaya, Joel	R	06	1.3	92	87%	17%	82%	162	207	174	228	183	188
		07	1.2	56	65%	20%	61%	141	241	200	156	271	135
		08	1.1	-67	86%	20%	50%	275	255	276	241	161	317
		09	1.1	-10	76%	14%	55%	300	250	321	172	344	206
		10	1.2	89	76%	33%	82%	288	315	293	333	286	316

Injuries

Off-Season Injury Report
by Rick Wilton

Andrew Bailey (RHP, OAK): A sore pitching elbow ended his year a bit early. Surgery cleaned out his elbow with good news that his ulnar collateral ligament was intact. If he avoids a setback in spring training, he should be good to go by Opening Day.

Scott Baker (RHP, MIN): Had his right elbow cleaned up at the end of October. He was expected to resume throwing before the end of the year. This minor procedure should not impact his 2011 season.

Jason Bay (OF, NYM): Suffered a concussion crashing into an OF wall in July. He missed the rest of the season and questions remain regarding his health going into 2011.

Carlos Beltran (OF, NYM): Has two problematic knees. He does not have much cartilage remaining in his right knee and micro-fracture surgery may be on the horizon at some point. Draft with caution as his SB and HR numbers will never approach 2008 levels again.

Mike Cameron (OF, BOS): A torn abdominal wall muscle cost him roughly two-thirds of the season. He underwent surgery in August and is expected to be healthy by the start of Spring Training.

Eric Chavez (3B, OAK): Serious cervical spine (neck) issues likely will force him to retire during the off-season.

Manny Corpas (RHP, FA): Underwent Tommy John surgery in September and will likely miss all but the last few weeks of the 2011 season.

Coco Crisp (OF, OAK): Knee and finger injuries cut into his playing time and effectiveness last year. His problems are chronic; expect more injury issues this season.

David Dejesus (OF, OAK): Suffered a torn ligament in his right thumb, costing him a chunk of the 2010 season. He is expected to be 100% for spring training with no residual effects from the injury.

Joey Devine (RHP, OAK): Missed all of the 2010 season recovering from Tommy John surgery. He was throwing well in instructional league action in the fall and he should not have any major restrictions in Spring Training.

Mark DeRosa (3B, SF): After needing a second identical surgery on his left wrist to repair damage to a torn tendon sheath, he was swinging a bat in the fall. He is expected back competing for a job in the spring though his power numbers could suffer as he rebuilds strength in his hand.

Jacoby Ellsbury (OF, BOS): Reportedly was recovered from the five fractured ribs in the anterior (front) part of his ribcage in the fall. Speculation suggested the posterior (in the back of the ribcage) rib fracture was not completely healed but should be by the end of the year.

Kelvim Escobar (RHP, NYM): In the past two years, he has suffered a torn labrum and anterior shoulder capsule in his pitching shoulder. It would be a miracle if he were able to recover from both this injuries and pitch effectively at the major league level.

David Freese (3B, STL): The Cardinals believe the surgery to his left ankle will allow him to be free of pain and restriction at the start of spring training.

Rafael Furcal (SS, LA): For the second time in three seasons, he battled back issues that cost him a considerable amount of playing time. Draft with caution as back problems will likely continue to plague him in the future.

Adrian Gonzalez (1B, SD): It wasn't supposed to be that serious, but the surgery on his right shoulder to correct a torn labrum could land him on the disabled list to start the 2011 season. How much of an impact will it have on his power numbers? Hanley Ramirez (SS, FLA) had similar surgery and did not suffer a drop-off. BJ Upton (OF, TAM) and Travis Hafner (DH, CLE) also had similar surgery but neither has regained their power. Odds are Gonzalez' offense will suffer somewhat due to this surgery and the long rehab that goes with the injury.

Josh Hamilton (OF, TEX): Returned for the post-season from a fractured rib, but his ability to remain healthy is in doubt. Though he recorded 514 AB in '10, rib, right knee (possibly arthritic) and hamstring issues plagued him most of the season. Heed the ongoing injury risk.

Conor Jackson (OF, OAK): Underwent sports hernia surgery in September and is expected to be 100% by March.

Bobby Jenks's (RHP, CHW): We never got the full story regarding his right forearm problems last season. Most likely, it was related to flexor mass tendon or muscle. Exercise caution until he proves he can pitch without further forearm problems this season.

Josh Johnson (RHP, FLA): The Marlins shut him down in September due to inflammation in his right shoulder and a sore back. An MRI ruled out any structural issues with his shoulder, and though he will be watched closely in the spring, don't back off him on draft day.

Chipper Jones (3B, ATL): Is attempting to come back from a torn ACL (anterior cruciate ligament) in his left knee, an injury he suffered in August. A near-40 year old recovering from this type of injury is not a good bet. We would not be surprised if he retired at some point in 2011.

Jair Jurrjens (RHP, ATL): Had surgery in the fall to repair cartilage damage in his right knee. The Braves expect him to be 100% recovered by the start of the season.

John Maine (RHP, NYM): Had surgery in July to clean out scar tissue that was causing him pain. His inability to remain healthy continues to be the trademark of his career.

Russell Martin (C, LA): A torn labrum and slight fracture in his right hip put him on the shelf for good in early August. While the Dodgers are optimistic, Martin still has some huge hurdles to overcome with this injury.

Joe Mauer (C, MIN): Elected not to have surgery on his troublesome left knee in the fall. They believe rest and rehab will help clear up the inflammation he battled most of the 2010 season.

Gil Meche (RHP, KC): Elected to bypass surgery on his pitching shoulder last summer. He worked out of the bullpen when he returned in September. It is likely the shoulder will act up again this season, especially if he moves back to the starting rotation.

Justin Morneau (1B, MIN): Back in early July, he suffered a concussion when his head struck the knee of an opponent at second base; he ended up missing 87 days. Early in November, the Twins were hopeful he would be ready at the start of spring training. But with concussions, you just don't know when the player will return. In addition, he is at greater risk for future head injuries. Exercise caution with players like him and Jason Bay.

Daniel Murphy (1B, NYM): Was diagnosed with a borderline grade three tear of the MCL (medial collateral ligament) in June. He elected to rehab rather than have it repaired via surgery. The Mets expect him back healthy at the start of spring training but his knee might not hold up with a tear that serious.

Joe Nathan (RHP, MIN): Had Tommy John surgery late in March and the Twins expect him to be ready at the start of the 2011 season.

Magglio Ordonez (OF, DET): The 37 year-old is coming off surgery to repair a fractured right ankle. He appears to be more susceptible to injuries as his career declines.

Jake Peavy (RHP, CHW): Tore his latissimus dorsi (lat) muscle up near the back edge of his shoulder. He had revolutionary surgery late in the year, the first of its kind for a Major League player. Any time a player suffers an injury where the tendon comes off the bone, it will be a long and difficult recovery. Everyone associated with the White Sox medical staff believes Peavy will return in 2011 and should pitch effectively. However, since his injury (and recovery) is the first of its kind, odds are he will struggle.

Dustin Pedroia (2B, BOS): Had surgery late in the season that included the insertion of a screw in the fractured navicular bone in his left foot. He is expected to be ready by March. Let's wait until we see him run.

Brad Penny (RHP, LA): A strained lat muscle, back and shoulder discomfort cost him most of the season. Staying healthy continues to be a big issue since 2007.

Francisco Rodriguez (RHP, NYM): A torn ligament in his right thumb, the result of a domestic dispute, cut short his 2010 season. The thumb should be healed by the time pitchers and catchers report.

Johan Santana's (LHP, NYM): His injury is a tear to the anterior portion (front) capsule in his left shoulder. The bad news was the surgeon was unable to do the procedure arthroscopically, meaning a much larger incision was needed to repair the damage. As such, his recovery will be longer than normal and he will have more scar tissue than typically would be expected. Factoring in the extent of the surgery and location of the damage, Santana is a good bet to start the year on the disabled list. He may not pitch effectively until the 2nd half of '11 or not at all next season.

Grady Sizemore (OF, CLE): Underwent micro-fracture surgery on his left knee in June. The Indians are encouraged by his recovery, but he may still start 2011 on the disabled list. Use caution on draft day.

Kevin Slowey (RHP, MIN): A triceps injury to his pitching arm cost him a spot on the Twins' post-season roster but he is expected to be 100% by January.

Geovany Soto (C, CHC): Underwent surgery in late September to repair damage to the A/C joint in his right shoulder. The Cubs indicated he can resume normal off-season workouts in January.

Stephen Strasburg (RHP, WAS): Underwent Tommy John surgery in late August and is likely to miss all but a few weeks of the 2011 season.

Huston Street (RHP, COL): Groin, shoulder and rib injuries cost him a good portion of last season. He is expected to be healthy for spring training.

Justin Upton (OF, ARI): Was already swinging a bat in the fall instructional league in October. He reported his left shoulder was strong and he did not feel any pain. Upton is a higher injury risk due to his left shoulder and the fact he has struggled with pain off and on the past few years.

Brandon Webb (RHP, ARI): Has started just one game the past two seasons. His career is in doubt as he works his way back from a serious right shoulder injury and surgery in September 2009.

Kevin Youkilis (1B, BOS): Underwent surgery on his right thumb in early August. He began swinging a bat in the fall and is expected to be ready for full-time duty at the start of spring training.

Chris Young (RHP, SD): A labrum injury and the follow-up surgery on his right shoulder in August 2009 cost him all but 20 IP last season. He was still not completely healthy in the fall and is a high-risk investment this season.

Joel Zumaya (RHP, DET): Another season and another surgery, this time to repair a serious fracture in his right elbow. He has broken down physically every year since 2007 and his career is in doubt after his latest injury.

Hidden Injuries: 2011 Speculations

by Ray Murphy

In addition to all of the documented injuries in this section, there are always other injuries that don't make it into our data set, because they aren't reported by team and player. Some aren't serious enough to shut players down, but manage to hamper performance. They may have been reported but under-emphasized this year, or perhaps they will be casually disclosed next spring. Others may never get confirmed. But here is a set of player that may have fought a hidden injury in 2010, and perhaps should have 2011 expectations adjusted accordingly.

John Lackey's disappointing first season in Boston obscured some real improvement in the 2nd half. In fact, his 2nd half BPV (86) was right in line with his career norms. With his longer-term BPV track record so stable, we have to consider undocumented causes for that outlier 1st half. And if we discount that performance blip, we can reset our 2011 expectations to include a sub-4.00 ERA.

Carlos Pena fell short of the 30 HR mark for the first time in his Tampa Bay career, and he finished with a sub-.200 BA to boot. Could either be injury-related? His PX and FB% both dipped precipitously in 2010, and his h% reached a new low. These indicators together all suggest the possibility of an injury. And while his xBA history suggests that a sub-.250 BA is his ceiling, a return to 35+ HR would follow just a minor uptick in FB%, if his health cooperates.

Ian Kinsler started the season on the DL due to an ankle sprain, and seemingly never found his power stroke when he returned. The ankle alone probably didn't keep him from repeating 2009's 31-HR output. But the ankle is likely what cost him from taking a run at the 20-SB level, which should be attainable in a full 2011 season if he has two good wheels under him.

BJ Upton has been teasing us with his power/speed skills for years now. We found out after 2009 that he was hampered all year by shoulder issues; could health have held him back in 2010 as well? Over his last 200 AB in 2010, he hit .261 with 10 HR and 14 SB. It's possible that those numbers are his healthy baseline, in which case we could triple them for an upside 2011 expectation.

Ben Zobrist may look like a flash in the pan after he regressed so far in 2010, but across 2008-09 he had a 700 AB sample with a PX of 147. In 2010, his PX plummeted to 83. He also lost almost 50 points off his xBA year-over-year. A hidden injury may not fully explain Zobrist's collapse, as regression to the mean is certainly a factor as well. But in coloring future expectations, if there is an injury that contributed to 2010, it might push our 2011 expectations a little closer to 2009 levels.

In **Javier Vazquez's** first stint in NY in 2004, it came out after the fact that his 2nd half (and playoff) collapse was injury-related. His 2010 stint in NY was a complete debacle, but it could have been injury-related as well? His velocity was off, and his Ctl/Dom/Cmd all went into free-fall. If better health in 2011 allows him to recapture his currently diminished arsenal, a strong rebound is possible.

Scott Rolen managed a vintage first half of 2010 (.300-17-53) before cratering over the balance of the season. If he were younger and didn't have a chronic back injury we might give him a pass on that 2nd half. Instead, it is more likely that the 1st half hot streak is the unrepeatable portion of his 2010 season.

Over his last six half-seasons, **Wandy Rodriguez** has posted the following BPV trend line: 96, 98, 76, 118, 40, 130. That next-to-last entry is from the first half of 2010, and clearly an outlier in that data set. Whether injury-driven or some other cause, like a mechanical issue, it certainly appears that the other five more consistent half-seasons represent Rodriguez's skill level, and as such we should set 2011 expectations against those near-elite levels.

Jonathan Broxton's massive 1H/2H BPV split (210/-17) also correlates perfectly with a period of abuse in late June, where he pitched four times in five days, culminating in a 48-pitch outing on the final night. While this is the second straight year that Broxton has faded in the second half, he

enters 2011 with a vote of confidence from new manager Don Mattingly, and that confidence plus a bit of more careful handling may be all that stands between Broxton and consecutive dominant half-seasons.

Andre Ethier landed on the DL in late May with a finger injury, but returned quickly thanks to a custom splint that allowed him to grip a bat sooner than expected. But the splint, or the injury, still hampered Ethier, as June was his worst month of the season (1 HR in 105 AB). He posted a 150 PX in 2009, and was ahead of that pace in 2010 before the injury. It took him until August to reach that level again. When setting expectations, we may need to think of Ethier as a multi-year 150+ PX performer, despite the fact that he "only" posted a 133 PX in 2010, due to the injury.

In 2009, **Raul Ibanez** tailed off badly after socking 22 first-half HR. At the conclusion of that season, he underwent surgery to repair a sports hernia. He was in the lineup to start 2010, but performed terribly in the first half. He finally recovered his swing in the 2nd half, to the tune of .307-10-47. Now at age 39, Ibanez isn't likely to have any more 23-HR half-seasons. But if health had eluded him for much of the prior year, then that second-half 2010 performance may be the right baseline against which to set our expectations going forward.

5-Year Injury Log

The following chart details the disabled list stints for all players during the past five years. For each injury, the number of days the player missed during the season is listed. A few DL stints are for fewer than 15 days; these are cases when a player was placed on the DL prior to Opening Day (only in-season time lost is listed). Abbreviations:

Lt = left	Rt = right	fx = fractured
R/C = rotator cuff		str = strained
surg = surgery		

TJS = Tommy John (ulnar collateral ligament reconstruction) surgery

x 2 = two occurrences of the same injury

x 3 = three occurrences of the same injury

All data provided by Rick Wilton of Baseball-Injury-Report.com and Fanball.com

---

The Extended Disabled List

The disabled list system is fairly accurate until the latter part of August. That is when teams greatly reduce placing players on the DL. Instead, teams will sit injured players until September 1, then use the expanded roster space to fill a void and never place legitimately injured players on the DL. The following are the estimated DL days for players who fell into this category in 2010.

Andrew Bailey (P, OAK): 16	Josh Hamilton (OF, TEX): 26
Scott Baker (P, MIN): 18	Bobby Jenks (P, CHW): 29
Michael Bourn (OF, HOU): 14	Josh Johnson (P, FLA): 29
Coco Crisp (OF. OAK): 15	Scott Podsednik (OF, LA): 24
Chris Getz (2B, KC): 21	F. Rodriguez (P, NYM): 50
Tom Gorzelanny (P, CHC): 22	Johan Santana (P, NYM): 31

BATTERS	Yr	Days	Injury
Abreu, Tony	08	184	Hip surgery 5/08
	10	21	Sprained left wrist
Amezaga, Alfredo	09	148	Strained left knee; lower back
Anderson, Brian	09	18	Strained right oblique
Anderson, Garret	07	96	Hip flexor x 2; right elbow
	09	15	Strained left quad muscle
Ankiel, Rick	06	182	Torn patella tendon
	09	19	Bruised shoulder
	10	80	Strained right quadriceps
Antonelli, Matt	10	155	Fractured hamate bone - left hand
Arias, Joaquin	10	32	Lower back strain x 2
Ausmus, Brad	10	102	Pinched nerve lower back
Aviles, Mike	09	134	Strained right forearm
Aybar, Erick	07	49	Strained left hamstring; bruised hand
	08	28	Dislocated right pinkie finger
Aybar, Willy	08	49	Strained left hamstring
Bailey, Jeff	09	58	High ankle sprain - left ankle
Baker, Jeff	07	21	Concussion
	09	66	Sprained left hand
Baker, John	10	143	Strained right elbow
Bako, Paul	06	31	Partially torn right oblique
Baldelli, Rocco	06	65	Left hamstring strain
	07	167	Strained left hamstring; Right groin
	08	133	Mitochondrial disorder
	09	31	Strained left hamstring; bruised left ankle
Barajas, Rod	07	29	Strained right groin
	10	26	Strained left oblique muscle
Bard, Josh	07	15	Strained left groin
	08	93	Sprained right ankle; strained right triceps
	10	33	Strained left calf muscle
Bartlett, Jason	08	20	Sprained right knee
	09	21	Sprained left ankle
	10	17	Strained right hamstring
Barton, Brian	08	55	Strained right oblique; Bruised right hand
Barton, Daric	08	17	Strained neck
	09	25	Strained right hamstring
Bates, Aaron	09	6	Sprained left ankle
Bautista, José	07	17	Puncture wound-left hand
Bay, Jason	10	69	Post concussion syndrome
Belliard, Ronnie	08	40	Strained left calf, Right groin
Beltran, Carlos	07	16	Strained abdominal muscle
	09	78	Bone bruise, right knee
	10	102	Recovery from surgery - right knee (1/10)
Beltre, Adrian	09	69	Surgery - right Shoulder; bruised testicle x 2
Berkman, Lance	09	20	Strained left calf
	10	32	Sprained ankle;LT knee surg
Bernadina, Roger	09	169	Fractured right ankle
Betancourt, Yuni	09	20	Strained right hamstring x 2
Betemit, Wilson	08	34	Strained right hamstring
Blake, Casey	06	48	Sprained right ankle; oblique
Blalock, Hank	07	107	Thoracic Outlet Syndrome
	08	108	Carpal tunnel right wrist; Inflam. right shoulder
Blanco, Andres	09	28	Strained left calf
Blanco, Henry	07	82	Herniated disc - neck
	09	24	Strained right hamstring
Blanks, Kyle	09	37	Strained arch-right foot
	10	138	Strained right elbow
Bloomquist, Willie	08	51	Strained right hamstring
Blum, Geoff	09	15	Strained left hamstring
	10	32	Bone chips right elbow
Boggs, Brandon	09	34	Dislocated left shoulder
Bourn, Michael	07	41	Sprained right ankle
Bradley, Milton	06	79	Sprained right knee; Left shoulder
	07	66	Calf; hamstring; wrist; oblique
	10	68	Tendinitis - right knee
Branyan, Russell	08	42	Strained right oblique muscle
	09	31	Herniated disc-lower back
	10	16	Herniated disc - lumbar spine
Bruce, Jay	09	64	Fractured right wrist
Buck, John	09	36	Herniated disc - lower back
	10	15	Laceration - right thumb
Buck, Travis	07	59	Strained left hamstring; Right thumb
	08	20	Shin splints
	09	15	Strained left oblique
	10	100	Strained right oblique
Burrell, Pat	09	32	Strained neck
Burriss, Emmanuel	09	34	Fractured left toe
	10	82	Fractured - left foot
Byrd, Marlon	08	27	Inflammation left knee

FIVE-YEAR INJURY LOG

BATTERS	Yr	Days	Injury
Byrnes, Eric	08	118	Strained right hamstring x 2
	09	71	Fractured left hand
Cabrera, Asdrubal	09	26	AC Joint sprain - left shoulder
	10	63	Fractured left forearm
Cabrera, Everth	09	60	Fractured hamate bone - left hand
	10	49	Strained right hamstring x 2
Cabrera, Orlando	10	31	Strained muscle - right ribcage
Cairo, Miguel	06	36	Strained left hamstring
Cameron, Mike	06	20	Strained left oblique
	10	100	Torn abdominal muscle x 2
Cano, Robinson	06	43	Strained left hamstring
Cantu, Jorge	06	43	Broken bone, left foot
Carroll, Brett	08	100	Separated right shoulder
	10	10	Strained left oblique
Carroll, Jamey	09	36	Fractured left hand
Cash, Kevin	10	16	Strained left hamstring
Casilla, Alexi	08	23	Torn ligament right thumb
	10	51	Bone spur in right elbow
Castillo, Luis	08	53	Strained left hip flexor
	10	47	Bruised right heel
Castillo, Wilkin	09	106	Torn labrum - right shoulder
Castro, Juan	07	84	Tendinitis right elbow x 2
Castro, Ramon	06	62	Strained left oblique
	07	49	Arthritis - lower back
	08	56	Strained right hamstring x 2
	10	29	Contusion - right heel
Chavez, Endy	07	82	Strained left hamstring
	09	107	Torn ACL - right knee
Chavez, Eric	07	66	Lower back spasms
	08	155	Inflammation of right shoulder; Back spasms
	09	163	Strained right forearm/elbow
	10	135	Neck spasms
Choo, Shin-Soo	08	61	Recovery from surgery on left elbow
	10	20	Sprained right thumb
Church, Ryan	08	70	Concussion x 2
	09	15	Strained right hamstring
Clement, Jeff	10	43	Left knee irritation
Clevlen, Brent	10	64	Sprained big right toe
Coghlan, Chris	10	69	Torn meniscus - left knee
Colvin, Tyler	10	13	Chest puncture wound
Copeland, Ben	09	30	Sprained right shoulder
Cora, Alex	08	25	Sore right elbow
	09	68	Torn lig. Right thumb; surgery both thumbs
Coste, Chris	07	7	Strained hamstring
	10	62	Strained right elbow
Cota, Humberto	07	27	Strained left shoulder
Crawford, Carl	08	47	Dislocated right index finger
Crede, Joe	07	118	Inflammation lower back
	08	34	Inflammation lower back
	09	17	Strained lower back
Crisp, Coco	06	49	Fractured left finger
	09	114	Sore right shoulder
	10	77	Fx finger; ribcage muscle
Crosby, Bobby	06	59	Lower back strain x 2
	07	68	Fractured left hand
	08	14	Strained left hamstring
	09	15	Strained left calf
Crowe, Trevor	09	18	Strained right oblique
Cruz, Nelson	09	16	sprained left ankle
	10	56	Strained RT & LT hammy
Cuddyer, Michael	07	15	Torn ligament-left thumb
	08	96	Dislocated right finger; Fx left foot; Left finger
Damon, Johnny	08	14	Sprained A/C joint right shoulder
DeJesus, David	06	40	Strained left hamstring
	10	72	Torn ligament - right thumb
Delgado, Carlos	09	147	Right hip impingement
Denorfia, Chris	07	183	Pending surgery - right elbow
	08	73	Lower back stiffness
DeRosa, Mark	06	15	Sprained left foot
	09	17	Sprained left wrist
	10	147	Neuritis - left wrist
Diaz, Matt	08	119	Strained ligament left knee
	10	45	Infected right thumb
Dickerson, Chris	09	52	Bruised right R/C; sprained left ankle
	10	101	Fractured hamate bone - right hand
Dobbs, Greg	09	25	Strained right calf

BATTERS	Yr	Days	Injury
Doumit, Ryan	06	100	Strained left hamstring x 2
	07	46	High ankle sprain; Left wrist sprain
	08	23	Fractured tip of left thumb
	09	80	Fractured scaphoid bone right wrist
	10	16	Concussion
Drew, J.D.	08	21	Herniated disc
Drew, Stephen	09	17	Strained left hamstring
Duffy, Chris	07	93	Sprained left ankle
	08	95	left shoulder surgery
Duncan, Chris	08	70	Pinched nerve -cervical spine
Eckstein, David	06	27	Torn oblique muscle
	07	28	Lower back spasms
	08	20	Strained right hip flexor
	09	22	Strained right hamstring
	10	31	Strained right calf
Edmonds, Jim	10	33	Strained RT & LT obliques
Ellis, Mark	06	30	Broken right thumb
	08	9	Torn labrum - right shoulder
	09	60	Strained left calf
	10	31	Strained left hamstring
Ellsbury, Jacoby	10	158	Fractured ribs x 3
Encarnacion, Ed	06	29	Sprained left ankle
	09	81	Fractured left wrist; left knee soreness
	10	48	Sprained RT wrist & shoulder
Escobar, Yunel	10	15	Strained left adductor
Estrada, Johnny	08	79	Sore right elbow; Neuritis right elbow
Ethier, Andre	10	16	Fractured pinkie finger - right hand
Everett, Adam	07	94	Fractured left fibula
	08	87	Strained right shoulder; tend. right shoulder
Feliz, Pedro	08	26	Inflammation lower back
Fields, Josh	10	150	Sore right hip flexor
Figgins, Chone	07	29	Fracture of two fingers - right hand
	08	37	Strained right hamstring x 2
Flores, Jesus	08	15	Sprained left ankle
	09	139	Torn labrum & bruised right shoulder
	10	182	Recovery from surgery - right shoulder
Fowler, Dexter	09	15	Bruised left knee
Frandsen, Kevin	06	15	Broken jaw
	08	181	Torn left Achilles tendon
Freese, David	10	97	Sprained right ankle
Furcal, Rafael	07	12	Sprained left ankle
	08	141	Back surgery 7/08
	10	58	Strained lower back; LT hammy
Gamel, Mat	10	61	Torn right lat muscle
Gardner, Brett	09	43	Fractured left thumb
Gentry, Craig	10	34	Fractured right wrist
German, Esteban	09	18	Strained right groin
Gerut, Jody	10	82	Bruised right heel
Getz, Chris	09	20	Strained right oblique
	10	15	Tight right oblique muscle
Giambi, Jason	07	68	Torn Plantar fascia tendon - Left foot
	09	18	Strained right quad
Gibbons, Jay	06	61	Sprained right knee; Left groin
	07	88	Torn labrum-lt shoulder; Bone bruise rt knee
Glaus, Troy	07	32	Left foot surgery; heel
	09	149	Recovery from surgery on rt pectoral muscle
	10	15	Sore left knee
Gload, Ross	07	47	Torn right quad muscle
	10	15	Strained right groin
Gomes, Jonny	06	41	Right shoulder surgery
Gomez, Carlos	07	64	Fractured hamate bone - left hand
	10	36	Concussion; Strained RT hip
Gonzalez, Alex	06	15	Oblique strain
	08	184	Compression fx left lower leg/surgery
	09	35	Bone chips - right elbow
Gordon, Alex	08	20	Torn right quadriceps
	09	91	Torn labrum - right hip / surgery
	10	13	Fractured tip of right thumb
Granderson, Curtis	08	24	Fractured 3rd metacarpal, right Hand
	10	26	Strained left groin
Greene, Tyler	10	16	Bruised right hand
Griffey Jr., Ken	06	28	Strained biceps tendon in right knee
Grudzielanek, Mark	07	23	Torn meniscus - left knee
	08	59	Torn deltoid ligament - right ankle
Guerrero, Vladimir	09	64	Torn right pectoral muscle; sore left knee
Guillen, Carlos	09	80	Inflammation right shoulder
	10	97	Lt hammy; RT calf; LT knee
Guillen, Jose	06	90	Left hamstring strain; Right elbow
	09	72	Torn lt LCL; str rt. hamstring; torn rt hip flexor
Gutierrez, Franklin	07	12	Strained left hamstring

FIVE-YEAR INJURY LOG

BATTERS	Yr	Days	Injury
Guzman, Cristian	06	182	Right shoulder surgery
	07	122	Strained left hamstring; left thumb
	09	15	Strained left hamstring
	10	18	Strained right quad
Gwynn, Tony, Jr.	08	19	Strained left hamstring
	10	25	Fractured hamate bone - right hand
Hafner, Travis	08	102	Strained right shoulder
	09	26	Sore and weak right shoulder
	10	17	Sore right shoulder
Hairston Jr., Jerry	07	73	Lower back soreness; neck
	08	50	Fractured rt hamstring x 2; Fractured lt thumb
	10	15	Sprained right elbow
Hairston, Scott	06	39	Left biceps strain
	07	29	Strained left oblique muscle
	08	32	Torn ligament - left thumb
	09	20	Strained left biceps
	10	17	Strained left hamstring
Hall, Bill	07	19	Sprained right ankle
Hamilton, Josh	07	51	Sprained right wrist; stomach ailment
	09	52	Strained ribcage; abdominal wall
Hanigan, Ryan	09	16	Concussion
	10	41	Fractured left thumb
Hannahan, Jack	10	26	Strained right groin
Hardy, J.J.	06	138	Right ankle surgery
	10	46	Sore left wrist
Harris, Willie	09	15	Strained left oblique
Hart, Corey	09	37	Appendicitis
Hawpe, Brad	08	16	Strained right hamstring
	10	15	Strained left quad muscle
Hayes, Brett	10	15	Bruised left wrist
Helton, Todd	06	15	Stomach ailment
	08	71	Sore lower back
	10	29	Stiff lower back
Hermida, Jeremy	06	40	Sore right hip flexor, groin strain
	07	43	Bruised right patellar
	08	9	Tight left hamstring
	10	42	Fractured ribs
Hernandez, Anderson	09	8	Strained left hamstring
Hernandez, Diory	10	81	Torn capsule - left shoulder surgery (2/10)
Hernandez, Ramon	07	33	Groin contusion; oblique
	09	64	Left knee surgery
	10	17	Inflammation - right knee
Heyward, Jason	10	18	Bone bruise - left thumb
Hicks, Brandon	10	13	Fractured right index finger
Hill, Aaron	08	123	Post concussion syndrome symptoms
	10	15	Strained right hamstring
Holliday, Matt	08	16	Strained left hamstring
Howard, Ryan	07	15	Strained left quad muscle
	10	19	Sprained left ankle
Hudson, Orlando	08	51	Dislocated left wrist
	10	33	Stained Rt oblique; sore LT wrist
Huff, Aubrey	06	23	Left knee sprain
Hundley, Nick	09	55	Bruised Left wrist
Hunter, Torii	06	15	Stress fracture, left foot
	09	39	Strained right adductor
Iannetta, Chris	09	16	Strained right hamstring
Ibanez, Raul	09	22	Strained left groin
Infante, Omar	08	54	Strained left hamstring; Fractured left hand
	09	82	Fractured 5th metacarpal - left hand
Inge, Brandon	08	17	Strained left oblique
	10	15	Fractured left hand
Iwamura, Akinori	07	34	Strained right oblique
	09	96	Torn ACL - left knee
Izturis, Cesar	06	93	Post elbow surgery; hamstring
	08	15	Strained right hamstring
	09	37	Appendicitis
Izturis, Maicer	06	46	Strained left hamstring
	07	63	Strained right hamstring x 2
	08	61	Strained back; torn thumb ligament
	10	85	Inflamed RT should. X2; Stra, LT forearm
Jackson, Conor	09	146	Valley fever
	10	108	Strained RT ham x 2; Ab strain
Jacobs, Mike	07	40	Fractured right thumb
Johnson, Chris	10	20	Strained intercostal muscle
Johnson, Kelly	06	182	Right elbow surgery
	09	20	Tendinitis - right wrist
Johnson, Nick	07	183	Fractured right femur + surgery x 2
	08	138	Torn tendon right wrist
	09	16	Strained right hamstring
	10	148	Inflamed tendon right wrist

FIVE-YEAR INJURY LOG

BATTERS	Yr	Days	Injury
Johnson, Reed	07	85	Herniated disc lower back
	08	15	Lower back spasms
	09	68	Fractured left foot; back spasms
	10	26	Lower back spasms
Jones, Adam	08	29	Fractured left foot
	09	33	Sprained left ankle
Jones, Andruw	08	82	Tendinitis - right patellar tendon
	09	15	Strained left hamstring
Jones, Chipper	06	44	Right ankle; oblique x 2
	07	20	Bone bruise right wrist/hand
	08	15	Strained left hamstring
	10	53	Torn ACL - left knee
Joyce, Matt	10	57	Strained right elbow
Kapler, Gabe	10	67	Spr. RT ankle; Stra. RT hip flexor
Kearns, Austin	08	78	Stress fx left foot; surgery right elbow
	09	62	Bruised right thumb
Kemp, Matt	07	17	Separated right shoulder
Kendall, Jason	10	30	Surgery - right rotator cuff
Kendrick, Howie	07	78	Fx index finger left hand x 2
	08	78	Strained left hamstring x 2
Kennedy, Adam	07	50	Torn cartilage - right knee
Keppinger, Jeff	07	21	Fractured right index finger
	08	39	Fractured left patellar (kneecap)
	10	15	Fractured big toe - left foot
Kinsler, Ian	06	43	Dislocated left thumb
	07	29	Stress fracture left foot
	08	43	Sports hernia
	09	16	Strained left hamstring
	10	61	Sprained RT ankle; Stra. LT groin
Konerko, Paul	08	23	Strained left oblique
Kotchman, Casey	06	146	Mononucleosis
	09	15	Bruised right lower leg
Kottaras, George	09	33	Strained lower back
Laird, Gerald	08	35	Strained left hamstring
Larish, Jeff	09	32	Recover from right wrist surgery
LaRoche, Adam	08	17	Right intercostal strain
LaRoche, Andy	08	34	Surgery right thumb
LaRue, Jason	06	15	Right knee surgery
	07	15	Contusion left shoulder
	10	75	Concussion; Stra. RT hammy
Lee, Carlos	08	51	Fractured left pink finger
Lee, Derrek	06	101	Inflammation, fx right wrist
Lewis, Fred	07	20	Strained right oblique
	10	11	Strained intercostal muscle - left side
Longoria, Evan	08	29	Fractured right hand
Lopez, Felipe	10	21	Strained right elbow
Lowell, Mike	08	42	Strained right oblique muscle; Right thumb
	09	19	Strained right hip
	10	41	Strained right hip
Lowrie, Jed	09	119	Fractured and strained left wrist
	10	108	Mononucleosis
Ludwick, Ryan	09	15	Strained right hamstring
	10	28	Strained left calf muscle
Lugo, Julio	06	31	Strained abdominal muscle
	08	80	Strained left quad
	09	22	Surgery to repair torn meniscus - right knee
Maldonado, Carlos	10	27	Fractured left thumb
Manzella, Tommy	10	57	Fractured left index finger
Marte, Andy	07	26	Strained left hamstring
	10	26	Non Baseball medical condition
Martin, Russell	10	60	Torn labrum - right hip
Martinez, Fernando	09	93	Inflammation behind right knee
Martinez, Ramon	09	124	Fractured pinkie finger - left hand
Martinez, Victor	08	78	Surgery - right elbow
	10	28	Fractured left thumb
Mathis, Jeff	10	58	Fractured right wrist
Matsui, Hideki	06	123	Broken left wrist
	07	15	Strained left hamstring
	08	56	Inflammation left knee
Matsui, Kaz	06	17	Sprained MCL, right knee
	07	36	Strained lower back
	08	54	Str rt hamstring; Anal fissures; Inflam disc
	09	21	Strained right hamstring
Matthews Jr., Gary	06	9	Ribcage strain
Mauer, Joe	07	34	Strained left quad muscle
	09	26	Inflamed right sacroiliac joint
McCann, Brian	06	16	Sprained right ankle
	09	15	Left eye infection
McDonald, John	06	15	Groin injury
	08	31	Sprained right ankle

FIVE-YEAR INJURY LOG

BATTERS	Yr	Days	Injury
McLouth, Nate	06	51	Left ankle sprain
	09	19	Strained-left hamstring
	10	41	Post concussion syndrome
Miles, Aaron	09	60	Strained right shoulder; right elbow
Milledge, Lastings	08	27	Strained groin
Molina, Jose	09	61	Grade two strain of the left hamstring
Molina, Yadier	07	29	Fractured left wrist
Montanez, Lou	09	119	Torn ligaments - right thumb
	10	53	Strained left oblique
Montero, Miguel	08	24	Fractured index finger right hand
	10	62	Torn meniscus - right knee
Moore, Adam	10	40	Sublexed left fibula
Mora, Melvin	07	23	Sprained left foot
	09	15	Strained left hamstring
Morales, Jose	07	22	Sprained left ankle
	10	39	Recovery from surgery on right wrist
Morales, Kendry	10	126	Fractured left leg
Morgan, Nyjer	09	38	Fractured left hand
	10	15	Strained right hip flexor
Morneau, Justin	10	87	Concussion
Morse, Michael	10	35	Strained left calf
Murphy, Daniel	10	50	Sprained right knee
Murphy, David	08	54	Sprained posterior cruciate ligament - rt knee
Murphy, Donnie	07	15	Strained oblique
	08	32	Inflammation right elbow
	10	31	Dislocated right wrist
Nady, Xavier	06	19	Appendectomy
	09	172	Torn ligament - right elbow
Napoli, Mike	07	51	Strained right hamstring; ankle
	08	32	Inflammation right shoulder
Navarro, Dioner	06	41	Bruised right wrist
	08	17	Lacerations of two fingers on right Hand
Nelson, Chris	09	27	Torn ligament - right wrist
Nix, Jayson	09	26	Strained right quad muscle
Nix, Laynce	09	15	Herniated disc-cervical spine
	10	23	Sprained right ankle
Ordonez, Magglio	08	18	Strained right oblique
	10	70	Fractured right ankle
Ortiz, David	08	54	Torn tendon sheath - left wrist
Overbay, Lyle	07	38	Fractured right hand
Pagan, Angel	06	75	Torn left hamstring
	07	54	Colitis
	08	140	Bruised labrum left shoulder
	09	80	Strained right groin; Right elbow surgery
Patterson, Eric	10	16	Strained neck
Paul, Xavier	09	137	Skin infection - left leg
Payton, Jay	07	19	Strained right hamstring
Pearce, Steve	10	131	Sprained right ankle
Pedroia, Dustin	10	97	Fx LT navicular bone; sore LT foot
Pena, Brayan	07	15	Concussion
	08	18	Lower back strain
Pena, Carlos	08	23	Fractured index finger left hand
	09	27	Fractured left index and ring finger
	10	15	Plantar Fasciitis - right foot
Pena, Tony	09	30	Fractured hamate bone left hand
Pence, Hunter	07	29	Chip fracture - right wrist
Perez, Fernando	09	149	Dislocated left wrist
Pettit, Chris	10	182	Recovery from surgery - right shoulder
Phillips, Brandon	08	18	Fractured right index finger & surgery
Pie, Felix	10	81	Strained left shoulder
Pierre, Juan	08	25	Sprained medial collateral ligament - lt knee
Podsednik, Scott	07	89	Strained left rib cage muscle; adductor
	08	25	Fractured left pinky finger
Polanco, Placido	06	37	Separated left shoulder
	10	21	Bone spur -right elbow
Posada, Jorge	08	108	Torn subscapularis muscle - right shoulder
	09	24	Strained right hamstring
	10	16	Stress fracture - right foot
Prado, Martin	08	59	Sprained left thumb
	10	17	Fractured right pinky finger
Pujols, Albert	06	18	Strained right oblique
	08	15	Strained left calf
Punto, Nick	08	40	Strained left hamstring x 2
	09	15	Strained right groin
	10	55	Strained LT hammy; hip flexor
Quentin, Carlos	07	45	Strained hamstring; torn labrum
	09	55	Plantar Fasciitis - left foot
Quintero, Humberto	09	17	Strained right shoulder
Ramirez, Aramis	07	15	Tendinitis - left patellar
	09	58	Dislocated left shoulder

FIVE-YEAR INJURY LOG

BATTERS	Yr	Days	Injury
Ramirez, Manny	10	65	Strained RT calf x 2; RT hammy
Reed, Jeremy	06	91	Fractured right thumb
Reimold, Nolan	09	17	Tendinitis - left Achilles tendon
Renteria, Edgar	07	34	Sprained right ankle x 2
	10	57	Strained RT groin; hammy; biceps
Reyes, Jose	09	137	Tendinitis right calf
	10	6	Recovery from hyperthyroidism
Rios, Alex	06	30	Staph infection in lower left leg
Rivera, Juan	06	21	Rib cage tightness
	07	154	Fractured left leg (1/07), surgery
Rivera, Mike	09	15	Strained left ankle
Roberts, Brian	06	24	Strained groin
	10	104	Str ab muscle; sore back (epidural injection)
Rodriguez, Alex	08	19	Grade 2 strain of right quad muscle
	09	33	Surgery to repair torn labrum - right hip
	10	15	Strained left calf
Rodriguez, Ivan	10	16	Strained lower back
Rohlinger, Ryan	10	30	Strained left hamstring
Rolen, Scott	07	33	Sore left shoulder
	08	41	Fractured finger; Inflammation right shoulder
	09	15	Postconcussion syndrome
Rollins, Jimmy	08	19	Sprained right ankle
	10	65	Strained RT calf x 2
Rosales, Adam	10	29	Stress fracture - right ankle
Ross, Cody	06	24	Bruised left pinky finger
	07	74	Strained left hamstring
Ross, David	06	18	Lower abdominal strain
	07	15	Concussion
	08	24	Back Spasms
	09	12	Strained left groin
Rowand, Aaron	06	56	Fx left ankle; Fx nose
	10	15	Fractured check bone
Ruiz, Carlos	09	21	Strained right oblique
	10	21	Concussion
Ryan, Brendan	08	24	Strained ribcage
	09	15	Strained left hamstring
Salazar, Oscar	10	33	Strained right Achilles tendon
Saltalamacchia, J	09	18	Numbness, fatigue-rt arm
	10	35	Strained upper back; infected leg
Sanchez, Angel	07	183	Strained elbow
	08	28	Sprained finger left hand
Sanchez, Freddy	07	6	Sprained MCL right knee
	09	20	Strained left shoulder
	10	45	Recovery from surgery - left shoulder
Santiago, Ramon	08	33	Separated left shoulder
Schafer, Jordan	09	30	Rehab from surgery - right wrist
	10	43	Recovery from surgery - left wrist
Schierholtz, Nate	09	16	Strained left hip
Schneider, Brian	06	15	Strained left hamstring
	09	42	Strained back muscle
	10	15	Strained right Achilles
Scott, Luke	09	16	Strained left shoulder
	10	18	Strained left hamstring
Shoppach, Kelly	10	54	Sprained right knee
Sizemore, Grady	09	54	Inflamed left elbow; torn ab. wall
	10	139	Bone bruise - left knee; microfracture surgery
Snider, Travis	10	63	Sprained right wrist
Snyder, Chris	08	19	Left testicular fracture
	09	81	Strained lower back x 2
Soriano, Alfonso	07	22	Strained right quad muscle
	08	56	Fx metacarpal - left hand; Strained right calf
	09	31	Surgery - left knee
Soto, Geovany	09	90	Strained left oblique
	10	30	Sprained RT shoulder; Shoulder Surgery
Span, Denard	09	15	Right ear infection
Spilborghs, Ryan	08	54	Strained left oblique
Stairs, Matt	10	24	Sore right knee
Stavinoha, Nick	10	19	Strained right shoulder
Stewart, Ian	10	28	Strained right oblique
Suzuki, Ichiro	09	10	Bleeding ulcer
Suzuki, Kurt	10	22	Intercostal strain
Sweeney, Mike	06	98	Bulging disc in upper back
	07	74	Cartilage damage right knee
	08	97	Inflammation - surgery on both knees 6/08
	09	15	Back spasms
	10	54	Back spasms; Inflamed back
Sweeney, Ryan	08	29	Sprained thumb; Bruised left foot
	09	15	Sprained left knee
	10	83	Pending surgery for patella tendinitis
Tatis, Fernando	10	90	Sprained right shoulder

FIVE-YEAR INJURY LOG

BATTERS	Yr	Days	Injury
Taveras, Willy	07	47	Strained right quad muscle
	09	34	Strained right quadriceps
Teahen, Mark	07	15	Strained left forearm
	10	73	Fractured right middle finger
Teixeira, Mark	07	34	Strained left quad muscle
Tejada, Miguel	07	35	Fractured radius left wrist
Thames, Marcus	07	21	Strained left hamstring
	09	46	Strained right oblique
	10	21	Strained right hamstring
Thome, Jim	07	22	Strained right ribcage
Tolbert, Matt	08	109	Torn ligament left thumb
	10	45	Sprained right middle finger
Torrealba, Yorvit	06	82	Right shoulder strain x 2
	08	31	Torn Meniscus - left knee/surgery 9/08
Torres, Andres	09	59	Strained left hamstring x 2
Tracy, Chad	07	57	Strained right knee; ribcage
	08	56	Recovery from microsurgery right knee
	09	31	Strained oblique
Treanor, Matt	06	15	Left shoulder
	08	28	Strained left hip
	09	166	Torn labrum - right hip
	10	30	Sprained right knee
Tulowitzki, Troy	08	67	Torn tendon right quad; Cut left hand
	10	39	Fractured left wrist
Upton, B.J.	07	34	Strained left quad
	09	8	Recovery from labrum surgery - rt shoulder
Upton Justin	08	55	Strained left oblique muscle
	09	20	Strained right oblique
Uribe, Juan	08	15	Strained left hamstring
Utley, Chase	07	31	Fractured right hand
	10	49	Sprained right thumb
Varitek, Jason	06	33	Cartilage damage, left knee
	10	67	Fractured 2nd metacarpal- left foot
Velez, Eugenio	10	18	Concussion
Venable, Will	10	19	Lower back pain
Victorino, Shane	07	22	Strained right calf
	08	16	Strained right calf
	10	15	Strained left abdominal muscle
Vizquel, Omar	08	40	Surgery left knee
Votto, Joey	09	24	Stress-related issue
Watson, Matt	10	18	Kidney stones
Weeks, Rickie	06	69	Right wrist surgery
	07	19	Tendinitis right wrist
	08	15	Sprained left knee
	09	140	Torn sheath left wrist.
Wells, Vernon	07	10	Left shoulder surgery (labrum & cyst)
	08	59	Fractured left wrist; Strained left hamstring
Werth, Jayson	06	182	Left wrist surgery
	07	33	Sprained last wrist
	08	15	Strained right oblique
Wieters, Matt	10	15	Strained right hamstring
Wigginton, Ty	06	33	Broken bone in left hand
	08	26	Fractured thumb left hand
Willingham, Josh	06	15	Strained ligament - left hand
	08	57	Back spasms
	10	48	Surgery - left knee
Willits, Reggie	08	17	Concussion
	10	10	Strained right hamstring
Wilson, Bobby	10	22	Bruised ankle; concussion
Wilson, Jack	08	51	Strained left calf
	09	17	Sprained left index finger
	10	101	Fx RT hand; Strained RT hammy
Wise, DeWayne	08	15	Strained left adductor
	09	61	Separated right shoulder; strained A/C joint
Wood, Brandon	10	22	Right Hip flexor strain
Worth, Danny	10	60	Bruised left heel
Wright, David	09	15	Concussion
Youkilis, Kevin	09	15	Strained left oblique
	10	61	Sprained right thumb
Young, Delmon	09	10	Recovery from elbow (right) surgery
Young, Eric	10	77	Stress Fracture; right tibia
Zaun, Gregg	06	5	Muscle pull, right calf
	07	44	Fractured right thumb
	08	19	Strained right elbow
	10	135	Strained right shoulder
Zimmerman, Ryan	08	57	Torn labrum - left shoulder
Zobrist, Ben	07	43	Strained left oblique muscle

FIVE-YEAR INJURY LOG

PITCHERS	Yr	Days	Injury
Aardsma, David	08	40	Strained right groin
Aceves, Alfredo	10	147	Herniated disk in lower back
Adams, Mike	09	90	Labrum surgery - rt shoulder; str shoulder
	10	26	Strained left oblique
Affeldt, Jeremy	10	28	Torn left oblique muscle
Albers, Matt	08	96	Torn labrum - pitching shoulder
Ambriz, Hector	10	36	Tendinitis - right elbow x2
Anderson, Brett	10	90	Left elbow inflammation x 2
Arias, Alberto	09	42	Strained right hamstring
	10	182	Impingement - right shoulder
Ascanio, Jose	09	54	Tendinitis - right shoulder
	10	182	Recovery from surgery - right shoulder
Atilano, Luis	10	74	Bone chips - right elbow
Baez, Danys	06	40	Appendectomy
	07	27	Tendinitis pitching forearm
	08	184	Tommy John surgery 9/2007
	10	15	Back spasms
Bailey, Andrew	10	32	Right intercostal strain
Bailey, Homer	10	83	Inflammation - right shoulder
Baker, Scott	08	32	Strained right groin
	09	10	Stiffness - right shoulder
Balfour, Grant	10	34	Strained intercostal muscle
Bannister, Brian	06	120	Strained right hamstring
	10	26	Tendinitis - right shoulder
Barrera, Henry	10	101	Recovery from TJS 6/09
Bastardo, Antonio	09	69	Strained right shoulder
	10	29	Ulnar Neuritis - left elbow
Bazardo, Yorman	10	19	Strained right shoulder
Beckett, Josh	07	15	Avulsion of skin - right index finger
	08	32	Back spasms; Sore pitching elbow
	10	65	Strained lower back
Bedard, Erik	07	22	Strained right oblique
	08	102	Torn labrum surgery 10/08; Sore hip
	09	100	Inflamed left shoulder x 2
	10	182	Recovery from surgery on left shoulder
Beimel, Joe	09	15	Strained left hip flexor
Belisario, Ronald	09	33	Strained right elbow
Belisle, Matt	06	71	Lower back strain x 2
	08	44	Sore right knee; sore right forearm
Beltre, Omar	10	30	Sprained right ankle
Benoit, Joaquin	08	34	Soreness - right shoulder
	09	183	Recovery from R/C surgery - right shoulder
Benson, Kris	06	17	Right elbow tendinitis
	07	183	Torn rotator cuff
	09	21	Tendinitis - right elbow
	10	157	Sore right shoulder
Bergesen, Brad	09	66	Contusion - left leg
Berken, Jason	10	51	Inflammation - right shoulder
Betancourt, Rafael	06	26	Right upper back strain
	09	38	Strained right groin
	10	15	Strained right groin
Billingsley, Chad	10	16	Strained right groin
Blanton, Joe	10	29	Strained left oblique
Bonderman, Jeremy	07	15	Blister right middle finger
	08	115	Thoracic outlet syndrome
	09	148	Recovery from thoracic outlet syndrome x 2
Bonser, Boof	09	185	Surgery - torn rotator cuff right shoulder
	10	64	Sore right shoulder; sore groin
Braden, Dallas	09	65	Infection - left foot
	10	27	Sore left elbow
Bradford, Chad	09	114	Recovery from strained back; elbow surgery
Bruney, Brian	08	97	Lisfranc injury right foot
	09	54	Strained right elbow x 2
Buchholz, Clay	08	18	Broken fingernail right hand
	10	24	Strained left hamstring
Buchholz, Taylor	09	183	Sprained UCL - right elbow
	10	129	Sore back; right elbow
Bulger, Jason	10	80	Sore right shoulder
Burnett, A.J.	06	73	Right elbow soreness x 2
	07	59	Sore pitching shoulder x 2
Bush, Dave	09	106	Fatigue - right arm
Butler, Josh	10	57	Impingement - pitching elbow
Byrdak, Tim	06	102	Bone spurs in left elbow
	07	26	Strained flexor tendon - pitching arm
	10	20	Strained right hamstring
Cabrera, Fernando	06	16	Bruised right heel
	08	88	Recovery from surgery on right elbow
Cahill, Trevor	10	16	Stress reaction - lt scapula (shoulder blade)
Capps, Matt	08	54	Bursitis - pitching shoulder

FIVE-YEAR INJURY LOG

PITCHERS	Yr	Days	Injury
Capuano, Chris	07	22	Strained left groin
	08	184	Tommy John surgery 5/08
Caridad, Esmailin	10	163	Strained Rt elbow; forearm
Carmona, Fausto	08	63	Strained left hip
Carpenter, Chris	06	15	Right shoulder bursitis
	07	182	Bone chips right elbow
	08	184	TJS recovery; Compressed nerve right arm
	09	35	Strained left ribcage muscle
Casilla, Santiago	08	33	Sore right elbow
	09	15	Sprained lateral collateral ligament - rt knee
Chamberlain, Joba	08	26	Tendinitis - right rotator cuff
Chen, Bruce	09	17	Torn left oblique muscle
Coffey, Todd	10	21	Bruised right thumb
Condrey, Clay	09	83	Strained left oblique x 2
	10	182	Strained flexor tendon - right elbow
Contreras, Jose	06	16	Pinched nerve in right hip
	08	74	Ruptured Achilles; Strained right elbow
Cook, Aaron	07	46	Strained right oblique
	09	34	Strained right shoulder
	10	54	Turf toe; Fx RT fibula
Corpas, Manuel	09	102	Bone spurs & surgery - right elbow
	10	38	Torn ulnar collateral ligament
Correia, Kevin	08	48	Strained left intercostals
Crain, Jesse	07	138	Torn R/C and Labrum
	09	16	Inflamed right shoulder
Cruz, Juan	06	29	Sore right shoulder
	07	18	Strained muscle - right shoulder
	08	27	Strained left oblique
	09	48	Strained right shoulder
Cueto, Johnny	09	15	Inflammation right shoulder
Daley, Matt	09	18	Sprained left foot
	10	87	Inflammation - right shoulder
Davies, Kyle	06	108	Strained right groin
Davis, Doug	08	23	Thyroid surgery
	10	141	Tend. LT elbow; Percarditis
Davis, Wade	10	18	Strained right shoulder
De La Rosa, Jorge	06	45	Blisters on left hand
	07	41	Strained pitching elbow
	10	74	Torn tendon - left middle finger
Delcarmen, Manny	10	16	Strained right forearm
Dempster, Ryan	07	27	Strained left oblique muscle
	09	25	Fractured right big toe
Detwiler, Ross	10	110	Rt hip strain; hip cartilage
Devine, Joey	08	67	Inflammation - right elbow setback 7/08
	09	183	Sprained right elbow
	10	182	Recovery from surgery - right elbow
Donnelly, Brendan	07	112	Strained pitching forearm
	09	16	Strained right calf
	10	22	Strained left oblique
Dotel, Octavio	06	135	Recovery from right elbow surgery
	07	94	Strained left oblique; shoulder
Downs, Scott	09	43	Bruised left toe; sprained left toe
Duchscherer, Justin	06	47	Right elbow tendinitis
	07	139	Strained right hip
	08	62	Str right hip; Strained right biceps tendon
	09	183	Recovery from surgery on right elbow
	10	156	Left Hip inflammation x 2
Duke, Zach	07	75	Tightness in pitching elbow
	10	25	Strained left elbow
Durbin, Chad	09	19	Strained lat muscle
	10	21	Strained right hamstring
Escobar, Kelvim	06	15	Right elbow irritation
	07	15	Irritation right shoulder
	08	184	Torn labrum - right Shoulder
	09	182	Recovery from labrum surgery
	10	182	Soreness - right shoulder
Estrada, Marco	10	124	Right shoulder fatigue
Eyre, Scott	06	16	Strained right hamstring
	08	66	Bone spur left elbow; Strained left groin
	09	23	Strained left calf
Eyre, Willie	09	64	Tightness right groin
Feldman, Scott	10	16	Bone bruise - right knee
Fister, Doug	10	24	Right shoulder fatigue
Flores, Randy	08	22	Tendinitis left ankle
Francis, Jeff	08	38	Inflammation - pitching shoulder
	09	183	Recovery from labrum surgery - left shoulder
	10	73	Soreness - LT shoulder x 2
Francisco, Frank	06	77	Recovery from right elbow surgery
	09	53	Tendinitis right shoulder x 2; pneumonia
	10	36	Strained right lat muscle

PITCHERS	Yr	Days	Injury
Fuentes, Brian	07	41	Strained left LAT muscle
	10	178	Mid-back strain (lat muscle)
Fulchino, Jeff	10	34	Tendinitis - right elbow
Gallagher, Sean	08	20	Fatigue - right shoulder
	10	24	Sprained left toe
Gallardo, Yovani	08	165	Two knee surgeries
	10	17	Strained oblique muscle
Garcia, Freddy	07	127	Tendinitis right biceps; R/C; labrum
Garcia, Jaime	09	137	Sore left elbow
Garza, Matt	08	16	Inflamed radial nerve in right arm
Gaudin, Chad	08	14	Left hip surgery (labrum)
Gervacio, Sammy	10	17	Posterior rotator cuff strain
Gonzalez, Miguel	09	183	Rehab from right elbow surgery
Gonzalez, Mike	06	38	Left arm fatigue
	07	138	Torn UCL
	08	80	Tommy John surgery 6/2008
	10	102	Strained left shoulder
Gorzelanny, Tom	06	29	Left elbow soreness
	08	19	Irritated left middle finger
Grabow, John	07	23	Inflamed pitching elbow
	10	15	Tendinitis - left knee
Green, Sean	06	50	Back spasms; strained side
	10	126	Strained right ribcage
Gregerson, Luke	09	28	Strained right shoulder
Greinke, Zack	06	79	Personal reasons
Guerrier, Matt	06	53	Fractured right thumb
Guthrie, Jeremy	08	21	Impingement - right rotator cuff
Gutierrez, Juan	10	15	Inflammation - right shoulder
Guzman, Angel	07	121	Strained right elbow
	08	155	Tommy John surgery 9/2008
	09	15	Strained right triceps
	10	182	Tornligament - right shoulder
Haeger, Charlie	10	43	Plantar fasciitis - RT foot x 2
Halladay, Roy	07	20	Appendectomy
	09	15	Right groin strain
Hamels, Cole	06	18	Left shoulder strain
	07	32	Strained pitching elbow
Hammel, Jason	10	18	Strained right groin
Hanrahan, Joel	10	8	Strained flexor tendon - right forearm
Happ, J.A.	10	81	Strained left forearm
Harang, Aaron	08	28	Strained pitching forearm
	09	45	Appendectomy
	10	61	Lower back spasms
Harden, Rich	06	146	Sprain right elbow; back strain
	07	151	Strained pitching shoulder x 2
	08	37	Strained right subscapularis muscle
	09	26	Strained lower back
	10	64	Tendinitis RT shoulder; Stra. LT glut muscle
Harrison, Matt	09	125	Inflamed left elbow; shoulder
	10	22	Left biceps tendinitis
Hawkins, LaTroy	07	31	Inflammation in pitching elbow
	09	16	Shingles
	10	136	Rt shoulder weakness x 2
Hendrickson, Mark	06	18	Left shoulder tightness
Hensley, Clay	07	34	Strained groin; Labrum surgery
	08	68	Strained right shoulder
	10	20	Strained left neck muscle
Hernandez, David	10	33	Sprained left ankle
Hernandez, Felix	07	26	Strained flexor muscle - right forearm
	08	16	Sprained left ankle
Hill, Shawn	06	95	Right elbow soreness
	07	94	Strained left (non-throwing) shoulder
	08	117	Right elbow (spurs) surgery 9/08; Forearm
	09	162	Inflammation - right elbow
Ho Park, Chan	10	33	Strained right hamstring
Hochevar, Luke	08	41	Ribcage contusion
	10	83	Strained right elbow
Hoffman, Trevor	09	21	Strained right oblique
Holland, Derek	10	62	Left rotator cuff inflammation
Howell, J.P.	10	182	Strained left shoulder
Hudson, Tim	08	65	Torn ulnar collateral ligament - right elbow
	09	150	Recovery from Tommy John surgery
Hughes, Phil	07	94	Strained left hamstring
	08	90	Fractured rib
Hunter, Tommy	10	24	Strained left oblique
Hurley, Eric	08	91	Strained left hamstring; sore right shoulder
	09	183	Torn rotator cuff - right shoulder
	10	182	Recovery from surgery x 2 - left wrist
Igarashi, Ryota	10	32	Strained left hamstring

PITCHERS	Yr	Days	Injury
Isringhausen, Jason	08	73	Torn flexor tendon; Lacerated right hand
	09	155	Torn UCL right elbow; surgery
Jakubauskas, Chris	10	115	Concussion
Janssen, Casey	08	184	Torn labrum - right shoulder (surgery 3/08)
	09	66	Sore right shoulder x 2
Jenks, Bobby	08	18	Bursitis - left scapula area
Jepsen, Kevin	09	15	Lower back spasms
Johnson, Jim	08	29	Impingement - right shoulder
	10	91	Small tear in right elbow
Johnson, Josh	07	166	Tight pitching elbow; nueritis
	08	102	Tommy John surgery 8/2007
Jurrjens, Jair	07	16	Sore pitching shoulder
	10	61	Strained left hamstring
Karstens, Jeff	07	104	Fractured right fibula; elbow
	08	50	Strained groin
	09	22	Strained lower back
Kazmir, Scott	06	55	Left shoulder sorenes x 2
	08	35	Strained Left elbow
	09	37	Strained right quadriceps
	10	36	Stra. RT hammy; Fatigue LT shoulder
Kelley, Shawn	09	58	Strained left oblique
	10	109	Right elbow inflammation
Kennedy, Ian	08	26	Strained right lat, bursitis, pitching shoulder
Kuo, Hong-Chih	07	126	Irritation - left elbow x 2
	09	85	Sore left elbow
	10	18	Sore left shoulder
Kuroda, Hiroki	08	19	Tendinitis - right shoulder
	09	72	Strained left oblique; concussion
Lackey, John	08	44	Grade 2 strain, right triceps
	09	41	Inflammation - right elbow
Laffey, Aaron	09	46	Strained right oblique
	10	42	Fatigued - left shoulder
Latos, Mat	10	15	Strained left oblique
League, Brandon	07	135	Strained lat; strained oblique
Leake, Mike	10	15	Fatigue - right shoulder
Lee, Cliff	07	32	Strained upper abdominal muscle
	10	26	Strained right abdominal muscle
Leroux, Chris	09	22	Inflamed right shoulder
	10	30	Strained right elbow
Lester, Jon	06	39	Lymphoma
	07	71	Recovery from lymphoma
Lewis, Rommie	10	18	Inflammation - left shoulder
Lewis, Scott	09	128	Strained left elbow
Lidge, Brad	07	23	Stained left oblique
	08	6	Surgery (cartilage damage) right knee
	09	19	Sprained right knee
	10	47	Inflamed rt elbow; Recov rt knee & elbow surg
Lilly, Ted	09	27	Inflamed left shoulder; surgery left knee
	10	20	Recovery from surgery - left shoulder
Lincoln, Mike	09	114	Herniated disc in neck
	10	124	Strained right latissimus dorsi muscle
Lindstrom, Matt	09	37	Strained right elbow
	10	15	Back spasms
Linebrink, Scott	08	40	Inflamed subscapularis muscle
Liriano, Francisco	06	34	Sore left elbow and forearm
	07	183	Torn UCL - pitching elbow and surgery
	09	22	Left arm fatigue
	09	174	Strained right forearm
Litsch, Jesse	10	128	TJS recovery; Torn labrum RT hip
Lohse, Kyle	09	54	Strained right forearm; left groin
	10	84	Exertional compartment syndrome - rt forearm
Lopez, Rodrigo	07	106	Torn flexor tendon-pitching arm x 2
Lowe, Mark	06	43	Right elbow tendinitis
	07	148	Sore right elbow; surgery
	10	148	Herniated lumbar disc
Madrigal, Warner	10	60	Strained right forearm
Madson, Ryan	07	81	Strained pitching shoulder; oblique
	10	70	Fractured right toe + surgery
Mahay, Ron	07	34	Strained ribcage muscle
	08	11	Plantar fasciitis - left foot
	10	42	Torn R/C right shoulder
Maine, John	06	40	Inflammation in right middle finger
	08	46	Strained R/C, bone spur right shoulder
	09	98	Weakness - right shoulder
	10	135	Arm fatigued - right shoulder
Marcum, Shaun	08	33	Strained pitching elbow
	09	183	Recovery from Tommy John surgery 9/08
	10	16	Inflammation - right elbow
Marinez, Jhan	10	70	Strained right elbow
Marmol, Carlos	06	16	Right shoulder fatigue

FIVE-YEAR INJURY LOG

PITCHERS	Yr	Days	Injury
Marquis, Jason	10	111	Debris in right elbow
Marshall, Sean	06	40	Strained left oblique muscle
Marte, Damaso	09	117	Tendinitis - left shoulder
	10	87	Inflammation - left shoulder
Martin, J.D.	10	70	Strained lower back
Martinez, Joseph	09	117	Concussion; skull fractures
Masset, Nick	09	15	Strained left shoulder
Mathieson, Scott	06	29	Right elbow surgery
	07	183	Tommy John surgery 9/2006
	08	184	Setbacks from TJ Surgery
	10	27	Strained back
Matsuzaka, Daisuke	08	24	Strained rotator cuff - right shoulder
	09	124	Weak and strained right shoulder
	10	44	Strained neck; RT forearm
Mazzaro, Vin	09	27	Tendinitis - right shoulder
McCarthy, Brandon	07	53	Stress fx - right shoulder blade; blister
	08	146	Inflammation right Forearm/setback 4/08
	09	88	Stress fracture - right scapula
	10	66	Recovery from shoulder surgery
McGowan, Dustin	08	83	Frayed labrum, surgery 7/08
	09	183	Recovery from labrum surgery - rt shoulder
	10	182	Sore right shoulder (60-day DL)
Meche, Gil	09	32	Back spasms
	10	105	Bursitis - right shoulder
Medders, Brandon	10	15	Right knee inflammation
Medlen, Kris	10	59	Partial tear of UCL- right elbow
Meek, Evan	09	54	Strained left oblique
Meloan, John	10	182	Tommy John surgery - right elbow (3/10)
Meyer, Dan	10	13	Strained left calf muscle
Mijares, Jose	10	58	Strained LT knee; blured vision
Miller, Andrew	07	20	Strained left hamstring
	08	49	Tendinitis in right patellar tendon
	09	25	Strained right oblique
Millwood, Kevin	07	50	Strained left hamstring x 2
	08	40	Strained right groin x 2
	10	16	Strained right forearm
Miner, Zach	07	23	Tendinitis pitching elbow
	10	182	Strained right elbow
Mitre, Sergio	06	88	Right shoulder inflammation
	07	17	Torn callus on pitching hand
	08	184	Strained right Forearm
	10	49	Strained left oblique
Mock, Garrett	10	145	Neck Pain (cervical spine);
Moehler, Brian	06	28	Sprained right ankle
	09	19	Sprained right knee
	10	87	Strained right groin
Monasterios, Carlos	10	18	Blister -right middle finger
Morales, Franklin	09	51	Strained left shoulder
	10	27	Left shoulder weakness
Morrow, Brandon	09	15	Tendinitis - right triceps
Morton, Charlie	09	7	Strained left oblique
	10	35	Right shoulder weakness
Moscoso, Guillermo	10	4	Blister - right index finger
Mota, Guillermo	09	15	Ingrown toenail
	10	15	IT band syndrome
Motte, Jason	10	27	Sprained right shoulder
Moyer, Jamie	10	74	Sprained Left elbow
Moylan, Peter	08	171	Soreness right Elbow, TJS 5/08
Myers, Brett	07	64	Soreness in pitching shoulder
	09	98	Torn and frayed labrum - right hip
Nathan, Joe	10	182	Tommy John surgery - right elbow (3/10)
Nelson, Joe	07	183	Shoulder surgery
Neshek, Pat	08	145	Partially torn UCL - right elbow
	09	185	Recovery from Tommy John surgery
	10	37	Inflamed right middle finger
Niemann, Jeff	10	21	Strained right shoulder
Niese, Jonathon	09	60	Torn right hamstring tendon
	10	19	Strained right hamstring
Nieve, Fernando	09	77	Torn right quadriceps
Nippert, Dustin	08	38	Blister - right foot
	09	93	Back spasms; inflammation in back
	10	45	Concussion
Nolasco, Ricky	07	119	Inflamed right elbow x 2
	10	35	Torn meniscus - right knee
Norris, Bud	10	35	Biceps tendinitis - right shoulder
Nunez, Leo	07	183	Hairline Fx - right wrist
	08	54	Strained left lat muscle
O'Flaherty, Eric	10	41	Viral infection
Ohlendorf, Ross	10	68	Strained RT lat; sore back
Ohman, Will	09	130	Inflammation - left shoulder

FIVE-YEAR INJURY LOG

PITCHERS	Yr	Days	Injury
Okajima, Hideki	10	22	Strained right hamstring
Oliver, Darren	09	11	Strained left triceps
Olsen, Scott	09	129	Tendinitis & torn labrum right shoulder
	10	68	Tightness left shoulder
Ortega, Anthony	10	122	Tendinitis - right triceps tendon
Oswalt, Roy	06	15	Strained middle back
	08	16	Strained left abductor muscle
	09	19	Lower back pain
Ottavino, Adam	10	87	Strained right shoulder
Outman, Josh	09	107	Sprained left elbow
	10	182	Recovery from surgery - left elbow
Padilla, Vicente	07	54	Strained right triceps
	08	30	Strained left hamstring; Strained neck
	09	16	Strained deltoid muscle - right shoulder
	10	75	Sore RT foreram; herniated disc
Park, Chan Ho	06	49	Abdominal pain; intestinal bleeding
Parra, Manny	07	21	Displaced chip fracture - left thumb
Parrish, John	06	182	Recovery from left elbow surgery
	10	51	Tendinitis - left rotator cuff
Paulino, Felipe	08	184	Pinched nerve in upper pitching arm
	09	19	Strained right groin
	10	83	Right shoulder tendinitis
Pavano, Carl	06	182	Back strain, bone chips in right elbow
	07	174	Torn ulnar collateral ligament
	08	145	Tommy John surgery 8/2007
Peavy, Jake	08	28	Strained right elbow
	09	101	Strained tendon - right ankle
	10	88	Detached lat muscle in right shoulder
Penny, Brad	08	95	Inflammation right shoulder
	10	134	Strained upper back
Perez, Oliver	07	18	Lower back stiffness
	09	105	Tendinitis right kneecap x 2
	10	50	Right knee patella tendinitis
Perkins, Glen	07	112	Strained teres major muscle
	09	52	Inflammation left shoulder; elbow
Perry, Ryan	10	26	Tendinitis upper right biceps
Pettitte, Andy	08	6	Backs spasms
	10	60	Strained left groin
Pineiro, Joel	07	15	Sprained right ankle
	08	36	Sore right shoulder; Sore right groin
	10	55	Strained left oblique
Pinto, Renyel	07	42	Strained left shoulder
	08	15	Strained left hamstring
	09	27	Tendinitis left elbow
	10	19	Sore left hip
Poveda, Omar	10	163	Recovery from Tommy John surgery
Purcey, David	10	19	Strained ligaments - right foot
Putz, J.J.	08	57	Costochondritis; Hyperextended right elbow
	09	122	Bone chips - right elbow
	10	15	Tendinitis - right knee
Qualls, Chad	09	35	Dislocated kneecap - left leg
Rapada, Clay	08	18	Biceps tendinitis left arm
Ray, Chris	07	72	Bone spur pitching elbow
	08	184	Tommy John surgery 8/2007
	09	25	Biceps tendinitis - right arm
	10	16	Strained right ribcage muscle
Resop, Chris	10	49	Strained left oblique
Reyes, Anthony	08	19	Strained pitching elbow
	09	135	Inflammation - right elbow
Reyes, Dennys	07	64	Inflamed elbow; shoulder
	10	16	Strained left elbow
Reyes, Jo-Jo	09	56	Strained left hamstring
	10	33	Strained right knee
Reynolds, Greg	09	34	Sore right shoulder
	10	70	Bruised right elbow
Richmond, Scott	09	28	Tendinitis - right shoulder
	10	78	Impingement - right shoulder
Riske, David	06	47	Lower back strain
	08	35	Hyperextended right elbow
	09	178	Tightness right elbow
	10	65	Recovery from Tommy John surgery
Robertson, Nate	07	20	Tired pitching arm
	09	77	Strained lower back; left elbow
Rodney, Fernando	07	56	Tendinitis right shoulder; biceps
	08	78	Tendinitis right shoulder
Rodriguez, Wandy	08	38	Strained left groin
Romero, J.C.	09	70	Strained left forearm
	10	18	Recovery from surgery on left elbow
Romero, Ricky	09	22	Strained left oblique
Rosales, Leo	10	124	Sprained right foot

PITCHERS	Yr	Days	Injury
Rowland-Smith, Ryan	09	69	Tendinitis - left triceps
	10	37	Strained lower back
Runzler, Dan	10	54	Dislocated left knee
Rzepczynski, Marc	10	45	Fractured middle finger - left hand
Sabathia, C.C.	06	30	Strained right oblique muscle
Saito, Takashi	08	31	Sprained pitching elbow
	10	18	Left hamstring strain
Sampson, Chris	07	29	Sprained ulnar collateral ligament
	09	15	Muscle Spasms - right shoulder
	10	21	Tendonitis - right biceps
Sanches, Brian	10	22	Strained right hamstring
Sanchez, Anibal	08	123	Labrum surgery - right Shoulder
	09	104	Sprained right shoulder x 2
Sanchez, Jonathan	07	23	Strained rib cage muscle
	08	20	Strained left shoulder
Santana, Ervin	09	60	Sprained MCL - right elbow; inflamed triceps
Santana, Johan	09	45	Bone spurs-left elbow - out for the year
Saunders, Joe	09	18	Tightness - left shoulder
Scherzer, Max	09	9	Sore right shoulder
Schlichting, Travis	09	35	Back Injury
	10	42	Inflammation - right shoulder
Schlitter, Brian	10	20	Right shoulder impingement
Schoeneweis, Scott	09	28	Depression
Seay, Bobby	10	182	Bursitis - left shoulder
Sheets, Ben	06	96	Right shoulder strain; tendinitis
	07	45	Sprained index finger right hand
	10	75	Strained right elbow
Sherrill, George	08	26	Inflammation left shoulder
	10	15	Back tightness
Shields, Scot	08	6	Strained right Shoulder
	09	131	Tendinitis - right patella tendon
Silva, Carlos	08	15	Tendinitis right shoulder
	09	131	Strained rotator cuff - right shoulder
	10	36	Irregular heart beat
Simon, Alfredo	09	173	Soreness right elbow
	10	21	Strained left hamstring
Slowey, Kevin	08	25	Strained biceps muscle right arm
	09	95	Strained right wrist
	10	15	Strained right triceps
Smith, Greg	09	34	Strained lower back
Smith, Joe	09	66	Sprained left knee; sore right R/C
Snell, Ian	08	15	Strained pitching elbow
Sonnanstine, Andy	10	16	Strained left hamstring
Soria, Joakim	07	15	Inflammation right shoulder
	09	25	Strained rotator cuff - right shoulder
Soriano, Rafael	06	15	Right shoulder fatigue
	08	154	Inflammation right elbow x 2
Sosa, Henry	09	61	Torn muscle-right shoulder
Sosa, Jorge	07	14	Strained left hamstring
Springer, Russ	08	16	Irritated ulnar nerve right elbow
	10	59	Strained left hip
Stauffer, Tim	08	184	Torn Labrum/surgery 5/08
	10	52	Appendectomy
Stokes, Brian	10	112	Shoulder fatigue
Strasburg, Stephen	10	61	Stiff RT shoulder; TJS surgery 9/10
Street, Huston	06	20	Strained right groin
	07	71	Irritated pitching elbow
	10	79	Strained right shoulder
Suppan, Jeff	08	15	Irritation right elbow
	09	28	Strained left oblique
	10	42	Strained neck; right groin
Talbot, Mitch	10	15	Strained back
Tallet, Brian	08	19	Fractured toe - right foot
	10	44	Sore left forearm
Taschner, Jack	10	15	Strained left hamstring
Tazawa, Junichi	09	14	Strained left groin
	10	182	Tommy John surgery (4/10) out for 2010
Tejeda, Robinson	09	30	Tendinitis - right rotator cuff
	10	30	Tendinitis - right biceps
Texeira, Kanekoa	10	27	Strained right elbow
Thatcher, Joe	10	18	Strained left shoulder

PITCHERS	Yr	Days	Injury
Thompson, Rich	10	20	Inflammation - right shoulder
Thornton, Matt	10	16	Inflammation left forearm
Threets, Erick	08	44	Intercostal strain -right side
	10	61	Turf toe; TJS pending
Uehara, Koji	09	121	Tendinitis right elbow; strained left hamstring
	10	70	Strained LT hammy; RT elbow
Valverde, Jose	09	47	Strained right calf
VandenHurk, Rick	09	60	Sore right elbow
Vargas, Claudio	07	15	Lower back spasms
	09	88	Tendinitis - right elbow
Vargas, Jason	07	9	Bone spur right elbow
	08	184	Left hip surgery (labrum) 3/08
Vizcaino, Luis	08	64	Strained right shoulder
Volquez, Edinson	09	140	Inflamed nerve right elbow; back spasms
	10	104	Recovery from Tommy John surgery 8/09
Wade, Cory	08	19	Inflammation right shoulder
	09	40	Strained & bursitis - right shoulder
	10	88	Surg on frayed labrum, rotator cuff & bursa sac
Wagner, Billy	08	58	Sprained left forearm
	09	137	Tommy John surgery 9/08
Wainwright, Adam	08	75	Sprained middle finger - right hand
Wakefield, Tim	06	57	Stress fracture in rib cage
	08	18	Soreness - pitching shoulder
	09	48	Lower back strain
Walker, Tyler	06	111	Right elbow surgery
	07	183	Tommy John surgery
	10	105	Sprained A/C joint - right shoulder
Wang, Chien-Ming	07	23	Strained right hamstring
	08	106	Lisfranc sprain, torn tendon - right foot
	09	125	Strained right shoulder; weak hip muscles
	10	182	Recovery from surgery - right shoulder
Weaver, Jeff	07	29	Inflammation in pitching shoulder
	10	34	Back tightness; tend. LT knee
Weaver, Jered	07	16	Tendinitis right biceps
Webb, Brandon	09	176	Bursitis - right shoulder
	10	182	Recovery from 8/2009 shoulder surgery
Wellemeyer, Todd	07	81	Sore pitching elbow
	09	29	Inflammation-right elbow
	10	55	Strained right quad
West, Sean	10	49	Inflammation - right knee
Westbrook, Jake	07	52	Strained left internal oblique muscle
	08	162	Tommy John surgery 06/08
	09	183	Recovery from TJ Surgery
White, Sean	09	20	Tendinitis - right shoulder
Willis, Dontrelle	08	38	Hyperextended right Knee
	09	152	Anxiety disorder
Wilson, C.J.	06	11	Right hamstring strain
	08	53	Bone spurs - left elbow, surgery 8/08
Wise, Matt	06	49	Right elbow surgery
	08	167	Bruise right forearm; weak right shoulder
Wolf, Randy	06	118	Recovery from left elbow surgery
	07	89	Soreness -pitching shoulder
Wood, Kerry	06	162	Post surgical; R/C tear
	07	124	Shoulder stiffness
	08	22	Blister on pitching hand
	10	52	Strained back; RT index finger
Wright, Jamey	07	66	Inflamed right shoulder
Wuertz, Michael	10	29	Tendinitis - right shoulder
Yates, Tyler	09	142	Inflammation - right elbow
Young, Chris	07	15	Strained left oblique
	08	89	Strained right forearm; nasal fractures
	09	112	Inflammation right shoulder
	10	164	Inflammation - right shoulder
Zambrano, Carlos	08	15	Strained right shoulder
	09	42	Strained left hamstring; strained back
Zimmermann, Jordan	09	78	Right elbow soreness
	10	119	Recovery from Tommy John surgery
Zumaya, Joel	07	107	Ruptured tendon right middle finger
	08	130	Recovery from surgery on right shoulder
	09	96	Sore right shoulder x 2
	10	96	Fractured olecranon process - right elbow

Prospects

Top Prospects for 2011

by Rob Gordon

Dustin Ackley (2B, SEA) got off to a slow start but rebounded nicely and made steady progress. He looked impressive in the Arizona Fall League (AFL). The only thing holding him back is the need for more repetition at second base.

Lars Anderson (1B, BOS) looks ready to see extended playing time in Boston after hitting .274/.349/.461 with 15 HR and some solid defense. He should develop more power as he matures and is worth watching in 2011.

Chris Archer (RHP, CHC) emerged as the Cubs' top pitching prospect. He breezed through two levels, going 15-3 with a 2.34 ERA, 65 BB / 149 K, and a sparkling .200 OBA in 142.1 IP. Archer will likely start the season in the minors, but could make a big impact in the 2nd half.

J.P. Arencibia (C, TOR) had his best season as a professional, hitting .301/.359/.626 with 32 HR. He remains stiff and below average defensively, but offers well above average power at a scarce position.

Brandon Allen (1B, ARI) got buried behind Adam LaRoche and then got off to a slow start. He eventually turned things around, hitting .261 with 25 HR and 83 BB for the year. Allen doesn't have much speed and is a so-so defender, but he does have the potential to hit for solid power and draw plenty of walks.

Yonder Alonso (1B, CIN) continues to improve defensively and is more athletic than he gets credit for. He had another solid season hitting 290/.362/.458 with 15 HR. Unfortunately, he is currently blocked at 1B by Joey Votto.

Brandon Beachy (RHP, ATL) emerged as a solid back-of-the-rotation guy. The Braves moved him from relief into a starting role and the results were excellent: 5-1, 1.73 ERA, and 28 BB / 148 K in 119.1 IP. Beachy has a nice four-pitch mix, throws strikes, and has plus command.

Brandon Belt (1B, SF) was arguably the biggest surprise in the minors. He reworked his swing and the results were outstanding: .352/.455/.620 with 23 HR and 22 SB. If Aubrey Huff departs in the off-season, Belt is the best in-house option to fill the 1B spot in 2011.

Andrew Brackman (RHP, NYY) was finally healthy and productive after having Tommy John surgery in 2007. He struggled with control in the past, but was solid in '10, going 10-11, 3.90 ERA, 39 BB / 126 K in 140.2 IP. The lanky Brackman is probably not ready for the Yankees starting rotation, but could carve out a role as a setup reliever.

Zach Britton (LHP, BAL) has a good low-90s sinking fastball, solid slider, and developing change. He gets plenty of ground balls and was 10-7 with a 2.70 ERA, 51 BB /124 K in 153.1 IP. He should get a chance to win a rotation spot.

Domonic Brown (OF, PHI) struggled in his brief stint in the majors, but has the tools to be an impact player. He just needs to refine his approach and get more experience.

Brown could start the '11 season in the minors but at some point he will get an extended chance to showcase his considerable skills.

Chris Carter (1B, OAK) has as much raw power as any player in the minors. He got off to a slow start, but hit .319/.421/.637 in the 2nd half. Carter is a "three true outcomes" guy as half of his hits went for extra bases and he struck out 138 times. Full-time AB in Oakland could result in some nice HR totals.

Simon Castro (RHP, SD) struggled when promoted to Triple-A, but has a good 90-95 MPH fastball, slider, and changeup. It isn't too hard to envision a scenario where the Padres' surprising staff struggles in 2011, and Castro would be the likely beneficiary.

Hank Conger (C, LAA) continued to do what he does best – hit. He is below average defensively, but hit .300/.385/.463 with 26 doubles, 11 HR, and 55 BB / 58 K in 387 AB.

Kyle Drabek (RHP, TOR) put together an impressive season and is in line to win a starting spot this spring. Using a plus 12-6 curveball and a low-to-mid 90s fastball, he went 14-9 with a 2.94 ERA, 68 BB / 132 K in 162 IP. Drabek doesn't have the size or late life on his fastball to overpower major league hitters, but he more than makes up for it by knowing how to pitch.

Scott Elbert (LHP, LA) desperately needs to get things back on track. He struggled with control and health issues, had one appearance in LA, and walked away from baseball when the Dodgers sent him down. After a four-month hiatus, Elbert returned to the AFL where his stuff looked sharp. He is still young, still talented, still wild, and still worth watching.

Danny Espinosa (SS/2B, WAS) has the valuable combination of power and speed. He strikes out a lot and may never hit for average, but he did manage to hit .268/.337/.464 with 22 HR and 25 SB. Espinosa will likely split time between SS and 2B for the Nationals.

Todd Frazier (OF, CIN) had a completely forgettable season, hitting just .258/.333/.448 with 17 HR and 127 K. At 25, he is no longer young and will need to put up some numbers in 2011 or risk becoming a super utility guy.

Freddie Freeman (1B, ATL) had a monster 2nd half. On the year, he hit .319/.378/.521 with 18 HR. Not the most fluid athlete, he still has good bat speed, makes solid contact, drives the ball well, and is an above-average defender.

Mat Gamel (3B, MIL) is still waiting for his chance to make an impact. The 25-year-old is a professional hitter (.304/.388/.496), but also is a player without a position. At this point, he needs a change of scenery, but he can definitely hit.

Kyle Gibson (RHP, MIN) flashed plus stuff and looked polished, going 11-6, 2.96 ERA, 39 BB / 126 K in 152 IP. He isn't going to blow hitters away, but he knows how to pitch, has solid command, and gets plenty of ground ball outs.

Greg Halman (OF, SEA) has tremendous raw power, but strikes out too much and may not ever hit for much average. He hit .243/.310/.545 with 33 HR, 15 SB, and 37 BB / 169 K. Love the power, hate the plate discipline.

Jeremy Hellickson (RHP, TAM) had to bide his time while waiting for a chance to contribute. To his credit, he never sulked and looked sharp when he finally got his chance (3.47 ERA, 8 BB / 33 K, and a .232 OBA). He has good command and has emerged as one of the more polished hurlers in the AL.

Eric Hosmer (1B, KC) got his eyesight corrected, was finally healthy, and had an offensive explosion. On the year he hit .338/.406/.571 with 23 HR and 59 BB / 66 K. Hosmer fields his position well, has a bit of speed, and is developing into an offensive force with the bat.

Desmond Jennings (OF, TAM) had a disappointing season, hitting just .278/.362/.393 with 3 HR. He missed time with a sore shoulder, a bad wrist, and was never 100%. Jennings did manage to steal 37 bases in 41 attempts. His power spike might still be a few years away, but for now he should see increased playing time.

Craig Kimbrel (RHP, ATL) was probably the most dominant reliever in the minors. He uses a mid-to-upper-90s fastball and a devastating slider to overpower hitters. Kimbrel was 3-2, 1.62 ERA, 35 BB / 83 K, 23 saves, and a .143 OBA in 55.2 IP. He was even more dominant in Atlanta and has to be considered the favorite to take over the Braves' closer role.

Jason Kipnis (OF, CLE) had a nice breakout season in 2010: .307/.386/.492 with 32 doubles and 16 HR. The 23-year-old isn't flashy but does everything well and should get a chance to see significant playing time for the rebuilding Indians.

Brett Lawrie (2B, MIL) had a solid sophomore season and is the best 2B power prospect in the minors. He is strong, athletic, and has a nice power/speed profile. He hit .285/.346/.451 with 36 doubles, 16 triples, 8 HR and 30 SB. He is currently stuck behind Rickie Weeks, but Weeks is about to get very expensive.

Corey Luebke (LHP, SD) mixes his three pitches well and possesses excellent command. He doesn't project to much of a strikeout pitcher but has the potential to become a dependable #3-4 starter. He should compete for a starting role in 2011.

Jordan Lyles (RHP, HOU) is the face of the future for the Astros and has solid stuff. In 2010, he was 7-12 with a 3.57 ERA, 46 BB / 137 K, and a .285 OBA in 158.2 IP. He could probably use a full season at Triple-A, but he's been rushed so far and that isn't likely to change in 2011.

Jake McGee (LHP, TOR) doesn't get a lot of attention but the results were hard to argue with: 4-8, 3.07 ERA, 36 BB / 127 K in 105.2 IP. He struggled two years ago and relies heavily on a 90-95 MPH fastball. McGee's secondary offerings lag behind the heater, prompting some scouts to project him as a future reliever.

Devin Mesoraco (C, CIN) finally had a nice breakout season. After hitting just .240/.311/.368 in his first three minor league seasons, he exploded, hitting .302/.377/.587 with 26 HR. Mesoraco was stronger and more fit this year, and it showed on the field. If the Reds opt not to bring back Ramon Hernandez, Mesoraco could see extended playing time behind the plate in 2011.

Mike Minor (LHP, ATL) reached the majors in his first season as a professional and showed better than anticipated velocity. He nibbled too much once he reached the majors, but his 90-94 MPH fastball, change-up, and curve give him the stuff to become a fixture in the Braves rotation.

Jesus Montero (C, NYY) started the season slowly but managed to hit .352/.396/.684 after the All-Star break. The only questions at this point are how many starts will he get behind the plate and how long will he have to wait to see full-time AB? Montero is a special hitter with plus power and the ability to be a middle of the order run producer. The move of Jorge Posada to DH creates the opening that Montero needs.

Mike Montgomery (LHP, KC) is working his way back from an elbow injury that caused him to miss 6 weeks of action. Prior to the injury, he was well on his way to establishing himself as one of the best LHP in the minors. If he can stay healthy, he should be ready to contribute in the 2nd half of 2011.

Mike Moustakas (3B, KC) is finally beginning to live up to the hype of being the 2nd overall pick. After hitting .262/.320/.444 in his first three seasons, the 22-year-old mashed his way to .322/.369/.630 with 36 HR. The move of Alex Gordon to the OF creates a potential opening for Moustakas in 2011.

Andy Oliver (LHP, DET) put up impressive numbers in his professional debut (9-8, 3.45 ERA, 50 BB / 119 K, .242 OBA in 130.1 IP). He struggled in Detroit, posting an ERA of 7.36, but he has a lively 90-95 MPH fastball and a good, if inconsistent, slider. If he can improve his control and develop a better off-speed pitch, he could log some productive innings in Detroit.

Jarrod Parker (RHP, ARI) finally looks to be healthy after having Tommy John Surgery in 2009. The surgery seems to have gone well and in October his fastball was sitting in the mid-90s in instructional league play. If completely healthy, look for him to contend for a rotation spot this spring.

Michael Pineda (RHP, SEA) continues to emerge as one of the more dominant hurlers in the minors. Over the past couple of seasons, he has filled out his 6'5" frame and his fastball now sits in the mid-to-upper 90s. He complements the fastball with a plus slider and has good control and a loose, easy delivery.

Wilson Ramos (C, WAS) was acquired from the Twins in the Matt Capps trade and will enter 2011 in a time-share with Ivan Rodriguez. Ramos has good raw strength but prefers to hit line drives instead of swinging for the fences. He sometimes struggles to make consistent contact, but in the past has shown an ability to hit for average.

Josh Reddick (OF, BOS) will have to battle for playing time in what is likely going to be a crowded OF situation in Boston, but Reddick has good athleticism and solid power potential. In 2010, he hit .266/.301/.466 with 18 HR in 451 AB.

Ben Revere (OF, MIN) is a hitting and on-base machine. The diminutive outfielder isn't going to hit for power, but he makes consistent contact (he's never struck out more than 41 times in any of his four minor league seasons), steals plenty of bases, and puts the ball into play.

Treyvon Robinson (OF, LA) is a solid, across-the-board contributor and put up respectable numbers - .300/.404/.438 with 9 HR, 38 SB, and 73 BB / 125 K. He is a good defender, gets on base near a .400 clip, has plus speed, and should add a bit of pop as he matures. The Dodgers have one OF opening and Robinson is their best in-house option.

Willin Rosario (C, COL) has as much power upside as any catching prospect in the NL. Strong and athletic, he continues to improve defensively and has a strong throwing arm, and good intensity. On the year, he hit .285/.342/.552 with 13 doubles and 19 HR in just 270 AB. A torn ACL puts his future somewhat in doubt and could result in a late start in 2011.

Tony Sanchez (C, PIT) was in the midst of a breakout season when he broke his jaw. Prior to the injury he was hitting .314/.416/.454. While Sanchez isn't likely to develop a ton of power, he has a good bat, nice plate discipline, and is a plus defender.

Tanner Scheppers (RHP, TEX) had a frustrating season as both a starter and reliever. His final numbers don't look that impressive (4.84 ERA), but his upper-90s fastball gives him the ability to dominate – most likely as a reliever.

Michael Taylor (OF, OAK) looked a bit lost at the plate in 2010, but still has solid long-term potential. On the year, he hit .272/.348/.392 with 6 HR and 16 stolen bases. If he can find a way to use his lower half more effectively and tap into his raw power (6'6", 260), he has a nice power/speed potential.

Julio Teheran (RHP, ATL) was finally healthy and showed the Braves what he could do. Featuring 93-96 MPH sinking fastball, a sharp breaking curveball, and a solid change-up, he dominated, going 9-8, 2.59, 40 BB / 159 K, and a .208 OBA in 142.2 IP, but might not see the majors until after the All Star Break.

Daryl Thompson (RHP, CIN) is finally healthy after a variety of ailments. He has as good 90-94 MPH fastball, a nice curveball, solid change, and throws strikes. He hasn't tossed over 100 innings since 2008, but if he can stay healthy he could work his way into the back end of the rotation.

Mark Trumbo (1B, LAA) tied for the minor league lead in home runs in 2010 with 36. Trumbo isn't a particularly fluid athlete, but he does have tremendous raw power. For the year, he hit .301/.368/.577 with 29 doubles and 36 HR. But he is currently blocked by Kendry Morales and can't really play the outfield.

Top Ranked 2011 Prospects

1. Jeremy Hellickson (RHP, TAM)
2. Domonic Brown (OF, PHI)
3. Jesus Montero (C, NYY)
4. Freddie Freeman (1B, ATL)
5. Brandon Belt (1B, SF)
6. Eric Hosmer (1B, KC)
7. Desmond Jennings (OF, TAM)
8. Danny Espinosa (SS/2B, WAS)
9. Craig Kimbrel (RHP, ATL)
10. Mike Minor (LHP, ATL)
11. Mike Moustakas (3B, KC)
12. Brandon Allen (1B, ARI)
13. Mat Gamel (3B, MIL)
14. Dustin Ackley (2B, SEA)
15. Michael Pineda (RHP, SEA)
16. J.P. Arencibia (C, TOR)
17. Wilson Ramos (C, WAS)
18. Tony Sanchez (C, PIT)
19. Andy Oliver (LHP, DET)
20. Zach Britton (LHP, BAL)
21. Kyle Drabek (RHP, TOR)
22. Jake McGee (LHP, TOR)
23. Michael Taylor (OF, OAK)
24. Jarrod Parker (RHP, ARI)
25 Tanner Scheppers (RHP, TEX)
26. Jason Kipnis (OF, CLE)
27. Jordan Lyles (RHP, HOU)
28. Brandon Beachy (RHP, ATL)
29. Lars Anderson (1B, BOS)
30. Chris Carter (1B, OAK)
31. Devin Mesoraco (C, CIN)
32. Hank Conger (C, ANA)
33. Kyle Gibson (RHP, MIN)
34. Corey Luebke (LHP, SD)
35. Mike Montgomery (LHP, KC)
36. Julio Teheran (RHP, ATL)
37. Yonder Alonso (1B, CIN)
38. Josh Reddick (OF, BOS)
39. Daryl Thompson (RHP, CIN)
40. Willin Rosario (C, COL)
41. Scott Elbert (LHP, LA)
42. Ben Revere (OF, MIN)
43. Andrew Brackman (RHP, NYY)
44. Chris Archer (RHP, CHC)
45. Mark Trumbo (1B, ANA)
46. Greg Halman (OF, SEA)
47. Simon Castro (RHP, SD)
48. Todd Frazier (OF, CIN)
49. Brett Lawrie (2B, MIL)
50. Treyvon Robinson (OF, LA)

Top Japanese Prospects

by Tom Mulhall

Shinnosuke Abe (C, Yomiuri Giants) has 30+ HR power and league-leading OPS. This Gold Glover is the highest paid catcher in Japan and is eligible for international free agency. However, he has never expressed any desire to play in the ML. *Possible ETA: 2012 but probably never.*

Norichika Aoki (OF, Yakult Swallows) is a Gold Glove winner with considerable experience in international play. Aoki has no power but consistently posts a .300+ BA with some speed. In 2010, he became the first player in Japanese history to post a second 200-hit season – a feat not even achieved by Ichiro. He is on track to become a free agent after 2011 and wants to play in the ML. At worst, he would make an excellent 4th OF for many ML teams and a source of cheap steals for his fantasy owner. At best, he could live up to his nickname of "mini-Ichiro." *Probable ETA: 2012.*

Yu Darvish (SP, Nippon Ham Fighters) had his usual stellar season with a 1.78 ERA and 1.05 WHIP. Still years away from attaining free agency, the rumors about his posting have increased in the past year. The only concern is innings – more than 200 IP for four straight years with 10 complete games in 25 starts in 2010. He has announced he will stay in Japan in 2011 but his time is coming. At worst, an above-average ML #3 SP. At best, Randy Johnson, only better looking. *Possible ETA: 50-50 for 2012.*

Kyuji Fujikawa (Closer, Hanshin Tigers) may finally be getting his wish as there are strong rumors his team has acquiesced to his long-time demands to be posted. If true, he could have an immediate impact in the right situation. Considered by many to be the best closer in Japan, he pitches in a relatively big stadium which should help his transition to the ML. Hope that your competitors have been burned on other recent Japanese imports, and bid an extra dollar on this power pitcher with an impressive K/9 rate. *Probable ETA: 2011.*

Hisashi Iwakuma (SP, Tohoku Rakuten Golden Eagles) has been posted, and if a ML team meets his organization's price, he will be pitching in the Majors in 2011. The 29-year-old could very well be the second best SP in Japan after Darvish. (His K/BB rate is even better than Darvish.) Iwakuma has had several solid seasons in a row, capped with a 2.82 ERA and 1.15 WHIP in 2010. Again, if your competitors have bought into the thinking that Japanese pitchers are overrated, a capable #3 SP could fall into your lap. *Probable ETA: 2011.*

Chang Yong Lim (Closer, Yakult Swallows) is a Korean who is among the best closers in Japan. He has often talked about playing in the ML; however, his team is dangling a three-year contract at him. Lim has a sidearm delivery with a mid-90s fastball complemented by a decent slider and forkball. He's hit 100 mph on the radar gun and in the right situation could be a decent ML closer. *Possible ETA: 2012.*

Munenori Kawasaki (SS, Fukuoka Softbank Hawks) is a speedy middle infielder nearing international free agency. He rebounded from a somewhat sub-par 2009 season and stole 30 bases with a .319 BA in 2010. A competent defender with international experience, the slap hitter was caught stealing 11 times and will have to improve his SB percentage, especially since he is completely lacking in power. *Possible ETA: 2012.*

Hiroyuki Kobayashi (Closer, Chiba Lotte Marines) posted a strong 2010 season but it still seems doubtful that a ML team will sign him as a closer. If he starts in middle relief, he could present a reasonable gamble for cheap saves. Hope that your competitors confuse him with Masahide Kobayashi (or maybe Kobayashi, the hot dog guy) and he slides to you for a buck. *Probable ETA: 2011.*

Shuichi Murata (3B, Yokohama Bay Stars) has an average BA but good power. At 5' 9", he may be too small to make the power transition to the ML, but he held his own in the WBC. He will be eligible for international free agency after the 2011 season and his team is currently in turmoil. *Possible ETA: 2012.*

Hiroyuki Nakajima (SS, Seibu Lions) is that rare Japanese middle infielder with a little pop to complement his speed and solid BA. The six-time All Star badly wants to test the ML waters and in the right park, he may even have 20-20 potential. *Possible ETA: 2012.*

Tsuyoshi Nishioka (2B, Chiba Lotte Marines) hit .346 to win the batting title and he has some speed to boot. His team unexpectedly posted the 26-year old switch-hitter several years early; he could pleasantly surprise. *ETA: 2011.*

Yuki Saito (SP, Waseda University) is a phenomenal young pitcher who, according to a Mets scout, could be "the next Pedro Martinez." Unfortunately, at the end of his stellar college career, Saito made himself eligible for the Japanese amateur draft and was claimed by the Nippon Ham Fighters. If he signs, a move to the ML won't come any time soon, although it's possible he could include an exit clause in his contract. What makes this most interesting is that if he pans out, the Ham Fighters may be more willing to let Darvish leave early. *Barely Possible ETA: 2016.*

Toshiya Sugiuchi (SP, Fukuoka Softbank Hawks) is getting close to free agency. In 2009, he was in the top four in his league in ERA, strikeouts, WHIP and wins. Coming off a sub-par 2010 with a 3.55 ERA, his team may decide to post him sooner rather than later. This could be a mistake since his underlying stats were as strong as ever, with an excellent K/BB ratio and a league-leading K/9 rate. The lefty former MVP and Sawamura Award winner could be a capable ML pitcher. *Possible ETA: 2012.*

Yoshinori Tateyama (RP, Nippon Ham Fighters) is now an international free agent who wants to pitch in the ML this season. The competent middle reliever has a 1.80 ERA, 1.02 WHIP, with over a K per inning. A reasonable longshot for cheap saves. *Probable ETA: 2011.*

Tsuyoshi Wada (SP, Fukuoka Softbank Hawks) is a left-hander with an excellent track record, finishing 2010 with a 3.04 ERA. Now eligible for domestic free agency, he probably will not be posted and will have to wait one more year for international free agency. *Probable ETA: 2012.*

Avoid: Yoshihiro Doi (Pitcher), Hichori Morimoto (OF), Naoyuki Shimizu (Pitcher).

Major League Equivalents

In his 1985 *Baseball Abstract*, Bill James introduced the concept of major league equivalencies. His assertion was that, with the proper adjustments, a minor leaguer's statistics could be converted to an equivalent major league level performance with a great deal of accuracy.

Because of wide variations in the level of play among different minor leagues, it is difficult to get a true reading on a player's potential. For instance, a .300 batting average achieved in the high-offense Pacific Coast League is not nearly as much of an accomplishment as a similar level in the Eastern League. MLEs normalize these types of variances, for all statistical categories.

The actual MLEs are not projections. They represent how a player's previous performance might look at the major league level. However, the MLE stat line can be used in forecasting future performance in just the same way as a major league stat line would.

The model we use contains a few variations to James' version and updates all of the minor league and ballpark factors. In addition, we designed a module to convert pitching statistics, which is something James did not originally do.

Do MLEs really work?

Used correctly, MLEs are excellent indicators of potential. But, just like we cannot take traditional major league statistics at face value, the same goes for MLEs. The underlying measures of base skill — contact rates, pitching command ratios, BPV, etc. — are far more accurate in evaluating future talent than raw home runs, batting averages or ERAs.

The charts we present here also provide the unique perspective of looking at two years' worth of data. These are only short-term trends, for sure. But even here we can find small indications of players improving their skills, or struggling, as they rise through more difficult levels of competition. Since players — especially those with any modicum of talent — are promoted rapidly through major league systems, a two-year scan is often all we get to spot any trends. Five-year trends do appear in the *Minor League Baseball Analyst*.

Here are some things to look for as you scan these charts:
Target players who...
- spent a full year in AA and then a full year in AAA
- had consistent playing time from one year to the next
- improved their base skills as they were promoted

Raise the warning flag for players who...
- were stuck at the same level both years, or regressed
- displayed marked changes in playing time from one year to the next
- showed large drops in BPIs from one year to the next

Players are listed on the charts if they spent at least part of 2009 or 2010 in Triple-A or Double-A and had at least 100 AB or 30 IP within those two levels. Each is listed with the organization with which they finished the season.

Only statistics accumulated in Triple-A and Double-A are included (players who split a season are indicated as a/a); Major League and Single-A (and lower) stats are excluded.

Each player's actual AB and IP totals are used as the base for the conversion. However, it is more useful to compare performances using common levels, so rely on the ratios and sabermetric gauges. Explanations of these formulas appear in the Encyclopedia.

Batters who had a BPV of at least 50, and pitchers who had a BPV of at least 90, and are less than 26 years of age (the "unofficial" break point between prospect and suspect) are indicated with an "a" after their age. This should provide a pool of the best rising prospects. Obvious prospects like Carlos Gonzalez and Jason Heyward were tagged as "a" in 2009. However, there were also lesser players tagged in last year's book who ended up getting significant playing time in 2010. Among them were Daric Barton, Jonathan Jay, Ryan Kalish, Jonathan Lucroy, Mitch Moreland, Logan Morrison, Cliff Pennington, Sean Rodriguez, Danny Valencia, Carlos Carrasco, Tyler Clippard and Doug Fister.

Also keep an eye on players over 26 but under 30, with similarly high BPVs. These are your "Bull Durham" prospects, indicated with a "b" after their age. Keep these players on your end-game or reserve list radar as there could be hidden short-term value here. Among the players tagged as "b" is last year's book were Shelley Duncan, Garrett Jones, Adam Rosales and Gaby Sanchez.

Major League Equivalent Statistics

BATTER	Yr	B	Age	Pos	Lev	Org	ab	r	h	d	t	hr	rbi	bb	k	sb	cs	ba	ob	slg	ops	bb%	ct%	eye	px	sx	rc/g	bpv
Abreu,Miguel	09	R	25	4	aa	BAL	489	53	135	29	1	4	43	12	53	24	8	277	293	363	657	2%	89%	0.22	66	105	3.79	47
	10	R	26	8	a/a	BAL	152	9	27	4	0	3	13	2	23	3	6	179	189	260	449	1%	85%	0.08	51	60	1.24	-17
Abreu,Tony	09	B	25 a	4	aa	LA	307	38	90	19	2	10	44	12	46	3	3	294	319	463	782	4%	85%	0.25	109	77	5.28	60
	10	B	26	6	aaa	ARI	94	10	27	6	1	1	13	3	14	1	0	290	311	400	711	3%	85%	0.20	77	89	4.61	11
Ackley,Dustin	10	L	23	4	a/a	SEA	501	61	115	29	5	5	39	60	64	8	4	230	312	337	649	11%	87%	0.94	76	104	3.76	33
Adams,David	10	R	23	4	aa	NYY	152	25	40	13	2	3	26	16	27	4	2	264	333	432	765	9%	83%	0.59	116	132	5.17	43
Adams,Russ	09	L	29	4	a/a	SD	207	22	43	10	2	1	15	14	34	2	2	208	257	287	544	6%	84%	0.41	58	92	2.45	23
	10	L	30	4	aaa	NYM	383	37	75	20	1	11	37	23	64	3	2	195	241	340	580	6%	83%	0.36	94	62	2.67	22
Adams,Ryan	10	R	23	4	aa	BAL	530	65	143	38	0	14	54	36	96	2	3	270	317	420	736	6%	82%	0.38	104	42	4.75	26
Adduci,James	09	L	24	8	aa	CHC	467	51	126	19	3	4	41	47	69	29	13	269	336	347	684	9%	85%	0.68	55	108	4.22	37
	10	L	25	8	aaa	CHC	367	40	74	8	1	2	22	18	61	15	10	202	239	243	483	5%	83%	0.29	28	106	1.82	-32
Affronti,Michael	09	R	26	4	aa	OAK	189	14	36	5	0	2	14	8	19	1	3	189	224	244	467	4%	90%	0.44	37	43	1.67	13
	10	R	27	6	a/a	HOU	377	30	79	9	3	3	32	14	62	5	6	210	238	271	509	4%	84%	0.22	39	82	2.00	-25
Aguila,Chris	10	R	32	8	aaa	FLA	337	29	60	18	1	6	24	19	79	2	2	179	222	290	512	5%	77%	0.24	76	60	2.06	-20
Albernaz,Craig	09	R	27	2	a/a	TAM	133	13	19	4	2	0	8	12	30	1	0	145	216	201	416	8%	77%	0.39	37	118	1.47	-8
	10	R	28	2	a/a	TAM	160	15	32	4	0	2	11	14	33	2	1	203	265	259	523	8%	79%	0.41	37	54	2.36	-36
Aldridge,Cory	09	L	30	8	aa	KC	354	32	87	17	3	14	48	16	78	0	1	245	278	430	708	4%	78%	0.21	112	49	4.10	27
	10	L	31	8	aaa	LAA	299	31	70	18	1	8	35	20	66	1	1	233	282	375	657	6%	78%	0.31	95	51	3.65	3
Alfonzo,Eliezer	09	R	31	2	aa	SD	204	19	45	8	0	9	25	5	52	1	0	221	240	383	623	2%	75%	0.10	98	38	3.08	-5
	10	R	32	2	aaa	SEA	174	15	32	7	1	6	15	5	45	0	1	186	209	337	546	3%	74%	0.11	92	58	2.19	-22
Allen,Brandon	09	L	24 a	3	a/a	ARI	447	57	120	23	4	16	55	37	62	5	2	267	324	441	764	8%	86%	0.60	107	92	5.18	75
	10	L	25	3	aaa	ARI	371	45	80	15	2	16	54	52	63	9	5	215	311	398	710	12%	83%	0.83	109	83	4.28	47
Almonte,Erick	09	R	32	3	aaa	MIL	247	20	54	9	0	2	21	20	52	3	0	220	277	275	553	7%	79%	0.38	41	51	2.73	-19
	10	R	33	0	aaa	MIL	325	27	77	16	1	2	26	20	61	3	0	238	281	309	590	6%	81%	0.32	54	62	3.09	-18
Alonso,Yonder	09	L	22 a	3	aa	CIN	105	10	29	10	0	2	12	12	13	1	0	276	350	429	779	10%	88%	0.92	114	36	5.72	75
	10	L	23	3	a/a	CIN	507	54	130	32	1	14	54	44	77	10	4	257	317	406	722	8%	85%	0.58	100	71	4.61	38
Alvarez,Pedro	09	L	23 a	5	aa	PIT	222	35	68	18	0	10	33	27	47	1	0	306	382	523	904	11%	79%	0.57	141	43	7.80	65
	10	L	24	5	aaa	PIT	242	32	58	14	2	10	41	24	52	3	5	239	306	433	740	9%	78%	0.45	120	88	4.37	30
Amarista,Alexi	10	L	21	4	a/a	LAA	256	29	72	7	2	1	22	10	14	6	4	280	307	335	643	4%	95%	0.73	38	97	3.63	18
Ambort,Michael	10	B	25	3	aa	SF	159	15	31	7	1	3	11	8	31	0	1	195	231	302	533	5%	81%	0.24	69	65	2.23	-11
Anderson,Bryan	09	L	23	2	aa	STL	163	17	35	6	2	3	9	8	32	1	0	215	251	331	583	5%	80%	0.25	72	103	2.84	21
	10	L	24	2	aaa	STL	270	27	60	10	0	8	30	19	40	0	0	221	272	345	616	6%	85%	0.47	77	25	3.23	18
Anderson,Drew	10	L	29	8	a/a	MIL	292	36	62	20	1	5	33	28	72	2	2	212	282	339	621	9%	75%	0.39	90	147	3.26	-7
Anderson,Drew M	09	L	27	4	aa	TAM	255	24	48	14	4	1	13	18	41	2	0	188	242	281	524	7%	84%	0.45	66	114	2.31	38
	10	L	28	4	aa	TAM	374	47	79	10	8	5	29	29	53	4	3	212	268	325	593	7%	86%	0.54	65	147	2.93	11
Anderson,Josh	10	L	28	8	aaa	ATL	142	14	21	4	0	0	2	4	25	9	2	149	169	174	343	2%	82%	0.14	22	137	0.99	-46
Anderson,Lars	09	L	22	3	aa	BOS	447	42	102	26	0	7	43	54	92	2	0	228	311	334	645	11%	79%	0.58	76	42	3.78	15
	10	L	23	3	a/a	BOS	471	47	120	40	2	11	53	38	96	2	3	254	310	416	726	8%	80%	0.40	115	52	4.53	27
Anderson,Leslie	10	R	28	8	a/a	TAM	303	28	76	13	1	6	28	17	47	3	1	250	289	360	649	5%	85%	0.36	73	60	3.67	9
Andino,Robert	10	R	26	6	aaa	BAL	546	53	122	25	3	11	57	21	93	12	3	224	253	340	593	4%	83%	0.23	76	103	2.93	2
Angle,Matthew	10	L	25	8	a/a	BAL	410	50	99	5	3	2	25	35	49	22	7	241	300	280	580	8%	88%	0.71	23	122	3.09	-11
Apodaca,Juan	09	R	23	2	aa	BOS	216	22	50	13	0	4	24	17	46	1	0	231	286	345	631	7%	79%	0.36	80	43	3.49	8
	10	R	24	2	a/a	CLE	250	20	50	8	0	4	14	29	55	1	0	200	282	276	559	10%	78%	0.52	51	33	2.77	-25
Arencibia,JP	09	R	24	2	aaa	TOR	466	49	94	28	1	17	55	19	91	0	1	202	233	374	607	4%	81%	0.21	111	44	2.83	34
	10	R	25 a	2	aaa	TOR	412	45	95	29	1	19	50	23	57	0	0	231	271	445	716	5%	86%	0.40	136	32	4.13	66
Armstrong,Cole	09	L	26	2	aaa	CHW	246	23	54	11	0	9	27	10	50	0	0	221	251	378	629	4%	80%	0.20	98	22	3.20	13
	10	L	27	2	aa	CHW	315	25	71	13	0	7	32	38	53	0	0	226	309	334	643	11%	83%	0.71	71	12	3.72	12
Arnal,Cristo	09	R	24	4	a/a	CLE	258	34	65	9	0	0	14	23	20	15	7	253	314	287	601	8%	92%	1.16	30	96	3.26	40
	10	R	25	6	aa	CLE	176	23	32	3	1	1	8	13	23	5	0	182	239	224	463	7%	87%	0.56	27	118	1.91	-16
Ashley,Nevin	09	R	25	2	aa	TAM	118	8	22	6	1	1	13	16	31	0	0	183	281	271	551	12%	74%	0.52	62	50	2.68	-14
	10	R	26	2	a/a	TAM	365	39	75	12	2	6	36	27	75	4	2	204	258	292	551	7%	79%	0.36	57	83	2.56	-21
Aubrey,Michael	09	L	27 b	3	aaa	BAL	376	34	94	24	1	7	43	16	37	2	2	249	280	376	656	4%	90%	0.44	89	50	3.62	57
	10	L	28 b	0	aaa	BAL	366	37	70	19	1	18	48	26	52	2	3	192	245	394	639	7%	86%	0.49	123	49	3.09	57
Auer,Tyson	10	R	25	8	a/a	LAA	232	27	59	9	2	2	9	12	30	10	10	252	288	331	619	5%	87%	0.38	53	113	2.93	2
Avery,Xavier	10	L	21	8	aa	BAL	107	8	24	5	0	3	14	5	25	8	0	221	257	356	613	5%	76%	0.20	87	91	3.44	-13
Baez,Edgardo	09	R	24	8	aa	WAS	323	36	75	12	3	8	24	24	72	5	11	232	285	360	645	7%	78%	0.33	79	91	3.13	17
	10	R	25	8	aa	WAS	270	22	61	10	1	3	24	23	66	6	3	226	286	303	589	8%	76%	0.34	53	72	3.01	-38
Bailey,Jeff	09	R	31	8	aaa	BOS	229	29	52	7	0	8	23	30	58	2	0	226	315	356	672	11%	75%	0.52	78	49	4.10	1
	10	R	32	8	aaa	ARI	478	48	101	25	4	7	43	35	69	2	1	212	265	324	589	7%	85%	0.50	76	81	2.93	18
Baisley,Jeff	09	R	27	5	aa	OAK	355	29	68	17	1	6	26	17	63	1	0	192	230	290	520	5%	82%	0.28	68	53	2.21	10
	10	R	28	5	a/a	OAK	376	33	86	25	1	6	45	25	77	3	3	230	278	352	630	6%	80%	0.33	87	54	3.32	3
Balentien,Wladimir	10	R	26	8	aaa	CIN	401	52	96	19	1	21	57	28	75	9	1	239	288	450	737	6%	81%	0.37	126	92	4.57	41
Bankston,Wes	09	R	26	5	aaa	CIN	457	46	107	23	2	16	60	24	81	2	1	234	273	397	670	5%	82%	0.30	101	59	3.72	40
	10	R	27	8	a/a	TEX	246	17	47	16	0	4	24	13	42	2	0	191	231	299	530	5%	83%	0.30	79	48	2.31	7
Barden,Brian	09	R	28	3	aa	STL	187	18	39	9	0	3	19	7	39	1	1	207	236	296	532	4%	79%	0.18	64	51	2.28	-7
	10	R	29	5	aaa	FLA	184	20	50	11	1	2	15	12	36	2	3	271	316	369	685	6%	80%	0.33	72	66	3.98	-6
Barfield,Josh	09	R	27	4	aaa	CLE	305	20	64	13	0	2	27	6	43	4	3	211	227	271	499	2%	86%	0.15	47	55	1.98	3
	10	R	28	4	aaa	SD	265	23	59	9	0	4	25	10	31	3	1	221	249	295	544	4%	88%	0.32	51	58	2.48	3
Barney,Darwin	09	R	24	6	aa	CHC	464	46	124	23	1	3	41	29	58	8	2	268	312	340	652	6%	87%	0.51	55	75	3.90	30
	10	R	25	6	aaa	CHC	479	50	120	21	2	2	34	16	39	8	4	251	275	315	590	3%	92%	0.42	49	86	2.99	15
Bates,Aaron	09	R	26	3	a/a	BOS	478	59	119	25	0	9	49	34	101	1	0	250	299	362	661	7%	79%	0.33	77	47	3.88	7
	10	R	27	8	aaa	BOS	429	37	90	16	1	9	41	44	103	0	1	210	284	315	599	9%	76%	0.43	67	29	3.10	-22
Baxter,Mike	09	L	25	8	aa	SD	505	60	131	32	4	7	61	48	84	11	9	259	323	376	699	9%	83%	0.57	83	93	4.26	47
	10	L	26	8	aaa	SD	482	66	113	23	6	12	54	44	69	16	12	234	298	380	679	8%	86%	0.64	91	127	3.74	34
Beerer,Scott	10	R	28	8	aa	COL	391	28	84	9	0	3	28	14	55	4	4	214	241	257	498	3%	86%	0.26	30	46	1.99	-23
Bell,Bubba	09	L	27	8	a/a	BOS	451	51	99	22	2	5	32	49	86	8	3	220	296	308	604	10%	81%	0.57	63	88	3.26	22
	10	L	28	8	aaa	BOS	351	34	89	17	1	5	36	31	56	10	7	254	314	346	660	8%	84%	0.55	65	73	3.76	7
Bell,Josh	09	B	23 a	5	aa	BAL	448	65	133	34	1	22	76	59	93	3	5	297	379	525	903	12%	79%	0.63	145	46	7.40	72
	10	B	24	5	aaa	BAL	316	34	79	22	0	12	40	18	63	2	5	251	291	431	722	5%	80%	0.28	118	40	4.13	27
Bellorin,Edwin	09	R	28	2	aa	COL	202	11	48	9	1	1	21	6	16	0	2	236	259	303	562	3%	92%	0.41	50	35	2.57	28
	10	R	29	2	aaa	HOU	250	10	38	6	0	1	8	13	39	0	0	151	194	187	380	5%	85%	0.34	27	12	1.17	-28
Belt,Brandon	10	L	22 a	3	a/a	SF	223	30	64	14	5	10	41	28	39	3	1	287	367	529	896	11%	83%	0.72	145	140	7.33	70
Beltre,Engel	10	L	21	8	aa	TEX	181	12	45	4	4	1	12	8	19	7	2	250	283	336	619	4%	89%	0.42	49	150	3.36	7

Major League Equivalent Statistics

BATTER	Yr B	Age	Pos	Lev	Org	ab	r	h	d	t	hr	rbi	bb	k	sb	cs	ba	ob	slg	ops	bb%	ct%	eye	px	sx	rc/g	bpv
Benson,Joe	10 R	23	8	aa	MIN	373	50	81	17	5	17	38	29	90	11	11	217	274	426	700	7%	76%	0.32	123	139	3.57	18
Bernier,Doug	09 B	29	6	aaa	NYY	227	27	34	8	1	0	16	28	78	1	0	148	240	189	429	11%	66%	0.35	34	78	1.60	-63
	10 B	30	5	aaa	PIT	200	16	36	11	0	1	10	11	42	4	1	179	222	247	468	5%	79%	0.26	55	76	1.83	-28
Berry,Quintin	09 L	25	8	aa	PHI	516	70	120	15	1	5	22	49	102	38	15	233	299	294	593	9%	80%	0.48	42	116	3.11	9
	10 L	26	8	aa	SD	348	38	59	8	2	2	26	36	76	22	8	170	247	221	469	9%	78%	0.47	35	127	1.89	-38
Bertram,Michael	09 L	26 a	3	aa	DET	123	17	30	6	2	7	24	10	27	0	0	245	303	481	785	8%	78%	0.39	137	94	5.15	69
	10 L	27	3	a/a	DET	467	43	98	25	2	10	50	24	107	4	1	209	247	335	582	5%	77%	0.22	84	75	2.78	-12
Betemit,Wilson	09 B	28	5	aaa	CHW	261	30	54	16	0	10	40	17	73	2	0	207	256	383	638	6%	72%	0.23	114	57	3.32	10
	10 B	29	6	aaa	KC	113	6	24	5	1	1	11	11	19	1	1	210	283	296	579	9%	83%	0.59	60	59	2.88	0
Bigley,Evan	10 R	24	8	aa	MIN	113	13	33	8	1	3	12	2	18	0	2	295	307	460	767	2%	84%	0.11	109	73	4.75	28
Bishop,Rawley	10 R	25	3	aa	DET	245	32	54	10	0	7	34	21	52	5	0	219	281	341	622	8%	79%	0.41	77	80	3.43	-5
Bixler,Brian	09 R	27	6	aa	PIT	403	54	93	20	5	6	33	26	111	10	3	231	277	352	628	6%	72%	0.23	79	145	3.39	11
	10 R	28	6	aaa	WAS	368	35	86	15	3	3	37	23	77	14	7	235	281	313	594	6%	79%	0.31	55	111	2.98	-26
Blackmon,Charles	10 L	24 a	8	aa	COL	337	41	91	21	3	10	42	24	33	14	8	271	319	436	755	7%	90%	0.72	107	113	4.81	61
Blalock,Hank	10 L	30	5	aaa	TAM	109	13	29	4	0	3	17	7	19	2	0	268	312	379	690	6%	83%	0.37	72	57	4.38	3
Blanco,Gregor	09 L	26	8	aaa	ATL	333	42	65	8	1	2	24	39	63	8	3	195	280	240	520	11%	81%	0.63	31	92	2.41	0
	10 L	27	8	aaa	ATL	154	20	36	6	0	1	8	18	26	7	1	233	315	293	608	11%	83%	0.71	46	91	3.56	-7
Bocock,Brian	10 R	26	6	aaa	PHI	380	30	74	9	2	4	25	39	82	10	7	195	271	260	531	9%	78%	0.48	42	83	2.38	-32
Boesch,Brennan	09 L	24 a	8	aa	DET	527	71	128	23	6	23	75	26	107	9	2	242	278	439	717	5%	80%	0.24	116	128	4.23	61
	10 L	25	8	aaa	DET	58	5	19	3	1	3	13	3	15	2	1	324	355	551	907	5%	74%	0.19	133	114	7.27	15
Boggs,Brandon	09 B	27	8	aa	TEX	332	34	75	13	2	6	35	44	88	6	2	224	316	333	648	12%	73%	0.50	69	85	3.83	0
	10 B	28	8	aaa	TEX	362	50	86	21	4	7	34	50	79	2	6	236	328	373	701	12%	78%	0.63	90	81	4.20	11
Bogusevic,Brian	09 L	26	8	aa	HOU	520	49	117	22	2	5	39	39	98	16	4	224	278	300	578	7%	81%	0.39	54	97	2.96	13
	10 L	27	8	aaa	HOU	502	63	113	21	1	9	40	47	92	17	1	225	292	326	618	9%	82%	0.51	67	106	3.50	-1
Bolivar,Luis	09 R	29	4	aaa	CIN	353	45	67	13	3	4	24	12	68	21	5	189	217	279	496	3%	81%	0.18	59	165	2.00	28
	10 R	30	6	a/a	ATL	343	29	65	9	3	3	22	15	85	10	4	188	223	258	481	4%	75%	0.18	44	117	1.86	-53
Bond,Brock	09 B	24	4	aa	SF	450	79	136	20	4	1	28	56	61	11	16	303	380	371	751	11%	86%	0.91	50	98	5.02	39
	10 B	25	4	a/a	SF	449	53	110	24	4	1	29	51	62	7	5	245	322	320	642	10%	86%	0.82	57	92	3.72	13
Bonifacio,Emilio	10 B	25	8	aaa	FLA	164	13	37	7	2	0	8	12	28	6	5	224	277	287	564	7%	83%	0.44	46	110	2.57	-15
Bonilla,Leury	10 R	26	8	aa	SEA	280	29	61	13	1	5	27	19	68	7	5	218	267	322	590	6%	76%	0.28	71	85	2.83	-26
Borchard,Joe	09 B	31	8	a/a	SF	346	36	61	16	3	9	37	16	85	0	1	177	214	319	533	4%	76%	0.19	90	75	2.16	7
	10 B	32	8	aaa	SF	423	40	83	20	3	10	40	27	89	1	3	197	245	334	579	6%	79%	0.30	87	68	2.63	-1
Boscan,Jean	09 R	30	2	a/a	ATL	294	19	60	13	0	0	24	27	60	1	1	205	271	249	520	8%	79%	0.44	39	30	2.35	-24
	10 R	31	2	aaa	ATL	220	14	42	9	0	3	14	16	51	1	0	189	245	274	519	7%	77%	0.32	58	32	2.27	-30
Botts,Jason	10 B	30	3	aaa	WAS	276	25	60	16	0	6	36	22	46	0	1	219	277	342	618	7%	83%	0.48	85	25	3.23	18
Bouchie,Andrew	10 R	25	2	a/a	DET	207	18	36	9	0	7	22	8	35	0	1	173	205	313	518	4%	83%	0.24	89	36	1.99	14
Bourgeois,Jason	09 R	28 b	8	aaa	MIL	424	44	107	14	4	2	30	17	37	26	7	253	282	316	598	4%	91%	0.47	44	132	3.17	50
	10 R	29	8	aaa	HOU	235	26	63	8	2	4	19	14	25	12	6	270	311	363	674	6%	89%	0.56	60	110	3.92	18
Bourjos,Peter	09 R	22 a	8	aa	LAA	437	65	117	16	10	5	46	43	68	29	13	268	333	384	718	9%	84%	0.63	70	188	4.56	70
	10 R	23	8	aaa	LAA	414	59	109	12	6	9	35	17	54	19	7	263	291	383	675	4%	87%	0.31	71	156	3.89	14
Bowker,John	09 L	26 b	8	aa	SF	366	66	108	20	3	16	67	60	60	8	6	294	393	493	886	14%	84%	1.00	122	95	7.29	91
	10 L	27	8	aaa	PIT	288	32	71	15	2	12	32	20	48	1	2	247	295	434	730	6%	83%	0.41	115	60	4.41	41
Bowman,Shawn	09 R	25	5	aa	NYM	347	33	86	21	2	7	35	20	85	0	0	249	290	379	669	5%	75%	0.24	89	46	3.88	-1
	10 R	26	5	aa	TOR	411	47	88	22	0	16	49	26	82	2	2	215	262	384	646	6%	80%	0.32	107	48	3.36	20
Boyer,Brad	09 L	26 a	5	aa	SF	367	40	96	21	8	2	34	24	63	9	6	261	306	379	685	6%	83%	0.37	78	162	4.03	57
	10 L	27	6	a/a	SF	255	28	48	10	2	2	22	29	46	2	5	188	272	263	535	10%	82%	0.64	53	77	2.33	-7
Bozied,Tagg	09 R	30	8	aa	PIT	215	22	48	14	1	3	13	14	56	3	2	225	274	344	618	6%	74%	0.26	84	75	3.19	-1
	10 R	31	3	aa	PHI	355	43	85	22	1	19	60	31	78	1	3	239	300	465	764	8%	78%	0.39	139	40	4.70	41
Brantley,Michael	09 L	22 a	8	aaa	CLE	457	66	110	19	1	5	30	51	40	38	6	241	317	319	636	10%	91%	1.28	56	125	3.95	69
	10 L	23	8	aaa	CLE	273	41	75	12	1	3	23	26	22	10	6	276	340	359	699	9%	92%	1.18	58	95	4.42	33
Brewer,Daniel	10 R	23	8	aa	NYY	508	67	119	28	2	9	68	45	98	24	12	233	296	349	645	8%	81%	0.46	80	110	3.51	5
Brown,Andrew	09 R	25	3	aa	STL	263	30	61	9	1	8	31	23	39	1	0	232	293	372	665	8%	85%	0.57	85	55	3.85	42
	10 R	26	3	aa	STL	361	47	84	14	1	14	45	29	82	1	2	232	290	390	680	8%	77%	0.36	95	53	3.88	3
Brown,Corey	09 L	24 a	8	aa	OAK	250	33	55	17	2	6	31	20	50	4	3	220	276	372	649	7%	80%	0.39	102	105	3.42	50
	10 L	25	8	a/a	OAK	466	61	108	14	7	11	50	46	100	16	3	231	300	358	658	9%	79%	0.46	75	153	3.89	-6
Brown,Domonic	09 L	22	8	aa	PHI	147	17	37	8	2	3	17	11	31	7	1	252	304	395	698	7%	79%	0.35	92	143	4.41	48
	10 L	23 a	8	a/a	PHI	343	52	101	20	3	18	55	29	62	14	8	294	350	523	873	8%	82%	0.47	138	114	6.52	55
Brown,Dusty	09 R	27	2	aaa	BOS	295	20	73	14	0	2	21	33	79	0	0	247	323	314	638	10%	73%	0.42	53	12	3.76	-39
	10 R	28	2	aaa	BOS	238	23	45	18	0	5	21	19	59	1	0	189	250	333	582	8%	75%	0.33	103	45	2.79	0
Brown,Jordan	09 L	26 a	8	aaa	CLE	417	51	120	30	1	11	52	24	57	2	5	289	328	446	774	6%	86%	0.43	108	47	5.19	58
	10 L	27	8	aaa	CLE	326	22	78	23	1	6	48	16	41	2	0	240	275	367	642	5%	87%	0.38	91	48	3.52	33
Brown,Matt	09 R	27	3	aa	LAA	388	46	81	24	0	10	56	35	90	5	5	209	274	348	622	8%	77%	0.39	95	60	3.16	20
	10 R	28	5	aaa	TEX	301	26	60	14	4	7	21	17	72	2	0	199	241	339	580	5%	76%	0.23	88	99	2.74	-12
Bruntlett,Eric	10 R	33	6	aaa	NYY	415	45	78	18	1	9	37	29	96	6	2	188	241	297	538	7%	77%	0.30	72	86	2.39	-21
Buck,Travis	09 L	26	8	aa	OAK	232	25	50	10	2	3	20	16	33	2	1	215	265	312	577	6%	86%	0.48	65	89	2.82	37
	10 L	27	8	aaa	OAK	121	15	28	6	1	2	11	7	21	2	3	228	272	335	607	6%	83%	0.36	71	97	2.88	2
Budde,Ryan	09 R	30	2	aa	LAA	273	25	51	14	1	5	24	23	76	1	1	187	250	299	549	8%	72%	0.30	76	54	2.49	-18
	10 R	31	2	aaa	LAA	172	14	31	5	0	1	8	12	46	1	1	178	231	222	453	6%	73%	0.26	34	48	1.70	-65
Buller,Dayton	10 R	29	2	aa	MIL	211	15	34	7	2	2	14	19	65	0	2	163	232	236	468	8%	69%	0.29	49	65	1.76	-66
Burke,Chris	09 R	30	6	a/a	ATL	312	34	69	16	1	3	27	22	59	11	3	221	273	303	576	7%	81%	0.38	62	103	2.92	19
	10 R	31	8	aaa	CIN	248	26	45	5	3	4	18	18	38	9	4	182	237	274	511	7%	85%	0.47	54	128	2.10	-2
Burke,Jamie	10 R	39	2	aaa	WAS	128	9	23	6	0	1	7	9	25	1	0	179	235	246	481	7%	81%	0.38	51	40	1.96	-20
Burns,Gregory	10 L	24	8	a/a	FLA	191	22	26	5	2	1	9	32	69	5	5	139	263	200	463	14%	64%	0.47	40	121	1.79	-83
Burriss,Emmanuel	10 B	26	6	aaa	SF	273	23	64	9	2	0	15	13	22	8	6	234	269	282	552	5%	92%	0.59	37	92	2.50	8
Burrus,Josh	10 R	27	8	aa	DET	203	19	34	4	2	5	20	14	51	5	5	168	220	284	504	6%	75%	0.26	65	112	1.83	-34
Buscher,Brian	10 L	29	5	aaa	CLE	162	13	32	7	1	3	17	12	9	0	0	196	252	297	549	7%	94%	1.29	67	40	2.53	46
Butler,Joey	10 R	25	8	aa	TEX	516	55	130	23	6	9	47	38	106	7	7	251	303	368	671	7%	79%	0.36	75	99	3.84	-6
Bynum,Seth	09 R	29	4	a/a	WAS	480	46	105	20	2	15	54	25	135	5	3	218	256	361	618	5%	72%	0.18	89	74	3.09	-8
	10 R	30	4	aaa	WAS	305	31	56	16	0	10	39	26	92	9	1	183	247	338	585	8%	70%	0.28	100	87	2.86	-23
Byrne,Bryan	09 L	25	3	aa	ARI	374	40	79	21	1	2	40	54	63	1	2	211	310	287	597	13%	83%	0.85	59	45	3.19	21
	10 L	26	3	aa	ARI	387	43	96	22	0	4	37	64	85	6	6	247	355	333	687	14%	78%	0.76	65	49	4.34	-5
Cabral,Marcos	10 R	26	6	a/a	HOU	243	16	52	7	0	4	18	14	33	2	3	216	258	292	549	5%	87%	0.42	50	34	2.46	-1

Major League Equivalent Statistics

BATTER	Yr	B	Age	Pos	Lev	Org	ab	r	h	d	t	hr	rbi	bb	k	sb	cs	ba	ob	slg	ops	bb%	ct%	eye	px	sx	rc/g	bpv
Cabrera,Willie	09	R	23	8	aa	ATL	371	39	94	18	2	7	47	30	49	3	8	254	310	367	677	8%	87%	0.62	75	58	3.79	42
	10	R	24	8	a/a	ATL	392	39	100	32	1	4	46	25	38	11	8	255	299	370	669	6%	90%	0.67	89	79	3.75	47
Cain,Lorenzo	09	R	23	8	aa	MIL	145	14	27	5	0	3	12	9	31	2	3	189	236	284	520	6%	79%	0.29	61	59	2.04	-4
	10	R	24	8	a/a	MIL	331	44	88	10	6	2	21	36	60	20	4	267	340	348	688	10%	82%	0.60	50	166	4.60	-11
Calderone,Adam	09	L	26	8	a/a	TOR	401	45	84	21	5	10	40	22	76	7	5	209	249	361	610	5%	81%	0.29	96	121	2.90	50
	10	L	27	8	a/a	TOR	496	43	94	25	5	12	47	21	102	6	10	189	222	330	553	4%	79%	0.21	90	97	2.17	0
Camp,Matt	09	L	25	8	aa	CHC	395	41	98	15	1	2	39	21	44	15	5	247	285	305	590	5%	89%	0.47	43	97	3.09	32
	10	L	26	4	aaa	CHC	436	32	92	13	1	1	26	29	32	8	6	211	259	251	511	6%	93%	0.90	31	67	2.19	10
Campana,Anthony	10	L	24	8	aa	CHC	489	55	133	19	3	0	28	33	65	34	24	273	318	324	642	6%	87%	0.51	40	112	3.37	-6
Campbell,Eric	10	R	23	5	aa	NYM	179	19	41	9	0	4	21	8	24	1	0	230	262	345	607	4%	86%	0.32	78	50	3.12	18
Canham,Mitchell	09	L	25	2	aa	SD	407	37	86	15	2	4	41	36	59	4	5	212	276	288	563	8%	85%	0.60	52	65	2.66	21
	10	L	26	2	a/a	SD	288	22	49	7	2	3	20	25	43	1	4	169	235	236	472	8%	85%	0.57	43	59	1.76	-8
Canizares,Barbaro	09	R	30	3	aaa	ATL	506	40	117	24	1	9	57	38	66	2	2	231	285	333	618	7%	87%	0.57	70	37	3.29	31
	10	R	31	0	aaa	ATL	425	42	111	21	1	9	55	30	54	2	0	262	310	382	692	7%	87%	0.55	80	48	4.31	28
Canzler,Russell	09	R	23	3	aa	CHC	233	23	55	14	0	6	29	25	37	2	6	236	311	370	681	10%	84%	0.69	91	35	3.75	42
	10	R	24	5	aa	CHC	356	49	87	25	2	16	47	34	74	4	5	245	310	464	774	9%	79%	0.45	138	77	4.89	46
Cardenas,Adrian	09	L	22 a	4	aa	OAK	508	59	130	35	2	3	59	40	51	6	8	256	311	352	663	7%	90%	0.78	74	69	3.77	56
	10	L	23	4	a/a	OAK	404	50	105	20	1	3	40	38	38	5	10	260	324	337	660	9%	91%	1.00	57	60	3.69	28
Carlin,Luke	09	B	29	2	aa	ARI	237	33	64	15	0	5	26	34	50	4	4	271	363	401	764	13%	79%	0.69	90	52	5.28	31
	10	B	30	2	aaa	CLE	243	21	44	8	1	3	19	23	55	3	2	180	252	251	503	9%	78%	0.42	48	72	2.15	-32
Carp,Mike	09	L	23	3	aa	SEA	413	58	101	23	1	13	56	53	95	0	1	244	330	396	726	11%	77%	0.56	98	42	4.74	24
	10	L	24	3	aaa	SEA	409	49	86	14	1	20	56	31	77	1	2	211	266	399	665	7%	81%	0.40	110	48	3.53	28
Carpenter,Matt	10	L	25	5	aa	STL	396	57	105	22	2	8	39	48	70	9	2	264	344	388	732	11%	82%	0.69	84	96	5.03	20
Carrera,Ezequiel	09	L	22	8	aa	SEA	329	61	103	11	3	2	34	55	59	24	15	313	411	383	794	14%	82%	0.93	47	126	6.02	34
	10	L	23	8	aaa	CLE	374	32	88	12	3	1	25	25	53	15	10	236	285	291	575	6%	86%	0.48	39	103	2.76	-11
Carrithers,Alden	10	L	26	4	aa	DET	210	21	46	6	0	1	8	25	23	6	5	219	304	260	563	11%	89%	1.08	31	61	2.75	4
Carroll,Brett	09	R	27	8	aa	FLA	103	13	20	3	1	4	10	6	23	0	1	197	244	348	592	6%	78%	0.28	87	89	2.69	21
	10	R	28	8	aaa	FLA	244	22	42	13	0	5	20	15	48	3	2	173	222	291	514	6%	80%	0.32	80	60	2.06	-1
Carroll,Sawyer	10	L	24	8	aa	SD	458	41	91	17	2	5	46	48	118	1	8	199	275	277	552	9%	74%	0.41	53	44	2.47	-39
Carson,Matt	09	R	28 b	8	aa	OAK	440	44	85	22	2	15	50	25	75	10	4	194	237	354	591	5%	83%	0.33	100	93	2.70	53
	10	R	29	8	aaa	OAK	244	33	52	13	1	8	22	15	47	8	4	215	259	370	629	6%	81%	0.31	99	107	3.10	16
Carter,Chris	10	L	28 b	8	aaa	OAK	113	11	28	7	1	4	14	5	7	0	0	249	283	421	703	4%	94%	0.77	110	54	4.15	75
	10	R	24	3	aaa	OAK	465	64	96	24	1	20	65	51	97	1	1	207	285	388	673	10%	79%	0.53	112	54	3.79	28
Carter,Yusuf	10	R	26	2	aa	OAK	131	9	22	4	1	1	6	9	31	3	0	165	221	230	451	7%	76%	0.30	43	95	1.75	-45
Cartwright,Albert	10	R	23	4	aa	HOU	140	13	30	4	1	0	6	10	36	6	4	214	267	257	524	7%	74%	0.28	32	109	2.24	-62
Castillo,Javier	09	R	26	5	a/a	NYM	442	31	90	21	2	6	31	23	83	1	2	204	243	298	541	5%	81%	0.28	65	47	2.38	3
	10	R	27	5	aaa	CHW	55	1	9	3	0	0	2	5	7	1	0	164	227	213	440	8%	88%	0.68	43	26	1.68	3
Castillo,Welington	09	R	22	2	aa	CHC	319	23	69	15	0	10	32	12	62	1	0	216	245	357	602	4%	81%	0.19	90	30	2.94	13
	10	R	23	2	aaa	CHC	239	25	52	15	1	10	41	14	42	0	3	217	260	410	670	5%	82%	0.33	122	46	3.38	40
Castillo,Wilkin	09	B	25	2	aaa	CIN	122	9	24	5	1	2	6	1	18	3	1	193	199	293	492	1%	85%	0.05	65	86	1.83	22
	10	B	26	2	aaa	CIN	317	33	67	14	2	7	26	9	45	8	4	212	234	337	571	3%	86%	0.21	80	109	2.54	15
Casto,Kory	09	L	28	5	aaa	WAS	447	44	101	19	1	6	45	34	79	3	4	226	281	314	595	7%	82%	0.43	61	52	3.00	10
	10	L	29	5	aa	ARI	167	17	35	5	0	6	23	20	43	1	1	211	296	353	649	11%	74%	0.47	85	33	3.62	-12
Castro,Jason	09	L	22	2	aa	HOU	239	29	62	10	1	2	22	19	27	2	1	259	314	335	649	7%	89%	0.70	54	70	3.82	36
	10	L	23	2	aaa	HOU	211	24	48	6	0	3	20	24	28	1	1	228	305	297	602	10%	87%	0.85	46	42	3.24	7
Castro,Jose	09	B	23	4	aa	CIN	333	25	83	12	1	1	25	10	26	2	5	249	271	300	571	3%	92%	0.38	39	47	2.66	22
	10	B	24	4	aa	CIN	357	19	73	12	0	0	25	11	32	1	0	203	226	236	463	3%	91%	0.34	29	34	1.78	-4
Castro,Ofilio	09	R	26	4	aa	WAS	301	26	78	14	1	3	30	31	48	0	4	260	329	339	669	9%	84%	0.65	57	28	3.95	12
	10	R	27	5	aa	WAS	196	16	34	5	2	1	13	16	24	1	0	174	238	230	467	8%	88%	0.66	36	79	1.86	-4
Castro,Starlin	09	R	19 a	6	aa	CHC	111	9	32	6	2	0	13	8	10	5	0	284	334	378	713	7%	91%	0.88	67	138	5.03	77
	10	R	21 a	6	aa	CHC	109	15	38	7	3	1	15	7	8	3	6	350	390	501	891	6%	93%	0.93	98	159	6.47	65
Cates,Chris	10	R	25	6	aa	MIN	290	18	46	4	0	0	9	12	17	3	1	159	193	172	365	4%	94%	0.72	11	59	1.08	-4
Caufield,Charles	09	R	26	8	aa	MIL	302	26	63	11	1	3	28	16	52	2	2	210	249	280	529	5%	83%	0.30	49	59	2.31	0
	10	R	27	8	a/a	MIL	187	18	41	9	1	3	18	17	49	2	0	221	287	322	609	8%	74%	0.35	69	71	3.30	-30
Cervenak,Mike	09	R	33	5	aaa	PHI	462	49	111	29	1	8	56	20	47	1	1	241	273	357	630	4%	90%	0.43	83	50	3.36	51
	10	R	34	5	aaa	NYM	433	31	79	18	0	5	26	7	53	2	1	183	195	259	454	2%	88%	0.13	55	51	1.60	0
Chalk,Bradley	10	L	25	8	a/a	SD	281	25	55	8	2	0	15	18	33	3	7	195	244	236	480	6%	88%	0.55	30	78	1.76	-9
Chambers,Adron	10	L	24	8	a/a	STL	321	46	76	8	4	4	25	29	51	11	6	238	302	324	626	8%	84%	0.58	51	134	3.40	-4
Chang,Ray	09	R	26 b	4	aa	PIT	127	17	31	13	0	2	15	11	14	1	2	246	307	391	698	8%	89%	0.78	112	56	4.06	80
	10	R	27	5	aa	BOS	440	38	109	29	1	5	37	34	51	0	1	248	302	354	656	7%	88%	0.67	79	29	3.79	33
Chavez,Angel	09	R	28	5	aaa	BOS	442	35	103	25	0	4	33	16	52	3	2	233	259	313	572	3%	88%	0.30	62	47	2.75	25
	10	R	29	5	aaa	TAM	411	32	86	13	1	6	38	22	64	3	3	209	250	289	539	5%	84%	0.35	52	53	2.37	-8
Chavez,Ozzie	09	B	26	6	aa	PHI	363	29	79	15	0	1	26	22	52	6	1	218	263	266	529	6%	86%	0.42	40	65	2.45	7
	10	B	27	4	a/a	PHI	389	33	69	13	0	4	23	27	64	5	5	178	231	238	470	6%	83%	0.42	43	58	1.77	-17
Chavez,Raul	10	R	38	2	aaa	TOR	200	9	28	9	0	2	12	6	16	0	0	140	165	213	378	3%	92%	0.36	55	20	1.08	18
Chen,Yung	09	R	26	4	aa	OAK	160	17	38	6	0	1	12	11	21	4	0	236	285	293	578	6%	87%	0.53	45	72	3.07	21
	10	R	27	4	aa	PIT	206	16	34	8	2	1	17	11	27	2	0	166	208	236	443	5%	87%	0.41	49	93	1.61	0
Chiang,Chih-Hsien	10	L	23 a	8	aa	BOS	438	40	106	37	1	8	48	23	46	1	0	242	280	386	666	5%	89%	0.50	105	47	3.77	54
Chirinos,Robinson	10	R	26 b	2	a/a	CHC	319	42	86	24	0	13	50	30	35	1	6	268	332	464	796	9%	89%	0.87	129	33	5.28	79
Chisenhall,Lonnie	10	L	22	5	aa	CLE	460	65	114	20	2	13	68	38	61	2	0	248	306	386	692	8%	87%	0.63	87	75	4.26	34
Christian,Justin	09	R	29	8	aaa	BAL	356	42	79	15	3	3	20	15	52	21	3	222	255	300	554	4%	85%	0.30	54	146	2.74	39
	10	R	30	8	a/a	NYY	409	54	90	15	3	8	40	37	56	16	5	220	284	326	611	8%	86%	0.65	68	119	3.25	17
Cipriano,William	09	R	25	4	aa	TAM	147	15	27	6	1	2	12	14	33	0	0	183	256	274	530	9%	77%	0.43	61	60	2.39	-4
	10	R	26	4	aa	TAM	233	29	55	9	2	3	20	25	55	3	1	234	309	327	636	10%	76%	0.46	62	95	3.66	-24
Ciriaco,Audy	10	R	23	5	a/a	DET	244	22	52	7	3	8	28	6	39	5	0	213	231	361	593	2%	84%	0.15	85	120	2.83	11
Ciriaco,Juan	10	R	27	6	a/a	SF	173	15	37	8	2	2	11	9	27	3	1	213	252	312	564	5%	85%	0.34	67	102	2.66	4
Ciriaco,Pedro	09	R	24	6	aa	ARI	469	46	129	15	3	4	44	14	58	32	11	276	296	345	641	3%	88%	0.24	46	121	3.63	31
	10	R	25	6	aaa	PIT	476	47	107	21	5	4	42	9	57	14	5	224	238	313	550	2%	88%	0.15	61	132	2.46	6
Clark,Douglas	09	R	28 b	2	aa	KC	199	25	50	12	0	5	22	12	24	1	2	252	296	394	689	6%	88%	0.52	96	47	3.99	57
	10	R	29	2	aaa	KC	220	18	44	11	1	3	16	15	30	1	1	199	249	293	542	6%	86%	0.48	67	55	2.43	13
Clark,Matthew	10	L	24	3	aa	SD	498	52	113	19	1	22	83	40	138	0	0	226	284	398	682	7%	72%	0.29	102	28	3.92	-12
Clemens,Koby	10	R	24	3	aa	HOU	452	65	101	21	2	24	74	59	133	8	3	223	313	434	746	12%	71%	0.44	125	89	4.76	7

Major League Equivalent Statistics

BATTER	Yr	B	Age	Pos	Lev	Org	ab	r	h	d	t	hr	rbi	bb	k	sb	cs	ba	ob	slg	ops	bb%	ct%	eye	px	sx	rc/g	bpv
Clement,Jeff	09	L	26	0	aa	PIT	470	62	109	31	2	15	69	40	93	2	1	231	292	399	691	8%	80%	0.43	111	68	4.07	48
	10	L	27	3	aaa	PIT	168	16	41	13	1	5	23	6	40	1	5	241	269	423	692	4%	76%	0.16	121	66	3.43	11
Clevenger,Steven	09	L	23	2	aa	CHC	307	27	81	16	3	1	30	21	35	3	3	265	311	345	656	6%	89%	0.59	59	79	3.80	40
	10	L	24 a	2	aa	CHC	271	27	74	21	0	4	34	14	22	0	7	273	309	393	703	5%	92%	0.66	91	27	3.95	53
Clevlen,Brent	09	R	26	8	aaa	DET	479	52	113	23	4	13	54	35	129	8	1	235	287	381	668	7%	73%	0.27	91	109	3.88	14
	10	R	27	8	aaa	ATL	191	15	40	6	0	2	22	17	57	2	0	212	278	275	553	8%	70%	0.31	45	45	2.73	-64
Clifford,Pete	09	L	26	8	aa	ARI	280	21	59	11	0	4	25	18	41	4	2	212	259	292	551	6%	85%	0.43	56	51	2.56	15
	10	L	27	8	aa	ARI	55	4	9	2	0	0	6	8	13	0	0	167	276	201	477	13%	76%	0.63	30	17	2.03	-43
Closser,JD	09	B	30	2	aa	LA	321	28	69	16	0	3	32	32	65	3	3	214	285	289	575	9%	80%	0.49	57	48	2.86	-1
	10	B	31	2	aaa	LA	254	18	45	6	0	2	14	12	36	2	1	177	214	221	435	4%	86%	0.33	31	49	1.54	-22
Coats,Buck	09	L	27 b	8	aaa	TOR	500	56	120	27	3	5	38	32	57	17	8	239	284	331	616	6%	89%	0.56	66	106	3.23	54
	10	L	28	8	a/a	CHW	442	42	104	18	1	5	34	32	70	6	1	235	286	317	603	7%	84%	0.45	57	74	3.24	-3
Colina,Alvin	09	R	28	2	aaa	ATL	225	23	48	10	0	6	32	19	52	1	1	212	273	340	613	8%	77%	0.36	82	41	3.16	3
	10	R	29	2	aaa	TAM	186	13	33	8	0	4	19	7	47	1	1	180	210	293	503	4%	75%	0.15	74	40	1.94	-31
Colina,Javier	09	R	31	3	aa	CHW	315	31	65	12	1	5	31	16	59	2	3	205	244	297	541	5%	81%	0.27	61	61	2.35	4
	10	R	32	4	aaa	CHW	132	6	19	7	0	3	10	3	26	0	1	142	163	270	434	3%	80%	0.13	85	22	1.28	-3
Collins,Michael	09	R	25	2	aa	SD	161	10	29	7	0	2	15	21	30	0	0	181	274	257	531	11%	81%	0.69	54	12	2.48	-2
	10	R	26	2	a/a	SD	154	18	31	6	2	2	19	11	28	1	0	203	256	305	561	7%	82%	0.39	66	107	2.68	-5
Colmenares,Carlos	10	B	25	5	a/a	LAA	275	27	65	5	2	0	12	22	43	7	7	237	294	269	563	7%	84%	0.52	22	89	2.66	-28
Colonel,Christian	09	R	28	5	aa	COL	391	41	93	14	2	5	51	29	50	2	3	237	289	325	614	7%	87%	0.58	58	59	3.24	29
	10	R	29	5	a/a	ATL	195	20	39	6	1	2	16	23	40	1	1	199	283	266	549	11%	80%	0.58	46	61	2.64	-22
Conger,Hank	09	B	22	2	aa	LAA	459	56	130	20	2	9	63	48	59	3	2	284	352	396	748	10%	87%	0.82	74	61	5.26	46
	10	B	23	2	aaa	LAA	387	39	99	23	1	8	34	38	39	0	3	256	322	382	705	9%	90%	0.97	87	29	4.36	49
Constanza,Jose	09	B	26	8	aa	CLE	486	83	120	13	5	0	39	66	66	41	14	246	337	292	628	12%	86%	1.00	32	150	3.77	42
	10	B	27	8	aaa	CLE	404	49	103	9	4	1	23	25	48	24	6	254	298	301	599	6%	88%	0.53	31	136	3.30	-9
Contreras,Anthony	09	L	26	4	aa	SD	221	14	43	8	2	1	21	9	26	2	2	196	228	259	488	4%	88%	0.37	44	76	1.90	22
	10	L	27	5	a/a	SD	193	17	40	6	0	3	17	6	29	2	1	205	230	280	510	3%	85%	0.22	51	58	2.11	-11
Contreras,Ivan	09	B	23	8	aa	LAA	142	14	35	4	1	0	8	9	27	4	3	246	291	289	580	6%	81%	0.33	31	95	2.86	-9
	10	B	24	4	aa	LAA	92	8	22	4	2	0	2	3	15	1	4	234	258	320	578	3%	83%	0.19	57	137	2.28	-13
Cook,David	09	R	28 b	8	a/a	CHW	447	70	97	19	1	23	67	52	94	7	7	217	298	417	715	10%	79%	0.55	119	76	4.13	57
	10	R	29	8	a/a	HOU	336	37	65	13	1	9	29	31	92	6	2	192	260	312	572	8%	73%	0.34	76	84	2.77	-30
Coon,Bradley	09	L	27	8	aa	LAA	442	65	107	14	2	3	30	50	72	19	8	241	318	300	618	10%	84%	0.69	41	110	3.48	23
	10	L	28	8	a/a	WAS	385	40	81	10	4	5	31	29	77	9	7	210	265	290	555	7%	80%	0.38	49	108	2.51	-24
Cooper,Craig	09	R	25	3	aa	SD	503	54	129	28	1	8	74	57	76	7	6	256	331	361	692	10%	85%	0.74	74	58	4.30	39
	10	R	26	8	a/a	SD	438	38	84	18	2	7	55	34	89	2	5	191	249	285	534	7%	80%	0.38	63	55	2.29	-15
Cooper,David	09	L	23	3	aa	TOR	473	60	119	32	0	10	63	57	93	0	0	252	332	383	715	11%	80%	0.61	93	28	4.68	27
	10	L	24	3	aa	TOR	498	44	109	27	1	16	58	39	60	0	0	218	275	372	647	7%	88%	0.65	99	24	3.53	48
Copeland,Benjamin	09	L	26	8	aa	SF	342	38	85	17	3	6	29	20	54	12	7	247	288	363	651	5%	84%	0.36	77	113	3.54	45
	10	L	27	8	aaa	SF	354	33	81	13	6	3	29	38	53	16	9	229	303	320	623	10%	85%	0.71	58	133	3.31	8
Corona,Reegie	09	B	23 a	4	a/a	NYY	467	66	115	27	1	6	38	62	67	15	4	246	335	347	681	12%	86%	0.93	73	95	4.36	55
	10	B	24	4	aaa	NYY	387	39	81	17	3	5	26	32	52	12	2	210	271	306	578	8%	87%	0.62	64	114	2.94	15
Coronado,Jose	09	B	23	4	aa	NYM	446	32	94	16	1	1	33	30	72	10	5	211	261	257	518	6%	84%	0.42	36	73	2.29	1
	10	B	24	6	aa	NYM	414	45	84	19	1	4	35	27	64	1	5	204	253	283	535	6%	85%	0.42	57	54	2.30	-1
Corporan,Carlos	09	B	26	2	aaa	MIL	179	7	29	8	1	1	13	7	37	0	1	163	192	231	424	4%	79%	0.18	50	40	1.36	-22
	10	B	27	2	aaa	ARI	286	23	66	17	3	7	29	15	43	3	3	232	269	386	655	5%	85%	0.34	100	80	3.45	31
Cortez,Fernando	09	L	28	0	aa	TAM	442	33	89	9	4	4	37	28	58	11	4	201	249	271	520	6%	87%	0.49	42	104	2.26	26
	10	L	29	4	a/a	CHW	262	22	63	12	1	1	18	14	21	4	5	240	278	302	580	5%	92%	0.66	49	65	2.74	19
Costanzo,Michael	09	L	26	5	a/a	BAL	272	29	49	14	2	3	32	34	78	0	2	179	271	274	545	11%	71%	0.43	67	64	2.50	-18
	10	L	27	5	a/a	CIN	319	35	69	18	1	9	36	26	80	5	0	217	276	364	640	8%	75%	0.33	96	85	3.55	-6
Coughlin,Sean	09	L	24 a	3	aa	ARI	161	19	45	8	0	6	16	29	16	0	0	280	389	435	825	15%	90%	1.84	98	15	6.65	76
	10	L	25	2	a/a	ARI	245	21	46	9	1	5	20	19	41	1	4	188	246	292	537	7%	83%	0.45	67	51	2.24	2
Cousins,Scott	09	L	25 a	8	aa	FLA	482	51	114	29	10	10	62	37	104	23	10	237	292	396	688	7%	78%	0.36	101	171	3.93	62
	10	L	26	8	aaa	FLA	410	53	97	17	3	9	35	24	66	8	5	236	278	360	638	5%	84%	0.36	78	107	3.38	11
Cowgill,Collin	10	R	24 a	8	aa	ARI	502	73	133	34	4	13	68	47	64	20	10	266	329	428	757	9%	87%	0.74	107	118	4.99	54
Cozart,Zachary	09	R	24	6	aa	CIN	463	59	108	26	1	10	48	52	78	8	2	232	310	355	664	10%	83%	0.66	83	81	3.96	46
	10	R	25	6	aaa	CIN	553	69	120	26	3	14	51	31	93	23	5	218	259	352	611	5%	83%	0.34	86	127	3.14	15
Crabbe,Callix	09	B	27	4	aa	SEA	356	38	63	12	3	3	27	44	48	6	7	176	267	248	515	11%	87%	0.92	49	88	2.16	36
	10	B	28	4	a/a	TOR	315	32	51	13	1	3	18	23	52	12	7	163	219	234	453	7%	83%	0.43	51	108	1.59	-10
Craig,Allen	09	R	25	8	aa	STL	472	58	126	22	1	18	62	27	78	2	0	267	307	430	737	5%	84%	0.35	101	57	4.77	45
	10	R	26	8	aaa	STL	306	39	76	19	1	8	55	23	47	1	0	250	302	400	702	7%	85%	0.49	100	58	4.32	35
Crawford,Brandon	09	L	23	6	aa	SF	392	33	95	25	2	3	27	17	85	10	8	242	274	339	613	4%	78%	0.20	73	88	3.03	8
	10	L	24	6	aa	SF	291	37	66	12	3	6	19	32	68	4	1	226	303	347	650	10%	77%	0.47	76	109	3.77	-11
Crowe,Trevor	09	B	26	8	aaa	CLE	185	21	47	9	1	2	15	24	28	11	8	254	341	346	687	12%	85%	0.88	65	96	4.07	46
	10	B	27	8	aaa	CLE	119	15	23	4	1	1	9	6	16	5	1	193	229	263	492	4%	86%	0.34	46	134	2.05	-7
Cruz,Arnoldi	09	R	23	2	aa	STL	405	33	75	22	1	7	36	26	65	1	0	186	236	295	531	6%	84%	0.41	75	50	2.32	25
	10	R	24	2	a/a	STL	163	20	37	9	0	5	15	12	24	0	0	230	284	371	656	7%	85%	0.52	93	33	3.68	31
Cruz,Lee	09	R	26	0	aa	CHW	227	23	50	15	0	6	29	10	49	0	1	219	252	357	609	4%	78%	0.21	95	37	2.97	11
	10	R	27	0	a/a	HOU	67	4	12	4	0	1	5	2	19	0	0	175	196	269	465	3%	72%	0.10	68	17	1.67	-51
Cruz,Luis	09	R	26	6	aa	PIT	229	22	50	13	0	2	18	5	22	2	3	218	233	300	533	2%	90%	0.21	64	61	2.20	36
	10	R	27	6	aaa	MIL	488	39	110	24	2	7	49	11	50	0	0	226	243	328	571	2%	90%	0.22	70	38	2.68	21
Cunningham,Aaron	09	R	23 a	8	aa	OAK	334	45	83	21	1	8	35	24	54	8	5	249	299	387	686	7%	84%	0.43	93	90	3.97	52
	10	R	24	8	aaa	SD	271	22	54	13	2	5	34	21	58	2	9	198	256	315	572	7%	78%	0.36	78	67	2.35	-8
Curry,Ryan	10	R	25	4	aa	FLA	387	36	84	19	1	5	29	14	34	4	5	216	244	306	550	4%	91%	0.41	64	66	2.38	25
Curtis,Colin	09	L	25	8	a/a	NYY	464	53	107	22	3	7	44	40	83	8	2	230	291	333	624	8%	82%	0.48	70	98	3.45	31
	10	L	26	8	aaa	NYY	239	24	59	20	0	5	23	18	36	1	2	248	300	389	689	7%	85%	0.49	104	37	4.04	38
Cusick,Matthew	10	L	24	5	a/a	NYY	284	23	59	11	2	3	28	28	33	3	1	206	277	287	564	9%	88%	0.84	55	73	2.79	17
Cust,Jack	10	L	32	0	aaa	OAK	110	13	21	4	0	3	11	20	27	0	0	193	319	301	621	16%	75%	0.75	70	23	3.53	-9
Cutler,Charles	10	L	24	2	aa	STL	119	8	22	3	0	0	6	11	13	0	0	186	252	210	462	8%	89%	0.84	21	20	1.84	-7
Daniel,Mike	09	L	25	8	a/a	WAS	423	43	94	15	6	6	37	29	79	10	5	222	272	324	597	6%	81%	0.37	64	128	3.01	30
	10	L	26	8	a/a	ATL	302	21	57	9	1	2	20	22	55	13	6	189	244	244	488	7%	82%	0.40	39	90	1.99	-27
Danielson,Sean	09	B	27	8	aaa	BOS	154	16	34	6	1	1	17	19	36	8	3	222	307	292	599	11%	77%	0.53	50	105	3.28	3
	10	B	28	8	aa	CIN	194	14	39	5	0	1	5	14	35	6	7	200	254	240	494	7%	82%	0.40	31	63	1.85	-32

Major League Equivalent Statistics

BATTER	Yr	B	Age	Pos	Lev	Org	ab	r	h	d	t	hr	rbi	bb	k	sb	cs	ba	ob	slg	ops	bb%	ct%	eye	px	sx	rc/g	bpv
Danks,Jordan	09	L	23	8	aa	CHW	284	43	63	11	1	6	17	32	65	6	3	221	300	328	628	10%	77%	0.50	69	94	3.46	14
	10	L	24	8	aaa	CHW	445	47	92	23	2	7	32	32	127	12	7	207	260	313	573	7%	71%	0.25	73	99	2.67	-41
D'Arnaud,Chase	10	R	24	6	aa	PIT	530	74	116	30	5	5	39	44	83	26	8	218	278	322	600	8%	84%	0.53	73	147	3.13	14
Darnell,James	10	R	24	5	aa	SD	373	39	83	18	1	8	43	39	60	2	0	223	297	339	636	10%	84%	0.65	77	57	3.60	18
Davis,Blake	09	L	26	6	aaa	BAL	180	18	34	4	1	1	12	11	37	3	2	188	236	235	471	6%	79%	0.30	31	90	1.82	-17
	10	L	27	6	a/a	BAL	265	25	54	12	1	4	18	15	38	2	5	205	247	299	545	5%	86%	0.39	65	62	2.29	7
Davis,Brad	09	R	27	2	aa	FLA	315	29	59	22	0	7	38	26	73	1	0	187	248	327	575	8%	77%	0.35	98	42	2.73	16
	10	R	28	2	aaa	FLA	244	23	55	12	0	6	23	17	47	1	2	225	276	350	626	7%	81%	0.37	82	36	3.25	5
Davis,Chris	09	L	24	5	aa	TEX	165	22	49	11	1	5	25	21	33	0	1	297	375	463	838	11%	80%	0.63	109	51	6.59	48
	10	L	25	5	aaa	TEX	398	50	113	27	2	11	60	28	84	2	2	285	331	441	773	7%	79%	0.33	105	6	5.35	14
Davis,Lars	10	L	25	2	aa	COL	128	17	34	5	0	2	9	14	24	0	2	263	337	345	682	10%	81%	0.60	56	38	4.10	-8
Davis,Leonard	09	L	26	8	a/a	WAS	440	42	105	18	5	13	46	30	99	11	2	239	288	391	679	6%	78%	0.30	92	119	3.99	34
	10	L	27	8	a/a	WAS	442	49	95	16	5	16	41	24	103	9	3	214	255	377	631	5%	77%	0.23	95	124	3.22	-5
Dawkins,Gookie	09	R	30	6	a/a	FLA	381	29	71	15	1	3	19	21	98	6	5	185	228	257	485	5%	74%	0.22	51	71	1.85	-28
	10	R	31	6	aaa	FLA	261	21	52	18	1	6	25	17	84	1	1	199	248	342	590	6%	68%	0.20	99	52	2.80	-35
De Aza,Alejandro	09	L	25 a	8	aa	FLA	267	38	71	19	5	7	28	24	53	9	6	264	324	444	767	8%	80%	0.44	116	154	4.97	77
	10	L	26	8	aaa	CHW	318	39	78	17	2	5	36	22	53	12	4	246	295	356	651	6%	83%	0.41	76	112	3.72	9
De Jesus,Ivan	10	R	23	4	aaa	LA	533	54	122	25	1	4	42	19	53	4	1	228	254	302	556	3%	90%	0.35	55	73	2.61	13
De La Cruz,Chris	09	B	27	6	aa	FLA	308	36	70	13	3	2	18	31	52	4	1	228	298	304	602	9%	83%	0.59	53	98	3.26	24
	10	B	28	6	aa	TAM	330	24	71	10	3	3	19	20	43	0	4	216	261	285	547	6%	87%	0.47	45	50	2.40	-2
De Los Santos,Est	10	B	24	6	aa	MIN	237	16	35	10	1	1	13	16	48	4	10	149	202	211	413	6%	80%	0.33	47	76	1.10	-29
De Los Santos,Jos	10	R	26	8	aa	PIT	150	11	25	4	0	0	9	4	29	7	3	169	190	194	384	2%	81%	0.13	22	98	1.15	-52
De Renne,Keoni	10	B	31	4	a/a	PHI	104	8	17	3	0	0	5	12	11	0	0	163	249	188	437	10%	90%	1.12	22	23	1.65	-1
de San Miguel,Alla	10	R	23	2	a/a	MIN	114	9	13	3	0	1	8	12	35	0	0	114	198	167	365	10%	69%	0.34	37	32	1.11	-72
Deeds,Douglas	09	L	28	8	aa	CHC	349	41	81	26	2	8	28	16	77	4	3	232	265	383	649	4%	78%	0.20	104	88	3.40	32
	10	L	29	8	aaa	ARI	480	48	108	31	5	7	31	36	86	6	11	226	280	355	635	7%	82%	0.42	89	93	3.14	15
DeJesus,Antonio	09	L	24	8	aa	STL	179	21	35	5	1	1	15	20	30	3	2	197	276	252	528	10%	83%	0.66	38	86	2.41	12
	10	L	25	8	aa	STL	189	23	32	8	3	1	15	19	35	6	0	168	244	254	498	9%	81%	0.54	57	158	2.22	-9
Delaney,Jason	09	R	27	3	aa	PIT	438	38	99	22	3	5	50	42	79	1	5	227	295	321	616	9%	82%	0.53	66	49	3.23	15
	10	R	28	3	aa	FLA	193	18	32	9	0	2	16	23	52	1	0	163	254	228	492	11%	73%	0.45	56	45	2.10	-40
Delarosa,Andersor	10	R	26	2	a/a	MIL	133	9	24	8	0	1	7	4	25	0	0	180	202	263	465	3%	81%	0.15	66	29	1.70	-15
DeLome,Collin	09	L	24	8	aa	HOU	467	59	103	16	7	16	45	27	112	11	10	220	264	384	648	6%	76%	0.24	95	141	3.19	35
	10	L	25	8	aaa	HOU	343	36	65	12	4	12	40	12	92	8	4	190	219	358	577	4%	73%	0.14	98	134	2.45	-19
Denker,Travis	09	R	24	4	a/a	BOS	404	38	93	28	1	5	39	42	80	3	3	230	303	340	643	9%	80%	0.53	81	52	3.61	22
	10	R	25	5	a/a	LA	102	5	17	4	0	1	5	5	14	1	3	166	203	230	433	4%	86%	0.34	47	41	1.29	-6
Denorfia,Chris	09	R	29	8	aa	OAK	432	40	84	13	3	5	31	20	43	9	7	195	230	273	503	4%	90%	0.46	50	97	1.98	40
	10	R	30	8	aaa	SD	121	11	26	7	3	1	8	9	18	5	1	218	269	337	606	7%	85%	0.48	79	160	3.20	20
Denove,Christophe	09	R	27	2	a/a	CIN	219	17	52	15	0	4	23	16	35	0	2	239	290	357	647	7%	84%	0.45	85	22	3.52	27
	10	R	28	2	a/a	CIN	257	27	61	12	0	5	25	20	40	3	0	238	293	336	629	7%	84%	0.50	67	58	3.54	8
Derba,Nicholas	09	R	24	2	aa	STL	108	7	12	4	0	1	5	15	26	0	1	107	218	169	387	12%	76%	0.59	45	28	1.22	-25
	10	R	25	2	a/a	STL	54	5	9	4	0	1	5	2	13	0	0	174	202	296	498	3%	76%	0.15	89	36	1.90	-15
Descalso,Daniel	09	L	23 a	4	aa	STL	438	55	115	26	3	7	54	37	48	2	1	263	320	384	704	8%	89%	0.77	83	75	4.47	63
	10	L	24	4	aaa	STL	468	62	110	26	2	6	51	33	35	6	5	235	285	337	623	7%	93%	0.96	73	85	3.28	44
Diaz,Argenis	09	R	23	6	aa	PIT	423	29	96	14	1	0	26	23	69	7	6	227	267	265	532	5%	84%	0.33	31	62	2.36	-9
	10	R	24	6	aaa	PIT	274	22	59	7	1	0	17	14	46	4	1	215	252	247	499	5%	83%	0.30	25	76	2.15	-35
Diaz,Jonathan	09	B	24	6	a/a	TOR	262	30	44	9	0	1	14	38	41	3	5	169	275	213	487	13%	84%	0.95	35	55	1.99	10
	10	B	25	6	a/a	TOR	406	43	74	19	1	1	27	39	50	4	3	183	254	241	495	9%	88%	0.77	47	72	2.07	7
Diaz,Robinzon	09	R	26	2	aa	PIT	149	14	33	4	0	2	11	6	11	0	1	222	255	284	539	4%	93%	0.59	41	37	2.39	25
	10	R	27	2	aaa	DET	251	22	52	14	2	1	15	4	11	0	0	208	219	287	506	1%	96%	0.32	59	61	2.05	35
Dillon,Joe	09	R	34	3	aaa	TAM	123	14	23	4	0	2	9	10	18	3	0	187	249	263	511	8%	86%	0.58	52	75	2.30	24
	10	R	35	4	aaa	TAM	351	40	69	17	0	6	39	23	54	3	0	196	245	295	541	6%	85%	0.42	69	74	2.47	8
Dinkelman,Brian	09	L	26	4	aa	MIN	459	53	118	34	2	7	55	44	71	4	7	258	323	383	706	9%	84%	0.62	91	60	4.31	48
	10	L	27	8	aaa	MIN	525	41	112	27	1	6	39	36	85	6	5	214	264	300	564	6%	84%	0.42	63	60	2.66	0
Dirks,Andy	09	L	24	8	aa	DET	361	37	82	13	1	5	36	29	50	9	6	228	286	309	596	8%	86%	0.59	55	78	3.01	29
	10	L	25	8	a/a	DET	476	60	123	26	2	12	49	29	58	17	5	258	300	399	700	6%	88%	0.49	92	107	4.28	38
Dlugach,Brent	09	R	27	6	aaa	DET	466	48	119	31	4	7	49	32	129	4	3	255	303	385	688	6%	72%	0.25	91	85	4.11	2
	10	R	28	6	aaa	DET	450	38	95	18	2	5	30	18	132	9	5	212	242	290	532	4%	71%	0.14	54	90	2.31	-64
Dolenc,Mark	10	R	26	8	aa	MIN	382	33	81	14	2	5	37	20	109	11	6	212	250	295	546	5%	72%	0.18	56	99	2.43	-57
Dominguez,Jeffrey	10	B	24	4	a/a	SEA	149	9	27	3	1	2	5	10	36	1	4	180	230	251	481	6%	76%	0.26	43	61	1.68	-50
Dominguez,Matt	10	R	21	5	aa	FLA	504	52	117	32	1	11	69	49	84	0	2	232	301	367	668	9%	83%	0.59	93	30	3.86	27
Donachie,Adam	09	R	26	2	aa	BAL	276	24	55	17	0	6	31	40	81	0	3	198	300	320	620	13%	71%	0.50	86	17	3.27	-16
	10	R	27	2	a/a	BAL	269	17	44	7	0	4	17	21	57	0	2	164	225	233	458	7%	79%	0.37	45	23	1.68	-31
Donald,Jason	09	R	25	6	aaa	CLE	243	27	49	14	1	2	13	14	56	6	0	201	245	290	535	5%	77%	0.25	67	109	2.48	6
	10	R	26	4	aaa	CLE	137	19	30	8	1	1	12	16	28	7	2	222	301	316	617	10%	79%	0.55	70	125	3.48	-4
Donaldson,Josh	09	R	24 a	2	aa	OAK	455	48	101	31	1	6	66	57	66	5	3	222	308	334	642	11%	85%	0.86	83	62	3.66	51
	10	R	25	2	aaa	OAK	294	35	55	11	1	12	45	31	56	2	1	186	263	346	609	9%	81%	0.55	95	65	3.06	21
Dopirak,Brian	09	R	26	3	a/a	TOR	546	61	151	38	2	23	81	38	112	1	3	277	324	477	801	6%	80%	0.34	128	40	5.54	47
	10	R	27	0	aaa	TOR	339	24	68	20	1	6	29	8	40	0	1	201	220	323	543	2%	88%	0.21	85	36	2.27	27
Dorn,Daniel	09	L	25	8	aaa	CIN	357	36	86	19	1	13	38	24	71	2	1	242	291	411	702	6%	80%	0.34	106	50	4.17	35
	10	L	26	8	aaa	CIN	275	37	70	20	1	11	34	29	72	0	0	254	324	455	779	9%	74%	0.40	130	42	5.34	21
Dorta,Melvin	09	R	28	5	a/a	BAL	431	44	103	18	1	4	30	30	52	10	10	238	287	309	596	6%	88%	0.57	52	73	2.93	30
	10	R	29	4	a/a	PHI	348	31	78	11	1	4	21	15	28	6	5	225	257	293	550	4%	92%	0.53	47	71	2.45	15
Douglas,Brandon	10	R	25 a	6	aa	DET	145	21	44	14	2	0	11	8	14	5	2	305	343	428	771	6%	90%	0.61	98	128	5.48	53
Downs,Matt	09	R	26 a	4	aa	SF	424	56	112	31	3	10	61	21	53	7	2	264	298	423	722	5%	87%	0.39	108	103	4.49	79
	10	R	27	5	aaa	HOU	216	26	42	8	1	6	21	18	32	3	6	196	259	319	578	8%	85%	0.58	77	77	2.52	21
Drennen,John	09	L	23	8	aa	CLE	325	40	82	22	3	7	36	20	56	0	2	253	296	401	697	6%	83%	0.35	99	72	4.10	45
	10	L	24	8	aa	CLE	440	34	112	23	3	5	44	26	47	2	4	255	297	353	650	6%	89%	0.55	69	53	3.62	26
Dubois,Jason	09	R	30	8	aa	NYM	377	33	77	18	1	11	43	26	106	2	1	205	256	345	600	6%	72%	0.24	89	50	2.96	-11
	10	R	32	8	aaa	CHC	223	29	50	9	1	13	36	17	52	0	0	225	280	446	726	7%	77%	0.33	129	44	4.29	27
Duda,Lucas	09	L	24	3	aa	NYM	395	38	96	25	1	7	42	49	76	2	2	243	327	365	691	11%	81%	0.65	86	44	4.31	30
	10	L	25 a	8	a/a	NYM	425	53	107	34	1	17	62	41	68	1	0	251	317	456	773	9%	84%	0.61	135	47	5.21	64
Duffy,Chris	10	L	30	8	aaa	PHI	346	35	66	14	3	4	26	19	102	9	3	192	233	285	518	5%	70%	0.18	62	120	2.17	-56
Duncan,Chris	10	L	29	3	aaa	WAS	262	18	39	6	0	5	20	22	66	3	5	148	215	230	444	8%	75%	0.34	51	42	1.48	-43

Major League Equivalent Statistics

BATTER	Yr	B	Age	Pos	Lev	Org	ab	r	h	d	t	hr	rbi	bb	k	sb	cs	ba	ob	slg	ops	bb%	ct%	eye	px	sx	rc/g	bpv
Duncan,Eric	09	L	25	5	aaa	NYY	323	32	60	11	1	4	22	14	68	1	0	187	222	262	483	4%	79%	0.21	50	67	1.91	-13
	10	L	26	4	aa	ATL	439	43	97	19	4	6	49	28	97	5	5	221	268	319	587	6%	78%	0.29	65	91	2.84	-22
Duncan,Shelley	09	R	30 b	8	aaa	NYY	452	69	103	25	1	26	81	52	103	2	0	228	307	459	766	10%	77%	0.50	139	61	4.98	60
	10	R	31	0	aaa	CLE	146	14	33	9	0	3	22	12	26	0	0	227	285	355	640	8%	82%	0.46	88	21	3.54	16
Dunigan,Joseph	10	L	24	8	aa	SEA	280	27	50	12	0	7	31	21	93	9	2	178	236	291	527	7%	67%	0.23	74	85	2.31	-58
Duran,German	09	R	25	4	aa	HOU	131	6	15	1	1	1	7	6	22	1	1	115	151	158	309	4%	83%	0.25	24	72	0.71	-17
	10	R	26	4	a/a	HOU	306	24	70	13	0	4	29	17	37	2	2	228	268	307	575	5%	88%	0.45	56	40	2.79	9
Durango,Luis	09	B	23	8	aa	SD	456	62	107	7	1	0	20	64	60	34	21	234	328	254	582	12%	87%	1.06	15	102	2.99	17
	10	B	24	8	aaa	SD	363	32	87	4	1	0	18	35	51	26	19	241	307	257	563	9%	86%	0.68	12	89	2.58	-27
Durham,Miles	09	R	27	3	aa	PIT	240	24	56	15	1	4	26	15	49	6	2	234	278	349	627	6%	80%	0.30	81	91	3.38	24
	10	R	28	8	aa	PIT	483	48	101	23	4	7	51	38	122	6	9	209	266	315	581	7%	75%	0.31	71	87	2.68	-28
Dyson,Jarrod	09	L	25	8	aa	KC	248	28	55	7	3	0	10	21	44	27	7	220	280	269	549	8%	82%	0.47	34	163	2.81	23
	10	L	26	8	a/a	KC	220	28	49	9	1	1	17	15	27	11	6	222	270	284	555	6%	88%	0.54	47	114	2.52	3
Easley,Edward	10	R	25	2	a/a	ARI	210	12	44	9	0	1	17	15	38	4	2	210	264	265	529	7%	82%	0.41	43	50	2.40	-21
Eldred,Brad	09	R	29	3	aaa	WAS	353	40	75	21	0	12	44	22	93	4	4	212	259	373	632	6%	74%	0.24	105	61	3.12	10
	10	R	30	3	aaa	COL	394	37	77	20	1	18	46	18	85	3	0	194	229	386	615	4%	79%	0.21	118	66	2.92	19
Eldridge,Rashad	09	B	28	8	a/a	TAM	469	51	113	21	2	3	42	49	81	20	10	240	311	309	620	9%	83%	0.60	51	96	3.41	21
	10	B	29	8	a/a	TAM	423	45	81	13	2	2	26	49	72	11	6	191	276	243	519	10%	83%	0.69	38	90	2.33	-15
Elmore,Jacob	10	R	23	4	aa	ARI	388	54	101	17	2	2	26	49	49	22	14	260	343	328	671	11%	87%	1.00	50	105	4.00	14
Emaus,Bradley	09	R	23 a	4	aa	TOR	505	63	123	27	2	10	63	56	71	10	3	243	318	363	681	10%	86%	0.78	82	88	4.20	57
	10	R	25	5	a/a	TOR	445	52	103	27	2	10	49	54	52	9	3	231	314	365	678	11%	88%	1.03	91	84	4.11	49
Errecart,Christophe	10	R	26	3	aa	MIL	158	12	29	8	1	4	14	3	34	1	0	184	199	321	520	2%	78%	0.08	89	75	2.04	-9
Escobar,Eduardo	10	B	22	6	aa	CHW	202	19	48	7	2	3	19	8	30	3	0	240	269	340	609	4%	85%	0.27	63	101	3.24	1
Espino,Damaso	09	B	26	2	a/a	CLE	247	20	51	12	1	2	18	13	16	0	1	205	244	283	527	5%	93%	0.79	58	45	2.28	45
	10	R	27	2	a/a	CLE	276	21	55	5	0	1	22	21	30	0	0	199	255	225	480	7%	89%	0.69	19	23	1.98	-12
Espinosa,Danny	10	B	23	6	a/a	WAS	481	69	117	17	4	19	59	35	100	22	12	242	294	410	704	7%	79%	0.35	98	128	4.00	11
Esposito,Brian	09	R	31	2	aa	HOU	260	15	48	7	1	3	25	6	38	0	0	183	201	255	456	2%	86%	0.16	46	32	1.64	-5
	10	R	32	2	a/a	HOU	197	9	31	5	1	2	13	3	40	0	0	155	170	216	385	2%	80%	0.09	40	37	1.13	-44
Evans,Nick	09	R	24	8	aa	NYM	342	33	68	19	2	10	30	26	63	2	0	198	255	350	605	7%	82%	0.42	98	73	3.02	42
	10	R	25 a	3	a/a	NYM	487	62	121	36	1	17	57	38	71	0	1	248	303	434	737	7%	85%	0.54	123	39	4.63	57
Evans,Terry	09	R	28	8	aa	LAA	537	85	133	30	4	20	74	32	144	23	5	248	290	427	717	6%	73%	0.22	112	144	4.39	38
	10	R	29	8	aaa	LAA	466	49	99	21	2	10	44	17	76	11	9	213	241	329	569	3%	84%	0.22	76	97	2.47	4
Everidge,Tommy	09	R	26 b	3	aa	OAK	430	55	113	27	1	13	64	35	53	0	1	263	319	419	738	8%	88%	0.66	103	39	4.81	62
	10	R	27	0	aaa	OAK	390	31	71	16	0	8	36	25	72	0	0	182	232	286	518	6%	81%	0.35	69	22	2.19	-5
Exposito,Luis	10	R	24	2	aa	BOS	473	47	113	41	1	8	68	39	67	1	2	238	297	379	676	8%	86%	0.58	104	41	3.92	44
Eymann,Eric	09	R	26	4	a/a	CIN	312	25	58	14	1	2	23	21	52	1	3	187	237	256	493	6%	83%	0.40	52	51	1.95	5
	10	R	27	3	a/a	CIN	379	32	83	18	2	5	32	17	59	6	5	218	251	313	564	4%	85%	0.28	66	78	2.56	1
Falu,Irving	09	B	26 b	4	aa	KC	465	46	105	17	3	1	29	39	28	8	6	226	285	281	566	8%	94%	1.37	42	85	2.77	52
	10	B	27	6	aaa	KC	503	52	112	13	4	1	32	30	31	11	5	222	265	267	532	6%	94%	0.95	31	104	2.44	13
Farris,Eric	10	R	25	4	aaa	MIL	230	21	53	8	1	2	12	7	22	11	2	230	251	296	548	3%	90%	0.31	46	109	2.61	7
Fedroff,Tim	10	L	24	8	aa	CLE	445	50	106	18	3	3	28	38	74	6	6	238	298	311	609	8%	83%	0.51	51	84	3.19	-8
Feliciano,Jesus	09	L	30	8	aa	NYM	495	39	116	23	1	1	29	18	42	9	5	234	260	288	549	3%	91%	0.42	45	73	2.53	33
	10	L	31	8	aaa	NYM	336	36	85	14	1	1	19	14	33	4	5	253	282	306	588	4%	90%	0.41	42	69	2.89	4
Felix,Jose	10	R	22	2	aa	TEX	105	6	26	3	0	1	5	1	5	0	1	248	255	305	559	1%	95%	0.20	40	24	2.52	17
Fernandez,Jair	10	R	24	2	a/a	MIN	210	18	45	11	1	3	19	16	31	0	0	215	269	317	587	7%	85%	0.51	71	39	2.94	15
Fields,Matthew	09	R	24	3	aa	TAM	284	34	62	12	1	5	28	16	81	1	0	220	262	321	583	5%	71%	0.20	68	70	2.89	-26
	10	R	25	3	aa	TAM	309	26	57	12	0	9	40	24	110	0	0	186	243	316	560	7%	65%	0.21	82	20	2.56	-60
Figueroa,Danny	09	R	27	8	aa	BAL	238	40	69	9	2	2	22	36	54	10	4	290	383	367	750	13%	77%	0.66	53	116	5.57	14
	10	R	28	8	a/a	BAL	264	24	45	5	1	1	15	31	47	7	3	170	257	208	465	10%	82%	0.66	26	87	1.90	-27
Figueroa,Franciscc	09	R	27 b	0	aa	BAL	226	29	63	17	4	0	26	27	39	12	3	277	353	383	736	11%	83%	0.68	79	152	5.23	63
	10	R	28	4	a/a	BAL	405	33	93	16	2	3	26	20	57	7	8	229	265	298	563	5%	86%	0.35	50	74	2.53	-5
Figueroa,Luis	09	B	36	4	aa	LAA	116	7	23	6	1	1	12	3	8	0	1	198	221	286	506	3%	93%	0.41	63	55	1.97	46
	10	B	37	6	aaa	LAA	457	31	106	20	2	3	43	14	15	2	3	232	256	307	563	3%	97%	0.94	54	45	2.62	38
Fixler,Jonathon	09	R	23 a	2	aa	HOU	115	11	19	4	1	7	18	8	21	0	2	162	215	392	607	6%	81%	0.37	130	67	2.44	65
	10	R	24	2	aa	HOU	98	11	24	4	2	5	12	11	31	1	2	245	318	470	789	10%	68%	0.34	128	133	4.98	-4
Florentino,Jhon	09	R	26	5	aa	HOU	399	30	86	13	4	4	30	21	60	5	1	214	254	293	547	5%	85%	0.35	51	93	2.55	21
	10	R	27	5	aa	HOU	316	24	68	14	2	4	29	22	56	2	2	216	267	308	574	6%	82%	0.39	63	61	2.77	-5
Florimon Jr.,Pedro	10	B	24	6	aa	BAL	120	13	20	3	0	1	10	9	24	3	1	163	221	212	433	7%	80%	0.36	34	84	1.57	-38
Flowers,Tyler	09	R	24	2	a/a	CHW	353	59	97	25	1	15	49	60	99	3	0	275	380	478	857	14%	72%	0.60	131	70	7.02	45
	10	R	25	2	aaa	CHW	346	33	65	18	1	13	40	43	101	2	1	189	279	363	642	11%	71%	0.43	109	49	3.45	-5
Folli,Mike	09	B	24 a	5	aa	STL	235	18	42	10	3	3	17	13	29	5	1	180	224	282	506	5%	88%	0.46	66	116	2.09	51
	10	B	25	4	a/a	TAM	220	15	37	7	2	3	16	19	33	2	0	167	232	252	484	8%	85%	0.57	54	78	1.98	1
Ford,Darren	10	R	25	8	aa	SF	463	55	107	18	8	4	34	32	96	32	15	230	279	328	607	6%	79%	0.33	62	172	3.01	-18
Ford,Shelby	09	B	25	4	aa	PIT	401	36	70	15	1	5	35	19	63	8	1	175	212	254	466	5%	84%	0.31	55	97	1.79	22
	10	B	26	4	aa	PIT	151	12	31	7	1	3	12	5	33	3	0	205	229	317	547	3%	78%	0.14	73	92	2.47	-21
Forsythe,Logan	09	R	23	5	aa	SD	244	30	58	7	2	2	25	33	53	4	0	238	329	307	636	12%	78%	0.62	45	100	3.86	5
	10	R	24	4	aa	SD	392	56	83	18	1	2	32	66	90	15	6	213	325	278	603	14%	77%	0.73	50	96	3.38	-21
Fowler,Dexter	10	B	25	8	aaa	COL	106	14	31	9	3	1	8	11	18	1	0	290	354	453	807	9%	83%	0.60	110	155	6.15	41
Fox,Adam	09	R	28	4	aa	TEX	364	36	80	11	2	14	38	18	77	5	3	220	257	378	635	5%	79%	0.23	92	80	3.23	25
	10	R	29	5	aa	WAS	150	14	19	6	1	2	11	11	34	3	1	129	191	217	408	7%	77%	0.34	60	107	1.33	-27
Francisco,Juan	09	L	22 a	5	a/a	CIN	529	69	146	29	2	26	79	21	99	5	2	276	304	486	789	4%	81%	0.21	128	76	5.27	60
	10	L	23	5	aaa	CIN	308	36	79	22	3	16	46	13	67	1	0	258	287	500	787	4%	78%	0.19	149	82	5.05	42
Frandsen,Kevin	09	R	27 b	6	aa	SF	427	53	106	16	2	9	43	18	32	3	4	249	279	358	637	4%	92%	0.56	70	71	3.39	57
	10	R	28	5	aaa	LAA	199	21	40	10	1	2	10	7	17	3	1	203	231	287	518	3%	91%	0.41	61	92	2.19	23
Frazier,Jeff	09	R	27	8	a/a	DET	486	50	127	29	1	10	52	21	58	1	3	261	291	385	676	4%	88%	0.36	86	40	3.89	43
	10	R	28	8	aaa	DET	477	52	99	27	2	19	52	23	81	5	1	207	243	393	636	5%	83%	0.28	117	86	3.18	37
Frazier,Todd	09	R	24 a	8	a/a	CIN	514	57	137	41	1	16	64	41	69	8	9	267	321	442	764	7%	87%	0.59	120	59	4.89	76
	10	R	25	8	aaa	CIN	480	55	108	29	3	14	51	36	108	11	5	226	279	388	667	7%	77%	0.33	105	101	3.68	9
Freeman,Freddie	09	L	20	3	aa	ATL	149	14	36	7	0	2	23	10	17	0	0	242	291	332	623	6%	88%	0.59	64	25	3.42	27
	10	L	21	3	aaa	ATL	461	62	133	31	1	15	74	38	71	5	2	289	344	460	804	8%	85%	0.54	113	67	5.91	46
Frey,Christopher	09	L	26	8	aa	COL	320	34	75	8	4	4	23	17	45	11	1	233	271	316	587	5%	86%	0.37	51	136	3.08	38
	10	L	27	8	aaa	COL	288	23	65	16	3	1	14	14	36	5	5	225	262	309	571	5%	88%	0.41	63	90	2.63	12

Major League Equivalent Statistics

BATTER	Yr	B	Age	Pos	Lev	Org	ab	r	h	d	t	hr	rbi	bb	k	sb	cs	ba	ob	slg	ops	bb%	ct%	eye	px	sx	rc/g	bpv
Frey,Evan	09	L	23	8	aa	ARI	506	51	126	21	6	1	42	48	64	25	16	250	315	320	634	9%	87%	0.75	49	122	3.47	45
	10	L	24	8	aa	ARI	517	72	137	23	5	1	39	56	77	28	13	266	337	334	671	10%	85%	0.72	51	128	4.10	2
Friday,Brian	09	R	24	6	aa	PIT	407	39	97	21	2	5	37	39	56	6	6	238	305	335	640	9%	86%	0.70	68	69	3.52	39
	10	R	25	4	aaa	PIT	288	31	62	16	3	1	21	28	54	8	8	217	286	303	589	9%	81%	0.51	64	109	2.82	-4
Frostad,Emerson	09	L	27	2	aa	TEX	252	24	51	12	2	3	21	34	42	0	1	201	296	296	592	12%	83%	0.80	65	54	3.08	27
	10	L	28	3	a/a	TEX	363	32	81	12	6	4	32	27	57	2	3	223	277	320	597	7%	84%	0.48	59	104	3.00	1
Fuld,Sam	09	L	28 b	8	aa	CHC	328	48	78	14	6	2	25	29	23	17	5	239	300	338	638	8%	93%	1.23	64	172	3.62	93
	10	L	29	8	aaa	CHC	368	43	77	12	4	3	17	42	30	13	10	208	290	287	577	10%	92%	1.43	51	120	2.78	32
Fuller,Clayton	10	B	23	8	aa	LAA	208	14	30	3	0	3	17	13	46	5	5	146	195	203	398	6%	78%	0.28	34	65	1.16	-47
Furmaniak,J.J.	09	R	30	4	aaa	PHI	378	26	68	15	1	4	35	16	73	3	3	180	213	259	472	4%	81%	0.22	55	57	1.74	-6
	10	R	31	4	a/a	TAM	326	39	67	14	2	1	19	30	60	7	4	206	272	269	541	8%	82%	0.50	48	98	2.49	-17
Gallagher,Jim	10	L	25	3	aa	CHW	503	56	127	30	1	9	42	60	82	3	3	252	332	372	704	11%	84%	0.73	84	48	4.50	25
Galvis,Freddy	10	B	21	6	aa	PHI	501	45	106	14	2	4	37	23	66	11	5	212	246	273	519	4%	87%	0.34	42	93	2.24	-9
Gamel,Mat	09	L	24	5	aaa	MIL	273	32	64	15	1	9	36	31	76	1	0	236	313	394	707	10%	72%	0.40	102	55	4.44	9
	10	L	25	5	a/a	MIL	339	45	89	23	0	10	54	33	65	2	1	263	329	421	750	9%	81%	0.51	106	49	5.06	28
Garcia,Emmanuel	09	L	24	8	aa	NYM	491	52	103	14	2	3	31	31	93	15	12	210	257	263	520	6%	81%	0.34	38	97	2.17	-3
	10	L	25	8	aaa	NYM	50	4	7	2	0	0	1	0	11	0	0	134	134	173	307	0%	77%	0.00	34	6	0.68	-62
Garcia,Harold	10	B	24	4	aa	PHI	231	21	57	8	1	4	24	11	45	9	6	246	280	339	619	4%	81%	0.24	60	88	3.10	-19
Garcia,Jose	10	R	23	4	aa	STL	263	27	59	7	1	3	21	15	36	7	4	224	266	293	559	5%	86%	0.42	45	89	2.61	-6
Garciaparra,Micha	09	R	26	6	a/a	MIL	189	6	34	5	0	1	9	17	39	0	0	180	250	219	469	8%	79%	0.45	29	2	1.89	-40
	10	R	27	3	a/a	HOU	71	8	18	5	0	0	7	5	16	0	0	254	298	330	628	6%	78%	0.29	67	35	3.52	-20
Gardenhire,Toby	09	B	27	4	aa	MIN	200	17	44	7	0	0	15	11	37	2	1	221	260	257	517	5%	82%	0.29	32	53	2.29	-20
	10	B	28	4	a/a	MIN	194	11	29	2	0	1	12	9	19	1	2	150	187	172	359	4%	90%	0.46	15	40	0.98	-17
Garko,Ryan	10	R	30	0	aaa	TEX	340	28	62	9	1	9	32	27	55	1	1	182	242	288	530	7%	84%	0.49	64	42	2.31	3
Garner,Cole	09	R	25 a	8	aa	COL	396	52	104	23	3	13	51	18	63	11	6	262	294	436	731	4%	84%	0.29	110	110	4.39	69
	10	R	26	8	aaa	COL	415	50	103	26	7	8	38	24	57	5	7	249	289	405	695	5%	86%	0.41	102	118	3.89	39
Gartrell,Maurice	09	R	26	8	a/a	CHW	474	72	118	26	3	22	74	45	121	5	2	248	313	452	765	9%	74%	0.37	125	93	5.03	45
	10	R	27	8	aaa	CHW	534	53	112	17	1	22	58	30	133	3	2	210	253	369	621	5%	75%	0.23	93	52	3.10	-12
Gaston,Jonathan	10	L	24	8	aa	HOU	460	56	104	15	6	12	44	40	98	11	5	226	288	360	648	8%	79%	0.41	79	129	3.57	-4
Gathright,Joey	09	L	28	8	aaa	BOS	332	43	98	11	2	0	18	24	45	21	7	294	341	339	681	7%	86%	0.52	35	116	4.41	24
	10	L	29	8	aaa	BAL	216	17	31	3	1	0	5	14	36	9	6	143	195	167	362	6%	83%	0.38	18	107	0.99	-39
Gentry,Craig	09	R	26 a	8	aa	TEX	512	77	134	19	6	7	40	38	56	38	7	263	313	360	673	7%	89%	0.67	62	159	4.27	69
	10	R	27	8	aaa	TEX	259	30	67	6	4	3	25	20	39	8	6	259	313	341	654	7%	85%	0.52	48	126	3.71	-6
German,Esteban	09	R	32	5	aa	TEX	389	44	97	12	3	3	41	45	61	25	9	249	327	317	644	10%	84%	0.74	45	123	3.85	33
	10	R	33	4	aaa	TEX	485	52	105	20	3	3	36	42	69	32	7	216	278	293	570	8%	86%	0.60	54	133	2.96	4
Giavotella,Johnny	10	R	23	4	aa	KC	522	69	149	33	3	6	48	46	49	10	9	285	343	394	738	8%	91%	0.94	79	84	4.88	44
Gibbons,Jay	10	L	34	8	aaa	LA	352	32	82	20	0	10	44	9	24	0	0	234	254	377	631	3%	93%	0.40	94	24	3.25	56
Gil,Jose	10	R	24	2	aa	NYY	106	15	21	5	1	5	19	8	20	0	0	199	253	398	652	7%	81%	0.39	118	82	3.37	35
Gilbert,Archie	09	R	26	8	aa	OAK	449	55	98	13	3	2	27	40	40	19	17	217	282	270	552	8%	91%	1.01	37	108	2.42	45
	10	R	27	8	aa	OAK	445	47	86	24	1	7	40	38	61	21	12	192	255	299	555	8%	86%	0.62	75	100	2.44	23
Giles,Thomas	09	L	26	8	aa	LA	179	23	38	9	0	9	24	26	57	0	1	211	310	416	726	13%	68%	0.46	125	27	4.45	9
	10	L	27	8	aa	LA	123	10	22	3	1	2	8	8	20	1	0	176	227	256	483	6%	84%	0.41	49	75	1.94	-12
Gillaspie,Conor	10	L	23	5	aa	SF	491	50	132	24	7	7	58	31	59	0	4	269	313	387	701	6%	88%	0.53	76	72	4.26	27
Gillespie,Cole	09	R	25 a	8	a/a	ARI	374	43	86	16	8	9	38	41	66	9	6	229	306	387	693	10%	82%	0.63	95	147	4.06	71
	10	R	26	8	aaa	ARI	264	32	61	12	5	5	29	27	34	5	6	230	301	362	663	9%	87%	0.79	82	124	3.56	35
Gillies,Tyson	10	L	22	8	aa	PHI	105	11	21	2	1	2	5	4	18	2	2	202	232	298	530	4%	83%	0.23	55	111	2.12	-14
Gimenez,Chris	09	R	27	2	aaa	CLE	136	15	27	6	0	5	11	12	36	0	0	196	261	345	606	8%	74%	0.33	94	28	3.05	-4
	10	R	28	8	aaa	CLE	196	23	42	8	0	6	23	14	33	1	1	216	269	354	623	7%	83%	0.43	86	47	3.22	17
Gimenez,Hector	09	B	27	5	aa	PIT	301	24	70	16	1	6	29	14	49	2	2	232	266	345	611	4%	84%	0.28	77	51	3.09	23
	10	B	28	2	aa	PIT	338	37	84	24	0	11	54	33	63	5	1	248	315	415	730	9%	81%	0.53	113	57	4.73	35
Gindl,Caleb	10	L	22	8	aa	MIL	463	49	111	30	1	7	48	46	65	8	6	240	308	354	663	9%	86%	0.71	83	67	3.81	30
Goedert,Jared	09	R	24	5	aa	CLE	313	30	63	20	1	4	33	31	46	1	0	202	274	310	583	9%	85%	0.67	79	53	2.95	40
	10	R	25	5	a/a	CLE	481	59	112	31	1	19	61	40	96	3	0	233	292	418	710	8%	80%	0.42	119	65	4.30	33
Golson,Greg	09	R	24	8	aa	TEX	457	36	104	15	7	2	32	23	98	15	5	227	264	302	566	5%	79%	0.24	49	139	2.75	7
	10	R	25	8	aaa	NYY	415	42	93	19	3	9	33	22	93	14	4	224	263	351	614	5%	78%	0.23	81	117	3.16	-12
Gomez,Mauro	10	R	26	3	aa	ATL	495	52	113	34	1	12	62	37	113	1	2	229	282	374	656	7%	77%	0.33	100	43	3.61	4
Gomez,Yasser	10	L	30	8	aa	ATL	127	7	31	3	0	0	7	14	9	1	3	248	324	268	592	10%	93%	1.54	18	23	2.96	7
Gonzalez,Edwar	09	R	27	8	aa	NYY	413	41	86	23	1	4	33	27	98	6	3	207	255	294	549	6%	76%	0.27	65	82	2.53	-4
	10	R	28	8	a/a	NYY	256	29	48	6	2	5	27	23	60	3	2	186	254	288	543	8%	77%	0.39	61	91	2.45	-26
Gonzalez,Juan	09	R	28	4	aa	LA	231	18	43	10	0	0	17	36	58	3	0	187	297	230	526	13%	75%	0.62	38	49	2.57	-26
	10	R	29	6	aa	ATL	102	5	17	3	0	0	9	11	25	0	0	164	242	190	432	9%	75%	0.42	23	15	1.60	-59
Gonzalez,Marwin	10	B	22	6	aa	CHC	305	18	67	10	2	3	31	13	31	4	5	219	251	295	546	4%	90%	0.43	51	66	2.35	10
Gordon,Alex	10	L	27	8	aaa	KC	260	42	68	18	2	9	31	37	58	5	2	262	353	453	806	12%	78%	0.64	124	98	5.93	37
Gorecki,Reid	09	R	29	8	aaa	ATL	371	42	84	21	4	6	36	26	70	11	7	228	277	353	631	6%	81%	0.36	84	117	3.23	42
	10	R	30	8	a/a	NYY	386	40	75	18	3	4	33	34	86	15	6	194	260	287	547	8%	78%	0.40	65	117	2.52	-19
Gorneault,Nick	09	R	30	8	aa	TOR	415	42	72	20	2	9	46	29	135	9	4	174	228	293	521	7%	67%	0.21	79	100	2.14	-22
	10	R	31	8	a/a	LAA	317	31	60	13	2	8	34	20	65	3	4	190	237	314	551	6%	80%	0.30	78	80	2.34	-6
Gosewisch,James	09	R	26	2	a/a	PHI	260	17	52	17	0	1	17	12	43	0	1	198	233	272	506	4%	83%	0.28	62	27	2.07	1
	10	R	27	2	aa	PHI	312	32	59	17	1	6	22	33	57	0	0	190	268	312	580	10%	82%	0.59	82	38	2.87	14
Gotay,Ruben	09	B	27 b	5	aa	ARI	371	50	89	27	2	9	44	80	60	2	4	241	375	397	772	18%	84%	1.34	106	51	5.54	74
	10	B	28	5	aaa	STL	473	55	103	23	1	7	46	62	92	0	5	217	308	316	624	12%	81%	0.67	69	31	3.34	2
Graham,Tyler	10	R	27	8	a/a	SF	349	45	100	20	2	2	26	17	50	27	12	287	321	372	693	5%	86%	0.35	64	124	4.18	6
Green,Andy	09	R	32	5	aa	NYM	174	16	33	5	1	3	14	13	31	2	0	191	246	274	519	7%	82%	0.42	53	75	2.30	10
	10	R	33	4	aaa	NYM	218	22	38	11	1	3	15	14	42	2	1	175	224	281	505	6%	81%	0.32	72	79	2.04	-6
Green,Nick	10	R	32	5	aaa	SD	242	21	40	12	2	3	20	11	51	1	4	165	202	260	461	4%	79%	0.22	66	83	1.51	-20
Green,Taylor	09	L	23	5	aa	MIL	306	28	71	14	0	4	35	29	32	0	1	232	299	317	616	9%	90%	0.91	61	24	3.34	33
	10	L	24	5	aa	MIL	393	40	88	25	1	11	64	37	57	0	2	224	292	377	668	9%	85%	0.65	102	33	3.76	43
Greene,Jonathan	10	R	25	8	aa	TEX	144	13	24	6	0	4	12	7	46	0	0	170	206	287	493	4%	68%	0.14	75	33	1.89	-56
Greene,Justin	10	R	25	8	aa	CHW	168	16	34	6	2	3	17	7	48	5	5	200	231	309	539	4%	71%	0.14	67	131	2.09	-51
Greene,Tyler	09	R	26	6	aa	STL	340	51	80	8	3	10	30	28	72	22	4	235	293	365	658	8%	79%	0.38	75	148	3.91	37
	10	R	27	6	aaa	STL	338	44	73	16	3	5	23	21	71	8	5	216	261	328	588	6%	79%	0.29	74	120	2.79	-11
Griffin,Michael	09	R	26	8	a/a	CIN	304	22	59	12	1	3	17	10	41	3	4	195	221	269	490	3%	86%	0.25	53	62	1.85	15
	10	R	27	8	a/a	CIN	238	19	51	17	1	6	23	6	37	1	5	213	230	375	605	2%	84%	0.15	110	56	2.56	33

Major League Equivalent Statistics

BATTER	Yr	B	Age	Pos	Lev	Org	ab	r	h	d	t	hr	rbi	bb	k	sb	cs	ba	ob	slg	ops	bb%	ct%	eye	px	sx	rc/g	bpv
Guez,Ben	10	R	24	8	a/a	DET	251	26	59	11	2	8	27	21	54	6	9	234	292	387	679	8%	78%	0.38	93	89	3.47	6
Guyer,Brandon	09	R	24	8	aa	CHC	189	18	32	12	1	1	12	8	30	6	6	171	204	259	463	4%	84%	0.26	68	115	1.48	36
	10	R	25 a	8	aa	CHC	369	56	109	35	4	10	42	20	41	22	4	297	333	489	822	5%	89%	0.50	132	150	6.17	74
Guzman,Carlos	10	L	24	8	aa	NYM	158	13	33	4	0	0	7	13	28	0	3	207	269	231	500	8%	82%	0.48	22	33	2.00	-36
Guzman,Jesus	09	R	25	3	aa	SF	452	62	128	24	4	12	58	30	76	0	2	283	328	435	762	6%	83%	0.40	97	65	5.17	45
	10	R	26	5	aaa	SF	445	45	117	24	1	12	50	26	54	4	5	263	303	401	704	5%	88%	0.47	91	50	4.20	37
Guzman,Joel	09	R	25	5	a/a	WAS	418	47	101	24	1	10	50	31	73	1	1	241	293	372	665	7%	83%	0.42	88	49	3.82	31
	10	R	26	0	aa	BAL	509	66	124	18	1	28	74	33	100	3	5	244	290	449	738	6%	80%	0.33	118	50	4.39	30
Hague,Matthew	10	R	25	3	aa	PIT	509	70	128	25	0	11	67	46	52	2	7	251	313	368	681	8%	90%	0.88	78	42	3.97	40
Hallberg,Marcus	09	R	24	4	aa	ARI	455	42	109	22	1	2	34	32	36	12	4	239	290	304	593	7%	92%	0.91	51	82	3.13	49
	10	R	25	4	aaa	ARI	384	35	84	21	2	1	27	32	30	3	5	218	277	290	567	8%	92%	1.05	57	62	2.69	31
Halman,Gregory	09	R	22	8	aa	SEA	457	57	87	16	1	22	64	27	172	8	8	190	236	374	610	6%	62%	0.16	107	88	2.69	-25
	10	R	23	8	aaa	SEA	424	61	86	18	2	24	60	28	138	11	5	203	253	421	674	6%	68%	0.21	127	116	3.45	-14
Hamilton,Mark	09	L	25	3	aa	STL	293	36	74	18	0	9	35	30	65	0	1	253	323	411	734	9%	78%	0.46	104	28	4.76	23
	10	L	26	3	aaa	STL	258	36	60	16	0	11	40	23	54	0	0	232	295	421	715	8%	79%	0.42	120	34	4.34	30
Hankerd,Kevin	09	R	25	8	aa	ARI	440	46	107	32	1	6	54	34	67	1	6	242	296	358	654	7%	85%	0.50	86	40	3.56	36
	10	R	26	3	a/a	ARI	207	15	45	11	0	3	23	19	23	1	1	218	283	313	596	8%	89%	0.80	69	31	3.07	29
Hannahan,Jack	10	L	31	5	aaa	BOS	334	33	65	16	1	6	31	35	76	2	0	193	270	300	570	9%	77%	0.46	73	59	2.81	-13
Harbin,Taylor	10	R	25	4	aa	ARI	433	39	106	27	3	5	37	20	67	9	9	244	278	353	630	4%	85%	0.30	78	87	3.18	12
Harris,Brendan	10	R	30	5	aaa	MIN	232	20	40	10	1	3	20	9	38	1	0	172	204	256	461	4%	84%	0.25	59	69	1.69	-8
Harrison,Joshua	10	R	23	5	aa	PIT	520	60	139	30	2	3	60	25	42	16	8	268	302	351	652	5%	92%	0.61	64	96	3.72	30
Harvey,Ryan	09	R	25 a	8	aa	COL	345	34	76	19	2	20	63	23	82	2	0	221	269	458	726	6%	76%	0.28	142	62	4.20	51
	10	R	26	8	aa	COL	239	22	44	11	0	9	27	12	59	3	2	185	224	346	570	5%	75%	0.20	100	57	2.45	-6
Hatcher,David	09	R	25 a	2	aa	FLA	156	24	31	9	3	7	23	12	42	1	0	197	256	418	675	7%	73%	0.30	132	154	3.60	62
	10	R	26	2	a/a	FLA	315	24	52	8	1	4	26	23	98	1	2	164	220	233	453	7%	69%	0.23	45	53	1.64	-73
Haveman,Brandon	10	L	24	8	aa	SEA	230	22	57	5	2	1	15	11	24	8	5	246	279	296	576	4%	90%	0.44	32	104	2.78	-5
Haydel,Lee	10	L	23	8	aa	MIL	452	48	111	17	5	0	28	28	84	18	7	245	290	304	593	6%	81%	0.34	42	130	3.10	-26
Hayes,Brett	09	R	26	2	aa	FLA	321	23	67	13	0	3	31	17	65	2	0	208	248	275	523	5%	80%	0.26	50	45	2.33	-15
	10	R	27	2	aaa	FLA	59	5	10	3	0	1	4	2	8	0	0	172	197	265	462	3%	87%	0.24	66	32	1.65	9
Head,Jerad	09	R	27	8	aa	CLE	327	41	80	20	3	5	40	20	73	5	2	245	289	366	655	6%	78%	0.28	84	108	3.70	24
	10	R	28	8	a/a	CLE	311	41	74	22	0	11	47	17	59	2	1	237	277	411	688	5%	81%	0.29	115	60	3.91	29
Hechavarria,Adeiny	10	R	21	6	aa	TOR	253	27	61	10	1	2	26	9	32	5	4	240	266	311	577	3%	87%	0.29	51	87	2.72	0
Heether,Adam	09	R	28	5	a/a	MIL	419	49	100	26	1	14	52	47	88	4	1	238	315	402	717	10%	79%	0.53	107	61	4.55	42
	10	R	29	5	aaa	OAK	329	35	55	11	1	6	26	33	53	4	4	169	245	262	507	9%	84%	0.63	60	75	2.11	3
Heisey,Chris	09	R	25 a	8	a/a	CIN	516	75	146	32	2	21	63	40	69	17	3	283	335	474	809	7%	87%	0.59	121	105	5.96	91
	10	R	26	8	aaa	CIN	79	5	16	3	0	4	9	6	20	2	0	202	255	381	636	7%	74%	0.28	105	34	3.36	-3
Henley,Paul	09	L	24 a	8	aa	STL	423	47	107	27	2	10	48	31	51	7	5	252	303	393	695	7%	88%	0.60	95	78	4.12	67
	10	L	25	8	a/a	STL	148	13	32	8	1	2	13	6	21	0	1	216	245	324	569	4%	86%	0.27	76	62	2.57	13
Henry,Jordan	10	L	22	8	aa	CLE	287	36	77	7	2	0	13	38	48	12	5	268	354	307	660	12%	83%	0.79	28	104	4.18	-19
Henry,Justin	10	L	25	4	a/a	DET	356	35	80	17	2	1	22	40	54	13	11	224	304	290	594	10%	85%	0.74	51	89	2.95	2
Henry,Sean	09	R	24 a	8	aa	CIN	420	54	102	20	1	11	31	34	58	18	10	242	298	370	669	7%	86%	0.58	83	97	3.75	57
	10	R	25	8	a/a	CIN	414	39	106	21	2	5	44	21	55	11	9	257	292	350	642	5%	87%	0.37	66	84	3.39	11
Henson,Bobby	10	R	23	8	aa	BAL	486	56	124	33	2	11	49	30	121	6	6	255	298	399	698	6%	75%	0.25	99	76	4.07	-7
Hernandez,Anders	10	B	28	6	aaa	HOU	200	13	37	4	0	1	13	9	26	3	5	185	220	216	436	4%	87%	0.35	23	50	1.41	-22
Hernandez,Diory	09	R	25	6	aaa	ATL	204	14	55	14	1	1	25	17	31	7	7	272	328	364	692	8%	85%	0.55	72	70	4.02	36
	10	R	26	6	aaa	ATL	116	10	30	6	1	0	13	4	20	3	1	262	284	325	610	3%	83%	0.19	49	94	3.27	-20
Hernandez,Gorkys	09	R	22	8	aa	PIT	556	65	144	24	3	2	41	31	103	17	18	259	298	324	622	5%	81%	0.30	49	96	3.12	6
	10	R	23	8	aa	PIT	368	36	86	10	2	2	21	25	77	14	3	234	284	288	572	6%	79%	0.33	37	108	2.96	-39
Hernandez,Luis	09	B	25	6	aa	KC	198	18	52	9	0	1	20	12	14	1	4	261	304	323	627	6%	93%	0.88	49	36	3.29	36
	10	B	26	6	a/a	NYM	414	36	95	17	6	2	30	17	51	4	6	229	260	311	571	4%	88%	0.34	56	98	2.63	6
Hernandez,Michel	10	R	32	2	aaa	BAL	190	17	39	3	0	3	15	14	22	2	1	206	262	264	526	7%	88%	0.65	37	49	2.37	-2
Herrera,Elian	10	B	26	8	a/a	LA	347	33	67	8	2	1	29	35	60	21	14	192	266	236	502	9%	83%	0.58	31	109	2.01	-24
Herrera,Jonathan	09	B	25	6	aa	COL	381	50	92	10	4	2	26	38	41	12	6	242	311	302	614	9%	89%	0.95	39	119	3.39	45
	10	B	26	6	aaa	COL	222	18	47	5	1	1	10	16	19	2	4	212	265	254	519	7%	91%	0.83	29	57	2.18	4
Hessman,Mike	09	R	32	5	aaa	DET	466	44	81	24	3	18	59	48	174	3	1	173	251	350	601	9%	63%	0.28	109	74	2.92	-19
	10	R	33	5	aaa	NYM	248	28	50	15	0	12	37	17	56	0	0	202	253	408	661	6%	77%	0.30	129	27	3.45	27
Hester,John	09	R	26 b	2	aa	ARI	329	47	96	29	5	7	51	17	57	10	3	291	327	473	799	5%	83%	0.31	124	145	5.69	86
	10	R	27 b	2	aaa	ARI	138	20	41	10	3	5	17	10	19	1	5	293	341	502	843	7%	86%	0.52	131	123	5.61	66
Hicks,Brandon	09	R	24	6	aa	ATL	464	56	99	22	3	9	42	47	127	15	1	213	286	329	615	9%	73%	0.37	76	124	3.42	9
	10	R	25	6	aaa	ATL	261	21	46	8	1	6	17	16	66	8	7	176	224	277	501	6%	75%	0.24	62	85	1.85	-38
Hill,Steven	09	R	25	2	aa	STL	464	47	109	22	1	13	48	27	84	1	2	236	278	374	652	5%	82%	0.32	89	42	3.55	24
	10	R	26	2	a/a	STL	395	44	86	23	1	15	65	29	79	1	0	217	270	393	663	7%	80%	0.37	112	51	3.64	25
Hodges,Wes	09	R	25	5	aaa	CLE	332	25	75	21	0	4	29	15	56	7	6	227	260	323	583	4%	83%	0.27	73	59	2.71	19
	10	R	26	3	aaa	CLE	493	46	107	23	2	10	42	22	83	2	0	216	250	332	582	4%	83%	0.27	76	64	2.81	5
Hoffmann,Jaime	09	R	25 a	8	aa	LA	358	55	88	20	3	8	52	45	52	12	12	247	331	389	720	11%	85%	0.87	92	107	4.28	72
	10	R	26	8	aaa	LA	545	52	123	27	1	5	42	23	70	10	9	226	258	304	561	4%	87%	0.33	58	75	2.53	5
Hoffpauir,Jarrett	09	R	26 b	4	aa	STL	358	39	84	17	2	9	39	26	23	3	1	234	285	370	655	7%	94%	1.13	88	71	3.69	81
	10	R	27 b	4	aaa	TOR	431	41	91	20	4	9	41	32	24	5	4	211	266	336	602	7%	94%	1.33	80	81	2.98	58
Hoffpauir,Micah	10	L	31	3	aaa	CHC	427	49	90	26	1	14	58	34	62	1	0	211	269	378	647	7%	85%	0.55	109	51	3.48	45
Holm,Steve	09	R	30	2	aa	SF	198	17	39	10	0	4	12	11	40	0	0	195	238	313	551	5%	80%	0.28	80	26	2.47	4
	10	R	31	2	aaa	SF	228	21	42	12	2	3	23	18	34	1	3	183	242	283	525	7%	85%	0.52	70	73	2.14	13
Holt,John	09	L	27	4	aaa	ATL	266	34	63	10	2	0	23	21	47	11	5	235	292	287	579	7%	82%	0.45	40	120	2.96	14
	10	L	28	4	a/a	OAK	246	21	41	3	1	1	14	10	41	7	2	165	197	194	391	4%	83%	0.24	19	107	1.26	-42
Hoover,Paul	09	R	33	2	aaa	PHI	245	19	48	13	1	1	20	20	67	1	2	198	259	267	527	8%	73%	0.30	54	51	2.32	-33
	10	R	34	2	aaa	PHI	255	17	50	10	2	2	15	19	67	0	0	197	252	270	522	7%	74%	0.28	52	47	2.31	-48
Hopper,Norris	09	R	31	8	aaa	WAS	409	36	91	11	2	0	26	26	25	17	8	222	268	258	526	6%	94%	1.03	28	98	2.37	41
	10	R	32	8	aaa	MIL	458	34	97	11	0	0	26	26	41	14	9	212	254	236	490	5%	91%	0.64	21	72	1.98	-6
Horton,Joshua	09	L	24	6	aa	OAK	510	58	110	18	4	3	45	46	47	7	4	215	280	282	563	8%	91%	0.98	46	95	2.75	47
	10	L	25	6	aa	OAK	420	47	101	15	2	2	39	33	42	3	4	240	295	299	594	7%	90%	0.78	43	67	3.07	12
Hosmer,Eric	10	L	21 a	3	aa	KC	195	31	57	14	2	9	28	11	18	2	1	291	329	528	858	5%	91%	0.61	148	102	6.35	94
House,J.R.	09	R	30	2	aa	KC	505	40	100	21	0	6	36	22	50	0	0	198	232	274	506	4%	90%	0.45	55	26	2.10	23
	10	R	31	2	aaa	NYM	225	13	42	10	0	3	19	9	29	0	0	185	215	264	479	4%	87%	0.29	58	17	1.84	3

Major League Equivalent Statistics

BATTER	Yr	B	Age	Pos	Lev	Org	ab	r	h	d	t	hr	rbi	bb	k	sb	cs	ba	ob	slg	ops	bb%	ct%	eye	px	sx	rc/g	bpv
Howard,Kevin	09	L	28 b	5	a/a	TOR	433	51	110	25	1	11	45	36	51	4	3	254	311	388	700	8%	88%	0.71	90	59	4.29	60
	10	L	29	5	aaa	STL	273	19	47	8	1	3	16	12	35	1	1	173	208	246	454	4%	87%	0.35	47	51	1.63	-3
Howell,Jeffery	09	R	26	2	aa	KC	195	16	42	9	1	3	17	12	29	0	2	217	262	316	578	6%	85%	0.41	68	45	2.71	21
	10	R	27	2	a/a	MIN	265	21	48	17	0	4	27	11	58	0	2	180	212	285	497	4%	78%	0.19	78	36	1.88	-15
Hu,Chin-lung	09	R	26	6	aa	LA	496	53	125	18	3	5	42	21	52	11	6	252	282	328	610	4%	89%	0.40	52	97	3.19	38
	10	R	27	6	aaa	LA	208	21	48	8	0	2	15	5	11	5	1	230	247	296	543	2%	95%	0.42	49	82	2.50	25
Hubbard,Marshall	09	L	27	3	aa	SEA	447	59	100	24	1	11	56	60	116	2	3	223	316	354	670	12%	74%	0.52	87	52	3.96	8
	10	L	28	0	a/a	NYM	349	34	62	15	0	6	33	27	60	1	0	179	239	275	513	7%	83%	0.45	65	47	2.20	0
Hudson,Robert	09	R	26	6	aa	CHW	315	32	67	6	1	3	23	12	36	12	3	213	242	263	505	4%	89%	0.33	32	108	2.19	21
	10	R	27	6	a/a	CHW	322	35	59	14	1	5	22	9	53	3	1	182	204	282	486	3%	83%	0.17	68	92	1.84	-4
Huffman,Chad	09	R	24	8	aa	SD	469	50	102	23	1	14	53	44	101	6	6	217	284	362	647	9%	78%	0.44	93	60	3.44	25
	10	R	25	8	aaa	NYY	368	39	87	16	0	9	38	35	76	0	2	238	303	358	661	9%	79%	0.46	78	25	3.79	0
Hughes,Luke	09	R	25	5	a/a	MIN	335	34	73	21	4	9	53	29	72	3	1	219	281	387	669	8%	78%	0.40	108	98	3.76	47
	10	R	26	4	aaa	MIN	74	8	16	6	0	1	5	4	15	2	0	211	249	336	584	5%	79%	0.24	96	80	2.91	6
Hughes,Rhyne	10	L	27	8	aaa	BAL	388	32	83	20	1	8	29	21	104	5	3	213	253	332	585	5%	73%	0.20	80	69	2.80	-32
Hulett,Tug	09	L	27 b	4	aa	KC	374	45	92	25	3	7	39	43	65	6	2	246	324	386	710	10%	83%	0.66	96	95	4.57	58
	10	L	28	4	aaa	SEA	350	33	59	21	1	5	28	42	66	5	5	170	259	273	532	11%	81%	0.65	75	65	2.30	8
Hunter,Cedric	09	L	22	8	aa	SD	541	58	121	16	4	1	43	20	36	10	4	224	252	274	526	4%	93%	0.57	36	109	2.34	44
	10	L	23	8	a/a	SD	541	63	131	22	4	5	53	40	39	12	10	242	294	325	620	7%	93%	1.03	57	96	3.24	32
Iglesias,Jose	10	R	21	6	aa	BOS	221	23	60	11	2	0	10	6	34	4	2	270	290	340	630	3%	85%	0.18	54	103	3.46	-11
Iorg,Cale	09	R	24	6	aa	DET	491	45	95	14	2	9	33	25	126	11	8	194	233	284	516	5%	74%	0.20	57	90	2.08	-19
	10	R	25	6	a/a	DET	493	42	89	24	2	8	31	14	132	9	7	181	204	288	492	3%	73%	0.11	72	97	1.79	-42
Iribarren,Hernan	09	L	25	4	aaa	MIL	379	35	99	16	3	2	40	23	55	9	8	260	302	332	634	6%	85%	0.41	52	90	3.43	23
	10	L	26	4	aaa	TEX	465	44	106	19	2	6	50	29	66	7	6	228	272	319	591	6%	86%	0.43	62	76	2.91	6
Ivany,Devin	10	R	28	2	a/a	WAS	220	22	41	8	2	4	19	20	60	4	3	188	256	288	544	8%	73%	0.34	64	102	2.45	-40
Iwamura,Akinori	10	L	32	5	aaa	PIT	163	17	32	8	1	2	10	25	28	0	2	198	303	287	590	13%	83%	0.87	62	50	3.01	9
Jackson,Anthony	09	B	25	8	aa	COL	422	47	82	9	3	4	26	33	48	21	6	194	252	256	508	7%	89%	0.69	39	128	2.25	41
	10	B	26	8	aa	COL	434	50	95	11	6	2	29	43	60	24	13	218	289	282	571	9%	86%	0.72	40	139	2.77	-3
Jackson,Brett	10	L	22	8	aa	CHC	228	35	56	12	3	5	21	23	47	14	5	246	315	390	705	9%	79%	0.49	92	157	4.34	12
Jacobs,Mike	10	L	30	3	aaa	TOR	469	41	87	21	2	11	48	26	65	1	0	185	228	308	536	5%	86%	0.40	79	55	2.30	20
Jaspe,Jonathan	10	B	25	2	aa	TOR	206	13	39	11	1	2	12	8	28	1	0	192	224	283	506	4%	87%	0.31	67	56	2.09	9
Jay,Jon	09	L	25	8	aa	STL	505	55	119	19	1	7	40	26	51	15	10	236	273	317	591	5%	90%	0.51	56	88	2.88	42
	10	L	26 a	8	aaa	STL	165	22	42	13	0	3	23	11	17	9	0	256	304	387	691	6%	90%	0.66	97	105	4.53	51
Jenkins,Andrew	09	R	26	3	aa	FLA	269	24	61	18	0	2	16	12	47	4	0	226	259	315	573	4%	83%	0.26	71	68	2.84	18
	10	R	27	5	a/a	TEX	439	39	87	18	2	8	41	29	83	4	5	199	248	303	552	6%	81%	0.35	68	64	2.43	-7
Jennings,Desmonc	09	R	23 a	8	a/a	TAM	497	83	147	29	8	10	56	61	61	47	8	296	373	447	819	11%	88%	1.00	97	175	6.70	105
	10	R	24	8	aaa	TAM	399	65	96	22	4	2	28	37	56	29	5	241	306	329	635	9%	86%	0.66	64	162	3.81	14
Jeroloman,Brian	09	L	24	2	aa	TOR	364	30	74	15	1	6	30	58	126	1	0	203	312	298	610	14%	65%	0.46	64	41	3.40	-46
	10	L	25	2	a/a	TOR	264	28	55	16	0	6	24	50	77	0	1	207	332	331	664	16%	71%	0.65	87	21	4.01	-13
Jimenez,D'Angelo	10	B	33	5	aaa	MIN	231	14	38	9	2	3	28	17	45	0	1	166	223	265	488	7%	81%	0.38	65	50	1.90	-10
Jimenez,Jorge	09	L	25	5	aa	BOS	498	50	131	24	2	9	70	41	61	3	2	262	319	374	693	8%	88%	0.68	74	55	4.32	45
	10	L	26	5	aaa	BOS	337	28	63	10	1	2	25	24	37	1	3	188	242	240	482	7%	89%	0.65	37	47	1.90	1
Jimerson,Charlton	10	R	31	8	aa	LAA	166	19	29	7	1	5	17	4	38	6	3	174	195	317	512	2%	77%	0.11	88	133	1.80	-13
Johnson,Chris	09	R	25	5	aa	HOU	384	36	92	17	4	11	31	15	73	2	1	240	269	388	657	4%	81%	0.21	91	83	3.57	32
	10	R	26 a	5	aaa	HOU	149	19	41	8	1	6	24	7	19	0	0	278	308	461	769	4%	87%	0.34	114	53	5.13	51
Johnson,Cody	10	L	22	8	aa	ATL	233	21	39	5	0	8	25	22	95	7	6	167	239	292	531	9%	59%	0.23	72	65	2.13	-86
Johnson,Dan	10	L	31	5	aaa	TAM	340	46	77	14	0	20	65	51	68	0	0	228	328	450	778	13%	80%	0.75	131	20	5.30	52
Johnson,Elliot	09	B	26	4	aaa	TAM	233	25	53	8	1	9	29	14	52	6	2	226	270	387	657	6%	78%	0.27	95	87	3.56	26
	10	B	27	6	aaa	TAM	427	53	111	20	4	8	41	28	82	22	6	261	306	384	689	6%	81%	0.34	80	132	4.21	1
Johnson,Joshua	09	B	24	5	aa	KC	132	20	23	3	0	0	7	23	18	2	2	171	292	193	485	15%	86%	1.23	20	69	2.07	12
	10	B	25	6	aa	WAS	223	36	57	14	2	4	26	24	33	5	6	254	326	387	714	10%	85%	0.72	91	107	4.27	35
Johnson,Michael	09	B	28	8	aa	LAA	248	27	45	14	2	4	23	20	43	3	4	181	242	298	540	7%	83%	0.46	80	93	2.27	39
	10	B	29	2	aaa	MIL	145	9	19	4	0	2	10	3	41	0	0	134	149	194	343	2%	72%	0.06	40	34	0.87	-75
Jones,Brandon	09	L	26	8	aaa	ATL	384	39	92	24	1	6	45	40	69	5	3	240	312	353	665	10%	82%	0.58	81	63	3.92	33
	10	L	27	8	a/a	DET	363	26	70	17	1	3	21	40	64	2	5	193	274	266	540	10%	82%	0.63	54	39	2.43	-5
Jones,Daryl	09	L	22	8	aa	STL	294	39	72	12	2	2	23	26	50	6	5	245	306	320	626	8%	83%	0.52	53	98	3.39	22
	10	L	23	8	aa	STL	451	51	93	15	4	6	36	39	73	12	11	206	270	296	565	8%	84%	0.53	57	108	2.56	-2
Jones,Jacque	10	L	35	8	aaa	MIN	339	24	71	19	0	3	20	12	79	3	0	208	235	286	521	3%	77%	0.15	60	53	2.26	-36
Jones,Mitch	09	R	32	8	aa	LA	387	52	89	20	2	26	75	30	107	7	3	231	286	496	782	7%	72%	0.28	156	89	4.83	57
	10	R	33	8	aaa	PIT	417	37	77	24	1	12	36	17	92	4	6	183	215	330	546	4%	78%	0.19	96	67	2.14	-1
Jones,Travis	09	R	24	4	aa	ATL	366	36	84	21	1	4	36	46	89	21	9	230	316	324	640	11%	76%	0.52	69	93	3.66	10
	10	R	25	4	aa	ATL	71	11	13	2	0	1	4	5	17	2	1	189	241	257	498	6%	77%	0.29	45	98	2.04	-43
Joseph,Caleb	10	R	24	2	aa	BAL	378	34	79	12	1	10	39	25	51	1	7	208	257	323	580	6%	86%	0.49	71	38	2.58	17
Joseph,Corban	10	L	22	4	aa	NYY	111	9	20	5	2	0	11	13	27	1	0	182	269	264	532	11%	76%	0.49	56	121	2.51	-28
Joyce,Matt	09	L	25 a	8	aaa	TAM	417	60	99	30	2	13	55	56	93	11	6	237	328	413	740	12%	78%	0.61	117	95	4.79	59
	10	L	26	8	aaa	TAM	92	14	22	6	0	2	9	17	18	1	4	240	356	370	726	15%	80%	0.90	93	50	4.33	26
Ka'aihue,Kila	09	L	25 a	3	aa	KC	441	61	95	25	1	12	42	77	68	0	1	215	332	360	692	15%	85%	1.13	96	38	4.34	58
	10	L	26 b	3	aaa	KC	323	48	85	15	1	16	56	63	55	2	0	262	383	459	842	16%	83%	1.15	118	53	6.79	60
Kahaulelio,Jacob	10	R	25	4	aa	CIN	408	45	88	23	1	11	39	32	66	4	4	217	273	359	633	7%	84%	0.48	94	63	3.28	27
Kaiser,Kody	10	B	25	8	aa	DET	182	15	39	7	2	3	15	12	47	5	5	212	261	315	576	6%	74%	0.26	65	106	2.57	-36
Kalish,Ryan	09	L	21 a	8	aa	BOS	391	54	103	21	3	10	47	36	70	12	3	263	326	411	737	9%	82%	0.52	95	115	4.93	58
	10	L	22 a	8	a/a	BOS	293	45	81	20	1	10	37	33	40	20	4	276	350	454	804	10%	86%	0.83	116	115	6.05	61
Kata,Matt	09	B	32	4	aa	HOU	227	14	46	8	1	2	14	8	24	5	0	202	228	266	494	3%	90%	0.33	45	83	2.09	28
	10	B	33	5	aaa	HOU	485	41	98	19	1	4	31	17	46	3	0	202	229	270	498	3%	91%	0.37	49	65	2.06	10
Katin,Brendan	09	R	27	8	aaa	MIL	459	49	91	28	4	17	67	27	147	2	0	198	242	389	631	5%	68%	0.18	119	92	3.13	8
	10	R	28	8	aaa	MIL	336	46	76	15	1	19	54	29	83	1	0	225	286	445	731	8%	75%	0.35	130	57	4.41	22
Kazmar,Sean	09	R	25	6	aa	SD	366	30	68	11	0	4	35	28	53	6	2	185	243	247	490	7%	85%	0.53	43	65	2.04	12
	10	R	26	6	aaa	SD	499	51	104	17	2	6	38	28	73	5	2	208	250	282	532	5%	85%	0.38	50	80	2.38	-6
Khoury,Ryan	09	R	26	4	aa	BOS	368	48	75	24	1	2	25	50	89	3	1	204	299	291	590	12%	76%	0.56	69	73	3.13	6
	10	R	27	5	a/a	BOS	289	24	62	18	3	1	15	17	43	3	2	213	258	306	564	6%	85%	0.40	70	89	2.65	9
Kieschnick,Roger	10	L	24	8	aa	SF	223	19	52	8	3	3	20	15	49	2	3	233	280	334	614	6%	78%	0.30	63	95	3.12	-23
Kindel,Jeff	09	L	26	3	aa	COL	463	47	106	23	2	5	49	51	73	6	6	229	305	316	620	10%	84%	0.69	63	66	3.35	29
	10	L	27	3	aa	COL	256	19	53	13	1	4	23	23	36	2	2	207	274	306	580	8%	86%	0.66	68	50	2.84	18

Major League Equivalent Statistics

BATTER	Yr	B	Age	Pos	Lev	Org	ab	r	h	d	t	hr	rbi	bb	k	sb	cs	ba	ob	slg	ops	bb%	ct%	eye	px	sx	rc/g	bpv
Kipnis,Jason	10	L	23	4	aa	CLE	315	49	85	18	3	7	33	25	51	6	1	271	323	411	734	7%	84%	0.48	92	119	4.91	25
Kleen,Steve	10	R	27	3	aa	OAK	132	9	20	5	0	3	14	10	29	1	1	150	209	245	455	7%	78%	0.34	62	41	1.62	-22
Koshansky,Joe	09	L	27	3	aaa	MIL	455	51	78	17	2	17	57	48	151	5	5	172	251	330	581	9%	67%	0.32	95	76	2.67	-13
	10	L	28	3	aaa	MIL	425	46	86	17	0	18	55	45	142	2	2	203	279	373	652	10%	67%	0.32	102	37	3.53	-31
Kozma,Peter	09	R	21	6	aa	STL	407	40	77	13	2	4	29	33	65	3	2	189	250	261	511	8%	84%	0.51	48	76	2.19	14
	10	R	22	6	aa	STL	503	53	105	24	1	9	56	43	84	10	2	209	271	314	585	8%	83%	0.51	72	86	2.97	8
Kratz,Erik	09	R	29	2	aa	PIT	319	32	69	25	0	7	31	22	66	5	0	216	265	359	624	6%	79%	0.32	103	73	3.32	36
	10	R	30	2	aaa	PIT	230	20	47	17	1	6	27	20	47	1	2	203	268	362	630	8%	80%	0.43	109	48	3.21	23
Kroeger,Josh	09	L	27	8	aaa	CHW	501	49	114	23	0	16	46	30	87	19	7	228	271	370	641	6%	83%	0.34	90	81	3.39	40
	10	L	28	3	aaa	CHW	442	36	70	17	1	11	37	32	76	11	7	159	216	279	494	7%	83%	0.42	75	82	1.86	7
Krum,Austin	09	L	24	8	aa	NYY	290	41	64	14	3	2	23	34	67	11	2	220	302	308	610	11%	77%	0.51	61	139	3.43	21
	10	L	25	8	aa	NYY	459	60	89	13	1	5	35	53	73	12	8	195	278	259	537	10%	84%	0.72	44	92	2.47	-6
Kuhn,Tyler	10	L	24	8	aa	CHW	384	42	93	14	3	5	40	30	68	5	6	243	297	333	629	7%	82%	0.44	59	84	3.36	-7
Kulbacki,Kellen	09	L	24	8	aa	SD	134	9	23	4	1	0	9	7	19	2	1	168	209	212	421	5%	86%	0.35	32	86	1.43	6
	10	L	25	8	aa	SD	135	12	24	5	1	2	10	12	21	1	0	178	242	270	513	8%	85%	0.55	60	73	2.23	4
Kunkel,Jeff	09	B	27	2	aa	DET	142	11	26	5	0	3	12	10	29	0	1	181	236	272	508	7%	79%	0.34	59	29	2.06	-12
	10	B	28	2	a/a	DET	230	20	48	5	2	3	18	14	42	1	1	207	251	278	529	6%	82%	0.32	42	72	2.34	-26
LaHair,Bryan	09	L	27	8	aa	SEA	457	59	111	24	1	21	70	39	120	0	6	244	303	439	741	8%	74%	0.32	120	34	4.46	19
	10	L	28	8	aaa	CHC	422	46	103	24	0	17	52	33	74	2	1	243	298	422	721	7%	82%	0.45	114	39	4.43	37
Laird,Brandon	10	R	23	5	a/a	NYY	531	72	133	24	1	24	85	36	96	2	2	251	299	432	731	6%	82%	0.38	109	54	4.52	30
Lalli,Blake	09	L	26	3	aa	CHC	373	39	101	22	0	5	40	25	48	0	2	271	317	368	684	6%	87%	0.52	71	26	4.18	28
	10	L	27	3	aa	CHC	453	42	113	19	0	3	35	47	44	0	2	250	321	310	630	9%	90%	1.05	46	21	3.61	18
Lamb,Mike	09	L	34	5	aa	NYM	440	30	87	22	1	3	37	14	33	0	0	197	223	274	497	3%	93%	0.44	58	31	2.00	34
	10	L	35	5	aaa	FLA	213	23	51	5	0	4	27	14	16	0	0	239	288	323	611	6%	92%	0.88	52	29	3.29	25
Lambin,Chase	10	B	31	5	aaa	WAS	488	39	95	22	2	11	43	33	122	6	3	195	246	315	562	6%	75%	0.27	78	72	2.58	-23
Lambo,Andrew	09	L	21	8	aa	LA	492	61	115	35	1	10	53	34	84	3	3	234	284	372	656	7%	83%	0.41	97	64	3.61	44
	10	L	22	8	aa	PIT	272	31	67	11	1	5	29	19	55	1	1	246	296	349	645	7%	80%	0.35	68	59	3.63	-12
Lane,Jason	09	R	33	8	aaa	TOR	411	41	78	31	3	9	30	37	65	3	2	190	256	341	598	8%	84%	0.56	105	76	2.91	62
	10	R	34	8	aaa	TOR	334	26	62	15	0	5	26	23	51	2	3	186	238	277	516	6%	85%	0.45	64	40	2.11	6
LaPorta,Matt	09	R	25 a	3	aaa	CLE	338	50	87	20	1	13	47	35	50	1	4	258	327	443	770	9%	85%	0.69	117	51	5.06	70
	10	R	26 a	8	aaa	CLE	69	6	21	4	0	4	12	9	9	0	1	300	384	518	901	12%	88%	1.10	133	9	7.34	83
Larish,Jeff	09	L	27	3	aaa	DET	211	31	49	11	0	5	21	34	53	2	2	231	338	349	687	14%	75%	0.64	80	52	4.28	9
	10	L	28	5	aaa	OAK	334	32	70	17	0	12	47	31	72	1	1	210	276	366	643	8%	78%	0.42	100	32	3.45	12
LaTorre,Tyler	09	L	26	2	aa	SF	181	22	41	8	1	1	19	23	33	1	2	229	316	300	616	11%	82%	0.71	53	65	3.36	14
	10	L	27	2	aa	SF	255	22	44	12	1	2	16	28	73	0	3	173	255	247	502	10%	71%	0.38	55	45	2.05	-50
Lavarnway,Ryan	10	R	23	0	aa	BOS	158	19	40	10	0	6	28	19	31	0	0	254	333	428	761	11%	81%	0.61	113	20	5.22	36
Lawrie,Brett	10	R	21	4	aa	MIL	554	74	143	34	10	7	52	41	96	25	16	258	310	396	706	7%	83%	0.43	91	163	4.09	19
Lawson,Matthew	10	R	25	4	aa	SEA	458	57	112	22	4	7	42	37	81	5	5	245	302	354	657	8%	82%	0.46	73	91	3.71	4
Lehmann,Daniel	09	R	24	2	aa	MIN	168	10	28	8	0	0	9	10	17	0	1	166	211	211	422	5%	90%	0.58	40	30	1.41	15
	10	R	25	2	a/a	MIN	182	14	37	7	1	1	9	11	20	0	0	201	248	263	511	6%	89%	0.56	45	44	2.21	5
Lemon,Marcus	09	L	21	4	aa	TEX	451	46	108	18	4	1	33	34	57	6	5	240	293	305	598	7%	87%	0.60	47	92	3.10	30
	10	L	22	8	aa	TEX	468	47	120	21	4	3	34	31	70	6	8	256	303	338	640	6%	85%	0.44	57	83	3.47	0
Leon,Maxwell	09	B	25	8	a/a	DET	265	32	56	9	3	7	30	21	46	5	3	213	270	344	614	7%	83%	0.45	79	113	3.10	45
	10	B	26	0	aaa	DET	298	28	60	8	5	3	20	17	51	2	1	201	245	287	532	6%	83%	0.34	53	113	2.35	-13
Lerud,Steven	09	L	25	2	aa	PIT	304	25	64	15	0	3	20	29	44	2	1	212	280	291	570	9%	86%	0.66	59	42	2.84	22
	10	L	26	2	a/a	BAL	174	15	28	7	1	5	12	18	44	0	0	162	240	292	532	9%	75%	0.41	80	45	2.33	-16
Liddi,Alex	10	R	22	5	aa	SEA	502	61	122	32	5	11	72	40	119	4	9	243	299	392	691	7%	76%	0.34	99	90	3.88	1
Lillibridge,Brent	09	R	26	6	aaa	CHW	246	29	53	7	2	3	20	25	57	14	1	217	289	295	584	9%	77%	0.44	50	132	3.24	8
	10	R	27	6	aaa	CHW	185	19	40	6	0	4	12	13	41	14	4	214	264	306	571	6%	78%	0.31	60	101	2.82	-26
Limonta,Johan	09	L	26	8	aa	SEA	438	47	109	27	5	5	43	46	76	6	6	250	321	363	685	10%	83%	0.60	79	94	4.09	43
	10	L	27	3	aa	SEA	486	58	115	32	1	10	59	40	96	2	4	237	295	369	663	8%	80%	0.41	92	50	3.73	12
Lin,Che-Hsuan	10	R	22	8	aa	BOS	458	65	115	18	3	1	25	53	45	19	15	251	329	310	639	10%	90%	1.18	44	106	3.53	19
Linares,Donell	10	R	27	5	aa	ATL	418	37	82	16	1	8	36	11	38	2	1	196	217	297	514	3%	91%	0.29	66	61	2.08	23
Lindsey,John	09	R	33	3	aa	FLA	443	40	87	18	1	14	62	30	124	1	2	196	246	332	578	6%	72%	0.24	85	41	2.68	-17
	10	R	34	3	aaa	LA	408	40	98	28	2	13	52	9	60	0	0	240	257	410	667	2%	85%	0.16	113	42	3.58	38
Linton,Ollie	10	L	24	8	aa	ARI	398	50	112	12	5	3	32	52	86	19	17	282	365	357	722	12%	78%	0.60	47	119	4.55	-24
Lis,Erik	09	L	26	0	aa	MIN	459	55	113	26	1	13	58	36	98	1	1	246	300	393	693	7%	79%	0.36	97	49	4.17	23
	10	L	27	3	a/a	MIN	449	30	80	16	0	11	51	24	100	0	1	178	220	287	507	5%	78%	0.24	69	19	2.03	-22
Liuzza,Matthew	10	R	27	2	aa	TOR	120	7	24	6	0	3	7	13	29	0	2	199	277	322	599	10%	76%	0.44	83	17	2.88	-10
Lo,Kuo Hui	10	R	25	8	aa	SEA	249	21	48	8	1	3	14	16	43	4	4	193	241	264	505	6%	83%	0.38	48	72	2.03	-16
Lobaton,Jose	09	B	25	2	aa	TAM	217	24	48	12	0	6	16	22	52	0	0	221	293	354	647	9%	76%	0.42	88	26	3.65	3
	10	B	26	2	a/a	TAM	265	23	58	10	0	6	27	24	51	1	0	220	283	323	606	8%	81%	0.46	67	33	3.22	-5
Locke,Andrew	09	R	27	8	aa	HOU	503	58	140	26	2	15	77	33	72	2	2	278	323	424	747	6%	86%	0.46	94	53	4.97	48
	10	R	28	8	aaa	HOU	477	49	105	28	3	13	50	29	80	5	1	221	265	370	635	6%	83%	0.36	98	84	3.36	24
Loewen,Adam	10	L	26	8	aa	TOR	459	49	90	26	2	9	49	46	124	12	6	196	270	321	590	9%	73%	0.37	84	94	2.89	-20
Lombardozzi,Steph	10	B	22 a	4	aa	WAS	105	17	29	5	2	4	11	11	13	4	2	276	345	476	821	9%	88%	0.85	118	150	5.88	66
Lopez,Jesus	09	R	22	6	aa	SD	259	22	50	11	1	1	18	18	29	2	0	193	245	255	500	6%	89%	0.62	47	70	2.15	29
	10	R	23	6	aa	SD	114	11	19	2	0	0	9	10	15	0	0	163	230	181	410	8%	87%	0.64	15	38	1.42	-24
Lopez,Pedro	09	R	25	4	aa	PIT	332	31	77	8	1	2	23	16	34	1	6	232	267	277	545	5%	90%	0.47	31	47	2.38	9
	10	R	26	6	a/a	WAS	217	15	37	10	0	1	12	16	33	4	4	170	225	229	454	7%	85%	0.48	48	58	1.62	-6
Lopez,Roberto	10	R	25	8	aa	LAA	276	27	58	12	1	6	32	22	43	0	6	209	267	320	587	7%	85%	0.52	72	42	2.65	13
Lormand,Ryan	10	R	25	6	a/a	SF	277	21	53	13	2	0	18	11	56	6	3	191	220	253	473	4%	80%	0.19	49	103	1.79	-33
Lough,David	09	L	24 a	8	aa	KC	236	32	70	13	1	7	25	10	23	10	5	295	323	444	767	4%	90%	0.42	96	101	5.07	78
	10	L	25	8	aaa	KC	460	48	111	14	8	8	43	30	55	11	6	242	288	357	645	6%	88%	0.54	68	131	3.53	21
Lowrance,Marvin	09	L	25	8	aa	WAS	361	40	77	20	2	12	39	35	83	1	2	214	283	380	663	9%	77%	0.42	105	59	3.64	30
	10	L	26	8	a/a	WAS	375	44	87	12	2	11	29	35	70	5	6	233	298	363	662	9%	81%	0.50	78	70	3.62	7
Lubanski,Chris	09	L	24	8	aa	KC	132	15	26	7	1	1	12	13	21	5	1	196	271	284	554	9%	84%	0.65	63	114	2.73	42
	10	L	26	8	aaa	TOR	355	41	78	19	4	10	33	24	65	2	1	220	268	381	650	6%	82%	0.36	101	96	3.47	22
Lucas,Edward	09	R	27	5	aa	KC	363	44	86	20	1	6	42	40	67	13	4	236	311	347	658	10%	82%	0.59	77	93	3.91	38
	10	R	28	6	aaa	KC	352	35	86	18	1	8	34	36	57	4	1	245	315	368	683	9%	84%	0.64	81	64	4.22	21
Lucroy,Jonathan	09	R	23 a	2	aa	MIL	419	49	99	28	1	8	53	67	57	1	1	236	341	365	706	14%	86%	1.17	91	42	4.60	60
	10	R	24	2	a/a	MIL	122	12	33	6	0	2	12	6	15	0	0	268	301	362	663	5%	88%	0.39	66	27	3.92	16

Major League Equivalent Statistics

BATTER	Yr	B	Age	Pos	Lev	Org	ab	r	h	d	t	hr	rbi	bb	k	sb	cs	ba	ob	slg	ops	bb%	ct%	eye	px	sx	rc/g	bpv
Lucy,Donny	09	R	27	2	a/a	CHW	222	16	41	7	0	2	10	10	60	2	2	182	217	239	457	4%	73%	0.17	41	51	1.65	-49
	10	R	28	2	aaa	CHW	204	17	35	8	1	2	8	7	48	2	2	173	200	246	446	3%	77%	0.15	52	81	1.52	-44
Luna,Aaron	10	R	24	8	a/a	STL	363	51	79	12	2	11	40	49	62	4	1	219	312	351	663	12%	83%	0.79	79	85	3.94	21
Luna,Hector	09	R	30 b	5	aa	LA	313	44	87	15	3	13	46	22	55	3	2	278	324	464	788	6%	83%	0.39	112	87	5.43	61
	10	R	31	5	aaa	FLA	354	36	77	13	0	10	46	28	60	4	1	219	276	341	617	7%	83%	0.47	76	59	3.27	10
Luna,Omar	10	R	24	6	a/a	TAM	149	14	38	5	1	1	8	2	24	3	2	257	266	322	588	1%	84%	0.08	45	90	2.87	-25
Lutz,Zachary	10	R	24	5	a/a	NYM	245	32	59	15	0	13	36	24	53	0	3	239	307	466	773	9%	78%	0.45	140	27	4.81	45
Machado,Alejandro	10	B	28	4	a/a	ATL	181	19	37	5	0	2	15	20	27	2	2	204	284	263	547	10%	85%	0.74	41	51	2.59	-5
Machado,Andy	09	B	29	6	aa	CHC	153	12	22	5	1	0	6	20	43	7	1	144	244	190	434	12%	72%	0.47	36	110	1.75	-26
	10	B	30	6	aa	MIL	249	15	50	15	1	1	21	28	65	0	1	200	280	280	560	10%	74%	0.42	63	33	2.71	-32
Macias,Drew	09	L	27	8	aa	SD	297	31	53	14	0	4	20	29	51	4	4	180	252	263	515	9%	83%	0.56	60	62	2.17	18
	10	L	28	8	aaa	ARI	274	29	54	9	4	4	16	30	37	5	11	197	276	296	571	10%	87%	0.81	61	106	2.43	17
Macri,Matt	09	R	27	3	aaa	MIN	365	44	67	21	2	8	32	25	82	4	5	182	235	316	551	6%	77%	0.31	89	90	2.30	23
	10	R	28	4	aaa	MIN	338	32	65	18	1	6	25	22	82	2	5	193	242	307	549	6%	76%	0.27	79	56	2.30	-19
Maddox,Marc	09	R	26	4	aa	KC	149	15	20	6	0	3	12	15	18	3	2	136	214	228	442	9%	88%	0.80	61	73	1.55	42
	10	R	27	4	aaa	KC	361	37	77	16	2	1	27	24	46	3	2	214	264	277	541	6%	87%	0.53	48	76	2.49	3
Mahar,Kevin	09	R	28	8	aa	PHI	407	43	104	15	1	10	40	18	77	5	3	255	287	368	655	4%	81%	0.24	71	69	3.69	12
	10	R	29	8	aa	PHI	364	33	72	12	1	9	34	28	80	4	4	198	255	314	569	7%	78%	0.34	72	60	2.60	-15
Mahoney,Joseph	10	L	24	3	aa	BAL	191	24	56	11	1	8	24	13	31	7	1	292	337	482	819	6%	84%	0.42	118	95	6.16	45
Majewski,Val	09	L	28	8	aa	LAA	131	14	26	4	1	3	14	11	22	4	1	195	259	296	555	8%	84%	0.53	61	100	2.64	31
	10	L	29	8	aa	OAK	302	25	59	14	0	6	39	26	64	3	2	196	260	302	562	8%	79%	0.40	71	50	2.65	-10
Maldonado,Brahiar	10	R	25	8	aa	NYM	250	27	56	16	3	9	25	12	67	5	3	226	262	425	687	5%	73%	0.18	125	120	3.64	4
Maldonado,Carlos	10	R	32	2	aaa	WAS	188	12	32	6	0	3	20	14	45	2	1	172	228	244	472	7%	76%	0.30	49	42	1.83	-40
Maldonado,Martin	10	R	24	2	a/a	MIL	277	21	59	13	0	7	29	18	59	1	4	211	260	333	593	6%	79%	0.31	80	28	2.76	-7
Malo,Jonathan	09	R	26	4	aa	NYM	366	31	67	8	2	1	24	27	55	8	4	182	239	221	460	7%	85%	0.49	27	91	1.77	4
	10	R	27	6	a/a	NYM	267	26	45	12	2	2	16	21	51	4	6	169	230	248	478	7%	81%	0.41	56	92	1.74	-15
Mangini,Matthew	09	L	24	5	aa	SEA	422	42	103	17	3	10	59	34	89	9	2	244	301	367	668	8%	79%	0.39	77	97	3.96	24
	10	L	25	5	aaa	SEA	447	54	116	26	2	12	47	20	81	2	0	260	292	410	702	4%	82%	0.25	98	71	4.26	17
Manzella,Tommy	09	R	26	6	aa	HOU	530	48	124	26	4	6	40	29	85	8	4	234	273	333	607	5%	84%	0.34	68	91	3.13	30
	10	R	27	6	a/a	HOU	41	6	13	3	0	1	4	2	6	0	2	307	336	439	775	4%	86%	0.32	92	61	4.59	30
Marrero,Chris	10	R	22	3	aa	WAS	524	65	142	27	0	15	73	38	88	1	3	271	320	408	729	7%	83%	0.43	90	34	4.68	20
Marrero,Christian	09	L	23 a	3	aa	CHW	229	25	64	14	1	11	34	16	45	1	1	278	324	488	812	6%	80%	0.35	130	48	5.72	55
	10	L	24	8	aa	CHW	488	44	114	24	2	7	54	60	76	10	6	234	317	332	650	11%	84%	0.78	68	70	3.77	16
Marson,Lou	09	R	23	2	aaa	CLE	314	33	77	16	1	2	26	33	50	3	1	247	319	321	640	10%	84%	0.67	57	64	3.77	22
	10	R	24	2	aaa	CLE	124	14	20	6	1	3	11	16	20	4	0	163	260	294	554	12%	84%	0.82	84	110	2.73	29
Marti,Amaury	10	R	36	8	aaa	STL	256	22	56	8	0	8	34	12	44	0	0	219	254	339	592	4%	83%	0.27	73	20	2.91	1
Martin,Dustin	09	L	25	8	aaa	MIN	422	47	91	14	4	4	42	29	85	21	8	216	267	294	561	6%	80%	0.34	51	133	2.65	15
	10	L	26	8	aaa	MIN	483	51	99	19	5	7	48	36	118	8	7	206	261	310	571	7%	75%	0.30	67	108	2.63	-28
Martinez,Fernando	09	L	21 a	8	aa	NYM	176	20	46	14	1	6	24	9	26	2	1	263	300	462	763	5%	85%	0.35	132	75	4.88	81
	10	L	22	8	aaa	NYM	257	30	57	14	0	9	25	13	51	1	0	220	258	381	639	5%	80%	0.26	103	52	3.34	14
Martinez,J.D.	10	R	23	8	aa	HOU	189	21	53	9	1	3	22	13	39	2	2	280	325	384	709	6%	79%	0.33	70	68	4.48	-11
Martinez,Luis	10	R	25	2	aa	SD	358	39	83	13	1	2	25	41	59	3	2	231	311	289	600	10%	84%	0.71	43	60	3.25	-8
Martinez,Michael	09	B	27	4	aa	WAS	188	18	36	6	2	1	6	16	33	0	3	191	256	259	514	8%	82%	0.49	46	75	2.11	6
	10	B	28	4	a/a	WAS	485	44	107	18	4	8	43	18	72	18	11	221	249	325	573	4%	85%	0.25	65	117	2.53	2
Martinez,Osvaldo	10	R	22	6	aa	FLA	516	75	143	27	3	4	45	43	57	11	10	277	333	364	697	8%	89%	0.75	63	93	4.30	24
Mastroianni,Darin	09	R	24	8	aa	TOR	247	36	62	10	2	1	23	36	47	36	8	253	349	319	668	13%	81%	0.78	47	150	4.55	35
	10	R	25	8	aa	TOR	525	72	130	22	5	3	33	56	83	33	11	247	320	322	642	10%	84%	0.68	53	136	3.79	0
Mather,Joe	09	R	27	8	aa	STL	194	14	28	7	1	3	17	10	32	5	4	144	185	232	417	5%	83%	0.31	58	92	1.26	20
	10	R	28	8	aaa	STL	335	35	69	13	2	6	29	24	60	4	4	205	258	310	568	7%	82%	0.39	68	78	2.58	-2
Mathews,Aaron	09	R	27	8	aaa	TOR	518	45	112	17	4	5	52	25	43	3	2	215	252	294	545	5%	92%	0.58	52	73	2.48	41
	10	R	28	8	aaa	TOR	327	26	77	19	1	6	26	14	40	2	0	234	266	355	621	4%	88%	0.35	84	53	3.27	29
Matsui,Kaz	10	B	35	4	aaa	COL	301	30	58	9	3	1	16	17	35	4	0	192	235	249	484	5%	88%	0.48	39	110	2.01	-3
Matthews Jr.,Gary	10	B	36	8	aaa	CIN	101	11	25	6	1	3	4	5	25	2	2	244	280	396	676	5%	76%	0.21	99	97	3.64	-7
Matulia,John	10	L	24	8	aa	TAM	475	44	112	20	6	8	49	28	107	3	5	236	279	352	630	6%	77%	0.26	73	91	3.28	-19
Maxwell,Justin	09	R	26	8	aaa	WAS	384	55	81	8	4	10	34	43	120	28	8	211	290	333	623	10%	69%	0.36	70	157	3.40	0
	10	R	27	8	aaa	WAS	230	28	56	15	0	5	17	28	68	13	7	244	325	368	693	11%	70%	0.40	88	82	4.11	-26
May,Lucas	09	R	25	2	aa	LA	235	26	63	15	1	5	26	26	54	2	1	270	342	404	747	10%	77%	0.48	93	60	5.14	22
	10	R	26	2	a/a	KC	375	45	89	19	2	10	42	26	66	3	2	238	288	381	669	7%	82%	0.40	91	75	3.80	18
Mayberry,John	09	R	26	8	aaa	PHI	316	36	71	18	1	11	35	26	86	5	2	223	283	393	675	8%	73%	0.31	108	76	3.81	17
	10	R	27	8	aaa	PHI	495	60	114	21	1	13	52	31	107	17	3	230	276	355	631	6%	78%	0.29	80	104	3.47	-8
Maybin,Cameron	09	R	22 a	8	aa	FLA	298	39	89	17	7	3	34	35	54	7	2	299	372	433	805	11%	82%	0.65	87	160	6.28	68
	10	R	23	8	aaa	FLA	130	16	38	5	1	3	17	10	19	4	1	294	343	415	758	7%	85%	0.51	75	95	5.41	16
Mayora,Daniel	09	R	24	4	aa	COL	441	48	114	21	1	6	38	31	65	16	9	259	307	350	658	7%	85%	0.48	65	87	3.76	34
	10	R	25 a	5	aa	COL	234	21	60	20	3	3	23	16	28	3	7	257	305	402	706	6%	88%	0.58	104	87	3.92	51
Mayorson,Manuel	09	R	27	4	a/a	TOR	399	36	82	12	2	1	20	14	27	11	5	205	232	251	483	3%	93%	0.51	34	103	1.92	40
	10	R	28	6	a/a	TOR	361	38	87	22	0	1	26	16	19	12	0	242	274	309	584	4%	95%	0.86	57	98	3.12	35
Maysonet,Edwin	09	R	28	4	aa	HOU	187	14	34	9	0	1	10	18	33	2	0	183	255	245	500	9%	82%	0.54	50	50	2.19	3
	10	R	29	6	aaa	HOU	302	19	59	11	1	2	24	17	56	2	2	195	237	254	491	5%	82%	0.30	43	51	1.98	-27
Maza,Luis	09	R	29	4	aa	LA	327	40	77	15	2	3	33	13	42	0	1	234	263	321	584	4%	87%	0.31	61	66	2.86	27
	10	R	30	4	aaa	HOU	199	14	33	5	1	1	9	14	27	1	0	167	220	214	433	6%	86%	0.50	33	60	1.57	-13
McAnulty,Paul	09	L	29	3	a/a	COL	381	26	69	18	1	10	36	33	76	0	1	180	245	310	554	8%	80%	0.43	84	26	2.50	13
	10	L	30	0	a/a	LAA	423	47	101	16	1	15	52	32	64	1	3	238	291	390	682	7%	85%	0.50	93	38	3.86	30
McBride,Matt	09	R	24 a	8	aa	CLE	361	42	81	27	0	11	55	16	41	1	1	223	257	386	643	4%	89%	0.40	111	51	3.32	70
	10	R	25	8	a/a	CLE	481	53	111	26	1	14	55	26	66	0	2	231	271	377	648	5%	86%	0.40	96	38	3.44	34
McBryde,Mike	09	R	25	8	aa	SF	376	58	100	21	3	4	36	15	56	18	12	266	294	368	662	4%	85%	0.27	72	135	3.52	48
	10	R	26	8	aaa	SF	74	8	15	4	0	2	6	1	13	0	2	203	213	330	544	1%	83%	0.07	84	12	1.95	3
McConnell,Chris	09	R	24	6	aa	KC	169	20	33	7	1	0	9	11	31	5	6	197	245	249	495	6%	82%	0.35	41	109	1.82	7
	10	R	25	6	aa	KC	359	32	71	17	3	2	28	36	56	8	8	198	270	278	548	9%	84%	0.63	58	91	2.44	4
McCoy,Mike	09	R	28 b	6	aa	COL	462	74	118	23	4	2	38	57	61	29	6	255	337	331	669	11%	87%	0.93	56	138	4.34	57
	10	R	29	6	aaa	TOR	213	26	46	10	1	3	14	20	23	9	3	214	281	319	600	8%	89%	0.85	71	107	3.16	32
McKenry,Michael	09	R	25 a	2	aa	COL	358	41	90	23	1	11	39	42	55	2	2	252	331	410	741	11%	85%	0.77	105	49	4.90	60
	10	R	26	2	aaa	COL	347	26	74	19	1	7	30	19	50	1	1	214	254	330	585	5%	86%	0.38	80	43	2.82	18
McLouth,Nate	10	L	29	8	aaa	ATL	128	13	24	1	0	4	13	14	20	5	0	186	266	296	562	10%	84%	0.69	59	77	2.88	5

Major League Equivalent Statistics

BATTER	Yr	B	Age	Pos	Lev	Org	ab	r	h	d	t	hr	rbi	bb	k	sb	cs	ba	ob	slg	ops	bb%	ct%	eye	px	sx	rc/g	bpv
McPherson,Dallas	10	L	30	0	aaa	OAK	318	30	59	12	1	12	45	19	82	1	0	184	230	339	569	6%	74%	0.23	93	52	2.56	-16
Mejia,Ernesto	10	R	25	0	aa	KC	261	26	60	16	0	8	35	16	64	1	0	228	273	379	652	6%	76%	0.26	101	40	3.59	-3
Melillo,Kevin	09	L	27	3	aa	MIL	385	44	77	18	2	7	39	47	64	3	3	201	288	313	601	11%	83%	0.73	74	68	3.10	37
	10	L	28	8	aaa	PIT	352	37	75	19	3	6	28	29	45	6	5	213	273	335	608	8%	87%	0.64	82	92	3.00	32
Mench,Kevin	10	R	33	8	aaa	WAS	281	20	54	13	0	3	30	26	29	3	1	194	261	266	527	8%	90%	0.87	54	45	2.39	20
Mendez,Carlos	10	R	24	3	aa	CIN	130	12	25	4	1	0	5	7	16	0	1	192	232	236	468	5%	88%	0.43	33	74	1.75	-10
Mercado,Orlando	09	R	25	2	aa	ARI	283	26	76	15	1	2	34	35	23	0	0	268	348	349	697	11%	92%	1.51	62	30	4.62	49
	10	R	26	2	a/a	ATL	291	26	65	8	0	1	20	35	35	2	2	223	306	258	564	11%	88%	0.99	28	40	2.86	-3
Mercer,Jordy	10	R	24	5	aa	PIT	485	53	119	28	1	2	52	24	57	6	1	245	281	319	600	5%	88%	0.42	59	81	3.18	11
Merchan,Jesus	09	R	28	4	a/a	CLE	141	14	35	5	1	0	9	8	20	1	0	250	290	300	589	5%	85%	0.39	39	71	3.12	7
	10	R	30	6	aaa	TOR	149	9	33	10	1	1	6	6	8	0	3	219	250	317	567	4%	95%	0.74	75	49	2.44	48
Mertins,Kurt	09	R	23	4	aa	KC	495	49	122	23	6	1	44	32	83	9	12	245	292	321	612	6%	83%	0.39	54	103	3.06	22
	10	R	24	4	a/a	KC	327	35	71	13	3	3	26	17	43	5	0	217	257	302	559	5%	87%	0.40	58	111	2.71	6
Mesoraco,Devin	10	R	22 a	2	a/a	CIN	239	37	61	13	2	14	35	19	41	1	1	255	310	502	812	7%	83%	0.46	146	84	5.47	65
Metcalf,Travis	09	R	27	5	aa	TEX	440	35	77	15	2	8	40	28	87	3	1	176	225	274	499	6%	80%	0.32	63	67	2.02	6
	10	R	28	5	aaa	COL	416	37	94	26	3	6	38	26	59	2	3	226	273	347	619	6%	86%	0.45	85	63	3.19	25
Meyer,Drew	09	L	28	4	aa	HOU	443	48	100	23	1	4	34	33	66	2	0	226	281	306	587	7%	85%	0.51	60	61	3.03	23
	10	L	29	4	aaa	LAA	261	18	49	9	2	2	15	20	40	3	1	188	245	257	502	7%	85%	0.50	48	74	2.13	-6
Miclat,Gregory	10	B	23	6	aa	BAL	228	27	50	8	1	1	13	19	41	3	7	219	278	275	553	8%	82%	0.46	41	77	2.39	-22
Mier,Jessie	10	R	26	2	aa	LA	145	11	31	5	0	1	10	8	20	2	1	214	257	266	523	6%	86%	0.42	39	51	2.32	-12
Miller,Corky	10	R	35	2	aaa	CIN	181	20	38	10	0	4	24	14	29	0	1	211	266	338	605	7%	84%	0.46	86	37	3.01	20
Miller,Jai	09	R	25	8	aa	FLA	343	47	88	22	2	12	44	34	103	5	3	257	324	442	766	9%	70%	0.33	118	88	5.10	21
	10	R	26	8	aaa	KC	345	34	73	22	1	12	41	27	102	4	4	213	270	387	657	7%	70%	0.27	113	62	3.43	-12
Miller,Matthew	09	R	27 b	8	aa	COL	523	63	145	34	6	7	75	38	66	3	1	278	327	410	736	7%	87%	0.57	90	98	4.94	66
	10	R	28	8	aaa	COL	507	53	129	18	1	6	48	38	63	1	0	254	306	330	636	7%	88%	0.60	52	46	3.66	8
Mills,Beau	09	L	23	3	aa	CLE	516	53	128	31	1	12	74	29	90	1	2	249	289	382	671	5%	83%	0.33	91	42	3.84	28
	10	L	24	3	aa	CLE	427	41	87	22	1	7	55	33	59	2	1	205	261	308	569	7%	86%	0.55	72	57	2.73	18
Miranda,Juan	09	L	26	3	aaa	NYY	438	64	112	27	1	17	72	48	104	1	0	256	329	441	771	10%	76%	0.46	118	54	5.32	37
	10	L	27	3	aaa	NYY	295	41	70	12	1	14	34	27	69	1	0	238	302	421	723	8%	77%	0.39	109	60	4.51	12
Mitchell,Jermaine	10	L	26	8	a/a	OAK	132	12	23	3	2	0	9	14	34	2	7	171	251	221	472	10%	74%	0.41	32	117	1.53	-57
Mitchell,Lee	09	R	27	5	aa	FLA	431	41	83	21	3	9	49	58	160	1	0	192	287	315	603	12%	63%	0.36	80	66	3.18	-39
	10	R	28	3	a/a	FLA	358	28	79	20	4	5	42	20	92	5	1	221	263	347	609	5%	74%	0.22	84	115	3.14	-23
Mitchell,Michael	10	R	25	8	aa	COL	152	13	31	4	3	2	8	12	29	8	1	204	263	303	566	7%	81%	0.43	57	157	2.86	-13
Mitchell,Russ	09	R	25	3	aa	LA	456	52	96	26	2	11	52	31	78	3	1	211	260	345	606	6%	83%	0.39	90	77	3.05	41
	10	R	26	5	aaa	LA	505	57	118	28	1	13	51	22	54	1	4	235	266	372	638	4%	89%	0.40	91	47	3.28	40
Molina,Gustavo	09	R	28	2	aaa	WAS	211	14	36	13	0	2	18	5	23	0	1	171	188	256	444	2%	89%	0.19	66	39	1.47	27
	10	R	29	2	aaa	BOS	112	9	23	5	0	5	13	5	20	0	0	204	240	393	633	5%	82%	0.26	115	10	3.12	30
Mollenhauer,Dale	10	L	24	4	aa	CHW	343	27	78	14	1	1	22	26	49	13	5	227	281	283	564	7%	86%	0.53	44	87	2.80	-6
Montanez,Lou	10	R	29	8	a/a	BAL	106	11	26	4	1	2	14	3	11	2	1	241	259	349	608	2%	89%	0.23	70	98	3.03	20
Montero,Jesus	09	R	20 a	2	aa	NYY	167	19	55	11	0	9	34	14	19	0	0	327	378	560	937	8%	89%	0.72	143	10	8.31	89
	10	R	21 a	2	aaa	NYY	453	60	125	30	2	22	68	44	78	0	0	275	340	493	833	9%	83%	0.57	136	41	6.20	60
Montz,Luke	09	R	26	2	a/a	WAS	320	27	50	13	0	7	29	38	64	1	4	155	244	265	509	11%	80%	0.59	71	30	2.07	9
	10	R	27	2	aa	NYM	110	6	15	3	0	1	10	7	27	0	3	139	192	188	380	6%	76%	0.27	34	37	1.00	-55
Moore,Adam	09	R	25	2	aa	SEA	435	46	108	21	0	9	47	37	72	1	1	249	307	361	668	8%	83%	0.51	76	35	3.96	22
	10	R	26	2	aaa	SEA	134	13	34	6	1	2	11	6	21	1	0	254	284	357	641	4%	85%	0.27	70	72	3.60	4
Moore,Jerome	10	L	23	8	aa	LAA	456	57	123	13	6	11	48	30	98	19	12	269	314	393	708	6%	79%	0.31	73	134	4.22	-13
Moore,Scott	09	L	26 a	5	aaa	BAL	123	16	28	7	0	7	18	7	20	1	0	229	268	443	712	5%	84%	0.33	130	54	4.10	67
	10	L	27	5	aaa	BAL	225	26	54	7	1	9	33	16	40	2	3	241	291	405	695	6%	82%	0.39	96	61	3.94	20
Morales,Jose	09	B	27	2	aaa	MIN	211	24	60	11	1	2	21	21	26	1	3	283	349	371	719	9%	88%	0.81	64	52	4.70	37
	10	B	28	0	aaa	MIN	258	21	53	15	1	2	18	23	56	0	0	206	272	293	565	8%	78%	0.42	66	36	2.76	-14
Morel,Brent	10	R	23	5	a/a	CHW	490	53	139	32	3	9	52	23	73	7	6	284	315	416	731	4%	85%	0.31	92	80	4.63	24
Moreland,Mitch	09	L	24 a	8	aa	TEX	301	40	86	17	3	7	46	18	36	1	1	287	328	431	758	6%	88%	0.50	94	81	5.18	64
	10	L	25	8	aaa	TEX	353	38	86	24	2	9	47	34	51	2	1	245	311	405	716	9%	86%	0.66	107	62	4.49	47
Morrison,Logan	09	L	22 a	3	aa	FLA	278	42	72	17	2	7	41	58	43	8	4	259	387	410	797	17%	85%	1.35	99	93	6.07	82
	10	L	23 a	3	aaa	FLA	238	26	63	15	3	4	33	37	29	1	2	264	363	399	763	14%	88%	1.30	91	75	5.39	54
Moss,Brandon	10	L	27	8	aaa	PIT	500	51	105	26	1	14	68	29	98	8	7	211	254	353	606	5%	80%	0.29	92	72	2.86	9
Mota,Jonathan	09	R	22	6	aa	CHC	320	27	71	15	1	2	19	29	51	2	7	222	287	294	580	8%	84%	0.57	54	46	2.72	12
	10	R	23	4	a/a	CHC	53	3	11	2	0	1	3	2	9	0	0	203	232	296	528	4%	83%	0.21	61	11	2.27	-11
Mount,Ryan	09	L	23	4	aa	LAA	305	31	72	16	0	3	27	18	58	5	8	235	276	315	591	5%	81%	0.30	60	59	2.75	3
	10	L	24	4	aa	LAA	308	28	61	12	2	8	32	12	65	6	5	199	231	324	555	4%	79%	0.19	77	93	2.32	-12
Moustakas,Michae	10	L	22 a	5	a/a	KC	484	72	140	40	0	25	95	26	49	2	1	289	325	527	852	5%	90%	0.53	153	51	6.28	94
Munson,Eric	09	L	32	2	aa	OAK	351	31	66	16	1	8	43	33	59	0	1	189	259	305	564	9%	83%	0.56	77	35	2.65	24
	10	L	33	3	aaa	SD	134	9	19	2	0	4	13	18	34	0	1	140	241	247	488	12%	75%	0.52	60	17	1.95	-28
Murphy,Donnie	10	R	28	6	aaa	FLA	206	21	45	10	1	8	23	12	37	0	0	218	260	393	654	5%	82%	0.32	107	40	3.47	27
Myrow,Brian	09	L	33	8	a/a	PIT	365	43	88	19	1	10	43	44	66	3	2	240	322	380	702	11%	82%	0.67	91	54	4.39	40
	10	L	34	3	aaa	PIT	301	28	50	9	1	4	28	35	64	3	1	167	253	246	499	10%	79%	0.55	52	65	2.14	-20
Nava,Daniel	09	B	27 b	8	aa	BOS	118	19	39	10	1	3	17	19	11	0	0	327	422	499	921	14%	91%	1.78	119	55	8.67	105
	10	B	28	8	aaa	BOS	284	31	71	16	1	7	36	21	57	3	2	250	301	390	691	7%	80%	0.37	93	63	4.12	10
Navarro Jr,Efren	10	L	24	3	aa	LAA	453	36	106	22	1	5	38	23	39	5	5	233	270	318	588	5%	91%	0.60	61	55	2.87	27
Navarro,Dioner	10	B	27	2	aaa	TAM	141	14	32	7	0	2	16	17	22	2	0	228	309	320	629	11%	85%	0.76	66	50	3.65	14
Navarro,Oswaldo	09	R	25	6	aa	SEA	349	31	79	12	1	1	21	36	76	7	3	226	299	272	571	9%	78%	0.48	36	72	2.94	-16
	10	R	26	6	aaa	HOU	288	29	65	20	1	5	26	24	56	2	4	225	286	349	635	8%	80%	0.43	89	56	3.32	10
Navarro,Yamaico	09	R	22	6	aa	BOS	135	13	24	7	1	2	9	12	23	4	1	180	247	292	539	8%	83%	0.53	76	106	2.45	44
	10	R	23	6	a/a	BOS	382	44	99	25	2	8	48	36	45	14	7	259	323	398	721	9%	88%	0.80	95	95	4.54	48
Nazario,Radames	10	R	23	6	aa	COL	192	13	43	9	0	2	17	20	33	1	1	225	296	301	598	9%	83%	0.60	56	28	3.15	-2
Neal,Thomas	10	R	23	8	aa	SF	525	60	144	38	1	10	60	39	84	10	5	274	325	407	732	7%	84%	0.47	95	73	4.78	28
Negron,Kristopher	10	R	25	6	a/a	CIN	491	61	114	18	4	10	32	39	88	27	11	233	290	344	634	7%	82%	0.45	70	130	3.43	2
Negron,Miguel	09	L	27	8	aaa	CHW	384	33	90	13	2	4	32	22	63	12	13	234	275	305	580	5%	84%	0.34	48	83	2.61	10
	10	L	28	8	aa	CHW	145	20	28	4	0	3	11	14	13	5	3	194	266	279	545	9%	91%	1.13	55	92	2.49	29
Negrych,James	09	L	25 a	4	aa	PIT	323	40	78	16	1	2	24	35	30	7	1	241	314	315	629	10%	91%	1.14	57	88	3.69	56
	10	L	26	4	a/a	PIT	396	44	94	16	3	3	40	39	65	8	8	237	305	313	618	9%	84%	0.59	53	88	3.27	-3
Nelson,Brad	09	L	27	0	aa	SEA	275	29	57	7	1	12	37	26	58	0	0	207	275	371	647	9%	79%	0.45	94	34	3.50	21
	10	L	28	0	aaa	SEA	409	41	82	20	0	12	41	43	69	2	2	200	277	334	611	10%	83%	0.63	87	39	3.15	23

Major League Equivalent Statistics

BATTER	Yr	B	Age	Pos	Lev	Org	ab	r	h	d	t	hr	rbi	bb	k	sb	cs	ba	ob	slg	ops	bb%	ct%	eye	px	sx	rc/g	bpv
Nelson,Chris	09	R	24 a	6	aa	COL	107	16	27	5	2	4	13	10	17	4	2	251	313	440	752	8%	84%	0.58	111	152	4.75	91
	10	R	25	6	aaa	COL	319	37	82	12	2	8	34	18	34	5	4	256	296	377	673	5%	89%	0.52	76	82	3.84	30
Nelson,Kevin	09	R	28	2	a/a	PHI	170	16	35	7	1	7	20	17	34	0	1	207	278	383	661	9%	80%	0.49	105	42	3.57	37
	10	R	29	2	aa	PHI	174	9	32	6	0	2	12	8	34	0	1	183	218	247	465	4%	81%	0.23	46	23	1.71	-30
Nickeas,Michael	10	R	28	2	a/a	NYM	293	19	62	13	0	4	22	32	43	1	1	212	290	292	582	10%	85%	0.75	57	24	2.99	8
Nicolas,Cesar	10	R	28	0	aa	DET	244	19	54	15	0	5	26	23	44	1	0	220	287	346	633	9%	82%	0.52	88	30	3.49	17
Nieuwenhuis,Kirk	10	L	23	8	a/a	NYM	514	66	119	36	2	14	56	28	104	10	9	231	271	389	660	5%	80%	0.27	107	93	3.41	17
Nieves,Abel	10	R	25	5	a/a	LAA	326	22	61	5	2	2	16	29	49	1	2	187	254	231	485	8%	85%	0.60	27	50	1.98	-20
Nivar,Ramon	09	R	30 b	4	aa	LA	171	22	40	13	2	3	15	3	20	10	6	231	247	372	619	2%	88%	0.17	99	156	2.75	86
	10	R	31	5	a/a	LA	178	16	37	11	1	1	14	3	14	5	6	205	217	291	508	1%	92%	0.18	67	105	1.75	26
Noonan,Nick	10	L	21	4	aa	SF	372	38	85	12	2	3	23	19	63	6	3	228	266	296	562	5%	83%	0.30	46	91	2.68	-19
Norman,Anthony	10	L	26	8	aa	PIT	191	22	36	7	1	3	15	21	41	3	2	187	266	276	542	10%	78%	0.50	58	84	2.49	-19
Nowak,Christopher	09	R	27	5	a/a	TAM	437	40	99	20	2	5	49	33	90	6	2	227	282	314	595	7%	79%	0.37	61	81	3.11	7
	10	R	28	3	aa	MIL	404	43	77	14	1	9	44	44	92	9	2	192	271	296	567	10%	77%	0.48	66	86	2.82	-17
Nowlin,Billy	10	R	24	0	aa	DET	142	14	33	10	1	4	20	2	32	0	0	235	245	400	645	1%	78%	0.06	110	58	3.30	4
Nunez,Eduardo	09	R	22	6	aa	NYY	497	68	156	25	1	9	54	21	61	19	7	314	342	423	764	4%	88%	0.34	74	96	5.42	49
	10	R	23	6	aaa	NYY	464	48	120	22	2	4	43	29	54	20	6	258	302	338	640	6%	88%	0.54	58	103	3.69	14
Nunez,Luis	10	R	24	6	aa	NYY	449	48	93	20	3	8	35	22	58	6	12	207	244	316	560	5%	87%	0.37	71	87	2.29	17
Oeltjen,Trent	09	L	27 b	8	aa	ARI	442	60	120	26	13	8	49	24	88	17	8	271	308	443	751	5%	80%	0.27	106	209	4.72	80
	10	L	28	8	aaa	LA	465	49	105	30	3	7	40	23	73	15	9	226	264	348	612	5%	84%	0.32	86	108	2.98	17
Olmedo,Ray	09	B	28	5	aaa	TAM	412	31	84	11	2	4	36	16	73	6	7	203	232	269	502	4%	82%	0.22	43	73	1.94	-5
	10	B	29	4	aaa	MIL	416	44	89	16	3	3	37	18	66	7	6	213	246	283	529	4%	84%	0.27	50	98	2.24	-14
O'Malley,Shawn	10	B	23	4	aa	TAM	144	15	24	1	2	0	6	13	27	8	1	167	236	201	437	8%	81%	0.48	18	157	1.77	-42
Orlando,Paulo	10	R	25	8	aa	KC	419	61	110	20	4	9	46	17	47	18	12	263	293	392	684	4%	89%	0.37	83	134	3.78	31
Orr,Pete	09	L	30	5	aaa	WAS	412	37	79	10	3	6	37	20	75	13	8	192	228	276	505	5%	82%	0.26	52	115	1.98	14
	10	L	31	8	aaa	WAS	489	46	100	26	5	9	33	24	89	19	9	205	242	330	572	5%	82%	0.27	82	133	2.57	4
Ortiz,Gabriel	10	R	25	2	aa	OAK	115	9	21	5	0	1	10	4	25	1	1	184	210	250	460	3%	78%	0.15	50	54	1.65	-39
Ortiz,Yancarlos	09	B	25	6	aa	MIN	327	26	63	6	2	0	22	30	66	2	3	193	261	221	482	8%	80%	0.46	20	64	1.96	-26
	10	B	26	6	a/a	MIN	229	14	33	4	1	1	14	12	43	2	0	145	187	181	368	5%	81%	0.28	24	70	1.11	-45
Osuna,Renny	09	R	24	6	aa	TEX	252	28	54	6	1	0	14	17	28	0	5	213	264	244	508	6%	89%	0.61	24	55	2.04	6
	10	R	25	5	aa	TEX	450	47	118	19	5	4	39	23	69	16	10	261	296	349	645	5%	85%	0.33	59	118	3.49	-3
Otness,John	09	R	28	2	a/a	BOS	118	9	26	9	0	1	12	11	18	0	0	224	292	321	613	9%	85%	0.63	78	17	3.32	25
	10	R	29	2	aa	FLA	116	8	22	5	0	1	12	9	13	0	1	185	242	252	494	7%	89%	0.67	51	29	1.98	12
Overbeck,Cody	10	R	24	5	aa	PHI	275	35	60	9	1	11	30	18	67	0	1	216	265	370	635	6%	76%	0.27	90	54	3.29	-10
Padilla,Jorge	09	R	30	8	aaa	WAS	311	43	91	14	2	3	15	18	32	10	10	292	331	374	705	5%	90%	0.56	59	96	4.20	48
	10	R	31	8	aaa	NYM	345	38	82	16	0	4	32	20	49	9	4	239	280	323	603	5%	86%	0.40	60	77	3.10	4
Padron,Jorge	10	L	24	8	aa	BOS	182	11	46	11	0	0	13	7	18	1	0	253	280	311	591	4%	90%	0.38	51	33	3.09	11
Pagnozzi,Matt	09	R	27	2	aa	STL	253	15	45	6	0	4	23	18	64	0	1	178	234	244	478	7%	75%	0.29	42	18	1.87	-47
	10	R	28	2	aaa	STL	207	13	38	8	0	1	14	17	39	0	0	183	245	235	480	8%	81%	0.44	41	17	1.96	-25
Pahuta,Tim	10	L	27	5	aa	WAS	283	28	50	12	1	8	30	13	64	4	0	175	210	308	519	4%	77%	0.20	84	90	2.12	-14
Paiml,Gregory	10	R	26	6	aa	CHW	232	22	46	7	1	2	17	8	50	4	1	198	226	262	488	3%	78%	0.17	44	92	1.96	-42
Paramore,Petey	10	B	24	2	aa	OAK	205	16	46	7	0	2	15	26	44	0	0	225	313	287	600	11%	79%	0.60	44	15	3.30	-25
Parejo,Freddy	09	R	25	8	a/a	MIL	300	24	60	12	1	2	20	13	49	2	4	198	233	266	498	4%	84%	0.27	50	60	1.94	3
	10	R	26	8	aa	HOU	170	12	45	7	1	0	14	6	30	6	1	265	289	315	604	3%	82%	0.19	39	90	3.33	-30
Parmelee,Chris	10	L	23	3	aa	MIN	411	40	99	22	1	5	34	33	55	2	2	241	297	336	633	7%	87%	0.60	68	50	3.51	18
Parraz,Jordan	09	R	25 a	8	aa	KC	273	32	84	22	2	5	36	26	31	3	12	309	369	457	826	9%	89%	0.83	105	62	5.61	76
	10	R	26	8	aaa	KC	432	42	98	24	1	8	44	28	61	6	6	226	274	339	613	6%	86%	0.47	79	64	3.08	21
Parrino,Andrew	10	B	25	6	aa	SD	410	59	83	23	3	9	41	59	110	3	2	201	301	335	636	12%	73%	0.53	89	91	3.54	-10
Pascucci,Val	09	R	31	3	aa	SD	436	43	77	17	1	12	53	45	118	2	0	175	253	300	553	9%	73%	0.38	78	55	2.57	-8
	10	R	32	8	aaa	NYM	190	26	37	8	0	11	25	27	61	0	0	192	294	407	701	13%	68%	0.44	126	25	4.12	-1
Pastornicky,Tyler	10	R	21	6	aa	ATL	134	19	31	4	1	2	12	14	18	9	2	231	305	323	628	10%	86%	0.78	58	129	3.66	13
Patchett,Gary	09	R	31	6	aa	LAA	313	30	62	8	1	3	20	15	64	0	7	198	236	253	488	5%	80%	0.24	37	48	1.77	-26
	10	R	32	6	aaa	LAA	196	10	36	3	1	1	14	8	40	0	3	182	213	221	434	4%	80%	0.19	26	42	1.42	-51
Paul,Xavier	09	L	25 a	8	aa	LA	116	11	34	9	1	2	13	9	21	7	2	290	339	430	769	7%	82%	0.41	99	106	5.45	55
	10	L	26	8	aaa	LA	228	27	55	15	0	7	23	10	29	4	4	243	276	396	672	4%	87%	0.36	103	67	3.57	43
Paulk,Michael	09	L	25	8	aa	COL	413	49	105	17	2	7	47	48	57	6	7	255	332	353	685	10%	86%	0.83	65	67	4.16	39
	10	L	26	3	aaa	COL	366	35	76	17	6	6	35	23	46	3	4	209	255	329	585	6%	88%	0.50	77	106	2.74	25
Payton,Jay	10	R	38	8	aaa	COL	439	34	105	27	3	3	41	14	34	7	3	240	263	341	604	3%	92%	0.40	74	89	3.03	36
Pearce,Steve	09	R	26 b	3	aa	PIT	273	29	65	17	1	9	41	25	40	2	7	239	303	408	710	8%	85%	0.62	109	47	3.91	61
	10	R	27	3	aaa	PIT	129	18	33	12	1	2	11	16	22	5	2	258	341	405	746	11%	83%	0.73	108	108	5.09	42
Pedroza,Jaime	10	B	24	4	aa	LA	411	38	94	17	2	5	27	43	83	8	10	229	302	315	618	10%	80%	0.52	59	70	3.18	-13
Peguero,Carlos	10	L	24	8	aa	SEA	488	66	105	20	3	17	56	44	149	5	11	215	280	370	649	8%	69%	0.30	94	84	3.27	-29
Pena,Wily Mo	09	R	28	3	aa	NYM	145	9	32	4	0	4	15	4	26	0	0	217	236	317	553	2%	82%	0.14	60	12	2.49	-12
	10	R	29	0	aaa	SD	142	19	33	4	0	5	24	11	43	0	1	235	288	378	666	7%	70%	0.24	85	42	3.72	-38
Perales,Daniel	10	L	26	8	a/a	TOR	271	29	55	15	1	7	24	11	39	4	1	205	236	340	576	4%	85%	0.29	90	89	2.66	24
Perez,Eduardo	09	B	25	3	aa	LA	292	37	71	19	1	9	38	24	69	0	2	241	300	409	709	8%	76%	0.35	110	47	4.22	25
	10	B	26	3	aa	LA	432	33	92	27	0	3	40	24	79	8	2	213	254	294	548	5%	82%	0.30	65	71	2.57	-9
Perez,Felix	10	L	26	8	aa	CIN	139	8	31	5	1	2	8	4	27	6	5	223	244	311	555	3%	81%	0.14	57	93	2.25	-24
Perez,Fernando	10	R	27	8	aaa	TAM	385	33	68	9	2	3	23	21	87	17	7	178	220	231	451	5%	77%	0.24	36	116	1.64	-49
Perez,Julio	10	R	25	8	aa	LAA	233	18	46	12	1	4	26	18	45	5	6	198	256	309	565	7%	81%	0.41	77	72	2.44	1
Perez,Kenny	09	B	28	3	aa	COL	315	26	78	18	2	3	36	23	37	2	1	249	301	343	643	7%	88%	0.64	69	60	3.68	42
	10	B	29	5	aa	COL	114	8	21	3	0	1	5	7	15	0	0	185	233	232	464	6%	87%	0.48	32	23	1.80	-12
Perez,Miguel	09	R	26	2	aa	PIT	106	12	23	5	0	2	10	7	26	0	1	213	259	310	569	6%	76%	0.26	67	47	2.62	-15
	10	R	27	2	aa	CLE	157	13	35	10	0	0	10	5	24	0	0	224	245	287	532	3%	84%	0.18	56	30	2.37	-10
Perez,Timo	10	L	35	8	a/a	PHI	276	26	58	11	1	4	24	16	29	5	1	209	253	302	555	6%	89%	0.55	62	84	2.63	20
Petersen,Bryan	09	L	23	8	aa	FLA	431	55	118	14	6	6	42	45	63	11	13	273	342	373	715	9%	85%	0.71	61	112	4.38	45
	10	L	24	8	aaa	FLA	322	34	68	12	1	4	19	26	52	4	5	212	270	289	560	7%	84%	0.50	53	68	2.58	-6
Peterson,Brock	09	R	26	3	aaa	MIN	316	39	82	16	2	8	35	26	72	0	0	259	316	393	708	8%	77%	0.36	87	54	4.50	11
	10	R	27	3	aaa	MIN	437	45	86	17	2	13	40	36	112	0	2	198	259	335	593	8%	74%	0.32	85	47	2.87	-17
Peterson,Shane	09	L	22	8	aa	OAK	228	19	54	12	1	3	18	13	30	4	0	235	276	337	613	5%	87%	0.44	72	79	3.32	42
	10	L	23	3	aa	OAK	460	49	106	21	3	4	48	47	86	10	2	230	302	315	617	9%	81%	0.55	60	101	3.46	-7
Petit,Gregorio	09	R	25	6	aa	OAK	357	32	70	14	0	3	22	18	60	0	3	196	235	261	496	5%	83%	0.30	48	34	1.96	-7
	10	R	26	6	aaa	TEX	471	42	100	17	1	6	39	29	78	8	4	212	257	287	545	6%	84%	0.38	52	76	2.50	-11

Major League Equivalent Statistics

BATTER	Yr B	Age	Pos	Lev	Org	ab	r	h	d	t	hr	rbi	bb	k	sb	cs	ba	ob	slg	ops	bb%	ct%	eye	px	sx	rc/g	bpv
Pham,Thomas	10 R	23	8	aa	STL	121	15	36	12	1	2	14	14	22	3	2	298	370	463	833	10%	82%	0.64	121	91	6.38	47
Phelps,Cord	10 B	24	4	a/a	CLE	442	51	118	25	4	6	42	31	56	3	7	266	315	379	694	7%	87%	0.56	77	75	4.10	26
Phillips,Kyle	09 L	25	5	a/a	TOR	317	30	78	11	0	8	24	25	57	0	0	246	302	353	655	7%	82%	0.44	68	20	3.82	5
	10 L	26	3	aaa	SD	242	20	57	8	1	2	26	14	33	0	0	236	277	300	577	5%	87%	0.42	45	38	2.91	-5
Phillips,Paul	09 R	32	2	aa	COL	123	8	27	5	2	1	10	3	16	0	0	221	237	311	548	2%	87%	0.15	60	70	2.45	21
	10 R	33	2	aaa	COL	122	9	21	6	1	0	5	7	8	1	1	174	218	237	455	5%	93%	0.83	49	73	1.65	25
Phipps,Denis	10 R	25	8	aa	CIN	372	32	71	19	2	4	25	24	73	6	10	192	242	283	525	6%	80%	0.33	65	77	2.03	-13
Pilittere,Peter	09 R	28	2	a/a	NYY	182	11	34	8	0	1	14	8	17	0	0	188	223	247	470	4%	91%	0.49	47	20	1.81	18
	10 R	29	2	aaa	NYY	56	4	17	4	0	1	4	4	14	0	0	299	350	409	758	7%	76%	0.32	80	12	5.45	-17
Pill,Brett	09 R	25 a	3	aa	SF	527	58	138	35	1	14	90	30	66	5	3	262	302	412	714	5%	87%	0.46	101	61	4.40	62
	10 R	26	3	aaa	SF	520	43	116	29	0	10	57	20	51	5	2	223	252	336	588	4%	90%	0.40	79	55	2.85	33
Pina,Manuel	09 R	22	2	aa	TEX	321	29	76	16	1	7	34	15	48	1	0	237	271	358	629	4%	85%	0.31	81	51	3.37	31
	10 R	23	2	a/a	KC	321	32	71	17	0	6	36	21	33	0	0	220	267	327	593	6%	90%	0.63	74	29	2.99	33
Pinckney,Brandon	09 R	27	5	a/a	BAL	295	26	76	11	1	2	23	5	42	0	3	256	270	317	587	2%	86%	0.13	45	42	2.84	-3
	10 R	28	5	aa	PHI	154	9	26	8	0	2	7	6	25	0	1	171	203	257	460	4%	84%	0.25	63	28	1.62	-5
Place,Jason	09 R	21	8	aa	BOS	141	18	36	7	0	3	14	14	43	1	2	258	326	372	698	9%	70%	0.33	78	47	4.24	-24
	10 R	22	8	aa	BOS	79	4	9	2	1	1	6	9	21	0	1	114	205	203	407	10%	73%	0.43	53	81	1.27	-41
Plouffe,Trevor	09 R	23	6	aaa	MIN	430	45	100	21	4	8	51	27	61	3	7	232	279	353	632	6%	86%	0.45	79	79	3.20	44
	10 R	24	6	aaa	MIN	402	39	82	19	3	11	36	19	74	4	6	203	239	344	583	5%	82%	0.26	89	84	2.56	9
Portes,Juan	09 R	24 a	8	aa	MIN	327	39	88	20	2	5	35	28	42	6	3	270	328	387	715	8%	87%	0.68	82	86	4.62	58
	10 R	25	5	aa	MIN	441	36	78	14	3	7	41	31	78	0	1	176	230	268	498	7%	82%	0.39	58	53	2.01	-9
Posey,Buster	09 R	22 a	2	aa	SF	131	18	39	8	1	4	19	15	20	0	1	298	370	466	836	10%	85%	0.75	108	60	6.46	66
	10 R	24 a	2	aaa	SF	172	23	53	12	2	4	24	20	22	1	1	308	378	467	846	10%	87%	0.87	106	81	6.82	55
Pounds,Bryan	10 R	25	5	aa	DET	185	18	45	8	1	5	22	15	42	1	2	244	302	374	675	8%	77%	0.37	82	57	3.87	-8
Presley,Alex	10 L	25	8	a/a	PIT	518	66	140	24	8	8	65	30	62	10	9	270	310	396	706	5%	88%	0.49	80	122	4.21	29
Price,Jared	09 R	28	2	aa	CHW	173	14	32	6	0	5	14	5	59	1	0	182	203	297	499	3%	66%	0.08	73	50	1.93	-56
	10 R	29	2	a/a	OAK	160	8	22	4	0	3	8	8	49	0	0	138	178	215	393	5%	69%	0.16	50	15	1.20	-71
Pridie,Jason	09 L	26	8	aaa	MIN	513	55	117	20	4	7	43	15	79	20	8	227	249	319	568	3%	85%	0.19	60	127	2.64	33
	10 L	27	8	aaa	NYM	164	12	37	5	1	2	13	8	32	6	4	224	262	297	559	5%	81%	0.26	47	91	2.54	-28
Quinlan,Robb	10 R	34	3	aaa	LAA	128	8	24	4	0	0	5	9	18	1	0	186	237	219	456	6%	86%	0.48	29	39	1.78	-17
Quintanilla,Omar	10 L	29	6	aaa	COL	119	8	23	5	1	1	9	6	17	1	1	192	232	274	506	5%	86%	0.36	57	70	2.05	0
Quiroz,Guillermo	09 R	28	2	aa	SEA	205	16	41	9	1	5	25	9	37	0	0	202	236	320	556	4%	82%	0.25	77	39	2.50	12
	10 R	29	2	a/a	SEA	325	26	71	17	1	4	32	19	69	0	2	219	263	317	580	6%	79%	0.28	69	35	2.78	-17
Raburn,John	09 B	31	6	a/a	MIL	235	24	47	4	1	2	13	30	29	4	4	199	289	246	535	11%	87%	1.01	30	69	2.45	19
	10 B	32	4	aaa	MIL	197	17	38	6	2	2	19	24	32	3	1	194	281	268	549	11%	84%	0.75	48	83	2.67	-3
Rahl,Christopher	09 R	26	8	aa	ARI	435	56	110	21	8	5	38	27	88	16	8	253	297	372	669	6%	80%	0.31	76	170	3.81	44
	10 R	27	8	a/a	ARI	302	38	75	15	3	6	28	15	57	6	10	247	282	378	660	5%	81%	0.26	84	107	3.25	4
Ramirez,Max	09 R	25	2	aa	TEX	274	23	56	12	0	4	34	27	73	1	0	203	274	287	562	9%	73%	0.37	59	36	2.76	-29
	10 R	26	2	aaa	TEX	189	17	46	8	0	2	21	20	41	0	0	244	315	313	629	9%	78%	0.48	51	20	3.62	-26
Ramirez,Wilkin	09 R	24	8	aaa	DET	434	61	104	17	5	15	45	35	127	29	11	239	297	402	698	8%	71%	0.28	96	159	4.07	25
	10 R	25	8	a/a	ATL	448	52	89	14	5	18	56	35	146	12	9	199	257	375	632	7%	67%	0.24	101	128	3.03	-33
Ramirez,Yordany	09 R	25	8	aa	HOU	457	29	97	19	1	8	34	8	53	10	9	212	225	313	537	2%	88%	0.14	67	68	2.12	33
	10 R	26	8	aaa	HOU	211	13	38	6	0	2	17	6	28	5	1	179	203	235	439	3%	87%	0.23	41	69	1.56	-13
Ramos,Wilson	09 R	22	2	aa	MIN	205	28	60	15	0	3	26	5	21	0	0	293	310	410	719	2%	90%	0.24	87	41	4.64	48
	10 R	23	2	aaa	WAS	357	33	82	16	1	7	32	13	52	1	2	231	257	338	595	3%	85%	0.24	71	50	2.89	7
Ransom,Cody	10 R	35	5	aaa	PHI	394	43	82	20	1	14	47	30	112	3	2	209	265	373	638	7%	72%	0.27	103	66	3.32	-15
Rapoport,James	09 L	24	8	aa	STL	458	52	98	13	4	3	43	54	57	9	8	214	296	279	575	11%	87%	0.94	43	94	2.85	36
	10 L	25	8	a/a	STL	492	52	110	15	2	3	32	38	54	6	6	224	279	279	558	7%	89%	0.69	39	72	2.64	4
Ratliff,Sean	10 L	24	8	aa	NYM	281	34	74	18	0	12	35	16	56	1	3	265	304	453	757	5%	80%	0.28	120	38	4.72	29
Raynor,John	09 R	26	8	aa	FLA	447	52	101	22	2	5	30	37	120	16	8	225	284	313	597	8%	73%	0.30	63	104	3.02	-9
	10 R	27	8	aaa	FLA	134	15	30	5	0	1	9	9	24	2	0	227	276	281	558	6%	82%	0.38	41	64	2.79	-24
Recker,Anthony	09 R	26	2	aa	OAK	329	28	68	12	1	9	37	24	78	1	0	207	261	333	593	7%	76%	0.31	78	45	2.96	-4
	10 R	27	2	a/a	OAK	288	30	60	14	1	7	31	20	61	1	1	209	260	341	601	6%	79%	0.32	86	56	2.98	-1
Reddick,Josh	09 L	23 a	8	a/a	BOS	327	44	79	20	4	11	32	33	66	5	6	242	311	428	739	9%	80%	0.50	117	110	4.47	66
	10 L	24	8	aaa	BOS	451	48	113	30	3	14	52	20	59	3	8	250	281	422	703	4%	87%	0.33	112	67	3.83	48
Redman,Prentice	09 R	30	8	aa	SEA	414	64	96	28	2	15	50	26	86	5	2	232	278	419	697	6%	79%	0.31	121	101	4.00	58
	10 R	31	8	aaa	LA	214	23	48	9	1	5	22	13	32	3	3	222	266	342	608	6%	85%	0.40	76	78	3.01	14
Reed,Jeremy	10 L	29	8	aaa	CHW	323	34	69	11	1	6	25	22	47	2	4	213	262	309	571	6%	86%	0.46	62	55	2.62	6
Reimold,Nolan	09 R	26 a	8	aaa	BAL	109	18	39	9	0	8	24	15	23	6	1	362	440	681	1121	12%	79%	0.64	196	67	12.68	118
	10 R	27	8	aaa	BAL	337	39	72	10	0	8	28	39	51	6	2	213	294	317	611	10%	85%	0.76	65	68	3.31	14
Repec,Matthew	10 R	27	5	aa	COL	240	17	40	14	1	1	16	20	46	0	1	165	229	244	472	8%	81%	0.43	62	45	1.82	-9
Repko,Jason	09 R	29	8	aa	LA	393	53	87	16	2	12	35	22	83	18	7	222	263	365	628	5%	79%	0.27	88	123	3.17	36
	10 R	30	8	aaa	MIN	228	26	48	6	1	4	19	20	45	7	3	211	274	302	576	8%	80%	0.44	56	92	2.81	-17
Restovich,Mike	09 R	31	8	aaa	CHW	489	65	115	28	2	19	48	46	126	0	1	235	300	414	714	9%	74%	0.36	113	48	4.35	21
	10 R	32	8	aaa	LA	321	27	65	15	2	6	26	17	58	1	1	204	244	318	562	5%	82%	0.29	76	59	2.57	1
Retherford,Chris	09 R	24 a	4	aa	CHW	478	60	126	40	2	10	64	26	64	3	3	263	301	416	717	5%	87%	0.41	109	69	4.39	67
	10 R	25	4	a/a	CHW	464	34	77	17	0	6	31	22	85	0	1	166	203	239	442	4%	82%	0.25	51	31	1.54	-22
Revere,Ben	10 L	22	8	aa	MIN	361	35	97	9	3	1	18	24	33	28	16	269	314	319	633	6%	91%	0.73	34	118	3.37	5
Reyes,Argenis	09 B	27	4	aa	NYM	379	32	86	16	2	2	23	22	40	7	4	228	271	294	564	6%	89%	0.55	48	83	2.72	34
	10 B	28	4	aaa	CLE	96	5	23	3	0	0	4	4	10	1	1	238	272	266	538	4%	89%	0.43	24	35	2.46	-12
Reyes,Raul	10 L	24	8	aa	NYM	211	17	40	7	1	6	18	6	48	1	0	190	212	316	528	3%	77%	0.12	76	63	2.18	-23
Rhinehart,William	09 L	25	3	aa	WAS	414	36	89	22	1	10	49	27	97	6	1	216	263	343	607	6%	77%	0.28	85	73	3.11	11
	10 L	26	8	a/a	WAS	101	8	17	8	0	3	9	6	22	1	1	168	212	326	537	5%	78%	0.25	109	56	2.12	11
Rhymes,Will	09 L	26	4	aaa	DET	404	40	91	15	5	3	34	29	54	17	8	225	278	305	583	7%	87%	0.54	53	125	2.87	42
	10 L	27	4	aaa	DET	364	43	92	16	5	2	26	26	31	16	5	252	302	341	643	7%	91%	0.84	60	144	3.69	29
Richar,Danny	09 L	26 b	4	aaa	CIN	169	16	42	9	1	4	13	8	16	2	3	250	285	381	666	5%	90%	0.51	87	66	3.59	62
	10 L	27	4	aaa	FLA	467	39	117	23	0	5	34	14	66	5	5	251	272	330	601	3%	86%	0.21	59	49	3.01	-1
Richard,Chris	09 L	35	3	aaa	TAM	365	42	75	17	0	18	56	39	86	2	1	205	282	398	680	10%	76%	0.46	117	41	3.83	33
	10 L	36	3	aaa	TAM	430	47	97	30	1	14	54	41	93	0	0	225	292	393	686	9%	78%	0.44	112	32	4.02	22
Richardson,Antoar	10 B	27	8	a/a	ATL	297	47	69	6	1	0	17	37	51	20	3	232	317	260	577	11%	83%	0.72	22	127	3.32	-27
Richardson,Kevin	09 R	29	2	aa	TEX	255	23	43	8	1	9	25	13	100	0	0	169	209	317	526	5%	61%	0.13	87	46	2.11	-62
	10 R	30	2	a/a	TEX	215	18	42	10	0	9	21	7	72	2	0	194	218	360	578	3%	67%	0.09	103	48	2.57	-43
Rivera,Mike	10 R	34	2	a/a	FLA	240	17	41	14	0	3	16	26	67	2	2	170	252	262	514	10%	72%	0.39	70	39	2.20	-34

Major League Equivalent Statistics

BATTER	Yr	B	Age	Pos	Lev	Org	ab	r	h	d	t	hr	rbi	bb	k	sb	cs	ba	ob	slg	ops	bb%	ct%	eye	px	sx	rc/g	bpv
Rivera,Rene	09	R	26	2	aa	NYM	239	17	45	11	0	6	22	9	58	0	0	189	219	316	534	4%	76%	0.16	83	17	2.24	-16
	10	R	27	2	a/a	NYY	162	13	39	10	0	6	22	6	32	0	0	239	267	417	684	4%	80%	0.20	114	11	3.82	21
Rivero,Carlos	09	R	21	6	aa	CLE	480	46	111	23	1	6	54	48	67	1	0	231	302	322	624	9%	86%	0.72	64	45	3.50	29
	10	R	22	6	aa	CLE	406	31	83	14	1	4	34	23	65	0	4	204	247	273	520	5%	84%	0.35	48	32	2.17	-13
Rizzo,Anthony	10	L	21	3	aa	BOS	414	49	102	32	0	14	60	33	71	5	1	246	303	427	729	7%	83%	0.47	122	64	4.60	46
Rizzotti,Matthew	10	L	25 a	3	a/a	PHI	311	37	93	25	0	13	52	36	60	1	1	299	371	509	881	10%	81%	0.59	138	28	7.22	55
Robbins,Whitney	09	L	25	3	aa	MIN	425	45	105	21	2	7	42	36	71	0	3	246	304	352	657	8%	83%	0.50	72	43	3.74	22
	10	L	26	3	aa	MIN	48	2	6	1	0	0	3	4	4	0	1	115	178	134	312	7%	91%	0.85	17	34	0.70	-6
Roberts,Brandon	09	L	25	8	aa	MIN	397	56	102	16	2	2	32	24	56	18	8	256	299	322	620	6%	86%	0.43	48	119	3.39	31
	10	L	26	8	a/a	MIN	267	34	72	10	2	2	23	22	32	12	4	271	326	345	671	7%	88%	0.68	51	114	4.18	10
Roberts,Ryan	10	R	30	4	aaa	ARI	347	34	67	20	2	6	31	31	54	9	7	194	259	311	570	8%	84%	0.57	81	89	2.58	20
Robinson,Chris	09	R	25	2	aa	CHC	310	29	89	20	2	2	39	10	41	8	3	288	311	382	693	3%	87%	0.25	71	91	4.31	39
	10	R	26	2	aaa	CHC	230	10	45	8	1	1	17	11	26	1	0	196	233	252	485	5%	89%	0.42	42	42	1.97	-1
Robinson,Clinton	10	L	26 a	3	aa	KC	477	64	135	38	3	19	71	42	66	3	4	284	342	493	835	8%	86%	0.64	136	65	6.12	72
Robinson,Derrick	10	B	23	8	aa	KC	511	56	131	25	5	1	36	34	62	38	21	256	303	331	633	6%	88%	0.55	55	134	3.32	10
Robinson,Shane	09	R	25 a	8	aa	STL	345	35	68	15	2	4	30	21	33	12	4	198	244	287	530	6%	90%	0.63	62	113	2.35	58
	10	R	26	8	aaa	STL	86	7	19	4	0	1	8	5	10	2	4	219	259	295	554	5%	89%	0.49	56	56	2.16	12
Robinson,Trayvon	10	B	23	8	aa	LA	434	60	109	20	3	7	43	52	101	28	19	251	331	357	688	11%	77%	0.51	70	120	3.97	-13
Rodriguez,Concep	09	R	23	8	aa	ATL	395	38	96	18	1	3	28	26	65	8	10	243	291	315	606	6%	83%	0.41	53	68	2.99	11
	10	R	24	8	aa	TOR	198	12	36	6	2	0	21	14	35	3	2	184	240	233	472	7%	82%	0.41	34	89	1.85	-29
Rodriguez,Guilder	09	B	26	6	aa	TEX	277	26	63	4	3	1	16	19	36	7	6	226	276	269	545	7%	87%	0.54	26	102	2.45	15
	10	B	27	6	a/a	TEX	390	44	86	5	3	0	23	29	43	14	6	219	273	247	520	7%	89%	0.66	18	112	2.34	-14
Rodriguez,Joshua	09	R	25	4	aa	CLE	105	15	29	4	0	0	11	21	29	2	3	274	396	311	707	17%	72%	0.72	32	51	4.71	-35
	10	R	26	6	a/a	CLE	380	44	94	25	1	9	42	39	72	5	5	247	317	393	710	9%	81%	0.53	100	62	4.34	24
Rodriguez,Luis	10	B	30	6	aaa	CHW	345	34	77	13	1	12	38	29	33	2	5	222	282	367	649	8%	90%	0.88	88	41	3.38	50
Rogers,Eddie	09	R	31	6	aa	ARI	254	31	58	15	0	3	30	10	40	7	3	228	257	328	585	4%	84%	0.26	74	93	2.84	34
	10	R	32	5	aaa	ARI	447	36	93	17	4	3	32	20	52	7	6	207	240	287	528	4%	88%	0.38	54	95	2.21	7
Rohlinger,Ryan	09	R	26 a	5	aa	SF	474	61	117	34	2	12	64	34	82	4	2	246	296	403	699	7%	83%	0.41	107	77	4.18	55
	10	R	27	6	aaa	SF	283	31	72	19	0	6	33	19	47	2	0	254	301	380	682	6%	83%	0.41	91	52	4.13	21
Rojas,Carlos	09	R	26	6	a/a	BAL	297	24	47	6	1	0	12	19	39	2	4	158	208	184	392	6%	87%	0.48	20	66	1.19	-4
	10	R	27	6	aa	BAL	306	26	62	10	1	1	29	21	49	1	3	201	253	250	503	6%	84%	0.43	37	50	2.08	-20
Roling,Kiel	10	R	24	3	aa	COL	329	34	69	17	0	10	31	22	77	0	0	209	257	349	606	6%	77%	0.28	91	28	3.03	-6
Romak,Jamie	09	R	24	3	aa	PIT	211	10	33	12	0	4	20	14	53	1	0	158	209	269	479	6%	75%	0.26	78	27	1.83	-16
	10	R	25	5	aa	KC	133	16	32	6	0	4	12	13	23	0	4	238	308	368	676	9%	83%	0.59	83	36	3.59	18
Romero,Alex	09	L	26 b	8	aa	ARI	279	31	86	18	3	2	36	25	23	6	5	307	363	412	776	8%	92%	1.09	77	89	5.57	74
	10	L	27	8	a/a	ATL	223	20	46	7	1	2	15	18	22	2	2	206	265	270	536	7%	90%	0.81	45	62	2.42	13
Romero,Niuman	09	B	25	6	a/a	CLE	367	38	78	12	1	1	29	29	42	11	6	212	269	259	528	7%	89%	0.69	36	89	2.38	27
	10	B	26	4	aaa	BOS	350	33	77	15	0	2	15	24	49	11	7	220	271	279	550	7%	86%	0.50	46	77	2.54	-4
Romine,Andrew	10	B	25	6	aa	LAA	383	42	94	13	2	2	26	37	54	16	11	246	313	306	619	9%	86%	0.69	43	96	3.32	-2
Romine,Austin	10	R	22	2	aa	NYY	455	51	110	26	0	9	58	32	76	2	0	242	292	360	652	7%	83%	0.42	82	52	3.74	14
Roof,Shawn	09	R	25	4	aa	DET	184	16	41	2	2	1	12	9	33	3	2	225	262	271	533	5%	82%	0.29	26	97	2.40	-10
	10	R	26	5	a/a	DET	272	29	59	8	2	0	17	16	51	9	7	216	259	260	520	5%	81%	0.31	33	109	2.15	-36
Rooney,Sean	09	B	23	2	aa	WAS	110	11	24	5	1	0	5	5	22	0	0	214	247	276	524	4%	80%	0.22	47	73	2.31	-11
	10	B	24	2	a/a	WAS	107	8	15	7	0	0	5	9	17	0	0	144	208	206	414	7%	84%	0.52	56	30	1.40	-1
Rosario,Alberto	10	R	24	2	aa	LAA	166	9	28	3	0	0	6	5	24	2	2	171	195	189	384	3%	85%	0.20	16	52	1.13	-39
Rosario,Wilin	10	R	22 a	2	aa	COL	270	34	74	13	1	17	42	17	43	1	0	273	317	520	837	6%	84%	0.40	145	51	5.98	67
Rottino,Vinny	09	R	29	3	aa	LA	414	46	83	14	0	3	40	46	55	10	2	201	282	260	542	10%	87%	0.85	42	83	2.67	28
	10	R	30	8	a/a	FLA	441	46	104	21	2	5	48	41	54	15	2	235	300	326	626	8%	88%	0.75	64	102	3.62	21
Ruggiano,Justin	09	R	27	8	aaa	TAM	471	56	98	23	1	12	57	41	144	18	4	208	272	334	607	8%	69%	0.29	82	105	3.19	-7
	10	R	28	8	aaa	TAM	457	55	102	25	0	11	50	30	119	17	6	223	271	347	618	6%	74%	0.25	83	94	3.19	-23
Russell,Kyle	10	L	24	8	aa	LA	273	26	55	19	1	7	20	20	93	2	2	200	255	352	607	7%	66%	0.22	103	66	2.95	-37
Russo,Kevin	09	R	25	4	aaa	NYY	353	45	103	16	1	5	27	38	55	11	7	293	361	383	744	10%	84%	0.68	63	80	5.17	33
	10	R	26	4	aaa	NYY	332	33	72	13	1	1	19	24	62	7	4	216	269	269	538	7%	81%	0.39	41	84	2.48	-26
Ryan,Dusty	09	R	25	2	aaa	DET	202	21	46	7	1	8	29	24	60	2	0	228	311	396	707	11%	71%	0.41	98	62	4.44	3
	10	R	26	2	aaa	SD	261	20	39	13	0	5	21	37	88	2	1	148	253	250	504	12%	66%	0.42	71	40	2.17	-51
Ryan,Mike	09	L	32	8	aa	FLA	367	46	87	20	0	10	49	37	71	2	1	236	307	375	682	9%	81%	0.53	92	48	4.10	32
	10	L	33	8	aaa	LAA	307	28	61	16	2	3	22	14	36	1	0	199	233	288	521	4%	88%	0.37	64	69	2.24	14
Saccomanno,Mark	09	R	29	3	aa	HOU	493	44	104	18	3	10	44	22	79	3	0	211	245	324	570	4%	84%	0.28	71	86	2.69	29
	10	R	30	3	a/a	FLA	451	37	86	17	3	8	40	20	104	0	4	190	224	290	514	4%	77%	0.19	65	51	2.02	-30
Salazar,Jeff	09	L	29	8	aa	PIT	315	32	68	6	2	7	28	21	51	11	0	215	264	313	577	6%	84%	0.41	57	113	3.00	29
	10	L	30	8	aaa	BAL	436	41	88	10	1	13	38	33	74	18	3	201	257	318	574	7%	83%	0.44	69	97	2.86	2
Salem,Emeel	10	L	26	8	a/a	TAM	530	57	117	21	5	3	34	38	61	18	12	220	272	293	564	7%	89%	0.62	51	115	2.61	10
Saltalamacchia,Jar	10	B	25	2	aaa	BOS	274	33	61	17	1	9	30	23	59	1	0	223	282	395	677	8%	79%	0.39	111	60	3.87	20
Sammons,Clint	09	R	26	2	aaa	ATL	299	26	53	10	0	6	29	16	57	6	0	178	219	277	496	5%	81%	0.28	63	77	2.04	10
	10	R	27	2	aaa	ATL	271	18	35	5	0	4	18	23	54	2	5	130	199	189	388	8%	80%	0.43	38	42	1.13	-32
Samson,Nathan	10	R	23	6	aa	CHC	233	19	53	6	1	1	16	11	28	1	5	227	261	273	535	4%	88%	0.39	33	52	2.23	-10
Sanchez,Angel	09	R	26	6	aaa	TOR	449	46	111	25	3	5	41	27	58	1	2	248	290	346	636	6%	87%	0.46	70	60	3.50	36
	10	R	27	6	aaa	BOS	223	19	53	10	1	0	13	18	27	5	1	238	295	291	586	7%	88%	0.68	43	77	3.12	3
Sanchez,Luis	09	B	22	6	aa	TOR	262	22	49	12	1	1	23	27	68	1	0	187	263	252	515	9%	74%	0.40	50	58	2.32	-26
	10	B	23	6	aa	TOR	98	6	15	3	0	0	8	6	20	1	0	150	198	180	378	6%	79%	0.29	27	50	1.19	-49
Sanchez,Salvador	10	R	25	8	aa	CHW	391	37	80	16	2	9	41	20	90	8	2	204	243	327	570	5%	77%	0.22	78	95	2.65	-19
Sanchez,Yunesky	09	B	25	4	aa	ARI	199	22	48	7	2	2	14	11	22	3	4	241	282	321	603	5%	89%	0.50	52	93	2.97	38
	10	B	26	5	aaa	ARI	338	25	75	15	2	5	31	16	30	3	5	223	258	318	576	4%	91%	0.51	64	59	2.64	26
Sandoval,Freddy	09	B	27 b	5	aa	LAA	277	38	71	14	3	5	38	21	39	10	3	257	308	377	685	7%	86%	0.53	80	127	4.20	62
	10	B	28	5	aaa	LAA	81	8	12	1	1	0	6	7	9	0	0	152	220	185	405	8%	89%	0.77	19	80	1.37	-12
Sands,Gerald	10	R	23	8	aa	LA	259	41	60	10	1	12	36	24	49	3	0	232	297	417	714	8%	81%	0.49	109	89	4.40	31
Santana,Carlos	09	B	23 a	2	aa	CLE	429	81	115	28	1	21	87	84	80	2	2	267	388	482	870	16%	81%	1.06	135	56	7.11	85
	10	B	24 a	2	aaa	CLE	196	29	52	12	1	9	38	35	32	5	0	264	375	470	845	15%	84%	1.07	129	85	6.87	69
Santangelo,Louis	09	R	27	2	aa	HOU	269	17	46	15	1	4	18	15	66	0	0	171	214	274	488	5%	75%	0.22	73	33	1.89	-18
	10	R	28	2	a/a	HOU	256	16	48	9	0	5	14	25	60	0	1	186	259	274	533	9%	77%	0.42	58	16	2.40	-27
Sappelt,David	10	R	24	8	a/a	CIN	438	51	137	25	7	9	55	29	49	15	17	313	356	461	817	6%	89%	0.60	95	119	5.60	45
Sardinha,Bronson	10	L	27 b	8	aa	COL	268	35	68	22	3	8	36	37	42	5	5	255	345	447	792	12%	84%	0.87	127	97	5.46	65

Major League Equivalent Statistics

BATTER	Yr B	Age	Pos	Lev	Org	ab	r	h	d	t	hr	rbi	bb	k	sb	cs	ba	ob	slg	ops	bb%	ct%	eye	px	sx	rc/g	bpv
Sardinha,Dane	09 R	30	2	aaa	DET	118	8	17	6	0	3	12	9	34	0	0	144	202	259	461	7%	71%	0.25	78	18	1.67	-32
	10 R	31	2	aaa	PHI	222	18	37	6	0	4	18	9	71	0	0	165	198	249	447	4%	68%	0.13	53	31	1.57	-74
Sarmiento,Elio	10 B	24	2	aa	TEX	204	16	36	7	3	2	17	13	38	2	0	174	225	264	489	6%	82%	0.36	56	112	1.99	-14
Satin,Joshua	10 R	26	4	aa	NYM	286	33	71	20	1	5	26	24	57	1	0	247	304	371	675	8%	80%	0.41	89	58	4.05	8
Saunders,Michael	09 L	23 a	8	aa	SEA	248	52	71	14	1	11	29	23	46	5	3	286	347	484	831	8%	81%	0.50	122	103	6.12	74
	10 L	24	8	aaa	SEA	80	5	14	1	0	0	4	9	13	3	0	172	254	184	438	10%	83%	0.66	11	61	1.81	-36
Savastano,Scott	10 R	24	8	aa	SEA	237	30	57	11	1	5	22	23	50	3	2	239	306	352	659	9%	79%	0.46	74	75	3.81	-5
Scales,Bobby	09 B	32	5	aa	CHC	306	30	67	13	1	4	28	33	62	6	8	219	296	308	604	10%	80%	0.53	61	64	3.00	8
	10 B	33	4	aaa	CHC	373	41	74	26	2	6	32	44	65	4	3	198	283	324	607	11%	83%	0.68	89	75	3.12	25
Schaeffer,Warren	10 R	26	6	a/a	COL	343	30	70	14	2	2	29	11	54	0	2	203	228	271	499	3%	84%	0.21	50	59	1.98	-15
Schafer,Jordan	10 L	24	8	a/a	ATL	252	18	41	7	1	1	11	18	51	8	10	164	220	210	430	7%	80%	0.36	33	85	1.32	-39
Schmidt,Konrad	10 R	26	2	aa	ARI	394	38	110	29	3	9	52	26	58	6	3	280	324	437	761	6%	85%	0.45	106	79	5.14	41
Schoop,Sharlon	09 R	22	5	aa	SF	320	31	72	15	0	2	31	17	54	5	6	225	264	291	555	5%	83%	0.31	51	62	2.47	4
	10 R	23	3	aa	SF	183	17	47	9	0	2	22	11	31	1	1	257	298	337	636	6%	83%	0.35	59	39	3.55	-6
Scott Jr.,Lorenzo	09 L	28	8	aa	FLA	400	51	88	11	4	7	36	50	129	16	13	221	308	320	627	11%	68%	0.39	60	121	3.28	-20
	10 L	29	8	a/a	FLA	303	47	63	11	3	5	26	32	110	5	4	209	284	314	598	9%	64%	0.29	66	126	3.04	-72
Scram,Deik	09 L	26 a	8	aa	DET	441	58	96	20	6	16	55	49	104	7	2	217	296	396	692	10%	76%	0.47	107	126	4.09	51
	10 L	27	8	a/a	DET	359	32	64	19	4	6	31	39	100	12	6	179	259	300	559	10%	72%	0.39	80	123	2.58	-26
Scruggs,Xavier	10 R	23	3	aa	STL	110	12	23	5	0	6	16	8	28	0	0	205	258	410	668	7%	75%	0.28	122	20	3.54	13
Sedbrook,Colt	09 R	24	4	aa	STL	174	16	35	4	0	2	12	17	24	6	2	199	271	254	525	9%	86%	0.72	37	72	2.43	16
	10 R	25	4	aa	STL	91	8	12	4	0	0	6	8	17	1	0	134	208	176	384	9%	81%	0.50	37	59	1.26	-27
Sellers,Justin	09 R	24	6	aa	LA	393	37	98	25	1	2	27	43	64	9	9	249	324	332	655	10%	84%	0.67	65	65	3.72	28
	10 R	25	6	aaa	LA	288	31	61	13	0	8	34	23	33	3	4	213	272	340	612	7%	88%	0.69	83	51	3.02	37
Sellers,Neil	09 R	27 b	5	aa	PHI	518	53	136	27	1	14	64	35	66	4	5	262	309	401	711	6%	87%	0.54	91	45	4.31	50
	10 R	28	5	a/a	PHI	410	25	76	20	1	5	30	26	80	0	3	185	234	277	511	6%	81%	0.33	66	25	2.08	-11
Seratelli,Anthony	10 B	28	5	aa	KC	299	28	61	8	2	2	26	33	51	10	6	205	284	262	546	10%	83%	0.65	39	93	2.55	-15
Sexton,Gregory	10 R	26	5	aa	TAM	113	8	21	7	0	1	10	15	19	0	2	183	279	266	545	12%	83%	0.79	64	27	2.43	9
Shealy,Ryan	10 R	31	0	aaa	BOS	286	29	54	21	1	10	38	31	76	0	0	190	270	377	648	10%	73%	0.41	124	35	3.46	14
Sheely,Matt	10 R	24	8	a/a	BOS	249	22	53	9	3	1	17	13	64	8	8	212	252	281	534	5%	74%	0.21	47	123	2.16	-52
Shelby III,John	09 R	24 a	8	aa	CHW	428	54	92	28	2	10	41	42	70	25	10	215	286	357	642	9%	84%	0.61	96	119	3.46	68
	10 R	25	8	aaa	CHW	398	50	84	15	4	9	34	20	101	12	9	210	248	338	585	5%	75%	0.20	78	134	2.59	-27
Shelton,Chris	09 R	29	5	aa	SEA	405	55	101	24	1	11	65	46	95	0	2	248	326	395	721	10%	76%	0.49	97	40	4.61	18
	10 R	30	3	aaa	HOU	285	17	54	9	0	7	27	19	71	0	0	188	238	289	527	6%	75%	0.26	63	10	2.29	-34
Shorey,Mark	09 L	25	8	aa	STL	258	15	62	10	0	4	20	12	40	2	2	240	275	324	599	5%	84%	0.30	58	31	3.03	4
	10 L	26	8	aaa	STL	156	14	32	6	0	2	13	6	28	1	0	206	234	277	511	3%	82%	0.20	50	51	2.17	-24
Shuck,Jack	10 L	23	8	a/a	HOU	528	54	138	15	3	2	28	49	61	13	14	262	324	312	636	8%	88%	0.80	35	78	3.50	1
Singleton,Steven	09 L	24	6	aa	MIN	158	12	41	10	2	1	15	6	22	1	1	261	287	365	652	4%	86%	0.26	74	84	3.63	38
	10 L	25	4	aa	MIN	502	50	110	36	3	5	37	28	48	2	6	219	261	330	590	5%	90%	0.59	82	63	2.79	40
Sizemore,Scott	09 R	25 a	4	a/a	DET	520	73	143	35	4	14	55	53	83	17	4	275	342	439	781	9%	84%	0.63	108	116	5.64	78
	10 R	26	4	aaa	DET	299	38	77	20	1	8	28	24	66	2	2	258	312	406	717	7%	78%	0.36	100	63	4.48	8
Smith,Corey	09 R	27	3	aa	KC	550	48	112	26	1	14	64	28	111	8	8	203	241	332	574	5%	80%	0.25	84	64	2.52	17
	10 R	28	5	aa	LA	402	39	84	26	1	9	57	25	66	4	2	208	254	344	597	6%	84%	0.37	94	71	2.92	23
Smith,Curt	10 R	24	3	aa	STL	319	29	74	16	1	6	35	12	49	2	1	232	259	343	602	3%	85%	0.24	76	60	3.00	8
Smith,Kevin	09 L	26	3	aa	NYY	158	17	36	7	1	2	13	9	46	0	1	226	270	315	585	6%	71%	0.21	61	67	2.85	-34
	10 L	27	3	aa	NYY	131	6	17	5	0	0	4	14	43	0	0	133	216	169	385	10%	67%	0.32	31	16	1.25	-87
Smith,Marquez	09 R	25	5	aa	CHC	411	45	104	32	1	9	39	27	75	3	0	252	298	397	695	6%	82%	0.36	103	66	4.25	43
	10 R	26	5	a/a	CHC	347	47	86	24	1	14	39	25	65	1	0	247	298	444	742	7%	81%	0.39	128	59	4.68	43
Smith,Timothy	09 L	23 a	8	aa	TEX	139	18	38	8	0	3	25	11	17	7	1	275	327	395	722	7%	88%	0.62	83	86	4.92	58
	10 L	24	8	aa	KC	307	37	81	16	0	6	36	24	31	11	6	263	316	372	688	7%	90%	0.77	76	77	4.13	37
Smoak,Justin	09 B	23	3	aa	TEX	380	45	99	20	0	9	43	61	66	0	0	261	363	384	747	14%	83%	0.92	83	20	5.33	33
	10 B	24	3	aaa	SEA	183	25	43	11	0	7	23	30	33	0	0	236	344	407	751	14%	82%	0.93	110	23	5.17	47
Snider,Travis	09 L	22 a	8	aaa	TOR	175	24	54	12	1	11	30	21	37	2	4	306	381	577	958	11%	79%	0.58	165	61	7.87	90
	10 L	23	8	aa	TOR	81	11	21	5	0	4	13	2	17	2	1	259	277	469	746	2%	79%	0.12	131	77	4.38	28
Snyder,Brad	09 L	27	8	aa	CHC	237	30	56	14	2	12	33	15	66	7	5	235	282	456	738	6%	72%	0.23	134	112	4.19	44
	10 L	28	8	aaa	CHC	477	62	114	29	3	17	67	36	102	12	4	238	292	415	707	7%	79%	0.35	113	106	4.19	21
Snyder,Brandon	09 R	23	3	a/a	BAL	463	57	130	35	2	13	84	47	100	3	2	281	347	449	796	9%	78%	0.47	114	63	5.79	44
	10 R	24	3	aaa	BAL	339	28	78	20	1	8	34	22	81	3	1	231	277	364	641	6%	76%	0.27	90	59	3.50	-10
Snyder,Justin	09 L	23	4	aa	NYY	262	24	48	9	0	3	27	27	48	1	2	183	261	251	511	9%	82%	0.57	47	38	2.20	-3
	10 L	24	4	a/a	NYY	267	46	57	11	1	3	23	42	39	2	1	212	320	291	611	14%	86%	1.10	55	80	3.43	15
Sogard,Eric	09 L	23 a	4	aa	SD	458	63	112	20	2	4	40	46	42	8	7	244	313	321	634	9%	91%	1.10	55	84	3.53	53
	10 L	24	4	aaa	OAK	514	56	122	22	4	3	44	52	49	10	12	237	307	312	619	9%	90%	1.06	53	84	3.24	25
Solano,Donovan	09 R	22	6	aa	STL	415	38	92	12	1	1	23	24	50	3	0	221	264	263	527	6%	88%	0.49	32	69	2.44	11
	10 R	23	6	aaa	STL	330	30	71	10	1	3	20	8	25	1	1	215	234	279	513	2%	92%	0.32	44	59	2.14	11
Solano,Jhonatan	09 R	24	2	a/a	WAS	276	20	57	15	0	2	24	10	35	2	1	205	232	282	514	3%	87%	0.27	60	50	2.15	20
	10 R	25	2	aa	WAS	317	24	70	13	0	5	35	17	27	1	1	219	259	305	564	5%	92%	0.64	60	32	2.67	26
Solarte,Yangervis	10 B	23	5	aa	MIN	127	11	30	8	0	2	15	2	14	1	1	239	251	347	598	2%	89%	0.14	79	49	2.87	23
Sosa,Ricardo	09 R	25	5	aa	ARI	443	48	103	24	0	10	55	30	69	3	1	233	282	356	639	6%	84%	0.44	83	54	3.51	35
	10 R	26	5	aa	ARI	36	3	9	1	0	1	6	3	8	0	0	256	309	358	666	7%	79%	0.36	62	11	3.99	-19
Spears,Nathaniel	09 L	24	5	aa	CHC	368	39	83	18	3	2	30	28	39	5	6	224	279	305	584	7%	90%	0.72	59	87	2.83	47
	10 L	25	4	aa	BOS	514	72	121	30	3	13	57	58	71	9	1	236	314	382	696	10%	86%	0.82	96	104	4.38	44
Spencer,Matthew	09 L	24	8	aa	OAK	371	43	90	25	2	6	45	19	54	1	4	243	279	367	646	5%	85%	0.34	88	64	3.41	43
	10 L	25	8	aa	CHC	377	44	86	13	1	12	47	25	67	7	2	229	277	369	646	6%	82%	0.37	85	83	3.54	12
Spidale,Michael	09 R	28	8	a/a	PHI	353	41	86	12	3	3	26	12	39	13	7	245	269	316	585	3%	89%	0.30	48	119	2.81	38
	10 R	29	8	aa	PHI	479	50	114	17	2	2	33	24	57	20	12	237	273	290	563	5%	88%	0.42	40	102	2.61	-4
Spring,Matthew	09 R	25	2	aa	TAM	224	20	39	12	0	7	29	19	71	0	0	176	241	317	558	8%	68%	0.27	92	23	2.53	-28
	10 R	26	2	aa	TAM	66	8	10	5	0	2	12	3	18	1	0	157	191	313	505	4%	73%	0.16	107	97	1.92	-14
St. Pierre,Max	09 R	29	2	a/a	DET	207	18	40	9	0	6	18	9	26	0	0	191	226	324	551	4%	88%	0.37	85	25	2.40	37
	10 R	30	2	a/a	DET	190	20	40	5	1	7	25	14	24	2	1	210	266	353	620	7%	88%	0.61	83	65	3.18	33
Stansberry,Craig	09 R	28	5	aa	SD	427	38	87	18	3	5	30	32	68	6	5	204	261	291	551	7%	84%	0.48	59	84	2.52	25
	10 R	29	5	aaa	SD	346	36	65	13	1	5	22	30	67	4	6	188	253	277	530	8%	81%	0.45	60	69	2.23	-12
Stanton,Mike	09 R	20	8	aa	FLA	299	45	67	15	2	14	49	30	88	1	1	225	296	425	721	9%	71%	0.35	120	85	4.35	25
	10 R	21 a	8	aa	FLA	192	36	57	12	1	18	45	40	46	1	0	295	417	644	1061	17%	76%	0.88	203	61	10.57	104

Major League Equivalent Statistics

BATTER	Yr	B	Age	Pos	Lev	Org	ab	r	h	d	t	hr	rbi	bb	k	sb	cs	ba	ob	slg	ops	bb%	ct%	eye	px	sx	rc/g	bpv
Statia,Hainley	09	B	24 a	6	aa	LAA	381	42	85	21	1	1	38	30	33	13	3	224	281	291	572	7%	91%	0.93	54	100	2.93	56
	10	B	25	4	a/a	LAA	108	9	25	5	1	0	12	12	11	1	4	231	305	293	599	10%	89%	1.01	47	70	2.82	17
Stavinoha,Nick	09	R	27	3	aa	STL	259	28	58	14	1	7	40	18	41	2	0	222	273	365	638	6%	84%	0.44	92	66	3.46	45
	10	R	28 b	3	aaa	STL	100	12	30	7	1	4	18	4	14	0	0	299	323	493	816	3%	86%	0.26	125	60	5.90	54
Stavisky,Brian	09	L	29	3	aa	PHI	394	39	87	25	1	9	47	42	81	2	2	220	296	354	649	10%	79%	0.52	92	46	3.64	26
	10	L	30	3	aa	PHI	105	9	22	3	0	2	7	7	22	1	1	210	258	291	550	6%	79%	0.30	54	46	2.51	-28
Steele,Thomas	10	R	24	8	aa	HOU	241	21	50	8	2	2	15	9	64	8	4	207	235	279	513	3%	74%	0.14	48	117	2.11	-58
Stern,Adam	09	L	30	8	a/a	MIL	488	53	107	16	3	3	28	34	62	22	11	219	269	282	551	6%	87%	0.54	44	118	2.53	35
	10	L	31	8	aaa	MIL	286	32	70	14	2	3	20	25	46	5	4	244	304	339	643	8%	84%	0.54	66	84	3.55	6
Stewart,Chris	09	R	28	2	aaa	NYY	232	28	56	10	0	1	15	21	30	1	1	241	303	295	598	8%	87%	0.69	44	48	3.20	16
	10	R	29	2	aaa	SD	266	21	48	10	1	4	26	21	35	1	0	179	239	271	510	7%	87%	0.60	61	51	2.18	12
Strait,William	09	R	26	8	aa	TAM	431	63	98	24	2	5	50	33	95	16	5	228	283	324	608	7%	78%	0.35	69	122	3.24	21
	10	R	27	8	aa	TAM	133	11	21	9	0	0	8	7	28	6	2	156	199	223	422	5%	79%	0.26	60	104	1.45	-23
Strange-Gordon,Dı	10	L	22	6	aa	LA	555	65	131	15	5	1	30	29	70	40	25	236	274	286	560	5%	87%	0.41	35	139	2.46	-11
Strieby,Ryan	09	R	24 a	3	aa	DET	294	52	79	15	1	15	47	45	68	2	0	268	365	483	848	13%	77%	0.67	130	69	6.70	61
	10	R	25	8	aaa	DET	290	23	61	13	0	8	38	25	72	1	1	211	274	344	618	8%	75%	0.35	85	27	3.21	-13
Stromsmoe,Skyler	10	B	26	8	aa	SF	142	9	29	3	1	2	6	6	32	5	0	207	237	279	516	4%	78%	0.18	43	95	2.33	-45
Sublett,Damon	10	L	25	8	aa	NYY	112	10	20	3	1	2	10	18	32	1	1	176	290	269	558	14%	72%	0.56	56	76	2.72	-40
Sucre,Jesus	10	R	22	2	aa	ATL	145	17	38	10	1	2	10	1	14	0	2	262	267	386	653	1%	90%	0.07	88	76	3.34	36
Sulentic,Matthew	09	L	22	8	aa	OAK	413	44	101	18	3	5	38	26	72	16	11	245	290	340	630	6%	82%	0.36	64	109	3.25	28
	10	L	23	8	aa	OAK	440	45	106	16	2	1	36	40	87	9	6	241	304	293	597	8%	80%	0.46	40	82	3.15	-29
Suomi,Richard	09	L	29	2	aa	KC	195	18	38	8	1	5	18	11	26	0	4	194	235	325	560	5%	87%	0.40	82	54	2.29	40
	10	L	30	2	a/a	PHI	194	16	40	4	0	3	16	7	38	2	3	204	231	279	510	3%	80%	0.18	47	51	2.02	-33
Sutil,Wladimir	09	R	25	6	aa	HOU	472	57	108	18	0	1	27	33	34	14	15	230	280	275	554	6%	93%	0.95	37	80	2.44	40
	10	R	26	6	a/a	HOU	420	44	94	11	0	1	23	29	38	18	7	224	274	257	532	6%	91%	0.76	27	92	2.49	0
Sutton,Drew	09	B	26	4	a/a	CIN	172	26	38	11	1	5	17	22	38	1	2	219	308	374	683	11%	78%	0.58	103	76	3.95	41
	10	B	27	8	aaa	CLE	359	32	77	19	1	4	29	44	81	6	4	216	301	303	605	11%	77%	0.54	64	65	3.23	-15
Sutton,Nathanael	09	L	27	8	aa	LAA	455	54	115	22	4	2	41	45	66	20	8	253	320	328	649	9%	86%	0.69	55	116	3.82	41
	10	L	28	4	aaa	LAA	397	39	77	15	4	1	23	27	55	8	8	193	245	255	500	6%	86%	0.50	45	104	1.97	-4
Swauger,Christoph	10	L	24	8	aa	STL	154	13	35	3	1	3	16	8	34	0	0	224	261	312	573	5%	78%	0.22	51	50	2.79	-37
Sweeney,Matthew	10	L	22	5	aa	TAM	163	11	29	6	0	2	21	10	45	1	0	178	225	252	477	6%	72%	0.22	52	41	1.89	-56
Tabata,Jose	09	R	21 a	8	aa	PIT	362	43	99	21	1	4	29	24	34	9	9	273	319	371	690	6%	91%	0.72	72	77	4.03	58
	10	R	22	8	aaa	PIT	224	33	61	12	1	2	15	18	26	20	7	272	326	362	688	7%	88%	0.69	65	128	4.29	23
Taveras,Willy	10	R	29	8	aaa	TEX	229	18	40	6	2	2	10	10	28	10	4	173	206	238	445	4%	88%	0.34	43	123	1.57	-6
Taylor,Michael	09	R	24 a	8	a/a	PHI	428	61	124	25	3	19	70	39	61	18	6	291	350	495	845	8%	86%	0.64	126	110	6.43	95
	10	R	25	8	aaa	OAK	464	54	99	20	4	4	53	35	67	11	7	213	268	298	566	7%	86%	0.52	59	111	2.66	5
Teagarden,Taylor	10	R	27	2	a/a	TEX	226	22	44	8	1	4	25	20	78	0	0	195	262	289	551	8%	65%	0.26	61	48	2.59	-71
Tejada,Ruben	09	R	20 a	6	aa	NYM	488	49	128	23	2	4	38	31	47	15	4	262	306	342	648	6%	90%	0.66	58	96	3.81	51
	10	R	21	6	aaa	NYM	218	19	54	10	0	1	12	10	29	1	4	246	279	306	585	4%	87%	0.35	48	39	2.76	-3
Tekotte,Blake	10	L	23	8	aa	SD	268	37	57	7	5	8	31	23	59	5	10	212	273	362	635	8%	78%	0.38	84	147	2.91	-4
Tenbrink,Nathaniel	10	L	24	8	aa	SEA	234	28	54	10	3	4	22	30	45	9	2	230	319	348	666	11%	81%	0.68	74	130	4.09	8
Terrero,Luis	10	R	30	8	a/a	CIN	237	25	52	15	0	9	32	13	62	5	1	219	259	402	660	5%	74%	0.20	118	72	3.54	2
Thames,Eric	10	L	24	8	aa	TOR	496	71	123	23	5	21	77	37	100	7	6	247	300	437	736	7%	80%	0.37	113	107	4.46	26
Thole,Josh	09	L	23 a	2	aa	NYM	384	39	111	26	1	1	37	36	28	6	5	289	350	370	720	9%	93%	1.29	66	61	4.79	61
	10	L	24 a	2	aaa	NYM	165	15	37	17	1	2	13	16	20	0	0	226	293	374	667	9%	88%	0.77	113	43	3.85	60
Thomas,Anthony	09	R	23	4	aa	CHC	427	55	98	23	1	10	34	41	94	11	15	230	297	356	653	9%	78%	0.44	84	78	3.32	22
	10	R	24	4	aa	CHC	402	48	94	26	6	9	53	24	78	11	2	234	277	392	669	6%	81%	0.31	103	148	3.80	18
Thomas,Clete	09	L	26	8	aaa	DET	175	23	45	15	1	1	14	22	46	15	3	258	339	371	710	11%	74%	0.47	89	127	4.89	29
	10	L	27	8	aaa	DET	71	10	11	2	1	3	9	9	27	6	0	155	252	324	576	11%	62%	0.34	95	182	3.03	-52
Thompson,Rich	09	L	30	8	aaa	PHI	445	50	93	17	3	3	26	27	74	19	4	208	254	279	533	6%	83%	0.37	49	134	2.47	27
	10	L	31	8	a/a	PHI	476	48	104	14	3	3	31	23	73	28	4	218	254	282	536	5%	85%	0.31	43	138	2.57	-16
Thorman,Scott	09	L	28	8	aa	KC	399	35	94	14	1	14	48	17	63	5	4	235	266	377	643	4%	84%	0.27	86	60	3.35	34
	10	L	29	3	aaa	KC	479	53	106	26	1	14	58	33	63	4	4	222	272	369	641	6%	87%	0.52	96	61	3.34	39
Thurston,Joe	10	L	31	4	aaa	ATL	465	37	97	14	3	9	48	24	64	5	7	208	247	309	556	5%	86%	0.37	62	67	2.42	7
Timmons,Wes	09	R	30	3	aaa	ATL	322	44	71	15	1	1	22	45	36	9	5	222	317	282	600	12%	89%	1.24	48	89	3.25	47
	10	R	31	5	aaa	ATL	386	48	86	17	1	4	31	45	33	14	8	222	304	304	608	10%	91%	1.37	58	88	3.22	35
Timpner,Clay	09	L	26	8	aa	SF	392	37	85	18	3	5	34	26	47	5	6	216	264	312	576	6%	88%	0.55	66	79	2.66	43
	10	L	27	8	aa	SF	417	32	104	16	2	3	41	27	61	5	4	250	296	317	613	6%	85%	0.44	48	61	3.29	-6
Tolbert,Matt	09	B	27 b	4	aaa	MIN	236	27	56	9	5	2	17	10	31	5	5	236	267	336	603	4%	87%	0.32	62	147	2.91	51
	10	B	28	4	aaa	MIN	173	13	38	7	2	1	8	9	27	4	1	219	257	295	552	5%	84%	0.32	53	106	2.62	-9
Tolleson,Steve	09	R	26	4	a/a	MIN	503	64	116	24	2	6	33	40	68	10	8	230	287	318	605	7%	86%	0.59	62	89	3.07	39
	10	R	27	6	aaa	OAK	292	34	75	13	2	6	29	25	38	6	3	255	314	369	682	8%	87%	0.65	74	88	4.13	25
Tomlin,James	09	R	27	8	aa	LA	387	42	100	19	2	2	26	43	73	9	10	258	333	330	663	10%	81%	0.59	55	76	3.82	13
	10	R	28	8	a/a	TEX	439	38	92	18	1	5	26	27	75	7	0	208	255	289	543	6%	83%	0.36	56	82	2.57	-10
Toregas,Wyatt	09	R	27	2	aaa	CLE	208	17	49	8	0	6	22	13	39	0	1	234	279	354	633	6%	81%	0.33	76	20	3.37	5
	10	R	28	2	a/a	CLE	109	5	17	4	0	2	8	5	14	0	0	157	197	239	436	5%	87%	0.37	55	7	1.50	2
Torres,Eider	09	B	27	6	aaa	CHW	359	30	74	10	1	1	24	20	62	11	7	205	247	246	493	5%	83%	0.33	31	86	1.97	-6
	10	B	28	6	a/a	COL	168	10	40	6	1	0	9	5	14	4	4	236	260	284	543	3%	91%	0.37	38	71	2.35	4
Torres,Tim	09	B	26	6	aa	FLA	224	21	44	8	2	1	23	21	57	7	1	197	265	260	525	8%	74%	0.36	44	114	2.47	-15
	10	B	27	4	a/a	FLA	369	43	83	16	3	10	36	49	90	9	4	224	315	364	679	12%	76%	0.54	87	100	4.09	-3
Tosoni,Rene	09	L	23	8	aa	MIN	425	56	104	24	3	12	63	37	91	7	9	244	305	397	702	8%	79%	0.41	98	90	4.02	38
	10	L	24	0	aa	MIN	185	16	42	7	3	3	18	18	43	2	1	228	298	342	640	9%	77%	0.43	70	109	3.59	-16
Tracy,Andy	09	L	36	3	aaa	PHI	453	55	92	18	1	21	70	53	112	5	1	203	286	387	672	10%	75%	0.47	109	70	3.83	32
	10	L	37	3	aaa	PHI	425	48	94	19	2	17	60	50	118	2	1	220	302	392	694	11%	72%	0.43	104	56	4.16	-4
Tracy,Chad	10	L	30	5	aaa	NYY	159	26	46	9	0	9	27	7	15	0	1	289	318	524	842	4%	90%	0.44	143	46	5.95	86
	10	R	25 a	0	aaa	NYY	281	42	65	11	1	16	45	30	48	4	2	231	305	448	753	10%	83%	0.63	127	46	4.75	54
Tripp,Brandon	10	L	25	8	aa	FLA	394	41	99	31	1	7	36	28	104	4	3	251	301	384	685	7%	74%	0.27	98	63	4.04	-12
Triunfel,Carlos	10	R	21	6	aa	SEA	470	41	108	10	1	5	34	10	43	2	10	230	247	289	536	2%	91%	0.24	38	46	2.16	1
Trumbo,Mark	09	R	24	3	aa	LAA	533	48	145	34	2	13	78	32	91	5	3	272	314	416	729	6%	83%	0.36	97	59	4.68	41
	10	R	25	3	aaa	LAA	532	69	132	25	3	25	82	38	89	2	5	247	298	446	744	7%	83%	0.43	119	60	4.52	44
Tucker,Jonathan	09	R	26 b	8	a/a	BAL	453	66	109	22	4	1	35	47	59	29	11	240	311	311	622	9%	87%	0.80	53	138	3.49	53
	10	R	27	8	a/a	BAL	347	34	63	14	1	2	21	31	40	18	5	182	248	241	489	8%	88%	0.77	45	109	2.08	8

Major League Equivalent Statistics

BATTERS

BATTER	Yr	B	Age	Pos	Lev	Org	ab	r	h	d	t	hr	rbi	bb	k	sb	cs	ba	ob	slg	ops	bb%	ct%	eye	px	sx	rc/g	bpv
Tuiasosopo,Matt	09	R	23	5	aa	SEA	226	37	53	14	0	10	30	32	80	3	1	234	330	425	755	13%	65%	0.41	121	65	5.07	2
	10	R	24	5	aaa	SEA	143	19	30	5	0	4	15	24	29	2	2	208	322	322	644	14%	80%	0.82	71	52	3.66	6
Turner,Justin	09	R	25 a	4	aaa	BAL	387	48	107	25	0	2	37	29	34	8	4	275	326	355	680	7%	91%	0.84	65	72	4.22	54
	10	R	26	4	aaa	NYM	396	50	102	24	1	9	31	24	44	5	4	259	300	396	697	6%	89%	0.54	93	71	4.14	44
Valaika,Chris	09	R	24	6	aaa	CIN	366	26	77	18	1	6	30	13	69	1	0	210	238	312	550	4%	81%	0.20	71	46	2.48	4
	10	R	25	4	aaa	CIN	424	38	110	24	1	4	40	15	63	2	4	259	285	348	633	3%	85%	0.24	67	47	3.38	3
Valdespin,Jordany	10	L	23	4	aa	NYM	112	6	22	7	0	0	6	1	17	3	3	196	204	259	462	1%	85%	0.06	55	70	1.50	-13
Valdez,Alexander	09	B	25	5	aa	OAK	275	30	61	12	3	3	32	23	32	3	4	222	281	318	599	8%	88%	0.71	64	92	2.98	50
	10	B	26	5	aa	OAK	526	61	110	23	5	9	55	29	107	7	1	210	252	324	575	5%	80%	0.28	74	120	2.78	-10
Valdez,Jesus	10	R	26	8	aa	WAS	527	51	125	27	3	8	54	23	76	2	2	237	269	342	611	4%	86%	0.30	73	65	3.14	11
Valencia,Danny	09	R	25 a	5	a/a	MIN	487	65	120	34	3	10	57	31	73	0	4	247	292	392	684	6%	85%	0.42	99	59	3.90	51
	10	R	26	5	aaa	MIN	185	16	43	12	0	0	17	10	29	2	0	234	273	298	572	5%	84%	0.34	57	54	2.89	-5
Vallejo,Jose	09	B	23	4	aa	HOU	412	35	88	12	4	2	28	20	72	8	4	214	250	276	526	5%	82%	0.27	41	107	2.30	6
	10	B	24	4	aa	HOU	99	5	10	0	0	0	2	6	34	1	1	97	147	97	244	5%	65%	0.17	0	56	0.45	-126
Van Kooten,Jason	10	R	26	4	aa	COL	398	52	95	28	3	14	42	25	84	8	7	238	283	425	708	6%	79%	0.30	121	103	3.92	27
Van Ostrand,Jame	09	R	25	3	aa	HOU	367	32	86	15	1	12	51	31	55	0	0	236	295	382	677	8%	85%	0.56	90	24	3.98	36
	10	R	26	3	aa	HOU	312	17	65	15	0	3	36	15	62	1	3	209	245	283	528	5%	80%	0.24	55	25	2.24	-24
Van Slyke,Scott	10	R	24	8	a/a	LA	255	21	48	9	1	3	22	12	32	3	3	188	223	264	487	4%	87%	0.36	51	72	1.85	1
Van Stratten,Nick	10	R	25	8	aa	KC	302	29	67	16	0	1	24	20	31	6	6	221	269	283	552	6%	90%	0.64	52	65	2.49	15
Vazquez,Jorge	09	R	28	3	aa	NYY	225	26	65	14	1	12	49	7	49	0	0	288	310	512	822	3%	78%	0.15	137	37	5.78	42
	10	R	29	3	a/a	NYY	334	38	77	18	0	16	51	14	99	0	0	229	260	427	687	4%	70%	0.14	122	27	3.77	-10
Vazquez,William	10	R	26	2	aa	BOS	131	11	18	2	0	1	6	10	32	0	1	136	200	172	372	7%	76%	0.32	24	46	1.09	-62
Vechionacci,Marco	09	B	23	5	aa	NYY	422	42	85	17	1	10	41	33	112	0	0	202	260	316	576	7%	73%	0.30	73	38	2.80	-20
	10	B	24	3	aa	NYY	406	44	99	14	2	10	43	34	95	5	2	244	301	359	661	8%	77%	0.35	72	77	3.85	-18
Velez,Eugenio	09	B	27 b	8	aa	SF	182	23	46	12	3	2	21	10	24	13	9	252	291	376	667	5%	87%	0.41	85	159	3.32	75
	10	B	28	8	aaa	SF	321	33	76	11	4	4	23	15	45	20	18	236	270	332	602	4%	86%	0.33	60	132	2.55	2
Viciedo,Dayan	09	R	21	5	aa	CHW	504	65	135	19	0	12	70	22	76	4	2	268	298	378	676	4%	85%	0.29	71	63	4.01	25
	10	R	22	3	aaa	CHW	343	33	86	13	0	18	37	9	62	1	1	250	270	448	717	3%	82%	0.15	116	29	4.12	27
Vitters,Joshua	10	R	21	5	aa	CHC	206	21	41	11	0	5	19	10	30	1	0	201	238	328	567	5%	86%	0.34	86	53	2.62	22
Wabick,David	09	L	25	8	aa	NYM	426	31	104	26	1	3	41	15	68	4	4	245	271	331	602	3%	84%	0.22	67	53	3.02	14
	10	L	26	8	a/a	NYM	180	15	43	14	1	1	17	6	28	1	4	240	263	342	605	3%	84%	0.20	80	63	2.80	9
Wagner,Mark	09	R	25 a	2	a/a	BOS	307	28	76	33	0	5	37	33	51	1	0	248	321	401	722	10%	83%	0.64	119	33	4.68	60
	10	R	26	2	aaa	BOS	127	9	23	6	0	2	12	7	22	0	0	181	226	268	494	5%	83%	0.34	61	23	1.99	-7
Walker,Brian	10	L	25	2	a/a	LAA	120	7	25	6	0	3	21	4	19	3	1	212	235	329	564	3%	84%	0.20	78	50	2.55	7
Walker,Neil	09	B	24 a	5	aa	PIT	356	30	83	29	1	11	55	20	50	4	2	232	273	407	680	5%	86%	0.40	120	59	3.78	70
	10	B	25 a	4	aaa	PIT	168	19	45	16	1	4	19	14	24	8	1	269	325	442	767	8%	85%	0.58	124	104	5.39	58
Wallace,Brett	09	L	23	5	aa	OAK	532	55	129	22	0	14	46	33	84	1	3	243	288	361	649	6%	84%	0.40	76	31	3.58	21
	10	L	24	3	aaa	TOR	385	37	88	19	1	11	36	16	56	1	1	229	261	367	627	4%	85%	0.29	89	49	3.23	23
Waring,Brandon	10	R	25	5	aa	BAL	472	54	101	27	1	19	55	44	144	0	1	214	281	397	677	9%	70%	0.31	115	36	3.80	-11
Watts,Kristopher	10	L	26	2	aa	PIT	173	19	39	11	0	3	15	23	18	0	0	223	314	335	650	12%	89%	1.24	81	26	3.82	48
Weeks,Jemile	09	B	23	4	aa	OAK	105	7	21	4	0	1	9	7	11	3	0	200	250	267	517	6%	90%	0.64	48	61	2.38	30
	10	B	24	4	aa	OAK	273	34	63	12	5	2	26	23	30	9	7	230	288	330	619	8%	89%	0.76	65	146	3.13	26
Weglarz,Nick	09	L	22 a	8	aa	CLE	339	64	73	16	1	14	60	73	71	2	3	215	353	393	747	18%	79%	1.02	109	64	5.02	60
	10	L	23 a	8	a/a	CLE	312	40	78	24	1	10	37	40	55	2	2	250	335	429	765	11%	82%	0.73	121	56	5.18	51
Wells,Casper	09	R	25	8	aa	DET	311	41	71	15	3	12	33	34	86	7	9	228	304	417	720	10%	72%	0.39	114	105	4.05	33
	10	R	26	8	aaa	DET	387	42	78	19	5	17	35	25	94	6	8	202	251	406	656	6%	76%	0.27	121	112	3.08	15
Wheeler,Zelous	10	R	24	6	aa	MIL	480	60	114	20	1	9	51	58	66	6	5	237	319	337	656	11%	86%	0.87	66	64	3.83	21
White,Christopher	10	B	23	8	a/a	DET	152	13	34	8	0	3	10	7	27	8	4	224	258	336	593	4%	82%	0.26	77	83	2.77	1
Whitesell,Josh	09	L	27	3	aa	ARI	225	26	57	13	1	6	44	31	43	1	1	252	342	400	742	12%	81%	0.71	96	50	5.01	41
	10	L	28	3	aaa	WAS	184	18	45	9	1	3	26	23	45	0	0	244	328	344	672	11%	75%	0.50	69	39	4.16	-20
Whiting,Boomer	10	B	27	8	aaa	WAS	310	43	66	10	2	0	13	40	78	29	12	214	304	258	563	12%	75%	0.52	34	136	2.84	-49
Whittleman,John	09	L	23	5	aa	TEX	438	49	89	26	1	8	46	65	90	3	2	203	306	322	628	13%	79%	0.72	83	56	3.50	29
	10	L	24	3	aa	TEX	259	20	48	13	1	4	25	34	62	1	2	185	281	288	568	12%	76%	0.55	70	44	2.75	-14
Widlansky,Robert	10	L	26	3	aa	BAL	279	22	65	13	0	5	22	13	41	0	0	232	267	330	597	5%	85%	0.32	68	19	3.04	6
Williams,Jackson	09	R	23	2	aa	SF	300	28	62	20	0	2	21	29	52	1	6	206	277	291	567	9%	83%	0.56	68	36	2.58	16
	10	R	24	2	a/a	SF	317	25	57	14	1	4	24	33	71	1	2	179	255	266	522	9%	78%	0.46	62	45	2.27	-19
Wilson,Josh	09	R	28	6	aa	SEA	103	11	21	4	1	2	11	7	15	2	1	205	256	316	572	6%	86%	0.48	72	100	2.70	45
	10	R	30	6	aaa	SEA	81	4	20	9	1	0	8	0	14	0	1	244	244	372	616	0%	83%	0.00	103	77	2.89	16
Wilson,Michael	09	B	26	8	aa	SEA	235	28	39	6	1	8	24	25	83	5	0	164	244	301	546	10%	65%	0.30	79	99	2.53	-27
	10	B	27	8	a/a	SEA	392	54	84	14	1	17	54	41	91	9	5	214	289	383	672	10%	77%	0.45	100	84	3.72	8
Wilson,Neil	10	R	27	2	a/a	FLA	138	11	25	6	0	5	15	9	30	0	0	180	231	320	551	6%	78%	0.30	87	18	2.43	-4
Wilson,Steffan	10	R	24	3	aa	MIL	206	16	36	10	0	5	23	15	55	2	1	172	230	289	519	7%	73%	0.28	77	49	2.16	-29
Wimberly,Corey	09	B	26	6	aa	OAK	297	39	70	8	2	0	20	17	23	15	9	234	275	275	551	5%	92%	0.72	31	123	2.49	43
	10	B	27	8	aaa	OAK	531	63	115	11	4	2	37	38	48	37	22	217	269	262	530	7%	91%	0.79	30	130	2.24	3
Winfree,David	09	R	24	8	aaa	MIN	422	39	100	28	2	11	51	22	80	0	2	237	275	387	661	5%	81%	0.28	101	43	3.59	30
	10	R	25	8	aaa	SEA	420	46	99	26	1	10	55	15	67	3	1	235	261	376	637	3%	84%	0.22	96	69	3.35	22
Wood,Brandon	09	R	25 a	5	aa	LAA	386	57	103	27	3	18	62	31	74	1	1	266	320	492	813	7%	81%	0.42	141	75	5.66	76
	10	R	26	5	aaa	LAA	51	3	8	0	0	1	1	2	12	0	0	147	178	203	381	4%	77%	0.16	29	18	1.13	-60
Worth,Danny	09	R	24	4	a/a	DET	436	35	91	19	3	0	24	31	97	6	7	209	262	265	527	7%	78%	0.32	44	81	2.28	-14
	10	R	25	5	aaa	DET	164	14	41	5	0	2	14	8	24	10	2	252	285	316	601	4%	85%	0.32	44	86	3.30	-12
Wright,Ty	09	R	25	8	aa	CHC	442	55	115	21	1	8	47	28	54	4	5	261	304	365	669	6%	88%	0.51	71	62	3.86	40
	10	R	26	8	a/a	CHC	464	50	106	24	1	8	46	14	46	5	3	229	252	332	584	3%	90%	0.31	72	75	2.79	26
Wrigley,Henry	10	R	24	5	aa	TAM	254	26	55	11	1	8	31	10	49	1	1	215	244	355	599	4%	81%	0.20	87	62	2.85	2
Yarbrough,Brandoı	09	L	25	2	aa	STL	119	11	29	6	1	1	9	16	33	0	1	242	333	331	664	12%	72%	0.49	62	59	3.98	-18
	10	L	26	2	aa	CIN	233	18	50	13	0	3	16	15	71	1	4	214	261	307	568	6%	69%	0.21	69	34	2.55	-53
Yepez,Jose	10	R	29	2	a/a	SEA	122	10	30	9	0	0	14	8	19	0	0	247	292	317	609	6%	85%	0.42	62	24	3.29	3
Young Jr.,Eric	09	B	24 a	4	aa	COL	472	93	129	19	8	6	34	43	64	45	15	273	334	382	716	8%	87%	0.68	69	191	4.65	78
	10	B	25	4	a/a	COL	136	15	29	5	1	1	6	10	24	7	0	214	270	283	553	7%	82%	0.42	47	122	2.87	-18
Young,Matt	09	L	27 b	8	a/a	ATL	486	70	118	19	6	4	29	80	62	35	17	242	349	331	681	14%	87%	1.29	59	142	4.21	69
	10	L	28	8	aaa	ATL	487	67	118	26	4	2	26	45	50	30	7	242	306	322	628	8%	90%	0.90	60	136	3.64	26
Zawadzki,Lance	09	B	24	6	aa	SD	346	46	82	14	4	4	34	35	66	11	1	236	305	333	638	9%	81%	0.53	64	136	3.77	36
	10	B	25	6	a/a	SD	373	42	67	11	1	4	25	27	84	9	7	179	235	244	479	7%	77%	0.32	45	97	1.84	-39

Major League Equivalent Statistics

PITCHERS

	Actual																Major League Equivalents									

PITCHER	Yr	Age Th		Lev	Org	w	l	g	sv	ip	h	er	hr	bb	k	era	whip	bf/g	oob	ctl	dom	cmd	hr/9	h%	s%	bpv
Abad,Fernando	10	25 L	a	a/a	HOU	4	3	19	0	46	61	14	4	8	35	2.82	1.50	10.7	312	1.6	6.8	4.2	0.8	37%	84%	98
Abreu,Erick	09	26 R		a/a	HOU	5	2	33	0	75	99	44	13	28	48	5.33	1.69	10.5	311	3.3	5.7	1.7	1.6	34%	73%	15
	10	27 R		a/a	HOU	4	6	36	0	99	122	47	15	28	65	4.28	1.51	12.2	296	2.5	5.9	2.4	1.4	33%	76%	40
Abreu,Juan	10	25 R		aa	ATL	4	2	39	11	44	51	19	2	24	39	3.85	1.71	5.2	284	5.0	7.9	1.6	0.5	36%	77%	65
Abreu,Winston	09	33 R		aaa	TAM	3	1	37	15	51	27	15	5	17	65	2.60	0.87	5.2	155	3.0	11.4	3.8	0.9	22%	76%	145
	10	33 R		aaa	TAM	0	4	51	23	55	40	16	1	21	67	2.58	1.11	4.4	199	3.4	10.9	3.2	0.2	30%	75%	142
Accardo,Jeremy	09	28 R		aaa	TOR	2	1	27	13	30	36	12	1	8	22	3.47	1.47	4.9	290	2.5	6.6	2.6	0.3	36%	76%	81
	10	29 R		aaa	TOR	3	2	42	24	44	53	15	1	14	21	3.08	1.52	4.6	291	2.9	4.4	1.5	0.2	33%	79%	49
Acosta,Manny	10	29 R		aaa	NYM	2	3	28	5	36	33	16	4	16	27	4.11	1.37	5.5	238	4.1	6.8	1.7	1.1	28%	73%	50
Additon,Nicholas	09	22 L		aa	STL	2	3	8	0	48	39	18	5	19	22	3.38	1.21	24.8	218	3.6	4.1	1.2	0.9	23%	75%	32
	10	23 L		aa	STL	9	6	28	0	150	165	78	19	49	93	4.68	1.43	23.3	273	2.9	5.6	1.9	1.1	31%	70%	39
Adkins,James	09	24 L		aa	LA	6	10	27	19	138	169	86	9	77	70	5.57	1.78	24.1	295	5.0	4.5	0.9	0.6	33%	68%	24
	10	25 L		a/a	LA	3	2	45	1	49	54	30	5	23	43	5.48	1.55	4.9	272	4.2	7.8	1.9	0.9	34%	65%	59
Adkins,Jon	10	33 R		aaa	CHW	2	6	48	10	53	81	36	4	18	16	6.08	1.87	5.3	344	3.0	2.7	0.9	0.7	37%	67%	0
Aguilar,Omar	10	25 R		aa	CLE	2	7	47	7	62	69	32	2	32	58	4.68	1.63	6.0	276	4.7	8.4	1.8	0.3	36%	70%	78
Albaladejo,Jonathan	09	27 R	b	aaa	NYY	3	0	27	11	36	31	10	5	3	21	2.58	0.95	5.2	227	0.8	5.3	6.9	1.3	24%	82%	148
	10	28 R	b	aaa	NYY	4	2	57	43	63	46	13	4	19	70	1.80	1.03	4.4	201	2.7	10.0	3.7	0.6	28%	86%	135
Albano,Marco	09	26 R		aa	LAA	6	6	30	0	88	101	55	13	44	64	5.64	1.64	13.4	282	4.5	6.5	1.5	1.3	32%	68%	29
	10	27 R		aaa	LAA	3	6	15	0	59	73	45	3	40	25	6.89	1.91	19.0	296	6.1	3.8	0.6	0.5	33%	62%	17
Alburquerque,Alberto	10	24 R		aa	COL	2	4	25	3	34	39	25	1	19	26	6.67	1.70	6.3	281	5.0	6.8	1.4	0.3	35%	57%	59
Alderson,Tim	09	21 R		aa	PIT	9	2	20	0	111	123	53	9	24	56	4.32	1.32	23.6	275	1.9	4.5	2.3	0.7	31%	68%	55
	10	22 R		aa	PIT	7	6	18	0	89	125	64	10	25	49	6.46	1.68	22.8	324	2.5	4.9	2.0	1.0	36%	61%	31
Allison,Jeff	10	26 R		aa	FLA	6	11	29	0	110	169	84	20	39	46	6.90	1.89	18.3	344	3.2	3.7	1.2	1.6	36%	66%	-16
Alvarez,Manuel	10	25 R	a	a/a	NYM	3	3	38	8	53	46	20	6	8	49	3.33	1.03	5.5	231	1.4	8.2	5.9	1.1	28%	72%	150
Alvarez,Mario	10	27 R		aa	LA	6	6	33	2	120	189	77	8	57	57	5.77	2.05	18.1	350	4.3	4.2	1.0	0.6	39%	71%	13
Anderson,Jason	09	30 R		a/a	PHI	3	3	51	8	70	80	41	11	29	32	5.29	1.55	6.2	281	3.7	4.1	1.1	1.4	29%	69%	4
	10	31 R		a/a	PHI	2	8	42	4	76	110	50	7	21	43	5.91	1.72	8.4	331	2.5	5.1	2.0	0.8	38%	65%	39
Anton,Michael	09	25 L		aa	LAA	3	8	20	0	81	104	63	7	47	51	7.00	1.87	19.4	305	5.3	5.7	1.1	0.8	35%	61%	26
	10	25 L		aa	LAA	5	12	27	0	138	176	100	27	67	82	6.52	1.75	23.9	303	4.3	5.3	1.2	1.7	33%	66%	0
Antonini,Michael	09	24 L		a/a	NYM	7	6	27	0	122	178	95	11	38	79	6.99	1.77	21.2	333	2.8	5.8	2.1	0.8	39%	59%	41
	10	25 L		a/a	NYM	8	12	29	0	168	194	88	23	32	105	4.73	1.34	24.7	283	1.7	5.6	3.3	1.2	32%	68%	64
Aquino,Greg	09	32 R		aaa	CLE	1	2	30	16	31	31	14	3	16	23	3.95	1.48	4.6	251	4.6	6.6	1.4	0.9	30%	76%	47
	10	33 R		aaa	CHW	1	6	40	10	49	54	39	14	24	41	7.14	1.59	5.5	272	4.4	7.5	1.7	2.5	29%	61%	6
Arbiso,Cory	10	24 R		aa	NYY	5	5	32	0	84	117	49	12	22	42	5.29	1.65	12.0	322	2.4	4.5	1.9	1.2	35%	70%	20
Archer,Chris	10	22 R		aa	CHC	8	2	13	0	70	53	16	2	38	58	2.06	1.30	22.7	206	4.9	7.5	1.5	0.3	27%	84%	83
Arguello,Douglas	09	25 L		aa	HOU	3	4	14	0	75	80	32	4	26	46	3.79	1.42	23.2	268	3.2	5.5	1.7	0.5	31%	73%	56
	10	26 L		aa	HOU	7	5	22	0	127	156	50	6	54	77	3.54	1.65	26.4	296	3.9	5.5	1.4	0.4	35%	78%	47
Arias,Santos	10	24 R		aa	MIN	0	7	23	0	37	45	23	5	20	20	5.50	1.75	7.5	295	4.8	4.9	1.0	1.3	32%	71%	10
Arias,Wilkin	09	29 L		aa	NYY	5	4	48	0	61	83	44	6	30	45	6.43	1.84	6.1	316	4.4	6.6	1.5	0.9	37%	65%	35
	10	30 L		aa	NYY	4	3	57	0	61	91	39	8	39	47	5.69	2.11	5.4	337	5.7	6.9	1.2	1.2	40%	75%	20
Arnesen,Erik	09	26 R		aa	WAS	8	6	22	0	123	179	82	14	30	71	6.01	1.70	25.8	332	2.2	5.2	2.4	1.1	37%	65%	38
	10	27 R		a/a	WAS	8	10	34	2	148	186	84	18	42	81	5.13	1.54	19.4	300	2.6	4.9	1.9	1.1	33%	68%	32
Arrieta,Jake	09	24 R		a/a	BAL	11	11	28	0	150	177	82	19	59	124	4.91	1.57	24.1	288	3.5	7.4	2.1	1.1	35%	71%	52
	10	25 R		aaa	BAL	6	2	12	0	73	55	18	4	33	54	2.22	1.21	25.1	205	4.1	6.7	1.6	0.5	25%	83%	73
Atkins,Mitch	09	24 R		aaa	CHC	8	12	27	0	146	188	131	32	54	109	8.07	1.66	24.8	306	3.3	6.7	2.0	2.0	34%	53%	17
	10	25 R		aaa	CHC	8	3	28	1	106	105	46	14	40	66	3.90	1.37	16.3	253	3.4	5.6	1.7	1.2	28%	76%	37
Augenstein,Bryan	09	23 R	a	a/a	ARI	7	5	17	0	81	78	31	2	14	57	3.44	1.13	19.4	248	1.6	6.3	4.1	0.2	31%	68%	122
	10	24 R		a/a	ARI	6	9	25	0	129	196	109	14	37	92	7.62	1.81	24.4	342	2.6	6.4	2.5	1.0	40%	57%	47
Aumont,Phillippe	10	22 R		aa	PHI	1	6	11	0	49	60	45	4	37	32	8.23	1.97	21.9	295	6.8	5.9	0.9	0.7	34%	56%	27
Avery,James	09	25 R		aa	CIN	2	3	10	0	56	71	30	4	22	25	4.82	1.67	25.7	303	3.6	4.1	1.1	0.7	33%	71%	21
	10	26 R		aa	CIN	2	3	8	0	46	73	37	11	18	20	7.17	1.98	28.2	353	3.5	3.9	1.1	2.2	36%	68%	-34
Axford,John	09	27 R		a/a	MIL	5	0	26	1	40	37	20	3	24	38	4.48	1.52	6.9	238	5.5	8.5	1.5	0.7	31%	71%	68
Ayala,Luis	10	33 R		aaa	COL	2	10	36	4	47	65	36	4	16	25	6.82	1.72	6.1	321	3.0	4.7	1.6	0.8	36%	59%	28
Baez,Federico	09	28 R		a/a	CIN	6	3	43	0	58	93	38	9	25	36	5.84	2.03	6.7	354	3.8	5.5	1.4	1.5	40%	74%	4
	10	29 R		a/a	CIN	1	2	38	5	56	68	27	6	34	22	4.30	1.83	7.0	294	5.5	3.6	0.6	1.0	31%	78%	2
Baez,Manauris	10	25 R		aaa	KC	2	2	8	0	33	47	29	4	16	15	7.99	1.93	20.0	330	4.4	4.1	0.9	1.1	36%	58%	0
Bailey,Homer	09	23 R		aaa	CIN	8	5	14	0	89	103	35	14	28	72	3.53	1.47	28.0	283	2.8	7.3	2.6	1.4	33%	82%	54
	10	24 R	a	aaa	CIN	2	0	4	0	19	17	6	0	5	13	2.84	1.16	19.4	235	2.4	6.2	2.6	0.0	30%	73%	100
Baker,Brian	09	27 R		aa	TAM	5	6	31	0	121	172	91	14	48	78	6.75	1.82	18.5	328	3.6	5.8	1.6	1.0	38%	63%	28
	10	28 R		aaa	TAM	9	5	37	0	105	115	53	11	44	59	4.51	1.51	12.6	272	3.8	5.0	1.3	0.9	31%	72%	32
Baldwin,Andrew	09	27 R		aaa	SEA	6	11	31	0	151	179	82	20	39	88	4.89	1.44	21.3	288	2.3	5.3	2.3	1.2	32%	69%	41
	10	28 R		aaa	SEA	9	7	32	1	117	152	71	13	38	73	5.42	1.62	16.6	307	2.9	5.6	1.9	1.0	35%	67%	39
Balester,Collin	09	23 R		aaa	WAS	7	10	20	0	107	150	67	5	37	61	5.63	1.75	25.0	324	3.1	5.1	1.6	0.4	38%	66%	43
	10	24 R		aaa	WAS	3	3	35	0	69	86	56	9	32	44	7.30	1.71	9.1	299	4.2	5.7	1.4	1.2	34%	57%	23
Ballard,Michael	09	26 L		a/a	TEX	8	8	28	0	151	200	88	21	33	79	5.26	1.54	24.1	312	1.9	4.7	2.4	1.3	34%	68%	34
	10	27 L		aaa	TEX	6	8	29	0	111	162	73	14	33	61	5.93	1.75	17.9	333	2.7	5.0	1.9	1.2	37%	67%	22
Banks,Josh	09	27 R		aaa	SD	7	7	26	0	125	135	54	5	37	78	3.87	1.37	20.6	270	2.7	5.6	2.1	0.4	32%	71%	68
	10	28 R		aaa	HOU	9	12	27	0	171	203	87	27	39	58	4.58	1.41	27.5	289	2.0	3.0	1.5	1.4	29%	72%	4
Banwart,Travis	09	24 R		a/a	OAK	10	6	28	0	145	184	85	11	40	68	5.28	1.54	23.1	303	2.5	4.2	1.7	0.7	34%	65%	35
	10	25 R		a/a	OAK	9	7	29	0	156	160	69	14	56	110	3.98	1.38	23.1	260	3.2	6.3	2.0	0.8	31%	73%	57
Barnes,Scott	09	22 L		aa	CLE	2	2	6	0	31	42	27	8	15	26	7.79	1.83	24.7	316	4.3	7.5	1.7	2.3	35%	61%	4
	10	23 L		aa	CLE	6	11	26	0	138	142	92	14	59	110	5.98	1.46	23.2	261	3.8	7.1	1.9	0.9	31%	59%	57
Bascom,Timothy	09	25 R		aa	BAL	3	7	15	0	81	111	62	6	33	47	6.88	1.76	25.4	318	3.6	5.2	1.4	0.7	36%	59%	31
	10	26 R		a/a	BAL	7	11	28	0	147	224	113	29	42	67	6.89	1.81	24.9	343	2.6	4.1	1.6	1.8	36%	65%	-9

Major League Equivalent Statistics

							Actual				Major League Equivalents																
PITCHER	Yr	Age	Th		Lev	Org	w	l	g	sv	ip	h	er	hr	bb	k	era	whip	bf/g	oob	ctl	dom	cmd	hr/9	h%	s%	bpv
Bass,Brian	10	29	R		aaa	PIT	4	4	41	2	69	86	29	3	23	41	3.79	1.57	7.6	299	2.9	5.3	1.8	0.4	35%	76%	53
Bastardo,Alberto	09	26	L		a/a	LA	6	3	14	0	73	85	40	6	32	49	4.92	1.60	23.6	285	3.9	6.1	1.6	0.8	33%	70%	44
	10	26	L		a/a	LA	12	8	27	0	139	190	88	12	47	85	5.68	1.70	23.8	319	3.0	5.5	1.8	0.8	37%	66%	38
Bateman,Joe	09	29	R		aaa	TAM	6	2	44	4	62	55	29	0	40	51	4.13	1.52	6.3	232	5.7	7.4	1.3	0.0	31%	70%	80
	10	30	R		aaa	TAM	7	0	54	4	76	69	17	3	27	50	1.97	1.26	5.9	237	3.2	6.0	1.9	0.4	29%	86%	71
Bautista,Denny	09	29	R		aaa	PIT	2	3	36	1	48	67	34	2	35	44	6.39	2.13	6.7	324	6.6	8.2	1.2	0.4	41%	68%	53
	10	30	R		aaa	SF	3	2	19	9	22	17	10	1	9	21	4.05	1.15	4.8	205	3.6	8.4	2.3	0.5	27%	64%	100
Bayliss,Jonah	09	29	R		aaa	TOR	7	2	38	5	50	46	25	5	26	37	4.55	1.45	5.8	240	4.7	6.7	1.4	1.0	28%	70%	47
	10	30	R		aaa	HOU	1	4	43	0	65	77	30	8	22	47	4.15	1.52	6.7	287	3.1	6.5	2.1	1.1	33%	76%	48
Bazardo,Yorman	09	25	R		aaa	HOU	9	6	23	0	135	140	60	18	33	68	3.97	1.29	24.7	263	2.2	4.6	2.0	1.2	28%	73%	36
	10	26	R		aaa	HOU	4	5	34	1	88	107	41	12	26	49	4.21	1.51	11.5	294	2.6	5.0	1.9	1.3	32%	76%	27
Beachy,Brandon	10	24	R	a	a/a	ATL	5	1	35	2	119	107	28	5	29	130	2.10	1.14	13.8	236	2.2	9.8	4.5	0.4	33%	83%	150
Beam,T.J.	09	29	R		aaa	TOR	8	4	39	0	119	160	84	12	32	69	6.31	1.61	13.9	316	2.4	5.2	2.2	0.9	36%	60%	41
	10	30	R		aaa	ARI	3	3	43	5	54	61	41	7	42	26	6.85	1.91	6.1	279	7.0	4.4	0.6	1.1	30%	64%	5
Beato,Pedro	09	23	R		aa	BAL	1	3	6	0	32	42	24	9	7	15	6.75	1.53	23.7	310	2.0	4.2	2.1	2.5	30%	63%	-13
	10	24	R		aa	BAL	4	0	43	16	59	58	18	5	19	41	2.66	1.29	5.8	250	2.8	6.2	2.2	0.8	29%	83%	65
Beavan,Blake	09	21	R		aa	TEX	4	4	15	0	89	123	47	5	12	30	4.71	1.52	26.4	321	1.2	3.1	2.5	0.5	35%	68%	47
	10	22	R	a	a/a	SEA	14	8	27	0	168	176	73	11	20	95	3.93	1.17	25.4	264	1.1	5.1	4.7	0.6	30%	66%	113
Bell,Robert	10	25	R		aa	TOR	3	2	10	0	49	74	40	12	13	27	7.35	1.79	23.1	342	2.4	5.0	2.0	2.2	36%	63%	-9
Bell,Trevor	09	23	R		a/a	LAA	7	7	22	0	140	136	49	6	34	75	3.15	1.21	26.3	250	2.2	4.8	2.2	0.4	29%	74%	69
	10	24	R		aaa	LAA	2	0	6	0	30	31	10	3	5	16	3.00	1.20	20.6	261	1.5	4.8	3.2	0.9	29%	79%	72
Below,Duane	10	25	L		aa	DET	7	12	28	0	126	161	84	20	37	84	6.02	1.57	20.2	304	2.6	6.0	2.3	1.4	34%	64%	35
Beltre,Omar	10	29	R		aaa	TEX	3	9	24	2	85	84	31	2	41	66	3.26	1.46	15.5	252	4.3	7.0	1.6	0.2	32%	77%	74
Benacka,Michael	09	27	R	b	a/a	OAK	3	1	55	4	79	70	26	0	38	67	3.01	1.37	6.2	233	4.3	7.6	1.8	0.0	31%	76%	91
	10	28	R		aaa	OAK	6	2	40	5	46	32	22	4	37	49	4.20	1.49	5.1	193	7.1	9.6	1.3	0.8	26%	73%	77
Berg,Justin	09	25	R		aaa	CHC	6	2	37	0	55	47	18	2	30	30	2.96	1.41	6.5	228	4.9	4.8	1.0	0.3	27%	79%	49
	10	26	R		aaa	CHC	4	1	21	0	29	27	13	2	11	14	4.13	1.31	5.9	239	3.5	4.2	1.2	0.6	26%	69%	38
Berger,Eric	09	23	L		aa	CLE	3	1	6	0	33	39	13	1	18	29	3.63	1.71	25.6	288	4.8	7.9	1.7	0.3	37%	78%	71
	10	24	L		a/a	CLE	5	6	23	0	112	122	69	10	72	78	5.55	1.73	22.6	271	5.8	6.2	1.1	0.8	32%	68%	36
Bergmann,Jason	10	29	R		aaa	WAS	6	4	43	0	50	54	22	8	21	44	3.94	1.49	5.1	269	3.7	7.8	2.1	1.4	32%	79%	51
Bibens-Dirkx,Austin	10	25	R		a/a	CHC	10	7	29	0	138	131	67	17	48	85	4.39	1.30	20.1	245	3.2	5.5	1.7	1.1	27%	69%	43
Bierbrodt,Nick	10	32	L		a/a	COL	1	1	35	1	37	56	33	9	26	24	8.11	2.19	5.4	340	6.2	5.9	1.0	2.2	37%	66%	-22
Bierd,Randor	09	26	R		aaa	BOS	3	1	25	0	61	89	48	9	23	48	7.14	1.84	11.6	333	3.4	7.0	2.0	1.3	39%	62%	33
	10	27	R		aaa	BOS	2	4	15	0	48	73	39	6	22	25	7.33	1.97	15.7	343	4.1	4.7	1.2	1.2	38%	63%	5
Billings,Bruce	10	25	R		aa	COL	11	6	34	1	109	105	54	7	44	81	4.42	1.37	13.8	248	3.6	6.7	1.8	0.6	30%	67%	65
Birkins,Kurt	09	29	L		a/a	COL	3	3	27	0	76	109	45	12	33	43	5.34	1.86	13.5	328	3.9	5.0	1.3	1.4	36%	75%	3
	10	30	L		aaa	COL	5	8	23	0	80	116	56	10	21	44	6.24	1.71	16.1	331	2.4	5.0	2.1	1.1	37%	64%	29
Bisenius,Joe	10	28	R		a/a	WAS	4	0	28	0	31	33	18	2	16	27	5.12	1.59	5.0	267	4.8	7.9	1.7	0.7	34%	68%	63
Blackley,Travis	09	27	L		aaa	ARI	4	7	38	3	111	143	63	11	34	86	5.09	1.60	13.2	306	2.8	7.0	2.5	0.9	37%	69%	61
	10	28	L		aaa	OAK	2	1	19	0	42	39	16	3	26	32	3.38	1.55	9.9	241	5.6	6.9	1.2	0.7	29%	80%	54
Bleich,Jeremy	09	22	L		aa	NYY	3	6	13	0	65	104	68	8	37	51	9.42	2.17	25.4	354	5.1	7.1	1.4	1.1	42%	55%	22
	10	23	L		aa	NYY	3	2	8	0	41	40	26	2	28	23	5.64	1.66	23.5	251	6.1	5.1	0.8	0.5	29%	64%	39
Bleier,Richard	10	23	L		aa	TEX	7	11	28	0	164	231	121	16	30	69	6.62	1.59	26.4	325	1.6	3.8	2.3	0.9	35%	57%	34
Blevins,Robert	10	26	R		a/a	LA	2	2	13	0	37	45	19	4	12	15	4.58	1.53	12.7	294	2.8	3.7	1.3	1.0	31%	72%	15
Bongiovanni,Vincent	10	28	R		aa	TOR	6	7	35	2	59	73	43	6	45	31	6.59	1.99	8.3	298	6.8	4.7	0.7	0.9	33%	67%	10
Bonser,Boof	10	29	R		aaa	OAK	2	3	14	0	56	61	35	4	24	34	5.69	1.51	17.8	272	3.8	5.5	1.5	0.7	32%	61%	44
Boone,Randy	09	25	R		a/a	TOR	9	10	27	0	137	171	85	8	51	80	5.60	1.61	23.0	299	3.3	5.2	1.6	0.6	35%	64%	43
	10	26	R		aa	TOR	5	10	24	0	133	156	71	9	44	73	4.82	1.50	24.5	287	3.0	4.9	1.7	0.6	33%	67%	44
Bowden,Michael	09	23	R		aaa	BOS	4	6	24	0	126	137	68	14	52	76	4.85	1.50	23.2	271	3.7	5.4	1.5	1.0	31%	69%	34
	10	24	R		aaa	BOS	6	4	31	1	105	98	55	14	37	66	4.71	1.28	14.3	242	3.2	5.6	1.8	1.2	27%	66%	42
Bowers,Cedrick	09	32	L		aaa	PHI	4	3	48	5	60	46	17	1	48	54	2.52	1.57	5.6	209	7.2	8.1	1.1	0.2	28%	83%	81
	10	33	L		aaa	OAK	2	1	29	0	32	25	13	1	23	42	3.55	1.51	4.9	213	6.5	11.8	1.8	0.3	33%	76%	112
Bowman,Michael	10	23	R		aa	MIL	9	13	26	0	131	168	94	14	54	82	6.44	1.69	23.2	305	3.7	5.7	1.5	1.0	35%	62%	31
Boxberger,Bradley	10	22	R		aa	CIN	1	4	22	0	29	39	32	5	22	35	9.86	2.09	6.6	314	6.8	10.8	1.6	1.5	42%	52%	44
Brackman,Andrew	10	25	R		aa	NYY	5	7	15	0	80	91	33	4	31	60	3.66	1.51	23.7	279	3.4	6.7	2.0	0.5	34%	76%	67
Brasier,Ryan	10	23	R		aa	LAA	7	12	28	0	142	147	96	31	67	78	6.08	1.51	22.5	262	4.2	4.9	1.2	2.0	27%	65%	-2
Braun,Ryan	10	30	R		aaa	CHW	1	3	52	18	57	57	19	6	38	49	2.98	1.65	5.0	254	6.0	7.7	1.3	0.9	31%	85%	51
Bray,Stephen	09	29	R		aa	SEA	7	8	26	0	144	188	76	16	45	64	4.76	1.61	25.1	308	2.8	4.0	1.4	1.0	33%	72%	17
	10	30	R		a/a	SEA	8	12	31	1	140	217	109	21	43	52	6.98	1.86	21.6	347	2.7	3.4	1.2	1.3	36%	63%	-8
Britton,Zachary	10	23	L		a/a	BAL	10	7	27	0	153	159	56	9	49	104	3.29	1.36	24.3	262	2.9	6.1	2.1	0.5	31%	76%	68
Broadway,Lance	09	26	R		aaa	NYM	5	9	19	0	100	145	92	9	41	47	8.24	1.86	25.2	332	3.7	4.2	1.1	0.8	37%	53%	12
	10	27	R		aaa	TOR	3	11	29	0	141	193	103	13	69	74	6.58	1.86	23.2	319	4.4	4.7	1.1	0.8	36%	64%	18
Broadway,Michael	10	23	R		a/a	ATL	5	1	40	1	53	57	30	3	25	52	5.08	1.54	5.9	269	4.2	8.8	2.1	0.5	36%	66%	83
Broderick,Brian	10	24	R		aa	STL	11	2	17	0	100	107	35	5	14	45	3.12	1.21	24.3	268	1.2	4.0	3.3	0.5	30%	75%	80
Bromberg,David	10	23	R		a/a	MIN	6	9	26	0	151	164	68	12	46	94	4.05	1.39	25.0	271	2.7	5.6	2.0	0.7	31%	72%	56
Brooks,Richard	09	25	R	a	aa	CHW	3	1	25	1	37	32	17	3	6	28	4.05	1.02	5.8	230	1.4	6.8	5.0	0.8	27%	61%	131
	10	26	R		aa	CHW	1	3	24	1	41	72	30	5	11	30	6.53	2.04	8.5	376	2.5	6.5	2.6	1.0	44%	68%	43
Brown,Andrew	10	30	R		aaa	STL	3	0	22	0	31	32	22	2	20	22	6.36	1.66	6.5	260	5.7	6.3	1.1	0.6	31%	60%	45
Brown,Brooks	09	24	R		a/a	DET	8	13	26	0	149	184	89	12	65	50	5.35	1.67	26.3	297	3.9	3.0	0.8	0.7	32%	68%	8
	10	25	R		aa	DET	12	9	28	2	128	149	76	10	41	66	5.31	1.48	20.1	285	2.9	4.6	1.6	0.7	32%	64%	38
Browning,Barret	09	25	L		aa	LAA	3	10	48	0	90	115	58	3	48	58	5.78	1.81	8.9	303	4.8	5.8	1.2	0.3	36%	66%	45
	10	26	L		a/a	LAA	7	5	51	0	88	112	58	7	42	68	5.91	1.74	8.1	302	4.3	7.0	1.6	0.8	37%	65%	48
Brummett,Tyson	09	25	R		a/a	PHI	3	10	27	2	102	153	80	17	29	59	7.05	1.78	17.8	339	2.6	5.2	2.0	1.5	37%	62%	16
	10	26	R		aa	PHI	1	2	28	1	55	83	39	2	16	25	6.37	1.79	9.3	339	2.6	4.1	1.6	0.4	38%	62%	34

Major League Equivalent Statistics

					Actual												Major League Equivalents									
PITCHER	Yr	Age	Th		Lev	Org	w	l	g	sv	ip	h	er	hr	bb	k	era	whip	bf/g	oob	ctl	dom	cmd	hr/9	h%	s%	bpv
Buchter,Ryan	10	24	L		aa	CHC	7	2	47	0	60	69	36	7	47	60	5.41	1.94	6.2	283	7.1	9.0	1.3	1.1	36%	74%	47
Buck,Dallas	09	25	R		aa	CIN	2	3	8	0	37	61	27	1	20	21	6.64	2.18	23.7	360	4.9	5.1	1.0	0.3	42%	67%	28
	10	26	R		aa	CIN	3	4	9	0	39	69	36	4	16	16	8.18	2.16	22.1	376	3.6	3.7	1.0	1.0	41%	61%	-7
Buckner,Billy	09	26	R		aaa	ARI	9	3	18	0	103	98	40	5	41	82	3.51	1.35	24.4	246	3.6	7.2	2.0	0.5	31%	74%	78
	10	27	R		aaa	DET	6	6	15	0	80	120	71	13	34	39	7.91	1.92	25.9	339	3.8	4.4	1.2	1.4	36%	59%	-5
Buente,Jay	09	26	R		a/a	FLA	5	2	51	2	83	96	38	8	50	65	4.10	1.75	7.6	283	5.4	7.0	1.3	0.8	34%	78%	43
	10	27	R		a/a	FLA	1	1	30	1	43	43	19	4	27	41	3.94	1.62	6.5	256	5.6	8.4	1.5	0.9	32%	78%	59
Bullington,Bryan	09	29	R	b	aaa	TOR	3	1	28	3	38	49	18	2	8	34	4.15	1.50	6.0	308	1.8	8.0	4.4	0.5	39%	72%	118
	10	30	R		aaa	KC	8	2	20	0	102	103	38	8	27	58	3.39	1.28	21.4	258	2.4	5.1	2.1	0.7	29%	75%	58
Bullock,William	10	23	R	a	aa	MIN	2	4	30	13	36	37	15	3	23	50	3.73	1.66	5.5	259	5.7	12.4	2.2	0.7	39%	79%	101
Bumgarner,Madison	09	20	L		aa	SF	9	1	20	0	107	90	28	6	29	62	2.32	1.10	21.5	223	2.4	5.2	2.2	0.5	26%	81%	73
	10	21	L		aaa	SF	7	1	14	0	82	85	28	5	18	54	3.09	1.26	24.5	263	2.0	5.9	3.0	0.5	31%	76%	85
Bump,Nate	09	33	R		aaa	DET	7	1	10	0	68	73	25	4	11	27	3.34	1.22	28.2	268	1.4	3.5	2.5	0.6	29%	73%	59
	10	34	R		aaa	PHI	8	4	20	0	107	153	54	9	27	44	4.51	1.68	24.6	328	2.3	3.7	1.6	0.8	36%	74%	21
Burke,Greg	10	28	R		aaa	SD	2	2	53	0	58	68	38	11	22	38	5.82	1.53	4.9	285	3.3	5.9	1.8	1.7	31%	66%	21
Burnett,Alex	09	22	R	a	aa	MIN	1	2	40	9	55	42	17	2	19	43	2.78	1.11	5.5	207	3.1	7.0	2.3	0.3	26%	75%	93
	10	23	R		aaa	MIN	0	2	14	2	19	28	13	1	8	15	6.09	1.88	6.6	333	3.8	7.0	1.9	0.5	41%	66%	56
Burres,Brian	09	29	L		aaa	TOR	6	7	19	0	107	139	65	12	31	68	5.42	1.58	25.4	307	2.6	5.7	2.2	1.0	35%	67%	44
	10	29	L		aaa	PIT	5	4	15	0	82	89	48	10	34	46	5.31	1.50	24.2	271	3.7	5.1	1.4	1.1	30%	66%	27
Burton,Jared	10	29	R		aaa	CIN	3	2	33	4	38	36	14	5	18	27	3.38	1.42	5.0	246	4.2	6.5	1.6	1.2	28%	82%	38
Burton,TJ	09	26	R		a/a	HOU	0	4	37	12	49	77	36	13	16	20	6.50	1.87	6.4	348	2.8	3.6	1.3	2.4	35%	72%	-39
	10	27	R		a/a	HOU	5	3	25	1	38	61	37	8	20	15	8.69	2.11	7.7	354	4.6	3.5	0.8	1.9	36%	60%	-36
Buschmann,Matthew	09	26	R		a/a	SD	5	11	35	0	140	181	96	15	44	67	6.16	1.61	18.1	307	2.8	4.3	1.5	0.9	34%	62%	22
	10	27	R		a/a	SD	2	6	40	0	91	100	58	7	47	76	5.70	1.61	10.3	273	4.6	7.5	1.6	0.7	34%	63%	59
Butler,Josh	09	25	R		a/a	MIL	3	2	11	0	56	60	23	4	14	43	3.65	1.33	21.6	268	2.3	6.9	3.0	0.7	33%	74%	85
	10	26	R		a/a	MIL	8	6	18	0	99	112	54	7	48	54	4.88	1.62	24.9	278	4.4	4.9	1.1	0.7	32%	70%	32
Butts,Brett	09	23	R		aa	ATL	7	3	53	5	73	77	28	6	39	58	3.43	1.59	6.2	266	4.8	7.2	1.5	0.8	32%	80%	53
	10	24	R	a	aa	ATL	0	1	15	3	23	21	5	0	6	24	2.04	1.18	6.3	237	2.5	9.2	3.8	0.0	34%	81%	142
Buursma,Jason	10	25	R		aa	STL	2	1	37	0	57	47	19	4	10	20	2.97	0.99	6.0	218	1.6	3.1	2.0	0.7	23%	72%	51
Buzachero,Edward	09	28	R		a/a	TOR	5	4	49	10	72	64	28	9	18	41	3.52	1.13	6.0	232	2.2	5.1	2.3	1.2	25%	74%	53
	10	29	R		a/a	HOU	8	1	39	1	93	150	89	17	40	39	8.61	2.04	11.8	356	3.9	3.8	1.0	1.7	37%	58%	-22
Cabrera,Alberto	10	22	R		aa	CHC	0	4	10	0	42	63	34	1	23	31	7.25	2.04	20.9	338	4.9	6.6	1.3	0.2	41%	61%	49
Cabrera,Fernando	09	28	R		aaa	BOS	0	3	43	22	52	55	17	4	25	42	2.90	1.53	5.4	264	4.4	7.2	1.7	0.7	32%	83%	58
	10	29	R		aaa	BOS	2	5	54	22	60	81	35	6	26	60	5.30	1.77	5.2	314	3.9	9.0	2.3	1.0	40%	71%	67
Caldera,Alexander	10	25	R		aa	KC	3	2	8	0	38	43	25	7	17	23	5.95	1.57	21.4	279	4.0	5.4	1.4	1.7	30%	66%	8
Calero,Kiko	10	36	R		aaa	LA	2	0	25	1	32	38	21	4	15	21	5.92	1.64	5.8	289	4.1	5.9	1.4	1.2	33%	65%	27
Cales,David	10	23	R		a/a	CHC	4	2	57	13	73	77	36	4	23	51	4.43	1.37	5.5	265	2.8	6.3	2.2	0.5	32%	67%	71
Capra,Anthony	10	23	L		aa	OAK	6	13	28	0	130	134	70	8	86	100	4.85	1.69	21.4	261	5.9	6.9	1.2	0.6	32%	71%	52
Carlson,Jesse	10	30	L		aaa	TOR	3	1	45	4	51	58	22	5	11	35	3.88	1.36	4.8	281	1.9	6.1	3.1	1.0	33%	74%	72
Carmona,Ysmael	10	26	R		a/a	LAA	5	3	44	12	61	45	20	2	39	48	2.95	1.38	6.0	203	5.7	7.0	1.2	0.3	26%	78%	73
Carpenter,Christopher	09	24	R		aa	CHC	0	3	7	0	32	36	23	0	12	20	6.38	1.51	20.3	279	3.5	5.7	1.6	0.0	34%	53%	68
	10	25	R		a/a	CHC	8	6	26	0	134	153	58	8	56	95	3.87	1.55	23.1	280	3.7	6.4	1.7	0.6	34%	75%	56
Carpenter,Drew	09	24	R		aaa	PHI	11	6	25	0	156	188	73	23	48	102	4.21	1.51	27.7	292	2.8	5.9	2.1	1.3	33%	77%	37
	10	25	R		aaa	PHI	8	11	27	0	151	181	88	23	57	90	5.24	1.57	25.1	291	3.4	5.8	1.7	1.4	32%	70%	27
Carr,Adam	10	26	R		a/a	WAS	6	2	53	14	72	77	31	3	27	51	3.89	1.44	5.9	267	3.3	6.4	1.9	0.4	33%	72%	68
Carrasco,Carlos	09	23	R	a	aaa	CLE	11	10	26	0	157	160	91	17	43	141	5.24	1.29	25.4	259	2.5	8.1	3.3	1.0	32%	60%	91
	10	24	R		aaa	CLE	10	6	25	0	150	150	66	15	44	118	3.96	1.29	25.3	255	2.6	7.1	2.7	0.9	31%	72%	76
Carrillo,Cesar	09	25	R		a/a	SD	8	7	25	0	150	168	82	11	47	68	4.92	1.44	26.2	278	2.8	4.1	1.4	0.6	31%	65%	35
	10	26	R		aaa	SD	5	14	27	0	151	174	93	15	56	82	5.53	1.52	24.8	283	3.3	4.9	1.5	0.9	32%	64%	31
Carrillo,Marco	09	23	R		aa	CHC	4	1	31	0	51	60	31	8	31	39	5.46	1.78	7.7	287	5.5	6.9	1.3	1.4	33%	72%	23
	10	25	R		a/a	CHC	5	1	29	2	53	63	28	5	18	43	4.74	1.52	8.1	289	3.0	7.3	2.4	0.8	35%	70%	66
Carroll,Scott	10	26	R		aa	CIN	3	9	20	0	117	154	63	8	34	50	4.86	1.61	26.5	311	2.7	3.9	1.5	0.6	34%	69%	28
Carson,Robert	10	22	L		aa	NYM	1	6	10	0	48	69	44	6	22	25	8.22	1.89	23.2	329	4.1	4.7	1.1	1.1	36%	55%	7
Carter,Anthony	10	24	R		aa	CHW	1	4	46	22	57	58	33	8	24	49	5.14	1.44	5.4	258	3.8	7.8	2.0	1.3	31%	67%	53
Cashner,Andrew	09	23	R		aa	CHC	3	4	12	0	58	55	29	0	30	34	4.47	1.46	21.2	244	4.6	5.3	1.1	0.0	30%	66%	62
	10	24	R	a	a/a	CHC	6	1	11	0	57	44	14	1	14	49	2.28	1.03	20.5	210	2.3	7.8	3.4	0.2	28%	77%	127
Cassel,Justin	09	25	R		a/a	CHW	7	11	27	0	126	184	93	19	53	67	6.61	1.88	22.4	333	3.8	4.7	1.3	1.4	36%	66%	3
	10	26	R		a/a	CHW	0	3	7	0	34	33	14	1	13	14	3.82	1.37	20.8	251	3.5	3.6	1.0	0.3	28%	71%	39
Cassevah,Bobby	09	24	R		aa	LAA	3	7	57	4	73	80	43	2	40	36	5.31	1.64	5.9	272	4.9	4.4	0.9	0.3	31%	65%	38
	10	25	R		aaa	LAA	3	4	45	5	59	72	28	6	22	32	4.31	1.59	5.9	294	3.4	4.8	1.4	0.9	33%	75%	27
Castaneda,Federico	10	27	R		a/a	KC	4	2	34	2	85	74	38	13	31	51	4.00	1.24	10.4	231	3.3	5.4	1.6	1.4	24%	73%	34
Castillo,Alberto	09	34	L		aaa	BAL	2	3	50	13	52	63	23	3	18	43	4.01	1.56	4.7	294	3.1	7.4	2.4	0.5	37%	74%	74
	10	35	L		aaa	BAL	1	2	39	4	39	56	25	5	15	34	5.80	1.80	4.7	328	3.4	7.9	2.3	1.2	40%	69%	49
Castillo,Jesus	09	25	R		aa	LA	7	9	29	0	150	191	97	12	66	71	5.80	1.71	24.0	304	3.9	4.3	1.1	0.7	34%	65%	21
	10	26	R		a/a	LA	5	15	25	0	127	176	71	11	50	59	5.04	1.78	23.9	321	3.5	4.1	1.2	0.8	35%	72%	17
Castro,Fabio	09	25	L		a/a	TOR	9	6	29	0	164	192	91	8	72	88	4.98	1.61	25.6	286	4.0	4.8	1.2	0.5	33%	68%	39
	10	26	L		aaa	BOS	7	9	31	0	104	133	73	10	51	86	6.29	1.77	15.7	305	4.4	7.5	1.7	0.9	37%	64%	48
Castro,Simon	10	22	R		a/a	SD	7	7	26	0	140	128	52	7	41	101	3.34	1.21	22.2	238	2.6	6.5	2.5	0.5	29%	72%	84
Cecil,Brett	09	23	L		aa	TOR	1	5	9	0	49	53	33	2	19	28	6.06	1.55	24.3	285	3.5	5.1	1.5	0.4	33%	58%	49
Ceda,Jose	10	24	R	a	aa	FLA	4	1	27	6	32	22	6	2	22	40	1.73	1.35	5.1	188	6.1	11.2	1.8	0.6	28%	90%	106
Chacin,Gustavo	09	29	L		a/a	PHI	9	4	20	0	115	154	59	14	53	48	4.60	1.80	27.2	314	4.1	3.7	0.9	1.1	34%	77%	0
	10	30	L		aaa	HOU	1	1	6	0	25	29	12	5	7	11	4.35	1.41	18.0	281	2.4	3.9	1.7	2.0	28%	78%	-2
Chacin,Jhoulys	09	22	R		a/a	COL	9	8	22	0	117	105	47	13	42	86	3.58	1.25	22.2	234	3.2	6.6	2.1	1.0	27%	75%	60
	10	23	R	a	aaa	COL	3	2	7	0	35	27	6	1	13	30	1.46	1.14	20.4	206	3.4	7.8	2.3	0.2	27%	88%	101

Major League Equivalent Statistics

PITCHERS

						Actual												Major League Equivalents								
PITCHER	Yr	Age	Th		Lev	Org	w	l	g	sv	ip	h	er	hr	bb	k	era	whip	bf/g	oob	ctl	dom	cmd	hr/9	h%	s%	bpv
Chapman,Aroldis	10	23	L	a	aaa	CIN	9	6	39	8	95	83	43	9	50	116	4.05	1.39	10.5	230	4.7	10.9	2.3	0.8	33%	72%	99
Chapman,Chance	09	26	R		aa	PHI	7	1	38	1	52	54	21	4	20	37	3.64	1.43	6.0	263	3.4	6.4	1.8	0.8	31%	76%	56
	10	27	R		aa	PHI	2	3	29	0	50	64	38	3	24	28	6.81	1.77	8.1	306	4.3	5.0	1.2	0.6	35%	59%	30
Chapman,Jaye	10	23	R		aa	ATL	1	4	36	0	50	68	34	1	26	47	6.11	1.87	6.7	317	4.6	8.4	1.8	0.2	41%	64%	74
Chatwood,Tyler	10	21	R		a/a	LAA	5	6	13	0	74	79	32	4	23	36	3.87	1.38	24.5	268	2.8	4.4	1.6	0.4	30%	71%	48
Chavez,Chris	10	26	R		aa	KC	2	0	20	0	32	49	32	6	22	16	9.05	2.23	8.2	346	6.1	4.4	0.7	1.6	37%	60%	-21
Chen,Hung-Wen	09	24	R		aa	CHC	8	11	27	0	142	201	94	16	35	81	5.94	1.66	24.1	326	2.2	5.2	2.3	1.0	37%	65%	38
	10	25	R		a/a	CHC	11	10	32	0	147	172	74	23	34	81	4.54	1.40	19.9	286	2.1	5.0	2.4	1.4	31%	72%	36
Chick,Travis	09	25	R		aa	LA	8	7	23	0	113	139	71	16	53	78	5.66	1.70	22.7	296	4.2	6.2	1.5	1.2	34%	69%	27
	10	26	R		a/a	TEX	2	2	6	0	21	40	26	1	13	14	10.85	2.52	19.2	393	5.7	6.1	1.1	0.5	46%	53%	22
Chico,Matt	09	26	L		aa	WAS	2	4	12	0	50	75	37	2	33	27	6.61	2.16	21.2	338	6.0	4.8	0.8	0.4	39%	67%	21
	10	27	L		a/a	WAS	7	9	26	0	141	197	83	18	47	64	5.27	1.73	25.2	323	3.0	4.1	1.4	1.2	35%	71%	9
Chulk,Vinnie	10	32	R		aaa	PIT	1	0	28	0	32	44	20	3	12	30	5.59	1.73	5.4	320	3.2	8.5	2.6	0.9	40%	68%	71
Cisco,Michael	09	22	R		aa	PHI	2	4	7	0	39	50	24	5	9	17	5.52	1.51	24.7	305	2.1	3.9	1.9	1.2	33%	65%	23
	10	23	R		a/a	PHI	4	11	17	0	97	122	63	14	21	57	5.83	1.47	25.1	301	1.9	5.3	2.7	1.3	33%	62%	45
Cishek,Steven	10	24	R	a	aa	FLA	3	1	22	2	31	37	19	0	12	29	5.48	1.56	6.3	289	3.4	8.5	2.5	0.0	39%	61%	102
Claggett,Anthony	09	25	R		aaa	NYY	7	7	39	4	82	96	39	8	34	37	4.32	1.59	9.5	286	3.8	4.0	1.1	0.9	31%	74%	18
	10	26	R		a/a	PIT	3	1	47	1	69	86	53	8	28	43	6.94	1.64	6.7	297	3.6	5.6	1.6	1.0	34%	57%	32
Clark,Craig	10	26	L		aa	SF	2	3	9	0	42	57	29	6	24	17	6.13	1.93	22.8	318	5.1	3.5	0.7	1.2	34%	70%	-10
Clark,Zachary	09	26	R		a/a	BAL	2	1	15	0	31	54	27	1	12	14	7.72	2.14	10.5	375	3.5	4.2	1.2	0.3	42%	61%	20
	10	27	R		a/a	BAL	1	6	20	1	65	92	38	7	17	25	5.24	1.68	15.0	326	2.4	3.5	1.5	1.0	35%	70%	13
Cobb,Alexander	10	23	R	a	aa	TAM	7	5	23	0	119	135	42	7	35	109	3.17	1.43	22.5	279	2.6	8.2	3.1	0.5	36%	79%	98
Cochran,Thomas	09	27	L		a/a	CIN	5	6	20	1	102	132	54	13	52	63	4.76	1.80	24.1	307	4.6	5.5	1.2	1.1	35%	76%	19
	10	28	L		aa	CIN	8	5	26	0	141	161	59	15	63	80	3.74	1.59	24.5	281	4.0	5.1	1.3	1.0	31%	79%	27
Cody,Chris	09	26	L		a/a	MIL	13	9	27	0	152	176	80	20	42	92	4.73	1.43	24.5	284	2.5	5.5	2.2	1.2	32%	70%	41
	10	27	L		aa	MIL	7	8	26	1	109	152	64	18	38	64	5.31	1.74	19.6	322	3.1	5.2	1.7	1.5	35%	73%	12
Coello,Robert	10	26	R		a/a	BOS	7	6	32	1	107	97	58	16	44	105	4.87	1.32	14.2	236	3.7	8.9	2.4	1.3	29%	66%	71
Cofield,Kyle	09	23	R		aa	ATL	10	5	26	0	140	145	80	11	94	77	5.14	1.70	24.9	262	6.0	4.9	0.8	0.7	30%	70%	28
	10	24	R		aa	ATL	1	3	18	0	55	67	32	4	24	33	5.22	1.65	14.0	294	3.9	5.4	1.4	0.7	34%	68%	38
Cohoon,Mark	10	23	L		aa	NYM	5	4	13	0	71	78	33	5	14	46	4.18	1.31	23.1	274	1.8	5.8	3.2	0.7	32%	68%	82
Coleman,Casey	09	22	R		aa	CHC	14	6	27	0	149	167	78	10	61	72	4.71	1.53	26.6	277	3.7	4.3	1.2	0.6	31%	69%	32
	10	23	R		aaa	CHC	10	7	21	0	117	114	57	10	33	51	4.38	1.26	23.3	250	2.5	3.9	1.5	0.8	27%	66%	38
Coleman,Louis	10	24	R	a	a/a	KC	7	3	42	7	92	69	25	6	24	87	2.42	1.01	8.6	205	2.3	8.5	3.7	0.6	27%	79%	124
Collazo,Willie	09	30	L		aaa	FLA	9	5	34	0	126	149	63	14	38	61	4.47	1.49	16.4	289	2.7	4.4	1.6	1.0	31%	72%	26
Collins,Tim	10	21	L	a	a/a	KC	3	1	56	15	71	41	16	5	23	99	2.05	0.90	4.8	165	2.9	12.5	4.3	0.6	26%	81%	170
Collmenter,Joshua	10	25	R		a/a	ARI	12	6	22	0	137	142	62	12	46	94	4.06	1.38	26.8	262	3.0	6.2	2.0	0.8	31%	72%	58
Concepcion,Alexander	09	25	R		a/a	PHI	2	3	38	3	95	102	44	13	13	45	4.18	1.21	10.3	269	1.2	4.2	3.5	1.2	29%	69%	65
	10	26	R		aaa	PHI	2	2	23	0	30	31	26	6	19	15	7.88	1.68	6.0	263	5.8	4.5	0.8	1.8	27%	55%	-9
Cooney,Brandon	10	25	R		aa	BAL	3	2	35	2	45	46	22	1	22	28	4.44	1.51	5.7	257	4.4	5.6	1.3	0.2	31%	68%	57
Corcoran,Roy	10	30	R		aaa	HOU	2	10	47	9	72	90	43	7	24	39	5.41	1.59	6.9	299	3.1	4.8	1.6	0.8	34%	66%	32
Corcoran,Tim	09	32	R		a/a	HOU	6	7	34	1	99	133	74	11	48	61	6.76	1.83	13.8	315	4.3	5.6	1.3	1.0	36%	63%	22
	10	32	R		aaa	LA	9	8	25	0	107	138	63	7	29	71	5.31	1.56	19.2	306	2.5	6.0	2.4	0.6	36%	65%	62
Cordero,Chad	10	29	R		aaa	NYM	1	2	34	6	35	39	13	2	10	28	3.30	1.37	4.2	274	2.5	7.1	2.9	0.6	34%	77%	87
Cordier,Erik	10	25	R		a/a	ATL	12	8	27	0	143	141	72	3	78	103	4.54	1.53	23.6	252	4.9	6.5	1.3	0.2	31%	68%	65
Cortes,Daniel	09	23	R		aa	SEA	7	11	26	0	135	147	79	8	91	101	5.27	1.76	24.3	272	6.1	6.7	1.1	0.5	33%	69%	48
	10	24	R		a/a	SEA	7	6	34	2	96	96	59	5	56	87	5.53	1.58	12.7	255	5.2	8.1	1.6	0.5	33%	63%	71
Cova,Rafael	10	29	R		aa	SF	0	6	48	23	57	46	25	4	46	46	3.94	1.62	5.4	217	7.3	7.2	1.0	0.6	27%	76%	58
Cox,Bryce	09	25	R		aa	BOS	1	5	45	12	56	84	26	2	31	29	4.10	2.06	6.2	340	5.0	4.6	0.9	0.4	39%	79%	23
	10	26	R		aa	BOS	1	6	42	12	53	67	38	3	30	29	6.43	1.82	6.0	301	5.1	4.9	1.0	0.6	34%	63%	27
Cox,James	10	26	R		aa	NYY	3	0	26	2	33	44	21	1	14	18	5.61	1.73	5.9	311	3.7	5.0	1.3	0.3	36%	65%	41
Cramer,Bob	09	30	L		a/a	OAK	4	5	18	0	57	91	32	1	22	37	5.01	1.99	15.5	355	3.5	5.8	1.7	0.2	42%	73%	49
	10	31	L		aaa	OAK	2	2	7	0	41	46	9	0	10	28	1.94	1.35	25.1	275	2.2	6.1	2.8	0.0	34%	84%	95
Crotta,Michael	09	25	R		aa	PIT	7	8	27	0	143	224	98	8	34	73	6.15	1.81	25.1	349	2.2	4.6	2.1	0.5	40%	64%	42
	10	26	R		a/a	PIT	7	10	28	0	156	212	96	10	41	79	5.51	1.62	25.3	318	2.4	4.6	1.9	0.6	36%	65%	42
Crow,Aaron	10	24	R		aa	KC	7	7	22	0	119	144	84	12	55	72	6.31	1.67	24.9	293	4.1	5.8	1.4	0.9	34%	62%	32
Culp,Nathanial	09	25	L		a/a	SD	8	9	28	0	158	200	83	13	31	53	4.74	1.46	24.7	302	1.8	3.0	1.7	0.8	32%	68%	26
	10	26	L		a/a	SD	5	11	30	1	136	185	81	9	33	65	5.36	1.60	20.5	318	2.2	4.3	2.0	0.6	35%	66%	40
Daigle,Casey	09	29	R		aaa	HOU	4	3	49	5	55	75	24	4	28	43	3.86	1.87	5.4	318	4.6	7.0	1.5	0.7	39%	80%	44
	10	29	R		aaa	HOU	2	3	35	8	44	64	27	7	14	27	5.62	1.77	5.9	332	2.9	5.6	1.9	1.3	37%	71%	22
Daley Jr.,Gary	10	25	R		aa	OAK	3	11	22	0	91	140	82	9	56	52	8.12	2.15	21.0	345	5.5	5.2	0.9	0.9	39%	61%	9
Davidson,Daniel	09	29	L		aaa	LAA	2	3	45	0	50	76	46	12	24	36	8.31	2.00	5.3	343	4.2	6.5	1.5	2.1	38%	61%	-6
	10	30	L		aaa	LAA	8	2	16	0	87	111	54	14	27	48	5.57	1.59	24.5	304	2.8	5.0	1.8	1.5	33%	68%	17
Davis,Erik	10	24	R	a	a/a	SD	5	0	8	0	44	33	14	2	14	37	2.86	1.07	22.0	204	2.9	7.6	2.6	0.4	26%	73%	103
Davis,Tony	10	23	L		aa	MIN	1	2	25	1	37	28	12	0	27	22	2.92	1.49	6.5	206	6.6	5.4	0.8	0.0	25%	78%	63
De La Cruz,Kelvin	10	23	L		aa	CLE	5	6	20	0	93	107	67	11	62	68	6.47	1.81	22.1	282	6.0	6.6	1.1	1.1	33%	65%	29
De La Rosa,Dane	10	28	R		aa	TAM	9	3	47	4	73	90	23	4	31	53	2.82	1.67	7.1	298	3.9	6.5	1.7	0.4	36%	84%	57
De La Rosa,Rubby	10	22	R		aa	LA	3	1	8	0	51	40	8	1	20	32	1.41	1.18	26.1	212	3.5	5.6	1.6	0.2	26%	88%	75
De La Rossa,Wilkins	09	25	L		aa	NYY	4	5	16	0	82	87	47	16	46	63	5.19	1.63	23.4	267	5.1	6.9	1.4	1.7	30%	73%	19
	10	26	L		aa	NYY	2	4	36	0	72	101	54	9	44	47	6.79	2.02	9.9	324	5.5	5.8	1.1	1.1	37%	67%	14
De La Torre,Jose	09	24	R	a	aa	NYM	3	2	18	2	30	26	11	1	17	31	3.15	1.43	7.3	230	5.0	9.4	1.9	0.3	32%	78%	95
	10	25	R		a/a	NYM	3	2	51	3	70	56	22	5	33	65	2.78	1.26	5.8	214	4.2	8.3	2.0	0.7	28%	80%	84
De La Vara,Gilbert	09	25	L		a/a	KC	6	2	38	2	71	107	54	6	35	36	6.80	2.00	9.2	341	4.4	4.6	1.0	0.8	38%	65%	12
	10	26	L		a/a	CIN	2	2	12	0	28	58	25	2	6	25	8.06	2.28	12.2	413	2.0	7.9	3.9	0.7	50%	63%	82
De Los Santos,Fautino	10	25	R	a	aa	OAK	1	5	25	0	31	36	26	1	16	42	7.59	1.65	5.7	282	4.6	12.1	2.6	0.3	43%	50%	117

Major League Equivalent Statistics

							Actual											Major League Equivalents									
PITCHER	Yr	Age	Th		Lev	Org	w	l	g	sv	ip	h	er	hr	bb	k	era	whip	bf/g	oob	ctl	dom	cmd	hr/9	h%	s%	bpv
De Los Santos,Richard	10	26	R		a/a	TAM	14	5	29	0	150	192	76	8	52	70	4.53	1.63	23.5	305	3.1	4.2	1.3	0.5	34%	71%	34
Deduno,Samuel	09	26	R		a/a	COL	12	5	25	0	138	123	54	3	78	100	3.55	1.46	24.2	234	5.1	6.5	1.3	0.2	29%	74%	68
	10	27	R		aaa	COL	3	1	6	0	30	22	11	3	16	24	3.14	1.25	21.0	200	4.7	7.1	1.5	0.9	24%	79%	61
DeHoyos,Gabe	09	30	R		a/a	SD	1	4	28	0	41	48	10	1	21	25	2.13	1.66	6.7	283	4.5	5.4	1.2	0.3	34%	87%	48
	10	30	R		aaa	LAA	5	1	38	1	82	82	31	4	32	61	3.41	1.39	9.3	255	3.5	6.7	1.9	0.5	31%	76%	69
Del Rosario,Enerio	09	24	R		a/a	CIN	1	0	19	5	30	32	5	1	6	17	1.54	1.27	6.6	267	1.8	5.2	2.8	0.3	31%	89%	83
	10	25	R		aaa	CIN	4	4	50	4	64	69	26	4	17	30	3.66	1.34	5.5	270	2.4	4.2	1.8	1.3	29%	78%	25
Delaney,Rob	09	25	R		a/a	MIN	8	4	62	7	83	91	41	6	22	61	4.44	1.35	5.7	271	2.4	6.6	2.8	0.7	33%	67%	77
	10	26	R		aaa	MIN	7	9	61	4	80	92	46	11	23	75	5.22	1.43	5.7	282	2.6	8.4	3.3	1.3	35%	66%	80
Delgado,Jesus	09	26	R		aaa	SEA	3	3	33	0	56	75	42	5	28	35	6.82	1.84	8.1	314	4.5	5.6	1.2	0.8	36%	62%	27
	10	26	R		a/a	CIN	3	2	36	1	64	92	34	4	28	35	4.83	1.87	8.5	330	3.9	4.9	1.3	0.6	38%	74%	26
Delgado,Randall	10	21	R	a	aa	ATL	3	5	8	0	43	38	26	2	19	40	5.36	1.32	22.9	232	4.0	8.3	2.1	0.4	31%	57%	91
DeMark,Mike	09	26	R		a/a	SD	2	3	60	1	64	66	24	2	39	45	3.44	1.63	4.9	260	5.5	6.3	1.2	0.3	32%	78%	56
	10	27	R		a/a	SD	1	0	42	0	56	54	23	6	26	40	3.69	1.43	5.8	248	4.2	6.4	1.5	0.9	29%	77%	48
Demel,Sam	09	24	R		a/a	OAK	2	5	55	14	61	52	15	2	26	50	2.21	1.27	4.7	225	3.8	7.4	1.9	0.3	29%	83%	86
	10	25	R	a	aaa	OAK	2	0	22	6	28	22	4	1	8	24	1.28	1.06	5.1	211	2.6	7.7	3.0	0.3	27%	90%	112
Detwiler,Ross	09	24	L		a/a	WAS	4	5	16	0	76	99	34	5	30	60	4.02	1.69	22.0	308	3.5	7.1	2.0	0.6	38%	77%	60
	10	25	L	a	a/a	WAS	3	2	8	0	37	52	13	1	8	27	3.24	1.61	21.1	322	2.0	6.6	3.3	0.2	39%	79%	92
DeVries,Cole	09	25	R		aa	MIN	7	14	26	0	137	196	95	17	49	70	6.21	1.79	24.8	328	3.2	4.6	1.4	1.1	36%	66%	14
	10	26	R		MIN	MIN	1	8	48	1	91	127	67	12	39	69	6.65	1.82	9.0	324	3.8	6.8	1.8	1.1	38%	64%	34
Diamond,Scott	09	23	L		aa	ATL	5	10	23	0	131	187	69	6	58	95	4.75	1.87	27.3	328	4.0	6.5	1.6	0.4	40%	74%	50
	10	24	L		a/a	ATL	8	7	27	0	158	191	72	6	57	108	4.11	1.56	26.3	292	3.2	6.1	1.9	0.4	35%	73%	63
Diamond,Thomas	09	27	R		a/a	TEX	2	3	38	1	55	71	37	6	50	45	5.98	2.19	7.4	306	8.2	7.3	0.9	0.9	37%	73%	30
	10	27	R		aaa	CHC	5	4	21	0	108	97	43	9	45	86	3.59	1.31	21.8	235	3.8	7.2	1.9	0.8	29%	75%	68
Diaz,Amalio	09	23	R		aa	LAA	3	7	36	0	113	140	62	11	35	68	4.92	1.55	14.0	298	2.8	5.4	1.9	0.9	34%	69%	41
	10	24	R		aa	LAA	5	6	38	3	110	135	68	6	38	70	5.57	1.57	13.0	296	3.1	5.7	1.8	0.5	35%	63%	53
Diaz,Jose	09	26	R		aa	TEX	3	1	36	10	39	38	21	2	26	29	4.85	1.62	4.9	248	5.9	6.6	1.1	0.5	30%	69%	53
	10	27	R		aa	BAL	1	0	19	4	25	25	8	1	13	18	2.90	1.52	5.8	257	4.6	6.6	1.4	0.4	32%	81%	61
Dickey,R.A.	09	35	R		aaa	MIN	2	1	5	0	33	46	23	1	9	14	6.30	1.69	30.5	324	2.6	3.9	1.5	0.3	36%	60%	36
	10	36	R		aaa	NYM	4	2	8	0	60	61	17	3	8	29	2.52	1.15	30.7	258	1.3	4.4	3.5	0.5	29%	79%	89
Dickson,Brandon	09	25	R		aa	STL	8	10	28	0	147	181	71	12	48	92	4.31	1.56	23.5	296	3.0	5.6	1.9	0.7	34%	73%	48
	10	26	R		aaa	STL	11	8	28	0	167	187	60	9	47	116	3.21	1.40	25.8	277	2.6	6.2	2.4	0.5	33%	78%	74
Dietz,Jeff	10	25	R		aa	ARI	3	3	35	2	51	69	34	8	26	39	5.93	1.87	7.0	318	4.6	6.9	1.5	1.5	37%	71%	19
Dillard,Tim	09	26	R		aaa	MIL	11	7	24	0	147	184	86	11	54	57	5.23	1.61	27.8	299	3.3	3.5	1.1	0.7	32%	67%	18
	10	27	R		aaa	MIL	5	7	41	1	109	112	57	6	34	70	4.69	1.33	11.3	259	2.8	5.8	2.1	0.5	31%	64%	66
DiNardo,Lenny	09	30	L		aaa	KC	10	5	29	2	151	181	80	7	42	101	4.76	1.48	22.9	291	2.5	6.0	2.4	0.4	35%	66%	71
	10	31	L		aaa	OAK	2	5	10	0	47	60	18	4	14	23	3.41	1.56	21.2	303	2.6	4.3	1.7	0.8	34%	80%	31
Dobies,Andrew	09	27	L		aa	BOS	2	3	27	0	39	44	24	1	15	30	5.57	1.50	6.4	277	3.4	6.8	2.0	0.3	35%	60%	74
	10	27	L		a/a	CHW	3	4	21	0	30	46	26	3	16	27	7.90	2.06	7.1	343	4.8	8.1	1.7	1.0	42%	61%	39
Dohmann,Scott	10	33	R		aaa	LA	1	2	47	16	51	63	28	6	18	32	5.02	1.59	4.9	298	3.2	5.7	1.8	1.1	34%	70%	34
Dolis,Rafael	10	23	R		aa	CHC	5	4	12	0	55	72	28	3	26	39	4.57	1.78	21.6	309	4.2	6.4	1.5	0.5	37%	74%	48
Dolsi,Freddy	09	27	R		aaa	DET	4	3	39	10	51	60	30	2	20	26	5.26	1.55	5.9	286	3.4	4.6	1.3	0.4	33%	64%	43
	10	28	R		aaa	CHW	3	7	46	0	91	111	62	19	47	60	6.13	1.73	9.2	293	4.7	5.9	1.3	1.9	32%	69%	2
Doolittle,Todd	10	28	R		a/a	FLA	4	4	50	2	76	84	32	7	31	63	3.80	1.51	6.7	274	3.7	7.4	2.0	0.8	34%	77%	63
Doubront,Felix	09	22	L		aa	BOS	8	6	26	0	121	140	58	8	52	87	4.31	1.59	21.0	284	3.9	6.5	1.7	0.6	34%	73%	54
	10	23	L		a/a	BOS	8	3	17	0	80	85	30	1	32	62	3.38	1.46	20.6	267	3.6	7.0	1.9	0.1	34%	75%	81
Downs,Darin	10	26	L		a/a	TAM	12	4	41	0	88	98	35	6	33	83	3.55	1.48	9.5	276	3.3	8.4	2.5	0.6	36%	77%	84
Drabek,Kyle	09	22	R		aa	PHI	8	2	15	0	96	105	47	11	31	64	4.40	1.42	27.8	272	2.9	6.0	2.1	1.0	31%	71%	49
	10	23	R		aa	TOR	14	9	27	0	162	134	56	12	67	115	3.11	1.24	25.0	221	3.7	6.4	1.7	0.7	26%	77%	65
Drucker,Scot	09	27	R		aaa	DET	8	3	29	0	113	145	83	17	41	63	6.62	1.65	17.8	306	3.3	5.0	1.5	1.3	33%	61%	16
	10	28	R		aaa	DET	4	5	42	1	86	131	70	13	30	55	7.30	1.87	9.8	343	3.1	5.7	1.8	1.3	39%	62%	19
Dubee,Michael	09	24	R		aa	PIT	3	0	26	1	34	45	13	5	9	22	3.55	1.61	5.9	314	2.5	5.9	2.4	1.4	35%	83%	37
	10	25	R	a	a/a	PIT	6	2	46	5	77	70	22	4	20	55	2.53	1.16	6.8	237	2.3	6.5	2.8	0.5	29%	80%	91
Duckworth,Brandon	09	34	R		aaa	KC	3	6	20	0	105	129	83	14	39	56	7.13	1.60	23.8	297	3.3	4.8	1.4	1.2	33%	55%	19
	10	35	R		aaa	PHI	5	4	25	0	105	117	53	6	49	83	4.50	1.58	18.9	276	4.2	7.1	1.7	0.5	34%	71%	61
Duff,Grant	09	27	R		aa	NYY	4	2	21	1	36	43	21	1	20	28	5.16	1.72	8.0	287	4.9	6.9	1.4	0.3	36%	68%	60
	10	28	R		a/a	NYY	1	4	32	8	37	49	20	6	21	35	4.73	1.88	5.6	313	5.0	8.4	1.7	1.4	38%	79%	37
Duffy,Daniel	10	22	L	a	aa	KC	5	2	7	0	39	41	14	3	8	36	3.21	1.25	23.4	264	1.8	8.3	4.5	0.7	34%	76%	126
Dumatrait,Phil	10	29	L		aaa	DET	4	1	8	0	42	51	20	3	20	14	4.22	1.67	24.2	291	4.2	2.9	0.7	0.7	31%	75%	8
Dunn,Mike	09	24	L		a/a	NYY	4	3	38	2	73	73	39	5	51	82	4.82	1.69	8.9	255	6.2	10.2	1.6	0.6	35%	71%	80
	10	25	L	a	aaa	ATL	2	0	38	7	47	35	9	1	25	57	1.74	1.29	5.2	204	4.8	11.0	2.3	0.2	31%	86%	122
Durden,Brandon	09	25	L		aa	COL	7	4	17	0	101	124	56	11	26	29	4.95	1.48	26.2	297	2.3	2.6	1.1	1.0	31%	68%	5
	10	26	L		a/a	COL	5	14	26	0	149	220	102	28	34	60	6.17	1.71	26.5	336	2.1	3.6	1.8	1.7	35%	67%	-4
Eager,Thomas	10	25	R		aa	STL	2	4	54	0	73	73	40	6	44	43	4.92	1.61	6.1	255	5.5	5.3	1.0	0.7	29%	69%	36
Edell,Ryan	09	26	L		a/a	CLE	4	7	32	0	136	193	78	19	39	104	5.15	1.71	19.7	327	2.6	6.9	2.7	1.3	38%	72%	50
	10	27	L		aa	OAK	11	5	26	0	147	217	81	8	27	80	4.94	1.65	25.9	336	1.6	4.9	3.0	0.5	38%	69%	65
Edlefsen,Steven	09	24	R		a/a	SF	7	0	28	2	41	37	14	3	24	26	3.16	1.48	6.5	236	5.2	5.7	1.1	0.7	27%	80%	45
	10	25	R		aaa	SF	7	2	49	6	64	60	18	6	31	42	2.55	1.42	5.7	242	4.4	5.8	1.3	0.9	28%	86%	44
Edwards,Justin	10	23	L		aa	CHW	3	10	20	0	106	168	92	27	36	41	7.78	1.92	25.7	351	3.1	3.5	1.1	2.3	35%	63%	-39
Egan,Patrick	10	26	R		a/a	BAL	7	2	49	5	83	100	41	4	16	33	4.44	1.39	7.3	292	1.7	3.6	2.1	0.5	32%	67%	49
Ekstrom,Mike	09	26	R		aaa	SD	4	2	42	0	62	48	13	2	16	36	1.94	1.05	5.9	211	2.4	5.2	2.2	0.3	25%	82%	81
	10	27	R		aaa	TAM	6	1	39	1	58	63	21	5	19	39	3.27	1.42	6.4	272	2.9	6.0	2.1	0.8	32%	79%	56
Elbert,Scott	09	24	L	a	a/a	LA	4	4	20	0	96	105	46	7	45	108	4.35	1.57	21.5	273	4.3	10.1	2.4	0.7	38%	73%	91
	10	25	L		aaa	LA	1	1	9	0	43	43	19	3	29	37	4.01	1.69	22.1	257	6.1	7.6	1.3	0.6	32%	77%	57

					Actual													Major League Equivalents									
PITCHER	Yr	Age	Th		Lev	Org	w	l	g	sv	ip	h	er	hr	bb	k	era	whip	bf/g	oob	ctl	dom	cmd	hr/9	h%	s%	bpv
Ellis,Joshua	09	25	R	a	a/a	ARI	7	3	40	1	61	67	32	2	20	56	4.66	1.43	6.6	274	3.0	8.3	2.8	0.3	36%	65%	99
	10	26	R		a/a	ARI	2	1	37	2	55	79	27	1	23	48	4.36	1.86	7.1	329	3.8	7.8	2.0	0.2	42%	75%	73
Ellison,Derrick	09	31	L		a/a	NYM	3	2	28	2	45	40	22	6	20	32	4.44	1.33	6.8	233	4.0	6.3	1.6	1.1	27%	69%	46
	10	32	L		aa	NYM	1	2	29	2	37	25	16	2	19	20	4.01	1.18	5.2	186	4.6	5.0	1.1	0.6	21%	66%	53
Ely,John	09	23	R		aa	CHW	14	2	27	0	156	172	67	12	54	107	3.86	1.45	25.2	274	3.1	6.2	2.0	0.7	32%	74%	57
	10	24	R		aaa	LA	5	4	13	0	68	65	38	7	25	46	5.03	1.32	22.2	247	3.3	6.1	1.8	0.9	28%	63%	53
Englebrook,Evan	09	27	R		a/a	HOU	3	1	30	9	36	43	23	3	14	18	5.75	1.56	5.4	288	3.4	4.6	1.3	0.9	32%	63%	27
	10	28	R		a/a	HOU	0	3	42	4	56	76	38	8	27	36	6.05	1.85	6.4	319	4.3	5.7	1.3	1.3	36%	69%	14
English,Jesse	09	25	L		aa	SF	7	7	26	0	100	128	67	10	63	55	5.99	1.91	18.6	304	5.7	4.9	0.9	0.9	34%	69%	15
	10	26	L		aaa	WAS	2	1	16	0	19	22	14	1	10	12	6.77	1.66	5.5	279	4.8	5.5	1.1	0.5	33%	57%	41
Ennis,John	10	31	R		a/a	PHI	2	0	19	2	34	51	24	9	13	20	6.29	1.88	8.6	340	3.3	5.3	1.6	2.3	36%	73%	-17
Enright,Barry	09	24	R		aa	ARI	10	9	27	0	156	208	93	22	38	88	5.35	1.58	26.0	314	2.2	5.1	2.3	1.2	35%	68%	34
	10	24	R	a	aa	ARI	4	1	14	0	93	103	43	12	16	68	4.17	1.28	27.9	275	1.5	6.6	4.3	1.2	32%	71%	97
Eppley,Cody	10	25	R		a/a	TEX	3	2	37	10	51	52	20	2	23	49	3.45	1.45	6.0	257	4.0	8.5	2.1	0.5	34%	77%	83
Erbe,Brandon	09	22	R		aa	BAL	5	3	14	0	73	56	29	8	37	52	3.58	1.27	21.9	208	4.6	6.4	1.4	1.0	24%	75%	52
	10	23	R		aaa	BAL	0	10	14	0	70	93	51	13	20	44	6.59	1.61	22.7	313	2.6	5.7	2.2	1.7	34%	62%	21
Escalona,Edgmer	09	23	R		aa	COL	1	2	31	4	36	40	13	6	11	26	3.33	1.42	5.1	276	2.8	6.5	2.3	1.5	31%	84%	41
	10	24	R		aaa	COL	3	5	57	1	69	68	45	17	27	63	5.87	1.38	5.2	252	3.5	8.2	2.3	2.2	28%	64%	36
Escalona,Sergio	09	25	L		a/a	PHI	2	3	47	14	60	63	27	6	23	43	4.10	1.44	5.6	280	3.5	6.4	1.8	0.9	31%	74%	51
	10	26	L		aa	PHI	4	8	50	10	54	57	29	7	24	39	4.78	1.51	4.8	267	4.0	6.5	1.6	1.1	31%	71%	40
Espineli,Geno	09	27	L		aaa	SF	3	4	52	19	59	77	25	2	13	26	3.85	1.51	5.0	308	1.9	3.9	2.0	0.3	35%	73%	50
	10	28	L		aaa	SF	5	5	53	12	60	76	25	5	17	30	3.70	1.55	5.1	303	2.6	4.4	1.7	0.8	34%	78%	33
Espino,Paolo	10	24	R		a/a	CLE	12	7	28	0	143	150	78	19	46	110	4.91	1.37	21.9	264	2.9	6.9	2.4	1.2	31%	67%	58
Espinosa,Sergio	10	25	L		aa	TAM	3	3	30	0	50	60	34	4	17	24	6.05	1.53	7.4	291	3.0	4.3	1.4	0.8	32%	59%	29
Estrada,Marco	09	26	R		aaa	WAS	9	5	27	0	136	160	71	11	34	82	4.70	1.42	21.9	287	2.2	5.5	2.4	0.7	33%	67%	59
	10	27	R	b	aaa	MIL	1	2	7	0	40	34	16	1	12	29	3.55	1.13	23.2	224	2.6	6.4	2.5	0.2	28%	67%	93
Etherton,Seth	09	33	R		aaa	ARI	11	8	28	0	160	208	97	28	37	99	5.44	1.53	25.5	308	2.1	5.6	2.7	1.6	34%	68%	35
	10	34	R		aaa	LA	5	7	19	0	103	118	52	12	21	74	4.51	1.35	23.1	282	1.8	6.5	3.5	1.0	33%	69%	81
Eveland,Dana	09	26	L		aaa	OAK	8	6	21	0	124	144	74	11	46	78	5.35	1.54	26.3	285	3.4	5.7	1.7	0.8	33%	65%	43
	10	27	L		aaa	PIT	0	2	11	0	26	45	26	5	5	21	8.92	1.94	11.5	374	1.8	7.4	4.1	1.8	44%	55%	58
Everts,Clinton	09	25	R		a/a	WAS	5	1	40	3	40	43	13	1	22	34	2.84	1.63	5.9	275	5.0	7.7	1.5	0.2	35%	82%	73
	10	26	R		aa	TOR	4	1	41	2	74	100	55	7	54	50	6.71	2.08	9.0	316	6.6	6.1	0.9	0.8	37%	67%	23
Eyre,Willie	09	31	R		aaa	TEX	0	0	19	2	34	29	11	1	14	21	2.78	1.27	7.5	228	3.6	5.5	1.5	0.3	27%	78%	66
	10	32	R		aaa	TEX	5	4	49	2	72	86	34	2	25	48	4.21	1.55	6.6	291	3.2	6.1	1.9	0.3	35%	71%	66
Fairel,Matthew	10	23	L		aa	CIN	5	3	10	0	61	59	32	13	25	38	4.72	1.37	26.2	248	3.7	5.6	1.5	2.0	25%	74%	12
Farquhar,Daniel	09	23	R		aa	TOR	1	4	37	15	45	38	17	1	34	44	3.38	1.59	5.5	224	6.8	8.8	1.3	0.2	31%	77%	84
	10	24	R		aa	TOR	4	3	53	17	76	55	32	7	42	67	3.77	1.27	6.0	197	5.0	7.9	1.6	0.9	24%	72%	71
Feierabend,Ryan	10	25	L		a/a	SEA	5	7	18	0	95	142	60	8	28	41	5.68	1.79	24.9	339	2.7	3.9	1.4	0.8	37%	68%	17
Fick,Charles	10	25	R		a/a	STL	5	1	32	0	76	75	34	6	23	52	4.03	1.29	10.0	253	2.7	6.2	2.3	0.7	30%	70%	68
Fields,Joshua	09	24	R		aa	SEA	2	2	31	1	33	39	31	2	24	30	8.30	1.91	5.2	287	6.6	8.3	1.3	0.6	37%	53%	56
	10	25	R		aa	SEA	1	1	21	6	28	22	12	0	20	23	3.90	1.50	5.9	213	6.4	7.2	1.1	0.0	28%	71%	79
Fien,Casey	09	26	R	b	aaa	DET	2	1	42	14	58	63	30	6	15	54	4.64	1.35	5.9	271	2.4	8.4	3.5	1.0	34%	67%	96
	10	27	R		aaa	DET	3	3	44	8	62	64	23	9	13	37	3.29	1.25	5.9	261	1.9	5.3	2.8	1.3	28%	80%	52
Fiers,Michael	10	25	R		aa	MIL	1	1	10	1	31	32	16	3	10	30	4.49	1.35	13.3	261	2.9	8.6	3.0	1.0	33%	69%	88
Fife,Stephen	10	24	R		aa	BOS	8	6	26	0	136	164	84	11	44	68	5.52	1.53	23.3	292	2.9	4.5	1.5	0.7	33%	63%	33
Figaro,Alfredo	09	25	R		aa	DET	6	3	16	0	80	86	43	10	24	53	4.88	1.38	21.5	268	2.8	6.0	2.2	1.1	30%	67%	49
	10	26	R		aaa	DET	10	6	23	0	124	167	71	13	39	93	5.16	1.66	24.7	316	2.8	6.8	2.4	1.0	37%	70%	53
Figueroa,Pedro	10	25	L		aa	OAK	1	6	13	0	71	95	48	6	28	48	6.13	1.73	25.4	313	3.6	6.0	1.7	0.8	37%	64%	40
Fish,Robert	10	23	L		aa	LAA	3	5	39	2	42	77	49	10	17	41	10.48	2.23	5.6	385	3.6	8.8	2.4	2.1	46%	54%	17
Fisher,Carlos	10	28	R	b	aaa	CIN	1	1	30	4	36	27	12	5	8	31	2.89	0.99	4.7	206	2.1	7.8	3.7	1.3	24%	79%	99
Flande,Yohan	09	24	L		aa	PHI	4	4	13	0	70	95	44	6	22	41	5.68	1.66	24.7	316	2.8	5.2	1.9	0.7	36%	65%	39
	10	25	L		aa	PHI	10	8	27	0	158	204	89	12	44	68	5.09	1.57	26.3	307	2.5	3.9	1.5	0.7	34%	67%	30
Flores,Adalberto	10	24	R		aa	TEX	3	4	38	4	60	74	38	4	22	51	5.71	1.60	7.1	297	3.2	7.7	2.4	0.6	37%	63%	73
Flores,Manuel	10	23	L		aa	LAA	1	5	9	0	48	73	37	2	12	21	6.96	1.78	25.1	343	2.3	4.0	1.7	0.4	38%	58%	35
Fox,Matt	09	27	R		aa	MIN	9	9	28	0	151	189	84	14	66	85	5.00	1.68	24.8	299	3.9	5.1	1.3	0.8	34%	71%	28
	10	28	R		aaa	MIN	6	9	35	0	123	141	61	17	52	83	4.47	1.57	15.8	282	3.8	6.0	1.6	1.2	32%	75%	32
French,Luke	09	24	L		aaa	DET	4	4	13	0	81	85	36	7	20	62	3.99	1.29	26.3	264	2.2	6.9	3.1	0.8	32%	70%	85
	10	25	L		aaa	SEA	11	3	17	0	113	116	38	6	22	55	3.05	1.22	27.6	260	1.8	4.4	2.5	0.5	29%	76%	67
Friedrich,Christian	10	23	L		aa	COL	3	6	18	0	87	121	64	12	35	64	6.60	1.79	22.8	322	3.6	6.6	1.8	1.3	37%	64%	30
Friend,Justin	10	24	R		aa	OAK	3	3	36	0	56	72	26	1	37	42	4.23	1.94	7.6	304	5.9	6.7	1.1	0.2	38%	76%	53
Frieri,Ernesto	09	24	R		aa	SD	10	9	27	0	140	138	60	12	63	97	3.85	1.44	22.6	252	4.1	6.2	1.5	0.7	30%	74%	52
	10	25	R	a	aaa	SD	3	1	39	17	37	14	6	2	17	44	1.47	0.84	4.7	115	4.2	10.5	2.5	0.6	16%	90%	134
Furbush,Charlie	10	24	L		a/a	DET	4	4	14	0	82	104	56	16	26	61	6.11	1.58	26.4	303	2.8	6.7	2.4	1.8	34%	65%	30
Gabino,Armando	09	26	R		aaa	MIN	6	4	38	1	98	93	38	7	25	51	3.50	1.20	10.6	245	2.3	4.7	2.1	0.7	28%	72%	58
	10	27	R		a/a	BAL	7	0	32	3	88	90	33	10	28	57	3.41	1.33	11.7	259	2.8	5.8	2.0	1.1	29%	78%	49
Gagnier,Lauren	10	26	R		a/a	DET	10	7	27	0	155	174	72	24	53	99	4.15	1.46	25.2	277	3.1	5.7	1.9	1.4	31%	77%	31
Galarraga,Armando	10	29	R		aaa	DET	4	2	8	0	44	49	24	5	15	32	4.83	1.46	24.2	278	3.1	6.5	2.1	1.1	32%	69%	49
Gamboa,Eduardo	10	26	R		aa	BAL	7	5	36	2	98	123	54	13	29	63	4.99	1.55	12.2	301	2.7	5.8	2.2	1.2	34%	70%	39
Garate,Victor	09	25	L		aa	LA	0	1	47	4	53	46	16	1	27	45	2.64	1.36	4.9	227	4.5	7.6	1.7	0.2	30%	80%	85
	10	26	L		a/a	WAS	1	2	40	5	46	37	22	4	23	45	4.34	1.30	4.9	214	4.6	8.8	1.9	0.9	27%	68%	79
Garceau,Shaun	10	23	R		aa	STL	0	6	7	0	33	44	22	2	18	20	5.90	1.87	22.6	315	4.8	5.6	1.2	0.6	37%	67%	33
Garcia,Angel	09	26	R		aa	OAK	2	0	21	1	38	43	19	1	24	24	4.46	1.78	8.5	280	5.8	5.7	1.0	0.3	34%	73%	46
	10	27	R		a/a	CHW	1	5	20	0	59	87	57	12	27	29	8.64	1.92	14.3	335	4.1	4.4	1.1	1.9	35%	56%	-19
Garcia,Justin	10	24	R		a/a	TAM	3	3	20	0	49	66	33	8	16	35	6.04	1.67	11.3	315	2.9	6.4	2.2	1.5	36%	66%	32

Major League Equivalent Statistics

PITCHER	Yr	Age	Th		Lev	Org	w	l	g	sv	ip	h	er	hr	bb	k	era	whip	bf/g	oob	ctl	dom	cmd	hr/9	h%	s%	bpv
Garcia,Ramon	09	25	L		aa	DET	4	4	35	2	92	159	81	14	22	36	7.92	1.97	12.9	371	2.2	3.5	1.6	1.3	39%	60%	-4
	10	26	L		a/a	DET	1	5	30	1	76	113	57	19	16	42	6.71	1.69	11.7	336	1.9	4.9	2.6	2.2	35%	65%	6
Garr,Brennan	09	26	R		aa	TEX	3	3	32	2	50	61	32	3	28	32	5.78	1.77	7.4	294	5.0	5.8	1.2	0.6	35%	66%	38
	10	27	R		a/a	TEX	8	5	43	0	65	96	49	9	28	50	6.77	1.90	7.3	335	3.8	6.9	1.8	1.2	39%	65%	30
Gaub,John	09	24	L	a	a/a	CHC	4	2	52	5	60	43	20	5	36	66	2.94	1.32	4.9	198	5.4	9.9	1.8	0.8	27%	81%	90
	10	25	L		aaa	CHC	3	4	30	3	29	29	23	1	24	33	7.21	1.85	4.6	257	7.5	10.1	1.3	0.3	37%	58%	83
Gayhart,Jared	10	24	R		aa	DET	0	4	22	1	32	34	26	3	20	23	7.20	1.66	6.7	266	5.5	6.5	1.2	0.9	31%	55%	40
Gearrin,Cory	10	24	R		aaa	ATL	3	5	52	0	80	80	35	6	32	60	3.93	1.40	6.7	255	3.6	6.7	1.9	0.7	31%	73%	64
Geary,Geoff	09	33	R		aaa	HOU	1	3	26	2	40	64	28	5	12	21	6.39	1.89	7.4	355	2.6	4.7	1.8	1.2	39%	67%	15
	10	34	R		aaa	LA	4	6	31	0	69	95	35	5	22	37	4.52	1.69	10.3	320	2.9	4.8	1.7	0.7	36%	74%	35
Gee,Dillon	09	23	R		aaa	NYM	1	3	9	0	48	56	28	6	17	37	5.24	1.52	23.7	285	3.2	6.9	2.2	1.1	34%	67%	52
	10	24	R		aaa	NYM	13	8	28	0	161	184	92	22	40	138	5.14	1.39	24.8	281	2.2	7.7	3.5	1.2	34%	65%	81
Geer,Josh	09	26	R		aaa	SD	2	5	9	0	52	66	28	4	14	17	4.80	1.54	25.9	302	2.5	3.0	1.2	0.7	32%	69%	17
	10	27	R		aaa	SD	11	11	29	0	171	226	103	23	32	75	5.43	1.51	26.1	312	1.7	3.9	2.4	1.2	33%	66%	30
George,Chris	09	30	L		aaa	BAL	2	1	17	0	49	64	26	7	10	22	4.67	1.51	12.8	310	1.8	4.0	2.2	1.2	33%	72%	26
	10	31	L		aaa	BAL	5	7	26	0	124	155	74	21	37	81	5.34	1.54	21.3	299	2.7	5.9	2.2	1.5	33%	69%	31
German,Matt	10	26	L		aa	PHI	1	2	43	0	46	57	38	6	25	28	7.42	1.80	5.0	300	4.9	5.4	1.1	1.1	34%	58%	17
Germano,Justin	10	28	R		a/a	CLE	5	3	24	1	72	85	33	8	16	40	4.11	1.40	13.0	287	2.1	5.0	2.4	1.0	32%	73%	48
Gibson,Kyle	10	23	R		a/a	MIN	7	5	19	0	108	111	44	5	26	72	3.66	1.27	23.8	260	2.2	6.0	2.8	0.4	31%	70%	85
Gil,Jerry	09	27	R		aa	CIN	3	4	24	0	49	72	70	14	60	22	12.81	2.70	11.5	335	11.0	4.0	0.4	2.7	33%	53%	-60
	10	28	R		a/a	CIN	5	6	47	7	63	82	46	9	67	40	6.55	2.35	7.1	307	9.5	5.7	0.6	1.3	34%	74%	1
Gleason,Sean	09	24	R		aa	BAL	3	5	10	0	51	97	54	6	25	17	9.46	2.39	27.1	394	4.4	3.0	0.7	1.1	42%	59%	-25
	10	25	R		aa	BAL	2	1	16	0	24	34	11	1	7	13	4.17	1.71	6.9	330	2.5	4.7	1.9	0.4	38%	75%	45
Godfrey,Graham	09	25	R		aa	OAK	11	8	28	0	159	174	67	8	49	85	3.77	1.40	24.6	273	2.8	4.8	1.7	0.4	31%	73%	52
	10	26	R		aaa	OAK	4	8	29	0	125	151	83	9	62	81	6.00	1.71	19.9	293	4.5	5.8	1.3	0.6	34%	64%	40
Gomes,Brandon	09	25	R	a	aa	SD	4	1	65	4	72	62	23	3	30	77	2.92	1.28	4.7	228	3.8	9.7	2.6	0.4	32%	78%	109
	10	26	R	b	aa	SD	7	2	51	1	72	64	18	2	29	72	2.30	1.29	6.0	234	3.6	9.0	2.5	0.3	32%	82%	106
Gomez,Jeanmar	09	22	R		aa	CLE	10	4	22	0	123	140	63	13	43	99	4.61	1.49	24.7	280	3.1	7.2	2.3	1.0	34%	71%	62
	10	23	R		aaa	CLE	8	8	20	0	116	132	69	14	38	72	5.32	1.47	25.5	281	3.0	5.6	1.9	1.1	32%	65%	39
Gomez,Mariano	09	27	L		aaa	ATL	8	4	47	8	72	61	20	3	31	30	2.50	1.27	6.4	225	3.8	3.8	1.0	0.4	25%	81%	42
	10	28	L		aaa	ATL	3	2	30	1	46	49	18	2	19	23	3.56	1.49	6.8	268	3.8	4.5	1.2	0.4	31%	76%	41
Gonzalez,Edgar	09	27	R		aaa	OAK	3	2	7	0	39	54	26	4	14	22	5.92	1.74	26.1	319	3.3	5.1	1.5	0.9	36%	66%	26
	10	28	R	b	aaa	LA	1	1	4	0	24	28	11	2	5	23	3.93	1.40	26.0	288	2.0	8.5	4.3	0.8	37%	73%	116
Gonzalez,Enrique	09	27	R		aaa	BOS	8	11	26	0	139	217	128	26	61	82	8.32	2.00	26.3	348	4.0	5.3	1.3	1.7	38%	59%	-6
	10	28	R		aaa	DET	4	5	12	0	66	85	32	11	17	43	4.40	1.55	24.6	306	2.3	5.8	2.5	1.5	34%	76%	37
Gonzalez,Reidier	09	24	R		aa	TOR	4	6	17	0	93	104	43	5	29	56	4.19	1.43	23.8	277	2.8	5.4	1.9	0.5	32%	70%	58
	10	25	R		a/a	TOR	8	10	25	0	133	223	116	16	54	70	7.88	2.08	26.6	364	3.6	4.7	1.3	1.1	40%	62%	4
Gordon,Brian	09	31	R		aaa	TEX	7	3	43	2	77	89	41	6	22	42	4.79	1.45	7.8	284	2.6	4.9	1.9	0.7	32%	67%	45
	10	32	R		aaa	PHI	1	3	40	0	78	91	41	3	21	70	4.74	1.43	8.5	284	2.4	8.1	3.3	0.4	37%	65%	106
Gordon,Derrick	10	27	L		aa	OAK	2	2	40	1	71	86	54	7	38	48	6.84	1.75	8.3	293	4.8	6.1	1.3	0.9	34%	60%	33
Gorgen,Matthew	10	24	R		aa	TAM	3	2	42	22	49	39	12	2	22	39	2.27	1.24	4.9	215	4.0	7.1	1.8	0.4	27%	82%	81
Gorgen,Scott	09	23	R		aa	STL	4	5	11	0	55	56	34	7	33	40	5.55	1.62	22.7	258	5.4	6.5	1.2	1.1	30%	67%	34
	10	24	R		aa	STL	5	1	12	0	50	37	7	3	18	38	1.30	1.09	16.7	203	3.2	6.8	2.2	0.6	25%	92%	84
Gosling,Mike	09	29	L		aaa	CLE	7	4	29	1	67	97	46	8	26	60	6.19	1.83	11.0	330	3.5	8.1	2.3	1.0	41%	67%	54
	10	30	L		aaa	CLE	3	0	13	0	27	27	11	2	10	19	3.69	1.35	8.9	252	3.3	6.3	1.9	0.7	30%	74%	60
Graham,Andrew	09	25	R		aa	COL	4	4	33	0	84	90	59	11	33	56	6.30	1.47	11.2	268	3.6	6.0	1.7	1.2	30%	57%	37
	10	26	R		a/a	COL	4	3	45	1	69	86	46	10	28	41	5.93	1.64	7.0	298	3.6	5.3	1.5	1.3	33%	66%	19
Graham,Connor	09	24	R		aa	CLE	1	3	8	0	38	49	29	4	28	34	6.82	2.03	23.6	308	6.6	8.0	1.2	1.0	38%	66%	38
	10	25	R		aa	CLE	3	6	43	2	78	85	35	5	52	55	4.00	1.75	8.5	272	5.9	6.3	1.1	0.6	33%	78%	43
Gray,Jeff	09	28	R	b	aaa	OAK	2	2	37	16	41	34	7	2	5	18	1.62	0.95	4.3	220	1.2	4.0	3.4	0.5	24%	86%	93
	10	29	R		aaa	CHC	3	1	25	1	35	52	26	2	15	20	6.64	1.90	6.8	336	3.9	5.3	1.4	0.4	39%	63%	31
Green,Nicholas	09	25	R		a/a	MIL	3	10	20	0	108	154	83	17	21	63	6.92	1.61	24.5	327	1.8	5.2	3.0	1.4	36%	58%	41
	10	26	R		aa	MIL	0	2	32	1	48	68	36	5	14	36	6.68	1.70	6.9	326	2.6	6.7	2.6	0.9	39%	60%	58
Grube,Jarrett	10	29	R		a/a	SEA	5	5	17	0	103	119	49	7	31	60	4.31	1.45	26.5	283	2.7	5.2	1.9	0.6	33%	70%	52
Guerra,Deolis	09	21	R		aa	MIN	6	3	12	0	62	68	42	4	17	42	6.06	1.36	22.2	271	2.5	6.1	2.5	0.6	32%	53%	72
	10	21	R		aa	MIN	2	13	24	0	127	167	92	17	41	75	6.54	1.63	24.1	310	2.9	5.3	1.8	1.2	35%	61%	27
Gustafson,Timothy	09	25	R		aa	ATL	2	3	20	0	61	72	36	4	36	41	5.26	1.75	14.3	286	5.3	6.0	1.1	0.6	34%	69%	39
	10	26	R		a/a	ATL	11	9	30	0	124	160	87	12	68	62	6.33	1.84	19.7	306	5.0	4.5	0.9	0.8	34%	65%	14
Gutierrez,Carlos	09	23	R		aa	MIN	1	3	22	0	52	73	45	6	26	25	7.84	1.90	11.4	325	4.5	4.4	1.0	1.1	36%	58%	5
	10	24	R		a/a	MIN	5	8	34	2	126	157	70	7	52	71	5.01	1.65	16.9	299	3.7	5.1	1.4	0.5	34%	69%	39
Hacker,Eric	09	27	R		a/a	PIT	6	7	27	0	147	212	96	10	60	77	5.84	1.85	26.0	331	3.7	4.7	1.3	0.6	37%	67%	25
	10	28	R		aaa	SF	16	8	29	0	165	204	94	21	60	103	5.10	1.60	25.2	301	3.3	5.6	1.7	1.1	34%	70%	31
Haeger,Charlie	09	26	R		aaa	LA	11	6	22	0	144	145	60	15	58	89	3.73	1.41	28.4	257	3.6	5.6	1.5	1.0	29%	76%	41
	10	27	R		aaa	LA	4	3	11	0	53	44	28	3	38	32	4.81	1.54	21.6	222	6.4	5.5	0.9	0.5	26%	68%	45
Hagadone,Nick	10	25	L		aa	CLE	2	2	19	1	48	51	28	5	35	37	5.33	1.78	11.9	265	6.5	6.9	1.1	1.0	32%	71%	36
Halama,John	09	38	L		aaa	ATL	4	7	16	0	90	109	56	8	35	46	5.57	1.60	25.5	294	3.5	4.6	1.3	0.8	33%	65%	26
	10	39	L		aaa	OAK	6	2	18	0	87	113	53	11	24	33	5.43	1.57	21.7	307	2.5	3.4	1.4	1.1	32%	67%	11
Hall,Jeremy	10	24	R		aa	TAM	6	9	27	0	148	183	83	14	73	66	5.05	1.73	25.5	297	4.5	4.0	0.9	0.9	32%	72%	12
Hamilton,Clayton	09	27	R		a/a	TEX	1	4	40	5	70	105	51	7	24	34	6.48	1.83	8.3	338	3.1	4.4	1.4	0.9	37%	64%	17
	10	28	R	b	aa	TEX	1	1	4	0	20	31	8	1	1	9	3.38	1.63	22.7	349	0.6	4.0	7.0	0.6	39%	80%	140
Hamilton,Cory	10	22	R		aa	DET	4	1	26	0	37	38	22	2	30	22	5.35	1.84	6.8	260	7.3	5.4	0.7	0.5	30%	70%	36
Hamman,Corey	09	30	L		a/a	PIT	1	5	55	1	59	90	56	4	27	36	8.53	1.98	5.3	343	4.1	5.5	1.3	0.6	40%	54%	31
	10	30	L		a/a	PIT	1	1	38	0	52	74	50	13	31	28	8.64	2.02	6.8	326	5.4	4.8	0.9	2.2	34%	59%	-27

Major League Equivalent Statistics

PITCHERS

						Actual											Major League Equivalents									
PITCHER	Yr	Age	Th		Lev	Org	w	l	g	sv	ip	h	er	hr	bb	k	era	whip	bf/g	oob	ctl	dom	cmd	hr/9	h%	s%	bpv
Hand,Donovan	09	24	R		aa	MIL	8	5	27	1	98	119	47	13	22	46	4.35	1.43	15.8	293	2.0	4.2	2.1	1.2	31%	73%	29
	10	24	R		a/a	MIL	4	1	48	2	75	96	33	4	13	43	3.95	1.45	6.9	304	1.6	5.1	3.2	0.5	35%	73%	77
Hankins,Derek	09	26	R		aa	PIT	3	4	19	1	71	90	47	7	28	48	5.97	1.65	17.1	302	3.5	6.1	1.7	0.9	35%	64%	41
	10	27	R		a/a	PIT	6	5	37	7	103	116	45	9	33	50	3.91	1.45	12.2	278	2.9	4.4	1.5	0.8	31%	75%	33
Happ,J.A.	10	28	L		a/a	PHI	1	1	8	0	34	57	31	8	22	23	8.17	2.32	22.4	365	5.7	6.2	1.1	2.1	40%	68%	-22
Hardy,Blaine	10	24	L		a/a	KC	4	4	40	7	93	82	31	8	26	56	3.00	1.16	9.5	232	2.5	5.4	2.2	0.8	26%	77%	63
Hardy,Rowdy	09	27	L		aa	KC	4	4	11	0	60	76	30	6	22	30	4.48	1.63	24.8	302	3.3	4.4	1.4	0.9	33%	74%	24
	10	28	L		aa	KC	4	3	36	3	81	114	40	5	19	42	4.42	1.65	10.3	326	2.1	4.6	2.2	0.5	37%	73%	47
Harrell,Lucas	09	24	R		a/a	CHW	12	4	25	0	146	169	74	10	75	80	4.58	1.67	26.8	284	4.6	4.9	1.1	0.6	32%	73%	31
	10	25	R		aaa	CHW	10	10	26	0	137	161	84	13	62	74	5.50	1.62	24.0	286	4.0	4.9	1.2	0.9	32%	66%	26
Harvey,Kris	10	27	R		aa	FLA	1	0	22	3	31	40	26	5	20	20	7.63	1.92	6.9	306	5.6	5.8	1.0	1.3	34%	60%	10
Hayes,Chris	09	27	R		a/a	KC	4	6	44	6	85	127	39	3	13	32	4.11	1.64	8.8	337	1.4	3.4	2.4	0.4	37%	74%	49
	10	28	R		aaa	KC	0	0	19	2	27	41	14	2	5	9	4.54	1.71	6.6	342	1.7	2.8	1.6	0.7	36%	74%	17
Haynes,Jeremy	10	24	R		aa	LAA	3	0	30	0	48	54	41	1	54	32	7.68	2.23	8.3	277	10.0	6.0	0.6	0.2	34%	62%	43
Hearne,Trey	09	26	R		a/a	STL	14	4	28	0	154	164	61	11	50	76	3.57	1.39	23.7	268	2.9	4.4	1.5	0.6	30%	75%	40
	10	27	R		a/a	STL	4	4	19	0	52	69	41	11	34	27	7.15	1.99	13.5	312	6.0	4.7	0.8	2.0	32%	68%	-23
Heath,Deunte	09	24	R		a/a	ATL	2	6	32	1	98	128	73	7	54	76	6.71	1.85	14.6	308	4.9	6.9	1.4	0.7	37%	62%	45
	10	25	R		aa	CHW	2	4	39	2	57	63	28	6	37	68	4.37	1.75	6.8	275	5.8	10.6	1.8	0.9	38%	76%	76
Hefner,Jeremy	10	25	R		aa	SD	11	8	28	0	167	177	62	11	54	93	3.34	1.38	25.7	266	2.9	5.2	1.8	0.6	31%	77%	54
Hellickson,Jeremy	09	23	R	a	a/a	TAM	9	2	20	0	114	84	39	9	30	116	3.08	1.00	22.3	201	2.4	9.2	3.9	0.7	27%	71%	130
	10	23	R	a	aaa	TAM	12	3	21	0	117	112	35	5	34	105	2.69	1.25	23.2	247	2.6	8.1	3.1	0.4	32%	79%	107
Henderson,Jim	10	28	R		aa	MIL	4	5	45	7	61	65	49	10	42	46	7.29	1.76	6.3	268	6.2	6.7	1.1	1.4	30%	59%	22
Henn,Sean	09	28	L		aaa	MIN	1	1	28	6	38	44	13	3	17	34	3.04	1.60	6.2	283	4.1	8.1	2.0	0.8	36%	83%	66
	10	29	L		aaa	TOR	3	4	38	2	97	113	46	5	51	52	4.28	1.69	11.8	286	4.7	4.8	1.0	0.5	33%	74%	33
Henry,Bryan	10	26	R		aa	ARI	4	6	32	0	100	140	59	10	30	45	5.29	1.70	14.5	324	2.7	4.0	1.5	0.9	35%	69%	19
Hensley,Steven	10	24	R		aa	SEA	7	11	22	0	117	130	66	7	51	70	5.08	1.54	23.7	275	3.9	5.4	1.4	0.6	32%	66%	45
Herges,Matt	10	41	R		aaa	KC	9	4	43	0	89	117	54	9	35	41	5.42	1.70	9.6	310	3.5	4.1	1.2	1.0	34%	69%	14
Hernandez,Carlos	09	30	L		aaa	TAM	7	6	21	0	112	126	55	10	47	65	4.42	1.55	23.8	279	3.8	5.2	1.4	0.8	32%	72%	35
	10	30	L		aaa	TAM	6	5	18	0	90	107	51	9	41	60	5.10	1.64	22.8	288	4.1	6.0	1.5	0.9	34%	70%	38
Hernandez,Fernando	09	25	R		a/a	CHW	3	4	57	20	69	57	19	3	28	59	2.46	1.23	5.0	220	3.7	7.7	2.1	0.4	28%	81%	88
	10	26	R		aa	OAK	5	6	45	4	77	85	39	6	23	55	4.57	1.39	7.4	273	2.6	6.5	2.4	0.7	33%	67%	69
Hernandez,Gabriel	09	23	R		aaa	SEA	10	9	26	0	146	165	86	14	47	88	5.30	1.45	24.6	279	2.9	5.4	1.9	0.9	32%	64%	45
	10	24	R		aaa	KC	10	6	31	0	144	152	87	29	51	99	5.43	1.41	20.1	265	3.2	6.2	1.9	1.8	29%	67%	25
Herold,Mitch	10	24	L		aa	BOS	3	4	26	0	51	66	36	2	13	35	6.32	1.55	8.8	308	2.2	6.2	2.8	0.4	37%	56%	78
Herrera,Daniel Ray	10	26	L	a	aaa	CIN	2	2	26	5	37	35	21	2	5	30	5.13	1.09	5.7	246	1.2	7.2	5.9	0.5	31%	50%	158
Herrmann,Frank	09	25	R		a/a	CLE	4	4	49	2	106	135	46	8	20	53	3.93	1.46	9.5	303	1.7	4.5	2.7	0.7	34%	74%	56
	10	26	R	b	aaa	CLE	3	0	19	2	28	16	1	0	8	19	0.33	0.88	5.6	167	2.6	6.2	2.4	0.0	22%	96%	108
Hill,Nicholas	09	25	L	a	a/a	SEA	5	6	36	2	95	101	42	5	27	86	3.98	1.35	11.3	267	2.6	8.1	3.1	0.5	34%	70%	101
	10	26	L		aa	SEA	2	1	28	1	42	56	23	3	20	30	4.98	1.79	7.1	311	4.3	6.3	1.5	0.7	37%	72%	41
Hill,Rich	10	31	L		aaa	BOS	7	4	42	0	99	104	62	10	66	78	5.66	1.72	10.9	265	6.0	7.1	1.2	0.9	32%	67%	42
Hinckley,Mike	09	27	L		aaa	TEX	1	1	33	0	49	66	25	5	25	27	4.62	1.86	7.1	316	4.6	4.9	1.1	1.0	35%	77%	14
	10	28	L		a/a	BAL	1	5	30	0	46	60	28	2	21	25	5.37	1.74	7.2	307	4.0	4.9	1.2	0.4	35%	68%	35
Hinshaw,Alex	09	27	L	b	aaa	SF	1	2	46	1	52	45	24	3	30	60	4.10	1.44	4.9	230	5.2	10.4	2.0	0.5	33%	71%	98
	10	28	L		aaa	SF	2	4	50	0	56	53	34	3	39	51	5.41	1.64	5.1	243	6.3	8.2	1.3	0.5	32%	65%	68
Hinton,Robert	09	25	R		a/a	MIL	0	6	53	12	75	83	44	6	40	65	5.31	1.64	6.5	275	4.8	7.8	1.6	0.8	34%	68%	58
	10	26	R		a/a	MIL	4	4	50	4	67	73	38	8	31	68	5.07	1.56	6.0	273	4.2	9.1	2.2	1.0	35%	69%	69
Hirsh,Jason	09	28	R		aaa	NYY	10	7	26	0	128	198	115	22	46	65	8.07	1.91	23.8	346	3.3	4.5	1.4	1.6	37%	58%	-4
	10	29	R		aaa	NYY	9	7	26	0	122	127	70	24	42	80	5.15	1.38	20.2	262	3.1	5.9	1.9	1.7	28%	68%	26
Hoey,Jim	09	27	R		aa	BAL	2	6	36	0	48	70	41	7	39	34	7.76	2.27	6.9	333	7.3	6.4	0.9	1.3	38%	66%	6
	10	28	R		a/a	BAL	0	6	42	0	52	48	26	1	38	51	4.56	1.65	5.7	241	6.5	8.9	1.4	0.2	33%	70%	82
Hoffman,Matthew	10	22	L		a/a	DET	1	2	29	0	31	49	30	5	22	23	8.85	2.27	5.6	349	6.4	6.7	1.1	1.4	41%	61%	6
Holland,Derek	10	24	L		aaa	TEX	6	2	11	0	62	55	15	5	17	44	2.17	1.16	23.1	232	2.5	6.4	2.6	0.7	28%	85%	79
Holland,Greg	09	24	R		a/a	KC	4	3	35	10	54	66	28	4	23	44	4.66	1.65	7.1	295	3.8	7.3	1.9	0.7	36%	72%	60
	10	25	R		aaa	KC	3	3	36	3	56	44	27	3	27	52	4.32	1.26	6.5	211	4.3	8.3	1.9	0.5	28%	65%	89
Holt,Bradley	09	23	R		aa	NYM	3	6	11	0	58	65	45	9	23	38	7.04	1.51	23.4	277	3.5	5.9	1.7	1.4	31%	54%	27
	10	24	R		aa	NYM	1	5	10	0	30	45	34	2	23	20	10.21	2.27	15.6	341	6.8	6.1	0.9	0.6	40%	52%	24
Hornbeck,Benjamin	10	23	L		aa	OAK	2	3	8	1	38	48	28	3	19	23	6.58	1.76	22.3	303	4.4	5.5	1.3	0.7	35%	61%	32
Horst,Jeremy	10	25	L	a	a/a	CIN	4	2	33	0	57	60	16	1	14	49	2.60	1.30	7.3	264	2.3	7.8	3.4	0.2	35%	79%	116
Hottovy,Thomas	10	29	L		a/a	BOS	3	3	41	0	75	120	60	15	50	39	7.16	2.26	9.5	353	6.0	4.7	0.8	1.8	38%	71%	-23
Houser,James	09	25	L		aaa	TAM	4	5	18	0	82	96	58	11	51	39	6.37	1.79	21.5	286	5.6	4.3	0.8	1.2	31%	65%	3
	10	26	L		a/a	FLA	1	4	28	1	56	81	39	7	26	42	6.24	1.91	9.7	331	4.2	6.7	1.6	1.2	39%	68%	27
Huber,Jon	09	28	R	b	aaa	ATL	4	0	27	1	42	54	26	3	8	34	5.52	1.46	6.8	304	1.6	7.4	4.6	0.7	37%	61%	114
	10	29	R		aaa	LA	3	3	39	18	47	52	16	3	16	30	3.06	1.45	5.3	275	3.1	5.7	1.9	0.5	32%	80%	59
Hudson,Dan	09	23	R	a	a/a	CHW	9	0	14	0	80	71	24	3	20	77	2.70	1.14	23.2	233	2.2	8.7	3.9	0.3	31%	76%	131
	10	24	R		aaa	CHW	11	4	17	0	93	91	43	16	31	96	4.16	1.31	23.2	251	3.0	9.3	3.1	1.5	31%	75%	79
Huff,David	09	25	L		aaa	CLE	5	1	7	0	39	39	22	5	16	29	5.12	1.42	24.2	257	3.7	6.6	1.8	1.2	30%	66%	46
	10	26	L		aaa	CLE	8	2	12	0	74	94	40	7	21	45	4.88	1.54	27.6	302	2.5	5.4	2.2	0.9	35%	69%	46
Hughes,William	09	24	R		aa	PIT	1	6	17	3	46	65	24	1	16	29	4.73	1.76	12.7	327	3.1	5.6	1.8	0.2	39%	71%	55
	10	25	R		aa	PIT	12	8	30	0	150	206	94	17	42	91	5.66	1.65	22.9	319	2.5	5.4	2.2	1.0	36%	66%	39
Humber,Philip	09	27	R		aaa	MIN	7	9	23	0	119	156	86	15	46	69	6.46	1.70	23.9	309	3.5	5.2	1.5	1.1	34%	62%	21
	10	28	R		aaa	KC	5	6	21	0	118	151	68	17	19	67	5.21	1.43	24.5	304	1.4	5.1	3.5	1.3	33%	66%	60
Hunter,Tommy	09	23	R		a/a	TEX	4	2	13	0	71	97	42	7	21	44	5.32	1.66	25.0	319	2.7	5.6	2.1	0.9	37%	68%	42
	10	24	R		aaa	TEX	1	2	6	0	26	31	14	2	11	12	4.81	1.60	19.8	288	3.8	4.1	1.1	0.7	32%	70%	24

Major League Equivalent Statistics

PITCHER	Yr	Age	Th	Lev	Org	Actual											Major League Equivalents								
						w	l	g	sv	ip	h	er	hr	bb	k	era	whip	bf/g	oob	ctl	dom	cmd	hr/9	h%	s%	bpv
Hunton,Jonathan	09	27	R		aa	OAK	4	4	40	4	54	53	22	2	13	34	3.64	1.21	5.6	251	2.1	5.7	2.7	0.4	30%	69%	84
	10	28	R		aaa	OAK	6	6	51	0	63	76	24	4	23	33	3.46	1.57	5.5	292	3.3	4.8	1.4	0.6	33%	79%	37
Hyde,Lee	10	26	L		a/a	ATL	4	6	51	8	60	78	28	4	25	45	4.25	1.71	5.5	307	3.8	6.7	1.8	0.6	37%	76%	52
Hynes,Colt	10	25	L		aa	SD	0	1	24	0	30	40	4	0	11	19	1.33	1.70	5.8	313	3.3	5.7	1.7	0.0	38%	91%	62
Hynick,Brandon	09	25	R		aaa	CHW	11	9	27	0	162	192	92	24	53	83	5.11	1.51	26.6	289	2.9	4.6	1.6	1.3	31%	69%	18
	10	26	R		a/a	CHW	4	5	21	0	112	157	71	21	37	68	5.66	1.73	24.8	324	3.0	5.5	1.9	1.7	35%	71%	11
Igawa,Kei	09	30	L		aaa	NYY	10	8	26	0	145	223	102	30	48	81	6.34	1.87	26.7	345	3.0	5.0	1.7	1.9	37%	70%	-4
	10	31	L		aaa	NYY	3	4	22	0	77	98	48	13	24	59	5.66	1.59	15.8	303	2.8	6.9	2.4	1.5	35%	67%	42
Inman,William	09	23	R		a/a	SD	7	9	27	0	150	163	83	17	44	86	4.98	1.38	23.9	271	2.6	5.2	2.0	1.0	30%	65%	42
	10	24	R		aaa	SD	2	4	11	0	62	55	24	5	25	46	3.48	1.29	23.8	233	3.6	6.7	1.8	0.7	28%	75%	65
Italiano,Craig	10	24	R		aa	SD	4	6	47	17	52	48	17	0	28	30	2.91	1.47	4.9	241	4.9	5.3	1.1	0.0	29%	78%	61
Jackson,Randy	09	22	R		a/a	CHC	6	5	17	0	88	87	42	10	42	72	4.28	1.46	22.7	252	4.3	7.4	1.7	1.0	30%	73%	56
	10	23	R		aaa	CHC	11	8	32	0	157	157	83	20	43	109	4.75	1.27	20.6	255	2.5	6.3	2.5	1.1	29%	65%	61
Jackson,Steven	09	28	R		aaa	PIT	1	0	19	1	32	46	20	2	8	20	5.61	1.71	7.8	331	2.4	5.6	2.4	0.6	39%	66%	54
	10	29	R		aaa	PIT	4	0	41	0	56	69	26	6	18	29	4.14	1.55	6.1	296	2.9	4.6	1.6	1.0	33%	76%	26
Jackson,Zach	09	26	L		aaa	CLE	4	8	30	0	99	148	81	14	34	59	7.39	1.84	15.7	339	3.1	5.4	1.7	1.3	38%	60%	17
	10	27	L		aaa	TOR	2	3	35	0	81	102	44	8	42	41	4.91	1.78	10.9	301	4.7	4.5	1.0	0.9	33%	74%	14
Jakubauskas,Chris	10	32	R		aaa	PIT	1	4	8	0	30	40	17	2	9	19	5.04	1.64	17.2	313	2.8	5.7	2.0	0.6	37%	69%	50
James,Chuck	10	29	L	b	a/a	WAS	10	1	26	2	66	71	26	7	13	50	3.53	1.27	10.6	268	1.8	6.8	3.9	1.0	32%	75%	95
James,Justin	10	29	R	b	a/a	OAK	2	1	28	5	39	32	10	1	17	35	2.25	1.25	5.8	217	3.9	8.1	2.1	0.3	29%	82%	95
Jarrett,Sean	10	27	R		aa	COL	3	1	18	0	30	41	10	2	10	12	2.89	1.69	7.7	319	2.9	3.7	1.3	0.7	35%	85%	19
Jennings,Daniel	10	23	L		aa	FLA	4	2	37	0	52	58	19	0	29	39	3.20	1.66	6.5	275	5.0	6.7	1.3	0.0	35%	79%	68
Jensen,Aaron	10	26	R		aa	SEA	3	1	42	3	59	103	36	1	18	30	5.43	2.06	7.0	375	2.8	4.5	1.6	0.2	43%	71%	36
Joaquin,Waldis	09	23	R	a	a/a	SF	5	5	44	2	64	45	18	0	28	48	2.53	1.14	5.9	194	3.9	6.8	1.7	0.0	25%	75%	93
	10	24	R		aaa	SF	1	2	23	2	34	47	20	4	20	28	5.26	1.96	7.3	320	5.3	7.4	1.4	1.1	39%	75%	33
Johnson,Alan	09	26	R		aaa	COL	10	6	26	0	143	187	99	24	48	62	6.23	1.64	25.1	309	3.0	3.9	1.3	1.5	32%	64%	-1
	10	27	R		aaa	COL	10	8	28	0	141	205	97	15	39	81	6.17	1.73	23.4	332	2.5	5.1	2.1	0.9	38%	64%	35
Johnson,Blake	09	24	R		aa	KC	8	8	24	0	122	174	75	12	40	51	5.51	1.75	23.7	328	3.0	3.8	1.3	0.9	36%	69%	13
	10	25	R		a/a	KC	5	4	29	1	88	118	49	4	24	45	5.05	1.61	13.8	314	2.5	4.6	1.8	0.4	36%	67%	45
Johnson,David	09	27	R		aaa	MIL	3	1	47	5	55	72	27	3	21	36	4.46	1.68	5.4	308	3.4	5.9	1.7	0.5	36%	73%	49
	10	28	R		aaa	MIL	2	2	48	0	65	73	38	11	31	56	5.21	1.60	6.1	278	4.3	7.7	1.8	1.5	33%	71%	39
Johnson,Jeremy	09	27	R		aaa	HOU	9	8	21	2	95	117	47	5	29	47	4.49	1.54	20.2	296	2.8	4.4	1.6	0.5	34%	70%	40
	10	28	R		aa	HOU	5	10	22	0	111	186	84	20	55	50	6.79	2.17	25.7	365	4.5	4.0	0.9	1.6	39%	71%	-24
Johnson,Kristofer	09	25	L		a/a	BOS	3	16	25	0	113	195	119	11	54	64	9.47	2.20	23.1	371	4.3	5.1	1.2	0.8	42%	54%	11
	10	26	L		aaa	BOS	6	13	28	0	132	180	92	17	53	67	6.26	1.76	22.1	318	3.6	4.6	1.3	1.2	35%	65%	11
Johnson,Steven	09	22	R		aa	BAL	4	3	9	0	48	41	21	6	21	44	3.92	1.29	22.5	226	3.9	8.2	2.1	1.1	28%	73%	70
	10	23	R		aa	BAL	7	8	28	0	145	169	103	31	77	104	6.40	1.70	23.9	285	4.8	6.4	1.3	1.9	31%	67%	7
Johnston,Andrew	09	26	R		aa	COL	2	4	56	31	53	82	31	4	21	29	5.26	1.94	4.6	346	3.6	4.9	1.4	0.8	39%	73%	21
	10	26	R		aaa	COL	3	3	55	1	55	70	31	5	15	29	5.04	1.55	4.5	303	2.5	4.7	1.9	0.8	34%	68%	37
Jones,Beau	09	23	L		aa	TEX	3	4	36	2	54	69	34	2	32	48	5.66	1.87	7.2	304	5.3	7.9	1.5	0.3	39%	68%	63
	10	24	L	a	aa	TEX	3	0	34	3	52	45	23	0	33	51	3.99	1.49	6.8	229	5.6	8.8	1.6	0.0	32%	70%	95
Jones,Hunter	09	26	L		aaa	BOS	4	3	36	2	53	59	39	9	26	34	6.69	1.60	6.7	275	4.5	5.7	1.3	1.5	30%	60%	15
	10	27	L		aaa	FLA	0	5	10	0	45	53	24	3	23	27	4.73	1.67	20.7	285	4.5	5.4	1.2	0.6	33%	71%	37
Jones,Jason	09	27	R		aaa	MIN	5	11	31	0	134	199	103	20	40	58	6.91	1.78	20.4	337	2.7	3.9	1.4	1.3	36%	62%	2
	10	28	R		a/a	WAS	2	8	14	0	54	90	61	15	18	22	10.13	2.00	19.0	362	3.1	3.6	1.2	2.5	36%	51%	-45
Jones,Mike	09	26	R		a/a	MIL	4	7	17	0	89	131	63	12	36	51	6.40	1.87	25.1	335	3.6	5.2	1.4	1.2	37%	67%	12
	10	27	R		a/a	MIL	1	1	19	0	40	41	16	0	33	20	3.62	1.87	10.1	262	7.5	4.5	0.6	0.0	31%	78%	42
Judy,Josh	09	24	R	a	aa	CLE	4	3	36	11	49	43	24	2	20	55	4.35	1.28	5.7	232	3.6	10.1	2.8	0.4	33%	64%	117
	10	25	R	a	a/a	CLE	3	0	40	2	49	61	18	5	14	49	3.22	1.54	5.5	298	2.7	9.1	3.4	0.9	39%	82%	93
Jukich,Benjamin	09	27	L		aaa	CIN	9	6	29	0	123	156	77	23	44	88	5.62	1.63	19.3	303	3.2	6.5	2.0	1.7	34%	70%	24
	10	28	L		aaa	CIN	7	4	29	1	115	128	62	11	48	86	4.86	1.54	17.7	276	3.8	6.8	1.8	0.8	33%	69%	53
Junge,Eric	10	34	R		aaa	LAA	5	3	14	0	80	100	47	9	21	48	5.32	1.51	25.4	299	2.4	5.4	2.3	1.1	34%	66%	44
Keating,Patrick	10	23	R	a	aa	KC	1	1	27	10	40	37	15	3	18	50	3.46	1.36	6.4	240	3.9	11.3	2.9	0.7	35%	76%	114
Kehrt,Jeremy	10	25	R		aa	BOS	3	11	20	0	105	143	73	12	36	48	6.21	1.70	24.3	318	3.1	4.1	1.3	1.0	35%	64%	14
Kelly,Casey	10	21	R		aa	BOS	3	5	21	0	95	124	60	10	31	72	5.68	1.63	20.6	309	3.0	6.9	2.3	0.9	37%	65%	56
Ketchner,Ryan	10	28	L		a/a	DET	7	6	30	2	137	181	85	28	47	73	5.56	1.66	21.0	311	3.1	4.8	1.6	1.9	33%	72%	-1
Keuchel,Dallas	10	22	L		aa	HOU	2	6	9	0	53	69	35	2	12	31	5.92	1.52	26.3	308	2.0	5.2	2.6	0.3	36%	58%	69
Kibler,Jonathan	09	23	L		aa	DET	6	9	27	0	161	198	92	16	68	72	5.12	1.65	27.3	296	3.8	4.0	1.1	0.9	32%	70%	14
	10	24	L		aa	DET	4	7	15	0	79	111	69	13	32	31	7.89	1.79	24.9	323	3.6	3.6	1.0	1.4	34%	56%	-11
Kiely,Tim	09	24	R		aa	LAA	4	3	15	0	94	131	71	18	19	38	6.74	1.59	28.3	322	1.8	3.6	2.0	1.7	33%	60%	3
	10	25	R		a/a	LAA	10	12	28	0	163	244	123	23	38	67	6.80	1.73	27.1	339	2.1	3.7	1.8	1.3	36%	61%	9
Kiker,Kasey	09	22	L		aa	TEX	7	7	25	0	126	124	65	10	67	104	4.64	1.52	22.4	252	4.8	7.4	1.6	0.7	31%	70%	60
	10	23	L		aa	TEX	1	4	14	0	40	33	43	1	47	36	9.68	2.00	14.1	220	10.6	8.1	0.8	0.2	29%	47%	69
Kimball,Cole	10	25	R		aa	WAS	5	1	38	12	54	43	20	6	34	57	3.33	1.44	6.2	216	5.7	9.5	1.7	0.9	28%	80%	75
Kimbrel,Craig	10	22	R	a	aaa	ATL	3	2	48	23	55	30	11	3	33	79	1.86	1.14	4.7	155	5.4	12.8	2.4	0.5	26%	86%	137
King,Blake	10	23	R	a	aa	STL	4	3	53	0	68	44	24	4	45	70	3.14	1.32	5.4	183	6.0	9.2	1.5	0.5	25%	77%	90
Kinney,Josh	09	31	R		aaa	STL	3	3	38	1	44	52	23	7	21	41	4.76	1.66	5.3	289	4.3	8.3	1.9	1.4	35%	75%	46
	10	31	R		aaa	STL	3	4	56	17	60	45	13	3	16	42	1.89	1.02	4.2	205	2.4	6.3	2.6	0.5	25%	84%	93
Kintzler,Brandon	09	25	R		aaa	MIL	1	2	9	0	35	51	23	6	10	26	5.97	1.74	18.2	332	2.6	6.7	2.6	1.4	38%	68%	41
	10	26	R	b	a/a	MIL	4	0	42	16	49	37	10	1	8	36	1.84	0.91	4.5	204	1.4	6.6	4.6	0.2	26%	79%	145
Kirkman,Michael	09	23	L		aa	TEX	5	7	18	0	96	109	57	10	44	53	5.30	1.60	24.1	280	4.1	5.0	1.2	1.0	31%	68%	25
	10	24	L		aaa	TEX	13	3	24	0	131	127	51	9	66	112	3.50	1.47	24.0	249	4.5	7.7	1.7	0.6	31%	77%	68
Klinker,Matthew	09	25	R		a/a	CIN	5	4	11	0	65	61	27	8	28	59	3.78	1.37	25.4	243	3.9	8.1	2.1	1.2	30%	77%	64
	10	26	R		a/a	CIN	11	10	28	1	163	186	84	23	47	116	4.64	1.43	25.4	281	2.6	6.4	2.4	1.3	32%	71%	50

Major League Equivalent Statistics

PITCHERS

PITCHER	Yr	Age	Th		Lev	Org	w	l	g	sv	ip	h	er	hr	bb	k	era	whip	bf/g	oob	ctl	dom	cmd	hr/9	h%	s%	bpv
											Actual							**Major League Equivalents**									
Kluber,Corey	09	24	R		aa	SD	2	4	9	0	45	48	24	4	34	29	4.74	1.83	23.8	269	6.8	5.8	0.9	0.8	31%	75%	29
	10	24	R		a/a	CLE	9	9	29	0	160	190	70	7	56	143	3.94	1.53	24.6	289	3.1	8.0	2.6	0.4	37%	74%	87
Koehler,Thomas	10	24	R		aa	FLA	16	2	28	0	158	169	60	13	52	124	3.41	1.40	24.4	268	2.9	7.1	2.4	0.7	33%	77%	73
Kohn,Michael	10	24	R	a	a/a	LAA	5	4	41	11	46	31	12	3	24	47	2.42	1.19	4.6	187	4.6	9.1	2.0	0.6	25%	82%	95
Kontos,George	09	24	R		a/a	NYY	4	5	13	0	71	79	36	8	33	52	4.57	1.58	24.6	277	4.2	6.6	1.6	1.0	32%	73%	41
	10	25	R		a/a	NYY	0	3	19	0	34	42	19	4	13	26	4.99	1.60	8.1	297	3.3	6.8	2.0	1.1	35%	71%	46
Koplove,Mike	09	33	R		aaa	SEA	4	4	55	11	72	63	19	4	28	59	2.37	1.27	5.5	231	3.5	7.4	2.1	0.5	29%	83%	81
	10	34	R		aaa	SD	0	1	32	1	43	49	25	5	21	27	5.29	1.64	6.1	283	4.4	5.6	1.3	1.1	32%	69%	25
Kopp,David	10	25	R		a/a	STL	12	9	26	0	145	177	67	11	46	75	4.16	1.54	24.9	295	2.9	4.6	1.6	0.7	33%	74%	36
Koronka,John	09	29	L		aaa	FLA	4	10	30	0	128	191	84	18	48	64	5.86	1.87	20.5	338	3.4	4.5	1.3	1.2	37%	70%	5
	10	30	L		a/a	LA	0	4	8	0	37	55	31	4	24	19	7.56	2.12	23.4	336	5.7	4.6	0.8	0.9	37%	63%	5
Korpi,Wade	10	25	L		a/a	FLA	0	3	38	0	42	51	26	3	26	33	5.52	1.82	5.2	292	5.5	7.1	1.3	0.7	36%	69%	46
Kown,Andrew	09	27	R		a/a	WAS	8	3	27	1	82	107	51	6	24	32	5.54	1.60	13.7	308	2.6	3.5	1.3	0.6	34%	64%	24
	10	28	R		a/a	WAS	8	8	30	1	146	201	87	23	40	65	5.38	1.65	22.3	320	2.5	4.0	1.6	1.4	34%	71%	7
Krebs,Eric	10	25	R		aa	LA	0	2	30	1	39	41	19	2	31	31	4.35	1.85	6.2	265	7.2	7.0	1.0	0.5	33%	76%	50
Krebs,Joseph	10	26	L		a/a	CIN	3	2	54	1	71	81	37	2	33	47	4.64	1.61	6.0	281	4.2	5.9	1.4	0.3	34%	69%	55
Kroenke,Zach	09	26	L		aaa	NYY	7	1	36	4	72	67	22	5	32	47	2.77	1.37	8.6	241	4.0	5.8	1.4	0.6	28%	82%	53
	10	26	L		aaa	ARI	7	3	40	2	97	100	38	5	35	58	3.54	1.39	10.5	261	3.2	5.4	1.7	0.5	31%	75%	56
Kulik,Ryan	09	24	L		aa	STL	6	10	24	0	125	173	84	15	40	46	6.01	1.71	24.1	322	2.9	3.3	1.1	1.1	34%	66%	1
	10	25	L		a/a	STL	8	9	33	1	129	139	67	12	55	57	4.67	1.50	17.3	270	3.8	4.0	1.0	0.9	29%	70%	21
Kunz,Eddie	09	24	R		aaa	NYM	4	5	40	1	61	64	44	9	32	33	6.49	1.57	6.9	264	4.7	4.9	1.0	1.3	28%	60%	13
	10	24	R		aa	NYM	7	8	42	3	111	124	67	7	67	50	5.46	1.72	12.3	277	5.5	4.1	0.7	0.6	31%	67%	22
Lahey,Timothy	09	28	R		aaa	MIN	2	3	41	1	56	82	44	6	22	34	7.08	1.85	6.5	333	3.5	5.5	1.5	1.0	38%	61%	23
	10	29	R		aaa	MIN	5	3	45	0	79	84	53	9	44	45	5.99	1.62	8.0	266	5.0	5.1	1.0	1.0	30%	63%	24
Lamb,John	10	20	L		aa	KC	2	1	7	0	33	38	21	2	11	24	5.71	1.50	20.8	283	3.1	6.6	2.1	0.5	34%	60%	67
Lamontagne,Andre	10	25	R		a/a	MIL	4	3	13	1	44	40	21	4	25	33	4.29	1.48	14.9	237	5.1	6.8	1.3	0.9	28%	72%	50
Lamura,BJ	10	30	R		a/a	TOR	5	6	31	0	95	73	44	10	55	59	4.16	1.35	13.1	209	5.2	5.6	1.1	0.9	23%	71%	42
Lanigan,Robert	10	23	R		aa	MIN	2	3	9	0	41	60	27	5	11	14	5.87	1.73	21.2	333	2.5	3.0	1.2	1.1	35%	67%	-2
Lannan,John	10	26	L		aa	WAS	1	4	7	0	40	64	27	3	11	22	5.97	1.88	27.6	354	2.5	4.8	1.9	0.7	40%	68%	32
Lansford,Jared	09	23	R		a/a	OAK	1	3	44	12	56	59	23	4	28	26	3.68	1.55	5.7	264	4.5	4.2	0.9	0.6	29%	77%	27
	10	24	R		a/a	OAK	5	3	46	12	54	55	25	1	24	38	4.17	1.46	5.1	259	4.0	6.3	1.6	0.2	32%	69%	70
Lara,Alexis	10	24	R		a/a	SD	4	5	45	0	72	61	31	3	32	51	3.87	1.29	6.7	225	4.0	6.4	1.6	0.4	28%	69%	71
Large,Terry	09	26	R		a/a	BOS	6	4	56	9	72	94	46	2	42	34	5.69	1.90	6.2	310	5.3	4.3	0.8	0.3	35%	68%	27
	10	27	R		a/a	BOS	5	1	24	0	41	51	45	7	29	18	9.79	1.93	8.3	296	6.3	4.0	0.6	1.5	31%	48%	-12
Lawrence,Brian	09	33	R		aaa	FLA	7	4	14	0	83	114	55	9	20	42	5.94	1.61	26.9	319	2.2	4.5	2.1	1.0	35%	64%	31
	10	34	R		aaa	FLA	11	8	26	0	142	191	80	20	41	99	5.06	1.63	24.9	315	2.6	6.3	2.4	1.3	36%	72%	42
Lawson,Donald	09	24	R		aa	BOS	3	12	23	0	115	154	103	12	60	47	8.07	1.86	23.9	314	4.7	3.6	0.8	0.9	34%	55%	3
	10	25	R		aa	BOS	6	5	33	2	78	99	41	6	41	29	4.73	1.79	11.2	302	4.7	3.3	0.7	0.6	33%	74%	10
Layne,Tom	09	25	L		aa	ARI	0	3	6	0	31	34	23	0	20	20	6.72	1.73	24.0	271	5.8	5.8	1.0	0.0	33%	57%	56
	10	26	L		aa	ARI	12	7	26	0	149	196	93	12	64	71	5.63	1.74	26.7	310	3.9	4.3	1.1	0.7	34%	67%	20
Leach,Brent	09	27	L		a/a	LA	2	1	27	2	31	36	19	3	27	30	5.45	1.99	5.7	281	7.7	8.6	1.1	1.0	36%	74%	45
	10	28	L		a/a	LA	10	5	39	0	104	128	63	7	55	64	5.46	1.75	12.5	295	4.8	5.5	1.2	0.6	34%	68%	35
LeCure,Sam	09	25	R		aaa	CIN	10	8	25	0	143	172	94	23	46	109	5.91	1.52	25.4	291	2.9	6.8	2.3	1.5	34%	64%	43
	10	26	R		aaa	CIN	8	3	15	0	98	113	48	10	24	75	4.45	1.40	28.2	284	2.2	6.9	3.1	0.9	34%	70%	77
Ledezma,Wil	09	29	L		a/a	TOR	1	3	26	1	35	65	21	1	22	28	5.41	2.47	7.3	386	5.7	7.2	1.3	0.3	47%	77%	38
	10	30	L	b	aaa	PIT	0	1	35	8	38	24	4	1	19	38	1.04	1.12	4.4	179	4.4	9.0	2.0	0.3	25%	92%	109
Lee,Chen	10	24	R	a	aa	CLE	5	4	44	0	72	67	30	6	22	71	3.73	1.23	6.8	241	2.7	8.8	3.3	0.8	31%	71%	105
Leesman,Charles	10	24	L		aa	CHW	5	2	11	0	63	57	25	1	22	44	3.52	1.24	23.9	235	3.1	6.2	2.0	0.1	29%	69%	83
Lehr,Justin	09	32	R		aaa	CIN	13	3	20	0	117	125	59	12	28	50	4.53	1.31	24.8	268	2.2	3.9	1.8	0.9	29%	67%	35
	10	33	R		aaa	CIN	1	3	7	0	37	71	34	2	13	12	8.19	2.25	27.3	395	3.1	3.0	1.0	0.5	43%	61%	-1
Lerew,Anthony	09	27	R		aa	KC	10	6	27	0	152	210	91	16	59	77	5.38	1.77	26.4	322	3.5	4.6	1.3	1.0	36%	70%	17
	10	28	R		aaa	KC	9	4	22	0	123	139	41	4	42	62	3.00	1.47	24.6	279	3.1	4.5	1.5	0.3	32%	79%	48
Leroux,Chris	09	26	R		aa	FLA	5	3	46	2	60	77	26	0	20	45	3.83	1.61	5.9	304	3.0	6.8	2.3	0.0	38%	74%	82
	10	27	R		aaa	FLA	0	3	21	1	22	29	20	2	7	17	8.01	1.64	4.8	310	3.0	7.1	2.4	0.8	38%	48%	61
Lewis,Jensen	10	26	R	b	aaa	CLE	2	1	24	2	30	32	10	2	8	26	3.08	1.34	5.3	267	2.5	7.8	3.2	0.6	34%	78%	97
Lewis,Rommie	10	28	L		aaa	TOR	1	5	24	5	53	73	40	5	20	33	6.74	1.76	10.4	320	3.5	5.7	1.6	0.9	37%	61%	32
Lincoln,Brad	09	24	R		a/a	PIT	7	7	25	0	136	157	62	11	27	86	4.09	1.35	23.2	283	1.8	5.7	3.2	0.7	33%	71%	78
	10	25	R		aaa	PIT	7	5	17	0	94	91	46	8	22	69	4.45	1.20	22.8	249	2.1	6.6	3.1	0.8	30%	63%	87
Lindblom,Joshua	09	22	R		a/a	LA	6	5	34	1	96	97	45	7	26	73	4.21	1.28	11.9	257	2.4	6.8	2.8	0.7	31%	67%	84
	10	23	R		aaa	LA	3	2	40	0	95	133	56	8	27	69	5.31	1.68	10.9	324	2.6	6.5	2.6	0.8	39%	68%	60
Lindsay,Shane	10	26	R		a/a	CLE	1	2	33	1	40	40	29	1	51	46	6.62	2.26	6.3	255	11.3	10.2	0.9	0.2	37%	68%	77
Link,Jon	09	26	R		aaa	CHW	1	2	48	13	56	68	35	7	29	57	5.67	1.73	5.4	292	4.7	9.2	2.0	1.1	38%	69%	59
	10	27	R		aaa	LA	3	2	45	4	60	63	21	4	19	44	3.08	1.35	5.7	263	2.8	6.5	2.4	0.6	32%	79%	72
Lively,Mitchell	10	25	R		aa	SF	2	4	23	3	32	42	20	1	20	19	5.61	1.94	6.8	311	5.6	5.3	0.9	0.3	36%	69%	35
Livingston,Bobby	09	27	L		a/a	PIT	9	7	27	0	156	229	97	9	39	53	5.57	1.72	26.8	334	2.3	3.1	1.4	0.5	36%	66%	19
	10	28	L		aaa	TAM	3	9	30	0	127	186	98	14	46	60	6.93	1.83	20.1	334	3.3	4.3	1.3	1.0	37%	62%	12
Liz,Radhames	09	26	R		a/a	BAL	4	4	25	0	92	141	67	4	30	58	6.51	1.86	17.6	344	2.9	5.6	1.9	0.4	40%	63%	47
	10	27	R		a/a	SD	8	8	25	0	123	134	65	15	37	94	4.75	1.39	21.2	272	2.7	6.9	2.5	1.1	32%	68%	61
Lo,Chia-Jen	09	24	R		aa	HOU	0	2	30	2	39	33	11	1	20	33	2.62	1.35	5.5	225	4.5	7.6	1.7	0.2	29%	80%	84
	10	25	R		aa	HOU	0	1	7	0	15	11	4	0	11	10	2.53	1.40	9.3	194	6.3	6.3	1.0	0.0	25%	80%	75
Lo,Ching	10	25	R		a/a	COL	3	5	33	0	78	84	38	9	25	35	4.37	1.40	10.2	270	2.9	4.1	1.4	1.1	29%	72%	22
Locke,Jeff	10	23	L	a	aa	PIT	3	2	10	0	57	64	26	5	11	47	4.09	1.31	24.2	277	1.7	7.4	4.3	0.8	34%	70%	110
Loe,Kameron	10	29	R		aaa	MIL	4	3	10	0	62	68	26	7	21	32	3.82	1.43	27.1	273	3.0	4.6	1.5	1.0	30%	76%	32

Major League Equivalent Statistics

PITCHER	Yr	Age Th		Lev	Org	w	l	g	sv	ip	h	er	hr	bb	k	era	whip	bf/g	oob	ctl	dom	cmd	hr/9	h%	s%	bpv
Lofgren,Charles	09	24 L		a/a	CLE	9	11	25	0	141	137	81	18	50	84	5.17	1.33	23.9	250	3.2	5.4	1.7	1.1	28%	63%	38
	10	25 L		aaa	MIL	7	8	28	0	131	154	82	24	74	83	5.63	1.74	21.8	287	5.1	5.7	1.1	1.6	31%	72%	6
Logan,Boone	09	25 L		aaa	ATL	4	2	29	2	35	29	15	2	17	34	3.87	1.32	5.1	222	4.4	8.6	2.0	0.5	29%	70%	88
	10	26 L	b	aaa	NYY	0	1	14	0	21	22	6	1	4	20	2.64	1.22	6.2	260	1.8	8.7	4.9	0.4	35%	79%	146
Long,Matthew	09	26 R		a/a	CHW	6	3	22	0	65	76	33	1	22	39	4.51	1.50	13.1	285	3.1	5.4	1.8	0.1	34%	67%	63
	10	27 R		aa	CHW	7	9	22	0	114	163	90	22	29	61	7.08	1.68	23.9	329	2.3	4.8	2.1	1.7	35%	60%	11
Loux,Shane	10	31 R		aaa	HOU	6	12	20	0	108	151	71	12	16	50	5.88	1.54	24.1	323	1.3	4.2	3.2	1.0	35%	62%	54
Lowe,Johnnie	10	26 R		aa	CHW	6	5	25	0	120	158	74	7	56	59	5.58	1.78	22.6	310	4.2	4.5	1.1	0.5	35%	67%	27
Luebke,Cory	09	25 L		aa	SD	3	2	9	0	41	42	18	2	15	37	3.92	1.38	19.7	260	3.2	5.8	1.8	0.5	31%	71%	62
	10	26 L		a/a	SD	10	1	19	0	114	92	36	7	29	74	2.83	1.06	23.9	216	2.3	5.9	2.5	0.6	25%	75%	82
Lueke,Joshua	10	26 R	a	a/a	SEA	3	1	33	7	43	40	14	2	11	49	2.86	1.17	5.3	241	2.2	10.3	4.7	0.4	34%	76%	154
Luetge,Lucas	10	24 L		aa	MIL	3	2	23	0	44	59	20	4	18	42	4.01	1.73	8.9	314	3.6	8.5	2.4	0.8	40%	79%	68
Lugo,Jose	09	26 L		a/a	MIN	4	2	59	4	67	74	38	2	39	52	5.09	1.68	5.2	274	5.2	7.0	1.3	0.3	34%	68%	62
	10	26 L		aaa	MIN	0	6	56	0	85	118	71	15	43	68	7.51	1.89	7.3	321	4.6	7.2	1.6	1.6	37%	62%	18
Lugo,Ruddy	09	29 R		aaa	DET	13	9	25	0	141	195	93	19	64	64	5.95	1.83	26.8	321	4.1	4.1	1.0	1.2	34%	69%	1
	10	30 R		aaa	DET	2	4	11	0	43	80	52	13	21	14	10.93	2.35	20.6	389	4.4	2.8	0.6	2.8	38%	56%	-76
Luis,Santo	10	27 R		a/a	BOS	6	2	38	1	67	76	40	1	40	50	5.36	1.72	8.2	278	5.4	6.6	1.2	0.1	35%	66%	61
Lujan,John	09	25 R		aa	CHW	3	5	37	1	58	68	42	1	32	41	6.53	1.72	7.3	285	5.0	6.3	1.3	0.2	35%	58%	57
	10	26 R		a/a	NYM	2	4	51	7	62	82	34	6	27	53	5.00	1.76	5.7	312	3.9	7.7	2.0	0.8	39%	72%	56
Lumsden,Tyler	09	26 L		a/a	HOU	2	4	30	0	62	90	43	10	41	19	6.29	2.11	10.4	332	6.0	2.7	0.5	1.5	34%	72%	-29
	10	27 L		aa	SD	5	13	29	0	141	196	93	7	66	45	5.91	1.86	23.3	323	4.2	2.9	0.7	0.5	35%	67%	8
Lyles,Jordan	10	20 R	a	a/a	HOU	7	12	27	0	158	175	63	11	40	135	3.56	1.36	25.1	275	2.3	7.7	3.4	0.6	34%	75%	97
Lyman,Jeff	09	23 R		a/a	ATL	5	9	38	0	98	94	45	3	55	78	4.13	1.52	11.5	247	5.1	7.2	1.4	0.3	31%	71%	70
	10	24 R		a/a	OAK	0	4	32	0	63	77	46	6	34	45	6.55	1.76	9.2	294	4.8	6.4	1.3	0.9	35%	62%	37
Lynn,Michael	09	22 R		a/a	STL	11	4	23	0	133	133	47	5	50	92	3.18	1.38	24.8	255	3.4	6.2	1.8	0.3	31%	76%	70
	10	23 R		aaa	STL	13	10	29	0	164	169	86	17	55	121	4.72	1.37	24.2	261	3.0	6.6	2.2	0.9	31%	67%	61
Mabee,Henry	10	25 R		aa	CHW	4	6	49	2	86	99	49	7	49	50	5.11	1.72	8.1	282	5.1	5.2	1.0	0.7	32%	70%	30
Macdonald,Michael	09	28 R		aaa	LAA	8	13	30	0	147	203	116	14	58	64	7.09	1.78	23.0	321	3.5	3.9	1.1	0.8	35%	59%	12
	10	29 R		aa	SF	5	8	27	0	134	230	95	14	40	52	6.38	2.01	24.5	370	2.7	3.5	1.3	0.9	40%	68%	2
MacDougal,Mike	10	34 R		a/a	STL	6	1	26	3	30	38	17	2	14	14	4.98	1.73	5.4	301	4.3	4.3	1.0	0.7	34%	71%	22
Machi,Jean	09	27 R		a/a	PIT	3	4	41	12	51	46	16	3	20	28	2.73	1.28	5.2	234	3.5	4.9	1.4	0.6	27%	80%	49
	10	28 R		aaa	PIT	5	5	58	23	59	58	29	6	31	47	4.48	1.49	4.5	251	4.6	7.1	1.5	1.0	30%	72%	51
Maclane,Evan	09	27 L		aaa	STL	8	11	27	0	165	221	87	23	23	80	4.72	1.47	26.9	314	1.2	4.3	3.5	1.2	34%	71%	55
	10	28 L		aaa	STL	8	7	24	0	147	177	76	18	20	67	4.63	1.34	26.1	291	1.2	4.1	3.3	1.1	31%	68%	58
Maday,Daryl	09	24 R		aa	SF	6	6	25	0	135	184	85	11	46	54	5.68	1.71	25.0	318	3.1	3.6	1.2	0.7	35%	66%	17
	10	25 R		a/a	SF	10	12	32	1	142	187	91	18	46	67	5.73	1.64	20.3	311	2.9	4.2	1.4	1.1	34%	66%	14
Madrigal,Warner	09	26 R		aaa	TEX	2	2	42	17	49	51	18	6	12	41	3.34	1.28	4.9	261	2.2	7.5	3.3	1.1	31%	79%	84
	10	27 R		a/a	TEX	5	2	35	3	50	52	28	8	16	32	4.98	1.35	6.1	263	2.8	5.8	2.1	1.4	29%	67%	39
Maestri,Alessandro	09	24 R		aa	CHC	4	2	54	3	85	87	47	11	58	59	5.01	1.71	7.3	260	6.1	6.2	1.0	1.1	30%	73%	28
	10	25 R		aa	CHC	2	3	28	2	40	53	36	3	22	25	7.98	1.88	6.9	313	5.0	5.7	1.1	0.7	36%	55%	28
Magnuson,Trystan	10	25 R	a	aa	TOR	3	0	46	5	73	82	24	1	11	50	3.01	1.28	6.7	278	1.4	6.1	4.5	0.1	34%	75%	125
Mahon,Reid	09	26 R		a/a	ARI	6	4	37	5	50	74	33	2	18	28	5.98	1.84	6.5	337	3.2	5.0	1.6	0.4	39%	65%	39
	10	27 R		aa	ARI	4	3	37	3	53	77	29	5	28	22	4.91	1.98	7.0	333	4.7	3.8	0.8	0.8	36%	76%	4
Maine,Scott	09	25 L		a/a	ARI	4	5	48	5	62	79	24	2	22	52	3.44	1.63	5.9	305	3.1	7.6	2.4	0.3	39%	78%	81
	10	26 L		a/a	CHC	2	2	45	10	57	52	23	5	25	51	3.65	1.35	5.4	236	4.0	8.1	2.0	0.8	30%	75%	74
Majewski,Gary	09	30 R		aaa	PHI	0	5	51	5	62	93	38	5	27	33	5.57	1.94	5.9	340	4.0	4.7	1.2	0.8	38%	71%	17
	10	31 R		aaa	HOU	4	5	40	2	53	82	43	8	19	31	7.34	1.90	6.4	347	3.2	5.2	1.6	1.3	38%	62%	11
Malone,Christopher	10	27 R		aa	COL	3	5	44	5	59	78	41	13	31	32	6.24	1.86	6.4	312	4.8	4.8	1.0	2.0	33%	71%	-18
Maloney,Matt	09	26 L		a/a	CIN	9	9	23	0	150	182	68	17	28	109	4.11	1.40	28.2	294	1.7	6.6	3.8	1.0	35%	73%	86
	10	27 L		aaa	CIN	10	7	24	0	134	154	61	11	29	89	4.08	1.36	23.9	282	1.9	6.0	3.1	0.8	33%	71%	77
Mandel,Jeff	09	24 R		aa	WAS	4	2	8	0	52	60	24	6	13	29	4.19	1.40	28.1	283	2.2	4.9	2.3	1.1	31%	73%	43
	10	25 R		a/a	WAS	6	10	32	0	134	193	89	11	48	70	6.00	1.80	19.8	330	3.2	4.7	1.5	0.7	37%	66%	27
Manship,Jeff	09	25 R		a/a	MIN	10	6	21	0	126	146	66	3	38	60	4.71	1.46	26.3	285	2.7	4.3	1.6	0.2	33%	65%	50
	10	26 R		aaa	MIN	3	8	19	0	98	146	62	12	21	69	5.65	1.71	23.9	338	1.9	6.4	3.3	1.1	39%	68%	61
Manuel,Robert	09	26 R		aaa	SEA	4	5	51	14	65	54	22	5	16	43	2.99	1.08	5.1	220	2.3	5.9	2.6	0.7	26%	75%	79
	10	26 R		aaa	BOS	8	2	45	13	64	57	16	4	14	39	2.22	1.10	5.7	233	1.9	5.5	2.8	0.6	27%	83%	83
Marek,Stephen	09	26 R		aaa	ATL	3	4	44	2	45	60	41	3	41	28	8.22	2.25	5.3	313	8.2	5.6	0.7	0.7	36%	61%	20
	10	27 R	b	a/a	ATL	6	2	60	13	63	57	10	5	23	58	1.48	1.28	4.4	238	3.3	8.3	2.5	0.7	31%	92%	91
Marquez,Jeff	09	25 R		aaa	CHW	2	8	11	0	45	89	70	17	23	24	13.88	2.48	22.2	402	4.6	4.7	1.0	3.4	41%	45%	-78
	10	26 R		aaa	CHW	8	9	27	0	144	187	88	18	51	77	5.47	1.64	24.4	307	3.2	4.8	1.5	1.1	34%	68%	21
Marte,Jose	09	26 R		aaa	ARI	4	1	47	2	71	73	38	3	31	53	4.82	1.46	6.6	260	3.9	6.7	1.7	0.4	32%	65%	68
	10	27 R		aaa	ARI	4	3	47	0	66	69	43	9	28	49	5.87	1.48	6.8	264	3.9	6.7	1.7	1.3	30%	62%	40
Marte,Luis	09	23 R		aa	DET	5	8	19	0	105	154	59	21	28	70	5.03	1.62	24.2	289	2.4	6.0	2.5	1.8	31%	71%	33
	10	24 R		a/a	DET	2	2	39	7	49	53	33	6	27	44	6.06	1.62	5.7	269	4.9	8.0	1.6	1.1	33%	63%	49
Marte,Victor	09	29 R		a/a	KC	3	5	39	8	64	67	22	1	28	40	3.14	1.49	7.2	264	4.0	5.6	1.4	0.2	32%	78%	61
	10	30 R		aaa	KC	4	1	25	3	40	48	19	3	15	23	4.18	1.59	7.2	292	3.4	5.1	1.5	0.7	33%	75%	36
Martin,Adrian	09	25 R		a/a	TOR	4	2	34	2	93	120	55	15	29	61	5.29	1.61	12.4	306	2.8	5.9	2.1	1.4	34%	70%	30
	10	26 R		aa	SF	6	1	37	1	61	87	38	7	30	41	5.59	1.92	8.0	329	4.4	6.0	1.4	1.0	38%	72%	24
Martin,J.D.	09	27 R	b	aaa	WAS	8	3	16	0	88	90	34	4	10	52	3.48	1.14	22.3	259	1.1	5.4	5.1	0.4	30%	69%	129
	10	28 R		aaa	WAS	2	2	7	0	41	48	21	3	8	20	4.62	1.39	25.2	288	1.8	4.4	2.4	0.7	32%	67%	53
Martin,Rafael	10	26 R		aa	WAS	5	4	47	0	67	75	40	7	30	44	5.40	1.56	6.4	276	4.0	5.8	1.5	0.9	32%	66%	38
Martinez,Cristhian	09	28 R		aa	FLA	9	3	17	0	104	135	52	10	29	46	4.48	1.58	27.5	308	2.5	4.0	1.6	0.8	34%	73%	26
	10	29 R	b	aaa	ATL	5	1	23	0	52	54	23	3	9	41	3.89	1.19	9.3	261	1.5	7.1	4.8	0.6	32%	67%	128

Major League Equivalent Statistics

						Actual											Major League Equivalents									
PITCHER	Yr	Age Th		Lev	Org	w	l	g	sv	ip	h	er	hr	bb	k	era	whip	bf/g	oob	ctl	dom	cmd	hr/9	h%	s%	bpv
Martinez,Joe	09	27 R		aaa	SF	0	2	7	0	35	42	20	1	7	18	5.04	1.41	21.7	293	1.9	4.7	2.6	0.3	34%	62%	71
	10	28 R		aaa	PIT	6	5	21	1	109	141	55	12	32	67	4.51	1.58	23.4	307	2.6	5.5	2.1	1.0	35%	73%	42
Martis,Shairon	09	23 R		aaa	WAS	4	4	13	0	74	100	49	10	17	37	5.90	1.58	25.7	316	2.1	4.5	2.1	1.2	34%	64%	29
	10	23 R		aaa	WAS	8	7	27	0	152	181	86	15	59	85	5.09	1.58	25.3	290	3.5	5.0	1.4	0.9	33%	68%	31
Mastny,Tom	10	30 R		aaa	FLA	4	5	18	0	86	107	49	10	37	49	5.17	1.67	22.0	298	3.9	5.1	1.3	1.0	33%	70%	23
Mata,Frank	09	26 R		aa	MIN	2	5	53	3	78	106	44	3	39	44	5.12	1.85	7.0	316	4.5	5.1	1.1	0.4	37%	71%	35
	10	27 R		aaa	BAL	5	3	36	8	42	40	19	2	20	24	3.96	1.42	5.1	246	4.2	5.2	1.2	0.4	29%	71%	50
Mateo,Marcos	09	26 R		aa	CHC	3	6	34	0	97	127	62	12	51	54	5.77	1.83	13.6	309	4.7	5.0	1.1	1.1	34%	70%	11
	10	26 R	b	a/a	CHC	0	1	25	4	33	42	14	2	8	34	3.93	1.51	5.9	304	2.1	9.3	4.4	0.6	40%	74%	124
Mathes,JR	09	28 L		aaa	CHC	12	8	26	0	129	181	67	14	16	42	4.70	1.52	22.1	324	1.1	2.9	2.6	1.0	34%	71%	35
	10	29 L		aaa	CHC	9	8	23	0	129	183	90	19	28	52	6.30	1.63	25.5	327	2.0	3.6	1.9	1.4	34%	63%	10
Mathieson,Scott	10	27 R		aaa	PHI	3	6	54	26	64	60	27	10	26	69	3.76	1.33	5.1	242	3.6	9.7	2.7	1.4	31%	78%	77
Mathis,Doug	09	26 R		aaa	TEX	4	2	11	0	57	78	25	4	16	32	3.91	1.66	23.8	320	2.6	5.1	1.9	0.7	37%	77%	43
	10	27 R		aaa	TEX	5	7	18	0	89	135	66	8	32	45	6.71	1.87	23.7	341	3.2	4.5	1.4	0.9	38%	63%	18
Matos,Osiris	09	25 R		aaa	SF	3	3	45	2	54	60	21	6	12	41	3.53	1.33	5.1	274	2.0	6.8	3.3	1.0	32%	77%	81
	10	26 R		aaa	SF	1	4	38	3	51	53	33	3	24	32	5.82	1.50	5.9	261	4.2	5.6	1.3	0.5	31%	59%	49
Maxwell,Blake	09	25 R		aa	BOS	7	8	32	0	111	172	94	11	37	46	7.64	1.88	16.7	347	3.0	3.7	1.3	0.9	38%	58%	7
	10	26 R		a/a	BOS	7	0	14	0	55	71	26	6	14	27	4.17	1.55	17.6	307	2.4	4.4	1.9	0.9	34%	75%	32
Mazone,Brian	09	33 L		aaa	PHI	7	2	24	0	70	106	47	6	18	37	6.09	1.77	13.7	342	2.3	4.8	2.1	0.8	38%	65%	34
	10	34 L		aaa	PHI	7	13	28	0	165	216	95	25	33	85	5.17	1.51	26.1	309	1.8	4.6	2.6	1.4	33%	69%	34
Mazzaro,Vin	09	23 R	a	aaa	OAK	2	2	10	0	56	45	16	2	15	38	2.56	1.07	22.4	215	2.4	6.1	2.5	0.3	26%	76%	92
	10	24 R		aaa	OAK	3	1	7	0	37	35	12	2	15	33	2.91	1.35	22.6	244	3.6	8.0	2.2	0.5	32%	79%	86
McAllister,Zachary	09	22 R		aa	NYY	7	5	22	0	121	121	43	5	36	82	3.20	1.30	23.2	255	2.7	6.1	2.3	0.4	31%	75%	77
	10	23 R		aaa	CLE	9	12	27	0	149	191	93	18	41	92	5.63	1.56	24.7	305	2.5	5.6	2.3	1.1	35%	65%	42
McAnaney,Patrick	10	25 L		aa	ARI	5	10	22	0	110	165	93	11	57	78	7.57	2.02	24.7	340	4.6	6.4	1.4	0.9	40%	61%	28
McCardell,Michael	09	25 R		aa	MIN	5	2	9	0	48	55	28	4	17	31	5.32	1.49	23.6	280	3.2	5.9	1.9	0.8	33%	64%	50
	10	25 R		aa	MIN	3	13	31	0	150	213	106	24	49	61	6.33	1.75	22.6	328	2.9	3.7	1.3	1.5	34%	66%	-6
McCarthy,Brandon	10	27 R		aaa	TEX	4	2	11	0	56	59	25	9	12	36	4.05	1.26	21.3	265	1.9	5.8	3.1	1.5	29%	74%	57
McClendon,Mike	09	25 R		aa	MIL	4	3	41	3	84	102	38	4	21	49	4.05	1.46	9.0	293	2.3	5.3	2.3	0.5	34%	72%	64
	10	25 R	a	a/a	MIL	5	4	32	2	70	68	18	1	16	51	2.30	1.20	9.0	251	2.0	6.6	3.2	0.1	32%	80%	109
McCulloch,Kyle	09	25 R		aa	CHW	9	9	28	1	149	233	106	12	35	53	6.42	1.79	25.1	348	2.1	3.2	1.5	0.7	38%	63%	16
	10	26 R		a/a	CHW	5	5	36	0	93	143	77	15	29	33	7.42	1.85	12.4	345	2.8	3.2	1.1	1.4	36%	61%	-14
McCutchen,Daniel	09	27 R		aaa	PIT	13	6	24	0	142	173	68	11	29	86	4.33	1.42	25.7	294	1.9	5.5	2.9	0.7	34%	70%	71
	10	28 R		aaa	PIT	4	8	13	0	79	83	41	12	18	31	4.65	1.28	25.5	264	2.1	3.5	1.7	1.3	27%	67%	18
McDonald,James	09	25 R	a	aaa	LA	1	0	6	0	30	22	11	2	14	36	3.32	1.21	20.7	202	4.2	10.7	2.5	0.6	29%	74%	113
	10	26 R		aaa	LA	6	1	12	0	63	61	25	3	20	47	3.60	1.28	22.1	248	2.9	6.6	2.3	0.4	30%	71%	81
Mcgee,Jacob	10	24 L	a	a/a	TAM	4	8	30	1	105	103	42	3	36	106	3.62	1.32	14.9	251	3.1	9.0	2.9	0.3	34%	71%	113
McGregor,Scott	10	24 R	a	aa	STL	6	5	15	0	80	91	34	6	8	41	3.82	1.23	22.2	279	0.9	4.6	4.9	0.7	31%	70%	109
McLeary,Marty	09	35 R		a/a	TOR	7	4	14	0	79	92	38	9	34	43	4.29	1.60	25.6	285	3.9	4.9	1.3	1.0	32%	75%	23
	10	36 R		a/a	MIL	8	10	26	0	116	217	109	22	56	68	8.45	2.35	23.5	390	4.3	5.3	1.2	1.7	43%	65%	-17
Medina,Ruben	09	23 R		aa	CIN	2	4	51	0	70	72	41	8	52	45	5.29	1.76	6.4	260	6.6	5.7	0.9	1.1	29%	71%	24
	10	24 R		aa	CIN	4	2	45	2	69	71	26	4	43	31	3.43	1.65	7.0	259	5.6	4.1	0.7	0.5	29%	80%	26
Mejia,Jenrry	09	20 R		aa	NYM	0	5	10	0	44	46	23	2	21	43	4.66	1.51	19.5	262	4.3	8.8	2.1	0.4	35%	68%	87
	10	21 R	a	aaa	NYM	2	0	7	0	35	23	5	1	13	32	1.17	1.01	19.7	181	3.3	8.2	2.5	0.2	25%	89%	113
Melancon,Mark	09	25 R	a	aaa	NYY	4	0	32	3	53	45	23	4	12	46	3.91	1.08	6.6	225	2.0	7.8	3.8	0.7	28%	64%	117
	10	26 R		aaa	HOU	7	1	43	7	60	74	24	5	31	50	3.62	1.75	6.5	296	4.7	7.5	1.6	0.8	37%	81%	52
Mendez,Adalberto	09	28 R		aa	FLA	2	4	27	0	36	41	22	2	20	24	5.42	1.71	6.2	280	5.1	6.0	1.2	0.6	33%	67%	42
	10	29 R		a/a	FLA	5	5	40	1	86	104	52	9	49	68	5.42	1.78	10.1	292	5.2	7.1	1.4	1.0	35%	70%	39
Mendoza,Luis	09	26 R		aaa	TEX	6	7	25	0	111	156	74	5	53	66	5.97	1.87	21.3	324	4.3	5.4	1.3	0.4	38%	66%	37
	10	27 R		aaa	KC	10	9	24	0	131	163	68	12	30	49	4.67	1.47	24.0	298	2.1	3.4	1.7	0.8	32%	69%	25
Mendoza,Thomas	09	22 R		a/a	LAA	9	8	24	0	150	166	64	13	41	80	3.84	1.38	26.9	275	2.5	4.8	2.0	0.8	31%	74%	46
	10	23 R		a/a	LAA	1	5	10	0	45	62	36	14	19	22	7.17	1.79	21.3	320	3.8	4.4	1.2	2.8	31%	67%	-42
Mercedes,Roque	10	24 R		aa	ARI	3	4	38	1	53	84	36	6	26	38	6.10	2.05	7.0	350	4.4	6.4	1.5	1.0	41%	71%	23
Merritt,Roy	09	24 L		aa	NYM	4	5	56	14	62	78	27	8	25	47	3.96	1.66	5.1	300	3.7	6.7	1.8	1.2	35%	80%	38
	10	25 L		a/a	NYM	4	6	64	9	86	92	44	7	28	54	4.63	1.40	5.8	267	3.0	5.7	1.9	0.8	31%	67%	52
Meszaros,Daniel	09	24 R		aa	HOU	3	3	37	1	61	72	26	7	17	39	3.87	1.44	7.2	286	2.5	5.7	2.3	1.1	32%	77%	48
	10	25 R		a/a	HOU	5	2	33	10	40	40	19	2	23	38	4.25	1.58	5.5	255	5.2	8.5	1.6	0.5	34%	72%	76
Meyer,Dan	10	29 L		a/a	FLA	1	2	33	2	42	45	21	5	23	21	4.44	1.63	5.8	269	5.0	4.4	0.9	1.0	29%	75%	15
Meyers,Bradley	09	24 R	a	aa	WAS	5	1	9	0	48	51	17	2	12	35	3.16	1.29	22.5	265	2.2	6.6	3.0	0.4	33%	75%	93
	10	25 R	a	aa	WAS	1	0	6	0	30	30	7	3	8	27	1.99	1.25	21.0	254	2.3	8.0	3.5	1.0	31%	90%	96
Mickolio,Kam	09	25 R		aaa	BAL	3	3	35	0	43	39	23	6	16	44	4.84	1.29	5.2	238	3.4	9.1	2.7	1.3	30%	65%	81
	10	26 R		aaa	BAL	4	3	30	0	35	52	31	5	16	39	7.93	1.94	5.7	335	4.2	9.9	2.4	1.3	44%	59%	58
Middleton,Kyle	09	29 R		aa	OAK	4	4	24	0	60	64	24	4	15	24	3.59	1.31	28.2	267	2.2	3.6	1.6	0.6	29%	73%	40
	10	30 R		aaa	OAK	6	8	23	1	102	109	44	9	46	54	3.91	1.51	19.7	267	4.0	4.8	1.2	0.8	30%	76%	31
Miley,Wade	10	24 L		aa	ARI	5	2	13	0	72	74	23	6	30	52	2.83	1.44	24.2	260	3.7	6.5	1.8	0.8	31%	83%	56
Miller,Andrew	10	25 L		aa	FLA	1	8	18	0	85	126	78	8	72	54	8.23	2.32	24.8	336	7.6	5.7	0.7	0.8	39%	63%	13
Miller,Jayson	10	25 L		aa	LAA	0	4	12	0	40	66	36	4	15	20	8.01	2.02	16.5	361	3.3	4.5	1.4	0.9	40%	59%	10
Miller,Jim	09	27 R		aaa	BAL	4	4	54	17	64	82	27	4	20	47	3.84	1.59	5.4	305	2.8	6.5	2.3	0.6	37%	76%	64
	10	28 R		aaa	BAL	1	0	33	6	57	74	40	12	18	41	6.26	1.62	7.9	308	2.9	6.4	2.2	1.9	34%	65%	23
Miller,Ryne	09	24 R		aa	BOS	2	2	14	1	39	35	16	2	14	31	3.63	1.24	11.6	233	3.1	7.2	2.3	0.5	29%	70%	85
	10	25 R		aa	BOS	2	6	27	0	84	109	76	22	58	56	8.10	1.98	15.3	307	6.2	6.0	1.0	2.4	32%	63%	-22
Mills,Adam	09	25 R		a/a	BOS	12	7	26	0	141	203	93	14	32	75	5.92	1.67	24.9	330	2.0	4.8	2.3	0.9	37%	64%	39
	10	26 R		aaa	BOS	4	10	25	0	131	207	103	19	25	50	7.07	1.77	24.6	351	1.7	3.4	2.0	1.3	37%	61%	7

Major League Equivalent Statistics

						Actual										Major League Equivalents									
PITCHER	Yr	Age Th		Lev	Org	w	l	g	sv	ip	h	er	hr	bb	k	era	whip	bf/g	oob	ctl	dom	cmd	hr/9	h%	s%	bpv
Mills, Brad	09	25 L		aaa	TOR	2	8	14	0	84	89	40	6	34	62	4.28	1.46	26.3	266	3.6	6.6	1.8	0.6	32%	71%	61
	10	26 L		aaa	TOR	8	6	20	0	112	112	52	11	38	86	4.14	1.34	23.9	255	3.1	6.9	2.2	0.9	31%	71%	66
Milone, Tom	10	24 L	a	aa	WAS	12	5	27	0	158	195	66	11	24	129	3.76	1.38	25.2	297	1.4	7.3	5.4	0.6	37%	74%	135
Minor, Mike	10	23 L	a	a/a	ATL	6	7	21	0	120	104	53	9	46	132	3.97	1.25	23.8	229	3.4	9.9	2.9	0.7	31%	69%	109
Misch, Pat	09	28 L		aaa	NYM	4	2	18	1	52	65	25	2	9	27	4.27	1.40	12.5	298	1.5	4.7	3.1	0.4	34%	68%	78
	10	29 L		aaa	NYM	11	4	23	0	150	175	62	12	25	76	3.69	1.33	27.8	285	1.5	4.5	3.0	0.7	32%	74%	66
Mitchell, Andy	09	31 R		aaa	BAL	11	5	37	0	113	161	95	19	56	47	7.54	1.92	14.8	328	4.4	3.7	0.8	1.5	34%	62%	-16
	10	32 R		aaa	BAL	0	1	16	0	32	76	32	0	7	13	8.83	2.58	11.1	446	2.1	3.7	1.8	0.0	49%	62%	26
Mitchell, William	10	23 R		a/a	NYY	13	4	26	0	150	166	80	14	63	102	4.79	1.52	25.7	275	3.8	6.1	1.6	0.8	32%	69%	46
Mixon, David	10	26 R		aa	SF	11	7	27	0	156	203	92	16	45	82	5.30	1.59	26.1	308	2.6	4.7	1.8	0.9	34%	67%	32
Mobley, Chris	09	26 R		a/a	FLA	3	3	44	3	61	99	39	6	26	37	5.72	2.03	6.9	356	3.8	5.4	1.4	0.8	41%	72%	22
	10	27 R		aa	TEX	2	2	14	0	28	35	17	1	17	18	5.40	1.84	9.6	299	5.4	5.8	1.1	0.4	36%	69%	42
Mock, Garrett	09	26 R	b	aaa	WAS	5	1	13	2	51	43	20	2	13	40	3.46	1.11	15.8	225	2.4	7.0	3.0	0.4	28%	68%	103
	10	27 R		a/a	WAS	1	2	3	0	16	23	13	1	6	4	7.11	1.80	25.2	330	3.2	2.4	0.8	0.6	35%	58%	0
Molleken, Dustin	09	25 R		aa	PIT	1	1	18	1	37	46	24	6	17	20	5.95	1.68	9.5	297	4.1	4.8	1.2	1.4	32%	67%	9
	10	26 R		aa	PIT	4	4	31	0	60	70	37	3	23	45	5.50	1.55	8.7	285	3.4	6.8	2.0	0.5	35%	63%	64
Montgomery, Michael	10	21 L		aa	KC	5	4	13	0	59	60	25	4	23	42	3.80	1.40	19.7	258	3.5	6.4	1.8	0.6	31%	73%	62
Morales, Franklin	09	24 L		aaa	COL	2	2	8	0	41	42	17	4	17	31	3.72	1.44	22.4	259	3.7	6.8	1.8	0.9	31%	76%	56
	10	25 L		aaa	COL	3	0	24	1	30	21	9	3	16	29	2.69	1.23	5.2	193	4.8	8.7	1.8	0.9	24%	82%	80
Morlan, Eduardo	09	24 R		aa	TAM	7	5	48	4	70	81	41	10	32	53	5.30	1.62	6.6	285	4.1	6.9	1.7	1.3	33%	70%	34
	10	25 R		aa	MIL	3	2	44	3	71	89	33	7	22	51	4.12	1.57	7.3	301	2.8	6.5	2.3	0.9	35%	76%	55
Morris, Bryan	10	24 R		aa	PIT	6	4	19	0	89	100	49	9	30	68	5.00	1.46	20.5	278	3.0	6.9	2.3	0.9	33%	67%	60
Mortensen, Clayton	09	25 R		aaa	OAK	9	8	23	0	137	154	72	12	43	86	4.73	1.44	26.0	278	2.8	5.6	2.0	0.8	32%	68%	52
	10	25 R		aaa	OAK	13	6	26	0	165	164	74	16	46	97	4.02	1.27	26.6	253	2.5	5.3	2.1	0.9	29%	70%	53
Morton, Charlie	09	26 R	a	aaa	PIT	7	2	11	0	71	64	21	3	16	50	2.68	1.12	26.2	234	2.0	6.4	3.1	0.4	29%	76%	101
	10	27 R		aaa	PIT	4	4	14	0	80	93	38	6	28	43	4.29	1.51	25.3	284	3.1	4.8	1.5	0.7	32%	72%	38
Moscoso, Guillermo	09	26 R		a/a	TEX	8	5	21	0	112	119	52	4	32	79	4.14	1.34	22.8	267	2.5	6.3	2.5	0.3	33%	68%	82
	10	27 R		aaa	TEX	7	7	23	0	123	162	82	20	48	89	6.03	1.71	24.8	310	3.5	6.5	1.8	1.4	36%	67%	28
Moseley, Dustin	10	29 R		aaa	NYY	4	4	12	0	72	103	45	9	19	47	5.63	1.70	27.8	329	2.4	5.8	2.4	1.1	38%	68%	42
Moskos, Daniel	09	23 L		aa	PIT	11	10	27	0	149	184	74	11	57	62	4.48	1.61	25.0	297	3.4	3.7	1.1	0.7	32%	73%	21
	10	24 L		a/a	PIT	3	6	56	22	58	59	31	3	34	49	4.78	1.59	4.7	257	5.3	7.7	1.5	0.5	33%	69%	66
Moss, Damian	09	33 L		aaa	COL	8	3	59	0	76	98	32	5	43	47	3.73	1.85	5.5	306	5.1	5.5	1.1	0.6	36%	81%	31
	10	34 L		aaa	COL	2	2	25	0	36	52	34	1	24	22	8.40	2.10	7.2	329	6.0	5.4	0.9	0.3	39%	56%	33
Muecke, Joshua	09	28 L		aaa	HOU	7	11	29	0	136	181	96	19	73	69	6.34	1.87	22.4	313	4.8	4.6	1.0	1.3	34%	67%	2
	10	29 L		aaa	COL	6	9	25	0	119	167	84	14	40	64	6.33	1.73	22.2	324	3.0	4.8	1.6	1.1	36%	64%	22
Mullins, Ryan	09	26 L		aa	MIN	11	11	28	0	145	223	88	14	41	97	5.45	1.82	24.6	345	2.6	6.0	2.4	0.9	40%	71%	45
	10	27 L		aaa	MIN	4	7	19	0	90	118	52	13	26	48	5.15	1.59	21.4	309	2.6	4.8	1.8	1.3	34%	71%	20
Mulvey, Kevin	09	24 R		aaa	MIN	5	8	24	0	149	172	76	12	54	93	4.59	1.52	27.5	283	3.3	5.6	1.7	0.7	33%	70%	46
	10	25 R		aaa	ARI	8	8	27	0	156	168	80	10	53	93	4.60	1.41	25.0	269	3.0	5.4	1.8	0.6	31%	67%	53
Munoz, Luis	09	28 R		a/a	SEA	8	10	27	0	140	178	89	20	68	82	5.69	1.76	24.3	304	4.4	5.3	1.2	1.3	34%	70%	13
	10	29 R		a/a	SEA	7	6	38	1	100	124	58	12	41	53	5.19	1.65	12.0	297	3.7	4.7	1.3	1.1	33%	70%	19
Munter, Scott	09	30 R		aaa	COL	4	6	46	1	55	66	35	3	27	27	5.74	1.70	5.5	291	4.5	4.5	1.0	0.5	33%	65%	28
	10	31 R		aaa	SD	4	1	49	0	71	64	22	2	33	54	2.82	1.38	6.2	237	4.2	6.8	1.6	0.3	30%	79%	74
Muschko, Craig	10	25 R		aa	CHC	9	3	26	1	143	173	76	20	29	81	4.75	1.41	23.8	293	1.8	5.1	2.8	1.3	32%	70%	48
Muyco, Jake	09	25 R		aaa	CHC	3	3	34	1	43	73	29	11	20	19	6.05	2.17	6.4	369	4.2	4.0	0.9	2.3	38%	78%	-45
	10	26 R		a/a	CHC	4	2	54	5	75	107	43	6	19	25	5.19	1.67	6.4	327	2.3	3.0	1.3	0.7	35%	69%	16
Narron, Sam	09	28 L		a/a	MIL	2	7	20	0	88	151	67	8	26	38	6.86	2.01	21.7	369	2.6	3.9	1.5	0.8	40%	65%	10
	10	29 L		aaa	MIL	9	7	17	0	104	148	57	8	23	45	4.94	1.65	28.0	328	2.0	3.9	1.9	0.7	36%	70%	33
Naylor, Drew	10	24 R		aa	PHI	12	10	27	0	167	198	99	14	44	92	5.33	1.45	27.0	289	2.4	5.0	2.1	0.7	33%	63%	49
Nelson, Joe	10	36 R		aaa	SEA	3	2	24	1	29	32	13	1	21	25	3.89	1.80	5.7	270	6.5	7.6	1.2	0.3	35%	78%	62
Neshek, Pat	10	30 R		aaa	MIN	5	1	30	1	39	48	20	4	13	19	4.60	1.56	5.8	295	3.1	4.4	1.4	1.0	32%	73%	21
Nevarez, Matthew	10	24 R		aa	HOU	2	1	36	1	38	36	21	1	49	34	4.87	2.25	5.5	245	11.7	8.0	0.7	0.2	32%	77%	61
Newby, Kyler	09	25 R		aa	ARI	2	3	42	4	65	83	40	14	25	40	5.53	1.67	7.1	304	3.5	5.5	1.6	1.9	33%	72%	4
	10	26 R		aa	ARI	4	3	31	0	88	101	51	16	32	81	5.22	1.51	12.6	282	3.3	8.3	2.5	1.6	34%	70%	53
Newmann, David	10	25 L		aa	TAM	3	9	23	0	114	171	76	8	50	61	5.96	1.94	24.1	340	3.9	4.8	1.2	0.6	39%	68%	23
Niesen, Eric	09	24 L		aa	NYM	4	7	16	0	83	85	49	6	41	71	5.36	1.52	23.0	260	4.5	7.7	1.7	0.7	33%	64%	65
	10	25 L		aa	NYM	4	6	33	0	77	91	48	8	62	44	5.58	1.99	11.5	288	7.3	5.2	0.7	0.9	33%	71%	16
Nieto, Arquimedes	10	21 R		aa	STL	1	3	7	1	35	38	22	5	17	26	5.63	1.56	22.5	270	4.3	6.6	1.5	1.3	31%	66%	35
Nieve, Fernando	09	27 R		a/a	NYM	3	1	9	0	42	44	28	3	18	32	5.88	1.47	20.6	262	3.9	6.9	1.8	0.7	32%	59%	59
	10	28 R		aaa	NYM	2	1	8	0	40	56	28	3	14	24	6.29	1.75	23.3	324	3.1	5.4	1.7	0.7	37%	63%	37
Noesi, Hector	10	24 R	a	a/a	NYY	9	5	20	0	117	128	52	10	22	91	4.00	1.28	24.6	272	1.7	7.0	4.1	0.8	33%	70%	106
Norrick, Floyd	09	26 L		a/a	STL	3	1	58	5	65	68	39	7	50	66	5.37	1.81	5.3	263	6.9	9.1	1.3	0.9	34%	71%	57
	10	27 L		a/a	STL	3	2	32	0	36	43	28	2	41	25	6.90	2.33	5.9	288	10.3	6.3	0.6	0.6	35%	69%	2
Nova, Ivan	09	23 R		a/a	NYY	6	8	24	0	139	168	80	9	63	77	5.18	1.66	26.5	293	4.1	5.0	1.2	0.6	34%	68%	35
	10	24 R		aaa	NYY	12	3	23	0	145	156	57	13	48	104	3.54	1.41	27.3	269	3.0	6.5	2.2	0.8	32%	77%	61
Novoa, Yunior	09	25 L		a/a	WAS	2	2	38	2	49	65	28	5	23	33	5.22	1.80	6.1	313	4.3	6.1	1.4	1.0	36%	72%	30
	10	26 L		aa	WAS	0	5	23	1	32	46	30	2	20	19	8.38	2.04	6.9	329	5.5	5.4	1.0	0.6	38%	56%	23
Nunez, Jhonny	09	24 R		a/a	CHW	5	0	42	4	70	69	27	8	27	70	3.46	1.37	7.2	252	3.5	9.0	2.6	1.0	32%	78%	82
	10	25 R		a/a	CHW	6	6	42	1	95	118	61	11	38	72	5.76	1.64	10.3	297	3.6	6.8	1.9	1.1	35%	66%	44
Nunez, Vladimir	09	35 R		a/a	ATL	3	2	45	5	83	82	25	7	39	67	2.74	1.46	8.1	253	4.2	7.2	1.7	0.8	31%	84%	60
	10	36 R		aaa	ATL	1	1	31	0	52	72	32	4	26	35	5.47	1.88	8.1	320	4.6	6.1	1.3	0.7	38%	71%	34
O'Connor, Mike	09	29 L		a/a	KC	3	10	26	0	90	162	83	12	29	46	8.27	2.12	17.5	381	2.9	4.6	1.6	1.2	42%	61%	3
	10	30 L		aaa	NYM	5	2	51	6	70	77	24	6	19	53	3.13	1.36	5.9	272	2.4	6.8	2.8	0.7	33%	79%	79
Ogando, Alexi	10	27 R	b	a/a	TEX	0	0	18	1	30	18	9	1	12	32	2.65	0.99	6.6	168	3.6	9.7	2.7	0.3	24%	73%	125

							Actual											Major League Equivalents									
PITCHER	Yr	Age	Th		Lev	Org	w	l	g	sv	ip	h	er	hr	bb	k	era	whip	bf/g	oob	ctl	dom	cmd	hr/9	h%	s%	bpv
Oland,Bryan	10	25	R		aa	SD	1	4	33	2	39	47	19	3	17	29	4.34	1.62	5.4	290	3.8	6.6	1.7	0.8	35%	74%	50
Olenberger,Kasey	09	32	R		aa	FLA	7	1	52	3	65	66	12	1	24	49	1.62	1.37	5.4	257	3.2	6.8	2.1	0.2	32%	88%	84
	10	33	R		aaa	ARI	2	3	47	6	56	66	37	8	16	42	5.91	1.46	5.2	288	2.5	6.7	2.6	1.4	33%	61%	53
Oliver,Andy	10	23	L		a/a	DET	9	8	23	0	130	132	59	15	48	102	4.08	1.38	24.3	258	3.3	7.1	2.1	1.0	31%	73%	59
Oliveros,Rayner	09	24	R		a/a	TAM	6	3	22	1	79	80	38	7	23	54	4.33	1.30	15.2	258	2.6	6.2	2.4	0.8	30%	68%	66
	10	25	R		aa	TAM	2	7	21	1	51	84	57	10	19	17	10.00	2.03	12.0	362	3.3	3.0	0.9	1.8	37%	50%	-33
Olson,Garrett	09	26	L		aaa	SEA	2	3	9	0	47	41	27	2	23	33	5.12	1.36	22.4	231	4.3	6.3	1.5	0.4	28%	69%	65
	10	27	L	b	aaa	SEA	2	5	12	0	46	39	21	4	15	43	4.02	1.18	15.8	225	3.0	8.3	2.8	0.8	29%	67%	94
Ondrusek,Logan	09	25	R		a/a	CIN	2	1	43	19	52	45	13	1	15	30	2.32	1.17	5.0	230	2.7	5.2	1.9	0.2	28%	79%	76
	10	26	R	a	aaa	CIN	0	1	14	1	19	24	11	0	3	12	5.21	1.42	6.0	302	1.4	5.6	3.9	0.0	36%	59%	110
Ortegano,Jose	09	22	L		aa	ATL	5	2	8	0	47	55	20	2	16	37	3.81	1.50	26.1	285	3.1	7.1	2.3	0.4	36%	74%	77
	10	23	L		aaa	ATL	3	11	21	0	103	136	82	13	44	77	7.17	1.75	22.9	311	3.8	6.7	1.8	1.1	37%	59%	36
Ortiz,Ramon	09	36	R		aaa	SF	5	6	35	0	129	137	47	9	33	92	3.30	1.31	15.6	266	2.3	6.4	2.8	0.7	32%	76%	80
	10	37	R		aaa	TAM	2	4	12	0	65	76	38	7	15	36	5.25	1.39	23.4	285	2.0	5.0	2.4	0.4	33%	66%	66
O'Sullivan,Sean	09	22	R		a/a	LAA	7	6	17	0	87	107	62	10	19	52	6.40	1.44	22.4	296	2.0	5.4	2.7	1.0	33%	55%	55
	10	23	R		aaa	LAA	5	5	15	0	85	98	45	7	27	49	4.76	1.47	24.9	283	2.9	5.2	1.8	0.7	32%	68%	45
Osuna,Edgar	09	22	L		aa	ATL	4	4	13	0	77	89	43	8	22	43	5.02	1.44	25.9	283	2.6	5.0	2.0	0.9	32%	66%	41
	10	23	L		a/a	KC	7	5	24	0	123	154	68	21	24	72	4.97	1.44	22.4	300	1.8	5.3	3.0	1.5	33%	70%	44
Ottavino,Adam	09	24	R		aa	STL	7	12	27	0	144	156	86	11	77	103	5.38	1.62	24.2	271	4.8	6.4	1.3	0.7	32%	66%	47
	10	25	R	a	aaa	STL	5	3	9	0	47	44	21	4	11	37	4.00	1.17	21.4	242	2.1	7.1	3.4	0.8	29%	67%	97
Ouellette,Ryan	09	24	R		aa	BAL	4	6	37	5	49	67	28	3	23	22	5.21	1.84	6.3	320	4.2	4.0	0.6	0.6	36%	71%	18
	10	25	R		aa	CHW	2	1	21	0	31	39	15	3	16	12	4.28	1.77	6.9	301	4.6	3.6	0.8	0.9	32%	78%	5
Owen,Dylan	09	23	R		aa	NYM	4	10	23	0	123	170	91	13	53	72	6.64	1.81	25.3	321	3.8	5.3	1.4	1.0	36%	63%	21
	10	24	R		a/a	NYM	7	8	36	0	126	140	73	15	52	87	5.22	1.52	15.6	276	3.7	6.2	1.7	1.1	32%	67%	40
Owens,Rudy	10	23	L	a	aa	PIT	6	2	26	0	150	138	47	11	22	111	2.82	1.07	23.0	240	1.3	6.7	5.0	0.7	29%	76%	133
Packer,Matt	10	23	L		aa	CLE	1	2	6	0	37	39	14	3	9	27	3.51	1.31	26.1	266	2.3	6.6	2.9	0.8	32%	75%	80
Palica,Thomas	10	23	L	a	aa	ATL	3	1	25	1	32	45	31	2	16	40	8.70	1.93	6.2	327	4.6	11.2	2.4	0.6	46%	52%	90
Palmer,Matt	10	32	R		aaa	LAA	2	3	13	2	46	35	15	4	18	29	2.88	1.14	14.4	205	3.5	5.6	1.6	0.8	23%	78%	56
Papelbon,Jeremy	09	26	L		a/a	CHC	6	6	33	0	108	161	61	12	32	61	5.08	1.79	15.4	338	2.7	5.1	1.9	1.0	38%	73%	27
	10	27	L		aa	CHC	1	2	31	1	76	136	64	11	18	42	7.55	2.03	12.1	380	2.1	5.0	2.3	1.3	42%	63%	20
Parcell,Garrett	09	25	R	a	aa	FLA	0	0	23	1	36	21	1	0	18	34	0.28	1.07	6.3	166	4.4	8.5	1.9	0.0	24%	97%	113
	10	26	R		aa	FLA	5	7	53	0	75	94	39	5	39	48	4.69	1.78	6.6	301	4.7	5.7	1.2	0.6	35%	73%	38
Paredes,Edward	10	24	L		a/a	SEA	2	3	45	3	55	63	30	2	30	42	4.91	1.69	5.6	282	4.9	6.9	1.4	0.3	35%	69%	59
Parise,Peter	09	25	R		a/a	STL	5	2	57	8	77	73	34	6	24	50	3.97	1.26	5.6	245	2.8	5.9	2.1	0.7	29%	69%	64
	10	26	R		aaa	STL	0	0	16	2	18	29	17	4	6	6	8.59	1.96	5.5	358	3.0	3.0	1.0	2.0	36%	58%	-39
Parker,Blake	09	24	R		a/a	CHC	2	3	55	25	63	53	25	4	38	64	3.53	1.44	5.0	222	5.4	9.1	1.7	0.6	30%	76%	83
	10	25	R		a/a	CHC	1	5	48	7	66	73	36	9	34	55	4.87	1.61	6.2	273	4.6	7.5	1.6	1.3	32%	73%	41
Parnell,Bobby	10	26	R		aaa	NYM	1	1	24	4	41	39	21	3	18	34	4.52	1.38	7.4	246	3.8	7.4	1.9	0.7	31%	67%	71
Paronto,Chad	09	34	R		aaa	HOU	2	1	44	24	51	41	11	1	15	32	1.85	1.09	4.7	215	2.6	5.7	2.2	0.2	26%	83%	86
	10	35	R		aaa	BOS	3	5	54	2	74	99	46	11	32	38	5.62	1.76	6.4	314	3.8	4.6	1.2	1.3	34%	70%	7
Parr,James	09	24	R		aaa	ATL	1	1	7	0	30	38	21	5	5	18	6.30	1.43	18.7	303	1.5	5.4	3.6	1.5	33%	58%	57
	10	25	R		aaa	ATL	2	5	9	0	45	60	30	6	17	25	5.99	1.71	23.2	313	3.4	5.0	1.5	1.2	35%	66%	17
Paterson,Joe	09	23	L	a	aa	SF	5	6	55	10	69	57	20	3	25	57	2.55	1.18	5.1	220	3.2	7.5	2.3	0.4	28%	79%	92
	10	24	L		aaa	SF	4	3	46	2	54	59	22	2	22	41	3.66	1.50	5.2	272	3.7	6.8	1.9	0.3	34%	75%	71
Patterson,Scott	09	30	R		aaa	OAK	3	4	58	1	63	73	33	4	44	56	4.75	1.86	5.2	284	6.3	7.9	1.3	0.6	36%	75%	53
	10	31	R		aaa	SEA	2	1	29	6	33	33	11	5	9	30	2.85	1.27	4.8	252	2.6	8.2	3.2	1.4	30%	86%	79
Patton,Troy	09	24	L		a/a	BAL	7	5	20	0	108	143	68	24	34	59	5.67	1.64	24.6	312	2.8	4.9	1.7	2.0	33%	71%	-1
	10	25	L		aaa	BAL	8	11	25	0	136	166	82	19	41	74	5.41	1.52	24.2	294	2.7	4.9	1.8	1.3	32%	67%	25
Pauley,David	09	26	R		aaa	BAL	9	12	27	0	152	214	104	22	47	87	6.16	1.72	26.1	326	2.8	5.2	1.8	1.3	36%	66%	21
	10	27	R		aaa	SEA	1	6	15	0	89	92	38	5	24	48	4.40	1.38	24.4	269	2.8	5.0	1.8	0.6	31%	71%	53
Paulino,Eduardo	10	25	R		aa	KC	8	5	28	0	113	134	58	6	60	70	4.60	1.71	18.7	288	4.8	5.6	1.2	0.5	34%	72%	40
Peacock,Bradley	10	23	R		aa	WAS	2	2	7	0	38	39	26	6	22	26	6.13	1.60	24.6	259	5.2	6.1	1.2	1.4	29%	64%	22
Peguero,Jailen	10	30	R		a/a	HOU	5	5	45	3	75	76	28	2	46	56	3.37	1.63	7.6	257	5.6	6.7	1.2	0.3	32%	79%	60
Pelzer,Wynn	10	24	R		aa	BAL	7	9	32	0	114	152	68	15	63	82	5.40	1.88	17.1	313	5.0	6.4	1.3	1.2	36%	73%	23
Pena,Hassan	10	26	R		aa	WAS	2	2	48	1	71	96	49	7	33	50	6.19	1.81	7.0	315	4.2	6.3	1.5	0.8	37%	65%	35
Pena,Tony	10	30	R		a/a	SF	3	2	53	6	76	106	50	5	34	43	5.91	1.84	6.8	323	4.0	5.0	1.2	0.6	37%	67%	30
Pendleton,Lance	09	26	R		aa	NYY	1	3	8	0	44	56	36	6	18	32	7.27	1.69	25.4	304	3.8	6.6	1.8	1.2	35%	57%	35
	10	27	R		a/a	NYY	12	5	29	0	154	161	85	22	64	105	4.96	1.46	23.3	263	3.8	6.1	1.6	1.3	30%	69%	35
Penn,Hayden	09	25	R		aaa	FLA	2	4	14	0	70	78	35	9	26	55	4.55	1.49	22.0	276	3.4	7.1	2.1	1.2	33%	72%	52
	10	26	R		aaa	PIT	4	4	12	0	65	83	37	3	21	47	5.17	1.60	24.5	303	2.9	6.4	2.2	0.4	37%	66%	66
Peralta,Joel	09	34	R		aaa	COL	6	0	31	4	36	35	12	3	11	26	2.88	1.25	4.9	247	2.6	6.4	2.4	0.8	29%	80%	71
	10	35	R		aaa	WAS	2	0	28	20	33	29	5	1	7	30	1.43	1.11	4.8	234	2.0	8.3	4.1	0.3	31%	88%	136
Peralta,Wily	10	21	R		aa	MIL	2	3	8	0	42	47	19	5	24	26	4.06	1.69	24.2	277	5.1	5.6	1.1	1.1	31%	79%	24
Perdomo,Luis	10	26	R		aaa	SD	4	6	58	1	82	79	31	5	33	43	3.39	1.37	6.1	249	3.6	4.7	1.3	0.6	28%	76%	44
Perez,Juan	09	31	L		aaa	ATL	2	4	47	1	57	47	27	7	38	49	4.32	1.50	5.4	222	6.0	7.8	1.3	1.2	26%	74%	50
	10	32	L		aaa	LA	4	3	45	1	45	37	13	3	18	41	2.52	1.21	4.1	218	3.6	8.1	2.3	0.6	28%	82%	89
Perez,Luis	09	25	L		aa	TOR	9	11	28	0	162	188	95	16	80	92	5.26	1.66	26.5	285	4.4	5.1	1.2	0.9	32%	69%	27
	10	26	L		a/a	TOR	10	11	28	0	160	182	93	9	82	87	5.21	1.65	26.1	280	4.6	4.9	1.1	0.5	32%	67%	35
Perez,Martin	10	19	L		aa	TEX	5	8	24	0	99	125	76	14	46	96	6.93	1.72	19.2	301	4.2	8.7	2.1	1.2	38%	60%	53
Perez,Oneli	09	26	R		aaa	STL	4	3	18	0	67	75	25	7	22	51	3.32	1.45	16.3	278	2.9	6.9	2.4	1.0	33%	80%	62
	10	27	R		aaa	STL	2	7	46	4	99	108	58	9	48	78	5.26	1.58	9.7	273	4.4	7.1	1.6	0.9	33%	67%	51
Perez,Sergio	09	25	R		aa	HOU	11	11	27	0	142	189	84	16	61	59	5.33	1.76	24.6	313	3.9	3.7	1.0	1.0	34%	71%	5
	10	26	R		a/a	HOU	5	7	22	0	107	142	64	11	53	48	5.40	1.82	23.1	313	4.4	4.0	0.9	0.9	34%	71%	9
Periard,Alexandre	10	23	R		aa	MIL	2	4	11	0	63	88	37	6	19	21	5.30	1.69	26.4	323	2.7	3.0	1.1	0.9	34%	69%	6

Major League Equivalent Statistics

						Actual											Major League Equivalents									
PITCHER	Yr	Age Th		Lev	Org	w	l	g	sv	ip	h	er	hr	bb	k	era	whip	bf/g	oob	ctl	dom	cmd	hr/9	h%	s%	bpv
Perkins,Glen	10	28 L		aaa	MIN	4	9	26	0	124	182	92	14	36	78	6.65	1.76	22.3	335	2.6	5.7	2.2	1.0	38%	62%	38
Pestano,Vinnie	09	25 R		aa	CLE	2	3	34	24	34	38	16	2	15	27	4.16	1.54	4.5	275	3.9	7.0	1.8	0.6	34%	73%	63
	10	26 R	a	aa	CLE	2	3	57	17	59	54	14	2	17	65	2.08	1.19	4.3	237	2.6	9.8	3.8	0.3	34%	83%	137
Peterson,Matthew	09	28 R		aa	FLA	4	4	56	37	58	70	37	4	35	40	5.79	1.80	4.9	292	5.4	6.2	1.1	0.6	35%	67%	41
	10	29 R		a/a	FLA	6	6	56	18	68	86	29	5	40	36	3.88	1.85	5.8	301	5.3	4.7	0.9	0.6	34%	80%	23
Petit,Yusmeiro	10	26 R		aaa	SEA	4	2	24	0	59	58	33	8	16	49	5.08	1.25	10.3	250	2.5	7.4	3.0	1.2	30%	62%	75
Pettyjohn,Adam	09	32 L		aaa	NYM	4	11	27	0	105	160	65	13	34	48	5.58	1.84	18.6	342	2.9	4.1	1.4	1.1	37%	71%	8
	10	33 L		aaa	NYM	2	4	44	2	62	74	37	6	33	37	5.35	1.75	6.6	289	5.0	5.3	1.1	0.9	33%	70%	24
Pfeiffer,David	10	25 L		LA		7	5	36	0	82	98	42	10	23	46	4.63	1.48	10.0	290	2.6	5.0	2.0	1.1	32%	71%	36
Phelps,David	10	24 R	a	a/a	NYY	10	2	26	0	158	157	52	7	36	129	2.96	1.22	25.2	254	2.0	7.3	3.6	0.4	32%	76%	112
Phillips,Heath	09	28 L		aaa	KC	8	7	27	0	149	217	112	14	52	93	6.73	1.80	26.1	332	3.1	5.6	1.8	0.8	38%	62%	35
	10	29 L		aaa	TAM	8	7	24	0	139	154	75	23	42	64	4.87	1.41	25.1	275	2.7	4.2	1.5	1.5	29%	70%	13
Phillips,Paul	09	26 R		a/a	TAM	3	3	31	7	44	33	14	1	19	34	2.79	1.17	5.8	202	3.9	7.0	1.8	0.2	26%	75%	88
	10	27 R		a/a	TAM	6	2	41	7	71	100	37	8	18	52	4.63	1.65	7.9	325	2.2	6.6	2.9	1.0	38%	74%	62
Phillips,Zachary	09	23 L		aa	TEX	0	0	20	2	33	32	7	1	20	24	1.96	1.55	7.4	248	5.3	6.6	1.2	0.3	31%	88%	62
	10	24 L		a/a	TEX	3	2	45	5	67	69	25	1	35	52	3.32	1.55	6.7	261	4.7	7.0	1.5	0.1	33%	77%	72
Pineda,Michael	10	22 R	a	a/a	SEA	11	4	25	0	139	123	52	9	31	144	3.39	1.11	22.4	232	2.0	9.3	4.6	0.6	32%	70%	144
Pino,Johan	09	26 R	a	a/a	CLE	9	3	42	0	127	135	53	11	32	105	3.73	1.31	12.8	267	2.2	7.5	3.3	0.7	33%	73%	94
	10	27 R		aaa	CLE	10	9	26	0	145	195	103	24	46	98	6.39	1.66	25.6	315	2.9	6.1	2.1	1.5	35%	64%	29
Pomeranz,Stuart	10	26 R		aa	COL	1	6	51	18	49	74	28	7	21	41	5.10	1.95	4.7	342	3.9	7.4	1.9	1.2	41%	76%	35
Pope,Ryan	09	23 R		aa	NYY	5	12	26	0	141	198	109	9	38	88	6.97	1.67	24.9	325	2.4	5.6	2.3	0.6	38%	56%	55
	10	24 R		aa	NYY	4	6	46	17	94	103	53	13	32	73	5.03	1.43	8.9	273	3.0	7.0	2.3	1.2	32%	67%	55
Poreda,Aaron	09	23 L		a/a	SD	5	7	20	0	107	88	49	3	73	93	4.12	1.50	23.7	220	6.1	7.8	1.3	0.3	29%	71%	77
	10	24 L		a/a	SD	1	2	39	0	54	32	23	1	62	42	3.83	1.74	6.5	169	10.3	7.0	0.7	0.2	22%	76%	72
Portice,Eammon	10	25 R		aa	BOS	3	7	40	0	93	124	60	10	26	74	5.81	1.61	10.5	314	2.5	7.1	2.9	1.0	38%	64%	67
Powell,Jeremy	09	33 R		aaa	PIT	4	7	34	2	98	136	52	9	26	48	4.73	1.65	13.2	321	2.4	4.4	1.8	0.9	36%	72%	30
	10	34 R		aaa	PIT	9	11	31	0	134	158	79	15	37	69	5.30	1.45	18.9	287	2.5	4.7	1.9	1.0	32%	64%	35
Price,Bryan	10	24 R		aa	CLE	6	3	40	1	69	85	29	7	22	59	3.76	1.54	7.7	295	2.8	7.7	2.7	0.9	36%	78%	71
Proctor,Scott	10	34 R		aaa	ATL	4	3	31	0	34	53	33	6	16	25	8.61	2.01	5.4	346	4.2	6.5	1.6	1.7	39%	58%	8
Province,Christopher	09	25 R		aa	BOS	2	4	43	1	79	89	32	3	34	46	3.59	1.56	8.2	279	3.8	5.2	1.4	0.4	33%	76%	48
	10	26 R		a/a	MIN	6	8	50	5	97	132	69	7	39	49	6.45	1.76	9.1	317	3.6	4.6	1.3	0.7	36%	62%	25
Pruneda,Benino	10	22 R	a	aa	ATL	0	4	25	0	34	33	16	2	23	45	4.21	1.64	6.2	248	6.1	11.8	2.0	0.5	38%	74%	102
Pucetas,Kevin	09	25 R		aaa	SF	10	6	28	0	159	181	91	13	45	82	5.15	1.42	24.7	280	2.5	4.6	1.8	0.7	31%	63%	43
	10	26 R		aaa	SF	5	7	26	0	136	186	93	16	57	79	6.15	1.78	24.6	319	3.7	5.2	1.4	1.1	36%	66%	20
Purcey,David	09	28 L		aaa	TOR	9	6	24	0	139	148	77	7	80	89	4.97	1.64	26.4	268	5.2	5.8	1.1	0.5	32%	69%	45
	10	29 L		a/a	TOR	2	2	20	0	21	20	12	4	18	20	5.02	1.78	5.0	245	7.5	8.7	1.2	1.5	30%	76%	37
Putnam,Zach	09	22 R	a	aa	CLE	4	2	33	2	56	71	35	2	19	52	5.60	1.60	7.7	302	3.0	8.3	2.7	0.3	39%	63%	92
	10	23 R	a	a/a	CLE	4	2	37	3	75	85	34	4	16	58	4.07	1.34	8.7	279	1.9	6.9	3.6	0.5	34%	69%	103
Rainwater,Josh	09	25 R		a/a	DET	3	4	39	5	71	80	40	5	26	45	5.09	1.49	8.0	279	3.3	5.7	1.7	0.7	33%	65%	50
	10	25 R		a/a	DET	2	4	49	1	80	122	56	9	24	48	6.26	1.82	7.8	343	2.7	5.3	2.0	1.1	39%	66%	28
Ramirez,Edgar	10	27 R		aa	NYM	6	1	41	1	76	99	47	10	31	46	5.57	1.70	8.6	308	3.7	5.4	1.5	1.2	34%	69%	21
Ramirez,Edwar	09	29 R	b	aaa	NYY	1	5	29	4	51	52	27	4	18	49	4.74	1.37	7.5	257	3.2	8.7	2.7	0.8	33%	66%	90
	10	30 R		aaa	OAK	3	4	36	0	49	53	21	4	22	28	3.82	1.52	6.1	269	4.0	5.2	1.3	0.8	30%	77%	35
Ramirez,Elizardo	09	27 R		aaa	TEX	9	11	28	0	142	201	98	21	39	62	6.21	1.69	23.4	327	2.5	3.9	1.6	1.3	35%	65%	7
	10	28 R		a/a	TEX	4	5	29	0	65	111	48	11	16	25	6.68	1.96	10.9	370	2.2	3.5	1.6	1.6	39%	68%	-13
Ramirez,J.C.	10	22 R		aa	PHI	3	4	13	0	77	96	51	12	23	51	5.95	1.54	26.5	299	2.7	5.9	2.2	1.4	34%	64%	36
Ramirez,Ramon	09	27 R		aaa	CIN	6	7	31	0	127	153	78	19	55	66	5.52	1.63	18.7	291	3.9	4.6	1.2	1.3	31%	69%	9
	10	28 R		aaa	BOS	5	5	28	0	97	132	72	19	39	63	6.68	1.76	16.2	318	3.6	5.9	1.6	1.8	35%	65%	7
Ramos,Cesar	09	25 L		aaa	SD	5	6	15	0	76	91	36	6	30	39	4.29	1.59	22.9	290	3.6	4.6	1.3	0.7	32%	74%	30
	10	26 L		aaa	SD	6	7	30	0	96	94	34	5	41	54	3.19	1.41	13.8	251	3.9	5.1	1.3	0.5	29%	78%	49
Rapada,Clay	09	29 L		aaa	DET	4	2	42	5	45	65	19	1	18	37	3.85	1.83	5.1	328	3.6	7.4	2.0	0.2	41%	78%	70
	10	30 L	b	aaa	TEX	1	2	50	2	59	38	15	1	22	48	2.34	1.02	4.7	182	3.3	7.3	2.2	0.2	24%	76%	104
Rasner,Jacob	10	24 R		aa	CHW	1	6	22	0	61	87	44	9	34	45	6.54	1.98	13.6	327	5.0	6.6	1.3	1.4	38%	69%	16
Ray,Jason	10	26 R		aa	OAK	3	3	24	0	34	46	22	5	23	13	5.75	2.02	7.0	315	6.0	3.4	0.6	1.2	33%	73%	-12
Ray,Robert	10	27 R		aaa	TOR	6	6	18	0	96	114	49	10	40	63	4.63	1.61	24.2	290	3.8	5.9	1.6	1.0	33%	73%	36
Ray,Ronald	09	25 R		aaa	SF	1	5	43	0	65	93	43	7	18	39	6.00	1.71	7.0	328	2.5	5.3	2.1	1.0	37%	65%	37
	10	26 R		aa	SF	2	3	48	4	80	101	47	6	21	50	5.30	1.52	7.4	302	2.3	5.7	2.4	0.6	35%	64%	60
Reckling,Trevor	09	20 L		aa	LAA	8	7	23	0	135	133	55	4	72	93	3.68	1.52	26.1	253	4.8	6.2	1.3	0.3	31%	75%	61
	10	21 L		a/a	LAA	7	13	28	0	148	177	109	14	74	96	6.59	1.70	24.4	290	4.5	5.8	1.3	0.9	34%	60%	33
Redding,Tim	10	33 R		aaa	NYY	8	5	18	0	109	124	45	5	23	71	3.74	1.35	25.9	281	1.9	5.9	3.1	0.4	33%	72%	86
Redmond,Todd	09	24 R		aaa	ATL	9	6	27	0	145	171	84	22	47	93	5.21	1.50	23.8	288	2.9	5.8	2.0	1.4	32%	68%	33
	10	25 R		aaa	ATL	9	10	28	0	162	176	90	22	44	128	4.99	1.36	24.8	271	2.5	7.1	2.9	1.2	32%	66%	67
Reed,Evan	10	25 R		a/a	FLA	2	1	32	5	42	42	9	1	15	33	1.98	1.37	5.7	255	3.3	7.0	2.1	0.2	35%	85%	84
Register,Steven	09	26 R		aaa	PHI	2	5	50	13	57	79	32	9	23	34	5.04	1.79	5.4	323	3.6	5.4	1.5	1.5	36%	76%	10
	10	27 R		aaa	TOR	1	4	48	1	82	97	42	7	23	48	4.62	1.46	7.5	288	2.5	5.3	2.1	0.8	33%	69%	49
Reid,Ryan	09	24 R		aa	TAM	0	1	42	1	58	81	37	4	31	42	5.71	1.92	6.7	323	4.7	6.5	1.4	0.7	39%	70%	38
	10	25 R		aa	TAM	3	3	43	2	72	89	43	2	43	47	5.41	1.83	8.0	297	5.4	5.8	1.1	0.3	36%	68%	45
Reifer,Adam	10	24 R	a	a/a	STL	4	1	52	17	55	58	19	2	14	43	3.04	1.31	4.5	264	2.4	7.0	3.0	0.3	33%	76%	96
Reineke,Chad	09	28 R		aaa	OAK	9	4	30	2	125	152	75	17	49	74	5.38	1.61	18.9	293	3.6	5.3	1.5	1.2	33%	69%	23
	10	28 R		aaa	CIN	9	9	32	1	131	165	72	23	39	68	4.95	1.55	18.3	301	2.7	4.7	1.8	1.6	32%	73%	13
Resop,Chris	10	28 R		aaa	ATL	6	3	17	0	86	75	28	5	38	73	2.88	1.31	21.4	229	4.0	7.6	1.9	0.5	29%	79%	81
Reyes,Jo-Jo	09	25 L		aaa	ATL	4	2	15	0	66	77	25	6	24	28	3.41	1.53	19.6	285	3.3	3.8	1.2	0.8	31%	80%	21
	10	26 L		a/a	TOR	2	6	14	0	61	67	33	7	19	49	4.81	1.41	18.9	274	2.8	7.3	2.6	1.1	33%	68%	66
Reynolds,Greg	10	25 R		aa	COL	7	6	17	0	89	137	73	13	16	34	7.40	1.71	24.3	344	1.6	3.5	2.2	1.3	36%	57%	13

Major League Equivalent Statistics

						Actual											Major League Equivalents									
PITCHER	Yr	Age	Th	Lev	Org	w	l	g	sv	ip	h	er	hr	bb	k	era	whip	bf/g	oob	ctl	dom	cmd	hr/9	h%	s%	bpv
Reynolds,Matt	10	26 L	a	aaa	COL	1	3	50	7	55	52	16	2	14	56	2.64	1.19	4.5	243	2.3	9.2	4.0	0.3	33%	78%	136
Reynoso,Ryne	09	25 R		a/a	ATL	7	10	26	0	153	160	80	14	65	76	4.73	1.47	25.8	263	3.8	4.5	1.2	0.8	29%	69%	28
	10	26 R		a/a	BOS	5	8	29	1	89	124	63	6	36	58	6.37	1.79	14.5	323	3.6	5.8	1.6	0.6	38%	63%	40
Rice,Jason	10	24 R		aa	BOS	3	2	48	13	60	53	22	6	29	58	3.32	1.37	5.4	231	4.4	8.7	2.0	0.9	29%	79%	74
Rice,Scott	10	29 L		a/a	COL	2	1	58	7	69	67	29	0	37	34	3.81	1.50	5.3	249	4.8	4.4	0.9	0.0	29%	72%	51
Richardson,Dustin	09	26 L	a	a/a	BOS	2	2	45	4	74	65	32	3	46	79	3.84	1.51	7.3	232	5.6	9.6	1.7	0.4	32%	74%	90
	10	27 L		aaa	BOS	3	0	32	2	44	31	16	4	32	47	3.37	1.43	6.0	194	6.5	9.5	1.5	0.8	26%	79%	79
Rincon,Juan	10	32 R		aaa	COL	4	4	47	8	45	63	42	4	33	34	8.38	2.12	4.8	324	6.5	6.8	1.0	0.8	39%	59%	28
Ring,Royce	09	29 L		aaa	STL	5	2	51	4	47	53	19	4	15	31	3.70	1.44	4.0	277	2.9	5.9	2.0	0.8	32%	76%	53
	10	30 L		aaa	NYY	2	1	52	2	42	44	12	3	12	32	2.59	1.33	3.4	264	2.6	6.8	2.6	0.7	32%	83%	77
Riordan,Cory	10	24 R		aa	COL	8	5	27	0	161	206	96	26	39	108	5.35	1.52	26.5	305	2.2	6.0	2.8	1.5	34%	68%	45
Rivas,Amaury	10	25 R		aa	MIL	11	6	25	0	141	149	62	7	58	98	3.96	1.47	24.8	266	3.7	6.2	1.7	0.5	32%	73%	61
Rivera,Mumba	09	29 R		aa	SEA	6	6	42	1	64	85	49	6	58	45	6.86	2.23	7.8	313	8.1	6.3	0.8	0.9	37%	69%	20
	10	30 R		a/a	SEA	0	4	39	6	51	56	34	6	28	31	6.01	1.65	6.0	273	4.9	5.5	1.1	1.1	31%	64%	24
Rivera,Saul	09	32 R		aaa	WAS	2	5	30	2	45	69	24	1	26	27	4.82	2.12	7.6	345	5.2	5.3	1.0	0.2	40%	76%	33
	10	33 R		aaa	CLE	2	2	32	5	38	40	17	1	18	17	3.99	1.52	5.3	265	4.2	4.1	1.0	0.2	30%	72%	39
Roark,Tanner	10	24 R		aa	WAS	11	6	28	0	141	179	78	15	43	89	5.00	1.58	22.7	303	2.8	5.7	2.1	1.0	35%	70%	42
Robertson,Tyler	10	23 L		a/a	MIN	4	14	28	0	149	202	97	16	56	81	5.85	1.73	24.8	317	3.4	4.9	1.4	1.0	35%	67%	22
Robles,Mauricio	10	22 L	a	a/a	SEA	9	7	27	0	142	123	63	10	67	144	3.98	1.33	22.4	229	4.2	9.1	2.2	0.7	30%	71%	89
Rodriguez,Aneury	09	22 R		aa	TAM	9	11	27	0	142	144	92	20	62	98	5.83	1.45	23.0	258	3.9	6.2	1.6	1.3	29%	61%	36
	10	23 R		a/a	TAM	7	5	29	0	123	126	58	10	50	86	4.24	1.43	18.5	259	3.7	6.3	1.7	0.7	31%	71%	55
Rodriguez,Fernando	09	25 R		a/a	LAA	4	2	49	4	79	76	45	5	45	62	5.15	1.53	7.2	247	5.2	7.0	1.4	0.6	30%	65%	58
	10	26 R		aaa	LAA	4	6	31	0	97	142	65	11	38	69	6.02	1.86	15.0	334	3.5	6.4	1.8	1.1	39%	68%	33
Rodriguez,Francisco	09	27 R		aaa	LAA	5	4	44	0	77	74	37	7	38	49	4.33	1.46	7.7	248	4.5	5.7	1.3	0.8	28%	72%	41
	10	28 R	b	aaa	LAA	2	1	13	0	22	21	9	0	5	15	3.86	1.19	7.0	246	2.1	6.2	2.9	0.0	31%	64%	104
Rodriguez,Henry	09	23 R	a	aaa	OAK	2	1	37	4	43	39	29	4	32	64	5.95	1.65	5.3	236	6.7	13.3	2.0	0.8	38%	63%	106
	10	24 R	a	aaa	OAK	0	2	20	11	21	10	4	1	8	27	1.71	0.85	4.0	140	3.4	11.5	3.4	0.4	22%	82%	154
Rodriguez,Jesus	09	24 R		aa	LA	6	5	46	1	80	103	39	12	22	35	4.38	1.56	7.8	306	2.5	3.9	1.6	1.3	32%	76%	12
	10	25 R		a/a	LA	4	2	42	0	62	73	36	6	25	28	5.20	1.58	6.6	286	3.7	4.0	1.1	0.9	31%	68%	17
Rodriguez,Rafael	09	25 R		aaa	LAA	1	0	22	3	34	29	7	3	9	19	1.87	1.13	6.3	228	2.4	5.0	2.1	0.8	25%	89%	59
	10	26 R		aaa	ARI	5	5	47	11	63	61	30	7	19	31	4.26	1.26	5.6	248	2.6	4.4	1.7	1.0	27%	69%	36
Roe,Chaz	09	23 R		aa	COL	7	3	20	0	117	128	55	9	43	63	4.20	1.46	25.6	272	3.3	4.9	1.5	0.7	31%	72%	39
	10	24 R		aaa	COL	9	13	27	0	158	217	104	18	45	97	5.92	1.66	26.8	320	2.6	5.5	2.2	1.0	36%	65%	39
Roemer,Wesley	09	23 R		aa	ARI	9	9	22	0	134	161	86	18	44	83	5.74	1.53	27.1	291	3.0	5.6	1.9	1.2	33%	64%	35
	10	24 R		a/a	ARI	4	7	22	0	124	157	80	23	47	86	5.80	1.64	25.7	302	3.4	6.2	1.8	1.7	34%	69%	20
Roenicke,Josh	10	28 R		aaa	TOR	9	1	36	1	59	61	22	5	24	44	3.27	1.44	7.2	262	3.6	6.7	1.8	0.8	31%	80%	57
Rogers,Esmil	09	24 R		a/a	COL	11	7	27	0	155	190	93	13	52	106	5.39	1.56	25.7	295	3.0	6.1	2.1	0.8	35%	65%	52
	10	25 R		aaa	COL	3	3	12	0	61	65	39	6	16	45	5.81	1.32	21.6	266	2.4	6.6	2.8	0.9	31%	55%	72
Rogers,Mark	10	25 R		a/a	MIL	6	8	25	0	116	100	53	3	74	100	4.08	1.50	20.5	228	5.8	7.8	1.3	0.2	30%	71%	77
Rohrbaugh,Robert	09	26 L		aa	SEA	3	3	9	0	47	60	24	6	14	34	4.66	1.58	23.6	303	2.8	6.5	2.4	1.1	36%	73%	51
	10	27 L		aa	SEA	4	2	31	2	73	102	37	5	13	48	4.53	1.57	10.6	324	1.6	5.9	3.8	0.6	38%	71%	88
Rollins,Heath	09	24 R		a/a	TAM	9	11	31	0	140	186	79	12	39	75	5.10	1.61	20.4	312	2.5	4.8	1.9	0.8	35%	68%	38
	10	25 R		a/a	TAM	5	3	44	2	82	98	58	7	41	44	6.35	1.69	8.6	290	4.5	4.8	1.1	0.8	33%	62%	24
Romero,Felix	09	29 R	b	aaa	SF	5	5	50	4	73	87	40	3	15	54	4.86	1.40	6.2	289	1.9	6.6	3.5	0.4	35%	63%	98
	10	30 R		a/a	SF	5	3	33	0	109	155	65	13	28	53	5.36	1.67	15.2	327	2.3	4.4	1.9	1.0	36%	69%	25
Rondon,Hector	09	22 R	a	a/a	CLE	11	10	27	0	146	158	66	11	29	130	4.05	1.28	22.7	270	1.8	8.0	4.6	0.7	34%	69%	124
	10	23 R		aaa	CLE	1	3	7	0	31	50	30	10	10	30	8.79	1.89	21.5	352	2.7	8.8	3.2	3.0	40%	59%	14
Rosa,Carlos	09	25 R		aaa	KC	2	8	43	7	71	82	46	7	32	69	5.89	1.61	7.5	283	4.1	8.8	2.1	0.9	36%	63%	69
	10	26 R		aaa	ARI	2	1	31	13	40	35	10	4	19	34	2.32	1.34	5.5	231	4.2	7.6	1.8	0.9	28%	88%	65
Rosario,Jose	10	25 R		a/a	FLA	5	5	18	0	85	102	43	8	42	61	4.57	1.69	21.8	291	4.5	6.5	1.4	0.9	34%	74%	40
Ross,Tyson	09	22 R		aa	OAK	5	4	9	0	50	41	21	3	17	27	3.78	1.16	22.7	219	3.1	4.9	1.6	0.5	25%	67%	57
	10	23 R	a	aaa	OAK	2	1	6	0	25	22	9	1	11	26	3.23	1.31	17.7	231	3.9	9.3	2.4	0.4	32%	75%	104
Rowland-Smith,Ryan	09	27 L		aaa	SEA	5	3	10	0	56	66	28	5	10	33	4.47	1.36	24.0	287	1.7	5.3	3.2	0.8	33%	68%	72
	10	28 L		aaa	SEA	2	4	6	0	37	51	23	4	5	20	5.63	1.51	27.3	319	1.3	4.9	3.8	1.0	35%	63%	69
Rundles,Rich	09	28 L		aaa	CLE	2	2	45	1	41	66	28	3	18	31	6.11	2.04	4.5	353	4.0	6.7	1.7	0.7	42%	69%	39
	10	29 L		aaa	STL	1	1	56	0	55	64	22	3	18	27	3.58	1.47	4.3	283	2.9	4.5	1.6	0.5	32%	76%	42
Rupe,Josh	09	27 R		aaa	TEX	5	7	24	1	89	144	91	6	45	51	9.15	2.13	18.7	357	4.6	5.2	1.1	0.6	41%	54%	19
	10	28 R		aaa	KC	2	4	40	10	52	58	20	5	23	40	3.53	1.55	5.8	276	3.9	6.9	1.8	0.9	33%	80%	51
Russell,Adam	09	27 R		aaa	SD	2	2	43	9	68	56	30	5	25	49	3.95	1.18	6.5	219	3.3	6.4	2.0	0.7	26%	67%	70
	10	27 R		aaa	SD	4	9	50	14	51	62	28	3	32	43	5.00	1.83	4.9	293	5.6	7.5	1.4	0.6	37%	72%	53
Rzepczynski,Marc	09	24 L	a	a/a	TOR	9	5	16	0	88	102	32	1	43	87	3.27	1.65	25.1	284	4.4	8.9	2.0	0.1	39%	79%	91
	10	25 L		aaa	TOR	5	5	12	0	67	77	37	8	24	52	5.02	1.51	24.7	282	3.3	7.0	2.2	1.1	33%	68%	54
Salas,Fernando	09	24 R		a/a	STL	4	2	34	0	38	36	18	4	11	26	4.14	1.24	4.7	245	2.7	6.2	2.3	1.0	28%	69%	62
	10	25 R	a	aaa	STL	1	0	34	19	35	27	15	2	8	38	3.87	1.00	4.1	210	2.1	9.6	4.7	0.5	29%	61%	153
Samardzija,Jeff	09	25 R		aaa	CHC	6	6	18	0	89	113	53	15	28	61	5.36	1.58	22.3	303	2.8	6.2	2.2	1.5	34%	70%	32
	10	26 R		aaa	CHC	11	3	35	0	111	93	59	9	64	88	4.75	1.41	13.7	223	5.2	7.1	1.4	0.7	27%	66%	60
Samuel,Francisco	09	23 R		aa	STL	3	4	52	22	47	39	32	2	42	51	6.10	1.72	4.2	221	8.0	9.7	1.2	0.4	31%	62%	83
	10	24 R		aaa	STL	3	0	35	6	34	27	15	2	31	32	3.97	1.71	4.5	214	8.2	8.5	1.0	0.5	28%	77%	69
Sanabia,Alex	10	22 R	a	a/a	FLA	6	1	16	0	98	76	24	2	20	63	2.20	0.98	23.9	210	1.8	5.8	3.2	0.2	26%	77%	108
Sanchez,Eduardo	09	21 R	a	aa	STL	2	0	41	10	50	32	15	4	17	50	2.74	0.99	4.8	182	3.1	9.1	2.9	0.7	24%	75%	114
	10	22 R	a	a/a	STL	1	1	50	14	53	41	13	3	17	53	2.26	1.10	4.3	209	2.9	8.9	3.1	0.5	28%	81%	116
Sanchez,Romulo	09	25 R		aaa	NYY	6	5	29	0	77	95	48	5	42	67	5.67	1.78	12.5	297	5.0	7.9	1.6	0.6	38%	67%	58
	10	26 R		aaa	NYY	10	8	31	0	104	104	59	10	62	84	5.08	1.59	15.2	255	5.3	7.3	1.4	0.9	31%	69%	50

Major League Equivalent Statistics

						Actual											Major League Equivalents									
PITCHER	Yr	Age	Th	Lev	Org	w	l	g	sv	ip	h	er	hr	bb	k	era	whip	bf/g	oob	ctl	dom	cmd	hr/9	h%	s%	bpv
Sanit, Amauri	09	30	R		a/a	NYY	1	5	40	10	45	60	30	5	20	22	6.08	1.76	5.3	312	3.9	4.4	1.1	1.0	34%	66%	14
	10	31	R		aaa	NYY	3	2	21	0	33	60	40	10	17	18	10.84	2.31	8.3	382	4.5	4.9	1.1	2.7	40%	55%	-51
Santeliz, Clevelan	09	23	R		aa	CHW	4	0	40	10	56	53	8	3	38	45	1.32	1.62	6.4	243	6.1	7.2	1.2	0.5	30%	94%	59
	10	24	R		aaa	CHW	1	4	38	2	54	45	33	11	34	44	5.50	1.46	6.2	222	5.7	7.3	1.3	1.8	24%	68%	27
Santiago, Mario	10	26	R		aa	KC	6	6	18	0	93	117	44	6	24	47	4.29	1.51	23.0	300	2.4	4.5	1.9	0.5	34%	71%	46
Sarfate, Dennis	10	29	R		aaa	BAL	2	2	47	20	56	41	23	5	29	55	3.71	1.24	5.0	199	4.6	8.8	1.9	0.9	25%	72%	81
Sartor, Matthew	09	25	R		aa	LA	4	6	49	11	71	82	46	9	32	61	5.76	1.61	6.6	283	4.1	7.7	1.9	1.1	34%	65%	51
	10	26	R		aa	LA	1	3	14	0	18	33	17	1	8	14	8.62	2.30	6.7	388	4.0	7.0	1.7	0.6	47%	60%	38
Satow, Joshua	10	25	L		aa	TAM	1	4	23	1	44	65	42	2	29	26	8.57	2.14	9.7	336	6.0	5.2	0.9	0.4	39%	57%	25
Sattler, Daniel	10	27	R		aa	OAK	1	2	33	1	45	56	26	5	25	29	5.28	1.81	6.5	300	5.0	5.7	1.1	0.9	34%	72%	26
Savery, Joseph	09	24	L		a/a	PHI	16	6	28	0	151	176	91	16	78	81	5.42	1.68	24.8	285	4.6	4.8	1.0	1.0	32%	68%	20
	10	25	L		aaa	PHI	1	12	28	0	127	181	85	16	53	57	6.02	1.84	21.6	328	3.8	4.0	1.1	1.1	35%	68%	2
Sborz, Jay	10	26	R		aaa	DET	6	6	43	19	43	43	28	9	23	36	5.89	1.54	4.5	256	4.8	7.4	1.5	1.9	28%	67%	24
Scheppers, Tanner	10	24	R		a/a	TEX	1	3	36	6	80	97	52	7	30	78	5.85	1.59	10.0	293	3.4	8.8	2.6	0.8	38%	63%	80
Scherer, Matthew	09	27	R		aaa	STL	3	4	52	1	73	90	34	8	18	42	4.18	1.46	6.2	296	2.2	5.1	2.4	1.0	33%	74%	46
	10	28	R		aaa	STL	4	2	33	0	47	47	22	6	12	29	4.22	1.25	6.0	256	2.2	5.6	2.5	1.2	28%	70%	55
Schlact, Michael	10	25	R		aa	TEX	1	5	12	0	53	91	57	7	22	21	9.63	2.12	22.3	369	3.7	3.5	0.9	1.2	39%	53%	-15
Schlereth, Daniel	10	24	L	a	aaa	DET	1	3	38	0	49	46	16	0	33	51	2.93	1.61	5.9	243	6.0	9.3	1.5	0.0	34%	80%	95
Schlichting, Travis	10	26	R		aaa	LA	3	0	27	1	47	52	20	4	11	24	3.86	1.33	7.4	272	2.1	4.5	2.1	0.8	30%	72%	49
Schlitter, Brian	09	24	R		aa	CHC	1	7	59	22	61	75	39	10	26	43	5.76	1.65	4.7	296	3.8	6.3	1.7	1.5	33%	68%	23
	10	25	R		aaa	CHC	2	1	37	13	45	47	17	3	20	37	3.38	1.48	5.4	263	4.0	7.4	1.9	0.6	33%	78%	68
Schmidt, Joshua	09	27	R		aa	NYY	8	4	46	3	83	80	24	3	47	71	2.61	1.53	8.1	249	5.1	7.7	1.5	0.4	32%	83%	72
	10	28	R		a/a	NYY	4	3	49	2	65	61	30	5	34	58	4.13	1.46	5.8	242	4.8	8.0	1.7	0.6	31%	72%	71
Schwimer, Michael	10	25	R	a	a/a	PHI	7	5	48	11	60	59	23	7	22	63	3.40	1.34	5.3	251	3.2	9.5	2.9	1.1	33%	79%	90
Schwinden, Chris	10	24	R		aa	NYM	4	7	11	0	79	107	49	7	19	55	5.63	1.60	21.0	317	2.2	6.3	2.9	0.8	37%	65%	65
Scribner, Evan	09	24	R	a	aa	SD	8	4	58	21	70	66	25	3	20	64	3.24	1.23	5.0	245	2.6	8.2	3.2	0.4	32%	73%	110
	10	25	R	a	aa	SD	4	5	57	16	66	61	23	6	17	65	3.18	1.18	4.7	241	2.3	8.8	3.9	0.8	31%	75%	119
Seddon, Chris	09	26	L		aaa	SEA	9	8	25	0	131	152	69	15	54	70	4.74	1.56	23.5	283	3.7	4.8	1.3	1.1	31%	72%	23
	10	27	L		aaa	SEA	10	4	18	0	101	103	39	6	29	56	3.49	1.31	23.7	259	2.6	5.0	1.9	0.6	30%	74%	58
Segovia, Zack	09	27	R		a/a	WAS	3	5	51	6	72	99	38	3	30	51	4.72	1.79	6.7	320	3.7	6.4	1.7	0.4	39%	73%	53
	10	27	R		aaa	NYY	3	2	44	4	62	82	38	8	15	44	5.49	1.56	6.3	312	2.1	6.3	3.0	1.2	36%	67%	56
Septimo, Leyson	10	25	L		a/a	ARI	3	2	42	4	45	36	41	3	53	47	8.19	1.96	5.2	214	10.5	9.3	0.9	0.6	29%	56%	68
Severino, Atahualpa	10	26	L		aaa	WAS	6	3	54	1	67	71	31	6	29	39	4.20	1.49	5.5	265	3.9	5.2	1.3	0.8	30%	73%	36
Sexton, Timothy	10	23	R		aa	LA	3	12	25	0	101	138	60	7	33	63	5.32	1.69	18.7	319	2.9	5.6	1.9	0.6	37%	68%	46
Shafer, Aaron	10	24	R		aa	CHC	2	2	25	2	34	39	23	3	10	25	6.00	1.46	6.0	283	2.7	6.7	2.4	0.8	34%	58%	65
Shaw, Bryan	10	23	R		aa	ARI	4	9	33	2	101	123	65	5	44	65	5.79	1.65	14.0	294	3.9	5.8	1.5	0.4	35%	63%	49
Shaw, Scott	10	24	R		aa	NYM	4	7	22	0	72	103	69	16	39	36	8.66	1.97	16.0	329	4.9	4.5	0.9	2.0	34%	58%	-23
Shawler, Anthony	10	23	R		aa	DET	5	4	28	0	102	126	64	18	22	69	5.63	1.44	15.9	297	1.9	6.1	3.2	1.5	33%	64%	53
Shell, Steven	09	27	R		a/a	SEA	6	3	22	1	61	79	40	11	23	35	5.90	1.68	12.7	307	3.4	5.2	1.5	1.6	33%	68%	7
	10	28	R		aaa	SEA	3	2	21	0	72	84	32	6	19	43	3.94	1.43	15.0	285	2.4	5.3	2.3	0.8	33%	74%	54
Shirek, Charles	09	24	R		aa	CHW	6	4	15	0	90	120	46	11	19	27	4.63	1.53	26.7	313	1.9	2.7	1.5	1.1	32%	72%	6
	10	25	R		a/a	CHW	2	3	15	0	74	105	44	3	22	35	5.39	1.71	22.9	327	2.6	4.2	1.6	0.4	37%	67%	38
Simons, Zachary	09	23	R		a/a	DET	4	2	42	4	69	63	27	5	25	54	3.52	1.27	6.9	238	3.3	7.0	2.2	0.7	29%	73%	75
	10	23	R		a/a	DET	3	4	44	3	70	61	25	7	27	62	3.21	1.26	6.6	230	3.5	8.0	2.3	0.9	29%	78%	78
Sinkbeil, Brett	09	25	R		aaa	FLA	2	8	47	0	83	116	62	9	45	47	6.72	1.94	8.6	324	4.9	5.1	1.0	1.0	36%	65%	13
	10	26	R		aaa	FLA	3	3	58	0	63	83	44	4	31	50	6.35	1.81	5.1	310	4.5	7.2	1.6	0.6	38%	63%	53
Sisco, Andy	10	28	L		aa	SF	4	4	48	1	66	81	51	6	45	52	6.88	1.89	6.6	295	6.1	7.1	1.2	0.8	36%	63%	39
Sisk, Brandon	10	25	L		aa	KC	4	6	40	9	68	88	41	7	28	50	5.43	1.69	7.9	306	3.7	6.5	1.8	0.9	36%	68%	44
Slama, Anthony	09	26	R	a	a/a	MIN	4	4	62	29	81	68	31	5	42	87	3.39	1.36	5.6	224	4.7	9.7	2.1	0.6	31%	76%	94
	10	27	R		aaa	MIN	2	2	54	17	65	45	18	5	32	60	2.42	1.19	5.0	193	4.4	8.3	1.9	0.7	25%	83%	84
Smit, Alexander	09	24	L		aa	CIN	4	3	21	0	71	67	33	13	46	61	4.14	1.60	15.3	245	5.9	7.7	1.3	1.6	28%	80%	32
	10	25	L		aa	CIN	1	5	10	0	43	65	54	7	31	32	11.21	2.22	22.2	341	6.4	6.7	1.1	1.5	39%	48%	3
Smith, Carlton	09	24	R		aa	CLE	6	2	37	3	79	85	33	6	26	35	3.75	1.39	9.2	268	2.9	4.0	1.4	0.7	29%	74%	33
	10	25	R		a/a	CLE	2	6	46	3	58	80	40	7	23	33	6.23	1.77	5.9	322	3.5	5.1	1.5	1.1	36%	66%	18
Smith, Chris	09	29	R	b	aaa	MIL	2	0	28	17	42	37	8	3	6	42	1.61	1.02	5.9	229	1.4	8.9	6.5	0.7	30%	89%	178
	10	29	R		aaa	MIL	3	4	47	26	48	56	23	8	23	51	4.33	1.65	4.7	286	4.3	9.6	2.2	1.4	36%	78%	58
Smith, Greg	09	26	L		a/a	COL	1	3	9	0	37	55	38	9	12	16	9.17	1.78	19.4	335	2.8	3.9	1.4	2.3	34%	50%	-28
	10	27	L		aaa	COL	2	5	15	0	75	94	52	14	26	40	6.19	1.59	22.6	300	3.1	4.8	1.5	1.7	32%	65%	4
Smith, Jordan	09	24	R		aa	CIN	5	3	13	0	73	94	37	5	23	33	4.57	1.59	25.4	305	2.8	4.1	1.5	0.6	34%	71%	30
	10	25	R		a/a	CIN	1	3	30	9	31	49	23	7	9	12	6.54	1.88	5.0	352	2.7	3.4	1.3	1.5	37%	67%	-14
Smith, William	10	21	L		a/a	LAA	3	6	13	0	71	100	49	9	25	43	6.14	1.75	25.6	325	3.1	5.4	1.7	1.1	37%	66%	27
Snell, Ian	09	28	R	b	aaa	PIT	2	2	6	0	37	34	5	0	13	37	1.28	1.25	25.8	237	3.1	9.0	2.9	0.0	33%	89%	123
	10	29	R		aaa	SEA	3	4	9	0	48	66	40	5	23	33	7.43	1.83	25.4	318	4.2	6.1	1.4	1.0	37%	58%	28
Snyder, Benjamin	09	24	L		aa	SF	4	4	34	1	97	101	41	4	40	70	3.81	1.45	12.5	263	3.7	6.5	1.8	0.4	32%	73%	67
	10	25	L		a/a	TEX	3	6	40	1	103	114	63	16	35	75	5.51	1.44	11.2	274	3.0	6.5	2.2	1.4	31%	64%	44
Socolovich, Miguel	10	24	R		a/a	CHW	7	6	51	2	78	66	36	5	47	66	4.16	1.45	6.7	224	5.5	7.6	1.4	0.6	28%	71%	67
Sommer, Luke	10	25	L		a/a	CHC	2	1	37	8	42	55	13	2	12	18	2.70	1.58	5.1	308	2.5	3.9	1.6	0.5	34%	84%	36
Sosa, Henry	09	24	R		aa	SF	6	0	14	0	72	75	25	4	26	36	3.15	1.40	22.3	262	3.3	4.5	1.4	0.5	30%	78%	43
	10	25	R		aaa	SF	7	8	36	0	115	122	56	19	52	69	4.35	1.51	14.2	267	4.0	5.4	1.3	1.5	29%	76%	17
Sosa, Jorge	09	32	R		aaa	WAS	1	2	20	3	48	49	20	3	14	44	3.74	1.31	10.2	260	2.6	8.2	3.2	0.6	33%	72%	101
	10	33	R		aaa	FLA	5	4	23	1	59	84	36	5	16	39	5.46	1.69	11.8	328	2.4	5.9	2.5	0.8	38%	68%	53
Souza, Justin	09	24	R		aa	OAK	6	8	25	0	98	111	53	4	25	62	4.83	1.39	16.9	280	2.3	5.7	2.5	0.4	33%	63%	75
	10	25	R		a/a	OAK	2	2	33	6	49	46	24	3	24	38	4.36	1.43	6.5	245	4.4	6.9	1.6	0.6	30%	69%	64

PITCHERS

PITCHER	Yr	Age	Th		Lev	Org	w	l	g	sv	ip	h	er	hr	bb	k	era	whip	bf/g	oob	ctl	dom	cmd	hr/9	h%	s%	bpv
Sowers,Jeremy	09	26	L		aaa	CLE	2	2	6		37	42	14	2	9	23	3.50	1.39	26.6	281	2.3	5.6	2.5	0.5	33%	75%	70
	10	27	L		aaa	CLE	2	6	27	0	52	62	39	2	18	25	6.73	1.54	8.6	290	3.1	4.3	1.4	0.4	33%	53%	41
Speigner,Levale	09	29	R		a/a	FLA	6	6	58	1	84	105	34	6	26	37	3.65	1.55	6.5	299	2.7	3.9	1.4	0.7	33%	77%	30
	10	30	R		aaa	SEA	5	7	45	10	65	88	41	8	22	36	5.69	1.69	6.7	316	3.1	5.0	1.6	1.1	35%	67%	23
Spoone,Chorye	10	25	R		aa	BAL	7	6	24	0	132	167	79	17	84	67	5.38	1.90	26.5	302	5.8	4.5	0.8	1.1	33%	73%	4
Spradlin,Jack	09	25	L		a/a	WAS	4	3	47	4	74	88	44	3	28	48	5.38	1.58	7.1	290	3.5	5.8	1.7	0.4	35%	64%	55
	10	26	L		a/a	WAS	1	1	47	1	60	86	42	8	28	41	6.31	1.88	6.2	327	4.2	6.1	1.5	1.2	38%	67%	22
St Clair,Allen	10	24	L		aa	LA	1	2	36	1	60	69	34	3	31	46	5.04	1.66	7.7	284	4.6	6.8	1.5	0.5	35%	68%	56
Stammen,Craig	09	26	R		aaa	WAS	4	2	7	0	40	38	10	4	8	12	2.27	1.16	23.3	247	1.8	2.7	1.5	0.9	25%	86%	25
	10	27	R		aaa	WAS	2	0	3	0	20	22	6	2	3	9	2.78	1.24	27.7	270	1.4	3.9	2.8	0.9	29%	82%	56
Stange,Daniel	09	24	R		aa	ARI	0	4	39	10	51	80	39	5	15	38	6.89	1.87	6.3	350	2.7	6.6	2.4	0.9	41%	63%	49
	10	25	R		a/a	ARI	8	4	49	15	55	49	26	4	21	28	4.21	1.27	4.7	235	3.4	4.6	1.4	0.7	26%	67%	44
Stetter,Mitch	10	30	L		aaa	MIL	3	2	41	0	42	55	38	10	20	43	8.24	1.78	4.8	309	4.2	9.2	2.1	2.1	37%	56%	30
Stevens,Jake	10	26	L		aa	SF	4	4	46	2	64	74	29	7	31	34	4.06	1.65	6.4	285	4.4	4.8	1.1	0.9	32%	78%	22
Stevens,Jeff	09	26	R	b	aaa	CHC	1	3	42	1	57	41	16	1	27	50	2.60	1.19	5.6	198	4.2	7.9	1.9	0.2	27%	77%	98
	10	27	R		aaa	CHC	0	2	36	10	42	35	17	3	25	36	3.59	1.42	5.1	220	5.4	7.7	1.4	0.7	28%	76%	67
Stewart,Zachary	09	23	R		a/a	TOR	3	0	27	2	62	66	14	2	25	53	2.03	1.46	10.1	267	3.6	7.7	2.1	0.3	34%	87%	84
	10	24	R		aa	TOR	8	3	26	0	136	143	60	13	55	89	3.95	1.45	22.9	265	3.6	5.9	1.6	0.9	31%	75%	45
Stiller,Erik	09	25	R		aa	CLE	8	3	41	0	69	74	37	2	36	56	4.77	1.59	7.6	269	4.6	7.3	1.6	0.3	34%	68%	69
	10	26	R		aa	HOU	1	0	23	0	38	47	28	11	9	22	6.52	1.48	7.3	298	2.2	5.1	2.4	2.7	29%	64%	-5
Stinson,Joshua	10	23	R		a/a	NYM	11	5	36	1	138	135	60	11	55	75	3.91	1.38	16.5	251	3.6	4.9	1.4	0.7	28%	73%	41
Stone,Bradley	09	25	R		a/a	FLA	6	3	34	0	96	101	36	4	25	46	3.35	1.31	12.0	265	2.4	4.3	1.8	0.4	30%	74%	54
	10	26	R		a/a	FLA	6	4	18	0	76	96	44	7	33	34	5.25	1.69	19.5	300	3.9	4.0	1.0	0.8	33%	69%	17
Stoner,Tobi	09	25	R		a/a	NYM	9	9	23	0	144	139	69	15	48	79	4.31	1.30	26.5	248	3.0	4.9	1.6	1.0	27%	69%	40
	10	26	R		aaa	NYM	10	10	23	0	120	169	84	18	42	69	6.28	1.76	24.4	325	3.2	5.2	1.6	1.4	36%	66%	15
Storey,Mickey	10	25	R		a/a	OAK	6	5	54	9	84	78	35	7	25	65	3.76	1.23	6.5	242	2.7	7.0	2.6	0.8	29%	71%	80
Stowell,Bryce	10	24	R	a	a/a	CLE	2	1	31	7	42	29	13	2	28	52	2.87	1.35	5.8	191	6.0	11.2	1.9	0.4	29%	79%	111
Strasburg,Stephen	10	22	R	a	a/a	WAS	7	2	11	0	55	36	10	1	13	56	1.63	0.89	19.1	183	2.1	9.1	4.3	0.2	26%	81%	159
Strickland,Scott	09	33	R		aaa	LA	2	1	50	32	48	44	17	5	23	48	3.15	1.40	4.2	239	4.3	9.1	2.1	1.0	31%	81%	76
	10	34	R		aaa	FLA	4	3	31	14	32	44	18	3	17	19	5.02	1.90	5.0	320	4.7	5.3	1.1	0.9	36%	75%	20
Strop,Pedro	09	24	R		aaa	TEX	6	6	47	5	64	73	46	4	35	51	6.52	1.69	6.3	281	4.9	7.2	1.5	0.6	35%	59%	55
	10	25	R	a	aaa	TEX	1	2	39	13	42	35	10	1	14	49	2.16	1.18	4.4	223	3.0	10.4	3.4	0.2	33%	81%	138
Stutes,Michael	09	23	R		aa	PHI	8	8	27	0	145	172	86	19	60	89	5.30	1.60	24.3	289	3.7	5.5	1.5	1.2	32%	69%	27
	10	24	R		a/a	PHI	7	1	53	3	76	66	35	8	45	66	4.15	1.46	6.3	229	5.4	7.8	1.5	1.0	28%	74%	57
Sues,Jeffrey	09	26	R		a/a	PIT	2	6	48	2	90	99	61	9	48	64	6.10	1.63	8.5	273	4.8	6.4	1.3	0.9	32%	62%	40
	10	27	R		aa	CHW	0	3	23	4	31	45	22	5	22	18	6.28	2.13	6.8	329	6.3	5.3	0.8	1.4	36%	73%	-3
Sullivan,Richard	10	23	L		aa	ATL	4	11	36	2	120	161	80	10	41	81	6.03	1.68	15.4	314	3.1	6.0	2.0	0.8	37%	63%	46
Swaggerty,Ben	09	27	L		aa	KC	4	1	26	1	43	71	29	4	23	40	6.02	2.18	8.5	360	4.8	8.3	1.7	0.8	45%	72%	47
	10	28	L		aa	KC	4	5	36	1	59	75	34	4	38	41	5.15	1.91	7.9	303	5.7	6.2	1.1	0.6	36%	72%	37
Swarzak,Anthony	09	24	R		aaa	MIN	4	5	13	0	79	89	34	4	21	37	3.86	1.39	26.3	278	2.4	4.2	1.8	0.5	31%	72%	48
	10	25	R		aaa	MIN	5	12	22	0	111	156	84	13	36	57	6.79	1.73	23.5	324	2.9	4.6	1.6	1.1	36%	60%	19
Swindle,R.J.	09	26	L		aaa	CLE	4	1	37	2	50	45	9	3	16	41	1.67	1.23	5.6	237	3.0	7.3	2.5	0.6	30%	89%	87
	10	27	L	b	aaa	TAM	2	4	40	2	55	52	15	6	11	45	2.41	1.13	5.6	243	1.7	7.3	4.2	1.0	29%	85%	108
Tabor,Lee	09	25	L		a/a	CIN	3	2	18	0	52	60	24	5	15	25	4.10	1.45	12.6	283	2.7	4.4	1.6	0.9	31%	74%	32
	10	26	L		a/a	CIN	4	4	41	1	68	88	44	6	28	53	5.85	1.72	7.7	308	3.8	7.0	1.9	0.8	37%	66%	50
Tanaka,Ryohei	09	27	R		aa	BAL	4	4	21	3	75	108	44	10	31	38	5.24	1.85	17.1	330	3.7	4.6	1.2	1.2	36%	74%	5
	10	28	R		aa	BAL	8	12	29	0	129	223	118	33	29	44	8.23	1.95	21.7	372	2.0	3.1	1.5	2.3	37%	61%	-37
Tanner,Clayton	10	23	L		aa	SF	9	9	27	0	149	178	80	11	65	66	4.83	1.63	25.1	290	3.9	4.0	1.0	0.7	32%	70%	22
Tatusko,Ryan	10	26	R		aa	WAS	12	3	30	0	136	162	57	6	59	72	3.74	1.62	20.6	290	3.9	4.8	1.2	0.4	33%	76%	40
Taubenheim,Ty	09	27	R		aaa	PIT	7	9	26	0	106	126	53	8	36	50	4.46	1.53	18.1	289	3.1	4.3	1.4	0.7	32%	71%	31
	10	28	R		a/a	PHI	6	6	21	1	83	114	57	14	34	44	6.23	1.79	18.6	320	3.7	4.7	1.3	1.5	34%	68%	1
Taylor,Andrew	10	24	L		aa	LAA	1	3	15	0	38	45	24	2	18	17	5.72	1.66	11.6	289	4.2	4.0	1.0	0.5	32%	64%	27
Teaford,Everett	09	25	L		aa	KC	3	7	16	0	81	107	59	13	36	33	6.54	1.76	23.7	311	4.0	3.7	0.9	1.5	32%	65%	-10
	10	26	L		a/a	KC	14	4	28	0	103	119	53	9	33	92	4.65	1.48	16.2	283	2.9	8.0	2.8	0.8	36%	69%	81
Teheran,Julio	10	20	R	a	aa	ATL	3	2	7	0	40	29	15	2	15	37	3.48	1.11	23.0	199	3.5	8.4	2.4	0.4	27%	68%	104
Thall,Chad	09	24	L		aa	BAL	2	2	53	1	60	64	28	5	32	44	4.26	1.59	5.1	268	4.7	6.5	1.4	0.8	32%	74%	46
	10	25	L		aa	BAL	2	1	39	1	40	49	24	8	17	30	5.49	1.63	4.7	295	3.7	6.7	1.7	1.7	33%	71%	21
Thayer,Dale	09	29	R		aaa	TAM	2	5	51	17	63	73	22	3	16	36	3.07	1.41	5.4	284	2.3	5.2	2.2	0.5	33%	79%	63
	10	30	R		aaa	TAM	4	1	46	3	60	81	27	3	26	43	4.12	1.79	6.1	317	4.0	6.4	1.6	0.5	38%	77%	49
Thomas,Justin	09	26	L		aaa	SEA	2	4	53	6	60	71	31	5	39	48	4.69	1.83	5.4	287	5.9	7.1	1.2	0.8	35%	75%	43
	10	27	L	b	aaa	PIT	5	0	40	4	54	37	16	4	9	42	2.74	0.86	5.1	190	1.5	6.9	4.5	0.7	23%	71%	132
Thompson,Aaron	09	23	L		aa	WAS	12	12	26	0	146	184	86	12	55	88	5.29	1.63	25.6	301	3.4	5.4	1.6	0.7	35%	67%	39
	10	24	L		a/a	WAS	5	13	27	0	141	197	113	18	56	85	7.20	1.79	24.6	323	3.6	5.4	1.5	1.1	36%	60%	20
Thompson,Brad	10	29	R		aaa	HOU	1	2	18	0	35	66	34	4	5	12	8.85	2.03	9.6	391	1.4	3.1	2.2	1.1	41%	55%	10
Thompson,Daryl	10	25	R	a	aa	CIN	0	5	12	0	51	44	25	4	12	44	4.46	1.09	17.1	229	2.0	7.7	3.8	0.7	29%	59%	112
Thompson,Jacob	10	24	R		aa	ATL	8	10	27	0	131	188	82	12	46	77	5.66	1.78	22.9	329	3.2	5.3	1.7	0.8	37%	68%	30
Thompson,Rich	09	25	R	a	aaa	LAA	3	1	29	0	43	44	16	6	10	43	3.37	1.27	6.2	261	2.1	8.9	4.2	1.3	33%	79%	107
	10	26	R	b	aaa	LAA	1	1	19	2	29	19	2	0	9	24	0.64	0.95	6.0	179	2.9	7.5	2.6	0.0	24%	93%	119
Thorne,Jeremy	10	25	R		aa	LAA	2	4	14	0	65	79	51	8	48	24	7.00	1.96	22.7	294	6.7	3.3	0.5	1.2	31%	65%	-9
Threets,Erick	09	28	L		aaa	LA	3	0	33	1	41	32	7	1	16	24	1.61	1.15	5.1	208	3.5	5.2	1.5	0.2	25%	86%	69
	10	29	L		aaa	CHW	1	0	17	2	21	15	2	0	5	8	0.92	0.97	4.8	197	2.3	3.6	1.6	0.0	23%	89%	70
Tillman,Chris	09	22	R	a	aaa	BAL	8	6	18	0	96	94	36	6	25	91	3.40	1.23	22.2	250	2.3	8.5	3.7	0.6	33%	73%	117
	10	22	R		aaa	BAL	11	7	21	0	121	130	51	11	28	83	3.82	1.31	24.4	270	2.1	6.2	3.0	0.8	32%	73%	76

Major League Equivalent Statistics

							Actual											Major League Equivalents									
PITCHER	Yr	Age	Th		Lev	Org	w	l	g	sv	ip	h	er	hr	bb	k	era	whip	bf/g	oob	ctl	dom	cmd	hr/9	h%	s%	bpv
Todd,Jesse	09	24	R	a	aaa	CLE	4	2	44	25	53	45	14	3	13	60	2.38	1.09	4.8	225	2.2	10.2	4.6	0.5	32%	80%	153
	10	24	R		aaa	CLE	4	2	44	4	49	50	19	5	17	47	3.49	1.37	4.8	259	3.1	8.6	2.8	0.9	33%	77%	86
Tomlin,Josh	09	25	R		aa	CLE	14	9	26	0	145	199	99	28	32	102	6.14	1.59	25.2	320	2.0	6.3	3.2	1.7	36%	65%	44
	10	26	R		aaa	CLE	8	4	20	0	107	91	35	10	32	70	2.97	1.15	21.8	225	2.7	5.9	2.2	0.8	26%	78%	66
Torra,Matthew	09	25	R		aa	ARI	10	13	28	0	180	252	108	34	31	92	5.39	1.57	28.9	324	1.6	4.6	3.0	1.7	34%	71%	28
	10	26	R		a/a	ARI	11	7	28	0	183	283	113	26	38	80	5.57	1.75	30.6	347	1.9	3.9	2.1	1.3	37%	70%	16
Torres,Alexander	09	22	L		aa	TAM	3	3	7	0	34	35	14	1	23	28	3.68	1.70	22.6	260	6.1	7.4	1.2	0.3	33%	77%	65
	10	23	L		aa	TAM	11	6	27	0	142	154	65	9	70	128	4.11	1.58	23.7	271	4.4	8.1	1.8	0.6	35%	74%	71
Torres,Carlos	09	27	R		aaa	CHW	10	4	23	1	128	121	48	6	62	112	3.41	1.43	24.2	244	4.3	7.8	1.8	0.4	31%	76%	78
	10	28	R		aaa	CHW	9	9	27	0	160	148	76	17	76	119	4.26	1.40	25.6	241	4.3	6.7	1.6	0.9	28%	72%	51
Towers,Josh	09	33	R		aaa	NYY	7	6	20	0	103	122	51	18	27	45	4.41	1.45	22.5	289	2.4	3.9	1.6	1.6	30%	75%	8
	10	34	R		aaa	LA	2	5	8	0	38	61	28	6	5	14	6.73	1.75	22.2	355	1.2	3.4	2.7	1.5	37%	63%	16
Trinidad,Polin	09	25	L		a/a	HOU	13	10	26	1	170	203	85	29	36	94	4.48	1.41	28.3	290	1.9	5.0	2.6	1.5	31%	74%	36
	10	26	L		a/a	HOU	4	11	28	0	149	218	97	17	42	76	5.84	1.74	24.8	333	2.5	4.6	1.8	1.0	37%	67%	23
Tucker,Ryan	10	24	R		aaa	FLA	0	5	7	0	33	44	25	3	17	17	6.78	1.84	22.6	312	4.6	4.6	1.0	0.8	35%	62%	17
Turpen,Daniel	10	24	R		aa	BOS	7	6	49	4	69	84	39	4	27	48	5.08	1.62	6.4	295	3.6	6.3	1.8	0.5	35%	68%	55
Ungs,Nick	09	30	R		aa	FLA	10	3	18	0	106	131	47	11	43	54	3.96	1.63	26.8	297	3.6	4.6	1.3	0.9	33%	78%	23
	10	31	R		aaa	FLA	1	2	7	0	33	45	28	6	14	15	7.70	1.78	22.3	318	3.7	4.1	1.1	1.7	33%	58%	-12
Urquidez,Jason	09	27	R		a/a	ARI	5	1	50	2	67	70	40	3	26	42	5.39	1.44	5.9	263	3.5	5.6	1.6	0.5	31%	60%	55
	10	28	R		aaa	ARI	5	4	51	5	71	95	41	6	22	57	5.16	1.63	6.4	313	2.7	7.2	2.6	0.8	38%	69%	66
Uviedo,Ronald	10	24	R		aa	TOR	5	5	41	1	80	75	45	15	39	79	5.10	1.43	8.5	244	4.4	8.8	2.0	1.7	29%	70%	49
Valdes,Raul	10	33	L		aaa	NYM	2	1	9	0	36	38	13	3	9	29	3.16	1.32	16.9	265	2.4	7.1	3.0	0.8	32%	79%	84
Valdez,Cesar	09	25	R		aaa	ARI	7	6	19	0	96	108	52	16	26	53	4.88	1.40	21.8	278	2.4	5.0	2.0	1.5	30%	69%	27
	10	26	R		aaa	ARI	6	10	20	0	97	114	64	11	43	78	5.89	1.62	22.1	287	4.0	7.2	1.8	1.0	34%	64%	48
Valdez,Merkin	10	29	R		aaa	TOR	3	5	39	0	58	92	45	4	25	29	7.01	2.02	7.3	353	3.8	4.5	1.2	0.7	40%	64%	16
Valiquette,Philippe	09	23	L		aa	CIN	1	1	27	3	32	29	13	3	21	24	3.63	1.55	5.3	236	5.9	6.7	1.1	0.8	28%	79%	47
	10	24	L		a/a	CIN	4	1	54	5	65	76	35	2	30	46	4.85	1.63	5.5	286	4.2	6.4	1.5	0.3	35%	68%	60
Van Hekken,Andy	09	30	L		a/a	HOU	8	6	33	0	123	191	79	11	33	52	5.76	1.82	17.7	347	2.4	3.8	1.6	0.8	38%	68%	17
	10	31	L		aaa	HOU	8	8	29	0	177	206	96	15	51	92	4.87	1.45	26.7	285	2.6	4.7	1.8	0.7	32%	67%	42
Van Mil,Loek	10	26	R		aa	LAA	1	2	24	0	30	52	29	1	25	16	8.56	2.55	6.9	370	7.5	4.7	0.6	0.3	42%	64%	12
VandenHurk,Rick	09	24	R	a	aaa	FLA	5	2	11	0	59	47	21	3	16	46	3.19	1.06	21.4	214	2.4	7.0	2.9	0.5	27%	70%	101
	10	25	R		aaa	BAL	9	5	22	0	118	132	69	14	42	78	5.23	1.48	23.6	277	3.2	6.0	1.8	1.1	32%	66%	42
Vargas,Claudio	10	32	R		aaa	LA	2	6	10	0	47	51	26	4	18	35	5.03	1.45	20.6	269	3.4	6.7	2.0	0.8	32%	66%	59
Varvaro,Anthony	09	25	R	a	aa	SEA	4	3	36	8	54	36	22	1	49	54	3.68	1.58	6.8	185	8.2	9.0	1.1	0.2	26%	75%	90
	10	26	R		a/a	SEA	1	3	50	9	65	57	32	3	36	61	4.37	1.43	5.6	230	5.0	8.4	1.7	0.4	30%	68%	82
Vasquez,Anthony	10	24	L	a	aa	SEA	2	3	7	0	38	49	13	2	5	23	2.99	1.44	23.7	308	1.2	5.4	4.3	0.5	36%	80%	102
Vasquez,Virgil	09	27	R		aaa	PIT	7	4	19	0	107	138	59	15	16	57	4.95	1.43	24.6	306	1.3	4.8	3.6	1.2	33%	68%	61
	10	28	R		aaa	TAM	6	2	12	0	66	87	43	10	16	32	5.86	1.56	24.7	311	2.2	4.3	2.0	1.3	33%	64%	20
Vaughan,Beau	09	28	R		a/a	TEX	7	2	46	8	62	80	39	5	27	42	5.64	1.73	6.3	306	3.9	6.0	1.5	0.7	36%	67%	42
	10	29	R		a/a	OAK	2	3	30	6	40	51	16	1	13	25	3.57	1.62	6.0	305	3.0	5.7	1.9	0.3	36%	77%	60
Veal,Donnie	10	26	L		aaa	PIT	3	2	9	0	49	46	27	3	22	33	4.90	1.38	23.5	244	4.0	6.0	1.5	0.6	29%	63%	57
Villanueva,Elih	10	24	R		aa	FLA	14	4	28	0	179	166	58	18	38	99	2.91	1.14	26.0	241	1.9	5.0	2.6	0.9	27%	79%	64
Villar,Henry	10	23	R		aa	HOU	4	7	36	5	102	114	61	13	45	56	5.37	1.57	12.7	278	4.0	5.0	1.2	1.2	30%	68%	20
Villarreal,Brayan	10	23	R		DET		0	4	8	0	43	42	22	7	15	38	4.51	1.34	23.0	251	3.2	7.9	2.4	1.5	29%	71%	58
Villarreal,Oscar	10	29	R		aaa	PHI	4	3	49	1	57	69	39	10	29	33	6.10	1.71	5.4	292	4.6	5.3	1.2	1.5	32%	67%	7
Villone,Ron	10	41	L		aaa	WAS	2	5	41	1	42	61	41	8	32	20	8.78	2.20	5.3	332	6.8	4.3	0.6	1.8	35%	61%	-27
Viola,Pedro	09	26	L		aaa	CIN	2	2	54	8	49	59	40	10	36	49	7.37	1.93	4.4	291	6.6	8.9	1.3	1.9	35%	65%	22
	10	27	L		a/a	BAL	3	6	35	0	72	105	59	4	32	53	7.32	1.90	9.9	332	4.0	6.6	1.6	0.6	40%	59%	46
Vogelsong,Ryan	10	33	R		aaa	LAA	3	8	33	1	95	117	53	7	57	88	4.98	1.83	13.7	296	5.4	8.4	1.5	0.7	38%	73%	58
Voss,Jay	09	22	L		aa	FLA	3	0	30	1	36	30	15	2	16	33	3.74	1.27	5.0	222	4.0	8.2	2.1	0.5	29%	70%	88
	10	23	L		aa	DET	2	3	33	1	48	70	37	7	25	27	6.96	1.98	7.1	333	4.6	5.1	1.1	1.4	37%	66%	1
Wagner,Neil	09	26	R		aa	CLE	1	3	46	2	61	64	30	4	38	57	4.43	1.68	6.1	266	5.6	8.4	1.5	0.7	34%	74%	64
	10	27	R		aa	OAK	7	3	46	5	63	90	38	1	37	45	5.42	2.01	6.7	328	5.3	6.5	1.2	0.2	40%	71%	49
Walden,Jordan	09	22	R		aa	LAA	1	5	13	0	60	86	46	4	30	48	6.90	1.93	22.4	329	4.5	7.2	1.6	0.6	40%	63%	48
	10	23	R		a/a	LAA	1	1	44	8	49	56	20	2	22	35	3.66	1.59	5.0	280	4.0	6.4	1.6	0.4	34%	76%	60
Waldrop,Steven	09	24	R		aa	MIN	2	3	31	0	55	60	11	2	19	24	1.85	1.42	7.7	271	3.0	4.0	1.3	0.3	31%	88%	42
	10	25	R		aaa	MIN	5	3	59	2	87	96	27	5	19	50	2.79	1.32	6.3	274	2.0	5.2	2.6	0.5	32%	80%	71
Walters,P.J.	09	25	R		aaa	STL	8	10	21	0	121	141	69	6	41	98	5.13	1.50	25.5	285	3.0	7.3	2.4	0.4	36%	64%	78
	10	26	R	a	aaa	STL	8	5	19	0	108	110	45	10	27	90	3.78	1.27	23.9	258	2.3	7.5	3.3	0.8	32%	72%	92
Warren,Adam	10	23	R	a	aa	NYY	4	2	10	0	54	56	23	2	16	52	3.77	1.33	23.0	261	2.7	8.7	3.2	0.3	35%	71%	112
Waters,Chris	09	29	L		aaa	BAL	9	7	29	0	114	153	86	19	53	54	6.76	1.80	18.6	314	4.2	4.2	1.0	1.5	33%	64%	-5
	10	30	L		aaa	MIL	5	10	21	0	105	121	62	20	62	50	5.33	1.73	21.3	283	5.3	4.2	0.8	1.7	29%	74%	-11
Watson,Anthony	10	25	L		aa	PIT	6	4	34	2	111	101	42	12	24	79	3.42	1.13	13.2	238	2.0	6.4	3.2	1.0	28%	74%	84
Webb,Ryan	09	24	R		aaa	SD	7	1	35	2	49	64	24	3	16	35	4.39	1.63	6.4	308	2.9	6.4	2.2	0.5	37%	73%	61
	10	25	R	a	aaa	SD	1	0	17	1	20	12	2	1	5	20	0.89	0.84	4.5	169	2.2	8.9	4.0	0.4	23%	94%	145
Webb,Travis	10	26	L		aa	CIN	6	10	23	0	118	161	86	20	72	72	6.56	1.97	25.2	318	5.5	5.5	1.0	1.5	35%	69%	1
Weber,Thad	09	25	R		aa	DET	7	3	13	0	75	99	46	9	20	34	5.46	1.58	26.0	311	2.4	4.1	1.7	1.1	34%	67%	21
	10	26	R		a/a	DET	11	13	28	0	189	225	99	23	45	105	4.71	1.43	29.4	290	2.2	5.0	2.3	1.1	32%	69%	43
Weiland,Kyle	10	24	R		aa	BOS	5	9	25	0	128	129	75	14	48	98	5.25	1.39	22.1	257	3.4	6.9	2.0	1.0	31%	63%	58
Weinhardt,Robbie	09	24	R		aa	DET	0	1	20	2	31	33	10	0	16	26	2.98	1.59	7.0	266	4.8	7.6	1.6	0.0	35%	79%	81
	10	25	R	a	aaa	DET	1	1	24	1	34	30	7	0	7	21	1.85	1.09	5.7	232	1.8	5.5	3.0	0.0	29%	81%	105
Weiser,Keith	09	25	L		aa	COL	9	15	27	0	156	256	130	32	31	74	7.49	1.84	27.5	359	1.8	4.3	2.4	1.9	38%	62%	3
	10	26	L		aa	COL	10	8	26	0	157	245	106	24	37	62	6.06	1.79	28.5	348	2.1	3.5	1.7	1.4	37%	68%	0

Major League Equivalent Statistics

						Actual											Major League Equivalents									
PITCHER	Yr	Age Th		Lev	Org	w	l	g	sv	ip	h	er	hr	bb	k	era	whip	bf/g	oob	ctl	dom	cmd	hr/9	h%	s%	bpv
Wells, Jared	09	28 R		a/a	SEA	2	0	30	1	38	46	25	6	30	25	5.97	1.99	6.2	292	7.1	6.0	0.8	1.4	33%	72%	9
	10	29 R		a/a	HOU	5	5	35	3	81	109	56	11	55	48	6.26	2.03	11.5	316	6.1	5.3	0.9	1.2	35%	70%	6
West, Sean	09	23 L		aa	FLA	7	3	12	0	64	81	44	13	31	57	6.23	1.76	24.9	304	4.3	8.0	1.9	1.9	36%	69%	25
	10	24 L		aaa	FLA	4	3	11	0	57	65	22	4	19	42	3.46	1.47	22.8	280	3.0	6.6	2.2	0.6	34%	78%	66
Westcott, Craig	10	25 R		aa	SF	3	3	13	0	66	95	53	11	31	38	7.16	1.89	24.5	329	4.2	5.2	1.2	1.4	36%	63%	3
Whelan, Kevin	09	26 R	a	a/a	NYY	4	0	44	3	67	58	29	1	46	69	3.95	1.55	6.8	228	6.2	9.3	1.5	0.1	32%	72%	92
	10	27 R		a/a	NYY	5	4	41	4	49	49	43	4	34	50	7.94	1.70	5.5	254	6.3	9.2	1.5	0.8	34%	51%	66
Whisler, Wes	09	27 L		aaa	CHW	10	12	26	0	152	209	98	14	62	66	5.79	1.78	27.5	320	3.7	3.9	1.1	0.9	35%	67%	11
	10	27 L		aaa	FLA	3	7	35	0	105	144	79	16	72	48	6.77	2.06	14.9	320	6.1	4.2	0.7	1.4	34%	68%	-10
Whitaker, Roger	10	26 R		a/a	SF	1	1	33	1	47	46	25	4	33	32	4.84	1.68	6.6	252	6.2	6.2	1.0	0.8	30%	72%	38
White, Alex	10	22 R		aa	CLE	8	7	18	0	106	99	30	8	26	68	2.54	1.18	24.2	242	2.2	5.8	2.6	0.7	28%	81%	76
Wilding, Taylor	10	26 R		aa	LAA	3	4	25	0	54	83	47	6	27	32	7.78	2.04	10.7	346	4.4	5.4	1.2	0.9	39%	61%	16
Wilhite, Matthew	09	28 R		aaa	COL	0	4	38	10	48	68	44	9	12	25	8.23	1.65	5.8	325	2.2	4.7	2.1	1.6	35%	50%	15
	10	29 R		aaa	COL	1	1	40	0	58	91	47	11	22	34	7.31	1.94	7.1	349	3.4	5.2	1.5	1.7	38%	65%	-2
Wilkie, Josh	09	25 R	a	a/a	WAS	7	5	51	5	71	84	28	2	18	53	3.59	1.43	6.1	288	2.3	6.7	3.0	0.3	36%	74%	92
	10	26 R		aaa	WAS	4	4	53	8	69	68	25	2	23	51	3.22	1.31	5.5	252	2.9	6.7	2.3	0.3	31%	74%	84
Williams, Matthew	10	24 R		aa	MIN	2	3	28	3	43	54	28	6	19	22	5.83	1.68	7.1	299	3.9	4.7	1.2	1.3	32%	67%	10
Williams, Randy	09	34 L		aaa	CHW	3	0	33	1	36	40	20	4	13	33	4.97	1.45	4.8	275	3.1	8.3	2.6	1.0	34%	67%	74
	10	35 L		aaa	CHW	1	0	21	2	32	31	12	1	9	19	3.26	1.25	6.4	246	2.7	5.3	2.0	0.3	29%	73%	71
Willinsky, Mark	10	24 R		aa	MIL	2	2	24	0	46	74	37	7	25	37	7.23	2.14	9.7	355	4.8	7.2	1.5	1.4	42%	67%	16
Wilson, Alex	10	24 R		aa	BOS	4	5	16	0	78	108	67	15	33	47	7.72	1.81	23.1	322	3.8	5.4	1.4	1.8	35%	59%	-1
Wilson, Justin	10	23 L		aa	PIT	11	8	27	0	142	125	58	4	68	109	3.65	1.36	22.5	231	4.3	6.9	1.6	0.3	29%	72%	76
Wise, Brendan	09	24 R		aa	DET	4	1	21	2	41	63	25	2	12	13	5.43	1.84	9.3	344	2.7	2.8	1.0	0.5	37%	69%	11
	10	25 R		a/a	DET	6	2	43	6	77	78	20	0	23	33	2.29	1.31	7.6	258	2.7	3.9	1.5	0.0	30%	81%	57
Withrow, Chris	10	21 R		aa	LA	4	9	27	0	129	153	88	12	66	98	6.13	1.70	22.1	289	4.6	6.8	1.5	0.8	35%	63%	44
Wolf, Ross	09	27 R		aaa	BAL	4	2	47	1	82	89	52	7	36	58	5.66	1.53	7.8	272	3.9	6.4	1.6	0.8	32%	63%	48
	10	28 R		aaa	OAK	0	3	35	8	48	44	15	2	17	30	2.76	1.27	5.7	240	3.2	5.7	1.8	0.4	29%	79%	67
Wood, Travis	09	23 L		a/a	CIN	13	5	27	0	167	143	43	8	55	119	2.31	1.18	25.4	227	3.0	6.4	2.2	0.4	28%	82%	81
	10	24 L	a	aaa	CIN	5	6	16	0	100	97	40	11	24	87	3.60	1.21	25.8	249	2.2	7.8	3.6	1.0	31%	74%	99
Woody, Abraham	09	27 R		a/a	ARI	1	3	43	0	65	106	66	11	38	21	9.08	2.21	7.7	357	5.2	2.9	0.5	1.5	37%	59%	-34
	10	28 R		aa	CIN	4	3	22	5	31	54	22	2	7	12	6.30	1.98	6.9	375	2.1	3.6	1.7	0.7	41%	67%	17
Wordekemper, Eric	09	26 R		a/a	NYY	3	2	38	2	58	68	34	8	18	34	5.33	1.47	6.7	285	2.7	5.3	1.9	1.2	32%	66%	34
	10	27 R		a/a	NYY	5	0	47	9	66	74	30	10	20	50	4.08	1.41	6.1	276	2.7	6.9	2.6	1.4	32%	76%	53
Worley, Vance	09	22 R		aa	PHI	7	12	27	0	153	186	109	21	49	85	6.41	1.53	25.3	294	2.9	5.0	1.7	1.2	32%	59%	26
	10	23 R		a/a	PHI	10	7	27	0	158	181	70	14	46	102	3.99	1.44	25.5	282	2.6	5.8	2.2	0.8	33%	74%	56
Worrell, Mark	10	28 R		aaa	SEA	2	4	29	0	37	45	26	5	15	29	6.40	1.62	5.8	295	3.6	6.9	1.9	1.3	35%	62%	40
Wright, Chase	09	27 L		aaa	MIL	9	7	26	0	131	172	76	15	52	50	5.23	1.71	23.3	310	3.5	3.5	1.0	1.1	33%	71%	2
	10	28 L		aaa	MIL	8	9	28	1	151	192	98	21	58	80	5.83	1.65	24.7	303	3.5	4.8	1.4	1.3	33%	66%	14
Wright, Matt	09	28 R		aaa	KC	1	5	9	0	40	58	40	3	16	25	9.00	1.84	21.2	331	3.6	5.6	1.6	0.7	38%	48%	34
	10	29 R		aa	OAK	7	3	15	0	78	120	39	9	14	30	4.46	1.71	24.1	344	1.6	3.5	2.2	1.0	37%	76%	23
Wright, Steven	09	25 R	a	a/a	CLE	10	0	38	2	87	94	32	1	22	59	3.27	1.33	9.7	269	2.3	6.1	2.7	0.1	33%	73%	90
	10	26 R		a/a	CLE	2	3	48	5	75	98	46	6	26	49	5.55	1.65	7.2	309	3.2	5.9	1.9	0.8	36%	66%	46
Wright, Wesley	10	26 L		aaa	HOU	4	1	15	0	69	82	38	8	32	35	4.99	1.65	21.1	288	4.2	4.5	1.1	1.1	31%	71%	15
Yourkin, Matt	09	28 L		aa	SF	6	2	50	8	63	76	28	6	33	50	3.92	1.72	5.9	293	4.6	7.1	1.5	0.9	35%	79%	44
	10	29 L		aaa	SF	7	8	29	0	136	173	75	14	40	84	4.95	1.56	21.0	303	2.6	5.5	2.1	0.9	35%	69%	44
Zagone, Richard	10	24 L		aa	BAL	5	5	13	0	76	95	46	10	23	33	5.48	1.54	26.2	299	2.7	3.9	1.5	1.2	32%	66%	13
Zagurski, Mike	09	27 L		aa	PHI	3	4	45	8	53	55	29	9	31	46	4.88	1.63	5.4	263	5.3	7.8	1.5	1.6	31%	75%	34
	10	28 L		aaa	PHI	2	3	52	3	52	55	25	4	29	58	4.36	1.62	4.5	265	5.1	10.0	2.0	0.7	36%	74%	82
Zaleski, Matthew	09	28 R		a/a	CHW	6	3	23	1	90	122	32	9	29	45	3.21	1.67	18.0	316	2.9	4.5	1.6	0.9	35%	84%	24
	10	29 R		aaa	CHW	7	8	28	1	139	168	102	30	49	71	6.61	1.56	22.3	292	3.2	4.6	1.4	1.9	30%	61%	-4
Zinicola, Zechry	09	25 R		a/a	WAS	1	2	43	5	54	81	43	2	20	40	7.22	1.87	6.0	341	3.3	6.6	2.0	0.3	41%	58%	59
	10	26 R		a/a	WAS	2	3	37	12	42	44	20	3	19	30	4.27	1.50	5.0	264	4.0	6.5	1.6	0.7	32%	72%	55

Ratings, Rankings & Cheat Sheets

Here is what you will find in this section:

Skills Rankings

We start by looking at some important component skills. For batters, we've ranked the top players in terms of pure power, speed, and batting average skill, breaking each down in a number of different ways to provide more insight. For pitchers, we rank some of the key base skills, differentiating between starters and relievers, and provide a few interesting cuts that might uncover some late round sleepers.

These are clearly not exhaustive lists of sorts and filters. If there is another cut you'd like to see, drop me a note and I'll consider it for next year's book. Also note that the database at BaseballHQ.com allows you to construct your own custom sorts and filters. Finally, remember that these are just tools. Some players will appear on multiple lists — even mutually exclusive lists — so you have to assess what makes most sense and make decisions for your specific application.

POWER

Top PX, 400+ AB: Top power skills from among projected full-time players.

Top PX, -300 AB: Top power skills from among projected part-time players. Possible end-game options are here.

Position Scarcity: A quick scan to see which positions have deeper power options than others.

Top PX, Ct% over 85%: Top power skills from among the top contact hitters. Best pure power options here.

Top PX, Ct% under 75%: Top power skills from among the worst contact hitters. These are free-swingers who might be prone to streakiness or lower batting averages.

Top PX, FB% over 40%: Top power skills from among the most extreme fly ball hitters. Most likely to convert their power into home runs.

Top PX, FB% under 35%: Top power skills from among those with lesser fly ball tendencies. There may be more downside to their home run potential.

SPEED

Top Spd, 400+ AB: Top speed skills from among projected full-time players.

Top Spd, -300 AB: Top speed skills from among projected part-time players. Possible end-game options here.

Position Scarcity: A quick scan to see which positions have deeper speed options than others.

Top Spd, OB% over .350: Top speed skills from among those who get on base most often. Best opportunities for stolen bases here.

Top Spd, OB% under .310: Top speed skills from among those who have trouble getting on base. These names may bear watching if they can improve their on base ability.

Top Spd, SBO% over 20%: Top speed skills from among those who get the green light most often. Most likely to convert their speed into stolen bases.

Top Spd, SBO% under 15%: Top speed skills from among those who are currently not getting the green light. There may be sleeper SBs here if given more opportunities to run.

BATTING AVERAGE

Top Ct%, 400+ AB: Top contact skills from among projected full-time players. Contact does not always convert to higher BAs, but is still strongly correlated.

Top Ct%, -300 AB: Top contact skills from among projected part-time players. Possible end-gamers here.

Low Ct%, 400+ AB: The poorest contact skills from among projected full-time players. Potential BA killers.

Top Ct%, bb% over 10%: Top contact skills from among the most patient hitters. Best batting average upside here.

Top Ct%, bb% under 6%: Top contact skills from among the least patient hitters. These are free-swingers who might be prone to streakiness or lower batting averages.

Top Ct%, GB% over 50%: Top contact skills from among the most extreme ground ball hitters. A ground ball has a higher chance of becoming a hit than a non-HR fly ball so there may be some batting average upside here.

Top Ct%, GB% under 40%: Top contact skills from among those with lesser ground ball tendencies. These players are making contact but hitting more fly balls, which tend to convert to hits at a lower rate than GB.

PITCHING SKILLS

Top Command: Leaders in projected K/BB rates.

Top Control: Leaders in fewest projected walks allowed.

Top Dominance: Leaders in projected strikeout rate.

Top Ground Ball Rate: GB pitchers tend to have lower ERAs (and higher WHIP) than fly ball pitchers.

Top Fly Ball Rate: FB pitchers tend to have higher ERAs (and lower WHIP) than ground ball pitchers.

High GB, Low Dom: GB pitchers tend to have lower K rates, but these are the most extreme examples.

High GB, High Dom: The best at dominating hitters and keeping the ball down. These are the pitchers who keep runners off the bases and batted balls in the park, a skills combination that is the most valuable a pitcher can own.

Lowest xERA: Leaders in projected skills-based ERA.

Top BPV: Two lists of top skilled pitchers here. For starters, those projected to be rotation regulars (180+ IP) and fringe starters with skill (-150 IP). For relievers, those projected to be frontline closers (10+ saves) and high-skilled bullpen fillers (9– saves).

Random Variance—Rebounds and Corrections

These charts list +/- 3, 4 and 5 Rand Var scores for players with a minimum 300 AB or 100 IP. The scores identify players who, in 2010, posted outlying levels of measures prone to regression. The +3, +4 and +5 scores are players we expect to rebound in 2011; –3, -4 and –5 scores are players due for a negative correction. Within each break, players are listed in alphabetical order.

Risk Management

Lists include players who've accumulated the most days on the disabled list over the past five years (Grade "F" in Health) and whose performance was the most consistent over the past three years. Also listed are the most reliable batters and pitchers overall, with a focus on positional and skills reliability. As a reminder, reliability in this context is not tied to skill level; it is a gauge of which players manage to accumulate playing time and post consistent output from year to year, whether that output is good or bad.

Position Scarcity Chart

There has been much discussion about position scarcity, its importance and how to leverage it in your draft. This chart provides a visual representation of the depth of talent for the top 45 players at each position and shows you why, in a snake draft league, it might make sense to draft a Brian McCann before you draft an Adrian Beltre.

Portfolio3 Plan

Players are sorted and ranked based on how they fit into the three draft tiers of the Portfolio3 Plan. A full description of how this plan works appears in the Encyclopedia.

Mayberry Method

Players are grouped based on how they score out in the Mayberry Method. A full description of how this plan works appears in the Gaming Research Abstracts section.

Rotisserie Auction Draft

This list is presented with both AL and NL players, mostly because we don't know who is going to end up on what team yet. The values are representative of standard 75%-plus depth leagues. However, remember that these values are for player-to-player comparative purposes only, and allow us to provide rankings. You should not use these as actual in-draft bid values (see the Consumer Advisory in the back of the book for a full explanation).

The free projections update in March will provide better estimates of playing time, and as such, better information for drafting purposes. The custom draft guides on Baseball HQ are available to those who wish to produce accurate valuations for their particular league configuration. But in the interim, you can still use this information to plan out the core of your draft. For those who subscribe to Baseball HQ, full projections begin appearing online in December.

Rotisserie Snake Draft

This ranking takes the previous auction list, re-sets it into rounds and adjusts the rankings based on position scarcity. Given the growing popularity of 15-team mixed leagues, like the National Fantasy Baseball Championship, we've set this list up for that type of format.

In the first eight rounds, your target players should be those that are shaded (though your first round pick may depend upon your seed). These are the position scarcity picks. Also pay attention to the bolded players; these are categorical scarcity picks (primarily steals and saves).

If you reach a point where there are still undrafted players from earlier rounds, you can judiciously target those. To build the best foundation, you should come out of the first 10 rounds with all your middle infielders, all your corner infielders, one outfielder, at least one catcher and two pitchers (at least one closer).

The reason we target scarce positions first is that there will be plenty of solid outfielders and starting pitchers later on. The Position Scarcity Chart shows you why. The 20th best catcher on the list is John Jaso; the 20th best starting pitcher is Tommy Hanson. Which one would you rather have on your team?

IMPORTANT CAVEAT ABOUT THESE LISTS

The auction and snake draft rankings do not represent average draft positions (ADP) or average auction values (AAV). They represent where each player's true value may lie. It is the variance between this true value and the ADP/AAV market values — or better, the value that your leaguemates place on each player — where you will find your potential for profit or loss.

That means *you cannot take these lists right into your draft with you.* You have to compare these rankings with your ADPs and AAVs, and build your draft list from there. In other words, if we project Dustin Pedroia as a first round pick but you know the other owners (or your ADP's) see him as a third-rounder, you can probably wait to pick him up in round 2. If you are in an auction league with owners who overvalue saves and Rafael Soriano (projected at $22) gets bid past $25, you will likely take a loss should you decide to chase the bidding.

Rotisserie 500 Rankings

This is a ranked list of batters and pitchers based on their 2009-2010 final values using the Roto500 categories. A full description is in the Gaming Research Abstracts section.

Simulation League Draft

Using Runs Above Replacement creates a more real-world ranking of player value, which serves simulation gamers well. Batters and pitchers are integrated, and value break-points are delineated.

BATTER SKILLS RANKINGS - POWER

TOP PX, 400+ AB

NAME	POS	PX
Dunn,Adam	3	204
Reynolds,Mark	5	189
Cruz,Nelson	9	180
Pena,Carlos	3	172
Howard,Ryan	3	172
Stanton,Mike	9	171
Votto,Joey	3	171
Cabrera,Miguel	3	168
Pujols,Albert	3	166
Ortiz,David	0	166
Werth,Jayson	89	165
Bautista,Jose	59	163
Gonzalez,Carlos	789	162
Youkilis,Kevin	3	162
Longoria,Evan	5	162
Napoli,Mike	23	159
LaRoche,Adam	3	157
Hamilton,Josh	78	156
Soriano,Alfonso	7	156
Teixeira,Mark	3	155
Hart,Corey	9	155
Scott,Luke	0	155
Uggla,Dan	4	154
Swisher,Nick	9	153
Fielder,Prince	3	153
Hawpe,Brad	9	153
Bruce,Jay	9	152
Young,Chris	8	152
Snider,Travis	79	151
Cust,Jack	0	151
Alvarez,Pedro	5	151
Soto,Geovany	2	150
Rodriguez,Alex	5	149
Stewart,Ian	5	148
Upton,Justin	9	148
Konerko,Paul	30	148
Wright,David	5	148
Willingham,Josh	7	147

TOP PX, -300 AB

NAME	POS	PX
Ross,David	2	174
Shoppach,Kelly	2	158
Duncan,Shelley	7	156
Francisco,Juan	5	156
Stairs,Matt	7	150
Hinske,Eric	37	145
Wells,Casper	9	144
Fox,Jake	0	142
Thames,Marcus	70	138
Varitek,Jason	2	136
Conrad,Brooks	5	134
Davis,Chris	3	134
Castro,Ramon	2	133
Duda,Lucas	7	132
Giambi,Jason	3	131
Wood,Brandon	56	130
Fields,Josh	5	129
Nix,Laynce	7	129
Michaels,Jason	7	128
Wise,DeWayne	8	128
Viciedo,Dayan	5	126
Edmonds,Jim	8	125
Gamel,Mat	5	125
Francisco,Ben	79	125
Johnson,Nick	0	124

POSITIONAL SCARCITY

NAME	POS	PX
Thome,Jim	DH	190
Ortiz,David	2	166
Scott,Luke	3	155
Cust,Jack	4	151
Lind,Adam	5	144
Fox,Jake	6	142
Ross,David	CA	174
Napoli,Mike	2	159
Shoppach,Kelly	3	158
Soto,Geovany	4	150
Iannetta,Chris	5	139
Posada,Jorge	6	138
Buck,John	7	138
Varitek,Jason	8	136
Dunn,Adam	1B	204
Branyan,Russell	2	195
Pena,Carlos	3	172
Howard,Ryan	4	172
Votto,Joey	5	171
Cabrera,Miguel	6	168
Pujols,Albert	7	166
Youkilis,Kevin	8	162
LaRoche,Adam	9	157
Teixeira,Mark	10	155
Uggla,Dan	2B	154
Weeks,Rickie	2	144
Hall,Bill	3	140
Johnson,Kelly	4	132
Lowrie,Jed	5	131
Nix,Jayson	6	125
Uribe,Juan	7	125
Utley,Chase	8	124
Reynolds,Mark	3B	189
Bautista,Jose	2	163
Longoria,Evan	3	162
Francisco,Juan	4	156
Alvarez,Pedro	5	151
Rodriguez,Alex	6	149
Stewart,Ian	7	148
Wright,David	8	148
Zimmerman,Ryan	9	134
Conrad,Brooks	10	134
Tulowitzki,Troy	SS	141
Lowrie,Jed	2	131
Wood,Brandon	3	130
Uribe,Juan	4	125
Ramirez,Hanley	5	117
Drew,Stephen	6	115
Gonzalez,Alex	7	112
Peralta,Jhonny	8	110
Cruz,Nelson	OF	180
Stanton,Mike	2	171
Werth,Jayson	3	165
Gonzalez,Carlos	4	162
Jones,Andruw	5	158
Hamilton,Josh	6	156
Hart,Corey	7	155
Swisher,Nick	8	153
Hawpe,Brad	9	153
Bruce,Jay	10	152
Young,Chris	11	152
Snider,Travis	12	151
Cameron,Mike	13	149
Upton,Justin	14	148
Hinske,Eric	15	145
Wells,Casper	16	144

TOP PX, Ct% over 85%

NAME	Ct%	PX
Pujols,Albert	88	166
Jones,Chipper	85	123
Wells,Vernon	87	123
Cano,Robinson	88	116
Posey,Buster	85	116
Kinsler,Ian	86	113
Sandoval,Pablo	86	112
Pedroia,Dustin	91	110
Martinez,Victor	88	108
Butler,Billy	86	107
Prado,Martin	86	106
Guerrero,Vladimir	88	104
Murphy,Daniel	87	103
Ruiz,Carlos	87	102
Sweeney,Mike	89	101
Lee,Carlos	91	101
Freeman,Freddie	85	101
Gload,Ross	88	99
Victorino,Shane	87	98
Rivera,Juan	88	97
Phillips,Brandon	86	96
Taylor,Michael	86	96
Rollins,Jimmy	90	95
Ordonez,Magglio	86	95
Mauer,Joe	89	94
Reyes,Jose	88	91
Ramirez,Alexei	87	90
Furcal,Rafael	85	89
Loney,James	85	87
Hernandez,Ramon	86	85
Suzuki,Kurt	89	84
Lopez,Jose	89	82
DeJesus,David	86	82
Pena,Brayan	89	81
Jackson,Conor	88	81
Kotchman,Casey	88	80
Ramos,Wilson	87	79
Betancourt,Y.	90	79

TOP PX, Ct% under 75%

NAME	Ct%	PX
Dunn,Adam	66	204
Branyan,Russell	65	195
Thome,Jim	69	190
Reynolds,Mark	60	189
Ross,David	73	174
Pena,Carlos	67	172
Howard,Ryan	69	172
Stanton,Mike	70	171
Werth,Jayson	73	165
Napoli,Mike	71	159
Shoppach,Kelly	61	158
Jones,Andruw	72	158
LaRoche,Adam	72	157
Duncan,Shelley	74	156
Uggla,Dan	74	154
Swisher,Nick	75	153
Hawpe,Brad	71	153
Young,Chris	74	152
Snider,Travis	74	151
Cust,Jack	64	151
Alvarez,Pedro	74	151
Cameron,Mike	70	149
Stewart,Ian	73	148
Upton,Justin	72	148
Hinske,Eric	73	145

TOP PX, FB% over 40%

NAME	FB%	PX
Dunn,Adam	49	204
Branyan,Russell	53	195
Reynolds,Mark	50	189
Cruz,Nelson	45	180
Ross,David	43	174
Pena,Carlos	46	172
Stanton,Mike	41	171
Cabrera,Miguel	40	168
Pujols,Albert	43	166
Ortiz,David	46	166
Werth,Jayson	43	165
Bautista,Jose	48	163
Youkilis,Kevin	43	162
Longoria,Evan	43	162
Napoli,Mike	45	159
Shoppach,Kelly	42	158
Jones,Andruw	44	158
LaRoche,Adam	43	157
Duncan,Shelley	54	156
Soriano,Alfonso	51	156
Teixeira,Mark	44	155
Hart,Corey	43	155
Scott,Luke	42	155
Uggla,Dan	45	154
Swisher,Nick	45	153
Fielder,Prince	41	153
Bruce,Jay	45	152
Young,Chris	50	152
Soto,Geovany	41	150
Stairs,Matt	42	150
Cameron,Mike	51	149
Stewart,Ian	44	148
Konerko,Paul	44	148
Wright,David	40	148
Willingham,Josh	45	147
Morneau,Justin	41	146
Hinske,Eric	45	145
Torres,Andres	42	143

TOP PX, FB% under 35%

NAME	FB%	PX
Francisco,Juan	29	156
Fields,Josh	34	129
Heyward,Jason	26	125
Pence,Hunter	33	121
Abreu,Bobby	34	121
Johnson,Chris	34	119
Fukudome,K.	34	117
Cano,Robinson	35	116
Posey,Buster	33	116
Hunter,Torii	35	113
Lewis,Fred	32	112
Jones,Adam	34	109
Bell,Josh	26	108
Cuddyer,Michael	35	108
Spilborghs,Ryan	33	107
Butler,Billy	34	107
Diaz,Matt	30	107
Morrison,Logan	32	106
Prado,Martin	33	106
Larish,Jeff	35	103
Ishikawa,Travis	34	102
Byrd,Marlon	33	101
Teahen,Mark	29	101
Maybin,Cameron	31	100
Young,Michael	32	100

BATTER SKILLS RANKINGS - SPEED

TOP Spd, 400+ AB

NAME	POS	Spd
Bourjos, Peter	8	173
Bourn, Michael	8	171
Jackson, Austin	8	160
Fowler, Dexter	8	152
Maybin, Cameron	8	152
Gardner, Brett	78	151
Suzuki, Ichiro	9	148
Drew, Stephen	6	148
Jennings, D.	9	147
Aybar, Erick	6	146
Podsednik, Scott	7	146
Morgan, Nyjer	8	146
McCutchen, A.	8	146
Granderson, Curtis	8	146
Borbon, Julio	8	144
Stubbs, Drew	8	142
Crawford, Carl	7	138
Escobar, Alcides	6	138
Victorino, Shane	8	136
Reyes, Jose	6	134
Pie, Felix	7	134
Tabata, Jose	7	134
Torres, Andres	789	133
Ellsbury, Jacoby	8	133
Theriot, Ryan	46	132
Colvin, Tyler	79	131
Castro, Starlin	6	131
Davis, Rajai	789	131
Pagan, Angel	789	131
Casilla, Alexi	46	129
Andrus, Elvis	6	128
Pierre, Juan	7	126
Infante, Omar	457	125
Span, Denard	8	124
Crisp, Coco	8	122
Pennington, Cliff	6	122
Cedeno, Ronny	6	121
Upton, Justin	9	121

TOP Spd, -300 AB

NAME	POS	Spd
Bonifacio, Emilio	8	144
Wise, DeWayne	8	141
Velez, Eugenio	7	136
Cain, Lorenzo	8	135
Lugo, Julio	46	135
Patterson, Eric	78	133
Santiago, Ramon	46	132
Pena, Ramiro	56	131
Inglett, Joe	9	127
Herrera, Jonathan	4	126
Gwynn, Tony	8	121
Guzman, Cristian	46	121
Rosales, Adam	4	120
Maier, Mitch	89	119
Wells, Casper	9	119
Ryal, Rusty	37	119
Bloomquist, Willie	9	116
Arias, Joaquin	4	116
Worth, Danny	6	113
Nelson, Chris	45	111
Francisco, Juan	5	110
Harris, Willie	79	110
Reddick, Josh	8	109
Dickerson, Chris	8	109
Valdez, Wilson	46	109

POSITIONAL SCARCITY

NAME	POS	Spd
Baldelli, Rocco	DH	98
Fox, Jake	2	83
Sweeney, Mike	3	66
Matsui, Hideki	4	64
Johnson, Dan	5	63
Scott, Luke	6	62
May, Lucas	CA	103
Mathis, Jeff	2	102
Jaso, John	3	102
Thole, Josh	4	96
Cervelli, Francisco	5	95
Hayes, Brett	6	95
Teagarden, Taylor	7	93
Whiteside, Eli	8	91
Ryal, Rusty	1B	119
Kelly, Don	2	102
Barton, Daric	3	101
Cuddyer, Michael	4	95
Marte, Andy	5	94
Davis, Ike	6	90
Youkilis, Kevin	7	90
Ishikawa, Travis	8	89
Pearce, Steve	9	85
Gload, Ross	10	84
Young Jr., Eric	2B	152
Lugo, Julio	2	135
Herrera, Jonathan	3	126
Rhymes, Will	4	126
Infante, Omar	5	125
Carroll, Jamey	6	124
Rosales, Adam	7	120
Ackley, Dustin	8	118
Francisco, Juan	3B	110
Inge, Brandon	2	104
Callaspo, Alberto	3	102
Polanco, Placido	4	99
Teahen, Mark	5	99
Vizquel, Omar	6	97
Stewart, Ian	7	96
Harris, Brendan	8	96
Marte, Andy	9	94
Cairo, Miguel	10	94
Drew, Stephen	SS	148
Aybar, Erick	2	146
Escobar, Alcides	3	138
Reyes, Jose	4	134
Cabrera, Everth	5	132
Theriot, Ryan	6	132
Santiago, Ramon	7	132
Castro, Starlin	8	131
Bourjos, Peter	OF	173
Bourn, Michael	2	171
Jackson, Austin	3	160
Fowler, Dexter	4	152
Maybin, Cameron	5	152
Gardner, Brett	6	151
Suzuki, Ichiro	7	148
Jennings, D.	8	147
Podsednik, Scott	9	146
Morgan, Nyjer	10	146
McCutchen, A.	11	146
Granderson, Curtis	12	146
Bonifacio, Emilio	13	144
Borbon, Julio	14	144
Stubbs, Drew	15	142
Venable, Will	16	141

TOP Spd, OB% over .350

NAME	OB%	Spd
Fowler, Dexter	354	152
Gardner, Brett	356	151
McCutchen, A.	362	146
Infante, Omar	353	125
Carroll, Jamey	363	124
Upton, Justin	360	121
Castillo, Luis	362	118
DeJesus, David	352	118
Figgins, Chone	352	118
Damon, Johnny	358	117
Furcal, Rafael	364	112
Gonzalez, Carlos	350	111
Bay, Jason	350	109
Zobrist, Ben	362	109
Tulowitzki, Troy	368	107
Heyward, Jason	398	106
Ramirez, Hanley	375	104
Markakis, Nick	365	104
Jaso, John	353	102
Werth, Jayson	379	101
Barton, Daric	371	101
Utley, Chase	370	100
Braun, Ryan	362	99
Roberts, Brian	359	99
Kinsler, Ian	356	97
Morrison, Logan	379	96
Pedroia, Dustin	368	95
Fukudome, Kosuke	387	94
Johnson, Kelly	355	94
Drew, J.D.	363	93
Bautista, Jose	369	91
Youkilis, Kevin	391	90
Beltran, Carlos	374	88
Jones, Chipper	385	86
Longoria, Evan	361	85
Ethier, Andre	361	85
Cruz, Nelson	356	84
Wright, David	356	82

TOP Spd, OB% under .310

NAME	OB%	Spd
Bourjos, Peter	299	173
Young Jr., Eric	309	152
Aybar, Erick	308	146
Venable, Will	306	141
Wise, DeWayne	267	141
Escobar, Alcides	299	138
Velez, Eugenio	282	136
Cain, Lorenzo	298	135
Gomez, Carlos	295	135
Patterson, Eric	293	133
Colvin, Tyler	298	131
Pena, Ramiro	286	131
Sanchez, Angel	295	129
Ryan, Brendan	301	124
Cedeno, Ronny	290	121
Guzman, Cristian	299	121
Rosales, Adam	309	120
Donald, Jason	295	119
Wells, Casper	308	119
Ryal, Rusty	279	119
Ackley, Dustin	309	118
Izturis, Cesar	289	118
Arias, Joaquin	289	116
Espinosa, Danny	291	115
Worth, Danny	287	113

TOP Spd, SBO% over 20%

NAME	SBO	Spd
Bourjos, Peter	33%	173
Bourn, Michael	33%	171
Fowler, Dexter	25%	152
Young Jr., Eric	34%	152
Gardner, Brett	32%	151
Jennings, D.	34%	147
Podsednik, Scott	27%	146
Morgan, Nyjer	35%	146
McCutchen, A.	23%	146
Bonifacio, Emilio	23%	144
Borbon, Julio	24%	144
Stubbs, Drew	29%	142
Venable, Will	23%	141
Wise, DeWayne	26%	141
Crawford, Carl	35%	138
Victorino, Shane	25%	136
Velez, Eugenio	44%	136
Gomez, Carlos	33%	135
Reyes, Jose	29%	134
Tabata, Jose	22%	134
Patterson, Eric	32%	133
Torres, Andres	24%	133
Ellsbury, Jacoby	38%	133
Cabrera, Everth	27%	132
Davis, Rajai	45%	131
Pagan, Angel	24%	131
Casilla, Alexi	25%	129
Andrus, Elvis	27%	128
Pierre, Juan	35%	126
Crisp, Coco	27%	122
Pennington, Cliff	25%	122
Gwynn, Tony	23%	121
Upton, B.J.	33%	118
Figgins, Chone	26%	118
Bloomquist, Willie	27%	116
Espinosa, Danny	26%	115
Bernadina, Roger	29%	112
Gonzalez, Carlos	20%	111

TOP Spd, SBO% under 15%

NAME	SBO	Spd
Maybin, Cameron	14%	152
Drew, Stephen	7%	148
Granderson, C.	12%	146
Santiago, Ramon	5%	132
Colvin, Tyler	9%	131
Sanchez, Angel	4%	129
Inglett, Joe	8%	127
Herrera, Jonathan	12%	126
Infante, Omar	6%	125
Carroll, Jamey	10%	124
Cedeno, Ronny	12%	121
Guzman, Cristian	6%	121
Rosales, Adam	11%	120
Donald, Jason	12%	119
Maier, Mitch	8%	119
Ryal, Rusty	8%	119
Ackley, Dustin	9%	118
Izturis, Cesar	15%	118
Castillo, Luis	13%	118
DeJesus, David	8%	118
Damon, Johnny	10%	117
Weeks, Rickie	10%	114
Jeter, Derek	13%	114
Worth, Danny	15%	113
Aviles, Mike	12%	112

BATTER SKILLS RANKINGS - BATTING AVERAGE

TOP Ct%, 400+ AB

NAME	Ct%	BA
Pierre,Juan	93	288
Callaspo,Alberto	93	282
Keppinger,Jeff	93	281
Polanco,Placido	92	296
Pedroia,Dustin	91	303
Molina,Yadier	91	278
Lee,Carlos	91	277
Brantley,Michael	90	260
Betancourt,Y.	90	262
Tejada,Miguel	90	276
Pierzynski,A.J.	90	277
Rollins,Jimmy	90	275
Thole,Josh	90	270
Mauer,Joe	89	334
Suzuki,Kurt	89	273
Lopez,Jose	89	268
Cano,Robinson	88	310
Suzuki,Ichiro	88	310
Martinez,Victor	88	300
Reyes,Jose	88	286
Pujols,Albert	88	317
Castro,Starlin	88	286
Escobar,Yunel	88	275
Tabata,Jose	88	283
Guerrero,Vladimir	88	289
Jaso,John	88	257
Ellsbury,Jacoby	88	290
Borbon,Julio	88	284
Scutaro,Marco	88	275
Jackson,Conor	88	277
Theriot,Ryan	87	270
Victorino,Shane	87	275
Ramirez,Alexei	87	285
Casilla,Alexi	87	263
Aybar,Erick	87	271
Wells,Vernon	87	280
Jennings,Desmond	87	260
Escobar,Alcides	87	257

TOP Ct%, -300 AB

NAME	Ct%	BA
Frandsen,Kevin	91	230
Sogard,Eric	90	246
Cora,Alex	90	247
Kendall,Jason	89	250
Kotsay,Mark	89	257
Bourgeois,Jason	89	248
Herrera,Jonathan	89	250
Miles,Aaron	89	250
Sweeney,Mike	89	270
Feliz,Pedro	89	237
Arias,Joaquin	88	265
Kotchman,Casey	88	257
Carter,W.Chris	88	263
Valdez,Wilson	88	267
Rivera,Juan	88	265
Blanco,Andres	88	258
Gload,Ross	88	286
Murphy,Daniel	87	273
Hairston,Jerry	87	256
Ramos,Wilson	87	250
Vizquel,Omar	87	253
Nelson,Chris	87	245
Counsell,Craig	86	248
Taylor,Michael	86	247
Cairo,Miguel	86	264

LOW Ct%, 400+ AB

NAME	Ct%	BA
Reynolds,Mark	60	223
Cust,Jack	64	245
Dunn,Adam	66	254
Pena,Carlos	67	235
Howard,Ryan	69	272
Stanton,Mike	70	262
Hawpe,Brad	71	278
Napoli,Mike	71	249
Upton,B.J.	71	248
Bay,Jason	71	265
Ankiel,Rick	71	233
Stubbs,Drew	72	250
LaRoche,Adam	72	270
Upton,Justin	72	280
Inge,Brandon	72	235
Stewart,Ian	73	252
Torres,Andres	73	251
Rodriguez,Sean	73	247
Weeks,Rickie	73	263
Werth,Jayson	73	284
Gomes,Jonny	73	247
Brown,Domonic	73	259
Snider,Travis	74	262
Alvarez,Pedro	74	275
Uggla,Dan	74	263
Young,Chris	74	253
Kemp,Matt	74	270
Blake,Casey	75	251
Swisher,Nick	75	272
Rasmus,Colby	75	258
Maybin,Cameron	75	267
Raburn,Ryan	75	268
Jackson,Austin	75	287
Bruce,Jay	75	272
Davis,Ike	75	261
Ludwick,Ryan	75	257
Saunders,Michael	75	250
Soto,Geovany	75	276
Ortiz,David	75	266
Headley,Chase	75	260
Wright,David	75	275
Soriano,Alfonso	76	267
Joyce,Matt	76	246
Granderson,Curtis	76	256
Sizemore,Grady	76	250
Gordon,Alex	76	259
Choo,Shin-Soo	77	298
Ross,Cody	77	266
Hart,Corey	77	279
Donald,Jason	77	240
Fielder,Prince	77	275
Willingham,Josh	77	269
Gutierrez,Franklin	77	255
Longoria,Evan	77	286
Overbay,Lyle	77	256
Fowler,Dexter	77	271
Cruz,Nelson	78	292
Johnson,Kelly	78	279
Colvin,Tyler	78	254
Lee,Derrek	78	286
Drew,J.D.	78	264
Bautista,Jose	78	270
Votto,Joey	78	318
Lind,Adam	78	273
Scott,Luke	78	264
Gonzalez,Carlos	78	302

TOP Ct%, bb% over 10%

NAME	bb%	Ct%
Mauer,Joe	12	89
Castillo,Luis	13	89
Pujols,Albert	16	88
Hanigan,Ryan	12	88
Jaso,John	13	88
Jackson,Conor	11	88
Ruiz,Carlos	12	87
Ordonez,Magglio	11	86
Counsell,Craig	11	86
Kinsler,Ian	11	86
Jones,Chipper	15	85
Furcal,Rafael	10	85
Zaun,Gregg	12	85
McCutchen,A.	10	85
LaRoche,Andy	10	85
Morrison,Logan	15	84
Huff,Aubrey	11	84
Damon,Johnny	11	83
Roberts,Brian	11	83
Holliday,Matt	11	83
Utley,Chase	12	83
Matsui,Hideki	12	83
Morneau,Justin	12	83
Martin,Russell	12	83
Ka'aihue,Kila	15	83
Beltran,Carlos	13	83
Barton,Daric	15	83
Gwynn,Tony	10	83
Schneider,Brian	12	83
McCann,Brian	11	82
Reimold,Nolan	10	82
Willits,Reggie	11	82
Punto,Nick	11	82
Nava,Daniel	11	82
Ramirez,Hanley	10	82
Cabrera,Miguel	12	82
Carroll,Jamey	11	82
Marson,Lou	11	82

TOP Ct%, bb% under 6%

NAME	bb%	Ct%
Polanco,Placido	5	92
Frandsen,Kevin	5	91
Izturis,Cesar	5	90
Betancourt,Y.	4	90
Molina,Bengie	4	90
Tejada,Miguel	4	90
Pierzynski,A.J.	4	90
Cabrera,Orlando	6	90
Pena,Brayan	6	89
Bourgeois,Jason	6	89
Lopez,Jose	4	89
Miles,Aaron	5	89
Feliz,Pedro	4	89
Suzuki,Ichiro	6	88
Arias,Joaquin	3	88
Borbon,Julio	5	88
Blanco,Andres	6	88
Ramirez,Alexei	6	87
Ramos,Wilson	3	87
Aybar,Erick	5	87
Escobar,Alcides	6	87
Aviles,Mike	4	86
Sanchez,Angel	6	86
Wilson,Jack	5	85
Sanchez,Freddy	6	85

TOP Ct%, GB% over 50%

NAME	GB%	Ct%
Pierre,Juan	55	93
Keppinger,Jeff	51	93
Frandsen,Kevin	55	91
Miles,Aaron	53	89
Castillo,Luis	66	89
Suzuki,Ichiro	57	88
Kotchman,Casey	54	88
Castro,Starlin	51	88
Escobar,Yunel	54	88
Tabata,Jose	59	88
Valdez,Wilson	61	88
Ellsbury,Jacoby	51	88
Borbon,Julio	56	88
Getz,Chris	51	88
Theriot,Ryan	53	87
Schumaker,Skip	59	87
Nelson,Chris	52	87
Hernandez,R.	50	86
Phillips,Brandon	51	86
Span,Denard	53	86
Gonzalez,Alberto	51	85
Denorfia,Chris	59	85
Velez,Eugenio	57	85
Jeter,Derek	61	85
Podsednik,Scott	51	85
Andrus,Elvis	59	84
Young Jr.,Eric	55	84
Bourjos,Peter	51	84
Guzman,Cristian	52	84
Morgan,Nyjer	53	83
Hernandez,A.	54	83
Kendrick,Howie	54	83
Gillespie,Cole	54	83
Nieves,Wil	56	83
Crowe,Trevor	54	83
Hudson,Orlando	51	83
Parra,Gerardo	52	82
Rodriguez,Ivan	58	82

TOP Ct%, GB% under 40%

NAME	GB%	Ct%
Lee,Carlos	38	91
Molina,Bengie	34	90
Pujols,Albert	39	88
Carter,W.Chris	39	88
Jackson,Conor	39	88
Hairston,Jerry	37	87
Ellis,Mark	40	86
Kinsler,Ian	37	86
Jones,Chipper	40	85
Kelly,Don	33	85
McDonald,John	36	85
Hill,Aaron	37	85
Janish,Paul	30	84
Moreland,Mitch	40	84
Sanchez,Gaby	37	84
Rolen,Scott	37	84
Pennington,Cliff	37	84
Craig,Allen	38	83
Roberts,Brian	37	83
Walker,Neil	37	83
Ramirez,Aramis	31	83
Tracy,Chad	35	83
Utley,Chase	38	83
Morneau,Justin	39	83
Ka'aihue,Kila	35	83

PITCHER SKILLS RANKINGS - Starting Pitchers

Top Command (k/bb)		Top Control (bb/9)		Top Dominance (k/9)		Top Ground Ball Rate		Top Fly Ball Rate	
NAME	**Cmd**	**NAME**	**Ctl**	**NAME**	**Dom**	**NAME**	**GB**	**NAME**	**FB**
Halladay,Roy	6.1	Halladay,Roy	1.2	Morrow,Brandon	10.0	Hudson,Tim	62	Young,Chris	54
Lee,Cliff	4.6	Slowey,Kevin	1.6	Lincecum,Tim	10.0	Mejia,Jenrry	61	Tomlin,Josh	50
Slowey,Kevin	4.5	Lee,Cliff	1.6	Strasburg,Stephen	9.9	Lowe,Derek	59	Lilly,Ted	50
Haren,Dan	4.4	Pineiro,Joel	1.7	Lester,Jon	9.8	Webb,Brandon	58	French,Luke	50
Nolasco,Ricky	4.0	Pavano,Carl	1.8	Gallardo,Yovani	9.7	Cook,Aaron	58	Enright,Barry	50
Anderson,Brett	3.7	Haren,Dan	1.9	Sanchez,Jonathan	9.6	Carmona,Fausto	57	VandenHurk,Rick	50
Hamels,Cole	3.7	Anderson,Brett	2.0	Minor,Mike	9.4	Drabek,Kyle	57	Hellickson,Jeremy	50
Shields,James	3.6	Fister,Doug	2.0	Harden,Rich	9.3	Westbrook,Jake	57	Slowey,Kevin	49
Lilly,Ted	3.5	Kuroda,Hiroki	2.0	Kershaw,Clayton	9.2	Masterson,Justin	56	Weaver,Jered	49
Greinke,Zack	3.5	Blackburn,Nick	2.0	Scherzer,Max	9.0	Garcia,Jaime	55	Chen,Bruce	48
Johnson,Josh	3.5	Sanabia,Alex	2.0	Volquez,Edinson	8.9	Carrasco,Carlos	55	Wood,Travis	48
Oswalt,Roy	3.5	Nolasco,Ricky	2.1	Liriano,Francisco	8.8	Romero,Ricky	55	LeBlanc,Wade	48
Weaver,Jered	3.4	Shields,James	2.1	Verlander,Justin	8.8	Pineiro,Joel	54	Minor,Mike	48
Kuroda,Hiroki	3.4	Enright,Barry	2.2	Johnson,Josh	8.7	Hernandez,Felix	54	Hudson,Dan	47
Hellickson,Jeremy	3.4	Oswalt,Roy	2.2	de la Rosa,Jorge	8.7	Carpenter,Chris	53	Harden,Rich	47
Wainwright,Adam	3.3	Buehrle,Mark	2.2	Nolasco,Ricky	8.6	Anderson,Brett	53	Vargas,Jason	46
Lewis,Colby	3.3	Lopez,Rodrigo	2.2	Hamels,Cole	8.6	Rogers,Esmil	53	Hughes,Phil	46
Lincecum,Tim	3.2	Bumgarner,Madison	2.2	Lewis,Colby	8.6	Cahill,Trevor	52	Lewis,Colby	46
Latos,Mat	3.2	Lilly,Ted	2.2	Latos,Mat	8.6	Porcello,Rick	52	Sanabia,Alex	45
Harang,Aaron	3.2	Dickey,R.A.	2.2	Hellickson,Jeremy	8.6	Lannan,John	52	Kazmir,Scott	45
Strasburg,Stephen	3.2	Carpenter,Chris	2.3	Parra,Manny	8.6	Maholm,Paul	52	Matusz,Brian	45
Baker,Scott	3.2	Tomlin,Josh	2.3	Wilson,C.J.	8.5	Marquis,Jason	52	Morrow,Brandon	45
Minor,Mike	3.1	Greinke,Zack	2.3	Norris,Bud	8.4	Halladay,Roy	52	Baker,Scott	45
Marcum,Shaun	3.1	Hamels,Cole	2.4	Weaver,Jered	8.4	Nova,Ivan	51	Cain,Matt	45
Hudson,Dan	3.1	Harang,Aaron	2.4	Jimenez,Ubaldo	8.4	Dickey,R.A.	51	Kennedy,Ian	45
Beckett,Josh	3.1	Wainwright,Adam	2.4	Hudson,Dan	8.4	Rzepczynski,Marc	51	Ohlendorf,Ross	45
Verlander,Justin	3.0	Baker,Scott	2.4	Peavy,Jake	8.3	Stauffer,Tim	51	Santana,Johan	44
Liriano,Francisco	3.0	Porcello,Rick	2.4	Beckett,Josh	8.3	Buchholz,Clay	51	Matsuzaka,Daisuke	44
Hernandez,Felix	3.0	Hill,Shawn	2.4	Gonzalez,Gio	8.3	Leake,Mike	51	Coke,Phil	44
Cain,Matt	3.0	Bergesen,Brad	2.4	Haren,Dan	8.3	Wilson,C.J.	51	Rowland-Smith,Rya	44
Rodriguez,Wandy	3.0	Braden,Dallas	2.4	Rodriguez,Wandy	8.3	Kuroda,Hiroki	50	Samardzija,Jeff	44

High GB, Low Dom			High GB, High Dom			Lowest xERA		Top BPV, 180+ IP		Top BPV, -150 IP	
NAME	**GB**	**Dom**	**NAME**	**GB**	**Dom**	**NAME**	**xERA**	**NAME**	**BPV**	**NAME**	**BPV**
Cook,Aaron	58	4.5	Hudson,Tim	62	5.8	Hernandez,Felix	2.87	Halladay,Roy	132	Strasburg,Stephen	119
Carmona,Faus	57	5.5	Mejia,Jenrry	61	7.1	Lincecum,Tim	2.94	Lincecum,Tim	122	Hellickson,Jeremy	101
Westbrook,Jak	57	5.4	Lowe,Derek	59	6.1	Lester,Jon	3.01	Haren,Dan	118	Peavy,Jake	91
Pineiro,Joel	54	4.9	Webb,Brando	58	6.8	Latos,Mat	3.11	Nolasco,Ricky	115	Harang,Aaron	87
Cahill,Trevor	52	5.4	Drabek,Kyle	57	6.5	Halladay,Roy	3.13	Johnson,Josh	113	Zimmermann,Jorda	83
Porcello,Rick	52	4.9	Masterson,Jus	56	7.3	Kershaw,Clayton	3.16	Hamels,Cole	112	Webb,Brandon	81
Lannan,John	52	5.0	Garcia,Jaime	55	7.1	Webb,Brandon	3.17	Lester,Jon	111	Rogers,Esmil	79
Maholm,Paul	52	5.3	Carrasco,Carl	55	7.3	Wainwright,Adam	3.20	Liriano,Francisco	108	Santana,Johan	75
Marquis,Jason	52	4.9	Romero,Ricky	55	7.3	Carpenter,Chris	3.26	Lee,Cliff	107	Rzepczynski,Marc	74
Dickey,R.A.	51	5.0	Hernandez,Fe	54	8.2	Jimenez,Ubaldo	3.27	Hernandez,Felix	106	Padilla,Vicente	73
Duensing,Bria	50	5.1	Carpenter,Chr	53	6.8	Verlander,Justin	3.33	Wainwright,Adam	105	Francis,Jeff	71
Bergesen,Brad	49	4.4	Anderson,Bret	53	7.2	Johnson,Josh	3.33	Greinke,Zack	103	Harden,Rich	64
Coleman,Case	49	4.1	Rogers,Esmil	53	7.0	Kuroda,Hiroki	3.34	Latos,Mat	102	Holland,Derek	64
Pelfrey,Mike	49	5.1	Halladay,Roy	52	7.6	Hanson,Tommy	3.36	Gallardo,Yovani	102	Mejia,Jenrry	63
Blackburn,Nic	49	4.2	Nova,Ivan	51	6.0	Morrow,Brandon	3.37	Oswalt,Roy	101	Sanabia,Alex	63
Volstad,Chris	49	5.3	Rzepczynski,N	51	8.0	Oswalt,Roy	3.37	Shields,James	100	Drabek,Kyle	62
Duke,Zach	48	5.1	Stauffer,Tim	51	5.8	Anderson,Brett	3.38	Beckett,Josh	100	Volquez,Edinson	62
Pavano,Carl	48	5.1	Buchholz,Clay	51	6.9	Cain,Matt	3.38	Lewis,Colby	99	Luebke,Cory	59
Hill,Shawn	46	5.2	Leake,Mike	51	5.9	Peavy,Jake	3.42	Verlander,Justin	98	Tillman,Chris	59
Buehrle,Mark	46	4.4	Wilson,C.J.	51	8.5	Scherzer,Max	3.46	Rodriguez,Wandy	97	Parra,Manny	57
Fister,Doug	46	5.2	Kuroda,Hiroki	50	6.8	Lee,Cliff	3.47	Weaver,Jered	96	LeBlanc,Wade	56
Kendrick,Kyle	45	4.0	Jimenez,Ubald	50	8.4	Sabathia,CC	3.49	Kuroda,Hiroki	96	Lopez,Rodrigo	56
Saunders,Joe	45	5.1	Lester,Jon	50	9.8	Weaver,Jered	3.49	Scherzer,Max	94	Penny,Brad	55
Lohse,Kyle	44	5.6	Luebke,Cory	50	6.1	Wilson,C.J.	3.50	Hanson,Tommy	93	Stauffer,Tim	53
Bannister,Bria	43	5.4	Wainwright,Ad	50	7.8	Billingsley,Chad	3.51	Carpenter,Chris	91	Iwakuma,Hisashi	53
Feldman,Scott	43	4.6	Liriano,Francis	49	8.8	Liriano,Francisco	3.52	Hudson,Dan	89	Morton,Charlie	53
Lopez,Rodrigo	42	5.3	de la Rosa,Jor	49	8.7	Greinke,Zack	3.52	Sabathia,CC	89	Silva,Carlos	53
Garcia,Freddy	42	5.5	Garland,Jon	49	5.8	Buchholz,Clay	3.54	Marcum,Shaun	87	Hill,Shawn	52
Guthrie,Jerem	41	5.3	Gonzalez,Gio	48	8.3	Hamels,Cole	3.61	Kershaw,Clayton	85	Garcia,Freddy	51
Hunter,Tommy	40	4.8	Morton,Charlie	48	5.9	Hudson,Tim	3.61	Morrow,Brandon	84	Tomlin,Josh	51
Hernandez,Liv	40	4.7	Billingsley,Cha	48	8.2	Gallardo,Yovani	3.61	Myers,Brett	83	Paulino,Felipe	51

PITCHER SKILLS RANKINGS - Relief Pitchers

Top Command (k/bb)

NAME	Cmd
Uehara,Koji	6.1
Mujica,Edward	5.6
Betancourt,Rafael	4.8
Lopez,Wilton	4.2
Romo,Sergio	4.1
Soria,Joakim	4.0
Street,Huston	3.8
Thatcher,Joe	3.8
Thornton,Matt	3.8
Soriano,Rafael	3.8
Benoit,Joaquin	3.7
Belisle,Matt	3.5
Oliver,Darren	3.5
Gregerson,Luke	3.5
Capps,Matt	3.4
Kuo,Hong-Chih	3.4
Peralta,Joel	3.4
Putz,J.J.	3.4
Madson,Ryan	3.3
Francisco,Frank	3.3
Papelbon,Jonathan	3.3
O'Day,Darren	3.3
Rivera,Mariano	3.3
Medlen,Kris	3.3
Maloney,Matt	3.2
Nathan,Joe	3.2
Bailey,Andrew	3.2
Saito,Takashi	3.1
Jenks,Bobby	3.1
Blevins,Jerry	3.1
Qualls,Chad	3.1

Top Control (bb/9)

NAME	Ctl
Uehara,Koji	1.4
Mujica,Edward	1.5
Belisle,Matt	1.8
Rivera,Mariano	1.9
Maloney,Matt	2.0
Germano,Justin	2.0
Herrmann,Frank	2.0
Capps,Matt	2.1
Betancourt,Rafael	2.2
O'Day,Darren	2.2
Lincoln,Brad	2.2
Martin,J.D.	2.2
Bonine,Eddie	2.3
Peralta,Joel	2.3
Litsch,Jesse	2.3
Oliver,Darren	2.3
Franklin,Ryan	2.3
Bell,Trevor	2.4
Qualls,Chad	2.5
Romo,Sergio	2.5
Soria,Joakim	2.5
Street,Huston	2.5
Soriano,Rafael	2.5
Medlen,Kris	2.5
Russell,James	2.5
Herrera,Daniel	2.5
Aceves,Alfredo	2.5
Hawkins,LaTroy	2.5
Karstens,Jeff	2.5
Mitre,Sergio	2.5
Sampson,Chris	2.5

Top Dominance (k/9)

NAME	Dom
Marmol,Carlos	13.5
Jansen,Kenley	11.7
Rodriguez,Henry	11.5
Robertson,David	11.4
Hanrahan,Joel	11.2
Braddock,Zach	11.1
Kimbrel,Craig	11.0
Thornton,Matt	11.0
Gonzalez,Mike	10.7
Chapman,Aroldis	10.6
Broxton,Jonathan	10.6
Ceda,Jose	10.6
Papelbon,Jonathan	10.5
Betancourt,Rafael	10.4
Putz,J.J.	10.4
Fujikawa,Kyuji	10.4
Axford,John	10.4
Kuo,Hong-Chih	10.3
Wilson,Brian	10.3
Dotel,Octavio	10.3
Thatcher,Joe	10.3
Romo,Sergio	10.2
Sipp,Tony	10.2
Benoit,Joaquin	10.2
Bard,Daniel	10.2
Bell,Heath	10.2
Wood,Kerry	10.1
Gregerson,Luke	10.1
Rodriguez,Francisco	10.1
Clippard,Tyler	10.1
Soria,Joakim	9.9

Top Ground Ball Rate

NAME	GB
Venters,Jonny	70
Moylan,Peter	65
Boyer,Blaine	61
Choate,Randy	61
League,Brandon	61
Webb,Ryan	61
Wright,Jamey	60
Lopez,Javier	60
Romero,J.C.	60
Walden,Jordan	60
Belisario,Ronald	60
Downs,Scott	59
Smith,Joe	59
Ziegler,Brad	59
Lopez,Wilton	58
Affeldt,Jeremy	58
Wang,Chien-Ming	57
Loe,Kameron	57
Herndon,David	57
Qualls,Chad	56
Meek,Evan	56
Jepsen,Kevin	56
Jenks,Bobby	56
Feliciano,Pedro	56
Baez,Danys	56
Badenhop,Burke	55
Troncoso,Ramon	55
Berg,Justin	55
Mitre,Sergio	54
Perez,Rafael	54
Runzler,Dan	53

Top Fly Ball Rate

NAME	FB
Frieri,Ernesto	62
Kelley,Shawn	57
Clippard,Tyler	56
Bastardo,Antonio	54
Ceda,Jose	54
Sipp,Tony	54
Uehara,Koji	54
Betancourt,Rafael	53
Tazawa,Junichi	53
Fuentes,Brian	53
Mijares,Jose	52
Hernandez,David	52
Purcey,David	52
Perez,Oliver	51
Tejeda,Robinson	51
Bowden,Michael	51
Sanches,Brian	51
Dotel,Octavio	51
Romo,Sergio	51
Soriano,Rafael	51
Marmol,Carlos	50
Braddock,Zach	50
Breslow,Craig	50
Marte,Damaso	50
Jansen,Kenley	50
Feliz,Neftali	50
Peralta,Joel	49
Balfour,Grant	49
Bautista,Denny	49
Wheeler,Dan	49
Benoit,Joaquin	49

High GB, Low Dom

NAME	GB	Dom
Boyer,Blaine	61	5.0
Wang,Chien-M	57	5.0
Herndon,David	57	4.7
Baez,Danys	56	5.5
Berg,Justin	55	4.1
Mitre,Sergio	54	5.1
Texeira,Kanek	53	5.3
Sampson,Chris	51	4.8
Smith,Jordan	51	4.6
Cormier,Lance	51	4.7
Pauley,David	51	5.2
Palmer,Matt	50	5.4
Laffey,Aaron	50	4.2
Thomas,Brad	50	4.3
Bonine,Eddie	48	3.6
Germano,Just	46	5.3
White,Sean	46	4.8
Harrison,Matt	46	5.1
Moseley,Dusti	45	5.2
Moehler,Brian	45	4.7

High GB, High Dom

NAME	GB	Dom
Venters,Jonny	70	8.7
Moylan,Peter	65	7.2
Choate,Randy	61	7.1
League,Brand	61	6.8
Webb,Ryan	61	6.7
Lopez,Javier	60	5.7
Romero,J.C.	60	7.1
Walden,Jorda	60	7.7
Belisario,Rona	60	6.5
Downs,Scott	59	7.4
Smith,Joe	59	7.4
Ziegler,Brad	59	5.9
Lopez,Wilton	58	5.7
Affeldt,Jeremy	58	7.9
Loe,Kameron	57	5.7
Qualls,Chad	56	7.5
Meek,Evan	56	7.6
Jepsen,Kevin	56	8.4
Jenks,Bobby	56	8.9
Feliciano,Pedr	56	8.1
Badenhop,Bur	55	6.3
Troncoso,Ram	55	5.9
Perez,Rafael	54	6.4
Runzler,Dan	53	9.7
O'Flaherty,Eric	53	6.9
Albers,Matt	53	5.9
Hensley,Clay	53	7.7
Camp,Shawn	53	6.5
Boggs,Mitchel	52	6.3
Reyes,Dennys	52	6.5
Demel,Sam	52	7.8

Lowest xERA

NAME	xERA
Kuo,Hong-Chih	2.40
Thornton,Matt	2.42
Bailey,Andrew	2.44
Bard,Daniel	2.47
Adams,Mike	2.55
Marmol,Carlos	2.64
Benoit,Joaquin	2.65
Soriano,Rafael	2.74
Balfour,Grant	2.74
Jansen,Kenley	2.77
Bell,Heath	2.80
Feliz,Neftali	2.81
Rodriguez,Francisco	2.84
Nathan,Joe	2.85
Putz,J.J.	2.87
Perez,Chris	2.89
Gregerson,Luke	2.89
Wilson,Brian	2.90
Papelbon,Jonathan	2.90
Thatcher,Joe	2.91
Frieri,Ernesto	2.92
Downs,Scott	2.94
Rivera,Mariano	2.96
Soria,Joakim	2.97
Ogando,Alexi	3.00
Braddock,Zach	3.02
Romo,Sergio	3.03
Venters,Jonny	3.04
Axford,John	3.05
Medlen,Kris	3.11
Frasor,Jason	3.12

Top BPV, 10+ Saves

NAME	BPV
Thornton,Matt	142
Soria,Joakim	135
Putz,J.J.	127
Kuo,Hong-Chih	122
Benoit,Joaquin	122
Uehara,Koji	121
Street,Huston	118
Papelbon,Jonathan	118
Bell,Heath	117
Jenks,Bobby	117
Broxton,Jonathan	117
Wilson,Brian	116
Nathan,Joe	114
Soriano,Rafael	111
Francisco,Frank	111
Hanrahan,Joel	109
Bailey,Andrew	108
Rodriguez,Francisco	97
Feliz,Neftali	96
Axford,John	96
Gonzalez,Mike	95
Capps,Matt	94
Venters,Jonny	93
Valverde,Jose	93
Marmol,Carlos	92
Nunez,Leo	91
Frasor,Jason	90
Motte,Jason	88
Jansen,Kenley	88
Perez,Chris	85
Rivera,Mariano	83

Top BPV, 9- Saves

NAME	BPV
Betancourt,Rafael	134
Thatcher,Joe	132
Gregerson,Luke	130
Romo,Sergio	130
Mujica,Edward	129
Madson,Ryan	115
Saito,Takashi	111
Oliver,Darren	110
Chamberlain,Joba	108
Chapman,Aroldis	104
Qualls,Chad	104
Farnsworth,Kyle	103
Marshall,Sean	103
Lopez,Wilton	102
Adams,Mike	101
Downs,Scott	100
Bard,Daniel	100
Medlen,Kris	99
Robertson,David	98
Bastardo,Antonio	96
Wuertz,Mike	95
Rodriguez,Henry	94
Parnell,Bobby	93
Sale,Chris	92
Burnett,Sean	91
Bray,Bill	91
Blevins,Jerry	91
Masset,Nick	89
Belisle,Matt	89
O'Day,Darren	88
Gervacio,Sammy	88

Rebounds and Improvements

BATTERS	Pos	+
Allen, Brandon	7	+5
Bautista, Jose	59	+5
Blanks, Kyle	7	+5
Bradley, Milton	70	+5
Castillo, Luis	4	+5
DeRosa, Mark	7	+5
Ellsbury, Jacoby	8	+5
Hill, Aaron	4	+5
Iannetta, Chris	2	+5
Lee, Carlos	37	+5
McLouth, Nate	8	+5
Pena, Carlos	3	+5
Reynolds, Mark	5	+5
Teixeira, Mark	3	+5
Arencibia, JP	2	+4
Berkman, Lance	30	+4
Encarnacion, Edwin	5	+4
Escobar, Alcides	6	+4
Jackson, Conor	7	+4
Lind, Adam	0	+4
Posada, Jorge	20	+4
Quentin, Carlos	90	+4
Ramirez, Aramis	5	+4
Reimold, Nolan	7	+4
Rodriguez, Alex	5	+4
Rollins, Jimmy	6	+4
Ryan, Brendan	6	+4
Smith, Seth	79	+4
Snider, Travis	79	+4
Valbuena, Luis	4	+4
Abreu, Bobby	79	+3
Ackley, Dustin	4	+3
Beltran, Carlos	8	+3
Escobar, Yunel	6	+3
Gordon, Alex	7	+3
Hawpe, Brad	9	+3
Izturis, Maicer	45	+3
Jeter, Derek	6	+3
Kouzmanoff, Kevin	5	+3
Lopez, Felipe	456	+3
Lopez, Jose	5	+3
Napoli, Mike	23	+3
Peralta, Jhonny	56	+3
Sandoval, Pablo	5	+3
Saunders, Michael	7	+3
Smoak, Justin	3	+3
Span, Denard	8	+3
Suzuki, Kurt	2	+3
Upton, B.J.	8	+3
Victorino, Shane	8	+3
Wigginton, Ty	345	+3

PITCHERS	+
Bannister, Brian	+5
Beckett, Josh	+5
Davis, Doug	+5
Duke, Zach	+5
Lohse, Kyle	+5
Marquis, Jason	+5
Morton, Charlie	+5
Parra, Manny	+5
Rogers, Esmil	+5
Shields, James	+5
Correia, Kevin	+4
Ely, John	+4
Rzepczynski, Marc	+4
Blackburn, Nick	+3
Blanton, Joe	+3
Bonderman, Jeremy	+3
de la Rosa, Jorge	+3
Francis, Jeff	+3
Hammel, Jason	+3
Harang, Aaron	+3
Masterson, Justin	+3
Rowland-Smith, Ryan	+3

Corrections/Declines

PITCHERS	-
Buchholz, Clay	-5
Hill, Shawn	-5
Stauffer, Tim	-5
Young, Chris	-5
Duensing, Brian	-4
Hellickson, Jeremy	-4
Johnson, Josh	-4
Price, David	-4
Sanabia, Alex	-4
Bumgarner, Madison	-3
Cahill, Trevor	-3
Cain, Matt	-3
Dickey, R.A.	-3
Figueroa, Nelson	-3
French, Luke	-3
Garcia, Jaime	-3
Hernandez, Felix	-3
Holland, Derek	-3
Iwakuma, Hisashi	-3
Luebke, Cory	-3
Mejia, Jenrry	-3
Palmer, Matt	-3
Sanchez, Jonathan	-3
Santana, Johan	-3
Tomlin, Josh	-3
Zambrano, Carlos	-3
Zimmermann, Jordan	-3

Corrections and Declines

BATTERS	Pos	-
Freese, David	5	-5
Gonzalez, Carlos	789	-5
Hamilton, Josh	78	-5
Infante, Omar	457	-5
Jackson, Austin	8	-5
Morneau, Justin	3	-5
Rasmus, Colby	8	-5
Buck, John	2	-4
Carroll, Jamey	46	-4
Johnson, Chris	5	-4
Morse, Mike	9	-4
Podsednik, Scott	7	-4
Ruiz, Carlos	2	-4
Venable, Will	789	-4
Aviles, Mike	4	-3
Brignac, Reid	46	-3
Butler, Billy	30	-3
Cameron, Mike	8	-3
DeJesus, David	9	-3
Ellis, Mark	4	-3
Hernandez, Ramon	2	-3
Konerko, Paul	30	-3
Manzella, Tommy	6	-3
Olivo, Miguel	2	-3
Pagan, Angel	789	-3
Swisher, Nick	9	-3
Uggla, Dan	4	-3
Votto, Joey	3	-3
Walker, Neil	4	-3
Zimmerman, Ryan	5	-3

Batters minimum 300 AB. PItchers minimuim 100 IP.

RISK MANAGEMENT

Pitchers	Pitchers
Aceves,Alfredo	Uehara,Koji
Adams,Mike	Vargas,Jason
Baez,Danys	Volquez,Edinson
Bedard,Erik	Wagner,Billy
Benoit,Joaquin	Walker,Tyler
Bonderman,Jeremy	Wang,Chien-Ming
Bray,Bill	Webb,Brandon
Capuano,Chris	Westbrook,Jake
Carpenter,Chris	Willis,Dontrelle
Ceda,Jose	Wood,Kerry
Chen,Bruce	Young,Chris
Davis,Doug	Zimmermann,Jordan
Duchscherer,Justin	Zumaya,Joel
Francis,Jeff	
Fuentes,Brian	
Gonzalez,Mike	
Harang,Aaron	**Batters**
Harden,Rich	Abreu,Tony
Harrison,Matt	Baker,John
Hawkins,LaTroy	Baldelli,Rocco
Hill,Shawn	Beltran,Carlos
Howell,J.P.	Bernadina,Roger
Hudson,Tim	Blanks,Kyle
Janssen,Casey	Bradley,Milton
Johnson,Josh	Chavez,Eric
Kelley,Shawn	Crisp,Coco
Kuo,Hong-Chih	DeRosa,Mark
Litsch,Jesse	Diaz,Matt
Lohse,Kyle	Dickerson,Chris
Lowe,Mark	Doumit,Ryan
Maine,John	Ellsbury,Jacoby
Marcum,Shaun	Fields,Josh
Marte,Damaso	Furcal,Rafael
Mathieson,Scott	Glaus,Troy
Matsuzaka,Daisuke	Gonzalez,Alex
Meche,Gil	Guillen,Carlos
Mitre,Sergio	Guzman,Cristian
Moehler,Brian	Izturis,Maicer
Moseley,Dustin	Jackson,Conor
Nathan,Joe	Johnson,Nick
Neshek,Pat	Johnson,Reed
Nippert,Dustin	Kinsler,Ian
Olsen,Scott	Kotsay,Mark
Padilla,Vicente	Lowrie,Jed
Paulino,Felipe	Morales,Kendry
Pavano,Carl	Morse,Mike
Peavy,Jake	Murphy,Daniel
Penny,Brad	Nady,Xavier
Perez,Oliver	Nelson,Chris
Putz,J.J.	Pagan,Angel
Ray,Chris	Pearce,Steve
Sanchez,Anibal	Sizemore,Grady
Sheets,Ben	Sweeney,Mike
Silva,Carlos	Treanor,Matt
Simon,Alfredo	Weeks,Rickie
Stauffer,Tim	Wilson,Jack
Tazawa,Junichi	Zaun,Gregg

CA	POS	Rel
McCann,Brian	2	AAA
Suzuki,Kurt	2	AAA
Molina,Bengie	2	ABB
Molina,Yadier	2	ABB
Pierzynski,A.J.	2	ABB
Kendall,Jason	2	BBA

1B/DH	POS	Rel
LaRoche,Adam	3	AAA
Loney,James	3	AAA
Dunn,Adam	3	AAB
Pujols,Albert	3	AAB
Teixeira,Mark	3	AAB
Butler,Billy	30	AAB
Cantu,Jorge	35	AAB
Cust,Jack	0	ABB
Howard,Ryan	3	BAB

2B	POS	Rel
Phillips,Brandon	4	AAA
Schumaker,Skip	4	AAB
Uggla,Dan	4	AAB
Theriot,Ryan	46	AAB
Barmes,Clint	46	ABB
Prado,Martin	45	BBA
Keppinger,Jeff	4	BBB

3B	POS	Rel
Headley,Chase	5	AAA
Kouzmanoff,Kevin	5	AAA
Longoria,Evan	5	AAA
Wright,David	5	AAA
Cantu,Jorge	35	AAB
Lopez,Jose	5	AAB
Peralta,Jhonny	56	AAB
Tejada,Miguel	56	AAB
Polanco,Placido	5	BAA
Zimmerman,Ryan	5	BAB
Inge,Brandon	5	BBA
Prado,Martin	45	BBA

SS	POS	Rel
Ramirez,Alexei	6	AAA
Theriot,Ryan	46	AAB
Peralta,Jhonny	56	AAB
Tejada,Miguel	56	AAB
Drew,Stephen	6	AAB
Ramirez,Hanley	6	AAB
Pennington,Cliff	6	ABA
Barmes,Clint	46	ABB
Andrus,Elvis	6	ABB
Betancourt,Yuniesk	6	ABB

OF	POS	Rel
Holliday,Matt	7	AAA
Abreu,Bobby	79	AAA
Victorino,Shane	8	AAA
Young,Chris	8	AAA
Werth,Jayson	89	AAA
Ethier,Andre	9	AAA
Braun,Ryan	7	AAB
Crawford,Carl	7	AAB
Damon,Johnny	70	AAB
Kemp,Matt	8	AAB
Span,Denard	8	AAB
Francoeur,Jeff	9	AAB
Hart,Corey	9	AAB
Markakis,Nick	9	AAB
Pence,Hunter	9	AAB
Suzuki,Ichiro	9	AAB
Ross,Cody	789	ABA
Young,Delmon	7	ABB
Winn,Randy	79	ABB
Byrd,Marlon	8	ABB
McCutchen,Andrew	8	ABB
Ibanez,Raul	7	BAB
Granderson,Curtis	8	BAB
Hunter,Torii	89	BAB
Murphy,David	79	BBA
Choo,Shin-Soo	9	BBA
Fukudome,Kosuke	9	BBA
Jones,Adam	8	BBB
Rowand,Aaron	8	BBB
Bruce,Jay	9	BBB
Upton,Justin	9	BBB

RP		Rel
Bell,Heath		AAA
Cordero,Francisco		AAA
Rivera,Mariano		AAA
Soria,Joakim		AAA
Wilson,Brian		AAA
Papelbon,Jonathan		AAB
Aardsma,David		ABA
Gaudin,Chad		ABA
Gregg,Kevin		ABA
Hendrickson,Mark		ABA
Lyon,Brandon		ABA
Franklin,Ryan		ABB
Sonnanstine,Andy		ABB
Takahashi,Hisanori		ABB
Rodriguez,Francisc		BAB
Valverde,Jose		BBA
Capps,Matt		BBB
Hoffman,Trevor		BBB
Jenks,Bobby		BBB

SP	Rel
Arroyo,Bronson	AAA
Billingsley,Chad	AAA
Blackburn,Nick	AAA
Blanton,Joe	AAA
Buehrle,Mark	AAA
Cain,Matt	AAA
Cueto,Johnny	AAA
Floyd,Gavin	AAA
Garland,Jon	AAA
Garza,Matt	AAA
Greinke,Zack	AAA
Halladay,Roy	AAA
Hamels,Cole	AAA
Haren,Dan	AAA
Hernandez,Felix	AAA
Hernandez,Livan	AAA
Jimenez,Ubaldo	AAA
Kershaw,Clayton	AAA
Lannan,John	AAA
Lewis,Colby	AAA
Lincecum,Tim	AAA
Maholm,Paul	AAA
Pelfrey,Mike	AAA
Richard,Clayton	AAA
Rodriguez,Wandy	AAA
Sabathia,CC	AAA
Sanchez,Jonathan	AAA
Saunders,Joe	AAA
Shields,James	AAA
Danks,John	AAB
Guthrie,Jeremy	AAB
Hammel,Jason	AAB
Jackson,Edwin	AAB
Lowe,Derek	AAB
Verlander,Justin	AAB
Weaver,Jered	AAB
Zito,Barry	AAB
Braden,Dallas	ABA
Correia,Kevin	ABA
Davies,Kyle	ABA
Galarraga,Armando	ABA
Gonzalez,Gio	ABA
Hanson,Tommy	ABA
Masterson,Justin	ABA
Volstad,Chris	ABA
Feldman,Scott	ABB
Kendrick,Kyle	ABB
Niemann,Jeff	ABB
Parra,Manny	ABB
Price,David	ABB
Baker,Scott	BAA
Bannister,Brian	BAA
Burnett,A.J.	BAA
Dempster,Ryan	BAA
Duke,Zach	BAA
Lee,Cliff	BAA
Lester,Jon	BAA
Lilly,Ted	BAA
Oswalt,Roy	BAA
Wainwright,Adam	BAA
Wolf,Randy	BAA
Zambrano,Carlos	BAA
Santana,Ervin	BAB
Bergesen,Brad	BBA
Buchholz,Clay	BBA
Carmona,Fausto	BBA

RISK MANAGEMENT

GRADE "A" in CONSISTENCY

Pitchers (min 120 IP)	Pitchers (min 120 IP)
Anderson,Brett	Nolasco,Ricky
Arroyo,Bronson	Ohlendorf,Ross
Bailey,Homer	Oswalt,Roy
Baker,Scott	Padilla,Vicente
Bannister,Brian	Paulino,Felipe
Beckett,Josh	Peavy,Jake
Bergesen,Brad	Pelfrey,Mike
Billingsley,Chad	Porcello,Rick
Blackburn,Nick	Richard,Clayton
Blanton,Joe	Rodriguez,Wandy
Braden,Dallas	Rzepczynski,Marc
Buchholz,Clay	Sabathia,CC
Buehrle,Mark	Sanchez,Jonathan
Bumgarner,Madison	Santana,Johan
Burnett,A.J.	Saunders,Joe
Bush,David	Scherzer,Max
Cain,Matt	Shields,James
Carmona,Fausto	Slowey,Kevin
Chen,Bruce	Tillman,Chris
Coke,Phil	Vargas,Jason
Cook,Aaron	Volstad,Chris
Correia,Kevin	Wainwright,Adam
Cueto,Johnny	Westbrook,Jake
Davies,Kyle	Wolf,Randy
Davis,Doug	Zambrano,Carlos
Davis,Wade	Zimmermann,Jordan
de la Rosa,Jorge	**Batters (min 400 AB)**
Dempster,Ryan	Abreu,Bobby
Duke,Zach	Brantley,Michael
Floyd,Gavin	Choo,Shin-Soo
Gallardo,Yovani	Crisp,Coco
Garcia,Freddy	Davis,Ike
Garland,Jon	Escobar,Alcides
Garza,Matt	Ethier,Andre
Gonzalez,Gio	Fowler,Dexter
Greinke,Zack	Gordon,Alex
Halladay,Roy	Headley,Chase
Hamels,Cole	Holliday,Matt
Hanson,Tommy	Infante,Omar
Happ,J.A.	Inge,Brandon
Harang,Aaron	Jackson,Austin
Haren,Dan	Kinsler,Ian
Hernandez,Felix	Kouzmanoff,Kevin
Hernandez,Livan	LaRoche,Adam
Hochevar,Luke	Loney,James
Hudson,Tim	Longoria,Evan
Hunter,Tommy	McCann,Brian
Jimenez,Ubaldo	Morrison,Logan
Johnson,Josh	Murphy,David
Jurrjens,Jair	Pedroia,Dustin
Kawakami,Kenshin	Pennington,Cliff
Kershaw,Clayton	Phillips,Brandon
Kuroda,Hiroki	Polanco,Placido
Lackey,John	Prado,Martin
Lannan,John	Ramirez,Alexei
Lee,Cliff	Rolen,Scott
Lester,Jon	Ross,Cody
Lewis,Colby	Sanchez,Freddy
Lilly,Ted	Santana,Carlos
Lincecum,Tim	Stewart,Ian
Maholm,Paul	Suzuki,Kurt
Marcum,Shaun	Tabata,Jose
Marquis,Jason	Thole,Josh
Masterson,Justin	Utley,Chase
Matusz,Brian	Victorino,Shane
McDonald,James	Werth,Jayson
Millwood,Kevin	Willingham,Josh
Morton,Charlie	Wright,David
Myers,Brett	Youkilis,Kevin
Niese,Jonathon	Young,Chris

TOP COMBINATION OF SKILLS AND RELIABILITY
Maximum of one "C" in Reliability Grade

BATTING POWER

PX over 120	PX	Rel
Dunn,Adam	204	AAB
Thome,Jim	190	ABC
Cruz,Nelson	180	CBB
Pena,Carlos	172	BAC
Howard,Ryan	172	BAB
Votto,Joey	171	AAC
Cabrera,Miguel	168	AAC
Pujols,Albert	166	AAB
Ortiz,David	166	BAC
Werth,Jayson	165	AAA
Youkilis,Kevin	162	CBA
Longoria,Evan	162	AAA
LaRoche,Adam	157	AAA
Teixeira,Mark	155	AAB
Hart,Corey	155	AAB
Scott,Luke	155	BBB
Uggla,Dan	154	AAB
Swisher,Nick	153	AAC
Hawpe,Brad	153	BBC
Bruce,Jay	152	BBB
Young,Chris	152	AAA
Cust,Jack	151	ABB
Rodriguez,Alex	149	CAB
Stewart,Ian	148	ACA
Upton,Justin	148	BBB
Konerko,Paul	148	AAC
Wright,David	148	AAA
Gonzalez,Adrian	144	AAC
Holliday,Matt	141	AAA
Ethier,Andre	138	AAA
Braun,Ryan	137	AAB
Drew,J.D.	136	ABC
Kemp,Matt	136	AAB
Upton,B.J.	135	AAC
Olivo,Miguel	134	ACB
Zimmerman,Ryan	134	BAB
Granderson,Curtis	133	BAB
Overbay,Lyle	133	AAC
Berkman,Lance	132	BAC
Ramirez,Aramis	132	BBC
Ibanez,Raul	129	BAB
Ramirez,Manny	129	CBB
Choo,Shin-Soo	128	BBA
McCann,Brian	127	AAA
Francisco,Ben	125	ACA
Utley,Chase	124	CAA
Wells,Vernon	123	BAC
Young,Delmon	122	ABB
Stubbs,Drew	122	ACB
Pence,Hunter	121	AAB
Abreu,Bobby	121	AAA

RUNNER SPEED

Spd over 100	SX	Rel
Bourn,Michael	171	AAC
Jackson,Austin	160	ACA
Fowler,Dexter	152	ACA
Maybin,Cameron	152	ACB
Gardner,Brett	151	BCB
Suzuki,Ichiro	148	AAB
Drew,Stephen	148	AAB
Aybar,Erick	146	BBC
McCutchen,Andrew	146	ABB
Granderson,Curtis	146	BAB
Bonifacio,Emilio	144	ACA
Stubbs,Drew	142	ACB
Venable,Will	141	ACA
Crawford,Carl	138	AAB
Escobar,Alcides	138	ACA
Victorino,Shane	136	AAA
Theriot,Ryan	132	AAB
Lewis,Fred	132	ACA
Andrus,Elvis	128	ABB
Pierre,Juan	126	ABC
Carroll,Jamey	124	BCA
Span,Denard	124	AAB
Pennington,Cliff	122	ABA
Upton,Justin	121	BBB
Maier,Mitch	119	ACA
Upton,B.J.	118	AAC
DeJesus,David	118	CBB
Damon,Johnny	117	AAB
Pence,Hunter	116	AAB
Hudson,Orlando	111	CBB
Ramirez,Alexei	110	AAA
Harris,Willie	110	ACB
Hart,Corey	109	AAB
Jones,Adam	107	BBB
Phillips,Brandon	105	AAA
Rollins,Jimmy	105	CAB
Ramirez,Hanley	104	AAB
Markakis,Nick	104	AAB
Brantley,Michael	104	ACA
Inge,Brandon	104	BBA
Gutierrez,Franklin	104	AAC
Callaspo,Alberto	102	BBC
Werth,Jayson	101	AAA
Barton,Daric	101	BBB
Utley,Chase	100	CAA

OVERALL PITCHING SKILL

BPV over 75	BPV	Rel
Thornton,Matt	142	ACA
Soria,Joakim	135	AAA
Halladay,Roy	132	AAA
Gregerson,Luke	130	ACB
Mujica,Edward	129	ACB
Lincecum,Tim	122	AAA
Haren,Dan	118	AAA
Papelbon,Jonathan	118	AAB
Bell,Heath	117	AAA
Jenks,Bobby	117	BBB
Broxton,Jonathan	117	ABC
Wilson,Brian	116	AAA
Nolasco,Ricky	115	CAA
Hamels,Cole	112	AAA
Lester,Jon	111	BAA
Oliver,Darren	110	ACB
Hanrahan,Joel	109	ACB
Chamberlain,Joba	108	ABC
Lee,Cliff	107	BAA
Hernandez,Felix	106	AAA
Wainwright,Adam	105	BAA
Qualls,Chad	104	BCB
Greinke,Zack	103	AAA
Marshall,Sean	103	ACB
Latos,Mat	102	ACB
Oswalt,Roy	101	BAA
Shields,James	100	AAA
Downs,Scott	100	BCA
Lewis,Colby	99	AAA
Medlen,Kris	99	BCB
Verlander,Justin	98	AAB
Rodriguez,Wandy	97	AAA
Rodriguez,Francisco	97	BAB
Weaver,Jered	96	AAB
Kuroda,Hiroki	96	CAA
Scherzer,Max	94	ACA
Capps,Matt	94	BBB
Valverde,Jose	93	BBA
Hanson,Tommy	93	ABA
Nunez,Leo	91	CBB
Lilly,Ted	91	BAA
Frasor,Jason	90	ACB
Masset,Nick	89	ACB
Sabathia,CC	89	AAA
Feliciano,Pedro	86	ACB
Kershaw,Clayton	85	AAA
Perez,Chris	85	ACA
Baker,Scott	84	BAA
Villanueva,Carlos	83	ACB
Billingsley,Chad	83	AAA
Rivera,Mariano	83	AAA
Wheeler,Dan	82	ACA
Carrasco,Carlos	82	ACB
League,Brandon	82	BCA
Cain,Matt	82	AAA
Vazquez,Javier	81	AAC
Dempster,Ryan	79	BAA
Takahashi,Hisanori	79	ABB
Lowe,Derek	77	AAB
Lackey,John	77	CAA
Fujikawa,Kyuji	76	ABC
Park,Chan Ho	76	BCA
Cueto,Johnny	75	AAA
Santana,Johan	75	CAA
Jimenez,Ubaldo	75	AAA
Floyd,Gavin	75	AAA

POSITION SCARCITY CHART

FIRST BASE	SECOND BASE	THIRD BASE	SHORTSTOP	CATCHERS	OUTFIELDERS	STARTERS	RELIEVERS
Pujols,Albert	Utley,Chase	Wright,David	Ramirez,Hanley	Mauer,Joe	Gonzalez,Carlos	Halladay,Roy	Bell,Heath
Cabrera,Miguel	Cano,Robinson	Longoria,Evan	Tulowitzki,Troy	Martinez,Victor	Crawford,Carl	Hernandez,Felix	Wilson,Brian
Votto,Joey	Pedroia,Dustin	Zimmerman,Ryan	Reyes,Jose	Posey,Buster	Braun,Ryan	Lester,Jon	Soriano,Rafael
Teixeira,Mark	Uggla,Dan	Rodriguez,Alex	Rollins,Jimmy	McCann,Brian	Holliday,Matt	Sabathia,CC	Papelbon,Jonathan
Fielder,Prince	Kinsler,Ian	Bautista,Jose	Ramirez,Alexei	Suzuki,Kurt	Werth,Jayson	Lincecum,Tim	Rodriguez,Francisco
Youkilis,Kevin	Phillips,Brandon	Young,Michael	Jeter,Derek	Santana,Carlos	Ellsbury,Jacoby	Verlander,Justin	Soria,Joakim
Gonzalez,Adrian	Johnson,Kelly	Ramirez,Aramis	Furcal,Rafael	Soto,Geovany	Cruz,Nelson	Wainwright,Adam	Feliz,Neftali
Howard,Ryan	Weeks,Rickie	McGehee,Casey	Bartlett,Jason	Napoli,Mike	Hamilton,Josh	Lee,Cliff	Axford,John
Morneau,Justin	Prado,Martin	Alvarez,Pedro	Andrus,Elvis	Montero,Miguel	Kemp,Matt	Weaver,Jered	Bailey,Andrew
Dunn,Adam	Zobrist,Ben	Beltre,Adrian	Drew,Stephen	Ruiz,Carlos	Choo,Shin-Soo	Haren,Dan	Perez,Chris
Konerko,Paul	Kendrick,Howie	Stewart,Ian	Castro,Starlin	Wieters,Matt	McCutchen,Andre	Oswalt,Roy	Aardsma,David
Morales,Kendry	Hill,Aaron	Reynolds,Mark	Desmond,Ian	Olivo,Miguel	Victorino,Shane	Cain,Matt	Marmol,Carlos
Huff,Aubrey	Walker,Neil	Headley,Chase	Peralta,Jhonny	Molina,Yadier	Pence,Hunter	Scherzer,Max	Hanrahan,Joel
Butler,Billy	Figgins,Chone	Sandoval,Pablo	Aybar,Erick	Posada,Jorge	Heyward,Jason	Greinke,Zack	Street,Huston
Lee,Derek	Infante,Omar	Polanco,Placido	Cabrera,Asdrubal	Buck,John	Ethier,Andre	Latos,Mat	Broxton,Jonathan
Lee,Carlos	Roberts,Brian	Encarnacion,Edwin	Theriot,Ryan	Doumit,Ryan	Rios,Alex	Price,David	Valverde,Jose
LaRoche,Adam	Rodriguez,Sean	Johnson,Chris	Pennington,Cliff	Martin,Russell	Suzuki,Ichiro	Hamels,Cole	Rivera,Mariano
Cuddyer,Michael	Beckham,Gordon	Rolen,Scott	Tejada,Miguel	Pierzynski,A.J.	Young,Delmon	Kershaw,Clayton	Jenks,Bobby
Sanchez,Gaby	Hudson,Orlando	Kouzmanoff,Kevin	Casilla,Alexi	Iannetta,Chris	Young,Chris	Jimenez,Ubaldo	Storen,Drew
Loney,James	Uribe,Juan	Lopez,Jose	Escobar,Yunel	Jaso,John	Hart,Corey	Hanson,Tommy	Capps,Matt
Davis,Ike	Espinosa,Danny	Cantu,Jorge	Scutaro,Marco	Hanigan,Ryan	Upton,Justin	Billingsley,Chad	Cordero,Francisco
Berkman,Lance	Aviles,Mike	Callaspo,Alberto	Hardy,J.J.	Snyder,Chris	Pierre,Juan	Johnson,Josh	Putz,J.J.
Pena,Carlos	Ellis,Mark	Blake,Casey	Escobar,Alcides	Thole,Josh	Bourn,Michael	Liriano,Francisco	Thornton,Matt
Jones,Garrett	Sanchez,Freddy	Freese,David	Lowrie,Jed	Pena,Brayan	Davis,Rajai	Lewis,Colby	Lyon,Brandon
Barton,Daric	Keppinger,Jeff	Jones,Chipper	Betancourt,Yuniesk	Avila,Alex	Upton,B.J.	Carpenter,Chris	Benoit,Joaquin
Freeman,Freddie	Izturis,Maicer	Inge,Brandon	Gonzalez,Alex	Torrealba,Yorvit	Hunter,Torii	Morrow,Brandon	Nathan,Joe
Smoak,Justin	Young Jr.,Eric	Viciedo,Dayan	Cabrera,Orlando	Hernandez,Ramo	Bruce,Jay	Anderson,Brett	Kimbrel,Craig
Overbay,Lyle	Hall,Bill	Francisco,Juan	Cedeno,Ronny	Barajas,Rod	Stubbs,Drew	Hudson,Dan	Kuo,Hong-Chih
Ka'aihue,Kila	Wigginton,Ty	Valencia,Danny	Brignac,Reid	Hundley,Nick	Wells,Vernon	Beckett,Josh	Lidge,Brad
Branyan,Russell	Schumaker,Skip	Mora,Melvin	Hairston,Jerry	Molina,Bengie	Stanton,Mike	Shields,James	Gregg,Kevin
LaPorta,Matt	Kennedy,Adam	Betemit,Wilson	Ryan,Brendan	Lucroy,Jonathan	Jackson,Austin	Rodriguez,Wandy	Nunez,Leo
Helton,Todd	Sizemore,Scott	Teahen,Mark	Cabrera,Everth	Arencibia,JP	Markakis,Nick	Marcum,Shaun	Venters,Jonny
Nady,Xavier	Carroll,Jamey	Bell,Josh	Donald,Jason	Varitek,Jason	Granderson,Curtis	Gallardo,Yovani	Uehara,Koji
Moreland,Mitch	Lopez,Felipe	Tracy,Chad	Renteria,Edgar	Rodriguez,Ivan	Pagan,Angel	Danks,John	Wheeler,Dan
Glaus,Troy	Castillo,Luis	Gamel,Mat	Izturis,Cesar	Saltalamacchia,Ja	Ibanez,Raul	Buchholz,Clay	Motte,Jason
Wallace,Brett	Rhymes,Will	Tejada,Ruben	Guzman,Cristian	Castro,Ramon	Fowler,Dexter	Cahill,Trevor	Frasor,Jason
Hinske,Eric	Nix,Jayson	Conrad,Brooks	Santiago,Ramon	Ross,David	Swisher,Nick	Slowey,Kevin	Franklin,Ryan
Murphy,Daniel	DeWitt,Blake	Fields,Josh	Manzella,Tommy	Moore,Adam	Jones,Adam	Kuroda,Hiroki	Fuentes,Brian
Davis,Chris	Guillen,Carlos	Cairo,Miguel	Janish,Paul	Schneider,Brian	Jennings,Desmon	Hughes,Phil	Meek,Evan
Kelly,Don	Getz,Chris	Vizquel,Omar	Wilson,Jack	Paulino,Ronny	Rasmus,Colby	Garza,Matt	League,Brandon
Kotchman,Casey	Rosales,Adam	LaRoche,Andy	Blum,Geoff	Shoppach,Kelly	Tabata,Jose	Lackey,John	Chapman,Aroldis
Clement,Jeff	Valbuena,Luis	Abreu,Tony	Sanchez,Angel	Castro,Jason	Gardner,Brett	Hudson,Tim	Jansen,Kenley
Kotsay,Mark	Baker,Jeff	Helms,Wes	Punto,Nick	Ramirez,Max	Quentin,Carlos	Wilson,C.J.	Bard,Daniel
Ishikawa,Travis	Barmes,Clint	Feliz,Pedro	Worth,Danny	Ramos,Wilson	Span,Denard	Hellickson,Jeremy	Gregerson,Luke
Giambi,Jason	Eckstein,David	Harris,Brendan	Valdez,Wilson	Marson,Lou	Soriano,Alfonso	Myers,Brett	Clippard,Tyler

PORTFOLIO3 PLAN

TIER 1
High Skill, Low Risk

BATTERS	Age	Bats	Pos	REL	Ct%	PX	Spd	R$
			Filters:	BBB	80	100	100	
Pujols, Albert	31	R	3	AAB	88	166	59	$37
Crawford, Carl	29	L	7	AAB	83	98	138	$33
Braun, Ryan	27	R	7	AAB	81	137	99	$32
Holliday, Matt	31	R	7	AAA	83	141	79	$32
Ramirez, Hanley	27	R	6	AAB	82	117	104	$32
Teixeira, Mark	30	B	3	AAB	80	155	64	$27
Zimmerman, Ryan	26	R	5	BAB	82	134	78	$27
McCutchen, Andrew	24	R	8	ABB	85	105	146	$26
Victorino, Shane	30	B	8	AAA	87	98	136	$25
Pence, Hunter	27	R	9	AAB	82	121	116	$25
Ethier, Andre	28	L	9	AAA	81	138	85	$24
Suzuki, Ichiro	37	L	9	AAB	88	55	148	$24
Young, Delmon	25	R	7	ABB	82	122	84	$24
Ramirez, Alexei	29	R	6	AAA	87	90	110	$22
Phillips, Brandon	29	R	4	AAA	86	96	105	$22
Hunter, Torii	35	R	89	BAB	81	113	70	$22
Prado, Martin	27	R	45	BBA	86	106	98	$21
Butler, Billy	24	R	30	AAB	86	107	54	$20
Markakis, Nick	27	L	9	AAB	84	103	104	$20
Span, Denard	27	L	8	AAB	86	60	124	$19
Andrus, Elvis	22	R	6	ABB	84	41	128	$19
Damon, Johnny	37	L	70	AAB	83	101	117	$18
McCann, Brian	27	L	2	AAA	82	127	47	$18
Byrd, Marlon	33	R	8	ABB	82	101	61	$18
Drew, Stephen	28	L	6	AAB	82	115	148	$17
Murphy, David	29	L	79	BBA	82	110	91	$17
Barton, Daric	25	L	3	BBB	83	102	101	$15
Theriot, Ryan	31	R	46	AAB	87	39	132	$14
Pennington, Cliff	26	B	6	ABA	84	66	122	$14
Kouzmanoff, Kevin	29	R	5	AAA	81	113	62	$14

TIER 2
High Skill, Mod Risk

BATTERS	Age	Bats	Pos	REL	Ct%	PX	Spd	R$
			Filters:	BBB	80	100	100	<$20
*Granderson, Curtis	30	L	8	BAB	76	133	146	$20
*LaRoche, Adam	31	L	3	AAA	72	157	65	$20
*Ibanez, Raul	38	L	7	BAB	80	129	82	$20
*Jones, Adam	25	R	8	BBB	79	109	107	$20
Abreu, Bobby	37	L	79	AAA	78	121	76	$19
Headley, Chase	26	B	5	AAA	75	102	87	$17
Loney, James	26	L	3	AAA	85	87	68	$17
Scott, Luke	32	L	0	BBB	78	155	62	$16
Polanco, Placido	35	R	5	BAA	92	62	99	$16
Suzuki, Kurt	27	R	2	AAA	89	84	77	$16
Peralta, Jhonny	28	R	56	AAB	80	110	78	$15
Tejada, Miguel	36	R	56	AAB	90	76	52	$14
Fukudome, Kosuke	33	L	9	BBA	80	117	94	$14
Ross, Cody	30	R	789	ABA	77	113	81	$13
Lopez, Jose	27	R	5	AAB	89	82	65	$13
Cust, Jack	32	L	0	ABB	64	151	46	$13
Cantu, Jorge	29	R	35	AAB	82	94	68	$12
Betancourt, Yuniesky	29	R	6	ABB	90	79	82	$12
Molina, Yadier	28	R	2	ABB	91	55	41	$12
Keppinger, Jeff	30	R	4	BBB	93	69	89	$11
Inge, Brandon	33	R	5	BBA	72	108	104	$10
Pierzynski, A.J.	34	L	2	ABB	90	74	49	$10
Schumaker, Skip	31	L	4	AAB	87	55	82	$10
Cabrera, Orlando	36	R	6	BAA	90	69	85	$10
Francoeur, Jeff	27	R	9	AAB	83	89	90	$8
Molina, Bengie	36	R	2	ABB	90	75	42	$8
Barmes, Clint	32	R	46	ABB	82	87	76	$6
Rowand, Aaron	33	R	8	BBB	77	100	81	$6
Kotchman, Casey	28	L	3	BBB	88	80	72	$5
Winn, Randy	36	B	79	ABB	84	75	99	$3
Kendall, Jason	36	R	2	BBA	89	35	80	$2

TIER 1
High Skill, Low Risk

PITCHERS	Age	Thrw	REL	BPV	R$
		Filters:	BBB	75	
Halladay, Roy	33	R	AAA	132	$31
Hernandez, Felix	24	R	AAA	106	$31
Lester, Jon	27	L	BAA	111	$28
Sabathia, CC	30	L	AAA	89	$27
Lincecum, Tim	26	R	AAA	122	$27
Verlander, Justin	28	R	AAB	98	$27
Wainwright, Adam	29	R	BAA	105	$26
Lee, Cliff	32	L	BAA	107	$26
Weaver, Jered	28	R	AAB	96	$25
Bell, Heath	33	R	AAA	117	$24
Haren, Dan	30	R	AAA	118	$24
Oswalt, Roy	33	R	BAA	101	$24
Cain, Matt	26	R	AAA	82	$24
Greinke, Zack	27	R	AAA	103	$23
Hamels, Cole	27	L	AAA	112	$23
Kershaw, Clayton	23	L	AAA	85	$22
Wilson, Brian	29	R	AAA	116	$22
Papelbon, Jonathan	30	R	AAB	118	$22
Rodriguez, Francisco	29	R	BAB	97	$21
Hanson, Tommy	24	R	ABA	93	$21
Soria, Joakim	26	R	AAA	135	$21
Billingsley, Chad	26	R	AAA	83	$21
Lewis, Colby	31	R	AAA	99	$20
Shields, James	29	R	AAA	100	$19
Rodriguez, Wandy	32	L	AAA	97	$19
Valverde, Jose	33	R	BBA	93	$17
Lilly, Ted	35	L	BAA	91	$17
Baker, Scott	29	R	BAA	84	$17
Cueto, Johnny	25	R	AAA	75	$16
Rivera, Mariano	41	R	AAA	83	$16
Jenks, Bobby	30	R	BBB	117	$16
Capps, Matt	27	R	BBB	94	$16
Dempster, Ryan	33	R	BAA	79	$16
Lowe, Derek	37	R	AAB	77	$15
Takahashi, Hisanori	35	L	ABB	79	$8

TIER 2
High Skill, Mod Risk

PITCHERS	Age	Thrw	REL	BPV	R$
		Filters:	BBB	50	<$20
*Price, David	25	L	ABB	67	$23
*Jimenez, Ubaldo	27	R	AAA	75	$21
Danks, John	25	L	AAB	66	$19
Buchholz, Clay	26	R	BBA	59	$19
Garza, Matt	27	R	AAA	58	$18
Gonzalez, Gio	25	L	ABA	63	$17
Arroyo, Bronson	34	R	AAA	55	$17
Niemann, Jeff	28	R	ABB	68	$17
Floyd, Gavin	28	R	AAA	75	$17
Santana, Ervin	28	R	BAB	64	$16
Gregg, Kevin	32	R	ABA	58	$15
Sanchez, Jonathan	28	L	AAA	68	$15
Braden, Dallas	27	L	ABA	52	$14
Franklin, Ryan	38	R	ABB	66	$13
Jackson, Edwin	27	R	AAB	60	$12
Burnett, A.J.	34	R	BAA	56	$11
Blanton, Joe	30	R	AAA	74	$11
Masterson, Justin	26	R	ABA	65	$10
Hammel, Jason	28	R	AAB	73	$9
Correia, Kevin	30	R	ABA	53	$8
Parra, Manny	28	L	ABB	57	$4
Hendrickson, Mark	36	L	ABA	57	$3
Gaudin, Chad	28	R	ABA	52	$3

* Tier 2 players should be less than $20 If you are going to spend more
  than $20 here, be aware of the added risk.

PORTFOLIO3 PLAN

TIER 3

High Skill, High Risk		Filters:		n/a	80	100	100	<$10
BATTERS	Age	Bats	Pos	REL	Ct%	PX	Spd	R$
Beltre,Adrian	31	R	5	CAF	85	123	53	$19
Bartlett,Jason	31	R	6	BBF	83	76	116	$19
Tabata,Jose	22	R	7	ADA	88	63	134	$19
Martinez,Victor	32	B	2	CBC	88	108	68	$19
Quentin,Carlos	28	R	90	CBD	83	142	61	$19
Cuddyer,Michael	32	R	39	CBC	83	108	95	$18
Posey,Buster	24	R	23	AFB	85	116	89	$18
Hill,Aaron	29	R	4	CBD	85	114	69	$18
Beltran,Carlos	33	B	8	FCC	83	130	88	$18
Walker,Neil	25	B	4	ADC	83	115	86	$17
Crisp,Coco	31	B	8	FDA	85	93	122	$17
Figgins,Chone	33	B	4	BAD	82	47	118	$17
Infante,Omar	29	R	457	DCA	86	63	125	$17
Morgan,Nyjer	30	L	8	BBD	83	44	146	$17
Sandoval,Pablo	24	B	5	ABD	86	112	61	$16
Podsednik,Scott	35	L	7	CCB	85	60	146	$16
Beckham,Gordon	24	R	4	ADD	81	121	84	$16
Bourjos,Peter	24	R	8	AFC	84	88	173	$16
Morrison,Logan	23	L	7	AFA	84	106	96	$16
Encarnacion,Edwin	28	R	5	DCB	81	130	56	$16
McLouth,Nate	29	L	8	CBD	80	104	93	$16
Castro,Starlin	21	R	6	AFB	88	75	131	$16
Borbon,Julio	25	L	8	ADB	88	42	144	$15
Santana,Carlos	24	B	2	AFA	82	116	71	$15
Freeman,Freddie	21	L	3	AFD	85	101	74	$14
Cabrera,Asdrubal	25	B	6	CBC	83	70	101	$14
Smith,Seth	28	L	79	ACD	82	133	93	$14
Pie,Felix	26	L	7	CDC	81	97	134	$14
Casilla,Alexi	26	B	46	CDC	87	54	129	$14
Hardy,J.J.	28	R	6	CBD	83	94	111	$13
Coghlan,Chris	25	L	7	CCD	81	78	110	$13
Lowrie,Jed	26	B	46	FFF	80	131	81	$13
Ruiz,Carlos	32	R	2	BCC	87	102	63	$12
Wieters,Matt	24	B	2	ADD	80	100	70	$12
Reimold,Nolan	27	R	7	ACF	82	108	94	$12
Gonzalez,Alex	34	R	6	FDC	81	112	60	$11
Aviles,Mike	30	R	4	DDF	86	66	112	$11
Kalish,Ryan	23	L	8	AFA	82	101	98	$11
Ka'aihue,Kila	27	L	3	ADF	83	115	65	$11
Izturis,Maicer	30	B	45	FDC	88	73	102	$11
Jones,Chipper	38	B	5	DBC	85	123	86	$10
Young Jr.,Eric	25	B	4	CDB	84	52	152	$10
Viciedo,Dayan	22	R	5	ADC	82	126	69	$10
LaPorta,Matt	26	R	3	ADB	81	109	70	$10
Crowe,Trevor	27	B	78	ADC	83	64	101	$10
Jay,Jon	26	L	89	ADD	87	69	105	$9
Moreland,Mitch	25	L	3	AFA	84	115	68	$9
Jaso,John	27	L	2	ADD	88	66	101.7	$9
Castillo,Luis	35	B	4	CCC	89	28	118.1	$9
Ryan,Brendan	29	R	6	ACD	86	50	124	$8
Rhymes,Will	28	L	4	ADB	89	59	125.7	$8
Renteria,Edgar	35	R	6	CCB	84	69	102.9	$8
Blanco,Gregor	27	L	8	ADF	80	46	123.8	$7
Murphy,Daniel	26	L	37	FDB	87	103	74	$7
Duda,Lucas	25	L	7	AFB	82	132	64	$7
Parra,Gerardo	23	L	79	ADB	82	76	101	$7
Bloomquist,Willie	33	R	9	BDA	84	57	116	$7
Gwynn,Tony	28	L	8	ADD	83	44	121	$6
Kelly,Don	31	L	37	ADB	85	74	102	$6
Arencibia,JP	25	R	2	AFC	83	132	64	$6
Tracy,Chad	30	L	5	CFA	83	100	62	$6
Izturis,Cesar	31	B	6	CCB	90	33	118	$6
Guzman,Cristian	33	B	46	FBB	84	59	121	$6
Schierholtz,Nate	27	L	9	ADB	82	99	100	$6
Cain,Lorenzo	24	R	8	AFF	80	56	135	$5
Santiago,Ramon	31	B	46	ADC	82	61	132	$5
Ackley,Dustin	23	L	4	AFF	87	74	118	$5
Denorfia,Chris	30	R	78	DDD	85	84	107	$5
Velez,Eugenio	28	B	7	ADB	85	81	136	$5

High Skill, High Risk		Filters:		n/a	75	<$10
PITCHERS	Age	Thrw	REL	BPV	R$	
Marcum,Shaun	29	R	FBA	87	$19	
Gallardo,Yovani	25	R	DBA	102	$19	
Slowey,Kevin	26	R	DBA	92	$18	
Hughes,Phil	24	R	DCB	75	$18	
Marmol,Carlos	28	R	ABD	92	$18	
Street,Huston	27	R	DBB	118	$18	
Hellickson,Jeremy	23	R	ADF	101	$17	
Myers,Brett	30	R	DAA	83	$17	
Putz,J.J.	34	R	FDD	127	$16	
Storen,Drew	23	R	AFF	81	$16	
Minor,Mike	23	L	ADF	101	$16	
Benoit,Joaquin	33	R	FDF	122	$15	
Nathan,Joe	36	R	FBA	114	$15	
Kuo,Hong-Chih	29	L	FCB	122	$15	
Peavy,Jake	29	R	FBA	91	$14	
Venters,Jonny	26	L	ADF	93	$14	
Uehara,Koji	35	R	FCC	121	$14	
Motte,Jason	28	R	ADB	88	$13	
de la Rosa,Jorge	29	L	DBA	76	$13	
Niese,Jonathon	24	L	CCA	78	$13	
Chapman,Aroldis	23	L	ACF	104	$12	
Jansen,Kenley	23	R	AFF	88	$12	
Bard,Daniel	25	R	ADA	100	$12	
Clippard,Tyler	26	R	ADA	77	$11	
Francisco,Frank	31	R	DCA	111	$11	
Zimmermann,Jordan	24	R	FDA	83	$11	
Capuano,Chris	32	L	FFF	77	$11	
Adams,Mike	32	R	FDB	101	$10	
Romo,Sergio	28	R	BDA	130	$10	
Harang,Aaron	32	R	FAA	87	$10	
Madson,Ryan	30	R	DCA	115	$10	
Balfour,Grant	33	R	CDB	87	$9	
Gonzalez,Mike	32	L	FDA	95	$9	
Betancourt,Rafael	35	R	CCB	134	$9	
Santos,Sergio	27	R	AFF	81	$8	
Wuertz,Mike	32	R	BDC	95	$8	
Burnett,Sean	28	L	ADB	91	$8	
Robertson,David	25	R	ADA	98	$8	
Parnell,Bobby	26	R	ADC	93	$8	
Demel,Sam	25	R	AFA	82	$8	
O'Day,Darren	28	R	ADA	88	$7	
Ogando,Alexi	27	R	AFF	86	$7	
Thatcher,Joe	29	L	AFC	132	$7	
Saito,Takashi	41	R	BCD	111	$7	
Lopez,Wilton	27	R	ADC	102	$7	
Rodriguez,Henry	24	R	AFD	94	$6	
Belisle,Matt	30	R	BDB	89	$6	
Camp,Shawn	35	R	ADA	77	$6	
Farnsworth,Kyle	34	R	ADA	103	$6	
Logan,Boone	26	L	ADA	78	$6	
Sale,Chris	22	L	AFF	92	$6	
Contreras,Jose	39	R	CCB	87	$6	
Peralta,Joel	35	R	ADB	87	$6	
Rogers,Esmil	25	R	ADD	79	$5	
Webb,Ryan	25	R	ADD	83	$5	
Bastardo,Antonio	25	L	AFF	96	$5	
Coffey,Todd	30	R	ADD	86	$5	
Linebrink,Scott	34	R	BDA	83	$5	
Blevins,Jerry	27	L	ADB	91	$5	
Maloney,Matt	27	L	ADB	76	$4	
Gee,Dillon	24	R	ADC	76	$4	
Gervacio,Sammy	26	R	AFD	88	$4	
Webb,Brandon	31	R	FCF	81	$4	
Howell,J.P.	27	L	FCA	82	$4	
Bray,Bill	27	L	FFA	91	$4	
Walker,Tyler	34	R	FDA	80	$3	
Mathieson,Scott	27	R	FFA	79	$3	
Strasburg,Stephen	22	R	CFF	119	$2	

MAYBERRY METHOD TOP 300 BATTERS Scores & Rankings

BATTERS	P	S	B	A	REL	M
Gonzalez,Carlos	5	3	5	5	ABF	90
Heyward,Jason	4	3	5	5	AFD	85
Cruz,Nelson	5	2	5	5	CBB	85
Werth,Jayson	5	3	3	5	AAA	80
Longoria,Evan	5	2	4	5	AAA	80
Drew,Stephen	3	5	3	5	AAB	80
Pujols,Albert	5	1	5	5	AAB	80
Pence,Hunter	4	3	4	5	AAB	80
Cabrera,Miguel	5	1	5	5	AAC	80
Votto,Joey	5	1	5	5	AAC	80
McCutchen,A	3	5	3	5	ABB	80
Granderson,C	4	5	2	5	BAB	80
Youkilis,Kevin	5	2	4	5	CBA	80
Tulowitzki,Troy	4	3	4	5	CBC	80
Hamilton,Josh	4	2	5	5	CBF	80
Ethier,Andre	4	2	4	5	AAA	75
Victorino,S	2	4	4	5	AAA	75
Braun,Ryan	4	2	4	5	AAB	75
Hart,Corey	4	3	3	5	AAB	75
Cano,Robinson	3	2	5	5	AAC	75
Young,Delmon	4	2	4	5	ABB	75
Bautista,Jose	5	2	3	5	ABD	75
Fowler,Dexter	3	5	2	5	ACA	75
Stubbs,Drew	4	5	1	5	ACB	75
Upton,Justin	4	4	2	5	BBB	75
Torres,Andres	4	4	2	5	BDD	75
Utley,Chase	4	3	3	5	CAA	75
Morneau,Justin	4	1	5	5	CBC	75
Pedroia,Dustin	3	2	5	5	DAA	75
Beltran,Carlos	4	2	4	5	FCC	75
Wright,David	4	2	3	5	AAA	70
Holliday,Matt	4	1	4	5	AAA	70
Crawford,Carl	2	4	3	5	AAB	70
Suzuki,Ichiro	1	5	3	5	AAB	70
Damon,Johnny	3	3	3	5	AAB	70
Markakis,Nick	3	3	3	5	AAB	70
Teixeira,Mark	4	1	4	5	AAB	70
Ramirez,Hanl	3	3	3	5	AAB	70
Konerko,Paul	4	1	4	5	AAC	70
Gonzalez,Adrian	4	1	4	5	AAC	70
Huff,Aubrey	4	1	4	5	AAF	70
Lind,Adam	4	1	4	5	AAF	70
Drew,J.D.	4	2	3	5	ABC	70
Maybin,Cameron	3	5	1	5	ACB	70
Beckham,Gordon	4	2	3	5	ADD	70
Morrison,Logan	3	2	4	5	AFA	70
Castro,Starlin	1	4	4	5	AFB	70
Posey,Buster	3	2	4	5	AFB	70
Bourjos,Peter	2	5	2	5	AFC	70
Brown,Domonic	4	3	2	5	AFD	70
Stanton,Mike	5	2	2	5	AFF	70
Zimmerman,R	4	1	4	5	BAB	70
Howard,Ryan	5	1	3	5	BAB	70
Ibanez,Raul	4	2	3	5	BAB	70
Wells,Vernon	4	1	4	5	BAC	70
Ortiz,David	5	1	3	5	BAC	70
Mauer,Joe	2	2	5	5	BAD	70
Prado,Martin	3	2	4	5	BBA	70
Choo,Shin-Soo	4	2	3	5	BBA	70
Jones,Adam	3	3	3	5	BBB	70
Barton,Daric	3	3	3	5	BBB	70
Scott,Luke	4	1	4	5	BBB	70
Johnson,Kelly	4	2	3	5	BBD	70
Zobrist,Ben	3	3	3	5	BBF	70
Rodriguez,Alex	4	1	4	5	CAB	70
Rollins,Jimmy	2	3	4	5	CAB	70
Beltre,Adrian	4	1	4	5	CAF	70
Pie,Felix	2	4	3	5	CDC	70
Reyes,Jose	2	4	3	5	DBB	70
Weeks,Rickie	4	3	2	5	FBB	70
Crisp,Coco	2	4	3	5	FDA	70
Abreu,Bobby	4	1	3	5	AAA	65
Young,Chris	4	2	2	5	AAA	65
Ramirez,Alex	2	3	3	5	AAA	65
Phillips,B	2	3	3	5	AAA	65
Kemp,Matt	4	2	2	5	AAB	65

BATTERS	P	S	B	A	REL	M
Span,Denard	1	4	3	5	AAB	65
Butler,Billy	3	1	4	5	AAB	65
Swisher,Nick	4	1	3	5	AAC	65
Upton,B.J.	4	3	1	5	AAC	65
Rios,Alex	3	2	3	5	AAC	65
Bourn,Michael	1	5	2	5	AAC	65
Jeter,Derek	1	3	4	5	AAD	65
Kubel,Jason	4	1	3	5	AAD	65
Young,Michael	3	2	3	5	AAD	65
Pierre,Juan	0	4	4	5	ABC	65
Sandoval,Pablo	3	1	4	5	ABD	65
Stewart,Ian	4	2	2	5	ACA	65
Rasmus,Colby	4	2	2	5	ACD	65
Tabata,Jose	1	4	3	5	ADA	65
Walker,Neil	3	2	3	5	ADC	65
Raburn,Ryan	4	2	2	5	ADD	65
Berkman,Lance	4	1	3	5	BAC	65
Lee,Derrek	4	1	3	5	BAF	65
Murphy,David	3	2	3	5	BBA	65
Fukudome,K	3	2	3	5	BBA	65
Bruce,Jay	4	2	2	5	BBB	65
Ramirez,Aramis	4	1	3	5	BBC	65
Ruiz,Carlos	3	1	4	5	BCC	65
Joyce,Matt	4	2	2	5	BDB	65
Guerrero,Vladimi	3	1	4	5	CBB	65
DeJesus,David	2	3	3	5	CBB	65
Hudson,Orlando	2	3	3	5	CBB	65
Cuddyer,Michael	3	2	3	5	CBC	65
Martinez,Victor	3	1	4	5	CBC	65
Soriano,Alfonso	4	2	2	5	CBD	65
Quentin,Carlos	4	1	3	5	CBD	65
Podsednik,Scott	1	5	2	5	CCB	65
Snider,Travis	4	1	3	5	CCB	65
Montero,Miguel	4	1	3	5	CDB	65
Willingham,Josh	4	1	3	5	DCA	65
Encarnacion,Edw	4	1	3	5	DCB	65
Soto,Geovany	4	1	3	5	DCF	65
Kinsler,Ian	3	2	3	5	FBA	65
Ellsbury,Jacoby	1	4	3	5	FBD	65
Sizemore,Grady	4	2	2	5	FBF	65
Morales,Kendry	3	1	4	5	FCD	65
Furcal,Rafael	2	3	3	5	FCF	65
Lowrie,Jed	4	2	2	5	FFF	65
McCann,Brian	4	0	3	5	AAA	60
Kouzmanoff,Kev	3	1	3	5	AAA	60
LaRoche,Adam	4	1	2	5	AAA	60
Dunn,Adam	5	0	2	5	AAB	60
Uggla,Dan	4	1	2	5	AAB	60
Overbay,Lyle	4	0	3	5	AAC	60
Reynolds,Mark	5	2	0	5	AAD	60
Fielder,Prince	4	0	3	5	AAD	60
Byrd,Marlon	3	1	3	5	ABB	60
Escobar,Alcides	1	4	2	5	ACA	60
Jackson,Austin	1	5	1	5	ACA	60
Brantley,Michael	1	3	3	5	ACA	60
Uribe,Juan	4	1	2	5	ACC	60
Desmond,Ian	2	3	2	5	ACD	60
Davis,Rajai	1	4	2	5	ACD	60
McGehee,Casey	3	1	3	5	ACD	60
Johnson,Chris	3	1	3	5	ADC	60
Thole,Josh	1	2	4	5	AFA	60
Davis,Ike	4	2	1	5	AFA	60
Smoak,Justin	3	1	3	5	AFB	60
Alvarez,Pedro	4	1	2	5	AFD	60
Freeman,Freddie	3	1	3	5	AFD	60
Jennings,Desmo	1	5	1	5	AFF	60
Donald,Jason	2	3	2	5	AFF	60
Hunter,Torii	3	1	3	5	BAB	60
Lee,Carlos	3	1	3	5	BAC	60
Pena,Carlos	5	1	1	5	BAC	60
Keppinger,Jeff	1	2	4	5	BBB	60
Callaspo,Alberto	1	3	3	5	BBC	60
Hawpe,Brad	4	1	2	5	BBC	60
Aybar,Erick	1	5	1	5	BBC	60
Morgan,Nyjer	0	5	2	5	BBD	60
Gardner,Brett	1	5	1	5	BCB	60

BATTERS	P	S	B	A	REL	M
Napoli,Mike	4	1	2	5	BCC	60
Rolen,Scott	3	1	3	5	CBA	60
Matsui,Hideki	3	1	3	5	CBB	60
Hardy,J.J.	2	3	2	5	CBD	60
Coghlan,Chris	1	3	3	5	CCD	60
Ordonez,Magglio	2	1	4	5	DBB	60
Infante,Omar	1	4	2	5	DCA	60
Pagan,Angel	2	4	1	5	FCC	60
Jackson,Conor	2	2	3	5	FDF	60
Headley,Chase	3	2	1	5	AAA	55
Suzuki,Kurt	2	1	3	5	AAA	55
Loney,James	2	1	3	5	AAA	55
Theriot,Ryan	0	4	2	5	AAB	55
Lopez,Jose	2	1	3	5	AAB	55
Peralta,Jhonny	3	1	2	5	AAB	55
Blake,Casey	3	1	2	5	AAC	55
Gutierrez,Franklin	2	3	1	5	AAC	55
Escobar,Yunel	1	2	3	5	AAC	55
Pennington,Cliff	1	4	1	5	ABA	55
Andrus,Elvis	0	4	2	5	ABB	55
Jones,Garrett	3	1	2	5	ABD	55
Sanchez,Gaby	3	1	2	5	ACB	55
Gomes,Jonny	4	1	1	5	ACF	55
Borbon,Julio	0	5	1	5	ADB	55
Crowe,Trevor	1	3	2	5	ADC	55
Jaso,John	1	3	2	5	ADD	55
Wieters,Matt	3	1	2	5	ADD	55
Rodriguez,Sean	3	2	1	5	ADF	55
Santana,Carlos	3	1	2	5	AFA	55
Carter,V.Chris	4	1	1	5	AFF	55
Polanco,Placido	1	2	3	5	BAA	55
Ludwick,Ryan	3	2	1	5	BAD	55
Inge,Brandon	3	3	0	5	BBA	55
Bartlett,Jason	1	3	2	5	BBF	55
Bay,Jason	3	3	0	5	CAC	55
Sanchez,Freddy	1	2	3	5	CBA	55
Kendrick,Howie	2	1	3	5	CBB	55
Cabrera,Asdrubal	1	3	2	5	CBC	55
McLouth,Nate	3	2	1	5	CBD	55
Hill,Aaron	3	1	2	5	CBD	55
Roberts,Brian	2	2	2	5	DAB	55
Gordon,Alex	3	1	2	5	DCA	55
Ankiel,Rick	4	1	1	5	DCC	55
Aviles,Mike	1	3	2	5	DDF	55
Gonzalez,Alex	3	1	2	5	FDC	55
Bernadina,Roger	2	3	1	5	FDF	55
Tejada,Miguel	1	1	3	5	AAB	50
Cantu,Jorge	2	1	2	5	AAB	50
Scutaro,Marco	1	2	2	5	AAC	50
Betancourt,Yunie	1	2	2	5	ABB	50
Saunders,Michael	2	3	0	5	ADB	50
LaPorta,Matt	3	1	1	5	ADB	50
Cust,Jack	4	0	0	5	ABB	45
DeWitt,Blake	1	2	1	5	ACB	45
Francisco,Juan	4	3	5	3	AFA	45
Figgins,Chone	0	3	1	5	BAD	45
Martin,Russell	1	1	2	5	CBB	45
Colvin,Tyler	4	4	3	3	ADC	42
Molina,Yadier	1	0	2	5	ABB	40
Wallace,Brett	2	1	0	5	AFC	40
Wells,Casper	4	3	3	3	AFB	39
Jones,Chipper	4	2	4	3	DBC	39
Lewis,Fred	3	4	2	3	ACA	36
Smith,Seth	4	2	3	3	ACD	36
Viciedo,Dayan	4	1	4	3	ADC	36
Morse,Mike	4	2	3	3	FFC	36
Thome,Jim	5	0	3	3	ABC	33
Venable,Will	3	5	0	3	ACA	33
Rosales,Adam	2	4	2	3	ADA	33
Rhymes,Will	1	4	3	3	ADB	33
Moreland,Mitch	3	1	4	3	AFA	33
Kalish,Ryan	3	2	3	3	AFA	33
Duda,Lucas	4	1	3	3	AFB	33
Wigginton,Ty	3	2	3	3	BBC	33
Ramirez,Manny	4	1	3	3	CBB	33
Young Jr.,Eric	1	5	2	3	CDB	33

BATTERS	P	S	B	A	REL	M
Cameron,Mike	4	3	1	3	DCB	33
Murphy,Daniel	3	1	4	3	FDB	33
Diaz,Matt	3	2	3	3	FDF	33
Ross,Cody	3	2	2	3	ABA	30
Olivo,Miguel	4	2	1	3	ACB	30
Cedeno,Ronny	2	4	1	3	ACC	30
Davis,Chris	4	1	2	3	ACC	30
Reimold,Nolan	3	2	2	3	ACF	30
Craig,Allen	2	2	3	3	ADA	30
Hinske,Eric	4	1	2	3	ADA	30
Nix,Jayson	4	2	1	3	ADB	30
Allen,Brandon	3	1	3	3	ADC	30
Iannetta,Chris	4	1	2	3	ADC	30
Jay,Jon	1	3	3	3	ADD	30
Arencibia,JP	4	1	2	3	AFC	30
Sizemore,Scott	3	2	2	3	AFC	30
Ackley,Dustin	1	3	3	3	AFF	30
Kotchman,Casey	2	1	4	3	BBB	30
Buck,John	4	1	2	3	BDB	30
Spilborghs,Ryan	3	2	2	3	BDD	30
Teahen,Mark	3	2	2	3	CBA	30
Branyan,Russell	5	1	1	3	CCB	30
Jones,Andruw	4	1	2	3	CDF	30
Posada,Jorge	4	1	2	3	DCC	30
Hafner,Travis	4	0	3	3	DCC	30
Guzman,Cristian	1	4	2	3	FBB	30
Izturis,Maicer	1	3	3	3	FDC	30
Schumaker,Skip	1	2	3	3	AAB	27
Cabrera,Melky	1	2	3	3	ABC	27
Bonifacio,Emilio	0	5	1	3	ACA	27
Valbuena,Luis	2	2	2	3	ACB	27
Hall,Bill	4	1	1	3	ACD	27
Ryan,Brendan	1	4	1	3	ACD	27
Valencia,Danny	2	2	2	3	ADA	27
Brignac,Reid	2	3	1	3	ADA	27
Parra,Gerardo	1	3	2	3	ADB	27
Betemit,Wilson	4	1	1	3	ADD	27
Ka'aihue,Kila	3	1	2	3	ADF	27
Boesch,Brennan	2	3	1	3	AFB	27
Espinosa,Danny	3	3	0	3	AFF	27
Bell,Josh	3	1	2	3	AFF	27
Rowand,Aaron	3	2	1	3	BBB	27
Mora,Melvin	2	2	2	3	BBC	27
Burrell,Pat	4	1	1	3	BBF	27
Hundley,Nick	3	2	1	3	BDB	27
Rivera,Juan	2	1	3	3	CCB	27
Castillo,Luis	0	3	3	3	CCC	27
Sanchez,Angel	0	4	2	3	CDB	27
Casilla,Alexi	1	4	1	3	CDC	27
Sweeney,Ryan	1	2	3	3	DCA	27
Hernandez,Ramor	2	1	3	3	DCB	27
Cabrera,Everth	1	4	1	3	DFF	27
Doumit,Ryan	3	1	2	3	FCB	27
Guillen,Carlos	2	2	2	3	FCB	27
Nady,Xavier	3	1	2	3	FDC	27
Francoeur,Jeff	2	2	1	3	AAB	24
Lopez,Felipe	1	2	2	3	ABD	24
Milledge,Lastings	1	2	2	3	ACB	24
Cunningham,Aaro	2	2	1	3	ADB	24
Kelly,Don	1	3	1	3	ADB	24
Blanco,Gregor	0	4	1	3	ADF	24
Pena,Brayan	2	0	3	3	AFB	24
Cain,Lorenzo	1	4	0	3	AFF	24
Cabrera,Orlando	1	2	2	3	BAA	24
Carroll,Jamey	0	4	1	3	BCA	24
Kennedy,Adam	1	2	2	3	BCB	24
Hanigan,Ryan	1	1	3	3	BDB	24
Manzella,Tommy	1	3	1	3	BDB	24
Helton,Todd	2	1	2	3	CBD	24
Gomez,Carlos	1	4	0	3	CCA	24
Izturis,Cesar	0	3	2	3	CCB	24
Hairston,Scott	3	2	0	3	CCB	24
Renteria,Edgar	1	3	1	3	CCB	24
Hairston,Jerry	1	2	2	3	CCC	24
Freese,David	2	1	2	3	DFA	24
Glaus,Troy	3	1	1	3	FCF	24

Power (PX)	
0-49	0
50-79	1
80-99	2
100-119	3
120-159	4
160+	5

Speed (Spd)	
0-49	0
50-79	1
80-99	2
100-119	3
120-139	4
140+	5

Expected BA	
.000 - .239	0
.240 - .254	1
.255 - .269	2
.270 - .284	3
.285 - .299	4
.300+	5

Plate App.	
0-99	0
100-249	1
250-449	3
450+	5

MM Score = (PX score + Spd score + xBA score + PA score) x PA score

Bolded players have high reliability scores.

MAYBERRY METHOD — TOP 300 PITCHERS — Scores & Rankings

PITCHERS	E	K	S	I	REL	M
Lincecum,Tim	5	5	0	5	AAA	100
Lester,Jon	5	5	0	5	BAA	100
Hernandez,F	5	4	0	5	AAA	95
Johnson,Josh	5	4	0	5	FAA	95
Halladay,Roy	5	3	0	5	AAA	90
Kershaw,C	4	5	0	5	AAA	90
Gallardo,Yovani	4	5	0	5	DBA	90
Hamels,Cole	4	4	0	5	AAA	85
Jimenez,U	4	4	0	5	AAA	85
Billingsley,C	4	4	0	5	AAA	85
Rodriguez,W	4	4	0	5	AAA	85
Haren,Dan	4	4	0	5	AAA	85
Greinke,Zack	4	4	0	5	AAA	85
Verlander,J	4	4	0	5	AAB	85
Scherzer,Max	4	4	0	5	ACA	85
Latos,Mat	4	4	0	5	ACB	85
Wilson,C.J.	4	4	0	5	BBC	85
Nolasco,Ricky	4	4	0	5	CAA	85
Beckett,Josh	4	4	0	5	DAA	85
Liriano,Francisco	4	4	0	5	DBC	85
Sabathia,CC	4	3	0	5	AAA	80
Carrasco,Carlos	4	3	0	5	ACB	80
Morrow,Brandon	3	5	0	5	ACC	80
Lee,Cliff	4	3	0	5	BAA	80
Wainwright,A	4	3	0	5	BAA	80
Oswalt,Roy	4	3	0	5	BAA	80
Bell,Heath	5	5	3	1	AAA	76
Hanrahan,Joel	5	5	3	1	ACB	76
Lewis,Colby	3	4	0	5	AAA	75
Weaver,Jered	3	4	0	5	AAB	75
Lowe,Derek	4	2	0	5	AAB	75
Gonzalez,Gio	3	4	0	5	ABA	75
Hanson,Tom	3	4	0	5	ABA	75
Hudson,Dan	3	4	0	5	ADB	75
Dempster,R	3	4	0	5	BAA	75
Kuroda,Hiroki	4	2	0	5	CAA	75
Carpenter,Chris	4	2	0	5	FAB	75
Cueto,Johnny	3	3	0	5	AAA	70
Shields,James	3	3	0	5	AAA	70
Floyd,Gavin	3	3	0	5	AAA	70
Cain,Matt	3	3	0	5	AAA	70
Danks,John	3	3	0	5	AAB	70
Romero,Ricky	3	3	0	5	AAC	70
Masterson,J	3	3	0	5	ABA	70
Price,David	3	3	0	5	ABB	70
Chacin,Jhoulys	3	3	0	5	ADC	70
Lackey,John	3	3	0	5	CAA	70
Niese,Jonathon	3	3	0	5	CCA	70
Myers,Brett	3	3	0	5	DAA	70
Hudson,Tim	4	1	0	5	FBA	70
Marcum,Shaun	3	3	0	5	FBA	70
Marmol,Carlos	4	5	3	1	ABD	68
Axford,John	4	5	3	1	AFD	68
Rodriguez,F	4	5	3	1	BAB	68
Valverde,Jose	4	5	3	1	BBA	68
Hammel,Jason	3	2	0	5	AAB	65
Niemann,Jeff	3	2	0	5	ABB	65
McDonald,James	2	4	0	5	ADA	65
Buchholz,Clay	3	2	0	5	BBA	65
Hochevar,Luke	3	2	0	5	DCA	65
Nunez,Leo	4	4	3	1	CBB	64
Jackson,Edwin	2	3	0	5	AAB	60
Matusz,Brian	2	3	0	5	ACA	60
Kennedy,Ian	2	3	0	5	ACC	60
Burnett,A.J.	2	3	0	5	BAA	60
Santana,Ervin	2	3	0	5	BAB	60
Carmona,Fausto	3	1	0	5	BBA	60
Storen,Drew	3	4	3	1	AFF	56
Richard,C	2	2	0	5	AAA	55
Blanton,Joe	2	2	0	5	AAA	55
Garza,Matt	2	2	0	5	AAA	55
Wolf,Randy	2	2	0	5	BAA	55
Jurrjens,Jair	2	2	0	5	CAA	55
Soria,Joakim	5	5	3	0	AAA	54
Wilson,Brian	5	5	3	0	AAA	54
Broxton,Jonathan	5	5	3	0	ABC	54

PITCHERS	E	K	S	I	REL	M
Nathan,Joe	5	5	3	0	FBA	54
Capps,Matt	3	3	3	1	BBB	52
Venters,Jonny	5	4	2	1	ADF	51
Jenks,Bobby	5	4	3	0	BBB	51
Saunders,Joe	2	1	0	5	AAA	50
Maholm,Paul	2	1	0	5	AAA	50
Garland,Jon	2	1	0	5	AAA	50
Arroyo,B	2	1	0	5	AAA	50
Braden,Dallas	2	1	0	5	ABA	50
Volstad,Chris	2	1	0	5	ABA	50
Cahill,Trevor	2	1	0	5	ABD	50
Duensing,Brian	2	1	0	5	ACB	50
Duke,Zach	2	1	0	5	BAA	50
Pavano,Carl	2	1	0	5	FAB	50
Papelbon,Jon	4	5	3	0	AAB	48
Jansen,Kenley	4	5	2	1	AFF	48
Bailey,Andrew	4	5	3	0	BCC	48
Soriano,Rafael	4	5	3	0	DBB	48
Street,Huston	4	5	3	0	DBB	48
Blackburn,Nick	2	0	0	5	AAA	45
Zito,Barry	1	2	0	5	AAB	45
Porcello,Rick	2	0	0	5	ACA	45
Davis,Wade	1	2	0	5	ACA	45
Dickey,R.A.	2	0	0	5	ACB	45
Arrieta,Jake	1	2	0	5	ADB	45
League,Brandon	5	2	2	1	BCA	45
Millwood,Kevin	1	2	0	5	CAA	45
Bush,David	1	2	0	5	DAA	45
de la Rosa,Jorge	4	4	0	3	DBA	45
Sanchez,J	3	5	0	3	AAA	42
Perez,Chris	3	5	3	0	ACA	42
Garcia,Jaime	4	3	0	3	ACD	42
Motte,Jason	3	5	2	1	ADB	42
Minor,Mike	3	5	0	3	ADF	42
Kimbrel,Craig	3	5	2	1	AFA	42
Meek,Evan	4	3	2	1	BDB	42
Lidge,Brad	3	5	3	0	CBC	42
Anderson,Brett	4	3	0	3	DCA	42
Guthrie,Jeremy	1	1	0	5	AAB	40
Lyon,Brandon	2	2	3	1	ABA	40
Vargas,Jason	1	1	0	5	FCA	40
Vazquez,Javier	3	4	0	3	AAC	39
Parra,Manny	3	4	0	3	ABB	39
Feliz,Neftali	3	4	3	0	ACC	39
Hellickson,Jerem	3	4	0	3	ADF	39
Rzepczynski,Mar	3	4	0	3	BDA	39
Peavy,Jake	3	4	0	3	FBA	39
Volquez,Edinson	3	4	0	3	FCB	39
Aardsma,D	2	5	3	0	ABA	36
Clippard,Tyler	2	5	2	1	ADA	36
Lilly,Ted	3	3	0	3	BAA	36
Pettitte,Andy	3	3	0	3	CAB	36
Bailey,Homer	3	3	0	3	CCA	36
Hensley,Clay	3	3	2	1	DDC	36
Harang,Aaron	3	3	0	3	FAA	36
Padilla,Vicente	3	3	0	3	FBA	36
Zimmermann,Jor	3	3	0	3	FDA	36
Capuano,Chris	3	3	0	3	FFF	36
Buehrle,Mark	1	0	0	5	AAA	35
Thornton,Matt	5	5	2	0	ACA	34
Gregerson,Luke	5	5	1	1	ACB	34
Chapman,Aroldis	5	5	1	1	ACF	34
Kuo,Hong-Chih	5	5	2	0	FCB	34
Putz,J.J.	5	5	2	0	FDD	34
Rivera,Mariano	3	2	3	0	AAA	33
Gregg,Kevin	2	4	3	0	ABA	33
Wells,Randy	3	2	0	3	ABC	33
Bumgarner,Madis	3	2	0	3	ADA	33
Drabek,Kyle	3	2	0	3	ADC	33
Norris,Bud	2	4	0	3	BDB	33
Matsuzaka,Daisu	2	4	0	3	FBB	33
Francis,Jeff	3	2	0	3	FCB	33
Paulino,Felipe	2	4	0	3	FDA	33
Marshall,Sean	5	4	1	1	ACB	32
Madson,Ryan	5	4	1	1	DCA	32
Cordero,F	2	3	3	0	AAA	30

PITCHERS	E	K	S	I	REL	M
Chamberlain,Joba	4	5	1	1	ABC	30
Narveson,Chris	2	3	0	3	ACB	30
Zambrano,C	2	3	0	3	BAA	30
Baker,Scott	2	3	0	3	BAA	30
Lindstrom,Matt	2	3	2	1	BCA	30
Santana,Johan	2	3	0	3	CAA	30
Holland,Derek	2	3	0	3	CCD	30
Rodney,Fernando	2	3	2	1	DBA	30
Francisco,Frank	4	5	2	0	DCA	30
Hughes,Phil	2	3	0	3	DCB	30
Sanchez,Anibal	2	3	0	3	FBB	30
Westbrook,Jake	3	1	0	3	FCA	30
Gonzalez,Mike	4	5	2	0	FDA	30
Benoit,Joaquin	4	5	2	0	FDF	30
Masset,Nick	4	4	1	1	ACB	28
Frasor,Jason	4	4	2	0	ACB	28
Burnett,Sean	4	4	1	1	ADB	28
Correia,Kevin	2	2	0	3	ABA	27
Cecil,Brett	2	2	0	3	ACB	27
Tillman,Chris	2	2	0	3	ADA	27
Mazzaro,Vin	2	2	0	3	ADB	27
Gomez,Jeanmar	2	2	0	3	ADB	27
Ely,John	2	2	0	3	ADB	27
Wood,Travis	2	2	0	3	ADF	27
Pineiro,Joel	3	0	0	3	CAB	27
Kawakami,Kenshin	2	2	0	3	CBA	27
Cook,Aaron	3	0	0	3	DAA	27
Slowey,Kevin	2	2	0	3	DBA	27
Parnell,Bobby	4	3	1	1	ADC	26
Demel,Sam	4	3	2	0	AFA	26
Santos,Sergio	3	5	2	0	AFF	26
Walden,Jordan	4	3	2	0	AFF	26
Lannan,John	2	1	0	3	AAA	24
Pelfrey,Mike	2	1	0	3	AAA	24
Coke,Phil	1	3	0	3	ACA	24
Fister,Doug	2	1	0	3	ACC	24
Gutierrez,Juan	1	3	3	0	ACF	24
Leake,Mike	2	1	0	3	ADF	24
Morton,Charlie	2	1	0	3	BCA	24
Gorzelanny,Tom	1	3	0	3	BCB	24
Kazmir,Scott	1	3	0	3	DAB	24
Davis,Doug	1	3	0	3	FBA	24
Bonderman,Jerem	2	1	0	3	FCB	24
Silva,Carlos	2	1	0	3	FCC	24
Uehara,Koji	3	4	2	0	FCC	24
Stauffer,Tim	2	1	0	3	FDB	24
Takahashi,H	3	3	1	1	ABB	22
Wheeler,Dan	3	3	2	0	ACA	22
Lopez,Wilton	4	1	1	1	ADC	22
Davies,Kyle	1	2	0	3	ABA	21
Bergesen,Brad	2	0	0	3	BBA	21
Ohlendorf,Ross	1	2	0	3	CBA	21
Marquis,Jason	2	0	0	3	DAA	21
Chen,Bruce	1	2	0	3	FDA	21
Janssen,Casey	3	2	1	1	FDC	20
Franklin,Ryan	3	1	2	0	ABB	18
Fujikawa,Kyuji	1	5	2	0	ABC	18
Talbot,Mitch	1	1	0	3	ACD	18
Perry,Ryan	2	3	1	1	ADA	18
Tomlin,Josh	1	1	0	3	ADF	18
Bannister,Brian	1	1	0	3	BAA	18
Garcia,Freddy	1	1	0	3	CCA	18
Bard,Daniel	5	5	1	0	ADA	16
Fuentes,Brian	1	4	2	0	FBC	16
Hernandez,Livan	1	0	0	3	AAA	15
Feldman,Scott	1	0	0	3	ABB	15
Kendrick,Kyle	1	0	0	3	ABB	15
Feliciano,Pedro	5	4	1	0	ACB	15
Hunter,Tommy	1	0	0	3	BDA	15
Robertson,David	4	5	0	1	ADA	14
Rodriguez,Henry	4	5	1	0	AFD	14
Downs,Scott	5	3	1	0	BCA	14
Qualls,Chad	5	3	1	0	BCB	14
Romo,Sergio	4	5	1	0	BDA	14
Wuertz,Mike	4	5	1	0	BDC	14
Betancourt,Rafael	4	5	1	0	CCB	14

PITCHERS	E	K	S	I	REL	M
Adams,Mike	4	5	1	0	FDB	14
Mujica,Edward	4	4	0	1	ACB	13
Jepsen,Kevin	4	4	1	0	ADB	13
Enright,Barry	0	1	0	3	ADD	12
Rogers,Esmil	4	3	0	1	ADD	12
Mejia,Jenrry	4	3	0	1	AFB	12
Affeldt,Jeremy	4	3	1	0	BCA	12
Dotel,Octavio	3	5	1	0	CCB	12
Wood,Kerry	3	5	1	0	FBB	12
Villanueva,Carlos	3	4	0	1	ACB	11
Gervacio,Sammy	3	4	1	0	AFD	11
Casilla,Santiago	3	4	1	0	BDB	11
Fulchino,Jeff	3	4	0	1	BDF	11
Bedard,Erik	3	4	0	1	FDB	11
Carrasco,D.J.	3	3	0	1	ACB	10
Veras,Jose	2	5	0	1	ADC	10
McClellan,Kyle	3	3	0	1	BCA	10
Sipp,Tony	2	5	1	0	CDB	10
Harden,Rich	2	5	0	1	FBB	10
Pena,Tony	3	2	0	1	ACA	9
Stammen,Craig	3	2	0	1	ACA	9
Camp,Shawn	3	2	0	1	ADA	9
Sanches,Brian	2	4	0	1	ADB	9
Hernandez,David	2	4	1	0	BCA	9
Badenhop,Burke	3	2	0	1	CDA	9
Ohman,Will	2	4	1	0	DDF	9
Breslow,Craig	2	3	1	0	ACA	8
Rauch,Jon	2	3	1	0	ACB	8
Cashner,Andrew	2	3	0	1	ADA	8
Wright,Wesley	2	3	0	1	ADA	8
Olson,Garrett	2	3	0	1	ADB	8
Gee,Dillon	2	3	0	1	ADC	8
Loe,Kameron	3	1	0	1	ADF	8
Oliver,Andrew	2	3	0	1	ADF	8
Lowe,Mark	2	3	1	0	FDB	8
Ceda,Jose	1	5	1	0	FFB	8
Iwakuma,Hisashi	2	2	0	1	AAF	7
Hendrickson,M	2	2	0	1	ABA	7
Boggs,Mitchell	2	2	0	1	ACA	7
Figueroa,Nelson	2	2	0	1	ACB	7
Luebke,Cory	2	2	0	1	ADA	7
Hawksworth,Blake	2	2	0	1	ADD	7
Nova,Ivan	2	2	0	1	ADD	7
Olsen,Scott	2	2	0	1	FBB	7
Sonnanstine,A	2	1	0	1	ABB	6
Guerrier,Matt	2	1	1	0	ACA	6
Monasterios,Carlos	2	1	0	1	ADB	6
Bell,Trevor	2	1	0	1	ADB	6
Sanabia,Alex	2	1	0	1	ADF	6
Pauley,David	2	1	0	1	ADF	6
Ondrusek,Logan	2	1	0	1	AFC	6
Lopez,Rodrigo	2	1	0	1	BCF	6
Bullington,Bryan	2	1	0	1	BDF	6
Penny,Brad	2	1	0	1	FBB	6
Young,Chris	1	3	0	1	FCB	6
Hill,Shawn	2	1	0	1	FDB	6
LeBlanc,Wade	1	2	0	1	ACB	5
Kirkman,Michael	1	2	0	1	ADC	5
VandenHurk,Rick	1	2	0	1	BDA	5
Happ,J.A.	1	2	0	1	CCA	5
Perez,Oliver	0	4	0	1	FBB	5
Galarraga,Arm	1	1	0	1	ABA	4
Palmer,Matt	1	1	0	1	ACD	4
O'Sullivan,Sean	1	1	0	1	ADA	4
Huff,David	1	1	0	1	ADB	4
Purcey,David	0	3	1	0	ADC	4
Moyer,Jamie	1	1	0	1	DAA	4
Detwiler,Ross	1	1	0	1	DDA	4
Lohse,Kyle	1	1	0	1	FBA	4
Harrison,Matt	1	1	0	1	FCA	4
Coleman,Casey	1	0	0	1	ADA	3
Samardzija,Jeff	0	2	0	1	ADA	3
Maya,Yunesky	0	1	0	1	AFF	2
Hoffman,Trevor	0	1	1	0	BBB	2
Wakefield,Tim	0	1	0	1	CAB	2
Robertson,Nate	0	1	0	1	CCB	2

Expected ERA	
0.00 - 3.19	5
3.20 - 3.59	4
3.60 - 3.99	3
4.00 - 4.39	2
4.40 - 4.79	1
4.80+	0

Dominance (K/9)	
0.0 - 4.9	0
5.0 - 5.9	1
6.0 - 6.9	2
7.0 - 7.9	3
8.0 - 8.9	4
9.0+	5

Saves potential	
0	0
1 - 9	1
10 - 24	2
25+	3

Innings Pitched	
0-69	0
70-129	1
130-179	3
180+	5

MM Score = ((xERA score x 2) + K/9 score + Sv score + IP score) x (IP score + Sv score)

Bolded players have high reliability scores.

ROTISSERIE AUCTION DRAFT

Top 560 players ranked for 75% depth leagues

NAME	POS	5x5	NAME	POS	5x5	NAME	POS	5x5	NAME	POS	5x5
Pujols,Albert	3	$37	Phillips,Brandon	4	$22	Ortiz,David	0	$19	Bay,Jason	7	$16
Cabrera,Miguel	3	$34	Upton,B.J.	8	$22	Cahill,Trevor	P	$19	DeJesus,David	9	$16
Gonzalez,Carlos	789	$34	Johnson,Kelly	4	$22	Abreu,Bobby	79	$19	Matsui,Hideki	0	$16
Crawford,Carl	7	$33	Hunter,Torii	89	$22	Damon,Johnny	70	$18	Dempster,Ryan	P	$16
Braun,Ryan	7	$32	Konerko,Paul	30	$22	Slowey,Kevin	P	$18	Bourjos,Peter	8	$16
Holliday,Matt	7	$32	Soriano,Rafael	P	$22	Kuroda,Hiroki	P	$18	Putz,J.J.	P	$16
Ramirez,Hanley	6	$32	Young,Michael	5	$22	Perez,Chris	P	$18	Storen,Drew	P	$16
Votto,Joey	3	$31	Ramirez,Aramis	5	$22	Cuddyer,Michael	39	$18	Berkman,Lance	30	$16
Halladay,Roy	P	$31	Bruce,Jay	9	$22	Aardsma,David	P	$18	Morrison,Logan	7	$16
Hernandez,Felix	P	$31	Stubbs,Drew	8	$22	Posey,Buster	23	$18	Suzuki,Kurt	2	$16
Werth,Jayson	89	$29	Papelbon,Jonathan	P	$22	Hill,Aaron	4	$18	Lyon,Brandon	P	$16
Utley,Chase	4	$28	Wells,Vernon	8	$21	Hughes,Phil	P	$18	Minor,Mike	P	$16
Wright,David	5	$28	Jeter,Derek	6	$21	McCann,Brian	2	$18	Pena,Carlos	3	$16
Longoria,Evan	5	$28	Rodriguez,Francisc	P	$21	Beltran,Carlos	8	$18	Encarnacion,Edwi	5	$16
Lester,Jon	P	$28	Jimenez,Ubaldo	P	$21	Garza,Matt	P	$18	McLouth,Nate	8	$16
Teixeira,Mark	3	$27	Hanson,Tommy	P	$21	Marmol,Carlos	P	$18	Gomes,Jonny	7	$16
Ellsbury,Jacoby	8	$27	Soria,Joakim	P	$21	Lackey,John	P	$18	Castro,Starlin	6	$16
Sabathia,CC	P	$27	Weeks,Rickie	4	$21	Willingham,Josh	7	$18	Bernadina,Roger	789	$16
Lincecum,Tim	P	$27	Feliz,Neftali	P	$21	Byrd,Marlon	8	$18	Johnson,Chris	5	$16
Cano,Robinson	4	$27	Morales,Kendry	3	$21	Hudson,Tim	P	$18	Borbon,Julio	8	$15
Cruz,Nelson	9	$27	Billingsley,Chad	P	$21	Hanrahan,Joel	P	$18	Desmond,Ian	6	$15
Verlander,Justin	P	$27	Johnson,Josh	P	$21	Street,Huston	P	$18	Benoit,Joaquin	P	$15
Zimmerman,Ryan	5	$27	Prado,Martin	45	$21	Raburn,Ryan	79	$18	Santana,Carlos	2	$15
Wainwright,Adam	P	$26	McGehee,Casey	5	$21	Wilson,C.J.	P	$18	Hawpe,Brad	9	$15
Hamilton,Josh	78	$26	Stanton,Mike	9	$21	Hellickson,Jeremy	P	$17	Nathan,Joe	P	$15
Tulowitzki,Troy	6	$26	Liriano,Francisco	P	$21	Broxton,Jonathan	P	$17	Carrasco,Carlos	P	$15
Pedroia,Dustin	4	$26	Jackson,Austin	8	$21	Walker,Neil	4	$17	Snider,Travis	79	$15
Fielder,Prince	3	$26	Huff,Aubrey	379	$21	Crisp,Coco	8	$17	Rolen,Scott	5	$15
Kemp,Matt	8	$26	Butler,Billy	30	$20	Stewart,Ian	5	$17	Bumgarner,Madis	P	$15
Rodriguez,Alex	5	$26	Markakis,Nick	9	$20	Myers,Brett	P	$17	Kimbrel,Craig	P	$15
Youkilis,Kevin	3	$26	Furcal,Rafael	6	$20	Gonzalez,Gio	P	$17	Davis,Wade	P	$15
Choo,Shin-Soo	9	$26	Axford,John	P	$20	Matusz,Brian	P	$17	Soto,Geovany	2	$15
Bautista,Jose	59	$26	Bailey,Andrew	P	$20	Figgins,Chone	4	$17	Lowe,Derek	P	$15
Gonzalez,Adrian	3	$26	Granderson,Curtis	8	$20	Valverde,Jose	P	$17	Pavano,Carl	P	$15
McCutchen,Andrew	8	$26	Lee,Derrek	3	$20	Kubel,Jason	90	$17	Kuo,Hong-Chih	P	$15
Lee,Cliff	P	$26	Lewis,Colby	P	$20	Lilly,Ted	P	$17	Romero,Ricky	P	$15
Victorino,Shane	8	$25	Lee,Carlos	37	$20	Baker,Scott	P	$17	Maybin,Cameron	8	$15
Howard,Ryan	3	$25	Carpenter,Chris	P	$20	Arroyo,Bronson	P	$17	Peralta,Jhonny	56	$15
Weaver,Jered	P	$25	Zobrist,Ben	49	$20	Reynolds,Mark	5	$17	Nunez,Leo	P	$15
Pence,Hunter	9	$25	Alvarez,Pedro	5	$20	Niemann,Jeff	P	$17	Aybar,Erick	6	$15
Heyward,Jason	9	$25	Kendrick,Howie	4	$20	Infante,Omar	457	$17	Nolasco,Ricky	P	$15
Ethier,Andre	9	$24	Morrow,Brandon	P	$20	Roberts,Brian	4	$17	Jones,Garrett	39	$15
Rios,Alex	8	$24	Pagan,Angel	789	$20	Drew,Stephen	6	$17	Ordonez,Magglio	9	$15
Suzuki,Ichiro	9	$24	LaRoche,Adam	3	$20	Murphy,David	79	$17	Napoli,Mike	23	$15
Morneau,Justin	3	$24	Ibanez,Raul	7	$20	Sanchez,Gaby	3	$17	Gregg,Kevin	P	$15
Bell,Heath	P	$24	Anderson,Brett	P	$20	Headley,Chase	5	$17	Barton,Daric	3	$15
Young,Delmon	7	$24	Fowler,Dexter	8	$20	Loney,James	3	$17	Sanchez,Jonathar	P	$15
Haren,Dan	P	$24	Swisher,Nick	9	$20	Chacin,Jhoulys	P	$17	Peavy,Jake	P	$14
Young,Chris	8	$24	Hudson,Dan	P	$20	Vazquez,Javier	P	$17	Freeman,Freddie	3	$14
Hart,Corey	9	$24	Jones,Adam	8	$20	Davis,Ike	3	$17	Sizemore,Grady	8	$14
Reyes,Jose	6	$24	Jennings,Desmond	9	$20	Floyd,Gavin	P	$17	Cabrera,Asdrubal	6	$14
Oswalt,Roy	P	$24	Beckett,Josh	P	$20	Morgan,Nyjer	8	$17	Lidge,Brad	P	$14
Cain,Matt	P	$24	Beltre,Adrian	5	$19	Sandoval,Pablo	5	$16	Guthrie,Jeremy	P	$14
Rollins,Jimmy	6	$24	Shields,James	P	$19	Cueto,Johnny	P	$16	Montero,Miguel	2	$14
Scherzer,Max	P	$23	Lind,Adam	0	$19	Brown,Domonic	9	$16	Theriot,Ryan	46	$14
Greinke,Zack	P	$23	Rasmus,Colby	8	$19	Rivera,Mariano	P	$16	Venters,Jonny	P	$14
Upton,Justin	9	$23	Bartlett,Jason	6	$19	Rodriguez,Sean	48	$16	Pennington,Cliff	6	$14
Uggla,Dan	4	$23	Rodriguez,Wandy	P	$19	Jenks,Bobby	P	$16	Colvin,Tyler	79	$14
Pierre,Juan	7	$23	Tabata,Jose	7	$19	Kennedy,Ian	P	$16	Smith,Seth	79	$14
Dunn,Adam	3	$23	Guerrero,Vladimir	0	$19	Scott,Luke	0	$16	Pie,Felix	7	$14
Mauer,Joe	20	$23	Martinez,Victor	2	$19	Podsednik,Scott	7	$16	Tejada,Miguel	56	$14
Latos,Mat	P	$23	Gardner,Brett	78	$19	Torres,Andres	789	$16	Fukudome,Kosuk	9	$14
Price,David	P	$23	Marcum,Shaun	P	$19	Gutierrez,Franklin	8	$16	Duensing,Brian	P	$14
Hamels,Cole	P	$23	Gallardo,Yovani	P	$19	Thornton,Matt	P	$16	Uehara,Koji	P	$14
Kershaw,Clayton	P	$22	Danks,John	P	$19	Santana,Ervin	P	$16	Casilla,Alexi	46	$14
Bourn,Michael	8	$22	Quentin,Carlos	90	$19	Beckham,Gordon	4	$16	Escobar,Yunel	6	$14
Ramirez,Alexei	6	$22	Span,Denard	8	$19	Capps,Matt	P	$16	Wood,Travis	P	$14
Wilson,Brian	P	$22	Andrus,Elvis	6	$19	Drew,J.D.	9	$16	Garcia,Jaime	P	$14
Kinsler,Ian	4	$22	Soriano,Alfonso	7	$19	Cordero,Francisco	P	$16	Wheeler,Dan	P	$14
Davis,Rajai	789	$22	Buchholz,Clay	P	$19	Polanco,Placido	5	$16	Braden,Dallas	P	$14

ROTISSERIE AUCTION DRAFT — Top 560 players ranked for 75% depth leagues

NAME	POS	5x5	NAME	POS	5x5	NAME	POS	5x5	NAME	POS	5x5
Kouzmanoff,Kevin	5	$14	Arrieta,Jake	P	$11	Hammel,Jason	P	$9	Hernandez,David	P	$8
Motte,Jason	P	$13	Kalish,Ryan	8	$11	Jay,Jon	89	$9	Burnett,Sean	P	$8
de la Rosa,Jorge	P	$13	Gregerson,Luke	P	$11	Sweeney,Ryan	9	$9	Betemit,Wilson	5	$8
Porcello,Rick	P	$13	Clippard,Tyler	P	$11	Allen,Brandon	7	$9	Robertson,David	P	$8
Smoak,Justin	3	$13	Sanchez,Freddy	4	$11	Zambrano,Carlos	P	$9	Bush,David	P	$8
Hudson,Orlando	4	$13	Doumit,Ryan	2	$11	Sanabia,Alex	P	$9	Parnell,Bobby	P	$8
Scutaro,Marco	6	$13	Richard,Clayton	P	$11	Nady,Xavier	39	$9	Demel,Sam	P	$8
Thome,Jim	0	$13	Blake,Casey	5	$11	Narveson,Chris	P	$9	Wood,Kerry	P	$8
Joyce,Matt	9	$13	Bailey,Homer	P	$11	Volstad,Chris	P	$9	Boesch,Brennan	79	$8
Ludwick,Ryan	9	$13	Holland,Derek	P	$11	Francisco,Ben	79	$9	Jepsen,Kevin	P	$7
Wolf,Randy	P	$13	Francisco,Frank	P	$11	Fister,Doug	P	$9	Getz,Chris	4	$7
Frasor,Jason	P	$13	Zimmermann,Jorda	P	$11	Millwood,Kevin	P	$9	Hill,Shawn	P	$7
Hardy,J.J.	6	$13	Burnett,A.J.	P	$11	Vargas,Jason	P	$9	Blanco,Gregor	8	$7
Coghlan,Chris	7	$13	Padilla,Vicente	P	$11	Stauffer,Tim	P	$9	O'Day,Darren	P	$7
Ramirez,Manny	70	$13	Capuano,Chris	P	$11	Cedeno,Ronny	6	$9	Murphy,Daniel	37	$7
Uribe,Juan	456	$13	Ka'aihue,Kila	3	$11	Wells,Casper	9	$9	Teahen,Mark	5	$7
Pineiro,Joel	P	$13	Morse,Mike	9	$11	Brignac,Reid	46	$9	Ogando,Alexi	P	$7
Franklin,Ryan	P	$13	Freese,David	5	$11	Francisco,Juan	5	$9	Qualls,Chad	P	$7
Espinosa,Danny	4	$13	Fujikawa,Kyuji	P	$11	Moreland,Mitch	3	$9	Oliver,Darren	P	$7
Escobar,Alcides	6	$13	Keppinger,Jeff	4	$11	Glaus,Troy	3	$9	Bell,Josh	5	$7
Ross,Cody	789	$13	Craig,Allen	9	$11	Balfour,Grant	P	$9	Rosales,Adam	4	$7
McDonald,James	P	$13	Saunders,Michael	7	$11	Bonderman,Jeremy	P	$9	Kawakami,Kenshi	P	$7
Niese,Jonathon	P	$13	Dickey,R.A.	P	$11	Hairston,Jerry	46	$9	Bedard,Erik	P	$7
Pettitte,Andy	P	$13	Izturis,Maicer	45	$11	Gonzalez,Mike	P	$9	Mujica,Edward	P	$7
Lowrie,Jed	46	$13	Diaz,Matt	7	$11	Marshall,Sean	P	$9	Gorzelanny,Tom	P	$7
Burrell,Pat	70	$13	Bradley,Milton	70	$11	Carroll,Jamey	46	$9	LeBlanc,Wade	P	$7
Lopez,Jose	5	$13	Downs,Scott	P	$11	Cabrera,Melky	789	$9	Kazmir,Scott	P	$7
Carmona,Fausto	P	$13	Branyan,Russell	30	$11	Jaso,John	2	$9	Valbuena,Luis	4	$7
Fuentes,Brian	P	$13	Blanton,Joe	P	$11	Hanigan,Ryan	2	$9	Rauch,Jon	P	$7
Jurrjens,Jair	P	$13	Masterson,Justin	P	$10	Walden,Jordan	P	$9	VandenHurk,Rick	P	$7
Cust,Jack	0	$13	Chamberlain,Joba	P	$10	Lopez,Felipe	456	$9	Thames,Marcus	70	$7
Ruiz,Carlos	2	$12	Jones,Chipper	5	$10	Castillo,Luis	4	$9	Dotel,Octavio	P	$7
Overbay,Lyle	3	$12	Saunders,Joe	P	$10	Rivera,Juan	79	$9	Chen,Bruce	P	$7
Carter,V.Chris	7	$12	Blackburn,Nick	P	$10	Snyder,Chris	2	$9	Garcia,Freddy	P	$7
Wieters,Matt	2	$12	Young Jr.,Eric	4	$10	Betancourt,Rafael	P	$9	Duda,Lucas	7	$7
Cantu,Jorge	35	$12	Ankiel,Rick	8	$10	Masset,Nick	P	$8	Nova,Ivan	P	$7
Garland,Jon	P	$12	DeRosa,Mark	7	$10	Ryan,Brendan	6	$8	Frieri,Ernesto	P	$7
Venable,Will	789	$12	Blanks,Kyle	7	$10	Iwakuma,Hisashi	P	$8	Dickerson,Chris	8	$7
Santana,Johan	P	$12	Hall,Bill	47	$10	Thole,Josh	2	$8	Parra,Gerardo	79	$7
Brantley,Michael	8	$12	Spilborghs,Ryan	79	$10	Cabrera,Everth	6	$8	Ely,John	P	$7
Gordon,Alex	7	$12	Martin,Russell	2	$10	Correia,Kevin	P	$8	Francis,Jeff	P	$7
Betancourt,Yuniesk	6	$12	Inge,Brandon	5	$10	Pena,Brayan	2	$8	Fox,Jake	0	$7
Cameron,Mike	8	$12	Hochevar,Luke	P	$10	Avila,Alex	2	$8	Baker,Jeff	45	$7
Volquez,Edinson	P	$12	Adams,Mike	P	$10	Santos,Sergio	P	$8	Thatcher,Joe	P	$7
Milledge,Lastings	79	$12	Bergesen,Brad	P	$10	Wuertz,Mike	P	$8	Bloomquist,Willie	9	$7
Jackson,Edwin	P	$12	Pierzynski,A.J.	2	$10	Torrealba,Yorvit	2	$8	Saito,Takashi	P	$7
Callaspo,Alberto	5	$12	Zito,Barry	P	$10	Rhymes,Will	4	$8	Lannan,John	P	$7
Lewis,Fred	7	$12	Wells,Randy	P	$10	Young,Chris	P	$8	Davis,Chris	3	$7
Hafner,Travis	0	$12	Viciedo,Dayan	5	$10	Hairston,Scott	7	$8	Lucroy,Jonathan	2	$7
Westbrook,Jake	P	$12	Jones,Andruw	9	$10	Wallace,Brett	3	$8	Duncan,Shelley	7	$7
Cecil,Brett	P	$12	Iannetta,Chris	2	$10	Donald,Jason	46	$8	Lopez,Wilton	P	$7
Meek,Evan	P	$12	Norris,Bud	P	$10	Pelfrey,Mike	P	$8	Rodney,Fernando	P	$7
League,Brandon	P	$12	LaPorta,Matt	3	$10	Nix,Jayson	45	$8	Gomez,Jeanmar	P	$7
Olivo,Miguel	2	$12	Gomez,Carlos	8	$10	Renteria,Edgar	6	$8	Bonifacio,Emilio	8	$7
Chapman,Aroldis	P	$12	Hensley,Clay	P	$10	Hernandez,Ramon	2	$8	Leake,Mike	P	$7
Jackson,Conor	7	$12	Wigginton,Ty	345	$10	Figueroa,Nelson	P	$8	Harris,Willie	79	$6
Jansen,Kenley	P	$12	Schumaker,Skip	4	$10	Mazzaro,Vin	P	$8	Gwynn,Tony	8	$6
Buehrle,Mark	P	$12	Gutierrez,Juan	P	$10	Valencia,Danny	5	$8	Heisey,Chris	789	$6
Reimold,Nolan	7	$12	Cabrera,Orlando	6	$10	DeWitt,Blake	4	$8	Cook,Aaron	P	$6
Molina,Yadier	2	$12	Tillman,Chris	P	$10	Guillen,Carlos	4	$8	Kelly,Don	37	$6
Drabek,Kyle	P	$12	Crowe,Trevor	78	$10	Harden,Rich	P	$8	Sipp,Tony	P	$6
Bard,Daniel	P	$12	Luebke,Cory	P	$10	Mora,Melvin	35	$8	Rodriguez,Henry	P	$6
Posada,Jorge	20	$12	Helton,Todd	3	$10	Barajas,Rod	2	$8	Barmes,Clint	46	$6
Sanchez,Anibal	P	$12	Romo,Sergio	P	$10	Hundley,Nick	2	$8	O'Flaherty,Eric	P	$6
Gonzalez,Alex	6	$11	Harang,Aaron	P	$10	Hunter,Tommy	P	$8	Feliciano,Pedro	P	$6
Buck,John	2	$11	Madson,Ryan	P	$10	Francoeur,Jeff	9	$8	Guillen,Jose	90	$6
Rzepczynski,Marc	P	$11	Kennedy,Adam	34	$9	Breslow,Craig	P	$8	Arencibia,JP	2	$6
Coke,Phil	P	$11	Sizemore,Scott	4	$9	Takahashi,Hisanori	P	$8	Tracy,Chad	5	$6
Aviles,Mike	4	$11	Matsuzaka,Daisuke	P	$9	Hinske,Eric	37	$8	Rowand,Aaron	8	$6
Ellis,Mark	4	$11	Tomlin,Josh	P	$9	Molina,Bengie	2	$8	Maier,Mitch	89	$6

ROTISSERIE SNAKE DRAFT — 15 TEAM MIXED LEAGUE

#	NAME	POS	#	NAME	POS	#	NAME	POS	#	NAME	POS
1	Pujols,Albert	3	5	Zobrist,Ben	49	9	Feliz,Neftali	P	13	Scott,Luke	0
	Cabrera,Miguel	3		Kendrick,Howie	4		Billingsley,Chad	P		Peralta,Jhonny	56
	Gonzalez,Carlos	789		Posey,Buster	23		Johnson,Josh	P		Torres,Andres	789
	Braun,Ryan	7		Hunter,Torii	89		Infante,Omar	457		Gutierrez,Franklin	8
	Holliday,Matt	7		Konerko,Paul	30		Roberts,Brian	4		Aybar,Erick	6
	Votto,Joey	3		Young,Michael	5		Soriano,Alfonso	7		Hughes,Phil	P
	Ramirez,Hanley	6		Rios,Alex	8		Andrus,Elvis	6		Drew,J.D.	9
	Utley,Chase	4		Suzuki,Ichiro	9		Liriano,Francisco	P		Garza,Matt	P
	Crawford,Carl	7		Ramirez,Aramis	5		Drew,Stephen	6		Marmol,Carlos	P
	Cano,Robinson	4		Bell,Heath	P		Ortiz,David	0		Polanco,Placido	5
	Tulowitzki,Troy	6		Bruce,Jay	9		Jackson,Austin	8		Bay,Jason	7
	Pedroia,Dustin	4		Haren,Dan	P		Abreu,Bobby	79		Lackey,John	P
	Werth,Jayson	89		McCann,Brian	2		Damon,Johnny	70		DeJesus,David	9
	Wright,David	5		Wells,Vernon	8		Santana,Carlos	2		Matsui,Hideki	0
	Halladay,Roy	P		Oswalt,Roy	P		Axford,John	P		Hudson,Tim	P
2	Longoria,Evan	5	6	Cain,Matt	P	10	Bailey,Andrew	P	14	Hanrahan,Joel	P
	Hernandez,Felix	P		Bartlett,Jason	6		Cuddyer,Michael	39		Street,Huston	P
	Teixeira,Mark	3		Scherzer,Max	P		Lewis,Colby	P		Cabrera,Asdrubal	6
	Mauer,Joe	20		Morales,Kendry	3		Carpenter,Chris	P		Wilson,C.J.	P
	Cruz,Nelson	9		Prado,Martin	45		Soto,Geovany	2		Bourjos,Peter	8
	Zimmerman,Ryan	5		McGehee,Casey	5		Rodriguez,Sean	48		Berkman,Lance	30
	Hamilton,Josh	78		Stanton,Mike	9		Morrow,Brandon	P		Morrison,Logan	7
	Fielder,Prince	3		Greinke,Zack	P		Pagan,Angel	789		Hellickson,Jeremy	P
	Kemp,Matt	8		Huff,Aubrey	379		Anderson,Brett	P		Broxton,Jonathan	P
	Rodriguez,Alex	5		Butler,Billy	30		Beltran,Carlos	8		Pena,Carlos	3
	Youkilis,Kevin	3		Markakis,Nick	9		Beckham,Gordon	4		Theriot,Ryan	46
	Choo,Shin-Soo	9		Pierre,Juan	7		Fowler,Dexter	8		Crisp,Coco	8
	Bautista,Jose	59		Granderson,Curtis	8		Willingham,Josh	7		Encarnacion,Edwin	5
	Gonzalez,Adrian	3		Latos,Mat	P		Byrd,Marlon	8		Myers,Brett	P
	Howard,Ryan	3		Price,David	P		Raburn,Ryan	79		Gonzalez,Gio	P
3	Pence,Hunter	9	7	Lee,Derrek	3	11	Hudson,Dan	P	15	McLouth,Nate	8
	Uggla,Dan	4		Lee,Carlos	37		Jennings,Desmond	9		Gomes,Jonny	7
	Lester,Jon	P		Hamels,Cole	P		Beckett,Josh	P		Bernadina,Roger	789
	Heyward,Jason	9		Kershaw,Clayton	P		Shields,James	P		Johnson,Chris	5
	Ramirez,Alexei	6		Bourn,Michael	8		Napoli,Mike	23		Matusz,Brian	P
	Ellsbury,Jacoby	8		Alvarez,Pedro	5		Stewart,Ian	5		Valverde,Jose	P
	Sabathia,CC	P		Wilson,Brian	P		Rodriguez,Wandy	P		Borbon,Julio	8
	Lincecum,Tim	P		LaRoche,Adam	3		Montero,Miguel	2		Lilly,Ted	P
	Ethier,Andre	9		Davis,Rajai	789		Gardner,Brett	78		Baker,Scott	P
	Kinsler,Ian	4		Ibanez,Raul	7		Kubel,Jason	90		Arroyo,Bronson	P
	Phillips,Brandon	4		Upton,B.J.	8		Marcum,Shaun	P		Niemann,Jeff	P
	Johnson,Kelly	4		Hill,Aaron	4		Reynolds,Mark	5		Hawpe,Brad	9
	Morneau,Justin	3		Swisher,Nick	9		Gallardo,Yovani	P		Snider,Travis	79
	Young,Delmon	7		Soriano,Rafael	P		Danks,John	P		Rolen,Scott	5
	Young,Chris	8		Jones,Adam	8		Castro,Starlin	6		Tejada,Miguel	56
4	Verlander,Justin	P	8	Beltre,Adrian	5	12	Figgins,Chone	4	16	Casilla,Alexi	46
	Hart,Corey	9		Lind,Adam	0		Desmond,Ian	6		Escobar,Yunel	6
	Wainwright,Adam	P		Stubbs,Drew	8		Murphy,David	79		Chacin,Jhoulys	P
	Reyes,Jose	6		Papelbon,Jonathan	P		Buchholz,Clay	P		Ruiz,Carlos	2
	Jeter,Derek	6		Rasmus,Colby	8		Sanchez,Gaby	3		Vazquez,Javier	P
	Rollins,Jimmy	6		Walker,Neil	4		Cahill,Trevor	P		Maybin,Cameron	8
	Weeks,Rickie	4		Tabata,Jose	7		Headley,Chase	5		Floyd,Gavin	P
	McCutchen,Andrew	8		Guerrero,Vladimir	0		Loney,James	3		Morgan,Nyjer	8
	Upton,Justin	9		Rodriguez,Francisco	P		Slowey,Kevin	P		Wieters,Matt	2
	Martinez,Victor	2		Jimenez,Ubaldo	P		Kuroda,Hiroki	P		Cueto,Johnny	P
	Lee,Cliff	P		Quentin,Carlos	90		Perez,Chris	P		Rivera,Mariano	P
	Victorino,Shane	8		Hanson,Tommy	P		Davis,Ike	3		Jenks,Bobby	P
	Weaver,Jered	P		Soria,Joakim	P		Sandoval,Pablo	5		Kennedy,Ian	P
	Dunn,Adam	3		Span,Denard	8		Aardsma,David	P		Podsednik,Scott	7
	Furcal,Rafael	6		Suzuki,Kurt	2		Brown,Domonic	9		Hudson,Orlando	4

ROTISSERIE SNAKE DRAFT — 15 TEAM MIXED LEAGUE

#	NAME	POS	#	NAME	POS	#	NAME	POS	#	NAME	POS
17	Scutaro,Marco	6	21	Cust,Jack	0	25	Saunders,Michael	7	29	Sweeney,Ryan	9
	Jones,Garrett	39		Overbay,Lyle	3		Jansen,Kenley	P		Saunders,Joe	P
	Ordonez,Magglio	9		Carter,V.Chris	7		Buehrle,Mark	P		Allen,Brandon	7
	Hardy,J.J.	6		Duensing,Brian	P		Izturis,Maicer	45		Blackburn,Nick	P
	Thornton,Matt	P		Cantu,Jorge	35		Diaz,Matt	7		Ryan,Brendan	6
	Santana,Ervin	P		Uehara,Koji	P		Bradley,Milton	70		Molina,Bengie	2
	Capps,Matt	P		Wood,Travis	P		Branyan,Russell	30		Nady,Xavier	39
	Barton,Daric	3		Garcia,Jaime	P		Drabek,Kyle	P		Cabrera,Everth	6
	Uribe,Juan	456		Aviles,Mike	4		Bard,Daniel	P		Hochevar,Luke	P
	Cordero,Francisco	P		Wheeler,Dan	P		Kennedy,Adam	34		Adams,Mike	P
	Freeman,Freddie	3		Martin,Russell	2		Jaso,John	2		Francisco,Ben	79
	Sizemore,Grady	8		Ellis,Mark	4		Jones,Chipper	5		Bergesen,Brad	P
	Espinosa,Danny	4		Venable,Will	789		Hanigan,Ryan	2		Zito,Barry	P
	Escobar,Alcides	6		Brantley,Michael	8		Sizemore,Scott	4		Wells,Randy	P
	Olivo,Miguel	2		Sanchez,Freddy	4		Sanchez,Anibal	P		Rhymes,Will	4
18	Dempster,Ryan	P	22	Gordon,Alex	7	26	Ankiel,Rick	8	30	Wells,Casper	9
	Putz,J.J.	P		Braden,Dallas	P		DeRosa,Mark	7		Donald,Jason	46
	Storen,Drew	P		Cameron,Mike	8		Blanks,Kyle	7		Norris,Bud	P
	Lyon,Brandon	P		Motte,Jason	P		Spilborghs,Ryan	79		Hensley,Clay	P
	Minor,Mike	P		Milledge,Lastings	79		Snyder,Chris	2		Francisco,Juan	5
	Molina,Yadier	2		de la Rosa,Jorge	P		Inge,Brandon	5		Moreland,Mitch	3
	Lowrie,Jed	46		Callaspo,Alberto	5		Rzepczynski,Marc	P		Renteria,Edgar	6
	Posada,Jorge	20		Porcello,Rick	P		Coke,Phil	P		Gutierrez,Juan	P
	Pennington,Cliff	6		Lewis,Fred	7		Thole,Josh	2		Glaus,Troy	3
	Colvin,Tyler	79		Pierzynski,A.J.	2		Arrieta,Jake	P		Cabrera,Melky	789
	Smith,Seth	79		Hafner,Travis	0		Gregerson,Luke	P		Tillman,Chris	P
	Pie,Felix	7		Wolf,Randy	P		Clippard,Tyler	P		DeWitt,Blake	4
	Benoit,Joaquin	P		Frasor,Jason	P		Viciedo,Dayan	5		Guillen,Carlos	4
	Nathan,Joe	P		Iannetta,Chris	2		Jones,Andruw	9		Luebke,Cory	P
	Carrasco,Carlos	P		Jackson,Conor	7		LaPorta,Matt	3		Romo,Sergio	P
19	Fukudome,Kosuke	9	23	Pineiro,Joel	P	27	Pena,Brayan	2			
	Buck,John	2		Franklin,Ryan	P		Gomez,Carlos	8			
	Bumgarner,Madison	P		Reimold,Nolan	7		Richard,Clayton	P			
	Kimbrel,Craig	P		Keppinger,Jeff	4		Cedeno,Ronny	6			
	Davis,Wade	P		McDonald,James	P		Bailey,Homer	P			
	Lowe,Derek	P		Niese,Jonathon	P		Avila,Alex	2			
	Pavano,Carl	P		Pettitte,Andy	P		Holland,Derek	P			
	Kouzmanoff,Kevin	5		Carmona,Fausto	P		Francisco,Frank	P			
	Kuo,Hong-Chih	P		Young Jr.,Eric	4		Brignac,Reid	46			
	Romero,Ricky	P		Fuentes,Brian	P		Torrealba,Yorvit	2			
	Smoak,Justin	3		Hall,Bill	47		Zimmermann,Jordan	P			
	Betancourt,Yuniesky	6		Jurrjens,Jair	P		Burnett,A.J.	P			
	Thome,Jim	0		Kalish,Ryan	8		Padilla,Vicente	P			
	Joyce,Matt	9		Garland,Jon	P		Capuano,Chris	P			
	Ludwick,Ryan	9		Blake,Casey	5		Hairston,Jerry	46			
20	Coghlan,Chris	7	24	Santana,Johan	P	28	Hernandez,Ramon	2			
	Ramirez,Manny	70		Volquez,Edinson	P		Carroll,Jamey	46			
	Doumit,Ryan	2		Jackson,Edwin	P		Crowe,Trevor	78			
	Nunez,Leo	P		Wigginton,Ty	345		Fujikawa,Kyuji	P			
	Nolasco,Ricky	P		Schumaker,Skip	4		Helton,Todd	3			
	Gregg,Kevin	P		Westbrook,Jake	P		Dickey,R.A.	P			
	Sanchez,Jonathan	P		Cabrera,Orlando	6		Downs,Scott	P			
	Ross,Cody	789		Cecil,Brett	P		Barajas,Rod	2			
	Peavy,Jake	P		Meek,Evan	P		Blanton,Joe	P			
	Lidge,Brad	P		Ka'aihue,Kila	3		Lopez,Felipe	456			
	Guthrie,Jeremy	P		Morse,Mike	9		Hundley,Nick	2			
	Venters,Jonny	P		Freese,David	5		Masterson,Justin	P			
	Burrell,Pat	70		League,Brandon	P		Chamberlain,Joba	P			
	Lopez,Jose	5		Chapman,Aroldis	P		Castillo,Luis	4			
	Gonzalez,Alex	6		Craig,Allen	9		Jay,Jon	89			

ROTISSERIE 500 — 2011 Draft - List Prices — Batters

BATTERS	'09	'10	R$
Pujols, Albert	54	49	$52
Crawford, Carl	38	40	39
Ramirez, Hanley	39	35	37
Cabrera, Miguel	30	43	37
Votto, Joey	25	47	36
Fielder, Prince	39	27	33
Choo, Shin-Soo	28	35	32
Werth, Jayson	31	32	32
Gonzalez, Adrian	32	30	31
Braun, Ryan	34	28	31
Holliday, Matt	30	31	31
Abreu, Bobby	35	26	31
Tulowitzki, Troy	31	27	29
Bourn, Michael	32	26	29
Wright, David	28	29	29
Mauer, Joe	36	21	29
Figgins, Chone	37	20	29
Longoria, Evan	24	29	27
Suzuki, Ichiro	25	28	27
Zobrist, Ben	33	20	27
Jeter, Derek	37	16	27
Gonzalez, Carlos	10	42	26
Utley, Chase	33	19	26
Teixeira, Mark	27	24	26
Dunn, Adam	28	21	25
Zimmerman, Ryan	23	25	24
Howard, Ryan	29	19	24
McCutchen, Andrew	17	30	24
Youkilis, Kevin	27	20	24
Rodriguez, Alex	28	19	24
Kemp, Matt	31	16	24
Bautista, Jose	6	39	23
Upton, Justin	25	20	23
Gardner, Brett	9	35	22
Konerko, Paul	12	32	22
Cano, Robinson	16	28	22
Pierre, Juan	12	31	22
Uggla, Dan	15	28	22
Davis, Rajai	20	22	21
Reynolds, Mark	30	12	21
Upton, B.J.	16	25	21
Cruz, Nelson	18	23	21
Victorino, Shane	20	21	21
Hunter, Torii	21	19	20
Kinsler, Ian	23	17	20
Hamilton, Josh	4	35	20
Lee, Derrek	27	12	20
Bay, Jason	31	8	20
Ellsbury, Jacoby	39	0	20
Span, Denard	25	13	19
Podsednik, Scott	17	20	19
Pence, Hunter	16	20	18
Swisher, Nick	17	19	18
Ethier, Andre	19	17	18
Pedroia, Dustin	25	11	18
Heyward, Jason	10	25	18
Butler, Billy	14	21	18
Morneau, Justin	17	18	18
Damon, Johnny	22	13	18
Berkman, Lance	24	11	18
Rios, Alex	8	26	17
Bartlett, Jason	28	6	17
Young, Chris	5	28	17
Pagan, Angel	8	25	17
Ortiz, David	10	23	17
Markakis, Nick	15	18	17
Martinez, Victor	21	12	17
Young, Michael	18	14	16
Roberts, Brian	27	5	16
Huff, Aubrey	3	28	16
Phillips, Brandon	17	14	16
Morgan, Nyjer	22	9	16
Helton, Todd	24	7	16
Ibanez, Raul	16	14	15
Jones, Chipper	19	11	15
Drew, J.D.	19	11	15
Scutaro, Marco	21	9	15
Granderson, Curtis	16	13	15
Pena, Carlos	18	11	15
Jackson, Austin	10	18	14
Thome, Jim	12	16	14
Matsui, Hideki	14	14	14

BATTERS	'09	'10	R$
McCann, Brian	11	17	14
Andrus, Elvis	12	16	14
Sandoval, Pablo	22	6	14
Johnson, Kelly	1	26	14
Cuddyer, Michael	15	12	14
Stubbs, Drew	3	23	13
Hart, Corey	7	19	13
Furcal, Rafael	9	17	13
Scott, Luke	9	17	13
Willingham, Josh	11	15	13
Cust, Jack	14	12	13
Fowler, Dexter	16	10	13
Kubel, Jason	17	9	13
Weeks, Rickie	2	23	13
Beltre, Adrian	3	22	13
Murphy, David	10	15	13
Fukudome, Kosuke	13	12	13
Barton, Daric	2	22	12
Rasmus, Colby	3	21	12
Torres, Andres	3	21	12
Wells, Vernon	9	15	12
LaRoche, Adam	14	10	12
Ramirez, Manny	15	9	12
Guerrero, Vladimir	5	18	12
Davis, Ike	10	13	12
Rolen, Scott	11	12	12
Gutierrez, Franklin	13	10	12
Loney, James	13	10	12
Lind, Adam	22	1	12
Prado, Martin	8	14	11
McGehee, Casey	9	13	11
Sanchez, Gaby	10	12	11
Hawpe, Brad	18	4	11
Morales, Kendry	19	3	11
Bruce, Jay	4	17	11
Crisp, Coco	4	17	11
Drew, Stephen	6	15	11
Ordonez, Magglio	10	11	11
Tabata, Jose	10	11	11
Ramirez, Alexei	11	10	11
Rollins, Jimmy	13	8	11
Coghlan, Chris	15	6	11
Headley, Chase	9	11	10
Posey, Buster	10	10	10
Overbay, Lyle	11	9	10
Posada, Jorge	11	9	10
Jones, Garrett	12	8	10
Lopez, Felipe	16	4	10
Castillo, Luis	18	2	10
Reyes, Jose	3	16	10
Jaso, John	10	10	10
Walker, Neil	10	9	10
Hudson, Orlando	11	8	10
Theriot, Ryan	12	7	10
Escobar, Yunel	14	5	10
Venable, Will	3	15	9
Byrd, Marlon	9	9	9
Stewart, Ian	9	9	9
Stanton, Mike	10	9	9
Jones, Adam	10	8	9
Desmond, Ian	10	8	9
Branyan, Russell	11	7	9
Lee, Carlos	13	5	9
Kennedy, Adam	13	5	9
Beltran, Carlos	15	3	9
Johnson, Nick	18	0	9
DeJesus, David	9	8	9
Bernadina, Roger	10	7	9
Colvin, Tyler	10	7	9
Castro, Starlin	10	7	9
Blake, Casey	13	4	9
Cabrera, Asdrubal	15	2	9
McLouth, Nate	17	0	9
Ross, Cody	8	8	8
Johnson, Chris	10	6	8
Boesch, Brennan	10	6	8
Aybar, Erick	10	6	8
Alvarez, Pedro	10	6	8
Smith, Seth	11	5	8
Hill, Aaron	16	0	8
Soriano, Alfonso	5	10	8
Valencia, Danny	10	5	8

BATTERS	'09	'10	R$
Young, Delmon	2	13	8
Pennington, Cliff	3	12	8
Ruiz, Carlos	5	10	8
Gomes, Jonny	6	9	8
Hafner, Travis	6	9	8
Kendrick, Howie	7	8	8
Napoli, Mike	8	7	8
Raburn, Ryan	8	7	8
Ludwick, Ryan	9	6	8
Morrison, Logan	10	5	8
Santana, Carlos	10	5	8
Soto, Geovany	2	12	7
Carroll, Jamey	4	10	7
Quentin, Carlos	4	10	7
Jones, Andruw	5	9	7
Polanco, Placido	7	7	7
Molina, Yadier	9	5	7
Ramirez, Aramis	9	5	7
Jay, Jon	10	4	7
Moreland, Mitch	10	4	7
Callaspo, Alberto	11	3	7
Izturis, Maicer	12	2	7
Infante, Omar	2	11	7
Burrell, Pat	3	10	7
Lewis, Fred	4	9	7
Uribe, Juan	6	7	7
Borbon, Julio	8	5	7
Martin, Russell	8	5	7
Conrad, Brooks	10	3	7
Freese, David	10	3	7
Young Jr., Eric	10	3	7
Diaz, Matt	13	0	7
Ellis, Mark	4	8	6
Schumaker, Skip	8	4	6
Cabrera, Melky	9	3	6
Tejada, Miguel	9	3	6
Rivera, Juan	9	3	6
Cervelli, Francisco	10	2	6
Herrera, Jonathan	10	2	6
Kalish, Ryan	10	2	6
Smoak, Justin	10	2	6
Sizemore, Grady	12	0	6
Cameron, Mike	12	0	6
Spilborghs, Ryan	4	7	6
Montero, Miguel	8	3	6
Francisco, Ben	8	3	6
Cabrera, Orlando	8	3	6
Beckham, Gordon	8	3	6
Saunders, Michael	10	1	6
Thole, Josh	10	1	6
Cain, Lorenzo	10	1	6
Cantu, Jorge	10	1	6
Kottaras, George	10	1	6
Brantley, Michael	10	1	6
Rhymes, Will	10	1	6
Brignac, Reid	10	1	6
Inge, Brandon	5	5	5
Sweeney, Ryan	7	3	5
Dye, Jermaine	10	0	5
Cabrera, Everth	10	0	5
Reimold, Nolan	10	0	5
Keppinger, Jeff	0	9	5
Aviles, Mike	0	9	5
Sanchez, Freddy	3	6	5
Olivo, Miguel	3	6	5
Francoeur, Jeff	5	4	5
Gwynn, Tony	6	3	5
Getz, Chris	7	2	5
Bradley, Milton	8	1	5
Betemit, Wilson	0	8	4
Patterson, Corey	0	8	4
Glaus, Troy	0	8	4
Peralta, Jhonny	3	5	4
Giambi, Jason	4	4	4
Suzuki, Kurt	6	2	4
Harris, Willie	7	1	4
Kearns, Austin	0	7	4
Hall, Bill	0	7	4
Hanigan, Ryan	1	6	4
Hairston, Scott	6	1	4
Bloomquist, Willie	6	1	4
DeRosa, Mark	7	0	4

BATTERS	'09	'10	R$
Torrealba, Yorvit	2	5	4
Maier, Mitch	3	4	4
Winn, Randy	6	1	4
Hermida, Jeremy	7	0	4
Punto, Nick	7	0	4
Denorfia, Chris	0	6	3
McDonald, Darnell	0	6	3
Wigginton, Ty	1	5	3
Hernandez, Ramon	1	5	3
Mora, Melvin	1	5	3
Hinske, Eric	2	4	3
Encarnacion, Edwin	2	4	3
Hairston, Jerry	3	3	3
Wieters, Matt	3	3	3
Bonifacio, Emilio	4	2	3
Barmes, Clint	5	1	3
Teahen, Mark	5	1	3
Roberts, Ryan	6	0	3
Ryan, Brendan	6	0	3
Dickerson, Chris	6	0	3
Buck, John	0	5	3
Blanco, Gregor	0	5	3
Vizquel, Omar	0	5	3
Joyce, Matt	0	5	3
Morse, Mike	0	5	3
Gomez, Carlos	1	4	3
Thames, Marcus	2	3	3
LaRoche, Andy	5	0	3
Lugo, Julio	5	0	3
Counsell, Craig	5	0	3
Baker, John	5	0	3
Lopez, Jose	5	0	3
DeWitt, Blake	0	4	2
Edmonds, Jim	0	4	2
Gonzalez, Alex	0	4	2
Crowe, Trevor	0	4	2
Lowrie, Jed	0	4	2
Guillen, Jose	0	4	2
Rodriguez, Sean	0	4	2
Snider, Travis	1	3	2
Milledge, Lastings	1	3	2
Kendall, Jason	1	3	2
Doumit, Ryan	1	3	2
Ross, David	2	2	2
Guillen, Carlos	3	1	2
Iannetta, Chris	4	0	2
Pierzynski, A.J.	4	0	2
Church, Ryan	4	0	2
Parra, Gerardo	4	0	2
Murphy, Daniel	4	0	2
Cairo, Miguel	0	3	2
Snyder, Chris	0	3	2
Renteria, Edgar	2	1	2
Pie, Felix	2	1	2
Velez, Eugenio	3	0	2
Belliard, Ronnie	3	0	2
Matthews Jr., Gary	3	0	2
Aybar, Willy	3	0	2
Gross, Gabe	3	0	2
Kapler, Gabe	3	0	2
Garko, Ryan	3	0	2
Ishikawa, Travis	3	0	2
Nix, Jayson	3	0	2
Kotchman, Casey	3	0	2
Rowand, Aaron	3	0	2
Tatis, Fernando	3	0	2

UNLISTED PLAYER PRICES:

Rookie eligible	$10
Previous MLB experience	$1

PITCHERS	'09	'10	R$
Hernandez,Felix	34	31	$33
Wainwright,Adam	32	32	32
Halladay,Roy	29	34	32
Lincecum,Tim	34	18	26
Verlander,Justin	27	20	24
Sabathia,CC	23	23	23
Carpenter,Chris	27	18	23
Jimenez,Ubaldo	19	25	22
Johnson,Josh	21	22	22
Lester,Jon	21	22	22
Greinke,Zack	37	5	21
Cain,Matt	22	17	20
Kershaw,Clayton	18	20	19
Weaver,Jered	15	22	19
Lee,Cliff	20	16	18
Haren,Dan	24	10	17
Bell,Heath	14	19	17
Rodriguez,Wandy	22	10	16
Wilson,Brian	12	18	15
Santana,Johan	16	14	15
Latos,Mat	10	19	15
Price,David	3	25	14
Vazquez,Javier	28	0	14
Oswalt,Roy	5	21	13
Wilson,C.J.	11	15	13
Gallardo,Yovani	15	11	13
Sanchez,Jonathan	7	18	13
Garcia,Jaime	10	15	13
Marmol,Carlos	11	14	13
Dempster,Ryan	13	12	13
Rivera,Mariano	16	9	13
Hamels,Cole	6	18	12
Hanson,Tommy	12	12	12
Lilly,Ted	16	8	12
Jurrjens,Jair	24	0	12
Soriano,Rafael	9	14	12
Buchholz,Clay	1	21	11
Soria,Joakim	9	13	11
Venters,Jonny	10	12	11
Danks,John	11	11	11
Bailey,Andrew	16	6	11
Wolf,Randy	16	5	11
Hudson,Tim	0	20	10
Billingsley,Chad	10	10	10
Axford,John	10	10	10
Thornton,Matt	11	9	10
Papelbon,Jonathan	13	7	10
Broxton,Jonathan	16	4	10
Scherzer,Max	7	12	10
Arroyo,Bronson	11	8	10
Hughes,Phil	11	8	10
Wagner,Billy	0	18	9
Cahill,Trevor	1	17	9
Adams,Mike	4	14	9
Romero,Ricky	7	11	9
Gregerson,Luke	7	11	9
Takahashi,Hisanori	10	8	9
Chacin,Jhoulys	10	8	9
Cordero,Francisco	11	7	9
Jackson,Edwin	14	4	9
Myers,Brett	0	17	9
Garland,Jon	6	11	9
Lyon,Brandon	7	10	9
Garza,Matt	9	8	9
Hudson,Daniel	10	7	9
Franklin,Ryan	11	6	9
Pineiro,Joel	13	4	9
Aardsma,David	14	3	9
Happ,J.A.	15	2	9
Beckett,Josh	17	0	9
Gonzalez,Gio	0	16	8
O Day,Darren	8	8	8
Zambrano,Carlos	8	8	8
Madson,Ryan	10	6	8
Guerrier,Matt	11	5	8
Wells,Randy	13	3	8
Nathan,Joe	16	0	8

PITCHERS	'09	'10	R$
Kuroda,Hiroki	4	11	8
Pettitte,Andy	8	7	8
Masset,Nick	9	6	8
Bumgarner,Madison	10	5	8
Kuo,Hong-Chih	1	13	7
Feliz,Neftali	2	12	7
Clippard,Tyler	3	11	7
Anderson,Brett	8	6	7
Moylan,Peter	8	6	7
Lopez,Wilton	10	4	7
Strasburg,Stephen	10	4	7
Niese,Jonathon	10	4	7
Liriano,Francisco	0	13	7
Cueto,Johnny	5	8	7
Rodriguez,Francisco	6	7	7
Lackey,John	8	5	7
Floyd,Gavin	8	5	7
Ogando,Alexi	10	3	7
Santos,Sergio	10	3	7
de la Rosa,Jorge	11	2	7
Wuertz,Mike	13	0	7
Dickey,R.A.	0	12	6
Capps,Matt	0	12	6
Duensing,Brian	1	11	6
Bard,Daniel	2	10	6
Richard,Clayton	3	9	6
Rhodes,Arthur	5	7	6
Betancourt,Rafael	6	6	6
Nunez,Leo	6	6	6
Breslow,Craig	6	6	6
Valverde,Jose	7	5	6
Feliciano,Pedro	7	5	6
Oliver,Darren	8	4	6
Zito,Barry	8	4	6
Wood,Travis	10	2	6
Jansen,Kenley	10	2	6
Kimbrel,Craig	10	2	6
Storen,Drew	10	2	6
Street,Huston	10	2	6
Webb,Ryan	10	2	6
Burnett,A.J.	12	0	6
Lewis,Colby	0	11	6
Sanchez,Anibal	1	10	6
Pavano,Carl	2	9	6
Braden,Dallas	4	7	6
Lowe,Derek	4	7	6
McClellan,Kyle	4	7	6
Fuentes,Brian	6	5	6
Niemann,Jeff	8	3	6
Baker,Scott	8	3	6
Buehrle,Mark	8	3	6
Frieri,Ernesto	10	1	6
Braddock,Zach	10	1	6
Leake,Mike	10	1	6
Gonzalez,Mike	11	0	6
Affeldt,Jeremy	11	0	6
Belisle,Matt	0	10	5
Marcum,Shaun	0	10	5
Marshall,Sean	0	10	5
Santana,Ervin	0	10	5
Hensley,Clay	0	10	5
Romo,Sergio	2	8	5
Sherrill,George	10	0	5
Hoffman,Trevor	10	0	5
Millwood,Kevin	10	0	5
Perez,Chris	0	9	5
Benoit,Joaquin	0	9	5
Burnett,Sean	2	7	5
Downs,Scott	2	7	5
Gregg,Kevin	3	6	5
Rodney,Fernando	5	4	5
Nolasco,Ricky	5	4	5
Rauch,Jon	5	4	5
Frasor,Jason	6	3	5
Feldman,Scott	9	0	5
Blanton,Joe	9	0	5
Correia,Kevin	9	0	5

PITCHERS	'09	'10	R$
Meek,Evan	0	8	4
Pelfrey,Mike	0	8	4
Shields,James	8	0	4
Howell,J.P.	8	0	4
Marquis,Jason	8	0	4
Casilla,Santiago	0	7	4
Kennedy,Ian	0	7	4
Carmona,Fausto	0	7	4
Hunter,Tommy	2	5	4
Balfour,Grant	2	5	4
Saito,Takashi	3	4	4
Sanches,Brian	3	4	4
Francisco,Frank	4	3	4
Dotel,Octavio	4	3	4
Ziegler,Brad	5	2	4
Ramirez,Ramon	5	2	4
Harden,Rich	7	0	4
Hawkins,LaTroy	7	0	4
Porcello,Rick	7	0	4
Peavy,Jake	7	0	4
Stauffer,Tim	0	6	3
League,Brandon	0	6	3
Hanrahan,Joel	0	6	3
Hernandez,Livan	0	6	3
Guthrie,Jeremy	0	6	3
Camp,Shawn	2	4	3
Coke,Phil	2	4	3
Chamberlain,Joba	2	4	3
Jenks,Bobby	4	2	3
Davis,Doug	6	0	3
Aceves,Alfredo	6	0	3
Washburn,Jarrod	6	0	3
Belisario,Ronald	6	0	3
Duke,Zach	6	0	3
Ohlendorf,Ross	6	0	3
Okajima,Hideki	6	0	3
Contreras,Jose	0	5	3
Vargas,Jason	0	5	3
Cecil,Brett	0	5	3
Motte,Jason	0	5	3
Loe,Kameron	0	5	3
Wood,Kerry	2	3	3
Jepsen,Kevin	2	3	3
Hammel,Jason	5	0	3
Grabow,John	5	0	3
Lannan,John	5	0	3
Lowe,Mark	5	0	3
Blackburn,Nick	5	0	3
Kawakami,Kenshin	5	0	3
Bedard,Erik	5	0	3
Morrow,Brandon	0	4	2
Davis,Wade	0	4	2
Figueroa,Nelson	0	4	2
Lidge,Brad	0	4	2
Crain,Jesse	0	4	2
Lopez,Javier	0	4	2
Chen,Bruce	0	4	2
Robertson,David	1	3	2
Thatcher,Joe	1	3	2
Slowey,Kevin	1	3	2
O Flaherty,Eric	2	2	2
Padilla,Vicente	3	1	2
Tejeda,Robinson	3	1	2
Wheeler,Dan	3	1	2
Medders,Brandon	4	0	2
Cook,Aaron	4	0	2
Harang,Aaron	4	0	2
Saunders,Joe	4	0	2
Bergesen,Brad	4	0	2
Bulger,Jason	4	0	2
Matusz,Brian	0	3	2
Perez,Rafael	0	3	2
Durbin,Chad	0	3	2
Gorzelanny,Tom	0	3	2
Westbrook,Jake	0	3	2
Perry,Ryan	0	3	2

PITCHERS	'09	'10	R$
Uehara,Koji	0	3	2
Veras,Jose	0	3	2
Weathers,David	3	0	2
Batista,Miguel	3	0	2
Herrera,Daniel	3	0	2
Qualls,Chad	3	0	2
Pinto,Renyel	3	0	2
Mujica,Edward	3	0	2
Farnsworth,Kyle	0	2	1
Peralta,Joel	0	2	1
Logan,Boone	0	2	1
LeBlanc,Wade	0	2	1
Silva,Carlos	0	2	1
Dessens,Elmer	0	2	1
Ohman,Will	0	2	1
Medlen,Kris	0	2	1
Carrasco,D.J.	1	1	1
Sipp,Tony	1	1	1
Weaver,Jeff	2	0	1
Condrey,Clay	2	0	1
Masterson,Justin	2	0	1
Eyre,Scott	2	0	1
Bruney,Brian	2	0	1
Vargas,Claudio	2	0	1
Gaudin,Chad	2	0	1
Maholm,Paul	2	0	1
Talbot,Mitch	0	1	1
Ray,Chris	0	1	1
Smith,Joe	0	1	1
Narveson,Chris	0	1	1
Norris,Bud	0	1	1
Blevins,Jerry	0	1	1
Volstad,Chris	0	1	1
Fister,Doug	0	1	1
Berken,Jason	0	1	1
Choate,Randy	0	1	1
Matsuzaka,Daisuke	0	1	1
Hernandez,David	0	1	1
Wuertz,Michael	0	1	1
Beimel,Joe	0	1	1
Lindstrom,Matt	0	1	1
Janssen,Casey	0	1	1
Zumaya,Joel	0	1	1
Kazmir,Scott	1	0	1
Wakefield,Tim	1	0	1
Heilman,Aaron	1	0	1
Moyer,Jamie	1	0	1
Penny,Brad	1	0	1
Bailey,Homer	1	0	1
McDonald,James	1	0	1
Rowland-Smith,Ryan	1	0	1

UNLISTED PLAYER PRICES:

Rookie eligible	$10
Previous MLB experience	$1

NAME	POS	RAR
Hernandez, Felix	P	37.0
Werth, Jayson	89	36.5
Cabrera, Miguel	3	36.1
Halladay, Roy	P	35.3
Mauer, Joe	20	34.8
Bautista, Jose	59	32.8
Pujols, Albert	3	32.0
Lester, Jon	P	31.2
Longoria, Evan	5	30.0
Lincecum, Tim	P	29.7
Tulowitzki, Troy	6	28.7
Holliday, Matt	7	28.3
Ramirez, Hanley	6	26.8
Santana, Carlos	2	26.2
Rodriguez, Alex	5	26.1
Heyward, Jason	9	25.8
Youkilis, Kevin	3	25.4
Hamilton, Josh	78	25.3
Soto, Geovany	2	24.9
Pedroia, Dustin	4	24.9
Votto, Joey	3	24.8
Liriano, Francisco	P	24.8
Utley, Chase	4	24.7
Wainwright, Adam	P	24.5
Cruz, Nelson	9	24.0
Martinez, Victor	2	23.1
Johnson, Josh	P	22.9
Gonzalez, Carlos	789	22.9
Haren, Dan	P	22.7
Cano, Robinson	4	22.5
Uggla, Dan	4	22.3
Anderson, Brett	P	21.9
Sabathia, CC	P	21.4
Teixeira, Mark	3	21.3
Zimmerman, Ryan	5	21.0
Hudson, Tim	P	20.9
Beckett, Josh	P	20.8
Greinke, Zack	P	20.7
Choo, Shin-Soo	9	20.3
Hamels, Cole	P	20.3
Verlander, Justin	P	20.3
Lee, Cliff	P	19.9
Morneau, Justin	3	19.8
Johnson, Kelly	4	19.7
Carrasco, Carlos	P	19.5
Lowe, Derek	P	19.4
Oswalt, Roy	P	19.2
Carpenter, Chris	P	19.1
Gallardo, Yovani	P	18.8
Scherzer, Max	P	18.7
Posey, Buster	23	18.2
Beltran, Carlos	8	18.0
Wright, David	5	18.0
Upton, Justin	9	18.0
Swisher, Nick	9	17.8
Ethier, Andre	9	17.6
Zobrist, Ben	49	17.5
Jimenez, Ubaldo	P	17.5
Rodriguez, Wandy	P	17.5
Braun, Ryan	7	17.4
Posada, Jorge	20	17.4
McCann, Brian	2	17.4
Kuroda, Hiroki	P	17.1
Ramirez, Manny	70	17.0
Hawpe, Brad	9	17.0
Ruiz, Carlos	2	17.0

NAME	POS	RAR
Romero, Ricky	P	16.8
Wilson, C.J.	P	16.2
Napoli, Mike	23	16.1
Dunn, Adam	3	16.1
Kinsler, Ian	4	16.0
Billingsley, Chad	P	15.9
McCutchen, Andrew	8	15.8
Shields, James	P	15.7
Lowrie, Jed	46	15.6
Montero, Miguel	2	15.4
Latos, Mat	P	15.3
Masterson, Justin	P	15.3
Weeks, Rickie	4	15.2
Stanton, Mike	9	15.1
Thome, Jim	0	14.6
Kershaw, Clayton	P	14.5
Drew, Stephen	6	14.4
Young, Chris	8	14.3
Venters, Jonny	P	14.0
Nolasco, Ricky	P	14.0
Lewis, Colby	P	13.7
Morrow, Brandon	P	13.6
Furcal, Rafael	6	13.6
Alvarez, Pedro	5	13.6
Garcia, Jaime	P	13.4
Myers, Brett	P	13.2
Buchholz, Clay	P	13.0
de la Rosa, Jorge	P	13.0
Dempster, Ryan	P	12.9
Abreu, Bobby	79	12.8
Willingham, Josh	7	12.8
Hanson, Tommy	P	12.8
Weaver, Jered	P	12.6
Pineiro, Joel	P	12.6
Drew, J.D.	9	12.4
Bruce, Jay	9	12.3
Thornton, Matt	P	12.3
Iannetta, Chris	2	12.3
Fukudome, Kosuke	9	12.2
Rollins, Jimmy	6	12.2
Konerko, Paul	30	12.0
Hart, Corey	9	11.9
Prado, Martin	45	11.9
Gonzalez, Gio	P	11.8
Fielder, Prince	3	11.8
Lackey, John	P	11.8
Floyd, Gavin	P	11.5
Morrison, Logan	7	11.4
League, Brandon	P	11.2
Westbrook, Jake	P	11.1
Chapman, Aroldis	P	10.9
Peavy, Jake	P	10.9
Reyes, Jose	6	10.8
Jeter, Derek	6	10.8
Gregerson, Luke	P	10.8
Jones, Chipper	5	10.7
Gonzalez, Adrian	3	10.7
Rzepczynski, Marc	P	10.6
Kemp, Matt	8	10.6
Ramirez, Alexei	6	10.5
Reynolds, Mark	5	10.5
Ortiz, David	0	10.4
Chacin, Jhoulys	P	10.4
Marcum, Shaun	P	10.4
Rasmus, Colby	8	10.3
Ramirez, Aramis	5	10.3

NAME	POS	RAR
Niese, Jonathon	P	10.3
Wieters, Matt	2	10.2
Bell, Heath	P	10.1
Drabek, Kyle	P	10.1
Downs, Scott	P	10.0
Marshall, Sean	P	9.9
Minor, Mike	P	9.7
Burrell, Pat	70	9.6
Broxton, Jonathan	P	9.6
Madson, Ryan	P	9.4
Carmona, Fausto	P	9.4
Crawford, Carl	7	9.3
Price, David	P	9.3
Mejia, Jenrry	P	9.3
Rogers, Esmil	P	9.3
Bard, Daniel	P	9.2
Soria, Joakim	P	9.2
Beltre, Adrian	5	9.2
Roberts, Brian	4	9.1
Zimmermann, Jorda	P	9.1
Putz, J.J.	P	9.1
Ross, David	2	9.0
Chamberlain, Joba	P	8.9
Robertson, David	P	8.8
Hudson, Dan	P	8.7
Fowler, Dexter	8	8.7
Papelbon, Jonathan	P	8.6
Wilson, Brian	P	8.6
Jenks, Bobby	P	8.5
Beckham, Gordon	4	8.5
Markakis, Nick	9	8.5
Scutaro, Marco	6	8.5
Hanrahan, Joel	P	8.5
Hardy, J.J.	6	8.4
Ibanez, Raul	7	8.4
Hellickson, Jeremy	P	8.4
Walden, Jordan	P	8.3
Axford, John	P	8.3
Webb, Ryan	P	8.2
Kuo, Hong-Chih	P	8.1
Volquez, Edinson	P	8.1
Benoit, Joaquin	P	8.1
Vazquez, Javier	P	8.1
Valverde, Jose	P	8.1
Pena, Carlos	3	8.1
Burnett, Sean	P	8.0
Damon, Johnny	70	8.0
Nathan, Joe	P	7.8
Quentin, Carlos	90	7.7
Oliver, Darren	P	7.7
Thatcher, Joe	P	7.6
Qualls, Chad	P	7.5
Parnell, Bobby	P	7.5
Marmol, Carlos	P	7.4
Berkman, Lance	30	7.4
Jepsen, Kevin	P	7.4
Lopez, Wilton	P	7.4
Rodriguez, Francis	P	7.3
Feliciano, Pedro	P	7.3
Young, Michael	5	7.2
Mujica, Edward	P	7.2
Sanchez, Jonathan	P	7.2
Bailey, Andrew	P	7.1
Wuertz, Mike	P	7.0
Danks, John	P	7.0
Masset, Nick	P	6.9

NAME	POS	RAR
Wells, Vernon	8	6.8
Bartlett, Jason	6	6.8
Granderson, Curtis	8	6.7
Niemann, Jeff	P	6.7
Cain, Matt	P	6.7
Hochevar, Luke	P	6.6
Pettitte, Andy	P	6.6
Jaso, John	2	6.5
Howard, Ryan	3	6.5
Choate, Randy	P	6.4
Snider, Travis	79	6.4
Buck, John	2	6.4
Johnson, Nick	0	6.4
Porcello, Rick	P	6.4
Sale, Chris	P	6.3
Soriano, Rafael	P	6.3
Raburn, Ryan	79	6.2
Frasor, Jason	P	6.2
Hammel, Jason	P	6.2
Hanigan, Ryan	2	6.2
Francisco, Frank	P	6.2
Farnsworth, Kyle	P	6.2
Saito, Takashi	P	6.2
Rodriguez, Henry	P	6.2
Encarnacion, Edwi	5	6.1
Cahill, Trevor	P	6.1
Murphy, David	79	6.0
Victorino, Shane	8	6.0
Pavano, Carl	P	6.0
Varitek, Jason	2	6.0
Ogando, Alexi	P	5.9
Smith, Joe	P	5.9
Camp, Shawn	P	5.8
Romo, Sergio	P	5.8
Betancourt, Rafael	P	5.7
Bedard, Erik	P	5.7
Suzuki, Kurt	2	5.6
Hughes, Phil	P	5.6
Adams, Mike	P	5.6
Jansen, Kenley	P	5.5
Hunter, Torii	89	5.4
Affeldt, Jeremy	P	5.4
Moylan, Peter	P	5.4
Street, Huston	P	5.4
Belisario, Ronald	P	5.4
Baker, Scott	P	5.4
Bradley, Milton	70	5.4
Nunez, Leo	P	5.3
Bailey, Homer	P	5.3
Smith, Seth	79	5.3
Meek, Evan	P	5.3
Stewart, Ian	5	5.2
Burnett, A.J.	P	5.2
Bumgarner, Madis	P	5.2
Logan, Boone	P	5.1
Capps, Matt	P	5.1
Cueto, Johnny	P	5.1
Branyan, Russell	30	5.1
Butler, Billy	30	5.0
Ordonez, Magglio	9	5.0
Gonzalez, Mike	P	5.0
Webb, Brandon	P	5.0
Balfour, Grant	P	4.9
Feliz, Neftali	P	4.8
Perez, Chris	P	4.8
Soriano, Alfonso	7	4.8

SIMULATION LEAGUE DRAFT   TOP 500

NAME	POS	RAR	NAME	POS	RAR	NAME	POS	RAR	NAME	POS	RAR
Coffey,Todd	P	4.8	Santana,Ervin	P	2.7	Fulchino,Jeff	P	1.2	Gaudin,Chad	P	-0.1
Janssen,Casey	P	4.8	Cook,Aaron	P	2.6	Walker,Tyler	P	1.2	Durbin,Chad	P	-0.1
Ziegler,Brad	P	4.8	McGehee,Casey	5	2.6	Zambrano,Carlos	P	1.2	Jackson,Conor	7	-0.2
Snyder,Chris	2	4.8	Hill,Shawn	P	2.5	Phillips,Brandon	4	1.2	Reimold,Nolan	7	-0.2
Rivera,Mariano	P	4.8	Correia,Kevin	P	2.5	Franklin,Ryan	P	1.1	Wood,Blake	P	-0.2
Joyce,Matt	9	4.6	Saltalamacchia,Jar	2	2.5	Meche,Gil	P	1.1	Sizemore,Scott	4	-0.2
Cust,Jack	0	4.6	Thole,Josh	2	2.5	Peralta,Joel	P	1.1	Corpas,Manny	P	-0.3
Santos,Sergio	P	4.6	Duensing,Brian	P	2.4	Hernandez,Ramon	2	1.1	Mijares,Jose	P	-0.3
Badenhop,Burke	P	4.5	Kubel,Jason	90	2.4	Byrd,Marlon	8	1.1	Marte,Damaso	P	-0.3
Hensley,Clay	P	4.4	Kennedy,Ian	P	2.4	Infante,Omar	457	1.1	Texeira,Kanekoa	P	-0.3
Rolen,Scott	5	4.4	Norris,Bud	P	2.4	Hawkins,LaTroy	P	1.1	Izturis,Maicer	45	-0.3
Howell,J.P.	P	4.4	Ross,Tyson	P	2.3	Perry,Ryan	P	1.0	Baker,John	2	-0.3
O'Flaherty,Eric	P	4.4	Lidge,Brad	P	2.3	Castro,Starlin	6	1.0	Zumaya,Joel	P	-0.3
Demel,Sam	P	4.4	Wright,Jamey	P	2.2	Germano,Justin	P	1.0	Hawksworth,Blake	P	-0.3
Jackson,Edwin	P	4.4	Crain,Jesse	P	2.2	Boggs,Mitchell	P	1.0	Sonnanstine,Andy	P	-0.3
Escobar,Yunel	6	4.3	Carrasco,D.J.	P	2.2	Sanchez,Anibal	P	1.0	Berken,Jason	P	-0.4
Padilla,Vicente	P	4.3	Bray,Bill	P	2.2	Guerrier,Matt	P	0.9	Molina,Yadier	2	-0.4
Lilly,Ted	P	4.2	Atchison,Scott	P	2.1	Pauley,David	P	0.9	Torres,Andres	789	-0.5
Capuano,Chris	P	4.2	Aceves,Alfredo	P	2.1	Doubront,Felix	P	0.9	Hernandez,David	P	-0.5
Pence,Hunter	9	4.2	Guillen,Carlos	4	2.1	Martin,Russell	2	0.9	Baez,Danys	P	-0.5
Uehara,Koji	P	4.2	Park,Chan Ho	P	2.1	McLouth,Nate	8	0.9	DeJesus,David	9	-0.5
Stammen,Craig	P	4.2	Morton,Charlie	P	2.1	Ely,John	P	0.9	Bowker,John	9	-0.5
Young,Delmon	7	4.1	Rodney,Fernando	P	2.1	Clippard,Tyler	P	0.8	Gamel,Mat	5	-0.6
Hudson,Orlando	4	4.1	Linebrink,Scott	P	2.1	Reyes,Dennys	P	0.8	Kendrick,Howie	4	-0.7
Lopez,Javier	P	4.1	Lecure,Sam	P	2.0	Ka'aihue,Kila	3	0.8	Harris,Willie	79	-0.7
McClellan,Kyle	P	4.1	Strasburg,Stephen	P	2.0	Olivo,Miguel	2	0.8	Wells,Casper	9	-0.7
Contreras,Jose	P	4.0	Stauffer,Tim	P	2.0	Upton,B.J.	8	0.8	Eveland,Dana	P	-0.7
Slowey,Kevin	P	4.0	Jones,Andruw	9	2.0	Lindstrom,Matt	P	0.8	Tejeda,Robinson	P	-0.7
Belisle,Matt	P	3.9	Tillman,Chris	P	2.0	Garland,Jon	P	0.8	Ambriz,Hector	P	-0.7
Loe,Kameron	P	3.9	Luebke,Cory	P	1.9	Slaten,Doug	P	0.8	Maloney,Matt	P	-0.7
O'Day,Darren	P	3.9	Baker,Jeff	45	1.8	Penny,Brad	P	0.8	Bonderman,Jerem	P	-0.7
Harang,Aaron	P	3.8	Castro,Ramon	2	1.8	Lowe,Mark	P	0.7	Dickerson,Chris	8	-0.8
Scott,Luke	0	3.8	Wang,Chien-Ming	P	1.8	Duda,Lucas	7	0.7	Simon,Alfredo	P	-0.8
Pena,Tony	P	3.7	Walker,Neil	4	1.8	Barton,Daric	3	0.7	Flores,Randy	P	-0.9
Sandoval,Pablo	5	3.7	Boyer,Blaine	P	1.8	Schneider,Brian	2	0.7	Figueroa,Nelson	P	-0.9
Storen,Drew	P	3.6	Mathieson,Scott	P	1.7	Breslow,Craig	P	0.7	Kawakami,Kenshi	P	-0.9
Cabrera,Asdrubal	6	3.6	Lewis,Fred	7	1.7	Silva,Carlos	P	0.6	Stubbs,Drew	8	-0.9
Nova,Ivan	P	3.5	Hafner,Travis	0	1.7	Hundley,Nick	2	0.6	Torrealba,Yorvit	2	-1.0
Doumit,Ryan	2	3.4	Oliver,Andrew	P	1.7	Slama,Anthony	P	0.6	Bullington,Bryan	P	-1.0
Wells,Randy	P	3.4	Duchscherer,Justin	P	1.6	Gee,Dillon	P	0.6	Lyon,Brandon	P	-1.0
Wood,Kerry	P	3.3	Maholm,Paul	P	1.6	Sipp,Tony	P	0.5	Blackburn,Nick	P	-1.0
Kimbrel,Craig	P	3.3	Balester,Collin	P	1.6	Zaun,Gregg	2	0.5	Morse,Mike	9	-1.0
Francis,Jeff	P	3.3	Gomez,Jeanmar	P	1.6	Thames,Marcus	70	0.5	Fields,Josh	5	-1.1
Casilla,Santiago	P	3.3	Stairs,Matt	7	1.6	Ohman,Will	P	0.5	Smith,Jordan	P	-1.1
Blevins,Jerry	P	3.3	Duncan,Shelley	7	1.6	Burnett,Alex	P	0.5	Viciedo,Dayan	5	-1.2
Holland,Derek	P	3.3	Troncoso,Ramon	P	1.6	Hill,Aaron	4	0.5	Moseley,Dustin	P	-1.2
Motte,Jason	P	3.3	Sizemore,Grady	8	1.5	Maybin,Cameron	8	0.4	Okajima,Hideki	P	-1.3
Wheeler,Dan	P	3.3	Aardsma,David	P	1.5	Richard,Clayton	P	0.4	Rodriguez,Francis	P	-1.3
Parra,Manny	P	3.2	Santana,Johan	P	1.5	Veras,Jose	P	0.3	Fuentes,Brian	P	-1.3
Mitre,Sergio	P	3.1	Herrera,Daniel	P	1.5	Cordero,Francisco	P	0.3	Romero,J.C.	P	-1.3
Schlereth,Daniel	P	3.1	Garza,Matt	P	1.5	Cashner,Andrew	P	0.3	Betemit,Wilson	5	-1.3
Hall,Bill	47	3.1	Gregg,Kevin	P	1.5	Bay,Jason	7	0.2	Kelley,Shawn	P	-1.3
Villanueva,Carlos	P	3.1	Medlen,Kris	P	1.5	Heilman,Aaron	P	0.1	Ellis,Mark	4	-1.4
Blanton,Joe	P	3.1	Leake,Mike	P	1.5	Rhodes,Arthur	P	0.1	Martin,J.D.	P	-1.4
Runzler,Dan	P	3.0	Bell,Trevor	P	1.4	Cecil,Brett	P	0.1	Mills,Brad	P	-1.4
Cameron,Mike	8	3.0	Braddock,Zach	P	1.4	Nava,Daniel	7	0.1	McDonald,Darnell	789	-1.5
Matusz,Brian	P	2.9	Dotel,Octavio	P	1.4	Nix,Laynce	7	0.1	Jurrjens,Jair	P	-1.5
Edmonds,Jim	8	2.9	Olson,Garrett	P	1.3	Sampson,Chris	P	0.0	Duke,Zach	P	-1.5
Perez,Rafael	P	2.9	Shoppach,Kelly	2	1.3	Albers,Matt	P	0.0	Ceda,Jose	P	-1.5
Avila,Alex	2	2.9	Hendrickson,Mark	P	1.3	Lewis,Jensen	P	0.0	Bergesen,Brad	P	-1.6
Matsui,Hideki	0	2.9	Keppinger,Jeff	4	1.3	Arroyo,Bronson	P	0.0	Marquis,Jason	P	-1.6
Gervacio,Sammy	P	2.8	Lannan,John	P	1.3	Acosta,Manny	P	0.0	Powell,Landon	2	-1.6
Fister,Doug	P	2.7	McDonald,James	P	1.3	Rapada,Clay	P	0.0	Francisco,Ben	79	-1.6
Harden,Rich	P	2.7	Takahashi,Hisanori	P	1.2	Ondrusek,Logan	P	0.0	Kapler,Gabe	9	-1.6
Dickey,R.A.	P	2.7	Bastardo,Antonio	P	1.2	Russell,Adam	P	-0.1	Crisp,Coco	8	-1.7
Gordon,Alex	7	2.7	Rauch,Jon	P	1.2	Herndon,David	P	-0.1	Kirkman,Michael	P	-1.7

2011 CHEATER'S BOOKMARK

BATTING STATISTICS / BENCHMARKS

Abbrv	Term	Formula / Descr.	BAD UNDER	'10 LG AVG AL	'10 LG AVG NL	BEST OVER
Avg	Batting Average	h/ab	250	260	255	300
xBA	Expected Batting Average	*See Encyclopedia*		261	259	
OB	On Base Average	(h+bb)/(ab+bb)	300	327	324	375
Slg	Slugging Average	total bases/ab	350	406	399	500
OPS	On Base plus Slugging	OB+Slg	650	733	723	875
bb%	Walk Rate	bb/(ab+bb)	5%	9%	9%	10%
ct%	Contact Rate	(ab-k) / ab	75%	80%	78%	85%
Eye	Batting Eye	bb/k	0.50	0.48	0.44	1.00
PX	Power Index	Normalized power skills	80	100	100	120
Spd	Statistically Scouted Speed	Normalized speed skills	80	100	100	120
SBO	Stolen Base Opportunity %	(sb+cs)/(singles+bb)		10%	9%	
G/F	Groundball/Flyball Ratio	gb / fb		1.16	1.22	
G	Ground Ball Per Cent	gb / balls in play		44%	45%	
L	Line Drive Per Cent	ld / balls in play		18%	18%	
F	Fly Ball Per Cent	fb / balls in play		38%	37%	
RC/G	Runs Created per Game	*See Encyclopedia*	3.00	4.53	4.35	7.50
RAR	Runs Above Replacement	*See Encyclopedia*	-0.0			+25.0

PITCHING STATISTICS / BENCHMARKS

Abbrv	Term	Formula / Descr.	BAD OVER	'10 LG AVG AL	'10 LG AVG NL	BEST UNDER
ERA	Earned Run Average	er*9/ip	5.00	4.14	4.02	4.00
xERA	Expected ERA	*See Encyclopedia*		4.20	4.07	
WHIP	Baserunners per Inning	(h+bb)/ip	1.50	1.35	1.35	1.25
BF/G	Batters Faced per Game	((ip*2.82)+h+bb)/g	28.0			
PC	Pitch Counts per Start		120	98	96	
OBA	Opposition Batting Avg	Opp. h/ab	290	258	257	250
OOB	Opposition On Base Avg	Opp. (h+bb)/(ab+bb)	350	325	326	300
BABIP	BatAvg on balls in play	(h-hr)/((ip*2.82)+h-k-hr)		299	305	
Ctl	Control Rate	bb*9/ip		3.2	3.3	3.0
hr/9	Homerun Rate	hr*9/ip		1.0	0.9	1.0
hr/f	Homerun per Fly ball	hr/fb		9%	9%	10%
S%	Strand Rate	(h+bb-er)/(h+bb-hr)		72%	72%	
DIS%	PQS Disaster Rate	% GS that are PQS 0/1		21%	21%	20%

Abbrv	Term	Formula / Descr.	BAD UNDER	'10 LG AVG AL	'10 LG AVG NL	BEST OVER
RAR	Runs Above Replacement	*See Encyclopedia*	-0.0			+25.0
Dom	Dominance Rate	k*9/ip		6.8	7.4	6.5
Cmd	Command Ratio	k/bb		2.1	2.2	2.2
G/F	Groundball/Flyball Ratio	gb / fb		1.15	1.21	
BPV	Base Performance Value	*See Encyclopedia*	50	54	62	75
DOM%	PQS Dominance Rate	% GS that are PQS 4/5		44%	46%	50%
Sv%	Saves Conversion Rate	(saves / save opps)		70%	69%	80%
REff%	Relief Effectiveness Rate	*See Encyclopedia*		66%	66%	80%

NOTES

2011 FANTASY BASEBALL WINNERS RESOURCE GUIDE

10 REASONS
why <u>winners</u> rely on
BASEBALL HQ PRODUCTS
for fantasy baseball information

1 **NO OTHER RESOURCE** provides you with more vital intelligence to help you win. Compare the depth of our offerings in these pages with any other information product or service.

2 **NO OTHER RESOURCE** provides more exclusive information, like cutting-edge component skills analyses, revolutionary strategies like the LIMA Plan, and innovative gaming formats like Rotisserie 500. Y*ou won't find these anywhere else on the internet, guaranteed.*

3 **NO OTHER RESOURCE** has as long and as consistent a track record of success in the top national competitions... Our writers and readers have achieved 24 first place, 8 second place and 13 third place finishes since 1997. *No other resource comes remotely close.*

4 **NO OTHER RESOURCE** has as consistent a track record in projecting impact performances. In 2010, our readers had surprises like Adrian Beltre, Robinson Cano, Brett Gardner, Carlos Gonzalez, Corey Hart, Kelly Johnson, Martin Prado, Joey Votto, Vernon Wells, Matt Capps, Jaime Garcia, Cole Hamels, Shaun Marcum and Brett Myers on their teams, *and dozens more.*

5 **NO OTHER RESOURCE** is supported by more than 50 top writers and analysts — all paid professionals and proven winners, not weekend hobbyists or corporate staffers.

6 **NO OTHER RESOURCE** has a wider scope, providing valuable information not only for Rotisserie, but for alternative formats like simulations, salary cap contests, online games, points, head-to-head, dynasty leagues and others.

7 **NO OTHER RESOURCE** is as highly regarded by its peers in the industry. Baseball HQ is the *only* three-time winner of the Fantasy Sports Trade Association's "Best Fantasy Baseball Online Content" award and Ron Shandler was a key subject in Sam Walker's *Fantasyland.*

8 **NO OTHER RESOURCE** is as highly regarded *outside* of the fantasy industry. Many Major League general managers are regular customers. We were advisors to the St. Louis Cardinals in 2004 and our former Minor League Director is now a scout for the organization.

9 **NO OTHER RESOURCE** has been creating fantasy baseball winners for as long as we have. Our 25 years of stability *guarantees your investment.*

10 Year after year, more than 90% of our customers report that Baseball HQ products and services have helped them improve their performance in their fantasy leagues. <u>That's the bottom line</u>.

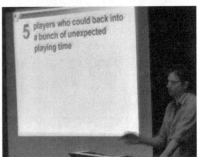

2011 MINOR LEAGUE BASEBALL ANALYST
By Rob Gordon and Jeremy Deloney

Available January 2011

The **Minor League Baseball Analyst** is the first book to integrate sabermetrics and scouting. For baseball analysts and those who play in fantasy leagues with farm systems, the *Analyst* is the perfect complement to the *Baseball Forecaster* and is designed exactly for your needs:

- *Stats and Sabermetrics...* Over three dozen categories for 1000 minor leaguers, including batter skills ratings, pitch repertoires and more
- *Performance Trends...* spanning each player's last five minor league stops, complete with leading indicators
- *Scouting reports...* for all players, including expected major league debuts, potential major league roles and more
- **Major League Equivalents...** Five year scans for every player
- *Mega-Lists...* The Top 100 of 2011, retrospective looks at the Top 100's of 2003-2010, organizational Top 15's, top prospects by position, power and speed prospects, and more
- *Additional Reports...* on international prospects, fantasy implications and more...
- *Player Potential Ratings...* Baseball HQ's exclusive system that evaluates each player's upside potential and chances of achieving that potential.

The *Analyst* was founded by Deric McKamey, a Bill James disciple and graduate of Major League Baseball's scout school. Deric is now a scout for the St. Louis Cardinals.

BOOKS

Art McGee's
HOW TO VALUE PLAYERS FOR ROTISSERIE® BASEBALL

Learn how to calculate the best player values for your draft or auction! Art McGee applies concepts from economics, finance, and statistics to develop a pricing method that far surpasses any other published. His method is highly sophisticated, yet McGee explains it in terms that any fantasy baseball owner can understand and apply.

In the 2nd Edition...
- Discover the power of Standings Gain Points (SGP)
- Learn how to adjust values for position scarcity, injury risk and future potential
- Set up your own pricing spreadsheet, as simple or sophisticated as you want
- Make better decisions on trades, free agents, and long-term contracts
- Apply these methods even if your league uses non-standard categories or has a non-standard number of teams
- PLUS... 10 additional essays to expand your knowledge base.

PQS Across America

Here's what happened...

It was time to renew the registration on my car and consider the annual question about vanity plates. I'm not real big on showing off how clever I am. It's much easier for eyewitnesses to remember cute monikers than random alpha-numerics, and that limits the types of acceptable felonies I can commit. But Sue had just gotten vanity tags on her car, and she and the girls were egging me on.

So I did what every good Dad does. I caved.

But what should it say? With a 7-character max, my options were limited. Nothing cute. No STATMAN or 4CASTER. Nothing with RON in it.

I finally settled on something that nobody would recognize. At least nobody in this neck of football country. A Pure Quality Start score of 5.

I am now the proud owner of a perfect pitching outing. Of course, I am not a pitcher, and if I was, I'd most likely post a PQS-0 than a PQS-5. But aren't vanity plates about being vain? About living the dream?

For the past month, I have been driving around southwest Virginia proclaiming — albeit surreptitiously — that I have pitched a masterful game. I might have hurled a 2-hit shut-out. I might have only gone 7 innings but struck out 8 and walked only 2. Heck, I might have even thrown a no-hitter. (I would have said perfect game, but I didn't want to shoot high.) Nobody knows except me. But it still feels oddly satisfying.

Perhaps more odd, though, is the fact that nobody has yet asked me what my license plate means. I did explain it to Sue and the girls... and it's okay, I'm used to blank stares in this house. But nobody else has inquired.

It could be anything, after all. It could be my monogram and my family size... if my name was Peter Quincy Smith and I had a wife and four kids. It could be my company's name... if I owned a company called Petrochemical Quality Systems... and if we had five satellite offices across the country. It could just be a name I gave my car, sort of like naming your dog Dog or naming a bridge Bob. It could just be a random assortment of letters and a number I like.

But it's not. I know what it is. If nobody else is interested, that's their loss.

So then I had this crazy idea. What if I challenged all my readers to go out and get a vanity plate with a PQS score on it? We could post all the photos on the Baseball HQ website and try to cover as many states as possible. If PQS-5 is

already taken (like in Virginia), then you could get any of the other PQS scores. I know, it's not great to be driving around with a PQS-0, but who would really know what that means? Heck, get PQS-6 or PQS-14 if the others are taken. Why not?

Now, I know that I can't expect people to go out and spend their money for something as stupid as this if I didn't make some sort of sweet offer. So how about a free subscription or extension to Baseball HQ? I don't know about other states, but vanity plates in Virginia cost just $20, so you would pay $20 to get a $99 product.

Here's what you need to do:

1. Purchase the vanity plate "PQS-5" in your state (or country!). If that plate is taken, purchase "PQS-4" or any PQS score down to 0. If you want to purchase a plate with a higher PQS score, go nuts.

2. Take a digital photograph of the plate and email the file to pqs@baseballhq.com. Make sure you identify yourself in the email and include your contact information.

3. When we receive your file, we will enter a one-year subscription (or extension) to BaseballHQ.com within 72 hours of receipt.

4. If anyone asks what PQS-5 means, tell them that it's a system for evaluating pitching performance used at BaseballHQ.com. A PQS-5 is the best you can be and it netted you a free $99 subscription. If they look at you funny, tell them you didn't do this because it was geeky; you did it because it was profitable.

By participating in this PQS Across America event, you are giving us permission to post the photo of your license plate on BaseballHQ.com, and possibly in next year's *Baseball Forecaster*.

This offer is for 2011 only, for now. If we start piling up state plates, we'll extend this exercise and provide additional freebies. You may have to send us a new photo each year, showing new date labels (or however it is done in your state). We'll make it worth your while if this takes off. If it doesn't, just revert back to your regular plates and you'll incur no more charges.

Of course, if this is all too much of a hassle, don't be putting your life on the line. I don't want to see PQS plates showing up in anyone's divorce settlement documents.

We're just having a little bit of fun.

CONSUMER ADVISORY

AN IMPORTANT MESSAGE FOR FANTASY LEAGUERS
REGARDING PROPER USAGE OF THE *BASEBALL FORECASTER*

This document is provided in compliance with authorities to outline the prospective risks and hazards possible in the event that the *Baseball Forecaster* is used incorrectly. Please be aware of these potentially dangerous situations and avoid them. Ron Shandler assumes no risk related to any financial loss or stress-induced illnesses caused by ignoring the items as described below.

1. The statistical projections in this book are intended as general guidelines, not as gospel. It is highly dangerous to use the projected statistics alone, and then live and die by them. That's like going to a ballgame, being given a choice of any seat in the park, and deliberately choosing the last row in the right field corner with an obstructed view. The projections are there, you can look at them, but there are so many better places to sit.

We have to publish those numbers, but they are stagnant, inert pieces of data. This book focuses on a *live forecasting process* that provides the tools so that you can understand the leading indicators and draw your own conclusions. If you at least attempt your own analyses of the data, and enhance them with the player commentaries, you can paint more robust, colorful pictures of the future.

In other words...

If you bought this book purely for the projected statistics and do not intend to spend at least some time learning about the process, then you might as well just buy an $8 magazine.

2. The player commentaries in this book are written by humans, just like you. These commentaries provide an overall evaluation of performance and likely future direction, but 40-word capsules cannot capture everything. Your greatest value will be to use these as a springboard to your own analysis of the data. Odds are, if you take the time, you'll find hidden indicators that we might have missed. *Forecaster* veterans say that this self-guided excursion is the best part of owning the book.

3. This book does not attempt to tackle playing time. Rather than making arbitrary decisions about how roles will shake out, the focus is on performance. The playing time projections presented here are merely to help you better evaluate each player's talent. Our online pre-season projections update provides more current AB/IP expectations based on how roles are being assigned.

4. The dollar values in this book are intended solely for player-to-player comparisons. They are not driven by a finite pool of playing time – which is required for valuation systems to work properly – so they cannot be used for bid values to be used in your own draft.

There are two reasons for this:

a. The finite pool of players that will generate the finite pool of playing time will not be determined until much closer to Opening Day. And, if we are to be brutally honest, there is really no such thing as a finite pool of players.

b. Your particular league's construction will drive the values; a $10 player in a 10-team mixed league will not be the same as a $10 player in a 13-team NL-only league.

Note that book dollar values also cannot be compared to those published at BaseballHQ.com as the online values *are* generated by a more finite player pool.

5. Do not pass judgment on the effectiveness of this book based on the performance of a few individual players. The test, rather, is on the collective predictive value of the book's methods. Are players with better base skills more likely to produce good results than bad ones? Years of research suggest that the answer is "yes." Does that mean that every high skilled player will do well? No. But many more of them will perform well than will the average low-skilled player. You should always side with the better percentage plays, but recognize that there are factors we cannot predict. Good decisions that beget bad outcomes do not invalidate the methods.

6. If your copy of this book is not marked up and dog-eared by Draft Day, you probably did not get as much value out of it as you might have.

7. This book is not intended to provide absorbency for spills of more than 6.5 ounces

8. This book is not intended to provide stabilizing weight for more than 15 sheets of 20 lb. paper in winds of more than 45 mph.

9. The pages of this book are not recommended for avian waste collection. In independent laboratory studies, 87% of migratory water fowl refused to excrete on interior pages, even when coaxed.

10. This book, when rolled into a cylindrical shape, is not intended to be used as a weapon for any purpose, including but not limited to insect extermination, canine training or to influence bidding behavior at a fantasy draft.